Buttress's
WORLD GUIDE TO
ABBREVIATIONS
OF ORGANIZATIONS

11th edition

Revised by

L. M. Pitman
Senior Assistant Librarian,
School of Slavonic and East European Studies,
University of London

BLACKIE ACADEMIC & PROFESSIONAL
An Imprint of Chapman & Hall
London · Weinheim · New York · Tokyo · Melbourne · Madras

Published by Blackie Academic and Professional, an imprint of Chapman & Hall, 2–6 Boundary Row, London SE1 8HN, UK

Chapman & Hall, 2–6 Boundary Row, London SE1 8HN, UK

Chapman & Hall GmbH, Pappelallee 3, 69469 Weinheim, Germany

Chapman & Hall USA, 115 Fifth Avenue, New York, NY 10003, USA

Chapman & Hall Japan, ITP-Japan, Kyowa Building, 3F, 2-2-1 Hirakawacho, Chiyoda-ku Tokyo 102, Japan

DA Book (Aust.) Pty Ltd, 648 Whitehorse Road, Mitcham 3132, Victoria, Australia

Chapman & Hall India, R. Seshadri, 32 Second Main Road, CIT East, Madras 600 035, India

Distributed in the United States, its possessions, Canada, Central and South America exclusively by Gale Research Inc., Penobscot Building, Detroit, Michigan 48226

First edition 1954
Second edition 1956
Third edition 1966
Fourth edition 1971
Fifth edition 1974
Sixth edition 1981
Seventh edition 1984
Eighth edition 1988
Ninth edition 1991
Tenth edition 1993
Eleventh edition 1997

© 1997 Chapman & Hall

Typeset in Times 10/12pt by Columns Design Ltd, Reading

Printed in Great Britain at the Alden Press, Oxford

ISBN 07514 0261 3

A catalogue record for this book is available from the British Library

Library of Congress Catalog Card Number: 96–86429

∞ Printed on permanent acid-free text paper, manufactured in accordance with ANSI/NISO Z39.48-1992 (Permanence of Paper)

Buttress's
**WORLD GUIDE TO
ABBREVIATIONS
OF ORGANIZATIONS**

JOIN US ON THE INTERNET VIA WWW, GOPHER, FTP OR EMAIL:

WWW: http://www.thomson.com
GOPHER: gopher.thomson.com
FTP: ftp.thomson.com
EMAIL: findit@kiosk.thomson.com

A service of I(T)P

Introduction

The previous edition of this directory extended its coverage of the Far East, Australasia and Latin America, areas previously under-represented. For this new edition emphasis has been given to increasing the number of entries for organizations from Britain, the United States and Australia, and particular attention has been paid to new political organizations in Central and Eastern Europe and the former Soviet Union.

The number of entries included has gone up to over 68,000 of which over 9,000 are new or amended. Cross-references from defunct organizations in the previous edition have been deleted, and references (indicated by *ex* and *now*) added for organizations which have changed their name since the previous edition.

As before, the range of organizations included is broad and only purely local organizations have been excluded. This directory therefore lists official and unofficial organizations, national and international, on all subjects: political, economic and social. Acronyms of parent bodies of subsidiary organizations are given where appropriate and equivalencies are used to link acronyms in different languages for the same organization. Further information about the organizations listed can be found in the sources listed in the bibliography.

I would like to thank Henry Heaney and Graeme Mackintosh for their advice, and David Grinyer for his technical support.

L. M. Pitman

Bibliography

Adams, R. (ed.) (1993) *Centres & Bureaux: A Directory of UK Concentrations of Effort, Information and Expertise*, 2nd edn, CBD Research, Beckenham.

Barrett, J.K. (1993) *Encyclopedia of Women's Associations Worldwide*, Gale, London.

Cichonski, T.J. (ed.) (1995) *International Research Centres Directory 1994–95*, 7th edn, Gale, London.

Europa World Yearbook 1995 (1995), Europa, London.

Greenslade, S. (1995) *Directory of European Professional and Learned Societies*, 5th edn, CBD Research, Beckenham.

Henderson, S.P.A. and Henderson, A.J.W. (eds) (1994) *Directory of British Associations and Associations in Ireland*, 12th edn, CBD Research, Beckenham.

HMSO (1996) *Britain 1996: An Official Handbook*, HMSO, London.

HMSO (1995) *Civil Service Yearbook 1995*, HMSO, London.

Mercer, P. (1994) *Directory of British Political Organizations*, Longman, Harlow.

Milner, J.E. (1994) *The Green Index: A Directory of Environmental Organizations In Britain and Ireland*, Cassell, London.

Research Centers Directory (1994), 18th edn, Gale, London.

Union of International Associations (1995) *Yearbook of International Organizations*, 32nd edn, K.G. Saur, München.

Shershukov, A. (1993) *Russian Trade Unions and Workers Organizations,* Panorama, Moscow.

Szajkowski, B. (ed.) (1994) *Political Parties of Eastern Europe, Russia and the Successor States*, Longman, Harlow.

Voluntary Agencies Directory (1995), 14th edn, NCVO, London.

Yearbook of the European Communities and of the Other European Organizations 94–95 (1995), 14th edn, Editions Delta SA, Brussels.

A

A&A	Art and Architecture
A&AFA	Asthma and Allergy Foundation of America
A&ECA	Anglican and Eastern Churches Association
A&P	Atlantic and Pacific (U.S.A.)
A&R	Arbeitgemeinschaft der Restauratoren-Museen Denkmalpflege, Grabungs Technik
A2	Société Nationale de Télévision en Couleur
A2LA	American Association for Laboratory Accreditation
AA	Addicts Anonymous (U.S.A.)
AA	Advertising Association
AA	Aerolineas Argentinas
AA	Agrarian Alliance (Hungary)
AA	Airship Association (U.S.A.)
AA	Akademisk Arkitektforening
AA	Alcoholics Anonymous
AA	Aluminum Association (U.S.A.)
AA	Aluminum Company of America
AA	American Airlines
AA	Analogue Addicts
AA	Arboricultural Association
AA	Architectural Association
AA	Arthrogryposis Association
AA	Association of Agriculture
AA	Astrological Association
AA	Atheists Association (U.S.A.)
AA	Automobile Association
AA	Avisenes Arbeidsgiverforening
AA	Congregatio Augustinianorum ab Assumptione
AA	Instituto de Astrofisica de Andalucia (Spain)
AAA	Action Against Abuse of Women and Girls
AAA	Action Against Allergy
AAA	Action on Alcohol Abuse
AAA	Actors and Artistes of America (AFL-CIO)
AAA	Agricultural Adjustment Administration (U.S.A.)
AAA	Air Affairs Afrique (Cameroon)
AAA	Alianza Anticomunista Argentina
AAA	Alianza por Acción Anticomunista (Honduras)
AAA	Allied Artists of America
AAA	Amateur Athletic Association
AAA	American Abstract Artists
AAA	American Academy of Achievement
AAA	American Academy of Actuaries
AAA	American Academy of Advertising
AAA	American Academy of Allergy
AAA	American Academy of Art
AAA	American Accordionists Association
AAA	American Accounting Association
AAA	American Aid for Afghans
AAA	American Airship Association
AAA	American Allergy Association
AAA	American Ambulance Association
AAA	American Angus Association
AAA	American Antarctic Association
AAA	American Anthropological Association
AAA	American Arbitration Association
AAA	American Arts Association
AAA	American Association of Anatomists
AAA	American Astronomers Association
AAA	American Australian Association
AAA	American Automobile Association
AAA	Americans Against Abortion
AAA	Anarchist Association of America
AAA	Anglo-Albanian Association
AAA	Anglo-American Associates (U.S.A.)
AAA	Antique Airplane Association (U.S.A.)
AAA	Appraisers Association of America
AAA	Architectural Aluminium Association
AAA	Archives of American Art
AAA	Army Audit Agency (U.S.A.)
AAA	ASEAN International Airports Association
AAA	Associated Agents of America
AAA	Association for Applied Artists
AAA	Association of Accounting Administrators (U.S.A.)
AAA	Association of Attenders and Alumni of the Hague Academy of International Law
AAA	Association of Authors Agents
AAA	Association of Average Adjusters
AAA	Australian Automobile Association
AAA	Federation for American Afghan Aid

AAA	1956 Anti-Fascist and Anti-Bolshevik Association (Hungary) = AAS	**AAACPA**	American Association of Attorney Certified Public Accountants
AAAA	Amateur Artists Association of America	**AAACU**	Asian Association of Agricultural Colleges and Universities
AAAA	American African Affairs Association	**AAAD**	American Athletic Association for the Deaf
AAAA	American Association for Affirmative Action	**AAAE**	American Association for Adult Education
AAAA	American Association for the Advancement of Atheism	**AAAE**	American Association of Academic Editors
AAAA	American Association of Advertising Agencies	**AAAE**	American Association of Airport Executives
AAAA	Army Aviation Association of America	**AAAE**	Australian Association of Adult Education
AAAA	Asian Amateur Athletic Association	**AAAÉA**	Association Africaine pour l'Alphabetisation et l'Éducation des Adultes = AALAE
AAAA	Asociación Argentina 'Amigos de la Astronomia'		
AAAA	Associated Actors and Artistes of America	**AAAÉÉNAA**	Association Amicale des Anciens Élèves de l'École Nationale Agronomique d'Alger
AAAA	Association for the Abolition of the Aberrant Apostrophe	**AAAÉINA**	Association Amicale des Anciens Élèves de l'Institut National Agronomique
AAAA	Association of Accredited Advertising Agencies (New Zealand, Singapore)		
AAAA	Australian Advertising Advisory Agency	**AAAF**	Association Aéronautique et Astronautique de France
AAAA	Australian Association of Advertising Agencies	**AAAH**	American Association for the Advancement of the Humanities
AAAAI	American Academy of Allergy, Asthma & Immunology	**AAAI**	Advertising Agencies Association of India
AAAAM	American Academy of Anti-Aging Medicine	**AAAI**	Affiliated Advertising Agencies International (U.S.A.)
AAAB	American Association of Architectural Bibliographers	**AAAI**	American Association for Artificial Intelligence
AAABA	All-American Amateur Baseball Association	**AAAIA**	All-India Automobile and Ancillary Industries Association (India)
AAAC	African Amateur Athletic Confederation (Senegal) = CAAA	**AAAID**	Arab Authority for Agricultural Investment and Development
AAAC	Alliance Atlantique des Anciens Combattants	**AAAIMH**	American Association for the Abolition of Involuntary Mental Hospitalization
AAAC	American Arab Affairs Council		
AAAC	American Association for the Advancement of Criminology	**AAAIWA**	Automobile, Aerospace and Agricultural Implementation Workers of America
AAAC	Australian Aboriginal Affairs Council		
AAAC	Australian Army Aviation Corps	**AAAJ**	Association Afro-Asiatique des Journalistes
AAACC	Association of Asian-American Chambers of Commerce	**AAAL**	American Academy of Arts and Letters
AAACE	Alianza Apostolica y Anti-Comunista de España	**AAAL**	American Association for Applied Linguistics
AAACE	American Association of Agricultural College Educators	**AAALAC**	American Association for Accreditation of Laboratory Animal Care
AAACI	American-Arab Association for Commerce and Industry		

AAAM	American Association for Automotive Medicine
AAAM	American Association of Aircraft Manufacturers
AAAN	American Academy of Applied Nutrition
AAAofE	Amateur Athletic Association of England
AAAOM	American Association for Acupuncture and Oriental Medicine
AAAP	American Association of Avian Pathologists
AAAP	Asian-Australian Association of Animal Production Societies
AAAR	American Association for Aerosol Research
AAAR	Association for the Advancement of Aging Research (U.S.A.)
AAARG	American Atheist Addiction Recovery Group
AAAS	American Academy of Arts and Sciences
AAAS	American Academy of Asian Studies
AAAS	American Association for the Advancement of Science
AAAS	Australian Association for the Advancement of Science
AAASA	Association for the Advancement of Agricultural Sciences in Africa
AAASA	Australian and Allied All Services Association
AAASS	American Association for the Advancement of Slavic Studies
AAAST	African Association for the Advancement of Science and Technology
AAASUSS	Association of Administrative Assistants and Secretaries to United States Senators
AAATC	Association of American Air Travel Clubs
AAATDC	Association for the Advancement of Appropriate Technologies in Developing Countries
AAATP	Asian Alliance of Appropriate Technology Practitioners
AAAUS	Association of Average Adjustors of the United States
AAAVYT	Associación Argentina de Agencias de Viajes y Turismo
AAB	Aircraft Accident Board (U.S.A.)
AAB	Alliance Agricole Belge
AAB	American Association of Bioanalysts
AAB	Association of Applied Biologists
AAB	Attendance Allowance Board
AABA	Associação Atletica Brasil Açucareiro
AABB	American Association of Blood Banks
AABB	Association des Archivistes et Bibliothécaires de Belgique = VABB
AABB	Association for the Advancement of British Biotechnology
AABB	Australian Association of Bush Regenerators
AABC	Afro-Asian Book Council (India)
AABC	American Amateur Baseball Congress
AABC	American Association of Bible Colleges
AABC	American Association of Biofeedback Clinicians
AABC	Association for the Advancement of Blind Children (U.S.A.)
AABD	Aid to the Aged, Blind and Disabled (U.S.A.)
AABDF	Allied Association of Bleachers, Printers, Dyers and Finishers
AABDFC	Association des Archivistes, Bibliothécaires et Documentalistes Francophones de la Caraïbe
AABE	Asian Association for Biology Education
AABEvK	Arbeitsgemeinschaft für das Archiv- und Bibliothekswesen in der Evangelischen Kirche
AABEVM	Association of American Boards of Examiners in Veterinary Medicine
AABGA	American Association of Botanical Gardens and Arboretums
AABH	Australian Association for Better Hearing
AABI	American Association of Bicycle Importers
AABI	Antilles Air Boats Inc.
AABL	Associated Australasian Banks in London
AABM	Association of American Battery Manufacturers
AABM	Australian Association of British Manufacturers
AABNF	African Association for Biological Nitrogen Fixation
AABP	American Association of Bovine Practitioners

AABP	Australian Association of Business Publications	**AAC**	Automotive Advertisers Council (U.S.A.)
AABPA	American Association for Budget and Program Analysis	**AACA**	American Association of Creative Artists
AABR	Association for the Advancement of the Blind and Retarded	**AACA**	Antique Automobile Club of America
AABS	Association for the Advancement of Baltic Studies	**AACA**	Asian and Australasian Congress of Anaesthesiology
AABT	Association for the Advancement of Behavior Therapy (U.S.A.)	**AACA**	Association of Certified and Corporate Accountants (Southern Africa)
AABTL	Amalgamated Association of Beamers, Twisters and Drawers (Hand and Machine)	**AACA**	Automotive Air Conditioning Association (U.S.A.)
AABTM	American Association of Baggage Traffic Managers	**AACAHPO**	American Association of Certified Allied Health Personnel in Opthalmology
AABTT	Association for Analytic & Bodymind Therapy & Training	**AACAP**	American Academy of Child and Adolescent Psychiatry
AABWA	Association of Accountancy Bodies in West Africa	**AACB**	Aeronautics and Astronautics Coordinating Board (U.S.A.)
AAC	Académia Argentina de Cirugia	**AACB**	Association of African Central Banks = ABCA
AAC	Aeronautical Advisory Council (U.S.A.)		
AAC	Affärsarbetsgivarnas Centralförbund	**AACB**	Australian Association of Clinical Biochemists
AAC	African Accounting Council		
AAC	African Advisory Council (Botswana)	**AACBC**	American Association of College Baseball Coaches
AAC	African Association of Cartography (Algeria)	**AACBP**	American Academy of Crown and Bridge Prosthodontics
AAC	Agrarische Adviescommissie (NIBEM)	**AACC**	Airport Associations Coordinating Council = CCAA
AAC	Agricultural Advisory Council for England and Wales	**AACC**	All Africa Conference of Churches = CETA
AAC	All-American Canal		
AAC	American Academy of Criminalistics	**AACC**	American Association for Contamination Control
AAC	American Adoption Congress		
AAC	American Alpine Club	**AACC**	American Association for Credit Counselors
AAC	American Archery Council		
AAC	American Association of Criminology	**AACC**	American Association for the Continuity of Care
AAC	Anglo American Corporation		
AAC	Anhui Agricultural College	**AACC**	American Association of Cereal Chemists
AAC	Armor and Arms Club (U.S.A.)		
AAC	Army Air Corps	**AACC**	American Association of Clinical Chemistry
AAC	Association des Amidonneries de Céreales de la CEE	**AACC**	American Association of Commercial Colleges
AAC	Association of American Choruses	**AACC**	American Automatic Control Council
AAC	Association of American Colleges	**AACC**	Arab Air Carriers Organization
AAC	Association of Analytical Chemists (U.S.A.)	**AACC**	Asociación Argentina de Criadores de Caprinos
AAC	Australian Agricultural Council *(now ARMCANZ)*	**AACC**	Asociación Argentina de Criadores de Cebú
AAC	Australian Air Corps		
AAC	Australian Association of Chiropractors	**AACC**	Asociación Argentina de Criadores de Cerdos
AAC	Austrian Alpine Club		

AACC	Asociación Argentina de Criadores de Corriedale	**AACI**	American Association for Conservation Information
AACC	Association for the Aid of Crippled Children (U.S.A.)	**AACI**	Association of Americans and Canadians in Israel
AACCC	All-American Conference to Combat Communism	**AACIA**	American Association for Clinical Immunity and Allergy
AACCH	American Association for Child Care in Hospital	**AACJC**	American Association of Community and Junior Colleges
AACCH	Asociación Argentina Criadores de Charolais	**AACK**	Asociación Argentina Criadores de Karakul
AACCLA	Association of American Chambers of Commerce in Latin America	**AACL**	Arab Association for Comparative Literature (Algeria)
AACCN	American Association of Critical Care Nurses	**AACL**	Association of American Correspondents in London
AACCP	American Association of Colleges of Chiropody-Podiatry	**AACLA**	Association of American Chambers of Commerce in Latin America
AACD	American Academy of Craniomandibular Disorders	**AACLI**	Australasian Advisory Committee on Land Information (of ANZLIC)
AACD	American Association for Counselling Development	**AACLS**	Association of American Collegiate Library Societies
AACD	Asian-American Caucus for Disarmament	**AACM**	American Academy of Compensation Medicine
AACDP	American Association of Chairmen of Departments of Psychiatry	**AACM**	Association for the Advancement of Creative Musicians (U.S.A.)
AACDT	Association of Advisers in Craft Design and Technology (*now* NAAIDT)	**AACN**	American Association of Colleges of Nursing
AACE	American Association for Cancer Education	**AACNP**	Asociación Argentina de Ciéncias Naturáles 'Physis'
AACE	American Association for Career Education	**AACO**	American Association of Certified Orthoptists
AACE	American Association of Cost Engineers	**AACO**	American Association of Correctional Officers
AACE	Association des Assureurs Coopératifs Européens = AECI	**AACO**	Arab Air Carriers Organization
AACE	Association for the Advancement of Computing in Education	**AACOM**	American Association of Colleges of Osteopathic Medicine
AACF	Afro-American Cultural Foundation	**AACP**	American Academy of Child Psychiatry
AACFO	American Association of Correctional Facility Officers	**AACP**	American Academy of Clinical Psychiatrists
AACG	American Association for Crystal Growth	**AACP**	American Association for Cerebral Palsy
AACGF	All-American Collegiate Golf Foundation	**AACP**	American Association of Colleges of Pharmacy
AACHSM	Afro-America Cultural and Historical Society Museum (U.S.A.)	**AACP**	American Association of Colleges of Podiatry
AACHT	American Association for Clinical Histocompatibility Testing	**AACP**	American Association of Commercial Publications
AACI	Airports Association Council International (Switzerland)	**AACP**	American Association of Convention Planners
AACI	American Academy of Crisis Interveners	**AACP**	American Association of Correctional Psychologists

AACP	Anglo-American Council for Productivity
AACP	Association des Agences Conseils en Publicité
AACPA	Asian Association of Certified Public Accountants
AACPA	Autoclaved Aerated Concrete Products Association
AACPDM	American Academy for Cerebral Palsy and Developmental Medicine
AACPM	American Association of Colleges of Podiatric Medicine
AACPP	Association of Asbestos Cement Pipe Producers (U.S.A.)
AACPR	American Association for Cleft Palate Rehabilitation
AACR	American Association for Cancer Research
AACR	American Association of Clinical Research
AACR	American Association of Conservators and Restorers
AACR	Association for the Advancement of Civil Rights (Gibraltar)
AACRAO	American Association of College Registrars and Admissions Officers
AACREA	Asociación Argentina de Consorcios Regionales de Experimentación Agricola
AACS	Aberdeen-Angus Cattle Society
AACS	American Association for Chinese Studies
AACS	American Association of Christian Schools
AACS	American Association of Cosmetic Surgeons
AACS	Asociación Argentina de la Ciencia del Suelo
AACS	Association of Art Centres in Scotland
AACS	Australian Amateur Cine Society
AACSA	Anglo American Corporation of South Africa
AACSB	American Assembly of Collegiate Schools of Business
AACSE	American Association of Classified School Employees
AACSL	American Association for the Comparative Study of Law
AACT	American Association of Clinical Toxicology
AACT	American Association of Commodity Traders
AACT	Association of Austrian Chemical Trades = BCG
AACTE	American Association of Colleges for Teacher Education
AACTP	American Association of Correctional Training Personnel
AACU	American Association of Clinical Urologists
AACUBO	American Association of College & University Business Officers
AACUO	Association for Affiliated Colleges and University Offices (U.S.A.)
AACVB	Asian Association of Convention and Visitor Bureaux
AAD	American Academy of Dermatology
AAD	American Academy of Diplomacy
AAD	Association of American Dentists
AAD	Australian Antarctic Division (DEST)
AAD	Australian Association of Dietitians
AADA	American Academy of Dramatic Arts
AADA	American Association of Deaf Athletes
AADA	Associated Antique Dealers of America
AADA	Australian Automobile Dealers Association
AADAA	Administración Autónoma de Almacenes Aduaneros (Bolivia)
AADAI	Arab Authority for Development and Agricultural Investment (Sudan)
AADC	American Association of Dental Consultants
AADE	American Academy of Dental Electrosurgery
AADE	American Association of Dental Editors
AADE	American Association of Dental Examiners
AADE	American Association of Diabetes Educators
AADFI	Association of African Development Finance Institutions = AIAFD
AADGB	American Association of District Governing Boards
AADGP	American Academy of Dental Group Practice
AADLA	Art and Antique Dealers League of America
AADM	American Academy of Dental Medicine
AADN	American Association of Doctors' Nurses

AADP	American Academy of Dental Prosthetics	**AAEE**	American Association of Economic Entomologists
AADPA	American Academy of Dental Practice Administration	**AAEE**	American Association of Electromyography and Electrodiagnosis
AADR	American Academy of Dental Radiology	**AAEE**	American-Asian Educational Exchange
AADR	American Association for Dental Research	**AAÉÉ**	Association pour l'Accueil des Étudiants Étrangers
AADS	American Academy of Dermatology and Syphilology	**AAEE**	Australian Association for Environmental Education
AADS	American Association of Dental Schools	**AAEF**	Australian American Educational Foundation
AADV	American Association of Dental Victims	**AAEH**	Asociation to Advance Ethical Hypnosis (U.S.A.)
AADW	Association of Artists and Designers in Wales	**AAEI**	American Association of Exporters and Importers
AAE	Agrupación Astronautica Española	**AAEKNE**	American Association of Elementary – Kindergarten – Nursery Educators
AAE	Alliance for Arts Education (U.S.A.)		
AAE	American Association of Endodontists	**AAEL**	American Association of Equipment Lessors
AAE	American Association of Engineers	**AAEM**	American Academy of Environmental Medicine
AAE	American Association of Esthetics		
AAE	Asociación Argentina de Electrotécnicos	**AAEM**	American Association of Electrodiagnostic Medicine
AAE	Association des Astronautes Européens = AEA	**AAEOCJ**	American Association of Ex-Offenders in Criminal Justice
AAE	Association for Adult Education	**AAEP**	American Association of Equine Practitioners
AAE	Association for Astronomy Education		
AAE	Associazione Archivistica Ecclesiastica (Vatican City)	**AAES**	American Association of Engineering Societies
AAE	National Association of Aeronautical Examiners (U.S.A.)	**AAÉS**	Association des Archivistes de l'Église de France
AAEA	American Academy of Equine Art	**AAES**	Association of Agricultural Education Staffs
AAEA	American Agricultural Economics Association	**AAES**	Australian Agricultural Economics Society
AAEA	American Agricultural Editors Association	**AAES**	Australian Army Education Service
AAEA	Arab Atomic Energy Agency	**AAÉSC**	Association pour l'Avancement des Études Scandinaves au Canada = AASSC
AAEC	Association Africaine pour l'Enseignement par Correspondance		
AAEC	Association of American Editorial Cartoonists	**AAESDA**	Association of Architects, Engineers, Surveyors and Draughtsmen of Australia
AAEC	Australian American Engineering Corporation	**AAESPH**	American Association for the Education of the Severely/ Profoundly Handicapped
AAEC	Australian Army Education Corps		
AAECP	ASEAN-Australian Economic Cooperation Program	**AAESU**	Allgemeine Arabische Eisen und Stahl Union
AAED	American Academy of Esthetic Dentistry	**AAETA**	Asociación Argentina Empresarios Transporte Automotor
AAEDC	American Agricultural Economics Documentation Center	**AAEU**	Arab Agricultural Engineers Union

AAF	Académie d'Agriculture de France	**AAFS**	American Association of Foot Specialists
AAF	Agricultural Aids Foundation (U.S.A.)	**AAFSD**	American Asociation of Food Stamp Directors
AAF	American Advertising Federation		
AAF	American Architectural Foundation	**AAFU Paris**	Association des Anciens Fonctionnaires de l'UNESCO
AAF	American Astronautical Federation		
AAF	Asociatia Artistilor Fotografi din Republica Socialista România	**AAG**	Afdeling Agrarische Geschiedenis
		AAG	Air Affaires Gabon
AAF	Association des Archivistes Français	**AAG**	Anthropological Association of Greece
AAF	Association for the Advancement of Feminism (Hong Kong)	**AAG**	Association of American Geographers
		AAG	Australian Association of Gerontology
AAFA	Anglo-American Families Association	**AAGB**	Aikido Association of Great Britain
AAFA	Architectural Aluminium Fabricators Association (U.S.A.)	**AAGBA**	American Angora Goat Breeders Association
AAFC	Association of Advertising Film Companies (U.S.A.)	**AAGC**	American Association for Gifted Children
AAFCO	Association of American Feed Control Officials	**AAGFE**	American Association of Gravity Feed Energy
AAFDBI	American Association of Fitness Directors in Business and Industry	**AAGFO**	America Academy of Gold Foil Operators
AAFE	Asociación Argentina de Fomento Equino	**AAGG**	Asociación Argentina de Geofisicos y Geodestas
AAFH	Academy of American Franciscan History	**AAGL**	American Association of Gynecological Laparoscopists
AAFI	Associated Accounting Firms International (U.S.A.)	**AAGO**	American Academy of Gnathologic Orthopedics
AAFI	Association des Anciens Fonctionnaires Internationaux = AFICS	**AÄGP**	Allgemeine Ärztliche Gesellschaft für Psychotherapie
AAFLI	Asian American Free Labor Institute (Philippines)	**AAGP**	American Association for Geriatric Psychiatry
AAFM	American Association of Feed Microscopists	**AAGREF**	Association Amicale de Génie Rural des Eaux et des Forêts
AAFMC	American Association of Foundations for Medical Care	**AAGS**	Association of African Geological Surveys = ASGA
AAFO	American Association of Functional Orthodontists	**AAGUS**	American Association of Genito-Urinary Surgeons
AAFP	American Academy of Family Physicians	**AAH**	Association for Applied Hypnosis
AAFP	American Association of Feline Practitioners	**AAH**	Association of Ancient Historians (Canada)
AAFP	American Association of Financial Professionals	**AAH**	Association of Art Historians
		AAH	Australian Academy of the Humanities
AAFPRS	American Academy of Facial Plastic and Reconstructive Surgery	**AAHA**	American Academy of Health Administration
AAFRC	American Association of Fund-Raising Counsel	**AAHA**	American Animal Hospital Association
AAFS	Academy of Ambulatory Foot Surgery (U.S.A.)	**AAHA**	American Association of Handwriting Analysts
AAFS	American Academy of Forensic Sciences	**AAHA**	American Association of Homes for the Aging

AAHC	American Association of Hospital Consultants	**AAHS**	American Association for Hand Surgery
AAHC	Association of Academic Health Centers (U.S.A.)	**AAHS**	American Aviation Historical Society
AAHC	Association of Agricultural and Horticultural Colleges (Éire)	**AAHSLM**	American Association of Hides, Skins and Leather Merchants
AAHCPA	American Association of Hispanic Certified Public Accountants	**AAI**	Académie des Affaires Internationales (U.S.A.)
AAHD	American Academy of the History of Dentistry	**AAI**	Accademia Archeologica Italiana
AAHD	American Association of Hospital Dentists	**AAI**	African-American Institute (U.S.A.)
AAHDS	American Association of Health Data Systems	**AAI**	Alliance of American Insurers
AAHE	American Association for Higher Education	**AAI**	Alternatives to Abortion International
		AAI	American Association of Immunologists
AAHE	American Association of Housing Educators	**AAI**	American Association of Inventors
AAHE	Association for the Advancement of Health Education	**AAI**	Architectural Association of Ireland
AAHGS	Afro-American Historical and Genealogical Society (U.S.A.)	**AAI**	Association Actuarielle Internationale = IAA
AAHL	Australian Animal Health Laboratory	**AAI**	Association of Advertisers in Ireland
		AAI	Association of Alabaster Importers
AAHM	American Association for the History of Medicine	**AAI**	Association of Art Institutions
		AAI	Association of Artists in Ireland
AAHM	Association of Architectural Hardware Manufacturers (U.S.A.)	**AAI**	Associazione Antiquari d'Italia
		AAI	Associazione Archivistica Ecclesiastica
AAHO	Afro-Asian Housing Organisation (Egypt)	**AAIA**	American Association for International Aging
AAHP	American Association for Hospital Planning	**AAIA**	Association of American Indian Affairs
AAHP	American Association of Homeopathic Pharmacists	**AAIAL**	American Academy and Institute of Arts and Letters
AAHP	American Association of Hospital Podiatrists	**AAIB**	Aircraft Accident Investigation Board
		AAIB	Albarake Algeria Islamic Bank
AAHPA	American Association of Hospital Purchasing Agents	**AAIC**	Agências Associadas de Investigação e Control de Creditos
AAHPERD	American Alliance for Health, Physical Education, Recreation and Dance	**AAIC**	American Amateur Inventors Club
		AAIC	ASEAN Aluminium Industry Club
AAHPRID	African Association for Human and People's Rights in Development (Botswana)	**AAIC**	Asian Association of Insurance Commissioners
		AAID	American Academy of Implant Dentistry
AAHPSSS	Australasian Association for the History, Philosophy and Social Studies of Science	**AAIE**	American Association of Industrial Engineers
		AAIE	Association for the Advancement of International Education (U.S.A.)
AAHQS	Australian Agricultural Health and Quarantine Service	**AAIE**	Association of Applied Insect Ecologists (U.S.A.)
AAHR	Australian Association for Humane Research	**AAIH**	American Association of Industrial Hygiene
		AAIH	Association Amicale des Ingénieurs Horticoles et des Élèves de l'École Nationale d'Horticulture de Versailles
		AAII	American Association of Individual Investors

AAIND	American Association of Independent News Distributors	**AALPP**	American Association for Legal and Political Philosophy
AAIP	Association of American Indian Physicians	**AALS**	American Association of Library Schools
AAIPS	American Association of Industrial Physicians and Surgeons	**AALS**	Association for Arid Lands Studies (U.S.A.)
AAIS	African Association of Insect Scientists (Kenya)	**AALS**	Association of American Law Schools
AAIS	American Association of Insurance Services	**AAM**	All-Armenia Movement
		AAM	American Academy of Mechanics
AAISW	American Association of Industrial Social Workers	**AAM**	American Academy of Microbiology
		AAM	American Association of Museums
AAIV	American Association of Industrial Veterinarians	**AAM**	Anglican Association of Musicians
		AAM	Asociación Argentina de Marketing
AAJ	American Association of Jurists	**AAM**	Association des Amidonneries de Maïs de la CEE
AAJR	American Academy for Jewish Research		
		AAM	Automobile Association of Malaysia
AAJWA	Asian Agricultural Journalists and Writers Association	**AAMA**	Acetic Acid Manufacturers' Association (Japan)
AAKF	American Amateur Karate Federation	**AAMA**	African American Museums Association
AAL	Académia Argentina de Létras		
AAL	Academy of Art and Literature	**AAMA**	American Academy of Medical Administrators
AAL	Association of Assistant Librarians		
AALA	American Agricultural Law Association	**AAMA**	American Agricultural Marketing Association
AALA	American Association of Laboratory Accreditation	**AAMA**	American Amusement Machine Association
AALA	American Automotive Leasing Association	**AAMA**	American Apparel Manufacturers Association
AALAE	African Association for Literacy and Adult Education (Kenya)	**AAMA**	American Architectural Manufacturers Association
AALAS	American Association for Laboratory Animal Science	**AAMA**	American Association of Medical Assistants
AALC	African-American Labor Centre (U.S.A.)	**AAMA**	Asociación de Amigos de Miguel Angel Asturias (France)
AALCC	Asian-African Legal Consultative Committee	**AAMA**	Automotive Accessories Manufacturers of America
AALDI	Association of Agricultural Librarians and Documentalists of India	**AAMAM**	Associação dos Amigos do Museu de Arte Moderna
AALGCSU	American Association of Land Grant Colleges and State Universities	**AAMBP**	Association of American Medical Book Publishers
AALL	American Association for Labor Legislation	**AAMC**	American Association of Medico-Legal Consultants
AALL	American Association of Law Libraries	**AAMC**	Association for the Advancement of Maternity Care
AALMA	Association Africaine pour la Liturgie, la Musique et les Arts (Zambia) = AFALMA	**AAMC**	Association of American Medical Colleges
AALMA	Associazione America Latina Messico Asia	**AAMC**	Australian Army Medical Corps
AALOCHNA	Centre for Documentation and Research on Women (India)	**AAMCCI**	African Association for Maternal and Child Care International

AAMCH	American Association for Maternal and Child Health	**AAMT**	American Association for Medical Transcription
AAMD	American Association of Medical Directors	**AAMT**	American Association for Music Therapy
AAMD	American Association on Mental Deficiency	**AAMTI**	Association of African Maritime Training Institutes (Egypt)
AAMD	Association of Art Museum Directors	**AAMVA**	American Association of Motor Vehicle Administrators
AAME	American Association of Microprocessor Engineers	**AAMW**	American Association of Medical Writers
AAMF	Association Aéromédicale de France	**AAN**	Akademiia Artilleriiskikh Nauk
AAMFT	American Association for Marriage and Family Therapy	**AAN**	American Academy of Neurology
		AAN	American Academy of Nursing
AAMHA	Association Africaine de Microbiologie et d'Hygiène Alimentaire (Tunisia)	**AAN**	American Academy of Nutrition
		AAN	American Association of Neuropathologists
AAMI	Association for the Advancement of Medical Instrumentation (U.S.A.)	**AAN**	American Association of Nurserymen
		AAN	Arkhiv Akademii Nauk
AAMI	Association of Allergists for Mycological Investigations (U.S.A.)	**AAN**	Assemblée de l'Atlantique Nord = NAA
		AAN	Australian Association of Neurologists
AAMMC	American Association of Medical Milk Commissions	**AANA**	American Anorexia Nervosa Association
AAMO	Asian Association of Management Organizations	**AANA**	American Association of Nursing Assistants
AAMOA	Afro-American Music Opportunities Association	**AANA**	Australian Association of National Advertisers
AAMP	American Academy of Maxillofacial Prosthetics	**AANG**	Association des Anciennes Normaliennes de Guinée
AAMP	American Academy of Medical Preventics	**AANII**	Arkticheskii i Antarkticheskii Nauchno-Issledovatelskii Institut
AAMP	American Association of Meat Processors	**AANII**	Arkticheskii i Antrakticheskii Nauchno Issledovatel'skii Institut Glavnogo upravleniia severnogo morskogo puti
AAMPR	American Association of Medico-Physical Research		
AAMR	American Academy on Mental Retardation	**AANO**	Albanian-American National Organisation
AAMRH	Association of Agricultural Medicine and Rural Health	**AANP**	American Association of Neuropathologists
AAMS	American Air Mail Society	**AANS**	American Academy of Neurological Surgery
AAMS	American Association of Meta-Science	**AANS**	American Agricultural News Service
AAMS	Arms, Armour and Militaria Society (Malta)	**AANS**	American Association of Neurological Surgeons
AAMS	Azienda Autónoma dei Monopoli di Stato	**AAO**	Abastumanskaia Astrofizicheskaia Observatoriia
AAMSE	American Association of Medical Society Executives	**AAO**	American Academy of Optometry
		AAO	American Academy of Organ
AAMSI	American Association for Medical Systems and Informatics	**AAO**	American Academy of Osteopathy
		AAO	American Association of Ophthalmology
AAMSU	All Assam Minority Students Union (Indonesia)		
AAMSW	American Association of Medical Social Workers	**AAO**	American Association of Orthodontists

AAO	Anglo-Australian Observatory	**AAP**	Associação dos Arquitectos Portugueses
AAÖ	Arbeitsgemeinschaft der Altphilologen Österreichs	**AAP**	Association des Administrateurs du Personnel de la Fonction Publique (Canada)
AAO	Association for the Advancement of Opthalmology	**AAP**	Association for Applied Psychoanalysis (U.S.A.)
AAOA	American Academy of Otolaryngologic Allergy	**AAP**	Association for the Advancement of Psychoanalysis (U.S.A.)
AAOEC	Afro-Asian Organization for Economic Cooperation	**AAP**	Association for the Advancement of Psychotherapy (U.S.A.)
AAOGAS	American Association of Obstetricians, Gynecologists and Abdominal Surgeons	**AAP**	Association of Academic Physiatrists
AAOGP	American Academy of Orthodontics for the General Practitioner	**AAP**	Association of American Physicians
		AAP	Association of American Publishers
AAOH	Asian Association of Occupational Health (Thailand)	**AAP**	Association of Aviation Psychologists (U.S.A.)
AAOHN	American Association of Occupational Health Nurses	**AAP**	Australasian Association of Philosophy
		AAP	Australian Associated Press
AAOM	American Academy of Occupational Medicine	**AAPA**	Advertising Agency Production Association
AAOM	American Academy of Oral Medicine	**AAPA**	Afro-Asian Philosophy Association
AAOM	American Academy of Orthopaedic Medicine	**AAPA**	American Academy of Physician Assistants
AAOMD	American Association on Mental Deficiency	**AAPA**	American Amateur Press Association
AAOMS	American Association of Oral and Maxillofacial Surgeons	**AAPA**	American Association of Pathologists Assistants
AAOO	American Academy of Ophthalmology and Otolaryngology	**AAPA**	American Association of Physical Anthropologists
AAOP	American Academy of Oral Pathology	**AAPA**	American Association of Port Authorities
AAOP	American Academy of Orthotists and Prosthetists	**AAPA**	American Association of Psychiatric Administrators
AAOS	American Academy of Orthopaedic Surgeons	**AAPA**	Asociación Argentina de Producción Animal
AAOS	American Association of Osteopathic Surgeons	**AAPA**	Asociación Argentina de Productores Agrícolas
AAOT	Australian Association of Occupational Therapists	**AAPA**	Association of Accredited Practitioners in Advertising (South Africa)
AAOU	Asian Association of Open Universities (Republic of Korea)	**AAPA**	Association of Authorised Public Accountants
AAP	Academy of American Poets	**AAPA**	Australian Asphalt Pavement Association
AAP	Albanian Agrarian Party		
AAP	American Academy of Pediatrics	**AAPAM**	African Association for Public Administration and Management
AAP	American Academy of Pedodontics		
AAP	American Academy of Periodontology	**AAPAP**	Anglo-American Press Association of Paris
AAP	American Academy of Psychoanolysis		
AAP	American Academy of Psychotherapists	**AAPC**	American Association of Pastoral Counselors
AAP	American Association of Pathologists		
AAP	American Association of the Professions	**AAPC**	American Association of Political Consultants
AAP	Art Association of the Philippines	**AAPC**	Asociación Argentina para el Progreso de las Ciencias

AAPCC	American Association of Poison Control Centers	**AAPLP**	American Academy of Pro-Life Physicians
AAPCO	Association of American Pesticide Control Officials	**AAPM**	American Association of Physicists in Medicine
AAPD	American Academy of Physiologic Dentistry	**AAPM**	Asian Association of Personnel Management
AAPE	American Academy of Physical Education	**AAPMA**	Association of Australian Port and Marine Authorities
AAPE	American Association for Paralegal Education	**AAPMR**	American Academy of Physical Medicine and Rehabilitation
AAPF	Asociación Argentina de Proteccion Familiar	**AAPNA**	Association of African Physicians in North America
AAPF	Association Algérienne pour la Planification Familiale	**AAPO**	All African Peoples' Organisation
AAPFCO	Association of American Plant Food Control Officials	**AAPO**	American Academy of Podiatry Administration
AAPG	American Association of Petroleum Geologists	**AAPO&S**	American Association for Pediatric Ophthalmology and Strabismus
AAPH	American Association for Partial Hospitalization	**AAPOR**	American Association for Public Opinion Research
AAPH	American Association of Professional Hypnologists	**AAPOS**	American Association for Pediatric Ophthalmology and Strabismus
AAPH	American Association of Professional Hypnotherapists	**AAPP**	American Association of Police Polygraphists
AAPHA-SEAN	Association for Planning and Housing	**AAPRCO**	American Association of Private Railroad Car Owners
AAPHD	American Association of Public Health Dentistry	**AAPRD**	American Academy for Plastics Research in Dentistry
AAPHP	American Association of Public Health Physicians	**AAPRDTW**	Association for the Advancement of Policy, Research and Development in the Third World
AAPHR	American Association of Physicians for Human Rights	**AAPRO**	Asociación Argentina de la Productividad
AAPI	Associazione Aziende Pubblicitarie Italiane	**AAPS**	African Association of Political Science
AAPICU	American Association of Presidents of Independent Colleges and Universities	**AAPS**	American Association for the Promotion of Science
AAPIER	American Association of Public Information, Education and Research	**AAPS**	American Association of Pharmaceutical Scientists
AAPL	Afro-American Police League	**AAPS**	American Association of Phonetic Sciences
AAPL	American Academy of Psychiatry and the Law	**AAPS**	American Association of Plastic Surgeons
AAPL	American Artists Professional League	**AAPS**	Association of American Physicians and Surgeons
AAPL	American Association of Petroleum Landmen	**AAPSC**	Afro-Asian Peoples Solidarity Council = CSPAA
AAPL	Association of Australian Parliamentary Librarians	**AAPSC**	American Association of Psychiatric Services for Children
AAPLE	American Academy for Professional Law Enforcement	**AAPSM**	American Academy of Podiatric Sports Medicine
AAPLOG	American Association of Pro-Life Obstetricians and Gynaecologists	**AAPSO**	Afro-Asian Peoples Solidarity Organisation (Egypt) = OSPAA

AAPSRO	American Association of Professional Standards Review Organisations	**AARO**	Association of Americans Resident Overseas
AAPSS	American Academy of Political and Social Sciences	**AAROI**	Associazione Anestesisti Rianimatori Ospedalieri Italiani
AAPT	American Association of Philosophy Teachers	**AARP**	American Association of Retired Persons
AAPT	American Association of Physics Teachers	**AARPAA**	American Association of Registered Patent Attorneys and Agents
AAPT	Association of Asphalt Paving Technologists (U.S.A.)	**AARRO**	Afro-Asian Rural Reconstruction Organisation = OASRR
AAPTS&R	Australian Association for Predetermined Time Standards and Research	**AARS**	American Association of Railway Superintendents
AAPWT	American Association of Public Welfare Attorneys	**AARS**	American Association of Railway Surgeons
AAPY	American Association of Professors of Yiddish	**AARS**	Asian Association on Remote Sensing (Japan)
AAR	American Academy of Religion	**AARS**	Association of American Rhodes Scholars
AAR	American Association of Rabbis	**AART**	Action Against Racism in Training
AAR	Artists Against Racism	**AART**	American Association for Rehabilitation Therapy
AAR	ASEAN Association of Radiologists		
AAR	Association Anakany Amin-Dreny (Madagascar)	**AART**	American Association for Respiratory Therapy
AAR	Association of American Railroads	**AART**	American Association of Religious Therapists
AARA	American Amateur Racquetball Association	**AARU**	Agricultural Aviation Research Unit
AARC	American-Arab Relations Committee	**AARU**	Association of Arab Universities = AUA
AARC	Asociación de Agricultores del Rio Caulicán (Mexico)	**AARZH**	Alians Amerikanskikh i Russkikh Zhenshchin
AARD	American Academy of Restorative Dentistry	**AAS**	Academy of Applied Science (U.S.A.)
AARDÉS	Association Algérienne pour la Recherche Démographique Économique et Sociale	**AAS**	African Academy of Sciences
		AAS	American Academy of Sanitarians
		AAS	American Amaryllis Society
AARDS	Australian Advertising Rate and Data Service	**AAS**	American Antiquarian Society
		AAS	American Association of Suicidology
AARF	Australian Accounting Research Foundation	**AAS**	American Astronautical Society
		AAS	American Astronomical Society
AARG	Aerial Archaeology Research Group	**AAS**	Ancient Astronaut Society (U.S.A.)
AARG	Association of Artist-Run Galleries (U.S.A.)	**AAS**	Archaeology Abroad Service
		AAS	Architectural Acoustics Society (U.S.A.)
AARHMS	American Academy of Research Historians of Medieval Spain	**AAS**	Association des Archivistes Suisses = VSA
AARINENA	Association of Agricultural Research Institutes in the Near East and North Africa	**AAS**	Association for Archery in Schools
		AAS	Association for Asian Studies (U.S.A.)
AARM	Association of Aquatic and Recreation Management	**AAS**	Association of Architects and Surveyors
		AAS	Australian Academy of Science
AARNet	Australian Academic and Research Network	**AAS**	Australian Acoustical Society

AAS	Austrian Academy of Sciences = OeAW	**AASHTO**	American Association of State Highway and Transportation Officials
AASA	Academy of the Arts and Sciences of the Americas	**AASIR**	Afro-American Society for International Relations
AASA	African Association for the Study of the Americas	**AASL**	American Association of School Librarians
AASA	Afro-American Student Association	**AASLD**	American Association for the Study of Liver Diseases
AASA	American Association of School Administrators	**AASLH**	American Association for State and Local History
AASA	Australian Association of Social Anthropologists	**AASM**	Association of American Steel Manufacturers
AASANA	Administración de Aeropuertos y Servicios Auxiliares a la Navegación (Bolivia)	**AASM**	Association of Aviation and Space Museologists
AASC	American Association of Small Cities	**AASND**	American Association for Study of Neoplastic Diseases
AASC	American Association of Specialized Colleges	**AASNS**	Asian-Australasian Society of Neurological Surgeons
AASC	American Association of State Climatologists	**AASP**	American Academy of Sports Physicians
AASC	Anglo-American Sporting Club	**AASP**	American Association of Senior Physicians
AASC	Association for the Advancement of Science in Canada	**AASP**	American Association of Social Psychiatry
AASC	Australian Accounting Standards Committee	**AASP**	American Association of Stratigraphic Palynologists
AASCO	Association of American Seed Control Officials	**AASP**	American Association of Swine Practitioners
AASCU	American Association of State Colleges and Universities	**AASP**	Association Arabe de Science Politique (Iraq)
AASD	American Academy of Stress Disorders	**AASP**	Association d'Agences Suisses de Publicité
AASDJ	American Association of Schools and Departments of Journalism	**AASP**	Association for the Advancement of Sports Potential
AASE	African Association of Science Editors	**AASR**	Asociatia Asistentilor Sociali din România
AASE	American Academy of Safety Education	**AASR**	Australian Association for the Study of Religions
AASE	American Association of Special Educators	**AASRC**	American Association of Small Research Companies (U.S.A.)
AASE	Australian Associated Stock Exchanges	**AASRI**	Arctic Antarctic Scientific Research Institute
AASECT	American Association of Sex Educators Counselors and Therapists	**AASS**	American Association for Social Security
AASF	Association des Architectes sans Frontières	**AASS**	Association Africaine de la Science du Sol = ASSA
AASG	Association of American State Geologists	**AASSC**	Association for the Advancement of Scandinavian Studies in Canada = AAESC
AASGP	American Association of Sheep and Goat Practitioners	**AASSREC**	Association of Asian Social Science Research Councils (India)
AASH	Australian Association of Speech and Hearing		
AASHFA	Association des Amis du Service Historique Forces Armées		
AASHG	Association of Assistant Secretaries and Higher Grades (Éire)		

AAST	American Association for the Surgery of Trauma	**AATRAA**	Association Argentina de Tecnicos de Refrigeración y Acondiciónamiento de Aire
AASU	All-Africa Students Union (Tanzania)	**AATS**	American Academy of Teachers of Singing
AASW	American Association of Scientific Workers	**AATS**	American Association for Thoracic Surgery
AASz	1956-os Antifasiszta és Antibolseviszta Szözvetség (Hungary) = AAA	**AATS**	American Association of Theological Schools
AAT	Administration de l'Assistance Technique (PNUD) = TAA	**AATS**	Australian Academy of Technological Sciences
AAT	American Academy of Thermology	**AATSE**	Australian Academy of Technological Science and Engineering
AAT	American Academy of Transportation	**AATSEEL**	American Association of Teachers of Slavic and East European Languages
AAT	Association of Accounting Technicians	**AATSP**	American Association of Teachers of Spanish and Portuguese
AATA	American Art Therapy Association	**AATT**	American Association for Textile Technology
AATA	American Association of Teachers of Arabic		
AATA	American Automobile Touring Alliance	**AATTA**	Arab Association of Tourism and Travel Agents
AATA	Anglo-American Tourist Association	**AATUF**	All-African Trade Union Federation
AATA	Animal Transport Association	**AAU**	Amateur Athletic Union (Éire, U.S.A.)
AATA	Association of African Tax Administrators	**AAU**	Armenian Artistic Union (Egypt)
AATB	American Association for Tissue Banks	**AAU**	Association of African Universities = AUA
AATCA	Austrian Air Traffic Controllers Association	**AAU**	Association of American Universities
AATCC	American Association of Textile Chemists and Colorists	**AAUA**	American Association of University Administrators
AATE	American Association of Teachers of Esperanto	**AAUL**	Atlantic Association of University Libraries
AATEA	American Association of Teacher Educators in Agriculture	**AAUOS**	Australian-Asian Universities Cooperation Scheme
AATF	American Association of Teachers of French	**AAUP**	American Association of University Professors
AATFS	Asian Association of Track and Field Statistics	**AAUP**	Association of American University Presses
AATG	American Association of Teachers of German	**AAUTA**	Australian Association of University Teachers of Accountancy
AATI	American Association of Teachers of Italian	**AAUW**	American Association of University Women
AATM	American Academy of Tropical Medicine	**AAV**	Association of American Vintners
AATNU	Administration de l'Assistance Technique des Nations Unies	**AAV**	Association of Avian Veterinarians (U.S.A.)
AATO	All Africa Teachers Organization = OPAPÉ	**AAV**	Nederlandse Vereniging van Algemene Aansprakelijkheids-Verzekeraars
AATP	American Academy of Tuberculosis Physicians	**AAVA**	American Association of Veterinary Anatomists
AATP	Arusha Appropriate Technology Project (Tanzania)		
AATPO	Association of African Trade Promotion Organizations = AOAPC	**AAVCC**	Australian Agricultural and Veterinary Chemicals Council

AAVD	American Academy of Veterinary Dermatology	**AAWU**	Afro-Asian Writers Union
AAVIM	American Association for Vocational Instructional Materials	**AAWU**	American Association of Wildlife Veterinarians
AAVLD	American Association of Veterinary Laboratory Diagnosticians	**AAYM**	American Association of Youth Museums
AAVMC	Association of American Veterinary Medical Colleges	**AAYPL**	Atlantic Association of Young Political Leaders
AAVN	American Association of Veterinary Nutrition	**AAYSO**	Afro-Asian Youth Solidarity Organisation
AAVP	American Association of Veterinary Parasitologists	**AAZK**	American Association of Zoo Keepers
AAVP	Association of American Volunteer Physicians	**AAZN**	American Association for Zoological Nomenclature
AAVPT	American Association of Veterinary Pharmacology and Therapeutics	**AAZPA**	American Association of Zoological Parks and Aquariums
AAVRPHS	American Association for Vital Records and Public Health Statistics	**AAZV**	American Association of Zoo Veterinarians
AAVS	Aroha Adivasis Vikas Sangh (India)	**AB**	Alpýdubandalag = PA
AAVSB	American Association of Veterinary State Boards	**AB**	Association of Bankrupts
AAVSO	American Association of Variable Star Observers	**AB**	Vereeniging der Antwerpsche Bibliophielen (Belgium)
AAVT	Association of Audio-Visual Technicians (U.S.A.)	**ABA**	Amateur Boxing Association
		ABA	American Bakers Association
AAVV	Autorité des Aménagements des Vallées des Voltas (Burkina Faso)	**ABA**	American Bankers Association
		ABA	American Bar Association
AAVYT	Asociación Argentina de Agencias de Viajes y Turismo	**ABA**	American Billiard Association
		ABA	American Birding Association
AAW	American Atheist Women	**ABA**	American Board of Anesthesiology
AAW	Athletics Association of Wales	**ABA**	American Booksellers Association
AAWA	Afro-Asian Writers' Association	**ABA**	American Bridge Association
AAWB	American Association of Workers for the Blind	**ABA**	Antiquarian Booksellers Association
		ABA	Arbeitsgemeinschaft für Betriebliche Alters-versorgung
AAWC	American Association of Workers for Children	**ABA**	ASEAN Bankers Association
AAWD	American Association of Women Dentists	**ABA**	Asian Bankers Association (Taiwan)
		ABA	Associação Brasileira de Antropologia
AAWE	Association of American Wives of Europeans	**ABA**	Association Belge des Aérosols
		ABA	Association of British Archaeologists
AAWH	American Association for World Health	**ABA**	Australian Biotechnology Association
AAWO	Association of Accommodation and Welfare Officers	**ABA**	Australian Booksellers Association
		ABA International	Association for Behavior Analysis International (U.S.A.)
AAWORD	Association of African Women for Research on Development = AFARD	**ABAA**	Antiquarian Booksellers Association of America
AAWP	American Association for Women Podiatrists	**ABAA**	Association of British Adoption Agencies
AAWPI	Association of American Wood Pulp Importers	**ABAA**	Association of Business Advertising Agencies

ABAC	Antiquarian Booksellers Association of Canada
ABAC	Association of British Aero Clubs
ABAC	Association of British Aviation Consultants (*now* BAAC)
ABAC	Association of Business and Administrative Computing
ABACC	Alcoholic Beverages Advertising Code Council (Australia)
ABACUS	Association of Bibliographic Agencies of Britain, Australia, Canada and the United States
ABADCAM	Association des Bibliothécaires, Archivistes, Documentalistes et Muséographers du Caméroun
ABAH	Asociación de Bibliotecarios y Archiveros de Honduras
ABAH	Australian Bureau of Animal Health
ABAI	American Board of Allergy and Immunology
ABAJP	Association Belge des Architectes de Jardins Publics = BVTL
ABAM	Association Belge des Assureurs Maritimes
ABAN	Algemene Bond van Autorijsschoolhouders in Nederland
ABANSA	Asociación de Banqueros de El Salvador
ABAO	Association des Banques de l'Afrique de l'Ouest (Sierra Leone) = WABA
ABAO	Association of British Abattoir Owners
ABAP	Associação Brasileira de Agencias de Propaganda
ABAPE	Associação Brasileira de Administração de Pessoal
ABAPRA	Asociación de Bancos de Provincia de la República Argentina
ABAPSTAS	Association of Blind and Partially Sighted Teachers and Students
ABARE	Australian Bureau of Agricultural and Resource Economics
ABARES	Australian Bureau of Agricultural and Resources Sciences
ABAS	Amateur Basketball Association of Scotland
ABAS	American Board of Abdominal Surgery
ABAS	Association of Business Administration Studies
ABASS	Assembly for Behavioral and Social Sciences (NRC) (U.S.A.)
ABAZ	Amateur Boxing Association of Zambia
ABB	Arbeitsgemeinschaft für Blitzschutz und Blitzableiterbau
ABB	Asociación Boliviana de Bibliotecarios
ABB	Association Belge des Banques = BVB
ABB	Association of Bloodhound Breeders
ABBA	Amateur Basket Ball Association
ABBA	American Bee Breeders Association
ABBA	Asociación de Bibliotecas Biomédicas Argentinas
ABBA	Association Belge des Brûleurs Automatiques
ABBC	Association of Bottled Beer Collectors
ABBE	Advisory Board on the Built Environment (NRC) (U.S.A.)
ABBF	Asian Bodybuilding Federation (Singapore)
ABBF	Association of Bronze and Brass Founders
ABBIM	Association of Brass and Bronze Ingot Manufacturers (U.S.A.)
ABBL	Association des Banques et Banquiers Luxembourg
ABBMM	Association of British Brush Machinery Manufacturers
ABBPR	Asociatia Bibliotecarilor din Bibliotecile Publice din România
ABBRA	American Boat Builders and Repairers Association
ABBS	Antigua and Barbuda Broadcasting Service
ABC	Academia Brasileira de Ciencias
ABC	Active Birth Centre
ABC	Africa Bibliographic Centre (Tanzania)
ABC	African Books Collective
ABC	African Boxing Confederation (Nigeria)
ABC	Agricultural Bank of China
ABC	American Bibliographical Center
ABC	American Blood Commission
ABC	American Broadcasting Company
ABC	Anarchist Black Cross
ABC	Anti-Bases Coalition (Philippines)
ABC	Antiquarian Booksellers Center (U.S.A.)
ABC	Arab Banking Corporation
ABC	ASEAN Brussels Committee
ABC	Asian Badminton Confederation
ABC	Asian Basketball Confederation

ABC	Asian Benevolent Corps (U.S.A.)	ABCD	Association of British Choral Directors
ABC	Associação Brasileira de Criadores	ABCD	Förbundet for Art, Bild, Copy och Design
ABC	Associación de Bibliotecarios de Catalunya	ABCEBLF	Australian Building Construction Employees' and Builders' Labourers' Federation
ABC	Association des Banquiers Canadiens = CBA	ABCH	American Boards of Clinical Hypnosis
ABC	Association of Biotechnology Companies (U.S.A.)	ABCHI	Association of British Health-Care Industries
ABC	Association of British Climatologists	ABCI	Amis Belges de la Coopération Internationale
ABC	Association of British Counties		
ABC	Association of British Parking Enforcement Companies	ABCIA	American Board of Clinical Immunology and Allergy
ABC	Association of Building Centres	ABCL	Association of British Container Lessors
ABC	Association of Business Centres	ABCM	Association of Building Component Manufacturers
ABC	Association of Business Communicators		
ABC	Audit Bureau of Circulations (Australia, India, South Africa, U.K., U.S.A.)	ABCN	Association of British Clinical Neurophysiologists
ABC	Australian Broadcasting Commission	ABCO	Association of British Conference Organisers
ABCA	American Building Contractors Association	ABCOC	Advance Booking Charter Operators Council
ABCA	American Business Communication Association	ABCOOP	Aliança Brasileira de Cooperativas
ABCA	Association Belge des Chefs d'Approvisionnement et Acheteurs	ABCP	Asian Buddhist Conference for Peace
ABCA	Association des Banques Centrales Africaines = AACB	ABCP	Associação Técnica Brasileira de Celulose e Papel
ABCA	Association of British Circus Artistes	ABCP	Association of Butter and Cheese Packers
ABCAR	Asociación Brasilena de Crédito y Asistensia Rural	ABCPA	Alberta Beef Cattle Performance Association (Canada)
ABCAT	Association of British Cutlers & Allied Trades	ABCPO	Association of British Professional Conference Organisers
ABCB	American Board of Clinical Biofeedback	ABCRP	Association Belge des Conseils en Relations Publiques
ABCB	Association of British Consortium Banks	ABCRS	American Board of Colon and Rectal Surgery
ABCC	American Board of Clinical Chemistry	ABCS	Association of British Chick Sexers
ABCC	Argentine-British Chamber of Commerce	ABCT	Association Belgo-Zaïroise du Textile
ABCC	Association of British Chambers of Commerce	ABCUL	Association of British Credit Unions Ltd.
		ABD	American Board of Dermatology
ABCC	Association of British Correspondence Colleges	ABD	Association Belge de Documentation = BVD
ABCC	Australian British Chamber of Commerce	ABD	Association Belge des Detectives
ABCD	Arab Board for Child and Development (Egypt) = ACCD	ABD	Association Belge du Diabète
ABCD	Association Belge de la Chaussure au Détail	ABD	Association of British Detectives
		ABD	Association of British Drivers
ABCD	Association for Bridge Construction and Design	ABDA	Arbeitsgemeinschaft der Berufsvertretungen Deutscher Apotheker

ABDI	Asociação Brasileira de Desenho Industrial	**ABEP**	Associação Brasileira de Estudos Populacionais
ABDIB	Asociação Brasileira para o Desenvolvimento das Industrias de Base	**ABEPAS**	Association Belge des Entreprises de Produits Alimentaires Surgelés
ABDO	Association of British Dispensing Opticians	**ABERT**	Associação Brasileira de Emissoras de Rádio e Televisão
ABDOSD	Arbeitsgemeinschaft der Bibliotheken und Dokumentationsstellen der Osteuropa-, Sudosteuropa- und DDR-Forschung (*now* ABDOS)	**ABES**	Asociación de Bibliotecarios de El Salvador
		ABES	Association for Broadcast Engineering Standards
ABDP	Association of British Directory Publishers	**ABES**	Australian Biological and Environmental Survey (ABRS, ERIN)
ABDPH	American Board of Dental Public Health	**ABESAO**	Association des Bibliothèques de l'Enseignement Supérieur de l'Afrique de l'Ouest Francophone
ABDR	Association Belge de Droit Rural		
ABDSA	Association of British Dental Surgery Assistants	**ABET**	Accreditation Board for Engineering and Technology (U.S.A.)
ABE	Asociação Brasileira de Exportadores	**ABET**	Advisory Board on Educational Technology
ABE	Association Bancaire pour l'ECU = EBA	**ABET**	Asociación Boliviana de Empresas Telefónicas
ABÉ	Association Belge de l'Éclairage	**ABETA**	Associação Brasileira de Estudos Técnicos de Agricultura
ABE	Association of British Editors		
ABE	Association of Building Engineers	**ABEX**	Association Belge des Experts
ABE	Association of Business Executives	**ABF**	Aerosolindustriens Brancheforening
ABEA	American Broncho-Esophagological Association	**ABF**	American Bar Foundation
		ABF	American Beekeeping Federation
ABEAS	Associação Brasileira de Educação Agricola Superior	**ABF**	Arbetarnas Bildningsförbund
		ABF	Army Benevolent Fund
ABEAS	Association Belge des Entreprises d'Alimentation à Succursales	**ABF**	Asian Baptist Federation
		ABF	Association Bois de Feu
ABEBD	Associação Brasileira de Escolas de Biblioteconomia e Documentação	**ABF**	Association des Bibliothécaires Français
		ABF	Association of British Factors
ABEC	Asociación Boliviana de Educación Catolica	**ABF**	Den Danske Antikvarboghandlerforening
ABECAFE	Asociación Salvadoreña de Beneficiadores y Exportadores de Café	**ABFACD**	Association Belge des Fabricants d'Appareils de Chauffage et de Cuisine Domestiques
ABECE	Associação Brasileira das Empresas Comerciais Exportadoras		
		ABFCFC	Association Belge des Filateurs de Coton et de Fibres Connexes
ABEDA	Arab Bank for Economic Development in Africa = BADEA	**ABFD**	Association of British Factors and Discounters
ABÉF	Association des Bibliothèques Écclésiastiques de France		
		ABFL	Association of British Foam Laminators
ABEGS	Arab Bureau of Education for the Gulf States	**ABFLO**	Association of Bedding and Furniture Law Officials (U.S.A.)
ABÉLF	Association Belge des Éditeurs de Langue Française	**ABFM**	American Board of Foreign Missions
ABÉM	Association Belge pour l'Étude, l'Essai et l'Emploi des Matériaux = BVSM	**ABFP**	American Board of Forensic Psychology
ABEMI	Associação Brasileira de Engenharia Industrial	**ABFSE**	American Board of Funeral Service Education

ABG	Associazione Italiana fra gli Industriali delle Acque e Bevande Gassate
ABGBI	Associated Booksellers of Great Britain and Ireland
ABGRA	Asociación de Bibliotecarios Graduados de la República Argentina
ABGSM	Association of British Generating Set Manufacturers (*now* AMPS)
ABGW	Aluminum, Brick and Glass Workers International Union (U.S.A.)
ABH	Association Belge des Hôpitaux = BVZ
ABH	Association for the Bibliography of History (U.S.A.)
ABH	Association of British Hairdressers
ABH	Association of Hispanists of Great Britain and Ireland
ABHC	Association of Bank Holding Companies (U.S.A.)
ABHI	Association of British Health Care Industries
ABHM	Association of Builders Hardware Manufacturers
ABHP	American Board of Health Physics
ABI	Akademickie Biuro Interwencji
ABI	American Butter Institute
ABI	Arnold Bergstraesser Institut für Kulturwissenschaftliche Forschung
ABI	Asociación de Bienestar Infantil (Guatemala)
ABI	Associação Brasiliera de Imprensa
ABI	Association des Bibliothèques Internationales
ABI	Association of British Insurers
ABI	Association of British Investigators
ABI	Associazione Bancaria Italiana
ABIA	Associação Brasileira das Industrias da Alimentação
ABIA	Association of British Introduction Agencies
ABIC	Association Belge d'Ingénieurs-Conseils et Experts = ABRI
ABIC	Association Belge de l'Industrie du Caoutchouc
ABICIT	Association Belge d'Ingénieurs-Conseils Diplomés Ingénieurs Techniciens
ABICTIC	Association Belge des Ingénieurs, des Chimistes et des Techniciens des Industries du Cuir
ABIEAS	Asociación Boliviana de Instituciones de Educación Agrícola Superior

ABIESI	Asociación de Bibiliotecarios de Institucions de Enseñanza Superior e Investigación (Mexico)
Abifarma	Associação Brasileira das Indústrias Farmacêuticas
ABIFT	Arab Bank for Investment in Foreign Trade
ABIH	American Board of Industrial Hygiene
ABIH	Association of British and International Hairdressers and Hairdressing Schools
ABIISE	Agrupación de Bibliotecas para la Integración de la Información Socio-Económica (Peru)
ABIM	American Board of Internal Medicine
ABIM	American Board of International Missions
ABIM	Association of British Insecticide Manufacturers
ABIOEC	Association of British Independent Oil Exploration Companies
ABIPAR	Asociación de Bibliotecarios del Paraguay
ABIR	Associação Brasileira de Informação Rural
ABIRA	Asociación de Bancos del Interior de la República Argentina
ABIS	Association of Burglary Insurance Surveyors
ABITA	Association Belge des Ingénieurs et Technicians de l'Aéronautique et de l'Astronautique
ABJ	Association of Brewers of Japan
ABJA	Association Belge des Journalistes Agricoles = BVLJ
ABJPAA	Association Belge des Journalistes Professionnels de l'Aéronautique et de l'Astronautique
ABJS	Association of Bone and Joint Surgeons (U.S.A.)
ABL	Associação Brasileira da Listas Telefónicas
ABL	Association Belge des Logopèdes
ABLA	Abortion Law Reform Association
ABLA	American Business Law Association
ABLA	Association Belge de Linguistique Appliquée = BVTL
ABLE	Action for Better Limb Engineering
ABLE	Association for Biology Laboratory Education (U.S.A.)
ABLGPL	Association Belgo-Luxembourgeoise des Gaz de Pétrole Liquéfies

ABLS	American Bryological and Lichenological Society	**ABN**	Association of British Neurologists
ABM	Asociación de Bancos de Mexico	**ABN**	Australian Bibliographic Network
ABM	Associação Brasileira de Matais	**ABNA**	Anorexia Bulimia Nervosa Association
ABM	Association Belge du Moulinage	**ABNEI**	Association Belge des Négociants Exportateurs et Importateurs
ABM	Association of Banks in Malaysia	**ABNM**	American Board of Nuclear Medicine
ABM	Association of Board Makers	**ABNOMS**	American Board of Neurological and Orthopaedic Medicine and Surgery
ABM	Association of Breastfeeding Mothers		
ABM	Association of British Maltsters	**ABNS**	American Board of Neurological Surgery
ABM	Association of British Music		
ABM	Association of Button Merchants	**ABNT**	Associação Brasiliera de Normas Técnicas
ABM	Australian Board of Missions		
ABMA	American Boiler Manufacturers Association	**ABO**	American Board of Ophthalmology
		ABO	American Board of Opticianry
ABMA	American Brush Manufacturers Association	**ABO**	American Board of Orthodontics
		ABO	American Board of Otolaryngology
ABMAC	American Bureau for Medical Advancement in China	**ABO**	Associação Brasileira de Odontologia
		ABO	Association of British Orchestras
ABMEC	Association of British Mining Equipment Companies	**ABO**	Association of British Orientalists
		ABOCF	Association of British Organic and Compound Fertilisers
ABMG	American Board of Medical Genetics		
ABMIT	Association Belgo-Méditerranéenne de Lutte contra la Thalassemie	**ABOCOL**	Abonos Colombianos S.A.
		ABOG	American Board of Obstetrics and Gynecology
ABMM	American Board of Medical Microbiology		
		ABOI	Association of British Offshore Industries
ABMP	Association Belge des Matières Plastiques		
		ABOMS	American Board of Oral and Maxillofacial Surgery
ABMP	Association of British Meat Processors		
ABMPCAE	Association of British Manufacturers of Photographic, Cine & Audio Equipment	**ABOP**	Algemene Bond van Onderwijzend Personeel
		ABOS	American Board of Orthopaedic Surgery
ABMPM	Association of British Manufacturers of Printers Machinery		
ABMRC	Association of British Market Research Companies	**ABP**	Agence Burundaise de Presse
		ABP	American Board of Pathology
ABMS	American Board of Medical Specialities	**ABP**	American Board of Pediatrics
ABMS	American Bureau of Metal Statistics	**ABP**	American Board of Pedodontics
ABMS	Associação Brasileira de Mecanica dos Solos	**ABP**	American Board of Periodontology
		ABP	American Board of Prosthodontics
		ABP	American Business Press
ABMSAC	Association of British Mountaineering Societies and Climbers	**ABP**	Arbeitgeberverband Bayerischer Papierfabriken
ABMT	American Board of Medical Toxicology		
ABN	African Biosciences Network (Senegal) = RAB	**ABP**	Asociación Bancaria de Panamá
		ABP	Association Belge des Paralysés
ABN	Algemene Bank Nederland	**ABP**	Ausschuss für Entwicklungsbezogene Bildung und Publizistik
ABN	Algemene Nederlandse Bond van Natuursteen-bewerkende Bedrijven		
		ABPA	Acoustical and Board Products Association (U.S.A.)
ABN	American Board of Nutrition		
ABN	Arbeitsgemeinschaft Beruflicher und Ehrenamtlicher Naturschutz	**ABPA**	Australian Book Publishers Association

ABPC	Associated British Picture Corporation	**ABR**	Association Belge de Radioprotection = BVS
ABPC	Association Belge de Photographie et de Cinématographie	**ABR**	Association for Biomedical Research (U.S.A.)
ABPC	Association of British Packing Contractors	**ABRA**	American Blood Resources Association
ABPC	Association of British Pewter Craftsmen	**ABRA**	Asociação Brasileira de Reforma Agraria
ABPCO	Association of British Professional Conference Organisers	**ABRA**	Asociación de Bancos de la República Argentina
ABPD	American Board of Podiatric Dermatology	**ABRACE**	Associação Brasileira de Computadores Electronicos
ABPE	Association Belgo-Luxembourgeoise de la Presse d'Entreprise	**ABRACO**	Associação Brasileira de Corrosão
ABPF	Association Beninoise pour la Promotion de la Famille	**ABRALIN**	Associação Brasileira de Lingüística
ABPHEF	Association Belge des Professeurs d'Histoire d'Expression Française	**ABRAM**	Associação Brasileira de Emprezas de Apoio Maritimo
ABPI	Association of the British Pharmaceutical Industry	**ABRAMO**	Associação Brasileira dos Mineradores de Ouro
ABPIS	Association of Book Publishers of the Independent States	**ABRAPEC**	Associação Brasileira de Orientação Agro Pecuária
ABPLA	American Board of Professional Liability Attorneys	**ABRAVA**	Associação Brasileira de Refrigeração, Aer-Condicionado, Ventilação e Aquecimento
ABPM	American Board of Preventive Medicine	**ABRC**	Association of British Research Councils
ABPMM	Association of British Preserved Milk Manufacturers	**ABRD**	Advisory Board for Redundant Churches
ABPMR	American Board of Physical Medicine and Rehabilitation	**ABRECSA**	Association of Black Reformed Christians in South Africa
ABPN	American Board of Psychiatry and Neurology	**ABREMIN**	Associação Brasileira de Entidades de Mineração
ABPN	Association of British Paediatric Nurses	**ABRF**	Association of Biomolecular Resource Facilities
ABPNL	Association Belge des Pilotes et Navigateurs de Ligne	**ABRFM**	Association of British Roofing Felt Manufacturers
ABPO	American Board of Podiatric Orthopedics	**ABRI**	Associatie van Belgische Raadgevende Ingenieurs en Experten = ABIC
ABPP	American Board of Professional Psychology	**ABRI**	Association Bretonne des Relais et Itinéraires
ABPR	Asociación de Bibliotecarios en Puerto Rica	**ABRO**	Army Base Repair Organization
ABPR	Association of British Picture Restorers	**ABRP**	Advisory Board on Restricted Patents
ABPS	American Board of Plastic Surgery	**ABRRM**	Association of British Reclaimed Rubber Manufacturers
ABPS	American Board of Podiatric Surgery	**ABRS**	Association of British Riding Schools
ABPS	Association of British Philatelic Societies	**ABRSAC**	Australian Biological Resources Study Advisory Council
ABPSA	Antigua and Barbuda Public Service Association	**ABS**	American Bible Society
ABPT	Association of Blind Piano Tuners	**ABS**	American Biological Society
ABPVM	Association of British Plywood and Veneer Manufacturers	**ABS**	American Board of Surgery
ABQ	Associação Brasileira de Quimica	**ABS**	American Bureau of Shipping
ABR	American Board of Radiology	**ABS**	American Burn Society

ABS	Anglo-Belgian Society	ABT	American Board of Trade
ABS	Animal Behavior Society (U.S.A.)	ABT	Arbeitstelle für Bibliothekstechnik
ABS	Architects' Benevolent Society	ABT	Association for Analytic and Bodymind Therapy and Training
ABS	ASEAN Banking Council		
ABS	Association des Bibliothécaires Suisses = VSB	ABT	Association of Banking Teachers
		ABT	Association of Beauty Teachers
ABS	Association of British Sailmakers	ABT	Association of Building Technicians
ABS	Association of British Spectroscopists	ABT	Australian Broadcasting Tribunal
ABS	Association of Business Schools	ABTA	Allied Brewery Traders Association
ABS	Auckland Botanical Society (New Zealand)	ABTA	Association of British Travel Agents
		ABTA	Australian Broadcasting Tribunal
ABS	Australian Bat Society	ABTAC	Australian Book Trade Advisory Committee
ABS	Australian Bureau of Statistics		
ABSA	African Baseball and Softball Association (Nigeria)	ABTAPL	Association of British Theological and Philosophical Libraries
ABSA	Associated Booksellers of Southern Africa	ABTCM	Association of British Textured Coating Manufacturers
ABSA	Association for Business Sponsorship of the Arts	ABTI	Association Bois Tropical Ivoirien
ABSA	Association of British Secretaries in America	ABTIR	Association des Bibliothéques de Théologie et d'Information Réligieuse
ABSAED	Association Belge des Secteurs de Alimentes de l'Enfance et Diététiques	ABTL	Association Belge des Technologues de Laboratoire = BVLT
ABSAM	Association of British Solid Fuel Appliance Manufacturers	ABTM	American Board of Tropical Medicine
ABSEL	Association for Business Simulation and Experimental Learning (U.S.A.)	ABTM	Association of British Transport Museums
ABSFAM	Association of British Solid Fuel Appliance Manufacturers	ABTR	Association for Brain Tumor Research (U.S.A.)
ABSFCE	Association of British Salted Fish Curers and Exporters	ABTS	American Board of Thoracic Surgery
ABSI	Association of the Boot and Shoe Industry	ABTT	Association of British Theatre Technicians
ABSM	Association of British Sterilizer Manufacturers	ABTUC	All-Burma Trade Union Congress
		ABU	Agrupación Bibliotecologica del Uruguay
ABSO	Association of British Security Officers	ABU	Algemene Bond Uitzendbureaus
ABSTD	Association of Basic Science Teachers in Dentistry	ABU	All-Bulgarian Union = OBS
ABSTECH	American Bureau of Shipping Worldwide Technical Services	ABU	Alliance Biblique Universelle = SBU, UBS, WBG
ABSTI	Advisory Board on Scientific and Technical Information (Canada)	ABU	American Board of Urology
ABSU	All Assam Bodo Students Union (India)	ABU	Asia Pacific Broadcasting Union
ABSU	Arab States Broadcasting Union (Egypt)	ABU	Asociación de Bibliotecarios del Uruguay
		ABU	Association des Bibliophiles Universels
ABSW	Association of British Science Writers	ABUEN	Asociación de Bibliotecas Universitarias y Especializadas de Nicaragua
ABSWAP	Association of Black Social Workers and Allied Professions		
ABSyM	Asociation Belge des Syndicates Médicaux = BVAS	ABURBEF	Cameroon National Association for Family Welfare
		ABV	Algemeen Belgisch Vlasverbond

ABVA	Association of British Veterinary Acupuncture	**ACA**	American Chiropractic Association
ABVMI	Suore Ancelle di Beata Vergine Maria Immacolata = SSMI	**ACA**	American College of Allergists
		ACA	American College of Anesthesiologists
ABVS	Advisory Board on Veterinary Specialities (U.S.A.)	**ACA**	American College of Angiology
		ACA	American College of Apothecaries
ABVT	American Board on Veterinary Toxicology	**ACA**	American Communications Association
		ACA	American Composers Alliance
ABVV	Algemeen Belgisch Vakverbond	**ACA**	American Correctional Association
ABWA	American Business Women's Association	**ACA**	American Council for the Arts
		ACA	American Council on Alcoholism
ABWA	Associated Business Writers of America	**ACA**	American Cryptogram Association
ABWAK	Association of British Wild Animal Keepers	**ACA**	American Crystallographic Association
		ACA	Anglers Cooperative Association
ABWARC	Australian Baptist World Aid and Relief Committee	**ACA**	Architectural Cladding Association
		ACA	ASEAN Contractors Organization
ABWE	Association of Baptists for World Evangelism (U.S.A.)	**ACA**	Asian Christian Association
		ACA	Asociación Centro-americana de Anatomia
ABYA	Association of Brokers and Yacht Agents	**ACA**	Asociación Colombiana de Apicultores
ABYC	American Boat and Yacht Council	**ACA**	Associação Civica Angolana
ABYDAP	Asociación de Bibliotecarios y Documentalistas Agricolas del Perú	**ACA**	Associated Chiropodists of America
		ACA	Association Canadienne d'Archaeologie = CAA
ABZ	Association of British Zoologists		
AC	Advertising Council (U.S.A.)	**ACA**	Association Canadienne d'Athlétisme
AC	Affärsarbetsgivarnas Centralförbund	**ACA**	Association Canadienne de l'Acoustique
AC	Akademikernes Centralorganisation		
AC	Alpine Club	**ACA**	Association des Compagnies d'Assurances agréés au Grand-Duché de Luxembourg
AC	Alpine Convention		
AC&R	American Cable and Radio Corporation		
		ACA	Association for Continence Advice
ACA	Accreditation Council for Accountancy (U.S.A.)	**ACA**	Association of Canadian Advertisers
		ACA	Association of Canadian Archivists
ACA	Acoustic Corporation of America	**ACA**	Association of Consultant Architects
ACA	Advertisement Contractors Association	**ACA**	Association of Consulting Actuaries
ACA	Advisory Committee on Advertising	**ACA**	Association of County Archivists
ACA	Afro-Caribbean Association	**ACA**	Asthma Care Association of America
ACA	Agence Camérounaise d'Assurances	**ACA**	Australian Coal Association
ACA	Agence Centrafricaine d'Assurances	**ACA**	Australian Consumers Association
ACA	Agence Congolaise d'Assurances	**ACA**	Australian Corrosion Association
ACA	Agricultural Computer Association (U.S.A.)	**ACA**	Australian Council for Aeronautics
		ACAA	Asian Christian Art Association
ACA	Agricultural Credit Administration (Philippines)	**ACAAI**	Air Cargo Agents Association of India
		ACABEF	Association Centrafricaine pour la Bien-Être
ACA	Agriculture Council of America		
ACA	Air Crews Association (Russia)	**ACABQ**	Advisory Committee on Administrative and Budgetary Questions (UN) = CCQAB
ACA	Aircrewmen Association		
ACA	Aluminium Costings Association		
ACA	American Cartographic Association	**ACAC**	American Christian Action Council

ACAC	Arab Civil Aviation Council	**ACAM**	Association des Compagnies d'Assurances Moyennes (Belgium)
ACAC	Australian Chemicals Advisory Committee	**ACAMAR**	Asociación Centroamericana de Armadores
ACACC	Asian Conference on Agricultural Credit and Cooperatives	**ACAN**	Action Committee Against Narcotics
ACACHE	Association of Career Advisers in Colleges of Higher Education	**ACAN**	Agencia Centro Americana de Noticias (Panama)
ACADEVIR	Collège Académique International de l'Environnement	**ACANZ**	Agricultural Council of Australia and New Zealand
ACADI	Arab Centre for Agricultural Documentation and Information (Sudan)	**ACAO**	Association of Chief Ambulance Officers
ACADI	Association des Cadres dirigeants de l'Industrie pour le Progrés Sociale et Économique	**ACAP**	Agence Camérounaise de Presse
		ACAP	Agence Centrafricaine de Presse
		ACAP	American Council on Alcohol Problems
ACADS	Association for Computer Aided Design	**ACAP**	Annapurna Conservation Area Project (Nepal)
ACAÉ	Ateliers et Chantiers de l'Afrique Équatoriale	**ACAP**	Asociación Colombiana de Agencias de Publicidad
ACAE	Australian Commission on Advanced Education	**ACAP**	Associação Central da Agricultura Portuguesa
ACAÉN	Association Canadienne pour l'Avancement des Études Neerlandaises = CAANS	**ACAP**	Associação do Comérico Automóvel de Portugal
ACAF	Aero-Club Air France	**ACAP**	Associazione Capi Aziende Pubblicitarie
ACAF	Alianza Civica de Asociaciones Femeninas (Guatemala)	**ACAQ**	Advisory Committee on Air Quality
		ACAR	Asociación Colombiana de Archivistas
ACAFADE	Asoción Centro Americana de Familiares de Detenidos Desaparecidos (Costa Rica)	**ACAR**	Associação de Credito e Assistencia Rural (Brazil)
ACAFAM	Asociación Centro Americana de Facultades de Medicina	**ACARA**	Asociación de Concesionarios de Automotores de la República Argentina
ACAHA	Association of Chief Administrators of Health Authorities	**ACARD**	Advisory Council for Applied Research and Development
ACAHN	Asociación Centro-Americano de Historia Natural (Guatemala)	**ACARMA**	Agricultural Chemical and Animal Remedies Manufacturing Association of New Zealand
ACAHR	American Council for the Advancement of Human Rights	**ACARPESC**	Serviço de Extensão de Santa Catarina
ACAI	Accademia Archeologica Italiana	**ACARTSOD**	African Centre for Applied Research and Training in Social Development (ECA) = CAFRADES
ACAI	Associazione Cristiana Artigiani Italiani		
ACAI	Associazione fra i Costruttori in Acciaio Italiani	**ACARU**	Association Canadienne d'Administeurs de Recherche Universitaire = CAURA
ACAIP	Advisory Committee on Animal Import Priorities	**ACAS**	Advisory, Conciliation and Arbitration Service
ACAIT	Asociación Centroamericana de Industrias Textiles (Guatemala)	**ACAS**	Asociación Centroaméricana de Sociología (Panama)
ACAL	Academia de Ciencias de América Latina	**ACAS**	Association Canadienne des Administrateurs Scolaires
ACALD	Association for Children and Adults with Learning Disabilities (U.S.A.)	**ACAS**	Association Centrale des Assistants Sociaux (Belgium)
ACALJ	Association Canadienne pour l'Avancement de la Littérature de la Jeunesse	**ACAS**	Association of African Sports Confederations = UCSA

ACAS	Association of Concerned African Scholars
ACASLA	Association of Chief Architects of Scottish Local Authorities
ACASS	Association of Chartered Accountant Students Societies
ACASSI	Association of Chartered Accountants Students Societies in Ireland
ACAST	Advisory Committee on the Application of Science and Technology to Development
ACAT	Action de Chrétiens pour l'Abolition de Torture
ACAT	Africa Cooperative Action Trust
ACATCM	All-China Association of Traditional Chinese Medicine
ACATEL	Central American Tourist Hotel Association
ACATS	Association of Civil Aviation Technical Staffs
ACAV	Agence Centrafrique de Voyage
ACAV	American Committee on Arthropod-borne Viruses
ACAVA	Association for Cultural Advancement through Visual Art
ACAVC	Advisory Committee on Agricultural and Veterinary Chemicals
ACB	Agricultural Cooperatives Bank of Iran
ACB	American Council of the Blind
ACB	Arab Central Bank
ACB	Asociación Costarricense de Bibliotecarios
ACB	Association Canadienne des Bibliothèques
ACB	Association de Conservateurs de Bibliothèques *(ex AENSB)*
ACB	Association of Certification Bodies
ACB	Association of Clinical Biochemists
ACB	Ateliers et Chantiers de Bretagne
ACBA	Aggregate Concrete Block Association
ACBB	American Council for Better Broadcasts
ACBC	Australian Catholic Bishops' Conference
ACBCC	Advisory Committee to the Board and to the Committee on Commodities (UNCTAD)
ACBCU	Association Canadienne des Bibliothèques de Collège et d'Université = CACUL
ACBD	Association Canadienne des Bibliothèques de Droit = CALL
ACBEF	Association Congolaise pour le Bien-Être Familial (Congo)
ACBF	African Capacity Building Foundation (Zimbabwe)
ACBIS	Association des Conseils en Brevets dans l'Industrie Suisse = VIPS
ACBLF	Association Canadienne des Bibliothécaires de Langue Française
ACBM	Association Canadienne des Bibliothèques, Archives et Centres de Documentation Musicaux = CAML
ACBM	Association of Cartonboard Makers
ACBOA	American Citizens Bank Operators Association
ACC	Aboriginal Coordinating Council
ACC	Academy of Canadian Cinema
ACC	Action for the Crippled Child
ACC	Administrative Committee on Co-ordination (UN) = CAC
ACC	Afghan Cart Company
ACC	Agricultural Credit Corporation (Éire, Jordan)
ACC	American Cars Corporation (Ivory Coast)
ACC	American Catholic Committee
ACC	American College of Cardiology
ACC	American College of Chemosurgery
ACC	American College of Cryosurgery
ACC	Anglican Consultative Council
ACC	Animal Christian Concern
ACC	Anti-Animal Carcass Campaign
ACC	Anti-Consumerism Campaign
ACC	Antique Collectors Club
ACC	Arab Cooperation Council (Jordan) = CCA
ACC	Asian Coconut Community
ACC	Asian Cultural Council (U.S.A.)
ACC	Asmara Chamber of Commerce (Ethiopia)
ACC	Asociación Comunal Campesina (El Salvador)
ACC	Associated Cement Companies (India)
ACC	Associated Communications Corporation
ACC	Association Canadienne des Communication = CCA
ACC	Association des Cartothèques Canadiennes = ACML
ACC	Association des Consommateurs du Canada = CCA

ACC	Association of Clinical Competence	ACCE	Advisory Committee on Chemicals in the Environment (ANZEC)
ACC	Association of Computer Clubs		
ACC	Association of Conservative Clubs	ACCE	African Council on Communication Education = CAEC
ACC	Association of County Councils		
ACC	Australasian Corrosion Centre (Australia)	ACCE	American Chamber of Commerce Executives
ACC	Australian Chamber of Commerce	ACCE	American Council for Construction Education
ACC	Australian Council of Churches		
ACC&CE	Association of Consulting Chemists and Chemical Engineers (U.S.A.)	ACCE	Association Canadienne des Chercheurs en Education = CERA
ACCA	Air Charter Carriers Association	ACCE	Association of Christian Centres in Europe (Germany)
ACCA	Air Conditioning Contractors of America	ACCE	Association of County Chief Executives
ACCA	American Clinical and Climatological Association	ACCE/ ICDR	ACCE Institute for Communication Development and Research (Kenya)
ACCA	American Cotton Cooperative Association	ACCEC	Australian Chambers of Commerce Export Council
ACCA	Animal Clinical Chemistry Association	ACCEFN	Academia Colombiana de Ciencias Exactas Fisicas y Naturales
ACCA	Associated Chambers of Commerce of Australia		
ACCA	Association des Caisses Communes d'Assurance	ACCEPT	Addictions Community Centre for Education, Prevention & Treatment
ACCA	Association of Chartered and Certified Accountants	ACCET	Asian Centre for Comparative Education
ACCAD	Advanced Computing Center for the Arts and Design, Ohio State University	ACCF	Agence Centrafricaine des Communications Fluviales
ACCAD	Advisory Committee for the World Climate Applications and Data Programmes	ACCF	Asian Christian Communications Fellowship
		ACCFA	Agricultural Credit and Co-operative Financing Administration (Philippines)
ACCADES	Asociación Cooperativa de Comerciantes, Aprovisionamiento y Consumo (El Salvador)	ACCFO	Association of County and City Finance Officers (Éire)
ACCAM	Société d'Accumulateurs du Caméroun	ACCG	American Committee for Crystal Growth
ACCART	Australian Council for Care of Animals in Research and Teaching	ACCH	Association for the Care of Children's Health (U.S.A.)
ACCBD	Advisory Committee on Conservation of Biological Diversity	ACCH	Australian Centre for Catchment Hydrology
ACCC	Advisory Committee to the Canada Centre for Inland Waters	ACCHAN	Allied Command Channel (NATO)
		ACCI	Abu Dhabi Chamber of Commerce and Industry
ACCC	American Council of Christian Churches	ACCI	Afghan Chamber of Commerce and Industry
ACCC	Association of Classic Car Clubs	ACCI	American Council on Consumer Interests
ACCCI	American Coke and Coal Chemicals Institute		
ACCD	American Coalition of Citizens with Disabilities	ACCI	ASEAN Chambers of Commerce and Industry
ACCD	Arab Council for Childhood and Development (Egypt) = ABCD	ACCI	Association of Chambers of Commerce of Ireland
		ACCI	Ateliers et Chantiers de la Côte-d'Ivoire
ACCDU	African Caribbean Community Development Unit	ACCI	Australian Chamber of Commerce and Industry

ACCIS	Advisory Committee for Coordination of Information Systems (UN)	**ACD**	American College of Dentists
ACCL	Alberta Council of College Librarians (Canada)	**ACD**	Association for Curriculum Development
ACCM	Advisory Council for the Church's Ministry	**ACDA**	American Choral Directors Association
ACCM	Association of Computer Cable Manufacturers	**ACDA**	American Component Dealers Association
ACCMLRI	Association des Caisses de Crédit Mutuel Libres à Responsabilité Illimitée	**ACDA**	Arms Control and Disarmament Agency (U.S.A.)
ACCN	Académia Chilena de Cióncias Naturales	**ACDB**	Agricultural and Cooperative Development Bank (Liberia)
ACCO	Algemene Classificatie Commissie voor de Overheidsadministratie	**ACDB**	Association du Catalogue Documentaire du Bâtiment
ACCO	American College of Chiropractic Orthopedists	**ACDE**	Advisory Committee on Dental Establishments (Scotland)
ACCO	Association of Child Care Officers	**ACDE**	Asociación Cristiana de Dirigentes de Empresa (Uruguay)
ACCO	Australian Council of Consumer Organisations	**ACDEGAM**	Asociación de Campesinos y Ganaderos del Magdalena Medio (Colombia)
ACCOSCA	African Confederation of Cooperative Savings and Credit Associations = ACEA	**ACDEPO**	Association of Civil Defence and Emergency Planning Officers (*now* EPS)
ACCP	American College of Chest Physicians	**ACDG**	Associazione Cristiana dei Giovani = ACJ, CVJM, UCJG
ACCP	American College of Clinical Pharmacology	**ACDHRS**	African Centre for Democracy and Human Rights Studies (Gambia)
ACCP	American College of Clinical Pharmacy	**ACDI**	Agence Canadienne de Développement International = CIDA
ACCP	Association of Child Psychology and Psychiatry	**ACDI**	Agricultural Cooperative Development International (U.S.A.)
ACCS	Associazione del Commercio dei Cereali e Semi	**ACDI-IMD**	Agencia Canadiense para el Desarrollo Internacional – Integracion de la Mujer en Desarrollo (Colombia)
ACCSA	Allied Communications and Computer Security Agency (NATO)	**ACDIMA**	Arab Company for Drug Industries and Medical Appliances (Kuwait)
ACCT	Agence de Coopération Culturelle et Technique = AGECOOP	**ACDO**	Association of Civil Defence Officers
ACCTI	American Chamber of Commerce for Trade with Italy	**ACDP**	Advisory Committee on Dangerous Pathogens
ACCTVS	Association of Closed Circuit Television Surveyors	**ACDP**	Albanian Christian Democratic Party = AKDS
ACCU	Asian Confederation of Credit Unions	**ACDP**	American Committee of Directors & Principals in Advanced Education
ACCU	Asian Cultural Centre for Unesco (Japan)	**ACDRI**	Advisory Committee on the Development of Research for Industry (CSIR) (South Africa)
ACCU	Association of Catholic Colleges and Universities (U.S.A.)	**ACDS**	Advisory Committee on Dangerous Substances
ACD	Advisory Committee on National Health Service Drugs	**ACDS**	Anglo Continental Dental Society
ACD	Alliance Centriste et Démocrate (Algeria)	**ACDST**	Agency of Cooperation for the Development through Sciences and Technology (Belgium)
ACD	Alliance for Cultural Democracy (U.S.A.)		

ACDTPN	Association pour le Contrôle de la Descendance des Taureaux Pie Noirs	**ACÉA**	Association Canadienne des Études Asiatiques = CASA
ACE	Académia de Cióncias Económicas (Argentina)	**ACÉA**	Association des Coopératives d'Épargne et de Crédit d'Afrique = ACCOSCA
ACE	Access Committee for England	**ACÉA**	Association des Éducateurs par Correspondance d'Afrique = AACE
ACE	Acción Católica Española		
ACE	Advisory Centre for Education		
ACE	Advisory Committee on Environment	**ACEA**	Association of Cost and Executive Accountants
ACE	Age Concern England	**ACEA**	Association of European Car Makers (Belgium)
ACE	Agricultural Communicators in Education		
ACE	Alliance for Beverage Cartons and the Environment	**ACEAA**	Advisory Committee on Electrical Appliances and Accessories
ACE	Allied Command Europe (NATO) = CAE	**ACÉAC**	Association des Conférences Épiscopales de l'Afrique Centrale
ACE	American College of Ecology	**ACÉAR**	Atelier Central d'Études d'Aménagement Rural
ACE	American Council on Education		
ACE	American Council on the Environment	**ACEB**	Asociación Colombiana de Empleados Bancarios
ACE	Amitiés Chrétiennes Européennes	**ACÉB**	Association Canadienne des Écoles de Bibliothécaires = CALS
ACE	Architects Council of Europe = CAE		
ACE	ASEAN Confederation of Employers (Philippines)	**ACEBA**	Asociación de Cultivadores de Especies Bioacuáticas (Ecuador)
ACE	Association des Compagnies Aériennes de la CEE	**ACEC**	American Consulting Engineers Council
ACE	Association for Coal in Europe	**ACEC**	Association of Consulting Engineers of Canada
ACE	Association for Copyright Enforcement (U.S.A.)	**ACEC**	Associazione Cattolica Esercenti Cinema
ACE	Association for Cultural Exchange	**ACÉC**	Ateliers de Constructions Électriques de Charleroi
ACE	Association for the Conservation of Energy	**ACÉCA**	Association des Coopératives d'Épargne et de Crédit d'Afrique = ACOSCA
ACE	Association of Caribbean Economists (Jamaica)	**ACÉCCT**	Association des Conférences Épiscopales du Congo, de la République Centrafricaine et du Tchad
ACE	Association of Children's Entertainers		
ACE	Association of Circulation Executives	**ACECDL**	Associação dos Comerciantes de Equipamentos Cientificos do Distrito de Lisboa
ACE	Association of Comics Enthusiasts		
ACE	Association of Conference Executives	**ACÉCO**	Association pour les Compensations d'Échanges Commerciaux
ACE	Association of Conservation Engineers (U.S.A.)	**ACÉÉ**	Association Canadienne des Études Écossaises = CASS
ACE	Association of Consulting Engineers		
ACE	Association of Cost Engineers	**ACéE**	Association Canadienne des Études Environnementales = ESAC
ACE	Association of the Chemical Industry (Japan)	**ACÉEDAC**	Association pour la Coopération des Églises, l'Environnement et le Développement de l'Afrique Centrale (Congo) = ROEDAC
ACE	Athens Centre of Ekistiks (Greece)		
ACE	Australian Christian Endeavour Union		
ACE	NATO Allied Command Europe		
ACE Centre	AIDS Communication Education Centre	**ACEFH**	Association Internationale contre l'Exploitation du Foetus Humain
ACEA	Asociación Costarricense de Economistas Agrícolas		

ACEG	Afghan Carpet Exporters' Guild	**ACÉRAC**	Association des Conférences Épiscopales de la Région de l'Afrique Centrale
ACEHI	Association of Canadian Educators of the Hearing-Impaired	**ACERP**	Asociación Cubana de Ejecutivos de Relaciones Públicas
ACEI	Association for Childhood Education International (U.S.A.)	**ACerS**	American Ceramic Society
ACEI	Association of Consulting Engineers of Ireland	**ACERT**	Advisory Committee for the Education of Romany and other Travellers
ACÉIB	Association des Centrales Électriques Industrielles de Belgique	**ACES**	Aerolíneas Centrales de Colombia
ACEID	Asian Centre of Educational Innovation for Development (Thailand)	**ACES**	American Catholic Esperanto Society
ACEJMC	Accrediting Council on Education in Journalism and Mass Communications	**ACES**	Applied Computational Electromagnetics Society
ACEL	Association des Chefs d'Entreprises Libres	**ACES**	Arab Center for Energy Studies (Egypt)
ACÉLA	Association Canadienne des Études Latino-Américaines et Caraïbes = CALAS	**ACES**	Asociación Cafetalera de El Salvador
ACEM	Association of Consulting Engineers of Manitoba = AICM	**ACES**	Association for Comparative Economic Studies (U.S.A.)
ACÉM-CI	Atelier de Construction Électromécanique de Côte-d'Ivoire	**ACESG**	American Council on Educational Simulation & Gaming
ACENVO	Association of Chief Executives of National Voluntary Organisations	**ACESIA**	American Council for Elementary School Industrial Arts
ACENZ	Association of Consultant Engineers of New Zealand	**ACESNA**	Agence Centrafricaine pour la Sécurité de la Navigation Aérienne
ACEO	Association of Chief Education Officers	**ACESW**	Association of Chief Education Social Workers
ACEOVEC	Association of Chief Executive Officers of Vocational Education Committees (Éire)	**ACET**	AIDS Care Education and Training
		ACET	Association of Consultants in Education and Training
ACEP	Advisory Committee on Export Policy (U.S.A.)	**ACETA**	Australasian Commercial and Economics Teachers Association
ACEP	American College of Emergency Physicians	**ACÉUM**	Association Canadienne des Écoles Universitaires de Musique
ACÉP	Association Canadienne des Études Patriotiques = CSPS	**ACF**	Académie Canadienne-Française
ACÉPE	Association pour le Développement d'Actions Collectives d' Éducation Permanent en Europe	**ACF**	Active Citizen Force (South Africa)
		ACF	Agricultural Co-operative Federation
		ACF	Anarchist Communist Federation
ACEPS	Associação Católico dos Enfermeiros e Profissionais de Saúde (Portugal)	**ACF**	Arab Co-operative Federation (Iraq)
		ACF	ASEAN Cardiologists Federation
ACEQ	Association of Consulting Engineers of Quebec (Canada)	**ACF**	ASEAN Constructors Federation (Indonesia)
ACER	Advisory Committee on Environmental Resources	**ACF**	Association of Charitable Foundations
		ACF	Australian Co-operative Foods
ACER	Afro-Caribbean Education Resource Centre	**ACF**	Australian Conservation Foundation
		ACF	Australian Cotton Foundation
ACER	Associazione Costruttori Edili di Roma e Provincia	**ACF**	Automobile Club de France
		ACFA	Air Charter Forwarders Association
ACER	Australian Council for Educational Research	**ACFA**	American Council for Free Asia
		ACFA	Army Cadet Force Association
		ACFA	Association of Cystic Fibrosis Adults

ACFAI	All China Federation of Automobile Industry
ACFAS	Association Canadienne Française pour l'Avancement des Sciences
ACFB	Associations Culturelles Franco-Brésiliennes (Brazil)
ACFC	Association Congolaise de Femmes Chercheurs
ACFC	Association of Canadian Film Craftspeople
ACFD	African Centre for Fertilizer Development (Nigeria)
ACFDH	Les Amis des Château-Forts et Demeures Historiques
ACFHE	Association of Colleges for Further and Higher Education
ACFM	Advisory Committee on Fisheries Management (ICES)
ACFM	Association Confédérale pour la Formation Médicale (France)
ACFM	Association of Cereal Food Manufacturers
ACFMO	Alliance de Constructeurs Français de Machines-Outils
ACFO	American College of Foot Orthopedists
ACFO	Association of Car Fleet Operators
ACFOA	Australian Council for Overseas Aid
ACFOD	Asian Cultural Forum on Development (Thailand)
ACFODE	Action for Development (Uganda)
ACFRA	Assureurs Conseils Franco-Africains (Gabon)
ACFS	American College of Foot Specialists
ACFS	American College of Foot Surgeons
ACFSS	Aged Christian Friend Society of Scotland
ACFT	Anhui College of Finance and Trade
ACG	American College of Gastroenterology
ACG	Anti-Counterfeiting Group
ACG	Arts Centre Group
ACG	Association Canadienne des Géographes = CAG
ACGA	American Cricket Growers Association
ACGB	Aircraft Corporation of Great Britain
ACGC	Asian Coordinating Group for Chemistry (Australia)
ACGF	Australian Citrus Growing Federation
ACGH	Association des Chauffeurs Guides d'Haiti
ACGIH	American Conference of Governmental Industrial Hygienists
ACGM	Advisory Committee on Genetic Manipulation
ACGPOMS	American College of General Practitioners in Osteopathic Medicine and Surgery
ACGR	Associate Committee on Geotechnical Research (Canada)
ACGRA	Australian Cotton Growers Research Association
ACH	Academia Colombiana de Historia
ACH	Association Canadienne des Hispanistes = CAH
ACH	Association for Comparative Haematology
ACH	Association for Computers and the Humanities (U.S.A.)
ACH	Association of Clinical Hypnotherapists
ACH	Association of Community Homes
ACH	Association of Contemporary Historians
ACHA	Acción Chilena Anticomunista
Acha	Alianza Chilena Anticomunista
ACHA	American Catholic Historical Association
ACHA	American College Health Association
ACHA	American College of Hospital Administrators
ACHA	Asociación Criadores de Holando Argentino
ACHAC	Association des Centres pour Handicapés de l'Afrique Centrale
ACHAN	Asian Community Health Action Network (India)
ACHAP	Asociación Chilena de Agencias de Publicidad
ACHAPI	Asociación Chilena de Apicultores
ACHAS	Acoustical Commission of the Hungarian Academy of Sciences
ACHCA	American College of Health Care Administrators
ACHCEW	Association of Community Health Councils for England and Wales
ACHCN	Academia Chilena de Ciencias Naturales
ACHEE	ASEAN Council for Higher Education in Environment
ACHET	Asociación Chilena de Empresas de Turismo

ACHI	Association for Childbirth at Home, International (U.S.A.)
ACHIF	Asociación Chilena de Ingenieros Forestales
ACHIGH	Asociación Chilena de Gastronomía
ACHIL	Association des Chimistes Luxembourgeois
ACHIP	Asociación Chilena de Investigaciones para la Paz
ACHM	Asociación Chilena Microbiologia
ACHP	Advisory Council on Historic Preservation (U.S.A.)
ACHPER	Australian Council for Health, Physical Education and Recreation
ACHR	Asian Coalition for Housing Rights (Thailand)
ACHRC	Alberta Children's Hospital Research Centre (Canada)
ACHRO	Asian Coalition of Human Rights Organisations
ACHS	American Catholic Historical Society
ACHS	Asociación Chilena de Seguridad Industrial
ACHSTS	African Council for the Training and Promotion of Health Sciences Teachers and Specialists
ACHSWW	American Committee on the History of the Second World War
ACHTR	Advisory Committee for Humid Tropics Research (UNESCO)
ACI	Actividade Nacional e Internacional de Investigação e Informação
ACI	African Cultural Institute = ICA
ACI	Agence Congolaise d'Information
ACI	Algemene Vereniging voor de Centrale Verwarmings- en Lucht-behandelingsindustrie
ACI	Alliance Coopérative Internationale = ICA, IGB, MICA
ACI	American Concrete Institute
ACI	Association Canadienne de l'Information = CIPS
ACI	Association Cartographique Internationale = ICA, IKV
ACI	Association for Conservation Information (U.S.A.)
ACI	Association of Chambers of Commerce of Ireland
ACI	Automobile Club d'Italia

ACI	Azione Cattolica Italiana
ACIA	Agricultural Construction Industry Association
ACIA	Asociación Centroamericana de Informaciones Agricolas
ACIA	Asociación Colombiana de Ingenieros Agrónomos
ACIA	Association of the Corporation of Insurance Agents
ACIAA	Australian Commercial and Industrial Artists Association
ACIAR	Australian Centre for International Agricultural Research
ACIAS	American Council of Industrial Arts Supervisors
ACIATE	American Council on Industrial Arts Teacher Education
ACIC	Aeronautical Charting and Information Center (U.S.A.)
ACIC	American Committee for International Conservation
ACIC	Asociación Costarricense para Información y Cultura
ACIC	Associació de Cantants i Intèrprets Professionals en Llengua Catalana
ACIC	Australian Chemical Industry Council
ACICAFÉ	Association du Commerce et de l'Industrie du Café dans la CEE
ACICST	Consortium for International Cooperation in Science and Technology
ACID	Association of Canadian Industrial Designers
ACID	Association of Colleges Implementing Dip HE Programmes
ACIEAS	Asociación Colombiana de Instituciones de Educación Agrícola Superior
ACIEL	Coordinating Action of Free Institutions of Commerce and Trade (Argentine)
ACIEM	Asociación Colombiana de Ingenieros Electricistas, Mecánicos y de Ramas Afines
ACIÉMP	Association Catholique Internationale d'Études Médico-Psychologiques
ACIESTI	Association Catholique Internationale des Enseignants et Chercheurs en Sciences et Techniques de l'Information
ACIF	Agricultural Construction Industry Association
ACIF	Asociación Católica Interamericana de Filosofía

ACIF	Asociación Colombiana de Ingenieros Forestales
ACIFA	Auxiliare Commerciale Immobilière Franco-Africaine
ACIG	Animal Cruelty Investigation Group
ACIJ	African Caribbean Institute of Jamaica
ACIL	American Council of Independent Laboratories
ACILÉCE	Association Coopérative Intersyndicale de Librairie et d'Édition de Corps Enseignant
ACIM	American Committee on Italian Migration
ACIMALL	Associazione Costruttori Italiani Macchine e Accessori per la Lavorazione de Legno
ACIMGA	Associazione Costruttori Italiani Macchine Grafiche e Affini
ACIMIT	Associazione Costruttori Italiani di Macchinario per l'Industria Tessile
ACIMO	Association de Coureurs Internationaux en Multicoques Océaniques
ACIN	Asociatia Cineastilor
ACINDAR	Industria Argentina de Aceros, S.A.
ACIN-DÉCO	Action Internationale de Développement Coopératif
ACIP	Agence Coopérative Interrégionale de Presse
ACIP	American College of International Physicians
ACIP	Asociación Colombiana de Investigadores Pesqueros
ACIPET	Asociación Colombiana de Ingenieros de Petróleos
ACIPHIL	Association of Consultants and Independents in the Philippines
ACIR	Advisory Commission on Intergovernmental Relations (U.S.A.)
ACIRL	Australian Coal Industries Research Laboratories
ACIS	African Church Information Service
ACIS	American Committee for Irish Studies
ACIS	American Council for International Studies
ACIS	American Council on International Sports
ACIS	Association of Contemporary Iberian Studies
ACISCA	Association of Christian Institutes for Social Concern in Asia (India)
ACISJF	Association Catholique Internationale des Services de la Jeunesse Féminine = ICGS
AcIT	Académie Internationale du Tourisme
ACIT	Asociación Colombiana de Ingenieros de Transportes y Vías
ACIT	Association des Chimistes de l'Industrie Textile
ACIUCN	Australian Committee for the International Union for the Conservation of Nature and Natural Resources
ACIVS	Association Internationale pour la Lutte contre la Violence Associée au Sport
ACIZ	Asociación de Comerciantes e Industriales del Zulia (Venezuela)
ACJ	Alianz Mundial de Asociaciones Christianas de Jóvenes = CVJM, UCJG, YMCA
ACJ	Ancillae Sacri Cordis Jesu
ACJA	All China Journalists Association
ACJA	American Criminal Justice Association
ACJS	Academy of Criminal Justice Sciences (U.S.A.)
ACKSA	All Cachar and Karingang Students Association (Indonesia)
ACL	Académia Carioca de Létras (Brazil)
ACL	Academia Chilena de la Lengua
ACL	Academia das Cióncias de Lisboa
ACL	American Classical League
ACL	Association Canadienne Linguistique = CLA
ACL	Association for Computational Linguistics (U.S.A.)
ACL	Automobile Club du Grand-Duché de Luxembourg
ACLA	American Clinical Laboratory Association
ACLA	American Comparative Literature Association
ACLALS	Association for Commonwealth Language and Literature
ACLAM	American College of Laboratory Animal Medicine
ACLANT	Allied Command Atlantic (NATO)
ACLC	Activity Centre of Lithuanian Catholics = KVC, LKVC
ACLC	Association Canadienne de Litterature Comparée = CCLA

ACLCA	Association of Christian Lay Training Centres in Africa (Zambia)	**ACMAF**	Association des Classes Moyennes Africaines
ACLEN	Asociación del Clero Nicaragüense	**ACMAR**	Ateliers de Construction de Matériels Routiers et de Travaux Publics
ACLI	American Council of Life Insurance		
ACLI	Associazione Cristiana Lavatori Italiana	**ACMC**	Advanced Composites Manufacturing Centre
ACLIJ	Asociación Colombiana del Libro Infantil y Juvenil	**ACMC**	American Common Market Club
ACLIS	Australian Council of Libraries and Information Services	**ACMC**	Association of Canadian Medical Colleges
ACLM	American College of Legal Medicine	**ACMD**	Advisory Council on the Misuse of Drugs
ACLM	Antigua Caribbean Liberation Movement	**ACME**	Advisory Council on Medical Education (U.S.A.)
ACLM	Association of Contact Lens Manufacturers	**ACME**	Advisory Council on Medical Establishments (Scotland)
ACLS	American Council of Learned Societies	**ACME**	Association of Consulting Management Engineers (U.S.A.)
ACLU	American Civil Liberties Union		
ACLVB	Algemene Centrale der Liberale Vakbonden van België = CGSLB	**ACME**	Association of Cotton Merchants in Europe
ACM	American College of Medicine	**ACMET**	Advisory Council on Middle East Trade
ACM	American College of Musicians	**ACMF**	American Corn Millers Federation
ACM	American Council on Marijuana and other Psychoactive Drugs	**ACMGA**	American College of Medical Group Administrators
ACM	Arab Common Market	**ACML**	Anti-Common Market League
ACM	Association for College Management	**ACML**	Arab Center for Medical Literature (Kuwait)
ACM	Association for Computing Machinery (U.S.A.)	**ACML**	Association of Canadian Map Libraries = ACC
ACM	Association of Clinical Microbiologists	**ACMP**	Amateur Chamber Music Players (U.S.A.)
ACM	Ateliers et Chantiers du Mali		
ACM	Australian Chamber of Manufactures	**ACMRR**	Advisory Committee on Marine Resources Research (FAO) = CAIRM, CCRRM
ACMA	Agricultural Co-operative Managers Association		
ACMA	Aluminium Coin Manufacturers' Association	**ACMS**	African Centre for Monetary Studies (Senegal)
ACMA	American Cutlery Manufacturers Association	**ACMS**	Association Interprofessionnelle des Centres Médicaux et Sociaux de la Région Parisienne
ACMA	Associated Chambers of Manufacturers of Australia	**ACMS**	Australasian Conference on the Mechanics of Structures and Materials
ACMA	Association des Chercheurs du Maïs en Afrique (Senegal) = AMRA	**ACMS**	Australian Clay Minerals Society
ACMA	Association of Cost and Management Accountants (South Africa)	**ACMT**	American College of Medical Technologists
ACMA	Association pour Combattre la Malnutrition par Algoculture Simplifiée	**ACN**	A Cuncolta Naziunalista (Corsica) = CCN
ACMA	Ateliers et Chantiers Maritimes d'Abidjan (Mali)	**ACN**	Action Christian National Party (Namibia)
ACMA	Athletic Clothing Manufacturers Association	**ACN**	Aid to the Church in Need
ACMAD	African Centre of Meteorological Applications for Development (Niger)	**ACN**	American College of Neuropsychiatrists

ACN	American College of Nutrition
ACN	Association Nationale Catholique de Nursing (Belgium)
ACNA	Association Profesionnelle du Caoutchouc Naturel en Afrique = ANRA
ACNA	Aziende Colori Nazionali Affini Spa
ACNFP	Advisory Committee on Novel Food Processes
ACNHA	American College of Nursing Home Administrators
ACNI	Arts Council of Northern Ireland
ACNM	American College of Nuclear Medicine
ACNM	American College of Nurse-midwives
ACNMA	Association des Compagnies Nationales de Navigation Maritime (Ivory Coast) = ANSL
ACNO	Association des Comités Nationaux Olympiques = ANOC
ACNOA	Association des Comités Nationaux Olympiques d'Afrique = ANOCA
ACNOE	Association des Comités Nationaux Olympiques Européens = AENOC
ACNP	American College of Neuropsychopharmacology
ACNP	American College of Nuclear Physicians
ACNS	Advisory Committee on Nuclear Safety (Israel)
ACNT	Australian Council of National Trusts
ACNUR	Alto Comisionado de los Naciones Unidas por los Refugiados = HCNUR, HCR, UNHCR
ACO	African Curriculum Organisation
ACO	American College of Orgonomy
ACO	American College of Otorhinolaryngologists
ACO	Arab Cities Organisation = OVA
ACO	ASEAN Cooperative Federation (Indonesia)
ACO	Association of Charity Officers
ACO	Association of Conservation Officers
ACO-HNS	American Council of Otolaryngology-Head and Neck Surgery
ACOA	Administrative and Clerical Officers' Association (Australia)
ACOA	American Committee on Africa
ACODA	Association Internationale pour la Coopération et le Développement en Afrique Australe (Belgium)
ACODEX	Asociación Colombiana de Exportadores
ACOEP	American College of Osteopathic Emergency Physicians
ACOEXA	Asociación Colombiana de Expertos Agrícolas
ACOFAL	Asociación Colombiana de Fabricantes de Alimentos para Animales
ACOFI	Asociación Colombiana de Facultades de Ingeniería
ACOG	American College of Obstetricians and Gynecologists
ACOGE	Asociación Colombiana de Geógrafos
ACOGUA	Asociación de Caficultores de Oriente de Guatemala
ACOH	Advisory Committee for Operational Hydrology (WMO) = CCHO
ACOHA	American College of Oesteopathic Hospital Administrators
ACOI	American College of Osteopathic Internists
ACOLECHE	Asociación Colombiana de Industriales de la Leche
ACOLF	Advisory Committee on Live Fish
ACOLFA	Asociación Colombiana de Fabricantes de Autopartes
ACOM	Asociación Colombiana de Museos, Institútos y Casas de Cultura (Colombia)
ACOMAG	Associazione per il Commercio delle Macchine ed Altrezzature per il Gelato
ACOMET	Asociación Cooperativa Metropolitana de Taxistas (El Salvador)
ACOMEX	Asociación Colombiana de Comercio Exterior
ACOMR	Advisory Committee on Oceanic Meteorological Research (WMO) = CAIMO, CCRMO
ACOMS	American College of Oral and Maxillofacial Surgeons
ACOOG	American College of Osteopathic Obstetricians and Gynecologists
ACOP	Advisory Committee on Pilotage (DOT)
ACOP	American College of Osteopathic Pediatricians
ACOP	Association of Chief Officers of Probation
ACOPAI	Asociación de Cooperativas de Producción Agropecuária Integradas (El Salvador)

ACOPE	Associação dos Comerciantes de Pescado	**ACP**	Agence Comores Presse
ACOPI	Asociación Colombiana Popular de Industriales	**ACP**	Albanian Communist Party = PKS
		ACP	American College of Pharmacists
ACOPLAST-ICOS	Asociación Colombiana de Industrias Plasticas	**ACP**	American College of Physicians
		ACP	American College of Podopediatrics
ACOPS	Advisory Committee on Oil Pollution of the Sea	**ACP**	American College of Prosthodontics
		ACP	American College of Psychiatrists
ACOPS	Advisory Committee on Protection of the Sea	**ACP**	Associated Church Press of the Western Hemisphere (U.S.A.)
ACOR	Advisory Committee on Own Resources (EU)	**ACP**	Association Canadienne de Philosophie = CPA
ACORBAT	Association for Co-operation in Banana Research in the Caribbean and Tropical America	**ACP**	Association Canadienne des Palynologues
		ACP	Association of Canadian Publishers
ACORD	Advisory Council on Research and Development for Fuel and Power	**ACP**	Association of Cheese Processors
		ACP	Association of Child Psychotherapists
ACORD	Agency for Cooperation and Research in Development (India)	**ACP**	Association of Circus Proprietors of Great Britain
ACORD	Agency for Cooperation in Rural Development (Switzerland)	**ACP**	Association of Clinical Pathologists
		ACP	Association of Computer Professionals
ACORD	Asian Center for Organization, Research and Development	**ACP**	Australian College of Paediatrics
ACORD	Euro Action-Agency for Cooperation and Research and Development	**ACPA**	American Capon Producers Association
ACOS	Advisory Committee on Safety (IEC)	**ACPA**	American Catholic Philosophical Association
ACOS	American College of Osteopathic Surgeons	**ACPA**	American Cleft Palate Association
		ACPA	American Concrete Pavement Association
ACOS	Arab Committee for Ottoman Studies (Tunisia)	**ACPA**	American Concrete Pipe Association
ACOS	Associazione Cattolica Operatori Sanitari	**ACPA**	ASEAN Consumer Protection Agency
		ACPA	Asociación Costarricense de Productores de Algodon
ACOSA	Aluminium Company of South Africa	**ACPA**	Association des Chefs de Publicité d'Annonceurs de Belgique
ACOSCA	Africa Cooperative Savings and Credit Association = ACECA		
		ACPA	Association of Christians in Planning and Architecture
ACOSS	Australian Council of Social Services	**ACPA**	Association of Computer Progammers and Analysts (U.S.A.)
ACOST	Advisory Committee on Science and Technology		
		ACPAC	AIDAB Centre for Pacific Development and Training
ACOT	Associate Committee on Tribology (NRC) (Canada)	**ACPC**	Arab Centre for Pharmaceutical and Chemical Industries (Jordan)
ACOT	Council for Development in Agriculture (Éire)		
		ACPC	Asian Christian Peace Conference (India)
ACOVEZ	Asociación Colombiana de Medicos Veterinarios y Zootecnistas	**ACPC**	Asian Council for People's Culture
ACP	Action Committee for Palestine	**ACPCC**	American Council of Polish Cultural Clubs
ACP	Advisory Committee on Pesticides		
ACP	African Comprehensive Party (Jamaica)	**ACPD**	Association Canadienne des Professeurs de Droit = CALT
ACP	African, Caribbean and Pacific States party to the Lomé Convention = AKP		
ACP	Agence Centrale Parisienne de Presse		

ACPE	Agrupación National Sindical de Constructores Promotores de Edificios Urbanos	ACR	Association for Consumer Research
		ACR	Association of Clinical Research
ACPE	American College of Physician Executives	ACR	Association of Countryside Rangers
		ACR	Australian Catholic Relief
ACPE	American Council on Pharmaceutical Education	ACR	Automobil Clubul Român
		ACRA	Aluminium Can Recycling Association
ACPE	Association for Clinical Pastoral Education (U.S.A.)	ACRA	American Constitutional Rights Association
ACPE	Association for Continuing Professional Education (U.S.A.)	ACRA	Aontacht Cumann Riartha Aitreabhthoiri
ACPES	Asociación Colombiana de Profesores de Enseñanza Secundaria	ACRA	Association Canadienne des Rédacteurs Agricoles de Langue Française
ACPF	Asia Crime Prevention Foundation (Japan)	ACRA	Association of College Registrars and Administrators
ACPF	Asociación del Congreso Panamericano de Ferrocarriles (Argentina) = PARCA	ACRA	Association of Company Registration Agents
ACPI	Association des Conseils en Propriété Industrielle	ACRA	Associazione Italiana Donne per lo Sviluppo
ACPI	Associazione Consulenti Pubblicitari Italiani	ACRA	Australian Cultivar Registration Authority
ACPM	Advisory Committee on Programme Management (EU)	ACRA	Central Body for Residents Associations (Éire)
ACPM	American College of Preventive Medicine	ACRC	Academia de Ciencias de la República de Cuba
ACPM	Association of Corrugated Paper Makers	ACRC	Afro-Caribbean Resource Centre
		ACRD	Ancient Culture Research Department (China)
ACPn	American College of Psychoanalysts		
ACPO	Association of Chief Police Officers	ACRE	Action with Communities in Rural England
ACPO	Association of the Chemical Profession of Ontario / Association des Chimistes Professionnels de l'Ontario	ACRE	Association for Consumer Research
		ACRE	Association of Community Councils in Rural England
ACPP	Association for Child Psychology and Psychiatry	ACRÉP	Association Canadienne de Recherche et d'Éducation pour la Paix = CPREA
ACPR	American College of Podiatric Radiologists	ACRÉQ	Association pour la Création et la Recherche en Électroacoustique du Québec
ACPS	American Color Print Society		
ACPS	Arab Company for Petroleum Services (OAPEC)	ACRES	American Council on Rural Special Education
ACPSM	Association of Chartered Physiotherapists in Sports Medicine	ACRES	Australian Centre for Remote Sensing (AUSLIG)
ACPSM	Australasian College of Physical Scientists in Medicine	ACRI	American Cocoa Research Institute
		ACRI	Associazione fra la Casse di Risparmio Italiano
ACPT	Asian Confederation of Physical Therapy	ACRILIS	Australian Centre for Research in Library and Information Science
ACQL	Association for Canadian and Quebec Literatures = ALCQ	ACRL	Association of College and Research Libraries (ALA)
ACQS	Association of Consultant Quantity Surveyors	ACRM	American Congress of Rehabilitation Medicine
ACR	American College of Radiology		

ACROA	Australian Council for Overseas Aid	**ACS**	Australian Customs Service
ACROSS	African Committee for the Relief of Southern Sudan	**ACS**	Automobil Club der Schweiz
ACROSS	Association for Christian Resource Organisation Serving Sudan	**ACSA**	Acoustical Society of America
		ACSA	Aerocarga SA (Mexico)
ACRO-TERRE	Association des Constructeurs pour la Réhabilitation et l'Optimalisation de la Terre	**ACSA**	Allied Communications Security Agency (NATO)
		ACSA	American Cotton Shippers Association
ACRP	Asian Conference on Religion and Peace	**ACSA**	Association Canadienne de Sociologie et d'Anthropologie = CSAA
ACRPI	Association for Clinical Research in the Pharmaceutical Industry	**ACSA**	Australian Collieries Staff Association
ACRPP	Association pour la Conservation et la Reproduction Photographique de la Presse	**ACSAA**	American Committee for South Asian Art
		ACSAD	Arab Centre for the Study of Arid Zones and Dry Lands (Syria)
ACRR	Advisory Council on Race Relations	**ACSE**	Association of Consulting Structural Engineers (Australia)
ACRR	American Council on Race Relations	**ACSÉDIA**	Association pour le Contrôle Sanitaire, l'Étude et le Développement de l'Insémination Artificielle
ACRSA	Association Canadienne de Recherches Sociales Appliqués = CAASR		
ACS	Additional Curates Society	**ACSEPLD**	Association Canadienne pour la Santé, l'Éducation Physique, le Loisir et la Danse
ACS	Age Concern Scotland		
ACS	American Camellia Society		
ACS	American Canal Society	**ACSHEE**	Advisory Committee of the Safety of Household Electrical Equipment
ACS	American Cancer Society		
ACS	American Carbon Society	**ACSI**	Association Canadienne des Sciences de l'Information = CAIS
ACS	American Celiac Society		
ACS	American Ceramic Society	**ACSI**	Association of Christian Schools International
ACS	American Cetacean Society		
ACS	American Chemical Society	**ACSIL**	Admiralty Centre for Scientific Information and Liaison
ACS	American College of Surgeons		
ACS	American Committee of Slavists	**ACSJ**	Agricultural Chemical Society of Japan
ACS	Armstrong Clan Society	**ACSL**	Church and Synagogue Libraries (U.S.A.)
ACS	Arumunian Cultural Society (Romania) = SCA		
ACS	ASEAN College of Surgeons	**ACSM**	American College of Sports Medicine
ACS	Association of Caribbean Studies (U.S.A.)	**ACSM**	American Congress on Surveying and Mapping
ACS	Association of Certified Secretaries of South Africa	**ACSO**	Association of County Supplies Officers
		ACSP	Advisory Council on Scientific Policy (U.S.A.)
ACS	Association of Chief Superintendents (Éire)		
ACS	Association of Clinical Scientists (U.S.A.)	**ACSP**	Association Canadienne de Science Politique = CPSA
		ACSPA	Australian Council of Salaried and Professional Associations
ACS	Association of Commonwealth Students		
ACS	Association of Consulting Scientists	**ACSPFT**	Asian Committee for Standardisation of Physical Fitness Tests
ACS	Association of Cricket Statisticians		
ACS	Australian Chamber of Shipping	**ACSR**	Association Cinématographique Suisse Romande
ACS	Australian Computer Society	**ACSS**	Australian Council of Social Services
ACS	Australian Construction Services	**ACSSM**	Associate Committee on Soil and Snow Mechanics (Canada)

ACST	Advisory Council on Science and Technology (Australia)	**ACTA**	Association of Cardiothoracic Anaesthetists
ACSTD	Advisory Committee on Science and Technology for Development (UN)	**ACTA**	Association of Chart and Technical Analysts
ACSTT	Advisory Committee on Scientific and Technical Training (EU) = BAWTA, CFFST	**ACTA**	Australian City Transit Authority
		ACTA	Australian Council on Tertiary Awards
ACSUS	Association for Canadian Studies in the United States	**ACTAC**	Association of Community Technical Aid Centres
ACSVD	Advisory Committee on Safety in Vehicle Design (ATAC) (Australia)	**ACTAF**	Association of Community Trusts and Foundations
ACSZ	Agricultural and Commercial Show Society of Zambia	**ACTE**	Approvals Committee for Telecommunications Equipment (CEC-DG XIII)
ACT	Action By Christians Against Torture		
ACT	Agricultural Central Trading	**ACTE**	Asociación para la Comunicatión y Tecnologia Educativa en Puerto Rico
ACT	Aid for Children with Tracheostomies		
ACT	American College of Theriogenologists	**ACTEA**	Accrediting Council for Theological Education in Africa (Nigeria) = COHETA
ACT	American College of Toxicology		
ACT	American Council on Transplantation	**ACTEC**	Association for Cultural, Technical and Educational Cooperation (Belgium)
ACT	Arts Counselling Trust		
ACT	Asian Community Trust (Japan)	**ACTFL**	American Council on the Teaching of Foreign Languages
ACT	Asian Confederation of Teachers		
ACT	Association des Communicateurs Techniques	**ACTH**	Association for Canadian Theatre History = AHTC
ACT	Association of Career Teachers	**ACTH**	Association for Cushing's Treatment and Help
ACT	Association of Christian Teachers		
ACT	Association of Commercial Televisions (France)	**ACTION**	Active Citizens to Improve Our Neighbourhood
ACT	Association of Corporate Treasurers	**ACTIS**	Auckland Commercial and Technical Information Service (New Zealand)
ACT	Association of Cycle Traders		
ACT	Association of Cytogenetic Technologists	**ACTL**	American College of Trial Lawyers
		ACTO	Association of Camping Tour Operators
ACT	Australian Capital Territory	**ACTO**	Association of Chief Technical Officers
ACT	Northern Ireland Advisory Committee on Travellers	**ACTR**	American Council of Teachers of Russian
ACT&UPC	Association of Charter Trustees and Urban Parish Councils	**ACTRA**	Association of Canadian Television and Radio Artists
ACT-UP	Aids Coalition to Unlease Power	**ACTRAM**	Advisory Committee on the Safe Transport of Radioactive Materials
ACTA	Alliance of Canadian Travel Associations		
ACTA	American Cardiology Technologists Association	**ACTS**	Action of Churches Together in Scotland
ACTA	American Corrective Therapy Association	**ACTS**	African Centre for Technology Studies (Kenya)
ACTA	Animal Consultants and Trainers' Association	**ACTS**	Australian Catholic Truth Society
		ACTSA	Action for Southern Africa (successor to the Anti-apartheid Movement)
ACTA	Association de Coordination Technique Agricole		
ACTA	Association des Commissionaires de Transports Aériens (Switzerland)	**ACTSS**	Association of Clerical, Technical and Supervisory Staffs (TGWU)
		ACTSU	Association of Computer Timer-sharing Users (U.S.A.)

ACTT	Association of Cinematograph, Television and Allied Technicians (Canada, U.K.) (*now* BECTU)
ACTU	Australian Council of Trade Unions
ACTUS	Action Tchadienne pour l'Unité et le Socialisme
ACTV	American Coalition for Traditional Values
ACTWU	Amalgamated Clothing and Textile Workers Union (Canada, U.S.A.)
ACU	Actors Church Union
ACU	Amalgamated Cooperatives Union (Russia)
ACU	Arbeitsgemeinschaft Christlicher Unternehmer
ACU	Asian Clearing Union (ESCAP)
ACU	Association of Commonwealth Universities
ACU	Association of Computer Users (U.S.A.)
ACU	Association of Cricket Umpires
ACU	Auto Cycle Union
ACU-I	Association of College Unions – International (U S A)
ACUA	Association of College and University Auditors (U.S.A.)
ACUC	Asociación Colombiana de Usuarios de Computadores
ACUCA	Association of Christian Universities and Colleges in Asia
ACUDE	Asociación de Consumidores y Usuarios de España
ACUE	American Committee on United Europe
ACUF	Association des Combattants de la Union Française
ACULE	Association of Credit Union League Executives (U.S.A.)
ACUM	Authors, Composers and Music Publishers Society (Israel)
ACUNOR	Empresa Acucareira Norte (Angola)
ACUP	Association of Canadian University Presses
ACUP	Association of College and University Printers (U.S.A.)
ACUPS	Association of Calendered UPVC Suppliers
ACURIL	Association of Caribbean University, Research and Institutional Libraries
ACURP	American College of Utilisation Review Physicians
ACUS	Atlantic Council of the United States
ACV	Algemeen Christelijk Vakverbond (Belgium) = CSC
ACV	Allgemeiner Cäcilian- Verband für die Länder der Deutschen Sprache
ACV	Association Centrale des Vétérinaires
ACV	Associazione Calzaturifici Valenzani
ACV	Stichting Afnemers Controle op Veevoeder
ACVD	American College of Veterinary Dermatology
ACVEN	Advisory Committee on Vehicle Emissions and Noise
ACVIM	American College of Veterinary Internal Medicine
ACVM	American College of Veterinary Microbiologists
ACVO	American College of Veterinary Opthalmologists
ACVP	American College of Veterinary Pathologists
ACVPF	Association des Créateurs de Variétés Potagères et Florales
ACVR	American College of Veterinary Radiology
ACVS	American College of Veterinary Surgeons
ACVT	American College of Veterinary Toxicologists
ACW	Age Concern Wales
ACW	Algemeen Christlijk Werkersverbond = CAB, MOC
ACW	Association of Catholic Women
ACW	Association of Community Workers
ACWCRP	Australian Committee for the World Climate Research Programme
ACWE	Advisory Commitee on Women's Employment
ACWF	All-China Women's Federation
ACWO	ASEAN Confederation of Women's Organizations
ACWO	Association of Community Welfare Officers (Éire)
ACWRTUK	American Civil War Round Table, United Kingdom
ACWTU	Association of Cooperative Workers Trade Unions (Russia)
ACWW	Associated Countrywomen of the World
ACYC	Association of Combined Youth Clubs

ACYPL	Atlantic Association of Young Political Leaders	**GALLE**	Activités de Product et de Format (Mali)
AD	Acción Democrática (Aruba, El Salvador, Venezuela)	**ADAGP**	Association pour la Diffusion des Arts Graphiques et Plastiques
AD	Action Directe	**ADAI**	Associazione degli Approvvigionatori Italiani
AD	Aliança Democrática	**ADAIP**	Alliance of Disability Advice and Information Providers
AD	Alianza Democrática (Chile, Paraguay)		
AD	American Defenders	**ADAIS**	Association pour le Développement Agro-Industriel du Sahel
AD	Australian Democrats		
ADA	Action for Dysphasic Adults	**ADAM**	American Defenders against Animal Mistreatment
ADA	Agrupament Democràtic d'Andorra	**ADAM**	Association Dauphinoise pour l'Aménagement de la Montagne
ADA	Allgemeiner Deutscher Automobile Club		
ADA	Aluminium Development Association	**ADAM**	Australian Data Archive for Meteorology
ADA	American Dairy Association	**ADAN**	Associazione degli Albergatori Napoletani
ADA	American Dehydrators Association		
ADA	American Dental Association	**ADAP**	Albanian Democratic Alliance Party
ADA	American Dermatological Association	**ADAPI**	Associação dos Armadores das Pescas Industriais
ADA	American Diabetes Association		
ADA	American Dietetic Association	**ADAPR**	Association des Aviculteurs Producteurs Romande
ADA	Anti-Dumping Authority		
ADA	Antique Dealers Association of America	**ADAPSO**	Association of Data Processing Service Organisations (Canada, U.S.A.) = ADPSO
ADA	Antiquities Dealers' Association		
ADA	Association of Drainage Authorities		
ADA	Associazione Direttori Albergo	**ADAPT**	Access for Disabled People in Arts Premises Today
ADA	Assotsiatsiia Dvizhenii Anarkhistov		
ADA	Atomic Development Authority (U.S.A.)	**ADAR**	Art and Design Admissions Registry
		ADARA	American Deafness and Rehabilitation Association
ADA	Australian Dental Association		
ADA	Ayuda del Automovilista	**ADAS**	Administratia Asigurarilor de Stat
ADAA	American Dental Assistants Association	**ADAS**	African Demonstration Centre on Sampling Agricultural Surveys (CCTA and FAO)
ADAA	Art Dealers Association of America		
ADAB	Australian Development Assistance Bureau		
		ADAS	Agricultural Development and Advisory Service
ADAC	Allgemeiner Deutscher Automobil Club		
ADAC	Association des Arts et de la Culture (Belgium)	**ADAS**	Army Dependants Assurance Trust
		ADAS	Associazione Nazionale Dettaglianti Articoli Sportivi
ADAC	Associazione degli Albergatori Capresi		
ADACÉS	Association pour le Développement des Activités Culturelles dans les Établissements Scolaires	**ADATIG**	Anglo-Dutch African Textiles Investigation Group
		ADB	African Development Bank
ADACI	Associazione degli Approvvigionatori e Compratori Italiani	**ADB**	Agricultural Development Bank (Ghana)
		ADB	Asian Development Bank (Philippines)
ADACI	Associazione Italiana di Management degli Approvvigionamenti		
ADAF	Arbeitskreis Deutscher Afrika-Forschungs- und Dokumentationsstellen	**ADB Group**	African Development Bank Group (Ivory Coast)
		ADBA	Agricultural Development Bank of Afghanistan
ADAF/	Association pour le Développement des		

ADBACI	Association pour le Développement de la Documentation, des Bibliothèques et Archives de la Côte d'Ivoire
ADBI	Agricultural Development Bank of Iran
ADBN	Agricultural Development Bank of Nepal
ADBP	Agricultural Development Bank of Pakistan
ADBPA	Association pour le Développement des Bibliothèques Publiques en Afrique
ADBR	Association pour le Développement des Bibliothèques des Religieuses
ADBS	Association des Documentalistes et des Bibliothécaires Spécialisés
ADBU	Association des Directeurs de Bibliothèques Universitaires
ADC	Aboriginal Development Commission (Australia)
ADC	Agricultural Development Corporation (Kenya,Pakistan)
ADC	Alternative Defence Commission
ADC	American-Arab Antidiscrimination Committee
ADC	Andean Development Corporation = CAF, SAD
ADC	Arbeitsgemeinschaft Deutscher Chorverbände
ADC	Arsenic Development Committee (France)
ADC	Asian Development Center (Philippines)
ADC	Asociación Demografica Costarricense (Costa Rica)
ADC	Association for Development Corporation (Austria)
ADC	Association of District Councils
ADC	Aviation Development Council (U.S.A.)
ADCA	Asociación de Dirigentes de Capacitacion de la Argentina
ADCA	Australian Department of Civil Aviation
ADCB	Abu Dhabi Commercial Bank
ADCE	Associação dos Dirigentes Cristãos de Empresas
ADCF	Association pour le Développement de la Culture Fourragère (Switzerland) = AGFF, APF
ADCI	American Die Casting Institute
ADCIS	Association for the Development of Computer-based Instructional Systems (U.S.A.)
ADCJ	Association of District Council Treasurers
ADCO	Abu Dhabi Company for Onshore Oil Operations
ADCO	Andean Development Company (Ecuador)
ADCOS	Australian Development Cooperation Scholarships
ADCT	Association of District Council Treasurers
ADCU	Association of Data Communications Users (U.S.A.)
ADD	Action on Disability and Development
ADD	Action on Drinking and Driving
ADD	Arbeitsgemeinschaft Deutscher Detektive
ADDA	Acción Democrática Ecuatorian
ADDA	Australian Database Development Association
ADDCAP	Abu Dhabi Drilling Chemicals & Products
ADDE	Association des Dépôts Dentaires Européens
ADDM	Association pour le Développement de la Documentation Médicale
ADDS	American Digestive Disease Society
ADDS	American Diopter and Decibel Society
ADE	African Institute for Economic Development and Planning (Senegal)
ADE	Association Européenne pour l'Étude de l'Alimentaire et du Développement de l'Enfant
ADEAC	Association d'Entrepôts en Afrique Centrale
ADÉARTA	Association pour le Développement de l'Équipement des Ateliers de Réparation des Tracteurs Agricoles
ADÉB	Association des Éditeurs Belges
ADEB	Association des Entrepreneurs Belges de Travaux de Génie Civil = VBA
ADEBA	Asociación de Bancos Argentinos
ADÉBD	Association des Diplômes de l'École de Bibliothécaires-Documentalistes
ADEBIO	Association pour le Développement de la Bioindustrie
ADÉC	Association pour le Développement de la Coopération Agricole
ADÉCAF	Agence de Développement Caféière (Central African Republic)

ADECEC	Asociación de Empresas Consultoras en Relaciones Públicas y Comunicación (Spain)	**ADES**	Association of Directors of Education in Scotland
ADECIN	Asociación Española de Comunicacion Interna (Spain)	**ADESG**	Associação dos Diplomados de Escola Superior de Guerra (Brazil)
ADECO	Acción Democrática Colorada (Paraguay)	**ADÉTEM**	Association Nationale pour le Développement des Techniques de Marketing
ADECO	Programa de Adiestramiento de Extensionistas en Comunicaciones, Latinoamérica	**ADÉTIM**	Association pour le Développement des Techniques des Industries Mécaniques
ADEE	Association for Dental Education in Europe = AEED	**ADETOM**	Association pour le Développement de l'Enseignement Technique Outre-Mer
ADEF	Association des Études Foncières	**ADEVIDA**	Asociación en Defensa de la Vida Humana
ADEGUI	Asociación Democrática Empresarial de Guipuzcoa	**ADEX**	Asociación de Exportadores (Peru)
ADÉIC-FÉN	Association d'Éducation et d'Information de Consommateur de l'Éducation National	**ADEXA**	Association pour le Développement des Exportations Agricoles
		ADEXMA	Asociación de Exportadores de Martinica
ADEIS	Association pour le Développement de l'Enseignement d'Image et Son	**ADEYA**	Asociación de Escritores y Artistas Españoles (Spain)
ADEK	Association of Former Trainees of the European Communities (Belgium)	**ADEZ**	Association des Entrepreneurs du Zaïre
ADEKRA	Arbeitsgemeinschaft Deutscher Kraftwagen-Spediteure	**ADÉZ**	Association pour le Développement des Études Zootechniques (Belgium)
ADELF	Association des Distributeurs Exclusifs de Livres en Langue Française (Canada)	**ADF**	Aerosolinteressenters Förening
ADÉLF	Association des Écrivains de Langue Française	**ADF**	African Development Fund = AfDF, FAD
ADÉLF	Association des Épidémiologistes de Langue Française	**ADF**	Aktion Demokratischer Fortschritt
ADEMA	Alliance pour la Démocratie au Mali	**ADF**	Albanian Democratic Front = FDSh
ADEMUPE	Asociación de Mujeres de Panama-Este	**ADF**	Arab Deterrent Force = FAD
		ADF	Arbeitsgemeinschaft Deutscher Filztuchfabriken
ADEMUSA	Asociación de Mujeres Salvadorenas	**ADF**	Asian Development Fund (ADB) = AsDF, FAD
ADENA	Asociación para la Defensa de la Naturaleza	**ADF**	Association Dentaire Française
ADEP	Agence Nationale pour le Développement de l'Éducation Permanente	**ADF**	Assotsiatsiia Dilerov Fondovogo Rynka
		ADF	Australian Defence Force
ADÉPA	Association pour le Développement de la Production Automatique	**ADF**	Automotive and Distributor Federation (*ex* MFA)
ADERI	American Disability Evaluation Research Institute	**ADFA**	Australian Defence Force Academy
ADERP	Association pour le Développement de L'Enseignement et des Recherches Scientifiques auprès des Universités de la Région Parisienne	**ADFA**	Australian Dried Fruits Association
		ADFAED	Abu Dhabi Fund for Arab Economic Development
		ADFAM	Aid for Addicts and Families
		ADFCIV	Association des Francophones au Centre International de Vienne
ADES	Asociación de Distribuidores de El Salvador	**ADFG**	Acao Democratico Feminina Gaucha (Brazil)
ADÉS	Association de la Documentation Économique et Sociale	**ADFIAP**	Association of Development Financing Institutions in Asia and the Pacific (Philippines)

ADFIMI	Association of National Development Finance Institutions in Member Countries of the Islamic Development Bank
ADFIP	Association of Development Financing Institutions in the Pacific (Fiji)
ADFL	Association of Departments of Foreign Languages (U.S.A.)
ADFS	American Dentists for Foreign Service
ADG	Action Démocratique Guyanaise
ADGA	American Dairy Goat Association
ADGAS	Abu Dhabi Gas Liquefaction Company = ADGLC
ADGFAD	Agrupación Diseño Grafico
ADGLC	Abu Dhabi Gas Liquefaction Company = ADGAS
ADGPF	Association pour le Développement des grands Ports Français
ADH	Association of Dental Hospitals of the United Kingdom
ADH	Hural of People's Deputies (Mongolia)
ADHA	American Dental Hygienists Association
ADHILAC	Asociación de Historiadores Latinoamericanos y del Caribe (Mexico)
ADHOC	Association of Departmental Heads of Catering
ADI	Académie Diplomatique International
ADI	Academy of Dentistry International (U.S.A.)
ADI	Agence d'Informatique
ADI	Agentsvo Delovoi Informatsii
ADI	Agrupación de Diseñadores Industriales
AdI	Alliance des Indépendants (Switzerland)
ADI	Alzheimer's Disease International (U.S.A.)
ADI	American Defense Institute
ADI	Anwenderverband Deutscher Informationsverarbeiter
ADI	Association pour le Développement International
ADI	Associazione Detectives Italiani
ADI	Associazione Italiana di Dietetica e Nutrizione Clinica
ADI	Associazione per il Disegno Industriale
ADI	Avtomobilno-dorozhnyi Institut
ADIA	Abu Dhabi Investment Authority
ADIA	Academy of Diplomacy and International Affairs (Germany)
ADIB	Abu Dhabi International Bank
ADIBBEL	Association des Dirigeants des Instituts de Beauté de Belgique
ADIC	Abu Dhabi Investment Company
ADIC	Association des Dirigeants et Cadres Chrétiens (Belgium)
ADIC	Association for Muslim-Christian Dialogue (France)
Adical	Associação das Industrias de Calcados (Brazil)
ADICE	Asociación de Industriales Conserveros del Ecuador
ADICEP	Association des Directeurs des Centres des Matières Plastiques
ADICIEL	Association de Diffusion de Cinéma Expression Latine
ADICT	Association Internationale de Documentation Information Culturelle Touristique
ADIFAL	Asociación para el Desarrollo de la Industria de los Fertilizante de América Latina
ADIG	Associazione per il Diabete Infantile e Giovanile
ADILINA	Association de Diffusion de Littérature Négro-Africaine
ADIM	Arbeitsgemeinschaft für Didaktik, Informatik und Mikroelektronik
ADIM	Asociación de Industriales Molineros (Bolivia)
ADIM	Asociación para el Desarrollo e Integracion de la Mujer (Peru)
ADIM	Associação para a Defesa dos Interesses de Macau
ADIMAGRO	Asociación de Importadores y Distribuidores de Maquinaria Agricola e Industrial (Colombia)
ADIMCE	Asociación de Industrias Manufactureras de Cereales (Colombia)
ADIMYF	Asociación para el Desarrollo Integral de la Mujer y la Familia (Guatemala)
ADIN	Asociación de Industrias Náuticas
ADIP	Association Nationale de Défense d'Élevage et du Commerce Rural Interprofessionnel
ADIP	Associazione Italiana dei Direttori del Personale
ADIPA	Associação dos Distribuidores de Produtos Alimentares
ADIPA	Association of Development, Research and Training Institutes of Asia and the Pacific

ADIPAR	Asociación de Bibliotecarios del Paraguay		**ADMARC**	Agricultural Development and Marketing Corporation (Malawi)
ADIR	Association des Déménageurs Internationaux Routiers (Belgium)		**ADMG**	Association of Deer Management Groups
ADIRI	Asociatia de Drept International si Relatii Internationale (Romania)		**ADMI**	American Dry Milk Institute
ADITES	Asociación de Investigación de la Tecnicas del Subsuelo		**ADMIG**	Australian Drug and Medical Information Group
ADIU	Armament Disarmament Information Unit (U.S.A.)		**ADMITRA**	Administration Travail (BIT)
ADK	Akademiia Deputatskogo Korpusa		**ADMK**	All-India Anna Dravida Munnetra Kazhagam
ADK	Alliance for Democracy in Korea		**ADMR**	Aide à Domicile en Milieu Rural
ADK	Arbeitgeberverband der Deutschen Kautschukindustrie		**ADMS**	American Donkey and Mule Society
ADK	Arbeitsgemeinschaft der Deutschen Kartoffelwirtschaft		**ADMSt**	Arbeitsgemeinschaft Deutscher Messerschmiede und Stahlwarenhändler
ADK	Arbeitsgemeinschaft des Deutschen Kunsthandwerks		**ADMT**	Association for Dance Movement Therapy
ADK	Arbeitsgemeinschaft Deutsches Krankenhaus		**ADMT**	Association of Dental Manufacturers and Traders of the United Kingdom
ADK	Ateliers de Kahankro (Mali)		**ADN**	Acción Democrática Nacional (Aruba)
ADKPZ	Arbeitskreis Deutscher Klein- und Pelztier- Züchter		**ADN**	Acción Democrática Nacionalista (Bolivia)
ADL	Verband für Informationsverarbeitung		**ADN**	Allgemeiner Deutscher Nachrichtendienst (DDR)
ADLA	Association Danoise de Linguistique Appliquée		**ADN**	Allgemeines Deutsches Nachrichtenbüro
ADLAD	Associazione Nazionale dei Datori di Lavoro al Personale Domestico		**ADN**	Alliance for National Dignity (Romania)
ADLAF	Arbeitsgemeinschaft Deutsche Lateinamerika-Forschung		**ADNATCO**	Abu Dhabi National Tanker Company
ADLF	Association des Diététiciens de Langue Française		**ADNOC**	Abu Dhabi National Oil Company
ADLP	Australian Democratic Labour Party		**ADO**	Alliantie voor Duurzame Ontwikkeling
ADLS	Association of Dunkirk Little Ships		**ADO**	Avdelningen für Driftsorganisation
ADM	Arbeitskreis Deutscher Marktforschungsinstitut		**ADOC**	Alianza Democrática de Oposición Civilista (Panama)
ADM	Artisans du Monde		**ADÖG**	Arbeitsgemeinschaft der Österreichischen Gemeinwirtschaft
ADM	Asociación Dental Mexicana		**ADP**	Agence de Distribution de Presse (Senegal)
ADM	Association of Domestic Management			
ADM	Association of Drum Manufacturers		**ADP**	Agence Djiboutienne de Presse
ADM	Association pour le Développement du Droit Mondial		**ADP**	Albanian Demo-Christian Party (Kosovo)
ADM	Associazione Nazionale Desegno di Macchine		**ADP**	Americans for Due Process
ADM-19	Alianza Democrática – Movimiento 19 de Abril (Colombia)		**ADP**	Anguilla Democratic Party
			ADP	Asociación de Diseñadores Profesionales
ADMA	American Drug Manufacturers Association		**ADP**	Association des Dirigeants du Personnel = VDP *(ex* CDSP)
ADMA	Association of Dance and Mime Artists		**ADP**	Association for Dental Prosthesis
ADMAOP-CO	Abu Dhabi Marine Operating Company		**ADP**	Association of Database Producers
			ADP	Association of Disabled Professionals

ADP	Australian Democrats Party	**ADRE**	Acción Democrática de Rescate Electoral (Mexico)
ADPA	American Defense Preparedness Association	**ADREPP**	Aircraft Accident Data Reporting Panel (ICAO)
ADPBA	Association Internationale pour le Développement des Bibliothèques en Afrique	**ADRI**	Animal Diseases Research Unit (Canada)
ADPC	Abu Dhabi Petroleum Company	**ADRI**	Association pour Développement Rural Integré (Rwanda)
ADPC	ASEAN Agricultural Development Plan Centre	**ADRI-PECHE**	Armement Dakarois pour le Regroupement de l'Industrie de la Pêche (Senegal)
ADPC	Asian Disaster Preparedness Center (Thailand)	**ADRIA**	Association pour le Développement de la Recherche dans les Industries Agricoles et Alimentaires
ADPH	Association Africaine pour le Développement du Palmier a l'Huile (Ivory Coast) = AFOPDA	**ADRIS**	Association for the Development of Religious Information Systems
ADPI	Association Internationale d'Études pour la Protection des Investissements	**ADRLT**	Association of Directors of Recreation, Leisure & Tourism
ADPIC	Abu Dhabi Pipeline Construction Company	**ADRRCP**	Association pour le Développement et la Recherches en Réanimation Chirurgicale et Pédiatrique
ADPPOC	Abu Dhabi Petroleum Port Operating Company	**ADS**	Alliance Démocratique Sénégalaise
ADPR	Agrarian Democratic Party of Romania	**ADS**	Alzheimer's Disease Society
ADPS	Azerbaidzhanskaia Demokraticheskaia Partiia Sobstvennikov	**ADS**	American Dialect Society
ADPSO	Association of Data Processing Service Organizations = ADAPSO	**ADS**	Arbeitsgemeinschaft Deutscher Schafzüchter
ADR	Alianza Democrática Revolucionaria (Bolivia)	**ADS**	Arbeitsgemeinschaft Deutscher Schweinezüchter
ADR	Arbeitsgemeinschaft Deutscher Rinderzüchter	**ADS**	Arbeitsgemeinschaft Deutscher Schwesternverbände
ADR	Arbeitsgemeinschaft Deutscher Rübenbauerverbünde	**ADS**	Arhivsko Društvo Slovenije
ADR	Association pour le Développement de la Recherche	**ADS**	Asociación Demografica Salvadorena
ADRA	Adressbuchausschuss der Deutschen Wirtschaft	**ADS**	Association of District Secretaries
ADRA	Adventist Development and Relief Agency International (U.S.A.)	**ADS**	Assotsiatsiia Delovogo Sotrudnichestva
ADRA	Animal Diseases Research Association	**ADS-LP**	Albanski Demokratski Sojuz-Liberalna Partija (Albania) = ADU-LP
ADRA	Association for the Study of Reptiles and Amphibia	**ADSA**	American Dairy Science Association
ADRAF	Agence de Développement Rural et d'Aménagement Foncier (New Caledonia)	**ADSA**	American Dental Society of Anesthesiology
ADRAI	Association pour le Développement de la Recherche et de l'Action Intégrée (Belgium)	**ADSA**	Art Deco Societies of America
		ADSA	Automated Door Suppliers' Association
ADRAO	Association pour le Développement de la Rizculture en Afrique de l'Ouest = WARDA	**ADSAI**	American Dermatologic Society of Allergy and Immunology
		ADSATIS	Australian Defence Science and Technology Information Service
ADRDI	Abra Diocesan Rural Development Inc. (Philippines)	**ADSCLAT**	Associations of Distributors to the Self-Service and Coin-Operated Laundry and Allied Trades
		ADSE	American Dental Society of Europe
		ADSET	Association for Database Services

ADSGM	Association of Deans of Southeast Asian Graduate Schools of Management (Philippines)	**ADVB**	Associação dos Diretores de Vendas do Brasil
ADSI	Agricultural Development Service, Inc. (Philippines)	**ADW**	Action Dritte Welt
		AdW	Akademie der Wissenschaften zu Göttingen
ADSOC	Administrative Support Operations Centre (U.S.A.)	**ADW**	Verband Deutscher Werbeagenturen und Werbemittlungen
ADsPH	Association of Directors of Public Health	**ADWA**	Atlantic Deeper Waterways Association (U.S.A.)
ADSRI	Animal and Dairy Science Research Institute (South Africa)	**AE**	African Enterprise (Australia)
ADSS	Association of Direct Speech Suppliers	**AE**	Alzheimer Europe (Belgium)
ADSS	Association of Directors of Social Services	**AE**	Associations Européennes
		AE	Assoziation Europa für Sozialen und Kulturellen Fortschritt
ADSS	Australian Defence Scientific Service	**AE**	I en Athinais Archaeologiki Etaireia
ADSSA	Association pour le Développement des Sciences Sociales Appliquées	**AEA**	Action on Elder Abuse
		AEA	Adult Education Association of the U.S.A.
ADSW	Association of Directors of Social Work		
ADT	Addictive Diseases Trust	**AEA**	Agence Européenne d'Approvisionnement
ADTA	American Dance Therapy Association		
ADTA	American Dental Trade Association	**AEA**	Agricultural Education Association (*now* REDA)
ADTC	Anglo-Dutch Trade Council		
ADTCB	Association des Directeurs de Théâtres Cinématographiques de Belgique	**AEA**	Agricultural Engineers' Association
		AEA	Aircraft Electronics Association (U.S.A.)
ADTD	Association of Data Terminal Distributors (U.S.A.)		
		AEA	Aluminium Extruders' Association
ADTM	Association pour le Diffusion des Techniques Ménagères	**AEA**	American Economic Association
		AEA	American Education Association
ADTSEA	American Driver and Traffic Safety Education Association	**AEA**	American Electrolysis Association
		AEA	American Electronics Association
ADTsISO	Tsentral'ni Institut Zaochnogo Obucheniia na Avtodorozhnom Transporte	**AEA**	American Entrepreneurs Association
		AEA	American Evaluation Association
		AEA	Anglican Evangelical Assembly
ADTV	Allgemeiner Deutscher Tanzlehrerverband	**AEA**	Asociación Española de Anunciantes
ADU	Adelaide University	**AEA**	Association d'Entreprises d'Affichage (Belgium)
ADU-LP	Albanian Democratic Union-Liberal Party = ADS-LP		
		AEA	Association Européenne d'Athlétisme = EAA
ADUSEC	Association des Diplômés Universitaires en Sciences Économiques, Commerciales, Politiques et Sociales (Luxembourg)		
		AEA	Association Européenne de l'Asphalte = EGV, EMAA
		AEA	Association Européenne des Audioprothésistes
ADV	Addressenverleger- und Direktwerbe-Unternehmerverband		
		AEA	Association for Environmental Archaeology
ADV	Arbeitsgemeinschaft Deutscher Verkehrsflughäfen		
		AEA	Association for European Astronauts = AAE
ADV	Arbeitsgemeinschaft für Datenverarbeitung (Austria)		
		AEA	Association of Electoral Administrators
ADV	Asociación de Dirigentes de Ventas y Mercadotechnica del Peré	**AEA**	Association of Established Agents (Éire)

AEA	Association of Estate Agents (Malta)	AEB	Associated Examining Board
AEA	Association of European Airlines	AÉB	Association des Écrivains Belges de Langue Française
AEA	Atomic Energy Authority		
AEA	Ayuda en Acción	AEB	Atomic Energy Bureau (Japan)
AEAA	Asociación de Escritores y Artistas Americanos (Cuba)	AEBH	Association of Emancipated Brazilian Homosexuals
AÉAC	Action Économique Arabe Commune (Egypt)	AEBIOM	Association Européenne pour la Biomasse
AEAC	Asociación Española de Amigos de los Castillos	AÉBPB	Association des Études Byzantines et Post-Byzantines
AEAC	Association for Euro-Atlantic Cooperation	AEBR	Association of European Border Regions = AGEG, ARFE, WVEG
AEAFM	Association d'Entraide des Agriculteurs Français du Maroc	AEBTRI	Association des Entreprises Bulgares des Transports Internationaux et de Routes
AEAI	Association Européenne des Assurés de l'Industrie		
AEAI	Association of Engineers and Architects in Israel	AEBU	Asociación de Bancarios del Uruguay
		AEC	African Economic Community
AEAIC	European Academy of Allergology and Clinical Immunology	AEC	Agence Européenne de Coopération = EAC, EAZ
AEALCD	Association Européenne des Administrateurs Locaux Chrétiens-Démocrates = EACDLA, AEALDC	AEC	Algemene Emigratie Centrale
		AEC	American Economic Council
		AEC	American Engineering Council
		AEC	Angola Emergency Campaign
AEALDC	Asociación Europea de Administradores Locales Democrata Cristianos = AEALCD, EACDLA	AEC	Asociación de Estudios del Caribe = CSA
		AEC	Asociación Española de la Carretera
AÉAM	Association des Évangéliques d'Afrique et de Madagascar	AEC	Asociación Europea de Coleopterologia
AEAM	Association of Entertainment and Arts Management	AEC	Associação Educação Católica (Brazil)
		AÉC	Association des Éditeurs Canadiens
AÉANC	Association des Éclaireurs de l'Armée Nationale Congolaise	AÉC	Association Épiscopale Catéchistique
		AEC	Association Européenne de Céramique
AEAP	Alliance Européenne des Agences de Presse = EANA	AEC	Association Européenne de Chimie
		AEC	Association Européenne des Cheminots
AEAP	Asociación Española de Agencias de Publicidad	AEC	Association Européenne des Conservatoires, Académies de Musique et Musikhochschulen
AEAS	Association of Educational Advisers in Scotland	AEC	Association Européenne des Enducteurs, Calandreurs et Fabricants de Revêtements de Sols Plastiques et Synthétiques
AEAZ	Adult Education Association of Zambia		
AEB	Agrupación Española de Bioingenieria	AEC	Association Européenne pour la Coopération
AEB	American Egg Board		
AEB	American Ethnology Bureau	AEC	Association of Ecclesiastical Caterers
AEB	Asiatische Entwicklungsbank = AsDB, BAsD	AEC	Associazione Europea per la Cooperazione = EAC, EAS, EGZ, ESS
AEB	Asociación Ecuatoriana de Bibliotecarios	AEC	Atlantic Education Committee = CAE
AEB	Asociación Española de Banca	AEC	Atomic Energy Commission of Syria
AEB	Associação dos Exportadores Brasileiras	AEC	Atomic Energy Corporation (South Africa)

AEC	Australian Education Council	**AECI**	Association of Electrical Contractors of Ireland
AEC	Australian Electoral Commission		
AEC	Australian Environment Council (= ANZEC)	**AECI**	Association of European Conjuncture Institutes (Belgium)
AECA	Association Européenne des Cadres de l'Assurance	**AECI**	Association of European Cooperative Insurers
AECA	Association Européenne des Centres d'Audiophonologie = EAPCA	**AECL**	Atomic Energy Canada Ltd
AECAL	Academia Europea de Ciencias, Artes y Letras = AESAL, EAASH	**AECM**	Association Européenne des Classes Moyennes; Asociación Europea de Clases Medias = EIBC, EMSBU
AECAP	Association of European Centres Against Poisons (Belgium)	**AECMA**	Association Européenne de Constructeurs de Matériel Aérospatial
AECAWA	Association of Episcopal Conferences of Anglophone West Africa (Liberia)	**AECNP**	Association Européenne des Centres Nationaux de Productivité = EANCP
AECB	Associação de Educação Católica do Brasil	**AECOPS**	Associação de Empresas de Construção e Obras Públicas do Sul
AECB	Association Européenne des Cadres de Banque	**AeCS**	Aero Club der Schweiz
AECB	Association for Environment Conscious Building	**AECS**	Association of European Correspondence Schools (Netherlands)
AECB	Association for the Export of Canadian Books	**AECS**	Australia Europe Container Services
AECB	Atomic Energy Control Board (Canada) = CCEA	**AECT**	Association of Educational Communications and Technology (U.S.A.)
AECC	Asociación Española contra el Cancer	**AECTS**	European Association for Cardio-Thoracic Surgery
AECC	Asociación Española para el Control de la Calidad		
AÉCC	Association des Éclaireurs Catholiques du Congo	**AECYA**	America-European Community Youth Association (Germany)
AECCG	African Elephant Conservation Coordination Group (Kenya)	**AED**	Association d'Entraide et de Developpement (Mali)
AECD	Asian Ecumenical Conference on Development	**AED**	Association of Engineering Distributors
AECDF	Association des Exploitatants de Cinéma et des Distributeurs de Films du Grand Duché de Luxembourg	**AÉD**	Association pour l'Étude et l'Évaluation Épidémiologiques des Désastres Pays en voie de Développement
AECE	Asociación Española de Comunicación Empresarial (Spain)	**AEDA**	American European Dietetic Association (France)
AECE	Asociación Española de Cooperación Europea	**AEDA**	Asociación Española de Aerosoles
AÉCEF	Association des Écrivains Croyants d'Expression Française	**AEDA**	Association Européenne des Dirigeants d'Associations = ESAE, GEV
AECEWA	Association of Episcopal Conferences of English-Speaking West Africa	**AEDA**	Association Européenne pour le Droit de l'Alimentation = EFLA
AeCF	Aero Club de France	**AEDAVE**	Asociación Empresarial de Agencias de Viaje
AECF	Association of European Christian Fraternities = EKV	**AEDBCS**	Association Européenne des Directeurs de Bureaux de Concerts et Spectacles
AECGV	Association Européenne du Commerce en Gros des Viandes	**AEDBF**	Association Européenne pour le Droit Bancaire et Financier (Belgium)
AECI	African Explosives and Chemical Industries	**AEDC**	Aboriginal Economic Development Corporation (Australia)
		AEDC	American Economic Development Council

AEDCL	Association of European Documentation Centre Libraries (*now* EDA)
AEDE	Association Européenne des Enseignants = EAT
AEDÉC	Association Européenne d'Études Chinoises = EACS
AEDEMO	Asociación Española de Estudios de Mercado y de Opinion Comercial
AEDF	Asian Economic Development Fund
AEDH	Association Européenne des Directeurs d'Hôpitaux = EAHM, EVKD
AEDIPE	Asociación Española de Direccion de Personal
AEDP	Aboriginal Employment and Development Program
AEDP	Association Européenne pour la Direction de Personnel = EAPM
AEDP	Association for Educational Data Processing (U.S.A.)
AEDRI	Airborne Equipment Design & Research Institute (China)
AEDS	Association for Educational Data Systems (U.S.A.)
AÉÉ	Agence pour les Économies d'Énergie
AEE	Asociación Electrotécnica Española
AEE	Association for Environmental Education
AEE	Association for Experiential Education
AEE	Association of Energy Engineers (U.S.A.)
AEE	Atomic Energy Establishment
AEEA	Association Européenne pour l'Enseignement de l'Architecture = EAAE
AEEA	European Association of Directory Publishers = EADP, EAV
AEEC	Airlines Electronic Engineering Committee (International)
AEEC	Animal Experimentation Ethics Committee
AEEC	Association of European Express Carriers (Belgium)
AÉECEEC	Association des Études de l'Europe Centrale et de l'Europe de l'Est du Canada = CEESAC
AEED	Association Européenne des Enseignants Dentaires = ADEE
AEÉD	Association Européenne pour l'Étude du Diabete = EASD

AEEE	Association of European Economics Education
AEÉEV	Association Européenne des Établissements d'Enseignement Vétérinaire = EAEVE
AEEF	Association Européenne de l'Ethnie Française
AEEF	Association Européenne des Exploitations Frigorifiques
AEEGS	American Electroencephalographic Society
AEÉMA	Association Européenne pour l'Éducation aux Médias Audiovisuels (Belgium)
AEEP	Associação das Enfermeiras e dos Enfermeiros Portugueses
AÉEPA	Association d'Études Européennes de Presse Agricole
AEEPJ	Association Européenne des Publications pour la Jeunesse
AÉÉRB	Association de l'Église Évangelique Reformée du Burkina
AEESA	Asociación Española de Economía y Sociología Agrarias
AEESCA	Association for Engineering Education in South and Central Asia
AEESEA	Association for Engineering Education in Southeast Asia
AEESEAP	Association for Engineering Education in Southeast Asia and the Pacific (New Zealand)
AEET	Atomic Energy Establishment Trombay (India)
AEETD	Association Européenne pour l'Enseignement de la Théorie du Droit (Belgium) = EATLT
AEEU	Amalgamated Engineering and Electrical Union (*ex* AEU)
AÉEVTPLF	Association des Établissements d'Enseignement Vétérinaire totalement ou partiellement de la Langue Française
AEEW	Atomic Energy Establishment Winfrith
AEEZ	Association des Entreprises de l'Est du Zaïre
AEF	Africa Evangelical Fellowship
AEF	Aircraft Engineering Foundation (U.S.A.)
AEF	Airfields Environment Federation
AEF	American Economic Foundation
AEF	American Euthanasia Foundation
AEF	Asfaltentreprenørenes Forening

AEF	Asociación Española de Financiadores	**AEI**	Airborne Equipment Institute (China)
AEFA	American Educational Finance Association	**AEI**	Alianza Espiritualista Internacional (Chile)
AEFA	Association Européenne des Films Animatiques (Belgium) = EAAF	**AEI**	American Enterprise Institute for Public Policy Research
AEFA	Association of European Federations of Agro-Engineers = CEIA, FAVE	**AEI**	Associated Electrical Industries
AEFJ	Asociación Española de Fabricantes de Juguetes	**AÉI**	Association des Écoles Internationales
AEFJ-Assoc	Association Européenne de Formation au Journalisme = EJTA	**AEI**	Associazione Educatrice Italiana
AEFM	Association Européenne des Festivals de Musique = EAMF	**AEI**	Associazione Elettrotecnica ed Elettronica Italiana
AEFMA	Association Européenne F. Matthias Alexander (Belgium)	**AEI**	Associazione Enotecnici Italiani
AEFNU-Mexico DF	Asociación de ex Funcionarios de las Naciones Unidas en Mexico = AFPNU Mexico DF	**AEIA**	Asociación Escuela de Ingenieria Agronomica (Ecuador)
AÉFS	Association des Éleveurs Française de Southdown	**AEIA**	Asociación Española de Informática y Automática
AEFTOP	Agrupación Española de Fabricantes de Transmisiones Oleo-Hidraulicas y Pneumatics	**AEIAAF**	Association Européenne de l'Industrie des Aliments pour Animaux Familiers
AEG	Albert-Einstein Gesellschaft	**AEIAR**	Association Européenne des Institutions d'Aménagement Rural
AEG	Allgemeine Elektrizitäts Gesellschaft	**AEIBS**	Association Européenne pour l'Information et les Bibliothèques de Santé = EAHIL
AEG	Asociación Española de Gemologia		
AEG	Association of Engineering Geologists (U.S.A.)	**AEIC**	Agence Européenne d'Information sur la Consommation
AEG	Association of Exploration Geochemists	**AEID**	Association Européenne des Instituts de Recherches et de Formation en Matière de Développement = EADI
AEG	Association pour l'Encouragement des Études Grecques en France		
AEGC	Association Européenne de Génie Civil	**AEIDC**	Arctic Environmental Information and Data Centre
AEGE	ASEAN Experts Group on the Environment	**AEIDL**	Association Européenne pour l'Information sur le Développement Local (Belgium)
AEGIS	Aid for the Elderly in Government Institutions		
AEGIS	American European Government Information Services	**AEIÉ**	Agence d'Examen de l'Investissement Étranger (Canada) = FIRA
AEGIS	Australian Electronic Government Information Service	**AEIE**	Association of Indian Engineering Industry (India)
AEGM	Anglican Evangelical Group Movement	**AEIH**	Association Européenne des Industries de l'Habillement
AEGPL	Association Européenne des Gaz de Pétrole Liquéfiés	**AEIII**	Association of the European Independent Informatics Industry
AEGRA-FLEX	Association Européenne des Graveurs et des Flexographes	**AEIPPR**	American Enterprise Institute for Public Policy Research
AEGS	Association of European Geological Societies	**AEIS**	Association of Electronic Industries in Singapore
AEHPL	Association Européenne pour l'Histoire de la Photographie = EGGPh, ESHPh	**AEIT**	Asociación Española de Ingenieros de Telecomunicación
AEI	Agéncia Europeia de Imprensa	**AEIU**	Asemblea de Estudiantes Independistas Universitarios
		AEJ	Association for Education in Journalism (U.S.A.)

AEJE	Association Européenne des Juristes d'Entreprises (Netherlands) = ECLA
AEK	Atomenergikommissionen (Denmark)
AEKI	Atomenergia Kutató Intézet
AELE	Association Européenne de Libre Échange (EFTA)
AELÉ	Association Européenne des Loteries d'État (Switzerland)
AELFA	Asociación Española de Logopedia, Foniatria y Audiologia
AELI	Asociación Europa de Libre Intercambio
AÉLIA	Association d'Études Linguistiques Interculturelles Africaines
AELLA	Association des Entrepreneurs Luxembourgeois des Lignes d'Autobus
AELLE	Association Européenne des Loteries et Lotos d'Etat (Switzerland)
AELTC	All England Lawn Tennis Club
AEM	Alianza Evangélica Mundial = UEM, WEF
AEM	Asociación Española de Marketing
AEMB	Association des Entrepreneurs de Montage de Belgique
AEMB	Association Européenne des Marchés aux Bestiaux
AEMC	Atomic Energy Minerals Centre (Pakistan)
AEMDA	Alliance Européenne des Associations de Myopathes = EAMDA
AEME	Association of Export and Marketing Executives
AEME	Association pour l'Enseignement Médical en Europe = AMEE, ASME
AEMH	Association Européenne des Médecins des Hôpitaux
AEMHSM	Association Européenne des Musées de l'Histoire des Sciences Médicales
AEMI	Association Européenne de Médecine Interne
AEMP	Association of European Management Publishers
AEMRI	Association of European Market Research Institutes
AEMS	American Engineering Model Society
AEMSM	Association of European Metal Sink Manufacturers
AEMT	Association of Electrical Machinery Trades
AEMT	Association of Emergency Medical Technicians
AEMTM	Association of European Machine Tool Merchants
AEMUS	Asociación de Estudiantes de Música (Uruguay)
AEN	Agence de l'OCDE pour l'Energie Nucléaire = NEA
AEN	Agentsvo Ekonomicheskikh Novostei
AENA	All England Netball Association
AENE	Association Européenne de Neuro-Endocrinologie = ENEA
AENOC	Association of European National Olympic Committees = ACNOE
AENOR	Asociación Española de Normalizacion
AÉNSB	Association de l'École Nationale Supérieure de Bibliothécaires (*now* ACB)
AEO	Arbeitsgemeinschaft für Elektronenoptik
AEO	Asociación Española de Orientalistas
AEO	Association of Education Officers
AEO	Association of Exhibition Organisers
AEO	Atomic Energy Organisation
AEOA	Adult Education Organisers' Association (Éire)
AEOI	Atomic Energy Organisation of Iran
AEOM	Association of European Open Air Museums
AEOPSP	Association Européenne des Officiers Professionnels Sapeurs-Pompiers
AEOZ	Association des Entreprises de l'Ouest du Zaïre
AEP	Academie Européenne des Écrivains Publics (Belgium)
AEP	Agence Européenne de Productivité (OECE)
AEP	Agencia Ecuadoriana de Prensa
AEP	Association Européenne de Podologues (Belgium)
AEP	Association Européenne de Psychiatrie (Luxembourg)
AEP	Association of Educational Psychologists
AEP	Association of Embroiderers and Pleaters
AEPA	All-Ethiopia Peasants Association
AEPB	Association pour l'Emploi des Plastiques dans le Bâtiment
AEPC	Asociación Española para el Progreso de las Ciencias
AEPCO	Association of Economic Poisons Control Officials (U.S.A.)

AEPE	Asociación Empresarial Publicidad Exterior	**AÉRALL**	Association d'Études et de Recherches sur les Aéronefs Allégés
AEPE	Asociación Establecimientos Privados de Enseñanza (Costa Rica)	**AERC**	African Economic Research Consortium (Kenya) = CREA
AEPE	Asociación Europea de Profesores del Español	**AERC**	Alcohol Education and Research Council
AEPE	Association pour l'Enseignement de la Pédiatrie en Europe = APEE	**AERC**	Applied Environmental Research Centre Ltd
AEPI	Agro-Environment Protection Institute (China)	**AERCE**	Asociación Española de Responsables de Compras y Existencias
AEPI	American Educational Publishers Institute	**AERCG**	African Environmental Research and Consulting Group (U.S.A.)
AEPIA	Agrupación Española de Plaguicidas	**AERDC**	Agricultural Extension and Rural Development Centre
AÉPIF	Association pour l'Étude et de Progrès de l'Irrigation Fertilisante	**AERDRI**	Agricultural Extension and Rural Development Research Unit (Egypt)
AEPLA	Asociación Española de Fabricantes de Agroquímicos para la Protección de las Plantas	**AERE**	Association of Environmental and Resource Economics (U.S.A.)
AEPP	Association of Existential Psychology and Psychiatry (U.S.A.)	**AERE**	Atomic Energy Research Establishment
AEPPC	Association Européenne des Practiciens des Procédures Collectives	**AERFC**	Association of European Regional Financial Centres
AEPS	Asociación Española de Prevención y Seguridad	**AERI**	Agricultural Economics Research Institute
AÉPS	Association des Établissements Publics de Soins (Belgium) = VOV	**AERL**	Association of Economic Representatives in London
AEPT	Asociación Española de Prensa Tecnica	**AERLS**	Agricultural Extension and Research Liaison Services (Nigeria)
AEQCT	Asociación Española de Químicos y Coloristas Textiles	**AERO**	Air Education and Recreation Association
AER	Asociación Ecuatoriana de Radiodifusora	**AEROBAL**	Association Européenne des Fabricants de Boîtes en Aluminium pour les Aérosols
AER	Asociación Española de Robotica	**Aerocivil**	Departamento Administrativo de Aeronáutica Civil (Colombia)
AER	Assembly of European Regions (Belgium)	**AERONICA**	Aerolineas Nicaragüenses
AER	Association Européenne de Radiologie = EAR, EGR	**AEROPA**	Intelligence Service for Air Transport in the European Community (Belgium)
AER	Association Européenne du Rhum = ERA, ERI, ERV	**AERP**	Agrupación Española de Relaciones Publicas
AÉR	Association Européenne pour l'Étude du Problème des Réfugiés	**AERP**	Association Européenne pour la Recherche sur le Pomme de Terre = EAPR
AER	Association for Education by Radio (U.S.A.)	**AERP**	Association of European Reiki Practitioners
AER	Association for Eye Research	**AERPF**	Association Européenne pour la Réduction de la Pollution due aux Fibres = EAFP
AERA	American Educational Research Association		
AÉRA	Association pour l'Étude et la Recherche Astronautique et Cosmique	**AERS**	Atlantic Estuarine Research Society (U.S.A.)
AERAC	Association Auxiliaire pour l'Enseignement Supérieur et la Recherche Agronomique en Coopération	**AERSG**	African Elephant and Rhino Specialist Group (Kenya)

AERTA	Association Européenne de Radio et Télévision Agricole
AERTEL	Association Européenne Rubans, Tresses, Tissus Elastiques
AERU	Agribusiness and Economic Research Unit (New Zealand)
AÉRZAP	Association pour les Études et Recherchess de Zoologie Appliquée et de Phytopathologie (Belgium) = VOFyToZ
AES	Abrasive Engineering Society (U.S.A.)
AES	Aerospace Electrical Society (U.S.A.)
AES	Agricultural Economics Society
AES	Amateur Entomologists Society
AES	American Electroencephalographic Society
AES	American Electromechanical Society
AES	American Electronical Society
AES	American Electroplaters Society
AES	American Endodontic Society
AES	American Entomological Society
AES	American Epidemiological Society
AES	American Epilepsy Society
AES	American Equilibration Society
AES	American Ethnological Society
AES	American Eugenics Society
AES	Asian Environmental Society (Philippines)
AES	Atlantic Economic Society
AES	Audio Engineering Society (U.K., U.S.A.)
AES	Australian Entomological Society
AES&S	Association of English Singers & Speakers
AES-CCC	Amici dello Stato Brasiliano dell' Espirito Santo - Centro di Collaborazione Comunitaria
AESA	Aerolineas de El Salvador SA
AESA	Agricultural Engineering Society (Australia)
AESA	American Educational Studies Association
AESA	Association pour l'Enseignement Social en Afrique = ASWEA
AESA	Astilleros Españoles
AESAU	Association of Eastern and Southern African Universities
AESC	Arab Economic and Social Council (Egypt) = CESA
AESCO	Association Européenne des Écoles et Colleges d'Optométrie
AESD	Association of Engineering and Shipbuilding Draughtsmen
AESE	American Educational Studies Association
AESE	Association of Earth Science Editors (U.S.A.)
AESÉD	Association Européenne de Sociétés d'Études pour le Développement
AÉSF	Association des Écrivains Scientifiques de France
AESG	Asian Elephant Specialist Group
AESGP	Association Européenne des Spécialités Pharmaceutiques Grand Public
AESI	Agricultural Economics Society of Ireland
AESIEAP	Association of the Electricity Supply Industry in East Asia and the Western Pacific (Australia)
AÉSIMP	Association pour l'Étude de la Stérilité et la Médicine Périnatale
AESIS	Australian Earth Sciences Information System Advisory Committee
AESM	All-Ethiopia Socialist Movement
AESOP	Association of European Schools of Planning
AESOR	Association Européenne de Sous-Officiers de Réserve
AÉSPRE	Association des Écoles de Santé Publique de la Région Européenne = ASPHER
AESR	Architects and Engineers for Social Responsibility
AESS	Association of English Singers and Speakers
AESSA	Aeronautical Society of South Africa
AESSEA	Agricultural Economics Society of South East Asia (Philippines)
AESTM	Association Européenne des Sciences et Techniques de la Mer
AESU	Arabische Eisen und Stahl Union = AISU, UAFA
AET	Association Européenne de Recherches sur la Glande Thyroïde = ETA
AET	Association Européenne de Thanatologie
AET	Association Européenne de Thermographie = EAT, ETA
AET	Association of Auto-Electrical Technicians

AETA	Association Européenne Tourisme Aérien
AETC	Alliance Européenne pour la Télévision et la Culture = EATC
AETEL	Asociación Española de Tecnicos de Laboratorio (Spain)
AÉTFAT	Association pour l'Étude Taxonomique de la Flore d'Afrique Tropicale (Belgium)
AETG	Association pour une Entraide avec les Touareg de Gossi (Mali)
AETR	Asociación Española de Tecnicos en Radiologia
AETS	Association for the Education of Teachers in Science (U.S.A.)
AETT	Association of Education and Training Technology
AETU	All-Ethiopia Trade Union
AEU	Amalgamated Engineering Union (*now* AEEU)
AEU	American Ethical Union
AEU	Arbeitskreis Evangelischer Unternehmer in der Bundesrepublik Deutschland
AEU	Asia Electronics Union (Japan)
AEV	Arbeitsgemeinschaft Erdölgewinnung und Verarbeitung (Germany)
AEV	Asociación de Escritores Venezolanos
AEVH	Association for the Education of the Visually Handicapped (U.S.A.)
AEVII	Federación de Veterinarios Europeos de la Industria y la Investigación
AEVPC	Association Européenne de Vente par Correspondance = EMOTA
AEWC	Alaska Eskimo Whaling Commission (U.S.A.)
AEWHA	All England Women's Hockey Association
AEWLA	All England Women's Lacrosse Association
AEWVH	Association for the Education and Welfare of the Visually Handicapped
AEYSC	All-European Youth and Student Cooperation = CPEJE
AF	Albino Fellowship
AF	Alliance Française
AF	Alternatief Forum (Suriname)
AF	Aluminium Federation
AF	Alpýduflokkurinn
AF	Angpanneföreningen
AF	Arkitektförbundet
AF	Association of Women (Moldova)
AFA	Access Flooring Association
AFA	Advocates For Animals
AFA	African Farmers Association
AFA	Air Freight Association of America
AFA	Amateur Fencing Association
AFA	Amateur Football Alliance
AFA	American Family Association
AFA	American Federation of Arts
AFA	American Federation of Astrologers
AFA	American Federation of Aviculture
AFA	American Finance Association
AFA	American Forensic Society
AFA	American Forestry Association
AFA	American Fracture Association
AFA	Anorexic Family Aid
AFA	Anti-Fascist Action
AFA	Arbeitsgemeinschaft für Abfallwirtschaft
AFA	ASEAN Federation of Accountants
AFA	Asociación Fisica Argentina
AFA	Asociación Folklorica Argentina
AFA	Assistance Forestière Africaine (Ivory Coast)
AFA	Association Française d'Astronomie
AFAA	Aerobics and Fitness Association of America
AFAA	ASEAN Federation of Advertising Associations
AFAA	ASEAN Federation of Automobile Associations
AFAA	Asian Federation of Advertising Associations (Japan)
AFAA	Association of Faculties of Agriculture in Africa
AFAA	Australian Federation of Advertising Agencies
AFAB	Association des Fédérations Africaines de Basketball (Egypt)
AFAB	Association Française d'Agriculture Biologique
AFAB	Associazione Food and Beverage
AFABA	Association des Fédérations Africaines de Basketball Amateur
AFAC	American Fisheries Advisory Committee
AFAC	Association des Fabricants d'Aliments Contrôlés pour le Bétail (Luxembourg)

AFACED	Association des Femmes d'Affaires et Entrepreneurs du Benin
AFACO	Association Française des Amateurs Constructeurs l'Ordinateurs
AFACPG	Association Française des Amateurs de Cactées et de Plantes Grasses
AFAEP	Association of Fashion Advertising and Editorial Photographers
AFAF	Asociación de Fabricantes de Articulos de Ferreteria (Venezuela)
AFAHA	Association Française des Amateurs Horlogerie Ancienne
AFAL	Association Francophone d'Accueil et de Liaison
AFALMA	Africa Association for Liturgy, Music and Arts (Zambia) = AALMA
AFAM	Action Familiale Africaine et Malagache
AFAMM	ASEAN Federation of Agricultural Machinery Manufacturers
AFAP	Association de la Femme Africaine Progressiste
AFAP	Association Française pour l'Accroissement de la Productivité
AFAQ	Association Française pour l'Expansion des Produits Agricoles de Qualité Garantie
AFAR	American Federation for Aging Research
AFAR	Asociación Feminia de Acción Rural (Argentina)
AFARD	Association des Femmes Africaines pour la Recherche sur le Développement = AAWORD
AFAS	American Fine Arts Society
AFAS	Anorexic Family Aid
AFAS	Association Française pour l'Avancement des Sciences
AFAS	Association France-Asie Sud
AFASIC	Association for all Speech Impaired Children
AFAT	Association Française de l'Assurance de Transports
AFB	Action for Bosnia
AFB	American Foundation of the Blind
AFB	Arbeitsgemeinschaft Fachärztlicher Berufsverbände
AFB	Arbeitsstelle für das Bibliothekswesen
AFB	Association Française du Béton
AFBA	Asociación Farmacéutica y Bioquímica Argentina

AFBC	Association of Football Badge Collectors
AFBD	Association of Futures Brokers and Dealers
AFBF	American Farm Bureau Federation
AFBS	American and Foreign Bible Society
AFBW	Algemene Fereratie van Bonaireaarise Werknemers (Netherlands Antilles)
AFC	African Football Confederation = CAF
AFC	African Forestry Commission
AFC	Agricultural Finance Corporation (Kenya)
AFC	Asian Football Confederation
AfC	Association for Colleges
AFC	Association Française de Chimiurgie
AFC	Association Française de Cristallographie
AFC	Association France-Containers
AFC	Association of Fish Canners
AFC	Australian Fisheries Council
AFC	Australian Forestry Council
AFC	Authors For Choice
AFC	Latin-American Forestry Commission (FAO)
AFCA	Association Française pour la Communauté Atlantique
AFCA	Association of Financial Controllers and Administrators
AFCA	Association pour la Formation des Cadres de l'Industrie et de l'Administration en Langue Française
AFCA	Association Professionelle des Fabricants de Compléments pour l'Alimentation Animale
AFCAC	African Civil Aviation Commission = CAFAC
AFCALTI	Association Française de Calcul et de Traitement de l'Information
AFCAM	Association of Fluorocarbon Consumers and Manufacturers
AFCAM	Ateliers Ferroviaires et Métallurgiques du Cameroun
AFCAPS	Association of Flexible PVC Suppliers
AFCASOLE	Association des Fabricants de Café Soluble des Pays de la CEE
AFCAT	Association Française de Calorimétrie et d'Analyse Thermique
AFCC	Association Française du Commerce des Cacaos
AFCCE	Association of Federal Communications Consulting Engineers (U.S.A.)

AFCEA	Armed Forces Communications and Electronics Association (U.S.A.)
AFCEL	Association Française pour la Connaissance de l'Ex-Libris
AFCÉT	Association Française pour la Cybernétique Économique et Technique
AFCFP	Arab Federation of Chemical Fertiliser Producers
AFCG	American Fine China Guild
AFCGC	Asociación Venezolana de Criadores de Ganada Cebé
AFCI	Association of Film Commissioners International (U.S.A.)
AFCIMAT	Asociación de Fabricantes de Conjuntos Importantes para la Mecanización del Agro y el Transporte (Argentina)
AFCIQ	Association Française pour le Contrôle Industriel de Qualité
AFCL	African Container Line
AFCL	Association Française des Conseils en Lobbying
AFCM	ASEAN Federation of Cement Manufacturers
AFCMA	Aluminium Foil Container Manufacturers Association
AFCMA	Asian Federation of Catholic Medical Associations
AFCMA	Australian Fibreboard Containers Manufacturers Association
AFCO	Asociación Española de Fabricantes de Carton Ondulado
AFCO	Australian Federation of Consumer Organizations
AFCOA	Australian Council for Overseas Aid
AFCOD	Association Française des Conseilleurs de Direction
AFCODI	Africaine Commerciale de Diffusion
AFCOFÉL	Association Française Comités Économiques Agricoles de Fruits et Légumes
AFCOM	Africaine de Constructions Mécaniques (Ivory Coast)
AFCOS	Association Française des Conseils en Organisation Scientifique
AFCOT	Association Française Cotonnière
AFCP	Association of Free Community Papers (U.S.A.)
AFCR	American Federation for Clinical Research
AFCS	Assocation Française des Chasseurs de Son

AFCU	American and Foreign Christian Union
AFCUD	Asia Fund for Credit Union Development (Thailand)
AFCWU	African Food and Canning Workers Union (South Africa)
AFD	Alliance of Free Democrats (Hungary)
AFD	Asociación de Familias de los Desaparecidos (Chile)
AFD	Associated Fashion Designers of London
AFDAC	Association Française de Documentation Automatique en Chimie
AfDB	African Development Bank
AFDC	Agriculture and Fishery Development Corporation (Republic of Korea)
AFDCS	Association of First Division Civil Servants (Éire)
AFDE	Association Française pour la Diffusion de l'Espagnol
AFDEC	Association of Franchised Distributors of Electronic Components
AFDET	Association Française pour le Développement de l'Enseignement Technique
AfDF	African Development Fund = ADF, FAD
AFDI	Agriculteurs Français et Développement International
AFDI	Association Française des Déménageurs Internationaux
AFDIN	Association Française de Documentation et d'Information
AFDIP	Association Africaine des Formateurs et Directeurs de Personnel
AFDO	Association of Food and Drug Officials (U.S.A.)
AFDP	Association of Former Political Prisoners (Moldova)
AFE	Administraçion de los Ferrocarriles del Estado (Uruguay)
AFE	American Association of Feed Exporters
AFE	Asociación de Forestales del Ecuador
AFE	Asociación de Futbolistas Españoles
AFÉ	Association Française de l'Éclairage
AFÉA	Association Française d'Études Américaines
AFÉC	Association Française pour l'Étude du Cancer
AFEC	Association Française pour le Contrôle de la Qualité des Hormones Désherbantes

AFÉC	Association Francophone d'Éducation Comparée	**AFEME**	Asociación de Facultades Ecuatorianas de Medicina
AFECI	Association des Fabricants Européens de Chauffebains et Chauff-Eau Instantanés et de Chaudières Murales au Gaz	**AFEMS**	European Association of Sporting Ammunition Manufacturers
AFECOR	Association des Fabricants Européens d'Appareils de Contrôle et de Régulation	**AFEO**	ASEAN Federation of Engineering Organisations (Indonesia)
AFECPAL	Asociación de Facultades y Escuelas de Contaduria Publica de America Latina	**ÁFEOSz**	Általános Fogyasztási Szövetkezetek Országos Szövetsége / National Federation of Consumer Cooperatives (Hungary)
AFEDÉF	Association des Fabricants Européens d'Équipements Ferroviaires	**AFÉQ**	Association Française pour l'Étude du Quaternaire
AFÉDÉS	Association Française pour l'Étude et le Développement des Applications de l'Énergie Solaire	**AFERA**	Association des Fabricants Européens des Rubans Auto-adhésifs
AFEE	Association for Evolutionary Economics (U.S.A.)	**AFÉRA**	Association Française des Études et Recherches d'Afrique
AFÉE	Association Française pour l'Étude des Eaux	**AFERO**	Asia and the Far East Regional Office (FAO)
AFEEC	ASEAN Federation of Electrical Engineering Contractors	**AFES**	ASEAN Federation of Endocrine Societies (Philippines)
AFEF	Association Française des Enseignants de Français	**AFÉS**	Association Française pour l'Étude du Sol
AFEI	Americans for Energy Independence	**AFESA**	Agrupación de Almacenistas de Ferretaria de España
AFEI	Arab Federation of Engineering Industries	**AFESD**	Arab Fund for Economic and Social Development = FADES
AFÉI	Association Française pour l'Étiquetage d'Information	**AFETT**	Association pour la Formation Européenne des Travailleurs aux Technologies (Belgium)
AFEI	Association of Finnish Electric Industries		
AFEI	Association of Freelance Editors and Indexers (Éire)	**AFETUK**	Anne Frank Educational Trust
AFÉID	Association Française pour l'Étude des Irrigations et du Drainage	**AFF**	Affischeringsföretagens Forening
		AFF	Allmänna Försvarsföreningen
AFEIEAL	Asociación de Facultades, Escuelas e Institútos de Investigaciones Económicas de America Latina	**AFF**	ASEAN Football Federation
		AFF	Association Française du Froid
		AFF	Australia Farmers Federation
AFEJ	Asian Forum of Environmental Journalists (Nepal)	**AFFA**	Association for Field Archaeology (U.S.A.)
AFELIES	Asociación del Fomento de la Educacion Laboral y Investigacion Economica y Social (Peru)	**AFFCO**	Alaska Forest Fire Council
		AFFCOD	Association Française des Firmes de Conseillers de Direction
AFÉLSH	Association des Facultés ou Établissements de Lettres et Sciences Humaines des Universités d'Expression Française (Senegal)	**AFFD**	Association of Fashion Fabric Distributors
		AFFF	American Fish Farmers Federation
		AFFHC	Australian Freedom from Hunger Campaign
AFEMA	Association des Fabricants Européens d'Emulsifiants Alimentaires	**AFFI**	American Frozen Food Institute
		AFFI	Arab Federation of Food Industries = FAIA
AFEMAC	Asociación de Fabricantes Españoles de Maquinas de Coser y para la Confección	**AFFMA**	ASEAN Federation of Furniture Manufacturers Association

AFFP	Arab Federation of Fish Producers = FAIP, FAPP		**AFIA**	Association Française Interprofessionelle des Agrumes
AFFPI	ASEAN Federation of Food Processing Industries		**AFIA**	Association Française pour l'Intelligence Artificielle
AFFR	Academy of Fire and Flood Restoration		**AFIC**	Asian Finance and Investment Corporation (Philippines)
AFFS	American Federation of Film Societies		**AFIC**	Association of Fashion and Image Consultants (U.S.A.)
AFFW	Arab Federation of Food Workers		**AFIC**	Australian Fishing Industry Council
AFG	Al-Anon Family Groups UK and Eire		**AFICAU**	Association de Fomento del Intercambio Commercial Anglo-Uruguayo
AFG	Association des Fabricants de Glucose de la CEE		**AFICCA**	Association pour la Fondation Internationale du Cinéma et de la Communication Audiovisuelle
AFG	Association Française de Gemmologie			
AFGA	Afghanistan Family Guidance Association		**AFICE**	Association Française des Ingénieurs et Chefs d'Entretien
AFGC	American Forage and Grassland Council		**AFICEP**	Association Française des Ingénieurs du Caoutchouc et des Plastiques
AFGE	American Federation of Government Employees		**AFICS**	Association of Former International Civil Servants = AAFI
AFGM	American Federation of Grain Millers		**AFICTIC**	Association Française des Ingénieurs, Chimistes et Techniciens des Industries du Cuir
AFGR	Association Française de Génie Rural			
AFGRED	Association des Femmes Guinéennes pour la Recherche et le Développement (Guinea)		**AFIDA**	Asociación de Ferais Internacionales de America
AFH	American Foundation for Homeopathy		**AFIDÉS**	Association Francophone Internationale des Directeurs d'Établissements Scolaires
AFHB	ASEAN Food Handling Bureau			
AFHRL	Australian Fish Health Reference Laboratory		**AFIEB**	Association Française des Ingénieurs et Experts en Bois Commerce et Industries de Bois
AFHS	Association of Family History Societies			
AFI	Acupuncture Foundation of Ireland		**AFIÉM**	Association Française pour l'Information en Économie Ménagère
AFI	Aid for India			
AFI	American Fiber Institute		**AFIF**	Association Suisse des Fournisseurs de l'Industrie pour la Ferraille
AFI	American Film Institute			
AFI	American Forest Institute		**AFIGAP**	Association Francophone Internationale des Groupes d'Animation de Paraplégie
AFI	Arbeidsforskningsinstituttet (Norway)			
AFI	Arthritis Foundation of Ireland		**AFIMAC**	Association des Fabricants et Importateurs de Matériel à Air Comprimé (Belgium)
AFI	Association for Futures Investment			
AFI	Association Fraternelle Internationale = ICA		**AFIMIN**	Association Française des Fabricants et Importateurs de Matériels et de Produits pour l'Industrie du Nettoyage
AFI	Association of Finnish Industries			
AFI	Association of Food Industries (U.S.A.)			
AFI	Associazione dei Fonografici Italiani		**AFIN**	Asociación de Compañias Financieras del Ecuador
AFI	Associazione Farmacisti dell'Industria			
AFI	Les Auxiliaires Féminines Internationales = ICA		**AFIN**	Association Française des Informaticiens
AFI-RAN	Africa, India Ocean Region Air Navigation		**AFINÉ**	Association Française pour l'Industrie Nucléaire d'Équipement
AFIA	American Foreign Insurance Association		**AFinLA**	Association Finlandaise de Linguistique Appliquée
AFIA	Apparel and Fashion Industry Association of Great Britain			

AFIP	Association Française des Indépendants du Pétrole	**AFLI**	Arab Federation for Libraries and Information (Tunisia)
AFIP	Association pour la Formation et l'Information Paysannes	**AFLR&L**	Association of Football League Referees and Linesmen
AFIP	Associazione Fotografi Italiani Professionisti	**AFM**	American Federation of Musicians of the United States and Canada
AFIPS	American Federation of Information Processing Societies	**AFM**	Asociación Española de Fabricantes de Maquinas-Herramienta
AFIR	Association Française des Industries de la Robinetterie	**AFM**	Association Forêt Méditerranéenne
AFIRD	Association Française des Instituts de Recherche sur le Développement	**AFM**	Association Française contre les Myopathies
AFIRÉC	Association Financière Internationale de Recherche Étude Cellulose	**AFM**	Association of Facilities Managers (*now* BIFM)
AFIRO	Association Française d'Informatique et de Recherche Opérationnelle	**AFM**	Aussenhandelsverband für Mineralöl
AFIS	Amministrazione Fiduciaria Italiana della Somalia	**AFMA**	Ámerican Federation of Medical Accreditation
AFISA	Aero Fletes Internationales SA (Panama)	**AFMA**	American Feed Manufacturers Association
AFISAC	Associazione Fabbricanti Italiani e Staniere di Macchinarie e Apparecchiature ad Aria Compressa	**AFMA**	American Film Marketing Association
		AFMA	American Fur Merchants Association
		AFMA	ASEAN Federation of Mining Associations
AFITAE	Association Française des Ingénieurs et Techniciens de l'Aéronautique et de l'Espace	**AFMA**	Association Française des Musées d'Agriculture
AFITE	Association Française des Ingénieurs et Techniciens de l'Environnement	**AFMA**	Association of Food Marketing Agencies in Asia and the Pacific
AFIUM	Associazione Fabbricanti Italiani di Utinsileria Meccanica	**AFMA**	Australian Fisheries Management Authority
AFJA	Association Française des Journalistes Agricoles	**AFMC**	Asian Fluid Mechanics Committee (Japan)
AFJB	Association des Femmes Juristes du Benin	**AFMC**	Association des Femmes Managers du Congo
AFJCC	American Forum for Jewish-Christian Cooperation	**AFME**	African Forum for Mathematical Ecology (Ethiopia)
AFJÉT	Association Française de Journalistes et Écrivains du Tourisme	**AFMÉ**	Agence Française pour la Maitrise de l'Énergie
AFJWG	Australia/France Joint Working Group on the Environment	**AFMH**	American Foundation for Mental Hygiene
AFK	Arbeitsgemeinschaft für Friedens-und Konfliktforschung	**AFMM**	United Kingdom Association of Fish Meal Manufacturers
AfK	Arbeitsgemeinschaft für Kommunikationsforschung	**AFMO**	Association Française de Constructeurs de Machines-Outils
AFL	Afar Liberation Front (Ethiopia)	**AFMP**	Association of Free Magazines and Periodicals
AFL	Armed Forces of Liberia		
AFL	Association Française Laitière	**AFMR**	African Music Rostrum (Ivory Coast) = TMAF
AFL	Association Française pour la Lecture		
AFL-CIO	American Federation of Labor and Congress of Industrial Organizations	**AFMR**	Asian Federation for Persons with Mental Handicap (Singapore)
AFLA	American Foreign Law Association	**AFMR**	Association pour la Formation en Milieu Rural

AFMS	American Federation of Mineralogical Societies	**AFP**	Anglican Pacifist Fellowship
AFMVM	Australasian Federation of Medical and Veterinary Mycology	**AFP**	Armed Forces of the Philippines
AFN	Aerosolforbundet Norge	**AFP**	Asociación Forestal del Perú
AFN	American Forces Network	**AFP**	Association Française de Psychiatrie
AFNA	Accordion Federation of North America	**AFP**	Associazione Fotoreporters Professionisti
AFNA	American Foundation for Negro Affairs	**AFP**	Australian Federal Police
AFNETA	Alley Farming Network for Tropical Africa (Nigeria)	**AFPA**	Advertising Film Producers Association
AFNIL	Agence Francophone pour la Numération Internationale du Livre	**AFPA**	Agence Nationale pour la Formation Professionelle des Adultes
AFNMS	Asian Federation of National Maintenance Societies	**AFPA**	Alcohol Fuels Producers' Association (U.S.A.)
AFNOR	Association Française de Normalisation	**AFPA**	American Fighter Pilots Association
AFO	Arab Family Organisation	**AFPA**	Anguilla Family Planning Association
AFOA	Aéro-Feu Ouest Afrique	**AFPA**	Association de Formation et Perfectionnement Agricole
AFOA	Antiques Fairs Organisers Association	**AFPA**	Association Française de la Presse de l'Automobile
AFOCA	Association Nationale pour la Formation Professionnelle suivant les Techniques de l'Industrie du Caoutchouc	**AFPA**	Association pour la Formation Professionnelle des Adultes
AFOCEL	Association Forêts-Cellulose	**AFPA**	Australian Fire Protection Association
AFOD	Arab Federation for the Organs of the Deaf	**AFPB**	Association Française pour la Préservation du Bois
AFODI	Atelier de Freinage de la Côte-d'Ivoire	**AFPC**	Afghan Fruit Processing Company
AFOÉV	Association Française des Observateurs d'Étoiles Variables	**AFPC**	Association for Fair Play for Children
AFOG	Asian Federation of Obstetrics and Gynaecology	**AFPCM**	Association of Fire Protection Contractors and Manufacturers
AFOHG	Anti-Fascist Organization of Hungarian Gypsies = MCASz	**AFPE**	American Foundation for Pharmaceutical Education
AFOMJ	Association of Fats and Oil Manufacturers of Japan	**AFPE**	American Foundation for Political Education
AFOPDA	African Palm Oil Development Association (Ivory Coast) = ADPH	**AFPE**	Association Française pour la Protection des Eaux
AFOPE	Association Française d'Organisateurs Permanents dans les Entreprises	**AFPEP**	Association Française des Producteurs Exportateurs de Pommes
AFORCOM	Société Africaine de Forages et de Constructions Mécaniques	**AFPF**	African Food and Peace Foundation (Uganda)
AFOREP	Association pour la Formation et la Recherche Psycho-Sociologiques	**AFPF**	Animation Parmi les Femmes pour la Promotion de la Famille (Benin)
AFOS	Agriculture Forestry and Other Human Activities Subgroup (RSWG)	**AFPF**	Association Française pour la Production Fourragère
AFOS	Arab Federation of Shipping (Iraq)	**AFPFL**	Anti-Fascist People's Freedom League (Burma)
AFOSR	Air Force Office of Scientific Research (U.S.A.)	**AFPH**	American Federation of the Physically Handicapped
AFOTEC	Service International d'Appui à la Formation et aux Technologies en Afrique de l'Ouest et au Sahel	**AFPI**	American Foreign Policy Institute
AFP	Agence France Presse	**AFPIA**	Association pour la Formation Professionelle dans les Industries de l'Ameublement

AFPIC	Association Nationale pour la Formation et la Promotion Professionelle dans l'Industrie et le Commerce de la Chaussure et des Cuirs et Peaux
AFPIC	Association pour la Formation Professionnelle dans les Industries Céréalières
AFPMCW	Arab Federation of Petroleum Mines and Chemical Workers
AFPMH	ASEAN Federation for Psychiatric and Mental Health
AFPNU-Mexico DF	Association of Retired United Nations Officials in Mexico = AEFNU Mexico DF
AFPP	Association Française de Producteurs de Plantes à Protéines Légumineuses à Grosses Graines = FAIP, FAPP
AFPPD	Asian Forum of Parliamentarians on Populations and Development (Japan)
AFPPT	Association pour la Formation et le Perfectionnement des Planteurs de Tabac
AfPU	African Postal Union = UPAF
AFPU	Association Française pour la Paix Universelle
AFPVA	Advertising Film and Videotape Producers Association
AFQ	Association Forestière Québecoise (Canada)
AFR	Asociatia Filatelistilor (Romania) (*now* FFR)
AFR	Association for a Free Russia
AFR	Auktoriserade Fastighetsmäklares Riksförbund
AFRA	Association Française de Régulation et d'Automatisme
AFRAA	African Airlines Association
AFRACA	African Regional Agricultural Credit Association
AFRAN	Association Française pour la Recherche de l'Alimentation Normale
AFRAT	Association pour la Formation des Ruraux aux Activités du Tourisme
AFRATC	African Air Tariff Conference (Kenya) = CAFTA
AFRC	Agriculture and Food Research Council
AFRC	Aluminium Foil Recycling Campaign
AFRC	Armed Forces Revolutionary Council (Ghana)
AFRC	Armed Forces Ruling Council (Nigeria)
AFRÉA	Association Française pour les Relations Économiques avec l'Allemagne
AFRÉC	Association Française pour les Recherches et les Études Camérounaises
AFREM	Association Française de Recherches et d'Essais sur les Matériaux et les Constructions
AFREP	Association Française des Relations Publiques
AFRÉSCO	Association Française de Recherches et Études Statistiques Commerciales
AFRF	American Fisheries Research Foundation
AFrI	Action From Ireland
AFRI	American Foundation for Resistance International
AFRI	Association Française de Robotique Industrielle
AFRIC	Agence Française de Representation et d'Industries au Caméroun
AFRIC	Société Africaine Française de Representations Industrielles et Commerciales
AFRIC-HOTELS	Industrie Hôtelière Africaine (Ivory Coast)
AFRIC-TRANSIT	Société Africaine de Transit, Transport, Tourisme (Ivory Coast)
AFRICA	Association pour la Formation, la Recherche et l'Information sur le Centre de l'Afrique
AFRICA Fund	Action For Resisting Invasion, Colonialism and Apartheid Fund
AFRICA RE	African Reinsurance Corporation (Nigeria)
AFRICA-PLAST	Industrie Africaine des Plastiques
AFRIGA	Armement Frigorifique Gabonais
AFRIMEX-CI	Africaine Import-Export Côte d'Ivoire
AFRIQUE-CONTACTS	Société Africaine de Promotion et de Services (Ivory Coast)
AFRIQUE-DéTER-GENTS	Société Africaine de Détergents (Senegal)
AFRISÉN	Armement Frigorifique Sénégalais
AFRO	African Regional Organisation of ICFTU
AFRO	Association des Fondeurs de Fromages (Belgium)
AFRO	Regional Office for Africa (WHO)

AFRO-FIET	African Regional Organization of the International Federation of Commercial, Clerical and Technical Employees
AFROFED-OP	African Regional Organization of the Public Services and Teachers
AFRONUS	African Council of Food and Nutrition Sciences (Zimbabwe) = CASAN
AFROSAI	African Organization of Supreme Audit Institutions
AFRTS	American Forces Radio and Television Service
AFS	American Fern Society
AFS	American Fertility Society
AFS	American Field Service
AFS	American Fisheries Society
AFS	American Folklore Society
AFS	American Foundrymens Society
AFS	Asian Fisheries Society (Philippines)
AFS	Association for Stammerers
AFS	Association of Football Statisticians
AFS	Australian Fishing Service
AFS	Auxiliary Fire Service
AFSA	African Statistical Association (Nigeria)
AFSA	Association des Fabricants Suisses d'Accumulateurs
AFSAT	Système Africain de Télécommunications Satellite
AFSAU	Association of Faculties of Science in African Universities (Kenya)
AFSB	American Federation of Small Business
AFSBO	Association des Fabricants Suisses de Bijouterie et d'Orfèvrerie
AFSC	American Friends Service Committee
AFSC	Australian Food Standards Committee
AFSCI	American Foundation for the Science of Creative Intelligence
AFSÉ	Association Française de Science Économique
AFSJER	Association Feminine pour le Sauvetage des Jeunes et Enfants de Rue (Congo)
AFSMAS	Association Francophone de Spectrométrie de Masses des Solides
AFSMI	Association of Field Service Managers International
AFSO	American Friends of Scottish Opera
AFSOA	Association Française pour la Sauvegarde de l'Orgue Ancien
AFSP	Association Française des Sciences Politiques
AFSP	Australian Foundation of Peoples of the South Pacific
AFSRB	ASEAN Food Security Reserve Board
AFSSP	Association de Fabricants Suisses de Spécialités Pharmaceutiques
AFSSRN	Asian Fisheries Social Science Research Network
AFST	Association of Food Scientists and Technologists (India)
AFSW	Arab Federation of Social Workers (Libya)
AFT	American Federation of Teachers
AFT	Association des Femmes de Tchakaloke (Benin)
AFT	Association for Family Therapy
AFTA	Andean Free Trade Association
AFTA	Arab Fund for Technical Assistance to Arab and African Countries = FAT
AFTA	ASEAN Free Trade Area
AFTA	Association of Finnish Travel Agents
AFTA	Association of French Teachers in Africa = APFA
AFTA	Atlantic Free Trade Area
AFTA	Australian Fishing Tackle Association
AFTAA	Association Française des Techniciens de l'Alimentation Animale
AFTAAC	Arab Fund for Technical Assistance to African Countries (Egypt)
AFTAM	Association pour la Formation Technique de Base des Africains et Malgaches
AFTC	Assistance Forestière Technique et Commerciale (Ivory Coast)
AFTCC	Association of Film and Television in the Celtic Countries
AFTE	Arab Federation for Technical Education = FAET
AFTEC	Association of Former Trainees of the European Communities
AFTERM	Association Française de Terminologie
AFTEX	ASEAN Federation of Textile Industries
AFTIM	Association Française des Techniciens et Ingénieurs de Sécurité et des Médecins du Travail
AFTM	American Foundation for Tropical Medicine
AFTN	Aeronautical Fixed Telecommunications Network (U.S.A.)
AFTO	Association of Flight Training Officers

AFTO	Islamic Agriculture and Food Technology Organization		**AG**	Andean Group
AFTP	Association Française des Techniciens du Pétrole		**AG**	Association for Gnotobiotics
			AG	Astronomische Gesellschaft
AFTPV	Association Française des Techniciens des Peintures, Vernis, Encres d'Imprimerie, Colles et Adhésifs		**AG-CNO**	Assemblée Générale des Comités Nationaux Olympiques (Mexico)
			AGA	Agricola Ganadera Antelana
AFTPVA	Association Française des Techniciens des Peintures, Vernis et Adhésifs		**AGA**	American Gas Association
			AGA	American Genetic Association
AFTRI	Association Française des Transporteurs Routiers Internationaux		**AGA**	Arab Geologists' Association
			AGA	Arbeitgeberverband Gross- und Aussenhandel
AFTS	Aeronautical Fixed Telecommunications Service		**AGA**	Arbeitsgemeinschaft Schadens abwicklung
AFTURD	Association des Femmes Tunisiennes pour la Recherche et le Developpement (Tunisia)		**AGA**	Architectural Granite Association
			AGA	Art Galleries Association (*now* VAGA)
AFTW	Arab Federation of Transport Workers (Libya)		**AGA**	Asociación General de Agricultores (Guatemala)
			AGA	Asparagus Growers' Association
AFTWUA	Amalgamated Footwear and Textile Workers' Union of Australia		**AGA**	Association de Géographes Africains (Ivory Coast)
AFU	Association Foncière Urbaine		**AGA**	Association de Géologues Arabes
AFUC	Association des Femmes Universitaires Catholiques		**AGA**	Association des Entreprises de Gros en Alimentation Générale (Belgium)
AFUCA	Asian Federation of Unesco Clubs and Associations		**AGA**	Australian Gas Association
			AGA	FAO Animal Production Health Division
AFULE	Australian Federated Union of Locomotive Enginemen		**AGAAC**	Acuerdo General Sobre Aranceles Aduaneros y Comercio = GATT
AFUNPI	Association of Former United Nations Personnel in and of India (India)		**AGAB**	Schweizerische Arbeitsgemeinschaft für Akademische Berufs- und Studienberatung
AFUPA	Advertising Film & Videotape Producers' Association			
AFUTT	Association Française des Utilisateurs du Téléphone et des Télécommunications		**AGAC**	American Guild of Authors and Composers
			AGACI	Association Française des Coureurs en Automobile
AFUW	Australian Federation of University Women		**AGADU**	Asociación General de Autores del Uruguay
AFVP	Association Française des Volontaires du Progrès		**AGAF**	Associazione Nazionale fra i Grossisti di Articoli Fotografici
AFW	Akademie für Führungskräfte der Wirtschaft		**AGAH**	FAO Animal Health Service
AfW	Arbeitskreis für Wehrforschung		**AGAK**	Aktionsgemeinschaft der Arbeitnehmer und Konsumenten
AFWA	Australian Federation for the Welfare of Animals		**AGAL**	Australian Government Analytical Laboratories
AFWC	African Forestry and Wildlife Commission (Ghana)		**AGAL**	FAO Livestock Policy Planning Unit
AFZ	Association Française de Zootechnie		**Agalev**	Anders Gaan Leven (Belgium)
AFZA	Australian Fishing Zone Authority		**AGAM**	FAO Meat Milk Service
AG	Action Group (Nigeria)		**AGANAPA**	Asociación de Ganaderos y Agricultores de la Panamericana (Venezuela)
AG	Actuarieël Genootschap			
AG	Adventurers' Guild			

AGAP	FAO Animal Production Service	**AGE**	Asian Information Centre for Geotechnical Engineering (Taiwan)
AGARA	Agrupación de Aseguradores de Riesgos de Aviación	**AGE**	Automotive Glazing Executive
AGARD	Advisory Group for Aerospace Research and Development (NATO)	**AGÉAM**	Association pour la Gérance des Écoles d'Apprentissage Maritime
AGAS	Arbeitsgemeinschaft für Angewandte Sozialforschung	**AGEC**	Arbeitsgemeinschaft Europäischer Chorverbände = EUROCHOR
AGASAL	Association des Grossistes en Appareils Sanitaires du Luxembourg	**AGECH**	Asociación Gremialista de Educatores de Chile
AGAV	Arbeitsgemeinschaft Alternativer Verlage und Autoren	**AGECO**	Agences Générales d'Exchanges Commerciaux
AGAV	Asociación Guatemalteca de Agencias de Viajes (Guatemala)	**AGECOOP**	Agency for Cultural and Technical Cooperation (France) = ACCT
AGB	Arbeitskreis Ganzheitliches Bauen	**AGED**	Association des Grandes Entreprises de Distribution de Belgique
AGB	Association Guillaume Budé (France)		
AGB	Association of Governing Boards of Universities and Colleges (U.S.A.)	**AGÉÉ-Europe**	Association des États Généraux des Étudiants d'Europe
AGB	Société d'Alimentation Générale du Bénin	**AGEG**	Arbeitsgemeinschaft Europäische Grenzregionen = AEBR, ARFE, WVEG
AGBEF	Association Guinéenne pour le Bien-Être Familial	**AGEHR**	American Guild of English Handbell Ringers
AGBI	Artists' General Benevolent Institution	**AGEI**	Associazione dei Geografi Italiani
AGBM	Association of Grey Board Makers	**AGEI**	Associazione Gerontologica Italiana
AGBOPRO-MOTION	Société Agbovilloise de Promotion de l'Habitat Urbain et Rural (Ivory Coast)	**AGÉLAF**	Association des Groupes Nationaux d'Éducation Nouvelle de Langue Française
AGBU	Animal Genetics and Breeding Unit (Australia)	**AGÉMA**	Association pour la Gérance des Écoles de Formation Maritime et Aquacole
AGC	African Groundnut Council = CAA	**AGEMI**	Association des Groupements d'Engraisseurs de Moutons d'Importation
AGC	Agricultural Genetics Company		
AGC	Ashanti Goldfields Corporation (Ghana)		
AGC	Associated General Contractors of America	**AGEMOS**	Associazione Nazionale Gestori di Magazzini di Vendita Generi Monopoli di Stato
AGCAS	Association of Graduate Careers Advisory Services	**AGEMOU**	Automobile, General Engineering and Mechanical Operatives' Union (Éire)
AGCCPF	Association Générale des Conservateurs des Collections Publiques de France	**AGEP-TIERS-MONDE**	Agence Européenne de Promotion et de Réalisations Tiers Monde
AGCD	Administration Générale Belge de la Coopération au Développement		
AGCD	Association of Green Crop Driers	**AGEPYM**	Asociación General de Empleados Publicos y Municipales (El Salvador)
AGChem-Dok	Arbeitsgemeinschaft Chemie-Dokumentation	**AGER**	Asociatia Generală a Economiştilor din România
AGCI	Associazione Generale delle Cooperative Italiane	**AGERA**	Association des Géophysiciens en Exploration et Recherches en Afrique de l'Ouest
AGCI	Assurances Générales de Côte d'Ivoire		
AGCS	Association of Golf Club Secretaries		
AGD	Allianz Deutscher Designer AGD e. V.	**AGERE**	Associazione Generale per l'Edilizia
AGDW	Arbeitsgemeinschaft Deutscher Waldbesitzerverbände	**AGERT**	Associação Gaucho de Emissoras de Radio e Televisão (Brazil)
AGE	American Aging Association	**AGET**	Advisory Group on Electron Tubes (U.S.A.)
AGE	Americans for Generational Equity		

AGETRAC	Agence Générale de Transit et de Consignation (Togo)		**AGIC**	Australian Goldmining Industry Council
AGETRAC-CI	Agence Générale de Transit et de Consignation en Côte - d'Ivoire		**AGICO**	Arabian General Investment Corporation
AGETRAN	Association Générale de Transport et de Tourisme		**AGICOA**	Association for the International Collective Management of Audiovisual Works (Switzerland)
AGEX	Agrupación de Exportadores Metalurgicos de Vizcaya		**AGID**	Association of Geoscientists for International Development
AGF	Akademische Gesellschaft für Finanzwirtschaft		**AGIF**	Automobilgummi-Importørernes Forening
AGF	Arbeitsgemeinschaft der Grossforschungs - Einrichtungen		**AGIFER**	Associazione Giornalisti Ferroviari
AGF	Arbeitsgemeinschaft Getreideforschung		**AGIFORS**	Airline Group International Federation of Operational Research Societies
AGF	Asian Games Federation		**AGIM**	Association Générale de l'Industrie du Médicament (Belgium)
AGF	Association de Géographes Français			
AGFAD	Association Gabonaise des Femmes d'Affaires et de Developpement		**AGIMEX**	Agence Générale d'Import-Export (Ivory Coast)
AGFF	Arbeitsgemeinschaft zur Förderung des Futterbaues (Switzerland) = ADCF, APF		**AGIP**	Agenzia Generale Italiana Petroli
			AGIP	Association for Group and Individual Psychotherapy
AGFF	Arbeitsgruppe Friedensforschung am Institut Politikswissenschaft		**AGIR**	Asociatia Generală a Inginerilor din România (*ex* CNIT)
AGFIS	Assemblée Générale des Fédérations Internationales de Sports = GAISF		**AGIR-ABCD**	Association Générale des Intervenats Retraites - Actions de Bénévolés pour la Coopération et le Développement
AGFUND	Arab Gulf Program of the U.N. Development Organisations			
AGGS	Allgemeine Geschichtsforschende Gesellschaft der Schweiz = SGSH, SGSS		**AGIRC**	Association Générale des Institutions de Retraites des Cadres
			AGIRT	Associazione Giornalisti Italiani della Radiotelevisione
AGH	Advisory Group on Hepatitis (JCVI)		**AGIS**	Afrikagrupperna i Sverige
AGH	American Guild of Hypnotherapists		**AGIS**	Asociación Guatemalteca de Instituciones de Seguros
AGH	Association of Germans in Hungary = MNSz		**AGIS**	Association of Ground Investigation Specialists
AGHG	Academia de Geografia e Historia de Guatemala		**AGIS**	Associazione Generale Italiana dello Spettacolo
AGHN	Asociación Guatemalteca de Historia Natural			
AGHS	Australian Garden History Society		**AGIT**	Action on Governors Information and Training
AGHTM	Association Générale des Hygiènistes et Techniciens Municipaux		**AGIT**	Asociación Guatemalteca de Interpretes y Traductores
AGHW	Association of Gardening and Hardware Wholesalers		**AGITRA**	Agence Ivoirienne de Transit
AGI	Alliance Graphique Internationale		**AGIV**	Aktiengesellschaft für Industrie und Verkehrswesen
AGI	American Geological Institute		**AGIVO**	Association des Groupements Industriels du Val-d'Oise
AGI	Arbeitsgemeinschaft Industriebau			
AGI	Association for Geographic Information		**AGJPB**	Association Générale des Journalistes Professionnels de Belgique = AVBB
AGI	Associazione Genetica Italiana			
AGI	Associazione Geofisica Italiana		**AGK**	Arbeitsgemeinschaft Korrosion
AGI	Associazione Geotecnica Italiana		**AGK**	Gesellschaft für Korrosion und Korrosionsschutz e. V.
AGI	Associazione Grafologica Italiana			

AGKER	Allami Gazdaságok Kereskedelmi	**AGOD**	International Association on the Genesis of Ore Deposits
AGKIBV	Arbeitsgemeinschaft Katholisch-Theologischer Bibliotheken	**AGOF**	Arbeitsgemeinschaft Ökologischer Forschungsinstitute
AGL	Aktionsgemeinschaft Luftfahrt	**AGÖF**	Arbeitsgemeinschaft Österreichischer Friedensvereine
AGL	Arbeitsgemeinschaft für Landschaftsentwicklung	**AGOFAO**	Agricultural Operations Division
AGLINET	Agricultural Libraries Information Network (UN)	**AGOR**	Advisory Group on Ocean Research (WMO)
AGLMH	Association for Great Lakes Maritime History	**AGOS**	American Gynaecological and Obstetrical Society
AGLOW	Association of Greater London Older Women	**AGP**	Agence Gabonaise de Presse
AGLS	FAO Soil Resources Development Conservation Service	**AGP**	Agencja Reklamy Handlu Zagranicznego
AGM	American Guild of Music	**AGP**	Albanian Green Party = PBS
AGMA	Amenity Grass Marketing Association	**AGP**	Arbeitgeberverband der Papieriudustrie Baden- Württemberg
AGMA	American Gear Manufacturers' Association	**AGP**	Arbeitsgemeinschaft zur Förderung der Partnerschaft in der Wirtschaft
AGMA	American Guild of Musical Artists	**AGP**	FAO Plant Production Protection Division
AGMANZ	Art Galleries and Museums Association of New Zealand	**AGP-CNO**	Assemblée Générale Permanente des Comités Nationaux Olympiques
AGMB	Association Générale des Meuniers Belges	**AGPA**	American Group Practice Association
AGMF	Association Généralé des Médecins de France	**AGPA**	American Group Psychotherapy Association
AGMG	Asociación General de Mercadologos de Guatemala	**AGPAEA**	Association de Gestion Portuaire de l'Afrique de l'Est et Australe = PMAESA
AGMI	Agrometeorologicheskii Institut	**AGPAOC**	Association de Gestion des Ports de l'Afrique de l'Ouest et du Centre = PMAWCA
AGMÖ	Arbeitsgemeinschaft der Musikerzieher Österreichs		
AGMS	Arbeitsgemeinschaft Massenspektroskopie	**AGPB**	Association Générale des Producteurs de Blé et autres Céréales (France)
AGMSA	American Gem and Mineral Suppliers Association	**AGPC**	FAO Crop Ecology Genetic Resources Unit
AGMU	Asociación Guatemalteca de Mujeres	**AGPCH**	Association of General Practitioner Community Hospitals (*now* CHA)
AGN	Advisory Group on Nutrition (UN)		
AGNIB	Association des Groupements du Négoce Intérieur du Bois Produit Derivé dans les Pays de la CEE	**AGPD**	Allgemeine Gesellschaft für Philosophie in Deutschland
		AGPH	Association Générale des Producteurs de Houblon
AGNK	Assembleia Gorskikh Narodov Kavkaza	**AGPL**	Association Générale des Producteurs de Lin
AGNVH	Association of Growers of the New Varieties of Hops	**AGPM**	Associated Glass and Pottery Manufacturers (U.S.A.)
AGO	American Guild of Organists		
AGO	Arbeitsgemeinschaft der Ordenshochschulen	**AGPM**	Association Générale des Producteurs de Maïs
AGÖ	Arbeitsgemeinschaft Österreicherischer Organisationsberater	**AGPNM**	Association of General Practitioners of Natural Medicine
AGO	Art Gallery of Ontario (Canada)		
AGO	Association of Gypsy and Romany Organisations		

AGPO	Association Générale des Producteurs d'Oléagineux
AGPOL	Foreign Trade Publicity and Publishing Enterprise (Poland)
AGPS	Australian Government Publishing Service
AGPV	Association Générale des Producteurs de Viande
AGR	Agences Générales Réunies (Ivory Coast)
AGR	Association of Graduate Recruiters
AGRA	Agence Générale de Renseignements Agricoles
AGRA	Association of Genealogists and Record Agents
AGRA-PRESSE	Agence Générale de Renseignements Agricoles
AGRAIR	Société Aérienne de Traitement Agricole (Cameroon)
AGRAN-DES	Agricola y Pecuaria de los Andes Ltda (Colombia)
AGRE	Atlantic Gas Research Exchange (France, U.K., U.S.A.)
AGREMCE	Agripación de Exportadores Metalurgicos del Centro de España
AGREXCO	Agricultural Export Company (Israel)
AGRHO-SUR	Agropecuária Horticola Suramericana (Colombia)
AGRI	American Genealogical Research Institute
AGRI-TP	Agriculture et Travaux Publics (Ivory Coast)
AGRI-PECHE-IVOIRE	Société Ivoire Sénégalaise d'Agriculture et de Pêche
AGRICHIM	Société des Produits pour l'Agriculture (Cameroon)
AGRIL-AGDO	Société Lagdo Agribusiness (Cameroon)
AGRINTER	Inter-American Information System for Agricultural Science (Costa Rica)
AGRIPOG	Société Agricole de Port-Gentil (Gabon)
AGRIS	International Formation System for Agricultural Sciences and Technology (Italy)
AGRO-GABON	Société pour le Développement de l'Agriculture au Gabon
AGRO-MASH	International Association for Vine, Fruit and Vegetable-growing Mechanization
AGROCAP	Société Agricole du Cap Vert
AGROLAC	Association des Groupements de Producteurs de Lait de Chèvre
AGROMAQ	Empresa Nacional de Maquinaria Agricola (Nicaragua)
AGROMEC	Empresa Nacional de Agromecanización
AGROPOL	Association pour le Développement International Agronomique et Industriel de Protéagineux et des Oléagineux
AGROSEM	Trustul pentru Asigurarea Productiei si Valorificarea Semintelor Agricole
AGROSUL	Empresa de Serviços Agropecuários do Mato Grosso do Sul (Brazil)
AGRR	Association Générale de Retraite par Répartition
AGRUSA	Agricultores Unidos S.A.
AGS	Aero Geophysical Survey (China)
AGS	Alpine Garden Society
AGS	American Gem Society
AGS	American Geographical Society
AGS	American Geriatrics Society
AGS	American Goat Society
AGS	American Gourd Society
AGS	American Graphological Society
AGS	Association for Gravestone Studies
AGS	Association of Garda Superintendents (Éire)
AGS	Association of Geotechnical Specialists
AGS	Assurances Générales Sénégalaises
AGS	FAO Agricultural Service Division
AGSBB	Atmospheric Geophysical and Space Sciences Branch, PAGASA (Philippines)
AGSD(UK)	Association for Glycogen Storage Disease (U.K.)
AGSE	FAO Agricultural Engineering Service
AGSG	Akademische Gesellschaft Schweizerischer Germanisten
AGSI	Association of Garda Sergeants and Inspectors (Éire)
AGSI	FAO Food Agricultural Industries Service
AGSIDC	Arab Gulf States Information and Documentation Centre (Iraq)
AGSM	FAO Marketing Credit Service
AGSO	Australian Geological Survey Organisation (*ex* BMR)
AGSP	FAO Farm Management Unit
AGSS	American Geographical and Statistical Society

AGSSV	Arbeitsgemeinschaft Schweizerischer Schweinezuchtverbände
AGT	Arbeitsgeververband Schweizerischer Transportunternehmungen
AGT	Association of Garden Trusts
AGT	Association of Geology Teachers (U.S.A.)
AGTA	Agence Générale de Transit en Afrique (Congo)
AGTE	Association of Group Travel Executives (U.S.A.)
AGTI	Association of Geography Teachers of Ireland
AGTO	Association of Group Tour Operators
AGU	American Geophysical Union
AGU	Arabian Gulf University (Bahrain)
AGU	Arbeitsgemeinschaft für Umweltfragen
AGUAI	Associação Guarani Independente (Brazil)
AGUIMEX	Agrupación de Exportadores Metalurgicos de Guipuzcoa
AGULF	Association Générale des Usagers de la Langue Française
AGUM	Association of Genito-Urinary Medicine
AGUSA	Artes Graficas Unidas, S.A. (Mexico)
AGV	Aachener Geschichtsverein
AGV	Arbeitgeberverband der Versicherungsunternehmungen in Deutschland
AgV	Arbeitsgemeinschaft der Verbraucher Verbände
AGVA	American Guild of Variety Artists
AGVO	Arbeitsgemeinschaft Vorderer Orient
AGVPS	Asociatia Generala a Vinatorilor si Perscarilor Sportivi (Romania)
AGVS	Autogewerbeverband der Schweiz
AGW	Anthropologische Gesellschaft in Wien (Austria)
AGW	Arbeitsgemeinschaft der Werbefachverbände
AGW	Association of Garden Wholesalers
AGW	Association of Golf Writers
AGZ	Antiquarische Gesellschaft in Zürich
AH	Academy of Humanism
AH&MA	American Hotel and Motel Association
AHA	American Heart Association
AHA	American Hepatitis Association
AHA	American Hereford Association
AHA	American Historical Association
AHA	American Hominological Association
AHA	American Hospital Association
AHA	American Humane Association
AHA	American Humanist Association
AHA	American Hypnotherapy Association
AHA	American Hypnotists Association
AHA	Arab Historians Association (Iraq)
AHA	Association des Historiens Africains (Senegal)
AHA	Association of Housing Aid Ltd
AHAS	Association of Heritage Approved Specialists
AHASCES	Association of Higher Academic Staff in Colleges of Education in Scotland
AHBA	Association of Hotel Booking Agents
AHC	Academia de Humanismo Cristiano (Chile)
AHC	American Horse Council
AHC	Animal Health Committee
AHC	Association of History and Computing
AHC	Australian Heritage Commission
AHC	Australian Horticultural Corporation
AHCA	American Health Care Association
AHCIET	Asociación Hispanoamericana de Centros de Investigacion y Empresas de Telecomunicaciones
AHCPA	Association of Health Centre & Practice Administrators (*now* AMGP)
AHCS	Association of Higher Civil Servants (Éire)
AHD	Arbeitsgemeinschaft für Hochschuldidaktik
AHD	Association of Household Distributors
AHDA	Animal Health Distributors' Association
AHDGA	American Hot Dip Galvanizers Association
AHDIS	Action Humaine pour le Développement Integre au Sénégal
AHDIVA	Asociación Hondureña de Distribuidores de Vehiculos, Automotores y Afines
AHDRI	Animal Husbandry and Dairy Research Institute (South Africa)
AHEA	American Home Economics Association
AHEC	American Hardwood Export Council
AHECS	United Kingdom Association of Home Economics and Consumer Studies in Higher Education (*ex* AHEIHE)

AHEIHE	Association of Higher Educational Institutions concerned with Home Economics
AHEM	Association of Hydraulic Equipment Manufacturers (U.S.A.)
AHES	American Humane Education Society
AHF	African Housing Fund (Kenya)
AHF	Allmänna Handelslagsförbundet
AHF	Arbeitsgemeinschaft Ausseruniversitärer Historischer Forschungseinrichtungen
AHF	Architectural Heritage Fund
AHF	Asia Handball Federation
AHF	Asia Hockey Federation (Pakistan)
AHF	Asian Hospital Federation (Philippines)
AHFC	American Hungarian Folklore Centrum (U.S.A.)
AHFSY	Association of Hungarians for Our Fatherland, Serbia and Yugoslavia (Serbia) = UMDSJ
AHGP	Australian Heritage Grants Program
AHGTC	Ancient and Honourable Guild of Town Criers
AHH	Association for Holistic Health (U.S.A.)
AHI	Afrikaanse Handelsinstituut
AHI	Asian Health Institute (Japan)
AHIBA	Asociación Hondureña de Instituciones Bancarias
AHIDC	Australian Housing Industry Development Council
AHILA	Asociación de Historiadores Latinoamericanistas Europeos (U.K.)
AHIOI	Association Historique Internationale de l'Océan Indien
AHIRA	African Human Rights Research Association
AHIRS	Australian Health Information and Research Service
AHIS	Association of Heads of Independent Schools
AHITI	Animal Health and Industry Training Institute (Kenya)
AHJRC	Alliance of Hungarian Jewish Religious Communities = MAZsiHiSz
AHL	Association for the History of Language (formerly known as the Melbourne Association for the History of Language)
AHM	Altos Hornos del Mediterraneo
AHM	Ateneo de Historia de la Medicina (Argentina)
AHMA	American Hardware Manufacturers Association
AHMCA	Asociación de Hombres de Mercadeo de Centro América (Guatemala)
AHME	Association of Hospital Medical Education (U.S.A.)
AHMSA	Altos Hornos de Mexico, S.A.
AHNOGB	Association of Head & Neck Oncologists of Great Britain
AHOEC	Association of Heads of Outdoor Education Centres
AHORRO-MET	Ahorros Metropolitanos (El Salvador)
AHOTEC	Asociación Hotelera Nacional del Ecuador
AHP	Associação dos Hotéis de Portugal
AHP	Association for Humanistic Psychology
AHPA	American Health Planning Association
AHPA	American Herbal Products Association
AHPADA	ASEAN Handicraft Promotion and Development Association
AHPCRC	Army High Performance Computing Research Center (U.S.A.)
AHPP	Association of Humanistic Psychology Practitioners
AHPRO-CAFÉ	Asociación Hondureña de Productores de Café
AHPWJC	Association of High Pressure Water Jetting Contractors
AHRA	ASEAN Hotel and Restaurant Association
AHRC	Alister Hardy Research Centre
AHRC	Asian Human Rights Commission (Hong Kong)
AHRI	Armauer Hansen Research Unit (Ethiopia)
AHRP	Australian Heritage Research Program
AHRTAG	Appropriate Health Resources and Technologies Action Group
AHS	Agricultural History Society (U.S.A.)
AHS	American Harp Society
AHS	American Helicopter Society
AHS	American Herb Association
AHS	American Horticultural Society
AHS	American Hypnodontic Society
AHS	Antiquarian Horological Society
AHS	Association for Humanist Sociology
AHS	Australian Herpitological Society
AHSA	African Heritage Studies Association

AHSA	American Horse Shows Association
AHSA	Art, Historical and Scientific Association (Canada)
AHSD	Authority Health and Safety Division
AHSI	Association Haïtienne des Spécialistes de l'Information
AHSO	Association of Home Safety Officers
AHSR	Association des Horticuleurs de la Suisse Romande
AHSS	Architectural Heritage Society for Scotland
AHSTI	Association of Heads of Science of Technical Institutes (Éire)
AHSZV	Allatforgalmi és Húsipari Szolgáltató Vállalat
AHT	Animal Health Trust
AHTA	Antigua Hotels and Tourist Association
AHTC	Association d'Histoire du Théâtre du Canada = ACTH
AHUA	Association of Heads of University Administrations
AHWA	Association of Hospital and Welfare Administrators
AI	Acción International
AI	Alianza Interamericana
AI	Altrusa International (U.S.A.)
AI	Amnesty International
AI	Asphalt Institute (U.S.A.)
AI	Association Interculturelle (Switzerland)
AIA	Abrasive Industries Association
AIA	Academy of Irish Art
AIA	Accuracy in Academic (U.S.A.)
AIA	Acupuncture International Association
AIA	Aerospace Industries Association of America
AIA	Africa Information Afrique (Zimbabwe)
AiA	Allergy-Induced Autism Support and Self-Help Group
AIA	American Institute of Architects
AIA	American Insurance Association
AIA	American Inventors Association
AIA	Anglo-Indian Association
AIA	Anglo-Israel Association
AIA	Archeological Institute of America
AIA	Artists International Association
AIA	Asbestos International Association
AIA	Asociación de Ingenieros Aeronáuticos
AIA	Asociación Ibero-Americano Atletismo
AIA	Associación de Ingenieros Agronomos (Uruguay)
AIA	Association for Industrial Archaeology
AIA	Association Internationale Africaine
AIA	Association of Automobile and Allied High Duty Ironfounders
AIA	Association of Insolvency Accountants (U.S.A.)
AIA	Association of International Accountants
AIA	Associazione Italiana Aerospaziali
AIA	Associazione Italiana Allevatori
AIA	Australian Insurance Association
AIA	Auto International Association
AIA	Aviation Industry Association (N.Z.)
AIA	International Association of Water Polo Referees = AIWP
AIA-EAC	EEC Advisory Council of the Asbestos International Association
AIAA	Aerospace Industries Association of America
AIAA	American Industrial Arts Association
AIAA	American Institute of Aeronautics and Astronautics
AIAA	Association Interprofessionnelle de l'Aviation Agricole
AIAA	Association of International Advertising Agencies
AIAB	Association Internationale des Anthropobiologistes
AIAC	Agricultural Industry Advisory Committe (HSE)
AIAC	Air Industries Association of Canada
AIAC	Artificial Intelligence Advisory Committee
AIAC	Association des Ingénieurs en Anticorrosion
AIAC	Association Internationale d'Archéologie Classique
AIAC	Association Internationale des Auteurs de Comics et de Cartoons
AIAC	Associazione Italiana Agenti di Cambio
AIAC	Associazione Italiana Analisti Chimici
AIAC	Associazione Italiana per le Attività Concertistiche
AIACE	Association Internationale des Anciens des Communautés Européennes
AIACI	Associazione Italiana Amminstratori Condomini e Immobili

AIACS	Association of International Air Courier Services	**AIAS**	Arbeitsgemeinschaft für Interdisziplinäre Angewandte Sozialforschung (Austria)
AIADA	American International Automobile Dealers Association	**AIAS**	Australian Institute of Aboriginal Studies
AIAE	Asociación de Ingenieros Aeronáuticos de España	**AIAS**	Australian Institute of Agricultural Science
AIAE	Association Internationale Autisme - Europe = IAAE	**AIASR**	Association des Ingénieurs Agronomes de la Suisse Romande
AIAE	Association Internationale des Anciens d'EUROCONTROL	**AIAT**	Association Internationale pour le Développement Économique et l'Aide Technique
AIAESD	American International Association for Economics and Social Development	**AIAU**	Atomic Institute of the Austrian Universities
AIAF	American Institute of Architects Foundation	**AIB**	Academy of International Business (U.S.A.)
AIAF	Association de l'Industrie et de l'Agriculture Française	**AIB**	African Immigrants Bureau
AIAF	Association Internationale des Archives Francophones	**AIB**	Agence d'Informations Burkinabo (Burkina Faso)
AIAF	Associazione Italiana degli Analisti Finanziari	**AIB**	Allied Irish Banks
AIAFD	Association des Institutions Africaines de Financement du Développement (Ivory Coast) = AADFI	**AIB**	American Institute of Baking
		AIB	American Institute of Banking
		AIB	Arab International Bank
AIAG	Aluminium Industrie Aktien Gesellschaft (Switzerland)	**AIB**	Association des Industries de Belgique
AIAG	Asociación de Industriales de Artes Graficas (Venezuela)	**AIB**	Association Internationale de Bibliophilie
AIAG	Association Internationale des Assureurs contre la Grêle	**AIB**	Association of Independent Businesses
AIAG	Association Italienne des Agents de Change	**AIB**	Association of Insurance Brokers
		AIB	Associazione Italiana per le Biblioteche
AIAH	Association of Irish Art Historians	**AIBA**	Agricultural Information Bank for Asia (Philippines)
AIAI	Agence Internationale d'Assurance des Investissements = IAIV, IIIA	**AIBA**	Asociación Interamericana de Bibliotecarios Agrícolas
AIAI	Artificial Intelligence Applications Institute	**AIBA**	Association Internationale de Boxe Amateur = IABA
AIAM	Associazione Italiana Amici della Medaglia	**AIBA**	Association Interprofessionnelle des Producteurs de Betteraves et d'Alcool de Betteraves
AIAP	Association Internationale des Arts Plastiques = IAA	**AIBA**	Association of International Border Agencies (U.S.A.)
AIAP	Associazione Italiana Architetti de Paesaggio	**AIBA**	Associazione Italiana Brokers di Assicurazioni
AIAP	Associazione Italiana Artisti e Grafici Pubblicitari	**AIBANIC**	Asociación de Instituciones Bancarias de Nicaragua
AIAP	Associazione Italiana Artisti Publicitori	**AIBC**	Architectural Institute of British Columbia
AIAP	Associazione Italiana Avvocati Tennisti		
AIAPP	Associazione Italiana di Architettura del Paesaggio	**AIBCM**	Association of Industrialized Building Component Manufacturers
		AIBD	American Institute of Building Design
AIAR	American Institute for Aerological Research	**AIBD**	Asia-Pacific Institute for Broadcasting Development (Malaysia)

AIBD	Association of International Bond Dealers (*now* ISMA)
AIBDA	Asociación Interamericana de Bibliotecarios y Documentalistas Agrícolas
AIBEA	All India Bank Employees' Association
AIBES	Associazione Italiana Barmen e Sostenitori
AIBGA	All Island Banana Growers Association (Jamaica)
AIBI	Association Internationale de la Bible et Informatique (Belgium)
AIBI	Association Internationale de la Boulangerie Industrielle
AIBM	Association Internationale des Bibliothèques, Archives et Centres de Documentation Musicaux = IAML, IVMB
AIBP	Association of Independent Biodynamic Psychotherapists
AIBS	American Institute of Biological Sciences
AIBS	Amnesty International: British Section
AIBS	Association Internationale de Bibliothéconomie Scolaire = IASL
AIBS	Association of Independent Beauty Schools
AIC	Académie Internationale de la Céramique = IAC
AIC	Agricultural Improvement Council
AIC	Agricultural Institute of Canada
AIC	Agrupacion Independiente Canaria
AIC	American Institute for Conservation of Historic and Artistic Works
AIC	American Institute of Chemists
AIC	American Institute of Constructors
AIC	American Institute of Cooperation
AIC	Appraisal Institute of Canada
AIC	Arab Investment Company (Saudi Arabia)
AIC	Asbestos Information Centre
AIC	ASEAN Insurance Council
AIC	Asociación Interamerican de Contabilidad = IAA
AIC	Asociación Panamericana de Contrabilitad = IAA
AIC	Association des Industries des Carrières (Belgium)
AIC	Association Internationale de Criminologie

AIC	Association Internationale de Cybernétique
AIC	Association Internationale de la Couleur = ICA
AIC	Association Internationale des Charités de St Vincent de Paul = AICVP
AIC	Association of Independent Cinemas
AIC	Association of Indian Communists
AIC	Associazione Italiana di Cartografia
AIC	Ateliers Informatiques du Centre
AICA	American Institute of Commemorative Art
AICA	American International Charolais Association
AICA	Association Internationale des Critiques d'Art = IACA
AICA	Associazione degli Industriali delle Conserve Animali
AICA	Associazione Italiana per l'Informatica ed il Calcolo Automatico
AICAF	Association for International Cooperation in Agriculture and Forestry (Japan)
AICARDES	Association of Arab Institutes and Centres of Research for Economic and Social Development
AICARR	Associazione Italiana Condizionamento dell'Aria, Riscaldamento Refrigerazione
AICB	Association Internationale contre le Bruit
AICC	All India Congress Committee
AICC	Asian Institute of Christian Communication (Singapore)
AICC	Association of Independent Crop Consultants
AICC	Associazione Italiana del Commercio Chimico
AICC	Associazione Italiana di Cultura Classica 'Atena e Roma'
AICC	Groupe des Chambres Syndicales et Unions Professionelles d'Agents Indépendants, Courtiers et Concessionnaires du Commerce et de l'Industrie (Belgium)
AICCF	Association Internationale du Congrès de Chemins de Fer (Belgium) = IEKV, IRCA
AICCP	Asociación de Ingenieres de Caminos, Canales y Puertos
AICD	Association Internationale des Compagnies de Dragage

AICE	American Institute of Chemical Engineers	**AICP**	Association Internationale des Circuits Permanents
AICE	American Institute of Crop Ecology	**AICP**	Association of Independent Commercial Producers (U.S.A.)
AICÉP	Association Internationale des Conseillers de l'Économie Privée	**AICPA**	American Institute of Certified Public Accountants
AICF	Action Internationale contre la Faim	**AICPA**	Associazione Italiana Concessionari Produzione Automobilistica
AICF	Ambassador International Cultural Foundation (U.S.A.)	**AICQ**	Associazione Italiana per il Controllo della Qualità
AICF	American Immigration Control Foundation	**AICR**	American Institute for Cancer Research
AICF	American-Israel Cultural Foundation	**AICR**	Amicale Internationale des Sous-Directeurs et Chefs de Réception des Grands Hôtels
AICF	Association Internationale de Coopération Francophones		
AICF	Associazione Italiana Chimica-Fisica	**AICRC**	Association of Independent Clinical Research Contractors
AICFO	Asociación Internacional para las Ciencias Fisicas del Océano = AISPO, IAPSO	**AICRIP**	All India Coordinated Rice Improvement Project
AICH	Amicale Internationale des Capitaines au Long Cours Cap Horniers	**AICS**	Alliance Internationale de Coopération Scolaire = IACS
AICH	Asociación Internacional de Hidrología Científica	**AICS**	Association Industrielle et Commerciale de la Savoie
AIChE	American Institute of Chemical Engineers	**AICS**	Association of Independent Computer Specialists
AICI	Association Interprofessionnelle des Employeurs de Côte d'Ivoire	**AICSJF**	Association Catholique Internationale des Services de la Jeunesse Féminine
AICI	Associazione Ingegneri Consultenti Italiani	**AICT**	Association Internationale contre la Torture
AICIS	Association Internationale du Cinéma Scientifique	**AICT**	Association Internationale des Critiques de Théâtre = IATC
AICK	Association Internationale pour la Conscience de Krishna = ISKCON	**AICTC**	Associazione Italiana di Chimica Tessile e Coloristica
AICL	Association Internationale des Critiques Littéraires = IALC	**AICU**	All India Cooperative Union
AICLF	Association Internationale des Criminologues de Langue Française	**AICU**	Association of International Colleges and Universities
AICM	Association des Ingénieurs-conseils du Manitoba	**AICV**	Association des Industries des Cidres et Vins de Fruits de la CEE
AICMÉS	Association Interprofessionelle des Constructeurs de Matériel d'Équipement Scientifique	**AICVF**	Association des Ingénieurs de Chauffage et de Ventilation de France
AICMR	Association Internationale des Constructeurs de Matériel Roulant	**AICVP**	Association Internationale des Charités de St Vincent de Paul = AIC
AICN	Asociación de Investigación de la Construcción Naval	**AICVS**	Association Internationale pour un Sport sans Violence = IANVS
AICO	Asociación Iberoamericana de Cámaras de Comercio	**AICYE**	Association of the International Christian Youth Exchange in Europe
AICO	Associazione Internazionale di Cultura Occidentale	**AID**	Agency for International Development (U.S.A.)
AICOS	Associazione per gli Interventi di Cooperazione allo Sviluppo	**AID**	Agricultural Information Division (Philippines)
		AID	Algemene Inspectiedienst

AID	Alliance Internationale de la Distribution par Cable	**AIDD**	American Institute for Design and Drafting
AID	Alternative for India Development	**AIDDA**	Associazione Imprenditrici e Donne Dirigenti d'Azienda
AID	Asociación Interamericana de Radiodifusion = IAAB	**AIDE**	Action Internationale pour les Droits de l'Enfant = IARC
AID	Associaçâo Internacional de Caprinos = IGA	**AIDE**	Agence Internationale pour le Développement
AID	Association for Improving the Downtrodden (India)	**AIDE**	Asociación Interamericana de Educación = IAEA
AID	Association Internationale de Développement = AIF, IDA	**AIDE**	Association Internationale de Dispacheurs Européens
AID	Land- und Hauswirtschaftlicher Auswertungs- und Informationsdienst	**AIDE**	Association Internationale de Distribution d'Eau = IWSA
AID	United States Agency for International Development	**AIDE**	Association Internationale de Droit des Eaux = AIDA, IAWL
AIDA	Asociación Internacional de Derecha de Aguas = AIDE, IAWL	**AIDÉ**	Association Internationale de Droit Économique
AIDA	Association Internationale de Droit Africain = IALA	**AIDEC**	Association for European Industrial Development and Economic Co-operation (Netherlands)
AIDA	Association Internationale de Droit des Assurances	**AIDEF**	All-India Defence Employees Federation
AIDA	Association Internationale de la Distribution des Produits Alimentaires et des Produits de Grande Consommation	**AIDELF**	Association Internationale des Démographes de Langue Française
		AIDEM	Associazione Italiana degli Editori di Musica
AIDA	Associazione Italiana di Aerotecnica	**AIDEP**	Association Interentreprises pour le Développement de l'Enseignement Programmé
AIDA	Associazione Italiana per la Documentazione Avanzata		
AIDA	Associazione Infermieri Diplomati Assistenza Infermi	**AIDESEP**	Asociación Inter-Étnica de la Selva Peruana
AIDA	Associazione Italiana di Aerofilateli	**AIDGUM**	Association for International Development of Natural Gums (France)
AIDAA	Association Internationale des Auteurs de l'Audiovisuel	**AIDH**	Association Internationale pour les Droits de l'Homme = IGM, ISHR, SIDH
AIDAA	Associazione Italiana di Aeronautica e Astronautica	**AIDI**	Associazione Industrie Dolciarie Italiane
AIDAB	Australian International Development Assistance Bureau	**AIDI**	Associazione Italiana degli Inventori
AIDAC	Association Internationale de Développment et d'Action Communautaires = IACD	**AIDI**	Associazione Italiana di Illuminazione
		AIDI	Associazione Italiana per la Documentazione e l'Informazione
AIDBA	Association Internationale pour le Développement de la Documentation, des Bibliothèques et des Archives en Afrique = IADLA	**AIDIC**	Associazione Italiana di Ingegneria Chimica
AIDC	Association Internationale de Droit Constitutionnel = IACL	**AIDIS**	Asociación Interamericana de Ingenieria Sanitaria y Ambiental
AIDC	Association Internationale pour le Développement du Coton = CDI	**AIDIS**	Associazione Italiana di Ingeneria Sismica
AIDC	Australian Industry Development Corporation	**AIDL**	Asociación Interamericana pro Democracia y Libertad = IADF
AIDCOM	Asian Institute for Development Communication (Malaysia)	**AIDL**	Auckland Industrial Development Laboratory (New Zealand)

AIDLAIT	Association Internationale de Défense des Producteurs de Lait, des Agriculteurs et des Industries de Transformation Connexes	**AIEC**	Agence Européenne d'Information sur la Consommation
AIDLCM	Association Internationale pour la Défense des Langues et Cultures Menacées	**AIECÉ**	Association d'Instituts Européens de Conjoncture Économique
AIDMO	Arab Industrial Development and Mining Organization (Iraq)	**AIÉCM**	Association Internationale d'Étude des Civilisations Méditerranéennes
AIDN	Association Internationale du Droit Nucléaire = INLA	**AIED**	Association Internationale d'Entreprises de Dragage = IADC
AIDO	Association Internationale des Directeurs d'Opéra = IAOD	**AIÉD**	Association Internationale des Étudiants Dentaires = IADS
AIDP	Association Internationale de Droit Pénal = IAPL	**AIÉE**	Association des Instituts d'Études Européennes
AIDP	Associazione Italiana per la Direzione del Personale	**AIÉÉ**	Association Internationale des Économistes de l'Énergie = IAEE
AIDR	Association de Développement Rural d'Outre-Mer	**AIÉÉ**	Association Internationale pour l'Évaluation Éducative = IAEA
AIDS	American Institute for Decision Sciences	**AIÉF**	Association Internationale des Études Françaises
AIDS	Association of Industrial Dental Surgeons	**AIÉGL**	Association Internationale d'Épigraphie Grecque et Latine (France)
AIDSEGA	Amitié Internationale des Scouts et Guides Adultes = IFOFSAG	**AIEH**	Australian Institute of Environmental Health
AIDT	Association Interparlementaire du Tourisme (Belgium)	**AIÉI**	Association Internationale des Études Industrielles
AIDUIM	Association Internationale pour le Développement des Universités Internationales et Mondiales = IADIWU	**AIÉI**	Association Internationale pour l'Éducation Intégrée = IAIE
AIÉ	Agence Internationale de l'Énergie = IEA	**AIÉI**	Association Internationale pour l'Éducation Interculturelle = IAIE
AIÉ	Association Internationale de l'Étancheite = IWA	**AIEI**	Association of Indian Engineering Industry
AIE	Association Internationale des Entreprises d'Équipement Électrique	**AIÉIA**	Association Internationale des Écoles et Instituts d'Administration (Belgium) = IASIA
AIE	Associazione Italiana Editori	**AIÉJI**	Association Internationale des Éducateurs de Jeunes Inadaptés = IAWMC
AIÉA	Agence Internationale de l'Énergie Atomique = IAEA, OIEA		
AIÉA	Association Internationale des Économistes Agronomiques = IAAE	**AIEL**	Asociación Internacional de Estructuras Laminares y Espaciales = AIVM, IASS, IVS
AIÉA	Association Internationale des Études Arméniennes (Israel)	**AIÉMA**	Association Internationale pour l'Étude de la Mosaïque Antique
AIÉA	Association Internationale des Étudiants en Agriculture = IAAS	**AIÉMPR**	Association Internationale d'Études Médicales Psychologiques et Religieuses
AIEA	Australian Institute of Engineering Associates	**AIÉNSAN**	Association des Ingénieurs de l'École Nationale Supérieure Agronomique de Nancy (France)
AIÉAS	Association Internationale des Études de l'Asia du Sud-Est	**AIÉO**	Association Internationale d'Études Occitanes
AIÉB	Association Internationale des Études Byzantines = IABS	**AIEP**	Association des Importateurs d'Essence et Pétroles

AIÉP	Association Internationale d'Études Patristiques
AIEP	Association Internationale des Usagers d'Embranchements Particuliers = IVA
AIÉP	Association Italienne d'Éditeurs de Périodiques
AIEP	Association of Independent Electricity Producers
AIEPAD	Asociación Iberoamericana de Estudio de los Problemas del Alcohol y la Droga (Argentina)
AIEPD	African Institute for Economic Planning and Development
AIÉPE	Association Internationale des Écoles Privées Européennes
AIÉPELF	Association Internationale des Écoles partiellement ou entièrement de Langue Française
AIÉPM	Association Internationale des Éducateurs pour la Paix Mondiale = IAEWP
AIER	American Institute of Economic Research
AIÉRI	Association Internationale d'Études et Recherches sur l'Information = IAMCR
AIES	Association Internationale d'Essais de Semences = ISTA
AIESAD	Asociación Iberoamericana de Educación Superior Distancia
AIÉSÉC	Association Internationale des Étudiants en Sciences Économiques et Commerciales
AIÉSEE	Association Internationale d'Études du Sudest Européen = IASEES
AIÉSÉP	Association Internationale des Écoles ou Instituts Supérieurs d'Éducation Physique
AIÉSI	Association Internationale des Écoles des Sciences de l'Information
AIESP	Arab Institute for Economic and Social Planning (Kuwait)
AIÉSS	Association Internationale des Écoles du Service Social = IASSW
AIEST	Association International d'Experts Scientifiques du Tourisme
AIETI	Asociación de Investigación y Especialización sobre Temas Iberoamericanos
AIÉV	Association International pour l'Étude de la Végétation = IAVS, IVV
AIF	Agenzia Internazionale Fides (Vatican City)
AIF	Alliance Internationale des Femmes = IAW
AIF	Apparel Industries Federation (Éire)
AIF	Arbeitsgemeinschaft Industrieller Forschungsvereinigungen
AIF	Arbejderbevaegelsens Internationale Forum
AIF	Asociación Internacional de Fomento = AID, IDA
AIF	Association des Industriels de France contre les Accidents du Travail
AIF	Association Internationale Futuribles = IAF
AIF	Association of Interchurch Families
AIF	Association of Invoice Factors
AIF	Associazione Italiana del Franchising
AIFA	Asociación Internacional de Fabricantes de Aceites
AIFA	Association Internationale Francophone des Aines (Canada)
AIFA	Associazione Italiana fra gli Importatori di Farine Animali
AIFE	American Institute for Exploration
AIFEA	All Indian Federation of Education Association (India)
AIFESPAC	Association Internationale du Festival Panafricain des Arts et Cultures (Senegal)
AIFF	International Association of Francophone Women
AIFLD	American Institute for Free Labor Development
AIFLV	Association des Industries des Fruits et Légumes au Vinaigre de la CEE
AIFM	Association Internationale des Femmes Médecins = MWIA
AIFM	Association of Independent Forest Managers
AIFO	Associazione Italiana Amici di Raoul Follerau
AIFOB	Association Internationale des Sylviculteurs et des Utilisateurs de Produits de la Forêt et du Bois
AIFP	Association Internationale de la Fonction Publique
AIFPAUR	Association Internationale pour la Formation Professionnelle en Aménagement Urbain et Régional

AIFR	American Institute of Family Relations	**AIGMF**	All India Glass Manufacturers Federation
AIFR	Vereinigung der Rumänischen Eisenbach-Ingenieure (Romania)	**AIGP**	Association Internationale de Gérontologie Psychoanalytique
AIFRB	American Institute of Fishery Research Biologists	**AIGR**	Associazione Italiana di Genio Rurale (*now* AIIA)
AIFRO	Association Internationale Francophone de Recherche Odontologique	**AIGREF**	Association des Ingénieurs du Génie Rural, des Eaux et des Forêts
AIFS	American Institute for Foreign Study	**AIGT**	Association for the Improvement of Geometrical Teaching
AIFS	Association Internationale des Fabricants de Superphosphate	**AIGx**	Association des Ingénieurs Issus de la Faculté des Sciences Agronomiques de l'État, Gembloux (Belgium)
AIFSM	Association of Industrial Filter and Separator Manufacturers	**AIGYPFB**	Asociación de Ingenieros y Geólogos de Yacimientos Petroliferos Fiscales Bolivianos
AIFSPR	Associazione Italiana di Fisica Sanitaria e di Protezione contro le Radiazioni		
AIFST	Australian Institute of Food Science and Technology	**AIH**	Académie Internationale d'Héraldique
AIFT	American Institute for Foreign Trade	**AIH**	American Institute of Homeopathy
AIG	Arbeitskreis Internationaler Gemeinschaftsdienste	**AIH**	American Institute of Hydrology
AIG	Association Internationale de Géodésie = IAG	**AIH**	Asociación Interamericana de Hoteles = IAHA
AIG	Association Internationale de Gérontologie = IAG	**AIH**	Asociación Internacional de Hispanistas
AIG	Association pour l'Information de Gestion	**AIH**	Association des Ingénieurs Horticoles
AIGA	American Institute of Graphic Arts	**AIH**	Association Internationale de l'Hôtellerie = IHA
AIGA	Association Internationale de Géomagnétisme et d'Aéronomie = IAGA	**AIH**	Association Internationale des Hydrogéologues = IAH
AIGA	Associazione Italiana Governanti d'Albergo	**AIH**	Association of Independent Hospitals
AIGAV	Associazione Internazionale de Giornalisti Accreditati Vaticano	**AIH**	Australian Institute of Horticulture
AIGC	Arab Investment Guarantee Corporation (Kuwait) = CIAGI, IAIGC	**AIH**	People's Great Hural (Mongolia)
AIGC	Association Internationale de Géochimie et de Cosmochimie = IAGC	**AIHA**	American Industrial Hygiene Association
AIGC	Association of International Garden Centres	**AIHC**	American Industrial Health Council
AIGCD	Association of Irish Grocery and Confectionery Distributors (Éire)	**AIHCE**	Association Internationale d'Histoire Contemporaine de l'Europe
AIGE	Asociación Interamericana de Gastroenterologia	**AIHD**	ASEAN Institute for Health Development
AIGI	Association Internationale de Géologie de l'Ingénieur = IAEG	**AIHDI**	Association Internationale d'Histoire du Droit et des Institutions
AIGLE	Association Internationale de Gerontologie, Législation et Ethique = EAGLE	**AIHE**	Association for Innovation in Higher Education (U.S.A.)
AIGM	Association Internationale de Grands Magasins = IADS, IWV	**AIHÉ**	Association Internationale d'Histoire Économique = IAEH
		AIHED	American Institute for Human Engineering and Development
		AIHJA	Association Internationale des Hautes Juridictions Administratives = IASAJ
		AIHP	American Institute of the History of Pharmacy
		AIHP	Association Internationale d'Histoire de la Psychanalyse = IAHP

AIHR	Association of International Health Researchers	**AIICE**	Association Internationale des Interprètes de Conférence
AIHS	Académie Internationale de l'Histoire des Sciences = IAHS	**AIIDAP**	Association Internationale d'Information et de Documentation en Administration Publique = IAIDPA
AIHS	American Indian Historical Society		
AIHS	American Irish Historical Society	**AIIE**	American Institute of Industrial Engineers
AIHTI	Association Internationale d'Histoire des Télécommunication et de l'Informatique	**AIIÉPT**	Association Internationale des Institutions d'Évaluation et de Prospective Technologique
AIHTTR	African Institute for Higher Technical Training and Research	**AIIG**	Associazione Italiana degli Insegnanti di Geografia
AIHV	Association Internationale pour l'Histoire du Verre	**AIIH**	Asociación Internacional de Investigaciones Hidráulicas = AIRH, IAHR
AII	Agentsvo Inostrannoi Informatsii		
AII	Association of International Irradiation (France)	**AIIHPH**	All-India Institute of Hygiene and Public Health
AII	Associazione Idrotecnica Italiana	**AIII**	Association of International Industrial Irradiation
AII	Associazione Italiana degli Inventori		
AII	Australian Insurance Institute	**AIIM**	Association for Information and Image Management
AIIA	American Institute for Islamic Affairs		
AIIA	Association of International Insurance Agents	**AIIM**	Association of Independent Investment Managers
AIIA	Associazione Italiana Industriali Abbigliamento	**AIIM**	Association of International Industrial Irradiation
AIIA	Associazione Italiana per l'Intelligenza Artificiale = IAAI	**AIIM**	Associazione Italiana di Informatica Medica
AIIA	Associazione Italiana di Ingegneria Agraria (*ex* AIGR)	**AIIMB**	Associazione Italiana di Ingegneria Medica e Biologica
AIIA	Australian Information Industry Association	**AIIMS**	All-Indian Institute of Medical Sciences
AIIA	Australian Institute of International Affairs	**AIIPA**	Associazione Italiana Industriali Prodotti Alimentari
AIIAA	Authorised Independent Investment Advisors' Association	**AIIPC**	American International Institute for the Protection of Childhood
AIIAD	Arab Institute for Investment in the Agricultural Development (Kuwait)	**AIIS**	American Institute for Imported Steel
AIIB	Allied Irish Investment Bank	**AIIS**	American Institute of Indian Studies
AIIBP	Association Internationale de l'Industrie des Bouillons et Potages	**AIIS**	American Institute of Iranian Studies (Canada)
AIIC	Actividade International de Investigação Comercial	**AIIS**	American Institute of Islamic Studies
		AIIS	Asian Institute of International Studies (Philippines)
AIIC	Association Internationale des Interprètes de Conférence; Asociación Internacional de Interpretes de Conferencias = IACI, IVKD	**AIIS**	Association Internationale pour l'Informatique Statistique (ISI) = IASC
AIICA	Asociación de Investigación de las Industrias del Curtido y Anexas	**AIISA**	Association des Ingénieurs de l'Institut Supérieur d'Agriculture
AIICA	Asociación Internacional para las Investigaciones sobre Contaminación de las Aguas = AIRPE, IAWPRC	**AIISP**	Associazione Italiana per l'Igiene e la Sanita Pubblica
		AIISUP	Association Internationale d'Information Scolaire, Universitaire et Professionnelle = IAEVI

AIIT	Association Internationale de l'Inspection du Travail = IALI	**AILC**	Association Internationale de Littérature Comparée = ICLA
AIIT	Associazione Italiana Ingegneri delle Telecomunicazioni	**AILÉ**	Association Internationale des Loteries d'État = IASL
AIJ	Asian Institute of Journalism	**AILF**	Association des Informaticiens de Langue Française
AIJA	Alliance Internationale Jeanne d'Arc = SJIA	**AILOG**	Associazione Italiana di Logistica
AIJA	Association Internationale des Jeunes Avocats	**AILSA**	Association of Insurance Loss Surveyors and Adjusters
AIJB	Association Internationale des Jardins Botaniques = IABG	**AIM**	Accuracy in Media (U.S.A.)
AIJD	Association Internationale des Juristes Démocrates = IADL, IVDJ, MAJD	**AIM**	Action in International Medicine
AIJE	Association des Industries du Jute Européennes = AEJI	**AIM**	Advanced Informatics in Medicine in Europe (Belgium)
AIJE	Association Internationale des Juges des Enfants	**AIM**	Africa Inland Mission International
AIJLF	Association Internationale des Journalistes de Langue Française	**AIM**	Agência de Informação de Moçambique
		AIM	Aid for International Medicine (U.S.A.)
AIJN	Association de l'Industrie des Jus et Nectars de Fruits et de Légumes de la CEE	**AIM**	American Indian Movement
		AIM	American Institute for Microminiaturization
AIJP	Association Internationale des Journalistes Philatéliques	**AIM**	American Institute of Management
AIJPF	Association Internationale des Journalistes de la Presse Féminine et Familiale = IAWHPJ	**AIM**	American Institute of Musicology
		AIM	Arbeitsgemeinschaft Information Meeresforschung und Meerestechnik
AIL	Academie Internationale Lutéce	**AIM**	Asian Institute of Management (Philippines)
AIL	Associação dos Industriais de Lacticiníos	**AIM**	Association des Ingénieurs Électriciens sortis de l'Institut Électrotechnique Montefiore, Liége (Belgium)
AIL	Association Internationale de Limnologie Théorique et Appliquée = IAL, IATAL, IVL, SIL	**AIM**	Association Européenne des Industries de Produits de Marque
AIL	Association Internationale pour la Lecture = IRA	**AIM**	Association Internationale de la Meunerie = IMA
AIL	Association of International Libraries	**AIM**	Association Internationale de la Mutualité
AILA	Agenzia Internazionale Letteraria Artistica	**AIM**	Association Internationale de Météorologie
AILA	Agrupación Ibero-Latinoamericana para el Estudio Científico de la Deficiencia Mental	**AIM**	Association Internationale des Marques (Belgium)
		AIM	Association of Independent Museums
AILA	American Immigration Lawyers Association	**AIM**	Association of Industrial Machinery Merchants
AILA	Asociación de Industriales Latinoamericanos	**AIM**	Association of Information Managers for Financial Institutions
AILA	Association Internationale de Linguistique Appliquée = IAAL	**AIM**	Association of Innovation Management
AILAE	Asociación Ibero-Latinamericana de Endodontistas	**AIM**	Association of Insulation Manufacturers
		AIM	Association of International Marketing
AILC	American Indian Law Center	**AIM**	Association pour les Applications de l'Informatique à la Médecine
		AIM	Associazione Italiana di Metallurgia

AIM	Atlantic International Marketing Committee	**AIMFR**	Association Internationale des Maisons Familiales Rurales
AIM	Australasian Institute of Metals	**AIMH**	Association Internationale du Maïs Hybride = INTERHYBRID
AIM	Australian Institute of Management		
AIM International	Africa Inland Mission International	**AIMI**	Association Internationale de Méditation Transcendentale
AIM UK	Automatic Identification Manufacturers and Suppliers Association	**AIMI**	Associazione di Informatica Musicale Italiana
AIMA	All India Management Association	**AIMJF**	Association Internationale des Magistrats de la Jeunesse et de la Famille = IAJFMC
AIMA	Asociación Iberoamericana de Medicina Aerospacial		
AIMA	Associação dos Industriais de Montagem de Automóveis	**AIMLC**	Association of Island Marine Laboratories of the Caribbean
AIMA	Association Internationale des Musées d'Agriculture	**AIMM**	Asociación de Industriales Metalurgicos y de Mineria de Venezuela
AIMA	Association of Incorporated Managers & Administrators	**AIMM**	Australian Institute of Mining and Metallurgy
AIMA	Azienda di Stato per gli Interventi nel Mercato Agricolo	**AIMMPE**	American Institute of Mining, Metallurgical and Petroleum Engineers
AIMAS	Académie Internationale de Médecine Aéronautique et Spatiale = IAASM		
AIMAS	Associazione Italiana di Medicina Aeronautica e Spaziale	**AIMMS**	Associação dos Industriais Metalurgicos e Metalomecanicos do Sul
AIMAV	Association Internationale pour la Communication Interculturelle = IACCC	**AIMO**	Accademia Italiana di Medicina Omeopatica
AIMB	Associazione Italiana di Ingegneria Medica e Biologica	**AIMO**	All-India Manufacturers Organisation
		AIMO	Association of Industrial Medical Officers
AIMBE	Association Internationale de Médecine et de Biologie de l'Environnement = IAMBE	**AIMO**	Associazione Italiana Manufatture Ombrelli
AIMC	American Institute of Medical Climatology	**AIMOH**	Accademia Italiana di Medicina Omeopatica Hahnemannia
AIMC	Associazione Internazionale Mosaicisti Contemporanei	**AIMP**	Archives Internationales de Musique Populaire (Switzerland) = IAFM
AIMC	Associazione Italiana Maestri Cattolici	**AIMP**	Associação da Indústria de Malte Portuguesa
AIMCF	African Inter-Ministerial Committee for Food (WFC)	**AIMP**	Association of Independent Music Publishers (U.S.A.)
AIME	American Institute of Mining, Metallurgical and Petroleum Engineers	**AIMPA**	Association Internationale de Météorologie et de Physique de l'Atmosphère = AIMFA, IAMAP
AIME	Asociación de Investigación para la Mejora de la Alfalfa		
AIME	Association Internationale des Magistrats de la Jeunesse	**AIMPE**	Australian Institute of Marine and Power Engineers
AIMETA	Associazione Italiana di Meccanica Teorica e Applicata	**AIMPES**	Associazione Italiana Manufatturieri Pelli Cuoio e Succedanei
AIMF	Association Internationale des Maires Responsables des Capitales et Métropoles partiellement ou entièrement Francophones	**AIMR**	Association for Investment Management and Research
		AIMRT	American Institute for the Medical Research of Trauma
AIMFA	Asociación Internacional de Meteorologia y Fisica Atmosfürica = AIMPA, IAMAP	**AIMS**	American Institute for Marxist Studies
		AIMS	American Institute for Mental Studies
		AIMS	American Institute for Musical Studies

AIMS	American Institute of Maritime Services		Navigants de Langue Française
AIMS	American Institute of Merchant Shipping	**AINOS**	Associazione Italiana di Anestesia Odonto-Stomatologica
AIMS	American International Managers Society	**AINP**	Association Internationale des Numismates Professionnels = IAPN
AIMS	American International Marchigiana Society	**AINS**	Administración Institucional Nacional de Sanidad
AIMS	Association for Improvements in the Maternity Services	**AINSE**	Australian Institute of Nuclear Science and Engineering
AIMS	Association for Improving Moral Standards	**AIO**	Academie Internationale Olympique
AIMS	Association for International Medical Study	**AIO**	African Insurance Organization (Cameroon) = OAA
AIMS	Association of Independent Motor Stores	**AIOA**	American Iron Ore Association
AIMS	Association of International Marathons and Road Races	**AIOA**	Aviation Insurance Officers Association
		AIOB	American Institute of Oral Biology
AIMS	Association of Irish Musical Societies	**AIOB**	Association Internationale pour l'Océanografie Biologique = IABO
AIMS	Australian Institute of Marine Sciences		
AIMSC	Australian Industry Marine Science Council	**AIOC**	Associazione Internazionale Insigniti Ordini Cavallereschi
AIMT	Association for Integrated Marketing Technology (U.S.A.)	**AIOCC**	Association Internationale des Organisateurs de Courses Cyclistes
AIMT	Association Internationale de Méditation Transcendentale	**AIOEC**	Association of Iron Ore Exporting Countries = APEF
AIMT	Association Internationale de Musées de Transports =IATM	**AIOFM**	Anhui Institute of Optics and Fine Mechanics (China)
AIMU	American Institute of Marine Underwriters	**AIOIS**	Asociación Interamericana de Ingenieria Sanitaria (Brazil)
AIN	Agencia de Información Nacional (Cuba)	**AIOM**	Associazione Italiana di Oncologia Medica
AIN	Agentsvo "Investitsii i Nedvizhimost"	**AIOP**	Association Internationale d'Orientation Professionnelle
AIN	American Institute of Nutrition		
AIN	Arab Institute of Navigation (Egypt)	**AIOPI**	Association of Information Officers in the Pharmaceutical Industry
AIN	Asociación de Ingenieros Navales		
AIN	Association of Interpretive Naturalists (U.S.A.)	**AIORMS**	Association Olympique Internationale pour la Recherche Médico-Sportive (Switzerland)
AIN	Association of Irish Nurserymen (Éire)	**AIORN**	Associação dos Industrias de Ourivesaria e Relojoaria do Norte
AIN	Australian Institute of Navigation		
AINA	Arctic Institute of North America (Canada)	**AIOSP**	Association Internationale d'Orientation Scolaire et Professionnelle = IAEVG, IVSBB
AINBN	Association for the Introduction of New Biological Nomenclature (Belgium) = NBN	**AIOTE**	Associazione Italiana Operatori Titoli Esteri
AINDT	Australian Institute for Non-Destructive Testing	**AIP**	Agence Ivoirienne de Presse
		AIP	American Independent Party
AINEC	All-India Newspaper Editors Conference	**AIP**	American Institute of Parliamentarians
		AIP	American Institute of Physics
AINF	Association Interprofessionnelle de France pour la Prévention des Accidents et de l'Incendie	**AIP**	Asociación Interamericana de Productividad
AINLF	Association Internationale des	**AIP**	Associação Industrial Portuguesa

AIP	Association Internationale de Papyrologues	**AIPCR**	Association Internationale Permanente des Congrès de la Route = AIPCC, PIARC
AIP	Association Internationale de Pédiatrie = IPA	**AIPE**	American Institute for Professional Education
AIP	Association Internationale de Photobiologie	**AIPE**	American Institute of Plant Engineers
AIP	Association Internationale des Ports =IAPH	**AIPE**	Association de l'Industrie des Produits d'Entretien (Belgium)
AIP	Association of Independent Producers	**AIPE**	Association de l'Industrie Pétrolière Européenne (Belgium) = EPIA
AIP	Associazione Italiana della Pellicceria	**AIPÉA**	Association Internationale pour l'Étude des Argiles
AIP	Associazione Italiana Prefabbricazione per l'Edilizia Industrializzata	**AIPEAPA**	Association Internationale de Psychiatrie de l'Enfant et de l'Adolescent et des Professions Associées = IACAPAP
AIP	Australian Institute of Packaging		
AIP	Australian Institute of Petroleum	**AIPEC**	Associação Iberoamericana de Portas e Costas = AIPYC
AIP	Australian Institute of Physics		
AIPA	Agence Panafricaine d'Information	**AIPF**	Association Internationale de la Presse Filmée = INA
AIPA	American Ionosphere Propagation Association	**AIPG**	American Institute of Professional Geologists
AIPA	Association Internationale de la Psychologie Adlérienne = IAIP, IVIP	**AIPH**	Association Internationale de Paléontologie Humaine
AIPA	Association Internationale de Psychologie Analytique = IAAP, IGFAP	**AIPH**	Association Internationale des Producteurs de l'Horticulture = IAHP
AIPA	Associazione Italiana per lo Studio della Psicologia Analitica	**AIPI**	Associazione Internazionale dei Professori d'Italiano
AIPA	Associazione Italiana Planificazione Aziendale	**AIPI**	Associazione Italiana Progettisti in Architetture d'Interni
AIPA	Australian Independent Publishers Association	**AIPLA**	American International Property Law Association
AIPA	Australian Institute of Park Administration	**AIPLE**	Asociación de Industriales de Productos Lacteos del Ecuador
AIPAD	Association of International Photography Art Dealers	**AIPLF**	Association Internationale des Parlementaires de Langue Française
AIPC	Accademia Internazionale de Propaganda Culturale	**AIPLU**	American Institute for Property and Liability Underwriters
AIPC	Asociación Iberoamericana Periodistos Cientificos	**AIPMA**	All-India Plastics Manufacturers Association
AIPC	Association Internationale de Prophylaxie de la Cécité = IAPB	**AIPnD**	Associazione Italiana Prove Non Distruttive Monitoraggio Diagnostica
AIPC	Association Internationale des Palais des Congrès = IACC	**AIPO**	African Intellectual Property Organization (Cameroon) = OAPI
AIPC	Association Internationale des Ponts et Charpentes = IABSE, IVBH	**AIPO**	ASEAN Interparliamentary Organisation
AIPCC	Asociación International Permanence Congresos Carreteras = AIPCR, PIARC	**AIPPh**	Association Internationale des Professeurs de Philosophie
AIPCEE	Association des Industries du Poisson de la CEE	**AIPPI**	Association Internationale pour la Protection de la Propriété Industrielle = IAPIP, IVFGR
AIPCN	Association Internationale Permanente des Congrès de Navigation = ISVSK, PIANC		

AIPS	American Institute of Pathologic Science	**AIRBM**	Associazione Italiana di Radiobiologia Medica
AIPS	Association Internationale de la Presse Sportive = ISPA	**AIRBO**	Association Internationale pour les Recherches au Bas Fourneau d'Ougrée
AIPS	Association Internationale pour la Prévention du Suicide = IASP, IVSP	**AIRBR**	Association Internationale du Registre des Bateaux du Rhin = IVR
AIPS	Association Internationale pour le Progrès Social = IASP	**AIRBS**	American Institute for Research in the Behavioral Sciences
AIPS	Associazione Italiana di Psicologia dello Sport	**AIRC**	Association Internationale de Réparateurs en Carrosserie (Netherlands)
AIPS	Australian Institute of Political Science	**AIRC**	Association of Independent Radio Contractors
AIPSA	Agro Industrias Peruanas S.A.	**AIRC**	Associazione Italiana per la Ricerca sul Cancro
AIPT	Association for International Practical Training	**AIRCAT**	Association Internationale des Régies et Commissions des Accidents du Travail = IAIABC
AIPT	Association Internationale de la Presse Touristique		
AIPT	Association Internationale pour la Promotion du Thé = ITPA	**AIRD**	Asian Institute for Rural Development
AIPU	Arab Inter-Parliamentary Union	**AIRD**	Australian Institute of Rural Development
AIPU	Association International de Pédagogie Universitaire	**AIRDO**	Association des Institutions de Recherche et Développement de l'Ocean Indien (Mauritius)
AIPU	Association International du Personnel de l'Unesco		
AIPYC	Asociación Iberoamericana de Puertos y Costas = AIPEC	**AIRE**	Association Internationale des Ressources en Eau = AIRH, IWRA
AIR	Action for Industrial Recycling (U.S.A.)	**AIRE**	Associazione Italiana per la Promozione degli Studie delle Ricerche per l'Edilizia
AIR	All-India Radio		
AIR	Alliance of Independent Retailers	**AIREA**	American Institute of Real Estate Appraisers
AIR	American Industrial Real-Estate Association	**AIREN**	American Institute for Research and Education in Naturopathy
AIR	American Institutes for Research in the Behavioural Sciences	**AIRF**	All India Railwaymen's Federation
AIR	Asociación Interamericana de Radiodifusión (Uruguay)	**AIRG**	Agency for Intellectual Relief in Germany
AIR	Asociación Interamericana de Redifusion	**AIRG**	Australian Industrial Research Group
AIR	Association des Instituteurs Réunis du Grande-Duché de Luxembourg	**AIRH**	Asociación Internacional Recursos Hidricos = AIRE, IWRA
AIR	Association Internationale de Radiodiffusion = IAB	**AIRH**	Association Internationale de Recherches Hydrauliques = AIIH, IAHR
AIR	Associazione Italiana Ragioneri	**AIRI**	Agenzia Informazioni Rapporti Internazionali
AIR	Australian Institute of Radiography		
AIR Ltd	Association of Independent Railways	**AIRI**	Animal Industry Research Institute (Australia)
AIRAC	Australian Ionising Radiation Advisory Council	**AIRI**	Associazione Italiana per la Ricerca Industriale
AIRAH	Australian Institute of Refrigeration, Air Conditioning and Heating	**AIRIA**	All India Rubber Industries Association
		AIRIEL	Associazione Italiana per la Ricerca nell'Impiego degli Elastomeri
AIRAPT	Association Internationale pour l'Avancement de la Recherche et de la Technologie aux Hautes Pressions	**AIRIT**	Association Internationale de Recherche en Informatique Toxicologique

AIRMA	All-India Radio Manufacturers Association	**AIS**	Association Internationale de Sociologie = ISA
AIRMÉC	Association Internationale pour la Recherche Médicale et les Échanges Culturels	**AIS**	Associazione Italiana degli Slavisti
		AIS	Associazione Italiana di Schermografia
AIRMIC	Association of Insurance and Risk Managers in Industry and Commerce	**AIS**	Associazione Italiana di Sociologia
		AIS	Associazione Italiana Sommeliers
AIRMN	Associazione Italiana di Radiologia e Medicina Nucleare	**AIS**	Australia Iron and Steel Pty
		AIS	Australian Information Service
AIRMOA	Association Internationale pour la Recherche Médicale dans Ouest Africain	**AIS**	Australian Institute of Sport
		AIS	Automobile-Importørernes Sammenslutning
AIRO	Associazione Italiana di Ricerca Operativa	**AIS**	Islamic Salvation Army (Algeria)
AIRP	Association Internationale de Receveurs de la Poste = ISP	**AISA**	Académie Internationale des Sciences Appliquées
AIRP	Association Internationale de Relations Professionnelles = AIRT, IIRA	**AISA**	Agence Islamique de Secours pour l'Afrique = IARA, ISRA
AIRP	Associazione Italiana per le Relazioni Pubbliche	**AISA**	Agricultural Information Society for Asia
AIRP	Associazione Italiana Ricostruttori Pneumatici	**AISA**	Association des Importateurs Suisses d'Automobiles
AIRPE	Association Internationale de Recherche sur la Pollution de l'Eau = AIICA, IAWPRC	**AISA**	Association Internationale pour la Sécurité Aérienne = IASA
		AISA	Association Internationale pour le Sport des Aveugles = IBSA
AIRPPAL	Association Interprofessionnelle Régionale Patronale des Pays de la Loire	**AISA**	Association of International Schools in Africa (Kenya)
		AISA	Associazione Italiana Studi Americanistici
AIRS	Aerobics International Research Society	**AISADC**	Association of Insurance Supervisory Authorities of Developing Countries (Philippines)
AIRSO	Association of Industrial Road Safety Officers		
AIRT	Asociación Internacional de Relaciones de Trabajo = AIRP, IIRA	**AISAM**	Association Internationale des Sociétés d'Assurance Mutuelle
AIRT	Association of the International Rubber Trade (*ex* RTA)	**AISB**	Association Internationale de Standardisation Biologique = IABS
AIRTO	Association of Independent Research and Technology Organisations	**AISB**	Society for the Study of Artificial Intelligence and the Simulation of Behavior
AIS	Action and Information on Sugars		
AIS	Akademio Internacia de la Sciencoj (San Marino)	**AISC**	American Institute of Steel Construction
		AISC	Assistenza Internazionale Servici di Congresso
AIS	Androgen Insensitivity Support Group		
AIS	Anglo-Italian Society	**AISC**	Association Internationale des Skål Clubs = IASC
AIS	Anglo-Ivorian Society		
AIS	Association for Information Systems	**AISC**	Association Internationale Sociale Chrétienne
AIS	Association for Integrative Studies		
AIS	Association Internationale de la Savonnerie et de la Détergence	**AISC**	Associazione Italiana Santa Cecilia per la Musica Sacra
AIS	Association Internationale de la Soie = ISA	**AISCAT**	Associazione Italiana Societé Concessionarie Autostrade e Traffori
AIS	Association Internationale de Sémiotique = IASS	**AISCO**	Arab Iron and Steel Company (Bahrain)

AISCO	Associazione Italiana Scuole per Corrispondenza	**AISP**	Associazione delle Imprese Svizzere di Perforazione
AISÉ	Association Internationale des Sciences de l'Éducation = IAAER	**AISP**	Associazione d'Italiana di Storia Postale
AISÉ	Association Internationale des Sciences Économiques = IEA	**AISPA**	Associazione Italiana Selezionatori Produttori Avicoli di Milano
AISE	Association Internationale des Statisticiens d'Enquêtes = IASS	**AISPIT**	Association Internationale de Seismologie et de Physique de l'Intérieur de la Terre = IASPEI
AISE	Association of Iron and Steel Engineers (U.S.A.)	**AISPO**	Association Internationale des Sciences Physiques de l'Océan = AICFO, IAPSO
AISEIT	Association of Institute and School of Education In-Service Tutors	**AISPS**	Associazione Italiana di Scienze Politiche e Sociali
AISFO	Associazione Italiana Sviluppo Foraggere	**AISRU**	Association Internationale pour la Statistique Régionale et Urbaine = IARUS
AISG	Accountants International Study Group	**AISS**	Administración Institucional de Servicios Socioprofesionales
AISH	Association Internationale des Sciences Hydrologiques = IAHS	**AISS**	Asociación Internacional Seguridad Social = ISSA
AISI	Advanced International Studies Institute	**AISS**	Association Internationale de la Science du Sol = IBG, ISSS, SICS
AISI	American Iron and Steel Institute	**AISS**	Association Internationale de la Sécurité Sociale = ISSA, IVSS
AISI	Associazione Italiana per lo Sviluppo Internazionale	**AISS**	Associazione Italiana Selezionatori Sementi e Costitutori Razze
AISIST	Australian Institute of Spatial Information Sciences and Technology	**AISSCAP**	Asociación de Instituciones de Seguridad Social de Centroamerica y Panama
AISJ	Association Internationale des Sciences Juridiques = IALS	**AISSF**	All India Sikh Students Federation
AISL	Association Internationale de l'Hôpital Schweitzer de Lambaréné	**AISSLI**	Associazione Internazionale per gli Studi di Lingua e Letterature Italiane = IASILL
AISL	Association of International Shipping Lines	**AIST**	Agency of Industrial Science and Technology (MITI)
AISL	Associazione Italiana di Studio del Lavoro	**AIST**	Agenzia Italiana Spettacolo e Turismo
AISLF	Association Internationale des Sociologues de Langue Française	**AIST**	Arbeitsgemeinschaft zur Förderung und Entwicklung des Internationalen Strassenverkehrs in der DDR
AISM	Association Internationale de Signalisation Maritime = IALA	**AIST**	Association Internationale pour la Sauvegarde de Tyr = IAST
AISM	Associazione Italiana per gli Studi di Mercato	**AISTS**	Associazione Italiana della Stampa Tecnica Scientifica e Periodica
AISMI	ASEAN Institute for Small Medium Industries	**AISU**	Arab Iron and Steel Union = AESU, UAFA
AISNA	Administración Institucional de la Sanidad Nacional	**AIT**	Agency for Instructional Technology (U.S.A.)
AISNA	Association des Ingénieurs en Sciences Nucléaires Appliquées	**AIT**	Alliance Internationale de Tourisme
AISÖ	Arbeitsgemeinschaft Internationaler Strassenverkehrsunternehmer Österreichs	**AIT**	Asian Institute of Technology (Thailand)
AISP	Association Internationale de Science Politique = IPSA	**AIT**	Asian Institute of Tourism (Philippines)
AISP	Association of Information Systems Professionals		

AIT	Asociación de Investigación del Transporte	**AITI**	Associazione Italiana Traduttori ed Interpreti
AIT	Association d'Interprètes et de Traducteurs	**AITIM**	Asociación de Investigación Técnica de las Industrias de la Madera y Corcho
AIT	Association of Inspectors of Taxes	**AITIT**	Association Internationale de la Teinture et de l'Impression Textiles = IATDP
AIT	Association of Insurance Teachers		
AIT	Associazione Italiana Teatri	**AITIVA**	Associazione Italiana Tecnici Industrie Vernici e Affini
AIT	Inter-American Association of Translators	**AITM**	Association of Irish Traditional Musicians
AITA	Air Industries and Transports Association (U.S.A.)	**AITO**	Association of Independent Tour Operators
AITA	Association Internationale des Transports Aériens	**AITO**	Associazione Italiana di Terapia Occupazionale
AITA	Association Internationale du Théâtre d'Amateurs = IATA	**AITOGA**	Associazione Italiana tra i Tecnici delle Industrie degli Oli, Grassi e Affini
AITA	Associazione Italiana Technici delle Attività Alberghiere	**AITPCI**	Association des Ingénieurs, Techniciens et Professionels du Contrôle Industrielle
AITAA	Asian Institute of Technology Alumni Association (Thailand)	**AITRC**	Applied Information of the Technologies Records Center (U.S.A.)
AITAL	Asociación Internacional de Transporte Aéreo Latinoamericana		
AITBM	Associazione Italiana dei Tecnici della Birra e del Malto	**AITS**	Association of Independent Tobacco Specialists
AITC	American Institute for Timber Construction	**AITSLT**	Association Internationale pour le Tourisme Social et les Loisirs des Travailleurs = IASTWL
AITC	Association Internationale des Traducteurs de Conférence	**AITT**	Association Internationale de Traitement Thermique et de l'Ingénierie des Matériaux = IFHT, IVW, MOTO
AITC	Association of Investment Trust Companies		
AITC	Australian Industry and Technology Commission	**AITT**	Association of Industrial Truck Trainers
AITE	Asociación de Industrias Textiles del Ecuador	**AITUC**	All-India Trades Union Congress
AITEC	Acción Internacional Tecnica = ACCION International	**AIU**	Alliance Israélite Universelle
		AIU	Association Internationale des Universités = IAU
AITEC	Association Internationale de Techniciens, Experts et Chercheurs	**AIU**	Association Internationale des Urbanistes = IGSRP, ISOCARP
AITEC	Associazione Italiana Tecnico Economica del Cemento	**AIU**	Association of Indian Universities
AITEL	Associazione Italiana Tecnici del Latte	**AIUÉALF**	Association Internationale des Universitaires, Écrivains et Artistes de Langue Française
AITeLaB	Associazione Italiana Tecnici di Laboratorio Biomedico		
AITEP	Association for International Technical Promotion (U.S.A.)	**AIUFFASS**	Association Internationale des Utilisateurs de Fils de Fibres Artificielles et Synthétiques et de Soie Naturelle
AITES	Association Internationale des Travaux en Souterrain = ITA	**AIULRE**	Associacion Internacionala per l'Usança de la Lengas Regionalas a l'Escola (Belgium) = SCOLARE
AITFA	Association des Ingénieurs et Techniciens Française des Aéroglisseurs		
AITha	Association Internationale de Thalassothérapie	**AIUM**	American Institute of Ultrasound in Medicine
		AIURA	American Institute of Urban and Regional Affairs

AIUS	Associazione Internazionale Uomo nello Spazis	**AIWRS**	Arctic International Wildlife Range Society
AIUS	Australian Institute of Urban Studies	**AIWS**	Hebei Institute of Weed Science
AIUTA	Association Internationale des Universités du Troisième Age	**AIYPC**	Asociación Iberoamericana de Puertos y Costas
AIV	Associazione Italiana del Vuoto	**AJ-MRDN**	And Jëf-Mouvement Révolutionnaire pour la Démocratie Nouvelle (Senegal) = AND JEF
AIVA	Association Internationale des Villes de l'Avenir		
AIVAC	Association Internationale pour le Vidéo dans les Arts et la Culture = IAVAC	**AJA**	African Jurists Association (Senegal)
AIVC	Association of Inter-Varsity Clubs	**AJA**	Amateur Judo Association of Great Britain
AIVCIT	Association Internationale de Volcanologie et de Chimie de l'Intérieur de la Terre = IAVCEI	**AJA**	American Judges Association
		AJA	American Judo Association
		AJA	Anglo-Jewish Association
AIVEMA	Asociación de Importadores de Vehiculos, Maquinaria y Afines (Costa Rica)	**AJA**	Associazione Jesolana Albergatori
		AJA	Australian Journalists Association
AIVF	Association des Ingénieurs des Villes de France	**AJAC**	Association Jeunesse Agriculteurs Casamance (Senegal)
AIVFC	Association Internationale des Villes Francophones de Congrès= IAFCT	**AJACS**	Association Jeunesse d'Actions pour le Coopération et la Solidarité
AIVM	Association Internationale pour les Voiles Minces et les Voiles Spatiaux = AIEL, IASS, IVS	**AJAP**	Association de la Jeunesse Africaine pour le Progrès
		AJBD	Arbeitsgemeinschaft für Juristisches Bibliotheks- und Dokumentationswesen
AIVN	Association Internationale des Villes Nouvelles = INTA	**AJBP**	Association of Jewish Book Publishers (U.S.A.)
AIVP	Association Internationale Villes et Ports = IACP	**AJC**	Asociación Judicial de Chile
AIVPA	Association Internationale Vétérinaire de Production Animale = ITVTP, IVAAP	**AJC**	Association des Journalistes de la Consommation
		AJC	Australian Jockey Club
AIVTs	Abonentskii Informatsionno-Vychislitel'nyi Tsentr	**AJCC**	American Jersey Cattle Club
		AJCC	American Joint Committee on Cancer
AIW	Arbeitkreis Fachagenturen und Berater für Industrie-Werbung	**AJCOR**	Australian Joint Council for Operational Research
AIW	Arbeitsgemeinschaft Industrieöffenbau- und Wärmeanlagen	**AJDC**	American Joint Distribution Committee
AIW	International Union of Allied Industrial Workers	**AJE**	Association des Journalistes Européens
		AJE	Association des Juristes Européens
AIWC	All India Women's Conference	**AJEF**	Association des Jeunes Européens Fédéralistes
AIWF	American Institute of Wine and Food		
AIWF	Assembly of International Winter Sports Federations	**AJÉF**	Association des Journalistes Économiques et Financiers
AIWFC	All India Women's Food Council	**AJEX**	Association of Jewish Ex-Servicemen and Women
AIWM	American Institute of Weights and Measures	**AJF**	Accueil des Jeunes en France
AIWO	Agudat Israel World Organisation = OMAI	**AJH**	Académie Internationale d'Héraldique (Luxembourg)
AIWP	All-Indonesian Workers' Party	**AJH**	Association des Journalistes de l'Horticulture
AIWP	Association Internationale des Arbitres de Water Polo = AIA	**AJHS**	American Jewish Historical Society

AJLAC	American Jewish League Against Communism	**AKDI**	Agentsvo Kommercheskoi i Delovoi Informatsii
AJMS	Association des Journalistes Médico-Sociaux	**AKDS**	Albanska Kršćanska Demokratska Stranka (Albania) = ACDP
AJNOC	Ajman National Oil Company	**AKE**	Arbeitskreis Entwicklungspolitik
AJP	Association des Journalistes du Pacifique (Fiji)	**AKEB**	Aktiengesellschaft für Kernenergie Beteiligungen (Switzerland)
AJPAA	Association des Journalistes Professionnels de l'Aéronautique et de l'Astronautique	**AKEL**	Anorthotiko Komma Ergazomenou Laou (Cyprus)
AJPAE	Association des Journalistes Professionnels de l'Aéronautique et de l'Espace	**AKEU**	Assotsiatsiia Konsultantov Po Ekonomike i Upravleniiu
		AKEW	Arbeitsgemeinschaft Kernkraftwerk der Elektrizitätswirtschaft (Austria)
AJPBÉ	Association des Journalistes Périodiques Belges et Étrangers	**AKF**	Aga Khan Foundation (Switzerland)
AJPF	Association Internationale des Journalistes de la Presse Féminine et Familiale	**AKF**	American-Korean Foundation
		AKF	Amternes og Kommunernes Forskningsinstitut (Denmark)
AJR	Association of Jewish Refugees in Great Britain	**AKF**	Arbeitsgemeinschaft für Konflikt- und Friedensforschung am Institut für Politische Wissenschaft
AJS	American Judicature Society	**AKI**	Afghanistan Karakul Institute
AJS	Association des Journalistes Sportifs	**AKI**	Arbeitsgemeinschaft Deutsche Kunststoffindustrie
AJSA	Association des Journalistes Suisses de l'Automobile = ASGA, SVAJ	**AKI**	Arbeitsgemeinschaft Keramische Industrie
AJSM	Association of Jute Spinners and Manufacturers	**AKIE**	Arbeitskreis Industrial Engineering
AJSPI	Association des Journalistes Scientifiques de la Presse d'Information	**AKKOR**	Assotsiatsiia Krestianskikh Khoziaistv i Selskokhoziaistvennykh Kooperativov Rossii
AJUSOL	Ajudûncia do Solimões (Brazil)		
AJV	Algemene Juweliers Vereniging	**AKL**	Autoalan Keskusliitto
AJWDFP	Arab-Jewish Women's Dialogue for Peace	**AKOD**	Arbeitsgemeinschaft Krankenpflegender Ordensschwestern Deutschlands
AJY	Association of Jewish Youth	**AKOÖ**	Kammer für Arbeiter und Angestellte für Oberösterreich
AK-BYGG	Nordiska Ambetsmannakommitten för Samarbete inom Byggsektorn = EK-BYGG	**AKOR**	Gesellschaft für Operations Research in Wirtschaft und Verwaltung
ÄK-LIVS	Nordiska Ämbetsmannakommittén för Livsmedelsfrågor	**AKPIRG**	Alaska Public Interest Research Group
		AKRS	Anarkho-Kommunisticheskii Soiuz
AKA	Alians Kazanskikh Anarkhistov	**AKS**	Amatorski Klub Sportowy
AKaP	Arbeitsgemeinschaft Katholischer Pflegeorganisationen	**AKT**	Ajia Komyuniti Torasuto (Japan)
		AKT	Auto-ja Kuljetusaian Työntekijäliitto
AKAVA	Akateemisten Järjestöjen Keskuselin	**AKThB**	Arbeitsgemeinschaft Katholisch-Theologischer Bibliotheken
AKB	Arbeitsgemeinschaft der Kunstbibliotheken	**AKTUR**	Action Front for the Retention of Turnhalle Principles (Namibia)
AKB	Association des Kinésithérapeutes de Belgique	**AKW**	Arbeitsgemeinschaft für Kunst und Wissenschaft (Austria)
AKBD	Arbeitsgemeinschaft der Kirchlichen Büchereiverbände Deutschlands	**AL**	Arab League
AKCLIS	Australian Key Centre in Land Information Studies	**Al-Anon**	Alcoholic Anonymous Family Groups (Éire, U.K.)

ALA	African Literature Association (U.S.A.)	**ALADA**	Asociación Latinoamericana del Algodon (Venezuela)
ALA	Agricultural Law Association	**ALADA**	Asociación Libreros Anticuarios de la Argentina
ALA	American Landrace Association		
ALA	American Laryngological Association	**ALADAA**	Asociación Latinoamericana de Estudios Afro-Asiáticos
ALA	American Library Association		
ALA	American Logistics Association	**ALADEFE**	Asociación Latinoamericana de Escuelas y Facultades de Enfermeria
ALA	American Lung Association		
ALA	Arbeitsgemeinschaft der Schweizerischen Aluminiumwaren-Fabrikanten	**ALADI**	Asociación Latinoamericana de Integración = LAIA
		ALADI	Association Latinoaméricaine de Dessein Industriel (Brazil)
ALA	ASEAN Law Association		
ALA	Asociación de Líneas Aéreas	**ALADIM**	Asociación Latinoamericana para el Desarrollo y la Integración de la Mujer (Chile) = LAADIW
ALA	Asociación Latinoamericana de Archivos		
ALA	Association of London Authorities	**ALAE**	Asociación Latinoamericana de Entomologia
ALA	Austral Lineas Aereas (Argentina)		
ALA	Authors League of America	**ALAE**	Association of Licensed Aircraft Engineers
ALA	Schweizerische Gesellschaft für Vogelkunde und Vogelschutz	**ALAETS**	Asociación Latinoamericana de Escuelas de Trabajo Social
ALABIC	Asociación Latinoamericana de Industrias de Bienes de Capital (Chile)	**ALAF**	Anglo-Latin American Foundation
		ALAF	Asociación Latino-Americana de Ferrocarriles
ALAC	AGHS Legal Cell (Pakistan)		
ALAC	Australian Land Administrators' Conference	**ALAF**	Asociación Latinoamericana de Fitotecnia
ALACA	Asociación Latinoamericana de Crédito Agricola	**ALAFACE**	Asociación Latinoamericana de Fabricantes de Cerveza (Peru)
ALACA	Association of Local Authority Chief Architects	**ALAFAR**	Asociación Latinoamericana de Fabricantos de Materiales Refractarios
ALACAT	Federación de Asociaciones Nacionales de Agentes de Carga de América Latina y del Caribe (Brazil)	**ALAFARPE**	Asociación Nacional de Laboratorios Farmaceuticos (Peru)
ALACE	Association of Local Authority Chief Executives	**ALAFEM**	Asociación Latinoamericana de Facultades y Escuelas de Medicina
ALACEM	Asociación Latinoamericana y del Caribe sobre Estudios de la Mujer (Costa Rica)	**ALAGRAN**	Latin American Association on Post-Harvest Grain Technology (Mexico)
ALACESE	Latin American Association of Export Credit Insurance Companies (Peru)	**ALAHUA**	Asociación Latinoamericana para la Promocion del Habitat, del Urbanismo y de la Arquitectura (Ecuador)
ALACF	Asociación Latinoamericana de Ciencias Fisiológicas	**ALAI**	Agence Latinoaméricaine d'Information (Ecuador)
ALAD	Arid Lands Agricultural Development Program	**ALAI**	Associação Latinoamericana de Immunologia (Brazil)
ALAD	Asociación Latinoamericana de Diabetes (Costa Rica)	**ALAI**	Association Littéraire et Artistique Internationale = ILAA
ALAD	Associação Latinoamericana de Dragages (Brazil)	**ALAIC**	Asociación Latinoamericana de Investigadores de la Communicación
ALADA	Asociación Latinoamericana de Derecho Aeronautico y Espacial	**ALAIH**	Asociación Latino-Americano de Ictiologos y Herpetologos
ALADA	Asociación Latinoamericana de Direito Agrario	**ALAINEE**	Asociación Latinoamércana de la Industria Electrica y Eletronica

ALALC	Asociación Latinoamericana de Libre Comercio
ALAM	Asociación Latinoamericana de Malezas
ALAM	Asociación Latinoamericana de Malhierbologia
ALAM	Association of Lightweight Aggregate Manufacturers
ALAMAR	Asociación Latinoamericana de Armadores = LASA
ALAMCTA	Latin American Association of Environmental Mutagens, Carcinogens and Teratogens
ALAMOC	Asociación Latinoamericana de Análisis y Modificación del Comportamiento (Uruguay)
ALANAM	Asociación Latinoamericana de Acadamias Nacionales de Medicina
ALANI	Association of Local Authorities of Northern Ireland
ALANZ	Applied Linguistics Association of New Zealand
ALAP	Agricultural Librarians Association of the Philippines
ALAPE	Asociación Latinoamericana de Pediatría
ALAPROVI	Asociación Latinoamericana de Productores de Vidrio (Uruguay)
ALAPROVI	Asociación Latinoamericana de Productores de Vino
ALAPSO	Asociación Latinoamericana de Psicología Social
ALAR	Association of Light Alloy Refiners
ALARS	Association of Light Alloy Refiners Ltd
ALAS	Asociación Latinoamericana de Sociologia (Argentina)
ALAS	Asociación Latinoamericana del Suelo
ALAS	Associazione Latiale Spedizionieri
ALASA	African Library Association of South Africa
ALASA	Asociación Latinoamericana de Aseguradoras Agropecuárias (Colombia)
ALASBIMN	Asociación Latinoamericana del Sociedades de Biología y Medicina Nuclear
ALASD	Asociación Latinoamericana Sindrome de Down (Mexico)
ALASECE	Asociación Latinoamericana de Organismos de Seguros de Creditos de Exportacion (Peru)
ALASEI	Agencia Latinoamericana de Servicios Especiales de Información
ALASRU	Asociación Latinoamericana de Sociología Rural
ALAT	Asociación Latinoamericana de Análisis Transaccional (Mexico)
ALAT	Association Latino-Américaine des Sociétés Commerciales Internationales (Brazil) = LAATC
ALATAC	Asociación Latinoamericana del Transporte Automotor por Carreteras
ALATIR	Asociación Latinoamericana de Recreación y Tiempre Libre
ALAV	Arbeitsgemeinschaft Literarischer Autoren und Verleger
ALB	Arbeitkreis Ladenbau im HDH
ALB	Arbeitsgemeinschaft Landwirtschaftliches Bauen
ALBA	Aluminium Bahrain
ALBAMA	Aliança Batista Missionária da Amazonia (Brazil)
ALBAMEX	Alimentos Balanceados de Mexico, S.A.
Albkontroll	Albanian Trade Supervisory Organization
ALBRSO	Association of London Borough Road Safety Officers
ALBSU	Adult Literacy Basic Skills Unit (NIACE)
ALC	Africa Literature Centre (Zambia)
ALC	Agricultural Land Commission
ALC	Alberta Livestock Co-operative (Canada)
ALC	Asociación Latinoamericana para la Calidad (Argentina)
ALCA	American Leather Chemists Association
ALCA	Associated Landscape Contractors of America
ALCAN	Aluminum Company of Canada
ALCASA	Almacenadora Centroamericana, S.A. (El Salvador)
ALCASA	Aluminio del Caroni, S.A. (Venezuela)
ALCATEL	Société Alsacienne de Constructions Atomiques, de Télécommunications et d'Électronique
ALCB	Association Luxembourgeoise contre le Bruit
ALCD	Association of Law Costs Draftsmen Ltd
ALCE	Asociación de Laboratorios Cinematograficos Españoles

ALCE	Associazione Ligure Commercio Estero	**ALEAS**	Asociación Latinoamericana de Educación Agrícola Superior
ALCEAPA	Asociación Latinoamericana y del Caribe de Empresas de Agua Potable y Alcantarillado	**ALEC**	Algemeen Landbouw Emigratie-Comité
ALCE COOP	Asociación Latinoamericana de Centros de Educación Cooperativa (Argentina)	**ALEC**	Arid Lands Environment Centre
ALCES	Association of Lecturers in Colleges of Education in Scotland	**ALEC**	Asian Labour Education Centre (Philippines)
ALCL	Association of London Chief Librarians	**ALEC**	Association of Language Excellence Centres
ALCLI	Asociación Latinoamericana de Centros de Lucha contra las Intoxicaciones (Venezuela)	**ALEC**	Associazione Laureati in Economia e Commercio
ALCOA	Aluminum Company of America	**ALECSO**	Arab League Educational, Cultural and Scientific Organization
ALCOM	Aquaculture for Local Community Development Programme (Zimbabwe)	**ALEEM**	Association of Loading and Elevating Equipment Manufacturers = ALEM
ALCOR-DES	Asociación Latinoamericana de Corporaciones Regionales de Desarrollo	**ALÉFPA**	Association Laïque pour l'Éducation et la Formation Professionnelle des Adolescents (Belgium)
ALCORSS	Australian Liaison Committee on Remote Sensing by Satellite	**ALÉJ**	Association Luxembourgeoise des Éditeurs de Journaux
ALCQ	Association des Littératures Canadienne et Québécoise = ACQL	**ALEM**	Association of Loading and Elevating Equipment Manufacturers =ALEEM
ALCS	Authors Licensing and Collecting Society	**ALEMAS**	Agrupación Nacional de Alquitrones, Emulsiones, Asfaltos Impermeabilizantes
ALD	Association Luxembourgeoise du Diabète		
ALDA	American Land Development Association	**ALEOA**	American Law Enforcement Officers Association
ALDA	Association de Liaison pour le Développement d'Agnam	**ALER**	Asociación Latinoamericana de Educación Radiofónica
ALDEASA	Almacenes, Depositos y Estaciones Aduaneros, SA	**ALERB**	Asociación Latinoamericana de Redactores de Revistas Biológicas (Mexico)
ALDEC	Asociación Latinoamericana de Derecho Constitucional	**ALERT**	All-Africa Leprosy and Rehabilitation Training Centre (Ethiopia)
ALDENIC	Almacenes Generales de Deposito de Nicaragua, S.A.	**aLERT**	Leeds European Refugee Trust
ALDEV	African Land Development Board (Kenya)	**ALES**	Aide aux Lépreux Emmaüs-Suisse
ALDHU	Asociación Latinoamericana para los Derechos Humanos	**ALESS**	Asociación Latinoamericana de Escuelas de Servicio Social
ALDICASA	Almacenes del Istmo Centroamericano, S.A. (El Salvador)	**ALEX**	Aluminium Extruders Association
		ALEXIA	Association of Arab Lexicology (Tunisia)
ALDIS	Action Locale pour un Développement International Solidaire	**ALF**	Afar Liberation Front (Ethiopia)
ALDOC	Arab League Documentation Centre	**ALF**	Animal Liberation Front
ALDU	Association of Lawyers for the Defence of the Unborn	**ALF**	Arab Liberation Front
		ALF	Arbeitsgemeinschaft der Lebensmittel-Filialbetriebe
ALE	Association for Liberal Education		
ALEA	Air Line Employees Association International	**ALF**	Asociación Latinoamericana de Farmacologia (Venezuela)
ALEA	American Law and Economics Association	**ALF**	Asociación Latinoamericana de Fitopatologia (Colombia)

ALF	Association Laitière Française pour le Développement de la Production et des Industries du Lait
ALF	Audiologopædisk Forening
ALFA	Aerolinea Federal Argentina
ALFAL	Asociación de Linguística y Filogia de América Latina
ALFE	Association Linguistique Franco-Européenne
ALFED	Aluminium Federation Ltd
ALFÉDIAM	Association de Langue Française pour l'Étude du Diabète et des Maladies Métaboliques
ALFI	American League of Financial Institutions
ALFORJA	Programa Regional Coordinado de Educación Popular (Costa Rica)
ALFSG	Animal Liberation Front Supporters' Group
ALGA	Australian Local Government Association
ALGES	Association of Local Government Engineers and Surveyors
ALGESA	Aerolineas Guinea Ecuatorial
ALGFO	Association of Local Government Financial Officers
ALGÖ	Arbeitsgemeinschaft Landwirtschaftlicher Geflügelzüchter Österreichs
ALGO	Association des Livres Généalogiques Ovins
ALGTB	Australian Local Government Training Board
ALGU	Association of Land Grant Colleges and Universities (U.S.A.)
ALGWE	Association of Lesbian and Gay Writers Living in Europe (Netherlands)
ALI	Alfa-Laval International (Sweden)
ALI	American Law Institute
ALI	American Library Institute
ALI	Association Luxembourgeoise des Ingénieurs
ALI	Associazione Librai Italiana
ALI	Latin American Exchange Association
ALIA	American Life Insurance Association
ALIA	Association of Lecturers in Accountancy
ALIA	Australian Library and Information Association
ALIANSA	Alimentos de Animales, S.A. (El Salvador)

ALIAZO	Aliança Angolana des Originarios do Zombo
ALIC	Australian Land Information Council (*now* ANZLIC)
ALICA	Asociación de Industriales de Conservas Alimenticias (Uruguay)
ALICA	Asociación Latinoamericana de Industriales y Cámaras de la Alimentación
ALICE	All-Africa Lutheran Churches Information Coordination Centre
ALICO	American Life Insurance Company (Suriname)
ALIDE	Asociación Latinoamericana de Instituciones Financieras de Desarrollo (Peru)
ALIFAR	Asociación Latinoamericana de Industrias Farmacéuticas
ALII	Association Luxembourgeoise des Ingénieurs et Industriels
ALIM	Association Linguistique Interméditerranéenne
ALIMDA	Association of Life Insurance Medical Directors of America
ALIMG	Australian Land Information Management Group
Alimport	Empresa Cubana Importadora de Alimentos
ALIN	Alianza de Liberación Nacional (Bolivia)
ALIO	Asociación Latino-Ibero-Americana de Investigación Operativa (Argentina)
ALIPLAST	Asociación Latinoamericana de Industrias Plásticas (Uruguay)
ALIPO	Alianza Liberal del Pueblo (Honduras)
ALISE	Association for Library and Information Science Education (U.S.A.)
ALIU	Animal Liberation Investigation Unit
ALJE	Association Luxembourgeoise des Juristes Européens
ALJHE	Association of Libraries of Judaica and Hebraica in Europe
ALJP	Association Luxembourgeoise des Journalistes Professionnels
ALKD	Association Luxembourgeoise des Kinésithérapeutes Diplômés
ALL	Association for Active Learning
ALL	Association for Language Learning
ALL	Association for Latin Liturgy
ALL	Astrological Lodge of London

ALLA	Allied Long Lines Agency (NATO)
ALLC	Association for Literary and Linguistic Computing
ALLC	Association of Larger Local Councils
ALLF	Académie Royale de Langue et de Littérature Française (Belgium)
ALLIANCE	Alliance of European Voluntary Service Organizations
ALM	American Leprosy Missions
ALM	Antillaanse Luchtvaart Maatschappij (Netherlands Antilles)
ALM	Asociación Latinoamericana de Microbiologia (Puerto Rico)
ALM	Asociación Latinoamericana de Microbiologia (Venezuela)
ALM	Association of Landscape Management (*ex* APFORLM)
ALM	Association of Lloyds Members
ALMA	Katholieke Academische Actie voor Internationale Samenwerking
ALMAP	Société Algéro-Mauritanienne de Pêche
ALMAR	Asociación Médico Latinoamericana de Rehabilitación
ALMC	Australian Labor Ministers Conference
ALMER-COM	European Chambers of Commerce Group for Trade with Latin America
ALMO	African Livestock Marketing Organisation
ALN	Armée de Libération Nationale (Algeria, Guadeloupe)
ALNUS	Association of Lough Neagh Users
ALÖ	Alternative Liste Österreich
ALO	Arab Labour Organization = OAT
ALO	Asian Labour Organisation
ALO	Association Libération Ondes
ALOP	Asociación Latinoamericana de Organizaciones de Promoción
ALOSEV	Asamblea Latinoamerica de Organizaciones de Servicio Voluntario
ALP	Afdeling Arbeidsfysiologie v. h. Laboratorium v. Fysiologie d. Dieren
ALP	Albanian Liberal Party = PLS
ALP	American Labor Party
ALP	Antigua Labor Party
ALP	Arakan Liberation Party (Burma)
ALP	Association Luxembourgeoise des Paysagistes
ALP	Association of Lithuanians in Poland = SLP
ALP	Association of Little Presses
ALP	Australian Labour Party
ALP	Australian League of Rights
ALPA	Asociación Latinoamericana para la Producción Animal
ALPA	Association Luxembourgeoise pour la Protection des Animaux
ALPAI	Air Line Pilots Association International
ALPAN	African Livestock Policy Analysis Network (Ethiopia)
ALPAR	Association Luxembourgeoise pour l'Alimentation et l'Hygiéne Rationnelles
Alpart	Aluminina Partners of Jamaica
ALPC	Agricultural Lime Producers Council
ALPDS	Association des Laboratoires de Prothèse Dentaire de Suisse = VZLS
ALPE-ADRIA	Association des Régions des Alpes Orientales (Italy)
ALPF	Algemeen Landbouw Pensioenfonds (Indonesia)
ALPI-CAM	Société Alpi Pietro et Fils Caméroun
ALPL	Association Luxembourgeoise des Pilotes de Ligne
ALPO	Association of Land and Property Owners (U.S.A.)
ALPO	Association of Lunar and Planetary Observers (U.S.A.)
ALPP	Asociación Latinoamericana de Paleobotanica y Palinologia
ALPRO	Alianza para el Progreso (OAS)
ALPSP	Association of Learned and Professional Society Publishers
ALR	Art Loss Register
ALR	Association of Lighting Retailers
ALR	Australian League of Rights
ALR	Société Luxembourgeoise de Radiologie
ALRA	Abortion Law Reform Association
ALRA	Adult Literacy Resource Agency
ALRANZ	Abortion Law Reform Association of New Zealand
ALRC	Anti-Locust Research Centre
ALROS	American Laryngological, Rhinological and Otological Society
ALS	Academy of Leisure Sciences
ALS	Algemeen Landbouw Syndicaat (Indonesia)
ALS	Alliance of Literary Societies
ALS	American Liszt Society
ALS	American Literary Society

ALS	American Littoral Society
ALS	Association of Legal Secretaries (*now* ILT)
ALS	Australian Littoral Society
ALSA	Amalgamated Labour Supporters Association
ALSA	American Legal Studies Association
ALSATEX	Société Alsacienne d'Étude et d'Exploitation
ALSB	Academy of Legal Studies in Business
ALSCI	Association of Lecturers in Scottish Central Institutions
ALSISS	Association of Learned Societies in the Social Sciences
ALSPI	Société Alsacienne de Participations Industrielles
ALSSOA	Amyotrophic Lateral Sclerosis Society of America
ALT	Amerikos lietuviu taryba = ALTas, CLA
ALT	Association of Law Teachers
ALTA	American Land Title Association
ALTA	American Library Trustee Association
ALTA	American Literary Translators Association
ALTA	Association of Local Transport Airlines (U.S.A.)
ALTas	Amerikos lietuviu taryba = ALT, CLA
ALTEC	Asociación Latinoamericana de Gestión Tecnologia (Brazil)
ALTER-SIAL	Alternatives Technologiques et Recherches sur les Industries Agricoles et Alimentaires (France)
ALTO	Association of Local Television Operators
ALTOUR	Société Nationale Algérienne de Tourisme et d'Hôtellerie
ALTSU	Association of Licensed TAP Software Users
ALTU	Association of Liberal Trade Unionists
ALU	Aboriginal Liaison Unit
ALU	Aluminium Can Recycling Association
ALUBOL	Aluminio Boliviano S.A.
ALUC	Association Luxembourgeoise des Universitaires Catholiques
ALUCAM	Compagnie Camérounaise de l'Aluminium
ALUCON-GO	Société pour la Transformation de l'Aluminium et autres Métaux du Congo
ALUPA	Association Luxembourgeoise pour l'Utilisation Pacifique de l'Énergie Atomique
ALUS	African Land Utilisation and Settlement Board
ALUV	Associazione Lombardo Uffici Viaggi
ALVA	Association of Leading Visitor Attractions
ALVAO	Association des Langues Vivantes pour l'Afrique Occidentale = WAMLA
ALYO	Association of Livery Yard Owners
ALZUCA	Almacenadora Azucarera, S.A. (El Salvador)
AM	Academy of Management
AM	Action Monégasque
AM	Arbeitsgemeinschaft Magnetismus
AM	Association of Montenegrins (Albania) = SM
AM	Australian Museum
AMA	Abstaining Motorists Association
AMA	Accumulator Makers Association
AMA	Adhesive Manufacturers Association (U.S.A.)
AMA	Aerial Manufacturers Association
AMA	African Mountain Association (Ethiopia)
AMA	African Music Association
AMA	Agricultural Marketing Association
AMA	Amateur Martial Association
AMA	Amateur Music Association
AMA	American Machinery Association
AMA	American Management Association International
AMA	American Maritime Association
AMA	American Marketing Association
AMA	American Medical Association
AMA	American Meteor Association
AMA	Architectural Metalwork Association
AMA	Arts Marketing Association
AMA	Association of Manufacturers Allied to the Electrical and Electronic Industry
AMA	Association of Metropolitan Authorities
AMA	Auckland Mathematical Association (New Zealand)
AMA	Australian Medical Association
AMA	CAM Assurance Mutuelle Agricole du Caméroun
AMABO	Association of Medical Advisers to British Orchestras

AMAC	Association Mondiale des Associés du Centre (U.S.A.) = WACA
AMADE	Association Mondiale des Amis de l'Enfance
AMAE	Associação Mineira de Administração Escolar (Brazil)
AMAFE	Association of Manufacturers of Animal Derived Food Enzymes (Denmark)
AMAI	Association of Municipal Authorities of Ireland (Éire)
AMAIS	Agricultural Materials Analysis Information Service (LGC)
AMAK	Aia Maea Ainen Kiribati / Kiribati Women's Federation
AMAMCO	Agence Mauritanienne et Marocaine de Coopération (Morocco)
AMANISSA	Entreprise Nigérienne de Bâtiments, Travaux Publics et Constructions
AMAP	Aerospace Medical Association of the Philippines
AMAPROP	Anglo American Properties Ltd
AMARC	Association Mondiale des Radiodiffuseurs Communautaires
AMAS	Association de Médecine Aéronautique et Spatiale = ASMA
AMAS	Association Mondiale d'Aviculture Scientifique
AMASC	Association Mondiale des Anciennes Élèves du Sacré Coeur
AMATÉCI	Agence Mauritanienne de Télévision et de Cinéma
AMAUS	Aero Medical Association of the United States
AMAV	Association Mondiale des Anatomistes Vétérinaires= WAVA, WV
AMB	Asociación Mexicana de Bancos
AMB	Asociación Mundial Buiatria = WAB, WGB
AMB	Asociación Mundial de Boxeo =WBA
AMB	Associação Medica Brasileira
AMB	Ateliers Métallurgiques du Bâtiment (Ivory Coast)
AMBA	Association of MBAs
AMBA	Auckland Master Bakers and Pastrycooks Association (New Zealand)
AMBAC	Asociación Mexicana de Bibliotecarios
AMBBA	Associated Master Barbers and Beauticians of America
AMBES	Association of Metropolitan Borough Engineers and Surveyors
AMBMO	Asociación Mediterrénea de Biología Marina y Oceanografia
AMBOP	American Board of Oral Pathology
AMBoV	Association of Members of Boards of Visitors
AMC	Advance Mission in Cambodia (UN)
AMC	Agricultural Mortgage Corporation
AMC	Alianza de Mujeres Costarricenses
AMC	American Mining Congress
AMC	Assemblée Mondiale des Citoyens = WCA
AMC	Association Médicale Canadienne = CMA
AMC	Association of Magistrates Courts
AMC	Association of Manufacturing Chemists
AMC	Association of Mercantile Clubs
AMC	Australian Manufacturing Council
AMC	Australian Maritime College
AMC	Entreprise Nationale des Appareils de Mesure et de Contrôle (Algeria)
AMC	Latin-Ibero American Society for Computational Methods in Engineering
AMCA	Academia Mexicana de Ciencias Agrícolas
AMCA	Air Movement and Control Association (U.S.A.)
AMCA	Amateur Motor-Cycle Association
AMCA	American Mosquito Control Association
AMCA	Association pour une Meilleure Connaissance de l'Asie
AmCAS	Centre for American & Commonwealth Arts & Studies
AMCAV	Association pour l'Amelioration et l'Amenagement du Cadre de Vie (Côte d'Ivoire)
AMCBT	Association of Midwest College Biology Teachers
AMCC	Association Mondiale pour la Communication Chrétienne= WACC
AMCCW	Association of Manufacturers of Chilled Car Wheels (U.S.A.)
AMCEN	African Ministerial Conference on the Environment
AMCHAM	American Chamber of Commerce in the Netherlands
AMCI	Associazione Medici Cattolica Italiana
AMCL	Association of Metropolitan Chief Librarians

AMCLI	Associazione Microbiologi Clinici Italiani	**AMEB**	Asociación Medica Española de Bioterapia
AMCO	Association of Management Consulting Organisations (Éire)	**AMEC**	Association of Mining and Exploration Companies Inc.
AMCOR	African Metals Corporation Ltd	**AMEC**	Australian Manufacturers Export Council
AMCOR	Romanian Management Consultants Association	**AMEC**	Australian Minerals and Energy Council
AMCOS	Association of Management Consulting of Slovenia	**AMECA**	Ateliers Métallurgiques du Bâtiment (Ivory Coast)
AMCS	Associated Male Choruses of America	**AMECAP**	Mexican Personnel Training Association
AMCSH	Assemblée Mondiale des Créateurs et Spécialistes de l'Humour = WATCH	**AMECD**	Association for Measurement and Evaluation in Counseling and Development (U.S.A.)
AMCSS	Agricultural Marketing and Credit Cooperative Societies (Sudan)	**AMECEA**	Association of Member Episcopal Conferences in Eastern Africa
AMCyT	Asociación Mexicana de Ciencia y Tecnologia	**AMECUSD**	Association of Manufacturers and Exporters of Concentrated and Unconcentrated Soft Drinks
AMD	Alliance pour une Mauritanie Démocratique		
AMD	Asociación Médica Dominicana	**AMED**	Association for Management Education and Development
AMDA	Association of Medical Doctors for Asia (Japan)	**AMEE**	Association for Medical Education in Europe = AEME
AMDA	Association of Minicomputer Dealers of America	**AMEE**	Association of Managerial Electrical Executives
AMDB	Agricultural Machinery Development Board	**AMEEF**	Australian Minerals and Energy Environmental Foundation
AMDCL	Association of Metropolitan District Chief Librarians	**AMEEGA**	American Medical Electroencephalographic Association
AMDE	Association of Medical Deans in Europe	**AMELA**	Aire Méditerranéenne et Latinoaméricaine (Belgium)
AMDEA	Association of Manufacturers of Domestic Electrical Appliances	**AMELEC**	Asociación Española de Fabricanto de Material Eléctrico
AMDEC	Agricultural Marketing Development Executive Committee	**AMEM**	Association of Miniature Engine Manufacturers
AMDEC	Associated Manufacturers of Domestic Electric Cookers	**AMÉN**	Association Mondiale pour l'Énergie Non-Polluante = PACE
AMDECL	Association of Metropolitan District Education and Children's Librarians	**AMER**	Associazione Micrologica ed Ecologica Romana
AMDEL	Australian Mineral Development Laboratories	**AMERSA**	Association for Medical Education and Research in Substance Abuse
AMDI	Associazione Medici Dentisti Italiani	**AMES**	Air Ministry Experimental Station
AMDISA	Association of Management Development Institutions in Asia (India)	**AMES**	Association for Media Education in Scotland
AME	Accord Monétaire Européen = EMA, EWA	**AMES**	Association of Marine Engineering Schools
AME	Asociación Meterológica Española	**AMETS**	Association for Management Education and Training in Scotland
AME	Association for Management Excellence (U.S.A.)		
AME	Association for Marriage Enrichment	**AMEU**	Association of Municipal Electricity Undertakings of Southern Africa
AME	Association of Municipal Engineers		
AMEA	Associazione Mediterranea di Educazione degli Adulti		

AMEWA	Associated Manufacturers of Electric Wiring Accessories	**AMI**	Applied Microelectronics Institute (Canada)
AMEWPR	Association for Medical Education in the Western Pacific Region	**AMI**	Arbeitsgemeinschaft Mahlkorkverarbeitender Industrie
AMEX	Agricultural Machinery Export Service	**AMI**	Arbejdsmiljoinstituttet (Denmark)
AMEX	American Express	**AMI**	Assistência Médica Internacional = IMA
AMF	Arab Monetary Fund = FMA	**AMI**	Association Montessori Internationale
AMF	Association des Maires de France	**AMI**	Association of Meat Inspectors
AMFA	Association Médicale Franco-Américaine	**AMI**	Association of Media Independents
AMFEP	Association of Microbial Food Enzyme Producers (EU)	**AMI**	Association of Medical Illustrators (U.S.A.)
AMFFA	American Medical Fly Fishing Association	**AMI**	Associazione Medica Italiana
AMFFBTV	Asociación Mundial de Fisiólogos, Farmacólogos, Bioquímicos y Toxicólogos Veterinarios = AMPPBTV, WAVPPBT	**AMIA**	American Medical Informatics Association
		AMIA	American Metal Importers Association
		AMIA	Anglian Marine Industries Association
		AMIA	ASEAN Music Industry Association
AMFORT	Association Mondiale pour la Formation Professionnelle Touristique = WAPTT	**AMIA**	Association Mondiale pour l'Union du Troisième Age (Switzerland)
AMG	Arbeitskreis Moderne Getränkeverpackung der Deutschen Erfrischungsgetränke Industrie	**AMIA**	Associazione Medica Italiana di Agopuntura
		AMIA	Australian Map Industry Association
AMGCI	Atelier de Mécanique Générale de la Côte-d'Ivoire	**AMIC**	Anglo American Industrial Corporation
AMGÉ	Association Mondiale des Guides et des Éclaireuses = AMGS, WAGGGS	**AMIC**	ASEAN Mass Communications Research and Information Centre (Singapore)
AMGI	Agence Multilatérale de Garantie des Investissements (IBRD) = MIGA	**AMIC**	Australian Mining Industrial Council
AMGI	Associazione Medici Geriatri Italiani	**AMICEE**	Asociación Mexicana de Ingenieros en Comunicaciónes Electricas y Electronicas
AMGP	Asociación Mexicana de Geólogos Petroleros		
AMGP	Association of Managers in General Practice (*ex* AHCPA)	**AMICI**	Association Mondiale des Interprètes de Conférences Internationales
AMGS	Asociación Mundial de las Guías Scouts = AMGE, WAGGGS	**AMIDEAST**	American - Mideast Educational and Training Service (U.S.A.)
AMGSR	Association des Marchands Grainiers de la Suisse Romande	**AMIE**	Aide Médicale Internationale à l'Enfance
AMH	Asociación Española de Almacenistas de Maquinas Herramientas	**AmIEE**	American Institute of Electrical Engineers
AMHMV	Association Mondiale d'Histoire de la Médecine Vétérinaire = WAHVM, WGGVM	**AMIEU**	Australasian Meat Industry Employees' Union (Australia)
		AMIÉV	Association Médicale Internationale pour l'Étude des Conditions de Vie et de la Santé
AMHSA	Automated Materials Handling Systems Association		
AMI	Agence Maritime Internationale	**AMIF**	American Marine Insurance Forum
AMI	Agence Mauritanienne de l'Information	**AMIF**	American Meat Institute Foundation
AMI	Alliance Médicale Internationale	**AmIME**	American Institute of Mining Engineers
AMI	American Meat Institute	**AMIN**	Advertising and Marketing International Network
AMI	Apostolat Militaire International	**AMIN**	Arab Medical Information Network (Kuwait)

AMINA	Association Mondiale des Inventeurs et Chercheurs Scientifiques (Belgium)
AMINOIL	American Independent Oil Company
AMINTA-PHIL	International Association for Philosophy of Law and Social Philosophy
AMIO	Arab Military Industrial Organization
AMIOF	Association Martiniquaise pour l'Information et l'Orientation Familiales (Martinique)
AMIP	Atmospheric Model Intercomparison Project
AMIRA	Associazione Maîtres Italiani Ristoranti e Alberghi
AMIRA	Australian Mineral Industries Research Association
AMIS	Asociación Mexicana de la Industria del Seguro
AMJ	Assemblée Mondiale de la Jeunesse = WAY
AMJD	Algerian Movement for Justice and Development
AMK	Arbeitsgemeinschaft "Die Moderne Küche"
AML	American Mail Line Ltd
AML	Applied Mathematics Laboratory (DSIR) (New Zealand)
AML	Association of Master Lightermen and Barge Owners
AML	Association of Mortgage Lenders
AML	Latvijas Medicinas Akademija
AMLA	African Medical Library Association (Congo)
AMLAR	Asociación Médico Latino-Americano de Rehabilitación
AMLAT-FEDOP	Latin American Federation of Employees in Public Service
AMLB	Australian Major League Baseball
AMLC	Australian Meat and Livestock Corporation
AMLF	Association des Microbiologistes de Langue Française
AMLFC	Association des Médecins de Langue Française du Canada
AMLRDC	Australian Meat & Livestock Research & Development Corporation
AMM	Aberdeen Maritime Museum
AMM	ASEAN Ministerial Meeting
AMM	Asociación Mexicana de Microbiología
AMM	Association Médicale Mondiale = WMA

AMM	Association of Macedonian Muslims = ZMM
AMM	Association of Manipulative Medicine
AMM	Association of Medical Microbiologists
AMM	Association of Mine Managers of South Africa
AMMA	American Mail-Order Merchants Association
AMMA	Art Metalware Manufacturers Association
AMMA	Assistant Masters and Mistresses Association (*now* ATL)
AMMA	Associazione Industriali Metallurgici Meccanici Affini
AMMA	Australian Margarine Manufacturers Association
AMMD	Association des Médecins et Médecins-Dentistes du Grand-Duché de Luxembourg
AMMF	Association Mondiale des Médecins Francophones (Canada)
AMMFI	Austrian Man-Made Fibres Institute
AMMLA	American Merchant Marine Library Association
AMMP	Association of Manufacturers of Medicinal Preparations
AMMPE	Asociación Mundial de Mujeres Periodistas y Escritoras
AMMRA	Arbeitsgemeinschaft Mittleständischer Mineralölraffinerien
AMMS	Academy of Military Medical Sciences (China)
AMN	Akademiia Meditsinskikh Nauk
AMN	Arquivo do Museu Nacional
AMN	Association of Makers of Newsprint
AMNASS	Amnesia Association
AMNH	American Museum of Natural History
AMNLAE	Asociación de Mujeres Nicaragüenses "Luisa Amanda Espinosa"
AMÖ	Arbeitsgemeinschaft Möbeltransport Bundesverband
AMO	Association of Magisterial Officers
AMO	Association of Mainframe Operators
AMOC	Aston Martin Owners Club
AMOCO-GABON	Amoco Gabon Petroleum Company
AMODEFA	Associação Mozambican para o Desenvolimento da Familia
AMOMO	Agricultural Machinery Operation and Management Office (China)

AMOP	Association of Mail Order Publishers (*now* DMA(U.K.))		**AMPP**	Association of Makers of Packing Papers
AMOPI	Associazione Medici Ospedali Psichiatrici Italiani		**AMPPA**	ASEAN Motion Pictures Association
AMOR	Asian Meeting of Religious (Japan)		**AMPPBTV**	Association Mondiale de Physiologistes, Pharmacologistes, Biochimistes et Toxicologistes Vétérinaires = AMFFBTV, WAVPPBT
AMORC	Ancient Mystical Order Rosae Crucis (U.S.A.)		**AMPPF**	Association Malienne pour la Protection et la Promotion de la Famille
AMOS	Australian Meteorological and Oceanographic Society		**AMPRA**	American Medical Peer Review Association
AMOSEAS	American Overseas Petroleum Limited		**AMPrA**	Association Nationale pour les Mutations Professionnelles en Agriculture
AMP	Associated Master Plumbers and Domestic Engineers			
AMP	Association for Molecular Pathology		**AMPRO-NAC**	Asociación de Mujeres ante la Problemética Nacional (Nicaragua)
AMP	Association Méditerranéenne de Psychiatrie		**AMPS**	Ananda Marga Pracarka Samgha
AMP	Association Mondiale de Phytothérapie = WPA		**AMPS**	Association Mondiale de Prospective Sociale
AMP	Association Mondiale de Psychiatrie = WPA		**AMPS**	Association of Management and Professional Staffs
AMP	Association of Massage Practitioners		**AMPS**	Association of Manufacturers of Power Generating Systems (*ex* ABGSM)
AMP	Association pour la Médiathèque Publique		**AMPS**	Association of Motorists Protection Service
AMP	Australian Mutual Provident Society		**AMPTC**	Arab Maritime Petroleum Transport Company (OAPEC)
AMP	Australian Mycological Panel		**AMPTP**	Association of Motion Picture and Television Producers (U.S.A.)
AMPA	Agence Malienne de Presse et de Publicité		**AMPV**	Asociación Mundial Patólogos Veterinarios = WAVP
AMPA	Agricultural Machinery Parts Association		**AMPW**	Association of Makers of Printings and Writings
AMPA	American Medical Publishers Association		**AMQUA**	American Quaternary Association
AMPA	Asociación Mundial de Producción Animal = AMZ, WAAP, WVT		**AMR**	Arbeitskreis für neue Methoden in der Regionalforschung (Austria)
AMPA	Centro Nazionale Applicazioni Materie Plastiche Agricoltura		**AMR**	Association de Médecine Rurale
AMPAS	Academy of Motion Picture Arts and Sciences (U.S.A.)		**AMR**	Association for Men's Rights (Malta)
AMPDE	Associated Master Plumbers & Domestic Engineers		**AMR**	Association of Minor Railway Companies
AMPEC	American Motion Picture Export Company		**AMR**	Société pour l'Aménagement du Milieu Rural (Ivory Coast)
AMPF	Association Marocaine de Planification Familiale		**AMRA**	American Medical Record Association
AMPF	Association Mauritanienne pour la Promotion de la Famille		**AMRA**	Ancient Mediterranean Research Association
AMPFAC	Asociación Mexicana de Profesionistas Forestales		**AMRA**	Association Belge des Maisons de Réforme Alimentaire
AMPM	Association of Malt Products Manufacturers		**AMRA**	Association of Maize Researchers in Africa (Senegal) = ACMA
AMPP	Asamblea Municipal de Poder Popular (Cuba)		**AMRA**	Automotive Manufacturers Racing Association

AMRC	Abadina Media Resource Centre (Nigeria)	**AMSA**	American Metal Stamping Association	
AMRC	Association of Medical Research Charities	**AMSA**	Asian Medical Students Association (Republic of Korea)	
AMRC	Association of Minor Railway Companies	**AMSA**	Association Mondiale des Sciences Agricoles	
AMRC	Australian Meat Research Committee	**AMSA**	Association of Medical Schools in Africa	
AMRCO	Association of Motor Racing Circuit Owners	**AMSA**	Australian Marine Sciences Association	
AMREF	African Medical Research Foundation (Kenya)	**AMSA**	Australian Maritime Safety Authority	
AMRF	African Medical and Research Foundation	**AMSAT**	Radio Amateur Satellite Corporation	
		AMSC	American Marine Standards Committee	
AMRIM	Association of Men Religious in Malawi	**AMSCV**	Associazione Medica dello Stato della Città del Vatticano	
AMRO	Association of Health Care Information and Medical Record Officers	**AMSÉ**	Association Mondiale des Sciences de l'Éducation = WAER	
AMROP	Association Mondiale pour l'Étude de l'Opinion Publique = WAPOR	**AMSE**	Australian Mining and Smelting Europe Ltd	
AMRP	Association Mondiale de Réadaptation PsychoSociale = WAPR	**AMSE**	International Association for the Advancement of Modelling and Simulation Techniques in Enterprises (France)	
AMRSM	Association of Major Religious Superiors of Men in the Philippines			
AMRSW	Association of Major Religious Superiors of Women in the Philippines	**AMSF**	Agricultural Managers and Services Foundation (Philippines)	
AMS	Agricultural Manpower Society	**AMSH**	Association for Moral and Social Hygiene	
AMS	Agricultural Marketing Service	**AMSME**	Association of Medical Schools in the Middle East (Egypt)	
AMS	American Magnolia Society			
AMS	American Mathematical Society	**AMSO**	Association of Market Survey Organisations	
AMS	American Meteorological Society	**AMSOC**	American Miscellaneous Society	
AMS	American Microchemical Society	**AMSOL**	Association d'Établissements Multiplicateurs de Semences Oléagineuses	
AMS	American Microscopical Society			
AMS	American Montessori Society			
AMS	American Musicological Society	**AMSP**	Association Médico-Sociale Protestante de Langue Française	
AMS	Ancient Monuments Society			
AMS	Arab Management Society (Egypt)	**AMSPAR**	Association of Medical Secretaries, Practice Administrators and Receptionists	
AMS	Association des Musiciens Suisses			
AMS	Association of Metal Sprayers			
AMS	Association of Missionary Societies	**AMSRI**	Anhui Machinery Scientific Research Institute (China)	
AMS	Associazione dei Musei Svizzeri = SMA, VMS	**AMSS**	American Milking Shorthorn Society	
		AMSS	Association of Muslim Social Scientists	
AMS	Associazione di Medicina Sociale	**AMSTAC**	Australian Marine Science and Technologies Advisory Council	
AMS	Assurance Medical Society			
AMS	Australian Mathematical Society	**AMSTP**	Association of Makers of Soft Tissue Papers	
AMS	Australian Musicology Society			
AMSA	American Meat Science Association	**AMSUS**	Association of Military Surgeons of the United States	
AMSA	American Medical Society on Alcoholism	**AMT**	Academy of Medicine Toronto (Canada)	
AMSA	American Medical Students Association	**AMT**	Association of Medical Technologists	

AMT	Ateliers Métallurgiques Togolais
AMTA	American Massage and Therapy Association
AMTA	Arab Maritime Transport Academy (Egypt)
AMTC	Apparel Manufacturing Technology Center (U.S.A.)
AMTDA	Agricultural Machinery and Tractor Dealers' Association
AMTDA	American Machine Tool Distributors Association
AMTDS	Agricultural Machinery Training Development Society
AMTE	Admiralty Marine Technology Establishment
AMTEC	Australian Meat Trades Export Group
AMTEG	Australian Metal Trades Export Group
AMTICP	Asociación Mexicana de Tecnicos de la Industrias de la Celulosa y del Papel
AMTIESA	Association of Management Training Institutions of Eastern and Southern Africa (Tanzania)
AMTIS	Arts Management Training Initiative
AMTRA	Animal Medicine Training Regulatory Authority
AMTRI	Advanced Manufacturing Technology Research Association
AMTU	Agence Mondiale pour les Problèmes de Circulation en Milieu Urbain
AMTV	Agrupación de Mujeres Tierra Viva (Guatemala)
AMTV	Allgemeiner Möbeltransportverband (Austria)
AMU	African Mathematical Union (Nigeria) = UMA
AMU	American Malacological Union
AMU	American Musicians Union
AMU	Anhui Medical University
AMU	Arab Maghreb Union = UMA
AMU	Associated Metalworkers Union
AMU	Association de Médecine Urbaine
AMU	Association of Master Upholsterers
AMU	Association of Minicomputer Users (U.S.A.)
AMUE	Association for the Monetary Union of Europe = AUME
AMUFOC	Association des Établissements Multiplicateurs de Semences Fourragères des Communautés Européennes
AMULP	Asociación de Mujeres Uruguayas Lourdes Pinto
AMURT	Ananda Marga Universal Relief Team
AMV	Association du Mérite Viticole
AMV	Association Mondiale Vétérinaire = WTG, WVA
AMVA	Asociación Mundial Veterinaria de Avicola = WVPA
AMVCB	Australian Motor Vehicle Certification Board
AMVES	Asociación de Médicos Veterinarios de El Salvador
AMVHA	Asociación Mundial Veterinarios Higienistas de los Alimentos = WAVFH
AMVL	Association des Médecins-Vétérinaires du Grand-Duché de Luxembourg
AMVMI	Association Mondiale des Vétérinaires Microbiologistes, Immunologistes et Spécialistes des Maladies Infectieuses = WAVMI
AMVPA	Asociación Mundial Veterinaria de Pequenos Animales = WSAVA
AMVR	Asociación Mundial de Vivienda Rural = IRHA
AMVR	Asociatia Medicilor Veterinari din România
AMVZ	Asociación de Médicos Veterinarios Zootecnistas (Colombia)
AMWA	Akina Mama Wa Afrika
AMWA	American Medical Women's Association
AMWA	American Medical Writers Association
AMWG	American Movement for World Government
AMZ	Association Mondiale de Zootechnie = AMPA, WAAP, WVT
AMZFI	Association Mondiale des Zones Franches Industrielles = WEPZA
AN	Action Nationale (Switzerland)
AN	Acuerdo Nacional (Paraguay)
AN	Agencia Nacional (Portugal)
AN	Australian National Railways Commission
AN	Avanzada Nacional (Chile)
ANA	Accademia Nazionale di Agricoltura
ANA	Aden News Agency
ANA	Afghan News Agency
ANA	Agence Nigérienne d'Assurances
ANA	All Nippon Airways (Japan)
ANA	American Naprapathic Association

ANA	American Narcolepsy Association
ANA	American Nature Association
ANA	American Neurological Association
ANA	American Newspaper Association
ANA	American Numismatic Association
ANA	American Nurses Association
ANA	Anguilla National Alliance
ANA	Article Number Association
ANA	Asociación Nacional de Agricultores
ANA	Association of National Advertisers (U.S.A.)
ANA	Association of Naval Aviation (U.S.A.)
ANA	Association of Nordic Aeroclubs
ANA	Association of Nurse Administrators
ANA	Associazione Nationale fra gli Agenti di Assicurazione
ANA	Associazione Nazionale Audio-Protesisti
ANA	Athenagence
ANA	Australian National Airways
ANAAS	Australian and New Zealand Society for the Advancement of Science
ANAB	Algemene Nederlandse Agrarische Bedrijfsbond
ANABAD	Asociación Nacional de Bibliotecarios, Archiveros, Arqueólogos y Documentalistas
ANABADS	Association Nationale des Bibliothécaires, Archivistes et Documentalistes Sénégalais
ANABIC	Associazione Nazionale Allevatori Bestiame Italiano da Carne
ANABo-RaPI	Associazione Nazionale Allevatori Bovini di Razza Piemontese
ANAC	Agence Nationale de l'Aviation Civile (Congo)
ANAC	Association Nationale des Acteurs de Cinématographie
ANAC	Associazione Nazionale Autoservizi in Concessione
ANACAFE	Asociación Nacional del Café (Guatemala)
ANACAMH	Asociasion Nacional de Campesinos Hondureños
ANACAP	Associazione Nazionale Aziende Concessionaire Affissioni e Pubblicité
ANACH	Asociación Nacional de Campesinos de Honduras
ANACNA	Associazione Nazionale Assistenti e Controllori della Navigazione Aerea

ANACR	Association Nationale des Anciens Combattants de la Résistance
ANADISME	Associazione Nazionale Aziende Distributrici Specialité-Medicinali e Prodotti Chimico-Farmaceutici
ANaDO	Associazione Nazionale Dirigenti Ospedalieri
ANAES	Asociación Nacional de Anunciantes de El Salvador
ANAF	Association Nationale des Avocats de France
ANAFEM	Asociación Nacional para el Fomento de las Exportaciones Mexicanas
ANAFEN	Associazione Nazionale Stampa Filatelica e Numismatica
ANAGENTI	Associazione Nazionale degli Agenti Rappresentanti di Caffé, Droghe, Coloniali
ANAGSA	Aseguradora Nacional Agricola y Ganadera (Mexico)
ANAH	Agence Nationale pour l'Amélioration de l'Habitat
ANAH	Association Nationale des Agronomes Haïtiens
ANAHL	Australian National Animal Health Laboratory
ANAHPS	Association Nationale Agricole et Horticole de Promotion Sociale
ANAI	African Network of Administrative Information
ANAI	Arab Network of Administrative Information
ANAI	Article Number Association of Ireland
ANAI	Associação Nacional de Apoio ao Indio (Brazil)
ANAI	Associazione Nazionale Amministratori Immobiliari
ANAI	Associazione Nazionale Archivistica Italiana
ANAIC	Asian Network for Analytical and Inorganic Chemistry (Australia)
ANAIP	Asociación Nacional Autónoma de Industriales de Plásticos
ANALAC	Asociación Nacional de Productores e Industriales Lácteos (Colombia)
ANALDEX	Asociación Nacional de Exportadores (Colombia)
ANALJA	Asociación Nacional de la Industria del Jabón (Colombia)
ANALPES	Asociación Nacional de Productores de Pesticidas (Colombia)

ANALTIR	Association Nationale des Entreprises Albanaises des Transports Routiers	**ANAV**	Academia Nacional de Agronomía y Veterinaria (Argentina)
ANAMPN	Associazione Nazionale Armatori Medio e Piccolo Naviglio	**ANAV**	Associazione Nazionale Avanspettacolo e Varieté
ANAMSO	Association Nationale des Agriculteurs Multiplicateurs de Semences Oléagineuses	**ANAVE**	Asociación de Navieros Españoles
		ANAVI	Asociación Nacional de Avicultores (Guatemala)
ANAMUC	Asociación Nacional de Mujeres Campesinas	**ANAVIP**	Asociación Nacional de Avicultores de Panama
ANAO	Australian Audit Office	**ANAVIT**	Asociación Nicaragüense de Agencias de Viajes
ANAOA	Association Nationale des Appellations d'Origine Agricole	**ANB**	Arab National Bank
ANAP	Anatavan Partisi (Turkey)	**ANB**	Associazione Nazionale Bieticoltori Italiani
ANAP	Asociación Nacional de Agricultores Pequeños (Cuba)	**ANB**	Austrian National Bank
ANAP	Associazione Nazionale Agenti di Pubblicité	**ANBE**	Asociación Nacional de Bananeros del Ecuador
ANAPAL	Association Nationale des Architectes Paysagistes Libéraux	**ANBEF**	Association Nationale des Bibliothécaires d'Expression Française (Belgium)
ANAPO	Alianza Nacional Popular (Colombia)		
ANARDE	Acil Navagarjan Rural Development Foundation (India)	**ANBG**	Australian National Botanic Gardens
		ANBI	Asociación de Bananeros Independientes (Honduras)
ANARE	Australian National Antarctic Research Expeditions	**ANBIMA**	Associazione Nazionale Bande Italiane Musicale Autonome
ANARE-MAGIC	ANARE Mapping and Geographic Information Committee	**ANBOS**	Algemene Nederlandse Bondvan Schoonheidsinstituten
ANAREC	Associação Nacional de Revendedores de Combustiveis	**ANBP**	Algemene Nederlandse Bond van Postordebedrijven
ANARLÉP	Association Nationale des Animateurs Ruraux de Loisirs et d'Éducation Populaire	**ANBS**	Asian Network of Biological Sciences (Singapore)
ANARPE	Associazione Nazionale Agenti Rappresentanti Propagandisti Editoriali	**ANC**	Academia Nacional de Ciencias (Mexico)
ANAS	Association Nationale des Assistants de Service Social	**ANC**	African National Congress (South Africa, Zambia)
ANAS	Associazione Nazionale Agenzie Stampa	**ANC**	Air Navigation Commission (ICAO)
ANAS	Azienda Nazionale Autonoma delle Strade Statali	**ANC**	Alianza Nacional Cristiana (Costa Rica)
ANASE	Association des Nations d'Asie du Sud-Est = ASEAN	**ANC**	Association of Neighbourhood Councils
ANASED	Associazione Nazionale Aziende Servizi Elaborazione Dati	**ANC**	Association of Noise Consultants
		ANC	Associazione Nazionale Cineoperatori
ANASIN	Associazione Nazionale Aziende Servizi Informatica	**ANC**	Associazione Nazionale Combattenti
ANASTA	Associazione Nazionale Aziende Saldatura e Techniche Affini	**ANC**	Australian Newspaper Council
		ANC-UNESCO	Australian National Commission for UNESCO
ANAT	Agence Nationale de l'Aménagement du Territoire (Algeria)	**ANCA**	Allied Naval Communications Agency (NATO)
ANATO	Asociación Colombiana de Agencias de Viajes y Turismo	**ANCA**	Antarctic Names Council of Australia
		ANCA	Asociación Nacional Cultivadores de Algodón (Venezuela)

ANCA	Associazione Nazionale Cooperative Agricole	**ANCI**	Associazione Nazionale Calzaturifici Italiani
ANCA	Australian National Coastal Authority	**ANCI**	Associazione Nazionale Coniglicultori Italiani
ANCA	Australian National Council on AIDS	**ANCI**	Associazione Nazionale dei Comuni Italiani
ANCA	Australian Nature Conservation Agency		
ANCAB	Algemene Nederlandse Christelijke Amptenaarsbond	**ANCI**	Ateliers Navals de Côte-d'Ivoire
ANCACA	American National Commission for the Accreditation of Colleges and Universities	**ANCIA**	Association Nationale des Centres d'Insemination Artificielle
		ANCIC	Associazione Nazionale Case di Informazioni Commerciali
ANCAD	Associazione Nazionale Commercianti Articoli Dentari	**ANCIGBP**	Australian National Committee, International Geosphere Biosphere Program
ANCAI	Association Nationale des Coureurs Automobiles Italiens		
ANCAP	Administración Nacional de Combustiles, Alcohol y Portland (Uruguay)	**ANCIPA**	Associação Nacional de Comerciantes e Industriais de Produtos Alimentares
		ANCIT	Associazione Nazionale dei Conservieri Ittici e delle Tonnare
ANCAR	Associação Nordestina de Credito e Assistencia Rural (Brazil)	**ANCLI**	Associazione Nazionale fra le Centrali del Latte d'Italia
ANCAR	Australian National Committee for Antarctic Research	**ANCMA**	Associazione Nazionale del Ciclo, Motociclo ed Accessori
ANCARSE	Associação Nordestina de Crédito e Assisténcia Rural de Sergipe (Brazil)	**ANCO**	Asociación Nacional de Criadores de Ovejas (Ecuador)
ANCAVE	Associação Nacional dos Centros de Abate e Indústrias Transformadores de Carne de Aves	**ANCO**	Associazione Nazionale dei Consorzi dell' Ortoflorofrutticoltura
ANCB	Association Nationale de Comptables de Belgique	**ANCOGAS**	Associazione Nazionale Commercianti Gas Liquefatti
ANCC	Associazione Nazionale per il Controllo della Combustione	**ANCOL**	Associated Newsagents Co-operative Ltd (Australia)
ANCCORW	Australian Consultative Committee on Refugee Women	**ANCOLD**	Australian National Committee on Large Dams
ANCCR	Association Nationale des Chanteurs et des Conteurs Ruraux	**ANCOM**	Agrupación Nacional Sindical Autónoma de Constructores de Maquinaria
ANCE	Associazione Nazionale Costruttori Edili		
		ANCOM	Andean Common Market
ANCE	Associazione Nazionale del Commercio con l'Estero	**ANCOMAG**	Associazione Nazionale Commercianti Macchine Grafiche Cartarie e Affini
ANCEC	Asociación Nacional Contra el Cancer (Panama)	**ANCOP**	Asociación Nacional de Constructores de Obras Publicas
ANCEF	Associazione Nazionale Commercianti Esportatori Fiori	**ANCOPI**	Association des Négociateurs-Conseils en Propriété Industrielle = LITCA, VDPW
ANCEFN	Académia Nacionál de Cióncias Exactas, Fisicas y Naturáles (Argentina)		
ANCEVE	Associação do Norte dos Comerciantes e Engarrafadores de Vinhos e Bebidas Espirituosas	**Ancor**	Associação Nacional das Corretoras de Valores (Brazil)
		ANCORA	Association Nationale pour la Coordination la Compensation des Restraites Complémentaires
ANCI	Asociación Nacional de Construcciones Industrializadas		
ANCI	Association Nationale des Constructeurs Immobiliers	**ANCPD**	Africa Network on Churches Participation in Development (Congo) = RAPED

ANCPEP	Association Nationale de Contrôle des Performances Porcines
ANCR	Associazione Nazionale Combattenti e Reducci
ANCRA	Associazione Nazionale Commercianti Radio, Televisione, Elettrodomestici ed Affini
ANCRI-GAP	Asociación Nacional de Criadores de Ganado Porcino (Venezuela)
ANCS	American Numerical Control Society
ANCS	Association Nationale des Clubs Scientifiques
ANCUN	Australian National Committee for the United Nations
AND	Associated National Distributors (Éire)
AND JEF	And Jëf-Mouvement Révolutionnaire pour la Démocratie Nouvelle (Senegal) = AJ-MRDN
ANDA	Administración Nacional de Acueductos y Alcantarillados (Salvador)
ANDA	Asociación Nacional de Actores (Mexico)
ANDA	Asociación Nacional de Anunciantes (Venezuela)
ANDA	Associação Nacional para Difusão de Adubos (Brazil)
ANDA	Associação Nordestina do Desenvolvimento Agrícola (Brazil)
ANDA	Association Nationale pour le Développement de l'Agriculture
ANDB	Algemene Nederlandse Drogistenbond
ANDBP	Association Nationale pour le Dévelopment des Bibliothèques Publiques
ANDCP	Association Nationale des Directeurs et Cadres de la Fonction Personnel
ANDCS	Académia Nacionál de Derécho y Ciéncias Sociales (Argentina)
ANDE	Administración Nacional de Electricidad (Paraguay)
ANDE	Asociación Nacional de Educadores (Costa Rica)
ANDE	Asociación Nacional de Empresarios (Ecuador)
ANDEA	African Network for the Development of Ecological Agriculture (Ghana)
ANDEBU	Asociación Nacional de Broadcasters Uruguayos
ANDEC	Acerías Nacionales del Ecuador
ANDECE	Agrupación Nacional de los Derivados del Cemento
ANDEN	Asociación Nacional de Educadores de Nicaragua
ANDES	Aerolineas Nacionales del Ecuador SA
ANDES	Asociación Nacional de Educadores Salvadoreños
ANDES	Associação Nacional dos Docentes do Ensino Superior (Brazil)
ANDESA	Almacenes Nacionales de Deposito, S.A. (Mexico)
ANDESA	Asociación Nacional de Directores de la Escuelas Superiores de Agricultura (Mexico)
ANDESÉ	Association Nationale des Docteurs des Sciences Économiques
ANDI	Asociación Nacional de Industriales (Colombia, Honduras)
ANDI	Associazione Nazionale degli Inventori
ANDIA	Asociación Nacional de Distribuidores de Insumos Agropecuários (Panama)
ANDIA-RIOS	Asociación de Diarios Colombianos
ANDIL	Associazione Nazionale degli Industriali dei Laterizi
ANDIMA	Asociación Nacional de Industriales Madereros (Venezuela)
ANDIN	Associazione Nazional di Ingegneria Nucleare
ANDIS	Associazione Nazionale di Ingegneria Sanitaria
ANDP	Albanian National Democratic Party
ANDP	Alliance National pour la Démocratie et le Progrès (Haiti)
ANDPVA	Association for Native Development in the Performing and Visual Arts (Canada)
ANDSCJR	Association Nationale pour le Développement Social et Culturel de la Jeunesse Rurale
ANDT	Association Nationale des Détaillants en Textile et en Habillement = NAVETEX
ANE	Asociación Numismatica Española
ANE	Associação Nacional dos Exportadores (Brazil)
ANEA	Asociación Nacional de Escritores y Artistas (Peru)
ANEB	Asociación Nacional Exportadores de Bolivia
ANEC	American Nuclear Energy Council
ANEC	Asociación Nacional de Enfermeras de Colombia

ANEC	Associação Nacional dos Exportadores de Cereais (Brazil)	**ANEP**	Asociación Nacional de Ex-Parlamentarios (Peru)
ANÉC	Association Nationale des Éleveurs de chinchillas	**ANEPLA**	Associazione Nazionale Estrattori, Produttori Lapidei ed Affini
ANEC	Associazione Nazionale Esercenti Cinema	**ANÉRA**	Association Normande d'Économie Rurale Appliquée
ANÉCÉA	Association Nationale d'Élevage du Cheval, d'Équitation et d'Agriculture	**ANERT**	Associazione Nazionale Esattori e Ricevitori delle Imposte Dirette e dei Tesorieri degli Enti Locali
ANÉDA	Association Nationale d'Études pour la Documentation Automatique	**ANES**	Asociación Nacional de Enfermeras Salvadoreñas
ANEF	Agrupación de Empleados Fiscales (Chile)	**ANESBWA**	Association of Non-English Speaking Background Women of Australia
ANEF	Associazione Nazionale di Educazioni Fisica	**ANESV**	Associazione Nazionale Esercenti Spettacoli Viaggianti
ANÉFÉ	Association Nationale des Écoles Françaises de l'Étranger	**ANET**	Associazione Nazionale Esercenti Teatri
ANEFHOP	Asociación Nacional Española de Fabricantes de Hormigon Preparado	**ANETA**	Algemeen Nieuws-en Telegraaf Agentschap
ANEFPR	Association Nationale d'Enseignement et de Formation Professionnelle Rurale	**ANEVEI**	Algemene Nederlandse Vereniging van Eierhandelaren
ANEFRYC	Asociación y Equipos para Producción de Frio y Climatización	**ANEXHON**	Asociación Nacional de Exportadores de Honduras
ANEGID	Associazione Nazionale Educatori Gioventù Italiana Disadattata	**ANEZA**	Association Nationale des Entreprises du Zaïre
ANEHOP	Agrupación Nacional Española de Fabricantes de Hormigon Preparado	**ANF**	Académia Nacionál de Farmácia (Brazil)
ANEIMO	Asociación Nacional de Empresas de Investigación de Mercados y de la Opinion Publica (Spain)	**ANF**	Agencia de Noticias Fides (Bolivia)
		ANF	Associação Nacional das Farmácias
ANÉJ	Association Nationale des Éducateurs de Jeunes Inadaptés	**ANF**	Association de la Noblesse Française
ANéLA	Association Néerlandaise de Linguistique Appliquée	**ANFAC**	Agrupación Nacional de Fabricantes de Automóviles y Camiones, Tractors y sus Motors
ANELEC	Asociación Nacional de Empresas Distribuidoras de Energia Electrica (Bolivia)	**ANFAC**	Asociación Colombiana de Fabricantes de Articulos de Caucho (Colombia)
ANÉM	Association Nationale d'Études Municipales pour la Promotion de la Fonction Communale	**ANFACE**	Asociación Nacional de Fabricantes de Cerveza
		ANFACI	Association Nationale des Fabricants de Colles Industrielles
ANÉMOM	Association Nationale des Écrivains de la Mer et de l'Outre-Mer	**ANFACO**	Asociación Nacional de Fabricantes de Conservas de Pescado y Marisco
ANEN	African NGOs Environment Network (Kenya)	**ANFAL**	Asociación Nacional de Fabricantes de Alcoholes y Licores (Guatemala)
ANEN	Australian NGO Environment Network	**ANFALA**	Asociación Nacional de Fabricantes de Ladrillos (Colombia)
ANÉNA	Association Nationale pour l'Étude de la Neige et des Avalanches	**ANFAMA**	Agrupación Nacional de Fabricantes de Maquinaria Agrícola
ANEP	Asociación Nacional de Empleados Públicos (Costa Rica)	**ANFAN**	Asociación para el Apoyo de la Nueva Familia en Nicaragua - Centros Ixchen
ANEP	Asociación Nacional de Empresa Privada (El Salvador)	**ANFAO**	Associazione Nazionale Fabbricanti Articoli di Occhialeria

ANFE	Asociación Nacional de Fomento Económico (Costa Rica)
ANFEL	Asociación Nacional de Fabricantes de Electrodomésticas
ANFFAS	Associazione Nazionale Famiglie di Fanciulli e Adulti Subnormali
ANFFE	Asociación Nacional de Fabricantes de Fertilizantes
ANFIA	Associazione Nazionale fra Industrie Automobilistiche
ANFIDA	Associazione Nazionale fra gli Industriali degli Acquedotti
ANFIH	Association Nationale pour la Formation Continue dans l'Industrie Hôtelière
ANFIIDÉ	Asociation Nationale Française des Infirmières et Infirmiers Diplômés et Élèves
ANFIMA	Associazione Nazionale fra i Fabbricanti di Imballagi Metallici ed Affini
ANFIO	Asociazione Nazionale fra i Fabbricanti di Impugnotore per Ombrelli
ANFMA	Association Nationale pour la Formation des Moniteurs Agricoles
ANFOCOP	Association Nationale pour la Formation Continue et Promotionnelle en Traitement de Surfaces
ANFOPAR	Association Nationale pour la Formation et le Perfectionnement Professionnel des Adultes Ruraux
ANFoV	Associazione Nazionale Fornitori di Videoinformazione
ANFP	Associação dos Fabricantes de Papel (Brazil)
ANFRENA	Agência Nacional de Frete e Navegação (Mozambique)
ANFRUT	Asociación Nacional de Fruticultores (Venezuela)
ANG	Academia Nacional de Geografía (Argentina)
ANG	Agencia Noticiosa da Guine
ANGA	Arbeitsgemeinschaft für Antennen und Kommunikationstechnik
ANGA	Associazione Nazionale Giovani Agricoltori
ANGAISA	Associazione Nazionale Grossisti Apparecchi Igienco-Sanitari
ANGAU	Australian New Guinea Administrative Unit
ANGEAT	Associazione Nazionale Giornalisti di Enogastronomia ed Agriturismo
ANGED	Asociación Nacional de Grandes Empresas de Distribución
ANGEM	Associazione Nazionale Gestori Mense
ANGG	Associazione Nazionale Giornalisti Giudiziari
ANGIP	Associazione Nazionale Grossisti Italiani Profumeria
ANGIS	Australian National Geoscience Information Service (of AGSO) (NGIS)
ANGO	Association du Négoce des Graines Oléagineuses, Huiles et Graisses Animales et Végétales et leurs Dérivés de la CEE
ANGOC	Asian Coalition of NGOs for Agricultural Reform and Rural Development
ANGOLO	Asian NGO Coalition for Agrarian Reform and Rural Development
Angomedica	Angolan Pharmaceutical Trading Organisation
ANGOP	Angolan News Agency
ANGOS	Air National Guard Optometric Society (U.S.A.)
ANGPVCC	Association Nationale des Groupements de Producteurs (Vins de Consommation Courante)
ANGR	Association Nationale des Grossistes Répartiteurs en Spécialités Pharmaceutiques (Belgium)
ANGRO	Associazione Nazionale Italiana Grossisti Orologiai
ANGV	Asociación Nacional de Ganaderos de Venezuela
ANH	Australian National Herbarium (CSIRO)
ANHG	Academia Nacional de Historia y Geografía (Mexico)
ANHP	Associação Nacional de Hospitalização Privada
ANHS	American Natural Hygiene Society
ANHSA	Aerovias Nacionales de Honduras SA
ANHSO	Association of National Health Service Officers
ANHSSO	Association of National Health Service Supplies Officers
ANHUL	Australian National Humanities Library
ANI	Academia de Negocios Internacionales (U.S.A.)
ANI	Agencia Nacional de Informações
ANI	Agentsvo Novostei i Informatsii

ANI	Australian Naval Institute
ANIA	Asociación Nacional de Ingenieros Agrónomos
ANIA	Association Nationale des Industries Agro-Alimentaires
ANIA	Association Nationale des Invalides de l'Armée
ANIA	Associazione Nazionale fra le Imprese Assicuratrici
ANIAA	Association Nationale des Industries Agricoles et Alimentaires
ANIACAM	Asociación Nacional de Importadores de Automoviles, Camiones Autobuses y Motorcicletas
ANIAD	Associazione Nazionale Industriali Alimentazione Dolciaria
ANIAF	Associazione Nazionale Imprese di Aerofotogrammetrica
ANIAI	Associazione Nazionale Ingegneri ed Architetti Italiani
ANIAMM	Associação Nacional dos Industriais de Aguas Mineromedicinais e de Mesa
ANIC	Association Nationale des Industriels et des Commerçants
ANIC	Associazione Nazionale dell'Industria Chimica
ANIC	Australian National Insect Collection
ANIC	Azienda Nazionale Idrogenazione Combustibili
ANICA	Associazione Nazionale fra gli Istituti di Credito Agrario
ANICA	Associazione Nazionale fra Industrie Cinematografiche ed Affini
ANICAF	Asociación Nacional de Industriales des Café (Venezuela)
ANICAV	Associazione Nazionale fra gli Industriali delle Conserve Alimentari Vegetali
ANICC	Association Nationale Interprofessionnelle du Champignon de Couché
ANICC	Associazione Nazionale Industriali e Commercianti Materiali Attrezzature Nautiche
ANICO-BECA	Associazione Nazionale Importatori e Commercianti di Bestiame e Carne
ANICTA	Associazione Nazionale Imprenditori Coibentazioni Termoacustiche
ANID	African Network for Integrated Development (Senegal) = RADI
ANID	Associazione Nazionale Insegnanti di Disegno
ANIDECOL	Federazione Nazionale Importatori Caffé, Coloniali e Droghe
ANIE	Associazione Nazionale Industrie Elettrotecniche ed Elettroniche
ANIECA	Associação Automóvel
ANIEL	Agrupación Nacional de Industries Electronicas
ANIELB	Association of Northern Ireland Education and Library Boards
ANIEM	Unione Nazionale Industrie Edili Minori
ANIEPI	Associazione Nazionale Importatori Esportatori Prodotti Ittici
ANIERM	Asociación Nacional de Importadores y Exportadores de la República Mexicana
ANIEST	Associazione Nazionale Italiana Esperti Scientifici del Turismo
ANIF	Asociación Nacional de Instituciones Financieras (Colombia)
ANIFOP	Association Nationale Interprofessionnelle pour le Formation Professionnelle et Technique dans l'Industrie des Plastiques
ANIFRMO	Association Nationale Interprofessionnelle pour la Formation Rationnelle de la Main-d'Oeuvre
ANIG	Associazione Nazionale Industriali Gas
ANILD	Associazione Nazionale Italiana Lavoratrici Domestiche
ANILEBE	Associação Nacional dos Industriais de Licores e Bebidas Espirituosas
ANILEC	Association Nationale Interprofessionnelle des Légumes de Conserve
ANILS	Associazione Nazionale Insegnanti di Lingue Straniere
ANIM	Asociación Nacional de Industriales Madereros (Venezuela)
ANIMA	Associazione Nazionale Industria Meccanica Varia ed Affine
ANIMEE	Associação Nacional dos Industriais de Material Elétrico eI Electrónico
ANIMeM	Associazione Nazionale Industriali Metalmeccanici Minori
ANIMOG	Associazione Nazionale Intaliana Medici ed Operatori Geriatrici
ANIMPEC	Associazione Nazionale Industriali Manufatturieri delle Pelli e del Cuoio
ANIN	Associated Northern Ireland Newspapers
ANIPA	Associazione Nazionale Imprese Pubblicité Audiovisiva

ANIPESCA	Associazione Nazionale Importatori Produtti della Pesca Conservati
ANIPLA	Associazione Nazionale Italiana per l'Automazione
ANIR	Asociación Nacional de Inovadores y Racionalizadores (Cuba)
ANIR	Associazione Nazionale Industrie Refrattari
ANIRP	Associação Nacional dos Industriais de Recauchutagem de Pneus
ANIRSF	Associação Nacional do Industriais de Refrigerantes e Sumos de Frutos
ANISA	Anglo Naval e Industrial SA (Spain)
ANISIG	Associazione Nazionale Imprese Specializzate in Indagini Geognostiche
ANISS	Associazione Nazionale Imprese Sistemi de Sicurezza
ANIT	Associazione Nazionale Imprese Teatrali
ANITA	Associazione Nazionale Imprese dei Trasporti Automobilistici
ANITAF	Associação Nacional das Industrias Texteis Algodoerias e Fibras
ANITI	Associazione Nazionale Italiana Traduttori ed Interpreti
ANITPAT	Associazione Nazionale Incegnanti Tecnico-Pratici e di Applicazioni Tecniche
ANIVEC	Associação Nacional das Industrias Vestuario e Confecções
ANJCA	Association Niortaise pour le Jumelage et la Coopération avec Atakpame
ANJIM	Association Nationale des Journalistes d'Information Médicale
ANK	Assotsiatsiia Nauchnogo Kommunizma
ANKO	Algemene Nederlandse Kappersorganisatie
ANL	Anti-Nazi League
ANL	Argonne National Laboratory (U.S.A.)
ANL	Australian National Line
ANLA	Association Norvégienne de Linguistique Appliquée
ANLF	Afghan National Liberation Front = JNMA
ANLM	Afar National Liberation Movement (Ethiopia)
ANM	Academía Nacionál de Medicína (Brazil)
ANM	Associazione Nazionale Magistrati
ANM	Australian Newsprint Mills Limited
ANMA	Association Nationale des Maîtres Agricoles et des Maîtresses Ménagères
ANMA	Associazione Nazionale Meccanizzazione Agraria
ANMA	Australian National Maritime Association Inc.
ANMB	Algemene Nederlandse Metaalbewerkersbond
ANMB	Algemene Nederlandse Molenaarsbond
ANMC	American National Metric Council
ANMÉR	Association Nationale de Migration et d'Établissement Ruraux
ANMF	Association Nationale de la Meunerie Française
ANMI	Associazione Nazionale dei Musei Italiani
ANMM	Asociación Nacional de Mineros Medianos (Bolivia)
ANMM	Australian National Maritime Museum
ANMP	Afghan National Movement Party
ANMRC	Australian Numerical Meteorology Research Centre
ANMW	Association of Newspaper & Magazine Wholesalers
ANN	Agencia Nicaragüense de Noticias
ANN	Anti-Nuclear Network
ANN	Asian-Pacific News Network
ANO	Abu Nidal Organisation
ANOC	Association of National Olympic Committees = ACNO
ANOCA	Association of National Olympic Committees of Africa = ACNOA
ANOF	Algemene Nederlandse Onderwijzers Federatie
ANOFPR	Association Nationale Ouvrière pour la Formation Professionnelle Rurale
ANOP	Agência Noticiosa Portuguesa
ANORAA	Association Nationale des Officers de Réserve de l'Armée de l'Air
ANÖV	Arbeitsgemeinschaft Niederösterreichischer Viehkaufleute
ANP	Acção Nacional Popular (Mozambique, Portugal)
ANP	Administración Nacional de Puertos (Uruguay)
ANP	Agence Nigérien de Presse
ANP	Algemeen Nederlands Presbureau
ANP	Andalusian National Party = PA
ANP	Assembleia Nacional Popular (Guinea-Bissau)

ANP	Assemblée Nationale Populaire (Congo)
ANP	Assembleia National Popular (Cape Verde)
ANP	Australian Nationalist Party
ANP	Awami National Party (Pakistan)
ANP	United Nations Applied Nutrition Programme
ANPA	American Newspaper Publishers Association
ANPA	Asociación Nacional de Productores de Arroz (Peru)
ANPAC	Associazione Nazionale Piloti Aviazione Commerciale
ANPAG	Associazione Nazionale Piloti Aviazione Generale
ANPAN	Associazione Nazionale Provveditori e Appaltatori Navali
ANPAT	Association Nationale pour la Prévention des Accidents du Travail (Belgium)
ANPC	Association Nationale des Promoteurs de Constructions
ANPC	Australian National Parks Council
ANPC	Australian Network for Plant Conservation
ANPCC	Asociación Nacional de Productores de Coco y Copra (Venezuela)
ANPCVW	Association of National Park and Countryside Voluntary Wardens
ANPE	Agence Nationale pour l'Emploi
ANPE	Asociación Nacional del Profesorado Estatal
ANPE	Association Nationale des Producteurs d'Endives
ANPEA	Association Nationale pour le Développement de l'Utilisation des Engrais et Amendements
ANPÉB	Association Nationale des Patrons Électriciens de Belgique
ANPED	Alliance of Northern People for Environment and Development (Germany)
ANPES	Associação Nacional de Programação Economica e Social (Brazil)
ANPI	Asociación Nacional de Pequeños Industriales (Honduras)
ANPI	Association Nationale des Partisans Italiens
ANPI	Association Nationale pour la Protection contre l'Incendie = NVBB
ANPIAS	Associazione Nazionale Presidi di Istituti Alberghiere di Stato
ANPIHF	Association Nationale des Planteurs Indépendants de Houblons Français
ANPLC	Association Nationale des Producteurs de Légumes Conservés
ANPO	Association of National Park Officers
ANPOCS	Associação Nacional de Pós-Graduação e Pesquisa em Cióncias Sociais, São Paulo (Brazil)
ANPP	Asamblea Nacional del Poder Popular (Cuba)
ANPP-DOSHR	Association Nationale Professionnelle des Personnels de Direction des Organismes Spécialisés d'Habitat Rural
ANPPCAN	African Network for Prevention and Protection Against Child Abuse and Neglect (Kenya) = RAPPANE
ANPPIA	Associazione Nazionale Perseguitati Politici Italiani Antifascisti
ANPPM	Association Nationale des Photographes de Publicité et de Mode
ANPPSA	Association Nationale pour la Promotion Professionnelle des Salaries de l'Agriculture
ANPRDPP	Association Nationale des Propriétaires Ruraux et Défenseurs de la Propriété Privée
ANPROCA	Asociación Nacional de Productores del Café (Bolivia)
ANPROS	Asociación Gremial Nacional de Productores de Semillas (Chile)
ANPROSE	Asociación Nacional de Productores de Semillas Certificadas (Venezuela)
ANPS	Asociación Nacional de Producción de Semillas (Chile, Colombia)
ANPSCAH	Association Nationale de Promotion Socio-Culturelle en Agriculture et en Horticulture
ANPUEP	Association Nationale des Propriétaires et Usagers d'Embranchements Particuliers
ANPUR	Associazione Nazionale Professori Universitari di Ruolo
ANPV	Algemene Nederlandse Pluimveeteelvereniging
ANPWS	Australian National Parks and Wildlife Service (*now* ANCA)
ANQUE	Asociación Nacional de Quimicos de España

ANR	Agrupación Nacional de la Recuperación
ANR	Aktion Neue Rechte (Austria)
ANR	Asociación Nacional Republicana (Paraguay)
ANR	Association Nationale de Révision de la Coopération Agricole
ANR	Association of Nursing Religious
ANR	Australian National Railways
ANR-PC	Asociación Nacional Republicana - Partido Colorado (Paraguay)
ANRA	Professional Association of Natural Rubber in Africa (Ivory Coast) = ACNA
ANRADIO	Asociación Nacional de Radio, Televisién y Cine de Colombia
ANRC	American National Red Cross
ANRC	Animal Nutrition Research Council (U.S.A.)
ANRC	Australian National Research Council
ANRCA	Association Nationale de Révision de la Coopération Agricole
ANRDGE	Alianza Nacional de Restauración Democrática de Guinea Ecuatorial
ANRÉD	Agence Nationale pour la Récupération et Élimination des Déchets
ANRFVC-NER	Association Nationale des Ruches Familiales de Vacances de la Confédération Nationale de la Famille Rurale
ANRPC	Association of Natural Rubber Producing Countries = APPCN
ANRSP	Agencja Nieruchomości Rolnych Skarbu Pañstwa
ANRT	Association Nationale de la Recherche Technique
ANS	Agencia Noticiosa Saporiti (Argentina)
ANS	Algemene Nederlandse Slagersbond
ANS	American Name Society
ANS	American Neuromodulation Society
ANS	American Neurotology Society
ANS	American Nuclear Society
ANS	American Numismatic Society
ANS	American Nutrition Society
ANS	Armée Nationale Sihanoukienne
ANS	Australian Numismatic Society
ANSA	Abbey National Staff Association
ANSA	Agenzia Nazionale Stampa Associata
ANSA	Aktiebolaget Nordiske Skinnauktioner
ANSA	Association Nationale des Sociétés par Action
ANSA	Australian National Sportsfishing Association
ANSD	Associazione Nazionale Sindicate Dirigenti
ANSDHA	Association Nationale pour le Développement des Sciences Humaines Appliquées
ANSE	Association Nationale des Services d'Eau (Belgium)
ANSEAU	Association Nationale des Services d'Eau (Belgium) = NAVEWA
ANSESAL	Agencia Nacional de Seguridad Salvadoreña
ANSI	American National Standards Institute
ANSI	Associazione Nazionale per la Scuola Italiana
ANSL	Association of African National Shipping Lines = ACNMA
ANSL	Australian National Standards Laboratory
ANSMO	Association des Négociants Suisses en Machines et Outils
ANSOL	Australian National Social Sciences Library
ANSP	Australian National Socialist Party
ANSPI	Agrupación Nacional Sindical de Pinturas
ANSR	Association for Nonsmokers Rights
ANSS	American Nature Study Society
ANSSMFE	Australian National Society of Soil Mechanics and Foundation Engineering
ANSTC	Australian Nuclear Science and Technology Council (DPIE)
ANSTEL	Australian National Scientific and Technological Library
ANSTI	African Network of Scientific and Technological Institutions (Kenya) = RAIST
ANSTO	Australian Nuclear Science and Technology Organization
ANSU	Asociación Nacional de Urbanizadores
ANT	Administracion Nacional de Telecomunicacións (Paraguay)
ANT	Armée Nationale Tchadienne
ANTA	Agence Nationale d'Information 'Taratra' (Madagascar)
ANTA	Associazione Nazionale Termotecnici e Aerotechnici
ANTAC	Associazione Nazionale Tecnici di Volo Aviazione Civile

ANTAI	Associazione Nazionale Tappezzieri e Arredatorie Italiani
ANTAR	Associazione Nazionale Autoriparatori e Autoricambisti
ANTAV	Association Nationale Technique pour l'Amélioration de la Viticulture
ANTC	Association of Nursery Training Colleges
ANTC	Australian National Television Council
ANTEL	Administración Nacional de Telecomunicaciónes (El Salvador, Uruguay)
ANTeL	Associazione Nazionale Tecnici di Laboratorio
ANTELCO	Administración Nacional de TeleCommunicaciónes (Paraguay, Peru)
ANTENNE-2	Société Nationale de Télévision en Couleur
ANTI	Associazione Nazionale Tributaristi Italiani
ANTL	Association Nationale des Tisseurs de Lin (Belgium)
ANTO	Antarctic Treaty Organization
ANTOR	Association of National Tourist Office Representatives in Great Britain
ANTRAL	Associação Nacional dos Transportadores Rodoviários em Automóveis Ligeiros
ANTRAM	Associação Nacional de Transportadores Publicos Rodoviários de Mercadorias
ANTROP	Associação Nacional de Transportadores Rodoviários de Pesados de Passageiros
ANTS	Anglo-Norman Texts Society
ANTSAL	Association Nationale des Techniciens Supérieurs Agricoles de Laiterie
ANTSH	Association Nationale des Techniciens Supérieurs Horticole
ANTZA	Associazione Nazionale fra i Tecnici dello Zucchero e dell'Alcole
ANU	Albanian National Union
ANU	Association des Nations-Unies = UNA
ANU	Australian National University
ANUC	Asociación Nacional de Usuarios Campesinos (Colombia)
ANUCAG	Asociación Nacional de Uniones de Crédito Agricola y Ganadero (Mexico)
ANUDÉ	Administration des Nations Unies pour le Développement Économique
ANUDE	Asamblea Nicaragüense de Unidad Democrática
ANUÉG	Association des Usagers de l'Électricité et du Gaz
ANUGA	Allgemeine Nahrungs und Genussmittel-Ausstellung
ANUIES	Asociación Nacional de Universidades e Institútos de Enseñanza Superior (Mexico)
ANUM	Algemene Nederlandse Unie van Muziekverenigingen
ANUP	Albanian National Unity Party = PUK
ANUTE	Administración Nacional de las Usinas y Transmissiones Eléctricas del Estado (Uruguay)
ANV	Asociación Nacional de Vitivinicultores (Mexico)
ANVA	Associazione Nazionale Venditori Ambulanti
ANVAR	Agence Nationale de Valorisation de la Recherche
ANVC	Algemene Nederlandse Vereniging van Contactlenzensspecialisten
ANVED	Associazione Nazionale Vendite per Corrispondenza e a Distenza
ANVG	Association Nationale des Volontaires de Guerre
ANVIDES	Associazione Nazionale di Vernicatura, Decorazione e Stuccatura
ANVO	Algemene Nederlandse Vereniging voor Optometristen
ANVR	Algemene Nederlandse Vereniging van Reisbureaus
ANVS	Algemene Nederlandse Vereniging van Speelgoedhandelaren
ANVSG	Algemene Nederlandse Vereniging voor Sociale Geneeskunde
ANVUMA	Association Nationale de Vulgarisation du Machinisme Agricole
ANVV	Algemene Nederlandse Vereniging voor Vreemdelingenverkeer
ANVW	Algemene Nederlandse Vereniging voor Wijsbegeerte
ANWB	Algemene Nederlandse Wielrijdersbond
ANWUNMV	Association of Nordic War and UN Military Veterans (Sweden)
ANZ	Air New Zealand
ANZ	Algemeen Nederlands Zangverbond
ANZ	Algemene Nederlandse Zuivelbond
ANZA	Association of New Zealand Advertisers

ANZAAS	Australian and New Zealand Association for the Advancement of Science
ANZAME	Australian and New Zealand Association for Medical Education
ANZAMRS	Australian and New Zealand Association for Medieval and Renaissance Studies
ANZASA	Australian and New Zealand American Studies Association
ANZAScA	Australia and New Zealand Architectural Science Association
ANZATS	Australia and New Zealand Association of Theological Schools
ANZCP	Australian and New Zealand College of Psychiatrists
ANZDEC	Asian-New Zealand Development Corporation
ANZEC	Australian and New Zealand Environment Council (*now* ANZECC)
ANZECC	Australian and New Zealand Environment and Conservation Council (*ex* ANZEC)
ANZECS	Australia-New Zealand-Europe Container Service
ANZFAC	Australian and New Zealand Fisheries and Aquaculture Council
ANZFAS	Australian and New Zealand Federation of Animal Societies
ANZHES	Australian and New Zealand History of Education Society
ANZLIC	Australia New Zealand Land Information Council (*ex* ALIC)
ANZM&S	Australian and New Zealand Merchants and Shippers Association
ANZMEC	Australian and New Zealand Minerals and Energy Council
ANZSES	Australian New Zealand Scientific Exploration Society
ANZSRLO	Australian and New Zealand Scientific Research Liaison Office
ANZTLA	Australian and New Zealand Theological Library Association
ANZUS	Australia, New Zealand, United States Pact
AO	Aide Olympique
AO	Association of Optometrists
AOA	Airport Operators' Association
AOA	Ambulance Officers' Association
AOA	American Ontoanalytic Association
AOA	American Optometric Association
AOA	American Orthopaedic Association
AOA	American Orthopsychiatric Association
AOA	American Osteopathic Association
AOA	ASEAN Orthopaedic Association (Singapore)
AOA	Asociación Odontológica Argentina
AOA	Association of Official Architects
AOAC	Association of Official Analytical Chemists (U.S.A.)
AOAD	Arab Organization for Agricultural Development (Sudan)
AÖAG	Arbeitsgemeinschaft der Österreichisch - Ausländischen Gesellschaften
AOAI	American Organist Association International
AOAO	American Osteopathic Academy of Orthopedics
AOAPC	Association des Organisations Africaines de Promotion Commerciale = AATPO
AOAS	American Osteopathic Academy of Sclerotherapy
AOAS	Arab Organization for Administrative Sciences = OASA
AÖB	Arbeitsgemeinschaft Österreichischer Bausparkassen
AOB	Association of Ballrooms
AOB	Association Ornithologique de Belgique
AOBO	Amigos del Orden Budista Occidental = FWBO, TBMSG
AÖBV	Allgemeiner Österreichischer Bauenverband
AOC	American Orthoptic Council
AOC	Arabian Oil Company (Japan)
AOC	Associação Operária Camponesa
AOC	Associated Overseas Countries (EU)
AOC	Association of Old Crows (U.S.A.)
AOCA	American Osteopathic College of Anesthesiologists
AOCAI	American Osteopathic College of Allergy and Immunology
AOCASS	Association Ouest et Centre Africaine de la Science du Sol = AWCACS
AOCD	American Osteopathic College of Dermatology
AOCI	Airport Operators Council International
AOCP	American Osteopathic College of Pathologists

AOCP	American Osteopathic College of Proctology	**AOGA**	Alaska Oil and Gas Association (U.S.A.)
AOCP	Asia Oceania Congress of Perinatology (Singapore)	**AOH**	Ancient Order of Hibernians
AOCP	Associated Owners of City Properties	**AOHA**	American Osteopathic Hospital Association
AOCPA	American Osteopathic College of Pathologists	**AOHC**	American Occupational Health Conference
AOCR	American Osteopathic Colege of Rheumatology	**AOHR**	Arab Organisation for Human Rights
AOCR	American Osteopathic College of Radiology	**AOI**	Aide Odontologique Internationale
AOCRM	American Osteopathic College of Rehabilitation Medicine	**AOI**	Aims of Industry
		AoI	Association of Illustrators
AOCRS	African Organization of Cartography and Remote Sensing (Algeria) = OACT	**AOI**	Association of Optometrists Ireland (Éire)
AOCS	American Oil Chemists' Society	**AOI**	Associazione Ottica Italiana
AOD	Ancient Order of Druids (U.S.A.)	**AOICC**	Association Internationale des Organisateurs de Courses Cyclistes
AODC	Association of Offshore Diving Contractors	**AOID**	Arab Organization for Industrial Development
AODC	Association of Offshore Drilling Contractors	**AOIP**	Association des Ouvriers en Instruments de Précision
AODC	Australian Oceanographic Data Centre	**AOIS**	Australian Overseas Information Service (DFAT)
AODRO	Australian Overseas Disaster Relief Organisation	**ÄOL**	Äidinkielen Opettajain Liitto
AODT	Association Européenne des Organisations Nationales de Commerçants Détaillants en Textiles	**AOLF**	Association d'Orthopédie de Langue Française
		AOM	Air Outre-Mer (France)
AOE	Allatorvostudomaáni Egyetem	**AÖM**	Arbeitsgemeinschaft Österreichischer Musikverleger
AÖE	Arbeitsgemeinschaft Österreichischer Entomologen	**AOMA**	American Occupational Medical Association
AOEC	Airways Operations Evaluation Center (U.S.A.)	**AOMA**	Apartment Owners and Managers Association of America
AOEHI	American Organization for the Education of the Hearing Impaired	**AOMA**	Arab Organization for the Manufacture of Armaments
AOÉS	Association Oecuménique pour l'Église et la Société = EACS	**AOMCL**	Association of Off-Machine Coaters and Laminators
AOF	Afrique Occidentale Française	**AONTAS**	National Association of Adult Education (Éire)
AOF	Association des Optométristes de France	**AOO**	American Oceanic Organisation
AOF	Australian Orchid Foundation	**AOOI**	Associazione Otologica Ospedalieri Italiana
AOFA	American Offshore Fishermens Association	**AOP**	Association of Optometrists
AOFAS	American Orthopaedic Foot and Ankle Society	**AOPA**	Aircraft Owners and Pilots Association
AOFD	African Organisation for Freedom and Democracy (Mauritius)	**AOPA**	American Orthotic and Prosthetic Association
		AOPA	Associazione Operatori e Piloti dell' Aviazione Generale d'Italia
AOFOG	Asia and Oceania Federation of Obstetrics and Gynecology (Singapore)	**AOPE**	Associated Organisations for Professionals in Education (U.S.A.)
AÖG	Arbeitsgemeinschaft Österreichischer Entomologen	**AOPEC**	Arab Organisation of Petroleum Exporting Countries

AOPI	Associazione Orticola Professionale Italiana	**AOTI**	Association of Tutors Incorporated
AOPL	Association of Oil Pipelines (U.S.A.)	**AOU**	American Ornithologists' Union
AOQC	Australian Organisation for Quality Control	**AOUD**	Alliance Universelle des Ouvriers Diamantaires
AORC	Association of Official Racing Chemists (U.S.A.)	**AOV**	Asfaltindustriens Oplysningskontor for Vejbygning
AORSA	Abnormal Occurrences Reporting System Association (EU)	**AP**	Acción del Pueblo (Costa Rica)
AORTIC	African Organisation for Research and Training in Cancer (Zaïre)	**AP**	Acción Popular (Peru)
		AP	Active Party (Hungary)
AOS	American Opthalmological Society	**AP**	Acuerdo Patriotico (Bolivia)
AOS	American Orchid Society	**AP**	Agrarian Party (Albania)
AOS	American Oriental Society	**AP**	Alianza Patriótica (Bolivia)
AOS	American Orthodontic Society	**AP**	Alianza Popular
AOS	American Otological Society	**AP**	Alliance for Progess (OAS)
AOS	Anglo-Orthodox Society	**AP**	Alliance Party (Fiji)
AOS	Apostleship of the Sea	**AP**	Associated Press (U.S.A.)
AOS	Asociatia Oamenilor de Stiinta	**AP**	Federación de Alianza Popular
AOS-R	Asociatia Oamenilor de Ştiinţa din România	**AP&PB**	Association of Print and Packaging Buyers
AOSA	American Optometric Student Association	**APA**	Airhawk Pilots Association
AOSA	American Orff-Schulwerk Association	**APA**	Aluminium Prefabs Association
AOSA	American Oxford Sheep Association	**APA**	American Pancreatic Association
AOSA	Association of Official Seed Analysts (U.S.A.)	**APA**	American Paralysis Association
		APA	American Pharmaceutical Association
AOSB	Arctic Ocean Sciences Board	**APA**	American Philological Association
AOSC	Association of Oilwell Servicing Contractors	**APA**	American Philosophical Association
		APA	American Physicists Association
AOSCA	Association of Official Seed Certifying Agencies (U.S.A.)	**APA**	American Planning Association
		APA	American Plywood Association
AOSCE	Asian and Oceania Society for Comparative Endocrinology (Hong Kong)	**APA**	American Polygraph Assocation
		APA	American Poultry Association
		APA	American Press Association
AOSD	Arab Organisation for Social Defence against Crime = OADS	**APA**	American Protestant Association
		APA	American Psychiatric Association
AOSSM	American Orthopaedic Society for Sports Medicine	**APA**	American Psychological Association
		APA	American Psychopathological Association
AOSTRA	Alberta Oil Sands Technology and Research Authority (Canada)	**APA**	American Psychotherapy Association
		APA	American Pulpwood Association
AOTA	American Occupational Therapy Association	**APA**	American PyroTechnics Association
		APA	Anthracite Producers Association (South Africa)
AOTA	Asian and Oceania Thyroid Association (Japan)	**APA**	Architectural Photographers Association (U.S.A.)
AOTA	Association Oecuménique des Théologiens Africains (Cameroon)		
		APA	Army Parachute Association
AOTC	Associated Offices Technical Committee	**APA**	Asociación Paleontológica Argentina
		APA	Asociación para la Prevención de Accidentes
AOTFA	American Old Time Fiddlers Association		

APA	Asociación para la Proteccion del Ambiente (Argentina)	**APAE**	Association of Public Address Engineers
APA	Asociación Peruana de Avicultura (Peru)	**APAF**	Association des Producteurs des Alpes Françaises
APA	Associação Portuguesa de Aerosois	**APAG**	American Photographic Artisans Guild
APA	Association des Producteurs Agricoles (Haiti)	**APAG**	Association Européenne des Producteurs d'Acides Gras
APA	Association for Prevention of Addiction Ltd	**APAG**	Association pour l'Appel de Genève
APA	Association for the Prevention of Addiction	**APAG**	Atlantic Policy Advisory Group (NATO)
APA	Association of Paediatric Anaesthetists	**APAH**	Associação Portuguesa de Administradores Hospitalares
APA	Association of Piping Adjudicators	**APAL**	Asociación Psiquiátrica de la América Latina (Venezuela)
APA	Association of Practising Accountants		
APA	Association of Preventive Medicine	**APALMS**	Asian-Pacific Association for Laser Medicine and Surgery (Singapore)
APA	Association of Professional Astrologers	**APAM**	Associação Portuguesa dos Aviários de Multiplicação
APA	Association of Public Analysts		
APA	Association of Publishing Agencies	**APAM**	Association Populaire des Amis des Musées
APA	Association Professionelle des Avocats		
APA	Australian Physiotherapy Association	**APAN**	Administración de los Parques Nacionales (Venezuela)
APA	Austria Presse Agentur		
APAA	American Physicians Art Association	**APANF**	Association des Pédiatres d'Afrique Noire Francophone (Ivory Coast)
APAA	Art Patrons Association of America		
APAA	ASEAN Port Authorities Association	**APAO**	Asia Pacific Academy of Opthalmology
APAA	Asian Patent Attorneys Association (Japan)	**APAO**	Association pour la Promotion des Produits Phosphates de l'Afrique de l'Ouest
APAC	Agricultural Policy Advisory Council (Japan)		
APAC	Appointment and Promotion Advisory Committee (FAO)	**APAP**	Asociación Peruana de Agencias de Publicidad
APAC	Asia-Pacific Agribusiness Club (Philippines)	**APAP**	Association of Professional Ambulance Personnel
APAC	Asociación Peruana para el Avance de la Ciencia	**APAPA**	Association for the Preservation of Anti-Psychiatric Artefacts (U.S.A.)
APAC	Association of African Communications Professionals (Senegal)	**APAR**	Association Parlementaire Agricole et Rurale (France)
APACE	Appropriate Technology for Community and Environment (Australia)	**APAS**	Association of Personal Assistants and Secretaries
APACS	Association for Payment Clearing Services	**APAS**	Association of Public Analysts of Scotland
APAD	Asia Pacific Academy of Ophthalmology (Japan)	**APAS**	Association Paritaire d'Action Sociale du Bâtiment et des Travaux Publiques
APAD	Association Euro-Africaine pour l'Anthropologie du Changement Social et du Développement	**APASP**	Association pour le Perfectionnement des Approvisionnements dans les Services Publics
APADA	Asociación de Productores Agrarios del Delta Argentino	**APAST**	Association Africaine pour Avancement des Sciences et Technique
APADI	Asosiasi Perpustakaan, Arsip dan Dokumentasi Indonesia	**APASWE**	Asian Pacific Association for Social Work Education
APAE	Asociación de Productores de Aceites Esenciales (Guatemala)	**APATS**	Asia Program for the Advancement of Theological Studies

APATS	Association of Appliance Testers and Servicers
APAUC	Association des Professeurs d'Allemand des Universités Canadiennes
APAVÉ	Associations de Propriétaires d'Appareils à Vapeur et Électriques
APAVIT	Asociación Panameña de Agencias de Viajes y Turismo
APAVIT	Asociación Peruana de Agencias de Viajes y Turismo
APAVT	Associação Portuguesa das Agencias de Viagens e Turismo
APB	Asociación Peruana de Bibliotecarios
APB	Associação Portuguesa de Biólogos
APB	Associação Paulista de Bibliotecarios
APB	Association de la Pierre Bleue
APB	Association Pharmaceutique Belge
APB	Association Professionelle des Banques (Burkina Faso, Ivory Coast)
APB	Auditing Practices Board
APBB	Arbeitsgemeinschaft der Parlaments- und Behördenbibliotheken
APBB	Asociaţia Pro-Basarabia şi Bucovina (Romania) = PBBA
APBC	Asian Pacific Bankers Club (Japan)
APBC	Association of Pet Behaviour Counsellors
APBC	Association of Professional Boardsailing Centres
APBD	Association Professionelle de Bibliothécaires et Documentalistes (Belgium)
APBÉF	Association Professionelle des Banques et des Établissements Financiers du Sénégal
APBF	Accredited Poultry Breeders Federation
APBG	Association des Professeurs de Biologie-Géologie de France
APBGPL	Association Professionelle Belge des Gaz de Pétrole Liquefiés
APBMM	Association of British Preserved Milk Manufacturers
APBS	Accredited Poultry Breeding Stations Scheme
APBU	Asia-Pacific Broadcasting Union
APC	African Groundnut (Peanut) Council
APC	All People's Congress (Sierra Leone)
APC	American Power Committee
APC	Andean Postal Committee (Colombia) = CPA
APC	Animal Procedures Committee

APC	Archives Publiques du Canada = PAC
APC	Asociación Peruana de Consultoria
APC	Associação Portuguesa de Cerámica
APC	Associação Portuguesa de Criatividade
APC	Association for Progressive Communications (U.S.A.)
APC	Association of Principals of Colleges
APC	Association of Professional Composers
APCA	Air Pollution Control Association (Canada, U.S.A.)
APCA	Anglo-Polish Catholic Association
APCA	Architectural Precast Cladding Association
APCA	Assemblée Permanente des Chambres d'Agriculture
APCA	Association des Palais de Congrès Africains (Senegal)
APCAC	Asia-Pacific Council of American Chambers of Commerce (Philippines)
APCADEC	Associação Portuguesa dos Chefes de Aprovisionamento e de
APCAS	Asia and Pacific Commission on Agricultural Statistics (Thailand)
APCB	Associação Paulista de Criadores de Bovinos (Brazil)
APCBU	Association of PC Business Users
APCC	Agricultural Planning and Coordinating Committee (MOEA) (Taiwan)
APCC	Animal Population Control Clinic
APCC	Asian and Pacific Coconut Community (Indonesia)
APCC	Asian-Pacific Corrosion Control Organization (Australia)
APCC	Assemblée des Présidents des Chambres de Commerce
APCC	Association for Pastoral Care and Counselling (BAC)
APCC	Association of Professional Computer Consultants
APCChE	Asian Pacific Confederation of Chemical Engineering
APCCI	Assemblée Permanente des Chambres de Commerce et d'Industrie
APCD	Association of Philippine Coconut Desiccators
APCEA	Association Parlementaire pour le Coopération Euro-Arabe = PAEAC
APCEI	Association pour le Perfectionnement Pratique des Cadres des Entreprises Industrielles

APCET	Associazione Pubblicté Cinematograffica e Televisivi	**APDAYC**	Asociación Peruana de Autores y Compositores
APCI	Advertising Press Club of Ireland	**APDC**	Apple and Pear Development Council
APCIM	Associação Portuguesa de Indéstria de Madeiras	**APDC**	Asian and Pacific Development Centre = CDAP
APCIMS	Association of Private Client Investment Managers and Stockbrokers	**APDCP**	Associação Portuguesa dos Directores e Chefes de Pessoal
APCK	Association for Promoting Christian Knowledge (Ireland)	**APDE**	Associação Portuguesa de Direito Europeu
APCM	Assemblée Permanente des Chambres de Métiers	**APDF**	Africa Project Development Facility (Kenya)
APCMF	Assemblée des Présidents des Chambres de Métiers de France	**APDF**	Asian Pacific Dental Federation = FDAP
APCMI	Association for the Pastoral Care of the Mentally Ill	**APDICT**	Associação Portuguesa para o Desenvolvimento da Informação Cientifica e Técnica
APCO	Asian Parasite Control Organization (Japan)	**APDILA**	Association des Pharmaciens Directeurs de Laboratoires d'Analyses Biologiques
APCO	Association of Pleasure-craft Operators on Inland Waterways	**APDIO**	Associação Portuguesa para o Desenvolvimento da Investigação Operacional
APCOL	All-Pakistan Confederation of Labour		
APCOM	International Symposium on the Application of Computers in the Mining Industry	**APDP**	Associação Protectora dos Diabéticos de Portugal
APCOR	Asia-Pacific Finance Corporation	**APDSA**	Asian Pacific Dental Student Association
APCP	Asociación Panamericana de Circurgia Pediátrica (Mexico)	**APDU**	Association of Public Data Users (U.S.A.)
APCP	Association of Pediatric Chartered Physiotherapists	**APE**	Afghanistan Plants Enterprise
APCS	Association de la Presse Cinématographique Suisse	**APE**	Asociación de Parasitológos Españoles
APCS	Association of Payment Clearing Services	**APE**	Assemblée Parlementaire Européenne = EP
APCT	Association for Psychological Counselling and Training	**APE**	Associação Portuguesa de Escritores
APCT	Association of Painting Craft Teachers	**APÉ**	Association de la Presse Étrangère
APCTT	Asian and Pacific Centre for Transfer of Technology (India)	**APEA**	Asociación Peruana de Economistas Agrícolas (Peru)
APCU	ASEAN Population Coordination Unit	**APEA**	Association de la Presse Eurafricaine
APD	Alianza por la Democracia (Dominican Republic)	**APEA**	Association de la Presse Europe - Tiers Monde
APD	Asistencia Pública Domiciliaria	**APEA**	Association of Petroleum and Explosives Administration
APD	Asociación para el Progreso de la Direccion	**APEA**	Association of Professional Engineers of Alberta (Canada)
APD	Associazione Aziende Italiane Pubblicità Diretta	**APEA**	Association of Professional Engineers, Australia
APDA	Asian People with Disabilities Alliance	**APEA**	Association Parlementaire Europe-Afrique
APDA	Asian Population and Development Association (Japan)	**APEA**	Australian Petroleum Exploration Association
APDA	Association for Professionals with Diplomas in Advertising (Finland) = FUR	**APEAI**	Alliance pour l'Expansion de l'Apiculture et ses Industries

APEAL	Association Professionnelle des Producteurs Européens d'Aciers pour Emballages (Belgium)
APEBC	Association of Professional Engineers of British Columbia (Canada)
APEC	Action on Pre-Eclampsia
APEC	Asia Pacific Economic Cooperation
APEC	Asia-Pacific Economic Cooperation Council
APEC	Asociación de Industriales de Puerto Rico
APEC	Asociación Paraguaya Enseñanza Católica
APEC	Associação Portuguesa de Economistas
APEC	Associação Portuguesa de Empresas Cinematográficas
APEC	Associação Portuguesa de Estudios Clássicos
APEC	Association des Professeurs pour la Promotion de l'Education Cinematographique dans l'Enseignement Officiel
APEC	Association of Professional Ergonomics Consultancies
APEC	Association pour l'Emploi des Cadres, Ingénieurs et Techniciens
APEC	Association pour la Participation des Employeurs à l'effort de Construction
APEC	Atlantic Provinces Economic Council (Canada)
APECITA	Association pour l'Emploi des Cadres, Ingénieurs et Techniciens de l'Agriculture
APECO	Asociación de Pequeños Comerciantes (Colombia)
APECOM	Associação Portuguesa das Empresas de Conselho em Comunicacao e Relaçoes Publicas
APÉCS	Association des Propriétaires et Éleveurs de Chevaux de Selle
APED	Alliance Panafricaine des ONG pour l'Environnement et du Développement (Ivory Coast)
APEDAC	Association Pédagogique Européenne pour la Diffusion de l'Actualité (Belgium)
APEDE	Asociación Panameña de Ejecutivos de Empresas
APEDIE	Association pour la Promotion et de Développement de Idée Européenne
APEE	Association for Pediatric Education in Europe = AEPE
APÉÉE	Association des Parents d'Élèves de l'École Européenne
APEF	Asociación pour la Promotion Économique de la Femme (Burundi)
APEF	Association des Pays Exportateurs de Minéral de Fer = AIOEC
APÉF	Association Professionelle des Établissements Financiers
APEGGA	Association of Professional Engineers, Geologists and Geophysicists of Alberta (Canada)
APEHC	Association of Professional Entertainment Hire Companies
APEID	Asian Programme of Educational Innovation for Development
APEIPQ	Associação Portuguesa das Empresas Industriais de Produtos Quimicos
APEJ	Agence de Presse Européenne Juive (Belgium)
APEL	Associação Portuguesa de Editores e Livreiros
APÉL	Association des Parents d'Élèves de l'Enseignement Libre
APÉL	Societé pour le Développement des Applications de l'Électricité
APÉLA	Association pour l'Étude des Littératures Africaines
APELCU	Asociación de Poetas y Escritores Libres de Cuba
APELL	Awareness and Preparedness for Emergencies at Local Level Network (France)
APÉLUX	Association des Patrons-Électriciens du Grand-Duché de Luxembourg
APEMI	Associação Portuguesa das Empresas de Mediação Imobiliaria
APEMIPE	Asociación de Pequeños y Medianos Industriales del Peru
APEMu	Association des Professeurs d'Éducation Musicale
APENPLAN	Asian Pacific Energy Planning Network (Malaysia)
APENS	Association of Professional Engineers of Nova Scotia
APEO	Association of Professional Engineers of Ontario (Canada)
APEPA	Association pour l'Encouragement de la Productivité Agricole
APEPM	Association of Professional Engineers of the Province of Manitoba (Canada)

APEPNB	Association of Professional Engineers of the Province of New Brunswick (Canada)	**APFA**	Associated Poultry Farmers of Australia
APEPO	Association of Professional Engineers of the Province of Ontario (Canada)	**APFA**	Association des Professeurs de Français en Afrique (Sudan) = AFTA
APER	Association of Publishers Educational Representatives	**APFACA**	Association Professionelle des Fabricants d'Aliments Composés pour Animaux (Belgium)
APERU	Applied Plant Ecology Research Unit	**APFAN**	Asia Pacific Food Analysis Network (Australia)
APERU	Asociación pro Enseñanza Rural Universitaria (Argentina)	**APFAV**	Association des Producteurs Suisses de Films et de Production Audio-Visuelle
APES	Asociace producentů ekologickych systémů	**APFC**	American Plant Food Council
APES	Association of Professional Engineers of Saskatchewan (Canada)	**APFC**	Asia-Pacific Forestry Commission (FAO)
APESA	Alliance des Producteurs et Exportateurs	**APFC**	Association of Professional Fire Consultants
APESC	Asia Pacific Energy Studies Consultative Group	**APFCB**	Asian & Pacific Federation of Clinical Biochemistry
APESCA	Asociación Colombiana de Pescadores e Industriales de Pesca	**APFE**	Association des Producteurs de Fibres de Verre Européens
APESEG	Asociación Peruana de Empresas de Seguros	**APFHRM**	Asian Pacific Federation of Human Resource Management (Hong Kong)
APESS	Association des Professeurs de l'Enseignement Secondaire et Supérieur du Grand-Duché de Luxembourg	**APFIRO**	Association des Producteurs de Femelles Issues de Béliers Finnois ou Romanov
APETI	Asociación Profesional Española de Traductores e Intérpretes	**APFO&LM**	Association of Playing Fields Officers and Landscape Managers (*now* ALM)
APEV	Association pour l'Étude de l'Email Vitrifié	**APFOCC**	Asian and Pacific Federation of Organisations for Cancer Research and Control
APEX	Agricultural Produce Exchange	**APFRI**	American Physical Fitness Research Institute
APEX	Ajia Minkan Kouryu Group		
APEX	Association of Professional Executive, Clerical and Computer Staff	**APFS**	African Peasant Farming Scheme
APEX	Institute for Astrophysics and Planetary Exploration (U.S.A.)	**APFTC**	Asian-Pacific Federation of Therapeutic Communities (Thailand)
APF	Afghanistan Peace Front	**APFUCA**	Asian Pacific Federation of UNESCO Clubs and Associations
APF	Anglican Pacifist Fellowship	**APG**	Arbeitskreis Pharmazeutischer Grosshandelsverbände
APF	Asian Packaging Federation (Philippines)	**APG**	Asociación de Periodistas de Guatemala
APF	Associação Portuguesa de Fundição	**APG**	Associação Portuguesa de Geografos
APF	Association for the Propagation of the Faith	**APG**	Association of Polish Geomorphologists = SGP
APF	Association of Professional Foresters	**APG**	Association of Professional Genealogists (U.S.A.)
APF	Associazione per il Promuovimento della Foraggicoltura (Switzerland) = ADCF, AGFF	**APGA**	American Personnel and Guidance Association
APF	Azerbaijan Popular Front	**APGA**	Asociación Professional de Galerias de Arte
APF	Pontifical Association for the Propagation of the Faith	**APGAM**	Associação Profissional dos Geólogos da Amazónia (Brazil)
APFA	American Production Finishers Association		

APGI	Association de Pharmacie Galénique Industrielle
APGI	Association of Professional Genealogists in Ireland
APGMEFE	Associação Portuguesa dos Grossistas de Material Elétrico Fotográfico e Electrónico
APGO	Association of Professors of Gynecology and Obstetrics (U.S.A.)
APGO	Associazione Piemontese Grossiti Ortoflorofrutticoli
APGPL	Associação Portuguesa de Gases de Petróleo Liquefeitos
APGTRH	Associação Portuguesa de Gestores e Tecnocos de Recursos Humanos
APH	Association for Public Health
APhA	American Pharmaceutical Association
APHA	American Polled Hereford Association
APHA	American Printing History Association
APHA	American Public Health Association
APHA	Association of Port Health Authorities
APHA	Australian Pneumatic and Hydraulic Association
APHB	American Printing House for the Blind
APHB	Association Patronale Horlogerie (Switzerland)
APHCA	Regional Animal Production and Health Commission for Asia, the Far East and the South-West Pacific (FAO)
APHD	Asia Partnership for Human Development
APHEDA	Australian People for Health, Education and Development Abroad
APHG	Association des Professeurs d'Histoire et de Géographie de l'Enseignment Publique
APHI	Association of Public Health Inspectors
APHIA	Association for the Promotion of Humour in International Affairs (France)
APHIS	Animal and Plant Health Inspection Service (U.S.A.)
APHS	American Poultry Historical Society
API	Agencja Publicystyczno Informacyjna
API	Aide aux Parents Isolés
API	AMECEA Pastoral Institute (Kenya)
API	American Paper Institute
API	American Petroleum Institute
API	Arab Planning Institute (Kuwait)
API	Asociación de Personal Investigador del CSIC

API	Asociación de Publicistas Industriales (Venezuala)
API	Associação Portuguesa de Informática
API	Associated Photographers International
API	Association of Pharmaceutical Importers
API	Association of Pharmaceutical Industries (Austria) = FCIOGP
API	Association of Physicians of India
API	Association of Play Industries
API	Association of Producers of Isoglucose of the EC
API	Association Phonétique Internationale = IPA
API	Associazione Pedagogica Italiana
API	Associazione Pescicoltori Italiani
API	Associazione Pioppicoltori Italiani
API	Indonesian Textile Association
API-PME	Agence pour la Promotion Internationale (PME)
API-MONDIA	Fédération Internationale des Associations d'Apiculture
APIA	Asociación Peruana de Ingenieros Agrónomos
APIA	Association pour la Promotion de l'Information Agricole
APIC	Africa Policy Information Centre (U.S.A.)
APIC	Asian Packaging Information Centre (Hong Kong)
APIC	Association for the Promotion of International Cooperation
APIC	Association Patronale Interprofessionnelle de Colmar et de sa Région
APICA	Association pour la Promotion des Initiatives Communautaires Africaines (Cameroon)
APICCAPS	Associação Portuguesa das Industrias de Calçado Componentes e Artigos de Pele e seus Sucedaneos
APICE	Asociación Panamericana de Instituciones de Crédito Educativo = PAAECI
APICE	Associazione fra Produttori Italiani di Calcestruzzi per l'Edilizia
APICORP	Arab Petroleum Investments Corporation (OAPEC)
APICP	Association for the Promotion of the International Circulation of the Press

APICS	American Production and Inventory Control Society
APIDC	Andhra Pradesh Industrial Development Corporation (India)
APIEAS	Asociación Peruana de Instituciones de Agrícola Superior
APIF	Associação Portuguesa da Industria Farmaceutica
APIFARMA	Associação Portuguesa da Indústria Farmacêutica
APIGTP	Associação Portuguesa das Indústrais Gráficas e Transformadoras do Papel
APIIP	Association Professionelle des Importateurs Indépendants des Produits du Pétrole
APIL	Association of Pacific Island Legislatures (Guam)
APIL	Association of Personal Injury Lawyers
APIL	Associazione Psicologica Italiane del Lavoro
APIM	Associação Portuguesa das Industria de Malha
APIM	Associação Portuguesa das Industrias Mineiras
APIM	Associação Portuguesa de Informatica Medica
APIM	Association Professionelle International des Médicins
APIMA	Associazione Provinciale Imprese di Meccanizzazione Agricola
APIMO	Associazione Professionale Italiana Medici Oculisti
APINESS	Asia-Pacific Information Network in Social Sciences (Thailand)
APINMAP	Asian and Pacific Information Network on Medicinal and Aromatic Plants
APIP	Associação Portuguesa da Indústria de Plasticos
APIS	Army Photographic Intelligence Service
APIT	Association for the Promotion of International Trade (Japan)
APIT	Association of Psychiatrists in Training
APITCO	Andhra Pradesh Industrial and Technical Consultancy Organization (India)
APIZ	Alliance des Prolétaires Indépendants du Zaïre
APJBF	Association des Producteurs de Jeunes Bovins de France
APJT	Association of Psychiatrists in Training
APJT	Association Professionelle des Journalistes du Tourisme
APK	Auto Pers Klub
APKK	An Party Kenethlegek Kernow
APL	Albanian Party of Labour
APL	American Poetry League
APL	Association des Professeurs de Lettres
APL	Association for Promoting Localisation
APL	Association of Pension Lawyers
APL	Association of Photographic Laboratories (*now* PMAInt)
APL	Association of Private Libraries
APL	Association of Programmed Learning
APLA	Antillan Public Library Association
APLA	Asociación Petroquímica Latinoamericana
APLA	Association of Parliamentary Librarians of Australia
APLA	Atlantic Provinces Library Association (Canada)
APLA	Azanian People's Liberation Army (S. Africa)
APLAFA	Asociación Panamena para el Planeamiento de la Familia
APLAR	Asia Pacific League Against Rheumatism
APLC	Association of Patent Licensing Consultants (GFR)
APLE	Asociacións de Palinologues de la Lengua Española
APLESA	Aplicaciones de Energia, SA
APLET	Association for Programmed Learning and Educational Technology
APLF	Association de Palynologues de la Langue Française
APLF	Association des Pédiatres de Langue Française
APLFD	Asian-Pacific League for Freedom and Democracy
APLIC	Association of Parliamentary Librarians in Canada
APLICI	Association for Population, Family Planning Libraries and Information Centers International (U.S.A.)
APLS	American Plant Life Society
APLS	American Psychology - Law Society
APLS	Association for Politics and the Life Sciences (U.S.A.)
APLUB	Associação do Profissionais Liberais Universitarios do Brasil

APLV	Association des Professeurs de Langues Vivantes de l'Enseignement Public
APM	Associação Portuguesa de Management
APM	Association for Palliative Medicine of Great Britain and Ireland
APM	Association of Project Managers
APM	Association Peuples Menacés = GfbV
APM	Australian Paper Manufacturers
APMA	American Pharmaceutical Manufacturers' Association
APMA	American Podiatric Medical Association
APMBFP	Association de la Petite et Moyenne Brasserie Familiale de Belgique
APMC	Allied Political and Military Commission
APMC	Andhra Pradesh Mining Corporation (India)
APMC	Association of Pioneer Motorcyclists
APMD	Associação Profissional dos Médicos Dentistas (Portugal)
APME	Associated Press Managing Editors (U.S.A.)
APME	Association de Producteurs de Matières Plastiques en Europe
APMEP	Association des Professeurs de Mathématiques de l'Enseignement Public
APMH	Association of Professions for the Mentally Handicapped
APMHC	Association of Professional Material Handling Consultants (U.S.A.)
APMI	American Powder Metallurgy Institute
APMI	Association of Printing Machinery Importers
APMO	Association of Private Market Operators
APMT	Association of Professional Music Therapists in Great Britain
APN	Academy of Pedagogical Sciences (Russia)
APN	Agentstvo Pechati Novosti
APN	Armée Populaire Nationale (Congo)
APN	Assemblée Populaire Nationale (Haiti)
APN	Assembleia Popular Nacional (Sao Tomé)
APNA	Association des Professionels Naviguants de l'Aviation
APNU	Administration Postale des Nations Unies = UNPA
APO	African People's Organisation
APO	Asian Productivity Organisation
APO	Associação Portuguesa de Odontologia
APO	Australian Patents Office
APO	Australian Purchasing Officers Association
APOA	Arctic Petroleum Operators Association (Canada)
APOAC	Asia-Pacific Office Automation Control (Taiwan)
APOB	Association Professionelle des Opticiens de Belgique
APOCB	Asian-Pacific Organization for Cell Biology (Japan)
APOI	Association of Palm Oil Importers
APÖM	Arbeitsgemeinschaft für PsychoTechnik in Österreich
APOPO	Association of Professional Opinion Poll Organisations
APOQ	Association des Producteurs d'Oeufs Québécois
APORS	Association of Asian-Pacific Operational Research Societies (Japan)
APOS	Association Professionelle des Opticiens Suisses de Formation Supérieure
APP	Associated Press of Pakistan
APP	Association of Polish Papermakers = SPP
APPA	African Petroleum Producers Association (Nigeria)
APPA	Aluminium Powder and Paste Association
APPA	Aluminium Primary Producers' Association
APPA	American Physicians Poetry Association
APPA	American Professional Practice Association
APPA	American Psychopathological Association
APPA	American Public Power Association
APPA	Antigua Planned Parenthood Association
APPA	Associação Brasileira de Pesquisas sobre Plantas Aromaticas e Oleos Essenciaias
APPA	Association de Propagande pour les Produits Agricoles
APPA	Association des Pilotes et Propriétaires d'Aéronefs

APPA	Association pour la Prévention de la Pollution Atmosphérique
APPAC	Aviation Petroleum Products Allocation Committee
APPAM	Association for Public Policy Analysis and Management (U.S.A.)
APPAVÉ	Association Parisienne des Propriétaires d'Appareils à Vapeur et Électriques
APPC	Associação Portuguesa de Projectistats e Consultores
APPC	Associação Portuguesa para o Progresso das Ciencia
APPCB	Association Professionelle de la Presse Cinématographique Belge
APPCN	Association des Pays Producteurs de Caoutchouc Naturel = ANRPC
APPCo	Association of Post Production Companies
APPE	Association for Practical and Professional Ethics
APPE	Association of Petrochemical Producers in Europe
APPEAL	Asia-Pacific Programme of Education for All (UNESCO)
APPEN	Asia-Pacific People's Environment Network (Malaysia)
APPI	International Association for the Promotion and Protection of Private Foreign Investments
APPIC	ASEAN Paper & Pulp Industry Club
APPIE	Amicale des Prisonniers Politiques et Internés d'Espagne
APPIMAF	Association pour la Protection de la Propriété Industrielle dans le Monde Arabe (Syria)
APPITA	Australian and New Zealand Pulp and Paper Industry Technical Association
APPM	Association of Publication Production Managers (U.S.A.)
APPM	Australian Pulp and Paper Mills
APPMA	American Pet Products Manufacturers Association
APPMSA	American Pulp and Paper Mills Superintendents' Association
APPP	Association of Planned Parenthood Physicians (U.S.A.)
APPPC	Asia Pacific Plant Protection Commission
APPPC	Asian Pulp and Paper and Paper-Products Council (Taiwan)
APPRO-TECH ASIA	Asian Alliance of Appropriate Technology Practitioners
APPS	Association pour la Promotion des Publications Scientifiques (Belgium)
APPS	Australian Plant Pathology Society
APPSA	Asian-Pacific Political Science Association (Thailand)
APPSGAN	Asian Pan-Pacific Association of Gastroenterology and Nutrition (Australia)
APPSS	Association of Police and Public Security Suppliers
APPTC	Asian-Pacific Postal Training Centre (Thailand)
APPTEA	Asia Pacific Physics Teachers and Educators Association (Philippines)
APPU	Asian-Pacific Parliamentarians Union
APPU	Asian-Pacific Postal Union
APPU	Australian Primary Producers' Union
APQCO	Asia Pacific Quality Control Organization (Philippines)
APQI	Associação Portuguesa para a Qualidade Industrial
APR	Agrarian Party of Russia
APR	Association for Promoting Retreats
APR	Association of Petroleum Re-refiners (U.S.A.)
APRA	Air Public Relations Association
APRA	Alianza Popular Revolucionaria Americana (Peru) = PAP
APRA	American Petroleum Refiners Association
APRA	Asian Peace Research Assocation
APRA	Associazione Provinciale Romana Albergatori
APRA	Australian Performing Rights Association
APRA	Australian Plastics Research Association
APRAC	Air Pollution Research Advisory Committee (U.S.A.)
APRACA	Asian and Pacific Regional Agricultural Credit Association
APRAGAZ	Assocation des Propriétaires de Récipients à Gaz Comprimés (Belgium)
APRCG	Asia Pacific Railway Cooperation Group
APRE	Alianza Popular Revolucionaria Ecuatoriana

APRÉFA	Association pour la Promotion des Recherches et Études Foncières en Afrique	**APROFE**	Asociación Probienestar de la Familia Ecuatoriana
APREP	Associação Portuguesa de Relações Publicas	**APROFIET**	Asian and Pacific Regional Organisation (FIET)
APRES	American Peanut Research and Education Society	**APROF-ONO**	Asociación Centroamericana de Productores Fonograficos (Costa Rica)
APRG	Air Pollution Research Group (South Africa)	**APROH**	Asociación para el Progreso de Honduras
APRI	African Peace Research Institute (Nigeria)	**APROMA**	Association des Produits à Marché Communauté Économique Européenne / Afrique - Caraïbes - Pacifique
APRI	Association pour la Protection contre les Rayonnements Ionisants	**APROPACA**	Asociación Venezolana de Productores de Pulpa, Papel y Carton
APRIA	Association pour la Promotion Industrie-Agriculture	**APROSC**	Agricultural Projects Services Centre (Nepal)
APRIGA	Agence pour la Promotion Industrielle de la Guadeloupe	**APROSE**	Associação Portuguesa dos Produtores de Seguros
APRISA	Ahorro Prestamos e Inversiones (El Salvador)	**APROTE-RRA**	Associação dos Proprietários de Terras Vizinhas às Reservas Indígenas (Brazil)
APRISA	Asociación de Ahorros Prestamos, Inversiones, S.A. (El Salvador)	**APRP**	Asociación Profesional de Relaciones Publicas (Spain)
APRL	Association for the Preservation of Rural Life	**APRR**	Association for Planning and Regional Reconstruction
APRO	Aerial Phenomena Research Organization (U.S.A.)	**APRS**	American Performing Rights Society
APRO	Airline Public Relations Organisation	**APRS**	Association for the Protection of Rural Scotland
APRO	Asian Pacific Regional Organisation (ICFTU)	**APRS**	Association of Professional Recording Studios
APRO-MAQUINA	Asociación Colombiana de Productores de Maquinas para Oficina	**APRS**	Australian Pattern Recognition Society
APRO-MUJER	Asociación Programa Nacional de Asesoria y Capacitacion para la Mujer Cooperativista (Costa Rica)	**APRU**	American Pigeon Racing Union
		APRU	Applied Psychology Research Unit (MRC)
APROBA	Association Professionelle pour l'Accroissement de la Productivité dans l'Industrie du Bâtiment	**APS**	Aborigines Protection Society
		APS	Acción Política Socialista (Peru)
APROB-ANA	Asociación de Productores Bananeros del Ecuador	**APS**	Agence Presse Sénégalaise
		APS	Algérie Presse Service
APRODÉC	Association pour la Promotion et la Diffusion des Études Créoles	**APS**	All Africa Press Service (Kenya)
		APS	American Peace Society
APRODEV	Association of Protestant Development Organizations in Europe (Belgium)	**APS**	American Pediatric Society
		APS	American Philatelic Society
APROFA	Asociación Chilena da Proteccion de la Familia	**APS**	American Philosophical Society
		APS	American Physical Society
APROFA	Associazione Provinciale Romana Organisini Facchinaggio	**APS**	American Physiological Society
		APS	American Phytopathological Society
APROFAM	Asociación Probienestar de la Familia de Guatemala	**APS**	American Polar Society
		APS	American Pomological Society
		APS	American Primrose Society
APROFAR	Asociación Profesional Española de Empresarios de Farmacia	**APS**	American Proctologic Society
		APS	American Prosthodontic Society

APS	American Psychological Society		**APSCE**	Association of Professional Staffs in Colleges of Education (Éire)
APS	American Psychosomatic Society		**APSDEP**	Asian and Pacific Skill Development Program
APS	Association de la Presse Suisse			
APS	Association of Pacific Systematists (U.S.A.)		**APSDIN**	Asian and Pacific Skill Development Information Network (Pakistan)
APS	Association of Plastics Societies		**APSE**	Asociación de Profesores de Segunda Enseñanza (Costa Rica)
APS	Association of Police Surgeons (*ex* APSGB)		**APSF**	Australian Pacific Science Foundation
APS	Association of Productivity Specialists		**APSF**	Australian Public Service Federation
APS	Association of Professional Staff (FAO/WFP)		**APSFC**	Andhra Pradesh State Financial Corporation (India)
APS	Association Patronale des Serigraphes (Switzerland)		**APSFO**	Association of Public Service Finance Officers
APS	Associazione Pubblicità Stampa		**APSG**	Association pour le Socialisme au Gabon
APS	Assoziazione per la Partecipazione allo Sviluppo		**APSG**	Australian Plant Specialists Group (IUCN)
APS	Australian Photogrammetric Society		**APSGB**	Association of Police Surgeons of Great Britain (*now* APS)
APS	Australian Psychological Society			
APS	Australian Public Service		**APSI**	Asian Pacific Statistical Institute (Japan)
APSA	Aerolineas Peruanas S.A.		**APSIA**	Association of Professional Schools of International Affairs (US)
APSA	African Purchasing and Supply Association		**APSIB**	Association Professionelle des Sociétiés Immobilières en Belgique
APSA	American Political Science Association			
APSA	Association for the Psychiatric Study of Adolescents		**APSLF**	Association de Psychologie Scientifique de Langue Française
APSA	Association of Payroll and Superannuation Administrators		**APSLLMD**	Association Professionelle Suisse des Laborantines et Laborants Médicaux Diplômés = SFDMLL
APSA	Association of Point of Sale Advertising			
APSA	Association of Professionals in Services for Adolescents		**APSM**	Association de Préhistoire et de Spéléologie de Monaco
APSA	Australian Pharmaceutical Science Association		**APSM**	Association for Physical and System Mathematics (U.S.A.)
APSA	Australian Political Studies Association		**APSO**	Afro-Asian Peoples' Solidarity Organisation
APSA	Australian Public Service Association		**APSO**	Agency for Personal Service Overseas (Éire)
APSA	Azufrera Panamericana,S.A. (Mexico)			
APsaA	American Psychoanalytic Association		**APSO**	Asia-Pacific Socialist Organization
APSACI	Associazione Piemontese degli Spedizionieri Autotrasportatori Corrieri e Ippotrasportatori		**APSP**	Agencja Powiernicza Skarbu Pa«nstwa
			APSRD	Association Professionelle des Exploitants de Services Réguliers Routiers de Transports de Détail
APSAI	Assemblée Plénière des Sociétiés d'Assurances contre l'Incendie			
APSAS	Association of Public Service Administrative Staff (*now* IPSA)		**APSRU**	Agricultural Production Systems Research Unit
APSC	Arab Petroleum Services Company (OAPEC)		**APSS**	Associação de Profissionais de Servicio Social (Portugal)
APSC	Asian-Pacific Society of Cardiology		**APSS**	Association for the Psychophysiological Study of Sleep (U.S.A.)
APSC	Association des Producteurs de Semence du Canada		**APSSEAR**	Association of Pediatric Societies of the Southeast Asian Region

APST	Association of Professional Scientists and Technologists		**APU**	Arab Postal Union = UPA
APSTC	Andhra Pradesh State Road Transport Corporation (India)		**APU/ATU**	African Postal and Telecommunications Union = UPA
APSW	Association for the Promotion of the Status of Women (Thailand)		**APUA**	Alliance for the Prudent Use of Antibiotics (U.S.A.)
APT	Asia Pacific Telecommunity		**APUA**	Association du Peuple pour l'Unité et l'Action (Algeria)
APT	Association for Practical Theology (U.S.A.)		**APUC**	Association for Promoting the Unity of Christendom
APT	Association for Preservation Technology		**APUMAG**	Asociación de Profesionales Universitarios del Ministerio de Agricultura y Ganaderia de la Nación (Argentina)
APT	Association of Pensioneer Trustees			
APT	Association of Personal Trainers			
APT	Association of Polytechnic Teachers			
APT	Association of Professional Therapists		**APUR**	Atelier Parisien d'Urbanisme
APT	Association of Psychiatrists in Training		**APV**	Arbeitsgemeinschaft für Pharmazeutische VerfahrensTechnik
APT	United Kingdom Association of Preservation Trusts		**APV**	Association de Propagande pour le Vin
APTA	American Physical Therapy Association		**APV**	Associazione Italiana Promozione Vendite e Pubblicità Punto Vendite
APTA	American Public Transit Association			
APTA	Asian Pineapple Traders Association		**APVC**	Association Protestante des Volontaires de la Coopération (Belgium)
APTA	Asociación de la Prensa Técnica Argentina		**APVD**	Association of Professional Video Distributors
APTA	Assocation pour la Promotion du Tourisme d'Affaires		**APVIC**	Association of Principals of Sixth Form Colleges
APTF	Associação Portuguesa de Terapeutas da Fala		**APVSCC**	Association of Principals of Vocational Schools and Community Colleges (Éire)
APTI	Arab Petroleum Training Institute		**APW**	Association of Printings and Writings
APTI	Association of Principals of Technical Institutions (Éire)		**APWA**	All Pakistan Women's Association
APTI	Associazione Produttori Tabacchi Italiani		**APWA**	American Public Welfare Association
			APWA	American Public Works Association
APTIC	African Pyrethrum Technical Information Centre		**APWLD**	Asia Pacific Forum on Women, Law and Development (Malaysia)
APTIRC	Asian Pacific Tax and Investment Research Centre		**APWSS**	Asian-Pacific Weed Science Society
APTLF	Association de Psychologie du Travail de Langue Française		**APYEF**	Asia-Pacific Youth Environmental Federation
APTO	Association of Psychiatric Treatment of Offenders		**APYF**	Asian Pacific Youth Forum
APTS	Association for the Prevention of Theft in Shops		**APYFL**	Asian Pacific Youth Freedom League (Republic of Korea)
APTS	Association of Primary Teaching Sisters (Éire)		**AQA**	Asociación Quimica Argentina
APTT	Association of Package Tour Travellers		**AQC**	Alaska Quaternary Center
APTU	Australian Postal and Telecommunications Union		**AQCH**	Association of Qualified Curative Hypnotherapists
APU	Aliança Povo Unido (Portugal)		**AQIS**	Australian Quarantine and Inspection Service
APU	Angkatan Perpaduan Ummah (Malaysia)		**AQMC**	Association of Quality Management Consultants
APU	Applied Psychology Unit (of MRC)		**AQRP**	Association of Qualitative Research Practitioners
			AQS	Association des Quincailliers Suisses

AQTE	Association Québécoise des Techniques de l'Eau (Canada)
AQUA	European Association of Water Meter Manufacturers
AQUA-EUROPA	Fédération Européenne du Traitement de l'Eau
AQUAM	Société Camérounaise d'Aquaculture
AQUREB	Aquatic Research Board
ARA	Accommodation for Recovery from Addiction
ARA	Aerial Ropeways Association
ARA	Aerospace Research Association (U.S.A.)
ARA	Aircraft Research Association
ARA	Amateur Riders' Association of Great Britain
ARA	Amateur Rocket Association (U.S.A.)
ARA	Amateur Rowing Association
ARA	American Revenue Association
ARA	American Rheumatism Association
ARA	American Rowing Association
ARA	American Royal Association
ARA	Anti-Racist Alliance
ARA	Arbeitsgemeinschaft Regenwald und Artenschutz
ARA	Armada de la Republica Argentina
ARA	Asian Recycling Association
ARA	Association of Relocation Agents
ARA	Association of River Authorities
ARA	Australian Robot Association
ARA	Les Amis de la Reliure
ARA	Society of American Registered Architects
ARAB	Académie Royale d'Archeologie Belgique
ARAB	Association Royale des Actuaires Belges = KVBA
Arab AIPU	Arab Inter-Parliamentary Union (Syria) = UIPA
AraBN	Arab Biosciences Network (Jordan)
ARABOSAI	Arab Organisation of Supreme Audit Institutions (Tunisia)
ARABSAT	Arab Satellite Communications Organization (Saudi Arabia)
ARAB-TERM	Arab Information Network for Terminology (Tunisia)
ARAC	Associação dos Industriais de Automóveis de Aluguer Sem Condutor
ARADO	Arab Administrative Development Organization (Jordan)
ARAF	Associated Regional Accounting Firms (U.S.A.)
Arafertil	Industria de Fertilizantes Araxa (Brazil)
ARAHE	Asian Regional Association for Home Economics
ARAI	Automotive Research Association of India
ARAL	Association to Repeal Abortion Laws (U.S.A.)
ARAM	Association of Railroad Advertising and Marketing (U.S.A.)
ARAMCO	Arabian-American Oil Company
ARAN	Associação do Ramo Automóvel do Norte
ARAN	Association for the Reduction of Aircraft Noise
ARANZ	Archives and Records Association of New Zealand
ARAR	Azienda Rilievo Alienazione Residuati
ARARI	Agean Regional Agricultural Research Institute (Turkey)
ARAS	Associação dos Reparadores de Automóveis do Sul
ARASWE	Asian Regional Association for Social Work Education
Aratrans	Arab Transport Company (Kuwait)
ARAVS	Asian Regional Association for Voluntary Sterilisation (India)
ARB	Airworthiness Requirements Board
ARB	Animal Rights Bureau
ARB	Armée Révolutionnaire Bretonne
ARB	Associação Rio-Grandense de Bibliotecários
ARB	Assotsiatsiya Rossiiskikh Bankov
ARBA	Amateur Rose Breeders' Association
ARBA	American Rabbit Breeders Association
ARBÉ	Académie Royale des Beaux-Arts et École Supérieure d'Architecture de Bruxelles
ARBE	Arbeitsgemeinschaft Bekleidungs Industrie
ARBEF	Association Rwandaise pour le Bien-Être Familial
ARBICA	Arab Regional Branch of the International Council on Archives
ARBIT	Arbeitsgemeinschaft der Bitumen-Industrie
ARBM	Association of Radio Battery Manufacturers
ARBRA	Associação Brasileira da Empresa do Reflorestamento
ARBS	Association for the Recognition of Business Schools

ARBS	Association pour la Recherche en Bioénergie Solaire	**ARCA**	American Rehabilitation Counseling Association
ARBUS	Arbeitnehmer- Radio- und Fernsehbund der Schweiz	**ARCA**	Asbestos Removal Contractors Association
ARC	Action for Renewal of the Church (Trinidad)	**ARCASIA**	Architects Regional Council for Asia (CAA)
ARC	Action Resource Centre	**ARCC**	African Regional Computer Confederation (Zambia)
ARC	Aeronautical Research Committee (CSIR) (India)	**ARCC**	African Regional Coordinating Committee for the Integration of Women in Development (Ethiopia)
ARC	Agricultural Refinance Corporation (India)		
ARC	Agricultural Research Centre (Egypt)	**ARCCA**	Agricultural Research Council of Central Africa
ARC	Agricultural Research Council		
ARC	Algerian Revolutionary Committee	**ARCCOH**	Asian Regional Coordinating Committee on Hydrology
ARC	Alliance Révolutionnaire Caraïbe (Guadeloupe)	**ARCE**	Associazione per le Relazioni Culturali con l'Estero
ARC	Animal Resources Centre	**ARCEA**	Association pour la Route Centre Europe-Atlantique
ARC	Animal Rights Coalition		
ARC	Anthropological Research Council	**ARCEDEM**	African Regional Centre for Engineering Design and Manufacturing (Nigeria) = CRACFT
ARC	Applied Research Corporation (Singapore)		
ARC	Arab Research Centre	**ARCES**	Association des Chargés de Communication de l'Enseignement Supérieur (France)
ARC	Architects Registration Council		
ARC	Arthritis and Rheumatism Council for Research in Great Britain and the Commonwealth	**ARCESP**	Associação Brasileira de Vendedores
		ARCH	Advice & Rights Centre for the Handicapped
ARC	Asbestosis Research Council		
ARC	Asociatia Româna pentru Calitate	**ARCH**	Association of Recreation Clubs for the Handicapped (Éire)
ARC	Association de Restauratrices et Cuisinières		
		ARCHI	Asociación de Radiodifusoras de Chile
ARC	Association for Residential Care	**ARCI**	Association de Recherche Coopérative Internationale
ARC	Association of Registered Childminders		
ARC	Association of Residential Communities for the Retarded	**ARCI**	Atelier de Rectification de Côte-d'Ivoire
		ARCIC	Anglican-Roman Catholic International Commission
ARC	Association of Rover Clubs Ltd		
ARC	Association pour la Recherche sur le Cancer	**ARCIS**	Africa Regional Centre for Information Science
ARC	Association Romande des Conseils en Publicité (Switzerland)	**ARCM**	Agricultural Research Council of Malawi
ARC	Assurances et Réassurances du Congo	**ARCN**	Agricultural Research Council of Norway
ARC	Asthma Research Council		
ARC	Asylum Rights Campaign	**ARCOA**	Asociación Rosarina de Criadores de Ovejeros Alemanes (Argentina)
ARC	Atlantis Research Centre		
ARC	Atma Jaya Research Center (Indonesia)	**ARCON**	Arctic Construction Company (Alaska)
ARC	Australian Research Council	**ARCOS**	Anglo-Russian Co-operative Society
ARC	Groupe Arc-en-Ciel	**ARCRL**	Agricultural Research Council Radiobiological Laboratory
ARC	Laboratory of Aquaculture and Artemia Reference Centre (Belgium)		
		ARCSS	UNESCO Centre for Social Science Research and Documentation of the Arab Region (Egypt)
ARC	Regional Conference for Africa (FAO)		
ARCA	Adult Residential Colleges Association		

ARCT	African Regional Centre for Technology (Senegal) = CRAT	**ARE**	Association of Religious in Education
ARCUK	Architects Registration Council of the United Kingdom	**AREA**	Aerovias Ecuatorianas, CA
		AREA	Airconditioning and Refrigeration European Association (Belgium)
ARD	American Radium Society	**AREA**	American Railway Engineering Association
ARD	Arbeitsgemeinschaft der Öffentlich-Rechtlichen Rundfunkanstalten der Bundesrepublik Deutschland	**AREA**	American Recreational Equipment Association
ARD	Association of Research Directors (U.S.A.)	**AREA**	Associação dos Armazenistas Refinadores e Exportadores de Azeite
ARDA	Action for Rational Drugs in Asia (Malaysia)	**AREA**	Association for Research and Environmental Aid (Australia)
ARDA	Agricultural and Rural Development Act (Canada)	**AREA**	Associazione Romana Esercenti Autorimesse
ARDA	American Railway Development Association	**AREA**	Australian Remedial Education Association
ARDA	Canadian Agricultural Rehabilitation and Development Association	**ARÉC**	Amitié Rurale des Étudiants Catholiques
ARDB	Australian Resources Development Bank	**AREC**	Arab Engineering Company (OAPEC)
ARDC	Agricultural and Rural Development Corporation (Burma)	**ARECSO**	Atelier de Rectification du Sud-Ouest (Ivory Coast)
ARDC	Agricultural Refinance and Development Corporation (India)	**AREG**	Antarctic Research Evaluation Group
ARDC	U.S. Air Research and Development Command	**AREK**	Amika Rondo de Esperantoj-Kolektantoj = ELF
ARDCS	Association of Rural District Council Surveyors	**ARELA**	Asociación de Reaseguradores Latinoamericanos (Uruguay)
ARDE	Alianza Revolucionaria Democrática (Nicaragua)	**ARELS-FELCO**	Association of Recognized English Language Schools; Federation of English Language Course Organisations
ARDE	Associazione Romana di Entomologia	**AREMA**	Avant-Garde de la Révolution Malgache (Madagascar)
ARDECO	Aluminium Resources Development Co. (Japan)		
ARDÉS	Association pour la Recherche Démographique, Économique et Sociale (Algeria)	**AREN**	Animal Rights Education Network
		ARENA	Alianza Republicana Nacionalista (El Salvador)
ARDI	Association of Registered Driving Instructors	**ARENA**	Asian Regional Exchange for New Alternatives (Hong Kong)
ARDI	Aviation Research and Development Institute (Belgium)	**ARÉR**	Association Régionale d'Économie Rurale
ARDIC	Association pour la Recherche et la Développement en Informatique Chimique	**ARÉRS**	Association Régionale pour l'Étude et la Recherche Scientifiques
		ARÉS	Association Sorgem pour la Recherche Économique et Sociale
ARE	Arbeitsgemeinschaft Regionaler Energie-versorgungs- Unternehmen	**ARÉSA**	Association pour le Recherche sur l'Énergie Solaire en Algérie
ARE	Assemblée des Régions d'Europe = AER	**ARETO**	Arab Republic of Egypt Telecommunications Organization
ARE	Association for Recurrent Education		
ARE	Association for Religious Education (U.S.A.)	**AREUEA**	American Real Estate and Urban Economics Association
ARE	Association for Research and Enlightenment (U.S.A.)	**ARF**	Advertising Research Foundation (U.S.A.)

ARF	Aeronautical Research Foundation (U.S.A.)	**ARI**	African Rehabilitation Institute (Zimbabwe)
ARF	Agricultural Research Foundation (U.S.A.)	**ARI**	Agricultural Research Institute (U.S.A.)
ARF	Alliance of Reform Forces (Bosnia-Hercegovina, Macedonia)	**ARI**	Aluminum Research Institute (U.S.A.)
ARF	Alliance of Reformed Forces (Yugoslavia-Montenegro)	**ARI**	American Refractories Institute
ARF		**ARI**	Animal Research Institute (Ghana)
ARF	Armenian Revolutionary Federation (Lebanon)	**ARI**	Asian Rural Institute (Japan)
ARF	ASEAN Regional Forum	**ARIA**	Accounting Researchers International Association
ARF	Asian Rowing Federation (China)	**ARIA**	Adult Reading Improvement Association (U.S.A.)
ARF	Association of Rehabilitation Facilities (U.S.A.)	**ARIA**	American Risk and Insurance Association
ARF	Autoriserte Reklambyåers Forening	**ARIAC**	Agricultural Research Institute and Agricultural College (South Africa)
ARFA	Allied Radio Frequency Agency (NATO)	**ARIAD**	Association pour la Recherche Information Aide Développement
ARFE	Association des Régions Frontalières Européennes = AEBR, AGEG, WVEG	**ARIAH**	Art Research Institute of Anhui (China)
ARFM	Alliance of Reform Forces for Montenegro	**ARIB**	Africa Research and Information Bureau
ARFU	Asian Rugby Football Union	**ARIC**	Association pour la Recherche Interculturelle (Switzerland)
ARGAS	Arabian Geophysical and Surveying Company (Saudi Arabia)	**ARIC**	Association Régionale d'Information Communale
ARGB	Association Royale des Gaziers Belges = KVBG	**ARIC**	Atmospheric Research & Information Centre
ARGC	Australian Research Grants Committee	**ARICD**	American Research Institute for Community Development
ARGCI	Agence de Representation Générale en Côte d'Ivoire	**ARICN**	Asian Regional Irrigation Communication Network
ARGE	Arbeitsgemeinschaft der Europäischen Schloss- und Beschlag-Industrie	**ARIDHE**	Arab Institute for the Development of Higher Education (Lebanon)
ARGE	Arbeitsgemeinschaft MeeresTechnik	**ARIE**	Associazione Ristoranti Italiani all'Estero
ARGE	Arbeitsgemeinschaft zur Förderung des Biologischen Landbaues	**ARIEL**	Asociación Reformista Independiente de Estudiantes de Letras (Peru)
ARGE	European Federation of Associations of Lock and Builders Hardware Manufacturers	**ARIFO**	Arab Industrial Information Bank (Iraq)
		ARIG	Arab Insurance Group (Bahrain)
ARGE ALP	Association des Régions des Alpes Centrales (Austria)	**ARILAIT**	Association pour la Recherche dans l'Industrie du Lait
ARGF	Automobildel- og Rekvisita-Grossistenes Forening	**ARIMA**	Association of Religious Institutes of Malawi
ARGK	Peoples Liberation Army of Kurdistan	**ARIMCI**	Automation Research Institute, Ministry of Chemical Industry (China)
ARGR	Association for Research in Growth Relationships (U.S.A.)	**ARIMMI**	Automation Research Institute, Ministry of Metallurgical Industry (China)
ARGS	American Rock Garden Society	**ARINFO**	Arab Industrial Information Bank
ARHA	American Rural Health Association	**ARINI**	Agricultural Research Institute of Northern Ireland
ARHAG	African Refugee Housing Action Group Ltd	**ARIOD**	Association pour la Recherche Informatisée et l'Organisation Documentaire
ARHS	Australian Railway Historical Society		
ARI	Acupuncture Research Institute (U.S.A.)		

ARIP	Alliance for the Rights of Indigenous Peoples	**ARLLF**	Académie Royale de Langue et de Littérature Française
ARIP	Association pour la Recherche et l'Intervention Psychosociologiques	**ARLO**	Arab Literacy and Adult Education Organization
ARIPO	African Regional Industrial Property Organisation (Zimbabwe)	**ARLOV**	Associazione Romana Locali con Orchestra, Varietà e Ballo
ARIS	Agrarian Research Intelligence Service (Italy)	**ARLP**	Authentic Radical Liberal Party (Paraguay) = PLRA
ARIS	Alcohol Research Information Service (U.S.A.)	**ARLT**	Association for the Reform of Latin Teaching
ARIS	Associazione Religiosi Istituti Spedalieri	**ARM**	African Reparations Movement
ARISBR	Asian Regional Institute for School Building Research	**ARM**	Afrikaner Resistance Movement = AWB
ARISE	Associates for Research into the Science of Enjoyment	**ARM**	Alliance of Radical Methodists
ARISF	Association of IOC-Recognised International Sports Federations	**ARM**	Alliance Reformée Mondiale = WARC
		ARM	Animal Rights Militia
ARIST	Agences Régionales de l'Information Scientifique et Technique	**ARM**	Aryan Resistance Movement
		ARM	Association de Recherche en Micro-biologie
ARIT	American Research Institute in Turkey	**ARM**	Association for the Rights of the Mentally Handicapped (Éire)
ARJA	Association Suisse Romande des Journalistes de l'Aéronautique et de l'Astronautique	**ARM**	Association of Radical Methodists
		ARM	Association of Radical Midwives
ARJES	Association des Rédacteurs de Journaux d'Entreprise de Suisse = SPRV	**ARM**	Association of Rooflight Manufacturers
		ARMA	Aluminium Radiator Manufacturers' Association
ARK	Animal Research Kills		
ARK	Ark Environmental Foundation	**ARMA**	American Rock Mechanics Association
ARKISYST	World Information System on Architecture and Urban Planning (UNESCO)	**ARMA**	Association of Records Managers and Administrators (U.S.A.)
		ARMA	Association of Residential Managing Agents
ARL	Admiralty Research Laboratory		
ARL	Aeronautical Research Laboratories (Australia, U.S.A.)	**ARMA**	Australian Rubber Manufacturers Association
ARL	Akademie für Raumsforschung und Landesplanung	**ARMA-LIBERI**	Associazione Armatori Liberi
ARL	Arabian Research Ltd (Cyprus)	**ARMB**	Académie Royale de Médécine de Belgique
ARL	Association of Research Libraries (U.S.A.)	**ARMCANZ**	Agricultural and Resource Management Council of Australia and New Zealand (ex AAC)
ARL	Australian Radiation Laboratory		
ARL	Autonrengasliitto	**ARMEF**	Association pour la Rationalisation et la Mécanisation de l'Exploitation Forestière
ARLA	Association of Residential Letting Agents		
ARLA-BANK	Banco Arabe Latinoamericano (Peru)	**ARMO**	Servicio Nacional de Adiestramiento Rápido de la Manode Obra en la Industria (Mexico)
ARLAC	African Regional Labour Administration Centre (Cameroon) = CRADAT	**ARMS**	Action for Research into Multiple Sclerosis
ARLC	All-Russia Labour Conference	**ARMS**	All-Russian Musical Society = SMR
ARLIS	Art Libraries Society (Australia, Éire, New Zealand, North America, U.K.)	**ARMS**	Amateur Radio Mobile Society

ARMS	Association of Researchers in Medicine and Science	**ARP**	Asociación de Radiodifusoras del Perú
ARMSA	Asian Regional Medical Students Association	**ARP**	Association of Retired Persons over 50
		ARP	Australian Republican Party
ARMSCOR	Armaments Development and Production Corporation (South Africa)	**ARPA**	Aluminium Rolled Products Association
ARN	Americas Resistance Network	**ARPA**	Asociación de Radiofusoras Privadas Argentinas
ARN	Association of Rehabilitation Nurses (U.S.A.)	**ARPA**	Associação dos Retalhistas de Produtos Alimentares do Distrito de Lisboa
ARN	Association pour la Renovation de la Noyeraie	**ARPANET**	Advanced Research Projects Agency Network (U.S.A.)
ARNI	Animal Rights National Index	**ARPCCA**	Association for Regional Parks and Countryside Commissions of Australia
ARNM	African Regional Network for Microbiology (Nigeria)	**ARPDP**	Association of Rehabilitation Programs in Data Processing (U.S.A.)
ARNMD	Association for Research in Nervous and Mental Diseases (U.S.A.)	**ARPE**	American Registry of Professional Entomologists
ARNO	Association of Royal Navy Officers	**ARPEL**	Asistencia Reciproca Petrolera Estatal Latinoamericana (Uruguay)
ARNTRA	Arthritis & Rheumatism Natural Therapy Research Association	**ARPLA**	Asian and Pacific Project for Labour Administration (Thailand)
ARO	Afrikagruppernas Rekryteringsorganisation	**ARPLOÉV**	Association des Rééducation de la Parole, du Langage Oral et Écrit et de la Voix
ARO	Agricultural Research Organisation (Israel)		
ARO	Army Research Office (U.S.A.)	**ARPMA**	Aluminium Rolled Products Manufacturers Association
ARO	Asian Regional Organisation	**ARPS**	Arab Physical Society (Lebanon)
ARO	Association for Research in Otolaryngology	**ARPS**	Association of Railway Preservation Societies
ARODFI	Afghan Raisin and Other Dried Fruits Institute	**ARPS**	Australian Royal Photographic Society
ARoENd	Asociatia Româna de Examinari Nedistructive	**ARR**	Association for Radiation Research
		ARRA	Amateur Radio Retailers Association
AROÉVÉN	Association Régionale des Oeuvres Éducatives et des Vacancies de l'Éducation Nationale	**ARRAG**	Anti-Racist Response and Action Group
		ARRB	Australian Road Research Board
AROL	Associazione Regionale Ospedali del Lazio	**ARRC**	Allied Rapid Reaction Corps (NATO)
		ARRC	Association of Road Racing Clubs
AROMA	Groupement des Fabricants d'Essences, Huiles Essentielles, Extraits, Produits Chimiques, Aromatiques et Colorants (Belgium)	**ARRCO**	Association des Régimes de Retraites Complémentaires
		ARRDO	Australian Railway Research and Development Organisation
AROMAR	Romanian Marketing Association	**ARREND-AVEN**	Arrendadora Industrial Venezolana, C.A.
AROWF	Association of Retailer Owned Wholesalers in Foodstuffs = UGAL, UGEL	**ARRG**	Association for Research into Restricted Growth (*now* RGA)
ARP	Agence Rwandaise de Presse	**ARRI**	Aboriginal Rural Resource Initiative
ARP	Agencja Rozwoju Przemysłu	**ARRI**	Automation and Robotics Research Institute (U.S.A.)
ARP	Albanian Republican Party = PRS		
ARP	Alcohol Recovery Project	**ARRL**	American Radio Relay League
ARP	Alternativa Revolucionaria del Pueblo (Bolivia)	**ARROW**	Active Resistance to the Roots of War
		ARROW	Asian-Pacific Research Centre for Women

ARRP	Animal Research Review Panel
ARRRI	Alligator Rivers Region Research Institute
ARRS	Aerospace Rescue and Recovery Service (U.S.A.)
ARRS	American Roentgen Ray Society
ARRU	Alligator Rivers Research Unit
ARS	American Radium Society
ARS	American Relief Society
ARS	American Rhinologic Society
ARS	American Rhododendron Society
ARS	Armenian Relief Society (U.S.A.)
ARSAC	Administration of Radioactive Substances Advisory Committee (DOH)
ARSAP	Agricultural Requisites Scheme for Asia and the Pacific
ARSBA	American Rambouillet Sheep Breeders Association
ARSC	Académie Royale des Sciences Coloniales (Belgium)
ARSC	African Remote Sensing Council (Mali) = CAT
ARSC	Association for Recorded Sound Collections (U.S.A.)
ARSC	Association for Research into Stammering in Childhood
ARSFC	Australian Recreation and Sport Fishing Confederation
ARSI	Amateur Radio Society of Ireland
ARSO	African Regional Standards Organization (Kenya) = ORAN
ARSO	Autorité pour l'Aménagement de la Région du Sud-Ouest (Ivory Coast)
ARSOM	Académie Royale des Sciences d'Outremer (Belgium)
ARSUBA	Société Française d'Archéologie Sub-Aquatique
ART	Agency for Rural Transformation (Grenada)
ART	Asociación de Relaciones de Trabajo de Venezuela
ARTA	American River Touring Association
ARTA	Autorité de la Route Trans-Africaine = TAHA
ARTAC	Association of Retail Travel Agents Consortia
ARTDO	Asian Regional Training and Development Organization
ARTEMAT	Chambre Syndicale Belge des Détaillants Spécialisés en Matériel pour le Dessin, les Beaux-Arts, les Arts Appliqués
ARTEP	Asian Regional Team for Employment Promotion
ARTF	Australian Road Transport Federation
ARTFP	Association de Recherche sur les Techniques de Forage et de Production
ARTGL-ACE	Confédération des Associations des Artisans Glaciers de la Communauté Européenne
ARTHENA	Association pour la Diffusion de l'Histoire de l'Art (France)
ARTI	Aeronautical Research and Test Institute (Czech Republic)
ARTI	Agrarian Research and Training Institute (Sri Lanka)
ARTI	Association of Remedial Teachers of Ireland
Article 19	International Centre Against Censorship
ARTL	Association for the Reform of Latin Teaching
ARTP	Association of Reclaimed Textile Processors
ARTSM	Association of Road Traffic Sign Makers
ARTU	African Radio and Television Union
ARU	Alliance of Ruthenians and Ukrainians (Serbia) = SRU
ARU	American Railway Union
ARU	Applied Research Unit, Ministry of Local Government and Lands (Botswana)
ARU	Asociación Rural del Uruguay
ARU	Australian Railways Union
ARUDSI	Asociación Regional de Universidades para el Desarrollo de Sistemas
ARULAT	Arab Union of Land Transport (Jordan)
ARVAC	Association of Researchers in Voluntary Action and Community Involvement
ARVO	Association for Research in Vision and Ophthalmology
AS	Academica Sinica (China)
AS	Aetherius Society
AS	Anatomical Society (Germany) = AG
AS	Aristotelian Society
AS	Association of Secretaries
AS	Association of Stammerers
AS	Association of Surgeons of Great Britain and Ireland
AS	Avicultural Society
AS	Independent Adoption Service
ASA	Acoustical Society of America

ASA	Advertising Standards Authority	**ASA**	Avicultural Society of America
ASA	Advice Services Alliance	**ASA of GB**	American Saddlebred Association of Great Britain
ASA	African Studies Association (U.S.A.)	**ASAAD**	American Society for Advancement of Anesthesia in Dentistry
ASA	Agricultural Science Association (Ireland)	**ASAAS**	Association of Suppliers to Airlines, Airports and Shipping
ASA	Alianza Socialista de Andalucia		
ASA	Alternative Socialist Association (Bulgaria)	**ASAB**	Association des Informaticiens de Belgique
ASA	Aluminium Stockholders Association	**ASAB**	Association des Professionels de l'Informatique en Belgique = VEBI
ASA	Amateur Swimming Association	**ASAB**	Association for the Study of Animal Behaviour
ASA	American Schools Association		
ASA	American Society for Aesthetics	**ASAB-IA**	ASAB-Informatic Assistance (Belgium)
ASA	American Society of Agronomy	**ASAC**	American Society of Agricultural Consultants
ASA	American Society of Anesthesiologists		
ASA	American Society of Appraisers	**ASAC**	Antarctic Scientific Advisory Committee
ASA	American Society of Artists		
ASA	American Sociological Association	**ASAC**	Asian Council of Securities Analysts (Japan)
ASA	American Soybean Association		
ASA	American Statistical Association	**ASACA-CHIB**	Association for the Study of African, Caribbean and Asian History and Culture in Britain
ASA	American Stockyards Association		
ASA	American Surgical Association		
ASA	Anglican Stewardship Association	**ASACH**	Asociación General de Supermercados y Autoservicio de Chile
ASA	Arbeitsgemeinschaft der Schweizerischen Altstoffwirtschaft		
ASA	Army Signal Association (U.S.A.)	**ASAE**	American Society for Aerospace Education (U.S.A.)
ASA	Artisan Staff Association (South Africa)	**ASAE**	American Society of Agricultural Engineers
ASA	Asian Students Association		
ASA	Asociación Salvadoreña Agropecuária	**ASAE**	American Society of Association Executives
ASA	Asociación Semilleros Argentinos		
ASA	Association der Schweizerischen Aerosolindustrie	**ASAE**	Association Suisse pour l'Aménagement des Eaux
ASA	Association des Statisticiens Agricoles	**ASAF**	Association Suisse des Analystes Financiers
ASA	Association of Sealant Applicators		
ASA	Association of Social Anthropologists of the Commonwealth	**ASAFÉD**	Association Africaine d'Éducation pour le Développement (Togo)
ASA	Association of Subscription Agents	**ASAG**	Association Suisse des Arts Graphiques
ASA	Association Suisse d'Aide aux Handicapés Mentaux = SHG	**ASAHP**	American Society of Allied Health Professions
ASA	Association Suisse des Annonceurs		
ASA	Associazione per le Scienze Astronautiche	**ASAI**	Advertising Standards Authority for Ireland
ASA	Astronomical Society of Australia	**ASAI**	American Society of Ancient Instruments
ASA	Atomic Scientists Association		
ASA	Australian Society of Accountants	**ASAI**	Arab Student Aid International (U.S.A.)
ASA	Australian Society of Anaesthetists	**ASAIC**	Asociación Argentina de Investigadores de la Comunicacion
ASA	Australian Society of Archivists		
ASA	Australian Society of Authors	**ASAIHL**	Association of South-East Asian Institutions of Higher Learning
ASA	Austrian Space Agency		

ASAIO	American Society for Artificial Internal Organs
ASAJA	Asociación Agraria -Jovenes Agricultores (Spain)
ASAJA	Asociación Sudamericana de Jueces de Atletismo
ASAL	Association for the Study of Australian Literature
ASALA	Armenian Secret Army for the Liberation of Armenia (Turkey)
ASALH	Association for the Study of Afro-American Life and History
ASANAL	Asian Association of National Languages (Malaysia)
ASAO	Association for Social Anthropology in Oceania (Hawaii)
ASAO	Association of Show and Agricultural Organisations
ASAO	Association Scientifique de l'Afrique Occidentale = WASA
ASAP	American Society for Adolescent Psychiatry
ASAP	American Society of Adlerian Psychology
ASAP	Arab Socialist Action Party
ASAP	Associazione Sindicale per le Aziende Petrolchimiche e Collegate a Partecipazione Statale
ASAP	Australian Society of Animal Production
ASAPE	Asian Society for Adapted Physical Education and Exercise (Japan)
ASAPHA	Association of Sea and Air Port Health Authorities
ASAPS	American Society for Aesthetic Plastic Surgery
ASARIN	Association Artistique Internationale
ASAS	Academia de Stiinte Agricole si Silvice
ASAS	Agostiniani Secolari Augustinos Seculares
ASAS	American Society of Abdominal Surgery
ASAS	American Society of Agricultural Sciences
ASAS	American Society of Animal Science
ASAS	Association of South-East Asian States
ASAS	Association Suisse des Assistants Sociaux et Éducateurs Diplômés = SBS
ASAT	Arbeitsgemeinschaft für Satellitentragersysteme
ASATA	Associazione Svizzera per le Attrezzature Tecniche Agricole = ASETA, SVLT
ASATEL	Asociación Salvadoreña de Hoteles y Restaurantes
ASATOM	Association pour les Stages et l'Accueil des Techniciens d'Outre-Mer
ASATR	Association Suisse des Assistants Techniques en Radiologie
ASATUR	Asociación Paraguaya de Agenices de Viajes y Turismo
ASAUK	African Studies Association of the United Kingdom
ASAVPA	Association de Salariés de l'Agriculture pour la Vulgarisation du Progrès Agricole
ASAWA	Association for the Advancement of Children in Africa (Zambia)
ASAZGUA	Asociación de Azucareros de Guatemala
ASB	Accounting Standards Board
ASB	Afrikaans Studentebond
ASB	Amalgamated Society of Boilermakers
ASB	American Society for Biotechnology
ASB	Arbeitsgemeinschaft für Wirtschaftliche Betriebsführung und Soziale Betriebsgestaltung
ASB	Association of Shell Boilermakers
ASB	Association of Southeastern Biologists (U.S.A.)
ASB	Australian Space Board
ASBA	American Southdown Breeders Association
ASBA	American Standardbred Breeders Association
ASBA	Australian Small Business Association
ASBAH	Association for Spina Bifida and Hydrocephalus
ASBANA	Asociación Bananera Nacional, S.A. (Costa Rica)
ASBC	American Society of Biological Chemists
ASBC	American Society of Biophysics and Cosmology
ASBC	American Society of Brewing Chemists
ASBCI	Association of Suppliers to the British Clothing Industry (*ex* BIMA)
ASBCL	Association of Strict Baptist Churches Limited
ASBE	American Society of Bakery Engineers
ASBE	American Society of Body Engineers

ASBEF	Association Sénégalaise pour le Bien-Être Familial
ASBI	Advisory Service for the Building Industry
ASBL	Groupement Luxembourgeois des Négociantes en Bois et Exploitants Forestiers
ASBMB	American Society for Biochemistry and Molecular Biology
ASBMT	Annales de la Société Belge de Médecine Tropicale
ASBORA	Asociación Boliviana de Radiodifusoras
ASBP	American Society of Bariatric Physicians
ASBPA	American Shore and Beach Preservation Association
ASBS	Association of Social and Behavioral Scientists (U.S.A.)
ASBS	Australian Systematic Botany Society
ASBU	Arab States Broadcasting Union
ASC	Aardappel Studie Centrum
ASC	Accounting Standards Committee
ASC	Acoustical Society of China
ASC	Adhesive and Sealant Council (U.S.A.)
ASC	Adorers of the Blood of Christ Sisters
ASC	Advice Advocacy and Representation Services for Children
ASC	Alcohol Studies Centre
ASC	Ambulance Services Council (Éire)
ASC	American Safety Council
ASC	American Sailing Council
ASC	American Security Council
ASC	American Society for Cybernetics
ASC	American Society of Cartographers
ASC	American Society of Cinematographers
ASC	American Society of Criminology
ASC	American Society of Cytology
ASC	Architectural Society of China
ASC	ASEAN Standing Committee
ASC	Asian Studies Centre
ASC	Association for Student Counselling
ASC	Association for the Study of Curriculum
ASC	Association of Serbs from Croatia = USH
ASC	Association of Speakers Clubs
ASC	Association of Systematics Collections (U.S.A.)
ASC	Association Suisse des Entreprises de Transport à Câbles
ASC	Associazione Svizzera dei Critici Cinematografica
ASC	Astronautical Society of Canada
ASC	Australian Seismological Centre
ASC	Australian Sports Commission
ASC&J	Amalgamated Society of Carpenters and Joiners
ASCA	Airline Sports and Cultural Association
ASCA	American Society for Conservation Archaeology
ASCA	American Society of Contemporary Artists
ASCA	Arab Society of Certified Accountants
ASCA	Asian Crystallographic Association (Taiwan)
ASCA	Association Suisse Codes des Articles = SACV
ASCAF	Association pour le Développement des Carburants par la Fermentation
ASCAME	Asamblea de las Camaras de Comercio e Industria del Mediterraneo
ASCAN	Asociación Canaria para Defensa de la Naturaleza (Canary Islands)
ASCAP	American Society of Composers, Authors and Publishers
ASCAP	Association Suisse pour le Commerce et l'Art Photographique
ASCAR	Associação Sulina de Crédito e Assisténcia Rural (Brazil)
ASCAT	Association Internationale des Éditeurs des Catalogues de Timbres-Poste
ASCATEP	Arab States Centre for Educational Planning and Administration
ASCB	American Society for Cell Biology
ASCB	Army Sport Control Board
ASCBF	Association pour la Sélection et la Création de Betteraves Fourragères
ASCC	Aeronautical Satellite Communications Center (U.S.A.)
ASCC	American Society of Concrete Constructors (U.S.A.)
ASCC	Association of Scottish Chambers of Commerce
ASCC	Australian Society of Cosmetic Chemists
ASCC	Australian Soil Conservation Council
ASCCP	American Society for Colposcopy and Cervical Pathology
ASCD	American Society of Computer Dealers

ASCD	Association for Supervision and Curriculum Development
ASCDH	Association Scientifique pour la Culture et le Développement de l'Hydroponique
ASCE	American Society of Civil Engineers
ASCE	Associazione Socialiste Cristiani Europei
ASCE	Sound and Communications Industries Federation Ltd
ASCEA	American Society of Civil Engineers and Architects
ASCER	Asociación Española de Fabricantes de Azulejos Pavimentos y Baldosas
ASCEW	International Water Supply Association of South-Central and West Asian Countries
ASCGD	American Society of Clinical Genetics and Dysmorphology
ASCH	American Society of Church History
ASCH	American Society of Clinical Hypnosis
ASCHB	Association for Studies in the Conservation of Historic Buildings
ASCHIM-ICI	Associazione Nazionale dell'Industria Chimica
ASCI	Administrative Staff College of India
ASCI	American Society for Clinical Investigation
ASCI	Association of Sport Climbers International (France)
ASCI	Association of Suppliers to the Care Industries
ASCI	Association Scientifique de Côte d'Ivoire
ASCIA	Agence de Synthèse et de Communication Interculturelle Appliquées aux Relations Économiques Mondiales
ASCIM	Association of Casing Importers
ASCIO	Asian Oceanic Computing Industry Organization (Republic of Korea)
ASCL	American Sugar Cane League of the U.S.A.
ASCM	Association of Ships Compositions Manufacturers
ASCM	Association of Steel Conduit Manufacturers
ASCMS	American Society of Contemporary Medicine and Surgery
ASCN	American Society for Clinical Nutrition
ASCN	Association Suisse des Constructeurs Navals

ASCNEB	Association des Stagiares du Collège National des Experts Compatable de Belgique
ASCNI	Advisory Committee on the Safety of Nuclear Installations
ASCO	American Society of Clinical Oncology
ASCO	American Society on Contemporary Ophthalmology
ASCO	Arab Satellite Communications Organisation
ASCO	Asian Science Communicators' Organization
ASCO	Association Suisse des Conseils en Organisation et Gestion
ASCO	Association Suisse des Tenaciers de Cafés-Concerts
ASCO	Verband Schweizerischer Konzertlokal-, Cabarets-, Dancing-, und Diskothek Inhaber
ASCO-FARVE	Associazione Nazionale Commercianti Farmaceutici Veterinari
ASCO-MACE	Association des Constructeurs de Machines à coudre de la CEE
ASCOBEL	Association Belge des Conseils en Organisation et Gestion
ASCOBIC	African Standing Conference on Bibliographic Control
ASCOFAME	Asociación Colombiana de Facultades de Medicina
ASCOLANE	Associazione Nazionale Commercie Laniero fra Commercianti e Rappresentanti di Materie Prime Tessili
ASCOLBI	Asociación Colombiana de Bibliotecarios
ASCOLMES	Asociación Colombiana de Medios de Comunicacion Social
ASCOLPA	Asociación Colombiana de Cultivadores de Papa
ASCOLSI	Asociación Colombiana de Sistemas
ASCOMAC	Associazione Nazionale Commercio di Macchine Agricole e da Cantiere
ASCOOP	Asociación Colombiano de Cooperativas
ASCOPE	ASEAN Council on Petroleum
ASCOTEC	Associazione Consultenti Tecnici
ASCP	American Society of Clinical Pathologists
ASCP	American Society of Consultant Pharmacists
ASCP	American Society of Consulting Planners

ASCP	Association Suisse de Contrôle des Installations sous Pression	**ASDA**	Association Suisse de Droit Aérien et Spatial = SVLR
ASCP	Association Suisse du Commerce de Gros en Papiers et en Matériaux d'Emballage	**ASDAN**	Association Suisse de la Diététique et de l'Alimentation
ASCPI	Association Suisse des Conseils en Propriété Industrielle = ASPA, VSP	**ASDAR**	Association pour la Selection et le Développement des Animaux de Race
ASCPT	American Society for Clinical Pharmacology and Therapeutics	**ASDB**	Asian Development Bank = AEB, BAsD
ASCRÉ-MON	Association Professionelle des Créateurs Belge et Monopolistes de Créateurs Étrangers de Variétés de Plantes	**ASDBAM**	Association Sénégalaise pour le Développement de la Documentation, des Bibliothéques, des Archives et des Musées
ASCRS	American Society of Cataract and Refractive Surgery	**ASDC**	American Society for Deaf Children
ASCRS	American Society of Colon and Rectal Surgeons	**ASDC**	American Society of Dentistry for Children
ASCS	Agricultural Stabilization and Conservation Service (U.S.A.)	**ASDC**	Association of Separated and Divorced Catholics
ASCS	American Society of Cosmetic Surgeons	**ASDD**	Association Suisse des Diététiciens Diplômés = SVERB
ASCS	Austrian Society for Cybernetic Studies = ÖSGK	**ASDE**	American Society of Danish Engineers
ASCSA	American School and Community Safety Association	**ASDER**	Asociación Salvadoreña de Radiodifusores
ASCT	American Society for Cytotechnology	**AsDF**	Asian Development Fund = ADF, FAD
ASCT	Association of String Class Teachers	**ASDF**	Association Suisse des Distributeurs de Films
ASCT	Atlantic Salmon Conservation Trust	**ASDIFLÉ**	Association de Didactique du Français Langue Étrangère
ASCTA	Association of Short-Circuit Testing Authorities	**ASDMA**	Architectural & Specialist Door Manufacturers' Association
ASCUE	Association of Small Computer Users in Education (U.S.A.)	**ASDOC**	Afrika Studie en Dokumentatie Centrum (Belgium) = CEDAF
ASCUN	Asociación Colombiana de Universidades	**ASDR**	American Society of Dental Radiographers
ASCUOIO	Associazione Nazionale Calzaturifici Italiani	**ASDS**	American Society for Dermatologic Surgery
ASCV	Association Suisse des Entreprises de Chauffage et de Ventilation	**ASDSFB**	Association of Scottish District Salmon Fishery Boards
ASCWSA	Association of Scientific Workers of South Africa	**ASDT**	Association Suisse des Détaillants en Textiles = STDV
ASD	Aktionsgemeinschaft Selbständiger Detaillisten der Schweiz	**ASDT**	Australian Society of Dairy Technology
ASD	Association Suisse de Documentation = SVD	**ASE**	Académie Syndicale Européenne = EGA, ETUCO, EVA
ASD	Association Suisse des Droguistes	**ASE**	Admiralty Signal Establishment
ASD	Association Suisse des Professionels de la Dance	**ASE**	Agence Spatiale Européenne = ESA, EWO
ASD	Association Suisse du Diabète = SDG	**ASE**	Amalgamated Society of Engineers
ASD	Partido Alianza Social Demócrata (Dominican Republic)	**ASE**	American Society for Social Economics
ASD	Social Democratic Alliance (Romania)	**ASE**	American Society of Echocardiography
		ASE	American Society of Educators
		ASE	American Society of Engineers
ASDA	American Student Dental Association	**ASE**	American Society of Enologists

ASE	American Society of Ethnohistory
ASE	Association for Science Education
ASE	Association of Space Explorers (U.S.A.)
ASÉ	Association Suisse des Économistes = VAV
ASÉ	Association Suisse des Électriciens = SEV
ASE	Association Suisse des Ergothérapeutes = VSE
ASE	Association Suisse des Experts-Comptables = ASP, VSB
ASE	Associazione degli Storici Europei
ASE	Astronomical Society of Edinburgh
ASE	Athens Stock Exchange
ASE	Australasian Society of Engineers
ASE	Australian Society of Endodontology
ASE	Australian Stock Exchange
ASE	Austrian Society for Ecology = ÖGÖ
ASEA	Agricultural Show Exhibitors Association
ASEA	Allmänna Svenska Elektriska Aktiobolaget
ASEA	American Society of Engineers and Architects
ASEA	American Solar Energy Association
ASÉA	Association Suisse des Électriciens sur Automobiles
ASÉA	Association Suisse pour l'Étude de l'Antiquité = SVA
ASEA	Associazione Svizzera di Economia delle Acque (Switzerland)
ASEA	Australian Society for Education through Art
ASEAI	Association Suisse des Experts Automobiles Indépendants
ASEAMS	Association of Southeast Asian Marine Scientists (Philippines)
ASEAN	Association of South East Asian Nations (Thailand) = ANASE
ASEAN-CUPS	ASEAN Countries Union of Polymer Science (Malaysia)
ASEANTA	ASEAN Tourist Association
ASEAS	Association Suisse pour l'Essai et l'Approvisionnement en Semenceaux des Pommes de Terre
ASEB	Assam State Electricity Board (India)
ASEC	Association des Seniors pour l'Europe Communautaire (Belgium)
ASEC	Association of Comoran Apprentices and Students
ASEC	Association Suisse pour l'Enseignement Commercial / Associazione Svizzera per l'Educazione Commerciale = SGKB, SSEB
ASECIC	Asociación Española de Cine Cientifico
ASECNA	Agence pour la Sécurité de la Navigation Aérienne en Afrique et à Madagascar
ASECO-LDA	Asociación Colombiana de Compañias de Seguros
ASECS	American Society for Eighteenth Century Studies
ASECUT	Asociación Ecuatoriana de Agencies de Viajes y Turismo
ASEDA	Aboriginal Studies Electronic Data Archive (ANU)
ASEE	American Society for Engineering Education
ASEE	American Society for Environmental Education
ASEE	Association of Supervisory and Executive Engineers
ASÉF	Association Suisse d'Économie Forestière = SVW
ASEF	Association Suisse des Entreprises de Forage = VSB
ASEFAPI	Asociación Española de Fabricantes de Pinturas
ASEFCA	Asociación Sindical Española de Fabricantes de Coias y Adhesives
ASEG	Association Suisse des Entrepreneurs Généraux = VSGU
ASEG	Associazione Svizzera degli Editori di Giornali
ASEH	American Society for Environmental History
ASEI	American Sports Education Institute
ASEIB	Asociación de Egresados de la Escuela Interamericana de Bibliotecologia (Colombia)
ASEICA	Asociación Ecuatoriana de Industrias del Cacao
ASEINCO	Asociación Española de Empresas de Ingenieria y Consultoras
ASÉJ	Association Suisse des Éditeurs de Journaux
ASELCA	Asociación Española de la Luche contra la Contaminación Ambiental
ASELF	Asociación Española de la Lucha contra el Fuego
ASÉLF	Association Suisse des Éditeurs de Langue Française

ASÉLT	Association Européenne pour l'Échange de la Littérature Technique dans le Domaine de la Sidérurgie
ASEM	American Society for Engineering Management
ASEM	Asociación Social y Educative de Marineros (U.S.A.)
ASEMOL-PRO	Asociación Nacional de Molineros de Arroz (Colombia)
ASENET	Association Suisse des Entreprises de Nettoyage à sec et d'Entretien des Textiles = VSCTU
ASEO	Associazione Svizzera per l'Economia de las Ovas
ASEP	American Society of Electroplated Plastics
ASEP	Asian Society for Environmental Protection (Thailand)
ASEP	Asociación Salvadoreña de Ejecutivos de Empresas Privadas
ASEP	Secretaría Permanente del Acuerdo Sudamericano sobre Estupefacientes y Psicotrépicos
ASÉPD	Association Suisse pour l'Étude des Problèmes Démographiques
ASEPÉLT	Association Scientifique Européenne pour la Prévision Économique à Moyen et Long Terme; European Scientific Association of Applied Economics
ASÉQUA	Association Scientifique pour l'Étude du Quaternaire Africain
ASER-PETROL	Asociacion de Empresas Refinadoras de Petroleo
ASERCCA	Asociación Europea de Estudios sobre el Caribe y Centro America Netherlands)
ASEREP	Association Européenne de Recherches et d'Échanges
ASÉRJ	Association Sénégalaise d'Études et de Recherches Juridiques
ASES	American Solar Energy Society
ASES	Asociación Salvadoreña de Empresas de Seguros
ASESA	Asfaltos Españoles
ASESP	African Social and Environmental Studies Programme (Kenya)
ASET	American Society of Electroencephalographic Technologists
ASET	Association for Sandwich Education & Training
ASÉT	Association Suisse pour l'Étude des Transports = ASST, SVWG
ASÉT	Association Suisse pour l'Étude du Travail = ASSL, SVBF
ASETA	Asociación de Empresas Estatales de Telecommunicaciones del Acuerdo Sub Regional Andino (Ecuador)
ASÉTA	Association Suisse pour l'Équipement Technique de l'Agriculture = ASATA, SVLT
ASEV	Aociation Suisse des Engraisseurs de Volaille
ASEVICO	International Association for Scientific Exchange on Violence and Human Coexistence
ASF	Agronomes sans Frontières
ASF	Albatros Superfosfaat-fabrieken N.V. te Utrecht
ASF	Alliance de Sociétés Féminines Suisses / Alleanza della Società Femminili Svizzere = BSF, NCWS
ASF	Alliance of Small Firms Trading as Individuals
ASF	American Scottish Foundation
ASF	American-Scandinavian Foundation
ASF	Arab Sugar Federation
ASF	Asian Squash Federation (Singapore)
ASF	Association des Selectionneurs Français
ASF	Association Suisse des Fonderies de Fer
ASF	Association Suisse des Forestiers = VSF
ASF	Atlantic Salmon Federation
ASF	Australian Speleological Federation
ASF	Aviation Sans Frontières (Belgium)
ASFA	American Science Fiction Association
ASFA	American Science Film Association
ASFA	Associatie van Surinaamse Fabrikanten
ASFA	Association des Sociétés Françaises d'Autoroutes
ASFA	Association Solidarité Franco-Arabe
ASFAC	Regional Centre for Functional Literacy in Rural Areas in the Arab States
ASFAD	Association of Stainless Fastener Distributors
ASFAID	American Association for Artificial Internal Organs
ASFAL-CHILE	Asfaltos Chilenos, S.A.
ASFALEC	Association des Fabricants de Laits de Conserve des Pays de la CEE
ASFB	Australian Society for Fish Biology
ASFBT	Association Suisse des Fabricants de Briques et Tuiles = VSZS

ASFC	Association Suisse des Fabricants de Cigarettes	**ASG**	Association of Socialist Greens
ASFCEW	Association of Sea Fisheries Committees of England and Wales	**ASG**	Association Suisse des Gravières
		ASG	Association Suisse des Grossistes et Importateurs de la Branche Automobile
ASFD	Azienda di Stato per le Foreste Demaniali	**ASG**	Associazione Svizzera dei Giudici = ASM, SRV
ASFE	Association of Soil and Foundation Engineers (U.S.A.)	**ASG**	Austrian Society for Surveying and Geoinformation = ÖVG
ASFEC	Arab States Regional Centre for Functional Literacy in Rural Areas	**ASGA**	Association des Services Géologiques Africains = AAGS
ASFEI	Association des Sociétés et Fonds Françaises d'Investissement	**ASGA**	Associazione degli Giornalisti del'Automobile = AJSA, SVAJ
ASFF	Association Suisse des Fabricants de Formulaires	**ASGA**	Associazione Svizzera dei Giornalisti Agricoli = ASJA, SVAJ
ASFI	Association of Suppliers to the Furniture Industry	**ASGAP**	Association of Societies for Growing Australian Plants
ASFIL-COTON	Association Belge des Filateurs de Coton et de Fibres Connexes	**ASGB**	Aeronautical Society of Great Britain
ASFIS	Aquatic Sciences and Fisheries Information System (FAO/IOC)	**ASGBI**	Anatomical Society of Great Britain and Ireland
ASFIT	Asociación de Funcionarios del Cuerpo de Ingenieros Técnicos en Topografía	**ASGBI**	Association of Surgeons of Great Britain and Ireland
ASFMRA	American Society of Farm Managers and Rural Appraisers	**ASGC**	Associazione Svizzera dei Giornalisti Cinematografici = ASJC, SVFJ
ASFO	American Society of Forensic Odontology	**ASGC**	Associazione Svizzera dei Grossisti di Carta
ASFO-MENTO	Asociación para el Fomento de la Producción (Colombia)	**ASGCA**	American Society of Golf Course Architects
ASFP	Association of Smoked Fish Processors (U.S.A.)	**ASGD**	American Society for Geriatric Dentistry
ASFP	Association of Specialised Film Producers	**ASGE**	American Society for Gastrointestinal Endoscopy
ASFP	Association Suisse des Facteurs et Accordeurs de Pianos	**ASGE**	American Society of Gas Engineers
ASFPCM	Association of Structural Fire Protection Contractors and Manufacturers	**ASGFM**	Association of Stillwater Game Fishery Managers
ASFPH	Association Suisse des Fabricants de Pierres d'Horlogerie et Scientifiques	**ASGP**	Association for the Study of German Politics
ASFSE	American Swiss Foundation for Scientific Exchange	**ASGP**	Association of Secretaries General of Parliaments
ASFT	Association Suisse des Fabricants de Tabac à fumer	**ASGP**	Association Suisse des Grossistes en Papier
ASG	Agrarsoziale Gesellschaft	**ASGP&P**	American Society of Group Psychotherapy and Psychodrama
ASG	American Society of Genealogists	**ASGROW**	Associated Seed Growers (U.S.A.)
ASG	American Society of Geolinguistics	**ASGS**	American Scientific Glassblowers Society
ASG	Arbeitsgemeinschaft der Schweizerischen Getränkebräuche	**ASGSB**	American Society for Gravitational and Space Biology
ASG	Arbeitsgemeinschaft Schweizer Grafiker (*now* SGD)	**ASH**	Action on Smoking and Health
		ASH	American Society of Hematology
ASG	Art Services Grants	**ASH**	Association Suisse des Horlogers

ASH	Association Suisse des Horticulteurs	**ASHSL**	Association of Scottish Health Sciences Librarians
ASH	Australian Society of Herpitologists Incorporated	**ASHT**	American Society of Hand Therapists
ASHA	American Saddlebred Horse Association	**ASHTAV**	Association of Small Historic Towns and Villages of the United Kingdom
ASHA	American School Health Association	**ASHVE**	American Society of Heating and Ventilating Engineers
ASHA	American Shire Horse Association	**ASI**	Adam Smith Institute
ASHA	American Social Health Association	**ASI**	Advances Systems Institute (NRIC)
ASHA	American Speech- Language- Hearing Association	**ASI**	Air Service Ivoirien
ASHA	American Spelean Historical Association	**ASÍ**	Alpyóusamband Íslands
ASHA	Association for the Application of Science in Human Affairs	**ASI**	Ambulance Service Institute
		ASI	American Society of Indexers
ASHCSP	American Society for Hospital Central Service Personnel	**ASI**	American Society of Interpreters
ASHE	American Society for Hospital Engineers (AHA)	**ASI**	American Society of Inventors
		ASI	Anti-Slavery International
ASHE	Association for the Study of Higher Education (U.S.A.)	**ASI**	Arbeitsgemeinschaft Sozialwissenschaftlicher Institut
ASHEA	Association pour la Sauvegarde de l'Hygiène de l'Eau et de l'Air (Switzerland) = ASIAA, VFWL	**ASI**	Architects' and Surveyors' Institute (Éire)
		ASI	Asian Social Institute (Philippines)
ASHFSA	American Society for Hospital Food Service Administrators (AHA)	**ASI**	Asian Statistical Institute
		ASI	Asociación Salvadoreña de Industriales
ASHG	American Society of Human Genetics	**ASI**	Association de la Sommelerie Internationale
ASHI	American Society for Histocompatibility and Immunogenetics	**ASI**	Association Soroptimiste Internationale = SIA
ASHNS	American Society for Head and Neck Surgery	**ASI**	Association Stomatologique Internationale
ASHON-PLAFA	Asociación Hondurena de Planificacion de Familia	**ASI**	Association Suisse des Infirmières et Infirmiers = SBK
ASHP	American Society of Hospital Pharmacists	**ASI**	Association Suisse des Inventeurs et des Détenteurs de Brevets = EVS
ASHPA	American Society for Hospital Personnel Administration	**ASI**	Associazione Sanitaria Internazionale
		ASI	Astronomy Society of India
ASHPR	American Society for Hospital Public Relations	**ASI**	Aviation Society of Ireland
ASHPS	American Scenic and Historia Preservation Society	**ASIA**	Airlines Staff International Association
		ASIA	American Spinal Injury Association
ASHR	African Society for Human Rights	**ASIA**	American Stone Importers Association
ASHR	Association Suisse des Ateliers d'Héliographie et de Reprographie	**ASIA**	Antiqui Societatis Jesus Alumni
		ASIA	Association Suisse de l'Industrie Aéronautique
ASHRAE	American Society of Heating, Refrigerating and Air-conditioning Engineers	**ASIA**	Association Suisse des Infirmières Assistantes et Infirmiers Assistants = SVK
ASHRM	American Society for Hospital Risk Management	**ASIA**	Australia Scientific Industries Association
ASHS	American Society for Horticultural Science	**Asia-Pacific-POPIN**	Asia-Pacific Population Information Network (Thailand)

ASIAA	Associazione per la Salvaguardia dell'Igiene dell'Acqua e dell'Aria (Switzerland) = ASHEA, VFWL
ASIAC	Australian Surveying Industry Advisory Committee
ASIAG	Association Interprofessionnelle de l'Aviation Agricole
Asian Re	Asian Reinsurance Corporation
ASIAT	Association Suisse des Ingénieurs Agronomes et des Ingénieurs en Technologie Alimentaire = SVIAL
ASIB	Association Suisse de l'Industrie du Bois
ASIC	Agricultural Science Information Centre (China)
ASIC	Association Scientifique Internationale du Café
ASIC	Association Suisse des Ingénieurs-Conseils
ASICA	Association Internationale pour le Calcul Analogique
ASICD	Association Suisse de l'Industrie et du Commerce Dentaire = SVDIDH
ASICEN	Association Syndicale de l'Industrie et du Commerce de l'Environnement Normand
ASICH	Confederación Cristiana de Trabajadores de Chile
ASICL	African Society of International and Comparative Law
ASID	American Society of Interior Designers
ASID	Association Suisse des Infirmières et Infirmiers Diplômés
ASIDIC	Association of Scientific Information Dissemination Centers (U.S.A.)
ASIE	American Society of International Executives
ASIES	Asociación de Sindicatos Independientes (El Salvador)
ASIF	Amateur Swimming International Federation
ASIF	ASEAN Iron and Steel Industry Federation
ASIFA	Association Internationale du Film d'Animation
ASIGI	Association des Écrivains Italiens pour la Jeunesse et l'Enfance
ASIGOM	Asociación Gremial de Industriales de la Goma (Chile)
ASIH	American Society of Ichthyologists and Herpetologists
ASIHG	Association Suisse des Importateurs d'Huiles de Graissage
ASII	American Science Information Institute
ASIL	American Society of International Law
ASIL	Associazione Italiana di Studio del Lavoro Civile (Switzerland)
ASILP	Associazione Svizzera degli Impresari di Lavori Pubblici e del Genio Civile = ASTP, VST
ASILS	Association of Student International Law Societies (U.S.A.)
ASIM	American Society of Internal Medicine
ASIM	Arbeitsgemeinschaft Simulation
ASIMAD	Asociación Gremial de Industriales de la Madera (Chile)
ASIMCO	Associazione Imbottigliatori Coca-Cola Italia
ASIMET	Asociación de la Industria Metalurgica y Metalmecanica (Chile)
ASIMPRES	Asociación de Impresores de Chile
ASIN	Acción de Sistemas Informativos Nacionales (Venezuela)
ASIN	Asociación de Sistemas de Informacion Nacionales (Mexico, Costa Rica)
ASINAPLA	Agrupación Sindical National de Plaguicidas
ASINCAL	Asociación Gremial de Industriales del Calzado (Chile)
ASINCE	Asociación Española de Consultores en Ingenieria (Spain)
ASINEL	Asociación de Investigacion Industrial Electrica
ASinGB	Anthroposophical Society in Great Britain
ASINTAC	Association of International Accountants
ASIO	Australian Security Intelligence Organisation
ASIP	Asociación Interamericana de Presupuesto Publico (Venezuela)
ASIP	Association Suisse des Fabricants d'Instruments de Pesage
ASIPI	Asociación Interamericana de la Propiedad Industrial = IAAIP
ASIPLA	Asociación de Industriales del Plastico (Chile)
ASIQUIM	Asociación Gremial de Industriales Quimicos (Chile)
ASIRA	Associazione Svizzera delle Imprese di Riscaldamento e di Aerazione

ASIS	American Society for Industrial Society
ASIS	American Society for Information Services
ASIS	Asociación Internacional de la Sintesis
ASIS	Association for the Study of Internal Secretions (U.S.A.)
ASIS	Associazione Internazionale per la Sintesi della Conoscenza
ASISS	Associazione Stampa Internazionale tra Giornalisti Accreditati presso la Sala Stampa delle Santa Sede
ASISTI	Asocio de Studado Internacia pri Spiritaj kaj Teologiaj Instruoj
ASIT	Africaine de Services Informatiques et Télétraitement (Ivory Coast)
ASIT	Asociatia Stiintifica a Inginerilor si Tehnicienilor (Romania)
ASIT	Association of Surgeons in Training
ASIWPCA	Association of State and Interstate Water Pollution Control Administrators (U.S.A.)
ASJ	Acoustical Society of Japan
ASJ	Association for Scientific Journals (U.S.A.)
ASJA	American Society of Journalists and Authors
ASJA	Association Suisse des Journalistes Agricoles = ASGA, SVAG
ASJC	Association Suisse des Journalistes Cinématographique = ASGC, SVFJ
ASJÉT	Association Suisse des Journalistes et Écrivains du Tourisme
ASJLP	Association Suisse de Journalistes Libres Professionnels
ASJS	Association Suisse des Journalistes Sportifs = VSSJ
ASJSA	American Society of Journalism School Administrators
ASJU	African Sports Journalists Union (Zaïre) = UJSA
ASK	Ain-o-Salish Kendra (Bangladesh)
ASK	Akshon Social Kristian (Netherlands Antilles)
ASK	Arbeitsgemeinschaft Schweizerischer Kongressorte
ASK	Association of Systematic Kinesiology
ASKI	Arbeitsgemeinschaft der Schweizerischen Kunststoff-Industrie
ASKU	Allgemeine Schweizerische Kranken und Unfallkasse
ASL	Association for Symbolic Logic (U.S.A.)
ASL	Association Suisse des Entreprises de Linoleum et des Sols Spéciaux
ASL	Australian Society for Limnology
ASL	Avelsföreningen för Svensk Låglandsboskap
ASLA	American Society of Landscape Architects
ASLA	Association Suédoise de Linguistique Appliquée
ASLA	Australian School Library Association
ASLAP	American Society of Laboratory Animal Practitioners
ASLAS	Australian Society for Laboratory Animal Science
ASLC	Association of Street Lighting Contractors
ASLDC	Association of Social and Liberal Democrat Councillors
ASLE	American Society of Lubrication Engineers
ASLE	Association for the Study of Literature and Environment
ASLEC	Association of Street Lighting Erection Contractors
ASLEF	Asssociated Society of Locomotive Engineers and Firemen
ASLH	American Society for Legal History
ASLHC	Association of Scottish Local Health Councils
ASLIB	Association for Information Management
ASLIC	Indian Association of Special Libraries and Documentation Centres
ASLK	Algemene Spaar-en Lijfrentekas (Belgium) = CGER
ASLM	American Society of Law and Medicine
ASLM	Association of Scissor Lift Manufacturers
ASLMS	American Society for Laser Medicine and Surgery
ASLO	American Society of Limnology and Oceanography
ASLO	American Society of Local Officials
ASLO	Associated Scottish Life Officers
ASLO	Australian Scientific Liaison Office
ASLP	Association of Special Libraries of the Philippines
ASLS	Association for Scottish Literary Studies
ASLT	Association Suisse des Entreprises de Linoléum, de Sols Spéciaux et de Tapis

ASM	Academia de Stiinte Medicale	**ASMCF**	Association for the Study of Modern & Contemporary France
ASM	Aktionsgemeinschaft Soziale Marktwirtschaft	**ASMD**	Association of Science Museum Directors (U.S.A.)
ASM	American Society for Metals	**ASME**	American Society of Magazine Editors
ASM	American Society for Microbiology	**ASME**	American Society of Mechanical Engineers
ASM	American Society of Mammalogists	**ASME**	Association for the Study of Medical Education = AEME
ASM	Arbeitgeberverband Schweizerischer Maschinen-und Metall-Industrieller	**ASME**	Association Suisse des Marchands d'Engrais
ASM	Association for Systems Management (U.S.A.)	**ASMECCA-NICA**	Associazione Nazionale di Meccanica
ASM	Association of Supervisors of Midwives	**ASMER**	Association for the Study of Man-Environment Relations (U.S.A.)
ASM	Association Suisse des Magistrats de l'Ordre Judiciare = ASG, SRV	**ASMET**	Arbeitsgemeinschaft Schweizerischer Metallmöbelfabrikanten
ASM	Australian Society for Microbiology	**ASMÉVEZ**	Asociación Nacional de Médicos Veterinarios Zootecnistas (Colombia)
AsMA	Aerospace Medical Association = AMAS	**ASMFA**	Association Suisse des Maîtres Ferblantiers et Appareilleurs
ASMA	American Society for Mass Spectrometry	**ASMFC**	Atlantic States Marine Fisheries Commission (U.S.A.)
ASMA	American Society of Maxillofacial Surgeons	**ASMFE**	International Association of Soil Mechanics and Foundation Engineering
ASMA	American Society of Music Arrangers	**ASMG**	Association Suisse des Marchands-Grainiers = SSV
ASMA	Arizona State Medical Association (U.S.A.)	**ASMH**	Association Suisse des Manufactures d'Horlogerie
ASMA	Association de Médecine Aéronautique et Spatiale	**ASMI**	Agudat Ha-Sifriyot Ha-Meyuhadot Umerkeze Ha-Meyda Beyisrael (Israel) = ISLIC
ASMAF	Association de Soutien de la Mission Évangélique Afrique-France	**ASMI**	Associazione Stampa Medica Italiana
ASMAF	Association Scientifique des Médecins Acupuncteurs de France	**ASMIC**	Association pour l'Organisation des Missions de Coopération Technique
ASMAIS	Association Suisse des Maisons d'Aménagement Intérieur et des Selliers = SVIMSA, USADIS	**ASMIC**	Australian Surveying and Mapping Industries Council
ASMAS	Association Professionnelle Suisse de Matériel de Soudage et de Coupage	**ASMM**	Association of Serbs and Montenegrins in Macedonia = ZSCM
ASMAS	Association Suisse des Magasins d'Articles de Sport	**ASMM**	Associazione Svizzera dei Maestri Meccanici
ASMB	Assemblée des Supérieurs Majeurs de Belgique	**ASMMA**	American Supply and Machinery Manufacturers Association
ASMB	Association of Sports Medicine of Balkans (Cyprus)	**ASMMB**	Association Suisse des Marchands de Machines à écrire et de Bureau
ASMB	Association Suisse des Marchands du Commerce Spécialisé en Machines à écrire et de Bureau	**ASMMC**	Association Suisse des Marchands de Matériaux de Construction = VSBH
ASMC	American Society of Music Copyists	**ASMO**	Association of Shared Mailing Organisers
ASMC	Association Suisse des Maîtres Coiffeurs (*now* SCMV)	**ASMP**	Académie des Sciences Morales et Politiques
ASMC	Association Suisse des Maîtres Couvreurs		
ASMCBO	Association Suisse des Maîtres-Cordonniers et Bottiers-Orthopédistes		

ASMP	American Society of Magazine Photographers
ASMP	Association Suisse des Marchands de Poissons
ASMPA	Association Suisse pour la Médecine des Petits Animaux
ASMPP	Association Suisse des Maîtres Plâtriers-Peintres = SMGV
ASMR	Asian Music Rostrum (France) = TMAS
ASMR	Australian Society for Medical Research
ASMS	American Society for Mass Spectroscopy
ASMS	American Society of Maxillofacial Surgeons
ASMS	Asian Society for Manpower Development
ASMT	American Society for Medical Technology
ASMT	American Society of Medical Technologists
ASMT	Association of Sexual & Marital Therapists (*now* BASMT)
ASMT	Association Suisse de Microtechnique = SGMT
ASMT	Association Suisse des Maîtres Tapissiers-Décorateurs, Revêtements de Sols et des Maisons d'Ameublements
ASN	American Society for Neurochemistry
ASN	American Society of Naturalists
ASN	American Society of Nephrology
ASN	American Society of Neuroimaging
ASN	American Society of Notaries
ASN	Amigas Sefaradies de Na'amat (Argentina)
ASNA	Arctic Slope Native Association (Alaska)
ASNE	American Society of Naval Engineers
ASNE	American Society of Newspaper Editors
ASNEF	Agrupación Sindical Nacional de Empresas de Financiación de Empresas de Financiación de Ventas a Plazos
ASNEF	Asociación Nacional de Entidades de Financiación
ASNEMGE	Association des Sociétés Nationales Européennes et Méditerranéennes de Gastroentérologie
ASNF	Association Suisse des Négociants en Fourrage
ASNHS	American Society for Neo-Hellenic Studies
ASNIBI	Asociación Nicaragüense de Bibliotecarios
ASNIP	Associazione Sindacale Nazionale dell'Industria Petrolifera
ASNK	Association Suisse des Négociants de Kiosques
ASNP	Association Suisse de Négociants en Timbres-Poste
ASNR	American Society of Neuroradiology
ASNT	American Society for Nondestructive Testing
ASO	African Students' Organisation (South Africa)
ASO	Air Sud Ouest (Ivory Coast)
ASO	Association for the Study of Obesity
ASO	Association Suisse des Opticiens = SOV
ASO	Australian Space Office
ASO	Australian Survey Office
ASO-CARNE	Asociación Española de Empresas de la Carne
ASO-CESAR	Association of Cotton Growers of Cesar (Colombia)
ASO-MEDIOS	Associación Nacional de Medios de Comunicación (Colombia)
ASOA	Association Scientifique de l'Ouest Africain = WASA
ASOA	Avicultural Society of America
ASOBAN	Asociación de Bancos e Instituciones Financieras de Bolivia
ASOC	Antarctic and Southern Ocean Coalition
ASOCANA	Asociación Nacional de Cultivadores de Caña de Azúcar (Colombia)
ASOCON	Asia Soil Conservation Network for the Humid Tropics (Indonesia)
ASODELFI	Asociación de Desarrollo Economico Laboral Femenino Integral (Costa Rica)
ASODOBI	Asociación Dominicana de Bibliotecarios
ASOE	Antarctic and Southern Ocean Environment
ASOE	ASEAN Senior Officials on the Environment
ASOF	Association of Summer Olympic Federations
ASOFARE	Asociación de Fabricantes de Remolques (Venezuala)
ASO-GRASAS	Asociación de Industriales de Aceites y Grasas Vegetales (Venezuela)
ASOIF	Association of Summer Olympic International Federations

ASOL	American Symphony Orchestra League	**ASP**	American Society of Primatologists
ASOLEP	Asociación de Industriales de Leche en Polvo (Venezuela)	**ASP**	Associated Schools Project in Education for International Cooperation and Peace = SEA
ASOM	Académie des Sciences d'Outre-Mer	**ASP**	Association for Software Protection (U.S.A.)
ASOMÉR	Association des Salaries des Organismes des Migration et d'Établissements Ruraux	**ASP**	Association of Service Providers
ASO-METAL	Asociación de Fabricantes Metalurgicos (Costa Rica)	**ASP**	Association Professionnelle Suisse des Commerçants en Peinture
ASO-NAGAF	Asociación Nacional de Grupos Asociativos Femeninos (Costa Rica)	**ASP**	Association Scientifique de la Précontrainte
ASO-NICMU	Asociación Nicaraguense pro Defensa de la Mujer	**ASP**	Association Suisse de Publicité
ASONIDA	Asociación Nacional de Industriales del Arroz (Venezuela)	**ASP**	Association Suisse des Podologues = SPV
ASO-PROFAR	Asociación Profesional de Fabricantes y Distribuidores de la Industria Farmaceutica Ecuatoriana	**ASP**	Association Suisse du Pneu
ASOQUIM	Asociación de Fabricantes de Productos Quimicos (Venezuela)	**ASP**	Associazione Svizzera dei Periti Contabili = ASE, VSB
ASOR	Australian Society for Operations Research	**ASP**	Astronomical Society of the Pacific (U.S.A.)
ASOS	American Society of Oral Surgeons	**ASP**	Australian Society of Prosthodontists
ASOS	Association Suisse d'Organisation Scientifique	**ASPA**	Alloy Steel Producers Association (India)
ASOSAI	Asian Organization of Supreme Audit Institutions	**ASPA**	American Self-Protection Association
ASOSP	Association Suisse pour l'Orientation Scolaire et Professionnelle	**ASPA**	American Society for Personnel Administration
ASO-TABACO	Asociación Nacional de Exportadores de Tabaco (Colombia)	**ASPA**	American Society for Public Adminstration
ASO-TRANS	Asociación Nacional de Transportadores (Colombia)	**ASPA**	American Society of Physician Analysts
ASOVAC	Asociación Venezolana para el Avance de la Ciencia	**ASPA**	American Society of Practicing Architects
ASP	Acción Sindical Panameña (Panama)	**ASPA**	Association of South Pacific Airlines
ASP	Afrikaanse Solidaire Partij	**ASPA**	Association of Swiss Patent Attorneys = ASCPI, VSP
ASP	Akademia Sztuk Pięknych	**ASPA**	Association Suisse des Propriétaires d'Autocamions
ASP	Albanian Socialist Party	**ASPA**	Association Suisse pour l'Automatique
ASP	Allmänna Svenska Prästföreningen	**ASPA**	Associazione Scientifica di Produzione Animale
ASP	Alternativa Solidaria-Plenty	**ASPA**	Australian Sugar Producers' Association
ASP	Alternative Social-Liberal Party (Bulgaria)	**ASPA**	Syndicat National des Fabricants d'Agents de Surface et Produits Auxiliaires Industriels
ASP	American Society for Photobiology	**ASPAC**	Asia Pacific Grouping of Consulting Engineers (Philippines)
ASP	American Society of Papyrologists	**ASPAC**	Asian and Pacific Council
ASP	American Society of Parasitologists	**ASPACA**	Asian and Pacific Cultural Association (Republic of Korea)
ASP	American Society of Pharmacognosy	**ASPAM**	Association des Producteurs d'Agrumes du Maroc
ASP	American Society of Photogrammetry	**ASPAN**	Association Suisse pour l'Aménagement National = VLP
ASP	American Society of Photographers		

ASPAS	Asociación Sindical de Pilotos Aviadores Salvadoreños
ASPAS	Association pour la Protection des Animaux Sauvage
ASPAU	African Scholarship Program of American Universities
ASPB	Algemene Schoorsteenvegers Patroonsbond
ASpB	Arbeitsgemeinschaft der Spezialbibliotheken
ASPBAE	Asian-South Pacific Bureau of Adult Education (India)
ASPC	American Sheep Producers Council
ASPC	Association Suisse des Philogues Classiques = SAV
ASPCA	American Society for the Prevention of Cruelty to Animals
ASPCC	Asian Socio-Pastoral Communications Centre (Philippines)
ASPD	Amalgamated Society of Painters and Decorators
ASPD	American Society of Podiatric Dermatology
ASPDM	American Society of Psychosomatic Dentistry and Medicine
ASPE	American Society of Plumbing Engineers
ASPE	American Society of Professional Ecologists
ASPE	American Society of Professional Estimators
ASPE	American Society of Psychopathology of Expression
ASPÉ	Association des Firmes Représentant en Suisse des Spécialités Pharmaceutiques Étrangères à Marques Déposées
ASPÉ	Association Suisse de Politique Étrangère = SGA
ASPEA	Association Suisse de Psychologues pour Enfants et Adolescents = SKJP
ASPÉA	Association Suisse pour l'Énergie Atomique = SVA
ASPEC	Association of Sorbitol Producers within the EC
ASPÉC	Association pour la Prévention et l'Étude de la Contamination
ASPÉE	Association Suisse des Professionnels de l'Épuration des Eaux = ASSPA, ASTEA, SWPCA, VSA
ASPEI	Association of South Pacific Environmental Institutions (Guam) = GOIAVE
ASPeI	Associazione Pedagogica Italiana
ASPEN	American Society for Parenteral and Enteral Nutrition
ASPEN	Asian Physics Education Network (Indonesia)
ASPEP	Association of Scientists and Professional Engineering Personnel (U.S.A)
ASPESCA	Asociación Colombiana de Pescadores
ASPET	American Society for Pharmacology and Experimental Therapeutics
ASPÉTS	Association Suisse des Professeurs des Écoles Techniques Supérieures = ASPSTS, SVDHTL
ASPEW	American Society of Professional and Executive Women
ASPF	Australian Society of Perfumers and Flavourists
ASPFAV	Associazione Svizzera dei Produttori di Filmi e Audiovisivi
ASPG	Association Suisse des Professeurs de Géographie = VSGg
ASPHER	Association of Schools of Public Health in the European Region = AESPRE
ASPI	American Society for Performance Improvement
ASPI	Arbeitgeberverband Schweizerischer Papier-Industrieller
ASPI	Asociación Publicitaria Internacional (Honduras)
ASPI	Associazione Psicoterapeuti Italiana
ASPIP	Arab Society for the Protection of Industrial Property (Egypt)
ASPIRE	Association for Spinal Injury Research, Rehabilitation & Reintegration
ASPL	American Society for Pharmacy Law
ASPLA	Agrupacion Sindical de Pilotes de Lineas Aéreas
ASPLF	Association des Sociétiés de Philosophie de Langue Française
ASPLP	American Society for Political and Legal Philosophy
ASPM	American Society of Paramedics
ASPM	American Society of Podiatric Medicine
ASPM	Association of Sanitary Protection Manufacturers
ASPM	Association of Surgeons and Physicians of Malta
ASPN	American Society for Pediatric Neurosurgery

ASPO	American Society for Psychoprophylaxis in Obstetrics	**ASR**	Association for the Sociology of Religion (U.S.A.)
ASPO	American Society of Plumbing Officials	**ASR**	Association Suisse des Romanistes
ASPOE	American Society of Petroleum Operations Engineers	**ASRA**	American Shropshire Registry Association
ASPORS	Asocjacja Polskich Towarzystw Badań Operacyjnych	**ASRA**	Anti-Shark Research Association (South Africa)
ASPP	American Society of Picture Professionals	**ASRA**	Association for the Study of Reptilia and Amphibia
ASPP	American Society of Plant Physiologists	**ASRCT**	Applied Scientific Research Corporation of Thailand
ASPP	Association for Sane Psychiatric Practices (U.S.A.)	**ASRD**	Astronomy, Space and Radio Division (SERC)
ASPP	Association Suisse de Photographes de Presse = SPV	**ASRDL**	Association Suisse Romande des Diffuseurs de Livres
ASPP	Australian Society of Plant Physiologists	**ASRE**	American Society of Refrigeration Engineers
ASPPC	Associação São Pedro de Pesquisas Cientificas (Brazil)	**ASRF**	Association Suisse Raoul Follereau
ASPPR	Association of Sugar Producers of Puerto Rico	**ASRI**	Academy of Sciences Research Institute (Ghana)
ASPQ	Association Suisse pour la Promotion de la Qualité = SAQ	**ASRLO**	Australian Scientific Research Liaison Office
ASPR	American Society for Psychical Research	**ASRO**	Association of Social Research Organisations
ASPRAM	Association des Producteurs d'Agrumes du Maroc	**ASRO**	Association Suisse de Recherche Opérationnelle =SVOR
ASPRIA	Association pour la Promotion Industrie - Agriculture	**ASRR**	American Society for Reformation Research
ASPROM	Association for the Study and Preservation of Roman Mosaics	**ASRR**	Association Suisse pour la Navigation du Rhône au Rhin
ASPRS	American Society for Photogrammetry and Remote Sensing	**ASRRC**	Australian Special Rural Research Council (*now* RIRDC)
ASPRS	American Society of Plastic and Reconstructive Surgeons	**ASRSC**	Atlantic Sea Run Salmon Commission
ASPS	African Succulent Plant Society	**ASRT**	American Society of Radiologic Technologists
ASPS	Association Suisse de Politique Sociale = SVSP	**ASRT**	Atlantic Salmon Research Trust
ASPSTS	Associazione Svizzera dei Professori delle Scuole Tecniche Superiori = ASPETS, SVD-HTL	**ASRWPM**	Association of Semi Rotary Wing Pump Manufacturers
		ASRY	Arab Shipbuilding and Repair Yard (Bahrain)
ASPT	American Society of Plant Taxonomists	**ASS**	African Supplies Service (Ivory Coast)
ASPU	Asian Sports Press Union	**ASS**	Anti-Slavery Society
ASPU	Asociación Sindical de Profesores Universitarios (Colombia)	**ASS**	Arbeitsgemeinschaft Schweizerischer Schulbuchverleger
ASQ	Deutsche Arbeitsgemeinschaft für Statistische Qualitatskontrolle	**ASS**	Asociación Salvadoreña de Sociologia
		ASS	Association Suisse des Selectionneurs
ASQC	American Society for Quality Control	**ASS**	Association Suisse pour la Technique du Soudage
ASR	Acción Socialista Revolucionara (Peru)		
ASR	Arbeitskreis Freier Sanitär-Röhrenhändler	**ASS**	Associazione degli Archivisti Svizzeri = AAS, VSA

ASS	Austrian Statistical Society = ÖSG
ASSA	Academy of the Social Sciences in Australia
ASSA	African Soil Science Association = AASS
ASSA	Association for Sociology in Southern Africa
ASSA	Assotsiatsiia Sektsii Svobodnykh Anarkhistov
ASSA	Astronomical Association of South Africa
ASSA	Astronomical Society of South Australia
ASSAGIP	Associazione Nazionale Agenti AGIP
ASSAL-ZOO	Associazione Nazionale fra i Produttori di Alimenti Zootecnici
ASSAP	Association for the Scientific Study of Anomalous Phenomena
ASSBANK	Associazione Nationale Aziende Ordinarie di Credito
ASSBB	Associazione per lo Sviluppo degli Studi di Banca e Borsa
ASSBRA	Association Belge des Brasseries
ASSBT	American Association of Sugar Beet Technologists
ASSC	Association of Scotland's Self-Caterers
ASSC-EMENTO	Associazione dell'Industria Italiana del Cemento, dell'Amiantocemento, della Calce e del Gesso
ASSCO	Association Européenne des Fabricants de Caisses d'Expedition en Carton Compact
ASSCO	Associazione fra Societé e Studi di Direzione ed Organizzazione Aziendale
ASS-COPHOs	Association of Country Public Health Officers
ASSD	Association of Stock and Share Dealers
ASSE	American Society of Safety Engineers
ASSE	American Society of Sanitary Engineering
ASSE	American Society of Swedish Engineers
ASSEA	Association of Surgeons of Southeast Asia
ASSEDIC-COOP-AGRI	Association pour l'Emploi dans les Coopératives Agricoles
ASSEFA	Friends of the Association for Sarva Seva Farms
ASSELEC-TO	Association des Multiplicateurs de Graines Selectionées de Tomates
ASSÉM	Association Suisse des Spécialists en Étude de Marché
ASSEPLAN	Assessoria de Planejamente e Acompanhamento, Recife (Brazil)
ASSERIT	Associazione Serigrafi Italiana
ASSET	American Society of Scientific and Engineering Translators
ASSET	Association of Health & Exercise Teachers
ASSET	Association of Supervisory Staff, Executives and Technicians
ASSET	Association Suisse des Journalistes du Tourisme
ASSET-ERIE	Associazione Italiana Fabbricanti Seterie
ASSFIBRE	Associazione Nazionale Produttori Fibre Tessili Artificiali e Siderurgiche Italiane
ASSFN	American Society for Stereotactic and Functional Neurosurgery
ASSG	Acne Sufferers Support Group
ASSG	Association of Scottish Shellfish Growers
ASSGB	Association of Ski Schools in Great Britain
ASSH	Académie Suisse des Sciences Humaines et Sociales = SAGW
ASSH	American Society for Surgery of the Hand
ASSI	Associazione Stampa Scolastica Italiana
ASSI-CREDITO	Associazione Sindicale fra le Aziende del Credito
ASSI-FONTE	Association de l'Industrie de la Fonte de Fromage de la CEE
ASSI-MAGRA	Associação Portuguesa dos Industriais de Mármores, Granitos e Ramos Afins
ASSI-MILOR	Association de la Sidérurgie et des Mines de Fer Lorraines
ASSIC	Shanghai Institute of Ceramics, Academia Sinica
ASSIDER	Associazione Industrie Siderurgiche Italiana
ASSIG	Aslib Social Sciences Information Group
ASSIGN	Association of Industrial Graphics and Nameplate Manufacturers
ASSILEC	Association de l'Industrie Laitière de la CEE
ASSIN-FORM	Associazione Costruttori Macchine, Attrezzature per Ufficio e per il Trattamento delle Informazione
ASSINDAL	Associazione Italiana Industriali Prodotti Alimentari

ASSINSEL	Association Internationale des Sélectionneurs pour la Protection des Obtentions Végétales
ASSIOT	Associazione Italiana Costuttiro Organi di Trasmissione e Ingranaggi
ASSIREME	Associazione fra gli Instituti Regionali di Mediocredito
ASSITEB	Association Internationale des Techniciens Biologistes de Langue Française
ASSITEJ	Association Internationale du Théâtre pour l'Enfance et la Jeunesse
ASSITOL	Associazione Italiana dell'Industria Olearia
ASSJU-TIERI	Associazione Italiana Industriali Jutieri
ASSL	Associazione Svizzera per lo Studio del Lavoro = ASET, SVBF
ASSLA	Associazione di Studi Sociali Latino-Americani (Venezuela)
ASSM	Académie Suisse des Sciences Humaines = SAGW
ASSM	Académie Suisse des Sciences Médicales / Academia Svizzera delle Scienze Mediche = SAMS, SAMW
ASSM	Association of Shopfront Section Manufacturers
ASSMB	Association des Sociétés Scientifiques Médicales Belges = VBMWG
ASSNAS	Associazione Nazionale Assistenti Sociali
ASSO	American Society for the Study of Orthodontics
ASSO-BIOTEC	Associazione Nazionale per lo Sviluppo delle Biotecnologie
ASSO-BOSCHI	Associazione Nazionale Forestale fra Proprietari di Boschi e Piantagioni Campestri de Legno
ASSO-CARTA	Associazione Italiana fra gli Industriali della Carta, Cartoni e Paste per Carta
ASSO-CASEARI	Associazione Nazionale Stagionatori e Grossisti de Prodotti Caseari
ASSO-CEMENTO	Associazione dell'Industria Italiana del Cemento, dell'Amiantocemento, della Celce e del Gesso
ASSO-CONSERVE	Associazione Nazionale Industriali Conserve Alimentari Vegetali
ASSO-DETER-GENZA	Associazione Nazionale dell'Industria della Saponeria, della Detergenza e dei Prodotti d'Igiene
ASSO-DOCKS	Associazione Italiana Magazzini Generali Frigoriferie e Depositari Conto Terzi
ASSO-FARMA	Associazione fra Industrie Chimico-Farmaceutiche
ASSO-FERMET	Associazione Nationale dei Commercianti in Ferro e Acciai, Metalli non Ferrosi, Ferramenta e Affini, Rottami
ASSO-FLUID	Associazione dei Costruttori Italiani di Apparecchiature Oleodrauliche e Pneumatiche
ASSO-GLACE	Association des Artisans Glaciers et des Fabricants de Mix pour Glace des Pays de la CEE
ASSO-GOMMA	Associazione Nazionale fra le Industrie della Gomma, Cavi Elettrici ed Affini
ASSO-GRASSI	Associazione Nationale Grassi Animali
ASSO-LATERIZI	Associazione Nazionale degli Industriali dei Laterizi
ASSO-LATTE	Associazione Italiana Lattiero-Casearia
ASSO-LIOSEMI	Associazione Nazionale fra gli Industriali degli Olii da Semi
ASSO-MARMI	Associazione dell'Industria Marmifera Italiana e delle Industrie Affini
ASSO-NOTAI	Associazione Nazionale dei Notai
ASSO-PETROLI	Associazione Nazionale Commercio Petroli
ASSO-PHOTO	International Organization for Photochemicals
ASSO-POMAC	Association of Common Market Potato Breeders (Germany)
ASSO-POTER	Associazione Nazionale Industriali Porcellane e Terraglie
ASSO-SPORT	Associazione Nazionale Produttori Articoli Sportivi
ASSO-UOVA	Associazione Nazionale fra Commercianti Grossisti Esportatori Importatori di Uova, Pollame e Affini
ASSO-VETRO	Associazione Nazionale degli Industriali del Vetro
ASSO-ZUCCH-ERO	Associazione Nazionale fra gli Industriali dello Zucchero
ASSOBAF	Société d'Intérêt Collectif Agricole (Guadeloupe)
ASSOBES-TIAME	Associazione Nazionale Commercianti Grossisti Esportatori Importatori di Bestiame e Carne

Assoc	Association of Service Sector Oil-Related Companies	**ASSO-RECO**	Association des Ressortissants du Haute et du Moyen Congo
ASSO-CHAM	Associated Chambers of Commerce and Industry (India)	**ASSOREL**	Associazione di Agenzie de RP a Servizio Completo
ASSOCO-MAPLAST	Associazione Nazionale Costruttori Macchine per Materie Plastiche e Gomma	**ASSOSPAZ-ZOLE**	Associazione Nazionale Fabbricanti Spazzole, Pennelli e Preparatori Relative Materie Prime
ASSOCOM	Association of Chambers of Commerce of South Africa	**ASSOT-TICA**	Associazione Nazionale Industriali dell'Ottica, Meccanica Fine e di Precisione
ASSOFER	Associação Portuguesa dos Armazenistas e Importadores de Aços, Tubos e Metais	**ASSP**	Academia de Stiinte Sociale si Politice
ASSOFER-LEGHE	Associazione Produttori Italiana di Ferroleghe ed Affini	**ASSP**	African Social Studies Programme
		ASSP	Association Suisse de Science Politique
ASSOFOND	Associazione Nazionale delle Fonderie	**ASSPA**	Association Suisse pour l'Automatisme = SGA
ASSOGIO-CATTOLI	Associazione Nazionale Fabbricanti Giocattoli	**ASSPA**	Associaziun Svizra dils Specialists dalla Purificaziun d'Aqua = ASPEE, ASTEA, SWPCA, VSA
ASSOIN-TERPRETI	Associazioni Nationale Interpreti di Congresso Professionisti		
ASSO-ISTAL	Associazione Nazionale Installatori d'Impianti e di Ventilazione, Idrici, Sanitari, Elettrici, Telefonici ed Affini	**ASSPLV**	Association des Sociétés Suisses des Professeurs de Langues Vivantes
		ASSR	American Society for the Study of Religion
ASSOITAL-PELLI	Associazione Italiana fra i Commercianti di Pelli Grezze	**ASSRI**	Associazione per lo Sviluppo delle Scienze Religiose in Italia
ASSOLAM-PADE	Associazione Nazionale Fabbricanti Lampade Elettriche, Valvole Termoioniche, Tubi Luminscenti, Bottiglie Isolanti, Apparecchi Termostatici	**ASSS**	American Suffolk Sheep Society
		ASSS	Astro Space Stamp Society
		ASSSI	Australian Society of Soil Science Incorporated
ASSOLOM-BARDA	Associazione Industriale Lombarda	**ASST**	Associazione Svizzera per lo Studio degli Trasporti = AASET, SVWG
ASSO-MECO	Associazione Nazionale Imprese Distrib'trici Metano Compresso	**ASST**	Azienda di Stato per i Servici Telefonici
ASSOMET	Associazione Nazionale Industrie Metalli non Ferrosi	**ASSTC**	Arab Security Studies and Training Center (Saudi Arabia)
ASSOMIN-ERARIA	Associazione Mineraria Italiana	**ASSUC**	Association des Organisations Professionnelles du Commerce des Sucres pour les Pays de la CEE
ASSO-MODA	Associazione Nazionale Italiana Rappresentanti Moda	**ASSUF-FICIO**	Associazione Nazionale Costruttori Macchine per Ufficio
ASSONAPA	Associazione Nazionale della Pastorizia	**ASSUR-LUX**	Assurances Reúnies de Luxembourg
ASSONAVE	Associazione Nazionale fra Costruttori di Navi d'Alto Mare	**AST**	Agencia Salvadoreña de Turismo
ASSONIME	Associazione fra le Società Italiane per Azione	**AST**	Association of Stress Therapists
		AST	Association of Swimming Therapy
ASSOPER	Associazione Operatori Economici Basso Lazio	**AST**	Association Suisse de Thanatologie
ASSOPIA-STRELLE	Associazione Nationale dei Produttori di Piastrelle di Ceramica	**AST**	Association Suisse des Marchands de Tapis
		AST	Astronomical Society of Tasmania
ASSORAM	Associazione Nazionale Rappresentanti Agenti Depositari Medicinali	**AST**	Atlantic Salmon Trust
		ASTA	American Seed Trade Association
		ASTA	American Society of Travel Agents

ASTA	American Spice Trade Association	**ASTI**	Association of Secondary Teachers, Ireland
ASTA	American Surgical Trade Association	**ASTI**	Association Suisse des Traducteurs et Interprètes = SÜDV
ASTA	Association of Shippers to Africa		
ASTA	Association of Short-Circuit Testing Authorities	**ASTIC**	Agrupación Sindical del Transporte Internacional por Carretera
ASTA	Auckland Science Teachers Association	**ASTIN**	Actuarial Studies in Non-Life Insurance (U.S.A.)
ASTA	Australian Science Teachers Association	**ASTIN-TORI**	Associazione Italiana Industriali Tintori, Stampatori e Finitori Tessili
ASTAG	Schweizerischer Nutzfahrzeugverband	**ASTINAVE**	Astilleros Navales Ecuatorianos
ASTC	Administrative Section for Technical Cooperation (UN)	**ASTINET**	Arab Scientific and Technical Information Network (Algeria)
ASTC	Associazione Svizzera dei Tecnici-Catastali	**ASTINFO**	Asian Scientific and Technological Network
ASTC	Australia Science and Technology Council	**ASTIS**	Australian Science and Technology Information Service
ASTD	American Society for Training and Development	**ASTISA**	Asesoramiento y Servicios Técnicos Industriales (Mexico)
ASTDD	Association of State and Territorial Dental Directors (U.S.A.)	**ASTM**	Action Solidarité Tiers Monde (Luxembourg)
ASTE	American Society of Test Engineers	**ASTM**	American Society for Testing and Materials
ASTE	Association pour le Développement des Sciences et Techniques de l'Environnement	**ASTM**	Association of Sanitary Towel Manufacturers
ASTEA	Associazione Svizzera Tecnici Epurazione Acque = ASPEE, ASSPA, SWPCA, VSA	**ASTMH**	American Society of Tropical Medicine and Hygiene
		ASTO	Arab Satellite Telecommunications Organizations (Saudi Arabia)
ASTEC	Australian Science and Technology Council	**ASTO**	Association of Sea Training Organisations
ASTED	Association pour l'Avancement des Sciences et des Techniques de la Documentation (Canada)	**ASTO**	Association of Sun Tanning Operators
ASTEF	Association pour l'Organisation des Stages en France	**ASTP**	Association des Entrepreneurs Suisses de Travaux Publiques = ASILP, VST
ASTEL	Association de Spécialistes de Techniques d'Enseignement du Langage	**ASTR**	American Society for Theatre Research
ASTEM	Association Scientifique et Technique pour l'Exploitation des Mers	**ASTR**	American Society of Therapeutic Radiologists
ASTEO	Association Scientifique et Technique pour l'Exploration des Océans	**ASTRA**	Association in Scotland for Research in Astronautics
ASTF	Association Suisse des Techniciennes et des Techniciens du Film = SFTV	**ASTRID**	Association Scientifique et Technique pour la Recherche en Informatique Documentaire (Belgium)
ASTG	Association Suisse des Techniciens-Géométres	**ASTRM**	Association Suisse des Techniciens en Radiologie Médicale = SVMTRA
ASTHEOL-CENTRAL	Association des Institutions d'Enseignement Théologique en Afrique Centrale (Cameroon)	**ASTRO**	International Association of State Trading Organisations of Developing Countries
ASTHEOL-WEST	Association des Institutions d'Enseignement Théologique en Afrique Occidentale (Zaïre)	**ASTRON - NFRA**	Netherlands Foundation for Research in Astronomy
ASTI	Arbeitgeberverband der Schweizerischen Textilveredlungs-Industrie	**ASTRU**	Associazione Italiana Strumenti ed Attrezzature Scientifiche

ASTS	American Society of Transplant Surgeons	**ASVS**	Anotera Scholi Viomichanikon Spouden
ASTS	Association Scientific and Technical Societies of South Africa	**ASW**	Aktionsgemeinschaft Solidarische Welt
		ASW	Allianz Schweizerischer Werbeberater
ASTS	Association Suisse pour la Technique du Soudage	**ASW**	Amalgamated Society of Woodworkers
ASTS	Association Suisse pour les Techniques Spatiales = SAST, SVWT	**ASWA**	American Society of Women Accountants
ASTT	Association Suisse des Techniciens de Théâtre = SVTB	**ASWA**	Anthropological Society of Western Australia
ASTTEL	Asociación Salvadoreña de Trabajadores de Telecomunicaciones	**ASWBM**	Association of Solid Woven Belting Manufacturers
AStV	Auschuss der Ständigen Vertreter = COREPER, PRC	**ASWDKW**	Amalgamated Society of Wire Drawers and Kindred Workers
ASTWKT	Amalgamated Society of Textile Workers and Kindred Trades	**ASWEA**	Association for Social Work Education in Africa (Ethiopia) = AESA
ASU	Acción Sindical Uruguaya	**ASX**	Australian Stock Exchange
ASU	Arab Socialist Union	**ASXU**	African Studies Institute, Xiangtan University
ASU	Arbeitsgemeinschaft Selbständiger Unternehmer	**ASYBEL**	Syndicat Belge de l'Acide Sulfurique
ASU	Association pour la Statistique et ses Utilisations	**ASZ**	American Society of Zoologists
		AT	Autotuojat
ASUA	Amateur Swimming Union of the Americas = UANA	**AT&P**	African Timber and Plywood (Ghana)
ASUC	American Society of University Composers	**AT&T**	American Telephone and Telegraph Company
ASUC	Association of Specialist Underpinning Contractors	**ATA**	Advanced Training Ltd.
		ATA	Advertising Typographers Association of America
ASUE	Arbeitsgemeinschaft für Sparsamen und Umweltfreundlichen Energieverbrauch	**ATA**	Africa Travel Association
ASUI	Associated Staffs for a United Ireland	**ATA**	African Technical Association (France)
ASUPA	Aluminium Sulphate Producers' Association (Belgium)	**ATA**	Agricultural Technologists of Australasia
ASV	Adalbert Stifter Verein e.V.	**ATA**	Air Transport Association
ASV	Arbeitsgemeinschaft Schweizer Volkstanzkreise	**ATA**	Air Transport Association of America
		ATA	Albania Telegraphic Agency
ASVA	Association of Scottish Visitor Attractions	**ATA**	American Taxation Association
ASVE	American Society of Veterinary Ethology	**ATA**	American Taxpayers Association
		ATA	American Theatre Association
ASVI	American Society for Value Inquiry	**ATA**	American Thyroid Association
ASVIL-MET	Associazione Italiani per lo Sviluppo degli Studi Sperimentali sulla Lavorazione dei Metalli	**ATA**	American Tinnitus Association
		ATA	American Topical Association
		ATA	American Translators Association
ASVO	American Society of Veterinary Ophthalmology	**ATA**	American Transport Association
		ATA	American Tree Association
ASVOSUD	Associazione Volontari Sud	**ATA**	American Trucking Association
ASVPC	Association Suisse de Vente par Correspondence	**ATA**	Angling Trade Association
		ATA	Animal Technicians Association
ASVPP	American Society of Veterinary Physiologists and Pharmacologists	**ATA**	Asia Theological Association (Taiwan)
		ATA	Asociación de Teleradiodifusoras Argentinas

ATA	Associazione Tecnica dell'Automobile
ATA	Atlantic Treaty Association
ATA Assn	Air Transport Auxiliary Association
ATAA	Air Transport Association of America
ATAB	Association des Détaillants en Tabacs (Belgium)
ATABW	American Trade Association for British Woolens
ATAC	Air Transport Advisory Council
ATAC	Air Transport Association of Canada
ATAC	American Transportation Advisory Council
ATAC	Asociación de Tecnicos Azucareros de Cuba
ATAC	Association des Transports Aériens par Charter
ATAC	Australian Transport Advisory Council
ATAF	Association International de Transporteurs Aériens
ATAFEG	Austria Tabakeinlöse und Fermentionsgesellschaft
ATAFM	American Teilhard Association for the Future of Man
ATAG	Air Transport Action Group (Switzerland)
ATAITKU	All The Acronyms In The Known Universe
ATALA	Association pour l'Étude et le Développement de la Traduction Automatique et de la Linguistique Appliquée
ATAM	Asociación de Técnicos en Alimentos de México
ATAM	Association of Teaching Aids in Mathematics
ATAN	Air Transport Association of the Netherlands
ATAR	Association des Transporteurs Aériens Régionaux
ATAS	Academy of Television Arts and Sciences (U.S.A.)
ATAS	Anatolian Refinery Company
ATAVE	Asociación de Técnicos Azucareros de Venezuela
ATAXIA	Friedrich's Ataxia Group
ATB	Agricultural Training Board
ATB	Arbeidertoeristenbond
ATB	Association for Tropical Biology (U.S.A.)
ATBEF	Association Togolaise pour le Bien-Être Familial
ATBOA	Australian Tuna Boat Owners Association
ATC	African Timber Company
ATC	Agence Transcongolaise des Communications
ATC	Aide au Travail des Cloîtres
ATC	Air Tanzania Corporation
ATC	Air Transport Committee (ICAO)
ATC	Alpine Tourist Commission = TGA
ATC	Argentina Televisora a Color, S.A.
ATC	Asociación de Trabajadores del Campo (Nicaragua)
ATC	Association of Therapeutic Communities
ATC	Association of Translation Companies
ATC	Australian Telecommunications Commission
ATC	Australian Tourist Commission
ATC	Vereniging van Automobieltechnici
ATCA	Air Traffic Conference of America
ATCA	Air Traffic Control Association (U.S.A.)
ATCA	Allied Tactical Communications Agency (NATO)
ATCA	American Theater Critics Association
ATCA	Australian Tuna Canners Association
ATCAS	African Training Centre for Agricultural Statistics (FAO)
ATCC	American Type Culture Collection
ATCEU	Air Traffic Control Experimental Unit
ATCHBEF	Association Tchadienne pour le Bien-Être Familial (Chad)
ATCI	Association of Town Clerks of Ireland (Éire)
ATCM	Association of Tank and Cistern Manufacturers (*ex* PTCMA)
ATCM	Association of Town Centre Management
ATCO	Association of Transport Coordinating Officers
ATCP	Antarctic Treaty Consultative Party
ATCP	Asociación Mexicana de Técnicos de las Industrias de la Celulosa y del Papel
ATCSG	Africa Tree Senta Wo Shien Suru Kai (Japan)
ATCV	Australian Trust for Conservation Volunteers
ATD	Association Tunisienne des Documentalistes, Bibliothécaires et Archivistes

ATDA	Appropriate Technology Development Association (India)	**ATEN**	Association Technique pour l'Énergie Nucléaire
ATDA	Australian Telecommunications Development Association	**ATENA**	Associazione Italiana di Tecnica Navale
ATDC	Asociacion Técnica de Derivados del Cemento	**ATEO**	Ateista Tutmonda Esperanto-Organizo
ATDF	Arab Towns Development Fund (Kuwait)	**ATEP**	Asociación Tecnica Española del Pretensado
ATDI	Appropriate Technology Development Institute (Papua New Guinea)	**ATEPO**	Association of Teachers of English to Pupils from Overseas (U.S.A.)
ATE	Asociación de Trabajadores del Estado (Argentina)	**ATESA**	Aerotaxis Ecuatorianos
ATE	Association of Tanzania Employers	**ATESEA**	Association for Theological Education in South East Asia
ATE	Association of Teachers of English	**ATESL**	Association of Teachers of English as a Second Language (U.S.A.)
ATE	Association of Therapeutic Education	**ATF**	Ardeiderpressens Tarifforening
ATE	Automatic Telephone and Electric Company	**ATF**	Association Technique de la Fonderie
ATEA	American Technical Education Association	**ATF**	Australian Teachers Federation
ATEA	Association for Teacher Education in Africa	**ATFAS**	Association of Teachers of Foundry and Allied Subjects
ATEA	Australian Telecommunications Employees Association	**ATFB**	Association Technique de Fonderie de Belgique = BTGV
ATeAC	Associazione Tecnica dell'Acciaio per Costruzioni Civili	**ATFCA**	Asian Track and Field Coaches Association
ATEC	Agence Transequatoriale des Communications (Central Africa)	**ATFP**	Arab Trade Financing Program
ATEC	Air Transport Electronics Council	**ATFS**	Association of Track and Field Statisticians
ATEC	Association pour le Développement des Techniques de Transport, d'Environnement et de Circulation	**ATG**	Appropriate Technology Group
		ATG	Association of Teachers of Geology
		ATG	Association of Teachers of German
ATECI	Asociación Tecnica Española de la Construcción Industrialzada	**ATG**	Association Technique de l'Industrie du Gaz en France
ATECMA	Agrupación Técnica Española de Constructores de Material Aeroespacial	**ATGC**	Asian Textile and Garments Council (Japan)
ATECYR	Asociación Ténica Española de Climatización y Refrigeración	**ATGWU**	Amalgamated Transport and General Workers Union
ATEE	Association for Teacher Education in Europe	**ATH**	International Association of Tracer Hydrology (Austria)
ATEFI	Associazione Tecnica delle Societé Finanziari	**ATHE**	Association of Teachers of Home Economics (Éire)
ATEG	Asociación Técnica Española de Galvanización	**ATI**	Aero Trasporti Italiani
		ATI	Air Transivoire (Ivory Coast)
ATEGIP	Association Technique pour l'Étude de la Gestion des Institutions Publiques et des Entreprises Privées	**ATI**	American Television Incorporated
		ATI	Appropriate Technology International
		ATI	Association of Teachers of Italian
ATEI	Amusement Trades Exhibition International	**ATI**	Associazione Termotecnica Italiana
		ATI	Associazione Trafiliere Italiani
ATEINSA	Aplicaciones Tecnicas Industriales, SA	**ATI**	Associazione Trasfilieri Italiani
ATEM	Asociación de Trabajo y Estudios de la Mujer (Argentina)	**ATI**	Australian Textile Institute
		ATI	Azienda Tabacchi Italiani
		ATIA	Australian Tourism Industry Association

ATIBT	Association Technique pour l'Importation des Bois Tropicaux = ITTTA
ATIC	Associação Tecnica da Indústria do Cimento
ATIC	Association Technique de l'Industrie du Chauffage de la Ventilation et des Branches Connexes (Belgium)
ATIC	Association Technique pour l'Importation du Charbon en France
ATIC	Associazione Tecnica Italiana per la Cinematografia
ATIC	Australian Tin Information Centre
ATICAM	Association Technique Internationale des Compagnies d'Assurances Maritimes et Transports
ATICCA	Australian Tertiary Institutions Consulting Companies Association
ATICELCA	Associazione Tecnica Italiana per la Cellulosa e la Carta
ATICPA	Asociación de Tecnicos de la Industria Papelara e Celulosa Argentina
ATIEA	Association of Theological Institutions in Eastern Africa
ATIEL	Association Technique de l'Industrie Européenne de Lubrifiants
ATIEP	Association of Telephone Information and Entertainment Providers
ATIF	Associazione Tecnici della Pubblicité
ATIF	Australian Timber Importers Federation
ATIFAS	Associazione Tessiture Italiana Fibre Artificiali e Sintetiche
ATIG	Alternative Technology Information Group
ATIM	Asociación de Investigación Tecnica de las Industrias de la Madera y Corcho
ATIME	Association of Theological Institutes in the Middle East (Lebanon)
ATIP	Association Technique de l'Industrie Papetière
ATIPCA	Asociación de Técnicos de la Industria Papelera y Celulósica Argentina
ATIPIC	Association des Techniciens de l'Industrie des Peintures et des Industries Connexes
ATIRA	Ahmedabad Textile Industry Research Association (India)
ATIS	Appropriate Technology Information Service
ATISA	Association des Techniciens et Ingénieurs Sanitaires Africains (Burkina Faso)
ATISCA	Association of Theological Institutions in Southern and Central Africa (Kenya)
ATISEA	Associazione Tappezzori in Stoffa e Affini
ATISM	Associazione Teologica Italiana per lo Studio della Morale
ATIT	Associazione Teatri Italiani di Tradizioni
ATITA	Air Transport Industry Training Association
ATITA	Association Technique des Industries Thermiques et Aérauliques
ATITRA	Association Technique Interministérielle des Transports
ATJ	Association of Teachers of Japanese (U.S.A.)
ATJL	Adriatico Tirreno Jonio Ligure
ATK	Akademia Teologii Katolickiej
ATK	Allattenyésztésztési és Takarmányozási Kutatóközpont
ATL	Alliance of Free Peasants (Moldova)
ATL	Association of Teachers and Lecturers (*ex* AMMA)
ATL	Autoriserte Trafikkskolers Landsforbund
ATLA	American Theological Library Association
ATLA	Association of Teachers of Lip Reading to Adults
ATLA	Association of Trial Lawyers of America
ATLACATL	Asociación de Ahorro y Préstamo (El Salvador)
ATLAS	Air France, Iberia, Lufthansa, Alitalia, Sabena
ATLAS	Association of Teachers of Latin American Studies (U.S.A.)
ATLAS	Association Technique des Laboratoires d'Analyse et de Synthèse
ATLF	Association des Traducteurs Littéraires de France
ATLIB	Air Transport Licensing Board
ATLU	Antigua Trades and Labour Union
ATM	Amici Thomae Mori
ATM	Association of Teachers of Mathematics (U.K., U.S.A.)
ATM	Association of Trailer Manufacturers
ATMA	Adhesive Tape Manufacturers Association
ATMA	American Textile Machinery Association

ATMA	American Textile Manufacturers Association
ATMA	American Tour Managers Association
ATMA	Association Technique, Maritime et Aéronautique
ATMCH	Association of Teachers of Maternal and Child Health (U.S.A.)
ATMI	American Textile Manufacturers Institute
ATMU	Automotive Tyre Manufacturing Association (India)
ATO	Afghan Tourist Organisation
ATO	African Telecommunications Union
ATO	African Timber Organization (Gabon) = OAB
ATO	Antarctic Treaty Organization
ATO	Arab Tourist Organisation (Jordan)
ATO	Arbeitskreis Topinambur
ATO	Australian Taxation Office
ATOA	Air Transport Operators Association
ATOA	Aviation Technical Officers' Association (Éire)
ATOCI	Association de Traducteurs et Réviseurs des Organisations et Conférences Intergouvernementales
ATOF	Australian Transport Officers Federation
ATOL	Aangepaste Technologie Ontwikkelingslanden (Belgium)
ATOM	Against Tests on Muroroa
ATOM	Association d'Aide aux Travailleurs d'Outre-Mer
ATOMKI	Atommag Kutató Intézete
ATONU	Assistance Technique de l'Organisation des Nations Unies
ATOS	American Theatre Organ Society
ATP	Agence Tchadienne de Presse
ATP	Association for Teaching Psychology
ATP	Association for Transpersonal Psychology (U.S.A.)
ATP	Association of Tennis Professionals (U.S.A.)
ATP	Association of Transportation Practitioners (U.S.A.)
ATPAS	Association of Teachers of Printing and Allied Subjects
ATPC	Association of Tin Producing Countries
ATPC	Australian Timber Producers Council
ATPF	Association Tunisienne du Planning Familial
ATPM	Association of Teachers of Preventive Medicine (U.S.A.)
ATPM	Association of Touring and Producing Managers
ATPsych	Association for Teaching Psychology
ATPT	Association of Tour Package Travellers
ATPUL	Association Technique pour la Production et l'Utilisation du Lin et autres Fibres Libériennes
ATR	Association of Teachers of Russian
ATR	Association of Teaching Religious
ATR	Association Technique de la Route
ATR	Avions de Transport Regional (France / Italy)
ATRAM	Africaine de Transit et de Manutention (Ivory Coast)
ATRC	Agricultural Tools Research Centre (India)
ATRCAD	African Training and Research Centre in Administration for Development = CAFRAD
ATRCW	African Training and Research Centre for Women (Ethiopia)
ATREG	African Technical Regional Environment Group
ATRÉM	Association Technique de la Réfrigération et de l'Équipement Ménager
ATRF	Australian Transport Research Forum
ATRI	Australian Turfgrass Research Institute
ATRIA	Association Technique de Recherches et d'Informations Audiovisuelles
ATRIC	Agence Togolaise de Réprésentations Industrielles et Commerciales
ATRIF	Air Transportation Research International Forum
ATRIH	Association des Transporteurs Routiers Internationaux en Hongrie (Hungary)
ATRIP	International Association for the Advancement of Teaching and Research in Intellectual Property
ATS	Agence Télégraphique Suisse
ATS	American Television Society
ATS	American Temperance Society
ATS	American Tentative Society
ATS	American Thermographic Society
ATS	American Thoracic Society
ATS	American Thyroid Society
ATS	American Tolkien Society
ATS	American Trauma Society

ATS	American Travel Service
ATS	Association of Theological Schools (U.S.A.)
ATS	Association Technique de la Sidérurgie
ATS	Atomiteknillinen Seura-Atomtekniska Sallskapet
ATS	Suomen Atomiteknillinen Seura
ATSA	Aero Transportes (Mexico)
ATSA	Association des Techniciens Supérieurs Agricoles
ATSC	Australian Tree Seed Centre (CSIRO)
ATSE-GWTU	All Trinidad Sugar Estates and General Workers Trade Union
ATSIC	Aboriginal and Torres Strait Islander Commission (Australia)
ATSO	Association of Trading Standards Officers
ATSP	Association of Teachers of Spanish and Portuguese
ATSS	Association for the Teaching of the Social Sciences
ATT	Association of Taxation Technicians
ATTA	American Tin Trade Association
ATTC	American Towing Tank Conference
ATTC	Anglo-Taiwan Trade Committee
ATTC	ASEAN Timber Technology Center
ATTC	Association of Travel Trades Clubs
ATTF	Arab Table Tennis Federation (Saudi Arabia)
ATTITB	Air Transport and Travel Industry Training Board
ATTO	Association of Tatars of Tiumen Oblast (Russian Federation)
ATTU	Asian Table Tennis Union (China)
ATU	African Telecommunication Union = UAT
ATU	Arab Telecommunications Union
ATU	Arab Tourism Union (Jordan)
ATU	Australian Teachers' Union
ATUA	All Trades Union Alliance
ATUC	African Trade Union Confederation
ATUC	Air Transport Users Committee (Éire)
ATUC	ASEAN Trade Union Council
ATUF	Agricultural Trade Union Federation (Albania) = FSB
ATV	Abonnee Televisie (Suriname)
ATV	Abwassertechnische Vereinigung
ATV	Agence de Transit et de Voyages (Central Africa)
ATV	Akademiet for de Tekniske Videnskaber
ATV	Asociación Textil Venezolana
ATV	Associated Television Corporation
ATV	Lydteknisk Institut
ATVF	Association Technique pour la Vulgarisation Forestière
ATW	Amalgamated Textile Workers (GMBATU)
ATWA	Association of Third World Affairs (U.S.A.)
ATWA	Association of Turkish Workers and Alevites
ATY	Apteekkitavara-Tukkukauppiaat ry
ATypI	Association Typographique Internationale
AU	Artists' Union (Afghanistan)
AUA	American Unitarian Association
AUA	American Urological Association
AUA	Association des Universités Africaines
AUA	Association des Universités Arabes = AARU
AUA	Association of Unestablished Agents (Éire)
AUA	Association of University Administrators (ex CUA)
AUA	Association of University Anaesthetists (U.S.A.)
AUA	Association of University Architects (U.S.A.)
AUA	Austrian Airlines
AUAI	Association for Uncertainty in Artificial Intelligence
AUALPA	Austrian Airline Pilots Association
AUAW	Amalgamated Union of Asphalt Workers
AUBRCC	Australian Uniform Building Regulations Coordinating Council
AUC	Air Transport Users Committee
AUC	American University in Cairo
AUC	Association of Underwater Contractors
AUC	Training University of the Mediterranean (Malta)
AUCAM	Association Universitaire Catholique pour l'Aide aux Missions
AUCAN-UKUS	Australia, Canada, United Kingdom, United States
AUCAS	Association of University Clinical Academic Staff
AUCBE	Advisory Unit for Computer Based Education

AUCBM	Arab Union for Cement and Building Materials (Syria)
AUCC	Association of Universities and Colleges of Canada
AUCCTU	All-Union Central Council of Trade Unions (Russia) (*now* GCTU)
AUCET	Association of University Chemical Education Tutors
AUCL	Association of University and College Lecturers
AUCM	Association pour l'Unification du Christianisme Mondial = HSA-UWC
AUCOLDI	Asociación Nacional de Autores de Obras Didácticas (Colombia)
AUD	Association for Union Democracy (U.S.A.)
AUDA	Interamerican Association of Environmental Law and Administration (Uruguay)
AUDAVI	Asociación Uruguaya de Agencias de Viajes Internacionales
AUDECAM	Association Universitaire pour le Développement de l'Enseignement et de la Culture en Afrique et à Madagascar
AUDI	Arab Urban Development Institute (Saudi Arabia)
AUDI	Société Internationale d'Audiologie
AUDIVIR	Conseil International pour l'Application des Moyens Audio-Visuels à l'Environnement
AUEBS	Association des Utilisateurs d'Eau du Bassin de la Somme
AUEF	Association Universités-Enterprises pour la Formation
AUEW	Amalgamated Union of Engineering Workers
AUFEMO	Administration Universitaire Francophone et Européenne en Médecine et Odontologie (France)
AUFM	Asociación Universal de Federalistas Mundiales = MUFM, WAWE
AUFO	Asian Union of Family Organisations
AUGB	Association of Ukrainians in Great Britain Ltd
AUI	Action d'Urgence Internationale = IEA
AUI	Associated Universities, Inc. (U.S.A.)
AUKML	Association of United Kingdom Media Librarians
AUKOI	Association of United Kingdom Oil Independents
AUKWPP	Association of UK Wood Pulp Producers
AULA	Arab University Library Association
AULLA	Australasian Universities Language and Literature Association
AULP	Associação das Universidades de Lingua Portuguesa
AULUVET	Association Umbro Laziale Uffici Viaggi e Turismo
AUMA	Ausstellungs- und Messe- Ausschuss der Deutschen Wirtschaf
AUME	Association pour l'Union Monétaire de l'Europe = AMUE
AUMP	Association pour les Urgences Médicales de Paris
AUMPC	Association of Unpasteurised Milk Producers and Consumers
AUMSA	Actuaciones Urbanas Municipales S.A.
AUO	African Unity Organisation
AUOD	Alliance Universelle des Oeuvriers Diamantaires = UADW
AUP	Agence Voltaïque de Presse
AUPAM	Arab Union of Pharmaceutical Manufacturers and Medical Appliance Manufacturers (Jordan)
AUPELF	Association des Universités partiellement ou entièrement de Langue Française
AUPFIRH	Asociación Uruguaya de Planificacion Familiar e Investigaciones sobre Reproduccion Humana
AUPS	Association des Universités Populaires Suisses = VSV
AUPTDE	Arab Union of Producers, Transporters and Distributors of Electricity (Jordan)
AUPTM	Architecture, Urbanisme, Paysage Tiers Monde (Martinique)
AUR	Arab Union of Railways = UACF
AUR	Armenian Union of Romania = UAR
AURA	Association of Universities for Research in Astronomy (U.S.A.)
AURA	Association of Users of Research Agencies
AUREG	Association de Recherches Géographiques et Cartographiques
AURIS	Aberdeen University Research and Industrial Services Ltd
AURISA	Australasian Urban and Regional Information Systems Association Inc.
AURP	American Universities Research Program
AURPO	Association of University Radiation Protection Officers

AUSAT	Australian Satellite Users Association
AUSC	Aberdeen Urban Studies Centre
AUSC	ASEAN University Sports Council
AUSD	African Union for Scientific Development (Ghana)
AUSDEC	Australasian Spatial Data Exchange Centre
AusIMM	Australian Institute of Mining and Metallurgy
AUSINET	The Australian Information Network (CSIRO)
AUSITRA	Federazione Nazionale Auxiliari del Traffico e Trasporti Complementari
AUSJAL	Asociación de Universidades Confiadas a la Compania de Jesus en America Latina (Colombia)
AUSLIG	Australian Surveying and Land Information Group
AUSSA	Alliance of Upper Silesian Societies and Associations = PGST
AUSSI	Australian Society of Indexers
AUSTA	Australian Studies Association
AUSTAT	Australian Society of Teachers of the Alexander Technique
AUST-CARE	Australian Care for Refugees
AUST-EMEX	Australian Environment Management Export Corporation Ltd
AUS-TRADE	Australian Trade Commission
AUS-TRAMA	Asociación de Usuarios del Transporte Maritimo de El Salvador
AUSTRI-ATOM	Österreichische Interessengemeinschaft für Nukleartechnik
AUSUDIAP	Association of United States University Directors of InternationalAgricultural Programs
AUT	Association of University Teachers
AUT(S)	Association of University Teachers (Scotland)
AUTE	Association of University Teachers of Economics
AUTEC	Atlantic Underwater Test Evaluation Centre
AUTIF	Association of Unit Trusts and Investment Funds
AUTIG	Auto-Tilbehørs Grossist-Foreningen
AUTM	Association of Unit Trust Managers
AUTM	Association of Used Tyre Merchants
Autoimport	Empresa Central de Abastecimiento y Venta de Equipos de Transporte Ligero (Cuba)
AUTOPUT-GABON	Société Africaine d'Études de Construction, de Génie Civil et de Travaux Publics (Gabon)
AUTOSAL	Automotores Salvadoreños, S.A.
AUTOVIA	Autotransport-Gewerbeverband der Schweiz
AUTRE	Associated Universities for Toxicology Research and Education (U.S.A.)
AUTS	Association of University Teachers Scotland
AUTWA	Association of University Teachers in West Africa
AUTY	Azatlyk Union of Tatar Youth (Russian Federation)
AUUA	American Univac Users Association
AUWE	Admiralty Underwater Weapons Establishment
AUXERAP	Société Auxiliaire de la Régie du Pétrole
AUXIMAD	Société Auxiliaire Maritime de Madagascar
AUXINI	Empresa Auxiliar de la Industria
AV	Afrikaner Volksunie
AV	Ecological Party "Green Alliance" (Moldova)
AV	Verein von Altertumsfreunden im Rheinlande
AVA	Aan en Verkoopbureau van Akkerbouwproducten
AVA	Academy of Visual Arts
AVA	Alberta Veterinary Association (Canada)
AVA	Algemene Vereniging voor de Nederlandse Aardewerken Glasindustrie
AVA	American Ventilation Association
AVA	American Vocational Association
AVA	Arbeitsgemeinschaft zur Verbesserung der Agrarstrukter in Hessen
AVA	ASEAN Valuers Association
AVA	Asociación Vitivinícola Argentina
AVA	Association des Viticulteurs d'Alsace
AVA	Association for Volunteer Administration (U.S.A.)
AVA	Association of Veterinary Anaesthetists
AVA	Atlantic Visitors Association (Belgium)
AVA	Audio Visual Association
AVA	Auror Vivar Association (Peru)
AVA	Australian Veterinary Association

AVAB	Automatic Vending Association of Britain
AVAE	Association for Voluntary Action in Europe (U.S.A.) = AVE
AVAL	Association pour les Ventes dans Alimentation
AVAMA	Audio Visual Aids and Allied Manufacturers Association
AVANT	Association of Voluntary Agencies on Narcotics Treatment (U.S.A.)
AVARD	Association of Voluntary Agencies for Rural Development (India)
AVAS	Association of Voluntary Action Scholars (U.S.A.)
AVASS	Association of Voluntary Aided Secondary Schools
AVB	Afdeling Agrarische Vertegenwoordiging Buitenland
AVB	Autorité pour l'Aménagement de la Vallée du Bandama (Ivory Coast)
AVBB	Algemeen Verbond Bouwbedrijft
AVBB	Algemene Vereniging van Beroepsjournalisten in Belgie = AGJPB
AVBM	Arbeitgeberverband der Berliner Metallindustrie
AVBM	Association Générale des Meuniers Belges
AVC	Alfaro Vive Carajo (Ecuador)
AVC	Asociación Venezolana de Caficultores (Venezuela)
AVC	Association of Vitamin Chemists (U.S.A.)
AVCA	Agriculture and Veterinary Chemicals Association
AVCAA	Agricultural and Veterinary Chemicals Association of Australia
AVCC	Australian Vice-Chancellors Committee
AVCFOM	Association des Villages Communautaires de France d'Outre-Mer
AVCI	Association of Vocational Colleges International
AVCL	Association des Villes et Communes Luxembourgeoises
AVCPT	Association of Veterinary Clinical Pharmacology and Therapeutics
AVCU	Agriculture and Veterinary Chemicals Unit
AVCZ	Algemeen Verbond der Cooperatieve Zuivelfabrieken (Belgium)
AVD	Automobilclub von Deutschland
AVDA	American Venereal Disease Association
AVDA	Asociación Venezolana de Derecho Agrario
AVDBAD	Association Voltaïque pour le Développement des Bibliothèques, des Archives et de la Documentation
AVDS	American Veterinary Dental Society
AVE	Arbeitgebervereinigung Energiewirtschafter Unternehmen
AVE	Asociación Venezolana de Ejecutivos
AVE	Association pour le Volontariat à l'Acte Gratuit en Europe = AVAE
AVE	Aussenhandelsvereinigung des Deutschen Einzelhandels
AVEC	Asociación Venezolana de Educación Católica
AVEC	Association des Centres d'Abbatage de Volailles et du Commerce d'Importation et d'Exportation de Volailles des Pays de la CEE
AVEC-	IFOS Audiovisual Education Committee IFOS
AVECI	Association des Voyageurs et Employés du Commerce et de l'Industrie
AVEFAM	Asociación Venezolana de Facultades de Medicina
AVEFIDE	Asociación Venezolana de Fabricantes de Instrumentos de Escritura
AVEM	Angola Verification Mission (UN)
AVEN-CULTA	Asociación Venezolana de Cultivadores de Tabaco
AVEN-EXCAF	Asociación Venezolana de Exportadores de Café
AVENSA	Aerovias Venezolanas
AVEPPA	Asociación Venezolana de Empresas Perforadores de Pozos de Agua y Afines
AVERA	American Vocational Education Research Association
AVÉRE	Association Européenne des Véhicules Électriques Routiers
AVERT	AIDS Education and Research Trust
AVEX	Asociación Venezolana de Exportadores
AVF	Académie Vétérinaire de France
AVF	Akademiia Vozdushnogo Flota
AVG	Asociación Venezolana de Ganaderos
AVGI	Algemene Vereniging van de Geneesmiddelenindustrie (Belgium)
AVGMP	Asociación Venezolana de Geología, Minas y Petróleo
AVHA	Association Vétérinaire d'Hygiène Alimentaire

AVI	Arbeitsgemeinschaft der Eisen- und Metallverarbeitenden Industrie	**AVMA**	Action for Victims of Medical Accidents
AVI	Association for Veterinary Informatics	**AVMA**	American Veterinary Medical Association
AVI	Association Universelle d'Aviculture Scientifique = WPSA	**AVMA**	Audio-Visual Management Association (U.S.A.)
AVIA	Fédération des Importateurs Suisses Indépendants en Produits Pétroliers	**AVMA**	Automatic Vending Machine Association
AVIACO	Aviación y Comercio	**AVMD**	Algemene Vereniging van Leraren bij Voorbereidend Wetenschappelijk en Algemeen Voortgezet Onderwijs
Aviaimport	Empresa Cubana Importadora y Exportadora de Aviación		
AVIANCA	Aerovías Nacionales de Colombia	**AVN**	Algemene Vereniging van Journalisten
AVIATECA	Empresa Guatemalteca de Aviación	**AVN**	Arbeitgebervereinigung Öffentlicher Nahverkehrsunternehmen
AVIB	Algemene Vereniging van Instellingen voor Bejaardenzorg	**AVNEG**	Algemene Vereniging van Nederlandse Gieterijen
AVICOSAN	Cooperativa Agricola-Avicola Santiago Ltda (Chile)	**AVNJ**	Algemene Vlaams-Nationaal Jeugdverbond (Belgium)
AVIEAS	Asociación Venezolana de Instituciones de Educación Agrécola Superior	**AVNOJ**	Anti-Fascist Council for the National Liberation of Yugoslavia
AVIEM	Asociación Venezolana de Ingeneiria Eléctrica y Mécanica	**AVOHV**	Algemeen Vlaams Oud-Hoogstudenten Verbond
AVIFIA	Congrès International sur les Applications Nouvelles du Vide et du Froid dans les Industries Alimentaires	**AVOL**	Algemene Vereniging van Ondernemers in het Loodgieters-, Sanitair- en Gasverwarmingsinstallatie- bedrijf
AVIH	Algemene Vereniging Inlands Hout		
AVIJ	Algemene Vereniging voor de Ijzerhandel	**AVORS**	Assotsiatsiia Vozroshdeniia Rossiiskogo Skautizma
AVIORNIS	Association Internationale pour la Protection d'Espéces en Péril	**AVOS**	Algemeen Verbond van Ondernemers in het Schildersbedrijf
AVIP	Association of Viewdata Information Providers (U.S.A.)	**AVP**	Arubaanse Volkspartij (Aruba)
AVIPLA	Asociación Venezolana de Industrias Plasticas	**AVPA**	Asociación Venezolana de Peritos Agropecuários
AVIS	Animal Husbandry and Veterinary Research Institute of Sichuan Province	**AVPC**	Asociación Venezolana de Productores de Cacao
AVIS	Associazione Volontari Italiani del Sangue	**AVPC**	Association of Vice-Principals of Colleges
AvJ	Arbeitsgemeinschaft von Jugendbuchvelegern in der Bundesrepublik Deutschland	**AVPES**	Asociación de Vendedores Profesionales de El Salvador
AVK	Arbeitsgemeinschaft Verstärke Kunststoffe	**AVR**	Assotsiatsiia Vrachei Rossii
AVL	Autovakuutusliitto	**AVRA**	Audio-Visual Research Foundation (U.S.A.)
AVLP	Association of Valuers of Licensed Property	**AVRC**	Applied Vision Research Centre
AVLP	Association Vive le Paysan (Burkina Faso)	**AVRDC**	Asian Vegetable Research and Development Centre
AVM	Algemene Vereeniging voor Melkvoorziening	**AVRE**	Association pour les Victimes de Repression en Exil
AVM	Asociación Venezolana de Mujeres	**AVRO**	Algemene Vereniging Radio-Omroep
AVM	Association des Fabricants de Verres de Montres (Switzerland)	**AVRO**	Animal Virus Research Organisation
		AVRO	Association of Vehicle Recovery Operators

AVRTC	Association of Victims of the Totalitarian Communist Regime (Moldova)
AVS	Algemene Vereniging van Schoolleiders bij het Voortgezet Onderwijs
AVS	American Vacuum Society
AVS	Autovermieter-Verband der Schweiz
AVSAB	American Veterinary Society of Animal Behaviour
AVSC	Association for Voluntary Surgical Contraception - Kenya
AVSI	Associazione Volontari per il Servizio Internazionale
AVT	Akademiia Vneshnei Torgovli
AVTRW	Association of Veterinary Teachers and Research Workers
AVÜ	Hungarian State Property Agency
AVV	Autorité des Aménagements des Vallées des Volta (Burkina Faso)
AVVA	Avtomobilnyi Vserossiiskii Alians
AVVC	Algemeen Verbond van Vrije Vakverenigen- Curaçao (Netherlands Antilles)
AVVL	Algemeen Verbond van Leerkrachten (Belgium) = FGPE
AVVN	Algemene Vereniging van Naaimachinenhandelaren
AVVS	Algemeen Verbond van Vakverenigingen in Suriname 'De Moederbond'
AVWV	Antilliaans Verbond van Werknemers Verenigingen
AVWW	Algemeen Verbond Vinkelbedrijven Woninginrichting
AVZ	Algemene Vereniging van Zeevarenden
AVZ	Algemene Vereniging voor de Teelt en Handel in Zaaizaad en Pootgoed
AW	Africa Watch
AWA	African Writers' Association (South Africa)
AWA	Alliance of Women in Architecture (U.S.A.)
AWA	Aluminium Window Association
AWA	Amalgamated Wireless Australasia
AWA	American Wine Association
AWA	Anarchist Workers Association
AWAC	Animal Welfare Advisory Council
AWACC	Anglophone West Africa Catechetical Commission (Ghana)
AWAG	Ahmedabad Women's Action Group (India)

AWAM	All Women's Action Society (Malaysia)
AWAM	Association of West African Merchants
AWAP	All-Wales Advisory Panel on the Development of Services with Mental Handicaps
AWARE	Action for Welfare and Awakening in the Rural Environment (India)
AWARE	Association of Women for Action and Research (Singapore)
AWAS	Australian Womens Army Service
AWB	Afrikaner Weerstandsbeweging = ARM
AWB	Agricultural Wages Board
AWB	Asian Wetland Bureau
AWB	Australian Wheat Board
AWB	Australian Wool Board
AWBA	American Wholesale Booksellers Association
AWC	American Women's Club - Argentina
AWC	American Wool Council
AWC	ASEAN Women's Circle
AWC	Assembly of Welsh Counties
AWC	Association for Women in Computing
AWC	Association of Women's Clubs (Zimbabwe)
AWC	Association of World Citizens (U.S.A.)
AWC	Australian Wool Corporation
AWCACS	West and Central African Association of Soil Science = AOCASS
AWCEBD	Association of Workers for Children with Emotional and Behavioural Difficulties (ex AWMC)
AWCH	Association for the Welfare of Children in Hospital (Éire)
AWCI	Association of Wall and Ceiling Industries International (U.S.A.)
AWCVIE	Ancient and Worshipful Company of Village Idiots
AWD	Association of Welding Distributors
AWE	Afghan Wool Enterprises
AWE	Association for World Education
AWEA	American Wind Energy Association
AWEBB	Association of Wholesale Electrical Bulk Buyers
AWEC	Albury-Wodonga Environment Centre
AWEPAA	Association of West European Parliamentarians for Action Against Apartheid (Netherlands)
AWES	Association of West Europe Shipbuilders

AWF	African Wildlife Foundation
AWF	Akademia Wychowania Fizycznego
AWF	American Wildlife Foundation
AWF	Anglican Women's Fellowship (South Africa)
AWF	Animal Welfare Foundation (BVA)
AWF	Asian Weightlifting Federation
AWF	Ausschuss für Wirtschaftliche Fertigung
AWF-International	Animals without Frontiers - International (Belgium) = DZG
AWG	Absatzwirtschaftliche Gesellschaft
AWG	Art Workers Guild
AWG	Association for Women GeoScientists (U.S.A.)
AWGC	Australian Woolgrowers and Graziers Council
AWHA	Australian Women's Home Army
AWI	American Watchmakers Institute
AWI	Animal Welfare Institute (U.S.A.)
AWI	Asian Women's Institute (Pakistan)
AWIA	American Wood Inspection Agency
AWID	Association of Women Industrial Designers
AWIS	Association for Women in Science (U.S.A.)
AWISE	Association for Women in Science and Engineering
AWIU	Animal Welfare Investigation Unit
AWL	Alliance for Workers Liberty
AWL	Association for a World Language (U.S.A.)
AWLA	Association of Welsh Local Authorities
AWLLA	All Wales Ladies Lacrosse Association
AWLN	Animal Welfare Liaison Network
AWLREM	Association of Webbing Load Restraint Equipment Manufacturers
AWMA	Asian Womens Management Association
AWMC	Association of Wardens of Mountain Centres
AWMC	Association of Workers for Maladjusted Children (now AWCEBD)
AWMF	Arbeitsgemeinschaft Wissenschaftlich-Medizinische Fachgesellschaften
AWMPF	Australian Wool and Meat Producers Federation
AWMS	Australasian Wildlife Management Society
AWN	Archaeologische Werkgemeenschap voor Nederland
AWNL	Australian Womens National League
AWO	Association of Water Officers (now IWO)
AWOJA	Association of Women's Organizations in Jamaica
AWP	Albanian Workers' Party = PPSh
AWPA	American Wire Producers Association
AWPA	American Wood-Preservers' Association
AWPA	American Word Processing Association
AWPA	Australian Women Pilots Association
AWPB	American Wood Preservers Bureau
AWPI	American Wood Preservers Institute
AWPR	Association of Women in Public Relations
AWR	Arbeitsgemeinschaft der Deutschen Werksredakteure
AWR	Association for the Study of the World Refugee Problem
AWR	Association for Women's Rights (Malta)
AWRA	American Water Resources Association
AWRA	Australian Welding Research Association
AWRA	Australian Wool Realisation Agency
AWRAC	Australian Water Research Advisory Council
AWRAN	Asian Women's Research and Action Network
AWRAP	Australian Wool Research and Promotion Organisation
AWRBIAC	Arkansas-White-Red Basins Inter-Agency Committee
AWRC	Arkansas Water Resources Center
AWRC	Asian Women's Resource Centre for Culture and Theology (Hong Kong)
AWRC	Australian Water Resources Council
AWRC	Australian Wool Realisation Commission
AWRE	Atomic Weapons Research Establishment
AWRT	American Women in Radio and Television
AWRTC	A Woman's Right to Choose
AWS	Agricultural Wholesale Society
AWS	Algemene Werkgeverorganisatie Schoonmaakbedrijven
AWS	American Watercolor Society
AWS	American Welding Society
AWS	American Wine Society

AWS	Arbeitsgemeinschaft Wissenschaftlicher Sortimentsbuchhandlungen	**AYC**	Asian Youth Council
AWS	Association of Women Solicitors	**AYD**	Alliance of Young Democrats (Hungary)
AWSA	Arab Women Solidarity Association (Egypt)	**AYDI**	Association for a Yugoslav Democratic Initiative (Serbia)
AWSCPA	American Women's Society of Certified Public Accountants	**AYE**	African Youth for Environment (Kenya)
AWSL	Asian Workers' Solidarity Link (Sri Lanka)	**AyEE**	Agua y Energía Eléctrica Sociedad del Estado (Argentina)
AWT	Animal Welfare Trust	**AYF**	Asian Yachting Federation
AWT	Arbeitsgemeinschaft für Wärmebehandlung und Werkstoff-Technik	**AYH**	Academia Yucateca de Historia (Mexico)
AWT	Arbeitsgemeinschaft für Wirkstoffe in der Tierernährung	**AYH**	American Youth Hostels
AWT	Association of Woodwind Teachers	**AYPAC**	Australian Youth Policy Action Coalition
AWTA	Australian Wool Testing Authority	**AYPC**	Asian Youth Population Coalition
AWTAO	Association of Water Transportation Accounting Officers (U.S.A.)	**AYRCGA**	All Year Round Chrysanthemum Growers Association
AWTCE	Association of World Trade Chamber Executives (U.S.A.)	**AYRO**	Action on Youth Rights and Opportunities
AWTE	Association of World Travel Exchange (U.S.A.)	**AYRS**	Amateur Yacht Research Society
AWU	Agricultural Workers Union (South Africa)	**AYSA**	American Yarn Spinners Association
AWU	Antigua Workers' Union	**AYU**	Ayuda Alemana a los Enfermos de Lepra = DAHW, GLRA
AWU	Association for the World University (U.S.A.)	**AYUSAL**	Association of Yugoslav Societies of Applied Linguistics
AWU	Australian Workers Union	**AZABDO**	Association Zaïroise des Archivistes, Bibliothécaires et Documentalistes
AWV	Algemene Werkgevers-Vereniging	**AZACCO**	Azanian Co-ordinating Committee (South Africa)
AWV	Amalgamated Wireless Valve Co. (Australia)	**AZaP**	Agence Zaïre Presse
AWV	Arbeitsgemeinschaft für Wirtschaftliche Verwaltung	**AZAPO**	Azania People's Organization (South Africa)
AWV	Association for Women Veterinarians (U.S.A.)	**AZBEF**	Association Zairoise pour le Bien-Être Familial
AWV	Ausschuss Wirtschaftliche Verwaltung	**Azerinform**	Azerbaijan Information Agency
AWWA	American Water-Works Association	**AZF**	American Zionist Federation
AWWA	Australian Water and Wastewater Association	**AZGN**	Artsen Zonder Grenzen Nederland
AWWM	Association of Wholesale Woollen Merchants	**AZI**	Association Zen Internationale
AWWT	Association of Welsh Wildlife Trusts	**Azinmash**	Azerbaijan Scientific, Research and Design Institute of Petroleum Engineering
AWWV	Arbeitsgemeinschaft der Wasserwirtschaftsverbande	**AZRC**	Arid Zone Research Centre (Australia)
AXrEM	Association of X-ray Equipment Manufacturers	**AZRI**	Arid Zone Research in Iraq
AYACL	Asian Youth Anti-Communist League	**AZS**	Akademicki Związek Sportowy
AYC	American Youth Congress	**AZSA**	Asturiana de Zinc
AYC	Asian Youth Centre (India)	**AZTAG**	Azerbaijan Telegraph Agency, Baku
		AZU	Aktionszentrum Umweltschutz
		AZURCA	Agroindustrias Zulia Ureña
		AZV	Autofahrlehrer-Zentralverband (Switzerland)

B

B&IHRC	Britain and Ireland Human Rights Centre
B&SCC	Billiard and Snooker Control Council
B-AS	Britain Australia Society
B-H Press	Bosnia-Herzegovina Press Association
BA	Banca Agricola (Romania)
BA	Benefits Agency (DSS)
BA	Biuro Avtomatizatsii
BA	Booksellers Association of Great Britain and Ireland
BA	British Academy
BA	British Airways
BA	British Association for the Advancement of Science
BA	Bundesanstalt für Arbeit
BAA	Bahamas Association of Architects
BAA	Biodynamic Agricultural Association
BAA	Booking Agents Association of Great Britain
BAA	Bremer Afrika Archiv
BAA	Brewers Association of America
BAA	British Accounting Association
BAA	British Acupuncture Association
BAA	British Agrochemicals Association
BAA	British Aikido Association
BAA	British Airports Authority
BAA	British Alsatian Association
BAA	British Anodising Association
BAA	British Archaeological Association
BAA	British Astronomical Association
BAA	Bundesausgleichsamt
BAA	Burlington Arcade Association
BAAA	British American Arts Association
BAAB	British Amateur Athletic Board
BAAC	Bank for Agriculture and Agricultural Co-operatives (Thailand)
BAAC	British Association of Aviation Consultants (*ex* ABAC)
BAAC	British Aviation Archaeological Council
BAACI	British Association of Allergy and Clinical Immunology
BAAEM	British Association of Airport Equipment Manufacturers and Services
BAAF	British Agencies for Adoption and Fostering
BAAG	British Aerospace Aircraft Group
BAAL	British Association of Applied Linguistics
BAALPE	British Association of Advisers and Lecturers in Physical Education
BAAM	Banque Arabe Africaine en Mauritanie
BAAO	British Association of Abattoir Owners
BAAP	British Association of Academic Phoneticians
BAAP	British Association of Audiological Physicians
BAAPS	British Association of Aesthetic Plastic Surgeons
BAAR	British Acupuncture Association and Register
BAARC	British Association of Automation and Robotics in Construction
BAAS	British Association for American Studies
BAAS	British Association for the Advancement of Science
BAASDC	British Association of American Square Dance Clubs
BAASO	British Afro-Asian Solidarity Organisation
BAAT	British Association of Art Therapists
BAB	Belgische Architectenbond
BAB	Berufsverband Freischaffender Architekten und Bauingenieure
BAB	Bond van Aannemers in de Bouwnijwerheid
BAB	British Aerospace Board
BAB	Bureau de l'Agriculture Britannique, Brussels (NFU)
BABA	British Air Boat Association
BABA	British Anaerobic and Biomass Association
BABA	British Artists Blacksmiths Association
BABCP	British Association of Behavioural and Cognitive Psychotherapy (*ex* BABP)
BABEL	European Foundation for Multilingual AV
BABEX	Bond van Aannemers met Bevoegdheid voor Explosieven
BABIE	British Association for Betterment of Infertility and Education
BABP	British Association for Behavioural Psychotherapy (*now* BABCP)
BABS	British Aluminium Building Service
BABS	British Association for Brazing and Soldering

BABS	British Association of Barbershop Singers	**BACE**	British Association of Consulting Engineers
BABT	British Approval Board for Telecommunications	**BACE**	British Association of Corrosion Engineers
BABTAC	British Association of Beauty Therapy and Cosmetology	**BACE**	Bureau of Agricultural Chemistry and Engineering (U.S.A.)
BABW	Beratender Ausschuss für Bildungs- und Wissenschaftspolitik	**BACEA**	British Airport Construction and Equipment Association
BAC	Biblioteca Agropecuária de Colombia	**BACEE**	British Association for Central and Eastern Europe
BAC	Block Advisory Committee (India)	**BACFI**	Bar Association for Commerce, Finance and Industry
BAC	Bois Africaines Contreplaques (Gabon)	**BACFID**	British Association of Canned and Preserved Food Importers and Distributors
BAC	British Accreditation Council for Independent Further and Higher Education		
BAC	British Aerospace Campaign	**BACG**	British Association of Crystal Growth
BAC	British Aircraft Corporation	**BACI**	British Association of Caving Instructors
BAC	British Animal Campaigns		
BAC	British Archives Council	**BACIE**	British Association for Commercial and Industrial Education
BAC	British Association for Counselling		
BAC	British Association of Chemists	**BACIS**	British Association of CIRP Industrial Sponsors
BAC	British Association of Choreographers		
BAC	British Atlantic Committee	**BACM**	British Association of Colliery Management
BAC	British Automatic Company		
BAC	Brouwtechnische Adviescommissie	**BACM**	Business and Commercial Management Group (MTIA)
BAC	Bureau Agricole Commun pour l'Étude de Conjoncture Économique	**BACMA**	British Artists Colour Manufacturers Association
BAC	Burma Airways Corporation		
BAC	Business Archives Council	**BACMI**	British Aggregate Construction Materials Industries
BAC	International Union of Bricklayers and Allied Craftsmen (U.S.A.)		
BAC/PFM	Bureau d'Assistance et de Coordination de la Femme Mauritanienne	**BACMM**	British Association of Clothing Machinery Manufacturers
BACA	Baltic Air Charter Association	**BACO**	Advisory Council (BASEEFA)
BACA	British Advisory Committee for Aeronautics	**BACPA**	British Africa, Caribbean and Pacific Association
BACA	British Agricultural Contractors' Association	**BACPFID**	British Association of Canned and Preserved Food Importers and Distributors
BACA	British Association of Clinical Anatomists		
BACA	British Association of Concert Agents	**BACR**	British Association for Cancer Research
BACAN	British Association for the Control of Aircraft Noise	**BACS**	British Association for Canadian Studies
BACC	British American Collectors Club (U.S.A.)	**BACS**	British Association for Chemical Specialists
BACC	British-American Chamber of Commerce	**BACS**	British Association for Chemical Specialities
BACCHUS	British Aircraft Corporation Commercial Habitat under the Sea	**BACS**	British Association for Chinese Studies
		BACS	British Association of Cosmetic Surgeons
BACCI	Béton Armé, Constructions Civiles et Industrielles	**BACSA**	British Association for Cemeteries in South Asia

BACT	British Association of Canoe Trades	**BAECON**	Bureau of Agricultural Economics (Philippines)
BACT	British Association of Conference Towns	**BAEE**	Benelux Association of Energy Economists
BACT	British Association of Creative Therapists	**BAEF**	Belgian-American Educational Foundation
BACTA	British Amusement Catering Trades Association	**BAeF**	British Aerophilatelic Federation
BACTE	British Association for Commercial and Technical Education	**BAEF**	British-American Educational Foundation
BACTV	British Action for Children's Television	**BAEM**	British Association of Accident and Emergency Medicine and Casualty Surgeons' Association (*ex* CSA)
BACUP	British Association of Cancer United Patients (and their Families and Friends)	**BAEng**	Bureau of Agricultural Engineering (U.S.A.)
BAD	Associação Portuguesa de Bibliotecários, Arquivistas e Documentalistes	**BAEQ**	Bureau d'Aménagement de l'Est du Québec (Canada)
BAD	Banque Africaine de Développement	**BAeS**	British Aerobatic Society (*ex* BAeA)
BAD	Banque Algérienne de Développement	**BAES**	British Association of Endocrine Surgeons
BAD	Banque Asiatique de Développement (Philippines)	**BAESC**	British Association of Executive Search Consultants
BAD	British Association of Dermatologists	**BAEU**	Beijing Agricultural Engineering University
BADA	British Antique Dealers' Association	**BAEXA**	British Agricultural Exhibitors' Association
BADA	British Audio Dealers Association	**BAF**	Beninese Armed Forces
BADC	Barbados Agricultural Development Corporation	**BAF**	British Abrasive Federation
BADCO	British Association of Domiciliary Care Officers (*ex* IHHO)	**BAF**	British Aerophilatelic Federation
BADÉA	Banque Arabe pour le Développement Économique en Afrique = ABEDA	**BAF**	British Allergy Foundation
		BAF	British Athletics Foundation
BADESUL	Banco de Desenvolvimento do Estado do Rio Grande do Sul	**BAF**	Bryggerienes Arbeidsgiverforening
BADR	Banque de l'Agriculture et du Développement Rural (Algeria)	**BAF**	Bundesarbeitsgemeinschaft der Fruchtimportmärkte
BADS	British Association for Day Surgery	**BäF**	Byggnadsämnesförbundet
BADT	British Association of Dental Therapists	**BAFA**	British Accounting and Finance Association
BAdW	Bayerische Akademie der Wissenschaften	**BAFA**	British American Football Association
BAE	Badminton Association of England Ltd.	**BAFA**	British Animated Film Association
BAE	British Academy of Experts	**BAFA**	British Arts Festivals Association
BAe	British Aerospace	**BAFATT**	British Association for Autogenic Training and Therapy
BAE	British Association of Electrolysists	**BAfD**	Banque Africaine de Développement
BAE	Bureau of Agricultural Economics (Australia)	**BAFE**	British Approvals for Fire Equipment
BAEA	British Actors Equity Association	**BAFI**	Bundesamt für die Anerkennung Ausländischer Flüchtlinge
BAeA	British Aerobatic Association (*now* BAeS)	**BAFM**	British Association of Forensic Medicine
BAEC	Bangladesh Atomic Energy Commission	**BAFM**	British Association of Friends of Museums
BAEC	British Agricultural Export Council	**BAFMA**	British and Foreign Maritime Agencies
BAECE	British Association of Early Childhood Education		

BAFOG	Bureau Agricole et Forestier Guyanais
BAFPA	British Association of Fencing and Pallet Agents
BAFRA	British Antique Furniture Restorers' Association
BAFS	Banque Americano-Franco-Suisse
BAFS	British Academy of Forensic Sciences
BAFSC	British Association of Field and Sports Contractors
BAFSM	British Association of Feed Supplement Manufacturers
BAFTA	British Academy of Film and Television Arts
BAFUNCS	British Association of Former United Nations Civil Servants
BAG	Bank Action Group (*now* IBAS)
BAG	British Artists in Glass
BAG	Bundesarbeitsgemeinschaft der Erzeugergemeinschaften
BAG	Bundesarbeitsgemeinschaft der Mittel- und Grossbetriebe des Einzelhandels
BAG	Bundesarbeitsgemeinschaft für das Schlacht- und Viehhofswesen
BAG	Burma Action Group
BAGA	British Amateur Gymnastics Association
BAGB	Baltic Association of Great Britain
BAGB	Bates Association of Great Britain
BAGB	Bicycle Association of Great Britain
BAGB	Bingo Association of Great Britain
BAGB	British Army Gurkha Battalion (Brunei)
BAGCC	British Association of Golf Course Constructors
BAGCD	British Association of Green Crop Driers
BAGDA	British Advertising Gift Distributors Association
BAGMA	British Agricultural and Garden Machinery Association
BAGS	British Association for Chemical Specialities
BAGUV	Bundesarbeitsgemeinschaft der Unfallversicherungsträger der Öffentlichen Hand
BAH	Biologische Anstalt Helgoland
BAH	British Airways Helicopters
Bah.FPA	Bahamas Family Planning Association
BAHA	British Activity Holiday Association
BAHA	British Association of Hotel Accountants
BAHM	British Association of Homeopathic Manufacturers (*ex* BHMA)
BAHO	British Association of Helicopter Operators
BAHOH	British Association of the Hard of Hearing
BAHP	British Association of Homoeopathic Pharmacists
BAHPA	British Agricultural and Horticultural Plastics Association
BAHS	British Agricultural History Society
BAHVS	British Association of Homeopathic Veterinary Surgeons
BAI	Bank Administration Institute (U.S.A.)
BAI	Bundesverband der Agraringenieure
BAI	Bureau des Affaires Indigènes
BAI	Bureau of Animal Industry (U.S.A.)
BAIC	Bahamas Agricultural and Industrial Corporation
BAIC	Bureau of Agricultural and Industrial Chemistry (U.S.A.)
BAIE	British Association of Industrial Editors
BAIF	Bharatiya Agro-Industries Foundation (India)
BAIL	Bulgarian Association of International Law
BAILER	British Association for Information and Library Education and Research
BAIR	British Airports Information Retrieval
BAIS	British Association for Irish Studies
BAJ	British Association of Journalists
BAK	Bundesapothekerkammer
BAK	Bundesarchitektenkammer
BAK	Bundesärztekammer
BAKDA	Bathroom and Kitchen Distributors' Association
BAKEB	Bundesarbeitsgemeinschaft für Rehabilitation
BAKER	Barisan Kemerdeka'an Rakyat (Brunei)
BAKR	Bulgarian Association of Kinesitherapists and Rehabilitators
BAL	Belize Airways Ltd
BALCO	Bahrain-Saudi Aluminium Company
BALCO	Bharat Aluminium Corporation (India)
BALD	British Association of Laser Dentistry
BALEXCO	Bahrain Aluminium Extrusion Company
BALF	Bendrasis Amerikos lietuviu fondas = BALFas, JLAF

BALFas	Bendrasis Amerikos lietuviu fondas = BALF, JLAF	**BAMER**	Banco de América (Nicaragua)
BALH	British Association for Local History	**BAMES**	Banque Malagasy d'Escompte et de Crédit
BALI	British Association of Landscape Industries	**BAMEX**	British Art Metal Manufacturers Export Group
BALM	Banque Arabe Libyenne-Mauritanienne pour le Commerce Extérieur et le Développement	**BAMI**	Beijing Agricultural Machinery Institute
		BAMIN	Banco Minero de Bolivia
BALM	Bundesanstalt für Landwirtschaftliche Marktordnung	**BAMM**	British Association of Manipulative Medicine (*now* BIMM)
BALPA	British Air Line Pilots' Association	**BAMM**	British Association of Medical Managers
BALPM	British Association of Lithographic Plate Manufacturers	**BAMMATA**	British Animal Medicine Makers and Allied Traders Association
BALPPA	British Association of Leisure Parks, Piers and Attractions	**BAMOTC**	Beijing Acupuncture-Moxibustion and Orthopedics-Traumatology College
BALR	British Association for Lung Research	**BAMP**	Barbados Association of Medical Practitioners
BALS	Bahamas Association of Land Surveyors	**BAMPA**	British Aeromedical Practitioners Association
BALT	British Association for Language Teaching	**BAMRG**	British Agricultural Marketing Research Group
BALTAP	Allied Forces Baltic Approaches (NATO)	**BAMS**	British Art Medal Society
BALTEX	Banque Arabe Libyenne Togolaise du Commerce Extérieur	**BAMTRI**	Beijing Aeronautical Manufacturing Technology Research Institute
BAM	Bacteriology and Applied Microbiology Division	**BAMW**	British Association of Meat Wholesalers
		BAN	British Association of Neurologists
BAM	Badminton Association of Malaysia	**BAN**	Bulgarska Akademiia na Naukite = BAS
BAM	Bank of Africa-Mali	**BAN-AFRIQUE**	Union de Banques en Côte d'Ivoire
BAM	British Association of Myasthenics (*now* MGA)	**BAN-RURAL**	Banco Nacional de Crédito Rural (Mexico)
BAM	Brothers to All Men International	**BANACRE**	Banco do Estado do Acre (Brazil)
BAM	Bundesanstalt für Materialprüfung	**BANADES**	Banco Nacional de Desarrollo (Nicaragua)
BAMA	British Aerosol Manufacturers Association	**BANADESA**	Banco Nacional de Desarrollo Agricola (Honduras)
BAMA	British Amsterdam Maritime Agencies	**BANAFI**	Banco Nacional de Fomento Industrial (El Salvador)
BAMA	British Army Motoring Association		
BAMAC	British Automobile Manufacturers Association in Canada	**BANAGAS**	Bahrain National Gas Company
		BANAMEX	Banco Nacional de México
BAMAG	Société Banguienne de Grands Magasins	**BANANIC**	Empresa Nicaragüense del Banano
BAMATM	British Association for the Medical Application of Transcendental Meditation	**BANC**	Biblioteca Agrícola Nacional de Colombia
		BANC	British Association of National Coaches
BAMB	Botswana Agricultural Marketing Board	**BANC**	British Association of Nature Conservationists
BAMB	Bureau of Administrative Management and Budget (UNDP)	**BANC-ATLAN**	Banco Atlántica (Honduras)
BAMDO	British Agricultural Marketing Development Organisation		
BAMEMA	Beama Ancillary Metering Equipment Manufacturers' Association	**BANCAHSA**	Banco La Capitalizadora Hondureña, S.A.

BANCO-MEXT	Banco Nacional de Comercio Exterior (Mexico)	**BANOCO**	Bahrain National Oil Company
BANCO-TRAB	Banco de los Trabajadores (Honduras)	**BANORO**	Banco del Noroeste (Mexico)
		BANORTE	Banco Nacional do Norte (Brazil)
BANCOCCI	Banco de Occidente (Honduras)	**BANPECO**	Banco Peruano de Comercio y Construcción
BANCOLAT	Banco de Latinoamerica, S.A. (Panama)	**BANPR**	British Association of Nursery and Pram Retailers
BANCO-MER	Banco Comercial de Panama		
BANCO-MER	Banco de Comercio (Honduras)	**BANS**	British Association of Numismatic Societies
BANCO-MERCIO	Banco del Comercio (Colombia)	**BANSDOC**	Bangladesh National Scientific and Documentation Centre
BANCON	Banco Continental (Honduras)	**BANT**	Belgian Association of Non-Destructive Testing
BANCON	Banco Latino de Fomento de la Construcción (Peru)	**BANTRAL**	Banco Central de Honduras
BANCOPAR	Banco Comercial (Paraguay)	**BANU**	Bulgarian Agrarian National Union
BAND	Book Action for Nuclear Disarmament	**BANUNP**	Bulgarian Agrarian Nation Union – Nikola Petkov
BANDAG	Société Gabonaise de Pneumatiques	**BANVI**	Banco Nacional de la Vivienda (Guatemala)
BANDA-GRO	Banco de Desarrollo Agropecuário (Venezuela)		
BANDECO	Banana Development Corporation of Costa Rica	**BAO**	Bayer Afrique de l'Ouest (Ivory Coast)
		BAO	Beijing Astronomical Observatory
BANDESCO	Banco de Desarrollo de la Construcción (Peru)	**BAO**	British Association of Orthodontists
BANDESCO	Banco del Desarrollo Economico Español	**BAODA**	British Association of Operating Department Assistants
BANDESA	Banco Nacional de Desarrollo Agricola (Guatemala)	**BAofE**	Badminton Association of England
		BAOL	British Association for Open Learning
BANDEVI	Banco de Desarrollo de la Vivenda (Chile)	**BAOL**	British Association of Otolaryngologists
BANERJ	Banco do Estado do Rio de Janeiro	**BAOM**	Bibliothèque d'Afrique et d'Outre-Mer
BANESPA	Banco do Estado de São Paulo (Brazil, Paraguay)	**BAOMS**	British Association of Oral and Maxillofacial Surgeons
BANEXI	Banque pour l'Expansion Industrielle	**BAOR**	British Army of the Rhine
BANFAIC	Banco de Fomento Agrícola e Industrial de Cuba	**BAOT**	British Association of Occupational Therapists
BANFFAA	Banco de las Fuerzas Armadas (Honduras)	**BAP**	Banco Agrario del Peru
		BAP	Biotechnology Action Programme (EU)
BANFINAN	Banco Financiera Hondureña, S.A.	**BAP**	British Association for Psychopharmacology
BANGAP	Société Centrafricaine de Distribution d'Appareils Électriques	**BAP**	British Association of Psychotherapists
BANHCAFE	Banco Hondureño del Cafe	**BAPA**	British Airline Pilots Association
BANI	National Arbitration Board (Indonesia)	**BAPA**	British Amateur Press Association
BANIC	Banco Nicaragüense	**BAPAM**	British Association of Performing Arts Medicine
BANIF	Banco Internacional do Funchal		
Bankcoop	Cooperative Credit Bank (Romania) = CCB	**BAPC**	British Aircraft Preservation Council
		BAPC	British Association of Paperback Collectors
BanKinter	Banco Intercontinental Espanol	**BAPC**	British Association of Parascending Clubs (*now* BHGPA)
BANMA	Banco Municipal Autónomo (Honduras)	**BAPC**	British Association of Print and Copyshops

BAPCO	Bahrain Petroleum Company	**BARB**	British Association Representing Breeders
BAPE	Barbados Association of Professional Engineers	**BARB**	Broadcasters Audience Research Board
BAPEPAM	Badan Pelaksana Pasar Modal	**BARC**	Bangladesh Agricultural Research Council
BAPEX	British Association of Paper Exporters		
BAPH	British Association of Paper Historians	**BARC**	Bhabha Atomic Research Centre (India)
BAPHE	British Association of Professional Hairdressing Employers	**BARC**	British Automobile Racing Club
BAPINDO	Bank Pembangunan Indonesia	**BARD**	Bangladesh Academy for Rural Development
BAPIP	British Association of Palestine-Israel Philatelists	**BARD**	British Association of Rally Doctors
		BARD	British Association of Record Dealers
BAPJR	British Association of Professional Jukebox Restorers	**BARD**	US-Israel Binational Agricultural Research and Development Fund
BAPLA	British Association of Picture Libraries and Agencies	**BAREMA**	British Anaesthetic and Respiratory Equipment Manufacturers Association
BAPMON	Background Air Pollution Monitoring Network (WMO)	**BARI**	Bangladesh Agricultural Research Institute
BAPN	British Association for Paediatric Nephrology	**Bari MAI**	Mediterranean Agronomic Institute of Bari = IAM Bari
BAPP	British Association of Pharmaceutical Physicians (*now* BrAPP)	**BARIF**	Banjarbaru Research Institute for Food Crops (Indonesia)
BAPP	British Association of Pig Producers	**BARIM**	Bureau d'Achats pour la République Islamique de Mauritanie
BAPPCo	British Automotive Parts Promotion Council	**BARLA**	British Amateur Rugby League Association
BAPPENAS	National Development Planning Agency (Indonesia)	**BARMA**	Boiler and Radiator Manufacturers Association
BApS	British Appaloosa Society		
BAPS	British Association of Paediatric Surgeons	**BARMA**	Bureau pour l'Application des Renseignements Météorologiques aux Activités Économiques et Agricoles
BAPS	British Association of Plastic Surgeons		
BAPS	British Astrological and Psychic Society	**BARNACS**	Barbados National Association of Co-operative Societies
BAPSA	Budget Annexe des Prestations Socials Agricoles	**BARR**	Board on Agricultural and Renewable Resources (U.S.A.)
BAPSC	Badeku Agricultural Production and Supply Company (Nigeria)	**BARRC**	Bicol Consortium for Agriculture and Natural Resources Research and Development (Philippines)
BAPSH	British Association for the Purebred Spanish Horse		
BAPT	British Association for Physical Training	**BARS**	British Association of Residential Settlements
BAPTO	British Association of Pool Table Operators	**BARSC**	British Association of Remote Sensing Companies
BAPW	British Association of Pharmaceutical Wholesalers (*ex* NAPD)	**BART**	Bishop Ambrose Reeves Trust
		BARTG	British Amateur Radio Teleprinter Group
BAQ	Bundesanstalt für Qualitätsforschung Pflanzlicher Erzeugnisse	**BARUK**	Board of Airline Representatives in the United Kingdom
BAR	British Association of Removers	**BAS**	Bangladesh Association Scotland
BAR	Bundesarbeitsgemeinschaft für Rehabilitation	**BAS**	Barbados Agricultural Society
BARA	Board of Airline Representatives	**BAS**	Brewers' Association of Scotland
BARB	British Association of Rose Breeders	**BAS**	British Alpine Society

BAS	British Ambulance Society
BAS	British Andrology Society
BAS	British Antarctic Survey
BAS	British Arachnological Society
BAS	British Association of Stammerers
BAS	Building Advisory Service (NFBTE)
BAS	Bulgarian Academy of Sciences = BAN
BAS	Bureau of Analysed Samples
BASA	Bahamas Association of Shipping Agents
BASA	Banco da Amazónia (Brazil)
BASA	British Adhesives and Sealants Association
BASA	British Air Survey Association
BASA	British Amputee and Les Autres Sports Association
BASA	British Architectural Students' Association
BASA	British Association of Seed Analysts
BASA	British Australian Studies Association
BASA	British Automatic Sprinkler Association
BASAF	British and South African Forum
BASAM	British Association of Grain, Seed, Feed and Agricultural Merchants
BASATA	British and South Asia Trade Association
BASBWE	British Association of Symphonic Bands and Wind Ensembles
BASC	British Association for Shooting and Conservation
BASC	British Association of Skin Camouflage
BASC	British Association of Sound Collections
BASCA	British Academy of Songwriters, Composers and Authors
BASCELT	British Association of State Colleges in English Language Teaching
BASCOL	Bauxite Alumina Study Company Ltd (Ghana)
BAsD	Banque Asiatique de Développement = AEB, AsDB
BASE	British Association for Service for the Elderly
BASÉ	Bureau Africain des Sciences de l'Éducation (Zaïre)
BASEA	British Airport Services and Equipment Association
BASEC	British Approval Service for Electric Cables
BASEEFA	British Approvals Service for Electrical Equipment in Flammable Atmospheres
BASEES	British Association for Slavonic and East European Studies (*ex* BUAS, BASSEES, NASEES)
BASES	British Association of Spectator Equipment Suppliers
BASF	Badische Anilin und Soda-Fabrik
BASI	British Association of Ski Instructors
BASI	Bundesarbeitsgemeinschaft für Arbeitssicherheit
BASIC	Bridge and Structures Information Center (U.S.A.)
BASIC	British American Security Information Centre
BASICS	British Association for Immediate Care Schemes
BASIS	British Agrochemicals Standards Inspection Scheme
BASIWU	Bahamas Airport, Service and Industrial Workers' Union
BASLC	British Association of Sports Ground and Landscape Contractors
BASM	British Association of Sport and Medicine
BASMA	Boot and Shoe Manufacturers Association and Leather Trades Protection Society
BASMA	British Adhesives & Sealants Manufacturers' Association
BASMM	British Association of Sewing Machine Manufacturers
BASMT	British Association of Sexual and Marital Therapy (*ex* ASMT)
BASO	British Association of Surgical Oncology
BASP	British Association for Social Psychiatry
BASPCAN	British Association for the Study and Prevention of Child Abuse and Neglect
BASR	Bureau of Applied Social Research (U.S.A.)
BASRA	British Amateur Scientific Research Association
BASS	Belgian Archives for the Social Sciences
BASS	British Association of Ship Suppliers
BASS	British Association of Sports Sciences
BASSA	British Airline Stewards and Stewardesses Association
BASSAC	British Association of Settlements and Social Action Centres
BASSEES	British Association for Soviet, Slavonic and East European Studies (*now* BASEES)

BASt	Bundesanstalt für Strassenwesen (Germany)	**BAURES**	Bangladesh Agricultural University Research System
BASW	British Association of Social Workers	**BAUS**	British Association of Urological Surgeons
BAT	British-American Tobacco Company		
BAT	Bureau de l'Assistance Technique (ONU) = TAB	**BAV**	Bureau Aardappelverbouw
		BAVA	British Amateur Video Awards
BATA	Bakery Allied Traders Association	**BAVP**	Bibliothèque Administrative de la Ville de Paris
BATA	British Air Transport Association		
BATAL	Banque Tchado-Arabe Libyenne pour le Commerce Extérieur et le Développement (Chad)	**BAW**	Basketball Association of Wales
		BAW	Bundesanstalt für Wasserbau
		BAWA	British Amateur Wrestling Association
BATAN	Badan Tenaga Atom Nasional (Indonesia)	**BAWAG**	Bank für Arbeit und Wirtschaft Aktiengesellschaft (Austria)
BATC	British Amateur Television Club	**BAWD**	British Association of Wheelchair Distributors
BATC	British Apparel & Textiles Centre		
BATC	British Apparel and Textile Confederation	**BAWE**	British Association of Women Entrepreneurs
BATC	British Arabian Technical Cooperation	**BAWLA**	British Amateur Weight Lifters Association
BATCLM	British Association of Trade Computer Label Manufacturers	**BAWM**	British Association of Wallcovering Merchants
BATD	British Association of Teachers of Dancing	**BAWRA**	British Australian Wool Realisation Association
BATELCO	Bahrain Telecommunications Company	**BAWTA**	Beartender Ausschuss für Wissenschaftlich Technische Ausbildung = ACSTT, CCFST
BATHC	British Amateur Treasure Hunting Clubs		
BATIMET-AL	Entreprise Nationale de Bâtiments Industrialisés (Algeria)	**BAWV**	Bundesarbeitsgemeinschaft Wirtschaftswissenschaftlicher Vereinigungen
BATMA	Bookbinding and Allied Trades Management Association	**BAYAN**	Bagong Alyansang Makabayan (Philippines)
BATO	British Association of Tourist Officers		
BATOD	British Association of Teachers of the Deaf	**BAYS**	British Association of Young Scientists
		BAYWA	Bayerische Warenvermittlung Landwirtschaftlicher Genossenschaften Aktiengesellschaft
BATR	British Association of Toy Retailers (*ex* NATR)		
BATRA-CI	Bâtiments et Travaux de Côte d'Ivoire	**BB**	Bando do Brasil
BATROE	British Association of Teachers and Researchers in Overseas Education	**BB**	Belgische Boerenbond
		BB	Boerenbond Belge
BATS	British Association of Tennis Supporters	**BB**	Boys' Brigade
		BB&PA	British Box and Packaging Association
BATS	British Association of Trauma in Sport	**BBA**	Bahamas Boatmen's Association
BATU	Brotherhood of Asian Trade Unionists	**BBA**	Barbados Builders' Association
BATU	Building and Allied Trades Union (Éire)	**BBA**	Belgian Bioindustries Association
BATVA	British All Terrain Vehicle Association	**BBA**	Biologische Bundesanstalt für Land- und Forstwirtschaft
BAU	Bangladesh Agricultural University		
BAU	Beijing Agricultural University	**BBA**	British Backgammon Association
BAU	Bundesanstalt für Arbeitsschutz und Unfallforschung	**BBA**	British Bankers' Association
		BBA	British Bingo Association
BAUA	Business Aircraft Users Association	**BBA**	British Biomagnetic Association
BAUBG	Bau-Berufsgenossenschaft	**BBA**	British Bison Association

BBA	British Board of Agrément		**BBFS**	British Bulgarian Friendship Society
BBA	British Bobsleigh Association		**BBG**	Algemene Nederlandse Bond van Binnenlandse Groothandelaren in Groente en Fruit
BBA	British Bonsai Association			
BBA	British Brazing Association			
BBA	British Buddhist Association		**BBG**	Bayerische Botanische Gesellschaft
BBA	British Burn Association		**BBGA**	British Broiler Growers Association
BBAA	Bureau Belge des Assureurs Automobiles		**BBGS**	British Business Graduates Society
			BBHG	British Branded Hosiery Group
BBAC	British Balloon and Airship Club		**BBI**	B'nai B'rith International
BBB	Bedrijfslaboratorium voor Grondonderzoek		**BBI**	Beijing Broadcasting Institute
			BBI	British Bottlers Institute
BBB	Blanke Bevrydingsbeweging (South Africa)		**BBK**	British Bank of Bahrain and Kuwait
			BBK	Bunderverband Bildender Künstler
BBBA	British Bird Breeders' Association		**BBKA**	British Beekeepers' Association
BBBA	British Boatbuilders' Association (*ex* FBBA)		**BBKC**	British Bee-keeping Centre
			BBKKP	Balai Besar Penelitian dan Pengembangan Industri Barang Kulit, Karet dan Plastik (Indonesia)
BBBIMA	British Bronze & Brass Ingot Manufacturers' Association			
BBBofC	British Boxing Board of Control		**BBL**	Bond Beter Leefmilieu – Vlaanderen vzw
BBC	British Bathroom Council		**BBL**	Bond van Bijzondere Leden
BBC	British Broadcasting Corporation		**BBL**	British Bridge League
BBC	Bureau du Bois Camérounais		**BBLO**	Belgische Bond voor Lichamelijke Opvoeding = FBEP
BBC-NHU	British Broadcasting Corporation Natural History Unit			
			BBM	Algemene Nederlandse Bond van Bierhandelaren en Mineraalwaterfabrikanten
BBCC	British Bottle Collectors Club			
BBCCS	British Beer Can Collectors Society			
BBCF	British Bacon Curers Federation		**BBM**	Bureau Bénélux des Marques
BBCFMA	British Baby Carriage and Furniture Manufacturers Association		**BBM**	Mandela Bush Negro Liberation Movement (Suriname)
BBCPF	British Ball Clay Producers' Federation		**BBMA**	British Bath Manufacturers' Association
BBCS	British Beer-mat Collectors Society		**BBMA**	British Battery Manufacturers' Association
BBCS	British Butterfly Conservation Society		**BBMA**	British Brush Manufacturers Association
BBD	Banque Béninoise pour le Développement			
			BBMA	British Button Manufacturers' Association
BBD	Bulgarska Botanichesko Druzhestvo			
BBDAWU	Bahamas Brewery, Distillers' and Allied Workers Union		**BBMA**	Building Board Manufacturers' Association of Great Britain
BBDM	Bureau Benelux des Dessins ou Modèles		**BBMC**	British Board of Marbles Control
			BBME	British Bank of the Middle East
BBEA	Brewery and Bottling Engineers Association (PPA)		**BBMRA**	British Brush Manufacturers Research Association
BBF	British Baseball Federation		**BBMS**	British Battery Makers Society
BBF	Brother's Brother Foundation (U.S.A.)		**BBN**	Belize Broadcasting Network
BBFA	British Binders and Finishers' Association		**BBN**	Bond voor Bedrijfs-autoverkeer in Nederland
BBFA	British Business Forms Association		**BBNA**	Black Bolt and Nut Association of Great Britain
BBFC	British Board of Film Classification			
BBFI	Baptist Bible Fellowship International (U.S.A.)		**BBO**	British Ballet Organisation

BBO	Gesamtverband Büromaschinen, Büromöbel und Organisationsmittel	**BBV**	Banco Bilbao Vizcaya
BBP	Beroepsvereniging van Bouwpromotors (Belgium)	**BBV**	Belgische Bodemkundige Vereniging = SBP
BBPA	British Bedding Plant Association	**BBW**	B'nai B'rith Women (U.S.A.)
BBPC	Basil Bunting Poetry Centre & Archive	**BBW**	Bildungswerk der Bayerischen Wirtschaft
BBQC	British Board of Quality Control	**BBW**	Bundersverband Bürowirtschaft in der Hauptgemeinschaft des Deutschen Einzelhandels
BBR	Belgische Beroepsvereniging van Reisbureaus		
BBRI	Boston Biomedical Research Institute	**BBW**	Bundesamt für Bildung und Wissenschaft (Switzerland)
BBRS	Blair Bell Research Society		
BBRU	Bituminous Binder Research Unit (South Africa)	**BBW**	Bundesausschuss Betriebswirtschaft
		BBWR	Non-Party Bloc for the Support of Reform (Poland)
BBS	Barbados Broadcasting Service		
BBS	Bartók Béla Szövetség	**BBYO**	B'nai B'rith Youth Organization (U.S.A.)
BBS	British Biophysical Society	**BC**	Backpackers Club
BBS	British Bison Society	**BC**	British Coal
BBS	British Blind Sport	**BC**	Builders' Conference
BBS	British Boomerang Society	**BC-ECOR**	British Committee for ECOR
BBS	British Brick Society	**BC-Net**	Business Cooperation Network (Belgium)
BBS	British Bromeliad Society		
BBS	British Bryological Society	**BCA**	Bahamas Contractors' Association
BBS	British Button Society	**BCA**	Banco Comercial dos Açores
BBS	Brittle Bone Society	**BCA**	Bliss Classification Association
BBS	Burma Broadcasting Service	**BCA**	Bomber Command Association
BBSA	British Blind and Shutter Association	**BCA**	Box Culvert Associaton
BBSATRA	British Boot, Shoe and Allied Trades Research Association	**BCA**	British Carton Association
		BCA	British Casino Association
BBSAWS	Babiker Badri Scientific Association for Women's Studies (Sudan)	**BCA**	British Cement Association
		BCA	British Chicken Association
BBSF	British Brain and Spine Foundation	**BCA**	British Chiropractic Association
BBSI	British Boot and Shoe Institution	**BCA**	British College of Accountancy
BBSLG	British Business Schools Librarians Group	**BCA**	British Colostomy Association
		BCA	British Confectioners' Association
BBSR	Bermuda Biological Station for Research	**BCA**	British Cookware Association
		BCA	British Crystallographic Association
BBSRC	Biotechnology and Biological Sciences Research Council	**BCA**	Business Council of Australia
		BCAA	Bristol Centre for the Advancement of Architecture
BBT	Barbados Board of Tourism		
BBT	Boulangerie, Biscuiterie Togolaise	**BCAB**	British Computer Association for the Blind
BBT	Byways and Bridleways Trust		
BBTA	British Bureau of Television Advertising	**BCAC**	Banque Centrale de l'Afrique Centrale
		BCAC	British Conference on Automation and Computation
BBTA	Bund Baugewerblich Tätiger Architekten		
		BCAI	British Columbia Artificial Insemination Centre
BBTK	Bond der Bedienden, Technicien Kaders van België = SETCa		
		BCAIE	Banco Centroamericano Integración Económica
BBTUA	British-Bulgarian Trade Union Association		
		BCAR	British Council for Aid to Refugees

BCAS	British Compressed Air Society
BCAWU	Black Community Against Women's Oppression
BCB	Banque Commerciale du Bénin
BCB	Belgisch Comité van Brandverzekeraars
BCB	British Consultants Bureau
BCB	Broadcasting Corporation of the Bahamas
BCB	Bureau Congolais des Bois
BCBC	British Cattle Breeders Club
BCBC	British Citizens Band Council
BCBD	British Council of Ballroom Dancing
BCBTE	Bór-, Cipó és Bórfeldolgozóipari Tudományos Egyesület (Hungary)
BCC	Badge Collectors' Circle
BCC	Bank of Credit and Commerce (UAE)
BCC	Banque Commerciale Congolaise
BCC	Beijing College of Commerce
BCC	Birth Control Campaign
BCC	Breast Cancer Care
BCC	British Caravanners Club
BCC	British Ceramic Confederation (*ex* NFCI)
BCC	British Chilean Council
BCC	British Cleaning Council
BCC	British Colour Council
BCC	British Communications Corporation
BCC	British Copyright Council
BCC	British Council of Churches
BCC	British Crafts Centre
BCC	British Cryogenic Council
BCC	Broadcasting Complaints Commission
BCC	Bureau Central de Compensation (UIC)
BCC	Burundi Coffee Company
BCC	Bus and Coach Council
BCC	Business Cooperation Centre (EU) = BRE
BCC	Bypost Collectors' Club
BCCA	Beer Can Collectors of America
BCCA	British Columbia Cattlemen's Association
BCCA	British Correspondence Chess Association
BCCA	British Cyclo-Cross Association
BCCB	British Coordinating Committee for Biotechnology
BCCC	British Chilean Chamber of Commerce
BCCCA	Biscuit, Cake, Chocolate and Confectionery Alliance
BCCCUS	British Commonwealth Chamber of Commerce in the United States
BCCF	British Calcium Carbonates Federation (*ex* BWF)
BCCF	British Cast Concrete Federation
BCCG	Bean Curd Canners' Group
BCCG	British Chamber of Commerce in Germany
BCCG	British Cooperative Clinical Group
BCCJ	British Chamber of Commerce in Japan
BCCM	Bureau Central de Compensation Maghrebine
BCCS	British Cheque Collectors' Society
BCCS	British Correspondence Chess Society
BCCSTI	Beijing Center of Space Science and Technology Information
BCCT	British Chamber of Commerce of Turkey
BCD	Banque Camérounaise de Développement
BCD	Belgisch Comité voor de Distributie
BCD	Benevolent Confraternity of Dissectologists
BCD	British Crop Driers, Ltd
BCD	Bureau du Commerce et du Développement (CNUCED)
BCDA	Barge and Canal Development Association
BCDA	British Chemical Dampcourse Association
BCDA	Bureau de Développement de Coopérative d'Assurance = CIDB, ODSC
BCDTA	British Chemical Distributors and Traders Association
BCE	Beijing College of Economics
BCE	Board of Customs and Excise
BCÉAO	Banque Centrale des États de l'Afrique de l'Ouest = CBWAS
BCECA	British Chemical Engineering Contractors Association
BCECC	British and Central-European Chamber of Commerce
BCECEC	British Conference and Exhibition Centres Export Council
BCEF	British Coal Exporters' Federation
BCEI	British Colour Education Institute (BCC)
BCÉI	Bureau Canadien d'Éducation Internationale = CBIE
BCEL	Banque du Commerce Extérieur Lao

BCEL	British Commonwealth Ex-Services League
BCEMA	British Combustion Equipment Manufacturers Association
BCEMB	British Columbia Egg Marketing Board
BCÉOM	Bureau Central d'Études pour les Équipements d'Outre-Mer
BCÉPS	Bureau de Coopération Économique du Pacifique Sud (Fiji)
BCET	British Coalition for East Timor
BCETEM	British Civil Engineering Test Equipment Manufacturers
BCF	Bacon Curers Federation
BCF	British Ceramic Confederation
BCF	British Chess Federation
BCF	British Coatings Federation (*ex* PMAGB, SBPIM)
BCF	British Concrete Federation
BCF	British Cycling Federation
BCFA	British Contract Furnishing Association
BCFA	British-China Friendship Association
BCFG	Burma Campaign Fellowship Group
BCFGA	British Columbia Fruit Growers' Association
BCFS	British Columbia Forestry Society
BCFSSA	Brake Cable and Fine Steel Strand Association
BCFTE	British Commonwealth Forest Translation Exchange
BCG	Biology Curators' Group
BCG	British Chelonia Group
BCG	Bundesgesinnung der Chemischen Gewerbe = AACT
BCGA	British Carrot Growers Association
BCGA	British Compressed Gases Association
BCGBA	British Crown Green Bowling Association
BCGLO	British Commonwealth Geographical Liaison Office
BCGMA	British Commercial Glasshouse Manufacturers' Association
BCGÖG	Bundesfraktion Christlicher Gewerschafter im Österreichischen Gewerkschaftsbund
BCGT	Banque Commerciale du Ghana (Togo)
BCGTMA	British Ceramic Gift and Tableware Manufacturers Association
BChA	British Chiropody Association
BCHAC	British Columbia Historical Arms Collectors (Canada)
BCHC	British Crane Hire Corporation
BCHE	Bath College of Higher Education
BCHFA	British-Canadian Holstein Friesian Association
BCHS	British Canadian Holstein Society
BCI	Banca Commerciale Italiana
BCI	Bat Conservation International (U.S.A.)
BCI	Battery Council International
BCI	Bedrijfsgroep Chemische Industrie
BCI	Bonsai Clubs International (U.S.A.)
BCI	Bureau Consultatif Interorganisational
BCIA	British Clothing Industry Association
BCIA	British Columbia Institute of Agrologists
BCIA	British Cooking Industry Association
BCIE	Banco Centroamericano de Integración Económica (CACM) = CABEI
BCIES	British Comparative and International Education Society
BCINA	British Commonwealth International Newsfilm Agency
BCIPPA	British Cast Iron Pressure Pipe Association
BCIRA	British Cast Iron Research Association
BCIS	Building Cost Information Service
BCIT	British Columbia Institute of Technology
BCIU	Business Council for International Understanding (U.S.A.)
BCK	Belgisch Centrum voor Kwaliteitszorg
BCLA	British Comparative Literature Association
BCLA	British Contact Lens Association
BCLDI	British Clayware Land Drain Industry
BCLMA	British Columbia Lumber Manufacturers' Association
BCM	Banque Centrale de Mauritanie
BCM	Banque Centrale du Mali
BCM	Bible Club Movement
BCM	Black Consciousness Movement (South Africa)
BCMA	BEAMA Capacitor Manufacturers Association
BCMA	Breast Care and Mastectomy Association
BCMA	British Canoe Manufacturers Association
BCMA	British Caramel Manufacturers Association
BCMA	British Carpet Manufacturers Association

BCMA	British Chain Manufacturers Association
BCMA	British Chip Board Manufacturers Association
BCMA	British Closure Manufacturers Association
BCMA	British Colour Makers Association
BCMA	British Columbia Medical Association
BCMA	British Complementary Medicine Association
BCMA	British Concrete Masonry Association
BCMA	British Cookware Manufacturers Association
BCMA	British Council of Maintenance Associations
BCMA	British Country Music Association
BCMA	British Crayfish Marketing Association
BCMC	British Cable Makers Confederation
BCME	Beverage Can Makers Europe (Belgium)
BCMÉA	Bureau Commun du Machinisme et de l'Équipement Agricole
BCMF	British Ceramic Manufacturers Federation
BCMI	Beijing Communications Management Institute
BCMM	Brunel Centre for Manufacturing Metrology
BCMN	Bureau Central de Mesures Nucléaires (Euratom) = CBNM
BCMS	Bible Churchmen's Missionary Society
BCMSB	Catholic Bishops Conference (Malaysia, Singapore and Brunei)
BCN	Banco Central de Nicaragua
BCN	Biblioteca del Congreso de la Nación (Argentina)
BCNI	Blind Centre of Northern Ireland
BCNO	British College of Naturopathy and Osteopathy
BCNZ	Broadcasting Corporation of New Zealand
BCO	Baseball Confederation of Oceania (Australia)
BCO	British College of Optometrists
BCO	British Council for Offices
BCOB	Bond van Christelijke Ondernemers in het Bakkersbedrijf
BCODP	British Council of Organisations of Disabled People
BCOG	British College of Obstetricians and Gynaecologists
BCOLATIN	Banco Latino (Peru)
BCP	Banco de Crédito Popular (Nicaragua)
BCP	Bangladesh Communist Party
BCP	Basotho Congress Party (Lesotho)
BCP	Basutoland Congress Party
BCP	Better Cities Program
BCP	Bulgarian Communist Party
BCP	Burmese Communist Party
BCPA	British Concrete Pumping Association
BCPA	British Council of Productivity Associations
BCPAA	British China and Porcelain Artists Association
BCPC	British Crop Protection Council
BCPCA	Beijing Centre of Physical and Chemical Analysis
BCPIT	British Council for the Promotion of International Trade
BCPMMA	British Ceramic Plant and Machinery Manufacturers Association
BCPO	British Commonwealth Producers' Organisation
BCPOU	Bahamas Communication and Public Officers' Union
BCPPC	British Christian Pen Pal Club
BCPR	Belgisch Centrum voor Public Relations = CBRP
BCPSA	British Columbia Political Studies Association
BCR	Bituminous Coal Research (U.S.A.)
BCR	British Ceramic Research
BCR	Bureau Communautaire de Référence (CE)
BCR	Bureau of Commercial Research
BCRA	British Cave Research Association
BCRA	British Ceramic Research Association
BCRA	British Coke Research Association
BCRA	British Commercial Rabbit Association
BCRC	British Cave Rescue Council
BCRC	British Columbia Research Council
BCRC-UK	Blissymbolics Communication Resource Centre
BCRG	Banque Centrale de la République de Guinée
BCRGA	British Cut Rose Growers Association
BCRI	Biological and Chemical Research Institute, Rydalmere
BCRP	Banco Central de Reserva del Peru
BCRU	British Committee on Radiological Units

BCRUM	British Committee on Radiation Units and Measurements
BCS	Biblical Creation Society
BCS	Bishops' Conference of Scotland
BCS	Black Country Society
BCS	Bond van Christelijke Slagerspatroons
BCS	British Calibration Service (DTI)
BCS	British Cardiac Society
BCS	British Cartographic Society
BCS	British Ceramic Society
BCS	British Clematis Society
BCS	British Computer Society
BCS	British Crossbow Society
BCSA	British College Sports Association
BCSA	British Constructional Steelwork Association
BCSA	British Cutlery and Silverware Association
BCSAA	British Computer Society ALGOL Association
BCSC	British Council of Shopping Centres
BCSC	British Cycle Speedway Council (*ex* CSC)
BCSD	Business Council for Sustainable Development (Switzerland)
BCSH	British Committee for Standards in Haematology
BCSI	British Campaign to Stop Immigration
BCSIR	Bangladesh Council of Scientific and Industrial Research
BCSLA	British Columbia School Librarians Association (Canada)
BCSS	British Cactus and Succulent Society
BCSS	British Charollais Sheep Society
BCT	Bat Conservation Trust
BCT	British Caspian Trust
BCT	Building Conservation Trust
BCTA	British Canadian Trade Association
BCTA	British Children's Theatre Association
BCTC	British Carpet Technical Centre
BCTC	British Ceramic Tile Committee
BCTCM	Beijing College of Traditional Chinese Medicine
BCTGA	British Christmas Tree Growers Association
BCTP	British Continental Trade Press
BCTS	British Connective Tissue Society
BCTWIU	Bakery, Confectionery and Tobacco Workers International Union (U.S.A.)
BCU	Banco Central del Uruguay
BCU	British Canoe Union
BCU	British Commonwealth Union
BCVA	British Cattle Veterinary Association
BCVA	British Columbia Veterinary Association
BCW	Botswana Council for Women
BCWA	British Car Wash Association
BCWLDI	British Clay Ware Land Drain Industry
BCWMA	British Clock and Watch Manufacturers Association (*now* BHF)
BCZ	Belgische Centrale Zuivelcommissie
BCZV	Bond van Coöperatieve Zuivelverkoopverenigingen
BDA	Banco de Desarrollo Agropecuário (Panama)
BDA	Basotho Democratic Alliance (Lesotho)
BDA	Brick Development Association (South Africa, U.K.)
BDA	British Darts Organisation
BDA	British Deaf Association
BDA	British Decorators Association
BDA	British Deming Association
BDA	British Dental Association
BDA	British Development Association
BDA	British Diabetic Association
BDA	British Dietetic Association
BDA	British Domestic Appliances, Ltd
BDA	British Dragon Boat Racing Association
BDA	British Drilling Association
BDA	British Dyslexia Association
BDA	Bulb Distributors' Association
BDA	Bund Deutscher Architekten
BDA	Bundesvereinigung der Deutschen Arbeitgeberverbände
BDA	Bundesvereinigung Deutscher Apothekerverbände
BDAA	Bio-dynamic Agricultural Association
BDABS	Blonde d'Aquitaine Breeders Society of Great Britain
BDAC	Biological Diversity Advisory Committee
BDACI	Bois d'Abidjan Côte-d'Ivoire
BDAF	British Defence and Aid Fund for Southern Africa
BDAMA	British Distributors of Animal Medicines Association
BDB	Bahamas Development Bank
BDB	Barbados Development Bank

BDB	Bibliotéca del Bibliotecário (Argentina)
BDB	Bund Deutscher Baumeister, Architekten und Ingenieure
BDB	Bund Deutscher Baumschulen
BDB	Bundesverband der Deutschen Briefmarkenversteigerer
BDB	Bundesverband der Deutschen Bürstenindustrie
BDB	Bundesverband Deutsche Beton- und Fertigteilindustrie
BDB	Bundesvereinigung Deutscher Bibliotheksverbände e.V.
BDBA	Bundesverband Deutscher Berufsausbilder
BDBL	Belgische Dienst voor Bedrijfsleven en Landbouw
BDC	Banco Desarrollo Caribe = CDB, Caribank
BDC	Banque de Développement des Comoros
BDC	Bentley Drivers Club
BDC	Berufsverband der Deutschen Chirurgen
BDC	Book Development Council
BDC	Building Data Council (Sweden)
BDC	Bureau International de Documentation des Chemins de Fer
BDCC	British Defence Coordinating Committee
BDD	Banque Dahoméenne de Développement
BDD	Bulgarsko Dermatologichno Druzhestvo
BDD	Bund Deutscher Detektive
BDD	Bundesverband Deutscher Detektive e.V.
BDDA	British Deaf and Dumb Association
BDDG	Bundesverband des Deutschen Düngemittelgrosshandels
BDDMG	Bundesverband des Deutschen Dental-Medizinischen Grosshandels
BDDRG	British Deep-Drawing Research Group
BDDSA	British Deaf Amateur Sports Association
BDDV	Bund Deutscher Dolmetscherverbände
BDE	Bundesverband Deutscher Einsenbahnen
BDÉAC	Banque de Développement des États de l'Afrique Centrale (Congo) = CASDB
BDÉGL	Banque de Développement des États des Grands Lacs
BDÉT	Banque de Développement Économique de Tunisie
BDF	Ballroom Dancers Federation
BDF	Banque de France
BDF	Barbados Defence Force
BDF	Belize Defence Force
BDF	Botswana Defence Force
BDF	British Digestive Foundation
BDF	Bund Deutscher Forstmänner
BDF	Bundesverband des Deutschen Güterfernverkehrs
BDFA	British Dairy Farmers' Association
BDFA	British Deer Farmers Association
BDFA	British Doll Artists Association
BDFA	Bundesverband der Finanz- und Anlageberater
BDFG	Bundesverband des Deutschen Farben-Tapeten- Bodenbelagsgrosshandels
BDFI	Bund Deutscher Fliesengeschäfte
BDG	Banque Gabonaise de Développement
BDG	Bloc Démocratique Gabonais
BDG	Bois Déroulés Gabon
BDG	Bund Deutscher Gebrauchsgrafiker
BDG	Bund Deutscher Grafik-Designer
BDG	Bundesverband Deutscher Gesangspädagogen
BDGA	British Dahlia Growers Association
BDH	British Drug Houses, Ltd
BDHA	British Dental Hygienists Association
BDHF	British Dental Health Foundation
BDI	British Dyslexia Institute
BDI	Bundesverband der Deutschen Industrie
BDI	Bureau de Développement Industriel (Gabon)
BDIA	Bund Deutscher Innerarchitekten
BDIC	Bibliothèque de Documentation Internationale Contemporaine
BDK	Bund der Deutscher Konsumgenossenschaften
BDK	Bundesvervand Deutscher Kosmetikerinnen
BDL	Banque de Développement Local (Algeria)
BDL	Bund der Deutschen Landjugend im Deutschen Bauernverband
BDL	Bundersverband Deutscher Leasing-Gesellschaften
BDL	Bundesverband Deutscher Lederhändler
BDLA	Bund Deutscher Landschaftsarchitekten
BDLI	Bundesverband der Deutschen Luftfahrt, Raumfahrt und Ausrüstungsindustrie

BDM	Banque de Développement du Mali	**BDS**	Bundesverband der Deutschen Schrottwirtschaft
BDMA	British Direct Marketing Association (*now* DMA(U.K.))	**BDS**	Bundesverband Deutscher Stahlhandel
BDMAA	British Direct Mail Advertising Association	**BDSA**	British Dental Students Association
BDMG	Banco de Desenvolvimento de Minas Gerais	**BDSC**	British Deaf Sports Council
BDMG	Bashkimi Demokratik i Minoritetit Grek "Omonia" = DUGM = OSO (Albania)	**BDSP**	Bundersverband Deutscher Samenkaufleute und Pflanzenzüchter
BDMH	Bundesverband des Deutschen Musikinstrumentenhersteller	**BdSW**	Bundesverband der Selbstbedienungs-Warenhäuser
BDMLR	British Divers Marine Life Rescue	**BDT**	Banque de Développement du Tchad
BDN	Bashkimi i të Drejtave të Njëriut (Albania) = UPHR	**BDTA**	British Dental Trade Association
BDN	Bundesverband des Deutschen Güternahverkehrs	**BDTA**	Bundesverband Deutscher Tabakwaren-Grosshändler und Automatenaufsteller
BDO	Bois Déroulés Océan	**BDU**	Bahamas Doctors' Union
BDO	British Darts Organisation	**BDU**	Belarusan Democratic Union (Poland) = BZD
BDO	Bund Deutscher Oenologen e.V.	**BDU**	Berufsverband der Deutschen Urologen
BDO	Bund Deutscher Orgelbaumeister	**BDU**	Bund Deutscher Unternehmensberater
BDP	Berufsverband Deutscher Psychologen	**BDÜ**	Bundesverband der Dolmetscher und Übersetzer
BDP	Bophuthatswana Democratic Party	**BDV**	Bundesverband der Versandschlachtereien
BDP	Botswana Democratic Party	**BDV**	Bundesverband Deutscher Volks- und Betriebswirte
BDP	Bundesverband der Pneumologen		
BDP	Bundesverband des Deutschen Personenverkehrsgewerbes	**BDV**	Bundesverband Deutscher Vorzugsmilcherzeuger
BDP	Bundesverband Deutscher Pflanzenzüchter	**BDVB**	Bundesverband Deutscher Volks- und Betriebswirte
BDPA	British Disposable Products Association	**BDVI**	Bund der Öffentlich Bestellten Vermessungsingenieure
BDPA	Bureau pour le Développement de la Production Agricole (Congo)	**BDVT**	Bund Deutscher Verkaufsförderer und Verkaufstrainer
BDPh	Bund Deutscher Philatelisten	**BDW**	Bund Deutscher Werbeberater
BDPK	Bundesverband Deutscher Privatkrankenanstalten	**BDWB**	Bundesverband Deutscher Wirtschaftsberater
BDR	Bangladesh Rifles	**BDWCA**	British Decoy Wildfowl Carvers' Association
BDRA	British Drag Racing Association (*now* BNDRA)	**BdWi**	Bund Demokratischer Wissenschaftlerinnen und Wissenschaftler
BdRB	Bundesverband der Reiseandenken-Branche		
BDRG	Bund Deutscher Rassegeflügelzüchter	**BDZ**	Bundesverband der Deutschen Zahnärzte (*now* BZAK)
BDRN	Banque de Développement de la République du Niger	**BdZ**	Bundesverband der Zigarrenindustrie
BDRS	British Double Reed Society	**BDZV**	Bundesverband Deutscher Zeitungsverleger
BDS	British Dam Society		
BDS	British Deer Society	**BE**	Bundesamt für Energiewirtschaft (Switzerland)
BDS	British Display Society	**BEA**	Banque Extérieure d'Algérie
BDS	British Dragonfly Society	**BEA**	British Egg Association
BDS	British Driving Society	**BEA**	British Energy Association
BDS	Bund Deutscher Sekretärinnen		

BEA	British Engineers' Association
BEA	British Entertainment Agencies
BEA	British Epilepsy Association
BEA	British Euchre Association
BEA	Bundesverband der Energie – Abnehmer
BEA	Business Equipment Association of South Africa
BEAB	British Electrotechnical Approvals Board
BÉAC	Banque des États de l'Afrique Centrale (UDEAC)
BEACON	British Electronic Auction Comparing Network
BEADA	British Export Accessory and Design Association
BEAG	British Egg Art Guild
BEAIRA	British Electrical and Allied Industries Research Association
BEAL	Banque Européenne d'Amérique Latine = EULABANK
BEAMA	Federation of British Electrotechnical and Allied Manufacturers Associations
BEAMATDA	BEAMA Transmission and Distribution Association
BEAS	British Educational Administration Society
BEB	British Export Board
BEC	Bahamas Employers' Confederation
BEC	Barbados Employers' Confederation
BEC	Batalhão de Engenharia Civil (Brazil)
BEC	Belgisch Elektrotechnisch Comité = CEB
BEC	Bermuda Employer's Council
BEC	Bourse Européenne des Collectionneurs
BEC	British Electrotechnical Committee
BEC	British Evangelical Council
BEC	Building Employers Confederation
BEC	Bureau Européen de Coordination des Organisations Internationales de Jeunesse = ECB
BEC	Business Executive Centre TEFRC
BECA	British Exhibition Contractors Association
BECC	British Empire Cancer Campaign
BECC	Bureau d'Études Coopérative et Communautaires
BECEB	Bedrijfs-Economisch Centrum voor de Elektrotechnische Bedrijfstak
BECETEL	Centre Belge d'Études Technologiques sur Tuyauteries et Accessoires
BECIBA	Société des Bétons et Ciments de Bassa (Cameroon)
BECIS	Bureau d'Études, de Conseils et d'Intervention du Sahel (Mali)
BECMA	British Electro-Ceramic Manufacturers Association
BECO	Banana Export Company (Jamaica)
BECOIJ	Bureau Européen de Coordination des Organisations Internationales de Jeunesse = ECBIYO
BECON	Bahamas Employees Federation
BECSA	Belgian Engineers and Constructors SA
BECT	Bureau Européen du Cinéma et de la Télévision (ACT, EBU)
BECTA	British Engineers' Cutting Tools Association
BECTO	British Electric Cable Testing Organisation
BECTU	Broadcasting, Entertainment, Cinematograph and Theatre Union (*ex* ACTT)
BECWLC	British Empire and Commonwealth Weight Lifting Council
BEDA	British Entertainment and Dancing Association
BEDA	Bureau of European Designers Associations
BEDCO	Basotho Enterprise Development Corporation (Lesotho)
BEDE	Banco de Desarrollo del Ecuador
BEDEK	Israel Aircraft Industries
BEDFPU	Brigada de Estudos da Defesa Fitossanitéria dos Produtos Ultramarinos (Portugal)
BEDU	Botswana Enterprises Development Unit
BEE	Bureau Européen de l'Environnement = EEB
BEE	Bureau of Educational Evaluation (U.S.A.)
BEEA	British Educational Equipment Association
BEEC	Buildings Energy Efficiency Confederation
BEÉP	Bureau Européen de l'Éducation Populaire = EBAE
BEF	Belga Esperantista Federacio
BEF	Beweging van Europese Federalisten
BEF	British Employees Federation
BEF	British Equestrian Federation
BEF	Bundesamt für Ernahrung und Forstwirtschaft

BEFAC	British Export Finance Advisory Council
BÉFS	Bureau d'Étude des Fluides et des Structures
BEG	Brush Export Group
BÉGÉBI	Bureau d'Études et de Gestion des Élevages Bovines Intensifs
BEGS	British and European Geranium Society
BEHA	British Export Houses Association
BEI	Banque Européenne d'Investissement = EIB, ETE
BEI	British Electricity International Ltd
BÉI	Bureau d'Éducation Ibéro-Américain = IABE, OEI
BEIC	British Egg Industry Council
BÉICIP	Bureau d'Études des Industrielles et de Coopération de l'Institut Français du Pétrole
BEIS	British Egg Information Service
BEITA	Business Equipment and Information Technology Association
BEJCE	Bureau d'Echange de Jeunes de la Communauté Européenne (Belgium) = ECYEB
BEL	Baha'i Esperanto-Ligo
BEL	Banque d'Expériences Linguistiques des Villes Jumelées
BEL	Bharat Electronics Ltd (India)
BELBAG-DRAGBEL	Fédération Belge des Dragueurs de Gravier et de Sable
BELC	Bureau pour l'Enseignement de la Langue et de la Civilisation Française à l'Étranger
BELCA	Bureau d'Études Ligier Caméroun
BELF	Bundesministerium für Ernährung, Landwirtschaft und Forsten
BELGA	Agence Télégraphique Belge de Presse
BELGO-DIDAC	Chambre Professionnelle du Matériel Didactique
BELGO-GALVA	Association Belge des Industries de la Galvanisation
BELGO-SPACE	Association Belge Interprofessional des Activities Spatiales
BELI-PECHE	Société Bénino-Arabe-Libyenne de Pêche Maritime
BELIN-FARM	Belta, Belarusan News Agency
BELMR	Bureau Européen des Langues moins Répandues
BELRA	British Empire Leprosy Relief Association
BELSRI	Beijing Electric Light Sources Research Institute
BELTAG	Belarusan Telegraph Agency, Minsk
BELU	Belgisch-Luxemburgse Economische Unie
BELVAC	Société Belge de Vacuologie et de Vacuotechnique
BEMA	Beroepsvereniging van Maatschappelijk Assistenten
BEMA	Bristol & West of England Engineering Manufacturers' Association
BEMA	British Essence Manufacturers' Association
BEMA	Business Equipment Manufacturers Association (U.S.A.)
BEMAC	British Export Marketing Advisory Committee
BEMAS	British Educational Management and Administration Society
BEMEKO	Belgian Measurement Confederation
BEMFAM	Sociedade Civil Bem Estar Familiar no Brasil
BEMI	Biciklista Esperantista Movado Internacia
BEMSA	British Eastern Merchant Shippers Association
BEMSEE	British Motor Cycle Racing Club Ltd.
BEN	Black Environment Network
BEN	British Naturalists Association
BEN	Bureau d'Études Nucléaires (Belgium)
BEN	Motor and Allied Trades Benevolent Association
BEN	National Executive Bureau of the CSON (Niger)
BENELUX	Belgium, Netherlands, Luxembourg Union
BENELUX-TUG	BENELUX Tandem User Group
BENHS	British Entomological and Natural History Society
BENS	British Electroless Nickel Society
BEO	Bureau d'Études Océanographiques
BEOA	British and European Osteopathic Association
BEOA	British Essential Oils Association
BEOC	Bureau Européen de l'Objection de Conscience = EBCO
BEP	Bosneger Eenheids Partij (Suriname)
BEPA	British Edible Pulses Association
BEPA	British Egg Products Association

BEPA	British European Potato Association
BEPC	British Electric Power Convention
BEPI	Bureau d'Études et de Participations Industrielles (Morocco)
BEPTOM	Bureau d'Études des Postes et Télécommunications d'Outre-Mer
BER	Bureau of Economic Research (Bangladesh)
BERA	Biomass Energy Research Association (U.S.A.)
BERA	British Educational Research Association
BERBOH	British Examining and Registration Board in Occupational Hygiene
BERC	Basic Education Research Centre (Kenya)
BERC	Biochemical Engineering Research Centre (India)
BERCO	British Electric Resistance Company
BERD	Banque Européen pour la Reconstruction et le Développement = EBRD, EBWE
BERJASA	Bersatu Rakyat Jelata Sabah (Malaysia)
Berne Union	International Union for the Protection of Literary and Artistic Works = Union de Berne
Berne Union	International Union of Credit and Investment Insurers = Union de Berne
Bersa	British Elastic Rope Sports Association
BES	Bioelectrochemical Society
BES	Biological Engineering Society
BES	British Ecological Society
BES	British Electrophoresis Society
BES	British Endodontic Society
BES	Bulgarsko Ekologichesko Druzhestvo – Svishtov
BESA	British Earth Sheltering Association
BESA	British Electrical Systems Association
BESA	British Esperanto Scientific Association
BESI	Bioprocess Engineering Society International
BESMA	British Electro-static Manufacturers' Association
BESO	British Executive Service Overseas
BESONU	Bureau des Affaires Économiques et Sociales des Nations Unies
BESPO	Fachverband Berufs-und Sportbekleidungsindustrie
BEST	Beit Ettamwil Saudi Tounsi (Tunisia)
BEST	Board of European Students of Technology (Hungary)

BET	Barbados External Telecommunicatiions
BET	Board of External Trade (Tanzania)
BET	British Electric Traction Company
BETA	British Equestrian Trade Association
BETA	Broadcast and Entertainment Trades Alliance
BETA	Bureau for Education Technology and Administration (U.S.A.)
BETA	Business Equipment Trade Association (U.S.A.)
BETAA	British Export Trade Advertising Association
Betlemitas	Orden de los Hermanos de Bélen
BETMA	Bureau Professionnel d'Études Techniques des Marchés Agricoles
BETRACO	Société Bénin Transit Cie
BETRACO-Niger	Niger Société Bénin-Niger de Transit et de Groupage
BETRO	British Export Trade Research Organisation
BETS	Business Ethics Teaching Society
BETURE	Bureau d'Études Techniques pour l'Urbanisme et l'Équipement
BEU	Benelux Economic Union = BRES
BEUC	Bureau Européen des Unions de Consommateurs
BEV	Bundesvereinigung Deutscher Einkaufsverbände
BEVA	British Equine Veterinary Association
BEVA	British Exhibition Venues Association
BEVA	Landsbond van de Belgische Varkensstamboeken
BEVABS	Bureau Éuropen des Vins, Alcools et Boissons Spiritueuses
BEVAG	Belgische Vereniging van de Atlantische Gemeenschap
BEVETAB	National Beroepsvereniging van Importeurs, Handelaars, Commissionairs, Makelaars en Agenten in Tabakken in Bladeren in België
BEVIA	Verband von Vieh-, Fleisch- und Fleischwarenimporteuren
BEVIFA	Vereninging der Belgische Vismeelfabrikanten
BEWA	British Effluent and Water Association
BEWAC	British West Indian Corporation
BEWAG	Berliner Kraft- und Licht AG
BEWEDIT	Belgische Comité voor Weverij en Diverse Textielindustrieén
BEWU	Bahamas Electrical Workers' Union

BEX	Banco Exterior de España	**BFD**	Société Beuglot Frères (Ivory Coast)
BExA	British Exporters' Association	**BFDG**	British Film Designers Guild
BF	Banque de France	**BFE**	Bedrijfsfederatie der Voortbrengers en Verdelers van Electriciteit in België
BF	Bibliotekarforbundet		
BF&VCA	British Fruit and Vegetable Canners Association	**BFE**	Bundesfachverband Edelmetallerzeugnisse und Verwandte Industrien
BFA	Battle of the Flowers Association (Jersey)		
BFA	Beijing Film Academy	**BFE**	Bundesstelle für Entwicklungshilfe
BFA	British Fabric Association	**BFEBS**	British Far Eastern Broadcasting Service
BFA	British Federation of Audio		
BFA	British Fellmongers Association	**BFEC**	British Food Export Council
BFA	British Film Authority	**BFES**	British Families Education Service
BFA	British Foundry Association	**BFF**	Born Free Foundation
BFA	British Fragrance Association	**BFF**	British Fishing Federation
BFA	British Franchise Association	**BFF**	Bund Freischaffender Foto-Designer
BFA	Bundestelle für Aussenhandelsinformation	**BFF**	Bundesverband der Deutschen Fischindustrie und des Fischgrosshandels
BfA	Bundesversicherungsanstalt für Angestellte		
		BFF	Bureau of Flora and Fauna
BFAC	British Federation of Aesthetics and Cosmetology	**BFFC**	British Federation of Folk Clubs
		BFFF	British Frozen Food Federation
BFACH	British Fundraising Association for Children in Hospitals	**BFFS**	British Federation of Film Societies
		BfG	Bank für Gemeinwirtschaft
BFACM	Banque Française de l'Agriculture et du Crédit Mutuel	**BfG**	Bundesanstalt für Gewässerkünde
		BFGH	Belgische Federatie voor Genealogie en Heraldiek = FGHB
BFAK	Bundesforschungsanstalt für Kleintierzucht		
		BFH	Bundesfinanzhof
BFAWU	Bakers, Food and Allied Workers Union = BU	**BFH**	Bundesforschungsanstalt für Forst- und Holzwirtschaft (Germany)
BFB	Bibliotheksforum Bayern		
BFB	Bundesverband der Freien Berufe	**BFH**	Bundesvereinigung der Fachverbände des deutschen Handwerks
BFBB	British Federation of Brass Bands		
BFBG	British Francophone Business Group	**BFHGH&-SCA**	British Federation of Hotel, Guest House and Self-Catering Associations
BFBN	Bond van Fabrikanten van Betonwaren in Nederland		
		BFHMF	British Felt Hat Manufacturers Federation
BFBPM	British Federation of Business and Professional Women		
		BFI	British Film Institute
BFBS	British and Foreign Bible Society	**BFI**	Verband der Schweizerischen Beutel- und Flexodruck-Industrie
BFBS	British Forces Broadcasting Service		
BFC	British Falconers' Club	**BFIA**	British Facsimile Industry Compatibility Committee (CCITT)
BFC	Bureau International de Film pour les Chemins de Fer		
		BFIA	British Flower Industry Association
BFCE	Banque Français du Commerce Extérieur	**BFIA**	British Forging Industry Association
BFCHP	British Federation of Care-Home Proprietors	**BFICC**	British Facsimile Industry Consultative Committee
		BFID	Brancheforeningen af Farmaceutiske Industrivirksomheder i Danmark
BFCMA	British Flue Chimney Manufacturers Association		
		BFISL	Búnadarfélag Íslands
BFCS	British Friesian Cattle Society	**BFISS**	British Federation of Iron and Steel Stockholders
BFD	Bund Freier Demokraten		

BFJD	Bundesverband Freier Juristen Deutschlands
BFL	Bahamas Federation of Labour
BFL	Betonforskningslaboratoriet
BFLA	Belize Family Life Association
BFM	British Furniture Manufacturers Federation
BFMA	British Farm Mechanization Association
BFMA	British Floorcovering Manufacturers Association
BFMA	Building Materials Factors Association
BFMC	British Friction Materials Council
BFMF	British Federation of Music Festivals
BFMF	British Footwear Manufacturers Federation
BFMF	British Furniture Manufacturers' Federation
BFMIRA	British Food Manufacturing Industries Research Association
BFN	Beroepsfotografen Nederland
BFNS	Benevolent Fund for Nurses in Scotland
BFÖ	Berufsverband Freiberufslichtierärzte Österreichs
BFP	Bureau of Freelance Photographers
BFPA	Barbados Family Planning Association
BFPA	British Fibreboard Packaging Association
BFPA	British Fluid Power Association
BFPDA	British Fluid Power Distributors' Association
BFPDRA	British Fluorospar Producers' Development & Research Association
BFPEA	British Fibreboard Packaging Employers' Association
BFPMS	British Federation of Printing Machinery and Supplies
BFPO	British Forces Post Office
BFPSA	British Fire Protection Systems Association
BFQ	Bibliothèque Fonds Quetelet (Belgium)
BFR	Banque Fédérative Rurale
BFR	Statens Rad for Byggnadsforskning
BFRC	British Flame Research Committee
BFRC	British Flat Roofing Council
BFS	Belarusan Farmers' Society (Poland) = BSR
BFS	Branded Furniture Society
BFS	British Fantasy Society
BFS	British Fluoridation Society
BFS	British Flute Society
BFS	British Fuchsia Society
BFS	Bundesanstalt für Flugsicherung
BFSA	British Fire Services Association
BFSLYC	British Federation of Sand and Land Yacht Clubs
BFSMEA	British Fishing and Small Vessel Equipment Association
BFSS	British Field Sports Society
BFST	Bundes-Fachgemeinschaft Schwimmbad-Technik
BFSU	Beijing Foreign Studies University
BFT	Bundesverband Freier Tankstellen und Unabhängiger Deutscher Mineralölhändler
BFTA	British Fur Trade Association
BFTPA	British Film and Television Producers Association
BFTSPA	British Film and Television Stunt Performers' Association
BFTT	British Federation of Textile Technicians
BFTU	Bahamas Federation of Trade Unions
BFU	Beijing Forestry University
BFUB	Bundesverband für Umweltberatung e.V.
BFUW	British Federation of University Women (*now* BFWG)
BFV	Banky Fampandrosoana ny Varotra (Madagascar)
BFV	Belgische Franchise-vereniging
BFV	Bundesamt für Verfassungsschutz
BFW	Bread for the World (U.S.A.)
BFWA	Bundesfachverband Wasseraufbereitung
BFWAU	Bakery and Food Workers' Amalgamated Union (Éire)
BFWG	British Federation of Women Graduates (*ex* BFUW)
BFYC	British Federation of Youth Choirs
BG	Bundesamt für Gesundheitswesen
BGA	Behavior Genetics Association
BGA	British Gaming Association
BGA	British Gear Association
BGA	British Gliding Association
BGA	British Go Association
BGA	British Grit Association
BGA	Bundesgesundheitsamt
BGA	Bundesverband des Deutschen Gross- und Aussenhandels

BGA	Irish Sugar Beet Growers' Association	**BGRIMM**	Beijing General Research Institute of Mining and Metallurgy
BGC	British Gas Corporation	**BGS**	Bashkimi i Gazetarëve të Shqipërisë (Albania)
BGC	British Glues and Chemicals Ltd		
BGCI	Britannic Gardens Conservation International	**BGS**	Bashkimi të Grave të Shqipërisë (Albania) = WUA
BGCS	Botanic Garden Conservation Secretariat	**BGS**	Bílgreinasambandid
BGD	Banque Gabonaise de Développement	**BGS**	Bodenkundliche Gesellschaft der Schweiz = SSP
BGD	Bureau voor Gemeenschappelijke Diensten	**BGS**	British Geological Service
BGE	Bórd Gáis Éireann	**BGS**	British Geological Survey
BGF	Banana Growers Federation (Australia)	**BGS**	British Geotechnical Society
BGF	Schweizerischer Verband der Berufs- und Geschäftsfrauen	**BGS**	British Geriatrics Society
		BGS	British Gladiolus Society
BGFS	British Grenada Friendship Society	**BGS**	British Goat Society
BGG/P	Berufsverband Geprüfter Graphologen / Psychologen e.V. = PACG	**BGS**	British Grassland Society
		BGS	Bulgarian Geological Society
BGGRA	British Gelatine and Glue Research Association	**BGS**	Bundesgrenzschultz
		BGS	Byggnadsgeologiska Sällskapet (Sweden)
BGH	Beroepsvereniging der Promoteurs voor Huisvesting en Ruimtelijke Ordening	**BGS**	Little Brothers of the Good Shepherd (Canada)
BGH	Bundesgerichtshof	**BGSA**	British Golf Supporters Association
BGI	Brasseries et Glacières Internationales	**BGTV**	Budapesti Geodéziai és Térképészeti Vállalat
BGI	Brewers' Grain Institute (U.S.A.)	**BGV**	Bergischer Geschichtsverein
BGI	Bureau Gravimétrique International (FAGS) = IGB	**BGV**	Bilgummiverkstedenes Landsforbound
BGIR	Belgisch Genootschap voor Internationaal Recht	**BGW**	Bundesverband der Deutschen Gas- und Wasserwirtschaft
BGIRA	British Glass Industry Research Association	**BGWF**	British Granite and Whinstone Federation
		BGWS	Boys' and Girls' Welfare Society
BGL	Bundesverband Garten- Landschafts- und Sportsplatzbau	**BGZL**	Bundesverband der Rein Gewerblichen Zahntechnischen Laboratorien
BGMA	British Gear Manufacturers Association	**BH&HPA**	British Holiday and Home Parks Association
BGMA	British Generic Manufacturers' Association	**BHA**	Bankcard Holders of America
BGMA	British Glass Manufacturers' Association	**BHA**	Barbados Hotel Association
BGMA	British Glucose Manufacturers Association	**BHA**	Black History for Action
		BHA	British Hamster Association
BGMC	British Glass Manufacturers' Confederation	**BHA**	British Handball Association
		BHA	British Hardmetal Association
BGMI	Beijing General Machinery Research Institute	**BHA**	British Homoeopathic Association
BGN	Board on Geographic Names (U.S.A.)	**BHA**	British Hospitality Association
BGPA	British Goose Producers Association	**BHA**	British Humanist Association
BGR	Bundesanstalt für Geowissebschaften und Rohstoffe- Tätigkeitsbericht	**BHA**	British Hyperlipidaemia Association
		BHA	British Hypnotherapy Association
BGRB	British Greyhound Racing Board	**BHAB**	British Helicopter Advisory Board
BGRF	British Greyhound Racing Federation	**BHAC**	British Horn of Africa Council
BGRG	British Geomorphological Research Group	**BHAFRA**	British Hat and Allied Feltmakers Research Association

BHAN	Black HIV and AIDS Network
BHB	British Horseracing Board
BHBA	British Hacksaw and Bandsaw Association (*ex* BHBMA)
BHBMA	British Hacksaw and Bandsaw Manufacturers Association (*now* BHBA)
BHC	Bahamas Hotels Corporation
BHC	Bois Hydrauliques du Caméroun
BHC	British Herdsmen's Club
BHC	Business History Centre
BHCA	British Health Care Association
BHCAWU	Bahamas Hotel Catering and Allied Workers' Union
BHCC	British Hellenic Chamber of Commerce (Greece)
BHCEC	British Health Care Export Council
BHCF	British Hexagonal Chess Federation
BHCF	British Hire Cruiser Federation
BHCIG	British Human-Computer Interaction Group
BHE	Bureau of Home Economics (U.S.A.)
BHEA	Bahamas Hotel Employers' Association
BHEC	British Health Care Export Council
BHEL	Bharat Heavy Electricals Ltd (India)
BHF	British Hardware Federation
BHF	British Horological Federation (*ex* BCWMA, WCIA)
BHFN	Banco Hipotecario de Fomento Nacional (Chile)
BHFP	Basque Homeland and Freedom Party = HB
BHFS	British Hungarian Friendship Society
BHFTA	British Health Food Trade Association
BHG	British Hat Guild
BHG	Bundesverband Holzgrosshandel
BHGA	British Hang Gliding Association
BHGPA	British Hang Gliding and Paragliding Association (*ex* BAPC)
BHGV	Bonner Heimat- und Geschichtsverein e. V.
BHHMA	British Hardware and Household Manufacturers Association
BHHS	British Hosta and Hemerocallis Society
BHI	British Horological Institute
BHIC	Bosnia-Herzegovina Information Centre
BHIF	Banco Hipotecario de Fomento Nacional (Chile)
BHIF	British Headware Industries Federation
BHIPA	British Honey Importers' and Packers' Association
BHKA	British Hand Knitting Association
BHKC	British Hand Knitting Confederation
BHKH	Bundesverband des Holz- und Kunststoffverarbeitenden
BHKS	Bundesvereinigung der Industrieverbände Heizungs-, Klima- und Sanitärtechnik
BHL	Bensinhandlernes Landsforbund
BHL	British Housewives League
BHM	Bandalag Háskólamanna
BHMA	British Herbal Medicine Association
BHMA	British Holistic Medical Association
BHMA	British Homeopathic Manufacturers' Association (*now* BAHM)
BHMEA	British Hard Metal Export Association
BHMRA	British Hydromechanics Research Association
BHPC	British Hardware Promotion Council
BHPR	British Health Professionals in Rheumatology
BHPS	British Hedgehog Preservation Society
BHR	British Hypnosis Research
BHRA	British Hydromechanics Research Association
BHRA	British Hypnosis Research Association
BHRC	British Harness Racing Club
BHS	Banque de l'Habitat du Sénégal
BHS	Barbados Horticultural Society
BHS	British Herpetological Society
BHS	British Holstein Society
BHS	British Home Stores
BHS	British Horse Society
BHS	British Hydrological Society
BHS	British Hypertension Society
BHSA	British Heavy Steel Association
BHSMA	British Hay and Straw Merchants Association
BHT	Brogdale Horticultural Trust
BHTA	British Herb Trade Association
BHTC	Book House Training Centre
BHTD	Bureau of Hygiene & Tropical Diseases
BHU	Bahamas Housekeepers' Union
BHU	Banaras Hindu University (India)
BHV	Banco Hipotecario de Venezuela
BHV	Bergshandteringens Vänner
BHVP	Bibliothèque Historique de la Ville de Paris
BI	Agricultural Society of Iceland

BI	Banca d'Italia
BI	Bank Indonesia
BI	Befrienders International = BI/SW
BI	Braille Institute (U.S.A.)
BI	Institute of Biology, Latvian Academy of Sciences
BI/SW	Befrienders International – Samaritans Worldwide = BI
BIA	Bakhtar Information Agency (Afghanistan)
BIA	Bankers' Institute of Australasia
BIA	Basketware Importers' Association
BIA	Bee Industries Association (U.S.A.)
BIA	Beijing Institute of Aerodynamics
BIA	Binding Industries of America
BIA	Bioindustry Association
BIA	Bossard International et Associés (Guinea)
BIA	Bouraq Indonesia Airlines = BOU
BIA	Brick Institute of America
BIA	British Institute of Acupuncture
BIA	British Irish Association
BIA	Brunei Investment Agency
BIA	Bureau International Afghanistan (France)
BIAC	British Institute of Agricultural Consultants
BIAC	Business and Industry Advisory Committee (OECD)
BIAE	British Institute of Adult Education
BIAG	Bangladesh International Action Group
BIAHP	British Institute for the Achievement of Human Potential
BIALL	British and Irish Association of Law Librarians
BIAO	Banque Internationale pour l'Afrique Occidentale
BIAP	Bureau International d'Audiophonologie = IBAP, IOAP
BIAPE	Banco Interamericano Ahorro Prestamo
BIAS	Belgian International Air Services
BIAS	Biomedical Instrumentation Advisory Service
BIAS	Brooklyn Institute of Arts and Sciences (U.S.A.)
BIAS	Bureau International Arabe des Stupéfiants (Jordan)
BIAS	Business and Industrial Agents' Society
BIAT	Banque Internationale pour l'Afrique au Tchad
BIAT	British Institute of Architectural Technicians
BIATA	British Independent Air Transport Association
BIAZ	Banque Internationale pour l'Afrique au Zaïre
BIB	Bank voor Internationale Betalingen
BIB	Banque Internationale de Burkina
BIBA	British Insurance Brokers' Association
BIBBA	British Island Bee Breeders Association
BIBBA	British Isles Bee Breeders' Association
BIBC	British Isles Bowling Council
BIBF	British and Irish Basketball Federation
BIBIC	British Institute for Brain Injured Children
BIBM	Bureau International du Béton manufacture
BIBRA	British Industrial Biological Research Association
BIBW	Belgisch Instituut voor Bestuurswetenschappen = IBSA
BIC	Baha'i International Community = CIB
BIC	Bahrain Insurance Company
BIC	Banco de la Industria de la Construcción (Peru)
BIC	Biodeterioration Information Centre
BIC	British Importers Confederation
BIC	Building Information Centre
BIC	Bureau International des Conteneurs = ICB
BiC	Business in the Community
BIC	Butter Information Council
BICA	Bahamas Institute of Chartered Accountants
BICA	Bizonal International Control Administration
BICAM	Catholic Biblical Centre for Africa and Madagascar (Kenya) = CEBAM
BICB	Bund der Ingenieure in Anwendungs- und Verfahrenstechnik der Chemischen Industrie
BICC	British Insulated and Callender's Cables Ltd
BICC	British-Israeli Chamber of Commerce
BICC	Bureau International des Chambres de Commerce = IBCC
BICE	Banco Industrial y de Comercio Exterior (Chile)
BICÉ	Banque Internationale pour la Coopération Économique = IBEC, MBES

BICE	Bureau International Catholique de l'Enfance = ICCB, IKBK, OICI
BICENGE	Biblioteca Complementar de Engenharia (Brazil)
BICERI	British Internal Combustion Engine Research Institute
BICI	Banque Internationale pour le Commerce et l'Industrie (Cameroon, Congo, Gabon, Ivory Coast, Niger, Senegal)
BICIA-BF	Banque Internationale pour le Commerce l'Industrie et de l'Agriculture de Burkina Faso
BICIT	Banque Internationale pour le Commerce et l'Industrie du Tchad
BICMA	British Industrial Ceramic Manufacturers Association
BICOM	Bénin International Compagnie
BICS	Bangkok Institute for Child Study (Thailand)
BICS	Banque Industrielle et Commerciale (France)
BICS	Barco Industries Creative Systems (Belgium)
BICS	British Institute of Cleaning Science
BICT	Banque Ivoirienne de Construction et de Travaux Publics
BICT	Beijing Institute of Chemical Technology
BICT	Beijing Institute of Clothing Technology
BICTA	British Investment Casting Trade Association
BID	Banco Interamericano de Desarrollo = IADB
BID	Banque Islamique de Développement
BIDAC	Biological Diversity Advisory Committee
BIDC	Banque Internationale du Congo
BIDC	Barbados Industrial Development Corporation
BIDE	Bangladesh Institute of Development Economics
BIDI	Banque Ivoirienne de Développement Industriel
BIDILC	Bureau International de la Didactique des Langues Classiques (Belgium)
BIDO	British Industrial Development Office
BIDS	Bangladesh Institute of Development Studies
BIE	Beijing Institute of Electromachining
BIE	British Institute of Embalmers
BIE	Bundesverband Industrieller Einkauf
BIÉ	Bureau International d'Éducation (Switzerland) = IBE, MBD, OIE
BIE	Bureau International de l'Environnement (Switzerland) = IEB
BIE	Bureau International des Expositions
BIE	Bureau Ivoirien d'Engineering
BIE	Bureau of Industry Economics
BIEA	Bond van Internationale en Europese Ambtenaren = SFE, UIECS, VIEB
BIEC	British Invisible Exports Council
BIEE	British Institute of Energy Economics
BIEET	British-Irish Exchange and Education Trust
BIÉF	Banque Internationale d'Information sur les États Francophones
BIÉM	Bureau International de l'Édition Mécanique =IBMR
BIEM	Bureau International des Sociétés Gérant les Droits d'Enregistrement et de Reproduction Mécanique
BIEN	Basic Income European Network (Belgium)
BIEN	Brigada de Investigaciones Especiales y Narcoticos (Guatemala)
BIÉS	Bureau Interprofessionnel d'Études Statistiques Sucrières
BIET	Board of Incorporated Engineers
BIET	British Institute of Engineering Technology
BIET	Bureau International de l'Enseignement Technique
BIF	British Industries Fair
BIFA	Banking Insurance and Finance Union
BIFA	British Independent Factors Association
BIFA	British Industrial Fasteners' Association
BIFA	British International Freight Association
BIFA	Bureau International de l'Heure
BIFAC	British Isles Federation of Agricultural Co-operatives
BIFAD	Board for International Food and Agricultural Development (AID)
BIFCA	British Industrial Furnace Construction Association
BIFD	British Institute of Funeral Directors
BIFEDSA	Building Industries Federation, South Africa = BIFSA
BIFF	British Industrial Fasteners Federation
BIFM	British Institute of Facilities Management (*ex* AFM)

BIFMA	British Industrial Floor Machine Association	**BILA**	British Insurance Law Association
BIFN	Banque Internationale pour le Financement de l'Énergie Nucléaire	**BILC**	Bureau for International Language Coordination
BIFOA	Betriebswirtschaftliches Institut für Organisation und Automation	**BILD**	British Institute of Learning Disabilities (*ex* BIMH)
BIFSA	Building Industries Federation of South Africa = BIFEDSA	**BILD**	Bureau International de Liaison et de Documentation (Germany)
BIFU	Banking Insurance and Finance Union	**BILETA**	British and Irish Legal Education Technology Association
BIG	Bank Inicjatyw Gospodarczych	**BILG**	Building Industry Libraries Group
BIG	Bois Industriels du Gabon	**BILI**	Beijing Institute of Light Industry
BIG	British Institute of Graphologists	**BILIPO**	Bibliothèque des Littératures Policières
BIG	Bund der Ingenieure des Gartenbaues und der Landespflege	**BIM**	Banco Industrial del Mediterraneo
		BIM	Beijing Institute of Meteorology
BIGA	British Iceberg Growers' Association Ltd	**BIM**	Bord Iascaigh Mhara (Éire)
BIGA	British Independent Garages Association	**BIM**	British Institute of Management (*now* IM)
BIGA	British Independent Grocers Association		
BIGA	Bundesamt für Industrie, Gewerbe und Arbeit (Switzerland)	**BIM**	British Insulin Manufacturers
		BIMA	Banque Internationale pour la Mauritanie
BIGCA	British Institute of Golf Course Architects	**BIMA**	British Industrial Marketing Association
BIGGA	British and International Golf Greenkeepers Association	**BIMA**	British Interactive Multimedia Association
BIGWU	Barbados Industrial and General Workers' Union	**BIMA**	British Interlining Manufacturers Association (*now* ASBCI)
BIHA	British Ice Hockey Association	**BIMAP**	Barbados Institute of Management and Productivity
BIHAS	Biological Institute, Henan Academy of Sciences (China)	**BIMAS**	Bimbingan Masyarakat (Indonesia)
BIHFS	British Institute of Hardwood Flooring Specialists	**Bimbo**	British Merchant Banking and Security Houses Association
BIHR	British Institute of Human Rights	**BIMCO**	Baltic and International Maritime Council (Denmark)
BII	British Institute of Innkeeping	**BIMH**	British Institute of Mental Handicap (*now* BILD)
BIIA	British Institute of Industrial Art		
BIIBA	British Insurance and Investment Brokers' Association	**BIML**	Bureau International de Métrologie Légale (OIML)
BIIC	British Insurers' International Committee	**BIMM**	British Institute of Muscoskeletal Medicine (*ex* BAMM)
BIIC	British-Irish Industry Circle	**BIMR**	Bureau International de Mécanique des Roches
BIICC	Bureau International d'Information des Chambres de Commerce	**BIMSA**	Beama Interactive & Mains Systems Association
BIICL	British Institute of International and Comparative Law	**BIMSOC**	British Institute of Management Secretariat for Overseas Countries
BIID	British Institute of Interior Design		
BIIT	British Institute of Industrial Therapy	**BIMT**	Bureau International de Mécanique des Terrains (WMC) = IBG, IBSM, MBMGP, OIMR
BIIT	Bureau International d'Information sur les Télécommunications (Switzerland)		
BIJS	British Institute of Jazz Studies	**BIN**	Banco Inmobilario (Nicaragua)
BIKA	British Institute of Kitchen Architecture	**BIN**	Belgisch Instituut voor Normalisatie = IBN
BIL	Bilmportoerenes Landsforening		

BIN	Bureau of Information on Nickel
BINA	Bangladesh Institute of Nuclear Agriculture
BINAGRI	Biblioteca Nacional de Agricultura (Brazil)
BINAME	Biblioteca Nacional de Medicina (Uruguay)
BINAS	Biosafety Information Network and Advisory Services
BINC	Building Industries National Council
BINE	Beijing Institute of Nuclear Engineering
BING	Federation of European Rigid Polyurethane Foam Associations
BINGO	Business International Non-Governmental Organisation
BINLAC	Biosciences Information Network for Latin America and the Caribbean (Venezuela) = RIBLAC
BINOP	Institut National d'Étude du Travail et d'Orientation Professionnelle
BInstNDT	British Institute of Non-Destructive Testing
BINTO	Boulangerie Industrielle Togolaise
BINZ	Bankers Institute of New Zealand
BIO	Bedford Institute of Oceanography (Canada)
BIO	Biologenes Interesseorganisasjon (Norway)
BIO	Brit Ivrit Olamit
BIO	Bureau Interorganisations pour les Systèmes d'Information et les Activités Connexes
BIO-POLYMER International	World Association of Food Grade Biopolymer Producers
Biobras	Bioquimica do Brasil
Biocentre	Biotechnology Centre, Wales
BIONET	Biodiversity Action Network (U.S.A.)
BIOP	Board of International Organisations and Programs (U.S.A.)
BiOS	Biomedical Optics Society
BIOS	British Institute of Organ Studies
BIOS	British Intelligence Objectives Sub-Committee
BIOSS	Brunel Institute of Organization & Social Studies
BIOSt	Bundesinstitut für Ostwissenschaftliche und Internationale Studien
BIOT	British Indian Ocean Territory
BIOTA	Biological Institute of Tropical America (U.S.A.)
Biotechnica	Association pour le Développement des Biotechnologies en Aquitaine
BIOTROP	Regional Center for Tropical Biology (SEAMEO)
BIP	Banco Industrial del Perú
BIP	Banco Internacional de Pagos
BIP	Botswana Independence Party
BIP	British Industrial Plastics
BIP	Union Belge des Installateurs Professionnels d'Antennes
BIPA	Bond van Importeurs van Pharmaceutische Artikelen
BIPAN	Banco Internacional de Panama
BIPAR	Bureau International des Producteurs d'Assurances et de Réassurances
BIPAVER	Bureau International Permanent des Associations des Vendeurs et Rechapeurs de Pneumatiques
BIPD	Beijing Institute of Packaging Design
BIPE	Bahamas Institute of Professional Engineers
BIPE	Beijing Institute of Physical Education
BIPE	Bureau d'Information et de Prévisions Économiques
BIPEA	British Independent Plastic Extruders Association
BIPEC	Boulangerie Industrielle de la Petite Côte
BIPED	Bureau International pour l'Étude de la Distribution
BIPG	Banque Internationale pour le Gabon
BIPL	Bureau International de la Paix
BIPM	Bureau International des Poids et Mesures = IBWM
BIPN	Banque Internationale pour le Niger
BIPO	British Institute of Public Opinion
BIPP	British Institute of Practical Psychology
BIPP	British Institute of Professional Photography
BIPPILA	Bureaux Internationaux Réunis pour la Protection de la Propriété Industrielle, Littéraire et Artistique
BIPS	British Institute of Persian Studies
BIPT	Banque Ivoirienne d'Épargne et de Développement des Postes et Télécommunications
BIPTM	Bureau International de Physique Thermique Minière (WMC) (Russia) = IBBW, IBMT, MBGT
BIR	Banque Internationale des Ressources (CCEI) = IRB

BIR	British Institute of Radiology	**BIS**	British Interplanetary Society
BIR	Bureau International de la Récupération	**BIS**	British Iris Society
BIR	Bureau of Immigration Research	**BIS**	British Italian Society
BIR	Bureau of Industrial Relations (U.S.A.)	**BIS**	British Ivy Society
BIR	Bureau of Industry Research	**BIS**	Bureau International du Scoutisme
BIRA	Belgisch Instituut voor Regeltechniek en Automatisatie = IBRA	**BIS**	Bureau of Indian Standards
		BIS	Bureau of Information Science
BIRA	British Institute of Regulatory Affairs	**BISA**	Banco Industrial S.A. (Bolivia)
BIRA	Bureau Interafricain pour les Ressources Animales = IBAR	**BISA**	British International Studies Association
		BISA	Bulgarian Industrial Association
BIRAS	British Inflammation Research Association	**BISAC**	Book Industry Systems Advisory Committee (U.S.A.)
BIRC	British Industry Roads Campaign	**BISAKTA**	British Iron and Steel and Kindred Trades Association
BIRD	Banque Internationale pour la Reconstruction et le Développement = BIRF, BIRS, IBRD World Bank	**BISCC**	British Iron and Steel Consumers Council
BIRD Centre	Centre for Brain Injury Rehabilitation & Development	**BISCOFA**	Schweizerischer Verband der Biscuits- und Confiseriefabrikanten
BIRDEM	Bangladesh Institute of Research and Rehabilitation in Diabetes, Endocrine, and Metabolic Disorders	**BISEC**	Board of Intermediate and Secondary Education (Pakistan)
BIRE	British Institution of Radio Engineers	**BISEE**	Beijing Institute of Satellite Environment Engineering
BIREME	Biblioteca Regional de Medicina (Uruguay)	**BISÉR**	Bureau Interafricain des Sols et de l'Économie Rurale
BIRF	Banco Internacional de Reconstrucción y Fomento = BIRD, BIRS, IBRD	**BISF**	British Iron and Steel Federation
BIRF	Brewing Industry Research Foundation	**BISFA**	Bureau International pour la Standardisation de la Rayonne et des Fibres Synthétiques (Switzerland)
BIRISPT	Bureau International de Recherche sur les Implications Socials du Progrès Technique		
		BISG	Book Industry Study Group (U.S.A.)
BIRMO	British Infra-Red Manufacturers Organization	**BISI**	British Iron and Steel Institute
		BISL	British Institute of Security Laws
BIROE	Bureau International de Recherches sur les Oiseaux d'Eau = IWRB	**BISM**	Balai Penelitian dan Pengembangan Industri Semarang (Indonesia)
BIRPS	Bitish Institutions Reflection Profiling Syndicate	**BISP**	British Institute of Sewage Purification
BIRS	Banca Internazionale per la Recostruzione et lo Sviluppo = BIRD, BIRF, IBRD, World Bank	**BISPA**	British Independent Steel Producers' Association
		BISRA	British Iron and Steel Research Association
BIRS	Bureau International de Recherches sur la Sauvagerie	**BIST**	British Institute of Surgical Technologists
BIRU	Basic Ideology Research Unit (U.K.)	**BISTI**	Bengbu Institute of Sci-Tech Information
BIRW	British-Irish Rights Watch	**BIT**	Beijing Institute of Technology
BIS	Bank for International Settlements (Switzerland) = BIZ, BRI	**BIT**	Beijing Institute of Tourism
		BIT	Board of Internal Trade (Tanzania)
BIS	Banking Information Service	**BIT**	Bureau International du Travail (ONU) = ILO
BIS	Bird Information Service		
BIS	British Ichthyological Society	**BIT**	Bureau International Technique de l'ABS (Belgium)
BIS	British Information Services		
BIS	British Interlingua Society	**BITA**	British Impact Treatment Association

BITA	British Industrial Truck Association	**BIWF**	British-Israel World Federation
BITA	British Industrial Tyre Manufactures Association	**BIWS**	Bureau of International Whaling Statistics = BSBI, OEBI
BITA	British Interior Textiles Association (*ex* HCFTA)	**BIZ**	Bank für Internationalen Zahlungsausgleich = BIS, BRI
BITAC	Bangladesh Industrial Technical Assistance Centre	**BJ&GF**	British Jewellery and Giftware Federation
BITC	Bureau International Technique du Chlore (Belgium)	**BJA**	British Jewellers Association
BITC	Business in the Community	**BJA**	British Judo Association
Bitco	Bahamas International Trust Company	**BJAEC**	Beijing Adult Education College
BITCO	Bihar Industrial and Technical Consultancy Organisation (India)	**BjB I**	Balkan-ji-Bari International
		BJC	British Junior Chamber
BITD	Bureau International des Tarifs Douaniers	**BJCC**	British Junior Chambers of Commerce
BITÉJ	Bureau International pour le Tourisme et les Échanges de la Jeunesse	**BJCEB**	British Joint Communications and Electronics Board
BITER	British Institute of Traffic Education Research	**BJGG**	British Joint Corrosion Group
		BJJA	British Jiu Jitsu Association
BITMA	British Industrial Tyre Manufacturers Association	**BJL**	British Jigsaw Library
BITO	British Institution of Training Officers	**BJOC**	Fédération Nationale de la Bijouterie, Joaillerie, Orfèvrerie, Cadeaux, Diamants, Pierres et Perles
BITOA	British Incoming Tour Operators Association		
BITOM	Bureau International de l'Information sur Toiles Métalliques	**BJP**	Bharatiya Janata Party
		BJPL	British Jigzaw Puzzle Library
BITOR	Bitúmenes Orinoco (Venezuela)	**BJRI**	Bangladesh Jute Research Institute
BITRAJU	Bureau International de Traductions Juridiques	**BJSM**	British Joint Services Mission (U.S.A.)
BITRI	Beijing International Trade Research Institute	**BJTRA**	British Jute Trades Research Association
		BJU	Bundesverband Junger Unternehmer
BITS	Birla Institute of Technology and Science	**BK**	Berliner Konferenz Europäischer Katholiken
BITS	Bureau International du Tourisme Social = IBST	**BKA**	British Karate Association
BITU	Bustamente Industrial Trade Union (Jamaica)	**BKA**	British Kodály Academy
		BKA	British Korfball Association
BIU	Bermuda Industrial Union	**BKA**	Bundeskriminalamt
BIU	British Import Union (Denmark)	**BKartA**	Bundeskartellamt
BIU	Bureau International des Universités	**BKBA**	British Kick Boxing Association
BIUNTI	Biuro Nauchnoi i Tekhnicheskoi Informatsii	**BKCA**	British Knitting and Clothing Association
BIUT CCI	Bureau International Usagers Transports	**BKCEC**	British Knitting and Clothing Export Council
BIV	Banque Internationale des Voltas	**BKDA**	Bund Katholischer Deutsche Akademikerinnen
BIV	Bayerischer Industrieverband Steine und Erden	**BKED**	Bund Katholischer Erzieher Deutschlands
BIV	Belgisch Instituut voor Verpakking	**BKF**	Bundeskonferenz der Kammern der Freien Berufe Österreichs
BIVEC	Benelux Interuniversitaire Groepering Vervoerseconomen = GIBET		
		BKFA	British Kidney Fund Association
BIW	Bund der Diplom- Ingenieure des Weinbaues, der Oenologie und der Getränketechnologie	**BKFA**	British Kite Fliers Association
		BKG	Bankenfachverband Konsumenten-und Gewerbliche Spezialkredite

BKJ	Bundesvereinigung Kulturelle Jugendbildung e.V.
BKKEN	National Family Planning Coordinating Board (Indonesia)
BKKL	Bányászati Kémiai Kutatólaboratóriuma
BKLF	Baker-og Konditormestrenes Landsförening
BKMF	Bageri-Konditori-og Molleriarbejdernes Forbund
BKMV	Velgische Kamer der Medische Voetverzorgers
BKO	Babak Khorramindin Organisation (Iran)
BKO	Bezpieczna Kasa Oszczedności
BKPA	British Kidney Patient Association
BKPM	Badan Koordinasi Pénanaman Modal
BKR	British Kendo Renmei
BKS	Bageri- och Konditoriarbetsgivareförbundet
BKS	Bildende Kunstneres Styre
BKSC	Société de Biscuiterie Koupan-Sohaing Caméroun
BKSK	Bundesverband Kunstoff- und Schwergewebekonfektion
BKSTS	British Kinematograph, Sound and Television Society
BKT	Bedrijfskadertraining
BKU	Bund Katholischer Unternehmer
BKV	Belgische Kunststoffen Vereniging
BKV/TF	Belgische Kamer van Vertalers, Tolken en Filologen = CBTIP
BKWSU	Brahma Kumaris World Spiritual University
BL	Basque Left = EE
BL	British Leyland
BL	British Library
BL	Broad Left
BL	Broilerprodusentenes Landslag
BL84	Broad Left 84
BLA	British Legal Association
BLA	British Lift Association
BLA	British Lime Association
BLA	Bureau de Liaison des Syndicats Européens des Produits Aromatiques (CE)
BLAC	British Light Aviation Centre
BLACC	British and Latin American Chamber of Commerce
BLADA	Bloque Latinoamericano de Actores (Uruguay)
BLADEX	Banco Latinoamericano de Exportaciones (Panama)
BLAR	British League Against Rheumatism
BLASA	Bantu Library Association of South Africa
BLAVA	British Laboratory Animals Veterinary Association
BLB	Brancheforeningen for Danske Leverandører af Butiksinventar
BLBA	British Lease Brokers' Association
BLBA	British List Brokers Association (*now* DMA(U.K.))
BLBEG	British Lawn Bowls Export Group
BLBS	Bundesverband der Lehrer an Beruflichen Schulen
BLBSD	British Library Bibliographic Services Division
BLC	British Leather Confederation
BLC	British Lighting Council
BLCC	Basic Law Consultative Committee (Hong Kong)
BLCCSA	BLC Cut Soles Association
BLCMP	Birmingham Libraries Cooperative Mechanisation Project
BLCS	British Limousin Cattle Society
BLdBG	Bundesinnung der Bangewerbe
BLDC	Basic Law Drafting Committee (Hong Kong)
BLDSA	British Long Distance Swimming Association
BLDSC	British Library Document Supply Centre
BLE	Budhana Ligo Esperantista (Belgium)
BLEC	Bureau de Liaison Européen du Cinéma = ECO
BLESMA	British Limbless Ex-Servicemen's Association
BLEU	Belgisch-Luxemburgse Economische Unie
BLF	Barnläkarföreningen
BLF	Brancheforeningen for Leverandører til Frisørstanden
BLF	British Lace Federation
BLF	British Laminated Plastics Fabricators Association = BLPFA
BLF	British Lubricants Federation
BLF	British Lung Foundation
BLF	Bundesministerium für Land- und Forstwirtschaft (Austria)
BLFAE	Bureau de Liaison France-Afrique-Europe

BLFC	British Leather Fashion Council
BLGA	Bayerische Landesgewerbeanstalt
BLGAMH	Black Lesbians and Gays Against Media Homophobia
BLH	British Legion Headquarters
BLHA	British Linen Hire Association
BLHSS	British Library – Humanities and Social Sciences
BLI	Bible Literature International
BLI	Birdlife International
BLI	Bureau Linguistique Interafricaine
BLIC	Bureau de Liaison des Industries du Caoutchouc de la C.E.E.
BLINDOC	Information Service on Rehabilitation and Employment of the Visually Handicapped (Switzerland)
BLISS	Baby Life Support Systems
BLIW	Belgisch-Luxemburgs Instituut voor de Wissel = IBLC
BLL	Bund für Lebensmittelrecht und Lebensmittelkunde
BLLA	British Luggage and Leathergoods Association
BLLV	Bayerischer Lehrer-und Lehrerinnenverband
BLMA	British Ladder Manufacturers' Association
BLMA	British Lead Manufacturers Association
BLMA	British Leathergoods Manufacturers Association
BLMA	British Lock Manufacturers' Association
BLMA	British Longwall Mining Association
BLMAS	Bible Lands Missions' Aid Society
BLMF	British Lawnmower Manufacturers Federation
BLMRA	British Lawn Mower Racing Association
BLNL	British Library Newspaper Library
BLO	Bureau Landelijke Opbouw (Suriname)
BLOF	British Lace Operatives Federation
BLOMEX	Association of Flower Exporters (Denmark)
BLORE	Bureau de Liaison des Organisations Régionales Européennes = CPMR
BLOWS	British Library of Wildlife Sounds
BLP	Barbados Labour Party
BLP	Botswana Liberal Party
BLPES	British Library of Political and Economic Science
BLPFA	British Laminated Plastics Fabricators Association = BLF
BLPS	British Landrace Pig Society
BLR	British League of Rights
BLR	Bundesverband der Luftfahrtzbehör- und RaketenIndustrie
BLR&D	British Library Research and Development
BLRA	Brewers' and Licensed Retailers' Association (*ex* BS)
BLRA	British Level Rating Association
BLS	Botswana, Lesotho, Swaziland
BLS	Branch Line Society
BLS	British Lichen Society
BLS	Bureau of Labor Statistics (U.S.A.)
BLSA	British Land Speedsail Association
BLSGMA	British Lamp Blown Scientific Glassware Manufacturers Association
BLT	Banque Libano-Togolaise (Togo)
BLT	Bundesfachverband Landwirtschaftlicher Trocknungsbetriebe
BLV	Bayerischer Landwirtschaftsverlag
BLVVG	Belgisch-Luxemburgse Vakgroep Vloeibaar Gas
BLWA	British Laboratory Ware Association
BLZ	Bundesverband Leichtbetonzuschlag-Industrie
BLZK	Bayerische Landeszahnärztekammer
BM	Bokaljska Mornarica (Montenegro) = BMA
BM	British Museum
BMA	Baby Milk Action
BMA	Bahrain Monetary Agency
BMA	Banke Milli Afghan
BMA	Barbados Manufacturers' Association
BMA	BEAMA Meter Association
BMA	Bible Memory Association International (U.S.A.)
BMA	Blanket Manufacturers' Association
BMA	Boka Mariners Association (Montenegro) = BM
BMA	British Majorette Association
BMA	British Manufacturers' Association
BMA	British Medical Association
BMA	British Midland Airways
BMA	Bundesministerium für Arbeit und Sozialordnung
BMA	Bundesverband der Möbelgrosshändler und Auslieferungslager

BMAA	British Marine Aquarists Association		**BMEG**	British Marine Equipment Council
BMAA	British Microlight Aircraft Association		**BMEG**	Building Materials Export Group
BMAPA	British Marine Aggregate Producers' Association		**BMEI**	Beijing Machinery and Electricity Institute
BMAS	British Medical Acupuncture Society		**BMEKK**	Budapesti Múszaki Egyetem Központi Könyvtára
BMATT	British Military Advisory and Training Team (Zimbabwe)		**BMELF**	Bundesministerium für Ernährung, Landwirtschaft und Forsten
BMAV	Belize Women Against Violence Movement		**BMES**	Beijing Mechanical Engineering Society
BMB	Baltic Marine Biologists (Sweden)		**BMES**	Biomedical Engineering Society
BMB	Bayerischer Müllerbund		**BMEU**	Bahamas Musicians' and Entertainers' Union
BMB	Bond van Maatkleding-bedrijven in Nederland		**BMF**	Bibliothecarii Medicinae Fennniae
BMB	Bundesministerium für Innerdeutsche Beziehungen		**BMF**	Black Management Forum (South Africa)
BMBA	British Merchant Banking and Securities Houses Association		**BMF**	British Microcomputer Federation
BMBA	British Motor Boat Association		**BMF**	British Motorcyclists Federation
BMBau	Bundesministerium für Raumordnung, Bauwesen und Städtebau		**BMF**	Builders Merchants Federation
BMBF	British Mountain Bike Federation		**BMF**	Building Materials Federation (Éire)
BMBW	Bundesministerium für Bildung und Wissenschaft		**BMF**	Bundesministerium der Finanzen
BMC	Banque de Madagascar et des Comores		**BMF**	Bundesverband Montagebau und Fertighäuser
BMC	Barbados Marketing Corporation		**BMFA**	British Men's Fashion Association
BMC	Bengbu Medical College		**BMFA**	Building Materials Factors' Association
BMC	Book Marketing Council (PA)		**BMFF**	British Man-made Fibres Federation
BMC	Botswana Meat Commission		**BMFSA**	British Metal Finishing Suppliers Association
BMC	British Match Corporation		**BMFT**	Bundesministerium für Forschung und Technologie
BMC	British Metal Corporation		**BMG**	Berliner Mathematische Gesellschaft
BMC	British Mountaineering Council		**BMG**	Berliner Medizinische Gesellschaft
BMCC	British Metal Castings Council		**BMG**	British Association of Mountain Guides
BMCD	Banque Malienne de Crédit et de Dépôts		**BMG**	British Measures Group
BMCRC	British Motor Cycle Racing Club		**BMG**	British Menswear Guild
BMCS	Bureau of Motor Carrier Safety (U.S.A.)		**BMGA**	British Mountain Guide Association
BMDA	Bahamas Motor Dealers' Association		**BMHA**	British Malignant Hyperthermia Association
BMDA	British Masonry Drill Association		**BMHB**	British Materials Handling Board
BMDC	Bimedicinska Dokumentationscentralen		**BMHF**	British Materials Handling Federation
BMDF	British Management Data Foundation		**BMHS**	British Morgan Horse Society
BMDH	Bihar Mineral Development Cooporation (India)		**BMHS**	British Music Hall Society
BME	Budapesti Müszaki Egyetem		**BMI**	Battelle Memorial Institute (U.S.A.)
BME	Bundesverband Materialwirtschaft und Einkauf		**BMI**	Bazgari Meli Ittehad (Afghanistan) = PNU
BMEA	British Marine Equipment Association		**BMI**	Belgische Maatschappij voor Internationale Investering = SBI
BMEC	British Marine Equipment Council		**BMI**	Birmingham and Midland Institute
BMEF	British Mechanical Engineering Federation		**BMI**	Building Maintenance Information Ltd
			BMI	Bundesministerium des Innern

BMI	Bureau Maritime International (ICC) = IMB
BMIC	British Music Information Centre
BMICPD	Beijing Municipal Institute of City Planning and Design
BMIF	British Marine Industries Federation
BMIFSA	BMIF Sailmakers' Association
BMJ	Bundesministerium der Justiz
BMJFG	Bundesministerium für Jugend, Familie und Gesundheit
BMK	Bond van Militair Kader (Suriname)
BML	British Maritime League
BML	Bundesministerium für Ernährung, Landwirtschaft und Forsten
BML	Föreningen Bekämpningsmedels-Leverantörer
BMLA	British Maritime Law Association
BMLA	British Medical Laser Association
BMLBS	British Matchbox Label and Booklet Society
BMLF	Bundesministerium für Land- und Forstwirtschaft (Austria)
BMLSS	British Marine Life Study Society
BMM	Association Benelux des Conseils en Marques et Modèles
BMM	Bundesfachverband der Marktmolkereien
BMMA	Bacon and Meat Manufactures Association
BMMA	Belgian Management and Marketing Association
BMMA	British Micrographic Manufactures Association
BMMFI	Bible and Medical Missionary Fellowship International
BMMG	British Microcomputers Manufacturers Group
BMMMA	British Mat and Matting Manufacturers Association
BMMPIC	Basic Metals and Mineral Processing Industry Council
BMNLF	Bangsa Moro National Liberation Front (Philippines)
BMP	Banco Minero del Peru
BMP	Bundesministerium für das Post- und Fernmeldewesen
BMP	National Council of Building Material Producers
BMPA	British Medical Pilots Association
BMPAWU	Bahamas Maritime Port and Allied Workers' Union
BMPCA	British Metallurgical Plant Constructors Association
BMPF	British Poultry Meat Federation (*ex* BPF)
BMR	Bundesverband der Maschinenringe (Germany)
BMR	Bureau of Market Research (South Africa)
BMR	Bureau of Mineral Resources, Geology and Geophysics (*now* AGSO)
BMR	Bureau of Municipal Research (Canada)
BMRA	British Maize Refiners Association
BMRA	British Medical Representatives Association
BMRB	British Marketing Research Bureau
BMRC	British Medical Research Council
BMRC	Bureau of Meteorology Research Centre (Australia)
BMRC	Business Management Research Center (Korea)
BMRDA	Bombay Metropolitan Region Development Authority (India)
BMRMC	British Motor Racing Marshals Club
BMRU	Blind Mobility Research Unit
BMS	Baptist Missionary Society
BMS	Birmingham Metallurgical Society
BMS	British Magical Society
BMS	British Malaysian Society
BMS	British Menopause Society
BMS	British Mexican Society
BMS	British Microcirculation Society
BMS	British Mule Society
BMS	British Museum Society
BMS	British Music Society
BMS	British Mycological Society
BMSA	British Medical Students Association
BMSE	Baltic Mercantile and Shipping Exchange
BMSOA	British Motor Ship Owners' Association
BMSS	British Model Soldier Society
BMSS	Butterfly and Moth Stamp Society
BMT	British Marine Technology
BMTA	British Measurement and Testing Association
BMTA	British Mining Tools Association
BMTA	British Motor Trade Association
BMTC	Bureau of Meterology Training Centre
BMTEC	British Management Training Export Council

BMTFA	British Malleable Tube Fittings Association
BMTI	Banque Mondiale des Termes Internationaux = WBIT
BMTI	Belgische Maatschappij van Technische Ingenieurs
BMU	Beijing Medical University
BMU	Board of Mission and Unity of the General Synod of the Church of England
BMUA	British Micro-Computers Users Association
BMUS	British Medical Ultrasound Society
BMV	Bolsa Mexicano de Valores
BMV	Bundesmarktverband für Vieh und Fleisch
BMV	Bundesministerium für Verkehr
BMVA	British Machine Vision Association and Society for Pattern Recognition
BMVg	Bundesministerium der Verteidigung
BMW	Bayerische Motoren Werke
BMWF	Bundesministerium für Wissenschaftliche Forschung
BMWi	Bundesministerium für Wirtschaft
BMWT	Vereniging van Fabrikanten van en Handelaren in Bouwmachines, Mijn- en Wegenbouwmachines en Transportmiddelen
BMWW	Biuro Międzynarodowej Wymiany Wydawnictw
BMZ	Baumusterzentrale (Austria)
BMZ	Bundesministerium für Wirtschaftliche Zusammenarbeit
BN	Banco de la Nacion (Peru)
BN	Bank Negara (Malaysia)
BN	Barisan Nasional (Malaysia)
BN	Biblioteca Nacional
BN	Biblioteka Narodowa
BN	Bibliothèque Nationale
BNA	Bakhtar News Agency
BNA	Baluch National Alliance (Pakistan)
BNA	Banco Nacional de Angola
BNA	Banque Nationale d'Algérie
BNA	Biblioteca Nacional de Angola
BNA	Bond van Nederlandsche Architecten
BNA	British Naturopathic Association
BNA	British Nuclear Associates
BNA	British Nursing Association
BNA	Bureau de la Nutrition Animale

BNA	Bureau of National Affairs (U.S.A.)
BNAC	British North American Committee
BNAE	Bureau de Normalisation de l'Aéronautique et de l'Espace
BNAPM	British National Association of Perry Makers
BNASEES	British National Association for Soviet and East European Studies (*now* BASEES)
BNAU	Bulgarian National Agrarian Union
BNB	Banco Nacional de Bolivia
BNB	Banque Nationale de Belgique = NBB
BNB	Barbados National Bank
BNB	Bond van Nederlandse Bandfabrikanten
BNC	Banco Nacional de Cuba
BNC	British Needlecraft Council
BNC	Bulgar National Congress (Russian Federation)
BNC	Bulgarian National Committee (U.S.A.)
BNC-ICC	British National Committee of the International Chamber of Commerce
BNCAR	British National Committee on Antarctic Research
BNCC	Banco Nacional de Crédito Cooperativo (Brazil)
BNCC	British National Committee for Chemistry
BNCCI	Bengal National Chamber of Commerce and Industry (India)
BNCD	Banque Nationale Centrafricaine de Dépôts
BNCE	Banco Nacional de Comercio Exterior (Mexico)
BNCE	British National Committee for Electroheat
BNCI	Banque Nationale pour le Commerce et l'Industrie (Belgium)
BNCIOI	Banque Nationale pour le Commerce et de l'Industrie "Océan Indien" (Mauritius)
BNCM	Bibliothèque Nationale du Conservatoire de Musique
BNCNDT	British National Committee for Non-Destructive Testing
BNCOE	British National Committee on Ocean Engineering
BNCOLD	British National Committee on Large Dams
BNCOR	British National Committee for Oceanographic Research

BNCS	British National Carnation Society
BNCSAA	British National Committee on Surface Active Agents
BNCSR	British National Committee for Scientific Radio
BNCSR	British National Committee on Space Research
BNCWO	Belgisch Nationaal Comité voor Wetenschappelijkes
BND	Banco Nacional de Desarrollo (Argentina, Nicaragua)
BND	Banque Nationale de Développement (Burkina Faso)
BND	Bundesnachrichtendienst
BNDA	Banque Nationale de Développement Agricole (Guinée, Ivory Coast, Mali)
BNDC	Banque Nationale de Développement du Congo
BNDC	British Nuclear Design and Construction Ltd
BNDD	Bureau of Narcotics and Dangerous Drugs (U.S.A.)
BNDE	Banco Nacional de Desenvolvimento Economico (Brazil)
BNDÉ	Banque Nationale de Développement Économique (Burundi, Morocco)
BNDES	Banco Nacional do Desenvolvimento Economico e Social (Brazil)
BNDO	Bureau National des Données Océaniques
BNDP	Brunei National Democratic Party
BNDRA	British Natural Drag Racing Association (ex BDRA)
BNDS	Banque Nationale de Développement du Sénégal
BNDU	Bulgarian National Democratic Union
BNEA	British Naval Equipment Association
BNÉC	Banque Nationale pour l'Épargne et le Crédit (Ivory Coast)
BNEC	British Nuclear Energy Council
BNES	British Nuclear Energy Society
BNÉTD	Bureau National d'Études Techniques de Développement (Ivory Coast)
BNF	Botswana National Front
BNF	British Nuclear Forum (now BNIF)
BNF	British Nutrition Foundation
BNF	Bulgarian National Front
BNF-Fulmer	BNF Metals Technology Centre
BNFA	British Narrow Fabrics Association
BNFL	British Nuclear Fuels plc
BNFMF	British Non-Ferrous Metals Federation
BNFMS	British Bureau of Non-Ferrous Metal Statistics
BNFSA	British Non-Ferrous Smelters' Association
BNG	Bayerische Numismatische Gesellschaft
BNG	British Neuroendocrine Group
BNGA	British Nursery Goods Association
BNGL	British National Gridiron League
BNH	Banco Nacional de Habitação (Brazil)
BNHPS	Belfast Natural History and Philosophical Society
BNHS	Birmingham Natural History Society
BNHS	British Natural Hygiene Society
BNI	Bankin'ny Indostria (Madagascar)
BNI	Beijing Neurosurgical Institute
BNI	Beroepsvereniging van Nederlandse Interieurarchitekten
BNIA	Bureau National Interprofessionnel de l'Armagnac
BNIC	Bureau National Interprofessionnel du Cognac
BNICEVCP	Bureau National Interprofessionnel des Calvados et Eaux-de-Vie de Cidre et de Poire
BNIF	British Nuclear Industry Forum (ex BNF)
BNIO	British National Institute of Oceanography
BNIP	Bureau National Interprofessionel du Pruneau
BNIST	Bureau National de l'Information Scientifique et Technique
BNITA	British Nautical Instrument Trade Association
BNL	Banca Nazionale del Lavoro
BNL	Brookhaven National Laboratory (U.S.A.)
BNM	Banque Nationale de Mauritanie
BNM	Bureau National de Métrologie
BNMA	British Nonwovens Manufacturers Association
BNMICN	Beijing Nonferrous Metals & Rare Earth Research Institute
BNMS	British Nuclear Medicine Society
BNMT	Britain-Nepal Medical Trust
BNNS	British Neural Network Society
BNO	Beroepsvereniging Nederlandse Ontwerpers

BNOA	British Naturopathic and Osteopathic Association	**BNUD**	Bund Natur- und Umweltschutz Deutschland
BNOC	Barbados National Oil Company	**BNUS**	Bureau des Nations Unies pour le Sahel = UNSO
BNOC	British National Opera Company		
BNOCL	Barbados National Oil Company Ltd	**BNV**	Belgische Natuurkundige Vereniging
BNOSP	Banco Nacional de Obras y Servicios Públicos (Mexico)	**BNVU**	Bond van Nederlandse Volksuniversiteiten
BNotK	Bundesnotarkammer	**BNZTC**	British – New Zealand Trade Council
BNP	Bangladesh National Party	**BOA**	Bank of Alexandria (Egypt)
BNP	Banque Nationale de Paris	**BOA**	Boliviana de Aviación
BNP	Basotho National Party (Lesotho)	**BOA**	British Octopush Association
BNP	Basque Nationalist Party = PNV	**BOA**	British Olympic Association
BNP	British National Party	**BOA**	British Oncological Association
BNPP	Barisan Nasional Pembebasan Pattani (Thailand)	**BOA**	British Orthopaedic Association
		BOA	British Osteopathic Association
BNQ	Bibliothèque Nationale du Québec (Canada)	**BOAC**	Bank of the Arab Coast (Dubai)
BNR	Bilbranches Nordiska Råd	**BOAD**	Banque Ouest-Africaine de Développement (Togo) = WADB
BNRP	Bulgarian National Radical Party / Bulgarska Natsionalna Radikalna Partiya	**BOAG**	British Overseas Aid Group
		BOAL	Basic Organization of Associated Labour
BNRS	British National Radio School	**BOBA**	British Overseas Banks Association
BNS	Baltic News Service	**BOBK**	Bank of Oman, Bahrain and Kuwait (Oman)
BNS	Bond van Nederlandsche Schilderspatroons	**BOBMA**	British Oat and Barley Millers Association
BNS	Bond van Nederlandse Stedebouwkundigen	**BOBMA**	British Oil-Burners Manufacturers Association
BNS	British Neuropathological Society	**BOC**	Belgisch Olympisch Comité
BNS	British Nuclear Energy Society	**BOC**	British Orchid Council
BNS	British Numismatic Society	**BOC**	British Ornithologists' Club
BNSA	Bethlehem Natural Science Association (U.S.A.)	**BOC**	British Oxygen Company
		BOCA	Building Officials and Code Administrators International (U.S.A.)
BNSC	British National Space Centre		
BNSM	British National Socialist Movement	**BOCBA**	British Overseas and Commonwealth Banks Association
BNSP	Brunei National Solidarity Party		
BNT	Banco Nacional de Trabajadores (Paraguay)	**BOCM**	British Oil and Cake Mills Ltd
BNT	Nederlandse Vereniging voor Tuin- en Landschapsarchitektuur	**BODC**	Barclays Overseas Development Corporation
		BODC	British Oceanographic Data Centre
BNTA	British Numismatic Trade Association	**BODEPA**	Bond van Detailisten in de Parfumeriehandel
BNTBC	British Nuclear Test Ban Coalition		
BNTEC	Beijing Numerical Control Technical Center	**BODMA**	British Oncology Data Managers' Association
BNTI	Belgisch Nationaal Tapijt Instituut = INBT	**BODS**	British Oceanographic Data Service (IOS)
BNTL	British National Temperance League	**BODY**	British Organ Donor Society
BNTU	Belize National Teachers Union	**BOEC**	British Oil Equipment Credits, Ltd
BNTVA	British Nuclear Test Veterans' Association	**BOF**	British Organic Farmers

BOF	British Orienteering Federation	**BOPAKO**	Bok- Pappers- och Kontorsvarförbundet
BOF	British Othello Federation	**BOPR**	Bureau d'Organisation des Programmes Ruraux (Congo)
BOF	British Overseas Fairs Ltd	**BORA**	British and Overseas Residents' Association
BOFED	Bond van Fabrikanten van Eetbare Dierlijke Vetten	**BORAD**	British Oxygen Research and Development Association
BOFS	British Orthopaedic Foot Surgery	**BORCO**	Bahamas Oil Refining Company
BOFSWU	Bahamas Oil and Fuel Services Workers' Union	**BORDA**	Bremer Arbeitsgemeinschaft für Uberseeforschung und Entwicklung
BOFWA	Botswana Family Welfare Association	**BORDA**	British Oriental Rug Dealers' Association
BOG	Bois Oeuvrés du Gabon	**BORIF**	Bogor Research Institute for Food Crops (Indonesia)
BOGA	British Onion Growers Association		
BOGA	British Orchid Growers Association	**BORM**	Bureau of Raw Materials for American Vegetable Oils and Fats Industries
BOGETA	Bond van Grossiers in Electrotechnische Artikelen	**BOS**	Biuro Odbudowy Stolicy
BOGMC	Bangladesh Oil, Gas and Mineral Corporation	**BOS**	Bloque Opositora del Sur (Nicaragua)
BOHS	British Occupational Hygiene Society	**BOS**	British Origami Society
BÖIA	Bund Österreicherischer Innenarchitekten	**BOS**	British Orthoptic Society
		BoS	Buildings of Scotland Trust
BOIL	British Overhead Irrigation Ltd	**BOS**	Bundesoberseeamt
BOLA	Betting Office Licensees Association	**BOS**	Stichting voor Nederlandse Bosbouw-Ontwikkelingssamenwerking
BOLEKA	Bond van Leveranciers aan de Kantoorboekhandel	**BOSCA**	British Oil Spill Control Association
BOLMADA	British Opthalmic Lens Manufacturers and Distributors Association	**BOSCAM**	Bouygués Offshore Caméroun
BOLSA	Bank of London and South America	**BOSS**	Bureau of State Security (South Africa)
BOM	Bureau of Meteorology	**BOSSF**	British Office Systems and Stationery Federation
BOM	Bureau of Mines (U.S.A.)	**BOSTI**	Buffalo Organization for Social and Technological Innovation (U.S.A.)
BOMA	British Overseas Mining Association		
BOMA	Building Owners and Managers Association International (U.S.A.)	**BOSTID**	Board on Science and Technology for International Development (U.S.A.)
BOMA	Business Owners Management Association	**BOT**	Biuro Obsługi Turystycznej
BOMMA	British Opthalmic Mass Manufacturers Association	**BOTAS**	Boru Hatlari ile Petrol Tasima (Turkey)
		BOTB	British Overseas Trade Board
BON	British Organisation of Non-Parents	**BOTGI**	British Overseas Trade Group for Israel
BONAC	Broadcasting Organizations of Non-Aligned Countries (Sierra Leone)	**BOTiI**	Biuro Obsługi Turystycznej i Informacji
BOND	British Overseas NGOs for Development	**BOTMA**	British Office Technology Manufacturers Alliance
BONEFO	Bond van Nederlandse Fotodetailhandelaren	**BOU**	Bouraq Indonesia Airlines = BIA
BOOBA	British Olive Oil Buyers' Association	**BOU**	British Ornithologists Union
BÖP	Berufsverband Österreichischer Psychologen	**BOV**	Belgische Ormithologische Vereniging
		BOVA	Nederlands Bond van Varkenshandelaren
BOP	Bureau of Operations and Programming (UNDP)	**BOVAG**	Bond van Automobiel-, Garage-en Aanwerwante Bedrijven
BOPA	Botswana Press Agency	**BOVAK**	Bond van Kermisbedrijfhouders
BOPA	British Outdoor Professionals Association	**BOVAL**	Bond van Loonbedrijven in Nederland

BOVEE	Nederlandse Bond voor Veehandelaren	**BPAO**	Société des Pétroles BP d'Afrique Occidentale
BOVESPA	Bolsa de Valores de São Paulo	**BPAS**	British Pregnancy Advisory Service
BOWAND	Belize Organization for Women and Development	**BpB**	Bundeszentrale für Politische Bildung
BOWI-SPORT	Bond van Winkeliers in Sportartikelen	**BPB**	Business Planning Board (U.S.A.)
BP	Bank Polski	**BPBA**	British Paper Box Association
BP	Body Positive	**BPBF**	British Paper Box Federation
BP	Boeren Partij	**BPBHA**	British Poultry Breeders and Hatcheries Association
BP	British Petroleum	**BPBIF**	British Paper and Board Industry Federation
BP-MA	British Pump Manufacturers Association	**BPC**	Basrah Petroleum Company
BP-MALI	Société Malienne des Pétroles BP	**BPC**	Black Peoples Convention (South Africa)
BPA	Baby Products Association	**BPC**	British Peace Committee
BPA	Banco Popular de Angola	**BPC**	British Peanut Council
BPA	Banco Portugués do Atlantico	**BPC**	British Pharmacopoeia Commission
BPÄ	Berufsverband der Praktischen Ärzte und Ärzte für Allgemeinmedizin Deutschlands	**BPC**	British Polarity Council
BPA	Biological Photographic Association (U.S.A.)	**BPCA**	British Pest Control Association
BPA	Book Packagers Association	**BPCC**	British Printing and Communication Corporation
BPA	British Paediatric Association	**BPCF**	British Postal Chess Federation
BPA	British Pantomime Association	**BPCF**	British Precast Concrete Federation
BPA	British Parachute Association Ltd	**BPDC**	Book and Periodical Development Council
BPA	British Paralympic Association	**BPE**	Bedrijfschap voor Pluimvee en Eieren
BPA	British Parking Association	**BPEAOA**	Bureau of Professional Education of the American Osteopathic Association
BPA	British Peace Assembly	**BPEAR**	Bureau for the Placement and Education of African Refugees (OAU) = OAU/BR
BPA	British Pétanque Association		
BPA	British Photographic Association	**BPEG**	British Photographic Export Group
BPA	British Pig Association	**BPF**	Belarusan Popular Front
BPA	British Ploughing Association	**BPF**	Borst- och Penselfabrikantföreningen
BPA	British Ports Association	**BPF**	British Philatelic Federation
BPA	British Professional Association	**BPF**	British Plastics Federation
BPA	British Psychodrama Association	**BPF**	British Polio Fellowship
BPA	British Pyrotechnists' Association	**BPF**	British Poultry Federation (*now* BMPF)
BPA	Broadcasting and Publications Authority (Kiribati)	**BPF**	British Property Federation
BPA	Bush Pilots Airways (Australia)	**BPF**	Buddhist Peace Fellowship
BPA	International Bridge Press Association	**BPFMA**	British Plumbing Fittings Manufacturers' Association
BPA	Presse- und Informationsamt der Bundesregierung	**BPG**	British Photodermatology Group
BPAA	British Poster Advertising Association	**BPGA**	British Potplant Growers' Association
BPAC	Book Publishers Association of Canada	**BPGMA**	British Pressure Gauge Manufacturers Association
BPAMA	"Bratska" Political Association of Macedonians in Albania = SBMS	**BPGS**	British Pelargonium and Geranium Society
BPAMT	British Performing Arts Medicine Trust		
BPANZ	Book Publishers Association of New Zealand	**BPH**	Balai Penelitian Hutan
		BPHH	Balai Penelitian Hutan Hasil (Indonesia)

BPHS	British Percheron Horse Society
BPHS	British Polled Hereford Society
BPI	Banco Portugués de Investimento
BPI	Belgisch Petroleum- Instituut
BPI	Bibliothèque Publique d'Information
BPI	British Phonographic Industry
BPIA	British Photographic Importers Association
BPICM	Bureau Permanent International des Constructeurs de Motorcycles
BPICS	British Production and Inventory Control Society
BPIF	British Printing Industries Federation
BPITT	Bureau Permanent International de la Tsétsé et de la Trypanosomiase
BPL	Bedrijfspensioenfonds voor de Landbouw
BPL	Bio-Products Laboratory
BPL	British Physical Laboratories Ltd
BPL	Bundesverband Personal-Leasing
BPM	Barbuda People's Movement
BPM	Birlik People's Movement (Uzbekistan)
BPMA	British Payroll Managers Association
BPMA	British Pottery Managers Association
BPMA	British Printing Machinery Association
BPMA	British Promotional Merchandise Association
BPMA	British Pump Manufacturers' Association
BPMC	Bauxite Parnasse Mining Company (Greece)
BPMF	British Postgraduate Medical Federation
BPMF	British Powder Metal Federation
BPMG	Book Production Managers Group
BPMMA	British Paper Machinery Makers' Association
BPMRI	Beijing Printing Machinery Research Institute
BPMTG	British Puppet and Model Theatre Guild
BPNMA	British Plain Net Manufacturers Association
BPO	Union Tarifare Balkan – Proche – Orient (Yugoslavia)
BPOS	British Pipe Organ Society
BPP	Belize Popular Party
BPP	Botswana Peoples Party
BPP	Brunei People's Party
BPP	Bulgarian People's Party
BPPA	British Pasta Products Association
BPPB	Balai Penelitian Perkebunan Besar (Indonesia)
BPPB	Banque de Paris et Pays-Bas
BPPF	British Pig Producers Federation
BPPGA	British Pot Plant Growers Association
BPPPG	Balai Penjelidikan Perusahaan Gula (Indonesia)
BPPT	Agency for Technology Assessment and Implementation (Indonesia)
BPR	Bloque Popular Revolucionario (El Salvador)
BPRA	Book Publishers' Representatives' Association
BPRA	British Pattern Recognition Association
BPRA	Bund der Public Relations Agenturen (Switzerland)
BPRI	British Polarographic Research Institute
BPRS	British Polarographic Research Society
BPRV	Brancheforeningen of Public Relations Virksomheder (Denmark)
BPS	Belgian Psychological Society = BVP, SBP
BPS	British Paper Stock Merchants Association, Ltd
BPS	British Pharmacological Society
BPS	British Photobiology Society
BPS	British Phrenological Society
BPS	British Phycological Society
BPS	British Postmark Society
BPS	British Printing Society
BPS	British Psychological Society
BPS	British Pteridological Society
BPS	Bundesverband Privater Sonderabfallbeseitiger
BPSA	British Pharmaceutical Students Association
BPSA	British Plastics Stockholders' Association
BPSA	British Polytechnics Sports Association
BPSA	Business Products Standards Association (U.S.A.)
BPSS	British Paraplegic Sports Society (*now* BWSF)
BPSU	Bahamas Public Services Union
BPT	Balai Penelitian Ternak (Indonesia)
BpT	Bundesverband Praktischer Tierärzte
BPT	Bureau de Promotion Touristique (Martinique)
BPT-GAZ	Société Butane et Propane Togolaise Gaz

BPTA	Briar Pipe Trade Association
BPTA	British Polyolefin Textiles Association
BPTA	British Property Timeshare Association
BPTRI	Beijing Printing Technical Research Institute
BPU	Beijing Polytechnic University
BPU	Botswana Progressive Union
BPU	British Powerboating Union
BPV	Buitenlandse Persvereniging in Nederland
BPW	United Kingdom Federation of Business & Professional Women
BPWA	British Public Works Association
BPWF	Black Panel World Foundation (Germany)
BPWG	British Plastic Windows Group
BPWT	Business and Professional Women's Association of Thailand
BQA	British Quality Association
BQHA	British Quarter Horse Association
BQKA	Bashkimi Qëndror i Kooperativave të Artizanatit (Albania)
BQKS	Bashkimi Qëndror i Kooperativave të Shit-Blerjes (Albania)
BQKT	Bashkimi Qëndror i Kooperativave Tregtare (Albania)
BQSRS	Beijing Qigong Scientific Research Society
BQVSA	British Quality Vegetable and Salad Association
BR	Benguela Railway (Angola)
BR	BetongvaruIndustrins Riksförbund
BR	British Rail
BRA	Bee Research Association
BRA	Bougainville Revolutionary Army (Papua New Guinea)
BRA	Brain Research Association
BRA	British Racketball Association
BRA	British Radiesthesia Association
BRA	British Records Association
BRA	British Reflexology Association
BRA	British Refrigeration Association
BRA	British Resorts Association
BRA	British Retailers' Association
BRA	British Rivet Association
BRA	British Robot Association
BRA	World War Two Battle Re-enactment Association Ltd
BRAB	Banque Belgo-Africaine du Burundi

BRAC	Bangladesh Rural Advancement Committee
BRACODI	Société des Brasseries de la Côte-d'Ivoire
BRADECO	Banco Brasileiro de Descontos
BRadPA	British Radiation Protection Association
BRADUNI	Société des Brasseries du Niger
BRAÉC	Bureau de Recherche et d'Action Économiques
BRAIN	Basic Research in Adaptive Intelligence and Neurocomputing (Belgium)
BRAIN	Bio-Oriented Technology Research Advancement Institution (Japan)
BRAK	Bundesrechtsanwaltskammer
BRALIMA	Brasseries Limonaderies et Malteries du Zaïre
BRALUP	Bureau of Resource Assessment and Land Use Planning (Tanzania)
BRAMA	British Rubber and Resin Adhesive Manufacturers Association
BRANIGER	Société des Brasseries et Boissons Gazeuses du Niger
BRANZ	Building Research Association of New Zealand
BrAPP	British Association of Pharmaceutical Physicians (*ex* AMAPI, BAPP)
BRAS-PETRO	Petrobrás Internacional (Brazil)
BRASCOOP	Fundação Brasileira de Cooperativismo
BRB	Banque de la République du Burundi
BRB	British Railways Board
BRBMA	Ball and Roller Bearing Manufacturers Association
BRC	Biological Records Centre
BRC	British Rabbit Council
BRC	British Record Centre
BRC	British Refugee Council
BRC	British Retail Consortium
BRCA	British Roller-Canary Association
BRCE	Banca Romana De Comert Exterior
BRCMA	Bitumen Roof Coatings Manufacturers Association
BRCP	British Register of Complementary Practitioners
BRCS	British Red Cross Society
BRCS	British Romagnola Cattle Society
BRD	Bundesrepublik Deutschland = GFR
BRDA	British Racing Drivers Association
BRDB	British Rubber Development Board

BRDC	British Racing Drivers' Club
BRDC	British Research and Development Corporation
BRDE	Banco Regional de Desenvolvimento do Extremo Sul
BRDS	British Red Deer Society
BRE	Building Research Establishment (DOE)
BRE	Bureau de Rapprochement des Entreprises (CE) = BCC
BREA	Bahamas Real Estate Association
BRÉDA	Bureau Régional pour l'Éducation en Afrique (UNESCO)
BREE-DANIA	Export Board for Breeding Cattle (Denmark)
BREG	British Rivet Export Group
BREMA	British Radio and Electronic Equipment Manufacturers Association
BRES	Benelux-Regionaal Ekonomische Samenwerking =BEU
BRÉS	Bureau de Recherches et d'Études Statistiques
BResMA	British Resin Manufacturers Association
BRF	Belgisches Rundfunk und Fernsehzentrum der Deutschsprachigen Gemeinschaft
BRF	Brewing Research Foundation
BRF	British Road Federation
BRFA	British-Romanian Friendship Association
BRFFI	Biochemical Research Foundation of the Franklin Institute (U.S.A.)
BRGA	British Reed Growers' Association
BRGM	Bureau de Recherches Géologiques et Minières
BRH	Biuro Radcy Handlowego
BRH	Bureau of Radiological Health (U.S.A.)
BRI	Banque des Règlements Internationaux = BIS, BIZ
BRI	Biosystematics Research Institute (Canada)
BRI	Bread Research Institute of Australia
BRI	Building Research Institute (Iceland, Japan, Poland, Turkey)
BRIB	Birmingham Royal Institution for the Blind
BRIC	Biotechnology Regulation Interservice Committee (EU)
BRIC	Bureau de Recherches pour l'Innovation et la Convergence
BRIC-ERAM	Société Centrafricaine de Briques et Céramiques
BRIDGE	Biotechnology Research for Innovation, Development and Growth in Europe (CEC) (Belgium)
BRIIRS	Beijing Research Institute for Information of Remote Sensing
BRIMAFEX	British Manufacturers of Malleable Tube Fittings Export Group
BRIMEC	British Mechanical Engineering Confederation
BRINCO	British Newfoundland Development Corporation
BRINDEX	Association of British Independent Oil Exploration Companies
BRINEX	British Newfoundland Exploration
BRIR	Bastou Research Institute of Rare Earth (China)
BRISCOM	British and Irish Subcommittee (FONASBA)
BRISMES	British Society for Middle Eastern Studies
BRITCHAM	British Chamber of Commerce Morocco
BritIRE	British Institution of Radio Engineers
BRL	Butterwick Research Laboratories
BRMA	Board of Registration of Medical Auxiliaries
BRMA	Boiler and Radiator Manufacturers' Association
BRMA	British Reinforcement Manufacturers Association
BRMA	British Rubber Manufacturers Association
BRMA	Bureau de Recherches Minières de l'Algérie
BRMCA	British Ready Mixed Concrete Association
BRMF	British Rainwear Manufacturers Federation
BRN	Barisan Revolusi Nasional (Thailand)
BROA	British Rig Owners' Association
BROCMA	British Roof Coatings Manufacturers Association
BRP	Bureau de Recherches de Pétrole
BRPF	Bertrand Russell Peace Foundation
BRPFA	British Retail and Professional Florists Association
BRPM	Bureau de Recherches et de Participations Minières (Morocco)
BRPRA	British Rubber Producers Research Association
BRPS	British Retinitis Pigmentosa Society

BRR	Bureau of Rural Resources	**BSA**	British Society of Aesthetics
BRRA	Bangladesh Rice Research Institute	**BSA**	British Society of Audiology
BRRA	British Rayon Research Association	**BSA**	British Sociological Association
BRRA	British Refractories Research Association	**BSA**	British Surfing Association
		BSA	Building Societies Association
BRRI	Bangladesh Rice Research Institute	**BSA**	Bund Schweizer Architekten = FAS
BRRI	Beijing Radio Research Institute	**BSA**	Bund Sozialistischer Arbeiter
BRRI	Building and Road Research Institute (Ghana)	**BSA**	Bundesortenamt
		BSA	Business Services Association
BRRU	Business Regulation Review Unit	**BSA**	Business Software Alliance
BRS	British Record Society	**BSA**	Business Spouses Association (Éire)
BRS	Bureau of Resource Sciences	**BSA**	Byzantine Studies Association
BRS	Burma Research Society	**BSAA**	British School of Archaeology at Athens
BRSCC	British Racing and Sports Car Club	**BSAC**	British Screen Advisory Council
BRT	Belgische Radio en Televisie = RTB	**BSAC**	British Society of Antimicrobial Chemotherapy
BRT	Brain Research Trust		
BRTA	British Racing Toboggan Association	**BSAC**	British Sub-Aqua Club
BRTA	British Regional Television Association	**BSAC**	Building Standards Advisory Committe
BRTDC	British Recorded Tape Development Committee	**BSACI**	British Society for Allergy and Clinical Immunology
BRTK	Bayrak Radio and TV Corporation (TRNC)	**BSAD**	British Sports Association for the Disabled
BRTTS	British Roll Turners Trade Society	**BSADP**	Bauchi State Aid Development Programme (Nigeria)
BRU	Bilharzia Research Unit (South Africa)	**BSAEM**	British Society for Allergy and Environmental Medicine
BRU	Building Research Unit (Tanzania)		
BRUFMA	British Rigid Urethane Foam Manufacturers Association	**BSAEM/ BSNM**	British Society for Allergy and Environmental Medicine, *with* the British Society for Nutritional Medicine
BRWS	British Rights of Way Society		
BS	Beaumont Society	**BSAF**	Berufsverband der Schweizer Augenoptiker mit Höherer Fachschulausbildung
BS	BeklodningsIndustriens Sammensluting		
BS	Biochemical Society		
BS	Biodeterioration Society	**BSAF**	British Sulphate of Ammonia Federation
BS	Biometric Society (U.S.A.)		
BS	Biophysical Society	**BSAIF**	British Sports and Allied Industries Federation
BS	Bloque Socialista (Dominican Republic)		
BS	Bookplate Society	**BSANZ**	Bibliographical Society of Australia and New Zealand
BS	Brewers Society (*now* BLRA)		
BS	British Shipbuilders	**BSAP**	British Society of Animal Production
BS	Budgerigar Society	**BSAS**	British Sausage Appreciation Society
BS	Ordo Basilianus Sanctissimi Salvatoris Melkitarum	**BSAT**	British Sporting Art Trust
		BSATA	Ballast, Sand and Allied Trades Association
BSA	Banwasi Seva Ashram (India)		
BSA	Bibliographical Society of America	**BSAVA**	British Small Animal Veterinary Association
BSA	Biofeedback Society of America		
BSA	Birmingham Small Arms Co.	**BSB**	Bahrani Saudi Bank
BSA	Boarding Schools Association	**BSB**	Bangladesh Shilpa Bank
BSA	Botanical Society of America	**BSB**	British Satellite Broadcasting
BSA	British Sandwich Association	**BSB**	British Society of Baking
BSA	British Sign Association		

BSB-FCE	Bruderschaft Sankt Benedikt für ein Christliches Europa = FSB-PEC, BSB-VCE
BSB-VCE	Broederschap St. Benediktus voor een Christelijk Europa = FSB-PEC, BSB-FCE
BSBA	British Starter Battery Association
BSBC	British Social Biology Council
BSBG	Binnenschiffahrts-Berufsgenossenschaft
BSBI	Botanical Society of the British Isles
BSBI	Bureau de Statistiques Baleinières Internationales = BIWS, OEBI
BSBMA	British Structural Bearings Manufacturers Association
BSBPR	British Society for Back Pain Research
BSBSPA	British Sugar Beet Seed Producers Association
BSBSW	Boilermakers, Shipwrights, Blacksmiths and Structural Workers (GMB)
BSC	Bibliographical Society of Canada
BSC	Bicycle Stamps Club
BSC	Biological Stain Commission (U.S.A.)
BSC	Biophysical Society of China
BSC	Botanical Society of China
BSC	British Safety Council
BSC	British Seeds Council
BSC	British Shippers Council
BSC	British Shoe Corporation
BSC	British Society of Cinematographers
BSC	British Society of Commerce
BSC	British Steel Corporation
BSC	British Sugar Corporation
BSC	British Sulphur Corporation
BSC	Broadcasting Standards Council
BSC	Building Societies Commission
BSCA	British Self Catering Association
BSCA	British Sulphate of Copper Association (Export) Ltd
BSCA	Building Service Contractors Association International
BSCA	Bureau of Security and Consular Affairs (U.S.A.)
BSCB	British Society for Cell Biology
BSCC	British Shell Collectors' Club
BSCC	British Society for Clinical Cytology
BSCC	British Steelmakers Creep Committee
BSCC	British Swedish Chamber of Commerce in Sweden
BSCC	British Synchronous Clock Conference
BSCC	British-Swiss Chamber of Commerce in Switzerland
BSCD	British Ski Club for the Disabled
BSCDA	British Stock Car Drivers Association
BSCE	Bird Strike Committee Europe
BSCMA	British Soluble Coffee Manufacturers Association
BSCN	British Society of Clinical Neurophysiology
BSCP	Biological Sciences Communication Project (U.S.A.)
BSCRA	British Slot Car Racing Association
BSCS	Biological Sciences Curriculum Study (U.S.A.)
BSCS	British Simmental Cattle Society
BSD	British Society of Dowsers
BSDA	British Sheep Dairying Association
BSDA	British Soft Drinks Association
BSDA	British Spinners and Doublers Association
BSDB	British Society for Developmental Biology
BSDH	British Society of Dentistry for the Handicapped
BSDP	Bulgarian Social Democratic Party
BSDR	British Society for Dental Research
BSE	British Shipbuilding Exports
BSEA	British Steel Export Association
BSEC	Black Sea Economic Cooperation Zone
BSECH	British Society of Experimental and Clinical Hypnosis
BSECS	British Society for Eighteenth Century Studies
BSEG	British Surgical Export Group
BSEM	British Society of Electronic Music
BSERI	Beijing Solar Energy Research Institute
BSES	British Schools Exploring Society
BSES	Building Services Engineering Society
BSF	Border Security Force (India)
BSF	British Scrap Federation
BSF	British Screen Finance
BSF	British Shogi Federation
BSF	British Society of Flavourists
BSF	British Softball Federation
BSF	British Spas Federation
BSF	British Stone Federation
BSF	Bund Schweizerischer Frauenorganisationen = ASF, NCWS
BSFA	British Sanitary Fireclay Association

BSFA	British Science Fiction Association	**BSIR**	Board for Scientific and Industrial Research (Israel)
BSFA	British Snail Farmers Association	**BSIRA**	Building Services Research Information Association
BSFA	British Steel Founders Association		
BSFC	Bihar State Finance Corporation (India)	**BSIU**	British Society for International Understanding
BSFMA	British Spectacle Frame Makers Association	**BSJA**	British Schools Judo Association
BSFP	British Society of Football Philately	**BSJA**	British Show Jumping Association
BSG	British Society of Gastroenterology	**BSK**	Banque Sénégalo-Koweitienne
BSG	British Society of Gerontology	**BSK**	Berghof Stiftung für Konfliktforschung
BSG	British Stickmakers Guild	**BSkyB**	British Sky Broadcasting
BSGB	Bead Society of Great Britain	**BSL**	Botanical Society of London
BSGE	British Society of Gynaecological Endoscopy	**BSL**	Bundesverband Spedition and Lageri
BSH	Berufsverband der Sozialarbeiter, Sozialpädagogen, Heilpädagogen Vereinigte Vertretung Sozialpädagogischer Berufe	**BSLA**	Bund Schweizer Landschaftsarchitekten = FSAP
		BSLPS	Société Belge de Logique et de Philosophie des Sciences
BSH	British Society for Haematology	**BSM**	British Society of Mycopathology
BSH	British Society of Hypnotherapists	**BSMA**	British Secondary Metals Association
BSH	Bundesamt für Seeschiffahrt und Hydrographie (Germany)	**BSMA**	British Skate Makers Association
		BSMA	British Strapping Merchants Association
BSHA	British Skater Hockey Association		
BSHC	Baltic Sea Hydrographic Commission	**BSMALTPS**	Boot and Shoe Manufacturers' Association and Leather Trades' Protection Society
BSHF	Building and Social Housing Foundation		
BSHK	Biophysical Society of Hong Kong	**BSMBEC**	Belgian Society for Medical and Biological Engineering and Computing
BSHM	British Society for the History of Mathematics	**BSMDH**	British Society for Medical and Dental Hypnosis
BSHP	British Society of the History of Pharmacy	**BSME**	British Society of Magazine Editors
BSHR	British Society for Horticultural Research	**BSMES**	British Society for Middle Eastern Studies
BSHS	British Society for the History of Science	**BSMGP**	British Society of Master Glass Painters
		BSMMA	British Sugar Machinery Manufacturers Association
BSHT	British Society of Hearing Therapists		
BSI	Bloody Sunday Initiative	**BSMOC**	Beijing Strong-Motion Observation Center
BSI	British Society for Immunology		
BSI	British Standards Institution	**BSMSP**	Bernoulli Society for Mathematical Statistics and Probability
BSIA	British Security Industry Association		
BSIA	British Starch Industry Association	**BSMT**	British Society of Music Therapy
BSIB	Boy Scouts International Bureau	**BSN**	British Society of Neuroradiologists
BSIC	British Ski Instruction Council	**BSN**	Bulgarian Society of Neurosurgery
BSIDA	British Starch Importer & Dealers Association	**BSNDT**	British Society for Non-Destructive Testing
BSIE	Banking Systems Information Exchange (U.S.A.)	**BSNNN**	British Society of Neuromedical and Neurosurgical Nurses
BSIP	Birbal Sahni Institute of Palaeobotany (India)	**BSO**	Bois du Sud-Ouest (Ivory Coast)
BSiP	Biuro Studiów i Projektów	**BSOEA**	British Stationery and Office Equipment Association

BSOM	British Society for Oral Medicine		**BSRA**	British Society for Research on Ageing
BSONT	British Society of Osteopaths and Natural Therapists		**BSRA**	British Sound Recording Association
BSOP	British Society for Oral Pathology		**BSRAE**	British Society for Research in Agricultural Engineering
BSOUP	British Society of Underwater Photographers		**BSRB**	Bandalag Starfsmanna Rikis og Baeja
BSP	British Society for Parasitology		**BSRC**	British Shoe Repair Council
BSP	British Society for Phenomenology		**BSRC**	British Sporting Rifle Club
BSP	British Society of Perfumers		**BSRD**	British Society for Restorative Dentistry
BSP	British Society of Periodontology		**BSRI**	Brewing Scientific Research Institute (Japan)
BSP	Bulgarian Socialist Party / Bulgarska Sotsialisticheska Partia		**BSRIA**	Building Services Research and Information Association
BSP	Bureau Sanitaire Panaméricain		**BSRM**	British Society of Rehabilitation Medicine
BSPA	Basic Slag Producers Association		**BSRN**	Baseline Surface Radiation Network
BSPA	British Speedway Promoters Association		**BSS**	Bangladesh Sangbad Sangstha
BSPA	British Sports Photographers Association		**BSS**	Berufsverband der Sozialarbeiter
BSPB	British Society of Plant Breeders		**BSS**	Bevera Sverige Svenskt
BSPD	British Society of Paediatric Dentistry		**BSS**	Bird Stamp Society
BSPEG	Bund der Sozialdemokratischen Parteien der Europäischen Gemeinschaft		**BSS**	Black Students' Society (South Africa)
BSPG	Binnenschiffahrts-Berufsgenossenschaft		**BSS**	Botanical Society of Scotland
BSPGR	British Society for Plant Growth Regulation		**BSS**	British Sailors Society
BSPOGA	British Society of Psychosomatic Obstetrics		**BSS**	British Sheep Society
			BSS	British Standards Society
BSPP	British Society of Plant Pathology		**BSS**	British Steam Specialities Limited
BSPP	Burmese Socialist Program Party		**BSS**	Broadcasting Support Services
BSpPS	British Spotted Pony Society		**BSSA**	British Shops and Stores Association (*ex* MAB)
BSPS	Bashkimi i Sindikatave të Pavarura të Shqipërisë (Albania) = UIATU		**BSSA**	British Sjögren's Syndrome Association
BSPS	British Show Pony Society		**BSSA**	British Stainless Steel Association (*ex* SSFA)
BSPS	British Society for the Philosophy of Science		**BSSAA**	British Snoring and Sleep Apnoea Association
BSR	Białoruskie Stowarzyszenie Rolników (Poland) = BFS		**BSSC**	British Shooting Sports Council
BSR	Board of Social Responsibility (Church of England)		**BSSEA**	British Special Ships Equipment Association
BSR	Brigade Socialiste Révolutionnaire (Belgium)		**BSSF**	British Students Sports Federation
BSR	British Society for Rheumatology		**BSSG**	British Society of Scientific Glassblowers
BSR	British Society of Rheology		**BSSH**	British Society for Surgery of the Hand
BSR	Bund Schweizerischer Reklameberater und Werbeagenturen		**BSSH**	British Society of Sports History
			BSSI	Beijing Stationery and Sporting Goods Institute
BSR	Church of England Board for Social Responsibility		**BSSI**	British Society for the Study of Infections
			BSSM	British Society for Strain Measurement
BSRA	British Shoe Repair Association (*ex* NAMSR)		**BSSMS**	British Society for the Study of Mental Subnormality
			BSSO	British Society for the Study of Orthodontics

BSSP	British Society of Sports Psychology
BSSPD	British Society for the Study of Prosthetic Dentistry
BSSR	Bureau of Social Science Research
BSSRS	British Society for Social Responsibility in Science
BSSS	British Society of Soil Science
BSSS	Bulgarian Soil Science Society
BSSSA	British Surgical Support Suppliers Association
BSSSC	Baltic Sea Salmon Standing Committee
BSSW	Bundesverband Schwimmbad, Sauna- und Wassertechnik
BST	Bharatha Seva Trust (India)
BST	British Sports Trust
BST	British Steel Technical
BST	Byggstandardiseringen
BSTA	British Surgical Trades Association
BStBK	Bundessteuerberaterkammer
BSTC	British Student Travel Centre
BSTF	British Student Tuberculosis Foundation
BSTI	Bangladesh Standards and Testing Institution
BSTP	British Society of Toxicological Pathologists
BSTSA	British Surface Treatment Suppliers' Association
BSTU	Barbados Secondary Teachers' Union
BSVI	Bundesvereinigung der Strassen- und Verkehrsingenieure
BSW	Botanical Society of Washington (U.S.A.)
BSWIA	British Steel Wire Industries Association
BT	Boissons et Glacières du Tchad
BT	Book Trust
BT	British Telecom
BTA	Blood Transfusion Association (U.S.A.)
BTA	Bois Transformés d'Afrique (Ivory Coast)
BTA	British Theatre Association
BTA	British Throwsters Association
BTA	British Tinnitus Association
BTA	British Tourist Authority
BTA	British Trade Association of New Zealand
BTA	British Triathlon Association
BTA	British Trout Association
BTA	British Tugowners Association
BTA	Bulgarian Telegraph Agency
BTA	Bulgarska Telegrafna Agentsia
BTAC	Banana Trade Advisory Committee (MAFF)
BTAF	British Tattoo Artists Federation
BTAO	Bureau of Technical Assistance Operations (UN)
BTASA	Book Trade Association of South Africa
BTB	Bundesverband der Tierzucht- und Besamungstechniker
BTBA	British Tchouk Ball Association
BTBA	British Teddy Bear Association
BTBA	British Tenpin Bowling Association
BTBA	British Textile By-Products Association
BTBA	British Twinning and Bilingual Association
BTC	Bhutan Tourism Corporation
BTC	Block Telethon Campaign
BTC	British Textile Confederation
BTC	British Transport Commission
BTC	British Travel Centre
BTCA	British Trade Council in Austria
BTCA	Business Travel Consumer Association
BTCC	Board of Transportation Commissioners of Canada
BTCD	Banque Tchadienne de Crédit et de Dépôts
BTCE	Bureau of Transport and Communications Economics
BTCI	Banque Togolaise pour le Commerce et l'Industrie
BTCI	Bâtiment et Technique de la Côte-d'Ivoire
BTCMPI	British Technical Council of the Motor and Petroleum Industries
BTCV	British Trust for Conservation Volunteers
BTD	Banque Togolaise de Développement
BTD	Bosnian Territorial Defence Force
BTDA	Beama Transmission & Distribution Association
BTDB	British Transport Docks Board
BTDR	Banque Tanzanienne de Développement Rural
BTE	Böripari Tudományos Egyesület
BTE	Bund Technischer Experten
BTE	Bundesverband des Deutschen Textil-Einzelhandels
BTE	Bureau of Transport Economics (Australia)

BTEA	British Textile Employers Association
BTEC	Brucellosis and Tuberculosis Eradication Campaign
BTEC	Business and Technology Education Council
BTECC	Book Trade Electronic Communication Committee
BTEMA	British Tanning Extract Manufacturers Association
BTF	British Tarpaviors Federation Ltd
BTF	British Trampoline Federation
BTF	British Turkey Federation
BTF	Bundesverband Freier Tankstellen und Unabhängiger Deutscher Mineralölhändler
BTFHA	British Touch for Health Association
BTFRA	British Trout Farmers' Restocking Association
BTG	British Technology Group
BTG	British Toymakers' Guild
BTG	Bundesverband des Deutschen Tankstellen und Garagengewerbes
BTGV	Belgische Technische Gieterijvereniging = ATFB
BTHMA	British Toy and Hobby Manufacturers' Association
BTI	Bekleidungstechnisches Institut e.V.
BTI	Board of Trade and Industries (South Africa)
BTI	British Theatre Institute
BTI	Bundesverband der Tabakwaren-Importeure
BTIA	British Tape Industry Association
BTIA	British Tar Industry Association
BTIA	British Turf Irrigation Association
BTIC	Barbados Tourism Investment Corporation
BTIDA	British Toy Importers' and Distributors' Association (*ex* TGIA)
BTIPR	Boyce Thompson Institute for Plant Research (U.S.A.)
BTK	Bundestierärztekammer, Gemeinschaft der Deutschen Tierärztekammern und Tierärztliche Vereinigungen e.V. (*ex* DT)
BTL	Bell Telephone Laboratories (U.S.A.)
BTLIA	British Turf and Landscape Irrigation Association
BTM	Bankin'ny Tantsaha Mpamokatra (Madagascar)
BTMA	British Textile Machinery Association
BTMA	British Theatre Museum Association
BTMA	British Timber Merchants Association
BTMA	British Turned-Parts Manufacturers Association
BTMA	British Typewriter Manufacturers' Association
BTN	Białostockie Towarzystwo Naukowe
BTN	Bydgoskie Towarzystwo Naukowe
BTO	Boeren-en Tuinders Onderlinge
BTO	British Trust for Ornithology
BTO	Bsemirnaja Turistskaja Organizatsija
BTOF	Federation of British Trawler Officers
BTOG	British Transport Officers Guild
BTPA	British Tractor Pullers' Association
BTPMA	British Turned Parts Manufacturers Association
BTPS	Bâtiments et Travaux Publics Sénégalaise
BTR	British Telecommunications Research Ltd
BTR	Bureau of Tourism Research
BTRA	Bombay Textile Research Association (India)
BTRA	British Truck Racing Association
BTRI	Beijing Textile Research Institute
BTRI	Blasting Techniques Research Institute (CCMRI) (China)
BTRUA	British Tennis Umpires' Association
BTS	Biuro Turystyki Sportowej
BTS	Blood Transfusion Service
BTS	Book Trust Scotland
BTS	British Tarantula Society
BTS	British Temperance Society
BTS	British Thoracic Society
BTS	British Titanic Society
BTS	British Toxicology Society
BTS	British Transplantation Society
BTS	British Trolleybus Society
BTS	British Trombone Society
BTS	British Tunnelling Society
BTS	Bureau Technique Syndical Européen pour la Santé et la Sécurité
BTS	Burma Translation Society
BTSA	British Tensional Strapping Association
BTTG	British Textile Technology Group
BTTMC	British Truck Trailer Manufacturers Association

BTTRI	Beijing Television Technology Research Institute		**BUIRA**	British Universities Industrial Relations Association
BTU	Bulgarian Translators Union = SPB		**BUJF**	Bundesministerium für Umwelt, Jugend und Familie (Austria)
BTUC	Bahamas Trade Union Congress		**BUKB**	Belgische Vereniging voor Klinische Biologie = SBBC
BTUC	British Telecommunications Union Committee		**BUKO**	Bundeskonferenz des Wissenschaftlichen und Künstlerischen Personals
BTV	Banco de los Trabajadores de Venezuela			
BTV	Bangladesh Television		**BULVA**	Belfast & Ulster Licensed Vintners' Association
BTZ	Biuro Turystyki Zagranicznej			
BU	Bakers Food and Allied Workers Union = BFAWU		**BUMICO**	Bureau Minier Congolais
			BUN	Biomass Users' Network
BU	Baptist Union of Great Britain and Ireland		**BUNAC**	British Universities North American Club
BU	Bundesamt für Umwelt (Switzerland)		**BUND**	Bund für Umwelt und Naturschutz Deutschland
BUA	British United Airways			
BUA	Koninklijke Beroepsunie der Architekten Gediplomeerd in de Hogere Architecktuurinstituten Sint-Lukas van Belgie = UPA		**BUOC**	British Union Oil Company
			BUP	Banque de l'Union Parisienne
			BUP	British United Press
			BUPA	British United Provident Association
BUAA	Beijing University of Aeronautics and Astronautics		**BUPT**	Beijing University of Posts and Telecommunications
BUAF	British United Air Ferries		**BUR**	Bundesverband Unabhängiger Betribs- und REFA-Berater
BUAS	Border Union Agricultural Society			
BUAS	British Universities Association of Slavists (*now* BASEES)		**BURA**	British Urban Regeneration Association
			BUREMI	Bureau de Recherches et d'Exploitation Minières (Niger)
BUAV	British Union for the Abolition of Vivisection		**BURISA**	British Urban and Regional Information Systems Association
BUD	Binnenlandse Veiligheidsdienst (Netherlands)			
			BURO	Bureau Universitaire de Recherche Opérationnelle
BUE	Belarusan Universal Exchange			
BUE	Buddhist Union of Europe = UBE		**BURTEC**	British Underwater Test and Evaluation Centre (MOD)
BUEN	Bureau of Unrepresented European Nations		**BUS**	Bureau Universitaire de Statistique et de Documentation Scolaire et Professionnelle
BUET	Bangladesh University of Engineering and Technology			
BUF	British Ultimate Federation		**BUSA**	British Universities Society of Arts
BUF	British Union of Fascists		**BUSA**	British Universities Sports Association
BUFCA	British Urethane Foam Contractors Association		**BUSAWU**	Bahamas Utilities Services and Allied Workers' Union
BUFO	British Union of Family Organisations		**BUSDOM**	Bureau Shell d'Outre-Mer
BUFOFI	Bundesforschung für Fischerei		**BUSF**	British Universities' Sports Federation
BUFORA	British Unidentified Flying Object Research Association		**BUSHCO**	Bushehr Petroleum Company
			BUSINET	Network for the Development of European Programmes in Higher Education
BUFOS	British Unidentified Flying Object Society			
BUFVC	British Universities Film and Video Council		**BUSTA**	British Universities Student Travel Association
BUI	Badminton Union of Ireland			
BUIC	Bureau Universitaire d'Information sur les Carrières		**BUSWE**	British Union of Social Work Employees

BUT	Bahamas Union of Teachers		**BVC**	British Vacuum Council
BUT	Barbados Union of Teachers		**BVCA**	British Venture Capital Association
BUTEC	British Underwater Testing Evaluation Centre		**BVD**	Belgische Vereniging der Detectives
BUTEC	British Universities Transatlantic Exchange Committee		**BVD**	Belgische Vereniging voor Documentatie = ABD
BUTYRA	Centrale Suisse de Ravitaillement en Beurre		**BVD**	Bundesverband Druck
BUVOHA	Vereningen Bureau voor Handelsinlichtingen		**BVDA**	British Veterinary Dental Association
BV	Betonvereniging		**BVDB**	Börsenverein des Deutscher Büchhandels
BVA	Berufsverband der Augenärzte Deutschlands		**BVDL**	Bundesverband Deutscher Leibeserzieher
BVA	Bond van Adverteerders		**BVDN**	Berufsverband Detuscher Nervenärzte
BVA	Bond van Vlaamse Architekten (Belgium)		**BVDR**	Bundesverband Deutscher Regisseure
BVA	Britain-Vietnam Association		**BVDRN**	Berufsverband der Deutschen Radiologen und Nuklearmediziner
BVA	British Veterinary Association		**BVE**	Basler Volkswirtschafts-bund (Switzerland)
BVA	British Videogram Association			
BVA	British Vigilance Association		**BVE**	Batallón Vasco Español
BVA	British Voice Association		**BVEB**	Bank for Foreign Economic Affairs (Belarus)
BVA	Bundesversicherungsamt			
BVA	Bundesverweltungsamt		**BVEM**	Belgische Vereniging voor Elektronen-Mikroskopie = SEME
BVAAWF	BVA Animal Welfare Foundation		**BVerfG**	Bundesverfassingsgericht
BVAB	Bedrijfsvereniging voor het Agrarisch Bedrijf		**BVERI**	Beijing Vacuum Electronics Research Institute
BVAMA	British Valve and Actuators Manufacturers' Association		**BVerwG**	Bundesverwaltungsgericht
BVAR	Belgische Vereniging voor Agrarische Recht		**BVF**	British Volleyball Federation
			BVFA	Bundesverband Feuerlöschgeräte und Anlagen-Industrie
BVAS	Belgische Vereniging van Artsen Syndikaten = ABSYM		**BVFI**	Bókavardafelag Islands
BVB	Belgische Vereniging der Banken = ABB		**BVG**	Nederlandse Bond voor het Glasbewerkings-, Glazeniers- en Glas-in Loodbedrijf
BVB	Belgische Vereniging voor Biochemie = SBB		**BVG**	Svenska Byggvarugrossistföreningen
BVB	Belgische Vereniging voor de Bedrijfspers		**BVH**	Bundesverband des Deutschen Versandhandels
BVB	Belgische Voetbalbond		**BVHA**	British Veterinary Hospitals Association
BVB	Beroepsvereniging voor Binnenhuisarchitekten		**BVI**	Belgisch Verpackingsinstituut = IBE
BVB	Boere Vryheidsbeweging (South Africa)		**BVI**	Bundergewerbeverband Snack- und Imbissbetriebe
BvB	Bond van Bontbedrijven		**BVI**	Bundesverband Deutscher Investment-Gesellschaften
BVB	Bundesverband der Büromaschinnen-Importeure		**BVIFLA**	British Virgin Islands Family Life Association
BVB	Bundesverband des Bodenlegerhandwerks		**BVIG**	Belgische Vereniging voor Indwenige Geneeskunde
BVB	Bundesverband Vertriebsunternehmen Büro- Organisations- und Kommunikationstechnik		**BVjA**	Bundesverband Junger Autoren und Autorinnen e.V.
			BVK	Bond van Kleermakerspatroons in Nederland

BVK	Bundesverband Deutscher Versicherungs-kaufleute	**BVR**	Bundesverband der Deutschen Volksbanken und Raiffeisenbanken
BVKS	Bundesverband Kunstoff- und Schwergewebe-Konfektion	**BVR**	Bundesverband der Lehrkräfte der Russischen Sprache
BVL	Bergverkenes Landssammenslutning	**BVRA**	British Veterinary Radiological Association
BVL	Bundesvereinigung Logistik e.V.		
BVLH	Bundervereinigung Lebenshilfe für Geistig Behinderte	**BVRFH**	Berufsverband der Reiseleiter, Fremdenführer und Hostessen Deutschlands
BVLJ	Belgische Vereniging van Landbouwjournalisten = ABJA	**BVRLA**	British Vehicle Rental and Leasing Association
BVLT	Belgische Vereniging van Laboratorium-technologen = ABTL	**BVS**	Belgische Vereniging van Stedebouwkyndigen
BVM	Berufsverband Deutscher Markt- und Sozialforscher e.V.	**BVS**	Belgische Vereniging voor Stralingsbescherming = ABR
BVM	Bundesverband Deutscher Marktforscher	**BVS**	Belgische Vereniging voor Suikerzieken
BVM	Bundesvereinigung Verbandmittel und Medicalprodukte = SDMA	**BVS**	Bundesverband des deutschen Seiler-, Segel- und Netzmacher-Handworks
BVMA	British Valve Manufacturers Association	**BVS**	Bundesverband Öffentlich Bestellter und Vereidigter Sachverständiger
BVMB	Bundesvereinigung Mittelständischer Bauunternehmunger	**BVSI**	Bundesverband Sargindustrie
BVMS	Biuro Vsemirnogo Soveta	**BVSK**	Bundesverband der Freiberuflichen und Unabhängigen Sachverständigen für das Kraftfahrzeugwesen
BVMSS	Biuro Vzaimozameniaemosti Ministerstva Stankostroeniia		
BVNA	British Veterinary Nursing Association	**BVSM**	Belgische Vereniging tot Studie, Beproefing en Gebruik der Materialen = ABEM
BVÖ	Berufsverband Bildender Künstler Österreichs		
BVÖ	Buchereiverband Österreichs	**BVSM**	Biuro Vsemirnogo Soveta Mira
BVÖ	Technisch-Wissenschaftlicher Verein Bergmännischer Verband Österreichs	**BVSW**	Bayerischer Verband für Sicherheit in der Wirtschaft
BVOP	Belgisch-Luxemburgse Vereniging van de Ondernemingspers	**BVT**	Belgische Vereniging van Transportverzekeraars
BVOT	Belgische Vereniging voor Orthopedie en Traumatologie	**BVT**	Bundesverband staatlich geprüfter Techiker
BVP	Banco de la Vivienda del Peru	**BVTA**	Bundesarbeitsgemeinschaft der Vereinigungen der Teer- und Asphaltmakadamherstellenden Firmen
BVP	Belgische Vereniging voor Psychologie = BPS, SBP		
BvP	Bond van Platenhandelaren	**BVTL**	Belgische Vereniging von Tuinarchitekten en Landschapsarchitekten = ABAJP
BVP	Bureau de la Vérification de la Publicité		
BVPA	Bundesverband der Pressebild-Agenturen, Bilderdienste und Bildarchive	**BVTL**	Belgische Vereniging voor Toegepaste Linguistiek Appliqués = ABLA
BvPA	Bundesverband der Pressedienste und Agenturen	**BVUIH**	Belgisch Vereniging van Uit- en Invoerhandelaars
BVPG	Belgische Vakgroep voor Petroleumgassen	**BVV**	Belgische Vereniging voor Verlamden
		BVV	Bükkvidéki Vendéglátó Vállalat
BVPO	Biuro Vnedreniia Programmnoi Obrabotki	**BVVB**	Belgische Vereniging der Voedingsbedrijven met Bijhuizen
BVR	Belgische Vereniging van de Rubberindustrie	**BVVK**	Beroepsvereniging der Vis Groothandelaars-Verzenders van de Kust
BVR	Biuro Vzaimnykh Raschetov		

BVVO	Beroepsvereniging Verzekerings-ondernemingen
BVW	Bundesverband der Wirtschaftsberater
BVWB	Belgische Vereniging voor Toepassing van Wetenschappelijke Methodes in het Bedrijsbeheer
BVWS	British Vintage Wireless Society
BVZ	Belgische Vereniging der Ziekenhuizen = ABH
BVZS	British Veterinary Zoological Society
BW	Bundesamt für Wirtschaft
BWA	Baptist World Alliance
BWA	Biuro Wystaw Zagranicznych
BWA	Black Watch Association
BWA	Bridge Deck Waterproofing Association
BWA	British Waterfowl Association
BWA	British Westeners Association
BWA	Bundesministerium für Wirtschaftliche Angelegenheiten (Austria)
BWAHDA	British Warm Air Hand Drier Association
BWB	British Waterways Board
BWBA	British Wild Boar Association
BWBF	British Wireless for the Blind Fund
BWBS	British Warm-Blood Society
BWC	Baltic Women's Council (U.S.A.)
BWC	Baltic World Council (U.S.A.)
BWC	Beauty Without Cruelty International
BWCC	Beauty Without Cruelty Charity
BWCC	British Weed Control Council
BWCI	Bahamas Workers' Council International
BWCMA	British Wood Chipboard Manufacturers Association
BWCMG	British Watch and Clock Makers Guild
BWCS	British White Cattle Society
BWDA	British Western Dance Association
BWEA	British Wind Energy Association
BWF	Belgische Wegenfederatie
BWF	Beratendes Weltkomitee des Freunde = FWCC, CCMA, CMCA
BWF	British Waterski Association
BWF	British Whiting Federation (now BCCF)
BWF	British Woodworking Federation
BWF	British Wool Federation
BWF	Bundesministerium für Wissenschaft und Forschung (Austria)
BWG	Braunschweigische Wissenschaftliche Gesellschaft
BWG	Österreichische Bankwissenschaftliche Gesellschaft an der Wirtschaftsuniversität Wien
BWI	Boating Writers International
BWIA	British West Indies Airways
BWIG	British Water Industries Group
BWISA	British West Indies Sugar Association
BWIUA	Building Workers' Industrial Union of Australia
BWJA	British Wholesale Jewellers Association
BWK	Bund der Wasser- und Kulturbauingenieure
BWKZ	Biuro Wspólpracy Kulturalnej z Zagranicą
BWMA	British Woodwork Manufacturers' Association
BWMB	British Wool Marketing Board
BWNMA	British Wire Netting Manufacturers Association
BWORF	Baptist World Relief (U.S.A.)
BWOY	British Wheel of Yoga
BWPA	British Waste Paper Association
BWPA	British Women Pilots Association
BWPA	British Wood Preserving Association
BWPA	British Wood Pulp Association
BWPUC	British Waste Paper Utilization Council
BWRE	Biological Warfare Research Establishment
BWRRA	British Wire Rod Rollers Association
BWS	British Water Colour Society
BWSA	British Wheat Starch Association
BWSF	British Water Ski Federation
BWSF	British Wheelchair Sports Foundation (ex BPSS)
BWSTA	British Welded Steel Tube Association
BWTA	British Wholesale Traders Association
BWTA	British Women's Temperance Association
BWTA	British Wood Turners Association
BWU	Barbados Workers' Union
BWV	Bundesverband Werkverkehr und Verlader
BWVS	Bundeswirtschaftsvereinigung Sportschiffahrt
BWW	Buses Worldwide
BWWA	British Waterworks Association
BWWEA	British Woven Wire Export Association
BWWFH	Black Women for Wages for Housework
BY	Suomen Betoniyhdistys

BYBA	British Youth Band Association
BYC	British Youth Council
BYF	British Yoseikan Federation
BYFO	Bygnings Fredrings Foreningen (Denmark)
BYGGDOK	Institutet für Byggdokumentation
BYNA	British Young Naturalists Association
BYPC	Beijing Youth Politics College
BYS	British Southern Slav Society
BYWCA	Botswana Young Women's Christian Association
BZ	Bedrijfschap voor Zuivel (Dairy Produce Corporation) (Netherlands)
BZA	British Zoelite Association
BZA	Bundesverband Zeitarbeit
BZAK	Bundeszahnärztekammer, Arbeitsgemeinschaft der Deutschen Zahnärztekammern e.V. (*ex* BDZ)
BZB	Verband der Deutschen Bauzubehörindustrie (HDH)
BZD	Białoruskie Zjednoczenie Demokratyczne (Poland) = BDU
BZG	Botanisch-Zoologische Gesellschaft Lichtenstein-Sargans-Werdenberg
BZG	Bundes-Zentralgenossen schaft Strassenverkehr
BZNS	Bulgarian National Agrarian Union
BZÖG	Bunderverband der Zahnärzte des Öffentlichen Gesundheitsdienstes – wissenschaftliche Gesellschaft zur Fürderung zahnärztlicher Social Hygiene
BZS	Britain-Zimbabwe Society
BZS	Bundesamt für Zivilschutz
BZTM	Biuro Zagranicznej Turystyki Młodziezy
BZV	Belarusan Association of Servicemen

C

C&E	HM Customs & Excise
C&PC	Corrosion & Protection Centre
C-CORE	Centre for Cold Ocean Resources Engineering (Canada)
C-FARR	Center for Fertility and Reproductive Research (U.S.A.)
C-MIST	Centre for Maritime & Industrial Safety Technology
C18	Combat 18

C2	Military Intelligence Service (Philippines)
C3FM	Case Center for Complex Flow Measurements (U.S.A.)
CA	Cadmium Association
CA	Camanachd Association
CA	Cat Association of Britain
CA	Chambre d'Agriculture (France)
CA	Champagne Association
CA	Church Army
CA	Civic Alliance (Serbia)
CA	Classical Action
CA	Classical Association
CA	Cockburn Association
CA	Coir Association
CA	Consumers Association
CA	Contributions Agency
CA	Cromwell Association
CA	Croquet Association
CA	Cruising Association
CA	Cultists Anonymous
CAA	Caisse Agropecuárome d'Amortissement (Benin, Ivory Coast)
CAA	Campaign for the Abolition of Angling
CAA	Canadian Archaeological Association = ACA
CAA	Canadian Authors' Association
CAA	Canadian Automobile Association
CAA	Caribbean Archives Association
CAA	Cathedral Architects' Association
CAA	Cement Admixtures Association
CAA	Central African Airways
CAA	Centro Azucarero Argentino
CAA	Chinese Aeromedical Association
CAA	Chinese Association of Automation
CAA	Chiropractic Advancement Association
CAA	Christian Adventure Association
CAA	Cigar Association of America
CAA	Cinema Advertising Association
CAA	Citizen Advocacy Alliance
CAA	Civil Aeronautics Administration (U.S.A.)
CAA	Civil Aviation Authority
CAA	Club for Acts and Actors (*ex* Concert Artistes Association)
CAA	Collection Agencies Association (*now* CSA)
CAA	Collectors of American Art (U.S.A.)

CAA	College Art Association of America	**CAARC**	Commonwealth Advisory Aeronautical Research Council
CAA	Commonwealth Association of Architects	**CAARI**	Cyprus American Archaeological Research Institute
CAA	Community Aid Abroad (Australia)	**CAARM**	Confederación de Asociaciones Algodoneras de la República Mexicana
CAA	Conseil Africain de l'Arachide = AGC		
CAA	Conseils Associés en Afrique (Ivory Coast)	**CAAS**	Canadian Association for American Studies
CAA	Cost Accountants' Association	**CAAS**	Canadian Association of African Studies
CAAA	Canadian Aberdeen Angus Association	**CAAS**	Center for Afro-American Studies, University of Michigan
CAAA	Canadian Association of Advertising Agencies	**CAAS**	Chinese Academy of Agricultural Sciences
CAAA	Chinese Acrobatic Artists Association	**CAAS**	Chinese Association for the Advancement of Science
CAAA	Commuter Airline Association of America	**CAAS**	Chinese Association of Applied Statistics
CAAA	Composers, Authors and Artists of America	**CAASA**	Centre Africain d'Application de Statistique Agricole (FAO)
CAAA	Confédération Africaine d'Athlétisme = AAAC	**CAASR**	Canadian Association of Applied Social Research = ACRSA
CAAB	Canadian Advertising Advisory Board	**CAASS**	Chinese Association of Agricultural Science Societies
CAABU	Council for the Advancement of Arab-British Understanding	**CAAT**	Campaign Against Arms Trade
CAAC	Civil Aviation Administration of China	**CAAV**	Central Association of Agricultural Valuers
CAACE	Comité des Associations d'Armateurs des Communautés Européennes	**CAAVS**	Chinese Association for Animal and Veterinary Sciences
CAACTD	Comite Asesor sobre la Aplicación de la Ciencia y la Tecnologia al Desarrollo (ONU)	**CAB**	Cabletelevision Advertising Bureau (U.S.A.)
CAADE	Campaign against Age Discrimination in Employment	**CAB**	Canadian Association of Broadcasters
		CAB	Chambre des Architectes de Belgique
CAADES	Confederación de Asociaciones Agricolas del Estado de Sinaloa (Mexico)	**CAB**	Christliche Arbeiterwegung = ACW, MOC
CAAE	Canadian Association for Adult Education	**CAB**	Citizens Advice Bureaux
CAAEO	Commission des Affaires d'Aise et d'Extrême-Orient de la Chambre de Commerce Internationale	**CAB**	Comité des Assurers Belges
		CAB	Compagnie Africaine des Bois (Ivory Coast)
CAAERP	Chinese Academy of Agricultural Engineering Research and Planning	**CAB**	Condensation Advisory Bureau
		CAB	Confédération Asiatique Billar = ABC
CAAIF	China Association for the Advancement of International Friendship	**CAB**	Corrosion Advice Bureau (BSC)
CAAIM	Coopérative Agricole d'Approvisionnement des Agriculteurs de la Marché	**CABAS**	City and Borough Architects Society
		CaBC	Caribbean Broadcasting Corporation
CAAK	Civil Aviation Administration of Korea	**CABE**	Christian Association of Business Executives
CAAMS	Chinese Academy of Agricultural Mechanisation Science	**CABEI**	Central American Bank for Economic Integration = BCIE
CAANS	Canadian Association for the Advancement of Netherlandic Studies = ACAEN	**CABEI**	Intergovernmental Committee on the River Plate Basin (Uruguay)
CAAP	Centro Andino de Acción Popular (Ecuador)	**CABET**	Canadian Association of Business Education Teachers

CABFAA	Coach and Bus First Aid Association		**CACAS**	Civil Aviation Council of the Arab States
Cabi	Commonwealth Agricultural Bureau International		**CACC**	Central Australian Conservation Council
CABM	Commonwealth of Australia Bureau of Meteorology		**CACC**	Civil Aviation Communications Centre
CABMA	Canadian Association of British Manufacturers and Agencies		**CACC**	Council for the Accreditation of Correspondence Colleges
CABNAVE	Cape Verde Naval Repair Company		**CACCI**	Committee on the Application of Computers in the Construction Industry
CABO	Centrum voor Agrobiologisch Onderzoek		**CACCI**	Confederation of Asian-Pacific Chambers of Commerce and Industry (Philippines)
CABO	Council of American Building Officials		**CACDP**	Council for the Advancement of Communication with Deaf People
CABO-PRESS	Cape Verde News Agency		**CACDS**	Commonwealth Advisory Committee on Defence Science
CABR	China Academy of Building Research		**CACE**	Central Advisory Council for Education
CABS	Conservation Association of Botanical Societies		**CACE**	Compania Andina de Comercio Exterior
CAC	Campaign Against Censorship		**CACED**	Central American Commission on Environment and Development (Guatemala)
CAC	Canada Arts Council			
CAC	Canterbury Agricultural College, Lincoln (N.Z.)		**CACEE**	Chinese Association for Continuing Education Engineering
CAC	Cathedrals Advisory Committee for England		**CACEF**	Centre d'Action Culturelle de la Communauté d'Expression Française
CAC	Central Arbitration Committee		**CACEP**	Société Camérounaise de Commercialisation et d'Exportation de Produits
CAC	Classical Association of Canada = SCEC			
CAC	Codex Alimentarius Commission (FAO/WHO)		**CACEPA**	Centre d'Actions Concertées des Entreprises de Produits Alimentaires
CAC	Colonial Advisory Council		**CACEU**	Central African Customs Economic Union = UDEAC
CAC	Comité Administratif de Coordination (ONU) = ACC		**CACEX**	Carteira de Comercio Exterior (Brazil)
CAC	Commonwealth Association of Architects		**CACFOA**	Chief and Assistant Chief Fire Officers Association
CAC	Community Advisory Committee		**CACGP**	Commission of Atmospheric Chemistry and Global Pollution
CAC	Conseil Africain de la Comptabilité = AAC		**CaCH**	Carmelite Sisters of Charity
CAC	Consumers Advisory Council (U.S.A.)		**CACH**	Central American Clearing House
CAC	Consumers Association of Canada = ACC		**CACI**	Catholic Alumni Clubs International (U.S.A.)
CAC	Council for Arms Control		**CACI**	Civil Aviation Chaplains International
CACA	Canadian Agricultural Chemicals Association		**CACI**	Société CentrAfricaine de Ciment
CACA	Cement and Concrete Association		**CACIA**	Compagnie d'Agriculture de Commerce et d'Industrie d'Afrique (Guinea)
CACA	Chartered Association of Certified Accountants		**CACIEL**	Comité de Acción para la Cooperacion y Concertacion Latinoamericana en el Sector Siderurgico (Caracas)
CACA	Chinese Anti-Cancer Association			
CACA	Chinese Arts and Crafts Association		**CACIF**	Comité Coordinador de Asociaciones Agrécolas Comerciales, Industriales y Financieras (Guatemala)
CACAC	Civil Aircraft Control Advisory Committee			
CACAS	Centre for American & Commonwealth Arts & Studies		**CACIP**	Central American Co-operative Corn Improvement Project

224

CACIP	Confederación Argentina de Comercio de la Industria y de la Producción
CACIRA	Chambre Syndicale des Constructeurs d'Appareils de Contrôle Industriel et de Régulation Automatique
CACISS	Comitato Assistenza Culturale Italiana Scolastica Scozia
CACJ	Comité de Asuntos Constitucionales y Jurídicos (FAO)
CACL	Canadian Association of Children's Librarians
CACLB	Churches Advisory Committee on Local Broadcasting
CACM	Central American Common Market = MCAC, MCCA
CACMF	Central American Common Market Fund (Honduras) = FCMC
CACOM	Central American Common Market
CACOM-IAF	Comptoir de l'Automobile et du Cycle, Outillage Matériel Industriel, Agricole et Forestier (Ivory Coast)
CACP	Chambre des Agences-Conseils en Publicité (Belgium)
CACP	Council for the Advancement of Consumer Policy (U.S.A.)
CACPU	China Association for Coal Processing and Utilization
CACR	Council for Agricultural and Chemurgic Research (U.S.A.)
CACRA	Caribbean Agricultural Credit Association (Jamaica)
CACRMA	Caisse Agropecuárome Centrale de Retraites Mutuelles Agricoles
CACS	Chinese Arts and Crafts Society
CACSA	Campaign Against the Child Support Act
CACSO	Central American and Caribbean Sports Organization = ODECABE
CACT	Caribbean Association of Catholic Teachers
CACTAL	Conference on the Application of Science and Technology to Latin America
CACU	Central Agricultural Co-operative Union (Egypt)
CACUL	Canadian Association of College and University Libraries = ACBCU
CAD	Centralforeningen of Autoreparatører i Danmark
CAD	Chinese Association for the Disabled (China)
CAD	Civil Aviation Department (India)

CAD	Comité Africain pour le Développement (Belgium)
CAD	Comité Agricole Départmental
CAD	Comité d'Aide au Développement (OCDE) = DAC
CAD	Commonwealth Association for Development
CADA	Campaign Against Drug Addiction
CADA	Compagnie Atlantique d'Assurances et de Réassurances (Morocco)
CADA	Compania Anonima Distribuidora de Alimentos (Venezuela)
CADA	Confederation of Art and Design Associations
CADAFE	Compania Anonima de Administración y Fomento Eléctrico (Venezuela)
CADAL	Centro di Azione e Documentazione sull'America Latina
CADAL	Compagnie Africaine Forestière et des Allumettes
CADAPSO	Canadian Association of Data Processing Service Organisations
CADAT	Caisse Algérienne d'Aménagement du Territoire
CADAUMA	Coopérative Agricole d'Achat et d'Utilisation de Matériel Agricole de l'Aveyron
CADC	Computer Aided Design Centre
CADD	Campaign Against Drinking and Driving
CADDET	Centre for Analysis and Dissemination of Demonstrated Energy Technologies
CADE	Coalition Against Dangerous Exports (BEUC)
CADEC	Christian Action for Development in the Caribbean
CADEC	Committee of the Dietetic Association of the Common Market
CADEF	Centro Argentino de Estudios Forestales
CADEICA	Confédération des Associations d'Écoles Indépendantes de la Communauté Européenne (Belgium)
CADER	Consejo Argentino de Estudios sobre la Reproducción
CADES	Centro Argentino de Estudios Sociológicos
CADESCA	Comité de Acción de Apoyo al Desarrollo Economico y Social de Centroamerica (Panama)
CADEZA	Caisse Générale d'Épargne du Zaïre
CADIA	Centro Argentino de Ingenieros Agrénomos

CADIB	Centre Africain de Documentation et d'Information en Matière de Brevets (Cameroon)	**CAEC**	County Agricultural Executive Committee
CADICA	Confederación Atlética del Istmo Centroamericano (Costa Rica)	**CAEDA**	Compressed Air Equipment Distributors Association
CADICEC	Association des Cadres et Dirigeants Chrétiens des Entreprises au Congo et au Rwanda-Burundi	**CAEE**	Committee on Aircraft Engine Emissions (ICAO)
CADIF	Cámara Argentina de la Industria Frigorífica	**CAEEB**	Companhia Auxiliar de Empresas Electricas Brasileiras
CADIN	Camara de Industrias de Nicaragua	**CAEES**	Centre Algérien d'Expansion Économique et Social
CADIPPE	Comité d'Action pour le Développement de l'Intéressement du Personnel à la Productivité des Entreprises	**CAEF**	Campaign Against Euro-Federalism
		CAEF	Comité des Associations Européennes de Fonderie
CADIRJ	Comité de Apoio aos Indígenas do Rio de Janeiro (Brazil)	**CAEI**	Compagnie Africaine d'Équipement Industriel (Ivory Coast)
CADIST	Centres d'Acquisition et de Diffusion de l'Information Scientifique et Technique	**CAEIT**	Chinese Academy of Electronics and Information Technology
CADL	Cámara Argentina de Destiladores	**CAEJ**	Communauté des Associations d'Éditeurs de Journaux de la CEE
CADM	Chinese Association of Discrete Mathematics	**CAEJC**	Commonwealth Association for Education in Journalism and Communication (Canada)
CADO	Central Air Documents Office (U.S.A.)		
CADP	Campaign Against Double Punishment	**CAEL**	Council for the Advancement of Experiential Learning (U.S.A.)
CADRE	Center for Aerospace Doctrine, Research and Education (U.S.A.)	**CAEM**	Campo Agrícola Experimental de Mexicali
CADSWES	Center for Advanced Decision Support for Water and Environmental Systems (U.S.A.)	**CAEM**	Centre Africain d'Études Monétaires = ACMS
CADU	Chilalo Agricultural Development Unit (Ethiopia)	**CAEM**	Centro Avanzado de Estudios Militares (Peru)
CADV	Campaign Against Domestic Violence	**CAeM**	Commission for Aeronautical Meteorology (WMO)
CADW	Welsh Historic Monuments	**CAEMC**	Comité d'Associations Européennes de Médecins Catholiques
CAE	Canadian Association of Exhibitions		
CAE	Chinese Aeronautics and Astronautics Establishment	**CAEND**	Centro Argentino de Ensayo no Destructivos de Materiales (Argentine)
CAE	Comité Atlantique de l'Éducation = AEC	**CAEP**	Chambre d'Agriculture et d'Élevage (French Polynesia)
CAE	Commandement Allié Europe (OTAN) = ACE	**CAEP**	Communauté des Associations d'Éditeurs de Périodique du Marché Commun
CAE	Conseil des Architectes d'Europe (Belgium) = ACE		
CAEA	Central American Economics Association	**CAEPC**	Comisión Asesora Europea sobre Pesca Continental
CAEC	Center for Analysis of Environmental Change (U.S.A.)	**CAEPE**	Centre d'Assemblage et d'Essais des Propulseurs et des Engins
		CAER	Centre for Alternative Education & Research
CAEC	Central American Economic Community	**CAER**	Conservative Action for Electoral Reform
CAEC	Committee of the Acta Endocrinologica Countries	**CAES**	Canadian Agricultural Economics Society
CAEC	Conseil Africain d'Enseignement de la Communication = ACCE		

CAES	Central Association of Experiment Stations (Indonesia)
CAES	Chiba Prefecture Agricultural Experiment Station (Japan)
CAESPCI	Central Association of Experimental Stations for Perennial Crops in Indonesia
CAESS	Compania de Alumbrado Electrico de San Salvador
CAETA	Commonwealth Association for the Education and Training of Adults
CAEU	Council of Arab Economic Unity = CUEA
CAEVR	Comité d'Action École et Vie Rurale
CAF	Central African Federation
CAF	Centralna Agencja Fotograficzna
CAF	Charities Aid Foundation
CAF	Chinese Academy of Forestry
CAF	Club Alpin Français
CAF	Comptoir Agricole Français
CAF	Confédération Africaine de Football = AFC
CAF	Conseil del l'Agriculture Française
CAF	Corporación Andina de Fomento = ADC, SAD
CAFA	Chambre Agricole Franco-Allemande
CAFAC	Commission Africaine del l'Aviation Civile = AFCAC
CAFADE	Comisión Nacional Administración del Fondo de Apoyo al Desarrollo Económico (Argentina)
CAFAL	Compagnie Africaine Forestière et des Allumettes
CAFAN-DINA	Cámara de Fabricantes de Autopartes Andina
CAFAN-GOL	Empresa de Rebenefício e Exportação do Café de Angola
CAFAP	Camara de Fabricantes de Autopartes del Peru
CAFAS	Council for Academic Freedom and Academic Standards
CAFC	Compagnie Agricole et Forestière du Caméroun
CAFCO	Caisse d'Allocations Familiales des Sociétés Coopératives de Consommation et de Production de la Suisse Romande
CAFCO	Compagnie Africaine de Commerce et de Commission
CAFE	Campaign Against Fascism in Europe
CAFE	Comité d'Action Féminine Européenne
CAFE	Companía Americana de Fomento Económico
CAFE	Council of American Forensic Entomologists
CAFE	Creative Activity For Everyone (Éire)
CAFEA-ICC	Commission on Asian and Far Eastern Affairs of the International Chamber of Commerce
CAFEC	Consortium Africain d'Exploitation de la Chaux (Senegal)
CAFEI	Central American Fund for Economic Integration (Honduras)
CAFESA	Central Ferretera, S.A. (El Salvador)
CAFESA	Companía Costarricense del Café
CAFI	Ceramic Art Federation International (U.S.A.)
CAFI	Commercial Advisory Foundation in Indonesia
CAFIC	Combined Allied Forces Information Centre
CAFIM	Confédération des Associations des Facteurs d'Instruments de Musique de la CEE
CAFIMA	Camara de Fabricantes de Implementos, Maquinarias Agricolas y Afines (Venezuela)
CAFISH-TRACO	Cameroon Fishing and Trading Company
CAFL	Compagnie des Ateliers et Forges de la Loire
CAFMHA	Camara Argentina de Fabricantes de Macquinas, Herramientas, Accesorios y Afines
CAFMNA	Compound Animal Feedingstuffs Manufacturers National Association
CAFOD	Catholic Fund for Overseas Development
CAFP	Chinese Association of Fire Protection
CAFP	Comisión Andina de Formación Profesional
CAFPTA	Comisión Aministradora del Fondo para la Promoción de la Tecnología Agropecuária (Argentina)
CAFRA	Caribbean Association for Feminist Research and Action (Barbados)
CAFRAD	Centre Africain de Formation et de Recherches Administratives pour le Développement (Morocco) = ATRCAD
CAFRADES	Centre Africain de Recherche Appliquée et de Formation en Matière de Développement Social (Libya)

CAFS	Canadian Association for Future Studies
CAFS	Center for Advanced Feminist Studies (U.S.A.)
CAFS	Centre for African Family Studies
CAFS	China Academy of Fishery Sciences
CAFTA	Central American Free Trade Association
CAFTA	Comisión Administradora para el Fondo de Tecnologia Agropecuária (Argentina)
CAFTA	Conférence Africaine des Tarifs Aériens = AFRATC
CAFTEL	Companie Africaine de Fabrication de Tableaux et d'Équipements Électriques (Ivory Coast)
CAFTEX	Compagnie Africaine de Textile (Ivory Coast)
CAFTRAC	Compagnie Africaine de Transactions Commerciales (Ivory Coast)
CAFTRAD	Centre Africain de Formation et de Recherche Administrative pour le Développement
CAFUM	Companhia de Fumigaçoes de Moçambique
CAG	Canadian Association of Geographers = ACG
CAG	Catholic Actors Guild (U.S.A.)
CAG	Community Architecture Resource Centre
CAG	Comparative Administrative Group of the American Society for Public Administration
CAGAC	Civil Aviation General Administration of China
CAGK	Ciurlionis Art Gallery of Kaunas = KCDM
CAGLS	Chinese Association of German Literature Studies
CAgM	Commission for Agricultural Meteorology (WMO)
CAGRIS	Caribbean Information System for the Agricultural Sciences (Trinidad-Tobago)
CAGS	Centre for Arab and Gulf Studies
CAGS	Chinese Academy of Geological Sciences
CAH	Canadian Association of Hispanists = ACH
CAH	Center for American History (U.S.A.)
CAH	Compagnie Africaine d'Hôtellerie (Congo)
CAHA	Christian Alliance Housing Association
CAHBI	Ad hoc Committee of Experts on Bioethics (Council of Europe)
CAHDA	Cámara Hondureña de Aseguradores
CAHI	Caribbean Association for the Hearing Impaired
CAHN	Central America Health Network
CAHN	Cooperative Agricole Haute Normandie
CAHOF	Canadian Aviation Hall of Fame
CAHPER	Canadian Association for Health, Physical Education and Recreation
CAHPERD	Canadian Association for Health, Physical Education, Recreation and Dance
CAHRC	Central America Human Rights Committee
CAHUMC	Commission on Archives and History of the United Methodist Church (U.S.A.)
CAI	Canadian Aeronautical Institute
CAI	Center for Archaeological Investigations (U.S.A.)
CAI	Cereals Association of Ireland
CAI	Club Alpino Italiano
CAI	Comité Arctique International
CAI	Compagnie Africaine pour l'Informatique (Ivory Coast)
CAI	Concrete Association of India
CAI	Confederation of Aerial Industries
CAI	Confederation of Australian Industry
CAI	Consejo Andino de Ingeniería
CAI	Consumers Association of Ireland
CAI	Container Aid International (Belgium)
CAI	Crochet Association International
CAIA	Centre for Armenian Information & Advice
CAIA	Centro Argentine de Ingeniéros Agrónomos
CAIA	Congreso Argentino de la Industria Aceitera
CAIAD	Campaign Against Immigration Act Detentions
CAIC	Caribbean Association of Industry and Commerce
CAIC	Children's and Adolescents' International Cooperation
CAIC	China Aero-Information Center
CAIC	Chinese Academy of International Culture
CAIC	Compagnie d'Agriculture d'Industrie et de Commerce (Madagascar)
CAICYT	Centro Argentino de Información Cientifica y Tecnologica
CAID	Centre for Adviser & Inspector Development

CAIE	Conseil des Associations des Immigrés en Europe
CAIFOM	Caisse de la France d'Outre-Mer
CAILS	Chinese Association of Indian Literature Studies
CAIM	Compagnie Agricole et Industrielle de Madagascar
CAIM	Syndicat National des Créateurs d'Architectures Intérieures et de Modèles
CAIMO	Comité Asesor de Investigaciones Meteorólogicas Oceánicas (WMO) = ACOMR, CCRMO
CAIO	Caribbean American Intercultural Organization
CAIP	Center for Computer Aids for Industrial Productivity (U.S.A.)
CAIPE	UK Centre for the Advancement of Interprofessional Education (in Primary Health and Community Care)
CAIR	Centre for Automotive Industry Research
CAIR	Comité d'Action Interallié de la Résistance
CAIRM	Comité Asesor sobre Investigaciones de los Recursos Marinos (FAO) = ACMRR, CCRRM
CAIRU	Colonial Agricultural Insecticides Research Unit
CAIS	Canadian Association for Information Science = ACSI
CAIS	Center for Applied Isotope Studies (U.S.A.)
CAIS	Central Abstracting and Indexing Service (API)
CAIS	Central American Integration Scheme
CAISS	Centre for Arms Control and International and Security Studies (U.S.A.)
CAISTAB	Caisse de Stabilisation et de Soutien des Prix des Productions Agricoles (Ivory Coast) = CSSPPA
CAIT	China Association of International Trade
CAIT	Citizen Advocacy Information and Training
CAITA	Compagnie Agricole et Industrielle des Tabacs Africains
CAITA-CI	Compagnie Agricole et Industrielle des Tabacs Côte-d'Ivoire
CAITS	Centre for Alternative Industrial and Technological Systems
CAITWM	Chinese Association of Integrated Traditional and Western Medicine
CAJ	Comisión Andina de Juristas (Peru)
CAJ	Committee on the Administration of Justice (Northern Ireland)
CAJ	Confederation of ASEAN Journalists
CAJ	Internationale Christliche Arbeiterjugend
CAJLS	Chinese Association of Japanese Literature Studies
CAJP	Clubes Agrícolas Juveniles del Perú
CAL	Catholic AIDS Link
CAL	Centro di Azione Latina
CAL	China Association of Land
CAL	Cocoa Association of London
CAL	Commonwealth Acoustic Laboratories (Australia)
CAL	Pontificia Commissione per l'America Latina
CALA	Canadian Association for Latin America
CALA	Chinese-American Librarians Association
CALA	Christiana Area Land Authority (West Indies)
CALAG	Citizens Against Lorries Action Group
CALAI	Conferencia de Autoridades Latinoamericanos de Informatica
CALANS	Caribbean and Latin American News Service
CALAS	Canadian Association of Latin American and Caribbean Studies = ACELA
CALAS	Chinese Association for Latin American Studies
CALC	Commonwealth Association of Legislative Counsel
CALCOFI	California Cooperative Oceanic Fisheries Investigations (U.S.A.)
CALF	Campaign Against Leather and Fur
CALFAA	Canadian Air Line Flight Attendants Association
CALG	Central America Labour Group
CALG	Compagnie des Landes de Gascogne
CALIP	Campaign Against Lead in Petrol
CALL	Canadian Association of Law Libraries = ACBD
CALL	Childhood Cancer and Leukaemia Link
CALNM	Chinese Association of Literature of National Minorities
CALNU	Cooperative Agropecuária Limitada Norte Uruguayo

CALO	Coopérative Agricole Lainière de l'Ouest
CALPA	Canadian Air Line Pilots Association
CALPOM	Committee for the Liberation of Prisoners of Opinion in Morocco
CALQ	Centro Académico "Luiz de Queiroz" (Brazil)
CALS	Canadian Association of Library Schools = ACEB
CALS	Centre for Applied Language Studies (Canada, U.K.)
CALT	Canadian Asociation of Law Teachers = ACPD
CALTECH	California Institute of Technology
CALTRAM	Compagnie Algéro-Libyenne de Transports Maritimes
CALVINOR	Cooperativa Agropecuária de Vitivinicultores del Norte (Uruguay)
CAM	Cameroon Anglophone Movement
CAM	Campaign Against Militarism
CAM	Center for Advanced Materials (U.S.A.)
CAM	Central Australian Museum, Alice Springs
CAM	Centro de Accion de las Mujeres (Ecuador)
CAM	Cercle Archéologique de Mons
CAM	Ceylon Association of Manufacturers (Sri Lanka)
CAM	Chinese Association of Musicians
CAM	Comision para los Asuntos de la Mujer (Puerto Rico)
CAM	Comité d'Action Muselman (Mauritius)
CAM	Commission for Agricultural Meteorology (WMO) = CMAg
CAM	Committee for Aquatic Microbiology (UN)
CAM	Commonwealth Association of Museums
CAM	Coordinadora Nacional de la Mujer (Panama)
CAM-I	Computer Aided Manufacturing International (U.S.A.)
CAMA	Civil Aviation Medical Association (Canada)
CAMA	Coated Abrasives Manufacturers Association
CAMA	Continental Advertising and Marketing Association
CAMA	Control and Automation Manufacturers' Association
CAMAA	Comptoir Africain de Matériels Abidjan (Ivory Coast)
CAMACOL	Cámara Colombiana de la Construcción
CAMAD	Société Camérounaise de Produits Alimentaires et Diététiques
CAMAG	Société Camérounaise de Grands Magasins
CAMAIR	Cameroon Airlines
CAMARCA	Caisse Mutuelle Agropecuárome de Retraites Complémentaires Agricoles
CAMAR-TEC	Center for Agricultural Mechanization and Rural Technology (Tanzania)
CAMAS	Confederation of African Medical Associations and Societies = CASMA
CAMAWA	Catholic Anglophone Media Association of West Africa (Ghana)
CAMB	Campaign Against Military Bases (Iceland)
CAMBOIS	Société Camérounaise des Bois
CAMC	Canadian Association of Management Consultants
CAMC	Central American Monetary Council
CAMC	Corporación Argentina de Productores Avícolas
CAMD	Council of Australian Museum Directors
CAMDA	Car and Motorcycle Drivers Association
CAMDEF	Société Camérounnaise de Déforestage
CAMDEV	Cameroon Development Corporation
CAME	Conference of Allied Ministers of Education
CAMEC	Catholic Missionary Education Centre
CAMEC	Compagnie Africaine de Métaux et de Produits Chimiques (Benin)
CAMECA	Centro Ajüjic Mejoracmiento Educación Superior América
CAMECO	Catholic Media Council
CAMEF	Communications Advertising & Marketing Education Foundation
CAMEL	Compagnie Algérienne du Méthane Liquide
CAMELEC	Compagnie Antillaise de Mécanique et d'Electricité (Guadeloupe)
CAMEN	Centro Applicazioni Militari Energia Nucleare
CAMEP	Société Camérounaise d'Études et de Promotion pour l'Afrique
CAMERI	Coastal and Marine Engineering Research (Israel)
CAMERIN-DUSTRIEL	Compagnie Camérounaise de Répresentations Industrielles
CAM-EROUN-CONSULT	Société Camérounaise d'Engineering et de Consultation

CAMES	Conseil Africain et Malgache pour l'Enseignement Supérieur (Burkina Faso)
CAMESA	Canadian Military Electronics Standards Agency
CAMFAX	Civil Aviation Meteorological Facsimile Network
CamFed	Cambridge Female Education Trust
CAMFORR	Campaign for Rent Reform
CAMGAZ	Société Camérounaise des Gaz Liquéfiés de Pétrole
CAMGOC	Gulf Oil Company of Cameroon
CAMHADD	Commonwealth Association for Mental Handicap and Developmental Disabilities
CAMI	Cameroon Motor Industries
CAMICO	Comptoir de l'Automobile, du Matériel Industriel, du Cycle et de l'Outillage (Burkina Faso, Niger)
CAMIG	Companhia Agricola de Minas Gerais (Brazil)
CAMILL-IANUM	Instítuto Internazionale di Teologia Pastorale Sanitaria
CAMIN-VEST	Société Holding Caméroun Investissement
CAM-INFOR	Société Camérounaise d'Informatique et de Services
CAMIRA	Comité d'Application des Méthodes Isotopiques aux Recherches Agronomiques (Belgium)
CAMJA	Comisión Nacional de Apoyo al Movimiento Juvenil Agrario (Uruguay)
CAML	Canadian Association of Music Libraries, Archives and Documentation Centres = ACBM
CAMLAP	Campaign for Law and Peace
CAMM	Centro de Apoyo a la Mujer Maltratada (Argentina)
CAMN	Committee of Australian Museum Directors
CAMNEWS	Cameroon News Agency
CAMOA	Société Camérounaise d'Oxygéne et d'Acétylène
CAMOBRA	Société des Brasseries Modernes de Caméroun
CAMOFI	Caisse Centrale do Mobilisation et de Financement (Burundi)
CAMP	Campaign Against Military Prostitution International (Philippines)
CAMP	Center for Advanced Management Programs (U.S.A.)
CAMP	Center for Advanced Manufacturing and Production (U.S.A.)
CAMP	Center for Advanced Materials Processing (U.S.A.)
CAMPC	Centre Africain et Mauricien de Perfectionnement de Cadres (Ivory Coast)
CAMPSA	Compañia Arrendatoria de Monopolio de Petróleos
CAMR	Centre for Applied Microbiology and Research (PHLS)
CAMRA	Campaign for Real Ale
CAMRDC	Central Africa Mineral Resources Development Centre (Congo)
CAMROC	Campaign Against Military Research on Campus
CAMRODD	Caribbean Association on Mental Retardation and Other Development Disabilities
CAMS	Chinese Academy of Medical Sciences
CAMS	Chinese Academy of Meteorological Sciences
CAMSI	Canadian Association of Medical Students and Interns
CAMSUCO	Cameroon Sugar Company
CAMT	Cámara Argentina Maderas Terciadas
CAMTEL	Société Camérounaise de Télécommunications
CAMVOY-AGES	Agence Camérounaise de Voyages
Camwork	Caribbean Association of Media Workers (Barbados)
CAN	Central Auténtica Nacionalista (Guatemala)
CAN	Centro Administrativo Nacional (Colombia)
CAN	Climate Action Network
CAN	Cocoa Association of Nigeria
CAN	Committee on Aircraft Noise (ICAO)
CAN	Correio Aéreo Nacional (Brazil)
CAN UK	Climate Action Network – UK
CAN-AM	Canadian-American Center, University of Maine
CANA	Caribbean News Agency (Barbados)
CANA	Centre for Advice on Natural Alternatives
CANA	Clergy Against Nuclear Arms
CANA	Cooperative Agricole la Noelle, Ancenis
CANACH	Asociación Nacional de Campensios de Honduras

CANAC-INTRA	Cámara Nacional de la Industria de Transformaçion (Mexico)
CANACO	Cámara Nacional de Comercio de la Ciudad de México
CANACO-MIND	Cámara Nacioinal de Comercio e Industrias de Managua (Nicaragua)
CANAI	Comiato Artistico Nazionale Acconciatori Italiani
CANAM-ECC	Cámara Nacional de Medios de Comunicación Colectiva (Costa Rica)
CANARA	Cámara Nacional de Radio (Costa Rica)
CANARI	Caribbean Natural Resources Institute
CANARIE	Canadian Network for the Advancement of Research, Industry and Education
CANCAM	Canadian Congress of Applied Mechanics
CANCEE	Canadian National Committee for Earthquake Engineering
CAN-DECAF	Campagnie Camérounaise de Décaféination
CANDELA	Alternative Trade of Non-Traditional Products and Development in Latin America (Peru)
CANDI	Caribbean Association of Nutritionists and Dieticians
CANE	Consumers Against Nuclear Energy
CANEFA	Comisión Asesora Nacional de Erradicación de la Fiebre Aftosa (Argentina)
CANEMTE	Camara Nacional de Empresas de Telecomunicacion y Afines (Venezuela)
CANF	Cuban-American National Foundation (U.S.A.)
CANGO	Committee for Air Navigation and Ground Organization
CANIRAC	Cámera Nacional de la Industria de Restaurantes y Alimentos Condimentados (Mexico)
CANMET	Canada Centre for Mineral and Energy Technology
CANOVAL	Coopérative Agricole du Noyonnaise et du Valois
CANSA	Compania Azucarera Nacional, S.A. (Nicaragua)
CANSAD	Caribbean Network of Cooperation in Small Animal Development (Chile)
CANSG	Civil Aviation Navigational Services Group
CANSM	Caisse Agropecuárome Nationale de la Sécurité dans les Mines
CANSM	Chinese Association of Natural Science Museums
CANSTAT	Canadian Society of Teachers of the Alexander Technique
CANTIER-MACCHINE	Associazione Commercianti Importatori Macchine da Cantiere ed Affini
CANTO	Caribbean Association of National Telecommunications Organisations
CANTV	Compañia Anonima Nacional Telefonos de Venezuela
CANU	Crnogorska Akademija Nauka i Umjetnosti
CANUC	Campaign Against the Namibian Uranium Contract
CANUKUS	Canada, United Kingdom, United States
CANUSPA	Canada, Australia, New Zealand and United States Parents Association
CANWEG	Canadian National Committee of the World Energy Conference
CAO	Canadian Association of Optometrists
CAO	Committee on Atmosphere and Oceans (U.S.A.)
CAO	Commonwealth Arts Organisation
CAOBISCO	Association d'Industries de Produits la Chocolaterie, Biscuiterie-Biscotterie et Confiserie de la CEE
CAOPRI	Central Arecanut and Oil Palm Research Institute (India)
CAORB	Civil Aviation Operational Research Branch
CAOSO	Coopérative Agricole Ovine du Sud-Ouest
CAOT	Canadian Association of Occupational Therapy
CAP	Campaign Against Pornography
CAP	Canadian Association of Palynologists
CAP	Canadian Association of Pathologists
CAP	Canadian Association of Physicists
CAP	Center for Academic Precocity (U.S.A.)
CAP	Central Agricultural Producers
CAP	Centres d'Alevinage Principaux (Zaïre)
CAP	Church Action on Poverty
CAP	College of American Pathologists
CAP	Commonwealth Association of Planners
CAP	Community Action Projects
CAP	Compagnie Africaine d'Armement à la Pêche
CAP	Compagnie d'Agences de Publicité
CAP	Compañia de Acero del Pacifico (Chile)
CAP	Confederação dos Agricultores de Portugal

CAP	Confederación Andina de Pobladores (Bolivia)	**CAPEB**	Confédération de l'Artisanat et des Petites Entreprises du Bâtiment
CAP	Congreso Agrario Permanente (Mexico)	**CAPECO**	Camara Peruana de la Construccion
CAP	Consumers' Association of Penang	**CAPEF**	Coopérative Agricole des Producteurs d'Endives de France
CAP	Cooperativa Agricolà de Productie (Romania)	**CAPEL**	CAPEL; the Chapels' Heritage Society
CAP	Corporation of Argentine Meat Producers	**CAPEL**	Centre pour l'Accroissement de la Productivité des Entreprises Laitières
CAPA	Canadian Association of Purchasing Agents	**CAPEM**	Comité d'Aménagement et du Plan d'Équipement de la Moselle
CAPA	Civil Rights Advice and Support Group	**CAPEMI**	Caixa de Pecúlio Militar (Brazil)
CAPA	Comisión Asesora de Politica Agraria (Venezuela)	**CAPER**	Caisse d'Accession à la Propriété et à l'Exploitation Rurales (Algeria)
CAPA	Commonwealth Association of Polytechnics in Africa (Kenya)	**CAPER**	Canadian Association of Publishers Educational Representatives
CAPA	Compagnie Africaine de Pêche Atlantique (Ivory Coast)	**CAPERAS**	Comité Argentino para el Estudio de la Regiones Aridas y Semiáridas
CAPA	Compagnie Africaine de Produits Alimentaires	**CAPEXIL**	Chemicals and Allied Products Export Promotion Council (India)
CAPA	Confederation of Asian and Pacific Accountants	**CAPF**	CE Comité Administrador del Programa Federal de Construción de Escuelas (Mexico)
CAPA	Council of Anglican Provinces of Africa	**CAPF**	Centre Administratif du Planning Familial (Guadeloupe)
CAPA	Selección y Comercio de la Patata de Siembra	**CAPF**	Council for Agricultural Planning and Development (Taiwan)
CAPAC	Composers' Authors' and Publishers Association of Canada	**CAPI**	Comisión de Administración Pública Internacional
CAPAM	Commonwealth Association for Public Administration and Management (ComSec)	**CAPIA**	Cámara Argentina de Productores Industriales Avicolas
CAPAP	Campaign Against Police Abuses of Power	**CAPIDE**	Centro Asesor y Planificador de Investigacion y Desarrollo (Chile)
CAPAR	Centre d'Animation et de Promotion Agricole et Rurale	**CAPIEL**	Comité de Coordination des Associations de Constructeurs d'Appareillage Industriel Électrique du Marché Commun
CAPC	Campaign Against Pornography and Censorship		
CAPC	Central African Power Corporation	**CAPIM**	Consortium Africain de Produits Industriels et Ménagers (Ivory Coast)
CAPC	Comité Ampliado del Programa y de la Coordinación (UNDP)	**CAPITA**	Center for Air Pollution Impact and Trend Analysis (U.S.A.)
CAPD	China Association for Promoting Democracy (China)	**CAPITB**	Chemical and Allied Products Industry Training Board
CAPD	Council for Agricultural Planning and Development (Taiwan)	**CAPITB**	Clothing and Allied Products Industry Training Board
CAPDI	China Aeronautical Project and Design Institute	**CAPL**	Canadian Association of Public Libraries
CAPE	Centre Africain de Promotion Économique	**CAPL**	Coastal Anti-Pollution League
CAPE	Children's Alliance for Protection of the Environment	**CAPLABAM**	Coopérative Agricole des Planteurs de Bamboutos (Cameroon)
CAPE	Council for American Private Education	**CAPLAME**	Coopérative Agricole des Planteurs de la Menoua (Cameroon)
CAPE	Cyprus Association for the Protection of the Environment		

CAPLAMI	Coopérative Agricole des Planteurs de la Misi (Cameroon)	**CAPSES**	Cooperativa Aragonesa da Productores de Semillas Selectas
CAPMA	Caisse d'Assurance et de Prévoyance Mutuelle des Agriculteurs	**CAPSOME**	Comité d'Action des Producteurs et Stockeurs d'Oléagineux pour les Marchés Extérieurs
CAPME	Centre National d'Assistance aux Petites et Moyennes Enterprises (Cameroon)	**CAPSW**	Chinese Association of Popular Science Writers
CAPMS	Central Agency for Public Mobilisation and Statistics (Egypt)	**CAPT**	Child Accident Prevention Trust
CAPP	Center for Applied Parallel Processing (U.S.A.)	**CAPT**	Comité "Association Pays Tiers" (CE)
CAPPI	Conference of Asian-Pacific Pastoral Institutes (Philippines)	**CAPTAC**	Conférence Africaine des Postes et Télécommunications de l'Afrique Centrale
CAPPS	Center for Aseptic Processing and Packaging Studies (U.S.A.)	**CAPTEAO**	Conférénce des Administrations des Postes et Télécommunications des Etats de l'Afrique de l'Ouest
CAPQ	Headquarters of Animal and Plant Quarantine Services (China)	**CAR**	Cadena Argentina de Radiodifusión
CAPRAL	Compagnie Africaine de Préparations Alimentaires (Ivory Coast)	**CAR**	Canadian Association of Radiologists
CAPRE	Comissão de Co-ordenação das Atividades de Processamento Electronico (Brazil)	**CAR**	Caribbean Action Plan (Jamaica)
		CAR	Center for Automotive Research (U.S.A.)
CAPRE	Comité Coordinador Regional de Instituciones de Agua Potable y Saneamiento, de Centroamerica, Panama y Republica Dominicana (Costa Rica)	**CAR**	Centre for the Advancement of Responsive Travel
		CAR	Centre of African Studies
		CAR	Chinese Association of Refrigeration
		CAR	Comité Agricole Régional
CAPRI	Center for Applied Polymer Research (U.S.A.)	**CAR**	Comités d'Action Républicaine
		CAR	Conferencia de Religiosos de Argentina
CAPRI	Centre d'Application et de Promotion des Rayonnements Ionisants	**CAR**	Corporación Autóctona Regional de la Sabana de Bogota y de los Valles de Ullate y Chinquinquirá (Colombia)
CAPRILAC	Comercializadora de Productos Caprinos (Chile)	**CAR**	Council for Aboriginal Reconciliation
CAPS	Captive Animals' Protection Society	**CARA**	Center for Applied Research in the Apostolate (U.S.A.)
CAPS	Center for Advanced Purchasing Studies (U.S.A.)	**CARAC**	Civil Aviation Radio Advisory Committee
CAPS	Center for AIDS Prevention Studies (U.S.A.)	**CARACOL**	Primera Cadena Radial Colombiana
CAPS	Center for Analysis and Prediction of Storms (U.S.A.)	**CARAF**	Christians Against Racism and Fascism
		CARAH	Centre Agronomique de Recherches Appliquées du Hainaut (Belgium)
CAPS	Chinese Association for Physiological Sciences	**CARAN**	Centre d'Accueil et de Recherche des Archives Nationales
CAPS	Civil Aviation Purchasing Service (ICAO)	**CARASE**	Centre Algérien de la Recherche Agronomique, Sociologique et Économique
CAPS	Confédération Agricole des Producteurs de Plantes Saccharifères	**CARATE**	Caribbean Association for the Teaching of English
CAPS	Confédération des Associations de Prévoyance Sociale	**CARAVA**	Christian Association for Radio and Audio-Visual Aid (India)
CAPSA	Compania Algodonera Paraguaya, S.A.		
CAPSC	Centre for the Applied Psychology of Social Care	**CARB**	Center for Advanced Research in Biotechnology (U.S.A.)

CARB	Instítuto de Carboquimica
CARBAP	Confederación de Asociaciones Rurales de Buenos Aires y La Lampa (Argentina)
CARBICA	Caribbean Regional Branch of the International Council on Archives
CARBOCOL	Carbones de Colombia
CARC	Canadian Arctic Resources Committee
CARC	Central Asian Research Centre (U.K.)
CARCAE	Caribbean Regional Council for Adult Education
CARCLO	Confederación de Asociaciones Rurales del Centro y Litoral Oeste (Argentina)
CARD	Campaign Against Racial Discrimination
CARD	Caribbean Association for the Rehabilitation of the Disabled
CARD	Center for Agricultural and Rural Development (U.S.A.)
CARD	Centre for Astrological Research and Development
CARDA	Caribbean Atlantic Regional Dental Association (Barbados)
CARDAN	Centre d'Analyse et de Recherche Documentaires pour l'Afrique Noire
CARDATS	Caribbean Agricultural Rural Development Advisory Training Service
CARDE	Canadian Armament Research and Development Establishment
CARDI	Caribbean Agricultural Research and Development Institute (Jamaica, Trinidad and Tobago)
CARDO	Centre for Architectural Research & Development Overseas
CARDPB	Civil Aviation Research and Development Programme Board
CARDRI	Committee Against Repression and for Democratic Rights in Iraq
CARE	Cancer Aftercare and Rehabilitation Society
CARE	Centre for Applied Research in Education
CARE	Christian Action Research and Education
CARE	Community Action in the Rural Environment
CARE	Cooperative for American Relief Everywhere
CARE	Cottage and Rural Enterprises Ltd
CARE-MED	Cooperativa Americana de Remesas al Exterior Mujeres en Desarrollo (Guatemala)
CAREBACO	Caribbean Regional Badminton Confederation
CAREC	Caribbean Epidemiology Centre (Trinidad and Tobago)
CARECE	Confédération des Associations de Résidents à l'Étranger de la Communauté Européenne
CAREF	Centre Algérien de Recherches et Expérimentations Forestières
CARENA	Compagnie Abidjanaise de Réparations Navales et de Travaux Industriels (Ivory Coast)
CARESS	Center for Analytic Research in Economics and the Social Sciences (U.S.A.)
CARF	Campaign Against Racism and Fascism
CARF	Canadian Advertising Research Foundation
CARF	Canadian Amateur Radio Federation
CARI	Central Agricultural Research Institute (Liberia)
CARI	Centro Analisi Relazioni Internazionali
CARI	Changchun Automobile Research Institute
CARI	Chinese Association of Relay and Installation
CARIBANK	Caribbean Development Bank = BDC, CDB
CARIBDOC	Caribbean Documentation Centre (Trinidad-Tobago)
Caribex	Empresa Exportadora del Caribe (Cuba)
CARIC	Compagnie Africaine de Représentations Industrielles et Commerciales (Cameroon, Congo, Gabon, Ivory Coast, Senegal)
CARICAD	Caribbean Centre for Development Administration
CARICAM	Société des Carrières du Caméroun
CARI-CARGO	Caribbean Air Cargo (Barbados)
CARICOM	Caribbean Commodity Market
CARI-FESTA	Caribbean Festival of Creative Arts (Guyana)
CARIFTA	Caribbean Free Trade Association
CARIMAC	Caribbean Institute of Mass Communication (Jamaica)
CARIPEDA	Caribbean People's Development Agency (St. Vincent-Grenadines)
CARIPLO	Cassa di Risparmio della Provincie Lombarde

CARIPOL	Caribbean Pollution Research and Monitoring Program	**CARS**	China Academy of Railway Sciences
CARIRI	Caribbean Industrial Research Institute (Trinidad)	**CARS**	Chinese Aerodynamics Research Society
CARIS	China Aviation Research Institute for Standardisation	**CARS**	Confederation Asia of Roller Skating (Japan)
CARIS	Christian Action and Response in Society	**CARSTIN**	Regional Network for the Exchange of Information and Experience in Science and Technology for Development in the Caribbean Region (Trinidad-Tobago)
CARIS	Current Agricultural Research Information System (FAO)		
CARIS-FORM	Caribbean Institute for Social Formation = CARISOV, INFORCAR, INFOSCAR	**CART**	Caribbean Association of Rehabilitation Therapists
CARISOV	Caribische Institut voor Social Vorming = CARISFORM, INFORCAR, INFOSCAR	**CART**	Community Alliance for Responsible Transport
CARIS-PLAN	Caribbean Information System for Economic and Social Planning (Trinidad-Tobago)	**CARTB**	Canadian Association of Radio and Television
		CARTE	Centre for Agrarian Research and Training and Education (India)
CARITAG	Caribbean Trade Advisory Group	**CARTE**	Industry Group for Collaboration on Aeronautical Research and Technology in Europe
CARITAS	Conférence Internationale des Charités Catholiques		
CARIWA	Caribbean Women's Association	**CARTG**	Canadian Amateur Radio Teletype Group
CARJ	Catholic Association for Racial Justice		
CARL	Campaign Against Racist Laws	**CARTONEX**	Conference for the Carton and Case Making Industry
CARL	Canadian Academic Research Libraries	**CARTOON**	Association Européenne du Film d'Animation
CARL	Computer Audio Research Laboratory		
CARNEID	Caribbean Network of Educational Innovation for Development	**CARVOLT**	Société de Cartoucherie Voltaïque
		ČAS	Česká Archeologická Společnost
CARNET	Canadian Aging Research Network	**CAS**	Academy of Sciences, Czech Republic = CAV
CARNI-VORE	International Carnivore Protection Society		
CARO	Société de Fabrication de Carrelages et Revêtements au Caméroun	**CAS**	California Academy of Sciences
		CAS	Canadian Anaesthetists Society
CaroLL	Caribbean Association of Law Librarians (Barbados)	**CAS**	Canadian Astronomical Society
		CAS	Caribbean Air Services
CAROSAI	Caribbean Organization of Supreme Audit Institutions (Trinidad-Tobago)	**CAS**	Catgut Acoustical Society
		CAS	Central Adjudication Services
CARP	Collegiate Association for the Research of Principles	**CAS**	Centre for African Studies
		CAS	Centre for Agricultural Strategy
CARP	Comprehensive Agrarian Reform Programme (Philippines)	**CAS**	Chicago Academy of Sciences
		CAS	China Archaeological Society
CARP	Cooperative Agricultural Research Program (U.S.A.)	**CAS**	China Association for Standardization
		CAS	Chinese Apicultural Society
CARPAS	Comisión Asesora Regional de Pesca para el Atlántico Sud-Occidental (FAO)	**CAS**	Chinese Archives Society
		CAS	Chinese Astronomical Society
CARRI	Chinese Aeronautical Rescue Research Institute	**CAS**	Church Adoption Society
		CAS	Club Alpin Suisse
CARS	Canadian Arthritis and Rheumatism Society	**CAS**	Commission for Atmospheric Sciences (WMO)
CARS	Central Agricultural Research Station (Somalia)	**CAS**	Commission on American Shipbuilding

CAS	Committee on Atlantic Studies		CASC	Committee on African Studies in Canada
CAS	Computer Arts Society (BCS)		CASC	Confederación Autónoma de Sindicatos Cristianos (Dominican Republic)
CAS	Consortium for Atlantic Studies (U.S.A.)		CASC	Conservatives Against Sex Censorship
CAS	Contemporary Art Society		CASCC	Canadian Agricultural Services Co-ordinating Committee
CAS	Council of Arbitration for Sport = TAD, TAS		CASD	Campaign Against Sea Dumping
CAS	Cypriot Advisory Service		CASDB	Central African States Development Bank (Congo) = BDEAC
CASA	Canadian Amateur Swimming Association		CASDS	Centre for Advanced Study in the Developmental Sciences
CASA	Canadian Asian Studies Association = ACEA		CASE	Campaign Against the Sale of Estates
CASA	Canadian Automatic Sprinkler Association		CASE	Campaign for the Advancement of State Education
CASA	Centre for Advanced Software Applications		CASE	Centre for Advanced Studies in Education
CASA	Centre for Advanced Study of Astronomy (Pakistan)		CASE	Centre for Advanced Studies in Environment (AA)
CASA	Ceylon Association of Steamer Agents (Sri Lanka)		CASE	Committee on Academic Science and Engineering (U.S.A.)
CASA	Chikyu Kankyo To Taimi Osen O Kangaeru Zenkoku Shimin Kaigi		CASE	Committee on the Atlantic Salmon Emergency
CASA	Computer and Automated Systems Association (U.S.A.)		CASE	Consumers Association of Singapore
CASA	Confederazione Artigiana Sindacati Agropecuáromi		CASEC	Confederation of Associations of Specialist Engineering Contractors
CASA	Construcción y Ahorro (El Salvador)		CASEMG	Companhia de Armazens e Silos do Estado de Minas Gerais (Brazil)
CASA	Construcciónes Aeronauticas S.A.		CASES	Center for Alternative Sentencing and Employment Services (U.S.A.)
CASA	Contemporary Art Society of Australia		
CASA	Société Centrale d'Achats Supermarché d'Afrique		CASHFI	Caribbean Association of Housing Finance Institutions
CASAC	Centre Against the Sexual Assault on Children		CASI	Canadian Aeronautics and Space Institute
CASAFA	Scientific Committee on the Application of Science to Agriculture, Forestry and Aquaculture		CASI	Commission Aéronautique Sportive Internationale
CASAN	Conseil Africain des Sciences de l'Alimentation et de la Nutrition (Zimbabwe) = AFRONUS		CASID	Center for Advanced Study of International Development (U.S.A.)
CASANZ	Clean Air Society of Australia and New Zealand		CASIDER	Comité de Acción para la Cooperación y Concertación Latinoamericana en el Sector Siderúrgico (Venezuela)
CASAR	Comité Acción para la Seguridad Alimentaria Regional (SELA) (Argentina)		CASIS	Canadian Association for Security and Intelligence Studies
CASAS	Commonwealth Association of Scientific Agricultural Societies		CASIS	Chartered Accountants Students Introduction Service
CASAW	Canadian Association of Smelter and Allied Workers		CASL	Confédération Africaine des Syndicats Libres
CASBO	Conference of American Small Business Organisations		CASLE	Commonwealth Association of Surveying and Land Engineering
CASC	Caisse d'Assurances des Coopératives Suisse de Consommation		CASLF	Comité d'Action pour la Sauvegarde des Libertés Forestières

CASLIS	Canadian Association of Special Libraries and Information Services	**CAST**	Council for Agricultural Science and Technology (U.S.A.)
CASLP	Conference on Alternative State and Local Policies (U.S.A.)	**CAST**	Creative and Supportive Trust
CASLS	Chinese Association of Soviet Literature Studies	**CASTA**	Center for Advanced Study in Theater Arts (U.S.A.)
CASMA	Caribbean Sports Medicine Association (Trinidad-Tobago)	**CASTD**	Committee on Application of Science and Technology to Development
CASMA	Confédération des Associations et Sociétés Médicales d'Afrique = CAMAS	**CASTIS**	Campaign Against State Terrorism in Sri Lanka
CASME	Commonwealth Association of Science and Mathematics Educators	**CASTME**	Commonwealth Association of Science, Technology and Mathematics Educators
CASMUS	Centre for Advanced Structural Materials	**CASU**	Co-operative Association of Suez Canal Users
CASNP	Canadian Alliance in Solidarity with the Native Peoples	**CASVAL**	Coopérative d'Approvisionnement des Syndicats Viticoles et Agricoles du Loire à Orléans
CASP	Centre for the Analysis of Social Policy	**CASW**	Committee on the Medical Aspects of the Contamination of Air, Soil and Water (DOH)
CASP	Community Aid and Sponsorship Programme (India)		
CASPLALS	Chinese Association of Spanish, Portuguese and Latin American Literature Studies	**CASW**	Contemporary Art Society for Wales
		CASW	Council for the Advancement of Scientific Writing
CASR	Centre for Applied Social Research	**CAT**	Centre for Alternative Technology
CASRO	Commission d'Achat de la Suisse Romande	**CAT**	Cercle des Arts et Techniques de la Coiffure Française (U.K.)
CASRO	Council of American Survey Research Organisations	**CAT**	Comisaría de Abastecimientos y Transportes
CASRSS	Centre of Advanced Study and Research in Social Sciences (Bangladesh)	**CAT**	Comité de l'Assistance Technique (ONU)
CASS	Canadian Association for Scottish Studies = ACEE	**CAT**	Communities Against Toxics
		CAT	Compagnie Africaine de Transformation (Togo)
CASS	Center for Atmospheric and Space Sciences (U.S.A.)	**CAT**	Compagnie Africaine de Transports
CASS	Center for Auditory and Speech Sciences (U.S.A.)	**CAT**	Compagnie Aluminium Togolais
		CAT	Conseil Africain de Télédétection (Mali) = ARSC
CASS	Chartered Accountant Students Society		
CASS	Chinese Academy of Social Science	**CAT**	Contracting and Trading Company (Lebanon)
CASS	Chongqing Academy of Social Sciences	**CAT**	Coordenacao Autonoma de Trabalhadores (Brazil)
CASS	Clarinet and Saxophone Society		
CASSH	Conseil Africain des Sciences Sociales et Humaines (Zimbabwe)	**CATA**	Canadian Air Transportation Administration
CAST	Centre d'Actualisation Scientifique et Technique	**CATA**	Center for Atmospheric Theory and Analysis (U.S.A.)
CAST	China Association for Science and Technology	**CATA**	Chinese Anti-Tuberculosis Association
		CATA	Commonwealth Association of Tax Administrators
CAST	Chinese Academy of Space Technology		
CAST	Confédération Africaine des Syndicats Libres	**CATA**	Compagnie Africaine de Transports Automobiles
CAST	Consolidated African Selection Trust (Ghana)	**CATANA**	Compania Anonima Tabacalera Nacional (Venezuela)

CATARC	China Automobile Technology and Research Centre	**CATI**	Conference of African Theological Institutions (Zimbabwe)
CATC	Caribbean Appropriate Technology Centre	**CATI**	Coordenadoria de Assisténcia Técnica Integral (Brazil)
CATC	Commonwealth Air Transport Council	**CATIAC**	Cotton and Allied Textiles Industry Advisory Committee
CATC	Confédération Africaine des Travailleurs Croyants	**CATIB**	Civil Air Transport Industry Training Board
CATCA	Canadian Air Traffic Control Association	**CATIC**	China National Aero-Technology Import and Export Corporation
CATCC	Canadian Association of Textile Colourists and Chemists	**CATIE**	Centro Agrónomico Tropical de Investigación y Enseñanza (Costa Rica)
CATCI	Compagnie Africaine de Transports Côte-d'Ivoire	**CATITB**	Cotton and Allied Textiles Industry Training Board
CATCN	Société Africaine de Transportes Caméroun	**CATP**	Compagnie Africaine de Travaux Publics (Ivory Coast)
CATCO	Caribbean Agricultural Trading Company (Barbados)	**CATPA**	Comité d'Action Technique contre la Pollution Atmosphérique
CATD	Confederación Auténtica de Trabajadores Democráticos (Costa Rica)	**CATPCE**	Comité d'Action des Transports Publics des Communautés Européennes
CATE	Center for Advanced Technology Education	**CATRA**	Cutlery and Allied Trades Research Association
CATE	Citizens for Alternatives to Trident and Elf (U.S.A.)	**CATRF**	Central Africa Tea Research Foundation (Malawi)
CATE	Committee for the Accreditation of Teacher Education	**CATS**	Canadian Association for Translation Studies
CATE	Confederación Argentina de Trabajadores del Espectaculo	**CATS**	Center for Applied Thermodynamic Studies (U.S.A.)
CATE-HUILSA	Compagnie Africaine Toutes Enterprises Huileries des Savanes (Ivory Coast)	**CATS**	Centre for Advanced Television Studies
CATECO	Société Camérounaise d'Automobile de Technique et du Commerce	**CATS**	Communities Against Toxics
CATED	Centre d'Assistance Technique et de Documentation du Bétiment et des Travaux Publics	**CATU**	Ceramic and Allied Trades Union
		CATU	Confederation of Albanian Trade Unions = KSS
CATEL	Compagnie Africaine de Télévision (Ivory Coast)	**CATU**	Confederation of Arab Trade Unions
CATER	Centro Andino de Tecnologia Rural (Ecuador)	**CATUD**	Central Autónoma de Trabajadores del Uruguay
CATES	Campaign Against Trade in Endangered Species	**CAU**	Consejo Academico Universitario (Mexico)
CATET	Centro Argentino de Técnicos en Estudios del Trabajo	**CAUL**	Council of Australian University Librarians
CATEX	Société Centrafricaine des Textiles pour l'Exportation	**CAURA**	Canadian Association of University Research Administrators = ACARU
CATH	Centrale Agropecuárome des Travailleurs Haïtiens	**CAUS**	Central de Acción y Unidad Sindical (Nicaragua)
CATI	Caribbean Aviation Training Centre	**CAUT**	Canadian Association of University Teachers
CATI	Central Auténtica de Trabajadores Independientes (Panama)	**CAUTG**	Canadian Association of University Teachers of German
CATI	Centres Administratifs et Techniques Interdépartementaux	**CAV**	Cámara Agricola de Venezuela
		CAV	Centro Antoonio Valdivieso (Nicaragua)
		CAV	Committee on Agricultural Valuation (MAFF)

CAVAL	Cooperative Action by Victorian Academic Libraries (Australia)
CAVEDINA	Cámara Venezolana de Industriales de Arroz
CAVEDIV	Camara Venezolana de Industria del Vestido
CAVENIC	Camara Venezolana de Industriales del Calzado
CAVI	Centre Audio-Visuel International
CAVIAR	Cinema and Video Industry Audience Research
CAVIC	Corporación Agroeconómica, Viticola, Industrial y Comercial (Argentina)
CAVIDEA	Camara Venezolana de Industria de Alimentos
CAVIM	Compania Anonima de Industrias Militares (Venezuela)
CAVINEX	Société Camérounaise d'Exploitation Vinicole
CAVN	C.A.Venezolana de Navegación
CAVN	Comité d'Aménagement de la Vallée du Niari
CAVN	Compania Anonima Venezolana de Navegacion
CAVO	Centralgenossenschaft für Alkoholfreie Verwertung von Obstprodukten (Switzerland)
CAVS	Center for Advanced Visual Studies (U.S.A.)
CAVV	Coöperatieve Aan-en Verkoop Vereniging
CAVY	Coopérative Agricole et Viticole du Département de l'Yonne
CAW	Campaign Against the Witchhunt
CAW	Committee for Asian Women (Hong Kong)
CAW	Coordinating Animal Welfare
CAWC	Central Advisory Water Committee
CAWCS	University of Wales Centre for Advanced Welsh Celtic Studies
CAWSS	Council of Australian Weed Science Societies
CAWTU	Church Action With The Unemployed
CAYA	Catholic Association of Young Adults
CAYC	Committee for ASEAN Youth Cooperation
CAZ	China Association of Zhenjiu
CAZ	Conservation Alliance of Zimbabwe
CAZF	Comité des Agrumes de la Zone Franc
CAZRI	Central Arid Zone Research Institute (India)
CAZS	Centre for Arid Zone Studies
CBA	Canadian Bankers' Association = ABC
CBA	Canadian Bar Association
CBA	Canadian Booksellers Association
CBA	Caribbean Atlantic Airways
CBA	Certified Bailiffs Association of England and Wales
CBA	Chambre Belge de l'Affichage et Média Connexes = CBAMC
CBA	Chinese Buddhist Association
CBA	Christian Booksellers Association
CBA	Citizens Band Association
CBA	Commercial Bank of Australia
CBA	Commonwealth Broadcasting Assiociation
CBA	Community Boats Association
CBA	Concrete Block Association
CBA	Confederation of British Associations
CBA	Council for British Archaeology
CBA	Criminal Bar Association
CBAAC	Centre for Black and African Arts and Civilization (Nigeria)
CBABG	Commonwealth Bureau of Animal Breeding and Genetics
CBAE	Commonwealth Board of Architectural Education
CBAE	Commonwealth Bureau of Agricultural Economics
CBAH	Commonwealth Bureau of Animal Health
CBAI	Comité Belge des Assureurs d'Incendie
CBAI	Contract Bridge Association of Ireland
CBAMC	Chambre Belge de l'Affichage et Média Connexes = CBA
CBAT	Central Bureau for Astronomical Telegrams (IAU)
CBAT	Centro de Biologia Aquática Tropical (Portugal)
CBB	Centrale Besturenbond v. Zuivelorganisaties in Nederland
CBB	Centre Belge du Bois
CBB	Centrum voor Bedrijfseconomie en Bedrijfseconometrie (Belgium)
CBB	Confédération des Betteraviers Belges
CBB	Confédération des Brasseries de Belgique
CBBA	Comissão Brasileira de Bibliotecarios Agrícolas

CBC	Canadian Broadcasting Corporation
CBC	Caribbean Broadcasting Corporation (Barbados)
CBC	Centro de Estudios Regionales Andinos "Bartolomé de las Casas" (Peru)
CBC	Chad Basin Commission
CBC	Confederation of Building Contractors
CBC	Cyprus Broadcasting Corporation
CBC	Société Commerciale des Bois du Caméroun
CBC	Société Royale Chambre Belge des Comptales
CBC-MSB	Catholic Bishops' Conference of Malaysia-Singapore-Brunei (Malaysia)
CBCC	Canada-British Columbia Consultative Board
CBCC	Chemical-Biological Co-ordination Centre (U.S.A.)
CBCI	Children's Book Council of Iran
CBCISS	Centro Brasileiro de Cooperação e Intercambio de Serviços Sociais
CBCS	Commonwealth Bureau of Census and Statistics (Australia)
CBCSD	Committee of Biological Control and Soil-Borne Disease (China)
CBCT	Council of British Cotton Textiles
CBD	Centralforeningen af Benzinforhandlere i Danmark
CBD	Comité Belge de la Distribution = BCD
CBD	Confederação Brasileira de Desportos
CBD	Convention on Biological Diversity
CBD	Corporación Boliviana de Desarrollo
CBDA	Comissão Brasileira de Documentação Agricola
CBDE	Chemical and Biological Defence Establishment
CBDG	Concrete Bridge Development Group
CBDIC	Centre Belge de Documentation et d'Information de la Construction
CBDN	Canadian Bacterial Diseases Network
CBDST	Commonwealth Bureau of Dairy Science and Technology
CBE	Commission for Biological Education (Germany)
CBE	Council for Basic Education (U.S.A.)
CBE	Council of Biology Editors (U.S.A.)
CBEA	Centro Brazileiro de Estatísticas Agropecuárias
CBEC	Caribbean Bananas Exporting Corporation
CBEET	Commonwealth Board on Engineering Education and Training (CEC)
CBEFEN	Comité Belge des Expositions et des Foires et d'Expansion Nationale
CBEMA	Canadian Business Equipment Manufacturers Association
CBEMA	Computer and Business Equipment Manufacturers Association (U.S.A.)
CBEN	Comisión Boliviana de Energia Nuclear
CBETS	Council of Biomass Energy Technology Sponsors (U.S.A.)
CBEVE	Central Bureau for Educational Visits and Exchanges
CBF	Catholic Bible Federation = FBC, FEBIC-LA, KBF
CBF	Confederação Brasileira de Futebol
CBF	Coras Beostoic agus Feola (Éire)
CBF	Corporación Boliviana de Fomento
CBF	Irish Livestock and Meat Board
CBFJRR	Central British Fund for Jewish Relief and Rehabilitation
CBFPEM	Council of British Fire Protection Equipment Manufacturers
CBG	Chambre Belge des Graphistes
CBG	Compagnie des Bauxites de Guinée
CBG	Companhia Brasileira de Geofísica
CBGA	Carpathian Balkan Geological Association
CBGS	Centrum voor Bevolkings- en Gezinstudiën (Belgium)
CBHA	Council for Biology in Human Affairs (U.S.A.)
CBHPC	Commonwealth Bureau of Horticulture and Plantation Crops
CBHV	Christlicher Bau-und Holzarbeiter-Verband
CBI	Cement och Betong Institutet (Sweden)
CBI	Central Bureau of Intelligence (India)
CBI	Chambre Belge des Inventeurs
CBI	Comisión Ballenera Internacional = CIB, IWC
CBI	Confederation of British Industry
CBI	Convention Bureau of Ireland
CBI	Cooperative Business International
CBI	Corriente Batelista Independiente (Uruguay)
CBIC	Canadian Biodiversity Informatics Consortium

CBIE	Canadian Bureau for International Education = BCEI
CBJ	Central Bank of Jordan
CBJO	Co-ordinating Board of Jewish Organizations
CBK	Centraal Brouwerij Kantoor
CBL	Centraal Bureau Levensmiddelenbedrijf
CBL	Cercle Belge de la Librairie
CBL	Commission Centrale Belge du Lait
CBLIA	Centro Belgo-Luxembourgeois d'Information de l'Acier
CBLT	Commission du Bassin du Lac Tchad = LCBC
CBM	Centrale Bond van Meubelfabrikanten
CBM	Centre for Bibliographic Management
CBM	Centre Technique et Scientifique de la Brasserie, Malterie et des Industries Connexes (Belgium)
CBM	Christoffel-Blindenmission
CBMA	Christian Bookstall Managers' Association
CBMA	Concrete Brick Manufacturers Association
CBMC	Christian Business Men's Committee (U.S.A.)
CBMC	Communauté de Travail des Brasseurs du Marché Commun
CBMPE	Council of British Manufacturers of Petroleum Equipment
CBN	Commission on Biochemical Nomenclature
CBN	Commonwealth Bureau of Nutrition
CBNIA	Cooperative Body of the Nordic Inventors' Associations = NOS
CBNM	Central Bureau for Nuclear Measurements (Euratom) = BCMN
CBO	Central Bank of Oman
CBO	Conference of Baltic Oceanographers
CBO&MGS	Centre for Byzantine, Ottoman & Modern Greek Studies
CBOB	Christelijke Bond van Ondernemers in de Binnenwaart
CBOE	Chicago Board Options Exchange
CBOI	Centro Biológico del Océano Indico
CBOT	Chicago Board of Trade
CBP	Chambre Belge des Podologues
CBPAE	Centro Brasileiro de Pesquisas Agricoles em Elano
CBPAH	Council for British Plastics in Agriculture and Horticulture
CBPAV	Chambre Belge des Publicités Audio-Visuelles
CBPBG	Commonwealth Bureau of Plant Breeding and Genetics
CBPC	Canadian Book Publishers Council
CBPC	Chambre Belge de la Publicité Cinématographique
CBPDC	Canadian Book and Periodical Development Council
CBPE	Centre for Business & Professional Ethics
CBPE	Centro Brasileiro de Pesquisas Educacionais
CBPF	Centro Brasileiro de Pesquisas Fisicas
CBPFC	Commonwealth Bureau of Pastures and Field Crops
CBPM	Chambre Belge des Pédicures Médicaux
CBPP	Committee of Biological Plant Pathogen (China)
CBPQ	Corporation des Bibliothécaires Professionnelles du Québec
CBPSE	Centre for Business & Public Sector Ethics
CBQ	Centre Belge pour la Gestion de la Qualité
CBR	Centraal Bureau voor de Rijweilhandel
CBR	Centre for Business Research
CBR	Conferéncia Boliviana de Religiosos
CBR	Consejo de Bienestar Rural (Venezuela)
CBRA	Chemical Biological Radiological Agency (U.S.A.)
CBRB	Centraal Bureau voor de Rijn-en Binnenvaart
CBRI	Central Bee Research Institute (India)
CBRI	Central Building Research Institute (India)
CBRP	Centre Belge des Relations Publiques = BCPR
CBRS	Coffee Board Research Station (India)
ČBS	Česká Botanická Společnost
CBS	(WMO) Commission for Basic Systems
CBS	Canadian Biochemical Society
CBS	Centraal Bureau Slachtveeverzekeringen
CBS	Centraal Bureau voor de Statistiek
CBS	Centraal Bureau voor Schimmelcultures
CBS	Central Bank of Seychelles
CBS	Chinese Biochemical Society
CBS	Christian Broadcasting System (Korea)

CBS	Columbia Broadcasting System (U.S.A.)
CBS	Commonwealth Bureau of Soils
CBSA	Catholic Bible Society of America
CBSA	Clay Bird Shooting Associations
CBSA	Council of Bank Staff Association
CBSE	Commonwealth Board of Surveying Education
CBSI	Catholic Boy Scouts of Ireland
CBSI	Chartered Building Societies Institute
CBSI	China Behaviour Science Institute
CBSL	Carnival Band Secretaries League
CBSN	Centraal Bureau voor de Schapenfokkerij in Nederland
CBSN	Christelijke Bond van Schoenwinkeliers
CBSO	City of Birmingham Symphony Orchestra
CBSS	Council of the Baltic Sea States
CBT	Centre Belge de Traductions
CBT	Centre for BioTechnology (Sweden)
CBT	Commission du Bassin du Tchad
CBT	Construction and Building Trades Section
CBTB	Nederlandse Christelijke Boeren-en Tuindersbond
CBTC	Confederação Brasileira de Trabalhadores Cristãos
CBTDC	China Building Technology Development Centre
CBTEC	Centro de Biotecnologia Agricola (Brazil)
CBTIP	Chambre Belge des Traducteurs, Interprètes et Philologues = BKV/TF
CBTS	Chinese Broadcasting & Television Society
CBTU	Companhia Brasileira de Trens Urbanos
CBTUC	Commonwealth of the Bahamas Trade Union Congress
CBU	Caribbean Broadcasting Union
CBU	Clearing Bank Union
CBURC	Computer Board for Universities and Research Councils
CBV	Centraal Bureau voor de Veilingen
CBV	Central Bureau voor de Varkensfokkerij in Nederland
CBV	Coopérative Suisse pour l'Approvisionnement en Bétail de Boucherie et en Viande
CBVN	Centraal Bureau voor de Varkensfokkerij in Nederland
CBWA	Centralne Biuro Wystaw Artystycznych
CBWAS	Central Bank of the West African States = BCEAO
CBWI	Committee for British Withdrawal from Ireland
CBWT	Confederation of British Wool Textiles
CC	Causa Común (Venezuela)
CC	Charity Commission
CC	Commission de Climatologie (OMM)
CC	Controllers Council (U.S.A.)
CC	Countryside Commission
CC	Craft Council
CC-EYE	Coordinating Committee for European Youth Exchanges (Belgium)
CCA	Canadian Centre for Architecture
CCA	Canadian Chemical Association
CCA	Canadian Communication Association = ACC
CCA	Canadian Construction Association
CCA	Caribbean Conservation Association
CCA	Carpet Cleaners Association
CCA	Cecchetti Council of America
CCA	Centre for Contemporary Arts, Glasgow
CCA	China Clay Association
CCA	Chinese Culture Association (U.S.A.)
CCA	Chitufuko Cha Amayi (Madagascar)
CCA	Christian Chiropractors Association (U.S.A.)
CCA	Christian Colportage Association
CCA	Christian Conference of Asia
CCA	Citizens Councils of America
CCA	Civic Catering Association
CCA	Coastal Cruising Association
CCA	Commission on Crystallographic Apparatus
CCA	Commonwealth Chess Association
CCA	Commonwealth Correspondents' Association
CCA	Compagnie Commerciale Africaine (Ivory Coast)
CCA	Company Chemists Association
CCA	Conférence Chrétienne d'Asie Orientale
CCA	Conseil de Coopération Arabe (Jordan) = ACC
CCA	Consejo de Cooperación Aduanera = CCC, CCD
CCA	Consortium of Caterers and Administrators (ex College Caterers Association)
CCA	Consultative Committee of Credit Associations (CEC)

CCA	Consumer Credit Association = CCAUK
CCA	Copper Conductors Association
CCA	Council of Chemical Associations (U.S.A.)
CCA	Covered Conductors Association
CCA	Cyprus Consumers Association
CCAA	Cement and Concrete Association of Australia
CCAA	Conseil de Coordination des Associations Aéroportuaires (Switzerland) = AACC
CCAAP	Central Committee for the Architectural Advisory Panels
CCAAP	Comisión Consultiva en Asuntos Administrativo y de Presupuesto (UN)
CCAB	Canadian Circulation Audit Board
CCAB	Consultative Committee of Accountancy Bodies
CCAC	Canadian Council on Animal Care
CCAC	Compagnie Commerciale de l'Afrique Centrale
CCAC	Consumer and Corporate Affairs Canada
CCAC	Coordinating Committee on Agricultural Chemicals
CCACC	Coordinating Committee of the EC Cooperative Associations
CCACU	Central Co-ordinating Allocation Committee for University Project Research (South Africa)
CCAF	Comité Central des Armateurs de France
CCAF	Compagnie Agricole et Forestière
CCAFMA	Caisse Centrale d'Allocations Familiales Mutuelles Agricoles
CCAHC	Central Council for Agricultural and Horticultural Co-operation
CCAI	Chambre de Commerce, d'Agriculture et d'Industrie (Mali, Togo)
CCAM	Canadian Congress of Applied Mechanics
CCAM	Centre de Conjoncture Africaine et Malgache
CCAM	Commission Consultative des Achats et de Marchés (CE)
CCAM	Council for Complementary and Alternative Medicine
CCAMAA	Caisse Centrale d'Assurances Mutuelles Agricoles contre les Accidents
CCAMAG	Caisse Centrale d'Assurances Mutuelles Agricoles contre la Grêle
CCAMAI	Caisse Centrale d'Assurances Mutuelles Agricoles contre l'Incendie
CCAMAMB	Caisse Centrale d'Assurances Mutuelles Agricoles contre la Mortalité du Bétail
CCAMLR	Commission for the Conservation of Antarctic Marine Living Resources
CCAO	Chambre de Compensation de l'Afrique de l'Ouest (AACB)(Sierra Leone) = WACH
CCAP	Citizens' Crusade Against Poverty (U.S.A.)
CCAP	Committee of Concerned Artists and Professionals (U.S.A.)
CCAP	Culture Centre of Algae and Protozoa
CCAPP	Coordinating Council of Albanian Political Parties (Serbia) = KVAPS
CCAQ	Consultative Committee on Administrative Questions (UN)
CCAR	Colorado Center for Astrodynamics Research
CCAR	Compagnie Camérounaise d'Assurances et de Réassurances
CCARI	China Chongqing Automobile Research Institute
CCARR	Coordinating Committee for the Alligators River Region
CCAS	Centre for Contemporary Asian Studies
CCAS	Consejo Co-ordinador Argentino Sindical
CCAS	Crisis Counselling for Alleged Shoplifters
CCAT	Central Council for the Amateur Theatre
CCAT	Comité de Coordination de l'Assistance Technique (ONU)
CCAU	Confederation of Central American Universities
CCAUK	Consumer Credit Association of the United Kingdom = CCA
CCAVMA	Caisse Centrale d'Assurance Vieillesse Mutuelle Agricole
CCB	Caribbean Council for the Blind (Antigua-Barbuda)
CCB	Centre Commercial du Bénin
CCB	Coalition Clean Baltic (Sweden)
CCB	Commision Canadienne du Blé = CWB
CCB	Commonwealth Geographical Bureau
CCB	Compagnie Camérounaise des Boissons
CCB	Conseil Canadien du Bois = CWC
CCB	Cooperative Centrale Boerenleenbank

CCB	Cooperative Credit Bank (Romania) = Bankcoop		**CCC**	Club Cricket Conference
			CCC	Club des Chefs des Chefs
CCBA	Centre de Calcul de Béton Armé (Ivory Coast)		**CCC**	Coalfield Communities Campaign
			CCC	Combatant Communist Cells (Belgium)
CCBAT	Comité Central Belge de l'Achèvement Textile		**CCC**	Commodity Credit Corporation (U.S.A.)
			CCC	Complexe Chimique Camérounais
CCBB	Comité Central de la Bonneterie Belge		**CCC**	Conseil de Coopération Culturelle (CE)
CCBD	Chambre de Commerce Belgo-Danoise		**CCC**	Conseil National du Credit (Cameroon)
CCBDA	Canadian Copper and Brass Development Association		**CCC**	Consumers Consultative Committee (EU)
			CCC	Copyright Clearance Center (U.S.A.)
CCBE	Commission Consultative des Barreaux Européens		**CCC**	Corporate Conservation Council
			CCC	Council for Cultural Cooperation (CE)
CCBET	Comité Central Belge de Textile l'Ennoblissement		**CCC**	Council for the Care of Churches
			CCC	Customs Co-operation Council (Belgium) = CCA, CCD
CCBI	Chambre de Commerce Belgo-Italienne			
CCBN	Central Council for British Naturism		**CCC-CA**	Confederación de Cooperatívas del Caribe y Centro América (Costa Rica)
CCBS	Cambridge Center for Behavioral Studies (U.S.A.)		**CCCA**	Comité Consultivo en Cuestiones Administrativas (UN)
CCBSA	Central Council of Bank Staff Associations		**CCCAM**	Centro de Cooperación Cientifica de Asia Meridional (India)
CCBV	Comité Professionnnel des Coopératives des Pays du Marché Commun pour le Bétail et la Viande		**CCCAS**	Centro de Cooperación Cientifica de Asia Sudoriental (Thailand) = SEASCO
			CCCB	Cámara de Comercio Colombo Británica
CCC	Calculator Collectors Club		**CCCB**	Commisão de Comércio do Cacau da Bahia (Brazil)
CCC	Camping & Caravanning Club of Great Britain and Ireland		**CCCBR**	Central Council of Church Bell Ringers
CCC	Campus Crusade for Christ		**CCCC**	Charity Christmas Card Council
CCC	Canadian Chamber of Commerce		**CCCCA**	Committee on Christian Communication in Africa (Switzerland)
CCC	Canadian Climate Centre		**CCCCN**	Commissão Coordenadora da Criação do Cavalo Nacional (Brazil)
CCC	Canadian Commercial Corporation			
CCC	Capricorn Conservation Council		**CCCE**	Caisse Centrale de Coopération Économique (Benin, Congo, Niger)
CCC	Caribbean Conference of Churches			
CCC	Caribbean Conservation Corporation		**CCCE**	Centre Congolais du Commerce Extérieur
CCC	Caribbean Consumer Committee (Jamaica)		**CCCFE**	Comité Consultatif de Coordination du Financement à moyen terme des Exportations
CCC	Caribbean Council of Churches			
CCC	Catholic Communications Centre		**CCCH**	Confédération des Cooperatives de Construction et d'Habitation
CCC	Cellules Communistes Combattantes (Belgium)		**CCCI**	Compagnie du Congo pour le Commerce et l'Industrie
CCC	Central Classification Committee			
CCC	Central Coordinating Council (Russia)		**CCCI**	Conseil Canadien pour la Coopération Internationale = CCIC
CCC	Centrale Cultuurtechnische Commissie			
CCC	Changsha Communications College		**CCCO**	Committee on Climatic Changes and the Ocean (SCOR/IOC)
CCC	Chemicals Consultative Committee (ANZECC)			
			CCCO	Joint SCOR/IOC Committee on Climatic Changes and the Ocean
CCC	Chinese Cultural Centre			
CCC	Citizens' Consultative Committee (Singapore)		**CCCP**	Committee for the Communication of Conservative Policies
CCC	City Communications Centre			

CCCR	Co-ordinating Committee for Cancer Research		**CCE**	Compagnie Camérounaise d'Entreprise
CCCS	Canadian Cooperative Credit Society		**CCÉ**	Compagnie Commercial d'Électronique
CCCSA	Conservation Centre and Conservation Council of South Australia		**CCE**	Conseil des Communes d'Europe = CEM, RGE
CCCU	Caribbean Confederation of Credit Unions		**CCE**	Consejo Coordinador Empresarial (Mexico)
CCCWA	Christian Consultative Council for the Welfare of Animals		**CCE**	Counsel and Care for the Elderly
CCCWU	Commonwealth Cement and Construction Workers' Union (Bahamas)		**CCE**	University of London Centre for Continuing Education
CCD	Centrale Contrôle Dienst		**CCÉA**	Commission de Contrôle de l'Énergie Atomique (Canada) = ACEB
CCD	Comité du Commerce et de la Distribution (CE) = CCA, CCC		**CCEA**	Commonwealth Council for Educational Administration
CCD	Conseil de Coopération Douanière (Belgium)		**CCEA**	County and City Engineers' Association (Éire)
CCDC	Capital City Development Corporation (Malawi)		**CCÉAC**	Comité de Coopération Économique de l'Amérique Centrale
CCDCG	Clinical Chemistry Data Communication Group (U.S.A.)		**CCÉAE**	Conférence des Chefs d'État de l'Afrique Equatoriale
CCDG	Société Commerciale du Gabon		**CCÉB**	Conseil Canadien des Écoles de Bibliothécaires
CCDLNE	Commission for Controlling the Desert Locust in the Near East (FAO) (Italy)		**CCEDA**	Chinese Chemical Exploration and Design Association
CCDLNWA	Commission for Controlling the Desert Locust in North-West Africa (FAO) = CLCPANO		**CCEE**	Caribbean Council for Europe
			CCEE	Consilium Conferentiarum Episcopalium Europae
CCDN	Cámara de Comercio, Agricultura e Industria del Distrito Nacional (Dominican Republic)		**CCEE**	Coordenadoria de Controle do Equilibrio Ecologico (Brazil)
CCDP	(WMO) Climate Change Detection Project		**CCEET**	Centre for Cooperation with European Economics in Transition (France)
CCDP	Comisión Centroamericana de Desarrollo Pesquero (Salvador)		**CCEG**	Confédération des Compagnonnages Européens
CCDP	Commission Canadienne de Droits de la Personne = CHRC		**CCÉI**	Comité Consultatif Économique et Industriel auprès de l'OCDE
CCDP	Compagnie Camérounaise de Dépôts Pétroliers		**CCÉI**	Conférence sur la Coopération Économique Internationale = CIEC
CCDR	Compagnie Camérounaise de Développement Regional		**CCEN**	Chilian Nuclear Energy Commission
CCDS	Canadian Council on Social Development		**CCEO**	Caribbean Council of Engineering Organisations (Jamaica)
CCDU	Croatian Christian Democratic Union		**CCÉP**	Commission Consultative des Études Postales (UPU) = CCPS
CCDVT	Caisse Centrale de Dépôts et Virements de Titres		**CCEP**	Coordinating Committee for Earthquake Prediction (Japan)
CCE	Comhaltas Ceoltoirí Eireann		**CCEPI**	Commission Consultative Européenne pour les Pêches dans les Eaux Intérieures
CCE	Comite de Cooperación Económica del Istmo Centroamericano		**CCEPTI**	Centrul de Cercetari Econimice pentru Promovarea Turismului International
CCE	Commission des Communautés Européennes = CEC		**CCÉRO**	Centre d'Études de Recherche Operationelle (Belgium)

CCERS	Comité Consultative Européenne de la Recherche sur la Santé = EACHR	**CCFI**	Constante Cameroon Fish Industry
CCES	Case Center for Electrochemical Sciences (U.S.A.)	**CCFM**	Council of Canadian Film Makers
		CCFOM	Caisse Centrale de la France d'Outre-Mer
CCES	China Civil Engineering Society	**CCFPI**	Comité Consultatif de la Fonction Publique Internationale
CCÉS	Conseil Consultatif Économique et Social de l'Union Économique (Benelux) = ESRA	**CCFR**	Coordinating Committee on Fast Reactors (Euratom) = CCRR
CCESP	Centre County Engineers' Society of Pennsylvania (U.S.A.)	**CCFST**	Comité Consultatif pour la Formation Scientifique et Technique = ACSTT, BAWTA
CCET	Centre for Computers Education & Training	**CCG**	Comic Creators' Guild
CCETI	Commission Consultative des Employés et des Travailleurs Intellectuels (OIT)	**CCG**	Commission Canadienne des Grains = CGC
CCETS	Canon Collins Educational Trust for Southern Africa	**CCG**	Communist Campaign Group
CCETSW	Central Council for Education and Training in Social Work	**CCG**	Conseil de Coopération du Golfe = GCC
CCÉTT	Centre Commun d'Études de Télévision et de Télécommunication	**CCGA**	Compagnie de Constructions Générales en Afrique
CCEUREA	Centre Coopératif d'Expansion et d'Utilisation Rationnelles d'Équipement Agricole	**CCGA**	Custom Clothing Guild of America
		CCGB	Cycling Council of Great Britain
CCF	Centrale Cultuurfondsen (Indonesia)	**CCGL**	Cooperativa Central Gaucha de Leite (Brazil)
CCF	Chinese Computer Federation	**CCGM**	Commission de la Carte Géologique du Monde = CGMW
CCF	Christian Children's Fund (U.S.A.)		
CCF	Christian Children's Fund of Great Britain	**CCGR**	Changchun Gold Research Institute
CCF	Co-operative Commonwealth Federation Montreal (Canada)	**CCGS**	Corpus Christi Geological Society (U.S.A.)
CCF	Commission for the Status of Women (Portugal)	**CCGTM**	Commonwealth Consultative Group on Technology Management (ComSec)
CCF	Congress for Cultural Freedom	**CCH**	Colegio de Ciencias y Humanidades (Mexico)
CCF	Conservative Centre Forward		
CCF	Crédit Commercial de France	**CCH**	Commerce Clearing House Inc. (U.S.A.)
CCF	Cumberland College Foundation (Australia)	**CCH**	Compagnie Commerciale Hollando
CCFA	Caribbean Cane Farmers Association	**CCHA**	Canadian Catholic History Association = SCHEC
CCFA	Chambre de Commerce Franco-Néerlandaise	**CCHA**	Compagnie Commerciale Hollando-Africaine
CCFA	Comando Conjunto de la Fuerza Armada (Peru)	**CCHD**	Catholic Committee against Hunger and for Development (France) =CCFD
CCFA	Combined Cadet Force Association	**CCHE**	Central Council for Health Education
CCFAN	Conseil de Commandement des Forces Armées du Nord (Chad)	**CChEN**	Comision Chilena de Energia Nuclear
		CCHF	Childrens Country Holidays Fund
CCFC	Christian Children's Fund of Canada	**CCHH**	Churches Council for Health and Heating
CCFD	Comité Catholique contre la Faim et pour le Développement = CCHD	**CCHMS**	Central Committee for Hospital Medical Services (BMA)
CCFE	Communauté des Chemins de Fer Européens = CER, GEB	**CCHO**	Comité Consultatif d'Hydrologie Opérationnelle (WMO) = ACOH

CCHR	Colombian Committee for Human Rights
ČCHS	Česká Chirurgická Společnost
CCHTS	Center for Carburization Heat Treatment Studies (U.S.A.)
CCI	Canadian Circumpolar Institute
CCI	Canadian Conservation Institute = ICC
CCI	Canadian Copyright Institute
CCI	Canadian Credit Institute
CCI	Canadian Crossroads International; Carrefour Canadien International
CCI	Central Campesina Independenti (Mexico)
CCI	Centre du Commerce Internationale (CNUCED/GATT) = ITC
CCI	Centro Común de Investigación (EURATOM) = CCR, GCO, GFS, JRC
CCI	Chambers of Commerce of Ireland
CCI	Chambre de Commerce et d'Industrie (France, New Caledonia)
CCI	Chambre de Commerce Internationale = ICC, IHK
CCI	Comités Consultatifs Internationaux
CCI	Compagnie Camérounaise Industrielle
CCI	Compagnie de Constructions Internationales
CCI	Confraternidad Carcelaria Internacional (U.S.A.) = PFI
CCI	Cotton Corporation of India
CCI	Cotton Council International (U.S.A.)
CCI	Crafts Council of Ireland
CCI	Crédit de la Côte d'Ivoire
CCI	Cross Cancer Institute (Canada)
CCI-EURO-TRAG	Compagnie de Constructions Internationales (Gabon)
CCIA	Camera di Commercio, Industria e Agricoltura di Rieti
CCIA	Chambre de Commerce, d'Industrie et d'Agriculture de Tananarive (Madagascar)
CCIA	Comité Cientifico de Investigaciones Antárticas (ICSU) = CSRA, SCAR
CCIA	Comité Consultivo Internacional del Algodón = CCIC, ICAC
CCIA	Commission of the Churches on International Affairs (WCC)
CCIA	Comptoir Commercial et Industriel Afrique
CCIA	Computer and Communications Industry Association (U.S.A.)
CCIA/WCC	Commission of the Churches on International Affairs of the World Council of Churches
CCIAESC	Coffee Commission of the Inter-American Economic and Social Council (U.S.A.)
CCIAS	Centre for Chemical Instrumental Analysis & Services
CCIASO	Chambre de Commerce, d'Industrie et d'Artisanat de la Région du Sénégal Oriental
CCIB	Chambre de Commerce et d'Industrie du Burundi
CCIC	Canadian Council for International Co-operation =CCCI
CCIC	Centre Catholique International pour l'Unesco
CCIC	Comité Catholique International de Coordination auprès de l'Unesco
CCIC	Comité Consultatif International du Coton = CCIA, ICAC
CCICMS	Council for the Co-ordination of International Congress of Medicine)
CCIEM	Catholic Committee for Intra-European Migration = CCMIE
CCIEM	Center for Computer Integrated Engineering and Manufacturing (U.S.A.)
CCIF	Centre Catholique des Intellectuels Français
CCIF	Comité Consultatif International Téléphonique
CCIIW	Canadian Council of the International Institute of Welding
CCIL	Canadian Co-operative Implements Ltd
CCIM	Chambre de Commerce et d'Industrie de la Martinique
CCIMCAT	Centro de Capacitacion e Investigacion de la Mujer Campesina Tarijena (Bolivia)
CCIO	Comité Cientifição de Investigaciones Oceánicas = CSRO, SCOR
CCIP	Chambre de Commerce et d'Industrie de Paris
CCIPB	Commission du Commerce International des Produits de Base (CNUCED) = CICT
CCIR	Catholic Council for International Relations
CCIR	Chambre de Commerce et l'Industrie de la Réunion
CCIR	Comité Consultative International des Radio-Communications (UIT)

CCIRN	Coordinating Committee for Intercontinental Research Networking (Netherlands)
CCIS	China Chemical Industry Society
CCIS	Compagnie Commerciale Industrielle du Sénégal
CCISM	Center for Creation and Interdisciplinary Study of Music
CCISUA	Coordinating Committee for Independent Staff Unions and Associations of the United Nations System
CCITT	Comité Consultatif International Télégraphique et Téléphonique (UIT)
CCITU	Coordinating Committee of Independent Trade Unions
CCIVS	Co-ordinating Committee for International Voluntary Service = CCSVI
CCIW	Canada Centre for Inland Waters
CCJ	Comité Européen de Coopération Juridique
CCJ	Council of Christians and Jews
CCJO	Consultative Council of Jewish Organisations (U.S.A.)
CCJS	Centre for Criminal Justice Studies
CCL	"Hospodar" Citizens' Circle of Lemkos (Poland) = OKŁ
CCL	Caribbean Congress of Labour
CCL	Centre for Construction Law & Management
CCL	Comité Central de la Laine
CCL	Commission Canadienne du Lait = CDC
CCL	Commission for Climatology (WMO)
CCL	Commonwealth Countries League
CCL	Conseil International de Continuation et de Liaison du Congrès Mondial des Forces de Paix
CCLA	Canadian Civil Liberties Association
CCLA	Canadian Comparative Literature Association = ACLC
CCLC	Comisión de la Cuenca del Lago Chad
CCLE	Caribbean Council of Legal Education (Jamaica)
CCLEPE	Consultative Committee for Local Ecumenical Projects in England
CCLF	Club des Congrès de Langue Française
CCLFA	Comité Central de la Laine et des Fibres Associées
CCLGF	Consultative Council on Local Government Finance
CCLIL	Fédération Française de la Filature de Laine Cardée et Autres Fibres
CCLLP	Campaign for Collective Leadership of the Labour Party
CCLM	Committee on Constitutional and Legal Matters (FAO) = CQCL
CCLM	Coordinating Council of Literary Magazines (U.S.A.)
CCLN	Council for Computerized Library Networks (U.S.A.)
CCLSD	Cooperative Centre for Local Sustainable Development
CCLU	Conference of Citizens Labor Unions (Philippines)
CCM	Caribbean Common Market (Guyana)
CCM	Centre de Coopération Maritime de la CCI = CMC, IMCC
CCM	Chama Cha Mapinduzi (Tanzania)
CCM	Comitatio Collaborazione Medica
CCM	Consejo Cultural Mundial (Mexico)
CCM	Cornish Chamber of Mines
CCMA	Caisse Centrale des Mutuelles Agricoles (France)
CCMA	Canadian Council of Management Association
CCMA	Comité Consultatif Mondial des Amis = CMCA, FWCCC
CCMA	Comite de Compradores de Material Aeronautico de America Latina
CCMA	Contract Cleaning and Maintenance Association (*now* CSSA)
CCMA	Corrugated Case Materials Association
CCMA	County and City Managers' Association (Éire)
CCMC	China Coal Monopoly Corporation
CCMC	City Capital Market Committee
CCMC	Committee of Common Market Automobile Constructors (Belgium)
CCMCU	Culture Collection of Microorganisms of Ciudad Universitaria Madrid
CCME	Churches' Committee for Migrants in Europe (Belgium)
CCMI	Centre for Construction Market Information
CCMIE	Comité Catholique pour les Migrations Intra-Européennes =CCIEM
CCML	Centro de Ciencias del Mar y Limnologia (Mexico)
CCMM	Compagnie Camérounaise de Mobilier Métallique

CCMMI	Council of Commonwealth Mining and Metallurgical Institutions	**CCO**	Comisión Colombiana de Oceanografia
CCMP	Coordinating Committee for the Moon and Planets (ICSU)	**CCO**	Conservative Central Office
CCMR	Center for Contemporary Music Research (Greece)	**CCOA**	Chinese Cereals and Oils Association
		CCOA	Christian Council on Ageing
CCMRC	Commonwealth Caribbean Medical Research Council (Jamaica)	**CCOC**	Comité de Coordination des Organisations des Consommateurs
CCMRG	Commonwealth Committee on Mineral Resources and Geology	**CCOD**	Christelijke Centrale van de Openbare Diensten
CCMRI	Central Coal Mining Research Institute (China)	**CCOD**	Concertacion Centroamericana de Organismos de Desarrollo (Costa Rica)
CCMS	Committee on the Challenges of Modern Society (NATO) = CDSM	**CCODP**	Canadian Catholic Organization for Development and Peace = OCCDP
CCMSC	Caribbean Common Market Standards Council	**CCofGB**	Cartoonists Club of Great Britain
CCMW	Churches Committee on Migrant Workers in Europe = CETME	**CCOL**	Coordinating Committee on the Ozone Layer (UNEP)
CCN	Civil Co-operation Bureau (South Africa)	**CCOO**	Comisiones Obreras
CCN	Community Computing Network	**CCOOA-CAL**	Comisión Coordinâdora de Organizaciones de Obreros Agricolas y Campesinos de América Latina
CCN	Compagnie Camérounaise du N'Goko		
CCN	Consulte des Comités Nationalistes (Corsica) = ACN	**CCOP**	Committee for Co-ordination of Joint Prospecting for Mineral Resources in Asian Offshore Areas (ESCAP)
CCN	Cruzada Civica Nacionalista (Venezuela)		
CCN	Cruzada Civilista Nacional (Panama)	**CCOP/ SOPAC**	Committee for the Coordination of Joint Prospecting for Mineral Resources in South Pacific Offshore Areas (ESCAP)
CCN	Cycle Campaign Network		
CCNA	Canadian Community Newspapers Association	**CCOPA**	Commissão Coordenadora da Obras Publicas de Alentejo
CCNA	Corfu Channel Naval Association	**CCOR**	Central Council of the Odinic Rite
CCNAA	Coordinating Council for North American Affairs	**CCOS**	China Cereals and Oils Society
CCND	Christian Concern for Nuclear Disarmament	**CCOTA-CAL**	Conseil Coordinateur des Organisations des Travailleurs Agricoles et des Paysans d'Amérique Latine
CCNDT	Canadian Council for Non-Destructive Technology		
CCNG	Computer Communications Networks Group (Canada)	**CCP**	Centre for Interdisciplinary Studies in Chemical Physics (Canada)
CCNR	Canadian Coalition for Nuclear Responsibility	**CCP**	Chinese Communist Party
		CCP	Comité Cafetalero del Perú
CCNR	Central Commission for the Navigation of the Rhine = CCR, ZKR	**CCP**	Commission on Comparative Planetology
CCNR	Consultative Committee for Nuclear Research (Council of Europe)	**CCP**	Committee on Commodity Problems (FAO)
CCNSC	Cancer Chemotherapy National Service Center (U.S.A.)	**CCP**	Compagnie des Caoutchoucs du Pakidié (Ivory Coast)
CCNUD	Cycle de la Coopération de Nations Unies pour le Développement	**CCP**	Confederação do Comércio Portugués
		CCP	Confederación Cientifica Panamericana (Argentina)
CCNY	Carnegie Coorporation of New York	**CCP**	Confederación de Campesinos Peruanos
CCNY	City College of New York	**CCP**	Confederation of Construction Professions
		CCP	Conférence Chrétienne pour la Paix = CFK, CPC, HMK

CCP	Consultative Committee on Publications (EU)	**CCPTP**	Comité Consultivo Pesquero Transpacífico = TPFCC
CCPA	Canadian Chemical Producers' Association	**CCPW**	Catholic Council for Polish Welfare
CCPA	Centrale Coopérative des Productions Animales	**CCPY**	Comissão pela Criação do Parque Yanomami (Brazil)
CCPA	Chinese Catholic Patriotic Association	**CCQAB**	Comité Consultatif pour les Questions Administratives et Budgétaires (ONU) = ACABQ
CCPALV	Centrul de Cercetari pentru Protecti Anticorozive, Lacuri si Vopsele, Bucaresti	**CCR**	Center for Conflict Resolution (U.S.A.)
CCPCI	Cuirs, Caoutchouc, Plastiques de Côte-d'Ivoire	**CCR**	Centrale Commissie voor de Rijnvaart = CCNR, ZKR
CCPD	Commission on the Churches' Participation in Development (WCC) (Switzerland)	**CCR**	Centre Commun de Recherche (Euratom) = JRC
CCPDH	Cuban Committee for Human Rights	**CCR**	Centre for Criminological Research (Canada)
CCPE	Council of European Conferences of Priests	**CCR**	Centre for Cultural Research (Germany)
CCPES	Canadian Council of Professional Engineers and Scientists	**CCR**	Council for Chemical Research (U.S.A.)
CCPF	Comité Central de la Propriété Forestière de la CEE	**CCRA**	Canadian Research Centre for Anthropology
CCPF	Comité de Coordination de la Production Frutière	**CCRB**	Coöperatieve Centrale Raiffeisen-Bank
CCPIT	China Committee for the Promotion of International Trade	**CCRE**	Conseil des Communes et Régions d'Europe = CEMR, CMRE, RGRE
CCPL	Cooperativa Central dos Productores de Leite (Brazil)	**CCRF**	Comité Central Rayonnement Français
CCPM	Consultative Committee for Programme Management (EU)	**CCRH**	Conseil Canadien de Recherches sur les Humanités = HRCC
CCPMA	Caisse Centrale de Prévoyance Mutuelle Agricole	**CCRI**	Central Coffee Research Institute (India)
CCPMNO	Comité de Coordination des Ports Méditerranéens Nord-Occidental	**CCRI**	Comité Consultatif de Recherche en Informatique
CCPMO	Comité de Coordinacion de los Puertos del Mediterraneo Nord-Occidental	**CCRMA**	Center for Computer Research in Music and Acoustics
CCPMO	Consultative Council of Professional Management Organisations	**CCRMO**	Comité Consultatif de la Recherche Météorologique Océanique (WMO) = ACOMR, CAIMO
CCPO	Comité Central Permanent de l'Opium (Switzerland)	**CCRN**	Centre Commun de Recherches Nucléaires (Euratom)
CCPP	Caisse Commune des Pensions du Personnel des Nations Unies	**CCRP**	Corporación Centro Regional de Población (Colombia)
CCPR	Central Council for Physical Recreation	**CCRR**	Center for Community and Regional Research (U.S.A.)
CCPR	Codex Committee on Pesticide Residues	**CCRR**	Comité de Coordination des Réacteurs Rapides (Euratom) = CCFR
CCPR	Cooperativa de Cafeteros de Puerto Rico	**CCRRM**	Comité Consultatif de la Recherche sur les Ressources de la Mer (FAO) = ACMRR, CAIRM
CCPS	Chinese Corrosion & Protection Society		
CCPS	Commission Permanente du Pacifique Sud	**CCRRMM**	Ordo Clericorum Regularium Melkitarum
CCPS	Consultative Committee for Postal Studies (UPU) = CCEP	**CCRS**	Canada Centre for Remote Sensing
		CCRS	Central Coconut Research Station (India)
		CCRSS	Conseil Canadien de Recherche en Sciences Sociales = SSRCC

CCRST	Comité Consultatif de la Recherche Scientifique et Technique
CCRT	Corporación Catalan de Radio y Televisión
CCRTD	Committee for Coordination of Cathode Ray Tube Development
CCRTL	Citizens Coalition for Rational Traffic Laws (U.S.A.)
CCRVDF	Codex Committee on Residues of Veterinary Drugs in Food
CCS	Canadian Cancer Society
CCS	Canadian Ceramic Society
CCS	Cancer Control Society (U.S.A.)
CCS	Center for Chinese Studies (U.S.A.)
CCS	Centre for Cartopedagogic Studies
CCS	Centre for Child Study
CCS	Centre for Cognitive Science
CCS	Centro de Capacitacion Social (Panama)
CCS	China Coal Society
CCS	Chinese Cancer Society
CCS	Chinese Ceramic Society
CCS	Chinese Chemical Society
CCS	Chocolate Chompers' Society
CCS	Comptoir Commercial du Sénégal
CCS	Confederation of Construction Specialists
CCS	Corporation of Secretaries
CCS	Council of Communication Societies (U.S.A.)
CCSA	Canadian Committee on Sugar Analysis
CCSA	Comité Chrétien de Service en Algérie
CCSA	Conservation Council of South Australia
CCSATU	Coordinating Council of South African Trade Unions
CCSB	Credit Card Service Bureau (U.S.A.)
CCSBSIF	Consejo Centroamericano de Superintendentes de Bancos, de Seguros y de otras Instituciones Financieras (Guatemala)
CCSC	Commercial Computer Security Centre
CCSC	Coordinating Committee for Satellite Communication
CCSD	Camadoam Council on Social Development
CCSDS	Consultative Committee for Space Data Systems
CCSERV	Conservation Council of the South East Region and Canberra
CCSL	Confédération Congolaise des Syndicats Libres
CCSM	Confédération Chrétienne des Syndicats Malgaches
CCSMA	Caisse Centrale de Secours Mutuels Agricoles
CCSMDG	Coordinating Committee of the Societies of Mineral-Deposits Geology
CCSO	Compagnie Commercial Sangha-Oubangui (Congo)
CCSPSL	Centre for Criminology & the Social & Philosophical Study of Law
CCSQ	Consultative Committee on Substantive Questions (UN)
CCSR	Canadian Consortium for Social Research
CCSR	Centre for Cosmology & (Space) Research
CCSS	Cambridge Centre for Sixth Form Studies
CCST	Conseil des Caraïbes pour la Science et la Technologie
CCST	Coordinating Committee on Science and Technology
CCSTAM	Comisión de Coordinacion para la Solidaridad entre los Trabajadores Azucareros del Mundo = ICCSASW
CCSU	Council of Civil Service Unions
CCSVI	Comité de Coordination du Service Volontaire International = CCIVS
CCT	CCI Comité Consultatif Transporteurs
CCT	Central Cristiana de Trabajadores (Paraguay)
CCT	Chamber of Coal Traders
CCT	Cockburn Conservation Trust
CCT	Comité Consultatif de Thermemotrie
CCT	Confederación Centroamericana de Trabajadores
CCT	Confederación Costarricense del Trabajo
CCT	Confrérie des Chevaliers du Tastevin
CCT	Consejo Centroamericana de Turismo
CCT	Consejo Coordinador de Trabajadores (Chile)
CCTA	Canadian Cable Television Association
CCTA	Central Computer and Telecommunications Agency
CCTA	Centrale Chemisch-Technische Afdeling (Indonesia)
CCTA	China Communications and Transport Association

CCTA	Comisión de Coordinación de Tecnologia Andina (Peru)	**CCWB**	Commission Consultative des Barreaux de la Communauté Européenne
CCTA	Consumer Credit Trade Association	**CCWC**	Catholic Child Welfare Council
CCTAN	Confederación de Campesinos y Trabajadores Agricolas de Nicaragua	**CCWCP**	Coordination Committee World Climate Programme
CCTD	Catholic Council of Thailand for Development	**CCWE**	Campaign for Cold Weather Credits
CCTD	Confederación Costarricense de Trabajadores Democráticos	**CCWGS**	China Council of Wind Generator Standardisation
CCTEM	Consejo Coordinador de Trabajadores Estatales y Municipales (El Salvador)	**CCWM**	Congregational Council for World Mission
CCTM	Centre de Collections de Types Microbiens (Switzerland)	**CCWU**	Clerical and Commercial Workers Union (Guyana)
CCTR	Centre for Cell & Tissue Research	**CCyDEL**	Centro Coordinador y Difusor de los Estudios Latinoamericanos (Mexico)
CCTS	Chicago Cluster of Theological Schools (U.S.A.)	**CD**	Cape Democrats (South Africa)
CCTS	Comité de Coordination des Télécommunications par Satellites (Switzerland)	**CD**	Centrum Demokraterne (Denmark)
		CD	Centrum Demokratyczne
		CD	Christian Democracy (Poland)
		CD	Co-operation for Development
CCTU	Comité de Coordination des Télécommunications (UNET)	**CD**	Coalición Democrática
CCTU	Czechoslovak Confederation of Trade Unions	**CD**	Commission du Danube
		CD	Convergencia Democrática (Peru)
CCU	Commonwealth Commercial Crime Unit (ComSec)	**CD**	Cultuurtechnische Dienst
		CD-ROM-SPRAG	CD-ROM Standards and Practices Action Group
CCU	Communication and Consultation Unit (MDBC)	**CDA**	Canadian Dental Association
CCU	Confederation of Canadian Unions	**CDA**	Canadian Department of Agriculture
CCU	Council for Communist Unity = MUC	**CDA**	Cattle Development Authority (Solomon Islands)
CCUA	Catholic Central Union of America		
CCUC	Central Council of the Union of Craftsmen (Afghanistan)	**CDA**	Centro de Defesa Amazónia (Brazil)
		CDA	Centro de Documentação Agrária (Mozambique)
CCUG	Church Computers Users Group		
CCUML	Comité Comunista Unificado Marxista-Leninista (Peru)	**CDA**	Centro di Documentazione Alpina
		CDA	Centro per la Documentazione Automatica
CCUN	Collegiate Council for the United States		
CCURR	Canadian Council on Urban and Regional Research	**CDA**	Chemists Defence Association
		CDA	Chinese Dancers' Association
CCUS	Chamber of Commerce of the United States	**CDA**	Christen Democratisch Appel
		CDA	Christian Democratic Action for Social Justice (Namibia)
CCV	Campaign for a Conservative Victory		
CCV	Cotonnière du Cap Vert (Senegal)	**CDA**	Commonwealth Dental Association
CCVM	Centrale Commissie voor Melk Hygiene	**CDA**	Compañia Dominicana de Aviación
CCW	Caribbean Church Woman	**CDA**	Computer Dealers Association (U.S.A.)
CCW	Council of Churches for Wales	**CDA**	Cooperative Development Agency
CCW	Countryside Council for Wales	**CDA**	Copper Development Association (BENELUX, U.K., U.S.A.)
CCW	International Committee on Chemical Warfare		
		CDAA	Churches Drought Action in Africa
CCWA	Conservation Council of Western Australia	**CDAC**	Centre for the Development of Advanced Computing (India)

CDAC	Civil Defense Advisory Council (U.S.A.)	**CdC**	Corte dei Conti
CDAE	Centro de Desarrollo Agrario del Ebro	**CDC**	Crop Development Centre (Canada)
CDAF	Compagnie des Dirigeants d'Approvisionnement et Acheteurs de France	**CDC**	Cyngor Defnyddwyr Cymru = WCC
		CDC Ltd	Chemical Dependency Centre Ltd
CDAH	Croatian Democratic Alliance in Hungary = MHSz	**CDCC**	Caribbean Development and Cooperation Committee (Trinidad-Tobago)
CDAP	Centre de Développement pour l'Asie et le Pacifique = APDC	**CDCC**	Conseil de la Coopération Culturelle (CCE)
CDAPSO	Canadian Data Processing Organisation	**CDCJ**	Comité Européen de Coopération Juridique (CCE)
CDARU	Christian Democratic Alliance of Romanians in Ukraine	**CDCR**	Centre for Documentation and Communication Research (U.S.A.)
CDAS	Centre for Developing-Area Studies (Canada)	**CDCT**	Centro de Documentação Cientifica e Técnica
CDAT	Comité Directeur pour Aménagement du Térritoire (CCE)	**CDCTM**	Centro de Documentación Cientifica y Tecnica de Mexico
CDATE	Centre for Design & Technology Education	**CDCU**	Centro de Documentação Cientifica Ultramarina (Portugal)
CDB	Caribbean Development Bank (Barbados) = BDC	**CDCW**	Cymdeithas Diogelu Cymru Wledig = CPRW
CDB	Commonwealth Development Bank	**CDD**	Catolicas por el Derecho a Decidir (Uruguay)
CDB	Compagnie de Bénin (Togo)		
CDB	Cyprus Development Bank	**CDDA**	Canadian Diamond Drilling Association
CDC	Cairo Demographic Centre (Egypt)	**CDDA**	Conseil Départemental de Développement Agricole
CDC	Caisse des Dépôts et Consignations		
CDC	Cameroon Development Corporation	**CDDC**	Comisión de Documentación Científica (Argentina)
CDC	Canadian Dairy Commission = CCL		
CDC	Canadian Development Corporation	**CDDH**	Comité Directeur pour les Droits de l'Homme (CCE)
CDC	Caribbean Documentation Centre		
CDC	Centro de Documentação Cientifica	**CDDR**	Campaign for Defence of Democratic Rights
CDC	Chemical Dependency Centre Ltd		
CDC	China Development Corporation	**CDDRT**	Campaign for the Defence of Democratic Rights in Turkey
CDC	Clearinghouse on Development Communication (U.S.A.)		
		CDdWC/ WFDS	Cymdeithas Ddawns Werin Cymru
CDC	Comisión de Documentación Cientifica (Argentina)	**CDE**	Center for Demography and Ecology (U.S.A.)
CDC	Committee for Development Cooperation	**CDÉ**	Centre de Documentation Économique (CCIP)
CDC	Commonwealth Development Corporation	**CDE**	Chemical Defence Establishment (MOD)
CDC	Compagnie des Compteurs	**CDE**	Club Dirigenti Esportazione
CDC	Comunidad Democrática Centroamericana	**CDE**	Coal Development Establishment
		CDE	Comissão Democrático Eleitoral
CDC	Concertación Democrática Cubana	**CDE**	Commission for Development and Exchange
CDC	Conselho de Desenvolvimento Comercial (Brazil)	**CDE**	Compagnie Dolisienne d'Entreprises (Congo)
CDC	Conservation for Development Centre		
CDC	Convergencia Democrática de Catalunya	**CDE**	Conselho de Desenvolvimento Economico (Brazil)

CDEC	Centro di Documentazione Ebraica Contemporanea	**CDI**	Centro de Documentação e Informação (Brazil)
CDEE	Canadian Defence Education Establishment (DRB)	**CDI**	Christian Democratic International = IDC
CDEJ	European Steering Committee for Intergovernmental Cooperation in the Youth Field (France)	**CDI**	Cobalt Development Institute
		CDI	Commission du Droit International (ONU) = ILC
CDEJ	Steering Committee for Employment and Labour (CE) (France)	**CDI**	Conselho de Desenvolvimento Industrail (Brazil)
CDÉLI	Centre de Documentation et d'Étude sur la Langue Internationale	**CDI**	Cotton Development International = AIDC
CDEP	Community Development Employment Projects	**CDI-BWA-MANDA**	Centrum voor Dorpsintegratie – Bwamanda – Belgie
CDET	Council for Dance Education and Training	**CDIAC**	Carbon Dioxide Information Analysis Center
CDEU	Christian Democratic European Union = ECDU, UEDC	**CDIAO**	Centre de Documentation et d'Information pour l'Afrique de l'Ouest (PADIS) = WADIS
CDF	Cameroon Democratic Front		
CDF	Capital Development Fund (UN)	**CDIC**	Canada Deposit Insurance Corporation
CDF	Centro de Datos sobre Fertilizantes (FAO)	**CDIC**	Canada Development Investment Corporation
CdF	Charbonnages de France	**CDICP**	Centrul de Documentare al Industriei Chimice si Petroliere (Romania)
CDF	Community Development Foundation		
CDF	Community Development Fund	**CDIÉA**	Centre de Développement Industriel pour les États Arabes, (Egypt)
CDF	Council for the Defense of Freedom (U.S.A.)	**CDIL**	Centro de Documentare Tehnica (Romania)
CDFC	Commonwealth Development Finance Corporation	**CDISA**	Centre de Documentation et d'Information de la Société des Africanistes
CDG	Campaign For Democracy in Ghana		
CDG	Carl Duisberg-Gesellschaft	**CDISS**	Centre for Defence & International Security Studies
CDH	Centralvereinigung Deutscher Handelsvertreter- und Handelsmakler Verbände	**CDIU**	Centrale Dienst voor de In- en Uitvoer
		CDIUPA	Centre de Documentation des Industries Utilisatrices des Produits Agricoles
CDH	Corte Interamericana Derechos Humanos		
CDH	Cour Européenne des Droits de l'Homme	**CDJA**	Cercle Départemental des Jeunes Agriculteurs
CDHAR	Comités Départementaux de l'Habitat et de l'Aménagement Rural	**CDL**	Centrala Drift Ledningen
		CDL	Comité de Liaison de l'Industrie du Tube d'Acier de la Communauté Européenne
CDHG	Guatemalan Commission for Human Rights		
CDHR	Comité Départemental de l'Habitat Rural	**CDL**	Comité de Liaison des Industries de Métaux Non-Ferreux de la Communauté Européenne
CDI	Centraal Diergeneeskunde Instituut		
CDI	Central za Dokumentaciju i Informacije	**CDL**	County and Democratic League (Australia)
CDI	Centre de Diffusion de l'Innovation (ANVAR)	**CDLDK**	Comité Liaison des Kinésithérapeutes de la CEE
CDI	Centre Économique Dévelopment Industriel Afrique, Caraïbes, Pacifique Communauté	**CDM**	Cable de Mexico, S.A.
CDI	Centre pour le Développement Industriel = CID	**CDM**	Central de Documentare Medicala (Romania)
CDI	Centro de Desarrollo Industrial (Honduras)		

CDM	Centro Democrático de Macau
CDM	Christian Democratic Movement (Slovakia) = KDH
CDM	Comité Directeur sur les Migrations Intraeuropéennes (CCE)
CDM	Commission on Dynamic Meteorology
CDM	Consolidated Diamond Mines (Namibia)
CDMF	Community Dance and Mime Foundation
CDMI	Centre de Documentation de Musique Internationale
CDMM	Comité Directeur sur les Moyens de Communication de Masse
CDN	Centro Dramático Nacional
CDN	Conselho Nacional de Defensa (Brazil)
CDN	Coordinadora Democrática Nicaragüense Ramiro Sacasa
CDNI	Committee for the Defense of National Interests (Bulgaria) = KZNI
CDNL	Conference of Directors of National Libraries
CDNPA	Canadian Daily Newspaper Publishers Association
CDOSTP	Coalizão Democrática de Oposição de São Tomé e Principe = CODO
CDP	Christian Democratic Party (Kiribati)
CDP	Civic Democratic Party (Bosnia-Herzegovina)
CDP	Committee of Directors of Polytechnics
CDP	Community Drug Project
CDP	Compagnie Camérounaise de Dépôts Petroliers
CDP	Convention Democratic Party (Liberia)
CDP	Coordinadora de Pobladores (Guatemala)
CDP-PPF	Constitutional Democratic Party – Party of People's Freedom (Russian Federation)
CDPC	Comité Européen pour les Problèmes Criminels (CE)
CDPE	Comité Directeur pour la Protection et le Gestion de l'Environnement et du Milieu Naturel
CDPH	Centre de Développement du Potential Humain (France)
CDPH	Comité Directeur pour la Conservation Intégrée du Patrimoine Historique
CDPI	Centro de Desarrollo y Productividad Industrial (Guatemala)

CDPO	Comité Européen sur la Population (CE)
CDPP	Christian Democratic People's Party (Hungary)
CDPPP	Centre for Development Planning, Projections and Policies (UN)
CDPR	Constitutional Democratic Party of Russia
CDPS	Centre for Development Planning Studies
CDPT	Centrul de Documentare si Propaganda Technica (Romania)
CDPU	Christian Democratic Party of Ukraine
CDR	Centre de Documentation Rurale
CDR	Centre for Development Research/ Center for Udviklingsforskning (Denmark)
CDR	Centre for Documentation on Refugees (Switzerland)
CDR	Coalition for the Defence of the Republic (Rwanda)
CDR	Comité de Defensa de la Revolución (Cuba)
CDR	Comités pour la Défense de la Révolution (Burkina Faso)
CDR	Conseil Démocratique Révolutionnaire (Chad)
CDR	Conventia Democratica din Romania
CDR	Council for Development and Reconstruction (Lebanon)
CDRA	Canadian Drilling Research Association
CDRB	Canadian Research Defence Board
CDRF	Canadian Dental Research Foundation
CDRI	Central Drug Research Institute (India)
CDRIA	Centre de Développement Rural Intégré pour l'Afrique (FAO)
CDRIAP	Centre de Développement Rural Intégré pour l'Asie et le Pacifique = CIRDAP
CDRL	European Steering Committee on Local and Regional Authorities (France)
CDRM	Comité Directeur pour les Questions Régionales et Municipales (CCE)
CDRS	Committees for the Defence of the Revolution (Ghana)
CDS	Center for Dredging Studies (U.S.A.)
CDS	Central Department of Statistics (Saudi Arabia)
CDS	Centre de Développements Sociaux (New Caledonia)
CDS	Centre de Documentation Sidérurgique
CDS	Centre de Données Stellaires

CDS	Centre des Démocrates Sociaux
CDS	Centre for Defence Studies
CDS	Centre for Development Studies (Ghana, India, U.K.)
CDS	Centro Democrático y Social
CDS	Centrul de Documentare Sciintifica (Romania)
CDS	Comité de Defensa Sandinista (Nicaragua)
CDS	Community Development Society (U.S.A.)
CDS	Conférénce des Directeurs des Écoles Professionnelles et de Métier de la Suisse
CDS	Conselho de Desenvolvimento Social (Brazil)
CDS	Consiglio di Stato
CDS	Cooperative Development Society (Éire)
CDS	Partido do Centro Democrático Social (Portugal)
CDS	Social Democratic Centre Party (France)
CDSC	Coal Dressing Special Council (China)
CDSC	Communicable Disease Surveillance Centre
CDSCC	Canberra Deep Space Communications Complex
CDSCE	Centro di Documentazione e Studi sulle Comunité Europea
CDSH	Centre de Documentation Sciences Humaines
CDSM	Comité sur les Défis de la Société Moderne (OTAN) = CCMS
CDSM	Committee on Dental and Surgical Materials (DOH)
CDSN	Comité Européen pour la Sauvegarde de la Nature et des Ressources Naturelles (CE)
CDSO	Commonwealth Defence Science Organisation
CDSP	Comité Européen de la Santé Publique
CDSP	Compagnie de Dirigeants de Services du Personnel (Belgium) (*now* ADP)
CDSS	Comité Directeur pour la Sécurité Sociale du Conseil de l'Europe (CE)
CDST	Centre de Documentaion Scientifique et Technique (CNRS)
CDSUE	Centro di Documentazione e Studi per l'Unione Europea
CDSVF	Comité de Défense Scientifique du Vin Français
CDT	Central Democrática de Trabajadores (Chile)
CDT	Confédération Démocratique du Travail (Morocco)
CDTC	Confédération Dahoméenne des Travailleurs Croyants
CDTG	Centrale Démocratique des Travailleurs de la Guyane
CDTI	Centro para el Desarrollo Tecnológico e Industrial
CDTPDC	Committee of Development of Technology in Plant Disease Control (China)
CDU	Caribbean Democratic Union
CDU	Christlich-Demokratische Union
CDU	Coligação Democrático Unitária
CDU	Convergencia Democrática en Uruguay
CDU	Croatian Democratic Union (Bosnia-Herzegovina, Croatia) = HDZ
CDU/CSU	Christlich-Demokratische Union / Christlich-Soziale Union (Germany)
CDUBH	Croatian Union of Bosnia and Herzegovina
CDUCE	Christian Democratic Union of Central Europe = UCDEC, UDCEC
CDUP	Committee for the Defense of the Unjustly Prosecuted (U.S.A.)
CDVEC	Curriculum Development Unit (Ireland)
CDVM	Club Dirigenti Vendite e Marketing
CDVPA	Comité Départemental de la Vulgarisation et du Progrès Agricole
CDVTPR	Centre de Documentation du Verre Textile et des Plastiques Renforcés
CDW	Centrum Derde Wereld (Belgium)
CDW	Committee for the Development of Women (St. Vincent)
CDWA	Christian Democratic Women of America (Venezuela) = MUDCA
CDWI	Christian Democratic Workers International (Germany)
CE	Christian Endeavour = CEUGBI
CE	Communautés Européennes = EC, EG (*ex* CEE)
CE	Community Economy
CÉ	Conseil d'État (Belgium, France)
CÉ	Conseil Économique
CE	Council of Europe
CEA	Canadian Education Association
CEA	Canadian Electrical Association
CEA	Canadian Export Association

CEA	Central Electricity Authority
CÉA	Centre d'Économique Alpine
CÉA	Centre de l'Étude de l'Azote
CÉA	Centre des Études Andines (France)
CEA	Centre Est Aéronautique
CÉA	Centres d'Études Architecturales (Belgium)
CEA	Centro de Estudios Africanos (Mozambique)
CEA	Centro de Estudos Agricolas (Brazil)
CÉA	Cercle d'Études Africaines
CEA	Cinematograph Exhibitors Association of Great Britain
CEA	Coal Exporters Association (U.S.A.)
CEA	Combustion Engineering Association
CEA	Comité Européen des Assurances = EAC, EIC
CÉA	Commissariat é l'Énergie Atomique (Belgium, France)
CÉA	Commission de l'Énergie Atomique (UN) = AEC
CÉA	Commission Économique pour l'Afrique (ONU) = CEPA, ECA
CEA	Commission Européenne des Arbitres (Portugal)
CEA	Compañia Ecuatoriana de Aviación
CEA	Confederación de Educadores Americanos
CEA	Confederación de Empresarios de Andalucia
CEA	Confédération Européenne de l'Agriculture (Switzerland)
CEA	Consejo Estatal de Azúcar (Dominican Republic)
CEA	Conservative Education Association
CEA	Coordination des Animaux Européens
CEA	Council for Educational Advance
CEA	Council of Economic Advisers
CEA	Cyriac Elias Voluntary Association (India)
CEAA	Centre Européen d'Aviation Agricole
CEAAL	Consejo de Educación de Adultos de América Latina
CEABH	Centre Eurafricain de Biologie Humaine
CEAC	Centro de Estudos de Antropologia Cultural (Portugal)
CEAC	Comisión de Energía Atómica Cuba
CEAC	Commission Européenne de l'Aviation Civile = ECAC
CEAC	Committee for European Airspace Coordination (NATO)
CEAC	Confédération Européenne des Anciens Combattants
CEAC	Consejo de Electrificacion de America Central
CEACRO	Comisión de Energia Atómica de Costa Rica
CEACS	Centre for East Asian Cultural Studies (Japan)
CEADO	Centro Argentino de Datos Oceanograficos
CEADS	Centro de Educación en Administración de Salud (Colombia)
CEADS	Confédération Européenne des Activités en Déchets Spéciaux
CÉAE	Conseil des Études Africaines en Europe = ECAS
CEAEECT	Chambre Européenne Arbitres Extrajudicaires et des Experts Conseillers Techniques
CÉAÉN	Centre d'Études pour les Applications de l'Énergie Nucléaire
CEAF	Comité Européen des Associations de Fonderies
CÉAI	Cercle d'Échanges Artistiques Internationaux
CEAL	Comité Europe-Amérique Latine (Belgium)
CÉAL	Commission Économique pour l'Amérique Latin (Chile)
CEALCO	Comisión Económica para Asia y Lejano Oriente (U.S.A.)
CEALDO	Comité de Expertos en Ajustes por Lugar de Destino Oficial (UN)
CEALL	Consejo de Educación de Adultos de América Latina
CÉAMP	Centrale d'Équipement Agricole et de Modernisation du Paysannat
CÉAN	Centre d'Étude d'Afrique Noire (France)
CÉAO	Commission Économique pour l'Asie Occidentale (ONU)
CÉAO	Communauté Économique de l'Afrique de l'Ouest (Burkina Faso)
CEAPIR	European Federation of Kidney Patients (Ireland)
CEAR	Comisión Española de Ayuda ad Refugiado
CEARC	Computer Education and Applied Research Centre

CEAS	Centre Écologique Albert Schweitzer (Switzerland)	**CEBCA**	Comisión Ecuatoriana de Bienes de Capital
CEAS	Centro de Estudos e Ação Social (Brazil)	**CEBEA**	Centre d'Étude Burundais des Énergies Alternatives
CEAS	Centro Erboristico Appenninico Sperimentale	**CEBÉA**	Centre Emile Bernheim pour l'Étude des Affaires (Belgium)
CEAS	Citizens' Europe Advisory Service	**CEBECO**	Nationale Coöperatieve Aan- en Verkoopvereniging voor Land- en Tuinbouw
CEAS	Cooperative Educational Abstracting Service (IBE)		
CEASC	Committee for European Airspace Coordination (NATO)	**CEBÉD-AIR**	Centrale Belge d'Études et de Documentation de l'Air
CEASE	Campaign for the Elimination of Acronyms in Scientific Exchange	**CEBÉD-EAU**	Centre Belge d'Étude et de Documentation des Eaux
CEASPA	Centro de Estudios y Acción Social de Panama	**CEBELA**	Centro Brasileiro de Estudos Latino-Americanos
CÉAT	Centre d'Études Aérodynamiques de Toulouse	**CEBEL-COR**	Centre Belge de l'Étude de la Corrosion
CÉAT	Centres d'Études Aérodynamiques et Thermiques	**CEBEMO**	Centrale voor Bemiddeling bij Medefinanciering van Ontwikkelingsprogramma's
CEAT	Coordination Européenne Amis de la Terre (FOEI)		
CEATM	Comité Estatal de Abastecimiento Tecnico Material (Cuba)	**CEBERENA**	Centre Belge de Recherches Navales
		CEBES	Centre for European Business Education Studies
CEB	Central Electricity Board (Mauritius, Malaysia, U.K.)	**CEBETID**	Comité Belge du Tissage et des Industries Textiles Diverses
CÉB	Comité Électrotechnique Belge = BEC	**CEBI**	Centre for European Business Information
CEB	Comité Euro-International du Béton		
CEB	Comité Européen des Constructeurs de Brûleurs	**CEBI**	Comité Européen des Bureaux d'Ingénierie
CEB	Comité Européen du Béton	**CEBI**	Société Forestière Tanoh Affing Louis de Commercialisation et d'Exploitation des Bois Ivoiriens
CÉB	Communauté Électrique Bénin		
CEB	Communauté Européenne des Cuisiniers		
CÉB	Compagnie Équatoriale des Bois (Gabon)	**CEBIAE**	Centro Boliviano de Investigación y Acción Educativas
CEB	Confédération Européenne de Billard	**CEBIS**	Centre for Environment and Business in Scotland
CÉBA	Comité Économique Belgo-Arabe		
CEBA	Confédération Européenne de Baseball Amateur	**CEBITUR**	Centro Brasileiro de Informação Turística
CEBAC	Comisión Especial Brasileño Argentina de Cooperación	**CEBJ**	Commission of Editors of Biochemical Journals
CEBAF	Continuous Electron Beam Accelerator Facility (U.S.A.)	**CEBLS**	Council of EEC Builders of Large Ships
CEBAM	Centre Catholique pour l'Afrique et Madagascar (Kenya) = BICAM	**CEBOSINE**	Centrale Bond van Scheepsbouwmeesters in Nederland
CEBANOR	Comité Régional d'Expansion Économique de la Basse-Normandie	**CEBP**	Association des Organisations Internationales de la Boulangerie, de la Pâtisserie, de la Confiserie, de la Chocolaterie Artisanales de la CEE
CEBAP	Centro de Estudios de Bosques Andino-Patagónicos (Argentina)		
CÉBAS	Centre d'Études Biologiques des Animaux Sauvages	**CEBRACO**	Centro Brasileiro de Informação de Cobre
CEBAS	Centro de Edafologia y Biologia Aplicada del Segura	**CEBRAP**	Centro Brasileiro de Análise e Planejamento

CEBRECNA	Centre Belge de Recherches Navales	**CEC**	Coopération par l'Education et la Culture (Belgium)
CEBS	Centro de Estudios del Bosque Subtropical, La Plata (Argentina)	**CEC**	Coordinación Educativa Centroamericana
CEBSO	Comité d'Expansion Économique Bordeaux Sud-Ouest	**CEC**	Council for Education in the Commonwealth
CÉBSP	Centre d'Étude Belge de Publicité	**CEC**	Council for Exceptional Children (U.S.A.)
CEBTP	Centre Expérimental de Recherches et d'Études du Bâtiment et des Travaux Publics (Algeria)	**CEC**	Fédération Européenne des Fabricants de Carreaux Céramiques
CEBUCO	Centraal Bureau voor Courantenpubliciteit van de Nederlandse Dagbladpers	**CECA**	Committee of European Coffee Associations
CÉBV	Communauté Économique du Bétail et de la Viande (Africa) = ECLM	**CECA**	Communauté Européenne du Charbon et de l'Acier = ECSC, EGKS, EKSG
CEC	Canada Employment Centre	**CECA**	Compagnie d'Exploitation des Carrières (Ivory Coast)
CEC	Caribbean Employers Confederation	**CECA**	Confederación Española de Cajas de Ahorro
CEC	Caribbean Examinations Council (Barbados)	**CECA**	Cyprus Employers Consultative Organisation
CEC	Catholic Education Council		
CEC	Central Executive Committee (PAP) (Singapore)	**CECA-GADIS**	Compagnie d'Exploitations Commerciales Africaines – Société Gabonaise de Distribution
CÉC	Centre d'Études du Commerce	**CECADE**	Centro de Capitación para el Desarrollo (Mexico)
CEC	Centre Européen de la Culture = ECC		
CEC	Centre for Economic Cooperation (UN)	**CECAF**	Committee for the Eastern Central Atlantic Fisheries (FAO) = COPACE, CPACE, CPACO
CEC	Cercle Européen de la Courtoisie		
CEC	Clarence Environment Centre	**CECAL**	Commission Episcopale de Coopération Apostolique Canada-Amérique Latine
CEC	Co-ordinating European Council for the Development of Performance Tests for Lubricants and Engine Fuels	**CECAPI**	Commission Européenne des Constructeurs d'Appareillage Électrique d'Installations
CEC	Collectif Européen de la Conscientisation		
CEC	Collectif Européen de la Culture	**CECAS**	Conference of East and Central African States
CEC	Comité Européen du Course	**CECAT**	Centre for Agricultural Education and Cooperation (Italy)
CEC	Commission Européenne des Industries de la Corsetrie	**CECATI**	Centros de Capacitación para el Trabajo Industrial (Mexico)
CEC	Commission of the European Communities = CCE	**CECAVI**	Confédération Européenne des Catégories Auxiliaires des Activités Viti-Vinicoles
CEC	Commission on Education and Communication		
CEC	Commonwealth Economic Committee	**CECC**	CENELEC Electronic Components Committee (EC) (Germany)
CEC	Commonwealth Education Cooperation		
CEC	Commonwealth Engineers Council	**CECC**	Communauté Européenne des Coopératives de Consummateurs = EMCC
CEC	Communauté Européenne des Cuisiniers		
CEC	Confédération Européenne de l'Industrie de la Chaussure	**CÉCC**	Compagnie d'Élevage et de Cultures du Caméroun
CEC	Confédération Européenne des Cadres	**CECC**	Coordinadora Educativa y Cultural Centroamericana (Nicaragua)
CEC	Conference of European Churches = CEE, KEC, KEK		
CEC	Consejo Economico Centroamericana (MCCA)		

CECCB	Chambres des Experts-Comptable et des Comptables de Belgique
CECCG	Confédération Européenne du Commerce de la Chaussure en Gros
CECCM	Confederation of European Community Cigarette Manufacturers (Belgium)
CECD	Confédération Européenne du Commerce de Détail
CECDC	Committee on Economic Cooperation among Developing Countries (UN)
CECE	Comisión Especial para la Formulación de Nuevas Medidas de Cooperation Económica Internacional
CECE	Comité Estatal de Colaboracion Economica (Cuba)
CECE	Comité Européen pour la Communication sur l'Environnement = ECEC
CECE	Committee for European Construction Equipment
CECÉC	Communauté Européenne Culturelle des Étudiants en Chimie
CECÉD	Conseil Européen de la Construction Électro-Domestique
CECF	China Export Commodities Fair
CECF	Commission Européenne des Communes Forestières et Communes de Montagne
CECG	Confédération Européenne du Commerce de la Chaussure en Gros (Belgium)
CECG	Consumers in the European Community Group
CECH	Comité Européen de la Culture du Houblon = EHGC
CÉCI	Centre d'Étude de Cooperation Internationale (Canada)
CECI	Centre Européen de Coopération Internationale (France) = ECIC
CECI	Centre Européen du Commerce International
CECI	Centro Empresarial de Comercio Internacional, S.A. (Costa Rica)
CECIF	Chambre Européenne pour le Développement du Commerce, de l'Industrie et des Finances
CECIMO	Comité Européen de Cooperation des Industries de la Machine-Outil (Belgium)
CECINE	Centro de Ensino de Ciencias do Nordeste (Brazil)
CECIOS	Conseil Européen du Comité International de l'Organisation Scientifique
CECIOS	European Council of Management
CECIP	Comité Européen des Constructeurs d'Instruments de Pesage
CECIRNA	Centro de Coordinación de Investigaciones de Recursos Naturales y su Aplicacion (Argentina)
CECLA	Comité Especial de Coordinación Latinoamericana
CECLB	Comité Européen de Contrôle Laitier-Beurrier
CECM	Convention Européenne de la Construction Métallique = ECCS, EKS
CECMA	Comité Européen des Constructeurs de Matériel Aéraulique
CÉCMAS	Centre d'Études des Communications de Masse
CECO	Centro de Estudios Costeira e Oceanica
CECOAP	Central de Cooperativas Agrarias de Produccion Azucarera del Peru
CECOCO	Chuo Boeki Goshi Kaisha (Central Commercial Co) (Japan)
CECOD	Comité de Fabricants Européens d'Installation et de Distribution de Pétrole
CECODE	Centre de Coopération au Développement (Belgium)
CECODE	Centre Européen du Commerce de Détail
CECODEC	Conseil Européen des Constructeurs de Cuisine
CECODHA	Comité Européen des Coopératives d'Habitation (Belgium)
CECODHAS	Comité Européen de Coordination de l'Habitat Social (Germany)
CECOF	Comité Européen des Constructeurs de Fours et d'Équipements Thermiques Industriels
CECOLDO	Centro Colombiano de Datos Oceanigraficos
CECOLFES	Centro Colombiano de Fertilidad y Esterilidad
CECOM	Central European Mass Communication Research Documentation Centre (Poland)
CECOMA	Confédération Européenne des Commerces de Mobilier, Machines de Bureau et Accessoires

CECOMAF	Comité Européen des Constructeurs de Matériel Frigorifique
CECON	Centre for Conservation Studies
CECON	Special Committee for Consultation and Negotiation (IA-ECOSOC) (U.S.A.)
CECOP	Centro de Comunicacion Popular (Panama)
CECOP	Comité Européen des Coopératives de Production et de Travail Associé
CECORA	Central de Cooperativas de Reforma Agraria (Colombia)
CECOTOS	Comité Européen de Coordination du Tourisme Social
CECOTRAD	Centrale d'Education et de Coopération des Travailleurs pour le Développement (Rwanda)
CECPA	Comité Européen du Commerce des Produits Amylacés et Dérivés
CECPI	Commission Européenne Consultative pour les Pêches dans les Eaux Intérieures = EIFAC
CÉCPRA	Centre d'Études de la Commission Permanente du Risque Atomique
CECRA	Comité Européen du Commerce et de la Réparation Automobiles (Belgium)
CECRI	Central Electrochemical Research Institute (India)
CECS	Centro de Estudios Científicos de Santiago
CECSA	Compania Exportadora de Cafe, S.A. (Honduras)
CECSA	Compañia Editorial Continental S.A. (Mexico)
CECT	Coleccion Española de Cultivos Tipo
CECT	Comité Européen de la Chaudronnerie et Tuyauterie
CECTAL	Centre for English Cultural Tradition and Language
CECTK	Committee for Electro-Chemical Thermodynamics and Kinetics (Belgium)
CECUA	Conference of European Computer User Association
CED	Centre Européen de Documentation Internationale
CED	Centro de Esploro Kaj Dokumentado pri la Monda Lingvo-Problemo (U.K.)
CED	Centro de Estudios del Desarrollo (Chile)
CED	Committee for Economic Development (U.S.A.)
CED	Confédération Européenne de la Droguerie
CÉDA	Caisse d'Équipement pour le Développement de l'Algérie
CEDA	Canadian Electrical Distributors Association
CEDA	Catering Equipment Distributors Association
CEDA	Central Dredging Association (Netherlands)
CEDA	Centre d'Edition et de Diffusion Africaines (Ivory Coast)
CEDA	Centre for Economic Development and Administration (Nepal)
CEDA	China Enterprise Director Association
CEDA	Chinese Exploration and Design Association
CEDA	Committee for the Economic Development of Australia
CEDA	Consumer Electronics Distributors' Association (Éire)
CEDADE	Cercle Européen des Amis de l'Europe
CEDADE	Circulo Ecuatoriano de Amigos de Europa
CEDADE	Circulo Español de Amigos de Europa
CÉDAF	Centre d'Étude et de Documentation Africaine (Belgium) = ASDOC
CÉDAG	Centre d'Études et de Diffusion de l'Agriculture de Groupe
CEDAG	Comité Européen des Associations d'Intérêt Général
CEDAL	Centro de Estudios Democráticos de América Latina (Costa Rica)
CEDAM	Casa Editrice Dott. Antonio Milani
CEDAM	Conservation, Explorations, Diving, Archaeology, Museums (U.S.A.)
CÉDAMEL	Centre d'Études et de Distribution des Appareils et du Matériel de l'Enseignement Linguistique
CEDAN	Conférence Européenne des Associations Nationales de Relations Publiques (CERP)
CÉDAOM	Centre d'Étude et de Documentation sur l'Afrique et l'Outre-Mer
CEDAP	Centro de Desarrollo de Administration Pública (Guatemala)
CEDAP	Comité Européen d'Application et de Développement des Relations Publiques (CERP)
CEDAR	Central European Data Request Facility
CEDAR	Centre for Educational Development, Appraisal & Research

CEDAR	Council for Educational Development and Research (U.S.A.)	**CEDEP**	Centro de Estudios para el Desarrollo y la Participacion (Peru)
CEDARS	Center for Entrepreneurial Development, Advancement, Research and Support (U.S.A.)	**CEDEP**	Centro de Pesquisas e Desenvolvimento (Brazil)
CEDATOS	Centro de Estudios y Datos	**CEDEP-LAR**	Centro de Desenvolvimento e Planejamento Regional, Belo Horizonte (Brazil)
CEDAW	Committee on the Elimination of Discrimination Against Women (UN) (Austria)	**CEDER**	Center for Environmental Design Education and Research (U.S.A.)
CEDB	Central Engineering and Design Bureau	**CÉDÉS**	Centre d'Étude du Développement Économique et Social (Morocco)
CEDC	Committee on Economic Cooperation among Developing Countries (UN)	**CEDES**	Centre d'Etudes Demographiques et Sociales (Mauritania)
CEDC	Community Education Development Centre	**CEDES**	Centro de Estudios de Estado y Sociedad, Buenos Aires (Argentina)
CEDDA	Centre for Experiment Design and Data Analysis (NOAA)	**CEDES**	Centro de Estudos de Educação e Sociedade, São Paulo (Brazil)
CEDDU	Centro de Estudios Demográficos y de Desarrollo Urbano (Mexico)	**CÉDÉS**	Corps Européen de Développement Économique et Social (Belgium)
CEDE	Centro de Estudios sobre Desarrollo Económico (Colombia)	**CEDESA**	Centre de Documentation en Sciences Sociales de l'Afrique (Belgium)
CEDE	Centro Europeo dell'Educazione (Italy)	**CEDÉSÉ**	Communauté Européenne des Étudiants en Sciences Économiques
CEDE	Conseil Européen du Droit de l'Environnement	**CEDH**	Convention Européenne des Droits de l'Homme
CEDE	European Council on Environmental Law	**CEDHAL**	Centro de Estudos de Demografía Historica da America Latina (Brazil)
CÉDÉAO	Communauté Économique des États de l'Afrique de l'Ouest = ECOWAS	**CEDI**	Centro Ecuménico de Documentação, São Paulo (Brazil)
CEDEC	Centro de Estudios de Cultura Contemporanea (Brazil)	**CEDI**	Confédération Européenne des Indépéndants
CEDEC	Confederacion Evangelica de Colombia	**CÉDIA**	Centre d'Études pour l'Extension des Débouchés Industriels de l'Agriculture
CEDECANI	Centro para el Desarrollo de la Capacidad Nacional de Investigaciones (Panama)	**CEDIA**	Centro de Estudio, Documentación e Información de Africa (Spain)
CEDEFOP	Centre Européen pour le Développement de la Formation Professionnelle	**CEDIA**	Comité Européen des Ingénieurs Agronomes de la CEE
CEDEFOP	European Centre for the Development of Vocational Training (EU)	**CEDIAL**	Centro de Estudios para el Desarrollo e Integración de América Latina
CEDEFT	Experimental Centre for the Development of Technical Training (Mexico)	**CÉDIAS**	Centre d'Études, de Documentation, d'Information et d'Action Sociales
CEDEIN	Centre Européen de Documentation et d'Information	**CEDIC**	Centro Española de Información de Cobre
CEDEL	Centro de Estudios Laborales (Argentina)	**CEDIC**	Comité Européen des Ingénieurs-Conseils du Marché Commun
CEDEM	Centro de Estudios para el Desarrollo de la Mujer (Chile)	**CEDIE**	Centro de Documentación e Investigación Educativa, Universidad Católica Madre y Maestra (Dominican Republic)
CEDEM	Centro para el Desarrollo de la Mujer (Panama)		
CEDÉP	Centre Européen d'Éducation Permanente (France)	**CÉDIES**	Centre d'Études, de Documentations et d'Informations Économiques et Sociales (Morocco)
CEDEP	Centro de Educación Popular (Ecuador)		

CEDIF	Compagnie Européenne pour le Développement Industriel et Financier (Belgium)
CEDIJ	Centre d'Information Juridique
CÉDIM	Centre d'Études de Droit International Médical
CÉDIM	Comité d'Études pour le Développement de l'Industrie Morutière
CEDIM	Comité Européen des Fédérations Nationales de la Maroquinerie, Articles de Voyages et Industries Connexes
CEDIMAR	Centro de Documentación e Información en Ciencias del Mar
CEDIME	Centro de Documentacion e Investigacion del Movimiento Social Ecuatoriano
CÉDIMÉS	Centre d'Études du Développement International et des Mouvements Économiques et Sociaux
CEDIMEX	Société Centrafricaine de Distribution-Importation-Exportation
CEDIMO	Centro Nacional de Documentação e Informação de Moéambique
CEDIP	Centro de Estudos de Dinamica Populacional (Brazil)
CEDIPAZ	Centro Internacional de Documentacion e Informacion para la Paz (Costa Rica)
CEDIS	Conferencia Española de Institútos Secularos
CEDITEC	Centro de Informacion Tecnica de la Construccion – Camaguey (Cuba)
CÉDJ	Centre d'Étude de la Délinquance Juvénile (Belgium)
CÉDLA	Centre d'Études et de Documentation Legislatives Africaines
CEDLA	Centro de Estudios y Documentación Latinoamericanos
CEDO	Centre for Educational Development Overseas (U.S.A.)
CEDO	Centro Español de Datos Oceanograficos
CEDOC	Centrale Dienst voor Onderwis- en Cultuurfilms
CEDOC	Centre Belge de Documentation et d'Information de la Construction
CEDOC	Centro de Documentación Cientifica (Argentina)
CEDOC	Confederación Ecuatoriana de Organizaciónes Clasistas
CEDOC-LI/ NETWORK	Network of Children's and Juvenile Literature Documentation Centers
CEDOCAR	Centre de Documentation de l'Armements
CEDOCOS	Centre de Documentation sur les Combustibles Solides (Belgium)
CEDODEC	Centre d'Études et de Documentation sur le Développement Culturel (Tunisia)
CEDOI	Episcopal Conference of the Indian Ocean (Reunion)
CEDOLASI	Centro Ecumenico de Documentacion Latinoamericana Sistematizada (Mexico)
CEDOM	Centre of Documentation and Teaching Materials (Peru)
CEDOPEX	Centro Dominicano de Promoción de Exportaciones
CÉDOPI	Centre d'Études Documentaires de Propriété Industrielle
CEDOR	Centre Démographique (ONU)
CEDORES	Centre de Documentation et de Recherche Sociales (Belgium)
CÉDP	Centre d'Études et de Documentation Paléontologique
CEDP	Centre Européen du Diamant et des Pierres Précieuses
CEDR	Centre For Dispute Resolution
CEDR	Comité Européen de Droit Rural
CEDR	Conference on Electron Device Research
CEDRA-SEMI	Centre de Documentation et de Recherches sur l'Asie du Sud-Est et le Monde Insulindien
CÉDRE	Centre d'Études de Documentation, de Recherche et d'Experimentation
CEDRE	Centre Européen du Développement Régional
CEDREFI	Centre de Documentation de Recherches et de Formation Indien Océaniques (Mauritius)
CEDRES	Centro di Documentazione e Ricerche Economiche e Sociali
CÉDRI	Centre d'Études et de Développement des Relations Internationales
CEDRI	Comité Européen pour la Défense des Refugiés
CÉDRIC	Centre d'Études de Documentation et de Recherches pour l'Industrie du Chauffage, du Conditionnement d'Air et des Branches Connexes
CEDSA	Centro de Documentación del Sector Agrario (Peru)
CÉDSI	Centre d'Études et de Défence de Sécurité International (France)
CEdT	Comité Européen du Thé

CEDT	Confédération Européenne des Organisations des Detaillants en Tabacs		**CEÉAS**	Centre Européen d'Études de l'Acide Sulfurique
CEDTA	Compania Ecuatoriana de Transportes Aéreos		**CEEBA**	Centre d'Études Ethnologiques de Bandundu (Zaïre)
CEDTT	Committee for Economic Development of Trinidad and Tobago		**CEEBIC**	Central and Eastern Europe Business Information Center
CEDUCEE	Centre d'Études et de Documentation sur l'URSS, la Chine, et l'Europe de l'Est (France)		**CEEC**	Comisión Episcopal de Evangelizacion y Catequesis (Peru)
CÉDUS	Centre d'Études et de Documentation pour L'Utilisation du Sucre		**CEÉC**	Comité Européen des Économistes de la Construction
CÉDVAR	Centre National d'Études, de Documentation, de Vulgarisation Technique de l'Artisanat Rural		**CEEC**	Comité Européen pour l'Enseignement Catholique
CEDYS	Centro de Estudios de Democracia y Sociedad (Peru)		**CÉÉC**	Commission Épiscopale pour l'École Catholique (Libya)
CEE	Centro de Estudios Educativos (Mexico)		**CEÉCO**	Comité d'Expansion Économique du Centre-Ouest
CEE	Comisión Estatal Electoral (Mexico)		**CEED**	Center for Entrepreneurship and Economic Development (U.S.A.)
CEE	Comité Estatal de Estadisticas (Cuba)		**CEED**	Centro de Estudios Económicos y Demográficos (Mexico)
CEE	Comité Européen d'Enterprise (CCE) = EBR		**CEEDI**	China Electronics Engineering Design Institute
CÉE	Commission Économique pour l'Europe (ONU) = CEPE, ECE, EEK		**CÉEDIA**	Centre d'Études pour l'Extension des Débouchés Industriels de l'Agriculture
CÉÉ	Commission Internationale de Réglementation en vue de l'Approbation de l'Équipement Électrique		**CEEE**	Centro de Estudios en Economia y Educacion (Mexico)
CÉE	Communauté Économique Européenne = EEC, EOF, EOK, EWG, MCE (*now* CE)		**CÉEEBA**	Centre d'Études Ethnologiques de Bandundu (Zaïre)
CÉE	Conférence des Églises Européennes = CEC, KEK		**CEEG**	Comité Européen pour l'Egalité des Chances entre les Femmes et les Hommes
CEE	Conference on English Education (U.S.A.)		**CÉÉGFP**	Centre d'Études d'Économie et de Gestion de la Forêt Privée
CEE	Council for Environmental Education		**CEÉH**	Centre Européen d'Écologie Humaine (Switzerland) = ECHE
CEE	International Commission for Conformity of Certification of Electrical Equipment (U.S.A.)		**CEELA**	Centro Experimental de Estudios Latinoamericanos (Venezuela)
CEEA	Centre Européen pour l'Étude de l'Argumentation (Belgium)		**CEEMA**	Centro de Ensenanza y Experimentación de la Maquinaria Agricola (Argentina)
CEEA	Centro de Estudios para Empressas Agricolas (Chile)		**CEEMA**	Committee for Engineering Education of Middle Africa (Nigeria)
CEEA	Centro de Estudos de Economia Agraria		**CEEMA**	Conférence Européenne des Experts Metéorologistes de l'Aeronautique
CEÉA	Communauté Européenne de l'Énergie Atomique (Euratom) = EAEC, EAG, EGA		**CEEMAC**	Certification of Electrical Equipment for Mining, Advisory Council (HSE)
CEEA	Confederation of European Economic Asociations		**CÉEMAT**	Centre d'Études et d'Expérimentation du Machinisme Agricole Tropical
CÉÉAC	Communauté Économique des États de l'Afrique Centrale = ECCAS		**CEÉN**	Centre Européen d'Études Nucleaires = NERC
			CEEOC	Commonwealth Equal Employment Opportunity Council

CEÉP	Centre Européen d'Études de Population = ECPS
CEEP	Centre Européen de l'Entreprise Publique
CEÉP	Confédération Européene d'Études de Phytopharmacie
CEEPP	Central and East European Publishing Project
CÉÉPPA	Centre d'Études Économiques pour les Produits Agricoles
CEÉPS	Communauté Européenne de l'Éducation Physique Scolaire
CEERA	Conférence Européenne des Experts Radiotélégraphistes de l'Aeronautique
CEERI	Central Electronics Engineering Research Institute (India)
CEES	Center for Energy and Environmental Studies (U.S.A.)
CEES	Center for Environmental and Estuarine Studies (U.S.A.)
CÉES	Centre d'Étude de Silicates (Belgium)
CEÉS	Comité Européen d'Étude du Sel = ECSS
CEESAC	Central and East European Studies Association of Canada = AEECEEC
CEESP	Centro de Estudios Economicos del Sector Privado (Mexico)
CEESTM	Centros Estudios Económicos y Sociales del Tercer Mundo (Mexico)
CÉÉT	Compagnie Énergie Électrique du Togo
CÉETA	Centre d'Étude et d'Expérimentation des Technologies Appropriées (Zaire)
CEÉTB	Comité Européen des Équipements Techniques du Bâtiment
CEF	Caixa Económica Federal (Brazil)
CEF	Campaign for Earth Federation (Malta)
CEF	Central European Federalists
CEF	Centre for Economic Forecasting
CEF	Centro de Estudios Filosóficos (Nicaragua)
CEF	Child Evangelism Fellowship (U.S.A.)
CEF	Childbirth Education Foundation (U.S.A.)
CEF	Circulo de Estudio Feminista (Dominican Republic)
CEF	College Employers Forum
CEF	Comité Estatal de Finanzas (Cuba)
CEF	Commission Européenne des Forêts = EFC
CEF	Conservation des Eaux et Forêts
CEF	Construction Employers' Federation (*ex* FBCEC)
CEF	Coordination Européenne des Femmes = ENOW
CEFA	Centro de Estudos de Fitosanidade do Armazenamento (Portugal)
CEFA	Comitatio Europeo di Formazione Agraria
CEFAC	Centre de Formations des Assistants Techniques du Commerce et des Consultants Commerciaux
CEFACD	Comité Européen des Fabricants d'Appareils de Chauffage et de Cuisine Domestique
CEFAT	European Centre for Professional Training in Environment and Tourism
CÉFB	Centre d'Études des Fontes de Bâtiment
CEFCA	Centre Française de Co-opération Agricole
CEFD	Centro de Estudios de Filosofíca del Derecho (Venezuela)
CEFDI	Compagnie d'Exploitation Forestière de Divo (Ivory Coast)
CEFEC	Confederation of European Firms, Employment Initiatives and Cooperatives for Psychically Disabled
CEFEMINA	Centro Feminista de Informacion y Acción (Costa Rica)
CEFER	DQ Agrupamento de Processos Químicos (Brazil)
CEFF	Confederation of English Fly Fishers
CEFIC	Conseil Européen des Fédérations de l'Industrie Chimique
CEFIF	Centre Européen du Conseil International des Femmes = ECICW
CEFIGRE	Centre de Formation Internationale pour la Gestion des Resources en Eau = ITCWRM
CEFIR	Training Centre for Regional Integration
CEFISEM	Centre de Formation et d'Information des Personnels concernés par la Scolarisation des Enfants de Migrants
CEFISTO	Centralförbundet för Finlands Svenska Teaterorganisationer (Finland)
CEFMR	Campaign To End Fraudulent Medical Research
CEFNO-MEX	Centro de Estudios Fronterizos del Norte de México
CEFOBI	Centro de Estudios Fotosintéticos y Bioquimicos (Argentina)
CEFPA	Centre Evangelique de Formation et de Production Artisanale (Central African Republic)

CEFPA	Centre for Population Activities (U.S.A.)
CEFRACOR	Centre Français de la Corrosion
CEFRÉS	Centre Européen Féminin de Recherche sur l'Évolution de la Société
CEFS	Centro de Estudio y Formacion Sindical (Argentina)
CEFS	Comité Européen des Fabricants de Sucre
CEFTRI	Central Food Technological Research Institute (India)
CEFV	Centro de Estudios del Futuro de Venezuela
CEG	Catholic Evidence Guild
CÉG	Centre d'Études de Gramat (DTAT)
CEG	Consumers in Europe Group
CEGA-GADIS	Compagnie d'Exploitations Commerciales Africaines, Société Gabonaise de Distribution
CEGAM	Confédération Européenne des Grandes Associations Musicales
CEGAN	Committee of High-Level Government Experts (ECLAC)
CEGAP	Comité Européen des Architectes Paysagistes
CEGAT	Centro de Estudios Ganaderos de Areas Tropicales (Argentina)
CEGB	Central Electricity Generating Board
CEGEP	Collége d'Enseignement Générale et Professionel (Canada)
CÉGÉT	Centre d'Études de Géographie Tropicale
CEGOC	Centro de Estudos de Gestão e Organização Cientifica (Portugal)
CÉGOS	Commission d'Études Générales de l'Organisation Scientifique
CEGROB	Communauté Européenne des Associations du Commerce de Gros Bière des Pays Membres de la CEE
CEGS	China Engineering Graphics Society
CEH	Centre on Environment for the Handicapped
CEH	Centro de Estudios Hidrograficos
CEH	Conférence Européenne des Horaires des Trains de Voyageurs = EFK
CEHA	Regional Centre for Environmental Health Activities (EMRO)
CEHI	Caribbean Environmental Health Institute (St. Lucia)
CEHILA	Comisión de Estudios de Historia de la Iglesia en America Latina
CEHMN	Collège Européen d'Hygiène et de Médecine Naturelles (Belgium)
CEHO	Compagnie Centrafricaine d'Exploitation Hôtelière
CEHP	Comité Européen de l'Hospitalisation Privée
CEHS	Canadian Economic History Society
CEHSMO	Centro de Estudios Historicos del Movimiento Obrero (Mexico)
CEI	Central European Initiative
CÉI	Centre d'Études Industrielles (Switzerland)
CEI	Centre for Education in International Management (Switzerland)
CEI	Centre for Environmental Information
CEI	Centre for Environmental Initiatives
CEI	Centre for Environmental Interpretation
CEI	Comitato Elettrotecnico Italiano
CEI	Comité Español de Iluminación
CEI	Commission Électrotechnique Internationale = IEC
CEI	Commission Europe de l'IOMTR = IEK
CEI	Committee for Environmental Information (UN)
CEI	Communauté des Etats Indépandants; Comunidad de Estados Independientes = CIS, GUS, SNG, WNP
CEI	Compagnia Editrice Italiana
CEI	Conference of the Electronics Industry
CEI	Cycling Engineers' Institute
CEI-Bois	Confédération Européenne des Industries du Bois
CEIA	Centre d'Entr'aide Intellectuelle Africaine
CEIA	Comité Especial de Investigaciones Antárticas
CEIA	Confédération Européenne d'Ingénieurs d'Agriculture = AEFA, FAVE
CÉIA	Coopérative d'Élevage et d'Insémination Artificielle
CEIBA	Corporacion Editorial Iberoamericana (Colombia)
CEIC	Centro Europeo d'Iniziative Culturali
CÉIC	Conseil Économique International du Cuir
CEICN	Centre Européen d'Information pour la Conservation de la Nature
CEIDER	Centro de Estudios y Desarrollo Rural
CÉIE	Centre d'Études et d'Information sur l'Enseignement

CEIF	Conseil des Fédérations Industrielles d'Europe = CFIE, REI
CEIF	Council of European Industrial Federations
CEIG	Christian Ethical Investment Group
CEIIC	Centro Estudiantil Internacional de Investigacion Cientifica (IUS) = CEIR, ISRC
CEIL	Centro de Estudios de Investigaciones Laborales (Argentina)
CÉIM	Centre d'Études Industrielles du Maghreb (Morocco)
CEIM	Conservative Evangelicals in Methodism
CEIN	Centril Experimental pentru Ingrasaminte Bacteriene (Romania)
CEINAR	Centro de Estudios Internacional Argentinos
CEIP	Carnegie Endowment for International Peace (U.S.A.)
CÉIPA	Comité d'Études et d'Informations sur les Produits Agricoles
CÉIPI	Centre d'Études Internationales de la Propriété Industrielle (France)
CEIR	Centre Étudiant International de Recherche (IUS) = CEIIC, ISRC
CEIR	Comité Européen de l'Industrie de la Robinetterie
CEIS	Caribbean Energy Information System (Jamaica)
CEIS	Centre for European Industrial Studies
CEIS	Centro de Investigaciones Sociales (Peru)
CEISA	Customs & Excise Indoor Staff Association (Éire)
CEISAL	Consejo Europeo de Investigaciones Sociales sobre América Latina
CEIST	Centro Europeo Informazione Scientifiche e Tecniche (Italy)
CEIT	Centro de Estudios e Investigaciones Tecnicas de Guipuzcoa
CÉITJA	Centre d'Étude Internationale sur le Travail des Jeunes dans l'Agriculture
CEJ	Centre Européen de la Jeunesse (CE) = EYC
CEJ	Confederación Española de Organizaciones de Empresarios del Juego
CEJ	Confédération Européenne du Jouet
CEJA	Conseil Européen des Jeunes Agriculteurs
CEJH	Communauté Européenne des Jeunes de l'Horticulture
CEKOM	Central European Mass Communication Research Documentation Centre
CEL	Centro Español de Logistica
CEL	China Esperanto-Ligo
CEL	Christian Ecology Link
CEL	Comisión Ejecutiva Hidroeléctrica del Río Lempa (El Salvador)
CEL	Commission on Environmental Law
CEL	Committee on Engineering Laws (U.S.A.)
CEL	Conseil Européen des Loisirs
CELA	Canadian Environmental Law Association
CELA	Centro Estudios Latinoamericanos (Mexico)
CELAC	Centre de Recherche et de Contrôle Lainier et Chimique
CÉLAC	Comité d'Études et de Liaison des Amendements Calcaires
CELAC	Committee for Exports to Latin America and the Caribbean (BNEC)
CELAD	Comité Européen de Lutte Antidrogue (Belgium)
CELADE	Centro Latinoamericano de Demograféa (Costa Rica)
CELADEC	Comisión Evangélica Latinoamérica de Educación Cristiana
CELAM	Consejo Episcopal Latino-Americano (Colombia)
CELAME	Comité de Liaison et d'Action des Syndicats Médicaux Européens
CELAP	Centro Latinoamericano de Población y Familia (Chile)
CÉLAT	Center for the Study of the Language, Art, and Culture of Francophones in North America (Canada)
CÉLAT	Centre d'Études sur la Langue, les Arts et les Traditions Populaires des Francophones en Amerique du Nord (Canada)
CELATS	Centro Latinoamericano de Trabajo Social
CELC	Commonwealth Education Liaison Committee
CELC	Fondation pour les Centres Européens Langues et Civilisations
CELCA	Centro Latinoamericano de Crédito Agricola (Mexico)

CELCAA	Comité Européen de Liaison des Commerces Agro-Alimentaires	**CELS**	Centre for European Legal Studies
CELCA-DEL	Centro Latinoamericano de Capacitacion y Desarrollo de los Gobiernos Locales (IULA)	**CELS**	Coalition for Education in the Life Sciences
CELCIT	Centro Latinoamericano de Creación e Ivestigación Teatral (Venezuela)	**CELSA**	Compania Ecuatoriana de Lubricantes S.A.
CELE	Centre for English Language Education	**CELT**	Centre for English Language Teaching
CELE	Centro Coordinamento Elettronica	**CELTA**	Centre de Linguistique Théorique et Appliquée (Zaire)
CELEH	Centro Latinamericano de Estadísticas Habitacionales	**CELTÉ**	Constructeurs Européens de Locomotives Thermiques et Électriques
CELEP	Latin American Evangelical Center for Pastoral Studies	**CELTS**	Centre for Leisure & Tourism Studies
CELESA	Centro de Exportación de Libros Españoles	**CELU**	Commonwealth Education Liaison Unit
CELETR-AMAZON	Centrais Electricas do Amazonas S.A. (Brazil)	**CÉLZA**	Cultures et Élevages du Zaïre
CÉLF	Centre d'Études Littéraires Francophones (France)	**CEM**	Centre d'Essais de la Méditerrannée
CÉLHTO	Centre d'Études Linguistiques et Historique par la Tradition Orale (Niger)	**CEM**	Centre for Environmental Mechanics (CSIRO)
CELI-BRIDE	Comité de Liaison Internationale des Broderies, Rideaux et Dentelles	**CEM**	Centro de Estudios para la Mujer
CÉLIB	Comité d'Études et de Liaison des Intérêts Bretons	**CEM**	Christian Education Movement
CELICA	Comité Européen de Liason des Cadres de l'Agriculture	**CEM**	Comité Européen sur les Migrations
CELiège	Confédération Européenne du Liège	**CEM**	Comité Exterior Mapuche
CÉLIHM	Comité d'Études et de Liaison Interprofessionnel de la Haute-Marne	**CEM**	Compagnie des Experts Maritimes et en Transports
CELIM	Comité Européen Lex Informatica Mercatoriaque	**CEM**	Confederación Evangélica Mundial = WEC, WEK
CELIMAC	Comité Européen de Liaison des Industries de la Machine à Coudre	**CEM**	Confédération Européenne de Maires
CELLU-CAM	Société Cellulose du Caméroun	**CEM**	Conférence Européenne des Horaires des Trains de Marchandises = EGK, EGTTC
CELME	Centro Sperimentale Lavorazione Metalli	**CEM**	Council of European Municipalities = CCE, RGE
CELNUCO	Comité Européen de Liaison des Négociants et Utilisateurs de Combustibles	**CEM**	Croisade d'Evangélisation Mondiale = CPM, WECI, WEF, WEK
CELOS	Centrum voor Landbouwkundig Onderzoek in Suriname	**CEM**	Curriculum, Evaluation & Management Centre
CELPA	Centro Espacial de Lanzamientos para la Prospección Atmosferica (Argentine)	**CEM-CI**	Compagnie des Experts Maritimes de Côte-d'Ivoire
CELPAP	Entreprise Nationale de Cellulose et de Papier (Algeria)	**CEM-BUREAU**	European Cement Association
CÉLPUF	Comité d'Études de Liaison du Patronat de l'Union Française	**CEMA**	Canadian Egg Marketing Agency
CÉLRA	Conférence des Évêques Latins dans les Régions Arabes (Israel)	**CEMA**	Canadian Electrical Manufacturers Association
		CEMA	Catering Equipment Manufacturers Association
		CÉMA	Centre d'Études et de Modernisation Agricoles
		CEMA	Centre for Education Management & Administration
		CEMA	Centro de Enlace para el Medio Ambiente (Kenya)
		CEMA	China Enterprise Management Association

CEMA	Cleaning Equipment Manufacturers Association (U.S.A.)	**CEMEC**	Centro Europeo per la Medicina della Catastrofi
CEMA	Comité Européen des Groupements de Constructeurs de Machinisme Agricole	**CEMEC**	Committee of European Associations of Manufacturers of Electronic Components
CÉMA	Comité pour l'Étude des Maladies et de l'Alimentation du Bétail (Belgium)	**CEMEDA**	Centro Multinacional de Educación de Adultos (Costa Rica)
CEMAA	Special Commission for the Amazonian Environment	**CEMEDETO**	Centro de Mejora y Demostración de las Técnicas Oleicolas (Spain)
CEMAFON	Comité Européen des Matérials et Produits de la Fonderie	**CEMENCO**	Liberia Cement Corporation
CÉMAG	Centre d'Étude de la Mécanisation en Agriculture de Gembloux (Belgium)	**CEMEN-TERA**	Fábrica Nacional de Cemento (Nicaragua)
CEMA-GREF	Centre National du Machinisme Agricole, du Génie Rural, des Eaux et des Forêts	**CEMEP**	European Committee of Manufacturers of Electrical Machines and Power Electronics
CEMAP	Commission Européenne des Méthodes d'Analyse des Pesticides	**CEMF**	Chambre Syndicale des Editeurs de Musique
CEMARSA	Centro de Maquinaria y Repuestos, S.A. (El Salvador)	**CEMI**	China-Europe Management Institute
CEMAT	Centre for Maghribi Studies in Tunis	**CEMI**	Conseil Européen pour le Marketing Industriel
CEMAT	Centro de Estudios Mesoamericano sobre Tecnologia Apropiada (Guatemala)	**CEMIE**	Centro Multinacional de Investigación Educativa (Costa Rica)
CEMAT	Conférence Européenne des Ministres Responsables de l'Aménagement du Territoire	**CEMINA**	Cemina – Centro de Projetos da Mulher (Brazil)
CEMAT	Società per la Construzione e l'Esercizio dei Mezzi Ausiliari del Transporte	**CEMLA**	Centro de Estudios Monetarios Latinoamericanos (Mexico)
CEMATEX	Comité Européen des Constructeurs de Matérial Textile	**CEMM**	Compagnie des Experts Maritimes de Madagascar
CEMB	Comité Européen de Mini-Basketball	**CEMN**	Compagnie des Experts Maritimes du Niger
CEMB	Compagnie des Exports Maritimes du Bénin	**CÉMO**	Commission Économique pour le Moyen-Orient (UN)
CEMBS	Committee for European Marine Biological Symposia (EMBA)	**CÉMO**	Conseil d'Églises du Moyen-Orient = MECC
CEMC	Canadian Engineering Manpower Council	**CÉMP**	Centre d'Étude des Matières Plastiques
CEMD	Centre for Enterprise and Management Development (University of Northumbria)	**CÉMP**	Centre d'Études et de Mesure de la Productivité
		CEMP	Centre for Environmental Management & Planning
CEMDOC	Centro Multinacional de Documentación Científica sobre Geologia, Geofisica de Colombia	**CEMP**	Ecosystem Monitoring Programme
		CEMPA	Comision Europea-Mediterrénea para el Estudio de la Organización de Aguas = CEMPE, EMCWP
CEME	Centro de Medicamentos (Brazil)		
CEME	Centro Italiano per Studio delle Relazioni Economiche e dei Mercati Esteri	**CEMPE**	Commission Europe-Méditerranée de Planification pour les Problèmes de l'Eau = CEMPA, EMCWP
CEME	Confederación Española de Mujeres Empresarias	**CEMPSA**	Clinical Engineering and Medical Physics Services Advisory Committee (Northern Ireland)
CEMEA	Centre d'Entraînement aux Méthodes d'Éducation Active (Belgium)	**CEMR**	Council of European Municipalities and Regions = CCRE, CMRE, RGRE

CÉMS	Centre d'Étude de la Météorologie Spatiale
CEMS	Centre for Ethnic Minority Studies
CEMS	China Electron Microscopic Society
CEMS	Church of England Men's Society
CEMS	Community of European Management Schools (France)
CEMS	Compagnie des Experts Maritimes du Sénégal
CEMSÉ	Comité Européen des Fabricants de Matériels de Soudage Électrique
CEMT	Compagnie des Experts Maritimes du Togo
CEMT	Conférénce Européenne des Ministres des Transports = ECMT
CEMU	Centro Sperimentale per le Macchine Utensili
CEMUBAC	Centre Médical de l'Université de Bruxelles au Congo
CEMUJER	Centro de Estudios de la Mujer "Norma Virginia Guirola de Herrera" (El Salvador)
CEMYC	Council of Europe Minority Youth Committees
CÉN	Centre d'Étude de l'Énergie Nucléaire (Belgium) = SCK
CÉN	Centre d'Études Nucleaires
CEN	Centro Nacionalista (Bolivia)
CÉN	Cercle d'Études Numismatiques (Belgium)
CEN	Comité Ejecutivo Nacional (Mexico)
CEN	Comité Européen de Normalisation
CÉN	Commissariat aux Énergies Nouvelles (Algeria)
CÉN	Commission pour l'Étude des Nuages (OMI)
CEN	Consejo de Economía Nacional
CÉNA	Centre d'Études Nord-Africaines
CENA	Centre d'Experimentation de la Navigation Aérienne
CENA	Centro de Energia Nuclearia Agricultura (Brazil)
CENAC	Centro Nacional de Estudios de la Construccion (Colombia)
CENACO	Centro Nacional de Computacion (Bolivia)
CENAD	Centre National d'Archives et de Documentation
CENADA	Centro Nacional de Datos Oceanograficos (Mexico)
CENADEC	Centre National de Développement des Entreprises Coopératives (Cameroon)
CENADEM	Centro Nacional de Desenvolvimento Micrografico (Brazil)
CENAFI	Centro Nacional de Formacion Integral (Bolivia)
CENAL	Comissão Executiva Nacional de Alcool (Brazil)
CENAMI	Centro Nacional de Ayuda a Mexicanos Indigenas
CENAN	Centro Nacional de Alimentacion y Nutricion
CENAPEC	National Centre for Promotion of Cooperative Enterprises (Ivory Coast)
CENAPIA	Centro Nacional de Promoción de la Pequeña Industria y Artesanía (Ecuador)
CENAR-BICA	Central African Regional Branch of the International Council on Archives
CENAR-EST	Centre National de la Recherche Scientifique et Technologique (Gabon)
CENAR-GEN	Centro Nacional de Recursos Genéticos (Brazil)
CENARP	Cercle National de Relations Publiques (Luxembourg)
CENATRA	Centre National d'Assistance Technique et de Recherche Appliquée (Belgium)
CENAZU-CAR	Centrales Azucareros (Venezuela)
CENCER	CEN Certification
CENCI	Centro de Estadisticas Nacionales y Comercio Internacional (Paraguay, Uruguay)
CENCIRA	Centro Nacional de Capitación y Investigación para la Reforma Agraria (Peru)
CEN-COMSA	Centro de Computo y Aplicaciones de Sistemas (Peru)
CENCOS	Centro Nacional de Comunicación Social (Mexico)
CENCRA	Centro Nacional de Capicitação em Reforma Agrária (Brazil)
CENDA	Centro Nacional de Desarrollo Agropecuário (Dominican Republic)
CENDEC	Centro de Treinamento para o Desenvolvimento (Brazil)
CENDES	Centro de Desarrollo Industrial del Ecuador
CENDES	Centro de Estudios del Desarrollo (Venezuela)
CEND-HRRA	Centre for the Development of Human Resources for Rural Areas (Philippines)

CENDIE	Centro Nacional de Documentación e Información Educativa (Argentina)	**CENIDS**	Centro Nacional de Información y Documentación en Salud (Mexico)
CENDIM	Centro Nacional de Documentación e Información en Medicina y Ciencias de la Salud (Uruguay)	**CENIET**	Centro Nacional de Información y Estadísticas de Trabajo (Mexico)
CENDIP	Centro Nacional de Documentación e Información Pedagégica (Colombia)	**CENIM**	Centro Nacional de Informação Científica en Microbiologia (Brazil)
CENDOC	Centro Nacional de Documentación (Colombia)	**CENIM**	Centro Nacional de Investigaciones Metalúrgicas
Cenebad	Centro Nacional de Educación Básica a Distancia	**CENIP**	Centro Nacional de Productividad (Peru)
CENECA	Centre National des Expositions et Concours Agricoles	**CENIS**	Center for International Studies (U.S.A.)
CENECA	Centro de Indagacion y Expresion Cultural y Artistica (Chile)	**CENITAL**	Centro Nacional de Inseminación Artificial (Colombia)
CENÉCO	Centre d'Entraînement à l'Économie	**CENMAC**	Centre for Micro-Assisted Communication
CENÉEMA	Centre National d'Étude et d'Expérimentation de Machinisme Agricole (Cameroon)	**CENP**	Committee of Food and Nutrition Policies (FAO)
CENÉLEC	Comité Européen de Normalisation Électrotechnique	**CENPAFAL**	Centro de Pastoral Familiar para America Latina (Colombia)
CENEP	Centro de Estudios de Poblacion (Argentina)	**CENPAR**	Centre National de Promotion de l'Artisanat Rural
CENET	Centro Nacional de Electronica y Telecommunicaciones	**CENPES**	Centro de Pesquisas e Desenvolvimento Leopoldo A. Miguez de Mello (Brazil)
CENFAM	Centro Nazionale di Fisica della Atmosfera e Meteorologia	**CENPES/RJ**	Centro de Pesquisa e Desenvolvimento (Brazil)
CÉNFAR	Centre d'Études Nucléaires de Fontenay-aux-Roses	**CENPHA**	Centro Nacional de Pesquisas Habitacionais (Brazil)
CEN-FOTUR	Centro Nacional de Formacion en Turismo (Peru)	**CENPLA**	Centro de Estudos, Pesquisa e Planejamento, (Brazil)
CÉNG	Centre d'Études Nucléaires de Grenoble	**CENPRO**	Centro de Promoción de Exportaciones e Inversiones (Costa Rica)
CENI	Caribbean Food and Nutrition Institute (Jamaica)	**CENRA**	Centro Nacional de Capacitación en Reforma Agraria (Peru)
CENI	Centro Nacional de Informatica (Honduras)	**CÉNS**	Centre d'Études Nucléaires de Saclay
CENIAP	Centro Nacional de Investigaciones Agropecuárias (Venezuela)	**CENSA**	Centro Nacional de Salud Animal (Cuba)
CEN-ICAÑA	Centro de Investigaciones Agropecuarias (Venezuela)	**CENSA**	Council of European and Japanese National Shipowners' Associations
CENICIT	Centro Nacional de Información Científica y Técnica (Venezuela)	**CENSH-ARE**	Center to Study Human-Animal Relationships and Environments (U.S.A.)
CENICOM	Centro Interamericano de Cooperación Municipal (U.S.A.)	**CENSIS**	Centre for Spatial Information Studies (Australia)
CENID	Centro Nacional de Información y Documentación (Chile)	**CENTA**	Centro Nacional de Technologia Agropecuraio (El Salvador)
CENIDE	National Centre for Educational Development and Research (Spain)	**CENTA**	Centro Nacional de Tecnificación Agricola (Salvador)
CENIDIM	Centro Nacional de Información, Documentación e Investigación Musicales (Mexico)	**CENTA**	Centro Nacional de Tecnologia Alimentaria (Peru)
		CENTA	Combined Edible Nut Trade Association

CENTEC	Gesellschaft für Centrifugentechnik
CENTED	Center for Technology, Environment and Development (U.S.A.)
CENT-EXBEL	Centre Scientifique et Technique de l'Industrie Textile Belge
CENTI	Centre pour le Traitement de l'Informatique
CENTOB	Centre National de Tri d'Océanographie Biologique
CENTRA-BOIS	Société Centrafricaine de Travaux du Bois
CENTRA-CUIRS	Société Centrafricaine des Cuirs
CENTRA-HYDRO	Société Centrafricaine des Hydrocarbures
CENTRA-MINE	Compagnie Centrafricaine des Mines
CENTRA-PALM	Société Centrafricaine des Palmaires
CENTRAGO	Société Centrafricaine pour le Développement de l'Agro-Industrie
CENTRA-NSPORT	Société Centrafricaine Arabe de Transport
Centre de Vienne	Centre Européen de Coordination de Recherche et de Documentation en Sciences Sociales = Vienna Centre
Centre ECDH	Centre d'Études et d'Initiatives pour l'Europe des Citoyens et des Droits de l'Homme (Belgium)
CENTR-EDIL	Centro Regionale dei Costruttori Edili Lombardil
CENTR-IFAN	Centre d'Institute Françaises d'Afrique Noire
CENTRO-BANCA	Banca Centrale di Credito Populare
CENTRO-CARTA	Centro Cartario Italiano per il Mercato Comune Europeo
CENTRO-COOP	Uniunea Centrala a Cooperativelor de Consum
CENTRO-MIDCA	Centro Taller Interamericano de Conservacion y Restauracion de Libros, Documentos y Material Fotografico (OAS) (Dominican Republic)
CENTRO-MIN	Empresa Minera del Centro de Perú
CENTR-OPEC	Center for OPEC Studies (Venezuela)
CENUSA	Centrales Nucleares S.A. (Spain)
CENWOR	Centre for Women's Research (Singapore)
CENYC	Council of European National Youth Committees

CEO	Centre for Earth Observation
CEO	Comité Européen de l'Outillage
CEO	Consulting Engineers of Ontario (Canada)
CEOA	Central European Operating Agency
CEOAH	Comité Européen de l'Outillage Agricole et Horticole
CEOBOL	Centro de Documentación (Bolivia)
CÉOC	Centre d'Études de l'Orient Contemporain
CEOC	Confédération Européenne d'Organismes de Contrôle
CÉOCOR	Comité d'Étude de la Corrosion et de la Protection des Canalisations
CEOE	Confederación Española de Organizaciones Empresariales
CEOS	Committee on Earth Observation Satellites (U.S.A.)
CEOS	County Education Officers Society
CEOSL	Confederación Ecuatoriana de Organizaciónes Sindicales Libres
CEOST	Committee on Equal Opportunities in Science and Technology (NSF)
CEP	Centre d'Essais des Propulseurs
CÉP	Centre d'Études des Matières Plastiques (Belgium)
CEP	Centro de Estudios y Publicaciones (Peru)
CÉP	Cercle d'Études Pédiatriques
CEP	Colloque Européen des Paroisses
CEP	Comité Estatal de Precios (Cuba)
CEP	Commission on Environmental Planning (IUCN)
CEP	Committee for Environmental Protection
CEP	Compagnie d'Exploration Petrolière
CÉP	Compagnie Équatoriale des Peintures (Cameroon)
CEP	Conférence Permanente Européenne de la Probation
CEP	Congregation for the Evangelization of Peoples (Italy)
CEP	Council on Economic Priorities (U.S.A.)
CEP	Council on Environmental Pollutants (U.S.A.)
CEP	Fédération des Organisations Nationales des Grossistes, Importateurs et Exportateurs en Poisson de la CEE

CÉPA	Centre d'Études des Problèmes Agricoles
CEPA	Centro de Educación y Promoción Agraria (Nicaragua)
CÉPA	Cercle d'Études de la Productivité Agricole
CEPA	Comisión Económica para Africa (ONU) = CEA, ECA
CEPA	Comisión Ejecutiva Portuaria Autónoma (El Salvador)
CEPA	Comité d'Experts pour les Ajustements (UN)
CEPA	Comité Européen de Patinage Artistique (Spain)
CÉPA	Commission d'Études Pratiques d'Aviation
CEPA	Commonwealth Environment Protection Agency (*now* EPA)
CEPA	Conference of Fire Protection Associations
CEPA	Consumers Education and Protective Association International (U.S.A.)
CEPAC	Centro di Producción Audiovisual para la Capacitación (Peru)
CEPAC	Confédération Européenne de l'Industrie des Pâtes, Papiers et Cartons
CÉPAC	Conférence des Évêques du Pacifique
CEPAC	Ecumenical Planning and Action in the Caribbean
CEPACC	Chemical Education Planning and Coordinating Committee (ACS)
CEPACS	Comité Episcopal Panafricain pour les Communications Sociales (SECAM)
CEPAD	Comité Evangelico Pro-Ayuda y Desarrollo (Nicaragua)
CEPADES	Centro Paraguayo de Estudios de Desarrollo Económico y Social
CEPAF	Comité Européen pour la Protection des Animaux à Fourrure
CEPAL	Cooperativa Esportazione Produtti Agricoli
CEPALC	Comisión Económica de las Naciones Unidas para América Latina y el Caribe = ECLAC
CEPALC	Comisión Económica para América Latina y el Caraibe (UN) = ECLAC
CEPAM	Centro Ecuatoriano para la Promoción y Acción de la Mujer
CEPANZO	Centro Panamericano de Zoonosis (PAHO, WHO) (Argentina)
CEPAO	Comisión Económica para el Asia Occidental (ONU) = ECWA
CEPAR	Centro de Estudios de Poblacion y de Paternidad Responsable (Ecuador)
CEPAS	Centro di Educazione Professionale per Assistenti Sociali
CÉPAZÉ	Centre d'Échange et Promotion Artisanal en Zones à Équiper
CEPB	Confederación de Empresarios Privados de Bolivia
CEPC	Central European Pipeline Committee
CEPC	Comité Elargi du Programme et de la Coordination (UNDP)
CEPC	Comité Européen pour les Problèmes Criminels = ECCP
CÉPCAM	Centre d'Études de Prévention Caméroun
CÉPCEO	Comité d'Étude des Producteurs de Charbon d'Europe Occidentale
CEPCH	Confederación de Empleados Particulares de Chile
CEPCIECC	Comisión Ejecutiva Permanente del Consejo Interamericano para la Educación, la Ciencia y la Cultura (CIC)
CEPCIES	Comisión Ejecutiva Permanente del Consejo Interamericano Economico y Social
CEPD	Committee of Epidemiology of Plant Disease (China)
CEPD	Council for Economic Planning and Development (Taiwan)
CÉPDAC	Comite d'Études pour la Défense et l'Amélioration des Cultures
CEPDEC-CLA	Comisión Especial de Programación y Desarrollo de la Educación, la Ciencia y la Cultura en America Latina (U.S.A.)
CÉPÉ	Centre d'Études des Programmes Économiques
CÉPÉ	Centre d'Études Phytosociologiques et Écologiques
CEPE	Comisión Económica para Europa = CEE, ECE, EEK
CEPE	Comité Eetbaar Plantaardig Eiwit
CEPE	Comité Européen des Associations de Fabricants de Peintures, d'Encres d'Imprimerie et de Couleurs d'Art
CÉPÉ	Compagnie d'Électronique et de Piezo-Électricité
CEPE	Corporación Estatal Petrolera Ecuatoriana
CEPEC	Centre for Professional Employment Counselling

CEPEC	Centro de Pesquisas do Cacau (Brazil)
CEPEC	Committee of European Associations of Manufacturers of Passive Electronic Components
CEPECE	Centre de Promotion de l'Enseignement Catholique en Europe (Belgium)
CEPED	Centro de Pesquisas e Desenvolvimento (Brazil)
CEPEIGE	Centro Panamericano de Estudios e Investigaciones Geográficas (Mexico) = PACGSR
CÉPEM	Centre d'Études Européennes pour les Problèmes de l'Environnement Marin
CEPEM	Centro Paraguayo de Estudios de la Mujer
CEPEO	Comité d'Étude des Producteurs de Charbon d'Europe Occidentale (Belgium)
CEPEP	Centro Paraguayo de Estudios de Población
CEPEP	European Centre for Parents of Pupils in State Schools
CÉPEPA	Comité Économique de la Prune d'Ente et du Pruneau d'Agen
CÉPER	Centre d'Études et de Perfectionnement (ANDCP)
CEPERN	Centro Panamericano de Entrenamiento para Evaluación de Recursos Naturales (Brazil)
CEPES	Centre Européen pour l'Enseignement Supérieur (Romania)
CEPES	Centre Européen pour la Promotion et la Formation en Milieu Agricole et Rural (Belgium)
CEPES	Centro de Estudios Politicos, Económicos y Sociales (Argentina)
CEPES	Centro Peruano de Estudios
CEPÉS	Comité Européen pour le Progrès Économique et Social
CEPES	European Centre for Higher Education (Romania)
CEPEX	Centre de Promotion des Exportations (Tunisia)
CEPEX	Centro de Promocion de las Exportaciones (Paraguay)
CEPEX	Centro Promotor de Exportadores de la Ficia
CEPFAR	Centre Européen pour la Promotion et la Formation en Milieu Agricole et Rural
CÉPGL	Communauté Économique des Pays des Grands Lacs
CÉPHR	Comité d'Étude pour la Promotion de l'Habitat Rural
CÉPI	Centre d'Études de Prévention Ivoirien
CÉPI	Centre d'Études et de Promotion Industrielles (Mali)
CEPI	China National Export Commodities Packaging Research Institute
CEPI	Circulo de Escritores y Poetas Iberoamericanos
CEPI	Confederation of European Paper Industries
CÉPIA	Centre d'Études Pratiques d'Informatique et d'Automatique
CEPIA	Centre Français de Promotion Industrielle en Afrique
CEPIECC	Comisión Ejecutiva Permanente Consejo Interamericano para la Educación, la Ciencia y la Cultura
CÉPII	Centre d'Études Prospectives et d'Information Internationale
CEPIS	Centro de Educação Popular Instítuto Sedes Sapientiae (Brazil)
CEPIS	Centro Panamericano de Ingenería Sanataria y Ciencias Ambientes
CEPITRA	Centre de Perfectionnement des Industries Textiles Rhône-Alpes
CEPL	Comité Español de Plásticos en Agricultura
CEPL	Conférence Européenne des Pouvoirs Locaux
CEPLA	Comisión de Estudios para la Promoción de la Lana Argentina
CEPLA	Commission on Environment Policy, Law & Administration (IUCN)
CEPLAC	Comissão Executiva do Plano da Lavoura Cacaueira (Brazil)
CEPLAES	Centro de Planificación y Estudios Sociales, Quito (Ecuador)
CEPLAN	Centro de Estudios de Planificación Nacional (Chile)
CEPM	Centre d'Exploitation Postal Metropolitain
CÉPM	Comité d'Études Pétrolières Marines
CEPMA	Consumer Electronic Product Manufacturers Association (Philippines)
CEPMAE	Centre d'Edition et de Production Manuels et d'Auxiliaires de l'Enseignement (Cameroon)
CEPMMT	Centre Européen pour les Prévisions Météorologiques à Moyen Terme = ECMWF

CEPO	County Emergency Planning Officers Society	**CEPU**	Confederación Ecuatoriana de Profesionales Universitarios
CÉPOI	Centre d'Études des Pays de l'Océan Indien	**CÉPVDVM**	Centre d'Étude des Problèmes Viticoles et de Défense des Vins Méridionaux
CÉPOM	Centre d'Études des Problèmes d'Outre Mer	**CEPYME**	Confederación Española de Pequeñas y Medianas Empresas
CEPPAF	Comité Européen pour la Protection des Phoques et autres Animaux à Fourrure	**CEQ**	Council on Environmental Quality (U.S.A.)
CEPPLE	Conference of Protestant Churches in the Latin Countries of Europe (France)	**CER**	Community of European Railways = CCFE, GEB
CEPR	Center for Energy Policy and Research (U.S.A.)	**CER**	Conferencia Ecuatoriana de Religiosos
CEPR	Centre For Economic Policy Research	**CER**	Conseil Economique et Régional (Central African Republic)
CEPR	Centre for Economic Policy Research (ANU)	**CERA**	Canadian Educational Researchers Association = ACCE
CEPRAP	Center for Engineering Plants for Resistance against Pathogens (U.S.A.)	**CERA**	Centrale Raiffeisenkas (Belgium)
CEPREM	Centre de Promotion et de Recherche pour la Monnaie Européenne	**CÉRA**	Centre d'Études des Recherches Arabe-Islamiques
CEPRIG	Centre de Perfectionnement pour la Recherche Industrielle et sa Gestion	**CÉRA**	Centre d'Études des Religions Africaines (Zaïre)
CÉPRO	Centre d'Étude des Problèmes Humains du Travail	**CÉRA**	Centre d'Études du Risque Atomique (Switzerland)
CEPRO-MUN	Centro de Promocion de la Mujer del Norte (Peru)	**CÉRA**	Centre d'Études et de Recherches sur l'Agriculture
CEPS	Center for Educational Policy Studies (U.S.A.)	**CÉRA**	Centre d'Études et de Recherches sur l'Aquaculture (Belgium)
CEPS	Central Europe Pipeline System (NATO)	**CÉRABATI**	Compagnie Générale de la Céramique du Bâtiment
CEPS	Centre for Enterprise Policy Studies	**CÉRAC**	Centre d'Études pour le Ruralisme et l'Aménagement des Campagnes
CEPS	Centre for European Policy Studies	**CERAC**	Comité d'Expansion Régionale et d'Aménagement de la Champagne
CEPS	Centro de Estudos e Pesquisas de Sociologia (Brazil)	**CERA-CHIM**	Centre de Recherche, d'Analyse et de Controle Chimiques (Belgium)
CEPS	Commission Européenne pour la Promotion de Soie	**CÉRAFER**	Centre National d'Études Techniques et de Recherches Technologiques pour l'Agriculture, les Forêts et l'Equipement Rural
CEPSA	Compania Española de Petroleos, S.A.		
CÉPSE	Centre d'Études Politiques et Sociales Européennes	**CERAG**	Caribbean Entry Refusals Action Group
CEPSÉ	Centre d'Execution des Programmes Sociaux et Économiques (Zaïre)	**CÉRAG**	Centre d'Études Régionales Antilles-Guyane
CÉPSI	Centre d'Études des Problèmes Sociaux Indigènes (Zaïre)	**CERAM**	Centre d'Enseignement et de Recherche en Analyse des Matériaux (France)
CEPT	Centro de Estudos de Pedologia (Portugal)	**CÉRAM-GABON**	Société Gabonaise de Céramique
CEPT	Centro de Estudos de Pedologia Tropical (Portugal)	**CÉRAME-UNIE**	Bureau de Liaison des Industries Céramiques du Marché Commun (Belgium)
CEPT	Conférence Européenne des Administrations des Postes et des Télécommunications		
CEPTA	Committee of Experts for the Prevention of Torture in the Americas (Uruguay)	**CÉRAO**	Conférence Épiscopale Régionale de l'Afrique de l'Ouest Francophone

CÉRAT	Centre d'Étude et de Recherche sur l'Administration Économique et l'Aménagement du Territoire
CÉRB	Conseil Économique Régional pour le Brabant (Belgium)
CERBE	Centrum voor Rationele Bedrijfsvoering Zuidhollandse Eilanden
CÉRBOM	Centre d'Études et de Recherches de Biologie et d'Océanographie Médicale
CÉRC	Centre d'Études des Revenus et des Cotes
CERC	Centro de Estudios de la Realidad Contemporanea (Chile)
CERC	Chemical Energy Research Centre
CERC	Civil Engineering Research Council
CERC	Comité Européen des Représentants de Commerce Group CEE
CERC	Continuing Education Research Centre
CERCA	Centre d'Enseignement Rural par Correspondance d'Angers
CÉRCA	Centre d'Études et de Recherches Catalanes des Archives
CÉRCA	Compagnie pour l'Étude et la Réalisation de Combustibles Atomiques
CÉRCHAR	Centre d'Études et Recherches des Charbonnages de France
CERCI	Centre for Educational Resources in the Construction Industry
CÉRCI	Compagnie d'Études et de Réalisations de Cybernétique Industrielle
CERCI	Cooperativa de Educação e Reabilitação das Crianças Inadaptadas
CÉRCLE	Centre d'Études et de Recherches sur les Collectivités Locales en Europe
CERCOL	Centre de Recherches Techniques et Scientifiques des Conserves de Légumes (Belgium)
CERCOR	Centre Européen de Recherches sur les Organisations et Ordres Religieux
CERD	Center for Educational Research and Development (U.S.A.)
CERD	Comité Européen de Recherche et de Développement (Belgium)
CÉRDAC	Centre d'Études et de Recherches Documentaires sur Afrique Centrale (Zaïre)
CERDAC	Centro Regional de Documentación para el Desarrollo Agrícola de América Central (Costa Rica)
CERDAS	Centre de Coordination des Recherches et de la Documentation en Sciences Sociales en Afrique Sub-Saharienne (UNESCO)
CERDEC	Center for Research and Documentation on the European Community (U.S.A.)
CÉRDI	Centre d'Études et de Recherches sur le Développement International
CERDIA	Centre de Documentation des Industries Utilisatices de Produits Agricoles
CERDIC	Centre de Recherche et de Documentation des Institutiones Chrétiennes
CERDO-TOLA	Centre Régional de Recherche et de Documentation pour les Traditions Orales et le Développement des Langues Africaines
CERDOT-OLA	Centre for Research and Documentation on Oral Traditions and the Development of African Languages (Cameroon)
CERE	Center for Environmental Research Education (U.S.A.)
CÉRE	Centre d'Études et de Recherches d'Environnement (Belgium)
CERÉ	Comité Européen pour les Relations Économiques
CERE	Consultation Européenne sur les Réfugiés et les Exiles = ECRE
CERÉA	Centre National de Recherches pour l'Étude des Animaux Nuisibles ou Utiles à l'Agriculture (Belgium)
CEREA	Comisión Especial de Representantes de Entidades Agropecuárias (Argentina)
CEREB	Centre for European Research in Economics and Business
CEREBE	Centre de Recherche sur le Bien-être
CEREC	European Committee for Business, Arts and Culture
CERÉD	Centre de Recherches d'Études Démographiques (Morocco)
CERÉÉQ	Centre Expérimentale de Recherches et d'Études pour l'Équipement (Senegal)
CEREFA	Comisión Ejecutiva de Repoblación Educación Forestal Agropecuária (Cuba)
CERÉGE	Centre de Recherches en Économie et Gestion des Entreprises (Belgium)
CEREL	Centro de Estudios de la Realidad Latinoamericana (Venezuela)
CERE-LAST – SA	Institutul de Cercetări pentru Prelucrarea Elastomerilor SA (Romania)
CÉRÉN	Centre d'Études Régionales sur l'Économie de l'Énergie

CÉRÉOPA	Centre d'Études et de Recherche sur l'Économie et l'Organisation des Productions Animales
CEREP	Centro de Estudios de la Realidad Puertorriqueña
CÉREQ	Centre d'Études et de Recherches sur les Qualifications
CÉRÉR	Comité d'Études et de Recherches Économiques Rurales
CERES	Center for Research and Education in Sexuality (U.S.A.)
CERES	Centre d'Assais et de Recherches d'Engins Spéciaux
CÉRÉS	Centre d'Études et de Recherches Économiques et Sociales (Tunis)
CÉRÉS	Centre d'Études et de Recherches et d'Éducation Socialiste
CERES	Centre de Recherches Socio-Religieuses (Burundi)
CERES	Centro de Estudios de la Realidad Económica y Social (Bolivia)
CÉRÉS	Comité d'Études Régionales Économiques et Sociales
CERES	Consumers For Ethics in Research Group
CERES	Controlled Environment Research Laboratory (CSIRO) (Australia)
CERESA	Central de Repuestos, S.A. (El Salvador)
CERESIS	Centro Regional de Sismologia para América del Sur (Peru)
CERET	Centre Européen de Réflexion et d'Étude en Thermodynamique (Switzerland)
CÉRF	Centre d'Études et de Recherches en Fonderies (Belgium)
CERFCI	Center for Studies, Research and Training in International Understanding and Cooperation (France)
CERGEC	Centre de Recherche Géographique et de Production Cartographique (Congo)
CÉRGIV	Centre d'Économie Rurale et de Gestion d'Ille et Vilaine
CERI	Canadian Energy Research Institute
CERI	Center for Earthquake Research and Information (U.S.A.)
CERI	Central Education Research Institute (Korea)
CÉRI	Centre d'Étude des Relations Internationales
CÉRI	Centre d'Études et de Recherche en Informatique (Algeria)
CÉRI	Centre d'Études sur la Recherche et l'Innovation
CERI	Centre Européen de Recherche sur l'Investissement Privé
CERI	Centre for Educational Research and Innovation (OECD)
CERI	Computational Engineering Research Institute
CERIA	Centre d'Enseignement et de Recherches des Industries Alimentaires et Chimiques (Belgium)
CÉRIB	Centre d'Études et de Recherche de l'Industrie du Béton
CÉRIC	Consortium d'Études et de Réalisations Industrielles et Commerciales (Benin)
CÉRICAM	Céramiques Industrielles du Caméroun
CÉRIN	Centre d'Études des Relations Interethniques de Nice
CERIS	Beijing Central Engineering and Research Incorporation of Iron and Steel Industry
CERIS	Centro de Estatistica Religiosa e Investigações Sociales (Brazil)
CERISIE	Laboratorio per la Certificazione e Ricerca sui Sistema Elastomerici (Italy)
CERJ	Consejo Etnico Runujel Junam (Guatemala)
CÉRK	Centre d'Études et de Recherches de Kara (Togo)
CERL	Central Electricity Research Laboratories
CERL	Computer-Based Education Research Laboratory (U.S.A.)
CERLAC	Centre for Research in Latin America and the Caribbean (Canada)
CERLALC	Centro Regional para el Fomento del Libro en América Latina y El Caribe (Colombia)
CÉRMA	Centre d'Études et de Recherches du Machinisme Agricole
CERMA-COM	Companie pour l'Exportation des Ressources Maritimes et le Commerce (Senegal)
CÉRMAP	Centre d'Études Mathématiques pour la Planification
CERMES	Centre de Recherches sur les Méningites et les Schistomiases (Niger)
CÉRMO	Centre d'Études et de Recherches de la Machine-Outil
CÉRMOC	Centre d'Étude et de Recherches sur le Moyen-Orient Contemporain (Lebanon)

CÉRMTRI	Centre d'Étude et de Recherches sur les Mouvements Trotskystes et Révolutionnaires Internationaux	**CERT**	Computer Emergency Response Team (U.S.A.)
CERN	CLES European Research Network	**CERT**	Council for Education Recruitment and Training for the Hotel Industry (Éire)
CERN	Organisation Européenne pour le Recherche Nucléaire	**CÉRTS**	Centre d'Études et Recherches en Technologie Spatiale
CÉRNA	Conférénce Épiscopale Régionale du Nord de l'Afrique	**CÉRTSM**	Centre d'Études et de Recherches Techniques Sous-Marines
CÉRP	Centre d'Études et de Recherches Psycho-techniques	**CERU**	Centro de Estudios Rurais e Urbanos (Brazil)
CERP	Centre Européen des Relations Publiques	**CERUR**	Centro de Estudios Regionales Urbanos y Rurales (Italy) = DSC
CERP-CON-SULTANTS	European Association of Public Relations Consultants	**CERUSS**	Comité Permanent International des Techniques et de l'Urbanisme Souterrains et Spatials
CERP-PRO	European Association of Public Relations Officers	**CERVA**	Consortium Européen de Réalisation et de Vente d'Avions
CÉRPA	Centre d'Étude et de Recherche sur la Pollution Atmosphérique (Belgium)	**CÉRVL**	Centre d'Étude et de Recherche sur la Vie Locale
CERPE	Centro de Reflexion y Planificación Educativa (Venezuela)	**CES**	Cadena de Emisoras Sindicales
		CES	Center for Energy Studies (U.S.A.)
CERPER	Empresa Pública de Certificaciones Pesqueras del Peré	**CES**	Center for Entrepreneurial Studies (U.S.A.)
CÉRPHOS	Centre d'Études et de Recherches des Phosphates Minéraux	**CES**	Center for Environmental Sciences (U.S.A.)
CERQUA	Centre de Développement des Certifications des Qualités Agricoles et Alimentaires	**CÉS**	Centre d'Études Sociologiques
		CES	Centre Européen des Silicones (Belgium)
CERR	Comité Européen de Réflexion sur les Retraites	**CES**	Centre for Educational Sociology
		CES	Centre for Environmental Studies
CÉRS	Centre d'Études et de Recherches Scientifiques	**CES**	Centre for Environmental Studies (Australia, UK)
CERS	China Energy Research Society	**CES**	Centre for European Studies (Sweden)
CERS	Coleção de Estirpes de Rhizobium (Brazil)	**CES**	Charities Evaluation Services
		CES	Chinese Electrotechnical Society
CERS	Confédération Européenne de Roller-Skating	**CES**	Christian Evidence Society
CÉRSÉ	Centre National d'Études et de Recherches Socio-Économiques (Belgium)	**CÉS**	Comité Économique et Social (CE) = ESC
		CES	Committee on Earth Science
CÉRT	Centre d'Études et de Recherche de Toulouse	**CES**	Commonwealth Employment Service
		CES	Communauté Européenne Sans-Abri
CERT	Charities Effectiveness Review Trust (NCVO)	**CES**	Confédération Européenne de Scoutisme
CERT	Comité de Roubaiz-Tourcoing d'Études et d'Actions Économiques et Sociales	**CES**	Confédération Européenne des Syndicats = EGB, ETUC
CERT	Comité Européen des Entreprises de Traitements de Surface	**CES**	Conference of European Statisticians (UN)
CERT	Committee on Energy, Research and Technology of the European Parliament	**CÉS**	Conseil Économique et Social (CE)
		CES	Consejo Económico y Social
CÉRT	Comptoir d'Études Radio Techniques	**CES**	Council for European Studies, Pittsburgh (U.S.A.)

CES	Crop Experiment Station (South Korea)
CESA	Catholic Ex-Servicemen's Association
CESA	Central Ecuatoriana de Servicios Agraria
CÉSA	Centre d'Études Sociales Africaines (Zaïre)
CESA	Comité Européen des Syndicats de l'Alimentation du Tabac et de l'Industrie Hôtelière (CE) = ETUCF
CESA	Conseil Economique et Social Arabe (Egypt) = AESC
CESA	Cooperative Educational Service Agency (U.S.A.)
CESA	Cultural Exchange Society of America
CESAG	Centre Africain d'Études Supérieures en Gestion (Senegal)
CESAI	Centro de Formação Profissional de Informática
CESAMP	Group of Experts on the Scientific Aspects of Marine Pollution
CÉSAO	Centre d'Études Économiques et Sociales de l'Afrique Occidentale
CESAO	Commission Economique et Sociale des Nations Unies pour l'Asie Occidentale = CESPAO, ESCWA
CESAP	Centro al Servicio de la Acción Popular (Venezuela)
CÉSAP	Commission Économique et Sociale des Nations Unies pour l'Asie et le Pacifique = CESPAP, ESCAP
CESB	Centre d'Enseignement Supérieur de Brazzaville
CESC	Conference on European Security and Cooperation
CESC	Continental Europe Simulation Council (SCSI)
CESCE	Comité Européen des Services de Conseillers d'Entreprises
CESCE	Compania Española de Seguros a la Exportacion
CESCJ	Conseil Européen des Services Communautaires Juifs = ECJCS
CESCO	Centro de Estudios del Cobre y la Mineria (Chile)
CESD	Centre Européen pour la Formation de Statisticiens-Économistes pour les Pays en Voie de Développement
CESDA	Confederation of European Soft Drinks Associations
CÉSÉ	Centre d'Études de la Socio-Économie
CESE	Comisión Ecuménica de Servicio (Brazil)
CESE	Comparative Education Society in Europe
CESE	Council for Environmental Science and Engineering
CESÉAR	Commission d'Entraide et de Service des Églises et d'Assurance aux Réfugiés = CICARWS
Ceseden	Centro Superior de Estudios de la Defensa Nacional
CÉSEM	Centre d'Études Supérieures Européennes de Management
CESEM	Centro de Estudios y Servicios sobre Migraciones Involuntarias (ACNUR) (Bolivia)
CESERFO	Centro Studi e Ricerche Fondiarie
CESG	Communications Electronics Security Group
CÉSH	Centre d'Études de Sciences Humaines (Zaïre)
CÉSI	Centre d'Études Supérieures Industrielles
CESI	Centre for Economic and Social Information (UN)
CESI	Chinese Electronics Standardisation Institute
CESI	Conseil Economique et Social Interaméricain = CIES, IA-ECOSOC
CESI	Council for Elementary Science International (U.S.A.)
CESIC	Catholic European Study and Information Centre (France)
CESID	Centro Superior de Información de la Defensa
CESIDE	Centro de Estudios Superiores para el Desarrollo (Colombia)
CÉSIGU	Comité pour l'Élaboration d'un Système Informatique de Gestion Universitaire (Canada)
CESII	Centro de Sociologia Industrial e do Trabalho (Brazil)
CESIN	Centro Economico Scambi Italo-Nipponici
CESIO	Comité Européen des Agents de Service et leurs Intermédiaires Organiques
CESIS	Centre d'Epidémiologie, Statistique et Information Sanitaire (Burkina Faso)
CESL	Conseil Européen de la Jeunesse Syndicale
CESLAMD	Comité de Liaison des Secrétariats Latino-Américaines des Moyens de Diffusion

CESMAD	Association des Transporteurs Routiers Internationaux Tschécoslovaques	**CESSTW**	Center for the Economic and Social Study of the Third World (Mexico)
CESME	Centro de Servicios Metalurgicos (Chile)	**CEST**	Centre for the Exploitation of Science and Technology
CESMEC	Centro de Estudios Medicion y Certificacion de Calidad (Chile)	**CESTA**	Centro Salvadoreno de Tecnologia Apropiada
CESNEF	Istituto di Ingegneria Nucleare, Centro di Studi Nucleari Enrico Fermi (Italy)	**CESTA**	Conference on Education and Scientific and Technical Training in Relation to Development in Africa
CESO	Canadian Executive Services Overseas	**CESTAS**	Centro di Educazione Sanitaria e Tecnologie Sanitarie Appropriate
CESO	Centre for the Study of Education in Developing Countries (Netherlands)	**CÉSTI**	Centre d'Études des Sciences et Techniques de l'Information (Tunisia)
CESO	Concorde Engines Support Organisation	**CESVITEM**	Centro Sviluppo Terzo Mondo
CESO	Council of Engineers and Scientists Organisations (U.S.A.)	**CET**	Centro de Empresas Transnacionales de las Naciones Unidas (U.S.A.)
CÉSP	Centre d'Études des Supports Publicitaires	**CET**	Commission Européenne du Tourisme = ETC
CESP	Commission on Environmental Strategy and Planning	**CET**	Commission on Education and Training (IUCN)
CESP	Confédération Européenne des Syndicats Nationaux et Associations Professionnelles de Pediatres (Belgium)	**CET**	European Ceramic Tile Manufacturers' Federation
CESP	Confederation of European Socialist Parties	**CÉTA**	Centres d'Études Techniques Agricoles
CESP	Conseil Européen des Syndicats de Police	**CETA**	Centro des Estudos Technicos de Automación
CESPA	Campaign for Equal State Pension Ages	**CÉTA**	Conference des Églises de Toute l'Afrique = AACC
CESPAO	Comisión Económica y Social para el Asia Ocidental (ONU) = CESAO, ESCWA	**CETA**	Conference of Engineering Trades Associations
CESPAP	Comisión Económica y Social para Asia y el Pacifico (ONU) = CESAP, ESCAP	**CETAC**	Careers, Education and Training Advice Centre
CESPQ	Compañia Ecuatoriana de Sal y Productos Químicos	**CETAL**	Centro de Estudios en Technologias Apropiadas para América Latina (Chile)
CESPROP	Centro de Estudios y Promoción Popular (El Salvador)	**CÉTAM**	Centre d'Études de Techniques Agricoles Ménagères
CESR	Canadian Electronic Sales Representatives	**CÉTAMA**	Commission d'Établissements des Méthodes d'Analyse
CÉSR	Centre d'Études Spatiales des Rayonnements	**CETAMEX**	Centro de Estudios de Technologia Apropriada para Mexico
CESRF	Christian Economic and Social Research Foundation	**CÉTASE**	Centre d'Études de l'Asie de l'Est (Canada)
CESSAC	Church of England Soldiers Sailors and Airmen's Clubs	**CÉTBGE**	Centre d'Étude et de Traitement des Bois Gorges d'Eau
CESSE	Council of Engineering and Scientific Society Executives (U.S.A.)	**CETC SPC**	Community Education Training Centre (Fiji)
CÉSSIM	Centre d'Études des Supports d'Information Médical	**CETCA**	Centre d'Enseignement Technique du Crédit Agricole
CESSP	China Editology Society of Science Periodicals	**CETCA**	Comité Especifico Tarifario Centro-Americano
CESSS	Council of Engineering and Scientific Society Secretaries (Canada, U.S.A.)	**CETDC**	China External Trade Development Council (Taiwan)

CETEC	Fundação Centro Tecnologia de Minas Geraïs (Brazil)	**CÉTME**	Comité des Églises auprès des Travailleurs Migrants en Europe = CCMWE
CETEC	Universidad Centro de Estudios Tecnicos (Dominican Republic)	**CETO**	Centre for Educational Television Overseas
CETEHOR	Centre Technique de l'Industrie Horlogère	**CETOP**	Comité Européen des Transmissions Oléohydrauliques et Pneumatiques
CETÉM	Centre d'Enseignement des Techniques d'Étude de Marché	**CÉTOPES**	Centre d'Études des Techniciens de l'Organisation Professionnelle
CETEM	Centro de Tecnologia Mineral (Brazil)	**CETOS**	Comité Européen de Coordination du Tourisme Social (Belgium)
CETENAL	Comisión de Estudios del Territorio Nacional (Mexico)	**CETP**	Confédération Européenne pour la Thérapie Physique = ECPT
CETEPA	Centre Professional Technique d'Études de la Pollution Atmosphérique	**CÉTRA**	Compagnie Équatoriale de Travaux (Gabon)
CETESB	Companhia de Tecnologia de Saneamento Ambiental (Brazil)	**CETRAC**	Centrale de Transports en Commun (Gabon)
CETEX	Comisión de Empresas Textiles Exportadoras (El Salvador)	**CETRA-MAR**	Consortium Européen des Transports Maritimes
CETEX	Committee on Extra-Terrestrial Exploration (NASA)	**CÉTRA-MET**	Compagnie Équatoriale pour la Transformation des Métaux en République Centrafricaine
CÉTF	Centre d'Études des Techniques Forestières	**CÉTRA-MÉT-CONGO**	Compagnie Équatoriale pour la Transformation des Métaux au Congo
CÉTHÉ-DEC	Centre d'Études Théoriques de la Détection et des Communications	**CETRI**	Centre Tricontinental (Belgium)
CETI	Committee for Energy Thrift in Industry (DOI)	**CÉTRIC**	Consortium d'Études Techniques et de Réalisations Industrielles du Caméroun
CETI	Coopérative d'Entreprises de Transport Internationaux	**CÉTSAP**	Centre d'Études Transdisciplinaires (Sociologie, Anthropologie, Politique) (France)
CETIE	Centre Technique International de l'Embouteillage et du Conditionnement	**CÉTSAS**	Centre d'Études Transdisciplinaires (Sociologie, Anthropologie, Sémiologie)
CETIEF	Centre Technique des Industries de l'Estampage	**CETSS**	Comité Estatal de Trabajo y Seguridad Social (Cuba)
CETIF	Consortium de Recherches d'Études pour l'Information et la Formation (Senegal)	**CETT**	Centro de Entreamiento para Tecnicos en Telecommunicaciónes (Venezuela)
CETIL	Committee of Experts for the Transfer of Information between Community Languages (EU)	**CETT**	Compagnie Européenne de Télétransmissions
CETIM	Centre Technique des Industries Mécaniques (France)	**CETTNA**	Centro Tecnico Tipolitografico Nacional (Honduras)
CETIOM	Centre Technique Interprofessionnel des Oléagineux Metropolitains	**CÉTU**	Centre d'Études des Tunnels (France)
CETIS	Centre Européen de Traitement de l'Information Scientifique (CCE)	**CETUC**	Centro de Estudos en Telecomunicacões da Universidade Catolica (Brazil)
CETISA	Compañia Española de Editoriales Tecnológicas Internacionales	**CEU**	Centre d'Études pour l'Evolution Humaine (Italy)
CETL	Centro Tecnologico de la Leche (Chile)	**CEU**	Centro de Estudios Universitarios
CETM	Centro de Estudios y Trabajos de la Mujer (Bolivia)	**CEU**	Ceuta Unida (Ceuta)
CETMA	Centre d'Ethno-technologie en Milieux Aquatiques	**CEU**	Construction Employees' Union (Afghanistan)
CÉTMA	Centre d'Études Techniques Ménagères et Agricoles		

CEUCA	Centro de Estudios Universitarios Colombo-Americanos		**CFA**	Chilled Food Association
CEUCORS	Centre Européen de Documentation en Sciences Sociales		**CFA**	China Film Association
			CFA	Circus Fans Association of Great Britain
CEUGBI	Christian Endeavour Union of Great Britain and Ireland = CE		**CFA**	Citizens for America
CEUMA	Christian European Visual Media Association		**CFA**	Comité Français des Aérosols
			CFA	Commercial Finance Association
CEUR	Centro de Estudios Urbanos y Regionales (Argentina)		**CFA**	Commission des Forêts pour l'Afrique (FAO)
CEUS	Centre for European Union Studies		**CFA**	Committee on Food Aid Policies and Programmes (FAO/WFP)
CEV	Centre d'Essais en Vol			
CEV	Confederación Empresarial Valenciana		**CFA**	Commonwealth Forestry Association
CEV	Coöperatieve Eierveiling van de ABTB		**CFA**	Communauté Financière Africaine
CEVE	Centro Experimental de la Vivienda Economica (Argentina)		**CFA**	Compagnie Forestière Africaine (Cameroon, Congo)
CEVECO	Centrale Organisatie van Veeafzet-en Vleesverwerkings-coöperaties		**CFA**	Compagnie France-Amérique (Ivory Coast)
CEVENE-MAC	Central Venezolana de Maquinas y Aceros, S.A.		**CFA**	Comptoir Français de l'Azote
			CFA	Confédération Française de l'Artisanat
CEVMA	Christian European Visual Media Association		**CFA**	Confédération Française de l'Aviculture
			CFA	Conférence des Femmes Africaines
CEVNO	Centrum voor Internationale Vorming		**CFA**	Congregatio Fratrum Cellitarum seu Alexianorum
CEVOI	Comptoir d'Exportation de Vanille de l'Océan Indien (Madagascar)			
			CFA	Consumer Federation of America
CEWC	Council for Education in World Citizenship		**CFA**	Contract Flooring Association
			CFA	Contract Furnishing Association
CEWU	Commonwealth Electrical Workers' Union (Bahamas)		**CFA**	Cookery and Food Association
			CFA	Corporación Frutícola Argentina
CEZ	Centre Européen pour la Formation dans l'Assurance (Switzerland)		**CFA**	Council for Acupuncture
			CFA	Council of Ironfoundry Associations
CEZ	Centro de Estudos de Zoonoses (Portugal)		**CFA**	Credit Foncier d'Afrique
			CFAC	Commercial Fisheries Advisory Committee (U.S.A.)
CEZA	Comité Européen des Études de Zoologie Agricole			
CEZMS	Church of England Zenana Missionary Society		**CFAD**	Consejo Fundaciones Americanas Desarrollo
			CFAE	Centre de Formation en Aérodynamique Expérimentale (Belgium)
CEZOO	Centre de Recherches Zoologiques Appliquées (Belgium)			
			CFAE	Council for Financial Aid to Education (U.S.A.)
CEZUS	Compagnie Européenne du Zirconium Ugine-Sandvik			
			CFAL	Comisión Forestal Latinoamericana
CF	Comité des Forêts		**CFAMG**	Communication Foundation for Asia Media Group (Philippines)
CF	Commonwealth Fund (U.S.A.)			
CF	Compassionate Friends		**CFAN**	Commission Forestière pour l'Amérique du Nord (FAO) = CFNA, NAFC
CF	Sveriges Civilingenjörsförbund = CF-STF			
CF-STF	Sveriges Civilingenjorsförbund = CF		**CFAO**	Compagnie Française de l'Afrique Occidentale (Benin, Cameroon, Central Africa, Congo, Gabon, Ivory Coast, Niger, Senegal, Togo)
CFA	Canadian Federation of Agriculture			
CFA	Canadian Forestry Association			
CFA	Cane Farmers' Association (Belize)		**CFAP**	Canadian Foundation for the Advancement of Pharmacy

CFAP	Commission des Forêts pour l'Asie et la Région du Pacifique	**CFDA**	Council of Fashion Designers of America
CFAT	Carnegie Foundation for the Advancement of Teaching (U.S.A.)	**CFDC**	Canadian Film Development Corporation
CFB	Cavity Foam Bureau	**CFDC**	Cane Farming Development Corporation (Guyana)
CFB	Commonwealth Forestry Bureau	**CFDC**	Centre Français de Droit Comparé
CFB	Conselho Federal de Biblioteconomia (Brazil)	**CFDE**	Centre de Formation et de Documentation sur l'Environnement
CFB	Council of the Corporation of Foreign Bondholders	**CFDT**	Compagnie Française pour le Développement des Fibres Textiles
CFBS	Canadian Federation of Biological Sciences	**CFDT**	Confédération Française Démocratique du Travail
CFC	Caribbean Food Corporation	**CFDT**	Union Départemental des Syndicats (Martinique)
CFC	Centre Français du Copyright	**CFE**	Comisión Federal de Electricidad (Mexico)
CFC	Co-operative Federation of Ceylon	**CFE**	Compagnie Belge de Chemins de Fer et d'Entreprises (Belgium)
CFC	Committee for a Free China		
CFC	Compagnie Forestière du Congo	**CFE**	Compagnie Forestière d'Eseka (Cameroon)
CFC	Confédération Générale des Cadres		
CFC	Congregatio Fratrum Christianorum	**CFE**	Compagnie Forestière de l'Equateur (Gabon)
CFC	Conservative Family Campaign		
CFC	Credit Foncier du Caméroun	**CFE**	Confédération Fiscale Européenne
CFCA	Canadian Federal Centre for AIDS	**CFE**	Confédération Française d'Encadrement
CFCA	China Fashion Colour Association	**CFEB**	Central Forestry Examination Board
CFCA	Confédération Française de la Coopération Agricole	**CFÉI**	Centre de Formation et d'Échanges Internationaux
CFCAM	Caisse Forestière de Crédit Agricole Mutuel et de Garantie Incendie Forestière	**CFEM**	Compagnie Française d'Entreprises Métalliques
CFCB	Compagnie Française de Crédit et de Banque	**CFEP**	Centre Français de Protection de l'Enfance
CFCCA	Centre de Formation des Cadres pour Coopératives Agricoles (Rwanda)	**CFÉS**	Comité Français d'Éducation pour la Santé
CFCD	Compagnie Foncière et Commerciale de Distribution	**CFESA**	Commercial Food Equipment Service Association (U.S.A.)
CFCD-CI	Compagnie Foncière et Commerciale de Distribution de Côte-d'Ivoire	**CFETCC**	China Foreign Economic and Trade Consultants Corporation
CFCE	Cathedrals Fabric Commission for England	**CFEU**	Conseil Français pour l'Europe Unie
CFCE	Centre Français du Commerce Extérieur	**CFF**	Chemins de Fer Fédéraux Suisse
CFCF	Comité Français contre la Faim	**CFF**	Civilforsvars-Forbundet
CFCIA	Chambre Française de Commerce et d'Industrie en Algérie	**CFF**	Commission For The Future
		CFF	Commission on Fossil Fuels
CFCO	Chemin de Fer Congo-Océan	**CFF**	Crédit Foncier de France
CFCPC	Comité des Fruits à Cidre et des Productions Cidricoles	**CFFA**	Commonwealth Families and Friendship Association
CFCS	Caribbean Food Crops Society	**CFG**	Compagnie Forestière du Gabon
CFD	Christlicher Friedensdienst = CMP, ICVD, MCP	**CFGAC**	Central Fire Brigades Advisory Council for England and Wales
CFDA	Cooperative Food Distributors of America	**CFGB**	Canadian Foodgrains Bank

CFGE	California Fruit Growers Exchange (U.S.A.)	**CFIUS**	Committee on Foreign Investment in the United States
CFGG	Compagnie Forestière du Golfe de Guinée	**CFJS**	China Federation of Journalism Societies
CFH	Canadian Federation for the Humanities = FCEH	**CFK**	Christliche Friedenskonferenz = CCP, CPC, HMK
CFH	International Information Centre of the Swiss Watchmaking Industry	**CFK**	Compagnie Forestière Kritikos (Cameroon)
CFHA	Colorado Forestry and Horticulture Association (U.S.A.)	**CFL**	Canadian Federation of Labour
CFHE	Consortium for Financing Higher Education (U.S.A.)	**CFL**	Chemins de Fer Luxembourgeois
CFHS	Catholic Family History Society	**CFL**	Confektionsfabrikanternes Landsforbund
CFI	Campaign for Freedom of Information	**CFL**	Creation for Liberation
CFI	Campaign for Industry	**CFLA**	Chinese Foreign Literature Association
CFI	Clothing and Footwear Institute	**CFLA**	Comisión Forestal Latinoamericana
CFI	Compagnie Forestière de l'Indénie (Ivory Coast)	**CFLAI**	Chinese Folk Literature and Art Institute
CFI	Confederation of Finishing Industries	**CFLF**	Comptoir des Filasses de Lin Françaises
CFI	Consejo Federal de Inversiones (Argentina)	**CFLP**	Central Fire Liaison Panel
CFI	Cooperative Fertilizers International (U.S.A.)	**CFM**	Centre for Facilities Management
		CFM	Centre for Franchise Marketing
CFI	Corporación de Fomento Industrial (Dominican Republic)	**CFM**	Comisión Femenil Mexicana Nacional
CFI	Corporación Financiera Internacional (UN) = IFC, SFI	**CFM**	Empresa dos Caminhos de Ferro de Moçambique
CFI	Council of the Forest Industries of British Columbia	**CFMA**	Chair Frame Manufacturers Association
CFI	Court of First Instance (EU)	**CFMC**	Caribbean Fishery Management Council (Puerto Rico)
CFI/BC	Crown Forest Industries of British Columbia	**CFME**	Compagnie Franco-Malgache d'Entreprises
CFIA	Comisión de Fomento e Investigaciones Agrícolas (Chile)	**CFMEU**	Construction, Forestry, Mining and Energy Union
CFIACE	Association Feminine d'Information and d'Aide a Creation d'Enterprise (Guinea)	**CFMM**	Congregatio Fratrum Beatae Mariae Virginis Misericordiae (Netherlands)
CFIB	Canadian Federation of Independent Business	**CFMMDRI**	Changsha Ferrous Metal Mine Design and Research Institute
CFIBC	Council of Forest Industries of British Columbia	**CFMR**	Comité Français de la Mécanique des Roches
CFIC	Canned Food Information Centre	**CFMSA**	Commonwealth Committee of Foreign Ministers on Southern Africa
CFIC	Congregatio Filii Immaculatae Conceptionis	**CFMU**	Compagnie Française des Minerais d'Uranium
CFIE	Conseil des Fédérations Industrielles d'Europe; Consejo de las Federaciones Industriales de Europa = CEIF, REI	**CFMVA**	Centre de Formation de Moniteurs et de Vulgarisateurs Agricoles
		CFN	Co-operative Federation of Nigeria
		CFN	Corporación Financiera Nacional (Ecuador)
CFIT	Committee for Industrial Technology (DTI)	**CfN**	Council for Nature
		CFNA	Comisión Forestal Norteamericana (FAO) = CFAN, NAFC
		CFNBS	Committee on the Formation of the National Biological Survey (U.S.A.)

CFNCL	Comité Fédéral National de Contrôle Laitier
CFNFMPR	Centre Familial National pour la Formation Ménagère Professionnelle Rurale
CFNI	Caribbean Food and Nutrition Institute
CFO	Algemeen Christelijke Federatie van Bonden van Personeel, Werkzaam bij de Overheid en in de Sectoren Gezondheidszorg en Maatschappelijk
CFOA	Chief Fire Officers Association
CFOCF	Commission For Our Common Future
CFP	Canadian Forest Products
CFP	Clube Filatelico de Portugal
CFP	Clube Filatélico de Portugal
CFP	Comissão de Financiamento da Produção (Brazil)
CFP	Compagnie Française des Pétroles
CFP	Concentración de Fuerzas Populares (Ecuador)
CFP	Confédération Française de la Photographie
CFP	Congregatio Fratrum Pauperum Sancti Francisci Seraphici
CFP	La Coordination du Front Populaire (Burkina Faso)
CFPA	Canadian Food Processors Association
CFPA	Caribbean Family Planning Affiliation
CFPA	China Family Planning Association
CFPC	Centre Chrétien des Patrons et Dirigeants d'Entreprise Française
CFPD	Compagnie Française Powell Duffryn
CFPFLC	Confédération Française des Producteurs de Fruits, Légumes et Champignons
CFPI	Central Family Planning Institute (India)
CFPI	Centro de Fomento y Productividad Industrial (Guatemala)
CFPI	Commission de la Fonction Publique Internationale = ICSC
CFPO	Commission des Forêts pour le Proche-Orient = NEFC
CFPO	Cornish Fish Producers Organisation
CFPPA	Cend de Formation et de Perfectionnement Professionnel Agricole
CFPPT	Centre de Formation et de Perfectionnement des Planteurs de Tabac
CFPRA	Campden Food Preservation Research Association
CFPS	Centre for Foreign Policy Studies (Canada)
CFPS	Confédération Française des Professions Sociales
CFR	Center for Field Research (U.S.A.)
CFR	Centre for Futures Research (U.S.A.)
CFR	Committee on Family Research (Belgium, Sweden)
CFRAI	Comité Français des Relations Agricoles Internationales
CFRI	Central Fuel Research Institute (India)
CFRO	Centre Français de Recherche Opérationnelle
CFRT	Colorado Foundation for Research in Tuberculosis (U.S.A.)
CFRTI	Centre Français de Renseignements Techniques Industriels
CFRTU	Chinese Federation of Railway Worker's Unions
CFRZ	Centre Fédéral de Recherches Zootechniques (Switzerland)
ČFS	Česká Farmaceutická Společnost
CFS	Canadian Forestry Service
CFS	Centre for Fiscal Studies
CFS	Chinese Foot Society
CFS	Committee on World Food Security (FAO)
CFS	Compagnie Forestière de Sangatanga (Gabon)
CFS	Comptoir Foncier du Sénégal
CFS	Comptoir Français des Superphosphates
CFS	Congregatio a Fraternitate Sacerdotali
CFSA	Charge Families' Support Association
CFSA	Cornish Federation of Sea Anglers
CFSAMAE	Chinese Federation of Societies for Agricultural Machinery and Agricultural Engineering
CFSC	Canadian Friends Service Committee
CFSG	Compagnie Forestière du Sud-Gabon
CFSI	Comité Français de la Semoulerie Industrielle
CFSL	Central Forensic Science Laboratory
CFSO	Compagnie Forestière Sangha-Oubangui (Cameroon)
CFT	Campaign Free Tibet
CFT	Children's Family Trust
CFT	Circle Foundation Trust Co. Ltd

CFT	Cystic Fibrosis Trust
CFTA	Celtic Film and Television Association
CFTC	Commodity Futures Trading Commission (U.S.A.)
CFTC	Commonwealth Fund for Technical Cooperation
CFTE	China Flight Test Establishment
CFTF	Centre Technique Forestier Tropical
CFTF	Children's Film and Television Foundation
CFTH	Compagnie Française Thomson-Houston
CFTRI	Central Food Technological Research Institute (India)
CFTV	Centre de Formation de Techniciens de Vulgarisation
CFTZ	Colón Free Trade Zone (Panama)
CFU	Caribbean Football Union
CFUP	Comité Français de l'Union Pan-Européenne
CFV	Corporación Venezolana de Fomento
CFW	Care for the Wild
CFW	Committee for the Free World (U.S.A.)
CFW	Concern for Family and Womanhood
CFWAA	China Folk Writers and Artists Association
CFX	Congregatio Fratrum a Sancto Francisco Xaverio
CFZ	Colon Free Zone (Panama)
CFZV	Centrala Farmaseutica Zoo-Veterinara (Romania)
CG	Caritas Gemeinschaft für Pflege- und Sozialberufe e.V.
CG	Coalicion Galega
CG	Coalition des Gauches
CG	Common Ground
CG	Contadora Group
CG18	GATT Consultative Group of Eighteen
CGA	Canadian Gas Association
CGA	Citrus Growers' Association (Belize)
CGA	Compagnie Générale d'Automatisme
CGA	Confédération Générale de l'Agriculture
CGA	Conseil Général de l'Agriculture
CGA	Country Gentlemen's Association
CGA	Cyprus Geographical Association =GOK
CGAD	Confédération Générale de l'Alimentation en Détail
CGADIP	Compagnie Gazière d'Afrique et de Distribution de Primagaz
CGAF	Confédération Générale de l'Artisanat Français
CGAF	Confédération Générale des Architectes Français
CGAP	Comité Général d'Action Paysanne
CGAPRPE	Consejo General de Asociaciones de Profesionales de Relaciones Publicas de España
CGAT	City Gallery Arts Trust
CGB	Christlicher Gewerkschaftsbund Deutschlands
CGB	Commonwealth Geographical Bureau (Sri Lanka)
CGB	Confédération Générale des Planteurs de Betteraves
CGBAPS	Cape Grim Baseline Atmospheric Pollution Station
CGBCE	Christliche Gewerkschaft Bergbau-Chemie-Energie
CGBD	Consultative Group on Biological Diversity (RBF)
CGBE	Christliche Gewerkschaft Bergbau und Energie
CGC	Canadian Grain Commission = CCG
CGC	Committee on Gynaecological Cytology (DOH)
CGC	Commonwealth Games Council
CGC	Confederación General de Cuadros
CGC	Confédération Générale des Cadres
CGC	Management and Co-ordination Advisory Committee (EU)
CGC-L	Consejo General de Castilla y Leon
CGCE	Centre Gabonais de Commerce Extérieur
CGCED	Caribbean Group for Cooperation in Economic Development
CGCI	Confédération Générale du Commerce et de l'Industrie
CGCRI	Central Glass and Ceramics Research Institute (India)
CGCS	Commonwealth Games Council for Scotland
CGCT	Compagnie Générale de Constructions Téléphoniques
CGD	Caixa Geral de Depésitos
CGD	Christliche Gewerkschaftbund Deutschland
CGD	Chronic Granulomatous Disease Research Trust and Support Group
CGDE	Christliche Gewerkschaft Deutscher Eisenbahner

CGDEM	Council of Gas Detection Equipment Manufacturers
CGDK	Coalition Government of Democratic Kampuchea
CGDLS	Confederazione Generale Democratica dei Lavoratori Sanmarinesi (San Marino)
CGDTS	Consejo General de Diplomados en Trabajo Social
CGE	Centre for Global Education
CGÉ	Compagnie Générale d'Électricité (Cameroon, France, Gabon, Senegal)
CGE	Confederación General Económica (Argentina)
CGÉ	Confédération Générale l'Épargne
CGE	Conservative Group for Europe
CGÉA	Confédération Générale Économique Algérienne
CGEC	Confederación General de Empleados de Comercio (Argentina)
CGÉCI	Compagnie Générale d'Électricité de Côte-d'Ivoire
CGEM	Confédération Général des Employeurs de Mauritanie
CGEM	Confédération Générale des Employeurs Marocains
CGÉM	Confédération Générale Économique Marocaine
CGÉR	Caise Générale d'Épargne et de Retraite (Belgium) = ASLK
CGÉR	Centre de Gestion et d'Économie Rurale
CGER	Centre for Global Environmental Research
CGF	Child Growth Foundation
CGF	Commonwealth Games Federation
CGFPI	Consultative Group on Food Production and Investment in Developing Countries (UN)
CGFTL	Confédération Générale des Filateurs et Tisseurs de Lin
CGG	Compagnie Générale de Géophysique
CGI	Catholic Guides of Ireland
CGI	Church Growth International (Republic of Korea)
CGI	Comitato Glaciologico Italiano
CGI	Commisione Geodetica Italiana
CGI	Compagnie Générale Industrielle (Ivory Coast)
CGI	Congrès Géologique International
CGIA	Center for Geographical Information and Analysis
CGIA	Confederazione Generale Italiana dell'Artigianato
CGIAR	Consultative Group on International Agricultural Research (FAO) = GCIAI, GCRAI
CGIC	Comité Général Interprofessionnel Chanvrier
CGIL	Confederazione Generale Italiana del Lavoro
CGL	Confédération Générale du Logement
CGLI	City and Guilds of London Institute
CGLO	Commonwealth Geological Liaison Office
CGLS	Confederazione General dei Lavoratori della Somalia
CGM	Compagnie Générale de Madagascar
CGMA	Casein Glue Manufacturers Association
CGMA	Compressed Gas Manufacturers' Association (U.S.A.)
CGMW	Commission for the Geological Map of the World = CCGM
CGOT	Compagnie Générale des Oléagineux Tropicaux
CGP	Caisse Générale de Péréquation des Prix des Produits et Marchandises de Grande Consommation (Burkina Faso)
CGP	Cámara Guatemalteca de Periodismo
CGP	Comando Guerrilleros del Pueblo (Guatemala)
CGP	Commissariat Général à la Productivité
CGP	Commissariat Général au Plan
CGPB	Confederação General dos Pescadores do Brasil
CGPB	Confédération Générale des Planteurs de Betteraves
CGPC	Canadian Government Publishing Centre
CGPCC	Confédération Générale des Planteurs de Chicorée à Café
CGPEL	Confédération Générale des Producteurs de Fruits et Légumes
CGPJ	Consejo General del Poder Judicial
CGPLBIR	Confédération Générale des Producteurs de Lait de Brebis et des Industriels de Roquefort
CGPM	Conférénce Générale des Poids et Mesures
CGPM	Conseil Général des Pêches pour la Méditerrannée (FAO) = GFCM
CGPME	Confédération Générale des Petites et Moyennes Entreprises

CGPP	Confederazione General dei Produttori di Patate = CGPPT	**CGT**	Central General de Trabajadores (Dominican Republic, El Salvador, Honduras, Venezuela)
CGPPO	Compagnie Générale des Plantations et Palmeraies de l'Ogooué	**CGT**	Centro de Geografía Tropical (Ecuador)
CGPPT	Confédération Général des Producteurs de Pommes de Terre = CGPP	**CGT**	Commissariat Général au Tourisme (Belgium)
CGPRT Centre	Regional Coordinating Centre for R & D of Coarse Grains, Pulses, Roots and Tuber Crops in the Humid Tropics of Asia and the Pacific (ESCAP) (Indonesia)	**CGT**	Compagnie Générale Transatlantique
		CGT	Confederação General dos Trabalhadores (Brazil)
		CGT	Confederación General de Trabajadores (Chile, Colombia, Honduras Venezuela)
CGPS	Canadian Government Purchasing Service	**CGT**	Confederación General del Trabajo (Argentina, Colombia, Nicaragua)
CGPT	Confédération des Paysans Travailleurs	**CGT**	Confédération Générale du Travail (France, Luxembourg, Martinique)
CGR	Center for Governmental Research Inc. (U.S.A.)	**CGT(I)**	Confederación General de Trabajo (Independiente) (Nicaragua)
CGR	Contraloria General de la Republica (Nicaragua)		
CGRA	Canadian Good Roads Association	**CGTB**	Canadian Government Travel Bureau
CGRA	China and Glass Retailers Association	**CGTB**	Confederación General de Trabajadores de Bolivia
CGRA	Consortium Général des Recherches Aéronautiques	**CGTC**	Central General di Trahadonan di Corsow (Netherlands Antilles)
CGRB	Capital Gains Research Bureau	**CGTC**	Confederación General de Trabajadores Costarricenses
CGRB	Combinatie Groningen v. Rationele Bedrijfsvoering	**CGTFB**	Confederación General de Trabajadores Fabriles de Bolivia
CGRI	Canadian Gas Research Institute		
CGRS	China Guanhanging Research Society	**CGTFO**	Confédération Générale du Travail Force Ouvrière
CGS	Canadian Geographical Society	**CGTG**	Confédération Générale du Travail de la Guadeloupe
CGS	Canadian Geotechnical Society		
CGS	Carolina Geological Society	**CGTL**	Confédération Générale des Travailleurs du Liban
CGS	Center for Government Service (U.S.A.)		
CGS	China Geography Society	**CGTP**	Confederación General de Trabajadores de Perú
CGS	Chinese Geophysical Society		
CGS	Clinical Genetics Society	**CGTP-IN**	Confederação General dos Trabalhadores Portugueses – Intersindical Nacional
CGS	Confederación General de Sindicatos (El Salvador)		
CGS	Cottage Garden Society	**CGTR**	Confédération Générale du Travail de la Réunion
CGSA	Computer Graphics Suppliers' Association	**CGTR**	Confédération Générale du Travail du Rwanda
CGSB	Canadian General Standards Board		
CGSB	Coordinadora Guerrillera Simon Bolivar (Colombia)	**CGTREO**	Compagnie Générale de Travaux de Recherches et d'Exploitation Océaniques
CGSCOP	Confédération Générale des Sociétés Coopératives Ouvrières de Production	**CGTS**	Confederación General de Trabajadores Salvadoreños
CGSI	Confédération Générale des Syndicats Indépendants	**CGTT**	Confederación General de Trabajadores del Transporte Terrestre y Afines de Chile
CGSLB	Centrale Générale des Syndicats Libéraux de Belgique = ACLVB	**CGTTA**	General Confederation of African Workers
CGSUS	Council of Graduate Schools of the United States		

CGTU	Confederación General de Trabajadores del Uruguay
ČGU	Česká Geologický Ústav
CGU	Canadian Geophysical Union
CGU	Confederación General Universitaria (Brazil)
CGUP	Comité Guatemalteca de Unidad Popular
CGV	Confédération Générale de la Vieillesse
CGV	Confédération Générale des Vignerons
CGV	Consejo General Vasco
CGVCO	Confédération Générale des Vignerons du Centre-Ouest
CGVSO	Confédération Générale des Vignerons du Sud-Ouest
CGWB	Canadian Government Wheat Board
CH	Centrala Handlowa
CH	European Regional Clearing House for Community Work (IEISW)
CH-AGRID	Association Nationale Suisse de Génie Rural, Irrigations et Drainage
CHA	Canadian Health Association
CHA	Canadian Historical Association
CHA	Caribbean Hotel Association
CHA	Catholic Headmasters' Association (Éire)
CHA	Catholic Health Association of the United States
CHA	Commercial Horticultural Association
CHA	Community Hospitals Association (*ex* AGPCH)
CHA	Countrywide Holidays Association
CHAC	Caribbean Hotel Advisory Council (Puerto Rico)
CHAC	Catholic Hospital Association of Canada
CHACONA	Chantier de Construction Navale
CHACRA	Champions for Action On Conservation and Rehabilitation in the Andes
CHAFC	Committee of Heads of Australian Fauna Collections
CHAFREC	Chambre Syndicale Française de l'Enseignement Privé par Correspondance
CHAH	Committee of Heads of Australian Herbaria
CHAIDIS	Chaine Africaine d'Importation, de Distribution et d'Exportation (Senegal)
CHAIS	Consumer Hazards Analysis Information Service
CHALUT-CAM	Société de Chalutage du Caméroun
CHAMCOM	Chambre de Commerce d'Agriculture et de l'Industrie de la République du Tchad
CHANCOM	Channel Committee (NATO)
CHAO	Commission Hydrographique de l'Asie Orientale (Monaco) = EAHC
CHAPS	Center for Health and Advanced Policy Studies (U.S.A.)
CHAR	Campaign for the Homeless and Rootless
CHAS	Catholic Housing Aid Society
CHAS	Children's Hospice Association Scotland
CHASYCA	Chambre Syndicale des Abattage et Confitionnement de Produits de Basse-Cour
ChAT	Chrześcijańska Akademia Teologiczna
CHB	Central Housing Board (Kenya)
CHB	Christlicher Holz- und Bauarbeiterverband der Schweiz
CHCC	Welsh Music Information Centre
CHCE	Comité Hospitalier de la Communauté Européenne = HCEC
CHCF	Catholic Handicapped Childrens Fellowship
CHD	Centre for Human Development
CHE	Campaign for Homosexual Equality
CHE	Centre for Health Economics, University of York
CHE	Comité d'Hygiène et d'Eau
CHE	IUAES Commission on Human Ecology (Poland)
CHÉAM	Centre des Hautes Études sur l'Afrique et l'Asie Modernes
CHEAR	Council on Higher Education in the American Republics
CHEC	Commonwealth Human Ecology Council
CHEEC	Committee on Higher Education in the European Community (EURASHE) (Belgium)
CHEEF	Center for Hydrogen Embrittlement of Electroplated Fasteners
CHEIRON	International Society of the History of Behavioral and Social Sciences (U.S.A.)
CHEK	Committee on the Human Environment
CHEMA	Container Handling Equipment Manufacturers' Association
CHEM-RAWN	Chemical Research Applied to World Needs
CHENOP	Companhia Hidro-Eléctrica do Norte de Portugal

CHER	Centre for Habilitation, Education and Research, University of Waterloo	**CHOCODI**	Chocolaterie, Confiserie de Côte-d'Ivoire
CHESF	Companhia Hidro-Elétrica do São Francisco	**CHOGM**	Commonwealth Heads of Government Meeting
CHESS	Cornell High Energy Synchroton Source (U.S.A.)	**CHPA**	Combined Heat and Power Association
CHEST	Combined Higher Education Software Teams	**CHPM**	Centrala Handłowa Przemysłu Muzycznego
CHETNA	Centre for Health Education, Training and Nutrition Awareness (India)	**CHPRS**	Chinese Handwriting and Painting Research (China)
CHF	Canadian Hunger Foundation	**CHR**	Centralforeningen af Hotelvoerter og Restauratærer i Danmark
CHF	Catholic Handicapped Fellowship	**CHR**	Collegium Heraldicum Russiae
CHF	Cooperative Housing Foundation (U.S.A.)	**CHR**	Commission Internationale de l'Hydrologie du Bassin du Rhin = KHR
CHFA	Consumer's Health Forum of Australia	**CHR**	Conférénce Haïtienne des Religieux
CHIA	Canadian Hovercraft Industries Association	**CHRAC**	Construction and Housing Research Advisory Council
CHIA	Craft and Hobby Industry Association	**CHRC**	Canadian Human Rights Commission = CCDP
CHIDRAL	Central Hidroelectrica del Rio Anchicaya, Limitada (Colombia)		
CHIDS	Cholistan Institute of Desert Studies (Pakistan)	**CHRDI**	Chinese Helicopter Research and Development Institute
CHIL-ECTRIA	Compañia Chilena de Electricidad	**CHRG**	Committee for Human Rights in Grenada
CHIMAF	Société Gabonaise de Produits Chimiques Industriels	**CHRH**	Committee for Human Rights in Honduras
ChIN	International Chemical Information Network (ICCS, PGI) = INCI	**CHRI**	Chongqing Highway Research Institute
CHIN-CHAN	Allied Commander in Chief, Channel (NATO)	**CHRI**	Commonwealth Human Rights Initiative
CHIP	Center for Human Information Processing, University of California, San Diego	**CHS**	Canadian Hydrographic Service
		CHS	Centre for Human Settlements (UN) (Kenya)
CHIPS	Christian International Peace Service	**ČHS**	Česká Hudebni Společnost
CHISS	Centre Haïtien d'Investigation en Sciences Sociales	**CHS**	Clarinet Heritage Society
CHIT	Child Head Injury Trust	**CHS**	Clydesdale Horse Society
CHIVE	Council for Hearing-Impaired Visits and Exchanges	**CHSA**	Chest Heart and Stroke Association
		CHSM	Centre for Health Services Management
CHLA	Canadian Health Libraries Association	**ChSS**	Chrześcijańskie Stowarzyszenie Społeczne
CHME	UK Standing Conference on Hospitality Management Education		
ChMF	Chernomorskaia Flota	**CHT**	Church Housing Trust
CHO	Confederation of Healing Organizations	**CHTA**	Contract Heat Treatment Association
CHO-BISCO	Chambre Syndicale des Grossiers en Confiserie Chocolaterie, Biscuits et Autres Dérivés du Sucre (Belgium)	**CHTI**	Caribbean Hospitality Training Institute
		CHTS	China Highway and Transportation Society
CHOCO-CAMC	Chocolaterie-Confiserie Camérounaise	**CHU**	Convenio Hipolito Unanue (Peru)
		CHULS	Committee of Heads of University Law Schools
CHOCO-SUISSE	Union de Fabricants Suisses de Chocolat	**CHy**	Commission for Hydrology (WMO)
		CHZ	Centrala Handłu Zagranicznego

CI	Caritas Internationalis, International Confederation of Catholic Organisations for Charitable Social Action	**CIAA**	Comité International d'Assistance Aéroportuaire
CI	Citizens' Initiative (Bulgaria)	**CIAA**	Comptoir Industriel et Agricole Abidjan (Ivory Coast)
CI	Combustion Institute	**CIAA**	Confédération des Industries Agro-Alimentaires de la CEE
CI	Commonwealth Institute		
CI	Congress of the Intelligentsia (Moldova)	**CIAA**	Consejo Internacional de Administración de Archivos (U.S.A.) = IRMC
CI	Conservation International (U.S.A.)		
CI	Consumer Interpol (IOCU) (Malaysia)	**CIAA-UNICE**	Commission des Industries Agricoles et Alimentaires de l'Union des Industries de la CEE
CI	Institutum Iosephitarum Gerardmontensium		
CI-AF	Comité Inter-Africain sur les Pratiques Traditionnelles ayant Effet sur la Santé des Femmes et des Enfants en Afrique = IAC	**CIAAU**	Comptoir Ivoirien d'Accessoires Automobiles = ICVA
		CIAB	Centro de Investigaciones Agricolas de El Bajio (Mexico)
CIA	Cancer Information Association	**CIAB**	Conseil International des Agences Bénévoles
CIA	Catering Institute of Australia		
CIA	Central Intelligence Agency (U.S.A.)	**CIABS**	Center for Inter-American and Border Studies, University of Texas at El Paso
CIA	Centre d'Insémination Artificielle		
CIA	Centre International d'Aviation Agricole	**CIAC**	Centrale Ivoirienne d'Achats et de Crédit
CIA	Centro de Inseminación Artificial (Puerto Rico)	**CIAC**	Centre International d'Action Culture (Belgium)
CIA	Centro de Investigaciones Agronómicas (Venezuela)	**CIAC**	Ceramics Industry Advisory Committee
		CIAC	Compagnie des Industries Africaines du Caoutchouc
CIA	Chartered Institute of Arbitrators		
CIA	Chemical Industries Association	**CIAC**	Corporación de la Industria Aeronaútica Colombiana
CIA	Chemical Institute of Australia		
CIA	Cigar Institute of America	**CIACA**	Commission Internationale d'Aéronefs de Construction Amateur (FAI)
CIA	Club International Aérophilatelistes		
CIA	Collegium Internationale Allergologicum	**CIACAM**	Compagnie Industrielle d'Automobiles du Caméroun
		CIACOL	Compañia de Ingenieros Agrénomos de Colombia
CIA	Comisión Internacional del Alamo (FAO)		
CIA	Comisión Internacional del Arroz (Thailand)	**CIACOP**	Centro Interamericano de Adiestramiento en Communicaciones para Población (Costa Rica)
CIA	Comitato Italiano Atlantico		
CIA	Comité International d'Auschwitz = IAK	**CIAD**	Association for Computer Applications in Engineering (Netherlands)
CIA	Commission Internationale d'Aérostation (FAI)	**CIAD**	Coalicion Internacional para Acciónes de Desarrollo = ICDA
CIA	Commonwealth Industries Association		
CIA	Compagnia Industriale Aerospaziale	**CIADFOR**	Centre Interafricain pour le Développement de la Formation Professionnelle (ILO)
CIA	Confederación Intercooperativa Agropecuária (Argentina)		
CIA	Confédération Internationale des Accordéonistes = ICA	**CIADI**	Centro Internacional de Arreglo de Diferencias Relativas a Inversiones = CIRDI, ICSID
CIA	Confédération Nationale Belge du Commerce Indépendant de l'Alimentation	**CIAE**	Central Institute of Agricultural Engineering (India)
CIA	Conseil International des Archives = ICA	**CIAE**	Chongqing Institute of Architecture and Engineering
CIA	Credit Insurance Association		

CIAECO-SOC	Consejo Interamericano Economico y Social	**CIAP**	Centre d'Information Agricole des Planteurs
CIAEM	Comité Interamericano Educación Matemática = IACME	**CIAP**	Centre d'Information de l'Aviation Privée
CIAF	Centro Interamericano de Fotointerpretación (Colombia)	**CIAP**	Centro de Investigaciones en Administracion Pública (Argentina)
CIAF	Centro Internazionale di Analisi Finanziaria	**CIAP**	Comité Interamericano de la Alianza para el Progreso (OAS)
CIAF	Congrès International d'Études Africaines = ICAS	**CIAP**	Commission Internationale de l'Atlas de Folklore Européen = SIEF
CIAFMA	Centre International de l'Actualité Fantastique et Magique	**CIAP**	Commission Internationale des Arts et Traditions Populaires
CIAG	Commission Internationale d'Aviation Générale (FAI)	**CIAP**	Compagnie Indusdtrielle et Agricole de l'Oubangui (Central Africa)
CIAG	Construction Industry Advisory Council	**CIAP**	Compagnie Ivoirienne d'Armement à la Pêche
CIAGA	Confederación Interamericana de Ganaderos = IACC	**CIAP**	Conseil Interafricain de Philosophie
CIAGI	Compagnie Inter-Arabe pour la Garantie des Invetissements = AIGC, IAIGC	**CIAPA**	Collectif International d'Appui a la Pêche Artisanale = ICSF
CIAGRAN	Camara de la Industria de las Artes Graficas de Nicaragua	**CIAPESC**	Companhia Amazônica de Pesca (Brazil)
CIAI	Coffee Industry Association of Ireland	**CIAPG**	Confédération Internationale des Anciens Prisonniers de Guerre = ICFPW
CIAI	Conférence International des Associations d'Ingénieurs		
CIAL	Credit Industriel d'Alsace et de Lorraine	**CIAPY**	Centro de Investigacion Agricolas de la Peninsula de Yucatan (Mexico)
CIALA	Inter-Faculty Centre for African Anthopology and Linguistics (Zaïre)	**CIAQ**	Centre d'Insémination Artificielle du Québec (Canada)
CIAM	Centro Internazionale di Animazione Missionario	**CIAR**	Canadian Institute for Advanced Research
CIAM	Colegio de Ingenieros Agrónomos de México	**CIARA**	Conférence Internationale sur l'Assistance aux Réfugiés en Afrique = ICARA
CIAM	Commission Internationale d'Aéromodelisme (FAI)	**CIARA**	Fundación para la Capacitación e Investigación Aplicada a la Reforma Agraria (Venezuela)
CIAM-LA	Centro de Investigacion y Accion de la Mujer Latinoamericana		
CIAMAN	Confédération Internationale des Associations des Médecines Alternatives Naturelles	**CIArb**	Chartered Institute of Arbitrators
		CIAS	California Institute for Asian Studies (U.S.A.)
CIAMÉ	Commission Interministérielle pour les Appareils de Mesures Électriques et Électroniques	**CIAS**	Centro de Investigación y Acción Social (Colombia)
		CIAS	Centro de Investigaciones Administrativas y Sociales (Venezuela)
CIAN	Comité International pour l'Afrique Noire	**CIAS**	Centro de Investigaciones Agrícolas de Sinaloa (Mexico)
CIANE	Centro de Investigaciones Agricolas del Noreste (Mexico)	**CIAS**	Comité Investigación Agua Subterránea (Argentina)
CIANE	Comité Interministerielle d'Action pour la Nature et l'Environnement	**CIAS**	Conference of Independent African States
CIANS	Collegium Internationale Activitatis Nervosae Superioris		
CIAO	Compagnie Industrielle Agricole Oubangui (Zaïre)	**CIAS**	Conseil International d'Action Sociale = ICSW

CIAS	Consejo Inter-Americano de Seguridad = IASC	**CIB**	Centrum voor Informatie Beleid
CIASA	Compania Internacional Aerea S.A. (Ecuador)	**CIB**	Chartered Institute of Bankers
		CIB	Chartered Institute of Builders
CIASE	Centro de Investigaciones Agrícolas del Sureste (Mexico)	**CIB**	Comité Interprofessional Bananier
		CIB	Commission Internationale de la Baleine = CBI, IWC
CIASE	China Institute of Aeronautic Systems Engineering	**CIB**	Communauté International Baha'ie = BIC
CIASI	Comité Interministériel pour l'Aménagement des Structures Industrielles	**CIB**	Confédération des Immobiliers de Belge
		CIB	Conseil Interfédéral du Bois
CIASTA	Cooperative Institute for Aerospace Science and Terrestrial Applications (U.S.A.)	**CIB**	Conseil International du Bâtiment pour la Recherche, l'Étude et la Documentation
CIASTR	Commission Internationale d'Astronautique (FAI)	**CIB**	Conseil International du Bétiment pour la Recherche, l'Étude el la Documentation
CIAT	Centro de Investigacion Agrícola Tropical (Bolivia)	**CIB**	Conseil International du Blé = CIT, IWC
CIAT	Centro Interamericano de Administración del Trabajo (ILO) (Peru)	**CIB**	Corporation of Insurance Brokers
CIAT	Centro Interamericano de Administradores Tributarios	**CIB**	ICC Counterfeiting Intelligence Bureau
CIAT	Centro Internacional de Agricultura Tropical (Colombia)	**CIB**	Société Congolaise Industrielle des Bois
CIAT	Comisión Interamericana del Atún Tropical = CITT, IATTC	**CIBAL**	Centre International de l'Information et Sources de l'Histoire Balkanique et Méditerranéenne (Bulgaria)
CIAT	Comité des Industries de l'Ennoblissement Textile des Pays de la CEE	**CIBC**	Canadian Imperial Bank of Commerce
CIATE	Cooperativa Industrial Agricola Tropical Ecuatoriana	**CIBC**	Confédération Internationale de la Boucherie et de la Charcuterie = IMV
CIATF	Comité International des Associations Techniques de Fonderie = ICFTA, IKGV	**CIBDOC**	International Council for Building Documentation
		CIBE	Confédération Internationale des Betteraviers Européens
CIATI	Centro de Investigación y Asistencia Técnica de la Industria (Argentina)	**CIBEP**	Association du Commerce International de Bulbes à Fleurs et de Plantes
CIATO	Centre Internationale d'Alcoologie/Toxicomanies	**CIBER**	Inter-African Centre for Information and Liaison in Rural Welfare
CIAV	Comisión Internacional de Ayuda y Verificacion (Nicaragua)	**CIBÉT**	Groupement Interuniversitaire Bénélux des Économistes des Transports (Belgium)
CIAV	Comité International pour l'Architecture Vernaculaire (ICOMOS)	**CIBIMA**	Centro de Investigacion de Biologia Marina (Argentina)
CIAVÉR	Centre International Audiovisuel d'Études et de Recherches (Belgium)	**CIBJO**	Confédération Internationale de la Bijouterie, Joaillerie, Orfèvrerie, des Diamants, Perles et Pierres
CIB	Campaign for an Independent Britain		
CIB	Central European International Bank	**CIBM**	Centro de Investigación de Biologia Marina (Argentina)
CIB	Centre Interaméricain de Biostatistique		
CIB	Centro de Investigaciones Básicas (Mexico)	**CIBPP**	Confédération Internationale de Jeu de Balle Pelote Paume
CIB	Centro de Investigaciones Biologicas	**CIBRA**	Comerico e Indústria de Produtos Agrícolas do Brasil
CIB	Centro Internacional Bibliografico	**CIBRAN**	Companhia Brasileira de Antibioticos

CIBRAZEM	Companhia Brasileira de Armazenamento		**CIC**	Corporacion de Ingenieros Consultores (Ecuador)
CIBS	Center for International Business Studies (U.S.A.)		**CIC**	Council for International Contact
			CIC	Crédit Industriel et Commercial
CIBSE	Chartered Institution of Building Services Engineers (Éire)		**CICA**	Canadian Institute of Chartered Accountants
CIBTC	China International Book Trading Corporation		**CICA**	Centre for International Co-operation Activities (Netherlands)
CIBV	Consejo Internacional de Buena Vecindad = IGNC		**CICA**	Centro Interamericano de Ciencias Administrativas
CIC	Capital Issues Committee		**CICA**	Chemical and Industrial Consultants' Association
CIC	Caribbean Investment Corporation			
CIC	Centre d'Information de la Couler		**CICA**	Comité Interconfédéral de Cordination de l'Artisanat
CIC	Centre d'Informations Catholiques			
CIC	Centre for International Communication (Netherlands)		**CICA**	Comité International Catholique des Aveugles
CIC	Chemical Institute of Canada = ICC		**CICA**	Comité International de la Croisade des Aveugles
CIC	China Institute of Communications			
CIC	Cinema International Corporation		**CICA**	Comité International des Critiques d'Architecture
CIC	Climate Impacts Centre (Australia)			
CIC	Cognac Information Centre		**CICA**	Comité International pour la Cité Antique
CIC	Collége Internationale des Chirurgiens = ICS		**CICA**	Comité Internationale de la Crise Alimentaire
CIC	Comité Intergubernamental de los Paises Coordinador de la Cuenca del Plata (Argentina)		**CICA**	Commerciale Italiane Cooperative Agricole
CIC	Comité International de Coordination = ICC		**CICA**	Compagnie Internationale de Commerce et d'Approvisionnement
CIC	Comité International de Coordination pour l'Initiation à la Science et le Développement des Activités Scientifiques Extra-Scolaires =ICC		**CICA**	Confédération Internationale du Crédit Agricole = ICAC, IVL
			CICA	Confederation of International Contractors Associations
CIC	Comité International de la Conserve		**CICA**	Conférence Internationale des Contrôles d'Assurances des États Africains
CIC	Comité International des Associations d'Analystes Financiers = ICC			
CIC	Comité International des Camps (UIRD) = ICCC		**CICA**	Construction Industry Computing Association
CIC	Commission Internationale du Châtaignier (FAO)		**CICA**	Société Commerciale et Industrielle de la Côte d'Afrique
CIC	Compagnie Immobilière du Congo		**CICAA**	Comisión Internacional para la Conservación del Atén del Atlántico = CICTA, ICCAT
CIC	Confédération Internationale de la Coiffure = ICHT			
CIC	Confédération Internationale des Cadres		**CICABE**	Centre International de la Culture Africaine et du Bien-être de l'Enfance
CIC	Conférence Internationale du Crédit		**CICAD**	Inter-American Drug Abuse Control Commission (OAS) = CILCAD (U.S.A.)
CIC	Conseil International de la Chasse et de la Conservation du Gibier = ICGWC			
CIC	Conseil Internationale des Compositeurs		**CICAD**	Inter-Parliamentary Commission for Environment and Development
CIC	Consejo Internacional de Curtidores = CIT, ICT, IG		**CICADES**	Centro Interamericano de Cooperación Académica para el Desarrollo Economico y Social
CIC	Construction Industry Council			

CICAE	Confédération International des Cinémas d'Art-et-Essai Européens
CICAF	Centre International de Création Audiovisuelle Francophone
CICAF	Compagnie Industrielle des Combustibles Atomiques Frittés
CICAF	International Committee for the Cinema and the Figurative Arts
CICAH	Comité de l'Industrie et des Activités Connexes de la Région Havraise
CICAIA	Comité International des Associations d'Industriels Aérospatiaux = ICCAIA
CICAJ	Centre International de Coordination de l'Assistance Juridique
CICAM	Cotonnière Industrielle du Caméroun
CICAP	Centre Interamericano de Capacitación en Administración Pública (Argentina)
CICAP	Consejo Internacional para la Colaboración en los Análisis de Plaguicidas = CIMAP, CIPAC
CICAR	Corporación Industrial Comercial Agropecuária (Argentina)
CICARWS	Commission on Inter-Church Aid, Refugee and World Service = CESEAR
CICAT	Centre for International Cooperation and Appropriate Technology (Netherlands)
CICATI	Division of the Exchange and Coordination of International Technical Assistance (Brazil)
CICATIRS	Comité International de Coordination et d'Action des Groupements de Techniciens des Industries de Revêtements de Surface = ICCATCI
CICATUR	Centro Interamericano de Capacitación Turistica (Argentina)
CICAV	Conseil International de Coordination des Associations d'Études et d'Action en Matière de Vieillissement
CICB	Chambre des Ingénieurs-Conseils de Belgique
CICB	Confederación Independiente de Campesinos de Bolivia
CICB	Criminal Injuries Compensation Board
CICB	Société Royale Chambre des Ingénieurs Conseils de Belgique = KRIB
CICBE	China Institute of Computer-Based Education
CICC	Centre International de Criminologie Clinique (Italy) = ICCC
CICC	Centre International de Criminologie Comparée (Canada) =ICCC
CICC	Centro Internazionale di Coordinazione Culturale
CICC	China International Chamber of Commerce
CICC	Compagnie Immobilière et Commerciale du Caméroun
CICCA	Centre International de Coordination pour la Célébration des Anniversaires
CICCA	Committee for International Cooperation between Cotton Associations
CICCC	Commission Internationale Contre les Camps de Concentration
CICCE	Comité des Industries Cinématographiques des Communautés Européennes
CICCH	Centre International Chrétien de la Construction d'Habilitation
CICCI	Centro Internacional de Criminologia Clinica (Italy) = ICCIC
CICCOPN	Centro de Formação Professional da Indústria de Construção e Obras Publicas do Norte
CICCYB	Centre International de Cyto-Cybernétique
CICD	Collegium Internationale Chirugiae Digestivae (Italy)
CICDA	Centre International de Coopération pour le Développement Agricole
CICE	Centre d'Information des Chemins de Fer Européens = ICER
CICÉ	Centre International de Calcul Électronique (ONU)
CICE	Centre Ivoirien du Commerce Extérieur
CICE	Centro de Investigaciones en Ciencias de la Educación (Argentina)
CICE	China Institute of Coal Economics
CICE	Comité de l'Industrie Cinématographique Européenne
CICÉ	Compagnie Industrielle des Céramiques Électroniques
CICE	Conférence Internationale des Courriers Express = IECC
CICE	Conferencia Internacional Católica de Escultismo = CICS, ICCS, IKKP
CICÉIPB	Comité Intérimaire de Coordination des Échanges Internationaux de Produits de Base
CICELA	Centre d'Informations et de Coordination des Eglises Lutheriennes d'Afrique = ALICE

CICELC	Comité International du Cinéma l'Enseignement et de Culture
CICELPA	Centro de Investigación de Celulosa y Papel (Argentina)
CICEP	Conseil Interaméricain du Commerce et de la Production = CICYP, IACCP
CICES	Camara de Industriales de la Confeccion de El Salvador
CICESE	Centro de Investigación Científica y Educación Superior de Ensenada (Mexico)
CICF	Centre International du Commerce de Gros
CICF	Chambre des Ingénieurs-Conseils de France
CICF	Confédération Internationale des Cadres Fonctionnaires
CICF	Cork International Choral Festival
CICFRI	Central Inland Capture Fisheries Research Institute (India)
CICG	Centre International de Conférences de Genève
CICG	Conférence Internationale Catholique du Guidisme = ICCG
CICG	Conférence Internationale du Commerce de Gros
CICH	Canadian Institute of Child Health
CICH	Centro de Información Cientifía y Humanistica (Mexico)
CICH	Comité Internationale de la Culture de Houblon = IHB, IHGC
CICHE	British Council Committee for International Cooperation in Higher Education
CICI	Centre Industriel Centrafricaino-Israélien
CICI	Commission Internationale de Coopération Intellectuelle
CICI	Confederation of Information Communication Industries
CICI	Consortium Ivoirien de Commerce et d'Industrie
CICIAMS	Comité International Catholique des Infirmières et Assistantes Médico-Sociales = ICCN
CICIBA	Centre International de Civilisations Bantoues (Gabon)
CICIG	Commissione Italiana del Comitato Internazionale di Geofisica
CICIH	Confédération Internationale Catholique des Institutions Hospitalières = ICCH
CICILS	Confédération Internationale du Commerce et des Industries des Légumes Secs = IPTIC
CICIRE-PATO	Committee for International Cooperation in Information Retrieval among Examining Patent Offices = ICIREPAT
CICITE	Conseil International du Cinéma et de la Télévision
CICL	Chambre des Ingénieurs-Conseils du Grand-Duché de Luxembourg
CICL	Consejo Internacional del Cobre Labrado = IWCC
CICM	Centre for International Christian Ministries
CICM	Centro de Investigación de Ciencias Marinas (Colombia)
CICM	Commission Internationale Catholique pour les Migrations = ICMC
CICM	Congregatio Immaculati Cordis Mariae
CICO	Conference of International Catholic Organisations
CICOLAC	Compañia Colombiana de Alimentos Lácteos
CICOM	Centro Interamericano de Capacitação e Comercialização
CICOMO	Companhia Industrial de Cordoarias de Moçambique
CICOPA	Comité International des Coopératives de Production et Artisanales
CICOTE-PHAR	Centre Technique International de Coordination Pharmaceutique
CICP	Comité International de Coordination des ONG sur la Question de la Palestine = ICCP
CICP	Confédération Internationale du Crédit Populaire =ICPC
CICPE	Comité d'Initiative pour le Congrès du Peuple Européen
CICR	Comité Internationale de la Croix-Rouge = ICRC, IKRK
CICRA	Centre International de Coordination des Recherches sur l'Autogestion
CICRA	Centre International pour la Coopération des Recherches en Agriculture
CICRA	Crohn's in Childhood Research Association
CICRC	Commission Internationale Contre le Régime Concentrationnaire
CICRED	Committee for International Cooperation in National Research in Demography (UNFPA) (France)

CICRIS	Co-operative Industrial and Commercial Reference and Information Service		**CID**	Centre Interinstitutionnel pour la Diffusion de Publications en Sciences Humaines
CICS	Center for Intelligent Computing Studies (U.S.A.)		**CID**	Centre International de Documentation des Producteurs de Scories Thomas (Belgium)
CICS	Centro Internazionale di Cooperazione allo Sviluppo		**CID**	Centre International pour le Développement (Switzerland)
CICS	Commission Internationale Catholique de la Santé		**CID**	Centro de Informacion y Documentacion (Argentina)
CICS	Committee for Index Cards for Standards (IOS)		**CID**	Centro de Investigacion Documentaria (Argentina)
CICS	Compagnie Industrielle et Commerciale du Sénégal		**CID**	Centro de Investigacion y Desarrollo
CICS	Conférénce Internationale Catholique du Scoutisme = CICE, ICCS		**CID**	Centro de Investigaciones para el Desarrollo (Colombia)
CICSA	Centro Información y Computo SA (Colombia)		**CID**	Centro Internacional para el Desarrollo
CICT	Commission on International Commodity Trade (UNCTAD) = CCIPB		**CID**	Comité International de la Détergence
			CID	Comité International du Dachau
CICT	Conseil International du Cinéma, de la Télévision et de la Communication Audiovisuelle= IFTC		**CID**	Conseil International de la Danse
			CID	Criminal Investigation Department
			CID	Croatian Independent Democrats
CICT	Criminal Injuries Compensation Tribunal (Éire)		**CID**	Cuba Independiente y Democrática (U.S.A.)
CICTA	Commission Internationale pour la Conservation des Thonidés de l'Atlantique = CICAA, ICCAT		**CIDA**	Canadian International Development Agency = ACDI
CICTP	Compagnie Industrielle de Constructions, d'Aménagements et de Travaux Publics (Ivory Coast)		**CIDA**	Centre d'Information de Documentation et de l'Alimentation
			CIDA	Centre d'Information et Documentation Atlantique
CICTRAN	Computer Information Centre for Transportation (South Africa)		**CIDA**	Centre d'Information et Documentation Automatique
CICY	Centre Internationale de Cyto-Cybernétique		**CIDA**	Centre International de Développement de l'Aluminium
CICYP	Consejo Interamericano de Comercio y Producción = CICEP, IACCP		**CIDA**	Centre International de Documentation Arachnologique
CICYT	Comité Interamericano de Ciencia y Tecnología		**CIDA**	Centro de Investigación y Difusión Aeronautico-Espacial (Uruguay)
CICYT	Comité Interministerial de Ciencia y Tecnología		**CIDA**	Centro de Investigaciones de Astronomía "Francisco J. Duarte" (Venezuela)
CID	Association des Consultants Internationaux en Droits de l'Homme		**CIDA**	Centro Interamericano de Desarrollo de Archivos (OAS)
CID	Central for Industrial Development (ACP) = CDI		**CIDA**	Comité Interamericano de Desarrollo Agricola
CID	Centre d'Information Documentation Moyen-Orient		**CIDA**	Comité Intergouvernemental du Droit d'Auteur = IGCC
CID	Centre d'Information et de Documentation du Congo et du Ruanda-Urundi		**CIDA**	Commission Internationale des Industries Agricoles
			CIDA	Companhia Industrial de Desenvolvimento da Amazônia (Brazil)
CID	Centre for Information and Documentation (Euratom)		**CIDA**	Confederazione Italiana dei Dirigenti di Azienda

CIDA	Inter-American Centre for Archives Development (Argentina)
CIDAA	Inter-American Commission for Environmental Law and Administration (Colombia)
CIDAC	Centre International de Documentation et Animation Culturelles
CIDADEC	Confédération Internationale des Associations d'Experts et de Conseils
CIDAF	Centro Italiano di Azione Forense
CIDAJAL	Centro Internacional de Desarrollo de Albergues Juveniles de America Latina (Argentina)
CIDAL	Centro de Información y Documentación para América Latina
CIDALC	Comité International pour la Diffusion des Arts et des Lettres par le Cinéma
CIDAMO	Centro de Informacion, Documentacion y Analisis del Movimiento Obrero Latinoamericano (Mexico)
CIDAP	Centro Interamericano de Artesanias Popular (Ecuador)
CIDAPAR	Companhia de Desenvolvimento Agropecuério, Industrial e Mineral do Estado do Pará (Brazil)
CIDAS	Centre d'Information et Documentation pour l'Agriculture et la Sylviculture (Romania)
CIDAT	Centre d'Informatique Appliquée au Développement et à l'Agriculture Tropicale (Belgium)
CIDB	Centre d'Information et du Documentation du Bâtiment
CIDB	Chemie-Information und Dokumentation Berlin
CIDB	Co-operative Insurance Development Bureau = BCDA, ODSC
CIDB	Conseil International de Documentation du Bâtiment
CIDBEQ	Centre d'Informatique Documentaire pour les Bibliothèques d'Enseignement du Québec (Canada)
CIDC	Centre Islamique pour le Développement du Commerce = ICDT
CIDC	Comité International de Droit Comparé = ICCL
CIDC	Consorci d'Informacio i Documentacio de Catalunya (Spain)
CIDC	Consortium Interafricain de Distribution Cinématographique (OCAM)
CIDCE	Centre International de Droit Comparé de l'Environnement
CIDD	Conseil International de la Danse
CIDE	Centro de Información y Documentación Económica
CIDE	Centro de Investigación y Desarrollo de la Educación, Santiago (Chile)
CIDE	Centro Informative de la Edificación
CIDE	Comisión de Inversiones y Desarrollo Económico (Uruguay)
CIDE	Commission Intersyndicale des Déshydrateurs Européens
CIDÉ	Confédération Internationale des Étudiants
CIDE	Conseil International pour le Droit de l'Environnement = ICEL
CIDEA	Centre for International Development Education and Action (New Zealand)
CIDEA	Consejo Interamericano de Educación Alimenticia (Venezuela)
CIDEAL	Centro de Comunicacion, Investigacion y Documentacion entre Europa, España y America Latina
CIDEC	Comité Interamericano de Cultura (U.S.A.)
CIDEC	Confederazione Italiana degli Esercenti e Commercianti
CIDECAF	Compagnie Ivoirienne de Decaféination
CIDECO	Consortium des Industries du Découpage et de l'Emboutissage du Centre-Ouest
CIDÉCT	Comité Internationale pour le Développement et l'Étude de la Construction Tubulaire
CIDEF	Centro Interamericano de Etnomusicologia y Folklore (Venezuela)
CIDÉF	Comité International des Études Françaises et du Dialogue des Cultures
CIDEFA	Conférence Internationale des Directeurs et Doyens des Etablissements d'Enseignement Supérieur et Facultés d'Expression Française des Sciences de l'Agriculture et de l'Alimentation
CIDEFÉG	Conférence Internationale des Doyens de Facultés et des Directeurs d'Écoles de Gestion
CIDEM	Centro de Informacion y Desarrollo de la Mujer (Bolivia)
CIDEM	Consejo Interamericano de Musica
CIDEM	Consejo Internacional de Mujeres = CIF, ICW, IFR
CIDEMS	Centro de Informacion y Documentacion en Educación Medica y Salud (PAFAMS)

CIDEN	Corporacion Internacional de Negocios, S.A. (Mexico)	**CIDIM**	Centro Italiano di Iniziativa Musicale (Italy)
CIDÉP	Centre International de Documentation et d'Études Pétrolières	**CIDISE**	Comité Interministériel pour le Développement de l'Investissement et de l'Emploi
CIDEP	Centre International de Formation et de Recherche en Population et Développement en Association avec les Nations Unies	**CIDITVA**	Centre International de Documentation de l'Inspection Techniques des Véhicles Automobiles
CIDER	Centro Interdisciplinario de Estudios Regionales (Colombia)	**CIDJ**	Centre d'Information et de Documentation Jeunesse
CIDES	Centre de Investigación para el Desarrollo Economico Social	**CIDMEF**	Conférence Internationale des Doyens des Facultés de Médecine d'Expression Française
CIDES	Centro de Informacion, Documentacion y Estudios Sociales (Costa Rica)	**CIDMY**	Centre International de Documentation Marguerite Yourcenar (Belgium) = IDCMY
CIDES	Centro de Investigación para el Desarollo Economico (Argentina)	**CIDO**	Conseil International de la Danse
CIDÉSA	Centre Internationale de la Documentation Économique et Sociale Africaine	**CIDOB**	Centro de Información y Documentación Boliviano
CIDESCO	Comité International d'Esthetique et de Cosmétologie	**CIDOB**	Centro de Información y Documentación, Barcelona
CIDGD	Centre International de Documentation "Georges Dopagne" (Belgium)	**CIDOC**	Centro Intercultural de Documentacion (Mexico)
CIDH	Comisión Interamericana de Derechos Humanos (U.S.A.) = IACHR	**CIDP**	Centre International de Documentation Parlementaire (Switzerland)
CIDHAL	Communicación Intercambio Desarrollo Humano Américano Latino	**CIDPA**	Chinese Industrial Development and Planning Association
CIDHEC	Centre Intergouvernmental de Documentation sur l'Habitat et l'Environnement pour les Pays de la Commission Économique pour l'Europe des Nations Unies = IDCHEC	**CIDR**	Compagnie International de Développement Rural
		CIDSÉ	Coopération Internationale pour le Développement et la Solidarité = ICDS
CIDI	Centre International de Documentation et d'Information	**CIDSP**	Centrule de Informare si Documentare in Stiinte Sociale si Politice (Romania)
CIDI	Centro de Información de Drogas y de Intoxicaciones (Dominican Republic)	**CIDSS**	Comité International pour l'Information et la Documentation en Sciences Sociales = ICSSD, ICSSDI
CIDI	Centro de Investigaciones para el Desarrollo Integral (Colombia)	**CIDST**	Committee for Scientific and Technical Information and Documentation (EU)
CIDI	Côte Ivoirienne d'Importation et de Distribution	**CIDT**	Compagnie Ivoirienne pour le Développement des Textiles
CIDIA	Centro Interamericano de Documentación y Información Agrícola (Costa Rica)	**CIDU**	Centro Interdisciplinario de Desarrollo Urbana y Regional (Chile)
CIDIA	Consejo Inter-Americano de Educación Alimenticia	**CIE**	Cartographie des Invertébrés Européens = EEW, EIS
CIDIAT	Centro Interamericano de Desarrollo Integral de Aguas y Tierras (Venezuela)	**CIE**	Centre for International Economics
CIDIC	Comité Interprofessionnel de Développement de l'Industrie Chevaline	**CIE**	Centre International de l'Eau
		CIE	Centre International de l'Enfance = CII, ICC
CIDIE	Committee of International Development Institutions on the Environment	**CIE**	Centre International de l'Environnement
		CIE	Centro de Investigaciones Económicas (Argentina, Colombia, Mexico)

CIE	Centro de Investigaciones Educativas
CIE	Chinese Institute of Electronics
CiE	Choice in Education
CIE	Comité Interafricain de Statistiques
CIE	Comité Interamericano de Educación
CIÉ	Comité International des Échanges
CIÉ	Commission Internationale de l'Éclairage
CIE	Compagnie Ivoirienne des Etiquettes
CIE	Consejo Interamericanode Escultismo (Costa Rica) = ISC
CIE	Consejo Internacional de Enfermeras = CII, ICN
CIE	Córas Iompair Éireann
CIE	Council for International Education
CIÉA	Centre International d'Études Agricoles
CIÉA	Centre International de l'Élevage pour l'Afrique
CIEA	College International des Experts Architectes (IUA)
CIEA	Commission Internationale de l'Enseignement Aéronautique et Spatial (FAI)
CIÉA	Conseil International d'Éducation des Adultes = ICAE
CIEC	Centre International Scientifique des Fertilisants
CIEC	Chemical Industry Education Centre
CIÉC	Comité International des Études Créoles
CIEC	Comité Nacional de Lucha contra el Cáncer (Colombia)
CIÉC	Commission Internationale de l'État Civil
CIEC	Confederación Interamericana de Educación Católica = IACCE
CIEC	Conference on International Economic Cooperation = CEI
CIéC	Conseil International d'Études Canadiennes = ICCS
CIECA	Commission Internationale des Examens de Conduite Automobile = IDTC
CIECC	Consejo Interamericano para la Educación, la Ciencia y la Cultura
CIÉCE	Centre d'Information et d'Études sur les Communautés Européennes (Belgium)
CIECOS	China International Economic Co-operation Society
CIEDA	Center for Immunity Enhancement in Domestic Animals (U.S.A.)
CIEDLA	Centro Interdisciplinario de Estudios sobre el Desarrollo Latinoamericano (Argentina)
CIEDUR	Centro Interdisciplinario de Estudios sobre el Desarrollo Uruguay
CIÉE	Centre Interuniversitaire d'Études Européennes (Canada)
CIEE	Consejo Internacional de Preparación para la Enseñanza = CIPE, ICET
CIEE	Council on International Educational Exchange (U.S.A.)
CIEE	Council for International Educational Exchange (U.S.A.)
CIEF	Centro de Investigaciones y Estudios Familiares
CIEF	Comité International d'Enregistrement des Frequences
CIEF	Conseil International d'Études Francophones (U.S.A.)
CIÉFR	Centre International d'Études de la Formation Réligieuse = LUMEN VITAE
CIEG	Cuerpo de Ingenieros del Ejercito de Guatemala
CIÉH	Comité Interafricain d'Études Hydrauliques = ICHS
CIÉHV	Conseil International pour l'Éducation des Handicapés de la Vue = ICEVH
CIEI	Centro de Investigaciones Economicas Internacionales (Universidad de La Habana) (Cuba)
CIEI	Centro de Investigaciones Educativas Indigenas (Ecuador)
CIEIA	Centro Internazionale per degli Studi sull Irrigazione
CIEIC	China International Economic Information Centre
CIEL	Centre for International Environmental Law
CIÉL	Centre International d'Études du Lindane (Belgium)
CIÉL	Centre International d'Études Latines
CIÉL	Centre International d'Études Loisir
CIEL	Comité des Intellectuels pour l'Europe des Libertés
CIEL	Commercial Importadora Exportadora S.A. (Canary Islands)
CIELAP	Canadian Institute for Environmental Law and Policy
CIEM	Comité Européen d'Études Morisques (Tunisia)

CIEM	Commission Internationale de l'Enseignement des Mathématiques = ICMI	**CIEPP**	Comité Illusionniste d'Expertise des Phénomènes Paranormaux
CIÉM	Confédération Internationale des Éditeurs de Musique = ICMP	**CIEPRC**	Confédération Internationale des Instituts Catholiques d'Éducation des Adultes Ruraux
CIÉM	Conseil International d'Éducation Mésologique des Pays de Langue Française	**CIEPS**	Centre International d'Enregistrement des Publications en Série
CIEM	Conseil International pour l'Exploration de la Mer = ICES	**CIEPS**	Centre International de l'ISDS
CIEMAL	Consejo de Iglesias Evangelicas Metodistas de America Latina	**CIÉPS**	Conseil Intergouvernemental pour l'Éducation Physique et le Sport = ICPES
CIEN	Centro de Investigaciones Económicas Nacionales (Guatemala)	**CIEPSS**	Conseil International pour l'Education Physique et la Science du Sport = ICSSPE
CIEN	Comisão Interamericano de Energia Nuclear = IANEC	**CIÉQE**	Comité International pour l'Étude des Questions Européennes
CIEN	Commissione Italiana per l'Europa Nucleare	**CIÉR**	Centre International d'Études Romanes
CIENER	Centro de Investigación Económica de la Energia (Spain)	**CIÉR**	Centre International d'Études Recherches (Belgium)
CIENES	Centro Interamericano de Ensenanza de Estadistica (Chile)	**CIER**	Centro Interamericano de Educación Rural
CIENTAL	Centro de Investigaciones y Estudios Internacionales para la América Latina (Ecuador)	**CIER**	Comisión de Integración Electrica Regional (Uruguay)
CIEO	Catholic International Education Office = OIEC	**CIER**	Commission for International Educational Reconstruction
CIEO	Centre International d'Exploitation des Océans = ICOD	**CIERA**	Center for International Education and Research in Accounting (U.S.A.)
CIÉP	Centre International d'Études Pédagogiques	**CIERA**	Chongquing International Economic Relations Association
CIEP	Centro de Investigación y Experimentación Pedagógica (Uruguay)	**CIÉRA**	Compagnie Ivoirienne d'Études et de Réalisations en Informatique et Automatisme
CIEP	Chinese Institute of Environmental Protection	**CIÉRE**	Centre International d'Études et de Recherches Européennes
CIEP	Commission Internationale de Enseignement de la Physique = ICPE	**CIÉRIÉ**	Compagnie Ivoirienne d'Études et de Réalisations Informatique et Économiques
CIEP	Consorcio dos Industriais de Equipaduento Pesado	**CIÉRP**	Centre Intersyndical d'Études et de Recherches sur la Productivité
CIEPAC	Centre International pour l'Education Permanente et l'Aménagement Concertée (Belgium)	**CIÉRRO**	Centre Interafricain d'Études en Radio Rural de Ouagadougou (Burkina Faso)
CIÉPAT	Centre Inter-États de Promotion de l'Artisanat d'Art et de Tourisme Culturels (Benin)	**CIERS**	Chinese Institute of Electronics Radar Society
CIÉPC	Commission Internationale d'Études de la Police de Circulation = ISCTP	**CIÉRSÉS**	Centre International d'Études et de Recherches en Socio-Économie de la Santé = IHCSERS
CIEPLAN	Corporación de Investigaciones Economicas para Latinoamérica	**CIÉS**	Centre d'Information Économique et Sociale des Nations Unies
CIEPO	Comité International d'Études Pré-Ottomanes et Ottomanes (U.S.A.)	**CIES**	Centre International d'Enseignement de la Statistique
		CIES	Centre International des Entreprises du Secteur Alimentaire = ICCFTI

CIES	Centro Informazione e Educazione allo Sviluppo	**CIÉU**	Centre Interdisciplinaire d'Études Urbaines
CIES	China Illuminating Engineering Society	**CIEU**	Centro de Investigaciones Económicas (Chile)
CIES	China Internal Combustion Engines Society	**CIEUA**	Congrès International de l'Enseignement Universitaire pour Adultes = ICUAE
CIES	Comité Inter-Unions de l'Enseignement des Sciences		
CIES	Comité International des Entreprises à Succursales	**CIF**	Canadian Institute of Forestry
CIÉS	Commission Internationale des Études Slaves	**CIF**	Centre Inter-Entreprises de Formation et d'Études Supérieures Industrielles
CIES	Comparative and International Education Society (U.S.A.)	**CIF**	Centro de Investigacion Forestal (Cuba)
CIES	Consejo Interamericano Económico y Social = CESI, IA-ECOSOC	**CIF**	Childhope International Foundation (Brazil)
CIES	Council for International Exchange of Scholars (U.S.A.)	**CIF**	Chinese Institute of Futurology
CIESC	Chemical Industry and Engineering Society of China	**CIF**	Commission Interaméricaine des Femmes = CIM, IACW
CIESE	Centro de Investigaciones y Estudios Socioeconomicos (Ecuador)	**CIF**	Committee on Industry and Finance (NEDC)
CIESÉF	Centre Interaméricaine d'Enseignement de Statistique Économique et Financière	**CIF**	Confédération Internationale de Fonctionnaires
CIESIN	Consortium for International Earth Science Information Network	**CIF**	Conseil International des Femmes = CIDEM, ICW, IFR
CIESJ	Centre International d'Enseignement Supérieur de Journalisme	**CIF**	Construction Industry Federation (Éire)
CIESM	Commission Internationale pour l'Exploration Scientifique de la Mer Méditerranée = ICSEMS	**CIF**	Cork Industry Federation
		CIF	Cultural Integration Fellowship (U.S.A.)
CIESPAL	Centro Internacional de Estudios Superiores de Periodismo para América Latina (Ecuador)	**CIF40**	Conseil International Formule 40
		CIFA	Comité International de Recherche et d'Étude de Facteurs de l'Ambiance = ICEF
CIÉSS	Centre Interaméricain d'Études de la Sécurité Sociale	**CIFA**	Committee for Inland Fisheries of Africa (FAO) = CPCA
CIÉST	Centre International d'Études Supérieures de Tourisme	**CIFA**	Consociazione Italiani Federazioni Autotrasporti
CIESU	Centro de Informaciones y Estudios del Uruguay	**CIFA**	Corporation of Insurance and Financial Advisers
CIESUL	Centro de Investigaciones Economicas y Sociales (Universidad de Lima)	**CIFAB**	Central Institute of Finance and Banking (China)
CIET	Center for Industrial and Engineering Technology (U.S.A.)	**CIFAC**	Confédération Internationale des Fabriques Artistiques et Créatives
CIET	Centro Interamericano Estudios Tributarios	**CIFAD**	Comité International des Femmes Africaines pour le Développement
CIETA	Calcutta Import and Export Trade Association (India)	**CIFAO**	Compagnie Industrielle et Financière d'Entreprises
CIÉTAP	Comité Interprofessionnel d'Études des Techniques Agricoles et Pesticides	**CIFAR**	Center for International Financial Analysis and Research (U.S.A.)
		CIFAVE	Camara de la Industria Farmaceutica Venezolana
CIETT	Confédération Internationale des Entreprises de Travail Temporaire	**CIFC**	Centre for Interfirm Comparisons
		CIFC	Centro de Investigação das Ferrugens do Cafeeiro (Portugal)

CIFC	Council for the Investigation of Fertility Control
CIFCA	Centro Internacional de Formación de Ciencias Ambientales para Paises de Habla Española
CIFDUF	Conférence Internationale des Facultés de Droit ayant en Commun l'Usage du Français
CIFE	Center for Integrated Facility Engineering (U.S.A.)
CIFE	Central Institute of Fisheries Education (India)
CIFE	Centre International de Formation Européenne
CIFE	Centro Italiano di Formazioine Europea
CIFE	Comision Interministerial de Fomento Económico (Peru)
CIFE	Conference for Independent Further Education
CIFÉG	Centre International pour la Formation et les Échanges Géologiques
CIFEI	Compagnia Italiana Forniture Elettro Industriali
CIFEJ	Centre International du Film pour l'Enfance et la Jeunesse = ICFCYP
CIFÉN	Compagnie Internationale pour le Financement de l'Énergie Nucléaire
CIFER	Colorado Institute for Fuels and High Altitude Engine Research
CIFES	Comité International du Film Ethnographique et Sociologique
CIFF	Centro Incremento Frutticoltura Ferraresa
CIFH	Comité International des Films de l'Homme
CIFI	Collegio Ingegneri Ferroviari Italiani
CIFI	Consorzio Industriali Fontomeccanici Italiani
CIFIM	Compagnie Ivoirienne de Financement Immobilier
CIFLS	China International Friendship and Liaison Society
CIFOR	Centre for International Forestry Research
CIFOS	Compagnie Immobilière et Foncière du Sénégal
CIFP	Comité International pour le Fair Play = IFPC
CIFPCA	Confederación Iberoamericana y Filipina de Productores de Cana de Azucar
CIFPEF	Conférence Internationale des Facultés, Instituts et Écoles de Pharmacie d'Expression Française
CIFPSE	Catholic International Federation for Physical and Sports Education = FICEP
CIFRÉS	Centre International de Formation, de Recherches et d'Études Séricicoles
CIFRI	Central Inland Fisheries Research Institute (India)
CIFST	Chinese Institute of Food Science and Technology
CIFT	Central Institute of Fisheries Technology (India)
CIFT	Committee on Invisibles and Financing Related to Trade (UNCTAD)
CIFTA	Comité International des Fédérations Théâtrales d'Amateurs de Langue Française
CIG	Cataloguing and Indexing Group (LA)
CIG	Centre d'Information Générale (Belgium)
CIG	Changchun Institute of Geography
CIG	Comité Intergouvernemental Nations Unies/FAO = IGC
CIG	Conférence Internationale du Goudron = ITC, ITK
CIG	Conference Interpreters' Group
CIG	Conserative Integration Group
CIG	International Helicopter Committee (FAI)
CIGA	Centro de Investigaciones de Grasas y Aceites (Argentina)
CIGA	Compagnia Italian dei Grandi Alberghi
CIGAS	Cambridge Intercollegiate Graduate Application Scheme
CIGB	Commission International des Grand Barrages (CME) = ICOLD
CIGC	Comité Intergouvernemental de Coordination pour la Planification de la Population et du Développement en Asie du Sud-Est = IGCC
CIGC	Comité Interprofessionnel du Gruyère du Comté
CIGDL	Chambre Immobilière du Grand-Duché de Luxembourg
CIGE	Centre Ivoirien de Gestion des Entreprises
CIGEB	Compagnie Ivoirienne de Gestion d'Entreprise de Boulangerie
CIGÉL	Compagnie Ivoirienne de Gestion et d'Études de Logements

CIGGT	Canadian Institute of Guided Ground Transport	**CII**	Chartered Insurance Institute
CIGH	Confédération Internationale de Généalogie et d'Héraldique = ICGH	**CII**	Compagnie Internationale pour l'Information
CIGI	Canadian International Grains Institute	**CII**	Conseil International des Infirmières = CIE, ICN
CIGiOC	Coordinamento Internazionale della Gioventù Operaia Cristiana = CIJOC, ICYCW	**CII**	Corporación Interamericana de Inversiones = ICC, SII
CIGMA	Compagnie Internationale des Grands Magasins	**CIIA**	Canadian Information Industry Association
CIGP	Conférence Internationale sur la Guerre Politique	**CIIA**	Canadian Institute of International Affairs = ICAI
CIGR	Commission Internationale du Génie Rurale = ICAE	**CIIA**	Commission Internationale des Industries Agricoles et Alimentaires
CIGRÉ	Conférence Internationale des Grands Réseaux Électriques à Haute Tension	**CIIA**	Council of Independent Inspecting Authorities
CIGS	Centre International de Gérontologie Sociale = ICSG	**CIIAA**	Commission Internationale des Industries Agricoles et Alimentaires
CIGV	Club International des Grands Voyageurs = IWTC	**Ciiagro**	Centro Integrado de Informações Agrometeorológicas (Brazil)
CIH	Central India Horse	**CIIAS**	Consejo Internacional para la Investigación en Agrosilvicultura (Kenya)
CIH	Comité Professionnel Interrégional de l'Horlogerie		
CIH	Commonwealth Institute of Health, Sydney University	**CIIC**	Centre d'Information de l'Industrie des Chaux et Ciments
CIH	Commonwealth Institute of Helminthology	**CIIC**	Centro Internacional de Investigaciones sobre el Cáncer = CIRC, IARC
CIHA	Comité Internationale d'Histoire de l'Art	**CIID**	Centro Internacional de Investigaciones para el Desarrollo (Canada) = CRDI, IDRC
CIHAN	Centraal Instituut ter Bevordering v.d. Buitenlandse Handel		
CIHCA	Cayman Islands Hotel and Condominium Association	**CIID**	Commission International des Irrigations et du Drainage = ICID
CIHE	Council for Industry and Higher Education	**CIIE**	Centre International de l'Industrie et pour l'Environnement = ICIE
CIHÉAM	Centre International des Hautes Études Agronomique Méditerranéennes (CE, OECD) = ICAMAS	**CIIG**	Construction Industry Information Group
		CIIM	Colorado Institute for Irrigation Management
CIHÉC	Commission Internationale d'Histoire Écclésiastique Comparée	**CIIME**	Committee for International Investment and Multinational Enterprises (OECD)
CIHL	Comisión Internacional de Historiadores Latinoamericanistas y del Caribe	**CIIMP**	Centro Internazionale di Ipnosi Medica Psicologica = ICMPH
CIHM	Commission Internationale d'Histoire Maritime	**CIINTE**	Centralny Instytut Informacji Naukowo-Techniczneji Ekonomicznej
CIHM	Commission Internationale d'Histoire Militaire =ICMH	**CIIPS**	Canadian Institute for International Peace and Security
CIHS	Commission Internationale d'Histoire du Sel (Austria)	**CIIR**	Catholic Institute for International Relations
CII	Camrose International Institute (Canada)	**CIIS**	Conferenza Italiana degli Istituti Secolari
CII	Centro Internacional de la Infancia = CIE, ICC	**CIITC**	Confédération Internationale des Industries Techniques du Cinéma

CIJ	Chartered Institute of Journalists (Éire)
CIJ	Commission International de Juristes = ICJ, IJK
CIJ	Cour International de Justice (ONU) = ICJ
CIJA	Centro para la Independencia de Jueces y Abogados = CIJL, CIMA
CIJAC	Club International des Journalistes Amateurs de Cigares
CIJF	Commission de l'Industrie des Jus de Fruits et de Légumes de la CEE
CIJL	Centre for the Independence of Judges and Lawyers = CIJA, CIMA
CIJM	Comité International des Jeux Méditerranéens (Greece)
CIJOC	Coordination Internationale de la Jeunesse Ouvrière Chrétienne; Coordinacion Internacionale de la Juventud Obrera Cristiana = CIGiOC, ICYCW
CIL	Centre for Independent Living
CIL	Comité Interprofessionel du Logement
CIL	Commissioners of Irish Lights
CIL	Confédération Nationale du Secteur Immobilier et du Logement (Belgium)
CILA	Centro Interamericano de Libros Academicos
CILA	Chartered Institute of Loss Adjustors
CILACC	Comité International de Lutte et d'Action contre le Communisme
CILAD	Colégio Ibero-Latino-Americano de Dermatologia (Portugal)
CILAF	Comité International de Liaison des Associations Féminines
CILAM	Compagnie Ivoirienne de Location Automobile et de Matériel
CILAS	Compagnie Industrielle des Lasers
CILB	Comité Interprofessional du Lait de Brebis
CILB	Commission Internationale de Lutte Biologique contre les Ennemis des Cultures
CILC	Confédération Internationale du Lin et du Chanvre
CILCAD	Commission Interaméricaine de Lutte contre l'Abus des Drogues = CICAD
CILÉCT	Centre International de Liaison des Écoles de Cinéma et de Télévision
CILEH	Centro de Investigaciones Literarias Españolas y Hispanoamericanas
CILF	Conseil International de la Langue Française = ICFL
CILG	CIRIA Information Liaison Group
CILICE	Centro Interbancario Latinoamericano de Información sobre Comercio Exterior (Colombia)
CILO	Centraal Instituut voor Landbouwkundig Onderzoek
CILRECO	Comité International de Liaison pour la Réunification Indépendante et Pacifique de la Corée = ILCRPK, INRRK
CILSS	Comité Permanent Inter-États de Lutte contre la Sécheresse dans le Sahel = ICDCS
CILT	Campaign to Improve London's Transport
CILT	Centre for Independent Transport Research in London
CILT	Centre for Information on Language Teaching
CILTADE	Centre International des Langues, Littératures et Traditions d'Afrique au Service du Développement (Belgium)
CIM	Canadian Institute of Mining and Metallurgy
CIM	Carte Internationale du Monde = IMW
CIM	Centro de Informação Mulher (Brazil)
CIM	Centro Internacional del Medio Ambiente
CIM	Chartered Institute of Marketing
CIM	Coetus Internationalis Ministrantium
CIM	Colloquio di Informatica Musicale
CIM	Comisión Interamericana de Mujeres = CIF, IACF
CIM	Comité Intergouvernemental pour les Migrations (Switzerland) = ICM
CIM	Comité International de Mauthausen = IMK
CIM	Comité International de Mini-Basketball
CIM	Commission for Industry and Manpower
CIM	Congregatio Iesu et Mariae (Eudistarum)
CIM	Congrès International des Fabrications Mécaniques
CIM	Conseil International de la Musique = IMC
CIM	Consorzio Italiano fra Macellatori Industriali Produttori Importatori Bestiame Carni e Affini

CIM	Convention Internationale Concernant le Transport des Merchandises par Chemins de Fer
CIM	Cooperative Investigation in the Mediterranean (IOC) = ECM
CIMA	Centre Interdisciplinaire d'Étude du Milieu Naturel et de l'Aménagement Rural
CIMA	Centre pour l'Indépendance des Magistrats et des Avocats = CIJA, CIJL
CIMA	Cereal Ingredients' Manufacturers' Association (*ex* RMA)
CIMA	Chartered Institute of Management Accountants
CIMA	Compagnie Industrielle de Miroiterie en Afrique (Cameroon, Congo, Gabon)
CIMA	Compagnie International des Machines Agricoles
CIMAC	Conseil International des Machines à Combustion
CIMADÉ	Comité Inter-Mouvement Auprès Des Évacués
CIMAE	Centro de Investigaciones Medicas Albert Einstein (Uruguay)
CIMAF	Centro de Cooperação dos Industriais de Maquinas e Ferramentas
CIMAFOR	Comité Interprofessionnel du Machinisme Forestier
CIMAG	Société des Grands Magasins de la Côte-d'Ivoire
CIMAL	Centro de Información sobre Migraciones en América Latina
CIMAN-GOLA	Empresa de Cimento de Angola
CIMAO	Les Cimenteries de l'Afrique de l'Ouest (Ghana, Ivory Coast, Togo)
CIMAP	Commission Internationale des Méthodes d'Analyse des Pesticides = CICAP, CIPAC
CIMAR	Centro de Investigaciones del Mar (Chile)
CIMAS	Conférence Internationale de la Mutualité et des Assurances Sociales
CIMB	Centre International d'Études Monétaires et Bancaires = ICMB
CIMB	Construction Industry Manpower Board
CIMC	Cercle International Massotherapie Chinoise
CIMC	Colombian Internal Medical Congress
CIMC	Committee for International Municipal Cooperation
CIMCEE	Comité des Industries de la Moutarde de la CEE

CIMCLG	Construction Industry Metric Change Liaison Group
CIME	Centro de Industriales Metalurgicos (Paraguay)
CIME	Centro de Investigación de Metodos y Technicas para Pequenos y Medianas Empresas (Argentine)
CIME	Comité Intergubernamental para las Migraciones Europeas
CIMÉ	Compagnie Industrielle des Métaux Électroniques
CIMÉ	Confédération Internationale de Musique Électronique
CIME	Conseil International des Moyens d'Enseignement = ICEM
CIME	Council of Industry for Management Education
CIMEA	Comité International des Mouvements d'Enfants et d'Adolescents = ICCAM
CIMÉC	Comité des Industries de la Mesure Électrique et Électronique de la Communauté (CE)
CIMEN-CAM	Société des Cimenteries du Caméroun
CIMES	Concours International du Meilleur Enregistrement Sonore
CIMEXA	Centro de Importaciones y Exportaciones, S.A. (Nicaragua)
CIMF	Centre International de Médecine pour la Famille (U.S.A.) = ICFM
CIMFM	Comité Internacional Medicina Farmacia Militares
CIMG	Construction Industry Marketing Group
CIMH	Caribbean Institute for Meteorology and Hydrology (Barbados)
CIMH	Comité International pour la Métrologie Historique = ICHM
CIMI	Centre of Industrial Microbiological Investigations (Argentina)
CIMI	Conselho Indigenista Missionário (Brazil)
CIMM	Canadian Institute of Mining and Metallurgy
CIMM	Centro de Investigacion Minera y Metalurgica (Chile)
CIMM	Chambre Internationale de la Marine Marchande
CIMM	Changcheng Institute of Metrology and Measurement
CIMM	Comité International de Médecine Militaire; Comite Internacional de Medicina Militar = ICMM

CIMMS	Cooperative Institute for Mesoscale Meteorological Studies (U.S.A.)	**CIMTE**	Centro de Investigaciones Multidisciplinarias en Tecnologia y Empleo (Colombia)
CIMMYT	Centro Internacional de Mejoramiento de Maéz y Trigo (Mexico)	**Cimtech**	National Centre for Information Management & Technology
CIMO	Centraal Instituut voor Materiaalonderzoek	**CIMTOGO**	Société des Ciments du Togo
CIMO	Commission des Instruments et des Méthodes d'Observation (OMM)	**CIMTP**	Congrès Internationaux de Médecine Tropicale et de Paludisme = ICTMM
CIMO	Confederation of Importers and Marketing Organizations in Europe of Fresh Fruit and Vegetables	**CIMUSET**	Comité International des Musées des Sciences et Technologies
		CIN	Chinese Institute of Navigation
CIMP	Commission Internationale de la Météorologie Polaire (AIMPA)	**CIN**	Commission International de Numismatique = INC, IKN
CIMP	Commission Internationale Médico-Physiologique (FAI)	**CINAB**	Comité des Instituts Nationaux des Agents en Brevets
CIMP	Committee on Igneous and Metamorphic Petrogenesis	**CINASE**	Centro de Investigacion y Asesoria Socioeconomica (Nicaragua)
CIMPA	Centre International de Mathematiques Pure et Appliquées = ICPAM	**CINAV**	Commission Internationale de la Nomenclature Anatomique Vétérinaire = ICVAN, IVANK
CIMPEC	Centro Interamericano para la Produccion de Material Educativo y Cientifico para la Prensa (Colombia)	**CINC**	Club International de Numismatique par Correspondance; Club Internacional de Numismática por Correspondencia = INCC
CIMPM	Comité International de Médecine et de Pharmacie Militaires = ICMMP		
CIMPO	Central Indian Medicinal Plants Organisation	**CINCC**	Coal Industry National Consultative Council
CIMPOR	Cimentos de Portugal, EP	**CINCWIO**	Cooperative Investigations in the North and Central Western Indian Ocean
CIMR	Changsha Institute of Mining Research		
CIMRST	Comité Interministériel de la Recherche Scientifique et Technique	**CINDA**	Centro Interuniversitario por Desarrollo Andino (Chile)
CIMS	Center for Innovation Management Studies	**CINDE**	Centre International pour le Développement Économique; Centro Internacional para el Desarrollo Económico = ICEG
CIMS	Center for Integrated Manufacturing Studies		
CIMS	Centro de Investigaciones Motivacionales y Sociales (Argentina)	**CINDE**	Costa Rican Investment and Development Co.
CIMS	Consociatio Internationalis Musicae Sacrae	**CINDER**	Centro Interamericano de Desarrollo Regional
CIMSCEE	Comité des Industries des Mayonnaises et Sauces Condimentaires de la CEE	**CINDOC**	Centro de Información y Documentación Científica
CIMT	Centre for Innovation in Mathematics Teaching	**CINE**	Council on International Nontheatrical Events (U.S.A.)
CIMT	Commission Internationale de la Médecine du Travail = CIMT, ICOH	**CINECA**	Co-operative Investigations of the Northern Part of the Eastern Central Atlantic (FAO)
CIMT	Compagnie Industrielle de Matériel de Transport		
CIMT	Conseil International de la Musique Traditionelle = ICTM	**CINEP**	Centro de Investigacion y Educación Popular (Colombia)
		CINF	Changsha Design and Research Institute of Non-Ferrous Metallurgy
CIMTAC	Committee for International Marine Telecommunications and Aviation Coordination	**CINF**	Commission Intersyndicale de l'Instrumentation et de la Mesure Nucléaire Française

CINFR	Central Institute for Nutrition and Food Research (Netherlands)	**CIO**	Confederation of Indian Organisations (U.K.)
CING	Commission Internationale des Neiges et Glaces = ICSI	**CIOA**	Centro Italiano Assidatori Anodici
CINIDREP	Centro Interamericano de Investigación y Documentación de Relaciones Públicas	**CIOAC**	Federación Independiente de Obreros Agricolas y Campesinos (Mexico)
		CIOB	Chartered Institute of Building
CINM	Cámara Internacional de Navegación Marítima	**CIOFF**	Comité International des Organisateurs de Festivals de Folklore et d'Arts Traditionnels
CINOA	Confédération Internationale des Négociants en Oeuvres d'Art = ICAD	**CIoH**	Chartered Institute of Housing (*ex* IOH)
CINP	Chambre Interdépartementale des Notaires de Paris	**CIOIC**	Centre d'Information des Organisations Internationales Catholiques
CINP	Collegium Internationale Neuro-Psychopharmacologicum	**CIOJ**	Centre d'Information et Documentation de la Jeunesse
CINP	Comité International de Liaison pour la Navigation de Plaisance = PNIC	**CIOM**	Chongqing Institute of Optics and Mechanics
CINPROS	Commission Internationale des Professionnels pour la Santé et les Droits de l'Homme = ICHP	**CIOM**	Confédération Internationale des Officiers-Médicins
		CIOMAL	Comité Exécutif International de l'Ordre de Malte pour l'Assistance aux lépreux
CINS	Collegium Internationale Activitatis Nervosae Superioris (Italy)	**CIOMR**	Comité Interallié des Officiers Médecins de Réserve
CINSA	Central de Industrias, S.A. (El Salvador)		
CINTAC	Compania Industrial de Tubos de Acero, S.A. (Chile)	**CIOMS**	Council for International Organization of Medical Sciences
CINTE	Centrum Informacij Naukowej, Technicznej i Ekonomicznej	**CIOPORA**	Communauté Internationale des Obtenteurs de Plantes Ornementales et Fruitières de Reproduction Asexuée
CINTECA	Centro de Información Tecnica Cafetalera (Brazil)		
CINTER-FOR	Centro Interamericano de Investigación y Documentación Formación Profesional (Uruguay) = IACRDVT	**CIOR**	Confédération Interalliée des Officiers de Réserve
		CIOS	Centro Italiano di Orientamento Sociale
CINTER-PLAN	Centro Interamericano de Estudios e Investigaciones para el Planeamiento de la Educación (Venezuela)	**CIOS**	Comité International pour l'Organisation Scientifique: World Council of Management
CINTERAD	Centre International d'Études, de Recherche et d'Action pour le Développement (Belgium)	**CIOSL**	Confederación Internacional de Organizaciones Sindicales Libres = CISL, IBFU, ICFTU, IVVV
CINTRA-FOR	Center for International Trade in Forest Products (U.S.A.)	**CIOSM**	Conseil International des Organisations des Sciences Médicales
CINU	Centre d'Information des Nations Unies = UNIC	**CIOSTA**	Comité International d'Organisation Scientifique du Travail en Agriculture = IOSTA
CINVA	Centro Interamericano de Vivenda (Colombia)		
CINVE	Centro de Investigaciones Económicas (Uruguay)	**CIOT**	Centro Internacional de Operación Telegrafica (Argentina)
CIO	Centar za Industrijsko Oblikovanje	**CIOT**	Compagnie Industrielle d'Ouvrages en Textiles (Central Africa)
CIO	Church Information Office	**CIP**	Caribbean Institute of Perinatology
CIO	Comité International Olympique = IOC, IOK	**CIP**	Catholic International Press = KIPA
		CIP	Centre d'Information de Presse (Belgium)
CIO	Commission Internationale d'Optique = ICO	**CIP**	Centre for International Policy

CIP	Centre International de la Pomme de Terre; Centro Internacional de la Papa	**CIPAC**	Collaborative International Pesticides Analytic Council = CICAP, CIMAP
CIP	Centre International de Paris	**CIPACI**	Société Commerciale et Industrielle des Produits Animaux en Côte d'Ivoire
CIP	Centro de Investigaciones Pesqueras (Venezuela)	**CIPAF**	Centro de Investigacion para la Acción Femenina (Dominican Republic)
CIP	Centro Información Preinversión América Latina Caribe	**CIPAIM**	Cellule d'Intervention contre la Pollution dans les Alpes-Maritimes
CIP	Centro Internacional de la Papa (Peru) = IPC	**CIPALP-DAMP**	International Centre for Information on Palestinian and Lebanese Prisoners, Deportees and Missing Persons
CIP	Club Internacional de Prensa		
CIP	Collège International de Podologie	**CIPAM**	Centro de Investigaciones de Plantas y Animales Medicinales (Mexico)
CIP	Comisión Internacional de Paz		
CIP	Commission Internationale de Phytopharmacie	**CIPASE**	Commission Internationale des Pêches pour l'Atlantique Sud-Est = CIPASO, ICSEAF
CIP	Commission Internationale du Peuplier = IPC	**CIPASH**	Committee on International Programs in Atmospheric Sciences and Hydrology (UN)
CIP	Commission Internationale Permanente pour l'Epreuve des Armes à Feu Portatives		
		CIPASO	Comisión Internacional de Pesquerías del Atlántico Sudoriental = CIPASE, ICSEAF
CIP	Comptoir Ivoirien des Papiers		
CIP	Confederação da Indústria Portuguesa	**CIPAT**	Conseil International sur les Problèmes de l'Alcoolisme et des Toxicomanies = ICAA
CIP	Confederation for an Independent Poland = KPN		
CIP	Confédération Internationale des Parents	**CIPB**	Commission du Commerce International des Produits de Base (CNUCED)
CIP	Congrès International de Psychomotricité = ICP	**CIPBC**	Centre National Interprofessionnel des Produits de Basse-Cour
CIP	Conselho Interministerial de Preços (Brazil)	**CIPC**	Centraal Instituut v. Physisch-Chemische Constanten
CIP	Council of International Programs (U.S.A.)	**CIPC**	Centro Internacional de Programacion de Computadoras (El Salvador)
CIP	Council of Iron Producers	**CIPC**	Comité International Permanent de la Conserve
CIPA	Canadian Industrial Preparedness Association		
CIPA	Canadian Institute of Public Affairs	**CIPCA**	Centro de Investigación y Promoción del Campesinado (Bolivia)
CIPA	Centre d'Information sur les Pratiques Associatives (Belgium)	**CIPCC**	Comité International Permanent du Carbon Carburant
CIPA	Centro de Investigación y Promoción Amazonica (Peru)	**CIPCE**	Information and Publicity Centre of the European Railways
CIPA	Chartered Institute of Patent Agents	**CIPCEL**	Comité International de la Pellicule Cellulosique
CIPA	Comité International des Plastiques en Agriculture		
CIPA	Comité Internationale de Photogrammétrie Architecturale = ICAP	**CIPCRO**	Comité Intersecretarial sobre Programas Científicos Relacionados con la Oceanografíca = CIPSRO, ICSPRO
CIPA	Compagnie Industrielle des Piles Électriques	**CIPE**	Collège International de Phonologie Expérimentale
CIPA	Confederazione Generale Italiana Professionisti e Artisti		
CIPA	Council on International and Public Affairs (U.S.A.)	**CIPE**	Comitato Inter-ministeriale per la Programmazione Economica

CIPE	Conseil International de la Préparation a l'Enseignement = CIEE, ICET
CIPÉA	Centre International pour l'Élevage en Afrique = ILCA
CIPEC	Consejo Intergubernamental de Países Exportadores de Cobre (Chile)
CIPEC	Consortium International Pharmaceutique et Chimique
CIPEC-	PT Centre International Perfectionnement Cadres Postes Télécommunications
CIPÉM	Comité International pour l'Études Myceniennes = ICMS
CIPÉPC	Commission Internationale Permanente d'Études de la Police de la Circulation
CIPET	Central Institute of Plastics Engineering and Technology (India)
CIPEXI	Compagnie Ivoirienne de Promotion pour l'Exportation et l'Importation
CIPF	Confédération Internationale du Commerce des Pailles, Fourrages, Tourbes et Dérivés
CIPFA	Chartered Institute of Public Finance and Accountancy
CIPH	Comité International Pharmaciens Homéopathes
CIPHP	Comisión Internacional de Pesquerias del Hipogloso del Pacifico
CIPI	Centre for International Public Issues
CIPI	Comité Interministériel de Politique Industrielle
CIPI	Compagnie Ivoirienne de Pêche et d'Industrie
CIPIC	Center for Image Processing and Integrated Computing (U.S.A.)
CIPIST	Centre International pour l'Information Scientifique et Technique = ICSTI, MCNTI
CIPL	Comité International de Paléographie Latine (ICHS)
CIPL	Comité International Permanent de Linguistes
CIPM	Comité International des Poids et Mesures = ICWM
CIPMA	Centro de Investigacion y Planificacion del Medio Ambiente (Chile)
CIPME	Committee on International Policy in the Marine Environment (U.S.A.)
CIPO	Comité International pour la Préservation des Oiseaux = ICBP
CIPO	Corporación Industrial de Productos Oleaginosos (Argentina)

CIPOL	Centre International de Publications Oecuméniques des Liturgies
CIPOM	Committee on Computers, Information Processing and Office Machines (CSA) (Canada)
CIPP	Conseil Indo-Pacifiques des Pêches (FAO) = IPFC
CIPPN	Commission Internationale des Pêcheries du Pacifique Nord
CIPPT	Centre International de Perfectionnement Professionnel et Technique
CIPQ	Centre International de Promotion de la Qualité
CIPR	Commission Internationale pour la Protection contre les Radiations = ICRP
CIPR	Commission Internationale pour la Protection du Rhin contre la Pollution = ICPRP, IKSR
CIPRA	Clothing Industry Productivity Resources Agency
CIPRA	Commission Internationale pour la Protection des Régions Alpines
CIPRE	Centre d'Initiative Progressiste Européen
CIPRO	Compagnie Ivoirienne de Produits
CIPRO-FILM	Centre Interafricain de Production de Films
CIPROVA	Comité Interprofessionnel pour la Promotion des Ventes des Produits Agricoles et Alimentaires
CIPS	Canadian Information Processing Society = ACI
CIPS	Chartered Institute of Purchasing and Supply
CIPS	China Industrial Property Society
CIPS	Chinese Information Processing Society
CIPS	Choice in Personal Safety
CIPS	Comité Interprofessionnel des Productions Saccharifères
CIPS	Commonwealth International Philatelic Society
CIPSH	Conseil International de la Philosophie et des Sciences Humaines = ICPHS
CIPSO	Compagnie Industrielles de Plastiques Semi- Ouvres
CIPSRO	Conseil Intersecrétariats des Programmes Scientifiques Relatifs à l'Océanographie = CIPCRO, ICSPRO

CIPT	Centre International de Physique Théorique (Italy) = ICTP
CIPV	Comité Permanent des Industries du Verre (CE)
CIR	Center for Immigrants' Rights (U.S.A.)
CIR	Centre International de Référence = WHO/IRC
CIR	Comité International de la Radioélectricité
CIR	Comité International Rom = RIJ
CIR	Commission for Industrial Relations
CIR	Commission International du Riz = IRC
CIR	Council of Industrial Relations
CIRA	Cast Iron Research Association
CIRA	Centre Interministériel des Enseignements Administratifs
CIRA	Centre International de Recherches sur l'Anarchisme
CIRA	Centro Interamericano de Recursos de Agua (IOHE)
CIRA	Centro Interamericano de Reforma Agraria (Colombia)
CIRA	Centro Italiano Radiatori Alluminio
CIRA	Commission Internationale pour la Réglementation des Ascenseurs et Monte-Charges = ICLR
CIRA	Confederation of Industrial Research Associations
CIRAD	Centre de Coopération Internationale en Recherche Agronomique pour le Développement = ICCARD
CIRAF	Conseil International pour la Recherche en Agroforesterie = ICRAF
CIRAS	Center for Industrial Research and Service (U.S.A.)
CIRB	Canadian Industrial Renewal Board
CIRB	Centre International de Recherche Biologique
CIRB	Centre International de Recherches sur le Bilinguisme (Canada) = ICRB
CIRC	Centre for International Research Cooperation
CIRC	Centre International de Recherche sur le Cancer = CIIC, IARC
CIRC	Comité International de Réglementation du Caoutchouc
CIRC	CSIRO International Relations Center (Australia)
CIRCCE	Confédération Internationale de la Représentation Commerciale de la Communauté Européenne

CIRCLE	Cultural and Information Research Centres in Europe
CIRCOM	Centre International de Recherches sur les Communautés Coopératives Rurales
CIRD	Centre International de Recherches Dermatologiques
CIRD	Centro Italiano Ricerche e Documentazione
CIRD	Comité Interservice de Recherche et de Développement (CE)
CIRD-	Africa Centre on Integrated Rural Development for Africa (FAO)
CIRDAP	Centre for Integrated Rural Development for Asia and the Pacific (FAO)
CIRDÉC	Centre International de Recherche et de Documentation en Éducation Continue
CIRDI	Centre International pour le Réglement des Différents Relatifs aux Investissements = CIADI, ICSID
CIRDOM	Centre Interuniversitaire de Recherche et de Documentation sur les Migrations
CIRE	Confederación Internacional de Remolacheros Europeos
CIRÉC	Centre International de Recherches et d'Études Chréiologiques
CIRECCA	Centre International de Recherches, d'Echanges et de Coopération entre la Caraïbe et les Amériques
CIRED	Centre International de Recherche sur l'Environnement et le Développement
CIRÉD	Congrès Internationale des Réseaux Électriques de Distribution
CIREN	Centro de Investigacion de la Realidad del Norte (Chile)
CIRÉS	Centre Ivoirien de Recherches Économiques et Sociales (Ivory Coast)
CIRES	Cooperative Institute for Research in Environmental Science (U.S.A.)
CIRÉSS	Centre International d'Études et de Recherches Socio-Sanitaires (Belgium)
CIRET	Centre for International Research on Economic Tendency
CIRF	Centre International d'Information et de Recherche sur la Formation Professionnelle
CIRF	Consejo Internacional de Recursos Fitogenéticos (FAO)
CIRFED	Centre International de Recherche et de Formation en vue du Développement Harmonisé

CIRFP	Centre International d'Information et de Recherche sur la Formation Policière
CIRFS	Comité International de la Rayonne et des Fibres Synthétiques = IRSFC
CIRG	Centre International de Recherches Glyptographique (Belgium)
CIRHO	Institut de Recherches pour les Huiles et les Oléagineux (CIRAD)
CIRIA	Construction Industry Research and Information Association
CIRIC	Centre International de Reportages et d'Information Culturelle (Switzerland)
CIRIÉC	Centre International de Recherches et d'Information sur l'Économie Publique, Sociale et Coopérative = IFIG
CIRIL	Centre Interdisciplinaire de Recherches avec des Ions Lourds (France)
CIRIOL	Comitato Italiano di Rappresentanza Internazionale per l'Organizzazione del Lavoro
CIRIT	Comité Interprofessionel de Renovation de l'Industrie Textile
CIRM	Centro Internazionale Radio-Medico
CIRM	Comité International Radiomaritime
CIRM	Conferencia de Institútos Religiosos de México
CIRMA	Centro de Investigaciones Regionales de Mesoamérica
CIRMES	Centre for Integrated Resource Management and Environmental Science
CIRMF	Centre International de Recherches Médicales(Gabon)
CIRN	Centre d'Information et de Recherches sur les Nuisances
CIRNA	Compagnie pour l'Ingénierie des Réacteurs au Sodium
CIRP	Collège International pour l'Étude Scientifique des Techniques de Production Mécanique
CIRPHO	Cercle International de Recherches Philosophiques par Ordinateur
CIRPO	Conférence Internationale des Résistants dans les Pays Occupés
CIRSA	Comité Internacional Regional de Sanidad Agropecuária (OIRSA)
CIRSE	Cardiovascular and Interventional Radiological Society of Europe
CIRSEA	Compagnia Italiana Ricerca Sviluppo Equipaggiamenti Aerospaziali
CIRSS	Centre International de Recherches Sahariennes et Sahéliennes
CIRSSE	Center for Intelligent Robotic System for Space Exploration (U.S.A.)
CIRST	Comité Interministériel de la Recherche Scientifique et Technique
CIRT	Centre International de Créations Théâtrales = ICTR
CIRT	Centre Ivoirien de Recherches Technologiques
CIRTEF	Conseil International des Radios-Télévisions d'Expression Française
CIRUISEF	Conférence Internationale des Responsables des Universités et Instituts à dominante Scientifique et Technique d'Expression Française
CIRVE	Conferenza Italiana dei Rappresentanti dei Vettori d'Emigrazione
CIRZ	Centro Italiano di Ricerche Zooeconomiche
CIS	Canadian Institute of Surveying
CIS	Center for Imaging Science (U.S.A.)
CIS	Center for International Studies (Canada)
CIS	Centre for Independent Studies (Australia)
CIS	Centre for Institutional Studies
CIS	Centre for International Security
CIS	Centre Interafricain de Sylviculture
CIS	Centre International d'Informations de Sécurité et d'Hygiéne du Travail
CIS	Centre International de Sémiologie
CIS	Centre International de Synthèse
CIS	Centre International des Stages
CIS	Centre International pour la Culture et l'Instruction par Image et le Son (Belgium)
CIS	Centro de Investigaciones Sociales (Bolivia)
CIS	Centro de Investigaciones Sociales (Colombia)
CIS	Centro de Investigaciones Sociológicas (Spain)
CIS	Centro Italiano di Sessuologia
CIS	China Instrument Society
CIS	China Investment Society
CIS	Coal Industry Society
CIS	Comité International de Sachsenhausen = ISK
CIS	Comité International du suivi du Sommet Francophone
CIS	Commonwealth of Independent States = CEI, GUS, SNG, WNP

CIS	Compagnie Ivoirienne de Sciages
CIS	Council for Inter-American Security (U.S.A.)
CIS	Cranbrook Institute of Science (U.S.A.)
CIS	Institute of Chartered Secretaries and Administrators
CIS	International Occupational Safety and Health Information Centre
CISA	Canadian Industrial Safety Association
CISA	Centro Italiano Studi Aziendali
CISA	Coach Industry Suppliers' Association
CISA	Commission Internationale de Secours Alpin = ICAR, IKAR
CISA	Confédération Internationale des Syndicats Arabes = ICATU
CISA	Congresos Internacionales SA
CISA	Consejo Indio de Sudamérica (Peru)
CISAC	Clinical Imaging Services Advisory Committee (Northern Ireland)
CISAC	Confédération Internationale des Sociétés d'Auteurs et Compositeurs
CISAD	Conseil International des Services d'Aide à Domicile = CISAF, ICHS, IRHD
CISAE	Congrès International des Sciences Anthropologiques et Ethnologiques
CISAL	Confederazione Italiana dei Sindacati Autonomi Lavatori
CISAVIA	Civil Service Aviation Association
CISC	Canadian Institute of Steel Construction
CISC	Citizens' Income Study Centre
CISC	Comité International de Sociologie Clinique = ICCS
CISC	Comité International pour la Solidarité avec Chypre (Finland)
CISC	Conférence Internationale du Scoutisme Catholique = ICCS
CISCE	Comité International pour la Sécurité et la Coopération Européennes = ICESC, ICEVS
CISCO	Centro Italiano Studi Containers
CISCO	Civil Service Catering Organization
CISCOM	Centro Internazionale Salesiano per le Communicazioni Sociali
CISCS	Centre International Scolaire de Correspondance Sonore Solidarité avec la Jeunesse Algérienne
CISDCE	Centro Internazionale Studi Documentazione sulle Comunité Europee
CISDEN	Centro Italiano di Studi di Diritto dell'Energia Nucleare
CISDI	Chongqing Iron & Steel Designing Institute
CISE	Centre for International Sports Exchanges
CISE	Centro Informazione Studi ed Esperienze
CISE	Consortium for International Studies in Education (U.S.A.)
CISE	Council of the Institution of Structural Engineers
CISE	Cuerpo Internacional de Servicios Ejecutivos (Peru)
CISEA	Centro de Investigaciones Sociales sobre el Estado y la Administración (Argentina)
CISEC	Centro de Investigaciones Socio-Economicas (Chile)
CISEPA	Centro de Investigaciones Sociales, Económicas, Politicas y Antropologicas (Peru)
CISER	Cornell Institute for Social and Economic Research
CISF	Central Industrial Security Forces (India)
CISF	Centro Internazionale Studi Famiglia
CISF	Confédération Internationale des Sages-Femmes
CISFEM	Centro de Investigacion Social, Formacion y Estudios de la Mujer (Uruguay)
CISGO	Commonwealth Interchange Study Group Operations
CISH	Comité International des Sciences Historiques = ICHS
CISH	Conseil International des Sports pour Handicapés = ISOD
CISHEC	Chemical Industry Safety and Health Council (CIA)
CISI	Centro Iniziative Studi Internazionali
CISI	Compagnie Internationale de Services et Informatique
CISIC	Centro Internazionale Sociale Istituzione Clero
CISIP	Centro Internazionale Studi Irrigazione a Pioggia
CISIR	Ceylon Institute of Scientific and Industrial Research (Sri Lanka)
CISJA	Comité International de Solidarité avec la Jeunesse Algérieene

CISL	Confédération Internationale des Syndicats Libres = CIOSL, IBFG, ICFTU, IVVV
CISL	Confederazione Italiana dei Sindacati Lavoratori
CISL	Groupe des Syndicats de l'Alimentation du Tabac et de l'Industrie Hôtelière dans la CEE
CISL-ORA	Organisation Régionale Asienne CISL
CISL-ORAF	Organisation Régionale Africaine CISL
CISL-ORE	Organisation Régionale Européenne de la CISL
CISLB	Comité International pour la Sauvegarde de la Langue Bretonne = ICDBL
CISLE	Central International des Syndicalistes Libres en Exil = ICFTUE
CISM	Canadian Institute of Surveying and Mapping
CISM	Centre International des Sciences Mécaniques
CISM	Centro de Investigación y Servicios Museológicos (Mexico)
CISM	Centro Informazione e Studi sul Mercato Comune Europeo
CISM	Conféderation Internationale des Sociétés Musicales
CISM	Conférence Internationale pour l'Étude Scientifique de la Méditerranée
CISM	Conferenza Italiana dei Superiori Maggiori
CISM	Conseil International du Sport Militaire
CISMI	Confederazione Italiana Sindacati Mutilati ed Invalidi
CISNAL	Confederazione Italiana dei Sindacati Nazionali dei Lavoratori
CISNR	Commission for Integrated Survey of Natural Resources (China)
CISO	Comité International des Sciences Onomastiques = ICOS
CISOC	Centro de Investigaciones Socio-Culturales (Chile)
CISOR	Centro de Investigaciones en Ciencias Sociales (Venezuela)
CISOR	Centro de Investigaciones Sociales y Sociorreligiosas (Venezuela)
CISP	Canadian Institute of Surveying and Photogrammetry
CISP	Centro Italiano Smalti Porcellanati
CISP	Comitatio Internazionale per lo Sviluppo dei Popoli

CISP	Comitato Italiano per lo Studio dei Probleme della Popolazione
CISPES	Committee in Solidarity with the People of El Salvador (U.S.A.)
CISPLAN	Caribbean Information System for Economic and Social Planning
CISPM	Confédération Internationale des Sociétés Populaires de Musique
CISPP	Centro Italiano di Studi e Programmazioni per la Pesca
CISPR	Comité International Spécial des Perturbations Radioélectriques
CISR	Center for Information Systems Research (U.S.A.)
CISR	Center for International Systems Research (U.S.A.)
CISRI	Central Iron & Steel Research Institute (China)
CISRI	Chongqing Iron & Steel Research Institute
CISRS	Christian Institute for the Study of Religion and Society (India)
CISS	Center for International and Strategic Studies (U.S.A.)
CISS	Centre for International and Strategic Studies (Canada)
CISS	Centre for International Security Studies (U.S.A.)
CISS	Centre for International Sports Studies
CISS	Comité International des Sports des Sourds = ICSD
CISS	Comité Permanente Interamericano de Seguro Social (Mexico)
CISS	Conférence Internationale de Service Social
CISS	Conferencia Interamericana de Seguridad Social = IACSS
CISS	Conseil International des Sciences Sociales = ISSC
CISS	Cooperazione Internazionale Sud-Sud
CISSAM	Centro Italiano per lo Studio e lo Sviluppo dell' Agopuntura Moderna e dell' altra Medicina
CISSEG	Centro Italiano per lo Studio e lo Sviluppo della Psicoterapia e dell'Autogenes Training
CISST	Center for Interdisciplinary Study of Science and Technology (U.S.A.)
CIST	Centro Internazionale della Stampa Turistica
CIST	Commission Internationale de la Santé du Travail = CIMT, ICOH

CISTC	Council on International Scientific and Technological Cooperation (U.S.A.)
CISTI	Canada Institute for Scientific and Technical Information = ICIST
CISTIP	Committee on International Scientific and Technical Information Programs (NAS, NRC) (U.S.A.)
CISTIT	Centre d'Information Scientifique et Technique et de Transferts Technologiques (Algeria)
CISTOD	Confederation of International Scientific and Technological Organizations for Development = COISTD
CISV	Children's International Summer Villages
CISWO	Coal Industry Social Welfare Organisation
CIT	Canberra Institute of Technology
CIT	Center for Irrigation Technology (U.S.A.)
CIT	Central Institute of Technology (New Zealand)
CIT	Central Istmeña de Trabajadores (Panama)
CIT	Centre for Information Technology
CIT	Centre International de Transactions (Benin)
CIT	Centre International du Tabac
CIT	Changsha Institute of Technology
CIT	Chartered Institute of Transport (South Africa, U.K.)
CIT	Coda International Training
CIT	Comité International des Transports Ferroviaires
CIT	Comité International Tzigane
CIT	Compagnie Industrielle des Télécommunications
CIT	Compagnie Italiana Transatlantica
CIT	Compagnie Italiana Turismo
CIT	Confédération Internationale du Travail
CIT	Congrès International Télétrafic = ITC
CIT	Congresos Interamericanos de Turismo = ITC
CIT	Conseil International des Tanneurs = CIC, ICT, IG
CIT	Consejo Internacional del Trigo = CIB, IWC
CITA	Centro de Investigacion en Tecnologia de Alimentos (Costa Rica)
CITA	Comité International de l'Inspection Technique Automobile
CITA	Consejo Interamericano de Archiveros (Mexico)
CITAB	Compagnie Industrielle des Tabacs de Madagascar
CITAG	Comité International Technique de l'Acide Glutamique = IGTC
CITAR	Center for Interactive Technology, Applications and Research (U.S.A.)
CITB	Carpet Industry Training Board
CITB	Construction Industry Training Board
CITC	Canadian Institute of Timber Construction
CITC	Caribbean Interim Tourism Committee
CITC	Confédération Internationale des Industries Techniques du Cinéma
CITD	Center for International Trade Development (U.S.A.)
CITE	Centro de Instrucciones de Tropas Especiales (Bolivia)
CITE	Confederacion Intersectorial de Trabajadores del Estado (Peru)
CITEC	Center for Industrial & Technological Co-operation
CITEC	Compagnie de l'Industrie Textile Cotonnière
CITÉC	Compagnie pour l'Information et les Techniques Électroniques de Contrôle
CITEC	Montreal Technology Initiative Centre
CITEF	Centro de Investigaciones de Tecnologia de Frutas y Hortalizas (Argentina)
CITEF	Conférence Internationale des Formations d'Ingénieurs et Techniciens d'Expression Française
CITEFA	Institúto de Investigaciones (Cientificas y Técnicas de las Fuerzas Armadas (Argentina)
CITEL	Comision Interamericana de Telecomunicaciones (U.S.A.)
CITELEC	Association Européenne des Villes Interessées par l'Utilisation de Véhicules Electriques (Belgium)
CITEN	Comité International de la Teinture et du Nettoyage à Sec
CITEP	Commonwealth Industrial Training and Experience Programme (ComSec)
CITÉPA	Centre Interprofessional Technique d'Études de la Pollution Atmosphérique
CITERE	Centre d'Information Tempi Réel Europe
CITES	Campaign Against International Trade in Endangered Species

CITES	Convention on International Trade in Endangered Species of Wild Fauna and Flora
CITG	Coal Industry Triparite Group
CITHA	Confederation of International Trading Houses Association
CITI	Center for Information Technology Integration (U.S.A.)
CITI	Centro de Informação Tecnica para a Indústria
CITI	Confédération Internationale des Travailleurs Intellectuels
CITIC	China International Trust and Investment Corporation
CITLA	Cámara Industrial Textil Lanera (Argentina)
CITLO	Centrum voor Informatieverwerking op het Gebied van Tropische Landbouw en Ontwikkeling (Belgium)
CITM	College International du Tiers-Monde
CITO	Centro de Investigaciones Tecnológicas de Oriente (Venezuela)
CITO	Conférence Internationale des Techniques Oléicoles
CITP	Conseil International des Télécommunications de Presse = IPTC
CITPPM	Confédération des Industries de Traitement des Produits des Pêches Maritimes
CITR	Canadian Institute for Telecommunications Research
CITR	Compagnie Ivoirienne de Transports Routiers
CITRA	Compagnie Industrielle de Travaux
CITRA	Conférence Internationale de la Table Ronde des Archives
CITRAP	Société de Construction de l'Immobilier et de Travaux Publiques (Ivory Coast)
CITS	China International Travel Service
CITS	Commission Internationale Technique de Sucrerie
CITS	Companhia Internacional Tratamentos de Superficies
CITT	Canadian International Trade Tribunal
CITT	Commission Interaméricaine du Thon Tropical (FAO) = CIAT, IATTC
CITTA	Confédération Internationale des Fabricants de Tapis Velours et Tissus d'Ameublement
CITU	Confederation of Insurance Trade Unions
CITYNET	Regional Network of Local Authorities for the Management of Human Settlements (Japan)
CiU	Convergéncia i Unió (Catalonia)
CIU	Workingmen's Club and Institute Union
CIUC	Consejo Internacional de Uniones Cientificas = CIUS, ICSU
CIUF	Conseil Interuniversitaire de la Communauté Française
CIUFFAS	Comitato Italiano Utilizzatori Filati di Fibre Artificali e Sintetiche
CIUL	Council for International Urban Liaison
CIUMR	Commission Internationale des Unités et Mesures Radiologiques
CIUP	Centro de Investigaciones Universidad Pedagógica (Colombia)
CIUPST	Commission Interunions de la Physique Solaire et Terrestre (CIUS) = SCOSTEP
CIUS	Canadian Institute of Ukrainian Studies
CIUS	Conseil International des Unions Scientifiques = CIUC, ICSU
CIUSS	Catholic International Union for Social Service = IKVSA, KIUMW, UCISS
CIUTI	Conférence Internationale Permanente de Directeurs d'Instituts Universitaires pour la Formation de Traducteurs et d'Interprètes
CIV	Centro de Investigaciones Veterinarias (Venezuela)
CIV	Commerce Industrie Voltaïque
CIV	Commission Internationale du Verre = ICG, IKG
CIV	Convention Internationale sur le Transport des Voyageurs et des Bagages par Chemins de Fer
CIV	Coöperatieve Centrale Landbouw In -en Verkoopvereniging
CIVA	Camara Venezolana de la Industria Automotriz
CIVA	Commission Internationale de Voltige Aérienne (FAI)
CIVAM	Centre d'Information et de Vulgarisation Agricole et Ménager
CIVAS	Comité Interprofessionnel des Vins d'Anjou- Saumur
CIVB	Comité Interprofessionnel des Vins de Bergerac
CIVB	Comité Interprofessionnel des Vins de Bordeaux
CIVC	Comité Interprofessionnel des Vins de Champagne

CIVCP	Comité Interprofessionnel des Vins des Côtes de Provence	**CJA & HSA**	Council of Justice to Animals and Humane Slaughter Association
CIVCR	Comité Interprofessionnel des Vins des Côtes-du-Rhône	**CJAIN**	Criminal Justice Archive and Information Network (U.S.A.)
CIVDN	Comité Interprofessionnel des Vins Doux Naturels	**CJCC**	Commonwealth Joint Communications Committee
CIVE	International Centre of Winter Maintenance (Italy)	**CJCCL**	Council of Jewish Communities in the Czech Lands = RŽOČZ
CIVÉM	Constructions Ivoiriennes Électromécaniques	**CJCE**	Cour de Justice de Communautés Européennes = CJEC
CIVEXIM	Compagnie Ivoirienne d'Exportation et d'Importation	**CJCI**	Conseil de la Jeunesse de Côte d'Ivoire
CIVG	Comité Interprofessionnel des Vins de Gaillac	**CJCS**	Centre for Jewish Community Studies (Israel)
CIVI	Central Institute for Industrial Development (Netherlands)	**CJD**	Centre des Jeunes Dirigeants d'Entreprise
CIVICIMA	Comité International du Vocabulaire des Institutions et de la Communication Intellectuelle au Moyen Age	**CJE**	Congrès Juif Européen (WJC) = EJC
		CJEC	Court of Justice of the European Communities = CJCE
CIVIJU	Association des Producteurs de Cidre, Vins, Jus de Fruits et des Embouteilleurs de Jus de Fruits (Belgium)	**CJEPC**	Central Joint Education Policy Committee
		CJF	Carl Johans Förbundet (Sweden)
		CJF	Council of Jewish Federations (U.S.A.)
CIVINEX	Société Ivoirienne d'Exploitation Vinicole	**CJHS**	Canadian Jewish Historical Association = SCHJ
CIVO	Centraal Instituut voor Voedingsonderzoek	**CJI**	Comité Juridico Interaméricano = IAJC
CIVPN	Comité Interprofessionnel des Vins du Pays Nantais	**CJIA**	Comité Juridique International de l'Aviation
CIVRES	Congrès International des Techniques du Vide en Recherche Spatiale	**CJM**	Congrès Juif Mondial = WJC
		CJP	Centre des Jeunes Patrons
CIVT	Comité Interprofessionel des Vins de Touraine	**CJP**	Comissão de Justica e Paz (Brazil)
CIVV	Centro Ittiologico Valli Venete	**CJR**	Study Centre for Christian-Jewish Relations
CIW	Carnegie Institute of Washington (U.S.A.)	**CJS**	Center for Japanese Studies (U.K., U.S.A.)
CIWA	Catholic Institute of West Africa (Nigeria) = ICAO	**CJSA**	Criminal Justice Statistics Association (U.S.A.)
CIWF	Clearinghouse International of the Women's Forum (U.S.A.)	**CJWP**	Committee for a Just World Peace (Japan)
CIWF	Compassion in World Farming	**CKB**	Christelijke Kruideniers Bond
CIWLT	Comité Permanent des Syndicats de Travailleurs de la Compagnie International des Wagon-Lits et du Tourisme	**CKF**	Centerkvinnorna
		CKH	Centrale Kamer van Handelsbevordering
		CKKP	Centralna Komisja Kontroli Partyjnej
		CKKR	Centralna Komisja Kontrolno Rewizyjna
CIYC	Church of Ireland Youth Council	**CKP**	Congress of the Karbadin People (Russian Federation)
CJ	Josephite Fathers		
CJA	Classic Jaguar Association (U.S.A.)	**CKS**	Centre for Korean Studies
CJA	Commonwealth Journalists Association	**CKSD**	Centralny Komitet Stronnictwa Demokratycznego
CJA	Conseil de la Jeunesse d'Afrique	**CL**	Celtic League

CL	Centre Lebret
CL	Communist League
CL&CGB	Church Lads' and Church Girls' Brigade
CLA	Canadian Library Association = ACB
CLA	Canadian Linguistic Association = ACL
CLA	Canadian Lung Association
CLA	Cantonese Language Association
CLA	Catholic Library Association (U.S.A.)
CLA	China Leprosy Association
CLA	Christian Liberation Army (Philippines)
CLA	Circolo dei Librai Antiquari
CLA	College Language Association (Barbados)
CLA	Commonwealth Lawyers Association
CLA	Commonwealth Library Association (Jamaica)
CLA	Computer Law Association (U.S.A.)
CLA	Computer Lessors Association (U.S.A.)
CLA	Confederación Lanera Argentina
CLA	Consejo Latinoaméricano y del Caribe para le Autogestión
CLA	Copyright Licensing Agency
CLA	Council of Lithuanian Americans = ALT, ALTas
CLA	Country Landowners' Association
CLAB	Centro Latino-Americano de Ciencias Biologicas
CLAB	Centro Latinoamericana de Automatización Bancaria (Colombia)
CLAB	Confederación Latinoamericana Box
CLABD	Congreso Latino-Americano de Biblioteconomía e Documentação (Brazil)
CLABE	Centre for Language & Business in Europe
CLAC	Caribbean Labour Administration Centre (Barbados)
CLAC	Comisión Latinoamericana Aviación Civil = LACAC
CLACE	Centro Latinoamericano de Coordinación de Estudios (Brazil)
CLACJ	Confederación Latinoamericana de Asociaciones Cristianas de Jóvenes
CLACPI	Comité Latinoamericano de Cine de Pueblos Indigenas
CLACSO	Consejo Latinoamericano de Ciencias Sociales (Argentina)
CLAD	Centro Latinoamericano de Administración para el Desarrollo (Venezuela)
CLADEA	Consejo Latinoamericano de Escuelas de Administración
CLADEM	Comité Latinamericano de Defensa de los Derechos de la Mujer – Costa Rica
CLADEM-H	Comité Latinoamericano para la Defensa de los Derechos de las Mujeres de Honduras
CLADER	Centre Latino-Américaine de Documentation Étude et Recherche
CLADES	Centro Latino Americano de Documentación Económica y Social (UN)
CLADES	Consorcio Latinoamericano sobre Agroecologia y Desarrollo
CLAEH	Centro Latino Americano Economia Humana
CLAEM	Coordinación Latinoamericano de Estudiantes de Medicina
CLAES	Centro Latinoamericano de Ecologia Social (Uruguay)
CLAF	Centro Latinoamericano de Fisica (Brazil)
CLAF	Commission Latino-Américaine des Forêts = LACFFP
CLAFIC	Confederación Latinoamericana de Fisioterapia y Kinesologia (Chile)
CLAG	Conference of Latin Americanist Geographers
CLAH	Conference on Latin American History (U.S.A.)
CLAI	Consejo Latinoaméricano de Iglesias = LACC
CLAID	Comision Latino Americano de Irigacion y Drenaje
CLAIET	Comité de Liaison des Associations Internationales d'Entreprises Touristiques
CLAIP	Consejo Latinoamericano de Investigacione para la Paz
CLAIS	Center for Latin American and Iberian Studies (U.S.A.)
CLAIS	Comisión Latinoamericana de Investigadores en Sorgo (Mexico)
CLAIS	Committee on Latin American and Iberian Studies (U.S.A.)
CLALB	College of Liberal Arts and Law, Beijing United Universities
CLALS	Centre for Latin American Linguistic Studies
CLAMOP	Centre Latino-Américain d'Opinion Publique

CLAMOR	Comité de Defensa dos Direitos Humanos para os Païses do Cone Sul (Brazil)	**CLATR-AMM**	Coordinación Latinoamericana de Trabajadores Metallúrgicos y Mineros
CLAMPI	Confederación Latinoamericana de la Pequeña y Mediana Industria (Colombia)	**CLATT**	Comité Latinoamericano de Textos Teologicos
CLAMUC	Consejo Latinoamericano Mujeres Católicas	**CLAUPAE**	Comité de Líneas Aéreas de la Unión Postal de las Américas y España
CLANN	College Library Activity Network in New South Wales	**CLAVA**	County Land Agents' and Valuers Association
CLAP	Centro Latinoamericano Perinatologia y Desarrollo Humano	**CLAW**	Consortium of Local Authorities in Wales
CLAPA	Cleft Lip and Palate Association	**CLAWS**	Community Land and Workspace Services Ltd
CLAPCS	Centro Latinamericano de Pesquisas en Ciencias Sociais (Brazil)	**CLB**	Centro do Livro Brasileiro
CLAPN	Comité Latinoamericano de Parques Nacionales	**CLB**	Communist League of Britain
CLAPTUR	Confederación Latinoamericano de Prensa Turística	**CLC**	Canadian Labour Congress = CTC
		CLC	Caribbean Labour Congress
CLAPU	Confederaçâo LatinoAmericana de Associações de Profissionais Universitários (Brazil)	**CLC**	Central Land Council
		CLC	Children's Legal Centre
CLAQ	Centro Latinoamericano de Quimica	**CLC**	Christian Life Community = CVX
CLAR	Confederación Latino Americana de Religiosos (Colombia)	**CLC**	Commonwealth Liaison Committee
		CLC	Consejo Latinoamericano de Cultura (Argentina)
CLARA	Centre for the Law of Rural Areas	**CLC**	Consolidated Leasing Corporation of America
CLARA	Comite Latinoamericano para las Regiones Aridas	**CLCA**	Comité de Liaison de la Construction Automobile des Pays des Communautés Européennes
CLARCFE	Consejo Latino Americano de Radiación Cósmica y Fisica del Espacio		
CLARTE	Centre de Liaison des Activités Régionales, Touristiques et Économiques	**CLCCR**	Comité de Liaison de la Construction de Carrosseries et de Remorques
CLAS	Center for Latin American Studies (U.S.A.)	**CLCPANO**	Commission de Lutte contre le Criquet Pèlerin en Afrique du Nord-Ouest (FAO) = CCDLNWA
CLAS	Centre for Latin American Studies	**CLD**	Agency for Christian Literature Development
CLASA	Confederación Latinoamericana de Sociedades de Anestesia	**CLD**	Comité de Liaison des Associations Européennes du Commerce de Détail
CLASEP	Comisión Latinoamericana Servidores Públicos	**CLE**	Caribbean Council for Legal Education
CLASP	Concerned Lawyers Association for Social Problems (Éire)	**CLE**	Centre de Liaison pour l'Environnement (Kenya) = ELC
CLASS	Concrete Lintel Association	**CLE**	Centre for Languages in Education
CLAT	Central Latinoamericana de Trabajadores	**CLE**	Committee of Liberal Exiles
		CLE	Comunidad Latinoamericana de Escritores (Mexico)
CLAT	Confederation of Latin-American Teachers (U.S.A.)	**CLE**	Council of Legal Education
CLATEC	Comisión Latinoamericana de Trabajadores de la Educación	**CLE**	Cumann Leabharfhoilsitheorí Éireann Teo = IBPA
CLATJUP	Confederación Latinoamericana de Trabajadores Pensionados y Jubilados (Venezuela)	**CLÉ**	Cumann Leabharfhoilsitheorí Éireann: Irish Book Publishers Association
		CLEA	Centro Latinoamericano de Educación de Adultos (Chile)

CLEA	Commonwealth Legal Education Association
CLEA	Council of Local Education Authorities
CLEAPSE	Consortium of Local Education Authorities for the Provision of Science Equipment
CLEAR	Campaign for Lead-Free Air
CLEAR	Center for Labor Education and Research (U.S.A.)
CLEAR	Center for Lake Erie Area Research (U.S.A.)
CLEAR	Criminal Law Education and Research Center (U.S.A.)
CLEARS	Cornell Laboratory for Environmental Applications of Remote Sensing
CLEC	Comité de Liaison de l'Engineering Chimique Français
CLECAT	Comité de Liaison Européen des Commissionnaires et Auxiliaries de Transports du Marché Commun
CLED-ESF	Comité Laïque pour l'Education au Développement – Educateurs sans Frontières
CLED-TIERRA	Centro Latinoamericano de Estudio y Difusion de la Construccion en Tierra (Peru)
CLEDIPA	Comité de Liaison Européen de la Distribution Indépendante de Pièces Automobiles (Belgium)
CLEI	Centro Latinoamericano Estudios Informática
CLÉIC	Comité de Liaison et d'Étude de l'Industrie de la Chaussure de la CEE
CLÉJFL	Centre de Liaison et d'Étude pour les Jus de Fruits et de Légumes
CLENE	Continuing Library Education Network and Exchange (U.S.A.)
CLEO	Comité de Liaison Européen des Ostéopathes
CLÉPA	Comité de Liaison de la Construction d'Équipements et de Pièces d'Automobiles
CLEPR	Council on Legal Education for Professional Responsibility
CLER	Comité de Liaison Énergies Renouvelables
CLES	Centre for Local Economic Strategies
CLETC	China Light Industrial Corporation for Foreign Economic and Technical Cooperation
CLETRI	China Leihua Electronic Technology Research Institute
CLF	Comité Linier de France
CLGW	Cement, Lime and Gypsum Workers International Union (U.S.A.)
CLHS	Centre for Left-Handed Studies
CLI	Centre de Liaison Interprofessionnel de l'Industrie, du Commerce et de l'Artisanat de l'Indre
CLI	Comann an Luchd-ionnsachaidh (Scotland)
CLIA	China Light Industry Association
CLIA	Cruise Lines International Association (U.S.A.)
CLIC	Cancer and Leukaemia in Childhood Trust
CLICE	European Cooperatives Intersectoral Liaison Committee (Belgium)
CLICÉC	Comité de Liaison International de la Coopération d'Épargne et de Crédit
CLIF	Comité Latinoamericano de Investigaciones Forestales (Chile)
CLIF	Commonwealth Land Information Forum (*now* CSDC)
CLIMEX	Information Exchange System on Country Activities on Climate Change
CLIMM	Commission de Liaison Inter-Nations Mars et Mercure
CLIMMAR	Centre de Liaison International des Marchands-Réparateurs de Machines Agricoles
CLIMO	Comité Européen de Liaison des Importateurs de Machines-Outils
CLINIMED	Société des Cliniques Médicales (Ivory Coast)
CLIP	Common Law Institute of Intellectual Property
CLIR	Center for Labor and Industrial Relations (U.S.A.)
CLIRP	Cercle Liegeois de l'Information et de Relations Publiques
CLISG	Commonwealth Land Information Support Group
CLITAM	Centre de Liaison des Industries de Traitement des Algues Marines de la CEE
CLITRAVI	Centre de Liaison des Industries Transformatrices de Viandes de la CEE
CLJP	Centre de Loisirs et des Jeunes de la Police
CLL	Copyright Licensing Limited (New Zealand)
CLLR	International Symposium on Computing in Literary and Linguistic Research

CLMA	Contact Lens Manufacturers Association (U.S.A.)
CLMC	Combined Loyalist Military Command (Northern Ireland)
CLMS	Centre for Labour Market Studies
CLNAI	Comitato di Liberazione Nazionale alta Italia
CLO	Campaign for Law and Order
CLO	Central Agricultural Organisation (Netherlands)
CLO	Centrale Landsdienaren Organisatie (Suriname)
CLO	Centrum Landbouwkundig Onderzoek (Belgium)
CLOA	Chief Leisure Officers Association
CLOING	Comité de Liaison des Organisations Internationales Non-Gouvernementales
CLOSP	Comité de Liaison des Organisations Syndicales et Professionnelles du Personnel des Communautés Européennes
CLP	Caja Laboral Popular
CLP	Club der Luftfahrtpublizisten (Austria)
CLP	Communal Liberation Party (TRNC)
CLP	Competition Law and Policy Committee (OECD)
CLPCE	Comité de Liaison des Podologues de la Communauté Européenne
CLPD	Campaign for Labour Party Democracy
CLPE	Centre for Language in Primary Education
CLPG	Central Laboratory of Petroleum Geology (China)
CLPR	Cooperative League of Puerto Rico
CLR	Canadian League of Rights
CLR	Council on Library Resources (U.S.A.)
CLRAE	Standing Conference of Local and Regional Authorities of Europe = CPL
CLRB	Canada Labour Relations Board
CLRI	Central Leather Research Institute (India)
CLRU	Cambridge Language Research Unit
CLS	Canon Law Society of America
CLS	Caribbean Labour Solidarity
CLS	Centre for Lebanese Studies
CLS	Christian Legal Society (U.S.A.)
CLS	Učená Společnost České Republiky
ČLS JEP	Česká Lékařská Společnost J E Purkyně
CLSA	Contact Lens Society of Australia
CLSB	Committee of London & Scottish Bankers
CLSP	Community Landcare Support Program
CLSS	Coast Life Saving Service (Éire)
CLT	Campaign for Local Television
CLT	Compagnie Libanaise de Télévision
CLT	Compagnie Luxembourgeoise de Télédiffusion
CLT	Cooperative League of Thailand
CLTA	Canadian Library Trustees Association
CLTC	Confederación Latinoamericana de Trabajadores de Comunicaciones
CLTRI	Central Leprosy Teaching and Research Institute (India)
CLU	Civil Liberties Union (U.S.A.)
CLU	Confederation of Labour Unions (Ethiopia)
CLUSA	Co-operative League of the USA
CLUW	Coalition of Labor Union Women (U.S.A.)
CLV	Coöperatieve Landbouwvereniging
CM	Carmelitane Missionarie
CM	Caroline Movement
CM	Chambre des Métiers
CM	Congregatio Missionis
CMA	Cable Makers' Association
CMA	Canadian Manufacturers Association
CMA	Canadian Medical Association = AMC
CMA	Canadian Museums Association
CMA	Carrot Marketing Association
CMA	Case Makers' Association
CMA	Casket Manufacturing Association of America
CMA	Castor Manufacturers' Association
CMA	Catering Managers Association of Great Britain
CMA	Cement Manufacturers Association (India)
CMA	Central Mapping Authority (New South Wales) (*now* LIC)
CMA	Centre de Transport International par Véhicules Automobiles (Yugoslavia)
CMA	Centre for Management Agriculture
CMA	Centre for Mathematical Analysis (ANU)
CMA	Centre for Multicultural Awareness (U.S.A.)
CMA	Chemical Manufacturers Association (U.S.A.)

CMA	Chinese Manufacturers Association of Hong Kong		**CMAR**	Comité Maghrebin d'Assurances et de Réassurance (Morocco)
CMA	Chinese Medical Association		**CMAS**	Confédération Mondiale des Activités Subaquatiques = WUF
CMA	Chocolate Manufacturers Association of the United States		**CMAV**	Coalition Mondiale pour l'Abolition de la Vivisection = WCV
CMA	Christian and Missionary Alliance (U.S.A.)		**CMB**	Centrale des Métallurgistes de Belgique
CMA	Christian Musicians' and Artists' Trust		**CMB**	Christian Mission to Buddhists
CMA	Church Music Association		**CMB**	Compagnie Maritime Belge
CMA	Civilian Military Assistance (U.S.A.)		**CMB**	Conseil Mondial de la Boxe = WBC
CMA	Comando Militar da Amazónia (Brazil)		**CMBES**	Canadian Medical and Biological Engineering Society
CMA	Commonwealth Medical Association		**CMBI**	Citrus Marketing Board of Israel
CMA	Communication Managers Association		**CMC**	California Advisory Commission on Marine and Coastal Resources (U.S.A.)
CMA	Compania Mexicana de Aviación		**CMC**	Canadian Marconi Company
CMA	Computer Management Association (U.S.A.)		**CMC**	Canadian Museum of Civilization
CMA	Conseil Mondial de l'Alimentation = WFC		**CMC**	Canadian Music Centre
			CMC	Catholic Media Council
CMA	Coopératives Marocaines Agricoles		**CMC**	Center for Marine Conservation (U.S.A.)
CMA	Corporacion de Mercadeo Agricola (Venezuela)		**CMC**	Central Manpower Committee (DOH)
CMA	Council for Museum Anthropology (U.S.A.)		**CMC**	Christian Medical Commission (Switzerland)
CMA	Country Music Association		**CMC**	Coöperatieve Melk Centrale
CMA	Countryside Management Association		**CMC**	Collective Measures Committee of the United Nations
CMA	Crédit Mutuel Agricole		**CMC**	Computer Maintenance Corporation (India)
CMAA	Cocoa Merchants Association of America		**CMC**	Conférence Mondiale sur le Climat (OMM) = WCC
CMAA	Crane Manufacturers Association of America		**CMC**	Congregation of Mother of Carmel
CMAAO	Confederation of Medical Associations in Asia and Oceania		**CMC**	Consejo Monetario Centroamericano (Guatemala)
CMAB	Centro Médico Argentino-Británico		**CMC**	Conservation Monitoring Centre (IUCN)
CMAC	Catholic Marriage Advisory Council		**CMC**	Culture Ministers Council
CMAE	Commission de Météorologie Aéronautique (OMM)		**CMC**	Curriculum Ministers Council
CMAÉC	Conseil Mondial des Associations d'Éducation Comparée = WCCES		**CMC**	ICC Centre for Maritime Cooperation = CCM, IMCC
CMAEHA	Coalition Mondiale pour l'Abolition de l'Expérimentation sur l'Homme et l'Animal		**CMC**	Syndicat National des Constructeurs de Matériel de Chauffage Central
CMAg	Commission de Météorologie Agricole (OMM) = CAM		**CMCA**	Comité Mundial de la Consulta de los Amigos = CCMA, FWCC
CMAI	Clothing Manufacturers Association of India		**CMCA**	Consejo Monetario Centroamericano (Costa Rica)
CMAI	Concrete Manufacturers' Association of Ireland		**CMCA**	Constructions Métalliques du Centrafrique
CMAO	Consejo Mundial de Artes y Oficios = WCC		**CMCÉ**	Comité Ministériel de Coordination Économique (Belgium)
CMAP	Comisión Mundial de Acción Professional = WCTA			

CMCEN-GRAIS	Comité Marché Commun de l'Industrie des Engrais Azotés et Phosphatés	**CMED**	Commission Mondiale de l'Environnement et du Développement (UN) = WCED
CMCÉS	Comité Ministériel de Coordination Économique et Sociale	**CMEH**	Council on Medication and Hospitals (U.S.A.)
CMCF/AD	Campagne Mondiale contre la Faim / Action pour le Développement = CMCH/AD, FFHCAD	**CMERA**	Centre Maghrébin d'Études et de Recherches Administratives
CMCH/AD	Campaña Mundial contra el Hambre/Acción pro Desarrollo = CMCF/AD, FFHCAD	**CMERI**	Central Mechanical Engineering Research Institute, Durgapur (India)
CMCM	Centre for Machine Condition Monitoring (Australia)	**ČMeS**	Česká Meteorologická Společnost (ex ČSMS)
CMCR	Centre for Mass Communication Research	**CMES**	Chinese Mechanical Engineering Society
CMCR	Compagnie Maritime des Chargeurs Réunis	**CMES**	Chinese Medical Educational Society
CMCSA	Canadian Manufacturers of Chemical Specialities Association	**CMET**	Committee for Middle East Trade
		CMF	Cast Metal Federation
CMCW	Christian Mission to the Communist World	**CMF**	Centro Nacional para el Desarrollo de la Mujer (Costa Rica)
CMD	Centrale Melkcontrôle Dienst	**CMF**	Coal Merchants Federation of Great Britain
CMD	Centralforeningen af Malermestre i Danmark	**CMF**	Coal Merchants' Federation
CMD	Chemicals and Mineral Division (Philippines)	**CMF**	Congregatio Missionariorum Filiorum Immaculati Cordis BMV "Claretiani"
CMDA	Caribbean Management Development Association (Barbados)	**CMFAD**	Council for Management Education and Development
CMDA	Cornish Mining Development Association	**CMFRI**	Central Marine Fisheries Research Institute (India)
CMDC	Central Milk Distributive Committee	**CMG**	Commission for Marine Geology (IUGS)
CMDF	Commonwealth Media Development Fund	**CMGM**	Comité du Monitoring des Grands Malades (CE)
CMDIK	Centrum Medycyny Doświadczalnej i Klinicznej Pań	**CMH**	Commission de Météorologie Hydrologique (OMM)
CMDP	Croatian Muslim Democratic Party = HMDS	**CMHA**	Canadian Mental Health Association
		CMHA	Chinese Mental Health Association
CMDT	Compagnie Malienne pour le Développement des Textiles (Mali)	**CMHC**	Canada Mortgage and Housing Corporation
CME	Centre for Medical Education	**CMHERA**	Community and Mental Handicap Educational and Research Association
CME	Centre for Multicultural Education		
CME	Chicago Mercantile Exchange (U.S.A.)	**CMHN**	Consejo Mexicano de Hombres de Negocios
CME	Compagnie Mauritanienne d'Entreprises	**CMHSD**	Centre for Mental Health Services Development, King's College London
CMÉ	Conférence Mondiale de l'Énergie = WEC	**CMI**	Canadian Mediterranean Institute
CMÉ	Conseil Mondial d'Éducation = WCCI, WFB	**CMI**	Caribbean Meteorological Institute
		CMI	Carmelites of Mary Immaculate
CME	Contracting Marine Engineering (UAE)	**CMI**	Centre Mondial d'Information (Switzerland) = WICC
CMEA	Council for Middle Eastern Affairs (U.S.A.)		
CMÉAOC	Conférence Ministérielle d'États Afrique Ouest Centre Transport Maritimes	**CMI**	Christian Michelsens Institutt for Videnskap og Andsfrihet (Norway)

CMI	Comité Maritime International = IMC
CMI	Comité Météorologique International
CMI	Commission Mixte Internationale pour la Protection des Lignes de Télécommunication et des Canalisations Souterraines
CMI	Communications et Media Internationaux
CMI	Computational Mechanics Institute
CMI	Congregatio Fratrum Carmelitarum Beatae Virginis Mariae Immaculatae
CMI	Consejo Mundial de Iglesias = COE, OeRK, WCC
CMI	Cordage Manufacturers' Institute
CMIDOM	Centre Militaire d'Information et de Documentation sur l'Outre-Mer
CMIÉB	Centre Mondiale d'Information sur l'Éducation Bilingue
CMIEC	China Metallurgical Import and Export Corporation
CMIM	Centre for Measurement & Information Medicine
CMIS	Conferenza Mondiale degli Istituti Secolari (Italy)
CMIST	Consultative Group on Marine Industries Science and Technology
CMIT	Committee on Capital Movements and Invisible Transactions (OECD)
CMITU	Centre Mondial d'Informations Techniques et d'Urbanisme (FMVJ)
CMJ	Church's Ministry Among the Jews
CMJA	Commonwealth Magistrates and Judges Association
CMJP	Centre Marocain des Jeunes Patrons et des Cadres Dirigeants
CML	Collegium Musicum di Latina
CML	Council of Mortgage Lenders
CMLA	Canadian Maritime Law Association
CMLA	Chief Martial Law Administrator (Pakistan)
CMM	Commission de Météorologie Maritime (OMM)
CMM	Compagnie Métallurgique et Minière
CMM	Congregatio Missionarium de Mariannhill
CMMA	Carpet Manufacturers Marketing Association (U.S.A.)
CMMA	Concrete Mixer Manufacturers Association
CMMC	Commonwealth Mining and Metallurgical Congress

CMMI	Commonwealth Mining and Metallurgical Institutions
CMMI	Council of Mining and Metallurgical Institutions (U.S.A.)
CMMS	Chemical, Metallurgical and Mining Society (South Africa)
CMN	Canadian Museum of Nature
CMN	Comisia pentru Ocrotirea Monumentelor Naturii
CMN	Compagnie Malienne de Navigation
CMO	Caribbean Meteorological Organisation (Trinidad-Tobago)
CMO	Central Melkhandelaren Organisatie
CMO	Colónia Militar de Oiapoque (Brazil)
CMO	Conference of Middle East Railways (Turkey)
CMOD	Centre Mondial d'Orientation Documentaire
CMOPE	Confédération Mondial des Organisations de la Profession Enseignante = WCOTP
CMP	Centre for Multiprocessors
CMP	Christian Movement for Peace = CFD, ICVD, MCP
CMP	Congrès Mondiaux du Pétrole = WPC
CMP	Conseil Mondial de la Paix = VSM, WFR, WPC
CMPA	Chinchilla Pelt Marketing Association
CMPAA	Certified Milk Producers Association of America
CMPC	Compañía Manufacturera de Papeles y Cartones (Chile)
CMPCO	Comité Mixta sobre Programas Cientificos Relacionados con la Oceanografíca
CMPE	Comité Medical Permanent Européen
CMPE	Contractors Mechanical Plant Engineers
CMPFT	Centro de la Mujer Peruana Flora Tristan
CMPI	Consejo Mundial de Pueblos Indigenos = WCIP
CMPO	Calcutta Metropolitan Planning Organisation (India)
CMPP	Comité Maghrebin Produits Pharmaceutiques
CMPR	Chambre Syndicale des Fabricants de Tuiles et de Briques du Poitou-Charentes-Limousin
CMPT	Comité Militaire du PCT (Congo)
CMR	Centre for Materials Research

CMR	Centre for Medicines Research	**CMS**	Cricket Memorabilia Society
CMR	Chrétiens dans le Monde Rural	**CMSB**	Confédération Mondial du Sport de Boules
CMR	Congresul Mondial Românesc = RWC		
CMRA	Chemical Marketing Research Association (U.S.A.)	**CMSER**	Commission on Marine Science, Engineering and Resources
CMRADR	Conférence Mondiale sur la Réforme Agraire et le Développement Rural (FAO) = WCARRD	**CMSF**	Congregatio Missionaria Sancti Francisci Assissensis
		CMSI	China Metallurgical Standardization Research Institute
CMRC	China Meat Research Center		
CMRC	Coal Mining Research Company (Canada)	**CMSM**	Conferencia Melitensis Superiorum Maiorum (Malta)
CMRC	Colonial Medical Research Committee	**CMSN**	Comité Militaire de Salut National (Mauritania)
CMRDI	Central Metallurgical Research and Development Institute (Egypt)		
		CMSS	Bohemian-Moravian Centre Party
CMRE	Committee for Monetary Research and Education (U.S.A.)	**CMT**	Comité Maghrebin du Tourism (Tunisia)
		CMT	Common Market Travel Association
CMRE	Consejo de Municipios y Regiones de Europa = CCRE, CEMR, RGRE	**CMT**	Confédération Mauricienne des Travailleurs
CMREF	Committee On Marine Research, Education and Facilities (U.S.A.)	**CMT**	Confédération Mondiale du Travail = WCL, WVA
CMRI	Chemical Machinery Research Institute (China)	**CMT**	Construction Métallique Tropicale
		CMT	MM/CMTFédération Mondiale de le Métallurgie
CMRI	Colonial Microbiological Research Unit (West Indies)		
CMRS	Central Mining Research Station (India)	**CMTC**	Companhia Municipal de Transportes Coletivos (Brazil)
CMRS	Conference of Major Religious Superiors	**CMTI**	Central Machine Tool Institute (India)
		CMTP	Canadian Manpower Training Program
CMRSHR	Chinese Medical Research Society of Health Recovery	**CMTR**	Compagnie Malienne de Transports Routiers
CMRT	Conférence Mondiale sur la Recherche dans les Transports = WCTR	**CMTT**	Commission Mixte pour les Transmissions Télévisuelles
CMS	Canadian Mathematical Society = SMC	**CMTU**	Confederation of Malta Trade Unions
CMS	Caribbean Meteorological Service	**CMU**	China Medical University
CMS	Catholic Missionary Society	**CMU**	Communication Managers' Union (Éire)
CMS	Centre for Medieval Studies (Canada)		
CMS	Centre for Mediterranean Studies	**CMU**	Community of Mediterranean Universities (Italy) = CUM
CMS	Chinese Mathematical Society		
CMS	Chinese Mechanical Society	**CMV**	Centrum voor Mondiale Vorming
CMS	Chinese Metal Society	**CMV**	Christlicher Metallarbeiterverband (BRD, Switzerland)
CMS	Church Missionary Society		
CMS	Church Monuments Society	**CMV**	Congregatione Mechitarista di Vienna
CMS	Clay Minerals Society	**CMW**	Council of Museums in Wales
CMS	Comboni Missionary Sisters (Italy)	**CN**	Circulo Nacional de Prensa (Guatemala)
CMS	Commission de Météorologie Synoptique (OMM)	**CN**	Coalition for Networked Information
CMS	Computational Mathematics Society (China)	**CN**	Conselho Nacional (Cape Verde)
		CNA	Campaign for Non-Alignment
CMS	Convention on the Conservation of Migratory Species (UNEP)	**CNA**	Carers National Association
		CNA	Central Neuropsychiatric Association (U.S.A.)
CMS	Corps Mondial de Secours		

CNA	Ceramisti Novesi Associati
CNA	Chinese Nursing Association
CNA	Coalition of National Agreement (Croatia)
CNA	Comisión Nacional del Arroz (Ecuador)
CNA	Comissão Nacional de Alimentacão (Brazil)
CNA	Comissão Nacional de Avicultura (Brazil)
CNA	Comité National pour l'Étude et la Prévention de l'Alcoolisme et des Autres Toxicomanies
CNA	Compagnie Nationale d'Assurances (Ivory Coast)
CNA	Confederação Nacional da Agricultura (Brazil, Portugal)
CNA	Confederación Nacional Agraria (Peru)
CNA	Confédération Nationale de l'Artisanat
CNA	Confederazione Nazionale dell' Artigianato
CNA	Consiliul National al Apelor
CNA	Corporación Nacional de Abastecimientos (Peru)
CNA	Cyprus News Agency
CNAA	Comité National d'Action Agricole
CNAA	Corporation Nationale de l'Agriculture et de l'Alimentation
CNAA	Council for National Academic Awards
CNAAG	Comité Nacional d'Astronomie d'Astrophysique et de Géographique (Algeria)
CNAB	Confédération Nationale de Administrateurs de Biens
CNABRL	Compagnie Nationale d'Aménagement du Bas-Rhône et Languedoc
CNAC	China National Aviation Corporation
CNAC	Comité National d'Action Communal
CNAD	Conference of National Armaments Directors (NATO)
CNAD	Conseil National des Arts Dramatiques
CNAE	Commisão Nacional de Actividades Especiais (Brazil)
CNAE	Companhia Nacional de Alimentação Escolar (Brazil)
CNAF	Confédération Nationale de l'Aviculture Française
CNAG	Centro Nacional de Agricultura y Ganadería (Honduras)
CNAG	Commission Nationale d'Amélioration Génétique

CNAG	Comunn na Gaidhlig
CNAH	Centre National pour l'Amélioration de l'Habitat
CNAIOS	Consociazione Nazionale delle Infermiere / Infermieri de Altri Operatorio Sanitorio Sociali
CNALCM	Comité National d'Action et de Liaison des Classes Moyennes
CNAM	Confédération Nationale de l'Artisanat et des Métiers
CNAM	Conservatoire National des Arts et Métiers
CNAN	Compagnie Nationale Algérienne de Navigation
CNAP	Centre National d'Animation et de Promotion
CNAPF	Centre National des Académies et Associations Littéraires et Savantes des Provinces Françaises
CNAPT	Ceylon National Association for the Prevention of Tuberculosis
CNAR	Caisse Nationale d'Assurance et de Réassurance (Mali)
CNAR	Confédération Nationale des Artisans Ruraux
CNAR	Confédération Nationale pour l'Aménagement Rural
CNAREM	Centre National des Recherches Métallurgiques
CNAS	Research Center for Nepal and Asian Studies (Nepal)
CNASA	Centre National d'Aménagements des Structures Agricoles
CNASEA	Centre National pour l'Aménagement des Structures des Exploitations Agricoles
CNAT	Commission Nationale de l'Aménagement du Territoire
CNAT	Confédération Nord-Africaine des Transports (Morocco)
CNAUK	Chemical Notation Association U.K.
CNAV	Christlinationaler Angestelltenverband der Schweiz
CNAVMA	Caisse Nationale d'Assurance Vieillesse Mutuelle Agricole
CNB	Centraal Normalisatiebureau
CNB	Comitato Nazionale per le Biotecnologie
CNB	Comité National Belge
CNB	Confédération Nationale de la Boulangerie et Boulangerie Pâtisserie

CNB	Confédération Nord-Américaine de Billard (U.S.A.)
CNBB	Confederação Nacional dos Bispos do Brasil
CNBDI	China Northeast Building Design Institute
CNBÉ	Comité National Belge de l'Éclairage
CNBF	Centre National des Blés de Force
CNBF	Centre National des Bureaux de Fret
CNBF	Confédération Nationale de la Boucherie Française
CNBMHI	China New Building Materials Industry Hangzhou Design Research Institute
CNBOS	Comité National Belge de l'Organisation Scientifique
CNBT	Conseil National de la Blanchisserie et de la Teinturerie
CNBVSL	Confédération Nationale Belge des Industries et du Commerce des Vins, Spiritueux et Liqueurs
CNBWMC	China National Building Waterproof Material Corporation
CNC	Captive Nations Committee (U.S.A.)
CNC	Central Nacional Campesina (Venezuela)
CNC	Centro Nacional de Cultura (Portugal)
CNC	Chambre Nationale de Commerce (Algeria)
CNC	Comisión Nacional Campesina (Chile)
CNC	Comisión Nacional del Cacao (Ecuador)
CNC	Comité National de la Consommation
CNC	Committee for Nature Conservancy (Northern Ireland)
CNC	Compagnie Nouvelle de Cadres
CNC	Confederação Nacional do Comércio (Brazil)
CNC	Confederación Nacional de Campesinos (Mexico)
CNC	Confederación Nacional de la Construccion
CNC	Confédération Nationale de la Construction (Belgium)
CNC	Confédération Nationale des Cadres (Belgium) = NCK
CNC	Conseil National de Commerce
CNC	Conseil National du Crédit
CNC	Conseil National du Cuir
CNC	Consejo Nacional Campesino (Costa Rica)
CNC	Conselho Nacional do Comércio (Brazil)
CNC	Conselho Nacional do Cooperativismo (Brazil)
CNC	Consiglio Nazionale dei Chimici
CNC	Consorzio Nazionale Canapa
CNC	Cumann Náisiúnta na gCór (Éire)
CNCA	Caisse Nationale de Crédit Agricole (Benin, Burkina Faso, Congo, France, Morocco, Niger, Senegal, Togo)
CNCA	Centre National de la Coopération Agricole
CNCA	Consejo Nacional de Conciliación Agraria (Peru)
CNCA	Consejo Nacional para la Cultura y las Artes (Mexico)
CNCA	Conselho Nacional Consultivo da Agricultura (Brazil)
CNCAF	Conseil National de la Coopération Agricole Française
CNCATA	Centre National Coopératif Agricole de Traitements Antiparasitaires
CNCBP	Centre National de Coopération des Bibliothèques Publiques
CNCC	Confédération Nationale du Commerce Charbonnier
CNCC	Council for Nature Conservation and the Countryside
CNCC	Czech National Committee for Chemistry = ČNKCH
CNCCEF	Comité National des Conseillers du Commerce Extérieur de la France
CNCCMM	Chambre Nationale des Constructeurs de Caravanes et de Maisons Mobiles
CNCD	Centre National de Coopération au Développement (Belgium)
CNCD	Confederazione Nationale dei Coltivatori Diretti
CNCE	Centre National du Commerce Extérieur
CNCF	Collège National des Chirurgiens Français
CNCF	Confédération Nationale de la Charcuterie de France
CNCI	Société Commerciale du Nord de la Côte-d'Ivoire
CNCIA	Confédération Nationale des Commerces et Industries de l'Alimentation
CNCIEC	China National Coal Import and Export Corporation
CNCL	Commission Nationale de la Communication et des Libertés

CNCM	Confédération Nationale du Crédit Mutuel	**CNDES**	Centre National de Documentation Économique et Sociale (Algeria)
CNCM	National Culture Collection of Microorganisms (France)	**CNDF**	Congress of National Democratic Forces (Ukraine)
CNCMCA	Confédération Nationale de la Coopération de la Mutualité et du Crédit Agricoles	**CNDH**	Centre National de Documentation Horticole
CNCP	Caisse Nationale de Crédit Professionnel	**CNDH**	Comisión Nacional de Derechos Humanos (Mexico)
CNCPIR	Chambre Nationale du Commerce du Pneumatique et de l'Industrie du Rechapage	**CNDI**	Caisse Nationale des Dépôts et Investissements (Burkina Faso)
CNCPT	Canadian National/Canadian Pacific Telecommunications	**CNDI**	Consiglio Nazionale Donne Italiane
CNCrA	Caisse Nationale de Crédit Agricole	**CNDM**	Consejo Nacional de los Derechos de la Mujer (Brazil)
CNCT	Consejo Nacional de Ciencia y Tecnologia (Mexico)	**CNDM**	Conselho Nacional dos Direitos da Mulher (Brazil)
CNCT	Coordenação Nacional das Classes Trabalhadores (Brazil)	**CNDP**	Centre National de Documentation Pédagogique
CNCV	Cape Verde National Council	**CNDRP**	Centre National de Documentation et de Recherche en Pédagogie
CNCV	Confederación Nacional de Cooperativas de Venezuela	**CNDS**	Council of Nordic Dental Students = NOS
CNCV	Confédération Nationale des Coopératives Vinicoles	**CNDST**	Centre National de Documentation Scientifique et Technique (Belgium, Senegal)
CND	Campaign for Nuclear Disarmament	**ČNDT**	Česká Společnost pro Nedestruktivní Testování
CND	Colegio Nacional de Decoradores y Diseñadores de Interior	**CNDV**	Confédération Nationale des Distilleries Vinicoles
CND	Comptoir National du Diamant (Central Africa)	**CNE**	Centre for the New Europe
CND	Conseil National de Développement (Niger)	**CNE**	Centro Nacional de Economía (Nicaragua)
CND	Conseil pour le Développement National (Rwanda)	**CNE**	Comisión Nacional de Energia (Chile)
		CNÉ	Confédération Nationale de l'Élevage
CND	Soeurs de la Congrégation de Notre-Dame	**CNE**	Conséjo Nacional de Educación (Bolivia)
CNDA	Angolan National Democratic Convention	**CNE**	Consejo Nacional de la Energía (Venezuela)
CNDA	Centre National de Documentation Agricole, Tunisia (AGRIS)	**CNEA**	Comisión Nacional de Energía Atomica (Argentina, Uruguay)
CNDA	Cherished Numbers Dealers Association	**CNEAF**	Comité National des Exploitants Agricoles Forestiers
CNDC	Comisión Nacional de Desarrollo Comunal (Peru)	**CNEAF**	Confédération Nationale des Experts Agricoles et Fonciers
CNDC	Consiglio Nazionale dei Dottori Commercialisti	**CNÉARC**	Centre National d'Études Agronomiques des Régions Chaudes
CNDCT	Centro de Documentacion Cientifica y Tecnologica (Bolivia)	**CNEASTA**	Irish Council for Training, Development and Employment for Persons with Disabilities
CNDE	Consejo Nacional de Desarrollo Económico (Peru)		
CNDEP	Conseil National des Détectives et Enquêteurs Privés	**CNÉAT**	Centre National d'Études d'Agronomie Tropicale

CNEC	Consórcio Nacional de Engenheiros Consultores (Brazil)
CNEC	National Commando Training Centre (Burkina Faso)
CNECA	Comisión Nacional de Estudio de la Cana y del Azucar (Bolivia)
CNECB	Collège National des Experts Compatables de Belgique = NCAB
CNÉÉJA	Centre National d'Études Économiques et Juridiques Agricoles
CNÉEMA	Centre National d'Études et d'Experimentation de Machinisme Agricole
CNEF	Cámara Nacional de Exploitación Forestal (Bolivia)
CNEF	Compagnie Nationale des Experts Forestiers
CNÉH	Centre National d'Études Historique (Algeria)
CNEIA	Comité National d'Expansion pour l'Industrie Aéronautique
CNÉIL	Centre National d'Études et d'Initiatives du Logement
CNEL	Chambre Nationale Syndicale des Experts du Grand-Duché de Luxembourg
CNEL	Consiglio Nazionale Economiche e Lavoro
CNEN	Comision Nacional de Energia Nuclear (Mexico)
CNEN	Comissão Nacional de Energia Nuclear (Brazil)
CNEN	Comitato Nazionale per l'Energia Nucleare
CNÉN	Conseil National de l'Énergie Nucléaire
CNÉP	Caisse Nationale d'Épargne et de Prévoyance (Algeria)
CNÉP	Centre National d'Étude Politique
CNEP	Comision Nacional para el Erradicacion del Paludismo
CNEP	Comptoir National d'Escompte de Paris
CNEPA	Centro Nacional de Ensino e Pesquisas Agronomicas (Brazil)
CNÉPDA	Comité National d'Étude des Problèmes du Développement Agricole
CNER	Campanha Nacional de Educaçao Rural (Brazil)
CNÉR	Centre National des Études Rurales
CNÉR	Conseil National des Économies Régionales

CNÉRA	Centre National d'Études et des Recherches Aéronautiques (Belgium)
CNÉRAD	Centre National pour l'Étude, la Recherche et l'Application du Développement
CNÉRIA	Centre National d'Études et de Recherches des Industries Agricoles
CNÉRNA	Centre National de Coordination des Études et Recherches sur la Nutrition Animale
CNÉRP	Centre National d'Étude et de Recherche au Paysage
CNÉRP	Conseil National des Économies Régionales et de la Productivité
CNERTP	Centre National d'Essais et de Recherches de Travaux Publics (Benin)
CNÉS	Centre National d'Études Spatiales
CNESER	Conseil National de l'Enseignement Supérieur et de la Recherche
CNÉT	Centre National d'Études de Télécommunications
CNÉTÉA	Centre National d'Études Techniques et Économiques de l'Artisanat
CNEWA	Catholic Near East Welfare Association
CNEXO	Centre National pour l'Exploitation des Océans
CNF	Canadian Nature Federation
CNF	Commonwealth Nurses Federation
CNF	Compagnie du Niger Français
CNFC	Centre National de Formation Coopérative (Cameroon)
CNFLRH	Comité National Français de Liaison pour la Réadaption des Handicapés
CNFM	Comité National Française des Mathématiciens
CNFP	Consejo Nacional de Fomento Pesquero (Venezuela)
CNFPT	Centre National de la Fonction Publique Territoriale
CNFR	Confédération Nationale de la Famille Rurale
CNFRA	Centre National Française de la Recherche Antarctique
CNFRE	Comité National Française de Recherches dans l'Espace
CNFRO	Comité National Française de Recherche Océanique
CNFTC	Centre National de Formation aux Techniques de Conditionnement des Boissons et Denrées Alimentaires

CNG	Catholic Needlework Guild
CNG	Children Need Grandparents
CNG	Christlichnationaler Gewerkschaftsbund der Schweiz
CNG	Confederación Nacional Ganadara (Mexico)
CNG	Conseil National du Gouvernement (Haiti)
CNG	Consiglio Nazionale dei Geometri
CNG	Coordinadora Nacional Guerrillero (Colombia)
CNGÉ	Conseil National des Grandes Écoles
CNGFF	Confédération Nationale des Groupes Folkloriques Français
CNGRDC	China National Garments Research and Designing Center
CNHC	Churches National Housing Coalition
CNHR	Comité National de l'Habitat Rural
CNHRAC	Confédération Nationale pour l'Habitat Rural et l'Aménagement des Campagnes
CNHS	Canada's National History Society
CNHS	Cherokee National Historical Society
CNI	Centre National de l'Informatique (Tunisia)
CNI	Compagnie Nationale de Navigation Intérieure (Gabon)
CNI	Confederação Nacional da Indústria (Brazil)
CNI	Conseil National des Ingénieurs
CNI	Consejo Nacional de Inversiones (Panama)
CNI	Consiglio Nazionale degli Ingegneri
CNIA	Centro Nacional de Investigaciones Agropecuárias (Argentina, Colombia, Dominica, Salvador)
CNIA	Comité National Interprofessionnel de l'Amande
CNIA	Compagnie Nordafricaine et Intercontinentale d'Assurances (Morocco)
CNIA	Conseil National Interprofessionnel de l'Aviculture
CNIA	Consejo Nacional de Investigaciones Agricolas (Venezuela)
CNIAA	Cámara Nacional de las Industrias Azucarera y Alcoholera (Mexico)
CNIB	Canadian National Institute for the Blind
CNIB	Confédération Nationale des Industries du Bois

CNIC	Centre National d'Information Chimique
CNIC	Centro Nacional de Investigaciones Cientificas (Cuba)
CNIC	Centro Nacional de Investigaciones de Café (Colombia)
CNIC	China Nuclear Information Center
CNIC	Conseil National de l'Industrie du Charbon
CNICI	Consejo Nacional de Investigaciones Cientificas y Técnicas (Argentina, Uruguay)
CNICT	Consejo Nacional de Investigaciones Cientificas y Técnicas
CNICTEI	Comitato Nazionale Italiano per la Cooperazione Tecnico Economico Internazionale
CNID	Comité National d'Initiative Démocratique (Mali)
CNIDICT	Centro Nacional de Información y Documentación Cientifica y Tecnologica
CNIDS	Cámara Nacional de las Industrias Derivadas de la Silvicultura (Mexico)
CNIE	Comisión Nacional de Investigaciones Espaciales (Argentine)
CNIEC	China National Import and Export Corporation
CNIÉL	Centre National Interprofessionnel d'Économie Laitière
CNIF	Conseil National des Ingénieurs Français
CNIH	Cámara Nacional de la Industria Hulera (Mexico)
CNIH	Comité National Interprofessionnel de l'Horticulture Florale et Ornementale et des Pépinières non Forestières
CNIH	Comité National Interprofessionnel du Houblon
CNIL	Comité National Interprofessionnel de la Laine
CNIL	Commission Nationale de l'Informatique et des Libertés
CNIM	Constructions Navales et Industrielles de la Méditerranée
CNIOS	Comitato Nazionale Italiana per l'Organizzazione Scientifica del Lavoro
CNIP	Centre National des Indépendants et Paysans
CNIP	Ciskei National Independence Party (South Africa)

CNIPA	Committee of National Institutes of Patent Agents	**CNMB**	Central Nuclear Measurements Bureau (EU)
CNIPBC	Comité National Interprofessionnel des Produits de Basse-Cour	**CNMCCA**	Confédération Nationale de la Mutualité, du Crédit et de la Coopération Agricoles
CNIPE	Centre National d'Information pour la Productivité des Entreprises	**CNMÉ**	Caisse Nationale des Marchés de l'État
CNIPT	Comité National Interprofessionnel de la Pomme de Terre	**CNMG**	Consejo Nacional de Mujeres de Guatemala
CNIR	Centre National Interprofessionnel du Rhum	**CNMHS**	Caisse Nationale des Monuments Historiques et des Sites
CNIR	Conferéncia Nacional dos Instítutos Religiosos	**CNMI**	Camera Nazionale della Moda Italiana
CNIRD	Caribbean Network for Integrated Rural Development (Trinidad-Tobago)	**CNMI**	Comité National de la Meunerie Industrielle
CNIT	Cámara Nacional de la Industria de Transformación (Mexico)	**CNMI**	Commonwealth of the Northern Mariana Islands
CNIT	Centre National des Industries et des Techniques	**CNMP**	Consejo Nacional de Mujeres del Paraguay
CNIT	Consiliul National al Inginerilor si Tehnicienilor (*now* AGIR)	**CNMV**	Comisión Nacional del Mercado de Valores
CNITE	Centro Nazionale Italiano per le Tecnologie Educative	**CNN**	Cable News Network (U.S.A.)
CNJA	Centre National des Jeunes Agriculteurs	**CNN**	Companhia Nacional de Navegação (Portugal)
CNJC	Centre National des Jeunes Cadres	**CNNC**	China National Non-Ferrous Corporation
CNJPHP	Cercle National des Jeunes Producteurs de l'Horticulture et des Pépinières	**CNNC**	China National Non-Ferrous Metals Industry Corporation
CNJT	Centre National Action Sociale pour les Jeunes Travailleurs	**CNO**	Comisión Nacional del Olivo (Mexico)
ČNKCH	Český Národní Komitet pro Chemii = CNCC	**CNO**	Conseil National des Opticiens
		CNO	Council of National Organisations
CNKi	Comité National du Kivu (Zaïre)	**CNOB**	Coordinating Committee of Burkinabe Workers (Burkina Faso)
CNL	Centre National des Lettres	**CNOE**	Comités Nationaux Olympiques Européens
CNL	Commonwealth National Library (Australia)	**CNOF**	Comité National de l'Organisation Française: Association Française de Management
CNL	Confédération Nationale Laitière		
CNL	Conseil National de la Libération (Chad)	**CNOOC**	China National Offshore Oil Corporation
CNLA	Centre Nationale de Lutte Antiparasitaire	**CNOP**	Confederación Nacional de Organizaciones Populares (Mexico)
CNLA	China Nordic Literature Association	**CNOP**	Conseil National de l'Ordre des Pharmaciens
CNLIA	Council of National Library and Information Associations (U.S.A.)	**CNOPAR**	Confédération Nationale des Organismes de Promotion Agricole et Rurale
CNLS	Centre for Nonlinear Studies	**CNOS**	Comitato Nazionale per l'Organizzazione Scientifica: Associazione per la Promozione del Managenent e della Technica
CNM	Confederação Nacional dos Metalurgicos (Brazil)		
CNM	Consejo Nacional de Magistros (Guatemala)		
CNMA	Comitato Nazionale di Meccanica Agraria		
CNMART	Comité National contre les Maladies Respiratoires et la Tuberculose	**CNOSA**	Centro Nazionale per l'Organizzazione Scientifica in Agricoltura (Italy)

CNOSF	Conseil National Olympique et Sportif Français
CNOUS	Centre National des Oeuvres Universitaires et Scolaires
CNOV	Comité National des Producteurs d'Oeufs à Couver et des Volailles dites d'un Jour
CNP	Comisión Nacional Permanente (Nicaragua)
CNP	Comitato Nazionale per la Produttività
CNP	Comité National des Prix
CNP	Consejo Nacional de Producción
CNP	Conselho Nacional do Petroleo (Brazil)
CNP	Cornish Nationalist Party
CNP	Corporation Nationale Paysanne
CNP	Council for National Parks
CNP	Croatian National Party
CNPA	Centro Nazional de Patología Animal (Peru)
CNPA	Comisión Nacional de Política Aeronáutica (Uruguay)
CNPA	Comissão Nacional de Politica Agraria (Brazil)
CNPAR	Centre National de Progrès Agricole et Rural
CNPB	Conseil Nordique de la Preservation du Bois = NTR, NWPC
CNPCC	Confédération Nationale des Planteurs de Chicorée à Café
CNPE	Caisse Nationale des Pensions pour Employés
CNPE	Consejo Nacional de Planificación Económica (Guatemala, Salvador)
CNPF	Confédération Nationale des Parachutistes Français
CNPF	Conseil National du Patronat Français
CNPFP	Comité National de Propagande en Faveur du Pain
CNPFV	Comité National de Propagande en Faveur du Vin
CNPGL	Centro Nacional de Pesquisa de Gado de Leite (Brazil)
CNPI	Comisión Nacional de Productividad Industrial
CNPIEC	China National Publications Import and Export Corporation
CNPIO	Comissão Nacional Portuguesa para Investigacéo Oceanografico
CNPITC	China National Publishing Industry Trading Corporation

CNPL	Comissão Nacional da Pecuária do Leite (Brazil)
CNPL	Confederação Nacional das Profissões Liberais (Brazil)
CNPP	Confederación Nacional de la Pequeña Propiedad (Mexico)
CNPPA	Commission on National Parks and Protected Areas (IUCN)
CNPPLF	Comité National de Propagande des Produits Laitiers Français
CNPQ	Conselho Nacional de Desenvolvimento Cientifico e Tecnologico (Brazil)
CNPq	Conselho Nacional de Pesquisa (Brazil)
CNPR	Centre National de Promotion Rurale
CNPRST	Centre National de Planification de la Recherche Scientifique et Technologique
CNPS	Confédération Nationale des Produits du Sol et Dérivés
CNPS	Conseil National de la Politique Scientifique (Belgium)
CNPSEPC	Confédération Nationale des Produits du Sol Engrais et Produits Connexes
CNPT	Centro Nacional de Pesquisa de Trigo (Brazil)
CNPTI	Centre National de Prevention et de Traitement des Intoxications
CNPU	Comissão Nacional de Regioes Metropolitanas e Politica Urbana (Brazil)
CNPV	Comité National des Producteurs de Viande
CNPVE-VAOC	Confédération Nationale des Producteurs de Vins et Eaux-de-Vie de Vin à Appellations d'Origine Contrôlées
CNR	Caisse Nationale de Réassurances (Cameroon)
CNR	Canadian National Railways
CNR	Coalición Nacional Republicana (Ecuador)
CNR	Conseil National de la Récupération (Switzerland)
CNR	Conseil National de la Révolution (Congo)
CNR	Consiglio Nazionale delle Ricerche
CNR	Czech National Council
CNRA	Centre National de Recherches Agronomiques
CNRA	Consejo Nacional de Reforma Agraria (Bolivia)

CNRC	Centro Nacional de Radiación Cosmica (Argentine)	**CNSNS**	Comisión Nacional de Seguridad Nuclear y Salvaguardias (Mexico)
CNRC	Conseil National de Recherches Canada = NRCC	**CNSO**	Confederación Nacional de Sindicatos Obreros (Chile)
CNRET	Centre for Natural Resources, Energy and Transport (UN)	**CNSP**	Comité Nicargüense por la Solidaridad con los Pueblos
CNRF	Centre National de Recherches Forestières	**CNSP**	Conselho Nacional de Seguros Privados (Brazil)
CNRG	Conseil National de la Résistance Guadeloupéenne	**CNT**	Canadian National Telecommunications
CNRI	Caribbean Natural Resources Institute	**CNT**	Central Nacional de Trabajadores (Guatemala)
CNRM	Centre National de Recherches Métallurgiques (Belgium)	**CNT**	Centre for Nutrition and Toxicology (Sweden)
CNRN	Comitato Nazionale per le Ricerche Nucleari	**CNT**	Comando Nacional de Trabajadores (Chile)
CNRRI	China National Rice Research Institute	**CNT**	Comisión Nacional del Trigo (Ecuador)
CNRS	Centre National de la Recherche Scientifique	**CNT**	Commission for the New Towns
CNRS/-PIRSEM	Programme Interdisciplinaire de Recherche sur les Énergies et Matières	**CNT**	Confederacion Nacional de Trabajadores (Costa Rica)
CNRSH	Centre Nigérien de Recherches en Sciences Humaines (Nigeria)	**CNT**	Confederación Nacional de Trabajadores (Peru, Uruguay)
CNRST	Centre National de la Recherche Scientifique et Technique	**CNT**	Confederación Nacional del Trabajo
CNRZ	Centre National de Recherches Zootechniques	**CNT**	Confédération Nationale des Travailleurs (Burkina Faso)
CNS	Canadian Nuclear Society	**CNTA**	Comptoir National Technique Agricole
CNS	Centre for Neuroscience	**CNTC**	Confederação Nacional dos Trabalhadores no Comércio (Brazil)
CNS	Chinese Nuclear Society	**CNTC**	Confederación Nacional de Transporte por Carretara Viajeros y Mercancias
CNS	Chinese Nutrition Society		
CNS	Cognitive Neuroscience Society	**CNTCB**	Confederación Nacional de Trabajadores Campesinos de Bolivia
CNS	Committee for National Salvation (Dominica)	**CNTD**	Confederación Nacional de Trabajadores Dominicanos
CNS	Conseil National des Syndicates (Luxembourg)	**CNTD**	Consejo Nacional de Trabajadores Democréticas (Guatemala)
CNS	Coordinadora Nacional Sindical (Chile)	**CNTE**	Compania Telefonica
CNS	Council for Name Studies in Great Britain and Ireland (*now* SNSBI)	**CNTE**	Coordinadora Nacional de Trabajadores de la Educación (Mexico)
CNS	Cyprus Numismatic Society	**CNTEEC**	Confederação Nacional dos Trabalhadores em Estabelecimentos de Educação e Cultura (Brazil)
CNS	National Council of Rubber Tappers		
CNSA	Comhairle nan Sgoiltean Araich = GPPA	**CNTG**	Confédération Nationale des Travailleurs Guinéens
CNSD	Confédération Nationale des Syndicats Dentaires	**CNTI**	Confederação Nacional dos Trabalhadores na Indústria (Brazil)
CNSF	Cornell National Supercomputer Facility	**CNTIB**	Confédération Nationale 'Les Travailleurs Indépendants' de Belgique
CNSM	Confédération Nationale des Syndicats de Mali	**CNTIC**	China National Technical Import Corporation
CNSM	Conservatoire National Supérieur de Musique	**CNTL**	National Council of Tourism in Lebanon

CNTMA	Chinese National Traditional Medical Association
CNTMR	Comité National contra la Tuberculose et les Maladies Respiratoires
CNTP	Central Nacional de Trabajadores de Panama
CNTR	Compagnie Nationale des Transports Routiers (Central Africa)
CNTS	Centre de Transfusion Sanguine
CNTS	Centre National des Techniques Spatiales (Algeria)
CNTS	Confédération Nationale des Travailleurs Sénégalais
CNTSM	Cooperación Nacional de Trabajadores de Servicios Multiplos (Venezuela)
CNTT	Confederação Nacional dos Transportes Terrestres (Brazil)
CNTT	Confédération Nationale des Travailleurs du Togo
CNTTMFA	Confederação Nacional dos Trabalhadores em Transportes Maritimos, Fluvais e Aéreos (Brazil)
CNTTT	Confederação Nacional dos Trabalhadores em Transportes Terrestres (Brazil)
CNTUR	Conselho Nacional de Turismo (Brazil)
CNTV	Confédération Nationale des Travailleurs Voltaïques
CNU	Christian National Union (Hungary) = KNU
CNU	Christian National Union (Poland) = ZChN
CNU	Coalition for National Unity (Solomon Islands)
CNU	Committee for National Unity (Burundi)
CNUAH	Centro de las Naciones Unidas para los Asentamientos Humanos = CNUEH, HABITAT
CNUCE	Centro Nazionale Universitario di Calcolo Elettronico
CNUCED	Conférence des Nations Unies pour le Commerce et le Développement = UNCTAD
CNUDCI	Commission des Nations Unies pour le Droit Commercial International = UNCITRAL
CNUDR	Centre des Nations Unies pour le Développement Régional (Japan) = UNCRD
CNUEH	Centre des Nations Unies pour les Etablissements Humains = CNUAH, HABITAT
CNUS	Comité Nacional de Unidad Sindical (Guatemala)
CNUT	Conférence Nationale des Usagers des Transports
CNUURC	Commission des Nations Unies pour l'Unification et le Relèvement de la Corée = UNCURK
CNV	Christelijk Nationaal Vakverbond in Nederland
CNV	Comisión Nacional de Valores (Mexico)
CNVF	Comité National des Vins de France
CNVPA	Conseil National de la Vulgarisation du Progrès Agricole
CNVS	Confédération Nationale des Industries et Commerces en Gros des Vins, Cidres, Sirops, Spiritueux et Liqueurs de France
CNWF	Council for a Nuclear Weapons Freeze (U.S.A.)
CNWRS	Centre for North-West Regional Studies
CO	Confoederatio Oratorii Sancti Philippi Nerii
COA	Cathedral Organists' Association
COA	China Orchid Association
COA	Commissie ter Bevordering v. het Kweken en het Onderzoek v. Nieuwe Aardappelrassen
COAC	Collège Ouest Africaine des Chirurgiens = WACS
COACAL	Centrum voor Onderzoek van het Arabisch en de Cultuur van de Arabisch Landen (Belgium) = CRACAC
COACH	Canadian Organisation for the Advancement of Computers in Health
COADC	Committee for Oceanographic Advice to Developing Countries
COADES	Confederación de Organismos Agricolas del Estado de Sonora (Mexico)
COAER	Union Costruttori Apparecchiature ed Impianti Aeraulici (Italy) (ANIMA)
COAG	Committee on Agriculture (FAO)
CoAG	Council of Australian Governments
COAG/NE	Near East Regional Commission on Agriculture
COALBRA	Companhia Coque e Alcool de Madeira (Brazil)
COAMA	Coordenação da Amazônia (FUNAI)
COAPI	Colegio Oficial de Agentes de la Propiedad Immobiliaria
COAS	Council of the Organisation of American States

COB	Central Obrera Boliviana
COB	Centre Océanologique de Bretagne (CNEXO)
COB	Colegio Oficial de Biólogos
COB	Commission des Opérations de Bourse
COB	Confederación Obrera Boliviana
COB	Coopérative Ouvrière Belge
COBAE	Comissão Brasileira de Atividades Espaciais
Cobaf	Committee on Biotechnology and Food
COBAFI	Companhia Baiana de Fibras (Brazil)
COBAL	Companhia Brasileira de Alimentos
COBAM	Confection-Bonneterie Africaine et Malgache
COBBA	Council of Brass Bands Association
COBCCEE	Comité des Organisations de la Boucherie et de la Charcuterie de la CEE
COBCOE	Council of British Chambers of Commerce in Continental Europe
COBECÉP	Comité Belge des Constructeurs d'Équipement Pétrolier
COBE-CHAR	Comptoir Belge des Charbons
COBEE	Compania Boliviano de Energia Electrica S.A.
COBEL-EXFO	Comité Belge des Expositions et des Foires et d'Expansion Nationale
COBEL-MIN	Compagnie Belge d'Entreprises Minières
COBELPA	Association des Fabricants de Pâtes, Papiers et Cartons de Belgique
COBEL-TOUR	Compagnie Belge de Tourisme
COBELDA	Compagnie Belge d'Électronique et d'Automation
COBENAM	Compagnie Béninoise de Navigation Maritime
COBI	Council on Biological Information
COBICA	Campanhia Brasileria de Industrialização da Castanha do Caju
COBIO-TECH	International Scientific Committee on Biotechnology (ICSU) (France)
COBOEN	Comisión Boliviana de Energia Nuclear (Bolivia)
COBOLCA	Comité Boliviano del Café
COBR	Centralny Ośrodek Badawczo-Rozwojowy
COBRA	Centre Oncologique et Biologique de Recherche Appliquée
COBRA	Computadoras e Sistemas Brasileiros S.A
COBRA	Cosmic Background Radiation Anisotropy Project (U.S.A.)
COBRAER	Confederação das Cooperativas de Electrificação Rural (Brazil)
COBRAG	Companhia Brasileira de Agricultura
COBRASA	Companhia Brasileira de Silos e Armazens
COBRECAF	Compagnie Bretonne de Cargos Frigorifiques
COBSEA	Coordinating Body on the Seas of East-Asia (Kenya)
COBSI	Committee on Biological Sciences Information (U.S.A.)
COBU	Crédit Libanais (Cyprus)
COC	Commission Officielle de Contrôle (des Semences et Plantes)
COC	Committee on Carcinogenicity in Chemicals in Food, Consumer Products and the Environment (DOH)
COC	Compagnie Ouest-Caméroun
COC	Conference of Omnibus Companies
COCADAC	Compagnie Camérounaise Danoise de Construction
COCAFER	Comisión Centroamericana de Ferrocarriles (Guatemala)
COCAM	Contreplaques du Caméroun
COCAP	Comissão Coordenadora da Alianca para o Progresso (Brazil)
COCAST	Council for Overseas Colleges of Arts, Science and Technology
COCA-TRAM	Comisión Centroamericana Transporte Maritimo
COCC	Confederación de Obreros y Campesinos Cristianos (Costa Rica)
COCDYC	Conservative and Christian Democratic Youth Community
COCEAN	Compagnie d'Études et d'Exploitation des Techniques Océans
COCEI	Coalición Obrero Campesina Estudiantil del Istmo (Mexico)
COCÉI	Compagnie Centrale d'Études Industrielles
COCEMA	Comité des Constructeurs Européens de Matériel Alimentaire et de Matériel de Conditionnement
COCENT-RAL	Cooperativa Central de Distribucion Ltda (Colombia)
COCEPRA	Comptoir Commercial d'Exchanges des Products Africains (Senegal)

COCERAL	Comité du Commerce des Céréales et des Aliments du Bétail de la CEE
COCESNA	Corporación Centroamericana de Servicios de Navegación Aerea (Honduras)
COCF	Centre for Our Common Future
COCI	Consortium des Agrumes et Plantes à Parfum de Côte d'Ivoire
COCI	Consortium on Chemical Information
COCIR	Comité Consultatif International des Radio-Communications
COCIR	Comité de Coordination des Industries Radiologiques et Electromédicales (Italy)
COCIS	Coordinamento delle ONG per la Cooperazione Internazionale allo Sviluppo
COCITAM	Compagnie Côte-d'Ivoirienne pour tous Appareillages Mécaniques
COCMM	Confédération des Organisations de Crédit Maritime Mutuel
COCO	Conference of Consumer Organizations (U.S.A.)
COCOBOD	Cocoa Marketing Board (Ghana)
COCOBRO	Coördinatie van Cultuur en Onderzoek van Broodgraan
COCODI	Compagnie de Commerce de la Côte-d'Ivoire
COCOES	Comité de Coordination des Enquêtes Statistiques
COCOM	Coordinating Committee on Export Controls (NATO)
COCOMAC	Comité de Coordination des Sociétés d'Orthopédie et de Traumatologie des Pays du Marché Commun Européen
COCONA	Conseil de Coopération de l'Atlantique Nord = NACC
COCOP	Red Latinoamérica de Coordinación y Promoción de Tecnologia Apropriada
COCOR	Commission de Coordination pour la Nomeclature des Produits Sidérurgiques (ECSC)
COCORP	Consortium for Continental Reflection Profiling (U.S.A.)
COCOS	Co-ordinating Committee for Manufacturers of Static Converters in the Common Market Countries
COCRIL	Council of City Research and Information Libraries
COCSA	Compañia Organizadora del Consumo,S.A.
COCSU	Council of Civil Service Unions
COCTA	Committee on Conceptual and Terminological Analysis (IPSA)
COCTI	Conférénce des Institutions Catholique de Théologie
COCU	Comisión Organizadora del Congreso Universitario (Mexico)
COCUSA	Chamber of Commerce of the United States
COD	Committee of Direction of Fruit Marketing (Australia)
CODA	Community Data
CODA	Council on Drug Abuse (Canada)
CODAL	Comptoir Industrial de Produits Alimentaires (Madagascar)
CODAR	Confédération des Associations Républicaines
CODAS	Council of Departments of Accounting Studies
CODASYL	Conference on Data Systems Languages
CODATA	Committee on Data for Science and Technology (ICSU)
CODATU	Conférences sur le Développement et l'Aménagement des Transports Urbains dans les Pays en Développement
CODC	Canadian Oceanographic Data Centre
CODE	Confederation of Dental Employers
CODE-AGRO	Amasonas Agricultural Development Company (Brazil)
CODECA	Corporation for Economic Development in the Caribbean
CODECAL	Corporación Integral de Desarrollo Cultural y Social (Colombia)
CODECI	Corporación para el Desarrollo de la Ciencia (Chile)
CODECO	Coordinadora Opositora Democrática Constitucional (Honduras)
CODEFI	Comité Interdépartementaux d'Examen des Problèmes de Fonctionnement des Entreprises
CODEH	Comité de Defensa de Derechos Humanos en Honduras
CODEH-UCA	Comisión de Defensa de los Derechos Humanos en Centroamérica
CODEL	Coordination in Development Inc. (U.S.A.)
CODELCO	Corporación Nacional del Cobre de Chile
CODEM	Comité de Defensa de los Derechos de la Mujer (Chile)

CODEMAC	Comité des Déménageurs du Marché Commun	**CODI-FINCI**	Compagnie Financière de la Côte d'Ivoire
CODEMIN	Panama Mining Organisation	**CODIA**	Comité de Industrialización de Algas (Argentina)
CODEMUH	Coordinadora para el Desarrollo de la Mujer Hondurena	**CODIAM**	Comité de Organisation et Développement d'Investissments Intellectuels d'Afrique
CODENA	Council for the Development of the North-East of Brazil	**CODICAF**	Conseil des Directeurs des Compagnies Aériennes en France
CODEPAR	Companhia de Desenvolvimento Económico do Paraná (Brazil)	**CODIÉSEE**	Réseau de Coopération en Matière de Recherche et de Développement pour l'Innovation Éducative dans le Sud-Est Européen (Unesco)
CODEPLAN	Companhia de Desenvolvimento do Planalto Central (Brazil)		
CODÉR	Commission de Développement Économique Régional	**CODIF**	Société Commerciale de Diffusion (Ivory Coast)
CODES	Centre for Ore Deposit and Exploration Studies (Australia)	**CODIFA**	Comité de Développement des Industries Françaises de l'Ameublement
CODES-AIMA	Companhia de Desenvolvimento de Roraima (Brazil)	**CODIFAC**	Comité de Développement d'Industrie de la Chaussure et des Articles Chaussants
CODESA	Confederación de Sindicatos Autónomas (Venezuela)		
CODESA	Congress of Democrats of South Africa	**CODIGAS**	Compania Distribuidora de Gas (Chile)
CODESA	Consejo de Desarrollo de Salta (Argentina)	**CODIMA**	Société Commerciale de Diffusion de Marques (Ivory Coast)
CODESA	Corporacion Costarricense de Desarrollo	**CODIMA**	Union Commerciale de Diffusion de Marques en Côte-d'Ivoire
CODESPA	Cooperacion al Desarrollo y Promocion de Actividades Asistenciales	**CODIMCA**	Consejo para el Desarrollo Integral de la Mujer Campesina (Honduras)
CODESRIA	Council for the Development of Economic and Social Research in Africa	**CODIMPA**	Compagnie Française Industrielle et Minière du Pacifique
CODESSER	Corporacion para el Desarrollo Social del Sector Rural (Chile)	**CODIP**	Conférence de La Haye de Droit International Privé = HCOPIL
CODEST	Committee for the European Development of Science and Technology	**CODIPLAM**	Comissão de Divulgação do Plano Global para a Amazônia (Brazil)
CODESUL	Companhia de Desenvolvimento de Sul (Brazil)	**CODIPRAL**	Compagnie de Distribution de Produits Alimentaires (Senegal)
CODÉTAF-CAM	Compagnie d'Étancheité Africaine au Caméroun	**CODIR**	Campaign for the Defence of Iranian People's Rights
CODÉTAF-CI	Compagnie d'Étancheité Africaine en Côte d'Ivoire	**CODIVAL**	Compagnie Ivoirienne de Sécurité
CODETOUR	Compagnie pour le Développement de l'Hôtellerie de du Tourisme	**CODO**	Coalizão Democrática de Oposição (Sao Tomé) = CDOSTP
CODEV	Communications for Development (Malta)	**Codos**	Commandos Rouges (Chad)
CODEVASF	Companhia de Desenvolvimento do Vale do São Francisco (Brazil)	**CODSIA**	Council of Defense and Space Industry Associations (U.S.A.)
CODEVI	Compagnie pour le Développement de l'Industrie Caméroun	**CODUSUCO**	Compania Distribuidora de Subsistenci, Conasupo (Mexico)
CODEVIN-TEC	Compagnie pour le Développement Industriel et Technique	**COE**	Chamber Orchestra of Europe
		CoE	Church of England
CODEXAL	Conseil Européen du 'Codex Alimentarius'	**COE**	Commission on Ecology (IUCN)
		COÉ	Conseil Oecuménique des Églises = CMI, OeRK, WCC

COÉB	Conseil d'Orientation Économique du Bas Saint-Laurent (Canada)
COÉC	Comité Central d'Océanographie et d'Étude des Côtes
COEFA	Comité d'Organisation Européen de la Fête des Arts (CE)
COEMA	Confederación de Obreros y Empleados Municipales de la Republica Argentina
CoEnCo	Council for Environmental Conservation
COES	Chinese Ocean Engineering Society
COESA	Committee on Extension to the Standard Atmosphere (U.S.A)
COEXPORT	Corporación de Exportadores de El Salvador
COF	Centro de Orientacion Familiar (Costa Rica)
COF	Comité Olympique Française
COF	Coordinadora de Organizaciones Feministas (Puerto Rico)
COFA	Commonwealth and Overseas Families Association
COFA	Comptoir Français Agricole
COFACE	Compagnie Française d'Assurance pour le Commerce Extérieur
COFACE	Confédération des Organisations Familiales de la Communautés Européennes
COFACICO	Entreprises Financières Cinématographiques et Commerciales (Congo)
COFADE	Comité de Familiares de los Desaperecidos de Honduras
COFADENA	Corporación de las Fuerzas Armadas para el Desarrollo Nacional (Bolivia)
COFAG	Comité des Fabricants d'Acide Glutamique de la CEE
COFAGRI	Société de Conditionnement et de Formulation Agricole (Cameroon)
COFALEC	Comité des Fabricants de Levure de Panification de la CEE
COFAMA	Comptoir Franco-Africaine de Matériaux
COFAP	Comité Française des Applications du Pyrèthre
COFAZ	Compagnie Française de l'Azote
COFCA	Coffee and Cacao Institute of the Philippines
COFCE	Comité pour l'Orientation et Formation des Cadres d'Entreprises
CofE	Church of England
COFEB	Centre Ouest-Africain de Formation et d'Études Bancaires (Senegal)
COFEB	Confédération Européenne des Fabricants de Baignoires
COFEDES	Coopération Française pour l'Étude et le Développement de l'Énergie Solaire
COFENAF	Commission des Fédérations et Syndicats Nationaux des Entreprises de Récupération des Ferrailles du Marché Commun
COFETRAG	Commission Nationale des Femmes Travailleuses de Guinée
Coffer	Coalition for Fair Electricity Regulation
COFHUAT	Confédération Française pour l'Habitation, l'Urbanisme et l'Aménagement du Territoire
CofI	Church of Ireland
COFI	Committee of Fisheries (FAO)
COFI	Council of Forest Industries of British Columbia
COFI-PECHE	Compagnie Industrielle Ivoirienne de Filets de Pêche
COFIAGRO	Corporatión Financiera de Fomento Agropecuário y Exportaciones (Colombia)
COFIBOIS	Nouvelle Compagnie Forestière et Industrielle du Bois (Congo)
COFICA	Compagnie pour le Financement de l'Industrie, du Commerce et de l'Agriculture
COFIDA	Comité pour les Fonds Internationaux de Droit d'Auteur (FIPC)
COFIDE	Corporacion Financiera de Desarrollo (Peru)
COFIE	Comissão de Fusão e Incorporação de Empresa (Brazil)
COFIEC	Compañia Financiera Ecuatoriana de Desarrollo
COFIFA	Compagnie Financière France-Afrique
COFIMER	Nouvelle Compagnie Financière pour l'Outre-Mer
COFIMPA	Compagnie Française Industrielle et Minière du Pacifique
COFINA	Corporación Financiera Nacional (Panama)
COFINAN-CIERA	Corporacuárin Financiera Colombiana
COFINCI	Compagnie Financière de la Côte d'Ivoire
COFIPE	Codigo Federal de Institutiones y Procedimientos Electorales (Mexico)

COFIRA	Confédération Française d'Ingénierie Rurale et Agricole
COFIREP	Compagnie Financière de Recherches Pétrolières
COFLA	Comisión Forestal Latinoamericana (Chile) = COFLAC, LAFC
COFLAC	Comisión Forestal Latinoamericana y del Caribe = COFLA, LAFC
COFNA	Comisión Forestal Norteamericana (Mexico)
COFO	Committee on Forestry (FAO)
COFORCÉS	Confédération Mondiale Forces Culturelles Économiques Sociales
COFORGA	Compagnie Forestière Gabonaise
COFORIC	Compagnie Forestière et Industrielle du Congo
COFRA-MINES	Compagnie Française des Mines
COFRA-NIMEX	Compagnie Française pour l'Exportation et l'Importation des Animaux Reproducteurs
COFRAL	Comité Français Agricole de Liaison pour le Développement International
COFRAL	Compagnie du Froid Alimentaire (Ivory Coast)
COFRA-MET	Compagnie Franco-Américaine des Métaux et Minérals
COFRATEL	Compagnie Française des Téléphones
COFRÉDA	Compagnie pour Favoriser la Recherche et l'Élargissement des Débouchés Agricoles
COFRÉM	Compagnie pour la Fabrication d'Éléments Mécaniques (Cameroon)
COFRÉNA	Comité Française de l'Équipement Naval
COFRÉND	Comité Française pour l'Étude des Essais Non Destructifs
COFRUCI	Coopérative Agricole de Production Bananière et Fruitière de Côte d'Ivoire
COFRUI-TEL	Coopérative des Producteurs pour la Commercialisation des Fruits et Légumes de la Côte d'Ivoire
COFSA	Commonwealth and Overseas Fire Services Asociation
COG	Canberra Ornothologists Group
COG	Combined Opposition Group (Bangladesh)
COG	Committee on Oceanography and GARP (SCOR)
COG	Consultant Orthodontists' Group
COG	Coordination Group of Non-Governmental Organisations in the field of the man-made environment
COG	Council of Australian Governments
COGATEL	Compagnie Gabonaise de Télécommunications
COGDEM	Council of Gas Detection Equipment Manufacturers
COGECA	Comité Général de la Coopération Agricole de la CEE
COGECI	Comptoir Général pour le Commerce et l'Industrie (Benin)
COGEDA	Compagnie Générale de Distribution et d'Approvisionnement (Ivory Coast)
COGEDRO	Comptoirs Généraux Réunis de Droguerie, Produits Chimiques, Peintures, Colorants (Ivory Coast)
COGÉFI	Conseil en Orgnaisation de Gestion Économique et Financière d'Entreprises
COGEI	Comitato dei Geografi Italiani
COGEI	Compagnie de Gestion d'Investissements Internationaux
COGEMA	Compagnie Générale des Matières Nucléaires
COGEMAT	Compagnie Générale de Matériels et de Matériaux (Gabon)
COGENE	Committee on Genetic Experimentation (ICSU)
COGEO-DATA	Committee on Storage, Automatic Processing and Retrieval of Geological Data (IUGS)
COGEO-DOC	Commission on Geological Documentation (IUGS)
COGEO-ENVIRON-MENT	Commission on Geological Sciences for Environmental Planning (IUGS)
COGEQUIN	Confédération Générale de la Quincaillerie
COGÉRAF	Compagnie Générale d'Études et Recherches pour l'Afrique
COGERCO	Comité de Gérance de la Reserve Cotonnière (Burundi)
COGET-EXIM	Compagnie Générale Togolais d'Export-Import
COGEXIM	Compagnie Générale Import-Export (Ivory Coast)
COGIM	Compagnie Générale Ivoirienne de Maintenance
COGIP	Compagnie Générale Ivoirienne de Piles Électriques
COGMA	Concrete Garage Manufacturers Association

COGRA	Compañia Colombiana de Grasas
CoGroWa	Commissie Grondwaterleidingsbedrijven
COGS	Computer Oriented Geological Society
COHA	Canadian Oral History Association = SCHO
COHATA	Compagnie Haïtienne de Transports Aériens
COHBANA	Corporación Hondureña del Banano
COHDEFOR	Corporación Hondureña de Desarrollo Forestal
COHEHRE	Consortium of Institutions of Higher Education in Health and Rehabilitation in Europe (Belgium)
COHEP	Consejo Hondureño de la Empresa Privada
COHETA	Conseil pour l'Homologation des Etablissements Théologiques en Afrique (Nigeria)
COHI	Caribbean Operational Hydrology Institute
COHSE	Confederation of Health Service Employees (*now* UNISON)
COI	Central Office of Information
COI	Commission de l'Océan Indien = IOC
COI	Commission Océanographique Intergouvernementale (ONU)= IOC, MOK
COI	Conseil Oléicole International = IOOC
COIC	Canadian Oceanographic Identification Centre
COIC	Careers and Occupational Information Centre (MSC)
COICA	Coordinadora de las Organizaciones Indigenas de la Cuenca Amazonica (Peru)
COID	Council of Industrial Design
COID	Council on International Development
COIDIEA	Conseil des Organisations Internationales Directement Intéressées à l'Enfance et à l'Adolescence
COIE	Committee on Invisible Exports
COIF	Control of Intensive Farming
COINASA	Consorcio de Inversiones y Administración, S.A. (Venezuela)
COINS	Committee on Improvement of National Statistics (IASI)
COIP	Caribbean Organization of Indigenous Peoples (Belize)
COIPM	Comité International Permanent pour la Recherche sur la Préservation des Matériaux en Milieu Marin (OECD)

COIS	Committee on International Standardization (ASTM)
COISM	Conseil des Organisations Internationales des Sciences Médicales
COISTD	Confédération des Organisations Internationales Scientifiques et Techniques pour la Développement = CISTOD
COITT	Colegio Oficial y Asociación Nacional Ingenieros Técnicos de Telecommunicación
COJE	Central Organisation for Jewish Education (U.S.A.)
COJEV	Comité des Organisations de Jeunesses Européennes Volontaires
COL	Commonwealth of Learning (CHOGM) (Canada)
COL COMP	Compania Colombiana de Computadores
COL-CIENCIAS	Fondo Colombiano para Investigaciones Científicas y Proyectos Especiales
COL-CULTURA	Istituto Colombiana de Cultura
COL-PUERTOS	Empresa Puertos de Colombia
COL-TABACO	Compañía Colombiana de Tabaco
COL-URANIO	Empresa Colombiana de Uranio
COLA	Camping and Outdoor Leisure Association
COLA-BIOCLI	Confederacion Latinoamericana de Bioquimica Clinica
COLA-TRADE	Comisión Latinoamericana de Trabajadores de la Energía
COLAC	Comité Latinoamericano de Manejo de Cuencas de Torrentes
COLAC	Confederación Latinoamericana de Cooperatives de Ahorro y Crédito
COLACOT	Confederación Latinoamericana de Cooperatives de Trabajadores
COLANCU	Comercializadora de Lanas y Cueros (Chile)
COLAPOM	Comisión Latinoamericana de Pobladores Marginados (Venezuela)
COLAT	Colectivo Latinoamericano de Trabajo Psicosocial
COLBAV	Colegio de Bibliteconomas y Archivistes de Venezuela
COLDI-GRASAS	Sociedad Colombiana de Industriales de Grasas Vegetales (Colombia)

Coleacp	Europe-ACP Liaison Committee for the Promotion of Tropical Fruit, Out-of-Season Vegetables, Flowers, Pot Plants and Spices (EU)	**COM-AGRICOLA**	Associazione Nationale Commercianti di Prodotti per l'Agricoltura
COLFIN	Compañía Colombiana de Financiamiento	**COM-CORDET**	Standing Committee for Coordination of Research, Development, Evaluation and Training (REC) (India)
COLGRO	Verband Schweizerischer Grossisten der Kolonialwarenbranche	**COM EUROCAFE**	Union des Cafetiers-Limonadiers de la Communauté Économique Européenne
COLIBI	Comité de Liaison des Fabricants de Bicyclettes	**COMA**	Coke Oven Managers Association
COLIÉR	Comité de Liaison des Intérêts Économiques de la Réunion	**COMA**	Committee on Medical Aspects of Food Policy (DOH)
COLIMO	Comité de Liaison des Constructeurs de Motorcycle des Pays de la CEE	**COMA**	Computer Operations Management Association (U.S.A.)
COLINAC	Comité de Liaison National des Associations Culturelles	**COMA-RINE**	Compagnie Marocaine d'Agences Maritimes (Morocco)
COLINCO	Compania Colombiana de Ingenieria y Construccion	**COMA-TRANSIT**	Compagnie Malienne de Transit
COLING	International Conference on Computational Linguistics	**COMABRA**	Companhia de Alimentos do Brasil S.A.
COLIPA	Comité de Liaison des Associations Européennes de l'Industrie de la Parfumerie, des Produits Cosmétiques et de Toilette	**COMACEE**	Comité CEE de l'Union Internationale des Agents Commerciaux et des Courtiers
COLIPÉD	Commission de Liaison des Pièces et Équipements de Deux Roues des Pays de la CEE	**COMACH**	Confederación Maritima de Chile
		COMACI	Société de Commission et d'Approvisionnement de la Côte d'Ivoire
COLMINAS	Colombiana de Minería		
COLN	Commissie Onderzoek Land-bouwwaterhuishouding Nederland	**COMACO**	Compagnie de Manutention et de Chalandage d'Owendo (Gabon)
COLOMB-EX	Compañía Colombiana de Comercio Exterior	**COMACOP**	Compagnie Mauritano-Coréenne pour la Pêche
COLP	Comité Latino Americano de Parques Nacionales y de Vida Silvestre	**COMAF**	Comité des Constructeurs de Matériel Frigorifique de la CEE
COLPRO SUMAH	Colegio Profesional de Superación Magisterial Hondureño	**COMAFCI**	Compagnie Maritime Africaine Côte d'Ivoire
COLSUB SIDIO	Caja Colombiana de Subsidio Familiar	**COMAL**	Compagnie Commerciale Camérounaise de l'Alumine et de l'Aluminium
COLT	Council on Library Technology (U.S.A.)	**COMALFA**	Comptoir Maghrebin de l'Alfa (Algeria)
COLTRAM	Comisión Latinoamericana de Transporte Maritimo (Caracas)	**COMALFI**	Sociedad Colombiana de Control de Malezas y Fisiologia Vegetal
COLUMA	Comité Français de Lutte contre les Mauvaises Herbes	**COMAMIDI**	Associazione Italiana dei Commercianti e degli Utilizzatori de Amidi, Fecole e Prodotti Derivati
Colvapores	Colombiana Internacional de Vapores	**COMA-NATRA**	Compagnie Mauritanienne de Navigation et de Transports
COM	Centraal Orgaan voor Melkhygiene	**COMANAV**	Compagnie Malienne de Navigation
COM	Commission on Ore Microscopy (IMA)	**COMANAV**	Compagnie Marocaine de Navigation
COM	Committee on Mutagenicity of Chemicals in Food, Consumer Products and the Environment (DOH)	**COMANOR**	Comité Maghrebin de Normalisation (Morocco)
		COMAPAC	Compania Manufacturera de Papeles y Cartones (Chile)
COM-AFRIQUE	Société Ivoirienne d'Expansion Commerciale	**COMAPI**	Comité d'Action pour l'Isolation et l'Insonorisation

COMA-POPE	Compagnie Mauritano-Portugaise des Pêches	**COMDESA**	Banco de Desarrolo del Paraguay
COMAR	Comando Aéreo Regional (Brazil)	**COMDEV**	Commonwealth Development Finance Company
COMAR	Committee on Man and Radiation (IEEE)	**COMÉ**	Conférence Mondiale d'Énergie
COMAR	Compagnie Mauritanienne des Armements	**COME-CAFCO**	Commerciale Européenne de Cafés et Cacaos
COMAR	Major International Project on Research and Training with a view to Integrated Management of Coastal Systems (UNESCO)	**COMÉCE**	Commission des Épiscopats de la Communauté Européenne
		COMEDA	Conseil Mondial d'Ethique des Droits de l'Animal
COMARAN	Compagnie Maritime de l'Afrique Noire	**COMELEC**	Official Elections Commission (Philippines)
COMARE	Committee on Medical Aspects of Radiation in the Environment (DOH)	**COMENER**	Comisión Centroamericana de Energía
COMARI	Confederación Mexicana de Relaciones Industriales	**COMEPP**	Cornell Manufacturing Engineering and Productivity Program
COMARS	Centro de Orientacion Radial para la Mujer Salvadorena	**COMER-NICSA**	Compania Mercantil Nicaragüense
COMASCI	Société Commerciale d'Applications Scientifiques (Belgium)	**COMERSA**	Corporacion Mercantil Venezolana, S.A.
		COMÉS	Comité de l'Énergie Solaire
COMASSO	Association of Plant Breeders of the EEC	**COMESA**	Committee on Meteorological Effect of Stratospherical Aircraft
COMATAM	Compagnie Malienne pour Tous Appareillages Mécaniques	**COMESA**	Common Market for Eastern and Southern Africa
COMATAS	Committee for Monitoring Agreements on Tobacco Advertising and Sponsorship	**COMET**	Collegium Medicorum Theatri
		COMÉT	Comité d'Organisation des Manifestations Économiques et Touristiques
COMATEX	Compagnie Malienne des Textiles		
COMATOR	Comité Maghrebin de Tourisme	**COMET**	Council of Mechanical and Metal Trade Association
COMAU-BEL	Chambre Syndicale du Commerce Automobile de Belgique		
		COMET	Council of Middle East Trade (BOTB)
COMAU-NAM	Compagnie Mauritanienne de Navigation Maritime	**COMÉTÉ**	Compagnie Mauritanienne d'Études Techniques et Économiques
COMAU-NAV	Compagnie Mauritano-Algérienne de Navigation Maritime	**COMÉTÉC-GAZ**	Comité d'Études Économiques de l'Industrie du Gaz
COMBAT	Association to Combat Huntington's Chorea	**COM-EURIM**	Commission Européenne Immigrés (Belgium)
COMBO-FLA	Comité Boliviano de Fomento Lanero	**COMEX**	Commonwealth Expedition
		COMEX	Compagnie Maritime d'Expertises
COMBOIS	Interessengemeinschaft führender Holzbe- und Verarbeitungsmaschinen-grosshändler	**COMEX**	Compagnie Mauritanienne d'Explosifs
		COMEX	Compañía Exportadora Española
		COMEX	Institut National Algérien du Commerce Extérieur
COMCEC	Standing Committee for Commercial and Economic Cooperation (OIC)		
COMCIAM	Climate Impacts Assessment and Management Program for Commonwealth Countries	**COMEX**	New York Commodity Exchange
		COMEXAZ	Comité de Mexico y Aztlan
		COMEXO	Comité d'Exploitation des Océans
COM-CORDE	Comisión Coordinadora para el Desarrollo Económico (Uruguay)	**COMFACI**	Compagnie Maritine Africain Côte d'Ivoire
COMDA	Canadian Office Machine Dealers Association	**COMFAD**	Council of Multinational Franchisors and Distributors (U.S.A.)

COMFER	Comité Federal de Radiodifusión (Argentina)	**COMNET**	International Network of Documentation Centres on Communication Research and Policies
COMGAS	Companhia de Gas de Sao Paulo (Brazil)	**COMNO-MET**	Complejo de la Mineria no Metalica (Nicaragua)
COMGE	Nederlandse Vereniging van Computer Gebruikers	**COMO**	Committee of Marketing Organisatioins
COMI-TEXTIL	Comité de Coordination des Industries Textiles de la CEE	**COMODAL**	Companhia de Transporte Intermodal (Brazil)
COMIAC	Islamic Standing Committee for Information and Cultural Affairs (OIC) (Saudi Arabia)	**COMOTEL**	Société Comorienne de Tourisme et d'Hôtellerie
COMIAO	Compagnie Commerciale et Industrielle de l'Afrique de l'Quest	**COMOUNA**	Compagnie Commerciale de l'Ouhamé-Nana (Central Africa)
COMIBOL	Corporación Minera de Bolivia	**COMPANIC**	Complejo Papelero Nicaragüense
COMIDES	Interstate Committee of Ministers on Desertification	**COMPESCA**	Companhia Brasileira de Pesca
COMIEX	Compagnie Ivoirienne d'Import-Export	**COMPETA**	Computer and Peripherals Equipment Trade Association
COMILOG	Compagnie Minière de l'Ogooué (Gabon)	**COMPLAN**	Comissão de Planejamento, Coordenação e Desenvolvimento Social e Económico e Produtividade (Brazil)
COMIN-FORM	Information Bureau of Communist Parties and Workers	**COMPRO**	Comité pour la Simplification des Procedures du Commerce International (CE)
COMINAK	Compagnie Minière d'Akouta (Niger)		
COMINOA	Comptoir des Mines et des Grands Travaux de l'Ouest Africain	**COMPRx**	Comprehensive Prescription House Association
COMINOR	Complexe Minier du Nord (Mauritania)	**COMPSAC**	International Computer Software and Applications Conference
COMINPLA-Mercosur	Comisión de Industrias Plasticas del Mercado Común del Sur (Argentina)	**COMPSTAT**	Conference on Computational Statistics
COMIPHOS	Compagnie Minière et Phosphatière	**COMPU-MAG**	Conference on Computations of Magnetic Fields
COMIREC	Comité Interprofessionnel de la Récupération et du Recyclage des Papiers et Cartons	**COMRATE**	Committee on Mineral Resources and the Environment (NRC) (U.S.A.)
COMISA	Compania Mercantil Intercontinental, S.A. (El Salvador)	**COMRED**	Comissao Coordenadora da Politica Nacional de Credito Rural (Brazil)
COMISA	Consultation Mondiale de l'Industrie de la Santé Animale (Belgium)	**COMSAT**	Communications Satellite Corporation (U.S.A.)
COMISE	Comptoir Industriel du Sénégal	**COMSC**	Caribbean Council of Quality Standards
COMIT	Banca Commerciale Italiana	**ComSec**	Commonwealth Secretariat
COMITAS	Compagnia Italiana di Assicurazioni	**COMSER**	Commission on Marine Science and Engineering Research (UN)
Comité de Dublin	Comité International Syndical pour la Paix et le Désarmement = Dublin Committee	**COMSTECH**	Standing Committee for Scientific and Technical Cooperation (OIC)
COMLA	Commonwealth Library Association	**COM-TECHSA**	Community Technical Services Agency Ltd
Commansat	Commonwealth Strategic Planning and Management of Science and Technology	**COMTEL**	Comision Nacional de Telecommunications (Chile)
COMMET	Council of Mechanical and Metal Trade Associations	**COMTEL-CA**	Comisión Técnica dela Telecomunicaciónes de Centroamerica (CACM)
COMNAP	Council of Managers of National Antarctic Programs		
COMNET	Community Network for European Education and Training (Belgium)	**COMUF**	Compagnie des Mines d'Uranium de Franceville (Gabon)

COMUN-BANA	Comercializadora Multinacional Banano
COMUR-HEX	Société pour la Conversion de l'Uranium en Métal et en Hexafluorure
COMUVIR	Institut d'Études Internationales de la Communication sur l'Environnement
COMVE	Committee on Motor Vehicle Emissions (ATAC)
CON-ALGODON	Confederación Colombiana del Algodon
CON-ANDINA	Confederación Andina Industrias
CONA-CINTRA	Camara Nacional de la Industria de la Transformacion (Mexico)
CONA-SEPUDEN	Council for Public Security and National Defence (Panama)
CONA TRADECO	Confederación Nacional de Federaciones y Sindicatos de Trabajadores del Comercio de Chile
CONAB	Conselho Nacional de Abastecimento (Brazil)
CONAC	Comisión Nacional de Acción Comunitaria (Uruguay)
CONAC	Consejo Nacional de la Cultura (Venezuela)
CONAC	La Continentale Agricole du Caméroun
CONACAJP	Comité Nacional de Clubes Agrícolas Juveniles Perú
CONACEX	Consejo Nacional de Comercio Exterior (Mexico)
CONACI	Confederación Nacional de Comunidades Industriales (Peru)
CONACO	Confederación Nacional de Comerciantes (Peru)
CONACOLT-NATORI	Confederazione Nazionale Coltivatori Diretti
CONACYT	Consejo Nacional de Cíencia y Technología (Argentina)
CONADE	Consejo Nacional de Desarrollo (Ecuador, Peru)
CONADE-CA	Comisión Nacional del Cacao (Mexico)
CONADEH	Comisión Nacional de Derechos Humanos (Peru)
CONADEP	Comisión Nacional sobre la Desaparación de Personas (Argentina)
CONADEP	Consejo Nacional de Desarrollo y Planificacion (Haiti)
CONADES	Comisión Nacional de Asistencia a la Poblacion Desplazada (El Salvador)
CONADI	Corporación Nacional de Inversiones (Honduras)
CONAE-CENID	Consejo Nacional de Educación, Centro Nacional de Información y Documentación (Uruguay)
CONAF	Corporación Nacional Forestal (Chile)
CONAFE	Comité Nacional de Ferias (Nicaragua)
CONAFE	Compania Nacional de Fuerza Electrica (Chile)
CONAFIB	Conseil National des Femmes Independants du Benin
Conafrut	Comisión Nacional de Fruticultura (Mexico)
CONAGE	Coordenação Nacional dos Geólogos (Brazil)
CONAHO-TU	Corporación Nacional de Hoteles y Turismo (Venezuela)
CONAIE	Confederación de Nacionalidades Indigenas de Ecuador
CONALTUR	Confederación Nacional de Transporte Urbano (Colombia)
CONAMAG	Comité Nacional de Mercadeo Agropecuário (Venezuela)
CONAMUS	Coordinadora Nacional de la Mujer Salvadorena
CONAN	Companhia de Navegação do Norte
CONANDEX	Consejo Andino Exportadores
CONAP	Corporación Nacional de Abastecimientos del Perú
CONAPAC	Companhia Nacional de Produtos Alimenticios Cearenses (Brazil)
CONAPAN	Confederación Nacional de Sindicatos de Trabajadores de la Industria del Pan, Ramos Conexos y Organismos Auxiliares (Chile)
CONAPE	Comisión Nacional del Petrôleo (El Salvador)
CONAPLAN	Consejo Nacional de Planificacio y Coordinación Economica (Salvador)
CONAPRO	Confederación Nacional de Profesionales
CONAPRO	Consejo Nacional de Produccion (Costa Rica)
CONAPRO-H Y M	Confederación Nicaraguense de Asociaciones de Profesionales "Heroes y Martires"
CONA-PROLE	Consejo Nacional de Produccion Lechera (Uruguay)
CONARE	Compania Nacional de Reforestacion (Venezuela)
CONAREX	Consortium Africain de Réalisation et Exploitation (Benin)
CONARG	Consejo Nacional de Registros Genealógicos (Nicaragua)

CONART	Consejo Nacional de Radiodifusion y Television (Argentina)
CONASE	Consejo Nacional de Seguridad (Argentina)
CONASEP	Confederación Nacional de Servidores Publicos (Ecuador)
CONASEV	Comisión Nacional Supervisora de Empresas y Valores (Peru)
CONASTIL	Compañia Colombiana de Astilleros Ltda
CONASUPO	Compañia Nacional de Subsistencias Populares (Mexico)
CONATEL	Conseil National des Télécommunications (Haiti)
CONATO	Consejo Nacional de Trabajadores Organizados (Panama)
CONAT-RACH	Confederación Nacional de Federaciones y Sindicatos de Interempresas de Trabajadores del Transporte Terrestre y Afines de Chile
CONATRAL	Confederación Nacional de Trabajadores Libres (Dominica)
CONATRAP	Confederación Nacional de Sindicatos de Trabajadores de la Industria del Plástico y Ramos Conexos (Chile)
CONAVI	Confederación Nacional de Viñateros (Argentina)
CONAVI	Consejo Nacional de la Vivienda (Bolivia)
CONAVI	Corporacion Nacional de Ahorro y Vivienda (Colombia)
CONAZA	Comisión Nacional de las Zonas Aridas (Mexico)
CONBA	Council of National Beekeeping Associations of the United Kingdom
CONBOS	Comité National Belge de l'Organisation Scientifique
CONCA	Comité Nacional de Comercialización de Arroz (Bolivia)
CONCACAF	Confédération d'Amérique du Nord, d'Amérique Centrale et des Caraïbes de Fútbal (Guatemala)
CONCAMIN	Confederación de Cámaras Industriales de los Estados Unidos Mexicanos
CONCAN-ACO	Confederación de Cámaras Nacionales de Comercio, Servicios y Turismo (Mexico)
CONCAP	Consejo de Iglesias Luteranas en Centroamérica y Panamá
CONCAWE	Oil Companies European Organisation for Environmental and Health Protection
CONCEN-TRANA-BANGUI	Compagnie Nationale Centrafricaine de Navigation Maritime
CONCERN	Care of the Neglected: Combining Education, Rehabilitation and Nursing
CONCERT	Consultative Group on Certification (CEN) (France)
CONCEX	Conselho Nacional do Comércio Exterior (Brazil)
CONCLAT	Congresso Nacional de Classe Trabalhadora (Brazil)
CONCO	Concrete Company (Saudi Arabia)
CONCOM	Constitutional Commission (Philippines)
CONCOM	Council of Nature Conservation Ministers = ANZEC
CONCOR-DE	Comision Coordinadora para el Desarrollo Economico (Uruguay)
CONCP	Conferência das Organizaçoes Nacionais de las Colónias Portuguesas
CONCY-TEC	Consejo Nacional de Ciencia y Tecnologia (Peru)
CONDAL	Comisión Nacional del Algodón (Ecuador)
CONDECA	Consejo de Defensa Centroamericana (Guatemala)
CONDEPA	Conciencia de Patria (Bolivia)
CONDEPE	Conselho Nacional de Desenvolvimento Pecuário (Brazil)
CONDESE	Conselho de Desenvolvimento Económico de Sergipe (Brazil)
CONDOR	Confederación Dominicana de Religiosos
CONEA	Confederation of National Educational Associations (U.S.A.)
CONECI	Consortium d'Entreprises de Côte-Ivoire
CONECOB	Comité National des Experts-Comptables de Belgique
CONELA	Confraternidad Evangelica Latinoamericana (Argentina)
CONEP	Consejo Nacional de la Empresa Privada (Panama)
CONEPLAN	Consejo Nacional de Economia y Planificación (Bolivia)
CONES	Consejo Nacional de Edificaciones Escolares (Bolivia)
CONES	Consejo Nacional Económiçoe Social (Argentina)
CONESCAL	Centro Regional de Construcciones Escolares para América Latina (Mexico)

CONESCAR	Convenio de Cooperación Tecnia, Estadistica y Cartograféa (Peru)
CONET	Consejo Nacional de Educación Técnica (Argentina)
CONF-CONSORZI	Confederazione Italiana Coltivatori
CONFAE-GUA	Conferencia de Religiosos y Religiosas de Guatemala
CONFAGRI-COLTURA	Confederazione Generale dell'Agricoltura Italiana
CONFAPI	Confederazione Italiana della Piccola e Media Industria
CONFCOM-MERCIO	Confederazione Generale Italiana del Commercio e del Turismo
CONFCOOP	Confederazione Cooperative Italiana
CONFE-METAL	Confederación Española de Organizaciones Empresariales del Metal
CONFE-RURAL	Confederación Rural de Venezuela
CONFECA-MARAS	Confederación Colombiana de Cámaras de Comercio
CONFEDI-LIZIA	Confederazione Italiana della Proprietà Edilizia
CONFEDO-RAFI	Unione Italiana delle Federazioni Nazionali ed Associazioni Territoriali di Categoria tra Fabbricani, Commerciani, Artigiani, Orafi, Gioiellieri, Argentieri, Orologiai, Banci Metalli Preziosi, Pietre Preziose
CONFEJES	Conférence des Ministres de la Jeunesse et des Sports des Pays d'Expression Française
CONF-ÉMÉN	Conférence de Ministres d'Éducation National des Pays d'Expression Française
CONFEN	Conselho Federal de Entorpecentes (Brazil)
CONFER	Confederación Española de Religiosos
CONFER	Conferencia de Religiosos de Nicaragua
CONFER	Consejo de Superioras Mayores de Argentina
CONFE-REMO	Conferência das Religiosas (Mozambique)
CONFERH	Conferencia de Religiosos de Honduras
CONFERRE	Conferencia de Religiosos de Chile
CONFERS	Confederación de Religiosos de El Salvador
CONFETRA	Confederazione Generale del Traffico e dei Trasporti
CONFI TARMA	Confederazione Italiana degli Armatori Liberi
CONFIARP	Confederacion Interamericana de Relaciones Publicas = IFPRA
CONFICO-MARC	Confederazione Italiana Commercianti Agenti Rappresentanti di Commercio
CONFIEP	Confederación Nacional de Instituciones de la Empresa Privada (Peru)
CONFIN	Consejo de Formento e Investigación Agrícola (Chile)
CONFIN-DUSTRIA	Confederazione Generale dell'Industria Italiana
CONFISIA	Confederazione Italiana dei Sindacati Ingegneri e Architetti
CONF-REGUA	Confederación de Religiosos de Guatemala
CONG	Coordinadora de Organizaciones no Gubernamentales de Mujeres (Venezuela)
CONGAD	Conseil des Organisations Non-Gouvernementales d'Appui au Développement (Senegal)
CONGE-MAR	Confederación de Gente de Mar, Marítimos, Portuarios y Pesqueros de Chile
CONGITA	Confédération Générale Italienne de la Technique Agricole
CONGO	Conference of Non-Governmental Organisations in Consultative Status with Unesco
CONGO-BOIS	Compagnie Congolaise des Bois
CONGO-LAP	Société Congolaise d'Appareillage Électrique
CONGO-MECA	Société Congolaise de Mécanographie
CONGOOD	Confederation of Non-governmental Organisations for Overseas Development (Éire)
CONGU	Council of National Golf Unions
CONI	Comitato Olimpico Nacionale Italiano
CONIA	Consejo Nacional de Investigaciones Agrícoles (Venezuela)
CONIAC	Construction Industry Advisory Committee (HSE)
CONIC	Conselho Nacional de Igrejas Cristas do Brasil
CONICET	Consejo Nacional de Investigaciones Científicas y Tecnológicas (Argentina)
CONICIT	Consejo Nacional de Investigaciones Científicas y Tecnológicas (Venezuela)
CONICYT	Comision Nacional de Investigación Cientifica y Tecnológia (Chile)

CONICYT	Consejo Nacional de Investigaciones Científicas y Tecnicas (Uruguay)
CONIDA	Comisión Nacional de Investigación y Desarrollo Aeroespacial (Peru)
CONIE	Comisión Nacional de Investigación de Espacio
CONIF	Confederacion de Instituciones Femeninas (Bolivia)
CONIF	Corporacion Nacional de Investigacion y Fomento Forestal (Colombia)
CONIN-AGRO	Confederación Intercooperativa Agropecuária (Argentina)
CONIN-DUSTRIA	Consejo Venezolaño de la Industria
CONIP	Consejo Nacional de la Iglesia Popular (El Salvador)
CONITAL	Consorzio Italiano Allevatori
CONITE	Comisión Nacional de Inversiones y Tecnologia Extranjeras (Peru)
CONLATIN-GRAF	Latin American Confederation of the Graphics Industry
CONLIS	Committee on National Library Information Systems (U.S.A.)
CONME-BOL	Confederación Sudamericana de Futbol (Peru)
CONPRO-BA	Consorcio de Productores Bananeros (Ecuador)
CONRAD	Contraceptive Research and Development Program
CONS-FETEMA	Confederación de Sindicatos y Federaciones de Trabajadores Electrometalurgicos, Mineros, Automotrices y Ramos Conexos (Chile)
CONS-TRONIC	Conference on Mechanical Aspects of Electronic Design
CONSAL	Conference of South-East Asian Librarians
CONSENA	Consejo de Seguridad Nacional (Uruguay)
CONSIDER	Conselho Nacional de Não-Ferrosos e de Siderurgica (Brazil)
CONSILP	Confederazione Sindicale Italiana Liberi Professionisti
CONSIN	Consejo Superior de Inteligencia (Peru)
CONSOB	Commissione Nazionale per le Società e la Borsa
CONSOM	Fédération Syndicale des Consommateurs
CONSOR-PESCA	Consorzio Nazionale fra Cooperative Pescatori ed Affini
CONSTRA-MET	Confederación de Sindicatos y Federaciones de Trabajadores de la Industria Metalurgica y Ramos Similares y Conexos (Chile)
CONSTROI	Empresa de Construção de Edificações (Angola)
CONSTRU BANCO	Banco de la Construccion, S.A. (Guatemala)
Constru import	Empresa Cubana Exportadora del Abastecimiento y Venta de Equipos de Construcción
CONSTRU-NAVES	Asociación de Constructores Navales Españoles
CONSU-BASQUET	Confederación Sudamericana de Basquetbol
CONSU PLANE	Consejo Superior de Planificatión Económica (Honduras)
CONSUÉL	Comité National Pour la Securité des Usagers de l'Électricité
CONSU-LOOP	Consejo Superior de Licitaciones y Contratos de Obras Publicas (Peru)
Consum import	Empresa Cubana Importadora de Artículos de Consumo General
CONSU-MED	Confederación Sudamericana de Medicina del Deporte (Argentina)
CONTAC	Conference on the Atlantic Community (U.S.A.)
CONTAG	Confederação Nacional dos Trabalhadores na Agricultura (Brazil)
CONTCOP	Confederação Nacional dos Trabalhadores em Communiçaoes e Publicidade (Brazil)
CONTEC	Confederação Nacional dos Trabalhadores nas Empresas de Crédito (Brazil)
CONTEL	Conselho Nacional de Telecomuniçãoes (Brazil)
CONTE-VECH	Confederación Nacional de Sindicatos de Trabajadores Textiles de la Confección, Vestuario y Ramos Conexos de Chile
CON-TEXTIL	Confederación Nacional de Federaciones y Sindicatos de Trabajadores Textiles y Ramos Similares y Conexos de Chile
CONTICyT	Comisión Nacional de Investigación Científica y Technológica (Chile)
CONTO-NAP	Société Béninoise de Distribution d'Appareils Électriques
CONTRA-LESA	Congress of Traditional Leaders of South Africa

CONTT-MAF	Confederação Nacional dos Trabalhadores em Transportes Marítimos, Fluviais e Aéreos (Brazil)
CONUB	Consejo Nacional de la Universidad Boliviana
CONUCOD	Conferencia de las Naciones Unidas sobre Comercio y Desarrollo = CNUCED, UNCTAD
CONUP	Consejo Nacional de la Universidad Peruana
CONUPIA	Confederación Gremial Nacional Unida de la Mediana y Pequeña Industria, Servicios y Artesanado (Chile)
CONUS	Comité Nacional de Unidad Sindical Guatemalteca
CONUTT	Confederación Nacional Unitaria de Trabajadores del Transporte (Chile)
CONVELE	Consejo Venezolano de la Leche (Venezuela)
CONVER	Conferencia Venezolana de Religiosos
CONVERTA	Suomen Paperin-J ja Kartonginjalostajain Yhdistys
CONVICO	Consejo Nacional de Vivienda de Empleados de Comercio (Bolivia)
CONZU-PLAN	Consejo Zuliano de Planificación y Promoción (Venezuela)
COOEDRC	China Offshore Oil Exploration & Development Research Center
COONA COVEN	Confederación Nacional de Cooperativas de Venezuela
COOP	Co-opérative pour le Développement des Oléagineux
COOP-LAINIERE	Coopérative Lainière de l'Île de France
COOP-CAHN	Coopérative des Planteurs de Café Arabica du Haut-Knam (Cameroon)
COOP-EFOR	Société Coopérative Forestière d'Administration et de Gestion
COOP-EFRUT	Cooperativa Agricola y Fruticola de Curico Ltda (Chile)
COOPEN-AGRO	Cooperativa Nacional de Mercadeo Agropecuário Limitada (Colombia)
COOPERE	Coordination et Promotion de l'Enseignement de la Religion en Europe (Belgium)
COOPI	Coopérative Ouvrière Publication Impression (Tunisia)
COOPIBO	Coopération en Développement-IBO (Belgium)
COOPRO-DUITS	Groupement Coopératif de Ventes Internationales des Produits du Burkina Faso
COp	Congregatio pro Operariis Christianis a Sancto Josepho Calasantio
COP	Contactgroep Opvoering Productiviteit
COP/FCCC	Conference of the Parties to the Framework Convention on Climate Change
COPA	Comité des Organisations Professionnelles Agricoles de la CEE
COPA	Committee for Agricultural Organisations in the European Community
COPA	Compania Panameña de Aviación
COPABA	Confederación Panamericana de Basquetbol
COPAC	Comité Mixte pour la Promotion de l'Aide aux Coopératives (FAO)
COPAC	Committee on Pollution Abatement and Control (U.S.A.)
COPAC	Community Patent Appeal Court (EU)
COPACA	Congresos Panamericanos de Carreteras
COPACAR	Corporación Paraguaya de Carnes
COPACE	Comité des Pêches pour l'Atlantique Centre-Est (FAO) = CECAF, CPACE, CPACO
COPACEL	Confédération Française de l'Industrie des Papiers, Cartons et Celluloses
COPACO	Commission de Pêches pour l'Atlantique Centre-Ouest (FAO) = WECAFC
COPAGRO	Companhia Paraense de Mecanização, Industrialização e Comercialização Agropecuária (Brazil)
COPAL	Cocoa Producers Alliance = CPA
COPAM	Comissão de Politica Ambiental (Brazil)
COPAMADE	Confederación Panamericana de Medicina Deportiva (Brazil)
COPAN	Consorzio Fabbricanti Compensati Paniforti Listellari e Affini
COPANT	Comisión Panamericana de Normas Técnicas (Argentina)
COPARCO	Société Congolaise de Perfumerie et Cosmétiques
COPARMEX	Confederación Patronal de la República Mexicana
COPARROZ	Cooperativa de Productores de Arroz de Tacuarembó (Uruguay)
COPATMEX	Confederación Patronal Mexicana
COPCIZ	Comité Permanent des Congrès Internationaux de Zoologie
COPCO	Committee on Consumer Policy (ISO)

COPE	Cadena de Ondas Populares Españolas	**Copextel**	Corporación Productora y Exportadora de Tecnología Electrónica (Cuba)
COPE	Committee on Political Education (U.S.A.)	**COPIA**	Centrala Obsługi Przedsi¿ebiórstw i Instytucji Artystycznych
COPE	Compagnie Orientale des Pétroles (Egypt)	**COPIBAT**	Compagnie de Promotion Immobilière et d'Industrialisation du Bâtiment (Ivory Coast)
COPEBRAS	Companhia Petroquimica Brasileira		
COPEC	Conference of Politics, Economics and Christianity	**COPICA**	Comité de Propagande pour les Industries et les Commerces Agricoles et Alimentaires
COPEC	Corporacion de Petroleos de Chile		
COPECIAL	Comité Permanent des Congrès Internationaux pour l'Apostolat des Laïcs	**COPIDER**	Comite de Promotores de Investigaciones para el Desarrollo Rural (Mexico)
COPECOD-ECA	Comisión Permanente del Consejo de Defensa Centroamericana (Guatemala)	**COPISEE**	Conférence Permanente des Ingénieurs du Sud-Est de l'Europe
COPEDIP	Compagnie Pétrolière d'Intérêts et de Participation	**COPL**	Center for Optics, Photonics and Lasers (Canada)
COPEFA	Compagnie des Pétroles France-Afrique	**COPLAN**	Development Planning Commission (Brazil)
COPEFA	Consejo Permanente de la Fuerza Armada (El Salvador)	**COPLAN-ARH**	Comisión del Plan Nacional de Aprovechamiento de los Recursos Hidráulicos (Venezuela)
COPEI	Comité de Organización Politica Electoral Independiente (Venezuela)		
COPEL	Companhia Paranaense de Energia Elétrica (Brazil)	**COPMEC**	Comité des Petites et Moyennes Entreprises Commerciales des Pays de la CEE
COPEMA	Compagnie Eburnéenne des Pêches Maritimes	**COPNEU**	Compagnie Industrielle du Pneumatique (Cameroon)
COPEMAR	Compagnie de Pêche et de Mareyage		
COPEMAR	Société Congolaise de Pêches Maritimes (Congo)	**COPO**	Centralny Ośrodek Przygotowań Olimpijskich
COPEMH	Colegio de Profesores de Educación Media de Honduras	**COPOL**	Council of Polytechnic Librarians
		COPORT-CHAD	Coopérative des Transportateurs Tchadiens (Chad)
COPENUR	Comité Permanent pour l'Enrichissement de l'Uranium (CCE)	**COPPEL**	Comité de Partidos Politicos por las Elecciones Libres (Chile)
COPÉP	Commission Permanente de l'Électronique au Commissariat Général du Plan	**COPPPAL**	Conferencia Permanente de Partides Políticos de América Latina
COPERE	Comite de Programación Económica y de Reconstrucción (Chile)	**COPPSO**	Conference of Professional and Public Service Organisations
Copersucar	Cooperativa Central dos Produtores de Acucar e Alcool do Estado de Sao Paulo	**COPQ**	Committee on Overseas Qualifications (Australia)
COPES	Coordination Office of Paediatric Endocrine Societies	**COPRA**	Conference of Private Residents Associations
COPESA	Corporacion Pesquera Ecuatoriana S.A.	**COPRA**	Les Constructeurs Professionnels Associés (Ivory Coast)
COPESCAL	Comisión de Pesca Continental para America Latina (FAO)	**COPRAI**	Comissão de Produtivadade da Asociação Industrial Portuguesa
COPESSOI	Conférence Permanente de l'Enseignement Supérieur du Sud-Ouest de l'Océan Indien	**COPRALIM**	Corporacion Procesadora de Alimentos (Nicaragua)
COPETAO	Compagnie des Pétroles Total Afrique Quest	**COPRAM**	Companhia Progresso do Amapa (Brazil)
COPEXO	Comité pour l'Expansion de l'Huile d'Olive	**COPRAPO-SE**	Confederación Panamericana de Productores de Seguros (Venezuela)

COPRAQ	Cooperative Programme of Research on Aquaculture (FAO)
COPRED	Consortium on Peace Research, Education and Development (U.S.A.)
COPREFA	Comité de Prensa de las Fuerzas Armadas (El Salvador)
Coprefil	Empresa Comercial y de Producciones Filatélicas (Cuba)
COPRIN	Comisión de Productividad Precios e Ingresos (Venezuela)
COPRO Niger	Société Nationale de Commerce et de Production du Niger
COPRODE	Consejo Provincial de Desarrollo (Argentina)
COPROMA	Compagnie des Produits du Mali
COPRONA	Compania Productora Nacional de Aceites (Chile)
COPS	College of Osteopathic Physicians and Surgeons (U.S.A.)
COPTAL	Comité Permanente Técnico para Asuntos del Asuntos del Trabajo, Latinoamerica
COPUL	Council of Prairie University Libraries (U.S.A.)
COPUOS	UN Committee on the Peaceful Uses of Outer Space
COPUS	Committee on the Public Understanding of Science
COPYME	Confederación General de las Pequeñas y Medianas Empresas del Estado Español
COQUINSA	Compania Quimica Nicaraguënse, S.A.
ČOR	Česká Odborová Rada
COR	Confederación Obrera Revolucionaria (Mexico)
COR	Conferencia de Religiosos de Puerto Rico
COR	The Club of Rome
CORA	Chemical and Oil Recycling Association (*ex* CRA)
CORA	Corporación de la Reforma Agraria (Chile)
CORAA	Council of Regional Arts Associations
CORADEP	Corporacion de Radiodifusion del Pueblo (Nicaragua)
CORAL	Corporation of Coastal Cotton Growers (Colombia)
CORAS	Centre for Operational Research & Applied Statistics
CORAT	Christian Organisations Research and Advisory Trust
CORC	Central Organisation for Rural Cooperatives (Iran)
CORCA	Committee of Registered Clubs Associations
CORCEMAR	Corporacion Cementera Argentina
CORDA	Coronary Artery Disease Research Organisation
CORDE	Corporación Dominicana de Empresas Estatales
CORDEPAZ	Corporación Regional de Desarrollo de la Paz (Bolivia)
CORDÉS	Comité d'Organisation des Recherches Appliquées sur le Développement Économique et Social
CORDI	Comité Consultatif pour la Recherche et le Développement Industriels (CCE)
CORDIS	The Community R&D Information Service (EU)
CORE	Caribbean Oceanographic Research Expedition
CORE	Center for Operations Research and Econometrics (Belgium)
CORE	Congress of Racial Equality (U.S.A.)
CORE	CSIR Committee on Research Expenditure (South Africa)
CORE	Cuban Organisation for the Representation of Exiles (U.S.A.) = RECE
CORE	International Centre of Operations Research and Econometrics
COREC	International Consultancy on Religion, Education and Culture
CORECA	Consejo Regional de Cooperación Agrícola en Centroamérica, México, Panamá y la República Dominicana
CORECI	Compagnie de Régulation et de Contrôle Industriel
CORÉDE	Communauté Romande de l'Économie d'Entreprise
COREDIAL	Comité Regional Encargado del Convenio de Convalidación de Estudios, Titulas y Diplomas de Educación Superior en America Latina y el Caribe
COREDIF	Compagnie de Réalisation d'Usines de Diffusion Gazeuse
COREE	Conference on Organic Environmental Economics
COREM	Conférences Régionales de Métiers
COREN	Council of Registered Engineers in Nigeria

COREP	Comité Régional de Pêche (Gabon)
COREPER	Comité des Représentants Permanents (CCE) = AStV, PRC
CORESTA	Centre de Coopération pour les Recherches Scientifiques Relatives du Tabac
CORFIN	Corporación Financiera de Nicaragua
CORFINA	Corporación Financiera Nacional (Guatemala)
CORFINO	Corporacion Forestal Industrial de Olancho (Honduras)
CORFO	Corporación de Formento de la Producción (Chile)
CORFOP	Corporacion Forestal del Pueblo (Nicaragua)
CORGI	Confederation for the Registration of Gas Installers
CORH	Committee on Operations Research – Hungary (MTA)
CORINCA	Corporacion Industrial Centroamericana (El Salvador)
CORINE	Coordinated Information on the European Environment
CORIP	Comité de Recherches de l'Industrie Pharmaceutique (Belgium)
CORKR	Campaign to Oppose the Return of the Khmer Rouge
CORMA	Corporación Chilena de la Mandera
COROI	Comptoir de Commerce et de Représentation pour l'Océan Indien
CORP	Corporación para el Fomento de Investigaciones Económicas (Colombia)
CORPA	Corporacion Publicitaria Nacional (Venezuela)
CORPAC	Corporación Peruana de Aeropuertos y Aviación Comercial
CORPINSA	Corporacion Inmobiliaria S.A. (El Salvador)
CORPO-FRUT	Corporación de Productores de Frutas de Rio Negro (Argentina)
CORPO-INDUSTRIA	Corporación de Desarrollo de la Pequeña y Mediana Industria (Venezuela)
CORPO-MERCADEO	Corporación de Mercadeo Agrícola (Venezuela)
CORPO-SANA	Corporación de Obras Sanitarias (Paraguay)
CORPO-TURISMO	Corporacion de Turismo de Venezuela
CORPORIN	Corporacion Industrial (El Salvador)
CORPSA	Corporación Papelera (Nicaragua)
CORS	Canadian Operational Research Society = SCRO
CORSAG	Corporación Santiagueña de Ganaderos (Argentina)
CORSAIN	Corporación Salvadoreña de Inversiones
CORSAL	Corporacion Salvadoreña de Calzado
CORSI	Operational Research Society of India
CORSI	Società Cooperativa per la Radiotelevisione nella Svizzera Italiana
CORSO	Council of Relief Services Overseas (New Zealand)
CORT	Council of Regional Theatres
CORT	Council of Repertory Theatres
CORTCO	Consortium of Retail Teaching Companies
COS	Canadian Otolaryngological Society
COS	Central Orchid Society
COS	Centralny Ośrodek Sportu
COS	Chinese Ophthalmological Society
COS	Chinese Optical Society
COS	Cinema Organ Society
COS	Community of Slovaks (Czech Republic) = SS
COS	Coordinadora de Organizaciones Sindicales
COSA	Cámaras Oficiales Sindicales Agrarias
COSALFA	Comisión Sudaméricana para la Lucha contra la Fiebre Aftosa
CoSAMC	Commission for Special Applications of Meteorology and Climatology (WMO)
Cosarese	Colectivo de Sacerdotes y Religiosos Secularizados
COSAS	Conference of South African Students
COSAT	Confederación Sudamericana de Tenis (Argentina)
COSATA	Co-operative Supply Association of Tanzania
COSATE	Commission Syndicale Technique (OEA)
COSATU	Congress of South African Trade Unions
COSAWR	Committee on South African War Resistance
COSBA	Computer Services and Bureaux Association
COSCA	Confederation of Scottish Counselling Agencies
COSCA	Council of Scottish Clan Associations (U.S.A.)

COSCO	China Ocean Shipping Company
COSDEGUA	Confederación de Sacerdotes Diocesanos de Guatemala
COSEAB	Compagnie Sénégalaise d'Exploitation d'Arachide de Bouche
COSEBI	Corporación de Servicios Bibliotecarios (Puerto Rico)
COSECO	Copperbelt Secondary Teachers Association (Zambia)
COSEDIA	Consortium Sénégalais pour la Diffusion de l'Automobile
COSEDIR	Compagnie Sénégalaise pour le Développement Industriel Rationnel
COSEELIS	Council on Slavonic and East European Library and Information Services
COSEM	Co-operative Seed Corn Society of Tunis
COSEM	Compagnie Générale des Semi-Conducteurs
COSEMCO	Comité des Semences du Marché Commun (Belgium)
COSEN	Comisión Salvadoreña de Energía Nuclear
COSENAM	Compagnie Sénégalaise de Navigation Maritime
COSEP	Consejo Superior de la Empresa Privada (Nicaragua)
COSEPRO	Corporacion de Servicios Profesionales (El Salvador)
COSEPUP	Committee for Science, Engineering and Public Policy (NAS) (U.S.A.)
COSETAM	Compagnie Sénégalaise pour Tous Appareillages Mécaniques
COSHEP	Committee of Scottish Higher Education Principals
COSIMEX	Compagnie Sénégalaise d'Importation et d'Exportation
COSINE	Cooperation for OSI Networking in Europe
COSIPA	Companhia Siderúgica Paulista (Brazil)
COSIRA	Council for Small Industries in Rural Areas
COSIRT	Comité Scientifique International pour la Recherche sur la Trypanosomiase
COSLA	Convention of Scottish Local Authorities
COSLASS	Comisión Sindical Latinoamericana de Seguridad Social, Higieno Industrial, Ecologia y Medio Ambiente en al Trabajo (CLAT) (Venezuela)
COSMA	Associazione Costruttori Macchine pe Cucire
COSMAT	Committee on the Survey of Materials Science and Engineering (NAC) (U.S.A.)
COSPAR	Committee on Space Research (ICSU)
COSPE	Cooperazione per lo Sviluppo dei Paesi Emergenti
COSPEC	Christian Organisations for Social, Political and Economic Changes
COSPIT	Centro Orientamento Studi e Propaganda Irrigua
COSPOIR	National Sports Council (Éire)
COSQUEC	Council for Occupational Standards and Qualifications in Environmental Conservation
COSRIMS	Committee on Research in the Mathematical Sciences (NAS) (U.S.A.)
COSSA	Commonwealth Office of Space Science and Applications (CSIRO)
COSSEC	Cambridge, Oxford and Southern School Examinations Council
COSSO	Vereniging Computer Service-en Software Bureaus
COST	Committee for Overseas Science and Technology
COST	Committee on Science and Technology (India)
COST	Coopération Européenne dans la Domaine de la Recherche Scientifique et Technique
COSTA	Council of Subject Teaching Associations
COSTED	Committee on Science and Technology in Developing Countries (ICSU)
COSTI	Centre on Scientific and Technical Information (Israel)
COSTI	Committee on Scientific and Technical Information (U.S.A.)
COSTIC	Comité Scientifique et Technique de l'Industrie du Chauffage de la Ventilation et du Conditionnement d'Air
COSTPRO	Canadian Organization for the Simplification of Trade Procedures
COSTRAR	Confédération Syndicale des Travailleurs de Rwanda
COSU	Co-ordination de l'Opposition Sénégalaise Unie
COSUMA	Conférence des Supérieurs Majeurs (Burundi, Rwanda)
COSUMAR	Compagnie Sucrière Marocaine et de Raffinage (Morocco)
COSUPI	Comissão Supervisora do Plano dos Institútos (Brazil)

COSV	Comitatio di Coordinamento delle Organizzazioni per il Servizio Volontario	**COTON-ANG**	Companhia Geral dos Algodões de Angola
COSWA	Conference on Science and World Affairs	**COTONCO**	Compagnie Cotonnière Congolaise
COSYGA	Confédération Syndicale Gabonaise	**COTONT-CHAD**	Société Cotonnière du Tchad
COT	Centrale Organisatie in de Tweewielerbranche	**COTRAM**	Compagnie Togolaise de Transit, Transport et Agence Maritime
COT	Centrum voor Onderzoek en Technisch Advies (Netherlands)	**COTRAM**	La Congolaise de Transport Maritime
COT	Committee on Toxicity of Chemicals in Food, Consumer Products and the Environment (DOH)	**COTRAM**	Union des Constructeurs de Matériel de Travaux Publics et de Manutention
COTA	Caribbean Organisation of Tax Administration	**COTRAMA**	Société Civile Coopérative d'Études des Transports et de Manutention
COTA	Collectif d'Echanges pour la Technologie Appropriée (Belgium)	**COTRAO**	Communauté de Travail des Régions des Alpes Occidentales
COTA	Commission on Theoretical Anthropology	**COTREL**	Comité d'Associations de Constructeurs de Transformateurs du Marché Commun
COTAC	Conference on Training Architects in Conservation	**COTRIJUI**	Cooperativa Regional Triticula Serra Ltda of Ijui (Brazil)
COTACEX	Comité Technique des Assureurs-Crédit à l'Exportation de la CEE	**COTRINAG**	Comissão de Organização de Triticultura Nacional e Armazenamento Geral (Brazil)
COTAL	Confederación de Organizaciones Turísticas de la América Latina	**COTS**	Childlessness Overcome Through Surrogacy
COTANCE	Confédération des Associations Nationales de Tanneurs et Megissiers de le CEE	**COTSOM**	Compagnie de Travaux Sous-Marins (Cameroon)
COTC	Canadian Overseas Telecommunications Corporation	**COTT**	Central Organization for Technical Training (South Africa)
COTCO	Committee on Technical Committee Operations (ASTM)	**COTTI**	Commission du Traitement et de la Transmission de l'Information
COTEF	Complexe Textile de Fès (Morocco)	**COTU**	Central Organisation of Trade Unions (Kenya)
COTEMA	Compagnie Technique Mauritanienne	**COTUNACE**	Compagnie Tunisienne pour l'Assurance du Commerce Extérieur
COTIF	Comité Technique International de Prévention et d'Extinction du Feu	**COTUR**	Corporacion de Turismo de Nicaragua
COTIRC	Comisión Técnica Interprovincial del Rio Colorado (Argentina)	**COTUSAL**	Compagnie Générale des Salines de Tunisie
COTIS	Confederation of Tape Information Services	**COV**	Christen Onderwijzers Verbond (Belgium)
COTIVO	La Cotonnérie Ivoirienne	**COVAS**	Coöperatieve Vereniging voor de Afzet van Suikerbieten
COTOA	Compagnie Textile de l'Ouest Africain (Senegal)	**COVECO**	Centrale Organisatie van Veeafzet-en Vleesverwerkings-coöperaties
COTOMET	Compagnie Togolaise des Métaux	**COVEG**	Stichting Centraal Orgaan voor de Voedings-en Genotmiddelenbranche
COTOMIB	Compagnie Togolaise des Mines du Bénin	**COVEMA**	Comando Vengadores de Martires (Chile)
COTON-FRAN	Société Cotonnière Franco Tchadienne	**COVEMI**	Compagnie Voltaïque d'Exploitation Minière
COTONA	La Cotonniere d'Antsirabe (Madagascar)	**COVENAL**	Corporación Venezolana de Aluminio

COVEN-EXTA	Cooperativa Venezolana de Exportadores de Tabaco	**CP**	Convention Patronale de l'Industrie Horlogère Suisse
COVENIN	Comisión Venezolana de Normas Industriales	**CP**	Royal College of Preceptors
COVENTA	Cooperativa Venezolana de Tabacaleros	**CPA**	Caja Postal de Ahorros
COVEP	Comisión Venezolana para la Productividad	**CPA**	California Pharmaceutical Association (U.S.A.)
COVEPRO	Cooperativa Venezolana de Productores	**CPA**	Canadian Pacific Airlines
COVINA	Companhia Vidreira Nacional	**CPA**	Canadian Petroleum Association
COVINCA	Corporación Venezolana de la Industria Naval CA	**CPA**	Canadian Pharmaceutical Association
COVINEX	Société Congolaise d'Exploitation Vinicole	**CPA**	Canadian Philosophical Association = ACP
COVO-DIAM	Compagnie Voltaïque de Distribution Automobile et de Matériel	**CPA**	Canadian Postmasters Association
COVON	Coéperatieve Vereniging van Ondernemers in het Natuursteenbedrijf	**CPA**	Canadian Psychiatric Association
		CPA	Canadian Psychological Association
COVOS	Groupes d'Études sur les Conséquences des Vols Stratosphériques	**CPA**	Carpet Planners Association
		CPA	Centre de Perfectionnement dans d'Administration des Affaires
COVP-DLO	DLO Centrum voor Onderzoek en Voorlichting voor de Pluimveehouderij "Het Spelderholt" (Netherlands)	**CPA**	Centre de Préparation aux Affaires
		CPA	Centre for Policy on Ageing
COW	Centrum voor Onderzoek Waterkeringen (Netherlands)	**CPA**	Chick Producers Association
		CPA	China Photographers' Association
COW	Committee of the Whole (UN General Assembly)	**CPA**	China Printing Association
		CPA	Chinese Pharmaceutical Association
COWA	Council for Old World Archaeology (U.S.A.)	**CPA**	Chinese Psychological Association
		CPA	Chipboard Promotion Association
CoWaBo	Commissie inzake Wateronttrekking aan de Bodem	**CPA**	City Property Association
		CPA	Cocoa Producers Alliance = COPAL
COWAN	Country Women Association of Nigeria	**CPA**	Comité Permanent Agricole (BIT)
COWAR	Coordinating Committee for Water Research (ICSU-UITA)	**CPA**	Comité Postal Andin (Colombia) = APC
		CPA	Commonwealth Parliamentary Association
COWSIP	Country Towns Water Supply Improvement Program	**CPA**	Commonwealth Pharmaceutical Association
COWT	Council of World Tensions (Switzerland)	**CPA**	Commonwealth Postal Administration
COYPSS	Coalition on Young People and Social Security	**CPA**	Commonwealth Professional Associations = OCA
COZAC	Conservation Zone Advisory Committee	**CPA**	Communist Party of Andalusia = PCE-PCA
CP	Centralkommitén for Produktivitetsfragor	**CPA**	Communist Party of Australia
		CPA	Communist Party of Azerbaijan
CP	Centrum Partij	**CPA**	Compagnie des Pétroles d'Algérie
CP	Coalición Popular	**CPA**	Concrete Pipe Association
CP	Comissão Politica (Cape Verde)	**CPA**	Construction Plant-hire Association
CP	Communist Party	**CPA**	Consumer Protection Agency (U.S.A.)
CP	Congregatio Passionis Iesu Christi	**CPA**	Contractors Plant Association
CP	Conservative Party (South Africa)	**CPA**	Cour Permanent d'Arbitrage (Netherlands)
CP	Contemplatives Passionistes	**CPA**	Craftsmen Potters Association

CPA	Credit Populaire d'Algérie	**CPB**	Communist Party of Britain
CPA	Credit Protection Association	**CPB**	Confederacion Panamericana de Badminton = PBC
CPA	Institute of Certified Public Accountants in Ireland	**CPB**	Corporation for Public Broadcasting (U.S.A.)
CPA	National Association of Creamery Proprietors and Wholesale Dairymen = NACEPE	**CPBA**	Caribbean Publishers and Broadcasting Association
CPA-ML	Communist Party of Australia – Marxist-Leninist	**CPBCA**	Coopérative des Planteurs Bamoun du Café Arabica (Cameroon)
CPAA	Centro de Pesquisa Agroflorestal da Amazônia Ocidental (Brazil)	**CPBF**	Campaign for Press and Broadcasting Freedom
CPAA	Certified Public Accountancy Associates (U.S.A.)	**CPBM**	Communist Party of Bohemia and Moravia = KSCM
CPAA	Colloquia for Presidents and Academic Administrators (U.S.A.)	**CPBP**	Comisión Protectora de Bibliotecas Populares (Argentina)
CPAA	Commission of the Prevention of the Abuse of Authority (Nepal)	**CPBP**	Comité Professional du Butane et du Propane
CPAA	Cultured Pearl Association of America	**CPBS**	Central Peoples Broadcasting Station (China)
CPAC	Centro de Pesquisa Agropecuária dos Cerrados (Brazil)	**CPBS**	Connemara Pony Breeders' Society (Éire)
CPAC	Consumer Protection Advisory Committee (DTI)	**CPC**	Campaign against Pornography and Censorship
CPAC	Corrosion Prevention Advisory Centre	**CPC**	Canadian Pension Commission
CPAC	International Collaborative Pesticides Analytical Committee	**CPC**	Caribbean Press Council
CPACE	Comité des Pêches pour l'Atlantique-Centre-Est (FAO) = CECAF, COPACE, CPACO	**CPC**	Caring Professions Concern
		CPC	Centre for Peaceful Change (U.S.A.)
		CPC	Centre for Plant Conservation (IUCN)
CPACO	Comité de Pesca de la FAO para el Atlántico Centro-Oriental = CECAF, COPACE, CPACE	**CPC**	Christian Peace Conference = CCP, CFK, HMK
		CPC	Coffee Promotion Council
CPACS	Centre for Peace and Conflict Studies (Sydney University)	**CPC**	Colectivo Pancha Carrasco (Costa Rica)
CPAD	Comité de Concertation sur l'Alcool et les Autres Drogues	**CPC**	Committee for Programme and Coordination (ECOSOC)
CPAF	Cambodian People's Armed Forces	**CPC**	Commonwealth Palaeontological Collection
CPAG	Child Poverty Action Group	**CPC**	Communist Party of the Crimea
CPAL	Canadian Pacific Air Lines	**CPC**	Community Patent Convention (EU)
CPAL	Centre de Productivité des Industries de l'Ameublement et de la Literie	**CPC**	Compagnie des Potasses du Congo
		CPC	Conservative Political Centre
CPAL	Creosote Producers Association	**CPC**	Cotton Public Corporation (Sudan)
CPANE	Commission des Pêches de l'Atlantique Nord-Est = NEAFC	**CPC/LAC**	Christian Peace Conference in Latin America and the Caribbean (Puerto Rico)
CPANT	Comité Panamericano de Normas Técnicas (Uruguay)	**CPCA**	Comision Permanente de Cooperativas de Autogestion – Programa Mujer en Autogestion (Costa Rica)
CPAR	Canadian Physicians for Aid and Relief		
CPAS	Church Pastoral Aid Society	**CPCA**	Comité des Pêches Continentales pour l'Afrique (FAO) = CIFA
CPB	Centraal Planbureau		
CPB	Communist Party of Bangladesh	**CPCA**	Cyprus Photogrammetric and Cartographic Association
CPB	Communist Party of Belarus		

CPCAM	Coopérative des Planteurs de Cafétiers de Mbouda (Cameroon)		**CPDR**	Committee of Plant Disease Resistance (China)
CPCAS	Commission Permanente de Coordination des Associations Spécialisées (FNSEA)		**CPDRI**	Coal Preparation Design and Research Institute (China)
CPCCI	Conférence Permanente des Chambers de Commerce et l'Industrie de la CEE		**CPDS**	Center for Policy and Development Studies (Philippines)
CPCE	Groupement Pharmaceutique de la Communauté Européenne = PGEC		**CPDS**	Centre for Product Development Services
CPCEA	Caisse de Prévoyance des Cadres d'Exploitations Agricoles		**CPE**	Caméroun Publi-Expansion
CPCG	Children's Panel Chairmen's Group		**CPE**	Centre de la Petite Enfance
CPCI	Centre de Perfectionnement Pratique des Cadres Commerciaux dans l'Industrie		**CPÉ**	Centre de Prospective et d'Évaluation
			CPE	Centrum voor Pastoraal in Europa
CPCIP	Commission Permanentede la Convention International des Pêches		**CPE**	Chamber of Professional Engineers (Malta)
CPCJ	United Nations Crime Prevention and Criminal Justice Branch		**CPÉ**	Comité de Politique Économique (OCDE) = EPC
CPCR	Congregatio Cooperatorum Paroeialium Christi Regis		**CPE**	Committee on Population and the Economy
CPCRI	Central Plantation Crops Research Institute (India)		**CPE**	Congrès du Peuple Européen
CPCS	Commissione Pontificiale per le Comunicazioni Sociali		**CPE**	Coopération Politique Européenne; Cooperacion Politica Europea; Cooperazione Politica Europea = EPC, EPS, EPZ, POCO
CPCV	Circulo de Periodismo Cientifico de Venezuela			
CPD	Concertación de los Partidos de la Democracia (Chile)		**CPE**	Coordination Paysanne Européenne
			CPE	Industry Council for Packaging and the Environment
CPDA	China Prospecting and Design Association		**CPE(M-L)**	Communist Party of England (Marxist-Leninist)
CPDA	Clay Pipe Development Association		**CPEA**	China Petroleum Equipment Association
CPDC	Caribbean Policy Development Centre (Barbados)		**CPEA**	Confederation of Professional and Executive Associations
CPDC	Committee on the Participation of Developing Countries		**CPEA**	Cyprus Professional Engineers' Association
CPDÉ	Commission Permanente de Développement de l'Élevage		**CPÉD**	Commission de la Participation des Églises au Développement (Switzerland)
CPDÉ	Compagnie Parisienne de Distribution d'Électricité			
CPDF	Caribbean Project Development Facility		**CPEF**	Christian Peace Education Fund
CPDL	Canadian Patents and Development Ltd		**CPEJÉ**	Coopération Paneuropéenne de la Jeunesse et des Étudiants = AEYSC
CPDM	Cameroon People's Democratic Front		**CPEPA**	Comité de la Prune d'Ente et du Pruneau d'Agen
CPDN	Comité Permanente del Debate Nacional por la Paz (El Salvador)		**CPEQ**	Corporation of Professional Engineers of Quebec (Canada)
CPDOC	Centro de Pesquisa e Documentação (Brazil)		**CPES**	Centro Paraguayo de Estudios Sociologicos
CPDP	Comissao Para os Direitos povo Maubere		**CPF**	Central Provident Fund (Singapore)
			CPF	Community Projects Foundation
CPDP	Comité Professionnel du Pétrole		**CPF**	Congregation for the Propagation of the Faith

CPF	Coopération Pharmaceutique Française
CPF	Cooperative Productive Federation
CPFC	Centre Panafricain de Formation Coopérative (Benin)
CPFC	Comisión de Protección Fitosanitaria para el Caribe (FAO) = CPPA
CPFE	Center for People, Food and Environment (U.S.A.)
CPFO	Centre de Promotion des Femmes Ouvrières (Haiti)
CPFRC	Central Pacific Fisheries Research Center (NMFS) (U.S.A.)
CPFS	Council for the Promotion of Field Studies
CPG	Bureau of Conference Planning and General Services (UNESCO)
CPG	Chemisch-Physikalische Gesellschaft (Austria)
CPG	Communist Party of Galicia = PCE-PCG
CPG	Coronary Prevention Group
CPGA	Comité Professionnel des Galeries d'Art
CPGB	Communist Party of Great Britain
CPGPA	Caisse Professionnele de Garantie des Producteurs Agricoles
CPGR	Commission on Plant Genetic Resources (FAO)
CPHA	Canadian Public Health Association
CPHA	Comprehensive Prescription House Association
CPHERI	Central Public Health Engineering Research Institute (India)
CPHL	Central Public Health Laboratory
CPHP	Confédération Patronale des Hautes-Pyrénées
CPHRF	Council for the Protection of Human Rights and Freedoms (Serbia) = VZLPS
CPI	Cerebral Palsy Ireland
CPI	Cinchona Products Institute (U.S.A.)
CPI	Commission Permanente Internationale Européenne des Gaz Industriels et du Carbure de Calcium
CPI	Communist Party of India
CPI	Confederation of Photographic Industries
CPI	Conseil Phytosanitaire Interafricain = IAPSC
CPI	Crop Protection Institute (U.S.A.)
CPI	Stichting Coöperatief Pluimveefokkers Institute
CPI(M-L)	Communist Party of India (Marxist-Leninist)
CPI-M	Communist Party of India – Marxist
CPI/AC	Comissão Pró-Indio do Acre (Brazil)
CPI/SP	Comissão Pró-Indio do São Paulo (Brazil)
CPIA	Cape Provincial Institute of Architects (South Africa)
CPIA	Conférence Pédagogique Internationale d'Approvisionnement
CPIC	Canadian Police Information Centre
CPIC	Comprehensive Pig Information Centre
CPIE	Centre de l'Information Européenne
CPIJ	Corrosion & Protection Institute of Japan
CPIP	Consejo de Pesca Indo-Pacifico
CPIRC	China Population Information & Research Center
CPISAA	Cape Provincial Institute of South African Architects
CPISRA	Cerebral Palsy International Sports and Recreation Association
CPISS	Comité Permanent Interaméricain Sécurité Sociale
CPITUS	Comité Permanent International des Techniques et de l'Urbanisme Souterrains
CPIUS	Comité Permanent Internacional de Tecnicos y de Urbanismo Subterráneo
CPIV	Comité Permanent des Industries de Verre de la CEE
CPIV	Comité Permanent International du Vinaigre (Marché Commun)
CPJ	Committee to Protect Journalists
CPJ	Communist Party of Jordan
CPK	Communist Party of Kazakhstan
CPKMU	CPK Mothers' Union (Kenya)
CPL	Cats Protection League
CPL	Centre Paritaire du Logement
CPL	Confédération des Professions Libérales
CPL-Lesotho	Communist Party of Lesotho
CPLiA	Centrala Przemysłu Ludowego i Artystycznego
CPLK	Comité Permanent de Liaison des Kinésithérapeutes de la CCE (Denmark) = SLCP
CPLRE	Conférence Permanente des Pouvoirs Locaux et Régionaux de l'Europe = CLRAE
CPM	Centre de Pyrolyse de Marienau (France)

CPM	Centre for Pest Management (Canada)	**CPO**	Centrum voor Plantenfysiologisch Onderzoek
CPM	College of Petroleum and Minerals (Saudi Arabia)	**CPO**	Commonwealth Producers Organisation
CPM	Comisión del Pacifico Meridional	**CPO**	County Planning Officers Society
CPM	Comité du Patrimoine Mondial = WHC	**CPOI**	Comisión de Pesca para el Océano Indico = IOFC
CPM	Communist Party of India – Marxist		
CPM	Conférence Permanente d'Études sur les Civilisations du Monde Méditerranéen	**CPOM**	Centro de Preclasificación Océanica de México
CPM	Congregatio Presbyterorum a Misericordia	**CPP**	Communist Party of Peru
		CPP	Communist Party of the Philippines
CPM	Corpo Policial de Moçambique	**CPP**	Croatian Peasants' Party
CPM	Corporación Pro-Crusada Mundial = CEM, WECI, WEK	**CPP-ML**	Communist Party of the Philippines – Marxist-Leninist
CPMC	Comité Permanent pour le Marché Commun de la Fédération Internationale de la Construction	**CPP-PFIP**	Kristeligt Folkeparti Framburds – og Fiskivinnuflokkarin (Faeroe Islands)
CPMC	Commission Permanente de Marché Commun de Bureau International des Producteurs d'Assurances et de Réassurances	**CPPA**	Cameria Political and Patriotic Association (Albania) = SPAC
		CPPA	Canadian Periodical Publishers Asociation
CPME	Conseil Parlementaire du Mouvement Européen = PCEM	**CPPA**	Canadian Pulp and Paper Association
CPME	Council on Podiatric Medical Education	**CPPA**	Coal Preparation Plant Association
CPMEA	China Printing Material & Equipment Association	**CPPB**	Comité de Problemos de Productos Básicos (FAO)
CPMÉÉ	Comité Permanent des Foires et Manifestations Économiques à l'Étranger	**CPPC**	Caribbean Plant Protection Committee (FAO) = CPFC
CPML	Centre for Petroleum & Mineral Law & Policy	**CPPCC**	Chinese People's Political Consultative Conference
CPMM	Comité de la Protection du Milieu Marin (OMCI) = MEPC	**CPPED**	Conseil Panafricain pour la Protection de l'Environnement et le Développement (Mauritania)
CPMP	Committee for Proprietary Medicinal Products (EU)	**CPPG**	Cable Programme Providers Group (*now* EPPG)
CPMR	Conference of Peripheral and Maritime Regions of the EEC = CRPM	**CPPPD**	Centre de la Planification, des Projections et des Politiques Relatives au Développement (UN)
CPN	Communist Party of Nepal		
CPN	Communist Party of the Netherlands	**CPPS**	Centre Panafricain de Prospective Sociale (Benin)
CPN	Cuerpo de la Policía Nacional	**CPPS**	Comisión Permanente del Pacifico Sur
CPNA	Commission Paritaire Nationale pour les Entreprises Agricoles	**CPPS**	Congregatio Missionariorum Pretiossimi Sanguinis
CPNA	Community Psychiatric Nurses' Association	**CPPS**	Sisters of the Most Precious Blood of O'Fallon (U.S.A.)
CPNB	Collectieve Propaganda van het Nederlandse Boek	**CPR**	Canadian Pacific Railway
CPNCÉP	Chambre Professionnelle Nationale des Conseillers de l'Économie Privée	**CPR**	Centre for Policy Research (India, U.S.A.)
		CPR	Centre of Polish Research (Canada)
CPNT	Comité Panamericano de Normas Técnicas (Argentina)	**CPR**	Comité de Politique Régionale (CE)
CPNZ	Communist Party of New Zealand	**CPR**	Committee of Permanent Representatives
		CPR	Conferencia Peruana de Religiosos

CPR	Croatian Party of Rights = HSP	**CPSA**	Canadian Political Science Association = ACSP
CPRA	Chinese Public Relations Association	**CPSA**	Civil and Public Services Association
CPRA	Comité Permanent de la Recherche Agricole (CE) = SCAR	**CPSA**	Clay Pigeon Shooting Association
CPRE	Council for the Protection of Rural England	**CPSA**	Comité Permanent des Structures Agricoles (CE)
CPREA	Canadian Peace Research and Education Association = ACREP	**CPSA**	Conservative Party of South Africa = KPSA
CPRF	Committee for the Peaceful Reunification of the Fatherland (Democratic People's Republic of Korea)	**CPSC**	Colombo Plan Staff College for Technician Education (Philippines)
		CPSC	Consumer Products Safety Commission (U.S.A.)
CPRF	Communist Party of the Russian Federation	**CPSE**	Committee on Plant Supply and Establishment
CPRH	Conférence on Peace Research in History (U.S.A.)	**CPSFA**	Comité Permanent de Soutien aux Femmes (Martinique)
CPRI	Canadian Peace Research Institute	**CPSG**	China Policy Study Group
CPRI	Central Potato Research Institute (India)	**CPSMA**	Catholic Primary School Managers' Association (Éire)
CPRI	Central Psi Research Institute (U.S.A.)	**CPSP**	Communist Party of the Spanish People = PCPE
CPRM	Companhia de Pesquisas de Recursos Minerais (Brazil)	**CPSR**	Computer Professionals for Social Responsibility
CPRM	Companhia Portuguesa Radio Marconi	**CPSSU**	Civil and Public Services Staff Union (Éire)
CPRO-DLO	DLO Centrum voor Plantenveredelings- en Reproduktieonderzoek (Netherlands)		
CPRPA	Cyprus Public Relations Professional Association	**CPST**	Comité de la Politique Scientifique et Technologie (OCDE) = CSTP
CPRS	Canadian Public Relations Society	**CPSU**	Civil and Public Service Union (Éire)
CPRW	Council for the Protection of Rural Wales = CDCW	**CPT**	Canadian Pacific Telecommunications
CPS	Canadian Phytopathological Society	**CPT**	Central Puertorriqueña de Trabajadores
CPS	Carnivorous Plant Society	**CPT**	Comissão Pastoral da Terra (Brazil)
CPS	Centre for Policy Studies	**CPT**	Communist Party of Tajikistan
CPS	Centre for Public Services	**CPT**	Communist Party of Thailand
ČPS	Česká Parazitologická Společnost = CSP	**CPT**	Communist Party of Turkey
CPS	China Planning Society	**CPT**	Confederación Paraguaya de Trabajadores
CPS	Chinese Pathophysiological Society		
CPS	Chinese Pediatric Society	**CPT**	Confederation of British Road Passenger Transport
CPS	Chinese Petroleum Society	**CPTA**	China Packaging Technology Association
CPS	Chinese Pharmacology Society		
CPS	Chinese Physical Society	**CPTB**	Clay Products Technical Bureau
CPS	Citizens Protection Society	**CPTC**	China Productivity and Trade Centre
CPS	Commission du Pacifique Sud = SPC	**CPTE**	Comité Permanent des Transports Européens
CPS	Committee for Penicillin Sensitivity		
CPS	Communist Party of Scotland	**CPTM**	Commissioner of Patents and Trade Marks (U.S.A.)
CPS	Communist Party of Spain = PCE	**CPTS**	Coalition for Peace Through Strength (U.S.A.)
CPS	Contemporary Photo Society (China)		
CPS	Crown Prosecution Service	**CPTT**	Central Panameña de Trabajadores del Transporte
CPS	Suore Missionarie del Preziosissimo Sangue		

CPU	China Pharmaceutical University	**CRA**	Chinese Rheumatology Association
CPU	Commonwealth Press Union	**CRA**	Commercial Rabbit Association
CPU	Communist Party of Ukraine	**CRA**	Community Radio Association
CPU	Corporacion de Promocion Universitaria (Chile)	**CRA**	Computing Research Association
		CRA	Concrete Repair Association
CPUSA	Communist Party of the United States of America	**CRA**	Confederaciones Rurales Argentinas
		CRA	County Registrars' Association (Éire)
CPUSTAL	Congreso Permanente de Unidad Sindical de los Trabajadores de América Latina	**CRA**	Crime Reporters Association
		CRA Terre	Centre International de Recherches et d'Application pour la Construction en Terre
CPV	Centrale Proefstations Vereniging		
CPWA	China Printing Workers Association	**CRAA**	Centre de Recherches Agro-Alimentaire (Zaïre)
CPWC	Central Peoples Workers Council (Burma)	**CRAAM**	Centro de Radio-Astonomia e Astrofisica Universidade Mackenzie (Brazil)
CPWD	Central Public Works Department (India)		
CQCA	China Quality Control Association	**CRAB**	Centre for Research Aquatic Biology
CQCJ	Comité des Questions Constitutionnelles et Juridiques (FAO) = CCLM	**CRAC**	Careers Research and Advisory Centre
		CRAC	Centre Régional d'Action Culturelle (ACI) = RCAC, RCCA
CQEE	Conseil du Québec de l'Enfance Exceptionnelle	**CRAC**	Centre Régional d'Action Culturelle (Togo)
CQRI	Centre Québécois de Relations Internationales	**CRACAC**	Centre for Research on Arabic and the Culture of the Arab Countries (Belgium) = COACAL
CQS	Chapter of Quantity Surveyors of the South African Institute of Architects		
		CRACCUS	Comité Régional de l'Afrique Centrale pour la Conservation et l'Utilisation des Sols
CQVB	Centre Québecois de Valorisation de la Biomasse		
CQYA	Chinese Quyi Artists Association	**CRACFT**	Centre Régional Africain de Conception et de Fabrication Techniques = ARCEDEM
CR	Cancer Research		
CR	Collegium Romanicum	**CRAD**	Centre de Recherche en Aménagement et en Développement (Canada)
CR	Comités Révolutionnaires (Burkina Faso)		
CR	Community of the Resurrection (CofE)	**CRAD**	Committee for Research into Apparatus for the Disabled
CR	Confédération de la Récupération (Belgium)	**CRADAT**	Centre Régional Africain d'Administration du Travail (Cameroon)
CR	Congregatio a Resurrectione		
CR	Coordination Rurale	**CRAE**	Center for Research and Application in Ergonomics (France)
CR	Council of Representatives (Russia)		
CR	Ordo Clericorum Regularium vulgo Theatinorum	**CRAÉ**	Centre de Recherches Agronomiques d'État (Belgium)
		CRAE	Committee for the Reform of Animal Experimentation
CR LTD	Community Regeneration Ltd		
CRA	Canadian Rheumatism Association	**CRAF**	Centre de Recherches Africaines
CRA	Centres de la Recherche Appliquée(Zaïre)	**CRAF**	Comité Régional d'Arboriculture Fruitière du Bassin Parisien
CRA	Centres de Recherches Agronomiques	**CRAG**	Cellular Radio Advisory Group
CRA	Chemical Recovery Association (*now* CORA)	**CRAIC**	Centre de Recherches Économiques, Agricoles, Industrielles et Commerciales
CRA	China Research Associates (U.S.A.)		

CRAM	Centre de Recherche sur l'Afrique Méditerranéenne
CRAM	Centre for Research into Asian Migration
CRAM	Collectivités Rurales Autochones Modernisées à Madagascar
CRAME	Compania Radio Aerea Maritima Española
Cramp	Concerned Residents Against Moral Pollution (Tasmania)
CRANN	Crann Sa Chathair (Woodland Management Trust)
CRAPE	Centre de Recherches Anthropologiques Préhistoriques et Ethnographiques (Algeria)
CRAQP	China Research Association of Qualified Personnel
CRAR	Committee for the Recovery of Archeological Remains (U.S.A.)
CRAS	Centre for Radiobiology and Radiation Protection (Netherlands)
CRAT	Centre Régional Africain de Technologie (Senegal) = ARCT
CRAT	Centre Rural d'Appui Technique (Cameroon)
CRATEMA	Centro di Ricerca di Assistenza Tecnica e Mercantile alle Aziende
CRATO	Centre Régionale de Recherche et de Documentation pour la Tradition Orale
CRAU	Centre de Recherches d'Architecture et d'Urbanisme (Belgium)
CRAV	Comisión de la Reforma Agraria y la Vivienda (Peru)
CRB	Centre Suisse de Rationalisation du Bâtiment
CRB	Confederação Rural Brasileira
CRB	Confederation of Roma in Bulgaria = KRB
CRB	Conferéncia dos Religiosos do Brasil
CRB	Conselho Regional de Biblioteconomia
CRBF	Commission Royale Belge de Folklore
CRBL	Campaign for a Real Broad Left
CRBM	Centre Régional de Biologie Marine = RMBC
CRC	Cancer Research Campaign
CRC	Centre d'Études et de Recherches des Chefs d'Entreprises
CRC	Centre de Recherches Techniques et Scientifiques Industries de la Tannerie, de la Chaussure, de la Pantoufle et des autres Industries Transformatrices du Cuir (Belgium)
CRC	Chemical Rubber Company
CRC	Clinical Research Centre
CRC	Confederation of Roofing Contractors Ltd
CRC	Conférence Religieuse Canadienne
CRC	Conferencia de Religiosos de Colombia
CRC	Constitutional Recommendation Committee (Nepal)
CRC	Constitutional Reform Centre
CRC	Cotton Research Corporation
CRC	Cuba Resource Center (U.S.A.)
CRCA	Caisse Régionale de Crédit Agricole
CRCA	Comissão Reguladora do Comércio de Arroz (Portugal)
CRCAM	Caisse Régionale de Crédit Agricole Mutuel
CRCC	Canadian Red Cross Committee
CRCE	Centre for Research into Communist Economies
CRCI	Car Rental Council of Ireland (Éire)
CRCP	Costa Rican Cocoa Products Co.
CRCPI	Coordinating Research Council of the Petroleum Industry (U.S.A.)
CRCS	Canadian Red Cross Society
CRCSHM	Cooperative Research Centre for Southern Hemisphere Meteorology
CRD	Centre de Recherches et de Documentation de l'Association Universelle pour l'Esperanto
CRD	Centre for Research and Documentation
CRD	Centre of Reviews and Dissemination (NHS)
CRD	Committee on Energy Research and Development (OECD)
CRD	Conservative Research Department
CRDB	Cooperative and Rural Development Bank (Tanzania)
CRDC	Cotton Research and Development Corporation
CRDÉ	Centre de Recherches en Développement Économique (Canada)
CRDF	Conseil de la Recherche et du Développement Forestiers (Canada)
CRDH	Centre de Recherche en Développement Humain (Canada)
CRDI	Cement Research and Development Institute (Pakistan)
CRDI	Centre de Recherches pour le Développement International (Canada) = CIID, IDRC

CRDLP	Centre for Research and Documentation of the Language Problem
CRDME	Committee for Research into Dental Materials and Equipment
CRDP	Centre de Recherche en Droit Public (Canada)
CRDS	Centre de Recherches et de Documentation du Sénégal
CRDTL	Caribbean Regional Drug Testing Laboratory (Jamaica)
CRDTO	Regional Documentation Centre for Oral Tradition (Niger)
CRE	Cadena Radial Ecuatoriana
CRE	Campaign for Real Education
CRE	Casse de Retraites de Expatriés
CRE	Centre Rencontres Européennes
CRE	Coal Research Establishment
CRE	Commercial Relations Export Department
CRE	Commission for Racial Equality
CRE	Conference of the Regions of Europe
CRE	Standing Conference of Rectors, Presidents and Vice-Chancellors of the European Universities (Switzerland)
CRÉA	Centre de Recherche Économiques Appliquées (Senegal)
CRÉA	Centre de Recherches et d'Études Agricoles
CREA	Centre for Anthropological Studies and Research (Cameroon)
CREA	Centre for Regional Economic Analysis (Australia)
CREA	Centro de Reconversión Económica del Austro (Ecuador)
CREA	Centro Regional de Educación de Adultos (Venezuela)
CREA	Consejo Nacional de Recursos para le Atención de la Juventud (Mexico)
CREA	Consorcio Regional de Experimentación Agrícola (Argentina)
CRÉA	Consortium pour la Recherche Économique en Afrique (Kenya) = AERC
CRÉA	Coopérative Régionale d'Équipement Agricole
CRÉAA	Conseil Régional d'Éducation et Alphabétisation des Adultes d'Afrique
CREACUS	Comité Régional de l'Afrique Orientale pour la Conservation et l'Utilisation du Sol =EARCCUS

CRÉAD	Centre d'Études et de Recherches en Économie Appliquée pour le Developpement (Algeria)
CREAGRAF	Centro Regional de Estudios Especializados Artes Gráficas (Costa Rica)
CREAI	Carteira de Credito Agricola e Industrial (Brazil)
CREAM	Centre Régional de l'Enseignement et de l'Apprentissage Maritimes (Ivory Coast)
CREATI	Centre de Recherches et d'Études pour l'Automatisation des Processus et Techniques Industrielles
CRECIT	Centre de Recherches Essais et Contrôles Scientifiques pour l'Industrie Textile (Belgium)
CRED	Campaign for Rational Economic Debate
CRED	Center for Research on Economic Development (U.S.A.)
CRED	Centre for Research on the Epidemiology of Disaster (Belgium)
CREDAF	Centre de Rencontres et d'Études des Dirigeants des Administrations Fiscales
CREDAL	Centre de Recherche et de Documentation sur l'Amerique Latine (France)
CREDEC	Centre Régional de Recherche et de Documentation pour le Développement Culturel (Senegal)
CREDI CODI	Crédit de la Côte d'Ivoire
CRÉDIF	Centre de Recherche et d'Étude pour la Diffusion du Français
CRÉDILA	Centre de Recherches d'Études et de Documentation sur les Institutions et la Législation Africaines (Senegal)
CREDIOP	Consorzio di Credito per le Opere Pubbliche
CREDISA	Asociación de Ahorro y Prestamo Credito Inmobiliario S.A. (El Salvador)
CREDISA	Crédito Inmobiliario (El Salvador)
CREDO	Center for Curriculum Renewal and Educational Development Overseas (U.S.A.)
CREDO	Network of Centres for Research, Education and Development of Organisations
CREDOC	Centre de Recherches et de Documentation sur la Consommation

CRÉDOP	Centre de Recherche d'Étude et de Documentation en Publicité (Belgium)	**CREPS**	Compagnie de Recherches et d'Exploitation de Pétrole du Sahara
CRÉE	Conseil des Relations Économique Extérieure (Lebanon)	**CRER**	Centre for Research on Ethnic Relations
CREÉA	Comité Régional d'Expansion Économique de l'Auvergne	**CRÉRMA**	Conseillers Régionaux d'Étude de la Rentabilité du Machinisme Agricole
CREÉGIM	Conseil Régional d'Expansion Économique de la Gaspérie et des Îles-de-la-Madeleine (Canada)	**CRÉS**	Centre de Recherches Économiques et Sociales
CREES	Centre for Russian and East European Studies (Canada, U.K.)	**CRES**	Centre for Research into Environmental Systems
CREFAL	Centro Regional de Educación Fundamental para la America Latina (Mexico)	**CRES**	Centre for Resource and Environmental Studies (ANU)
CREFOGA	Crédit Foncier du Gabon	**CRÉS**	Centre Régional d'Énergie Solaire (Mali)
CREG	Centre for Research & Education on Gender	**CRES**	Chinese Rare Earth Society
CREI	Centro Regional para la Enseñanza de la Informática (Spain)	**CRÉSA**	Centre de Recherches Économiques et Sociales Appliquées
CRÉIPAC	Centre de Rencontres et d'Échanges Internationaux du Pacifique Sud	**CRESA**	Centro Ricerca per l'Economia, l'Organizzazione e l'Amministrazione della Sanita
CRÉL	Centre de Recherches et d'Études Linguistiques	**CRESAL**	Centre de Recherches et d'Études Sociologique Appliquées de la Loire (France)
CREMER-CA	Continental de Creditos Mercantiles, C.A. (Venezuela)	**CRESALC**	Centro Regional de Educación Superior en America Latine y el Caribe (UNESCO)
CREN	Corporation for Research and Educational Networking	**CRESALC**	Comité Régional de Educación Sexual para Latinoamerica y el Caribe (Colombia)
CRENO	Conférénce des Régions de l'Europe du Nord-Ouest = CRENWE, CRONWE, KRENWE	**CRESHS**	Centre de Recherches en Sciences Humaines et Sociales (Haiti)
CRENWE	Conference of Regions of North-West Europe = CRENO, CRONWE, KRENWE	**CRÉSM**	Centre de Recherches et d'Études sur les Sociétés Méditerranéennes
CRÉO	Centre de Recherches et d'Études Océanographiques	**CRÉSM**	Centre de Recherches et d'Études sur les Sociétés Musulmanes
CREOC	Centro Ricerche Economiche ed Operative della Cooperazione	**CRESME**	Centro Richerche Economiche Sociologiche e di Mercato nell'Edilizia
CREOEC	China Rural Export-Oriented Economy Society	**CRÉSPA**	Centre Régional d'Études Supérieures pour la Préparation aux Affaires
CRÉP	Centre de Recherche Économique sur l'Épargne	**CRESR**	Centre for Regional & Social Research
		CRÉSR	Centre Régional d'Études Socio-Religieuses
CREPA	Centre Régional pour l'Eau Potable et l'Assainissement à Faible Coût (ICHS) (Burkina Faso)	**CRESS**	Centre for Research in Earth and Space Science (Canada)
CREPCO	Consejo de Reajuste de los Precios de la Construccion (Peru)	**CREST**	Comité de la Recherche Scientifique et Technique (CE)
CRÉPÉM	Centre de Recherches et d'Études pour une Éducation Mondialiste	**CReSTeD**	Council for the Registration of Schools Teaching Dyslexic Pupils
CREPLA	Centre Régional de Promotion de Livre en Afrique (Cameroon)	**CRET**	Commission Régionale Européenne de Tourisme
CREPS	Centre Régional d'Éducation Physique et Sportive	**CRETC**	Comisión Reguladora de Tarifas de Comunicaciones (Peru)

CRETÉ	Association des Correspondants des Radios et des Télévisions Étrangères
CRETT	Comisión Reguladora de Tarifas de Transporte (Peru)
CRETUR	Credito de Turismo, S.A. (Honduras)
CREW	Centre for Research on European Women (Belgium)
CRF	Calendar Reform Foundation (U.S.A.)
CRF	Conservation and Research Foundation (U.S.A.)
CRFA	Canadian Restaurant and Foodservers Association
CRFB	Centre de Recherches du Fer-Blanc
CRFESC	Commission de la République Française pour l'Education, la Science et la Culture
CRFM	Comité de Coordination de la Recherche Forestière Méditerranéenne
CRFT	Comitetul Român de Fotogrammetrie si Teledetectie
CRG	Centre de Recherches de Gorsem
CRGM	Centre de Recherches Géologiques et Minières (Zaire)
CRGM	Comité de la Recherche Géologique et Minière (FEGECE)
CRHCS	Commonwealth Regional Health Community Secretariat for East Central and Southern Africa (Tanzania)
CRHRE	Centre for Research of Human Resources and the Environment (Indonesia)
CRI	Caribbean Research Institute
CRI	Cement Research Institute (India)
CRI	Central Research Institute (India)
CRI	Centre de Recherches Industrielles (Belgium)
CRI	Centre for the Study of Regulated Industries
CRI	Children's Relief International
CRI	Clinical Research Institute (South Korea)
CRI	Coconut Research Institute (Sri Lanka)
CRI	Comité de Recherche en Informatique
CRI	Conference of Religious of India
CRI	Cotton Research Institute (China)
CRI	Croce Rossa Italiana
CRI	Croix Rouge Internationale = IRC, IRK
CRI	National Criminal Intelligence Service (Netherlands)
CRIA	Caisse de Retraite Interentreprises Agricoles
CRIA	Centre de Recherches sur les Trypanosomiases Animales (Central Africa)
CRIA	Council on Religion and International Affairs (U.S.A.)
CRIAA	China Research Institute of Aero-Accessories
CRIAA	Collectif de Recherche et d'Information sur Afrique Australe
CRIABD	Centre International Chrétien de Recherche d'Information et d'Analyse de la Bande Dessinée = ICCC
CRIAC	Centre de Recherches Industriales de l'Afrique Centrale
CRIBC	Central Research Institute of Building and Construction (China)
CRIC	Centre de Recherches de l'Industrie Belge de la Céramique
CRIC	Centre de Recherches Industrielles sur Contrats
CRIC	Centre de Relations Internationales Culturelles
CRIC	Centre National de Recherches Scientifiques et Techniques pour l'Industrie Cimentière (Belgium)
CRIC	Centro Regionale d'Intervento per la Cooperazione
CRIC	Commercial Radio International Committee
CRIC	Congregatio Canonicorum Regularium Immaculatae Conceptionis Beatae Virginis Mariae
CRIC	Consejo Regional Indígena del Cauca (Colombia)
CRICCAL	Centre de Recherches Interuniversitaire sur les Champs Cultures en Amérique Latine
CRICT	Centre for Research into Innovation & Culture Technology
CRID	Centre de Recherche et d'Information pour le Développement (France)
CRID	Centre pour la Recherche Interdisciplinaire sur le Développement (Belgium)
CRIDAOL	Centro Regional de Investigación y Desarrollo Agraria de Galicia
CRIDÉ	Centre de Recherches Interdisciplinaires Droit-Économie (Belgium)
CRIDÉ	Centre de Recherches Interdisciplinaires pour le Développement de l'Éducation (Zaïre)

CRIDEV	Centre Rennais pour le Développement et la Libération des Peuples
CRIDON	Centre de Recherches d'Information et de Documentation Notariales
CRIE	Centro Regional de Informaciones Ecuménicas (Mexico)
CRIEL	Comité Interprofessional des Eaux-de-vie du Languedoc
CRIEPI	Central Research Institute of the Electrical Power Industry (Japan)
CRIES	Coordinadora Regional de Investigaciones Económicas y Sociales (Nicaragua)
CRIET	Comités Réunis de l'Industrie d'Ennoblissement Textile dans le CE
CRIF	Centre de Recherches Scientifiques et Techniques de l'Industrie des Fabrications Métalliques (Belgium)
CRIF	Conseil Représentatif des Institutions Juives de France
CRIFC	Central Research Institute for Food Crops (Indonesia)
CRIG	Cocoa Research Institute of Ghana
CRII	Centre de Recherches sur les Institutions Internationales (Switzerland)
CRIJAF	Central Research Institute for Jute and Allied Fibres (India)
CRILA	Circulo de Radioterapeutas Ibero-Latinoamericanas (Caracas)
CRILC	Canadian Research Institute of Launderers and Cleaners
CRILJ	Centre de Recherche et d'Information sur la Littérature de Jeunesse
CRIM	Centro Regional de Informática de la Mujer (Chile)
CRIM	Clinical Research Institute of Montreal
CRIMES	Child Rape and Incest Merit Effective Sentencing
CRIMM	Changsha Research Institute of Mining and Metallurgy
CRIN	Cacao Research Institute of Nigeria
CRINA	Centre de Recherche International de Nutrition Animale
CRIPSA	Centre for Research into Primary Science & Technology
CRIPST	China Research Institute of Printing Science and Technology
CRIQ	Centre de Recherche Industrielle de Québec (Canada)
CRISA	Car Radio Industry Specialists' Association
CRISOL	Corriente de Renovacion Independiente y Solidaridad Laboral (Bolivia)
CRISOL	Cristianos Solidarios (Nicaragua)
CRISP	Car Radio Industry Specialists Association
CRISP	Centre de Recherche et d'Information Sociopolitiques (Belgium)
CRIT	Centre for Research into Teaching
CRIT	Co-ordinating Centre for Regional Information Training (Kenya)
CRIWI	Research Institute of the Wood Industry (China)
CRJ	Commission for Racial Justice
CRK	Centraal Registratie-Kantoor Detailhandel-Ambacht
CRL	Canonici Regolari della Congregazione del Sanctissimo Salvatore Lateranense
CRL	Cholera Research Laboratory (Bangladesh)
CRLC	Coopérative Régionale Lainière du Centre
CRLS	Coastguard Radio Liaison Station
CRM	Centrale Raad voor de Milieuhygiène
CRM	Centre de Recherches Métallurgiques (Belgium)
CRM	Committee on the Review of Medicines (DOH)
CRM	Compagnie Radio-Maritime
CRM	Coordinadora Revolucionaria de Masas (El Salvador)
CRM Soc	Charles Rennie Mackintosh Society
CRMAC	Centre de Recherche sur le Monde Arabe (Belgium)
CRMÉ	Centre Régional de Mouvements d'Énergie
CRME	Committee on Research in Medical Economics (U.S.A.)
CRME	Council for Research in Music Education
CRMP	Coastal Resources Management Project (ASEAN/U.S.A.)
CRMS	Centro Ricerche Malattie della Selvaggina
CRN	Co-op Reform Network
CRN	Countryside Recreation Network
CRNA	Campaign for the Restoration of the National Anthem and Flag
CRNL	Chalk River Nuclear Laboratories (AECL)
CRO	Cave Rescue Organization of Great Britain

CRO	Citizens' Rights Office		**CRPG**	Centre de Recherches Pétrographiques et Géochimiques (France)
CRO	Commissie voor Rassenonderzoek van Groenvoedergewassen		**CRPG**	Conseil Régional du Patronat de la Guadeloupe
CRO	Companies Registration Office		**CRPL**	Central Radio Propagation Laboratory (U.S.A.)
CRO	Conseil de la Recherche Océanologique			
CROACUS	Comité Régional de l'Afrique Occidentale pour la Conservation et l'Utilisation du Sol		**CRPL**	Centre for Research into Philosophy & Literature
			CRPLF	Communauté des Radios Publiques de Langue Française
CROC	Confederación Revolucionaria de Obreros y Campesinos (Mexico)		**CRPM**	Conférence des Régions Periphériques Maritimes de la CEE = CPMR
CRODT	Centre de Recherches Océanographiques de Dakar-Thiaroye (Senegal)		**CRPP**	Centre de Recherches en Physique des Plasmas (Switzerland)
CROM	Confederación Regional Obrera Mexicana		**CRPPH**	Committee on Radiation Protection and Public Health (OECD/NEA)
CROMAR	Croatian Marketing Association		**CRPQF**	Comissão Reguladora dos Productos Químicos e Farmacéuticos (Portugal)
CRONWE	Conferentie voor Regionale Ontwikkeling in Noord-West Europa = CRENO, CRENWE, KRENWE		**CRR**	Centre de Recherches Rizicoles de Djibelor (Senegal)
CROSS	Comprehensive Rural Operations Service Society (India)		**CRR**	Centre de Recherches Routières (Belgium)
CROSSA	Centre Régional Opérationnel de Surveillance et de Sauvetage pour l'Atlantique		**CRRAG**	Countryside Recreation Research Advisory Group
			CRREL	Cold Regions Research and Engineering Laboratory (U.S.A.)
CROSSMA	Centre Régional Opérationnel de Surveillance et de Sauvetage pour la Manche		**CRRI**	Central Rice Research Institute (India)
			CRRI	Central Road Research Institute (India)
CROWC	Central Rights of Way Committee		**CRRL**	Central Reference and Research Library (Ghana)
CROWD	Central Registry of World Dancers (U.S.A.)		**CRRP**	Community Rainforest Reforestation Program
CRP	C. Rudolf Poensgen Stiftung zur Förderung von Führungskraften in der Wirtschaft e. V.		**CRRS**	Central Rainlands Research Station (Sudan)
CRP	Canonici Regolari Premonstratensi = OPraem		**CRS**	Catholic Record Society
			CRS	Catholic Relief Services (U.S.A.)
CRP	Central Reserve Police (India)		**CRS**	Centrala Rolnicza Spódzielni "Samopomoc Chłopska"
CRP	Centre de Recherche Physique			
CRP	Christian Republican Party (Bulgaria)		**CRS**	Centre for Resource Studies (Canada)
CRP	Civil Rights Party (Korea)		**CRS**	Centre for Retail Studies (Éire)
CRP	Comandos Revolucionarios del Pueblo (Peru)		**CRS**	Cereals Research Station
			CRS	China Railway Society
CRP	Community Rights Project		**CRS**	Christian Rescue Service
CRP	Constitutional Rights Project (Nigeria)		**CRS**	Compagnies Républicaines de Sécurité
CRPAO	Comisión Regional de Pesca para el Africa Occidental		**CRS**	Conflict Research Society
			CRS	Council for Resolution and Settlement (Afghanistan)
CRPB	Clyde River Purification Board			
CRPE	Centre de Recherches en Physique de l'Environnement Terrestre et Solaire		**CRS**	Ordo Clericorum Regularium a Somascha
CRPE	Centre for Research into Primary Education		**CRSA**	Centre of Research in Administrative Sciences (Canada)

CRSA	Cold Rolled Sections Association		**CRTC**	Clay Roofing Tile Council
CRSA	Ordo Canonicorum Regularium Sancti Augustini		**CRTK**	Centre Régional de Télédetection, Kinshasa (Zaïre)
CRSÉSFPI	Centre de Recherches Statistiques, Économiques et Sociales et de Formation pour les Pays Islamiques (Turkey) = SESRTCIC		**CRTPB**	Canadian Radio Technical Planning Board
			CRTU	Congress of Russian Trade Unions
			CRTUA	Confederation of Russian Trade Union Associations
CRSFS	Chinese Research Society for Future Studies		**CRTV**	Cameroon Radio and Television
CRSIM	Centre de Recherches Scientifiques, Industrielles et Maritimes		**CRU**	Centre de Recherche d'Urbanisme
			CRU	Co-Operatives Research Unit
CRSLE	Chinese Research Society of Land Economics		**CRUCH**	Consejo de Rectores de Universidades Chilenas
CRSMM	Chinese Research Society for Modernization of Management		**CRUEA**	Centre de Recherche des Utilisations des Énergies Alternatives (Burundi)
CRSN	Centre de Recherche en Sciences Neurologiques (Canada)		**CRUESI**	Centre de Recherches pour l'Utilisation de l'Eau Salée en Irrigation (Tunisia)
CRSOA	County Road Safety Officers Association		**CRUFA**	Conférence des Recteurs des Universités Francophones d'Afrique
CRSP	Centre for Research into Social Policy		**CRULIFE**	Crusade for Life (Nigeria)
CRSQS	Chinese Research Society of Qigong Science		**Cruse**	National Organisation for the Widowed and their Children
CRSSA	Centre de Recherches du Service de Santé des Armées		**CRUTAC**	Centro Rural Universitario de Treinamento e de Acao Comunitaria (Brazil)
CRST	Commission de Recherches Scientifiques et Techniques (OUA) = STRC		**CRWPC**	Canadian Radio Wave Propagation Committee
CRSTE	Chinese Research Society of Technology Economics		**CRWRC**	Christian Reformed World Relief Committee (U.S.A.)
CRSV	Centre de Recherches Science Vie		**CRYM**	Comisión Reguladora de la Produción y Comercio de la Yerba Mate (Argentina)
CRSVI	Conférence Régionale du Service Volontaire International = RCIVS		**CRZZ**	Centralna Rada Związków Zawodowych
CRT	Centre de Recherche sur les Transports (Canada)		**CS**	Café Society
CRT	Centre for Rural Transport		**CS**	Chocolate Society
CRT	Centro di Ricerca per il Teatro		**CS**	Chromatography Society
CRT	Confederación Revolucionaria de Trabajadores (Mexico)		**CS**	Cliometric Society
			CS	Coleopterists Society
CRT	Conférence Rail Tourisme		**CS**	Commonwealth Secretariat
CRT	Shipowners' Refrigerated Cargo Research Association		**CS**	Concrete Society
CRTA	Centre de Recherche sur les Trypanosomoses Animales (Burkina Faso)		**CS**	Congregatio Missionariorum a Sancto Carolo 'Scalabriniani'
			CS	Congregatio Missionariorum a Sancto Carolo = PSSC
CRTA	Colombo Rubber Traders Association (Sri Lanka)		**CS**	Conservation Society
CRTA	Conselho Regional Tecnicos Administração (Brazil)		**CS**	Constantian Society (U.S.A.)
			CS	Cultural Survival
CRTC	Canadian Radio Television and Telecommunications Commission		**CS**	Cyclamen Society
			CSA	Campaign for a Scottish Assembly

CSA	Canadian Standards Association	CSAC	Catholic Scout Advisory Council
CSA	Caribbean Shipping Association (Jamaica	CSAC	Pallottine Sisters of the Catholic Apostolate
CSA	Caribbean Studies Association (U.S.A.) = AEC	CSAE	Canadian Society of Agricultural Engineering = SCGR
CSA	Casualty Surgeons Association (*now* BAEM)	CSAE	Chinese Society of Agricultural Engineering
CSA	Centralförbundet för Socialt Arbete	CSAEP	Chinese Society of Agro-Environmental Protection
CSA	Centro Studi Adriatici	CSAF	Centro di Sperimentazione Agricola e Forestale
ČSA	Československá Aerolinie		
CSA	Chambre Syndicale de l'Amiante	CSAI	Italian Automobile Sporting Commission
CSA	Channel Swimming Association		
CSA	Chemical Structure Association	CSALT	Canadian Society for the Advancement of Legal Technology
CSA	Child Support Agency		
CSA	Chinese Society of Agronomy	CSAM	Chinese Society of Agricultural Machinery
CSA	Chinese Society of Anatomy		
CSA	Chinese Society of Anesthesiology	CSAM	Conseil Supérieur de l'Aviation Marchande
CSA	Chinese Society of Astronautics		
CSA	Chinese Sports Association	CSAO	Shaanxi Astronomical Observatory
CSA	Choir Schools' Association	CSAP	Canadian Society of Animal Production
CSA	Civil Service Alliance (Éire)	CSAR	Compagnie Sénégalaise d'Assurance et de Réassurances
CSA	Civil Service Assembly (Canada, U.S.A.)	CSARE	Centro di Studi Applicazioni Risorse Energetiche
CSA	Civil Service Association (Guyana)		
CSA	Collectif Strategies Alimentaires	CSAS	Centre for Southern African Studies
CSA	Communauté Suisse de Travail pour l'Aphasie = SAA	CSAT	Colegio Superior de Agricultura Tropical (Mexico)
CSA	Computer Science Association (Canada)	CSATA	Centro Studi e Applicazioni in Tecnologie Avanzate
CSA	Computing Services Association		
CSA	Computing Systems Services Association (U.S.A.)	CSATCO	Child Support Appeal Central Office
		CSATM	Confédération Sud-Américaine de Tennis de Table (Uruguay)
CSA	Confédération Syndicale des Avocats		
CSA	Conseil Supérieur d'Audio Visuel	ČSAZ	Česká Akademie Zemědělská
CSA	Conseil Supérieur de l'Agriculture	CSB	Centre for Structural Biochemistry (Sweden)
CSA	Costume Society of Scotland		
CSA	Council for Scottish Archaeology	CSB	Confédération Syndicale Burkinabê (Burkina Faso)
CSA	Creative Services Association		
CSA	Credit Services Association (*ex* CAA)	CSB	Congregation of Saint Basil
CSA	Cryogenic Society of America	CSB	Conseil Supérieur des Bibliothèques
CSAA	Canadian Sociology and Anthropology Association = ACSA	CSB	Consejo Superior Bancario
		CSBC	Canadian Society for Cell Biology
CSAA	China Society of Aeronautics and Astronautics	CSBE	Chinese Society of Biomedical Engineering
CSAA	China Sulphuric Acid Association	CSBF	Civil Service Benevolent Fund
CSAA	Confederación Sudamericano de Atletismo	CSBNTP	Chambre Syndicale Belge des Négociants en Timbres Poste
CSAB	Civil Service Appeal Board	CSBP	Chambre Syndicale des Banques Populaires de France
CSAC	Alliance Cocoa Scientific Advisory Committee	CSBS	Canadian Society of Biblical Studies = SCEB

CSBTA	Civil Service Blind Telephonists' Association (Éire)	**CSCE**	Canadian Society for Civil Engineering
CSBVF	Chambre Syndicale de la Boulonnerie et de la Visserie Forgées	**CSCE**	Coffee, Sugar and Cocoa Exchange
CSC	Canadian Saltfish Corporation	**CSCE**	Conference on Security and Co-operation in Europe (NATO) (*now* OSCE)
CSC	Canadian Society for Chemistry = SCC	**CSCF**	Cast Stone and Concrete Federation
CSC	Catholic Students Council	**CSCFE**	Civil Service Council for Further Education
CSC	Centro Sperimentale di Cinematografia		
CSC	Chambre Syndicale Nationale des Industries de la Conserve	**CSCH**	Canadian Society of Church History = SCHE
CSC	Chinese Society of Cardiology	**ČSCH**	Česká Společnost Chemická
CSC	Christian Service Centre	**CSChE**	Canadian Society for Chemical Engineering = SCGC
CSC	Civil Service Commission		
CSC	Comité Suisse de la Chimie	**CSCN**	Chambre Syndicale des Constructeurs de Navires et de Machines Marines
CSC	Commercial Solvents Corporation (U.S.A.)		
		CSCNWW	Centre for the Study of Christianity in the Non-Western World
CSC	Commission Syndicale Consultative auprès de l'OCDE = TUAC	**CSCo**	Caisse de Stabilisation Cotonnière (Zaïre)
CSC	Commonwealth Science Council		
CSC	Commonwealth Scientific Committee	**CSCP**	Chinese Society of Corrosion and Protection
CSC	Compagnie Sénégalaise de Carrières		
CSC	Computer Society of Canada	**CSCR**	Central Society for Clinical Research (U.S.A.)
CSC	Confédération des Syndicats Chrétiens (Belgium) = ACV	**CSCS**	Centre for the Study of Comprehensive Schools
CSC	Confédération des Syndicats Chrétiens de la Suisse	**CSCS**	China Society of Cotton Science
CSC	Confédération Syndicale Congolaise	**CSCS**	China Steel Construction Society
CSC	Congregatio a Sancto Cruce	**CSCS**	Chinese Society for Crop Sciences
CSC	Congregatio Servorum a Charitate = SC, SdC	**CSCS**	Commonwealth Students Children Society
CSC	Construction Safety Campaign	**CSCSI**	Canadian Society for Computational Studies of Intelligence = SCEIO
CSC	Cuba Solidarity Campaign		
CSC	Cycle-Speedway Council (*now* BCSC)	**CSCT**	Canadian Society for Chemical Technology = SCTC
CSCA	Chambre Syndicale des Constructeurs d'Automobiles	**CSD**	Centre for Sustainable Development
		CSD	Chartered Society of Designers
CSCA	Consejo Superior de los Colegios de Arquitectos de España	**CSD**	Civil Service Department
		CSD	Commission on Sustainable Development (IUCN)
CSCAW	Catholic Study Circle for Animal Welfare		
CSCB	Chinese Society for Cell Biology	**CSD**	Commonwealth Society for the Deaf
CSCB	Committee of Scottish Clearing Bankers	**CSD**	Conférence Suisse des Directeurs des Écoles Professionnelles et des Métiers = SDK
CSCC	Centre for the Study of Communication and Culture		
CSCC	Council of State Chambers of Commerce (U.S.A.)	**CSD**	Consejo Superior de Deportes
		CSD	Consultative Sub-Committee on Surplus Disposal (FAO)
CSCCEFP	Chinese Society of Chemistry and Chemical Engineering of Forest Products	**CSD**	Convergencia Social Democrática (Equatorial Guinea)
CSCE	Canadian Society for Chemical Engineering	**CSD**	Correctional Services Department (Hong Kong)

CSD	United Nations Commission on Sustainable Development		**CSEÉ**	Compagnie des Signaux et d'Entreprises Électriques
CSDC	Commonwealth Spatial Data Committee		**CSÉERI**	Comité Scientifique pour l'Étude des Effets des Radiations Ionisantes (International)
CSDÉM	Chambre Syndicale de l'Édition Musicale		**CSEG**	Canadian Society of Exploration Geophysicists
CSDF	Cold Storage and Distribution Federation (*ex* NCSF)		**CSEI**	Centro Studi di Economia Applicata all'Ingegneria
CSDH	Council of Societies in Dental Hypnosis (U.S.A.)		**CSEI**	Chambre Syndicale des Esthéticiens Industriels
CSDHA	Centre for Social Development and Humanitarian Affairs (UN)		**CSELT**	Centro Studi e Laboratori Telecommunicazioni
CSDI	Changjiang Ship Design Institute		**CSEM**	Centre Séismologique Européo-Méditerranéen = EMSC
CSDN	Chinese Society for Dialectics of Nature		**CSEM**	Chinese Society of Emergency Medicine
CSDPP	Chambre Syndicale de la Distribution des Produits Pétroliers		**CSEMP**	Chambre Syndicale des Emballages en Matières Plastiques
CSDS	Centre for Social and Development Studies (South Africa)		**CSEN**	Centro Superior de Estudios Nucleares (Peru)
CSE	Campaign for State Education		**CSÉP**	Conseil Supérieur de l'Éducation Populaire
CSE	Centre de Sociologie Européenne			
CSE	Centre for Software Engineering		**CSEPE**	Comité Syndical Européen des Personnels Enseignants
ČSE	Česká Společnost Ekonomická		**CSER**	Centre for the Study of Economics and Religion (Canada)
CSE	Chinese Society of Education			
CSE	Chinese Society of Endocrinology		**CSER**	Committee on Solar Electromagnetic Radiation
CSE	Commission Seismologique Européenne = ESC			
CSE	Compagnie Sénégalaise d'Entreprises		**CSERB**	Computer Science and Electronics Requirements Board
CSE	Conférence des Statisticiens Européens		**CSES**	Chinese Society of Environmental Science
CSE	Conference of Socialist Economists		**CSES**	Chinese Solar Energy Society
CSE	Conférence Spatiale Européenne =ESC		**CSES**	Council for Social and Economic Studies (U.S.A.)
CSEA	Chinese Society of Experimental Animals		**CSESP**	Comité Syndical Européen des Services Publiques = EPSC
CSEA	Committee of Student European Associations		**CSÉSS**	Conseil Suisse des Écoles de Service Social = SASSA
CSEABC	Chambre Syndicale des Entreprises Artisanales du Bâtiment		**CSESS**	Cooperative State Experiment Station Service (U.S.A.)
CSÉB	Chambre Syndicale des Électriciens Belges		**CSET**	Chinese Society of Engineering Thermophysics
CSEC	Centre for the Study of Environmental Change		**CSEU**	Civil Service Executive Union (Éire)
CSED	Chinese Society of Endemic Diseases		**CSEU**	Confederation of Shipbuilding and Engineering Unions
CSEDB	Chambre Syndicale des Entrepreneurs de Déménagements Belgique		**CSF**	Canadian Studies Foundation = FEC
CSEE	Canadian Society of Electrical Engineers		**CSF**	China Society of Fisheries
CSEE	Chinese Society of Electrical Engineering		**CSF**	Chinese Society of Forestry
CSEE	Comité Syndical Européen de l'Education = ETUCE			
CSEÉ	Comité Syndical Européen des Personnels de l'Éducation = ETUCE			

CSF	Coil Spring Federation
CSF	Comité des Salines de France
CSF	Compagnie Générale de Télégraphie sans Fil
CSF	Confederación Sudamericana de Fútbol
CSF	Congregatio a Sacra Familia
CSFA	Canadian Scientific Film Association
CSFA	Confédération des Sociétés Françaises d'Architectes
CSFB	Cartophilic Society of Great Britian
CSFC	Central South Forestry College (China)
CSFCO	Co-ordination Staff Foreign and Commonwealth Office
CSFE	Canadian Society of Forest Engineers
CSFIFF	Chambre Syndicale Française des Industriels Fondeurs de Fromage
CSFN	Centro Siciliano de Fisica Nucleare
CSFN	Sisters of the Holy Family of Nazareth; Suore della Sacra Famiglia di Nazareth
CSFP	Commonwealth Scholarship and Fellowship Plan
CSFRA	Coil Spring Federation Research Organisation
CSFSBA	Chambre Syndicale des Fabricants de Supports en Béton Armé Destinés aux Canalisations Aériennes
CSFTI	Committee on Southern Forest Tree Improvement (U.S.A.)
CSFVA	China Science Film and Video Association
CSG	Catholic Stage Guild
CSG	Cetacean Specialist Group (SSC)
CSG	Chinese Society of Gastroenterology
CSG	Chinese Society of Geriatrics
CSGA	Canadian Seed Growers Association
CSGB	Cartophilic Society of Great Britain
CSGPC	Chinese Society of Geodesy, Photogrammetry and Cartography
CSH	Centralna Skladnica Harcerska
CSH	Chambre Suisse de l'Horlogerie
CSH	Chambre Syndicale Horticole
CSHAE	Caribbean Society of Hotel Association Executives (Puerto Rico)
CSHAM	Chinese Society of High Altitude Medicine
CSHB	Chambre Syndicale de l'Horticulture Belge
CSHE	Chinese Society of Chemical Engineering
CSHE	Chinese Society of Hydraulic Engineering
CSHE	Chinese Society of Hydroelectric Engineering
CSHL	Centre for the Study of Human Learning
CSHM	Chinese Society of Hospital Management
CSHPM	Canadian Society for the History and Philosophy of Mathematics = SCHPM
CSHPS	Canadian Society for the History and Philosophy of Science = SCHPS
CSHS	Chinese Society for Horticultural Science
CSHSD	Centre for the Study of Health, Sickness & Disablement
CSHST	Chinese Society of History of Science and Technology
CSI	Canadian Society for Immunology
CSI	Cartel des Syndicats Indépendants des Services Publics (Belgium)
CSI	Center for Science Information (U.S.A.)
CSI	Centrala Spółdzielni Inwalidów
CSI	Centro Sviluppo Settori d'Impiego S.r.l. (Italy)
CSI	Centro Sportivo Italiano
CSI	Chartered Surveyors Institution
CSI	Chinese Society for Instrumentation
CSI	Christian Solidarity International (U.S.A.)
CSI	Cinémathèque Scientifique Internationale = ISFL
CSI	Coeliac Society of Ireland
CSI	Commission Séricicole Internationale = ISC, ISK
CSI	Commission Sportive International = ISC
CSI	Computer Society of India
CSI	Conférence Suisse sur l'Informatique = SIK
CSI	Congregatio Sancti Ioseph
CSI	Construction Surveyors Institute
CSI	Convenção de Segurança
CSIA	Chambre Syndicale des Importateurs d'Automobiles, Cycles et Industries Annexes
CSIA	Comité Scientifique International de l'Arctique = IASC
CSIC	China Standards Information Centre
CSIC	Consejo Superior de Investigaciónes Cientificas

CSICC	Canadian Steel Industries Construction Council	**CSIRT**	Comité Scientifique International de Recherches sur les Trypanosomiases
CSICC	China Statistical Information and Consultancy Centre	**CSIS**	Canadian Security Intelligence Service
CSICE	Chinese Society for Internal Combustion Engines	**CSIS**	Center for Strategic and International Studies (Indonesia, U.S.A.)
CSICOP	Committee for the Scientific Investigation of Claims of the Paranormal	**CSIS**	Centre for Spatial Information Systems (CSIRO)
CSID	Centro de Servicios de Información y Documentación (Mexico)	**CSIS**	Comisia de Stat pentru Incercarea Soiurilor
CSID	Centro Superior de Información de la Defensa (Panama, Spain)	**CSIT**	Comité Sportif International du Travail = IWSC
CSIDDD	Chambre Syndicale des Industries de Désinfection, Désinsectisation et Dératisation	**CSIT**	Labour Sports International
		CSITSL	Comité Syndical International du Tourisme Social et des Loisirs = ITUCSTL
CSIE	Centre for Studies on Inclusive Education	**CSJ**	Chemical Society of Japan
CSIE	Centre for the Studies of Integration in Education	**CSJ**	Confraternity of Saint James
CSIE	Centro Studi Ingegneria Economica	**CSJ**	Corte Suprema de Justicia (Nicaragua)
CSIER	Centre for the Study of International Economic Relations (Canada)	**CSJC**	Chartered Societies Joint Committee
		CSK	Comité Spécial du Katanga (Zaïre)
CSIF	Confederación Sindical Independiente de Funcionarios	**CSK**	Cooperative Study of Kuroshio and Adjacent Regions (UNESCO) = ECK
CSIH	Canadian Society for International Health = SCSI	**ČSKI**	Czech Society for Cybernetics and Informatics / Česká Společnost pro Kybernetiku a Informatiku
CSII	Centre for the Study of Industrial Innovation		
CSIJ	Comité Sportif International de la Jeunesse	**CSL**	Central Science Laboratory
		CSL	Chinese Society of Luminescence
CSIL	Chinese Society of International Law	**CSL**	Circle of State Librarians
CSIM	Chinese Society of Internal Medicine	**CSL**	Commonwealth Serum Laboratories (Australia)
CSIMV	Chambre Syndicale des Industriels Métallurgistes du Vimeu	**CSL**	Compagnie Sénégalaise des Lubrificants
		CSL	Confédération des Syndicats Libres
CSIO	Central Scientific Instruments Organisation (India)	**CSLA**	Canadian School Library Association
CSIP	Chambre Syndicale des Industries de la Piscine	**CSLATP**	Canadian Society of Landscape Architects and Town Planners
CSIPD	Chinese Society of Infectious and Parasitic Diseases	**CSLB**	Confédération des Syndicats Libéraux de Belgique
CSIR	Centre for the Study of International Relations, Stockholm	**CSLO**	Canadian Scientific Liaison Office
		CSLP	Croatian Social Liberty Party
CSIR	Council for Scientific and Industrial Research (Ghana, India, South Africa)	**CSLS**	China Society of Library Science
		CSLT	Canadian Society of Laboratory Technologists
CSIRO	Commonwealth Scientific and Industrial Research Organisation (Australia)	**CSLT**	College of Speech and Language Therapists
CSIRO - OSSA	CSIRO Office of Space Science and Applications	**CSM**	Cambridge Society of Musicians
		CSM	Canadian Society of Microbiologists
CSIRODIT	Commonwealth Scientific and Industrial Research Organisation Division of Information Technology	**CSM**	Centrale Suikermaatschappij
		CSM	Centro Sperimentale Metallurgico
		ČSM	Česká Společnost pro Mechaniku

CSM	Chinese Society for Measurement
CSM	Chinese Society for Microbiology
CSM	Chinese Society of Mechanics
CSM	Chinese Society of Metals
CSM	Christian Socialist Movement
CSM	Climate System Monitoring Project (WMO/WCP)
CSM	Commission for Synoptic Meteorology (WMO)
CSM	Committee on the Safety of Medicines (DOH)
CSM	Compagnie Sénégalaise de Métallurgie
CSM	Conférence Française des Supérieures Majeures
CSM	Conselho Superior de Minas (Brazil)
CSMA	Caisse de Secours Mutuels Agricoles
CSMA	Chemical Specialities Manufacturers Association (U.S.A.)
CSMA	Civil Service Motoring Association
CSMA	Communications Systems Management Association
CSMA	Congregatio Sancti Michaelis Archangeli (Poland)
CSMCRI	Central Salt and Marine Chemicals Research Institute (India)
CSME	Canadian Society for Mechanical Engineers
CSME	Chinese Society of Medical Ethics
CSME	Confédération Syndicale Mondiale des Enseignants = WCT, WVL, WVOP
CSMF	Confédération des Syndicats Médicaux Français
CSMF	Conférence des Supérieurs Majeurs de France
CSMFF	Chambre Syndicale des Mines de Fer de France
ČSMG	Česká Společnost pro Mineralogii a Geologii
CSMG	Chinese Society of Medical Genetics
CSMH	Chinese Society of Medical History
CSMI	Chinese Society for Microbiology and Immunology
CSMI	Commission for Small and Medium Industries (Philippines)
CSMIRMA	Conferência dos Superiores Maiores dos Institútos Religiosos Masculinos de Angola
CSML	Centre for the Study of Management Learning
CSMPG	Chinese Society of Mineralogy, Petrology and Geochemistry
CSMPTE	Chinese Society of Motion Picture and Television Engineering
CSMRS	Central Soil Mechanics Research Station (India)
CSMSRM	Chinese Society of Medical Science Research Management
CSMTE	Chinese Society for Modern Technical Equipments
CSMTS	Card Setting Machine Tenters Society
CSMV	Chinese Society of Medical Virology
CSN	Comité de Salut National (Benin)
CSN	Companhia Siderúrgica Nacional (Brazil)
CSN	Confédération des Syndicats Nationaux (Canada)
CSN	Conseil Supérieur du Notariat
CSN	Consejo de Seguridad Nuclear
CSN	Conselho de Segurança Nacional
CSN	Coordinadora Sindical de Nicaragua
CSN	Office for Standards and Measurements (Czech Republic)
CSNA	Chambre Syndicale Nationale de l'Agencement
CSNA	Classification Society of North America
CSNA	Commonwealth Society of North America (U.S.A.)
CSNAME	Chinese Society of Naval Architecture and Marine Engineering
CSNC	Chambre Syndicale des Constructeurs de Navires et de Machines Marines
CSNCRA	Chambre Syndicale Nationale du Commerce et de la Réparation de l'Automobile
CSNDP	Chambre Syndicale Nationale des Agencies Privées de Recherches et Mandataires en Obtention de Renseignements et de Preuves
CSNDT	Canadian Society for Non-Destructive Testing
CSNÉ	Chambre Syndicale Nationale de l'Étanchéité
CSNÉ	Chambre Syndicale Nationale des Fabricants d'Équipements
CSNEIMB	Chambre Syndicale des Entrepreneurs d'Installations de Magasins et Bureaux et Activités Annexes
CSNÉSA	Chambre Syndicale Nationale des Électriciens et Spécialistes de l'Automobile
CSNFEI	Chambre Syndicale Nationale des Fabricants d'Encres d'Imprimerie

CSNHP	Chambre Syndicale Nationale des Entreprises et Industries de l'Hygiène Publique
ČSNI	Český Normalizační Institut
CSNI	Committee on the Safety of Nuclear Installations (NEA) (OECD)
CSNIGR	Chambre Syndicale Nationale des Industries Graphiques de Reproduction
CSNIP	Chambre Syndicale Nationale des Industries de Protection
CSNISE	Chambre Syndicale Nationale des Installateurs de Stands et d'Expositions
CSNL	Chambre Syndicale Nationale de la Literie
CSNLVI	Chambre Syndicale Nationale des Loueurs de Véhicules Industriels
CSNM	Chambre Syndicale Nationale du Motorcycle
CSNM	Chinese Society of Nautical Medicine
CSNMPH	Chambre Syndicale Nationale de la Mécanique de Haute Précision
CSNR	Chinese Research Society of Natural Resources
CSNRRM	Chambre Syndicale Nationale des Rectifieurs et Reconstructeurs de Moteurs
CSNU	Chambre Syndicale des Fabricants d'Uniformes
CSO	Central Seismological Observatory (India)
CSO	Central Selling Organisation of Diamond Producers
CSO	Central Statistical Office (Ethiopia, U.K.)
CSO	Central Statistical Office of Finland
CSO	Central Statistical Organization (India)
CSO	Central Statistics Office (Éire, Iraq)
CSO	Centre de Sociologie des Organisations
CSO	Chief Scientist Office (Scotland)
CSO	Chinese Society of Otolaryngology
CSO	Committee of Senior Officials (EC)
CSOG	Chinese Society of Obstetrics and Gynecology
CSOL	Chinese Society of Oceanology and Limnology
CSOMI-KERT	Csongrád Megyei Kertészeti Vállalat
CSON	Higher National Orientation Council (Niger)
ČSOP	Český Svaz Ochrancu Prirody
CSOP	Commission to Study the Organization of Peace (U.S.A.)
CSOPE	Comité de Solidarité avec les Opposants des Pays de l'Est (Switzerland)
CSOPMEM	Chinese Society of Optimization Planning Methodology and Economic Mathematics
CSP	Chambre Syndicale de la Phytopharmacie et de la Protection des Plantes
CSP	Chartered Society of Physiotherapy
CSP	Chinese Society of Particuology
CSP	Chinese Society of Pathology
CSP	Chinese Society of Psychology
CSP	Cuerpo Superior de Policía
CSP	Czech Society for Parasitology = ČPS
CSP	International Council for Science Policy Studies
CSP	Societas Sacerdotum Missionariorum a Sancto Paulo Apostolo
CSPA	Congress of Catholic Secondary School Parents Associations (Éire)
CSPAA	Conseil de Solidarité des Pays Afro-Asiatiques = AAPSC
CSPBI	Comité Spécial du Programme Biologique International
CSPCA	Canadian Society for the Prevention of Cruelty to Animals
CSPE	Comité Scientifique pour les Problèmes de l'Environnement (ICSU) = SCOPE
CSPEC	Confederation of the Socialist Parties of the European Community
CSPECVM	Chambre Syndicale Patronale des Enseignants de la Conduite des Véhicules à Moteur
CSPEFF	Chambre Syndicale des Producteurs et Exportateurs de Films Français
CSPES	Centro Studi per la Programmazione Economica e Sociale
CSPFLC	Confédération Nationale des Producteurs de Fruits, Legumes et Champignons
CSPG	Canadian Society of Petroleum Geologists
CSPI	Centre for Science in the Public Interest (U.S.A.)
CSPI	Citizens Committee on Infant Nutrition (U.S.A.)
CSPM	Chinese Society of Perinatal Medicine
CSPMR	Chinese Society of Physical Medicine and Rehabilitation
CSPN	Conselho Superior de Política Nuclear (Brazil)

CSPO	Centre for the Study of Public Order
CSPOA	Civil Service Professional Officers Association (Northern Ireland)
CSPODP	Canada South Pacific Ocean Development Project
CSPP	Center for the Study of Power and Peace (U.S.A.)
CSPP	Centre for the Study of Public Policy
CSPP	Centro di Studi sui Problemi Portuali
CSPP	Chinese Society for Plant Pathology
CSPP	Chinese Society of Plant Physiology
CSPPA	Caisse de Stabilisation de Prix des Produits Agricoles (Burkina Faso)
CSPPN	Caisse da Stabilisation des Prix des Produits du Niger
CSPS	Canadian Society of Patristic Studies = ACEP
CSPS	Chinese Society of Pediatric Surgeons
CSPS	Chinese Society of Plastic Surgery
CSPSE	Chinese Society of Photographic Science and Engineering
CSPT	Compagnie Sénégalaise des Phosphates de Taiba
CSPVA	Committee on Student Placement in Voluntary Agencies
CSQ	Croatian Society for Quality = HDK
CSQ	Czech Society for Quality
CSR	Centre for Software Reliability
CSR	Chinese Society of Radiology
CSR	Circolo Speleologico Romano
CSR	Conférence Suisse de Sécurité dans le Trafic Routier = SKS
CSR	Conseil Suprême de la Révolution (Chad)
CSR	Convenio Simón Rodriguez (Ecuador)
CSR	Council on the Study of Religion (Canada)
CSR	Cykel-och Sporthandlarnas Riksförbund
CSRA	Comité Scientifique pour les Recherches Antarctiques (ICSU) = CCIA, SCAR
CSRA	Committee of Secretaries of Research Associations
CSRA	Copper Smelters and Refiners Association
CSRC	Cognitive Science Research Centre
CSRD	Chinese Society of Respiratory Diseases
CSRE	Chinese Society of Rare Earth
CSRF	Civil Service Retirement Fellowship
CSRG	Centre for Remote Sensing in Geology (China)
CSRI	Computer Systems Research Institute (Canada)
CSRME	Chinese Society for Rock Mechanics and Engineering
CSRO	Chinese Society of Radiation Oncology
CSRO	Comité Scientifique pour les Recherches Océaniques (ICSU) = CCIO, SCOR
CSROH	Revolucniho Odborového Hnuti
CSRP	Chambre Syndicale du Raffinage du Pétrole
CSRS	Canadian Society for Renaissance Studies = SCER
CSRS	Central Sericulture Research Station (India)
CSRS	Centre Suisse de Recherches Scientifiques en Côte d'Ivoire
CSRS	Cooperative State Research Service (USDA)
CSRSOM	Conseil Supérieur des Recherches Sociologiques Outre-Mer
CSS	Centre for Social Studies (Bangladesh)
CSS	China Stereology Society
CSS	Chinese Silicate Society
CSS	Chinese Society of Stomatology
CSS	Chinese Sociological Society
CSS	Clan Stewart Society
CSS	Compagnie Sucrière Sénégalaise
CSS	Congregatio a Sanctissimi Stigmatibus
CSS	Conseil Supérieur de Statistique (Belgium)
CSS	Convention of Social Solidarity (Romania)
CSS	Costing and Statistical Society (South Africa)
CSS	Council for Science and Society
CSS	County Surveyors Society
CSS	Zentralverband Schweizerischer Schneidermeister
CSSA	Cactus and Succulent Society of America
CSSA	Campaign for a Socialist South Africa
CSSA	Chambre Syndicale Suisse de l'Automobile et Branches Annexes
CSSA	Cleaning and Support Services Association (*ex* CCMA)
CSSA	Computer Society of South Africa
CSSA	Concrete Society of Southern Africa
CSSA	Conseil Supérieur pour le Sport en Afrique (Cameroon) = SCSA

CSSA	Crop Science Society of America	**CST**	Confédération Syndicale du Tchad
CSSAR	Centre of Space Science and Applied Research (China)	**CST**	Coordinadora de Solidaridad de los Trabajadores (El Salvador)
ČSSB	Česká Společnost Biochemická	**CSTA**	Canadian Society of Technical Agriculturists
CSSC	China State Shipbuilding Corporation	**CSTA**	Catholic Secondary Teachers Association (Northern Ireland)
CSSC	Civil Service Sports Council		
CSSD	Czech Social Democratic Party	**CSTA**	Consejo Sindical de Trabajadores Andinos
CSSE	Canadian Society for the Study of Education = SCEE	**CSTAL**	Confederación Sindical de los Trabajadores de América Latina
ČSSE	Česká Společnost Entomologická při AVČR	**CSTAM**	Chinese Society of Theoretical and Applied Mechanics
CSSE	Compagnie Sénégalaise du Sud-Est	**CSTB**	Canadian Society for Theoretical Biology = SCBT
CSSE	Conference of States Sanitary Engineers (U.S.A.)	**CSTB**	Centre Scientifique et Technique du Bâtiment
CSSF	Chambre Syndicale de la Sérigraphic Française	**CSTC**	Centre Scientifique et Technique de la Construction (Belgium)
CSSF	Chambre Syndicale de la Sidérurgie Française	**CSTC**	Chinese Society of Tropical Crops
CSSF	Confédération des Sociétés Scientifiques Français	**CSTC**	Consejo Sindical de Trabajadores del Caribe
CSSIMS	Central States Society of Industrial Medicine and Surgery (U.S.A.)	**CSTCS**	Consejo Sindical de Trabajadores del Cono Sur (Argentina)
CSSME	Centre for the Studies of Science & Mathematics Education	**CSTD**	Committee on Science and Technology for Development (UNCSTD)
CSSP	Committee of Scientific Society Presidents (U.S.A.)	**CSTE**	Centro di Studio par la Termodinamica ed Elettrochimica dei Sistemi Salini Fusi e Solidi (Italy)
CSSp	Congregatio Sacrissimi Spiritus		
CSSPPA	Caisse de Stabilisation et de Soutien des Prix des Productions Agricoles (Ivory Coast) = CAISTAB	**CSTEC**	Commission of Socialist Teachers of the European Community (Netherlands)
		CSTFTAB	Confederación Sindical de Trabajadores Ferroviarios, Ramas Anexas y Transportes Aéreos de Bolivia
CSSR	Centro Studi Sociologia Religiosa		
CSSR	Chinese Society of Space Research	**CSTG**	International Coordination of Space Techniques for Geodesy and Geodynamics (IAG)
CSSR	Congregatio Sanctissimi Redemptoris		
CSSRC	China Ship Scientific Research Centre		
CSSRO	Chambre Syndicale des Soies et Rayonnes Oeuvrées	**CSTI**	Council of Science and Technology Institutes
CSSS	Canadian Soil Science Society	**CSTIV**	Chambre Syndicale Nationale de la Transformation Industrielle du Verre Plat
CSSS	China Sports Science Society		
CSSS	Chinese Society of Sericultural Science		
CSSS	Czech and Slovak Simulation Society	**CSTL**	IARI Central Seed Testing Laboratory (India)
CSST	Coordination Committee for Science and Technology	**CSTM**	Calcutta School of Tropical Medicine (India)
CSSTI	China Society for Scientific and Technical Information	**CSTM**	Centro Studi Terzo Mondo
CSSTLP	Chinese Society for Science and Technology of Labor Protection	**CSTM**	Compagnie Sénégalaise pour la Transformation des Métaux
CST	Central Sandinista de Trabajadores (Nicaragua)	**CSTP**	Comité Scientifique et Technique de la Pêche (CE) = STFC
CST	Committee on Science and Technology (U.S.A.)		

CSTP	Committee for Scientific and Technological Policy (OECD) = CPST
CSTR	Centre for Speech Technology Research
CSTT	Comité Supérieur des Transports Terrestres du Conseil de l'Entente (Niger)
CSU	Christlich-Soziale Union
CSU	Combined State Unions (New Zealand)
CSU	Companhia Siderurgica Nacional (Brazil)
CSU	Confédération des Syndicats Unitiés de Belgique
CSUCA	Consejo Superior Universitario Centroamericano (Costa Rica)
CSULA	California State University, Los Angeles (U.S.A.)
CSUM	Chinese Society of Urological Medicine
CSUS	Chinese Society of Urban Studies
CSUSA	Copyright Society of the U.S.A.
CSUT	Central South University of Technology
CSUT	Confederación de Sindicatos Unitarios de Trabajadores
CSUTCB	Confederación Sindical Unica de los Trabajadores Campesinos de Bolivia
CSV	Centraal Stikstof Verkoopkantoor
CSV	Chreschtlech-Sozial Vollekspartei (Luxembourg) = PCS
CSV	Community Service Volunteers
CSV	Congregatio Clericorum Parochialium seu Catechistarum Sancti Viatoris
CSVE	Chinese Society of Vibration Engineering
CSVS	Chartered Surveyors Voluntary Service
ČSVTS	Český Svaz Vědeckotechnických Společnosti
CSVW	Conservation Volunteers Northern Ireland
CSW	Central Scotland Woodlands
CSW	Christlicher Studenten-Weltbund = FUACE, FUMEC, WSCF
CSW	Council for the Status of Women (Éire)
CSW	United Nations Commission on the Status of Women
CSWDB	Central Scotland Water Development Board
CSWE	International Commission of the Council on Social Work Education
CSWG	Church of Scotland Women's Guild
CSWRI	Central Sheep and Wool Research Institute (Indonesia)
ČSZP	Česká Společnost pro Životní Prostředí
CT	Cambodia Trust
CT	Congreso del Trabajo (Mexico)
CT	Conseil de Tutelle (ONU)
CTA	Cable Television Association
CTA	Canadian Tuberculosis Association
CTA	Catering Teachers Association
CTA	Centre Technique de Coopération Agricole et Rurale (Netherlands)
CTA	Centro de Trabalhadores do Acre (Brazil)
CTA	Centro Tecnico Aereospacial (Brazil)
CTA	Chain Testers Association of Great Britain
CTA	Channel Tunnel Association
CTA	Children's Theatre Association
CTA	Cinema Theatre Association
CTA	Coffee Trade Association
CTA	Collegio dei Tecnici dell'Acciaio
CTA	Commercial Trailer Association
CTA	Commercial Travellers' Association
CTA	Computer Traders Association
CTA	Consorcio Técnica de Aeronáutica (Angola)
CTA	Conurbation Transport Authority
CTAA	Centro de Tecnologia Agricola e Alimentaria (Brazil)
CTAA	Children's Theatre Association of America
CTAC	Comité des Transporteurs Aériens Complémentaires
CTACG	Committee on Financial Aspects of Corporate Governance
CTAF	Comité des Transporteurs Aériens Français
CTAISB	Canadian Transportation Accident Investigation and Safety Board
CTAL	Confederación de Trabajadores de América Latina
CTAM	Cable Television Administration and Marketing Society (U.S.A.)
CTAMBJO	Syndicat National des Cadres, Techniciens, et Agents de Maîtrise de la Bijouterie, Joaillerie Orfèvrerie et des Activités qui s'y Rattachent
CTAP	Centre of Theoretical and Applied Physics (Jordan)
CTAPI	China Technical Association of Paper Industry

CTAS	Centre Technique des Applications de Soudage (SAF)		**CTCC**	Central Transport Consultative Committee
CTAT	Centre Technique d'Agriculture Tropicale		**CTCD**	Centre Technique pour le Contrôle de la Descendance
CTAVI	Centre Technique Audio Visuel International		**CTCÉ**	Comité de Thermodynamique et de Cinétique Électrochimique (Belgium)
CTB	Central de Trabajadores Bolivianos		**CTCEE**	Comisão Tecnica de Cooperação Economica External
CTB	Centre Technique du Bois		**CTCG**	Centrale des Travailleurs Chrétiens de La Guyane (French Guiana)
CTB	Commonwealth Telecommunications Bureau		**CTCH**	Central de Trabajadores de Chile
CTB	Companhia Telefonica Brasileira		**CTCI**	Classic Thunderbird Club International (U.S.A.)
CTBA	Centre Technique du Bois et de l'Ameublement (France)		**CTCMI**	Chinese Technical Committee of Manganese Industry
CTBLV	Christlicher Textil- Bekleidungs- und Lederarbeiter-Verband		**CTCPA**	Centre Technique de la Conservation des Produits Agricoles (France)
CTC	Canadian Transport Commission		**CTCR**	Confederación de Trabajadores de Costa Rica
CTC	Central de Trabajadores Costarricenses		**CTCRI**	Central Tuber Crops Research Institute (India)
CTC	Central de Trabajadores de Cuba			
CTC	Central Training Council (DOE)		**CTCSG**	Centre Technique de la Canne et du Sucre de la Guadeloupe
CTC	Centre on Transnational Corporations (UN)		**CTCSM**	Centre Technique de la Canne du Sucre de la Martinique
CTC	Centre Technique de Conserves des Produits Agricoles		**CTD**	Centre for Telecommunications Development (Switzerland)
CTC	Centre Technique du Cuir		**CTD**	Centre Technique de Développement de Sénégal
CTC	Centro Tecnológico do Calçado			
CTC	Clothing Technology Centre		**CTD**	Commission Technique Documentation (UIC)
CTC	Coach Tourism Council		**CTD**	Confederación de Trabajadores Dominicanos
CTC	Compagnie de Transport et de Commerce (Cameroon)			
CTC	Compañia de Teléfonos de Chile		**CTDC**	Confederación de Trabajadores Democráticos de Colombia
CTC	Confederación de Trabajadores Costarricenses		**CTE**	Confederación de Trabajadores del Ecuador
CTC	Confederación de Trabajadores de Colombia			
CTC	Confederación de Trabajadores de Cuba		**CTEB**	Council of Technical Examining Bodies
CTC	Confederación de Trabajadores del Cobre (Chile)		**CTEC**	Commonwealth Tertiary Education Commission
CTC	Congrès du Travail du Canada = CLC		**CTEF**	Comité Technique Européen du Fluor
CTC	Consejo de Trabajadores del Caribe (Guyana)		**CTEI**	Centro Tropical de Enseñanza e Investigación (Costa Rica)
CTC	Consumers' Transport Council		**CTERAM**	China Techno-Economic Research Association for Mines
CTC	Cyclists Touring Club			
CTCA	Canadian Telecommunications Carriers Association		**CTES**	China Textile Engineering Society
CTCA	Confederación de Trabajadores Centroamericanos (Honduras)		**CTETOC**	Council for Technical Education and Training for Overseas Countries
CTCB	Centre Technique du Cuir Brut		**CTEU**	Commerce and Transport Employees' Union (Afghanistan)
CTCB	Confederación de Trabajadores de Comercio de Bolivia			

CTEX	Centro Tecnológico do Exército (Brazil)
CTF	Canadian Teachers Federation
CTF	Catholic Teachers Federation
CTF	Central de Trabajadores Federados (Guatemala)
CTF	Coffee Trade Federation
CTF	Comité de Tourisme et des Fêtes
CTF	Communauté des Télévisions Francophones (Switzerland)
CTF	Children's Tropical Forests UK
CTFA	Cosmetic, Toiletry and Fragrance Association (U.S.A.)
CTFL	Centre Technique des Fruits et Légumes
CTFM	Comité des Transports Ferroviares du Maghreb
CTFMA	Copper Tube Fittings Manufacturers Association
CTFT	Centre Technique Forestier Tropical (Ivory Coast)
CTG	Confédération des Travailleurs de Guiné
CTGA	Ceylon Tea Growers Association
CTGREF	Centre Technique du Génie Rural des Eaux et des Forêts
CTGWE	Christmas Tree Growers of Western Europe
CTH	Confederación de Trabajadores de Honduras
CTHCM	Confederation of Tourism, Hotel and Catering Management
CTHS	Comité des Travaux Historiques et Scientifiques
CTI	Centraal Technisch Instituut TNO
CTI	Centre de Traitement de l'Information (Belgium)
CTI	Centro de Trabalho Indigenista (Brazil)
CTI	Comitato Termotechnico Italiano
CTI	Confédération des Travailleurs Intellectuels
CTI	Container Transport International (U.S.A.)
CTIA	Conseil Technique Interaméricain Archives = ITCA
CTIB	Centre Technique de l'Industrie du Bois (Belgium)
CTIC	Comisiones Técnicas Inter-Crea (Argentina)
CTICG	CTI Centre for Geography
CTICH	CTI Centre for History Archaeology & Art History
CTICM	Centre Technique Industriel de la Construction Métallique
CTICMS	CTI Centre for Mathematics & Statistics
CTIF	Centre Techniques des Industries de la Fonderie
CTIF	Comité Technique International de Prévention et Extinction du Feu
CTIFL	Centre Technique Interprofessionnel des Fruits et Légumes
CTIM	Centro de la Tribuna Internacional de la Mujer = IWTC
CTIO	Observatorio Interamericano de Cerro Tololo
CTIOM	Centre Technique Interprofessionnel des Oléagineux Métropolitains
CTIP	Compagnia Tecnica Industrie Petrole
ČTK	Česká Tisková Kancelár
CTL	Centre de Tourisme et de Loisirs (Cameroon)
CTLS	Council Tax Legal Services
CTM	Centre for Traditional Chinese Medicine
CTM	Companhia Portuguesa de Transportes Maritimos
CTM	Concordia de Telecomunicações de Macau
CTM	Confederación de Trabajadores de Mexico
CTM	Conférence Technique Mondiale
CTM-LN	Compagnie de Transports au Maroc "Lignes Nationales"
CTMA	British Civil Engineering Test Equipment Manufacturers Association
CTMA	Centre Technique du Machinisme Agricole
CTMB	Canal Transport Marketing Board
CTMC	Compagnie pour la Transformation des Métaux au Caméroun
CTMO	Community Trade Marks Office (EU)
CTN	Central de Trabajadores Nicaragüenses
CTNC	Committee on Transnational Corporations (UN)
CTNE	Compañia Telefónica Nacional de España
CTNRC	Centre for Thai National Reference Collections
CTNSS	Centre for Thai National Standard Specifications
CTO	Caribbean Tourism Organization (Barbados)
CTO	Central Tractor Organisation (India)
CTO	Comité Technique de l'Olivier
CTO	Commonwealth Telecommunications Organisation

CTP	Centre Technique de l'Industrie des Papiers, Cartons et Celluloses	**CTSP**	Transition Committee for the Safety of the People (Mali)
CTP	Communauté de Travail des Pyrénées	**CTT**	Centrum voor Tuinbouwtechniek
CTP	Conféderación de Trabajadores Peruanos	**CTT**	Córas Trachtála (Éire)
CTPA	Cosmetic Toiletry and Perfumery Association	**CTT**	Council for Travel and Tourism
		CTTA	Colombo Tea Traders Association
CTPI	Centre for Theology & Public Issues	**CTTH**	Cathedrals Though Touch and Hearing
CTPL	Centre Technique et de Promotion des Laitiers de Haut Fourneau	**CTTN-IREN**	Cleaning Technical Centre (France)
		CTU	Caribbean Telecommunications Union (Trinidad-Tobago)
CTPL	Centre Technique et de Promotion des Laitiers Sidérurgiques	**CTU**	China Textile University
CTPS	Permanent Technical Committee for Plant Breeding (France)	**CTU**	Commonwealth Transport Union (Bahamas)
CTPTA	Centro Tropical de Pesquisas e Tecnologia de Alimentos (Brazil)	**CTU**	Communist Trade Unionists
		CTU	Conservative Trade Unionists
CTR	Comision de Telecomunicaciones Rurales (Mexico)	**CTU**	Croatian Teachers Union
		CTUC	Commonwealth Trade Union Council
CTRG	Charities' Tax Reform Group	**CTUY**	Confederation of Trade Unions of Yugoslavia
CTRI	Catholic Tape Recorders International (U.S.A.)	**CTUYM**	Caribbean Trade Union Youth Movement
CTRI	Central Tobacco Research Institute (India, South Africa)	**CTV**	Centro Televisio Vaticano
CTRL	Cotton Technological Research Laboratory (India)	**CTV**	Confederación de Trabajadores de Venezuela
CTRM	Compagnie de Transports Routiers et de Messageries	**CTVM**	Centre for Tropical Veterinary Medicine
		CU	Casualties Union
CTRN	Conseil Transitionel de Redressement National (Guinea)	**CU**	Catholic Union of Great Britain
		CU	Centralny Urząd
CTRP	Central de Trabajadores de la Revolución Peruana	**CU**	Civic Union (Russia)
		CU	Colombia Unida
CTRP	Confederación de Trabajadores de la República de Panamá	**CU**	Commercial Union
		CU	Communications Unit (IUCN)
CTRU	Colonial Termite Research Unit (Nigeria)	**CUA**	Canadian Urological Surgeons
		CUA	Catering Utensils Association
CTS	Canadian Theological Society = SCT	**CUA**	Conference of University Administrators (*now* AUA)
CTS	Canadian Thoracic Society		
CTS	Centre for Transportation Studies (Canada)	**CUAC**	Community and Union Action Campaign
		CUAG	Computer Users Association Group
CTS	Committee on the Teaching of Science (ICSU)	**CUB**	Confederación Universitaria Boliviana
CTS	Coopération Technique Suisse	**Cuba-equipos**	Empresa Cubana Importadora de Productos Mecánicos y Equipos Varios
CTS	Incorporated Catholic Truth Society		
CTSA	Catholic Theological Society of America	**Cuba-industria**	Empresa Cubana Exportadora de Productos Industriales
CTSA	Crucible and Tool Steel Association	**Cubaelectr-ónica**	Empresa Importadora y Exportadora de Productos de la Electrónica (Cuba)
CTSCCV	Centre Technique de la Salaison de la Charcuterie et des Conserves de Viande	**Cubaexport**	Empresa Cubana Exportadora de Alimentos y Productos Varios
CTSIBV	Centre Technique et Scientifique de l'Industrie Belge du Verre	**Cubafrutas**	Empresa Cubana Exportadora de Frutas Tropicales

CUBALSE	Empresa para la Prestacion de Servicios a Extranjeros (Cuba)	**CUKT**	Carnegie United Kingdom Trust
		CULPAVAL	Cultivadores de Patata Valdivia
CUBANA	Empresa Cubana de Aviación	**CULTIMAR**	Cultivos Marinos Tongoy (Chile)
Cubatur	Empresa de Turismo Internacional (Cuba)	**CUM**	Communauté des Universités Méditerranéens; Communità delle Università Mediterranee (Italy)
CUBE	Concertation Unit for Biotechnology (CCE)		
CUC	Coal Utilization Council	**CUM**	Cooperative Union of Malaysia
CUC	Comité de Unidad Campesina (Guatemala)	**CUMA**	Canadian Urethane Manufacturers Association
CUC	Computers Users' Committee (UNDP)	**CUMA**	Coopérative d'Utilisation de Matériel Agricole
CUCB	Chambre des Urbanistes- Conseils de Belgique	**CUMATEX**	Associazione Nazionale Rappresentanti Commercianti Macchine e Accessori per l'Industria Tessile, Maglierie e per Cucire
CUCÉS	Centre Universitaire de Coopération Économique et Sociale		
CUD	Cités Unies Développement	**CUMS**	Council of University Management Schools
CUD	Coopération Universitaire au Développement		
		CUMT	China University of Mining and Technology
CUE	Committee for University English		
CUÉA	Conseil de l'Unité Économique Arabe = CAEU	**CUN**	Congress of Ukrainian Nationalists
		CUNA	Commissione Technica di Unificazione nell' Autoveicolo
CUEBS	Commission on Undergraduate Education in the Biological Sciences (AIBS)	**CUNA**	Consejo Unitario Nacional Agrario (Peru)
CUED	National Council for Urban Economic Development (U.S.A.)	**CUNA**	Credit Union National Association (U.S.A.)
CUEES	Car User Entrapment Extrication Society	**CUNY**	City University of New York (U.S.A.)
		CUPE	Canadian Union of Public Employees
CUEP	Central Unit on Environmental Pollution (DOE)	**CUPR**	Centre for Urban Policy Research (U.S.A.)
CUEP	Christian Union for the Estate Profession	**CUPRA**	Confederazione Unitaria della Produzione Agricole
CUEPACS	Congress of Unions of Employees in the Public and Civil Services (Malaysia)	**CUPW**	Canadian Union of Postal Workers
		CUR	Comando Urbano Revolucionario (Guatemala)
CUF	Catholicarum Universitatum Foederatio		
CUF	Companhia União Fabril (Portugal)	**CUR**	Commisse voor Uitvoering van Research
CUFLET	Empresa Cubana de Fletes		
CUG	China University of Geoscience	**CUR**	Det Centrale Uddanneisesråd
CUGC	Conference of Unions in Government Corporations (Philippines)	**CURAC**	Coal Utilization Research Advisory Committee (Australia)
CUGW	Centralny Urząd Gospodarki Wodnej	**CURB**	Campaign on the Use and Restriction of Barbiturates
CUHK	Chinese University of Hong Kong		
CUHSAW	Commonwealth Union of Hotel Services and Allied Workers (Bahamas)	**CURDS**	Centre for Urban & Regional Development Studies
Cuica	Comité Unitario del Cine	**CURE**	Citizens United for Racial Equality (U.S.A.)
CUIDES	Consejo Universitario Interamericano para el Desarrollo Economico y Social = IUCESD		
		CUREI	Centre Universitaire de Recherche Européenne et Internationale
CUIROP	Confédération Européenne du Commerce de Cuir en Gros	**CURL**	Consortium of University Research Libraries

CURLA	Centro Universitario Regional del Litoral Atlantico (Honduras)	**CUTMA**	Consejo Colombiano de Usuarios del Transporte de Carga
CURPHAM-ETRA	Centre Universitaire de Recherche Européene et Internationale (France)	**CUTS**	Canadian Universities Travel Service
CURS	Centre for Urban & Regional Studies	**CUTS**	Coalition for Urban Transport Sanity
CURS	Centre Universitaire de Recherche Scientifique (Morocco)	**CUTV**	Central Unitaria de Trabajadores de Venezuela
CUS	Confederación de Unificación Sindical (Nicaragua)	**CV**	Congregatio Vincentiana
CUS	Conférence Universitaire Suisse = SHK	**CVAC**	Comites Voluntarios de Autodefensa Civil (Guatemala)
CUSA	Council for United States Aid (China)	**CVAIT**	Cantina Viticultori
CUSA	Council of Unions of South Africa	**CVB**	Centraal Veevoederbureau in Nederland
CUSEA	Council for University Students of East Africa (Tanzania)	**CVBC**	Cámara Venezuelano-Britanica de Comercio y Industria
CUSG	Confederación Unidad de Sindicatos de Guatemala	**CVC**	Campaign for Vietnam Cinema
CUSIC	Comité Unitario de Sindicalistas Cristianos de Venezuela	**CVC**	Corporación Autónima Regional del Valle del Cauca (Colombia)
CUSO	Canadian University Service Overseas = SUCO	**CVCC**	Classic Vehicles Clubs Committee
CUSRPG	Canada-United States Regional Planning Group (NATO)	**CVCP**	Committee of Vice-Chancellors and Principals of the Universities of the United Kingdom
CUSS	Centre Universitaire des Sciences de la Santé (Cameroon)	**CVCS**	Centro Volontari Cooperazione allo Sviluppo
CUST	Centre Universitaire des Sciences et Techniques	**CVF**	Corporación Venezolana de Fomento
CUST	Chengdu University of Science and Technology	**CVFA**	Conseil de la Vie Française en Amérique
CUSURDI	Council of United States Universities for Rural Development in India	**CVG**	Corporación Venezolana de Guayana
CUSUS-WASH	Council of U.S. Universities for Soil and Water Development in Arid and Sub-humid Areas	**CVHO**	Vereniging van Docenten bij het Christelijk Voorbereidend Wetenschappelijk en Hogen Algemeen Voortgezet Onderwijs
CUT	Caribbean Union of Teachers	**CVI**	Centraal Veevoeder Instituut
CUT	Central Unica dos Trabalhadores (Brazil)	**CVI**	Croix Verte Internationale = IGC
CUT	Central Unitaria de Trabajadores (Chile, Colombia, Dominican Republic)	**CVJF**	Christlicher Verband Junger Frauen = UCJF, YWCA
CUT	Chartered Union of Taxpayers	**CVJM**	Christlichen Vereine Junger Männer = ACDG, ACJ, UCJG, YMCA
CUT	Comité Pro-Confederación Unica (Colombia, Dominican Republic)	**CVJR**	Centre de Voyages de la Jeunesse Rurale
CUT	Confederación Unitaria de Trabajadores (Costa Rica)	**CVL**	Central Veterinary Laboratory
CUTA	Canadian Urban Transport Association	**CVLB**	Christelijke Veenkoloniale Landbouwbond
CUTA	Conducción Unica de los Trabajadores Argentinos	**CVM**	Centro Volontari Marchigiani
CUTAL	Confédération Unique des Travailleurs de l'Amérique Latine	**CVM**	Comissão de Valores Mobiliáros (Brazil)
CUTI	Chinese Underwater Technology Institute	**CVM**	Controlestation voor Melkproducten
		CVM	Corporación Autónima Regional de los Valles de Magdalena y Siné (Colombia)
		CVMA	Canadian Veterinary Medical Association
		CVMP	Committee for Veterinary Medicinal Products (EU)

CVNI	Conservation Volunteers Northern Ireland	**CWAI**	Confederation of West Australian Industry
CVNW	Centrale Vereniging van Nederlandse Wijnhandelaren	**CWARC**	Canadian Workplace Automation Research Centre
CVO	Centre for Voluntary Organisation	**CWAS**	Centre for West African Studies
CVP	Christelijk Volkspartij (Belgium) = PSC	**CWAS**	Committee of Women in Asian Studies
CVP	Comité Vétérinaire Permanent (CE) = SVA, SVC	**CWB**	Canadian Welding Bureau
CVP	Corporación Venezolana del Petróleo	**CWB**	Canadian Wheat Board = CCB
CVPCEE	Comité des Ventes Publiques de Cuirs et Peaux Verts des Pays de la CEE	**CWB**	Commonwealth Writers of Britain
		CWC	Canadian Welfare Council
CVRD	Companhia Vale do Rio Doce (Brazil)	**CWC**	Canadian Wood Council = CCB
CVRDE	Combat Vehicle Research and Development Establishment (India)	**CWC**	Catering Wages Commission
		CWC	Comenius World Council (U.S.A.)
CVRS	Centre Voltaïque de la Recherche Scientifique (Burkina Faso)	**CWC**	Commonwealth of World Citizens (U.S.A.) = RCM
CVRTC	Commercial Vehicle and Road Transport Club	**CWC**	Congress Working Committee (India)
CVS	Chinese Vacuum Society	**CWCA**	China Wildlife Conservation Association
CVSM	Central-Verband Schweizerishcher Mobeltransporteurs	**CWCC**	Childrens World Community Chest
ČVSM	Česká Vědecká Společnost pro Mykologii	**CWCT**	Countrywide Workshops Charitable Trust
CVT	Camphill Village Trust Ltd	**CWD**	Caribbean Women for Democracy
CVT	Centrale Vakgroep Tuinbouw van de Belgische Boerenbond	**CWD**	Centre for Women and Development (Nepal)
CVT	Committee on Vacuum Techniques (U.S.A.)	**CWD**	Council of Welsh Districts
		CWDC	Canadian Wood Development Council
CVTM	Compagnie Voltaïque pour la Transformation des Métaux	**CWDE**	Centre for World Development Education
CVV	Coöperatieve Veeafzetvereniging v. Noord-en Zuid-Holland	**CWDI**	Canadian Welding Development Institute
CVV	Coöperatieve Venlose Veiling Vereniging	**CWDS**	Centre for Women's Development Studies (India)
CVV	Curaçaosche Verbond van Vakverenigingen (Netherlands Antilles)	**CWE**	Co-operative Wholesale Establishment (Sri Lanka)
CVWW	Council of Voluntary Welfare Work	**CWF**	Canadian Wildlife Federation
CVX	Communauté Mondiale de Vie Chrétienne; Communità Mondiale di Vita Cristiana; Comunidad de Vida Cristiana (Italy) = WCLC, GCL	**CWF**	Centrala Wynajmu Filmów
		CWF	Commonwealth Weightlifting Federation
		CWF	Conservative Way Forward
CVZ	Christelijke Vereniging van Ziekenhuizen en Diakonessenhuizen	**CWFP**	Concerned Women for Family Planning (Bangladesh)
CWA	Campaign for a Welsh Assembly	**CWG**	Comrades for a Workers Government
CWA	Comedy Writers' Association of Great Britain	**CWG**	Cooperative Women's Guild
		CWGC	Commonwealth War Graves Commission
CWA	Communications Workers of America		
CWA	Country Women's Association (Australia, U.S.A.)	**CWI**	Centrum voor Wiskunde en Informatica (Netherlands)
CWA	Crime Writers Association	**CWI**	Clean World International
CWAAL	Chinese Women's Anti-Aggression League (Taiwan)	**CWID**	Coalition of Women for International Development

CWINC	Central Waterways, Irrigation and Navigation Commission (India)
CWINRS	Central Waterpower, Irrigation and Navigation Research Station (India)
CWKS	Centralny Wojskowy Klub Sportowy
CWL	Catholic Women's League
CWL	Children with Leukaemia Charitable Trust
CWM	Caribbean Workers Movement
CWM	Contactgroep van Werkgevers in de Mataalindustrie
CWM	Council for World Mission
CWMA	Country Wool Merchants Association
CWME	Commission on World Mission and Evangelism (WCC)
CWN	Catholic Women's Network
CWN	City Women's Network
CWO	Communist Workers' Organization
CWP	Coordinating Working Party on Atlantic Fishery Statistics (FAO)
CWPC	Central Water and Power Commission (India)
CWPRS	Central Water and Power Research Station (India)
CWPS	Center for War/Peace Studies (U.S.A.)
CWPU	Central Water Planning Unit (DOE)
CWR	Centre for Women's Resources (Philippines)
CWR	Conference of Women Religious (Papua New Guinea)
CWR	Crusade for World Revival
CWRA	Canadian Water Resources Association
CWRAWU	Commonwealth Wholesale, Retail and Allied Workers Union (Bahamas)
CWRL	Citrus Wastage Research Laboratory (Australia)
CWS	Canadian Welding Society
CWS	Church World Service (U.S.A.)
CWS	Co-operative Wholesale Society
CWSA	Contract Work Study Association
CWTG	Computer World Trade Group
CWU	Chemical Workers Union (U.S.A.)
CWU	Christian Workers' Union (Belize)
CWU	Church Women United (U.S.A.)
CWU	Communication Workers' Union (Éire)
CWVA	Commonwealth Veterinary Association
CWVYS	Council for Wales Voluntary Youth Services
CWWA	Coloured Workers Welfare Association

CWY	Canada World Youth
CXC	Caribbean Examinations Council
CXOI	Xi'an Oils and Fats Research Institute
CYAC	Commonwealth Youth Affairs Council
CYATCA	Cyprus Air Traffic Controllers Association
CyBC	Cyprus Braodcasting Corporation
CYC	Catholic Youth Council (Éire)
CYEC	Commonwealth Youth Exchange Council
CYFA	Church Youth Fellowships Association
CYI	Chinese Yinglian Institute
CYL	Communist Youth League
CYM	Centre for Young Musicians
CYM	Commonwealth Youth Movement
CYMS	Catholic Young Men's Society
CyNA	Cyprus Nurses Association
CyNS	Cyprus Numismatic Society
CYP	Clubs for Young People (ex NABC)
CYP	Commonwealth Youth Programme
CYS	Catholic Youth Services
CYS	Centre for Youth Studies
CYSA	Cape York Space Agency
CYSA	Community Youth Services Association
CYSC	Churches Youth Service Council (Northern Ireland)
CYTA	Cyprus Telecommunications Authority
CYTED-D	Programa Iberoamericana de Ciencia y Tecnologia para el Desarrollo
CYWU	Community Youth Workers Union
CZA	Chinese Zhusuan Association
CZC	Centrale Zuivelcommissie
CZL	Contrôlestation voor Zuivelproducten
CZM	Coastal Zone Management
CZMS	Coastal Zone Management Subgroup (IPCC)
CZOZ	Coöperatieve Zuid- Nederlandse Organisatie van Zuivelvervaardigers
CZPA	Comisia de Zonare a Produselor Agricole
CZS	China Zoological Society

D

D&HAA	Dock and Harbour Authorities Association
DA	Dalmatian Action / Dalmatinska Akcija
DA	Danmarks Apotekerforening
DA	Dansk Agronomforening

DA	Dansk Arbejdsgiverforening = DAF
DA	Demokratischer Aufbruch
DA	Depressives Anonymous
DA	Design Austria
DA	Despatch Association
DA	Deutsche Akademie für Sprache und Dichtung
DA	Dingake Association (Botswana)
DA	Directio Administrativa (Romania)
DA	Direktorate for Arbejdstilsynet
DA'91	Democratisch Alternatief 1991 (Suriname)
DAA	Defence Accounts Agency
DAA	Democratic Alliance of Albanians (Bosnia-Herzegovina) = DSA
DAAD	Deutscher Akademischer Austauschdienst
DAAE	Dansk Andels Aegexport
DAARE	Disabled Against Animal Research and Exploitation
DAB	Da Afghanistan Bank
DAB	Democratic Alliance for the Betterment of Hong Kong
DAB	Deutsche Athletiek-Bund
DABEI	Deutsche Aktionsgemeinschaft Bildung, Erfindung und Innovation e. V.
DABIS	Gesellschaft für Datenbank Informationssysteme
DAC	Defence Animal Centre
DAC	Development Assistance Committee (OECD) = CAD
DAC	Drought Action Committee (UNDP) (Somalia)
DACA	Institute for the Development of Agricultural Cooperation Asia (Japan)
DACE	Dutch Association of Cost Engineers
DACHO	Dachorganisation des Filschaffenden in Deutschland
DACS	Design and Artists Copyright Society Ltd
DACT	Directorate of Administrative and Computer Training (Australia)
DACV	Democratic Alliance of Croats in Vojvodina = DSHV
DAD	Department Administratiewe Dienste (South Africa)
DADA	Designers and Art Directors Association of London
DADJ	Den Almindelige Danske Jordemoderforening
DAE	Department of Atomic Energy (India)
DAE	Direccion de Arquitectura Educativa (El Salvador)
DAEK	Danmark Atomenergikommissionen
DAEP	Directorate of Aircraft Equipment Production
DAEP	Division of Atomic Energy Production
DAER	Departmento Autónomo de Estradas do Rodagem (Brazil)
DAERA	Disability Alliance Educational and Research Association
DAF	Danmarks Automobil-Forhandler-Forening
DAF	Dansk Annoncær-Forening
DAF	Dansk Arbejdsgivereforening = DA
DAFECO	Direction des Affaires Extérieures et de la Coopération d'Électricité de France
DAFFA	Delicatessen and Fine Foods Association
DaFFO	Dansk Forening til Fremme af Opfindelser
DAFS	Department of Agriculture and Fisheries for Scotland
DAFS	Department of Agriculture, Fisheries and Forestry (Isle of Man)
DAfStb	Deutscher Ausschuss für Stahlbeton
DAG	Debendox Action Group
DAG	Democratic Alliance of Ghana
DAG	Deutsche Angestellten Gewerkschaft
DAG	Development Assistance Group (U.S.A.)
DAG	Divorce Action Group (Éire)
DAGA	Deutsche Arbeitsgemeinschaft für Akustik
DÄGFA	Deutsche Ärztegesellschaft für Akupunktur
DAGK	Deutschen Arbeitsgemeinschaft Kybernetic
DAGV	Deutsche Arbeitsgemeinschaft Genealogischer Verbände
DAGV	Deutsche Arbeitsgemeinschaft Vakuum
DAGV	Deutscher Automaten-Grosshandels-Verband
DAH	Danmarks Aktive Handelsrejsende
DAH	Deutsche Medizinische Arbeitsgemeinschaft für Herd- und Regulations-forschung
DAHE	Department of the Arts, Heritage & Environment (*now* DEST)
DAHG	Democratic Alliance of Hungarian Gypsies = MCDSz

DAHW	Deutsches Aussätziger – Hilfswerk = AYU, GLRA
DAI	Deutscher Architekten- und Ingenieur-Verband
DAI	Deutsches Anwaltsinstitut e.V.
DAI	Deutsches Archäologisches Institut
DAIA	Delegación de Asociaciones Israelitas Argentinas
DAIC	Dominica Association of Industry and Commerce
DAIR	Dansk Arbejdsgiverforenings og Industrirådetsforbindelseskontor ved De Europaeiske Fællesskaber
DAIS	District Agricultural Improvement Stations (China)
DAK	Dansk Atomreaktor Konsortium
DAK	De Samvirkende Danske Andels-Kreatureskportforeninger
DAK	Deutsche Angestellten Krankenkasse
DAK	Deutsche Atomkommission Geschaftsführung (BMWF)
DAKOFO	Danske Korn- Og Foderstof Im- Og Eksportørers Fællesorganisation
DAKS	Danske Automobil Komponentfabrikkers Sammenslutning
DAL	Danske Arkitekters Landsforbund
DAL	Deutsche Akademie der Landwirtschafts Wissenschaften
DAL	Deutscher Arbeitsring für Lärmebekämpfung
DAL/AA	Danske Arkitekters Landsforbund/Akademisk Arkitektforening
DALA	Departmento de Asuntos Latinoamericanos (Cuba)
DALIA	Distribuidora Argentina Libro Ibero-Americano
DALPA	Danish Air Line Pilots Association
DAM	Democratic Alliance of Montenegro = DSCG
DAM	Direct Action Movement
DAMAG	Société Dakaroise de Grands Magasins (Senegal)
DAMDA	Dairy Appliance Manufacturers and Distributors Association
Dame-Inglesi	Istituto della Beata Vergine Maria
DAMW	Deutsches Amt für Material- und Warenprüfung
DAN	Direct Action Network
DAN-PATATAS	Danske Kartoffelavleres og Kartoffeleksportørers Faellesorganisation
DANA	Andelsslagteriernes Konserveseksport
DANATOM	Danish Association for Industrial Development of Atomic Energy
DANBIF	Danske Boghandleres Importørforening
DANCOOP	Departamento Administrativo Nacional de Cooperativas (Colombia)
DANDOK	Danish Committee for Scientific and Technical Information and Documentation
DANE	Departmento Administrativo Nacional de Estadistica (Colombia)
DANFIP	Dansk Føderation for Informationbehandling og Virksomhedsstyring
DANHORS	Danish Farmers Export Union
DANI	Department of Agriculture (Northern Ireland)
DANIDA	Danish International Development Agency
DANPRO	Danish Committee on Trade Procedures
DANR	Department of Agriculture and Natural Resources (Philippines)
DANRIC	Department of Agriculture and Natural Resources Information Council (Philippines)
DANVAK	DANVAK – VVS Teknisk Forening
DAP	Democratic Action Party (Malaysia)
DAP	Deutsche Akademie für Psychoanalyse
DAP	Drought Action Programme (UNDP) (Somalia)
DAP	Servicio de Divulgación Agrícola de Panamá
DAPD	Directorate of Aircraft Production Development
DAPIS	Danish Agricultural Products Information Service
DAR	(CSIRO) Division of Atmospheric Research
DAR	Daughters of the American Revolution
DARA	Deutsche Arbeitsgemeinschaft für Rechenanlagen
DARC	Deutscher Amateur Radio Club
DARG	Discourse Analysis Research Group (Canada)
DARH	Democratic Association of Romanians in Hungary = MRDS
DARPA	Defence Advanced Research Projects Agency (U.S.A.)

DARPA	Defense Advanced Research Projects Agency (*ex* ARPA)	**DAu**	Dansk Automations Selskab
DAS	Dansk Akustisk Selskab	**DAU**	Dansk Kunst- og Antikvitetshandler-Union
DAS	Dansk Anaesthesiologisk Selskab	**DAU**	Direcciones Municipales de Arquitectura y Urbanismo (Cuba)
DAS	Den Danske Arktiske Station	**DAV**	Deutscher Alpenverein
DAS	Departamento Administrivo de Seguridad (Colombia)	**DAV**	Deutscher Altphilologenverband
DAS	Department of Administrative Services (Australia)	**DAV**	Deutscher Anwaltverein
DAS	Deutscher Allgemeiner Sängerbund	**DAV**	Deutscher Apotheker-Verein
DASA	Defence Analytical Services Agency	**DAV**	Deutscher Automaten- Verband
DASA	Dental Association of South Africa	**DAV**	Deutscher Autorenverband
Dasa	Deutsche Aerospace	**DAVID**	Group for the Development of an Audiovisual Identity for Europe (Belgium)
DASA	Domestic Appliance Service Association		
DASD	Deutsche Akademie für Sprache und Dichtung	**DAVR**	Democratic Alliance of Vojvodina Romanians = DSRV
DASET	Department of the Arts, Sport, the Environment and Territories (*now* DEST) (Australia)	**DAW**	Deutsche Akademie der Wissenschaften zu Berlin
		DAW	Deutscher Arbeitskreis Wasserforschung
DASETT	Department of the Arts, Sport, the Environment, Tourism and Territories (*now* DEST) (Australia)	**DAW**	Drama Association of Wales
		DAWN	Development Alternatives with Women for New Era (Barbados)
DASF	Dansk Arbejdsmands- og Specialarbjderforbund	**DAWS**	Danish Animal Welfare Society
DASIAC	Defense Atomic Support Agency Information and Analysis Centre (U.S.A.)	**DAZ**	Deutsche Ärztegemeinschaft für Medizinische Zusammenarbeit
DASP	Departmento Administrativo do Servico Público (Brazil)	**DB**	Danmarks Biblioteksforening
		DB	Dansk Blomsterhandlerforening
DASP	Deutscher Ausschuss für Spektralanalyse	**DB**	Deutsche Bücherei
		DB	Deutsche Bundesbahn
DASS	Depressives Associated	**DBA**	Design Business Association
DASt	Deutscher Ausschuss für Stahlbau	**DBA**	Deutsche Bauakademie
DASUCH	Department of Social Action, University of Chile	**DBA**	Dutch Barge Association
DATA	Design and Technology Association (*ex* EIDCT)	**DBAE**	Doctors in Britain Against Animal Experiments
		DBB	Deutscher Beamtenbund
DATAR	Délégation à l'Aménagement du Territoire et à l'Action Régionale	**DBC**	Deaf Broadcasting Council
DATCA	Danish Air Traffic Controllers Association	**DBCE**	(CSIRO) Division of Building, Construction and Engineering
DATCO	Disability Appeal Tribunal Central Office	**DBCP**	Drifting Buoy Cooperation Panel
		DBE	Development Bank of Ethiopia
DATE	Danish Association of Teachers of English	**DBF**	Danmarks Blomsterlogavler – Forening
		DBF	Dansk Biogasteknisk Forening
DATE	Debreceni Agrártudományi Egyetem	**DBF**	Den Danske Boghandlerforening
DATF	Danske Apotekstekuikeres Forening	**DBfK**	Deutscher Berufsverband für Krankenpflege
DAtF	Deutsches Atomforum		
DATUM	Dokumentions und Ausbidungszentrum für Theorie und Methode der Regionalforschung	**DBfK**	Deutscher Berufsverband für Pflegeberufe – Bundesverband e.V.
		DBG	Design Business Group

DBG	Deutsche Bodenkundliche Gesellschaft
DBG	Deutsche Botanische Gesellschaft
DBG	Deutsche Bunsen- Gesellschaft für Physikalische Chemie
DBI	Dansk Beton Industriforening
DBI	Deutsches Bibliothekinstitut
DBIU	Dominion Board of Insurance Underwriters (Canada)
DBIV	Deutsche Braunkohlen-Industrieverein
DBJUN	Dokumentationszentrum des Bunds Judischer Verfolger des Naziregimes (Austria)
DBK	Dansk Bradvoernskomité
DBL	Danske Bankfunkbionaerers Landsforening
DBMC	Danish Bacon and Meat Council
DBMC	Dominica Banana Marketing Corporation
DBNMA	Disposable Baby Napkin Manufacturers Association
DBP	Deutsche Bundespost
DBR	Deutscher Bildungsrat
DBR	Directorate of Biosciences Research (DRB) (Canada)
DBR	Division of Building Research (Canada)
DBS	Det Danske Bibelselskab
DBS	Deutsche Berufsverband der Sozialarbeiter und Sozialpädagogen
DBS	Development Bank of Singapore
DBS	Donkey Breed Society
DBS	Društvo Bibliotekarjev Slovenije
DBSH	Deutscher Berufsverband der Sozialarbeiter / Sozialarbeiterinnen, Sozialpädagogen / Sozialpädagoginnen, Heilpädagogen, Heilpädagoginnen e.V.
DBSS	Dutch Benelux Simulation Societies
DBTI	Dansk Beklaednings og Textil Institut
DBV	Deutsche Binnentankreedervereinigung
DBV	Deutsche Burgenvereinigung e.V. zur Erhaltung der Historischen Wehr- und Wohnbauten
DBV	Deutscher Bäderverband
DBV	Deutscher Bauernverband
DBV	Deutscher Betonverein
DBV	Deutscher Biblioteksverband
DBV	Deutscher Büchereiverband
DBV	Deutscher Bund für Vogelschutz
DC	Congregatio Patrum Doctrinae Christianae
DC	Daughters of Charity of Saint Vincent de Paul
DC	Democratic Coalition (Hungary, Montenegro)
DC	Democratic Coalition = CD
DC	Partito della Democrazia Cristiana
DCA	Defense Communications Agency (*now* DISA)
DCAS	Divorce Conciliation and Advisory Service
DCB	Dignity and Charity Bloc (Russian Federation)
DCBS	Devon Cattle Breeders' Society
DCC	Development Capital Corporation (Éire)
DCCA	Dessert and Cake Mixes Association
DCCC	Domestic Coal Consumers' Council
DCDSTF	Digital Cartographic Data Standards Task Force
DCE	Diretório Central de Estudantes (Brazil)
DCF	Dansk Cerealforening
DCF	Disabled Christians Fellowship
DCF	Fédération Nationale des Directeurs Commerciaux de France
DCFRN	Developing Countries Farm Radio Network = RRRPD
DCG	Democracia Cristiana Guatemalteca
DChIV	Deutscher Chemie-Ingenieur-Verband
DCI	Defence for Children International = DEI, DNI
DCI	Directorate of Chemical Inspection
DCIB	Dry Cleaning Information Bureau
DCIOO	Import Opportunities Office for Developing Countries
DCIS	Delaware Country Institute of Science (U.S.A.)
DCL	Distillers Company Limited
DCMA	Dessert & Cake Mixes Association
DCN	Partido de Concialicación Nacional (El Salvador)
DCP	Democratic Centre Party (Latvia)
DCPAC	Desertification Control Program Activity Centre
DCPE	Dominion Council of Professional Engineers (Canada)
DCPO	Dana Center for Preventive Ophthalmology (U.S.A.)
DCPU	Data Communication Protocol Unit (DTI)
DCR	Democratic Convention of Romania

DCRF	Die Casting Research Foundation of the American Die Casting Institute
DCS	Dansk Cardiologisk Selskab
DCS	Diecasting Society
DCSC	Dependable Computing Systems Centre
DCSH	Department of Community Services and Health
DCSHJ	Daughters of Charity of the Sacred Heart of Jesus of La Salle-de-Vihiers = FCSCJ
DCSM	Danish Council for Scientific Management
DCT	Drapers Chamber of Trade
DCTPB	Dubai Commerce and Tourism Promotion Board
DCV	Deutscher Caritasverband
DCVH	Democratic Community of Vojvodina Hungarians = DZMV
DCW	Dance Council for Wales
DCWAB	Diplomatic and Commonwealth Writers Association of Britain
DD	Data for Development International Association = DFD, DPD
DD	Democratic Departure (Germany) = DA
DDA	Delhi Development Authority (India)
DDA	Deutchers Dampfkessel-Ausschuss
DDA	Disabled Drivers Association
DDA	Dominion Department of Agriculture (Canada)
DDASS	Direction Départmentale de l'Action Sanitaire et Sociale
DDB	Den Danske Bankforening
DDB	Deutscher Diabetiker Bund
DDB	Deutscher Dolmetscherbund
DDBF	Den Dansk Bagerstands Foellesorganisation
DDC	Defense Documentation Centre (U.S.A.)
DDC	Desert Development Centre (Egypt)
DDC	Diamond Distributors Centrafrique
DDC	FAO Investment Centre
DDCB	FAO/IBRD Cooperative Programme
DdD	Den Danske Dyrlægeforening
DDF	Danske Dagblades Forening
DDF	Dental Documentary Foundation (Belgium)
DDF	Dominica Defence Force
DDF	FAO Field Liaison Division
DDG	Deutsche Dendrologische Gesellschaft
DDG	Deutsche Dermatologische Gesellschaft
DDG	Deutsche Diabetes-Gesellschaft
DDH	Det Danske Hedeselskab
DDI	FAO Industry Cooperative Programme
DDK	Demokraticheskoe Dvizhenie Kommunistov
DDK-Rossii	Demokraticheskoe Dvizhenie Kommunistov Rossii
DDL	Det Danske Luftfart-Selskab
DDMC	Disabled Drivers Motor Club
DDN	Defense Data Network
DDN NIC	Defense Data Network Network Information Center
DDR	Dvizhenie Demokraticheskikh Reform
DDRI	Daqing Drilling Research Institute
DDS	Dansk Dermatologisk Selskab
DDS	De Dansk Sukkerfabrikker
DDS	Department of Defence and Security (Mozambique)
DDT	Democratic Labour Confederation (Morocco)
DDT	Department of Development and Technology (ESTEC)
DDV	Deutsche Diabetiker-Verband
DDV	Deutscher Detektiv-Verband e.V.
DE	Dansk Erhvervsfrugtavl
DE³	Groupe Développement-Énergie-Environnement-Économie (IEPF)
DEA	Dachverband der Schweizerischen Industrie Elektrischer Apparate und Geräte für den Haushalt
DEA	Dairy Executives Association (Éire) (*ex* ICMA)
DEA	Dance Educators of America
DEA	Development Education Association (*ex* NADEC)
DEA	Drug Enforcement Agency (U.S.A.)
DEAIC	Dirección de Educación Artesanal, Industrial y Comercial (Venezuela)
DEALC	Desarrollo y Educación en América Latina
DEB	Društvo Ekonomista Beograda
DEBEG	Deutsche Betriebsgesellschaft für Dratlose Telegraphie
DEBRA	Dystrophic Epidermolysis Bullosa Research Association
DEBRIV	Deutscher Braunkohlenindustrieverein
DEC	Denmark Environment Centre
DEC	Disasters Emergency Committee
DEC	Dollar Exports Council

DECAM	Departamento de Conservação Ambiental (Brazil)
DECAT	Departamento de Conservación y Asistencia Técnica del Ministerio de Agricultura (Chile)
DECC	Disciples Ecumenical Consultative Council (U.S.A.)
DECEE	Dirección de Estadística, Catastro y Estudios Económicos (Peru)
DECHEMA	Deutsche Gesellschaft für Chemisches Apparatewesen, Chemische Technik und Biotechnologie
DECIEM	Defence and Civil Institute of Environmental Medicine (DRB) (Canada)
DECO	Associação Portuguesa para a Defesa do Consumidor
DECP	Division de la Coordination Économique et du Plan (Morocco)
DECSA	Departmento de Conservación de Suelos y Agua (Chile)
DECTA	Developing Countries Trade Agency
DECUS	Digital Equipment Computer Users
Decus-Europe	Digital Equipment Computer Users Society
DED	Department of Economic Development (Northern Ireland)
DED	Deutscher Entwicklungs-Dienst
DEET	Department of Employment, Education and Training (Australia)
DEF	Danske Elværkers Forening
DEF	Directia Economiei Forestiere (Romania)
DEFD	Dynamique Entreprenariale Feminine pour le Développement (Congo)
DEFI	Det Europeiske Fagforeningsinstitut = EGI, ETUI, EVI, ISE
DEFRA	Vereinigung zur Förderung der Wirtschaftsbeziehungen Zwischen Deutschland und Frankreich
DEG	Danske Erhvervsgartnerforening
DEG	Deutsche Entomologische Gesellschaft
DEG	Deutsche Exlibris-Gesellschaft
DEG	Deutsche Gesellschaft für Wirtschaftliche Zusammenarbeit
DÉG	Direction des Études Générales (Morocco)
DEG	Directorate of Environmental Geology (Indonesia)
Degebo	Deutsche Forschungsgesellschaft für Bodenmechanik
DEGUSSA	Deutsche Gold- und Silber Scheideanstalt
DEH	Danske Ejendomshandlerforening
DEHOGA	Deutscher Hotel- und Gaststättenverband
DEHR	Direction de l'Hydraulique et de l'Équipement Rural (Algeria)
DEI	Défense des Enfants-International = DCI, DNI
DEI	Departmento Ecuménico de Investigaciones (Costa Rica)
DEIP	Division de Exploraciones e Introducción de Plantas (Argentina)
DEJIMAS	Entreprise Nationale de Développement des Industries d'Articles de Sport, Jouets et Instruments de Musique (Algeria)
DEK	Dansk Elektroteknisk Komité
DEKRA	West German Motor Vehicle Standards Institution
DELGA	Liberal Democrats for Lesbian and Gay Action
DEMA	Data Entry Management Association (U.S.A.)
DEMKO	Dansk Elektrische Materielkontrol
DEMLAB	Democratic Labour Party (Dominica)
DEMOS	Democratic Opposition of Slovenia
DEMOS	Demokratska Opozicija Slovenije (Slovenia) = DOS
Demotex	Nederlandse Bond van Christelijke Detailhandelaren in Textiel-en Mode-Artikelen
DEMYC	Democratic Youth Community of Europe
DENACAL	Departamento Nacional de Acueductos y Alcantarillados (Nicaragua)
DENAGEO	Departamento Nacional de Geologia (Bolivia)
DENI	Departamento Nacional de Investigaciones (Panama)
DENI	Department of Education for Northern Ireland
DENIP	Union Professionnelle des Importateurs en Fourniteurs Dentaires (Belgium)
DENTEL	Departamento Nacional de Telecomuncações (Brazil)
DEOC	Department of Economic and Organised Crime (Russia)
DÉP	Département Fédéral de l'Économie Publique (Switzerland)

DEP	Department of Environment and Planning (Australia)
DEP	Groupe des Démocrates Européens de Progrès (CCE) = EPD
DEPANA	Lliga per a la Defensa del Patrimoni Natural
DEPCA	International Study Group for the Detection and Prevention of Cancer
DEPO	Nederlands Vereniging van Detailhandelaren in Pootaardappelen
DEPOS	Democratic Movement of Serbia
DER	Departmento de Estrados de Rodagem (Brazil)
DER	Deutscher Erfinderring
DERC	Development Economics Research Centre
DERE	Dounreay Experimental Reactor Establishment
DEREL-VANS	Département d'Enseignement et de Recherche Langues Vivantes aux Non-Spécialistes
DERI	Dalian Electronics Institute
DERL	Defence Electronics Research Laboratory (India)
DÉRT	Divison Électronique, Radioélectricité et Télécommunications (SEE)
DERZH-STANDART	State Committee of Ukraine for Standardisation, Metrology and Certification
DES	Dansk Endokrinologisk Selskab
DES	Department of Education and Science
DESAL	Centro para el Desarrollo Económico y Social de América Latina (Chile)
DESC	Development Education Support Centre (Éire)
DESCO	Centro de Estudios y Promoción del Desarrollo (Peru)
DESCONAP	Research and Training Centres on Desertification Control in Asia and the Pacific
DESEC	Centro para el Desarrollo Social y Economico (Bolivia)
DESG	Deutsch-Europäische Studiengesellschaft
DESIDOC	Defence Scientific Information and Documentation Centre (India)
DEST	Department of the Environment, Sport and Territories (Australia) (*ex* DAHE, DASETT, DHAE)
DESU	Delhi Electric Supply Undertaking (India)
DESWOS	Deutsche Entwicklungshilfe für Soziales Wohnungs- und Siedlungswesen
DESY	Deutsches Elektronen Synchrotronen (Germany)
DETC	Defence Engineering Terminology Committee (MOD)
DETEX	Stichting Detailhandel in Textielgoederen
DETI	Drents Economisch Technologisch Instituut
DETRAN	Departamento de Transportes (Brazil)
DEU	Democratic Union (Czech Republic)
DEULA	Deutsche Landmaschinenschulen
DEULA	Deutsche Lehranstalten für Agrartechnik
DEUPRO	Auschuss für die Vereinfachung Internationaler Handelsverfahren
DEV	Derecha Emergente de Venezuela
DEV	Deutscher Erfinderverband
DEV	Directia Economiei Vínatului (Romania)
DEV-SOL	Devrimci-Sol (Turkey)
DEVCO	Committee for Standardisation in the Developing Countries (ISO)
DEVCO	State Agencies Development Corporation Organisation (Éire)
DeVg	Deutsche Vereinigung für die Rehabilitation Behinderter
DevIs	Devrimei Isci Sendikalari Federasyonu (TRNC)
DEZAPA	Algemene Nederlands Bond van Detailhandelaren in Zaden en Aanverwante Artikelen
DF	Danmarks Forskningsbiblioteksforening
DF	Danske Fysioterapeuter
DF	Deutscher Frauenrat
DF	Landsforeningen Dansk Frugtavl
DFA	Deutscher Fuszballbund
DFAT	Department of Foreign Affairs and Trade
DFB	Deciduous Fruit Board (South Africa)
DFB	Deutsche Frauenbewegung
DFBO	Deutsche Forschungsgesellschaft für Blechverarbeitung und Oberflüchenbehandlung
DFC	Development Finance Company (Trinidad and Tobago)
DFC	Development Finance Corporation (Belize, New Zealand)
DFC	Duty Free Confederation

DFCK	Development Finance Company of Kenya
DFCU	Development Finance Company of Uganda
DFD	Data for Development International Association = DD, DPD
DFD	Democratischer Frauenbund Deutschlands (DDR)
DFD	Département Fédéral des Finances et des Douanes (Switzerland)
DFD	Dogs for Disabled
DFDS	Det Forenede Dampskibs-Selskab
DFE	Danmarks Fiskeindustri-og Eksportforening
DFE	Dansk Forening for Europaret
DFE	Delegationen für Energiforskning
DfEE	Department for Education and Employment
DFF	Dansk Forstkandidaters Forening
DFF	Dansk Fotografisk Forening
DFF	Den Danske Forlaeggerforening
DFFA	Delicatessen and Fine Food Association
DFFF	Demokratiska Förbundet av Finlands Folk
DFG	Deutsche Forschungsgemeinschaft
DFGH	Danske Fotogrossisters Handelsforening
DFGR	Democratic Forum of Germans in Romania = FDGR
DFH	Danmarks Farmaceutiske Hæjskole
DFI	Delegationen för Vetenskaplig och Teknisk Informations Försörjning
DFI	Disability Federation of Ireland
DFIK	Dansk Forening for Industriel Kvalitetskontrol
DFIN	Department of Finance
DFK	Dansk Flaskegas Komité
DFK	Dansk Forening for Kvalitetsstyring
DFL	Danske Forsikringsfunktionaerers Landsforening
DFL	Deutsche Forschungsanstalt für Luftfahrt (*now* DLR)
DFLP	Democratic Front for the Liberation of Palestine
DFM	Dansk Institut for Fundamental Metrologi
DFMF	Dansk Forening for Medicinsk Fysik
DFO	Deutsche Forschungsgesellschaft für Oberflächenbehandlung
DFOM	Départements Français d'Outre-Mer

DFP	Dominica Freedom Party
DFR	Deutscher Fernschulrat
DFR	Diplomerade Företagsekonomers Rijksförbund
DFRC	Distillers Feeds Research Council (U.S.A.)
DFRF	Democratic Front for the Reunification of the Fatherland (Democratic People's Republic of Korea)
DFRRI	Directorate of Feeder Roads and Rural Infrastructure (Nigeria)
DFS	Danmarks Farmaceutiske Selskab
DFS	Dansk Fysiurgisk Selskab
DFS	Democratic Federation of Serbs (Hungary) = SzDSz
DFSS	Democratic Front for the Salvation of Somalia
DFU	Deutsche Friedens Union
DFV	Deutsche Feuerwehrverband
DFV	Deutscher Fischereiverband
DFV	Deutscher Forstverein
DFVLR	Deutsche Forschungs-und Versuchsanstalt für Luft- und Raumfahrt
DFWG	Deutsche Farbwissenschaftliche Gesellschaft
DFWR	Deutscher Forstwirtschaftsrat
DG	Deutsche Gesellschaft für Galvanotechnik
DG	Directorate General (EU)
DG	Directors Guild of Great Britain = DGGB
DGA	Deutsche Gesellschaft für Amerikastudien = DGfA
DGA	Deutsche Gesellschaft für Anaesthesia
DGA	Deutsche Gesellschaft für Angiologie
DGA	Deutsche Gesellschaft für Asienkunde
DGA	Direction Générale de l'Agriculture
DGA	Durum Growers Association of the United States
DGAA	Dirección General de Asuntos Agrarios (Guatemala)
DGAA	Distressed Gentlefolks Aid Association
DGaaE	Deutsche Gesellschaft für Allgemeine und Angewandte Entomologie
DGAB	Direction de la Gestion Administrative et du Budget (UNDP)
DGAC	Direction Génération de l'Aviation Civile (Spain, Uruguay)
DGAI	Deutsche Gesellschaft für Anästhesiologia und Intensivmedizin

DGAO	Deutsche Gesellschaft für Angewandte Optik
DGAP	Deutsche Gesellschaft für Analytische Psychologie
DGAP	Deutsche Gesellschaft für Auswärtige Politik
DGAP	Dirección de la Gestión Administrativa y Presupuesto (UNDP)
DGAR	Deutsche Gesellschaft für Agrarrecht
DGAS	Double Glazing Advisory Service (GGF)
DGAW	Deutsche Gesellschaft für Anästhesie und Wiederbelebung
DGB	Deutsche Gesellschaft für Betriebswirtschaft
DGB	Deutscher Gewerkschaftbund
DGBK	Deutsche Gesellschaft für Baukybernetik
DGBW	Deutsche Gesellschaft für Bewasserungswirtschaft
DGC	Deutsche Gesellschaft für Chronometrie
DGCI	Direcção-Geral das Contribuções e Impostos
DGD	Deutsche Gesellschaft für Dokumentation
DGDDI	Direction Générale des Douanes et Droits Indirects
DGDP	Deutsche Gesellschaft für Dynamische Psychiatrie
DGE	Deutsche Gesellschaft für Elektronenmikroskopie
DGE	Deutsche Gesellschaft für Endokrinologie
DGE	Deutsche Gesellschaft für Ernährung
DGE	Dirección General de Electricidad (Mexico)
DGEA	Dirección General de Extensión Agropecuária (Ecuador)
DGEC	Dirección General de Estadistica y Censos (Nicaragua)
DGEF	Direction Générale des Eaux et Forêts
DGEG	Deutsche Gesellschaft für Eisenbahngeschichte
DGEG	Deutsche Gesellschaft für Erd- und Grundbau
DGemG	Deutsche Gemmologische Gesellschaft
DGEMP	Direction Générale de l'Énergie et des Materières Premiers
DGER	Direction Générale des Enquêtes et Recherches
DGEW	Deutsche Gesellschaft für Erzielhungs Wissenschaft
DGF	Danmarks Gummiteknologiske Forening
DGF	Dansk Geofysisk Forening
DGF	Dansk Geologisk Forening
DGF	Dansk Geoteknisk Forening
DGF	Deutsche Gesellschaft für Fachkrankeupflege
DGF	Deutsche Gesellschaft für Fettwissenschaft
DGF	Deutsche Gesellschaft für Flugwissenschaften
DGfA	Deutsche Gesellschaft für Amerikastudien = DGA
DGfA	Deutsche Gesellschaft für Arbeitschutze
DGFA	Dirección General de Fomento Agrícola (Argentina)
DGfB	Deutsche Gesellschaft für Betriebswirtschaft
DGfBUI	Deutsche Gesellschaft für Bluttransfusion und Immunohaematologie
DGfdB	Deutsche Gesellschaft für das Badewesen
DGfE	Deutsche Gesellschaft für Erziehungswissenschaft
DGfF	Deutsche Gesellschaft für Flöte e.V.
DGfH	Deutsche Gesellschaft für Hochschulkunde
DGfH	Deutsche Gesellschaft für Holzforschung
DGfH	Deutsche Gesellschaft für Hopfenforschung
DGfHK	Deutsche Gesellschaft für Heereskunde
DGFI	Deutsches Geodätisches Forschungsinstitut (DGK)
DGFK	Deutsche Gesellschaft für Friedens- und Konfliktforschung
DGfK	Deutsche Gesellschaft für Kartographie
DGfL	Deutsche Gesellschaft für Logistik e. V.
DGfM	Deutsche Gesellschaft für Mykologie e.V.
DGFMA	Decorative Gas Fire Manufacturers' Association
DGfP	Deutsche Gesellschaft für Personalführung
DGfP	Deutsche Gesellschaft für Pilzkunde
DGfP	Deutsche Gesellschaft für Psychologie
DGFP	Dirección General de Fomento Pecuario (Ecuador)
DGfPs	Deutsche Gesellschaft für Psychologie

DGfS	Deutsche Gesellschaft für Sexualforschung	**DGK**	Deutsche Gesellschaft für Kybernetik
DGfZ	Deutsche Gesellschaft für Züchtungskunde	**DGK**	Deutsche Gesellschaft für Wissenschaftliche und Angewandte Kosmetik
DGG	Deutsche Gartenbau-Gesellschaft	**DGKCh**	Deutsche Gesellschaft für Klinische Chemie
DGG	Deutsche Geologische Gesellschaft		
DGG	Deutsche Geophysikalische Gesellschaft	**DGKH**	Deutsche Gesellschaft für Kinderheilkunde
DGG	Deutsche Gesellschaft für Gerontologie	**DGLR**	Deutsche Gesellschaft für Luft- und Raumfahrt
DGG	Deutsche Glastechniche Gesellschaft		
DGG	Deutsche Gruppenpsychotherapeutische Gesellschaft	**DGLRM**	Deutsche Gesellschaft für Luft- und Raumfahrtmedizin
DGG	Dirección General de Ganadería (Salvador)	**DGM**	Deutsche Gesellschaft für Metallkunde
DGGB	Directors Guild of Great Britain = DG	**DGMA**	German Society for Measuring Technique and Automation
DGGL	Deutsche Gesellschaft für Gartenkunst und Landschaftspflege	**DGMK**	Deutsche Gesellschaft für Mineralölwissenschaft und Kohlechemie
DGGM	Dirección General de Geografica y Meteorología (Mexico)		
DGGR	Direction Générale du Génie et de l'Hydraulique Agricole	**DGMK**	Deutsche Wissenschaftliche Gesellschaft für Erdöl, Erdgas und Kohle e.V.
DGGTOT	Directia Generala Geo-Topografica si de Organizare a Teritoriului (Romania)	**DGMKG**	Deutsche Gesellschaft für Mund-, Kiefer- und Gesichtschirurgie
DGGV	Deutsche Gesellschaft für Gesundheitsvorsorge	**DGMP**	Deutsche Gesellschaft für Medizinische Physik
DGH	Deutscher Grosshändlerverband für Heizungs-, Lüftungs- und Klimadedarf	**DGMR**	Deutsche Gesellschaft für Medizinische Tumortherapie
DGHK	Deutsche Gesellschaft für Hydrokultur	**DGMR**	Directorate of Petroleum and Mineral Resources (Saudi Arabia)
DGHM	Deutsche Gesellschaft für Hygiene und Mikrobiologie	**DGMS**	Deutsche Gesellschaft für Medizinische Soziologie
DGHST	Direcção Geral de Higiene e Segurança do Trabalho	**DGMU**	Dirección General de Meteorología del Uruguay
DGHT	Deutsche Gesellschaft für Herpetologie und Terrarienkunde	**DGMW**	Deutsche Gesellschaft für Missionswissenschaft
DGI	Danish Geotechnical Institute	**DGN**	Deutsche Gesellschaft für Neurologie
DGI	Direction Générale des Impôts	**DGN**	Deutsche Gesellschaft für Nuklearmedizin
DGIA	Dirección General de Infrastructura Aeronáutica (Uruguay)		
DGIA	Dirección General de Investigaciones Agrícolas (Salvador)	**DGN**	Dirección de Geológia de la Nación (Argentina)
DGIAA	Direccion General de Industrias Agrarias y Alimentarias	**DGN**	Dirección General de Normas (Mexico)
DGICA	Direccion General de Investigacion y Capacitacion Agrarias	**DGNch**	Deutsche Gesellschaft für Neurochirurgie
DGIEA	Dirección General de Investigación y Extensión Agrícola (Guatemala)	**DGO**	Deutsche Gesellschaft für Galvano- und Oberflächentechnik (ex DGG)
DGIFLC	Directia Generala de Imbunatatiri Funciare si Constructii Agricole	**DGO**	Deutsche Gesellschaft für Osteuropakunde
DGIP	Direction Générale de l'Information et de la Documentation (Madagascar)	**DGOH**	Direccion General de Obras Hidraulicas
DGK	Deutsche Geodätische Kommission	**DGON**	Deutsche Gesellschaft für Ortung and Navigation

DGOR	Deutsche Gesellschaft für Operations Research
DGOSM	Dirección General de Oceanografia y Senalamiento Maritimo (Mexico)
DGOT	Deutsche Gesellschaft für Orthopédie und Traumatologie
DGP	Danmarks Gasmateriel Prøvning
DGP	Deutsche Gesellschaft für Parasitologie
DGP	Deutsche Gesellschaft für Parodontologie
DGP	Deutsche Gesellschaft für Pathologie
DGP	Deutsche Gesellschaft für Personalwesen
DGP	Deutsche Gesellschaft für Pflanzenernährung
DGPA	Dirección General de Planificación y Administración (Panama)
DGPA	Direccion General del Patrimonio del Estado
DGPA	Directia Generala a Productiei Animale
DGPF	Deutsche Gesellschaft für Phänomenologische Forschung e.V.
DGPF	Deutsche Gesellschaft für Photogrammetrie und Fernerkundung (*ex* DGP)
DGPh	Deutsche Gesellschaft für Photographie
DGPL	Deutsche Gesellschaft für Polarforschung
DGPM	Deutsche Gesellschaft für Psychosomatische Medizin
DGPM	Direction de la Géologie et de la Prospection Minière (Ivory Coast)
DGPMR	Deutsche Gesellschaft für Physikalische Medizin und Rehabilitation
DGPN	Deutsche Gesellschaft für Psychiatrie und Nervenheilkunde
DGPP	Deutsche Gesellschaft für Phoniatrie und Pédaudiologie
DGPPA	Dirección General de la Pequeña Propriedad Agrícola (Mexico)
DGPPP	Dirección General de Planeación y Promoción Pesqueras (Mexico)
DGPPT	Deutsche Gesellschaft für Psychotherapie, Psychosomatik und Tiefenpsychologie
DGPs	Deutsche Gesellschaft für Psychologie
DGPT	Deutsche Gesellschaft für Pharmacologie und Toxikologie (*ex* DPhG)
DGPT	Deutsche Gesellschaft für Psychotherapie und Tiefenpsychologie
DGPuK	Deutsche Gesellschaft für Publizistik- und Kommunikationswissenschaft
DGPV	Directia Generala a Productiei Vegetale (Romania)
DGQ	Deutsche Gesellschaft für Qualität
DGQ	Direcção-Geral da Qualidade (Portugal)
DGR	Deutsche Gesellschaft für Rehabilitation
DGRA	Dirección General de Reforma Agraria (Panama)
DGRh	Deutsche Gesellschaft für Rheumatologie
DGRH	Dirección General de Recursos Hidráulicos (Ecuador)
DGRM	Deutsche Gesellschaft für Rechtsmedizin
DGRN	Dirección General de Recursos Naturales (Honduras)
DGRR	Deutsche Gesellschaft für Raketentechnik und Raumfahrt
DGRST	Délégation Générale à la Recherche Scientifique et Technique
DGRV	Deutscher Genossenschafts- und Raiffeisenverband
DGS	Dansk Grafologisk Selskab
DGS	Det Grönlandske Selskab
DGS	Deutsche Gesellschaft für Sonnenenergie
DGS	Deutsche Gesellschaft für Soziologie
DGS	Deutsche Gesellschaft für Sprachheilpädagogik
DGS	Directia Generala Silvica
DGSE	Direction Générale de la Sécurité Extérieure
DGSF	Deutsche Gesellschaft für Sexualforschung
DGSFMM	Direcção General dos Serviços de Fomento Maritimo Marinho
DGSMP	Deutsche Gesellschaft für Sozialmedizin und Prävention (*ex* DGS)
DGSMT	Directio Generala a Statiunilor de Masini si Tractoare
DGSNM	Dirección General del Servicio Nacional Meteorológico (Argentina)
DGSP	Deutsche Gesellschaft für Soziale Psychiatrie
DGSS	Deutsche Gesellschaft für Sprechwissenschaft und Sprecherziehung
DGSS	Direccion General de la Seguridad Social (Uruguay)

DGSV	Dirección General de Sanidad Vegetal (Mexico)		**DHEW**	Departments of Health, Education and Welfare (U.S.A.)
DGTD	Directorate General of Technical Development (India)		**DHF**	Dag Hammarskjold Foundation
			DHF	Danmarks Harfiskeri-forening
DGTE	Direccion General de Transacciones Exteriores		**DHG**	Deutsche Hämophiliegesellschaft zur Bekämpfung von Blutungskrankheiten
DGTII	Direzione Generale delle Tasse e delle Imposte Indirette		**DHG**	Dungekalk-Hauptgemeinschaft
DGTP	Dirección General de Tecnologia Pesquera (Mexico)		**DHH**	Deutscher Hochseesportverband Hansa
			DHHS	Department of Health and Human Services (U.S.A.)
DGTS	Directio Generala Tehnica Stiintifica		**DHI**	Dansk Hydraulisk Institut
DGU	Dansk Geologiske Undersogelse		**DHI**	David Hume Institute
DGU	Deutsche Gesellschaft für Unternehmensforschung		**DHI**	Deutsches Hydrographisches Institut
			DHI	Door and Hardware Institute (U.S.A.)
DGUT	Deutsche Gesellschaft für Verhaltungstherapie		**DHKD**	Dogal Hayati Koruma Dernegi
DGV	Deutsche Gesellschaft für Volkerskunde		**DHKT**	Deutsche Handwerkskammertag
DGV	Deutsche Graphologische Vereinigung		**DHM**	Daughters of the Heart of Mary
DGV	Deutscher Genossenschaftsverband		**DHMT**	District Health Management Team (Zambia)
DGV	Deutscher Germanistenverband		**DHMV**	Deutscher Holzmastenverband
DGV	Deutscher Giessereiverband			
DGVN	Deutsche Gesellschaft für die Vereinten Nationen		**DHN**	Dirección de Hidrográfia y Navegación (Peru, Venezuela)
DGVS	Deutsche Gesellschaft für Verdauungs- und Stoffwechselkrankheiten		**DHN**	Directoria de Hidrografia e Navegação (Brazil)
DGVT	Deutsche Gesellschaft für Verhaltenstherapie		**DHR**	International Commission for the Hydrology of the River Rhine Basin
DGW	Deutsche Gesellschaft für Windenergie e.V.		**DHRC**	Documentation and Humanities Research Centre (Qatar)
DGW	Deutsche Gesellschaft für Wirtschaftliche Fertigung und Sicherheitstechnik		**DHRC**	Douglas Hospital Research Centre (Canada)
			DHRD	Department of Housing and Regional Development (Australia)
DGW	Deutsche Gesellschaft für Wohnungsmedizin		**DHRE**	Organising Committee for the Decade of Human Rights Education (U.S.A.)
DGWT	Deutsche Gesellschaft für Warenkunde und Technologie		**DHS**	Dansk Haematologisk Selskab
DGZfP	Deutsche Gesellschaft für Zerstörungsfreie Prüfverfahren		**DHS**	Design History Society
			DHS	Deutsche Haupstelle gegen die Suchtgefahren
DGZMK	Deutsche Gesellschaft für Zahn-, Mund- und Kieferheilkunde		**DHS**	Division of History of Science (IUHPS)
DH	Dansk Hortonomforening		**DHS**	Domestic Heating Society
DH	Department of Health		**DHSA**	Diaphragmatic Hernia Support Association
DH	Deutsche Heilpraktikerschaft			
DHAE	Department of Home Affairs and Environment (*now* DEST)		**DHSH**	Department of Human Services and Health (Australia)
DHAEMAE	Disposable Hypodermic and Allied Equipment Manufacturers Association of Europe		**DHSp**	Deutscher Ausschuss für Spektroskopie
			DHT	Disabled Housing Trust
DHC	Domestic Heating Council		**DHV**	Deutscher Handels- und Industrieangestelltenverband
DHDS	Dolmetsch Historical Dance Society		**DHV**	Deutscher Hochschulverband

DHV	Deutscher Hugenottenverein
DHWR	Deutscher Holzwirtschafts Rat
DI	Danmarks Ingeniorakademi
DI	Dansk Idroetsloerforening
DI	Démocrates Indépendants (Morocco)
DI	Dyslexia Institute
DIA	Danmarks Ingeniørakademi
DIA	Danske Interieur Arkitekter
DIA	Defence Industry Association
DIA	Departmento de Investigación Agropecuária (Colombia)
DIA	Design and Industries Association
DIA	Deutscher Innen- und Aussenhandel
DIA	Difusiones Inter-Americanas
DIA	Documentation et Informations Africaines
DIA	Driving Instructors Association
DIAA	Direction des Industries Agricoles et Alimentaires
DIAKONIA	World Federation of Diaconal Associations and Sisterhoods
DIAL	Danske Indendørs Arkitekters Landsforbund
DIAL-UK	National Association of Disablement Information and Advice Lines
DIAMA	Société de Distribution Automobile Malienne
DIANA	Komma Dimokratikis Ananeosis (Greece)
DIAS	Disability Information and Advice Service Ltd
DIAS	Dublin Institute of Advanced Studies (Éire)
DIASEN	Société de Distribution Automobile Sénégalaise
DIAUP	Democratic Islamic Arab Unity Party (Algeria)
DIB	Deutscher Imkerbund
DIB	Deutsches Institut für Betriebswirtschaft
DIB	Development Industrial Bank (Egypt)
DIC	Diamond Information Centre
DICA	Direction des Carburants (MIR)
DICE	Dairy and Ice Cream Equipment Association
DICE	Durrell Institute of Conservation and Ecology
DICI	Design Institute of Chemical Industry (Vietnam)
DICOPA	Société de Distribution de Cosmétiques et Parfumerie (Senegal)

DICORE	División de Conservación de Recursos (Chile)
DICP	Dalian Institute of Chemical Physics
DICR	Dutch Institute for Consumer Research
DICSA	División de Investigación de Conservación de Suelos y Aguas (Puerto Rico)
DICTA	District Council Technical Association
DICTO	Development of Islamic Countries Transport Organisation (Malaysia)
DID	Drainage and Irrigation Department (Malaysia)
DID	Verband Deutscher Industrie-Designer
DIDA	Dirección de Inspección y Defensa Agraria (Peru)
DIDEFA	División de Defensa Agropecuária (Chile)
DIE	Danish Institute for the International Exchange of Scientific and Literary Publications
DIEESE	Departamento Intersindical de Estatisticas e Estudos Sócio-Económicos (Brazil)
DIEL	Advisory Committee on Telecommunications for Disabled and Elderly People
DIÉLCI	Diffusion Électrique de la Côte d'Ivoire
DIÉLI	Direction des Industries Électroniques et de l'Informatique
DIESA	Department of International Economic & Social Affairs (UN)
DIF	Dansk Idraets Forbund
DIF	Dansk Ingeniørforening
DIF	Dekk Importoørenes Forening
DIF	Deutsches Institut zur Förderung des Industriellen Führungsnachwuches
DIFCA	La Diffusion du Caoutchouc
DIFF	Development Import Finance Facility
DIFPOA	Divisão de Inspeção e Fiscalização de Produtos de Origem Animal (Brazil)
DIFS	Dalian Institute of Forestry Science
DIfU	Deutsches Institut für Urbanistik
DIG	Disablement Income Group
DIG	Drinks Industry Group (Éire)
DIGA	Dynamics International Gardening Association (U.S.A.)
DIGAASES	Direccion General de Aprovechamiento de Aguas Salinas y Energia Solar (Mexico)
DIGAP	Direct Investigation Group on Aerial Phenomena

DIGÉC	Direction du Gaz, de l'Électricité et du Charbon
DIGEDE-COM	Direccion General para el Desarrollo de la Comunidad (Panama)
DIGERE-NARE	Direccion General de Recursos Naturales Renovables (Honduras)
DIGESA	Direccion General de Servicios Agricolas (Guatemala)
DIGI	Deutsche Interessengemeinschaft Internet
DIGOS	Direzione Investigazione Generali Operazioni Speciali
DIGS	Disablement Income Group Scotland
DIHT	Deutscher Industrie- und Handelstag
DII	Direction Interdepartementale de l'Industrie
DIICA	Departamento Técnico Interamericano de Cooperación Agrícola (Chile)
DIJIN	Direccion de Policia Judicial e Investigacion (Colombia)
DIKO	Demokratiko Komma (Cyprus)
DILAPSA	Distribuidora Latinoamericana de Publicaciones (Chile)
DILF	Danske Indkøbschefers Landsforening
DILGEA	Department of Immigration, Local Government and Ethnic Affairs (Australia)
DIM	Deutsches Institut für Marktforschung
DIMA	Derechos Iguales para Las Mujeres Argentinas
DIMAC	Distribuidora de Materials de Construção (Mozambique)
DIMDI	Deutsches Institut für Medizinische Dokumentation und Information
Dimed	Divisão Nacional de Vigilância Sanitária e Medicamentos (Brazil)
DIMÉLEC	Direction des Industries Mécaniques, Électriques et Électroniques
DIMERCA	Distribucion y Mercadeo Centroamericano (Nicaragua)
DIMÉS	Distribution de Matériel Électrique au Sénégal
DIMEX	Centre Français du Commerce Extérieur
DIMIN	Departamento de Inteligencia del Ministro del Interior (Peru)
DIMINCO	National Diamond Mining Company (Sierra Leone)
DIMO	Danske Interne Medicineres Organisation
DIN	Demograficheskii Institut Akademii Nauk

DIN	Deutsches Institut für Normung
DINA	Chilean Directorate of National Intelligence
DINA	Diesel Nacional (Mexico)
DINA-COPRIN	Dirección General de Costos, Precios y Ingresos (Uruguay)
DINACOS	Dirección Nacional de Comunicación Social (Chile)
DINADECO	National Directorate of Community Development (Costa Rica)
DINAR	Dirección Narcótica (Paraguay)
DINFIA	Dirección Nacional de Fabricaciones e Investigaciones Aeronáuticas (Argentina)
DIO	Dienst voor Internationale Ontwikkeling
DIPA	Diamond Industrial Products Association
DIPA	Ductile Iron Producers Association
DIPAN	Directoria da Produção Animal (Brazil)
DIPC	Ductile Iron Producers' Association
DIPR	Deutsches Institut für Public Relations e.V.
DIPRA	Ductile Iron Pipe Research Association (U.S.A.)
DIPROA	División de Producción Agropecuária (Chile)
DIPROBAS	Distribuidora de Productos Basicos (Nicaragua)
DIPUVEN	Distribuidora de Publicaciones Venezolanas
DIQUI-VENJA	Distribuidora Química Venezolana
DIR	Department of Industrial Relations (Australia)
DIRA	Danish Industrial Robot Association
DIREL	Federazione Italiana Dirigenti Enti Pubblici Locali
DIRI VENTAS	Asociación de Dirigentes de Ventas y Mercadotecnia (Colombia)
DIRMEN	Associazione Tecnia Italiana Dirigenti Mensa
DIRSTAT	Federazione fra le Associazioni e i Sindacati Nazionali dei Quadri Direttivi dell'Amministrazione dello Stato
DIS	Danmarks Internationale Studenterkomité
DIS	Development Information System (UN)
DISA	Defense Information Systems Agency (*ex* DCA)
DISA	Direção de Informação a Segurança de Angola

DISCON	Defence Integrated Secure Communications Network (Australia)
DISCS	Domestic International Sales Corporations (U.S.A.)
DISCUS	Distilled Spirits Council of the United States
DISEDE	Direccion de los Seguros de Desempleo (Uruguay)
DISGRA	Association des Distributeurs et Importateurs de Sable et Gravier
DISI	Dairy Industries Society International (U.S.A.)
DISIP	Venezuelan Political Police
DISK	Confederation of Progressive Trade Unions (Turkey)
DISMA	Deutsches Institut für Statistik und Meinungsforschung
DISPER	Distribuidora de Productos Perecederos (Nicaragua)
DIST	Department of Industry, Science and Technology (Australia)
DISTRI-PRESS	Fédération Internationale des Distributeurs de Presse
DISY	Demokratikos Synagemos (Cyprus)
DIT	Division of Information Technology (CSIRO)
DITAC	Department of Industry, Technology and Commerce (Australia)
DITB	Distributive Industry Training Board
DITC	Department of Industry, Trade and Commerce (Canada)
DITURIS	Direccion Nacional de Turismo (Ecuador)
DIU	Democratic Independent Union (Belize)
DIVENAZ	Distribuidora Venezolana de Azúcares
DIVERSI-TAS	IUBS/SCOPE/UNESCO Programme on Biological Diversity
DIW	Deutsches Institut für Wirtschaftforschung
DIZ	Deutsches Institut für Zeitgeschichte
DJ	Dansk Journalistforbund
DJ	Daughters of Jesus of Kermaria = FJ, HJ
DJ	Democracy Now (Germany)
DJBFA	Danske Jazz, Beat og Folkemusikautorer
DJF	Disc Jockeys Federation
DJOØF	Danmarks Jurist- og Oøkonomforbund
DJP	Départment Fédéral de Justice et Police (Switzerland)
DJT	Deutscher Juristentag

DJV	Deutsche Journalistenverband
DJV	Deutscher Jagdschutzverband
DJVK	Danmarks Jordbrugsvidenskabelige Kandidatforbund
DK	Dansk Kedelforening
DK	Democratic Kampuchea (Cambodia)
DK	Demokraticheskii Kongress
DK	Dunajskaja Komissija (Hungary)
DK-U	Dansk Kæreloerer-Union
DKB	Deutscher Konditorenbund
DKDGS	Kongelige Danske Geografiske Selskab
DKE	Deutsche Elecktrotechnische Kommission
DKF	Dansk Kiropraktorforening
DKF	Dansk Kor Forbund
DKF	Danske Konsummoelkmejeriers Foelesreproesentation
DKF	Dyskusyjny Klub Filmowy
DKFZ	Deutsches Krebsforschungszentrum
DKG	Deutsche Kautschukgesellschaft
DKG	Deutsche Keramische Gesellschaft
DKG	Deutsche Kinotechnische Gesellschaft für Film und Fernsehen
DKG	Deutsche Krankenhausgesellschaft
DKI	Deutsches Krankenhausinstitut
DKI	Deutsches Kunststoff Institut
DKI	Deutsches Kupferinstitut
DKI	Dvizhenie Kommunisticheskoi Initsiativy
DKIN	Deutsches Komitee Instandhaltung
DKM	Dansk Kulturhistorisk Museumsforening
DKNVS	Det Kongelige Norske Videnskabers Selskab
DKOSRTs	Dvizhenie za Kulturno, Obrazovatelno i Sotsialno Razvitie na Tsiganite (Bulgaria) = MCESDG
DKP	Danmarks Kommunistiske Parti
DKP	Democratic Korea Party
DKP	Deutsche Kommunistische Partei = KPD
DKS	Dansk Kartografisk Selskab
DKS	Dansk Kerneteknisk Selskab
DKS	Dansk Kirurgisk Selskab
DKV	Deutscher Kaffee-Verband
DKV	Deutscher Kalte- und Klimatechnisher Verein
DKVS	Kongelige Danske Videnskabernes Selskab

DL	Democratic Left (Czech Republic)
DL	Deutscher Lehrerverband
DL	Foreningen af Danske Landskabsarkitekter
DL/SWA	Commission for Controlling the Desert Locust in the Eastern Region of its Distribution Area in South West Asia (FAO) (Italy)
DLA	Decorative Lighting Association
DLA	Dental Laboratories Association
DLA	Deutsche Landjugend-Akademie, Fredeburg
DLC	Distance Learning Centre
DLCC	Disabled Living Centres Council
DLCO-EA	Desert Locust Control Organization for Eastern Africa = OLCP-EA
DLF	Dagligvaruleverantoerers Förbund
DLF	Danmarks Lærerforening
DLF	Dansk Lokalhistorisk Forening
DLF	Danske Landboforenings Frøforskning
DLF	Défense de la Langue Française
DLF	Deutschlandfunk
DLF	Disabled Living Foundation
DLF	Foreningen af Danske Lysreklame Fabrikanter
DLG	Deutsche Landwirtschaftsgesellschaft
DLG-EKO	Democratic League of Greens – EKO (Bulgaria)
DLH	Deutsche Lufthansa AG
DLI	Department of Labour and Industry (Australia)
DLI	Fachverband der Deutschen Laborbau-Industrie
DLIS	Desert Locust Information Service (FAO)
DLK	Danske Landbrugeres Kreatursalgsforening
DLK	Democratic League of Kosovo = DSK
DLL	Direction du Livre et de la Lecture
DLM	Democratic Labour Movement (Guyana, Netherland Antilles)
DLMA	Dominica Liberation Movement Alliance
DLMPS	Division of Logic, Methodology and Philosophy of Science (IUHPS)
DLO	Direct Labour Organisation
DLP	Democratic Labour Party (Australia)
DLP	Democratic Labour Party (Barbados)
DLP	Democratic Liberal Party (Korea)
DLP	Democratic Liberal Party of Armenia
DLP	Dominica Labour Party
DLPA	Dry Lining and Partition Association
DLR	Dansk Landbrugs Realkreditfond
DLR	Deutsche Forschungsanstalt für Luft- und Raumfahrt e. V.
DLR	Syndicat National des Distributeurs, Loueurs et Réparateurs de Matériel de Bâtiment, de Travaux Publics et de Manutention
DLRG	Deutsche Lebensrettungs- Gesellschaft
DLRI	Dalian Diesel Locomotive Research Institute
DLSRT	Dunkirk Little Ships Restoration Trust
DLT	Deutscher Landkreistag
DLV	Deutsche Lehrmittelverband
DLV	Deutscher Ladenbau- Verband
DLV	Deutscher Landfrauenverband
DM	Dansk Magisterforening
DM	Daughters of Our Lady of Mercy
DM	Demokraticheskaia Moskva
DM	Union Démocratique Mauricienne (Mauritius)
DMA	Dance Masters of America
DMA	Defence Manufacturers Association
DMA	Defense Mapping Agency (U.S.A.)
DMA	Délégation Ministérielle pour l'Armament
DMA	Dominion Marine Association (Canada)
DMA	Direct Marketing Association (*ex* AMOP, BDMA, BLBA, DMPA)
DMAC	Diving Medical Advisory Committee (AODC)
DMALIC	Die & Mould Association of Light Industry of China
DMB	Deutscher Mieterbund
DMB	Deutscher Museumsbund
DMBF	Dansk Musikbiblioteksforening
DMC	Dalian Medical College
DMD	Democratic Movement of the Donbas (Ukraine)
DMDS	Deutsche Gesellschaft für Medizinische Dokumentation und Statistik
DME	Directorate of Mechanical Engineering
DMF	Dansk Markedsførings Forbund
DMF	Dansk Mathematisk Forening = DMS
DMF	Dansk Møbeltransport Forening
DMF	Danske Mineralbandsfabrikanters

DMF	Dialogo Mujer Foundation (Colombia)		**DMSG**	Deutsche Multiple Sklerose Gesellschaft
DMF	Disabled Motorists Federation		**DMSP**	Defense Meteorological Satellite Program (U.S.A.)
DMG	Deutsche Malako-zoologische Gesellschaft		**DMSPC**	Defence Material Standardization Policy Committee (MOD)
DMG	Deutsche Meteorologische Gesellschaft		**DMSSB**	Direct Mail Services Standards Board
DMG	Deutsche Mineralogische Gesellschaft		**DMTS**	Department of Mines and Technical Surveys (Canada)
DMG	Deutsche Morgenländische Gesellschaft		**DMU**	Dalian Marine University
DMG	Deutsche Mozart-Gesellschaft		**DMU**	Dansk Magasinpresses Udgiverforening
DMG	Foreningen af Danske Manufaktur-Grossiter		**DMV**	Deutsche Marketing Vereinigung
DMHV	Deutscher Mobilheimverband		**DMV**	Deutsche Mathematikervereinigung
DMI	Danske Meteorologiske Institut		**DMV**	Deutscher Markscheiderverein
DMI	Department of Manpower and Immigration (Canada)		**DMV**	Deutscher Marmorverband
DMI	Department of Manufacturing Industry (Australia)		**DMV**	Deutscher Musiker Verband
DMI	Directorate of Military Intelligence (South Africa)		**DMVA**	Dublin Master Victuallers Association (Éire)
DMIAA	Diamond Manufacturers and Importers Association of America		**DMyG**	Deutschsprachige Mykologische Gesellschaft
DMJ	Daughters of Mary and Joseph		**DMYV**	Deutscher Motoryachtverband
DMK	Dravida Munnetra Kazhagam (India)		**DMZ**	Demilitarized Zone (Democratic People's Republic of Korea)
DML	Danske Malermestres Landssekretariat		**DNA**	Deutsche Normenausschuss
DMMTRI	Dalian Modular Machine Tool Research Institute		**DNA**	Dirección Nacional del Antartico (Argentina)
DMN	Direction de la Météorologie Nationale		**DNA**	Direction de la Navigation Aérienne
DMP	Normenausschuss Materialprüfung im DIN		**DNA**	District Nursing Association
DMPA	Direct Mail Producers Association (*now* DMA) (U.K.)		**DNA**	Norwegian Labour Party
DMPA	Disinfectant and Maintenance Products Association		**DNB**	Deutsches Nachrichtenbro
			DNB	Dirección Nacional del Banano (Ecuador)
DMpF	Dansk Musikpædagogisk Forening		**DNB**	Vereniging 'De Nederlandse Baksteen-industrie'
DMPRI	Dalian Marine Product Research Institute		**DNBF**	De Norske Blikemballagefabrikers Forening
DMR	Demokraticheskaia Molodezh Rossii		**DNBV**	Koninklijke Nederlandse Brandweervereniging
DMR	Deutscher Musikrat			
DMRC	Defence Maintenance and Repair Committee (MOD)		**DNCP**	Dirición Nacional de Construcciónes Portuarias y Vias Navegables (Argentina)
DMRL	Defence Metallurgical Research Laboratory (India)			
DMS	Danish Mathematical Society = DMF		**DNCW**	Dominica National Council of Women
DMS	Danmarks Mejeritekniske Selskab		**DND**	Den Norske Dataforening
DMS	Danmarks Mikrobiologiske Selskab		**DND**	Department of National Defence (Canada)
DMS	Dansk Medicinsk Selskab			
DMS	Dansk Medikoteknisk Selskab		**DNDR**	Dirección Nacional de Desarrollo (Bolivia)
DMS	Dansk Metallurgisk Selskab			
DMSA	Domestic Manufacturing Stationers' Association		**DNEF**	Departamento Nacional de Estradas de Ferro (Brazil)

DNER	Departamento Nacional de Estradas de Rodagem (Brazil)	**DNPM**	Departamento Nacional de Produção Mineral (Brazil)
DNF	Dansk Naturhistorisk Forening	**DNPV**	Departamento Nacional de Produção Vegetal (Brazil)
DNF	Dansk Numismatisk Forening		
DNF	Deutscher Naturschutzring e.V. – Bundesverband für Umweltschutz	**DNPVN**	Departamento Nacional de Portos e Vias Navegáveis (Brazil)
DNF	Norske Forsikringsforening	**DNR**	Den Norske Reisebyråforening
DNFB	De Norske Blikemballagefabrikers Forening	**DNR**	Department of National Revenue (Canada)
DNFF	Den Norske Fagpresses Forening	**DNR**	Deutsche Naturschutzring
DNFS	Direccion Nacional de Fauna Silvestre (Argentina)	**DNS**	Dalmatinska Narodna Stranka (Croatia) = DNP
DNG	Deutsche Numismatische Gesellschaft – Verband der Deutschen Münzvereine e.V.	**DNS**	Dansk Neurologisk Selskab
		DNS	Den Norske Sykehusforening
		DNSE	Dirección Nacionál del Servicio Estadístico (Argentina)
DNGE	Dirección Nacional de Granos y Elevadores (Argentina)	**DNSF**	Democratic National Salvation Front (Romania)
DNH	Den Norske Husflidsforening		
DNH	Department of National Heritage	**DNSL**	De Norske Saltfisekspørters Landsforening
DNH	Udgiverselskab for Danmarks Nyeste Historie	**DNSU**	Dansk Nasjonal Sosjalistisk Ungdom
DNI	Dana Normalisasi Indonesia	**DNSU**	Domovinsko Nepartije Srpske Udruženje (Serbia) = HNPSA
DNI	Defensa de los Niños – International = DCI, DEI		
		DNT	Det Norske Travselskap
DNIBR	Danish National Institute of Building Research	**DNTF**	De Norske Teatres Forening
		DNU	Directorio Nacional Unido (Honduras)
DNJ	Den Norske Jordmorforening	**DNV**	Den Norske Veterinærforening
DNJ	Det Norske Justervesen	**DNV**	Det Norske Veritas
DNKL	De Norske Klippfiskeksportorers Landsforening	**DNV**	Deutscher Nautischer Verein
		DO	(CSIRO) Division of Oceanography
DNL	Det Norske Luftfartsselskab	**DO-G**	Deutsche Ornithologen-Gesellschaft
DNLF	Den Norske Lægeforening	**DOAC**	Defence Operational Analysis Centre
DNM	Den Norske Mikrobionom-forening	**DOAL**	Deutsche Ost Afrika Linie
DNM	Det Norske Jorg- og Myrselskap	**DOAT**	Direction des Opérations de l'Assistance Technique (UNDP) = TAO
DNM	Foreningen af Danske Naturvidenskabelige Museer		
		DOB	Verband der Damenober Bekleidungsindustrie
DNMF	Det Norske Maskinist-forbund		
DNN	Det Norske Nitridaktieselskap	**DOBETA**	Domestic Oil Burning Equipment Testing Association
DNO	Danske Nervelægers Organisation		
DNOCS	Departamento Nacional de Obras contra las Secas (Brazil)	**DOBG**	Dansk Online Brugergruppe
		DOC	Department of Communications (Canada)
DNOS	Departamento Nacional de Obras de Saneamento (Brazil)		
		DOC	Dépôts Océan Congo
DNP	Dalmatian National Party (Croatia) = DNS	**DOCA**	Automatic Documentation Section (CETIS)
DNP	Departamento Nacional de Planeación (Colombia)	**DOCA-PESCA**	Grémio dos Armadores da Pesca de Arrasto
DNP	Direcção Nacional das Pescas (Cape Verde)	**DOCCEN**	Centro de Documentacion Central (Nicaragua)

DOCEGEO	Rio Doce Geologia e Mineração (CVRD) (Brazil)
DOCENAVE	Vale do Rio Doce Navegação (Brazil)
DOCENT	Documentation Centrale pour le Développement (Belgium)
Docomomo	International Working Party for the Documentation and Conservation of Buildings, Sites and Neighbourhoods of the Modern Movement
DOCPAL	Sistema de Documentación sobre Población en América Latina
DOD	Dansk Organisation of Detailhandelskoeder
DOD	Department of Defense (U.S.A.)
DOD	Deutsches Ozeanographisches Datenzentrum
DOE	Department of Electronics (India)
DOE	Department of Energy (U.S.A.)
DoE	Department of the Environment
DoE	Department of the Environment (U.S.A.)
DOE (NI)	Department of the Environment (Northern Ireland)
DOF	Dansk Ornithologisk Forening
DØF	Danske Økonomers Forening
DOF	Department of Finance (Australia)
DOFUNGE	Sociedade Tecnica de Fundições Geraïs S.A. (Brazil)
DOG	Deutsche Ophthalmologische Gesellschaft
DOG	Deutsche Orient-Gesellschaft
DoH	Department of Health
DOI	Department of Industry (Canada)
DOI	Department of the Interior (U.S.A.)
DOKP	Dyrekcja Okręgowa Kolei Państwowych
DOKS	Dansk Optometri og Kontaktlinse Selskab
DOM-TOM	Départements d'Outremer – Territoires d'Outremer
DOMAINS	Deep Ocean Manned Instrumented Station
DOMEI	Zen Nihon Rodo Sodomei (Japan)
DOMITOR	Association Internationale pour le Développement de la Recherche sur le Cinéma des Premiers Temps
DOMMDA	Drawing Office Material Manufacturers and Dealers Association
DOMO	Dispensing Opticians Manufacturing Organisation

DOMOS	Centro de Desarrollo de la Mujer (Chile)
DONGAS	Dansk Olie og Naturgas
DONS	Department of National Security (South Africa)
DOP	Direction des Opérations et de la Programmation (UNDP)
DOPIE	Department of Primary Industries and Energy = DPIE
DOPS	Dansk Optisk Selskab
DOPS	Departamento da Ordem Política e Social (Brazil)
DOR	Departamento de Orientacion Revolucionaria (Cuba)
DORDEC	Domestic Refrigeration Development Committee
DORIS	Société de Développement Opérationnel des Richesses Sous-Marines
DORS	Danish Operations Research Society
DOS	Dansk Ortopoedisk Selskab
DOS	Dansk Otolaryngologisk Selskab
DOS	Democratic Opposition of Slovenia = DEMOS
DOS	Directorate of Operational Services
DOS	Directorate of Overseas Surveys (ODA)
DOSCO	Dominion Steel and Coal Corporation (Canada)
DOSLI	Department of Survey and Land Information (New Zealand)
DOSME	Dirección de Obra Social y Ministerio de Educación (Argentina)
DoT	Department of Telecommunications (India)
DoT	Department of Tourism
DOT	Department of Trade
DOT	Department of Transport (Canada, UK)
DOTAC	Department of Transport and Communications
DOUAL'AIR	Société d'Exploitation des Bars et Restaurants de l'Aérogare de Douala (Cameroon)
DOUALAP	Société Camérounaise de Diffusion d'Appareils Électriques
DOV	Deutsche Orchestervereinigung
DOZ	Deutsches Olympia Zentrum
DP	Danske Psykologforening
DP	Democracy Party (Burma, Egypt, Kenya)
DP	Democratic Party (Albania, Bulgaria, Hungary, Macedonia, Serbia, Slovenia)

DP	Democratic Party (Montenegro) = DS		DPG	Deutsche Physikalische Gesellschaft
DP	Democratic Party (South Africa, Uganda)		DPG	Deutsche Physiologische Gesellschaft
DP	Democratische Partij (Netherlands Antilles)		DPG	Deutsche Phytomedizinische Gesellschaft
DP	Democrazia Proletaria		DPG	Deutsche Psychoanalytische Gesellschaft
DP	Demokraticheskaia Partiia		DPhG	Deutsche Pharmazeutische Gesellschaft
DP	Deutsches Patentamt		DPhV	Deutscher Philologenverband
DP-NSF	Democratic Party – National Salvation Front (Romania)		DPI	Department of Primary Industries = DPIE
DP-UDC	Democracia Popular – Unión Democrata Cristiana (Ecuador)		DPI	Department of Public Information (UN)
DPA	Dartmoor Preservation Association		DPI	Diretoria do Património Indígena (Brazil)
DPA	Data Protection Agency		DPI	Disabled Peoples International = OMPH, OMPI
DPA	Democratic Party of Albania = PDS			
DPA	Democratic Party of Albanians (Serbia)		DPIE	Department of Primary Industries and Energy = DPI
DPA	Deutsche Presse Agentur		DPIO	Democracy and Peace Interim Organisation (Burma)
DPA	Dewan Pertimbangan Agung (Indonesia)		DPIS	Derby Porcelain International Society
DPA	Diary Publishers Association		DPJ	Departamento de Polícia Judiciária (Brazil)
DPA	Directory Publishers' Association			
DPA	Disabled Persons Assembly (New Zealand)		DPK	Democratic Party of Kurdistan
DPA	Duck Producers Association		DPK	Deutsche Pappelkommission
DPAA	Draught Proofing Advisory Association		DPK	Deutsche Pudel-Klub
DPAG	Dangerous Pathogens Advisory Group		DPKR	Demokraticheskaia Partiia Kommunisticheskov Rossii
DPAS	Discharged Prisoners' Aid Society		DPM&C	Department of Prime Minister and Cabinet
DPC	Defence Planning Committee (NATO)			
DPC	Democratic Party of the Crimea		DPMA	Dairy Products Manufacturers Association (South Africa)
DPC	Dubai Petroleum Company		DPMA	Data Processing Management Association (U.S.A.)
DPCSD	Department for Policy Coordination and Sustainable Development (UN)		DPMNU	Democratic Party for Macedonian National Unity
DPD	Association Internationale Données pour le Développement = DD, DFD		DPMOAP	Society of Data Processing Machine Operators and Programmers (U.S.A.)
DPEA	Departamento de Pesquisa e Experimentação Agropecuárias (Brazil)		DPN	Democratic Party of Nauru (Burma)
DPERPLA	Delegacion del Parlamento Europeo para las Relaciones con los Paises de Latinoamerica = ELAIA		DPO	Dansk Privatopdager Organization
			DPOM	Directia Planificarii si Organizarii Muncii
DPET	Directoria de Pesquisas e Ensino Tecnico (Brazil)		DPOS	District Planning Officers Society
DPF	Dansk Pilotforening		DPP	Democratic Progress Party (Taiwan)
DPF	Danske Papiringeniorers Forening		DPP	Democratic Progressive Party (South Africa)
DPF	Departamento da Polícia Federal (Brazil)			
DPF	Départment Politique Fédéral (Switzerland)		DPP	Development Resources Panel (UNDP)
DPF	Directia Plan Financiar (Romania)		DPP	Directia Propagandei si Presei (Romania)
DPFGR	Demersal and Pelagic Fisheries Research Group		DPP	Direction de la Prévention des Pollutions

DPPA	Dominica Planned Parenthood Association
DPPC	Development and Project Planning Centre
DPPR	Democratic Political Party of Roma / Demokratska Politička Partija Roma (Serbia)
DPPRM	Democratic Progressive Party of Roma in Macedonia / Demokratska Progresivna Partija na Romite vo Makedonija
DPR	Demokraticheskaia Partiia Rossii
DPR	Dewan Perwakitan Raykat (Indonesia)
DPRF	Dansk Public Relations Forening
DPRG	Deutsche Public-Relations-Gesellschaft
DPRI	Disaster Prevention Research Institute (Japan)
DPRK	Dansk Public Relations Klub
DPRK	Democratic Peoples Republic of Korea
DPRTF	Drought Policy Review Task Force
DPS	Dales Pony Society
DPS	Dansk Pediatrisk Selskab
DPS	Dansk Psykiatrisk Selskab
DPS	Democratic Party of Serbia
DPS	Democratic Party of Serbs / Demokratska Partija na Srbite (Macedonia)
DPS	Democratic Party of Socialists (Bulgaria)
DPS	Democratic Party of Socialists / Demokratska Partija Socijalista (Montenegro)
DPS	Disabled Photographers' Society
DPS	Dvizhenie za Prava i Svobodi (Bulgaria) = MRF
DPSC	Detainees' Parents' Support Committee (South Africa)
DPSCA	Department of Political and Security Council Affairs (UN)
DPSPA	Display Producers and Screen Printers Association
DPSSC	Drugs and Poisons Schedule Standing Committee
DPT	CSIR Division of Production Technology (South Africa)
DPT	Democratic Party of Tajikistan
DPT	Democratic Party of Turkmenistan
DPT	Democratic Party of Turks / Demokratska Partija na Turcite (Macedonia)
DPTAC	Disabled Persons Transport Advisory Committee
DPTG	Deutsche Paul Tillich Gesellschaft
DPTRI	Drilling and Production Technology Research Institute
DPU	Democratic Party of Ukraine
DPU	Demokraticheskaia Partiia Uzbekistana
DPU	Development Planning Unit
DPUH	Društvo Povjesničara Umjetnosti Hrvatske
DPV	Dansk Patent-og Varemaerkekonsulentforening
DPV	Deutsche Psychoanalytische Vereinigung
DPV	Deutscher Palästina Verein
DPWV	Deutscher Paritaetischer Wohlfahrtsverbande
DPZ	Deutsches Primatenzentrum
DR	Danmarks Radio
DR	Danmarks Retsforbund
DR	Deutsche Reichsbahn
DR	Groupe des Droites Européennes
DRA	Danish Robot Association
DRA	Defence Research Agency
DRAE	Defence Research Analysis Establishment (Canada)
Dragbel	Fédération Belge des Dragueurs de Gravier et de Sable
DRATEX-CONFECAM	Société de Confection de Linge de Maison et de Vêtement au Caméroun
DRB	Danske Reklamebureauers Brancheforening
DRB	Defence Research Board (Canada)
DRB	Deutscher Richterbund
DRC	Dada Research Centre (Germany)
DRC	Dictionary Research Centre
DRDC	Democratic Rights Defence Campaign
DRDO	Defence Research and Development Organization (India)
DRE	Department of Resources and Energy
DREA	Defence Research Establishment Atlantic (DRB)
DREO	Defence Research Establishment Ottawa (DRB)
DREP	Defence Research Establishment Pacific (DRB)
DRET	Defence Research Establishment Toronto (DRB)
DRF	Dansk Rationaliserings Forening

DRF	Decency Research Foundation (U.S.A.)	**DRTT**	CSIR Division of Roads and Transport Technology (South Africa)
DRG	Defence Research Group (NATO)	**DRU**	Dirección Revolucionario Unida (El Salvador)
DRG	Deutsche Rheologische Gesellschaft		
DRG	Deutsche Röntgengesellschaft – Gesellschaft für Medizinische Radiologie, Strahlenbiologie und Nuklearmedizin	**DRV**	Deutscher Raiffeisenverband
		DRV	Deutscher Reifenhändlerverband
		DRV	Deutscher Reisebüroverband
DRI	CSO Demographic Research Institute (Hungary)	**DS**	Danmarks Sprogloererforening
		DS	Dansk Samling
DRI	Denver Research Institute (U.S.A.)	**DS**	Dansk Socialrådgiverforening
DRIC	Defence Research Information Centre	**DS**	Dansk Standardiseringsråd
DRIE	Department of Regional Industrial Expansion (Canada)	**DS**	Delphinium Society
		DS	Demokraticheskii Soiuz
DRIRC	Defence Research and Intramural Resources Committee (MoD)	**DS**	Demokratska Stranka (Montenegro) = DP
DRIVE	Dedicated Road Infrastructure for Vehicle Safety on Europe (CEC)	**DS**	Dhamma School
		DS	Diecasting Association
DRK	Dansk Røde Kors	**DSA**	Bureau Européen d'Information pour le Développement de la Santé Animale
DRK	Deutsches Rötes Kreuz		
DRL	Deutscher Rat für Landespflege	**DSA**	Democratic Socialists of America
DRMA	De re militari Association	**DSA**	Demokratski Savez Albanaca (Bosnia-Herzegovina) = DAA
DRME	Direction des Recherches et Moyens d'Essais		
DRML	Defence Research Medical Laboratories (DRET)	**DSA**	Direct Selling Association
		DSA	Direction des Services Agricoles
DRN	Departamento de Recursos Naturais (Brazil)	**DSA**	Door and Shutter Association
		DSA	Down's Syndrome Association
DRNR	Dirección de Recursos Naturales Renovables (Venezuela)	**DSA**	Dozenal Society of America
		DSA	Drilling and Sawing Association
DRO	Danske Radiologers Organisation	**DSA**	Driving Standards Agency
DROGA	Schweizerischer Verband Angestellter Drogisten	**DSA**	Dviženje za Semakendonska Akcija (Macedonia) = MPMA
DRP	Development Resources Panel (UNDP)	**DSAA**	Defense Security Assistance Agency (U.S.A.)
DRP/M	Demokraticheskaia Rabochaia Partiia (Marksistov)		
		DSAB	Deutscher Sportärztebund
DRPC	Defence Research Policy Committee	**DSABRO**	District Surveyors' Association (*ex* SCBRO)
DRPLC	Département des Recherches des Plantations Lever au Congo		
		DSAC	Defence Scientific Advisory Council (MOD)
DRPM	Democratic Reform Party of Muslims (Serbia)	**DSAI**	Down's Syndrome Association of Ireland
DRS	Dansk Radiologisk Selskab		
DRS	Direzione Richerche e Studi	**DSAM**	Dansk Selskab for Almen Medicin
DRST	Direction de la Recherche Scientifique-Technique (GIN)	**DSB**	Dachverband der Schweizerischen Bekleidungsindustrie
DRT	Disability Resource Team	**DSB**	Danske Statsbaner
DRTC	Documentation Research and Training Centre, Bangalore (India)	**DSB**	Deutsche Schaustellerbund
		DSB	Deutscher Sängerbund e.V.
DRTE	Defence Research Telecommunications Establishment (Canada)	**DSB**	Deutscher Sauna-Bund
DRTPC	Development Research and Technological Planning Centre (Egypt)	**DSB**	Deutscher Sportbund

DSB	Drug Supervisory Body (Switzerland)	**DSIS**	Defence Scientific Information Services (DRB)
DSBA	Dalesbred Sheep Breeders Association	**DSK**	De Samvirkende Kobmandsforeninger i Danmark
DSBJ	Demokratski Savez Bugarina Jugoslavije (Serbia) = DUBY	**DSK**	Demokratski Savez Kosova (Serbia) = DLK
DSBy	Dansk Selskab for Bygningsstatik	**DSKFNM**	Dansk Selskab for Klinisk Fysiologi og Nuklear Medicin
DSC	Dangerous Sports Club		
DSC	Desert Society of China	**DSKV**	Den Danske Sammenslutning af Konsulenter i Virksomhedsledelse
DSC	Development Study Center (Israel)		
DSC	Development Study Center = CERUR	**DSL**	Dansk Svejseteknisk Landsforening
DSCG	Demokratski Savez Crne Gore (Montenegro) = DAM	**DSL**	Danske Slagtermestres Landsforening
		DSL	Danske Sprog- og Litteraturselskab
DSD	Dansk Selskab for Datalogi= Danish Society for Computer Science	**DSL**	Deutsche Strassenliga e.V., Vereinigung zur Förderung des Strassen- und Verkehrswesens
DSD	Duales System Deutschland		
DSDC	Defence Source Definition Committee (Australia)	**DSLF**	Dansk Selskab for Logopaedi og Foniatri
DSE	Deutsche Stiftung für Internationale Entwicklung	**DSLV**	Deutscher Sportlehrer Verband
		DSM	Dansk Selskab for Materialprøvning og- forskning
DSF	Danmarks Skolebiblioteks-Forening		
DSF	Dansk Skattevidenskabelig Forening	**DSM**	Deutsche Sammlung von Mikroorganismen und Zellkultureen
DSF	Dansk Skibshandlerforening		
DSF	Dansk Skuespillerforbund	**DSMA**	Door and Shutter Manufacturers Association
DSF	Dansk Socialrådgiverforening		
DSF	Danske Salgslederes Foellesråd	**DSMP**	Daughters of St Mary of Providence
DSF	Danske Studerendes Faellesråd	**DSNA**	Dictionary Society of North America
DSF	Deutsch-Sowjetische Freundschaft	**DSO**	Dansk Selskab for Optometri
DSF	Dirección de Seguridad Federal (Mexico)	**DSOG**	Dansk Selskab for Obstetrik og Gynaekologi
DSFL	Dansk Selskab for Fotogrammetri og Landmåling		
		DSOM	Dansk Selskab for Oldtids- og Middelalderforskning
DSfL	Dansk Selskab for Logistik		
DSFL	Danske Sparekassefunktionaerers Landsforening	**DSOV**	Dansk Selskab for Opvarmings- og Ventilationsteknik
DSG	Defence Science Group (MOD)	**DSP**	Democratic Smallholders and Citizens' Party (Hungary)
DSG	Deutsche Schillergesellschaft		
DSG	Deutsche Schlafwagen- und Speisewagen Gesellschaft	**DSP**	Democratic Socialist Party (Éire, India, Japan, Korea, Morocco)
DSG	Deutsche Statistische Gesellschaft	**DSP**	Democratik Sol Parti (Turkey)
DSGB	Dozenal Society of Great Britain	**DSP**	Društvo Slovenskih Pisateljev
DSHV	Demokratski Savez Hrvata u Vojvodini (Serbia) = DACV	**DSpÄB**	Deutscher Sportärzebund
		DSPAC	Danish Society of Pathological Anatomy and Clinical Cytology
DSI	Dairy Society International (U.S.A.)		
DSI	Defence Services Intelligence (Burma)	**DSPCA**	Dublin Society for the Prevention of Cruelty to Animals
DSI	Down's Syndrome International (U.S.A.)		
		DSR	Dansk Sygeplejeråd
DSI	General Directorate of State Hydraulic Works (Turkey)	**DSRF**	Dansk Salgs-og Reklameforbund
		DSRV	Demokratski Savez Rumuna Vojvodin (Serbia) = DAVR
DSIM	Dansk Selskab for Intern Medicin		
DSIR	Department of Scientific and Industrial Research (New Zealand)	**DSS**	Danmarks Skolebiblioteksforening

DSS	Department of Social Security
DSS	Department of Social Service (Australia)
DSS	Department of Supply and Services (Canada)
DSS	Drustvo Slovenskih Skladateljev
DSSA	Dental System Suppliers' Association
DSSA	Direct Sales and Service Association
DSSV	Deutschschweizerischer Sprachverein (*now* SVDS)
DST	Deutscher Städtetag
DST	Direction de la Surveillance de la Territoire
DST	Directorate for Territorial Security (Ivory Coast)
DStB	Deutscher Städtebund
DStG	Deutsche Statistische Gesellschaft
DStGB	Deutscher Städte- und Gemeindebund
DSTI	Division of Scientific and Technical Information (IAEA)
DSTM	Dansk Selskab for Trafikmedicin og Ulykkesforebyggelse
DSTO	Defence Sciences and Technology Organization (Australia)
DSTS	Dansk Selskab for Teoretisk Statistik
DSTV	Deutscher Stahlbauverband
DStV	Deutscher Steuerberaterverband
DSU	Deutsche Soziale Union
DSV	Dansk Selskab for Virksomhedsledelse
DSV	Deutsche Schrottverband
DSV	Deutscher Schädlingsbekämpfer-Verband
DSV	Deutscher Sekretärinnen-Verband
DSV	Deutscher Stahlbau-Verband
DSV	Deutscher Syndici-Verband
DSV	Direction des Services Vétérinaires
DSV	German Swimming Federation
DSWA	Dry Stone Walling Association of Great Britain
DT	Deutsche Tierärzteschaft (*now* BTK)
DT	Direktorate for Tolduaesenet
DTA	Democratic Turnhalle Alliance (Namibia)
DTA	Development Trusts Association
DTA	Dominion Traffic Association (Canada)
DTAG	Development Training Advisory Group
DTAT	Direction Technique des Armaments Terrestres
DTB	Danmarks Tekniske Bibliotek
DTB	German Tennis Federation
DTC	Département des Transports et Communications et de l'Énergie (Switzerland)
DTC	Department of Technical Co-operation
DTC	Department of Transport and Communications (Australia)
DTCA	Direction Technique des Constructions Aéronautiques
DTCD	Department of Technical Cooperation for Development (UN)
DTE	Direction Technique des Engins
DTF	Dairy Trade Federation
DTF	Dansk Tandlægeforening
DTF	Domestic Textiles Federation
DTG	Deutsche Tropenmedizinische Gesellschaft
DTH	Danmarks Tekniske Højskole
DTI	Dansk Teknologisk Institut
DTI	Dansk Textil Institut
DTI	Department of Trade and Industry
DTICA	Departamento Tecnico Interamericano de Cooperación Agricola (Chile)
DTL	Dansk Forening for Information og Dokumentation
DTL	Dansk Teknisk Lærerforening
DTL	Dansk Teknisk Litteraturselskab
DTO	Dansk Teknisk Oplysningstjeneste
DTp	Department of Transport
DTREO	Département des Travaux, Recherches et Exploitation Océaniques
DTRI	Dairy Training and Research Institute (Philippines)
DTRU	Demographic Training and Research Unit (Sri Lanka)
DTSY	Department of the Treasury
DTTAC	Distributive Trades Technology Advisory Centre
DTU	Dansk Textil Union
DTV	Deutsche Textilreinigungs- Verband
DTV	Deutscher Transport- Versicherungs- Verband
DU	Distriktenes Utbyggingsfond
DUA	Direccion General de Urbanizacion y Arquitectura (El Salvador)
DUBAL	Dubai Aluminium Company
Dublin Committee	International Trade Union Committee for Peace and Disarmament = Comité de Dublin
DUBY	Democratic Union of Bulgarians in Yugoslavia = DSBJ

DUC	Dansk Undergrunds Consortium	**DVFA**	Deutsche Vereinigung für Finanzanalyse und Anlageberatung
DUGAS	Dubai National Gas Company		
DUGG	Deutsche Union für Geodésie und Geophysik	**DVFB**	Deutscher Vieh- und Fleischhandelsbund
DUGM	Democratic Union of the Greek Minority = OSO = BDMG (Albania)	**DVFFA**	Deutscher Verband Forstlicher Forschungsanstalten
DUHR	Democratic Union of Hungarians in Romania = UDMR	**DVFG**	Deutscher Verband für Flüssiggas
DUKŽ	Društvo za Unapredenje Kvalitete Živlenja	**DVfVW**	Deutscher Verein für Versicherungswissenschaft
DUMV	Democratic Union of Magyars of Vojvodina (Serbia)	**DVG**	Deutsche Veterinärmedizinische Gesellschaft
DUP	Democratic Unionist Party (Northern Ireland)	**DVG**	Deutsche Volkswirtschaftliche Gesellschaft
DUP	Democratic Unity Party (Romania)	**DVGI**	Deutsche Vereinigung der Erdölgeologen and Erdölingenieure
DURG-AFRO	Groupe Africain de Recherche sur l'Utilisation des Médicaments (Zimbabwe)	**DVGW**	Deutscher Verein des Gas- und Wasserfachs
DURR	Democratic Union of Roma in Romania = UDRR	**DVIS**	Deutscher Verein für Internationales Seerecht
DURS	Democratic Union of Roma in Slovakia = DZRS	**DVJB**	Danish Veterinary and Agricultural Library
DUS	Democratic Union of Serbs (Romania) = UDS	**DVKJ**	Deutsche Vereinigung für Kinder- und Jugendpsychiatrie
DUS	Udenrigspolitiske Selskab = FPS	**DVL**	Deutsche Versuchsanstalt für Luftfahrt
DUSC	Democratic Union of Slovaks and Czechs (Romania) = UDSC	**DVLA**	Driver and Vehicle Licensing Agency
DUSH	Democratic Union of Slovaks in Hungary = MSzSz	**DVM**	Deutsche Verband für Materialprüfung
DUW	Dijksdienst voor de Uitvoering van Werken	**DVMD**	Deutsche Medizinischer Bibliothekare
DVA	Danske Vognmaends Arbejdsgiversammenslutning	**DVMF**	Dansk Vulkanisør- Mester-Forening
DVA	Deutsche Versicherungs Akademie	**DVMLG**	Deutsche Vereinigung für Mathematische Logik und Grundlagenforschung der Exakten Wissenschaften
DVA	Dunkirk Veterans Association		
DVA	German Peoples Party	**DVN**	Diabetes Vereniging Nederland
DVAG	Deutscher Verband für Angewandte Geographie	**DVO**	Danske Veterinærhygienikeres Organisation
DVB	Deutscher Bäderverband	**DVOH**	Deutsche Verband für Oberflachenveredlung und Härtung
DVB	Deutscher Büchereiverband		
DVBF	Deutscher Verband Berufstätiger Frauen	**DVPW**	Deutsche Vereinigung für Politische Wissenschaft
DVC	Damodar Valley Corporation (India)	**DVRG**	Deutsche Vereinigung für Religiongeschichte
DVD	Denture Vereinigung für Datenschutz		
DVEB	Deutscher Verband Evangelischer Büchereien	**DVS**	Deutscher Verband für Schweisstechnik
		DVS	Deutscher Versicherungs-Schutzverband
DVF	Dansk Vandteknisk Forening	**DVT**	Deutscher Verband Technisch-Wissenschaftlicher Vereine
DVF	Dansk Veterinærhygiejnisk Forening		
DVF	Danske Vandvarkers Forening	**Dvta**	Deutscher Verband Technischer Assistenten in der Medizin
DVF	Deutsche Verband Farbe	**DVTWV**	Deutscher Verband Technisch-Wissenschaftlicher Verbands
		DVU	Deutsche Volksunion

DVV	Deutsche Vereinigung zur Bekämpfung der Viruskrankheiten
DVV	Deutsche Vereiningung für Vermögensberatung
DVV	Deutscher Verzinkerei Verband
DVV	Deutscher Volkshochschul Verband
DVW	Deutscher Verein für Vermessungswesen
DVWG	Deutsche Verkehrswissenschaftliche Gesellschaft
DVWK	Deutsche Verband für Wasserwirtschaft und Kulturbau
DW	Daughters of Wisdom = FdlS, FdS, HdlS
DW	Deutsche Welthungerhilfe
DWA	Drystone Walling Association
DWAS	Doctor Who Appreciation Society
DWAW	Distillery Wine and Allied Workers International
DWB	Deutscher Weinbauverband
DWB	Deutscher Werkbund
DWB	Doctors Without Borders = MSF
DWC	Democratic Workers' Congress (Sri Lanka)
DWG	Deutsche Weltwirtschaftliche Gesellschaft
DWG	Deutsche Werbewissenschaftliche Gesellschaft
DWHH	Deutsche Welthungerhilfe
DWK	Deutsche Wissenschaftliche Kommission für Meersforschung
DWK	Deutsches Woll-Komitee
DWP	Democratic Workers Party (South Africa)
DWP	Verband Deutscher Werbefilmproduzenten
DWR	Division of Water Resources (CSIRO)
DWS	Deutsches Wetterdienst Seewetteramt
DWT	CSIR Division of Water Technology (South Africa)
DWT	Deutsche Gesellschaft für Wehrtechnik
DWV	Deutsche Waren- Vertriebsgesellschaft
DWV	Deutscher Wäscherei Verband
DWV	Deutscher Weinbauverband
DYN	Diarios y Noticias (Argentina)
DYP	Dogru Yol Partisi (Turkey)
DZB	Development Bank of Zambia
DZF	Deutsche Zentrale für Fremdenverkehr
DZfCH	Deutscher Zentralausschuss für Chemie
DZG	Deutsche Zoologische Gesellschaft
DZI	State Insurance Institute (Bulgaria)
DZK	Deutsches Zentralkomitee zur Bekämpfung der Tuberkulose
DZL	Deutsche Zentralinstitut für Lehrmittel
DZMV	Demokratska Zajednica Madžara Vojvodine (Serbia) = DCVH
DZRS	Demokratický Zväz Rómov na Slovensku (Slovakia) = DURS
DZT	Deutsche Zentrale für Tourismus
DZV	Deutsche Zentrale für Volkesgesundheitspflege
DZVHÄ	Deutscher Zentralverein Homöopathischer Ärzte
DZW	Deutsche Dokumentations Zentrale Wasser

E

E and P-Forum	Oil Industry International Exploration and Production Forum
E&F	Eaux et Forêts
E-AG	European-Atlantic Group
EA	Elektriska Arbetsgivareföreningen
EA	Environmental Agency (Japan)
EA	Eusko Alkartasuna
EA	Evangelical Alliance
EAA	East African Association
EAA	East Asian Assistancy (SJ) = JCEA
EAA	Electrical Appliance Association
EAA	Electricity Arbitration Association
EAA	Entertainments Agents Association
EAA	Euro Action – ACORD
EAA	European Accounting Association
EAA	European Aluminium Association
EAA	European Athletic Association = AEA
EAAA	European Association of Advertising Agencies
EAAC	European Association of Audiophonological Centres (France)
EAACI	European Academy of Allergology and Clinical Immunology
EAAE	European Association of Agricultural Economists
EAAE	European Association of Architectural Education = AEEA
EAAF	European Association of Animated Film (Belgium) = AEFA
EAAJ	Engineering Advancement Association of Japan
EAAM	European Association for Aquatic Mammals (Netherlands)

EAAMC	Euro-Asian Association of Mountaineering and Climbing (Russia)
EAAP	European Association for Animal Production = EAZ, EVT, FEZ
EAAS	East Anglian Aviation Society
EAAS	European Association for American Studies
EAASH	European Academy of Arts, Sciences and Humanities = AECAL, AESAL
EAATEE	East Africa Association for Theological Education by Extension (Tanzania)
EAB	Esperanto Asocio de Britujo
EAB	Europäische Akademie Berlin
EABA	European Amateur Boxing Association
EABS	European Association for Bioeconomic Studies (Italy)
EABT	European Association for Behaviour Therapy
EAC	East African Community
EAC	East Asiatic Company (Denmark) = ØK
EAC	Egyptian Association of Citizens (Macedonia) = ZE
EAC	Elderly Accommodation Counsel
EAC	Electro-Agricultural Centre
EAC	Engineering Advisory Council
EAC	Engineering Applications Centre
ÉAC	Études Agricoles par Correspondance
EAC	European Agency for Cooperation = AEC, EAZ
EAC	European Agriculture Confederation
EAC	European Amino-Carboxylates Association
EAC	European Association for Cooperation = AEC, EAS, EAZ, EGZ, ESS
EAC	European Astronaut Centre (ESA)
EAC	European Banks Advisory Committee
EAC	Europees Assurantie Comité = CEA, EIC
EAC	Evangelical Association of the Caribbean
EAC	Expedition Advisory Centre
EAC	External Affairs Canada
EAC	INSEAD Euro-Asia Centre
EACA	European Air Carrier Assembly
EACA	European Association of Charter Airlines (Netherlands)
EACACT	East Africa Centre for Agricultural Credit Training (Tanzania)
EACC	Edinburgh Airport Consultative Committee
EACC	Société Eurafricaine Café, Cacao (Ivory Coast)
EACDLA	European Association of Christian Democratic Local Administrators = AEALCD, AEALDC
EACE	European Association for Cancer Education
EACE	European Association for Cognitive Ergonomics
EACEM	European Association of Consumer Electronics Manufacturers
EACHR	European Advisory Committee on Health Research = CCERS
EACL	European Association for Chinese Law
EACLALS	European Branch of the Association for Commonwealth Literature and Language Studies
EACME	European Association of Centers of Medical Ethics (Belgium)
EACMFS	European Association for Cranio-Maxillo-Facial Surgery
EACN	European Air Chemistry Network
EACPA	East Asia Catholic Press Association (Hong Kong)
EACR	European Association for Cancer Research
EACRO	European Association of Contract Research Organisations
EACRO-TANAL	East African Centre for Research on Oral Tradition and African National Languages
EACRP	European American Committee on Reactor Physics (ENEA)
EACS	Ecumenical Association for Church and Society (Belgium) = AOES
EACS	European Association for Chinese Studies = AEDEC
EACS	European Association of Classification Societies
EACT	European Advisory Council for Technology Trade
EACTA	European Association of Cardiothoracic Anaesthesiologists
EAD	Europäischer Austauschdienst
EADA	Eastern Dredging Association
EADB	East African Development Bank
EADE	European Association of Diabetes Educators
EADI	European Association of Developmental Research and Training Institutions = AEID

EADK	Europäische Autorenvereinigung "Die Kogge"
EADP	European Association of Directory Publishers = AEEA, EAV
EADTU	European Association of Distance Teaching Universities (Netherlands)
EAE	Eastern Association of Electroencephalographers (U.S.A.)
EAE	Elliniki Astronautiki Etaireia = HAS
EAE	Estacion Agricola Experimental de Leon
EAEBP	European Association of Editors of Biological Periodicals
EAEC	East Africa Engineering Consultants (Kenya)
EAEC	East African Extract Corporation
EAEC	East Asian Economic Caucus
EAEC	European Airlines Electronic Committee
EAEC	European Atomic Energy Community (Euratom) = CEEA, EAG, EGA
EAECMI	Export Association of the Electric Cable Making Industry
EAEE	European Association of Earthquake Engineering
EAEE	Evangelische Arbeitsgemeinschaft für Erwachsenenbildung in Europa
EAEEIE	European Association for Education in Electrical and Information Engineering
EAEG	European Association of Exploration Geophysicists
EAEM	Escola de Agronomica Eliseu Maciel (Brazil)
EAEN	Eastern Africa Environmental Network (IUCN) (Kenya)
EAERE	European Association of Environmental and Resource Economists
EAES	European Atomic Energy Society
EAESP	European Association of Experimental Social Psychology
EAET	East African External Telecommunications Company
EAEVE	European Association of Establishments for Veterinary Education = AEEEV
EAF	Elektrokemiske Arbeidsgiverforening
EAFA	European Aluminium Foil Association
EAFE	European Association of Fisheries Economists (Belgium)
EAFORD	International Organization for the Elimination of all Forms of Racial Discrimination
EAFP	European Association against Fibre Pollution = AERPF
EAG	Environmental Assessment Group Ltd
EAG	Europäische Atomgemeinschaft (Euratom) = CGEA, EAEC, EGA
EAG	European Atherosclerosis Group
EAGA	Expert Advisory Group on AIDS (DoH)
EAGB	Executives Association of Great Britain
EAGB	Eyecare Association of Great Britain
EAGE	European Association for Gastroenterology and Endoscopy
EAGFL	Europäischer Ausrichtung- und Garantiefonds für die Landwirtschaft = EAGGF, EGTPE, EOGFL, EUGFL, FEOGA
EAGGF	European Agricultural Guidance and Guarantee Fund = AEGFL, EGTPE, EOGFL, EUGFL, FEOGA
EAGLE	European Association for Grey Literature Exploitation
EAGLE	Exchange on Ageing, Law and Ethics = AIGLE
EAGO	European Association of Gynaecologists and Obstetricians
EAGS	European Association of Exploration Geophysicists
EAHC	East Asia Hydrographic Commission (Monaco) = CHAO
EAHE	European Association of Human Ecology (Belgium)
EAHIL	European Association of Health Information and Libraries = AEIBS
EAHM	European Association of Hospital Managers = AEDH, EVKD
EAHMA	European Aluminium Holloware Manufacturers Association = FEAMA, VEAWI
EAHP	European Association for Haematopathology (Denmark)
EAHP	European Association for Humanistic Psychology
EAHP	European Association of Hospital Pharmacists
EAHTMA	Engineers and Allied Hand Tool Makers Association
EAIA	Early American Industries Association
EAIC	East Asian Insurance Corporation
EAIE	European Association for International Education (Netherlands)
EAJS	European Association for Japanese Studies

EAK	Cyprus Farmers Union
EAL-IUL	Europäischer Ausschuss der Lebens-, Genussmittel- und Gastgewerbegewerkschaften in der IUL = ECF-IUF, SETA-UITA
EALA	European Air Law Association
EALE	European Association of Labour Economists (Italy)
EALE	European Association of Law and Economics (Netherlands)
EALIS	Egyptian Association of Archives, Librarianship and Information Science
EALM	European Association of Livestock Markets
EAM	Entreprises Ali Mheni (Tunisia)
EAMDA	European Alliance of Muscular Dystrophy Associations = AEMDA
EAMF	European Association of Music Festivals = AEFM
EAN	European Abortion Network = ENWRAC
EAN	International Article Numbering Association
EANA	Esperanto Association of North America
EANA	Europäische Arbeitsgemeinschaft der Niedergelassenen Ärzte
EANA	European Alliance of News Agencies = AEAP
EANHS	East Africa Natural History Society
EANI	Energy Action Northern (Ireland)
EANM	European Association of Nuclear Medicine
EANN	European Association of Neuroscience Nurses
EANPC	European Association of National Productivity Centres = AECNP
EANPG	European Air Navigation Planning Group
EANS	European Association of Neurosurgical Societies
EAO	Egyptian Agricultural Organization
EAO	Egyptian Antiquities Organisation
EAO	Europäische Akademie Otzenhausen
EAO	European Architects Organisation
EAOA	European Association of Osteo-Arthrology = EGOA
EAOI	East Asia Open Institute (Hong Kong)
ÉAP	École Européenne des Affaires
EAP	Environment Actions Plan
EAP	Environment Assistance Program
EAP	Europäische Arbeiter Partei
EAP	European Advertising Press
EAPA	English Apples and Pears Association
EAPA	European Alliance of Press Agencies
EAPA	European Asphalt Pavement Association
EAPAC	Eggs Authority Producer Advisory Committee
EAPC	Europäischer Aero-Philatelisten-Club
EAPCA	European Audio Phonological Centres Association = AECA
EAPE	European Association for Evolutionary Political Economy
EAPG	European Association of Petroleum Geoscientists and Engineers (Netherlands)
EAPHSS	European Association of Programmes in Health Service Studies
EAPI	East Asian Pastoral Institute (Philippines)
EAPM	European Association for Personnel Management = AEDP
EAPM	European Association of Perinatal Medicine
EAPM	Greek Personnel Management Association
EAPN	European Anti-Poverty Network
EAPR	European Association for Potato Research (Netherlands) = AERP
EAPS	European Association for Population Studies
EAPS	European Association of Professional Secretaries
EAR	Elliniki Aristera
EAR	European Association of Radiology = AER, EGR
EARAC	East Anglian Regional Advisory Council
EARAPA	European Association for Research into Adapted Physical Activity (Belgium)
EARB	Electronics and Aviation Requirements Board
EARCCUS	East African Regional Committee for the Conservation and Utilisation of the Soil = CREACUS
EARDHE	European Association for Research and Development in Higher Education
EARE	European Action for Racial Equality
EARIE	European Association for Research in Industrial Economics

EARLI	European Association for Research on Learning and Instruction (Netherlands)	**EASST**	European Association for the Study of Science and Technology
EARN	European Academic Research Network (*now* TERENA)	**EASTC**	Eastern Africa Statistical Training Centre (Tanzania)
EAROPH	East Asia Regional Organisation for Planning and Housing (India)	**EASVO**	European Association of State Veterinary Officers = UEVF
EARSeL	European Association of Remote Sensing Laboratories	**EAT**	Employment Appeals Tribunal (Éire)
Earthkind	Earthkind Humane Education Centre	**EAT**	Entreprise Africaine de Travaux
ÉAS	Électronique Aéro-Spatiale	**EAT**	Environmental Awareness Trust
EAS	Epilepsy Association of Scotland (ex SEA)	**EAT**	Europäische Vereinigung für Thermographie = AET, ETA
EAS	European Aquaculture Society	**EAT**	European Advertising Tripartite
EAS	European Atherosclerosis Society	**EAT**	European Association of Teachers = AEDE
EAS	Europese Associaties voor Samenwerking = AEC, EAZ	**EATA**	East Asia Travel Association
EASA	Ecclesiastical Architects & Surveyors Association	**EATA**	European Association of Transactional Analysis
EASA	Engineers Association of South Africa	**EATB**	East Anglia Tourist Board
EASD	European Association for the Study of Diabetes = AEED	**EATC**	European Alliance for Television and Culture = AETC
EASD	European Association for the Study of Dreams (Belgium)	**EATCS**	European Association for Theoretical Computer Science
EASE	Electronic Auction Systems Europe	**EATJP**	European Association for the Trade in Jute Products
EASE	European Association for Special Education	**EATLT**	European Association for the Teaching of Legal Theory (Belgium) = AEETD
EASE	European Association of Science Editors	**EATP**	European Association for Textile Polyolefins
EASHP	European Association of Senior Hospital Physicians	**EATPC**	European Technical Association for Protective Coatings
EASI	European Association for Shipping Informatics	**EATS**	European Air Transport Service
EASIT	European Association for Software Access and Information Transfer	**EATWOT**	Ecumenical Association of Third World Theologians (Nigeria)
EASL	East African School of Librarianship	**EAV**	Europäischer Adressbuchverleger Verband = AEEA, EADP
EASL	Electricity Association Services (*ex* EC)	**EAVA**	Ethnographic Audio Visual Archive
EASL	European Association for the Study of the Liver	**EAVA**	European Association of Veterinary Anatomists
EASL	European Association of Sinological Libraries	**EAVA**	European Audio Video Association
EASOB	European Association for the Study of Bioprostheses	**EAVE**	European Audio Visual Enterpreneurs; Entrepreneurs de l'audiovisuel Européen
EASS	Editura Agro-Silvica de Stat (Romania)	**EAVPT**	European Association for Veterinary Pharmacology and Toxicology
EASSG	European Accountancy Students Study Group	**EAVSOM**	European Association for the Visual Studies of Man (Italy)
EASSI	European Association of the Surgical Suture Industry	**EAW**	Electrical Association for Women
EASSP	European Association for the Study of Safety Problems in the Production and use of Propellant Powders	**EAWAG**	Eidgenössischen Anstalt für Wasserversorgung, Abwasserreinigung und Gewässerschutz (Switzerland)

EAWL	East Africa Women's League
EAWLS	East African Wild Life Society (Kenya)
EAY	European Alliance of YMCAs
EAZ	Economic Association of Zambia
EAZ	Europäische Agentur für Zusammenarbeit = AEC, EAC, EAS, EGZ, ESS
EAZ	Evropeyskaia Assotsiatsiia po Zhivotnovodstvu = EAAP, EVT, FEZ
EB & RA	Engineer Buyers' and Representatives' Association
EBA	ECU Banking Association = ABE
EBA	Electric Boat Association
EBA	English Basketball Association
EBA	English Bowling Association
EBA	European Boardsailing Association
EBA	European Burns Association
EBA	European Business Associates On-line
EBA	European Heating Boilers Association = EHV, UEC
EBAA	European Business Aviation Association (Belgium)
EBAA	Eye Bank Association of America
ÉBAD	École des Bibliothécaires, Archivistes et Documentalistes (Senegal)
EBAE	European Bureau of Adult Education = BEEP
EBAG	Europäische Bildungs- und Aktionsgemeinschaft
EBBA	English Basket Ball Association
EBBH	Europese Bond van Bouw- en Houtarbeiders = EFBH, EFBT, EFBWW, FELEDL, FETBB
EBBS	European Brain and Behaviour Society
EBC	Educational Broadcasting Council (ex SBCUK)
EBC	English Bowls Council
EBC	European Brewery Convention
EBCC	Egyptian British Chamber of Commerce
EBCD	European Bureau for Conservation and Development
EBCG	European Biotechnology Coordination Group (CEC, CEFIC) (Belgium)
EBCo	European Bureau of Conscientious Objection = BEOC
EBCT	Empresa Brasileira de Correios e Telegrafos
EBD	Estacion Biologica de Donana
EBDS	European Bureau of Deaf Students
EBEA	Economics and Business Education Association
EBEA	Electronic and Business Equipment Association
EBEN	European Business Ethics Network
EBES	Sociétés Réunis d'Énergie du Bassin de l'Escaut (Belgium)
EBF	English Bowling Federation
EBF	European Baptist Federation
EBIAMS	Executive Board of the International Association of Microbiological Societies
EBIC	EFTA Brewing Industry Council
EBIC	European Banks International Company (Belgium)
EBIF	European Button Industries Federation
EBIS	ESCAP Bibliographic Information Systems (Thailand)
EBIS	European Brain Injury Society (Belgium)
EBL	European Bridge League
EBLIDA	European Bureau of Library, Information and Documentation Associations
EBLUL	European Bureau for Lesser Used Languages (EC)
EBM	Estación de Biologia Marina (Chile)
EBM	European Association of Business and Management Teachers
EBM	European Baptist Mission
EBM	Wirtschaftsverband Eisen, Blech und Metall- Verarbeitende
EBMA	Electric Battery Manufacturers Association
EBMA	European Butylated Hydroxytoluene – BHT – Manufacturers' Association
EBMT	European Bone Marrow Transplant Group
EBN	Empresa Brasileira de Notícias
EBN	European Business Innovation Centre Network (CEC)
EBNB	European Business and Innovation Centres Network
EBNI	Electricity Board for Northern Ireland
EBO	European Communities Baroque Orchestra
EBOA	Export Buying Offices Association
EBPS	European Baptist Press Service
EBR	Europäischer Betriebsrat = CEE
EBRD	European Bank for Reconstruction & Development = BERD, EBWE

EBS	Educational Broadcasting Services Trust
EBS	Emergency Bed Service
EBS	European Book Society
EBS	European Business School
EBSA	Estuarine and Brackish-Water Sciences Association
EBSC	Equine Behaviour Study Circle
EBSC	European Bird Strike Committee
EBTU	Empresa Brasileira de Transportes Urbanos
EBU	English Bridge Union
EBU	Europäische Bestatter-Union
EBU	European Badminton Union = UEB
EBU	European Blind Union = UEA
EBU	European Boxing Union
EBU	European Broadcasting Union (Switzerland) = UER
EBWE	Europäische Bank für Wiederaufbau und Entwicklung = BERD, EBRD
EBY	European Blue Cross Youth Association (Switzerland)
EBYC	European Bahá'í Youth Council
EBZ	Europäische Bildungs- und Begegnungszentren
EC	Earth Council (Costa Rica)
EC	Electricity Council (*now* EASL)
EC	Engineering Council
EC	Esquerra de Catalunya
EC	Euro-Caritas
EC	EuroCity (IUR)
EC	European Communities = CE, EG
EC	European Council of Ministers
EC	International Eurocheque Secretariat
EC-Fund	Mutual Aid and Loan Guarantee Fund of the Entente Council (Ivory Coast) = FEGECE
EC4	European Committee for Cultural Co-operation
ECA	Ecology Council of America
ECA	Economic Commission for Africa (UN) = CEA, CEPA
ECA	Educational Centres Association
ECA	Electrical Contractors Association
ECA	Employment Conditions Abroad
ECA	Empresa de Comercio Agrícola de Chile
ECA	English Clergy Association (*ex* PCA)
ECA	English Curling Association
ECA	Entreprise de Centre Afrique (Burkina Faso)
ECA	Environmental Contaminants Authority
ECA	Europe China Association
ECA	European Camac Association
ECA	European Catering Association
ECA	European Claimants Association
ECA	European Cockpit Association
ECA	European Commission on Agriculture (FAO)
ECA	European Congress of Accountants
ECA/ ATRCW	Inter-African Committee on Traditional Practices affecting the Health of Women and Children
ECAC	European Civil Aviation Conference = CEAC
ECACC	European Council of American Chambers of Commerce
ECAFE	Economic Commission for Asia and the Far East
ECAI	European Conference on Artificial Intelligence
ECAM	Employers Consultative Association of Malawi
ECAM	Enseignement Catholique au Maroc
ECAM	Euro-China Association for Management
ECAMA	European Citric Acid Manufacturers' Association
ECAP	Environmental Cooperation with Asia Program
ECARBICA	East and Central African Regional Branch of the International Council on Archives
ECAS	Edinburgh Cripple Aid Society
ECAS	Electrical Contractors Association of Scotland
ECAS	Euro Citizen Action Service
ECAS	European Council of African Studies = CEEA
ECASAAMA	European Solidarity with Mozambique and Angola
ÉCAT	École Coloniale d'Agriculture de Tunis
ECAT	Emergency Committee for American Trade
ECATRA	European Car and Truck Rental Association
ECAZA	European Community Association of Zoos and Aquaria
ECB	Environment Coordination Board (UNEP)
ECB	European Congress of Biotechnology

ECB	European Coordination Bureau for International Youth Organisations = BEC
ECBA	European Community Biologists Association
ECBC	European Carbon Black Centre
ECBIYO	European Coordination Bureau for International Youth Organizations = BECOIJ
ECBL	European Confederation of Associations of Manufacturers of Insulated Wires and Cables
ECBO	European Cell Biology Organisation = OEBC
ECBO	European Community Baroque Orchestra
ECBO	European Conference of British Bus and Coach Operators
ECC	Economic Council of Canada
ECC	Electricity Consumers Council
ECC	End Conscription Campaign (South Africa)
ECC	Energy Conservation Council (U.S.A.)
ECC	English Ceramic Circle
ECC	Ethiopian Chamber of Commerce
ECC	European Crystallographic Committee
ECC	European Cultural Centre (Switzerland) = CEC, EKZ
ECCA	European Coil Coating Association
ECCAI	European Coordinating Committee for Artificial Intelligence
ECCAS	Economic Community of Central African States = CEEAC
ECCASA	Empresa de Curtidos Centro Americana, S.A.
ECCB	Eastern Caribbean Central Bank
ECCC	English Country Cheese Council
ECCC	European Communities Chemistry Committee
ECCE	European Committee for Civil Engineers
ECCIS	European Committee for Iron and Steel Standardisation (Belgium)
ECCLS	European Committee for Clinical Laboratory Standards
ECCO	European Conference of Conscript Organisations
ECCO	European Culture Collections' Organization
ECCOFEX	European Commission Coordinating Committee of Options and Future Exchanges
ECCP	European Committee on Crime Problems = CEPC
ÉCCR	Études, Courtage, Commerce, Representation en Afrique (Ivory Coast)
ECCS	European Convention for Constructional Steelwork = CECM, EKS
ECCS	European Union of Christian-Democratic and Conservative Students
ECCSEC	Ecumenical Commission for Church and Society in the European Community
ECCT	European Council for Certification and Testing
ECCTO	European Community Cocoa Trade Organisation
ECCU	English Cross Country Union
ECCW	European Council for Cooperation in Welding
ECDPM	European Centre for Development Policy Management
ECDS	Eastern Caribbean Drug Service = SPCO
ECDS	European Contact Dermatitis Society
ECDU	Environmental Conservation and Development Unit
ECDU	European Christian Democratic Union = CDEU, UEDC
ECE	Economic Commission for Europe (UN) = CEE, CEPE, EEK
ECE	Empresa de Comercio Exterior (Ecuador)
ECE	European Congress of Epilepsy
ECE	Export Council for Europe
ECEC	European Centre for Environmental Communication = CECE
ECEHBP	Economic Commission for Europe Committee on Housing, Building and Planning
ECEL	European Council for Environmental Law
ÉCÉM	Études et Construction Électro-Mécaniques et Médicales
ECEMEX	Empresa de Comercio Exterior Mexicana, S.A.
ECEPLAN	Escritório Central de Planejamento e Contrôle (Brasil)
ECerS	European Ceramic Society (Germany)
ECES	European Centre of Environmental Studies

ECETOC	European Chemical Industry Ecology and Toxicology Centre
ECF	East China Fair
ECF	Eastern Counties Farmers
ECF	European Caravan Federation
ECF	European Chimay Foundation
ECF	European Coffee Federation
ECF	European Commission on Forestry and Forest Products (FAO)
ECF	European Cultural Foundation = ECS, EKS, FEC
ECF	European Cyclists Federation
ECF-IUF	European Committee of Food, Catering and Allied Workers' Unions within the IUF = EAL-IUL, SETA-UITA
ECFA	European Children's Film Association (Belgium)
ECFA	European Committee for Future Accelerators
ECFCI	European Centre of Federations of the Chemical Industry
ECFFP	European Commission on Forestry and Forest Products
ECFI	East Caribbean Farm Institute
ECFMS	Educational Council for Foreign Medical Students
ECG	Ecosystem Conservation Group (UNEP)
ECG	European College of Gerodontology
ECG	European Contact Group on Urban Industrial Mission
ECGC	Export Credit and Guarantee Corporation (India)
ECGD	Export Credits Guarantee Department
ECGS	European Center for Geodynamics and Seismology (Belgium)
ECHE	European Centre for Higher Education (Romania)
ECHE	European Centre for Human Ecology = CEEH
ECHG	English Churches Housing Group
ECHO	Equipment for Charity Hospitals Overseas
ECHO	European Communities Host Organisation
ECHO	European Community Humanitarian Office
ECI	European Construction Institute
ECI	European Federation of Trade Unions for Energy, the Chemical Industry and Miscellaneous Industries

ECIAF	Eastern Caribbean Institute of Agriculture and Forestry (Trinidad-Tobago)
ECIC	European Centre for International Cooperation = CECI
ECIC	Export Credit Insurance Cooperation (Singapore)
ECICW	European Centre of the International Council of Women = CEFIF
ECID	Centro de Estudios Centroamericanos de Investigación y Desarrollo (Guatemala)
ECIEL	Programa de Estudios Conjuntos sobre Integración Económica Latinoamericana
ECIF	Electronic Components Industry Federation
ECIL	Electronics Corporation of India Ltd
ECIM	East China Institute of Metallurgy
ECIM	European Christian Industrial Movement
ECIM	European Council of Integrated Medicine
ECIMACT	Empresa Comercial de la Industria de Materiales, Construccion y Turismo (Cuba)
ECIMETAL	Empresa Comercial para la Industria Metalurgica y Metal-mecanica (Cuba)
ECIMOT	European Central Inland Movements of Transport
ECIP	European Community Investment Partners
ECIP	European Cooperation in Information Processing
ECIPL	East China Institute of Politics and Law
ECIQUIM	Empresa Comercial para Industrias Quimicas (Cuba)
ECIS	European Centre for Infrastructure Studies
ECIS	European Colloid and Interface Society (Italy)
ECIS	European Community Information Service
ECIS	European Council of International Schools
ECISS	European Committee for Iron and Steel Standardisation
ECIT	East China Institute of Technology
ECITB	Engineering Construction Industry Training Board
ECITS	Ente Conzorziale Interprovinciale Toscano Sementi

ECJCS	European Council of Jewish Community Services = CESCJ	**ECMCS**	European Conference on Mixing and Centrifugal Separation
ÉCK	Étude en Commun du Kuro-shio et des Régions Adjacentes (UNESCO) = CSK	**ECME**	Economic Commission for the Middle East (UN)
ECKO	Europees Centrum voor Kernonderzoek (CERN)	**ECMEA**	European Conference of Meteorological Experts for Aeronautics
ECL	Association of European Cancer Leagues (Denmark)	**ECMF**	Electric Cable Makers Federation
ECLA	European Company Lawyers Association (Netherlands) = AEJE	**ECMG**	Electronic Components Manufacturers' Group (Éire)
ECLA	Institúto para el Estudio de la Ciencia Latinoamericana (Argentina)	**ECMI**	European Consortium for Mathematics in Industry
ECLAC	Economic Commission for Latin America and the Caribbean (UN) = CEPALC	**ECMMR**	European College of Marketing and Marketing Research (U.K.)
		ECMRA	European Chemical Marketing Research Association
ECLAIR	European Collaborative Linkage of Agriculture and Industry through Research (EU)	**ECMT**	European Conference of Ministers of Transport = CEMT
ECLAT	European Computer Lessors and Trading Association	**ECMWF**	European Centre for Medium-Range Weather Forecasting = CEPMMT
ECLATEL	Empresa Commercial Latinoamericana de Telecommunicaciónes	**ECN**	Energieonderzoek Centrum Nederland
		ECN	European Counter Network
ECLE	European Centre for Leisure and Education = CELE	**ECN**	European Curriculum Network
ECLG	European Consumer Law Group	**ECNAIS**	European Council of National Associations of Independent Schools
ECLIPS	European Convention of Library Suppliers and Information Providers	**ECNAP**	Eastern Caribbean Natural Area Management Program
ECLM	European Community for Livestock and Meat = CEBV	**ECNC**	Economic Committee of the Nordic Council
ECLO	Emergency Centre For Locust Operations (FAO)	**ECNC**	European Centre for Nature Conservation
ECLOF	Ecumenical Church Loan Fund (U.S.A.)	**ECNP**	European College of Neuropsychopharmacology
ECLSO	European Contact Lens Society of Ophthalmologists	**ECNR**	European Council for Nuclear Research
ÉCM	Étude en Commun de la Méditerranee = CIM	**ECNU**	East China Normal University
		ECO	Earth Communications Office
ECM	European Christian Movement	**ECO**	Economic Cooperation Organisation (Iran, Pakistan, Turkey)
ECM	European Conference of Mixing		
ECMA	European Carton Makers Association	**ECO**	English Channel Organisation
ECMA	European Catalysts Manufacturers Association	**ECO**	Environmental Communication Organisation
ECMA	European Collectors and Modellers Association	**ECO**	European Cinematographic Office = BLEC
ECMA	European Computer Manufacturers Association	**ECO**	European Coal Organisation (UN)
		ECO	Irish Environmental Conservation Organisation for Youth
ECMB	European Conference on Molecular Biology		
		ECO	Malta Ecological Society
ECMBR	European Committee on Milk-Butterfat Recording	**ECO**	Partido de Empresarios, Campesinos y Obreros (El Salvador)
ECMC	European Container Manufacturers Committee	**ÉCO**	Société d'Études et de Contrôle Technique (Ivory Coast)

ECO-DEV	Association d'Aide au Développement Économico-Écologique de l'Est de l'Afrique et de l'Océan Indien	**ECOSAL**	Equipo de Conferencias Sindicales de América Latina
ECO/FIN	Economic and Financial Council of Ministers (EU)	**ECOSEC**	European Cooperation Space Environment Committee
ECO/PAHO/ WHO	Pan American Center for Human Ecology and Health (PAHO, WHO)	**ECOSOC**	Economic and Social Council (OAS, UN)
ECOCEN	Economic Cooperation Centre for the Asian and Pacific Region (Thailand)	**ECOSOL**	European Centre of Studies on Linear Alkylbenzene
ECOCO	Ecological Consortium	**ECOSY**	European Confederation of Socialist Youth
ECOD	European Consortium for Ocean Drilling	**ECOTAL**	Equipo de Conferencias de Trabajadores de América Latina
ECODU	European Control Data Users Group	**ECOTEX**	Entreprise Nationale des Industries de Confection et de Bonneterie (Algeria)
ECOFAM	Women in Support for Ecological Projects (Russia)	**ECOTROP**	Laboratory of Tropical Ecology (France)
ECOFILM	Empresa Colombiana de Microfilmacion	**ECOVAST**	European Council for the Village and Small Town
ECOLINC	Environmental Network in the Community	**ECOWAS**	Economic Community of West African States = CEDEAO
ECOLOS	Ecological Coalition on the Law of the Sea	**ECOZOEK**	Stichting tot Bevordering van het Onderzoek in de Economische Wetenschappen
ECOM	Centro de Computadoras del Gobierno de Chile	**ECP**	Egyptian Communist Party
ECOM	Empresa de Computación e Informática (Chile)	**ECP**	English Collective of Prostitutes
ECOMA	European Computer Measurement Association	**ECP**	European Confederation for Plant Protection Research
ECOMINAS	Empresa Colombiana de Minas	**ECP**	European Organisation for Cooperation in Cancer Prevention Studies
ECONI- QUEL	Empresa Colombiana de Niquel	**ECPA**	European Clinical Pharmacists Association (Netherlands)
ECOP	Extension Committee on Organisation and Policy (U.S.A.)	**ECPA**	Evangelical Christian Publishers Association (U.S.A.)
ECOPE- MAR	Empresa Conservera de Pescados y Mariscos (Cuba)	**ECPA**	Expert Committee on Post Adjustments (UN)
ECO- PETROL	Empresa Colombiana de Petróleos (Colombia)	**ECPAT**	End Child Prostitution in Asian Tourism (Thailand)
ECOPOP	Association Écologie et Population (Switzerland)	**ECPC**	Enlarged Committee for Programme and Coordination (UNDP)
ECOPS	European Committee on Ocean and Polar Sciences (CEC, ESF)	**ECPE**	European Centre for Public Enterprises
ECOR	Engineering Committee on Ocean Resources (IOC)	**ECPR**	European Consortium for Political Research
ECOR	Engineering Committee on Oceanic Resources (CEI, Royal Society)	**ECPRD**	European Centre for Parliamentary Research and Documentation
ECOROPA	European Group for Ecological Action	**ECPS**	English Connemara Pony Society
ECOS	European City Co-operation Unit	**ECPS**	European Centre for Population Studies (Netherlands) = CEEP
ECOSA	European Conference on Optical Systems and Applications	**ECPS**	European Council for Payment Systems
ECOSA	European Consumer Safety Association (Netherlands)	**ECPT**	European Confederation of Physical Therapy = CETP

ECPTO	East Caribbean Popular Theatre Organization (St. Vincent-Grenadines)
ECQAC	Electronic Components Quality Assurance Committee (CECC)
ECRA	Electric Car Racing Association (U.S.A.)
ECRA	Ethical Consumer Research Association
ECRAM	Euro-China Research Association in Management (Belgium)
ECRC	Electricity Council Research Centre
ECRC	European Computer-Industry Research Centre GmbH (Germany)
ECRCBC	Euro-China Research Centre for Business Cooperation
ECRE	European Consultation on Refugees & Exiles = CERE
ECREA	European Conference of Radiotelegraphy Experts for Aeronautics
ECRI	Emergency Care Research Institute (U.S.A.)
ECRIB	European Commissary Resale Items Board
ECRIM	Engineering, Construction and Related Industries Manpower Committee (TSA)
ECRJ	Evangelical Christians for Racial Justice
ECRL	Eastern Caribbean Regional Library
ECRO	European Chemoreception Research Organization
ECRT	European Confederation of Retail Tobacconists
ECRX	European Committee on Racism and Xenophobia
ECS	Electrochemical Society (U.S.A.)
ECS	European Cetacean Society
ECS	European Chemical Society
ECS	European Committee for Standardisation
ECS	European Components Service (DTI)
ECS	Europese Culturele Stichting = ECF, EKS, FEC
ECSA	Estuarine and Coastal Studies Association
ECSA	European Chips and Snacks Association
ECSA	European Chlorinated Solvents Association
ECSA	European Community Shipowners' Association
ECSA	European Community Studies Association (U.S.A.)
ECSA	European Computing Services Association
ECSACON	East, Central and Southern African College of Nursing (Tanzania)
ECSAM	European Commission Safeguards Analysis and Measurement Working Group
ECSC	Energy Conservation and Solar Centre
ECSC	European Coal and Steel Community = CECA, EGKS, EKSG
ECSERI	East China Sea Fisheries Research Institute
ECSF	European Civil Service Federation = FFPE
ECSG	European Community Services Group
ECSIM	European Centre of Study and Information on Multinational Corporations
ECSITE	European Collaborative for Science Industry Technology Exhibitions
ECSMA	European Copper Sulphate Manufacturers' Association
ECSMU	European Center for Strategic Management of Universities
ECSO	European Cooperation and Solidarity
ECSS	European Committee for the Study of Salt = CEES
ECSSID	European Cooperation in Social Science Information and Documentation
ECSWPR	European Centre for Social Welfare Policy and Research
ECT	Empresa Brasileira de Correios e Telégrafos
ECTA	Electrical Contractors' Trading Association
ECTA	European Communities Trade Mark Association
ECTA	European Cutting Tools Association
ECTAA	Group of National Travel Agents Associations within the EEC
ECTARC	European Centre for Traditional and Regional Cultures
ECTCI	Entreprise Commerciale et de Transports en Côte d'Ivoire
ECTEL	European Telecommunications and Professional Electronics Industry
ECTF	Edinburgh Centre for Tropical Forests
ECTG	European Channel Tunnel Group
ECTI	Electro-Technical Council of Ireland
ECTMAC	East Coast Trawl Management Advisory Committee

ECTP	European Council of Town Planners
ECTPO	East Caribbean Popular Theatre Organisation
ECTUA	European Council of Telecommunications Users Associations (Belgium)
ECTUN-AMAC	East Coast Tuna Management Advisory Committee
ECTWT	Ecumenical Coalition on Third World Tourism (Thailand)
ECU	English Church Union
ECU	Environmental Change Unit
ECU	European Chiropractors Union
ECU	European Credit Union
ECU	Experimental Cartography Unit (NERC)
ECUA-QUIMICA	Ecuatoriana de Productos Quimicos
ECUA-GRAN	Ecuatoriana de Granos S.A.
ECUCT	East China University of Chemical Technology
ECUM	Evangelical Coalition for Urban Mission
ECUMESA	Ecuatoriana de Metales S.A.
Ecusa	Episcopal Church of the United States
ECUTOR-IANA	Compania Ecuatoriana de Aviación (Ecuador)
ECVM	European Council of Vinyl Manufacturers (Belgium)
ECWA	Economic Commission for Western Asia (United Nations)
ECWF	European Council for World Freedom
ECWS	English Civil War Society
ECWS	European Centre for Work and Society
ECYC	European Confederation of Youth Clubs
ECYEB	European Communities Youth Exchange Bureau = BEJCE
ECYO	European Community Youth Orchestra = OJCE
ECYTU	European Confederation of Youth Travel Organisations (FIYTO)
ÉCZ	Église du Christ au Zaïre
ED	European Democratic Group in the European Parliament
ED	European Dialogue (formerly contained END)
ED	European Dialogue (HCA U.K.)
ED'H	Electricité d'Haiti
EDA	British Electrical Development Association = BEDA
EDA	Eating Disorders Association
EDA	Ecological Design Association
EDA	Economic Development Association (Puerto Rico)
EDA	Educational Development Association
EDA	English Draughts Association
EDA	Eniasa Dimokratiki Aristera
EDA	European Democratic Alliance
EDA	European Demolition Association
EDA	European Dyslexia Association
EDAC	Electronics Development Analysis Centre (Korea)
EDAC	Engineering Design Advisory Committee of the Design Council
EDAMA	European Domestic Appliance Manufacturers Association
EDANA	European Disposables and Nonwovens Association
EDB	Economic Development Board (Fiji, Singapore)
EDB	Export Development Board (Sri Lanka)
EDC	Early Dance Circle
EDC	Economic Development Commission (Canada)
EDC	Education Development Centre
EDC	Engineering Design & Quality Research Centre
EDC	EROS Data Centre (USGS)
EDC	European Conference of Associations of Data and Control Cables Industries – EURODATACAB
EDC	European Documentation Centres (EC)
EDC	Export Development Corporation (Canada)
EDCC	Environmental Dispute Coordination Commission (Japan)
EDCCI	Economic Development Committee for the Chemical Industry
EDCF	Economic Development Co-operation Fund (Republic of Korea)
EDCS	Ecumenical Development Co-operative Society
ÉDÉ	Établissements d'Utilité Agricole d'Élevage
EDE	European Association for Directors of Residential Care Homes for the Elderly
EDECN	European Development Education Curriculum Network = RIEDE
EDEK	Ethniki Demokratiki Enosi Kyprou (Cyprus)

EDEKA	Purchasing Cooperative of German Merchants	**EDMA**	European Direct Marketing Association
EDELCA	Electrificacion del Caroni (Venezuela)	**EDMMA**	European Dessert Mixes Manufacturers Association
EDEN	European Distance Education Network	**EDNES**	Earth Data Network for Education and Scientific Exchange (Russia)
EDEU-CHEM	Association of Editors of European Chemistry Journals	**EDO**	Europese Defensie Organisatie
EDF	Economic Development Foundation (Philippines)	**EDON**	Eniaia Demokratiki Organosis Neolaias (Cyprus)
ÉdF	Électricité de France	**EDP**	Electricidade de Portugal
EDF	European Development Fund (EU) = EEF, EOF, EUF, FED, FES	**EDP**	Erk Democratic Party (Uzbekistan)
EDG	Employment Department Group	**EDPA**	European Dichromate Producers Association (Germany)
EDHASA	Editora y Distribuidora Hispano Americana S.A.	**EDPAA**	Electronic Data Processing Auditors Association (U.S.A.)
EDI	Economic Development Institute (IBRD) = IDE	**EDPRESS**	Educational Press Association of America
EDI	Entraide pour le Développement Intégral	**EDR**	Experimenterende Danske Radiomatorer
EDI-GABON	Européenne du Diamant d'Investissement au Gabon	**EDRA**	Environmental Design Research Association (U.S.A.)
EDIA	EDI Association	**EDRC**	Economic and Development Review Committee (OECD)
EDICA	Egyptian Documentation and Information Centre for Agriculture	**EDS**	European Democrat Students (Austria)
EDICESA	Ecumenical Documentation and Information Centre for Eastern and Southern Africa (Zimbabwe)	**EDSA**	European Down's Syndrome Association (Belgium)
EDICON	Electronic Data Interchange (Construction) Ltd	**EDSO**	European Deaf Sports Organisation
EDIDGPAB	Exploration & Development Institute, Dagang Petroleum Administrative Bureau (China)	**EDSP**	Environment and Development Support Program (Canada)
EDIK	Enose Demokratikou Kentrou	**EDT**	Economic Diversification and Trade (Canada)
EDIL	Entreprise Nationale d'Engineering et de Développement des Industries Légères (Algeria)	**EDTA**	European Dialysis and Transplant Association
ÉDIM	Éditions Imprimeries du Mali	**EDTC**	European Diving Technology Committee
EDIMEL	Entreprise Nationale de Développement du Materiel Eléctrique (Algeria)	**EDTNA**	European Dialysis and Transplant Nurses Associationwith ERCA
EdinTox	Edinburgh Centre for Toxicology	**EDU**	European Democratic Union; Europäische Demokratische Union = UDE
EDIPSA	Editora de Publicaciones, S.A. (Nicaragua)	**EDU**	Europol Drugs Unit
EDISG	European Distributed Intelligence Study Group (ECA, ESONE, EWICS)	**EDU-CREDITO**	Fondo de Garant¡a para el Crédito Educativo (El Salvador)
ÉDITOGO	Établissement National des Éditions du Togo	**EDUC-International**	Association of Advisers on Education in International Religious Congregations (Italy)
EDLS	European Divine Life Society	**EDUCA**	Editorial Universitaria Centroamericana
EDM	Ethiopian Democratic Movement	**EDUP**	Ethiopian Democratic Unionist Party
ÉDM	Société Énergie du Mali	**EDV**	Eisendrahtvereinigung
EDMA	European Diagnostic Manufacturers' Association	**EE**	English Estates
		EE	Euskadiko Ezquerra (Spain)

EE	Euzkadiko Ezquerra	**EECOD**	European Ecumenical Organisation for Development
EE AA	European Evangelical Accrediting Association (Germany)	**EECS**	Electrical Equipment Certification Service
EEA	Association of the Electronics, Telecommunications & Business Equipment Industries	**EED**	European Enterprises Development Company (Luxembourg)
EEA	Dirección de Econom¡a y Estadistica Agropecuária (Venezuela)	**EEDC**	East European Documentation Centre on Naturism and Related Subjects (Greece)
EEA	Educational Equipment Association	**EEDC**	Electronics Economic Development Committee (NEDC)
EEA	Employment Equality Agency (Éire)	**EEE**	Ellinki Edafologiki Etaireia = HSSS
EEA	Empresa Ecuatoriana de Aviación	**EEE**	Ellinki Etaireia Epicheirisiakon Erevnon
EEA	Estación Experimental de Agricultura (Bolivia)	**EEE**	Entente Européenne pour l'Environnement = EEA
EEA	European Economic Area = EEE	**EEE**	Espace Économique Européen; Espacio Economico Europeo = EAA
EEA	European Economic Association	**EEE-YFU**	European Educational Exchange – Youth For Understanding
EEA	European Energy Association		
EEA	European Environment Agency	**EEF**	Engineering Employers' Federation
EEA	European Environmental Alliance = EEE	**EEF**	Europäische Entwicklungsfond = EDF, EOF, EUF, FED, FES
EEA	European Evangelical Alliance		
EEAA	Environmental Education Advisors Association	**EEF**	European Environment Foundation = FEE
EEAT	Estación Experimental Agrícola de Tucumán (Argentina)	**EEFNIA**	Engineering Employers' Federation Northern Ireland Association
EEB	Eastern Electricity Board	**EEG**	Electroencephalographic Society
EEB	Electrification Engineering Bureau (China)	**EEG**	Essence Export Group
EEB	Europäischer Erziehungsbund	**EEG**	Europese Economische Gemeenschap = CEC, EEC, EOF, EOK, EWG, MCE
EEB	European Environmental Bureau (EU) = BEE	**EEGS**	Environmental and Engineering Geophysical Society
EEBB	East Europe Boxing Bureau		
EEBP	Estação Experimentál de Biologia e Piscicultura (Brazil)	**EEI**	Edison Electric Institute (U.S.A.)
EEC	English Electric Company	**EEIA**	Electrical and Electronic Insulation Association (BEAMA)
EEC	Eurocontrol Experimental Centre (France)	**EEIBA**	Electrical and Electronics Industries Benevolent Association
EEC	Europa Esperanto-Centro	**EEIC**	Environmental Education and Information Committee
EEC	European Economic Community = CEE, EEG, EOF, EOK, EWG, MCE (*now* EC, EU)	**EEIG**	European Economic Interest Grouping = EESV, EWIV, GEIE
EEC-TEDIS	Trade Electronic Data Interchange System (CEC) = TEDIS	**EEK**	Evropeiskaia Ekonomicheskaia Komissiia OON = CEE, CEPE, ECE
EECA	European Electronic Component Manufacturers Association		
EECC	European Environmental Consumers Coordination	**EEMA**	European Electronic Mail Association
		EEMAC	Electrical and Electronic Manufacturers Association of Canada
EECCS	European Ecumenical Commission for Church and Society	**EEMJEB**	Electrical and Electronic Manufacturers Joint Education Board
ÉÉCI	Énergie Électrique de la Côte d'Ivoire		
EECMB	Electrical Equipment Certification Management Board	**EEML**	Elliniki Etaireia Metafraston Logotechnias

EEMS	European Environmental Mutagen Society
EEMUA	Engineering Equipment and Material Users Asociation (*ex* OCMA)
EEO	European Electro Optics Conference and Exhibition
EÉOA	Compagnie des Eaux et Électricité de l'Ouest Africaine
EEOA	European Electro-Optics Association
EEOC	Equal Employment Opportunity Commission (U.S.A.)
EEP	East European Partnership
EEP	East European Program (IUCN)
EEPC	Eastern Export Promotion Council (India)
ÉEPFL	École Polytechnique Fédérale de Lausanne (Switzerland)
EEPG	European Educational Publishers' Group
EEPhM	Hellenike Hetaireia Philosophikon Meleton = HSPhS
EEPV	Elliniki Etaireia Protasias tis Vusezs = HSPN, SHPN
EEQ	Empresa Electrica Quito (Ecuador)
EERI	Earthquake Engineering Research Institute (U.S.A.)
EERI	Environmental and Ecological Research Institute (Thailand)
ÉÉRM	Établissement d'Études et de Recherches Météorologiques
EERO	European Environmental Research Organisation
EES	Egypt Exploration Society
EES	Energy Efficiency Service (Northern Ireland)
EESA	Electrical and Engineering Staffs Association (EETPU)
EESV	Europeses Economische Samenwerkingsverbanden = EEIG, EWIV, GEIE
EETC	East European Trade Council
EETPU	Electrical, Electronic, Telecommunications and Plumbing Union
EETS	Early English Text Society
EEU	Emergency Engineering Unit (Bosnia)
EEU	Europa Esperanto-Unio
EEUA	Engineering Equipment Users Association (U.S.A.)
EEVC	English Electric Valve Company
EEVC	European Experimental Vehicle Committee
EEW	Erfassung der Europäischen Wirbellosen
EEZ	Exclusive Economic Zone (Seychelles)
EF	Elektroteknisk Forening
EF	Engineering Foundation (U.S.A.)
EF	Europäische Frauen- Union
EF!	Earth First!
EFA	Association Européenne des Moniteurs d'Auto-École
ÉFA	École Française d'Afrique
EFA	Electrical Floorwarming Association
EFA	Elevatorfabrikantforeningen
EFA	Empresa Ferrocarriles Argentinos
EFA	Epilepsy Foundation of America
EFA	Eton Fives Association
EFA	European Federation of Agricultural Workers Trade Unions
EFA	European Finance Association
EFA	European Free Alliance
EFA	Evangelical Fellowship of Asia
EFA	Federation of European Accountants = FEE
EFAA	English Field Archery Association
EFACI	Société d'Exploitations Forestières et Agricoles de la Côte-d'Ivoire
EFAD	European Federation of the Associations of Dieticians
EFAPIT	Euromarket Federation of Animal Protein Importers and Traders
EFAR	European Federation for AIDS Research = FERS
EFATCA	European Federation of Air Traffic Controllers Associations
EFB	European Federation of Biotechnology; Europäische Federation Biotechnologie = FEGB
EFBA	Entreprise Forestière des Bois Africains (Ivory Coast)
EFBA	European Food Brokers Association
EFBACA	Entreprise Forestière de Bois Africains Centrafrique
EFBH	Europäische Föderation der Bau- und Holzarbeiter = EBBH, EFBT, EFBWW, FELEDL, FETBB
EFBPW	European Federations of Business and Professional Women
EFBS	European Federation of Building Societies

EFBT	Europaeisk Federation af Bygnings- og Treindustriarbejdere = EBBH, EFBH, EFBWW, FELEDL, FETBB
EFBTE	Eastern Federation of Building Trades' Employers
EFBWW	European Federation of Building and Wood Workers = EBBH, EFBH, EFBT, FELEDL, FETBB
EFC	Entreprise Forestière Camérounaise
EFC	European Federation of Corrosion = EFK, FEC
EFC	European Forestry Commission = CEF
EFC	European Foundation Centre (ECF)
EFC	European Freedom Council
EFCE	European Federation of Chemical Engineering = EFCIW
EFCEM	European Federation of Catering Equipment Manufacturers
EFCG	Europäische Föderation der Chemiegewerkschaften = EFCGWU, FESCID
EFCGWU	European Federation of Chemical General Workers Unions = EFCG, FESCID
ÉFCIS	Société pour l'Étude et la Fabrication de Circuits Intégrés Spéciaux
EFCIW	Europäische Föderation für Chemie-Ingenieur-Wesen = EFCE
EFCNS	European Federation of Child Neurology Societies
EFCO	European Federation of Camping Site Organisations = FEHPA
EFCS	European Federation for Company Sport
EFCS	European Federation of Cytology Societies
EFCT	European Federation of Chemical Trade (Belgium)
EFCT	European Federation of Conference Towns = EVK, FEVC
EFCTC	European Fluorocarbon Technical Committee (Belgium)
EFCVC	European Federation of Cell Virus Collections
EFDA	European Federation of Data Processing Associations
EFDA	European Formula Drivers Association
EFDF	European Flying Disc Federation
EFDO	European Film Distribution Office
EFDR	European Federation of Dairy Retailers = UNECOLAIT
EFDSS	English Folk Dance and Song Society
EFEC	European Fashion Export Council
EFEC	European Financial Engineering Company = SEFI
EFECOT	European Federation for the Education of Children of Occupational Travellers (Belgium)
EFECW	Ecumenical Forum of European Christian Women
EFEM	European Federation of Energy Management Associations = FEAGE
EFEMA	European Food Emulsifiers Manufacturers Association
EFEN	Equipe Feminine d'Education Nutritionelle (Madagascar)
EFEO	European Flight Engineers Organization
EFEP	European Federation of Environmental Professionals (Belgium) = EVUB, FEPE
EFER	European Foundation for Entrepreneurship
EFF	Electronic Frontier Foundation
EFF	Elektronikfabrikantforeningen
EFF	European Furniture Federation = EMV, UEA
EFFAS	European Federation of Financial Analysts Societies = FEAAF
EFFEI	European Federation of Financial Executives Institutes
EFFHA	European Federation of Finance House Associations = EUROFINAS
EFFOST	European Federation for Food Science and Technology
EFFTA	European Fishing Tackle Trade Association
EFG	Economic Forestry Group
EFGA	English Farmers Growers Association
EFH	Elizabeth Fitzroy Homes
EFI	Ekonomiska Forskningsinstitutet (Sweden)
EFI	Electronic Forum for Industry
EFI	Elektrisitetsforsyningens Forskningsinstitutt (Norway)
EFI	Employers Federation of India
EFI	Equestrian Federation of Ireland
EFIA	European Fertiliser Import Association
EFIBCA	European Flexible Intermediate Bulk Container Association
EFIC	European Fuel Information Centre (Belgium)

EFICS	European Forestry Information and Communications System
EFIFC	European Federation of Investment Funds and Companies
EFIL	European Federation for Intercultural Learning
EFIM	Ente Partecipazione e Finanziamento Industria Manifatturiera
EFIS	European Federation of Immunological Societies
EFJC	Europäische Föderation Junger Chöre = EFYC
EFK	Europäische Föderation Korrosion = EFC, FEC
EFK	Europäische Reisezugfahrplan Konferenz = CEH
EfL	Enterprise for Labour
EFL	Explosion and Flame Laboratory
EFLA	Educational Film Library Association (U.S.A.)
EFLA	European Food Law Association = AEDA
EFLA	European Foundation for Landscape Architecture
EFLC	European Fund for Library Cooperation
EFLE	European Foundation for Law Economics
EFLF	European Federation of Left Feminists
EFM	European Federalist Movement = MFE
EFMA	European Fertiliser Manufacturers Association
EFMA	European Financial Marketing Association
EFMA	European Fittings Manufacturers' Association
EFMA	Evangelical Foreign Missions Association (U.S.A.)
EFMC	European Federation for Medicinal Chemistry
EFMD	European Foundation for Management Development
EFMI	European Federation for Medical Informatics
EFMK	European Federation of Masseurs-Kinesitherapeutes
EFN	European Federation of Naturopaths
EFNA	European Federation for Nature and Animals
EFNEA	European Federation of National Engineering Associations = FEANI
EFNEP	Expanded Food and Nutrition Education Program (U.S.A.)
EFNMS	European Federation of National Maintenance Societies
EFNS	Educational Foundation for Nuclear Science (U.S.A.)
EFNS	European Federation of Neurological Societies
EFO	Elektroforeningen (Norsk Elektrogrossister Agentur og Producenter)
EFOA	European Federation of Outdoor Advertising
EFOA	European Fuel Oxygenates Association
EFOMP	European Federation of Organisations for Medical Physics
EFORT	European Federation of National Associations of Orthopaedics and Traumatology
EFOTES	International Federation Telephonic Emergency Services
EFP	Ecoforum For Peace (Bulgaria)
EFP	Europäische Föderalistische Partei (Austria, Germany)
EFP	European Federation of Parasitologists
EFPA	Egyptian Family Planning Association
EFPA	European Federation of Psychologists Associations
EFPA	European Food Phosphates Producers Associations
EFPA	European Food Service and Packaging Association
EFPIA	European Federation of Pharmaceutical Industries Associations
EFPS	European Federation of Productivity Services
EFPW	European Federation for the Protection of Waters = FEG, FEPE
EFQCA	European Federation of Quality Circles and Quality Management Associations
EFQM	European Foundation for Quality Management
EFRA	European Flame Retardants Association
EFRC	Elm Farm Research Centre
EFRE	European Federation for Renewable Energy = FEER
EFRP	European Federation for Retirement Provision
EFS	Eesti Folkloori Selts
EFS	Eesti Füüsika Selts

EFSA	England Football Supporters' Association
EFSC	European Federation of Soroptimist Clubs
EFSI	Employers Federation of Southern India
EFSS	Emergency Food Supply Scheme (WFP) = SAAU
EFSUMB	European Federation of Societies for Ultrasound in Medicine and Biology
EFT	European Foundation for Tourism = FET
EFTA	European Fair Trade Association (Netherlands)
EFTA	European Family Therapy Association
EFTA	European Flexographic Technical Association
EFTA	European Free Trade Association = AELE
EFTA	European Technological Forecasting Association
EFTAMALT	EFTA Malting Industry Association
EFTC	Electrical Fair Trading Council
EFTC	European Federation of Therapeutic Communities
EFTTA	European Fishing Tackle Trade Association
EFTU	Engineering and Fastener Trade Union
EFU	Europäische Frauenunion = EUW, UEF
EFVA	Education Foundation for Visual Aids
EFVA	European Federation of Vending Associations
EFWPSA	European Federation of Branches of the World's Poultry Science Association (Netherlands)
EFWZ	Europäischer Fonds Währungspolitische Zusammenarbeit = EMCF, FECOM
EFYC	European Federation of Young Choirs = EFJC
EG	Engineers' Guild
EG	Esquerda Galega (Spain)
EG	Eurographics
EG	Europäische Gemeinschaft = EC, CE (*ex* EEG)
ÉGA	Électricité et Gaz d'Algérie
EGA	Entreprise Générale Atlantique
EGA	Europäische Gewerkschaftsakademie = ASE, ETUCO, EVA
EGA	Europese Gemeenschap voor Atomenergie = CEEA, EACE, EAG
EGAC	Export Guarantees Advisory Council
EGAKU	Europäischer Gewerkschaftsausschuss für Kunst, Medien und Unterhaltung (ETUC)
EGAS	Education Grants Advisory Service
EGAS	European Group for Atomic Spectroscopy
EGASF	European General Aviation Safety Foundation
EGAT	Electricity Generating Authority of Thailand
EGATS	EUROCONTROL Guild of Air Traffic Services
EGB	Europäischer Gewerkschaftsbund = CES, ETUC
EGCAP	Entreprise Générale du Cap-Vert de Travaux Publics et Particuliers (Senegal)
EGCI	Export Group for the Constructional Industries
EGCM	Entreprise Gabonaise de Constructions Métalliques
EGCM	European Group for Co-operation in Management
EGCS	English Guernsey Cattle Society
EGED	Entreprise Nationale Guinéenne d'Exploitation du Diamant
EGEE	Entente des Générations pour l'Emploi et l'Entreprise
EGF	European Go Federation
EGF	European Graphical Federation
EGF	European Grassland Federation
EGF	European Group on Fracture
EGF	European Society of Handwriting Psychology = EGS, ESHP
EGF	Europeiska Grafologförbundet = EGS, ESHP, ESS, EVS, SEG, SEPS
EGFI	European Group of Financial Institutions (Belgium)
EGGA	European General Galvanizers Association
EGGPh	Europäische Gesellschaft für die Geschichte der Photographie = AEHPh, ESHPh
EGI	Edward Grey Institute of Field Ornithology
EGI	Energiagazdálkodási Intézet
EGI	Europäisches Gewerkschaftsinstitut = DEFI, ETUI, EVI, ISE
EGIG	Expédition Glaciologique Internationale au Groenland

EGIM	Entreprise Générale de Maçonnerie (Ivory Coast)	**EGS**	European Geophysical Society
EGK	Entreprise Générale Korhogolaise (Ivory Coast)	**EGSC**	Eastern Group Supply Council
		EGSF	Equine Grass Sickness Fund
EGK	Europäische Gesellschaft für Kur und Erholung	**EGSG**	Eastern German Studies Group
EGK	Europäische Güterzugfahrplankonferenz = CEM, EGTTC	**EGSL**	European Group for the Study of Lysosomes
EGKS	Europäische Gemeinschaft für Kohle und Stahl = CECA, ECSC, EKSG	**EGSMA**	Egyptian Geological Survey and Mining Authority
EGLEI	European Group for Local Employment Initiatives = GEPILE	**EGT**	Entreprise Générale des Travaux (Ivory Coast)
EGLI	Esperantista Go-Ligo Internacia	**EGT - CENTRE**	Entreprise de Gestion Touristique du Centre (Algeria)
EGM	European Glass Container Manufacturers' Committee	**EGTA**	Entente Générale des Teinuriers et Apprêteurs de Lainages
EGN	Elisheva Group Na'amat (Australia)	**EGTA**	European Group of TV Advertising
EGNGG	Europäischer Gewerkschaftsausschuss Nahrung Genuss Gaststätten Gemeinschaft	**EGTO**	Egyptian General Trade Organisation
		EGTPE	Evropaiko Georgiko Tamio Prosanatolismuke Engviseon = EAGFL,EAGGF, EOGFL, EUGFL, FEOGA
EGOA	Europäische Gesellschaft für Osteo-Arthrologie = EAOA	**EGTR**	Entreprise Générale de Travaux Routiers (Congo)
EGOLF	European Group of Official Laboratories for Fire Testing	**EGTTC**	European Goods Trains Timetable Conference = CEM, EGK
EGOS	European Group for Organisational Studies	**EGTYF**	European Good Templar Youth Federation
EGOTH	Egyptian General Organization for Tourism and Hotels	**EGU**	English Golf Union
EGOTI	Egyptian General Organization for Trade and Industry	**EGV**	Europäische Gussasphalt-Vereinigung = AEA, EMAA
EGP	Ejército Guerrillero de los Pobres (Guatemala)	**EGZ**	Europäische Gesellschaft für Zusammenarbeit = AEC, EAC, EAS, ESS
EGP	Entreprise Guinéenne de Préfabrication (Guinea)	**EHA**	Economic History Association
EGPA	European Group of Public Administration = GEAP	**EHA**	English Hockey Association
		EHA	Environmental Health Officers Association
EGPC	Egyptian General Petroleum Corporation	**EHA**	European Helicopter Association
EGPC	Emirates General Petroleum Corporation	**EHB**	Europäisches Hopfenbaubüro
		EHB	European Homograft Bank
EGPGC	Exército Guerrilheiro do Pobo Galego Ceibe	**EHC**	European Homologation Committee
		EHC	European Hotel Corporation
EGPW	European General Practice Workshop	**EHCI**	Every Home for Christ International
EGR	Europäische Gesellschaft für Radiologie = AER, EAR	**EHF**	European Hockey Federation = FEH
		EHGC	European Hop Growers Committee = CECH
EGRSA	Edible Gelatin Research Society of America	**EHI**	Europäisches Hochschulinstitut = EUI, IUE
EGS	English Goethe Society		
EGS	Europäische Gesellschaft für Schriftpsychologie und Schriftexpertise = EGF, ESHP, ESS, EVS, SEG, SEPS	**EHIA**	European Herbal Infusions Association
		EHIBCC	European Health Industry Business Communications Council

EHL	Eesti Heliloojate Liit	**EIAB**	Escuela Interamericana de Biblioteconomia
EHL	Elektriska Hushållsapparatleverantörer	**EIAC**	Electronics Industries Association of Canada
EHL	Entente des Hôpitaux Luxembourgeois		
EHLASS	European Home and Leisure Surveillance Systems	**EIAC**	Ergonomics Information Analysis Centre
EHMA	European Healthcare Management Association	**EIAG**	Environmental Impact Analysis Group
EHMA	European Hotel Managers Association	**EIAJ**	Electronic Industry Association of Japan
EHÖ	Technisch-Wissenschaftlicher Verein "Eisenhütte Österreich"	**EIAJ**	Engineering Industries Association of Japan
EHOA	Environmental Health Officers' Association (Éire)	**EIAS**	Institut Européen Inter-Universitaire de l'Action Sociale
EHOC	European Helicopter Operators Committee	**EIASM**	European Institute for Advanced Studies in Management (Belgium)
EHOHU	European Hard of Hearing Union (IFHOH)	**ÉIB**	École Internationale de Bordeaux
EHOTN	Europäische Hilfeorganisation für Tiere in Not	**EIB**	Economisch Instituut voor de Bouwijverheid
EHPF	European Health Policy Forum	**EIB**	Entreprise et Industrie du Bois (Ivory Coast)
EHPM	European Federation of Associations of Health Product Manufacturers	**EIB**	Environmental Information Bureau
EHPRG	European High Pressure Research Group	**EIB**	Europäische Investitionsbank (EU) = BEI, ETE
EHPRN	European Health Policy Research Network	**EIB**	European International Business Association
EHPS	Endurance Horse and Pony Society of Great Britain	**EIB**	European Investment Bank = BEI, ETE
EHRC	European Humanities Research Centre	**EIBA**	Electrical Industries Benevolent Association
EHS	Ecclesiastical History Society	**EIBA**	English Indoor Bowling Association
EHTA	European Holiday Timeshare Association	**EIBA**	European International Business Association
EHTF	English Historic Towns Forum	**EIBC**	European Independent Business Confederation = AECM, EMSBU
EHV	Edelstahlhandels-Vereinigung		
EHV	Europäische Heizkessel Vereinigung = EBA, UEC	**EIBIS**	Engineering in Britain Information Services
EHV	Europäischer Holzhandelsverband = ETA, FEBO	**EIBIS**	European International Burn Injuries Society
EI	Emmaus International (France)	**EIBM**	Escuela Interamericana de Bibliotecologia (Colombia)
EIA	Ebénisterie Ivoirienne d'Abidjan (Ivory Coast)	**EIC**	Energy Industries Council
EIA	Electronic Industries Association (U.S.A.)	**EIC**	Energy Information Centre
		EIC	Engineering Institute of Canada
EIA	Engineering Industries Association	**EIC**	Environment Information Centre
EIA	Engineering Industry Association (Éire)	**EIC**	European Insurance Committee = CEA, EAC
EIA	Environment Institute of Australia		
EIA	Environmental Investigation Agency	**EIC**	European International Contractors
EIA	European Documentation Association (*ex* AEDCL)	**EICA**	East India Cotton Association
		EICA	Egyptian International Centre for Agriculture
EIA	European Information Association	**EICF**	European Investment Casters' Federation

EICs	Euro Information Centres	**EIL**	Elektroinstallatorenes Landsforbund
EID	Empresa de Investigação e Desenvolvimento Electronica SARL (Portugal)	**EIL**	Experiment in International Living
		EIM	Europanel-Études Internationales de Marchés
EIDCT	Educational Institute of Design, Craft and Technology (*now* DATA)	**EIM**	European Institute for the Media
EIEC	English Industrial Estates Corporation	**EIMCU**	Electronic Imaging and Media Communication Unit, University of Bradford
EIEC	European Institute of Environmental Cybernetics	**EIMM**	Estacion de Investigaciones Marinas de Margarita (Venezuela)
EIEI	General Directorate of Electrical Surveys Administration (Turkey)	**EIMMA**	East India Metal Merchants Association (India)
EIEMA	Electrical Installation Equipment Manufacturers Association	**EIMRS**	European Industrial Marketing Research Society
ÉIÉR	École Inter-États d'Ingénieurs de l'Équipement Rural (Burkina Faso)	**EIMU**	Environmental Information Management Unit
EIESP	European Institute of Education and Social Policy	**EIN**	Escuéla Industriál de la Nación (Argentina)
EIF	European Investment Fund	**EIO**	Economische Voorlichtingsdienst
EIF	Exhibition Industry Federation	**EIO**	Elektriska Installatörganisationen
EIFAC	European Inland Fisheries Advisory Commission (FAO) = CECPI	**ÉIP**	Association Mondiale pour l'École Instrument de Paix
ÉIFC	Établissement International de Financement et de Crédit (Ivory Coast)	**EIP**	Energy Information Programme (UNESCO)
EIFEL	European Group for the Ardennes and the Eifel	**EIPA**	European Information Providers Association
EIFF	Europäisches Institut für Fernstudium	**EIPA**	European Institute of Public Administration = IEAP
EIFFA	English International Fly Fishing Association	**EIPC**	European Institute for Printed Circuits
EIFI	Electrical Industries Federation of Ireland	**EIPDAS**	Educational Innovations Programme for Development in the Arab States
EIFI	European Industrial Fasteners Institute	**EIPG**	Energy Investment Promotion Group (EU)
EIFLG	Engineering Institutions Foreign Language Group	**EIPPA**	European Isopropanol Producers' Association (Belgium)
EIG	Ethical Investors' Group	**EIR**	Eidgenossisches Institut für Reaktorforschung (Switzerland)
EIGA	Engineering Industry Group Apprenticeship		
EIGA	European Industrial Gases Association	**EIRB**	European Investment Research Bureau
EIGS	Ethiopian Institute of Geological Surveys	**ÉIRC**	Équipes Internationales de Renaissance Chrétienne
EIHSA	Envases Industriales Hondureños, S.A.	**EIRD**	Engineering Institute for Research and Development (Thailand)
EIIA	European Information Industry Association (*ex* EHOG)	**EIRENE**	European Information Researchers Network
EIICA	European International Institute for Consumer Affairs = IEIC	**EIRENE**	International Christian Service for Peace
EIII	Association of the European Independent Informatics Industry	**EIRIS**	Ethical Investment Research Information Service
EIILC	Electrical Installation Industry Liaison Committee	**EIRMA**	European Industrial Research Management Association (France)
EIJC	Engineering Institutions Joint Council		
EIJHE	East Indian Jute and Hessian Exchange	**EIS**	Educational Institute of Scotland

EIS	Elektroniikkainsinöörien Seura
EIS	Engineering Integrity Society
EIS	Enterprise Investment Scheme
EIS	Environmental Information Services Ltd
EIS	European Institute for Security Matters
EIS	European Invertebrate Survey = CIE, EEW
EISA	European Independent Steelworks Association
EISCAT	European Incoherent Scattering Scientific Organisation
EISM	Emei Research Institute of Semiconductor Materials (China)
ÉISMV	École Inter-États des Sciences et Médicine Vétérinaires (Senegal)
EISN	Environmental Information and Support Network (ANU)
EISSWA	Experimental Information Service in Turo Social Welfare Agencies
EISW	Inter-University European Institute on Social Welfare
EIT	European Institute for Trans-National Studies in Group and Organisational Development (Denmark)
EIT	European Institute of Technology (France)
EIT	Federation of European Information Technology Associations
EITM	European Institute of Tourism Management (France)
EITR	Ecumenical Institute for Theological Research
EIU	Economist Intelligence Unit
EIUF	European ISDN User Forum
EIVT	European Institute for Vocational Training
EIZ	Engineering Institute of Zambia
EJC	European Jewish Congress (WJC) = CJE
EJCS	English Jersey Cattle Society
EJCSC	European Joint Committee of Scientific Cooperation (CE)
EJJU	European Jujitsu Union (Austria)
EJMA	English Joinery Manufacturers' Association
EJSBA	European Jet Ski Boat Association
EJT	Ejercito Juvenil de Trabajo (Cuba)
EJTA	European Journalism Training Association = AEFJ-Assoc
EJU	Exports to Japan Unit (DTI)
EK	Enosi Kentrou (Cyprus)
EK-BYGG	Nordisk Embetsmannkomité for Samarbeid innen Byggesektoren = AK-BYGG
EKC	English Karate Council
EKD	Evangelische Kirche in Deutschland (BRD)
EKE	Elliniki Ktiniatriki Etaireia = HVMS, SVH
EKESO	Europees Korps voor Ekonomische en Sociale Ontwikkeling (Belgium)
EKI	Institúto por Esperanto en Komerco kaj Industrio (Netherlands)
EKKE	Ethniko Kentro Koinonikon Erevnon (Greece)
EKL	Eesti Kirjanike Liit
EKRIS	Enosis Katastimatarchon Radiofonon & Illektrikon Syskevon
EKS	Eesti Keemia Selts
EKS	Eesti Kirjanduse Selts
EKS	Etaireia Kypriakon Spoudon (Cyprus)
EKS	Europäische Konvention für Stahlbau = CECM, ECGS
EKS	Europäische Kulturstiftung = ECF, ECS, FEC
EKSG	Europese Kolen en Staal Gemeenschap = CECA, ECSC, EGKS
EKU	Evangelische Kirche der Union
EKV	Europäischer Kartellverband Christlicher Studentenverbände (Austria) = AECF
EKV	Europese Kunstverdienste
EKV	Schweizerischer Energie-Konsumenten-Verband von Industrie und Wirtschaft
EKWC	European Ceramics Work Centre
EKZ	Europäisches Kulturzentrum = CEC, ECC
EL	Economic League
EL	Entreprenørenes Landssammenslutning
ELA	Elicottero Lavoro Aereo
ELA	Equipment Leasing Association
ELA	Estonian Librarians Association = ERU
ELA	Ethiopian Library Association
ELA	European Laser Association
ELA	European Logistics Association
ELA	Revolutionary Popular Struggle (Greece)
ELA-IFE	Federación de Enseñanza de ELA
ELA-STV	Euzko Langilleen Alkartasuna-Solidaridad de Trabajadores Vascos

ELA/STV	Eusko Langilleen Alkartasuna	**ELENA**	European Legal Network on Asylum (ECRE)
ELAA	Egyptian Library and Archives Association	**ELEOUR-GIKI**	Central Cooperative Union of Olive and Olive Oil Producers of Greece
ELAG	European Library Automation Group	**ELEPAC**	Société Hellion Emballages Plastiques pour l'Afrique Centrale
ELAIA	European Parliament Delegations for Latin America = DPERPLA	**ELETRO-BRAS**	Centrais Elétricas Brasileiras
ELAN	Environment in Latin-America Network	**ELETRO-NORTE**	Centrais Elétricas do Norte (Brazil)
ELANE	Electronics Association for the North East	**ELF**	Earth Liberation Front
ELB	Environment Liaison Board	**ELF**	Elimination of Leukaemia Fund
ELBS	English Language Book Society	**ELF**	Environmental Law Foundation
ELC	Employer-Labour Conference (Éire)	**ELF**	Esperanto-Ligo Filatelista = AREK
ELC	Environment Liaison Centre (Kenya) = CLE	**ELF**	Essences et Lubrifiants de France
ELC	Environmental Law Centre (IUCN)	**ELF-PLF**	Eritrean Liberation Front – Popular Liberation Forces
ELC	European Industrial Food Additives and Food Enzyme Liaison Committee (Netherlands)	**ELFA**	Educational Film Library Association
		ELFA	Electric Light Fittings Association
ELC	European Lighting Council (Belgium)	**ELFO**	Elektroinstallatørernes Landsforening
ELC	Europese Landbouw-Confederatie	**ELFSE-REPCA**	Société Elf de Recherches et d'Exploitation des Pétroles du Cameroun
ELCA	European Landscape Contractors Association		
ELCI	Environment Liaison Centre International	**ELG**	European Liaison Group (IFFJ) (U.K.)
		ELGA	English Ladies Golf Association
ELCON	Electricity Consumers Resource Council (U.S.A.)	**ELGA**	European Liaison Group for Agriculture
ELCSA	Evangelical Lutheran Church in Southern Africa	**ELGI**	Magyar Allami Eötrös Loránd Geofizikai
ELD	European Liberals and Democrats = LDE	**ELI**	Environmental Law Institute (U.S.A.)
		ELI	European Lawyers Institute = IEA
ELDC	European Lead Development Committee	**ELIA**	European League of Institutes of the Arts (Netherlands)
ELDO	European Launcher Development Organization	**ELIC**	Electric Lamp Industry Council
ELDOK	Elektronisk Dokumentations- og Patentforening	**ELIF**	Sveriges Elektroindustriförening
		ELKEPA	Ellenikon Kentron Paragogikotitos
ELDR	Federation of Liberal, Democratic and Reform Parties of the European Community	**ELLA**	European Long Lines Agency (NATO)
		ELLI	European Lifelong Learning Initiative Project
ELEC	English Language Education Council (Japan)	**ELMA**	Electric Lamp Manufacturers' Association
ELEC	English Language Exploratory Committee (Japan)	**ELMA**	Empresa Líneas Maritimas Argentinas
ELEC	European League for Economic Cooperation = LECE	**ELMA**	European Association for Length Measuring Instruments and Machines
ELECTRO-LIMA	Electricidad de Lima (Peru)	**ELMAF**	Emballages Légers Métalliques Africains
ELECTRO-PERU	Empresa de Electricidad del Peru	**ELMO**	European Laundry and Dry Cleaning Machinery Manufacturers Organisation
ELEKTRIM	Polish Foreign Trade Company for Electrical Equipment	**ELMU**	Environment Law and Machinery Unit (UNEP)

ELN	Ejercito de Liberación Nacional (Bolivia, Colombia, Nicaragua, Peru)	**EMA**	Environmental Management Association (U.S.A.)
ELNA	Esperanto League for North America	**EMA**	European Marketing Association
ELO	European Landowning Organizations Group	**EMA**	European Medical Association (Belgium)
ELO	European Leisure Organisation	**EMA**	European Monetary Agreement = AME, EWA
ELOT	Ellinikos Organismos Tupopoiesseos	**EMA**	European Motorcycle Association
ELP	Working Group of European Librarians and Publishers (CEC) (Netherlands)	**EMA**	Evangelical Missionary Alliance
		EMA	Evaporated Milk Association (U.S.A.)
ELPA	Automobile Association of Greece	**EMA**	Excavator Makers Association
ÉLPA	Éleveurs Limousin Plein Air	**EMA**	Executives and Managers Association of Great Britain and Ireland
ELPESA	Electroquimica Penwalth SA (Nicaragua)	**EMAA**	European Mastic Asphalt Association = AEA, EGV
ELRA	European Language Resources Association	**EMAB**	Entreprise Malienne du Bois
ELRA	European Leisure and Recreation Association	**ÉMAC**	École Africaine de la Météorologie et de l'Aviation Civile (ASECNA)
ELSA	Estonia Learned Society of America	**EMAC**	Educational Media Association of Canada
ELSA	European Law Students Association (Finland)	**EMAC**	Entreprise Publique Économique des Manufactures de Chaussures et Maroquinerie (Algeria)
ELSA	European Lead Stabilizers Association (Belgium)		
ELSA	European League of Stuttering Associations	**EMAC**	European Marketing Academy
		EMAC	Extra-Mural Activity Association
ELSI	Esso Lubrication Service to Industry	**EMACO**	Electromedicinsk Apparat Compagni
ELSPA	European Leisure Software Producers' Association	**EMAIA**	Electrical Meter and Allied Industries Association (Australia)
ELSSOC	El Salvador Solidarity Campaign	**EMANI**	European Mutual Assurance for Nuclear Insurance
ELTA	Lietuvos telegramu agentura		
ELTAC	European Largest Textile and Apparel Companies (Belgium)	**EMAP**	European Marketing and Advertising Press
ELU	English Lacrosse Union	**EMARC**	Escola Média de Agricultura da Região Cacaueira (Brazil)
ELWCHG	European Labor and Working Class History Group (U.S.A.)	**EMAS**	Electro-Acoustic Music Association of Great Britain
ELWW	European Laboratory Without Walls	**EMASE**	Entrepôts Maliens au Sénégal
EM	Escuadrón de la Muerte (Guatemala)	**EMATEC**	Empresa Abastecimento Tecnico Material (Angola)
EM	European Movement = ME		
EMA	CSIR Division of Earth, Marine and Atmospheric Science and Technology (South Africa)	**EMATER**	Emprésa de Assisténcia Técnica e Extensão Rural (Brazil)
		EMB	Europäischer Metallgewerkschaftsbund Gemeinschaft = EMF, FEM
EMA	Eesti Arstide Liit	**EMBA**	European Marine Biological Association
EMA	Egyptian Medical Association		
EMA	Electronic Mail Association (U.S.A.)	**EMBA**	European Methylbromide Association
EMA	Employment Management Association (U.S.A.)	**EMBAL-GROS**	Chambre Syndicale des Négociants en Papiers d'Emballage et Cartons en Gros (Belgium)
EMA	Empreza de Mecanisação Agricola (Brazil)		
EMA	Energy Management Association (Éire)	**EMBAL-PACK**	Groupement Européen des Fabricants de Papiers d'Emballage
EMA	Engineers and Managers Association		

ÉMBC	Équipement et Mobilier de Bureau du Caméroun	**EMECA**	European Major Exhibitions Centres Association
EMBC	European Molecular Biology Conference	**EMECS**	Environmental Management of Enclosed Coastal Seas
EMBL	European Molecular Biology Laboratory	**EMEP**	Cooperative Programme for Monitoring and Evaluation of the Long-range Transmission of Air Pollutants in Europe (UNEP, WHO)
EMBO	European Molecular Biology Organisation = OEBM		
EMBOC	Empresa Boliviana de Construcciones	**ÉMF**	Association d'Échanges Musicaux Francophones
EMBRAER	Empresa Brasileira de Aeronáutica		
EMBRAMIL	Empresa Brasileira de Misseis	**EMF**	Environmental Medicine Foundation
EMBRAPA	Empresa Brasiliera de Pesquisa Agropecuária	**EMF**	European Management Forum
		EMF	European Meeting on Ferroelectrics
EMBRATEL	Empresa Brasileira Telecomunicaçãoes	**EMF**	European Metalworkers Federation = EMB, FEM
EMBRATER	Empresa Brasileira de Assistência Técnica e Extensão Rural	**EMF**	European Missionary Fellowship
EMBRATUR	Empresa Brasileira de Turismo	**EMF**	European Motel Federation = FEM
EMC	Early Music Centre	**EMF-FCP**	Central and East European Media Center Foundation (Poland)
EMC	Entreprise Minière et Chimique		
EMC	Environmental Management Committee	**EMF-RCA**	Association Education à la Maitrise de la Fecondité (Central African Republic)
EMC	European Marketing Council		
EMC	European Multimedia Centre	**EMFA**	Estado Maior das Forças Armadas (Brazil)
EMC	European Muscle Club		
EMCA	Electronic Motion Control Association (U.S.A.)	**EMG**	Elektronikus Mérókészülékek Gyára
		EMG	Euro Media Garanties
EMCA	European Marketing Consultants Association	**EMGCU**	East Mengo Growers Co-operative Union (Uganda)
EMCAFLET	Empresa Centroamericana de Fletes, S.A. (Nicaragua)	**EMGE**	European Medical Graduate Exchange
		EMGI	Ethiopian Mapping and Geography Institute
EMCAPA	Empresa Capixaba de Pesquisa Agropecuária (Brazil)		
		EMI	Electric and Musical Industries Ltd
EMCCC	European Military Communications Coordinating Committee (NATO)	**EMI**	Entraide Missionnaire Internationale
		EMI	Environment Management Industries
EMCDDA	European Centre for Drugs and Drug Addiction (EU)	**EMI**	European Monetary Institute
		EMIAA	Environment Management Industry Association of Australia
EMCF	European Monetary Cooperation Fund = EFWZ, FECOM		
EMCON	European Congress on Electron Microscopy	**EMIC**	Environmental Mutagen Information Center (U.S.A.)
		EMIC	Export Market Information Centre
EMCOPER	Empresa de Comercialización de Productos Perecederos (Colombia)	**EMINWAR**	Environmentally Sound Management of Inland Waters
EMCRF	European and Mediterranean Cereal Rusts Foundation	**EMIS**	Electronic Materials Information Service (IEE)
EMCWP	European Mediterranean Commission on Water Planning = CEMPA, CEMPE	**EMIS**	European Medical Informatics Society
		EMIS	International Elecromagnetic Isotope Separators Conference
EMCY	European Union of Music Competitions for Youth	**EMIT**	Xi'an Institute of Electro-Mechanical Information
EMDG	Euromissile Dynamics Group		
EME	Elliniki Mathimatiki Etaireia		
EMEA	European Agency for the Evaluation of Medicinal Products (EU)	**EMLB**	Elektronmikroskopisk Laboratorium for de Biologiske Fag (Norway)

EMLC	Ethnic Minorities Law Centre	**EMR**	Department of Energy, Mines and Resources (Canada)
EMLD	Ethnic Minority Liberal Democrats		
ÉMLR	Église Methodiste Libre au Rwanda	**EMRB**	Engineering Materials Requirements Board (DTI)
EMM	Entente Médicale Méditerranéenne		
EMMA	European Manufactured Marble Association	**EMRB**	European Marketing Research Board
		EMRC	Group of European Medical Research Councils (ESF)
EMMSA	Envelope Makers and Manufacturing Stationers Association	**EMRO**	Regional Office Eastern Mediterranean (WHO)
EMN	European Museums Network		
EMO	Elektrik Mühendisleri Odasi	**EMRS**	European Materials Research Society
EMO	Emergency Measures Organisation (Canada)	**EMRSA**	Eastern Mediterranean Region Staff Association, Alexandria (WHO)
EMOSE	Empresa Moçambicana de Seguros	**EMS**	Econometric Society (U.S.A.)
EMOTA	European Mail Order Traders Association = AEVPC	**EMS**	Edinburgh Mathematical Society
		EMS	Eesti Matemaatika Selts
EMP	Association des Étudiants de l'European Management Programme	**EMS**	Eesti Mikrobioloogia Selta
		EMS	Entomological Monitoring Services
EMP	Empresa Nacional de Petroleos, SA	**EMS**	Environmental Mutagen Society (U.S.A.)
EMP	Environment Management Program	**EMS**	Etaireia Makedonikon Spoudon
EMP	Ethnikon Metsovion Polytechneion	**EMS**	European Mariculture Society (Belgium)
EMP	European Society of Mathematical Physics	**EMS**	European Mathematical Society
		EMS	European Monetary System = EWS, SME
EMPA	Eidgenössische Materialprüfungs- und Forschungsanstalt (Switzerland)		
		EMS	Express Mail Service (Brussels)
EMPA	Eidgenössische Materialprüfungsanstalt (Switzerland)	**EMSA**	Electron Microscopy Society of America
EMPA	Empresa Pública de Abastecimentos (Cape Verde)	**EMSA**	Entreprenadmaskinleverantörernas Samarbetsorgan
EMPA	European Marine Pilots Association	**EMSA**	Europees Bureau voor Milieu en Systeem Analyse
EMPA	European Military Press Association		
EMPA	European/Mediterranean Planetarium Association (Greece)	**EMSAL**	Empresa de la Sal (Peru)
		EMSBU	European Medium and Small Business Union = AECM
EMPAC	Conference on Electricity for Materials Processing and Conservation	**EMSC**	Europe – Mediterranean Seismological Centre (Belgium) = CSEM
EMPAGRI	Empresas Agricolas (Costa Rica)		
EMPCO	English Metal Powder Company	**EMSOS**	European Musculo-Skeletal Oncology Society
EMPE	European Network for Development of Multiprofessional Education in Health Sciences	**EMSP**	École Multinationale Supérieure des Postes (Congo)
		EMSR	État Majeur Spécial Révolutionnaire (Congo)
EMPEX	Empresa de Comercio Exterior (Bolivia)		
EMPG	European Mathematical Psychology Group	**EMSS**	Elisha Mitchell Scientific Society (U.S.A.)
EMPOR-CHI	Empresa Portuaria de Chile	**EMSU**	Europäische Mittelstands-Union
		EMT	Empresa Municipal de Transportes
EMPOWER	Education means Protection of Women engaged in Re-creation (Thailand)	**EMTA**	Electro Medical Trade Association
		EMTEL-CUBA	Empresa de Telecomunicaciones Internacionales de Cuba
EMPRE-CAM	Empresa Comercializadora de Camoines Ltda (Chile)		
EMPRE-MAR	Empresa Maritima del Estado (Chile)	**EMU**	Europäische Musikschul-Union

EMU	European Economic and Monetary Union = UEM	**ENAEX**	Empresa Nacional de Explosivos (Chile)
EMU	European Malacological Union = UME	**ÉNAF**	École Nationale Agronomique Féminine
EMV	Empresa Metalurgica Vinto	**ENAF**	Empresa Nacional de Fundiciones (Bolivia)
EMV	Europäischer Möbel-Verband = EFF, UEA	**Enafer**	Empresa Nacional de Ferrocarriles del Perú
EMWP	Esperantist Movement for World Peace = MEM	**ENAFER-PERU**	Empresa Nacional de Ferrocarriles del Peru
EMYC	European Methodist Youth Council	**ENAFLA**	Entreprise Nationale d'Approvisionnement et de Régulation en Fruits et Légumes (Algeria)
ÉNA	École Nationale d'Administration		
ÉNA	École Nationale d'Agriculture	**ENAFOOD**	European NGOs Network on Agriculture, Food and Development = RONGEAD
ÉNA	Émaillerie Nouvelle Afrique		
ENA	English Newspaper Association		
ENA	Ethiopia News Agency	**ENAFOR**	Entreprise Nationale de Forage (Algeria)
ENA	European Needlemakers Association	**ENAFRI**	Empresa Nacional de Frigorificos (Chile)
ENA	European Neurosciences Association		
ENA	European Nitrators' Association	**ENAG**	Escuela Nacional de Agricultura y Ganadería (Nicaragua)
ENA-PECHES	Entreprise Nationale des Pêches (Algeria)	**ENAGAS**	Empresa Nacional del Gas, SA
ÉNAA	École Nationale d'Agriculture d'Alger	**ENAGEO**	Entreprise Nationale de Géophysique (Algeria)
ENAAT	European Network Against the Arms Trade	**ENAJUC**	Entreprise Nationale des Jus et Conserves Alimentaires (Algeria)
ENAB	Entreprise Nationale d'Approvisionnement en Bois et Dérivés (Algeria)	**ENAL**	Empresa Nicaragüense del Algodón
		ENAL	Ente Nazionale Assistenza Lavoratori
ENABAS	Empresa Nicaragüense de Alimentos Básicos	**ENAL**	Entreprise Nationale du Livre (Algeria)
ENABIN	Empresa Nacional de Autobuses Inter-Urbanos (Nicaragua)	**ENAM**	Entreprise Nationale de Métallurgie (Burkina Faso)
ENABOL	Empresa Naviera Boliviana	**ENAMER**	Asociación Nacional de Medicos Rurales (Ecuador)
ENABUS	Empresa Nacional de Buses (Nicaragua)		
ÉNAC	École Nationale d'Aviation Civile	**ENAMI**	Empresa Nacional de Minería (Chile)
ENAC	Empresa Nacional de Almacenamiento y Comercializacion de Productos Agropecuários (Ecuador)	**ENAMM**	Escuela Nacional de Marina Mercante Almirante Miguel Grau (Peru)
		ENAOC	Entreprise Nationale d'Approvisionnement en Outillage et Produits de Quincaillerie Générale (Algeria)
ENAC	Entreprise Nationale de Canalisation (Algeria)		
ENAC	Entreprise Nationale de Confection (Cameroon)		
		ENAP	Empresa Nacional de Petróleo (Chile)
ENACAR	Empresa Nacional del Carbón (Chile)	**ENAP**	Escuela Nacional de Administración Pública (El Salvador)
ENACE	Empresa Nacional de Edificaciones (Peru)		
ENACO	Empresa Nacional de Construções (Brazil)	**ENAPAL**	Entreprise Nationale d'Approvisionnement en Produits Alimentaires (Algeria)
ENACOMO	Empresa Nacional de Comercialização (Mozambique)		
ENACT	Advisory Committee on Telecommunications for England	**ENAPC**	Entreprise Nationale des Emballages en Papier et Cartons (Algeria)
		ENAPI	Ente Nazionale Artigianato e Piccole Industrie
ENADIMSA	Empresa Nacional Adaro de Investigaciones Mineras S.A. (Spain, Peru)	**Enapu**	Empresa Nacional de Puertos (Peru)

ENASA	Empresa de Navegação da Amazônia (Brazil)	**ENCEL**	Empresa Nacional de Construções Electricas (Angola)
ENASA	Empresa Nacional de Autocamiones SA	**ENCG**	Entreprise Nationale des Corps Gras (Algeria)
ENASAL	Empresa Nacional de la Sal (Nicaragua)	**ENCI**	Empresa Nacional de Comercialización de Insumos (Peru)
ENASC	Entreprise Nationale d'Ascenseurs (Algeria)		
ENAT	Entreprise Africaine de Travaux (Ivory Coast)	**ENCIME**	Empresa Nacional de Cimento (Angola)
		ENCK	Eerste Nederlandse Coöperatieve Kunstmestfabriek
ENATB	Entreprise Nationale d'Ammeublement et de Transformation du Bois (Algeria)	**ENCO-NIQUEL**	Empresa Colombiana de Niquel Ltda
ENATRU-PERU	Empresa Nacional de Transporte Urbano del Peru	**ENCODIPA**	Empresa Nacional de Comercialização e Distribuição de Produtos Agricolas (Angola)
ENAVES	Empresa Nacional del Vestuario (Nicaragua)		
ENAVI	Empresa Nacional de Avicultura (Cape Verde)	**ENCONA**	Environmental Coalition for North America
		ENCOTEL	Empresa Nacional de Correos y Telégrafos (Argentina)
ENAZUCAR	Empresa Nicaragüense del Azucar		
ENB	English National Board for Nursing, Midwifery and Health Visiting	**ENCPT**	Entreprise Nationale de Travaux Publics (Mauritania)
ENBC	Eastern Nigeria Broadcasting Corporation	**END**	Equipes Notre-Dame
		END	European Network for Dolphins
ENBRI	European Network of Business Research Institutes	**ENDA**	Environnement et Développement du Tiers-Monde (Senegal)
ENBS	European Network of Bangladesh Studies	**ENDASA**	Empresa Nacional de Aluminio, SA
ÉNC	École Nationale de la Coopération (Tunisia)	**ENDC**	Eastern Nigeria Development Corporation
ENC	Ente Nazionale Circhi	**ENDE**	Empresa Nacional de Electricidad (Bolivia)
ENCA	European Natural Casing Association = ENSCA	**ENDEF**	Estudo Nacional da Despesa Familiar (Brazil)
ENCA	European Naval Communications Agency (NATO)	**ENDES**	Empresa Nacional de Semen (Ecuador)
ENCAFE	Empresa Nicaragüense del Cafe	**ENDESA**	Empresa Nacional de Electricidad (Chile, Spain)
ENCAR	Empresa Nicaragüense de la Carne		
ENCASA	Empacadora Nacional de Carnes, S.A. (Honduras)	**ENDEV**	Eastern Nigeria Development Finance Co.
ENCATM	Entreprise Nationale de Consignation et d'Activités Annexes aux Transports Maritimes (Algeria)	**ENDEX**	Empresa Nacional de Explosivos (Chile)
		ENDIAMA	Empresa Nacional de Diamentes de Angola (ex DIAMANG)
ENCB	Escuela Nacional de Ciencias Biológicas (Mexico)	**ENDIASA**	Empresa Nacional para el Desarrollo de la Industria Alimentaria, SA
ENCC	Ente Nazionale per la Cellulose e per la Carta	**ENDIMAR**	Empresa Nicaragüense Distribuidora de Productos del Mar y Lagos
ENCC	Entreprise Nationale de Charpentes et de Chaudronnerie (Algeria)	**ENDLF**	Eelam National Democratic Liberation Front (Sri Lanka)
ENCC	Environmental Noise Control Committee	**ENDMC**	Entreprise Nationale de Développement et de Recherche Industriels des Matériaux de Construction (Algeria)
ENCDP	Entreprise Nationale de Commercialisation et de Distribution des Produits Pétroliers (Algeria)		
		ENDS	Empresa Nacional de Semillas (Chile)

ENDS	Environmental Data Services Ltd
ENDU-PLAST	Société d'Enduction Plastique (Ivory Coast)
ENE	Empresa Nacional de Electricidade (Angola)
ENEA	Comitato Nazionale per la Ricerca e per lo Sviluppo dell'Energia Nucleare e dell'Energie Alternative
ENEA	European Neuro-Endocrine Association = AENE
ENEC	Encuentro Nacional Eclesial Cubano
ENEDIM	Entreprise Nationale de Développement des Industries Manufacturières (Algeria)
ENEE	Empresa Nacional de Energie Electrica (Honduras)
ÉNEF	École Nationale des Eaux et Forêts
ENEF	English New Education Fellowship
ENEL	Ente Nazionale per l'Energia Elettrica
ENÉLEC	Entreprises Électriques et Industrielles (Gabon)
ÉNEMA	École Nationale d'Enseignement Ménager Agricole
ENEP	Entreprise Nationale d'Engineering Pétrolier (Algeria)
ENERGAS	Empresa Nacional de Gas
ENESA	Empresa Nacional de Electricidad, S.A.
ENESA	Empresa Nacional de Seguros Agrarios
ENEX	Engineering Export Association of New Zealand
ÉNFA	École Nationale de Formation Agronomique
ÉNFA	École Nationale Féminine d'Agronomie
ENFE	Empresa Nacional de Ferrocarriles (Bolivia)
ENFERSA	Empresa Nacional de Fertilizantes, S.A.
ENFO	The Environmental Information Service (Éire)
ÉNFPPM	École Nationale de Formation et de Perfectionnement de Patrons de Pêche et de Mécaniciens
ENG	European Nursing Group = GNE
ENGA	Entreprise Générale Africaine (Benin)
ENGACO	Entreprises Gabonaises de Constructions
ENGAM	Entreprise Gabonaise de Montage
ENGANET	Entreprise Gabonaise de Nettoyage, Entretien et Travaux
ENGCB	Entreprise Nationale de Génie Civil et Bâtiments (Algeria)
ENGENICO	Entreprise Générale Nigérienne de Construction
ENGI	Entreprise Nationale des Gaz Industriels (Algeria)
ÉNGREF	École Nationale du Génie Rural, des Eaux et des Forêts
ENGTP	Entreprise Nationale des Grands Travaux Pétroliers (Algeria)
ÉNH	École Nationale d'Horticulture
ÉNH	École Nationale des Haras
ENHER	Empresa Nacional Hidroelectrica del Ribagorzana
ENHR	European Network for Housing Research
ÉNI	École Nationale d'Ingénieurs
ENI	Ente Nazionale Idrocarburi
ENI	Ethiopian Nutrition Institute
ÉNIA	École Nationale des Industries Agricoles et Alimentaire
ENIA	Empresa Nicaragüense de Insumos Agropecuários
ENIAL	Entreprise Nationale de Développement et de Coordination des Industries Alimentaires (Algeria)
ENIARES	Empresa Nicaragüense de Artistas y Espectaculos
ENICAB	Empresa Nicaragüense de Cabotaje
ENICAB	Entreprise Nationale des Industries du Câble (Algeria)
ENIEM	Entreprise Nationale des Industries de l'Electro-Ménager (Algeria)
ENIEPSA	Empresa Nacional de Investigacion y Explotacion de Petroleos, S.A.
ÉNIL	Écoles Nationales d'Industries Laitières
ENIMPORT	Empresa Nicaragüense de Importación
ENIP	Estonian National Independence Party
ENIPREX	Empresa Nicaragüense de Promoción de Exportaciones
ÉNISA	École Nationale d'Ingénieurs Spécialisés en Agriculture
ENIT	Ente Nazionale Italiano per il Turismo
ÉNITA	École Nationale des Ingénieurs de Travaux Agricoles
ÉNITAA	École Nationale d'Ingénieurs des Techniques des Industries Agricoles et Alimentaires
ÉNITAH	École Nationale d'Ingénieurs des Travaux Agricoles, Option Horticulture
ÉNITEF	École Nationale des Ingénieurs des Travaux des Eaux et Forêts
ÉNITRTS	École Nationale des Ingénieurs des Travaux Ruraux et des Techniques Sanitaires

ENIU	Ente Nazionale Italiano di Unification
ENLF	Eelam National Liberation Front (Sri Lanka)
ENMAR	Empresa Nicaragüense de Productos del Mar
ENMC	European Neuromuscular Center (EAMDA)
ENMS	European Nuclear Medicine Society
ENN	Environmental Network for Nicaragua
ENNA	Eerste Surinaams – Nederlandse Levensverzekering
ENNICO	Entreprise Nigérienne de Confiserie
ENO	Comité Hellénique de Normalisation
ENO	English National Opera
ENOC	European National Olympic Committees
ENOF	Entreprise Nationale de Produits Miniers Non-Ferreux et des Substances Utiles (Algeria)
ENOP	European Network of Organisational and Work Psychologists
ENOW	European Network of Women = CEF
ENP	English National Party
ENPA	Ente Nazionale Protezione Animali
ENPAS	Ente Nazionale di Previdenza e Assistenza per i Dipendenti Statali
ENPC	Entreprise Nationale des Plastiques et de Caoutchouc (Algeria)
ENPE	Entreprise Nationale de Pétrochimie et d'Engrais (Algeria)
ENPI	Ente Nazionale per la Prevenzione degli Infortuni
ENPROVIT	Empresa Nacional de Productos Vitales (Ecuador)
ÉNPS	École Nationale de Promotion Sociale (Madagascar)
ENR	Emissora Nacional de Radiodifusão
ENR	Ente Nazionale Risi
ENRC	European Nuclear Research Centre
ENRDP	Entreprise Nationale de Raffinage et de Distribution des Produits Pétroliers (Algeria)
ÉNRÉA	École Nationale de Radiotechnique et d'Électricité Appliquée
ENRI	Electronic Navigation Research Institute (Japan)
Enrich	European Network for Research in Global Change
ENS	European Neurology Society (France)
ENS	European Nuclear Society
ÉNSA	École Nationale Supérieure Agronomique
ENSA	Empresa de Navegação da Amazônia (Brazil)
ENSA	Empresa Nacional de Seguros e Resseguros de Angola
ENSA	Equipos Nucleares S.A.
ÉNSAD	École Nationale Supérieure des Arts Décoratifs
ÉNSAÉ	École Nationale de la Statistique et de l'Administration Économique
ÉNSAE	École Nationale Supérieure de l'Aéronautique et de l'Espace
ÉNSAIA	École Nationale Supérieure d'Agronomie et Industries Alimentaires
ÉNSAIS	École Nationale Supérieure des Arts et Industrie de Strasbourg
ÉNSAJF	École Nationale Supérieure d'Agronomie pour Jeunes Filles
ÉNSAN	École Nationale Supérieure Agronomique de Nancy
ÉNSAT	École Nationale Supérieure Agronomique de Toulouse
ÉNSB	École Nationale Supérieure de Bibliothécaires
ÉNSBANA	École Nationale Supérieure de Biologie Appliquée à la Nutrition et à l'Alimentation
ENSCA	European Natural Sausage Casings Association = ENCA
ENSEME	Entreprise Sénégalaise des Mousses et Plastiques
ÉNSFA	École Nationale Supérieure Féminine d'Agronomie
ÉNSH	École Nationale Supérieure d'Horticulture
ENSH	European Natural Hygiene Society = GHN
ENSI	Environment and School Initiatives Project
ÉNSIA	École Nationale Supérieure des Industries Agricoles et Alimentaires
ENSIC	Environmental Sanitation Information Center (AIT)
ENSIDESA	Empresa Nacional Siderurgia S.A.
ÉNSMIC	École Nationale Supérieure de Meunerie et des Industries Céréalières
ÉNSP	École Nationale de la Santé Publique
ÉNSP	École Nationale Supérieure du Paysage
ENSP	Entreprise Nationale de Service aux Puits (Algeria)

ÉNSPM	École Nationale Supérieure du Pétrole et des Moteurs	**EOA**	English Orienteering Association
ÉNSSAA	École Nationale Supérieure des Sciences Agronomiques Appliquées	**EOA**	Essential Oil Association of the United States
ÉNST	École Nationale Supérieure des Télécommunications	**EOAAD**	Wildpeace – European Organization for Aid to Animals in Distress
ENSU	Union Européenne des Classes Moyennes	**EOAC**	European Ornithological Atlas Committee
ÉNSV	École Nationale des Services Vétérinaires	**EOARDC**	European Office of the U.S. Air Research and Development Command
ENT	Empresa Nacional de Turismo (Mozambique)	**EOB**	Eastern Orchestral Board
ENTA	European Network for the Treatment of AIDS	**EOC**	Entidades Oficiales de Credito
		EOC	Equal Opportunities Commission
ENTEC	Esfahan Nuclear Technology Centre (Iran)	**EOCCD**	European Organisation for the Control of Circulatory Diseases
ENTEL	Empresa Nacional de Telecommunicaciónes (Argentina, Bolivia, Chile, Peru)	**EOCHAP**	Empresa Publica de Comercializacion de Harina y Aceite de Pescado (Peru)
ENTELEC	Energy, Telecommunications and Electrical Association (U.S.A.)	**EODA**	Eastern Ontario Development Association (Canada)
ENTEX	Empresa Texteis de Angola	**EODC**	Earth Observation Data Centre
ENTMV	Entreprise Nationale de Transport Maritime de Voyageurs Algérie Ferries	**EOF**	Europaeiske Okonomiske Faellesskab = CEE, EEC, EEG, EOK, EWG, MCE
ENTO	CSIRO Division of Entomology	**EOF**	Europees Ontwikkelingsfonds = EDF, EEF, EUF, FED, FES
ENTP	Entreprise Nationale des Travaux aux Puits (Algeria)	**EOGFL**	Europees Orientatie- en Garantiefonds voor de Landbouw = EAGFL, EAGGF, EGTPE, EUGFL, FEOGA
ENTPL	Entreprise Nationale de Transformation de Produits Longs (Algeria)		
Entra	Engineering Training Authority	**EOHDN**	Europese Organisatie voor Hulpverlening aan Dieren in Nood
ENTRÉ-LEC	Compagnie d'Entreprises Électriques (Cameroon)	**EOI**	Entr'aide Ouvrière Internationale = IAM
ENTTPP	Entreprise Nationale de Tubes et de Transformation de Produits Plats (Algeria)	**EOK**	Evropaiki Ikonomiki Kinotita = CEE, EEC, EEG, EOF, EWG, MCE
		EOLAS	Irish Science and Technology Agency (ex IIRS, NBST)
ENTUR-PERU	Empresa Nacional de Turismo (Peru)	**EOM**	Ellinikos Organismos Marketing
ENU	European Network of the Unemployed	**EONR**	European Organisation for Nuclear Research
ENUSA	Empresa Nacional del Uranio S.A.	**EONS**	European Oncology Nursing Society
ÉNV	Écoles Nationales Vétérinaires	**ÉOPGS**	École et Observatoire de Physique du Globe de Strasbourg (Switzerland)
ENVIRO-PROTECT	International Association for the Protection of the Environment in Africa		
ENVITEC	International Fair and Congress on Engineering in Environmental Protection	**EOQ**	European Organization for Quality= OEC
		EORTC	European Organisation for Research on Treatment of Cancer = OERTC
ENWRAC	European Network for Women's Right to Abortion and Contraception = EAN	**EOS**	Egyptian Organization for Standardization
EO	Education Otherwise	**EOS**	Europäische Organisation der Sagewerke = EOZ, OES
EO	Evangelische Omroep		
EO-WCL	European Organisation of the World Confederation of Labour	**EOS**	European Ophthalmological Society = SOE

EOS	European Optical Society
EOS	European Orthodontic Society
ÉOS	Société Anonyme d'Énergie de l'Ouest Suisse
EOSC	Employments Occupational Standards Council
EOTA	European Organisation for Technical Approvals
EOTC	European Organisation for Testing and Certification (CEC, CEN/CENELEC)
EOUCH	Empresa de Omnibus Urbanos de Ciudad de La Habana (Cuba)
EOWA	English Olympic Wrestling Association
EOZ	Europese Organisatie der Zagerijen = EOS, OES
EP	Ecology Party (Albania) = PE
EP	Entrepreneurs' Party (Hungary)
EP	European Parliament = APE
EPA	Economic Planning Agency (Japan)
EPA	English Pool Association
EPA	Environment Planning Authority
EPA	Environment Protection Agency (Australia)
EPA	Environmental Protection Agency (U.S.A.)
EPA	Europäische Patentamt = EPO, OEB, UEB
EPA	European Parents Association
EPA	European Petrochemical Association (Belgium)
EPA	European Photochemical Association
EPA	European Playworkers Association (Germany)
EPA	European Prosthodontic Association
EPABA	Empresa de Pesquisa Agropecuária da Bahia (Brazil)
EPAC	Economic Planning Advisory Council
EPACCI	Economic Planning and Advisory Council for the Construction Industries
EPACT	European Promotion Association for Composite Tanks and Tubulars
EPAMIG	Empresa de Pesquisa Agropecuária do Estado de Minas Geraïs (Brazil)
EPASA	Electron Probe Analysis Society of America
EPB	Economic Planning Board (Rep. of Korea)
EPB	Ejercito Popular de Boricua (Puerto Rica)
EPB	Export Promotion Bureau (Pakistan)

EPBA	Export Promotion Bank of Afghanistan
EPBP	European Partners for Blindness Prevention
EPC	Economic Policy Committee (OECD) = CPE
EPC	Educational Publishers Council (PA)
EPC	Ejército del Pueblo Costarricense
EPC	Emergency Preparedness Canada
EPC	Ethiopian Petroleum Corporation
EPC	European Conference of Associations of Power Cables Industries = EUROPOWER CAB
EPC	European Pancreatic Club
EPC	European Plastics Converters (Belgium) = EuPC
EPC	European Political Cooperation = CPE, EPS, EPZ, POCO
EPC	European Publishers' Council
EPC	Export Publicity Council
EPCA	Economic Planning and Coordination Authority (Hawaii)
EPCA	European Petrochemical Association
EPCA	European Polyolefin Clingfilm Association
EPCAA	European Pharmaceutical Congress Advisory Association (Switzerland)
EPCC	Edinburgh Parallel Computing Centre
EPCC	Environment Policy Coordinating Committee (DEST)
EPCIA	Expanded Polystyrene Cavity Insulation Association
EPCRI	Electrical Power Construction Research Institute (China)
EPCS	English Playing Card Society
EPD	Eidgenössisches Politisches Department (Switzerland)
EPD	Environmental Protection Division
EPD	European Progressive Democrats (EU) = DEP
EPDA	Ethiopian Peoples Democratic Alliance
EPDA	European Plastics Distributors' Association
EPDC	Electric Power Development Corporation (Japan)
EPE	Europese Partij; Parti Européen (Belgium)
EPEA	Electrical Power Engineers' Association (EMA)
EPEG	Europa Parlamenta Esperanto-Grupo
EPEMA	Environment Protection Equipment Manufacturers Association

EPEP	Environmental Protection Research Institute for Electric Power (China)	**EPIM**	European Professional Indemnity Mutual
EPESA	Empresa Paraguaya de Electrificacion	**EPITEL**	Association for European Public Information by Television (Belgium)
EPETMA	European Polyester Terephthalate Film Manufacturers Association	**EPIU**	Electrical and Plumbing Industries Union
ÉPF	École Polytechnique Fédérale (Switzerland)	**ÉPK**	Écoles Populaires Kanaks (New Caledonia)
EPF	European Packaging Federation	**EPK**	Euskadiko Partidu Komunista (Spain)
EPF	European Planning Federation	**EPL**	Ejercito Popular de Liberación (El Salvador)
EPF	European Policy Forum		
EPF	European Polymer Federation	**EPL**	European Petrochemical Luncheon
EPFCL	Esso Pakistan Fertilizer Co. Ltd	**EPLAF**	European Planning Federation
EPFT	Environmental Problems Foundation of Turkey = TSV	**EPLF**	Eritrean People's Liberation Front
		EPLP	European Parliamentary Labour Party
EPFTR	Expert Panel for the Facilitation of Tuna Research (FAO)	**EPM**	Escola Paulista de Medicina (Brazil)
EPHA	European Public Health Alliance (ECAS)	**EPMA**	European Powder Metallurgy Association
ÉPHÉ	École Pratique des Hautes Études	**EPNA**	Empresa Pesquera Nacional (Ecuador)
EPhE	Elliniki Pharmakeutiki Etaireia	**EPNS**	English Place-Name Society
EPhMRA	European Pharmaceutical Marketing Research Association	**EPO**	Earthnet Programme Office (ESRIN)
		EPO	Education Partners Overseas
EPhS	European Physical Society	**EPO**	European Patent Office = EPA, OEB, VEB
EphSoc	Ephemera Society		
EPI	Employment Policy Institute	**EPOA**	East Coast Petroleum Operators Association (Canada)
EPI	European Peace Initiative		
EPI	European Photographic Chemicals Industry Group (Belgium)	**EPOA**	European Property Owners Association
		EPOC	Earthquake Prediction Observation Centre (ERI) (Japan)
EPI	European Policy Institute		
EPI	Institute of Profesional Representative before the European Patent Office (Germany)	**EPOC**	ESCAP Pacific Operations Centre
		EPOCH	End Physical Punishment of Children
EPI -Centre	Emergency Planning Information Centre	**EPP**	European People's Party = EVP, PPE
		EPPAPA	European Pure Phosphoric Acid Producers' Association
EPIA	European Petroleum Industry Association (Belgium) = AIPE		
		EPPAPERU	Empresa Peruana de Promocion Artesanal
EPIA	European Photovoltaic Industries Association	**EPPCo**	Emirates Petroleum Products Company (UAE)
EPIC	Educational Policy Information Centre (NFER)		
		EPPG	European Programme Providers' Group (*ex* CPPG)
EPIC	Electronic Properties Information Center (U.S.A.)		
		EPPMA	Expanded Polystyrene Product Manufacturers Association
EPIC	Empresa Paraguaya de Intercambio Comercial		
		EPPMP	European Power Press Manufacturers Panel
EPIC	European Parliament Industry Council		
Epic	European Philosophical Inquiry Centre	**EPPO**	European and Mediterranean Plant Protection Organisation = OEPP
EPIC	European Proliferation Information Centre		
		EPR	WHO Panafrican Centre for Emergency Preparedness and Response (Ethiopia)
EPIC	Export Payment Insurance Corporation (Australia)		
		EPRC	European Policies Research Centre

EPRDF	Ethiopian People's Revolutionary Democratic Front
EPRI	Electric Power Research Institute (China)
EPRL	Environmental Physics Research Laboratories (CSIRO) (Australia)
EPRLF	Eelam People's Revolutionary Liberation Front (Sri Lanka)
EPRO	European Pentecostal Relief Organization
Eproyiv	Empresa de Proyectos para Industrias Varias (Cuba)
EPRP	Ethiopian People's Revolutionary Party
EPRS	European Paediatric Respiratory Society
EPS	Ejército Popular Sandinista (Nicaragua)
EPS	Emergency Planning Society (*ex* ACDEPO)
EPS	Environmental Protection Service, Pacific and Yukon Region (Canada)
EPS	European Palm Society
EPS	European Physical Society = EPhS
EPS	European Pineal Society
EPS	Europese Politieke Samenwerking; Evropaiki Politiki Sinergasia = CPE, EPC, EPZ, POCO
EPS	Experimental Psychology Society
EPSA	Empresa Publica de Servicios Agropecuário (Peru)
EPSC	European Public Service Industry Committee = CSESP
EPSEP	Empresa Peruana de Servicios Pesqueros
EPSF	European Paintball Sports Federation
EPSG	Epiphytic Plant Study Group
EPSG	European Pineal Study Group
EPSG	European Production Study Group
EPSMA	European Association for Manufacturers of Self-Adhesive Materials
EPSO	European Peace and Security Office
EPSRC	Engineering and Physical Sciences Research Council
EPSU-JET	European Public Service Union – JET
EPT	Exploring Parenthood Trust
EPTA	Electrophysiological Technologists Association
EPTA	European Paltrusion Technology Association
EPTA	European Pentecostal Theological Association (Germany)
EPTA	European Piano Teachers Association
EPTA	European Power Tool Association
EPTEL	Empresa Publica de Telecomunicações (Angola)
EPTISA	Estudios y Proyectos Technicos Industriales SA
EPTRIZP	Electric Power Test and Research Institute of Zhejiang Province
EPTRS	Export Promotion Techniques Research Service (GATT)
EPU	Economic Planning Unit (Malaysia)
EPU	European Picture Union
EPU	European Press Photo Union
EPW	East Prussian Wolves (Poland) = WPW
EPYC	European Political Youth Council (DEMYC, EYCD) (Belgium)
EPZ	Europäische Politische Zusammenarbeit = CPE, EPC, EPS, POCO
EPZA	Export Processing Zones Authority (Mauritius, Pakistan, Taiwan)
EQA	European Quality Alliance
EQUAM	European Committee on Quality Assurance and Medical Devices in Plastic Surgery
ÉRA	École Régionale d'Agriculture
ERA	Educational Recording Agency
ERA	Electrical Research Association
ERA	Electronic Research Association
ERA	Empresarios Radiodifusores Asociados (Costa Rica)
ERA	Eritrean Relief Association
ERA	European Recreation Association
ERA	European Regional Airlines Organisation
ERA	European Renal Association
ERA	European Retail Alliance
ERA	European Rifle Association (Luxembourg)
ERA	European Rotogravure Association
ERA	European Rum Association = AER, ERI, ERV
ERA	Expérience Rurale Alternative (Switzerland)
ERA Club	English Racing Automobiles Club
ERAD	Eradication of Animal Diseases Board (Éire)
ERAF	Europ-Afric pour l'Importation et l'Exportation (Ivory Coast)
ERAP	Entreprise de Recherches et d'Activités Pétrolières

ERASMUS	European Community Action Scheme for Mobility of University Students	**ERDO**	European Research and Development Organization
ERASS	European Rheumatoid Arthritis Surgical Society (Switzerland)	**ERECC**	Economic Research and Engineering Consulting Centre of the Aviation Industry (China)
ERB	Educational Records Bureau (U.S.A.)		
ERBE	Erómú Beruházási Vállalat	**ERENAV**	Entreprise Nationale de Réparations Navales (Algeria)
ERC	Earth Resources Centre		
ERC	Economic Research Council	**ERES**	European Rare Earth and Actinide Society
ERC	Economics Research Centre (Philippines)	**ERF**	European Rotorcraft Forum
ERC	Educational Research Centre (Éire)	**ERFA**	Conference on Economics of Route Air Navigation Facilities and Airports
ERC	Energy Research Centre (ANU)		
ERC	Esquerra Republicana Catalana	**ERFA**	Estuarine Research Federation of America
ERC	European Registry of Commerce (Belgium)	**ERFMI**	European Resilient Flooring Manufacturers' Institute (Switzerland)
ERC	Evaluation Review Committee		
ERC	Regional Conference for Europe (FAO)	**ERG**	Endocrine Research Group (Canada)
ERCA	Educational Research Council of America	**ERG**	Enrichment Reprocessing Group (Japan)
ERCA	European Renal Care Association with EDTNA	**ERG**	European Regional Group for Social Work Education (IASSW) (Finland)
ErCam	Congregatio Eremitarum Camaldulensium Montis Coronae	**ERG**	European Right Group
		ERGOMAS	European Research Group on Military and Society
ERCIM	European Research Consortium for Informatics and Mathematics	**ERI**	Earthquake Research Institute, Tokyo (Japan)
ERCO	Electrical Reduction Company of Canada	**ERI**	Elm Research Institute (U.S.A.)
ERCOFTAC	European Research Community on Flow, Turbulence and Combustion	**ERI**	Europäischen Rum-Industrie = AER, ERA, ERV
ERD	Group of the European Democratic Alliance = RDE	**ERIA**	Estudios y Realizaciónes en Informatica Aplicada
ERDA	Electrical and Radio Development Association (Australia)	**ERIC**	Educational Resources Information Center (U.S.A.)
ERDA	Energy Research and Development Agency (U.S.A.)	**ERIC**	Enuresis Research and Information Centre
ERDA	European Research and Development Agency	**ERIC**	Environmental Research and Information Centre
ERDC	Eastern Region Development Corporation (Nigeria)	**ERICA**	European Research into Consumer Affairs
ERDC	European Research and Development Committee	**ERICO**	European Research and Information Centre for Obesity
ERDC	PNOC Energy Research and Development Center (Philippines)	**ERIDO**	European Regional Industrial Development Organization (Belgium)
ERDE	Electronics and Radar Development Establishment (India)	**ERIL**	Earthquake Research Institute of Lanzhou (China)
ERDF	European Regional Development Fund = FEDER	**ERIME**	Economic Research Institute for the Middle East (Japan)
ERDIC	Energy Research Development and Information Centre (Australia)	**ERIS**	Escuela Regional de Ingenieria Sanitaria (Guatemala)
ERDL	Explosives Research and Development Laboratory (India)	**ERIW**	European Research Institute for Welding

ERL	Electronics Research Laboratory (Australia)
ERL	Energy Research Laboratories
ERM	Enfants Refugiés du Monde
ERMA	Ernest Read Music Association
ERMA	European Resin Manufacturers' Association
ERMCO	European Ready Mixed Concrete Organization
ERN	Ejercito de Resistencia Nicaragüense
ERN	European Regionalist Network
ERNO	Entwicklungsring Nord
ERO	Ethiopian Relief Organization
ERO	European Radiocommunications Office
ERO	European Regional Organisation of the Fédération Dentaire Internationale (IDF/FDI)) (Germany) = ORE
EROPA	Eastern Regional Organization for Public Administration (Philippines) = ORAP
EROS	Eelam Revolutionary Organisation of Students (Sri Lanka)
EROS	European River Ocean System 2000
ERP	Ejército Revolucionario del Pueblo (Argentina, El Salvador)
ERP	Estonian Reform Party
ERP	European Recovery Programme = PRE
ERP	European Rehabilitation Partners
ERPDB	Eastern Regional Production Development Board (Nigeria)
ERPM	East Rand Proprietary Mines
ERR	Earth Resources Research
ERRA	European Recovery and Recycling Association (Belgium)
ERRL	Eastern Regional Research Laboratory (U.S.A.)
ERS	Economic Research Service (U.S.A.)
ERS	Electoral Reform Society
ERS	Electric Railway Society
ERS	European Respiratory Society
ERSDAC	Earth Resources Satellite Data Analysis Center (Japan)
ERSO	Electronics Research and Service Organization (Taiwan)
ERT	Elliniki Radiophonia Tileorassi
ERT	Ente de Radiotelevisión (Argentina)
ERT	European Round Table of Industrialists
ERT	Explosivos Río Tinto (Spain)
ERT	Union Explosivos Río Tinto S.A.

ERTI	Erdészeti Tudományos Intézet
ERTV	Egyptian Radio and Television Corporation
ERU	Eesti Raamatukoguhoidjate Ühing = ELA
ERU	English Rugby Union
ERU	Environmental Research Unit (Éire)
ERU	Europese Radio Unie
ERV	Europese Rum Vereniging = AER, ERA, ERI
ERVA	Erhvervsaskeriernes Branc
ERYICA	Association Européenne pour l'Information et le Conseil des Jeunes
ES	Econometric Society
ES	Endocrine Society (U.S.A.)
ES	Ergonomics Society
ESA	Department of Economic and Social Affairs (UN)
ÉSA	École Supérieure d'Agriculture et de Viticulture d'Angers (Belgium)
ESA	Ecological Society of Australia
ESA	Economic Science Association
ESA	Ejército Secreto Anticomunista (El Salvador, Guatemala)
ESA	Electrolysis Society of America
ESA	Employment Services Agency
ESA	Endocrine Society of Australia
ESA	Entomological Society of America
ESA	Ethnological Society of America
ESA	Euratom Supply Agency
ESA	European Sightseeing and Tours Association
ESA	European Society of Agronomy (France)
ESA	European Sociological Association
ESA	European Space Agency = ASE, EWO
ESA	European Spice Association
ESA	European Strasbismological Association
ÉSAA	École Supérieure d'Agriculture d'Angers
ESAA	Electricity Supply Association of Australia
ESAA	English Schools Athletic Association
ÉSAAT	École Supérieure d'Application d'Agriculture Tropicale
ESAB	Elektriska Svetsningsaktiebolaget
ESAC	Endangered Species Advisory Committee
ESAC	Environmental Studies Association of Canada = ACéE

ÉSACG	École Supérieure d'Application des Corps
ESACT	European Society for Animal Cell Technology
ESAE	European Society of Association Executives = AEDA, GEV
ESAFS	East and Southeast Asia Federation of Soil Science Societies (Japan)
ESAG	Escalator Safety Action Group
ESAI	Educational Studies Association of Ireland
ESAL	Escola Superior de Agricultura de Lavras (Brazil)
ESALQ	Escola Superior de Agricultura "Luiz de Queiroz" (Brazil)
ESAMI	Eastern and Southern African Management Institute
ESAMRDC	Eastern and Southern African Mineral Resources Development Centre (Tanzania)
ESAN	Escuela de Administración de Negocios para Graduados (Peru)
ESAN	European Social Action Network
ESANZ	Economic Society of Australia and New Zealand
ESAO	European Society for Artificial Organs
ÉSAP	École Supérieure d'Agriculture de Purpan
ESAP	Egyptian Society of Animal Production
ESAP	Escuela Superior de Administración Pública (Colombia)
ESAPTA	Eastern and Southern African Preferential Trade Area = PTA, ZEP
ESARBICA	Eastern and Southern African Regional Branch of the International Council on Archives
ESARDA	European Safeguards Research and Development Association
ESARIPO	Industrial Property Organization for English-Speaking Africa
ÉSAT	École Supérieure d'Agronomie Tropicale
ESAURP	Eastern and Southern African Universities Research Programme
ESAURP	Escola Superior de Agricultura da Universidade Rural de Pernambuco (Brazil)
ESAV	Escola Superior de Agricultura e Veterinaria (Brazil)
ESB	Economic Stabilisation Board (China)
ESB	Electricity Supply Board (Éire)
ESB	English-Speaking Board
ESB	European Settlement Board
ESB	European Society for Biomaterials
ESB	European Society of Biomechanics
ESB	Export Services Branch (DTI)
ESBA	English Schools Badminton Association
ESBBA	English Schools Basket Ball Association
ESBG	European Savings Banks Group = ESV, GECE
ESBOA	Electricity Supply Board Officers Association (Éire)
ESBRA	European Society for Biomedical Research on Alcoholism
ESBVM	Ecumenical Society of the Blessed Virgin Mary
ESC	Ecological Society of China
ESC	Economic and Social Committee (EU) = CES
ESC	Economic Security Committee (Jordan)
ESC	Energy Strategy Commission (Japan)
ESC	English Ski Council
ESC	Entomological Society of Canada
ESC	Entomological Society of China
ESC	Ethiopia Solidarity Campaign
ESC	European Pharmaceutical Students Committee
ESC	European Seismological Commission = CSE
ESC	European Shippers' Council
ESC	European Society of Cardiology = SEC
ESC	European Society of Chronobiology (Netherlands)
ESC	European Society of Contraception = SEC
ESC	European Society of Culture = SEC
ESC	European Space Conference = CSE
ESC	Executive Secretaries Club
ESCA	East of Scotland College of Agriculture
ESCA	English Schools Cricket Association
ESCA	European Speech Communication Association
ESCAP	Economic and Social Commission for Asia and the Pacific (UN) = CESAP, CESPAP
ESCAP - CGPRT Centre	Regional Coordination Centre for Research and Development of Coarse Grains, Pulses, Roots and Tuber Crops in the Humid Tropics of Asia and the Pacific

ESCAP/TIS	Trade Information Service
ESCB	European System of Central Banks
ESCES	Experimental Satellite Communication Earth Centre (India)
ESCGTA	European Standing Conference of Geography Teachers' Associations
ESCH FAO	Sugar Beverages and Horticultural Crops Service
ESCI	European Society for Clinical Investigation
ESCM	European Society for Clinical Microbiology (Germany)
ESCMID	European Society of Clinical Microbiology and Infectious Diseases
ESCO	European Satellite Consulting Organisation
ESCO	European Sterility and Conception Organization
ESCOM	Electricity Supply Commission (South Africa)
ESCOP	European Scientific Cooperative for Phytotherapy
ESCOP	Experiment Station Committee on Organization and Policy (U.S.A.)
ESCOR	Advisory Committee for Economic and Social Research Overseas (FCO)
ESCORENA	European System of Cooperative Research Networks in Agriculture
ESCOW	East Sepik Council of Women
ESCOW	Engineering and Scientific Committee on Water (New Zealand)
ESCP	European Society of Clinical Pharmacy
ESCPB	European Society of Comparative Physiology and Biochemistry
ESCRS	European Society of Cataract and Refractive Surgeons
ESCSB	European Society for Comparative Skin Biology
ESCVS	European Society for Cardiovascular Surgery
ESCWA	Economic and Social Commission for Western Asia = CESAO, CESPAO
ESD	Environment Strategies Division (DEST)
ESD	European Society of Dacryology
ESD	WHO Epidemiological Information Service
ESDA	European Social Development Associates
ESDEN	Ethnikos Syndesmos Diplomatouchon Ellinidon Nosokomon
ESDERC	European Semiconductor Device Research Conference
ESDERC	European Solid State Device Research Conference
ESDP	Estonian Social Democratic Party
ESDP	European Social Development Programme
ESDP	European Society for Developmental Pharmacology
ESDR	European Society for Dermatological Research
ESDREMA	European Surgical Dressings Manufacturers' Association
ESDSC	Ecologically Sustainable Development Steering Committee
ESDU	Engineering Sciences Data Unit
ESDUCK	Egyptian Society for the Dissemination of Universal Culture and Knowledge
ESE	European Society of Endodontology
ESEE	European Society for Engineering Education = SEFI
ESEF	Electrotyping and Stereotyping Employers' Federation
ESEN	Empresa del Seguro Estatal Nacional (Cuba)
ESER	Einheits-System für Elektronische Rechentechnik = IGCCT
ESF	Egyptologiska Sällskapet i Finland
ESF	Ekonomiska Samfundet i Finland
ESF	European Science Foundation = FES
ESF	European Script Fund
ESF	European Security Forum
ESF	European Social Fund = FSE
ESF	European Surfing Federation
ESFA	English Schools Football Association
ESG	Engineers and Scientists Guild (U.S.A.)
ESG	Escola Superior de Guerra (Brazil, Mexico)
ESG	Euphorbia Study Group
ESG	European Seal Group
ESGA	English Schools Gymnastics Association
ESGCP	European Study Group for Cell Proliferation
ESGE	European Society of Gastrointestinal Endoscopy
ESGLD	European Study Group on Lysosomal Diseases
ESGO	European Society of Gynaecological Oncology

ESGR	European Society for Gastrointestinal Radiologists
ESH	European Society of Haematology
ESH	European Society of Hypnosis
ESH	Human Resources Institutions Agrarian Reform Division
ESHA	European Secondary Heads Association (Netherlands)
ESHH	FAO Home Economics Social Programmes Service
ESHP	European Society of Handwriting Psychology = EGF, EGS, ESS, EVS, SEG, SEPS
ESHPh	European Society for the History of Photography = AEHPh, EGGPh
ESHRE	European Society for Human Reproduction and Embryology
ESHSI	Economic and Social History Society of Ireland
ESI	Ecological Studies Institute
ESI	Education Standards Institute
ESI	Empresa de Suministros Industriales (Cuba)
ESIB	European Student Information Bureau
ÉSIC	Association d'Études et de Statistiques de l'Industrie Cotonnière
ESIC	Employees State Insurance Corporation (India)
ESIC	Environmental Science Information Center (NOAA)
ESICUBA	Empresa de Seguros Internacionales de Cuba
ESID	European Society for the Study of Infant Deaths
ESIDOG	European Society for Infectious Diseases in Obstetrics and Gynaecology (Italy)
ÉSIÉ	École Supérieure Interafricaine de l'Électricité = ICEE, IEEC
ESIF	European Service Industries Forum
ÉSIJY	École Supérieure Internationale de Journalisme Yaoundé (Cameroon)
ESIP	Engineering Societies International Publications Committee
ESIS	European Shielding Information Service (Euratom)
ESIS	European Structural Integrity Society
ESIT	Egyptian Society for Information Technology
ESITC	Electricity Supply Industry Training Committee

ÉSITEX	Association d'Études et de Statistiques de l'Industrie Textile
ÉSITPA	École Supérieure d'Ingénieurs et Techniciens pour l'Agriculture
ESJ	Entomological Society of Japan
ESK	Europäische Schnellbrüter-Kernkraftwerksgesellschaft
ESKA	European Society of Knee Surgery and Arthroscopy (Switzerland)
Eskom	Electricity Supply Commission (South Africa)
ESLA	Egyptian School Library Association
ESLI	Esperanto Sak-Ligo Internacia
ESLO	European Satellite Launcher Organisation
ESM	Entreprise Sénégalaise du Mobilier
ESM	European Society for Microcirculation
ESM	European Society for Mycobacteriology
ESMA	Electrical Sign Manufacturers' Association
ESMG	Electric Steel Makers' Guild
ESMO	European Society of Medical Oncology
ESMOC	European Solar Meeting Organizing Committee
ESMS	European Society of Medical Sociology
ESMST	European Society of Membrane Science and Technology
ESN	European Sensory Network
ESN	European Society for Neurochemistry
ESN	European Society of Nematologists
ESN	FAO Food Policy Nutrition Division
ESNA	European Society of Nuclear Methods in Agriculture
ESNA-CIFOR	Escuela Nacional de Ciencias Forestales (Honduras)
ESNE	Engineering Societies of New England (U.S.A.)
ESNF	FAO Food Policy Food Science Service
ESNICVD	European Society for Non-Invasive Cardiovascular Dynamics
ESNN	FAO Nutrition Programmes Research Service
ESNR	European Society of Neuradiology
ESNS	FAO Food Standards Food Control Service
ESNSW	Entomological Society of New South Wales
ESNZ	Entomological Society of New Zealand
ESO	Entomological Society of Ontario

ESO	European School of Oncology	**ESPR**	European Society for Paediatric Research
ESO	European Shipmasters Organisation; Europäische Schiffer Organisation = OEB	**ESPR**	European Society of Pediatric Radiology
ESO	European Society of Osteoarthrology	**ESPRI**	European Economic and Social Policy Research Institute = IRPES
ESO	European Southern Observatory	**ESPRIT**	European Strategic Programme for Research and Development in Information Technology
ESOA	European Society of Osteoarthrology		
ESOC	European Space Operations Centre		
ESOMAR	European Society for Opinion and Marketing Research (Netherlands)	**ESPU**	European Society for Paediatric Urology
ESONE	European Standards on Nuclear Electronics Committee	**ESQ**	Entomological Society of Queensland
ESORIB	European School of Oral Rehabilitation, Implantology and Biomaterials	**ESQA**	English Slate Quarries Association
		ESR	Europa Saaten Dienst
ESOT	European Society for Organ Transplantation	**ESRA**	Economische en Sociale Raad van Advies der Benelux Economische Unie = CCES
ESOTCM	European Society of Ophthalmology and Traditional Chinese Medicine		
ESP	European Society of Pathology	**ESRA**	European Safety and Reliabiity Association
ESP	FAO Policy Analysis Division		
ESPACI	European Society of Paediatric Allergy and Clinical Immunology	**ESRA**	European Society of Regional Anaesthesia
ESPD	European Association for Pediatric Dermatology	**ESRA**	European Synthetic Rubber Association
		ESRANGE	European Space Launching Range
ESPD	Export Services and Promotions Division (DTI)	**ESRB**	European Society for Radiation Biology
ESPE	European Society for Pediatric Endocrinology	**ESRC**	Economic and Social Research Council
		ESRC	Environmental Science Research Centre (China)
ESPE	European Society for Population Economics (Germany)	**ESRC**	Permanent Committee of European Science Research Councils
ESPEN	European Society of Parenteral and Enteral Nutrition	**ESRC**	West European Science Research Council
ESPGAN	European Society for Paediatric Gastroenterology	**ESRF**	Economic and Scientific Research Foundation (India)
ESPHI	European Society for Paediatric Haematology and Immunology	**ESRF**	European Squash Rackets Federation
		ESRF	European Synchrotron Radiation Facility
ESPI	Ente Siciliano per la Promozione Industriale	**ESRI**	Economic and Social Research Institute (Éire)
ESPIC	European Society of Pediatric Intensive Care (Belgium)	**ESRI**	Engineering and Statistical Research Institute (Canada)
ESPKU	European Society for Phenylketonuria and Allied Disorders	**ESRI**	European Systems Research Institute (Belgium)
ESPLAF	European Strategic Planning Federation	**ESRIN**	European Space Research Institute
ESPN	European Society for Pediatric Nephrology	**ESRO**	European Space Research Organization
		ESRS	European Sleep Research Society
ESPN	European Society of Paediatric Neurosurgery	**ESRS**	European Society for Rural Sociology = SESR
ESPO	European Society for Psychosocial Oncology	**ESRS**	European Synchrotron Radiation Society
ESPOL	Escuela Politecnica Nacional (Ecuador)	**ESS**	Eastern Searoad Service (Australia)

ESS	Eastern Surgical Society (U.S.A.)
ESS	Europaeisk Sammenslutning for Smaerbejde = AEC, EAC, EAS, EGZ
ESS	Europaeisk Selskab for Skriftpsykologi = EGF, EGS, ESHP, EVS, SEG, SEPS
ESS	FAO Statistics Division
ESSA	Electricity Supply Association of Australia
ESSA	English Schools Swimming Association
ESSA	Europäischer Salzstudien-Ausschuss
ESSA	European Single Service Association (Switzerland)
ESSC	Earth Systems Science Committee
ESSC	European Society for Soil Conservation
ESSCIRC	European Solid State Circuits Conference
ESSCS	European Society for the Study of Cognitive Systems
ESSE	European Society for Surgery of Shoulder and Elbow
ÉSSÉC	École Supérieure des Sciences Économiques et Commerciales
ESSFA	Essens Fabrikant Foreningen
ESSI	European Software and Systems Initiative
ESSIR	European Society for the Study of International Relations = SEPERI
ESSO	European Society of Surgical Oncology
ESSOP	European Society for Social Pediatrics
ESSR	European Society for Surgical Research
ESSRA	Economic and Social Science Research Association
EST	European Society of Toxicology
ESTA	Earth Science Teachers' Association
ESTA	Energy Systems Trade Association
ESTA	Europäische Schwertransporte- und Automobilkranarbeiten
ESTA	European Security Transport Association
ESTA	European String Teachers Association
ESTA	European Surgical Trade Association
ESTAC	Eastern Africa Statistical Training Centre
ESTB	Entreprise Sénégalaise de Transportes Bellassées
ESTEC	European Space Technology Centre
ESTHER	École Inter-États des Techniciens Supérieurs de l'Hydraulique et de l'Equipement Rural (Burkina Faso) = ETSHER
ESTI	European Society of Transport Institutes
ESTI	European Solar Test Installation
ESTI	European Space Technology Institute
ESTL	European Space Tribology Laboratory
ESTOC	European Smokeless Tobacco Council
ESTRA	English Speaking Tape Respondents Association
ESTRO	European Society of Therapeutic Radiation and Oncology
ESU	Endangered Species Unit (ANCA)
ESU	Energy Studies and Sustainable Technology Unit (Scotland)
ESU	Energy Studies Unit
ESU	English Speaking Union
ESU	Europäische Schausteller-Union
ESU	European Showmen's Union = UFE
ESUR	European Society for Uroradiology
ESV	Europaische Sparkassenvereinigung = ESBG, GECE
ESVA	English Schools Volleyball Association
ESVD	European Society of Veterinary Dermatology
ESVV	European Society for Veterinary Virology
ESW	Europese Stichting voor Wetenschappen
ESWM	Együttëles, Spoluzitie, Wspólnota, Souziti; Madersko Křest'anskodemokratické hnutie
ESWTR	European Society of Women in Theological Research
ET	Ejército de Tierra
ETA	Educational Television Association
ETA	Eesti Teaduste Akadeemia / Academia Scientiarum Estoniae / Estonian Academy of Sciences
ETA	Environment Teachers' Association
ETA	Environmental Transport Association
ETA	Esperanto Teachers Association
ETA	Estonian Telegraph Agency
ETA	Ethiopian Tourism Commission
ETA	European Tallying Association
ETA	European Taxpayers Association
ETA	European Teachers Association
ETA	European Tennis Association
ETA	European Thermographic Association = AET, EAT
ETA	European Thyroid Association = AET
ETA	European Timber Association = EHV, FEBO

ETA	European Truckowners Association	**ETE**	Épitéstudományi Egyesület (Hungary)
ETA	European Tube Association	**ETE**	Evropaiki Trapeza Ependiseon = EIB, BEI
ETA	European Tugowners Association		
ETA	Euskadi Ta Askatasuna (Spain)	**ETE**	Experimental Tunnelling Establishment
ETA-I	Electronic Technicians Association International	**ETENE**	Escritório Técnico de Estudos Económicos do Nordeste (Brazil)
ETA-P-M	ETA Politico-Militar	**ETEPE**	Escritório Técnico de Planejamento (Brazil)
ETAA	Empresa de Transportes Aereos de Angola	**EtF**	Ergoterapeutforeningen
ETAC	Environment Technical Advisory Committee	**ETF**	European Telemarketing Federation
		ETF	European Training Foundation
ETAD	Ecological and Toxicological Association of the Dyestuffs Manufacturing Industry	**ETFRN**	European Tropical Forest Research Network
		ETG	Environment and Training Group
ÉTAF	École d'Enseignement Technique Féminine	**ETH**	Eidgenössische Technische Hochschule (Switzerland)
ETAG	European Tourist Action Group	**ETHIC**	Electric Trace Heating Industry Council
ETAN	European Technology Assessment Network (EU)	**ETI**	Emballage and Transportinstituttet (Denmark)
ETAN	Jugoslovenskí Savez za Elektroniku, Telekomunikacije Automatizaciju i Nuklearnu Tehniku	**ÉTI**	Építéstodományi Intézet
		ETI	Expert Center for Taxonomic Identification (The Netherlands)
ETAP	Expanded Technical Assistance Programme (UN)	**ETIA**	European Tape Industry Association
		ETIC	English-Teaching Information Centre
ETAPC	European Technical Association for Protective Coatings (Belgium)	**ETIF**	Economisch-Technologisch Instituut Friesland
ÉTAS	Établissement d'Expériences Techniques d'Angers (DTAT)	**ETIMEX**	Ethiopian Import and Export Corporation
ETB	English Tourist Board	**ETIO**	Economisch-Technologisch Instituut Overijssel
ÉTBS	Établissement d'Expériences Techniques de Bourges (DTAT)	**ETIU**	Economisch-Technologisch Instituut Utrecht
ETC	Ecological Trading Company Plc		
ETC	European Conference of Associations of Telecommunication Cables Industries = EUROTELCAB	**ETIYRA**	El Toro International Yacht Racing Association (U.S.A.)
		ETJC	Engineering Trades Joint Council
ETC	European Tea Committee	**ÉTK**	Épitésügyi Tájkékoztatási Központ
ETC	European Travel Commission = CET	**ETL**	Eesti Teadlaste Liit
ETC	Experimental Techniques Centre	**ETL**	Electotechnical Laboratory (Japan)
ETC	Stichting ETC Consultants for Development Programmes	**ETL**	Elintarviketeollisuusliitto
		ETM	Association Europe – Tiers Monde
ÉTCA	Études Techniques et Constructions Aérospatiales (Belgium)	**ETMA**	English Timber Merchants Association
		ETMA	European Television Magazines Association
ETCI	Electro-Technical Council of Ireland		
ETCI	Euro Travellers Cheque International	**ETMC**	European Transport Maintenance Council
ETCS	European Tissue Culture Society		
ETDÉ	Entreprise Transport et Distribution d'Électricité	**ETMI**	European Technology Management Initiative (EFMD, EUROPACE)
ETDS	Electric Transport Development Society	**ETO**	European Transport Organisation
ETE	Energiagazdálkadási Tudományos Egyesület	**ETP**	European Training Programme in Brain and Behaviour Research

ETPC	Entreprise de Travaux Publiques Caméroun
ETPC	European Thermophysical Properties Conferences
ETPI	Eastern Telecommunications Philippines Inc
ETPM	Société Entrepose pour les Travaux Pétroliers Maritimes
ETPO	Entreprise de Travaux Publics de l'Ouest
ETPO	European Trade Promotion Organisation
ETRA	European Textile Rental Association
ETRAC	Educational Television and Radio Association of Canada
ETRB	Electrical Technology Requirements Board (DTI)
ETRI	Electronics and Telecommunications Research Institute (South Korea)
ETRTO	European Tyre and Rim Technical Organization
ETS	Electrodepositors' Technical Society
ETS	Elintarviketieteiden Seura ry
ETS	European Teratology Society
ETS	Evangelical Tract Society and Prayer Union
ETSA	English Table Soccer Association
ETSAB	Escuela Tecnica Superior de Arquitectura de Barcelona
ETSAM	Escuela Tecnica Superior de Arquitectura de Madrid
ETSHER	Organisation Inter-États des Techniciens Supérieurs de l'Hydraulique et d'Étude de l'Equipement Rural (Burkina Faso) = ESTHER
ETSI	European Telecommunications Standards Institute (France)
ETSICCPB	Escuela Tecnica Superior de Ingenieros de Caminos, Canales y Puertos
ETSIIB	Escuela Tecnica Superior de Ingenieros Industriales de Barcelona
ETSIIT	Escuela Tecnica Superior de Ingenieros Industriales de Terrassa (Barcelona)
ETSIN	Escuela Tecnica Superior de Ingenieros Navales
ETSITB	Escuela Tecnica Superior de Ingenieros de Telecomunicacion
ETSMA	European Tyre Stud Manufacturers Association
ETSU	Energy Technology Support Unit
ETT	Education Today and Tomorrow
ETTA	Eastern Townships Textile Association (Canada)
ETTA	English Table Tennis Association
ETTDC	Electronics Trade and Technology Development Corporation (India)
ETTIC	Education and Training Technology International Convention
ETTU	European Table Tennis Union
ETU	Ethiopian Trade Union
ETUA	Electrical Trades Union of Australia
ETUC	European Trade Union Confederation = CES, EGB
ETUCE	European Trade Union Committee for Education = CSEE
ETUCF	European Trade Union Committee of Food and Allied Workers = CESA
ETUCO	European Trade Union College = ASE, EGA, EVA
ETUF	Egyptian Trade Union Federation
ETUF	European Trade Union Federation
ETUI	European Trade Union Institute = DEFI, EGI, EVI, ISE
ETV	Europäischer Tabakwaren-Grosshandels-Verband
ETV	European Ready Mixed Concrete Organisation
ETVG	European Tumour Virus Group
ETWA	English Tiddlywink Association
ETY	Energiataloudellinen Yhdistys
EU	European Union / Europäische Union = UE, EC, CE (*ex* EEC, CEE, EEG)
EUAIS	European Union of Arab and Islamic Studies = UEAI
EUATB	Escuela Universitaria de Arquitectura Tecnica
EUBCA	Escuela Universitaria de Bibliotecnologia y Ciencias Afines (Uruguay)
EUBS	European Undersea Bio-medical Society
EUC	European Union of Customs
EUCA	Fédération Européenne des Associations de Torrefacteurs de Café
EUCAPA	European Capsules Association
EUCARPIA	European Association for Research on Plant Breeding
EUCC	European Union of Coastal Conservation
EUCD	Europäische Union Christlicher Demokraten = CDEU, UEDC

EUCDA	Europäische Union Christlich Demokratischer Arbeitsnehmer = EUCDW, UELDC, UETDC
EUCDW	European Union of Christian Democratic Workers = EUCDA, UELDC, UETDC
EUCEPA	European Liaison Committee for Pulp and Paper
EUCHEM	European Chemical Congress
EUCHEM-AP	European Committee of Chemical Plant Manufacturers
EUCID	European Union of Clinicians in Implant Dentistry (Belgium)
EUCLID	Centre for Legal Interdisciplinary Development
EUCLID	European Association for Library and Information Education and Research
EUCOFEL	Union Européenne du Commerce de Gros d'Expédition, d'Importation et d'Exportation en Fruits et Légumes
EUCOFF	European Conference on Flammability and Fire Retardants
EUCOLAIT	Union Européenne du Commerce des Produits Laitiers et Dérivés
EUCOMED	European Confederation of Medical Suppliers Associations
EUCONEC	European Conference on Industrial Electrical Capacitors
EUCPS	European University Centre for Peace Studies
EUCT	Association 'Eurotourisme' Culture Folklore Tourisme de l'Europe Unie
EUD	European Union of Dentists = EUZ, UEMD, UEPMD
EUDAT	European Association for the Development of Databases in Education and Training (Germany)
EUDEBA	Editorial Universitaria de Buenos Aires (Argentina)
EUDIFF	Association Européenne pour le Développement de l'Information et de la Formation des Femmes (Belgium)
EUDISED	European Documentation and Information System for Education
EUEMAIL	Ständige Konferenz der Europäischen Emaillewarenindustrie
EUF	Europaeische Udviklingsfonds = EDF, EEF, EOF, FED, FES
EUF	European Union of Federalists (France)
EUFMD	European Commission for the Control of Foot and Mouth Disease
EUFOS	European Federation of Societies for ORL, Head and Neck Surgery
EUFTW	European Union of Film and Television Workers
EUG	European Union of Geosciences
EUGFL	Europaeiske Udviklings- og Garantifond for Landbruget = EAGFL, EAGGF, EGTPE, EOGFL, FEOGA
EUGROPA	Union Européenne des Commerce de Gros en Papiers, Cartons et Emballages
EUHOFA	Association Européenne des Directeurs d'Écoles Hôtelières
EUI	European Insurance Committee
EUI	European University Institute = EHI, IUE
EUITIB	Escuela Universitaria de Ingenieria Tecnica Industrial de Barcelona
EUJCD	Europäische Union Junger Christlicher Demokraten = EUYCD, UEJDC
EUJS	European Union of Jewish Students (Belgium) = UEEJ
EULA-BANK	Banco Euro-Latinoamericano = BEAL
EULAC	Asociación de Editoriales Universitarias de América Latina y el Caribe (Peru)
EULAR	European League Against Rheumatism
EULAS	European Union of Local Authority Staffs = UEFPC
EULEP	European Late Effects Project = SUM, WUS
EUMABOIS	Comité Européen des Constructeurs de Machines à Bois
EUMA-PRINT	European Committee of Associations of Printing and Paper Converting Machinery Manufacturers
EUMC	Entr'aide Universitaire Mondiale de Canada = WUSC
EUMETSAT	European Organisation for the Exploitation of Meteorological Satellites
EUMT	Europäische Union gegen den Missbrauch der Tiere = UEMTA
EUNC	Eritrean Unified National Council (Ethiopia)
EUPA-GRAPH	European Association of Manufacturers of Printing and Writing Papers (France)
EuPC	European Plastics Converters (Belgium) = EPC
EUPE	European Union for Packaging and the Environment
EUPG	Escuela Universitaria Politecnica de Girona

EUPM	Escuela Universitaria Politecnica de Manresa (Barcelona)	**EURAL**	Centro de Investigaciones Europeo-Latinoamericanas (Argentina)
EUPO	European Community University Professors in Ophthalmology	**EUR-ALARM**	European Association of Fire and Intruder Alarm Systems
EUPONEM	European Association of Netting Manufacturers	**EURANUT**	European Association of Nut Growers, Packagers and Distributors
EUPRA	European Peace Research Association (Germany)	**EURAPS**	European Association of Plastic Surgeons (France)
EUPRIO	Association of European University Public Relations and Information Officers (Belgium)	**EURAS**	European Anodisers Association
		EURASAP	European Association for the Science of Air Pollution
EUPRISO	European Union of Public Relations = UERP	**EURASCO**	European Agricultural Society and Show Organizers Consultative Committee
EUPSA	European Union of Paediatric Surgical Associations		
EUPSYCA	European Working Group for Psychosomatic Cancer Research	**EURASHE**	European Association for Institutions of Higher Education
		EURASIP	European Association for Signal Processing
EUPV	Escuela Universitaria Politecnica de Vilanova (Barcelona)	**EURATOM**	European Atomic Energy Community = CEEA, EAEC, EAG, EGA
EUR	Europäische Union der Rechtspfleger		
EUR	European University Research	**EUREAU**	Union des Associations des Distributeurs d'Eau de Pays Membres des Communautés Européennes
EUR-ACOM	European Association of Coalfield Local Authorities		
EUR-OP	Office for Official Publications of the European Communities (CEC)	**EUREC**	Société Coopérative Européenne
		EUREG	European Association for Interregional Cooperation
EUR-P	European Union for Retired People		
EUR-ELECTRIC	European Committee of the Electricity Supply Industry	**EUREKA**	European Research and Coordination Agency
EUR-OPTICA	West European Optical Societies	**EUREL**	Convention of National Societies of Electrical Engineers of Western Europe
EURA	Energy Users Research Association		
EURA	European Renderers Association	**EUREMAIL**	Conférence Permanente de l'Industrie Européenne Productrice d'Articles Émaillés
EURABC	Europäische Gemeinschaft auf Absprache für Atomaren, Biologischen und Chemischen Umweltschutz		
		EUREPRO	International Association for the Prepress Industry
EURABIA	European Coordinating Committee of Friendship Societies with the Arab World	**EURES**	European Reticulo-Endothelial Society
		EURESCO	Conseil de Coopération Culturelle Européenne
EURACA	European Air Carriers Association		
EURACS	European Association of Classification Societies	**EURET**	European Research for Transport
		EURIM	European Conference on Research into the Management of Information Systems and Networks
EURADA	Association Européenne des Agences de Développement (Belgium)		
EURAFREP	Société de Recherches et Exploitation de Pétrole (Mauritania)	**EURIMA**	European Insulation Manufacturers Association
EURAG	European Federation for the Welfare of the Elderly	**EURING**	European Union for Bird Ringing
EURAGRI-TOUR	Bureau Européen de l'Agriculture (Belgium)	**EURISOL**	European Federation of the Electro-Ceramic Industry
EURAGRI-TOUR	European Office for Green Tourism	**EURO**	Association of European Operational Research Societies

Euro AFIS	Europäische Arbeitsgemeinschaft zur Forderung des Informations Austausches über Suchtgefahren Rhein-Maas-Mosel (CE, CEC) = GEERMM
EURO-AIM	European Association for an Audiovisual Independent Market (CEC)
EURO-HKG	European High Temperature Nuclear Power Stations Society
Euro-MDF	European Federation of the Medium Density Fibreboard Manufacturers (Germany)
EURO-BITUME	European Bitumen Association
EURO-BUILD	European Organisation for the Promotion of New Techniques and Methods in Building
EURO-CENTRES	Foundation for European Language and Educational Centres
EURO-CHAMB-RES	Association of European Chambers of Commerce and Industry
EURO-CLAMP	European Clamping Tools Association
EURO-CONTROL	European Organisation for the Safety of Air Navigation
EURO-COPCOST	European Cooperation and Coordination in the Field of Scientific and Technical Research
EURO-COTON EEC	Committee for the Cotton and Allied Textile Industries
EURO-DATACAB	European Conference of Associations of Data and Control Cables Industries
EURO-FEDOP	European Federation of Employees in Public Service
EURO-FINAS	European Federation of Finance House Associations = EFFHA
EURO-FORGE	European Committee of Forging and Stamping Industries
EURO-GLACES	Association of the Ice Cream Industries of the EEC
EURO-GRAPHICS	European Association for Computer Graphics (Switzerland)
EURO-GROPA	Union des Distributeurs de Papiers et Cartons
EURO-GYPSUM	Association Européenne de l'Industrie du Plâtre
EURO-MAISIERS	Groupement des Associations des Maïsiers de la CEE
EURO-METAUX	Association Européenne de Métaux
EURO-MICRO	European Association for Microprocessing and Microprogramming
EURO-MINERALS	Confederation of Learned/Engineering Societies in the Mineral Industry
EURO-PECHE	Association des Organisations Nationales d'Entreprises de Pêche de la CEE
EURO-PHYSICS	European Physics Congress
EURO-PILOTE	European Organization of Airline Pilots Association
EURO-PLANT	Comité Européen des Constructeurs de Grand Ensembles Industriels
EURO-PLATE	European Registration Plate Association
EURO-POWER-CAB	European Conference of Associations of Power Cables Industries = EPC
EURO-PREFAB	Europäische Organisation für den Fertigibau
EURO-PRESSE FAMILIA	Association Européenne des Éditeurs de la Presse Périodique d'Information Féminine ou Familiale
EURO-SPACE	European Industrial Space Study Group
EURO-STRUCT PRESS	European Association of Publishers in the Field of Building and Design
EURO-TALENT	Comité Européen pour l'Education des Enfants et Adolescents Précoces, Doués, Talentueux
Euro-tecnet	Community Action Programme in the Field of Vocational Training and Technological Change (EU)
EURO-TELCAB	European Conference of Associations of Telecommunication Cables Industries = ETC
EURO-THERM	European Federation of Associations of Central Heating Materials Manufacturers
EURO-TOQUES	European Community of Cooks
EURO-TRANS	Comité Européen des Associations de Constructeurs d'Engrenages et d'Eléments de Transmission
EURO-VISION	Union Européenne de Radio-Diffusion
EURO-WINDING WIRES	European Conference of Associations of Winding Wires Industries = EWW
EuroACE	European Association for the Conservation of Energy

EUROAD-SAFE	European Road Safety Equipment Federation	**EUROGAS**	European Union of the Natural Gas Industry
EUROAVIA	Association of European Aeronautical and Astronautical Students	**EURO-GRAF**	Group of Federations of Graphics Industries in the EEC
EUROBAT	Association of European Accumulator Manufacturers	**EURO-GRAM**	Société Européenne de Recherches et d'Études Programmées
EUROBIT	European Association of Manufacturers of Business Machines Data Processing	**EURO-LABO**	European Association for Comparative Testing (Belgium)
EUROBOIS	European Group of Woodworking Journals	**EUROLAT**	European Network on Lateritic Weathering and Global Environment
EUROCAE	European Organisation for Civil Aviation Equipment	**Eurolib**	European Library Project
EUROCAT	European Association on Catalysis	**EUROLIPID**	Fédération Européenne pour l'Étude des Corps Gras
EURO-CHOR	Federation of European Choirs = AGEC	**EUROLUX**	European Group for Rooflights and Smoke Ventilation
Euroco	European Postgraduate Education in Polymer and Composites Engineering	**EUROM**	European Federation of Precision Mechanical and Optical Industries
EUROCOM	Gesellschaft für Europäische Kommunikation	**EUROM**	European Photographic Manufacturers Association
EUROCOM	Union Européenne des Négociants en Combustibles	**EURO-MALT**	Comité de Travail des Malteries de la CEE
EURO-COMP	European Computing Congress	**EUROMAP**	European Committee of Machinery Manufacturers for the Plastics and Rubber Industries
EURO-COOP	European Community of Consumer Cooperatives	**EUROMAT**	Vereinigung der Europäischen Verbande der Automatenwirtschaft
Eurocop	European Co-Production Association (Germany)	**EUROMDF**	Fédération Européenne des Fabricants de Panneaux de Moyenne Densité
EUROCOPI	European Computer Programme Institute	**EURO-MEAS**	Conference on Precise Electrical Measurement
EUROCOR	European Congress on Metallic Corrosion	**EURO-MECH**	European Mechanics Committee
EURO-CORD	Fédération des Industries de Corderie-Ficellerie de l'Europe Occidentale	**EUROMED**	European Council of American Chambers of Commerce
EURODATA	Eurodata Foundation	**EUROMET-REC**	Fédération du Négoce et de l'Industrie de la Récupération et du Recyclage des Métaux Nnon-Ferreux de la CE (Belgium)
EURODOC	Joint Documentation Service (ESA/EUROSPACE)		
EURO-DUCKS	European Waterfowl Habitat Fund	**EUROMIL**	European Organization of Military Associations
EUROFER	European Confederation of Iron and Steel Industries	**EUROMOT**	European Committee of Internal Combustion Engine Manufacturers Association
EUROFEU	European Committee of the Manufacturers of Fire Protection Equipment	**EURONAD**	Eurogroup Committee of National Armaments Directors
EUROFIET	Organisation Régionale Européenne de la Fédération Internationale des Employés, Techniciens et Cadres	**EURONEM**	European Association of Netting Manufacturers
EUROFIMA	Société Européenne pour le Financement de Matériel Ferroviaire	**EURONET**	European Telecommunications Network
EUROFUEL	Société Européenne de Fabrication de Combustibles à Base d'Uranium pour Réacteurs à Eau Légère	**Euronet-Diane**	Direct Information Access Network for Europe
		EUROP	European Railway Wagon Pool

EUROP-ADRESS	European Association of Direct Mail Houses	**EUROTAS**	European Transpersonal Association (Belgium)
EUROPA CLUB	Association for a European Understanding across Linguistic Frontiers	**EUROTEST**	European Association of Testing Institutions
EUROPACE	European Programme of Advanced Continuing Education	**EUROTOX**	Comité Européen Permanent de Recherches sur la Protection des Populations contre les Risques de Toxicité à Long Terme
EUROPE-TODAY	International Press Agency specialized in such Themes as Environment, Quality of Life and Health	**EURO-VENT**	European Committee of Manufacturers of Air Handling Equipment
EUROPEC	European Offshore Petroleum Conference and Exhibition	**EURP**	European Union of Public Relations
EUROPERI-NATALE	Société Belge du Congrès Européen de Médecine Périnatale	**EURRN**	European Urban and Regional Research Network
Europex	European Information Centre for Explosion Protection	**EURYDICE**	Education Information Network in the European Community
EUROPILE	Association des Fabricants Européens de Piles Électriques	**EURYICA**	European Youth Information and Counselling Service
EUROPMI	Comité de Liaison des Petites et Moyennes Entreprises Indépendentes (CE)	**EURYSN**	European Youth Science Network (Éire)
EUROPOL	European Police Service	**EUSA**	Europese Unie van de Sociale Apoteken = EUSMCP, EUSP, UEFS, UEPS, VESA
EUROPSO	European Federation of National Psoriasis Patients Associations (Netherlands)	**EUSA**	Evangelical Union of South America (U.K.)
EURO-PUMP	European Committee of Pump Manufacturers	**EUSAFEC**	Eastern United States Agricultural and Food Export Council
EUROPUR	European Association of Flexible Foam Block Manufacturers	**EUSARF**	European Scientific Association for Residential and Foster Care of Children and Adolescents
EURORAD	European Association of Manufacturers of Radiators	**EUSD**	European Union for Scientific Development (Germany)
EUROSA	Europe-Afrique Australe	**EUSE**	European UNIVAC Scientific Exchange
EUROSAC	Fédération Européenne des Fabricants de Sacs en Papier à Grande Contenance	**EUSI**	Ente Unitario Segretariato Italiano
EUROSAG	European Salaried Architects Group	**EUSIDIC**	European Association of Information Services
EUROSAI	European Organisation of Supreme Audit Institutions	**EUSIREF**	European Network of Scientific Information Referral Centres
EUROSAT	European Application Satellite Systems	**EUSMCP**	European Union of Social, Mutual and Cooperative Pharmacies = EUSA, EUSP, UEFS, UEPS, VESA
EUROSIM	Federation of European Simulation Societies	**EUSOMA**	European Society of Mastology (Italy)
EURO-SOLAR	European Solar Energy Association	**EUSP**	European Union of Social Pharmacies = EUSA, EUSMCP, UEFS, UEPS, VESA
EUROSTAT	Statistical Office of the European Communities = OSCE, SOEC	**EUSUG**	European Unix System Users Group
EUROSTEP	European Association of Users of Satellites in Training and Education Programmes	**EUSUHM**	European Union of School and University Health and Medicine = UEHMSU
Eurostep	European Solidarity Towards Equal Participation of People	**EUTDS**	Europäische Union der Tapezierer, Dekorateure (Raumausstatter) und Sattler
EUROTALC	Scientific Association of European Talc Industry (Belgium)	**EUTECA**	European Technical Caramel Association (Belgium)

EUTELSAT	European Telecommunications Satellite Operation
EUTO	European Union of Tourist Officers
EUVEPRO	European Vegetable Protein Federation
EUW	European Union of Women = EFU, UEF
EUWEP	European Union of Wholesale trade in Eggs, Egg-Products, Poultry and Game
EuWiD	Europäischer Wirtschaftsdienst
EUYCD	European Union of Young Christian Democrats = EWJCD, UEJDC
EUZ	Europäische Union der Zahnärtze = EUD, UEMD, UEPMD
EV	Edelstahl-Vereinigung
EV	Erdöl-Vereinigung (Switzerland)
EVA	Electric Vehicle Association of Great Britain
EVA	Elektrisitetsverkenes Arbeidsgiverforening
EVA	English Vineyards Association
EVA	English Volleyball Association
EVA	Esperantlingua Verkista Asocio
EVA	Europese Vakbondsakademie = ASE, EGA, ETUCO
EVA	Europese Vrijhandels-Associatie
EVAA	Electric Vehicle Association of the Americas
EVAAP	Electric Vehicle Association of Asia Pacific
EVATMI	European Vinyl Asbestos Tile Manufacturers Institute
EVB	Erklarung von Bern
EVB	Europese Verzamelaarsbeurs
EVBK	Europäische Vereinigung Bilender Kunstler aus Eifel und Ardennen
EVC	Eurovision Control Central (EBU)
EVCA	European Venture Capital Association
EVD	Economische Voorlichtingsdienst
EVD	Eidgenössiches Volkswirtschaftsdepartement (Switzerland)
EVDF	Environmental Volunteering Development Forum
EVDG	Electrical Vehicle Development Group
EVE	Espace Video Européen
EVEA	Estonian Small Business Association
EVHA	Europese Vereniging voor Haveninformatica
EVI	Europees Vakbondsinstituut = DEFI, EGI, ETUI, ISE
EVI	Ex-Volunteers International
EVK	Europäische Vereinigung der Kongressstädte = EFCT, FEVC
EVKD	Europäische Vereinigung der Krankenhausdirektoren = AEDH, EAHM
EVKI	Europäische Vereinigung der Keramik-Industrie
EVMAC-MEX	Ejecutivos de Ventas y Mercadotecnia de México
EVMF	Europäische Vereinigung de Musikfestspiele
EVO	Algemene Verladers- en Eigen Vervoerders Organisatie
EVO	Eisenbahn-Verkehrsordnung
EVP	Europäische Volkspartei = EPP, PPE
EVS	Energie-Versorgung Schwaben
EVS	Erfinder- und Patentinhaber-Verband der Schweiz = ASI
EVS	Europees Verbond voor Schiftpsychologie = EGF, EGS, ESHP, ESS, SEG, SEPS
EVS	National Standards Board of Estonia
EVSE	Enosis Viomichanon Sporelaiourgon Ellados
EVSz	Erdélyi Világszövetség (Hungary) = WFT
EVT	Europäische Vereinigung für Tierproduktion = EAPP, EAZ, FEZ
EVU	European Vegetarian Union
EVUB	Europäische Vereinigung der Umweltwissenschaftlichen Berufe (Belgium) = EFEP, FEPE
EVUS	Einkaufsvereinigung Unabhängiger Schuhhändler
EWA	Educational Writers Association (U.S.A.)
EWA	Entwicklungswerkstatt Austria
EWA	Europäisches Währungsabkommen = AME, EMA
EWA	European Welding Association
EWAC	Effluent and Water Advisory Committee (WRA)
EWAC	European Wheat Aneuploid Co-operative
EWBA	English Women's Bowling Association
EWBF	English Women's Bowling Federation
EWC	East-West Center (U.S.A.)
EWC	Europese Werkgroep Conscientisatie
EWCA	East-West Center Association
EWCI	Estonian World Council
EWEA	European Wind Energy Association
EWF	Electrical Wholesalers' Federation

EWF	European Wax Federation
EWF	European Weightlifting Federation
EWG	Ethics Works Group (IUCN)
EWG	Europäische Wirtschaftsgemeinschaft = CEE, EEC, EEG, EOF, EOK, MCE
EWGAE	European Working Group on Acoustic Emission
EWGCF	European Working Group for Cystic Fibrosis
EWGLI	European Working Group on Legionella Infections
EWGPO	European Working Group in Pediatric Otorhinolaryngology (Italy)
EWI	Executive Women International (U.S.A.)
EWIA	External Wall Insulation Association
EWIBA	English Womens Indoor Bowling Association
EWIF	External Wall Insulation Association
EWIV	Europäische Wirtschaftliche Interessenvereinigung = EEIG, EESV, GEIE
EWL	European Women's Lobby = LEF
EWMD	European Women's Management Development Network
EWN	Education Workers Network
EWO	Europäische Weltraumorganisation = ASE, ESA
EWOS	European Workshop for Open Systems
EWPCA	European Water Pollution Control Association
EWPI	East-West Population Institute (EWC)
EWPM	European Wood Preservatives Manufacturing Group
EWRS	European Weed Research Society
EWS	English Westerners Society
EWS	Europäische Wissenschaftsstiftung
EWS	Europäisches Währungssystem = EMS, SME
EWSLA	East-West Sign Language Association (Japan)
EWW	European Conference of Associations of Winding Wires Industries = EUROWINDINGWIRES
EXBOA	Export Buying Offices Association
EXCA	Groupement Syndical des Exportateurs de Caséine
EXCO	Express Coach Operators' Association (Ireland)
EXCOM	Executive Committee (UNHCR)

EXI	Syndicat National des Industriels Exportateurs Importateurs de Produits Laitiers
EXIBA	European Extruded Polystyrene Insulation Board Association
EXICASA	Exportadora e Importadora Centroamericana, S.A. (El Salvador)
EXIMBANK	Export-Import Bank (U.S.A.)
EXIMHSA	Exportadora e Importadora Hondureña, S.A.
EXPAINSO	Société Développement du Sud-Ouest
EXPAN-ENTRE	Société pour l'Expansion Économique de la Région du Centre
EXPLORIS	Exploration of the North Sea
Exportang	Angolan Export Organisation
EXPS	Exmoor Pony Society
EXTEB-ANDES	Banco Exterior de los Andes y España (Colombia, Peru, Venezuela)
EXTEL	Exchange Telegraph
EYA	Ecumenical Youth Action
EYA	European Youth Aclist = JAE
EYC	European Young Conservatives
EYC	European Youth Centre = CEJ
EYCD	European Young Christian Democrats = JDCE
EYCE	Ecumenical Youth Council in Europe
EYCW	European Young Christian Workers = JOC
EYE	European Youth Exchange
EYF	European Youth Foundation = FEJ
EYFA	European Youth Forest Action
EYHG	European Young Homeless Group
EYPF	European Youth Press Federation
EZE	Evangelische Zentralstelle für Entwicklungshilfe
EZI	European Zinc Institute (Netherlands)
EZLN	Zapatista National Liberation Army
EZN	Estação Zootecnica Nacional (Portugal)
EZS	Elektrotehniska Zveza Slovenije
EZU	Europäische Zahlungs-Union

F

FA	Families Anonymous
FA	Ferroalloys Association (U.S.A.)
FA	Ferrocarriles Argentinos
FA	Flora of Australia (ABRS)

FA	Football Association		**FABES**	Vereniging van Fabrikanten van Betonstraatstenen
FA	Forretningsbankenes Arbeidsgiverforening		**FABI**	Fédération Royale d'Associations Belges d'Ingénieurs Civils et d'Ingénieurs Agronomes
FA	Freedom Association			
FAA	Federación Agraria Argentina		**FABI**	Federazione Autonoma Bancari Italiana
FAA	Federal Aviation Administration (U.S.A.)		**FABIS**	Faba Bean Information Service (Syria)
FAA	Film Artistes Association		**FABRI-METAL**	Fédération des Entreprises de l'Industrie des Fabrications Métalliques, Mécaniques, Électriques et de la Transportation des Matières Plastiques (Belgium)
FAA	Finnish Aerosol Association			
FAA	Frontier Areas Administration (Burma)			
FAACE	Fight Against Animal Cruelty in Europe			
FAAFI	Fédération des Associations Anciens Fonctionnaires Internationaux = FAFICS			
			FAC	Confédération Africaine de Football
FAAPF	Federación Argentina de Asociaciones de Productores Forestales		**FAC**	Fédération Autonome des Cadres
			FAC	Federation of Agricultural Cooperatives
FAAR	Friends of American Art in Religion		**FAC**	Feminists Against Censorship
FAAS	Fujian Academy of Agricultural Sciences		**FAC**	Fonds d'Aide et de Coopération
			FAC	Food Advisory Committee (MAFF)
FAAVCA	Federación de Asociaciones de Agencias de Viajes de Centro América		**FAC**	Food Aid Convention (FAO)
			FAC	Forschungsgemeinschaft Arthrologie und Chirotherapie
FAAW	Federation of Arab Agricultural Workers			
			FAC	Fujian Agricultural College
FAB	Farm Apprenticeship Board (Éire)		**FAC-UK**	Federation of Agricultural Co-operatives
FAB	Fédération Nationale des Auto-Écoles Professionnelles de Belgique		**FACA**	Federación Argentina de Cooperativas Agrarias
FAB	Fédération Royale des Sociétés d'Architectes de Belgique		**FACA**	Fédération Algérienne de la Coopération Agricole
FAB	Feline Advisory Bureau		**FACACH**	Federación de Cooperativas de Ahorro y Crédito de Honduras
FAB	Feminist Audio Books			
FAB	Flour Advisory Bureau		**FACC**	Federación Argentina de Cooperativas de Consumo
FAB	Força Aérea Brasileira			
FAB	Foreningen af Byplanlaeggere (Denmark)		**FACC**	Federation of African Chambers of Commerce
FAB	Forschungs Institüt für Arbeit und Bildung		**FACCI**	Federation of Afghan Chambers of Commerce and Industry
FAB	Société Franco-Africaine des Bois (Ivory Coast)		**FACCO**	Chambre Syndicale des Fabricants d'Aliments Préparés pour Chiens, Chats, Oiseaux et Autres Animaux Familiers
FAB	Stichting Opleiding Federatie Adviserende Beroepen			
FABADEF	Fédération des Associations de Bibliothécaires, Archivistes, Documentalistes des États Membres du Sommet Francophone		**FACE**	Fédération des Associations de Chasseurs de la CEE
			FACE	Fondo Andino de Comercio Exterior (Venezuela)
FABASEN	Société de Fabrication d'Articles Sanitaires et d'Emballages (Cameroon)		**FACE**	International Federation of Associations of Computer Users in Engineering, Architecture and Related Fields
FABC	Federation of Asian Bishops Conferences			
			FACE	International League of Folk Arts for Communication and Education
FABDEN	Fédération des Amicales de Documentalistes et Bibliothécaires de l'Education Nationale			
			FACÉJ	Forges et Ateliers de Construction Électrique de Jeumont

FACETS	Franco-American Committee for Educational Travel and Study
FACFF	Fédération des Associations de Communes Forestières Françaises
FACH	Fuerzas Armadas de Chile
FACIM	Fondation pour l'Action Culturelle Internationale en Montagne
FACOGAZ	Union des Fabricants Européens de Compteurs de Gaz
FACOMED	Syndicat des Fabricants et Constructeurs des Industries Médico-Chirurgicales
FACO-PHAR	Syndicat National de la Fabrication et du Commerce des Produits à l'Usage Pharmaceutique et Parapharmaceutique
FACP	Food and Agriculture Council, Pakistan
FACPB	Federación de Asociaciones de Comerciantes en Productos Basicos = FCA
FACRI	Flight Automatic Control Research Institute (China)
FACS	Fédération des Amis des Chemins de Fer Secondaires
FACS	Federation of American Controlled Shipping
FACS	Federation of Asian Chemical Societies
FACSS	Federation of Analytical Chemistry and Spectroscopy Societies (U.S.A.)
FACT	Federation Against Copyright Theft
FACT	Fertilisers and Chemicals Travancore (India)
FACT	Food Additives Campaign Team
FACT	Foundation for Advanced Computer Technology (U.S.A.)
FACTS	Federation of Australian Commercial Television Stations
FACTU	Federation of Air Controllers Trade Unions (Russia)
FACTU	Föreningen Svensk Fachpress
FAD	Federatie van de Automobiel Distributie (Belgium) = FDA
FAD	Fonds Africain de Développement = ADF, AfDF
FAD	Fonds Asiatique de Développement = ADF, AsDF
FAD	Force Arabe Dissuasion = ADF
FADA	Federation of Automobile Dealer Associations of Canada
FADALTEC	Fabrica de Alambres Tecnicos S.A. (Colombia)
FaDB	Foreningen af Danske Biologer
FADBEN	Fédération des Associations de Documentalistes-Bibliothécaires de l'Education Nationale
FADEAC	Federación Argentina de Entidades Empresarias de Autotransporte de Cargas
FADEN	Federación de Asociaciones de Empresarios de Navarra
FADEP	Fondo Andino Desarrollo Empresarial Andino
FADES	Fonds Arabe pour le Développement Économique et Social = AFESD
FADH	Haitian Armed Forces
FADI	Frente Amplio de la Izquierda (Ecuador)
FADINAP	Fertilizer Advisory Development and Information Network for Asia and the Pacific (ESCAP/IFCD)
FADN	EU Farm Accountancy Data Network
FADSP	Federación de Asociaciones para la Defensa de la Sanidad Publica
FAE	Federación de Amigos de la Enseñanza
FAE	Federation of Arab Engineers
FAE	Fondation Archives Européennes (ECC)
FAE	Forum Atomico Español
FAE	Foundation for Accounting Education (U.S.A.)
FAE	Foundation on Automation and Employment
FAE	Fuerza Aérea Ecuatoriana
FAEA	Federation of ASEAN Economic Associations (Indonesia)
FAEAB	Federações dos Engenheiros Agrónomos do Brasil
FAeB	Force Aérienne Belge
FAEB	Fuerza Aérea Boliviano
FAEC	Force Aérienne Congolaise
FAECF	Fédération des Associations Européennes des Constructeurs de Fenêtres
FAEG	Fuerza Aérea Guatemalteca
FAEMI	Federação das Associações dos Engenheiros de Minas (Brazil)
FAÉP	Fédération des Associations d'Éditeurs de Périodiques de la CEE
FAEPLA	Fedaración de Asociaciones Educativas Privadas Latinoamericanas y del Caribe
FAET	Fédération Arabe pour l'Enseignement Technique = AFTE
FAET	Forum for the Advancement of Educational Therapy

FAETT	Forum for the Advancement of Educational Therapy and Therapeutic Teaching
FAF	Fachverband der Audiovisions- und Filmindustrie (Austria)
FAF	Famille Adoptive Française
FAF	Financial Accounting Foundation (U.S.A.)
FAF	Finska Antikvariatforeningen
FAF	Forum Atomique Français
FAFGE	Foreningen af Fabrikanter, Grossiter, Importoører og Agenter i El-Branchen
FAFH	Federación de Asociaciones Femenistas Hondureñas
FAFICS	Federation of Associations of Former International Civil Servants = FAAFI
FAFPAS	Fédération des Associations de Fabricants de Produits Alimentaires Surgelés de la CEE
FAFPIC	Forestry and Forest Products Industry Council
FAFS	Farm and Food Society
FAFS	Federation des Associations Feminines du Senegal
FAG	Forces Armées Gabonaises
FAG	Friedreichs Ataxia Group
FAGA	Force de l'Air Gabonaise
FAGACE	Fonds Africain de Garantie et de Coopération Économique (Benin)
FAGAM	Groep Fabrieken van Gasmeters
FAGANIC	Federación de Asociaciones Ganaderas de Nicaragua
FAGAR	Groep Fabrieken van Gasdrukregelaars
FAGC	Federation of Arab Gulf Chambers (Saudi Arabia)
FAGÉC	Fédération d'Associations et Groupements pour les Études Corses
FAGIC-TMAT	Ferme Agro-Industrielle et Commerciale des Tabacs et du Mais du Togo
FAGIHT	Fédération Autonome Général de l'Industrie Hôtelière
FAGLACI	Fabrique de Glaces Alimentaires de Côte d'Ivoire
FAGS	Federation of Astronomical and Geophysical Data Analysis Services (ICSU)
FAGT	Federation of Agricultural Group Traders
FAH	Forschungsinstitut für Absatz und Handel (Switzerland)
FAH	Fuerza Aérea Hondureña
FAHACIB	Société Fawaz Hammond pour le Commerce et l'Industrie du Bénin
FAI	Fédération Abolitionniste Internationale = IAF
FAI	Fédération Aéronautique Internationale = IAF
FAI	Federazione Apicoltori Italiani
FAI	Federazione Autorimesse Italiane
FAI	Federazione Autotrasportatori Italiani
FAI	Fertiliser Association of India
FAI	Football Association of Ireland
FAIA	Fédération Arabe des Industries Alimentaires = AFFI
FAIA	Food Additives Industry Association
FAIAO	Fédération des Associations des Industriels de l'Afrique de l'Ouest = FEWAMA
FAIAT	Federazione delle Associazioni Italiane Alberghi e Turismo
FAIB	Fédération des Associations Internationales Établies en Belgique
FAIBP	Fédération des Associations de l'Industrie des Bouillons et Potages de la CEE
FAIC	Federación Argentina de la Industria del Caucho
FAIC	Federation of Australian Investment Clubs
FAID	Federazione Associazioni Imprese Distribuzione
FAILCLEA	Federazione Autonoma Italiana Lavoratori Cemento, Legno, Edilizia ed Affini
FAILE	Federazione Autonoma Italiana Lavoratori Elettrici
FAILM	Federazione Autonoma Italiana Lavoratori Metalmeccanici e Siderurgici
FAIM	Federation of Asian Institute of Management Alumni Associations (Philippines)
FAIMA	Federación Argentina de la Industria de la Madera y Afines
FAIP	Fédération Arabe des Industries de la Pêche = AFPP, FAPP
FAIR	Family Action Information and Rescue
FAIR	Federation of Afro-Asian Insurers and Reinsurers
FAIR	Union Professionnelle des Fabricants et Importateurs de Matériel Électronique (Belgium)
FAIRT	Suomen Kansainvälisten Muuttokuljetusliikkeiden Liitto

FAIS	Federación Argentina de Industrias de la Sanidad	**FAMH**	Foederatio Analyticorum Medicinalium Helveticorum
FAIS	Finnish Artificial Intelligence Society = STES	**FAMHM**	Federation of Associations of Materials Handling Equipment Manufacturers
FAIT	Fakul'tet Avtomatiki i Telemekhaniki	**FAMID**	Foreningen af Mineralvandsfabrikanter i Danmark
FAIT	Families Against Intimidation and Terror (Northern Ireland)	**FAMMAC**	Fédération des Amicales d'Anciens Marins et de Marins Anciens Combattants
FAITA	Federación de Asociaciones Industriales Textiles del Algodón (Mexico)		
FAITA	Federazione delle Associazionei Italiane dei Complessi Turistico- Ricettivi all'Aria Aperta	**FAMOS**	Flexible Automatisierte Montagesysteme
		FAMPA	Ferro Alloys and Metals Producers Association
FAJ	Federation of Arab Journalists = FJA	**FAMSA**	Federation of African Medical Students Associations
FAK	Federasie van Afrikaanse Kultuurverenigings		
FAK	Finlands Automobiklubb	**FAMW**	Federation of African Media Women
FAL	Bundesforschungsanstalt für Landwirtschaft (Germany)	**FAN**	Federación Agraria Nacional (Costa Rica)
FAL	Folkeakademiens Landsforbund	**FAN**	Federation of Arab News Agencies
FAL	Frente Anti-imperialista de Liberación (Peru)	**FAN**	Forces Armées Nigériennes
		FANA	Federation of Arab News Agencies
FAL	Fuerzas Armadas de Liberación (El Salvador)	**FANADA**	Federazione Autonoma Nazionale delle Associazioni Dipendenti Alberghi, Bar, Ristoranti
FALA	Armed Forces for the Liberation of Angola		
FALCRI	Federazione Autonoma Lavoratori Casse di Risparmio Italiane	**FANAF**	Fédération des Sociétés d'Assurance de Droit National Africaines (Senegal)
FALK	Föreningen Arkivverksamma i Landsting och Kommum	**FANAL**	Federación Agraria Nacional (Colombia)
FALN	Fuerzas Armadas de Liberación Nacional (Puerto Rica)	**FANATEX**	Fábrica Nacional de Textiles (Nicaragua)
FALPRO	Special Programme for Trade Facilitation (UNCTAD/ECE)	**FANCIF**	Fondo Antárquico National para la Capacitación e Investigación Forestal (Argentina)
FAMA	Fachverband Messen und Ausstellungen		
FAMA	Federal Agricultural Marketing Authority (Malaysia)	**FANOA**	Fédération des Appellations et Noms d'Origine Agricole
FAMAB	Fachverband Messe- und Ausstellungsbau	**FANS**	Federatio of Asian Nutrition Societies
FAMASUL	Federação da Agricultura do Mato Grosso do Sul (Brazil)	**FAO**	Food and Agriculture Organisation = OAA (UN)
FAMD	Foundation for Asian Management Development (Japan)	**FAO**	Forces Armées de l'Ouest (Chad)
		FAO/RAF	FAO Regional Office for Africa
FAMED	Vereinigung Schweizerischer Fabriken der Medizinischen Technik	**FAO/RAPA**	Regional Office for Asia and the Pacific (FAO)
FAMEM	Federation of Associations of Mine Equipment Manufacturers	**FAO/REU**	FAO Regional Office for Europe
		FAO/RLAC	FAO Regional Office for Latin America and the Caribbean
FAMEX	Foreningen af Danske Mælkekonservesfabrikker med Landbrugsministeriel Autorisation til Fremstilling af Mælkekonserves for Export	**FAO/RNEA**	FAO Regional Office for the Near East
		FAO/WFP-FSA	Field Staff Association of FAO and WFP
		FAO/WHO/FNAF	Joint FAO/WHO OAU Regional Food and Nutrition Commission

FAOB	Federation of Asian and Oceanian Biochemists	**FAR**	Federal Department of Agricultural Research (Nigeria)
FAOE	Federation of African Organizations and Engineers (WFEO)	**FAR**	Fondo Andino de Reservas (JUNAC)
FAP	Federación de Alianza Popular	**FAR**	Föreningen Auktoriserade Revisorer
FAP	Forces Armées Populaires (Chad)	**FAR**	Foundation for Australian Resources
FAP	Forschungsausschuss für Planungsfragen (Switzerland)	**FAR**	Foundation of Applied Research (U.S.A.)
FAP	Freiheitliche Arbeiterpartie	**FAR**	Fuerzas Armadas Rebeldes (Guatemala)
FAP	Fuerza Aérea del Perú	**FAR**	Fuerzas Armadas Revolucionarias (Cuba)
FAPA	Federation of Asian Pharmaceutical Associations	**FARA**	Federation of Active Retirement Associations (Éire)
FAPA	Federation of Asian Photographic Art	**FARB**	Federation of Australian Radio Broadcasters
FAPAL	Groep Fabrieken van Aktieve en Passieve Elektronische Bouwelementen	**FARC**	Fuerzas Armadas Revolucionarias de Colombia
FAPC	Fédération Française des Associations de Photographes Créateurs	**FAREC**	Unione Fabbricanti Apparecchi di Riscaldamento e Cucine
FAPCO	Fayoum Petroleum Company (Egypt)	**FAREGAZ**	Union des Fabricants Européens de Régulateurs de Pression du Gaz
FAPE	Federación de Asociaciones de la Prensa de España	**FARGRO**	Farmers' and Growers' Industries
FAPEA	Fuerzas Armadas Populares Eloy Alfaro (Ecuador)	**FARM**	Filipino Agrarian Reform Movement
FAPEB	Fédération des Artisans et des Petites Entreprises du Bâtiment	**FARM-AFRICA**	Food and Agricultural Research Management – Africa
FAPEL	Groep Fabrieken van Aktieve en Passiere Elektronuische Bouwelementen i Nederland	**FARM-INDUSTRIA**	Associazione Nazionale dell'Industria Farmaceutica
FAPES	Fundacion Argentina para la Promocion del Desarrollo Económico y Social	**FARM-UNIONE**	Associazione Nazionale dell'Industria Farmaceutica Italiana
FAPESP	Fundação de Amparo à Pesquisa do Estado de São Paulo (Brazil)	**FARMIN**	Farmatsevticheskii Institut
FAPLA	Forças Armadas Populares de Libertação de Angola	**FARN**	Fuerzas Armadas de la Resistencia Nacional (El Salvador)
FAPNUU	Federation of the Staff Associations of the United Nations and its Specialized Agencies in Uruguay	**FARO**	Frente Agrícola de la Region Oriental (El Salvador)
FAPP	Federación Arabe de Productores Pesqueros = AFFP, FAIP	**FARON**	Fabrieken van Röntgen en Andere Elektromedische Apparatuur in Nederland
FAPRA	Federation of African Public Relations Associations	**FARP**	Forças Armadas Revolucionarias do Povo (Guinea-Bissau)
FAPRO	Federation of ASEAN Public Relations Organisations	**FARP**	Fuerzas Armadas de Resistencia Popular (Chile)
FAPSNUBA	Federación de Asociaciones de Personal del Sistema de Naciones Unidas en Buenos Aires	**FARP**	People's Revolutionary Armed Forces (Cape Verde)
FAPTA	Fédération Suisse des Associations des Planteurs de Tabac	**FAS**	European Federation of Associations of Industrial Safety and Medical Officers
FAPU	Frente de Acción Popular Unificado (El Salvador)	**FAS**	Faculty of Architects and Surveyors
FAR	British Foundation for Age Research	**FAS**	Fédération des Architectes Suisses = BSA
		FAS	Federation of American Scientists
		FAS	Federation of Astronomical Societies
		FAS	Foras Aiseanna Saothar (Éire)

FAS	Foreign Agricultural Service (U.S.A.)		**FASM**	Fundusz Akcji Socjalnej Młodziezy
FAS	Forschungsgemeinschaft für Altersfragen in der Schweiz		**FASME**	Federación de Asociaciones Sidero-Metalurgicas Españolas
FAS	Fuerza Aérea Salvadoreña		**FASNUDS**	Fonds d'Affectation Spéciale des Nations Unies pour le Développement Social = FFNUDS, UNTFSD
FAS	Funding Agency for Schools			
FAS	International Federation of Associations of Specialists in Occupational Safety and Industrial Hygiene		**FASNUPPD**	Fonds d'Affectation Spéciale des Nations Unies pour la Planification et les Projections en Matière de Développement = FFNUPPD, UNTFDPP
FAS	Verband Schweizerischer Firmen für Artz- und Spitalbedarf			
FASA	Federación Argentina de Sindicatos Agrarios		**FASOMG**	Fédération Avicole du Sud-Ouest et du Midi Garonnais
FASA	Federación Argentina de Sociedades Apícolas		**FASP**	Fédération Autonome des Syndicats de Police
FASA	Federation of ASEAN Shipowners Association		**FASPA**	Fédération Africaine des Syndicats du Pétrole et Affinage
FASAB	Front Autonomiste et Socialiste Autogestionnaire Bretonne		**FASRC**	Federation of Arab Scientific Research Councils
FASAS	Federation of Asian Scientific Academies and Societies		**FASS**	Federation of Associations of Specialists and Sub-contractors
FASASA	Fonds d'Action Sociale pour l'Aménagement des Structures Agricoles		**FASST**	Farming for Agriculturally Sustainable Systems in Tasmania
FASC	Federation of ASEAN Shippers Councils		**FASST**	Federation of Americans Supporting Science and Technology
FASE	Federação de Orgãos para Assistência Social e Educação (Brazil)		**FASST**	Forum for the Advancement of Students in Science and Technology (U.S.A.)
FASE	Federation of Acoustical Societies of Europe		**FASST**	Friends of Aerospace Supporting Science and Technology
FASE	Forum of African Science Educators (Zambia)		**FAST**	Federation Against Software Theft
FASE-COLDA	Unión de Aseguradores Colombianos		**FAST**	Federazione delle Associazioni Scientifiche e Tecniche
FASEB	Federation of American Societies for Experimental Biology		**FAST Programme**	Forecasting and Assessment in the Field of Science and Technology (CEC)
FASÉM	Fédération Nationale des Professionnels Spécialistes de l'Équipement Ménager et de l'Électronique Domestique		**FASTS**	Federation of Australian Scientific and Technical Societies
			FAT	Federation of Arab Teachers
FASFID	Fédération des Associations et Sociétés Françaises d'Ingénieurs Diplômés		**FAT**	Fonds Arabe pour l'Assistance Technique = AFTA
FASGUA	Federación Autónoma Sindical de Guatemala		**FAT**	Forces Armées Tchadiennes
FASH	Federación Auténtica Sindical de Honduras		**FAT**	Föreningen Auktoriserade Translatorer
			FAT	Forschungsvereinigung Automobiltechnik
FASI	Friedreich's Ataxia Society of Ireland		**FAT**	Frente Auténtico de los Trabajadores (Mexico)
FASII	Federation of Associations of Small Industries in India			
FASL	Farm Assured Scotch Livestock		**FAT**	Société Forestière Africaine de Transports (Ivory Coast)
FASM	Fédération Africaine des Syndicats des Mines (Algeria)		**FATA**	Federation of ASEAN Travel Associations
			FATA	Fondo Assicurativo tra Agricoltori

FATAA	Federation of Arab Travel Agents' Associations
FATCh	Foreningen af Amtskommunernes Tekniske Chefer
FATE	Federation of Automatic Transmission Engineers
FATG	Fine Art Trade Guild
FATIPEC	Fédération des Associations de Techniciens des Industries des Peintures, Vernis, Émaux et Encres d'Imprimerie de l'Europe Continentale
FATIS	Food and Agriculture Technical Information Service (OECD)
FATMA	Fundação de Amparo a Tecnologia e ao Meio Ambiente (Brazil)
FATME	Fabbrica Apparecchiature Telefoniche e Materiale Elettrico
FATRE	Federación Argentina de Trabajadores Rurales y Estibadores
FATS	Federation of Arab Teachers Syndicates
FATTA	Federation of Arab Travel Agents' Associations
FATUREC	Federation of Air Transport User Representatives in the European Community
FAUNA	Friends of Animals under Abuse
FAV	Fuerzas Aéreas Venezolanas
FAVA	Federation of Asian Veterinarian Associations
FAVAD	Vereniging van Fabrikanten van Zwakalcoholhoudende en Alcoholvrije Dranken
FAVDO	Forum of African Voluntary Development Organizations (ANID) = FOVAD
FAVE	Forum der Agrar-Ingenieur-Verbände Europas = AEFA, CEIA
FAVENPA	Camara de Fabricantes Venezolanos de Productos Automotores
FAVF	Fédération des Associations Viticoles de France
FAW	Fachverband Aussenwerbung
FAW	Federation of Army Wives
FAWA	Federation of Asian Women's Associations
FAWAC	Farm Animals Welfare Advisory Committee
FAWC	Farm Animal Welfare Council
FAWC	Federation of African Women's Clubs
FAWCE	Farm Animal Welfare Co-Ordinating Executive

FAWCO	Federation of American Women's Clubs Overseas
FAWN	Farm Animal Welfare Network
FAWTU	Federation of Aircraft Workers Trade Unions (Russia)
FAY	Friends of the Ankerwyke Yew
FB	Fachverband der Bauindustrie (Austria)
FB	Fachverband der Bekleidungsindustrie (Austria)
FB	Faculty of Building
FB	Federation of Bakers
FB	Forskningsberedningen
FB	Fribaptistsamfundet = SIBU
FB	Fundación Bariloche
FB(SA)	Faculty of Bookkeeping (South Africa)
FBA	Farm Buildings Association
FBA	Federal Bar Association (U.S.A.)
FBA	Federation of Bloodstock Agents
FBA	Federation of British Artists
FBA	Federation of British Astrologers
FBA	Federation of British Audio
FBA	Foreign Banks Association
FBA	Freshwater Biological Association
FBA	Fur Breeders Association
FBA	Société Forces et Boulonneries d'Abidjan (Ivory Coast)
FBAA	Fédération Belge des Exploitants d'Autobus et Autocars
FBAF	Fédération Belge des Alliances Françaises
FBAS	Federation of British Aquatic Societies
FBBA	Fishing Boat Builders Association (*now* BBBA)
FBBF	Fibre Building Board Federation
FBBS	Federation of British Bonsai Societies
FBC	Fédération Biblique Catholique; Federação Biblica Catolica; Federazione Biblica Cattolica = CBF, FEBIC-LA, KBF
FBC	Fiji Broadcasting Commission
FBC	Finnish Business Club (Éire)
FBC	Fox Broadcasting Company (U.S.A.)
FBCA	Federation of British Cremation Authorities
FBCAEI	Federation of Builders Contractors and Allied Employers of Ireland
FBCCI	Franco-British Chamber of Commerce and Industry (France)
FBCE	Fellowship of British Christian Esperantists

FBCEC	Federation of Building and Civil Engineering Contractors (Northern Ireland) (*now* CEF)
FBCMA	Fibre Bonded Carpet Manufacturers Association
FBCN	Fundação Brasileira para e Conservação da Natureza
FBCS	Federation of British Craft Societies
FBCSM	Fédération Belge des Chambres Syndicales des Médicins
FBDB	Federal Business Development Bank (Canada)
FBEI	Fachverband der Bergwerke und Eisenerzeugenden Industrie (Austria)
FBEP	Fédération Belge d'Education Physique = BBLO
FBETM	Federation of British Engineers' Tool Manufacturers
FBF	Fate Bene Fratelli = OH
Fbf	Folkbildningsförbundet
FBF	Forskningsbibliotekernes Fællesrad
FBFC	Franco-Belge de Fabrication de Combustibles
FBFM	Federation of British Film Makers
FBG	Fachverband Bürobedarf für Grossverbraucher
FBG	Federation of British Growers
FBH	Fachgruppe für Brückenbau und Hochbau (Switzerland) = GPC
FBH	Fédération Belge des Horticoles Semences
FBH	Federation of Bulgarians in Hungary = MBSz
FBHE	Federation of British Horticultural Exporters
FBHO	Federation of Black Housing Organisations
FBHTM	Federation of British Hand Tool Manufacturers
FBHVC	Federation of British Historic Vehicle Clubs
FBI	Federal Bureau of Investigation (U.S.A.)
FBI	Federatie der Belgische Industrieën
FBI	Fonds du Bien-être Indigène (Belgium)
FBIC	Farm Buildings Information Centre
FBIS	Foreign Broadcast Information Service (U.S.A.)
FBIT	Fédération Belge des Ingénieurs Techniciens

FBM	Fachvereinigung der Bunt- und Metallpapierfabriken
FBMA	Finnish Boat and Motor Association
FBMA	Food and Beverage Managers Association
FBMA	Union Suisse des Entreprises de Forge, du Bois, du Métal et de la Machine Agricole
FBMV	Federación Boliviana de Médicos Veterinarios
FBP	Fortschrittliche Bürgerpartei (Liechtenstein)
FBPCS	Federation of Behavioral, Psychological and Cognitive Sciences
FBPP	Federation of British Plant Pathologists
FBPS	Forest and Bird Protection Society of New Zealand
FBPWFMA	Federation of British Port Wholesale Fish Merchants Association
FBR	Forskningsbiblioteksrådet
FBR	Foundation for Business Responsibilities
FBRAM	Federation of British Rubber and Allied Manufacturers
FBRC	Federation of British Racing Clubs
FBS	Fire Brigade Society
FBSA	Foreign Banks and Securities Houses Association
FBSC	Federation of British Scooter Clubs
FBSC	Federation of Building Specialist Contractors
FBSI	Federasi Buruh Seleruh Indonesia
FBTO	Federation of British Trawler Officers
FBTR	Federation of British Tape Recordists
FBU	Federation of Broadcasting Unions
FBU	Fire Brigades Union (Éire, U.K., U.S.A.)
FBU	Fraternité Blanche Universelle = UWB
FBUA	Franco-British Union of Architects
FBUI	Federation of British Umbrella Industries
FBVA	Forstliche Bundesversuchsanstalt (Austria)
FBVL	Fonds ter Bevordering van de Veredeling van Landbouwgewassen
FBW	Forschungsgemeinschaft Bauen and Wohnen
FC	Federación Campesina (Venezuela)
FC	Filiae Crucis Leodiensis (Belgium)
FC	Filii Caritatis

FC	Forestry Commission
FC	Fratres a Caritate
FC	Front Calédonien
FCA	Farm Credit Administration (U.S.A.)
FCA	Federation of Canadian Artists
FCA	Federation of Commodity Associations (U.K., U.S.A.) = FACPB
FCA	Fellowship of Christian Athletes (U.S.A.)
FCA	Fencing Contractors Association
FCA	Fishing Clubs of Australia
FCA	Foncière de la Côte d'Afrique
FCA	Food Casings Association
FCA	Franchise Consultants Association
FCAA	Federación de Cooperativas Arroceras Argentinas
FCAATSI	Federal Council for the Advancement of Aborigines and Torres Strait Islanders (Australia)
FCAC	Fédération des Coopératives Agricoles de Céréales
FCACV	Federación de Cooperativas de Ahorro y Crédito de Venezuela
FCAI	Federal Chamber of Automotive Industries (Australia)
FCAM	Fédération Cotonnière d'Afrique Francophone et de Madagascar
FCAS	Federation of Charity Advice Services
FCAT	Société Franco-Centrafricaine des Tabacs
FCB	Fédération Nationale des Coopératives Agricoles de Transformation de la Betterave Industrielle
FCB	Food Corporation of Bhutan
FCBA	Friesland Cattle Breeders' Association of South Africa
FCBG	Federation of Children's Book Groups
FCBM	Federation of Clinker Block Manufacturers
FCC	Federación Cristiana Campesina (Paraguay)
FCC	Federal Communications Commission (U.S.A.)
FCC	Federation of Crafts and Commerce
FCCA	Christian Federation of Craftsmen and Apprentices (Luxembourg)
FCCAC	Fédération des Chambres de Commerce de l'Afrique Centrale (Congo)
FCCAM	Fédération Centrale du Crédit Agricole Mutuel
FCCAO	Fédération des Chambres de Commerce d'Afrique de l'Ouest = FWACC
FCCBÉ	Fédération des Chambres de Commerce Belges à l'Étranger = VBKKB
FCCC	Farm Credit Corporation (Canada)
FCCC	Federación de Cámaras de Comercio del Istmo Centroamericano (El Salvador)
FCCD	Foundation for Cultural Cooperation and Development (France)
FCCI	Fondation pour la Communication de la Culture Internationale
FCCI-Océan Indien	Fédération des Chambres de Commerce de l'Industrie de l'Océan Indien
FCCSET	Federal Co-ordinating Council for Science, Engineering and Technology (U.S.A.)
FCD	First Chief Directorate
FCD	Fonds Communautaire de Développement (Burkina Faso)
FCD	Frente Cívico Democrático (Guatemala)
FCD	Front Congolaise pour le Restauration de la Démocratie (Zaïre)
FCDA	Federal Capital Development Authority (Nigeria)
FCDC	Fertilizer and Chemical Development Council (Israel)
FCDE	Federation of Clothing Designers and Executives
FCDRC	Family & Community Dispute Research Centre
FCE	Association Belge des Femmes Chefs d'Entreprises
FCE	Femmes Chefs d'Entreprises Mondiales = WAWE
FCEC	Federation of Civil Engineering Contractors
FCECA	Fishery Committee for the Eastern Central Atlantic
FCÉH	Fédération Canadienne des Études Humaines = CFH
FCEM	Femmes Chefs d'Entreprises Mondiales = WAWE
FCEP	Christian Federation of Employees and Civil Servants (Luxembourg)
FCEV	Fédération des Clubs Européens de Formules IV
FCF	Faculty of Community Finance
FCF	Footwear Components Federation
FCFC	Free Church Federal Council

FCGB	Ferrocarril General Belgrano (Argentina)
FCGBM	Ferrocarril General Bartolome Mitre(Argentina)
FCGSM	Ferrocarril General San Martin (Argentina)
FCGU	Ferrocarril General Urquiza (Argentina)
FCH	Flower Council of Holland
FCh	Fundación Chile
FCHPE	Federación de Choferes Profesionales del Ecuador
FCI	Fachverband der Chemischen Industrie (Austria)
FCI	Factors Chain International
FCI	Federated Chamber of Industries (South Africa)
FCI	Fédération Colombophile Internationale
FCI	Fédération Cynologique Internationale
FCI	Federazione Colombofila Italiana
FCI	Fertiliser Corporation of India
FCI	Finance Corporation for Industry
FCI	Fondo de Compensacion Interterritorial
FCI	Food Corporation of India
FCI	Fundación Cientifica Internacional
FCI	South African Federated Chamber of Industries
FCIA	Foreign Credit Insurance Association (U.S.A.)
FCIC	Federation of Consultants from Islamic Countries (Turkey)
FCIO	Fachverband der Chemischen Industrie Österreichs
FCIOGP	Fachverband der Chemischen Industries Österreichs Gruppe Pharmazeutika = API
FCJ	Faithful Companions of Jesus
FCJ	Fédération Internationale des Journalistes Catholiques
FCK	Central Organisation of Farmers' Cooperatives (Hungary)
FCLA	Fisheries Council for Latin America
FCM	Faculty of Community Medicine
FCM	Fellowship of Christian Magicians (U.S.A.)
FCM	Friends of Cathedral Music
FCMA	Fibre Cement Manufacturers Association
FCMC	Fondo Centroamericano del Mercado Comun (Honduras) = CACMF

FCMH	Fraternité Catholique des Malades et Infirmes
FCML	Christian Federation of Luxembourg Metalworkers
FCMRF	Fédération des Centres Musicaux Ruraux de France
FCN	Federal Convention/Namibia
FCNL	Friends Committee on National Legislation
FCO	Farmers Central Organization
FCO	Foreign and Commonwealth Office
FCOBC	Christian Federation of Building and Quarry Workers (Luxembourg)
FCOMF	Fédération des Coopératives Oléicoles du Midi de la France
FCOT	Fellowship of Cycling Old-Timers
FCOUL	Christian Federation of Luxembourg Factory Workers
FCPO	Fellowship of Christian Peace Officers (U.S.A.)
FCPO	Fundação Centro de Pesquisa de Oncologia (Brazil)
FCPSP	Christian Federation of Public Service Workers (Luxembourg)
FCR	Association des Fabriques de Chaudières et Radiateurs (Switzerland) = KRW
FCRA	Fabric Care Research Association
FCRC	Federal Contract Research Centers (U.S.A.)
FCRI	Financial Control Research Institute
FCRIMS	Freight Committee of the Rubber Industry of Malaysia and Singapore
FCS	Family Conciliation Scotland
FCS	Federation of Communication Services
FCS	Federation of Conservative Students
FCS	Forces Comoriennes de Sécurité
FCSA	Football Council of South Africa
FCSCJ	Filles de la Charité du Sacré-Coeur de Jésus = DCSHJ
FCSI	Foodservice Consultants Society International (U.S.A.)
FCSU	Federation of Civil Service Unions (Mauritius)
FCTA	Fédération Suisse des Travailleurs du Commerce des Transports et de l'Alimentation
FCTPAS	Christian Federation of Social Insurance Pensioners (Luxembourg)
FCTU	Federation of Associations of Catholic Trade Unionists

FCTV	Federación de Cooperativas de Transporte de Venezuela	**FDD**	Fundación Dominicana de Desarrollo (Dominica)
FCUA	Federal Clerks' Union of Australia	**FDE**	Fachverband Deutscher Eisenwaren- und Hausrathändler
FCV	Federación de Campesinos de Venezuela	**FDEA**	Femmes Développement Entreprise en Afrique
FCWE(NI)	Forum for Community Education Work	**FDÉS**	Fonds de Développement Économique et Social
FCWU	Food and Canning Workers Union (South Africa)	**FDF**	Fachverband Deutscher Floristen
FCWV	Federatie van de Katholieke en Protestants- Christelijke Werkgeversverbonden	**FDF**	Food and Drink Federation
		FDF	Footwear Distributors Federation
		FDF	Front Démocratique des Francophones (Belgium)
FCX	Farmers Cooperative Exchange (U.S.A.)		
FD	Front Démocratique (Comoros)	**FDFR**	Federal Department of Forestry Research (Nigeria)
FDA	Association of First Division Civil Servants		
FDA	Fédération de la Distribution Automobile (Belgium) = FAD	**FDFU**	Federation of Documentary Film Units
		FDGB	Freier Deutscher Gewerkschaftsbund
FDA	Fellowship of Depressives Anonymous	**FDGPA**	Fédération Départementale des Groupements de Productivité Agricole
FDA	Food and Drug Administration (U.S.A.)		
FDA	Footwear Distributors' Federation	**FDGR**	Forumul Democratic al Germanilor din România (Romania) = DFGR
FDA	Forum Democrático Angolana		
FDA	Freier Deutscher Autorenverband Schulzverband Deutscher Schriftsteller	**FDGV**	Fédération des Grands Vins de Bordeaux à Appellation Controlée
		FDH	Farmaceutsko Drustvo Hrvatske
FDA	Freight Distribution Association (Éire)	**FDH**	Forum for Databehandling i Helsesektoren
FDAA	Federal Disaster Assistance Administration (U.S.A.)		
		FDH	Frères des Hommes
FDAP	Fédération Dentaire Asie Pacifique = APDF	**FDI**	Fédération Dentaire Internationale = IDF
FDAR	Federal Department of Agricultural Research (Nigeria)	**FDI**	Fonds pour le Développement Industriel = IDF
FDB	Fællesforeningen for Danmarks Brugsforeninger	**FDI**	Food and Disarmament International
		FDI	Fundación para el Desarrollo Integral del Valle de Cauca (Colombia)
FDBR	Fachverband Dampfkessel-, Behälter- und Rohrleitungsbau		
		FDIC	Federal Deposit Insurance Corporation (U.S.A.)
FDC	Federación Demócrata Cristiana		
FDC	Federation of Dredging Contractors	**FDIF**	Fédération Démocratique Internationale des Femmes = FDIM, IDFF, MDFZ, WIDF
FDC	Fertilizer Data Centre (FAO)		
FDC	Fiji Development Co.		
FDC	Filles de la Divine Charità (Italy)	**FDIM**	Federación Democrática Internacional de Mujeres = FDIF, IDFF, MDFZ, WIDF
FDC	Foreningen af Dansk Civiløkonomer		
FdCC	Congregatio Filiorum a Caritate "Canossiani"		
		FDJ	Freie Deutschland Jugend
FDCÉTA	Fédération Départementale des Centres d'Études Techniques Agricoles	**FDK**	Fachverband der Krankenpflege
		FDK	Fachverband Deutsche Klavierindustrie
FDCR	Frente Democrático Contra la Represión (Guatemala)	**FDK**	Foreningen af Danske Kunstmuseer
		FDKI	Foreningen af Danske Kemiske Industrier
FDD	Fondation Documentaire Dentaire (Belgium)		
		FDLD	Front Démocratique pour la Libération de Djibouti
FDD	Foro Democrático y Doctrinario (Mexico)		

FdlS	Filles de la Sagesse = DW, FdS, HdlS
FDLUQ	Fronte Democrática Liberale dell'Uomo Qualcunque
FDM	Fachverband des Deutschen Maschinen- und Werkzeug-Grosshandels
FDM	Foreningen af Danske Medicinfabrikker
FDM	Fratelli di Nostra Signora della Misericordia
FDMS	Federation of Deer Management Societies
FDN	Frente Democrático Nacional (Peru)
FDN	Fuerzas Democráticas Nicaragüenses
FDO	Federatie van Nederlandse Danslerarenorganisaties
FDO	Fédération Départementale Ovine
FDO	Foreningen af Danske Osteproducenter
FDOMEZ	Frente Democrático Oriental de México Emiliano Zapata
FDP	Fathers of Divine Providence "Don Orione"
FDP	Freie Demokratische Partei
FDPA	Furniture Design Protection Association
FDR	Federation of Drum Reconditioners
FDR	Frente Democrático Revolucionario (El Salvador)
FDRS	Food Distribution Research Society (U.S.A.)
FDS	Fachverband der Deutschen Schulmöbelindustrie
FDS	Fairbridge Drake Society
FDS	Félag Dráttarbrauta og Skipasmidja
FdS	Figlie della Sapienza = Dw, FdlS, HdlS
FDS	Forschungszentrum des Deutschen Schiffbaus
FDSEA	Fédération Départementale des Syndicats d'Exploitants Agricoles
FDSh	Fronti Demokratik Shqipërisë = ADF
FDT	Fachverband des Deutschen Tapethandels
FDTF	Food, Drink and Tobacco Federation (Éire)
FDTITB	Food, Drink and Tobacco Industry Training Board
FDU	Fudau University
FDVR	Federal Department of Veterinary Research (Nigeria)
FDW	Fachverband Film- und Diapositiv-Werbung
FE-MA	Fédération Nationale des Unions Professionnelles de Négociants en Matériaux de Construction de Belgique
FEA	Fair Employment Agency (Northern Ireland)
FEA	Federación Española de Automovilismo
FEA	Fédération des Experts d'Automobiles de Suisse = VAE
FEA	Federation of European Aerosol Associations (Switzerland)
FEAAF	Fédération Européenne des Associations d'Analystes Financiers = EFFAS
FEAB	Fair Employment Appeals Board (Northern Ireland)
FEAC	Federation of African Consultants = FECA
FEACO	Fédération Européenne des Associations de Conseils en Organisation
FEAD	Fédération Européenne des Activités du Déchet
FEAE	Fuerza Especial Antiterrorista de Elite (Bolivia)
FEAEP	Fédération Européenne des Associations d'Enseignement Privé
FEAÉP	Fédération Européenne des Associations d'Étudiants en Psychologie
FEAGE	Fédération Européenne des Associations pour la Gestion de l'Énergie = EFEM
FEAI	Fédération Européenne pour l'Apprentissage Interculturel
FEAJA	Federation of East African Journalists' Associations
FEAL	Fédération Nationale des Groupements de Labels Agricoles
FEALC	Federación Espeleológica de America Latina y el Caribe
FEAM	Fédération Européenne des Associations de Mécanographes
FEAMA	Fédération Européenne des Fabricants d'Articles de Ménage et Professionnels en Aluminium = EAHMA, VEAWI
FEAMC	Fédération Européenne des Associations des Médicales Catholiques
FEAN	Fédération des Enseignante d'Afrique Noire
FÉANF	Fédération des Étudiants d'Afrique Noire Française
FEANI	Fédération Européenne d'Associations Nationales d'Ingénieurs = EFNEA
FEANTSA	Fédération Européenne d'Associations Nationales Travaillant avec les Sans-Abri (Belgium)

FEAO	Federation of European American Organisations
FEAP	Federación Española de Asociaciones de Peleteria
FEAPS	Federación Españolas des Asociaciones Protectoras de Subnormales
FEASIES	Federación de Asociaciones Sindicales Independientes de El Salvador
FEB	Fachgemeinschaft der Einrichter von Bildungsstätten
FEB	Federación de Empleados Bancarios (Peru)
FÉB	Fédération des Éditeurs Belges
FEB	Fédération des Entreprises Belges = VBO
FEB	Fédération des Expéditeurs de Belgique
FEBA	Far East Broadcasting Association (Singapore)
FEBAB	Federação Brasiliera de Associações de Bibliotecários
FEBAN-COOP	Federación de Bancos Cooperativos de la República Argentina
FeBe	Fédération de l'Industrie du Béton (Belgium)
FEBE	Fédération Européenne des Banques Alimentaires
FEBECA	Fédération Belge du Commerce Alimentaire
FEBECOOP	Fédération Belge des Coopératives
FEBEDIB	Federatie van Belgische Diamantbeurzen
FEBEL-BOIS	Fédération Belge des Entreprises de la Transformation du Bois = FEBELHOUT
FEBEL-HOUT	Belgische Federatie der Ondernemingen van de Houtverwerking = FEBELBOIS
FEBEL-QUIN	Fédération Belge des Quincailliers
FEBELCAR	Fédération Belge de la Carrosserie et des Métiers Connexes
FEBELGRA	Fédération Belge des Industries Graphiques
FEBELTEX	Fédération de l'Industrie Textile Belge
FEBES	Fédération Belge du Spectacle
FEBEVO	Federatie van de Belgische Voedingshandel
FEBIAC	Chambre Syndicale des Constructeurs d'Automobiles et de Motocycles de Belgique et Fédération Belge des Industries de l'Automobile et du Cycle "Réunies"
FEBIC	Fédération Belge de l'Industrie de la Chaussure
FEBIC-LA	Federación Biblica Catolica = CBF, FBC, KBF
FEBLAN-SEC	Fédération Nationale Belge de la Blanchisserie, du Nettoyage à Sec et de la Teinturerie
FEBMA	Federation of European Bearing Manufacturers Associations
FEBO	Fund for Experimental Concrete Research (Netherlands)
FEBS	Federation of European Biochemical Societies
FEC	Arbeitskreis Kulinarischer Fachjournalisten – Food Editors Club Deutschland e.V.
FEC	Fair Employment Commission (Northern Ireland)
FEC	Farm Electric Centre
FEC	Federación Española de Cuadros
FEC	Fédération Européenne de la Corrosion = EFC, EFK
FEC	Federation of the European Cutlery and Flatware Industries
FEC	Fluid Engineering Centre
FÉC	Fondation d'Études du Canada = CSF
FEC	Fondation Européenne de la Culture = ECF, ECS, EKS
FEC	Fonds Européen de Coopération (ECF) (Belgium)
FEC	Foundation for Environmental Conservation (Switzerland)
FEC	Free Europe Committee
FÉC	La Forestière Équatoriale du Caméroun
FEC-FO	Fédération des Employés et Cadres-Force Ouvrière
FECA	Fédération des Consultants Africains = FEAC
FECAF	Fédération Européenne des Collectionneurs et des Amateurs de Curiosités, Antiquités et Folklore (Belgium)
FECAICA	Federación de Cámaras y Asociaciones Industriales Centroamericanas
FECAMCO	Federación de Cámaras de Comercio del Istmo Centroamericano (Panama)
FECAMO	Fédération Belge des Entrepreneurs Carreleurs et Mosaïquistes
FECANIC	Federación Nicaragüense de Cooperativas de Ahorro y Crédito

FECAUBEL	Fédération des Concessionaires de l'Automobile de Belgique
FECAVA	Federation of European Companion Animal Veterinary Associations
FECB	Foreign Exchange Control Board
FECC	Federación Campesina Cristiana Costarricences
FECC	Fédération Européenne du Commerce Chimique
FECC	Foundation of European Carnival Cities (Netherlands)
FECCAS-UTC	Federación Campesina Cristiana de El Salvador – Unión de Trabajadores del Campo
FECCOO	Federación de Enseñanza de CCOO
FECDBA	Foreign Exchange and Currency Deposit Brokers Association
FECE-SITLIH	Federación Central de Sindicatos de Trabajadores Libres de Honduras
FECÉP-	Fédération Européenne des Constructeurs d'Équipement Pétrolier = FEPEM
FECETRAG	Federación Central de Trabajadores de Guatemala
FECHIMIE	Fédération des Industries Chimiques de Belgique
FECMA	Federation of European Credit Managers' Associations
FECMS	Federation of Catering Equipment Manufacturers and Suppliers
FECODE	Federación Colombiana de Educadores
FECOL-TRACOM	Federación Colombiana de Trabajadores
FECOLAC	Fundación Educativa de la Confederación Latinoamericana de Cooperativas de Ahorro y Credito
FECOM	Fonds Européen de Coopération Monétaire = EFWZ, EMCF
FECOPAL	Fédération des Coopératives Agricoles et Services de Commercialisation (Belgium)
FECOPAM	Federación Nacional de Cooperativas de Produccion Agrícola y Mercadeo (Ecuador)
FECORAH	Federación de Cooperativas Agropecuárias de la Reforma Agraria de Honduras
FECOSA	Ferrocarriles de Costa Rica
FECO-TRIGO	Federação dos Cooperativas Brasileiras de Trigo e Soja
FECOVE	Federación de Cooperativas de Consumo de Venezuela
FECOVI	Fédération Nationale des Fabricants de Conserves de Viandes
FECRO	Federation of European Credit Reporting Organisations
FECS	Fédération Européenne des Fabricants de Céramiques Sanitaires (Switzerland)
FECS	Federation of European Cancer Societies
FECS	Federation of European Chemical Societies
FECTD	Federation of European Chemical Traders & Distributors
FECTO	Federation of European Cities' Tourist Offices = FEOT
FECTS	Federation of European Connective Tissue Societies
FECUTI-ANDINA	Federación Subregional Andina de Consejos de Usuarios del Transporte Internacional de Carga (Ecuador)
FED	Federation of European Paediatric Research Societies
FED	Fondation Européenne Dragan
FED	Fonds Européen de Développement = EDF, EEF, EOF, EUF, FES
FED-EXPORT	Federazione Italiana dei Consorzi Agrari
FEDA	Fédération des Syndicats de la Distribution Automobile
FEDA	Further Education Development Association
FEDAAS	Federación Española de Asociaciones de Asitentes Sociales
FEDAC	Fédération Européenne des Anciens Combattants
FEDAI	Foreign Exchange Dealers Association of India
FEDAL	Federación de Entidades Democráticas de America Latina
FEDAN-FARBIO	Federación Andina de Farmacia y Bioquímica
FEDAR-LINEA	Associazione Italiana dell'Armamento di Linea
FEDAS	Federación Española de Actividades Subacuáticas
FEDAS	Fédération des Associations Commerciales Européennes des Fournisseurs de Laboratoires Scientifiques
FEDC	Federation of Engineering Design Companies
FEDÉ	Fédération Européenne des Écoles

FEDE	Fédération Européenne des Fabricants d'Enveloppes
FEDE-CACAO	Federación Nacional de Cacaoteros (Colombia)
FEDE-CAMARAS	Federación Venezolana de Cámaras y Asociaciones de Comercio y Producción
FEDE-CREDITO	Federación de Cajas de Crédito (El Salvador)
FEDE-FARMA	Federación Centroamericana de Laboratorios Pharmacéuticos (Guatemala)
FEDE-METAL	Federación Ecuatoriana de Trabajadores Metalurgicos y Afines
FEDE-METAL	Federación Metalúrgica Colombiana
FEDE-PALMA	Federación Nacional de Cultivadores de Palma Africana
FEDE-PETROL	Federación de Trabajadores Petroleros (Colombia, Venezuela)
FEDE-POMTER	Fédération Nationale des Syndicats de Négociants en Pommes de Terre et Légumes en Gros
FEDE-PRICAP	Federación de Empresas Privadas de Centroamérica y Panamá
FEDE-PUERTOS	Federación Nacional de Trabajadores Portuarios de Colombia
FEDE-STRUC TURAS	Federación Colombiana de Fabricantes de Estructuras Metalicas
FEDE-SYNDI	Union Professionnelle des Agents Concessionnaires, Courtiers et Distributeurs en Vins et Spiritueux
FEDEAGRO	Federación Nacional de Asociaciones de Productores Agropecuários (Venezuela)
FEDÉAR	Fédération d'Équipes Apostoliques de Religieuses
FEDE-ARROZ	Federación Nacional de Arrozeros (Colombia)
FEDEAU	Fédération pour le Développement de l'Artisanat Utilitaire
FEDEBON	Federación Boneria di Trabao (Netherlands Antilles)
FEDEC	Belgische Federatie van de Distributie in Huishoudelijke Uitrusting en Elektronica
FEDE-CACES	Federación de Asociaciones Cooperativas de Ahorro y Crédito de El Salvador
FEDECAFE	Federación Nacional de Cafeteros (Colombia)
FEDECAM	Federación Nacional de Cámaras de Comercio del Peru

FedeCámara	Federación de Cámaras de Comercio e Industria de Honduras
FEDECAPP	Federazione Italiana degli Industriali del Cappello
FEDECAR	Fédération des Caisses Rurales (Belgium)
FEDECCON	Federación Guatemalteca de Cooperativas de Consumo
FEDECHAR	Fédération Charbonnière de Belgique
FEDECO-MELEGNO	Federazione Nazionale dei Commercianti del Legno e del Sughero
Fedecrédito	Federación Nacional de Cooperativas de Ahorro y Crédito y de Servicios Múltiples (Costa Rica)
FEDEFAM	Federación Latinoamericana de Asociaciones de Familiares de Detenidos Desaparecidos
FEDEGAN	Federación Colombiana de Ganaderos (Colombia)
FEDEJCO	Federación Desarrollo Juvenil Comunitario (Honduras)
FEDÉL	Fédération Française des Syndicats d'Éleveurs de Chevaux de Selle
FEDEMAC	Fédération des Entreprises de Déménagement du Marché Commun
FEDEMAR	Fédération Belge des Exploitants Forestiers et Marchands de Bois de Mine et Papeterie
FEDEMOA	Federación Mexicana de Organizaciones Agrícolas
FEDEMOL	Federación Nacional de Molineros de Trigo (Colombia)
FEDENAGA	Federación Nacionale de Ganaderos (Venezuela)
FEDENTEL	Fédération Nationale des Dentelles, Tulles, Broderies, Guipures et Passementeries
FEDEPAPA	Federación Colombiana de Productores de Papa
FEDEPAS	Federación Nacional de Fabricantes de Pastas Alimenticias (Colombia)
FEDER	Fonds Européen de Développement Régional = ERDF
FEDER-AGENTI	Federazione Nazionale Agenti Raccomandatori Marittimi, Agenti Aerei e Pubblici Mediatori Marittimi
FEDER-ALGODON	Federación Nacional de Algodoneros (Colombia)
FEDER-CHIMICA	Federazione Nazionale dell'Industria Chimica
FEDER-CONSORZI	Federazione Italiana dei Consorzi Agrari

FEDER-FARMA	Federazione Nazionale Unitaria dei Titolari di Farmacia Italiani
FEDER-FIORI	Federazione Nazionale Fioristi
FEDER-GROSSISTI	Federazione Nazionale del Commercio Alimentare all'Ingrosso
FEDER-HOUT	Nationale Federatie van Houthandelaars (Belgium)
FEDER-LEGNO	Federazione Italiana delle Industrie del Legno, del Sughero e dell' Arredamento
FEDER-LIBRO	Federazione Italiana Lavoratori del Libro
FEDER-LINEA	Associazione Italiano dell' Armamento di Linea
FEDER-LOM-BARDA	Federazione Regionale fra le Associazioni Industriale della Lombardia
FEDER-NATURA	Federazione Nazionale Pro Natura
FEDER-OTTICA	Federazione Nazionale degli Ottici-Optometristi
FEDER-PESCA	Federazione Nazionale delle Imprese di Pesca
FEDER-RADIO	Federación Nacional de Radio (Colombia)
FEDER-SARTI	Federazione Nazionale Sarti e Sarte d'Italia
FEDER-SINDAN	Federazione dei Sindicati Dipendenti Aziende di Navigazione
FEDER-TERME	Federazione Nazionale delle Industrie Idro-Termali
FEDER-TESSABB	Federazione Nazionale Operatori Commerciali Ingrosso e Trasformatori Tessile, Abbigliamento, Mercerie ed Affini
FEDER-TESSILE	Federazione fra le Associazioni delle Industrie Tessili e Abbigliamento
FEDERA	Fédération des Sociétés Commerciales Pharmaceutiques Belges
FEDERA-BOIS	Fédération Nationale des Négociants en Bois (Belgium)
FEDERA-CAFE	Federación Nacional de Cafeteros (Colombia)
FEDERA-HOUT	Nationale Federatie van Houthandelaars (Belgium)
FEDERA-ICPA	Federazione Associazioni Italiane Concessionari Produzione Automobilistica
FEDE-RADIO	Federación Nacional de Radio (Colombia)
FEDERAG-RONOMI	Federazione Nazionale Dottori i Scienze Agrarie e Forestali
FEDE-RATEL	Federación Nacional de Trabajadores de Radio, Teatro, Cine, TV y Afines (Venezuela)
FEDER-BRAC-CIANTI	Federazione Nazionale Braccianti, Salariati, Tecnici
FEDER-COLT IVATORI	Federazione Italiana Coltivatori Diretti Mezzadri e Coloni
FEDER-COM LEGNO	Federazione Nazionale dei Commercianti del Legno e del Sughero
FEDERDIA	Federazione Italiana Dipendenti Impiegati dell' Agricoltura
FEDEREC	Fédération Nationale des Syndicats des Industries et Commerces de la Récupération
FEDERFISA	Federazione Nazionale tra Fabbricanti ed Esportatori Italiani di Fisarmoniche ed Altri Strumenti Musicali
FEDERGAS	Federazione Nazionale Commercianti di Gas Liquido in Bombole e Kerosene
FEDER-MAGAZ-ZINI	Federazione Italiana Magazzini Generali
FEDER-MAR	Fédération Maritime de la Côte-d'Ivoire
FEDER-MECCAN-ICA	Federazione Sindicale dell'Industria Metalmeccanica
FEDER-OLIO	Federazione Nazionale del Commercio Oleario
FEDERPOL	Federazione Nazionale degli Istitut di Polizia Privata
FEDERPRO	Federazione Professionale della Pubblicità
FEDERVINI	Federazione Italiana Industriali Produttori, Esportatori ed Importatori di Vini, Acquaviti, Liquori, Sciroppi, Aceti ed Affini
FEDES	Fédération Européenne de l'Emballage Souple
FEDES	Federazione Europea dei Fabbricanti di Sachetti di Carta
FEDES-ARROLLO	Fundación por la Educación Superior y el Desarrollo (Colombia)
FEDESA	Fédération Européenne de la Santé Animale
FEDE-SPEDI	Federazione Nazionale Spedizionieri
FEDETA	Federación de Trabajadores de Antioquia (Colombia)

FEDETAB	Fédération Belgo Luxembourgeoise des Industries du Tabac	**FEDORA**	Forum Européen de l'Orientation Académique (Greece)
FEDETAN	Federatie der Leerlooierijen en Aanverwante Nijverheden	**FEDPA**	Federación de Cooperativas de Ahorros y Créditos de Panamá
FEDETAN	Fédération de la Tannerie et des Industries Connexes	**FEDSA**	Federation of European Direct Selling Associations
FEDETAV	Federación de Trabajadores del Valle (Colombia)	**FEE**	Fachverband der Elektro- und Elektronikindustrie (Austria)
FEDETEL	Federación Democrática de Empleados y Trabajadores de Telecomunicaciones (Ecuador)	**FÉE**	Fédération des Électeurs Européennes
		FEE	Fédération des Experts-Comptables Européens
FEDE-TEXTIL	Federación Nacional de Industriales Textiles (Colombia)	**FEE**	Federation of European Publishers
FEDE-TRAM	Federazione Nazionale Aziende Municipalizzate di Trasporto	**FEE**	Fondation Européenne pour l'Environnement = EEF
FEDE-TRANS-PORTE	Federación de Trabajadores del Transporte (Venezuela)	**FEÉCA**	Fédération Européenne pour l'Éducation Catholique des Adultes
FEDEVNEP	Federación de Empleados Publicos (Venezuela)	**FEEE-B**	Fondation pour l'Education à l'Environnement en Europe-Belgique
FEDHOTEL	Fédération Nationale de l'Hôtellerie Belge	**FEEM**	Federación de Estuiantes de Enseñanza Media (Cuba)
FEDIA	Fédération des Ingénieurs Agronomes de Belgique	**FEEM**	Federation of European Explosive Manufacturers
FEDIAF	Fédération Européenne de l'Industrie des Aliments pour Animaux Familiers	**FEEMA**	Fundação Estadual de Engenharia do Meio Ambiente (Brazil)
FEDICA	Fédération des Associations de l'Industrie et du Commerce de l'Automobile (Belgium)	**FEER**	Fédération Européenne des Énergies Renouvelables = EFRE
		FEF	Full Employment Forum
FEDICER	Fédération des Industries Céramiques de Belgique et du Luxembourg	**FEFA**	Federación Española de Fotógrafos de Publicidad y Moda
FEDIL	Fédération des Industries Luxembourgeois	**FEFA**	Federazione Nazionale Enti per la Fecondazione Animale
FEDIMA	Fédération des Industries de Matières Premières et des Améliorants pour la Boulangerie et la Pâtisserie dans la CEE	**FEFA**	Fondo Especial para Financiamientos Agropecuários (Mexico)
		FEFAC	Fédération Européenne des Fabricants d'Aliments Composés pour Animaux (Belgium)
FEDIOL	Fédération de l'Industrie de l'Huilerie de la CEE	**FEFAF**	Fédération Européenne des Femmes Actives au Foyer (Belgium)
FEDIPAC	Fédération Nationale des Distributeurs de Produits Alimentaires et de Grande Consommation	**FEFANA**	Fédération Européenne des Fabricants d'Adjuvants pour la Nutrition Animale
FEDIS	Fédération Belge des Entreprises de Distribution	**FEFC**	Further Education Funding Council
		FEFCA	Fédération Européenne des Fabricants de Céramique d'Art
FEDIVER	Fédération de l'Industrie du Verre (Belgium)	**FEFCO**	Fédération Européenne des Fabricants de Carton Ondulé
FEDO FACT	Engineering and Design Organization (India)	**FEFE**	Fédération Européenne des Fabricants d'Enveloppes
FEDOLIVE	Fédération de l'Industrie de l'Huile d'Olive de la CEE	**FEFG**	Far East Fracture Group (Japan)
FEDOM	Fonds Européen de Développement pour les Pays et Territoires d'Outremer	**FEFIM**	Fédération Française des Industries du Médicament

FEFPEB	Fédération Européenne des Fabricants de Palettes et Emballages en Bois
FEG	Fachverband von Elektrogeräte-Lieferanten (Switzerland)
FEG	Föderation Europäischer Gewässerschutz = EFPW, FEPE
FEGAP	Fédération Européenne de la Ganterie de Peau
FEGARBEL	Fédération des Garagistes de Belgique
FEGARLUX	Fédération des Garagistes-Réparateurs du Grand-Duché de Luxembourg
FEGAZLIQ	Fédération Nationale des Centres de Liaison Régionaux de Concessionaires de Gaz Liquefiés
FEGB	Fédération Européenne du Génie Biologie = EFB
FEGC	Fédération Européenne du Génié Chimique
FEGECE	Fonds d'Entraide et de Garantie des Emprunts du Conseil de l'Entente (Ivory Coast) = EC-Fund
FEGOMEE	Fédération Européenne des Groupements d'Outre-Mer et d'Expulsés de l'Est
FEGOZI	Federatie Goud en Zilver
FEGRAB	Fédération des Industries Graphiques de Belgique
FEGUA	Ferrocarriles de Guatemala
FEH	Fédération Européenne de Hockey = EHF
FEHA	Foreningen af Fabrikanter og Importører af Elektriske
FEHCIL	Federación Hondureña de Cooperativas Industriales Ltda
FEHCOCAL	Federación Hondureña de Cooperativas Cafetaleras
FEHCOVIL	Federación Hondureña de Cooperativas de Vivienda
FEHMUC	Federación Hondureña de Mujeres Campesinas
FEHPA	Fédération Européenne de l'Hôtelerie de Plein Air = EFCO
FÉI	Fédération Équestre Internationale
FEI	Federation of the Electronics Industry
FEI	Forschungskreis der Ernährungsindustrie e.V.
FEIA	Flight Engineers International Association (U.S.A.)
FEIBP	Fédération Européenne de l'Industrie de la Brosserie et Pinceauterie
FEIC	Fédération Européenne de l'Industrie du Contreplaqué
FEICA	Fédération Européenne des Industries de Colles et Adhésifs
FEICADE	Federación de Instituciones Centroamericanas de Desarrollo (Guatemala)
FEICC	Foundation for the Establishment of an International Criminal Court (U.S.A.)
FEICRO	Federation of European Industrial Cooperative Research Organizations
FEIG	Federación Empresarial Internacional de Ginebra = FIPGE, IEFG
FEII	Federation of Electronic and Informatic Industries (Éire)
FEILAT	Fundación de Estudios e Investigaciones Latinoamericanas (Costa Rica)
FEIM	Fédération Européenne des Importateurs de Machines et d'Equipements de Bureau (Belgium)
FEIM	Fundación para las Encuentras Internacionales en las Montanas
FEIQUE	Federación Empresarial de la Industria Quimica Española
FEISEAP	Federation of Engineering Institutions of South-East Asia and the Pacific
FEITIS	Fédération Européenne des Industries Techniques de l'Image et du Son
FEJ	Fonds Européen Jeunesse = EYF
FEJB	Forum of Environmental Journalists of Bangladesh
FEJOL	Federación de Jovenes Latinoamericanos Liberales Radicales Progresistas (Paraguay)
FEKÍ	Félag Enskukennara à Íslandi
FEKO	Federatie van Kleinhandelsorganisaties
FEKS	Factory of the Eccentric Author (Russia)
FEL	Association des Femmes Européennes Libérales (Luxembourg)
FEL	Full Employment League
FEL-CAMGIE	Groupement des Exploitants Forestiers Camérounais
FELA-TRABAS	Federación Latinoamericana de Trabajadores Bancarios y de Seguros
FELABAN	Federación Latinoamericana de Bancos (Colombia)
FELAC	Federación Latinoamericana de Asociaciones de Consultores
FELAC	Federación Latinoamericana de Cirurgia (Colombia)

FELACUTI	Federación Latinoamericana de Consejos de Usuarios de Transporte Internacional
FELAFACS	Federación Latinoamericana de Facultades de Comunicacion Social (Peru)
FELAH	Federación Latinoamericana de Hospitales
FELAINCO	Federación Latinoamericana de las Industrias de la Confección
FELAP	Federación Latinamericana de Periodistas
FELASA	Federation of European Laboratory Animal Science Associations
FELATRAP	Federación Latinoamericana de Trabajadores de Prensa
FELCN	Fuerza Especial del Lucha Contra el Narcotrafico (Bolivia)
FELCOOP	Fédération Française de la Coopération Fruitière, Légumière et Horticole
FELCRA	Federal Land Consolidation and Rehabilitation Authority (Malaysia)
FELCSA	Federation of Evangelical Lutheran Churches of Southern Africa
FELDA	Federal Land Development Authority (Malaysia)
FELEBAN	Federación Latino-Americana de Bancos (Colombia)
FELEDL	Federazione Europea dei Lavatori Edil e del Ligno = EBBHA, EFBH, EFBTA, EFBWW, FETBB
FELS	Further Education Labour Students
FELTACA	Federación Latinoamericana de Trabajadores Campesinos y de la Alimentación (Venezuela)
FEM	Fédération Européenne de la Manutention
FEM	Fédération Européenne des Metallurgistes = EMB, EMF
FEM	Fédération Européenne des Motels = EMF
FEM	Feminists on the March (Puerto Rico)
FEM	Fondation Européenne pour le Management
FEM	Forschungsinstitut für Edelmetalle und Metallchemie e.V.
FEMA	Federal Emergency Management Agency (U.S.A.)
FEMAC	Federación Mesoamericana de Asociaciones Conservacionistas No-Gubernamentales
FEMAC	Fédération Mondiale des Anciens Combattants
Femaco	Federación Mexicana Anticomunista
FEMANU	Fédération Mondiale des Associations pour les Nations Unies
FEMAR	Fondação de Estudos do Mar
FEMAS	Far East Merchants Association (U.S.A.)
FEMB	Fédération Européenne du Mobilier du Bureau
FEMB	Federazione Europea Costruttori Mobili Ufficio
FEMC	Fédération Européenne des Médecins de Collectivités
FEMC	Federation of Earth Moving Contractors
FEMCIECC	Special Multilateral Fund of the Inter-American Council for Education, Science and Culture
FEMEB	Fédération Médicale Belge
FEMEDICA	Federación Medica Gremial de la Capital Federal (Argentina)
FEMETAL	Federación Española de Empresarios del Metal
FEMFM	Federation of European Manufacturers of Friction Materials
FEMGED	Fédération Européenne des Moyennes et Grandes Entreprises de Distribution
FEMIB	Fédération Européenne des Syndicats de Fabricants de Menuiseries Industrielles de Bâtiment
FEMIBE	Fédération Mondiale des Dirigeants des Instituts de Beauté et de l'Esthétique (Belgium)
FEMIDE	Fédération Mondiale des Institutions Financières de Développement = WFDFI
FEMIPI	Fédération Européenne des Mandataires de l'Industrie en Propriété Industrielle
FEMK	Fédération Européenne des Masseurs-Kinésithérapeutes Praticiens en Physiothérapie
FEMNET	African Women Development and Communication Network (Kenya)
FEMO	Fachverband der Eisen- und Metallwarenindustrie Österreichs
FEMO	Fédération de l'Enseignement Moyen Officiel du Degré Supérieur de Belgique = FOMO
FEMOSI	Fédération Mondiale des Syndicats d'Industries = FEMUSI, WIG, WOFIWU

FEMP	Federación Española de Municipios y Provincias
FEMPI	European Federation of Agents of Industry in Industrial Property
FEMRA	Federation of European Market Research Associations
FEMS	Federation of European Materials Societies
FEMS	Federation of European Microbiological Societies
FEMSA	Fabrica Española Magnetos, S.A.
FeMTAA	Fédération Mondiale des Travailleurs de l'Agriculture et de l'Alimentation = WFAFW, WFALA, WFLVA
FEMUSI	Federación Mundial de Sindicatos de Industrias = FEMOSI, WIG, WOFIWU
FÉN	Fédération de l'Éducation Nationale
FEN	Fédération Européenne des Narcotics
FEN	Fédération Européenne des Nars
FENA	Fédération Européenne du Négoce de l'Ameublement
FENA	Fédération Européenne du Négoce en Gros du Verre Plat
FENA-DESAL	Ferrocarriles Nacionales de El Salvador
FÉNA-SYCOA	Fédération Nationale des Syndicats du Commerce Ouest-Africain
FENA-TRIADE	Federación de Trabajadores de Institútos Autónomos (Venezuela)
FENA-TRILIH	Federación Nacional de Tribus para la Libertad del Indio Hondureño
FENAB	Fédération Nationale des Agriculteurs Belges
FÉNACÉM	Fédération Nationale du Commerce de l'Équipement Ménager
FÉNACÉR	Fédération Nationale des Syndicats du Commerce Électronique Radio-Télévision
FENACLE	Federación Nacional de Campesinos Libres del Ecuador
FENACOA	Federación Nacional de Cooperativas Agropecuárias (Uruguay)
FENACOAC	Federación Nacional de Cooperativas de Ahorro y Crédito de Guatemala
Fenacocal	Federación Nacional de Cooperativas de Cañeras (Honduras)
FENACOMI	Federación Nacional de Comerciantes Minoristas (Ecuador)
FÉNADAG	Fédération Nationale des Détaillants en Alimentation Générale (Belgium)
FENAGH	Federación Nacional de Agricoltores y Ganaderos de Honduras
FENAJ	Federação Nacional dos Jornalistas Profissionais (Brazil)
FENAL	Federación Nacional Agraria (Colombia)
FENAL	Federazione Esercenti Latterie e Derivati del Latte
FENALAC	Federación Nacional de Ligas Agrarias Cristianas (Paraguay)
FENALCE	Federación Nacional de Cultivadores de Cereales (Colombia)
FENALCO	Federación Nacional de Comerciantes (Colombia)
FENALT-RASE	Federación Nacional de Trabajadores al Servicio del Estado (Colombia)
FENALTRA-CONCEM	Federación Nacional de Trabajadores de la Construcción y del Cemento (Colombia)
FENAPES	Federación Nacional de Empresas Pequeñas Salvadoreñas
FENAPI	Federación Nacional de la Pequeña Industria (Ecuador)
FENAPI	Federazione Nazionale Perita Industriali
FENAPRO	Federazione Nazionale Profumieri e Bigottieri
FÉNARUM	Fédération Nationale des Producteurs de Rhum
FENAS-TRAS	Federación Sindical de Trabajadores Salvadoreños
FENASA-TREV	Federación Nacional de Sindicatos Autónomos de Trabajadores de la Educación de Venezuela
FENASI-BANCOL	Federación Nacional de Sindicatos Bancarios Colombianos
FENASTEG	Public Workers' Union (Guatemala)
FÉNASYDA	Fédération Nationale des Syndicats de la Distribution des Équipements et Outillages pour l'Automobile et Activités Annexes
FENATEX	Federación de Trabajadores Textiles y del Vestuario (Chile)
FeNATO	Federazione Nazionale Tecuici Ospedaleiri e Sanitari
FENATRA-CISTAS	Federación de Trabajadores Cigarrilleros, Tabaqueros y Similares (Venezuela)
FENATRAP	Federación Nacional de Trabajadores de los Servicios Públicos (Costa Rica)
FENA-TRAPEC	Federación Nacional de Trabajadores de las Autoridades Portuarias del Ecuador

FENATS	Federación Nacional de Trabajadores de Salud (Chile)
FÉNAVIAN	Fédération Nationale des Fabricants de Produits et Conserves de Viandes
FÉNAVINO	Fédération Nationale de la Viticulture Nouvelle
FENCAP	Federación Nacional de Campesinos del Perú
FENCO	Foundation of Canada Engineering Corporation
FENEAL	Federazione Nazionale Lavoratori Edile Affini e del Legno
FENEC	Federación Nicaragüense Educación Católica
FENECAFE	Federación Nacional de Cooperativas Cafetaleras (Ecuador)
FÉNEDAG	Fédération Nationale des Détaillants en Alimentation Générale
FENEDEX	Federatic voor de Nederlandse Export
FÉNEMA	Fédération des Négociants de Machines Agricoles (Luxembourg)
FÉNETEC	Fédération des Syndicats de Négociants Techniques
FENEWOL	Federatie Nederlandse Wolindustrie
FENEX	Federatie van Nederlandse Expediteursorganisaties
FÉNFIRO	Fédération Nationale des Groupements de Femelles Prolifiques Issues de Béliers Finnois ou Romanov
FÉNIÉ	Fédération Nationale des Industries Électroniques
FENIOF	Federazione Nazionale Imprese Onoranze Funebri
FENIT	Federazione Nazionale Imprese Trasporti
FENLAI	Federazione Nazionale Lavoratori Auto-Ferrotramvieri e Internavigatori
FENNO-BOARD	Finnish Wallboard Industry Association
FENOC	Federación Nacional de Organizaciones Campesinos (Ecuador)
FENODE	Federación de Obreros del Estado
FENOSA	Fuerzas Electricas del Noroeste, S.A.
FENOT	Federación Nacional de Obreros del Transporte (Guatemala)
FENPROF	Federação Nacional dos Professores
FENS	Federation of European Nutrition Societies
FENSA	Federación Nacional de Sindicatos Agrícolas (Colombia)
FÉNSCOPA	Fédération Nationale des Syndicats de Commerce en Gros de Produits Avicoles
FENSIL	Federación Nacional Sindical Libre (Guatemala)
FÉNU	Fonds d'Équipement des Nations Unies = FNUDC, UNCDF
FENUDE	Fondo Especial de las Naciones Unidas para el Desarrollo Económico = SUNFED
FEO	Fishmeal Exporters Organization
FEO	Flora Europaea Organisation = OFE
FEOF	Foreign Exchange Operations Fund (Laos)
FEOGA	Fonds Européen d'Orientation et de Garantie Agricole = EAGFL, EAGGF, EGTPE, EOGFL, EUGFL
FEOST	Fédération Européenne des Organisations Syndicales du Personal des Transports (Belgium)
FEOT	Fédération Européenne des Offices de Tourisme = FECTO
FEOTC	Federal Exporters Oversea Transport Committee (Australia)
FEP	Federación Española de Pesca
FEP	Fédération des Employés Privés (Luxembourg)
FEP	Fédération Européenne des Syndicats de Fabricants de Parquets
FEP	Foundation for Education with Production (Botswana)
FEPA	Fédération de l'Enseignement Privé Agricole
FEPA	Fédération Européenne des Fabricants de Produits Abrasifs
FEPA	Federation of European Philatelic Associations
FEPA-FARBIO	Federación Panamericana de Farmacia y Bioquémica
FÉPACI	Fédération Panafricaine des Cinéastes
FEPAFEM	Federación Panamericana de Asociaciones de Facultades Escuelas de Medicina (Venezuela) = PAFAMS
FEPAN-DOSA	Federación Panamericana pro Donación Voluntaria de Sangre
FEPAPHAM	Pan African Federation of Associations for Persons with Mental Handicap (Morocco)
FEPAR	Federación Panameña de Religiosos y Religiosas
FÉPASA	Fédération Panafricaine des Syndicats de l'Agriculture = FAFATU

FEPD	Fédération Européenne des Parfumeurs Détaillants
FÉPE	Fédération des Écoles Privées d'Europe
FEPE	Fédération Européenne de la Publicité Extérieure
FEPE	Fédération Européenne des Professionels de l'Environnement = EFEP, EVUB
FEPE	Fédération Européenne pour la Protection des Eaux = EFPW, FEG
FEPEDICA	Fédération Européenne du Personnel d'Encadrement des Productions, des Industries, des Commerces et des Organismes Agro-Alimentaires (Belgium)
FEPEM	Federation of European Petroleum Equipment Manufacturers = FECEP
FEPER	Federación Peruana de Relacionistas Publicos
FEPF	Fédération Européenne des Industries de Porcelaine et de Faïence de Table et d'Ornementation
FEPF	Fédération Européenne des Producteurs de Fibres-Cement
FEPIA	Fondation Européenne pour la Promotion des Industries Agro-Alimentaires
FEPIEC	Federación Panamericana de Ingenieria Económica y de Costos (Argentina)
FEPMA	Federation of European Pencil Manufacturers Associations
FEPOW	Far East Prisoners of War Association
FEPPD	Fédération Européenne de Patrons Prothésistes Dentaires
FEPPR	Federacion de Enfermeria Practica de Puerto Rico
FÉPRABEL	Fédération des Producteurs d'Assurances de Belgique
FEPRANAL	Federación Nacional del Sector Privado Para la Acción Comunal (Colombia)
FEPRINCO	Federación de la Producción, la Industria y el Comercio (Paraguay)
FEPRO	Federación de Asociaciones de Profesionales Academicos de El Salvador
FEPS	Federation of European Physiological Societies
FEPSAC	Fédération Européenne de Psychologie des Sports et des Activités Corporelles
FEPT	Fédération Européenne de la Presse de la Télévision
FEQUINAL	Federación Nacional de Trabajadores de la Industria Quimica (Colombia)
FER	Federation of Engine Re-manufacturers
FER	Frente Estudiantil Revolucionario (Nicaragua)
FERA	Fédération Européenne des Réalisateurs de l'Audiovisuel
FERA	Föreningen för Elektricitetens Rationella Användning
FERA	Further Education Research Association
FERC	Regional Conference for Asia and the Far East (FAO)
FERCO	Fédération Européenne de la Restauration Collective
FERE	Federación Espanola de Religiosos de Enseñanza
FERE	Fondation Egyptologique Reine Elisabeth (Belgium)
FERELPAR	Federación de Religiosos del Paraguay
FERES	Fédération Internationale des Instituts Catholiques de Recherches Socio-Religieuses
FeRFA	Federation of Resin Formulators and Applicators
FERG	Frente Estudiantil Revolucionario Robin García (Guatemala)
FERI	Fishery Engineering Research Institute (China)
FEROPA	Fédération Européenne des Syndicats de Panneaux de Fibres
FERP	Fédération des Entreprises de Récupération du Papier et du Carton = VPRB
FERPHOS	Entreprise Nationale du Fer et du Phosphate (Algeria)
FERPI	Federazione Relazioni Pubbliche Italiana
Ferpress	Union Internationale de Presse Ferroviaire (Austria)
FERR-ANGOL	Empresa Nacional de Ferro de Angola
FERROCAR	Instítuto Autónomo de Ferrocarriles del Estado (Venezuela)
Ferronor	Empresa de Transporte Ferroviario (Chile)
FERS	Federación Española de Religiosas Sanitarias
FERS	Fédération Européenne de Recherche sur le SIDA = EFAR
FERT	Commission on Fertilisers (FAO)

FERTI-BRAS Petrobrás Fertilizantes (Brazil)

FERTICA Fertilizantes de Centroamerica (Honduras)

FERTIL Ruwais Fertilizers Industries (Abu Dhabi)

FERTIMEX Fertilizantes Mexicanos S.A.

FERTISA Fertilizantes Ecuatorianos S.A.

FERTISUL Fertilizantes do Sul (Brazil)

FES Fachverband der Elektrizitätsversorgung des Saarlandes

FÉS Fédération des Éditeurs Suisses

FES Fédération Européenne de la Salmoniculture

FES Fondation Européenne de la Science = ESF

FES Fondo Europeo de Sviluppo = EDF, EEF, EOF, EUF, FED

FES Friedrich-Egbert-Stiftung

FES-CAST Federation of Engineering Societies of China Association for Science and Technology

FESA Foundry Equipment and Suppliers Association

FESABID Federación Española de Sociedades de Archivista, Biblioteconomía y Documentación

FESAC Fondation de l'Enseignement Supérieur en Afrique Centrale

FeSAPI Federazione Sindacati Avvocati e Procuratori Italiani

FESCID Fédération Européenne des Syndicaats de la Chimie et des Industries Diverses = EFCG, EFCGWU

FESEB Federación Sindical de Empleados Bancarios (Guatemala)

FESFP Fédération Européenne des Syndicats de Fabricants de Parquets

FESI Federación Española de Sociedades de Informática = Spanish Federation of Computer Societies

FESI Fédération Européenne des Syndicats d'Entreprises d'Isolation

FESI-TRANH Federación Sindical de Trabajadores Nacionales de Honduras

FESIAN Federación Sindical Agraria Nacional (Costa Rica)

FESIN-CONTRANS Federación de Sindicatos de la Industria de Construcción, Similares, Transporte y de Otras Actividades (El Salvador)

FESIN-TEXSICA Federación de Sindicatos Textiles, Similares y Conexos y Otras Actividades (El Salvador)

FESITRA-UCAMC Federación de Sindicatos de Trabajadores de las Universidades de Centroamerica, Mexico y el Caribe (Nicaragua)

FESODEBU Femmes Solidaires pour le Développement au Bushi (Zaïre)

FESPA Federation of European Screen Printers Associations

FESPO Federation of European Science Policy Organizations

FESPP Federation of European Societies of Plant Physiology

FESRI Fushun Education Science Research Institute (China)

FÉSSCAP Fédération d'Étudiants Sociaux-Chrétiens d'Amérique Centrale et Panamá

FESSH Federation of European Societies for Surgery and Rehabilitation of the Hand

FEST Fédération Européenne des Sociétés de Toxicologie

FEST Forschungsstätte de Evangelischen Studiengemeinschaft (Germany)

FEST Foundation for Education, Science and Technology (South Africa)

FÉSTAL Fédération Syndicale du Teillage Agricole du Lin

FESTRAC Federación Sindical de Trabajadores de Cudinamarca (Colombia)

FESV Fédération Européenne pour le Droit à la Stérilisation Voluntaire

FÉSYGA Fédération des Syndicats Gabonais

FESYP Fédération Européenne des Syndicats de Fabricants de Panneaux de Particules

FET Fair Employment Tribunal (Northern Ireland)

FET Federación Española de Tenis

FET Fédération Européenne des Associations des Téléspectateurs

FET Fondation Européenne du Tourisme = EFT

FET Foundation on Economic Trends (U.S.A.)

FET Future of Europe Trust

FETA Federation of Environmental Trade Associations

FETA Fire Extinguishing Trades Association

FETAB Federación Dominicana de Cooperativas Agropecuárias del Tabaco

FETAC	Foreign Economic and Trade Arbitration Committee (China)
FETAEMG	Federação dos Trabalhadores na Agricultura de Minas Gerais (Brazil)
FETAGRI	Federação dos Trabalhadores da Agricultura (Brazil)
FÉTANOR	Fédération des Industries du Blanchiment, de la Teinture et de Apprêts de la Région du Nord
FETAP	Fédération Européenne des Transportes Aériens Privés
FETBB	Fédération Européenne des Travailleurs du Bâtiment et du Bois = EBBH, EFBH, EFBT, EFBWW, FELEDL
FETCM	Federación Europea de los Trabajadores de la Construccion y la Madera = EBBH,EFBH, EFBT, EFBWW, FELEDL, FETBB
FETE-UGT	Federación de Trabajadores de la Enseñanza de la Union General de Trabajadores
FETENTEL-PERU	Federación de Trabajadores de la Empresa Nacional de Telecomunicaciones del Perú
FETIG	Federación de Trabajadores de la Industria Grafica de Venezuela
FETIMP	Federación de Trabajadores de la Industria Metalérgica del Perú
FETOURAG	Fédération du Tourisme Agricole (Belgium)
FETP	Far East Trade Press (Hong Kong)
FÉTRA	Fédération des Industries Transformatrices de Papier et de Carton (Belgium)
FETRA-BANCA	Federación de Trabajadores Bancarios (Venezuela)
FETRA-CADE	Federación de Trabajadores de Cana de Azucar (Venezuela)
FETRA-COSIC	Federación de Trabajadores de la Aviacion Comercial (Venezuela)
FETRA-EDUCA-CION	Federación de Trabajadores Educaciónales (Venezuela)
FETRA-ELECTRIC	Federación de Trabajadores Electricos (Venezuela)
FETRA-HIDROCAR-BUROS	Federación de los Trabajadores de Hidrocarbura de Venezuela
FETRA-HOSIVEN	Federación de Trabajadores Hoteleros y Similares (Venezuela)
FETRA-METAL	Federación Nacional de Trabajadores Metalúrgicos (Venezuela)
FETRA-PESCA	Federación de Trabajadores de la Pesca (Venezuela)
FETRA-PETROL	Federación Ecuatoriana de Trabajadores Petroleros, Gas y Afines
FETRA-SCAP	Federación de Trabajadores de la Salud de Centroamerica y Panamá
FETRAB-TAS	Federación de Trabajadores de Alimento, Bebida, Tabaco y Asociados Sindicatos (Guatemala)
FETRABAN	Federación de Trabajadores Bancarios del Paraguay
FETRA-COM	Federación Ecuatoriana de Trabajadores de la Construccion, Madera y Materiales de Construccion y Afines
FETRAL-DC	Frente de Trabajadores Democrata Cristianos de America (Venezuela)
FETRAL-COS	Federación de Trabajadores Latinoamericanos de Comercio, Oficinas y Similares (Venezuela)
FETRALIS	Federación Ecuatoriana de Trabajadores de la Alimentacion, Bebidas, Tabacos y Similares
FETRAN-JAS	Federación de Trabajadores Agropecuários, Jardineros y Similares
FETRASUR	Federación de Trabajadores del Sur (Honduras)
FETRATEL	Federación de Trabajadores de Telecomunicaciones (Venezuela)
FETRATEX	Federación de Trabajadores Textiles (Venezuela)
FETSALUD	Federación de Trabajadores de la Salud (Nicaragua)
FETTVIC	Federación Ecuatoriana de Trabajadores Textiles y del Vestido, Calzado y Cuero
FETULIA	Federación de Trabajadores Unidos de la Industria Azucarera (Guatemala)
FEU	Federación Estudiantil Universitaria (Cuba)
FEU	Further Education Unit
FEUC	Federación de Estudiantes Universidad Católica (Chile)
FEUCA	Federación de Estudiantes Universitarios de Centroamérica
FEUCAL	Federación de Estudiantes Universitarios Católicos de America Latina
FEUGRES	Fédération Européenne des Fabricants de Tuyaux en Grés
FEUPF	Fédération Européenne des Unions Professionelles des Fleuristes

FEVA	Federacion Venezolana de Abrogadas Todos Juntas
FEVAP	Federación Venezolana de Agencias Publicitarias
FEVC	Fédération Européene des Villes de Congrès (Belgium) = EFCT, EVK
FEVE	European Glass Container Federation
FEVE	Fédération Européenne du Verre d'Emballage
FEVE	Ferrocarriles de Via Estrecha
FEVEL	Fédération Européenne du Velours
FEVE-TRAPH	Federación Venezolana de Asociaciones de Transportistas Distribuidora de Derivados de Hidrocarburo
FEVIR	Federation of European Veterinarians in Industry and Research
FEW	Freemen of England and Wales
FEWAMA	Federation of West African Manufacturers Associations = FAIAO
FEWIA	Federation of European Writing Instruments Associations (Spain)
FEWITA	Federation of European Wholesale and International Trade Associations
FEZ	Fédération des Entreprises du Zaïre
FEZ	Fédération Européenne de Zootechnie = EAAP, EAZ, EVT
FF	Feminist Forum
FF	Fianna Fáil
FF	Filosofisk Forum (Denmark)
FF	Finlands Fysioterapeutförbund
FFA	Fédération Française d'Athlétisme
FFA	Federation of Financial Associations (Korea)
FFA	Flygtekniska Försöksanstalten
FFA	Föreningen för Arbetarskydd
FFA	Foundation for Foreign Affairs (U.S.A)
FFA	Future Farmers of America
FFA	South Pacific Forum Fisheries Agency
FFAC	Société Fiduciaire France Afrique (Cameroon, Congo)
FFACI	Société Fiduciaire France Afrique Côte-d'Ivoire
FFAÉAF	Fédération Française des Associations d'Élevages d'Animaux à Fourrure
FFAG	Fiduciaire France-Afrique-Gabon
FFAJ	Fédération Français des Auberges et de la Jeunesse
FFAS	Fiduciaire France-Afrique-Sénégal
FFB	Fédération Française de la Brosserie
FFB	Food From Britain
FFC	Fédération Française de la Carrosserie
FFC	Finlands Fachföreningars Centralförbund = SAK
FFC	Forests Forever Campaign
FFCAA	Fédération Française des Coopératives Agricoles d'Approvisionnement
FFCAC	Fédération Française des Coopératives Agricoles de Céréales
FFCAT	Fédération Française des Commissionnaires et Auxiliaires de Transport, Commissionnaires en Douane, Transitaires, Agents Maritimes et Aériens
FFCB	Federal Farm Credit Board (U.S.A.)
FFCB	Fédération Française de Coopération entre Bibliothèques
FFCC	Farms for City Children
FFCFLH	Fédération Française de la Coopération Fruitière, Légumière et Horticole
FFCFP	Fédération Française de Cadres de la Fonction Publique
FFCG	Fédération Française du Commerce des Grains
FFCSO	Fédération Française des Coopératives de Stockage d'Oléagineux
FFCVN	Fédération Française des Chaines Volontaires Nationales
FFDA	Flying Funeral Directors of America
FFDoA	Federated Funeral Directors of America
FFE	Fondation Friedrich Ebert
FFÉA	Fédération Française d'Économie Alpestre
FFEF	Fédération des Foires-Expositions de France
FFÉM	Fédération Française d'Économie Montagnarde
FFEMA	Federacion Femenina Evangelica Metodista (Argentina)
FFÉPGV	Fédération Française d'Éducation Physique et de Gymnastique
FFÉSSM	Fédération Française d'Études et de Sport Sous-Marins
FFF	Farmaceutiska Foreningen i Finland
FFF	Fashion and Footwear Federation (Éire)
FFF	Fédération de Foires-Expositions de France
FFF	Fédération Française de Football
FFF	Finlands Farmaceutförbund
FFF	Fish Friers' Federation

FFF	International Federations of Performers
FFFF	Foreningen af Fabrikanter af Farmaceutisk-Kemiske Tilsaetningsstoffer til Foderstofindustrien
FFFLCAF	Fédération Française de la Filature de Laine Cardée et Autres Fibres
FFHB	Fédération Française de Handball
FFHC	Fédération Française des Haltérophiles et Culturistes
FFHC/AD	Freedom From Hunger Campaign/Action for Development (FAO) = CMCF/AD, CMCH/AD
FFHS	Federation of Family History Societies
FFI	Fachverband Faltschachtelindustrie
FFI	Forsvarets Forskningsintsinstitutt
FFIC	Fédération Française des Industries de Corseterie
FFIIG	Fédération Française de l'Imprimerie et des Industries Graphiques
FFINTEL	Fédération Française des Importateurs Négociants-Transformateurs et Exportateurs de Laines
FFIPPBT	Fédération Française de l'Industrie des Produits de Parfumerie, de Beauté et de Toilette
FFITP	Fédération Française d'Instituts Techniques du Pétrole
FFITP	Fédération Française des Industries Transformatrices des Plastiques
FFIVM	Fédération Française des Industries du Vêtement Masculin
FFJP	Internation Federation of Fruit-Juice Producers
FFMA	Flavour and Fragrance Manufacturers' Association (Japan)
FFMA	Funeral Furnishing Manufacturers Association
FFMC	Freshwater Fish Marketing Corporation (U.S.A.)
FFMI	Fédération Française du Matériel d'Incendie
FFMIN	Fédération Française des Marches d'Intérêt National
FFMKR	Fédération Française des Masseurs Kinésithérapeutes Rééducateurs
FFMU	Forschungsgesellschaft für Feingeräte, Mikro und Uhrentechnik
FFMW	Federation of Fresh Meat Wholesalers
FFN	Fédération Française de Natation
FFNFPMAP	Fédération Familiale Nationale pour la Formation Professionnelle et Ménagère Agricole Privée
FFNUDS	Fondo Fiduciario de las Naciones Unidas para el Desarrollo Social = FASNUDS, UNTFSD
FFNUPPD	Fondo Fiduciario de las Naciones Unidas para Planificación y Proyecciones del Desarrollo = FASNUPPD, UNTFDPP
FFOA	Association of Former FAO and WFP Staff Members (Italy)
FFOPS	Fédération Française des Organismes de Prévention et de Sécurité
FFP	Farm Forestry Program
FFP	Fédération Française de Publicité
FFP	Fédération Française du Paysage
FFP	Forests for the People (Sri Lanka)
FFP	Fund for Peace (U.S.A.)
FFPAF	Forest and Forest Products Policy Advisory Forum
FFPAM	Federation of Family Planning Associations of Malaysia
FFPE	Fédération de la Fonction Publique Européenne = ECSF
FFPLB	Fédération Française des Producteurs de Lait de Brebis
FFPN	Française Frisonne Pie Noire (race bovine)
FFPRI	Forest and Forest Product Research Institute (Ghana)
FFPS	Fauna and Flora Preservation Society
FFR	Fédération Française de Rugby
FFR	Feratia Filatelică Română (*ex* AFR)
FFRC	Food Freezer Refrigeration Council
FFRC	Freshwater Fisheries Research Center (China)
FFRI	Fujian Fisheries Research Institute
FFRP	Fédération Française des Relations Publiques
FFRSA	Fondation pour Favoriser les Recherches Scientifiques (Belgium)
FFS	Farm & Food Society
FFS	Fédération Française de Spéléologie
FFS	Félag Forstöðumanna Sjúkrahúsa á Íslandi
FFS	Föreningen för Samhällsplanering
FFS	Foundation for Fiscal Studies (Éire)
FFS	Front des Forces Socialistes (Algeria)
FFSA	Fédération Française des Sociétés d'Assurances

FFSAM	Fédération Française des Sociétés d'Amis de Musées	**FFVV**	Fédération Française de Vol à Voile
FFSB	Fédération des Foires et Salons du Benelux	**FFW**	Federation of Free Workers (Philippines)
FFSC	Institutum Fratrum Franciscalium a Santa Cruce loci Waldbreitbach	**FFW**	Foundation for Women (Thailand)
FFSÉ	Fédération Française des Sports Équestres	**FFWAG**	Farming, Forestry & Wildlife Advisory Group
FFSF	Fédération Française des Semences Fourragères, Grandes Cultures, Gazons, et Espaces Verts	**FFWF**	Fonds zur Foederung der Wissenschaftlichen Forschung
FFSHB	Fédération Française des Sociétés d'Homéopathie et de Biothérapie	**FFWFRI**	Fujian Fresh-Water Fisheries Research Institute
FFSI	Institutum Fratrum Filiorum Sancti Ioseph, vulgo Bayo Zefiti (Rwanda)	**FFYV**	Fédération Française du Yachting à Voile
FFSJ	Fédération Française des Sociétés de Journalistes	**FFZ**	Fédération Française de Zootechnie
FFSL	Fédération Française des Syndicats de Librairies	**FG**	Fíne Gael
FFSM	Fédération des Fondations pour la Santé Mondiale = FWHF	**FGA**	Fachgemeinschaft Antriebstechnik (VDMA)
FFSPBPV	Fédération Française des Syndicats de Producteurs de Bois et Plants de Vigne	**FGA**	Fachgruppe für Architektur
FFSPIG	Fédération Française des Syndicats Patronaux de l'Imprimerie et des Industries Graphiques	**FGA**	Fédération Générale de l'Agroalimentaire
FFSPN	Fédération Française des Sociétés de Protection de la Nature	**FGAA**	Fédération Générale Arabe d'Assurance = GAIF, UGAA
FFSSN	Fédération Française des Sociétés de Sciences Naturelles	**FGAE**	Family Guidance Association of Ethiopia
FFSU	Fédération Française des Stations Uvales	**FGAF**	Fraunhofer-Gesellschaft zur Forderung des Angewandten Forschung = FhG
FFTA	Finnish Foreign Trade Association	**FGAT**	Fédération des Unions Professionnelles des Grossistes en Articles Tréfilés (Belgium)
FFTB	Fédération des Fabricants de Tuiles et de Briques de France		
FFTC	Food and Fertilizer Technology Centre, Taipei (China)	**FGB**	Federation of Associations of Wholesale Dealers in Building Materials (Netherlands)
FFTL	Fédération Française du Tissage de Laine et Autres Fibres		
FFTRI	Fruit and Food Technology Research Institute (South Africa)	**FGBI**	Federation of Soroptimist Clubs of Great Britain and Ireland
FFTS	Fédération Française des Travailleurs Sociaux	**FGBMFI**	Full Gospel Business Men's Fellowship International (U.S.A.)
FFU	Forskningens Fællesudvalg	**FGBPW**	Federation of Gambia Business and Professional Women
FFU	Forskningsrodense Fellesutvag	**FGC**	Fédération Genevoise de Coopération
FFU	Front Uni (Central African Republic)	**FGC**	Flat Glass Council
FFVIB	Fresh Fruit and Vegetable Information Bureau	**FGCA**	Fédération Générale des Cadres de l'Agriculture
FFVMA	Fire Fighting Vehicle Manufacturers Association	**FGD**	Forschungsgesellschaft Druckmaschinen
		FGDC	Federal Geographic Data Committee (U.S.A.)
		FGDS	Fédération de la Gauche Démocrate et Socialiste
		FGE	Organisatie van Fabrikanten van Grafische Eindproducten
		FGEI	Fédération des Géomètres-Experts Indépendants (Belgium)

FGF	Fachgruppe der Forstingenieure (Switzerland) = GSF
FGG	Fränkische Geographische Gesellschaft
FGGM	Federation of Gelatine and Glue Manufacturers
FGH	Forschungsgemeinschaft für Hochspannungs- und Hochstromtechnik
FGHB	Fédération Généalogique et Héraldique de Belgique = BFGH
FGHS	Vereniging van Fabrikanten en Groothandelaren in Sportbenodigheden
FGI	Fédération Graphique Internationale
FGI	Front des Générations de l'Indépendance (Algeria)
FGIF	Finlands Gymnastik och Idrottsförbund
FGIL	Fédération Générale des Instituteurs Luxembourgeois
FGIPCI	Federation of Government Information Processing Councils Incorporated (U.S.A.)
FGK	Forschungsgesellschaft Kunststoffe
FGL	Fondation Giovanni Lorenzini
FGL	Foreningen af Grossister i Landbrugsmaskiner
FGMA	Flat Glass Marketing Association (U.K., U.S.A.)
FGMÉÉ	Fédération Nationale des Syndicats de Grossistes en Matériel Électrique et Électronique
FGMI	Federation of Gujarat Mills and Industries (India)
FGMOPA	Fonds de Garantie Mutuelle et d'Orientation de la Production Agricole
FGÖD	Fachwissenschaftliche Gesellschaft Österreichischen Dentisten
FGOLF	Fédération des Gynécologues et Obstétriciens de Langue Française
FGP	Fuerza de Guerrilleros de los Pobres (Guatemala)
FGPE	Fédération Générale du Personnel Enseignant (Belgium) = AVVL
FGR	Fachgemeinschaft Gusseieme Rohre
FGS	Federation of Genealogical Societies (U.S.A.)
FGS	Forschungsgesellschaft für das Strassen- und Verkerswesen
FGSV	Forschungsgesellschaft für Strassen- und Verkehrswesen
FGT	Fachverband der Garagen-, Tankstellen- und Service-Stations Unternehmungen (Austria)
FGTB	Fédération Générale du Travail de Belgique
FGTI	Fédération Générale des Travailleurs Indépendants
FGU	Fachgruppe für Untertagbau
FGV	Fachgruppe für Verfahrens- und Chemieingenieurtechnik (Switzerland) = GGC
FGV	Fundação Getúlio Vargas (Brazil)
FGW	Forschungsgesellschaft für Wohnen, Bauen und Planen (Austria)
FGYA	Franco-German Youth Agency
FH	Fédération Horlogère Suisse
FH	Fédération Suisse des Associations de Fabricants d'Horlogerie
FHA	Family Heart Association
FHA	Federal Highway Administration (U.S.A.)
FHA	Federal Housing Administration (U.S.A.)
FHA	Félag Husgagnarkitekta
FHA	Finance Houses Association
FHA	Future Homemakers of America
FHA	Institúto de Fomento de Hipotecas Aseguradas (Guatemala)
FHB	Farm Holiday Bureau
FHC	Food Hygiene Centre
FHD	Foreningen af Herreekviperings- handlere i Danmark
FHD	Fundación Humanismo y Democracia
FHF	Fédération Hospitalière de France
FHF	Federation of Hardware Factors
FHF	International Federation of Health Funds
FHFW	Federation of High Frequency Welders
FhG	Fraunhofer-Gesellschaft zur Forderung der Angewandten Forschung = FGAF
FHH	Fachhandelsverband Fasern und Haare
FHI	Fachverband der Holzverarbeitenden Industrie (Austria)
FHI	Family Health International (U.S.A.)
FHI	Fédération Haltérophile Internationale
FHI	Félag Húsgagna -og Innanhússarkitekta
FHI	Food for the Hungry International (Switzerland)
FHIA	Fundación Hondureña de Investigación Agrícola (Honduras)
FHKI	Federation of Hong Kong Industries
FHLBB	Federal Home Loan Bank Board (U.S.A.)

FHPL	Fédération Horticole Professionnelle Luxembourgeoise
FHR	Fachvereinigung Hartpapierwaren und Rundgefässe
FHRC	Flood Hazard Research Centre
FHRF	Finney-Howell Research Foundation (U.S.A)
FHS	Filologisk-Historiske Samfund
FHS	Finlands Hundstambok
FHS	Finska Hushållnings-Säkkskapet
FHS	Furniture History Society
FHSR	Foundation for Health Services Research
FHTA	Federated Home Timber Associations
FHWA	Federation Highway Administration (U.S.A.)
FI	FAO Fisheries Department
FI	Front Indépendantiste (New Caledonia)
FI	Frontiers International
FIA	Faribabad Industries Association (India)
FIA	Federación Interamericana de Abogados = IABA
FIA	Federated Ironworkers Association of Australia
FIA	Fédération des Industries Agricoles et Alimentaires (Belgium)
FIA	Fédération Internationale d'Aikido = IAF
FIA	Fédération Internationale de l'Artisanat = IFC, IFH
FIA	Fédération Internationale de l'Automobile = IAF
FIA	Fédération Internationale des Acteurs = IFA
FIA	Fédération Nationale des Syndicates des Industries de l'Alimentation
FIA	Federation of Islamic Associations in the United States and Canada
FIA	Federazione Italiana Autorimesse
FIA	Fibreoptic Industry Association
FIA	Fitness Industry Association
FIA	Friends of Israel Association
FIA	Fruit Importers Association
FIA	International Federation of Master-Craftsmen
FIAA	Federated Ironworkers' Association of Australia
FIAA	Fédération Internationale d'Athlétisme Amateur = IAAF
FIAAF	Fédération Internationale des Associations d'Auteurs de Film
FIAB	Fédération Internationale des Associations de Bibliothécaires et des Bibliothèques = IFLA
FIABCI	Federazione Internazionale delle Professioni Immobiliarii Capitolo Italiano
FIABGRAL	Federação Internacional de Associações de Bibliotecarios-Grupo Regional América Latina
FIABP	Fédération des Associations de l'Industrie des Bouillons et Potages de la CEE
FIABV	Federación Iberoamericana de Bolsas de Valores (Argentina) = IAFSE
FIAC	Federación de Ingenieros Agronomos de Colombia
FIAC	Fédération Interaméricaine des Automobile Clubs
FIAC	Fédération Internationale Amateur de Cyclisme = IACF
FIAC	Fédération Internationale de l'Artisanat de la Chaussure
FIAC	Fédération Internationale des Agences Catholiques de Presse
FIAC	Federation of Independent Advice Centres
FIAC	Federation of International American Clubs
FIAC	Fertilizer Industry Advisory Committee (FAO)
FIAC	Foundries Industry Advisory Committee (HSC)
FIACAT	Fédération Internationale des ACAT: Action des Chrétiens pour l'Abolition de la Torture = IFACAR
FIACC	Five International Associations Co-ordinating Committee
FIACP	Fédération Internationale des Agences Catholiques de Presse
FIACTC	Fédération Internationale des Associations des Chémistes du Textile et de la Couleur
FIAD	Fédération Internationale des Associations des Distributeurs de Films
FIAD	Fondation Internationale Autre Développement
FIAÉM	Fédération Internationale des Associations des Étudiants en Médecine = IFMSA

FIAÉT	Fédération Internationale des Associations pour l'Éducation des Travailleurs = IFWEA, IVA
FIAF	Federación Interamericana de Filatelia (Mexico)
FIAF	Fédération Internationale des Archives du Film = IFFA
FIAI	Fédération Internationale des Associations d'Instituteurs = IFTA, IVL
FIAIVT	Federazione Italiana delle Associazioni delle Imprese Viaggi et Turismo
FIAJ	Fédération Internationale des Auberges de la Jeunesse = IYHF
FIAJA	Fédération Internationale des Associations de Journalistes Automobiles
FIALEC	Federazione Italiana fra le Associazioni Laureati in Economia e Commercio
FIAM	Fédération Internationale des Associations de Mécanographes
FIAMC	Fédération Internationale des Associations des Médicales Catholiques
FIAN	Foodfirst Information and Action Network (Germany)
FIANATM	Fédération Internationale des Associations de Négociants en Aciers, Tubes et Métaux
FIANE	Fonds d'Intervention et d'Action pour la Nature et l'Environnement
FIANI	Fédération Internationale d'Associations Nationales d'Ingénieurs
FIAP	Federación Ibero-Americana de Asociaciones de Periodistas
FIAP	Fédération Internationale de l'Art Photographique
FIAP	Fédération Internationale des Architectes Paysagistes = IFLA
FIAP	Fédération Internationale des Associations Pédagogiques
FIAP	Federation of Inter-Asian Philately (Singapore)
FIAP	Federazione Italiana Autotrasportatori Professionali
FIAPA	Fédération Internationale de l'Activité Physique Adaptée = IFAPA
FIAPA	Fédération Internationale des Associations de Chefs de Publicité d'Annonceurs
FIAPA	Fédération Internationale des Associations de Personnes Agées
FIAPÉ	Fédération Internationale des Associations de la Presse de l'Église
FIAPF	Fédération Internationale des Associations de Producteurs de Films = IFFPA
FIAPL	Fédération Internationale des Associations des Pilotes de Ligne
FIAPP	Fédération Internationale des Anciens Prisonniers Politiques
FIAPS	Fédération Internationale des Associations de Professeurs de Sciences = ICASE
FIAR	Vereniging van Fabrikanten, Importeurs en Agenten op Electronicagebied
FIARBC	Federal Interagency River Basin Committee (U.S.A.)
FIARO	Federazione Italiana Associazioni Regionali Ospedaliere
FIARVEP	Federazione Italiana Agenti Rappresentanti Viaggiatori e Piazzisti
FIAS	Federación Interamericana de Asociaciones de Secretarias
FIAS	Fédération Internationale Amateur de Sambo = IASF
FIAS	Flinders Institute for Atomic Studies (Australia)
FIAS	Foreign Investment Advisory Service (MIGA)
FIAS	Formation Internationale Aéronautique et Spatiale
FIASA	Financiera Industrial y Agropecuária (Guatemala)
FIASE	Fondo Interamericano Asistencia Situaciones Emergencia
FIAT	Fabbrica Italiana Automobile Torino
FIAT	Fédération Internationale des Archives du Télévision = IFTA
FIAT	Fédération Internationale des Associations de Thanatopraxie = IFAT
FIAT	Field Information Agency, Technical (U.S.A.)
FIAT	Forest Industries Association of Tasmania
FIATA	Fédération Internationale des Associations de Transitaires et Assimilés
FIATC	Fédération Internationale des Associations Touristiques de Cheminots
FIATÉ	Fédération Internationale des Associations de Travailleurs Évangéliques
FIAV	Fédération Internationale des Artistes de Variétés = IFVA

FIAV	Fédération Internationale des Associations de Veuves et Veufs = IFWWO
FIAV	Fédération Internationale des Associations Vexillologiques
FIAVET	Federazione Italiana dello Associazioni degli Uffici Viaggio e Turismo
FIB	Fachgruppe für Industrielles Bauen (Switzerland)
FIB	Fédération des Industries Belges
FIB	Fédération Française de l'Industrie du Béton
FIB	Fédération Internationale de Boules
FIB	Federazione Italiana Bancari
FIB	Félag Islanskra Bifreiðæigenda
FIBA	Banque Française Intercontinentale
FIBA	Fédération Internationale de Basketball = IBF
FIBA	Federation of Irish Bee-keepers' Associations
FIBA	Federazione Italiana Bancari e Assicuratori
FIBAFIN	Federación Iberoamericana de Asociaciones Financieras (Chile)
FIBCA	Flexible Intermediate Bulk Container Association
FIBEP	Fédération Internationale des Bureaux d'Extraits de Presse
FIBEPA	Fachverband für Imprägnierte und Beschichtete Papiere
FIBKA	Federation of Irish Beekeepers' Association
FIBMA	National Federation of Ironmongers and Builders Merchants Staff Associations
FIBO	Federation of Independent British Optometrists
FIBP	Federazione Italiana delle Biblioteche Popolari
FIBR	Fujian Institute of Building Research
FIBT	Fédération Internationale de Bobsleigh et de Tobogganing
FIBTP	Fédération Internationale du Bâtiment et des Travaux Publics
FIBV	Fédération Internationale des Bourses de Valeurs = IFSE
FIBWA	Free Inter-Branch Workers Association (Russia)
FIC	Congregatio Fratrum Immaculatae Conceptionis (Belgium)
FIC	Fédération de l'Industrie Cimentière (Belgium)

FIC	Fédération des Instituteurs Chrétiens (Belgium)
FIC	Fédération Internationale de Canoë = ICF, IRK
FIC	Fédération Internationale des Chronométreurs
FIC	Fédération Internationale des Entreprises de Couverture
FIC	Federazione Italiana Caccia
FIC	Federazione Italiana Cuochi
FIC	Fire Industry Council
FIC	Foundation for International Cooperation
FICA	Fédération Internationale des Cadres de l'Agriculture
FICA	Fédération Internationale des Cheminots Antialcooliques = IEAV, IRTU
FICA	Fédération Internationale des Coopératives d'Assurances = FISC, ICIF, IGVF
FICA	Forest Industries Campaign Association
FICA	Formula 1 Constructors Association
FICAC	Fédération Internationale des Corps et Associations Consulaires (Denmark)
FICB	Federal Intermediate Credit Bank (U.S.A.)
FICB	Fédération des Industries Chimiques de Belgique
FICC	Fédération des Industries Complémentaires de la Construction
FICC	Fédération Internationale de Camping et de Caravanning = IFCC
FICC	Fédération Internationale de Chimie Clinique = IFCC
FICC	Fédération Internationale de Choeurs d'Enfants
FICCI	Federation of the Indian Chambers of Commerce and Industry
FICCIA	Fédération Internationale des Cadres de la Chimie et des Industries Annexes
FICE	Fédération Internationale des Choeurs d'Enfants (U.S.A.)
FICE	Fédération Internationale des Communautés d'Enfants = IFCC
FICÉ	Fédération Internationale des Communautés Éducatives
FICEMÉA	Fédération Internationale des Centres d'Entraînement aux Méthodes d'Éducation Active
FICENSA	Financiera Centroamericana, S.A. (Honduras)

FICEPA	Federación Tecnica Iberoamericana de la Celulosa y el Papal (Brazil)	**FIDA**	Falkland Islands Development Agency
FICÉPS	Fédération Internationale Catholique d'Éducation Physique et Sportive = CIFPSE	**FIDA**	Federación Internacional de Abogadas = IFWL
FICF	Fédération des Industries Condimentaires	**FIDA**	Federal Industrial Development Authority (Malaysia)
FICF	Fédération Internationale Culturelle Féminine = WICF	**FIDA**	Federation of Industrial Development Associations
FICI	Federation of Irish Chemical Industries	**FIDA**	Federazione Italiana Dettaglianti dell'Alimentazione
FICICA	Fédération Internationale du Personnel d'Encadrement des Industries et Commerces Agricoles et Alimentaires	**FIDA**	Fondo Internacional Desarrollo Agrícola (ONU) = IFAD
FICM	Fédération Internationale des Clubs de Motorhomes	**FIDA**	Nederlandse Vereniging van Fabrikanten, Importeurs en Detaillisten van Audiologische Apparatuur
FICME	Fédération Internationale des Cadres des Mines et de l'Énergie	**FIDACA**	Fédération Internationale des Associations Catholiques pour les Aveugles
FICOB	Fédération des Industries et du Commerce des Équipements de Bureau et d'Informatique	**FIDAE**	Federazione Istituti Dipendenti della Autorité Ecclesiastica
FICOM-J	Fédération Internationale des Organismes Missionnaires de Jeunes	**FIDAE**	Federazione Italiana Dipendenti Aziende Elettriche
FICP	Fédération Internationale du Cyclisme Professionnel	**FIDAF**	Federación Internacional de Asociaciones de Ferreteros y Almacenistas de Hierros = FIDAQ, IFIA, IVE
FICP	Institutum Fratum Instructionis Christianae de Ploërmel	**FIDAF**	Fédération Internationale Action Familiale = IFFLP
FICPI	Fédération Internationale des Conseils en Propriété Industrielle	**FIDAF**	Federazione Italiana Dottori in Agraria e Forestali
FICPM	Fédération Internationale des Centres de Préparation au Mariage	**FIDAL**	Federación Interamericana del Algodón (Mexico)
FICS	Fédération Internationale de Chiropratique Sportive (U.S.A.)= IFSC	**FIDAL**	Federation of Italian Amateur Athletics
FICS	Fédération Internationale des Chasseurs de Son	**FIDAP**	Federación Interamericana de Administración de Personal
FICSA	Federation of International Civil Servants Associations	**FIDAP**	Federazione Italiana dell Aziende di Pulimento
FICT	Fédération Internationale de Centres Touristiques = IFTC	**FIDAPA**	Federazione Italiana Donne Arti Professioni Affari
FICT	Fédération Internationale des Cadres des Transports	**FIDAQ**	Fédération Internationale des Associations de Quincailliers et de Fer = FIDAF, IFIA, IVE
FICTS	Fédération Internationale du Cinéma et de la Télévision Sportifs (Tunisia)	**FIDAS**	Fondation Internationale d'Art Sacré
FICU	Fonds International pour Coopération Universitaire	**FIDASE**	Falkland Islands and Dependencies Aerial Survey Expedition
FICUR	Fédération Interprofessionnelle de la Congélation Ultrarapide	**FIDAT**	Federazione Italiana Dependenti Aziende Telecomunicazioni
FID	Fédération Internationale d'Information et de Documentation = IFD	**FIDC**	Falkland Islands Development Corporation
FID	Fédération Internationale du Diabète = IDF	**FIDCA**	Fédération Internationale des Cadres de l'Agriculture
FID	Frente de Izquierda Dominicano	**FIDCLA**	Latin American Commission (FID)

FIDE	Federación de Colegios Católicos (Chile)	**FIDO**	Frazer Island Defenders Organisation
FIDE	Fédération de l'Industrie Dentaire en Europe	**FIDOF**	Fédération Internationale des Organisateurs de Festivals
FIDÉ	Fédération Internationale des Échecs = FIE	**FIDOM**	Fonds d'Investissement et de Développement Économique des Départements d'Outre-Mer
FIDE	Fédération Internationale pour le Droit Européen	**FIDONET**	International FidoNet Association = IFNA
FIDE	Fundación de Investigacion para el Desarrollo (Argentina)	**FIDOR**	Fibre Building Board Development Organization
FIDE	Fundación para la Investigacion y Desarrollo Empresarial (Honduras)	**FIDS**	Falkland Islands Dependencies Survey
FIDEA	Federación Interamericana de Educación de Adultos = IFAE	**FIDUBEL**	Union des Filatures Belges de Fibres Dures
FIDECO	Fishing Development Company (Seychelles)	**FIE**	Fédération Internationale d'Escrime
FIDEL	Frente Izquierda de Liberación (Uruguay)	**FIÉ**	Fédération Internationale des Échecs = FIDE
FIDÉLF	Fédération Internationale d'Écrivains de Langue Française	**FIEA**	Fédération Internationale des Experts en Automobile
FIDÉPS	Fonds International pour le Développement de l'Éducation Physique et du Sport = IFDPES	**FIEALC**	Federación Internacional de Estudios sobre America Latina y el Caribe
FIDES	Federación Interamericana de Empresos de Seguros	**FIEB**	Fédération des Industries des Eaux de Boisson
FIDÉS	Fonds d'Investissement pour le Développement Économique et Sociale de la France d'Outre-Mer (ONU)	**FIEB**	Fédération Royale de l'Industrie des Eaux des Boissons Raffraîchissants (Belgium) = VIWF
FIDES	Fonds International de Développement	**FIÉC**	Fédération Internationale des Associations d'Études Classiques = IFSCS
FIDES	Frente Intersecretarial para la Defensa del Empleo y el Salario (Mexico)	**FIEC**	Fédération Internationale Européenne de la Construction
FIDESZ	League of Young Democrats (Hungary)	**FIEC**	Fellowship of Independent Evangelical Churches (U.S.A.)
FIDETO	Fideicomiso para el Turismo Obrero (Mexico)	**FIEDA**	Fondation Internationale pour l'Enseignement du Droit des Affaires
FIDH	Fédération Internationale des Droits de l'Homme = IFHR	**FIEDC**	Faculté Internationale pour l'Enseignement de Droit Comparé
FIDI	Fédération Internationale des Déménageurs Internationaux = IFIFR	**FIEDO**	Federazione Italiana Exercizi Dettaglianti Ortofrutticoli
FIDIA	Fédération Internationale des Intellectuels Aveugles	**FIÉÉ**	Fédération des Industries Électriques et Électroniques
FIDIC	Fédération Internationale des Industries du Cinema de Film Etroit	**FIEEA**	Fédération Internationale pour les Echanges Educatifs d'Enfants et d'Adolescents = IFECYE, IVAB
FIDIC	Fédération Internationale des Ingénieurs-Conseils = IFCE	**FIÉF**	Fédération Internationale pour l'Économie Familiale = IFHE, IVHW
FIDJC	Fédération Internationale des Directeurs de Journaux Catholiques	**FIEG**	Federazione Italiani Editori Giornali
FIDO	Film Industry Defence Organisation	**FIEGA**	Fédération Internationale d'Eutonie Gerda Alexander = IGAEF
FIDO	Fondation Internationale pour le Développement, l'Organisation et l'Éducation Permanente	**FIEHAN**	Vereniging Fabrikanten en Importeurs van Elektrische Huishoudelijke Apparaten in Nederland
FIDO	Forklift Independent Distributors Organisation		

FIÉJ	Fédération Internationale des Éditeurs de Journaux
FIEL	Fundación de Investigaciones Económicas Latinoamericanas (Argentina)
FIELD	Foundation for International Environmental Law and Development
FIEM	Fédération Internationale de l'Encadrement des Industries Métallurgiques
FIEM	Fédération Internationale de l'Enseignement Ménager
FIEM	Fonds International d'Entr'aide Musicale = MIMAF
FIEN	Forum Italiano dell'Energia Nucleare
FIEO	Federation of Indian Export Organizations
FIÉP	Fédération Internationale d'Éducation Physique
FIÉP	Fédération Internationale des Étudiants en Pharmacie
FIEP	Fédération Internationale pour l'Éducation des Parents et d'Éducateurs = IFPE
FIER	Fédération Internationale des Enseignants de Rythmique
FIERGS	Federação das Industrias do Estado do Rio Grande do Sul (Brazil)
FIERP	Federazione Italiana Esperti Relazioni Pubbliche
FIES	Federazione Italiana Esercizi Spirituali
FIESCA	Federation of Institutions of Engineers of South and Central Asia
Fiesp	Federação das Indústrias do Estado de São Paulo (Brazil)
FIÉSP	Fédération Internationale des Étudiants en Sciences Politiques = IFSPS
FIET	Facultad de Ingenieria Electronica y Telecommunicaciones (Colombia)
FIET	Fédération Internationale des Employés, Techniciens et Cadres
FIÉV	Fédération des Industries des Équipements pour Véhicles
FIF	Félag Islenzkra Ferdaskrifstofa
FIF	Félag Islenzkra Flugumferdarstjora
FiF	Forward in Faith
FIFA	Fédération Internationale de Football Association
FIFA	Fédération Internationale du Film d'Art

FIFAPA	Fondo de Inversiones Financieras para Aguas Potables y Alcantarillado (Mexico)
FIFARMA	Federación Latinoamericana de la Industria Farmaceutica (Argentina)
FIFAS	Fédération Françaises des Industries des Sports et des Loisirs
FIFCH	Federación Industrial Ferroviaria de Chile
FIFCJ	Fédération Internationale des Femmes des Carrières Juridiques = IFWLC
FIFCLC	Fédération Internationale de Femmes de Carrières Libérales et Commerciales = FIMNP, IFBPW
FIFDU	Fédération Internationale des Femmes Diplômées des Universités = FIMU, IFUW
FIFE	Fédération Internationale des Associations de Fabricants de Produits d'Entretien
FIFe	Fédération Internationale Féline
FIFS	Federation of Irish Film Societies
FIFSP	Fédération Internationale des Fonctionnaires Supérieurs de Police = IFSPO
FIFTA	Federazione Italiana Facchini Transportatori ed Ausiliari
FIG	Fédération Internationale de Gymnastique = IGF, ITB
FIG	Fédération Internationale des Géomètres = IFS
FIG	Fraud Investigation Group
FIGA	Food Institute of Greater Arizona
FIGA	Fretted Instrument Guild of America
FIGADI	Financière Gabonais de Développement Immobilier
FIGAPE	Fondo de Financiamiento y Garantía para la Pequeña Empresa (El Salvador)
FIGAS	Chambre Syndicale des Fabricants, Importateurs et Grossistes en Articles de Sports
FIGAWA	Technische Vereinigung der Firmen im Gas- und Wasserfach
FIGAZ	Fédération de l'Industrie du Gaz (Belgium)
FIGIEFA	Fédération Internationale des Grossistes et Importateurs et Exportateurs en Fournitures Automobiles
FIGIJ	Fédération Internationale de Gynécologie Infantile et Juvénile = IFIJG

FIGISC	Federazione Italiana Gestori Impianti Stradali Carburanti
FIGL	Fédération Internationale de Gymnastique Ling
FIGO	Bond van Fabrikanten en Importeurs van en Groothandelaren in Gas- en Oliebranders
FIGO	Fédération Internationale de Gynécologie et d'Obstétrique = IFGO
FIGSA	Financiera Guatemalteca
FIH	Fédération Internationale de Handball = IHF
FIH	Fédération Internationale de Hockey = IHF
FIH	Fédération Internationale des Hôpitaux = IHF, IKV
FIH	Fédération Interntionale Hôtellière
FIHBJO	Fédération Internationale des Horlogers, Bijoutiers, Joailliers, Orfèvres, Détaillants des États Membres de la CEE
FIHC	Fédération Internationale des Hommes Catholiques = ICCM
FIHMPS	Fédération Internationale d'Hygiène de Médecine Préventive et Sociale = IFHPSM
FIHP	Federazione Italiana Hockey e Pattinaggio
FIHPA	Forum International de l'Hôtellerie de Plein Air
FIHUAT	Fédération Internationale pour l'Habitation, l'Urbanisme et l'Aménagement des Territoires = FIVU, IFHP, IVWSR
FII	Fachgruppe der Ingenieure der Industrie (Switzerland) = GII
FII	FAO Fishery Industries Division
FII	Federation of Irish Industries
FII	Felag Islenzkra Idnrekenda
FIIC	Federación Interamericana de la Industria de la Construcción = IAFCI
FIICPI	Fédération Internationale Ingénieurs-Conseils en Propriété Industrielle
FIIDOT	Fédération Internationale pour l'Information sur le Don d'Organes et de Tissus Humains
FIIEE	Federación Internacional de Instituciones para la Enseñanza del Español
FIIG	Fédération des Institutions Internationales Semi-Officielles et Privées Établies à Genève
FIIG	Fédération Internationale des Industries Graphiques = IFGI
FIIH	Fédération Internationale d'Ingénierie Hospitalière = IFHE
FIIM	Fédération Internationale de l'Industrie du Médicament = IFPMA
FIIM	Fédération Internationale des Ingénieurs Municipaux = IFME
FIINSEI	Federazione Italiana Institute Non Statale di Educazione ed IstruzioneI
FIIP	Fédération Internationale de l'Industrie Phonographique
FIIR	Federal Institute of Industrial Research (Nigeria)
FIIRO	Federal Institute of Industrial Research Oshodi (Nigeria)
FIIS	Fondation Internationale de l'Innovation Sociale = IFSI
FIJ	Fédération Internationale de Judo = IJF
FIJ	Fédération Internationale des Journalistes = FIP, IFL, IJF
FIJ	Fédération Internationale du Jazz = IJF
FIJA	Fédération Internationale des Journalistes Agricoles = IFAJ
FIJC	Fédération Internationale Jeunes Coopérateurs
FIJÉT	Fédération Internationale des Journalistes et Écrivains du Tourisme = IFTJW
FIJL	Fédération Internationale des Journalistes Libres = IFFJ
FIJLR	Fédération Internationale des Jeunesses Libérales et Radicales = IFLRY
FIJM	Fédération Internationale des Jeunesses Musicales
FIJU	Fédération Internationale des Producteurs de Jus de Fruits = FIJUG, IFJU
FIJUG	Federación Internacional de Productores de Jugos de Frutas = FIJU, IFJU
FIKIN	Foire Internationale de Kinshasa (Zaïre)
FIL	Fédération des Industriels Luxembourgeois
FIL	Fédération Internationale de Laiterie = IDF, IMV
FIL	Fédération Internationale de Luge de Course
FIL	Fédération Internationale des Librairies = IBF, IBV
FIL	Feira Internacional de Lisbõa

FIL	Félag Íslenskra Leikara (Iceland)
FIL	Félag Íslenskra Leikskókakennara (Iceland)
FIL	Fondation International pour la Liberté = IFF
FILA	Fédération Internationale de Lutte Amateur = IAWF
FILA	Federation of Indian Library Associations
FILA	Föreningen Importörer av Lantbruksmaskiner
FILB	Fédération des Industries Lourdes du Bois
FILCA	Federazione Italiana Lavoratori delle Costruzioni e Affini
FILCAMS	Federazione Italiana Lavoratori Commercio, Albergo, Mensa e Servizi
FILCOTEX	Société Industrielle de Filature, Confection et Textiles (Ivory Coast)
FILDIR	Fédération Internationale Libre des Déportés et Internes de la Résistance
FILE	Federazione Italiana Lavatore Essatoriale
FILET	Federazione Italiana Libere Emittenti Teleradio
FILFP	Forum International de Liaison des Forces de Paix = ILF
FILIS	Federazione Italiana Lavatori Informazione Spettacolo
FILISBÉL	Syndicat Belge des Canalisations Électriques
FILK	Forschungsinstitut für Leder- und Kunstledertechnologie
FILLEA	Federazione Italiana Lavoratori del Legno, Edili ed Affini
FILLM	Fédération Internationale des Langues et Littératures Modernes = IFMLL
FILM	Federazione Italiana Lavoratori del Mare
FILM	Irish Film Institute
FILT	Fédération Internationale de Lawn Tennis = ILTF
FILTA	Federazione Italiana dei Lavoratori Tessili e Abbigliamento
FILTAT	Federazione Italiana Lavoratori Trasporti e Ausiliari del Traffico
FILTEA	Federazione Italiana Lavoratori Tessili e Abbigliamento, Calzaturieri
FILTISAC	Filatures, Tissages, Sacs Côte d'Ivoire S.A.
FIM	Fairness in Media (U.S.A.)
FIM	Fédération Internationale des Musiciens
FIM	Fédération Internationale Mineurs = IBV, MIF
FIM	Fédération Internationale Motocycliste
FIM	Federazione Italiana Metalmeccanici
FIM	Finnish Institute of Management
FIMA	Federazione Italiana Mercanti d'Arte
FIMA	Feria Técnica Internacional de la Maquinaria Agricola
FIMA	Fischwirtschaftliches Marketing-Institut
FIMA	Food Industries of Malaysia
FIMAA	Federazione Italiana Mediatori e Agenti di Affari
FIMAIA	Fondo para la Creacion y Fomento de Centrales de Maquinaria y Equipo Agrícola de la Industria Azucarera (Mexico)
FIMARC	Fédération Internationale des Mouvements d'Adultes Ruraux Catholiques
FIMBRA	Financial Intermediaries, Managers and Brokers Regulatory Association
FIMC	Fédération Internationale de la Musique Chorale = IFCM
FIMCAP	Fédération Internationale des Communautés de Jeunesse Catholique Paroissiales
FIME	Fédération Internationale des Maisons de l'Europe = IFEH
FIME	Fédération Internationale Musique Espérance
FIMÉM	Fédération Internationale des Mouvements d'École Moderne
FIMFR	Federación Internacional de Medicina Fisica y Rehabilitación
FIMIGCEE	Fédération de l'Industrie Marbrière et del'Industrie Granitière de la Communauté Économique Européenne
FIMITIC	Fédération Internationale des Mutilés et Invalides du Travail et des Invalides Civils
FIMK	Fédération Internationale des Masseurs-Kinésithérapiques Practiciens et Physiothérapie
FIMM	Fédération des Importeurs de la Métallurgie et de la Mécanique
FIMM	Fédération Internationale de Médecine Manuelle
FIMNP	Federación Internacional de Mujeres de Negocios y Profesionales = FIFCLC, IFBPW

FIMOP	Chambre Syndicale Belge des Fabricants et Importateurs de Matériel de Transmission Oléo-Hydraulique et Pneumatique
FIMPR	Fédération Internationale de Médecine Physique et Réadaptation = FIMFR, IFPMR
FIMS	Fédération Internationale Médecine Sportive = IFSM
FIMTM	Fédération des Industries Mécaniques et Transformatrices des Métaux
FIMU	Federación Internacional de Mujeres Universitarias = FIFDU, IFUW
FIMU	Free and Independent Miners' Union (Albania) = SLPM
FIN	Fédération des Industries Nautiques
FIN	Food Irradiation Network = FINI
FIN	Futures Information Network (U.S.A.)
FIN-AFRICA	Centre for Financial Assistance to African Countries
FIN-SOCIAL	Fundo De Investimento Social (Brazil)
FINA	Fédération Internationale de Natation Amateur = IASF
FINANDES	Financiera Andina S.A. (Ecuador)
FINANSA	Financiera Nacional S.A. (Ecuador)
FINANSUR	Financiera del Sur (Ecuador)
FINASA	Financiera Nacional Azucarera (Mexico)
FINAT	Fédération Internationale des Fabricants et Transformateurs d'Adhésifs et Thermo-Collants sur Papiers et autres Supports
FINATA	Fédération Internationale des Associations de Transporteurs et Assimilés
FINATA	Financiera Nacional de Tierras Agrícolas (El Salvador)
FINAVI	Financiera Nacional de la Vivienda (Honduras)
Finbiotec	Finanzia per lo Sviluppo delle Biotecnologie
FINCEC	Fédération des Syndicats de Cadres et Agents de Maîtrise de l'Importation et du Négoce des Combustibles et de l'Exploitation de Chauffage
FINCO	Finance Corporation of the Bahamas
FINDECO	State Finance and Development Corporation (Zambia)
FINÉBEL	Entente Économique Franco-Italo-Néerlandaise-Belgo-Luxembourgeoise
FINEFTA	Finland – European Free Trade Association
FINEP	Financiadora de Estudos e Projetos (Brazil)
FINI	Food Irradiation Network International = FIN
FINIWAX	Société de Finition de Tissue Wax (Central Africa)
FINN-BOARD	Finnish Board Mills Association
FINN-BROKER	Finlands Skeppsmäklareförbund
FINN-METAL	Suomen Metalliteollisuusyhdstys
FINNCELL	Finska Cellulosaföreningen
FINNIDA	Department for International Cooperation (Finland)
FINNIDA	Finnish International Development Agency
FINNPAP	Finnish Paper Mills' Association
FINPRO	Finnish Committee on Trade Procedures
FINRRAGE	Feminist International Network of Resistance to Reproductive and Genetic Engineering
FINS	Fishing Industry News Service (Australia)
FINSIDER	Società Finanziaria Siderurgica
FINUL	Force Intérimaire des Nations Unies du Liban = FPNUL, UNIFIL
FINUMA	Fabrique Ivoirienne de Nuoc Mam
FIO	Fédération Internationale d'Oléiculture
FIO	Food Investigation Organisation
FIO	Fujian Institute of Oceanology
FIOCÉS	Fédération Internationale des Organisations de Correspondances et d'Échanges Scolaires
FIODS	Fédération Internationale des Organisations de Donneurs de Sang Bénévoles = IFBDO
FIOH	Future in Our Hands
FIOM	Fédération Internationale des Organisations des Travailleurs de la Métallurgie = FISM, FITIM, IMB, IMF
FIOM	Federazione Italiane Operai Metallurgici
FIOPI	Federação Interamericana de Organizações des Profissionais da Imprensa = FIOPP
FIOPM	Fédération Internationale des Organismes de Psychologie Médicale = IFPMO, IVPMO

FIOPP   Federación Interamericana de Organizaciones de Periodistas Profesionales = FIOPI

FIOSS   Fédération Internationale des Organisations des Sciences Sociales = IFSSO

FIOST   Fédération Internationale des Organisations Syndicales du Personnel des Transports = IFTUTW

FIOT   Fédération Internationale des Oeuvriers du Transport = ITF

FIP   Federación Internacional de Periodistas = FIJ, IFJ, IJF

FIP   Fédération Internationale de la Précontrainte

FIP   Fédération Internationale de Philatélie = IPF

FIP   Fédération Internationale de Phonothèques

FIP   Fédération Internationale de Podologie

FIP   Fédération Internationale des Piétons = IFP

FIP   Fédération Internationale Pharmaceutique = IPF

FIP   Fédérations Internationales Professionnelles = ITF

FIP   Federazione Italiana della Pubblicità

FIP   Félag Islenzkra Prentidnadarins

FIP   Forum Inżynierów Polskich

FIP   Fundusz Inicjatyw Prasowych "Solidarność"

FIPA   Fédération Internationale des Producteurs Agricoles = IFAP

FIPA   Fédération Internationale des Professionnels de l'Assistance

FIPA   Federation of International Poetry Associations

FIPA   Federazione Italiana Periti Agrari

FIPA   Federazione Italiana Portieri Albergo "Le Chiavi d'Oro"

FIPAD   Fondation Internationale pour un Autre Développement = IFDA

FIPAGO   Fédération Internationale des Fabricants de Papiers Gommés

FIPC   Fédération Internationale des Pharmaciens Catholiques = IFCP

FIPC   Fonds International pour la Promotion de la Culture

FIPCO   Fédération Internationale pour la Philatélie Constructive

FIPDU   Fédération Internationale des Femmes Diplômées des Universités

FIPÉ   Fédération Internationale des Associations de la Presse d'Église

FIPE   Federazione Italiana Pubblici Esercizi

Fipe   Fundação Instítuto de Pesquisas Económicas (USP) (Brazil)

FIPEC   Fédération des Industries des Peintures, Vernis et Couleurs

FIPEC   Fundo Incentivo Pesquisa Technico Cientifico (Brazil)

FIPESO   Fédération Internationale des Professeurs de l'Enseignement Secondaire Officiel = IFST

FIPET   Federación Interamericana de Periodistas y Escritores de Turismo

FIPF   Fédération Internationale des Professeurs de Français = IFTF

FIPFI   Fédération Internationale des Producteurs de Films Indépendants = IFPIA

FIPG   Fédération de l'Industrie du Petit Granit

FIPGE   Fondation Internationale de Genève pour la Promotion de l'Entreprise = FEIG, IEFG

FIPIF   Finnish Plastics Industry Federation

FIPJP   Fédération Internationale de Petanque et Jeu Provençal

FIPLV   Fédération Internationale des Professeurs de Langues Vivantes = WFFLTA

FIPM   Fédération Internationale de Psychothérapie Médicale = IFMP, IGAP

FIPMEC   Fédération Internationale des Petites et Moyennes Entreprises Commerciales = IFSMC, IVKMH

FIPMI   Fédération Internationale des Petites et Moyennes Entreprises Industrielles = IFSMI, IVKMI

FIPO   Fédération Internationale de Philatélie Olympique

FIPOI   Fondation des Immeubles pour les Organisations Internationales

FIPOL   Fonds International d'Indemnisation pour les Dommages Dus à la Pollution par les Hydrocarbures = IOCF, IOPC Fund

FIPP   Fédération Internationale de la Presse Périodique

FIPP   Fédération Internationale Pénale et Pénitentiare = IPPF

FIPREGA	Fédération Internationale de la Presse Gastronomique, Vinicole et Touristique = FISGV, IFGVP, IVGWP
FIPRESCI	Fédération Internationale de la Presse Cinématographique = IFCP
FIPS	FAO Fisheries Statistics Unit
FIPS	Fédération Internationale de la Presse du Sport
FIPTP	Fédération Internationale de la Presse Technique et Périodique
FIPV	Federación Internacional de Pelota Vasca
FIQ	Fédération Internationale des Quilleurs
FIR	Fédération Internationale des Résistants
FIR	Fédération Internationale Routière
FIR	Federation of Irish Renderers (Éire)
FIR	Forschungsinstitut für Rationalisierung (Germany)
FIRA	Fédération Internationale de Rugby Amateur = IARF
FIRA	Fideicomisos Instituídos en Relación con la Agricultura (Mexico)
FIRA	Foreign Investment Review Agency (Canada) = AEIE
FIRA	Furniture Industry Research Association
FIRAD	Federazione Italiana Religiose di Apostolato Diretto
FIRAS	Federazione Italiana Religiose Assistenti Sociali
FIRC	Fishing Industry Research Council
FIRDC	Fishing Industry Research and Development Council
FIRE	Federazione Italiana Religiose Educatrici
FIRE	Feminist International Radio Endeavour (Costa Rica)
FIREC	Fédération Internationale des Rédacteurs en Chef
FIRHF	Fédération Internationale pour la Recherche de l'Histoire des Femmes (Norway) = IFRWH
FIRI	Fishing Industry Research Institute (South Africa)
FIRI	Food Industry Research Institute (China)
FIRILITE	Federation of International Research Institutes on Law and Information Technology in Europe
FIRM	Fédération Internationale des Reconstructeurs de Moteurs
FIRMS	Fonds d'Intervention et de Régularisation du Marché du Sucre
FIRN	Foreningen af Importorer af Raavarer til Naeringsmiddelindustrien (Denmark)
FIRP	Federazione Italiana Relazioni Pubbliche
FIRS	Fédération Internationale de Roller-Skating
FIRS	Fonds d'Intervention et de Regularisation du Marché du Sucre (CE)
FIRSM	Fujian Research Institute of the Structure of Matter
FIRST	Forum of Incident Response and Security Teams
FIRT	Fédération Internationale pour la Recherche Théâtrale = IFTR
FIRT	Fertilizer Industry Round Table (U.S.A.)
FIRTO	Fire Insurers Research and Testing Organisation
FIS	Federación Internacional de Softbol = ISF
FIS	Fédération Internationale de Sauvetage Aquatique = ILSF
FIS	Fédération Internationale de Ski
FIS	Fédération Internationale des Centres Sociaux et Communautaires = IFSNC
FIS	Fédération Internationale des Settlements
FIS	Fédération Internationale du Commerce des Semences = IFST
FIS	Federation of Irish Societies
FIS	Federazione Informazione Spettacolo
FIS	Federazione Italiana della Strada
FIS	Federzione Italiana Sementi
FIS	Félag Islenskra Stórkaupmanna
FIS	Fellowship of Independent Schools
FIS	Fondation Internationale pour la Science (UNESCO) = IFS
FIS	Fonds d'Intervention Sidérurgique
FIS	Foundation for International Studies (Malta)
FIS	Front Islamique du Salut (Algeria)
FISA	Federación Independiente de Sindicatos Agrarios
FISA	Fédération Internationale des Sociétés Aérophilatéliques
FISA	Fédération Internationale des Sociétés d'Aviron = IRF
FISA	Fédération Internationale du Sport Automobile

FISA	Federation of Insurance Staffs Associations
FISA	Feria Internacional de Santiago (Chile)
FISA	Fianakaviana Sambatra (Madagascar)
FISA	Financiera Industrial S.A. (Guatemala)
FISA	Footwear Institute of South Africa
FISAC	Federazione Nazionale Assicuratori
FISAE	Fédération Internationale des Sociétés d'Amateurs Exlibris
FISAM	Federazione Italiana delle Scienze e delle Attività Motorie
FISAP	Federazione Italiana Sindacti Artisti Professionisti
FISAR	Federal Institute for Snow and Avalanche Research (U.S.A.)
FISB	Fédération Internationale de Ski-bob
FISB	Fujian Institute of Subtropical Botany
FISBA	Federazione Italiana Salariati Braccianti Agricoli e Maestranze Specializzate
FISC	Federación Internacional de Seguros Cooperatives = FICA, ICIF, IGVF
FISC	Fédération Internationale des Chasseurs du Son
FISC	Federation of Information Systems Centres (*ex* FMS)
FISC	Foundation for International Scientific Coordination
FISC	Fund for International Student Cooperation
FISCC	Fruit Industry Sugar Concession Committee (Australia)
FISCIT	Foundation for International Exchange of Scientific and Cultural Information by Telecommunications (U.S.A.)
FISCOBB	Fédération Internationale des Syndicats Chrétiens d'Ouvriers du Bâtiment et du Bois = IFCTUBWW
FISD	Fédération Internationale de Sténographie et de Dactylographie = IFKM, IFST, INTERSTENO
FISÉ	Fédération Internationale des Sociétés d'Électroencéphalographie
FISE	Fédération Internationale Syndicate de l'Enseignement
FISE	Fonds International de Secours à l'Enfance (UN) = UNICEF
FISEC	Fédération Internationale Sportive de l'Enseignement Catholique (OE)= IFSCE
FISÉM	Fédération Internationale des Sociétés d'Écrivains Médecins
FISF	Fédération Internationale de Scrabble Francophone
FISF	Fédération Internationale des Société de Fertilité
FISGV	Federazione Internazionale della Stampa Gastronomica e Vinicola = FIPREGA, IFGVP, IVGWP
FISH	Forskningsinstituted vid Svensk Handleshogskolan
FISIÉR	Fédération Internationale des Sociétés et Instituts pour l'Étude de la Renaissance = IFSISR
FISITA	Fédération Internationale des Sociétés d'Ingénieurs des Techniques de l'Automobile
FISM	Fédération Internationale des Sociétés Magiques = IFMS
FISM	Federazione Internationale dei Sindicati Metalmeccani = FIOM, FITIM, IMB, IMF
FISMA	Federazione Italiana Strumenti Musicali ed Accessori
FISNAL	Federazione Italiana Sindacati Nazionali Assicuratori Lavoratori
FISOS	Federazione Italiana Sindicati Ospedalieri
FISP	Fédération Internationale des Sociétés de Philosophie = IFPS
FISP	Fédération Internationale des Sports Populaires = IFPS, IVV
FISPIU	Federazione Italiana Servizi Pubblici Igiene Urbana
FISPT	Fédération Internationale Sport Pour Tout
FISS	Fédération Internationale de Sauvetage et de Secourisme
FISS	Fédération Internationale des Sociétés Scientifiques
FIST	Fédération de l'Industrie Suisse du Tabac
FIST	Federazione Italiana Sindicati dei Trasporti
FISTAV	Fédération Internationale des Syndicats des Travailleurs de l'Audio-Visuel = IFAVWU, IFTUAVW
FISTED	Fondation Islamique pour la Science, la Technologie et le Développement (OIC) = IFSTAD
FISTH	Fédération Internationale des Syndicats du Textile et de l'Habillement = IFTUTCI

FISU	Fédération Internationale du Sport Universitaire = IUSF	**FITIM**	Federación Internacional de Trabajadores de las Industrias Metalurgicas = FIOM, FISM, IMB, IMF
FIT	Fédération Internationale de Tennis = ITF	**FITIM**	Société de Filature et de Tissage de Madagascar
FIT	Fédération Internationale de Trampoline = ITF	**FITITHC**	Fédération Internationale des Travailleurs des Industries du Textile de l'Habillement et du Cuir = ITBLAV, ITBLF, ITGLWF
FIT	Fédération Internationale des Traducteurs = IFT		
FIT	Fédération Internationale Triathlon = IFT, ITU	**FITITVC**	Federación Interamericana de Trabajadores de la Industria Textil, Vestuario, Cuero y Calzado (Mexico)
FIT	Federation of International Traders		
FIT	Federazione Italiana Tabaccai	**FITIVC**	Federación Interamericana de Trabajadores de la Industria Textil, Vestuario y Cuero (Colombia)
FIT	Federazione Italiana Trasporti		
FIT	Félag Islenzkra Tryggingastaerdfraedinga	**FITPAS**	Federación Internacional de los Trabajadores de las Plantaciones, Agricolas y Similares = FITPASC, IFPAAW, IFPLAA
FIT	Foundation for International Training for Third World Countries		
FITA	Fédération Internationale de Tir à l'Arc = IAF	**FITPASC**	Fédération Internationale des Travailleurs des Plantations, de l'Agriculture et des Secteurs Conncxes = FITPAS, IFPAAW, IFPLAA
FITA	Fédération Internationale des Techniciens Agronomes		
FITAC	Federación Interamericana de Touring y Automóvil Clubes = IFTAC	**FITPC**	Fédération Internationale des Travailleurs du Pétrole et de la Chimie = FITPQ, IFPCW, IVPC
FITAC	Film Industry Training and Apprenticeship Council		
FITAM	Fédération de l'Industrie Textile Africaine et Malagache	**FITPQ**	Federación Internacional de Trabajadores Petroleros y Químicos = FITPC, IFPCW, IVPC
FITB	Fédération de l'Industrie Textile Belge		
FITBB	Fédération Internationale des Travailleurs du Bâtiment et du Bois = FITCM, IBBH, IBTU, IFBWW	**FITS**	Fédération Internationale du Tourisme Social = ISTF
		FITT	Fédération Internationale de Tennis de Table = ITTF
FITC	Fédération Internationale du Thermalisme et du Climatisme	**FITT**	Fédération Internationale des Travailleurs de la Terre
FITC	Foundry Industry Training Committee	**FITTHC**	Fédération Internationale des Travailleurs des Industries du Textile de l'Habillement et du Cuir = ITBLAV, ITBLF, ITGLWF
FITC	Fujian Research Institute of Tropical Crops		
FITCE	Fédération des Ingénieurs des Télécommunications de la Communauté Européenne		
		FITUG	Federation of Independent Trade Unions in Guyana
FITCH	Federación Industrial Ferroviaria de Chile	**FITV**	Federación Internacional Textil, Vestido (CMT) = FITH, IFTC
FITCM	Federación Internacional de Trabajadores de la Construcción y la Madera = FITBB, IBBH, IBTU, IFBWW	**FIU**	Florida International University
		FIUC	Fédération Internationale des Universités Catholiques = IFCU
FITE	Federación Interamericana de Trabajores del Espectáculo = IFEW	**FIV**	Fédération de l'Industrie du Verre (Belgium)
FITEC	Fédération Internationale du Thermalisme et du Climatisme = IFTC	**FIV**	Fédération Internationale des Vespas Clubs (Italy)
FITH	Fédération Internationale du Textile et d'Habillement (CMT) = FIIV, IFTC	**FIV**	Fédération Internationale Vieillesse = IFA

FIV	Fondo de Inversiones de Venezuela	**FKI**	Federation of Korean Industries
FIVA	Fédération Internationale des Véhicules Anciennes	**FKI**	Förderungs für Konsumenten-Information (Switzerland)
FIVA	Federazione Italiana Venditori Ambulanti e Giornalai	**FKM**	Forschungskuratorium Maschinenbau
FIVB	Fédération Internationale de Volleyball = IVBF	**FKS**	Vereniging van Handelaren in Fourage-, Kunstmest-, Hooi-, Stro en Ruwvoeders
FIVS	Fédération des Importateurs de Vins et Spiritueux	**FKSL**	Förbundet Kristna Lärare och Seminarister
FIVS	Fédération Internationale des Vins et Spiritueux	**FKT**	Fyns Kommune Telefonselskab
FIVU	Federación Internacional de Vivienda y Urbanismo = FIHUAT, IFHP, IVWSR	**FKTG**	Fernseh- und Kinotechnische Gesellschaft
FIVZ	Fédération Internationale Vétérinaire de Zootechnie = IVFZ	**FKTU**	Federation of Korean Trade Unions
FIYTO	Federation of International Youth Travel Organisations	**FKV**	Fachgruppe der Kultur- und Vermessungsingenieure (Switzerland) = GRG
FIZ	Fachinformationszentrum	**FLA**	Federación Lanera Argentina
FJ	Filles de Jesus de Kermaria = DJ, HJ	**FLA**	Fiji Library Association
FJ	Fuerza Joven	**FLA**	Film Laboratory Association
FJA	Fédération des Journalistes Arabes = FAJ	**FLA**	Finance and Leasing Association
FJCE	Forum Jeunesse des Communautés Européennes = YFEC	**FLA**	Free Lebanese Army
		FLA	Frente de Liberação dos Açores
FJCEE	Fédération des Jeunes Chefs d'Enterprises d'Europe	**FLAA**	Federación Latino Americana de Agrimensores (Uruguay)
FJEE	Fédération des Jeunes Écologistes Européens (Belgium)	**FLAC**	Free Legal Advice Centres (Éire)
FJF	Finlands Journalistförbund	**FLACPO**	Fondo Latinoamericano de Cultura Popular (Venzuela)
FJK	Flyjournalisternas Klubb	**FLACSO**	Facultad Latinoamericana de Ciencias Sociales (Chile)
FJL	Frente Juvenil Lautaro		
FJMI	Federation of Jewellery Manufacturers of Ireland	**FLAD**	Fundação Luso-Americana para Desenvolvimento
FJN	Front Jeności Narodu	**FLAEI**	Federazione Lavoratori Aziende Elettriche Italiane
FJR	Frente Juvenil del Partido Revolucionario Institucional (Mexico)	**FLAFEET**	Federación Latinoamericana de las Feminas Ejutivas de Empresas Turisticas
FJRO	Federation of Jewish Relief Organisations	**FLAJA**	Federación Latinoamericana de Jóvenes Ambiantalistas (Colombia)
FKCBS	Frantisek Kmoch Czech Bands Society	**FLAM**	Forces de Libération Africaine de Mauritanie
FKCO	Finlands Kennel Centralorgan		
FKE	Federation of Kenya Employers	**FLAMES**	Fabrication Labour and Material Estimating Service
FKF	Finlands Kommunal-förbund	**FLAPF**	Federación Latinoamericana de Productores de Fonograms y Videograms
FKG	Foreningen af Kommunale Gasvæker		
FKGB	Independent Smallholders' Party (Hungary)	**FLAR**	Fondo Latinoamericano de Reservas = LARF
FKGP	Független Kisgazda Párt – Torgyán Frakció = ISP	**FLASA**	Fundación La Salle de Ciencias Naturales (Venezuela)
FKH	Forschungskommission für Hochspannungsfragen (Switzerland)	**FLASCA**	Federación Latinoamericana de Sociedades de Cancerologia (Venezuela)
FKI	Fachvereinigung der Deutschen Kartonagen-Industrie		

FLASOES	Federación Latinoamericana de Sociedades de Escritores (Venezuela)
FLAT-GRAPA	Federación Latinoamericana de Trabajadores Gráficos, Papelero y Afines
FLATE-VECU	Federación Latinoamericana de Trabajadores del Textil, Vestido, Calzado, Cuero y Conexos
FLATEC	Federación Latinoamericana de Trabajadores de la Educación y la Cultura (Venezuela)
FLATI	Federación Latinoamericana de Trabajadores de la Industria (Argentina)
FLATICOM	Federación Latinoamericana de Trabajadores de la Industria de la Construcción y la Madera (Venezuela)
FLATT	Federación Latinoamericana de Trabajadores del Transporte
FLB	Federal Land Bank (U.S.A)
FLBA	Family Law Bar Association
FLC	Federazione Lavatori delle Costruzioni
FLCAE	Federación Latinoamericana del Cariba de Asociaciones de Exportadores (Venezuela)
FLCAK	Family Life Counselling Association of Kenya
FLCS	Front de Libération de la Côte des Somalis (Djibouti)
FLD	Friends of the Lake District
FLDA	Federal Land Development Authority (Malaysia)
FLE	Félag Löggiltra Endurskodenda (Iceland)
FLEAA	Fédération Luxembourgeoise des Exploitants d'Autobus et d'Autocars
FLEC	Federatie van Land-en Tuinbouwwerktuigen Exploiterende Coöperatie
FLEC	Frente para a Libertação de Enclave de Cabinde (Angola)
FLECE	Federación Libre de Escuelas de Ciencias de la Empresa
FLESA	Football League Executive Staff Association
FLEURO-SELECT	European Organisation for Testing New Flowerseeds
FLEXI-FOAM	Société Africaine de Produits Plastiques (Burkina Faso)
FLF	Finlands Läkarforbund = SLL
FLGEB	Fédération des Livres Généalogiques de l'Espèce Bovine
FLGEC	Fédération des Livres Généalogiques de l'Espèce Chevaline
FLGEP	Fédération des Livres Généalogiques de l'Espèce Porcine
FLI	Fachverband der Ledererzeugenden Industrie (Austria)
FLI	Fédération Lainière Internationale = IWTO
FLIC	Federal Library and Information Center Committee (U.S.A.)
FLIC	Film Library Information Council
FLIDEPEC	Federation of Liberal and Democratic Parties in the European Community
FLING	Frente para a Libertação da Guiné Portuguesa (Guinea-Bissau)
FLKF	Finlands Landskommuners Förbund
FLM	Family Life Mission (Germany)
FLM	Fédération Luthérienne Mondiale
FLN	Frente de Liberación Nacional (Peru)
FLN	Front de la Libération Nationale (Algeria)
FLNC	Front de la Libération Nationale de la Corse
FLNKS	Front de Libération Nationale Kanake Socialiste (New Caledonia)
FLO-PETROL	Société Auxiliaire des Producteurs de Pétrole
FLOAG	Front for the Liberation of the Occupied Arabian Gulf
FLOMIC	Flow Measurement & Instrumentation Consortium
FLOPAC	Flight Operations Advisory Committee (IATA)
FLOPEC	Flota Petrolera Ecuatoriana
FLP	Fiji Labour Party
FLP	Forest Products Laboratory (U.S.A)
FLRA	Federal Labor Relations Authority (U.S.A.)
FLRFA	Federation of Land Reform Farmers Association (Philippines)
FLS	Family Life Services (Montserrat)
FLS	Fiji Library Service
FLS	Finska Läkaresällskapet
FLS	Folklore Society
FLS	Front Line African States (Zambia)
FLS	Fundación La Salle de Ciencias Natureles (Venezuela)
FLT	Fachverband Landwirtschaftlicher Trocknungswerke

FLT	Forschungsvereinigung für Luft- und Trocknungstechnik
FLTA	French Lawn Tennis Association
FLTPR	Federación Libre de los Trabajadores de Puerto Rico
FLUG	Flugfelag Islands
FLW	International Fur and Leather Workers Union of the United States and Canada
FM	Félag Menntaskólakennara
FM	Fraternité Mondiale WB
FMA	Fabrica Militar de Aviones (Argentina)
FMA	Family Mediators Association
FMA	Fan Manufacturers' Association
FMA	Fédération Mondiale des Annonceurs = WFA
FMA	Federation of Management Associations
FMA	Fertilizer Manufacturers' Association
FMA	Filiae Mariae Auxiliatricis
FMA	Fond Monétaire Arabe = AMF
FMA	Fondajo Monda Alternativo (Netherlands)
FMA	Fondo Monetario Andino
FMA	Fonds Monétaire Arabe = AMF
FMA	Football Membership Authority
FMAA	Furniture Manufacturers' Association of Australia
FMAC	Fédération Mondiale des Anciens Combattants = WVF
FMACU	Fédération Mondiale des Associations et Clubs Unesco = WFUCA
FMAEM	Federazione Nazionale Aziende Elettriche Municipalizzate
FMAM	Fédération Mondiale des Amis de Musées = WFFM
FMANU	Fédération Mondiale des Associations pour les Nations Unies = WFUNA
FMB	Fédération Genevoise des Métiers du Bâtiment
FMB	Federation of Master Builders
FMBRA	Flour Milling and Baking Research Association
FMBSA	Farmers' and Manufacturers' Beet Sugar Association (U.S.A.)
FMC	Families of Murdered Children
FMC	Fatstock Marketing Corporation
FMC	Federación de Mujeres Cubanas
FMC	Federal Maritime Commission (U.S.A.)
FMC	Federation of Microsystems Centres (*now* FISC)
FMC	Finnish Management Council
FMC	Fleuristes du Marché Commun (FEUPF)
FMC	Fujian Medical College
FMCB	Fédération Mondiale des Organisations de Construction et du Bois = FMTCM, WFBWU, WFWBI, WVBH
FMCC	Fédération Mondiale des Collections de Cultures = WFCC
FMCEC	Federation of Manufacturers of Construction Equipment and Cranes
FMCIM	Fédération Mondiale des Concours Internationaux de Musique = WFIMC
FMCP	Federation of Manufacturers of Contractors Plant
FMCU	Federación Mundial de Ciudades Unidas = FMVJ
FMD	Foreningen af Markedsanalyse-Institutter i Danmark
FMD	Friends of Medieval Dublin
FMDF	Foreningen af Medarbejdere ved Danmarks Forskningsbiblioteker
FMDIYR	Federation of Multiple DIY Retailers
FMDM	Franciscan Missionaries of the Divine Motherhood
FME	Federatie Metaal- en Electrotechnische Industrie
FME	Fédération Mondiale des Employés = WFCW
FME	Foundation for Management Education
FMEM	Federación Mundial Educación Médica = WFME
FMF	Fachverband Moderne Fremdsprachen
FMF	Fédération des Médecins de France
FMF	Food Manufacturers Federation
FMF	Forest Management Foundation
FMFA	Federal Ministry for Foreign Affairs (Austria)
FMFC	Francisco Morazan Frente Constitucional (Honduras)
FMFMCB	Fédération Nationale des Fabricants de Menuiseries, Charpentes et Bâtiments Industrialisés
FMFR	Fédération Mondiale des Femmes Rurales
FMFSGP	Fédération Mondiale des Fabricants de Spécialitiés Pharmaceutiques Grand Public = WFPMM
FMG	Food Machinery Group
FMGPL	Forum Mondial des Gaz de Pétrole Liquéfiés = WLPGF

FMGPL	Forum Mondial des GPL = WLPGF
FMH	Foederatio Medicorum Helveticorum (Switzerland)
FMHW	Federation of Mental Health Workers
FMI	Congregatio Filiorum Mariae Immaculatae
FMI	Fachverband Metallwaren- und verwandte Industrien
FMI	Fachverband Mineral-Faserindustrie
FMI	Federation of Malta Industries
FMI	Federation of Music Industries
FMI	Fondo Monetario Internacional; Fonds Monétaire Internationale = IMF, IWF
FMI	Société France Media International
FMIG	Food Manufacturers Industrial Group
FMJD	Fédération Mondiale de la Jeunesse Démocratique = WFDY
FMJD	Fédération Mondiale du Jeu de Dames = WDF
FMJLR	Fédération Mondiale des Jeunesses Libérales et Radicales = WFLRY
FMLH	Frente Morazanista de Liberación Nacional (Honduras)
FMLN	Farabundo Marti National Liberation Front
FMLN	Frente Farabundo Martí de Liberación Nacional (El Salvador)
FMM	Fédération des Chambres Syndicales des Minérais et des Métaux Non Ferreux
FMM	Fratres de Misericordia
FMM	Fundación Mundo Mujer (Colombia)
FMMA	Fratres Misericordiae Mariae Auxiliatricis
FMMB	Fédération des Chambres Syndicales des Métaux
FMMCSF	Fédération des Maisons Médicales
FMME	Fund for Multinational Management Education (U.S.A.)
FMN	Fédération Mondiale de Neurologie = WFN
FMN	Fédération Motocycliste Nationale
FMNH	Field Museum of Natural History, Chicago, USA
FMO	Federation of Manufacturing Opticians
FMO	Fédération Professionnelle Agricole pour la Main-d'Oeuvre Saisonnière
FMO	Financieringsmaatschaappij voor Ontwikkelingslanden
FMOB	Federation of Master Organ Builders
FMOI	Fédération Mondiale des Organisations d'Ingénieurs = WFEO
FMPC	Federation of Motion Picture Councils (U.S.A.)
FMPS	Federation of Modern Painters and Sculptors (U.S.A.)
FMPTE	Federation of Municipal Passenger Transport Employers
FMPVE	Fédération Mondiale de Promotion des Véhicules Electriques (Canada) = WEVA
FMRA	Fertilizer Manufacturers' Research Association (New Zealand)
FMRA	Foreign Media Representatives Association (U.S.A.)
FMRC	Financial Management Research Centre (Australia)
FMS	Fachverband der Maschinen- und Stahlbauindustrie (Austria)
FMS	Family Mediation Scotland
FMS	Fédération Mondiale des Sourds = WFD
FMS	Institutum Fratrum Maristarum a Scholis
FMSAR	Fédération Marocaine des Sociétés d'Assurances et de Réassurances
FMSC	Fédération Mondiale des Sociétés de Cuisiniers = WACS, WDK
FMSE	Federation of Medium and Small Employers
FMSI	Federazione Medicosportiva Italiano
FMSM	Fédération Mondiale pour la Santé Mentale = WFMH
FMSPA	Fish and Meat Spreadable Products Association
FMSR	Fédération des Mouvements Socialistes Régionalistes (Réunion)
FMT	Federation of Merchant Tailors
FMTA	Farm Machinery and Tractor Trade Association of New South Wales
FMTCM	Federación Mundial de Trabajadores de la Construcción y la Madere = FMCB, WFBWU, WFWBI, WVBH
FMTI	Federación Mundial de Trabajadores de la Industria; Fédération Mondiale des Travailleurs de l'Industrie = WAI, WFIW, WIB
FMTNM	Fédération Mondiale des Travailleurs Non Manuels = WFNMW
FMTS	Fédération Mondiale des Travailleurs Scientifiques = WFSW, WFW
FMV	Finommechanikai Vállalat

FMVI	Fachverband Metallwawren- und Verwandte Industrien
FMVJ	Fédération Mondiale des Villes Jumelées = FMCU
FMW	Federacja Młodzieży Walczącej
FMWB	Federation of Methodist Women in Bolivia
FMWUA	Federated Miscellaneous Workers' Union of Australia
FN	Congregatio Sacrae Familiae a Nazareth
FN	Front National (France, French Guiana, New Caledonia)
FN	Fuerza Nueva
FNA	Federation of National Associations (U.S.A.)
FNA	Federazione Nazionale Assicuratori
FNA	Finnish News Agency
FNAA	Federazione Nazionale Artigiani dell'Abbigliamento
FNAAPDAV	Fédération Nationale des Associations Agricoles pour le Développement de l'Assurance-Vie
FNAARC	Federazione Nazionale fra la Associazioni Agenti e Rappresentanti di Commercio
FNAB	Fédération Nationale des Artisans du Bâtiment et des Branches Professionnelles Annexes
FNAC	Fédération Nationale d'Achats des Cadres
FNACÉ	Fédération Nationale des Agents sous Contrat de l'État (Zaïre)
FNAD	Fédération Nationale des Activities du Déchet
FNADE	Fédération Nationale des Docteurs d'État et Diplômes des Universités de France
FNAÉ	Fédération Nationale de l'Équipement Électrique
FNAEM	Federatione Nazionale Aziende Elettriche Municipalizzate
FNAF	Fédération Nationale Agroalimentaire et Forestière
FNAF	Fédération Nationale des Associations Françaises d'Inventeurs
FNAFI	Fédération Nationale des Associations Françaises d'Inventeurs
FNAFO	Fédération Nationale de l'Agriculture Force Ouvrière
FNAFU	Fonds Nationale d'Aménagement Foncier et d'Urbanisme
FNAH	Fonds National de l'Amélioration de l'Habitat
FNAI	Federazione Nazionale Autoferrotranvieri Internavigatori
FNAIM	Fédération Nationale des Agents Immobiliers, Mandataires en Vente de Fonds de Commerce, Administrateurs de Biens, Syndicats de Copropriété, Marchants de Biens et Experts
FNALA	Federazione Nazionale Artigiani del Legno e dell' Arredamento
FNAM	Federazione Nazionale Artigiani Metalmeccanici
FNAMAC	Fédération Nationale Artisanale des Métiers d'Art et de Création du Bijou et de l'Horlogerie
FNAMGAV	Federazione Nazionale Aziende Municipalizzate Gas, Acqua, Varie
FNAMI	Fonds National Assurance-Maladie-Invalidité
FNAMS	Fédération Nationale des Agriculteurs Multiplicateurs de Semences
FNAO	Fédération Nationale des Commerces de l'Antiquité, de l'Occasion et des Objets de Collection
FNAP	Fédération Nationale des Agences de Presse
FNAR	Fédération Nationale des Artisans et Petites Entreprises en Milieu Rural
FNARÉR	Fédération Nationale des Associations Régionales d'Économie Rurale
FNARH	Fédération Nationale des Associations de Personnel des Postes et Télécommunications pour la Recherche Historique
FNAROA	Fédération Nationale des Artisans Restaurateurs d'Objets d'Art
FNAS	Fédération Nationale des Chambres Syndicales des Grossistes et Équipements Sanitaires, Chauffage et Canalisation
FNAS	Fondo Nacional de Asistencia Social
FNASAVPA	Fédération Nationale des Associations des Salariés de l'Agriculture pour la Vulgarisation du Progrès Agricole
FNASBA	Federation of National Associations of Ship Brokers & Agents
FNASSEM	Fédération Nationale de Sauvegarde des Sites et Ensembles Monumentaux
FNB	Fédération Nationale Bovine
FNB	Fédération Nationale des Boissons

FNB	Fédération Nationale du Bâtiment	**FNCBF**	Fédération Nationale des Commerçants en Bestiaux de France
FNB	Fédération Nationale du Bois		
FNB	Food and Nutrition Board (U.S.A.)	**FNCBPV**	Fédération Nationale du Commerce du Bétail, Porcs et Viande (Belgium)
FNBB	Fédération Nationale Belge de la Blanchisserie	**FNCBV**	Fédération Nationale de la Coopération Bétail et Viande
FNBC	Fédération Nationale des Bibliothèques Catholiques (Belgium)	**FNCC**	Fédération Nationale de Conserveries Coopératives
FNBTR	Fédération Nationale Belge des Transporteurs Routiers = NBFBV	**FNCC**	Fédération Nationale des Coopératives Chrétiennes
FNC	Federación Nacional de Cafeteros (Colombia)	**FNCC**	Fédération Nationale des Coopératives Cidricoles
FNC	Federación Nacional del Campesino (Bolivia)	**FNCC**	Fédération Nationale des Coopératives de Céréales
FNC	Federal Networking Council	**FNCC**	Fédération Nationale des Coopératives de Consommation
FNC	Fédération Nationale Chevaline		
FNC	Fédération Nationale de la Coiffure	**FNCC**	Fondo Nacional del Café y del Cacao (Venezuela)
FNC	Fédération Nationale des Cressiculteurs		
FNC	Frente Nacional Constitucionalista (Ecuador)	**FNCCIB**	Fédération Nationale des Chambres de Commerce et d'Industrie de Belgique = NFKHNB
FNC	Front National de Concertation (Haiti)	**FNCCRÉ**	Fédération Nationale des Collectivités Concédantes de Régies Électriques
FNCA	Fédération Nationale des Coopératives Apicoles	**FNCD**	Front Nasyonal pou Chanjman ak Demokrasie (Haiti)
FNCA	Fédération Nationale des Coopératives Artisanales de France et d'Outre-Mer	**FNCÉRVO**	Fédération Nationale des Comités Économiques Régionaux de la Volaille
FNCA	Fédération Nationale du Crédit Agricole = FNCrA	**FNCÉTA**	Fédération Nationale des Centres d'Études Techniques Agricoles
FNCA	Federazione Nazionale della Cooperazione Agricola	**FNCF**	Fédération Nationale des Cinémas Français
FNCAA	Fédération Nationale du Commerce et de l'Artisanat de l'Automobile	**FNCFI**	Federazione Nazionale Commercianti Filatelici Italiani
FNCAM	Fédération Nationale du Crédit Agricole Mutuel	**FNCFP**	Fédération Nationale des Coopératives Agricoles de Fruits, Primeurs, Fleurs et Autres Produits Agricoles
FNCASEF	Fédération Nationale des Coopératives Agricoles de Semences Fourragères		
FNCAST	Fédération Nationale de la Coopération Agricole Scientifique et Technique	**FNCG**	Fédération Nationale des Centres de Gestion
FNCATBI	Fédération Nationale des Coopératives Agricoles de Transformation de la Betterave Industrielle	**FNCG**	Fédération Nationale du Commerce des Grains
		FNCH	Fédération Nationale des Coopératives d'Huilerie
FNCATS	Fédération Nationale de la Coopération Agricole Technique et Scientifique	**FNCHR**	Fédération Nationale des Coopératives d'Habitat Rural
FNCAUMA	Fédération Nationale des Coopératives d'Achat et d'Utilisation de Matériel Agricole = FNCUMA	**FNCIA**	Fédération Nationale des Coopératives d'Insémination Artificielle
FNCAv	Fédération Nationale de la Coopération Avicole	**FNCIB**	Fédération Nationale des Chambres Immobilières de Belgique
FNCB	Fédération Nationale des Coiffeurs de Belgique = NVHB	**FNCIVAMA**	Fédération Nationale des Centres d'Information et de Vulgarisation Agricoles et Ménagères Agricoles
FNCB	Fédération Nationale des Coopératives Agricoles de Transformation de la Betterave Industrielle		

FNCL	Fédération Nationale des Coopératives Lainières
FNCL	Fédération Nationale des Coopératives Laitières
FNCL	Fundación del Nuevo Cine Latinoamericano (Cuba)
FNCO	Federazione Nazionale dei Collegi delle Ostetriche
FNCP	Federación Nacional de Cooperativas de Producción (Venezuela)
FNCP	Fédération Nationale des Centres de Préformation
FNCP	Fédération Nationale des Constructeurs Promoteurs
FNCPA	Fédération Nationale des Syndicats de Conserveurs de Produits Agricoles
FNCPBV	Fédération Nationale des Coopératives de Producteurs de Bétail et de Viande
FNCPLA	Fédération Nationale du Commerce des Produits Laitiers et Avicoles
FNCPSA	Fédération Nationale des Coopératives de Producteurs de Sel de l'Atlantique
FNCPV	Fédération Nationale des Coopératives de Producteurs de Viande
FNCPVRT	Fédération Nationale des Coopératives de Production et de Vente des Raisins de Table
FNCR	Fédération Nationale des Coopératives Rizicoles
FNCRA	Fédération Nationale des Comités Régionaux de Propagande et l'Expansion de Produits Agricoles
FNCrA	Fédération Nationale du Crédit Agricole = FNCA
FNCRM	Fédération du Commerce et de la Réparation du Cycle et du Motocycle
FNCRP	Fédération Nationale des Comités Régionaux de Propagande
FNCSD	Fédération Nationale des Chambres Syndicales Dentaires (Belgium)
FNCSM	Fédération Natonale des Chambres Syndicales de Médecins
FNCSO	Fédération Nationale des Coopératives de Stockage d'Oléagineux
FNCTB	Fédération Nationale des Coopératives Agricoles de Transformation de la Betterave
FNCTSA	Fédération Nationale de la Coopération Technique Scientifique Agricole
FNCTTFEL	National Federation of Railwaymen, Transport Workers, Civil Servants and Employees of Luxembourg
FNCUMA	Fédération Nationale des Coopératives d'Achat et d'Utilisation de Matériel Agricole = FNCAUMA
FNCV	Federación Nacional de Cooperatives de Vivienda (Venezuela)
FNCV	Fédérative Nationale des Coopératives Vinicoles
FNCV	Federazione Nazionale del Commercio Vinicolo
FNCV	Field Naturalists Club of Victoria (Australia)
FND	Fonds Nationale de Développement (Mauritania)
FND	Frente Nacional Democrático (Venezuela)
FNDAB	Fédérative Nationale de Défense de l'Agriculture Biologique
FNDC	Fédération Nationale des Dramatiques Catholiques
FNDCV	Fédération Nationale des Distilleries Coopératives Vinicoles
FNDE	Fondo Nacional de Desarrollo Económico (Peru)
FNdesUPA	Fédération Nationale des Unions Professionales Agricoles de Belgique
FNDF	Federal National Democratic Front (Burma)
FNDF	Fédération Nationale des Distributeurs de Films
FNDL	Fratres Nostrae Dominae Lurdensis; Freres de Notre Dame de Lourdes
FNDPL	Fédération Nationale des Détaillants en Produits Laitiers
FNDR	Front National pour la Défense de la Révolution Socialiste (Madagascar)
FNDSC	Filles de Notre-Dame du Sacré Coeur = FNSSC
FNE	Faisceaux Nationalistes Européens
FNEAA	Fédération Nationale des Exploitants d'Autobus et Autocars
FNÉAF	Fédération Nationale des Éleveurs d'Animaux à Fourrure
FNEB	Fédération Nationale des Fabricants de Caisses et Emballages en Bois de France
FNEB	Institute of First Navigation Engineering Bureau (China)
FNÉC	Fédération Nationale des Éleveurs de Chèvres
FNECC	Fédération Nationale des Employés Commerciaux et Cadres (Zaïre)

FNECFP-FO	Fédération de l'Enseignement Force Ouvrière
FNÉD	Fédération Nationale des Étudiants en Droits et en Sciences Politiques
FNÉÉ	Fédération Nationale de l'Équipement Électrique
FNÉÉGA	Fédération Nationale de l'Énergie Électrique et du Gaz d'Algérie
FNÉF	Fédération Nationale des Étalonniers de France
FNÉF	Fédération Nationale des Étudiants de France
FNEM	Fondo Nacional de Exploración Minera (Bolivia)
FNÉMF	Fédération Nationale des Étudiants en Médecine en France
FNENF	Fédération Nationale des Entrepreneurs de Nettoyage de France
FNETAR	Fédération Nationale des Entrepreneurs de Travaux Agricoles Ruraux
FNF	Families Need Fathers
FNF	Fédération Nationale de la Fourrure
FNF	Föreningarna Nordens Förbund = NYL
FNFC	Fédération Nationale des Fabricants de Cravates
FNFC	First National Finance Corporation
FNFF	Fédération Nationale des Fleuristes de France
FNFFAC&M	Fédération Nationale des Fabricants de Fournitures Administratives Civiles et Militaires
FNFHFTM	Federation of Needle, Fish Hook and Fishing Tackle Makers
FNFPVEI	Fédération Nationale des Fabricants de Peintures, Vernis et Encres d'Imprimerie
FNFR	Fédération Nationale de la Famille Rurale
FNFR	Fédération Nationale des Foyers Ruraux
FNFT	Fédération Nationale des Fabricants-Transformateurs de l'Industrie Cotonnière
FNG	Fédération Nationale du Genêt
FNGAA	Fédération Nationale des Groupements Agricoles d'Approvisionnement
FNGDSB	Fédération Nationale des Groupements de Défense Sanitaire du Bétail
FNGÉDA	Fédération Nationale des Groupes d'Études et de Développement Agricoles
FNGH	Fédération Nationale de l'Horlogerie en Gros
FNGPA	Fédération Nationale des Groupements de Productivité Agricole
FNGPC	Fédération Nationale des Groupements de Protection des Cultures
FNGPPTP	Fédération Nationale des Groupements et Producteurs de Pommes de Terre de Primeur
FNGVPA	Fédération Nationale des Groupements de Vulgarisation et du Progrès Agricole
FNHG	Fédération Nationale de l'Horlogerie en Gros
FNHM	Friends of the Natural History Museum
FNHMID	Fédération Nationale des Huileries Métropolitaines et Industries Dérivées
FNHPV	Fédération Nationale des Herbagers et Producteurs de Viande
FNHRATR	Fédération Nationale de l'Habitat Rural et de l'Aménagement du Territoire Rural
FNI	Fédération Nationale des Infirmières et Infirmiers
FNI	Fédération Naturiste Internationale = INF
FNI	Fonds National d'Investissement (Niger)
FNIA	Fondo Nacional de Investigaciones Agropecuárias (Venezuela)
FNIB	Fédération Nationale de l'Injection des Bois
FNIB	Fédération Nationale des Infirmières Belges
FNIBN	Fédération Française des Importateurs de Bois du Nord
FNIC	Fédération Nationale des Industries du Corset
FNIC	Food and Nutrition Information and Educational Materials Center (U.S.A.)
FNICF	Fédération Nationale del'Industrie de la Chaussure de France
FNICG	Fédération Nationale de l'Industrie des Corps Gras
FNICGV	Fédération Nationale des Industries et Commerces en Gros des Viandes
FNIE	Fédération Nationale de l'Industrie des Engrais
FNIÉ	Fédération Nationale des Industries Électroniques
FNIÉBI	Fédération Nationale des Installateurs-Électriciens du Bâtiment et de l'Industrie

FNIÉÉG	Fédération Nationale des Syndicats des Industries de l'Énergie Électrique et du Gaz	**FNM**	Free National Movement (Bahamas)
FNIEF	Federazione Nazionale Insegnanti Educazione Fisica	**FNMA**	Fédération Nationale de la Mutualité Agricole
FNIF	Független Nemzeti Ifjúsági Front (Hungary) = INYF	**FNMBC**	Fédération Nationale des Négociants en Gros en Bonneterie, Mercerie, Chaussures et Négoces Connexes de France
FNIH	Fédération Nationale de l'Industrie Hôtelière de France et d'Outre-Mer	**FNMC**	Federación Nacional Minera de Chile
FNIL	Federação Nacional dos Industriais de Lanifícios	**FNMCB**	Federación Nacional de Mujeres Campesinas de Bolivia
FNIL	Fédération Nationale des Syndicats d'Industriels Laitiers	**FNMCCA**	Fédération Nationale de la Mutualité du Crédit et de la Coopération Agricoles
FNIM	Federação Nacional dos Industriais de Moagem	**FNMF**	Fédération Nationale de la Marbrerie Funéraire
FNIMMÉ	Fédération Nationale des Importateurs de la Métallurgie, de la Mécanique et de l'Électronique	**FNMIP**	Fédération Nationale des Malades, Infirmes et Paralysés
FNINF	Fédération Nationale Interprofessionnelle de la Noix Française (CFPFL)	**FNMT**	Fábrica Nacional de Moneda y Timbre
		FNMTTB	Fédération Nationale des Maîtres Tailleurs et Tailleuses de Belgique
FNIP-VEICF	Fédération Nationale des Industries des Peintures, Vernis, Encres d'Imprimerie et Couleurs Fines	**FNMV**	Fédération Nationale des Entreprises de Miroiterie-Vitrerie
FNIRF	Federação Nacional dos Institútos Religiosos Femininas	**FNNBEB**	Fédération Nationale des Négociants en Bières et Eaux de Boisson (Belgium)
FNISCGCV	Fédération Nationale de l'Industrie de la Salaison, de la Charcuterie en Gros et des Conserves de Viandes	**FNNMC**	Fédération Nationale des Négociants en Matériaux de Construction
		FNNPE	Federation of Nature and National Parks of Europe
FNISM	Federazione Nazionale Insegnanti Scuole Medie	**FNO**	Fédération Nationale Ovine
FNITCE	Fédération Nationale des Ingénieurs, Techniciens, Cadres et Employés	**FNOA**	Fédération Nationale des Organisations Agricoles
FNJAP	Fédération Nationale des 'Jeunes Alliances Paysannes'	**FNOCPAB**	Fédération Nationale des Organismes de Contrôle des Performances des Animaux de Boucherie
FNKE	Fachnormenausschuss Kerntechnik	**FNOFPCCA**	Fédération Nationale des Organismes de Formation et de Promotion des Conseillers et Cadres de l'Agriculture
FNL	Friends of the National Libraries		
FNLA	Frente Nacional de Liberação de Angola		
FNLAV	Federazione Nazionale Lavoratori Arti Visive	**FNOGA**	Fédération Nationale des Organismes de Gestion Agricole
FNLF	Fédération Nationale des Logis de France	**FNOM**	Federazione Nazionale degli Ordini dei Medici
FNLG	Fédération Nationale des Livres Zootechniques	**FNOMCEO**	Federazione Nazionale degli Ordini dei Medici Chirurghi e degli Odontoiatria
FNLG	Fo nou Libere la Guyane (French Guiana)	**FNOMÉR**	Fédération Nationale des Organismes de Migration et d'Établissement Ruraux
FNLP	Fédération Nationale des Producteurs de Lait	**FNOMI**	Fédération Nationale des Organismes de Migrations Intérieures
FNLV	Fédération Nationale des Loueurs de Véhicules	**FNOOMM**	Federazione Nazionale degli Ordeni dei Medici
		FNOP	Federatie van Nederlandse Organisaties voor het Personenvervoer
FNLVPT	Fédération Nationale des Loueurs de Voitures de Place à Taximètre	**FNOSAD**	Fédération Nationale des Organisations Sanitaires Apicoles Départementales

FNOSS	Fédération Nationale des Organismes de Sécurité Sociale	**FNPRCM**	Fédération Nationale des Producteurs de Reinette Canada de Montagne
FNOT-SI	Fédération Nationale des Offices de Tourisme et Syndicats d'Initiative	**FNPRT**	Fédération Nationale des Producteurs des Raisins de Table
FNOVI	Federazione Nazionale degli Ordini dei Veterinari Italiani	**FNPSA**	Fédération Nationale de Producteurs de Sel de l'Atlantique
FNP	Fédération Nationale de la Pisciculture	**FNPSMS**	Fédération Nationale des Producteurs de Semences de Maïs et de Sorgho
FNP	Fédération Nationale des Podologues	**FNPT**	Federação Nacional dos Productores de Trigo (Portugal)
FNP	Fédération Nationale Porcine		
FNP	Federazione Nazionale Pensionati	**FNPT**	Fédération Nationale des Planteurs de Tabac
FNP	Fiji National Party	**FNPT**	Fédération Nationale des Producteurs de Topinambours
FNPA	Fédération Nationale de la Propriété Agricole		
FNPBRF	Fédération Nationale des Producteurs de Bois et Reboiseurs Français	**FNPT**	Fédération Nationale des Producteurs de Truffes
FNPC	Fédération Nationale des Producteurs de Chanvre	**FNPT**	Fondo Nacional de Protección del Trabajo
FNPC	Fédération Nationale des Promoteurs-Constructeurs	**FNPT**	Front National Progressiste Tunisien
FNPÉCSF	Fédération Nationale des Propriétaires et Éleveurs du Cheval de Selle et de Sport Français	**FNPTC**	Fédération Nationale des Groupements de Producteurs de Pommes de Terre de Consommation
FNPF	Fédération Nationale de la Pisciculture Française	**FNPVCC**	Fédération Nationale des Producteurs de Vins de Consommation Courante
FNPF	Fédération Nationale des Producteurs de Fraises	**FNPVDQS**	Fédération Nationale des Producteurs de Vins de Qualité Supérieure
FNPF	Fédération Nationale des Producteurs de Fruits	**FNQ**	Fédération Nationale de la Quincaillerie
FNPFB	Fédération Nationale des Entrepreneurs de Pompes Funèbres de Belgique	**FNR**	Fachnormenausschus Radiologie
FNPFC	Fédération Nationale des Producteurs de Fruits à Cidre	**FNR**	Front National de Renouvellement (Algeria)
FNPHP	Fédération Nationale des Producteurs de l'Horticulture et des Pépinières	**FNRC**	Food and Nutrition Research Centre (Philippines)
FNPL	Fédération Nationale des Producteurs de Lait	**FNRS**	Fonds National de la Recherche Scientifique (Belgium) = NFWO
FNPL	Fédération Nationale des Producteurs de Légumes	**FNS**	Fédération Nationale des Scieries (Belgium)
FNPLL	Fédération Nationale des Producteurs de Lavande et de Lavandin	**FNS**	Frente Nacional Sindical (Guatemala)
FNPP	Fédération Nationale de la Photographie Professionnelle (Belgium)	**FNS**	Friedrich Nietzsche Society
		FNSA	Fédération Nationale des Sinistrés Agricoles
FNPPPT	Fédération Nationale des Producteurs de Plantes de Pommes de Terre	**FNSA**	Fédération Nationale des Syndicats Agricoles (Belgium, France)
FNPPTI	Fédération Nationale des Producteurs de Pommes de Terre Industrielles	**FNSACC**	Fédération Nationale des Syndicats Agricoles des Cultivateurs de Champignons
FNPPTP	Fédération Nationale des Producteurs de Pommes de Terre de Primeur	**FNSAESR**	Fédération Nationale des Syndicats Autonomes de l'Enseignement Supérior et de la Recherche
FNPR	Federatsiia Nezavisimykh Profsoiuzov Rossii	**FNSAFER**	Fédération Nationale des Sociétés d'Aménagement Foncier et d'Etablissement Rural

FNSAGA	Fédération Nationale des Syndicats d'Agents Généraux
FNSBS	Fonda Nacional de Saud y Bienestar Social (Peru)
FNSC	Fédération pour une Nouvelle Société Calédonienne
FNSCC	Fédération Nationale des Sociétés Coopératives de Commerçants
FNSCC	Federation of Nuclear Shelter Consultants and Contractors
FNSCCF	Fédération Nationale des Syndicats de Confituriers et Conserveurs de Fruits
FNSCE	Fédération Nationale des Syndicats de Société de Commerce Extérieur
FNSDPL	Fédération Nationale des Syndicats de Détaillants en Produits Laitiers
FNSEA	Fédération Nationale des Syndicats d'Exploitants Agricoles
FNSÉCSF	Fédération Nationale des Syndicats d'Éleveurs de Chevaux de Selle Français
FNSÉLC	Fédération Nationale des Syndicats d'Éleveurs de Lapins de Chair
FNSÉR	Fédération Nationale des Élus Socialistes et Republicains
FNSFPA	Fédération Nationale des Syndicats de Fabricants de Pâtes Alimentaires
FNSHEE	Fédération Nationale des Syndicats d'Gerbagers, Emboucheurs et Engraisseurs
FNSI	Federazione Nazionale della Stampa Italiana
FNSIA	Fédération Nationale des Syndicats de Industries de d'Alimentation
FNSIAA	Fédération Nationale des Syndicats des Industries de l'Alimentation Animale
FNSIC	Fédération Nationale des Syndicats d'Ingénieurs et de Cadres
FNSICAÉ	Fédération Nationale des Sociétés d'Intérêt Collectif Agricole d'Électricité
FNSIL	Fédération Nationale des Syndicats d'Industriels Laitiers
FNSIOT	Fédération Nationale des Syndicats d'Initiative et Offices de Tourisme
FNSIT-CEOAA	Fédération Nationale des Syndicats d'Ingénieurs, Techniciens, Cadres Administratifs et Employés des Organisations Agricoles de l'Agriculture
FNSL	Fédération Nationale des Syndicats du Liège
FNSNCF	Fédération Nationale des Syndicats de Négociants en Combustibles et Carburants de France
FNSOAI	Fédération Nationale des Syndicats Ouvriers Agricoles Indépendants
FNSP	Federação Nacional dos Sindicatos de Professores
FNSP	Fédération Nationale des Sapeurs-Pompiers Français
FNSPF	Fédération Nationale des Sociétés Photographiques de France (*now* FPF)
FNSPFS	Fédération Nationale des Syndicats de Propriétaires Forestiers Sylviculteurs
FNSPPT-CQC	Fédération Nationale des Syndicats des Producteurs de Pommes de Terre de Consommation de Qualité Contrôlée
FNSPT	Fédération Nationale des Syndicats Producteurs de Topinambours
FNSPV	Fédération Nationale des Syndicats de Pépiniéristes Viticulteurs
FNSSA	Field Naturalists Society of South Australia
FNSSC	Figlie di Nostra Signora del Sacro Cuore = FNDSC
FNSSN	Fédération des Sociétés de Sciences Naturelles
FNT	Federación Nacional de Tabacaleros (Colombia)
FNTA	Federación Nacional de Trabajadores de Azucar (Cuba)
FNTA	Fédération Nationale des Transporteurs Auxiliaires
FNTAF	Fédération Nationale des Travailleurs de l'Agriculture et des Forêts de France et d'Outremer
FNTAL	Fédération Nationale du Teillage Agricole du Lin
FNTC	Frente Nacional de Trabajadores y Campesinos (Peru) = FRENATRACA
FNTCA	Fédération Nationale des Techniciens et Cadres de l'Agriculture (CGA)
FNTDP	Fédération Nationale des Transports de Denrées Périssables et Assimilés
FNTM	Federação Nacional dos Trabalhadores Maritimos (Brazil)
FNTM	Federación National de Transportes de Mercancías
FNTMMS	Federación National de Trabajadores Mineros, Metalúrgicos y Siderérgicos (Peru)
FNTMPE	Federación Nacional de Trabajadores Maritimos y Portuarios del Ecuador

FNTP	Federação Nacional dos Productores de Trigo
FNTP	Fédération Nationale des Transformateurs de Papier
FNTR	Fédération Nationale des Transports Routiers
FNTT	Fédération Nationale des Travailleurs de la Terre (Algeria)
FNU	Fujian Normal University
FNUAP	Fonds des Nations Unies pour les Activités en Matière de Population = UNFPA
FNUDC	Fondo de las Naciones Unidas para el Desarrollo de la Capitalización = FENU, UNCDF
FNUDIO	Fonds des Nations Unies pour le Développement de l'Irian Occidental
FNUF	Fijian Nationalist United Front
FNUK-UNIKOM	Front National Uni des Komores – Union des Komoriens
FNULAD	Fonds des Nations Unies pour la Lutte contre l'Abus des Drogues = UNFDAC
FNUMAB	Fédération Nationale Unifiée des Maîtres-Artisans du Bâtiment
FNUNF	Fédération Nationale pour l'Utilisation Naturelle des Fruits
FNUOD	Force des Nations Unies Chargée d'Observer le Dégagement = FNUOS, UNDOF
FNUOS	Fuerza de las Naciones Unidas para la Observación de la Separación = FNUOD, UNDOF
FNUPA	Fédération Nationale des Unions Professionnelles Agricoles (Belgium)
FNV	Federación Nacional de la Vivienda (El Salvador)
FNV	Federación Nacional Velasquista (Ecuador)
FNV	Federatie Nederlandse Vakbeweging
FNV	Forbundet Nordisk Vuxenupplysing
FNVPA	Fonds National de la Vulgarisation et du Progrès Agricoles
FNW	Fundusz Niezależnych Wydawnictw
FO	Faculty of Opthalmologists
FO	Force Ouvrière (France, French Guiana)
FO	Frente Obrero (Nicaragua)
FOA	Farmers Organization Authority (Malaysia)
FOA	Försvarets Forskningsanstalt
FOAA	Flying Optometrists Association of America
FOAD	Fédération des Organisations Agricoles Diverses
FOAL	Friends of Animals League
FOAPH	Fédération Ouest-Africaine des Associations pour la Promotion des Personnes Handicappées = WAFAH
FOAS	Friends of Afghanistan Society
FOB	Federatie van Onderlinge Brandwaaborgmaatschappij in Nederland
FOB	Friends of Blue
FOBB	Fédération Suisse des Ouvriers sur Bois et du Bâtiment
FOBBS	Federation of British Bonsai Societies
FOBFO	Federation of British Fire Organisations
FOBID	Federatie van Organisaties op het gebied van Bibliotheek- Informatie- en Dokumentatie- wezen
FOCA	Formula One Constructors' Association
FOCAP	Federacion Odontologica de Centro America y Panama
FOCC	Friends of the Clergy Corporation
FOCCO	Fomento y Cooperacion Comunal (El Salvador)
FOCEM	Fondo Centroamericano de Establización Monetaria
FOCEP	Frente Obrero, Campesino, Estudiantil y Popular (Peru)
FOCOEX	Fomento de Comercio Exterior
FOCOL	Federation of Coin-Operated Launderettes
FOCUS	Foreign Ophthalmological Care from the United States
FOCWA	Nederlandse Vereniging van Ondernemers in het Carosseriebedrijf
FOD	Field Operations Division (IUCN)
FODE-RUMA	Fondo de Desarrollo Rural Marginal (Ecuador)
FODO	Federation of Opthalmic Dispensing Opticians
FOE	Friends of the Earth
FOEGIN	Vereniging voor Fabrieken op Electrotechnisch Gebied in Nederland
FOEI	Friends of the Earth International
FOESSA	Fundación Fomento de Estudios Sociales y de Sociologia Aplicada
FOEXP	Export Expansion Group (Brazil)
FOFATUSA	Federation of Free African Trade Unions of South Africa
FOFI	Federazione degli Ordini dei Farmacisti Italiani

FOFTA	Fédération Odontologique de France et des Territoires Associés		**FOMO**	Servicio Nacional de Formacion de Mano de Obra
FOGA	Fonds d'Orientation de Garantie Agricole (CE)		**FOMODA**	Fonds de Modernisation et de Développement de l'Artisanat
FOGAIN	Fondo de Garantia y Fomento a la Industria Mediana y Pequeña (Mexico)		**FOMRE**	Stichting Fundamenteel Onderzoek der Materie met Röntgen- en Electronenstralen
FOGAPE	Fonds d'Aide et de Garantie des Crédits aux Petites et Moyennes Entreprises Camérounaises		**FOMRHI**	Federation of Makers and Restorers of Historical Instruments
FOGRA	Deutsche Gesellschaft für Forschung im Graphischen Gewerbe		**FOMTUR**	Sociedad Financiera para el Fomento del Turismo y de Recreo Público (Venezuela)
FOGRA	Forschungsgesellschaft für Druck- und Reproduktionstechnik		**FOMWAN**	Federation of Muslim Women's Associations of Nigeria
FOI	Federation of Industries (Malta)		**FONACC**	Federación Obrera Nacional del Cuero y El Calzado (Chile)
FOI FAO	Forest Industries Trade Division		**FONADE**	Fondo Nacional de Desarrollo (Ecuador)
FOIC	Freedom of Information Clearinghouse (U.S.A.)			
FOICA	Fondo de Obras para la Iglesia Católica		**FONADE**	Fondo Nacional para el Desarrollo (Colombia)
FOIE	FAO Forest Economics Statistics Branch		**FONADER**	Fonds National de Développement Rural (Cameroon)
FOIM	FAO Mechanical Wood Products Branch		**FONAIAP**	Fondo Nacional de Investigaciones Agropecuárias (Venezuela)
FOIP	FAO Pulp Paper Branch		**FONAPRE**	Fondo Nacional de Preinversión (Ecuador)
FOL	Frente Obrero de Liberashon (Netherlands Antilles)		**FONARES**	Fonds National de la Recherche Scientifique
FOLA	Federación Odontológica Latino-Americana		**FONART**	Fondo Nacional para el Fomento de las Artesanias (Mexico)
FOLACL	Federation of Local Authority Chief Librarians		**FONAS**	Fondo Nacional de Asistencia Social
FOLUSA	Friends of Libraries, U.S.A.		**FONASBA**	Federation of National Associations of Ship Brokers and Agents
FOM	Federatie Organisaties in de Machinehandel		**FONATUR**	Fondo Nacional de Fomento al Turismo (Mexico)
FOM	Stichting voor Fundamenteel Onderzoek der Materie		**FONAVI**	Fondo Nacional de la Vivienda (Argentina)
FOM RCP	Faculty of Occupational Medicine		**FONDAD**	Forum on Debt and Development (Netherlands)
FOMA	Flake Oatmeal Millers' Association (Éire)		**Fondation HYGIE**	Fondation Internationale pour la Promotion de l'Hygiène (Switzerland)
FOMC	Federal Open Market Committee (U.S.A.)		**FONDEM**	Fondo Interamericano de Asistencia para Situaciones de Emergencía
FOMCA	Federation of Malaysian Consumers Association		**FONDE-PORT**	Fondo Nacional para los Desarrollos Portuarios (Mexico)
FOMEX	Fondo para el Fomento de las Exportaciones (Mexico)		**FONDESCA**	Fondo para el Desarrollo Económico y Social de Centroamerica (CABEI)
FOMH	Fédération Suisse des Ouvriers sur Métaux et Horlogers		**FONDUR**	Fondo Nacional de Desarrollo Urbano (Venezuela)
FÖMI	Földmérési Intézet			
FOMIZ	Federation des Ouvriers des Mines du Zaïre		**FONEI**	Fondo de Equipamiento Industrial (Mexico)
FOMO	Federatie van het Officieel Middelbaar Onderwijs van de Hogere Graad van België			

FONICA	Federación Obrera Nacional de la Industria del Vestido y Afines (Argentina)
FONOLA-SOL	Asociación Nordica de Intercambio en Educación Popular con America Latina (Sweden)
FONPLATA	Financial Fund for the Development of the River Plate Basin
FONUBEL	Forum Nucléaire Belge
FOOF	Federación Obrera de Organizaciones Femeniles (Mexico)
FOP	Föreningen för Oförstörande Provning (Sweden)
FOPADESC	Fondation Panafricaine Développement Économique Social et Culturel
FOPDAC	Federation of Overseas Property Developers, Agents & Consultants
FOPERDA	Fondation Père Damien
FOPERDIC	Association for the Development of Further Professional Training in the Foundry and Related Industries (France)
FOPEX	Fondo de Promoción de Exportaciones (Ecuador)
FOPEX	Fondo de Promoción de Exportaciones No Tradicionales (Peru)
FOPS	Fair Organ Preservation Society
FOPS	National Federation of Playgoers Societies
FOPSA	Federation of Productivity Services Associations
FOPTUR	Fondo de Promoción Turística (Peru)
FoR	Fellowship of Reconciliation
FOR	Forest Resources Division (FAO)
FORALAC	Société Forestière Agricole, Industrielle et Commerciale en Afrique Équatoriale
FORATOM	Forum Atomique Européen
FORC	Financial Options Research Centre
FORCE	Task Force for Human Resources, Education, Training and Youth (CEC)
Ford	Forum for the Restoration of Democracy (Kenya)
FORDS	Floating Ocean Research and Development Station
FORE	Forestry Institutions Education Branch (FAO)
FOREAMI	Fonds Reine Elizabeth pour l'Assistance Médicale aux Indigènes (Belgium)
FOREST	Freedom Organisation for the Right to Enjoy Smoking Tobacco
FOREX	International Association of Exchange Dealers
FOREXI	Société pour la Réalisation de Forages d'Exploitation en Côte d'Ivoire
FORINDI	Société Forestière d'Irindi (Gabon)
FORJA	Fuerza de Orientación Radical de la Joven Argentina
FORL	FAO Forest Logging Transport Branch
FORM	FAO Forest Management Branch
FORMA	Fonds d'Orientation et de Régularisation des Marchés Agricoles
FORPPA	Fondo de Ordenación y Regulacion de Productos y Precios Agrarios
FORR	Fundusz Obrotowy Reformy Rolnej
FORS	Finnish Operations Research Society
FORSTAD	Forum for Research in Science, Technology and the Arts for Development (Sierra Leone)
FORTRA	Federation of Radio and Television Retailers Association
FORW	Forest Conservation Wildlife Branch (FAO)
FORWARD	Foundation for Women's Health Research and Development
FOS	Fédération Ouvriers Syndicats (Haiti)
FOS	Field of Science
FOS	Fifth of October Society (Bulgaria) = OPO
FOS	Fisheries Organisation Society
FOS	Föreningen för Orientaliska Studier
FOSATU	Federation of South African Trade Unions
FOSC	Federation of Sidecar Clubs
FOSEP	Fondo Salvadoreño para Estudios de Preinversion
FOSFA	Federation of Oils, Seeds and Fats Associations
FOSIDEC	Fonds de Solidarité et d'Intervention pour le Développement (CEAO)
FOSKOR	Phosphate Development Corporation (South Africa)
FOSS	Federation of Scottish Skateboarders
FOSS	Föreningen Ostra Sveriges Skogsarbeten
FOSSSA	Federation of Scottish School Sports Associations
FOTIA	Federación Obrera de Trabajadores de la Industria Azucarera (Argentina)
FOTIM	Fotobranchens Importsorforening
FOV	Federatie van Onderlinge Verzekeringmaatschappijen in Nederland

FOVAD	Forum des Organisations Africaines Volontaires de Développement (ANID) = FAVDO
FOW	Friends of Women Foundation (Thailand)
FOWP	Fertilisers from Organic Wastes Program
FP	Federación Progresista
FP	Federazione della Funzione Pubblica
FP	Film Polski
FP	Fremskridtspartiet
FP	Front Populaire (Burkina Faso)
FP-25	Forças Populares de 25 Abril
FP-31	Frente Popular 31 de Enero (Guatemala)
FPA	Family Planning Association
FPA	Fédération de la Propriété Agricole
FPA	Federation of Professional Associations
FPA	Film Production Association of Great Britain
FPA	Fire Protection Association
FPA	Flexible Packaging Association (U.K., U.S.A.)
FPA	Flowers and Plants Association
FPA	Foreign Press Association
FPA	Formación Professional Acelerada
FPA	Foyers de Progrès Agricole
FPA	Free Pacific Association
FPAA	Federación Panamericana de Asociaciones de Arquitectos
FPAB	Family Planning Association of Bangladesh
FPAF	Family Planning Association of Fiji
FPAHK	Family Planning Association of Hong Kong
FPAI	Family Planning Association of India
FPAK	Family Planning Association of Kenya
FPAL	Family Planning Association of Liberia
FPAN	Family Planning Association of Nepal
FPAP	Family Planning Association of Pakistan
FPAPNG	Family Planning Association of Papua New Guinea
FPAS	Frank Patterson Appreciation Society
FPASL	Family Planning Association of Sri Lanka
FPATT	Family Planning Association of Trinidad and Tobago
FPAU	Family Planning Association of Uganda
FPB	Federation of Professional Bodies (Malta)
FPB	Fédération Pétrolière Belge
FPB	Forum of Private Business
FPBAI	Federation of Publishers' and Booksellers' Association of India
FPC	Fédération des Patrons Catholiques
FPC	Flowers Publicity Council
FPC	Fondation pour la Protection des Consommateurs (Switzerland)
FPC	Food Production Corporation (Ghana)
FPC	Frente Popular Costarricense
FPC	Fresh Produce Consortium (*ex* PPMA)
FPCEA	Fibreboard Packing Case Employers Association
FPCMA	Fibreboard Packing Case Manufacturers Association
FPCP	Fratres Piae Congregationis a Praesantatione = FPM
FPCS	Farm Planning Computer Service
FPD	Forum of People with Disabilities (Éire)
FPDA	Federación de Periodistas Deportivos de América (Cuba)
FPDA	Finnish Plywood Development Association
FPDC	Federation of Plastering & Drywall Contractors (*ex* NFPC)
FPDC	Food Products Development Centre (Bangladesh)
FPÉ	Fédération Professionnelle des Producteurs et Distributeurs d'Électricité de Belgique
FPEP	Fédération des Pupilles de l'Enseignement Public
FPF	Federação Portuguesa de Futebol
FPF	Fédération Photographique de France
FPF	Finska Pappersingeniörsföreningen
FPFA	Family Planning Federation of Australia
FPFC	Fair Play For Children Association
FPFJ	Family Planning Federation of Japan
FPFRÉ	Fédération des Professeurs Français Résidents à l'Étranger
FPFSG	Federation of Prisoners' Families Support Groups
FPGAUS	Federated Pecan Growers Associations of the United States
FPH	Fondation pour le Progrés de l'Homme (France)
FPH	Frente Patriótico Hondureño
FPI	Front Populaire Ivoirien
FPIA	Family Planning International Assistance

FPIAA	Fire Protection Industry Association of Australia	**FPPB**	Fédération de la Presse Périodique de Belgique
FPIP	Fédération Professionelle Independante de la Police	**FPPE**	Fédération du Prêt à Porter Féminin
FPIS	Family Planning International Assistance	**FPPM**	Federación del Partido del Pueblo Mexicano
FPL	Fatherland Party of Labor (Bulgaria) = OPT	**FPPTE**	Federation of Public Passenger Transport Employers
FPL	Frente Popular Libertador (Guatemala)	**FPR**	Frente Patriótico para la Revolución (Nicaragua)
FPL	Fuerzas Populares de Liberación (Guatemala, El Salvador)	**FPR**	Front Patriotique Rwandais
FPLM	Forças Populares de Liberação de Moçambique	**FPR**	Frontul Popular Român (Romania) = RPF
FPM	Fachverband Pulver-Metallurgie	**FPR**	Fuerzas Populares Revolucionarias Lorenzo Zelaya (Honduras)
FPM	Fédération Patronal Monégasque	**FPR**	Nordisk Forskningspolitisk Rad
FPM	Fratres Praesentationis Mariae = FPCP	**FPRA**	Federation of Private Residents Associations
FPMA	Federation of Pharmaceutical Manufacturers' Associations (Japan)	**FPRA**	Finnish Peace Research Association
FPMCHA-DPRK	Family Planning and MCH Association of the Democratic People's Republic of Korea	**FPRC**	Flying Personnel Research Committee
		FPRDI	Forest Products Research and Development Institute (Philippines)
FPMI	Forest Pest Management Institute (Canada)	**FPRI**	Forest Products Research Division
FPMR	Manuel Rodriguez Patriotic Front (Chile)	**FPRI**	Forest Products Research Institute (Ghana, Philippines)
FPMR-A	Frente Patriotico Manuel Rodriguez – Autónomo (Chile)	**FPRL**	Forest Products Research Laboratory
FPMR-P	Frente Patriótica Manuel Rodriguez – Partido (Chile)	**FPRP**	Asociación Puertorriquena pro Bienestar de la Familia
FPMT	Foundation for the Preservation of the Mahayana Tradition = IMI	**FPRP**	Foundation for the Promotion of Responsible Parenthood (Aruba)
FPN	Front Porozumienia Narodowego	**FPRS**	Forest Products Research Society (U.S.A.)
FPNUL	Fuerza Provisional de las Naciones Unidas en El Libano = FINUL, UNIFIL	**FPS**	Federación de Partidos Socialistas
FPO	Federation of Professional Organisations	**FPS**	Federación Panamericana de Squash
		FPS	Federation of Petroleum Suppliers
FPO	Federation of Prosthodontic Organizations (U.S.A.)	**FPS**	Federation of Piling Specialists
FPÖ	Freiheitliche Partei Österreichs	**FPS**	Fell Pony Society
FPO-PT	Front Patriotique Oubanquien – Parti de Travail (Central African Republic)	**FPS**	Finnish Physical Society = SF
		FPS	Foreign Policy Society (Denmark) = DUS
FPOP	Family Planning Organization of the Philippines	**FPS**	Fotografi Professionisti Svizzeri = SBF, PpS
FPP	Federación de Periodistas del Perú	**FPS**	Free Painters and Sculptors
FPP	Fondul Proprietatii Private (Romania) = NAP	**FPS**	Friedenspolitische Studien Gesellschaft
		FPS	Front Patriotique de Salut (Chad)
FPP	Free Peasants' Party (Uzbekistan)	**FPS**	Koninklijke Vereniging 'Het Friesch Paardenstamboek'
FPP	Patriotic Front for Progress		
FPPB	Family Planning and Population Board (Singapore)	**FPSC**	Family Policy Studies Centre
		FPSG	Food Processors' and Suppliers' Group (Éire)

FPSR	Finnish Physicians for Social Responsibility	**FRCN**	Federal Radio Corporation of Nigeria
FPT	Federazione Poste e Telecomunicazioni	**FRD**	Fédération Romande des Détaillants
FPU	Frente del Pueblo Unido (Bolivia)	**FRD**	Forbrugerrådet
FPV	Farmers' Party of Vojvodina (Serbia) = SSV	**FRD**	Foundation for Research Development (South Africa)
FPV	Front Progressiste Voltaïque (Burkina Faso)	**FRDC**	Fisheries Research and Development Corporation
FPWP	Female Prisoners Welfare Project/Hibiscus	**FRDC**	Forest Research and Development Centre (Indonesia)
FR	Fotohandlaranas Riksförbund	**FRDP**	Frente Revolucionario de Defensa del Pueblo (Peru)
FR	Fuerza Republicana (Argentina)	**FRÉ**	Fédération Romande des Écoles de Conduite
FR3	France Régions 3	**FREC**	Forestry Research and Education Centre (Sudan)
FRA	Federación Rural Boliviana		
FRA	Federal Railroad Administration (U.S.A.)	**FREColl**	Forest Resources and Environment Collective
FRA	Flexible Roofing Association	**FRED**	Fund for Rural Economic Development (Canada)
FRA	Frente Radical Alfarista (Ecuador)		
FRAC	Food Research and Action Center (U.S.A.)	**FREDEMO**	Frente Democrático (Peru)
FRAE	Istituto di Fotochimica e Radiazioni d'Alta Energia (Italy)	**FREEZE**	Nuclear Weapons Freeze Ltd
		FREGG	Free Range Egg Association
FRAMA-TOME	Société Franco-Américaine de Constructions Atomiques	**FREI**	Forest Research and Education Institute (Sudan)
FRAME	Fund for the Replacement of Animals in Medical Experiments (U.K., U.S.A.)	**Frejudepa**	Frente Renovador, Justicia, Democracia y Participacion (Argentina)
FRAMPO	Partido Front Amplio Popular (Panama)	**FREJULI**	Frente Justicialista do Liberacion (Argentina)
FRANA	Groupement des Fabricants et Représentants des Adjuvants en Nutrition Animale (Belgium)	**FREJUPO**	Front Justicialista de Unidad Popular (Argentina)
		FRELIMO	Frente de Libertação de Moçambique
FRANCE-VIN	Société les Bons Vins de France (Cameroon)	**FREM**	Federación de Religiosas Enfermeras Mexicanas
FRANCO-SIM	Société Francophone de Simulation	**FREN**	Frente Revolucionario Nacionalista (Chile)
FRAP	Frente Revolucionario Antifascista y Patriótico	**FRENA-TRACA**	Frente Nacional de Trabajadores y Campesinos (Peru) = FNTC
FRAP	Frente Revolucionario Armado y Popular (Chile, Mexico)	**FRENO**	Frente Nacional Opositóra (Panama)
FRAP	Front Révolutionnaire d'Action Prolétarienne (Belgium)	**FRENOA**	Frente Nacional de Organizaciones Autónomas (Chile)
FRB	Federation of Radical Booksellers	**FRENP**	Foundation for Research and Editions of Neohellenic Philosophy = IEENPh
FRB	Fédération Routière Belge		
FRB	Fisheries Research Board of Canada	**FREPEBO**	Frente Peronista Bonaerense (Argentina)
FRB	Frente de la Revolución Boliviana		
FRBC	Farm & Rural Buildings Information Centre	**FREPNH**	Foundation for Research and Editions of Neohellenic Philosophy (Greece)
FRCAB	Flat Roofing Contractors Advisory Board	**FRES**	Federation of Recruitment and Employment Services
FRCC	Fell and Rock Climbing Club	**Fretilin**	Frente Revolucionário de Este Timor Independente
FRCID	Fédération Romande du Commerce Indépendant du Détail (Switzerland)		

FRETRASC	Frente de Trabajadores Socialcristiano (Nicaragua)
FRFI	Fight Racism, Fight Imperialism
FRG	Family Rights Group
FRG	Federal Republic of Germany = BRD, GFR
FRGEI	Fédération Royale des Géomètres-Experts Indépendants = KFZLE, KFSLE, RFISE
FRH	Federation of Romanians in Hungary = MRSz
FRH	Fédération pour le Respect de l'Homme et de l'Humanité
FRHB	Federation of Registered House-Builders
FRI	Federation of Reclamation Industries
FRI	Fédération Romande Immobilière (Switzerland)
FRI	Fédération Routière Internationale = IRF
FRI	Fisheries Research Institute (U.S.A.)
FRI	Flowers Research Institute (China)
FRI	Food Research Institute (Canada)
FRI	Foreningen af Rådgivende Ingeniører
FRI	Forest Research Institute (India)
FRI	Frente Revolucionario de Izquierda (Bolivia)
FRIA	Compagnie Internationale pour la Fabrication de l'Aluminium (Africa)
FRICA	Frutera Industrial, C.A. (Venezuela)
FRICO	Friesche Coöperatieve Zuivel-Export Vereniging
FRIDA	Fund for Research and Investment for the Development of Africa
FRIFS	Fujian Research Institute of Forestry Science
FRIGO-BRAS	Companhia Brasileira de Frigorificos
FRIJP	Forestry Research Institute of Jiangsu Province
FRIM	Forest Research Institute of Malawi
FRIMPT	Fifth Research Institute, Ministry of Posts and Telecommunications (China)
FRIN	Forest Research Institute of Nigeria
FRIPT	First Research Institute of the Ministry of Posts and Telecommunication (China)
FRISA	Fuel Research Institute of South Africa
FRITALUX	Union Économique France, Italie, Benelux
FRITU	Federation of Russian Independent Trade Unions
FRL	Fédération Romande des Locataires
FRL	Fisheries Research Laboratory Marine Department (New Zealand)
FRLSU	Forum for Research into the Languages of Scotland and Ulster
FRLT	Federation of Retail Licensed Trades NI
FRLTNI	Federation of the Retail Licensed Trade of Northern Ireland
FRM	Federation of Recorded Music Societies (*ex* NFGS)
FRM	Fédération Romande des Maîtres Menuisiers Ebenistes, Fabricants de Meubles, Charpentiers et Parqueteurs (Switzerland)
FRMMP	Fédération Romande des Maîtres Plâtriers-Peintres
FRN	Forskningsrådsmämnden
FRN	Frente de Reconstrucción Nacional (Ecuador)
FRN	Frente de Resistencia Nacionalista (Chile)
FRN	Furniture Recycling Network
FRNSTP	Frente de Resistência Nacional de Sao Tomé e Principe
FRNSTP-R	FRNSTP-Renovada
FRO	Fire Research Organisation
FRO	Fundusz Restrukturyzacji i Oddłuzenia
FROLINAT	Front de Libération Nationale du Tchad
FRONTIER	Society for Environmental Exploration
FRP	Fédération Romande de Publicité (Switzerland)
FRP	Fuerzas Populares Revolucionarias (Honduras)
FRPL	Fuerzas Rebeldes y Populares Lautaro (Chile)
FRR	Foreningen af Registrerede Revisorer
FRS	Federal Reserve System (U.S.A.)
FRS	Fédération Routière Suisse
FRS	Fire Research Station (BRE)
FRS	Frente Revolucionaria Sandinista (Nicaragua)
FRS	Fruit Research Station (DSIR) (New Zealand)
FRSÉB	Fédération Régionale des Syndicats des Éleveurs de Brebis
FRSKGD	Fauna Research Section of the Kenya Game Department
FRSL	Ffestiniog Railway Society

FRSP	Fédération Romande des Syndicats Patronaux (Switzerland)	**FSASR**	Fédération des Sociétés d'Agriculture de la Suisse Romande
FRSWG	Fast Reactor Safety Working Group (EU)	**FSAV**	Fédération Suisse des Agences de Voyages
FRTC	Fast Reactor Training Centre (UKAEA)	**FSAW**	Federation of South African Women
FRTRA	Federation of Radio and Television Retailers Association	**FSB**	Fachverband Schweizerischer Betonvorfabrikanten
FRU	Fachgruppe für Raumplanung und Umwelt	**FSB**	Falange Socialista Boliviana
FRU	Federación de Religiosis del Uruguay	**FSB**	Federata Sindikale e Bujgesise (Albania) = ATUF
FRU	Free Representation Unit	**FSB**	Federation of Small Businesses
FRUBO	Nederlandse Bond van Grossiers in Zuidvruchten	**FSB**	Fédération Spéléologique de Belgique Francophone
FRUCOM	Fédération Européenne des Importateurs de Fruits Secs, Conserves, Epices et Miels	**FSB**	Föreningen Sveriges Byggnadsinspektörer
FRUIDEM	Front de Résistance pour l'Unité, l'Indépendance et la Démocratie en Mauritanie	**FSB-PEC**	Fraternitas Sancti Benedicti pro Europa Christiana = BSB-FCE, BSB-VCE
FRUTTIN-GROSSO	Sindicato Nazionale Commercianti Grossisti e Commissionari di Prodotti Ortofrutticoli	**FSBI**	Falange Socialista Boliviana de la Izquierda
		FSBI	Fisheries Society of the British Isles
FRV	Fédération Romande des Vignerons (Switzerland)	**FSC**	Fédération Suisse des Consommateurs
		FSC	Field Studies Council
FRV	Félag Rédgjafarverkfrædinga	**FSC**	Fiji Sugar Corporation
FRY	Federal Republic of Yugoslavia	**FSC**	Forest School Camps
FS	Fachverband für Strahlenschutz (Switzerland)	**FSC**	Forestry Safety Council
		FSC	Forestry Stewardship Council
FS	Federation of Synagogues	**FSC**	Institutum Fratrum Scholarum Christianarum
FS	Ferrovie dello Stato-Italia		
FS	Fertiliser Society	**FSCC**	Federal Surplus Commodities Corporation (U.S.A.)
FS	Fountain Society		
FSA	Fédération Suisse des Avocats = SAV	**FSCC**	Federation of Syndicate Credit Companies
FSA	Filipino Shipowners Association	**FSCÉ**	Fonds de Solidarité des Céréaliculteurs et des Éleveurs
FSA	Finlands Svenska Andelsförbund		
FSA	Fonds de Solidarité Africain (Niger)	**FSCRH**	Fédération Suisse des Cafetiers, Restaurateurs et Hôteliers
FSA	Football Supporters Association		
FSA	Föreningen Svenska Margarintillverkare	**FSCSM**	Fédération Belge des Chambres Syndicales de Médecine
FSA	Föreningen Sveriges Arbetsterapeuter	**FSD**	Fédération des Socialistes Démocrates
FSAA	Family Service Association of America		
FSAC	Folia Scientifica Africae Centralis	**FSD**	Foreningen af Skatterådgivere i Danmark
FSAC	Food Safety Advisory Centre		
FSAD	Föreningen af Sygehausadministratores i Danmark	**FSD**	Frente Sindical Democrático (Colombia, Peru)
FSAI	Fédération Suisse des Architectes Indépendants	**FSE**	Fédération des Sociétés Suisses d'Employés
FSAP	Fédération Suisse des Architectes Paysagistes = BSLA	**FSE**	Fonds Social Européen = ESF
		FSE	Föreningen Sveriges Energirådgivare
FSAS	Family Squatting Advisory Service	**FSÉA**	Fédération Suisse pour l'Éducation des Adultes = SFAE, SVEB

FSEC	Federal Software Exchange Center (U.S.A.)	**FSK**	Fachverband Schaumkunstoffe im GKV
FSF	Fédération Suisse du Franchising	**FSK**	Federal Service of Counter-intelligence (Russia)
FSF	Federazione Svissera dei Fisioterapisti Diplomati	**FSK**	Finlands Svenska Kommunförbund
FSF	Finlands Sjuksköterskeförbund = SSL	**FSK**	Finlands Svenska Köpmannaförbund
FSF	Finlands Stadförbund	**FSK**	Föreningen Svenska Konservtillverkare
FSF	Flight Safety Foundation (U.S.A.)	**FSK**	Schweizerischer Fachverband für Sand und Kies = ASG
FSF	Föreningen Svensk Form	**FSKG**	Finlands Svenska Kninnozgymnastikörbund
FSF	Free Software Foundation (U.S.A.)	**FSL**	Fédération des Syndicats Libres des Travailleurs Luxembourgeois
FSF	Institutum Fratrum a Sancta Familia de Bellicio	**FSL**	Finlands Svenska Lärarförbund
FSFA	Federation of Specialised Film Associations	**FSLJ**	Föreningen Skogs- och Lantbruksjournalister
FSFF	Finlands Svenska Författareföreningen	**FSLN**	Frente Sandinista de Liberación Nacional (Nicaragua)
FSFPI	Fédération Syndicale de la Fonction Publique Internationale	**FSLTT**	Fédération des Syndicats Libres des Travailleurs de la Terre
FSFRL	Far Seas Fisheries Research Laboratory (Japan)	**FSM**	Federación Sindical Mundial; Fédération Syndicale Mondiale = VFP, WFTU, WGB
FSG	Factoring Services Group		
FSG	Föreningen Svenska Glasstillverkare	**FSM**	Federated States of Micronesia
FSG	Fortress Study Group	**FSM**	Fédération Sephardite Mondiale = WSF
FSG	Franz Schmidt-Gesellschaft (Austria)	**FSM**	Fédération Socialiste de la Martinique
FSG	Institutum Fratrum Instructionis Christianae a Sancto Gabriele	**FSM**	Filles de Sainte-Marie de la Présentation
FSGC	Fratelli de San Giuseppe Benedetto Cottolengo	**FSM**	Finlands Svenska Mejeriförbund
FSGD	Federation of Sports Goods Distributors (*now* SRGB)	**FSM**	Foreningen Svenska Marknadsundersokningsinstitut
FSGVB	Fédération des Syndicates des Grands Vins de Bordeaux	**FSM**	Franciscan Sisters of Mary (U.S.A.)
FSH	Federation of Slovenes in Hungary = MSzSz	**FSMF**	Furnishing Spring Makers Federation
FSI	Fachverband Schneidwarenindustrie	**FSMG**	Vereniging van Fabrikanten van Stempels, Matrijzen, Mallen en Andere Speciale Gereedschappen
FSI	Fédération Spirite Internationale		
FSI	Fédération Suisse d'Informatique = SVI	**FSMGB**	Federation of Small Mines of Great Britain
FSI	Föreningen Sveriges Industri-förnönodenhetsleverantörer	**FSMI**	Congregatio Filiorum Sanctae Mariae Immaculatae
FSI	Frente Sindical Independiente (Mexico)	**FSMT**	Fédération Suisse des Marchands de Tabacs
FSI	International Society of Fire Service Instructors	**FSN**	Fachverband Schweizerischer Neonfirmen
FSIA	Financial Services Industry Association (Éire)	**FSN**	Federatie van Schoenwinkeliers-verenigingen
FSID	Foundation for the Study of Infant Deaths	**FSN**	Federation of Student Nationalists
FSIE	Federación de Sindicatos Independientes de la Enseñanza	**FSN**	Fédération Suisse des Notaires = SNV
		FSN	Front Syndical National (Mauritius)
		FSN-PD	Partidul Democrat (Romania)
FSIS	Finnish Society for Information Services	**FSNRIC**	Fédération Syndicate Nationale de la Répresentation Commerciale

FSNT	Federazione Svizzera dei Negozianti in Tabacchi	FSSF	Finlands Svenska Scoutförbund
FSNTJ	Fédération Suisse des Négociants en Tabacs, Journaux et Articles Divers	FSSR	Fundacja Społeczna Solidarności Robotniczej
FSNV	Fédération Suisse des Négociants en Vins	FSSS	Föreningen Sveriges Sjöfart och Sjöförsvar
FSP	Congregatio Fratrum a Sancto Patricio (Ireland)	FST	Federatie Steen-, Cement-, Glas- en Keramische Industrie
FSP	Fédération Suisse des Physiothérapeutes	FST	Fédération Suisse du Tourisme
FSP	Foreningen Sveriges Plastfabrikanter	FST	Foreningen Svenska Tonsättare
FSP	Foundation for the Peoples of the South Pacific	FSTAL	Fédération Syndicale du Teillage Agricole du Lin
FSPA	Farm Shop and Pick your own Association	FSTII	Fushun Scientific and Technical Information Institute
FSPD	Fachverband Schweizerischer Privat-Detektive	FSTL	Föreningen Svenska Tradgärds- och Landskapsarkitekter
FSPE	Federation of Societies of Professional Engineers (South Africa)	FSTMB	Federación Sindical de Trabajadores Mineros Bolivianos
FSPF	Fédération des Sociétiés Philatéliques Françaises	FSTPB	Federación Sindical de Trabajadores Petroleros Bolivianos
FSPF	Fédération des Syndicats Pharmaceutiques de France	FSTSE	Federación de Sindicatos de Trabajadores al Servicio del Estado (Mexico)
FSPG	Fire Service Preservation Group		
FSPI	Foundation for the Peoples of the South Pacific International (Fiji)	FSTSGEM	Federación Sindical de Trabajadores al Servicio del Gobierno, Estados y Municipios (Mexico)
FSPS	Federation of Sailing and Powerboat Schools	FSU	Finlands Scoutunion
FSPSP	Fédération Suisse du Personnel des Services Publics	FSV	Fondo Social para la Vivienda (El Salvador)
FSPYOA	Farm Shop and Pick Your Own Association	FSZMP	Federacja Socjalistycznych Związków Młodzieży Polskiej
FSR	Federación Sindical Revolucionaria (El Salvador)	FT	Félag Tónlistarskólakennara (Iceland)
FSR	Fédération Suisse de la Relieure = VBS	FTA	Fair Trials Abroad
FSR	Foreningen af Statsautoriserede Revisorer	FTA	Federación de Trabajadores Arubanos (Aruba)
FSRI	Foreign Service Research Institute (U.S.A.)	FTA	Federation of Trade Associations
		FTA	Flotation Tank Association
FSRP	Forum Suisse des Relations Publiques	FTA	Fördergesellschaft Technischer Ausbau
FSS	Fédération Suisse des Sélectionneurs = SZV	FTA	Foreign Trade Association
		FTA	Freight Transport Association
FSS	Fédération Suisse du Commerce des Spiritueux = VSS	FTAA	Free Trade Area of the Americas
		FTAT	Furniture, Timber and Allied Trades Union
FSS	Finnish Sauna Society (U.K.)		
FSS	Föreningen Sveriges Skirvmaterielleverantörer	FTBA	Furnishing Trades Benevolent Association
FSS	Föreningen Sveriges Stadsarkitekter	FTC	Fair Trade Commission (Japan)
FSS	Forensic Science Service	FTC	Federación de Trabajadores Copeyanos (Venezuela)
FSSA	Fertilizer Society of South Africa	FTC	Feed the Children
FSSE	Fédération des Sociétés Suisses d'Employés	FTC	Forestry Training Council
		FTC(E)	Feed the Children (Europe)

FTDA	Florists Transworld Delivery Association (U.S.A.)
FTDC	Federación de Trabajadores Demócrata Cristiana (Chile)
FTDF	Federación de Trabajadores del Departamento del Distrito Federal (Mexico)
FTÉC	Fédération des Travailleurs de l'Éducation et de la Culture (Algeria)
FTESA	Foundry Trades Equipment and Supplies Association
FTF	Fibre Trade Federation
FTF	Flygtekniska Föreningen – Svensk Förening für Flygteknik och Rymdteknik
FTF	Funktionśvrrernes og Tjenestemśndened Fśllesråd (Denmark)
FTFI	Fiskeriteknologisk Forskningsinstitutt (Norway)
FTG	Federación de Trabajadores de Guatemala
FTG	Forschungensgemeinschaft für Technisches Glas
FTGB	Federatie Textiel Groothandelsbonden
FTHA	Fork Truck Hire Association
FTI	Fiziko-Tekhnicheskii Institut
FTI	Fundação de Tecnologia Industrial (Brazil)
FTITB	Furniture and Timber Training Board
FTM	Forum du Tiers Monde = TWF
FTMA	Federated Textile Manufacturers Associations
FTMTA	Farm Tractor & Machinery Trade Association (Éire)
FTN	Federación de Trabajadores Nicaragüenses
FTN	Forces Terrestres et Navales (Gabon)
FTO	Fruit Traffic Organisation
FTPAA	Film and Television Production Association of Australia
FTPR	Federación del Trabajo de Puerto Rico
FTPS	Food Trades Protection Society
FTSC	Federal Telecommunications Standards Committee (U.S.A.)
FTSKO	Federation of Textile Societies and Kindred Organisations
FTU	Federación de Trabajadores Urbanos (Paraguay)
FTU	Federation of Trade Unions (Hong Kong)
FTU	Fishing Technology Unit (Israel)
FTUC	Fiji Trades Union Congress
FTUN	Federación de Transportadores Unidos Nicaragüense
FTUO	Federation of Trade Union Organisations (Russia)
FTWN	Farmers' Third World Network
FU	Formes Utiles
FU	Freie Universität Berlin
FU	Fuzhou University
FU.SA.DES	Fundación Salvadoreña para el Desarrollo Económico y Social
FUA	Federación Universitario Argentina
FUAAV	Fédération Universelle des Associations d'Agencies de Voyages = UFTAA
FUACÉ	Fédération Universelle des Associations Chrétiennes d'Étudiants = CSW, FUMEC, WSCF
FUAJ	Fédération Unie des Auberges de Jeunesse
FUAPO	Front Uni des Associations et Partis de l'Opposition (Gabon)
FUAR	Frente Unido de Acción Revolucionaria (Colombia)
FUCE	Fédération des Universités Catholiques Européennes (Poland)
FUCI	Federazione Universitari Cattolica Italiani
FUDANREN	Federation of Japanese Women's Organizations
FUDECO	Fundación para el Desarrollo de la Región Centro-Occidental de Venezuela
FUDFYFA	Fideicomiso Unico para el Desarrollo de la Flora y Fauna Acuaticat (Mexico)
FUE	Federated Union of Employers (Éire)
FUEN	Federal Union of European Nationalities = FUEV, UFCE, UFNE
FUEV	Féderalistische Union Europäischer Volksgruppen = FUEN, UFCE, UFNE
FUGB	Federation of Ukrainians in Great Britain
FUGE	Federated Union of Government Employees (Éire)
FUINCA	Fundación de la Red de Información Cientifica Automatizada
FULC	Federazione Unitaria Lavoratori Chimici
FULK	Front Uni de Libération Kanak (New Caledonia)
FULREAC	Foundation de l'Université de Liège pour les Recherches Scientifiques en Afrique Centrale

FULS	Federation of Ulster Local Studies
FUMEC	Federación Universal de Movimentos Estudiantiles Cristianos = CSW, FUACE, WSCF
FUMOA	Société Fûts Métalliques de l'Ouest Africain
FUMPO	Federated Union of Managerial and Professional Officers
FUN	Frente de Unidad Nacional (Guatemala)
FUN	Frente Unido Nacionalista (Venezuela)
FUN	Friends United Network
FUNA-CAMH	Frente de Unidad Nacional Campesino de Honduras
FUNAI	Fundação Nacional do Indio (Brazil)
FUNAP	Federation of Staff Associations of United Nations and its Specialized Agencies in the Philippines
FUNARTE	Fundação Nacional de Arte (Brazil)
FUNCIN-PEC	Front Uni National pour Cambodge Indépendent, Neutre, Pacifique et Coopératif
FUNDA-COMUN	Fundación para el Desarrollo de la Comunidad
FUNDAR	Fundación para el Desarrollo Regional (Argentina)
FUNDAYA-CUCHO	Fundación Gran Mariscal de Ayacucho (Venezuela)
FUNDE	Fundación Nicaragüense de Desarrollo
FUNDEAL	Fundación para el Desarrollo Algodonero (Peru)
FUNDEF	Fundación de Etnomusicologia y Folklore
FUNDE-MUN	Fundacion Salvadorena para el Desarrollo de la Mujer y el Nino
FUNDEP	Fundação de Desenvolvimento da Pesquisa (Brazil)
FUNDESCO	Fundación para el Desarrollo de la Función Social de las Comunicaciones
FUNPLATA	Fondo Fiduciario para el Desarrollo de la Cuenca del Plata
FUNRURAL	Fundo de Assistência e Previdência ao Trabalhador Rural (Brazil)
FUNVES	Fundación Vicente Giulio Soho (Venezuela)
FUNVISIS	Fundación Venezolana de Investigaciones Sismológicas
FUP	Força de Unidade Popular
FUP	Frente Unido del Pueblo (Colombia)
FUPAD	Fundación Panamericana de Desarrollo = PADF
FUPIAL	Fédération des Unions Patronales Interprofessionnelles de l'Artois et du Littoral
FUR	Föreningen för Udbildade Reklamkonsulenter (Finland) = APDA
FUR	Frente Unido Revolucionario (Guatemala)
FURC	Fonds pour l'Utilisation Rationelle des Combustibles
FURC	Foundation for Underdeveloped Regions in China
FURD	Frente Unido Revolucionario Democrático (Guatemala)
FURY	Fellowship of Reformed Youth
FUS	Fédération des Urbanistes Suisses
FUS	Fruit-Union Suisse
FUSE	Federation for Unified Science Education (U.S.A)
FUSEP	Fuerza de Seguridad Publica (Honduras)
FUSS	Federación Unitaria Sindical de El Salvador
FUT	Frente Unitario de Trabajadores (Ecuador)
FUTD-CUT	United Front of Democratic Workers (Columbia)
FUTH	Federación Unitaria de Trabajadores de Honduras
FUTT	Federación Unitaria de Trabajadores del Transporte (Colombia)
FUW	Farmers Union of Wales
FUWN	Fundusz Ubezpieczeniowy Wydawnictw Niezależnych
FUYL	Frente de Unidad Liberal (Honduras)
FVAV	Fédération Vaudoise des Sociétés d'Agriculture et de Viticulture (Switzerland)
FVB	Fabrikanten-Verband für Beleuchtungskörper
FVC	Fachgruppe für Verfahren-und Chemieingenieururtechnik
FVD	Federação dos Vinicultores do Dão
FVD	Foellersreproesention for Private Vandvoerker i Danmark
FVE	Federation of Veterinarians of the EEC
FVG	Fachverband für das Güterbeförderungsgewerbe Österreiche
FVH	Föreningen för Vattenhygien
FVK	Landelijke Vereniging van Kaashandelaren
FVL	Fachverband Lichtwerbung

FVM	Federación Venezolana de Maestros
FVM	Föreningen Svenska Verktygmaskintillverkare
FVNH	Federatie Verbond Nederlands Houtindustrie
FVPC	Federation of Visual Planning Consultants
FVPG	Film and Video Press Group
FVPRA	Fruit and Vegetable Preservation Research Association
FVR	Federal Department of Veterinary Research (Nigeria)
FVS	Fachvereinigung Soda
FVS	Forschungsgesellschaft für das Verkehrs- und Strassenwesen im ÖIAV (Austria)
FVTDV	Groep Fabrikanten en Vertegenwoordigers van Toevoegingsmiddelen voor de Dierlijke Vocding
FVV	Forschungsvereinigung Verbrennungskraftmaschine
FVVK	Facherband Verpackung und Verpackungsfolien aus Kunststoff
FVVNNB	Fremdenverksverband Nordsee-Niedersacken-Bremen
FVVTW	Verkehrsverband Teutoburger Wald
FWA	Family Welfare Association
FWACC	Federation of West African Chambers of Commerce (Nigeria) = FCCAO
FWAPSA	Federation of West African Pharmaceutical Students Associations (Ghana)
FWAT	Forest Workers Association of Tasmania
FWBO	Friends of the Western Buddhist Order = AOBO, TBMSG
FWC	Fourth World Council
FWC	Friends World College (U.S.A.)
FWCC	Friends World Committee for Consultation = BWF, CCMA, CMCA
FWD	Federation of Wholesale Distributors
FWEA	International Federation of Workers Educational Associations
FWERI	Finnish Water and Environment Research Institute
FWG	Facherband Werkzeug-Grosshandel
FWG	Forschungsanstalt der Bundeswehr für Wasserschall und Geophysik
FWHF	Federation of World Health Foundations
FWI	Federation of the West Indies
FWI	Freshwater Institute (Canada)
FWID	Federation of Wholesale and Industrial Distributors
FWN	Farmers' World Network
FWPA	Finnish Wood Preserving Association
FWPRDC	Forest and Wood Products Research and Development Corporation
FWRAP	Federal Water Resources Assistance Program
FWRM	Fiji Women's Rights Movement
FWRMGB	Federation of Wire Rope Manufacturers of Great Britain
FWT	Farming and Wildlife Trust
FWU	Institut für den Film und Bild Wissenschaft und Unterricht Gemeinnützige
FWVFA	Federation of World Volunteer Firefighters Associations
FWWCP	Federation of Worker Writers and Community Publishers
FYC	Family & Youth Concern
FYDEP	Empresa Nacional de Fomento y Desarrollo Económico de El Petén (Guatemala)
FYF	Find Your Feet
FYF	Finlands Yrkeskvinnors Förbund = SLVL
FYSiF	Suomen Fyysikkojen Seura / Fysikersamfundet i Finland
FZ	Franc Zone
FZA	Fernmeldetechnisches Zentralamt (Austria)
FZD	Finanz- und Zolldepartment (Switzerland)
FZG	Federation of Zoological Gardens of Great Britain and Ireland
FZLE	Federatie der Zelfstandige Landmeters-Experten (Belgium)
FZÖ	Fachverein der Zuckerfabriken Österreichs
FZY	Federation of Zionist Youth
FZZG	Federacja Związków Zawodowych Górników

G

G&SS	Gilbert & Sullivan Society
G-10	Group of Ten (GAB)
G-11	Group of 11
G-15	Group of Fifteen
G-19	Group of 19

G-2	Army Intelligence Network (Guatemala)
G-2	Army Intelligence Unit (Panama)
G-2	Group of 2
G-24	Group of Twenty Four
G-3	Group of Three
G-30	Group of 30
G-33	Group of 33
G-5	Group of Five
G-6	Group of 6
G-7	Group of Seven
G-77	Group of 77
G-8	Group of Eight
G-8	Grupo de 8 (Argentina)
G-9	Group of 9
G-ESP	Greens – Ecological Social Party (Slovenia)
GA	Galvanizers Association
GA	Gamblers Anonymous
GA	Gemmological Association of Great Britain
GA	General Assembly of the United Nations
GA	Geographical Association
GA	Geologists Association
GA	Gesellschaft für Arzneipflanzenforschung
GA	Giftware Association
GA	Grafiska Arbetsgivareförbundet
GA	Green Alliance
GA	Greening Australia
GA	Gypsum Association (U.S.A.)
GA-NOC	General Assembly, National Olympic Committees
GAA	Gaelic Athletic Association (Ireland)
GAA	Greenhouse Action Australia
GAA	Grupo de Acción Anticomunista (Paraguay)
GAAA	Greek Advertising Agencies Association
GAAA	Groupement Atomique Alsacien Atlantique
GAAM	Ghana Association for the Advancement of Management
GAAS	Guangdong Academy of Agricultural Sciences
GAAS	Guangxi Academy of Agricultural Sciences
GABA	Global Agricultural Biotechnology Association
GABA	Nederlandse Vereniging van Bedrijven in de Gemende Branche (Glas, Aardewerk en Bijbehorende Artikelen)
GABCC	Great Australian Bight Consultative Committee
GABIA	Great Australian Bight Industry Association
GABIM	La Gabonaise Immobilière
GABOA	Société Gabonaise d'Oxygène et d'Acétylène
GABOMA	Société Gabonaise des Grands Magasins
GABOMER	Société Gabonaise de Pêche en Mer (Gabon)
GABONAP	Société Gabonaise de Diffusion d'Appareils Électriques
GABONEX	Société Gabonaise d'Exploitation Vinicole
GABOSEP	Société Gabonaise de Sepultures
GABRIELA	General Assembly Binding Women for Reforms, Integrity, Equality, Leadership and Action (Philippines)
GABTRANS	Société Gabonaise de Transports Internationaux
GAC	Geological Association of Canada
GAC	Government Art Collection
GAC	Guangxi Agricultural College
GACIFAL	Groupe Consultatif de la Recherche et de l'Enseignement Forestier pour l'Amérique Latine
GACOA	Groupe Commercial Africain (Central Africa)
GACRI	Guangdong Arts and Crafts Research Institute (China)
GAD	Government Actuary's Department
GAD	Groupe Africaine de Distribution
GAD	Groupe d'Aide au Développement
GADA	Gemeinschaft Aktiver Deutsche Apotheker und Apothekerinnen
GADAR	Guild of Antique Dealers & Restorers
GADEF	Groupement des Associations Dentaires Francophones
GAE	Groupe Spécialisé pour l'Aménagment du Territoire et l'Environnement
GAE	Groupements Agricoles d'Exploitation
GAE	Grupo Aéreo Embarcado
GAE	Grupo Anticomunista Español
GAEC	Ghana Atomic Energy Commission
GAEC	Greek Atomic Energy Commission
GAEC	Groupements Agricoles d'Exploitation en Commun

GAF	Gesellschaft für Aerosolforschung		**GAL**	Grupos Antiterroristas de Liberación
GAF	Glasmästeribranchens Arbetsgivareförbund		**GAL**	Guild of American Luthiers
GAF	Gulvbeloegningsbranchens Arbejdsgiverforning		**GALA**	Greek Applied Linguistics Association
			GALA	Grupo de Acústicos Latinoamericanos
GAFICA	Grupo Asesor de la FAO para la Integración Económica Centroamericana (Guatemala)		**GALC**	European Booksellers Association
			GALF	Groupement des Anthropologistes de Langue Française
GAFOR	Société Gabonaise de Forage		**GALHA**	Gay and Lesbian Humanist Association
GAFRO	Ghana Association for Research on Women		**GALIAF**	Société Gaz Liquéfiés d'Afrique
GAFTA	Grain and Feed Trade Association		**GALOP**	Gay London Policing
GAG	Gays Against Genocide		**GAM**	Groupement des Aciers Moulés (Belgium)
GAG	Georg-Agricola-Gesellschaft zur Förderung der Geschichte der Naturwissenschaften und der Technik e.V.		**GAM**	Groupement des Associations Meunières des Pays de la CEE
			GAM	Grupo de Apoyo Mutuo por el Aparecimiento con Vida de Nuestros Familiares (Guatemala)
GAGBI	Grenfell Association of Great Britain and Ireland		**GAMA**	Gas Appliance Manufacturers Association (U.S.A.)
GAGTL	Gemmological Association and Gem Testing Laboratory of Great Britain		**GAMA**	Guitar and Accessory Manufacturers Association of America
GAI	Associazione dei Gruppi Archeologici d'Italia		**GAMBICA**	Association for the Instrumentation Control and Automation Industry in the United Kingdom
GAI	Guild of Architectural Ironmongers			
GAIA	Graphic Arts Industries Association (U.S.A.)		**Game Coin**	Game Conservation International
			GAMF	Gépipari és Automatizálási Müszaki Föiskola
GAIF	General Arab Insurance Federation (Egypt) = FGAA, UGAA		**GAMI**	Groupement pour l'Avancement de la Mécanique Industrielle
GAIF	General Assembly of International Sports Federations		**GAMIF**	Groupement d'Acceptations Maritimes Internationales en France
GAIIA	Global Alliance of International Information Industry Associations (U.S.A.)		**GAMM**	Gesellschaft für Angewandte Mathematik und Mechanik
			GAMMA	Gender and Mathematics Association
GAILL	Groupement des Allergologistes et Immunologistes de Langues Latines		**GAMMA**	Institute of Advanced Research Long-range Planning
GAIN	Grupo de Apoio ao Indio (Brazil)		**GAMNA**	Gambian News Agency
GAISF	General Association of International Sports Federations = AGFIS		**GAMO**	Glavnyi Arkhiv Ministerstva Oborony
			GAMS	Group for the Advancement of Spectroscopic and Physiochemical Analysis Methods
GAIU	Graphic Arts International Union			
GAJ	Guild of Agricultural Journalists (U.S.A.)		**GAMS**	Groupement pour l'Avancement des Sciences Analytiques
GAJES	Groupe d'Action pour la Justice et l'Egalité Sociale (Benin)		**GAMTA**	General Aviation Manufacturers and Traders Association
GAK	Gemeinschafsausschuss Kaltformgebung		**GAN**	Green Academic Network
GAK	Gesellschaft für Aktuelle Kunst e.V.		**GANPAC**	German-American National Political Action Committee (U.S.A.)
GAL	Gesellschaft für Angewandte Linguistik		**GANVAM**	Asociación Nacional de Vendedores y Reparadores de Vehículos a Motor, Recambios Accesorois y Afines
GAL	Gesellschaft für Arbeitswissenschaft im Landbau			
GAL	Greening Australia Limited			

GAO	General Accounting Office (U.S.A.)
GAO	Gruppo Amici dell'Organizzazione
GAO	Réseau Groupements – Associations Villageoises – Organisations Paysannes
GAP	Girls Alone Project
GAP	Global Action Plan for the Earth (U.K., U.S.A.)
GAP	Groupement d'Action Populaire (Burkina Faso)
GAP	Southeast Anatolia Project (Turkey)
GAP UK	Global Action Plan UK
GAPAN	Guild of Air Pilots and Air Navigators (U.K., U.S.A.)
GAPAVÉ	Groupement des Associations de Propriétaires d'Appareils à Vapeur et Électriques
GAPEX	General Agricultural Products Export Corporation (Tanzania)
GAPINDO	Perkumpulan Koperasi Gabungan Pembelian Importir Indonesia
GAPMB	Ghana Agricultural Produce Marketing Board
GAPS	German Association for Political Science
GAPT	Guild of Anatomical Pathology Technicians
GAR	Groupements d'Artisans Ruraux (Burkina Faso)
GAR	Grupos Antiterroristas Rurales
GAR	Grupos Armados Revolucionarios
GAR	Guangxi Research and Design Institute of Architectural Science (China)
GARDEN-EX	Federation of Garden and Leisure Equipment Exporters
GARF	Graphic Arts Research Foundation (U.S.A.)
GARP	Global Atmospheric Research Programme
GARTEur	Group for Aeronautical Research and Technology in Europe
GAS	General Aviation Services (Canada)
GAS	Glasgow Archaeological Society
GAS	Group Analytic Society
GAS-EUROSOUD	European Committee of Manufacturers of Gas-Welding Equipment
GASBINDO	Gabungan Serikat Buruh Islam Indonesia
GASC	German-American Securities Corporation
GASCO	Abu Dhabi Gas Industries Limited

GASCO	General Aviation Safety Committee
GASERC	Gulf Arab States Educational Research Center (ABEGS) (Kuwait)
GASGA	Group for Assistance on Systems Relating to Grain Afterharvest (Netherlands)
GASLAB	Global Atmospheric Sampling Laboratory
GAT	Gabon Air Transport
GaT	Gemeinschaftsausschuss der Technik
GAT	Groupement Africain des Travaux au Caméroun
GAT	Guyane Air Transport
GATA	Glass and Allied Trades Association
GATCO	Guild of Air Traffic Control Officers
GATE	Agrártudományi Egyetem, Gödölló
GATE	Germany Appropriate Technology Exchange
Gateway	National Federation of Gateway Clubs
GATF	Graphic Arts Technical Foundation (U.S.A.)
GATL	Group Aérien de Transport et de Liaison (Ivory Coast)
GATPRO-CO	German-American Trade Promotion Company
GATRA-MAR	Société Gabonaise de Transports Maritimes
GATT	General Agreement on Tariffs and Trade (UN) (*now* WTO)
GAU	Glavnoye Artilleriiskoe Upravleniie
GAUFCC	General Assembly of Unitarian and Free Christian Churches
GAV	Gemeinschaftsausschuss Verzinken
GAVA	Guild of Aviation Artists
GAW	Gay Authors Workshop
GAW	Global Atmosphere Watch (WMO)
GAWF	General Arab Women Federation
GAWF	Greek Animal Welfare Fund
GAWI	Gesellschaft für Abwicklung Wirtschaftlicher Angelegenheiten
GAWU	Guyana Agricultural Workers Union
GB	Girls Brigade
GBA	Governing Bodies Association
GBAEV	Gesellschaft für Biologische Anthropologie, Eugenik und Verhaltensforschung
GBARC	Great Britain Aeronautical Research Committee
GBC	Ghana Broadcasting Corporation

GBC	Gibraltar Broadcasting Corporation
GBCC	Beijing Compruter Centre
GBCh	Gesellschaft für Biologische Chemie
GBCRMWU	Grand Bahama Construction, Refinery and Maintenance Workers' Union
GBCT	Guild of British Camera Technicians
GBDL	Gesellschaft für Bibliothekswesen und Dokumentation des Landbaues
GBE	Groupe Bois-Énergie (IEPF)
GBÉ	Groupement Belge des Banques d'Épargne
GBEU	Grand Bahama Entertainers' Union
GBF	Gesellschaft für Biotechnologische Forschung mbH (Germany)
GBF	Grafiske Bedrifters Felleskontor
GBFE	Guild of British Film Editors
GBGSA	Governing Bodies of Girls Schools Association
GBH	Gewerkschaft Bau und Holz (Switzerland)
GBI	Gesamtverband Besteckindustrie
GBI	Groupe des Bois Ivoiriens
GBIGAS	Institute of Geochemistry, Guangzhou Branch, Academia Sinica
GBK	Gemeenschap Beeldende Kunstenaars (Netherlands)
GBK	Gesellschaft Bildender Küntter Österreichs
GBL	Grafiske Bedrifters Landsforening
GBM	Gulf Building Materials (UAE)
GBMA	Garden Building Manufacturers Association
GBMA	Golf Ball Manufacturers Association (U.S.A.)
GBMPC	Great Britain Map Postcard Club
GBMR	Groupement Belge de Mécanique des Roches
GBNE	Guild of British Newspaper Editors
GBO	Groepering van de Vloer- en Muurbekledingsondernemigen (Belgium)
GBO	Groupement Belge des Omnipraticiens = VBO
GBP	Gay Bereavement Project
GBRA	Gas Breeder Reactor Association
GBRCC	Great Barrier Reef Consultative Committee
GBRF	Great Britain Racquetball Federation
GBRMPA	Great Barrier Reef Marine Park Authority
GBRS	Groupe Belge de Recherche Sous-Marine
GBS	British Guillain Barré Syndrome Support Group
GBS	Groupement des Unions Professionnelles Belges de Médecins Spécialistes = VBS
GBSS	Governesses' Benevolent Society of Scotland
GBST	Global Blood Safety Initiative (Switzerland)
GBTA	Guild of Business Travel Agents
GBTCU	Grand Bahama Telephone and Telecommunications Union
GBTSF	Great Britain Target Shooting Federation
GC	Game Conservancy Trust
GCA	Garden Centre Association
GCA	Gasket Cutters' Association
GCA	Genealogy Club of America
GCA	Geophysics Corporation of America
GCA	Global Commission on AIDS (WHO)
GCA	Grains Council of Australia
GCA	Graphic Communications Association (U.S.A.)
GCA	Groep Fabrieken van Apparaten voor de Chemische Industrie
GCB	Greyhound Consultative Body
GCB	Guernsey Cattle Breeders' Association
GCBS	General Council of British Shipping
GCBW	General Committee for Bahrain Workers
GCC	Game Conservancy Council
GCC	Gas Consumers Council
GCC	Grandes Carrières du Caméroun
GCC	Great Council of Chiefs (Fiji)
GCC	Grid Cooperating Centre
GCC	Gulf Cooperation Council (Saudi Arabia) = CCG
GCCA	Greeting Card and Calendar Association
GCCC	General Council of County Councils (Éire)
GCCF	Governing Council of the Cat Fancy
GCCIP	Global Climate Change Information Programme
GCCNI	General Consumer Council for Northern Ireland
GCDP	Grupo Coordinador do Desenvolvimento da Pesca (Brazil)

GCDRA	Green Crop Driers Research Association
GCEC	Gold Coast Environment Centre
GCECWCR	Gypsy Council for Education, Culture, Welfare & Civil Rights
GCFI	Gulf and Caribbean Fisheries Institute
GCFP	Guild of Conservation Food Producers
GCGB	Golf Club – Great Britain
GCH	Guild of Curative Hypnotherapists
GCHQ	Government Communications Headquarters
GCI	Génie Climatique International
GCI	Global Commons Institute
GCI	Groupe Chaudronnerie Ivoirienne
GCI	Groupe Spécialisé de la Construction Industrialisée dans le Bâtiment et le Génie Civil (Switzerland)
GCI	Guangzhou Communications Research Institute (China)
GCIAI	Grupo Consultivo sobre Investigación Agrícola International = CGIAR, GCRAI
GCIC	Gifted Children's Information Centre
GCIC	Groupement Cinématographique International de Conciliation = IFCG
GCICUK	German Chamber of Industry and Commerce in the UK
GCIRC	Glass Container Industry Research Corporation (U.S.A.)
GCIRC	Groupe Consultatif International de Recherche sur le Colza
GCL	Guild of Cleaners & Launderers
GCL	Weltgemeinschaft Christlichen Lebens = CVX, WCLC
GCM	Guild of Church Musicians
GCMB	Ghana Cocoa Marketing Board
GCME	Gomel Regional Commodity and Raw Materials Exchange (Belarus)
GCO	Gemeenschappelijk Centrum voor Onderzoek (EURATOM) = CCI, CCR, GFS, JRC
GCÖD	Gesamtverband der Christlichen Gewerkschaften Öffenlicher Dienst Bahn und Post
GCOS	Global Climate Observing System (ICSU,IOC, UNEP, WMO)
GCP	Groupe Consultatif des Protéines et Calories du Système des Nations-Unies = PAG
GCP	Guild of Computer Practitioners
GCPPI	Gifted Children's Pen Pals International (U.S.A.)
GCRAI	Groupe Consultatif de la Recherche Agricole Internationale (FAO) = CGIAR, GCIAI
GCRCH	General Council & Register of Consultant Herbalists Ltd
GCRI	Glasshouse Crops Research Institute (*now* HRA)
GCRI	Grain Crops Research Institute (South Africa)
GCRN	General Council and Register of Naturopaths
GCRO	General Council and Registrar of Osteopaths
GCS	Game Conservation Society (U.S.A.)
GCS	Greek Society of Computer and Information Scientists
GCS	Guernsey Conservation Society
GCSP	Government Communications Staff Federation
GCT	Confederación General de Trabajadores (Costa Rica)
GCT	Game Conservancy Trust
GCT	Groupe Consultatif Technique (UN)
GCTU	General Council of Trade Unions (Russia)
GCU	Guyana Cooperative Union
GCVAW	Gabriela Commission on Violence against Women (Philippines)
GCVM	Confédération Générale des Vignerons du Midi
GCW	Gesellschaft der Chirurgen in Wien (Austria)
GCWT	Golf Course Wildlife Trust
GD	Grupos Dinamizadores (Mozambique)
GD CV INSTIT	Guangdong Cardiovascular Institute (China)
GDA	Gas Distribution Administration
GDA	Global Dialog Association (U.S.A.)
GDA	Grafik-Design Austria
GDAPS	Grémio dos Armadores da Pesca da Sardinha
GdB	Gesellschaft des Bauwesens
GdB	Gesellschaft des Bibliophilen
GDBA	Genossenschaft Deutscher Bühnen Angehöriger
GDBA	Guide Dogs for the Blind Association
GDBH	Gesellschaft Deutscher Berg- und Hüttenleute

GDC	General Dental Council		**GEA**	Greek Ecologists Association
GDCh	Gesellschaft Deutscher Chemiker		**GEA**	Groupe d'Études des Problèmes des Grandes Entreprises Agricoles
GDDA	General Desert Development Authority (Egypt)		**GEAC**	Groupement d'Entreprises au Caméroun
GDE	Gemeinschaft Deutscher Einkaufskontore des Nahrungsmittelgrosshandels		**GEAE**	Groupement Européen des Ardennes et de l'Eifel
GDF	Gaz de France		**GEAF**	Grupo Executivo do Abastecimento de Fertilizantes (Brazil)
GDF	Guyana Defence Force		**GEAMR**	Groupement Européen des Associations des Maisons de Réforme
GDG	Gemeinschaft Deutscher Gross-Messen			
GDICMM	Guangdong Institute of Chinese Materia Medica		**GEAP**	Groupe Européen d'Administration Publique = EGPA
GDL	Gazodinamicheskaia Laboratoriia		**GEB**	Gemeinschaft der Europäischen Bahnen = CCFE, CER
GDL	Gemeinschaft Deutscher Lehrerverbände		**GEBAM**	Grupo Executivo do Baixo Amazonas (Brazil)
GDL	Gesamtverband des Deutschen Leder-Gross- und -Aussenhandels		**GEBANA**	Arbeitsgemeinschaft Gerechten Bananenhandel (Switzerland)
Gdl	Gesellschaft der Ingenieure der Schweizerischen Bundesbahnen		**GEBCO**	General Bathymetric Chart of the Oceans
GDL	Gewerkschaft Deutscher Lokomotivführer und Anwärter		**GEBE-COMA**	Groupement Belge des Constructeurs de Matériel Aérospatial
GDM	Gesamtverband Deutscher Metallgiessereien		**GEBO**	Golventreprenörernas Branschorganisation
GDM	Gesamtverband Deutscher Musikfachgeschäfte		**GEBRA**	Vereniging Centrale Organisatie Gemengde Branche
GDM	Ghana Democratic Movement		**GEBRAM**	Gespreksgroep Fabrikanten van Brandweervoertuigen- Apparaten en-Material
GDMB	Gesellschaft Deutscher Metallhütten- und Bergleute			
GDMK	Gewerkschaft Deutscher Musikerzieher und Konzertierender Künstler		**GEC**	General Electric Company
GdO	Gesellschaft der Orgelfreunde		**GEC**	Groupe Européenne de Curiethérapie
GDPA	General Dental Practitioners Association		**GEC**	Groupement Européen des Fabricants de Celluloses
GDPF	Groupement des Directeurs Publicitaires de France		**GECA**	Groupement National d'Exploitation des Conserves Agricoles (France)
GDPS	Government Document Publishing Service (U.S.A.)		**GECA-MINES**	La Générale des Carrières et des Mines (Zaïre)
GDRICS	Guangdong Research Institute of Cereal Science (China)		**GECACI**	Générale Cafétière et Cacaoyère de Côte-Ivoire
GDS	Gesamtverband Deutscher Spielwarenexporteure		**GECE**	Groupement Européen des Caisses d'Epargne = ESBG, ESV
GDSI	Global Development Studies Institute (U.S.A.)		**GECICAM**	Entreprise de Génie Civil et Construction au Caméroun
GDTI	Gender Dysphoria Trust International		**GECOM**	Générale Camérounaise de Constructions Métalliques
GDV	Gesamtverband der Deutschen Versicherungswirtschaft		**GECOMIN**	General Congolese Ore Company (Zaïre)
Ge-TM	Genève – Tiers-Monde		**GECO-PHAM**	General Organisation for Phosphate and Mines (Syria)
GEA	Garage Equipment Association			
GEA	Ghana Employers Association		**GÉCUS**	Groupe d'Études et de Coordination de l'Urbanisme Souterrain
GEA	Global Education Associates (U.S.A.)			

GEDA	Guam Economic Development Authority
GEDAG	Gesamtverband Deutscher Angestellten-Gewerkschaften
GEDC	Ghanaian Enterprises Development Commission
GEDÉO	Groupement d'Équipement et d'Outillage (Central Africa)
GEDIP	Grupo Executivo do Desenvolimento da Industria de Pesca
GEDIS	Groupement Européen des Entreprises de Distribution Integrée
GEDÖK	Gemeinschaft Deutscher und Österreichischer Kunstlerinnen
GEDRT	Groupe Européen d'Échange d'Expérience sur la Direction de la Recherche Textile
GEE	Group of Economic Experts (OECD)
GEEDA	Groundnut Extractions Export Development Association (India)
GEEI	Grupo Especial de Estudos Indigenistas (Brazil)
GEEP	Group of Experts on Environmental Pollutants
GÉÉR	Groupement d'Étude pour l'Équipement Rural
GEERMM	Groupe Européen d'Echanges Rhin-Meuse-Moselle – Drogues et Dépendances (CE, CEC) = Euro AFIS
GÉERS	Groupe d'Études Européens des Recherches Spatiales
GEEUP	Glasgow Environmental Education Urban Projects
GEF	Global Environment Facility (U.S.A.)
GEFA	Gulf-European Freight Association
GEFACS	Groupement des Fabricants d'Appareils Sanitaires en Céramique de la CEE
GEFAM	Gesellschaft der Freunde Alter Musikinstrumente (Switzerland)
GEFAP	Groupement Européen des Associations Nationales de Fabricants de Pesticides
GEFCA	Groupement Européen des Financiers du Cinéma et de l'Audiovisuel
GEFCO	Griqualand Exploration and Finance Company
GEFDU	Groupe Européen des Femmes Diplômées des Universités = UWE
GEFIU	Gesellschaft für Finanzwirtschaft in der Unternehmensführung
GEGEN	Gesellschaft für Geschichte der Neuzeit
GEGZ	Geographische-Ethnographische Gesellschaft, Zurich
GEHI	Guangzhou Environmental Health Institute (China)
GEIA	Groupo Executivo da Industria Automobilistica (Brazil)
GEIAO	German Export-Import Advisory Office
GEID	Groupe Européen des Industries de Défense (IEPG) (Portugal)
GEIDA	Grupo Executivo de Irrigação para o Desenvolvimento Agrícola (Brazil)
GEIE	Groupement Européen d'Intérêt Économique = EEIG, EESV, EWIV
GEIP	Greenhouse Education and Information Program
GEIP	Groupe Européen Indépendant de Programme (NATO) = IEPG
GEIPOT	Empresa Brasileira de Planejamento de Transportes
GEJ	Groupe Européen des Journalistes (IFJ)
GEL	Groupement Européen de Lymphologie
GÉLC	Groupe des Éditeurs de Livres des Communautés Européennes
GÉLNA	Groupe d'Études sur la Littérature Néo-Africaine
GELP	Groupement d'Exploitation de Laboratoire Photo-Cinéma (Ivory Coast)
GELRE	Vereniging tot Beoefening van Geldersche Geschiedenis Oudheidkunde en Recht
GELTSPAP	Group of Experts on Long-Term Scientific Policy and Planning (UNESCO)
GEM	Group Education Museums
GEM	Groupes Evangile et Mission
GEM	Guild of Experienced Motorists
GEMA	Gesellschaft für Musikalische Aufführungs und Mechanische Vervielfältigungsrechte
GEMA	Gymnastic Equipment Manufactures Association
GEMAS	Groupement Européen des Maisons d'Alimentation et d'Approvisionnement à Succursales
GEMC	Grupo de Estudos para o Desenvolvimento Comunitário de Macau
GEMEC	Grupo de Estudio para el Mejoramiento de la Enseñanza de las Ciencias (Honduras)

GEMFOR	Groupe d'Études des Méthodes de Formation (IEPF)
GEMI	Bureau de la Géologie et des Mines (Burkina Faso)
GEMM	Groupement Européen du Mobilier Métallique
GEMMA	Gilt Edge Market Makers Association
GÉMP	Groupe d'Études et de Mesures de la Productivité (AFAP)
GEMPA	Grupo de Estudios de la Mujer Paraguaya
GEMS	Gilevi Exploration and Mining Syndicate (Tanzania)
GEMS	Global Environment Monitoring System (UNEP)
GEMWU	General Engineering and Metalworkers Union (Zimbabwe)
GEN	Group of European Nutritionists
GÉNAVIR	Groupement d'Intérêt Économique pour la Gestion des Navires Océanologiques
GÉNCO	Société Générale de Construction au Caméroun
GENCOR	General Mining Union Corporation (South Africa)
GENECO	Genootschap van Nederlandse Componisten
GENEMA	Groupement d'Exportation des Navires et Engins de Mer et Acier
Geneva - Association	International Association for the Study of Insurance Economics = Association de Genève; Genfer Vereinigung
GENI	Gestalt Education Network International
GÉNICIAT	Génie Civil en Afrique Tropicale (Ivory Coast)
GENS	Gestioni Esercizio Navi Sicilia
GENUNG	Groupe d'Exports des Nations Unies sur les Noms Géographiques = UNGEGN
GEO	Glosa Education Organisation
GEO	Grupos Especiales de Operaciones
GEOAR	General Egyptian Organization for Aquatic Resources
GEOBOL	Servico Geológico de Bolivia
GEOMIN	Entreprise de Coopération pour l'Industrie Minière et la Géologie (Romania)
GEP	Grasslands Ecology Program
GÉP	Groupement Intersyndical pour l'Équipement des Industries du Pétrole, du Gaz Naturel et de la Pétrochimie
GEP	Organização das Mulheres Gestoras de Empresas em Portugal

GEPA	Gulf-European Freight Association (U.S.A.)
GEPA	Study, Research and Analysis Office (Angola)
GEPHA	Bundesverband des Genossenschaftlichen Pharmazeutischen Grosshandels in Deutschland
GEPI	Gestion e Partecipazioni Industriali
GEPI	Groupement National Technique des Entrepreneurs de Peinture Industrielle
GEPILE	Groupement Européen pour la Promotion des Initiatives Locales pour l'Emploi = EGLEI
GEPLACEA	Grupo de Paises Latinoamericanos y del Caribe Exportadores del Azucar
GEPLASE	Grupo de Estudos para o Plantio da Seringueira (Brazil)
GEPMS	Groupement Européenne des Papiers Minces Spéciaux
GEPNA	Groupe Européen de Planification de la Navigation Aérienne
GEPOC	Gesellschaft für Polymerchemie
GÉPS	Groupe d'Études des Protéines de Soja
GEPS	Groupe Européen de Presse Spécialisée
GEPSA	Empresa Guineano-Española de Petróleos (Equatorial Guinea)
GEPTI	Groupement d'Entreprises pour Travaux Internationaux
GEPVP	Groupement Européen des Producteurs de Verre Plat
GER	Group of European Radiotherapists
GER	Groupement des Entreprises de Revêtements de Sols et Murs (Belgium)
GER	Guilde Européenne du Raid
GERAKAN	Parti Gerakan Rakyat Malaysia
GERCA	Grupo Executivo de Racionalização da Cafeicultura (Brazil)
GÉRCOS	Groupement d'Études et de Réalizations des Compresseurs Spéciaux
GÉRDAT	Groupement d'Études et de Recherches pour de Développement de l'Agronomie Tropicale
GÉRDEC	Groupe d'Études et de Recherches pour le Développement Culturel
GÉRDES	Groupe d'Études et de Recherches pour le Développement des Sciences Sociales
GÉREC	Groupement pour l'Étude et la Réalisation d'Ensembles Contrôle-Commande
GÉRES	Groupe Énergies Renouvelables

GERG	Groupe Européen de Recherches Gazières
GÉRICO	Groupement d'Études et de Réalisations Industrielles et Commerciales (Ivory Coast)
GÉRIP	Groupe d'Études et de Recherches des Infirmiers Psychiatriques
GERISIC	Groupe Européenne de Recherche et d'Information sur l'Italie Contemporaine
GÉRS	Groupe d'Études et de Recherches Sous-Marines
GÉRSPPA	Group d'Études et de Recherches pour les Solutions aux Problèmes des Personnes Âgées
GÉRT	Groupement d'Études et de Réalisations Techniques
GES	Gesellschaft für Elektronische Systemforschung
GES	Global Epidemiological Surveillance and Health Situation (WHO)
GES	Government Economic Service
GESAMP	Group of Experts on Scientific Aspects Marine Pollution
GESAMP	Group of Experts on the Scientific Aspects of Marine Pollution (UN)
GESC	Government Electronic Data Processing Standards Committee (Canada)
GESEM	Groupement Européen des Sources d'Eaux Minérales Naturelles
GESM	Group for Educational Services in Museums
GÉSMA	Groupe d'Études Sous-Marines de l'Atlantique
GÉSOL	Groupe Intersyndical de l'Énergie Solaire
GETAT	Grupo Executivo das Terras do Araguaia/Tocantins (Brazil)
GETB	Groupement des Entrepreneurs de Travaux Publics et de Bâtiments (Ivory Coast)
GETT	Group of European Manufacturers for the Advancement of Turbine Technology
GEURR	Group of Experts on Urban and Regional Research (Switzerland)
GEV	Gesellschaft Europäischer Verbandsleiter = AEDA, ESAE
GÉVES	Groupe d'Étude et de Contrôle des Variété et des Semences
GEVF	Gesellschaft für Wirtschafts-und Verkehrswissenschaftliche Forschung
GEW	Gewerkschaft Erziehung und Wissenschaft
GEWINA	Genootschap voor Geschiedenis der Geneeskunde, Wiskunde, Natuurwetenschappen en Techniek
GEWR	Groupement des Exploitants de Wagons-Réservoirs et de Containers Citernes à Vins Alcools et Boissons autres que la Bière
GEX	Groupement des Exportateurs (Cameroon)
GEXPICA	Groupement d'Exportateurs Ivoiriens de Café et de Cacao
GF	Genealogiska Föreningen
GF	Geografiska Förbundet
GF	Geologiska Föreningen
GF	Glassbransjeforbundet i Norge
GF	Guarda Fiscal (Portugal)
GFA	Gesellschaft für Arbeitswissenschaft
GfA	Gesellschaft für Arzneipflanzenforschung
GFA	Gesellschaft für Forschungen zur Auffuhrungspraxis (Austria)
GFA	Groupement Foncier Africain
GFA	Groupement Français d'Assurances
GFAA	Game Fishing Association of Australia
GFB	Gemeinschaft Fachärztlicher Berufsverbände
GFB	Schweizerische Gesellschaft für Bauforschung
GFBG	Gesellschaft für Forschung auf Biophysikalischen Grenzgebieten (Switzerland)
GfbV	Gesellschaft für Bedrohte Völker = APM
GFC	German Friendship Circles (Poland) = KPN
GFC	Gesellschaft für Chemiewirtschaft
GFC	Groep Fabrikanten van Compressoren
GFCI	Groupement Foncier de la Côte d'Ivoire
GFCM	General Fisheries Council for the Mediterranean (FAO) = CGPM
GfdS	Gesellschaft für Deutsche Sprache
GfE	Gesellschaft für Erdkunde zu Berlin
GfE	Gesellschaft für Ernährungsphysiologie
GfEaH	Gesellschaft für Ernährungsphysiologie de Haustiere
GFF	Gesellschaft zur Förderung der Forschung (Switzerland)
GFFC	Groupement Français des Fabricants de Carton

GFFIL	Groupement Français des Fournisseurs d'Information en Ligne
GFFSA	German Federal Flight Security Agency
GfG	Gesellschaft für Ganzheitsforschung (Austria)
GfG	Gesellschaft für Gerontologie
GFI	Glas Forsknings Institutet
GFI	Green Flag International
GFI	Groupement Français d'Informatique
GFII	Groupement Français de l'Industrie de l'Information
GFJTU	General Federation of Jordanian Trade Unions
GfK	Gesellschaft für Kernforschung
GfK	Gesellschaft für Konsum-, Markt- und Absatzforschung
GfKl	Gesellschaft für Klassifikation e.V.
GFM	Gesellschaft für Musikforschung
GFM	Schweizerische Gesellschaft für Marketing
GfÖ	Gesellschaft für Ökologie
GFP	Gesellschaft zur Förderung der Photographie
GFPA	Gambia Family Planning Association
GFPE	Gesellschaft für Praktische Energiekunde
GFPF	Gesellschaft zur Förderung Pädagogischer Forschung
GfPhDDR	Gesellschaft für Photogrammetrie in der Deutschen Demokratischen Republik
GFR	German Federal Republic = BRD
GFRCA	Glass Fibre Reinforced Cement Association
GFS	Gemeinsame Forschungsstelle (EURATOM) = CCI, CCR, GCO, JRC
GFS	Gesellschaft zur Förderung der Segelflugforschung
GFS	Girls Friendly Society
GFS & TF	Girls Friendly Society and Townsend Fellowship
GFSA	Gold Fields of South Africa
GFSAÉPCS	Groupement Fédératif des Syndicats et Associations d'Éleveurs et Propriétaires de Chevaux de Sang
GFSMA	Ground Flat Stock Manufacturers' Association
GFSTU	General Federation of Somali Trade Unions
GfT	Gesellschaft für Tribologie
GFTHTA	Glazed & Floor Tile Home Trade Association

GFTU	General Federation of Trade Unions
GFU	Gemeinschaft Freier Unternahmensberater
GFU	Gesellschaft zur Förderung des Unternehmernachwuchses
GfW	Gesellschaft für Wehrkunde
GfW	Gesellschaft für Weltraumforschung
GFWC	General Federation of Womens Clubs
GFZFF	Gesellschaft zur Förderung von Zukunfts- und Friedensforschung
GG	Gesundheitstechnische Gesellschaft
GG	Gutenberg-Gesellschaft, Internationale Vereinigung für Geschichte und Gegenwart der Druckkunst
GGA	Ghana Geographical Association
GGA	Girl Guides Association
GGA	Good Gardeners Association
GGA	Guernsey Growers Association
GGB	Gesellschaft für die Geschichte und Bibliographie Brauwesens
GGC	Groupe Spécialisé du Génie Chimique (Switzerland) = FGV
GGDPAC	Government Geoscience Database Policy Advisory Committee
GGE	Guild of Glass Engravers
GGF	Glass and Glazing Federation
GGFI	Gosudarstvennyi Geofizicheskii Institut
GGG	Gesellschaft für Geistesgeschichte
GGGI	Gosudarstvennyi Geologo-Geodezicheskii Institut
GGGS	Golden Guernsey Goat Club
GGL	Guild of Guide Lecturers
GGLF	Gewerkschaft Gartenbau, Land- und Forstwirtschaft
GGMC	Guyana Geology and Mines Commission
GGPÖ	Gesellschaft fur die Geschichte des Protestantismus in Österreich
GGT	Geographische Gesellschaft Trier
GGTI	Générale de Grands Travaux Ivoiriens
GGW	Gesellschaft für Geologische Wissenschaften
GGW	Gesellschaft für Geschichte des Weines e.V.
GGW	Groep Gereedschapswerktuigen van de Vereniging van Metalindustrieén
GH	Guild of Hairdressers
GHA	Gartnerneriets og Hagebrukets Arbeidsgiverforening

GHB	Ghaqda Bibljotekarji (Malta)
GHCN	Global Historical Climate Network
GHECO	Greening of Higher Education Council
GHEN	Northern Hydrographic Group (Sweden) = NHF, NHG
GhLM	Ghaqda Letteraja Maltija
GHM	Groep Houtbewerkingsmachines
GHN	Groupe Hygiène Naturelle = ENSH
GHP	Groep Farbrikanten van Hydraulische et Pneumatische
GHP	Guild of Hospital Pharmacists
GHRA	Guyana Human Rights Association
GHS	Garden History Society
GHT	Gesellschaft für Hochtemperatur-Reaktor-Technik
GI	Gesellschaft für Informatik
GI	Gideons International (U.S.A.)
GI	Gold Institute
GI	Grafisk Institutt
GIA	Gemological Institute of America
GIA	Groupement Ivoirien d'Assurances
GIA	Groups of Agrarian Investigations (Chile)
GIA	Gummed Industries Association (U.S.A.)
GIA	Islamic Armed Group (Algeria)
GIAC	Gioventà Italiana di Azione Cattolica
GIAC	Groupement des Industries Agricoles, Alimentaires et de Grande Consommation
GIAM	Conference on Global Impacts of Applied Microbiology
GIAMR	Guangdong Institute of Agricultural Machinery Research (China)
GIAN	Gruppo Italiano Arricchimento Uranio
GIANA	Groupement International des Analystes de l'Alimentation
GIAPEC	Groupement International des Associations de Parents d'Élèves de l'Enseignement Catholique (Belgium) = IGCPA
GIASTA	Groupement International pour l'Avancement des Sciences et Techniques Alimentaires
GIAT	Groupement d'Industries Atomiques
GIAT	Groupement Industrial des Armements Terrestres
GIB	Gibraltar Information Bureau
GIB	Gulf International Bank
GIBA	Groupement Interprofessionnal des Entreprises du Bénin
GIBACLIM	Générale Ivoirienne de Bâtiment et de Climatisation
GIBAIR	Gibraltar Airways
GIBAT	Groupement pour l'Industrialisation du Bâtiment (Algeria)
GIBÉT	Groupement Interuniversitaire Benelux des Économistes des Transports = BIVEC
GIBI	Gabungan Importir Buku Indonesia
GIBSO	Groupement des Industriels de la Banlieue Sud-Ouest
GIBV	Gesellschaft für Bedrohte Volker
GIC	General Industry Corporation (Abu Dhabi)
GIC	General Insurance Corporation of India
GIC	Ghana Investment Centre
GIC	Gulf Investment Corporation (Kuwait)
GICA	Groupement Patronal des Industriels et des Commerçants de l'Ain
GICAM	Groupment Interprofessionnel pour l'Étude et le Coordination des Intérêts Économiques du Caméroun
GICCW	Government-Industry Conference against Chemical Weapons
GICE	Groupement Interprofessionnel des Chefs d'Entreprise de la Haute-Loire
GICIC	German-Irish Chamber of Industry and Commerce (Éire)
GID	Gesellschaft für Information und Dokumentation
GIDAS	Gidrotekhnicheskaia Assotsiatsiia
GIDAVI	Groupement Interprofessionel pour la Défense et l'Amélioration des Vins de Consommation Courante
GIDC	Gujarat Industrial Development Corporation (India)
GIDIM	Groupement Interentreprises pour le Financement du Développement Immobilier
GIDNT	Główny Instytut Dokumentacji Naukowo-Technicznej
GIDOTOM	Groupement Interprofessionel pour le Développement de la Product des Oléagineux dans les Territoires d'Outre-Mer
GIDRO-NITO	Vsesoiuznoe Nauchnoe Inzhenerno-Tekhnicheskoe Obshchestvo Gidrotekhnikov
GIE	Grupo Interamericano de Editores (Argentina)

GIÉFCA	Groupement d'Intérêt Économique pour Favoriser le Développement du Crédit Automobile et Industriel en Afrique	**GIM**	Geneva Informal Meeting of International Non-Governmental Youth Organizations (Switzerland)
GIÉL	Groupement des Industries Électroniques	**GIM**	Gosudarstvennyi Institut Makhorkovedeniia
GIEPS	Guangzhou Institute for Environmental Protection Sciences (China)	**GIM**	Groupe Internationale Möbelspediteure
GIEWS	Global Information and Early Warning System on Food and Agriculture (FAO)	**GIM**	Gruppe Internationaler Möbelspediteur
GIF	Garden Industry Federation	**GIM-IC**	Genetics of Industrial Microorganisms – International Commission (Switzerland)
GIF	Grafiska Industriförbundet	**GIMA**	Garden Industries Manufacturers Association
GIFAM	Groupement des Industries Françaises des Appareils d'Équipement Ménager	**GIMA**	Grupo Independente de Macau
GIFAP	Groupement des Industriels Français d'Articles de Pêche	**GIMAT**	Groupement des Industries de Matériaux de Construction
GIFAP	Groupement International des Associations Nationales de Fabricants de Produits Agrochimiques	**GIMCI**	Groupement des Industries de la Métallurgie en Côte d'Ivoire
GIFAS	Groupement des Industries Françaises Aéronautiques et Spatiales	**GIMD**	Gosudarstvennyi Institut Muzykalnoi Dramy
GIFCO	Gruppo Italiano Fabbricanti Cartone Ondulato	**GIMEC**	Groupement des Importateurs et Réparateurs de Matériel
GIFFAT	Groupement d'Industriels Français de Fournitures Administratives Textiles	**GIMECA**	Groupement des Industries Mécaniques
		GIMÉÉ	Groupement Syndical des Industries de Matériels d'Équipement Électrique
GIFPA	Groupement Interprofessionel des Fleurs et Plantes Aromatiques	**GIMÉLEC**	Groupement des Industries de Matériels d'Équipement Électrique et de l'Électronique Industrielle Associée
GIG	Genetic Interest Group	**GIMÉM**	Groupement Intersyndical du Matériel d'Équipement Minier
GIGN	Groupe d'Intervention de la Gendarmerie Nationale	**GIMESKh**	Gosudarstvennyi Nauchno-Issledovatel'skii Institut Mekhanizatsii i Elektrifikatsii Sel'skogo Khoziaistva
GIHOC	Ghana Industrial Holdings Corporation		
GII	Fachgruppe der Ingenieure der Industrie (Switzerland) = FII	**GIMIP**	Gosudarstvennyi Institut Mer i Izmeritel'nykh Priborov
GIIC	Gulf International Investment Company (Bahrain)	**GIMMON**	Groupement des Industries Minières et Métallurgiques d'Outre-Mer
GIIGNL	Groupe International des Importateurs de Gaz Naturel Liquéfié	**GIMPA**	Ghana Institute of Management and Public Administration
GIII	Gosudarstvennyi Institut Istorii Iskusstv	**GIMRA**	General Insurance Market Research Association
GIIIZ	Gosudarstvennyi Institut Inzhenernykh Izyskanii	**GIMRADA**	U.S. Army Geodesy, Intelligence and Mapping Research and Development Agency
GIIL	Gosudarstvennoe Izdatel'stvo Inostrannoi Literatury		
GIIN	Groupe Intersyndical de l'Industrie Nucléaire	**GIN**	Geological Institute of the Russian Academy of Sciences
GIL	Gesellschaft für Informationsverarbeitung in der Landwirtschaft	**GINA**	Gaufretterie Industrielle Africaine
		GINETEX	Groupement International d'Etiquetage pour l'Entretien des Textiles
GILA	Government of India Librarians Association	**GINMASh**	Gosudarstvennyi Nauchno-Issledovatel'skii Institut Neftianogo Mashinostroeniia
GILA	Gruppo Italiano di Linguistica Applicata		
GILS	Grémio dos Industrials de Lanifícios do Sul (Portugal)	**GINMP**	Gansu Institute of New Medicine and Pharmacology (China)

GINSI	Gabungan Importir Nasional Seluruh Indonesia
GINZ	Gosudarstvennyi Nauchnyi Institut Narodnogo Zdravookhraneniia
GIOC	Giovenà Italiana Operaia Cattolica
GIOM	Groupement Interprofessionel des Oléagineux Métropolitains
GIOP	Główny Inspektorat Ochrony Pracy
GIOT	Gosudarstvennyi Institut Okhrany Truda
GIP	Gosudarstvennyi Institut Psikhiatrii
GIPA	Groupement Interprofessionnel de l'Automobile (Ivory Coast)
GIPCEL	Groupement des Industries du Polyurethane Cellulaire
GIPEC	Groupe d'Études International pour Utilizations de Profils Creux dans la Construction (Switzerland)
GIPFA	Groupement Interprofessionnel des Plantes à Parfum et Aromatiques
GIPGS	Greenhouse Information Program Grants Scheme
GIPI	Gosudarstvennyi Inzhenerno-Proektnyi Institut
GIPICO	Groupement Interprofessionnel Patronal de l'Industrie et du Commerce de l'Orne
GIPME	Global Investigation of Pollution in the Marine Enviroment
GIPP	Gremio dos Industriais de Planificação do Porto
GIPRO-TsMO	Gosudarstvennyi Nauchno-Issledovatel'skii i Proektnyi Institut Splavov i Obrabotki Tsvetnykh Metallov
GIPROMEZ	Gosudarstvennyi Institut Proektirovaniia Metallurgicheskikh Zavodov
GIQOM	Groupement Intersyndical de la Quincaillerie, de l'Outillage et du Ménage
GIRA	German Industrial Relations Association
GIRA	Groupement de l'Industrie de la Radio et de l'Électricité (Belgium)
GIRCA	Groupement Interprofessionel pour l'Étude et de Développement de l'Économie Centrafricaine
GIRCÉ-TAPE	Groupement Interrégional des Centres d'Études Techniques Agricoles pour les Problèmes d'Entreprise
GIRÉP	Groupe International du Rêve-Éveille en Psychanalyse

GIREP	Groupe International pour la Recherche sur l'Enseignement de la Physique
GIRGV	Groupe International des Ressources Génétiques Végétales = IBPGR
GIRIO	Government Industrial Research Institute, Osaka (Japan)
GIROQ	Groupe Interuniversitaire des Recherches Océanographiques du Québec
GIRP	Groupement International de la Répartition Pharmaceutique des Pays de la Communauté Européenne
GIRPIA	Groupements Interprofessionnels de Répartition des Produits Indispensables à l'Agriculture
GIRSO	Groupement International pour la Recherche Scientifique en Stomatologie et Odontologie
GIS	Geoscience Information Society
GIS	Główny Inspektorat Sanitarny
GIS	Government Information Service
GIS	Government Information Services (Éire)
GIS	Groupement de l'Industrie Sidérurgique
GIS	Gruppo Intervente Speciale (Italy)
GIS	Guild of Incorporated Surveyors
GISA	Vereniging van Groothandelaren in Sanitaire Artikelen
GISECA	Groupement Ivoirien des Sociétés d'Exportation et Coopératives Agricoles
GISEM	Groupement International des Sources d'Eaux Minérales Naturelles
GISL	Groupement des Industries Sidérurgiques Luxembourgeoises
GISPRI	Global Industrial and Social Progress Research Institute
GISRA	Guyana Institute for Social Research and Action
GISS	Gansu Institute of Sports Science (China)
GISS	Goddard Institute for Space Studies
GISTI	Guangdong Institute of Scientific and Technical Information (China)
GIT	Generación Intermedia Tradicionalista (Paraguay)
GITA	Grémio dos Industriais de Transportes em Automóveis
GITB	Gas Industry Training Board
GITCE	Gecaga Institute of Tropical Comparative Endocrinology (Kenya)
GITÉ	Groupe Internationale de Travail sur l'Éducation = IWGE

GITÉ	Groupe Internationale pour la Technologie de l'Énergie (OCDE) = IETG
GITÉR	Groupe Internationale Technique sur l'Électrification Rurale (IEPF)
GITL	Government/Industry Technical Liaison Committee
GITO	Groupement Interprofessionel des Entreprises du Togo
GITOM	Guangdong Institute of Tropical and Oceanic Meteorology (China)
GITRAM	Groupement Industriel pour la Transformation des Métaux (Cameroon)
GITT	Groupement des Industries du Transport et du Tourisme
GIU	General Importers Union (Malta)
GIVD	Gosudarstvennyi Institut Veterinarnoi Dermatologii
GIVTs	Glavnyi Informatsionno-Vychislitel'nyi Tsentr
GIZO	Gosudarstvennyi Institut po Izucheniiu Zasishlivykh Oblastei
GJEPC	Gem and Jewellery Export Promotion Council (India)
GKAE	Gosudarstvennyi Komitet po Ispolzovaniiu Atomnoi Energii
GKC	Gesellschaft Deutscher Kosmetik-Chemiker
GKE	Geodéziai és Kartográfiai Egyesület
GKF	Beroepsvereniging van Interieurarchitecten
GKI	Gazdaságkutató Intétet (Hungary)
GKKF	Główny Komitet Kultury Fizycznej
GKKFiS	Główny Komitet Kultury Fizycznej i Sportu
GKKFiT	Główny Komitet Kultury Fizycznej i Turystki
GKN	Gemeenschappelijke Kerneenergiecentrale in Nederland
GKNT	Gosudarstvennyi Komitet po Nauke i Tekhnike
GKR	Grazhdanskii Komitet Rossii
GKS	Górnicy Klub Sportowy
GKSC	Greek Kurdish Solidarity Committee
GKSS	Gesellschaft für Kernenergieverwertung in Schiffbau und Schiffahrt
GKT	Groep Kranen en Transportinrichtingen (Netherlands)
GKV	Gesamtverband Kunstsoffverarbeitende Industrie
GKVD	Gesamterband der Kraftfahrzeugvermieter Deutschlands
GKWW	Gesprächskreis Wissenschaft und Wirtschaft
GL	Gael-Linn Teoranta (Éire)
GL	Glassmestrenes Landsforening
GL	Green League (Germany)
GL	Gymnasieskolernes Lærerforening
GLA	German Landowners' Assembly (Czech Republic) = ZSN
GLA	Ghana Library Association
GLA	Groupe Libération Armée (Guadeloupe)
GLA	Guyana Library Association
GLAAD	Gay and Lesbian Alliance Against Defamation (U.S.A.)
GLAAS	Greater London Association of Alcohol Services
GLABC	Government Libraries Association of British Columbia
GLACSEC	Group of Latin American and Caribbean Sugar Exporting Countries = GEPLACEA
GLAD	Gay and Lesbian Legal Advice
GLAD	Greater London Association for Disabled People
Glafo	Glasforskningsinstitutet (Sweden)
GLAR	Grupo Lationoamericano de RILEM
GLARILEM	Grupo Latinoamericano de la Réunion Internacional de Laboratorios de Ensayos e Investigaciones sobre Materiales y Estructuras
GLARP	Grupo Latinoamericano de Rehabilitación Profesional
GLCI	Guangdong Leather Chemical Institute (China)
GLE	Gesellschaft für Logotherapie und Existenzanalyse (Austria)
GLÉCS	Groupe Linguistique d'Études Chamitosémitiques
GLEN	Gay and Lesbian Equality Network (Éire)
GLF	Grammofonleverantörernas Förening
GLFC	Great Lakes Fishery Commission (U.S.A.)
GLFC	Grupo Lesbico Feminista Costarricense Entendidas
GLIAS	Greater London Industrial Archaeological Society
GLINT	Gospel Literature International
GLM	Gesellschaft für Lehr-und Lernmethoden (Switzerland)

GLM	Grundejernes Landsorganisation
GLOBE	Global Legislators Organization for a Balanced Environment International
GLOCOPH	Global Continental Palaeohydrology Project
GLP-AACR	Gibraltar Labour Party and Association for the Advancement of Civil Rights
GLPA	Ground Limestone Producers' Association (Éire)
GLRA	German Leprosy Relief Association = AYU, DAHW
GLRC	Grain Legume Research Council
GLS	Gypsy Lore Society
GLSA	Greater London Staff Association
GLSM	Gruppen Lufttenik inom Sveriges Mekanförbund
GLU	Guyana Labor Union
GLV	Graphische Lehr-und Versuchsanstalt (Austria)
GM	Vereniging Fabrikanten van Gebruiksartikelen in de Metaalindustrie
GMA	Gesellschaft Mess- und Automatisierungstechnik (VDI/VDE)
GMA	Ghana Manufacturers Association
GMA	Glasgow Mathematical Association
GMA	Gospel Music Association
GMA	Greek Management Association
GMA	Grocery Manufacturers of Australia
GMAA	Gold Mining Association of America
GMAC	Genetic Manipulation Advisory Committee
GMB	General Municipal, Boilermakers and Allied Trades Union = GMBATU
GMBA	Gibraltar Master Bakers' Association
GMBATU	General Municipal, Boilermakers and Allied Trades Union = GMB
GMBF	Gesellschaft für Molekularbiologische Forschung
GMBMU	General Municipal and Boilermakers Union
GMBS	Verband Schweizerischer Grossisten der Mercerie, Bonneterie und Strickgarne
GMC	General Medical Council
GMC	General Military Council (Philippines)
GMC	Gesellschaft für Mathematik und Datenverarbeitung
GMC	Guild of Memorial Craftsmen
GMC	Guiyang Medical College
GMC	La Générale Matières Colorants
GMCC	Geophysical Monitoring for Climate Change (NOAA)
GMD	Gemeenschappelijke Medische Dienst (Netherlands)
GMD	Gesellschaft für Mathematik und Datenverarbeitung
GMDS	Deutsche Gesellschaft für Medizinische Dokumentation, Informatik und Statistik
GMDSS	Global Maritime Distress and Safety System = SMDSM
GME	Gelatine Manufacturers in Europe (Belgium)
GMÉA	Groupement Médicale d'Études sur l'Alcoolisme
GMEL	Groupement des Mathématiciens d'Expression Latine = GMRL
GMF	Glasmästeriförbundet
GMF	Glass Manufacturers Federation
GMF	Grus-och Macadam-föreningen
GMFA	Gay Men Fighting AIDS
GMG	Gouvernement Mondial Géniocrate (Switzerland)
GMHT	Glasite Meeting House Trust
GMI	Mobile Intervention Group (Senegal)
GMIAL	Groupement pour l'Aménagement et l'Exploitation des Infrastructures
GMITPM	Gorgas Memorial Institute of Tropical and Preventive Medicine (U.S.A.)
GML	Gemeinschaft der Milchwirtschaftlichen Landesvereinigungen
GMP	Guild of Metal Perforators
GMPA	Greater Manchester Police Authority
GMPC	Guangdong Medical and Pharmaceutical College
GMPCA	Groupe des Méthodes Physiques et Chimiques de l'Archéologie
GMR	Great Man-made River Authority (Libya)
GMrhKG	Gesellschaft für Mittelrheinische Kirchengeschichte
GMRI	General Machinery Research Institute (China)
GMRITI	Guangzhou Municipal Research Institute of Textile Industry (China)
GMRL	Group of Mathematicians of the Romance Languages = GMEL
GMSC	General Medical Services Council (BMA)
GMSC	Grant Maintained Schools Centre
GMST	Grant Maintained Schools Trust

GMT	Société des Générale des Moulins du Togo
GMTRI	Guangzhou Machine Tool Research Institute (China)
GMU	Guyana Mineworkers Union
GMV	Genootschap voor Muzikale Volkenkunde
GMV	Groep Fabrieken van Machines voor de Voedings- en Genotmiddelenindustrie
GMW	General and Municipal Workers (GMBATU)
GNA	Ghana News Agency
GNA	Grand National Assembly (Bulgaria)
GNA	Groupement National d'Achat
GNA	Gulf News Agency
GNAPO	Groupement National d'Achat des Produits Oléagineux
GNAPR-CAR	Groupement National de Association Professionnelles Régionales des Commissionnaires Affréteurs-Routiers
GNAS	Grand National Archery Society
GNAVT	Grémio Nacional das Agências de Viajens e Turismo
GNB	Groupement National Bulbicole
GNC	General Nursing Council
GNC	National Consultative Council (Chad)
GNCB	Groupement National du Cuir Brut (Belgium)
GNCC	Ghana National Chamber of Commerce
GNDÄ	Gesellschaft Deutscher Naturforscher und Ärzte
GNE	Groupement du Nursing Européen = ENG
GNECI	Groupement National des Entrepreneurs Constructeurs
GNEL	Grémio Nacional des Editores e Livreiros
GNÉLPC	Groupement National des Éleveurs Professionnels de Lapins de Chair
GNÉRFEA	Groupement National des Éleveurs "Reine de France" et Essaims d'Abeilles
GNERI	Gneri Natural Energy Research Institute
GNÉSLRP	Groupement National Éleveurs Selectionneurs de Lapins de Race Pure
GNET	Gremio Nacional dos Exportadores de Téxteis
GNF	Grémio Nacional das Farmácias
GNGG	Gewerkschaft Nahrung-Genuss-Gaststätten
GNIAA	Groupement National des Industries de l'Alimentation Animale
GNIBC	Groupement National Interprofessionnel de la Betterave, de la Canne et des Industries Productrices de Sucre et d'Alcool
GNIC	Grémio Nacional dos Industrials de Calçado
GNICTMP	Grémio Nacional dos Industriais de Composição e Transformação de Matérias Plásticas
GNIFC	Groupement National Interprofessional des Fruits à Cidre
GNIJR	Groupement National Interprofessionnel des Jus de Raisins et Dérivés
GNIL	Groupement National Interprofessionel Linier
GNIMFVA	Grémio Nacional dos Industriais de Montagem e Fabricação de Veículos Automóveis
GNIN	Groupement National des Importateurs et du Négoce de Laine (Belgium)
GNIPTIT	Groupement National Interprofessionnel de la Pomme de Terre Industrielle et des Industries de Transformation
GNIS	Groupement National Interprofessionel de Production et d'Utilisation des Semences Graines et Plantes
GNIT	Gremio Nacional dos Industriais de Tomate
GNIT	Groupement National Interprofessionel du Topinambour
GNITC	Groupement National de l'Industrie de la Terre Cuite (Belgium)
GNLF	Gorkha National Liberation Front (India)
GNPP	Great Nigerian People's Party
GNR	Guarda Nacional Republicana (Portugal)
GNRS	Great Northern Railway Society
GNT	Gesellschaft für Nuklear-Transporte
GNTC	Ghana National Trading Corporation
GNTC	Girls Nautical Training Corps
GNUT-SEARCH	National Research Centre for Groundnuts (India)
GNV	Gesellschaft für Nukleare Verfahrenstechnik
GOAC	Greek Orthodox Archdiocesan Council of North and South America
GOBR	Group of Officials on Biotechnology Regulation
GOC	General Optical Council
GOC	Gesellschaft Österreichischer Chemiker

GOCA	Groupement des Organismes de Contrôle Automobiles
GÖCh	Gesellschaft Österreichischer Chemiker
GODA	Guild of Drama Adjudicators
GODB	Gal Oya Development Board (Sri Lanka)
GODE	Gulf Organization for Developement of Egypt
GOEDEB	General Organisation for the Exploitation and Development of the Euphrates Basin (Syria)
GOETO	Grand Order of European Tour Operators
GOFTA	Golf Facilities Trades Association
GOGECA	Comité Générale de la Coopération Agricole de la CEE
GOHBPR	General Organization for Housing, Building and Planning Research (Egypt)
GOIAVE	Groupement Océanien des Instituts à Vocation Environnementale (Guam) = ASPEI
GOIC	Gulf Organisation for Industrial Consulting
GOIEF	Cairo International Fair
GOK	Geographikos Omilos Kyprou = CGA
Golkar	Sekber Golongan Karyu (Indonesia)
GOMAC	Groupement des Opticiens du Marché Commun
GOMPCI	Groupement Outre-Mer Pharmaceutique (Ivory Coast)
GOONS	Guild of One-Name Studies
GOPR	Górskie Ochotnicze Pogotowie Ratunkowe
GOPR	Groupement pour l'Opération de Productivité Rizicole (Madagascar)
GOS	Global Observing System (WMO)
GOS	Guild of Surveyors
GOSEAC	Group of Specialists on Environmental Affairs and Conservation
Gosekonom-komissiia	Gosudarstvennaia Nauchno-Ekonomicheskaia Komissiia
Gosstroi	Gosudarstvennyi Komitet po Delam Stroitel'stva
GOST	Committee of the Russian Federation for Standardisation, Metrology and Certification
GOU	Vereniging Gezamenlijke Onafhankelijke Uitgevers
GOVPF	Groupement Obligatoire des Viticulteurs et Producteurs de Fruits (Tunisia)
GÖWG	Gesellschaft für Öffentliche Wirtschaft und Gemeinwirtschaft
GP	Gesellschaft für Psychologie
GP	Green Party (Germany)
GPA	Garden Products Association
GPA	Garlic Processors Association
GPA	Gewerkschaft der Privatangestellten (Austria)
GPA	Global Programme on AIDS (WHO)
GPA	Goat Producers Association
GPA	Groupement de Pharmaciens d'Afrique
GPA	Groupement de Productivité Agricole
GPAFI	Groupement de Prévoyance et d'Assurance des Fonctionnaires Internationaux
GPAM	Groupement des Producteurs d'Ananas de la Martinique
GPARAFN	Green Party Anti-Racist and Anti-Fascist Network
GPB	Groupement Professionnel des Bitumes
GPBA	General Produce Brokers Association
GPBN	Groupement Pharmaceutique Bénin-Niger
GPC	General Peoples Congress (Libya)
GPC	General Petroleum Company (Egypt)
GPC	Global Processing Center
GPC	Greek Productivity Centre
GPC	Groupe Spécialisé des Ponts et Charpentes (Switzerland) = FBH
GPC	Groupement des Pharmaciens du Caméroun
GPC	Groupements de Producteurs de Ciment (Belgium)
GPCC	Global Precipitation Climatology Centre
GPCC	Grand Prix Contact Club
GPCSA	General Practice Computer Suppliers Association
GPD	Generals for Peace and Disarmament
GPDA	Gypsum Plasterboard Development Association
GPDA	Gypsum Products Development Association
GPDST	Girls Public Day School Trust
GPE	Guided Projectile Establishment
GPECC	Groupement Professionnel des Exportateurs de Café et de Cacao (Ivory Coast)
GPEI	Gabungan Perusahaan Ekspor Indonesia
GPFC	General Practice Finance Corporation

GPI	Gesellschaft für Pädagogik und Information
GPI	Grupo Parlamentario Independiente
GPIC	Gulf Petrochemical Industries Company (Bahrain)
GPIN	Groupement Professionnel de l'Industrie Nucléaire (Belgium)
GPLS	Groupement Professionnel des Commerçants et Industriels Libanais du Sénégal
GPMA	Grocery Products Manufacturers Association (Canada)
GPMH	Good Practices in Mental Health
GPMU	Graphical, Paper & Media Union (*ex* NGA, SOGAT)
GPNI	Groupement Professionnel National de l'Informatique
GPO	Association Générale des Producteurs d'Oléagineux
GPO	Government Printing Office (U.S.A.)
GPOI	General Public Organization for Industrialization (Libya)
GPP	Gambian Peoples Party
GPP	Guild of Pastoral Pyschology
GPPA	Gaelic Pre-School Playgroups Association = CNSA
GPPA	Grenada Planned Parenthood Association
GPPEPA	Groupement des Producteurs de la Prune d'Ente et du Pruneau d'Agen
GPPIP	Groupement Professionnel des Pharmaciens de l'Industrie PharmaceutiqueI de la CEE
GPRA	Gesellschaft Public Relations Agenturen
GPRMC	Groupement des Plastiques Renforcés du Marché Commun
GPrÖ	Gesellschaft für die Geschichte des Protestantismus in Österreich
GPS	German Pacific Society
GPS	Gibraltar Philatelic Society
GPSCO	Global Position System Consortium (UNSW, ANU, TAFE, LIC)
GPTC	Gambia Public Transport Corporation
GPTI	Guangdong Posts & Telecommunications Institute (China)
GPU	Green Party of Ukraine
GPV	Gereformeerd Politiek Verbond
GPV	Gesellschaft Pro Vindonissa (Switzerland)
GPV	Groep Fabrieken van Pompen voor Vloeistoffen
GPV	Schweizerischer Glas- und Propzellanhandels-Verband
GPWA	General Practitioners Writers Association
GPWM	Guild for the Promotion of Welsh Music
GR	Direction du Génie Rurale
GR	Green Realignment
GR	Grupo da Reflexão (Sao Tomé)
GRA	Garda Representative Association (Éire)
GRA	Gesellschaft für Rechnergesteuerte Analgen
GRADE FRB	Groupe de Recherche et d'Action pour un Developpement Engogene Rurale (Burkina Faso)
GRAE	Gouvernement Révolutionnaise de l'Angola en Exil
GRAFD	Groupe de Recherche-Action Femme et Developpement (Benin)
GRAIN	Genetic Resources Action International (ICDA) (Spain)
GRAIN-UNION	Société Commerciale de l'Union Générale des Coopératives Agricoles de Céréales
GRAMA-COP	Grain Marketing Cooperative of the Philippines
GRAM-OVEN	Grandes Molinas de Venezuela, S.A.
GRANIL	Grand Accelerator National d'Ions Lourds (France)
GRAPA	Grupo Antimarxista (Chile)
GRAPO	Grupos de Resistencia Antifascista Primero de Octubre
GRB	Gas Research Board
GRBS	Gardeners' Royal Benevolent Society
GRBS	Groupe de Recherche en Biologie Spatiale
GRCA	Glassfibre Reinforced Cement Association
GRCDA	Government Refuse Collection and Disposal Association (U.S.A.)
GRCESD	Guizhou Provincial Research Centre of Economic & Social Development (China)
GRCÉTA	Groupement Régional de Centre d'Études Techniques Agricoles
GRD	Groupe des Ressources pour le Développement (UNDP)
GRD	Gruppe für Rustungsdienst (Switzerland)
GRDA	Gin Rectifiers and Distillers Association (*now* GVA)

GRDC	Geological Research and Development Centre (Indonesia)
GRDC	Grains Research and Development Corporation
GRDP	Groupement National des Transporteurs Routiers de Denrées et Produits Périssables
GRDQ	Groupe de Recherche sur la Demographie Québecoise (Canada)
GRDR	Groupe de Recherche et de Réalisation pour le Développement Rural dans le Tiers Monde
GREACAM	Guardian Royal Exchange Assurance Caméroun
GRÉCAS	Groupement d'Études et de Courtages d'Assurances
GRÉCE	Groupement de Recherche et d'Étude pour la Civilisation Européenne
GRECMU	Grupo de Estudios sobre la Condición de la Mujer en Uruguay
GREDES	Grupo de Estudios para el Desarrollo (Peru)
GREFA	Groupement des Exportateurs Français de l'Ameublement
GRÉM	Groupement Romand pour l'Étude du Marketing (Switzerland)
GREMA-DEIRAS	Grémio dos Exportadores de Madeiras (Portugal)
GREMPA	Mediterranean Cooperative Research and Study Group on the Almond Tree (MAIZ)
GRÉP	Groupe de Recherche et d'Éducation pour la Promotion
GREPFA	Groupe de Recherche Européen en Placement Familial (Belgium)
GRÉPR	Groupe de Recherches et d'Études pour la Promotion Rurale
GREQUI	Grupo de Estudos da Questão Indígena (Brazil)
GRESO	Groupement pour l'Expansion des Sociétés Commerciales à Exportation du Sud-Ouest
GRÉT	Groupe de Recherches et d'Échanges Technologiques
GRF	Graphic Reproduction Federation
GRF	Greek Road Federation = ODOMEL
GRF	Gummiringsfüreninger
GRG	Groupe Spécialisé des Ingénieurs du Génie Rural et Géomètres (Switzerland) =FKV
GRG	International Committee on General Relativity and Gravitation
GRGS	Groupe de Recherche de Géodesie Spatiale
GRI	Geophysical Research Institute (China)
GRI	Groupe de Recherches Ionosphériques
GRICAAS	Grassland Research Institute, Chinese Academy of Agricultural Sciences
GRIE	Grupo Regional Centroamericano sobre Interconexión Eléctrica
GRIMM	Groupe de Recherche Interdisciplinaire sur les Materiaux Moleculaires (France)
GRIN	Guarda Rural Indígena (Brazil)
GRINM	General Research Institute for Non-Ferrous Metals (China)
GRIP	Gay Rights in Prison
GRL	Grain Research Laboratory (Canada)
GRL	Groupe de Réflexion de la Librarie
GRLA	Grupul Român de Linguistica Aplicata = RWCAL
GRO	General Register Office (Scotland)
GROFOR	Deutscher Verband des Grosshandels mit Oelen, Fetten und Oelrohstoffen
GROHAD	Vereniging van Nederlandse Groothandelaren in Gedistilleerd en Likeuren
GROMO	Bundesverband des Gross- und Aussenhandels mit Molkereiprodukten
GRONTMIJ	Grondverbetering- en Ontginningsmaatschappij (Netherlands)
GROPACA	Chambre Syndicale des Grossistes en Papiers et Cartons pour Écriture et Impression (Belgium)
GROPO	Nederlandse Vereniging voor de Binnenlandse Groothandel in Pootaardappelen
GROQUI-FAR	Associação de Grossistas de Produtos Químicos e Farmacéuticos
GROUP-AROMA	Syndicat National des Fabricants et Importateurs d'Huiles Essentielles et Produits Aromatiques Naturels
GROUPE-GAMMA	Comité Européen d'Action Gérontologique
GROUP-ISOL	Association of EEC Manufacturers of Technical Ceramics for Electronic, Electrical, Mechanical and other Applications
GRP	Greater Romania Party = PRM
GRPA	Guyana Responsible Parenthood Association
GRPA	Guyana Rice Producers Association
GRPÉ	Groupe de Rapporteurs sur la Pollution et l'Énergie (ONU)

GRPF	Gesellschaft zur Förderung Pädagogischer Forschung
GRS	Gesellschaft für Reaktorsicherheit
GRS	Groupe Révolution Socialiste (Martinique)
GRTU	General Retailers and Traders Union (Malta)
GRUCA	Grupo de Embajadores Centroamericanos ante la CEE
GRUFEPRO-MEFAM	Grupo Femenino pro Mejoramiento Familiar (Guatemala)
GRULA	Grupa de Embajadores de America Latina ante las Comunidades Europeas
GRUR	Deutsche Vereinigung für Gewerblichen Rechtsschutz und Urheberrecht
GRUSZAG	Georgian Telegraphic Agency, Tbilisi
GRV	Gesellschaft für Rationale Verkehrspolitik
GS	Genetical Society
GS	Glassbransjens Servicekontor
GS – HG	Geological Society – Hydrogeology Group
GSA	Genetics Society of America
GSA	Geological Society of Africa = SGA
GSA	Geological Society of America
GSA	Geological Society of Australia
GSA	Girls Schools Association
GSA	Groupe Spécialisé de l'Architecture (Switzerland)
GSAM	Guangdong Society of Agri-Machinery
GSB	Ghana Standards Board
GSBI	Gesamtverband der Schweizerischen Bekleidungsindustrie
GSBK	Gesellschaft Schweizerischer Bildender Künstlerinnen
GSC	Genetics Society of China
GSC	Geographical Society of China
GSC	Geological Society of China
GSC	Gerontological Society of China
GSCCMF	Gujarat State Co-operative Cotton Marketing Federation (India)
GSCSCERS	Geographical Society of China Sub-Commission on Environmental Remote Sensing
GSD	Guild of Software Distributors
GSD	Law Society Group for Solicitors with Disabilities
GSÉCI	Groupement Socio-Économique Communautaire Islamique (Senegal)
GSEE	Geniki Synomospondia Ergaton Ellados
GSF	Gesellschaft für Strahlen-und Umweltforschung
GSF	Groupe Spécialisé des Ingénieurs Forestiers (Switzerland)
GSF	Institut für Gesundheits – System – Forschung
GSF	Schweizerische Genossenschaft für Schlachtvieh und Fleischversorgung
GSFC	Gujarat State Fertilizers Company (India)
GSFC	Gujarat State Financial Coporation (India)
GSG	Grosshandelszentralverband für Spielwaren und Geschenkartikel
GSG	Guild of St Gabriel
GSGB	Golf Society of Great Britain
GSI	Geographical Society of Ireland
GSI	Geographical Survey Institute
GSI	Geological Society of Israel
GSI	Gesellschaft für Schwerionenforschung
GSIC	Gujarat Small Industries Corporation (India)
GSK	Gesellschaft für Schweizerische Kunstgeschichte = SHAS, SSAS
GSL	Geological Society of London
GSL	Gesellschaft Schweizerischer Landwirte
GSL	Vereniging "De Gezamenlijke Steenkolenmijnen in Limburg"
GSLK	Gesellschaft für Salzburger Landeskunde
GSM	Gesellschaft für Selbstspielende Musikinstrumente e.V.
GSM	Greek Society for Microbiology
GSMAMP	Groupement Suisse des Marchands d'Aciers Spéciaux, Métaux et Plastique
GSMBA	Gesellschaft Schweizerischer Maler, Bildhauer und Architekten = SPSAS
GSMBE	Gesellschaft Schweizerischer Malerinnen, Bildhauerinnen und Kunstgewerblerinnen
GSN	Green Student Network
GSN	Groupement des Soufflantes Nucléaires
GSNMS	Groupement des Syndicats Nationaux de Médecins Spécialisés
GSoA	Gerontological Society of America
GSoA	Gruppe für eine Schweiz ohne Armee
GSOI	Groupe Spécial sur les Organisations Internationales (OCDE)
GSP	Geographical Society of Philadelphia (U.S.A.)

GSP	Guild of Software Developers
GSPIA	University of Pittsburgh's Graduate School of Public and International Affairs
GSPLAJ-BC	Great Socialist People's Libyan Arab Jamahiriyah Broadcasting Corporation
GSPMR	Greek Society of Physical Medicine and Rehabilitation
GSRP	Gambian Socialist Revolutionary Party
GSRTST	German Society for Rocket Technology and Space Travel
GSS	Ghost Story Society
GSS	Gono Shahajjo Sangstha (Bangladesh)
GSS	Government Statistics Service
GSSA	Geological Society of South Africa
GSSA	Grassland Society of Southern Africa
GSSOS	Groupement des Sociétiés Scientifiques Odonto-Stomatologiques
GST	Gesellschaft Schweizerischer Tierärtze = SVS
GSU	General Service Union (UN) = SSG
GSU	General Service Unit (Kenya)
GSU	German Social Union = DSU
GSV	Grassland Society of Victoria (Australia)
GSV	Güteschutzverband Stahlgerüstbau
GSWG	Gesellschaft für Sozial- und Wirtschaftsgeschichte
GSZ	Gesellschaft Schweizerischer Zeichenlehrer = SSMD
GTA	Gesellschaft für Gestalttheorie und ihre Anwendung
GTA	Gibraltar Teachers Association
GTA	Glass Textile Association
GTA	Graduate Teachers' Association (Malta)
GTA	Grain Transportation Agency (Canada)
GTA	Groupement Togolais d'Assurance
GTA	Gun Trade Association
GTAV	Geography Teachers' Association of Victoria
GTC	Ghana Tobacco Company
GTCS	Groupe de Travail Intergouvernmental du Contrôle ou de la Surveillance (ONU) = GTIV
GTD	Gesellschaft Deutscher Tierfotografer
GTDA	Groupement pour le Développement de la Télédetection Aérospatiale
GTE	Gépipari Tudományos Egyesület
GTF	Gesellschaft für Technologiefolgenforschung
GTFT	Groupement du Théâtre et du Folklore Togolais
GTICM	Grupo de Trabajo Intergubernamental sobre Contaminación de los Mares (IMCO)
GTIV	Grupo de Trabajo Intergubernamental sobre Vigilancia o Supervisión (ONU) = GTCS
GTL	Groupement National des Entreprises de Taxis et de Voitures de Location (Belgium)
GTM	Groep Textielmachinesz van de Vereniging van Metaal-Industrieén
GTMA	Gauge and Tool Makers Association
GTMB	Ghana Timber Marketing Board
GTME	Grupo de Trabalho de Missionários Evangélicos (Brazil)
GTN	Gdańskie Towarzystwo Naukowe
GTN	Global Trends Network (U.S.A.)
GTO	Grønlands Tekniske Organisation
GTOS	Global Terrestrial Observing System
GTR	Green Teacher Resources
GTRE	Gas Turbine Research Establishment (India)
GTS	Gesellschaft für Tribologie und Schmierungstechnik
GTS	Global Telecommunications System (WMO)
GTSPP	Global Temperature and Salinity Pilot Project
GTUC	Grenada Trade Union Council
GTUC	Guyana Trades Union Council
GTW	Gesellschaft der Tierärzte in Wien (Austria)
GTW	Guild of Travel Writers
GTZ	Deutsche Gesellschaft für Technische Zusammenarbeit
GUALO	General Union of Associations of Loom Overlookers
GUAS	General Union of Arab Students
GUAT-EXPRO	Centro Nacional de Promoción de las Exportaciones (Guatemala)
GUATEL	Empresa Guatemalteca de Telecomunicaciones (Guatemala)
GUBI	Gemeinschaft Unabhangiger Beratender Ingenieurbüros
GUC	Główny Urząd Cel
GUCCIAAC	General Union of Chambers of Commerce Industry and Agriculture for Arab Countries

GUE	Groupe pour la Gauche Unitaire Européenne
GUG	Gesellschaft für Unternehmensgeschichte
GUGiK	Główny Urząd Geodezji i Kartografii
GUI	Golfing Union of Ireland
GUIMAG	Société Guinéenne de Grands Magasins
GUINÉLEC	Société Guinéenne d'Installations Électriques
GUKPPiW	Główny Urząd Kontroli Prasy, Publikacji i Widowisk
GULERPE	Grupo Universitário Latinamericano de Estudios para la Reforma y Perfeccionamiento de la Educación
GULP	Grenada United Labour Party
GUM	Główny Urząd Miar
GUM	Gesellschaft für Umwelt-Mutationsforschung
GUMR	Groupement des Utilisateurs de Matériaux Réfractaires (Belgium)
GUNT	Gouvernement d'Union Nationale Transitoire (Chad)
GUPCG	Genito-Urinary Physicians Colposcopy Group
GUPCO	Gulf of Suez Patroleum Company (Egypt)
GUPIRI	Guangzhou Pharmaceutical Industry Research Institute (China)
GUPS	General Union of Palestine Students
GUPW	General Union of Palestinian Women
GUPW	General Union of Palestinian Workers
GUS	Główny Urząd Statystyczny
GUS	Gemeinschaft der Unabhangigen Staaten = CIS, CEI, SNG, WNP
GUS	Gruppo Nazionale Giornalisi Uffici Stampa
GUSS	Gulf Centre for Strategic Studies
Gutenberg Society	International Association for Past and Present History of the Art of Printing
GUTM	Główny Urząd Telekomunikacji Międzymiastowej
GUVU	Gesellschaft für Ursachenforschung bei Verkehrsunfällen
GUYMINE	Guyana Mining Enterprise
GUYSTAC	Guyana State Corporation
GUYSUCO	Guyana Sugar Corporation
GV	Gesellschaft für Versuchstierkunde = SOLAS
GV-NOK	Gererormeerd Politiek Verbond
GVA	Gin & Vodka Association of GB (*ex* GRDA, VTA)
GVAM	Groupement de Vulgarisation Agricole et Ménagère
GVB	Gesellschaft für Verkehrsbetriebswirtschaft e.V.
GVC	Gesellschaft Verfahrenstechnik und Chemieingenieurwesen
GVC	Girls Venture Corps
GVCAC	Girls' Venture Corps Air Cadets
GVG	Gesellschaft für Versicherungswissenschaft und Gestaltung
GVK	Gesellschaft für Vergleichendekunstforschung (Austria)
GVM	Groep Fabrieken van Verbrandingsmotoren
GVN	Beroepsvereniging Grafisch Vormgevers Nederland
GVOM	Groupe Volontaire Outre Mer (Switzerland)
GvR	Genootschap voor Reclame
GVS	Gesellschaft für die Volksmusik in der Schweiz
GVS	Goat Veterinary Society
GVS	Grosshandelsverband Schreib-Papierwaren und Bürobedarf
GVST	Gesamtverband des Deutschen Steinkohlen Bergbaus
GVT	Forschungs-Gesellschaft Verfahrens-Technik
GWA	Gesellschaft Werbeagenturen
GWA	Ghana Welfare Association
GWC	Gippsland Waters Coalition
GWCG	General Wiring Cables Group
GWDB	Ground Water Development Bureau (Taiwan)
GWDU	General Workers Development Union (Belize) (*now* UGWU)
GWF	General Workers' Federation (Mauritius)
GWF	Gesellschaft für Werkzeugmaschinenbau und Fertigungstechnik (Switzerland)
GWG	Gesellschaft für Wissenschaftliche Gesprächspsychotherapie
GWI	Gaswärme Institut
GWIS	German Wine Information Service
GWK	Gesellschaft zur Wiederaufarbeitung von Kernbrennstoffen

GWK	Grenwisselkantoren
GWL	Gesellschaft für Wissenschaft und Leben im Rheinisch-Westfälischen Industriegebiet
GWLG	Gottfried-Wilhelm-Leibniz-Gesellschaft
GWR	Gesellschaft für Weltraumforschung und Raumfahrt
GWRDC	Grape and Wine Research and Development Corporation
GWS	Great Western Society
GWTUF	Government Workers Trade Union Federation (Sri Lanka)
GWU	Gambia Workers Union
GWU	General Workers Union (Malta)
GWUCC	Garment Workers Union Consultative Committee
GWUSA	Garment Workers Union of South Africa
GXAAS	Guangxi Academy of Agricultural Sciences (China)
GXAPI	Guangxi Applied Physics Institute (China)
GXCC	Guangxi Computer Centre (China)
GXOI	Guangxi Institute of Oceanography
GZ	Gesellschaft für Zukunstsfragen
GZ	Girozentrale und Bank der Österreichischen Sparkassen
GZB	Genossenschaftliche Zentralbank (Austria)
GZG	Gutegemeinschaft Zinngerat
GZPWP	Główny Zarząd Polityczny Wojska Polskiego
GZSTII	Guangzhou Scientific & Technical Information Institute (China)

H

H-e A	Hezbollah-e Afghanistan
HA	Hermanitas de la Asunción = IA, LSA, PSA
HA	Herpes Association
HA	Historical Association
HA	Hockey Association
HA-UK	Historical Artillery
HAA	Herpetological Association of Africa
HAA	Historic Aircraft Association
HAA	Homeless Action and Accommodation Ltd

HAA	Hungarian Astronomical Association = MCSE
HAAFS	Hebei Academy of Agricultural and Forestry Sciences (China)
HAAS	Hunan Academy of Agricultural Sciences (China)
HAB	Hessische Akademie für Bürowirtschaft
HABITAT	United Nations Centre for Human Settlements = CNUAH, CNUEH
HAC	Horticultural Advisory Council for England and Wales
HACF	Hellenic Association of Consulting Firms
HACSG	Hyper Active Children's Support Group
HACT	Housing Association Charitable Trust
HAD	Hrvatsko Arhivističko Društvo
HADC	Helen Arkell Dyslexic Centre
HAE	Hire Association Europe
HAES	Hawaii Agricultural Experiment Station
HAF	Handverkernes Arbeidsgiverforening
HAF	Hellenic Air Force (Greece)
HAF	Helsetjenestens Administrajonsförbund
HAFRA	British Hat and Allied Feltmakers Research Association
HAFS	Heilungkiang Academy of Forestry Sciences (China)
HAG	Hauptarbeitsgemeinschaft des Landmaschinen-Handels und -Handwerks
HAG	Historische und Antiquarische Gesellschaft zu Basel
HAGD	Hauptvereinigung des Ambulanten Gewerbes und der Schausteller in Deutschland
HAHMRI	Hohhot Animal Husbandry Machinery Research Institute (China)
HAHP	Health Action for Homeless People
HAI	Health Action International
HAI	Helicopter Association International
HAI	Hellenic Aerospace Industries (Greece)
HAI	Help Age International
HAI	Historical Association of Ireland
HAIA	Hearing Aid Industry Association
HAIG	Helsinki Agreements Implementation Group (Belgium)
HAIL	Hague Academy of International Law (Netherlands)
HAKA	Verband der Deutschen Herren- und Knaben-Oberbekleidungsindustrie

HAKAF	Vereniging van Groothandelaren in Katoenen Kunstzijdeafvallen
HAL	Heathrow Airport Limited
HAL	Hindustan Aeronautics Ltd (India)
HALO	Housing Association Liaison Office
HALOW	Help and Advice Line for Offenders' Wives
HAMCHAM	Chambre de Commerce et d'Industrie Haïtiano-Américaine
HANA	Halibut Association of North America
HANA	Haveeru News Agency (Maldives)
HAOJAF	Handelns Arbetsgivareorganisation Järnhandlarnas Arbetsgivareförening
HAPA	Handicapped Adventure Playground Association
HAPM	Hollands-Amerikaanse Plantage Maatschappij
HAPPA	Horses and Ponies Protection Association
HARAKAT	Harakat-e Enqelab-e Eslami-e Afghanistan = IRMA
HARC	Hester Adrian Research Centre
HarGIN	Harmonious Groupings in Nature
HAS	Hawaiian Academy of Science
HAS	Head Teachers Association of Scotland
HAS	Hellenic Astronautical Society (Greece) = EAE
HAS	Hospital Advisory Service for England and Wales
HAS	Vereniging van Leveranciers van Huishoudelijke Artikelen, Speelgoedere Speelgoederen, Houtwaren en Soortgelijke Artikelen
HASA	Editorial Hispanoamericana S.A.(Argentina)
HASCO	Haitian American Sugar Corporation
HASL	Hawaii Association of School Librarians
HASRI	Hangzhou Aquatic Science Research Institute (China)
HASS	Hunan Academy of Social Sciences (China)
HASTE	Helicopter Ambulance Service to Emergencies
HAT	History of Advertising Trust
HATCA	Hungarian Air Traffic Controllers Association
HATCMP	Hubei Academy of Traditional Chinese Medicine (China)
HATIS	Hide and Allied Trades Improvement Society
HATRA	Hosiery and Allied Trades Research Association
HATTA	Hellenic Association of Tourist and Travel Offices
HAVYW	Humanitarian Appeal for Victims of the Yugoslav War
HB	Herri Batasuna (Spain)
HBA	Herring Buyers Association
HBAA	Human Betterment Association of America
HBAMS	Hebei Academy of Medical Sciences (China)
HBC	Historic Buildings Council (Scotland, Wales)
HBC	Historic Buildings Council for Northern Ireland
HBC	Hudson's Bay Company (Canada)
HBD	Hrvatsko Bibliotekarsko Drustvo
HBD	Hrvatsko Biolosko Drustvo
HBEF	Health and Beauty Employers Federation
HBES	Human Behavior and Evolution Society
HBF	House Builders Federation
HBI	Vereniging van Handelaren in Plantenziekten-Bestrijdingsmiddelen en Landbouw-Insecticiden
HBLB	Horse Race Betting Levy Board
HBMC	Historic Buildings and Monuments Commission for England; English Heritage
HBPF	High Blood Pressure Foundation
HBR	Herbário Barbosa Rodrigues (Brazil)
HBS	Havergal Brian Society
HBS	Hawaiian Botanical Society
HBS	Henry Bradshaw Society
HBS	Historic Brass Society
HBSA	Historical Breechloading Smallarms Association
HBTI	Harcourt Butler Technological Institute (India)
HBV	Christelijke Bedrifsbond voor de Handle, het Banken Verzekeringswesen de Adminstratieve Kantoren en de Vrije Beroepen
HBV	Gewerkschaft Handel, Banken und Versicherungen
HBWB	Home Beer and Winemaking Bureau
HBWMA	Home Brewing and Winemaking Manufacturers Association
HBWTA	Home Brewing and Winemaking Trade Association

HC	Hairdressing Council	HCPT	Handicapped Childrens Pilgrimage Trust
HC	Headmasters Conference		
HCA	Hospital Caterers Association	HCPT	Historic Churches Preservation Trust
HCA	Hypertrophic Cardiomyopathy Association	HCR	Haut Commissariat des Nations Unies pour les Réfugiés = ACNUR, UNHCR
HCAR	Higher Committee for Agrarian Reform (Egypt)	HCR	Haut-Comissariat à la Recherche (Algeria)
HCB	Hidroeléctrica de Cabora Bassa (Mozambique)	HCR	Haut-Commissaire des Nations Unies pour les Réfugiés
HCB	Huileries du Congo Belge	HCR	Nordiska Unionen für Hotell- Café och Restauanagaställda
HCC	Hospital Chaplaincies Council		
HCC	Housing Consultative Council for England	HCRC	Hotel & Catering Research Centre
		HCRC	Human Communication Research Centre
HCC	Hovermail Collectors' Club		
HCC	Hyderabad Commercial Corporation (India)	HCS	Hebei Crop Society
		HCS	Hellenic Chamber of Shipping
HCCC	Hyderabad Co-operative Commercial Corporation (India)	HCS	Holy Crown Society (Hungary) = SzT
		HCSA	Hospital Consultants and Specialists Association
HCDM	Hungarian Christian Democratic Movement (Slovakia) = MKDH		
		HCT	Herpetological Conservation Trust
HCEC	Hospital Committee of the European Community = CHCE	HCTA	Health Careers Tutors' Association
		HCVC	Historic Commercial Vehicle Society
HCFTA	Home and Contract Furnishing Textiles Association (now BITA)	HCWU	Hotel and Catering Workers Union (GMBATU)
HCGB	Helicopter Club of Great Britain	HDA	Hodgkin's Disease Association
HCGB	Hoverclub of Great Britain	HDA	Holistic Dental Association
HCI	Hotel and Catering Institute (South Africa)	HDA	Horticultural Dealers Association
		HDA	Hospital Doctors Association
HCIH	Hubei Cancer Institute and Hospital (China)	HDAI	Huntington's Disease Association of Ireland
HCIMA	Hotel Catering and Institutional Management Association	HDDU	Hrvatsko Društvo Dramskih Umjetnika
HCITB	Hotel and Catering Industry Training Board	HDE	Hauptgemeinschaft des Deutschen Einzelhandels
HCJA	High Court Journalists' Association	HDF	Hauptverband Deutscher Filmtheater
HCLF	Haut Comité de Langue Française	HDF	Hungarian Democratic Forum = MDF
HCME	United Hatters, Cap and Millinery Workers International Union	HDGA	Hot Dip Galvanisers Association
		HDGECP	Human Dimensions of Global Environmental Change Programme (IFIAS, ISSC, UNU)
HCNM	High Commissioner on National Minorities (EU)		
HCNN	Hoofdcommissie voor de Normalisatie in Nederland	HDH	Hauptverband der Deutschen Holzindustrie und Verwandter Industriezweige
HCNUR	Haut Commissariat des Nations Unies pour les Réfugiés = ACNUR, UNHCR	HDI	Henry Dunant Institute (Switzerland) = IHD
HCOPIL	The Hague Conference on Private International Law = CODIP	HdIS	Hijas de la Sabiduria = DW, FdlS, FdS
		HDK	Hrvatsko Društvo za Kakvoću = CSQ
HCP	Healthy Cities Project		
HCP	Hungarian Civic Party (Slovakia) = MOS	HDKI	Hrvatsko Društvo Kemijskih Inženjera i Tehnologa
HCPRU	Hot Climate Physiological Research Unit (Nigeria)	HDKKT	Hrvatsko Društvo Kazališnih Kritičara i Teatrologa

HDLP	Hermanitas de los Pobres = IDP, LSP, PSDP
HDLU	Hrvatsko Društvo Likovnih Umjetnika
HDP	Hauptverband für Zucht und Prüfung Deutscher Pferde
HDP	Human Dimensions of Global Environmental Change Programme
HDRA	Henry Doubleday Research Association
HDRBG	Heissdampfreaktor Betriebsgesellschaft
HDS	Hauptverband der Deutschen Schuhindustrie
HDS	Historical Diving Society
HDS	Hnutie za Demokratické Slovensko (Slovakia) = MDS
HDS	Hrvatsko Društvo Skladatelja
HDUR	Hungarian Democratic Union of Romania
HDZ	Croatian Democratic Union
HDZ	Hrvatska Demokratska Zajednica (Bosnia-Herzegovina) = CDU
HE	Hidroeléctrica Española
HEA	Hairdressing Employers Association
HEA	Health Education Authority
HEA	Heating Engineering Association
HEA	Higher Education Authority (Éire)
HEA	Horticultural Education Association
HEA	Horticultural Exhibitors Association
HEAA	Home Economics Association for Africa
HEAA	Home Economics Association of Australia
HEAC	Higher Education Accommodation Consortium
HEATH	Higher Education and the Handicapped (U.S.A.)
HEBA	Home Extension Building Association
HEBS	Health Education Board for Scotland
HÉC	École des Hautes Études Commerciales
HEC	Health Education Council
HECSA	Hidroelectrica de Cataluña S.A.
HED	Hrvatsko Ekološko Društvo
HED	Hrvatsko Etnološko Društvo
HEDCO	Higher Education for Development Cooperation (Éire)
HEFA	Hospital Employees' Federation of Australia
HEFA	Human Embryo and Fertilisation Authority
HEFCE	Higher Education Funding Council for England
HEI	Health Effects Institute
HEI	Higher Education International
HEIA	Hydrogen Energy Industry Association (U.S.A.)
HEIST	Higher Education Information Services Trust
HEIX	Home Economics Information Exchange (FAO)
HELCOM	Baltic Marine Environment Protection Commission – Helsinki Commission (Finland)
HELINAS	Elleniko Instituto Allilengyis ke Synergasias me tis Anaptyssomenes Chores
HELIOS	Handicapped People in Europe Living Independently in Open Society (CEC)
HELMEPA	Hellenic Marine Environmental Protection Association
HELOA	Higher Education Liaison Officers Association
HELORS	Hellenic Operational Research Society (Greece)
HELP	Help End Lead in Petrol
HELP	Holiday Endeavour for Lone Patients
HELP	Home, Education, Livelihood Program (U.S.A.)
HEPC	Handloom Export Promotion Council (India)
HEPC	Hydro-Electric Power Commission (Canada)
HEPCC	Heavy Electrical Plant Consultative Council
HÉPI	Haute École Populaire Internationale (Denmark)
HEPRA	Hellenic Public Relations Association
HEQC	Higher Education Quality Council
HERA	High Energy Reaction Analysis Group (Switzerland)
HERCASA	Hércules de Centroamérica (Nicaragua)
HERE	Home Economics Resources in Education (*now* THERE)
HERE	Hotel Employees and Restaurant Employees International Union
HERI	Henan Energy Research Institute
HERO	Hidroeléctrica Industria y Comercio (Brazil)
HERRA-MEX	Fabricantes Exportadores de Herramientas Manuales
HERU	Health Eonomics Research Unit (Scotland)

HES	Hawaiian Entomological Society
HESC	International Congress of Scientists on the Human Environment
HESCA	Health Sciences Communications Association (U.S.A.)
HET	Haldane Educational Trust
HET	Heritage Education Trust
HETMA	Heavy Edge Tool Manufacturers' Association
HEUNI	Helsinki Institute for Crime Prevention and Control affiliated with the United Nations
HEURAS	Secretariat of the European Associations in Higher Education
HEVAC	Heating, Ventilating and Air Conditioning Manufacturers Association
HEW	Hamburgische Elektrizitäs Werke
HFA	Housing Finance Agency (Éire)
HFAC	Hill Farming Advisory Committee (MAFF)
HFD	Hrvatsko Filozofsko Društvo
HFD	Hrvatsko Fizikalno Društvo
HFDA	High Fidelity Dealers Association
HFEA	Human Fertilisation and Embryology Authority
HFES	Human Factors and Ergonomics Society
HFFF	Hungarian Freedom Fighters Federation
HFH	Home from Hospital
HFI	Hemmens Forskningsinstitut
HFI	Hjúkrunarfélag Islands
HFI	Hubei Fisheries Science Research Institute (China)
HFIAW	International Association of Heat and Frost Insulators and Asbestos Workers
HFMA	Hardwood Flooring Manufacturers' Association
HFMA	Health Food Manufacturers Association
HFMA	Healthcare Financial Management Association
HFO	De Danske Handelsforenings Foelles-Organisation
HFRO	Hill Farming Research Organisation
HFS	Holstein Friesian Society of Great Britain and Northern Ireland
HFS	Hrvatski Filatelisticki Savez
HFSJG	Internationale Stiftung Hochalpine Forschungsstationen Jungfraujoch und Gornergrat (Switzerland)
HFT	Home Farm Trust

HFT	International Symposium on Human Factors in Telecommunications
HFVOA	Hull Fishing Vessel Owners' Association
HFW	Housing for Women
HGA	Hop Growers of America
HGCA	Home Grown Cereals Authority
HGD	Hrvatsko Geodetsko Društvo
HGD	Hrvatsko Geografsko Društvo (*ex* SGDG)
HGGA	Heraldische-Genealogische Gesellschaft 'Adler' (Austria)
HGHSC	Home Grown Herbage Seeds Committee
HGP	Hungarian Green Party
HGP	Hungarian Gypsy Party = MCP
HGPD	Gewerkschaft Hotel, Gastgewerbe, Persönlicher Dienst (Austria)
HGS	Harness Goat Society
HGS	Hurdy-Gurdy Society
HGSDP	Hungarian Gypsy Social Democratic Party = MCSzP
HGTAC	Home Grown Timber Advisory Committee
HGTMC	Home Grown Timber Marketing Corporation
HGUÖ	Hauptverband des Graphischen Unternehmungen Österreichs
HGV	Hohenzollischer Geschichtsverein
HHA	Historic Houses Association
HHG	Heinrich Heine-Gesellschaft
HHH	Hash House Harriers International
HHIA	Headway Head Injuries Association
HHLA	Handkerchief & Household Linens Association
HHLGCS	(Department of) Health, Housing, Local Government and Community Services
HHMT	Helene Harris Memorial Trust
HHN	Honger Hoeft Niet
HHS	Hawaiian Historical Society
HHS	Helpers of the Holy Souls (France) = SA
HHS	Historical Harp Society
HHS	Huguenot Historical Society (U.S.A.)
HHY	Henkilöstöhallinnollinen Yhdistys
HI	Handicap International (Belgium)
HI	Hizb-i Islami (Afghanistan) = IP
HI	Hotline International (U.S.A.)
HIA	Hawaiian Irrigation Authority

HIA	Housing Industry Association (Australia)
HIAS	Hebrew Immigrant Aid Society (U.S.A.)
HIB	Herring Industry Board
HIBIN	Vereniging van Handelaren in Bouwmaterialen in Nederland
HIC	Habitat International Coalition
HICSS	Hawaii International Conference on System Sciences
HID	Halkla Iliskiler Dernegi
HIDB	Highlands and Islands Development Board
Hidrandina	Energía Hidroeléctrica Andina (Peru)
Hidronor	Hidroeléctrica Norpatagónica (Argentina)
HIER	Hungarian Institute for Educational Research
HIERRO-PERU	Empresa Minera Hierro del Perú
HII	Harakat-i-Inquilab-i-Islami (Afghanistan) = MIR
HII	Housing Institute of Ireland (Éire)
HIK	Hið Islenska Kennarafélag
HIK	Statens Handels- och Industrikommission
HIMAPBU	Himpunan Maskyurakat Pencinta Buku
HIMAT	Instítuto Colombiano de Hidrología, Meteorología y Adecuación de Tierras
HIMI	Heilongjiang Institute of Medical Information (China)
HinD	Housewives in Dialogue
HINDALCO	Hindustan Aluminium Corporation (India)
HIOW	Hoger Institut v. Opvoedkundige Wetenschappen (Belgium)
HIP	Homeless Information Project
HIPA	Honey Importers and Packers Association
HIPH	High Institute of Public Health, Alexandria University (Egypt)
HIRC	Head Injuries Rehabilitation Centre
HIS	Hospital Infection Society
HIS	Hunters' Improvement and National Light Horse Breeding Society
HISGS	Human Insulin Solicitors' Group Scotland
HISHA	Highlands and Islands Sheep Health Association
HISP	Historic Independent Smallholders' Party (Hungary)
HISWA	Nederlandse Vereniging voor Handel en Industrie op het Gebied van Scheepbouw en Watersport
HITA	Hamper Industry Trade Association
HITAHR	Hawaii Institute of Tropical Agriculture and Human Resources
HITHA	Historic Irish Tourist Houses and Gardens Association
HIUS	Hispanic Institute in the United States
HIVA	Hoger Instituut voor de Arbeid (Belgium)
HIVOS	Humanistisch Instituut voor Ontwikkelingssamenwerking (Netherlands)
HJ	Hijas de Jesus de Kermaria = DJ, FJ
HJCF	Hungarian Jewish Cultural Federation = MZsKE
HJLP	Hungarian Justice and Life Party
HJSA	Hamburger Jute- und Sisal Association
HK	Handels- og Kontorfunktionaerernes Forbund i Danmark
HKCEC	Hong Kong Catholic Education Council
HKCW	Hong Kong Council of Women
HKG	Hochtemperatur-Kernkraftwerk GmbH
HKI	Fachverband Heiz- und Kochgeräte-Industrie
HKI	Helen Keller International
HKIA	Hong Kong Institute of Architects
HKJSMA	Hong Kong Jade and Stone Manufacturers Association
HKLA	Hong Kong Library Association
HKMA	Hong Kong Management Association
HKMS	Hong Kong Mathematical Society
HKNMA	Hong Kong National Musicology Association
HKNMRS	Hong Kong National Music Research Society
HKP	Hong Kong Polytechnic
HKPC	Hong Kong Productivity Council and Centre
HKTDC	Hong Kong Trade Development Council
HKU	University of Hong Kong
HLA	Hawaii Library Association
HLA	Hungarian Logistics Association = MLBKT, UVL
HLCC	Home Laundering Consultative Council
HLCF	Holy Land Conservation Fund (U.S.A.)
HLG	Historic Landscapes Group

HLI	Human Life International
HLISRDI	Hubei Light Industrial Scientific Research Design Institute (China)
HLRA	Handbag Liners and Repairers Association
HLZ	Hrvatski Liječnički Zbor
HMA	Hawaii Medical Association
HMA	Hellenic Marketing Association
HMA	Hop Merchants Association
HMAC	Hazardous Material Advisory Council (U.S.A.)
HMC	Headmasters Conference
HMC	Health Ministers Council
HMC	Horticultural Marketing Council
HMC	Royal Commission on Historical Manuscripts
HMCA	Hospital and Medical Care Association
HMCI	Her Majesty's Chief Inspector of Schools
HMDS	Her Majesty's Diplomatic Service
HMDS	Hrvatska Muslimanska Demokratska Stranka (Croatia) = CMDP
HMFI	Hárgreiðslumeistarafélag Íslands
HMFI	Her Majesty's Factory Inspectorate
HMGCC	Her Majesty's Government Communications Centre
HMI	Hahn-Meitner-Institut für Kernforschung
HMI	Her Majesty's Inspectorate of Schools
HMIP	HM Inspectorate of Pollution
HMIPI	Her Majesty's Industrial Pollution Inspectorate
HMK	Hristianshaja Mirnaja Konferencija = CCP, CFK, CPC
HMNFE	Her Majesty's Norfolk Flax Establishment
HMOCS	Her Majesty's Overseas Civil Service
HMPA	Hawaii Macadamia Producers Association
HMRI	Hubei Mechanical Research Institute (China)
HMRS	Historical Model Railway Society
HMS	Hind Mazdoor Sabha (India)
HMS	Historical Metallurgy Society
HMSI	Hebei Machinery Science Institute (China)
HMSO	Her Majesty's Stationery Office
HMT	Her Majesty's Treasury
HMU-CMS	Harmonie Mondiale Universelle – Conseil Mondiale du Service = UWH/WCS

HMvL	Hollandsche Maatschappij van Landbouw
HMW	Hollandsche Maatschappij der Wetenschappen
HMWA	Hairdressing Manufacturers and Wholesalers' Association
HMWG	Huma Multipurpose Women's Group (Kenya)
HMY	Hedelmänja Marjanviljelijät
HNA	Hungarian National Alliance = MNSz
HND	Hrvatsko Numizmaticko Društvo
HNEPI	Hunan Environmental Protection Institute (China)
HNF	Hungarian National Front = MNF
HNG	Hulpkomitee voor Nationalistiche politieke Gevangenen (Belgium)
HNGNA	Hellenic National Graduate Nurses Association (Greece)
HNHIA	Headway National Head Injuries Association
HNO	Österreichische Gesellschaft für Hals-Nasen- und Ohrenheilkunde, Kopf- und Halschirurgie
HNP	Herstigte Nasionale Party (South Africa)
HNP	Hungarian National Party
HNPSA	Homeland Non-Party Serbian Association = DNSU
HNR	Nordic Council of Organisatons for the Disabled
HNS	Hnutie za Nezávislé Slovensko (Slovakia) = MIS
HNU	Hainan University
HNU	Henan University
HNW	Vereniging "Het Nederlandse Wegencongres"
HO	Hovedorganisationen af Mesterforeninger i Byggefagene i Danmark
HOA	Huileries de l'Ouest Africain
HOAC	Hermandad Obrera de Acción Catolica
HOC	Holland Organizing Centre (Netherlands)
HOCRE	Home Office Central Research Establishment
HOF	Horizons of Friendship (Canada)
HOG	Harley-Davidson Owners Group
HOG	Hermann-Oberth-Gesellschaft
HOI!	Hands off Ireland!
HOKÉV	Horgászcikk Készító és Értékesító Vállalat

HOMA	Heads of Marine Agencies
HONDUTEL	Empresa Hondureña de Telecomunicaciones (Honduras)
HONSA	Hotelera Nacional, S.A. (Chile)
HOP	Holidays One-Parents
HOPE	Healthcare Opposed to Euthanasia
HOPE	Hellenic Organisation for the Promotion of Exports
HOPE	Help Organise Peaceful Energy
HOPECO	Hormoz Petroleum Company (Iran)
HORECA	International Organisation of Hotel and Restaurant Associations
HORECAF	Nederlandse Bond van Werkgevers in Hotel-, Restaurant-, Café- en Aanverwante Bedrijven
HORESCA	Fédération Nationale des Hôteliers, Restaurateurs et Cafetiers du Grande-Duché de Luxembourg
HORSC-ERA	House of Representatives Standing Committee on the Environment, Recreation and the Arts (Australia)
HORSEC	House of Representatives Standing Committee on Environment and Conservation (Australia)
HORU	Home Office Research Unit
HOS	Hrvatske Obrambene Snage
HOST	Hosting for Overseas Students
HOT	Hawk and Owl Trust
HOTAFRIC	Société de Développement Hôtelier et Touristique de l'Afrique de l'Ouest (Ivory Coast)
HOTREC	Comité de l'Industrie Hôtelière de la CEE
HOW	Hands off Our Water
HP	Homeland Party (Afghanistan) = HW
HPA	Handley Page Association
HPA	Health Projects Abroad
HPA	Hen Packers Association
HPA	Hospital Physicists Association
HPA	Hurlingham Polo Association
HPC	Hindustan Paper Corporation (India)
HPC	Horticultural Policy Council
HPCA	Hiroshima Peace Centre Associates (U.S.A.)
HPCI	Himpunan Pustakawan Chusus Indonesia
HPCL	Hindustan Petroleum Corporation Limited (India)
HPD	Hrvatsko Prirodoslovno Društvo
HPEC	Handicraft Promotion and Export Centre (Afghanistan)
HPF	Horace Plunkett Foundation for Cooperative Studies
HPI	Heifer Project International (U.S.A.)
HPI	Hellenic Purchasing Institute
HPIC	Health Promotion Information Centre
HPMA	Heat Pump Manufacturers' Association
HPMIDC	Himachul Pradesh Mineral and Industrial Development Corporation (India)
HPP	Hernieuwde Progressieve Partij (Suriname)
HPP	Hungarian People's Party (Croatia), = MNS = MLS (Slovakia)
HPPA	High Performance Pipe Association
HPPA	Horses and Ponies Protection Association
HPRA	Hungarian Public Relations Association = MPRSZ
HPRILIM	Hangzhou Project and Research Institute of Light Industry Machinery (China)
HPRP	Human Potential Research Project
HPRS	Hellenic Public Relations Society (Greece)
HPRS	Houghton Poultry Research Station
HPRU	Handicapped Persons Research Unit
HPS	Hardy Plant Society
HPS	Health Physics Society
HPS	Hellenic Philatelic Society = SPH
HPS	Hellenic Physical Society
HPS	Highland Pony Society
HPSEB	Himachal Pradash State Electricity Board (India)
HPTA	High Pressure Technology Association
HPTA	Hire Purchase Trade Association
HPV	Hauptverband der Papier, Pappe und Kunststoffe Verarbeitenden Industrie
HPY	Helsingin Puhelinyhdistys
HR	Hydraulics Research Ltd
HRA	Harbin Railway Administration (China)
HRA	Horse Rangers' Association
HRA	Horticultural Research Association (*ex* GCRI)
HRA	Hotell- och Restaurangarbetsgivare-föreningen
HRAI	Human Rights Advocates International (U.S.A.)

HRB	Health Research Board (Éire)
HRB	Hotell- och Restaurangbranchföreningen
HRC	Humanities Research Centre (Australia)
HRC	Huntingdon Research Centre
HRC	Nordiska Unionen för Hotell-, Café- och Restauranganställda
HRCC	Humanities Research Council of Canada = CCRN
HRDG	Commonwealth Human Resource Development Group
HRDU	Housing and Building Research Institute (Kenya)
HREBIU	Hotel and Restaurant Employees and Bartenders International Union
HREOC	Human Rights and Equal Opportunity Commission
HRGB	Handbell Ringers of Great Britain
HRHL	Hotelli- ja Ravintolahenkilökunnan Liitto
HRI	Horticultural Research International
HRI	Human Rights Internet (Canada)
HRIS	Highway Research Information Service (AAHSO)
HRK	Hochschulrektorenkonferenz
HRN	Hotelli-ja Ravintolaneuvosto
HRS	Human Rights Society
HRSCGR	Hebei Research Society of Crop Germplasm Resources
HRSP	Association of Human Resource Systems Professionals (U.S.A.)
HRT	Humane Research Trust
HRTK	Hoger Rijksinstituut voor Textiel en Kunststoffen (Belgium)
HRW	Human Rights Watch
HS	Hume Society
HSA	Herb Society of America
HSA	Hospital Saving Association
HSA	Humane Slaughter Association
HSA	Hunt Saboteurs Association
HSA-UWC	Holy Spirit Association for the Unification of World Christianity = AUCM
HSAC	Hebridean Spinners Advisory Committee
HSB	Hochleistungs-schnellbau Studiengesellschaft
HSBA	Herdwick Sheep Breeders Association
HSBS	Hunt Servants Benefit Society
HSC	Haiti Solidarity Campaign
HSC	Health and Safety Commission
HSC	Health Services Centre
HSC	High State Committee (Algeria)
HSCL	Hindustan Steel Construction Limited (India)
HSD-SMS	Hnutí a samosprávnou demokracie – Společnost pro Moravu a Slezsko
HSDMS	Hnutíza Samosprávnou Demokracii Moravy a Slezka (Czech Republic) = MSDMS
HSDP	Hungarian Social Democratic Party
HSE	Health and Safety Executive
HSE	Human Scale Education Movement
HSEI	Harbin Shipbuilding Engineering Institute (China)
HSES	Hungarian Solar Energy Society = MNT
HSF	Hospital Saturday Fund
HSFK	Hessische Stiftung für Friedens- und Konfliktsforschung
HSG	Haiti Support Group
HSGB	Haflinger Society of Great Britain
HSGV	Hanseatischer Sparkassen-und Giroverband
HSI	Hungarian Society for Immunology = MIT
HSM	Societatea Hidrobiologicâ din Moldova
HSMC	Health Services Management Centre
HSMS	Holy Spirit Missionary Sisters = SSPS
HSN	Hysterectomy Support Network
HSP	Croatian Party of Rights
HSP	Hrvatska Stranka Prava (Croatia) = CPR
HSP	Hungarian Socialist Party
HSPA	Hawaiian Sugar Planters' Association
HSPHS	Hellenic Society for Philosophical Studies (Greece) = EEPhM
HSPN	Hellenic Society for the Protection of Nature (Greece) = EEPV, SHPN
HSPRS	Hellenic Society of Photogrammetry and Remote Sensing (Greece)
HSQ	Historical Society of Queensland (Australia)
HSRC	Health Sciences Resource Centre (CISTI)
HSRC	Human Sciences Research Council (South Africa)
HSRIES	Hangzhou Scientific Research Institute for Environmental Sanitation (China)
HSS	Henry Sweet Society for the History of Linguistic Ideas

HSS	History of Science Society (U.S.A.)
HSSL	Haldane Society of Socialist Lawyers
HSSL	Historical Society of Sierra Leone
HSSMFE	Hellenic Society of Soil Mechanics and Foundation Engineering
HSSS	Hellenic Society of Social Science = EEE
HST	Hawaiian Sugar Technologists
HSTAG	Hungarian Simulation Tools and Application Group
HSWP	Hungarian Socialist Workers' Party
HT	Society for Horticultural Therapy
HTA	Harris Tweed Association
HTA	Help The Aged
HTA	Horticultural Trades Association
HTA	Humanist Teachers Association
HTB	Hospitals Trust Board (Éire)
HTCI	Hangzhou Termite Control Institute (China)
HTE	Hiradástechnikai Tudományos Egyesület
HTFS	Heat Transfer and Fluid Flow Service
HTG	Hafenbautechnische Gesellschaft
HTG	Hemtextilgrossisterna
HTI	Henan Tumour Institute (China)
HTLDC	Hsinchu Tidal Land Development Planning Commission (Taiwan)
HTMA	Hawaii Territorial Medical Association
HTMA	Home Timber Merchants Association
HTRP	Humid Tropics Research Programme (UNESCO)
HTS	Helen Television System (St Lucia)
HTTA	Highway and Traffic Technicians Association
HU	Hangzhou University
HUAI	Harbin Underwater Acoustics Institute (China)
HUDCO	Housing and Urban Development Corporation (India)
HUGO	Human Genome Organisation
HUICOMA	Huileries Cotonnières du Mali
HUILCO	Huilerie du Congo
HUK	Verband der Haftpflicht- Unfall- und Kraftverkehrs- Versicherer
HUMEX	Hules Mexicanos, S.A.
HUMRRO	Human Resources Research Office
HUMUCI	Société Humus Côte- d'Ivoire
HUNGALU	Hungarian Aluminium Corporation
HUNOSA	Empresa Nacional Hulleras del Norte
HURACA	Huilerie, Raffinerie du Caméroun
HURIDOCS	Human Rights Information and Documentation System, International
HUSAT	Human Sciences and Advanced Technology Research Institute
HV	Hochschulverband
HVA	Health Visitors Association
HVACMA	Heating, Ventilating & Air Conditioning Manufacturers' Association
HVCA	Heating and Ventilating Contractors' Association
HVFL	Historischer Verein für das Fürstentum Liechtenstein
HVG	Hüttentechnische Vereinigung der Deutschen Glasindustrie
HVK	Hrvatska Veterinarska Komora (*ex* SDVIVT)
HVMS	Hellenic Veterinary Medical Society = EKE, SVH
HVO	Hrvatske Vijece Obrane
HVRA	Hawaiian Volcano Research Association
HW	Hezb-e-Watan (Afghanistan) = HP
HWCRI	Hadassah WIZO Canada Research Institute (Israel)
HWI	Herdisconteringen Waarborginstituut = IRG
HWMV	Schweizerischer Hartweizenmüller- Verband
HWWA	Hamburgisches Weltwirtschaftsarchiv
HYA	Hydro-og Aerodynamisk Laboratorium
HYDRO-CONGO	Société Nationale de Recherche et d'Exploitation Petrolières
HYPECO	Hybrid Poultry Breeding Corporation (Belgium-Netherlands)
HYSACAM	Hygiène et Salubrité du Caméroun
HYTASA	Hilaturas y Tejidos Andaluces
HZD	Hessische Zentrale für Datenverarbeitung
HZFRD	Hrvatska Zajednica Računovoda i Financijskih Djelatnika

I

I-CL	International-Communist League
I-GOOS	IOC Committee for Global Ocean Observing System
I-i-A	Ittehad-i-Ansarollah

I-S	Ingeniør Sammenslutningen (*now* IDA)
I3W	Informationsdienst 3. Welt (Switzerland)
IA	Ileostomy Association of Great Britain and Ireland
IA	Institute of Actuaries
IA	Inter Aide (France)
IA	International Affiliation of Independent Accounting Firms = IA International
IA	International Alert
IA	Inuit Ataqatigiit (Greenland)
IA	Irmazinhas da Assunçâo = HA, LSA, PSA
IA International	Independent Accountants International (U.S.A.) = IA
IA RAN	Institute of Archaeology, Russian Academy of Sciences
IA-ECOSOC	Inter-American Economic and Social Council = CESI, CIES
IAA	Institut Agricole d'Algérie
IAA	Institute of Administrative Accountants
IAA	Institute of African Alternatives
IAA	Instcustúto Antártica Argentino
IAA	Institúto do Açúcar e do Alcool (Brazil)
IAA	Inter-American Accounting Association = AIC
IAA	Interamerican Accounting Association = AIC
IAA	International Academy of Architecture (IUA)
IAA	International Academy of Astronautics
IAA	International Actuarial Association = AAI
IAA	International Advertising Association
IAA	International Aerosol Association
IAA	International Arthroscopy Association
IAA	International Association for Aerobiology
IAA	International Association of Agriculturists
IAA	International Association of Art (Painting, Sculpture, Printmaking) = AIAP
IAA	International Association of Astacology
IAA	International Astronautical Academy
IAA	Ireland-Australia Association
IAA	Irish Aquaculture Association
IAA	Irish Architectural Archive
IAA	Israel Archives Association

IAAA	International Airforwarder and Agents Association (U.S.A.)
IAAA	Irish Amateur Athletic Association
IAAA	Irish Association of Advertising Agencies
IAAALD	Inter-American Association of Agricultural Librarians and Documentalists (Costa Rica)
IAAAM	International Association for Aquatic Animal Medicine
IAAATDC	International Association for the Advancement of Appropriate Technology for Developing Countries
IAABO	International Association of Approved Basketball Officials
IAAC	Institúto Argentino de Control de la Calidad
IAAC	International Antarctic Analysis Centre
IAAC	International Association of Art Critics = AICA
IAACI	International Association of Allergology and Clinical Immunology = AIA
IAACR	Institúto Agrario Argentino de Cultura Rurál
IAADFS	International Association of Airport Duty Free Stores (U.S.A.)
IAAE	Institute for Application of Atomic Energy (China)
IAAE	International Association Autism – Europe = AIAE
IAAE	International Association of Agricultural Economists = AIEA
IAAE	Israel Association of Agricultural Engineering
IAAEE	International Association for the Advancement of Ethnology and Eugenics
IAAEES	International Association for the Advancement of Earth and Environmental Sciences
IAAER	International Association for the Advancement of Educational Research = AISE
IAAF	International Agricultural Aviation Foundation
IAAF	International Amateur Athletic Federation = FIAA
IAAH	International Association for Adolescent Health
IAAI	International Airports Authority of India

IAAI	International Association of Arson Investigators	**IAB**	ICSU Abstracting Board = ICSUAB
IAAI	Italian Association for Artificial Intelligence = AIIA	**IAB**	Industrial Advisory Board (OECD)
		IAB	Institut Agricole de Beauvais
IAAIP	Inter-American Association of Industrial Property = ASIPA	**IAB**	Institut für Arbeitsmarkt und Berufsforschung
IAAJ	International Association of Agricultural Journalists	**IAB**	International Aquatic Board
IAAL	International Association of Applied Linguistics = AILA	**IAB**	International Association of Boards of Examiners in Optometry (U.S.A.)
IAALD	International Association of Agricultural Librarians and Documentalists	**IAB**	International Association of Book-keepers
		IAB	International Association of Broadcasting = AIR
IAAM	International Association of Auditorium Managers	**IAB**	Internationale Akademie für Bäder-, Sport-, und Freizeitbauten
IAAMRH	International Association of Agricultural Medicine and Rural Health	**IAB**	Internet Architecture Board
IAAO	International Association of Assessing Officers (U.S.A.)	**IAB**	Irish Association for the Blind
		IABA	Inter-American Bar Association = FIA
IAAP	International Association for Analytical Psychology = AIPA, IGFAP	**IABA**	International Amateur Boxing Association = AIBA
IAAP	International Association of Applied Psychology = AIPA	**IABA**	International Association of Aircraft Brokers and Agents
IAAPA	International Association of Amusement Parks and Attractions (U.S.A.)	**IABA**	Irish Amateur Boxing Association
IAAPEA	International Association Against Painful Experiments on Animals	**IABBE**	International Association for Better Basic Education
IAARC	International Administrative Aeronautical Radio Conference	**IABC**	International Association of Building Companions = IBO
IAAS	Immigrants Appeals Advisory Service	**IABC**	International Association of Business Communicators (U.S.A.)
IAAS	Incorporated Association of Architects and Surveyors	**IABE**	Ibero-American Bureau of Education = BEI, OEI
IAAS	Institute of Acoustics, Academia Sinica	**IABEM**	International Association for Boundary Element Methods
IAAS	Institute of African Asian Studies	**IABG**	International Association of Botanic Gardens = AIJB
IAAS	Institute of Auctioneers and Apprentices in Scotland	**IABG**	International Association on Biomedical Gerontology (U.S.A.)
IAAS	International Association for Atmospheric Science	**IABM**	International Academy of Biological Medicine
IAAS	International Association of Agricultural Students = AIEA	**IABM**	International Association of Broadcasting Manufacturers
IAASM	International Academy of Aviation and Space Medicine = AIMAS	**IABMS**	International Association of Botanical and Mycological Societies
IAASP	International Association of Airport and Seaport Police	**IABN**	Institúto Autónomo, Biblioteca Nacional y Servicios de Bibliotecas de Venezuela
IAATI	International Association of Auto Theft Investigators	**IABO**	International Association for Biological Oceanography = AIOB
IAATM	International Association for Accident and Traffic Medicine	**IABO**	International Association of Biblicists and Orientalists
IAAW	International Association of African Writers	**IABP**	International Association of Businessmen and Professionals

IABS	International Association for Biological Standardization = AISB		**IACA**	Irish American Cultural Association
IABS	International Association for Business and Society		**IACAAN**	International Committee on Avian Anatomical Nomenclature
IABS	International Association of Buddhist Studies		**IACAC**	Inter-American Commercial Arbitration Commission
IABS	International Association of Byzantine Studies = AIEB		**IACAHP**	Inter-African Advisory Committee for Animal Health and Production
IABSE	International Association for Bridge and Structural Engineering = AIPC, IVBH		**IACAPAP**	International Association for Child and Adolescent Psychiatry and Allied Professions = AIPEAPA
IABSF	International Amateur Boat Surfing Federation		**IACB**	Inter-Agency Consultative Board (UN)
IABSOIW	International Association of Bridge, Structural and Ornamental Iron Workers		**IACB**	International Advisory Committee on Bibliography
IABTI	International Association of Bomb Technicians and Investigators		**IACBC**	International Advisory Committee on Biological Control
IAC	Indian Airlines Corporation		**IACBD**	International Academy for Child Brain Development (U.S.A.)
IAC	Industries Assistance Commission (*now* IC)		**IACBDT**	International Advisory Committee on Bibliography, Documentation and Terminology
IAC	Industry Advisory Committee on Survey and Mapping		**IACC**	Instituto de Aeronaútica Civil de Cuba
IAC	Institut d'Affaires Culturelles (Belgium)		**IACC**	Inter-American Confederation of Cattlemen = CIAGA
IAC	Institute of Administration and Commerce of South Africa		**IACC**	International Agricultural Coordination Commission
IAC	Institute of Amateur Cinemaphotographers		**IACC**	International Anti-Counterfeiting Coalition (U.S.A.)
IAC	Instituto de Astrofisica de Canarias		**IACC**	International Association for Cell Culture
IAC	Instituto de Campinas (Brazil)		**IACC**	International Association of Congress Centres = AIPC
IAC	Inter Afrique Charters			
IAC	Inter-African Committee on Traditional Practices Affecting the Health of Women and Children in Africa = CI-AF		**IACCA**	Irish Association of Company and Commercial Accountants (Éire)
			IACCC	International Association for Cross-Cultural Communication = AIMAV
IAC	Internationaal Agrarisch Centrum (Netherlands)		**IACCE**	Inter-American Association for Catholic Education = CIEC
IAC	International Academy of Ceramics = AIC		**IACCHE**	Inter-American Confederation of Chemical Engineering
IAC	International Academy of Cytology		**IACCI**	International Association of Computer Crime Investigators
IAC	International Aerobatic Club			
IAC	International Alpine Conference		**IACCI**	International Association of Credit Card Investigators
IAC	International ANTOR Committee		**IACCP**	Inter-American Council for Commerce and Production = CICEP, CICYP
IAC	International Artists Cooperation			
IAC	International Athletes Club		**IACCP**	International Association for Cross-Cultural Psychology
IACA	Associação Portuguesa dos Industrias de Alimentos Compostos para Animals			
IACA	Inter-American College Association		**IACD**	International Association for Community Development = AIDAC
IACA	International Air Carrier Association			
IACA	International Air Charter Association (Switzerland)		**IACD**	International Association of Clothing Designers
IACA	International Association of Consulting Actuaries			

IACD	Irish Association for Curriculum Development	**IACMAG**	International Association for Computer Methods and Advances in Geomechanics
IACDB	International Action Committee for Democracy in Burma	**IACME**	Inter-American Committee of Mathematical Education = CIAEM
IACDT	International Advisory Committee for Documentation and Terminology	**IACME**	International Association of Coroners and Medical Examiners
IACE	Institut Africain des Caisses d'Epargne (Benin)	**IACME**	International Association of Crafts and Small and Medium-sized Enterprises = IGU, UIAPME
IACED	Interagency Committee on Environment and Development	**IACNET**	Inter-American Citrus Network (FAO/RLAC) (Chile)
IACEE	International Association for Continuing Engineering Education	**IACO**	Inter-African Coffee Organisation = OIAC
IACES	International Air Cushion Engineering Society	**IACO**	Inter-American Coffee Organisation = OIC
IACESR	Irish Association for Cultural, Economic and Social Relations	**IACODLA**	International Advisory Committee on Documentation, Libraries and Archives (UNESCO)
IACF	International Amateur Cycling Federation = FIAC	**IACOMS**	International Advisory Committee on Marine Sciences
IACFA	International Adult Cystic Fibrosis Association (Netherlands)	**IACP**	Inter-African Council for Philosophy = CIAP
IACH	International Association of Colour Healers	**IACP**	International Association of Chiefs of Police
IACHEI	International Association of Consultants in Higher Education Institutions	**IACP**	International Association of Cities and Ports = AIVP
IACHR	Inter-American Commission on Human Rights = CIDH	**IACP**	International Association of Computer Programmers
IACI	Inter-American Children's Institute (OAS) = IIE, IIN	**IACP**	Investment Advisory Centre of Pakistan
IACI	Inter-American Copyright Institute = ICI, IIDA	**IACPP**	International Association for Cross-Cultural Psychology
IACI	International Association of Conference Interpreters = AIIC, IVKD	**IACPS**	International Academy of Chest Physicians and Surgeons
IACI	Irish American Cultural Institute	**IACQ**	Institúto Argentino de la Calidad
IACID	Inter-American Centre for Integral Development (OAS)	**IACR**	Institute of Arable Crops Research (AFRC)
IACIS	International Association of Colloid and Interface Scientists	**IACR**	International Association for Cryptologic Research
IACJ	Inter-American Council of Jurists	**IACR**	International Association of Cancer Registries
IACL	International Academy of Comparative Law	**IACRDVT**	Inter-American Centre for Research and Documentation on Vocational Training = CINTERFOR
IACL	International Association of Constitutional Law = AIDC	**IACRLRD**	International Association for Comparative Research on Leukemia and Related Diseases
IACL	International Association of Criminal Law		
IACM	Institute of Applied and Computational Mathematics (Greece)	**IACS**	Indian Association for the Cultivation of Science
IACM	International Association for Computational Mechanics	**IACS**	International Academy of Christian Sociologists
IACM	International Association of Circulation Managers		

IACS	International Academy of Cosmetic Surgery	**IADF**	Inter-American Association for Democracy and Freedom = AIDL
IACS	International Alliance for Cooperation among Schools = AICS	**IADH**	Institut Arabe des Droits de l'Homme (Tunisia)
IACS	International Association of Classification Societies	**IADH**	International Association of Dentistry for the Handicapped
IACS	International Association of Counselling Services (U.S.A.)	**IADIS**	Irish Association for Documentation and Information Services
IACSAC	Inter-American Catholic Social Action Confederation	**IADIWU**	International Association for the Development of International and World Universities = AIDUM
IACSS	Inter-American Conference of Social Security = CISS	**IADL**	International Association of Democratic Lawyers = AIJD, IVDJ, MAJD
IACST	International Association for Commodity Science and Technology = IGWT	**IADLA**	International Association for the Development of Documentation, Libraries and Archives in Africa = AIDBA
IACT	International Association for Clean Technology		
IACVB	International Association of Convention and Visitors Bureaux	**IADMFR**	International Association of Dento-Maxilli-Facial Radiology
IACVF	International Association of Cancer Victims and Friends	**IADO**	Institúto Agroindustrial de Oleaginosos (Argentina)
IACW	Inter-American Commission of Women = CIF, CIM	**IADO**	Institúto Argentino de Oceanográfica
IACW	International Association of Crime Writers	**IADO**	Iran Agriculture Development Organisation
IAD	Institúto Agrario Dominicano	**IADP**	Intensive Agricultural District Programme (India)
IAD	International Association of Documentalists and Information Officers	**IADPÉ**	Institut Asiatique pour le Développement et la Planification Économique (Thailand)
IAD	Internationale Arbeitsgemeinschaft Donauforschung	**IADR**	International Association for Dental Research
IAD	Internationaler Zivildienst		
IADA	Internationale Arbeitsgemeinschaft der Archiv-, Bibliotheks- und Graphikrestauratoren	**IADRS**	International Association of Dive Rescue Specialists (U.S.A.)
		IADS	International Agricultural Development Service (U.S.A.)
IADAP	Institúto Andino de Artes Populares (Ecuador)	**IADS**	International Association of Dental Students = AIED
IADB	Inter-American Defense Board = JID, OID	**IADS**	International Association of Department Stores = AIGM, IWV
IADB	Interamerican Development Bank = BID, IDB	**IADSL**	Instituto Interamericano para el Desarrollo del Sindicalismo Libre (Argentina)
IADC	Inter-American Defense College		
IADC	Inter-American Development Commission	**IADT**	Irish Association of Distributive Trades
IADC	International Association of Dredging Companies = AIED	**IAE**	Institut d'Administration des Entreprises
IADC	International Association of Drilling Contractors	**IAE**	Institute for the Advancement of Engineering (U.S.A.)
IADE	Instituto Argentino para el Desarrollo Economico	**IAE**	Institute of Atomic Energy of China
		IAE	Institute of Automobile Engineers
IAdEM	Internacia Asocio de Esperantistoj Matematiskoj (France)	**IAE**	International Academy of Education (Belgium)

IAE	International Association for Ecology	**IAES**	International Academy of Environmental Safety
IAE	International Association of Egyptologists	**IAESM**	International Association for the Economics of Self Management
IAEA	Indian Adult Education Association	**IAESP**	Instítuto Agronómico de Estado de São Paulo (Brazil)
IAEA	Institute of Automobile Engineer Assessors	**IAESR**	Institute of Applied Economic and Social Research
IAEA	Inter-American Educational Association = AIDE	**IAESTE**	International Association for the Exchange of Students for Technical Experience
IAEA	International Agricultural Exchange Association = AIEE		
IAEA	International Association for Educational Assessment = AIEE	**IAET**	International Association for Enterostomal Therapy
IAEA	International Association of Empirical Aesthetics = AIEE	**IAEVG**	International Association for Educational and Vocational Guidance = AIOSP, IVSBB
IAEA	International Atomic Energy Agency (Austria) = AIEA, OIEA	**IAEVI**	International Association for Educational and Vocational Information = AIISUP
IAEA	Iraqi Atomic Energy Authority		
IAEAC	International Association of Environmental Analytical Chemistry	**IAEWP**	International Association of Educators for World Peace = AIEPM
IAEAL	Instítuto Altos Estudios América Latina	**IAF**	Indian Air Force
IAEB	Institute of Account Executives and Book-keepers	**IAF**	Institut Armand Frappier (Canada)
IAEC	International Association of Electrical Contractors (France)	**IAF**	Inter-American Foundation (U.S.A.)
		IAF	International Abolitionist Federation = FAI
IAEC	International Association of Environmental Coordinators = IPRE	**IAF**	International Aeronautical Federation = FAI
IAEC	Israel Atomic Energy Commission	**IAF**	International Aikido Federation = FIA
IAEDB	International Association for Education of the Deaf-Blind	**IAF**	International Apparel Federation
IAEDEN	Instituto de Altos Estudios de la Defensa Nacional (Venezuela)	**IAF**	International Arab Federation
		IAF	International Archery Federation = FITA
IAEE	International Association for Earthquake Engineering	**IAF**	International Association Futuribles = AIF
IAEE	International Association for Energy Economics = AIEE	**IAF**	International Association of Falconry and Conservation of Birds of Prey
IAEE	International Association of Elevator Engineers	**IAF**	International Astronautical Federation
IAEG	International Association of Engineering Geology = AIGI	**IAF**	International Automobile Federation
		IAF	Internationale Athletiekfederatie
IAEI	International Association of Electrical Inspectors	**IAF**	Société Interafricaine de Financement (Ivory Coast)
IAEMS	International Association of Environmental Mutagen Societies	**IAF RAN**	Institute of Africa, Russian Academy of Sciences
IAEN	Instituto de Altos Estudios Nacionales (Ecuador)	**IAFAE**	Inter-American Federation for Adult Education
IAEP	Institute of Agro-Environmental Protection (China)	**IAFC**	Inter-American Freight Conference
IAES	Institute of Aeronautical Sciences	**IAFC**	International Association of Fire Chiefs (U.S.A.)
IAES	Institute of Aerospace Sciences (U.S.A.)	**IAFCI**	Inter-American Federation of the Construction Industry = FIIC

IAFCT	International Association of French-speaking Congress Towns = AIVFC	**IAG**	Ionist Art Group
IAFE	International Association of Fairs and Expositions	**IAGA**	Instítuto Argentino de Grasas y Aceites
IAFEI	International Association of Financial Executives Institutes	**IAGA**	International Association of Geomagnetism and Aeronomy = AIGA
IAFESM	International Association for the Economics of Self-Management (Yugoslavia)	**IAGASA**	Associazione Italiana Gestori Aeroporti e Servici Aeroportuali
IAFF	International Advertizing Film Festival	**IAGB**	Institut für Anwendungen der Geodäsie im Bauwesen (Germany)
IAFF	International Art Film Federation	**IAGB&I**	Ileostomy Association of Great Britain and Ireland
IAFF	International Association of Fire Fighters	**IAGC**	International Association of Geophysical Contractors
IAFFE	International Association For Feminist Economics	**IAGC**	International Association on Geochemistry and Cosmochemistry = AIGC
IAFM	International Archives of Folk Music (Switzerland) = AIMP	**IAGFA**	International Association of Government Fair Agencies
IAFMM	International Association of Fish Meal Manufacturers	**IAGLL**	International Association of Germanic Languages and Literatures = IVG
IAFP	Instítuto de Anatomia y Fisiologia Patólogicas (Argentina)	**IAGLP**	International Association of Great Lakes Ports
IAFP	International Association of Financial Planners (U.S.A.)	**IAGLR**	International Association for Great Lakes Research
IAFRV	Internationale Arbeitsgemeinschaft für Forschung zum Romanischen Volksbuch	**IaGMI**	Iaroslavskii Gosudarstvennyi Meditsinskii Institut (Russia)
IAFS	International Association of Family Sociology	**IAGOD**	International Association on the Genesis of Ore Deposits
IAFS	International Association of Forensic Sciences	**IAGP**	International Antarctic Glaciological Project
IAFSE	Ibero-American Federation of Stock Exchanges = FIABV	**IAGP**	International Association of Group Psychotherapy
IAFSS	International Association for Fire Safety Science	**IAgrE**	Institution of Agricultural Engineers
IAFT	International Association of Forensic Toxicologists	**IAgS**	Institute of Agricultural Secretaries
		IAGS	International Association of Gandhian Studies (U.S.A.)
IAFWA	International Association of Fish and Wildlife Agencies	**IAgSA**	Institute of Agricultural Secretaries & Administrators
IAG	Institute of American Genealogy	**IAGUSP**	Instítuto de Astronomia e Geofisica da Universidade de São Paulo (Brazil)
IAG	Institute of Applied Geology (Saudi Arabia)	**IAH**	Institute for Animal Health (AFRC)
IAG	Institute of Australian Geographers	**IAH**	International Arabian Horse Association (U.S.A.)
IAG	International Association of Geodesy = AIG	**IAH**	International Association of Hydrogeologists = AIH
IAG	International Association of Geomorphologists	**IAH**	International Association of Hydrology
IAG	International Association of Gerodontology	**IAH**	Internationale Arbeitsgemeinschaft für Hymnologie = IFRH
IAG	International Association of Gerontology = AIG	**IAHA**	Inter-American Hotel Association = AIH
IAG	Internationale Arbeitsgemeinschaft f.d. Unterrichtsfilm	**IAHA**	International Association of Historians of Asia (Singapore)

IAHA	International Association of Hospitality Accountants (U.S.A.)
IAHA	International Association of Hypno-Analysts (U.S.A.)
IAHA	Internationales Arbeiter-Hilfswerk
IAHAIO	International Association of Human-Animal Interaction Organizations (U.S.A.)
IAHB	International Association of Human Biologists
IAHCCJ	International Association for the History of Crime and Criminal Justice
IAHCSM	International Association of Hospital Central Service Management
IAHD	International Association of Hillel Directors
IAHE	International Association for Hydrogen Energy
IAHE	International Association of Handicapped Esperantists
IAHECL	International Association of Humanist Educators, Counsellors and Leaders (IHEU)
IAHHP	International Asociation of Holistic Health Practitioners
IAHIC	International Association of Home Improvement Councils
IAHM	Incorporated Association of Headmasters
IAHM	International Academy of the History of Medicine
IAHMS	International Association of Hotel Management Schools
IAHP	International Academy of the History of Pharmacy
IAHP	International Association for the History of Psychoanalysis = AIHP
IAHP	International Association of Health Policy (U.S.A.)
IAHP	International Association of Heart Patients
IAHP	International Association of Horticultural Producers = AIPH
IAHR	International Association for Hydraulic Research = AIIH, AIRH
IAHR	International Association for the History of Religions
IAHRC	Inter-American Human Rights Commission
IAHS	International Academy of History of Sciences = AIHS
IAHS	International Association for Hospital Security
IAHS	International Association for Housing Science
IAHS	International Association of Hydrological Sciences = AISH
IAHSSJH	International Association of Historical Societies for the Study of Jewish History (Israel)
IAHU	International Association of Health Underwriters
IAI	Ibero-Amerikanisches Institut
IAI	Institut Africain Informatique (Gabon)
IAI	Institute of Architectural Ironmongers
IAI	Instituto de Automatica Industrial
IAI	International African Institute
IAI	International Anthropological Institute
IAI	International Apple Institute (U.S.A.)
IAI	International Association for Identification
IAI	Israel Aviation Industries
IAI	Istituto Affari Internazionali
IAIA	Institute of American Indian Arts
IAIA	International Association for Impact Assessment
IAIABC	International Association of Industrial Accident Boards and Commissions = AIRCAT
IAIAF	International Affiliation of Independent Accounting Firms
IAIB	International Asociation of Islamic Banks
IAIC	International Association of Insurance Counsel (U.S.A.)
IAICM	International Association of Ice Cream Manufacturers
IAICU	International Association of Independent Colleges and Universities (U.S.A.)
IAIDEC	Institúto Argentino de la Industria y Exportación de Carnes
IAIDPA	International Association of Information and Documentation in Public Administration = AIIDAP
IAIE	Inter-American Institute of Ecology (ESA)
IAIE	International Association for Integrative Education = AIEI
IAIE	International Association for Intercultual Education (Netherlands) = AIEI

IAIE	International Association of Institutes of Export		**IAL**	International Association of Linguistics
IAIGC	Inter-Arab Investment Guarantee Corporation (Kuwait) = AIGC, CIAGI		**IAL**	International Association of Theoretical and Applied Limnology = AIL, IATAL, IVL, SIL
IAII	Inter-American Indian Institute (OAS) = III		**IAL**	International Hospitals Group
IAIL	International Association for Insurance Law		**IAL**	Internationale Artiesten Loge
			IAL	Irish Academy of Letters
IAIM	Irish Association of Investment Managers (Éire)		**IALA**	International African Law Association = AIDA
IAIN	International Association of Institutes of Navigation		**IALA**	International Association of Lighthouse Authorities = AISM
IAIP	International Association of Independent Producers		**IALANA**	International Association of Lawyers Against Nuclear Arms (Sweden)
IAIP	International Association of Individual Psychology = AIPA, IVIP		**IALB**	Internationalen Arbeitskreises Landwirtschaftlicher Berater
IAIR	International Association of Industrial Radiation		**IALC**	International Arid Lands Consortium
IAIR	Irish Association for Industrial Relations (Éire)		**IALC**	International Association of Lions Clubs
IAIS	International Association of Independent Scholars		**IALC**	International Association of Literary Critics = AICL
IAITO	International Association of Independent Tanker Owners		**IALE**	International Association for Landscape Ecology
IAIU	Insurance Agents International Union		**IALEIA**	International Association of Law Enforcement Intelligence Analysts
IAIV	Internationaler Agentur für Investitions-versicherung = AIAI, IIIA		**IALHI**	International Association of Labour History Institutions
IAJ	International Association of Judges		**IALI**	International Association of Labour Inspection = AIIT
IAJC	Inter-American Juridical Committee = CJI		**IALL**	International Association for Labor Legislation (U.S.A.)
IAJE	Internacio Asocio de Juristoj-Esperantistoj		**IALL**	International Association of Law Librarians
IAJFCM	International Association of Juvenile and Family Court Magistrates = AIMJF		**IALL**	International Association of Learning Laboratories
IAJRC	International Association of Jazz Record Collectors		**IALP**	International Association of Logopedics and Phoniatrics (U.S.A.)
IAK	Internationales Auschwitz-Komitee = CIA		**IALRW**	International Association of Liberal Religious Women = UFLC
IAKS	Internationalen Arbeitskreis Sport und Freizeiteinrichtungen		**IALS**	International Association of Legal Science = AISJ
IAL	Danske Indendørsarkitekters Landsforbund		**IAM**	Institut Agronomique Méditerranéen
			IAM	Institute of Administrative Management
IAL	Imperial Arts League		**IAM**	Institute of Advanced Motorists
IAL	Indian Airlines		**IAM**	Institute of Applied Mathematics (Canada)
IAL	Institut Archéologique du Luxembourg			
IAL	Institut Archéologique Liégeois		**IAM**	Institute of Aviation Medicine
IAL	Instituto Adolfo Lutz (Brazil)		**IAM**	International Academy of Management (Netherlands)
IAL	International Anti-Prohibitionist League		**IAM**	International Academy of Metabology (U.S.A.)
IAL	International Arbitration League = LIA			
IAL	International Association of Laryngectomees		**IAM**	International Academy of Myodontics

IAM	International Afro-American Museum (U.S.A.)	**IAMCR**	International Association for Mass Communication Research = AIERI
IAM	International Association of Machinists and Aerospace Workers	**IAME**	Inter-American Musical Editions (OAS)
IAM	Internationale Arbeitsgemeinschaft für Müllforschung	**IAMFE**	International Association on Mechanisation of Field Experiments
IAM	Internationaler Arbeitskreis für Musik	**IAMFES**	International Association of Milk, Food and Environmental Sanitarians (U.S.A.)
IAM	Internationales Arbeiter-Hilfswerk = EOI	**IAMFS**	International Association for Maxillo-Facial Surgery
IAM	Istituto Agronómico Mediterraneo	**IAMG**	International Association for Mathematical Geology
IAM Montpellier	Institut Agronomique Méditerranéen de Montpellier (ICAMAS) = Montpellier MAI	**IAMHIST**	International Association for Audio-Visual Media in Historical Research and Education
IAM Bari	Institut Agronomique Méditerranéen de Bari	**IAML**	International Association of Master Locksmiths
IAMA	Incorporated Advertising Managers Association	**IAML**	International Association of Music Libraries, Archives and Documentation Centres = AIBM, IVMB
IAMA	International Abstaining Motorists Association		
IAMA	International Agribusiness Management Association	**IAML-UK**	International Association of Music Libraries, Archives and Documentation Centres – UK Branch
IAMA	Irish Association of Municipal Authorities		
IAMACS	International Association for Mathematics and Computers in Simulation	**IAMLT**	International Associaton of Medical Laboratory Technologists
		IAMM	Institut Agronomique Méditerranéen à Montpellier
IAMAM	International Association of Museums of Arms and Military History	**IAMM**	Irish Association of Master Mariners
IAMANEH	International Association for Maternal and Neonatal Health = MCI	**IAMMA**	Irish Agricultural Machinery Manufacturers' Association
IAMAP	International Association of Meteorology and Atmospheric Physics = AIMFA, AIMPA	**IAMN**	Institutul de Cercetari Inginerie Technologica Proiectare si Productie pentru Industria Anorganica si Metale Neferoase, Bucuresti
IAMAS	International Association of Meteorology and Atmospheric Sciences	**IAMO**	Inter-American Municipal Organisation = OICI
IAMAT	International Association for Medical Assistance to Travellers	**IAMO**	International Association for Medical Oceanography
IAMB	Institut Africain et Mauricien de Bilinguisme (Mauritius)	**IAMOT**	International Association for the Management of Technology
IAMB	International Association of Macrobiologists	**IAMP**	International Association of Mathematical Physics
IAMB	International Association of Microbiologists	**IAMP**	International Association of Mercury Producers
IAMB	Irish Association of Master Bakers	**IAMPTH**	International Association of Master Penmen and Teachers of Handwriting
IAMBE	International Association for Medicine and Biology of Environment = AIMBE		
IAMC	Institute for the Advancement of Medical Communication (U.S.A.)	**IAMR**	Institute of Applied Manpower Research (India)
IAMC	Israel Association of Management Consultants	**IAMRC**	International Antarctic Meteorological Research Centre
IAMCA	International Association of Milk Control Agencies	**IAMS**	International Advanced Microlithography Society

IAMS	International Association for Mission Studies	**IAOE**	International Association of Optometric Executives
IAMS	International Association for Mongol Studies (Mongolia)	**IAOHRA**	International Association of Official Human Rights Agencies
IAMSÉA	Institut Africain Mauricien Statistique Économie Appliquée	**IAOL**	International Association of Orientalist Librarians
IAMSLIC	International Association of Marine Science Libraries and Information Centres	**IAOM**	International Academy of Osteopathic Medicine
IAMTI	International Aviation Management Training Institute (Canada) = IIFGA	**IAOMO**	International Association of Olympic Medical Officers
IAMZ	Institut Agronomique Méditerranéen de Saragosse (ICAMAS) = MAIZ	**IAOMS**	International Association of Oral and Maxillofacial Surgeons
IAN	Institúto Agrario Nacional (Venezuela)	**IAOO**	Irish Agricultural Officers Organisation
IAN	Institúto Agronómico de Norte (Brazil)	**IAOPA**	International Council of Aircraft Owner and Pilot Associations
IAN	Internationale des Amis de la Nature = IFN, NFI	**IAOS**	International Association for Official Statistics
IANA	Internet Assigned Numbers Authority	**IAOS**	International Association of Ocular Surgeons
IANC	Institúto de Asuntas Nucleares de Colombia	**IAOS**	Irish Agricultural Organisation Society
IANC	International Academy of Nutrition Consultants	**IAOT**	International Association of Organ Teachers
IANC	International Anatomical Nomenclature Committee	**IAOUG**	International Association of Underwater Games
IANDS	International Association for Near-Death Studies	**IAP**	Institute of Analysts and Programmers
IANE	Institute of Advanced Nursing Education of the Royal College of Nursing	**IAP**	Institute of Animal Physiology
		IAP	Institute of Australian Photographers
IANEC	Inter-American Nuclear Energy Commission (OAS) = CIEN	**IAP**	Institúto Argentino del Petróleo
IANLS	International Association for Neo-Latin Studies	**IAP**	Institúto dos Actuarios Portugueses
		IAP	Insurance Association of Pakistan
IANOS	International Assembly of National Organizations of Sport (Australia)	**IAP**	International Academy of Pathology
		IAP	International Academy of Poets
IANSA	Industria Azucarena Nacional (Chile)	**IAP**	International Academy of Proctology
IANVS	International Association for Non-Violent Sport (Monaco) = AICVS	**IAP**	International Association of Parapsychologists
IAO	Incorporated Association of Organists	**IAP**	International Association of Photoplatemakers (U.S.A.)
IAO	Institúto Agronómica per l'Oltremare	**IAP**	International Association of Planetology
IAO	International Association of Orthodontics (U.S.A.)	**IAP**	International Association of Pteridologists
IAO	Internationale Arbeitsorganisation = ILO, OIT	**IAP-RAS**	Institute of Atmospheric Physics, Russian Academy of Sciences
IAOC	International Athletic Olympic Committee	**IAPA**	Instituto de Alimentacion y Productividad Animal
IAOD	International Academy of Optimum Dentistry	**IAPA**	Inter-American Press Association = SIP
		IAPA	International Airline Passengers Association
IAOD	International Association of Opera Directors = AIDO	**IAPA**	International Association of Physicians in Audiology
		IAPA	Irish Airline Pilots Association

IAPA	Irish Association of Professional Archaeologists	**IAPIP**	International Association for the Protection of Industrial Property = AIPPI, IVFGR
IAPAR	Fundação Instítuto Agronomico do Parana (Brazil)	**IAPL**	International Association of Penal Law = AIDP
IAPAS	Institute of Atmospheric Physics, Academia Sinica	**IAPM**	International Academy of Preventive Medicine (U.S.A.)
IAPB	International Association for the Prevention of Blindness = AIPC	**IAPM**	Irish Association of Paper Merchants
IAPBT	International Association of Piano Builders and Technicians (U.S.A.)	**IAPMA**	International Association of Hand Papermakers and Paper Artists
IAPC	Institute for the Advancement of Philosophy for Children	**IAPMEI**	Instítuto de Apoioàs Pequeñas e Médias Empresas Industriais
IAPC	International Association of Political Consultants	**IAPMO**	International Association of Plumbing and Mechanical Officials
IAPC	International Auditing Practices Committee (IFAC)	**IAPN**	International Association of Professional Numismatists = AINP
IAPC	Internationaler Aero-Philatelisten Club	**IAPO**	International Association of Physical Oceanography
IAPCM	Institute of Applied Physics and Computational Mathematics (China)	**IAPP**	Indian Association for Plant Physiology
IAPCO	International Association of Professional Congress Organisers	**IAPP**	International Association of Plant Physiologists
IAPD	International Association of Paediatric Dentistry	**IAPP**	International Association of Police Professors (U.S.A.)
IAPD	International Association of Parents of the Deaf	**IAPP**	International Association of Prevention Programs (U.S.A.)
IAPEC	International Agency for the Promotion of Ear Care (IFOS)	**IAPP**	Irish Association of Pigmeat Processors
IAPES	International Association of Personnel in Employment Security	**IAPPLT**	Inter-American Program for Linguistics and Language Teaching
IAPESGW	International Association of Physical Education and Sports for Girls and Women	**IAPPW**	International Association of Pupil Personnel Workers (U.S.A.)
IAPF	Irish Association of Pension Funds (Éire)	**IAPR**	International Association for Pattern Recognition
IAPG	Inter-American Parliamentary Group on Population and Development	**IAPRG**	Institute of Animal Physiology & Genetics Research (AFRC)
IAPG	International Association of Psychoanalytic Gerontology	**IAPRI**	International Association of Packaging Research Institutes
IAPGR	AFRC Institute of Animal Physiology and Genetics Research	**IAPS**	Incorporated Association of Preparatory Schools
IAPH	International Association of Ports and Harbours = AIP	**IAPS**	International Affiliation of Planning Societies
IAPh	Internationale Assoziation von Philosopinen	**IAPS**	International Association for the Properties of Steam
IAPHC	International Association of Printing House Craftsmen	**IAPS**	International Association of Pathology Societies
IAPI	Institute of Advertising Practitioners in Ireland	**IAPS**	International Association of Physics Students (Hungary)
IAPI	Instítuto Argentino de Promoción del Intercambio	**IAPSC**	Inter-African Phytosanitary Council = CPI
IAPIC	International Association of Personal Image Consultants	**IAPSC**	International Association of Pipe Smokers Clubs

IAPSC	International Association of Professional Security Consultants	**IARC**	Independent Assessment & Research Centre
IAPSC	Investigation of Air Pollution Standing Conference	**IARC**	International Action for the Rights of the Child = AIDE
IAPSO	Inter-Agency Procurement Services Office (IAPSU)	**IARC**	International Agency for Research on Cancer (WHO) = CIIC, CIRC
IAPSO	International Association for the Physical Sciences of the Ocean = AICFO, AISPO	**IARC**	International Agricultural Research Center (U.S.A.)
IAPSRS	International Association for Psychosocial Rehabilitation Services	**IARCB**	International Asian Research Conference Board
IAPSUN	International Association of Political Scientists for the United Nations (Austria)	**IARCS**	Institut Asiatique de Recherche sur les Constructions Scolaires (Sri Lanka)
IAPT	International Association for Plant Taxonomy	**IARE**	International Association of Railway Employees
IAPTA	International Allied Printing Trades Association	**IAREP**	International Association for Research in Economic Psychology
IAPTC	International Association of Plant Tissue Culture	**IARF**	International Amateur Rugby Federation = FIRA
IAPTE	International Academy of Pediatric Transdisciplinary Education (Greece)	**IARF**	International Association for Religious Freedom
IAPUP	International Association on the Political Use of Psychiatry	**IARHH**	International Association for Research in Hospital Hygiene
IAPW	International Association for Personnel Women	**IARI**	Indian Agricultural Research Institute
IAPWS	International Association for the Properties of Water and Steam	**IARIGAI**	International Association of Research Institutes for the Graphic Arts Industry
IAQ	International Academy for Quality	**IARIW**	International Association for Research in Income and Wealth
IAQC	International Association of Quality Circles	**IARM**	Institúto Argentino de Racionalización de Materiales
IAQR	Indian Association for Quality and Reliability	**IARM**	International Academy of Reproductive Medicine
IAR	Institut für Angewandte Reaktorphysik	**IARM**	International Association of Ropeway Manufacturers
IAR	Institute for Aerodynamics Research (China)	**IARP**	Indian Association for Radiation Protection
IAR	Institute of Agricultural Research (Ethiopia)	**IARP**	International Association for Religion and Parapsychology (Japan)
IAR	Institute of Asian Research (Canada)	**IARR**	International Association for Radiation Research
IAR	Instituto Argentino de Radioastronomia		
IAR	International Association of Radiopharmacology	**IARS**	Institute of Agriculture Research Statistics (India)
IAR	Internationaler Archivrat	**IARS**	International Anesthesia Research Society
IARA	Inter-Allied Reparations Agency		
IARA	International Aerosol Research Assembly	**IARU**	International Amateur Radio Union
		IARUS	International Association for Regional and Urban Statistics = AISRU
IARA	International Association of Rebekah Assemblies	**IARW**	International Association of Refrigerated Warehouses
IARA	Islamic African Relief Agency = AISA, ISRA	**IAS**	Indian Administrative Services
IArb	Institute of Arbitrators	**IAS**	Institute for African Studies (Zambia)

IAS	Institute of Accounting Staff	**IASC**	International Accounting Standards Committee (IFA)
IAS	Institute of Advanced Studies (ANU)	**IASC**	International Arctic Science Committee = CSIA
IAS	Institute of Aeronautical Sciences		
IAS	Institute of African Affairs (Germany)	**IASC**	International Association for Statistical Computing = AIIS
IAS	Institute of Alcohol Studies		
IAS	Institute of Andean Studies (U.S.A.)	**IASC**	International Association of Seed Crushers
IAS	Inter-American Society		
IAS	Interafricaine Socialiste = IASD, SDIA, SIA	**IASC**	International Association of Skal Clubs = AISC
IAS	International Absorption Society	**IASC**	Irish Association of Songwriters and Composers
IAS	International Aircraft Services (Éire)		
IAS	International Association of Sedimentologists (IUGS)	**IASCCA**	International Association for the Study of Cultures of Central Asia
IAS	International Association of Siderographers	**IASCE**	International Association for the Study of Cooperation in Education
IAS	International Atherosclerosis Society	**IASCO**	International Association of Service Companies
IAS	International Audiovisual Society		
IAS	International Ayurveda Society	**IASD**	Interafricaine Socialiste et Démocratique = IAS, SDIA, SIA
IAS	Internationaler Arbeitskreis Sicherheit beim Skilauf	**IASDSC**	International Association for the Study and Dissemination of Slav Cultures
IAS	Irish Archaeological Society		
IAS	Irish Astronomical Society	**IASDW**	International Association to Stop the Destruction of the World
IAS	Irish-Arab Society		
IAS	Islamic Academy of Science	**IASE**	Instytut Automatyki Systemów Energetycznych (Poland)
IAS	Istituto di Astrofizica Spaziale (Italy)		
IASA	International Academy of Sciences and Arts	**IASE**	Inter-American Association of Sanitary Engineering
IASA	International Air Safety Association = AISA	**IASE**	International Amateur Surfing Federation
IASA	International Alliance for Sustainable Agriculture	**IASE**	International Association for Statistics Education
IASA	International Association of Sound Archives	**IASEE**	International Association for Solar Energy Education
IASA	Irish Amateur Swimming Association	**IASEES**	International Association of South-East European Studies = AIESEE
IASAIL	International Association for the Study of Anglo-Irish Literature	**IASEI**	Instítuto Ajijo Sobre Educación Internacional (Mexico)
IASAJ	International Association of Supreme Administrative Jurisdictions = AIHJA	**IASF**	International Amateur Sombo Federation = FIAS
IASAP	International Association for Social Progress	**IASF**	International Amateur Surfing Federation (U.S.A.)
IASAP	International Association for the Study of the Alcohol Problem	**IASF**	International Amateur Swimming Federation = FINA
IASB	International Aircraft Standard Bureau	**IASFEC**	Arab States Centre for Functional Literacy in Rural Areas (Egypt)
IASBS	International Association of Shin Buddhist Studies (Japan)	**IASH**	International Association of Scientific Hydrology
IASC	Inter-American Safety Council = CIAS		
IASC	Inter-American Society for Cardiology (Mexico)	**IASH**	Israeli Academy of Sciences and Humanities
IASC	Inter-American Society for Chemotherapy	**IASI**	Institutul de Chimie Macromoleculara pentru Pon' Iasi

IASI	Inter-American Statistical Institute (OAS) = IIE
IASI	International Association for Sports Information
IASIA	International Association of Schools and Institutes of Administration = AIEIA
IASILL	International Association for the Study of the Italian Language and Literature = AISLLI
IASL	Inter-American School of Librarianship (Colombia)
IASL	International Association for the Study of the Liver
IASL	International Association of School Librarianship = AIBS
IASL	International Association of State Lotteries = AILE
IASLC	International Association for the Study of Lung Cancer
IASLIC	Indian Association of Special Libraries and Information Centres
IASM	Istituto per l'Assistenza allo Sviluppo del Mezzogiorno
IASMAL	International Academy of Social and Moral Sciences, Arts and Letters
IASMIRT	International Association for Structural Mechanics in Reactor Technology
IASOC	International Association for the Study of Organised Crime
IASOS	Institute of Antarctic and Southern Ocean Studies
IASP	Inter-American Society of Psychology = SIP
IASP	International Association for Social Progress = AIPS
IASP	International Association for Suicide Prevention = AIPS, IVSP
IASP	International Association for the Study of Pain
IASP	International Association in Support of Perestroika = MAPP
IASP	International Association of Scholarly Publishers
IASP	International Association of Science Parks (France)
IASP	International Association of Space Philatelists
IASPEI	International Association of Seismology and Physics of the Earth's Interior = AISPIT
IASPER	International Association for the Study of Prehistoric and Ethnologic Religions
IASPM	International Association for the Study of Popular Music
IASPS	International Association for Statistics in Physical Sciences
IASRI	Indian Agricultural Statistics Research Institute
IASS	Institute of Advanced Architectural Studies
IASS	Instrumento Andino de Seguridad Social
IASS	International Association for Scandinavian Studies
IASS	International Association for Semiotic Studies = AIS
IASS	International Association for Shell and Spatial Structures = AIEL, AIVM, IVS
IASS	International Association of Sanskrit Studies
IASS	International Association of Security Services (U.S.A.)
IASS	International Association of Soil Science
IASS	International Association of Survey Statisticians = AISE
IASSIST	International Association for Social Science Information Service and Technology
IASSMD	International Association for the Scientific Study of Mental Deficiency
IASSW	International Association of Schools of Social Work = AIESS
IAST	International Association to Save Tyre = AIST
IAST	Irish Association for Sail Training
IASTE	International Association for the Study of Traditional Environments
IASTED	International Association of Science and Technology for Development
IASTG	International Association of Structural / Tectonic Geologists
IASTWL	International Association for Social Tourism and Workers Leisure = AITSLT
IASUS	International Association of Satellite Users and Suppliers
IASW	Irish Association of Social Workers (Éire)
IASWG	Inter-Country Adoption Social Workers Group
IASWS	International Association for Sediment Water Science (Switzerland)

IAT	Institute of Agricultural Technology (Vietnam)
IAT	Institute of Air Transport = ITA
IAT	Institute of Animal Technology
IAT	Institute of Asphalt Technology
IAT	International Association for Time-Keeping
IAT	International Association of Trichologists
IATA	Institúto de Agroquimica y Tecnologia de Alimentos
IATA	Institúto de Aperfeiçoamento Técnico Acelerado
IATA	International Air Transport Authority
IATA	International Amateur Theatre Association = AITA
IATAFI	International Association for Technology Assessment and Forecasting Institutions
IATAL	International Association of Theoretical and Applied Limnology = AIL, IAL, IVL, SIL
IATC	International Association of Theatre Critics = AICT
IATC	International Association of Tool Craftsmen
IATDP	International Association of Textile Dyers and Printers = AITIT
IATE	International Association for Temperance Education – IVES
IATEFL	International Association of Teachers of English as a Foreign Language
IATEM	Institúto Agrotécnico Económico de Misiones (Argentina)
IATF	International Airline Training Fund
IATG	International Association of Teachers of German = IDV
IATH	Institute for Advanced Technology in the Humanities
IATL	International Academy of Trial Lawyers
IATLIS	Indian Association of Teachers of Library Science
IATM	International Association of Tour Managers
IATM	International Association of Transport Museums = AIMT
IATMO	International Academy of Tumor Marker Oncology
IATN	International Association of Telecomputer Networks
IATO	International Air Transport Organization
IATP	International Agricultural Training Programme
IATP	International Association of Tungsten Producers
IATR	International Association for Tamil Research (Malaysia)
IATR	International Association of Teachers of Russian
IATROS	Organisation Mondiale des Médecins Indépendants (Australia)
IATS	Institute for Advanced Talmudic Studies (Canada)
IATS	Institúto de Acuicultura de Torre de la Sal
IATS	International Association for Tibetan Studies
IATSS	International Association of Traffic and Safety Sciences
IATSW	Indian Association of Trained Social Workers
IATT	Inter Africaine de Transit et de Transport (Ivory Coast)
IATTC	Inter-American Tropical Tuna Commission = CIAT, CITT
IATU	Inter-American Telecommunications Union
IATUL	International Association of Technical University Libraries
IATVPM	International Association of Teachers of Veterinary Preventive Medicine
IAU	Institute for American Universities (France)
IAU	International Academic Union
IAU	International Association of Universities = AIU
IAU	International Astronomical Union = UAI
IAU	Internationale Armbrustsehutzen Union
IAUD	International Association for the Union of Democracies
IAUEC	International Association of Underwater Engineering Contractors
IAUL	Inter-African Union of Lawyers
IAUP	International Association of University Presidents
IAUPE	International Association of University Professors of English
IAUPL	International Association of University Professors and Lecturers

IAUR	Instítuto de Antibióticos da Universidade do Recife (Brazil)
IAURRE	International Association for Urban and Regional Research and Education
IAUS	International Association of University Students
IAUSD	Inter-American Union for Scientific Development (IOSCD) (Germany)
IAV	Vidion/International Association of Video (U.S.A.)
IAVAC	International Association for Video in Arts and Culture = AIVAC
IAVCEI	International Association of Volcanology and Chemistry of the Earth's Interior = AIVCIT
IAVCM	International Association of Visual Communications Management
IAVE	International Association for Volunteer Effort
IAVFH	International Association of Veterinary Food Hygiene
IAVG	International Association for Vocational Guidance
IAVI	Irish Auctioneers and Valuers Institute
IAVPF	Irish Audio-Visual Production Federation
IAVRS	International Audiovisual Resource Service
IAVS	International Association for Vegetation Science = AIEV, IVV
IAVS	Irish Anti-Vivisection Society
IAVS	Irish Association for Victim Support
IAVSD	International Association for Vehicle Systems Dynamics
IAVTC	International Audio-Visual Technical Centre (Belgium)
IAW	Institut für Angewandte Wirtschaftsforschung (Germany)
IAW	International Alliance of Women = AIF
IAWA	Incorporated Advertising Managers Association
IAWA	Independent American Whiskey Association
IAWA	International Animal Welfare Alliance
IAWA	International Association of Wood Anatomists
IAWCM	International Association of Wiping Cloth Manufacturers
IAWE	International Association for Wind Engineering
IAWF	International Amateur Wrestling Federation = FILA
IAWGD	Inter-Agency Working Group on Desertification (Kenya)
IAWHPJ	International Association of Women and Home Page Journalists = AIJPF
IAWID	Institute of Agriculture and Women in Development (Sri Lanka)
IAWL	International Association for Water Law = AIDA, AIDE
IAWM	Industrial Association of Wales and Monmouthshire
IAWM	International Alliance for Women in Music
IAWM	International Association of Wholesale Markets
IAWM	International Association of Women Ministers
IAWMC	International Association of Workers for Maladjusted Children = AIEJI
IAWP	International Association of Women Philosophers
IAWPRC	International Association on Water Pollution Research and Control = AIRPE, AIICA
IAWQ	International Association on Water Quality
IAWR	Internationale Arbeitsgemeinschaft der Wasserwerke im Rheineinzugsgebiet
IAWRT	International Association of Women in Radio and Television
IAWS	International Academy of Wood Science
IAWS	Irish Agricultural Wholesale Society
IAYP	International Association of Young Philosophers (Russia)
IAYSG	Irish Association of Youth Science Groups
IAZ	Instítuto de Agricultura y Zootecnia (Peru)
IB	Iberia, Líneas Aéras de España
IB	Institute of Biology
IB	Institute of Brewing
IB	Instituut voor Bodemvruchtbaarheid
IB	Intervention Board
IB-CC	International Business Contact Club
IB-DLO	DLO Instituut voor Bodemvruchtbaarheid Onderzoek (Netherlands)
IBA	Independent Broadcasting Authority
IBA	Indian Banks' Association

IBA	Industrial Biotechnology Association (U.S.A.)	**IBAS**	Independent Banking Advisory Service (*ex* BAG)
IBA	Institute of British Architects	**Ibase**	Institúto Brasileiro de Análises Sociais Económicas
IBA	Institution of Business Agents		
IBA	Institúto de Biologia Andina (Peru)	**IBASS**	International Bond & Share Society
IBA	International Backgammon Association (U.S.A.)	**IBB**	Institute of Biochemistry and Biophysics (Iran)
IBA	International Banana Association	**IBB**	Institute of British Bakers
IBA	International Bankers Association	**IBB**	International Bank of Brunei
IBA	International Bar Association	**IBB**	International Bowling Board
IBA	International Bartenders Association	**IBB**	Invest in Britain Bureau
IBA	International Baseball Association = FIBA	**IBB**	Irish Business Bureau (CCI, CII, FIE)
IBA	International Bauxite Association	**IBBA**	Institúto Boliviano de Biologia de la Altura (Bolivia)
IBA	International Biographical Association	**IBBA**	International Brangus Breeders Association
IBA	International Bridge Academy		
IBA	International Bryozoology Association	**IBBA**	International Business Brokers Association
IBA	Irish Brewers' Association (Éire)	**IBBA**	Irish Basket Ball Association
IBA	Irish Brokers' Association	**IBBA**	Irish Bread Bakers' Association (Éire)
IBA	Israel Broadcasting Authority	**IBBA**	Irish-Belgian Business Association
IBAA	Independent Bankers Association of America	**IBBC**	Instituut voor Bouwmaterialen en Bouwconstructies
IBAB	Institut Belge pour l'Amélioration de la Betterave	**IBBD**	Institúto Brasileiro de Bibliografia e Documentação
IBAC	Industrial Biotechnology Association of Canada	**IBBH**	Internationaler Bund der Bau- und Holzarbeiter = FITBB, IFBWW
IBAC	Institute of Business Analysts and Consultants	**IBBW**	Internationales Büro für Bergbauwarmephysik (WMC) (Russia) = BIPTM, IBMT, MBGT
IBAC	International Business Aviation Council		
IBAE	Institution of British Agricultural Engineers	**IBBY**	International Board on Books for Young People
IBAHP	Inter-African Bureau for Animal Health and Production (Kenya)	**IBC**	Institute of Barristers Clerks
		IBC	Institute of Building Control
IBAM	Institute of Business Administration and Management (Japan)	**IBC**	Institute of Business Counsellors
		IBC	Institutional Biosafety Committees
IBAM	Institúto Brasileiro de Administração Municipal	**IBC**	Institúto Bacteriológico de Chile
		IBC	Institúto Brasileiro do Café
IBAMA	Institúto Brasileiro do Meio Ambiente e Recursos Naturais Renováveis	**IBC**	Insurance Bureau of Canada
		IBC	International Biographical Centre (U.K.)
IBAN	Institut Belge pour l'Alimentation et la Nutrition		
		IBC	International Book Committee
IBANA	Institut de Biologie Appliquée la Nutrition et l'Alimentation	**IBC**	International Borzoi Council
		IBC	International Botanical Congress
IBAP	Internationales Büro für Audiophonologie = BIAP, IOAP	**IBC**	International Boundary Commission (U.S.A.)
IBAP	Intervention Board for Agricultural Produce	**IBC**	International Broadcasting Convention
IBAR	Interafrican Bureau for Animal Resources = IBAR	**IBC**	International Old Catholic Bishops Conference (Netherlands)

IBC	World Institute of Buddhist Culture	**IBEE**	International Builders Exchange Executives (U.S.A.)
IBCA	Institute of Burial and Cremation Administration	**IBEG**	International Book Export Group
IBCA	Instítuto Boliviano de Cultivos Andinos	**IBEG**	Internationaler Bund der Erziehungsgemeinschaften
IBCA	International Braille Chess Association	**IBELCO**	Institut Belge de Coopération Technique
IBCAM	Institute of British Carriage and Automobile Manufactures	**IBEPEGE**	Instítuto Brasileiro de Estudos e Pesquisas de Gastroenterologia
IBCC	International Bird Census Committee	**IBERSOM**	Institut Belge pour l'Encouragement de la Recherche Scientifique Outre-Mer
IBCC	International Bureau of Chambers of Commerce = BICC	**IBERTO**	Société Industrielle et Commercial Ibéro-Togolaise
IBCE	International Bureau for Cultural Exchange	**IBES**	International Broncho-Esophagological Society
IBCIN	International Biologisch Contact- en Informatiebureau voor Nederland	**IBET**	Instítuto de Biologia Experimental e Tecnologica (Portugal)
IBCS	International Bureau of Commercial Statistics	**IBETA**	Irish Business Equipment Trade Association
IBCTA	Irish Bakery and Confectionery Trades Association	**IBETEX**	Industrie Béninoise des Textiles
IBD	Incorporated Institute of British Decorators and Interior Designers	**IBEW**	International Brotherhood of Electrical Workers
IBDA	Instítuto Brasileiro de Direito Agrário	**IBF**	Frauenhofer-Institut für Betriebsfestigkeit (Germany)
IBDC	Institut Belge de Droit Comparé	**IBF**	Institute of British Foundrymen
IBDC	International Buchenwald-Dora Committee	**IBF**	International Badminton Federation
IBDF	Instítuto Brasileiro de Desenvolvimento Florestal	**IBF**	International Balint Federation
		IBF	International Balut Federation
IBDI	International Bureau of Documentation and Information in Sport	**IBF**	International Bandy Federation
IBDISFS	Institute of British Detective, Investigative Security and Forensic Specialists	**IBF**	International Basketball Federation = FIBA
		IBF	International Bicycle Fund (U.S.A.)
IBE	Institut für Bildungs- und Entwicklungsforschung (Austria)	**IBF**	International Bodysurfing Federation
		IBF	International Booksellers Federation =FIL, IBV
IBE	Institute Belge de l'Emballage = BVI		
IBE	Institute of Business Ethics	**IBF**	Irish Bankers' Federation (Éire)
IBE	International Bureau for Epilepsy	**IBF**	Irish Banking Foundation (Éire)
IBE	International Bureau of Education = BIE, MBD, OIE	**IBFAN**	International Baby Food Action Network
IBEAS	Instítuto Boliviano de Educación y Acción Social	**IBFCC**	International Border Fancy Canary Club
		IBFD	Instítuto Brasileiro de Direito Financeiro
IBEC	Indo-British Economics Committee		
IBEC	International Bank for Economic Cooperation = BICE, MBES	**IBFD**	International Bureau of Fiscal Documentation (Netherlands)
IBEC	International Basic Economy Corporation (U.S.A.)	**IBFG**	Internationaler Bund Freier Gewerkschaften = CIOSL, CISL, ICFTU, IVVV
IBEC	International Business Engineering Company		
IBEC	Irish Business & Employers' Confederation	**IBFI**	International Business Forms Industries (U.S.A.)
IBECC	Brazilian Institute of Education, Science and Culture	**IBFMP**	International Bureau of the Federations of Master Printers

IBFO	International Brotherhood of Firemen and Oilers
IBFR	Inter-African Bureau for Forestry Resources
IBG	Incorporated Brewers Guild (U.K., U.S.A.)
IBG	Institute of British Geographers
IBG	International Boxing Guild
IBG	Internationale Begegnung in Gemeinschaftsdiensten
IBG	Internationale Bodenkundliche Gesellschaft = AISS, ISSS, SICS
IBG	Internationales Büro für Gebirgsmechanik (WMC) = IBSM, MBMGP, OIMR
IBGE	Institúto Brasileiro de Geografia e Estatística
IBH	Institut für Bibliothekswissenschaft und Wissenschaftliche Information der Humboldt- Universität zu Berlin
IBH	Institúto Bibliographico Hispanico
IBH	Institúto Brasileiro de Habitação
IBHA	Insulation, Building and Hard Board Association
IBHA	International Buckskin Horse Association (U.S.A.)
IBHP	Institut Belge des Hautes Pressions
IBI	Institut International des Châteaux Historiques
IBI	Institute of Bankers in Ireland
IBI	Institute of Biology of Ireland
IBI	Intergovernmental Bureau for Informatics (Italy)
IBI	International Biomass Institute (U.S.A.)
IBI	Internationales Burgen Institut = ICI
IBI	Investment Bank of Ireland
IBIA	Institute of British Industrial Art
IBIB	Instytut Biocybernetyki i Inzynierii Biomedycznej (Poland)
IBIC	International Buffalo Information Centre (Thailand)
IBICT	Institúto Brasileiro de Informação en Ciencia e Technologia
IBIE	International Brewing Industries Exposition
IBIIR	Independent Board of Inquiry into Informal Repression (South Africa)
IBION	Issue Based Indian Ocean Network
IBIS	Indonesian Biodiversity Information System (Indonesia)
IBIS	International Book Information Service
IBIS	International Burn Injuries Society
IBIS	Irish Banks' Information Service (Éire)
IBISCO	Société Ivoirienne de Biscuiterie et Confiserie
IBIT	Institúto Brasileiro para Investigação da Tuberculose
IBJ	Industrial Bank of Japan
IBJ	Instytut Badań Jadrowych
IBK	Institut für Bauen mit Kunstoffen
IBK	Internationale Beleuchtungs-Kommission
IBKO	International Bureau van het Katholik Onderwijs
IBL	Independent Business League
IBL	Institute of British Launderers
IBL	Instytut Badań Literackich
IBL	Instytut Badawczy Lesnictwa
IBL	International Brotherhood of Longshoremen
IBLA	Institut des Belles-Lettres Arabes (Tunis)
IBLA	Inter-American Bibliographical and Library Association = IABLA
IBLC	Institut Belgo-Luxembourgeois du Change = BLIW
IBLM	International Bureau of Legal Metrology
IBM	Indian Bureau of Mines
IBM	Institúto de Biológia Marina (Argentina)
IBM	Institúto de Biológia Maritima (Portugal)
IBM	Instytut Budownictwa Mieszkaniowego
IBM	International Brotherhood of Magicians
IBM	International Business Machines Corporation (U.S.A.)
IBM	Internationale Büro Maschinen Gesellschaft
IBM	Istituto di Biologia del Mare
IBMARNR	Brazilian Institute of Environment and Renewable Natural Resources
IBME	Institute of Biomedical Engineering (Canada)
IBME	Institúto de Biológia y Medicína Experimental (Argentina)
IBMER	Instytut Budownictwa Mechanizacji i Elektryfikacji Rolnictwa (Poland)
IBMP	International Board of Medicine and Psychology

IBMR	International Bureau for Mechanical Reproduction = BIEM
IBMS	Institute of Bar Management & Stewardship
IBMS	Institute of Biomedical Science (*ex* IMLS)
IBMT	International Bureau of Mining Thermophysics (WMC) (Russia) = BIPTM, IBBW, MBGT
IBN	Indigenous Biodiversity Network
IBN	Institut Belge de Normalisation = BIN
IBN	International Biosciences Networks (ICSU, UNESCO)
IBNS	International Bank Note Society
IBO	Instituut voor Bosbouwkundig Onderzoek
IBO	International Association of Building Companions
IBO	International Baccalaureate Office = OBI
IBO	International Broadcasting Organization
IBO	International Butchers' Organization (Belgium)
IBO	Internationale Bouworde
IBOA	Irish Bank Officials' Association
IBOB	International Brotherhood of Old Bastards
IBOO	International Bureau voor Onderwijs en Opvoeding
IBOPC	Institúto Brasileiro de Oftalmologia e Prevenção da Cegueira
IBP	Institut Belge du Pétrole
IBP	Institute for Black Peoples = IPN
IBP	Institute for Business Planning
IBP	Institute of British Photographers
IBP	Institúto Boliviano del Petroleo
IBP	Institúto Brasileiro de Petroleo
IBP	Institúto Brasileiro de Potasa
IBP	International Biological Programme = PBI
IBP	Internationaler Bund der Privatangestellten
IBPA	International Bridge Press Association
IBPA	International Business Press Associates
IBPA	Irish Book Publishers' Association = CLE
IBPAT	International Brotherhood of Painters and Allied Trades
IBPC	Institut Biologique Physico-Chimique
IBPCS	International Bureau for Physico-Chemical Standards
IBPF	International Black Peoples Foundation
IBPGR	International Board for Plant Genetic Resources = GIRGV
IBPI	International Bureau for Plant Taxonomy and Nomenclature (Netherlands)
IBPT	Industrial Buildings Preservation Trust
IBPT	Institúto de Biologia e Pesquisas Tecnológicas (Portugal)
IBR	Institúto de Bienestar Rural (Paraguay)
IBR	Instituut der Bedrijfsrevisoren (Belgium) = IRE
IBR	Interregional Bloc for Reforms (Ukraine)
IBRA	Institut Belge de Régulation et d'Automatisme = BIRA
IBRA	Institúto Brasileiro de Administração
IBRA	Institúto Brasileiro de Reforma Agraria
IBRA	International Bee Research Association
IBRA	International Bible Reading Association
IBRADES	Institúto Brasileiro de Desenvolvimento
IBRAM	Institúto Brasileiro de Mineração
IBRAPE	Industria Brasileira de Produtos Electronicos e Electricos
IBRAR	Institúto Brasileiro de Reforma Agrária Regional
IBRASA	Institução Brasileira de Difusão Cultural
IBRC	Insurance Brokers' Registration Council
IBRC	International Bird Rescue Centre (U.S.A.)
IBRD	International Bank for Reconstruction and Development (World Bank) = BIRD, BIRF, BIRS
IBRE	Institúto Brasileiro de Economia
IBRG	International Biodeterioration Research Group
IBRI	Institúto Brasileiro de Relações Internacionais
IBRM	Institute of Baths and Recreation Managment (*now* ISRM)
IBRO	International Brain Research Organisation
IBS	Institut Belge de la Soudre
IBS	Institute of Bankers in Scotland
IBS	Institute of Broadcast Sound
IBS	Institute of Building Societies (South Africa)
IBS	Instituto Brasileiro de Siderurgia (Brazil)

IBS	Instituut voor Biologisch en Scheikundig Onderzoek van Landbouwgewassen	**IBTE**	International Bureau of Technical Education
IBS	International Bach Society	**IBTEN**	Institúto Boliviano de Ciencia y Technología Nuclear
IBS	International Bible Society	**IBTS**	International Beer Tasting Society
IBS	International Brecht Society	**IBTT**	International Bureau for Technical Training
IBS	International Bronchoesophagological Society	**IBTTA**	International Bridge and Tunnel-Turnpike Association (U.S.A.)
IBS	Internationale Biometrische Gesellschaft	**IBTU**	International Bureau of Transport Users (ICC)
IBSA	Institut Belge des Sciences Administratives = BIBW	**IBTU**	Internationella Byggnads-och Träindustriar-Unionen = FITBB, FITCM, IBBH, IFBWW
IBSA	International Biotechnology Suppliers Association (U.S.A.)	**IBU**	International Broadcasting Union
IBSA	International Blind Sports Association = AISA	**IBU**	Internationale Binnenschiffahrts Union = IUIN, UINF
IBSA	International Board Sailing Association	**IBU**	Internationale Bürgermeister-Union
IBSA	Irish Building Societies Association	**IBUPL**	International Bureau for the Unification of Penal Law
IBSCC	International Bureau for the Suppression of Counterfeit Coins	**IBUSZ**	Idegenforgalmi, Beszerzési Utazási es Szállitasi
IBSCF	International Baltic Sea Fishery Commission	**IBV**	Internationale Buchhändler-Vereinigung = FIL, IBF
IBSEFO	Société Ivoirienne de Bois, Scieries et Exploitations Forestières	**IBV**	Internationaler Bergarbeiterverband = FIM, MIF
IBSFC	International Baltic Sea Fishery Commission	**IBVEA**	International Bureau of Veterinary Educational Aids (Australia)
IBSI	Conference of Religious in Indonesia	**IBVL**	Instituut voor Bewaring en Verwerking van Landbouwprodukten
IBSL	Irish Blind Sports Limited		
IbSN	Iberoamerican Society for Neurochemistry	**IBVT**	Instituut voor Bewaring en Verwerking van Tuinbouwprodukten
IBSNAT	International Benchmark Sites Network for Agrotechnology Transfer	**IBW**	Instituut voor Bestuurwetenschappen
IBSREM	International Board for Soil Resources Management	**IBW**	Instytut Budownictwa Wodnego
IBST	Institute of British Surgical Technicians	**IBWA**	International Bank for West Africa Ltd
IBST	International Bureau of Social Tourism; Internationales Büro für Sozialtourismus = BITS	**IBWA**	International Bottled Water Association
		IBWA	International Business Women's Association
IBT	Institute of Behaviour Therapy	**IBWC**	International Boundary and Water Commission (USA-Mexico)
IBT	International Broadcasting Trust		
IBT	International Brotherhood of Teamsters, Chauffeurs, Warehousemen and Helpers of America	**IBWM**	International Bureau of Weights and Measures = BIPM
		IBWO	International Bureau voor de Wederopbouw en de Ontwikkeling
IBTA	Independent Business Training Association (ex ISTA)	**IBWS**	International Bureau of Whaling Statistics
IBTA	Institúto Boliviano de Tecnologia Agropecuária	**IC**	Industry Commission (ex IAC)
IBTA	International Baton Twirling Association of America and Abroad	**IC**	Institute of Carpenters
		IC	Institute of Ceramics
IBTA	International Business Travel Association	**IC**	Institutum Caritatis "Rosminiani"

IC	Intercooperation (Switzerland)	ICA	International Confederation of Associations
IC	International Chapters	ICA	International Congress of Acarology
IC	International Company Transport	ICA	International Congress of Africanists
IC	Islamic Congress	ICA	International Congress of Americanists
IC	Izquierda Comunista	ICA	International Congress on Acoustics
IC	Izquierda Cristiana (Chile)	ICA	International Control Agency
ICA	Ice Cream Alliance	ICA	International Cooperative Alliance = ACI, IGB, MKA
ICA	Imprimerie Centrale d'Afrique		
ICA	Incultural Association (Switzerland)	ICA	International Copper Association
ICA	Industria y Comercio de Alimentación	ICA	International Council for ADP in Government Administration
ICA	Industrial Catering Association		
ICA	Information Centre for Aeronautics (India)	ICA	International Council on Archives = CIA
		ICA	Irish Cinemas Association
ICA	Institut Culturel Africain = ACI	ICA	Irish Countrywomen's Association
ICA	Institute of Chartered Accountants of England and Wales	ICA	Islamic Cement Association (Turkey)
		ICAA	Insulation Contractors Association of America
ICA	Institute of Consumer Advisers		
ICA	Institute of Contemporary Arts	ICAA	International Civil Airports Association
ICA	Institute of Cultural Affairs (Belgium)	ICAA	International Civil Aviation Authority
ICA	Instítuto Colombiano Agropecuário	ICAA	International Classified Advertising Association
ICA	Instítuto Colombiano de Antropología		
ICA	Institutul de Cercetari Alimentare	ICAA	International Council of Accrediting Agencies for Evangelical Theological Education (WEF)
ICA	Insurance Council of Australia		
ICA	Inter-Cultural Association = AFI		
ICA	Inter-Cultural Cooperation Association	ICAA	International Council on Alcohol and Addictions = CIPAT
ICA	Interarab Cambist Association		
ICA	Interfaculty Committee Agraria (Belgium)	ICAAN	International Committee on Avian Anatomical Nomenclature
		ICAAS	International Campaign Against Apartheid in Sports
ICA	Intergovernmental Council for Automatic Data Processing		
		ICAB	Industries Camérounaises des Annexes du Bâtiment
ICA	International Caribbean Airways		
ICA	International Cartographic Association = ACI	ICAB	International Cargo Advisory Bureau
		ICAC	Independent Commission Against Corrruption (Hong Kong)
ICA	International Catholic Auxiliaries = AFI		
ICA	International Chefs Association	ICAC	Institute of Chartered Accountants of the Caribbean (Jamaica)
ICA	International Chianina Association		
ICA	International Chiropractors Association	ICAC	International Civil Aviation Committee
ICA	International Claim Association	ICAC	International Confederation for Agricultural Credit = CICA, IVL
ICA	International College of Angiology (U.S.A.)		
		ICAC	International Cotton Advisory Committee = CCIA, CCIC
ICA	International Colour Association = AIC		
ICA	International Commission on Acoustics	ICAC	Islamic Civil Aviation Council (OIC) (Saudi Arabia)
ICA	International Communication Agency (Dominican Republic, Guyana, Mexico)		
		ICACGP	International Commission on Atmospheric Chemistry and Global Pollution (IAMAP)
ICA	International Communications Association		
ICA	International Confederation of Accordionists = CIA	ICAD	Inter-American Committee for Agricultural Development

ICAD	International Confederation of Art Dealers = CINOA	**ICAIR**	International Centre for Antarctic Information and Research
ICADA	International Congress on Alcohol and Drug Abuse	**ICAIRR**	Independent Care after Incestuous Relationship and Rape
ICADA	Irish Computer Aided Design Association	**ICAITI**	Instítuto Centroamericano de Investigación y Tecnología Industrial (Guatemala)
ICADD	International Congress on Alcohol & Drug Dependency	**ICALPE**	International Centre for Alpine Environments
ICADF	International Commission for Agreement on Danube Fishing	**ICAM**	Institut Catholique d'Arts et Métiers
ICADI	Inter-American Center for Agricultural Documentation and Information	**ICAM**	Institut Culturel Africain, Malgache et Mauricien
ICADIS	Instítuto Centroamericano de Documentación e Investigación Social	**ICAM**	International Confederation of Architectural Museums
ICADTS	International Committee on Alcohol, Drugs and Traffic Safety	**ICAMAS**	International Centre for Advanced Mediterranean Agronomic Studies (CE, OECD) = CIHEAM)
ICAE	International Commission of Agricultural Engineering = CIGR	**ICAME**	International Commission on the Applications of the Mossbauer Effect (Denmark)
ICAE	International Commission on Atmospheric Electricity (IAMAP)		
ICAE	International Council for Adult Education = CIEA	**ICAMI**	International Committee Against Mental Illness
ICAEC	International Confederation of Associations of Experts and Consultants	**ICAN**	Instítuto Colombiano de Antropologia
ICAES	Instítuto Centroamericano de Estudios Sociales (Costa Rica)	**ICAN**	International College of Applied Nutrition (U.S.A.)
ICAEW	Institute of Chartered Accountants in England and Wales	**ICAN**	International Conservation Network
		ICAN	Invalid Children's Aid Nationwide
ICAF	Institut de Coopération Audiovisuelle Francophone	**ICANA**	Instítuto Cultural Argentina Norte-Americano
ICAF	International Center on Adolescent Fertility (CPO)	**ICANAS**	International Congress of Asian and North African Studies
ICAF	International Commission on the Anthropology of Food and Food Problems (U.S.A.)	**ICAO**	Institut Catholique de l'Afrique de l'Ouest (Nigeria) = CIWA
ICAF	International Committee on Aeronautical Fatigue	**ICAO**	International Civil Aviation Organisation (UN) = MOGA, OACI
ICAFFH	International Committee for the Anthropology of Food and Food Habits	**ICAP**	Instítuto Centroamericano de Administración Pública (Costa Rica)
ICAI	Institut Canadien des Affaires Internationales = CIIA	**ICAP**	Instítuto Cubano de Amistad con los Pueblos
ICAI	Institute of Chartered Accountants in Ireland	**ICAP**	Instítuto de Crédito Agrícola y Pecuario (Venezuela)
ICAI	Institute of Cultural Affairs International	**ICAP**	International Committee of Architectural Photogrammetry = CIPA
ICAI	Instítuto Católico de Artes e Industrias	**ICAP**	International Congress of Applied Psychology
ICAI	International Committee for Aid to Intellectuals	**ICAPF**	Instítuto Centroamericano de Población y Familia (Guatemala)
ICAIC	Instítuto Cubano del Arte e Industria Cinematográficos	**ICAPR**	Inter-Department Committee on Air Pollution Research
ICAIE	International Committee Against Involuntary Exile	**ICAPR**	International Committee for Animal Performance Recording

ICAPRO-MUPA	Instituto de Capacitacion y Promocion de la Mujer Panamena
ICAQMH	International Commission for the Application of Quantitative Methods in History
ICAR	Indian Council of Agricultural Research
ICAR	Information Caraïbe (Guadeloupe)
ICAR	Institutul de Cercetari Agronomice al României
ICAR	International Commission for Alpine Rescue = CISA, IKAR
ICARA	International Conference on Assistance for Refugees = CIARA
ICARDA	International Centre for Agricultural Research in the Dry Areas
ICARE	Instítuto Chileno de Administración Racional de Empresas (Chile)
ICARE	International Centre for the Advancement of Research and Education (Italy)
ICAROEC	Regional Office and Education Centre for South-East Asia (ICA)
ICAS	Commission on Anti-Fungal Susceptibility Testing (IUMS)
ICAS	Institute of Chartered Accountants of Scotland
ICAS	Interdepartment Committee for Atmospheric Science (U.S.A.)
ICAS	International Conference on Acoustics, Speech and Signal Processing
ICAS	International Congress of African Studies = CIAF
ICAS	International Council of Air Shows
ICAS	International Council of Associations of Surfing
ICAS	International Council of the Aeronautical Sciences
ICASALS	International Centre for Arid and Semi-arid Land Studies (U.S.A.)
ICASE	Instítuto Centroamericano de Administración y Supervisión de Educación (Panama)
ICASE	International Council of Associations for Science Education = FIAPS
ICASSI	International Committee for Adlerian Summer Schools and Institutes
ICAT	Industrie Centrafricaine du Textile
ICAT	International Convention of Amateurs in Television
ICATU	International Confederation of Arab Trade Unions = CISA
ICAVE	International Coalition Against Violent Entertainment (U.S.A.)
ICAW	International Conference on Automation in Warehousing
ICAZ	International Council for Archeozoology
ICB	Indian Coffee Board
ICB	Industrial Co-ordination Bureau
ICB	Institutul de Constructii, Bucuresti
ICB	International Centrum voor de Bosbouw
ICB	International Congress of Biochemistry
ICB	International Container Bureau = BIC
ICB	International Convention Bureau (Belgium)
ICB	International Council for Building Research Studies and Documentation
ICB(SA)	Institute of Certified Bookkeepers of South Africa
ICBA	International Community of Booksellers Associations
ICBB	International Commission for Bee Botany
ICBBA	International Cornish Bantam Breeders Association
ICBD	International Council of Ballroom Dancing
ICBDMS	International Clearinghouse for Birth Defects Monitoring Systems
ICBERG	International Community Epilepsy Research Group
ICBF	Instítuto Colombiano de Bienestar Familiar
ICBG	International Cooperative Biodiversity Groups (NSF)
ICBH	Institute of Contemporary British History
ICBL	International Conference on the Biology of Lipids
ICBLB	International Committee for Breaking the Language Barrier
ICBO	International Conference of Building Officials
ICBP	International Council for Bird Preservation = CIPO, IRV
ICBRSD	International Council for Building Research Studies and Documentation
ICBT	Interdepartmental Committee on Biotechnology (DTI)
ICBT	Irish Children's Book Trust
ICBTC	International Citizens Band Truckers Club

ICBY	International Council on Books for Young People	**ICC**	Islanders Co-Ordinating Council (Torres Strait) (Australia)
ICC	Imprimerie Commerciale du Cameroun	**ICC-CAPA**	Commission on Asian and Pacific Affairs of the International Chambers of Commerce
ICC	Indian Central Coconut Committee		
ICC	Industrial Credit Corporation (Éire)	**ICC-CCI**	International Chamber of Commerce – Commission on Environment (France)
ICC	Institut Canadien de Conservation = CCI		
ICC	Institut de Chimie du Canada = CIC	**ICCA**	Independent Computer Consultants Association (U.S.A.)
ICC	Institute of Clinical Chiropractic	**ICCA**	Industrie Cotonnière Centrafricaine
ICC	Institute of Coal Chemistry (China)	**ICCA**	Instítuto Centroamericano de Ciencias Agricolas
ICC	Inter-American Investment Corporation = CII, SII		
		ICCA	International Computer Chess Association
ICC	Intergovernmental Consultative Committee	**ICCA**	International Congress and Convention Association
ICC	International Association of Cereal Science and Technology	**ICCA**	International Consumer Credit Association (U.S.A.)
ICC	International Cello Centre		
ICC	International Centre for Pure and Applied Chemistry (ICTP) (Italy)	**ICCA**	International Correspondence of Corkscrew Addicts
ICC	International Chamber of Commerce = CCI, IHK, IKK	**ICCA**	International Corrugated Case Association
ICC	International Children's Care (SDA)	**ICCA**	International Council for Commercial Arbitration
ICC	International Children's Centre CIE, CII	**ICCA**	International Council of Chemical Associations
ICC	International Climatological Commission	**ICCA**	Islamic Coalition Council of Afghanistan
ICC	International Coffee Council	**ICCAD**	International Centre for Computer-Aided Design (Italy)
ICC	International Committee for Coordination = CIC		
ICC	International Communist Current	**ICCAIA**	International Coordinating Council of Aerospace Industries Associations = CICAIA
ICC	International Computing Centre (UN)		
ICC	International Congress of Carboniferous Stratigraphy and Geology	**ICCAM**	International Committee of Children's and Adolescents Movements = CIMEA
ICC	International Control Commission (Laos)	**ICCARD**	International Commission for Central American Recovery and Development
ICC	International Coordinating Committee for the Presentation of Science and the Development of Scientific Out-of-School Activities = CIC	**ICCARD**	International Cooperation Centre of Agricultural Research for Development = CIRAD
ICC	International Coordinating Committee of Financial Analysts Associations = CICC	**ICCAS**	International Conference on Computer Applications in the Automation of Shipyard Operation and Ship Design
ICC	International Coordinating Committee of World Sports Organisations for the Disabled (Netherlands)	**ICCAT**	International Commission for the Conservation of Atlantic Tunas = CICAA, CICTA
ICC	International Corrosion Council	**ICCATCI**	International Committee to Coordinate Activities of Technical Groups in the Coatings Industry = CICATIRS
ICC	International Creative Centre (Switzerland) = RCI		
ICC	International Cricket Council	**ICCB**	Instítuto Cultural Colombo-Británico
ICC	Inuit Circumpolar Conference	**ICCB**	International Catholic Child Bureau = BICE, IKBK, OICI
ICC	Irish Council of Churches		

ICCBC	International Committee for Colorado Beetle Control	**ICCET**	Centre for Environmental Technology (Imperial College)
ICCBD	Intergovernmental Committee on the Convention on Biological Diversity	**ICCF**	Institutul de Cercetari Chimico-Farmaceutice
ICCC	Caritas Internationalis (International Confederation of Catholic Charities) = CI	**ICCF**	International Committee on Canned Food
ICCC	International Centre for Clinical Criminology (Italy) = CICC	**ICCF**	International Correspondence Chess Federation
ICCC	International Centre for Comparative Criminology = CICC	**ICCFAA**	International Coordinating Committee of Financial Analysts Associations (U.S.A.)
ICCC	International Christian Centre for Comics = CRIABD	**ICCFS**	Centre Fusion Studies
ICCC	International Christian Chamber of Commerce	**ICCFTI**	International Center for Companies of the Food Trade and Industry = CIES
ICCC	International Cocoa Council	**ICCG**	International Catholic Conference of Guiding = CICG
ICCC	International Concentration Camp Committee = CIC	**ICCG**	International Conference on Crystal Growth
ICCC	International Conference of Catholic Charities = CICC	**ICCH**	International Commodity Clearing House
ICCC	International Conference on Co-ordination Chemistry	**ICCIC**	International Centre for Clinical Criminology (Italy) = CICCI
ICCC	International Conference on Computer Communication	**ICCICE**	Islamic Chamber of Commerce and Industry and Commodity Exchange (Pakistan)
ICCC	International Congress on Construction Communications	**ICCIDD**	International Council for Control of Iodine Deficiency Disorders (Australia)
ICCC	International Council for Computer Communication	**ICCIR**	International Coordination Committee for Immunology of Reproduction = MKKIR
ICCC	International Council of Christian Churches	**ICCJ**	International Council of Christians and Jews
ICCC	International Cybernetics Congress Committee	**ICCL**	International Commission on Climate (IAMAP)
ICCD	Institute of Chocolate and Confectionery Distributors	**ICCL**	International Committee of Comparative Law = CIDC
ICCD	International Committee for a Community of Democracies (U.S.A.)	**ICCL**	International Committee on Computational Linguistics
ICCDA	Inter-Regional Coordinating Committee of Development Association (Senegal)	**ICCL**	Irish Council for Civil Liberties
ICCE	Institúto Colombiano de Construcciones Escolares	**ICCLA**	International Centre for the Co-ordination of Legal Assistance
ICCE	International Centre for Conservation Education	**ICCM**	International Committee for the Conservation of Mosaics
ICCE	International Commission on Continental Erosion	**ICCM**	International Conference on Composite Materials
ICCE	International Council for Computers in Education	**ICCM**	International Conference on the Conservation of Molluscs
ICCE-OIDE	Institutul Central de Cercetari Energetice Officiul de Informare Documentara pentru Energetica	**ICCM**	International Council of Catholic Men = FIHC
ICCEE	International Classification Commission for Electrical Engineering	**ICCN**	International Committee of Catholic Nurses = CICIAMS

ICCNA	International Center for the Control of Nutritional Anaemia (U.S.A.)
ICCO	Interkerkelijke Coördinatie Commissie voor Ontwikkelingsprojekten
ICCO	International Carpet Classification Organization
ICCO	International Cocoa Organization
ICCP	Institute for the Certification of Computer Professionals
ICCP	Institutul de Cercetari pentru Cultura Porumbului (Rumania)
ICCP	International Camp Counsellor Program (YMCA) (U.S.A.)
ICCP	International Commission on Cloud Physics (IAMAP)
ICCP	International Committee for Coal Petrology
ICCP	International Coordinating Committee for NGOs on the Question of Palestine = CICP
ICCP	International Council for Children's Play
ICCPT	Institutul de Cercetari pentru Cereale si Plante Tehnice
ICCR	Indian Council for Cultural Relations
ICCR	International Committee for Coal Research
ICCRA	Associazione Nazionale Importatori Carni Congelate, Refrigerate ed Affini
ICCRA	Investigaciones Cooperatives en el Mar Caribe y Regiones Adjacentes (FAO)
ICCREA	Istituto di Credito delle Casse Rurali e Artigiane
ICCROM	International Centre for the Study of the Preservation and RestorationI of Cultural Property (Italy)
ICCS	Institute of Cereal Science of Shanghai
ICCS	Inter-European Commission on Church and School
ICCS	Internatinal Committee on Clinical Sociology = CISC
ICCS	International Catholic Conference of Scouting = CICE, CICS, IKKP
ICCS	International Centre for Chemical Studies (UNESCO)
ICCS	International Centre for Child Studies
ICCS	International Committee of Contamination Control Societies
ICCS	International Container and Chassis Services (Belgium)
ICCS	International Council for Canadian Studies = CIéC
ICCSASW	International Commission for the Coordination of Solidarity Among Sugar Workers = CCSTAM
ICCSTI	Inter-Departmental Co-ordinating Committee for Scientific and Technical Information
ICCTA	International Consultative Council of Travel Agents
ICCU	International Cross-Country Union
ICCU	Istituto Centrale per il Catalogo Unico delle Biblioteche Italiane per le Informazione Bibliografiche
ICCW	Indian Council for Child Welfare
ICD	Institute of Civil Defence (*now* ICDDS)
ICD	Institute of Community Development
ICD	Institute of Crustal Dynamics (China)
ICD	International Center for the Disabled (U.S.A.)
ICD	International Centre for Development (Africa)
ICD	International College of Dentists (U.S.A.)
ICD	International Committee of Dermatology
ICD	International Congress of Dietetics
ICD	International Cooperation for Development
ICD	Internationale des Coiffeurs de Dames
ICDA	Indian Cotton Development Council
ICDA	International Catholic Deaf Association
ICDA	International Cheese Deli Association
ICDA	International Coalition for Development Action = CIAD
ICDA	International Committee of Dietetic Associations
ICDB	Islamic Co-operative Development Bank (Sudan)
ICDBL	International Committee for the Defence of the Breton Language = CISLB
ICDC	Industrial and Commercial Development Corporation (Kenya)
ICDC	International Child Development Centre (UNICEF)
ICDCS	Interstate Permanent Committee for Drought Control in the Sahel = CILSS
ICDDRB	International Centre for Diarrhoeal Diseases Research (Bangladesh)
ICDDS	Institute of Civil Defence & Disaster Studies (*ex* ICD)

ICDE	International Council for Distance Education	**ICEA**	International Childbirth Education Association (U.S.A.)
ICDECAA	International Committee for the Development of Educational and Cultural Activities in Africa	**ICEA**	International Christian Esperanto Association
ICDL	International Centre for Distance Learning (ICDE, OU, UNU)	**ICEA**	International Community Education Association
ICDLI	International Committee for the Decorative Laminate Industry (EEC)	**ICEA**	International Consulting Economists Association
ICDM	International Commission on Dynamic Meteorology (IAMAP)	**ICEA**	International Consumer Electronics Association
ICDO	International Civil Defence Organisation = OIPC	**ICEAM**	International Committee for Economic and Appled Microbiology
ICDOA	Irish Civil Defence Officers' Association	**ICEATCA**	Icelandic Air Traffic Controllers Association
ICDP	International Committee for Dermatopathology (U.S.A.) = ILDS	**ICEB**	Indonesian Commodity Exchange Board
ICDR	International Confederation of Dairy Retailers	**ICEC**	International Cost Engineering Council
ICDRG	International Contact Dermatitis Research Group	**ICEC**	International Cryogenic Engineering Committee
ICDS	International Cooperation for Development and Solidarity = CIDSE	**ICECC**	Information Centre for European Culture Collections (Germany)
ICDSI	Independent Commission on Disarmament and Security Issues	**ICECHIM**	Institutul de Cercetari Chimice
		ICECOOP	Instítuto Chileno de Educación Cooperativa
ICDT	Islamic Centre for the Development of Trade (Morocco) = CIDC	**ICECSA**	Islamic Commission for Economic Cultural and Social Affairs
ICE	Institute for Consumer Ergonomics	**ICECU**	Instítuto Centroamericano de Extensión y Cultura (Costa Rica)
ICE	Institute of Ceramic Engineers (U.S.A.)	**ICED**	Institute for Community Education Development (U.S.A.)
ICE	Institute of Chemical Engineers		
ICE	Institution of Chemical Engineers (U.S.A.)	**ICED**	International Council for Educational Development
ICE	Institution of Civil Engineers	**ICED**	Interprofessional Council on Environmental Design
ICE	Instítuto Costarricense de Electricidad	**ICEE**	Interafrican College of Electrical Engineering = ESIE, IEEC
ICE	Instítuto de Ciencias de la Educación		
ICE	Instítuto de Ciencias Económicas	**ICEED**	International Research Center for Energy and Economic Devolopment (U.S.A.)
ICE	Instítuto de Comercio Exterior (Peru, Venezuela)		
ICE	International Congress of Ecology	**ICEF**	Coordinating Committee of Chemical and General Workers Unions in the European Community
ICE	International Council of Ethologists		
ICE	International Council on Electrocardiology	**ICEF**	International Committee for Research and Study on Environmental Factors = CIFA
ICE	International Cultural Exchange		
ICE	IOMTR Committee for Europe	**ICEF**	International Federation of Chemical, Energy and General Workers' Unions
ICE	Istituto Nazionale per il Commercio Estero	**ICEG**	International Center for Economic Growth = CINDE
ICÉA	Institut Canadien d'Éducation des Adultes		
		ICEH	International Centre for Eye Health
ICEA	Insulated Cable Engineers Association (U.S.A.)	**ICEI**	Institute of Civil Engineers of Ireland

ICEI	Instituto Cooperazione Economica Internazionale
ICEJ	International Christian Embassy Jerusalem
ICEL	Instituto Colombiano de Energía Eléctrica
ICEL	International Committee for Ethnic Liberty
ICEL	International Committee on English in the Liturgy
ICEL	International Council of Environmental Law = CIDE
ICEM	International Centre for Earth, Environmental and Marine Sciences and Technologies (ICS)
ICEM	International Council for Educational Media = CIME
ICEM	Irish Council of the European Movement
ICEMES	International Cooperation on Marine Engineering Systems
ICEMET	Institutul de Cercetari Metalurgic
ICEMGCNY	International Congress of EMG and Clinical Neurophysiology
ICEMIN	Institutul de Cercetari Miniere
ICEMU	Instituto Centroamericano de Estudios de la Mujer
ICEN	International Committee on Embryological Nomenclature
ICEP	Instituto do Comércio Externo de Portugal
ICEPHEW	Institution of Civil Engineers Panel for Historical Engineering Works
ICEPS	Istituto Cooperazione Economica Internazionale e i Problemi di Sviluppo
ICER	Industry Council for Electronic and Electrical Equipment Recycling
ICER	Information Centre of the European Railways = CICE
ICER	Institute for Central European Research (U.S.A.)
ICES	Institution of Civil Engineering Surveyors
ICES	International Centre for Ethnic Studies
ICES	International Commission for Erosion and Sedimentation
ICES	International Conference of Engineering Societies
ICES	International Council for the Exploration of the Sea = CIEM

ICES	Interuniversity Centre for European Studies
ICES	Istituto per la Cinematografia Educativa Scientifica e Sociale
ICESA	International Commission for the Earth Sciences in Africa (ICL, IASPEI)
ICESA	International Conference on Environment Sensing and Assessment
ICESC	International Committee for European Security and Cooperation = CISCE, ICEVS
ICESD	Intergovernment Committee on Ecologically Sustainable Development
ICET	International Centre for Earth Tides
ICET	International Centre for Economy and Technology (Belgium)
ICET	International Council on Education for Teaching = CIEE, CIPE
ICETEX	Instituto Colombiano de Especializacion Tecnica en el Exterior (Colombia)
ICEU	Irish Customs & Excise Union (Éire)
ICEUM	International Conference on Energy Use Management
ICEVH	International Council for Education of the Visually Handicapped = CIEHV
ICEVS	Internationaal Comite voor Europese Veiligheid en Samenwerking = CISCE, ICESC
ICEX	Instituto Español de Comércio Exterior
ICF	Ice Cream Federation
ICF	Industrial Careers Foundation
ICF	Industry Churches Forum (*ex* Industrial Christian Fellowship)
ICF	Institute of Chartered Foresters
ICF	Institutul de Cercetari Forestiere (Romania)
ICF	International Canoe Federation = FIC
ICF	International Cardiology Foundation
ICF	International Casting Federation
ICF	International Cheerleading Foundation (U.S.A.)
ICF	International Chess Federation
ICF	International Christian Federation = ICFPADA
ICF	International Congregational Fellowship
ICF	International Congress on Fracture
ICF	International Consultants Foundation (U.S.A.)
ICF	International Crane Foundation
ICF	International Cremation Federation

ICF	International Cultural Foundation		**ICFS**	Ireland-Cuba Friendship Society
ICF	International Curling Federation		**ICFTA**	International Committee of Foundry Technical Associations = CIATF, IKGV
ICF	Islamic Charter Front (Sudan)			
ICF	Société des Ingénieurs Civils de France		**ICFTU**	International Confederation of Free Trade Unions = CIOSL, CISL, IBFG, IVVV
ICF/M/A	International Cystic Fibrosis /Mucoviscidosis/ Association			
ICFA	International Committee on Fine Arts (ICOM)		**ICFTUE**	International Centre of Free Trade Unionists in Exile = CISLE
ICFA	International Committee on Future Accelerators (ICSU)		**ICG**	Institute of Careers Guidance (*ex* ICO)
			ICG	Inter-Union Commission on Geodynamics
ICFAD	International Council of Fine Arts Deans		**ICG**	International Commission on Glass = CIV, IKG
ICFC	International Council of Fan Clubs			
ICFCYP	International Centre of Films for Children and Young People = CIFEJ		**ICG**	International Congress of Genetics
			ICGA	Imperial Continental Gas Association
ICFES	Instítuto Colombiana para el Formento de la Educación Superior		**ICGA**	International Carnival Glass Association
			ICGA	International Classic Guitar Association
ICFG	International Cold Forging Group		**ICGA**	Irish Craft and Giftware Association
ICFG	International Commission on Fungal Genetics		**ICGB**	International Cargo Gear Bureau
			ICGEB	International Centre of Genetic Engineering and Biotechnology
ICFG	International Crusade for Filipino Greatness			
			ICGEBnet	International Centre for Genetic Engineering and Biotechnology Network
ICFI	International Committee of the Fourth International			
ICFID	Inter-Church Fund for International Development (Canada)		**ICGEL**	International Crushing and Grinding Equipment Limited
			ICGH	International Confederation of Genealogy and Heraldry = CIGH
ICFL	International Council of the French Language = CILF			
ICFM	Institute of Charity Fundraising Managers		**ICGI**	International Council of Goodwill Industries
			ICGI	Unione Cattolica Giuristi Italiana
ICFM	International Center for Family Medicine (U.S.A.) = CIMF		**ICGP**	Irish College of General Practitioners
ICFM	International Commission on Food Mycology		**ICGS**	International Catholic Girls Society = ACISJF
ICFM	Islamic Conference of Foreign Ministers		**ICGVAN**	International Committee on Gross Veterinary Anatomical Nomenclature (Switzerland)
ICFMDS	International Centre of Methodology for Future and Development Studies (Romania)			
			ICGW	International Commission on Ground Water
ICFMH	International Committee on Food Microbiology and Hygiene		**ICGWC**	International Council for Game and Wildlife Conservation = CIC
ICFOST	International Committee for Food Science Technology		**ICH**	Institute of Curative Hypnotherapists
			ICH	Instítuto Cubano de Hidrografía
ICFP	International Conservation Financing Project (WRI)		**ICH**	Instítuto de Cultura Hispanica
ICFPADA	International Christian Federation for the Prevention of Alcoholism and Drug Addiction = ICF		**ICHA**	Instituto Chileno del Acero
			ICHA	Irish Commercial Horticultural Association
ICFPW	International Confederation of Former Prisoners of War = CIAPG		**ICHC**	International Committee for Histochemistry and Cytochemistry
ICFS	International Conference on Fluid Sealing		**ICHC**	International Committee for Horticultural Congresses

ICHCA	International Cargo Handling Co-ordination Association	**ICHT**	International Committee on Haemostasis and Thrombosis
ICHD	Inter-Society Commission for Heart Disease Resources (U.S.A.)	**ICHT**	International Confederation of the Hairdressing Trade = CIC
ICHÉC	Institut Catholique des Hautes Études Commerciales (Belgium)	**ICHV**	Institutul de Cercetari Horti-Viticole (Romania)
ICHEH	Instituto Chileno de Estudios Humanisticos	**ICI**	Imperial Chemical Industries
IChemE	Institution of Chemical Engineers	**ICI**	Inképscentralemas Aktiebolag
IChF	Instytut Chemii Fizycznej	**ICI**	Institut pour la Coopération Internationale (Austria)
ICHHS	International Council of Home-Help Services = CIOTF, IRHD	**ICI**	Instítuto de Colonización (Colombia)
ICHM	Institute of Care Home Managers	**ICI**	Instítuto de Cooperación Iberoamericana
ICHM	Interest Community of the Hungarian Minority (Slovenia) = ISMM	**ICI**	Inter-American Co-operative Institute (Panama)
ICHM	International Commission on the History of Mathematics (IMU, IUHPS)	**ICI**	Inter-American Copyright Institute (Brazil) = IACI, IIDA
ICHM	International Committee for Historical Metrology = CIMH	**ICI**	International Castles Institute (Netherlands) = IBI
ICHMT	International Centre for Heat and Mass Transfer	**ICI**	International Conference on Intelligence
IChN	Instytut Chemii Nieorganicznej	**ICI**	International Congress Institute
IChO	Instytut Chemii Ogólnej	**ICI**	International Correspondence Institute
ICHOHYP	International Committee of Hard of Hearing Young People (Denmark)	**ICI**	Istituto Cotoniero Italiana
ICHP	International Commission of Health Professionals for Health and Human Rights = CINPROS	**ICIA**	Information & Communication Industry Association
ICHPER	International Council on Health, Physical Education and Recreation	**ICIA**	International Centre of Information on Antibiotics (Belgium)
IChPW	Instytut Chemicznej Przeróbki W¿egla	**ICIA**	International Communications Industries Association
ICHR	Indian Council for Historical Research	**ICIA**	International Credit Insurance Association
ICHS	Interafrican Committee for Hydraulic Studies = CIEH	**ICIANZ**	Imperial Chemical Industries of Australia and New Zealand
ICHS	International Clinical Hyperthermia Society	**ICIASF**	International Congress on Instrumentation in Aerospace Simulation Facilities
ICHS	International Committee of Historical Sciences = CISH	**ICIB**	Indian Commercial Information Bureau
ICHS	International Committee on the History of the Second World War	**ICIB**	International Council for Building Research, Studies and Documentation
ICHS	International Council of Home-Help Services = CISAD, IRHD	**ICIBI**	International Cargo Inspection Bureau
ICHSLTA	International Council of Hides, Skins and Leather Traders Associations	**ICIC**	International Cancer Information Center (NCI) (U.S.A.)
ICHSMSS	International Commission for the History of Social Movements and Structures	**ICIC**	International Copyright Information Centre (UNESCO)
ICHSPP	International Congress on High-Speed Photography and Photonics	**ICIC**	Islamic Commission for the International Crescent (OIC) (Saudi Arabia)
ICHSWW	International Committee on the History of the Second World War	**ICICI**	Industrial Credit and Investment Corporation of India
		ICID	International Commission on Irrigation and Drainage (India) = CIID

ICIDCA	Institúto Cubano de Investigaciones de los Derivados de la Caña de Azucar	**ICITPR**	Institutul de Cercetari Inginerie Tehnologica si Proiectare pentru Rafinarii, Ploesti
ICIDI	Independent Commission on International Development Issues	**ICIV**	Institúto Cooperativo Interamericano de la Vivienda (Guatemala)
ICIE	International Centre for Industry and the Environment = CIIE	**ICIW**	International Confederation of Professional and Intellectual Workers
ICIE	International Council for Innovation in Higher Education	**ICJ**	International Commission of Jurists = CIJ, IJK
ICIF	International Co-operative Insurance Federation = FICA, FISC, IGVF	**ICJ**	International Court of Justice = CIJ
ICIHI	Independent Commission on International Humanitarian Issues	**ICJA**	International Criminal Justice Association (U.S.A.)
ICIM	Internationale des Cadres des Industries Métallurgiques	**ICJC**	International Council of Jews from Czechoslovakia
ICIMOD	International Centre for Integrated Mountain Development (Nepal)	**ICJCE**	Instituto de Censores Jurados de Cuentas de España
ICIP	Institúto Colombiano de la Investigación Pedagógica	**ICJIB**	International Coalition for Justice in Bhopal
ICIPÉ	Informateur Centre International de Propagation du Jeu d'Échecs (France)	**ICJP**	Irish Commission for Justice and Peace
ICIPE	International Centre of Insect Physiology and Ecology (Kenya)	**ICJW**	International Council of Jewish Women
ICIPEC	Istituto per la Cooperazione Politica, Economica e Culturale Internazionale	**ICKL**	International Council of Kinetography Laban
ICIPU	Istituto di Credito per le Imprese di Pubblica Utilité	**ICL**	Industrie de la Chassure de Luxe (Ivory Coast)
ICIRA	Institúto de Capacitación e Investigación en Reforma Agraria (Chile)	**ICL**	International Cancer League
		ICL	International Computers Limited
ICIREPAT	Committee for International Cooperation in Information Retrieval among Examining Patent Offices	**ICL**	Interunion Commission on the Lithosphere
		ICLA	Institúto Catequistico Latinoamericano
ICIS	International Center for Integrative Studies (U.S.A.)	**ICLA**	International Comparative Literature Association = AILC
ICIS	International Centre for Industrial Studies	**ICLA**	Investigadores de Cafe de Latino America
ICIS	International Centre for Islamic Studies	**ICLAM**	International Committee for Life, Disability and Health Assurance Medicine
ICIS	International Conference on Ion Sources		
ICIS	International Council for Infant Survival (U.S.A.)	**ICLARM**	International Center for Living Aquatic Resources Management (Philippines)
ICIST	Institut Canadien de l'Information Scientifique et Technique = CISTI	**ICLAS**	International Council for Laboratory Animal Science
ICIT	Institúto Cubano de Investigaciones Tecnológicas (Cuba)	**ICLC**	International Centre for Local Credit (Netherlands)
ICIT	International Centre for Island Technology	**ICLC**	International Congress on Lightweight Concrete
ICITA	International Chain of Industrial and Technical Advertising Agencies	**ICLC**	International Criminal Law Commission (FEICC)
ICITA	International Co-operative Investigations of the Tropical Atlantic = RICAT	**ICLCO**	International Contact Lens Council of Ophthalmology (Japan)
		ICLCUA	ICL Computer Users Association
		ICLD	International Center for Law in Development (U.S.A.)

ICLD	International Commission on Large Dams	**ICMA**	International Congresses for Modern Architecture
ICLE	Institute of Continuing Legal Education (U.S.A.)	**ICMA**	Irish Cable Makers Association
ICLEI	International Council for Local Environment Initiatives	**ICMART**	International Council of Medical Acupuncture and Related Techniques (Belgium)
ICLES	International Common Law Exchange Society	**ICMB**	Instituto de Ciencias del Mar
ICLM	International Christian Leprosy Mission	**ICMB**	International Center for Monetary and Banking Studies = CIMB
ICLPA	Irish Cream Liqueur Producers' Association	**ICMBE**	International Conference on Medical and Biological Engineering
ICLR	International Committee for Lift Regulations = CIRA	**ICMC**	International Catholic Migration Commission = CICM
ICLS	International Centre of Legal Science (Netherlands)	**ICMC**	International Christian Media Commission
ICLS	International Courtly Literature Society = SILC	**ICMC**	International Circulation Managers Commission
ICLS	Irish Central Library for Students	**ICMC**	International Committee on Medicinal Chemistry
ICLY	International Council on Lethal Yellowing	**ICMC**	International Conference on Metallurgical Coatings
ICM	Institute of Chemical Metallurgy (CNH)	**ICMCST**	International Conference on Microelectrics Circuits and System Theory
ICM	Institute of Commercial Management		
ICM	Institute of Construction Management	**ICME**	International Commission for Mathematical Education
ICM	Institute of Credit Management	**ICME**	International Contemporary Music Exchange
ICM	Intergovernmental Committee for Migration = CIM	**ICME**	International Council on Metals and the Environment (Canada)
ICM	International Confederation of Midwives	**ICMEA**	Institutul de Cercetari pentru Mecanizarea si Electrificarea Agriculturii (Romania)
ICM	International Congress on Mechanical Behaviour of Materials		
ICM	Islamic Constitutional Movement (Kuwait)	**ICMEDC**	International Council of Masonry Engineering for Developing Countries
ICM	Missionary Sisters of the Immaculate Heart of Mary	**ICMEE**	Institution of Certificates for Mechanical and Electrical Engineers (South Africa)
ICMA	Indian Chemical Manufacturers Association		
ICMA	Institute for Computational Mathematics and Applications (U.S.A.)	**ICMES**	International Conference Marine Engineering Systems
ICMA	Institute of Certified Management Accountants (U.S.A.)	**ICMF**	Indian Cotton Mills Federation
		ICMFDS	International Center of Methodology for Future and Development Studies (Romania)
ICMA	Instituto de Ciencia de Materiales de Aragon (Spain)		
ICMA	International Center of Medieval Art	**ICMG**	International Commission for Microbial Genetics
ICMA	International Christian Maritime Association	**ICMH**	International Commission of Military History = CIHM
ICMA	International Circulation Managers Association (U.S.A.)	**ICMI**	Association of Muslim Intellectuals
ICMA	International City Management Association	**ICMI**	International Commission on Mathematical Instruction
ICMA	International Computer Music Association (Russia)		

ICMICA	International Catholic Movement for Intellectual and Cultural Affairs = MIIC
ICMID	International Committee for Microbiological and Immunological Documentation
ICMLT	International Congress of Medical Laboratory Technologists
ICMM	International Committee of Military Medicine = CIMM
ICMM	International Committee of Military Medicine and Pharmacy = CIMPM
ICMM	International Congress of Maritime Museums
ICMMA	Industrial Cleaning Machine Manufacturers Association
ICMMA	International Council of the Museum of Modern Art (U.S.A.)
ICMMB	International Conference on Mechanics in Medicine and Biology
ICMOD	International Conference on Management of Data
ICMP	International Confederation of Music Publishers = CIEM
ICMP	International Conference on Medical Physics
ICMPH	International Centre of Medical and Psychological Hypnosis (Italy) = CIIMP
ICMR	Indian Council of Medical Research
ICMR	International Committee for Mountain Racing
ICMRD	International Center for Marine Resource Development (U.S.A.)
ICMREF	Interagency Committee on Marine Science, Research, Engineering and Facilities (U.S.A.)
ICMRT	International Center for Medical Research and Training (NIH) (U.S.A.)
ICMS	International Centre for Mathematical Sciences
ICMS	International Committee for Mycenaean Studies = CIPEM
ICMSA	Irish Creamery Milk Suppliers Association
ICMSF	International Commission on Microbiological Specifications for Foods
ICMT	International Commission on Mycotoxicology
ICMUA	International Commission on the Meteorology of the Upper Atmosphere (IAMAP)
ICN	Instítuto de Ciencias Naturales (Colombia)
ICN	Instítuto para la Conservación de la Naturaleza
ICN	International Chemical and Nuclear Corporation
ICN	International Communes Network
ICN	International Conference on Nutrition
ICN	International Council of Nurses = CIE, CII
ICNACO	Investigaciones Cooperativas en la Parte Norte del Atlantico Centro-Oriental (FAO)
ICNAF	International Council for North West Atlantic Fisheries
ICNARC	Intensive Care National Audit and Research Centre
ICNATVAS	International Council of the National Academy of Television Arts and Sciences
ICNCP	International Commission for the Nomenclature of Cultivated Plants
ICNDT	International Committee for Non-Destructive Testing
ICNND	Interdepartmental Committee on Nutrition for National Defense (U.S.A.)
ICNT	International Committee for Natural Therapeutics
ICNV	International Committee for the Nomenclature of Viruses
ICO	Institut Canadien des Oceans
ICO	Institute of Careers Officers (*now* ICG)
ICO	Instítuto de Crédito Oficial
ICO	Intergovernmental Commission on Oceanography
ICO	International Carbohydrate Organisation
ICO	International Chemistry Office
ICO	International Coastal and Ocean Organization (U.S.A.)
ICO	International Coffee Organisation = OIC
ICO	International Commission for Optics = CIO
ICO	International Commission on Oceanography
ICO	International Commodity Organisation (UNCTAD)
ICO	International Congress of Orientalists
ICO	International Congress of Otolaryngology
ICO	International Consultancy Organisation = OCI

ICO	International Council of Ophthalmology (IFOS)
ICO	Irish Chiropodists Association
ICO	Islamic Circle Organization
ICOA	International Castor Oil Association (U.S.A.)
ICOBA	International Confederation of Book Actors
ICOC	Indian Central Oilseeds Committee
ICOD	International Centre for Ocean Development (Canada) = CIEO
ICOD	International Council on Disability
ICODES	Instítuto Colombiano de Desarrollo Social
ICODI	Société des Impressions sur Tissus de Côte d'Ivoire
ICOF	Industrial Common Ownership Finance Ltd
ICOFTA	Indian Council of Foreign Trade
ICOGRADA	International Council of Graphic Design Associations
ICOH	International Commission on Occupational Health = CIMT, CIST
ICOHM	International Committee on Occupational Mental Health
ICOHTEC	International Committee for the History of Technology Committee
ICOI	International Congress of Oral Implantologists
ICOLD	International Commission on Large Dams = CIGB
ICOLPE	Instítuto Columbiano de Pedagogia
ICOM	Industrial Common Ownership Movement
ICOM	Institute of Computational Mathematics (U.S.A.)
ICOM	International Council of Museums
IComA	Institute of Company Accountants (*ex* SCCA)
ICOME	International Committee of Microbial Ecology
ICOMI	Industria et Commercio de Minerios (Brazil)
ICOMIA	International Council of Marine Industry Associations
ICOMIDC	Conseil International sur les Mathématiques dans les Pays en voie de Développement (Tunisia)
ICOMON	Conseil International des Monuments
ICOMOS	International Council of Monuments and Sites
ICOMP	International Council on the Management of Population Programmes
ICON	Inter-Institutional Committee on Nutrition (U.S.A.)
ICON	Investment Company of Nigeria
ICONA	Instítuto para la Conservación de la Naturaleza
ICONTEC	Instítuto Colombiano de Normas Tecnicas
ICOO	Iraqi Company for Oil Operations
ICOP	Instítuto Colombiano de Opinión Pública
ICOPA	International Congress on Parasitology
ICOPRAPA	International Conference of Peace Researchers and Peace Activities
ICOR	Interagency Commission on Ocean Resources (U.S.A.)
ICOR	Intergovernmental Conference on Oceanic Research
ICOREC	International Consultancy on Religion, Education and Culture
ICorrST	Institution of Corrosion Science and Technology
ICORS	Icelandic Operational Research Society
ICOS	Institute of Comparative Overseas Studies (Germany)
ICOS	International Committee of Onomastic Sciences = CISO
ICOS	Irish Cooperative Organisation Society
ICOS	Irish Council for Overseas Students
ICOSA	International Council of Seamen's Agencies (U.S.A.)
ICOSI	International Committee on Smoking Issues
ICOSO	International Committee for Outer Space Onomastics
ICOTAF	Industrie Cotonnière Africaine
ICP	Institut za Celulozo in Papir, Ljubljana<FIELD 00>ţPRIVATE ţţ
ICP	Institutul de Cercetari pentru Pesticide
ICP	International Center of Photography (U.S.A.)
ICP	International Commission on Penicillium and Aspergillus
ICP	International Committee for Learning by Participation
ICP	International Committee on Photobiology
ICP	International Communist Party
ICP	International Congress of Psychomotricity = CIP

ICP	International Cooperative Program
ICP	International Council of Parliamentarians on Alcohol and Drug Policy
ICP	International Council of Psychologists
ICP	International Institute of Cellular and Molecular Pathology (Belgium)
ICP	Investment Corporation of Pakistan
ICP	Iraqi Communist Party
ICP	Israel Cable Programming
ICPA	Institutul de Cercetari pentru Pedologie si Agrochimie
ICPA	International Co-operative Petroleum Association
ICPA	International Commission for the Prevention of Alcoholism and Drug Dependency
ICPA	International Cotton Producers' Association
ICPA	Irish Corrugated Packaging Association
ICPAE	International Commission on Planetary Atmospheres and their Evolution (IAMAP)
ICPAM	International Centre for Pure and Applied Mathematics (France) = CIMPA
ICPAO	Institutul de Cercetari pentru Prodise Auxiliare Organice, Medias
ICPAS	Institute of Certified Public Accountants of Singapore
ICPBR	International Commission for Plant-Bee Relationships
ICPC	Institutul de Cercetari si Productie a Cartofului
ICPC	International Cable Protection Committee
ICPC	International Confederation of Popular Credit = CIOP
ICPC	International Criminal Police Commission
ICPCB	Institutul de Cercetari si Productie pentru Cresterea Bovinelor
ICPCC	International Council for Pastoral Care and Counselling
ICPCE	International Great Plains Conference of Entomologists
ICPCH	Institutul de Cercetari si Proiectare pentru Industria Celulizei si Hîrtiei
ICPCI	International Conference on the Performance of Computer Installations
ICPCMP	Institutul de Cercetari pentru Prelucrarea Cauciucului si Maselor Plastice
ICPCP	Institutul de Cercetari si Productie pentru Cultura Pajistilor
ICPD	International Commission on Physics for Development
ICPD	International Conference on Population and Development
ICPDD	Institutul de Cercetari si Proiectari Delta Dunarii
ICPDP	International Committee for Pollution Damage to Plants
ICPE	Institutul de Cercetari Stiintifica si Inginerie Tehnologica pentru Industria Electrotehnica
ICPE	International Catholic Programme of Evangelisation (Malta)
ICPE	International Centre for Public Enterprises in Developing Countries (Yugoslavia)
ICPE	International Commission on Physics Education = CIEP
ICPEAC	International Conference on the Physics of Electronic and Atomic Collisions
ICPEAR	Institutul de Cercetari si Proiectare pentru Epurarea Apelor Reziduale
ICPEMC	International Commission for Protection against Environmental Mutagens and Carcinogens (Netherlands)
ICPES	Inter-Governmental Committee for Physical Education and Sport
ICPFR	International Committee for Physical Fitness Research
ICPGA	Institutul de Cercetari si Proiectari pentru Gospodarirea Apelor
ICPHS	International Council for Philosophy and Humanistic Studies = CIPSH
ICPI	Institúto Colombiano de Planeación Integral
ICPIC	International Cleaner Production Information Clearinghouse
ICPIC	International Council for Philosophical Inquiry with Children (IAPC)
ICPICH	International Commission for the Preservation of Islamic Cultural Heritage (OIC) (Turkey)
ICPIGP	Internationale Chrétienne Professionelle pour les Industries Graphiques et Papetières = IFCTUGPI
ICPIN	International Crime Prevention Information Network = RIIPD

ICPL	International Centre for Protected Landscapes	**ICPU**	International Catholic Press Union = IUKP, UCIP
ICPL	International Committee of Passenger Lines	**ICPU**	International Cities for Peace Union = UMVP, WUCP, WUPT
ICPLA	International Clinical Phonetics and Linguistics Association	**ICPVT**	International Council for Pressure Valve Technology
ICPM	Institute of Corrosion and Protection of Metals (China)	**ICQC**	International Conference on Quality Control
ICPM	International College of Psychosomatic Medicine (Mexico)	**ICR**	Institute for Computer Research (Canada)
ICPM	International Commission for Plant Raw Materials	**ICR**	Institute for Cosmic Ray Research (Japan)
ICPM	International Committee on Polar Meteorology (IAMAP)	**ICR**	Institute of Cancer Research
ICPM	International Congress of Physical Medicine	**ICR**	Institute of Chemical Reagents (China)
ICPMS	International Council of Prison Medical Services (U.S.A.)	**ICR**	Institute of Cultural Research
ICPN	International Committee on Plant Nutrition	**ICR**	International Collective Resistance
ICPO	International Criminal Police Organisation = IKPO, Interpol, OIPC	**ICR**	International Committee on Rheology
ICPO	Irish Commission for Prisoners Overseas	**ICR**	International Congress of Radiology
ICPP	Institutul de Cercetari pentru Proiectia Plantelor	**ICR**	Irish Consumer Research Limited
ICPP	International Conference on the Internal and External Protection of Pipes	**ICRA**	Indo-Chinese Refugee Association
ICPP	International Congress of Paedriatric Pathology	**ICRA**	Industrial Chemical Research Association
ICPR	Indian Council of Peace Research	**ICRA**	Industrial Copyright Reform Association
ICPR	International Conference on Production Research	**ICRA**	Institúto Costarricense de Defensa Agraria
ICPRP	International Commission for the Protection of the Rhine against Pollution = CIPR, IKSR	**ICRA**	International Catholic Rural Association
ICPRR	International Council on Public Relations in Rehabilitation	**ICRA**	International Centre for Research in Accounting (U.K.)
ICPS	Institute of Cost and Production Surveyors	**ICRA**	Irish Civil Rights Association
ICPS	International Cerebral Palsy Society	**ICRAF**	International Council for Research in Agro-Forestry (Kenya) = CIRAF
ICPS	International Conference on the Properties of Steam	**ICRAFON**	Société Industrielle des Crayons et Fournitures (Cameroon)
ICPS	International Congress of Photographic Science	**ICRB**	International Center for Research on Bilingualism (Canada) = CIRB
ICPS	Trade Unions International of Chemical Oil and Allied Workers	**ICRB**	International Cooperative Reinsurance Bureau
ICPSA	Irish Conference of Professional and Service Associations	**ICRC**	Indian Cancer Research Centre
ICPSR	Inter-University Consortium for Political and Social Research (U.S.A.)	**ICRC**	International Committee of the Red Cross = CICR, IKRK
		ICRCM	International Center on Recent Crustal Movement (CRCM, IAG)
		ICRCP	International Centre for Relief to Civilian Population
		ICRDB	International Cancer Research Data Bank (U.S.A.)
		ICRE	International Commission on Radiological Education and Information (Italy)

ICREP	Instítuto Chileno de Relaciones Publicas	**ICS**	Internationaal Congres van Schoonheidsspecialisten
ICRET	International Centre for Research into Economic Transformation (Russia)	**ICS**	International Camellia Society
ICRF	Imperial Cancer Research Fund	**ICS**	International Centre for Science and High Technology (TWAS, UNIDO)
ICRH	Institute for Computer Research in the Humanities (U.S.A.)	**ICS**	International Chamber of Shipping = CIMM
ICRH	International Congress on Religious History	**ICS**	International Churchill Society (U.S.A.)
ICRIP	International Circle for Research into Philosophy (U.S.A.)	**ICS**	International Cogeneration Society
		ICS	International College of Surgeons = CIC
ICRISAT	International Crop Research Institute for the Semi-Arid Tropics (India)	**ICS**	International Commission on Stratigraphy (IUGS)
ICRM	Instítuto Cubano de Recursos Minerals	**ICS**	International Committee of Slavists
ICRM	Instítuto de Crédito para la Reconstrucción Nacional	**ICS**	Internationaal Conrad Society (U.S.A.)
		ICS	International Coronelli Society
ICRM	International Committee for Radionuclide Metrology	**ICS**	International Correspondence School (U.S.A.)
ICRO	International Cell Research Organisation	**ICS**	International Crocodilian Society (U.S.A.)
ICRO	Irish Cave Rescue Organisation	**ICS**	Investors' Compensation Scheme
ICRP	International Commission on Radiological Protection = CIPR	**ICS**	Irish Chamber of Shipping
		ICS	Irish Computer Society
ICRS	International Cannabis Research Society	**ICS**	Irish Concrete Society
ICRS	International Commission on Radium Standards	**ICS**	Israel Crystallographic Society
		ICS	Istituto Centrale di Statistica
ICRSC	International Council for Research in the Sociology of Cooperation	**ICS/CI**	International Clarinet Society / ClariNetwork International
ICRSDT	International Committee on Remote Sensing and Data Transmission (IAHS)	**ICSA**	Information and Computing Services Association (Éire)
ICRT	Instítuto Cubano de Radio y Television	**ICSA**	Institute of Chartered Secretaries and Administrators
ICRU	International Commission on Radiation Units	**ICSA**	International Christian Studies Association
ICRUM	International Commission on Radiation Units and Measurements	**ICSA**	International Civil Service Agency
		ICSA	Internationaal Committee against Apartheid, Racism and Colonialism in Southern Africa
ICRW	International Centre for Research on Women (U.S.A.)		
ICS	Indian Chemical Society	**ICSA**	International Correspondence Society of Allergists (U.S.A.)
ICS	Industrial Computing Society		
ICS	Industries Chimiques du Sénégal	**ICSA**	International Council for Scientific Agriculture
ICS	Institut de Cinématographie Scientifique		
ICS	Institute of Caribbean Sciences (Puerto Rico)	**ICSA**	International Council of Securities Associations
ICS	Institute of Chartered Shipbrokers	**ICSAB**	International Civil Service Advisory Board
ICS	Institute of Child Study (Canada)		
ICS	Institute of Computer Science	**ICSB**	International Committee on Systematic Bacteriology
ICS	Institute of Computer Science (Greece)		
ICS	Institute of Cornish Studies	**ICSB**	International Council for Small Businesses (U.S.A.)
ICS	Instítuto Catalan de la Salud		
ICS	Intensive Care Society	**ICSC**	Indian Central Sugarcane Committee

ICSC	Inter-Ocean Canal Study Commission (U.S.A.)	**ICSIT-MUA**	Institutul de Cercetare, Proiectare si Inginerie Tehnologica pentru Masini si Utilaje Agricole
ICSC	International Civil Service Commission = CFPI	**ICSK**	International Cultural Society of Korea
ICSC	International Committee for Silent Chess	**ICSM**	Intergovernmental Committee on Surveying and Mapping (*ex* IGACSM)
ICSC	International Committee on Soil Conditioning	**ICSM**	International Committee of Scientific Management = CIOS
ICSC	International Council of Shopping Centers	**ICSMA**	International Conference on Strength of Metals and Alloys
ICSC	Irish Christian Study Centre	**ICSO**	Institut Ciezkiej Syntezy Organicznej (Poland)
ICSD	International Committee of Sports for the Deaf = CISS	**ICSOBA**	International Congress on Bauxite-Alumina-Aluminium
ICSE	International Committee for Sexual Equality	**ICSOG**	International Correspondence Society of Obstetricians and Gynecologists (U.S.A.)
ICSE	International Committee for Solvent Extraction Chemistry and Technology (ISEC)	**ICSOM**	International Conference of Symphony and Opera Musicians
ICSEAF	International Commission for the Southeast Atlantic Fisheries = CIPASE, CIPASO	**ICSP**	International Committee for the Science of Photography
ICSEB	International Congress of Systematic and Evolutionary Biology	**ICSP**	International Council of Societies of Pathology
ICSEE	International Committee for the Study of Educational Exchange	**ICSPFT**	International Committee for the Standardisation of Physical Fitness Tests
ICSEI	International Cooperation System for the Examination of Inventions (WIPO)	**ICSPHR**	International Centre of Studies for the Protection of Human Rights (U.S.A.)
ICSEM	International Council for the Scientific Exploration of the Mediterranean	**ICSPRO**	Inter-Secretariat Committee on Scientific Programmes Relating to Oceanography = CIPCRO, CIPSRO
ICSEMS	International Commission for the Scientific Exploration of the Mediterranean Sea = CIESM	**ICSPS**	International College of Spiritual and Psychic Sciences
ICSEP	International Center for the Solution of Environmental Problems (U.S.A.)	**ICSPS**	International Council for Science Policy Studies
ICSF	International Collective in Support of Fishworkers = CIAPA	**ICSR**	Institute for Cultural Studies and Research (Iran)
ICSG	International Centre of Social Gerontology = CIGS	**ICSS**	Institúto Colombiano de Seguros Sociales
ICSH	International Committee for Standardisation in Haematology	**ICSS**	International Committee for the Sociology of Sport
ICSH	International Congress Services Holland	**ICSS**	International Congress of Soil Science
ICSH	Irish Council for Social Housing	**ICSSCO**	International Collaborative Society for Supportive Care in Oncology
ICSI	International Commission of Snow and Ice = CING	**ICSSD**	International Committee for Social Science Information and Documentation = CIDSS
ICSI	International Conference on Scientific Information		
ICSID	International Centre for Settlement of Investment Disputes (UN) = CIADI, CIRDI	**ICSSID**	International Committee for Social Sciences Information and Documentation = CIDSS
ICSID	International Council of Societies of Industrial Design	**ICSSPE**	International Council of Sport Science and Physical Education = CIEPSS

ICSSR	Indian Council of Social Science Research
ICST	Institution of Corrosion Science and Technology
ICSTI	International Centre for Scientific and Technical Information (Russia) = CIPIST, MCNTI
ICSTIS	Independent Committee for the Supervision of Telephone Information Standards
ICSTO	International Civil Service Training Organization
ICSU	International Council of Scientific Unions = CIUC, CIUS
ICSU-CODATA	ICSU Committee on Data for Science and Technology = CODATA
ICSU-PWDC	ICSU Panel on World Data Centers
ICSUAB	International Council of Scientific Unions Abstracting Board = IAB
ICSUIA	Instistúto de Ciencias Sociales de la Universidad Iberoamericana (Mexico)
ICSV	International Committee for the Study of Viruses
ICSV	Internationale Christlich-Soziale Vereinigung (Belgium)
ICSW	International Commission on Surface Water
ICSW	International Committee on Seafarers' Welfare
ICSW	International Council on Social Welfare = CIAS
ICSWOA	International Centre for Scientific Work Organisation in Agriculture
ICT	Frauenhofer-Institut für Chemische Technologie (Germany)
ICT	Institute of Circuit Technology
ICT	Institute of Clay Technology
ICT	Institute of Computer Technology (U.S.A.)
ICT	Institute of Concrete Technology
ICT	Instistúto de Crédito Territorial (Colombia)
ICT	International Commission on Trichinellosis (Poland)
ICT	International Council of Tanners = CIC, CIT, IG
ICTA	Imperial College of Tropical Agriculture (West Indies)
ICTA	Instistúto de Ciencia y Tecnologia Agricola (Guatemala)

ICTA	International Centre for Technical Aids, Housing and Transportation (Sweden)
ICTA	International Centre for Tropical Agriculture
ICTA	International Confederation for Thermal Analysis
ICTA	International Confederation of Technical Agriculturists
ICTA	International Council for Travel Agents
ICTA	Ivory Coast Travel Agency
ICTAA	Institut Technique Coopératif des Aliments pour Animaux
ICTAM	International Congress of Theoretical and Applied Mechanics
ICTB	International Customs Tariffs Bureau
ICTC	Indian Central Tobacco Committee
ICTC	International Cooperative Training Center (U.S.A.)
ICTED	International Cooperation in the Field of Transport Economics Documentation (ECMT)
ICTF	International Cocoa Trades Federation
ICTF	International Commission on the Taxonomy of Fungi (IUMS)
ICTF	International Conference on Thin Films
ICTH	International Commission for the Teaching of History
ICTI	International Committee of the Toy Industries
ICTM	International Centre for High Technology and Advanced Materials (ICS)
ICTM	International Council for Traditional Music = CIMT
ICTME	International Conference on Tribo-Terotechnology and Maintenance Engineering
ICTMM	International Congresses on Tropical Medicine and Malaria = CIMTP
ICTP	International Centre for Theoretical Physics (Italy) = CIPT
ICTPDC	Imperial College Thermophysical Properties Data Centre
ICTR	International Centre of Theatre Research (France) = CIRT
ICTRM	Interagency Committee on the Transportation of Radioactive Materials (U.S.A.)
ICTS	International Catholic Truth Society
ICTS	International Congress of the Transplantation Society

ICTT	Internacional del Personal de los Servicios de Correos, Télegrafos y Teléfonos = IPTT, PTTI	**ICW**	Institute of Clerks of Works of Great Britain
ICTTC	International Consultative Telegraph and Telephone Committee	**ICW**	Instituut voor Cultuurtechniek en Waterhuishouding
ICTU	International Conference of Trade Unionists	**ICW**	International Chemical Workers Union (U.S.A.)
ICTU	Irish Congress of Trade Unions	**ICW**	International Council of Women = CIDEM, CIF, IFR
ICTV	International Committee on Taxonomy of Viruses (IUMS)	**ICWA**	Indian Council of World Affairs
ICTVTR	Islamic Centre for Technical and Vocational Training and Research (OIC)	**ICWA**	International Coil Winding Association
		ICWA	Israel Centre for Waterworks Appliances
ICU	Institut pour la Coopération Universitaire	**ICWAI**	Institute of Cost and Works Accountants of India
ICU	International Christian University (Japan)	**ICWDP**	International Committee for World Day of Prayer
ICU	International Cycling Union = UCI	**ICWES**	International Conference of Women Engineers and Scientists
ICUAE	International Congress of University Adult Education = CIEUA	**ICWL**	International Creative Writers League
ICUE	International Committee on the University Emergency	**ICWM**	International Committee of Weights and Measures = CIPM
ICUMSA	International Commission for Uniform Methods of Sugar Analysis	**ICWQ**	International Commission on Water Quality
ICUP	International Catholic Union of the Press = UCIP	**ICWRS**	International Commission on Water Resource Systems
ICUS	International Conference on the Unity of the Sciences	**ICWS**	International Centre of Water Studies (IWT)
ICV	International Commission of Viticulture	**ICWS**	International Co-operative Wholesale Society
ICVA	International Council of Voluntary Agencies = CIAB	**ICWTD**	International Committee for World Trade Development
ICVAN	International Committee on Veterinary Anatomical Nomenclature (Austria) = CINAV, IVANK	**ICWU**	International Chemical Workers Union (U.S.A.)
ICVB	Institutul de Cercetari Veterinare si Biopreparate Pasteur	**ICY**	International Christian Youth
		ICYCW	International Coordination of Young Christian Workers = CIJOC, GIGiOC
ICVD	Internationale Christelijke Vredesdient = CFD, CMP, MCP	**ICYE**	Federation of National Committees in the International Christian Youth Exchange
ICVEN	International Committee on Veterinary Embryological Nomenclature (U.S.A.)	**ICYF**	Institute for Children, Youth and Families (U.S.A.)
ICVG	International Council for the Study of Viruses and Virus Diseases of Grapevines	**ICYT**	Instítuto de Información y Documentación en Ciencia y Tecnología
ICVHN	International Committee on Veterinary Histological Nomenclature (U.S.A.)	**ICYYLM**	International Commission on Yeasts and Yeast-like Microorganisms
ICVR	Interuniversitair Centrum voor Rechtsvergelijking	**ICZ**	Institutul de Cercetari Zootehnice
ICVS	International Cardiovascular Society	**ICZN**	International Commission for Zoological Nomenclature
ICVV	Institutul de Cercetari pentru Viticultura si Vinificatie	**ID**	Izquierda Democrática (Ecuador)
ICW	Institute of Clayworkers	**IDA**	Industrial Development Authority (Éire)

IDÉRIC	Institut d'Études et de Recherches Interethniques et Interculturelles
IDÉRPC	Institut de Développement Économique de la République Populaire du Congo
IDERT	Institut d'Enseignement et de Recherches Tropicales
IDES	Institúto de Desarrollo Económico y Social (Argentina)
IDESAC	Institúto para el Desarrollo Económico y Social de América Central (Guatemala)
IDÉT	Institut pour le Développement Économique et Technique
IDEVI	Institúto de Desarrollo del Valle Inferior del Rio Negro (Argentina)
IDEX	Société Ivoirienne de Distribution et d'Exportation
IDF	Industrial Development Fund = FDI
IDF	Institut pour le Développement Forestier
IDF	International Dairy Federation = FIL, IMV
IDF	International Democratic Fellowship
IDF	International Dental Federation = FDI
IDF	International Development Foundation
IDF	International Diabetes Federation = FID
IDF	Israeli Defence Force
IDFA	Infant and Dietetic Foods Association
IDFA	Interessengemeinschaft Deutscher Fachmessen und Ausstellungsstädte
IDFA	Irish Deer Farmers' Association (Éire)
IDFA	Irish Duty Free Association (Éire)
IDFB	International Down and Feather Bureau
IDFC	International Duty Free Confederation (Belgium)
IDFF	Internationale Demokratische Frauenföderation = FDIF, FDIM, WIDF
IDG	Institut für Dampf- und Gasturbinen (Germany)
IDG	Istituto per la Documentazione Giuridica (Italy)
IDGTE	Institution of Diesel and Gas Turbine Engineers
IDGUK	India Development Group Ltd
IDHCA	International District Heating and Cooling Association (U.S.A.)
IDHE	Institute of Domestic Heating and Environmental Engineers
IDHÉC	Institut des Hautes Études Cinématographiques
IDHF	Irish Dental Health Foundation
IDHS(GB)	Irish Draught Horse Society (Great Britain)
IDI	Indian Development Institute
IDI	Information and Documentation Institute (Belgium)
IDI	Institut de Développement Industriel
IDI	Institut de Droit International = IIL
IDI	Institúto Dominicano de Investigaciones (Dominican Republic)
IDI	International Diabetes Institute
IDI	International Disaster Institute
IDIA	Industrial Design Institute of Australia
IDIA	Irish Dairy Industries Association
IDIADA	Institúto de Investigacion Aplicada del Automovil
IDIAP	Institúto de Investigaciones Agropecuários de Panamá
IDIB	Industrial Diamond Information Bureau
IDIC	Industrial Development and Investment Centre (Taiwan)
IDIC	Institúto de Investigaciones y Control Tecnoci del Ejercito (Chile)
IDICT	Institúto de Documentación e Información Cientifica y Técnica (Cuba)
IDIEM	Institúto de Investigaciones y Ensayes de Materiales (Chile)
IDILF	Information et Diffusion Internationale du Livre de Langue Française
IDIN	International Development Information Network (OECD)
IDIS	Institut für Dokumentation und Information über Socialmedizin und offtenliches Gesundheitswesen
IDIS	International Dairy Industries Society
IDIT	Institut du Droit International des Transports
IDJC	International Dressage Judges' Club (Belgium)
IdK	Internationaler der Kriegsdienstgegner = IOT, IRG, WRI
IDLA	Inversiones y Desarrollo Los Andes
IDLG	Infant Drinks Litigation Group
IDLG	Information Development and Liaison Group (DoE)
IDLI	International Development Law Institute
IDLSG	International Drycleaners and Launderers Study Group
IDLV	Institut de la Vie
IDM	Institute of Defence Management (India)

IDM	Institute of Development Management (AMTIESA) = IDM-BLS	**IDRC**	Industrial Development Research Council (U.S.A.)
IDM	Instítuto de Desarrollo Municipal (Paraguay)	**IDRC**	International Development Research Centre (Canada) = CIID, CRDI
IDM	International Dental Manufacturers	**IDRC**	Irish Dairy Records Co-operative
IDM-BLS	Institute of Development Management – Botswana, Lesotho and Swaziland (AMTIESA) = IDM	**IDRÉM**	Institut de Documentation de Recherches et d'Études Maritimes (Ivory Coast)
IDMA	Indian Drug Manufacturers Association	**IDRF**	International Disaster Relief Force
IDMA	International Destination Management Association	**IDRI**	Information and Data Research Institute (China)
IDMA	International Diamond Manufacturers Association	**IDRIART**	Institut pour le Développement des Relations Interculturelles par l'Art
IDMA	International Doll Makers Association	**IDRO**	Industrial Development and Renovation Organization (Iran)
IDMA	Irish Direct Marketing Association (Éire)	**IDRS**	International Double Reed Society (U.S.A.)
IDN	International Directory Network	**IDS**	Incomes Data Services
IDO	Industrial Development Organisation (UN)	**IDS**	India Development Service
IDO	Instítuto de Denominaciones de Origen	**IDS**	Industrieverband Deutscher Schmieden
IDO	International Dental Organisation	**IDS**	Industry Department For Scotland
IDOC	International Documentation and Communication Centre (Italy)	**IDS**	Institute for Development Studies (Kenya)
IDOC	International Documentation on the Contemporary Church (U.S.A.)	**IDS**	Institute of Development Studies
		IDS	International Dendrology Society
IDOCO	Internationale des Organisations Culturelles Ouvrières (Austria)	**IDS**	International Development Services
IDORT	Instítuto de Organização Racional do Trabalho (Brazil)	**IDS**	International Dostoevsky Society
		IDS	Irish Deaf Society
IDOSARCS	Institute of Development of Southern African Red Cross Societies	**IDS**	Istarski Demokratski Sabor (Croatia) = IDA
IDP	International Development Programme of Australian Universities and Colleges	**IDSA**	Indian Dairy Science Association
		IDSA	Industrial Designers Society of America
IDP	Irmazinhas dos Pobres = HDLP, LSP, PSDP	**IDSA**	Infectious Diseases Society of America
IDPL	Indian Drugs and Pharmaceuticals Ltd (India)	**IDSA**	International Development Service of America
IDPM	Institute of Data Processing Management	**IDSA**	International Diving Schools Association (U.S.A.)
IDPT	International Donkey Protection Trust	**IDSA**	Irish Deaf Sports Association
IDPT	Islamic Democratic Party of Tatarstan	**IDSAGB**	Independent Democratic Socialist Association of Gypsies (Bulgaria) = NDSATsB
IDR	Institute for Development Research (Denmark)		
IDR	Institute of Development Research (Ethiopia)	**IDSO**	International Diamond Security Organization
IDR	International Dental Relief	**IDSTM**	Institute of Distribution, Sales, Technology and Management
IDRA	Intercultural Development Research Association (U.S.A.)	**IDT**	Institutul de Documentare Technica
		IDTA	International Dance Teachers' Association
IDRAS	Institute of Desert Research, Academia Sinica	**IDTA**	Irish Dental Trade Association (Éire)

IDTC	Industrial Development Technical Centre (Qatar)
IDTC	International Driving Tests Committee = CIECA
IDU	Industrial Development Unit
IDU	International Democratic Union = UDI
IDU	International Dendrology Union
IDV	Interessengemeinschaft Deutscher Versandbier-Grosshändler
IDV	Internationaler Deutschlehrerverband = IATG
IDV RAN	Institute of the Far East, Russian Academy of Sciences
IdW	Institut der Wirtschaftsprüfer in Deutschland
IDW	Institut für Dokumentationwesen
IDW	International Dolphin Watch
IE	Iarnród Éireann = IR
IE	Institute of Energy
IE	Institute of Engineers
IE	Institute of Export
IE	Institution of Electronics
IE	Institution of Engineers (India)
IE RAN	Institute of Economics, Russian Academy of Sciences
IE/PAC	Industry and Environment Program Activity Centre (UNEP)
IEA	Indian Engineering Association
IÉA	Institut Économique Agricole (Belgium)
IEA	Institut Européen des Affaires
IEA	Institut Européen des Avocats = ELI
IEA	Institute of Applied Economics (Canada)
IEA	Institute of Economic Affairs
IEA	Institute of Engineers, Australia
IEA	Institute of Environmental Assessment
IEA	Institúto de Energia Atomica (Brazil)
IEA	Institúto de Experimentaciones Agropecuárias (Argentina)
IEA	Instytut Energii Atomowej
IEA	International Assocation for the Evaluation of Education Achievement
IEA	International Economic Association = AISE
IEA	International Electrical Association
IEA	International Emergency Action
IEA	International Energy Agency = AIE
IEA	International Entomological Association
IEA	International Entrepreneurs Association
IEA	International Epidemiological Association
IEA	International Ergonomics Association
IEA	International Executives Assocation
IEA	Irish Epilepsy Association
IEA	Irish Exporters Association
IEA	Istituto Europeo delle Acque = IEE
IEA CR	IEA Coal Research
IEAA	European Institute of Architecture and Planning = INEAA
IEAA	Institute of Estate Agents and Auctioneers of South Africa
IEAA	International Educational Accreditations Association
IÉAAC	Institut d'Études Agronomiques d'Afrique Centrale
IEAB	Internacia Esperanto-Asocio de Bibliotekistoj
IEACS	Institut Européen des Armes de Chasse et de Sport
IEAG	Institúto Ecuatoriano de Antropolgía y Geografica
IEAJ	Internacia Esperanto Asocio de Juristo
IEAL	Independent Educational Association Limited
IEAM	Institute of Entertainment & Arts Management
IEAP	Institut Européen d'Administration Publique = EIPA
IEAR	Internacia Esperanto-Amikaro Rotarianoj
IEARC	International Exhibitors Association Radiological Congress
IEAS	Institute of Electronics, Academia Sinica
IEAS	International Economic Appraisal Service
IEASMA	International Electronic Article Surveillance Manufacturers' Association
IEAust	Institution of Engineers (Australia)
IEAV	Internationales Eisenbahn Alkoholgegner Verband = FICA, IRTU
IEAZ	Institúto Experimental de Agricultura Zootécnica
IEB	Institution of Engineers (Bangladesh)
IEB	Institúto de Estudos Brasileiros
IEB	International Education Board
IEB	International Energy Bank
IEB	International Environmental Bureau (Switzerland) = BIE

IEC	Information Exchange Centre (CISTI)
IÉC	Institut d'Études Centrafricaines
IEC	Institut des Experts-Comptables (Belgium) = IDAC
IEC	Institute of Employment Consultants
IEC	Instítuto de Electronica de Comunicaciones
IEC	International Edsel Club
IEC	International Egg Commission
IEC	International Electrotechnical Commission = CEI
IEC	International Energy Cooperative (U.S.A.)
IEC	International Everesters Club
IEC	International Extension College (U.K.)
IEC	Irish Equine Centre (Éire)
IEC	Israel Electric Corporation
IECA	Industry Education Councils of America
IECA	International Erosion Control Association
IECAIM	Instituto Ecuatoriano de Investigaciones y Capacitacion de la Mujer (Ecuador)
IECB	Institutul de Energetica Chimica si Biochimica
IECBSHM	International Editorial Committee for Book Series on Hydraulic Machinery (China)
IECC	International Express Carriers Conference = CICE
IECEE	IEC System for Conformity Testing to Standards for Safety of Electrical Equipment
IECEJ	Institute of Electronics and Communication Engineers of Japan
IECF	International European Construction Federation (France)
IECI	Institute for Esperanto in Commerce and Industry (Netherlands)
IECIC	International Engineering and Construction Industries Council (U.S.A.)
IECLB	Igreja Evangélica de Confissão Luterana no Brasil
IECN	Instítuto Ecuatoriano de Ciencias Naturales
IECQA	International Electrotechnical Commission on Quality Assessment
IECS	Institute of Estuarine and Coastal Studies
IÉD	Institut d'Études du Développement (Switzerland)
IED	Institut Européen de Développement (Belgium)
IED	Institution of Engineering Designers
IÉDA	Institut d'Études du Développement Africain
IEDC	International Energy Development Corporation
IEDD	Institution of Engineering Draughtsmen and Designers
IÉDÉS	Institut d'Étude de Développement Économique et Social
IEDO	Institution of Economic Development Officers
IEDP	Institute of Economic Development and Policy (EWC)
IEDR	Institute of Economic Development and Research (Philippines)
IEDS	International Environment and Development Service (USAID/WEC)
IEDSS	Institute of European Defence and Strategic Studies
IEDW	Communauté d'Intérêts des Anciens Résistants dans les Pays Occupés par le Fascisme
IEE	Institut Européen de l'Eau = IEA
IÉE	Institute d'Écologie Européenne
IEE	Institute of Earth Education
IEE	Institute of Explosives Engineers
IEE	Institution of Electrical Engineers
IEE	Instítuto de Estudios Economicos
IEE	Instítuto Español de Emigración
IEE	International Institute for Hyraulic and Environmental Engineering (Netherlands)
IEE-CASS	Institute of Industrial Economics, Chinese Academy of Social Sciences
IEEC	Integrated Electronics Engineering Center (U.S.A.)
IEEC	Interafrican Electrical Engineering College = ESIE, ICEE
IEEE	Institute of Electrical and Electronic Engineers (U.S.A.)
IEEE	Instítuto Español del Envase y Embalaje
IEEI	Instituto de Estudos Estratégicos e Internacionais (Portugal)
IEEIE	Institute of Electrical and Electronic Incorporated Engineers
IEEJ	Institute of Electrical Engineers of Japan
IEEM	Institute of Ecology and Environmental Management

IEENPh	Hidryma Ereunes kai Ekdoseon Neohellenikes Philosophias = FRENP	**IEI**	International Environment Institute (FIS)
IEEO	Institute of Executive Engineers and Officers	**IEI**	International Esperanto Institute = IIE
IEEP	Institute for European Environmental Policy = IPEE	**IEI**	Israel Export Institute
		IEI	Istituto Ecologico Internazionale
IEEP	International Environmental Education Programme (UNESCO/UNEP) = IPEE	**IEI**	Istituto Erpetologico Italiano
		IEIAS	Institut Européen Interuniversitaire de l'Action Sociale (Belgium) = IEISW
IEF	Institúto de Estudios del Futuro (Chile)	**IEIC**	Institut Européen Interrégional de la Consommation = EIICA
IEF	Inst1túto Ecuatoriano del Folklore		
IEF	International Ecumenical Fellowship	**IEIC**	Institution of Engineers-in-Charge
IEF	International Environment Facility	**IEICE**	Institute of Electronics, Information and Communication Engineers
IEF	International Environment Forum (U.S.A.)	**IEIP**	Institut Européen des Industries de la Pectine (Belgium)
IEF	International Eye Foundation		
IEF	Irish Equine Foundation (Éire)	**IEISW**	Inter-University European Institute on Social Welfare = IEIAS
IEFA	International Europese Federale Aktie	**IEK**	Internacia Ekzamenoj
IEFE	Istituto di Economia delle Fonti di Energia	**IEK**	IOMTR-Europakommission = CEI
IEFG	International Enterprise Foundation of Geneva = FEIG, FIPGE	**IEKA**	Internacia Esperanto-Klubo Automobilista
IEFP	Institut Européen pour la Formation Professionnelle	**IEKV**	Internationale Eisenbahn-Kongress-Vereinigung = AICCF, IRCA
IEFR	International Emergency Food Reserve = RAIU	**IEL**	Inst14úto Euvaldo Lodi (Brazil)
		IEL RAS	A N Frumkin Institute of Electrochemistry of the Russian Academy of Sciences
IEG	Immunopatholgy Exchange Group		
IEGA	Instituto de Economía y Geografía Aplicadas (Spain)	**IELA**	International Exhibition Logistics Associations
IEGHP	Institute of Economic Geography, Hunan Province (China)	**IEM**	Institute of Engineering Mechanics (China)
IÉGSP	Union Intercommunale pour l'Étude et la Gestion des Services Publics à Caractère Industriel et Communal	**IEM**	Instituto de Enseñanza Media
		IEM	Institúto Emissor de Macau
		IEMA	International Eightmetre Association (Canada)
IEH	Institution of Environmental Health Officers	**IEMCS**	Industrial Estates Management Corporation for Scotland
IEHA	International Economic History Association = AIHE	**IEME**	Inspectorate of Electrical and Mechanical Engineering
IEHASS	Institute of Economics, Hubei Academy of Social Sciences (China)	**IEME**	Instituto Español de Moneda Extranjera
IEHÉI	Institut Européen des Hautes Études Internationales	**IEME**	Instituto Español de San Francisco Javier para Misiones Extranjeras
IEHO	Institution of Environmental Health Officers	**IÉMVT**	Institut d'Élevage et de Médecine Vétérinaire des Pays Tropicaux
IEHV	Internationaler Eishockey Verband = IIHF, LIHG	**IEMW**	Internacia Esperanto-Museo, Wien (Austria)
IEI	Industrial Education International	**IÉN**	Institut d'Études Nucléaires (Algeria)
IEI	Institute of Electrical Inspectors (Australia)	**IEN**	Instituto de Engenharia Nuclear (Brazil)
		IEN	Instituto Elettrotecnico Nazionale
IEI	Institution of Engineers of Ireland	**IENN**	International Environmental Negotiation Network (U.S.A.)
IEI	Instituto de Educación y Investigación		

IENS	Indian and Eastern Newspaper Society (India)
IEnvSc	Institution of Environmental Sciences
IEO	Industry and Environment Office (UNEP)
IEO	Institut de l'Europe Occidentale pour l'Imprégnation du Bois = WEI
IEO	Instítuto Español de Oceanografica
IEOS	International Earth Observation System
IEOSM	International Earth Observation Satellite Missions
IEP	Industry and Environment Office (IUCN)
IEP	Institut für Europäische Politik e.V.
IEP	Instítuto de Estudios Peruanos (Peru)
IEP	International Economic Publishers (U.S.A.)
IEPA	International Economic Policy Association (U.S.A.)
IEPA	Irish Educational Publishers Association
IEPAL	Instítuto de Estudios Políticas para América Latina
IEPC	International Environmental Programs Committee (NAS) (U.S.A.)
IEPE	Instítuto de Estudos e Pesquisas Económicas (Brazil)
IEPES	Instítuto de Estudios Politicos, Económicos y Sociales (Mexico)
IEPESA	Industria Ecuatoriana de Productos Electronicos S.A.
IEPF	Institut de l'Énergie des Pays ayant en Commun l'Usage du Français (ACCT)
IEPFC	International Elvis Presley Fan Club
IEPG	Independent European Programme Group (NATO) = GEIP
IEPGE	Instítuto de Economia y Producciones Ganaderas del Ebro
IEPI	Institut Européen de Recherche et Réadaption en Psychiatrie Infantile
IEPRC	International Electronic Publishing Research Centre
IEPS	International Electronics Packaging Society (U.S.A.)
IER	Institut Ekonomiki Rolnej
IER	Institute for Economic Research (Iran)
IER	Institute for Educational Research (U.S.A.)
IER	Institute of Education and Research, University of Dacca
IER	Institute of Employment Rights
IER	Institute of Engineering Research
IER	Organization for International Economic Relations (UN)
IÉRA	Institut d'Études et Recherches d'Arabisation (Morocco)
IERAC	Instítuto Ecuatoriano de Reforma Agraria y Colonización
IERB	Islamic Economics Research Bureau
IERD	International Exposition of Rural Development (Belgium)
IERE	Institution of Electronic and Radio Engineers
IERE	International Electrical Research Exchange
IERÉT	Institut Européen de Recherches et d'Études Touristiques
IERH	Instítuto Ecuatoriano de Recuros Hidráulicos
IERHAS	Institute of Energy Resources, Hebei Academy of Sciences (China)
IERPS	Institut des Énergies Renouvelables pour le Pacifique Sud (Polynesia, Tahiti) = SPIRE
IÉRS	Institut d'Études et de Recherches Sociales (Iran)
IERS	International Earth Rotation Service
IERS	International Education and Refugee Service
IERS	International Educational Reporting Service (IBE)
IERT	Institute of Engineering and Rural Technology (India)
IES	Illuminating Engineering Society (U.S.A.)
IES	Institute for Environmental Studies (Canada, U.S.A.)
IES	Institute of Ecosystem Studies (U.S.A.)
IES	Institute of English Studies
IES	Institution of Engineers and Shipbuilders in Scotland = IESS
IES	Institution of Environmental Sciences
IES	International Ecology Society (U.S.A.)
IES	International Endotoxin Society
IES	Israel Exploration Society
IESA	Illuminating Engineering Society of Australia
IESA	Institut d'Etudes Supérieures des Arts
IESA	Instítuto de Estudios Superiores de Administración (Venezuela)
IESA	Instítuto Español del Envase y Embalaje (Spain)

IESA	International Esperantists Scientific Association		**IETC**	UNEP International Environment Technology Centre
IESBS	Institute of Engineers and Ship Builders in Scotland		**IETCC**	Institúto de la Construccion y del Cemento "Eduardo Torroja"
IESC	Information Exchange Steering Committee (DOF)		**IETE**	Institution of Electronics and Telecommunication Engineers (India)
IESC	International Executive Service Corps (U.S.A.)		**IETEJ**	Institute of Electronics and Telecommunications Engineers of Japan
IESE	Institúto de Estudios Sociales y Económicos (Bolivia)		**IETEL**	Institúto Ecuatoriano de Telecomunicaciónes
IESE	Institúto de Estudios Superiores de la Empresa		**IETF**	Internet Engineering Task Force
IESG	Internet Engineering Steering Group		**IETG**	International Energy Technology Group (OECD) = GITE
IESI	International Economic Studies Institute (U.S.A.)		**IETM**	Informal European Theatre Meeting (Belgium)
IÉSIÉL	Institut d'Études Supérieures de l'Industrie et de l'Économie Laitières		**IETN**	International Environment Television Network
IESIS	Institution of Engineers & Shipbuilders in Scotland		**IETS**	International Embryo Transfer Society (U.S.A.)
IESL	Institute of Electronic Structure and Laser (Greece)		**IETTAB**	International Environment Technology Transfer Advisory Board
IESNA	Illuminating Engineering Society of North America		**IEU**	Forum International-International Ecosystems University (U.S.A.)
IESNEC	Institution of Engineers and Shipbuilders of of North-East Coast		**IEV**	Institúto Experimental de Veterinária (Brazil)
IESOE	Interconnexion de l'Electricité du Sud-Ouest de l'Europe		**IEVR RAN**	Institute of Europe, Russian Academy of Sciences
IESRI	Institut Européen d'Études et de Relations Intercommunales (Switzerland)		**IEX**	Institute of Export
			IExpE	Institute of Explosives Engineers
IESS	Institution of Engineers and Shipbuilders in Scotland = IES		**IEZ**	Institut Européen du Zinc (France) = EZI
IESS	Institúto Ecuatoriano de Seguridad Social (Ecuador)		**IF**	Institute of Foresters
IESS	Internet Entrepreneurs Support Association		**IF**	Institute of Fuel
			IF	Institutet för Framtidsstudier (Sweden)
IESSA	Institute of Economic Studies and Social Action (Philippines)		**IF RAN**	Institute of Philosophy, Russian Academy of Sciences
IESSÉ	Institut d'Enseignement Supérieur Social de l'État (Belgium)		**IFA**	Independent Film Makers Association
IESTIS	Institúto Ecuatoriano de Sociología y Técnica, Transculturación, Integración e Investigación Social		**IFA**	Industrial Forestry Association (U.S.A.)
			IFA	Industries et Forêts Africaines (Cameroon, Central Africa, Congo)
IÉSTO	Institut d'Études Supérieures des Techniques d'Organisation		**IFA**	Institut Français de l'Alcool
IET	Institute of Engineering Thermophysics (China)		**IFA**	Institute of Field Archaeologists
			IFA	Institute of Financial Accountants
IET	Institute of Engineers and Technicians		**IFA**	Institute of Foresters of Australia
IET	Institute of Exploration Techniques (China)		**IFA**	Institúto de Fomento Algodonero (Colombia)
			IFA	International Federation of Actors = FIA
IETAL	Institúto de Estudios Turísticos de América Latina		**IFA**	International Federation of Airworthiness

IFA	International Federation of Aromatherapists
IFA	International Federation on Ageing =FIV
IFA	International Fertilizer Industry Association
IFA	International Festivals Association (U.S.A.)
IFA	International Fiscal Association
IFA	International Florists Association
IFA	International Footprint Association
IFA	International Franchise Association
IFA	International Fructose Association
IFA	Irish Farmers Association
IFA	Irish Football Association
IFA	Israel Futorologist Association
IFA	Istituto di Fisica dell'Atmosfera
IFA	Istituto Nazionale per la Formazione Professionale Assicurativa
IFA	Majma'a al-Fiqh al-Islami (OIC)
IFA	Schweizerischer Interverband für Film und Audiovision
IFAA	Institute for African Alternatives
IFAA	International Federation of Advertising Agencies
IFAA	International Flight Attendants Association (U.S.A.)
IFAA	International Fossil Algae Association
IFABC	International Federation of Audit Bureaux of Circulations
IFAC	Institut des Fruits et Agrumes Coloniaux
IFAC	Institut Français d'Action Coopérative
IFAC	International Federation of Accountants
IFAC	International Federation of Advertising Clubs = FICP
IFAC	International Federation of Automatic Control
IFACAT	International Federation of ACAT = FIACAT
IFACS	Irish Farm Accounts Co-operative Society (Éire)
IFAD	International Fund for Agricultural Development = FIDA
IFADAP	Institúto Financeiro de Apoio ao Desenvolvimento da Agricultura e Pescas (Portugal)
IFAE	Interamerican Federation for Adult Education = FIDEA
IfAG	Institut für Angewandte Geodäsie
IFAJ	International Federation of Agricultural Journalists = FIJA
IfAL	Institut für Ausländische Landwirtschaft
IFAL	Institúto Frances de America Latina (Mexico)
IFALDA	International Federation of Air Line Despatchers Associations
IFALPA	International Federation of Air Line Pilots Associations
IFALS	International Federation of Arts, Letters and Sciences
IFAM	Institúto de Fomento y Asesoria Municipal (Costa Rica)
IFAM	Istituto di Fizica Atomica e Molecolare (Italy)
IFAN	Institut Fondamental d'Afrique Noire (Senegal)
IFAN	Institut Français d'Afrique Noire
IFAN	Internationale Föderation der Ausschusse Normenpraxis
IFAP	Industrie Africaine de Filets de Pêche
IFAP	Industrielle pour la Fabrication d'Articles en Plastiques (Ivory Coast)
IFAP	International Federation of Agricultural Producers = FIPA
IFAPA	International Federation of Adapted Physical Activity = FIAPA
IFAPA	International Foundation of Airlines Passengers Associations
IFAPAO	International Federation of Asian and Pacific Associations of Optometrists
IFAPO	Institut Français d'Archaeologie du Proche-Orient (Lebanon)
IFAPP	International Federation of the Associations of Pharmaceutical Physicians
IFAR	International Foundation for Art Research (U.S.A.)
IFARHU	Institúto para a Formación y Aprovechamiento de Recursos Humanos (Panama)
IFARSD	International Federation of Agricultural Research Systems for Development
IFAS	International Federation of Aquarium Societies
IFAS	International Federation of Associations of Specialists in Occupational Safety and Industrial Hygiene
IFAS	International Financial Advisory Service
IFAT	Institut Français d'Amérique Tropical (ORSTOM)

IFAT	International Federation of Alternative Trade (Netherlands)	**IFCC**	Intergovernmental Follow-Up and Coordination Committee of the Group of 77 on ECDC (U.S.A.)
IFATCA	International Federation of Air Traffic Controllers Associations	**IFCC**	International Federation of Camping and Caravanning = FICC
IFATCC	International Federation of Associations of Textile Chemists and Colourists	**IFCC**	International Federation of Children's Communities = FICE
IFATSEA	International Federation of Air Traffic Safety Electronic Associations	**IFCC**	International Federation of Clinical Chemistry = FICC
IFATU	International Federation of Arab Trade Unions	**IFCC**	Ireland-France Chamber of Commerce
IFAVWU	International Federation of Audio Visual Workers Unions = FISTAV, IFTUAVW	**IFCD**	International Federation of Catholic Dailies
IFAW	International Fund for Animal Welfare	**IFCE**	Institut Française des Combustibles et de l'Énergie
IFAWPCA	International Federation of Asian and Western Pacific Contractors Associations	**IFCE**	International Federation of Consulting Engineers = FIDIC
IFB	Independent Forward Block (Mauritius)	**IFCES**	International Federation of Comparative Endocrinological Societies
IFB	International Film Bureau	**IFCF**	Institut Français des Conseils Fiscaux
IFB	International Forum for Biophilosophy	**IFCG**	International Film Conciliation Group = GCIC
IFBA	International Fire Buff Associates		
IFBB	International Federation of Body Builders	**IFCH**	International Foundation for Cultural Harmony
IFBBF	Imported Fibre Building Board Federation	**IFCI**	Industrial Finance Corporation of India
IFBDO	International Federation of Blood Donors Organisations = FIODS	**IFCJ**	International Federation of Catholic Journalists
IFBE	International Federation of Asssociations of Business Economists	**IFCLA**	International Federation of Computer Law Associations (Belgium)
IFBPW	International Federation of Business and Professional Women = FIFCLC, FIMNP	**IFCM**	International Federation for Choral Music = FIMC
IFBSO	International Federation of Boat Show Organisers	**IFCMU**	International Federation of Christian Miners Unions = FISCM
IFBWW	International Federation of Building and Wood Workers = FITBB, FITCM, IBBH, IBTU	**IFCO**	International Fan Club Organization
		IFCO	International Fisheries Cooperative Organization
IFC	Industrial Finance Corporation (India)	**IFCO**	International Foster Care Organisation = OIPF
IFC	Institut Français du Caoutchouc		
IFC	International Facilitating Committee	**IFCO**	Interreligious Foundation for Community Organization (U.S.A.)
IFC	International Federation of Master-Craftsmen = FIA, IFH	**IFCP**	International Federation of Catholic Pharmacists = FIPC
IFC	International Finance Corporation (UN) = CFI, SFI	**IFCP**	International Federation of the Cinematographic Press = FIPRESCI
IFC	International Foundry Congress	**IFCPC**	International Federation for Cervical Pathology and Colposcopy
IFC	Irish Film Centre		
IFCA	International Federation of Catholic Alumnae	**IFCR**	International Foundation for Cancer Research
IFCAA	International Fire Chiefs Association of Asia	**IFCS**	International Federation for Computer Science
IFCB	International Federation of Cell Biology		
IFCC	Institut Français du Café, du Cacao et d'Autres Plantes Stimulantes (Ivory Coast)	**IFCS**	International Federation of Chopin Societies (Poland)

IFCS	International Federation of Classification Societies
IFCT	Industrial Finance Corporation of Thailand
IFCT	Institut Française de Coopération Technique
IFCTU	International Federation of Christian Trade Unions
IFCTU-BWW	International Federation of Christian Trade Unions of Building and Woodworkers = FISCOBB
IFCTUGPI	International Federation of Christian Trade Unions of Graphical and Paper Industries = ICPIGP
IFCU	International Federation of Catholic Universities = FIUC
IFCU	Irish Federation of Computer Users (Éire)
IFCW	International Forum for Child Welfare
IFCWAP	International Federation for Charming Worms and Allied Pastimes
IFD	International Federation for Documentation = FID
IFD	International Foundation for Dermatology (ILDS)
IFD	Internationale Föderation des Dachdeckerhandwerks = IFRC
IFDA	Independent Film Distributors Association
IFDA	Instock Footware Distributors Association
IFDA	International Federation of Data Processing Associations
IFDA	International Food Service Distributors Association (U.S.A.)
IFDA	International Foundation for Development Alternatives = FIPAD
IFDA	International Franchised Dealers Association
IFDAS	International Federation of Dental Anesthesiology Societies
IFDC	International Fertilizer Development Center (U.S.A.)
IFDO	International Federation of Data Organizations for the Social Sciences
IFDPES	International Fund for the Development of Physical Education and Sport = FIDEPS
IFE	Institut Français de l'Énergie
IFE	Institut für Technische Forschung und Entwicklung (Austria)
IFE	Institute of Fence Engineers
IFE	Institute of Freshwater Ecology
IFE	Institution of Fire Engineers
IFE	Institúto de Fomento Economico (Panama)
IFE	Institutt for Energiteknikk
IFE	Internationale Föderaton für Eisstockschiessen = IIFE
IFEA	Institut Français d'Études Andines (Peru)
IFEA	International Federation of Endodontic Associations (Mexico)
IFEA	International Federation of National Engineering Associations
IFEAT	International Federation of Essential Oils and Aroma Trades
IFEB	Institut Français d'Études Byzantines
IFEC	Institut Français de l'Emballage et du Conditionnement
IFEC	Institut Français des Experts Comptables
IFEC	International Foodservice Editorial Council (U.S.A.)
IFEC	International Foundation for Earth Construction (U.S.A.)
IFEC-UNCC	Institut Français des Experts-Comptables – Union Nationale des Commissaires aux Comptes
IFECYE	International Federation for Educative Children and Youth Exchanges = FIEEA, IVAB
IFEES	International Federation of Electro-Encephalographic Societies
IFEF	Internacia Fervojista Esperanto Federacio
IFEH	International Federation of Environmental Health
IFEH	International Federation of Europe Houses = FIME
IFEI	Institut Français d'Esthétique Industrielle
IFEIA	Institúto Franco-Ecuatoriano de Investigaciónes Agronómicas
IFEMS	International Federation of Electron Microscope Societies
IFEN	International Far-Eastern Numismatics (Belgium)
IFEO	International Federation of Eugenic Organizations
IFEP	Danish Electronics Reliability Institute

IFEPT	International Federation for Enteric Phage Typing
IFER	Fédération Internationale des Sociétés de Publicité Ferroviaire
IFER	Institute of Family & Environmental Research
IFER	Internationale Föderation des Eisenbahn-Reklame-Gesellschaften (Switzerland)
IFERS	International Flat Earth Society
IFES	Institute for Far Eastern Studies (South Korea)
IFES	International Federation of Exhibition Services
IFES	International Fellowship of Evangelical Students
IFES	International Flat Earth Society
IFET	International Federation of Employers and Technicians
IFET	International Federation of Equestrian Tourism
IFETI	Ipari Formatervezési és Ergonómiai Tanács Irodája (Hungary)
IFEW	Inter-American Federation of Entertainment Workers = FITE
IFF	Industriens Forskningsforening
IFF	Industrifarmaceutforeningen
IFF	Institut für Festkörperforschung
IFF	Institute for the Future (U.S.A.)
IFF	Institute of Freight Forwarders
IFF	Instrumenttekuiska Föreningen
IFF	International Fencing Federation
IFF	International Flying Farmers (U.S.A.)
IFF	International Freedom Foundation = FIL
IFFA	Immobilière et Financière France-Afrique
IFFA	Indigenous Flora and Fauna Association
IFFA	Institut for Fortstliche Arbeitswissenschaft
IFFA	Institut Français de la Fièvre Aphteuse
IFFA	International Federation of Film Archives = FIAF
IFFA	International Frozen Food Association
IfFANG	Institut für Fangtechnik
IFFCO	Indian Farmers Fertilizer Co-operative
IFFE	International Freedom Fund Establishment
IFFEC	International Federation of Free Evangelical Churches = IBFEG
IFFET	Institut Français du Film Educatif et Technique
IFFF	Internationale Frauenliga für Frieden und Freiheit = LIFPL, LIMPL, WILPF
IFFH	International Federation for Family Health
IFFI	Institut Français du Froid Industriel
IFFI	Institute of Freight Forwarders of Ireland
IFFJ	International Federation of Free Journalists = FIJL
IFFLP	International Federation for Family Life Promotion = FIDAF
IFFM	Institute of Fluid Flow Machinery (Poland)
IFFPA	International Federation of Film Producers' Associations = FIAPF
IFFS	International Federation of Fertility Societies
IFFS	International Federation of Film Societies
IFFSI	International Family Food Services
IFFTU	International Federation of Free Teachers' Unions = IVFL, SPIE
IFG	Instituto de Fisiografia y Geológica (Argentina)
IFG	International Federation of Glucose Industries
IFGA	International Federation of Grocers Associations = IVLD, UIDA
IFGI	International Federation of the Graphic Industries = FIIG
IFGMA	International Federation of Grocery Manufacturers Associations
IFGO	International Federation of Gynecology and Obstetrics = FIGO
IFGVP	International Federation of Gastronomical, Vinicultural and Touristic Press = FIPREGA, FISGV, IVGWP
IFH	Instituto de Filologia Hispánica
IFH	Internationale Föderation des Handwerks = FIA, IFC
IFHA	Irish Finance Houses Association (Éire)
IFHBT	International Federation of Health & Beauty Therapists
IFHE	International Federation of Home Economics = FIEF, IVHW
IFHE	International Federation of Hospital Engineering = FIIH

IFHOH	International Federation of the Hard of Hearing	**IFIC**	Irish Forests Industry Chain
IFHP	International Federation for Housing and Planning = FIHUAT, FIVU, IVWSR	**IFIE**	Instítuto Forestal de Investigaciones y Experiencias
IFHP	International Federation of Health Professionals	**IFIEC**	International Federation of Industrial Energy Consumers
IFHPSM	International Federation for Hygiene, Preventive and Social Medicine = FIHMPS	**IFIEC-Europe**	International Federation of Industrial Energy Consumers, Europe (Belgium)
		IFIF	International Feed Industry Federation
IFHR	International Federation of Human Rights = FIDH	**IFIF**	International Foundation for Inner Freedom
IFHRO	International Federation of Health Records Organisation	**IFIF**	Internationale Föderation von Industriegewerkschaften und Fabrikarbeiterverbänden
IFHSB	International Federation for Hydrocephalus and Spina Bifida	**IFIFR**	International Federation of International Furniture Removers = FIDI
IFHT	International Federation for Heat Treatment and Surface Engineering = AITT, IVW, MOTO	**IFIG**	Internationales Forschungs- und Informationszentrum für Gemeinwirtschaft = CIRIEC
IFHTM	International Federation for the Heat Treatment of Materials	**IFIJG**	International Federation of Infantile and Juvenile Gynaeology = FIGIJ
IFHTP	International Federation for Housing and Town Planning	**IFIP**	International Federation for Information Processing
IFI	Institut de Finance Internationale = IIF	**IFIPAC**	International Federation of Centers for Puppetry Arts
IFI	Instítuto de Fomento Industrial (Colombia)	**IFireE**	Institution of Fire Engineers
IFI	International Fabricare Institute (U.S.A.)	**IFIS**	International Food Information Service
IFI	International Federation of Interior Architects/ Interior Designers	**IFISRR**	International Federation of Institutes for Socio-Religious Research
IFI	International Film Institute (U.S.A.)	**IFITU**	Indian Federation of Independent Trade Unions
IFI	Islamic Foundation of Ireland	**IFJ**	Instytut Fizyki Jądrowej
IFI	Israel Furniture Industry	**IFJ**	International Federation of Journalists = FIJ, FIP, IJF
IFIA	Instítuto Forestal de Industrialización y Administración (Argentina)	**IFJU**	International Federation of Fruit Juice Producers = FIJU, FIJUG
IFIA	International Federation of Inventors' Associations	**IFK**	Industrieverbank Füllhalter und Kugelschreiber
IFIA	International Federation of Ironmongers and Iron Merchants Associations = FIDAF, FIDAQ, IVE	**IFKM**	Internationale Föderation für Kurzschrift und Maschinenschreiben = FISD, IFST, INTERSTENO
IFIA	International Fence Industry Association	**IFKT**	International Federation of Knitting Technologists = FITB, IFWS
IFIA	International Fertilizer Industry Association (France)	**IFKWVA**	International Federation of the Korean War Veterans' Associations (Republic of Korea)
IFIAS	International Federation of Institutes for Advanced Study		
IFIAT	International Federation of Independent Air Transport	**IFL**	Icelandic Federation of Labour
		IFL	Institute of Fluorescent Lighting
IFIC	International Ferrocement Information Centre (Thailand)	**IFL**	Institutet för Företagsledning
IFIC	International Fire Information Conference	**IFL**	International Federational of Lithographers, Process Workers and Kindred Trades

IFL	International Friendship League	**IFMI**	Irish Federation of Marine Industries
IFLA	Institúto Forestal Latinoamericano (FAO) (Venezuela)	**IFMLL**	International Federation for Modern Languages and Literatures = FILLM
IFLA	International Federation of Landscape Architects = FIAP	**IFMMS**	International Federation of Mining and Metallurgical Students
IFLA	International Federation of Library Associations and Institutions = FIAB	**IFMP**	International Federation for Medical Psychotherapy = FIPM, IGAP
IFLA	International Finance and Leasing Association	**IFMP**	International Federation of Maritime Philately
IFLAIC	Institúto Forestal Latinoamericano de Investigación y Capacitación	**IFMS**	International Federation of Magical Societies = FISM
IFLB	Islamic Front for the Liberation of Bahrain	**IFMSA**	International Federation of Medical Student Associations = FIAEM
IFLRY	International Federation for Liberal Radical Youth = FIJLR	**IFMSS**	International Federation of Multiple Sclerosis Societies
IFLS	Institut Français de Libre Service	**IFN**	Institut Français de Navigation
IFLV	Institut Français de Langues Vivantes	**IFN**	International Feminist Network
IFM	Initiative for Peace and Human Rights (Germany)	**IFN**	International Friends of Nature = IAN, NFI
IFM	Institute of Factory Management	**IFNA**	International Federation of Netball Associations
IFM	Institute of Fisheries Management	**IFNA**	International Federation of Nonlinear Analysts
IFM	Instytut Fizyki Molekularnej (PAN)	**IFNA**	International FidoNet Association = FIDONET
IFM	International Association of Infant Food Manufacturers	**IFNAES**	International Federation of the National Associations of Engineering Students = FIANEI
IFM	International Falcon Movement		
IFM	International Federation of Musicians	**IFNGO**	International Federation of Non-Governmental Organisations for the Prevention of Drug and Substance Abuse
IFM	International Fund for Monuments		
IFM-SEI	International Falcon Movement/ Socialist Educational International = MIF/IES	**IFNSA**	International Federation of the National Standardizing Association
IFMA	Independent Furniture Manufacturers' Association	**IFO**	Institut für Wirtschaftforschung
IFMA	Institutional Fund Managers Association	**IFO**	Institute for Fermentation (Japan)
IFMA	International Farm Management Association	**IFO**	International Farmers Organization
		IFO	International Fortran Organisation
IFMA	International Federation of Margarine Associations	**IFO**	Irish Fishermen's Organisation (Éire)
IFMA	International Foodservice Manufacturers Association (U.S.A.)	**IFOAD**	International Federation of Original Art Diffusers
IFMA	Internationale Fahrrad- und Motorrad-Ausstellung	**IFOAM**	International Federation of Organic Agricultural Movements
IFMA	Irish Fireplace Manufacturers' Association (Éire)	**IFOCAP**	Institut de Formation pour des Cadres Paysans
IFMA	Irish Flour Millers Association	**IFOFSAG**	International Fellowship of Former Scouts and Guides = AIDSEGA
IFMAP	Irish Federation of Musicians and Associated Professions	**IFOG**	International Federation of Olive Growers
IFMBE	International Federation for Medical and Biological Engineering		
IFME	International Federation of Municipal Engineers = FIIM	**IFOMT**	International Federation of Orthopaedic Manipulative Therapists

Ifona	Instítuto Forestal Nacional (Argentina)	**IFPI**	International Federation of Phonogram and Videogram Producers
IFOP	Institut Français d'Opinion Publique	**IFPI**	International Federation of the Phonographic Industry
IFOP	Instítuto de Fomento Pesqueras (Chile)		
IFOR	International Fellowship of Reconciliation = MIR	**IFPIA**	Independent Film Producers International Association = FIPFI
IFORD	Institut de Formation et de Recherche Démographique (RIPS) (Cameroon)	**IFPLAA**	Internationale Föderation der Plantagen, Land- und Anverwandten Arbeiter = FITPAS, FITPASC, IFPLAA
IFORS	International Federation of Operational Research Societies	**IFPMA**	International Federation of Pharmaceutical Manufacturers Associations = FIIM
IFOS	International Federation of Opthalmological Societies		
IFOS	International Federation of Oto-Rhino-Laryngological Societies	**IFPMM**	International Federation of Purchasing and Materials Management
IFOSA	International Federation of Stationers Associations	**IFPMO**	International Federation of Psychological-Medical Organizations = FIOPM, IVPMO
IFOTES	International Federation of Telephonic Emergency Services	**IFPMR**	International Federation of Physical Medicine and Rehabilitation = FIMFR, FIMPR
IFP	Institut Français de Polémologie		
IFP	Institut Français du Pétrole	**IFPO**	Irish Fish Producers' Organisation (Éire)
IFP	International Federation of Pedestrians = FIP	**IFPP**	International Federation of the Periodical Press
IFP	International Federation of Periodicals		
IFPA	Industrial Fire Protection Association of Great Britain	**IFPRA**	Inter-American Federation of Public Relations Associations = CONFIARP
IFPA	Information Film Producers of America	**IFPRA**	International Federation of Park and Recreation Administration
IFPA	Inter-American Federation of Personnel Administration	**IFPRI**	International Food Policy Research Institute (U.S.A.)
IFPA	International Federation of Photographic Art	**IFPS**	International Federation of Palynological Societies
IFPA	International Federation of Psoriasis Associations	**IFPS**	International Federation of Philosophical Societies = FISP
IFPA	International Fire Photographers Association	**IFPS**	International Federation of Popular Sports = IVV
IFPA	International Physical Fitness Association	**IFPS**	International Federation Psychoanalytic Societies
IFPA	Irish Family Planning Association		
IFPAAW	International Federation of Plantation, Agricultural and Allied Workers = FITPAS, FITPASC, IFPLAA	**IFPTE**	International Federation of Professional Technical Engineers
		IFPTO	International Federation of Popular Travel Organisations
IFPC	International Fair Play Committee = CIFP	**IFPWA**	International Federation of Public Warehousing Associations
IFPCS	International Federation of Unions of Employees in Public and Civil Services	**IFR**	Indian Famine Relief
IFPCW	International Federation of Petroleum and Chemical Workers = FITPC, FITPQ, IVPC	**IFR**	Institute of Food Research
		IFR	International Federation for Robotics
		IFR	International Federation of Religious
IFPE	International Federation for Parent Education = FIEP	**IFR**	International Federation of Ropemakers (Germany)
IFPEA	Irish Fish Processors' and Exporters' Association (Éire)	**IFR**	Internationaler Frauenrat = CIDEM, CIF, ICW

IFRA	INCA-FIEJ Research Association	**IFRWH**	International Federation for Research in Women's History (ICHS) (Norway) = FIRHF
IFRA	Independent Footware Retailers Association	**IFS**	Institute for Fiscal Studies
IFRA	International Fragrance Association (Switzerland)	**IFS**	International Family Service for Overseas Students
IFRA	International Fund-Raising Association (U.S.A.)	**IFS**	International Federation of Settlements and Neighbourhood Centres
IFRAA	International Federation of Regional Airlines Associations	**IFS**	International Federation of Surveyors = FIG
IFRAC	Intenational Federation of Railway Advertising Company	**IFS**	International Fertilizers Supply Scheme
IFRACI	Institut de Formation et de Recherches Appliquées en Côte d'Ivoire	**IFS**	International Film Seminars
IFRB	Institute of Food and Radiation Biology (Bangladesh)	**IFS**	International Foundation for Science (UNESCO) = FIS
IFRB	International Frequency Registration Board (ITU)	**IFSA**	Institut Français des Sciences Administratives
IFRC	Independent Food Retailers' Confederation	**IFSA**	Instock Footware Suppliers Association
IFRC	International Federation of Roofing Contractors = IFD	**IFSA**	International Federation of Sports Acrobatics
IFRC	International Fusion Research Council	**IFSA**	International Fuzzy Systems Association
IFREMER	Institut Française de Recherche pour l'Exploitation de la Mer	**IFSA**	Intumescent Fire Seals Association
IFRF	International Flame Research Foundation	**IFSA**	Irish Federation of Sea Anglers (Éire)
IFRH	International Fellowship for Research in Hymnology = IAH	**IFSC**	International Federation of Sports Chiropractic (U.S.A.) = FICS
IFRI	Institut Français des Relations Internationales	**IFSCC**	International Federation of Societies of Cosmetic Chemists
IFRI	Islamic Federation of Research Institutes	**IFSCE**	International Federation of Sport in Catholic Education = FISEC
IFRIMA	International Federation of Risk and Insurance Management Associations (U.S.A.)	**IFSCS**	International Federation of the Societies of Classical Studies (Switzerland) = FIEC
IFRINF	Iraqi Front of Revolutionary Islamic and National Forces	**IFSD**	International Fund Sports Disabled
IFRM	Institute of Fund Raising Managers	**IFSDA**	International Federation of Stamp Dealers Associations
IFROA	Institut Français de Restauration des Oeuvres d'Art	**IFSDP**	International Federation of the Socialist and Democratic Press
IFRP	International Fertility Research Program	**IFSE**	International Federation of Scientific Editors
IFRPD	Institute of Food Research and Product Development (Thailand)	**IFSE**	International Federation of Stock Exchanges = FIBV
IFRRO	International Federation of Reproduction Rights Organisations	**IFSEA**	International Food Service Executives Association (U.S.A.)
IFRS	International Fisheries Research Society (Japan)	**IFSECN**	International Federation of Societies for Electroencephalography and Clinical Neurophysiology
IFRU	Institut Français du Royaume-Uni	**IFSEM**	International Federation of Societies for Electron Microscopy
IFRW	International Federation of Resistance Workers	**IFSH**	Institut für Friedensforschung und Sicherheitspolitik, Hamburg

IFSHC	International Federation of Societies of Histochemistry and Cytochemistry
IFSHT	International Federation of Societies of Hand Therapists
IFSI	International Foundation for Social Innovation = FIIS
IFSISR	International Federation of Societies and Institutes for the Study of the Renaissance = FISIER
IFSL	Irish Foundry Services Ltd
IFSM	International Federation of Sportive Medicine = FIMS
IFSMA	International Federation of Ship Master Associations
IFSMC	International Federation of Small Medium-Sized Commercial Enterprises = FIPMEC, IVKMH
IFSMI	International Federation of Small Medium-Sized Industrial Enterprises = FIPMI, IVKMI
IFSMP	International Federation of Serious Music Publishers
IFSP	International Federation of Societies of Philosophy
IFSPO	International Federation of Senior Police Officers = FIFSP
IFSPS	International Federation of Students in Political Science = FIESP
IFSR	International Federation for Systems Research
IFSRC	International Financial Services Research Center (U.S.A.)
IFSS	International Federation of Sled-dog Sports = ISDRA
IFSSH	International Federation of Societies for Surgery of the Hand
IFSSO	International Federation of Social Science Organizations = FIOSS
IFST	Institute of Food Science and Technology
IFST	International Federation of Secondary Teachers = FIPESO
IFST	International Federation of Shorthand and Typewriting = FISD, IFKM, INTERSTENO
IFST	International Federation of the Seed Trade = FIS
IFSTA	International Fire Service Training Association
IFSTAD	Islamic Foundation for Science, Technology and Development (OIC) = FISTED
IFSTD	Interim Fund for Science and Technology for Development
IFSW	International Federation of Social Workers
IFT	Institute for Family Therapy
IFT	Institute of Food Technologists (U.S.A.)
IFT	Institute of Foreign Trade (Éire)
IFT	International Federation of Translators = FIT
IFT	International Federation of Triathlon = FIT, ITU
IFTA	International Federation of Teachers Associations = FIAI, IVL
IFTA	International Federation of Television Archives = FIAT
IFTA	International Federation of Thanatologists Associations = FIAT
IFTA	International Fine Technics Association
IFTAC	Interamerican Federation of Touring and Automobile Clubs = FITAC
IFTC	International Council for Film Television and Audiovisual Communication = CICT
IFTC	International Federation of Thermalism and Climatism = FITEC
IFTC	International Federation of Tourist Centres = FICT
IFTC	International Federation Textile and Clothing (WCL) = FIIV, FITH
IFTDH	International Federation Terre des Hommes
IFTDO	International Federation of Training Development Organizations
IFTF	International Federation of Teachers of French = FIPF
IFTF	International Fur Trade Federation
IFTIM	Institut de Formation des Techniques d'Implantation et Manutention
IFTJW	International Federation of Travel Journalists and Writers = FIJET
IFTM	International Federation for Tropical Medicine
IFTO	International Federation of Tour Operators
IFTOMM	International Federation for the Theory of Machines and Mechanisms
IFTPP	International Federation of the Technical and Periodical Press
IFTR	Institute of Fundamental Technological Research POL)

IFTR	International Federation for Theatre Research = FIRT		**IFWTA**	International Federation of Workers Travel Associations
IFTS	Institut Français des Transports Aériens		**IFWTO**	International Federation of Women's Travel Organisations
IFTTA	International Forum of Travel and Tourism Advocates		**IFWWO**	International Federation of Widows' and Widowers' Organizations = FIAV
IFTUAVW	International Federation of Trade Unions of Audio-Visual Workers = FISTAV, IFAVWU		**IFYC**	International Federation of Young Cooperators
IFTUTCI	International Federation of Trade Unions for the Textile and Clothing Industries = FISTH		**IFYE**	International Farm Youth Exchange
			IG	Institute of Groundsmanship
IFTUTW	International Federation of Trade Unions of Transport Workers = FIOST, IFVV		**IG**	Institution of Geologists
			IG	Instytut Geologiczny
IFU	Industrialiseringsfonden for Udviklingslandene		**IG**	Interessengemeinschaft Deutschprachiger Sudwester (Namibia)
IFUC	Interprovincial Farm Union Council (Canada)		**IG**	International Graphics
			IG	Internationale Gerbervereinigung = CIC, CIT, ICT
IFUNA	Indian Federation of United Nations Associations		**IG&GA**	International Grooving and Grinding Association
IFUT	Irish Federation of University Teachers		**IGA**	Industrie-Gemeinschaft Aerosole
IFUW	International Federation of University Women = FIFDU, FIMU		**IGA**	Inspection Générale de l'Agriculture
			IGA	Institute of Group Analysis
IFUW	Irish Federation of University Women		**IGA**	Interessen-Gemeinschaft Aerosole
IFUWA	Indian Federation of University Women's Associations		**IGA**	International Gay Association
			IGA	International General Aviation
IFV	Internationaler Faustball Verband		**IGA**	International Geneva Association (U.S.A.)
IFVA	International Federation of Variety Artistes = FIAV		**IGA**	International Geographical Association
IFVHSF	International Federation of Voluntary Health Service Funds		**IGA**	International Geothermal Association
			IGA	International Glaucoma Association
IFVPA	Independent Film, Video and Photographers Association		**IGA**	International Goat Association = AID
IFVTCC	Internationale Föderation der Vereine der Textilchemiker und Coloristen		**IGA**	International Gold Association
			IGA	International Golf Association
IFVV	Internationale Federatie van Vakorganisaties van Vervoerspersoneel = FIOST, IFTUTW		**IGA**	International Grenfell Association
			IGA	Irish Gas Association (Éire)
			IGA	Irish Grassland Association
IFW	Institut für Fertigungstechnik und Spanende Werkzeugmaschinen (Germany)		**IGAC**	Instituto Geográfico "Augustín Codazzi" (Colombia)
IFWC	Irish Federation of Women's Clubs		**IGACSM**	Intergovernmental Advisory Committee on Surveying and Mapping (*now* ICSM)
IFWEA	International Federation of Workers Educational Associations = FIAET, IVA		**IGADD**	Intergovernmental Authority of Drought and Development (Djibouti)
IFWL	International Federation of Women Lawyers = FIDA		**IGAE**	Intervencion General del Estado
IFWLC	International Federation of Women in Legal Careers = FIFCJ		**IGAEA**	International Graphic Arts Education Association (U.S.A.)
IFWRI	Institute of Furniture Warehousing and Removal Industry		**IGAEF**	International Gerda Alexander Eutony Federation = FIEGA
IFWS	Internationale Föderation von Wirkerei- und Strickerei-Fachleuten = FITB, IFKT		**IGAeM**	Internationale Gesellschaft für Aerosole in der Medizin = ISAeM, ISAM

IGAFA	Internationale Gastronomie-und Fremdenverkehrs-Austellung
IGAL	Welt Interessen Gemeinschaft Alterer Langstveeken Läufer
IGAM	Internationale Gesellschaft für Allgemeinmedizin = ISGP, SIMG
IGAP	Institute for Grassland and Animal Production (AFRC)
IGAP	Internationale Gesellschaft für Ärztliche Psychotherapie = FIPM, IFMP
IGAPHE	Instit́uto de Gestão e Alienação do Patŕimonio Habiticional do Estado
IGAS	Institute of Geochemistry, Academia Sinica
IGAS	International Graphoanalysis Society
IGB	International Gravimetric Bureau (FAGS) = BGI
IGB	Internationaler Genossenschaftsbund = ACI, ICA, MKA
IGBA	Irish-German Business Association
IGBE	Institut Gosudarstvennykh Bukhgalterov-Ekspertov
IGBP	Scientific Committee for the International Geosphere-Biosphere Programme (Sweden)
IGC	Institute for Global Communications
IGC	Institute for Graphic Communication (U.S.A.)
IGC	Institute of Guidance Counsellors (Éire)
IGC	Institutional Grants Committee
IGC	Instit́uto Geografico e Cadastral (Portugal)
IGC	Inter-Government Copyright Committee
IGC	International Garden Centre Association
IGC	International Garden Club
IGC	International Geoid Commission (IAG)
IGC	International Glaucoma Committee
IGC	International Glaucoma Congress
IGC	International Grassland Congress
IGC	International Green Cross = CVI
IGC	International Guides Club
IGC	Irish Goods Council
IGC	UN/FAO Intergovernmental Committee = CIG
IGCA	International Garden Centres Association
IGCAGS	Institute of Geology, Chinese Academy of Geological Sciences
IGCAS	Institute of Geology, Academia Sinica
IGCC	Intergovernmental Coordinating Committee for Population and Family Planning in Southeast Asia = CIGC
IGCC	Intergovernmental Copyright Committee = CIDA,
IGCC	University of California Institute on Global Conflict and Cooperation
IGCCT	Inter-Governmental Commission for Cooperation of Socialist Countries in the field of Computer Technology = ESER
IGCESTD	Intergovernmental Committee of Experts on Science and Technology Development (ECA)
IGCI	Industrial Gas Cleaning Institute (U.S.A.)
IGCI	Internationale Gesellschaft für Chemo- und Immunotherapie
IGCJAP	International Guild of Craft Journalists Authors and Photographers
IGCO	Intergovernmental Copper Organisation
IGCP	International Geological Correlation Programme (IUGS and UNESCO) = PICG
IGCPA	International Group of Catholic Parents' Associations = GIAPEC
IGCPES	Intergovernmental Committee for Physical Education and Sport (UNESCO)
IGCR	Instit́uto Geográfico de Costa Rica
IGCS	International Gynecologic Cancer Society
IGCSTD	Intergovernmental Committee on Science and Technology for Development (UN)
IGD	Institute of Grocery Distribution
IGDP	Institut Gigieny Detei i Podrostkov
IGE	Institution of Gas Engineers
IGE	International Guiding Eyes (U.S.A.)
IGEGM	Internationale Gesellschaft zur Erforschung von Grenzgebieten der Medizin
IGEME	Ihracati Gelistirme Etüd Merkezi (Export Promotion Research Centre) (Turkey)
IGEN	Institut Genetiki
IGEPA	Internationall Gewerkschaft im Europäischen Patentamt = SUEPO, USOEB
IGER	Institut Nationale de Gestion et d'Économie Rurale

IGER	Institute of Grassland and Environmental Research (AFRC)
IGF	International Foundation for the Conservation of Wildlife
IGF	International Genetics Federation
IGF	International Graphical Federation = FGI
IGF	International Gymnastic Federation = FIG, ITB
IGFA	International Game Fish Association
IGFA	International Group of Funding Agencies for Global Change Research
IGFA	Irish Grain and Feed Association (Éire)
IGFAP	International Gesellschaft für Analytische Psychologie = AIPA, IAAP
IGFP	International Gemeinschaft für Psychologie (Switzerland)
IGFRI	Indian Grassland and Fodder Institute
IGG	Institute of Geodesy and Geophysics (China)
IGG	Instituut voor Grondwater en Geo-Energie TNO (Netherlands)
IGGD	Institut Geologii i Geokhronologii Dokembriia
IGGE	Institute of Geophysical and Geochemical Exploration (China)
IGGI	Intergovernmental Group on Indonesia
IGGT	Institute for Guided Ground Transport (Canada)
IGI	Groupement International des Fabricants de Revétements Muraux
IGIA	Institut de Gestion Internationale Agro-Alimentaire
IGiK	Instytut Geodezji i Kartografii
IGiO	Instytut Głuchoniemych i Ociemniałych
IGIP	Internationale Gesellschaft für Ingenieurpädagogik (Austria)
IGJ	Internationale Gesellschaft für Jazzforschung
IGK	Ingenieurgemeinschaft Kernverfahrenstechnik
IGK	Instytut Gospodarki Komunalnej
IGL	Institut Gramme de Liège (Belgium)
IGLA	International Gay and Lesbian Association
IGLD	International Grand Lodge of Druidism
IGLS	Institute of Government Land Surveyors
IGLU	Institute of University Management and Leadership; Institúto de Gestion y de Lideração (IOME)
IGLYO	International Lesbian and Gay Youth Organization (Netherlands)
IGM	Institúto Geográfico Militar (Argentina)
IGM	Institúto Geografico Militare (Italy)
IGM	Institúto Geográfico Militare (Paraguay)
IGM	Internationale Gesellschaft für Menschenrechte = AIDH, ISHR, SIDH
IGM	Internationale Gesellschaft für Moorforschung
IGM/WCP	Intergovernmental Negotiating Committee for Framework Convention on Climate Change
IGMAA	International Gas Model Airplane Association (U.S.A.)
IGMB	Insituut voor Graan, Meel en Brood
IGME	Institute of Geology and Mineral Exploration (Greece)
IGMER	International Genootschap voor Medische Endoskopie en Röntgenkinematografie
IGMG	Internationale Gustav Mahler Gesellschaft = IGMS
IGMR	Tianjin Institute of Geology and Mineral Resources
IGMS	International Gustav Mahler Society = IGMG
IGMW	Internationale Gesellschaft für Musikwissenschaft = IMS, SIM
IGN	Institut Géographique National
IGN	Institúto Geográfica Nacional (El Salvador, Guatemala, Honduras, Panama, Peru)
IGN	Institúto Geológico Nacional (Colombia)
IGNC	International Good Neighbour Council = CIBV
IGNiG	Instytut Gornictwa Naftowego i Gazownictwa (Poland)
IGNM	Internationale Gesellschaft für Neue Musik
IGNOU	Indira Gandhi National Open University (India)
IGO	International Guild of Opticians
IGOSS	Integrated Global Ocean Services System = SGIEO, SGISO, SMISO
IGÖV	Interessengemeinschaft Öffentlicher Verkehr
IGP	Grossistforeningen for Isenkram-, Glas- og Porcelænstranchen
IGP	Institute of State and Law, Russian Academy of Sciences

IGP	Instítuto Geofisico del Perú	**IGT**	Institute of Gas Technology (U.S.A.)
IGP	International Guild of Prestidigitators	**IGTC**	International Gas Turbine Center
IGPA	International General Produce Association	**IGTC**	International Glutamate Technical Committee = CITAG
IGPAI	Inspeção-General dos Produtes Agricolas e Industrias	**IGTechE**	Institution of General Technician Engineers
IGPF	Internationale Gesellschaft für Photogrammetrie und Fernerkundung = ISPRS, SIPT	**IGTI**	ASME International Gas Turbine Institute (U.S.A.)
IGPHA	Instítuto Goiano de Pré-História e Antropologia (Brazil)	**IGU**	International Gas Union = UIIG
IGPP	Institute of Geophysics and Planetary Physics	**IGU**	International Geographical Union = UGI
IGPRAD	Intergovernmental Panel on Radioactive Waste	**IGU**	International Geophysical Union
IGQL	Internationale Gesellschaft für Quantitative Linguistik = IQLA	**IGU**	Internationale Gewerbeunion = IACME, UIAPME
IGR	Instytut Genetyki Roślin	**IGUS**	International Group of Experts on the Explosion Risks of Unstable Substances (OECD)
IGROF	International Rorschach-Gesellschaft = IRS, SIR		
IGRS	Irish Genealogical Research Society	**IGV**	Internationaler Gemeindeverband = IULA, UIV
IGS	Association de l'Industrie Graphique Suisse	**IGVF**	Institut Grazhdanskogo Vozdushnogo Flota
IGS	Institute of General Semantics (U.S.A.)	**IGVF**	Internationale Genossenschaftliche Versicherungs-Föderation = FICA, FISC, ICIF
IGS	Institute of Geological Studies (NERC)		
IGS	Instytut Gospodarstwa Społecznego	**IGW**	Instytut Gospodarki Wodnej
IGS	Interessengemeinschaft Schweizerischer Standbaufirmen	**IGW**	Interessengemeinschaft für Weltraumforschung
IGS	Interessengemeinschaft Silberwaren	**IGWF**	International Garment Workers' Federation
IGS	International Geosynthetics Society		
IGS	International Geotextile Society	**IGWMC**	International Ground Water Modelling Center (U.S.A.)
IGS	International Geranium Society	**IGWT**	Internationale Gesellschaft für Warenkunde und Technologie = IACST
IGS	International Glaciological Society		
IGS	International Graphoanalysis Society	**IGZa**	Institut Géographique du Zaïre
IGS	International Graphonomics Society	**IH**	Institute of Horticulture
IGS	Irish Georgian Society	**IH**	Institute of Hydrology (NERC)
IGS	Irish Graphical Society	**IH**	Instítuto Hidrografico (Chile, Portugal)
IGS	Israel Geographical Society	**IHA**	Independent Healthcare Association
IGS	Israel Gerontological Society	**IHA**	Independent Hospitals Association
IGSC	International Group for Scientific Coordination (U.S.A.)	**IHA**	Instítuto Hidrografico de la Armada (Chile)
IGSP	Internationale Gesellschaft der Schriftpsychologie = IHPS, SIPE, SIPS	**IHA**	International H-Boat Association
		IHA	International Horse Association
IGSQ	Institute of Geological Sciences, Qinghai Province (China)	**IHA**	International Hotel Association = AIH
		IHA	Irish Hardware Association
IGSRP	Internationale Gesellschaft der Stadt und Regionplaner = AIU, ISOCARP	**IHA**	Issuing Houses Association
		IHAIO	International Historical Association of the Indian Ocean
IGSS	Instítuto Guatemalteco de Seguridad Social	**IHAN**	International Health Awareness Network

IHAP	International Human Assistance Programs	**IHEA**	Industrial Heating Equipment Association (U.S.A.)
IHAR	Instytut Hodowli i Aklimatyzacji Roślin	**IHEA**	Institut des Hautes Études Agraires
IHAROA	IHA Regional Organization of Africa = ORAIHA	**IHEA**	Irish-Hungarian Economic Association (Éire)
IHAS	Institute for the History of Arabic Science (Syria)	**IHEB**	International Heat Economy Bureau
		IHEc	Institute of Home Economics
IHASA	International Hotel Association South Asia (IHA)	**IHEDREA**	Institut des Hautes Études de Droit Rural et d'Économie Agricole
IHB	Internationale Hopfenbaubüro = CICH, IHGC	**IHEES**	Institut Européen des Hautes Études Économiques et Sociales
IHBA	Individual House Builders' Association	**IHEG-CAGS**	Institute of Hydrogeology and Science Engineering Geology, Chinese Academy of Geological Science
IHBA	Irish Home Builders' Association (Éire)		
IHBC	International Health and Beauty Council	**IHES**	Illinois Horticultural Experiment Station (U.S.A.)
IHBPA	International Hepato-Biliary-Pancreatic Association (U.S.A.)	**IHEU**	International Humanist and Ethical Union = UIHL
IHBR	Institut Historique Belge de Rome	**IHF**	International Handball Federation = FIH
IHBS	International Hajji Baba Society	**IHF**	International Health Foundation
IHBS	Irish Hereford Breed Society	**IHF**	International Helsinki Federation for Human Rights
IHC	Industrieele Handelscombinatie		
IHC	Infantile Hypercalcaemia Foundation	**IHF**	International Hockey Federation = FIH
IHC	International Health Council	**IHF**	International Hospital Federation = FIH, IKV
IHC	International Help for Children		
IHC	International Hydrochemical Commission	**IHF**	Irish Hairdressers Federation
		IHF	Irish Heart Foundation
IHCA	Instítuto Histórico Centroamericano	**IHF**	Irish Hotels Federation (Éire)
IHCA	International Hobie Class Association	**IHFA**	Industrial Hygiene Foundation of America
IHCA	Irish Hospital Consultantss Association		
IHCAFE	Instítuto Hondureño del Café	**IHFC**	International Heat Flow Commission (IAPSO, IASPEI, IAVCEI)
IHCI	Irish Hotel and Catering Institute		
IHCSERS	International Health Centre of Socio-Economic Research and Studies = CIERSES	**IHFHR**	International Helsinki Federation for Human Rights
		IHFPA	Instítuto de Higiene y Fomento de la Producción Animal (Chile)
IHD	Institut Henry-Dunant (Switzerland) = HDI		
		IHFR	Institute of Health Food Retailing
IHD	Institute Of Human Development (U.S.A.)	**IHG**	Industrieverband Hausgeräte
		IHG	Institute on the Holocaust and Genocide
IHD	International Hydrological Decade (UNESCO)	**IHGB**	Instítuto Histórico e Geográfico Brasileiro
IHDER	Instítuto Hondureño de Desarrollo Rural	**IHGC**	International Hop Growers Convention = CICH, IHB
IHDP	Independent Hungarian Democratic Party		
		IHGS	Institute of Heraldic and Genealogical Studies
IHE	Industry, Human Settlements and Environment Division (ESCAP)	**IHHA**	International Halfway House Association (U.S.A.)
IHE	Institute of Health Education		
IHE	International Institute for Hydraulic and Environmental Engineering	**IHHO**	Institute of Home Health Organisers (*now* BADCO)
IHE	International Institute for Hydrologic and Environmental Engineering	**IHIE**	Institute of Highway Incorporated Engineers

IHJHCA	International Messianic Jewish/Hebrew Christian/Alliance	**IHRMA**	Irish Hotel and Restaurant Managers' Association
IHK	Internationale Handelskammer = CCI, ICC	**IHS**	Indiana Historical Society
IHKM	Instytut Historii Kultury Materialnej	**IHS**	Institute of Human Sciences (U.S.A.)
IHL	International Hockey League	**IHS**	International Headache Society
IHL	International Homeopathic League = LHI	**IHS**	International Health Society
		IHS	International Herpetological Society
IHLADI	Instítuto Hispano-Luso-Americano de Derecho Internacional	**IHS**	International Horn Society
		IHS	International Hydrofoil Society
IHM	Sisters Servants of the Immaculate Heart of Mary of Scranton	**IHSA**	Institute of Health Service Administrators
IHMA	Instítuto Hondureña de Mercadeo Agrícola (Honduras)	**IHSA**	Inversiones Husascaran S.A. (Peru)
		IHSGB	Icelandic Horse Society of Great Britain
IHMB	Industrie des Huiles Minérales de Belgique	**IHSM**	Institute of Health Services Management
IHN	International Heart Network	**IHSM**	Institute of Hotel Security Management
IHO	International Hydrographic Organisation = OHI	**IHSMI**	Irish Health Services Management Institute (Éire)
IHOA	Independent Hostel Owners Association	**IHSPRG**	International Herbage Seed Production Research Group
IHospE	Institute of Hospital Engineering		
IHP	Intergovernmental Council of the International Hydrological Programme (UNESCO) = PHI	**IHSRC**	International Heat Stress Research Centre (Sudan)
		IHT	Institution of Highways and Transportation
IHPA	Irish Hydro Power Association (Éire)	**IHTA**	International Health and Temperance Association
IHPC	International Pacific Halibut Commission (Canada and U.S.A.)	**IHU**	Irish Hockey Union
IHPMI	International Health Policy and Management Institute	**IHW**	Instytut Handlu Wewnętrznego
		IHW	International Herpes-virus Workshop
IHPRS	International Husserl & Phenomenological Research Society	**II**	Ikebana International
IHPS	International Handwriting Psychology Society = ISSP, SIPE, SIPS	**II**	Inheritance International (Switzerland)
		II	Institute of Inventors
IHPST	Institute for the History and Philosophy of Science and Technology (AN)	**II**	Ittehad-i Islami (Afghanistan) = IU
		IIA	Information Industry Association
IHPVA	International Human Powered Vehicle Association	**IIA**	Institut International d'Anthropologie
		IIA	Institute of Industrial Archaeology
IHR	Institute for Historical Review (U.S.A.)	**IIA**	Institute of Internal Auditors (Éire, U.K., U.S.A.)
IHR	Institute of Historical Research (South Africa, U.K.)	**IIA**	Institute of International Auditors
IHR	Institute of Horticultural Research (AFRC)	**IIA**	Instituto de Investigaciones Agronomicas (Guatemala)
IHRA	Indonesian Hotel and Restaurant Association	**IIA**	Instítuto de Investigaxiones Agropecuárias (Chile)
IHRA	International Hot Rod Association	**IIA**	International Imagery Association
IHRB	International Hockey Rules Board	**IIA**	International Institute for Africa
IHRC	Immigration History Research Center (U.S.A.)	**IIA**	International Institute of Andragogy (IFAE) (Venezuela) = INSTIA
IHRIP	International Human Rights Internship Programme	**IIA**	International Investments Association
		IIA	Irish Insurance Association

IIA	Istituto Italiano degli Attuari	**IIBEM**	Indian Institute of Biochemistry and Experimental Medicine
IIa RAN	Institute of Linguistics, Russian Academy of Sciences	**IIBH**	International Institute of Biological Husbandry
IIAA	Independent Insurance Agents of America	**IIBR**	Israel Institute for Biological Research
IIAA	Institute of Inter-American Affairs (UN)	**IIC**	India International Centre
IIAA	InstIt́uto de Investigação Agronomica de Angola	**IIC**	Institute of Insurance Consultants
		IIC	InstIt́uto de Ingeneiros de Chile
IIAA	Instit́uto International de Asuntos Ambientales	**IIC**	Instituto de Investigación Cientifica (Mexico)
IIAC	Industrial Injuries Advisory Council	**IIC**	International Indigenous Commission
IIACE	Instituto de Investigaciones Aplicades de Ciencias Espaciales (Argentina)	**IIC**	International Institute for Cotton (U.S.A.)
IIAG	Institut für Angewandt Geodesie	**IIC**	International Institute for the Conservation of Historic and Artistic Works
IIAI	Indian Institution of Art in Industry		
IIAI	Instit́uto de Investigaciones Agroindustriales (Peru)	**IIC**	International Institute of Communications
IIAI	International Institute of American Ideals	**IIC**	Istituto Internazionale delle Communicazioni
IIALM	International Institute of Adult Literacy Methods	**IICA**	Institute of Instrumentation and Control, Australia
IIAM	Institut de la Recherche Agronomique Mozambique	**IICA**	Instit́uto de Investigação Cientifica de Angola
IIAP	Institut International d'Administration Publique	**IICA**	Instit́uto Interamericano de Ciencias Agrícolas, San José (Costa Rica)
IIAR	International Institute of Ammonia Refrigeration (U.S.A.)	**IICA**	Instit́uto Internacional de Ciencias Administrativas = IIAS, IISA, IIVW
IIAS	Indian Institute of Asian Studies		
IIAS	Institute of Inter-American Studies (U.S.A.)	**IICA**	Instit́uto Internacional de las Cajas de Ahorro
IIAS	Inter-American Institute of Agricultural Sciences	**IICA**	Interamerican Institute for Cooperation on Agriculture
IIAS	International Institute of Administrative Sciences (Belgium) = IICA, IISA, IIVW	**IICAT**	Investigación Internacional Cooperativa del Atlántico Tropical
IIASA	International Institute for Applied Systems Analysis	**IICCI**	International Information Center of Cosmetic Industries
IIB	Institut International de Bibliographie	**IICE**	Institut International des Caisses d'Epargne = IIE, IIS, ISB
IIB	Institut International de Brevets = IPI		
IIB	Instit́uto de Investigaciones Biomedicas	**IICG**	International Institute of Comparative Government
IIB	International Institute of Biotechnology	**IICHAW**	International Institute for the Conservation of Historic and Artistic Works
IIBA	International Institute for Bioenergetic Analysis (U.S.A.)		
IIBA	Irish Indoor Bowling Association	**IICHEE**	Indian Institute of Chemical Engineers
IIBA	Irish-Italian Business Association	**IICL**	Institute of International Container Lessors
IIBB	Institute of Independent British Business		
IIBC	International Institute of Biological Control	**IICM**	Instit́uto de Investigação Cientifica de Moçambique
IIBCE	Instituto de Investigaciones Biológicas "Clemente Estable" (Uruguay)	**IICM**	Irish Institute of Credit Management (Éire)

IICMFA	Integrated Information Centre of the Ministry of Foreign Affairs (Saudi Arabia)	**IIE**	Instituto de Investigaciones Eléctricas (Mexico)
IICO	International Islamic Charitable Organisation	**IIE**	Instítuto de la Ingenieria de España
		IIE	Instítuto do Investimento Estrangeiro
IICS	Institut International de Chimie Solvay	**IIE**	Instítuto Interamericano de Estadística = IASI
IICSP	Instítuto Internacional Ciencias Sociales Politicas	**IIE**	Instítuto Internacional de Estadística = IIS, ISI
IICT	Instítuto de Investigação Científica Tropical	**IIE**	International Institute of Entomology
IICT	Instítuto de Investigaciónes Cientificas y Technologicas (Argentina)	**IIEA**	Irish Institute for European Affairs
		IIEB	Institut International d'Études Bancaires
IICY	International Independent Christian Youth = JICI	**IIEC**	International Institute for Energy Conservation (U.S.A.)
IICY	International Investment Corporation for Yugoslavia	**IIEC**	Istituto Internazionale di Educazione Cinematografica
IID	Institut Internationale de Documentation	**IIED**	International Institute for Environment and Development
IIDA	Instítuto Interamericano de Direito de Autor = IACI, ICI	**IIEDH**	Institut International d'Études des Droits de l'Homme, Trieste
IIDAL	Instítuto Internacional de Derecho Administrativo Latino	**IIEE**	Institut International d'Études sur l'Education (Belgium)
IIDARA	Instítuto Iberoamericano de Derecho Agrario y Reforma Agraria	**IIEH**	Institut International d'Études Hebraïques
IIDC	Instítuto de Investigaciones Económicas (Mexico)	**IIEIC**	International Institute Examinations Inquiry Committee
IIDD	Institut Internationale du Développement Durable – IISD (WCED)	**IIEJ**	Instítuto Intermericano de Estudios Jurídicos Internacionales
IIDES	Instituto de Investigaciones para el Desarrollo de la Salud (Ecuador)	**IIEL**	Institut International d'Études Ligures = IISL
IIDH	Institut International de Droit Humanitaire = IIDU, IIHL	**IIEL**	Instítuto Internacional de Estudios Laborales (ILO) (Switzerland) = IIES, IILS
IIDH	Instítuto Interamericano de Derecho Humanos = IIHR	**IIEM**	Indian Institute of Experimental Medicine
IIDP	Institut International du Droit Public	**IIEP**	International Institute for Educational Planning = IIPE
IIDRA	Instítuto Iberoamericano de Derecho Agrario y Reforma Agraria (Venezuela)	**IIER**	International Institute for Economic Research
IIDU	Istituto Internazionale di Diritto Umanitario = IIDH, IIHL	**IIES**	Institut International d'Education Spécialisé (Belgium)
IIE	Institut Interaméricain de l'Enfance = IACI, IIN	**IIES**	Institut International d'Études Sociales (ILO) (Switzerland) = IIEL, IILS
IIE	Institut International d'Esperanto = IEI	**IIES**	International Institute for Environmental Studies
IIE	Institut International d'Etiopathie		
IIE	Institut International de l'Environnement = IIGD	**IIESDM**	International Institute of Environmental Studies and Disaster Management
IIE	Institut International de l'Epargne = IICE, IIS, ISBI	**IIESES**	Instituto de Investigaciones y Estudios Superiores Económicos y Sociales (Mexico)
IIE	Institute of Incineration Engineers		
IIE	Institute of Industrial Engineers (Éire)		
IIE	Institute of International Education (U.S.A.)		

IIET RAN	Vavilov Institute of the History of the Natural Sciences and Technology, Russian Academy of Sciences
IIExE	Institution of Incorporated Executive Engineers
IIF	Institut International du Froid = IIR
IIF	Institute of International Finance = IFI
IIF	Internationales Institut für den Frieden = IIP
IIF	Irish Insurance Federation
IIFCOOP	Instítuto Interamericano de Financiamienta Cooperativo (Chile)
IIFE	International Icing Federation = IFE
IIFET	International Institute of Fisheries Economics and Trade
IIFGA	Institut International de Formation en Gestion Aéronautique Civile = IAMTI, IIFGAC (Canada)
IIFP	Institut International des Finances Publiques (Belgium) = IIPF
IIFSO	International Islamic Federation of Student Organizations
IIFT	Indian Institute of Foreign Trade
IIG	Instítuto de Investigaciones Geologicas (Chile)
IIGEAG	Instítuto de Investigaciones Geologicas Edafologicas y Agrobiologicas de Galicia
IIHF	International Ice Hockey Federation = IEHV, LIHG
IIHL	International Institute of Humanitarian Law = IIDH, IIDU
IIHN	Institut International d'Histoire du Notariat
IIHR	Indian Institute of Horticultural Research
IIHR	Interamerican Institute of Human Rights = IIDH
IIHR	International Institute of Human Rights
III	Imprimerie Industrielle Ivoirienne
III	Institut Isostatique International
III	Instítuto Indigenista Interamericana (Mexico)
III	Instítuto Interamericano Indigenista (OAS) = IAII
III	Instítuto Internacional de Integración del Convenio 'Andrés Bello' (Colombia)
III	Insurance Institute of Ireland
III	Inter-American Indian Institute (OAS)
III	International Independence Institute (U.S.A.)
III	International Institute of Interpreters (U.S.A.)
III	International Isocyanates Institute (U.S.A.)
III	Internationales Institut für Industrieplanung (Austria)
III	Investors in Industry
III	Istituto Italiano Imballaggio
IIIA	International Investment Insurance Agency = AIAI, IAIV
IIIA	Israeli Institute of International Affairs
IIIC	International Institute of Intellectual Cooperation
IIIC	International Irrigation Information Centre
IIIE	Indian Institute of Industrial Engineers
IIIHS	International Institute of Integral Human Sciences (Canada) = IISHI
IIJM	Istituto Internazionale "Jacques Maritain"
IIJP	Instítuto de Investigaciónes Juridico-Politicas (Argentina)
IIL	Institute of International Law (Netherlands) = IDI
IIL	Instítuto Italo-Latinamericano
IIL	Insurance Institute of London
IILA	Instítuto Italo-Latino-Americano = ILAI
IILC	Internationaal Instituut voor Landaanwinning en Cultuurtechniek
IILE	Irish Institute of Legal Executives (Éire)
IILFSC	International Institute of Law of the French Speaking Countries = IDEF
IILI	Instítuto Internacional de Literatura Iberoamericana
IILP	Institute of International Licensing Practitioners
IILR	Institute of International Labor Research
IILS	International Institute for Labour Studies (ILO) (Switzerland) = IIEL, IIES
IIM	Indian Institute of Management
IIM	Indian Institute of Metals
IIM	Institut International du Médiateur = IOI
IIM	Institut National de la Marionnette
IIM	Institution of Industrial Managers (now IM)
IIM	Instítuto de Investigaciónes Microquímicas (Argentina)

IIM	Istituto Idrografico della Marina
IIMA	Indian Institute of Management
IIMC	Institut International de Musicologie Comparée
IIMC	Institúto Interamericano de Mercados de Capital (Venezuela)
IIMC	International Institute of Municipal Clerks (U.S.A.)
IIMH	Irish Institute of Materials Handling (Éire)
IIMI	International Irrigation Management Institute (Sri Lanka)
IIMM	Institúto de Investigaciones Minero-Metalurgicas (Bolivia)
IIMP	Institúto de Investigaciónes de Materias Primas (Chile)
IIMT	International Institute of Milling Technology
IIN	Institúto Indigenista Nacional (Guatemala)
IIN	Institúto Interamericano del Niño = IACI, IIE
IIN	Istituto Italiano di Navigazione
IIN	Istituto Italiano di Numismatica
IINA	International Islamic News Agency
IINA	Ireland International News Agency
IINCE	International Institute of Noise Control Engineering (U.S.A.)
IINREN	Interagency Interim National Research and Education Network
IINSE	Interuniversity Institute of Nuclear Sciences and Engineering (Belgium) = IISN
IINTE	Instytut Informacji Naukowej, Technicznej i Ekonomicznej
IIO	Institúto de Investigaciones Oceanologicas (Mexico)
IIO	International Islamic Organization
IIOR	Institut Issledovaniia Organizovannykh Rynkov
IIOST	Institut International d'Organisation Scientifique du Travail (Switzerland)
IIP	Indian Institute of Packaging
IIP	Indian Institute of Petroleum
IIP	Institut International de la Presse = IPI
IIP	Intergovernmental Informatics Programme (UNESCO) = PII
IIP	International Ice Patrol
IIP	International Institute for Peace (Austria) = IIF
IIP	International Institute of Parasitology
IIP	International Institute of Philosophy
IIP	Irish Independence Party
IIP	Israel Institute of Petroleum
IIP	Israel Institute of Productivity
IIP	Istituto Italiano dei Plastici
IIPA	Indian Institute of Public Administration
IIPA	Institute of Incorporated Practitioners in Advertising
IIPA	Institute of Incorporated Public Accountants (Éire)
IIPC	Industrielle Ivoirienne de Plastiques et de Caoutchouc
IIPE	Institut International de Planification de l'Education = IIEP
IIPE	Institution of Incorporated Plant Engineers
IIPER	International Institution of Production Engineering Research = CIRP
IIPF	International Institute for Public Finance = IIFP
IIPFT	International Institute of Protein Food Technology (U.S.A.)
IIPM	Irish Institute of Pensions Managers
IIPMM	Irish Institute of Purchasing and Materials Management
IIPO	International Institute of Physical Oceanography
IIPP	Institut Internationale de Promotion et de Prestige
IIPR	Istituto Internazionale Psicologia Religiosita (Italy)
IIPS	International Institute for Population Studies (India)
IIPU	Istituto Italiano di Paleontologia Umana
IIR	Deutsches Institut für Interne Revision
IIR	Institut Islamique de Recherche = IRI
IIR	Institute of International Relations (China, Taiwan, Trinidad and Tobago)
IIR	Institute of International Relations (Czech Republic)
IIR	Institute of International Relations for Advanced Studies on Peace and Development in Asia (Japan)
IIR	International Institute for Robotics
IIR	International Institute of Refrigeration = IIF
IIRA	International Industrial Relations Association = AIRP, AIRT
IIRB	Institut International de Recherches Betteravières (Belgium)

IIRE	International Institute for Resource Economics (U.S.A.)	**IISA**	Irish Institute of Secretaries and Administrators
IIRG	Institut International de Recherches Graphologiques	**IISCO**	Indian Iron and Steel Company
IIRG	Istituto Internazionale per la Ricerca Geotermiche (Italy)	**IISD**	International Institute for Sustainable Development = IIDD (WCED)
IIRI	International Industrial Relations Institute	**IISE**	International Institute of Social Economics
IIRM	Irish Immigration Reform Movement (U.S.A.)	**IISEE**	International Institute of Seismology and Earthquake Engineering (Japan)
IIRR	International Institute for Rice Research (Philippines)	**IISG**	International Instituut voor Sociale Geschiedenis
IIRR	International Institute of Rural Reconstruction (U.S.A.)	**IISHI**	Institut International des Sciences Humaines Intégrales (Canada) = IIIHS
IIRS	Institute for Industrial Research and Standards (Éire, U.S.A.)	**IISHR**	International Institute for the Study of Human Reproduction (U.S.A.)
IIRSDA	Institut International de Recherche Scientifique pour le Développement en Afrique (Côte d'Ivoire)	**IISI**	International Iron and Steel Institute (Belgium)
IIRSM	International Institute of Risk and Safety Management	**IISIA**	Israeli Institute for the Study of International Affairs
IIS	Indian Institute of Science	**IISL**	Institúto Internazionale di Studi Liguri (Italy) = IIEL
IIS	Indonesian Institute of Sciences	**IISL**	International Institute for the Sociology of Law (ISA)
IIS	Institut International de la Soudure = IIW	**IISL**	International Institute of Space Law (France)
IIS	Institut International de Sociotechnique (IADIWU)	**IISM**	Istituto Italiano per la Storia della Musica
IIS	Institut International de Statistique = IIE, ISI	**IISN**	Institut Interuniversitaire des Sciences Nucléaires (Belgium) = IINSE
IIS	Institute for Intercultural Studies (U.S.A.)	**IISO**	International Institute for Site Planning
IIS	Institute of Industrial Selling	**IISPS**	International Institute of Social and Political Science (Switzerland) = IISSP
IIS	Institute of Information Scientists	**IISR**	Indian Institute of Sugar-cane Research
IIS	Institute of Information Scientists (Japan)	**IISR**	Institute for International Social Research (U.S.A.)
IIS	Instituut voor Internationale Studien (Netherlands)	**IISR**	International Institution of Submarine Research
IIS	International Institute of Security	**IISRP**	International Institute of Synthetic Rubber Producers
IIS	International Institute of Sociology	**IISS**	International Institute for Strategic Studies
IIS	International Institute of Stress (Canada)	**IISS**	International Institute for the Science of Sintering
IIS	International Insurance Society (U.S.A.)	**IISSP**	Institut International des Sciences Sociales et Politiques = IISPS
IIS	Internationales Institut der Sparkassen = IICE, IIE, ISBI	**IIST**	Institut International des Sciences Théoriques = IITS
IIS	Irish Institute of Secretaries	**IIST**	International Institute for Safety in Transportation
IIS	Istituto Italiano dello Saldatura	**IISWM**	Institute of Iron and Steel Wire Manufacturers
IISA	Independent Immigration Support Agency		
IISA	Institut Interaméricain des Sciences Agricoles (Costa Rica)		
IISA	Institut International des Sciences Administratives (Belgium) = IIAS, IICA, IIVW		

IIT	Indian Institute of Technology
IIT	Institut International du Théâtre = ITI
IIT	Institute of Industrial Technicians
IIT	Institute of Information Technology (Japan)
IIT	Institúto de Investigaciones Tecnológicas (Colombia)
IIT	Instituto de Investigaciones Tecnológicas (Ecuador)
IIT	International Investment Trust (Africa)
IIT	Israel Institute of Technology
IITA	International Institute of Tropical Agriculture (Nigeria)
IITC	Insurance Industry Training Council
IITC	International Indian Treaty Council
IITD	Irish Institute of Training and Development
IITF	International Investment Trust Fund (UN)
IITF	Internationales Institut für Terminologieforschung
IITJ	IOJ Budapest International Institute for Training of Journalists
IITM	International Institute for Traditional Music
IITPIC	Institutul de Inginerie Tehnologica si Proiectare pentru Industria Chimica
IITS	International Institute of Theoretical Sciences = IIST
IITT	Institut International du Travail Temporaire = IITW
IITW	International Institute for Temporary Work = IITT
IIU	International Islamic University, Petaling Jaya (OIC)
IIUG	International Institut für Umwelt und Gesellschaft
IIUPL	International Institute for the Unification of Private Law = UNIDROIT
IIVG	Internationales Institut für Vergleichende Gesellschaftsforschung
IIVRS	International Institute for Vital Registration and Statistics
IIVW	Internationales Institut für Verwaltungswissenschaften = IIAS, IICA, IISA
IIW	Indian Institute of Welders
IIW	International Inner Wheel
IIW	International Institute of Welding = IIS

IIWG	International Industry Working Group
IIWPA	International Information and Word Processing Association
IIZ	Institut für Internationale Zusammenarbeit (Austria)
IJA	Institute of Jewish Affairs
IJA	International Jugglers Association
IJAB	Internationaler Jugendaustausch und Besucherdienst
IJAN	Internationale des Jeunes Amis de la Nature = IYNF, NFJI
IJB	Internationale Jugendbibliothek = IKJ, IYL
IJC	International Joint Commission (Canada/U.S.A.)
IJCAII	International Joint Conference on Artificial Intelligence Inc.
IJCIC	International Jewish Committee on Interreligious Consultations
IJCR	Institute for Jewish-Christian Relations (U.S.A.)
IJE	Institute of Jewish Education
IJEA	Ireland-Japan Economic Association
IJF	International Jazz Federation = FIJ
IJF	International Judo Federation = FIJ
IJF	Internationale Journalisten-Föderation = FIJ, FIP, IFJ
IJG	Contactcentrum Fabrikanten Ijzerwaren en Gereedschappen
IJGD	Internationale Jugendgemeinschaftsdienste
IJI	International Juridical Institute
IJI	Islam Jamhoori Ittehad (Pakistan)
IJIRA	Indian Jute Industry's Research Association
IJJF	International Ju Jitsu Federation
IJK	Internationale Juristen-Kommission = CIJ, ICJ
IJMA	Indian Jute Mills Association
IJMARI	Indian Jute Mills Association Research Institute
IJNPS	Institúto Joaquim Nabuco de Pesquisas Sociais (Brazil)
IJO	International Juridical Organization
IJO	International Jute Organization
IJOA	International Juvenile Officers Association
IJPU	International Jewish Peace Union (France)
IJS	Institute of Jazz Studies (U.S.A.)

IJTU	Independent Journalists Trade Union (Russia)	**IKPO**	Internationale Kriminalpolizeiliche Organisation = ICPO, Interpol, OIPC
IJVS	International Jewish Vegetarian Society	**IKRA**	International Kirlian Research Association (U.S.A.)
IJWU	International Jewelry Workers Union	**IKRK**	Internationales Komitee vom Roten
IK	Iparretarrak (France)		Kreuz = CICR, ICRC
IKA	Catholic Information Agency (Croatia)	**IKS**	Interkantonale Kontrolstelle für Heilmittel (Switzerland)
IKA	International Kitefliers Association	**IKS**	International Kodály Society (Hungary)
IKA	Internationale Kochkunst Ausstellung	**IKS**	Internationales Kautschukbüro, Sektion
IKA	Ireland-Korea Association		Schweiz
IKA	Irish Kidney Association	**IKSJ**	Internationale Katholische Studierende
IKAPI	Ikatan Penerbit Indonesia		Jugend = IYCS, JECI
IKAR	"Nezavisimost" – Initsiativnyi Komitet Assotsiatsiia Rabochikh	**IKSR**	Internationale Kommission zum Schutze des Rheins Gegen Verunreinigung = CIPR, ICPRP
IKAR	Internationale Kommission für Alpines Rettungswesen = CISA, ICAR	**IKU**	Institutt for Kontinentalsokkelundersokelser og Petroleumsteknologi a.s. (Norway)
IKBK	Internationales Katholisches Bureau für das Kind = BICE, ICCB, OICI		
IKC	Instytut Koniunktur i Cen Handlu Zagranicznego	**IKUE**	Internacia Katolika Unuigo Esperantista
IKD	Internationale Kommission der Detektivverbände	**IKUP**	Internationale Katholischen Union der Presse = ICPU, IUKP, UCIP
IKEF	Internacia Komerca kaj Ekonomia Fakgrupo	**IKV**	Institut für Kunststoffverarbeitung
IKEL	Internacia Komitato por Etnaj Liberecoj	**IKV**	Internationaler Krankenhausverband = FIH, IHF
IKEO	Internacia Kooperativa Esperanto Organizo	**IKVSA**	Internationale Katholische Vereinigung für Soziale Arbeit = CIUSS, KIUMW, UCISS
IKF	International Kart Federation		
IKF	International Korfball Federation	**IKW**	Industrieverband Körperpfledge- und Waschmittel
IKG	International Gift Commission	**IKWN**	Instytut Krajowych Włókien Naturalnych (Poland)
IKG	Internationale Kommission für Glas = CIV, ICG	**IL**	Insinöörilitto
IKGV	Internationales Komitee Giessereitechnischer Vereinigungen = CIATF, ICFTA	**IL**	Institut für Leichte Flächentragwerke (Germany)
IKH	Interkantonalen Kontrollstelle für Heilmittel (Switzerland)	**IL**	Institute of Linguists
		IL	Internationale Libérale = LI
IKI	Internationales Kali-Institut = IPI	**ILA**	All India Library Association
IKJ	Internationales Kuratorium für das Jugendbuch = IJB, IYL	**ILA**	Independent Living Alternatives
		ILA	Insolvency Lawyers Association
IKK	Internationale Kamer van Koophandel = CCI, ICC, IHK	**ILA**	International Laundry Association
		ILA	International Law Association
IKKP	Internationale Katholische Konferenz des Pfadfindertums = CICE, CICS, ICCS	**ILA**	International Leading Association
		ILA	International Leprosy Association = SIL
IKN	Internationale Kommission für Numismatik = CIN, INC	**ILA**	International Listening Association
		ILA	International Longshoremen's Association
IKO	Instituut voor Kernphysisch Ondersoek	**ILA**	International Lupin Association
IKPE	Interministerielles Komitee für Entwicklungshilfe (Austria)	**ILA**	Iranian Library Association
IKPiD	Izba Książki, Papieru i Druku	**ILA**	Israel Library Association

ILA RAN	Institute of Latin American Studies, Russian Academy of Sciences
ILAA	International Literary and Artistic Association = ALAI
ILAB	International League of Antiquarian Booksellers = LILA
ILAC	International Laboratory Accreditation Conference
ILACDE	Instítuto Latinoamericano de Cooperación y Desarrollo
ILACDE	Instítuto Latinoamericano de Doctrina y Estudios Sociales
ILACIF	Latin American Institute for Auditing Sciences (Colombia)
ILACO	International Land Development Consultants (Netherlands)
ILACPS	Instítuto Latinoamericano de Ciencias Politicas y Sociales (Peru)
ILADES	Instítuto Latinoamericano de Ciencias Políticas y Sociales
ILADES	Instítuto Latinoamericano de Doctrinas y Estudios Sociales (Chile)
ILAE	International League Against Epilepsy
ILAFA	Instítuto Latinoamericano del Fierro y el Acero (Chile)
ILAFIR	Instítuto Latinoamericano de Fisología y Reproducción
ILAI	Italian-Latin American Institute = IILA
ILAIS	Institute of Latin American and Iberian Studies (U.S.A.)
ILAM	Institute of Leisure and Amenity Management
ILAMA	International Life-Saving Appliance Manufacturers Association
ILANUD	Instítuto Latinoamericano de las Naciones Unidas para el Prevención del Delito y Tratamiento del Delincuente (Costa Rica)
ILAP	Institute Latinoamericano del Plastico
ILAPES	Instítuto Latinoamericano de Planificación Económica y Social
ILAR	Institute of Laboratory Animal Resources (U.S.A.)
ILAR	International League against Rheumatism
ILARI	Instítuto Latinoamericano de Relaciones Internacionales
ILAS	Institute of Latin American Studies (China)
ILAS	International Linear Algebra Society
ILASE	Internacia Ligo de Agrikulturaj Specialistoj – Esperantistoj
ILAT	Instítuto Latinoamericano de Teatro
ILATID	Instítuto Latinoamericano de Alta Tecnologia, Informática y Derecho
ILB	Instituut voor Landbouwbedrijfsgebouwen
ILB	International Labour Board (U.S.A.)
ILB	International Liaison Bureau
ILBE	International League of Blind Esperantists
ILC	Inner Light Consciousness (U.K.)
ILC	Institute of Legal Cashiers
ILC	International Catholic-Jewish Liaison Committee
ILC	International Law Commission (UN) = CDI
ILC	International Life-Boat Conference
ILCA	Institute of Legal Cashiers & Administrators
ILCA	Insurance Loss Control Association (U.S.A.)
ILCA	International Lightning Class Association
ILCA	International Livestock Centre for Africa = CIPEA
ILCAA	Institute for the Study of Languages and Cultures of Asia and Africa (Japan)
ILCATUR	Instítuto Latinoamericano de Capacitación Turística
ILCE	Instítuto Latinoamericano de Cinematografíca Educativa (Mexico)
ILCE	Instítuto Latinoamericano de la Comunicación Educativa
ILCMP	International Liaison Committee on Medical Physics
ILCOP	International Liaison Committee of Organizations for Peace
ILCRPK	International Liaison Committee for Reunification and Peace in Korea = CILRECO, INRRK
ILCS	International Liquid Crystal Society
ILCTA	International League of Commercial Travellers and Agents = LI
ILCU	Irish League of Credit Unions
ILD	Instítuto Libertad y Democracia (Peru)
ILDA	International Lutheran Deaf Association
ILDAV	International League of Doctors Against Vivisection
ILDES	Instítuto Latinoamericano de Desenvolvimento Económico e Social (Brazil)

ILDIS	Institúto Latinoamericano de Investigaciones Sociales (Ecuador)
ILDM	Institute of Logistics and Distribution Management
ILDS	International League of Dermatological Societies = ICDP
ILDU	Industria Lanera del Uruguay, S.A.
ILDV	Instituto Libertad y Democracia de Venezuela
ILE	Institut für Lateinamerikaforschung und Entwicklungszusammenarbeit (Switzerland)
ILE	Institute of Legal Executives
ILE	Institution of Lighting Engineers
ILE	Institution of Locomotive Engineers
ILEA	Inner London Education Authority
ILEA	International League of Electrical Asociations
ILÉC	Institut de Liaisons et d'Études des Industries de Consommation
ILEC	Institúto Latinoamericana para le Educación por la Comunicación (Mexico)
ILEC	International Lake Environment Committee (Japan)
ILECC	Inner London Education Computing Centre
ILEF	Internacia Ligo de Esperantistaj Fotoiano-Magnetofon-Amatoroj
ILEI	Internacia Ligo de Esperantistaj Instruistoj
ILEIA	Information Centre for Low-External-Input and Sustainable Agriculture (Netherlands)
ILEP	International Federation of Anti-Leprosy Associations
ILEPES	Institúto Latinoamericano de Planificación Economica y Social (Chile)
ILERA	Internacia Ligo de Esperantistaj Radio-Amatoroj
ILERI	Institut Libre d'Étude des Relations Internationales
ILESA	Institute of Lighting Engineers of South Africa
ILESA	International Law Enforcement Stress Association
ILET	Institúto Latinoamericano de Estudios Transnationales (Mexico) = LAITS
ILEX	Institute of Legal Executives

ILF	Industrial Leathers Federation
ILF	International Liaison Forum of Peace Forces = FILFP
ILF	International Lifeboat Federation
ILF	International Loan Fund
ILF	Intreprindere de Lucrari Forestiere
ILFCAAE	International League for Child and Adult Education = LIEEP
ILG	Irish Linen Guild
ILGA	International Lesbian and Gay Association (Sweden)
ILGPNWU	International Leather Goods, Plastic and Novelty Workers Union (U.S.A.)
ILGU	Irish Ladies' Golf Union
ILGWU	International Ladies' Garment Workers Union (U.S.A.)
ILGYO	International Lesbian and Gay Youth Organisation
ILHMFLT	International Laboratory of High Magnetic Fields and Low Temperatures (Poland)
ILHR	International League for Human Rights
ILI	Institute for Land Information (U.S.A.)
ILI	International Law Institute (U.S.A.)
ILI	International Linguistics Institute
ILI	Irish Landscape Institute
ILI RAN	Institute of Linguistic Studies, Russian Academy of Sciences
ILIC	International Library Information Center (U.S.A.)
ILICED	Institúto Latinoamericano en Educación a Distancia
ILID	Institut für Landwirtschaftliche Information und Dokumentation
ILIS	International Lesbian Information Service (Netherlands)
ILITA	International Literaire en Toneelagentschap
ILKE	Internacia Libro-Klubo Esperanta
ILL	Institut Max von Laue – Paul Langevin (France)
ILLA	Irish Ladies Lacrosse Association
ILLL	International Lutheran Laymen's League
ILM	Groep Internationale Laboratoria Onderzoek Industrie Medicamenten
ILM	Internationaler Landmaschinenmarkt
ILMA	Independent Lubricant Manufacturers Association (U.S.A.)
ILMA	International Licensing and Merchandisers Association

ILMB	Irish Livestock and Meat Board
ILMO	International Legal Metrology Organisation = OIML
ILNA	Indian Languages Newspapers Association
ILO	Instituut voor Landhouwhuishoudkundig Onderzoek
ILO	International Labour Organisation = IAO, OIT
ILO	International Latitude Observatory (Japan)
ILO-CIS	International Occupational Safety and Health Information Centre
ILOB	Instituut voor Landbouwkundig Onderzoek van Biochemische Producten
ILOC	International Lunar Occultation Centre (Japan)
ILocoE	Institution of Locomotive Engineers
ILP	Independent Labour Party
ILP	Islamic Liberation Party (Tunisia)
ILPA	Immigration Law Practitioners Association
ILPA	International Labor Press Association (U.S.A.)
ILPA	International Leisure and Professional Association (Belgium)
ILPC	International League for the Protection of Cetaceans
ILPE	Industria Lobera y Pesquera del Estado (Uruguay)
ILPEC	Instítuto Latinoamericano de Pedagogía de la Comunicación (Costa Rica)
ILPES	Instítuto Latinoamericano de Planificación Económica y Social (ECLAC)
ILPH	International League for the Protection of Horses
ILPNR	International League for the Protection of Native Races (U.S.A.)
ILR	Instituut voor Landbouwtechniek en Rationalisatie
ILRA	International Laboratory of Marine Radioactivity (IAEA)
ILRAC	Italian Literature Research Association of China
ILRAD	International Laboratory for Research on Animal Diseases (Kenya) = ILVR
ILRC	International Lasar Radar Conference

ILRCO-CSA	International Red Locust Control Organization for Central and Southern Africa
ILRI	Indian Lac Research Institute
ILRI	International Institute for Land Reclamation and Improvement (Netherlands)
ILRS	International League of Religious Socialists
ILS	Incorporated Law Society
ILS	Industrial Locomotive Society
ILS	Institute for Life Sciences
ILS	Institute of Labor Studies (Lesotho)
ILS	Institute of Legal Secretaries
ILS	International Latitude Service
ILS	International Lilac Society
ILS	International Limnological Society (ICSU)
ILS	International Lunar Society (U.S.A.)
ILS	Irish Literary Society
ILSA	Inspection des Lois Sociales en Agriculture
ILSA	Inter-American Legal Services Association (Colombia)
ILSA	International Lung Sounds Association
ILSC	International Learning Systems Corporation
ILSF	International Life-Saving Federation = FIS
ILSGB	International Language (Ido) Society of Great Britain
ILSI	International Life Sciences Institute
ILSi Europe	International Life Science Institute, European Branch
ILSLB	Information and Library Services Lead Body
ILSMH	International League of Societies for the Mentally Handicapped
ILT	Institute of Local Television
ILT	Institute of Paralegal Training (*ex* ALS)
ILTAM	Institute for Literature and Mass Artistic Techniques
ILTS	Institute of Licensed Trade Stocktakers (*ex* ISLTS)
ILTTA	International Light Tackle Tournament Association
ILU	Institute of London Underwriters
ILU	International Legal Union
ILV	Frauenhofer-Institut für Lebensmitteltechnologie undd Verpackung (Germany)

ILVES	Institúto Latinoamericano Vicente Emilio Solo (Venezuela)
ILVR	International Laboratory of Veterinary Research (Kenya) = ILRAD
ILWC	International League of Women Composers
ILWML	International Lutheran Women's Missionary League
ILWP	International Leninist Workers Party
ILWU	International Longshoremen's and Warehousemen's Union
ILZRO	International Lead Zinc Research Organisation
ILZSG	International Lead and Zinc Study Group
IM	Institute of Management (*ex* IIM, BIM)
IM	Institute of Marketing
IM	Institute of Metals
IM	Institute of Micrographics
IM	Institutet for Metalforskning
IM	International Medicine (U.S.A.)
IM	International Missions
IM	Svenska Leverantöföreningen för Instrument och Mätteknik
IMA	Independent Midwives Association
IMA	Indian Medical Association
IMA	Indonesian Mining Association
IMA	Industrial Marketing Association
IMA	Industrial Mission Association
IMA	Institut du Monde Arabe
IMA	Institut Madeleine Aulina
IMA	Institute for Mediterranean Affairs (U.S.A.)
IMA	Institute of Management Accountants (Éire)
IMA	Institute of Marine Affairs (Trinidad and Tobago)
IMA	Institute of Mathematics and its Applications
IMA	Institúto de Matemática Aplicada (Argentina)
IMA	International Magnesium Association
IMA	International Management Association
IMA	International Medical Assistance = AMI
IMA	International Military Archives
IMA	International Milling Association = AIM
IMA	International Mineralogical Association
IMA	International Mohair Association
IMA	International Molybdenum Association
IMA	International Music Association
IMA	International Mycological Association
IMA	Irish Medical Association
IMA	Islamic Medical Association (Tunisia)
IMA	Israel Medical Association
IMA	Schweizerisches Institut für Landmaschinenwesen und Landarbeitstechnik
IMA	Stjornunarfélag (Icelandic Management Association)
IMAA	Institute for Mediterranean Art and Archaeology (U.S.A.)
IMAA	International Maine-Anjou Association (U.S.A.)
IMAAN	International Muslim Association for Animals and Nature
IMAC	Institúto de Mediacion, Arbitraje y Conciliacion
IMAC	International Movement of Apostolate of Children = MIDADE, MIDADEN
IMACA	International Mobile Air Conditioning Association (U.S.A.)
IMACE	Association des Industries Margarinières des Pays de la CEE
IMACS	International Association for Mathematics and Computers in Simulation
IMACY	Industrie Malienne du Cycle et du Cyclomoteur (Mali)
IMADE-FOLK	Institute Malagache des Arts Dramatiques et Folkloriques (Madagascar)
IMADR	International Movement Against All Forms of Discrimination and Racism (Japan) = MIDRA
IMAF	International Martial Arts Federation
IMAG	Instituut voor Mechanisatie Arbeid en Gebouwen
IMAG	International Mail-Art Group
IMAG	Internationaler Messe und Ausstellungsdienst GmbH
IMAGE	Institute for Molecular and Agricultural Genetic Engineering (U.S.A.)
IMAJ	International Management Association of Japan
IMAL	Industries Maghrebines de l'Aluminium (Tunisia)
IManF	Institute of Manufacturing
IMAP	Institute of Materials and Advanced Processes (U.S.A.)

IMAPEC	Industries Mauritaniennes de Pêche
IMAR	Inner Mongolian Autonomous Region
IMarE	Institute of Marine Engineers
IMARPE	Instítuto del Mar del Perú
IMARSAT	International Maritime Satellite Organization
IMART	International Medical Association for Radio and Television
IMAS	Institute of Microbiology (China)
IMAS	Instítuto Mixto de Ayuda Social (Costa Rica)
IMAS	International Marine and Shipping Conference
IMASA	Irish Match Angling and Surfcasting Association
IMAT	Istituto di Microbiologia Agraria e Tecnica
IMATA	International Marine Animal Trainers Association (U.S.A.)
IMATEC	Société Internationale de Matériel Technique (Senegal)
IMAU	International Movement for Atlantic Union
IMAWU	International Molders and Allied Workers Union (U.S.A.)
IMB	Institute of Marine Biochemistry (NERC)
IMB	Institute of Medicinal Biotechnology (China)
IMB	International Maritime Bureau (ICC) = BMI
IMB	Internationaler Metallgewerkschaftsbund = FIOM, FISM, FITIM, IMF
IMBA	Insurope – Multinational Benefits Association (Belgium)
IMBA	Internationale Motorsportbond Amateurs
IMBA	Irish-Mexican Business Association
IMBB	Institute of Molecular Biology and Biotechnology (Greece)
IMBDC	International Marine Biodiversity Development Corporation (Canada)
IMBEC	Importadora de Bens de Consumo (Mozambique)
IMBEX	International Mens and Boys Exhibition
IMBI	Institute of Medical and Biological Illustration
IMBiGS	Instytut Mechanizacji Budownictwa i Górnictwa (Poland)
IMBISA	Inter-regional Meeting of Bishops of Southern Africa
IMBM	Institute of Maintenance and Building Management
IMC	Industrial Marketing Council
IMC	Information Management Centre
IMC	Iniciativa de Mujeres Cristianas (El Salvador)
IMC	Institute of Management Consultants
IMC	Institute of Measurement and Control
IMC	Institute of Medicine of Chicago (U.S.A)
IMC	Institute of Motorcycling
IMC	Institutum Missionum a Consolata
IMC	International Information Management Congress
IMC	International Mailbag Club
IMC	International Management Council (U.S.A.)
IMC	International Maritime Committee = CMI
IMC	International Materials Conference
IMC	International Meat Council
IMC	International Meteorological Committee
IMC	International Minerals and Chemical Corporation (U.S.A)
IMC	International Monetary Conference
IMC	International Music Council = CIM
IMC	Irish Manuscripts Commission
IMCA	Insurance Marketing Communications Association
IMCA	International Motor Contest Association (U.S.A.)
IMCAHO	Importadora Centroamericana de Honduras
IMCARY	International Movement of Catholic Agricultural and Rural Youth (Belgium) = MIJARC
IMCC	International Maritime Cooperation Centre (ICC) = CCM, CMC
IMCE	Instítuto Mejicano de Comercio Exterior
IMCE	Inter-Ministerial Committee for Environment
IMCEA	International Military Club Executives Association
IMCI	Industries Métallurgiques de la Côte d'Ivoire
IMCL	International Movement of Catholic Lawyers = MIJC
IMCO	Intergovernmental Maritime Consultative Organisation

IMCOBEL	Groupement Professionnel Belge des Importateurs-Concessionnaires d'Usines d'Outillages	**IMEC**	Institut Mondiale d'Écologie et de Cancérologie = WIEC
IMCOM	Institut Meditérranéen de la Communication	**IMEC**	Interuniversity Microelectronics Center (Belgium)
IMCoS	International Map Collectors Society	**IMechE**	Institution of Mechanical Engineers
IMCOS	International Meteorological Consultant Service	**IMechIE**	Institution of Mechanical Incorporated Engineers
IMCS	International Movement of Catholic Students – Pax Romana = MIEC	**IMÉDE**	Institut pour l'Étude des Méthodes de Direction de l'Entreprise (Switzerland)
IMCYC	Instítúto Mexicano del Cemento y del Concreto	**IMEG**	Irish Mining & Exploration Group
IMCyP	Instituto de Madera, Celulosa y Papel (Mexico)	**IMEHA**	International Maritime Economic History Association
IMD	Indian Meteorological Department	**IMEKO**	International Measurement Confederation
IMD	Institut für Maschinelle Dokumentation (Austria)	**IMELSA**	Importaciones y Exportaciones Literarias (Nicaragua)
IMD	Instytut Medycyny Doświadczalnej	**IMEMME**	Institution of Mining Electrical and Mining Mechanical Engineers
IMD	International Institute for Management Development	**IMEMO**	Institut Mirovoi Ekonomiki i Mezhdunarodnykh Otnoshenii
IMD	International Methods-Time-Measurement Directorate	**IMEMO-RAN**	Institute of World Economy and International Relations, Russian Academy of Sciences
IMDA	International Magic Dealers Association	**IMEN**	International Mother-Tongue Education Network
IMDA	International Mail Dealers Association		
IMDA	International Map Dealers Association	**IMENUR**	Institut Mondial des Cités Unies pour l'Environnement et l'Urbanisme
IMDE	Chengdu Institute of Mountain Disaster and Environment (China)	**IMEPI RAN**	Institute of International Economic and Political Studies, Russian Academy of Sciences
IMdFS	International Marie de France Society		
IMDI	International Management and Development Institute	**IMER**	Institute for Marine Environmental Research (NERC)
IME	Institut Mondial de l'Environnement = WEI	**IMER**	Instytut Mechanizacji i Elektryfikacji Rolnictwa
IME	Institute of Makers of Explosives (U.S.A.)	**IMERFA**	Institut Mondiale d'Études, de Recherches, de Formations et d'Action en Matière Psycho-Sociale et Juridique
IME	Institute of Marine Engineers		
IME	Institute of Mechanical Engineers = MechE	**IMERNAR**	Instítúto Mexicano de Recursos Naturales Renovables
IME	Institute of Medical Ethics	**IMES**	Instítúto Mexicano de Estudios Sociológicos
IME	Institute of Mining Engineers	**IMES**	Internacia Minista Esperanto-Societo
IME	Instítúto de Médicos Especialistas (Brazil)	**IMES**	Irish Marine Emergency Services
IME	Instítúto Militar de Engenharia (Brazil)	**IMESA**	Institution of Municipal Engineers of South Africa
IME	International Medical Exchange		
IME	International Metal Exchange	**IMESCIAL**	Institut Mondial des Structures Communales et d'Information sur l'Administration Locale (France)
IMEA	Incorporated Municipal Electrical Association		
IMÉA	Institut d'Études Métallurgiques et Électroniques Appliquées (Switzerland)	**IMET**	Institute of Modern Educational Technology (China)
IMEA	Irish Meat Exporters Association		

IMETU	Irish Municipal Employees Trade Union	**IMHV**	Interessengemeinschaft Musikwissenschaftlicher Herausgeber und Verleger
IMEXGRA	Chambre Syndicale pour le Commerce d'Importation et d'Exportation de Graines et Aliments pour le Bétail (Belgium)	**IMI**	Imperial Metal Industries
		IMI	Institute of Machine Tools and Instruments (Vietnam)
IMEXIN	Empresa Importadora y Exportadora de Infraestructura (Cuba)	**IMI**	Institute of Medical Illustrators
IMEXPAL	Importadora y Exportadora de Plantas Alimentarias, sus Complementos y Derivados (Cuba)	**IMI**	Institute of the Motor Industry
		IMI	International Mahayana Institute = FPMT
IMF	Institut de Mécanique des Fluides	**IMI**	International Maintenance Institute (U.S.A)
IMF	Institute of Metal Finishing		
IMF	International Marketing Federation	**IMI**	International Management Institute (Switzerland)
IMF	International Meeting on Ferroelectricity	**IMI**	International Market Intelligence (Norway)
IMF	International Metal Workers' Federation = FIOM, FISM, FITIM, IMB	**IMI**	International Marketing Institute (U.S.A.)
IMF	International Monetary Fund = FMI, IWF	**IMI**	International Masonry Institute (U.S.A.)
		IMI	International Metaphysical Institute
IMF	International Myomassethics Federation	**IMI**	International Mycological Institute (CABI)
IMF	Irish Marine Federation		
IMFBC	Institutul de Medicina si Farmacie, Biblioteca Centrala	**IMI**	Irish Management Institute
		IMI	Israel Military Industries
IMFC	Inner Mongolia Forestry College	**IMI**	Istituto Mobiliare Italiano
IMFT	Institute of Maxillofacial Technology	**IMIA**	Institúto Mexicano de Information Avicola
IMG	Industrial Marketing Group		
IMG	International Marxist Group	**IMIA**	International Machinery Insurers Association (IFIP)
IMG	Internationale Mosel-Gesellschaft	**IMIA**	International Medical Informatics Association
IMG	Islamic Missionaries Guild of the Caribbean and South America (Trinidad – Tobago)	**IMIA**	Irish Meat Industries Association
		IMICI	Industries Métallurgiques de la Côte d'Ivoire
IMGC	Instituto di Metrologia "Gustavo Colonnetti" (Italy)	**IMiD**	Instytut Matki i Dziecka
IMGE	Société Commerciale d'Importation Marchandises Générales (Ivory Coast)	**IMIE**	Institúto Mexicano de Investigaciones Económicas
IMGF	International Minigolf Federation (Germany)	**IMIF**	International Maritime Industries Forum
		IMinE	Institution of Mining Engineers
IMGRE	Institut Mineralogii Geokhimii i Kristallokhimii Redkikh Elementov (Russian Federation)	**IMINOCO**	Iranian Marine International Oil Company
		IMIQ	Institúto Mexicano de Ingenieros Quimicos
IMGTechE	Institution of Mechanical and General Technician Engineers	**IMIS**	Institute of Medical Illustrators in Scotland
IMH	Institutul de Meteorologie si Hidrologie	**IMIS**	International Marketing Information Service (U.S.A.)
IMH	International Medical Help		
IMHB	Institut Médical d'Homeópathie et de Biothérapie	**IMIT**	Institute for Management of Innovation and Technology (Sweden)
IMHE	Programme on Institutional Management in Higher Education (France)	**IMIT**	Institute of Musical Instrument Technology
IMHS	Indian Military Historical Society		

IMIT	Institúto Mexicano de Investigaciones Tecnológicas		**IMNDA**	Irish Motor Neurone Disease Association
IMK	Internationales Mauthausen Komitee = CIM		**IMO**	Inşaat Mühendisleri Odasi (Turkey) = TCCE
IMktM	Institute of Marketing Management (South Africa)		**IMO**	Information Market Observatory (CEC)
IML	Institut Monétaire Luxembourgeois		**IMO**	Institut Mezhdunarodnykh Otnosheniy
IML	Institúto Médico Legal (Brazil)		**IMO**	Institute of Market Officers
IMLA	Indian Medical Library Association		**IMO**	Instytut Materiałów Ogniotrwałych
IMLA	International Maritime Lecturers Association		**IMO**	Inter-American Municipal Organisation
IMLA	Irish Maritime Law Association		**IMO**	International Maritime Organization = OMI
IMLGM	Institute of Medical Laboratory Glassware Manufacturers		**IMO**	International Mennonite Organization
IMLI	IMO International Maritime Law Institute (Malta)		**IMO**	International Meteorological Organisation
IMLI RAN	Gorky Institute of World Literature, Russian Academy of Sciences		**IMO**	International Miners Organization = OIM
IMLO	Internationale Maatschappij v. Landbouwkundige Ontwikkeling		**IMO**	Irish Medical Organisation
IMLS	Institute of Medical Laboratory Sciences (*now* IBMS)		**IMOA**	Irish Multichannel Operators' Association
IMM	Institute of Massage and Movement (*ex* Institute of Male Masseurs)		**IMOB**	Industrie van Minerale Oliën van België
IMM	Institute of Master Mariners (Éire)		**IMP**	Institut za Mehanizaciju Poljoprivrede
IMM	Institute of Materials Management		**IMP**	Institute of Modern Physics, Academia Sinica
IMM	Institute of Molecular Medicine		**IMP**	Institúto Mexicano del Petróleo
IMM	Institution of Mining and Metallurgy		**IMP**	Instytut Mechaniki Precyzyjnej
IMM	Instytut Maszyn Matematycznych		**IMPA**	Information Management Professional Association (AIT) (Thailand)
IMM	Instytut Medycyny Morskiej		**IMPA**	International Maritime Pilots Association
IMMA	International Motorcycle Manufacturers Associations		**IMPA**	International Master Printers Association
IMMAPI	International Meeting of Medical Advisers in the Pharmaceutical Industry		**IMPA**	International Meat Processors Association
IMMCAMS	Institute of Materia Medica, Chinese Academy of Medical Sciences		**IMPA**	International Motor Press Association
IMMI	International Mass Media Institute (Norway)		**IMPA**	International Museum Photographers Association (U.S.A.)
IMMINE	Institúto Nicaragüense de la Minería		**IMPA**	International Myopia Prevention Association (U.S.A.)
IMMK	Interkultura Monda Movado Kommunomej		**IMPA**	International Personnel Management Association (U.S.A.)
IMMRAN	International Meeting of Marine Radio Aids to Navigation		**IMPA**	Irish Master Printers Association
IMMRC	International Mass Media Research Centre (France)		**IMPA**	Irish Meat Processors' Association
IMMRRI	Idaho Mining and Mineral Resources Research Institute (U.S.A.)		**IMPACT**	Implementing Agency for Cooperation and Training (U.S.A.)
IMMS	International Material Management Society (U.S.A.)		**IMPACT**	International Initiative Against Avoidable Disablement (UNDP, UNICEF, WHO)
IMN	Institúto Meteorológico Nacional (Costa Rica)		**IMPACT**	International Marketing Program for Agricultural Commodities and Trade Center (U.S.A.)

IMPACT	Irish Municipal, Public & Civil Trade Union (Éire)	**IMRA**	Industrial Marketing Research Association
IMPAE	Institute of Meteorology and Physics of the Atmospheric Environment (Greece)	**IMRA**	International Mission Radio Association (U.S.A.)
IMPBA	International Model Power Boat Association (U.S.A.)	**IMRA**	Irish Mountain Rescue Association
IMPC	International Mineral Processing Congress	**IMRAMN**	International Meeting on Radio Aids to Marine Navigation
IMPC	International Municipal Parking Congress	**IMRB**	Indian Market Research Bureau
IMPC	Istituto di Arte Mineraria	**IMRC**	International Metropolitan Railway Committee
IMPCA	International Methanol Producers and Consumers Association	**IMRI**	International Marian Research Institute (U.S.A.)
IMPE	Institúto de la Mediana y Pequeña Empresa	**IMRIC**	International Management Research Centre
IMPEX	Société Ivoirienne pour l'Industrie, l'Importation et l'Expo	**IMRNR**	Institúto Mexicano de Recursos Naturales Renovables
IMPGA	Institut de Métérologie et de Physique du Globe d'Algérie	**IMRO**	Investment Management Regulatory Organisation
IMPHOS	Institut Mondial du Phosphate	**IMRO**	Irish Music Right Organisation
IMPHQA	Institut Mondial pour la Protection de la Haute Qualité Alimentaire	**IMRO-DP**	Internal Macedonian Revolutionary Organization-Democratic Party = VMRO-DP
IMPI	International Microwave Power Institute	**IMRO-DPMNU**	Internal Macedonian Revolutionary Organization – Democratic Party for Macedonian National Unity = VMRO-DPMNE
IMPIEL	Industrias Mediterraneas de la Piel		
IMPiHW	Instytut Medycyny Pracy i Higieny Wsi		
IMPLAD	Institute of Medicinal Plant Development (China)	**IMRO-I**	Internal Macedonian Revolutionary Organization-Independent (Bulgaria) = VMRO-N
IMPM	Institut de Recherches Médicales et d'Études des Plantes Médicinales (Cameroon)	**IMRO-UMS**	Internal Macedonian Revolutionary Organization of Macedonian Societies in Bulgaria = VMRO-OMD
IMPORT-PESCA	Associazione Nationale Importatori Grossisti Prodotti Ittici Freschi e Congelati	**IMS**	Indian Medical Service
		IMS	Industrial Management Society (U.S.A.)
Importang	Angolan Import Organisation	**IMS**	Institut Mondial des Sciences (Belgium) = WIS
IMPPA	Independent Motion Picture Producers Association		
IMPRECO	Impressions de Textiles de la République Populaire du Congo	**IMS**	Institut za Ispitivanje Materijala SR Srbije
		IMS	Institute for Mediterranean Studies (Greece)
IMPRESIT	Imprese Italiane all'Estero		
IMPRIGA	Imprimerie Centrale d'Afrique (Gabon)	**IMS**	Institute for Mesoamerican Studies (U.S.A.)
IMPRO-MER	Société Ivoirienne d'Importation de Produits de la Mer	**IMS**	Institute of Management Sciences (U.S.A.)
IMPS	International Micro Programmers Society	**IMS**	Institute of Management Services
IMQ	Istituto Italiano del Marchio di Qualité	**IMS**	Institute of Management Specialists
IMQS	Irish Mining and Quarrying Society	**IMS**	Institute of Manpower Studies
IMR	Institute for Medical Research (Malaysia, U.S.A.)	**IMS**	Institute of Mathematical Statistics (U.S.A.)
IMR	Institute of Metal Research, Academia Sinica	**IMS**	Institute of Meteorological Science (China)

IMS	Institute of Metropolitan Studies
IMS	Institute of Museum Services (U.S.A.)
IMS	Institute on Man and Science
IMS	International Meat Secretariat = OIV, OPIC
IMS	International Meditation Society
IMS	International Metallographic Society
IMS	International Mountain Society
IMS	International Multihull Society
IMS	International Musicological Society = IGMW, SIM
IMSA	Industria Metalmecanica S.A. (Bolivia)
IMSA	International Medical Sciences Academy (India)
IMSA	International Motor Sports Association
IMSA	International Municipal Signal Association (U.S.A.)
IMSCO	Initial Maritime Satellite Consortium (U.K. and U.S.A.)
IMSI	International Maple Syrup Institute (Canada)
IMSL	International Mathematical and Statistical Libraries
IMSM	Institute of Marketing and Sales Management
IMSO	Institute of Municipal Safety Officers
IMSoP	International Medical Society of Paraplegia = IMSP
IMSP	International Medical Society of Paraplegia
IMSS	Instítúto Mexicano del Seguro Social
IMSSA	Institute of Mine Surveyors of South Africa
IMST	Institut de Mécanique Statistique de la Turbulence (France)
IMST	International Mushroom Society for the Tropics (Hong Kong)
IMSTI	Institute of Marine Sci-Tech Information (SOA) (China)
IMT	Institute of Municipal Transport
IMTA	Imported Meat Trade Association
IMTA	Institute of Municipal Treasurers and Accountants (South Africa)
IMTA	International Meat Trade Association
IMTEC	Institute of Marine and Terrestrial Ecology (Canada)
IMTEC	International Movements Towards Educational Change (Norway)
IMTG	Internationale Moor und Torf-Gesellschaft
IMTI	Instítúto del Minifundio y de las Tierras Indivisas (Argentina)
IMTMA	Indian Machine Tool Manufacturers Association (India)
IMTPA	Institut de Médecine Tropicale Princesse Astrid (Belgium)
IMTRA	Associazione Importatori Organi di Trasmissione
IMTU	Independent Miners Trade Union (Russia)
IMU	Instituto de Investigacion, Capacitacion y Desarrollo de la Mujer "Norma Virginia Guirola de Herrera" (El Salvador)
IMU	International Mailers Association (U.S.A.)
IMU	International Mathematical Union = UMI
IMU	International Metal Union
IMU	International Monarchist Union = UIM
IMUP	International Movement for Universal Peace
IMUZ	Instytut Melioracji i Użytków Zielonych
IMV	Internationaler Metzgermeisterverband = CIBC
IMV	Internationaler Milchwirtschaftsverband = FIL, IDF
IMVS	Institute of Medical and Veterinary Science (Australia)
IMW	Institute of Masters of Wine
IMW	International Map of the World = CIM
IMWA	International Mine Water Association (U.S.A.)
IMWIC	International Maize and Wheat Improvement Centre (Mexico)
IMWOO	Instituut voor Maatschappij-Wetenschappelijk Onderzoek in de Ontwikkelingslanden
IMWoodT	Institute of Machine Woodworking Technology
IMWU	International Molders' and Allied Workers' Union
IMZ	Instytut Metalurgii Żelaza
IMZ	Internationales Musikzentrum (Austria)
IMZA	Association Professionnelle des Importateurs et Exportateurs Belges de Semences Fourragères
INA	Industrias Nacionales Agrícolas, S.A. (Nicaragua)
INA	Information Networking Alliance

INA	Institut National Agronomique	**INAFEC**	Institut Africain d'Education Cinématographique
INA	Institut National de l'Audiovisuel		
INA	Institute of National Affairs (Papua New Guinea)	**INAFOR**	Institúto Nacional Forestal (Guatemala)
		INAFORM	International Association of Forest Resources Management
INA	Institute of Nautical Archaeology (U.S.A.)		
		INAGHEI	Institut National d'Administration de Gestion et des Hautes Études Internationales (Haiti)
INA	Institution of Naval Architects		
INA	Institúto Nacional Agrario (Honduras)		
INA	Institúto Nacional de Abastecimientos (Colombia)	**INAGRISA**	Iniciativas Agricolas, S.A.
		INAH	Institúto Nacional de Antropogia e Historia (Mexico)
INA	Institúto Nacional de Aprendizaje (Costa Rica)		
		INAIL	Istituto Nazionale per l'Assicurazione contro gli Infortuni sul Lavoro
INA	Iraqi News Agency		
INA	Irish Naturist Association (INF)	**INAIR**	Internacional de Aviación SA (Panama)
INA	Istituto Nazionale delle Assicurazioni	**INAISE**	International Association of Inventors in the Social Economy
INA	Verenigung van Fabrikanten en Importeurs van Naaimachines		
		INAIT	Institúto Nacional de Investigacion del Transporte (Peru)
INAA	Institúto Nicaragüense de Acueductos y Alcantarillados		
		INAL	Indian National Agricultural Library
INAA	Institúto Nicaragüense de Agua y Alcantarillado	**INALCO**	Institúto Nacional de Cooperativas (Bolivia)
INABIM	Incorporated National Association of British and Irish Millers	**INALI**	Institúto Nacional de Limnologia (Argentina)
INABU	Imprimerie Nationale du Burundi	**INALI**	Istituto Nazional Assistenza Lavoratori Italiani
INAC	Institúto Nacional de Carnes (Uruguay)		
INAC	Istituto Nazionale per le Applicazioni del Calcolo	**INALPRE**	Institúto Nacional de Preinversión (Bolivia)
INACAP	Institúto Nacional de Capacitación Professional (Chile)	**INAM**	Institut National d'Assurance contre la Maladie
INACEB	Industrie Alimentaire du Centre et de Bouaké (Ivory Coast)	**INAM**	Istituto Nazionale per l'Assicurazione contro le Malattie
INACG	International Nutritional Anemia Consultative Group (U.S.A.)	**INAME**	International Newspaper Advertising and Marketing Executives
INACH	Institúto Antartico Chileno (Chile)	**INAMI**	Institut National d'Assurance Maladie-Invalidité
INACOL	Institut National pour l'Amélioration des Conserves de Légumes (Belgium)		
		INAMPS	Institúto Nacional de Assistencia Médica da Previdência Social (Brazil)
INACP	Institut de Nutrition pour l'Amérique Centrale et Panama (Guatemala)		
		INAN	Institúto Nacional de Alimentação e Nutrição (Brazil)
INAD	Institúto Nacional de Administracion para el Desarrollo (Guatemala)		
		INANDEP	Institúto Andino de Estudios en Poblacion y Desarrollo (Peru)
INADE	Institúto Nacional de Desarrollo (Peru)		
INADES	Institut African pour le Développement Économique et Social	**INANDES**	Institúto Andino de Estudios Sociales (Peru)
INADUR	Institúto Nacional de Desarrollo Urbano (Peru)	**INANTIC**	Institúto Nacional de Normas Tecnicas Industriales y Certificacion (Peru)
INAEICM	Institut Nationale Agricole d'Études et d'Initiatives Coopératives et Mutualistes	**INAO**	Institut National d'Appellation d'Origine
INAF	Industrie Alimentaire d'Afrique (Senegal)	**INAOE**	Institúto Nacional de Astrofisica, Optica y Electronica (Mexico)
INAF	Institúto Nacional De Ampliacion de la Frontera Agrícola (Peru)	**INAP**	Institúto Nacional de Acción Poblacional e Investigación (Chile)

INAP	Instítuto Nacional de Administración Pública (Guatemala, Spain)
INAPA	Instítuto Nacional de Aquas Potables y Alcantarillados (Dominica)
INAPE	Instítuto Nacional de Asistencia y Promocion del Estudiante
INAPE	Instítuto Nacional de Pesca (Uruguay)
INAPG	Institut National Agronomique Paris-Grignon
INAPI	Institut Algérien de Normalisation et de Propriété Industrielle (Algeria)
INARBEL	Industries Ardoisières Belges
INARC	Institut Nord-Africain de Recherches Cotonnières
INARCH	Istituto Nazionale di Architettura
INARI	International Agency for Rural Industrialisation (Italy)
INARS	Istituto Nazionale per le Regioni Storiche
INAS	Institut Nationale d'Administration Scolaire et Universitaire
INAS	Instítuto Nacional de la Asistencia Social
INAS-FMH	International Sports Federation for Persons with Mental Handicap
INASA	Industrias Nacionals Agricolas (Nicaragua)
INAT	Institut National Agronomique de Tunisie
INAT	Institut National d'Assistance Technique (Belgium)
INATA-PROBU	International Association of Professional Bureaucrats
INATEIA	Istituto Nazionale di Assistenza Tecnico-Economica per Imprenditori Agricoli
INAUM	Istituto Nazionale di Architettura e Urbanistica Montana
INAZUCAR	Instítuto Azucarero Dominicana
INB	Institut National du Bois
INB	Instítuto Nacional de Bachillerato
INB	Instytut Naukowo Badawczy
INB	Internazionale Natrium-Brutreaktorbaugesellschaft
INBA	Instítuto Nacional de Bellas Artes (Mexico)
INBA	Instítuto Nacional de Biologia Animal (Bolivia, Peru)
INBA	Irish-Nigerian Business Association
INBF	Imprimerie Nationale du Burkina Faso
INBH	Institut National Belge du Houblon
INBio	Instituto Nacional de Biodiversidad (National Biodiversity Institute) (Costa Rica)
INBOCI	Industries du Bois en Côte d'Ivoire
INBOLCA	Instítuto Boliviano del Café
INBOLPEX	Instítuto Boliviano de Promoción de Exportaciones
INBOPIA	Instítuto Boliviano de la Pequeña Industria y Artesania
INBT	Institut National Belge du Tapis = BNTI
INC	Iglesia Ni Cristo (Philippines)
INC	Institut National de la Consommation
INC	Institut Nicaragüense de Café
INC	Instítuto Nacional de Canalizaciónes (Venezuela)
INC	Instítuto Nacional de Colonización (Ecuador, Spain, Uruguay)
INC	Instítuto Nacional de Consumo
INC	Instítuto Nacional de Cultura (Peru)
INC	International Nickel Company
INC	International Numismatic Commission = CIN, IKN
INC	International Nut Council
INC	Iraqi National Congress
INC	Ironfounders National Confederation
INC/FCCC	Intergovernmental Negotiating Committee for a Framework Convention on Climate Change
INCA	Independent National Computing Association
INCA	Industria Nacional de Clavos y Alambres (Nicaragua)
INCA	Institut National de Crédit Agricole (Belgium)
INCA	International Committee for Andean Aid
INCA	International Newspaper in Colour Association (Switzerland)
INCA	Istituto Nazionale Confederale di Assistenza
INCAE	Instítuto Centroamericano de Administracion de Empresas
INCAFE	Instítuto Nacional del Café (El Salvador)
INCAP	Instítuto de Nutrición de Centroamérica y Panamá (Guatemala)
INCAR	Instítuto Nacional del Carbon
INCAR	International Committee Against Racism

INCASUR	Instítuto de Capacitación Social del Cono Sur (Argentina)
INCATEL	Instítuto Centroamericano de Telecommunicaciones (El Salvador)
INCB	International Narcotics Control Board = JIFE, OICS
INCC	International Newspaper Collectors Club
INCC	International Numismatic Club by Correspondence = CINC
INCE	Instítuto Nacional de Cooperación Educativa (Venezuela)
INCE	Instítuto Nacional para la Calidad de la Edificación
INCEI	Instítuto Nacional de Comercio Exterior e Interior (Nicaragua)
INCERC	Institutul de Cercetari în Constructii si Economia Constructiilor
INCF	International New Course Faction
INCI	International Network for Chemical Information (ICCS, PGI) = ChIN
INCIBA	Instítuto Nacional de Cultura y Bellas Artes (Venezuela)
INCIE	Instítuto Nacional de las Ciencias de Educación
INCINC	International Copyrights Information Centre (U.S.A.)
INCINE	Instítuto Nicaragüense de Cine
INCIS	Istituto Nazionale Case per gli Impiegati dello Stato
Incité	Company and Industry Information for Research and the City
INCITEC	Fundación Instítuto de Investigacion Cientificas y Tecnicas (Colombia)
INCLEN	International Clinical Epidemiology Network
INCN	Institut National pour la Conservation de la Nature (Zaïre)
INCO	International Chamber of Commerce
INCOCAL	Industria de Componentes para Calçado
INCOFER	Instítuto Costarricense de Ferrocarriles
INCOLDA	Instítuto Colombiano de Administración
INCOMAQ	Industria Constructora de Maquinaria (Ecuador)
INCOMAS	International Conference on Marketing Systems for Developing Countries
INCOME	Industriale Cotonicola Meridionale
INCOMEX	Instítuto Colombiano de Comercio Exterior
INCOMI	Indústria e Comércio de Minerios S.A. (Brazil)
INCON-CRYO	International Conference on Cryogenics (India)
INCOOP	Instítuto Nacional de Cooperativas (Peru)
INCOP	Industria Costruzione Oper Pubbliche
INCOP	Instítuto Costarricense de Puertos del Pacifico
INCOR	Indian National Committee on Oceanic Research
INCOR	Intergovernmental Conference on Oceanographic Research
INCOR	Israeli National Committee for Oceanographic Research
INCORA	Instítuto Colombiano de la Reforma Agraria
INCORET	Interdepartementale Coördinatiecommissie voor de Openlucht- recreatie en het Toerisme
INCOSAI	International Congress of Supreme Adult Institutions
INCOSPAR	Indian National Committee for Space Research
INCOTEC	International Co-operative Training and Education Committee (ICA)
INCP	Institut International des Collectivités Publiques
INCP	Instítuto Nacionál de Ciéncia Politica (Brazil)
INCPEN	Industry Committee for Packaging and the Environment
INCQS	Instítuto Nacional de Controle de Qualidad en Saude (Brazil)
INCRA	Instítuto Nacional de Colonização e Reforma Agrária (Brazil)
INCRAE	Instítuto de Colonización de la Région Amazónica (Ecuador)
INCRET	Instítuto de Capacitacion y Recreacion de los Trabajadores (Venezuela)
INCUBAR	Asociación Colombiana de Incubadores
INCYTH	Instítuto Nacional de Ciencia y Tecnica Hidricas (Argentina)
IND	Instítuto Nacional de Deportes (Venezuela)
IND	Instítuto Nicaragüense de Deportes
INDA	Instítuto de Investigacion y Desarrollo de Autogestion (Peru)
INDA	Instítuto International Investigación Acción Desarrollo
INDA	Instítuto Nacional do Desenvolvimento Agrério (Brazil)

INDA	Istituto Nazionale di Dramma Antico
INDAC	Integral Nuclear Data Centre (U.S.A)
INDAF	Instítuto Nacional de Desarrollo y Aprovechamiento Forestales (Cuba)
INDAG	Industrial and Agricultural Co. Ltd (Nigeria)
INDAL	Indian Aluminium Co.
INDAL	Industria de Almidones y Alimentos (Ecuador)
INdAM	Istituto Nazionale di Alta Matematica Francesco Severi
INDAP	Instítuto de Desarrollo Agropecuário (Chile)
INDC	International Nuclear Data Committee (IAEA)
INDCAM	Société Indocamerounaise
INDDA	Instítuto Nacional de Desarrollo Agroindustrial (Peru)
INDE	Instítuto Nacional de Desarrollo (Peru)
INDE	Instítuto Nacional de Electrificación (Guatemala)
INDE	Instítuto Nicaragüense de Desarrollo
INDEC	Instítuto Nacional de Estadéstica y Censos (Argentina)
INDECO	Industrial Development Corporation (Zambia)
INDECO	Instítuto Nacional para el Desarrollo de la Comunidad Rural y de la Vivienda Popular (Mexico)
INDEF	Instítuto Nacional de Financiamiento (Bolivia)
INDEHI	Instituto de Investigación y Desarrollo Hidrobiológico (Peru)
INDELEC-SA	Industrias Electricas, S.A. (Nicaragua)
INDER	Instítuto Nacional de Deportes, Educación Fisica y Recreación (Cuba)
INDERENA	Instítuto de Desarrollo de Recursos Naturales Renovables y del Ambiente (Colombia)
INDES	Instítuto Nacional de los Deportes de El Salvador
INDESIT	Industria Elettrodomestici Italiana
INDEVCO	ndustrial Development Company (Lebanon)
INDEX	Centre for Industrial Development (Suriname)
INDI	Instítuto de Desenvolvemento Industrial de Minas Gerais (Brazil)
INDI	Instítuto Nacional del Indigena (Paraguay)
INDIS	Industrial Information System (UNIDO)
INDITEC-NOR	Instítuto Nacional de Investigaciones Tecnologicas y Normalización (Chile)
INDO	Instítuto Nacional de Denominaciones de Origen de los Vinos Españoles
INDOC	Indonesisch Documentatie en Informatie Centrum
INDOMUL	Industria Militar (Colombia)
INDOSUEZ	Banque de l'Indochine et de Suez
INDOTA	Indonesian Timber Association
INDPRO	Indian Committee for Simplification of External Trade Documents (India)
INDRHI	Instítuto Nacional de Recursos Hidráulicos (Dominica)
INDRP	Institut Nacional de Recherches et de Documentation Pédagogiques
INDU-ARROZ	Federación de Industriales del Arroz (Colombia)
INDU-NARES	Servicio Comercial y Técnico de Industrias Auxiliares de la Construcción Naval
INDU-QUINISA	Industrias Quimicas de Nicaragua, S.A.
Indubán	Banco de Finación Industrial
INDUMIL	Industria Militar (Colombia)
INDUPERU	Empresa Estatal de Industrias del Perú
INDUSTRI-RÅDET	Federation of Danish Industries
INE	Initiative for Nonprofit Entrepreneurship (U.S.A.)
INE	Institution of Nuclear Engineers
INE	Instítuto Nacional de Energia (Ecuador)
INE	Instítuto Nacional de Estadística (Peru, Spain)
INE	Instítuto Nicaragüense de Energia
INE	Istituto Nazionale di Ecologia
INEA	Ethnobiological Institute of Australia
INEA	International Electronics Association
INEA	Istituto Nazionale di Economia Agraria
INEAA	Institut Européen d'Architecture et d'Aménagement du Territoire = IEAA
INEAC	Institut National pour l'Étude Agronomique du Congo (Belgium)
INEC	Institut Européen d'Écologie et de Cancerologie (Belgium)
INEC	Institut Européen de Cancérologie
INEC	Institut Européen des Industries de la Gomme de Caroube
INEC	Instítuto Nacional de Estadísticas y Censos (Ecuador, Nicaragua)

INEC	Instítuto Nacional para el Mejoramiento de la Enseñanza de las Ciencias (Argentina)
INECAFE	Instítuto Ecuatoriano del Café
INECEL	Instítuto Ecuatoriano de Electrificación
INECOOP	Istituto Nazionale per l'Educazione Cooperativa
INÉD	Institut National d'Études Démographiques
INED	International Network for Educational Information (IBE)
INEDECA	Industria Ecuatoriana Elaboradora de Cacao
INEDES	Instítuto Ecuatoriano de Planificación para el Desarrollo Social
INEE	International Excellence Exchange Foundation (Belgium)
INEFOS	Instítuto Ecuatoriano de Formacion Social
INEGI	Instítuto Nacional de Estadistica, Geografia e Informatica (Mexico)
INEHRI	Instítuto Ecuatoriana de Recursos Hidraúlicos
INEL	Instituto Nacional de Estudios Lingüísticos (Bolivia)
INEM	Instítuto Nacional de Empleo
INEM	Instítuto Nacional de Enseñanza Media
INEMIN	Instítuto Ecuatoriano de Mineria
INEMO	Chambre Syndicale des Importateurs et Négociants en Machines-Outils et Outillages de Belgique
INEMO	Istituto Nazionale di Economia Montana
INEN	Instítuto Ecuatoriano de Normalizacion
INEN	Instítuto National de Energia Nuclear (Guatemala)
INENCO	Center for International Environmental Cooperation (Russia)
INEOA	International Narcotic Enforcement Officers Association
INÉP	Institut National d'Éducation Populaire
INEP	Institut National d'Études Politiques (Zaïre)
INEP	Institut za Primenu Nuklearne Energije u Poljoprivredi, Veterinarstru i Sumartsvu
INEP	Instítuto Nacional de Estudos e Pesquisas Educacionais (Brazil)
INER	Institute of Nuclear Energy Research (Taiwan)
INER	Instítuto Nacional de Electrificacion Rural (Bolivia)
INERA	Institut National pour l'Étude et la Recherche Agronomique (Zaïre)
INERHI	Instítuto Ecuatoriano de Recursos Hidraulicos
INERIS	Institut National de l'Environnement Industriel et des Risques (France)
INERM	Instítuto National d'Études Rurales Montagnardes
INERYCYT	Instituto Nacional de Enfermedades Respiratorias y Cirugía Torácica (Chile)
INES	International Network of Natural Engineers and Scientists for Global Responsibility
INESC	Institut de Estudos Socio-Económicos (Brazil)
INESPAL	Industria Española del Aluminio
INESPRE	Instítuto de Estabilización de Precios (Dominican Republic)
INETOP	Institut National de l'Enseignement Technique d'Orientation Professionnelle
INEUT	Istituto Nazionale di Economia Urbana e Territoriale
INF	Instítuto Nacionál de Farmacologia (Brazil)
INF	International Naturist Federation = FNI
INF	Islamic National Front (Sudan)
INFA	International Federation of Aestheticians
INFA	Vereinigung Spezialisierter Innenarchitekturfirmen
INFACT	Irish National Federation Against Copyright Theft
INFAS	Institut für Angewandte Sozialwissenschaft
INFCO	Information Committee of ISO
INFCSV	Institut National de Formation des Cadres Supérieurs de la Vente
INFE	Instítuto Nacional de Fomento de la Exportación
INFEDOP	International Federation of Employees in Public Service
INFI	Instítuto Nacional de Fomento Tabacalero (Colombia)
INFI	Investment and Finance Bank (Lebanon)
INFIC	International Network of Feed Information Centres (FAO)
INFIR	Istituto Nazionale per il Finanziamento della Ricostruzione
INFN	Istituto Nazionale de Fisica Nucleare

INFO	International Fortean Organization
INFO	International Information Management Exposition and Conference
INFO-NAVIT	Instítuto del Fondo Nacional de la Vivienda para los Trabajadores (Mexico)
INFO-PACHS	Incorporated Association for Food Packaging Health Safety
INFO-TERRA	International Environmental Information System (Kenya)
INFOC	Instítuto Nacional de Formacion Campesina (Ecuador)
INFOFISH	Intergovernmental Organisation for Marketing Information and Technical Advisory Services for Fishery Products in the Asia-Pacific (FAO)
INFOL	Instítuto Nacional de Fomento Lanero (Bolivia)
INFOLAC	Information for Latin American Countries Project (UN)
INFONAC	Instítuto de Fomento Nacional (Nicaragua)
INFOODS	International Network of Food Data Systems (UNU)
INFOP	Instítuto de Fomento de la Producción (Guatemala)
INFOPAL	Population Information and Technology Area (ECLAC)
INFO-PESCA	Center for Marketing Information and Advisory Services for Fishery Products in Latin America and the Caribbean
INFOPLAN	Sistema de Información para la Planificación de América Latina y el Caribe (Chile)
INFOR	Information Network and File Organization
INFORAV	Istituto Nazionale per lo Sviluppo e la Gestione Avanzata dell'Informazione
INFORCAR	Institut de Formation Sociale des Caraïbes = CARISFORM, CARISOV, INFOSCAR
INFORM	Information Network Focus on Religious Movements
INFORMS	Institute for Operations Research and the Management Sciences
Informstal	International System of Scientific and Technical Information on Ferrous Metallurgy (Russia)
INFORP	Instítuto Nacional de Formacion Profesional (Honduras)
INFORSA	Industrias Forestales, S.A. (Chile)
INFOS	Informationszentrum für Schnittwertemachning
INFOSA-MAK	Fish Marketing Information, Promotion and Technical Advisory Services for Arab Countries (FAO)
INFOSCAR	Instítuto Formación Social Caribe = CARISFORM, CARISOV, INFORCAR
INFOSTAT	Institute of Informatics and Statistics (Slovakia)
INFOTAB	International Tobacco Information Center (Belgium)
INFOTEC	Fondo de Informacion y Documentacion para la Industria (Mexico)
INFOTERM	International Information Centre for Terminology (Austria)
INFU.S.A.	International Network for a UN Second Assembly (MAPW)
ING	Institut National de Gestion (Niger)
ING	Instítuto Nacional de Geografíca (Brazil)
ING	Instituut voor Nederlandse Geschiedenis
INGALA	Instítuto Nacional Galapagos (Ecuador)
INGC	Istituto Nazionale de Genetica per la Cerealicoltura
INGE	Instítuto Nacional de Granos y Elevadores (Argentina)
INGEBA	International Cooperative Bank Company (Switzerland)
INGEO-MINAS	Instítuto Nacional de Investigaciones Geológico-Mineras (Colombia)
INGEOMIN	Instítuto de Geologia y Mineria (Peru)
INGRAF	Instituut for Grafisk Forskning
INGUAT	Instítuto Guatemalteca de Turismo
INH	Institut National d'Hygiène
INH	Instítuto Nacional de Hidrocarburos
INHF	Institut National Homéopathique Français
INHIGEO	International Committee on the History of the Geological Sciences
INI	Institut National de l'Industrie
INI	Instítuto Nacional de Indústria
INI	Instítuto Nacional de Inversiones (Bolivia)
INI	Instítuto Nacional de Investigaciones (Chile)
INI	Instítuto Nacional Indigenista (Mexico)
INI	Istituto Nazionale dell'Informazione
INIA	Instítuto de Investigaciones Aropecuarias (Chile)
INIA	Instítuto Nacional de Investigaciones Agrarias (Mexico, Spain)

INIA	Instítuto Nacional de Investigaciones Agronómicas
INIA	International Institute on Aging (ECOSOC)
INIAG	Institut National des Industries et des Arts Graphiques
INIAG	Instítuto de Investigaciones Agrarias (Colombia)
INIAP	Instítuto Nacional de Investigaciones Agropecuárias (Ecuador)
INIASA	Istituto Nazionale per l'Instruzione e l'Addestramento nel Settore Artigiano
INIBAP	International Network for the Improvement of Banana and Plantain
INIBP	Instítuto Nacional de Investigaciones Biológico
INIC	Instítuto Nacional de Imigração e Colonização (Brazil)
INIC	Instítuto Nacional de Investigação Científica
INIC	Instítuto Nacional de Investigaciones Cientificas (Paraguay)
INIC	Instítuto Nacional de la Investigación Cientifica (Mexico)
INICHAR	Institut National de l'Industrie Charbonnière (Belgium)
INICTEL	Instítuto Nacional de Investigaciones y de Capacitacion de Telecomunicaciones (Peru)
INID	Institutul Nacional de Informare si Documentare Stiintifica si Tehnica
INIDE	Instítuto Nacional de Investigación y Desarrollo de la Educación (Peru)
INIDEP	Instituto Nacional de Investigación y Desarollo Pesquero (Argentina)
INIDIEC	Empresa Nicaragüense de Distribucion y Exhibicion Cinematografica
INIDIN	Indonesian National Information and Documentation Network
INIE	Instítuto de Investigaciones Energeticas y Servicio de Ingenieria Electronica (Peru)
INIE	Instítuto Nacional de Ingenieria España
INIE	Instítuto Nacional de Investigaçãos Espaciais (Brazil)
INIED	Instítuto Nacional de Infraestructura Educativa (Peru)
INIEX	Institut National des Industries Extractives (Belgium) = NIEB
INIF	Industria Nacional de Insecticidas e Fertilizantes (Brazil)
INIF	Institut National des Industries de Fermentation
INIF	Instituto Nacional de Investigaciones Forestales (Mexico)
INIFAT	Instítuto de Investigaciones Fundamentales en Agricultura Tropical A.Humboldt (Cuba)
INII	Instítuto Nacional de Investigação Industrial (Portugal)
INIL	Institut National des Industries Légères (Algeria)
ININ	Instítuto Nacional de Investigaciones Nucleares (Mexico)
ININCO	Instítuto de Investigaciones de la Comunicacion (Venezuela)
ININVI	Instítuto Nacional de Investigacion y Normalizacion de la Vivienda (Peru)
INION RAN	Institute of Scientific Information in the Social Sciences, Russian Academy of Sciences
INIP	Instítuto Nacional de Investigação das Pescas (Portugal)
INIP	Instítuto Nacional de Investigaciones Pecuarias (Mexico)
INIP	Instítuto Nacional per l'Incremento della Produttività
INIP	Istituto Nazionale per l'Incremento della Produttività
INIPA	Instítuto Nacional de Investigacion y Promocion Agropecuária (Peru)
INIRC	International Non-Ionizing Radiation Committee (IRPA)
INIREB	Instituto Nacional de Investigaciones sobre Recursos Bióticos (Mexico)
INIRO	Indonesisch Instituut voor Rubber Onderzoek
INIS	International Nuclear Information System (IAEA)
INISA	Instítuto de Investigaciones en Salud (Costa Rica)
INISER	Instítuto Nicaragüense de Seguros y Reaseguros
INISM	Istituto Nazionale Italiano per lo Studio del Microclima
INISTE	International Network for Information in Science and Technology Education
INIT	Instítuto Nacional de Industria Turística (Cuba)
INITE	Instituto de Ingenieros Técnicos de España
INITO	Société Initiative Togolaise

INIVA	Institute of International Visual Arts
INKA	Internationale Nederlandse Kultuuraktie
INKATHA	Inkatha ye Nkululeko yeSizwe
INL	Institut National dụ Logement
INL	Institúto Nacional do Livro
INLA	International Nuclear Law Association = AIDN
INLA	Irish National Liberation Army
INLAP	Institute for Law and Peace
INLASA	Industria Nacional Laminadora, S.A. (Uruguay)
INLCO	Institut National des Langues et Civilisations Orientales
INLD	Institúto Nacional do Livro e do Disco (Mozambique)
INLE	Institúto Nacional del Libro Español
INLOGOV	Institute of Local Government Studies
INM	Imbokodvo National Movement (Swaziland)
INM	Institut National de Marketing
INM	Institute of Naval Medicine (MOD)
INM	Institúto Nacional de Meteorologia
INM	Institúto Nacional do Mate (Brazil)
INMA	Institut National de Médecine Agricole
INMARSAT	International Maritime Satellite Organization
INMAS	Institute of Nuclear Medicine and Allied Sciences (India)
Inmecafe	Institúto Mexicano del Cafe
INMETRO	Institúto Nacional de Metrologia, Normalização e Qualidade Industrial (Brazil)
INMG	Institúto Nacional de Meteorologia e Geofisica (Portugal)
INMV	Institúto Nacional de Medicina Veterinaria (Cuba)
INN	Imprimerie Nationale du Niger
INN	Institúto Nacional de la Nutrición (Argentina, Colombia, Ecuador, Venezuela)
INN	Institúto Nacional de Normalización (Chile)
INN	International Negotiation Network
INNA-NEWS	International Newsreel and News Film Association = AIPF
INNATE	Irish Network for Non-violent Action Training and Education
INNERTAP	Information Network on New and Renewable Energy Resources and Technologies for Asia and the Pacific (UNESCO) (Philippines)
INNFA	Institúto Nacional del Niño y la Familia (Ecuador)
INNOTECH	Regional Centre for Educational Innovation and Technology (SEAMEO)
INNS	International Neural Network Society
INO	Irish Nurses Organisation
INO	Istituto Nazionale d'Ottica
INOC	Inter-Islamic Network on Oceanography (Comstech, OIC) (Turkey)
INOC	Iraq National Oil Company
INOCAR	Institúto Oceanografico de la Armada (Ecuador)
INODEP	Institut Oecuménique pour le Développement des Peuples (Switzerland)
INOE	Internacia Naturista Organizo Esperantista
INOGE	Inter-Islamic Network on Genetic Engineering and Biotechnology (COMSTECH, OIC) (Egypt)
INOR	Organisation Internationale Restitutions
INORCOL	Institúto de Normas Colombiana
INOS	Institúto Nacional de Obras Sanitarias (Venezuela)
INOTEX	Industrie Nouvelle Textile (Cameroon)
INOU	Irish National Organisation of the Unemployed
INP	Institute of National Planning (Egypt)
INP	Institúto Nacional de la Productividad (Argentina)
INP	Institúto Nacional de Pesca (Mexico)
INP	Institúto Nacional de Pinho (Brazil)
INP	Institúto Nacional de Planificación (Peru)
INP	Institúto Nacional de Prevision
INP	Instytut Nauk Politycznych
INP RAN	Institute of National Economic Forecasting, Russian Academy of Sciences
INP ROSSII	Informatsionno-Narodnaia Partiia Rossii
INPA	Institúto Nacional de Pesquisas de Amazónia (Brazil)
INPA	International Newspaper Promotion Association
INPABO	Institúto Paraguense de Botanica
INPADOC	International Patent Documentation Center (EPO)

INPAR	Institut National de Promotion Agricole de Rennes	**INQUA**	International Union for Quaternary Research
INPC	Irish National Petroleum Corporation	**INR**	Institut National de Radio-diffusion (Belgium)
INPC	Irish National Productivity Committee	**INRA**	Institut National de la Recherche Agronomique
INPDTU	Irish National Painters' and Decorators' Trade Union (Éire)	**INRA**	Institute for Natural Resources in Africa (UNU) = UNU/INRA
INPE	Institut National pour la Promotion de l'Entreprise	**INRA**	Institúto Nacional de Reforma Agraria (Cuba)
INPE	Institúto Nacional de Pesca del Ecuador	**INRA**	Institúto Nicaragüense de Reforma Agraria
INPE	Institúto Nacional de Pesquisas Espaciais (Brazil)	**INRA**	International Network for Religion and Animals
INPED	Institut National de la Production et du Développement Industriel (Algeria)	**INRA-VISION**	Institúto Nacional de Radio y Televisión (Colombia)
INPEP	Institúto Nacional de Pensiones de los Empleados Publicos (El Salvador)	**INRAB**	Institut National de Recherches Anti-arcticaux de Belgique
INPES	Institúto Nacional de Salud (Colombia)	**INRAN**	Institut National de Recherches Agronomiques au Niger
INPESCA	Institúto Nicaragüense de la Pesca	**INRAT**	Institut National de le Recherche Agronomique de Tunisie
INPET	Institúto Peruano de Empresas de Propiedad Exclusiva de sus Trabajadores	**INRDG**	Institut National de Recherche et de Documentation de Guinée
INPFC	International North Pacific Fisheries Commission	**INRDM**	Interdisciplinary Natural Resources Development and Management Program (AIT) (Thailand)
INPFL	Independent National Patriotic Front of Liberia	**INRDP**	Institut National de Recherche et de Documentation Pédagogiques
INPI	Insitut National de la Propriété Industrielle	**INRE**	Institute of Natural Resources and Environment (CSIRO)
INPI	Institúto Nacional da Propriedade Industrial (Brazil, Portugal)	**INRE**	Institúto Nacionale de Reforma Económica (Cuba)
INPI	Institúto Nacional de Promoción Industrial (Peru)	**INRETS**	Institut National de Recherche sur les Transports et leur Sécurité (France)
INPPARES	Instituto Peruano de Paternidad Responsable	**INRF**	Institut National de Recherches Forestières (Tunis)
INPPSS	Institúto Nacional para le Producción de Semillas Selectas	**INRH**	Institúto Nacional de Recursos Hidráulicos (Cuba)
INPROA	Institúto de Promición Agraria (Chile)	**INRIA**	Institut National de Recherche en Informatique et en Automatique
INPRODE	Institúto Profesional para el Desarrollo (Colombia)	**INRIC**	International Network of Resource Information Centers
INPRUHU	Institúto para la Promoción Humana (Nicaragua)	**INRN**	Institúto Nacional de Racionalización y Normalización
INPS	Institut National de la Prévoyance Sociale	**INRO**	International Natural Rubber Organisation = OICN
INPS	Institúto Nacional da Previdência Social (Brazil)	**INRO**	International Naval Research Organization
INPS	Istituto Nazionale della Previdenza Sociale	**INRP**	Institut National de la Recherche Pédagogique
INPSA	Industria Nacional de Plasticos, S.A. (Panama)		
INPSA	Institut National de Promotion Supérieure Agricole		
INPV	Institut National de la Protection des Végétaux (Algeria)		

INRRK	International Network for Reconciliation and Reunification of Korea = CILRECO, ILCRPK
INRS	Institut National de Recherche et de Sécurité pour la Prévention des Accidents du Travail et de Maladies Professionelles
INRS	Institut National de Recherche Scientifique (Rwanda, Togo)
INRT	Instítuto Nacional de Racionalizatición del Trabajo
INRV	Institut National de Recherche Vétérinaire (Belgium)
INS	Immigration and Naturalisation Service
INS	Institut National de Sécurité
INS	Institut National des Sports
INS	Institute for Nuclear Study (Japan)
INS	Institute National de Statistique
INS	Institute of Nuclear Sciences (DSIR) (New Zealand)
INS	Instítuto Nacional de Seguros (Costa Rica)
INS	Instytut Nauk Społecznych
INS	International Neuromodulation Society
INS	International Neuropsychology Society
INSA	Indian National Science Academy
INSA	Indonesian National Shipowners Association
INSA	Institut National des Sciences Appliquées
INSA	International Service Association for Health
INSA	International Shipowners' Association
INSAB	International Numismatic Society Authentication Bureau
INSAE	Institut National de la Statistique et de l'Analyse Économique (Benin)
INSAFI	Instítuto Salvadoreño de Fomento Industrial
INSAFOP	Instítuto Salvadoreño de Fomento de la Producción
INSAG	International Nuclear Safety Advisory Group
INSAH	Institut du Sahel (Mali)
INSALUD	Instítuto Nacional de la Salud
INSANICA	Industrias Sanitarias de Nicaragua
INSBA	Institut National Supérieur des Beaux-Arts
INSC	Irish National Stud (Éire)
INSCA	International Sausage Casing Association
INSDC	Indonesian National Science Documentation Centre
INSDOC	Indian National Scientific Documentation Centre
INSEA	Informatic Services Association (Belgium)
INSEA	Institut National de Statistiques et d'Économie Appliquée (Morocco)
INSEA	International Society for Education through Art
INSEAD	Institut Européen d'Administration des Affaires
INSEAN	Istituto per Studi ed Esperenze di Architettura Navale
INSEE	Institut National de la Statistique et des Études Économiques
INSEM	Institut Européen de Management
INSERM	Institut National de la Santé et de la Recherche Médicale
INSERSO	Instítuto Nacional de Servicios Sociales
INSFO-PAL	Instítuto National de Fomento Municipal (Colombia)
INSINCA	Industrias Sinteticas de Centroamerica (El Salvador)
INSIVU-MEH	Instítuto Nacional de Sismologia, Vulcanologia, Meteorologia e Hidrologia (Guatemala)
INSJ	Institute for Nuclear Study (Japan)
INSNA	International Network for Social Network Analysis
INSO	Instítuto Nacional de Salud Ocupacional (Bolivia)
INSOC	Institut Universitaire d'Information Sociale et Économique
INSONA	International Society of Naturalists (India)
INSORA	Instítuto de Organización y Administración (Chile)
INSPEC	International Information Services for the Physics and Engineering Communities
INSPIRE	Integrated Spinal Rehabilitation Foundation
INSS	Instítuto Nacional de Seguridad Social
INSSBI	Instítuto Nicaragüense de Seguridad Social y Bienestar
INSTA	Internordisk Standardiseringssamarbejde
INSTAAR	Institute of Arctic and Alpine Research (U.S.A.)

INSTAB	Information Service on Toxicity and Biodegradability (WPRL)	**INTABS**	International Terminal Accounting and Banking Service
InstBE	Institution of British Engineers	**INTAF**	International Task Force for the Rural Poor
InstE	Institution of Electronics	**INTAGRO**	Instítuto Agrario de Estudios Económicos (Chile)
InstF	Institute of Fuel		
INSTIA	Instítuto Nacional de Andragogia (IFAE) (Venezuela) = IIA	**INTAL**	Instítuto para la Integración de America Latina (IDB)
InstMC	Institute of Measurement and Control	**INTAMEL**	International Association of Metropolitan City Libraries
InstME	Institute of Media Executives	**INTAMIC**	International Association for Microcircuit Cards
InstMP	Institute of Management in Printing		
INSTN	Institut National des Sciences et Techniques Nucléaires	**INTAS**	International Association for the Promotion of Co-operation with Scientists from the Independent States of the Former Soviet Union
InstofP	Institute of Piping		
INSTOP	Institut National Scientifique et Technique d'Océanographie et de Pêche (Tunisia)		
		INTAVA	International Aviation Association
InstP	Institute of Physics	**INTC**	Isfahan Nuclear Technology Centre (Iran)
InstPC	Institute of Public Cleansing	**INTD**	Institut National des Techniques de la Documentation
InstPS	Institute of Public Supplies		
InstR	Institute of Refrigeration	**INTE**	Instítuto de Investigación Técnica (Chile)
InstRA	Institute of Registered Architects		
INSTRAW	International Research and Training Institute for the Advancement of Women (Dominican Republic)	**INTE**	Instítuto de Tecnicas Energeticas
		INTEC	Comité de Investigaciones Tecnológicas de Corfo (Chile)
InstSMM	Institute of Sales Management and Marketing	**INTEC**	Instítuto Tecnologico de Computacion (Panama)
InstWP	Institute of Word Processing		
INSURF	International Network on Soil Fertility and Sustainable Rice Farming	**INTEC**	International Naval Technology Expo and Conference
		INTECA	Instítuto Tecnico Aeronautico (Nicaragua)
INSz	Instytut Nawozów Sztucznych		
INT	Institute of New Technologies of Education (Russia)	**INTECNOR**	Instítuto Nacional de Tecnologia y Normalizacion (Paraguay)
INT	Instítuto Nacionál de Tecnologia (Brazil)	**INTECOF**	International Economic Functions (Cameroon)
INT	Instítuto Nazionale Trasporti		
INT-WORLSA	International Third World Legal Studies Association	**INTECOL**	International Association for Ecology (IUBS)
		INTECOM	International Council for Technical Communication
INTA	Instítuto de Nutricion y Tecnologia Alimenticia (Chile)		
INTA	Instítuto Nacional de Técnica Aerospacial	**INTED**	Instítuto Técnico de Distribucion y Libreservicio
		INTEL	Instítuto Nacional de Telecommunicaciónes (Panama)
INTA	Instítuto Nacional de Tecnologia Agropecuário (Argentina)		
INTA	Instítuto Nacional de Transformación Agrária (Guatemala)	**INTEL-SAT**	International Telecommunications Satellite Organisation
INTA	International Association for the Development and Management of Existing and New Towns = AIVN	**INTELCAM**	Société des Télécommunications Internationales du Caméroun
		INTELCI	Télécommunications Internationales de la Côte d'Ivoire
INTA	International New Thought Alliance		
INTA-SAFCON	International Tanker Safety Conference	**INTELCO**	International Electronic Company (Ivory Coast)

INTELCO	Office des Télécommunications Internationales du Congo	**COOP**	Society (Netherlands)
INTELCOM	Ingenieria de Telefonos y Comunicaciones (Honduras)	**INTER-COOP**	International Organization for Consumer Co-operative Distributive Trades
INTELEC	International Telecommunications Energy Conference	**INTER-COSMOS**	Council on International Cooperation in Research and Uses of Outer Space
INTEM	Instítuto Interamericano de Educación Musical	**INTER-DOC**	Centre International de Documentation et d'Information (Belgium)
INTEMA	Institute of Materials Science and Technology (Argentina)	**INTER-ELECTRO**	International Organisation for Electrical Equipment
INTEPHIL	International Standing Conference on Philanthrophy	**INTER-ELEKTRO**	International Organisation for Economic, Scientific and Technical Cooperation for Electrical Engineering
INTER-SU	Bureau de Liaison des Sanatoriums Universitaires et de Protection Antituberculeuse des Étudiants	**INTER-EXPERT**	International Association of Experts
INTER-ALUMINA	Interamericana de Alumina (Venezuela)	**INTER-EXPO**	Committee of Organisers of National Participations in International Economic Displays
INTER-ASMA	International Association of Asthmology	**INTER-FAST**	International Industrial Fastener Engineering Exhibition and Conference
INTER-BANCA	Banca per Finanziamenti a Medie e Lungo Termine	**INTER-FILM**	International Inter-Church Film Centre
INTER-BANQUE	Banque Intercontinentale du Gabon	**INTER-FINISH**	International Union for Electrodeposition and Surface Finishing
INTER-BASE	Empresa Caboverdeana das Infrastruturas de Pescas (Cape Verde)	**INTER-FORST**	International Exposition of the Technology of Forestry and Forest Industries (Germany)
INTER-BRANT	Union Intercommunale des Centrales Electriques du Brabant (Belgium)	**INTER-FRIGO**	International Railway-owned Company for Refrigerated Transport
INTER-BRAS	Petrobrás Comércio Internacional (Brazil)	**INTER-GALVA**	International Galvanizing Conference
INTER-CARGO	International Association of Dry Cargo Shipowners	**INTER-GASTRA**	International Trade Fair for the Hotel and Catering Industry
INTER-CENTRE	International Centre for the Terminology of the Social Sciences (Switzerland)	**INTER-GEOTECH-NIKA**	International Organization for Technical Cooperation in Geology
INTER-CHIM	International Organization for Cooperation in Small Volume Chemicals Production	**INTER-HYBRID**	Association Intercontinentale du Maïs Hybride = AIMH
INTER-COLOR	Commission Internationale pour la Couleur dans la Mode et de Textile	**INTER-KAMA**	Internationaler Kongress mit Ausstellung für Messtechnik und Automatik
INTER-COM	Société Intercommunale Belge de Gas et d'Electricité	**INTER-LAINE**	Comité des Industries Lainières de la CEE
INTER-COMSA	Intercontinental de Comunicaciónes per Satellite SA (Panama)	**INTER-LAIT**	Société Interprofessionnelle de Lait
INTER-CON	Intercontinental Church Society	**INTER-MARGEO**	International Organization for Marine Geology
INTER-CON	International Convention and Exposition (IEEE)	**INTER-METAL**	Organization for Cooperation in the Field of Heavy Metallurgy (Hungary)
INTER-CON-TAINER	International Company for Transport by Transcontainers	**INTER-METALL**	Organisation for Cooperation in the Iron and Steel Industry
INTER-	International Agricultural Cooperative		

INTER-MICRO	International Conference on Microscopy	**INTERFAIS**	International Food Aid Information System
INTER-NEPCON	International Congress on Project Planning by Network Analysis	**INTERFAM**	International Independent Information and Advertising Agency of Women in Russia
INTER-OCEAN	International Conference and Exhibition for Marine Technology	**INTER-GRAF**	International Confederation for Printing and Allied Industries
INTER-PHIL	International Standing Conference on Philanthropy	**INTERGU**	Internationale Gesellschaft für Urheberrecht
INTER-PIPE	International Pipeline Technology Convention	**Interights**	International Centre for the Legal Protection of Human Rights
INTER-PLAN	International Group for Studies in National Planning	**INTERMA**	Instítuto de Terras do Maranhão (Brazil)
INTER-PLAS	International Plastics Exhibition and Conference	**INTERMAC**	International Association of Merger and Acquisition Consultants (U.S.A.)
INTER-PORT	International Organization for Seaports	**INTERMAG**	International Association of Television Political Magazines
INTER-PROPO	Sociedade de Propaganda International de Produtos Portugueses	**INTERMAN**	International Management Development Network (ILO, UNDP)
INTER-QUANT	International Commission for the Application of Quantitative Methods in History	**INTERMAT**	Instítuto de Terras de Mato Grosso (Brazil)
INTER-SHOE	International Federation of the Independent Shoe Trade	**INTERNET**	International Project Management Association
INTER-SPUR	Instítuto Interconexión Fluvial Suramericana	**INTERNET**	Scientific and Technical Information Network (UNESCO)
INTER-SPUTNIK	International Organization of Space Communications	**INTEROPS**	Commission pour la Coopération Multilatérale dans l'Observation des Satellites Artificiels de la Terre
INTER-STENO	International Federation of Shorthand and Typewriting = FISD, IFKM, IFST	**INTERPAP**	Société Interafricaine de Participation (Ivory Coast)
INTER-TANKO	International Association of Independent Tanker Owners	**INTERPAVE**	Concrete Block Paving Association
INTER-VICO	Inter-American Organization of Cooperative Housing Technical Service Organizations (Colombia)	**INTERPOL**	International Criminal Police Organisation = ICPO, IKPO, OIPC
		INTERRAD	International Association for the Study of Radiolarians
INTER-WOOL-LABS	International Association of Wool Textile Laboratories	**INTERTEL**	International Legion of Intelligence (U.S.A)
INTERAF	Société Interafricaine d'Import-Export Côte d'Ivoire	**INTER-TOTO**	International Association of Toto and Lotto Organisations
INTERAN	International Conference on the Analysis of Geological Materials	**INTERVIS**	Polish Organisation for the Export-Import of Tools
INTERBA	Instítuto de Terra da Bahía (Brazil)	**INTERZUM**	International Fair of Accessories and Materials for Woodworking and Furniture
INTERBOR	Union Internationale des Techniciens Orthopédistes		
INTERCO	International Council on Jewish Social and Welfare Services	**INTESCA**	Internacional de Ingenieria y Estudios Technicos SA
INTER-COOP EUROPE	International Society of European Agricultural Cooperatives (Switzerland)	**Intevep**	Instítuto Venezolana Tecnologico del Petróleo (Venezuela)
		INTEXTAR	Instítuto de Investigacion Textil y Cooperacion Industrial
INTEREG	Internationales Institut für Nationalitätenrecht und Regionalismus	**INTG**	Intersindical Nacional de Trabajadores Gallegos

INTI	Instítuto Nacional de Tecnologia Industrial (Argentina)
INTIB	Industrial and Technological Information Bank (UNIDO)
INTINTEC	Instítuto de Investigación Tecnológica Industrial y de Normas Tecnicas
Intirub	Indonesian Tyre and Rubber Works
INTIST	International Institute of Science and Technology (U.S.A.)
INTN	Instítuto Nacional de Tecnología y Normlización (Paraguay)
INTO	Irish National Teachers Organisation
INTOSAI	International Organisation of Supreme Audit Institutions
INTP	Institut National des Télécommunications et des Postes
INTRA	Instítuto Nacional del Transporte (Colombia)
INTRACO	International Trading Company (Togo)
INTRADEP	Cabinet Interafricain d'Études, de Pilotage et de Promotion de Travaux (Ivory Coast)
INTRANED	Internationale Transport Agenturen "Nederland"
INTROP	Information Centre of Tropical Plant Protection (Germany)
INTS	International Nuclear Track Society
INTSH	Institut National Tchadien pour les Sciences Humaines (Chad)
INTSHU	Institut Togolais des Sciences Humaines
INTSOR-MIL	International Sorghum and Millet Program
INTSOY	International Soybeam Program (U.S.A.)
INTSOY	International Soybean Program (Puerto Rico)
INTUC	Indian National Trade Union Congress
INTUG	International Telecommunications Users Group
INTUR	Instítuto Nacional de Turismo (Cuba)
INTURIS-MO	Instítuto Nicaragüense de Turismo
INU	Institute Nazionale di Urbanistica
INU	Istituto Nazionale di Urbanistica (Italy)
INUA	Instítuto Nazionale di Ultracustica
INucE	Institution of Nuclear Engineers
INUOV	Internationale Unie van let Openbaar Vervoer
INUTOM	Institut Universitaire des Territoires d'Outremer (Belgium)
INUVGATA	Irish National Union of Vintners, Grocers and Allied Trades Association
INV	Institut National du Verre (Belgium)
INV	Instítuto Nacional de la Vivenda
INV	Instítuto Nacional de Vitivinicultura (Argentina)
INV	Instítuto Nacional de Vivienda (Cuba)
INVA	Industri Vaskerienes Forbund
INVA	Instítuto de la Vivienda (Honduras)
INVE	Instítuto Nacional de Viviendas Ecónomicas (Uruguay)
INVEMA	Asociación de Investigación Industrial de la Maquina-Herramienta
INVEMAR	Instituto de Investigaciones Marinas de Punta de Betín (Colombia)
INVESTI	Instítuto Venezolano de Investigaciones Tecnológicas e Industriales
INVI	Instítuto Nacional de la Vivienda (Dominica)
INVSL	Indian National Veterinary Science Library
INVU	Instítuto Nacional de Vivienda y Urbanismo (Costa Rica)
INVUFLEC	Institut National de Vulgarisation des Fruits, Légumes et Champignons
INWAR-DAM	Islamic Network of Water Resources Development and Management (OIC)
INWAT	International Network of Women Against Tobacco
INYF	Independent National Youth Front (Hungary) = FNIF
IO	Institut Océonographique
IOA	Indian Optometric Association (India)
IOA	Institute of Acoustics
IOA	Insurers' Offices Association
IOA	International Office for Audiophonology (Belgium)
IOA	International Olympic Academy = AIO
IOA	International Omega Association (U.S.A)
IOA	International Orthoptic Association (U.S.A.)
IOA	International Osteopathic Association
IOA	International Ostomy Association
IOA	International Ozone Association (U.S.A.)
IOAP	International Office for Audiophonology = BIAP, IBAP
IOAT	International Organisation Against Trachoma

IOB	Chartered Institute of Bankers
IOB	Institute of Biology
IOB	Institute of Brewing
IOB	Institution of Buyers
IOB	Insurance Ombudsman Bureau
IOBB	International Organization of Biotechnology and Bioengineering
IOBC	International Organisation for Biological Control of Noxious Animals and Plants = OILB
IOBI	Institute of Bankers in Ireland
IOBP	International Organization of Plant Biosystematists
IOBS	Institute of Bankers in Scotland
IOC	Indian Ocean Commission
IOC	Indian Oil Corporation
IOC	Institute of Carpenters
IOC	Institute of Ceramics
IOC	Institute of Commerce
IOC	Institúto Oswaldo Cruz (Brazil)
IOC	Intergovernmental Oceanographic Commission (UN) = COI, MOK
IOC	International Oceanographic Commission
IOC	International Olympic Committee = CIO, IOK
IOC	International Organising Committee of World Mining Congresses
IOC	International Ornithological Congress
IOC	International Ozone Commission (IAMAP)
IOCARIBE	IOC Association for the Caribbean and Adjacent Regions
IOCC	Institute for Customer Care
IOCC	International Optical Computer Conference
IOCCC	International Office of Cocoa, Chocolate and Sugår Confectionery = OICCC
IOCD	International Organisation for Chemical Sciences in Development = OICD
IOCF	International Oil Compensation Fund = FIPOL, IOPC Fund
IOCG	International Organization on Crystal Growth
IOCHC	International Organisation for Cooperation in Health Care = MMI, OICS
IOCN	Institutul Oncologic Cluj Napoca
IOCU	International Organization of Consumers Unions = OIUC
IOCV	International Organisation of Citrus Virologists
IOD	Institute of Directors
IoD	Institute of Directors
IOD	International Institute for Organizational and Social Development (Belgium)
IÖD	Internationale der Öffentlichen Dienste = ISKA, ISP, PSI
IODE	International Oceanographic Data Exchange
IODMM	International Office of Documentation on Military Medicine = OIDMM
IOE	Institut d'Observation Économique
IOE	Institute of Offshore Engineering
IOE	International Office of Epizootics = OIE
IOE	International Organisation of Employers = OIE
IOEAS	Institute of Optics and Electronics, Academia Sinica
IOF	Institut für Organische Forschung und Dokumentation
IOF	Institutet för Optisk Forskning (Sweden)
IOF	International Oceanographic Foundation
IOF	Internationale Orientierungslauf Föderation
IOFC	Indian Ocean Fisheries Commission = CPOI
IOFGA	Irish Organic Farmers and Growers Association (Éire)
IOFI	International Organisation of the Flavour Industry
IOG	Institute of Groundsmanship
IOGT	International Order of Good Templars
IOH	Institute of Horticulture
IOH	Institute of Housing (now CIoH)
IOH	Institute of Occupational Hygienists
IOHE	Inter-American Organization for Higher Education (IAU) = OUI
IOHE	International Organization for Human Ecology
IOI	International Ocean Institute (Malta)
IOI	International Ombudsman Institute = IIM
IOIC	International Oil Investment Company (Libya)
IOIE	International Organisation of Industrial Employers
IOJ	Institute of Journalists
IOJ	International Organisation of Journalists = MOZ, OIJ, OIP

IOJD	International Organization – Justice and Development	**IOOC**	Iranian Offshore Oil Company
IOK	International Order of Kabbalists	**IOOF**	Independent Order of Oddfellows
IOK	Internationales Olympisches Komitee = CIO, IOC	**IOOL**	International Optometric and Optical League
IOKSZ	Union of Handicrafts Co-operatives (Hungary)	**IOOTS**	International Organisation of Old Testament Scholars
IOL	Institute of Librarians (India)	**IOP**	Institute of Packaging
IOL	Institute of Logistics	**IOP**	Institute of Painters in Oil Colours
IOL	International Old Lacers (U.S.A.)	**IOP**	Institute of Physics
IOLR	Israel Oceanographic and Limnological Research Ltd	**IOP**	Institute of Plumbing
IOM	Institut für Österreichische Musikdokumentationen	**IOP**	Institute of Printing
		IOP	Institute of Pyramidology
IOM	Institute of Meat	**IOP**	International Organisation of Palaeobotany = OIP
IOM	Institute of Metals		
IOM	Institute of Occupational Medicine	**IOP**	International Organisation of Psychophysiology = OIP
IOM	Instit́uto Oncologico de Madrid		
IOM	Instit́uto y Observatorio de la Marina	**IOP**	Iranian Oil Participants
IOM	International Organisation for Migration = OIM	**IOPAB**	International Organisation for Pure and Applied Biophysics
IOM	International Organisation for Mycoplasmology	**IOPB**	International Organisation of Plant Biosystematists
IOMA	International Oxygen Manufacturers Association	**IOPC**	Institute of Paper Conservation
IOMAC	Indian Ocean Marine Affairs Cooperation (UNCTAD) (Sri Lanka)	**IOPC Fund**	International Oil Pollution Compensation Fund = FIPOL, IOCF, IOPCF
IOMC	International Organisation for Medical Co-operation	**IOPCF**	International Oil Pollution Compensation Fund = FIPOL, IOPC Fund, IOCF
IOMEP	International Office of Mechanical Paving	**IOPEC**	Iranian Oil Exploration and Production Company (Iran)
IOMP	International Organisation for Medical Physics	**IOPH**	International Office of Public Health
IOMS	International Organisation for Masoretic Studies	**IOPI**	International Organization for Plant Information
IOMTR	International Organisation for Motor Trades and Repairs	**IOPIDDS**	International Organization for Plant Data Standards Group
ION	Institute for Optimum Nutrition	**IOPIISC**	International Organization for Plant Information Information Systems Committee
ION	Institute of Navigation (U.S.A.)		
ION	Institute of Neuroscience (U.S.A.)		
ION	Ionosphere and Aural Phenomena Advisory Committee (ESA)	**IOPNZ**	Institute of Physics in New Zealand
		IOQ	Institute of Quarrying
IONA	International Organisation for the New Acropolis = OINA	**IOR**	Institut za Oceanografiju i Ribarstvo
		IOR	Institute of Roofing
IONS	Institute of Noetic Sciences	**IOR**	Istituto per le Opere di Religione (Vatican)
IOOC	International Conference on Integrated Optics and Optical Fibre Communication	**IOR-TOCC**	Technical and Operational Control Centre in the Indian Ocean Region (INTELSAT)
IOOC	International Olive Oil Council (Spain) = COI	**IORS**	Operations Research Society of Ireland
		IOS	Institute of Ocean Science (Canada)

IOS	Institute of Oceanographic Sciences (NERC)	**IOUTN**	International Organization for the Unification of Terminological Neologisms = MOUNT, OIUNT
IoS	Institute of Statisticians	**IOV**	Institute of Virology (NERC)
IOS	International Offshore Services (U.K.)	**IOV**	Instítuto Oceanográfico de Valparaiso (Chile)
IOS	International Oleander Society	**IOV**	Internationale Organisation für Volkskunst (Austria)
IOS	International Organisation for Succulent Plant Study	**IOVST**	International Organisation for Vacuum Science and Technology = OISTV
IOS	Iraqi Organisation for Standardization	**IOWC**	International One World Crusade
IOSA	Incorporated Oil Seed Association	**IOWME**	International Organisation of Women and Mathematics Education (U.S.A.)
IOSA	International Oil Scouts Association	**IOZV**	Internationale Organisation für Zivilverteidigung
IOSA	Irish Offshore Services Association	**IP**	Institute of Packaging
IOSCD	International Organization for Scientific Cooperation and Development	**IP**	Institute of Petroleum
IOSCO	International Organisation of Securities Commissions = OICV	**IP**	Institute of Physics, Academia Sinica
		IP	Institute of Plumbing
IOSCS	International Organization for Septuagint and Cognate Studies	**IP**	Islamic Party (Afghanistan) = HI
		IP	Istiqlal Party (Morocco)
IOSDL	Institute of Oceanographic Sciences Deacon Laboratory	**IP RAN**	Institute of Psychology, Russian Academy of Sciences
IOSGT	International Organization for the Study of Group Tensions	**IPA**	Frauenhofer-Institut für Produktsiontechnik und Automatisierung (Germany)
IOSH	Institution of Occupational Safety and Health	**IPA**	Independent Petroleum Association
IOSHD	International Organization for the Study of Human Development	**IPA**	Indian Pharmaceutical Assocation
		IPA	Industrial Participation Association
IOSOT	International Organization for the Study of the Old Testament	**IPA**	Industrie des Pêches Algériennes
IOST	International Organization of Study Tours for Teachers (Belgium)	**IPA**	Information Processing Association (Israel)
IOSTA	International Committee of Work Study and Labour Management in Agriculture = CIOSTA	**IPA**	Insolvency Practitioners Association
		IPA	Institut de Préparation aux Affaires
		IPA	Institut Pédagogique Africain
IOSTE	International Organisation for Scientific and Technical Education	**IPA**	Institute for Policy Analysis (Canada)
IOSTTA	International Organization of Scenographers, Theatre Technicians and Architects = OISTAT	**IPA**	Institute of Incorporated Public Accountants in Greece
		IPA	Institute of Practitioners in Advertising
IOT	Internationale van Oorlogstegenstanders = IdK, IRG, WRI	**IPA**	Institute of Public Administration (Éire, U.S.A.)
IOTA	Institut d'Ophthalmologie Tropicale Africaine	**IPA**	Institute of Public Affairs (Australia)
IoTA	Institute of Transport Administration	**IPA**	Instítuto de Pesquisas Agronómicas (Brazil)
IOTA	International Occultation Timing Association	**IPA**	Instítuto de Petroquimica Aplicada
IOTA	Irish Overseas Transport Association	**IPA**	Interamerican Press Association
IOTCG	International Organisation for Technical Cooperation in Geology	**IPA**	International Association for the Child's Right to Play
IOTO	Industrie des Oléagineux du Togo	**IPA**	International Palaeontological Association
IOTTSG	International Oil Tanker Terminal Safety Group		

IPA	International Peace Academy	**IPAL**	Instítuto para America Latina (Peru)
IPA	International Peach Academy	**IPAL**	Integrated Program on Arid Lands
IPA	International Pediatric Association = AIP	**IPALMO**	Istituto per le Relazioni tra Italia e Paesi dell'Africa, America Latina e Medio Oriente
IPA	International Permafrost Association		
IPA	International Phonetic Association = API	**IPAM**	Institut Pédagogique Africain et Malgache
IPA	International Photographers Association	**IPAR**	Institut de Pédagogie Appliqué à Vocation Rurale
IPA	International Pinball Association		
IPA	International Platform Association	**IPART**	Institute of Photographic Apparatus Repair Technicians
IPA	International Police Association		
IPA	International Psycho-Analytical Association	**IPAS**	Institute of Psychology, Academia Sinica
IPA	International Psychogeriatric Association	**IPAS**	International Projects Assistance Services
IPA	International Psychohistorical Association (U.S.A.)	**IPAT**	Instítuto Panameño de Turismo
		IPAT	International Conference on Ion Plating and Allied Techniques
IPA	International Publishers Association = IVU, UIE		
		IPAT	International Porcelain Artist Teachers
IPA	International Publishers Audio-Visual Association	**IPAV**	Institute of Professional Auctioneers and Valuers (Éire)
IPA	Involvement & Participation Association	**IPAVS**	International Project of the Association for Voluntary Sterilization
IPAA	Independent Petroleum Association of America	**IPB**	Institute of Practitioners in Beauty
		IPB	Institutul Politehnic Bucuresti
IPAA	International Prisoners' Aid Association	**IPB**	International Peace Bureau (Switzerland)
IPAC	Independent Petroleum Association of Canada		
		IPBA	India, Pakistan and Bangladesh Association (U.K.)
IPAC	Institut Polytechnique de l'Afrique Centrale		
		IPBA	Irish Paper Box Association
IPAC	Institute of Public Administration of Canada	**IPBMM**	International Permanent Bureau of Motor Manufacturers
IPAC	International Peace Academy Committee (U.S.A.)	**IPC**	Indicative Planning Council
IPAC	Women's International Policy Action Committee on Environment and Development	**IPC**	Industrial Production Corporation (Sudan)
		IPC	Institute of Philippine Culture
IPACA	Industria Papelera Centroamericana (Honduras)	**IPC**	Institute of Production Control
		IPC	Institute of Pure Chiropractic
IPACK	International Packaging Material Suppliers Association	**IPC**	Instítuto de Plasticos y Caucho
		IPC	Instítuto Panameña de Café
IPADE	Instítuto de Promocion y Apoyo al Desarrollo	**IPC**	Instytut Przemysłu Cukrowniczego
IPAE	Instítuto Peruano de Administración de Empresas (Peru)	**IPC**	Inter-African Phytosanitary Commission (U.K.)
IPAF	International Powered Access Federation	**IPC**	International Paralympic Committee
		IPC	International People's College in Denmark
IPAFRIC	Inter-Pêches Afrique (Senegal)		
IPAG	Institut Panafricain de Géopolitique	**IPC**	International Pepper Community
IPAI	International Primary Aluminium Institute	**IPC**	International Petroleum Cartel
		IPC	International Photographic Council

IPC	International Poplar Commission = CIP	IPDC	Instituto Puertorriqueno de Derechos Civiles
IPC	International Potato Centre (Peru) = CIP	IPDC	International Programme for the Development of Communication (UNESCO) =PIDC
IPC	International Press Centre		
IPC	International Prison Commission		
IPC	International Publishing Corporation (U.K.)	IPDiR	Instytut Przemysłu Drobnego i Rzemiosła
IPC	Iraq Petroleum Company	IPE	Asociación de Investigación Tecnica de la Industria Papelera Española
IPC	Irish Peace Council		
IPC	Irish Productivity Centre	IPE	Incorporated Plant Engineers
IPC	Islamic Peace Committee (OIC)	IPE	Institute of Petroleum Engineers
IPC Union	Union for International Patent Classification	IPE	Institute of Production Engineers
		IPE	Institute of Public Enterprise (India)
IPCA	International Petroleum Co-operative Alliance	IPE	Institúto Papelero Español
		IPE	Institúto Português de Embalagem
IPCA	International Postcard Collectors Association	IPE	International Petroleum Exchange
		IPE	Istituto di Politica Estera
IPCC	Intergovernmental Panel on Climatic Change	IPEA	Institut Pontifical d'Études Arabes et d'Islamologie = PISAI
IPCC	International Peace Communication and Coordination Centre	IPEA	Institúto de Planejamento Económico e Social (Brazil)
IPCC	Irish Peatland Conservation Council	IPEA	Ireland-Poland Economic Association
IPCCIOS	Inter-Pacific Council (CIOS)	IPEAAD	Institúto de Pesquisas e Experimentação Agropecuárias da Amazónia Ocidental (Brazil)
IPCI	Islamic Propagation Centre International		
IPCL	India Petrochemicals Ltd	IPEACO	Institúto de Pesquisas e Experimentação Agropecuárias do Centro-Oeste (Brazil)
IPCL	Institut du Pétrole, des Carburants et Lubrifiants	IPEACS	Institúto de Pesquisas e Experimentação Agropecuárias do Centro Sul (Brazil)
IPCR	Institute for Physical and Chemical Research (Japan)		
IPCRA	Irish Professional Conservators and Restorers Association	IPEAL	Institúto de Pesquisas e Experimentação Agropecuárias do Leste (Brazil)
IPCRSIAA	Institut Professionnel de Contrôle et de Recherches Scientifiques des Industries de l'Alimentation Animale (France)	IPEAME	Institúto de Pesquisas e Experimentação Agropecuárias do Meridional (Brazil)
		IPEAN	Institúto de Pesquisas e Experimentação Agropecuárias do Norte (Brazil)
IPCS	Institution of Professional Civil Servants	IPEANE	Institúto de Pesquisas e Experimentação Agropecuárias do Nordeste (Brazil)
IPCS	International Playing-Card Society		
IPCS	International Programme on Chemical Safety (WHO) = PISC	IPEAS	Institúto de Pesquisas e Experimentação Agropecuárias do Sul (Brazil)
IPCTT	Internacional del Personal de Correos, Telegrafos y Telefonos (Costa Rica)	IPEC	Institúto Peruano de Estudios Cooperativos
IPCWN	Irish Permaculture Worknet	IPEE	Institut pour une Politique Européenne de l'Environnement = IEEP
IPD	Institut Panafricain pour le Développement = PAID		
		IPEE	International Programme on Environmental Education (UNESCO/UNEP) = IEEP
IPD	Institut Prumyslového Designu		
IPD	Institute of Professional Designers		
IPD	Institúto de Pesquisas e Desenvolvimento (CTA) (Brazil)	IPEL	International Pipeline Engineering Ltd (Canada)
IPDA	International Periodical Distributors Association (U.S.A.)	IPEN	Institúto Peruano de Energía Nuclear (Peru)

IPEN	Pan-American Naval Engineering Institute	**IPGCU**	International Printing and Graphic Communications Union
IPENZ	Institution of Professional Engineers New Zealand	**IPGH**	Institúto Panamericano de Geografia e Historia (OAS)(Mexico) = PAIGH, PIGH
IPEONGC	Institute of Petroleum Exploration Oil and Natural Gas Commission (India)	**IPGMR**	Institute of Postgraduate Medicine and Research (Bangladesh)
IPEP	Institúto de Promocion y Educación Popular (Peru)	**IPGRI**	International Plant Genetic Resources Institute (Italy)
IPEPO	Institúto para la Propaganda Exterior de los Productos del Olivar	**IPGS**	International Philatelic Golf Society
IPES	Institúto Paraguayo de Estudios Sociales	**IPGSA**	International Plant Growth Substance Association
IPES/GB	Institúto de Pesquisas e Estudos Sociais, Guanabara (Brazil)	**IPH**	Institute of Public Health (Japan)
IPESA	Industria Pesquera Ecuatoriana S.A.	**IPH**	International Association of Paper Historians
IPESUL	Institúto de Pesquisas Económicas e Sociais do Rio Grande do Sul (Brazil)	**IPHAME-TRA**	Institut de Pharmacopée et de Médecine Traditionelles (Gabon)
IPEX	International Printing Machinery and Allied Trades' Exhibition	**IPHAN**	Institúto de Património Histórico e Artístico Nacional (Brazil)
IPF	Institut Française du Pétrole, des Carburants et Lubrifiants	**IPharmM**	Institute of Pharmacy Management
IPF	International Peace Forest	**IPHC**	International Pacific Halibut Commission
IPF	International Pen Friends (Ireland)	**IPHF**	Illinois Poultry and Hatchery Federation (U.S.A.)
IPF	International Pharmaceutical Federation = FIP	**IPI**	Ikatan Pustakawan Indonesia
IPF	International Philatelic Federation = FIP	**IPI**	Institute of Patentees and Inventors
IPF	International Powerlifting Federation	**IPI**	Institute of Professional Investigators
IPF	International Prayer Fellowship	**IPI**	International Patent Institute = IIB
IPF	Irish Printing Federation	**IPI**	International Pesticide Institute
IPF	Isolerglassproducentenes Farening	**IPI**	International Petroleum Institute
IPFA	Institute of Public Finance and Accountancy	**IPI**	International Potash Institute (Switzerland) = IKI
IPFA	International Physical Fitness Association	**IPI**	International Press Institute = IIP
IPFC	Indo-Pacific Fisheries Commission (Thailand) = CIPP	**IPI**	Irish Planning Institute
IPFE	Institúto Peruano de Fomento Educativo	**IPIA**	Institutul de Patologia si Igiena Animala (Romania)
IPFEO	Institut des Producteurs de Ferro-alliages d'Europe Occidentale	**IPIC**	International Petroleum Investment Company (Abu Dhabi)
IPFR	Institute of Plasma and Fusion Research (U.S.A.)	**IPICOL**	Industrial Promotion and Investment Corporation of Orissa (India)
IPG	Independent Publishers Guild	**IPIE**	Institut de Politique Internationale et Européenne (France)
IPG	Industrial Policy Group (OECD)	**IPIE**	Institute of Profit Improvement Executives
IPG	Information Policy Group (OECD)		
IPG	Institute of Petroleum Geology (China)	**IPIECA**	International Petroleum Industry Environmental Conservation Association
IPG	Institute of Professional Goldsmiths		
IPG	Institutul de Petrol si Gaze Ploiesti		
IPG	Instytut Przemysli Gumowego	**IPIN**	Institúto Panamericano de Ingenieria Naval (Brazil)
IPG	International Piano Guild (U.S.A.)		
IPGC	Institúto de Pesca del Golfo de Mexico y el Caribe	**IPIN**	International Peace Information Service

IPIRA	Indian Plywood Industries Research Association
IPIRTI	Indian Plywood Industries Research and Training Institute
IPiSS	Instytut Pracy i Spraw Społecznych
IPJAE	Institúto Politecnico Jose A. Echeverria (Cuba)
IPK	Interessengemeinschaft für Pharmazeutische und Kosmetische Produkte (Switzerland)
IPKO	International Information Centre on Peacekeeping Operations (France)
IPLA	Institute of Public Loss Assessors
IPLA	Institúto de Productos Lacteos de Asturias
IPLA	Institúto Pastoral Latinoamericano (Chile)
IPLAN	Institúto de Planejamento Económico e Social (Brazil)
IPlantE	Institution of Plant Engineers
IPLCA	International Pipeline Contractors Association
IPLIC	International Pro-Life Information Centre
IPLO	Irish Peoples Liberation Organisation
IPLOCA	International Pipe Line and Offshore Contractors Association
IPM	Institut de Physique Météorologique (Senegal)
IPM	Institut Pasteur du Maroc (Morocco)
IPM	Institute of Personnel Management (Éire, South Africa, U.K.)
IPM	Institute of Printing Management
IPM	Institute of Psychosexual Medicine
IPM	Instytut Prawa Międzynarodowego
IPM	Statens Institut för Psykosocial Miljömedecin (Sweden)
IPMA	International Personnel Management Association
IPMA	International Primary Market Association
IPMAS	Institute of Sci-Tech Policy & Management, Academia Sinica
IPMER	Institute of Post-Graduate Medical Education and Research (India)
IPMI	International Precious Metals Institute
IPMP	Integrated Pest Management Programs
IPMS	Institution of Professionals, Managers and Specialists
IPMS	International Plastic Modellers Society
IPN	Institut des Peuples Noirs = IBP
IPN	Institúto Politecnico Nacional (Mexico)
IPNA	International Pediatric Nephrology Association
IPNCB	Institut des Parcs Nationaux du Congo Belge
IPO	Institut voor Plantenziektenkundig Onderzoek
IPO	International Parents Organization
IPO	International Progress Organization
IPO	International Projects Office (NATO)
IPO	Istituto per l'Oriente C.A. Nallino
IPOD	International Program of Ocean Drilling
IPOL	Institute of Polarology
IPOS	International Psych-Oncology Society
IPOSTEL	Institúto Postal Telegráfico (Venezuela)
IPP	Institut für Plasmaphysik
IPP	Institute of Plant Protection (China)
IPPA	Independent Programme Producers Association
IPPA	Indo-Pacific Prehistory Association (Australia)
IPPA	Indonesian Planned Parenthood Association
IPPA	International Paediatric Pathology Association
IPPA	International Pectin Producers' Association
IPPA	International Pentecostal Press Association
IPPA	International Prisoners Aid Association
IPPA	Irish Pre-School Playgroups Association
IPPA	Irish Professional Photographers Association
IPPA	Islamic Party of the People of Afghanistan
IPPC	Industrial Promotion and Productivity Centre (Nepal)
IPPC	Institúto Português do Património Cultural
IPPC	International Plant Protection Congress
IPPC	International Population Policy Consortium
IPPESG	Irish Political Prisoners in Europe Solidarity Group
IPPF	International Penal and Penitentiary Foundation = FIPP
IPPF	International Planned Parenthood Federation

IPPJ	Institute of Plasma Physics Japan
IPPL	International Primate Protection League = LIPP
IPPLM	Institute of Plasma Physics and Laser Microfusion (Poland)
IPPM-L	Instytut Podstawowej Problemy Marksizmu-Leninizmu
IPPM-L	Instytut Podstawowych Problemów Technik
IPPMA	Irish Plastic Pipe Manufacturers' Association
IPPNO	International Philosophers for the Prevention of Nuclear Omnicide
IPPNW	International Physicians for the Prevention of Nuclear War
IPPP	Independent People's Progressive Party (Malaysia)
IPPP	Institute of Plant Production and Processing (CSIRO)
IPPR	Institute for Public Policy Research
IPPR	Institute of Project Planning and Research (China)
IPPS	Institute for Public Policy Studies (Republic of Korea)
IPPS	International Plant Propagators Society
IPPSA	Institute of Property Practitioners of South Africa
IPPTA	Indian Pulp and Paper Technical Association
IPPV	Institúto para la Promocion Publica de la Vivienda
IPQ	Instituto Português da Qualidade
IPqM	Institúto de Pesquisas da Marinha (Brazil)
IPR	Institut Pierre Richet (IRTO)
IPR	Institute for Policy Research
IPR	Institute for Puerto-Rican Policy, Inc. (U.S.A.)
IPR	Institute of Pacific Relations (U.S.A.)
IPR	Institute of Population Registration
IPR	Institute of Psychophysical Research
IPR	Institute of Public Relations
IPR	Institúto de Pesquisas Rodoviarias (Brazil)
IPR	International Public Relations Group of Companies Inc. (U.S.A.)
IPR	Istituto per le Pubbliche Relazioni
IPR RAN	Institute of Market Studies, Russian Academy of Sciences
IPRA	Indian Painting Research Association
IPRA	International Peace Research Association
IPrA	International Pragmatics Association
IPRA	International Public Relations Association
IPRAO	Institut de Prévoyance et de Retraite de l'Afrique Occidentale
IPRC	Israel Plastics & Rubber Centre
IPRE	International Professional Association for Environmental Affairs = IAEC
IPREIG	Institut Professional de Recherches et d'Études des Industries Graphiques
IPRI	International Plant Research Institute (U.S.A.)
IPRI	Italian Peace Research Institute
IPRiS	Instytut Przemysłu Rolnego i Spożywczego
IPRO	International Pallet Recycling Organisation
IPRO	International Patent Research Office
IProdE	Institution of Production Engineers
IPRS	International Confederation for Plastic and Reconstructive Surgery
IPRU	Institúto de Planeamiento Regional y Urbano (Argentina)
IPS	Incorporated Phonographic Society
IPS	Indian Phytopathological Society
IPS	Indian Police Service
IPS	Industrieverband Pflanzenschutz
IPS	Institut voor Pluimveeteelt
IPS	Institute for Palestine Studies (Lebanon)
IPS	Institute for Planetary Synthesis (Switzerland)
IPS	Institute for Policy Studies
IPS	Institute of Pacific Studies (USP) (Fiji) = PIC
IPS	Institute of Population Studies (Peru)
IPS	Institute of Professional Sport
IPS	Institute of Purchasing and Supply
IPS	Inter-Press Service (Italy)
IPS	International Confederation for Plastic Surgery
IPS	International Palm Society
IPS	International Peat Society = IMTG, MTO
IPS	International Perimetric Society
IPS	International Phenomenological Society
IPS	International Phycological Society
IPS	International Planetarium Society

IPS	International Police Security
IPS	International Primatological Society
IPS	Interpolimetrics Society (U.S.A.)
IPS	Intractable Pain Society of Great Britain and Northern Ireland
IPSA	Independent Postal System of America
IPSA	Institute for the Psychological Study of the Arts (U.S.A.)
IPSA	Institute of Public Service Administrators (*ex* APSAS)
IPSA	International Political Science Association = AISP
IPSA	International Professional Security Association
IPSCI	Industrial Promotion Services en Côte d'Ivoire
IPSF	International Pharmaceutical Students Federation
IPSF	International Professional Surfthion Federation (U.S.A.)
IPSG	Immigration Prisoners Support Group
IPSI	Institute of Professional Secretaries in Ireland
IPSJ	Information Processing Society of Japan
IPSM	Institute of Physical Sciences in Medicine
IPSM	Institute of Purchasing and Supply Management (Australia)
IPSOA	Istituto Post-universitario per lo Studio dell'Organizzazione Aziendale
IPSOC	Information Processing Society of Canada
IPSRA	International Professional Ski Racers' Association
IPSSG	International Printers Supply Salesmen's Guild (U.S.A.)
IPST	Israel Programme for Scientific Translations
IPT	Institúto de Pesquisas Tecnológicas (Brazil)
IPTA	International Patent and Trademark Association
IPTC	International Press Telecommunications Council = CITP
IPTEA	Internacia Postista Kaj Telekomunistka Esperanto-Asocio
IPTEC	Division of Inter-institutional Cooperation in Science and Technology (Indonesia)
IPTEC	International Piano Teachers Consultants
IPTIC	International Pulse Trade Industry Confederation = CICILS
IPTO	International Pet Trade Organisation
IPTPA	International Professional Tennis Players' Association
IPTT	Internationale du Personnel des Postes, Télégraphes et Téléphones = ICTT, PTTI
IPU	Igreja Presbiteriana Unida do Brasil
IPU	Inter-Parliamentary Union = UIP
IPU	International Peasant Union
IPU	Irish Pharmaceutical Union
IPU	Irish Print Union
IPV	Idegenforgalmi Propaganda és Kiadó Vállalat
IPV	Industrieverband Papier- und Plastikverpackung
IPVS	International Pig Veterinary Society
IPVU	Institúto Paraguayo de Vivienda Urbanismo
IPW	Institüt für Internationale Politik und Wirtschaft
IPWH	International Organisation for the Provision of Work for Handicapped Persons
IPZ	Instytut Przemysłu Zielarskiego
IPZ RAN	Institute of Employment Studies, Russian Academy of Sciences
IQ	Institute of Quarrying (South Africa, U.K.)
IQ	International Quorum of Film and Video Producers
IQA	Institute of Quality Assurance
IQA	Institúto de Químico Agricola (Brazil)
IQA	Irish Quality Association
IQB	Institúto Químico Biológico (Brazil)
IQC	International Quality Centre (EOQC)
IQCA	Irish Quality Control Association
IQEC	International Quantum Electronics Conference
IQLA	International Quantitative Linguistics Association = IGQL
IQPR	Institute of Qualified Personnel Resources (China)
IQPS	Institute of Qualified Private Secretaries
IQS	Institute of Quantity Surveyors
IQS	Institúto Quimico de Sarria
IQSA	International Quantum Structures Association

IR	Board of Inland Revenue
IR	Industrirådet
IR	Institut Rízení
IR	Institute of Refrigeration
IR	Institute of Roofing
IR	Irish Rail = IE
IR	Izquierda Revolucionaria
IRA	Institute de la Recherche Agronomique (Cameroon)
IRA	Institúto de Relaciones Agrarias
IRA	International Racquetball Association
IRA	International Reading Association = AIL
IRA	International Reprographics Association
IRA	International Rodeo Association
IRA	International Rubber Association
IRA	Investment Recovery Association (U.S.A.)
IRA	Irish Republican Army
IRA	Istituto di Ricerca sulle Acque = IRSA
IRAA	Independent Refiners Association of America
IRAB	Institut de Recherches Appliquées du Bénin
IRABA	Institut de Recherche Appliquée du Béton Armé
IRABOIS	Institut de Recherches Appliqués au Bois
IRAC	Institut pour le Redressement des Arts Classiques (Belgium)
IRAC	Institúto de Reforma Agraria y Colonización (Ecuador, Peru)
IRAC	Interdepartment Radio Advisory Committee (U.S.A.)
IRADES	Istituto Ricerche Applicate, Documentazione e Studi
IRAF	Institut de Recherches Agronomiques et Forestières (Gabon)
IRAG	Centre International de Recherche des Aptitudes à la Gestion
IRAM	Institut de Recherche Appliquée du Metal
IRAM	Institut de Recherches Agronomiques de Madagascar
IRAM	Institut de Recherches et d'Application de Méthodes de Développement
IRAM	Institut für Radioastronomie im Millimeterwellenbereich
IRAM	Institúto Argentino de Racionalización de Materiales
IRAMM	Institut de Recherche et d'Action contre la Misère Mondiale
IRAN	Industries Réunies de l'Afrique Noire (Ivory Coast)
IRAN-SENCO	Société Irano-Sénégalaise des Pétroles et des Mines
IRANDOC	Iranian Documentation Centre
IRANOR	Institúto Nacional de Racionalización y Normalización
IRAP	Industrial Research Assistance Program (NRC) (Canada)
IRAP	Organisation Internationale pour l'Avancement de la Recherche aux Hautes Pressions
IRAS	Industriforbundets Rasjonaliseringskontor
IRASA	International Radio Air Safety Association
IRAT	Institut de Recherches Agronomiques Tropicales et des Cultures Vivrières
IRATA	Industrial Rope Access Trades Association
IRATRA	Institúto Nacional de Racionalización del Trabajo
IRAZ	Institut de Recherche Agronomique et Zootechnique (Zaïre)
IRB	Informationszentrum Raum und Bau
IRB	Institut Rudjer Boskovic
IRB	Institute of Radiation Breeding (Japan)
IRB	Institúto de Resseguros do Brazil
IRB	International Resources Bank = BIR
IRB	Istituto Ricerche Breda (Italy)
IRBG	Irish in Britain Representation Group
IRC	Industrial Relations Center (U.S.A.)
IRC	Industrial Relations Centre (New Zealand)
IRC	Industrial Relations Committee (Australia)
IRC	Industrial Reorganisation Corporation
IRC	Information Resource Centre
IRC	Institut de Recherches sur le Cancer
IRC	International Radiation Commission (IAMAP)
IRC	International Red Cross = CRI, IRK
IRC	International Reference Centre (WHO) = CIR
IRC	International Relations Club
IRC	International Rescue Committee
IRC	International Research Council

IRC	International Resources Offices		**IRCS**	Irish Red Cross Society
IRC	International Rice Commission = CIR		**IRCT**	Institut de Recherches du Coton et des Textiles Exotiques
IRC	International Rights Centre		**IRCT**	Institut Recherche Coloniale Tropicale
IRC	International Rubber Conference		**IRCT**	International Council for Torture Victims (RCT)
IRC	International Water and Sanitation Centre (Netherlands)		**IRCWD**	International Reference Centre for Waste Disposal (WHO, EAWAG)
IRC	Istituto Internazionale Ricerca Camping-Caravanning		**IRD**	Institute of Radiation Dosimetry (Czech Republic)
IRC	SCI International Resource Centre		**IRD**	Instítuto de Radioproteção e Dosimetria (Brazil)
IRCA	Institut de Recherche de la Chimie Appliquée		**IRD**	Irish Resource Development Trust
IRCA	Institut de Recherches sur le Caoutchouc en Afrique		**IRDA**	Industrial Research and Development Authority
IRCA	Institution de Retraites Complémentaires Agricoles		**IRDA**	Inter-Church Relief and Development Agency (WEF) (Hong Kong)
IRCA	International Radio Club of America		**IRDABI**	Institute for Research and Development of Agro-Based Industry (Indonesia)
IRCA	International Railway Congress Association = AICCF, IEKV		**IRDAC**	Industrial Research and Development Advisory Commitee (EU)
IRCAM	Institut de Recherche et de Acoustique Musique		**IRDC**	International Road Documentation Center (U.S.A.)
IRCAM	Institut de Recherches Scientifiques (Cameroon)		**IRDCLI**	Institute for Research and Development of Cellulose Industries (Indonesia)
IRCC	Institut de Recherches du Café, du Cacao et Autres Plantes Stimulantes		**IRDE**	Instruments Research and Development Establishment (India)
IRCC	Instrument Repair and Calibration Centre (Thailand)		**IRDECE**	Institut de Recherche pour le Développement de l'Espace Culturel Européen – Fondation Européenne Yehudi Menuhin (Belgium)
IRCCOPR	Inter-Research Council Committee on Pollution Research			
IRCE	Istituto Nazionale per le Relazioni Culturali con l'Estero		**IRDG**	Inter-Regional Deputies Group (Russia)
IRCHA	Institut National de Recherche Chimique Appliquée		**IRDHBI**	Institute for Research and Development of Handicraft and Batik Industries (Indonesia)
IRCHMB	International Research Centre on Hydraulic Machinery (IECBSHM) (China)		**IRDP**	Institut Romand de Recherches et de Documentation Pédagogiques (Switzerland)
IRCI	Industrial Reconstruction Corporation of India			
IRCICA	Research Centre for Islamic History, Art and Culture (Turkey)		**IRE**	Institut des Reviseurs d'Entreprises (Belgium) = IBR
IRCIHE	International Referral Centre for Information Handling Equipment (UNESCO)		**IRE**	Institut National des Radioéléments / Nationaal Instituut voor Radioelementen (Belgium)
IRCN	Institut de Recherches de la Construction Navale		**IRE**	Institute of Refractories Engineers
IRCO	International Rubber Conference Organisation		**IRE**	Istituto per il Rinnovamento Economico
IRCOBI	International Research Committee on the Biokinetics of Impacts		**IREA**	Institut de Recherches de l'Économie Alimentaire
			IREA	Irish Refrigeration Enterprises Association
IRCP	International Research Centre for Precancer Conditions		**IREAN**	Initsiativa Revoliutsionnykh Anarkhistov

IREC	Irrigation Research and Extension Advisory Committee (Australia)	**IRET**	Institut de Recherches en Écologie Tropicale (Gabon)
IRECA	International Rescue and Emergency Care Association	**IRET**	Institute for Research on the Economics of Taxation (U.S.A.)
IRECUS	Institut de Recherche et d'Enseignement pour les Cooperatives (Canada)	**IRETA**	Institute for Research, Extension and Training in Agriculture (USP) (Samoa)
IRED	Innovations et Réseaux pour le Développement	**IREX**	Institut pour la Recherche Appliquée et l'Experimentation en Génie Civil
IREDA	International Radio and Electrical Distributors Association	**IREX**	International Research and Exchanges Board
IREE	Institut de Recherches et d'Études Européens	**IRF**	Institute de Recherche Fondamentale (CEA)
IREE	Institute of Radio and Electronic Engineers (Australia)	**IRF**	International Racquetball Federation
IREF	International Real Estate Federation	**IRF**	International Re-education Foundation (U.S.A.)
IREF	Istituto di Ricerche Educative e Formative	**IRF**	International Reform Federation
IREI	International Rare Earth Institute (China)	**IRF**	International Religious Fellowship
IRELA	Instítuto de Relaciones Europeo – Latinoamericanas	**IRF**	International Road Federation = FRI
IREM	Institut de Recherche sur l'Enseignement des Mathématiques	**IRF**	International Rowing Federation = FISA
		IRF	Island Resources Foundation (U.S.A.)
IREM	International Rostrum of Electroacoustic Music (IMC)	**IRF**	Svenska Institutet för Rymdfysik, Kiruna (Sweden)
IREMAM	Institut de Recherche et d'Études sur le Monde Arabe et Musulman	**IRFA**	Imprimerie Relieure Franco-Africaine (Ivory Coast)
IREN	Institut de Recherche sur les Énergies Nouvelles (Côte d'Ivoire)	**IRFA**	Institut de Recherches sur les Fruits et Agrumes
IRENA	Instítuto Nicaragüense de Recursos Naturales y del Ambiente	**IRFA**	Istituto di Ricerche e Formazione in Agricultura
IRENE	International Restructuring Education Network Europe	**IRFAN**	International Rain Forest Action Network = RAN, TRAN
IREP	Institut de Recherche Économique et de Planification	**IRFEC- Europe**	Institut de Recherche et de Formation pour l'Education et la Communication – Europe (Belgium)
IREP	Institut de Recherches et d'Etudes Publicitaires	**IRFED**	Institut Internationale de Recherches et de Formation en Vue du Développement Harmonisé
IREQ	Institut de Recherche d'Hydro-Québec	**IRFF**	International Relief Friendship Foundation
IRES	Institut de Recherches Economiques et Sociales (Belgium)	**IRFIS**	International Research Forum in Information Science
IRES	Institut de Recherches Économiques et Sociales (Zaïre)	**IRFIS**	Istituto Regionale per il Finanziamento alle Industrie in Sicilia
IRES	Instítuto de Reinserción Social	**IRFRH**	Institut de Recherche et de Formation aux Relations Humaines (France)
IRESCO	Institut de Recherche sur les Sociétés Contemporaines (France)	**IRFU**	Irish Rugby Football Union
IRESD	Institut Régional pour l'Enseignement Supérieur et le Développement (Singapore) = RIHED	**IRFV**	Internationaler Regenmantelfabrikantenverband
		IRG	Institut de Réescompte et de Garantie = HWI
IRESP	Institut de Recherches Économiques, Sociales et Politiques (Belgium)	**IRG**	International Research Group on Wear of Engineering Materials

IRG	International Research Group on Wood Preservation	**IRIB**	Islamic Republic of Iran Broadcasting
IRG	Internationale des Résistants à la Guerre = IdK, IOT, WRI	**IRIC**	Institut des Relations Internationales du Cameroon
IRGA	Irish Retail Grocers Association	**IRIDE**	Istituto per le Ricerche e le Iniziative Demografiche
IRGC	International Rice Germplasm Center (IRRI) (Philippines)	**IRIEC**	Institut de Recherche en Informatique et en Économie
IRGC	Islamic Revolutionary Guards Corps (Iraq)	**IRIFIP**	International Research Institute for Immigration and Emigration Politics
IRGCP	International Research Group for Carcinoembryonic Proteins	**IRIJ**	Institut de Recherche d'Informatique Juridique
IRGCVD	International Research Group on Colour Vision Deficiencies	**IRIMS**	International Research Institute for Management Sciences (Russia)
IRGM	Institut de Recherches Géologiques et Minières (Cameroon)	**IRIPS**	Institúto di Ricerche e di Interventi Psico-Sociali
IRGOD	International Council for Research in Cooperative Management	**IRIS**	European Network of Training Schemes for Women
IRGRD	International Research Group on Refuse Disposal	**IRIS**	Incorporated Research Institutions for Seismology (U.S.A.)
IRH	Institut de Recherches Hydroliques	**IRIS**	Industrial Relations Information Service (BRD)
IRHA	International Rural Housing Association = AMVR	**IRIS**	Industrial Research and Information Service
IRHA	Irish Road Haulage Association	**IRIS**	Institut de Recherches de l'Industrie Sucrière
IRHD	Internationaler Rat der Hauspflegedienste = CISAD, ICHS	**IRIS**	Institute for Regional and International Studies (U.S.A.)
IRHE	Institúto de Recursos Hidráulicos y Electrificación (Panama)	**IRIS**	Institute for Research in Information and Scholarship (U.S.A.)
IRHO	Institut de Recherches pour les Huiles et Oléagineux	**IRIS**	Institute for Robotics and Intelligent Systems (Canada)
IRHP	Institute for Research in Hypnosis and Psychotherapy (U.S.A.)	**IRIS**	International Reporting Information Systems
IRHT	Institut de Recherche et d'Histoire des Textes (France)	**IRIS**	International Rest Investigators Society
IRI	Industrial Research Institute (Canada, Japan)	**IRISL**	Islamic Republic of Iran Shipping Lines
IRI	Interuniversity Reactor Institute (Netherlands)	**IRISS**	Institute for Research in the Social Sciences
IRI	Investment Research Institute (China)	**IRK**	Institute of Kiswahili Research (Tanzania)
IRI	Islamic Research Institute = IIR	**IRK**	International Rood Kruis = CRI, IRC
IRI	Istituto per la Ricostruzione Industriale	**IRK**	Internationale Representantschaft Kanusport = FIC, ICF
IRI RAN	Institute of Russian History, Russian Academy of Sciences	**IRK**	Internationales Ravensbruck-Kommitee
IRIA	Indian Rubber Industries Association	**IRK**	Internationales Rotes Kreuz = CRI, IRC
IRIA	Institut Recherche d'Information et d'Automatique	**IRL**	Institute of Rural Life at Home and Overseas
IRIA	Institúto Regional de Investigaciones del Algogón (Salvador)	**IRL**	Internationaler Ring für Landarbeit
IRIA	Société Ivoirienne de Représentation Industrielle et Automobile	**IRLA**	Independent Record Labels Association
IRIa RAN	Institute of the Russian Language, Russian Academy of Sciences	**IRLA**	International Religious Liberty Association

IRLCO-CSA	International Red Locust Control Organisation for Central and Southern Africa
IRLF	International Right to Life Federation
IRLI RAN	Institute of Russian Literature, Russian Academy of Sciences
IRM	Institut Européen de Recherche et d'Information sur les Multinationales
IRM	Institut Suisse de Recherches Ménagères
IRM	Institute of Builders' Merchants
IRM	Institute of Recreation Management
IRM	Institute of Religion and Medicine
IRM	Institute of Risk Management
IRMA	International Rehabilitation Medicine Association
IRMA	Islamic Revolution Movement of Afghanistan = HARAKAT
IRMB	Institut Royal Météorologique de Belgique
IRMC	International Records Management Council (U.S.A.) = CIAA
IRMMH	Institute of Research into Mental and Multiple Handicap
IRMRA	Indian Rubber Manufacturers' Research Association
IRN	Independent Radio News
IRNA	Islamic Republic News Agency (Iran)
IRNU	Institut de Recherches des Nations Unies pour le Développement Social = UNRISD
IRNUDS	Institut de Recherche des Nations Unies sur la Défense Sociale (Italy)
IRNWAD	International Resource Network of Women of African Descent
IRO	Industriele Raad voor de Oceanologie (TNO)
IRO	Institute of Rent Officers
IRO	Internationale Radio-Organisatie
IRO	Istarska Radikalna Organizacija / Istrian Radical Organization (Croatia)
IRO-FIET	Inter-American Regional Organization of the International Federation of Commercial, Clerical and Technical Employees
IROAA	Instítuto de Recursos Odontológicos del Area Andina (Peru)
IROPCO	Iranian Offshore Petroleum Company
IRP	International Records Productions
IRP	International Rostrum of Young Performers (IMC) = TIJI
IRP	Islamic Renaissance Party (Tajikistan, Uzbekistan)
IRPA	International Radiation Protection Association
IRPA	International Retinitis Pigmentosa Association (Germany)
IRPA	Irrigation Pump Administration (Philippines)
IRPEM	Istituto di Ricerche sulla Pesce Marittima (Italy)
IRPEPS	Inspectorans Rerum Publicarum Europaeorum Pharmacopopularum Societas (France)
IRPES	Institut Européen de Recherche sur les Politiques Économiques et Sociales = ESPRI
IRPSE	Institute for Research and Planning in Science and Education
IRPTC	International Register of Potentially Toxic Chemicals (UNEP) = RIPQPT, RISCPT
IRQPC	International Rubber Quality and Packing Conferences
IRR	Institute for Risk Research (Canada)
IRR	Institute of Race Relations
IRRA	Industrial Relations Research Association (U.S.A.)
IRRC	Investor Responsibility Research Center (U.S.A.)
IRRDB	International Rubber Research and Development Board
IRRI	Institut Royal des Relations Internationales (Belgium)
IRRI	International Rice Research Institute
IRRPA	International Road Racing Press Association (France)
IRRS	Irish Railway Records Society
IRRV	Institute of Revenues, Rating & Valuation (*ex* R&VA)
IRS	Independent Review Service for the Social Fund
IRS	Inland Revenue Service (U.S.A.)
IRS	Institut de Recherche Scientifique (Zaire)
IRS	Institut de Recherches Sahariennes
IRS	Institut für Reaktorsicherheit
IRS	Institutul Roman de Standardizare
IRS	Instituut voor Rationele Suikerproductie
IRS	International Referral System (UNEP)
IRS	International Reynard Society = SIR

IRS	International Rhinologic Society
IRS	International Rorschach Society = IGROF, SIR
IRS	Irrigation Research Station (New Zealand)
IRSA	International Rett Syndrome Association
IRSA	International Rural Sociological Association
IRSA	Irish Research Scientists' Association
IRSA	Istituto di Ricerca Sulle Acque = IRA
IRSAC	Institut pour la Recherche Scientifique en Afrique Centrale
IRSC	Institut de Recherches Scientifiques au Congo
IRSC	Institut de Recherches Scientifiques sur le Cancer
IRSCL	International Research Society for Children's Literature
IRSE	Institut Robert Schuman pour l'Europe
IRSE	Institution of Railway Signal Engineers
IRSF	Inland Revenue Staff Federation
IRSFC	International Rayon and Synthetic Fibres Committee = CIRFS
IRSG	International Rubber Study Group
IRSG	Internet Research Steering Group
IRSH	Institut de Recherches en Sciences Humaines
IRSI	Istituto Ricerca Sicurezza Industriale
IRSIA	Institut pour l'Encouragement de la Recherche Scientifique dans l'Industrie et l'Agriculture (Belgium)
IRSID	Institut de Recherches de la Sidérurgie
IRSM	Institut de Recherches Scientifiques de Madagascar
IRSO	Institute of Road Safety Officers
IRSP	Irish Republican Socialist Party
IRSS	Institute for Research in Social Science (U.S.A.)
IRSTA	International Roller Skating Trainers Association
IRSUR	Institut de Recherche en Sociologie Urbaine et Rurale
IRT	Institut de Reboisement de Tunis
IRT	Institut de Recherche des Transports
IRT	Institut de Recherches Technologiques (Gabon)
IRT	Institute for Research on Teaching (U.S.A.)
IRT	Institute of Reprographic Technology

IRTA	International Reciprocal Trade Association
IRTA	International Road Racing Teams Association (Switzerland)
IRTAC	International Round Table for the Advancement of Counselling = TRIDO
IRTC	Independent Radio and Television Commission (Éire)
IRTC	International Road Tar Conference
IRTCES	International Research and Training Centre on Erosion and Sedimentation (UNESCO) (China)
IRTDA	Indian Roads and Transport Development Association (India)
IRTE	Institute of Road Transport Engineers
IRTF	Internet Research Task Force
IRTIRA	Institut de Recherches sur la Tuberculose et les Infections Respiratoires Aiguës
IRTIS	Inter Regional Training Information System (ILO) (Switzerland)
IRTO	Institut de Recherche Scientifique au Togo
IRTS	International Radio and Television Society = SIRT
IRTS	Irish Radio Transmitters Society
IRTU	International Railway Temperance Union = FICA, IEAV
IRU	Institute de Recherche d'Urbanisme
IRU	International Raiffeisen Union
IRU	International Railway Union
IRU	International Relief Union = UIS
IRU	International Road Transport Union
IRU	International Rugby Union
IRU	Internationale Rijnvaartunie = UIR, UNIR
IRV	Internationale Rat für Vogelschutz = CIPO, ICBP
IRWA	Iranian Refugee Workers Association
IRWA	Irish Racing Writers' Association
IRWC	International Registry of World Citizens = RICM
IRWCU	Inter-Republican Work Collectives Union (Russia)
IRYDA	Instítuto Nacional de Reforma y Desarrollo Agrario
IRZ	Institut de Recherches Zootechniques (Cameroon)
IRZA	Institut de Recherches sur la Zone Aride en Arabia Saoudite

IS	Industrial Society
IS	Institut za Stocarstvo
IS	International Socialists
IS	International Society of Sculptors, Painters and Gravers
IS	Irish Skeptics
IS	Islamic Society (Afghanistan) = JI
IS RAN	Institute of Sociology, Russian Academy of Sciences
ISA	Independent Telecommunications Suppliers Association
ISA	Indian Society of Advertisers
ISA	Industrie Siderurgiche Associate (Italy)
ISA	Information South Africa
ISA	Instituto de Investigaciones de Arquitectura y Sistemas Ambientales (Venezuela)
ISA	Instrument Society of America
ISA	Interconexión Eléctrica (Colombia)
ISA	International Schools Association
ISA	International Seabed Authority = ISBA
ISA	International Seaweed Association
ISA	International Settlement Authority
ISA	International Shakespeare Association
ISA	International Silk Association = AIS
ISA	International Silo Association
ISA	International Skateboard Association
ISA	International Skating Association
ISA	International Society of Acupuncture
ISA	International Society of Appraisers
ISA	International Society of Arboriculture
ISA	International Sociological Association = AIS
ISA	International Soling Association
ISA	International Songwriters Association (Éire)
ISA	International Studies Association (U.S.A.)
ISA	International Sunflower Association
ISA	International Surfing Association
ISA	International Sweeteners Association (Belgium)
ISA	Irish Sailing Association
ISA	Irish Society for Archives
ISA	Irish Society for Autism
ISA	ISA – The International Society for Measurement and Control
ISA	Islamic Shipowners' Association (Saudi Arabia)
ISA 21	International Society of Women Airline Pilots
ISA RAN	Institute of Systems Analysis, Russian Academy of Sciences
ISAA	Institute of South African Architects
ISAA	Irish Ship Agents' Association
ISAA	Israel Society of Aeronautics and Astronautics
ISAAC	International Society for Augmentative and Alternative Communication (Canada)
ISAB	Institute for the Study of Animal Behaviour
ISABU	Institut des Sciences Agronomiques du Burundi
ISAC	International Scientific Agricultural Council
ISAC	International Security Affairs Committee (U.S.A.)
ISAC	International Society for Autistic Children
ISAC	Interuniversity South-East Asia Committee (U.S.A.)
ISAC	Irish Society for Autistic Children
ISACOM	Institut Supérieur Africain de la Communication, Abidjan (Ivory Coast)
ISADA	Industries et Savonneries du Dahomey
ISAE	Indian Society of Agricultural Economics
ISAE	Indian Society of Agricultural Engineers
ISAE	Internacia Scienca Asocio Esperantista
ISAE	International Society for Applied Ethology
ISAeM	International Society for Aerosols in Medicine = IGAeM, ISAM
ISAG	International Scientific Group on the Renin Angiotensin System and its Inhibition
ISAG	International Society for Animal Genetics (*ex* ISABR)
ISAGA	International Simulation and Gaming Association
ISAHM	International Society for Animal and Human Mycology
ISAI	Independent Schools Association Inc.
ISAID	Institute for the Study and Application of Integrated Development (Canada)
ISAK	International Society for the Advancement of Kinanthropometry
ISAL	Iglesia y Sociedad en América Latina

ISAL	International Society of African Lawyers	**ISAW**	Institution of Social Affairs and Welfare (Israel)
ISALC	International Society of Animal Licence Collectors	**ISB**	Institut für Selbstbedienung
ISAM	Institute for Studies in American Music	**ISB**	Institute of Scientific Business
ISAM	International Society for Aerosols in Medicine (Austria) = IGAeM, ISAeM	**ISB**	Institute of Small Business
ISAMA	International Scientific Association for Micronutrients in Agriculture	**ISB**	International Society of Bassists
ISAO	International Society for Artificial Organs	**ISB**	International Society of Biometeorology
ISAP	Institut de Statistique pour l'Asie et le Pacifique (Japan) = SIAP	**ISB**	International Society of Biorheology
ISAP	Institúto Superior de Administración Publica (Argentina)	**ISB**	Internationaler Studentenbund = IUS, MSS UIE
ISAP	International Society for Adolescent Psychiatry	**ISB RAN**	Institute of Slavic and Balkan Studies, Russian Academy of Sciences
ISAP	International Society of Art and Psychopathology =SIPE	**ISBA**	Incorporated Society of British Advertisers
ISAPL	International Society of Applied Psycholinguistics	**ISBA**	Independent Schools Bursars Association
ISAPS	International Society for Aesthetic Plastic Surgery	**ISBA**	International Seabed Authority = ISA
ISAR	Institut des Sciences Agronomiques du Rwanda	**ISBA**	International Society for Bayesian Analysis
ISAR	International Society for Animal Rights	**ISBA**	Irish-Swedish Business Association
ISAR	International Society for Astrological Research	**ISBB**	International Society of Bioclimatology and Biometeorology
ISAS	Institute of Software, Academica Sinica	**ISBC**	International Society of Bible Collectors
ISAS	Institute of Space and Aeronautical Science (India, Japan)	**ISBGA**	Irish Sugar Beet Growers Association
ISAS	International Screen Advertising Services	**ISBI**	International Savings Banks Institute = IICE, IIE, IIS
ISAS	International Society for Advancement of Science	**ISBI**	International Society for Burn Injuries
ISAS	Istituto di Scienze Amministrative e Socio-Economiche	**ISBM**	Institute for the Study of Business Markets (U.S.A.)
ISASC	International Society of Antique Scale Collectors	**ISBM**	International Bureau of Strata Mechanics (WMC) = BIMT, IBG, MBMGP, OIMR
ISASI	International Society of Air Safety Investigators	**ISBM**	International Schools of Business Management
ISAST	International Society for Arts, Sciences and Technology	**ISBM**	International Society of Behavioural Medicine (Sweden)
ISAT	International Society of Analytical Trilogy = SITA	**ISBO**	Institúto de Sociologia Boliviana
ISATT	International Study Association on Teacher Thinking	**ISBO**	Islamic States Broadcasting Organization
ISAU	International Staff Association of Unesco = AIPU	**ISBRA**	International Society for Biomedical Research on Alcoholism
ISAUST	Institute of Surveyors, Australia	**ISBT**	International Society for Blood Transfusion = SITS
		ISC	Industrial Structure Council (Japan)
		ISC	Institut Scientifique Chrétien (Morocco)
		ISC	Institute for the Study of Conflict
		ISC	Institutional Shareholders' Committee
		ISC	Inter-State Commission
		ISC	Interamerican Scout Committee = CIE

ISC	Interamerican Society of Cardiology	**ISCE**	Institute of Sound and Communications Engineers
ISC	International Sculpture Centre		
ISC	International Seismological Centre	**ISCE**	Instítuto Salvadoreño de Comercio Exterior
ISC	International Sericultural Commission = CSI, ISK	**ISCE**	International Society for Clinical Enzymology
ISC	International Society for Chronobiology		
ISC	International Society of Cardiology = SIC	**ISCE**	International Society of Chemical Ecology
ISC	International Society of Chemotherapy	**ISCE**	International Society of Christian Endeavour
ISC	International Society of Citriculture	**ISCED**	International Society of Continuing Education in Dentistry = SIECD
ISC	International Society of Cryosurgery		
ISC	International Society of Cryptozoology	**ISCES**	International Society of Complex Environmental Studies (Finland)
ISC	International Sporting Commission = CSI	**ISCET**	International Society of Certified Electronics Technicians
ISC	International Student Conference		
ISC	International Supreme Council of World Masons	**ISCEV**	International Society for Clinical Electrophysiology of Vision
ISC	International Surfing Committee	**ISCFB**	International Society of Cranio-Facial Biology
ISCA	Independent Safety Consultants Association		
ISCA	Indian Science Congress Association	**ISCHE**	International Standing Committee for the History of Education (Finland)
ISCA	Industrial Speciality Chemicals Association	**ISCLT**	International Society for Clinical Laboratory Technology
ISCA	International Sailing Craft Association		
ISCA	International Save the Children Alliance	**ISCM**	International Society for Contemporary Music = SIMC
ISCA	International Secretariat of Christian Artists = SIAC	**ISCN**	International Society of Non-Invasive Cardiology
ISCA	International Senior Citizens Association	**ISCO**	Independent Schools Careers Organisation
ISCA	International Society of Copier Artists	**ISCO**	International Soil Conservation Organization
ISCA	International Standards Co-ordination Association		
ISCA	International Standards Steering Committee for Consumer Affairs (ISO)	**ISCO**	Istituto Nazionale per lo Studie della Congiuntura
ISCA	International Sunfish Class Association (U.S.A.)	**ISCONG**	International Society of Computers in Obstetrics, Neonatology and Gynecology (Japan)
ISCAIP	International Society for Child and Adolescent Injury Prevention	**ISCOR**	South African Iron and Steel Industrial Corporation
ISCB	International Society for Classical Bibliography	**ISCOS**	Institute for Security and Cooperation in Outer Space (U.S.A.)
ISCC	Inter-Society Color Council (U.S.A.)	**ISCOS**	Inter-governmental Standing Committee on Shipping (Kenya)
ISCC	International School for Cancer Care		
ISCC	International Sporting Club de Cannes	**ISCP**	International Society for Chinese Philosophy
ISCCA	International Student Centre for Cultural Activities	**ISCP**	International Society for Comparative Psychology
ISCCF	International Study Center for Children and Families	**ISCP**	Irish Society of Chartered Physiotherapists
ISCCP	International Satellite Cloud Climatology Program	**ISCPES**	International Society on Comparative Physical Education and Sport

ISCS	Institute for the Study of Christianity and Sexuality	**ISDEE**	Istituto di Studi e Documentazione sull' Est Europeo (Italy)
ISCS	International Scientific Co-operative Service	**ISDG**	International Society of Dynamic Games
ISCS	International Society of Communications Specialists (U.S.A.)	**ISDI**	International Social Development Institute
ISCS	Italian Society for Computer Simulation	**ISDI**	International Special Dietary Food Industries
ISCSC	International Society for the Comparative Study of Civilizations	**ISDIBER**	Instítuto de Sociologia y Desarrollo del Area Iberica
ISCT	Institute of Science Technology	**ISDIC**	Islamic Documentation and Information Centre
ISCTC	Inter-Service Components Technical Committee	**ISDM**	Institute for the Study of Drug Misuse (U.S.A.)
ISCTP	International Study Commission for Traffic Police = CIEPC	**ISDM**	International Society of Disaster Medicine = SIMC
ISCTR	International Scientific Committee for Trypanosomiasis Research	**ISDN**	Institute for the Study of Developing Nations (U.S.A.)
ISCTRC	International Scientific Committee for Trypanosomiasis Research and Control	**ISDN**	International Society for Developmental Neuroscience = SIND
ISCUS	Indo-Soviet Cultural Society (India)	**ISDO**	Istituto Superiore di Organizzazione
ISCVS	International Society for Cardiovascular Surgery	**ISDP**	International Society for Developmental Psychobiology (U.S.A.)
ISCWA	Institute for the Study of Cycles in World Affairs	**ISDRA**	International Sled Dog Racing Association = IFSS
ISCYRA	International Star Class Yacht Racing Association (U.S.A.)	**ISDS**	International Serials Data System = CIEPS
ISCZA	Institute of Subtropical Crops, Zhejiang Academy of Sciences	**ISDS**	International Sheep Dog Society
ISD	Institute of Sustainable Development (Tatura)	**ISDS**	International Society for Dermatolgic Surgery
ISD	International Society for Development	**ISE**	Institut Syndical Européen = DEFI, EGI, ETUI, EVI
ISD	International Society of Dermatology: Tropical, Geographical and Ecological	**ISE**	Institute for Software Engineering (U.S.A.)
ISD	International Society of Differentiation	**ISE**	Institute of Systems Engineering (China)
ISD	Internationaler Suchdienst = ITS, SIR	**ISE**	Institution of Structural Engineers
ISDA	International SinoDance Association (Hong Kong)	**ISE**	Instítuto de Seguros del Estado (Chile)
ISDB	International Society of Developmental Biologists	**ISE**	Instítuto de Superación Educaciónal (Cuba)
IsDB	Islamic Development Bank (OIC)	**ISE**	Instítuto per gli Studi di Economia
ISDC	Industrial Studies and Development Centre (Saudi Arabia)	**ISE**	Intergovernmental Meeting of Scientific Experts on Biological Diversity
ISDCA	International Secretariat for Data Communication Applications	**ISE**	International Society for Endoscopy
ISDCI	International Society of Developmental and Comparative Immunology	**ISE**	International Society of Electrochemistry = SIE
ISDD	Institute for the Study of Drug Independence	**ISE**	International Society of Endocrinology
ISDE	Instítuto Superior de Dirección de Empresas	**ISE**	International Society of Ethnobiology (U.S.A.)
ISDE	International Society for Diseases of the Esophagus	**ISE**	Irish School of Ecumenics

ISEA	Independent Steel Employers Association
ISEA	Industrial Safety Equipment Association (U.S.A.)
ISEA	Institut de Science Économique Appliquée
ISEA	Inter-american Society for Educational Administration = SIAE
ISEA	Inter-Society for the Electronic Arts
ISEA	Internacia Scienca Asocio Esperantista
ISEA	Ireland-Spain Economic Association
ISEA-AN	Institut de Science Économique Appliquée, Centre d'Afrique du Nord (Tunisia)
ISEAS	Institute of South-East Asian Studies (China, Singapore)
ISEC	International Securities and Exchange Commission
ISEC	International Solvent Extraction Conference
ISEC	International Statistics Educational Centre (India)
ISECS	International Society for Eighteenth Century Studies = SIEDS
ISECSI	International Society for Educational, Cultural and Scientific Interchanges
ISEE	International Society for Ecological Economics
ISEE	International Society for Environmental Education (U.S.A.)
ISEE	International Society for Environmental Ethics
ISEH	International Society for Experimental Hematology
ISEI	Interdisciplinaire Studiegroep Europese Integratie
ISEIU	International Society of Ergonomics for Information Users
ISEK	International Society of Electrophysiological Kinesiology
ISEL	Institute for Studies in Environmental Law
ISÉLP	Institut Supérieur pour l'Étude du Langage Plastique (Belgium)
ISEM	Institute for the Study of Earth and Man (U.S.A.)
ISEM	International Society for Ecological Modelling
ISENCY	Industrie Sénégalaise du Cycle
ISEP	International Society for Ecological Psychology

ISEP	International Society for Educational Planning
ISEP	International Society for Evolutionary Prostitology
ISEP RAN	Institute of Socioeconomic Studies, Russian Academy of Sciences
ISEPAPK - RAN	Institute of Socioeconomic Studies of the Development of the Agroindustrial Complex, Russian Academy of Sciences
ISEPN RAN	Institute of Socioeconomic Studies of Population, Russian Academy of Sciences
ISEPSA	Industria de Seda Paraguaya, S.A.
ISER	Institut Supérieur d'Économie Rurale
ISER	Institute for Sex Education & Research
ISER	Institute of Social and Economic Research (Canada, U.S.A.)
ISER	Institute of Social and Economic Research (West Indies)
ISERI	Institut Supérieur d'Etude et de Recherche Islamiques (Mauritania)
ISERP	Institut Supérieur d'Etudes et de Recherches Pédagogiques
ISES	Institut des Sciences Économiques et Sociales (Switzerland)
ISES	International Ship Electric Service Association
ISES	International Society of Explosives Specialists
ISES	International Solar Energy Society
ISESCO	Islamic Educational, Scientific and Cultural Organisation
ISESP	Istituto Superiore Europeo di Studi Politici (Italy)
ISETC	International Society for Environmental Toxicology and Cancer
ISETU	International Secretariat of Arts, Communications Media and Entertainment Trade Unions = ISGKU, SISE, SISS
ISF	Ingénieurs sans Frontières
ISF	International School Sport Federation
ISF	International Science Foundation
ISF	International Shipping Federation
ISF	International Socialist Foundation
ISF	International Society for Fat Research
ISF	International Society of Financiers
ISF	International Softball Federation = FIS
ISF	International Solidarity Fund
ISF	International Spiritualist Federation = FSI

ISF	International Surfing Foundation		**ISGD**	International Study Group on Diabetes in Children and Adolescents
ISF	International Surfthion Federation		**ISGE**	International Society for Geothermal Engineering
ISF	Islamic Salvation Front (Algeria) = FIS			
ISF	Islamic Solidarity Fund (OIC)		**ISGE**	International Society for Group Activity in Education
ISF	Svenska Ingenjörssamfundet			
ISFA	International Scientific Film Association		**ISGE**	International Society of Gastoenterology
ISFA	International Society of Financial Analysts		**ISGHPM**	International Study Group for the Relations between the History and Pedagogy of Mathematics
ISFA	Irish Small Farmers Association			
ISFAACTU	Inter-State Federation of Civil Aviation Air Crews Trade Unions (Russia)		**ISGI**	International Service for Geomagnetic Indices (Netherlands)
ISFAHSIG	International Society for the Advancement of Humanistic Studies in Gynaecology		**ISGKU**	Internationales Sekretariat der Gewerkschaft für Kunst und Unterhaltung = ISETU, SISE, SISS
ISFAS	Institúto Social de las Fuerzas Armadas			
ISFC	Institut Scientifique Franco-Canadienne (Canada)		**ISGO**	International Society of Geographic Ophthalmology
ISFC	International Society and Federation of Cardiology = SFIC		**ISGP**	International Society of General Practice = IGAM, SIMG
ISFGW	International Society of Friendship and Good Will (U.S.A.)		**ISGP**	International Society of Geographical Pathology = SIPG
ISFL	Interessengemeinschaft Schweizerischer Foto-Kino-Lieferanten		**ISGP**	International Society of Gynaecological Pathologists (U.S.A.)
ISFL	International Scientific Film Library = CSI		**ISGRCM**	International Study Group for Research in Cardiac Metabolism
ISFL	International Society of Family Law		**ISGS**	International Society for General Semantics
ISFNR	International Society for Folk-Narrative Research		**ISGSH**	International Study Group for Steroid Hormones
ISFR	International Society for Fluoride Research		**ISGSR**	International Society for General Systems Research (U.S.A.)
ISFSI	International Society of Fire Service Instructors		**ISH**	International Society of Haematology = SIH
ISG	Inland Shipping Group		**ISH**	International Society of Homeric Studies
ISG	Institut für Sozialforschung und Gesellschaftspolitik (Germany)		**ISH**	International Society of Hypertension
ISG	Institúto Superior de Gestão		**ISH**	International Society of Hypnosis
ISG	Interessengemeinschaft der Schweizerischen Gärungsessig-Industrie		**ISHA**	Islamic Shipowners Association (Saudi Arabia)
ISG	International Signifisch Genootschap		**ISHAM**	International Society of Human and Animal Mycology = SIMHA
ISG	International Socialist Group			
ISG	International Spice Group		**ISHC**	International Society for Heterocyclic Chemistry (Austria)
ISG	Internationale Heinrich Schütz-Gesellschaft		**ISHE**	International Society for Human Ethology
ISGA	International Stained Glass Association		**ISHI**	International Society for the History of Ideas
ISGA	International Study Group of Aerogrammes		**ISHL**	International Society for Historical Linguistics
ISGA	Irish Salmon Growers' Association			
ISGC	International Society of Guatemala Collectors		**ISHM**	Institut des Sciences Humaines du Mali

ISHM	International Society for Hybrid Microelectronics
ISHM	International Society of the History of Medicine = SIHM
ISHOBSS	International Society for the History of the Behavioral and Social Sciences
ISHPES	International Society for the History of Physical Education and Sport (Sweden)
ISHR	International Society for Heart Research
ISHR	International Society for Human Rights = AIDH, IGM, SIDH
ISHRA	Iron and Steel Holding and Realisation Agency
ISHS	International Society for Horticultural Science = SICH, SISH
ISHSAA	Institute of Shops Health and Safety Acts Administration
ISI	Frauenhofer-Institut für Systemtechnik und Innovationsforschung (Germany)
ISI	Indian Social Institute
ISI	Indian Standards Institution
ISI	Indian Statistical Institute
ISI	Informatics Society of Iran
ISI	Initiative for Scottish Insects
ISI	Institute for Scientific Information (U.S.A.)
ISI	Inter-Services Intelligence (Afghanistan)
ISI	International Statistical Institute = IIS
ISI	Israel Standards Institute
ISIA	International Snowmobile Industry Association (U.S.A.)
ISIA	Irish Security Industry Association
ISIA	Irish Sugar Intervention Agency
ISIC	Instítuto Salvadoreño de Investigaciónes de Café
ISIC	International Solvay Institute of Chemistry
ISICIB	Centro Internazionale Bibliografico dell' Istituto di Studi sul Lavoro
ISID	International Society of Interior Designers
ISID	Research Institute of the Iron and Steel Industry (France)
ISIDA	Irish Sudden Infant Death Association
ISIDOG	International Society for Infectious Diseases in Obstetrics and Gynaecology (U.S.A.)
ISIFI	International Scientific Institute for Feminine Interpretation (Netherlands)
ISIFM	International Society of Industrial Fabric Manufacturers
ISIG	Institute of Standards and Industrial Research (Ghana)
ISIG	Instítuto di Sociologia Internazionale, Gorizia
ISIL	Indian Society of International Law
ISIM	International Society of Internal Medicine
ISIME	Istituto Storico Italiano per il Medio Evo
ISIMM	International Society for the Interaction of Mechanics and Mathematics
ISINI	International Society for Intercommunications of New Ideas (U.S.A.)
ISIO	Institute for the Study of International Organisations
ISIP	Instítuto Italiano di Polemologia e di Recerche sui Conflitti
ISIP	Internacianalna Stalna Izlozbo Publikacija (Yugoslavia)
ISIP	International Society of Immunopharmacology
ISIR	Institute of Standards and Industrial Research (Ghana)
ISIR	International Society for Invertebrate Reproduction
ISIR	International Society for the Immunology of Reproduction
ISIRI	Institute of Standards and Industrial Research of Iran
ISIS	Independent Schools Information Service
ISIS	Indian School of International Studies
ISIS	International Science Information Service (U.S.A.)
ISIS	International Security Information Service
ISIS	International Student Information Service (U.S.A.)
ISIS	Servicio de Información y Comunicación de las Mujeres (Chile)
ISIS Association	International Student Insurance Services Association (ISTC)
ISITB	Iron and Steel Industry Training Board
ISIUA	Institut Supérieur et International d'Urbanisme Appliqué (Belgium)
ISJC	Independent Schools Joint Council
ISJP	International Society for Japanese Philately

ISK	International Seidenbau Kommission	**ISM**	Institute of Spiritualist Mediums
ISK	International Society of the Knee	**ISM**	Institute of Sports Medicine
ISK	Internationales Sachsenhausen-Komitee = CIS	**ISM**	Institute of Supervisory Management
ISK RAN	Institute of the United States and Canada, Russian Academy of Sciences	**ISM**	Instítuto Social de la Marina
		ISM	International Society for Mesotherapy
ISKA	Internasjonalen for Stats-og Kommunalansatte = IÖD, ISP, PSI	**ISM**	International Society for Metaphysics
		ISM	Irish Sovereignty Movement
ISKCON	International Society for Krishna Consciousness = AICK	**ISM**	Istituto di Struttura della Materia (Italy)
ISKO	International Society for Knowledge Organization (Germany)	**ISMA**	Industrie Sénégalaise de Marbre et d'Agglomérés
ISKO	International Student Korfball Organisation (IKF)	**ISMA**	Institute for the Study of Man in Africa (South Africa)
ISL	International Soccer League (U.S.A.)	**ISMA**	International Securities Market Association (*ex AIBD*)
ISL	International Society of Literature		
ISL	International Society of Lymphology	**ISMA**	International Shipmasters Association of the Great Lakes
ISL	International Surfing League (U.S.A.)		
ISL	Irish Steel Limited (Éire)	**ISMA**	International Stress Management Association
ISL	Istituto di Studi sul Lavoro		
ISLA	Information Services on Latin America (U.S.A.)	**ISMA**	International Symposium on Musical Acoustics
ISLA	International Sign Linguistics Association	**ISMA**	Istituto Sperimentale per la Meccanizzazione Agricola (Italy)
ISLA	Islamic Library Association	**ISMAL**	Institut National des Sciences de la Mer et de l'Amenagement du Littoral (Algeria)
ISLE	Istituto per la Documentazione e gli Studi Legislativi		
ISLEWTT	International Post conference Symposium on Low Cost and Energy Saving Wastewater Treatment Technologies	**ISMAM**	International Society for Medical and Applied Malacology (U.S.A.)
		ISMCM	Institut Supérieur des Matériaux et de la Construction Mécanique
ISLIC	Israel Society of Special Libraries and Information Centres = ASMI	**ISME**	Institute of Sheet Metal Engineering
		ISME	International Society for Music Education
ISLIMA	Industrie Sénégalaise pour le Linge de Maison	**ISME**	International Survey of Management Education (U.S.A.)
ISLL	Irish Society for Labour Law		
ISLSCP	International Satellite Land Surface Climatology Project	**ISMEBC**	International Society for Molecular Electronics and BioComputing
ISLT	International Snow Leopard Trust (U.S.A.)	**ISMED**	International Society on Metabolic Eye Diseases
ISLTC	International Society of Leather Trades Chemists	**ISMEO**	Istituto Italiano per il Medio ed Estremo Oriente
ISLTS	Incorporated Society of Licensed Trade Stocktakers (*now* ILTS)	**ISMES**	Istituto Sperimentale Modelli e Structure
ISLU	Israel Special Libraries Union	**ISMEX**	International Shoe Machinery Exhibition
ISLWG	International Shipping Legislation Working Group (UNCTAD)	**ISMFE**	International Society of Soil Mechanics and Foundation Engineering
ISM	Incorporated Society of Musicians	**ISMG**	International Scientific Management Group (GARP)
ISM	Institute of Sales and Marketing Management	**ISMH**	International Society of Medical Hydrology and Climatology

ISML	Istituto per la Storia del Movimento Liberale		**ISNVP**	International Society for Non Verbal Psychotherapy
ISMM	Institute of Sales & Marketing Management		**ISO**	Interdisciplinary Students of Organizations
ISMM	Interesna Skupnost Madžarske Manjšine (Slovenia) = ICHM		**ISO**	International Organisation for Standardisation
ISMM	International Society for Mountain Medicine (Switzerland)		**ISO**	International Self-service Organisation
ISMM	International Society of Mini- and Micro- Computers		**ISO**	International Shopfitting Organisation
ISMOG	Instituut voor Sociaal-Economische Studie van Minder Ontwikkelde Gebieden		**ISO**	International Society of Organbuilders (Germany)
			ISO	International Stevedore Organisation
ISMOH	Irish Society of Medical Officers of Health (Éire)		**ISO**	International Sugar Organisation = OIA, OIS
ISMPH	International Society for Medical and Psychological Hypnosis (U.S.A.) = SIIMP		**ISO**	International Systemics Organisation (Finland)
			ISOA	Indian Society of Oriental Art
ISMRC	Inter-Services Metallurgical Research Council		**ISOA**	International Support Vessel Owners' Association
ISMS	International Society for Mushroom Science		**ISOB**	Incorporated Society of Organ Builders
			ISOB	International Society of Barristers
ISMUN	International Student Movement for the United Nations		**ISOBM**	International Society of Oncodevelopmental Biology and Medicine
ISMWSF	International Stoke Mandeville Wheelchair Sports Federation		**ISOC**	Instítuto de Información y Documentación en Ciencias Sociales
ISN	International Society for Neurochemistry		**ISOC**	Internet Society
ISN	International Society of Nephrology		**ISOCARP**	International Society of City and Regional Planners = AIU, IGSRP
ISN	International Society of Neuroendocrinology		**ISOD**	International Society for Orbital Disorders
ISN	International Society of Neuropathology (Canada)		**ISOD**	International Sports Organisation for the Disabled = CISH
ISNA	Indian Science News Association		**ISODARCO**	International School on Disarmament and Research on Conflicts (Italy)
ISNA	Istituto di Studi Nucleari per l'Agricoltura		**ISODOC**	International Centre for Standard in Information and Documentation (ISO)
ISNAR	International Service for National Agricultural Research (Germany)		**ISOF**	International Society for Ocular Fluorophotometry = SIFO
ISNET	Inter-Islamic Network on Space Sciences and Technology (COMSTECH, OIC) (Pakistan)		**ISOMED**	International Society of Mediterranean Ecology (MEDECOS) (France)
ISNIM	International Society for Neuroimmunomodulation		**ISONET**	International Standards Information Network (ISO)
ISNO	International Society for Neuro-Ophthalmology = SINO		**ISONEVO**	Instituut voor Sociaal Onderzoek van het Nederlandse Volk
ISNP	International Society of Naturopathic Physicians		**ISOPA**	European Di-isocyanate Producers' Association (Belgium)
ISNP	Russian Independent Institute of Social and National Problems		**ISORID**	International Information System on Research in Documentation (UNESCO)
ISNS	International Society for Neoplatonic Studies		**ISOSC**	International Society for Soilless Culture

ISOU	International Society for Ophthalmic Ultrasound
ISP	Independent Smallholder, Land Labourer and Citizens' Party (Hungary)
ISP	Independent Smallholders' Party Torgyan Faction (Hungary) = FKGP
ISP	Institute for the Study of Peace (U.S.A.)
ISP	Institute of Sales Promotion
ISP	Institute of Sewage Purification
ISP	Institute of the Sociology of Parliamentarism
ISP	Interessengemeinschaft der Schweizerischen Parkettindustrie
ISP	International Society for Pathophysiology (Russia)
ISP	International Society for Photogrammetry
ISP	International Society for Psychophysics
ISP	International Society of Planters (Malaysia)
ISP	International Society of Postmasters = AIRP
ISP	Istituto di Sperimentazione per la Pioppicoltora (Italy)
ISP	Société Internationale des Services Publiques = IÖD, ISKA, PSI
ISPA	Institutul de Studii si Proiectari Agricole
ISPA	International School Psychology Association
ISPA	International Screen Publicity Association
ISPA	International Skat Players Association
ISPA	International Small Printers' Association
ISPA	International Society of Parametric Analysts
ISPA	International Software Products Association
ISPA	International Sporting Press Association = AIPS
ISPA	International Squash Players Association
ISPA	Istituto di Studi Politici ed Amministrativi
ISPAA	International Society of Performing Arts Administrators
ISPAA	International Society of Plastic and Audio-visual Art
ISPAS	International Foundation "Pro Arte Spirituali" (Belgium)
ISPAS	International Society of Professional Ambulance Services (U.S.A.)
ISPCA	Irish Society for the Prevention of Cruelty to Animals
ISPCA	Ironmaking and Steelmaking Plant Contractors Association
ISPCAN	International Society for Prevention of Child Abuse and Neglect
ISPCC	International Ship Painting and Corrosion Conference
ISPCC	Irish Society for the Prevention of Cruelty to Children
ISPD	International Society of Peritoneal Dialysis
ISPDSAMS	Institute of Antiparasitic Diseases, Sichuan Academy of Medical Sciences
ISPE	Institute and Society of Practitioners in Electrolysis
ISPE	Institute of Swimming Pool Engineers
ISPE	Institutel de Studii si Proiectari Energetice (Romania)
ISPE	International Society for Philosophical Enquiry
ISPE	International Society of Pharmaceutical Engineers
ISPE	International Society of Planetarium Educators
ISPE	Istituto di Studi per la Programmazione Economica
ISPE	Istituto per lo Studio dei Problemi dell'Emigrazione
ISPEMA	Industrial Safety (Protective Equipment) Manufacturers Association
ISPER	Istituto per la Direzione del Personale
ISPES	Istituto per la Promozione dello Sviluppo Economico e Sociale
ISPH	International Society for Professional Hypnosis
ISPH	International Society of Psychology of Handwriting = IGSP, IHPS, SIPE, SIPS,
ISPHS	International Society for Phenomenology and Human Sciences
ISPhS	International Society of Phonetic Sciences
ISPI	Istituto per gli Studi di Politica Internazionale
ISPI RAN	Institute of Sociopolitical Studies, Russian Academy of Sciences
ISPIC	International Society for the Prevention of Iatrogenic Complications (Denmark)

ISPL	International Society for Phenomenology and Literature
ISPM	International Society of Plant Morphologists
ISPMB	International Society for the Protection of Mustangs and Burros
ISPMB	International Society of Plant Molecular Biology (U.S.A.)
ISPN	International Society for Parenteral Nutrition (U.S.A.)
ISPN	International Society for Pediatric Neurosurgery
ISPO	Information Society Project Office (EU)
ISPO	International Society for Preventive Oncology
ISPO	International Society for Prosthetics and Orthotics
ISPOG	International Society of Psychosomatic Obstetrics and Gynecology
ISPP	Indian Society for Plant Pathology
ISPP	Institute of Safety and Public Protection
ISPP	International Society for Plant Pathology
ISPP	International Society for Portuguese Philately
ISPP	International Society of Political Psychology
ISPP	International Society of Pre-retirement Planners
ISPP	Internationale Studiengemeinschaft für Pränatale Psychologie
ISPROM	Istituto di Studi e Programmi per il Mediterraneo
ISPRS	International Society for Photogrammetry and Remote Sensing = IGPT, SIPT
ISPS	Institutul de Studee si Proiectari Silvice (Romania)
ISPWP	International Society for the Prevention of Water Pollution
ISQ	Institúto de Soldadura e Qualidade (Portugal)
ISQA	International Association for Quality Assurance in Health Care
ISQA	Israel Society for Quality Assurance
ISR	Institute for Social Research (South Africa)
ISR	International Society of Radiology
ISRA	International Seabed Research Authority
ISRA	International Society for Research on Aggression
ISRA	International Study Centre of Rheumatic Diseases
ISRA	Islamic Relief Agency = AISA, IARA
ISRAIN	Institut Supérieur de Recherche Appliquée pour les Industries Nucléaires (Belgium)
ISRB	Inter-Services Research Bureau
ISRC	International Student Research Centre (IUS) = CEIIC, CEIR
ISRCA	Institute for Scientific Research in Central Africa
ISRCDVS	International Society for Research on Civilization Diseases and Vital Substances = SIRASVI, SIRMCE
ISRCSC	Inter-Service Radio Components Standardization Committee
ISRD	International Society for Rehabilitation of the Disabled
ISRE	Istituto di Studi e Ricerche Ecologiche
ISREC	Institut Suisse de Recherches Expérimentales sur le Cancer (Switzerland)
ISRF	International Squash Rackets Federation
ISRF	International Sugar Research Foundation (U.S.A.)
ISRFCTC	Inter-Services Radio-Frequency Cables Technical Committee
ISRI	Israel Shipping Research Institute
ISRI	Istituto di Studi sulle Relazioni Industriali
ISRI WUSC	Iron & Steel Research Institute, Wuhan Iron & Steel Company
ISRIC	International Soil Reference and Information Centre (Netherlands)
ISRIN	Istituto per le Ricerche sull'Informatica
ISRIXISC	Iron and Steel Research Institute of Xiangtan Iron and Steel Company
ISRM	Institute of Sport & Recreation Management (*ex* IBRM)
ISRM	International Society for Rock Mechanics
ISRM	International Society of Reproductive Medicine
ISRN	Incorporated Society of Registered Naturopaths
ISRO	Indian Space Research Organisation
ISRO	International Society of Radiation Oncology (U.S.A.)

ISRP	International Society for Respiratory Protection
ISRRT	International Society of Radiographers and Radiological Technicians
ISRS	International Society for Reef Studies
ISRSA	International Synthetic Rubber Safety Association
ISRT	International Spinal Research Trust
ISS	Inn Sign Society
ISS	Institute of Social Studies (Netherlands)
ISS	Institute of Sports Sponsorship
ISS	Instítuto de Seguros Sociales (Colombia)
ISS	Inter-Republic Security Service (Russia)
ISS	International Institute of Sociology (Denmark)
ISS	International Schools Services (U.S.A.)
ISS	International Scotist Society = SIS
ISS	International Seaweed Symposium
ISS	International Seismological Summary
ISS	International Social Service = SSI
ISS	International Society for Stereology
ISS	International Society of Significs
ISS	International Society of Surgery = SIC
ISS	International Softbill Society
ISS	International Sports Committee for Seafarers
ISS	International Student Service (U.S.A.)
ISS	International Sunshine Society
ISS	Israel Surgical Society
ISS	Istituto Superiore di Sanità
ISSA	Institute for Social Studies and Action (Philippines)
ISSA	International Sailing Schools Association
ISSA	International Sanitary Supply Association (U.S.A.)
ISSA	International Ship Suppliers Association
ISSA	International Shirt Stylists Association
ISSA	International Slurry Seal Association
ISSA	International Social Security Association = AISS, IVSS
ISSA	International Society of Securities Administrators (Switzerland)
ISSA	International Swimming Statisticians Association (Canada)
ISSAS	Institute of Solid State Physics, Academia Sinica
ISSB	Inter-Service Security Board
ISSBD	International Society for the Study of Behavioural Development
ISSC	International Ship Structures Congress
ISSC	International Social Science Council = CISS
ISSCL	Social Service Institution for Housing for Workers (Italy)
ISSCT	International Society of Sugar Cane Technologists
ISSD	International Society for Social Defence = SIDS
ISSD	International Society for the Study of Dissociation
ISSE	International School to School Experience (U.S.A.)
ISSE	International Society for the Study of Expressionism
ISSEA	Institut Sous-Régional de Statistique et d'Économie Appliquée (CACEU)
ISSEI	International Society for the Study of European Ideas
ISSEP	Institut Scientifique de Service Public (Belgium)
ISSER	Institute of Statistical, Social and Economic Research (Ghana)
ISSF	International Service of the Society of Friends
ISSFAM	Instítuto de Seguro Social de las Fuerzas Armadas Mexicanas
ISSGD	Institute of Soil Science of Guangdong Province
ISSK	International Socialists of South Korea
ISSLS	International Society for the Study of the Lumbar Spinal
ISSM	Institute of Sterile Services Management
ISSMC	Institute for Social Studies in Medical Care
ISSMFE	International Society of Soil Mechanics and Foundation Engineering
ISSMO	International Society for Structural and Multidisciplinary Optimization
ISSO	International Self-Service Organisation
ISSO	International Side-Saddle Organisation
ISSOCO	Istituto per lo Studio della Società Contemporanea
ISSOL	International Society for the Study of the Origin of Life
ISSP	Institute for Solid State Physics (Japan)
ISSP	International Society of Sports Psychology = SIPS

ISSP	Irish Society for Surveying and Photogrammetry
ISSR	Institute for Social Science Research (U.S.A.)
ISSR	International Society for the Sociology of Religions = SISR
ISSR	International Society of Root Research (Sweden)
ISSR	Istituti Superiori di Scienze Religiose (Vatican)
ISSRC	International Society for Study of Religion and Culture (Hong Kong)
ISSRS	Institut de Service Social et de Recherches Sociales
ISSS	International Society for Skiing Safety
ISSS	International Society for the Study of Symbols (U.S.A.)
ISSS	International Society of Soil Science = AISS, IBG, SICS
ISSSA	International Society for Strategic Studies on Africa
ISSSE	International Society of Statistical Science in Economics
ISST	Institut des Sciences Sociales du Travail
ISST	Institute for Space Science and Technology (U.S.A.)
ISST	International Society for the Study of Time
ISST	International Society of Skilled Trades
ISST	Istituto Scientifico Sperimental dei Tabacchi
ISSTD	International Society for the Study of Trophoblastic Diseases (U.S.A.)
ISSTDR	International Society for Sexually Transmitted Disease Research
ISSTIP	International Society for the Study of Tension in Performance
ISSUE	Issue (the National Fertility Association) (*ex* NFA)
ISSVD	International Society for the Study of Vulvar Diseases (U.S.A.)
IST	Institute of Science Technology
IST	International Society on Toxinology
IST-EUROPA	Istituto per l'Economia Europea
ISTA	Independent Secretarial Training Association (*now* IBTA)
ISTA	Indian Scientific Translators Association
ISTA	Industrial Science and Technology Agency (MITI) (Japan)
ISTA	Institut Sous-Régional Multisectoriel de Technologie Appliquée, de Planification et d'Evaluation des Projets (Gabon)
ISTA	Instítuto Salvadoreño de Transformación Agraria
ISTA	Instítuto Salvadoreño de Transformación Agraria
ISTA	International School of Theatre Anthropology
ISTA	International Schools Theatre Association
ISTA	International Seed Testing Association = AIES
ISTA	International Sight-Seeing and Tours Association
ISTA	International Special Tooling Association
ISTA	International Statistiche Agrarinformationen
ISTA	International Steel Trade Association
ISTA	Irish Seed Trade Association
ISTAHC	International Society of Technology Assessment in Health Care (Netherlands)
ISTAM	Israel Society for Theoretical and Applied Mechanics
ISTAT	Istituto Centrale di Statistica
ISTB	International Squash Tournament Board = WSC
ISTC	Indo-Swiss Training Centre (India)
ISTC	Industry, Science and Technology Canada
ISTC	Institute of Scientific and Technical Communicators
ISTC	Institute of Swimming Teachers & Coaches
ISTC	International Society for Terminal Care (Austria)
ISTC	International Stress and Tension Control Association
ISTC	International Student Travel Confederation
ISTC	International Switching and Testing Centre (U.K.)
ISTC	Iron and Steel Trades Confederation
ISTCL	International Scientific and Technical Committee on Laundering
ISTD	Imperial Society of Teachers of Dancing
ISTD	Institute for the Study and Treatment of Delinquency

ISTD	Inter-Services Topographical Department
ISTE	International Society for Technology in Education
ISTE	International Society of Tropical Ecology
ISTEA	Iron and Steel Trades Employers Association
ISTED	Institut des Sciences et des Techniques de l'Equipement et de l'Environnement pour le Développement
ISTERH	International Society for Trace Element Research in Humans (Japan)
ISTESU	International Secretariat for Teaching Educational Sciences in Universities
ISTF	International Social Travel Federation = FITS
ISTF	International Society of Tropical Foresters
ISTFA	International Society for Testing and Failure Analysis (U.S.A.)
ISTH	International Society on Thrombosis and Haemostasis
ISTI	International Science Technology Institute (U.S.A.)
ISTIC	Institute of Scientific and Technical Information of China
ISTIC	Instítuto de Servicios Sociales para Trabajadores de la Industria de la Construccion (Argentina)
ISTIF	Institute of Scientific and Technological Information, Chinese Academy of Forestry
ISTIHB	Institute of Sci-Tech Informations, Hebei Province (China)
ISTIS	International Science and Technology Information Service
ISTNA	International Seminars on Training for Nonviolent Action
ISTOR	Istituto per la Storia del Risorgimento Italiano
ISTP	International Society of Tropical Pediatrics (Philippines)
ISTPM	Institute Scientifique et Technique des Pêches Maritimes
ISTRA	Interplanetary Space Travel Research Association
ISTRAK	International Strassenteer Konferenz
ISTRC	International Society for Tropical Root Crops
ISTRO	International Soil Tillage Research Organisation

ISTROS	International Institute for Intercultural Contacts (Bulgaria)
IStructE	Institution of Structural Engineers
ISTS	Institute for Space and Terrestrial Science (U.S.A.)
ISTS	International Society for Twin Studies
ISTU	Instítuto Salvadoreño de Turismo
ISTVS	International Society for Terrain-Vehicle Systems
ISU	Immigration Services Union
ISU	International Salon der Uitvinders
ISU	International Salvage Union
ISU	International Skating Union = UIP
ISU	International Society of Urology = SIU
ISU	International Stereoscopic Union
ISUDO	International Society for Ultrasonic Diagnostics in Ophthalmology = SIDUO
ISUE	International Society of Urological Endoscopy
ISUH	Institute for the Study of Universal History though Arts and Artifacts (U.S.A.)
ISUNAM	Instítuto de Investigaciones Sociales (Mexico)
ISUOG	International Society for Ultrasound in Obstetrics and Gynecology
ISUSE	International Secretariat for the University Study of Education
ISV	Interessengemeinschaft Schweizerischer Verleger
ISV	International Society for Vibroacoustics
ISV	International Society of Videographers (U.S.A.)
ISV	Istituto Sperimentale per la Viticoltura
ISVA	Incorporated Society of Valuers and Auctioneers
ISVA	Institutett for Stromningsmekanik og Vandbygning (Denmark)
ISVA	International Satellite Verification Agency (U.S.A.)
ISVBM	International Society of Violin and Bow Makers
ISVE	Istituto di Studi per lo Sviluppo Economico
ISVEE	International Society for Veterinary Epidemiology & Economics (U.S.A.)
ISVEIMER	Istituto per lo Sviluppo Economico dell'Italia Meridionale
ISVET	Istituto per gli Studi sullo Sviluppo ed il Progresso Tecnico

ISVI	Istituto di Formazione e Ricerca sui Problemi Sociali dello Sviluppo		**ITA**	International Taxicab Association (U.S.A.)
ISVO	Interdisciplinary Research and Training Center for Development Cooperation (Belgium)		**ITA**	International Thermographers Association (U.S.A.)
ISVR	Institute of Sound & Vibration Research		**ITA**	International Tire Association
ISVSK	Internationaler Ständiger Verband für Schiffahrt-Kongresse = AIPCN, PIANC		**ITA**	International Transpersonal Association
			ITA	International Triticale Association (Australia)
ISW	Institute of Social Welfare		**ITA**	International Tube Association
ISW	Interessengemeinschaft für den Schweizerischen Weinimport		**ITA**	International Tunnelling Association = AITES
ISWA	International Science Writers Association		**ITA**	International Turquoise Association
ISWA	International Solid Wastes and Public Cleansing Association		**ITA**	International Twins Association
			ITA	International Typographic Association
ISWC	International Secretariat of World Citizens = SICM		**ITA**	Ireland-Taiwan Association
			ITA	Irish Translators' Association
ISWM	Institute of Solid Waste Management (South Africa)		**ITAA**	International Theatrical Agencies Association
ISWNE	International Society of Weekly Newspaper Editors (U.S.A.)		**ITAA**	International Transactional Analysis Association
ISWT	International Society of Wine Tasters (U.S.A.)		**ITAA**	Irish Travel Agents' Association
			ITABIA	Italian Biomass Association
ISY	Ilmansuojeluyhdistys		**ITAC**	Inter Action Groupe
ISYF	International Sikh Youth Federation		**ITACAB**	Instítuto de Transferencia de Tecnologias Apropiadas para Sectores Marginales (Panama)
ISYVC	International Sivananda Yoga Vedanta Center (Canada)			
ISZ	Industrieverband Schreib-und Zeichengeräte		**ITAI**	Institute of Traffic Accident Investigators
ISzM	Ifjúság Szervezet "Mladost" (Hungary) = MYA		**ITAL**	Institute of Food Technology (Brazil)
			ITAL	Instituut voor Toepassing van Atoomenergie in de Landbouw
IT	Institute of Trichologists			
IT&T	International Telegraph and Telephone Corporation		**ITALMOPA**	Associazione degli Industriale Mugnari e Pastoi d'Italia
ITA	European Federation of International Trade Advisers		**ITALPRO**	Comitato Italiano per la Semplificazione delle Proceduro del Commercio Internazionale
ITA	Independent Television Authority			
ITA	Indian Tea Association		**ITALSIEL**	Società Italiana Sistemi Informativa Eletronica
ITA	Initial Teaching Alphabet Foundation			
ITA	Institut du Transport Aérien = IAT		**ITALTEL**	Societa Italiana Telecomuniazioni
ITA	Institut Technique de l'Aviculture des Produits de Basse-cour et des Élevages de Petites Animaux		**ITALTOGO**	Société Italo-Togolaise
			ITAMA	Information Technology Acquisition and Marketing Association (U.S.A.)
ITA	Institute of Transactional Analysis		**ITAP**	Institut Technique des Administrations Publiques
ITA	Institute of Transport Administration			
ITA	Institute of Travel Agents		**ITAR-TASS**	Informatsionnoe Telegrafnoe Agentsvo Rossii – Telegrafnoe Agentsvo Suverennykh Stran
ITA	Instituto Tecnológico de Aeronáutica (Brazil)			
			ITAS	Industrial Training Association (Scotland)
ITA	International Tape Association		**ITAU**	Compania Itaú des Transportes Acéros (Brazil)
ITA	International Tax Academy (IBFD)			

ITAVI	Institut Technique de l'Aviculture, des Productions de Basse-Cour et des Élevages de Petits Animaux
ITAVI	Servizio Telecommunicazioni e Meteorológico dell' Aeronautica
ITB	Institut Français de la Betterave Industrielle
ITB	Instytut Techniki Budowlanej
ITB	Internationaler Turnerbund = FIG, IGF
ITBA	International Toy Buff's Association
ITBA	Irish-Turkish Business Association
ITBA	Istituto di Tecnologie Biomediche Avanzate (Italy)
ITBLAV	Internationale Textil-, Bekleidungs und Lederabeiter Vereinigung = FITITHC, ITBLF, ITGLWF
ITBLF	Internationella Textil-Beklädnads Läderbetarefederationen = FITITHC, ITBLAV, ITGLWF
ITBTP	Institut Technique du Bâtiment et des Travaux Publiques
ITC	Imperial Tobacco Compnay
ITC	Independent Television Commission
ITC	Independent Theatre Council
ITC	Indian Tobacco Company
ITC	Industrial Training Council
ITC	Information Technology Committee
ITC	Inland Transport Commission
ITC	Institute of Town Clerks (South Africa)
ITC	Instytut Techniki Cieplnej
ITC	Inter-American Travel Congress = CIT
ITC	International Institute for Aerial Survey and Earth Sciences (Netherlands)
ITC	International Instituut voor Training en Consulting (Belgium)
ITC	International Tar Conference = CIG, ITK
ITC	International Tea Committee
ITC	International Teletraffic Congress = CIT
ITC	International Thyroid Conference
ITC	International Tin Council
ITC	International Trade Centre (UNCTAD/GATT) = CCI
ITC	International Trade Commission (U.S.A.)
ITC	International Training Centre for Aerial Survey (Netherlands)
ITC	International Training Centre for Post-Graduate Soil Scientists (UNESCO) (Belgium)
ITC	International Training in Communication
ITC	International Translations Centre
ITC	International Transport Committee
ITC	International Tribology Council
ITC	International Trotsky Committee
ITC	International Typeface Corporation
ITC	Irish Timber Council
ITC	Société Ivoirienne de Transactions Commerciales
ITCA	Inter-American Technical Council of Archives = CTIA
ITCABIC	Inter-Territorial Catholic Bishops Conference (Sierra Leone)
ITCAS	International Training Centre for Aerial Survey
ITCB	International Textiles and Clothing Bureau = OITP
ITCC	International Technical Cooperation Centre (Israel)
ITCCA	International Tai Chi Chuan Association
ITCF	Institut Technique des Céréales et des Fourrages
ITCF	Institúto de Terra, Cartografia e Floresta (Brazil)
ITCH	Institute of Transcultural Health Care
ITCI	International Tree Crops Institute (U.S.A.)
ITCPN	International Technical Conference on Protection of Nature
ITCRA	International Textile Care and Rental Association
ITCS	International Transport Compagnies Syndicate
ITCVD	Tianjin Institute of Cardiovascular Disease
ITCWRM	International Training Centre for Water Resource Management (UNEP) = CEFIGRE
ITD	Institute of Training and Development (*now* IPD)
ITD	Instytut Technologii Drewna
ITDA	Irish Tyre Distributors' Association
ITDC	International Trade Development Committee (U.S.A.)
ITDG	Intermediate Technology Development Group
ITDI	Industrial Technology Development Institute (Philippines)
ITDP	Institute for Transportation and Development Policy (U.S.A.)

ITÉ	Institiúid Teangeolaíochta Éireann
ITE	Institute of Television Engineers (Japan)
ITE	Institute of Terrestrial Ecology (NERC)
ITE	Institute of Traffic Engineers (U.S.A.)
ITE	Institute of Transportation Engineers
ITE	Institution of Telecommunication Engineers (India)
ITE/EIC	Environmental Information Centre
ITEA	International Esperanto Tourist Association
ITEA	International Test and Evaluation Association (U.S.A.)
ITEB	Institut Technique d'Élevage Bovin
ITEC	Institúto Tecnologico de Electronica y Comunicaciónes (Colombia)
ITEC	International Therapy Examination Council
ITEC	International Total Energy Congress
ITECO	Coopération Technique Internationale-Centre de Formation pour le Développement
ITEI	International Technology & Economy Institute (China)
ITEMA	Industrie Textile du Mali
ITEME	Institution of Technician Engineers in Mechanical Engineering
ITEO	International Trade and Employment Organisation
ITEPMAI	Institut Technique des Plants Médicinales, Aromatiques et Industrielles
ITER	International Thermonuclear Experimental Reactor
ITERAM	Institúto de Terras do Amazonas (Brazil)
ITERG	Institut Technique d'Études et des Recherches des Corps Gras
ITERPA	Institúto de Terras do Pará (Brazil)
ITES	Institute of Terrestrial Ecology (South)
ITESC	International Tanker Equipment Standing Committee
ITESM	Institúto Technológico y de Estudios Superieres de Monterrey (Mexico)
ITESSA	Institute of Topographical and Engineering Surveyors of South Africa
ITF	Committee of Transport Workers Unions in the EEC
ITF	Industrial and Trade Fairs International
ITF	Institut Textile de France
ITF	Institutet för Träteknisk Forskning (Sweden)
ITF	Instrumenttekniska Föreningen
ITF	International Technology Foundation
ITF	International Tennis Federation = FIT
ITF	International Trade Federations = FIP
ITF	International Trampoline Federation = FIT
ITF	International Transport Federation
ITF	International Transport Workers' Federation = FIOT
ITF	Irish Tax Federation
ITF	Irish Textiles Federation
ITFCA	International Track and Field Coaches Association (U.S.A.)
ITFCS	International Task Force for Child Survival
ITFL	International Task Force on Literacy
ITG	Informationstechnische Gesellschaft in VDE
ITG	Institut Technique du Gruyère
ITG	Instituto Tecnologico de Gas (Portugal)
ITG	International Trumpet Guild
ITGA	International Tobacco Growers Association
ITGA	Irish Timber Growers Association
ITGLIC	International Tropical Grain Legume Information Centre (Nigeria)
ITGLWF	International Textile and Garment and Leather Workers Federation = FITITHC, FITTHC, ITBLAV
ITH	Internationale Tagung der Historiker derArbeiterbewegung
ITHA	International Tourist Health Association (Italy)
ITI	Iceberg Transport International (Saudi Arabia)
ITI	Indian Telephone Industries
ITI	Institute for Technical Interchange (Hawaii)
ITI	Institute of Translation and Interpreting
ITI	International Tax Institute (U.S.A.)
ITI	International Technology Institute (U.S.A.)
ITI	International Theatre Institute = IIT
ITI	International Thrift Institute
ITI	International Training Institute
ITI	Irish Telecommunications Investments
ITI	Irish Timber Industries
ITI	Islands Teknologische Institut
ITIA	International Tungsten Industry Association

ITIC	International Toxicology Information Centre (Spain)
ITIC	International Tsunami Information Centre (Hawaii)
ITIC	Irish Tourist Industry Confederation
ITICA	Chambre Syndicale Nationale d'Isolation Thermique, de l'Insonorisation et de la Correction Acoustique
ITIPAT	Institut pour la Technologie et l'Industrialisation des Produits Agricoles Tropicaux (Ivory Coast)
ITIRC	IBM Technical Information Retrieval Center (U.S.A.)
ITIS	Industrial Technical Information Service (Singapore)
ITIS	Insect Toxicologists Information Service (Netherlands)
ITIS	Intermediate Technology Industrial Services (ODA)
ITIUS	International Theatre Institute of the United States
ITJ	Instytut Techniki Jądrowej
ITK	Internationale Teerkonferenz = CIG, ITC
ITKF	International Traditional Karate Federation (U.S.A.)
ITL	Institute of Tape Learning
ITLR	Institut für Thermodynamik der Luft- und Raumfahrt (Germany)
ITM	Institute of Travel Managers in Industry and Commerce
ITM	Institute of Tropical Meteorology (India)
ITM	Institúto di Tecnologia Meccanica
ITM	Irish Traveller Movement
ITMA	Imported Tyre Manufacturers' Association
ITMA	Institute of Trade Mark Agents
ITMA	International Tanning Manufacturers Association (U.S.A.)
ITMA	Irish Transport Manufacturers' Association (Éire)
ITMAR	Information Technology Marketing Association
ITMEB	International Tea Market Expansion Board
ITMF	International Textile Manufactures Federation
ITMRC	International Travel Market Research Council
ITN	Independent Television News
ITN	International Training Network for Water and Waste Management (U.S.A.)
ITO	Indian Tourist Office
ITO	Institute of Traffic Officers of South Africa
ITO	International Trade Organisation
ITOCY	Industrie Togolaise du Cycle et du Cyclometer
ITOPF	International Tanker Owners Pollution Federation
ITOU	Irish Tax Officials' Union
ITOVIC	Institut Technique de l'Élevage Ovin et Caprin
ITP	Industrie Togolaise des Plastiques
ITP	Institut Technique de la Pomme de Terre
ITP	Institut Technique du Porc
ITPA	Independent Track Promoters Association
ITPA	Institut Technique de Pratique Agricole
ITPA	International Tax Planning Association
ITPA	International Tea Promotion Association = AIPT
ITPA	Irish Trade Protection Association
ITPAC	Imported Tobacco Product Advisory Council
ITPC	International Tree Project Clearinghouse (UN)
ITR	Instytut Tele- i Radiotechnicznej
ITRA	International Truck Restorers Association
ITRABO	Société Ivoirienne de Transactions du Bois
ITRC	Industrial Toxicology Research Centre (India)
ITRC	International Tin Research Council
ITRI	Industrial Technology Research Institute (Taiwan)
ITRI	International Tin Research Institute
ITRI	International Trade Research Institute (China)
ITRMLM	Institut Territorial de Recherche Médicale Louis Malardé
ITRPF	International Tyre, Rubber and Plastics Federation
ITRU	Industrial Training Research Unit
ITS	Compagnie Internationale de Services de Télécommunications
ITS	Institute for Transport Studies

ITS	Instituut voor Toegepaste Sociologie
ITS	Instytut Tworzyw Sztucznych
ITS	International Technogeographical Society
ITS	International Telecommunications Society
ITS	International Thespian Society
ITS	International Tracing Service = ISD, SIR
ITS	International Trade Secretariats = SPI
ITS	International Turfgrass Society
ITS	Irish Texts Society
ITS	Islamic Texts Society
ITSA	Independent Tank Storage Association
ITSA	Information Technology Services Agency
ITSA	Institute of Trading Standards Adminstration
ITSC	International Telephone Service Centres
ITSC	International Tyre Specialists Congress
ITSG	International Tin Study Group
ITSM	Institut für Thermische Strömungsmaschinen und Maschinenlaboratorium (Germany)
ITSSAR	Independent Training Scheme & Register
ITSTC	Information Technology Steering Committee
ITSU	International Coordination Group for the Tsunami Warning System in the Pacific (IOC) (U.S.A.)
ITT	Industrie Textile Togolaise
ITT	Institute of Textile Technology (U.S.A.)
ITT	Institute of Travel and Tourism
ITT	Instítúto Torcuato di Tella (Argentina)
ITT	Instituut voor Tuinbouwtechniek
ITT	Société Ivoirienne de Technologie Tropicale
ITTA	Insurance Technology Trade Association
ITTA	International Teachers Temperance Association
ITTC	International Towing Tank Conference
ITTEHAD	Ittehad-e Islami-e Afghanistan
ITTF	International Table Tennis Federation = FITT
ITTID	International Trust for Terminal and Incurable Diseases
ITTO	International Timber Trade Organisation

ITTO	International Tropical Timber Organisation = OIBT OIMT
ITTTA	International Technical Tropical Timber Association = ATIBT
ITU	International Technological University = UIT
ITU	International Telecommunications Union = UIT
ITU	International Telegraphic Union
ITU	International Temperance Union
ITU	International Triathlon Union = FIT, IFT
ITU	International Typographical Union
ITUAC	Independent Trade Union Action Council (Jamaica)
ITUCPD	International Trade Union Committee on Peace and Disarmament
ITUCSTL	International Trade Unions Committee of Social Tourism and Leisure = CSITSL
ITUG	International Tandem Users' Group (U.S.A.)
ITUS	Independent Trade Union of Servicemen (Russia)
ITUSA	Information Technology Users Standards Asociation
ITUSC	International Trade Union Solidarity Campaign
ITV	Institut Technique du Vin
ITV	Instítúto Técnico Vocacional (Guatemala)
ITV	Internationaler Trampolin-Verband
ITVA	International Industrial Television Association
ITVTP	Internationale Tierärzliche Vereinigung für Tierproduktion = AIVPA, IVAAP
ITVV	Internationaler Transport-Versicherungs-Verband
ITWKA	Inland Tea Warehouse Keepers Association
ITZN	International Trust for Zoological Nomenclature
IU	Interlingue Union
IU	International Environmental Protection Union
IU	Islamic Unity (Afghanistan) = II
IU	Izquierda Unida (Bolivia, Chile, Peru, Spain)
IU.S.A.	Industrias Unidas (El Salvador)
IUA	Instytut Urbanistyki i Architektury
IUA	International Union Against Alcoholism = UIA

IUA	International Union of Academies (Belgium) = UAI	**IUCESD**	Interamerican University Council for Economic and Social Development = CUIDES
IUA	International Union of Advertising	**IUCFA**	Inter-Union Committee for Frequency Allocations for Radio Astronomy and Space Science
IUA	International Union of Angiology		
IUA	International Union of Architects = UIA		
IUAA	International Union of Alpine Associations = UIAA	**IUCH**	International Union for Circumpolar Health (U.S.A.)
IUAA	International Union of Alpinist Associations	**IUCI**	International Union of the Ionosphere
IUAC	International Union Against Cancer = UICC	**IUCISD**	Inter-University Consortium for International Social Development
IUACE	Indian University Association for Continuing Education	**IUCM**	Inter-Union Commission for Studies of the Moon
IUAES	International Union of Anthropological and Ethnological Sciences = UISAE, UNICAE	**IUCME**	International University Contact for Management Education
		IUCN	World Conservation Union (formerly International Union for the Conservation of Nature and Natural Resources)
IUAI	International Union of Aviation Insurers = UIAA		
IUAJ	International Union of Agricultural Journalists = UIJA	**IUCN**	World Conservation Union = UICN
		IUCNGA	IUCN General Assembly
IUAM	Islamic Union of Afghan Mujaheddin	**IUCOG**	Inter-Union Commission of Geodynamics
IUAO	International Union for Applied Ornithology	**IUCPA**	Union Internationale de Chimie Pure et Appliquée
IUAPPA	International Union of Air Pollution Prevention Associations = UIAPPA	**IUCr**	International Union of Crystallography
IUATLD	International Union against Tuberculosis and Lung Disease = UICTMR	**IUCRC**	Industry – Univ. Cooperative Research Center (U.S.A.)
		IUCRG	Inter Union Committee on Radio Geophysics
IUB	International Union of Biochemistry = IUBMB, UIB	**IUCRM**	Inter-Union Committee on Radio Meteorology
IUB	International Universities' Bureau	**IUCRO**	Inter Union Committee on Radio Oceanography
IUBMB	International Union of Biochemistry and Molecular Biology	**IUCS**	Inter-Union Commission on Spectroscopy
IUBS	International Union of Biological Sciences = UICB, UISB	**IUCST**	Inter-Union Commission on Science Teaching
IUBSSA	International Union of Building Societies and Saving Associations = IUHFI	**IUCSTP**	Inter-Union Commission on Solar-Terrestrial Physics
IUC	Inter-University Centre of Post-Graduate Studies (Yugoslavia)	**IUCSTR**	Inter-Union Commission on Solar and Terrestrial Relationships
IUC	Inter-University Council for East Africa (Uganda)	**IUCW**	International Union for Child Welfare
IUC	International Union Against Cancer	**IUDC**	International Union for Development Cooperation = UNICOS
IUC	International Union of Crystallography		
IUCAB	International Union of Commercial Agents and Brokers	**IUDSE**	Internationale Union Demokratisch Sozialistischer Erzieher = IUSDT
IUCAF	Inter-Union Commission on Frequency Allocations for Radio Astronomy and Space Science (COSPAR, ICSU)	**IUDZG**	International Union of Directors of Zoological Gardens = UIDJZ
IUCE	International Union of Cinematograph Exhibitors = UIEC	**IUE**	Institut de l'Unesco pour l'Education (Germany) = UIE, UIP

IUE	Institut Universitaire Européen = EHI, EUI	**IUHR**	International Union of Hotel, Restaurant and Bar Workers
IUE	International Union for Electro-heat = UIE	**IUHS**	International Union of History of Sciences = UIHS
IUE	International Union of Electrical, Radio and Machine Workers	**IUI**	Industriens Utredningsinstitut
IUEC	Inter-Universitare Efficiency Commissie	**IUI**	International Union of Interpreters
IUEC	International Union of Elevator Constructors	**IUIH**	International Union of Independent Hospitals = IUPH, IUPNH, UIHP
IUEE	Institut Universitaire d'Études du Développement (Switzerland)	**IUIN**	International Union for Inland Navigation (Belgium) = IBU, UINF
IUEE	Institut Universitaire d'Études Européennes (Switzerland)	**IUIR**	Italian Union for Istria and Rijeka (Slovenia) = IZIR
IUEFI	Internacia Unuigo de la Esperantistoj Filologoj = IUEP	**IUIS**	International Union of Immunological Societies
IUEM	International Union of Esthetics Medicine	**IUJCD**	Internationale Union Junger Christlicher Demokraten = IUYCD, UIGDC, UIJDC
IUEP	International Union of Esperantist Philologists = IUEFI	**IUKP**	Internationale Union der Katholischen Presse = ICPU, IKUP, UCIP
IUEW	International Union of Electrical Workers	**IUL**	International Union der Gewerkschaften der Lebens- und Genussmittelarbeiter Gewerkschaften = IUF, UITA
IUF	International Unicycling Federation		
IUF	International Union of Food and Allied Workers' Association = IUL, UITA	**IUL**	International University in Lugano (Switzerland)
IUFDT	International Union of Food, Drink and Tobacco Workers' Associations = UIAT	**IULA**	International Union of Local Authorities = IGV, UIV
IUFO	International Union of Family Organisations = UIOF	**IULCW**	International Union of Liberal Christian Women = UFLC
IUFoST	International Union of Food Science and Technology	**IULEC**	Inter-University Labor Education Committee (U.S.A.)
IUFRO	International Union of Forest Research Organisations	**IULIA**	International Union of Life Insuance Agents
IUG	Insurers Union of Greece	**IULN**	International Union of Latin Notaries = UINL
IUGB	International Union of Game Biologists	**IULTCS**	International Union of Leather Technologists and Chemists Societies
IUGE	Internationale Union für Gesundheitserziehung = IUHE, UIES	**IULVT**	International Union for Land Value Taxation and Free Trade
IUGG	International Union of Geodesy and Geophysics = UGGI	**IUMH**	International Union for Mental Health = IU.S.A.MH
IUGS	International Union of Geological Sciences = UICG, UISG	**IUMI**	International Union of Marine Insurance
IUHE	International Union for Health Education = IUGE, UIES	**IUMP**	International Union of Master Painter = UNIEP
IUHEI	Institut Universitaire de Hautes Études Internationales (Switzerland)	**IUMRS**	International Union of Materials Research Societies
IUHFI	International Union of Housing Finance Institutions	**IUMS**	International Union for Moral and Social Action = UIAMS
IUHHA	International Union of Historic House Associations	**IUMS**	International Union of Microbiological Societies = UISM
IUHPS	International Union of the History and Philosophy of Science = UIHPS	**IUMSWA**	International Union of Marine and Shipbuilding Workers of America

IUNA	Irish United Nations Association	**IUPT**	International Union of Public Transport =UITP
IUNG	Instytut Uprany, Nawozenia i Głeboznawstwa	**IUQR**	International Union of Quarternary Research
IUNS	International Union of Nutritional Sciences = UISN	**IUR**	International Union of Radioecologists (Belgium) = UIR
IUNT	Instítúto Uruguayo de Normas Tecnicas	**IUR**	International Union of Railways = UIC
IUO	International Union of Oenologists	**IUR**	International University of Radiophonics (France)
IUOE	International Union of Operating Engineers	**IURA**	International Union of Radio Amateurs
IUOTO	International Union of Official Travel Organizations	**IURC**	International Union for Research of Communication (Switzerland)
IUP	Association of Independent Unionist Peers	**IURD**	Institute of Urban and Regional Development (U.S.A.)
IUP	International Union of Phlebology	**IURES**	International Union of Reticuloendothelial Societies
IUPA	International Union of Police Associations = UISP	**IURMS**	International Union of Radio Medical Services = UIMC
IUPA	International Union of Practitioners in Advertising = UIP	**IURN**	Institut Unifié de Recherches Nucléaires
IUPAB	International Union of Pure and Applied Biophysics = UIBPA	**IURN**	International Union of Registered Nurses = UIIDE
IUPAC	International Union of Pure and Applied Chemistry = UICPA, UIQPA	**IURP**	Imprensa da Universidade Rural de Pernambuco (Brazil)
IUPAP	International Union of Pure and Applied Physics = UIPPA	**IURPC**	International Union of Roofing and Plumbing Contractors =UICP
IUPC	Inter-University and Polytechnic Council for Higher Education Overseas	**IURS**	International Union of Radio Science = URSI
IUPERJ	Instítúto Universitário de Pesquisas do Rio de Janeiro (Brazil)	**IUS**	Inter-University Seminar on Armed Forces and Society (U.S.A.)
IUPESM	International Union for Physical and Engineering Sciences in Medicine	**IUS**	International Union of Speleology = UIS
IUPH	International Union of Private Hospitals = IUIH, IUPH, IUPNH	**IUS**	International Union of Students = ISB, MSS, UIE
IUPHAR	International Union of Pharmacology	**IUSA**	International Underwater Spearfishing Association
IUPIP	International Union for the Protection of Industrial Property = UIPPI	**IUSA**	International Union for Slavonic Archeology (Poland)
IUPIW	International Union of Petroleum and Industrial Workers	**IUSAMH**	International Union of Societies for the Aid of Mental Health = IUMH
IUPLAW	International Union for the Protection of Literary and Artistic Works	**IUSDT**	International Union of Social Democratic Teachers = IUDSE
IUPN	International Union for the Protection of Nature	**IUSF**	International Union of Societies of Foresters = UISIF
IUPNH	International Union of Private Nursing Homes = IUIH, IUPH, UIHP	**IUSF**	International University Sports Federation = FISU
IUPO	International Union of Property Owners = UIPI	**IUSG**	International Uveitis Study Group
IUPPS	International Union of Prehistoric and Protohistoric Sciences = UISPP	**IUSM**	International Union for Surveys and Mapping
IUPS	International Union of Physiological Science = UICF, UISP	**IUSO**	Institute of University Safety Officers
IUPsyS	International Union of Psychological Science	**IUSO**	International Union of Security Officers

IUSP	International Union of Scientific Psychology
IUSS	International Union for Social Studies
IUSSI	International Union for Study of Social Insects = UIEIS
IUSSP	International Union for the Scientific Study of Population = UIESP
IUSUHM	International Union of School and University Health and Medicine = UIHMSU
IUSY	International Union of Socialist Youth = UIJS
IUT	Industrial Unit of Tribology
IUT	Instit́uto de Utilidade Turística
IUT	International Union of Tenants
IUT	International Union of Therapeutics = UTI
IUTAD	Instit́uto Universidade do Tras-0s-Montes e Alto Douro
IuTAKE	Iuzhno-Turkmenistanskaia Arkheologicheskaia Kompleksnaia Ekspeditsiia
IUTAM	International Union of Theoretical and Applied Mechanics = UITAM
IUTCA	International Union of Technical Cinematograph Associations = UNIATEC
IUTCT	International Union for Thermal Medicine and Climatothalassotherapy = UIMTCT
IUTOX	International Union of Toxicology
IUVDT	International Union against the Venereal Diseases and the Treponematoses = UIMVT
IUVFTA	Internationale Union für Vakuum-Forschung, -Technik und- Anwendung = IUVSTA, UISTAV
IUVSTA	International Union for Vacuum Science, Technique and Applications = IUVFTA, UISTAV
IUWA	International Union of Women Architects = UIFA
IUWDS	International Ursigram and World Days Service (FAGS)
IUYCD	International Union of Young Christian Democrats = IUJCD, UIGDC, UIJDC
IV	Institut Virusologii
IV	Institute of Valuers (South Africa)
IV RAN	Institute of Oriental Studies, Russian Academy of Sciences
IVA	Ingenjörsvetenskapsakademien
IVA	Instit́uto de Vacuna Antivariolosa (Bolivia)
IVA	International Veterinary Auxiliary
IVA	Internationale Vereinigung der Anschlussgeleise-Benützer = AIEP
IVA	Internationaler Verband für Arbeiterbildung = FIAET, IFWEA
IVA	Irish Veterinary Association
IVAAP	International Veterinary Association for Animal Production = AIVPA, ITVTP
IVAB	Internationaler Verband für Austausch und Bildung von Kindern und Jugendlichen = FIEEA, IFECYE
IVAC	Instit́uto Venezolano de Acción Communitaria
IVACG	International Vitamin A Consultative Group
IVACL	International Voluntary Action on Child Labour
IVADM	International Veterinary Academy on Disaster Medicine
IVANK	International Veterinär-Anatomische Nomenklatur-Kommission = CINAV, ICVAN
IVAS	Institute of Valuers and Auctioneers in Scotland
IVBA	International Veteran Boxers Association
IVBF	International Volleyball Federation = FIVB
IVBH	Internationale Vereinigung für Brückenbau and Hochbau = AIPC, IABSE
IVBS	Industriele Vereniging tot Bevordering van de Stralingsveiligheid
IVBV	Internationale Vereinigung der Bergführerverbände = UIAGM
IVC	Industrievereinigung Chemiefaser
IVC	International Vacuum Congress
IVC	Permanent Committee for the International Veterinary Congresses
IVCA	International Visual Communications Association
IVCA	Irish Venture Capital Association
IVCC	Institut des Vins de Consommation Courante
IVCF	Intervarsity Christian Fellowship
IVCS	Indian Volunteers for Community Service
IVD	Industrievereinigung Chemiefaser

IVDJ	Internationale Vereinigung Demokratischer Juristen = AIJD, IADL, MAJD
IVE	Institute of Vitreous Enamellers
IVE	Institúto Veterinario Ecuatoriano
IVE	Internationale Vereinigung des Eisenwaren- und Eisenhändlerverbände = FIDAQ, IFIA
IVE	Internationale Vereinigung von Einkaufsverbänder
IVEA	Irish Vocational Education Association
IVEI RAN	Institute of Foreign Economic Studies, Russian Academy of Sciences
IVEL	Institúto Veterinario Ecuatoriano del Litoral
IVEM	Institute of Virology & Environmental Microbiology (NERC)
IVES	Internationaler Verband für Erziehung zu Suchmittelfreiem Leben = IATE
IVF	Industrieverband Friseurbedarf
IVF	Institutet för Verkstadsteknisk Forskning
IVFGR	Internationale Vereinigung für Gewerblichen Rechtsschultz = AIPPI, IAPIP, IVR
IVFL	Internationale Vereinigung für Freier Lehrergewerkschaften = IFFTU, SPIE
IVFT	Instituut voor Veterinaire Farmacologie en Toxicologie der Rijksuniversiteit Utrecht
IVFZ	International Veterinary Federation of Zootechnics = FIVZ
IVG	Industrievereinigung Gartenbedarf
IVG	Internationale Vereinigung für Germanische Sprach- und Literaturwissenschaft = IAGLL
IVGWP	Internationaler Verband der Gastronomie-und Weinbau-Presse = FIPREGA, FISGV, IFGVP
IVH	Industrieverband für Heimtierbedarf
IVH	Internationale Vereinigung des Handwerks
IVHW	Internationaler Verband für Hauswirtschaft =FIEF, IFHE
IVI	Institut Vseobshchei Istorii
IVI RAN	Institute of World History, Russian Academy of Sciences
IVI(MO)-RAN	Institute of Military History of the Ministry of Defence of Russia and the Russian Academy of Sciences
IVIA	Instituto Valenciano de Investigaciones Agrarias (Spain)
IVIA	International Videotex Industry Association (France)
IVIC	Instituto Venezolano de Investigaciones Cientificas
IVIO	Instituut voor Individueel Onderwijs
IVIP	Internationale Vereinigung für Individual-Psychologie = IAIP, AIPA
IVIPA	International Videotext Information Providers Association
IVITA	Institúto Veterinario de Investigaciones Tropicales y de Altura (Peru)
IVK	Industrieverband Kunststoffbahnen
IVK	Institut Vrachebnoi Kosmetiki
IVK	Institutet för Växtforskning och Kyallagring (Sweden)
IVKBJ	International Verbond van de Katholieke Boerenjeugdbeweginen
IVKD	Internationaler Verband der Konferenz-Dolmetscher = AIIC, IACI
IVKDF	Institut von Karman de Dynamique des Fluides (Belgium)= VKIFD
IVKh	Institut Vodnogo Khoziaistva
IVKM	Internationaler Verband der Katholischen Mädchenschutzvereine
IVKMH	International Vereinigung der Klein- und Mittelbetriebe des Handels = FIPMEC, IFSMC
IVKMI	Internationale Vereinigung der Klein- und Mittelbetriebe der Industrie = FIPMI, IFSMI
IVL	Institutet für Vatten-och Luftvardsforskning
IVL	Institutet voor Veredeling van Landbouwgewassen
IVL	Internationale Vereinigung der Lehrerverbände = FIAI, IFTA
IVL	Internationale Vereinigung für Landwirtschaftskredit = CICA, ICAC
IVL	Internationale Vereinigung für Theoretische und Angewandte Limnologie = AIL, IAL, IATAL, SIL
IVLA	International Visual Literacy Association
IVLD	Internationale Vereinigung der Organisationen von Lebensmittel-Detaillisten = IFGA, UIDA
IVM	Industrievereinigung Möbelzubehör
IVMB	International Vereinigung der Musikbibliotheken, Musikarchive und Musikdokumentationszentren = AIBM, IAML

IVN	Internationale Vereniging voor Nederlandistiek	**IVSB**	Industrieverband Schneidwaren und Bestecke
IVND	Institut Vysshei Nervnoi Deiatel'nosti	**IVSBB**	Internationale Vereinigung für Schul- und Berufsberatung = AIOSP, IAEVG
IVO	Instituut voor Ontwikkelingsvraagstukken (Netherlands)	**IVSKMTB**	Industrieverband Sand, Kies, Mörtel, Transportbeton Novel
IVO	Instituut voor Veeteelkundig Onderzoek (TNO)	**IVSP**	Internationale Vereinigung für Selbstmordprophylaxe = AIPS, IASP
IVO	Internationaler Verband der Orthopädieschuhteknik	**IVSS**	Institúto Venezolano de los Seguros Sociales
IVP	Industrie des Vernis et Peintures, Mastics, Encres d'Imprimerie et Couleurs d'Art	**IVSS**	International Varna Sociological School (Bulgaria)
IVP	Institut Vodnykh Problem	**IVSS**	International Vereinigung für Soziale Sicherheit = AISS, ISSA
IVP	Institúto Venezolano de Petroquímica	**IVSS**	Internationaler Verband für Schwerhörigenseelsorge
IvP	Instituut voor Plantenveredeling	**IVSU**	International Veterinary Students Union
IvP	Instituut voor Pluimveeteelt	**IVT**	Industrieverband Textil (Switzerland)
IVP	Instituut voor Visserijprodukten	**IVT**	Institut Vneshnei Torgovli
IVPC	Internationaler Verband der Petroleum- und Chemie-arbeiter = FITPC, FITPQ, IFPCW	**IVT**	Instituut voor de Veredeling van Tuinbouwgewassen
IVPMO	Internationaler Verband Psychologisch-Medizinischer Organisationer = FIOPM, IFPMO	**IVT**	International Visual Theatre Research Community
		IVT	Internationale Vereinigung der Textileinkaufs-verbände
IVPP	Institute of Vertebrate Palaeontology & Palaeoanthropology (China)	**IVT**	Internationaler Verband der Tarifeure
IVR	Internationale Vereinigung des Rheinschiffsregisters = AIRBR	**IVTAN**	Institut Vysokikh Temperatur (Russian Federation)
IVR	Internationale Vereinigung für Gewerblichen Rechtsschultz = AIPPI, IAPIP, IVFGR	**IVTE**	Institut Vrachebno Trudovoi Ekspertizy
		IVTs	Informatsionnyi Vychislitel'nyi Tsentr
IVR	Internationale Vereinigung für Rechts- und Sozialphilosophie	**IVU**	Institúto de Vivienda Urbana (El Salvador)
IVRA	International Veterinary Radiology Association	**IVU**	Institúto Veterinario Uruguay
IVRG	International Verticillium Research Group	**IVU**	International Vegetarian Union
		IVU	Internationaler Verleger-Union = IPA, UIE
IVRI	Indian Veterinary Research Institute	**IVU**	Irish Veterinary Union
IVRO	Instituut voor Rassenonderzoek van Landbouwgewassen	**IVV**	Internationale Vereinigung für Vegetationskunde = AIEV, IAVS
IVS	Industrie Vereinigung Schaffhausen	**IVV**	Internationaler Verband für Verkehrsschulung und Verkehrseziehung
IVS	Industrieverband Stahlschornsteine		
IVS	Institut Vaktsin i Syvorotok	**IVV**	Internationaler Volkssportverband = IFPS
IVS	Institúto Venezolano de los Seguros Sociales (Venezuela)	**IVVO**	Research Institute for Livestock Feeding and Nutrition (Netherlands)
IVS	International Voluntary Service	**IVVV**	International Verbond van Vrije Vakverenigingen = CISL, CIOSL, IBFG, ICFTU
IVS	Internationale Verbindung für Schalentragwerke und Raumtragwerke = AIEL, AIVM, IASS		
IVSA	International Veterinary Students Association	**IVW**	Internationaler Verband für Die Wärmebehandlung und Randschittechnik = AITT, IFHT, MOTO

IVWSR	Internationaler Verband für Wohnungswesen, Städtebau und Raumordnung = FIHAUT, FIVU, IFHP
IWA	Independent Warranty Association
IWA	Indian Workers Association
IWA	Inland Waterways Association
IWA	International Waterproofing Association = AIE
IWA	International Wheat Agreement
IWA	International Woodworkers of America
IWA	International Word Association
IWA	International Workers Aid
IWA	Irish Wheelchair Association
IWAAC	Inland Waterways Amenity Advisory Council
IWAAS	Institute of West Asian and African Studies (China)
IWAC	International Women's Anthropology Conference (U.S.A.)
IWAHMA	Industrial Warm Air Heater Manufacturers Association
IWAI	Inland Waterways Association of Ireland
IWB	International Waterpolo Board
IWBDC	International Workers Bosnian Defence Committee
IWBP	Intergration with Britain Party (Gibraltar)
IWC	Institute for Workers Control
IWC	Institute for World Concern
IWC	Interim Wilderness Committee
IWC	International Whaling Commission = CBI, CIB
IWC	International Wheat Council = CIB, CIT
IWC	International Wildlife Coalition
IWC	International Windglider Class
IWC	Irish Wildbird Conservancy
IWC	Irish Wildlife Conservancy
IWCA	International World Calendar Association
IWCC	International Women's Cricket Council
IWCC	International Wrought Copper Council = CICL
IWCS	International Wood Collectors Society
IWCT	International War Crimes Tribunal
IWDA	International Women's Development Agency (Australia)
IWEM	Institution of Water and Environmental Management
IWEP	Institute of World Economics and Politics (China)
IWES	Institution of Water Engineers and Scientists
IWF	Institut für den Wissenschaftlichen Film Gemeinnützige
IWF	Institut für Werkzeugmaschinen und Fertigungstechnik (Germany)
IWF	International Weightlifting Federation = FHI
IWF	Internationaler Währungsfonds = FMI, IMF
IWF	Irish Wildlife Federation
IWFA	International Women's Fishing Association
IWFMA	Irish Wholesale Fruit Merchants Association
IWFS	International Wine and Food Society
IWG	Impacts Working Group (IPCC)
IWG	International Writers Guild = SIARCT
IWG	Internationale Werbegesellschaft
IWGA	International Wheat Gluten Association (U.S.A.)
IWGA	International World Games Association
IWGDMGC	International Working Group on Data Management for Global Change
IWGE	International Working Group on Education = GITE
IWGE	International Working Group on Ergometry (ICSSPE)
IWGGE	Interdepartmental Working Group on the Greenhouse Effect
IWGIA	International Work Group for Indigenous Affairs
IWGLV	International Working Group of Legume Virologists (Canada)
IWGM	Intergovernmental Working Group on Monitoring of Surveillance (UN)
IWGMP	Intergovernmental Working Group on Marine Pollution (IMO)
IWGNSRD	International Working Group on Nuclear Structure and Reaction Data
IWGUG	International Working Group on Urban Geology (Norway)
IWHC	International Wages for Housework Campaign
IWHM	Institution of Works and Highways Management
IWHR	Institute of Water Conservancy and Hydroelectric Power Research (China)

IWHTE	Institution of Works and Highways Technician Engineers		**IWS**	International Wool Secretariat
IWIBA	Irish Women's Indoor Bowling Association		**IWS**	International World Services (Belgium)
			IWSA	International Water-Supply Association = AIDE
IWIEF	Inventors Workshop International Educational Foundation		**IWSAW**	Institute for Women's Studies in the Arab World (Lebanon)
IWIM	Institut für Wissenschaftsinformation in der Medizin		**IWSc**	Institute of Wood Science
IWIS	Instituut TNO voor Wiskunde, Informatieverwerking en Statistiek		**IWSC**	International Weed Science Council (IWSS)
IWIU	Inland Waterways International Union		**IWSC**	International Workers Sport Committee = CSIT
IWIU	Insurance Workers International Union		**IWSF**	International Water Ski Federation
IWKI	Internationales Wissenschaftliches Kongress-Institut (Austria)		**IWSG**	International Wool Study Group
			IWSI	Irish Work Study Institute
IWL	Institut für Gewerbliche Wasserwirtschaft und Luftreinhaltung		**IWSOE**	International Weddell Sea Oceanographic Expedition
IWLA	Izaak Walton League of America (U.S.A.)		**IWSOM**	Institute of Work Study Organisation and Methods
IWLC	International Water Lily Club		**IWSP**	Institute of Work Study Practitioners (South Africa)
IWM	Imperial War Museum		**IWSS**	Instytut Włokien Sztucznych i Syntetycznych
IWM	Institute of Wastes Management			
IWMA	International Wire and Machinery Organisation		**IWSS**	International Weed Science Society (U.S.A.)
IWNI	Inland Waterways Northern Ireland		**IWSV**	Ingenieurverband der Wasser-und Schifffahrtsverwaltung
IWO	Institute for Works Order (U.S.A.)			
IWO	Institution of Water Officers (*ex* AWO)		**IWT**	International Water Tribunal (Netherlands)
IWOC	International Wizard of Oz Club (U.S.A.)		**IWTA**	Inland Water Transport Authority (Pakistan)
IWOCA	Instituut voor Wetenschappelijk Onderzoek in Centraal Africa		**IWTC**	International Women's Tribune Center = CTIM
IWP	Indicative World Plan for Agricultural Development (FAO) = PIM		**IWTC**	International World Travellers' Club = CIGV
IWP	Instytut Wzornictwa Przemysłowego		**IWTF**	International Wheelchair Tennis Federation
IWPA	International Information and Word Processing Association		**IWTF**	Intractable Wastes Task Force
IWPC	Institute of Water Pollution Control (South Africa, U.K.)		**IWTO**	International Wool Textile Organisation = FLI
IWPPA	Independent Waste Paper Processors Association		**IWU**	Irish Writers' Union
IWPR	Institute for War and Peace Reporting		**IWV**	Internationale Warenhaus-Vereinigung = AIGM, IADS
IWRA	International Water Resources Association = AIRE, AIRH		**IWVA**	International War Veterans Alliance
IWRAW	International Women's Rights Action Watch		**IWW**	Industrial Workers of the World (U.S.A.)
IWRB	International Waterfowl and Wetlands Research Bureau = BIROE		**IWWA**	International Wild Waterfowl Association
IWRPF	International Waste Rubber and Plastic Federation		**IWWA**	Internationale Wirtschafts- und Werbundsausstellung
IWS	Industrial Water Society		**IWWG**	International Women's Writing Guild (U.S.A.)
IWS	Institute of Water Study			

IWYF	International World Youth Friendship
IXS	International XAFS Society
IYA	Irish Yachting Association
IYAS	International Years of the Active Sun
IYCHE	International Youth Conference on the Human Environment
IYCS	International Young Catholic Students = IKSJ, JECI
IYCW	International Young Christian Workers = JOCI
IYDU	International Young Democratic Union
IYF	International Youth Federation for Environmental Studies and Conservation
IYFF	International Youth Federation for Freedom
IYFM	International Yoga Fellowship Movement
IYHA	Irish Youth Hostels Association
IYHF	International Youth Hostel Federation = FIAJ
IYL	International Youth Library (Germany) = IJB, IKJ
IYM	International Youth Movement
IYNF	International Young Nature Friends = IJAN, NFJI
IYRU	International Yacht Racing Union
IYS	International Youth Service
IYTA	International Yoga Teachers Association
IZA	Internationaal Zeemanshuis Antwerpen
IZA	International Zeolite Association
IZA	International Zinc Association
IZB	Industries Zaïroises des Bois
IZE	International Association of Zoo Educators
IZhT	Institut Zheleznodorozhnogo Transporta
IZI	Interdisziplinäres Zentrum für Forschung und Entwicklung in der Intensivmedizin (Austria)
IZIP	Instítúto de Zoonosis e Investigación Pecuaria (Peru)
IZIR	Italijanska Zveza za Istro in Reko (Slovenia) = IUIR
IZiZ	Instytut Żywności i Żywienia
IZMIRAN	Institut Zemnogo Magnetizma, Ionosfery i Rasprostraneniya Radiovoln (Russian Federation)
IZO NKP	Otdel izobrazitel'nykh Iskusstv (Narodny Komissariat Prosveshcheniia)

IZVV	Internationales Zentrum für Verbrechens- und Verkehrsunfallverhüttung (IFSPO)
IZWTI	Internationales Zentrum für Wissenschaftliche und Technische Information
IZWO	Instituut voor Zeewetenschappelijk Onderzoekyrzw (Belgium)

J

J2	Military Intelligence Service (Philippines)
JA	Japan Agriculture
JA	Jordbrukets Arbeidsgiverforening
JAA	Japan Aeronautic Association
JAA	Japan Asia Airways
JAA	Joint Aviation Authorities
JAAA	Japan Amateur Athletic Association
JAAC	Amilcar Cabral African Youth Organization (Guinea-Bissau)
JAAC-CV	Juventude Africana Amilcar Cabral – Cabo Verde
JAALD	Japanese Association of Agricultural Librarians and Documentalists
JAAS	Jewish Academy of Arts and Sciences (U.S.A.)
JAAS	Jiangsu Academy of Agricultural Science
JAAS	Jilin Academy of Agricultural Sciences (China)
JABC	Japan Audit Bureau of Circulation
JABPPC	Joint Animal By-Products Parliamentary and Advisory Committee
JAC	Jeunesse Agricole Chrétienne
JAC	Jewellery Advisory Centre
JAC	Joint Advisory Committee (UN)
JACA	Japan Air Cleaning Association
JACARI	Joint Action Committee Against Racial Interference
JACES	Joint Advisory Committee for Engineering Services
JACF	Jeunesse Agricole Catholique Féminine
JACL	Japan American Citizen League
JACOLA	Joint Airports Committee of Local Authorities
JACRD	Joint Committee for Agricultural Research and Development (U.S.A.)

JACT	Joint Association of Classical Teachers	**JANIS**	Joint ANZECC/MCFFA NFPS Implementation Sub-Committee
JADE	Jeunes pour une Action Démocratique en Europe	**JANSA**	Janatorial Supplies Association
JADE	Jewish-Arab Dialogue in Europe	**JAP**	Fédération Nationale des Jeunes Alliances Paysannes (Belgium)
JAE	Jeunesse Acliste Européenne = EYA	**JAP**	Jamaica American Party
JAE	Junta Autónoma de Estradas	**JAPA**	Japan Aircraft Pilots Association
JAEC	Japan Atomic Energy Commission	**JAPATIC**	Japan Patent Information Center
JAEC	Joint Atomic Energy Commission (U.S.A.)	**JAPCo**	Japan Atomic Power Company
JAEIP	Japan Atomic Energy Insurance Pool	**JAPDEVA**	Junta de Administración Portuaria y de Desarrollo Económico de la Vertiente Atlántica (Costa Rica)
JAERI	Japan Atomic Energy Research Institute	**JAPEX**	Japan Petroleum Exploration Company
JAES	Japan Atomic Energy Society	**JAPIA**	Japan Auto Parts Industries Association (U.S.A.)
JAF	Japan Automobile Federation		
JAFC	Japan Atomic Fuel Corporation	**JAPIO**	Japan Patent Information Organisation
JAFS	Japan Asian Association and Asian Friendship Society	**JAPRRCC**	Japan Authors' and Publishers' Reprographic Rights Clearance Centre
JAFZA	Jebel Ali Free Zone Authority (Dubai)	**JAPRW**	Japanese Association of Photosynthesis Research Workers
JAGB	Jockeys Association of Great Britain		
JAICC	Joint Arab-Irish Chamber of Commerce	**JARA**	Japan Antibiotics Research Association
JAICI	Japanese Association for International Chemical Exchange	**JARDOR**	Comité Français pour les Jardins et l'Horticulture
JAIEG	Joint Atomic Information Exchange Group (U.S.A.)	**JARE**	Japanese Antarctic Research Expedition
JAIF	Japan Atomic Industrial Forum	**JARI**	Japanese Association of Railway Industries
JAIMS	Japan-America Institute of Management Science (Hawaii)	**JARI**	Jiangsu Automation Research Institute (China)
JAIS	Japan Aircraft Industry Society	**JARI**	Jute Agricultural Research Institute (India)
JAL	Japan Air Lines		
JALC	Japan American Lumber Conference	**JARL**	Japan Amateur Radio League
JALMA	Japan Leprosy Mission for Asia	**JARRP**	Japan Association for Radiation Research on Polymers
JAMA	Japan Automobile Manufacturers Association	**JARTS**	Japan Railway Technical Service
JAMAL	Jamaican Movement for the Advancement of Literacy	**JAS**	Jamaica Agricultural Society
		JAS	Japan Association of Shipbuilders
JAMC	Japan Aircraft Manufacturing Corporation	**JAS**	Jewish Agricultural Society (U.S.A.)
		JAS	Junior Astronomical Society
JAMINTEL	Jamaica International Telecommunications	**JAS**	Jysk Arkaeologisk Selskab
JAMPRESS	Jamaican Government News Agency	**JASDF**	Japan Air Self-Defence Force
JAMSAT	Japan Radio Amateur Satellite Corporation	**JASNA**	Jane Austen Society of North America
		JASPA	Jobs and Skills Programme for Africa (ILO) = PECTA
JAMSTEC	Japan Marine Science and Technology Centre		
JAMTS	Japan Association of Motor Trade and Service	**JASSCC**	Japan Academic Society System for Copyright Clearance
JANA	Jamahiriya News Agency (Libya)	**JAST**	Jamaican Association of Sugar Technologists
JANE	Journalists Against Nuclear Extermination	**JAT**	Jugoslovenski Aerotransport
JANET	Joint Academic Network	**JAT**	Junta de Asistencia = TAB (UNDP)

JATC	Japan Association for Tissue Culture
JATCC	Joint Aviation Telecommunications Coordination Committee
JATEC	Japan Technical Committee to Aid US Anti-War Deserter
JATES	Japan Techno-Economics Society
JATMA	Japan Automobile Tyre Manufacturers Association
JAUW	Japanese Association of University Women
JAVIC	Japan Audio-Visual Information Centre
JAWC	Joint Animal Welfare Council
JAWG	Joint Airmiss Working Group (NATS)
JAWS	Japan Animal Welfare Society (U.K.)
JAWS	Joint Action for Water Services
JBA	Japan Bankers Association
JBA	Japanese Bioindustry Association
JBAS	Jussi Björling Appreciation Society
JBC	Jamaica Broadcasting Corporation
JBC	Japanese Broadcasting Corporation
JBCSA	Joint British Committee for Stress Analysis
JBF	Japan Booksellers' Federation
JBG	Svenska Järn- och Balkgrossiters Förening
JBHCPIUA	Journeymen Barbers, Hairdressers, Cosmetologists and Proprietors' International Union of America
JBI	Jamaica Bauxite Institute
JBIA	Jewish Braille Institute of America
JBMS	Bolyai Jànos Matematikai Tarsulat
JBPA	Japan Book Publishers Association
JBPVE	Joint Board for Pre-Vocational Education
JBS	Japanese Biochemical Society
JBS	John Birch Society (U.S.A.)
JBTB	Jongeren-Boeren- en Tuindersbond
JCA	Japan Container Association
JCA	Jewish Colonization Association
JCAB	Japan Civil Aviation Bureau
JCADR	Japan Centre for Area Development
JCAM	Joint Commission on Atomic Masses
JCAP	Joint Committee on Aviation Pathology
JCAPI	Junta Consultiva de Administración Publica Internacional
JCB	Joint Coal Board
JCBMI	Joint Committee for the British Memorial Industry
JCBSF	Joint Commission for Black Sea Fisheries
JCBSSA	Jersey Cattle Breeders Society of South Africa
JCC	Joint Consultative Council of the Fresh Fruit and Vegetable Industry
JCCBI	Joint Committee for the Conservation of British Insects
JCCBI	Joint Committee for the Conservation of British Invertebrates
JCCF	Jamaica Combined Cadet Force
JCCI	Japan Chamber of Commerce and Industry
JCCMI	Joint Committee for Church Music in Ireland
JCDT	Jamaica Conservation and Development Trust
JCEA	Jesuit Conference of East Asia = EAA
JCEA	Junta de Control de Energía Atómica (Peru)
JCEC	Joint Communication Electronics Committee (U.S.A.)
JCEE	Jeunesse des Communautés Ethniques Européennes = JEV, YEN
JCEM	Joint Center for Energy Management (U.S.A.)
JCEPF	Fédération des Jeunes Chambres Économiques des Pays Utilisant le Français dans leurs Relations Communes
JCF	Jamaican Constabulary Force
JCFA	Japan Chemical Fibres Association
JCFBS	Joint Commission on the Fisheries in the Black Sea
JCHPME	Joint Committee on Higher Professional Medical Education (WACP, WACS) (Nigeria)
JCI	Junior Chamber International
JCIAMR	Joint Commission on International Aspects of Mental Retardation (IASSMD, ILSMH)
JCII	Japan Camera and Optical Instruments Inspection and Testing Institute
JCJ	Journalist Committee of Japan
JCLI	Joint Council for Landscape Industries
JCMC	Joint Conference on Medical Conventions
JCMD	Joint Committee on Mobility for the Disabled
JČMF	Jednota Československych Matematiku a Fysiku

JCMWA	Joint Christian Ministry in West Africa = MICCAO
JCP	Jamaican Communist Party
JCP	Japan Communist Party/Nikon Kyosanto
JCP	Joint Committee for Palestine
JCPDS	Joint Comittee on Power Diffraction Standards (U.S.A.)
JCPI	Japan Cotton Promotion Institute
JCPS	Joint Center for Political Studies (U.S.A.)
JCR	Junta for Revolutionary Coordination (Argentina)
JCS	James Connolly Society
JCS	Jersey Cattle Society of the United Kingdom
JCS	Joint Commonwealth Societies
JCS	Justices Clerks Society
JCSA	Joseph Conrad Society of America
JCSS	Jaffee Center for Strategic Studies (Israel)
JCSTR	Joint Commission on Solar and Terrestrial Relationships
JCT	Joint Contracts Tribunal for the Standard Form of Building Contract
JCT	Junta de Cooperación Técnica
JCTND	Jugoslovenski Centar za Tehniku i Naucnu Dokumentaciju
JCUDI	Japan Computer Usage Development Institute
JCUNQ	James Cook University of North Queensland (State)
JCUSD	Joint Committee on Urban Storm Drainage (IAHR/IAWPRC)
JCVI	Joint Committee on Vaccination and Immunisation
JCWA	Japan Clock and Watch Association
JCWI	Joint Council for the Welfare of Immigrants
JD	Janata Dal
JD	Junta Democrática
JD	Justicia Democrática
JDA	Japan Defence Agency
JDA	Jewellery Distributors Association of the United Kingdom
JDB	Japan Development Bank
JDC	Jewish Documentation Centre
JDC	The American Jewish Joint Distribution Committee
JDCA	Japan Designer and Craftsman Association
JDCE	Jeunes Démocrates Chrétiens Européens = EYCD
JDF	Jamaica Defence Force
JDL	Jewish Defence League
JDM	Jugoslovensko Drustvo za Mehaniku
JDMA	Japan Diet Marketing Association
JDPT	Jugoslovensko Drustvo za Poljoprivrednu Tehniku
JDREMC	Joint Departmental Radio and Electronics Measurements Committee
JE	Journalistes en Europe
JEA	Jamaica Exporters Association
JEA	Japan Electric Association
JEAC	Junta de Exportação do Algodão Colonial
JEB	Jewish Education Bureau
JEB	Joint Examining Board
JEC	Jeunesse Étudiante Catholique Internationale = KSJ, YCS
JEC	Joint European Committee of Paper Exporters
JECC	Japan Electric Computer Corporation
JECC	Joint Egyptian Cotton Committee
JECFA	Joint FAO/WHO Expert Committee on Food Additives
JECFI	Joint Expert Committee on Food Irradiation
JECI	Jeunesse Étudiante Catholique Internationale = IKSJ, IYCS
JECMA	Japan Export Clothing Makers Association
JECs	Junta de Exportação dos Cereais
JECS	Nepal Kyoiku Kyokai
JEDEC	Joint Electron Device Engineering Council (U.S.A.)
JEF	Jeunesse Européenne Fédéraliste = YEF
JEI	Japan Economic Institute (U.S.A.)
JEIA	Japan Electronic Industries Association
JEIDA	Japan Electronic Industry Development Association
JEL	Jackson Estuarine Laboratory (U.S.A.)
JEL	Jeunesses Européennes Libérales = LEY
JEMIC	Japan Electric Meters Inspection Corporation
JEMIMA	Japan Electric Measuring Instrument Manufactures Association
JEMRB	Joint European Medical Research Board (EURIMA)

JEN	Junta de Energia Nuclear	**JFS**	Jamaica Freight and Shipping Company
JENDRPC	Joint Euratom Nuclear Data and Reactor Physics Committee	**JFSEO**	Japan Federation of Smaller Enterprises
JENER	Joint Establishment for Nuclear Energy Research (Netherlands & Norway)	**JFT**	Juridiska Föreningen i Finland rf
		JFTC	Japan Foreign Trade Council
JEOL	Japan Electron Optics Laboratory Company	**JFTC**	Joint Fur Trade Committee
		JFW	Jamaica Federation of Women
JEPIA	Japan Electronic Parts Industry Association	**JGA**	Japan Gas Association
		JGA	Japan Golf Association
JERC	Japan Economic Research Centre	**JGC**	Jugoslovenski Gradjevinski Centar
JERI	Japan Economics Research Institute	**JGOFS**	Joint Global Ocean Flux Study
JERS	Japan Ergonomics Research Society	**JGSDF**	Japan Ground Self Defence Force
JES	Japanese Electroplating Society	**JHDA**	Junior Hospital Doctors Association
JESA	Japanese Engineering Standards Association	**JHEA**	Junta de Historia Eclesiástica (Argentina)
JESC	Japanese Engineering Standards Committee	**JHI**	Jeffreys Henry International
		JHS	John Hampden Society
JESC	Joint Electronics Standardisation Committee	**JHSE**	Jewish Historical Society of England
		JHSF	Japan Health Sciences Foundation
JESSI	Joint European Submicron Silicon Initiative (EUREKA)	**JHWLI**	Jianghan Well Logging Institute
		JI	Jamiat-i Islami (Afghanistan) = IS
JET	Joint European Torus	**JIA**	Jute Importers Association
JETRO	Japan External Trade Relations Organisation	**JIB**	Joint Intelligence Bureau
		JIBA	Japanese Institute of Business Administration
JETS	Institute for Japanese-European Technology Studies	**JIBECI**	Joint Industry Board for the Electrical Contracting Industry
JETSB	Joint European Torus Supervisory Board (EU)	**JIBICO**	Japan International Bank and Investment
JEUR	Joint ECE/FAO Agriculture Division	**JIC**	Joint Industrial Council
JEV	Jesuit European Volunteers	**JIC**	Juventudes Inconformes de Colombia
JEV	Jugend Europäischer Volksgruppen = JCEE, YEN	**JICA**	Japan International Co-operation Agency
JF	Jordbrukets Förskiningsrad	**JICA**	Jiangsu Provincial Institute of Culture and Art
JFA	Japan Fishery Agency		
JFC	Jugend für Christus = JPC, YFCI	**JICC**	Japan Information & Cultural Centre
JFCC	Japanese Federation of Culture Collections of Microorganisms	**JICI**	Jeunesse Indépendante Chrétienne Internationale = IICY
JFEA	Japanese Federation of Employers Associations	**JICMARS**	Joint Industry Committee of Medical Advertisers for Readership Surveys
JFEO	Japanese Federation of Economic Organisations	**JICNARS**	Joint Industry Committee for National Readership Surveys
JFEW	Federation of Electric Worker Union of Japan	**JICPAR**	Joint Industry Committee for Postal Audience Research
JFPA	Jamaica Family Planning Association	**JICRAR**	Joint Industry Committee for Radio Audience Research
JFPS	Japan Fire Prevention Society		
JFRCA	Japanese Fisheries Resources Conservation Association	**JICS**	Joint Interpreting and Conference Service (EU)
JFRI	Jiangxi Forestry Research Institute	**JICST**	Japan Information Centre of Science and Technology
JFRO	Joint Fisheries Research Organisation (Malawi, Zambia)		

JID	Junta Interamericana de Defensa = IADB, OID	**JKA**	Jugoslavenski Komitit za Aerosole
JIDA	Japan Industrial Designers Association	**JKF**	Jednota Klasickych Filologu
JIDC	Jamaica Industrial Development Corporation	**JKF**	Jednota Klasických Filologů
		JKFC	Japan-Korea Joint Fisheries Commission
JIEA	Japan Industrial Explosives Association	**JKLF**	Jammu and Kashmir Liberation Front
JIEE	Japan Institute of Electrical Engineers	**JKNC**	Jammu and Kashmir National Congress
JIFA	Japanese Institute for Foreign Affairs	**JLA**	Japanese Library Association
JIFE	Junta Internacional de Fiscalización de Estupefacientes = INCB, OICS	**JLA**	Jewish Law Association
		JLA	Jordan Library Association
JIFS	Jerusalem Institute for Federal Studies	**JLAF**	Joint Lithuanian-American Fund = BALF, BALFas
JII	John Innes Institute		
JIIA	Japan Institute of International Affairs	**JLB**	Jewish Labour Bund
JIII	Japan Institute of Invention and Innovation	**JLCD**	Joint Liaison Committee on Documents used in the International Carriage of Goods
JIIST	Japan Institute for International Studies and Training		
		JLG	Joint Liaison Group (Sino-British)
JILA	Japanese Institute of Landscape Architects	**JLIA**	Japan Lumber Importers Association
		JLIRI	Jinan Light Industry Research Institute
JILA	Joint Institute for Laboratory Astrophysics (U.S.A.)	**JLP**	Jamaica Labour Party
		JLU	Jilin University
JIMA	Japan Industrial Management Association	**JMA**	Jamaica Manufacturers Association
		JMA	Jamara Memorial Association
JIMA	John Innes Manufacturers Association	**JMA**	Japan Management Association
JIMC	Japan Immuno-Monitoring Centre	**JMA**	Japan Meteorological Agency
JIN	Japanese Institution of Navigation	**JMC**	Japan Monopoly Corporation
JINR	Joint Institute for Nuclear Research = OIJAI	**JMC**	Jewish Marriage Council
		JMC	Jiangxi Medical College
JIO	Joint Intelligence Organization	**JMC**	Joint Mathematical Council of the United Kingdom
JIOA	Joint Intelligence Objectives Agency (U.S.A.)		
		JMEA	Japan Machinery Exporters Association
JIRA	Japan Industrial Robot Association	**JMF**	Jeunesses Musicales de France
JIRAMA	Jiro sy Rano Malagasay (Madagascar)	**JMG**	Järnmanufakturgrossisternas Förening
JIRP	Juneau Icefield Research Program (U.S.A.)	**JMI**	Japan Management Institute
		JMIA	Japan Mining Industry Association
JIS	Jamaica Information Service	**JMIF**	Japan Motor Industrial Federation
JISC	Japan Industrial Standards Committee	**JML**	Jern- og Metallvare-fabrikkenes Landsforening
JISC	Joint Information Services Committee		
JISEA	Japan Iron and Steel Exporters Association	**JMM**	Jamaica Merchant Marine
		JMMA	Japan Materials Management Association
JISF	Japan Iron and Steel Federation		
JISHA	Japan Industrial Safety and Health Association	**JMMA**	Japan Microscope Manufacturers Association
JITA	Japan Industrial Technology Association	**JMMII**	Japan Machinery and Metals Inspection Institute
JITPA	Japanese International Trade Promotion Association		
		JMPLA	MPLA-Youth (Angola)
JIU	Joint Inspection Unit (UN)	**JMPR**	Joint FAO/WHO Meeting on Pesticide Residues
JIU	Junta de Investigação de Ultramar		
JJSS	Juventudes Socialistas		

JMRP	Joint Meteorological Radio Propagation Sub-Committee	**JOC**	Jeunesse Ouvrière Chrétienne = YCW
JMS	Jydsk Medicinsk Selskab (Denmark)	**JOC**	Joint Organizing Committee for GARP
JMSDF	Japan Maritime Self Defence Force	**JOC**	Juventud Obrera Católica (Paraguay)
JMTBA	Japan Machine Tool-Builders Association	**JOCI**	Jeunesse Ouvrière Chrétienne Internationale; Juventud Obrera Católica Internacional = IYCW
JMU	Liverpool John Moores University	**JODC**	Japanese Oceanographic Data Centre
JNA	Jordan News Agency = PETRA/JNA	**JODCO**	Japan Oil Development Company
JNA	Junta Nacional de Algodón (Argentina)	**JOERA**	Japan Optical Engineering Research Association
JNAU	Jawaharlal Nehru Agricultural University (India)	**JOI**	Joint Oceanographic Institutions, Inc. (U.S.A.)
JNC	Junta Nacional de Carnes (Argentina)	**JOIA**	Japan Ocean Industries Association
JNCC	Joint Nature Conservation Committee	**JOICFP**	Japanese Organisation for International Cooperation in Family Planning = OJCIPF
JNE	Association des Journalistes-Écrivains pour la Nature et l'Écologie		
JNEC	Jamaica National Export Corporation	**JOIDES**	Joint Oceanographic Institutions for Deep Earth Sampling (U.S.A.)
JNF	Japan Nuclear Fuel Company	**JOMA**	Japan Oriental Music Association
JNF	Jewish National Fund	**JONAH**	Jews Organised for A Nuclear Arms Halt
JNFI	Japan's Nuclear Fuel Industries		
JNG	Junta Nacional de Granos (Argentina)	**JONDE**	Joven Orquesta Nacional de España
JNIB	Jamaica National Investment Bank	**JONSIS**	Joint North Sea Information System
JNICT	Junta Nacional de Investigação Cientifica e Tecnologica (Portugal)	**JOPP**	Joint Venture Phare Programme (EU)
		JORC	Jeddah Oil Refinery Company (Saudi Arabia)
JNIP	Jamaica National Investment Promotions	**JPA**	Jamaica Press Association
JNMA	Jebha-i-Nejat-i-Melli Afghanistan = ANLF	**JPA**	Japan Petroleum Association
		JPA	Japan Procurement Agency
JNNS	Japanese Neural Network Society	**JPA**	Jesuit Philosophical Association of the United States and Canada
JNOC	Japan National Oil Corporation		
JNP	Junta Nacional de Planeamiento (Bolivia)	**JPC**	Japan Productivity Centre
		JPC	Jeunesse pour Christ = JFC, YFCI
JNPC	Junta Nacional de Planificación y Coordinación (Dominican Republic)	**JPCA**	Japan Petrochemical Industry Association
JNPCE	Junta Nacional de Planificación y Coordinación Económica (Ecuador)	**JPDC**	Japan Petroleum Development Corporation
JNPP	Junta Nacional dos Produtos Pecuários	**JPEG**	Joint Photographics Experts Group
JNR	Japanese National Railways	**JPFFI**	Jiangsu Provincial Freshwater Fisheries Institute
JNSC	Japan Nuclear Safety Commission		
JNSP	Joint WHO/UNICEF Nutrition Support Programme	**JPI**	Japan Packaging Institute
		JPI	Jianghan Petroleum Institute
JNSRDA	Japan Nuclear Ship Research and Development Agency	**JPIA**	Japan Plastics Industry Association
		JPIC	World Convocation on Justice, Peace and the Integrity of Creation
JNTA	Japan National Tourist Association		
JNTO	Japan National Tourist Organization	**JPMA**	Japan Plywood Manufactures Association
JNU	Jiangnan University		
JNU	Jiangxi Normal University	**JPMO**	Jersey Potato Marketing Organisation
JNUL	Jewish National and University Library (Israel)	**JPPRI**	Jewish Planning Policy and Research Institute (U.S.A.)
JNV	Junta Nacional de la Vivienda (Peru)		

JPPW	Japanese Federation of Paper Pulp Workers Unions	**JS-19**	Juventud Sandinista 19 de julio (Nicaragua)
JPRA	Japanese Phonograph Record Association	**JSA**	Japan Silk Association
JPRA	Juventud Peronista de la República Argentina	**JSA**	Japan Spinners' Association
		JSA	Jesuit Seismological Association (U.S.A.)
JPRG	Japan Peace Research Group	**JSAE**	Japan Society of Automotive Engineering
JPRS	Joint Publications Research Service (U.S.A.)	**JSAE**	Society of Automotive Engineers of Japan
JPS	Jean Piaget Society: Society for the Study of Knowledge and Development	**JSAP**	Japan Society of Applied Physics
JPS	Joint Planning Staff for the World Climate Research Programme	**JSAWC**	Joint Services Amphibious Warfare Centre
JPSA	Jewish Pharmaceutical Society of America	**JSB**	Japan Satellite Broadcasting Co.
		JSB	Judicial Studies Board
JPSCo	Jamaica Public Service Company	**JSC**	Japan Science Council
JPSSIRI	Jilin Province Sugar Beet & Sugar Industry Research Institute	**JSC**	Johnson Space Center (U.S.A.)
		JSC	Joint Scientic Committee of the World Climate Research Programme (WMO/ICSU)
JPT	Japan Publications Trading Company		
JRA	Japanese Red Army		
JRB	Joint Radio Board (U.S.A.)	**JSC**	Joint Sites Committee
JRC	Jamaica Railway Corporation	**JSCFA**	Steel Castings and Forgings Association of Japan
JRC	Japan Red Cross		
JRC	Joint Research Centre (EURATOM) = CCI, CCR, GCO, GFS	**JSD**	Jatiya Samajtantrik Dal =Bangladesh National Socialist Party
JRCI	Jewish Representative Council of Ireland	**JSD**	Jugoslovensko Statisticko Drustvo
		JSDA	Japanese Self-Defense Agency (U.S.A.)
JRCT	Joseph Rowntree Charitable Trust	**JSE**	Johannesburg Stock Exchange
JRDA	Jeunesse du Rassemblement Démocratique Africain	**JSE**	Juventudes Socialistas de España
		JSEA	Japan Ship Exporters Association
JRDC	Japan Research and Development Corporation	**JSEE**	Japanese Society for Engineering Education
JREA	Japanese Railway Engineering Association	**JSEM**	Japan Society for Electron Microscopy
		JSEM	Japan Society of Electrical Discharge Machining
JRF	Janssen Research Foundation (Belgium)	**JSF**	Japan Skating Federation
JRF	Joseph Rowntree Foundation	**JSFC**	Japanese-Soviet Fisheries Commission for the Northwest Pacific
JRIA	Japan Radioisotope Association		
JRIA	Japan Rocket Industry Association	**JSFK**	Jydsk Selskab for Fysik og Kemi
JRIA	Japan Rubber Industry Association	**JSG**	Jewish Socialist Group
JRP	Jeunesse Rurale Protestante	**JSG**	Joint Space Group (UKISC, DTI)
JRR	Jeunesse Révolutionnaire Rwagasore (Burundi)	**JSIA**	Japan Software Industry Association
		JSICI	Japan Society for International Chemical Information
JRSMA	Japan Rolling Stock Manufacturers Association		
		JSL	Johnson Society of London
JRT	Jugoslovenska Radiotelevizija	**JSLA**	Japan Special Libraries Association
JRTV	Jordanian Radio and Television Corporation	**JSLE**	Japan Society of Lubrication Engineers
		JSLS	Japan Society of Library Science
JRW	Jeunesse Révolutionnaire Rwagasore (Burundi)	**JSMDA**	Japan Ship Machinery Development Association

JSME	Japan Society of Mechanical Engineers	**JTSMA**	Jennifer Trust for Spinal Muscular Atrophy
JSMEA	Japan Ship Machinery Export Association	**JTTRE**	Joint Topical Trials Research Establishment (Australia, U.K.)
JSMI	John Stuart Mill Institute	**JTUAC**	Joint Trade Union Advisory Committee
JSNDI	Japan Society for Non-Destructive Inspection	**JUC**	Joint University Council
JSNP	Japan Satellite News Pool	**JUC**	Juventud Universitaria Católica (Brazil)
JSP	Junta Superior de Precios	**JUCEPLAN**	Junta Central de Planificación (Cuba)
JSPB	United Nations Joint Staff Pension Board	**JUDCA**	Juventud Demócrata Cristiana de América
JSPF	United Nations Joint Staff Pension Fund	**JUF**	Jamaica United Front
JSPP	Japan Society for Plant Pathology	**JUF**	Jordbruksare-Ungdomen Forbunds
JSPS	Japan Society for the Promotion of Science	**JUGL**	JANET User Group for Libraries
JSQC	Japan Society for Quality Control	**JUGO-KOMORA**	Jugoslawische Bunderwirtschaftkammer
JSS	Jacob Sheep Society	**JUJEM**	Junta de Jefes del Estado Mayor
JSS	Japan Society of Scotland	**JUKL**	Jugoslovensko Udruzenje Kontrolora Letenja
JSS	Jathika Sevaka Sangamaya (Sri Lanka)	**JUMA**	Jugoslovensko Udruzenje za Marketing
JSSA	John Steinbeck Society of America	**JUMV**	Jugoslovensko Brustvo za Motore i Vozila
JSSF	Japanese Society of Scientific Fisheries		
JSTC	Joint Scientific and Technical Committee (GCOS)	**JUN**	Jordbrukets Upplysningsnamand
JSTPPC	Joint Services Technical Publication Policy Committee (MOD)	**JUNAC**	Junta del Acuerdo de Cartagena (Pacto Andino)
JSWB	Java Suiker Werkgevers Bond	**JUNAL**	Junta Nacional de Algodão (Brazil)
JSZS	Japanese Society of Zootechnical Science	**JUNAPLA**	Junta Nacional de Planificación y Coordinación Económica (Ecuador)
JTA	Japan Trucking Association	**JUNIC**	Joint United Nations Information Committee
JTA	Jewish Telegraphic Agency		
JTAC	Joint Technical Advisory Committee (U.S.A.)	**JUP**	Association Internationale des Journées Universitaires de la Paix (Belgium)
JTAS	Jydsk Telefon Aktieselskab	**JUREMA**	Jugoslavensko Udruzenje za Mjerenja, Regulaciju i Automaciju
JTB	Jamaica Tourist Board		
JTB	Japan Travel Bureau	**JUS**	Jugoslavenski Zavod za Standardizaciju
JTC	Japan Tobacco Corporation	**JUS**	Jurist-och Samhällsvetareförbundet
JTC	Joint Trade Committee	**JUSB**	Japan University Sports Board
JTCMF	Joint Technical Commission of the Marine Fruit (Uruguay)	**JUSE**	Japanese Union of Scientists and Engineers
JTES	Japan Techno-Economics Society	**JUSEK**	Förbundet för Jurister, Samhällsvetare och Ekonomer
JTF	Japan Textile Federation (U.S.A.)		
JTG	Jordan Technology Group	**JUSK**	Jugoslovenski Savez Organizacija za Unapredenje Kvaliteta i Pouzdanosti
JTI	Jordbrukstekniska Institutet (Sweden)		
JTI	Jydsk Teknologisk Institut (Denmark)	**JUSMAP**	Joint United States Military Advisory and Planning Group
JTLS	Joint Technical Language Service (GCHQ)	**JUSTIS**	Japan-United States of America Textile Information Service
JTRL	Jute Technological Research Laboratory (India)		
		JUVENTO	Mouvement de la Jeunesse Togolaise
JTS	Japan Tobacco and Salt Public Corporation	**JUWATA**	Union of Tanzania Workers
		JVC	Japan Victor Company

JVC	Japan Volunteer Center
JVC	Jorvik Viking Centre
Jvf	Järnverksföreningen
JVI	Joint Vienna Institute
JVP	Janatha Vimukthi Peramuna (Sri Lanka)
JVS	Jewish Vegetarian and Natural Health Society (U.K., U.S.A.)
JVSA	Japan Video Stores Association
JWAHK	Jewish Women's Association of Hong Kong
JWB	Jewish Welfare Board
JWCA	Japan Watch and Clock Association
JWDS	Japan Work Design Society
JWEF	Joinery and Woodwork Employers' Federation
JWG	Joint Working Group between the Roman Catholic Church and the World Council of Churches
JWIC	Japan Whaling Information Center (U.S.A.)
JWIC	Japan Wood Industry Conference
JWP	Joint Women's Programme (India)
JWPAC	Joint Waste Paper Advisory Council
JWS	Japan Welding Society
JXPREI	Jiangxi Provincial Rare Earth Institute
JYARRI	Jiang You Aerial Ropeway Research Institute (China)
JZS	Jamarska Zveza Slovenije

K

K-Door	Keep Death Off Our Roads
K/A	Knights of the Altar International
K4	Commission for the Study of the Quaternary (Russia)
KÄB	Kneippärztebund
KAB	Nederlandse Katholieke Arbeidersbeweging
KAC	Kuwait Airways Corporation
KACB	Koninklijke Automobiel Club van België
KACST	King Abdul Aziz City for Science and Technology (Saudi Arabia)
KADIN	Kamar Dagang dan Industri Indonesia
KADU	Kenya African Democratic Union
KAERI	Korea Atomic Energy Research Institute (South Korea)

KAF	Kenya Air Force
KAF	Konfeksjonsfabrikkenes Arbeids-giverforening
KAFAB	Verband Schweizerischer Kartonfabrikanten
KAI	Keep America Independent
KAIST	Korea Advanced Institute of Science and Technology
KAK	Kungliga Automobil Klubben
KAL	Korean Air Lines
KAL	Suomen Kuorma-Autolitto
KALME	Communication Committee of the Lutheran Minority Churches in Europe
KAMA	Korea Automobile Manufacturers Association (Republic of Korea)
KAMEDO	Swedish Organizing Committee for Disaster Medicine
KAMPEXIM	Kampuchean Export Import (Cambodia)
KAN	Club of Committed Non-Party Members (Czech Republic)
KANTAFU	Kenya African National Traders and Farmers Union
KANTL	Koninklijke Academie voor Nederlandse Taal-en Letterkunde
KANU	Kenya African National Union
KANUPP	Karachi Nuclear Power Project
KANZEKO	Kahama Nzega Co-operative Union (Tanzania)
KAP	Kommunustik Arbejderparti (Denmark)
KAP	Kuwait Action Plan
KAPI	Kasetsart University Agricultural and Agro-Industrial Product Improvement Institute (Thailand)
KAPSh	Kruglaia Arkticheskaia Palatka Sistemy Inzhinera Shaposhnikova
KAPWA	Kite Aerial Photography Worldwide Association
KAR	Korpusnoy Artilleriiskii Rezerv
KAR	Krajowa Agencja Robotnicza
KARI	Keshan Agricultural Research Institute
KARNA	Kweekbedrijf v. Aardappelrassen d. Nederlandse Aardappelmeelindustrie
KARS	Kansas Applied Remote Sensing Program (U.S.A.)
KARTO-FLEX	Vereniging van Nederlandse Fabrikanten van Kartonnagesen
KAS	Kansas Academy of Science
KAS	Kentucky Academy of Science
KAS	Konfederatsiia Anarkho-Sindikalistov

KASEF	Katholisches Sekretariat für Europäische Fragen = OCIPE	**KCC**	Kenya Cooperative Creameries
KASKA	Koninklijke Academie voor Schoone Kunsten Antwerpene	**KCC**	Kurdish Cultural Centre
		KCDM	Kauno Ciurlionio dailes muziejus = CAGK
KASLIB	Kanagawa Association of Special Libraries and Information Bureaux	**KCDQ**	Key Centre for Design Quality (Univ. of Sydney)
KATL	Kansas Augmented Telerobotics Laboratory (U.S.A.)	**KCI**	Key Club International (U.S.A)
KATY	Kemikalialan Tukkukauppiasyhdistys	**KCIA**	Korean Central Intelligence Agency
KAV	Katholischer Akademiker-Verband	**KCL**	Finnish Pulp and Paper Research Institute
KAVB	Koninklijke Algemene Vereniging voor Bloembollencultuur	**KCN**	Kids Clubs Network
KAW	Krajowa Agencja Wydawnicza	**KCNA**	Korean Central News Agency (KPDR)
KAZTAG	Kazakh Telegraph Agency	**KCS**	Korean Chemical Society
KB	Kulturbund	**KCSA**	Kerr Centre for Sustainable Agriculture (U.S.A.)
KBBM	Koninklijke Belgische Bosbouwmaatschappij = SRFB	**KDA**	Katholischer Deutscher Akademikerinnen
KBC	Kenya Broadcasting Corporation	**KDA**	Kenya Dental Association
KBCV	Koninklijke Belgische Comissie voor Volkskunde	**KDA**	Kwazulu Department of Agriculture (South Africa)
KBE	Katholische Bundesarbeitsgemeinschaft für Erwachsenenbildung	**KDB**	Kenya Dairy Board
		KDC	Katholiek Documentatiecentrum
KBF	Katholische Bibelföderation = CBF, FBC, FEBIC-LA	**KDD**	Kokusia Denshin Denwa (Japan)
		KDF	Københavns Detailhandlerforening
KBF	Kommunale Bibliotekarers Forening	**KDF**	Kuwait Democratic Forum
KBG	Kerkraftwerks Betriebsgesellschaft	**KDH**	Christian Democratic Movement (Slovakia)
KBI	Kritiko-bibliograficheskii Institut		
KBM	Katholieke Bond Metallbewerkingsbedrijven	**KDH**	Krest'anskodemokratické Hnutie (Slovakia) = CDM
KBN	Komitet Badań Naukowych	**KDI**	Korea Development Institute
KBO	Organisation for the Management and Development of the Kagera River Basin = OBK	**KDI**	Stichting Kwaliteitsdienst
		KDNP	Christian Democratic People's Party (Hungary)
		KDP	Kalabagh Dam Project
KBOF	Kansai Bangladesh Orphans' Fund (Japan)	**KDP**	Kansallinen Demokraattinen Puolue (Finland)
KBS	Korean Broadcasting System	**KDP**	Kurdish Democratic Party (Iran)
KBV	Kassenaertzliche Bundesvereinigung	**KDP**	Kurdistan Democratic Party
KBV	Nederlandse Katholieke Bond van Vervoers-Personaal	**KDP-PNS**	Konstitutsionno-Demokraticheskaia Partiia – Partiia Narodnoi Svobody
KBVE	Koninklijke Belgische Vereniging der Elektrotechnici = SRBE	**KDS**	Christian Democratic Party (Czech Republic)
KBVFGR	Koninklijke Belgische Vereniging voor Fysische Geneeskunde en Rehabilitatie = SRBMPR	**KDS**	Kassem Darwish Fakhroo & Sons (Qatar)
		KDS	Khuzistan Development Service
KBVT	Koninklijke Belgische Vereniging voor Tandheelkunde = SRBMD	**KDS**	Komma Demokratikon Sosialismou
KBW	Korpus Bezpieczeństwa Wewnętrznego	**KDS**	Kristen Democratisk Samling
KC	Foreningen af Kommunale Chefer (Denmark)	**KDS**	Latvian Christian Democratic Union
KC	Kennel Club	**KDT**	Kammer der Technik

KDU	Křesťanská a Demokratická Unie	**KES**	Kwaliteitsbureau voor te Exporteren Schapen
KDU-CSL	Christian Democratic Union – Czechoslovak People's Party (Czech Republic)	**KESC**	Karachi Electric Supply Corporation
		KESH	State Electricity Cooperative of Albania
KDUN	Kristen Demokratisk Ungdom i Norden	**KEST**	Studiengesellschaft zur Förderung der Kernenergiewertung in Schiffbau und Schiffahrt
KDVS	Det Kongelige Danske Videnskabernes Selskab		
KEC	Konferentsiia Evropeyskikh Tserkvei = CEC, CEE, KEK	**KETA**	Kenya External Trade Authority
KECO	Korea Electric Company	**KF**	Kemisk Forening
KED	Kirchlicher Entwicklungsdienst der evangelischen Kirche in Deutschland	**KF**	Kødbranchens Faellesråd
		KF	Konservative Folkeparti
		KF	Kooperativa Forbundet
KEDI	Korean Education Development Institute	**KF**	Kristeligt Folkeparti (Denmark)
KEE	Kallitechnikon Epimelitirion Ellados	**KFA**	Kammer für Aussenhandel
KEEN	Komitet Ekspertów ds Edukacji Narodowej	**KFA**	Keep-Fit Association
		KFA	Kenya Farmers Association
KEGME	Kendro Grevnon ya tis Ginekes tis Mesoyiou	**KFA**	Kernforschungsanlage Julich des Landes Nordrhein Westfalen
KEIA	Korea Economic Institute of America	**KFAED**	Kuwait Fund for Arab Economic Development
KEIDAN-REN	Keizaiddantai Rengo-kai (Japan)	**KFAS**	Kuwait Foundation for the Advancement of Science
KEIDA-NREN	Federation of Economic Organizations, Japan	**KFAT**	National Union of Knitwear, Footwear and Apparel Trades (*ex* NUFLAT, NUHKW)
KEIZAI DOYUKAI	Japan Federation of Corporate Executives		
KEK	Kolektivo Esperantista Komunista	**KFC**	Korea Friendship Committee
KEK	Konferenz Europäischer Kirchen = CEC, CEE	**KFD**	Kooperative Faellesforbund i Danmark
		KFEA	Korean Federation of Educational Associations
KEKE	Kallitechniki Enosis Kommoton Ellados		
KeKe	Keksijäyhdistysten Keskusjärjestö	**KFEANI**	Keep Fit & Exercise Association NI
KÉKI	Központi Élelmiszeripari Kutató Intézet	**KFH**	Kuwait Finance House
KELI	Kristina Esperantista Ligo Internacia	**KFK**	Kernforschungszentrum, Karlsruhe
KEMA	Keuring van Electrotechnische Materialen	**KFKI**	Központi Fizikai Kutató Intézete (MTA)
		KFKL	Kristályfizikai Kutatólaboratórium
KEMRI	Kenya Medical Research Institute	**KFL**	Kenya Federation of Labour
Kemya	Al-Jubail Petrochemical Co. (Saudi Arabia)	**KFL**	Kosmetikkfabrikkenes Landsforening
		KFN	Kristne for Nedrustring (Denmark)
KENATCO	Kenya National Transport Company	**KFP**	Kristelig Folkpart (Norway)
KENGO	Kenya Energy and Environment Organisations	**KFSB**	Korean Federation of Small Businesses
		KFSLE	Königliche Föderation Selbständiger Landmesser-Experten = FRGEI, KFZLE, RFISE
KENPRO	Kenyan Committee on Trade Procedures		
KEOSOE	Kentriki Enosis Oinopoietikon Synetairikon Organoseon Ellados	**KFTCIC**	Kuwait Foreign Trading, Contracting and Investment Company
KEPA	Kehitysyhteistyön Palvelukeskus	**KFU**	King Faisal University (Saudi Arabia)
KERM	Komitet Ekonomiczny Rady Ministrów	**KfW**	Kreditanstalt fur Wiederaufbau (Germany)
KES	Karg-Elert Society		
KES	Kvakera Esperantista Societo	**KfW**	Kuratorium für Wasserwirtschaft

KFZLE	Koninklijke Federatie der Zelfstandige Landmeters-Experts = FRGEI, KFSLE, RFISE
KG	Kolloid-Gesellschaft
KGAA	Kungliga Gustav Adolfs Akademien
KGB	Komitet Gosudarstvennoi Bezopasnosti
KGH	Den Kongelig Grønlandske Handel
KGS	Kurt Gödel Society
KGvL	Koninklijk Genootschap voor Landbouwwetenschap
KGYV	Kohászati Gyárépító Vállalat
KH	Komitet Helsinski (Poland)
KHAD	Khedamat-e-Etela'at Dawlati (Afghanistan)
KHD	Kartner Heimatdienst (Austria)
KhDSR	Khristiansko-Demokraticheskii Soiuz Rossii
Khlebo-produkt	Vserossiiskoe Aktsionernoe Obshchestvo po Torgovle Khlebom, Zernom i Sel'skokhoziaistvennym Produktami (Russia)
KHRP	Kurdish Human Rights Project
KhV	Soiuz "Khristianskoe Vozrozhednie"
KHVS	Kunsthandelsverband der Schweiz
KI	Kennarasamband Islands (Iceland)
KI	Konjunkturinstitutet
KI-SAM	Kunsttørings Industriens Sammenslutningen
KIA	Kachin Independence Army (Burma)
KIA	Kenya Institute of Administration
KIA	Kibbutz Industries Association (Israel)
KIB	Arbeitskreis Selbstandiger Kunstsoff-Ingenieure und- Berater
KIC	Kurdistan Information Centre
KIC	Kuwait Insurance Company
KID	Confédération d'Unité Démocratique (Haiti)
KIDA	Korean International Development Agency (Republic of Korea)
KIEMP	Kenya Industrial Energy Management Program
KIER	Korea Institute of Energy and Resources
KIET	Korea Institute for Economics and Technology
KIF	Knitting Industries Federation
KIF	Konfektionsindustriföreningen
KIF	Kvarnindustriföreningen
KIFP	Korean Institute for Family Planning
KIHASA	Korea Institute for Health and Social Affairs
KIIB	Koninklijk Instituut voor Internationale Betrekkingen (Belgium) = IRRI
KIIC	Kuwait International Investment Company
KIK	Klub Inteligencji Katolickiej
Kilamco	Kilwa Ammonia Company (Tanzania)
KIM	Kenya Institute of Management
KIMMA	Kongres Indian Muslim Malaysia
KINT	Nederlandse Vereniging voor Kwaliteitstoezicht, Inspectie en Niet-Destructief Techniek
KIO	Kenya Information Office
KIO	Kring Industriële Ontwerpers
KIO	Kuwait Investment Office
KIPA	Katholische Internationale Press-Agentur = CIP
KIPIC	Kuwait International Petroleum Investment Company
KIRBS	Korean Institute for Research in the Behavioural Sciences
KIRDI	Kenya Industrial Research and Development Institute
KIRTAK	Kirghiz Telegraph Agency, Frunze
KIS	Kenya Inspection Service
KISA	Korean International Steel Associates
KISAN	Union of Coastal Indians (Nicaragua)
KISOSZ	Kiskereskedágos Szervezete
KISR	Kuwait Institute for Scientific Research
KIST	Korean Institute of Science and Technology
KISZ	Magyar Kommunista Ifjusáki Szövetség
KIT	Koninklijk Instituut voor de Tropen
KITA	Kesatuan Insaf Tanah Ayer (Malaysia)
KITCO	Kenala Industry and Technical Consultancy Organisation (India)
KITLV	Koninkijk Instituut voor Taal-, Land- en Volkenkunde
KIUMW	Katholieke Internationale Unie voor Maatschappelijk Werk = CIUSS, IKVSA, UCISS
KIV	Karten Industrie Verlags Verband
KIvI	Koninkijk Instituut van Ingenieurs
KIWA	Keuringsinstituut voor Waterleidingartikelen
KIY	Kirjastoieteen ja Informatiikan Yhdistys
KIZ	Kunming Institute of Zoology
KJA	Kargaran-e Jawan-e Afghanistan
KJG	Kärntner Juristische Gesellschaft (Austria)

KJV	Kartell Jüdischer Verbindungen in Great Britain
KJVD	Kommunistischer Jugenverband Deutschlands
KK	Kabushiki Kaisha
KK	Kemian Keskusliito
KK	Kisebbségi Kerekasztal (Hungary) = NMR
KK	Komisja Krajowa
KK	Kulutusosuuskuntien Keskusliitto
KKE	Kommunistiko Komma Ellados
KKF	Komitet Kultury Fizycznej
KKG	Krajowa Komisja Gornictwa
KKK	Kapunngan sa Kalipay ug Kasakit (Philippines)
KKK	Ku Klux Klan (U.S.A.)
KKKK	Knights of the Ku Klux Klan (U.S.A.)
KKL	Kalatalouden Keskusliitto
KKL	Kommunale Kinematografers Landsforbund
KKN	Komitet Kultury Niezależnej
KKP	Krajowa Komisja Porozumiewawcza
KKR	Kohlberg Kravis Roberts (U.S.A.)
KKS	Kolejowy Klub Sportowy
KKW	Krajowa Komsja Wykonawcza
KL	Koninklijke Landmacht
KLA	Karachi Library Association (Pakistan)
KLA	Kenya Library Association
KLA	Korean Library Association
KLA	Kungliga Lantbruksakademien
KLB	Korea Longterm Credit Bank
KLBV	Verband der Konzertlokalbesitzer und aller Veranstalter Österreiche
KLD	Kongres Liberalno-Demokratyczny
KLF	Kjøttbransjens Landsforbund
KLF	Kosmetikkleverandørenes Forening
KLFI	Központi Légförfizikai Intézete (Hungary)
KLH	Kingdom of Lesotho Handicrafts
KLIAU	Korea Land Improvement Association Union
KLM	Koninklijke Luchtvaart Maatschappij
KLME	Kuala Lumpur Metal Exchange
KLNITE	Knitting, Lace and Net Industry Training Board
KLSS	Korean Library Science Society
KLTV	Katholieke Vereniging van Land-en Tuin-bouwonderwijzers
KLY	Konttorikoneliikkeiden Yhdistys
KM	Koncessionamnden for Miljoskydd
KMA	Kauno medicinos akademija
KMA	Kungliga Musikaliska Akademien
KMB	Katholieke Bond Metaalbewerkingsbedrijven
KMBA	Koninklijke Maatschappij voor Bouwmeesters van Antwerpen
KMBB	Koninklijke Maatschappij tot Bevordering der Bouwkunst
KMC	Kenya Meat Commission
KMDA	Koninklijke Maatschappij voor Dierkunde van Antwerpen (Belgium) = SRZA
KMF	Kontomaskin-och Kontorsmöbelhandlarnas Förening
KMFB	Gewerkschaft Kunst, Medizin, Freie Berufe (Austria)
KMI	Kansanmusiikki-Instituutti (Finland)
KMK	Klub Miłośników Książki
KMK	Standige Konferenz der Kulturministers der Länder
KML	Kauppamallastamojen Liitto
KMMC	Kerala Minerals and Metals Corporation (India)
KMO	Koulujen Musiikinopettajat
KMPiK	Klub Międzynarodowej Prasy i Książki
KMRI	Kunming Metallurgy Research Institute (China)
KMS	Kort-Og Matrikelstyrelsen (Denmark)
KMSO	Kansainvälisen Maaperäseuran Suomenosasto
KMT	Klub Miłośniów Teatru
KMT	Kuo Min Tang (Taiwan)
KMTNC	King Mahendra Trust for Nature Conservation (Nepal)
KMTP	Koninklijke Maatschappij Tuinbouw en Plantkunde
KMU	Kilusan Mayo Uno (Philippines)
KMW	Klub Młodzieży Wiejskiej
KMZGZLP	Komisja Młodzieżowa Zarządu Głównego Związku Literatów Polskich
KNA	Kenya News Agency
KNAC	Koninklijke Nederlandse Automobiel Club
KNAG	Koninklijk Nederlands Aardrijkskundig Genootschap
KNAK	Kongelik Norsk Automobilklubb

KNAN	Koninklijke Nederlandse Adademie voor Naturwetenschappen	**KNMP**	Koninklijke Nederlandse Maatschappij ter Bevordering der Pharmacie
KNAS	Kenya National Academy of Arts and Sciences	**KNMvD**	Koninklijke Nederlandse Maatschappij voor Diergeneeskunde
KNAU	Koninklijke Nederlandse Athletiek Unie	**KNNP**	Katholieke Nederlands Nieuwsblad Pers
KNAV	Koninklijke Nederlandse Alpen-Vereniging	**KNNV**	Koninklijke Nederlandse Natuurhistorische Vereniging
KNAW	Koninklijke Nederlandse Akademie van Wetenschappen	**KNOB**	Koninklijke Nederlandse Oudheidkundige Bond
KNBB	Katholieke Nederlandse Boerinnenbond	**KNOV**	Koninklijke Nederlandse Organistenvereniging
KNBTB	Katholieke Nederlandse Boeren- en Tuinders-bond	**KNOV**	Koninklijke Nederlands Ondernemersverband
KNBV	Koninklijke Nederlandse Botanische Vereniging	**KNP**	Katholiek Nederlands Persbureau
KNC	Karenni National Council (Burma)	**KNP**	Klub Niezależnych Posłów
KNCCI	Kenya National Chamber of Commerce and Industry	**KNPC**	Korea National Party
		KNPC	Kuwait National Petroleum Company
KNCV	Koninklijke Nederlandse Centrale Vereniging tot Bestrijding der Tuberculose	**KNPV**	Koninklijke Nederlandse Planteziektenkundige Vereniging
KNCV	Koninklijke Nederlandse Chemische Vereniging	**KNR**	Kalaallit Nunaata Radioa – Grønlands Radio
KNDP	Katholieke Nederlandse Dagbladpers	**KNRG**	Kwame Nkrumah Revolutionary Guards (Ghana)
KNFC	Kenya National Federation of Cooperatives	**KNRV**	Koninklijke Nederlandse Redersvereniging
KNGMG	Koninklijk Nederlands Geologisch Mijnbouwkundig Genootschap	**KNS**	Koninklijke Nederlandse Schouwburg
KNGMP	Koninklijk Nederlands Genootschap voor Munt- en Penningkunde	**KNSM**	Koninklijke Nederlandse Stoomboot Maatschappij
KNHM	Vereniging Koninklijke Nederlandische Heidemaatschappij	**KNTC**	Kenya National Trading Corporation
		KNTC	Korea National Tourism Corporation
KNHMV	Koninklijke Nederlandsche Heidemaatschappij Vereniging	**KNTV**	Koninklijke Nederlandse Toonkunstenaars-Vereniging
KNI	Kalaallit Nieuerfiat (Greenland)	**KNU**	Karen National Union (Burma)
KNI	Kantorberita Nasional Indonesia	**KNU**	Kereztény Nemzeti Unió (Hungary) = CNU
KNiT	Komitet Nauki i Techniki		
KNJBTB	Katholieke Nederlandse Jonge Boere-en Tuinderbond	**KNUB**	Koninklijke Nederlandse Uitgeversbond
KNK	Komitet Narodnogo Kontrolia	**KNVD**	Koninklijk Nederlands Verbond van Drukkerijen
KNL	Klub Nowoczesnego Liberalizmu	**KNVL**	Koninklijke Nederlandse Vereniging voor Luchtvaart
KNLC	Koninklijk Nederlands Landbouw Comité		
KNLS	Kenya National Library Service	**KNVTO**	Koninklijke Nederlandse Vereniging van Transport-Ondernemingen
KNMBP	Koninklijke Nederlandse Maatschappij ter Bevordering der Pharmacie	**KNVvL**	Koninklijke Nederlandse Vereniging voor Luchtvaart
KNMG	Koninklijke Nederlandsche Maatschappij tot Bevorderung der Geneeskunst	**KNZ**	Koninklijke Nederlandse Zuivelbond
		KO	Komitet Obywatelski
		KOC	Kuwait Oil Company
KNMI	Koninklijk Nederlandse Meteorologisch Instituut	**KODA**	International Forbund til Beskyttelse af Komponistrettigheder i Danmark
		KODISO	Komma Dimokratikou Sosialismou

KOG	Koninklijk Oudheidkundig Genootschap		**KPB**	Kommunistische Partij van België = PCB
KOICA	Korea International Cooperation Agency		**KPC**	Korea Productivity Centre
KOK	Kansallinen Kokoomus (Finland)		**KPC**	Kuwait Petroleum Corporation
KOK	Komitet Obrony Kraju		**KPCU**	Kenyan Planters Co-operative Union
KOKO	Internacia Naturprotektada Asocio de Esperantistoj		**KPD**	Klub Pisarzy Demokratycznych
KOL	Kuvaamataidon Opettajain Liitto		**KPD**	Kommunistische Partei Deutschlands = DKP
KOMEITO	Clean Government Party (Japan)		**KPDR**	Korean People's Democratic Republic
KONAKOM	Kongre Nasyonal Mouvman Demokratik (Haiti)		**KPF**	Kenya Patriotic Front
KONPAPP	Kontors- och Pappersvaruleverantörernas Förening		**KPGBF**	Komisja Polityki Gospodarczej, Budżietu i Finansów
KOO	Koordinierungstelle der Österreichischen Bischofskonferenz für Internationale Entwicklung und Mission (Austria)		**KPI**	Kuwait Petroleum International
			KPICO	Kuwait Pharmaceutical Industries Company
KOP	Komisja Ochrony Pracy		**KPJN**	Katholiede Plattelands Jongeren Nederland
KOPERiN	Komitet Obrony Praw Emerytów, Rencistów i Niepełnosprawnych		**KPK**	Communist Party of Kazakhstan
			KPL	Khao San Pathet Lao = LNA
KOPKAM-TIB	Command for the Restoration of Order (Indonesia)		**KPN**	Koła Przyjaźni Niemieckiej (Poland) = CIP
KOPTARI	Konferensi Pemimpim Tarekat Religius Indonesia		**KPN**	Komunistyczna Partia Narodowa
KOR	Komitet Obrony Robotników		**KPN**	Konfederacja Polski Niepodległej (Poland) = GFC
KORDI	Korean Ocean Research and Development Institute		**KPNLF**	Khmer Peoples National Liberation Front (Kampuchea)
KORSTIC	Korean Scientific and Technological Information Centre		**KPNO**	Kitt Peak National Observatory (U.S.A.)
KOS	Kanalizatsionno-Ochistnyie Sorucheniya		**KPÖ**	Kommunistische Partei Österreichs
KOSLO	Konferenz Schweizerischer Lehrerorganisationen		**KPOH**	Komisja Porozumiewawcza Organizacji Harcerskich
KOTA	Magyar Kórusok és Zenekarok Szövetsége		**KPP**	Komunistyczna Partia Polski
KOTC	Kuwait Oil Tanker Company		**KPPA**	Kosovo Patriotic and Political Association = SPAK
KOTRA	Korea Trade Promotion Corporation		**KPR**	Krestianskaia Partiia Rossii
KÖTUKE	Kózuti Kózlekedési Tudományos Kutató Intézet		**KPRP**	Kampuchean Peoples Revolutionary Party
KOUD-PROFIEL	Vereniging van Handelaren in Koudgevormde Profielen		**KPSA**	Konserwatiewe Party vab Suid-Afrika = CPSA
KOV	Katholieke Onderwijsers Vakorganisatie		**KPSTiTN**	Komitet Porozumiewawczy Stowarzyszeń Twórczych i Towarzystw Naukowych
KP	Keskustapuolue			
KP	Klub Poselski		**KPTC**	Kuwait Public Transport Company
KP	Konservativnaia Partiia		**KPU**	Kaszubian Pomeranian Union (Poland) = KZP
KPA	Korean People's Army (Democratic People's Republic of Korea)		**KPWU**	Korean Port Worker's Union
KPAWU	Kenya Plantation and Agricultural Workers Union		**KQC**	London University King's College
			KRAB	Kamer van Reclame-Adviesbureaus (Belgium)
KPB	Kenya Pyrethrum Board			

KRAOMA	Kraomita Malagasay	**KSEPL**	Koninklijke Shell Exploratie en Produktie Laboratorium
KRB	Konfederatsiya na Roma v Bulgaria = CRB	**KSF**	Kashmiri Students Federation
KREDITTIL-SYNET	Banking, Securities, Insurance and Exchange Commission (Norway)	**KSF**	Kungliga Svenska Flygrapnet
KREIC	Kuwait Real Estate Investment Consortium	**KSFC**	Karnataka State Financial Corporation (India)
KREMU	Kenya Department of Resources Surveys and Remote Sensing	**KSGB**	Kite Society of Great Britain
KRENWE	Konferenz für Regionalentwicklung in Nordwesteuropa = CRENO, CRENWE, CRONWE	**KSHR**	Konferenz Schweizerischer Handelsschutrektoren
		KSHS	Kansas State Historical Society
KRF	Kristeligt Folkeparti	**KSJ**	Internationale Katholische Studierende Jugend = JEC, YCS
KRG	Konsultacyjna Rada Gospodarcza	**KSJ**	Knights of St. John (U.S.A.)
KRIB	Koninklijke Vereniging Kamer van Raadgevend Ingenieurs van België = CICB	**KSLA**	Kungliga Skogs- och Lantbruksakademien
KRIPA	Korean Research Institute of Public Administration	**KSM**	Koresponda Servo Mondskala
		KSMA	Keats-Shelley Memorial Association
KRISO	Korea Research Institute of Ship and Ocean	**KSN**	Kongres Solidarności Narodowej
KRL	Vereniging Katoen Rayon- Linnen- en Jute-Industrie	**KSO**	Klaedergrossisternes of Skraedderfagets Oplysningsudvalg
KRN	Krajowa Rada Narodowa	**KSP**	Konfederatsiia Svobodnykh Profsoiuzov
KRO	Katholieke Radio Omroep	**KSPC**	Kuwait Spanish Petroleum Company
KRO	Konstnärernas Rijksorganisation	**KSPR**	Konfederatsiia Svobodnykh Profsoiuzov Rossii
KROM	Norsk Forening for Kriminalreform		
KRS	National Council for the Judiciary (Poland)	**KSRC**	Kuwait Shipbuilding and Repairyard Company
		KSRL	Konwent Seniorów Ruchu Ludowego
KRW	Vereinigung der Kessel- und Radiatoren-Werke (Switzerland) = FCR	**KSRTC**	Karnataka State Road Transport Corporation (India)
KS	Co-ordinating Council of Public Associations (Kazakhstan)	**KSS**	Eidgenossisches Kommission zur Stahlenschutz (Switerland)
KS	Kübel-Stiftung	**KSS**	Keep Sunday Special Campaign
KSA	Eidgenossisches Kommission für die Sicherheit von Atomlagen (Switzerland)	**KSS**	Konfederata e Sindikatave të Shqipërisë (Albania) = CATU
		KSSE	Kurdish Students' Society in Europe
KSA	Kitchen Specialists Association	**KSSM**	Konferenza tas Superjuritas – Sorijiet Maltin (Malta)
KSA	Klinefelter's Syndrome Association		
KSAA	Keats-Shelley Association of America	**KSSS**	Kungl. Svenska Segelsällskapet
KSAC	Kingston and Saint Andrew Corporation (Jamaica)	**KSSU**	KLM, SAS, Swissair, UTA
		KSU	Christian Social Union (Slovakia)
KSAK	Kungliga Svenska Aeroklubben	**KSZ**	Komitet Sotsialnoi Zashchity
KSC	Knights of St Columbanus (Éire)	**KT**	Konfederatsiia Truda
KSC	Komitet Samoobrony Chłopskiej	**KTAS**	Københavns Telefon Aktieselskab
KSCM	Komunisticka Strana Cech a Moravy	**KTBL**	Kuratorium für Technik und Bauwesen in der Landwirtschaft
KSDIC	Kerala State Industrial Development Corporation (India)	**KTCCA**	Kotwali Thana Central Cooperative Association (Bangladesh)
KSE	Korean Stock Exchange (Republic of Korea)	**KTCWAO**	Kenya Thirsty Child and Women Aid Organisation
		KTDA	Kenya Tea Development Authority

714

KTDC	Kenya Tourist Development Corporation		**KUVV**	Katholieke Unie van Verpleegkunden en Verzorgenden
KTE	Kozlekedéstudományi Egyesület		**KV**	Kartográfiai Vállalat
KTF	Kemisk-Tekniska Leverantörförbundet		**KVA**	Koninklijke Vlaamse Academie voor Wetenschappen, Letteren en Schone Kunsten van België
KTG	Kerntechnische Gesellschaft im Deutschen Atomforum		**KVA**	Kungliga Vetenskaps-Akademien
KTGA	Kenya Tea Growers Association		**KVAB**	Koninklijke Vlaamse Adademie voor Wetenschappen van België
KTH	Kungliga Tekniska Högskolan (Sweden)		**KVAN**	Koninklijke Vereniging van Archivarissen in Nederland
KTIBF	Kibris Turk Ischi Birlikleri Federasyonu (TRNC)		**KVAPS**	Koordinirano Veće Albanske Političke Stranke (Serbia) = CCAPP
KTiR	Klub Techniki i Racjonalizacji		**KVARN**	Sveriges Kvarnyrkesförbund
KTK	Kommission des Technischen Kommunicationsystem		**KVBA**	Koninklijke Vereniging van Belgische Aktuarissen = ARAB
KTL	Keep the Link		**KVBG**	Koninklijke Vereniging der Belgische Gasvaklieden = ARGB
KTL	Kuratorium für Technik in der Landwirtschaft		**KVC**	Lietuvos kataliku veikimo Centras = ACLC, LKVC
KTM	Pertasbiran Keretapi Tanah Melayu (Malaysia)		**KVCV**	Koninklijke Vlaamse Chemische Vereniging
KTMMOB	Kibris Türk Mühendis ve Mimar Odalari Birligi (Turkey)		**KvF**	Svenska Draftverksföreningen
KTN	Kieleckie Towarzystwo Naukowe		**KVGN**	Koninklijke Vereniging van Gasfabrikaaten in Nederland
KTP	Kommunistinen Tyovaenpuolue (Finland)		**KVHAA**	Kungliga Vitterhets Historie och Antikvitets Akademien
KTPI	Kerukanan Tulodo Pranatan Ingil (Suriname)		**KVIV**	Koninklijke Vlaamse Ingenieursvereniging
KTS	Kerntechnische Sektion der Schweizerischen Vereinigung für Atomenergie		**KVL**	Den Kongelige Veterinaer- og Landbohojskole
KTS	Kirjallisuudentutkijain Seura ry		**KVNT**	Koninklijke Vereniging 'het Nederlands Trekpaard
KTU	Kauno technologijos Universitetas			
KTUC	Kiribati Trades Union Congress		**KVO**	Katholiede Vervoeders Organisatie
KTV	Kafee-und Teeverband (Austria)		**KVO**	Koninklijke Verbond van Ondernemers in het Klein en Middelgrote Bedrijf
KTV	Kunnallisten Työntekiläin ja Viranhaltijain Liitto (Finland)		**KVOB**	Katholiede Vereniging van Ondernemers in het Bloembollenbedrijf
KUF	Kabul Union of Furriers (Afghanistan)			
KUFNCD	Kampuchean United Front for National Construction and Defence		**KVOB**	Katholieke Vereniging van Ondernemers in het Bakkersbedrijf
KUFPEC	Kuwait Foreign Petroleum Exploration Company		**KVS**	Kansanvalistusseura
KUiA	Komitet Urbanistyki i Architektury		**KVS**	Koninklijke Vlaamse Schouburg
KUK	Konfederace Umeni a Kulturu (Czech Republic)		**KVV**	Kungliga Vetenskaps och Vitterhets-Samhället i Göteborg
KUL	Katholieke Universiteit Leuven (Belgium)		**KVWM**	Katholiede Vereniging van Werkgevers in het Metaalindustrie
KUL	Katolicki Uniwersytet Lubelski		**KVZ**	Katholieke Vereniging van Ziekeninrichtingen
KUNA	Kuwait News Agency			
KUP	Kwacha United Press (Angola)		**KW**	Komitet Wojewódzki
KURRI	Kyoto University Research Reactor Institute (Japan)		**KWAU**	Korea Women's Associations United

KWDI	Korean Women Development Institute
KWF	Kommission zur Föderung der Wissenschaftlichen Forschung (Switzerland)
KWF	Kuratorium für Waldarbeit und Forsttechnik (Germany)
KWF-NOK	Stichting Koningin Wilhelmina Fonds-Nederlandse Organisatie voor de Kankerbestrijding
KWFA	Kenya Women Fellowship Association
KWFT	Kenya Women Finance Trust
KWP	Korean Workers Party (KPDR)
KWP	Kurdish Workers Party (Turkey)
KWV	Kooperatieve Wijnbouwers Vereniging van Zuid-Afrika
KWWA	Korean Women Workers Association
KY	Kansantaloudellinen Yhdistys
KY	Sveriges Kvarnyrkesförbund
KYAE	Kentron Ygiinis ke Asfalias tis Ergassias (Greece)
KYBE	Kentron Hydrobiologikon Ereynon (Greece)
KYDEP	Home Products Handling Administration (Greece)
KZ	Komitet Zakładowy
KZ-M	Klub Zachowawczo – Monarchistyczny
KZA	Komitee Zuidelijk Afrika (Netherlands)
KZBV	Kassenzahnärztliche Bundesvereinigung
KZhK	Komitet Zhenshchin Kirgyzstana
KZMP	Komunistyczny Związek Młodzieży Polskiej
KZNI	Komiteta Zashtita na Natsionalnite Interesi (Bulgaria) = CDNI
KZP	Kaszubski Związek Pomorski (Poland) = KPU
KZWZZ	Komitet Założycielski Wolnych Związków Zawodowych

L

L-DPN	Liberalno-Demokratyczna Partia "Niepodległość"
LA	Läderindustriernas Arbestsgivareförbund
LA	Lard Association
LA	Lebanese Army
LA	Lemko Association (Poland) = SŁ
LA	Library Association

LA	Livsforsikringsselskapenes Arbeidsgiverforening
LAA	Laboratoire d'Anthropologie Appliquée (France)
LAA	Latin American Association
LAA	Library Association of Alberta (Canada)
LAA	Library Association of Australia
LAA	Libyan Arab Airlines
LAA	Lithuanian Agriculture Academy = LZUA, ZUA
LAAD	Latin American Agribusiness Development Corporation
LAADIW	Latin American Association for the Development and Integration of Women
LAAF	Libyan Arab Air Force (Libya)
LAAS	Laboratoire d'Automatique et d'Analyse des Systèmes (France)
LAAS-CNRS	Laboratoire d'Automatique et de ses Applications Spatiales du CNRS
LAATC	Latin American Association of Trading Companies (Brazil) = ALAT
LAB	Laboratorio Municipal de Barcelona
LAB	Laboratory Animals Bureau
LAB	Langile Abertzaleen Batzordea (Spain)
LAB	Latin America Bureau
LAB	Legal Aid Board
LAB	Library Association of Barbados
LAB	Lloyd Aéreo Boliviano
LABA	Laboratory Animals Breeders Association (U.S.A.)
LABAK	Landssamband Bakarameistrara (Iceland)
LABAN	Lakas ng Bayan (Philippines)
LABBS	Ladies Association of British Barbershop Singers
LABEN	Laboratori Elettronici e Nucleari
LABOR-ELEC	Laboratoire de l'Industrie Électrique (Belgium)
LABORIA	Laboratoire de Recherche en Informatique et en Automatique
LabPU	Labour Party of Ukraine
LABRE	Liga de Amadores Brasilieros de Radio Emissão (Brazil)
LAC	Laboratory Animals Centre (MRC)
LAC	Landscape Advisory Committee
LAC	Latin American Center (U.S.A.)
LAC	Latvian Academy of Culture = LKA
LAC	Library Association of China
LAC	Ligas Agrarias Cristianas (Paraguay)

LAC	Linea Aerea del Caribe (Colombia)	**LAFU**	Ladies Amateur Fencing Union
LACA	Latin America Coffee Agreement	**LAG**	Legal Action Group
LACA	Local Authority Caterers Association (*ex* NASMO)	**LAGB**	Linguistics Association of Great Britain
LACAC	Latin American Civil Aviation Commission = CLAC	**LAGE**	Lineas Aéreas Guinea Ecuatorial
		LAGEMAR	Laboratorio de Geologia Marinha (Brazil)
LACASA	Latin American and Caribbean Solidarity Association	**LAGER**	Lesbian and Gay Employment Rights
LACC	Latin-American Council of Churches = CLAI	**LaH**	Landssammenslutningen af Hospitalslaboranter
LACE	Linkage Assistance and Cooperation for the European Border Regions (AEBR, CEC)	**LAHRC**	Libyan Arab Human Rights Committee
		LAI	Library Association of Ireland
		LAI	Linee Aeree Italiane
LACFFP	Latin-American Commission on Forestry and Forestry Products = CLAF	**LAIA**	Latin American Integration Association = ALADI
LACIM	Les Amis d'un Coin de l'Inde et du Monde	**LAIC**	Latin America Information Centre
LACIMAR	Laboratorio de Ciencias do Mar (Brazil)	**LAIC**	Les Argiles Industrielles du Caméroun
LACITO	Laboratoire de Langues et Civilisations à Tradition Orale (France)	**LAIC**	Lesbian Archive & Information Centre
		LAICA	Lineas Aereas Interiores de Catalina (Colombia)
LACMA	Latin American and Caribbean Movers Association	**LAIG**	Library Association Industrial Group
LACOTS	Local Authorities Co-ordinating Body on Training Standards	**LAIICS**	Latin American Institute for Information and Computer Sciences (Chile)
LACS	League Against Cruel Sports	**LAITS**	Latin American Institute of Transnational Studies = ILET
LACSA	Lineas Aéreas Costarricenses S.A.		
LACSAB	Local Authorities Conditions of Service Advisory Board	**LAJC**	Latin American Jewish Congress
		LAKMIDA	Lietuvos Anglu Kanglos Mokytoju ir Destytoju Asociacija (Lithuania)
LACUS	Linguistic Association of Canada and the United States	**LAL**	Lietuvos avialinijos
LADB	Lesotho Agricultural Development Bank	**LAL**	Linja-Autoliitto
		LALIT	Linite Travayer Lavil Lakanpayn (Mauritius)
LADE	Lineas Aéreas del Estado (Argentine)		
LADECO	Linea Aérea del Cobre (Chile)	**LAM**	Liberal Alliance of Montenegro = LSCG
LADH	Liga Argentina de Derechos Humanos		
LADH	Ligue Algérien pour Droits Humains	**LAM**	Library Association of Malaysia = PPM
LADIMA	Laboratorio Andino de Mederas (Peru) = Andean Group	**LAM**	Linhas Aéreas de Moçambique
		LAM	Lithuanian Academy of Music
LAE	London Association of Engineers	**LAMA**	Latin American Manufacturers Association
LAEE	Lithuanian Association for Energy Economics = LEEA	**LAMA**	Light Aircraft Manufacturers Association (U.S.A.)
LAF	Landskabsarkitekternes Fagforening (Denmark)	**LAMA**	Local Authority Members Association (Éire)
LAFANISA	Laboratorios Farmaceuticos de Nicaragua, S.A.	**LAMAS**	London and Middlesex Archaeological Society
LAFB	Libyan Arab Foreign Bank		
LAFC	Latin American Forestry Commission = COFLA, COFLAC	**LAMC**	Livestock Auctioneers Market Committee for England and Wales
Lafico	Libyan Arab Foreign Investment Company	**LAMCO**	Liberian-American-Swedish Minerals Co.

LAMD	Lietuvos Antropologu Moksliné Draugija	**LARIA**	Local Authorities Research and Intelligence Association
LAMDA	London Academy of Music and Dramatic Art	**LARO**	Latin American Regional Office (FAO)
LAMEL	Istituto di Chimica e Tecnologia dei Materiali e dei Componenti per l'Ellectronica (Italy)	**LARRIE**	Local Authorities Race Relations Information Exchange
		LARS	Laboratory for Applications of Remote Sensing (U.S.A.)
LAMINO-PLAST	Associazione Italiana Industria Laminati Plastici	**LARSA**	Latinoamericana de Reaseguros, S.A. (Panama)
LAMP	Latin America Mass Media Project	**LAS**	Land Agents Society
LAMP	Latin American Market Planning Centre (U.S.A.)	**LAS**	Latvijas Arhitektu Savieniba
		LAS	League of Arab States = LEA
LAMPA	Lampleverantörernas Förening	**LAS**	Library Association of Singapore
LAMSAC	Local Authorities Management Services and Computer Committee	**LAS**	Ligne Aerienne Seychelles
		LAS	Lithuanian Academy of Sciences = LMA, MA
LAN	Linea Aérea Nacional (Chile)		
LANAP	Latin American Natural Areas Program	**LAS**	London Appreciation Society
LANCAFA	Libera Associazione Nazional Commerciani, Artiginai, Floricoltori, Albergatori	**LASA**	Laboratory Animals Science Association
		LASA	Latin American Shipowners Association = ALAMAR
LANDATA	Land Division Data Base (Victoria) (Australia)	**LASA**	Latin American Studies Association (U.S.A.)
LANICA	Lineas Aéreas de Nicaragua		
LANS	Latin America News Service	**LASA**	London Advice Services Alliance
LANSA	Lineas Aéreas Nacionales S.A. (Honduras, Peru)	**LASCO**	Latin American Science Co-operation Office (UNESCO)
LAP	Labour Action for Peace	**LASEDECO**	Land Settlement and Development Corporation (Philippines)
LAP	Liberian Action Party		
LAP	Lineas Aéreas Paraguayas	**LASER**	London and South East Advisory Council
LAP	Líneas Aéreas Petroleras (Colombia)		
LAPA	Líneas Aéreas Privadas Argentinas	**LASER**	London and South East Library Region
LAPADA	London and Provincial Antique Dealers Association	**LASHST**	Latin American Society for the History of Sciences and Technology = SLHCT
LAPCO	Lavan Petroleum Company (Iran)	**LASIM**	Los Angeles Society of Internal Medicine (U.S.A.)
LAR	Landskapsarkitekternas Riksforbund		
LAR	Libyan Arab Republic	**LASL**	Los Alamos Scientific Laboratory (U.S.A.)
LAR	Liniile Aeriene Române	**LASMO**	London and Scottish Marine Oil
LARA	Land Access Rights Association	**LASO**	Latin American Solidarity Organization
LARAC	Local Authority Recycling Advisory Council	**LASPAU**	Latin American Scholarship Program of American Universities
LARC	Association for Library Automation Research Communications (U.S.A.)	**LASRA**	Leather and Shoe Research Association (New Zealand)
LARC	Libyan-American Reconstruction Commission	**LASS**	Liaoning Academy of Social Sciences
		LASSA	Licensed Animal Slaughterers and Salvage Association
LARC	Lindheimer Astronomical Research Center (U.S.A.)		
LARC	Regional Conference for Latin America (FAO)	**LASSI**	Latin American Secretariat of the Socialist International
LARF	Latin American Reserve Fund = FLAR	**LASST**	Laboratory for Surface Science and Technology (U.S.A.)

LASWMMR	London Association of Scale & Weighing Machine Manufacturers & Repairers
LAT	Liga Argentina contra la Tuberculosis
LATA	London Amenity and Transport Association
LATAG	Latin American Trade Advisory Group (BOTB)
LATINAH	Latin America Human Settlements Information Network
LATN	Líneas Aéreas de Transporte Nacional (Paraguay)
LATS	Latin-America Thyroid Society = SLAT
LATT	Library Association of Trinidad and Tobago
LATTU	Latin American Table Tennis Union = ULATEM
LATU	Laboratorio Tecnológico del Uruguay
LATUF	Latin America Trade Union Federation
LAU	Lithuanian Artists' Union = LDS
LAUA	Lloyds Aviation Underwriters Association
LAUTRO	Life Assurance and Unit Trust Regulatory Organisation
LAV	Landmaschinen- und Ackerschlepper-Vereinigung (VDMA)
LAV	Lëtzebuerger Arbechter-Verband
LAV	Lineas Aéropostal Venezolana
LAVA	Local Authorities Videotex Association
LAVA	Local Authority Valuers Association
LAVE	Association Volcanologique Européenne
LAW	Land Authority for Wales
LAW	Legal Action for Women
LAW	Loyalist Association of Workers
LAWASIA	Law Association for Asia and the Western Pacific
LAY	Look After Yourself Project Centre
LB	Levý Blok
LBA	Legião Brasileira de Assistência
LBA	London Boroughs Association
LBA	Luftfahrt Bundesamt
LBB	Latvijas Bibliotekăru Biedriba
LBC	Les Bois du Congo
LBD	Lietuvos Bibliotekininku Draugija
LBD	Lietuvos Biotechnologu Draugija
LBDI	Liberian Bank for Development and Investment
LBES	Lifeboat Enthusiasts Society
LBF	Lantbruksförbundets Byggnadsförening
LBF	Lithuanian Basketball Federation = LKF
LBF	Lunds Botaniska Förening
LBG	Ludwig Boltzmann Gesellschaft (Austria)
LBL	Lawrence Berkeley Laboratory (U.S.A.)
LBO	Liberal Bosnian Organization / Liberalna Bošnjaèka Organizacija
LBP	Liga dos Bombeiros Portugueses
LBRI	Lake Biwa Research Institute
LBSG	Letter Box Study Group
LBT	Landesverband Bayerischen Transportunternehmen
LBWG	Landelijke Beroepsorganisatie van Werkers in de Gezondheidszorg
LC	Congregatio Legionariorum Christi
LC	Lárarnas Centralförbund
LC	Liaison Committee of Rector's Conferences of Member States of the European Communities
LC	Library of Congress (U.S.A.)
LC	Locomotive & Carriage Institute
LC	Lutheran Council of Great Britain
LC&TPA	Lighting Column and Transmission Pole Association
LC-MY	League of Communists – Movement for Yugoslavia (Serbia)
LC-SDP	League of Communists – Social Democratic Party (Bosnia-Hercegovina)
LCA	Laboratoire Centrale de l'Armament (DTAT)
LCA	Landelijk Centrum voor Amateurdans
LCA	Lead Contractors Association
LCA	Liverpool Cotton Association
LCA-GB	Lightweight Cycle Association of Great Britain
LCAS	Lithuanian Catholic Academy of Sciences = LKMA
LCB	Literarisches Colloquium Berlin
LCBC	Lake Chad Basin Commission (Chad) CBLT
LCC	Labour Co-ordinating Committee
LCC	Legalise Cannabis Campaign
LCC	London Cycling Campaign
LCC-PDC	League of Communists of Croatia – Party of Democratic Change
LCCEB	London Chamber of Commerce Examinations Board
LCCI	London Chamber Commerce & Industry
LCD	Lord Chancellor's Department

LCDASS	Labour Committee on Democratic Accountability of Secret Services
LCDP	Lithuanian Christian Democratic Party
LCDTU	Liaison Committee for the Defence of Trade Unions
LCDU	Lithuanian Christian Democratic Union = LKDS
LCER	Labour Campaign for Electoral Reform
LCF	Laboratoire Central de Fitopatologia (Argentina)
LCF	Law Centres Federation
LCF	Librarians Christian Fellowship
LCG	Harvard Laboratory for Computer Graphics (U.S.A.)
LCGB	Letzeburger Chreschtleche Gewerkschaftsbond (Luxembourg)
LCGB	Locomotive Club of Great Britain
LCGIL	Libera Confederazione Generale Italiana dei Lavoratori
LCHRC	London Chinese Health Resource Centre
LCI	Labour Committee on Ireland
LCI	Library for Cultural Initiation (Spain)
LCIE	Laboratoire Central des Industries Électriques
LCIGB	Locomotive and Carriage Institution of Great Britain and Ireland
LCIHR	Lawyers Committee for International Human Rights (U.S.A.)
LCIR	London Centre for International Relations
LCIRI	Liaoning Chemical Industry Research Institute
LCLA	Lutheran Church Library Association (U.S.A.)
LCLGR	Labour Campaign for Lesbian and Gay Rights
LCM	League of Communists of Montenegro
LCM	Little Company of Mary = SNDM
LCMA	Lightweight Cycle Manufacturers Association
LCMSC	Labour Common Market Safeguards Committee
LCOS	London Conference on Overseas Students
LCP	London Centre for Psychotherapy
LCPC	Laboratoire Central des Ponts et Chaussées
LCPRC	Liquid Crystalline Polymer Research Center (U.S.A.)

LCR	La Causa R (Venezuela)
LCR	Liga Comunista Revolucionaria
LCR	Ligue Communiste Révolutionnaire
LCS-PDR	League of Communists of Slovenia – Party of Democratic Reform
LCSC	Legislative Council Select Committee
LCT	Laboratoire Central de Télécommunications
LCTCM	Liaoning College of Traditional Chinese Medicine
LCTR	Labour Campaign for Travellers Rights
LCTUI	Liaison Commission for Trade Unions in Iran
LCU	Labour Congress of Ukraine
LCU	Libya Constitutional Union
LCU	Lithuanian Cinematographers' Union = LKDS
LCWE	Lausanne Committee for World Evangelisation
LCWIO	Liaison Committee of Women's International Organisation
LD-MPT	Ligue Démocratique – Mouvement pour le Parti du Travail
LDA	Landsforeningen af Danske Anlægsgartnermestre
LDA	Lead Development Association
LDA	Lietuvos dailes akademija
LDA	Lithuanian Dental Association
LDDC	London Docklands Development Corporation
LDDP	Lietuvos demokratine darbo partija = LDLP
LDE	Libéraux et Démocrates Européens = ELD
LDEUG	Liberal Democrat Eastern Europe Group
LDFPA	Laboratorio de Defesa Fitossanitária dos Produtos Armazenados (Portugal)
LDK	Lietuvos Didzioji Kunigaikstyste
LDLA	Liberal Democrat Lawyers Association
LDLF	Libyan Democratic Liberation Front
LDLP	Lithuanian Democratic Labour Party = LDDP
LDM	Lietuvos dailes muziejus
LDOS	Lord's Day Observance Society
LDP	Lakas ng Demokratikong Pilipinas
LDP	Landsforeningen af Danske Plantehandlere
LDP	Liberal Democratic Party (Belarus, Bulgaria, Slovenia)

LDP	Liberal-Democratic Party Jiyu-Minshuto (Japan)
LDP	Lietuvos demokratu partija
LDPAS	Long Distance Paths Advisory Service
LDPD	Liberal Demokratische Partei Deutschlands
LDPR	Liberal Democratic Party of Russia
LDPU	Liberal Democratic Party of Ukraine
LDR	European Parliament Liberal, Democratic and Reform Group
LDRC	Libel Defense Resource Center (U.S.A.)
LDRTA	Long Distance Road Transport Association of Australia
LDS	Latvijas Dizaineru Savieniba
LDS	Library and Documentation Service for Asia and the Pacific = UNESCO/LDS
LDS	Lietuvos dailininku sajunga = LAU
LDS	Lietuvos darbininku sajjunga = LWU
LDTA	Large Diameter Tube Association
LDV	Landsforeningen Danske Vognmænd
LDV	Loyalist Defence Volunteers
LDWA	Long Distance Walkers Association
LDYS	Liberal Democrat Youth and Students
LEA	Laboratorio de Engenharia de Angola
LEA	Leasehold Enfranchisement Association
LEA	Lietuvos Ekonomistu Asociacija
LEA	Ligue des États Arabes = LAS
LEA	Lithuanian Engineers Association = LIS
LEAD	Laboratories d'Électronique et d'Automatique Dauphinois
LEAD	Linking Education and Disability
LEADR	Lawyers Engaged in Alternative Dispute Resolution
LEAF	Linking Environment and Farming
LEAG	Legislative Extended Assistance Group (U.S.A.)
LEAN	Local Established Auctioneer Network
LEANORD	Laboratoire d'Électronique et d'Automatique du Nord de la France
LEAP	Landcare and Environment Action Program
LEAP	Large Experimental Aquifer Program (U.S.A.)
LEAP	Loan and Educational Aid Programme (Nigeria)
LEAS-EUROPE	European Federation of Equipment Leasing Company Associations
LEAT	International Institute of Legal, Economic and Administration Terminology (France)
LEB	Landesarbeitsgemeinschaft für Ländliche Erwachsenenbildung
LEC	Landbrugers EDB-Center (Denmark)
LEC	Launceston Environment Centre
LEC	Liberia Electricity Corporation
LECÉ	Ligue Européenne de Co-opération Économique = ELEC
LECT	League for the Exchange of Commonwealth Teachers
LEDU	Local Enterprise Development Unit (Northern Ireland)
LEEA	Lietuvos Energetiku Ekonomistu Asociacija = LAEE
LEEA	Lifting Equipment Engineers' Association
LEEC	London Environmental Economics Centre
LEEF	London Environmental Education Forum
LEES	Laboratory for Electromagnetic and Electronic Systems (U.S.A.)
LEF	Landbouw Egalisatie Fonds
LEF	Lantbruksakademiens Kommitté for Ekonomisk Forskning
LEF	Lobby Européen des Femmes = EWL
LEFTA	Labour Economic Finance and Taxation Association
LEG	Loteria Estadual de Goiás (Brazil)
LEGA-COOP	Lega Nazionale delle Cooperative e Mutue
Legco	Legislative Council (Hong Kong)
LEGPA	Laboratory of Engineering and Applied Physics
LEI	Landbouw Economisch Instituut
LEI	Landsforeningen for Elektroteknisk Industri
LEKKJ	Lutherische Europäische Kommission für Kirche und Judentum (LWF)
LEKNAS	National Institute of Economic and Social Research (Indonesia)
LELA	Leverantörföreningen för Lantbruksmaskiner
LELESA	Société Pétrolière d'Élé (Cameroon)
LEMA	Lifting Equipment Manufacturers Association
LEMI	Laboratorio de Ecologia Marina (Chile)
LEMIT	Laboratorio de Ensayo de Materiales e Investigaciones Technológicas (Argentina)
LEN	Ligue Européenne de Natation

LEN	Living Economy Network	**LFDA**	Ligue Française des Droits de l'Animal
LENA	Laboratorio Energia Nucleare Applicata	**LFEEP**	Ligue Française de l'Enseignement et de l'Education Permanente
LENA	Lesotho News Agency	**LFEM**	Laboratoire Fédéral d'Essai de Matériaux (Switzerland)
LENTA	London Enterprise Agency		
LEO	Lyons Electronic Office	**LFF**	Land-und Forstwirtschaftlicher Forschungsrat e.v. Bonn
LEOK	Laboratorium voor Electronische Ontwikkelingen voor de Krijsmacht (Netherlands)		
		LFF	Lietuvos futbolo federacija
LEP	Laboratoires d'Électronique Philips (France)	**LFG**	London Freshwater Group
		LFI	Labour Friends of Israel
LEPRA	British Leprosy Relief Association	**LFI**	Laxforskningsinstitutet
LERN	Learning Resources Network (U.S.A.)	**LFI**	Let's Face It
LERT	Libertarian Education and Research Trust	**LFÍ**	Lyfjafræðingafélag Íslands
		LFIG	Labour Finance and Industry Group
LES	Laboratorio de Energia Solar (Brazil)	**LFL**	Landøkonomisk Forsøgslaboratorium
LES	Licensing Executives Society International	**LFLU**	Liberian Federation of Labour Unions
		LFMA	Letter File Manufacturers' Association
LES	Livestock Experiment Station (South Korea)	**LFNC**	Lao Front for National Construction
		LFNSA	Low Frequency Noise Sufferers Association
LET	Laboratoire d'Économie des Transports (France)		
		LFR	Liechtenstein Förderkreis für Raumfahrt
LET	Laboratoire Électrotechnique de Tokyo	**LFS**	Landscentralen for Småindustri
LETA	Latvian Telegraph Agency	**LFS**	Lietuvos Fotomeninku Sajunga
LETATA	Light Edge Tool and Allied Trades Association	**LFSA**	Landesverband freier Schweizer Arbeiter
LETI	Laboratoire d'Électronique et de Technologie de l'Informatique	**LFSEP**	Ligue Française Contre la Sclérose en Plaques
LETII	Liaoning Electronics Technical Information Institute	**LFT**	Liszt Ferenc Társaság
		LFT	Lufttraffikkledelsens Forening
LETS	Local Employment and Trading Schemes	**LFTD**	Stichting Landbouw Fysisch-Technische Dienst
LEU	London Ecology Unit	**LFTU**	Lao Federation of Trade Unions
LEV	Liechtensteinischer Arzteverein	**LFTY**	Laaketieteellisen Fysikan ja Tekniikan Yhdistys
LEVS	Levnedsmiddelselskabet		
LEY	Liberal European Youth = JEL	**LFU**	Lithuanian Farmers' Union = LZS
Lf	Lanstingsförbundet	**LG&PSU**	Local Government and Public Services Union (Éire)
LF	Lebanese Front		
LF(IOC)	Legion of Frontiersmen – Independent Overseas Command	**LGA**	Leek Growers' Association
		LGA	Lietuvos Geotermijos Asociacija
LFAJ	Ligue Française pour les Auberges de Jeunesse	**LGA**	Liptako-Gourma Integrated Development Authority
LFAN	Lesbian Feminist Action Network	**LGA**	Local Government Agency
LFC	London Food Commission	**LGA**	Local Government Authority
LFCB	Ligue Française contre le Bruit	**LGAO**	Laboratorie de Géophysique Appliquée a l'Océanographie
LFCMA	Liquid Food Carton Manufacturers' Association		
		LGBC	Local Government Boundary Commission for England
LFD	League of Free Democrats (Germany) = BFD	**LGC**	Laboratory of the Government Chemist
LFD	Lietuvos Fiziku Draugija	**LGC**	Local Government Commission

LGCARF	Lesbian and Gay Campaign Against Racism and Fascism
LGCE	Local Government Commission for England
LGCM	Lesbian and Gay Christian Movement
LGCSB	Local Government Computer Services Board (Éire)
LGDP	Local Government Development Program
LGEB	Local Government Examinations Board
LGEIES	Local Government Environmental Information Exchange Scheme
LGFA	Lattice Girder Floor Association
LGIB	Local Government International Bureau
LGIC	Laminated Glass Information Centre
LGIU	Local Government Information Unit
LGMB	Local Government Management Board
LGNM	Luxemburger Gesellschaft für Neue Musik
LGOG	Limburgs Geschied- en Oudheidkundig Genootschap
LGP	Lithuanian Green Party = LZP
LGPA	Lesbian and Gay Police Association
LGSC	Liquified Gas Shipping Company (Abu Dhabi)
LGSNB	Local Government Staff Negotiations Board (Éire)
LGSP	Local Government Staff Panel (Éire)
LGTA	Ligue Générale des Travailleurs de l'Angola
LGTB	Local Government Training Board
LGU	Ladies Golf Union
LGU	Liechtensteinische Gesellschaft für Umweltschutz
LGWU	Lesotho General Workers Union
LGYFI	Lesbian and Gay Youth Federation of Ireland
LGYM	Lesbian and Gay Youth Movement
LH	Lingkugan Hidup (Ministry of State for Environment) (Indonesia)
LHC	London Hazards Centre
LHCH	Laboratoires d'Hydraulique Appliquée et de Constructions Hydrauliques et Navales (Belgium)
LHDH	Ligue Haïtienne de Droits Humains
LHE	London Health Emergency
LHF	Landbo- of Husmandsforeningernes
LHI	Lefthanders International (U.S.A.)
LHI	Ligue Homéopathique Internationale = IHL
LHU	London Housing Unit
LHV	Luchtvaart Historische Vereniging
LI	Landscape Institute
LI	Liberal International = IL
LI	Liberty International
LI	Ligue Internationale de la Représentation Commerciale = ILCTA
LIA	International Union of Life Assurance Agents
LIA	Laser Institute of America
LIA	Lead Industries Association (U.S.A.)
LIA	Lianyungang Institute of Apitherapy
LIA	Life Insurance Association
LIA	Ligue Internationale d'Arbitrage = IAL
LIA	Línea Internacional Aérea (Ecuador)
LIA	Linhas Aéreas da Guinée-Bissau
LIAC	Liberian International American Corporation (U.S.A.)
LIADA	Liga Iberoamericana de Astronomía
LIASA	Ligas de Aluminio S.A. (Brazil)
LIAT	Leeward Islands Air Transport Services
LIB	Landbrugsmaskin-Importørernes Branchforening
LIBA	Lloyd's Insurance Brokers Association
LIBC	Lloyd's Insurance Brokers Committee
LIBE	Ligo Internacia de Blindaj Esperantistoj = ILBE
LIBER	Ligue des Bibliothèques Européennes de Recherche
LibPU	Liberal Party of Ukraine
LIBRA	Linhas Brasileiras de Navegação
LIC	International Debt Recovery Organisation
LIC	League International For Creditors
LIC	Library and Information Commission
LIC	Life Insurance Corporation (India)
LICA	Land Improvement Contractors of America
LICCA	Liga Internationalis Catholica Contra Alcoholismus
LICCO	Ligue Internationale Contre la Concurrence Malhonnête
LICOSA	Libreria Commissionaria Sansoni
LICOTRA	L'Essor Ivoirien de Construction et de Travaux Publics
LICOVI	L'Ivoirienne de Confection Industrielle
LICP	Lanzhou Institute of Chemical Physics
LICR	Ludwig Institute for Cancer Research

LICRA	Ligue Internationale Contre le Racisme et l'Antisémitisme	**LIH**	Laboratory of Industrial Hygiene (China)
LICWIO	Liaison Committee of Women's International Organizations	**LIHG**	Ligue Internationale d'Hockey sur Glace = IEHV, IIHF
LIDA	Ligue Internationale des Droits de l'Animal	**LII**	Lietuvos Informacijos Institutas
LIDA	Tanzania Livestock Development Authority	**LIL**	Laboratoire International de la Lune
LIDC	Lead Industries Development Council	**LILA**	Ligue Internationale de la Librairie Ancienne = ILAB
LIDC	Ligue Internationale du Droit de la Concurrence	**LIM**	Groupement des Laboratoires Internationaux de Recherche et d'Industrie du Médicament
LIDE	Liga de Activación de la Región del Delta (Argentina)	**LIMA**	Lietuvos Respublikos Istorijos Mokytoju Asociacija
LIDH	Ligue Internationale des Droits de l'Homme = ILHR	**LIMBA**	Les Industries Manufacturères du Bois Africain (Ivory Coast)
LIDLIP	Ligue Internationale pour les Droits et la Libération des Peuples	**LIMC**	Fondation pour le Lexicon Iconographicum Mythologiae Classicae
LIEÉP	Ligue Internationale de l'Enseignement de l'Éducation et de la Culture Populaire = ILFCAAE	**LIMEX**	L'Ivoirienne d'Import-Export
LIÉF-ÉSAP	Laboratoire d'Informatique de l'Économie Financière de l'École Supérieure d'Agriculture de Purpan	**LIMPL**	Liga Internacional de Mujeres pro Paz y Libertad = IFFF, LIFPL, WILFP
LIEM	Lietuvos istorijos ir etnografijos muziejus	**LIMRA**	Life Insurance Management and Research Association (U.S.A.)
LIEN	Ligue Internationale pour l'Éducation Nouvelle = WEF	**LINA**	Liberian News Agency
LIF	Läkemedelsindustriföreningen	**LINABOL**	Lineas Navieras Bolivianos
LIF	Lighting Industry Federation	**LINAR**	Larkana Institute of Nuclear Medicine and Radiotherapy (Pakistan)
LIFE	League for International Food Education (U.S.A.)	**LINC**	Library and Information Cooperation Council
LIFFE	London International Financial Futures and Options Exchange	**LINK**	British Centre for Deafened People
LIFIM	Liikkeenjohdon Instituutti	**LINK**	International Leisure Information Network (WLRA)
LIFL	Laboratoire d'Informatique Fondamentale de Lille	**LINK**	Let's Increase Neurofibromatosis Knowledge
LIFMA	Leather Importers, Factors and Merchants Association	**LINOCO**	Libyan National Oil Corporation
LIFPL	Ligue Internationale de Femmes pour la Paix de la Liberté = IFFF, LIMPL, WILPF	**LINS**	Labrador Institute of Northern Studies (Canada)
LIFT	Local Initiatives Foundation for Training	**LIO**	Laboratorium voor Insekticidenonderzoek
LIFZA	Liberia Industrial Free Zone Authority	**LIP**	London International Press
LIGAVRAC	Ligue Internationale des Associations de Voyageurs, Représentants et Agents de Commerce	**LIPAD**	Ligue Patriotique pour le Développement (Burkina Faso)
LIGG	Lanzhou Institute of Glaciology and Geocryology	**LIPAP**	Lanzhou Institute of Plateau Atmospheric Physics
LIGNUM	Schweizerische Arbeitsgemeinschaft für das Holz	**LIPI**	Lembaga Ilmu Pengetahuan Indonesia
		LIPP	Ligue Internationale pour la Protection des Primates = IPPL
		LIPT	Ladies' International Polo Tournament
		LIPU	Liga Italiana della Protezione Uccelli
		LIQC	Laboratorio de Investigaciones sobre la Quimica del Café (Colombia)

LIR	Lakemedelsinformationsradet		**LITTT**	Luoyang Institute of Tracking and Telecommunication Technology
LIRA	Lambeg Industrial Research Association (Northern Ireland)		**LIVI**	Lämpöinsinööriyhdistys
LIRA	Liberal Industrial Relations Association		**LIVOTEX**	L'Ivoirienne de Textiles
LIRAR	Les Ingénieurs Radio Réunis		**LJA**	Lady Jockeys Association
LIRC	Lebanese Information and Research Center (U.S.A.)		**LJA**	Latvijas Juras Akademija = LMA
			LJA	Liga de la Juventud Comunista
LIRDP	Luangwa Integrated Resource Development Project		**LJA**	London Jute Association
LIRI	Leather Industries Research Institute (South Africa)		**LJEWU**	Lanka Jathika Estate Workers Union (Sri Lanka)
LIRM	Laboratorie International de Pollution Marine		**LJK**	Liikkeenjohdon Konsultit
			LJL	Lietuvos juru laivininkyste = LN
LIRMA	Laboratoire International de Recherche sur les Maladies des Animaux		**LJS**	Lithuanian Journalists' Society = LZD
LIRMA	London Insurance & Reinsurance Market Association		**LJST**	Library of Japanese Science and Technology (U.K.)
LIRR	Luoyang Institute of Refractories Research		**LJU**	Lithuanian Journalists' Union = LZS
LIRS	Lutheran Immigration and Refuge Service (U.S.A.)		**LJUSA**	Ljusarmatujrleverantorerna
			LK	Liiketyönantajain Keskusliitto
LIS	Lesbian Information Service		**LKA**	Latvijas Kulturas Akademija = LAC
LIS	Lietuvos Inžinieriu Sajunga = LEA		**LKD**	Leverantörföreningen Kontors-och Datautrustning
LIS	Light Industries Services (Singapore)			
LIS	List and Index Society		**LKD**	Lietuviu kulturos draugija = SLC
LISA	Laboratory for Information Science in Agriculture, Colorado (U.S.A.)		**LKD**	Lietuvos Kraštotyros Draugija
			LKDP	Lietuvos krikscioniu demokratu partija = LCDP
LISA	Leather Industry Suppliers Association		**LKDS**	Lietuvos kinematografijos darboutoju sajunga = LCU
LISC	Library and Information Services Council			
LISC	Lions International Stamp Club		**LKDS**	Lietuvos krikscioniu demokratu sajunga = LCDU
LISCO	Liberian Iron and Steel Corporation			
LISE	Librarians of Institutes and Schools of Education		**LKF**	Landsforeningen til Kiropraktikkens Fremme
LISH	Laboratoire d'Informatique pour les Sciences de l'Homme (France)		**LKF**	Lietuvos krepsinio federacija = LBF
			LKMA	Lietuviu kataliku mokslo akademija = LCAS
LISNAVE	Estaleiros Navais de Lisboa			
LIST	Ligue International de Sécurité des Transports		**LKP**	Liberaalinen Kansanpuolue
			LKS	Latvijas Komponistu Savieniba
LISU	Library and Information Statistics Unit		**LKS**	Liberation Kanake Socialiste (New Caledonia)
LIT	Ludwig Boltzmann Forschungsstelle für Informationstechnologische Systemforschung			
			LKS	Lietuvos kino studija
			LKS	Lietuvos Kompozitoriu Sajunga
LITC	Library Information Technology Centre		**LKT**	Landsforeningen af Kliniske Tandteknikere
LITCA	Licensing Innovation and Technology Consultants Association = ANCOPI, VDPW		**LKTP**	Lembaga Kemajuan Tanah Persekutuan (Malaysia)
			LKVC	Lietuvos kataliku veikimo Centras = ACLC, KVC
LITES	Lietuvos Šiluminés Inžinieriu Sajunga		**LLA**	Lebanese Library Association
LiTG	Lichttechnische Gesellschaft		**LLA**	Lesotho Liberation Army
LITINT	Literacy International (U.S.A.)		**LLA**	Lietuvos laisves armija

LLA	Louisiana Library Association	**LMDH**	Mauritanian Human Rights League
LLAOR	Langues et Langages en Afrique Orientale (France)	**LME**	London Metal Exchange
		LMEC	Labour Middle East Council
LLE	Laboratory for Laser Energetics (U.S.A.)	**LMFA**	Light Metal Founders Association
		LmK	Landsforeningen mot Kreft
LLEPO	Ligue Luxembourgeoise pour l'Étude et la Protection des Oiseaux	**LMM**	Laboratoire de Métallurgie Mécanique (Switzerland)
LLG	Labour Life Group	**LMMA**	Lietuvos Matematikos Mokytoiu Asociacija
LLG	Landcare Liaison Group		
LLH	Leverantörföreningen for Lek- och Hobbyartikler	**LMMU**	Latin Mediterranean Medical Union = UMML
LLI	Laubach Literacy International (U.S.A.)	**LMN**	Live Music Now!
LLI	Life Line International (Australia)	**LMPA**	Methodist Local Preachers Mutual Aid Association
LLL	Labour Left Liaison		
LLL	Lietuvos laisves lyga	**LMRI**	Laboratoire de Métrologie des Rayonnements Ionisants
LLLI	La Leche League International		
LLNE	Law Librarians of New England (U.S.A.)	**LMS**	Laboratory for Mathematics and Statistics (U.S.A.)
LLNL	Lawrence Livermore National Laboratory	**LMS**	Landslaget Musikk i Skolen (Norway)
		LMS	Latin Mass Society
LLP	Liberian Liberal Party	**LMS**	Lietuvos Mokslininku Sajunga
LLS	Lietuvos lenku sajunga = PUL	**LMS**	Lietuvos Muziku Draugija
LLS	Lietuvos liberalu sajunga = LLU	**LMS**	London Mathematical Society
LLSBA	Leicester Longwool Sheep Breeders Association	**LMS**	London Medieval Society
		LMS	Riksföreningen för Lärarna i Moderna Språk
LLSP	Ligue Luxembourgeoie de la Sclérose en Plaques		
LLU	Lithuanian Liberal Union = LLS	**LMT**	Laboratoire de Mécanique et Technologie (France)
LMA	Latvian Maritime Academy = LJA	**LMUA**	Lloyds Motor Underwriters Association
LMA	Lebanese Management Association	**LMV**	La Mala Vida (Venezuela) = TBL
LMA	Lietuvos mokslu akademija = LAS, MA	**LMX**	London Market Excess of Loss
LMA	Linoleum Manufacturers Association	**LN**	Lithuanian Navigation = LJL
LMA	London Mayors Association	**LNA**	LAO News Agency = KPL
LMAGB	Locomotive Manufacturers Association of Great Britain	**LNA**	League for National Advancement (Papua New Guinea)
LMB	Latvijas Muzikas Biedriba	**LNA**	Libyan National Alliance
LMC	Lanzhou Medical College	**LNB**	Landsforbundet Norsk Brukskunst
LMC	Liga Maritima de Chile	**LNBEE**	Laboratoire National Belge d'Électrothermie et d'Électrochimie
LMC	London Mennonite Centre		
LMCA	Long-Term Medical Conditions Alliance	**LNBTP**	Laboratoire National du Bâtiment et des Travaux Publics (Burkina Faso)
LMCA	Lorry Mounted Crane Association	**LNDB**	Lesotho National Development Bank
LMCNI	Livestock Marketing Commission for Northern Ireland	**LNDC**	Lesotho National Development Corporation
LMCPA	London Motor Cab Proprietors Association (ex TFOF)	**LNDI**	Liga Nazional Donne Italiana
		LNEC	Laboratório Nacional de Engenharia Civil
LMD	Lietuviu mokslo draugija = LSS		
LMDC	Laboratoire Matériaux et Durabilité des Constructions (France)	**LNETI**	Laboratório Nacional de Engenharia e Tecnologia Industrial

LNF	Laboratori Nazional di Frascati
LNF	Latvian National Foundation (Sweden)
LNHS	London Natural History Society
LNLC	Ladies Naval Luncheon Club
LNLF	Lao National Liberation Front
LNNK	Latvian National Independence Movement
LNOC	Lithuanian National Olympic Committee = LTOK
LNRM	Libyan National Rally Movement
LNS	Laboratoire National Saturne (France)
LNSASURI	Saline and Alkaline Soil Utilization Research Institute of Liaoning Province
LNSP	Liberal National Social Party (Czech Republic)
LNT	National Youth League (Moldova)
LNTP	Laboratoire National des Travaux Publics (Mauritania)
LNU	Landsradet for Norske Ungdomsorganisasjoner
LNU	Lithuanian Nationalist Union = LTS
LNVL	Létzebuerger Natur- a Vuelleschutzliga (Liechtenstein)
LO	Land-organisationen i Sverige
LO	Landsorganisasjonen i Norge
LO	Landsorganisationen i Danmark
LO	Lutte Ouvrière
LOAS	Loyal Order of Ancient Shepherds
LOB	Landelijke Organisatie van Bedrijfspluimveehouders
LOB	Location of Offices Bureau
LOBB	Vereniging Landbouwkundig Overleg Bemestings Beleid
LOBE	Landelijke Organisatie van Bedrijfseendenhouders
LOC-AFRIQUE	Compagnie Ouest Africaine de Crédit-bail (Senegal)
LOCI	Ligue des Originaires de Côte d'Ivoire
LOCIG	Limited Overs Cricket Information Group
LOF	Landelijke Organisatie van Fokkers
LOFA	Leisure and Outdoor Furniture Association
LOG	Landbrukets Emballasjeforretning og Gartnernes Felleskjop
LOI	Loyal Orange Institution
LOK	Landelijke Organisatie van Kuikenmesters
LOK	Liga Obrony Kraju

LOMNER	Liga Organizaţülor Minorităţilor Naţionale şi Etnice România = LONEMR
LONACI	Loterie Nationale de Côte d'Ivoire
LONASE	Loterie Nationale Sénégalaise
LONEMR	League of Organizations of National and Ethnic Minorities in Romania = LOMNER
LONRHO	London and Rhodesian Mining and Land Co.
LONT	Leber's Optic Neuropathy Trust
LOOK	National Federation of Families with Visually Impaired Children
LOP	Landelijke Organisatie van Piepkuikenfokkers
LOP	Liga Ochrony Przyrody
LORC	Liaoning Ornithological Research Centre
LORCS	League of Red Cross and Red Crescent Societies = LSCR
LOROM-BOIS	Société Centrafricano-Roumaine pour l'Exploitation, l'Industrialisation et la Commercialisation du Bois
LOS	Landelijke Organisatie van Pluimveeselecteurs
LOS PrepCom	UN Preparatory Commission on the International Sea-Bed Authority and for the International Tribunal for the Law of the Sea
LOT	Polskie Linie Lotnicze
LOV	Landelijke Organisatie van Vermeerderaars
LOV	League of Vlachs (Macedonia) = LV
LP	Labour Party (Israel, New Zealand, South Africa)
LP	Liberal Party (Australia, Philippines)
LP	Liberal Party of Macedonia
LP-28	Ligas Populares del 28 de Febrero (El Salvador)
LPA	Lao People's Army
LPA	Leather Producers Association
LPA	Liberal Party of Australia
LPA	Livestock Producers' Association (Belize)
LPA	Loyalist Prisoners Aid
LPA	Loyalist Prisoners Association
LPAB	Nederlandse Bond van Logies- Pension- en Aanverwante Bedrijven
LPAC	London Parallel Applications Centre
LPAC	London Planning Advisory Committee

LPAI	Ligue Populaire Africaine pour l'Indépendance (Djibouti)
LPBS	Labour Party Black Section
LPC	League of Professional Craftsmen
LPCCOA	Laser Professional Commission of China Optics Association
LPCS	Laboratoire de Physique des Composants à Semiconducteurs (France)
LPD	Labour Party of Dominica
LPDM	Liga Paraguaya de los Derechos de la Mujer
LPDR	Lao People's Democratic Republic = SPPL
LPF	Lao Patriotic Front = NLHS
LPFA	Laminated Plastics Fabricators Association
LPG	Le Parti de la Guadeloupe
LPGA	Ladies Professional Golf Association
LPGITA	Liquefied Petroleum Gas Industry Technical Association
LPI	Life and Peace Institute (Sweden)
LPI	Lunar and Planetary Institute (U.S.A.)
LPIS	Labour Party Irish Society
LPL	Lasi-jo Posliinityöväen Liitto
LPM	Littéraire Populaire du Mali
LPMC	Liberian Produce Marketing Corporation
LPN	Liga para a Protecção da Natureza (Portugal)
LPO	Ligue Française pour la Protection des Oiseaux
LPO	London Philharmonic Orchestra
LPP-ITB	Lembaga Penelitian Perencanaan Wilayah dan Kota (Indonesia)
LPRA	Low Power Radio Association
LPRC	Liberia Petroleum Refining Corporation
LPRP	Lao People's Revolutionary Party (Laos)
LPRYU	Lao People's Revolutionary Youth Union
LPS	Labour Party Socialists
LPT	Landsforeningen af Praktiserende Tandteknikere i Danmark
LPTF	Laboratoire Primaire du Temps et des Fréquences (BNM)
LPU	Low Pay Unit
LPUINM	Libera Post-Université Internazionale Nuova Medicina
LPV	Laboratorio de Patologia Veterinaria (Portuguese)
LPWA	Loyalist Prisoners Welfare Association
LQFE	Laboratório Quimico Farmacéutico de Exército (Brazil)
LR	Lärarnas Riksförbund
LR	Lietuvos Respublika
LRA	Lace Research Association
LRAT	Lietuvos Respublikos Auksciausioji Taryba = SCRL
LRB	London Residuary Body
LRC	International Chemical Employers' Labour Relations Committee
LRC	Labour Relations Commission (Éire)
LRC	Law Reform Commission (Éire)
LRC	Lithuanian Red Cross = LRK
LRC	London Research Centre
LRCC	Laboratoire de Recherches et de Contrôle du Caoutchouc
LRCI	League for a Revolutionary Communist International
LRCS	League of Red Cross Societies and Red Crescent Societies
LRCS	Lincoln Red Cattle Society
LRD	Labour Research Department
LRDC	Land Resources Development Centre (ODA)
LRDC	Learning Research and Development Center (U.S.A.)
LRDE	Technical Information Centre of the Electronics and Radar Development Establishment (India)
LRDG	Learning Resources Development Group
LRF	Lantbrukarnas Riksförbund
LRG	Landscape Research Group
LRH	Laboratórium Rybárstva a Hydrobiológie
LRI	Legiforgalmi Repuloteri Igazgatosag (Hungary)
LRK	Lietuvos Raudonasis Kryzius = LRC
LRP	Society for Long Range Planning
LRRA	Litter and Recycling Research Association
LRS	Lietuvos Rasytoju Sajunga = LWU
LRS	Lietuvos Respublikos Seimas = LS
LRTA	Light Rail Transit Association
LRTMA	London Rubber Terminal Market Association

LRU	Lithuanian Riflemen Union = LSS
LRV	Lietuvos Respublikos Vyriausybe
LS	Labologists' Society
LS	Liberalnyi Soiuz
LS	Lietuvos Sajudis
LS	Lietuvos Seimas = LRS
LS	Linnaean Society
LSA	Land Settlement Association
LSA	Law Services Association
LSA	Lead Sheet Association
LSA	Leisure Studies Association
LSA	Leukemia Society of America
LSA	Linguistic Society of America
LSA	Lithuanian State Archives = LVA
LSA	Little Sisters of the Assumption = IA, LSA, PSA
LSA	London Sisal Association
LSA	Lowe's Syndrome Association (United Kingdom Contact Group)
LSA	Lute Society of America
LSAC	Laboratory Services Advisory Committee (Northern Ireland)
LSAP	Letzeburger Sozialistesch Arbechterpartei (Luxembourg) = POSL
LSBA	Lonk Sheep Breeders Association
LSC	Lanthushållnigs- Sállskapens Centralförbund
LSCÉ	Ligue Suisse Contra l'Épilepsie = SLgE
LSCG	Liberalni Savez Crne Gore (Montenegro) = LAM
LSCR	Ligue des Sociétés de la Croix-Rouge et du Croissant-Rouge = LORCS
LSD	Lietuvos Sociologu Draugija
LSDP	Lietuvos Socialdemokratu Partija
LSDV	League of Social Democrats of Vojvodina = LSV
LSE	London School of Economics and Political Science
LSEO	Landelijk Steunpunt Educatie Ontwikkelingssamenwerking
LSEW	Law Society of England and Wales
LSF	Lithuanian Society of Foresters
LSFPM	Liga de Solidaritate cu Frontul Popular al Moldovei / League of Solidarity with the People's Front of Moldova
LSG	La Societe Guernesiaise
LSG	League of St. George
LSG	Ligo de Samseksamaj Geesperantistoj
LSHTM	London School of Hygiene and Tropical Medicine
LSIRI	Liaoning Standards Information Research Institute
LSL	Lårvare-og Sportsartikkelfabrikantenes Landsforening
LSL	Latuijas Sieviesu Liga = WLL
LSL	Linnaean Society of London
LSMB	Lint and Seed Marketing Board, Tanzania
LSNSW	Linnaean Society of New South Wales
LSNY	Linnaean Society of New York (U.S.A.)
LSP	Liberal Socialist Party (Egypt)
LSP	Little Sisters of the Poor = HDLP, IDP, PSDP
LSPN	Ligue Suisse pour la Protection de la Nature = SBN
LSRA	Lead Smelters and Refiners Association
LSRE	Labour Supporters for Real Equality
LSRH	Laboratoire Suisse de Recherches Horologères
LSRI	Life Science Research Israel Ltd
LSS	Landslaget for Språklig Sammling
LSS	Law Society of Scotland
LSS	Lietuvos sauliu sajunga = LRU
LSS	Lietuvos skautu sajunga = LSU
LSS	Lithuanian Scientific Society = LMD
LSSA	Limnological Society of Southern Africa
LSSA	London Subterranean Survey Association
LSSC	Lithuanian Society of Saint Casimir (Poland) = LTSwK
LSSO	Lietuvos Slaugos Specialistu Organizacija
LSSP	Lanka Sama Samaja Party (Sri Lanka)
LSTA	London Shellac Trade Association
LSU	Liberální Sociální Unie
LSU	Lithuanian Scout Union = LSS
LSV	Lääkärin Sosiaalinen Vastuu
LSV	Landelijke Specialisten Vereniging
LSV	Lëtzebürger Schriftsteller-Verband (Luxembourg)
LSV	Liga Socialdemokrata Vojvodine (Serbia) = LSDV
LSWF	Light of Salvation Women's Fellowship (Nigeria)
LT	Lantbrukssallskapets Tidskriftsaktiebolag
LT	Lucis Trust
LTA	Latvian Telegraphic Agency

LTA	Lawn Tennis Association
LTA	Lawn Tennis Writers Association
LTA	Linen Trade Association (U.S.A.)
LTA	Livestock Traders' Association of Great Britain
LTAVR	Lowland Territorial Army Volunteer Reserve
LTB	Katholieke Land-en Tuinbouwbond
LTC	Land Tenure Center (U.S.A.)
LTC	Law Technology Centre
LTC	Les Transports au Congo
LTCDA	Low Temperature Coal Distillers' Association
LTD	Lietuvos teatro draugija = LTS
LTD	Lietuvos techniku draugija = LTS
LTDA	Licensed Taxi Drivers Association
LTF	Lufttraffikkledelsens Forening
LTG	Little Theatre Guild of Great Britain
LTIB	Lead Technical Information Bureau
LTJ	Land-en Tuinbouw Jongeren
LTK	Liiketyönantajain Keskuslitto
LTL	Learning Through Landscapes
LTLMB	Latviešu Tautas Lietiškǎs Mǎkslǎs Biedriba (Latvia)
LTN	Lódzkie Towarzystwo Naukowe
LTN	Lubelskie Towarzystwo Naukowe
LTN	Lubuskie Towarzystwo Naukowe
LTO	Land Titles Office
LTOK	Lietuvos tautinis olimpinis komitetas = LNOC
LTOM	London Traded Options Market
LTŚwK	Litewskie Towarzystwo Św. Kazimierza (Poland) = LSSC
LTPCI	La Lorraine des Travaux Publics de Côte d'Ivoire
LTRC	Louisiana Transportation Research Center (U.S.A.)
LTS	Lietuviu tautininku sajunga = LNU
LTS	Lithuanian Technicians' Society = LTD
LTS	Lithuanian Theatre Society = LTD
LTS	London Topographical Society
LTS	Lysteknisk Selskab
LTSI	Laboratoire Traitement du Signal et Instrumentation (France)
LTSI	Liaoning Tussah Silk Institute
LTT	Leninist-Trotskyist Tendency
LTT	Société des Lignes Télégraphiques et Téléphoniques
LTTE	Liberation Tigers of Tamil Eelam (Sri Lanka)
LTTEPF	Liberation Tigers of Tamil Eelam People's Front (Sri Lanka)
LTU	Lufttransport-Unternehmen
LTUA	Lawn Tennis Umpires Association
LTUG	Labour and Trade Union Group
LTV	Lietuvos televizija
LTY	Lääketeollisuuyhistys
LU	Lemko Union (Poland) = ZŁ
LU	Liaoning University
LU	Ligue Universelle
LUA	Lloyds Underwriters Association
LUASA	Life Underwriters' Association of South Africa
LUBEREF	Petromin Lubricating Oil Refining Company (Saudi Arabia)
LUBP	Ligue Universelle du Bien Public
LUC	London Underwriting Centre
LUC	Luteranos Unidos in Communicação (Brazil)
LUCE	Language for Cooperation in Europe (EIESP)
LUCIA	Lutheran Communications in Asia
LUCT	Liga Uruguaya contra la Tuberculosis
LUDP	Lesotho United Democratic Party
LUEMA	Land Use and Environmental Management Authority
LUF	Ligue Universelle de Francs-Maçons
LUMEN-VITAE	International Centre for Studies in Religious Education (SJ) = CIEFR
LUNA	Lloyd's Underwriters' Non-Marine Association
LUP	Liberia Unification Party
LURS	London Underground Railway Society
Lusa	Portuguese Press Agency
LUSES	Foundation for the Promotion of Finnish Music
LUT	Loge Unie des Théosophes
LUTCH	Computer-Human Interface Research Centre
LUV	Land Use Volunteer Service
LUXAIR	Société Anonyme Luxembourgeoise de Navigation Aérienne
LUXATOM	Syndicat Luxembourgeois pour l'Industrie Nucléaire
LV	Liga na Vlasite (Macedonia) = LOV
LV	Línea Aéropostal Venezolana
LVA	Landversicherungsanstalt

LVA	Licensed Victuallers' Association
LVA	Licensed Vintners Association (Éire)
LVA	Lietuvos valstybinis archyvas = LSA
LVA	Lietuvos veterinarijos akademija = LVA
LVCB	London Visitor and Convention Bureau
LVCC	Landelijk Verbond der Christelijke Coöperatieven (Belgium)
LVECC	Light Vehicles Energy Consumption Committee
LVFS	Lake Victoria Fisheries Service (Kenya)
LVM	Limburgse Vinyl Maatschappij (Belgium)
LVMEB	Landelijke Vereniging der Meesters Elektriekers van België
LVMW	Landelijke Vereniging van Maatschappelijk Werkers
LVRI	Lanzhou Veterinary Research Institute
LVRS	Lowveld Research Stations (Zimbabwe)
LVS	Literarischer Verein Stuttgart e.V.
LVSC	London Voluntary Service Council
LWA	London Welsh Association
LWAC	Labour Womens' Action Committee
LWB	Lutherischer Weltbund = FLM, LWF
LWC	London Women's Centre
LWF	Lutheran World Federation = FLM, LWB
LWI	Labour Women for Ireland
LWIU	Leather Workers International Union of America
LWM	Lutheran World Ministries
LWN	Labour Womens' Network
LWP	Ludowe Wojsko Polskie
LWR	Lutheran World Relief
LWRRDC	Land and Water Resources Research and Development Corporation
LWS	Landbouw Winter Scholen
LWT	London Weekend Television
LWT	London Wildlife Trust
LWTC	London World Trade Centre
LWTCA	London World Trade Centre Association
LWU	Lithuanian Workers' Union = LDS
LWU	Lithuanian Writers' Union = LRS
LWU	Regional Commission on Land and Water Use in the Near East
LWVPR	League of Women Voters of Puerto Rico
LYF	Lutheran Youth Fellowship (U.S.A.)
LYMEC	Liberal Youth Movement of the European Community

LYSIS	Lesbian Youth Support Information Service
LZB	Landeszentralbank
LZD	Lietuvos zurnalistu draugija = LJS
LZP	Lietuvos zalioji partija = LGP
LZS	Lietuvos zemdirbiu sajunga = LFU
LZS	Lietuvos zurnalistu sajunga = LJU
LZS	Ludowe Zespoły Sportowe
LZT	Beurs voor Landbouw Zuivel en Techniek
LZUA	Lietuvos zemes ukio akademija (Congo) = LAA, ZUA

M

M&ETA	Marine & Engineering Training Association (*ex* MTA)
M-19	Movimiento 19 de Abril (Colombia)
M-20	Movimiento 20 de Diciembre (Panama)
M-22	Mouvement du 22 fevrier
MA	Lietuvos mokslu akademija = LAS, LMA
MA	Maternity Alliance – Australia
MA	Mathematical Association
MA	Mazurian Association (Poland) = SM
MA	Melanesian Alliance (Papua New Guinea)
MA	Microwave Association
MA	Millers Association (Malta)
MA	Ministère de l'Agriculture
MA	Miscarriage Association
MA	Museums Association
MAA	Maison de l'Agriculture Algérienne
MAA	Manitoba Association of Architects (Canada)
MAA	Manufacturers Agents Association of Great Britain and Ireland
MAA	Mathematical Association of America
MAA	Medical Artists Association of Great Britain
MAA	Medieval Academy of America
MAA	Money Advice Association
MAA	Motor Agents Association (*now* RMI)
MAAC	Mastic Asphalt Advisory Council
MAAGB	Medical Artists Association of Great Britain
MAAI	Modeling Association of America International

MAAK	Movement for Pan-Macedonian Action		**MACEN**	Manufacturera Centroamericana (Nicaragua)
MAAL	Microfilm Association of Australia		**MACI**	Ministerio de Agricultura, Comercio e Industria (Panama)
MAB	Man and the Biosphere Programme (UNESCO)		**MACINTER**	International Network of Psychology-Based Man-Computer Interaction Research (IUPsyS) = NMCIR
MAB	Memorial Advisory Bureau			
MAB	Menswear Association of Britain (*now* BSSA)		**MACOMA**	Matériaux de Construction de Madagascar
MAB-NSN	MAB Northern Sciences Network		**MACS**	Maharashtra Association for the Cultivation of Science (India)
MABCO	Manufacturing and Building Company Limited (Saudi Arabia)		**MACWUSA**	Motor Assemblers and Component Workers Union (South Africa)
MABECO	Manufacture Béninoise de Confiserie		**MAD**	Mali Democratic Alliance = ADEMA
MABI	Groep Nederlandse Fabrikanten van Magazijn-, Archief- end Bibliotheekinrichtingen		**MADA**	Muda Agricultural Development Authority (Malaysia)
MABIC	Movement against Bats in Churches		**MADASS**	Motivation and Determination Achieves Self-Satisfaction
MABOSE	Manufacture de Bonneterie Sénégalaise		**MADEC**	Martial Arts Development Commission
MABRI	Conference of the Major Superiors of Brothers Congregations in Indonesia		**MADECO**	Manufacturas de Cobre (Chile)
MAC	Magyar Acélárugyár		**MADEPA**	Movimiento Apolitico de Productores Agropecuários (Uruguay)
MAC	Maritime Arbitration Commission (China)		**MADI**	Moskovskii Avtomobil'no-dorozhny (avtodorozhnu) Institut
MAC	Martial Arts Commission		**MADINPA**	Maderera Industrial Paraguaya, S.A.
MAC	Mineralogical Association of Canada		**MADO**	Mezhregionalnoe Assotsiatsiia Demokraticheskikh Organizatsii
MAC	Ministerio de Agricultura y Cria (Venezuela)		**MAE**	Magyar Agrártudományi Egyesület
MAC	Mobile Advice Centre		**MAE**	Manchester Association of Engineers
MAC	Movimiento de Autenticad Colorado (Peru)		**MAE**	Maritime Advisory Exchange
MAC	Mozambique Angola Committee		**MAE**	Mérite Artistique Européen
MAC	Museums Association of Canada		**MAÉ**	Ministère des Affaires Étrangères
MAC	Museums Association of the Caribbean (CCA)		**MAE**	Ministerio de Asuntos Exteriores
MAC	National Microelectronics Applications Centre (Éire)		**MAE**	Ministero degli Affari Esteri
MACA	Medical After-Care Association		**MAEE**	Marine Aircraft Experimental Establishment
MACA	Mental After-Care Association		**MAES**	Society of Mexican American Engineers and Scientists
MACACI	Manufacture de Caoutchouc de la Côte d'Ivoire			
MACATW	Mothers and Children Against Toxic Waste		**MAF**	Ministero dell'Agricoltura e della Foreste
MACC	Madison Academic Computing Center (U.S.A.)		**MAF**	Ministry of Agriculture and Forestry (Japan)
MACC	Manufacture d'Armes et de Cartouches Congolaises		**MAF**	Missionary Aviation Fellowship
MACDATA	Materials & Components Developing & Testing Association		**MAF**	Motorbranschens Arbetsgivareförbund
MACE	Mechanical and Civil Engineering Contractors (Abu Dhabi)		**MAFA**	Maison des Agriculteurs Français d'Algérie
			MAFERSA	Material Ferroviario S.A. (Brazil)
MACEF	Mastic Asphalt Council and Employers Federation		**MAFES**	Mississippi Agricultural and Forestry Experiment Station
			MAFF	Ministry of Agriculture, Fisheries and Food

MAFF	Ministry of Agriculture, Forestry and Fisheries (Japan)
MAFI	Magyar Allami Földtani Intézet
MAFILM	Magyar Filmgyárto Vállalat
MAFIS	Management Farm Information Service
MAFKI	Magyar Asványolaj és Földgáz Kísérleti Intézet
MAfr	Societas Missionariorum Africae = PB, WF
MAFREMO	Malawi Freedom Movement
MAFRIMA	Manufacture Centrafricaine de Matelasserie
MAFVA	Miniature Armoured Fighting Vehicle Association
MAG	Ministerio de Agricultura y Ganaderia (Costa Rica)
MAG	Motorcycle Action Group
MAGA-PLAST	Manufacture Gabonaise de Produits d'Étanchéité
MAGATE	Mercados, Silos y Frigorificos del Distrito Federal (Venezuela)
MAGB	Maltsters Association of Great Britain
MAGB	Microform Association of Great Britain
MAGDA	Mobility Aid and Guide Dog Alliance
MAGLI-CALZE	Associazione Italiana Produttori Maglierie e Calzetterie
MAGMA	Empresa Nacional de Minas (Mozambique)
MAGS	Medical Action for Global Security
MAGUK	Motorcycle Action Group
MAGZI	Mission d'Aménagement et de Gestion des Zones Industrielles (Cameroon)
MAHART	Magyar Hajózási Rt
MAHAZ	Mahaz-e Meli-e Eslami-e Afghanistan = NIFA
MAHIR	Magyar Hirdetó
MAHISSA	Maices Hibridos y Semillas, S.A.
MAHN	Mongolian People's Revolutionary Party
MAI	Manufacturers Association of Israel
MAI	Medical Aid for Iraq
MAI	Museums Association of India
MAI	Music Association of Ireland
MAIB	Marine Accident Investigation Board
MAIC	Maine Aquaculture Innovation Center (U.S.A.)
MAIC	Major Analytical Instrumentation Center (U.S.A.)
MAICh	Mediterranean Agronomic Institute of Chania (ICAMAS)
MAIF	Major Analytical Instruments Facility (U.S.A.)
MAIG	Matsushita Atomic Industrial Group (Japan)
MAILL-EUROP	Comité des Industries de la Maille des Pays de la CEE
MAITA	Marine and Allied Industries Training Association
MAIU	Marine Accident Investigation Unit
MAIZ	Mediterranean Agronomic Institute of Saragossa (ICAMAS) = IAMZ
MAJ	Medical Association of Jamaica
MAJD	Mezhdunarodnaia Assotsiatsiia Iuristov-Demokratov = AIJD, IADL, IVDJ
MAKIT	Magyar Allergologiai és Klinikai Immunológiai Tírsaság
MAKL	Mezhdunarodnaia Assotsiatsiia Kvantitativnoi Lingvistiki
MALAS	Midwestern Association for Latin American Studies (U.S.A.)
MALDEF	Mexican American Legal Defense and Educational Fund
Malév	Hungarian Airlines
MALÉV	Magyar Légikozlekedési Vállalat
MALIGAZ	Société Malienne des Gaz Industriels
MALRY	Malaysian Leprosy Relief Association
MAM	Medical Association of Malta
MAM	Museo de Arte Moderno (Mexico)
MAMA	Meet-a-Mum Association
MAMAA	Mothers Against Murder and Aggression
MAMBO	Mediterranean Association for Marine Biology and Oceanography
MAMDC	Multipurpose Arthritis and Muscoskeletal Diseases Center (U.S.A.)
MAMSA	Managing and Marketing Sales Association
MAMSER	Mass Mobilisation for Self Reliance, Social Justice and Economic Recovery (Nigeria)
MAN	Mandato de Acción y Unidad Nacional (Bolivia)
MAN	Manufacturers Association of Nigeria
MAN	Mouvement pour une Alternative Nonviolente (France)
MAN	Movimentu Antiyas Nobo (Netherlands Antilles)
MAN	Movimiento de Acción Nacional (Chile)
MAN	Movimiento de Acción Nacionalista (Uruguay)

MANA	Malawi News Agency	**MAPP**	Moskovskaia Assotᶜiatsiia Proletarskikh Pisatelei
MANA	Music Advisers National Association		
MANA	Musicians Against Nuclear Arms	**MAPRIAL**	Mezhdunarodnaia Assotsiatsiia Professorov Russkogo Iazyka i Literatury
MANATEX	Manufacture Nationale Textile (Morocco)		
MANH	Mouvement Autonomiste des Nouvelles Hébrides	**MAPS**	Middle Atlantic Planetarium Society (U.S.A.)
MANLA	Malawi National Liberation Army	**MAPS**	Mouvement d'Action Politique et Social (Switzerland)
MANR	Ministry of Agriculture and Natural Resources (Nigeria)	**MAPW**	Medical Association for the Prevention of War (*now* MEDACT)
MANU	Makedonska Akademija na Naukite i Umetnostite	**MAR**	Mouvement d'Action Rurale
MANU-CACIG	Manufacture Centrafricane de Cigares	**MAR**	Movimiento de Acción Revolucionaria (Mexico)
MANU-CONGO	Société Congolaise de Manutention	**MARA**	Majlis Amanah Rakyat (Malaysia)
MANU-TECNICA	Empresa Nacional de Manutenção (Angola)	**MARAIR-MED**	Maritime Air Forces Mediterranean (NATO)
MANZ	Medical Association of New Zealand	**MARBA**	Mid-American Regional Bargaining Association
MAO	Movimiento de Autodefensa Obrera (Colombia)	**MARC**	Maastricht Referendum Campaign
MAOL	Matemaattisten Aineiden Opettajien Liitto	**MARC**	Methodist Archives & Research Centre
MAOTE	Magyar Altalános Orvosok Tudományos Egyesülete	**MARC**	Micronesian Area Research Center – University of Guam
MAP	Management Association of the Philippines	**MARC**	Mining and Reclamation Council of America
MAP	Manufacture Abijanaise de Plastiques (Ivory Coast)	**MARC**	Missions Advanced Research and Communication Center (U.S.A.)
MAP	Medical Aid for the Palestinians	**MARC**	Monitoring and Assessment Research Center (U.S.A.)
MAP	Mediterranean Action Plan = MEDU		
MAP	Middle Atmosphere Programme	**MARC**	Movimiento Agrario Revolucionario del Campesinado Boliviano
MAP	Movimiento de Acción Popular (Mexico)	**Marcelline**	Suore di Santa Marcellina
MAP-ML	Movimiento de Acción Popular – Marxista Leninista (Nicaragua)	**MARCH**	National Association for Mental After-Care in Residential Care Homes
MAP-TV	Memory – Archives – Programmes	**MARCO-GAZ**	Organisation de l'Industrie du Gaz Canalise du Marché Commun
MAPA	Mexican American Political Association		
MAPA	Ministerio de Agricultura, Pescas y Alimentacion	**MARDB**	Mountain Agricultural Resources Development Bureau (Taiwan)
MAPAM	United Workers Party	**MARDEC**	Malaysian Rubber Development Corporation
MAPBIN	Mauritian Action for Promotion of Breast-Feeding and Infant Nutrition	**MARDI**	Malaysian Agricultural Research and Development Institute
MAPDA	Mid-America Periodical Distributors Association (U.S.A.)	**MAREWA**	Movimenti de Apoio à Resistência Waimiri-Atroari (Brazil)
MAPI	Machinery and Allied Products Institute (U.S.A.)	**MARI**	Microelectronics Application Research Institute
MAPI	Mitsubishi Atomic Power Industries (Japan)	**MARIF**	Malang Research Institute for Food Crops (Indonesia)
MAPP	Mezhdunarodnaia Assotsiatsiya v Podderzhku Perestroiki = IASP	**MARIN**	Maritiem Research Instituut Nederland
		MARIN-ALG	World Association of Seaweed Processors (France)

MARINCO	Arabian Marine Petroleum Company (Saudi Arabia)
MARINCO	Marketing International Consultants
MARINTEK	Norsk Marinteknisk Forskningsinstitutt a.s.
MARKFED	Punjab State Co-operative Supply and Marketing Federation (India)
MARM	Mensa Animal Rights Movement
MARPIC	Marine Pollution Information Centre
MARQUES	Association of European Trade Mark Proprietors
MARSA	Microfilm Association of the Republic of South Africa
MARSAV-CO	Compagnie des Margarines, Savons et Cosmétiques au Zaïre
MARSIM	International Conference on Marine Simulation
MARU	Medical Architecture Research Unit
MARU	Middle America Research Unit
MAS	Malaysian Airline System = MH
MAS	Manchester Astronomical Society
MAS	Microbeam Analysis Society
MAS	Military Agency for Standardization (NATO)
MAS	Mississippi Academy of Sciences
MAS	Monetary Authority of Singapore
MAS	Money Advice Scotland
MAS	Movimiento al Socialismo (Argentina, Mexico, Venezuela)
MAS	Movimiento de Acción Socialista (Peru)
MAS	Muerte a Secuestradros (Colombia)
MASA	Mail Advertising Service Association International (U.S.A.)
MASA	Medical Association of South Africa
MASC	Movimiento Agrario Social-Cristiano (Venezuela)
MASEAN	Medical Association of South East Asian Nations
MASI	Media Association of the Solomon Islands
MASI	Molinera Argentina Sociedad Industrial
MASPEC	Istituto Materiali Speciali per Elettronica e Magnetismo (Italy)
MASPED	Magyar Altalános Szállátumányozási Vállalat
MASS	Money Advice Support Services
MaST	Management and Skills Training
MASTA	Medical Advisory Service for Travellers Abroad
MASU	Mediterranean and African Society of Ultrasound (France)
MAT	Magyar Allerológiai Társaság
MAT	Magyar Aluminiumipari Troszt
MAT	Ministerio de Administración Territorial
MAT-SULFUR	Companhia do Materiais Sulfurosos (Brazil)
MATA	Museums Association of Tropical Africa
MATAC	Money Advice Trust Advisory Committee
MATCH	Mothers Apart from their Children
MATE	Méréstecknikai és Automatizélási Tudományos Egyesület
MATEL-AFRIC	Matériel Électrique Africain (Senegal)
MATELCA	Société Marocaine de Telecommunications par Cable Sous-marin (Morocco)
MATELO	Maritime Air-Radio Telegraph Organization (RAF)
MATEX	Manufacturera Textil, S.A. (El Salvador)
MATFA	Meat and Allied Trades Federation of Australia
MATFORM	Syndicat des Constructeurs Français de Matériel pour la Transformation des Matières Plastiques et du Caoutchouc
MATFORSK	Norwegian Food Research Institute
MATIF	Marché à Terme des Instruments Financiers
MATRA	Mauritanienne de Transit Transport Representation Assurances
MATRANS	Société Matériels et Transports (Ivory Coast)
MATSA	Managerial, Administrative, Technical and Supervisory Association (GMBATU)
MATTRA	Société Mauritanienne de Transit, Transport Représentation et Assurances
MAUK	Mining Association of the United Kindgom
MAUR-ÉLEC	Société d'Eau d'Électricité
MAURINAP	Société Mauritanienne de Diffusion d'Appareils Électriques
MAUS	Movimiento de Acción y Unidad Socialista (Mexico)
MAV	Magyar Allamvasutak
MAV	Verband der Münzautomatenwirtschaft

MAVAD	Magyar Vadkereskedelmi Szövetkezeti Vállalat
MAVEG	Materiae Vegetabiles (Netherlands)
MAVOCI	Manufacture Voltaïque de Cigarettes (Burkina Faso)
MAW	Młodziezowa Agencja Wydawnicza
MAW	Mauritius Alliance of Women
MAWEV	Verband der Maschinen- und Werkzeughändler (Austria)
MAYASA	Minas de Almaden y Arrayanes, S.A.
MAYC	Methodist Association of Youth Clubs
MAZsiHiSz	Magyarországi Zsidó Hitközségek Szövetsége (Hungary) = AHJRC
MB	Muslim Brotherhood (Jordan)
MBA	Malta Broadcasting Authority
MBA	Management Buy-out Association
MBA	Marine Biological Association of the United Kingdom
MBA	Master Builders' Association (South Africa)
MBAA	Master Brewers Association of the Americas
MBAUK	Marine Biological Association of the United Kingdom
MBC	Mediterranean Burns Club
MBC	Middle East Broadcasting Centre
MBC	Mountain Bike Club
MBC	Munhwa Broadcasting Corporation (Republic of Korea)
MBCA	Ministero per i Beni Culturali e Ambientali
MBD	Mezhdunarodnoie Biuro Prosveshchenie = BIE, IBE, OIE
MBDA	Metal Building Dealers Association (U.S.A.)
MBES	Mezhdunarodnyi Bank Ekonomicheskogo Sotrudnichestva = BICE, IBEC
MBF	Multiple Births Foundation
MBF	Musicians' Benevolent Fund
MBFT	Magyar Biofizikai Társaság
MBG	Mission Biologique du Gabon
MBGT	Mezhdunarodnoie Biuro po Gornoi Teplofizike (WMC) (Russia) = BIPTM, IBBW, IBMT
MBH	Movimiento de Bases Hayistas (Peru)
MBIA	Malting Barley Improvement Association (U.S.A.)
MBL	Movimiento Bolivia Libre
MBLE	Manufacture Belge de Lampes et de Materiel Électronique (Belgium)
MBMA	Master Boiler Makers' Association (U.S.A.)
MBMA	Metal Building Manufacturers Association (U.S.A.)
MBMGP	Mezhdunarodnoie Biuro po Mekhanike Gornykh Porod (WMC) = BIMT, IBG, IBSM, OIMR
MBO	Liberal Bosnian Organization
MBO	Muslim Bosnian Organization / Muslimanska Bošnjačka Organizacija (Bosnia – Herzegovina)
MBOA	Motor Barge Owners Association
MBOR	Międzynarodowy Bank Odbudowy i Rozwoju
MBP	Międzynarodowe Biuro Pracy
MBPM	Maurice Bishop Patriotic Movement (Grenada)
MBPP	Movimiento Blanco Popular y Progresista (Uruguay)
MBR	Minerações Brasileiras Reunidas S.A.
MBRC	Marine Biology Research Centre (Canada)
MBS	Malta Board of Standards
MBS	Manchester Business School
MBS	Mutual Broadcasting System (U.S.A.)
MBSI	Musical Box Society International
MBSOGB	Musical Box Society of Great Britain
MBSz	Magyarországi Bolgárok Szövetsége (Hungary) = FBH
MBT	Magyar Biológiai Társaság
MBW	Międzynarodowe Biuro Wychowania
MBW	Movement for a Better World = MMM
MC	Consolata Missionary Sisters
MC	Department of Mass Communication (France)
MC	Manganese Center (U.S.A.)
MC	Manpower Council (Northern Ireland)
MC	Ministère de la Coopération
MC	Movimiento Comunista
MCA	Malaysian Commercial Association (U.K.)
MCA	Malaysian-Chinese Association (Malaysia, U.S.A.)
MCA	Management Consultancies Association
MCA	Marché Commun Arabe (Jordan) = ACM
MCA	Marquee Contractors Association (*now* SEMCA)

MCA	Mason Contractors Association of America
MCA	Master Carvers Association
MCA	Master Craftsman's Association
MCA	Meat Carriers Association
MCA	Medical Council on Alcoholism
MCA	Medicines Control Agency
MCA	Microfilming Corporation of America
MCA	Milling Cutter and Toolbit Association
MCA	Motor Cycle Association (*now* MCIA)
MCA	Mug Collectors' Association
MCA	UK Module Constructors Association
MCAA	Mechanical Contractors Association of America
MCAC	Marché Commun de l'Amérique Centrale; Mercado Común de la América Central = CACM, MCCA
MCANW	Medical Campaign Against Nuclear Weapons (*now* MEDACT)
MCAP	Medical Commission on Accident Prevention
MCASz	Magyar Cigányok Antifasiszta Szervezete (Hungary) = AFOHG
MCB	Management Center do Brazil
MCBA	Magnesite Chrome Brickmakers Association
MCBSF	Mixed Commission for Black Sea Fisheries (FAO)
MCC	Manufacturers Camérounaises du Caoutchouc
MCC	Marylebone Cricket Club
MCC	Mennonite Central Committee (U.S.A.)
MCC	Moscow Coordinating Council
MCC	Motor Caravanners' Club
MCCA	Conference of the Methodist Church in the Caribbean and the Americas
MCCA	Mercado Común Centroamericano = CACM, MCAC
MCCA	Minor Counties Cricket Association
MCCC	Maghreb Community Consultative Committee (Morocco)
MCCC	Marie Curie Cancer Care
MCCI	Missionarii Comboniani Cordis Iesu
MCCIM	Malaysian National Chamber of Commerce and Industry
MCCM	Movimiento Contra el Cáncer Marxista (Chile)
MCCN	Marine and Coastal Community Network
MCCO	Mercado Común del Caribe Oriental
MCD	Movement for Christian Democracy
MCD	Movimiento por el Cambio Democrático (Mexico)
MCDSz	Magyarországi Cigányok Demokratikus Szövetsége (Hungary) = DAHG
MCE	Management Centre Europe
MCE	Mercado Común Europeo = CEE, EEC, EEG, EOF, EOK, EWG
MCE	Moscow Commodity Exchange
MCE	Movimiento Comunista de España
MCEI	Marketing Communication Executives International (U.S.A.)
MCESDG	Movement for the Cultural, Educational, and Social Development of Gypsies (Bulgaria) = DKOSRTs
MCF	Movement for Colonial Freedom
MCFFA	Ministerial Council of Forestry, Fisheries and Aquaculture (Australia)
MCFTU	Mauritius Confederation of Free Trade Unions
MCG	Mains Cable Group
MCHAP	Maternal and Child Health Association of the Philippines
MCI	Mercado Común Iberoamericano
MCI	Mother and Child International = IAMANEH
MCI	Mountaineering Council of Ireland
MCIA	Motor Cycle Industry Association Ltd (*ex* MCA)
MCIE	Midland Counties Institution of Engineers
MCIS	Maison du Commerce International de Strasbourg
MCK	Międzynarodwy Czerwony Krzyz
MCL	Movement for Compassionate Living
MCL	Movimiento Cristiano dei Lavoratori
MCLA	Monetary Centre for Latin America
MCLN	Mouvement Centrafricain pour la Libération Nationale (Central African Republic)
MCM	Ministerial Council Meeting (OECD)
MCMI	Ministry of the Coal Mining Industry (Russia)
MCN	Movimiento de Conciliación Nacional (Dominican Republic)
MCNTI	Mezhdunarodniy Tsentr Nauchnoi i Tekhnicheskoi Informatsii = CIPIST, ICSTI
MCNU	Magyarországi Cigányok Nemzetiségi Uniója (Hungary) =NCGH

MCofS	Mountaineering Council of Scotland	**MDAA**	Muscular Dystrophy Associations of America
MCP	Magyar Cigány Párt (Hungary) = HGP	**MDAS**	Malt Distillers Association of Scotland
MCP	Malawi Congress Party	**MDB**	Movimento Democrático Brasileiro
MCP	Malaysian Communist Party	**MDB**	Multilateral Development Bank
MCP	Medical Campaign Project	**MDBC**	Murray-Darling Basin Commission
MCP	Mouvement Chrétien pour la Paix = CFD, CMP, ICVD	**MDBMC**	Murray-Darling Basin Ministerial Council
MCPS	Mechanical Copyright Protection Society	**MDC**	Malawi Development Corporation
		MDC	Malta Development Corporation
MCR	Movimiento Comunista Revolucionario (Argentina)	**MDC**	Management Development Centre (Sudan)
MCR	Movimiento de Campesinos Revolucionarios (Chile)	**MDC**	Merseyside Development Corporation
		MDC	Mint Directors Conference
MCRF	Motorcykelbranschens Riksförbund	**MDC**	Mwanachi Development Corporation (Tanzania)
MCRIAISC	Mine Company's Research Institute of Anshan Iron and Steel Complex	**MDD**	Międzynarodowy Dzień Dziecka
MCRSSA	Mid Cold Rolled Steel Strip Association	**MDDUS**	Medical & Dental Defence Union of Scotland
MCS	Malaysian Civil Service		
MCS	Marine Conservation Society	**MDE**	Dansk Ejendomsmaeglerforening
MCS	Marriage Counselling Service (Éire)	**MDF**	Magyar Democratic Forum
MCS	Mechanical Cultivation Services (Greece)	**MDF**	Magyar Demokrata Fórum (Hungary) = HDF
MCS	Military College of Science	**MDF**	Manic Depression Fellowship
MCS	Mountaineering Council of Scotland	**MDF**	Meubles de France (Ivory Coast)
MCSE	Magyar Csillagászati Egyesület = HAA	**MDFRC**	Murray-Darling Freshwater Research Centre
MCSI	HM Magistrates' Courts Service Inspectorate	**MDFZ**	Mezdunarodnaia Demokraticheskaia Federatsiia Zhenshchin = FDIF, FDIM, IDFF, WIDF
MCSIB	Management Consulting Services Information Bureau (BIM)		
MCSU	Melkcontrolestation Utrecht	**MDG**	Major Donors Group
MCSzP	Magyar Cigány Szociáldemokrata Párt (Hungary) = HGSDP	**MDG**	Mezhregionalnaia Deputatskaia Gruppa
MCT	Missão de Combate as Tripanosomiasis	**MDHA**	Masters of Deerhounds Association
MCTA	Milling Cutter and Toolbit Association	**MDI**	Muscular Dystrophy Ireland
MCU	Mauritius Cooperative Union	**MDLC**	Movement in Defence of the Liberian Constitution
MCU	Modern Churchpeople's Union		
MCWAP	Maternity and Child Welfare Association of Pakistan	**MDM**	Mass Democratic Movement (South Africa)
MCZ	Museum of Comparative Zoology, Harvard University	**MDN**	Mobilisation pour le Développement National (Haiti)
MD	Mouvement des Démocrates	**MDN**	Movimiento Democrático Nacional (Colombia)
MDA	Maize Development Association		
MDA	Medical Devices Agency	**MDN**	Movimiento Democrático Nicaragüense
MDA	Millinery Distributors Association	**MDP**	Malta Democratic Party = PDM
MDA	Mine Design Association (China)	**MDP**	Milliyetçi Demokrasi Partisi (Turkey)
MDA	Mouvement pour la Démocratie en Algérie	**MDP**	Mongolian Democratic Party
		MDP	Mouvement de la Paix
MDA	Museum Documentation Association	**MDP**	Mouvement Démocratique Populaire (Senegal)
MDA	Music Distributors Association (U.S.A.)		

MDP	Movimento Democrático Português
MDP	Movimiento Democrático Peruano
MDP	Movimiento Democrático Popular (Chile)
MDP	Muslim Democratic Party (Bosnia – Herzegovina) = MDS
MDPA	Mines Domaniales de Potasse d'Alsace
MDPNE	Ministère de la Protection de la Nature et de l'Environnement
MDPS	Movement for Democracy and Progress
MDR	Ministério Desenvolvimento Regional (Brazil)
MDRA	Mouvement Démocratique du Renouveau Algérien
MDRC	Manpower Demonstration Research Corporation (U.S.A.)
MDS	Mouvement des Démocrates Socialistes (Tunisia)
MDS	Movement for a Democratic Slovakia = HDS
MDS	Muslimanska Demokratska Stranka (Bosnia-Herzegovina) = MDP
MDSPJ	Movement for Democracy, Social Progress and Justice (Belarus)
MDT	Moviment de Defensa de la Terra
MDU	Medical Defence Union
MDU	Mongolian Democratic Union
MDUSSE	Manufacturers of Domestic Unvented Supply Systems Equipment
MÉ	Ministère de l'Économie
MÉ	Ministère de l'Éducation
ME	Mouvement Européen = EM
ME	Myalgic Encephalomyelitis Association
ME-TUR-EX	Mediterranean Tourism Fair (Turkey)
MEA	Marketing Executives Association of Belgium
MEA	Medical Equestrian Association
MEA	Middle East Airlines (Lebanon)
MEA	Middle East Association
MEA	Myalgic Encephalomyelitis Association
MEAC	Manufacturing Engineering Applications Center (U.S.A.)
MEAG	Mayo Environmental Awareness Group (Éire)
MÉAN	Mission d'Étude et d'Aménagement du Niger (Nigeria)
MEASE	Middle East Association of Science Editors (IFSE)
MEAU	Missão de Estudos Agronómicos do Ultramar
MEAUP	Missão de Estudos Apícolas do Ultramar Portugues
MEB	Movimento de Educação de Base (Brazil)
MEBCO	Middle East Banking Company (Lebanon)
MEBPA	Missão de Estudos Broceanólogicas e de Pesca de Angola
MEC	Microbiological Education Committee
MEC	Mineral Exploration Company (India)
MEC	Ministério de Educação e Cultura (Brazil)
MEC	Ministerio de Educación y Ciencia
MEC	Movimiento Emergente de Concordia (Guatemala)
MEC	Music Education Council
MECA	Medical Eye Centre Association
MECANEM-BAL	Société Africaine d'Emballages Métalliques (Ivory Coast)
MECAS	Middle East Centre for Arab Studies
MECC	Middle East Council of Churches = CEMO
MECCA	Missionary and Ecumenical Council of The Church Assembly
MechE	Institute of Mechanical Engineers = IME
MECON	Metallurgical and Engineering Consultants (India)
MECON	Mideast Constructors Limited (Qatar)
MECV	Ministère de l'Environnement et Cadre de Vie
MEDACT	Medical Action for Global Security (ex MCANW, MAPW)
MEDC	Microelectronics Educational Development Centre
MEDI	Marine Environmental Data Information Referral System (IOC)
MEDIA-CULT	International Institute for Audio-Visual Communication and Cultural Development (Austria)
MEDICA-EURO-PRESS	Comité Permanent de la Presse Médicale Européenne
MEDICOR	Centre for Offshore and Remote Medicine (Canada)
MEDIF	Medicinalimportorforening
MEDISPA	Medical Sterile Products Association
MEDO	International Institute "Mater Ecclesiae Domesticae" (Netherlands)

MEDOSZ	Magyar Mezögazdasági, Erdészeti és Vizügyi Dologozók Szakszervezete	**MEMA**	Marine Engine and Equipment Manufacturers' Association
MEDTAP	Battle Medical Technology Assessment & Policy Research Centre	**MEMAC**	Machinery and Equipment Manufacturers Association of Canada
MEDU	Mediterranean Action Plan = MAP	**MEMAC**	Marine Emergency Mutual Aid Centre (ROPME)
MEE	Magyar Elektrotechnikai Egyesület		
MEECI	Mechanical and Electrical Engineering Construction Industry	**MEMACO**	Metal Marketing Corporation (Zambia)
		MEMCH	Movimiento Pro Emancipacion de la Mujer Chilena
MEEI	Hungarian Institute for Testing and Certification of Electrical Equipment	**MEMIC**	Medical Microbiology Interdisciplinary Commission (Japan)
MEEMA	Marine Engine & Equipment Manufacturers' Association	**MEMIN**	Mediterranean Environmental Management Training Network (UNDP)
MEETA	Maintenance Energy and Environment Technology Association (Éire)	**MEMMI**	Mém Müszaki Intézet
MEEU	Missão de Estudos Económicos do Ultramar	**MEMO**	Middle East Media Operations Limited (Cyprus)
MEF	Malaysian Employers Federation	**MEMOR-IAL**	"Memorial" – Vsesoiuznoe Dobrovolnoe Istoriko-Prosvetitelskoe Obshchestvo
MEF	Maskinentreprenorenes Forbund		
MEF	Mauritius Employers Federation		
MEFA	Foreningen af Danske Medicinfabrikker	**MEN**	Ministerstwo Edukacji Narodowej
Mefasa	Mecanizaciones y Fabricaciones	**MENA**	Middle East News Agency (Egypt)
MEFF	Mercado Español de Futuros Financieros	**MENCAP**	Royal Society for Mentally Handicapped Children and Adults
MEFI	Mezögépfejlesztö Intézet	**MENOFER**	Fédération des Unions Professionnelles des Distributeurs de Métaux Non-Ferreux et Appareils Sanitaires (Belgium)
MEG	Max-Eyth-Gesellschaft für Agrartechnik		
MEG	Movimento Eucaristico Giovanile		
MEG	Münchner Entomologische Gesellschaft		
MEGJR	Mitteleuropäischer Guttempler Jugendrat	**MENS**	Middle East Neurosurgical Society
		MENTEC	Menai Technology Enterprise Centre
MEGS	Meeting of European Geological Societies	**MEOA**	Malaysian Estate Owners Association (Malaysia)
MEH	Mères et Enfants d'Haiti	**MEOC**	Middle East Oil Company
MEHSA	Materiales Electricos de Honduras, S.A.	**MEP**	Movimento Electoral del Pueblo (Venezuela)
MEI	Ministerio de Industria y Energia		
MEIC	Myanma Export-Import Corporation (Burma)	**MEP**	Movimentu Electoral di Pueblo (Aruba)
		MÉP	Société des Missions – Étrangères de Paris
MEIU	Medical Education Information Unit (BIM)		
MEJ	Mouvement Eucharistique des Jeunes = MEG	**MEPA**	Missão de Estudos de Pesca de Angola
		MEPARC	Middle East Policy and Research Center (U.S.A.)
MEKOG	N.V. Maatschappij tot Exploitatie van Kooksovengassen	**MEPC**	Malawi Export Promotion Council
MÉL	Ministère de l'Équipement et du Logement	**MEPC**	Marine Environment Protection Committee (IMO) = CPMM
MEL	Muzika Esperanto-Ligo	**MEPI**	Middle East Peace Institute (Israel)
MELA	Middle East Librarians Association	**MEPP**	Société Mauritanienne d'Entreposage de Produits Pétroliers
MELCO	Mitsubishi Electric Corporation (Japan)		
MELM	Middle East Lutheran Ministry	**MEPRA**	Misión de Estúdios de Patológia Regionál Argentina
MEM	Mondpaca Esperantista Movado = EMWP	**MEPZA**	Mauritius Export Processing Zones Association

MEQ	Quebec Ministry of Environment
MER	Romanian Ecological Movement
MERADO	Mechanical Engineering Research and Development Organization (India)
MERALCO	Manila Electric Company (Philippines)
MERB	Myanmar Education Research Bureau (Myanwar)
MERC	Meat Export Research Center (U.S.A.)
MERC	Music Education Research Council (U.S.A.)
MERCA-TOR	European Network for Information, Documentation and Research on Regional and Minority Languages and Education
MERCOR-SA	Mercados en Origen de Productos Agrarios, S.A.
MERCO-SUR	Sectorial Committee for the Common Market of the South
MERECEN	Movimiento Estable Republicano Centrista (El Salvador)
MERG	Macroeconomic Research Group (South Africa)
MERI	Mining and Excavation Research Institute (U.S.A.)
MERIP	Middle East Research and Information Project (U.S.A.)
MERL	Materials Engineering Research Laboratory Ltd
MERNU	Missão de Estudo do Rendimento Nacional do Ultramar
MERRCAC	Middle Eastern Radioisotope Centre for the Arab Countries (IAEA)
MERT	Minoségi Ellenorzo Rt
MERU	Maharishi European Research University
MERU	Mechanical Engineering Research Unit (South Africa)
MERU	Medical Engineering Research Unit
MES	Malaysian Economic Society
MES	Minerals Engineering Society
MES	Movimento de Esquerda Socialista (Portugal)
MESA	Marine Education Society of Australia
MESA	Middle East Studies Association of North America
MESC	Middle East Solidarity Council (Turkey)
MESC	Ministry of Education Science and Culture (Japan)
MESCO	Middle East Science Co-operation Office (UNESCO)
MESIRES	Ministère de l'Enseignement Supérieur de l'Informatique et de la Recherche Scientifique (Cameroon)
MESOT	Middle East Society for Organ Transplantation
MESPF	Malaysian Estates Staff Provident Fund
MESR	Mysore Engineering Research Station (India)
MESRS	Ministry of Higher Education and Scientific Research (Algeria)
MESS	Türkiye Metal Sanayicileri Sendikai
MESZ	Magyar Epitómüvészek Szövetsége
MET	Medical Educational Trust
META	Model Engineering Trade Association
METAN-GOL	Empresa Angolana de Embalagens
METAROM	Romanian Agency for Foreign Trade
METASA	Metales y Estructuras S.A. (Nicaragua)
METCOM	Mechanical & Metal Trades Confederation
Metcon	Metal & Mechanical Confederation
MÉTE	Magyar Élelmezésipari Tudományos Egyesület
METEOSAT	European Organisation for the Development of Meteorological Satellites
METLA	Finnish Forest Research Institute (Finland)
METO	Metsäalan Toimihenkilöliitto
METRO-BER	Metró Közlekedésztési és Beruházási Vállalat
Metropolis	World Association of the Major Metropolises (France)
METROVIN	Société Métropolitaine des Vins
METU	Middle East Technical University (Turkey)
MEUC	Major Energy Users' Council
MEV	Mikroelektronikai Vállalat
MEVA	Missão Evangélica de Amazônia (Brazil)
MEWAC	Mediterranean Europe, West Africa Conference
MEWU	Metals and Engineering Workers' Union (Australia)
MEXE	Military Engineering Experimental Establishment
MEXICANA	Compania Mexicana de Aviación
MEZÖGÉP	Mezögazdasági és Élelmiszeripari Gépgyártó Vállalat
MEZU	Missão de Estudos Zoológicos do Ultramar

MF	Magazines for Friendship (U.S.A.)
MF	Ministero delle Finanze
MF	Ministerstwo Finansów
MF	Morris Federation
MFA	Maize and Forage Association
MFA	Menningar-og Frædslusamband Althýdu (Iceland)
MFA	Metal Finishing Association
MFA	Motor Factors Association (now ADF)
MFALDA	Marginal Farmers and Agricultural Labourers Development Agency (India)
MFAR	Maison Familiale d'Apprentissage Rural
MFBRO	Międzynarodowa Federacja Bojowników Ruchu Oporu
MFC	Movimiento Familiar Cristiano (Uruguay)
MFD	Malerforbundet i Danmark
MFD	Mennonietischer Freiwilligen Dienst
MFDC	Mouvement des Forces Démocratiques de Casamania
MFDS	Movement for a Democratic Slovakia
MFE	Magyar Fogorvosok Egyesülete
MFE	Magyar Fögorvosok Egyesülete
MFE	Mouvement Fédéraliste Européen
MFECS	Mediterranean Far East Container Service
MFHA	Masters of Foxhounds Association
MFI	Malmö Flygindustri
MFJ	Movement for Freedom and Justice (Ghana)
MFKI	Müszaki Fizikai Kutató Intézet
MfL	Movement for London
MFLA	Midwest Federation of Library Associations
MFM/MKM	Mouvement pour le Pouvoir Prolétarien/Monoma Ka Mivimbio (Madagascar)
MFME	Movement for Middle England
MFME	Verband der Führungskräfte der Metall- und Electroindustrie
MFMI	Men for Missions International (U.S.A.)
MFO	Multinational Force and Observers
MFP	Maremathou Freedom Party (Lesotho)
MFP	Mothers For Peace
MFPA	Mouth and Foot Painting Artists
MFPB	Malta Federation of Professional Bodies
MFPC	Man-made Fibres Producers' Committee
MFQ	Mouvement Français pour la Qualité

MFR	Movement for Freedom and Rights (Bulgaria)
MFR	Movement for Romania = MPR
MFRA	Multiple Food Retailers Association
MFSA	Metal Finishing Suppliers Assiciation (U.S.A.)
MFSM	Międzynarodowa Federacja Schronisk Młodziezowych
MFT	Magyar Farmakolóiai Társaság
MFT	Magyar Földrajzi Társaság
MFT	Medizinischer Fakultätentag der Bundesrepublik Deutschland
MFT	Svensk Föreningen för Medicinsk Fysik och Teknik
MFTI	Moscow Institute of Physics and Technology
MFVPA	Music, Film and Videotape Producers Association
MFVRC	Mezhdunarodniy Fond za Vyzhivaniie i Razvitiie Chelovechestva
MG	Mainosgrafikot
MG	Meibion Glyndwr
MG	Misioneros de Guadalupe
MGA	Ministerio de Ganaderia y Agricultura (Uruguay)
MGA	Missão Geográfica de Angola
MGA	Mushroom Growers Association (U.K., U.S.A.)
MGA	Myasthenia Gravis Association (ex BAM)
MGAGB	Mounted Games Association of Great Britain
MGC	Museums and Galleries Commission
MGE	Magyar Geofizikusok Egyesület
MGE	Mouvement Gauche Européenne
MGF	Musikkgrossistenes Förening
MGFHU	Missão de Geográfia Fisica e Humana do Ultramar
MGGGS	Midland Geranium, Glasshouse and Garden Society
MGI	Mapping and Geography Institute (Ethiopia)
MGI	Marine Geological Institute of Indonesia
MGiE	Ministerstwo Górnictwa i Energetyki
MGIMO	Moskovskii Gosudarstvenny Institut Mezhdunarodnykh Otnoshenii
MGK	Ministerstwo Gospodarki Komunalnej
MGM	Magasins Gabonais de Vêtements
MGM	Magyar Gördüloisapágy Muvek

MGM	Metro Goldwyn Meyer (U.S.A.)	**MHS**	Military Historical Society
MGM	Missão Geografica de Moçambique	**MHSz**	Magyarországi Horvátok Szövetsége (Hungary) = CDAH
MGMI	Mining, Geological and Metallurgical Institute of India	**MHT**	Magyar Hidrológiai Társaság
MGMR	Ministry of Geology and Mineral Resources (China)	**MHW**	Ministry of Health and Welfare (Japan)
MGN	Mirror Group Newspapers	**MHWiU**	Ministerstwo Handlu Wewnętrznego i Usług
MGP	Mouvement Gaulliste Populaire	**MHZ**	Ministerstwo Handlu Zagranicznego
MGPiB	Ministerstwo Gospodarki Przestrzennej i Budownictwa	**MI**	Militia Immaculatae
		MI	Ministère de l'Industrie
MGR	Marina de Guerra Revolucionaria (Cuba)	**MI**	Mondharmoniga Instituto (Italy)
		MI	Multimedia International Corporation
MGR	Mouvement de le Gauche Reformatrice	**MI**	Ordo Clericorum Regularium Ministratium Infirmis "Camilliani"
MGS	Malta Geographical Society		
MGS	Movimiento Giovanile Salesiano = MJS, SYM	**MIA**	Maldive International Airlines
		MIA	Malleable Ironfounders' Association
MGU	Moskovskii Gosudarstvennyi Universitet	**MIA**	Malta Institute of Accountants
		MIA	Manitoba Institute of Agrologists (Canada)
MGyT	Magyar Gyermekorvosok Társasága		
MGYT	Magyar Gyógyszerészeti Társaság	**MIA**	Manufacture Ivoirienne d'Ameublement
MGZMK	Mitteldeutsche Gesellschaft für Zahn-, Mund und Kieferheilkunde zu Erfurt e.V.	**MIA**	Marine Industries Association (U.S.A.)
		MIA	Maritime Information Association (*ex* MLA)
MH	Malaysian Airline System = MAS		
MH	Musiklärarnas Riksförening	**MIA**	Meetings Industry Association
MHA	Manila Hemp Association	**MIA**	Music Industries Association
MHA	Mental Health Association (Éire, U.S.A.)	**MIAA**	Missão de Inquerítos Agricólas de Angola
MHAC	Mental Health Act Commission	**MIAC**	Manufacturing Industries Advisory Council (Australia)
MHEA	Mechanical Handling Engineers Association		
		MIAF	Mauritanian Islamic Air Force
MHEDA	Material Handling Equipment Distributors Association (U.S.A.)	**MIAG**	Matériel Industriel et Automobile Gabonais
MHFC	Mental Health Film Council	**MIAM**	Fédération Nationale du Matériel Industriel, Agricole et Ménager en Bois
MHG	Materialhenteringsgruppen inom Sveriges Mekanförbund		
		MIAM	Manufacture Ivoirienne d'Articles de Ménage
MHI	Materials Handling Institution (China)		
MHM	Mental Health Media	**MIAMSI**	Mouvement International d'Apostolat des Milieux Sociaux Indépendants
MHM	Societas Missionariorum Sancti Joseph de Mill Hill		
		MIAS	Marine Information and Advisory Service (IOS)
MHN	Museo Histórico Nacionál (Argentina)		
MHO	Metropolitan Home Ownership	**MIAT**	Mongolian Civil Air Transport
MHP	Milliyetçi Hareket Partisi (Turkey) = NAP	**MIATCO**	Mid-America International Agri-Trade Council
MHRA	Modern Humanities Research Association	**MIB**	Metal Information Bureau
		MIB	Motor Insurers' Bureau
MHS	Malta Heraldic Society	**MIB**	Mustard Information Bureau (U.S.A.)
MHS	Malta Historical Society	**MIBA**	Société Minière de Bakwanga (Zaïre)
MHS	Meat Hygiene Service	**MIBCI**	Manufacture de Brosserie de Côte d'Ivoire

MIC	Congregatio Clericorum Marianorum sub titulo Immaculatae Conceptionis Beatae Virginis Mariae		**MIDA**	Movimiento de Integración Democrática (Dominican Republic)
MIC	Dansk Musik Informations Center		**MIDADE**	Mouvement International d'Apostolat des Enfants = IMAC
MIC	Magnesium Industry Council		**MIDADEN**	Movimiento Internacional de Apostolado de los Niños = IMAC
MIC	Malaysian-Indian Congress			
MIC	Materials Information Centre		**MIDAS**	Meat Industry Development and Advisory Service (ARC/MLC)
MIC	Military Industries Commission (Iraq)			
MIC	Millinery Information Centre		**MIDC**	Metal Industries Development Centre (Taiwan)
MIC	Movimento Italiano di Cultura			
MIC	Movimiento de Integracion Colorada (Paraguay)		**MIDCOM**	Centre for the Development of the Metals Industry of Malaysia
MICAUCB	Ministero dell'Industria de Commercio e dell'Artigianto Ufficio Centrale Brevetti		**MIDEC**	Middle East Industrial Development Projects Corporation
			MIDEM	Marché International du Disque et de l'Édition Musicale
MICCAO	Ministère Chrétien Commun en Afrique Occidentale = JCMWA		**MIDEVIV**	Mission de Développement des Semences et des Cultures Vivrières Maraîchères et Fruitières Autour des Centres Urbains (Cameroon)
MICCI	Malaysian International Chamber of Commerce and Industry			
MICE	Manufacture Ivoirienne de Confection Enfantine		**MIDF**	Malaysian Industrial Development Finance
MICE	Ministerio de Comercio Exterior (El Salvador, Nicaragua)		**MIDH**	Mouvement pour l'Instauration de la Démocratie en Haiti
MICEB	Missão Cristão Evangélica do Brasil		**MIDIA**	Media Information Department of Islamic Afghanistan
MICI	Manufacture d'Imprimerie et de Cartonnage Ivoirienne		**MIDIRS**	Midwives Information and Resource Service
MICOIN	Ministerio de Comercio Interior (Nicaragua)		**MIDIST**	Mission Interministérielle d'Information Scientifique et Technique
MICONS	Ministerio de la Construccion (Cuba, Nicaragua)		**MIDRA**	Mouvement International contre Toutes les Formes de Discrimination et le Racisme (Japan) = IMADR
MICRO	Microelectronics Innovation and Computer Science Research Program (U.S.A.)			
			MIDS	Madras Institute of Development Studies (India)
MICRO	Multinational Initiative for the Use of Computers in Research Organisations		**MIE**	Ministerio de Industria y Energía
MICTQ	Quebec Ministry of Industry, Trade and Technology		**MIE**	Mouvement International Pro-Esperanto
MICUMA	Société des Mines de Cuivre de Mauritanie		**MIE**	Mouvement pour l'Indépendance de l'Europe
MID	Ministerstvo Innostrannykh Del (Russia)		**MIEC**	Meteorological Information Extraction Centre (ESOC)
MID	Movimiento de Integracion Democrática (Cuba)		**MIEC**	Moscow International Energy Club (Russia)
MID	Movimiento de Integración y Desarrollo (Argentina)		**MIÉC**	Pax Romana, Mouvement International des Étudiants Catholiques = IMCS
MID	Movimiento Independiente Democrático (Panama)		**MIECC**	Motor Industry Education Consultative Committee
MIDA	Malaysian Industrial Development Authority		**MIEM**	Moscow Institute of Electronic-Mechanical Engineering
MIDA	Ministerio de Desarrollo Agropecuário (Panama)		**MIEU**	Mines and Industries Employees' Union (Afghanistan)

MIF	Miners' International Federation = FIM, IBV	**MIM**	Malaysian Institute of Management
MIF	Motor Industries Federation	**MIM**	Malta Institute of Management
MIF	Task Force on the Multinational Information Framework	**MIM**	Mediterranean Institute of Management (Cyprus)
MIF/IÉS	Mouvement International Faucons – International Éducative Socialiste = IFM/SE	**MIM**	Mouvement Indépendantiste Martiniquais
MIFED	International Film and TV Film Documentary Market	**MIMAF**	Musicians International Mutal Aid Fund (France) = FIEM
MIFERMA	Société Anonyme des Mines de Fer de Mauritanie	**MIMC**	Marconi International Marine Communication Company
MIFERSO	Société des Mines de Fer du Sénégal Oriental	**MIMC**	Ministerio de la Industria de Materiales de la Construccion (Cuba)
MIFIN	Ministerio de Finanzas (Nicaragua)	**MIMO**	Moskovskii Institut Mezhdunarodnykh Otnoshenii
MIFU	Margarine-Industriens Foelles-Udvalg	**MIMOS**	Malaysian Institute of Microelectronic Systems
MIGA	Multilateral Investment Guarantee Agency (IBRD)	**MIMR**	Ma'anchan Institute of Mining Research
MIGB	Millinery Institute of Great Britain	**MIN**	Movimiento de Integración Nacional (Venezuela)
MIGMGMR	Institute of Marine Geology, Ministry of Geology and Mineral Resources (China)	**MIN**	Movimiento de la Izquierda Nacional (Bolivia)
MII	Maritime Institute of Ireland	**MINAG**	Ministry of Agriculture (Cuba)
MII	Mediators' Institute of Ireland	**MINAGRI**	Ministerio de Agricultura (Cuba)
MII	Muslim Intellectuals International (Pakistan)	**MINAL**	Ministerio de la Alimentacion (Cuba)
MIIA	Mouvement contre l'Insécurité et l'Immigration Abusive (Belgium)	**MINAZ**	Ministerio del Azucar (Cuba)
MIIC	Mouvement International des Intellectuels Catholiques = ICMICA	**MINBAS**	Ministerio de la Industria Basica (Cuba)
MIIGA	Moskovskii Institut Inzhenerov Grazhdanskoi Aviatsii	**MINCEX**	Ministerio de Comercio Exterior (Cuba)
MIIGAiK	Moskovskii Institut Inzhenerov Geodezii, Aerofotos'emki i Kartografii	**MINCON-MAR**	Ministerial Conference of West and Central African States on Maritime Transport (Ivory Coast)
MIIVT	Moskovskii Institut Inzhenerov Vodnogo Transporta	**MIND**	National Association for Mental Health
MIIZ	Moskovskii Institut Inzhenerov Zemleustroistva	**MINDECO**	Mining Development Corporation (Zambia)
MIIZhT	Moskovskii Institut Inzhenerov Zheleznodorozhnogo Transporta	**MINED**	Ministerio de Educación (Cuba)
MIJARC	Mouvement International de la Jeunesse Agricole et Rurale Catholique = IMCARY	**MINERO-PERU**	Empresa Minera del Perú
MIJC	Mouvement International des Juristes Catholiques = IMCL	**MINESLA**	Conference of Ministers of Education and those Responsible for the Promotion of Science and Technology in Relation to Development in Latin America and the Caribbean
MIK	Menuiseries Industrielles du Kouilou (Congo)	**MINESPOL**	Conference of Ministers responsible for Science and Technology Policy in the European and North American Region
MIL	Maanmittausinsinöörien Liitto	**MINETRAS**	Syndicat des Constructeurs de Matériels pour Mines et Travaux Souterrains
MILF	Moro Islamic Liberation Front (Philippines)	**MINFAR**	Ministerio de las Fuerzas Armadas (Cuba)
MILSET	International Movement for Leisure Activities in Science & Technology	**MINIL**	Ministerio de la Industria Ligera (Cuba)
		MININT	Ministerio del Interior (Cuba)

Miniusta	Ministerstvo Iustitsii (Belarus)
MINKH	Plekhanov Moscow Institute of the National Economy
MINOM	Mouvement International pour une Nouvelle Muséologie
MINPECO	Empresa Comercializadora de Productos Mineros (Peru)
MINPOREN	National Association of Commercial Broadcasters in Japan
MINRA	Miniature International Racing Association (U.S.A.)
MINREX	Ministerio de Relaciones Exteriores (Cuba)
MINSA	Ministerio de Salud (Cuba)
MINSAP	Ministerio de Salud Publica (Cuba)
MINSE	Ministerio de Seguridad do Estado (Angola)
MINSHATO	Democratic Socialist Party (Japan)
MINTER	Ministério do Interior (Brazil)
MINURSO	Mission des Nations Unies pour le Referendum au Sahel Occidental
MIO	Mediterranean Information Office
MIPA	Manufacture Ivoirienne des Plastiques Africains
MIPCOM	Marché International des Films et des Programmes pour la Télévision, la Vidéo, le Câble et le Satellite
MIPE	Moscow Institute of Power Engineering
MIPEM	Marché International des Professionels de l'Immobilier
MIPI	Madjelis Ilmu Pengetahaun Indonesia
MIPN	Mouvement Italien pour la Protection de la Nature
MIPPT	McMaster Institute for Polymer Production Technology (Canada)
MIPRENUC	Mission Préparatoire des Nations Unies au Cambodge = UNAMIC
MIPSA	Moscow Institute of Painting, Sculpture and Architecture
MIPTC	Men's International Professional Tennis Council
MIPTES	Movimiento Independiente de Profesionales y Técnicos de El Salvador
MIR	Ministère de l'Industrie et de la Recherche
MIR	Mouvement International de la Réconciliation = IFOR
MIR	Mouvement pour l'Indépendance de la Réunion
MIR	Movement for Islamic Revolution (Afghanistan) = HII
MIR	Movimiento de Izquierda Revolucionaria (Bolivia, Chile, Peru, Venezuela)
MIRA	Monterey Institute for Research in Astronomy
MIRA	Motor Industry Research Association
MIRAD	Ministério da Reforma e Desenvolvimento Agrário (Brazil)
MIRAL	Société de Miroiterie et d'Aluminium (Gabon)
MIRCEN	UNEP/UNESCO/ICRO Microbiological Resource Centre (Sweden)
MIRE	Microcomputers in Religious Education
MIRF	Myopia International Research Foundation (U.S.A.)
MIRI	Mitsubishi Sogo Kenkyusho (Japan)
MIRINZ	Meat Industry Research Institute, New Zealand
MIRL	Mechanical Industry Research Laboratories (Taiwan)
MIRN	Movimento Independente da Reconstucão Nacional (Portugal)
MIRO	Mineral Industry Research Organisation
MIRT	Meteorological Institute for Research and Training (Egypt)
MIS	Milieu Information Service (U.S.A)
MIS	Mining Institute of Scotland
MIS	Mobility Information Service
MIS	Movement for an Independent Slovakia = HNS
MISEREOR	Bischöfliches Hilfswerk Misereor
MISIS	Moscow Institute of Steel and Alloys
MISO	Mostra Internazionale Scambi Occidente
MISON	Mezhdunarodnaia Informatsionnaia Sistema Obshchestvennym Naukam
MISR	Makerere Institute of Social Research (Uganda)
MISR	Malawi Institute of Social Research
MISSAMBE	Mission d'Étude d'Aménagement de la Vallée Supérieure de la Benoú (Cameroon)
MISSIO	Internationales Katolisches Missionswerk
MIST	Music In Scotland Trust
MIT	Magyar Immunológiai Társaság = HSI
MIT	Massachusetts Institute of Technology (U.S.A.)
MIT	Society of Management Information Technology

MITA	Microcomputer Industry Trade Association	**MKDH**	Mad'arské Krest'ansodemokratické Hnutie (Slovakia) = HCDM
MITA	Schweizerischer Verband des Mineral- und Tafelwasserhandels	**MKDP**	Meziparlamentní klub demokratické pravice
MITEBI	Manufacture Ivoirienne de Matériaux pour le Bâtiment et l'Industrie	**MKE**	Magyar Kémikusok Egyesülete
MITEX	Federatie van Middenstandsorganisaties in de Textildetailhandel	**MKE**	Magyar Könyvtárosok Egyesülete
		MKFE	Magyarországi Nemzetközi Közúti Fuvarozók Egyesülete
MITI	Ministry for International Trade and Industry (Japan)	**MKhG**	Moskovskaia Khelsinskaia Gruppa
MITKA	Movimiento Indio Tupaj Katari (Bolivia)	**MKI**	Mikroelektronikai Kutató Intézet
MITP	Movimiento Intersindical de Trabajadores de Paraguay	**MKiS**	Ministerstwo Kultury i Sztuki
		MKISZ	Magyar Képzö-és Iparmüvészek Szövetsége
MITRA	Management Institute for Training and Research in Asia	**MKKE**	Magyar Könyvkiadök és Könyvterjesztok Egyesúlése
MITRANS	Ministerio de Transporte	**MKKFiT**	Miejski Komitet Kultury Fizycnej i Turystyki
MIU	Maharishi International University		
MIU	Microalgae International Union	**MKKIR**	Mezhdunarodnyi Koordinatsionnyi Komitet po Immunologii Reproduktsii = ICCIR
MIV	Melk-Inkoop-Vereniging		
MIV	Milchindustrie-Verband	**MKKL**	Moskovskii Klub Kommunistov-Lenintsev
MIVI	Ministerio de Vivienda (Panama)		
MIVICO	Marché International des Villes de Congrès	**MKL**	Maaseutukeskusten Liito
		MKL	Maatalouskeskusten Liitto
MIWAC	Marine and Inland Waters Advisory Committee (ANZECC)	**MKL**	Maskin- og Konstruktions-verkstedenes Landsforening
MIZEN	Metalurski Institut Hasan Brkic, Zenica	**MKMA**	Machine Knife Manufacturers Association (U.S.A.)
MJ	Societas Misionariorum a Sancti Josephi	**MKNS**	Moskovskii Komitet Novykh Sotsialistov
MJA	Medical Journalists Association		
MJA	Movement of Algerian Journalists	**MKO**	Międzyzakładowy Komitet Organizacyjny
MJA	Movimiento de la Juventud Agraria (Uruguay)		
		MKS	Międzyzakładowy Komitet Strajkowy
MJAA	Messianic Jewish Alliance of America	**MKSZ**	Magyar Képzomüvészek Szövetsége
MJAC	Midlands Joint Advisory Council for Environmental Protection	**MKWZZ**	Międzynarodowa Konferencja Wolnych Zwiazków Zawodowych
MJL	Movimiento Juvenil Lautaro (Chile)	**ML**	Ministerstwo Lacznósci
MJR	Markkinointijohdon Ryhmä	**MLA**	Malawi Library Association
MJS	Movimiento Juvenil Salesiano = MGS, SYM	**MLA**	Malta Library Association
		MLA	Manitoba Library Association (Canada)
MJSA	Mouvement des Jeunesses Socialistes Africaines	**MLA**	Marine Librarians Association (U.K., U.S.A.) (*now* MIA)
MJSK	Magyar Jogász Svövetség	**MLA**	Master Locksmiths Association
MJSZ	Magyar Jogász Svövetség	**MLA**	Medical Library Association (U.S.A.)
MK	Ministerstwo Komunikacji	**MLA**	Modern Language Association
MKA	Mezhdunarodnyi Kooperativnyi Alians = ACVI, ICA, IGB	**MLA**	Music Library Association (U.S.A.)
MKBT	Magyar Karszt- és Barlangkutató Társulat	**MLAF**	Mainostajien Liitto Annonsörernas
MKCK	Międzynarodowy Komitet Czerwonego Krzyza	**MLAGB**	Muzzle Loaders Association of Great Britain

MLBKT	Magyar Logisztikai Egyesület = HLA, UVL	**MMA**	Meter Manufacturers Association
MLC	Comoran Liberation Movement	**MMA**	Microtome Manufacturers' Association
MLC	Maori Language Commission	**MMA**	Music Masters and Mistresses Association
MLC	Meat and Livestock Commission	**MMAAS**	Movement for Montenegro's Autonomous Accession to Serbia = PAPCGS
MLC	Modern Language Centre (Canada)		
MLD	Marineluchtuaardienst (Netherlands)	**MMAC**	Marine Mechanics Academic Committee (China)
MLD	Mouvement pour la Libération de Djibouti	**MMAI**	Margarine Manufacturers' Association of Ireland
MLDG	Militant Labour Disability Group		
MLEU	Mouvement Libéral pour l'Europe Unie	**MMAJ**	Metal Mining Agency of Japan
MLG	Midwifery Legislation Group	**MMB**	Medicus Mundi Belgium
MLI	Ministry of Light Industry (China)	**MMB**	Mercedarian Missionaries of Bérriz
MLIDER	Movimiento Liberal Democrático Revolucionario (Honduras)	**MMC**	Monopolies and Mergers Commission
		MMCS	Mediterranean Marine Sorting Centre
MLK	Lithological Committee of the Russian Academy of Sciences	**MMD**	Makedonsko Mladezhko Druzhestvo (Bulgaria) = MYS
MLN	Movimiento de Liberación Nacional (Guatemala, Uruguay)	**MMD**	Movement for Multiparty Democracy (Zambia)
MLP	Malta Labour Party	**MME**	Magyar Madártani és Természetvédelmi Egyesület
MLP	Mauritius Labour Party		
MLP	Militant Labour Party	**MME**	Ministério de Minas e Energia (Brazil)
MLP	Ministero dei Lavori Pubblici	**MMEA**	Metallic Mineral Exploration Agency (MITI)
MLP	Movimiento Nacional Revolucionario (El Salvador)		
		MMEI	Chengdu Research Institute of Electric Welding Machinery
MLPC	Mouvement pour la Libération du Peuple Centrafricain (Central African Republic)	**MMFITB**	Man-made Fibres Producing Industry Training Board
MLR	Movimiento Liberal Rodista (Honduras)	**MMI**	Foreninger af Mobelarkitekter og Indretningsarkitekter i Danmark
MLS	Mad'arská Ludová Strana (Slovakia) = HPP	**MMI**	Mahaz-i-Melli-i-Islami (Afghanistan) = NIF
MLSTP	Movimento de Liberação de São Tomé e Príncipe	**MMI**	Medicus Mundi Internationalis = IOCHC
MLSTP-PSD	MLSTP-Partido Social Democrático (Sao Tomé)	**MMI**	Ministry of Metallurgical Industry (China)
MLTA	Modern Language Teachers' Association (Éire)	**MMI**	Movimiento Monarchico Italiano
MLURI	Macaulay Land Use Research Institute	**MMIJ**	Mining and Metallurgical Institute of Japan
MLV	Ministerie van Landbouwen Visserij	**MML**	Marx Memorial Library
MM	International Society for the Interaction of Mechanics and Mathematics	**MMLS**	Moskovskii Molodezhnyi Liberalnyi Soiuz
MM	Maryknoll Missionaries: Catholic Foreign Mission Society of America	**MMM**	International Association of Margaret Morris Method
MMA	Macaroni Manufacturers Association (Malta)	**MMM**	Medical Missionaries of Mary
		MMM	Mouvement Militant Mauricien
MMA	Maldives Monetary Authority	**MMM**	Mouvement Mondial des Mères = WMM
MMA	Mauritius Marine Authority		
MMA	Meat Manufacturers Association	**MMM**	Mouvement pour un Monde Meilleur = MBW
MMA	Medical Missionary Association		

MMM	Movimiento por un Mundo Mejor = MBW
MMMA	Metalforming Machinery Makers Association
MMMA	Milking Machine Manufacturers Association
MMO	Makina Mühendisleri Odasi (Turkey)
MMP	International Organization of Masters, Mates and Pilots
MMP	Master Music Printers and Engravers Association
MMPS	Commission Médico-Pédagogique et Psycho-Sociale (BICE)
MMRA	Maritime Marshland Rehabilitation Administration (Canada)
MMRI	Metallurgy and Materials Science Research Institute (Thailand)
MMRS	Metal and Minerals Research Service
MMS	Magyar Marketing Szövetség
MMS	Marist Missionary Sisters = SMSM
MMS	Massachusetts Medical Society
MMS	Methodist Missionary Society
MMS	Mexican Mathematical Society = SMM
MMS	Moravian Missionary Society
MMSA	Medical Mycological Society of the Americas
MMSA	Mining and Metallurgical Society of America
MMSC	Movimiento Magisterial Social-Cristiano (Venezuela)
MMSG	Molecular Manufacturing Shortcut Group
MMT	Magyar Meteorológiai Társaság
MMT	Magyar Mikrobiológiai Társaság
MMTA	Minor Metals Traders Association
MMTC	Marine Mineral Technology Center (U.S.A.)
MMTC	Minerals and Metals Trading Corporation of India
MMTC	Mouvement Mondial des Travailleurs Chrétiens = WBCA, WMCW
MMTO	Multiple Mirror Telescope Observatory (U.S.A.)
MN	Movimiento Nacional (Costa Rica)
MNA	Mouvement National Algérien
MNA	Multiple Newsagents Association
MNAM	Musée National d'Art Moderne
MNBA	Multinational Business Association (U.S.A.)
MNC	Mouvement National du Congo
MNC	Movimiento Nacional Conservador (Colombia)
MNCA	Mouvement d'Intégration de la Culture Autochtone
MNCP	Mbandzeni National Convention Party (Swaziland)
MNDA	Missionary Sisters of Our Lady of the Angels
MNDA	Motor Neurone Disease Asociation
MNDID	Mouvement National Djiboutien pour l'Instauration de la Démocratie
MNÉ	Mouvement National pour la Défense et le Développement d'Épargne
MNF	Magyar Nemzeti Front (Hungary) = HNF
MNF	Millers' National Federation (U.S.A.)
MNF	Miso National Front (India)
MNF/FASA	Union of Conscientious Objectors/Association of Anti-Militarist Socialists (Denmark)
MNFU	Manx National Farmers Union (IOM)
MNHN	Museo Nacional de Historia Natural (Uruguay)
MNL	Maatschappij der Nederlandse Letterkunde
MNLF	Moro National Liberation Front (Philippines)
MNO	Mauritanian Nationalist Organisation
MNOT	Magyar Nök Országos Tanácsa
MNP	Moravian National Party (Czech Republic) = MNS
MNP	Movimento Nacional Parlamentarista (Brazil)
MNP	Movimiento Nacional Progresista (Colombia)
MNP	Movimiento Nacional y Popular (Paraguay)
MNP	Movimiento Nacionalista Popular (Chile)
MNP	Movimiento No Partidarizado (Peru)
MNP-28	Mouvement National Patriotique – 28 Novembre (Haiti)
MNPD	Movimiento Nacional por la Paz y la Democracia (Guatemala)
MNR	Mouvement Nationaliste Révolutionnaire
MNR	Movimento Nacional da Resistência de Moçambique = RENAMO
MNR	Movimiento Nacional Revolucionario (El Salvador, Spain)

MNR	Movimiento Nacionalista Revolucionario Histórico (Bolivia)
MNRI	Movimiento Nacionalista Revolucionario de Izquieda (Bolivia)
MNRP	Movimiento Nacionalista Revolucionario del Pueblo (Bolivia)
MNRV	Movimiento Nacionalista Revolucionario Vanguardia (Bolivia)
MNS	Madjarska Narodna Stranka (Croatia) = HPP
MNS	Malayan Nature Society
MNS	Manitoba Naturalists Society (Canada)
MNS	Moravian National Party
MNS	Moravská Národní Strana (Czech Republic) = MNP
MNS	Movimiento Nacional de Salvación (Dominican Republic)
MNSD	Mouvement National de la Société de Développement (Niger)
MNSP	Movimiento Nacional Socialista del Perú
MNSz	Magyar Nemzeti Szövetség (Hungary) = HNA
MNSz	Magyarországi Németek Szövetsége (Hungary) = AGH
MNT	Magyar Napenergia Társaság = HSES
MNT	Magyar Néprajzi Társaság
MNTB	Merchant Navy Training Board
MNTB	Missão Novas Tribos do Brasil
MNU	Movement for National Unity (St Vincent)
MNUOM	Mision de las Naciones Unidas en el Oriente Medio = UNMEM
MNyT	Magyar Nyelvtudományi Társaság
MO	Institutum Missionariorum Opificium
MO	Milicja Obywatelska
MOA	Microwave Oven Association
MoA	Museum of Australia
MOAC	Ministry of Agriculture and Cooperatives (Thailand)
MOAF	Ministry of Agriculture and Forests (Republic of Korea)
MOBRAL	Movimento Brasileiro de Alfabetização
MOC	Melkhygiënisch Onderzoek Centrum
MOC	Ministry of Constructions (Republic of Korea)
MOC	Mouvement Ouvrier Chrétien = ACW, CAB
MOCAF	Motte-Cordonnière-Afrique (Central African Republic)

MOCAPT	Missouri Center for Agricultural Products Technology
MOCARGO	Empresa Moçambicana de Cargas
MOCHI	Moniteur du Commerce International
MOCI	Ministry of Commerce and Industry (Republic of Korea)
MOD	Międzynarodowa Organizacja Dziennikarzy
MOD	Ministry of Defence
MODEF	Mouvement de Défense des Exploitations Agricoles Familiales
MODELH-PRDH	Mouvement Démocratique pour la Liberté d'Haiti – PRDH
Modena	Movimiento Democratizador Nacionalista (Honduras)
MOD-EUROP	Europäischer Modeausschuss Schuhe
Modin	Movimiento por la Dignidad y la Independencia (Argentina)
MODSA	Ministry of Defence Staff Association
MODUR	Movimiento de Unidad Ruralista (Uruguay)
MODUSSE	Manufacturers of Domestic Unvented Supply Systems Equipment
MOE	Ministry of the Environment (Bulgaria)
MOEA	Ministry of Economic Affairs (Taiwan)
MOED	Movimiento Etico y Democrática (Paraguay)
MOF	Ministry of Finance (Japan)
Mofert	Ministry of Foreign Economic Relations and Trade (China)
Moftec	Ministry of Foreign Trade and Economic Co-operation (China)
MOGA	International Conference on Microwave and Optical Generation and Amplification
MOGA	Mezhdunarodnaia Organizatsiia Grazhdanskoi Aviatsii (UN) = ICAO, OACI
MOI	Monaco Oceanographic Institute
MOI	Moskovskoe Obedinenie Izbiratelei
MOI	Mouvement Ouvrier International
MOIR	Movimiento Obrero Independiente Revolucionario (Colombia)
MOJA	Movement for Justice in Africa (Gambia, Liberia)
MOJMRP	Meteorological Office, Joint Meteorological Radio Propagation Sub-Committee

MOK	Mezhpravitel'stvennaia Okeanograficheskaia Komissiia = COI, IOC
MOLARA	Motoring Organizations Land Access & Rights Association
MOLICA	Movimento para a Libertação de Cabinda (Angola)
MOLIRENA	Movimiento Liberal Republicano Nacionalista (Panama)
MOLISV	Movimento Liberazione e Sviluppo
MOM	Magyar Optikai Muvek
MOM	Musée Océanographique de Monaco
MOMI	Museum of the Moving Image
MOMIMTS	Military & Orchestral Musical Instrument Makers' Trade Society
MON	Ministerstwo Obrony Narodowej
MON-3	Universitaris Pel Tercer Mon
MONALI	Movement for National Liberation (Barbados)
MONARCA	Movimiento Nacional de Reivindicación Callejista (Honduras)
MON-BUSHO	Ministry of Education (Japan)
MONEG	(TOGA) Monsoon Numerical Experimental Group
MONGOL-TELEVIDZ	Mongolian Television
MONIMA	Mouvement National pour l'Indépendance de Madagascar
MONOTAR	Mouvement National des Travailleurs Agricoles Ruraux
Montpellier MAI	Mediterranean Agronomic Institute of Montpellier (ICAMAS) = IAM Montpellier
MONTRAC	Movimiento Nacional de Trabajadores de Comunicaciones
MONTRAL	Movimiento Nacional de Trabajadores para la Liberación (Venezuela)
MONTREV	Movimiento Nacional de Trabajadores Estatales de Venezuela
MONT-SAME	Mongolyn Tsahilgaan Medeeniy Agentiag (Mongolia)
MONUIK	Mission d'Observation de l'ONU en Irak et au Kuwait = UNIKOM
MONUMO	Mission de l'Organisation des Nations Unies au Moyen-Orient
MOP	Międzynarodowa Organizacja Pracy
MOP	Mouvement d'Organisation de Pays (Haiti)
MOP	Mouvement Ouvrier Paysan (Haiti)
MOPA	Mail Order Publishers' Authority
MOPALI	Movimiento Paraguayo de Liberación
MOPC	Ministerio de Obras Publicas y Comunicaciones (Paraguay)
MOPCh	Mezhdunarodnoe Obshchestvo Prav Cheloveka
MOPI	Moskovskii Oblastnoi Pedagogicheskii Institut
MOPOCO	Movimiento Popular Colorado (Paraguay)
MOPS	Mail Order Protection Service
MOPTSLKP	Mezhdunararodnoe Obedinenie Profsoiuzov Trudiashchikhsia Selskogo i Lesnogo Khoziaistva i Plantatsii= TUIAFPW, UISTABP, UISTAFP
MOPU	Ministerio de Obras Publicos y Urbanismo
MOPUL	Movimiento Popular para la Union Latinoamericana
MOR	Movimiento Obrero Revolucionario Salvado Cayetano (El Salvador)
MORENA	Mouvement de Redressement National (Gabon)
MORENA	Movimiento de Renovación Nácional (Venezuela)
MORENA	Movimiento de Restauracion Nacional (Colombia)
MORI	Market and Opinion Research International
MOROP	Verband der Modelleisenbahner und Eisenbahnfreunde Europas
MOS	Mad'arská Občianska Strana (Slovakia) = HCP
MOS	Malta Ornithological Society
MOS	Medical Disability Society
MOSA	Medical Officers of Schools Association
MosGIK	Gosudarstvennaia Inskektsiia pri Minsel'khoz
MOSICP	Movimiento Sindical Cristiano del Perú
MOsiSW	Mnisterstwo Oświaty i Szkolnictwa Wyzszego
MOSiZN	Ministerstwo Ochrony Środowiska i Zasobów Naturalnych
MOSSAD	Israeli Secret Service
MOSST	Ministry of State for Science and Technology (Canada)
MOST	Association for Preventative and Voluntary Work (Yugoslavia)
MOST	Ministry of Science and Technology (Republic of Korea)
MOSTiW	Miejski Ośrodek Sportu, Turystyki i Wypoczynku

MOSZ	Mezógazdasági Szövetkezók és Termelók Országos Szövetsége	**MPAA**	Motion Picture Association of America
MOSZK	Central Union of Hungarian Co-operative Societies	**MPAGB**	Modern Pentathlon Association of Great Britain
MOT	Magyar Onkológusok Társasága	**MPAIAC**	Movimento para la Autodeterminacion y Independencia del Archipielago Canario
MOTA	Mail Order Traders Association		
MOTCD	Magyar Onkológusok Társasága Cytodiagnosztikai Sectio	**MPAS**	Mobile Projects Association Scotland
MOTESZ	Magyar OrvosTudományi Társaságok és Egyesületek Szovetsege	**MPAU**	Mahatma Phule Agricultural University (India)
MOTNE	Meterological Operational Telecommunications Network Europe	**MPBA**	Model Power Boat Association
		MPBP	Metal Polishers, Buffers, Platers and Helpers International Union (U.S.A.)
MOTO	Mezhdunarodnoe Obshchestvo po Termicheskoi Obrabotke i Tekhnologii Obrabotki Poverkhnosti = AITT, IFHT, IVW	**MPC**	Ministerstwo Przemysłu Ciezkiego
		MPC	Multi-Party Conference (Namibia)
		MPC	Mysore Power Corporation (India)
MOTOR-AGRI	Société pour le Développement de la Motorisation de l'Agriculture (Ivory Coast)	**MPCA**	Manpower Citizens' Association (Guyana)
		MPCD	Mouvement Populaire Constitutionnel et Démocratique (Morocco)
MOTT	Men of the Trees	**MPCh**	Ministerstwo Przemysłu Chemicznego
MOUN-CORE	Mouvement Nigérien des Comités Révolutionnaires	**MPCRI**	Management Promotion Council of the Ryukyu Islands
MOUNT	Międzynarodowa Organizacja Unifikacji Neologizmów Terminologicznych = IOUTN, OIUNT	**MPCU**	Marine Pollution Control Unit
		MPD	Movimiento para la Democracia (Cape Verde)
MOW	Ministerstwo Oświaty i Wychhowania	**MPD**	Movimiento Popular Democrático (Ecuador)
MOW	Movement for the Ordination of Women		
MOW	Movement for the Ordination of Women (Australia)	**MPD**	Movimiento Popular Dominicano
		MPDL	Movimiento por la Paz, el Desarme y la Libertad
MOWD	Ministry of Works and Development (New Zealand)	**MPE**	Ministry of Planning and Environmen
MOZ	Mezhdunarodnaia Organizatsiia Zhurnalistov = IOJ, OIJ, OIP	**MPEAA**	Motion Picture Export Association of America
MP	Milicia do Povo (Cape Verde)	**MPEDA**	Marine Products Export Development Authority
MP	Ministerstwo Przemysłu		
MP	Mouvement Populaire (Morocco)	**MPEG**	Museu Paraense Emílio Goeldi
MPA	Magazine Publishers Association (U.S.A.)	**MPF**	Maîtresses Pieuses Filippini
		MPF	Metallurgical Plantmakers Federation
MPA	Major Projects Association	**MPF**	Methodist Peace Fellowship
MPA	Marketing and Promotion Association	**MPG**	Managerial, Professional and Staff Liaison Group
MPA	Master Photographers Association of Great Britain	**MPG**	Max-Planck-Gesellschaft zur Förderung der Wissenschaften = MPIAS
MPA	Master Printers' Association (Singapore)	**MPG**	Mezhrespublikanskaia Parlamentskaia Gruppa
MPA	Modern Poetry Association		
MPA	Mortar Producers Association	**MPGA**	Metropolitan Public Gardens Association
MPA	Motherland Political Association (Albania) = SPM	**MPGI**	Mouvement Populaire pour une Guadeloupe Indépendante
MPA	Music Publishers Association (U.K., U.S.A.)	**MPGK**	Miejskie Przedsiębiorstwo Gospodarki Komunalnej

MPGWU	Marine, Port and General Workers' Union (Éire)
MPHEC	Maritime Provinces Higher Education Commission (Canada)
MPI	Meeting Planners International (U.S.A.)
MPI	Middle Path International (Buddhism)
MPI	Ministero della Pubblica Istruzione
MPI	Missions Professionnelles Internationales
MPI	Movimiento por Independencia (Puerto Rico)
MPIA	Max-Planck Institut für Astronomie
MPIA	Miejskie Przedsiębiorstwo Imprez Artystycznych
MPIAS	Max Planck Institute for the Advancement of Science = MPG
MPiPS	Ministerstwo Pracy i Polityki Socjalnej
MPJ	Mouvement Panafricain de la Jeunesse = PAYM, PYM
MPK	Miejskie Przedsiębiorstwo Komunikacyjne
MPL	Ministerstwo Przemysłu Lekkiego
MPL	Møbelprodusentenes Landsforening
MPL	Montoneros Patria Libre (Ecuador)
MPLA-PT	Movimento Popular de Liberação de Angola – Partido do Trabalho
MPLC	Movimiento Popular de Liberación Cinchonero (Honduras)
MPLT	Mouvement Populaire pour la Libération du Tchad
MPM	Milli Prodüktivite Merkezi (Turkey)
MPM	Mouvement Populaire Mahorais (Mayotte)
MPMA	Metal Packaging Manufacturers Association
MPMA	Movement for Pan-Macedonian Action = DSA
MPMR	Movimiento Patriótico Manuel Rodríguez
MPO	Federation Union of Managerial & Professional Officers
MPO	Managerial and Professional Officers (*ex* FUMPO)
MPO	Miejskie Przedsiębiorstwo Oczyszczania
MPPF	Malaysian Planters Provident Fund
MPPP	Mauritius People's Progressive Party
MPR	Majelis Permusyawaratan Rakyat (Indonesia)
MPR	Mişcarea Pentru România (Romania) = MFR
MPR	Mongolian People's Republic = BNMAU
MPR	Mouvement Populaire de la Révolution (Zaïre)
MPR	Movement for Romania
MPRP	Mongolian Peoples Revolutionary Party
MPRSZ	Magyar Public Relations Szövetség = HPRA
MPS	Malta Photographic Society
MPS	Mathematical Programming Society
MPS	Medical Protection Society Limited
MPS	Medizinisch Pharmazeutische Studiengesellschaft
MPS	Mervyn Peake Society
MPS	Mont Pelerin Society
MPS	Mouvement Populaire Sénégalais
MPS	Movimiento Patria Socialista
MPS	Society for Mucopolysaccharide Diseases
MPSA	Midwest Political Science Association
MPSC	Movimiento Popular Social Cristiano (El Salvador)
MPSIC	Madhya Pradesh State Industries Corporation (India)
MPT	Magyar Parazitológusok Társasága
MPT	Miejskie Przedsiębiorstwo Taksówkowe
MPT	Ministry of Posts and Telecommunications (Japan)
MPTA	Municipal Passenger Transport Association
MPU	Mediterranean Phytopathological Union
MPUT	Ministry of Public Utilities and Transport (Jamaica)
MQB	Mining Qualifications Board
MQM	Muhajir Qaumi Movement (Pakistan)
MQV	Ministère de la Qualité de la Vie
MR	Milicias Rodrigistas (Chile)
MR	Ministerstwo Rolnictwa
MRA	Marketing Research Association (U.S.A.)
MRA	Misiones Rurales Argentinas
MRA	Moral Re-Armament
MRA	Motorcycle Retailers Association
MRA	Music Retailers Association
MRAP	Mouvement contre le Racisme, l'Antisémitisme et pour la Paix
MRBI	Market Research Bureau of Ireland
MRC	Medical Research Council (Canada, U.K.)

MRC	Migrants Resource Centre	**MRIS**	Maritime Research Information Service (NAS) (U.S.A.)
MRC	Model Railway Club	**MRJC**	Mouvement Rural de la Jeunesse Catholique
MRC	Mountain Rescue Committee		
MRC CC	Medical Research Council Collaborative Centre	**MRJCF**	Fédération du Mouvement Rural de Jeunesse Chrétienne Féminine
MRCC	Mineral Resources Consultative Committee	**MRK"S"**	Międzyzakładowy Robotniczy Komitet "Solidarność"
MRCD	Movement for Responsible Coastal Development	**MRKT**	Movimiento Revolucionario Tupaj Katari (Bolivia)
MRCI	Medical Research Council of Ireland	**MRL**	Materials Research Laboratory (Australia)
MRCMC	Murrumbidgee Regional Catchment Management Committee	**MRL**	Ministère de la Reconstruction et du Logement
MRCNZ	Medical Research Council of New Zealand	**MRL**	Movimiento Revolucionario Liberal (Colombia)
MRCO	Manufacturing Research Corporation of Ontario	**MRLiGZ**	Ministerstwo Rolnictwa, Lesnictwa i Gospodarki Zywnościowej
MRD	Movement for the Restoration of Democracy (Nepal, Pakistan)	**MRLT**	Mouvement Révolutionnaire pour la Libération de la Tunisie
MRDE	Mining Research and Development Establishment (BC)	**MRM**	Movimiento Revolucionario del Magisterio (Mexico)
MRDP	Movimiento Revolucionario de Defensa del Pueblo	**MRM**	Mozambique Resistance Movement
MRDSz	Magyarországi Románok Demokratikus Szövetsége (Hungary) = DARH	**MRND**	Mouvement Revolutionnaire National pour le Développement (Rwanda)
MRE	Malaysian Rubber Exchange	**MRO"SW"**	Mlodziezowy Ruch Oporu "Solidarności Walczącej"
MRELB	Malaysian Rubber Exchange and Licensing Board	**MRP**	Magyarországi Romaparlament (Hungary) = RP
MRf	Malaremästarnas Riksförening i Sverige		
MRF	Metering Research Facility (U.S.A.)	**MRP**	Marksistskaia Rabochaia Partiia
MRF	Motorbranschens Riksförbund	**MRP**	Mouvement Révolutionnaire du Peuple (Chad)
MRF	Movement for Rights and Freedoms (Bulgaria) = DPS	**MRP**	Movimiento Revolucionario Popular (Venezuela)
MRFB	Malaysian Rubber Fund Board	**MRP-IXIM**	Movimiento Revolucionario del Pueblo – Ixim (Guatemala)
MRG	Management Research Groups		
MRG	Minority Rights Group	**MRPMA**	Malaysian Rubber Products Manufacturers Association
MRG	Mouvement des Radicaux de Gauche (France, Réunion)	**MRPRA**	Malaysian Rubber Producers Research Association (U.K.)
MRI	Meat Research Institute	**MRRC**	Magnetic Resonance Research Centre
MRI	Medical Records Institute	**MRRDB**	Malaysian Rubber Research and Development Board
MRI	Meuse Rhine Issel Cattle Society of the United Kingdom of Great Britain and Northern Ireland	**MRRTC**	Maligaya Rice Research and Training Center of the Philippines
MRI	Midwest Research Insitute (U.S.A.)		
MRI	Mineral Resources Institute (U.S.A.)	**MRS**	Market Research Society
MRI	Ministerio de Relaciones Interiores (Venezuela)	**MRS**	Materials Research Society
MRI	Mitsubishi Research Institute (Japan)	**MRS**	Mechanical Rights Society
MRI	Motivation Research Institute	**MRS**	Media Resource Service
MRI	Movimiento Revolucionario Internacional	**MRS**	Medical Research Society

MRS	Mouvement Républicain Sénégalais	**MSA**	Mouvement Socialiste Africain
MRS	Mouvement Républicain Suisse = SRB	**MSA**	Movement for Silesian Autonomy (Poland) = RNRAS
MRSC	Mississippi Remote Sensing Center	**MSA**	Musicological Society of Australia
MRSz	Magyarországi Románok Szövetsége (Hungary) = FRH	**MSA**	Mutualité Sociale Agricole
MRT	Mary Rose Trust	**MSA**	Mycological Society of America
MRT	Ministère de la Recherche et de la Technologie	**MSAN**	Multiport Ship Agencies Network (Netherlands)
MRTA	Movimiento Revolucionario Tupac Amarú (Peru)	**MSAVLC**	Medical and Scientific Aid for Vietnam, Laos and Cambodia
MRTB	Medical Radiological Technicians Belgium	**MSBA**	Malaysia, Singapore and Brunei Association (U.K.)
MRTC	Maritime Radio Technical Committee (DTI)	**MSC**	IMO Maritime Safety Committee
MRTK	Movimiento Revolucionario Tupac Katenri (Bolivia)	**MSC**	Mediterranean Society of Chemotherapy
MRU	Mano River Union	**MSC**	Meteorological Service of Canada
MRUA	Mobile Radio Users Association	**MSC**	Meteorological Society of China
MRW	Ministerstwo Rynku Wewn¿etrznego	**MSC**	Meteorological Synthesising Centre (EMEP)
MRYL	Mongolian Revolutionary Youth League = Revsomol	**MSC**	Military Staff Committee (UN)
MS	Mammal Society	**MSC**	Ministerio de Sanidad y Consumo (Spain)
MS	Mandala Society (Canada, U.S.A.)	**MSC**	Missionarii Sacratissimi Cordis Iesu
MS	Manpower Society	**MSC**	Missionary Sisters of the Most Sacred Heart of Jesus of Hiltrup
MS	Matica Slovenská (Slovakia) = SM		
MS	Media Society	**MSC**	Missionary Sisters of the Sacred Heart
MS	Mellemfolkeligt Samvirke (Denmark)	**MSC**	Movimiento Social Cristiano (Chile)
MS	Men of the Stones (U.S.A.)	**MSCA**	Moravian-Silesian Citizens' Assembly = OSMS
MS	Ministère de la Santé		
MS	Ministerstwo Sprawiedliwości	**MSD**	Międzynarodowe Stowarzyszenie Drzeworytników
MS	Missionarii Dominae Nostrae a La Salette	**MSD**	Mines Safety Department (Zambia))
MS	Mongolia Society	**MSD-OPS**	Programa Mujer, Salud, y Desarrollo – Organizacion Panamericana de la Salud (Honduras)
MS	Movement for Survival		
MS	Movimiento Studentesco (Italy)		
MS	Multiple Sclerosis Society of Great Britain and Northern Ireland	**MSDMS**	Movement for the Self-Governing Democracy of Moravia and Silesia = HSDMS
MS AGRO-PROM-INFORM	Mezhdunarodnyi Sistem Nauchno-Tekhnicheskoi Informatsii po Sel'skomu i Lesnomu Khoziaistvu	**MSDN**	International Microbial Strain Data Network (UNEP)
		MSDP	Mongolian Social Democratic Party
MSA	Marine Safety Agency	**MSE**	Mouvement Socialiste Européen
MSA	Media Studies Association	**MSEB**	Maharashtra State Electricity Board (India)
MSA	Mellan- och Sydsvenska Skogbrukets Arbetsstudier		
MSA	Metaphysical Society of America	**MSF**	Congregatio Missionariorum a Sancta Familia
MSA	Microscopy Society of America		
MSA	Mineralogical Society of America	**MSF**	Manufacturing, Science and Finance Union
MSA	Modern Studies Association		
MSA	Motor Schools Association of Great Britain	**MSF**	Médecins Sans Frontières = DWB
		MSF	Mouvement Sioniste de France

MSF	Multiple Shops Federation	**MSR**	Movement for Serbian Renewal
MSFS	Missionarii Sancti Francisci Salesii de Annecia	**MSRA**	Multiple Shoe Retailers' Association
		MSRG	Medieval Settlement Research Group
MSG	Mexico Solidarity Group	**MSRG**	Moated Site Research Group
MSGB	Manorial Society of Great Britain	**MSRI**	Malaysian Sociological Research Institute
MSH	Maison des Sciences de l'Homme		
MSHG	Nederlandse Vereniging van Agenten in Metaalwaren, Sanitaire, Huishoudelijke en Aanverwante Artikelen en Galanterieën	**MSS**	Maharogi Sewa Samiti (India)
		MSS	Mezhdunarodnyi Slavianskii Sobor
		MSS	Mezhdunarodnyi Soiuz Studentov; Mezinárodní Svaz Studentstva = ISB, IUS, UIE
MSHG	Nederlandse Vereniging van Zelfstandige Handelsagenten		
		MSSA	Mid-South Sociological Association
MSHR	Missionary Sisters of the Holy Rosary	**MSSA**	Missionary Sisters of St. Augustine
MSHS	Medical Sciences Historical Society	**MSSC**	Mine Surveying Special Council (China)
MSI	Marie Stopes International		
MSI	Marine Science Institute (Philippines)	**MSSCC**	Congregatio Missionariorum a Sanctissimis Cordibus Iesu et Mariae
MSI	Mathematical Sciences Institute (U.S.A.)		
		MSSGB	Motion Study Society of Great Britain
MSI-DN	Movimento Sociale Italiano-Destra Nazionale	**MSSP**	Missionalis Societas Sancti Pauli (Malta)
MSIA	Movement of Spiritual Inner Awareness	**MSSR**	Medical Society for the Study of Radiesthesia
MSIRI	Marmara Scientific and Industrial Research Institute (Turkey)		
		MSSST	Congregatio Missionariorum Servorum Sanctissimae Trinitatis = ST
MSIRI	Mauritius Sugar Industry Research Institute		
		MSSVD	Medical Society for the Study of Venereal Diseases
MSJ	Meteorological Society of Japan		
MSL	Marine Sciences Laboratory	**MST**	Magyar Sebész Társaság
MSM	Mouvement Socialiste Mauricien	**MST**	Movimento dos Trabalhadores Rurais Sem Terras (Brazil)
MSM	Movimiento Salvadoreno de Mujeres (Costa Rica)		
		MSTC	Management Systems Training Council
MSMA	Margarine and Shortening Manufacturers Association	**MSTCL**	Metal Scrap Trade Corporation Ltd (India)
MSMA	Master Sign Makers Association	**MSTK**	Mezhrespublikanskii Soiuz Trudovykh Kollektivov
MSMA	Membrane Switch Manufacturers' Association		
		MSU	Migrant Support Unit
MSMA	Metal Sink Manufacturs Association	**MSUSM**	Medical Society of the United States and Mexico
MSMEA	Multiwall Sack Manufacturers Employers Association		
		MSW	Ministerstwo Spraw Wewn¿etrznych
MSN	Movimiento de Salvación Nacional (Colombia)	**MSWEG**	Mild Steel Wire Export Group
		MSZ	Ministerstwo Spraw Zagranicznych
MSP	Association Suisse des Marchands de Papier Peints = VST	**MSZH**	Magyar Szabványügyi Hivatal
		MSZKI	Mérés- és Számítás- technikai Kutató Intézet
MSP	Congregatio Missionariorum Servorum Pauperium		
		MSzKSz	Magyar Szent Korona Szövetség
MSP	Milli Selamet Partisi (Turkey) = NSP	**MSzSz**	Magyarországi Szlovákok Szövetsége (Hungary) = DUSH
MSPA	Mauritian Sugar Producers' Association		
MSPA	Medical Sterile Products Association	**MSzSz**	Magyarországi Szlovenek Szövetsége (Hungary) = FSH
MSpS	Missionarii a Spiritu Sancto		
MSPT	Manufacture Sénégalaise de Papiers Transformés	**MT**	Internacia Asocio Monda Turismo

MT	Ministère des Transports	**MTI**	Museum Training Institute
MTA	Magyar Tudományos Akadémia	**MTIAA**	Metal Trades Industry Association of Australia
MTA	Marine Trades Association (*now* M&ETA)	**MTK**	Maatalouden Tutimuskeskus Kirjasto
MTA	Master Tanners Association	**MTK**	Maataloustuottajain Keskusliitto
MTA	Mica Trades Association	**MTK**	Międzynarodowe Targi Ksiazki
MTA	Mineral Research and Exploration Institute of Turkey	**MTKI**	Magyar Tejgazdasági Kisérleti Intézet
MTA	Mobel- og Trearbeidings- industriens Arbeidsgiverforening	**MTL**	Mainostoimistojen Liitto
		MTM	Methods-Time Measurement Association for Standards and Research (U.S.A.)
MTA	Movimiento Teresiano de Apostolado = TAM		
MTA-BKKL	Bányászati Kémiai Kutatólaboratóriuma (MTA)	**MTMA-UK**	Methods-Time Measurement Association of the United Kingdom
MTA-TAKI	Talajtani és Agrokémiai Kutatóintézete (MTA)	**MTO**	Mezhdunarodnoe Obshchestvo po Torfu
		MTO	Multilateral Trade Organization (GATT)
MTAA	Motor Trades Association of Australia	**MTO Shah-maghsoudi**	Maktab Tarighat Oveyssi Shahmaghsoudi
MTAC	Mid-Atlantic Technology Applications Center (U.S.A.)	**MTOA**	Manufacture de Tabacs de l'Ouest Africain (Senegal)
MTB	Malaysian Tin Bureau (U.S.A.)		
MTC	Migrant Training Company	**MTOA**	Motor Transport Owners Association of South Africa
MTC	Ministerio de Transpores y Comunicaciones		
MTC	Movimiento Tradicionalista Colorado (Paraguay) = TRADEMO	**MTOC**	Movimiento de Trabajadores y Obreros de Clase (Peru)
		MTP	Manufacture Togolaise des Plastiques
MTD	Mouvement Togolais pour la Démocratie	**MTP**	Międzynarodowe Targi Poznańskie
MTDC	Management Teacher Development Centre	**MTP**	Movimiento Todos por la Patria (Argentina)
MTDR	International Machine Tool Design and Research Conference	**MTPS**	Syndicat National des Industries d'Équipement
MTDUR	Muslim Turkish Democratic Union of Romania = UDMTR	**MTRB**	Marine Technology Requirements Board (DTI)
MTE	International Association of Research in Mother Tongue Education = PLM	**MTRB**	Maritime Transportation Research Board (U.S.A.)
		MTRC	Mass Transit Railway Corporaton (Hong Kong)
MTESZ	Müszaki és TermészetTudomány Egyesületek Szövetsége	**MTS**	Marine Technology Society (U.S.A.)
MTF	Materialteknisk Forening	**MTS**	Międzynarodowy Trybunal Sprawiedliwości
MTF	Militærteknisk Forening		
MTFCI	Model T Ford Club International	**MTsFB**	Moskovskaia Tsentral'naia Fondovaia Birzha (Russia)
MTFP	Marema Tlou Freedom Party (Lesotho)	**MTSZ**	Magyar Természetbarát Szövetség
MTHL	Metalliteollisuudenharjoittajain Liitto	**MTT**	Milicias de Tropas Territoriales (Cuba)
MTI	Magyar Távirati Iroda	**MTTA**	Machine Tools Trades' Association
MTI	Meinatoeknafélag Islands	**MTTI**	Maszaki Tudomanyos Tajekoztato Intezetben (Hungary)
MTI	Metal Treating Institute (U.S.A.)		
MTI	Ministry of Trade and Industry (Republic of Korea)	**MTTK**	Maatalouden Tutkimuskeskus (Finland)
		MTU	Motoren- und Turbinen- Union
MTI	Mouvement de la Tendance Islamique (Tunisia)	**MTU Association**	Mongolian Trade Unions Association

MTUC	Malaysian Trades Union Congress
MTV	Magyar Televizio
MTV	Music Television
MTVSZ	Magyar Természetvédók Szövetsége
MTZiL	Ministerstwo Transportu, Zeglugi i Lacznośći
MU	Mothers Union
MU	Musicians Union
MUA	Machinery Users Association
MUA	Mail Users Association
MUA	Mujeres Unidas en Accion (Puerto Rico)
MUBA	Schweizer Mustermesse in Basel
MUC	Mesa para la Unidad de los Comunistas
MUC	Movimiento Unidad y Cambio (Honduras)
MUCECH	Movimiento Unitario Campesino y Etnias de Chile
MUCG	Management-Union Consultative Group (DEST)
MUD	Mouvement d'Union Démocratique (Monaco)
MUDCA	Mujeres Demócrata Cristianas de America (Venezuela) = CDWA
MUDE	Mujeres en Desarrollo Dominicana
MUDECHI	Asociación de Mujeres de Chile
MUDRA	Training and Research Centre for the Performing Arts (Belgium)
MUF	Malta Union of Farmers
MUF	Melanesian United Front (Papua New Guinea)
MUFACE	Mutualidad General de Funcionarios Civiles del Estado
MUFM	Mouvement Universel pour une Fédération Mondiale = AUFM, WAWF
MUFON	Mutual UFO Network (U.S.A.)
MUI	Council of Muslim Ulemas
MUKKI	Muszaki Kémiai Kutató Intézet
MUL	Marxist University of London
MULC	Mando Unificando para la Luche Contraterrorista
MULPOC	Multinational Programming and Operational Centres (ECA)
MULT	Movimiento de Unificación y Lucha Triqui (Mexico)
MULTICOR	Multinational Finance Corporation (Indonesia)
MULTI-FERT	Empresa Multinacional Latinoamericana de Comercialización de Fertilizantes S.A. (Panama)

MUNFLA	Folklore and Language Archive – Memorial University of Newfoundland
MUNL	Maharishi University of Natural Law
MUNPAL	Mutualidad Nacional de Prevision de la Administración Local
MUNT	Magyar Urológusok és Nephrológusok Társasága
MUOSZ	National Association of Hungarian Journalists / Magyar Újaságírók Országos Szövetsége
MUP	Malta Union of Pharmacists
MUP	Mouvement de l'Unité Populaire (Tunisia)
MUP	Movimento da Unidade Progressiva (Brazil)
MUR	Movimiento de Unidad Revolucionaria (Honduras, Panama)
MUR	Movimiento Universitario Reformista (Colombia)
MURA	Midwestern Universities Research Association (U.S.A.)
MURC	Murrumbidgee Users Rehabilitation Committee
MURS	Mouvement Universel de la Responsabilité Scientifique
MUSA	Mujeres Unidas de Sarapiqui (Costa Rica)
MUSADE	Mujeres Unidad en Salud y Desarrollo (Costa Rica)
MUSIC	Multimedia Systems Institute of Crete
MUSINI	Mutualidad de Seguros del Instítuto Nacional de Industria
MUSZI	Mezogazdasági Ugyvitelszervezési és Számítástechnikai Közös Vállalat
MUT	Magyar Urbanisztikai Társaság
MUT	Malta Union of Teachers
MUTA	Made-up Textiles Association
MUZ	Institute for International Collaboration in Agriculture and Forestry (Czechoslovakia)
MUZ	Maatschappij ter Uitvoering der Zuiderzeewerken
MV	Mijnbouwkundige Vereeniging
MV	Movement of Volunteers (Moldova)
MVA	Makelaarsvereniging Amsterdam
MVA	Missouri Valley Authority (U.S.A.)
MVD	Ministerstvo Vnutrennikh Del
MVDA	Motor Vehicle Dismantlers Association of Great Britain
MVKIIIa	Moskovskii Vechernii Komsomol'skii Institut Inostrannykh Iazykov

MVL	Mekaniske Verksteders Landsforening
MVL	Musikkens Venners Landsforbund
MVMT	Magyar Villiamos Muvek Tröszt
MVRG	Medieval Villages Research Group
MVRIS	Motor Vehicle Registration Information Service (SMMT)
MVS	Mennonite Voluntary Service
MVSofSA	Mine Ventilation Society of South Africa
MVSz	Magyarok Világszövetsége (Hungary) = WFH
MVT	Military Vehicle Trust
MVWGS	Multi-Vintage Wine Growers Society
MWA	Married Women's Association
MWA	Muslim Women's Association (Kenya)
MWA	Mystery Writers of America
MWAA	Movers and Warehousemen's Association of America
MWC	Mennonite World Conference
MWC	Mental Welfare Commission
MWCT	Ministry of Wildlife, Conservation and Tourism (Namibia)
MWF	Medical Womens Federation
MWF	Methodist Women's Fellowship – Ghana
MWG	Międzynarodowa Współpraca Geofizyczna
MWIA	Medical Women's International Association = AIFM
MWIA-A	Medical Women's International Association – Australia
MWIA-B	Medical Women's Internation Association – Bolivia
MWIA-B	Medical Women's International Association – Brazil
MWIA-C	Medical Women's International Association – Cameroon
MWIA-C	Medical Women's International Association – Colombia
MWIA-E	Medical Women's International Association – Ecuador
MWIA-E	Medical Women's International Association – Egypt
MWIA-G	Medical Women's International Association – Georgia
MWIA-G	Medical Women's International Association – Ghana
MWIA-G	Medical Women's International Association – Guatemala
MWIA-I	Medical Women's International Association – India

MWL	Muslim World League
MWP-PDP	Marxist Workers Party – Party of the Dictatorship of the Proletariat (Russian Federation)
MWR	Ministry of Water Resources (China)
MWRAF	Muslim Women's Research and Action Front (Sri Lanka)
MWTCo	Marconi's Wireless Telegraph Co. Ltd
MWU	Maccabi World Union (Israel)
MWV	Mineralölwirtschaftsverband
MXD	Mujeres por la Democracia (Paraguay)
MXY	Institutum Yarumalense pro Missionibus ad Exteras Gentes (Colombia)
MY	Muoviyhdistys
MYA	"Mladost" Youth Association (Hungary) = ISzM
MYA	Model Yachting Association
MYM	Muslim Youth Movement
MYP	Malawi Young Pioneers
MYRAA	Model Yacht Racing Association of America
MYS	Macedonian Youth Society = MMD
MYWO	Maendeleo Ya Wanawake Organization (Kenya)
MZBM	Miejski Zarząd Budynkow Mieszkalnych
MZH	Miejski Zarząd Handlu
MZiOS	Ministerstwo Zdrowia i Opieki Spolecznej
MZK	Miejski Zakłady Komunikacyjne
MZO	Miejski Zakłady Oczyszczania
MZS	Hungarian Standards Office
MZS	Międzynarodowy Związek Spóldzielczy
MZsKE	Magyar Zsidók Kulturális Egyesülete (Hungary) = HJCF
MZV	Mineralól Zentralverband

N

N&S	Koninklijke Vereniging voor Natuur- en Stedeschoon
N.I. 2000	Northern Ireland 2000
NA	Napoleonic Association
NA	Narcotics Anonymous
NA	Nation Party (Turkey)
NA	Nationale Aktion für Volk und Heimat (Switzerland) = AN
NA	Nordisk Amatørteaterrad

NA	Norsk Arkivrad	**NAAD**	National Association of Aluminum Distributors (U.S.A.)
NA	Noticias Argentinas	**NAADI**	National Association of Approved Driving Instructors
NA	Nueva Alternativa (Venezuela)		
NAA	National Academy of Arbitrators (U.S.A.)	**NAADO**	National Association of Administrative Dental Officers
NAA	National Aeronautic Association (U.S.A.)	**NAAE**	National Association of Agricultural Employees (U.S.A.)
NAA	National Arborist Association (U.S.A.)	**NAAF**	Norges Astma- og Allergiforbund
NAA	National Archery Association (U.S.A.)	**NAAH**	National Association of Advisers in History
NAA	National Artists Association		
NAA	National Association of Accountants (U.S.A.)	**NAAIDT**	National Association of Advisers & Inspectors in Design and Technology (*ex* AACDT)
NAA	National Automobile Association (U.S.A.)	**NAAJS**	National Academy for Adult Jewish Studies (U.S.A.)
NAA	Neckware Association of America		
NAA	Nederlandse Aardappel-Associatie	**NAALD**	Nigerian Association of Agricultural Librarians and Documentalists
NAA	Normenausschuss Armaturen im DIN	**NAAMM**	National Association of Architectural Metal Manufacturers (U.S.A.)
NAA	North Atlantic Assembly = AAN		
NAAA	National Aerial Applicators Association (U.S.A.)	**NAAMSA**	National Association of Automobile Manufacturers of South Africa
NAAA	National Agricultural Aviation Association (U.S.A.)	**NAAN**	National Advertising Agency Network (U.S.A.)
NAAA	Nordic Association of Advertising Agencies (Denmark)	**NAAO**	North Africa Area Ofice (UNICEF)
NAAAS	National Association for Applied Arts and Sciences (U.S.A.)	**NAAOSE**	National Association of Advisory Officers for Special Education
NAAB	National Architectural Accrediting Board (U.S.A.)	**NAAP**	National Association for Accreditation in Psychoanalysis (U.S.A.)
NAAB	National Association of Animal Breeders (U.S.A.)	**NAAP**	National Association of Advertising Publishers (U.S.A.)
NAABC	National Association of American Business Clubs	**NAAR**	National Association of Advertising Representatives
NAAC	National Association of Agricultural Contractors	**NAAS**	National Association of Academies of Sciences (U.S.A.)
NAAC	National Association of Arts Centres	**NAAS**	News Afro-Asian Service
NAACC	National Association for American Composers and Conductors	**NAAS**	Ningxia Academy of Agro-Forestry Sciences
NAACIE	National Association of Agricultural, Commercial and Industrial Employees (Guyana)	**NAAS**	Nordic Association for American Studies
NAACLS	National Accrediting Agency for Clinical Laboratory Sciences (U.S.A.)	**NAASR**	National Association for Armenian Studies and Research (U.S.A.)
NAACLT	North American Association for Celtic Language Teachers	**NAASRA**	National Association of Australian State Road Authorities
NAACOG	Nurses Association of the American College of Obstetricians and Gynecologists	**NAATS**	National Association of Air Traffic Specialists (U.S.A.)
		NAAW	National Association of Amateur Winemakers
NAACP	National Association for the Advancement of Coloured Peoples (U.S.A.)	**NAAWER**	National Association of Arc Welding Equipment Repairers
		NAAWP	National Association for the Advancement of White People (U.S.A.)

NAB	National Apex Body (India)	**NABPULP**	National Book Pulping Centre
NAB	National Association of Bookmakers	**NABS**	National Advertising Benevolent Society
NAB	National Association of Broadcasters (U.S.A.)	**NABS**	National Association of Bank Servicers (U.S.A.)
NAB	News Agency of Burma	**NABS**	National Association of Bereavement Services
NAB	Nordiska Rådgivarde Nämnden för Energiiformation	**NABS**	National Association of Breeder Services
NABA	National Association of Black Accountants (U.S.A.)	**NABS**	Nordic Association for British Studies
NABARD	National Bank for Agricultural and Rural Development (India)	**NABSE**	National Alliance of Black School Educators (U.S.A.)
NABAS	National Association of Balloon Suppliers	**NABT**	National Association of Biology Teachers (U.S.A.)
NABB	National Association for Better Broadcasting (U.S.A.)	**NABT**	National Association of Black Professors (U.S.A.)
NABB	Nationale Associatie des Compatables de Belgique	**NABT**	National Association of Blind Teachers (U.S.A.)
NABBA	National Amateur Body Building Association	**NABTE**	National Association for Business Teacher Education (U.S.A.)
NABC	National Association of Boys' Clubs (*now* CYP)	**NABU**	Naturschutzbund Deutschland e.V.
NABCO	National Association of Building Cooperatives (Éire)	**NABU**	Vereniging van Nederlandse Aannemers met Belangen in het Buitland
NABD	National Association of Blood Donors	**NABWU**	North American Baptist Women's Union
NABD	Normenausschuss Bibliotheks- und Dokumentationswesen im DIN	**NAC**	National Abortion Campaign
NABE	National Association for Bilingual Education (U.S.A.)	**NAC**	National Accelerator Centre (South Africa)
NABE	National Association of Bar Executives (U.S.A.)	**NAC**	National Agricultural Council
NABE	National Association of Biological Engineering (U.S.A.)	**NAC**	National Air Charters (Zambia)
NABE	National Association of Business Economists (U.S.A.)	**NAC**	National Amusements Council
		NAC	National Anglers Council
NABET	National Association of Broadcast Employees and Technicians (U.S.A.)	**NAC**	National Archives Council
NABF	Norsk Antikvarbokhandlerforening	**NAC**	National Arts Centre (Canada)
NABF	North American Baptist Fellowship	**NAC**	National Association for the Childless (*now* ISSUE)
NABIL	Nepal Arab Bank Limited	**NAC**	National Association of Choirs
NABIM	Incorporated National Association of British and Irish Millers	**NAC**	National Association of Conveyancers
NABISCO	National Biscuit Company	**NAC**	National Asthma Campaign
NABL	National Association of Bond Lawyers (U.S.A.)	**NAC**	National Aviation Club (U.S.A.)
NABM	National Association of Biscuit Manufacturers	**NAC**	Nederlandse Akkerbouw Centrale
		NAC	Nederlandse Astronomen Club
NABMA	National Association of British Market Authorities	**NAC**	New Assembly of Churches
NABO	National Association of Boat Owners	**NACA**	National Academy of Code Administration (U.S.A.)
NABP	National Associations of Boards of Pharmacy (U.S.A.)	**NACA**	National Agricultural Chemicals Association (U.S.A.)
		NACA	National Air Carrier Association (U.S.A.)
		NACA	National Association for Clean Air (South Africa)

NACA	National Athletic and Cycling Association	**NACE**	National Advisory Committee on Electronics (India)
NACA	Network of Aquaculture Centres in Asia (FAO/UNDP)	**NACE**	National Association of Corrosion Engineers (U.S.A.)
NACAA	National Association of Country Agricultural Agents (U.S.A.)	**NACEBO**	Nationale Centrale voor Metaal- Hout- en Bouwvakondernemingen
NACAB	National Agricultural Centre Advisory Board	**NACED**	National Advisory Council on the Employment of Disabled People
NACAB	National Association of Citizens Advice Bureaux	**NACEHC**	National Accreditation Council for Environmental Health Curricula (U.S.A.)
NACAE	National Advisory Council on Art Education	**NACEPE**	National Association of Creamery Proprietors and Wholesale Dairymen = CPA
NACAM	National Association of Corn and Agricultural Merchants	**NACEW**	National Advisory Council on the Employment of Women (New Zealand)
NACAO	National Association of County Arts Officers	**NACF**	National Agricultural Cooperative Federation (Republic of Korea)
NACAR	National Advisory Committee on Aeronautical Research (South Africa)	**NACF**	National Art Collections Fund
NACAS	National Advisory Committee on Agricultural Services (Canada)	**NACF**	National Association of Church Furnishers
NACB	National Association of Catering Butchers	**NACFRC**	North Atlantic Coastal Fisheries Research Centre (U.S.A.)
NACBC	National Advisory Centre on the Battered Child	**NACGPs**	National Association of Commissioning GPs
NACC	National Aboriginal Consultative Committee (Australia)	**NACGT**	National Association of Careers Guidance Teachers
NACC	National Association for Colitis and Crohn's Disease	**NACHA**	National Automated Clearing House Association (U.S.A.)
NACC	North Atlantic Cooperation Council = COCONA	**NACHC**	National Association of Community Health Centers (U.S.A.)
NACCA	National Association for Creative Children and Adults (U.S.A.)	**NACHP**	National Association of Counsellors, Hypnotherapists and Psychotherapists (*ex* NAHP)
NACCAM	National Co-ordinating Committee for Aviation Meteorology (U.S.A.)	**NACISA**	NATO Communications and Information Services Agency
NACCAN	National Association of Christian Councils and Networks	**NACK**	National Advisory Committee on Kangaroos (*now* NCCK, SACK)
NACCC	Network of Access and Child Contact Centres	**NACL**	Nippon Aviotronics Company Ltd (Japan)
NACCSS	National Association of Commodity Cargo Superintendents and Surveyors	**NACLA**	North American Congress on Latin America (U.S.A.)
NACCU	National Association of Canadian Credit Unions	**NACLE**	National Association of Chimney Lining Engineers
NACCW	National Advisory Centre of Careers for Women	**NACM**	National Association of Charcoal Manufacturers
NACCWO	National Association of Civil Court Welfare Officers	**NACM**	National Association of Cider Makers
NACD	National Association of Chemical Distributors (U.S.A.)	**NACM**	National Association of Colliery Managers
NACDET	National Association of Colleges in Distributive Education and Training	**NACM**	National Association of Cotton Manufacturers (U.S.A.)
NACDS	National Association of Chain Drug Stores (U.S.A.)		

NACM	National Association of Credit Management (U.S.A.)	**NACSS**	National Association of Clerical and Supervisory Staffs
NACMA	NATO ACCS Management Agency	**NACT**	National Alliance of Cardiovascular Technologists (U.S.A.)
NACMC	National Association of Christian Marriage Counselors (U.S.A.)	**NACT**	National Association of Clinical Tutors
NACMO	National Association of Cigarette Machine Operators	**NACT**	National Association of Cycle Traders
NACO	National Agricultural Company (Tanzania)	**NACTA**	National Association of Colleges and Teachers of Agriculture (U.S.A.)
NACO	National Agricultural Corporation (St Christopher and Nevis)	**NACTST**	National Advisory Council on the Training and Supply of Teachers
NACO	National Agricultural Credit Office (Vietnam)	**NACTU**	National Affiliation of Carpet Trade Unions
NACO	National Association of Consumer Organizations (U.S.A.)	**NACTU**	National Council of Trade Unions (South Africa)
NACO	National Association of Cooperative Officials	**NACUA National**	Association of College and University Attorneys (U.S.A.)
NACO-BROUW	National Comité voor Brouwgerst	**NACUBO**	National Association of College and University Business Officers (U.S.A.)
NACOA	National Advisory Committee on the Oceans and Atmosphere (U.S.A.)	**NACUFS**	National Association of College and University Fund Services (U.S.A.)
NACOA	National Association for Children of Alcoholics	**NACUSIP**	National Congress of Union in the Sugar Industry of the Philippines
NACODS	National Association of Colliery Overmen, Deputies and Shotfirers	**NACVS**	National Association of Councils for Voluntary Service
NACOLADS	National Council on Libraries, Archives and Documentation Services (Jamaica)	**NAD**	National Academy of Design (U.S.A.)
		NAD	National Association of the Deaf (Éire)
NACOSH	National Advisory Committee on Occupational Safety and Health (U.S.A.)	**NAD**	Nordiska Nämnden för Alkohol och Drogforskning
NACOSS	National Approval Council for Security Systems	**NADA**	National Association of Dealers in Antiques (U.S.A.)
NaCoVo	National Comité van Voederbouw	**NADA**	National Automobile Dealers Association (U.S.A.)
NACPCC	National Advisory Committee for Pig Carcase Competitions	**NADALT**	Nationale Dienst voor Afset van Land-en Tuinbouwprodukten
NACPDE	National Advice Centre for Postgraduate Dental Education	**NADAP**	National Association on Drug Abuse Problems (U.S.A.)
NACRC	National Association of Community Relations Councils	**NADASO**	National Association of Design and Art Service Organisations (U.S.A.)
NACRO	National Association for the Care and Resettlement of Offenders	**NADASO**	National Association of Drug and Allied Sales Organizations (U.S.A.)
NACS	National Association of Chimney Sweeps	**NADBRH**	National Association for Deaf-Blind and Rubella Handicapped
NACS	National Association of Computer Stores (U.S.A.)	**NADC**	National Animal Data Centre
NACS	National Association of Cosmetology Schools (U.S.A.)	**NADC**	National Animal Disease Center (U.S.A.)
		NADC	National Association of Dredging Contractors (U.S.A.)
NACS	Nordic Association for Clinical Sexology	**NADC**	Northern Region Agricultural Development Centre (Thailand)
NACSCC	National Association of Community Schools, Colleges and Centres	**NADCO**	National Agricultural Development Company (Saudi Arabia)

NADCORP	National Development Corporation (Éire)	**NAEA**	National Aerospace Education Association (U.S.A.)
NADD	National Association of Deputising Doctors	**NAEA**	National Art Education Association (U.S.A.)
NADE	National Association for Design Education	**NAEA**	National Artists Equity Association (U.S.A.)
NADEC	National Agricultural Development Company (Saudi Arabia)	**NAEA**	National Association of Estate Agents
NADEC	National Association of Development Education Centres (*now* DEA)	**NAEA**	Newspaper Advertising Executives Association of Canada
NADECO	National Development Company (Ghana)	**NAEB**	National Association of Educational Broadcasters (U.S.A.)
NADECT	National Association for Drama in Education and Children's Theatre	**NAEBM**	Normenausschuss Eisen- Blech- und Metallwaren im DIN
NADEE	National Association of Divisional Executives for Education	**NAEC**	National Aboriginal Education Committee
NADEEC	NATO Air Defence Electronic Environment Committee	**NAEC**	National Aeronautical Establishment, Canada
NADEFCOL	Defense College (NATO) = NDC	**NAEC**	National Aerospace Education Council (U.S.A.)
NADEPA	National Democratic Party (Solomon Islands)	**NAEC**	National Agricultural Engineering Corporation (China)
NADFAS	National Association of Decorative and Fine Art Societies	**NAEC**	National Association for Educational Computing (U.S.A.)
NADGE	NATO Air Defence Ground Environment	**NAECOE**	National Academy of Engineering, Committee on Ocean Engineering (U.S.A.)
NADITEX	Nationale Distribution des Textiles (Ivory Coast)	**NAECON**	National Aerospace Electronics Conference (U.S.A.)
NADJ	National Association of Disk Jockeys	**NAEd**	National Academy of Education (U.S.A.)
NADL	National Animal Disease Laboratory (Japan, U.S.A.)	**NAED**	National Association of Engravers and Diestampers
NADP	National Association of Deafened People	**NAEE**	National Association for Environmental Education
NADP	National Atmospheric Deposition Program (U.S.A.)	**NAEGA**	North American Export Grain Association
NADPAS	National Association of Discharged Prisoners' Aid Societies	**NAEGS**	National Association of Educational Guidance Services for Adults
NADSA	National Agricultural Diversification and Settlement Authority (Sri Lanka)	**NAEHMO**	National Association of Employers on Health Maintenance Organizations (U.S.A.)
NADSA	National Association of Dramatic and Speech Arts (U.S.A.)	**NAEIAC**	National Association of Educational Inspectors, Advisers & Consultants (*ex* NAIEA)
NADUS	National Association of Doctors in the United States	**NAEMB**	National Academy of Engineering Marine Board (U.S.A.)
NADVH	National Association of Drama with the Visually Handicapped	**NAEMT**	National Association of Emergency Medical Technicians (U.S.A.)
NADW	National Association of Disabled Writers	**NAEN**	National Association of Educational Negotiators (U.S.A.)
NAE	National Academy of Engineering (U.S.A.)	**NAEOM**	National Association of Electronic Organ Manufacturers
NAE	National Aeronautical Establishment (NRC) (Canada)		

NAEP	National Association of Environmental Professionals (U.S.A.)	**NAFCO**	National Agricultural and Food Corporation (Tanzania)
NAEPS	National Academy of Economics and Political Science (U.S.A.)	**NAFD**	National Association of Funeral Directors
NAESA	North American Economic Studies Association (U.S.A.)	**NAFD**	Nigerian Association for Family Development
NAEST	National Archive for Electrical Science and Technology	**NAFE**	National Association for Film in Education
NAET	National Association of Educational Technicians (U.S.A.)	**NAFEC**	National Aviation Facilities Experimental Center (U.S.A.)
NAEW	NATO Airborne Early Warning and Control Force	**NAFED**	National Agricultural Co-operative Marketing Federation (India)
NAEWVH	National Association for the Education and Welfare of the Visually Handicapped	**NAFED**	National Association of Fire Equipment Distributors (U.S.A.)
NAEYC	National Association for the Education of Young Children (U.S.A.)	**NAFEKAV**	National Federatie der Kleinhandelaars in Algemene Voedingswaren (Belgium)
NAF	Nederlands Atoomforum	**NAFEM**	National Association of Food Equipment Manufacturers (U.S.A.)
NAF	Nigerian Air Force	**NAFEO**	National Association for Equal Opportunity in Higher Education (U.S.A.)
NAF	Nordisk Anaesthesiologisk Förening		
NAF	Nordisk Andelsforbund		
NAF	Nordiske Administrative Forbund	**NAFEP**	National Association of Frozen Egg Packers
NAF	Norges Apotekerförening		
NAF	Norsk Arbeitsgiverförening	**NAFF**	National Association for Freedom
NAF	Norsk Astronautisk Förening	**NAFFD**	North American Federation of Freedom and Democracy
NAF	Norske Annonsørers Förening		
NAFA	Nordic Anthropological Film Association	**NAFHE**	National Association of Further and Higher Education
NAFA	Nordic Association for Andrology	**NAFI**	National Association of Flight Instructors (U.S.A.)
NAFA	Normenausschuss Fahrräder im DIN		
NAFAC	National Association for Ambulatory Care (U.S.A.)	**NAFI**	National Association of Forest Industries
NAFAG	NATO Air Force Armaments Group	**NAFINSA**	Nacional Financiera SNC (Mexico)
NAFAS	National Association of Flower Arrangement Societies of Great Britain	**NAFIPS**	North American Fuzzy Information Processing Society
NAFB	National Association of Farm Broadcasters (U.S.A.)	**NAFM**	National Association of Furniture Manufacturers
NAFB & AE	National Association of Farriers, Blacksmiths & Agricultural Engineers	**NAFO**	National Association of Fire Officers
		NAFO	Northwest Atlantic Fisheries Organization
NAFBRC	National Association of Family Based Respite Care	**NAFP**	National Association of Fund Holding Practices
NAFC	National Anti-Fluoridation Campaign		
NAFC	National Association of Farmwork Contractors	**NAFPD**	National Association of Family Planning Doctors
NAFC	National Association of Financial Consultants (U.S.A.)	**NAFRC**	North Atlantic Fisheries Research Center (NMFS)
NAFC	North-American Forestry Commission (FAO) = CFAN, CFNA	**NAFS**	National Association of Fastener Stockholders
		NAFS	North America Fertility Society
NAFC	North-East Atlantic Fisheries Commission (U.K.)	**NAFSA**	National Association of Foreign Student Advisers (U.S.A.)

NAFSA	National Fire Services Association of Great Britain
NAFSCA	National Automatic Sprinkler and Fire Control Association
NAFSO	National Association of Field Study Officers
NAFTA	North American Free Trade Agreement
NAFTC	National Agri-Food Technology Centre (Canada)
NAFTRAC	National Foreign Trade Council (U.S.A.)
NAFUO	Normenausschuss Feinmechanik und Optik im DIN
NAFV	National Association of Federal Veterinarians (U.S.A.)
NAG	National Acquisitions Group
NAG	National Association of Gagwriters (U.S.A.)
NAG	National Association of Goldsmiths of Great Britain and Ireland
NAG	National Association of Groundsmen
NAG	Nederlands Akoestisch Genootschap
NAG	Nystagmus Action Group
NAGA	North American Gamebird Association
NAGARD	NATO Advisory Group for Aeronautical Research and Development
NAGC	National Association of Gifted Children
NAGC	National Association of Girls Clubs (U.S.A.)
NAGIS	Natal/KwaZulu Association for Geographical Information Systems (South Africa)
NAGLO	National Association of Government Labor Officials (U.S.A.)
NAGM	National Association of Glove Manufacturers (U.K., U.S.A.)
NAGM	National Association of Governors and Managers
NAGPM	National Association of Grained Plate Makers (U.S.A.)
NAGS	National Association for Girls and Women in Sport (U.S.A.)
NAGS	National Association of Hospital Management Committee Group Secretaries
NAGT	National Association of Geology Teachers (U.S.A.)
NAGUI-CAVE	Companhia Nacional de Navegação Arca Verde
NAHA	National Association of Health Authorities in England and Wales (*now* NAHAT)
NAHA	North American Highway Association
NAHA	Norwegian-American Historical Association
NAHAT	National Association of Health Authorities & Trusts (*ex* NAHA)
NAHB	National Association of Home Builders (U.S.A.)
NAHBO	National Association of Hospital Broadcasting Organisations
NAHC	National Association of Holiday Centres
NAHCSM	National Association of Health Care Supplies Managers
NAHD	National Association for Human Development (U.S.A.)
NAHE	National Alliance for Hydroelectric Energy (U.S.A.)
NAHE	National Association for Humanities Education (U.S.A.)
NAHEM	National Association of Health Estate Managers
NAHEMA	NATO Helicopter (NH90) Design, Development, Production and Logistics Management Agency
NAHFO	National Association of Hospital Fire Officers (U.K., U.S.A.)
NAHG	National Association of Homoeopathic Groups
NAHHRM	National Association of Healthcare Human Resources Management
NAHI	Nederlands Agronomisch Historisch Instituut
NAHO	National Association of Homeowners
NAHP	National Association of Hypnotists and Psychotherapists (*now* NACHP)
NAHPS	National Association of Hospital Play Staff
NAHRI	National Animal Husbandry Research Institute (Denmark)
NAHRO	National Association of Housing and Redevelopment Officials (U.S.A.)
NAHRW	National Association of Human Rights Workers (U.S.A.)
NAHS	National Association of Health Stores
NAHSA	National Association for Hearing and Speech Action (U.S.A.)
NAHSE	National Association of Health Services Executives (U.S.A.)
NAHSL	North Atlantic Health Sciences Libraries
NAHSPO	National Association of Health Service Personnel Officers

NAHSSO	National Association of Health Service Security Officers
NAHT	National Association of Head Teachers
NAI	Nanjing Aeronautical Institute (China)
NAI	National Association of Instructors
NAI	Nordiska Afrikaninstitutet (Sweden) = SIAS
NAIBD	National Association of Industries for the Blind and Disabled
NAIC	National Advice & Information Centre for Outdoor Education
NAIC	National Association of Investment Clubs
NAIC	National Astronomy and Ionosphere Center (U.S.A.)
NAICC	National Association of Independent Computer Companies (U.S.A.)
NAICJA	National American Indian Court Judges Association
NAICU	National Association of Independent Colleges and Universities (U.S.A.)
NAICV	National Association of Ice Cream Vendors (U.S.A.)
NAID	National Association of Industrial Distributors
NAIDM	National Association of Insecticide and Disinfectant Manufacturers (U.S.A.)
NAIEA	National Association of Inspectors and Educational Advisers (*now* NAEIAC)
NAIES	National Association of Interdisciplinary Ethnic Studies (U.S.A.)
NAIF	National Association for Irish Freedom (U.S.A.)
NAIF	Nordens Akademiska Idrotts-förbund
NAIG	Nippon Atomic Industry Group (Japan)
NAIL	National Agro Industries Limited (Seychelles)
NAIL	Neurotics Anonymous International Liaison (U.S.A.)
NAIOP	National Association of Industrial and Office Parks (U.S.A.)
NAIPRC	Netherlands Automatic Information Processing Research Centre
NAIR	National Association of Independent Retailers (Éire)
NAISS	National Association of Iron and Steel Stockholders
NAITA	National Association of Independent Travel Agents
NAITTE	National Association of Industrial and Technical Teacher Educators (U.S.A.)
NAIWC	National Association of Inland Waterway Carriers
NAIY	National Association of Indian Youth (U.K.)
NAJAKS	Nordic Association for Japanese and Korean Studies
NAK	Nederlandse Algemene Keuringsdienst voor Landouwzaden en Aardappelpootgoed
NAK	Nordiska Ambetsmannakommittén Konsumentfragor = NCCA, NEK
NAKB	Nederlandse Algemene Keuringsdienst voor Boomkwekerijgewassen
NAKBA	National Association to Keep and Bear Arms (U.S.A.)
NAKG	Nederlandse Algemene Keuringsdienst voor Groente en Bloemzaden
NAKMAS	National Association of Karate & Martial Arts Schools
NAKN	National Anti-Klan Network (U.S.A.)
NAKS	Nederlandse Algemene Keuringsdienst voor Siergewassen
NAL	National Acoustic Laboratory (Australia)
NAL	National Aeronautical Laboratory (India, U.S.A.)
NAL	National Aerospace Laboratory (Japan)
NAL	National Agricultural Library (U.S.A.)
NAL	National Air Lines (U.S.A.)
NAL	Normenausschuss Lebensmittel und Landwirtschaftliche Produkte im DIN
NAL	Norske Agenters Landsforbund
NAL	Norske Arkitekters Landsforbund
NAL	Norske Avisers Landforbund
NALA	National Adult Literacy Agency (Éire)
NALA	National Association of Language Advisers
NALAA	National Assembly of Local Arts Agencies (U.S.A.)
NALAC	National Association of Local Arts Councils
NALC	National Association of Ladies Circles of Great Britain and Ireland
NALC	National Association of Laryngectomee Clubs
NALC	National Association of Lawyers for Children
NALC	National Association of Local Councils

NALCC	National Automatic Laundry Cleaning Council	**NAMARCO**	National Marketing Corporation (Philippines)
NALCD	National Agricultural Library and Centre for Documentation (Hungary)	**NAMB**	National Agricultural Marketing Board (Canada, Zambia)
NALD	National Association of Limbless Disabled	**NAMB**	National Association of Master Bakers, Confectioners and Caterers
NALF	Norsk Arbeidslederforbund	**NAMBLA**	North American Men-Boy Love Association
NALGO	National and Local Government Officers Association (*now* UNISON)	**NAMC**	Nihon Aeroplane Manufacturing Company (Japan)
NALGWC	National Association of Local Government Women's Committees	**NAMCO**	North American Management Council (CIOS)
NALHF	National Association of Leagues of Hospital Friends	**NAMCO**	North Atlantic Marine Cooperative Commission
NALHM	National Association of Licensed House Managers	**NAMCW**	National Association for Maternal and Child Welfare
NALI	National Association of the Launderette Industry	**NAMD**	National Association of Market Developers (U.S.A.)
NALIC	National Association of Loft Insulation Contractors	**NAME**	National Anti-Racist Movement in Education
NALM	National Association of Lift Makers	**NAME**	National Association of Management/ Marketing Educators (U.S.A.)
NALO	National Association of Launderette Owners	**NAME**	National Association of Marine Enginebuilders
NALR	North American Liturgy Resources	**NAME**	National Association of Marine Engineers of Canada
NALRET	National Association for Learning Resources Educational Technology	**NAME**	National Association of Medical Examiners (U.S.A.)
NALS	National Association of Legal Secretaries (U.S.A.)	**NAME**	New American Music in Europe
NALSAT	National Association of Land Settlement Association Tenants	**NAMF**	National Association of Metal Finishers (U.S.A.)
NALSI	National Association of Life Science Industries (U.S.A.)	**NAMFREL**	National Citizens' Movement for Free Elections (Philippines)
NALSO	National Association of Labour Student Organisations	**NAMG**	National Association of Multiple Grocers
NAM	National Association of Manufacturers (U.S.A.)	**NAMHI**	National Association for the Mentally Handicappped of Ireland
NAM	Nederlandse Aardolie Maatschappij	**NAMHO**	National Association of Mining History Organisations
NAM	Non-Aligned Movement		
NAM	Normenausschuss Maschinenbau im DIN	**NAMI**	National Association of Malleable Ironfounders
NAM-A	National Association of Mathematics Advisers	**NAML**	National Association of Marine Laboratories
NAMA	National Account Marketing Association (U.S.A.)	**NAMM**	National Association of Margarine Manufacturers (U.S.A.)
NAMA	National Agri-Marketing Association (U.S.A.)	**NAMM**	National Association of Master Masons
NAMA	National Assistance Management Association (U.S.A.)	**NAMM**	National Association of Mirror Manufacturers (U.S.A.)
NAMA	National Automatic Merchandising Association (U.S.A.)	**NAMMA**	NATO Multi Role Combat Aircraft Development and Production Management Agency
NAMA	North American Mycological Association		

NAMMC	Natural Asphalt Mine-Owners' and Manufacturers' Council
NAMMC	North Atlantic Marine Mammal Commission
NAMO	National Agricultural Marketing Officials (U.S.A.)
NAMP	National Association of Meat Purveyors (U.S.A.)
NAMPUS	National Association of Master Plumbers of the United States
NAMPW	National Association of Meat Processors and Wholesalers (U.S.A.)
NAMS	National Association of Marine Services (U.S.A.)
NAMSA	NATO Maintenance and Supply Agency
NAMSB	National Association of Mutual Savings Banks (U.S.A.)
NAMSO	NATO Maintenance and Supply Organisation
NAMSR	National Association of Multiple Shoe Repairers (*now* BSRA)
NAMT	National Association for Music Therapy (U.S.A.)
NAMT	Norwegian Association of Microbiological Technologists
NAMUCAR	Naviera Multinacional del Caribe (Costa Rica)
NAN News	Agency of Nigeria
NANA	Northwest Alaska Natives Association (U.S.A.)
NANAP	Non-Aligned News Agency Pool
NANAWO	Namibia National Women's Organization
NANCIE	Centre International de l'Eau
NANCO	National Association of Noise Control Officials (U.S.A.)
NANFM	National Association of Non-Ferrous Scrap Metal Merchants
NANFPT	National Association of Natural Family Planning Teachers
NANGOF	Namibian NGO Forum
NANICA	Naviera Nicaragüense
NANN	National Association of Nursery Nurses
NANP	National Association of Naturopathic Physicians (U.S.A.)
NANS	National Association of Nigerian Students
NANU	National Association of Non-Unionists
NAO	National Accordion Organisation of the United Kingdom
NAO	National Audit Office
NAO	Nautical Almanac Office (RGO)
NAOE	National Association for Outdoor Education
NAOMI	National Association of Ovulation Method Instructors
NAON	National Association of Orthopaedic Nurses (U.S.A.)
NAOO	National Association of Optometrists and Opticians (U.S.A.)
NAOP	National Association of Operative Plasterers
NAOSH	National Authority for Occupational Safety and Health (Éire)
NAP	National Action Party (Turkey) = MHP
NAP	National Afforestation Program
NAP	National Agency for Privatisation (Romania) = FPP
NAP	National Alliance Party (Sierra Leone)
NAP	National Association of Parliamentarians (U.S.A.)
NAP	National Awami Party (Bangladesh)
NAP	Niger Agricultural Project (Nigeria)
NAP	Northern Agricultural Producers
NAPA	National Agricultural Plastics Association (U.S.A.)
NAPA	National Agricultural Press Association (U.S.A.)
NAPA	National Alcohol Producers' Association (U.S.A.)
NAPA	National Association of Press Agencies
NAPAEO	National Association of Principal Agricultural Education Officers
NAPAP	National Acidic Precipitation Assessment Program (U.S.A.)
NAPARE	National Association for Perinatal Addiction Research and Education
NAPB	National Agricultural Products Boards (Tanzania)
NAPB	Nederlandse Aannemersbond en Patroonsbond voor de Bouwbedrijven in Nederland
NAPCA	National Association of Pension Consultants and Administrators (U.S.A.)
NAPCA	National Association of Pipe Coating Applicators (U.S.A.)
NAPCAE	National Association of Public Continuing and Adult Education (U.S.A.)

NAPCE	National Association for Pastoral Care in Education	**NAPMA**	NATO Airborne Early Warning & Control Programme Management Agency
NAPCE	National Association of Professors of Christian Education (U.S.A.)	**NAPMECA**	National Association of Postgraduate Medical Education Centre Administrators
NAPCEPE	North Aegean Petroleum Company EPE (Greece)	**NAPNES**	National Association for Practical Nurse Education and Service (U.S.A.)
NAPD	National Association of Pharmaceutical Distributors	**NAPO**	National Association of Probation Officers
NAPD	National Association of Plastics Distributors (U.S.A.) (*now* BAPW)	**NAPO**	National Association of Property Owners
NAPDEA	North American Professional Driver Education Association (U.S.A.)	**NAPP**	National Association for Patient Participation
NAPE	National Association of Port Employers	**NAPP**	National Association for the Protection of Punters
NAPE	National Association of Power Engineers (U.S.A.)	**NAPPH**	National Association of Private Psychiatric Hospitals (U.S.A.)
NAPE	National Association of Primary Education	**NAPPO**	North American Plant Protection Organization (Canada)
NAPE	National Association of Professional Educators (U.S.A.)	**NAPR**	National Association of Pram Retailers
NAPE	National Association of Professional Engravers (U.S.A.)	**NAPR**	National Association of Publishers Representatives (U.S.A.)
NAPEHE	National Association for Physical Education in Higher Education (U.S.A.)	**NAPRECA**	Natural Products Research Network for Eastern and Central Africa (UNESCO) (Ethiopia)
NAPF	National Association of Pension Funds	**NAPRI**	National Animal Production Research Institute (Nigeria)
NAPGC	National Association of Public Golf Courses	**NAPROLE**	Société Industrielle Métallique et Produits Souples Bernard Nau, Daniel Provence et Claude Leclerc (Ivory Coast)
NAPH	National Association of Professors of Hebrew (U.S.A.)		
NAPH&MSC	National Association of Plumbing, Heating and Mechanical Services Contractors	**NAPS**	National Association for Premenstrual Syndrome
NAPIM	National Association of Printing Ink Manufacturers (U.S.A.)	**NAPS**	National Association of Personal Secretaries
NAPL	National Association of Printers and Lithographers (U.S.A.)	**NAPS**	National Auricula and Primula Society
NAPLIB	National Association of Aerial Photographic Libraries	**NAPS**	Nationwide Association of Preserving Specialists
NAPLO	National Association of Power Loom Overlookers	**NAPSA**	National Association of Public Service Advertisers
NAPM	National Association of Paper Merchants	**NAPSAC**	National Association for the Protection from Sexual Abuse of Adults and Children with Learning Disabilities
NAPM	National Association of Pastoral Musicians (U.S.A.)	**NAPT**	National Association of Percussion Teachers
NAPM	National Association of Perry Makers		
NAPM	National Association of Pharmaceutical Manufactures (U.S.A.)	**NAPT**	National Association of Physical Therapists (U.S.A.)
NAPM	National Association of Photographic Manufactures (U.S.A.)	**NAPTW**	National Association of Pet Trade Wholesalers
NAPM	National Association of Purchasing Management (U.S.A.)	**NAPV**	National Association of Prison Visitors

NAPWPT	National Association of Professional Word Processing Technicians (U.S.A.)	**NARIC**	National Rice and Corn Corporation (Philippines)
NAQP	National Association of Quick Printers (U.S.A.)	**Narkom-zdrav**	Narodnyi Komissariat Zdravokhraneniia
NAR	National Alliance for Reconstruction (Trinidad and Tobago)	**Narkom-zem**	Narodnyi Komissariat Zemledeliia
NAR	Nationale Adviesraad voor Ontwikkelingssamenwerking	**NARM**	National Association of Relay Manufacturers (U.S.A.)
NAR	Nordisk Amatørteaterrad	**NARMC**	National Association of Regional Media Centers (U.S.A.)
NAR	Nordiska Akademikerrådet	**NARO**	Naval Aircraft Repair Organisation
NAR	Nouvelle Action Royaliste	**NARO**	North American Regional Office (FAO)
NAR	Nuclei Armati Rivoluzionari	**NARP**	National Association of Railroad Passengers (U.S.A.)
NARA	National Amateur Rowing Association	**NARP**	Nordiska Ambetsmanna-Kommittén Regionalpolitik
NARA	National Animal Rescue Association	**NARPD**	National Association for the Relief of Paget's Disease
NARA	National Archives and Records Administration (U.S.A.)	**NARPO**	National Association of Retired Police Officers
NARC	National Association for Retarded Children (U.S.A.)	**NARPS**	National Association of UK River Protection Societies
NARCOM	North American Research Group on Management	**NARPV**	National Association for Remotely Piloted Vehicles (U.S.A.)
NARE	National Association for Remedial Education (*now* NASEN)	**NARRA**	National Resettlement and Rehabilitation Administration (Philippines)
NAREC	National Association of Racial Equality Councils	**NARS**	National Archives and Records Service (U.S.A.)
NARES	National Association of Re-enactment Societies	**NARS**	National Association of Radiator Specialists
NARF	National Association of Rehabilitation Facilities (U.S.A.)	**NARS**	Nordic Working Group on Reactor Safety
NARF	National Association of Retail Furnishers	**NARSAD**	National Alliance for Research on Schizophrenia and Depression (U.S.A.)
NARGC	National Association of Regional Game Councils (Éire)	**NARSC**	National Association of Reinforcing Steel Contractors (U.S.A.)
NARGN	National Association of Retail Grocers of Norway	**NARSIS**	National Association for Road Safety Instruction in Schools
NARGUS	National Association of Retail Grocers of the United States	**NARST**	National Association for Research in Science Teaching (U.S.A.)
NARI	Nanjing Automation Research Institute	**NARTAR**	National Association for Race Relations Teaching and Action Research
NARI	Natal Agricultural Research Institute (South Africa)	**NARTM**	National Association of Rope and Twine Merchants
NARI	National Agricultural Research Institute (Japan)	**NARU**	North Australia Research Unit (of ANU)
NARI	National Agricultural Research Institute of Guyana	**NAS**	National Academy of Sciences (U.S.A.)
NARI	National Association of Recycling Industries (U.S.A.)	**NAS**	National Association of Shopfitters
NARIC	European Community Network of the National Academic Recognition Information Centres (ERASMUS)	**NAS**	National Association of Shopkeepers of Great Britain and Northern Ireland
NARIC	National Academic Recognition Information Centre		

NAS	National Audubon Society (U.S.A.)	**NASC**	National Association of Scaffolding Contractors
NAS	National Autistic Society	**NASC**	National Association of Solar Contractors (U.S.A.)
NAS	Nautical Archaeology Society		
NAS	Nebraska Academy of Sciences	**NASC**	National Association of Student Councils (U.S.A.)
NAS	Noise Abatement Society		
NAS	Nordisk Akustik Selskab	**NASC**	National Aviation Security Committee
NAS	Nordisk Audiologisk Selskab	**NASCAS**	National Academy of Sciences Committee on Atmosphere Sciences (U.S.A.)
NAS	Norges Akademikersamband		
NAS	Normenausschuss Schweisstechnik im DIN		
NAS/UWT	National Association of Schoolmasters / Union of Women Teachers	**NASCH**	National Association of Swimming Clubs for the Handicapped
		NASCID	National Society for Children with Intestinal Disorders
NASA	National Advertising Sales Association		
NASA	National Aeronautics and Space Administration (U.S.A.)	**NASCMVE**	National Academy of Sciences Committee on Motor Vehicle Emissions (U.S.A.)
NASA	National Association of Schools of Art (U.S.A.)		
		NASCO	National Academy of Sciences Committee on Oceanography (U.S.A.)
NASA	National Settlement Authority (Libya)		
NASA	Nigerian Anthropological and Sociological Association	**NASCO**	National Agricultural Supply Company (U.S.A.) = OCSAN
NASA	Nordic Association for South Asian Studies	**NASCO**	North Atlantic Salmon Conservation Organisation
NASA	North Atlantic Seafood Association (U.S.A.)	**NASCOM**	NASA Communications Network
		NASD	National Amalgamated Stevedores and Dockers
NASAA	National Assembly of State Arts Agencies (U.S.A.)		
NASAA	National Association for Sustainable Agriculture in Australia	**NASD**	National Association for Staff Development in Further and Higher Education
NASAB	National Association of Shippers Advisory Boards (U.S.A.)	**NASD**	National Association of Securities Dealers (U.S.A.)
NASACO	National Shipping Agencies Company (Tanzania)	**NASDA**	National Space Development Agency (Japan)
NASAD	National Association of Sport Aircraft Designers (U.S.A.)	**NASDEC**	National Assets and Services Development Export Consortium
NASAE	National Association of Supervisors of Agricultural Education (U.S.A.)	**NASDU**	National Amalgamated Stevedores and Dockers Union
NASAP	North American Society of Adlerian Psychology	**NASDVE**	National Association of State Directors of Vocational Education (U.S.A.)
NASAR	National Association for Search and Rescue (U.S.A.)	**NASEAS**	Nordic Association for Southeast Asian Studies
NASBA	National Automobile Safety Belt Association	**NASEES**	National Association of Soviet and East European Studies (*now* BASEES)
NASBE	National Association of State Boards of Education (U.S.A.)	**NASEN**	National Association for Special Educational Needs (*ex* NARE, NCSE)
NASBE	National Association of Supervisors of Business Education (U.S.A.)	**NASF**	National Association of State Foresters (U.S.A.)
NASBOSA	National Academy of Sciences Board on Ocean Science Affairs (U.S.A.)	**NASFW**	National Association of Solid Fuel Wholesalers
NASC	National Association for the Salvation of the Country (Sudan)	**NASG**	National Association of Specimen Groups

NASH	National Association of Specimen Hunters	**NASSTIE**	National Association of State Supervisors of Trade and Industrial Education (U.S.A.)
NASHAC	National Associations for Safety and Health in the Arts and Crafts (U.S.A.)	**NASU**	National Adult School Union
NASHAW	National Association for Statewide Health and Welfare (U.S.A.)	**NASUA**	National Associations of State Units on Ageing (U.S.A.)
NASIS	National Association for State Information Systems (U.S.A.)	**NASULGC**	National Association of State Universities and Land-Grant Colleges (U.S.A.)
NASK	Normenausschung Siebböden und Kornmessung im DIN	**NASW**	National Association of Science Writers (U.S.A.)
NASL	North American Soccer League	**NASW**	National Association of Social Workers (U.S.A.)
NASMHPD	National Associations of State Mental Health Program Directors (U.S.A.)	**NASWE**	National Association of Social Workers in Education
NASMO	National Association of Schools Meals Organisers (*now* LACA)	**NAT**	Nämnden för Avkommeundersökning av Tjurar
NASO	National Adult School Organisation	**NAT**	National AIDS Trust
NASO	National Association of Sports Officials (U.S.A.)	**NAT**	National Association of Toastmasters
NASO	National Astrological Society (U.S.A.)	**NAT**	National Association of Tripe Dressers
NASO	Network of African Scientific Organisations (AAS) (Kenya)	**NAT**	Nordiska Aembetsmanna-Kommittén Transportfrágor
NASOL	Norske Symfoni-Orkestres Landsforbund	**NATA**	National Air Transportation Association
NASP	National Association of School Psychologists (U.S.A.)	**NATA**	National Association of Testing Authorities (Australia)
NASPAA	National Association of Schools of Public Affairs and Administration (U.S.A.)	**NATA**	National Aviation Trades Association (U.S.A.)
NASPCS	National Advisory Service for Parents of Children with a Stoma	**NATAS**	National Academy of Television Arts and Sciences (U.S.A.)
NASPE	National Association for Sport and Physical Education (U.S.A.)	**NATCO**	Northern Advanced Technologies Corporation (U.S.A.)
NASPHV	National Association of State Public Health Veterinarians (U.S.A.)	**NATCOL**	Natural Food Colours Association
NASPM	National Association of Seed Potato Merchants	**NATD**	National Association for the Teaching of Drama
NASPO	National Association of Senior Probation Officers	**NATD**	National Association of Teachers of Dancing
NASPO	National Association of State Purchasing Officials (U.S.A.)	**NATD**	National Association of Tile Distributors
NASS	National Ankylosing Spondylitis Society	**NATD**	National Association of Tobacco Distributors (U.S.A.)
NASS	National Association of Semen Suppliers	**NATD**	National Association of Tool Dealers
NASS	National Association of Steel Stockholders	**NATD**	National Association of Tripe Dressers
NASSH	North American Society for Sport History	**NATE**	National Association for the Teaching of English
NASSS	National Association for the Support of Small Schools	**NATEC**	Institut für Naturwissenschaftlich-Technische Dienste
		NATEC	Naval Air Technical Evaluation Centre
		NATECLA	National Association for the Teaching of English and other Community Languages to Adults

NATESA	National Alliance of Television and Electronics Servicers of America	**NATU**	National Association of Trade Unions (Philippines)
NATESLA	National Association for the Teaching of English as a Second Language to Adults	**NATURA**	Réseau des Universités Agronomiques Européennes à Orientation Tropicale et Subtropicale en Rélation avec le Développement Agricole
NATEX	National Textile Industries Corporation Ltd (Tanzania)		
NATF	Norsk Apoteknikerforbund	**NatVALA**	National Viewers & Listeners Association
NATFHE	National Association of Teachers in Further and Higher Education	**NAU**	Nordiska Unionen för Arbetsledare, Tekniska Functionårer och Andra Chefer
NATFHE	National Association of Teachers of Further and Higher Education		
NATG	National Association of Training Groups (*now* NTF)	**NAUA**	Nordic Association of University Administrators (Finland)
NATGA	National Amateur Tobacco Growers' Association	**NAUI**	National Association of Underwater Instructors (U.S.A.)
NATHE	National Association of Teachers of Home Economics	**NAUMP**	National Association of Uniform Manufacturers and Distributors (U.S.A.)
NATIE	National Association for Trade and Industrial Education (U.S.A.)	**NAUS**	National Association for Urban Studies
NATMAC	National Air Traffic Management Advisory Committee	**NAUT**	Nordisk Arbeidsmarkedsutvalg = NLMC
NATMAP	Division of National Mapping (*now* AUSLIG)	**NAUTT**	National Association of Unions in the Textile Trade
NATMH	National Association of Teachers of the Mentally Handicapped	**NAUW**	National Association of University Women (U.S.A.)
NATN	National Association of Theatre Nurses	**NAV**	Nederlandse Aerosole Vereniging
NATO	National Association of Temperance Officials	**NAV**	Nederlandse Anthropogenetische Vereniging
NATO	National Association of Tenants Organisations (Éire)	**NAV**	Nederlandse Architekten Vereniging
NATO	North Atlantic Treaty Organisation = OTAN	**NAV**	Normenausschuss Vakuumtechnik im DIN
NATPS	National Association of Trade Protection Societies	**NAVA**	National Association for Vetrinary Acupuncture (U.S.A.)
NATR	National Association of Tenants and Residents	**NAVA**	National Audio-Visual Association
NATR	National Association of Toy Retailers (*now* BATR)	**NAVAS**	Nederlandse Aannemers Vereniging van Afbouw-en Stukadoorswerken
NATS	National Air Traffic Services (CAA, MOD)	**NaVAST**	Nationaal Verbond der Aannemers-Schrijnwerkers en Timmerlieden
NATS	National Association of Teachers of Singing (U.S.A.)	**NAVB**	National Association of Volunteer Bureaux
NATS	National Associaton of Textile Supervisors (U.S.A.)	**NAVBC**	National Agricultural and Veterinary Biotechnology Centre (Éire)
NATS	Nordisk Avisteknisk Samarbetsnémned	**NAVBO**	North American Vascular Biology Organization
NATT	National Association of Teachers of Travellers	**Navecaribe**	Empresa de Navegación Caribe (Cuba)
NATTA	Network for Alternative Technology and Technology Assessment	**NAVEG**	Nederlandse Agentenvereniging op Verlichtings-en Electrotechnisch Gebied
NATTS	National Association of Trade and Technical Schools (U.S.A.)	**NAVEMHA**	Nationaal Verbond der Melk-en Zuivelhandelaars van België
		NAVETEX	Nationaal Verbond der Textiel- en Kledingdetaillanten (Belgium) = ANDT

NAVEWA	Nationale Vereniging der Waterleidingbedrijven (Belgium) = ANSEAU	**NAWG**	National Association of Wheat Growers (U.S.A.)
NAVF	Norges Almenvitenskapelige Forskningsråd	**NAWGA**	National-American Wholesale Grocers Association
NAVGRA	Navy and Vickers Gearing Research Association	**NAWICS**	National Anglo-West Indian Conservative Society
NAVH	National Association of Voluntary Hostels	**NAWK**	National Association of Warehouse Keepers
NAVHO	National Association of Voluntary Help Organisers (*now* NAVSM)	**NAWL**	National Association of Women Layers (U.S.A.)
NAVIGA	World Organisation for Modelship Building and Modelship Sport	**NAWO**	National Alliance of Women's Organizations
NAVISAL	Compania Naviera Salvadoreña S.A.	**NAWP**	National Association of Women Pharmacists
NAVL	National Anti-Vaccination League	**NAWPM**	National Association of Wholesale Paint Merchants
NAVM	Nurses Anti-Vivisection Movement		
NAVP	National Association of Veal Producers	**NAWPU**	National Association of Water Power Users
NAVROM	Navigatia Maritima si Fluviala Romana		
NAVS	National Anti-Vivisection Society	**NAWU**	National Agricultural Workers Union (U.S.A.)
NAVSA	Syndicat National de Vente et Services Automatiques	**NAYC**	National Association of Young Cricketers
NAVSM	National Association of Voluntary Service Managers (*ex* NAVHO)	**NAYC**	National Association of Youth Clubs
NAVSS	National Association of Victims Support Schemes	**NAYCEO**	National Association of Youth and Community Education Officers
NAW	National Assembly of Women	**NAYE**	National Association of Young Entrepreneurs (India)
NAW	National Association of Wholesaler – Distributors (U.S.A.)	**NAYO**	National Association of Youth Orchestras
NAW	National Association of Widows		
NAW	Normenausschuss Wasserwesen um DIN	**NAYPCAS**	National Association of Young Peoples Counselling and Advisory Services
NAWA	Namibian Women's Association	**NAYPIC**	National Association of Young People In Care
NAWA	National Association of Women Artists (U.S.A.)	**NAYSO**	National Association of Youth Service Officers
NAWAFA	North Atlantic Westbound Freight Association	**NAYT**	National Association of Youth Theatres
NAWAPA	North American Water and Power Alliance	**NB**	Nordiska Bowlingförbundet
NAWB	National Association of Wine and Beermakers	**NB**	Norges Byforbund
		NB	Norsk Betongforening
NAWB	National Association of Workshops for the Blind Incorporated	**NBA**	National Bar Associations (U.S.A.)
		NBA	National Beekeepers Association of New Zealand
NAWBM	National Association of Wine & Beer Makers	**NBA**	National Benzole and Allied Products Association
NAWC	National Association of Womens' Clubs		
NAWCH	National Association for the Welfare of Children in Hospital	**NBA**	National Blood Authority
		NBA	National Braille Association
NAWDC	National Association of Waste Disposal Contractors Ltd	**NBA**	National Brassfoundry Association
		NBA	National Broadcasting Authority (Bangladesh)
NAWF	North American Wildlife Foundation (U.S.A.)	**NBA**	National Building Agency (Éire, U.K.)

NBA	Niger Basin Authority	**NBCW**	National Board of Catholic Women
NBAA	National Business Aircraft Association (U.S.A.)	**NBD**	National Bank for Development (Egypt)
		NBD	Nederlandse Bond van Dansleraren
NBAB	Nederlandse Bond van Architecten, Bouwvakpatroons	**NBD**	Nordisk Byggedag
		NBDA	National Bicycle Dealers Association
NBAD	National Bank of Abu Dhabi	**NBDC**	National Broadcasting Development Committee
NBAD	National Bank of Bahrein		
NBAD	National Bank of Brunei	**NBDF**	Norsk Bedriftsykepleier-Diakonforening
NBAPA	National Benzole and Allied Products Association	**NBEA**	National Business Education Association (U.S.A.)
NBB	Nationale Bank van België = BNB	**NBEET**	National Board of Employment, Education and Training (Australia)
NBB	Nederlandse Boekverkopersbond		
NBB	Nederlandse Bond van Bouwondernemers	**NBEO**	National Board of Examiners in Optometry (U.S.A.)
NBB	Vereniging Nederlandsch Binnenvaartbureau	**NBER**	National Bureau of Economic Research (U.S.A.)
NBBE	National Board for Bakery Education	**NBF**	National Bedding Federation
NBBFP	Nationale Bond der Belgische Filmproducenten	**NBF**	National Boccia Federation
		NBF	Nederlandse Bond van Filmers
NBBL	Norske Boligbyggelags Landsforbund	**NBF**	Nordisk Barnkirurgisk Förening = ScAPS
NBBR	Nordens Blåkors- och Blåbandsråd		
NBBS	Nederlands Bureau voor Buitenlandse Studentenbetrekkingen	**NBF**	Norges Bilbransjeforbund
		NBF	Norsk Bedriftsoøkonomisk Forening
NBBZ	Nederlandse Bond van Bad-en Zweminrichtingen	**NBF**	Norsk Bibliotekforening
		NBF	Norsk Blomsterhandlerforbund
NBC	National Bank of Commerce (Tanzania)	**NBF**	Norsk Botanisk Forening
NBC	National Black Caucus	**NBF**	Norsk Brannvern Forening
NBC	National Book Council (Australia)	**NBF**	Norske Byggevareprodusenters Forening
NBC	National Broadcasting Company (U.S.A.)		
		NBFA	National Benevolent Fund for the Aged
NBC	Nigerian Broadcasting Corporation	**NBFA**	National Business Forms Association (U.S.A.)
NBC	Nordens Bondeorganisationers Centralråd		
		NBFBV	Nationale Belgische Federatie der Baanvervoerders = FNBTR
NBCC	National Book Critics Circle (U.S.A.)		
NBCC	National Buildings Construction Corporation (India)	**NBFFO**	National Board of Fur Farm Organizations (U.S.A.)
NBCC	Nigerian-British Chamber of Commerce	**NBFGR**	National Bureau of Fish Genetic Resources (India)
NBCDA	National Business Computer Dealers Association	**NBFMA**	National Building Frame Manufacturers Association
NBCDI	National Black Child Development Institute (U.S.A.)	**NBFV**	Nederlandse Bond van Filatelisten Verenigingen
NBCI	Nigerian Bank for Commerce and Industry	**NBG**	Neue Bachgesellschaft
		NBGA	National Bingo Game Association Ltd
NBCK	Nederlandse Bond van Copieerders en Klein-Offsetdrukkers	**NBHS**	National Bureau for Handicapped Students
NBCP	National Book Council of Pakistan		
NBCRC	National Biological Control Research Centre (Thailand)	**NBI**	National Benevolent Institution
		NBI	Norges Byggforskningsinstitutt
NBCS	Nederlandse Bond van Christelijke Schilderpatroons	**NBIF**	Norsk Bergindustriforening

NBIN	National Biodiversity Information Network (Indonesia)	**NBRU**	National Bus and Rail Union (Éire)
NBIRN	National Bureau of Industrial Research, Nanking (China)	**NBS**	National Broadcasting Service (New Zealand, Trinidad and Tobago)
NBK	National Bank of Kazakhstan	**NBS**	Nauru Broadcasting Service
NBK	National Bank of Kuwait	**NBS**	Nordiska Byggforskningsorganens Samarbetsgrupp
NBK	Nederlandse Bond van Kunstenaars	**NBS**	Norsk Bedriftsoøkonomisk Samfunn
NBK	Nordisk Bilteknisk Komité	**NBS**	Norsk Biokjemisk Selskap
NBKV	Nederlandse Bond van Konijnenfokkersverenigingen	**NBS**	Norske Bonde-og Småbrukarlag
NBL	Norsk Bibliotekarlag	**NBSB**	National Biological Standards Board
NBL	Norsk Blomsterdyrkerlag	**NBSGB**	National Bonsai Society of Great Britain
NBLC	Nederlands Bibliotheek en Lektuur Centrum	**NBSI**	National Bible Society of Ireland
NBM	Nederlandse Bond van Makelaars in Onroerende Goederen	**NBSL**	National Biological Standards Laboratory (Australia)
NBM	Nordisk Byggforskningsmöte	**NBSS**	National Bible Society of Scotland
NBME	National Board of Medical Examiners (U.S.A.)	**NBSS**	National British Softball Society
		NBT	National Book Trust, India
NBNA	National Benchmark Network for Agrometeorology	**NBTA**	National Baton Twirling Association
NBNI	Nasionale Bounavorsingsinstituut (South Africa)	**NBTF**	Nordiska Byggnads- och Tråabetarefederationen
NBO	National Bank of Oman	**NBTPI**	National Book Trade Provident Institution
NBO	National Buildings Organization (India)	**NBU**	National Busworkers Union (Éire)
NBO	Nordisk Byggnads-Kooperativ Organisation	**NBU**	Nordiska Bankmannaunionen
NBO	Nordiska Kooperativa och Allmännyttiga Bostadsföretags Organisation = NHCO, ONCPUHE	**NBV**	Nederlandse Biotechnologische Vereniging
		NBV	Nederlandse Bodemkundige Vereniging
NBOV	Nederlandse Banketbakkers Ondernemers Vereniging	**NBvA**	Nederlandse Bond van Assurantie-Agenten
NBP	Narodwy Bank Polski	**NBvFV**	Nederlandse Bond van Filatelisten-Verenigingen
NBP	New Britain Party	**NC**	Nepali Congress
NBPA	National Back Pain Association	**NC**	Nordic Council = NR, PN
NBPGR	National Bureau of Plant Genetic Resources (India)	**NC**	Norsk Cementforening
NBPS	National Backgammon Players Society of Great Britain	**NCA**	Nationaal Comité voor Studie en Preventie van het Alkoholisme en andere Toxicomanieën
NBPS	Nederlandse Bon van Patroons in het Steen- Houtgraniet- en Kunststeenbedrijf	**NCA**	National Campaign for the Arts Limited
		NCA	National Cancer Alliance
NBR	National Bank of Romania	**NCA**	National Carpet Association (China)
NBR	National Board of Roads and Water (Finland)	**NCA**	National Caving Association
		NCA	National Coal Association (U.S.A.)
NBR	Norske Bedriftavisers Redaktøklubb	**NCA**	National Coffee Association of the USA
NBRI	National Building Research Institute (South Africa)	**NCA**	National Commission of Agriculture (India)
		NCA	National Commission on Accreditation (U.S.A.)
NBRT	National Board for Respiratory Therapy (U.S.A.)	**NCA**	National Committee on Agrometeorology

NCA	National Communications Association (U.S.A.)		**NCASI**	National Council of the Paper Industry for Air and Stream Improvement (U.S.A.)
NCA	National Confectioners Association of the United States		**NCAT**	National Center for Appropriate Technology (U.S.A.)
NCA	National Council of Aviculture		**NCAT**	National Centre for Alternative Technology
NCA	National Council on Alcoholism (U.K., U.S.A.)		**NCATC**	Nigerian Civil Aviation Training Centre
NCA	National Cranberry Association (U.S.A.)		**NCATE**	National Council for Accreditation of Teacher Education (U.S.A.)
NCA	National Cricket Association		**NCAVAE**	National Committee for Audio-Visual Aids in Education
NCA	National Crimes Authority (Australia)		**NCAW**	National Campaign Against Workfare
NCA	Nationale Commissie tegen het Alcoholisme en Andere Verslavingen		**NCAW**	National Council for Animal Welfare
NCA	Nordic Concrete Association		**NCB**	National Children's Bureau
NCAA	National Center for the Arts and the Aging (U.S.A.)		**NCB**	National Coal Board
NCAA	National Children Adoption Association		**NCB**	National Commercial Bank (Jamaica, Saudi Arabia)
NCAB	National Citizen's Advice Bureaux		**NCB**	Nationale Confederatie van het Bouwbedrijf (Belgium)
NCAB	National College der Accountants van België = CNECB		**NCB**	Nederlandse Consumentenbond
NCACC	National Civil Aviation Consultative Committee		**NCB**	Nordic Copyright Bureau
NCAD	National College for Art and Design (Éire)		**NCB**	Stichting Nederlandse Centrale voor het Begrafenisbedrijf
NCAE	National College of Agricultural Engineering		**NCBA**	National Catholic Bandmaster Association (U.S.A.)
NCAEE	National Committee on Art Education for the Elderly (U.S.A.)		**NCBA**	National Cattle Breeders' Association
NCAEG	National Confederation of American Ethnic Groups (U.S.A.)		**NCBC**	North Carolina Biotechnology Center
NCAER	National Council of Applied Economic Research (India)		**NCBE**	National Clearinghouse for Bilingual Education (U.S.A.)
NCAFMW	National Council of Associations of Fresh Meat Wholesalers		**NCBE**	National Council for Baking Education
NCAI	National Congress of American Indians		**NCBE**	National Council for Better Education (U.S.A.)
NCAIR	National Center for Automated Information Retrieval (U.S.A.)		**NCBEA**	National Catholic Business Education Association (U.S.A.)
NCAJ	National Center for Administrative Justice (U.S.A.)		**NCBI**	National Council for the Blind of Ireland
NCAL	National Centre for Athletics Literature		**NCBMP**	National Council of Building Material Producers
NCAR	National Centre for Atmospheric Research (New Zealand, U.S.A.)		**NCBNP**	Network for the Chemistry of Biologically Important Natural Products (IDP) (Australia)
NCAR	National Committee for Antarctic Research		**NCBO**	Nederlandse Christelijke Bond van Werknemers in de Hout- en Bouwnijverheid
NCAR	National Conference on the Advancement of Research (U.S.A.)		**NCBP**	National Council of the Balkan Peoples (Russian Federation)
NCARB	National Council of Architectural Registration Boards (U.S.A.)		**NCBRM**	Nederlandse Christelijke Bond van Rijwiel en Motorhandelaren
NCASI	National Campaign Against Solvent Abuse		**NCBT**	National Convention of Black Teachers

NCBT	Nationale Confederatie van de Belgische Textielreiniging		**NCCCare**	National Childcare Campaign
NCBTB	Nederlandse Christelijke Boeren- en Tuindersbond		**NCCD**	National Council on Crime and Delinquency (U.S.A.)
NCC	National Capital Commission (Canada)		**NCCE**	National Commission for Cooperative Education (U.S.A.)
NCC	National Caravan Council		**NCCED**	National Congress for Community Economic Development (U.S.A.)
NCC	National Cavy Club			
NCC	National Climatic Center (NOAA)		**NCCED**	National Council for Carers and their Elderly Dependents Ltd
NCC	National Computing Centre			
NCC	National Construction Corporation (Kenya)		**NCCEE**	Netherlands Committee for the Common Market
NCC	National Consultative Committee (ANCA)		**NCCFN**	National Coordinating Committee on Food and Nutrition (Philippines)
NCC	National Consultative Council		**NCCG**	National Council on Compulsive Gambling (U.S.A.)
NCC	National Consultative Council of the Building and Civil Engineering Industries		**NCCI**	National Committee for Commonwealth Immigrants
NCC	National Consumer Council		**NCCI**	North Central Computer Institute (U.S.A.)
NCC	National Council of Churches in New Zealand			
NCC	National Curriculum Council (*now* SCAA)		**NCCIJ**	National Catholic Conference for Interracial Justice (U.S.A.)
			NCCJ	National Conference of Christians and Jews (U.S.A.)
NCC	Nature Conservancy Council		**NCCK**	National Christian Council of Kenya
NCC-LAW	North Carolina Center for Laws Affecting Women		**NCCK**	National Consultative Committee on Kangaroos (ANCA)
NCCA	Inter-Scandinavian Committee on Consumer Matters (Norway) = NAK, NEK		**NCCK**	Nederlandse Club voor Chefkoks
			NCCL	National Council for Civil Liberties
NCCA	National Carpet Cleaners Association		**NCCL**	National Council of Canadian Labour
NCCA	National Club Cricket Association		**NCCLS**	National Committee for Clinical Laboratory Standards (U.S.A.)
NCCA	National Cotton Council of America			
NCCA	National Council for Curriculum Assessment (Éire)		**NCCM**	National Community of Croatian Montenegrins = NZCH
NCCA	National Council of Chartered Accountants (South Africa)		**NCCM**	National Council of Catholic Men (U.K., U.S.A.)
NCCA	National Council of Critical Analysis (U.S.A.)		**NCCM**	National Council of Concentrate Manufacturers
NCCA	Nordic Committee of Senior Officials for Consumer Affairs = NÄK, NEK		**NCCMCR**	National Co-ordinating Committee for Mountain and Cave Rescue (Éire)
NCCAE	National Consultative Committee for Agricultural Education		**NCCMHC**	National Council of Community Mental Health Centers (U.S.A.)
NCCAN	National Center on Child Abuse and Neglect (U.S.A.)		**NCCMHS**	National Consortium for Child Mental Health Services (U.S.A.)
NCCAS	National Committee for Climate Change and Atmospheric Sciences		**NCCNSW**	Nature Conservation Council of New South Wales
NCCAT	National Committee for Clear Air Turbulence (U.S.A.)		**NCCPA**	National Council of College Publications Advisers (U.S.A.)
NCCAW	National Consultative Committee on Animal Welfare		**NCCPAP**	National Conference of Certified Public Accountancy Practitioners (U.S.A.)
NCCB	National Council of Catholic Bishops (U.S.A.)		**NCCPB**	National Council of Commercial Plant Breeders (U.S.A.)

NCCPG	National Council for the Preservation of Plants and Gardens	**NCEA**	North Central Electric Association (U.S.A.)
NCCS	National Council of Corrosion Sciences	**NCEB**	National Council for Environmental Balance (U.S.A.)
NCCS	Nordic College of Caring Sciences	**NCEC**	National Chemical Emergency Centre
NCCV	Nederlandse Cacao en Cacaoproducten Vereniging	**NCEC**	National Christian Education Council
NCCW	National Chamber of Commerce for Women	**NCEC**	North Coast Environment Centre
		NCECA	National Council on Education for the Ceramic Arts (U.S.A.)
NCCW	National Council of Catholic Women	**NCED**	Norwegian Campaign for Environment and Development
NCD	National Commission for Democracy (Ghana)		
NCD	National Council on Drugs (U.S.A.)	**NCEER**	National Center for Earthquake Engineering Research (U.S.A.)
NCD	Nederlands Centrum van Direkteuren en Commissarissen	**NCEP**	National Council on Employment Policy (U.S.A.)
NCD	Nordic Committee on Disabilities = NNH	**NCEPC**	National Committee on Environmental Planning and Co-ordination (India)
NCDB	National Development Credit Agency (Tanzania)	**NCEPC**	National Council for Environmental Pollution Control (India)
NCDB	Nederlandse Christelijke Drogistenbond	**NCER**	National Committee for Electoral Reform
NCDC	National Climate Data Center		
NCDC	National Coal Development Corporation (India)	**NCERD**	National Council for Educational Research and Development (U.S.A.)
NCDC	National Cooperative Development Corporation (India)	**NCERT**	National Council of Educational Research and Training (India)
NCDI	National Committee for Democratic Initiatve (Mali) = CNID	**NCES**	National Center for Educational Statistics (U.S.A.)
NCDL	National Canine Defence League	**NCET**	National Council for Educational Technology
NCDP	National Coconut Development Programme (Tanzania)		
NCDP	National Commission for Development Planning (Zambia)	**NCF**	National Cancer Foundation (U.S.A.)
		NCF	National Clayware Federation
NCDRC	National Catholic Disaster Relief Committee (U.S.A.)	**NCF**	National Clothing Federation of South Africa
NCDS	National Centre for Development Studies (ANU)	**NCF**	National Coaching Foundation
NCDS	National Centre for Down's Syndrome	**NCF**	National Cooperage Federation
NCDS	National Community Development Service (U.S.A.)	**NCF**	Nordisk Cerealistförbund
		NCF	Nordiska Centerungdomens Förbund = NCY
NCDS	National Council for the Divorced and Separated	**NCF**	Norges Colonialgrossisters Forbund
NCE	National Commission on Education	**NCFA**	National Council of Forestry Association Executives (U.S.A.)
NCE	National Committee for the Environment	**NCFB**	National Collection of Food Bacteria (AFRC)
NCE	National Council for the Elderly (Éire)	**NCFC**	National Council of Farm Cooperatives (U.S.A.)
NCEA	National Catholic Education Association (U.S.A.)	**NCFI**	Nurses Christian Fellowship International
NCEA	National Community Education Association (U.S.A.)	**NCFL**	National Catholic Forensic League (U.S.A.)
NCEA	National Council for Educational Awards (Éire)	**NCFM**	National Commission on Food Marketing (U.S.A.)

NCFR	National Campaign for Firework Reform	**NCHP**	Nederlandse Centrale van Hoger Personeel
NCFR	National Council on Family Relations (U.S.A.)	**NCHS**	National Center for Health Statistics (U.S.A.)
NCFS	National College of Foot Surgeons (U.S.A.)	**NCHSE**	National Centre for Human Settlements and Environment (India)
NCFS	National Conference of Friendly Societies	**NCHSO**	National Committee of Hungarian Students Organization
NCG	National Contractors Group	**NCHV**	Nederlandse Vereniging van Christelijke Handelsreizigers en Handelsagenten
NCG	National Council on Gambling		
NCGA	National Computer Graphics Association (U.S.A.)	**NCI**	National Cancer Institute (Egypt)
		NCI	National Cancer Institute (U.S.A.)
NCGA	National Corn Growers Associaton (U.S.A.)	**NCIA**	National Cavity Insulation Association
NCGA	National Cotton Ginners' Association (U.S.A.)	**NCIC**	National Cancer Institute of Canada
		NCIC	National Cartographic Information Center (U.S.A.)
NCGCP	National Climate and Global Change Program	**NCIC**	National Construction Industry Council (U.S.A.)
NCGE	National Council for Geographic Education (U.S.A.)	**NCIC**	National Crime Information Center (FBI) (U.S.A.)
NCGEB	National Center for Genetic Engineering and Biotechnology (Thailand)	**NCIES**	National Committee for International Education through Satellites (U.S.A.)
NCGG	National Committee for Geodesy and Geophysics (Éire, Pakistan)	**NCIGBP**	National Committee for IGBP
NCGGO	National Centrum voor Grasland- en Groenvoederonderzoek	**NCIH**	National Conference of Industrial Hydraulics (U.S.A.)
NCGH	Nationality Council of Gypsies in Hungary = MCNU	**NCIH**	National Council for International Health (U.S.A.)
NCGIA	National Center for Information and Analysis (U.S.A.)	**NCIMB**	National Collection of Industrial and Marine Bacteria
NCGR	National Council for Geocosmic Research (U.S.A.)	**NCIS**	National Criminal Intelligence Service
		NCISS	National Council of Investigation and Security Services (U.S.A.)
NCGT	National Council of Geography Teachers (U.S.A.)	**NCIT**	National Council on Inland Transport
NCGV	Nationaal Centrum voor de Geestelijke Volksgezondheid	**NCITD**	National Committee on International Trade Documentation (U.S.A.)
NCH	National Campaign for the Homeless (Éire)	**NCITO**	National Council of Industry Trading Organizations
NCH	National Center for Homeopathy (U.S.A.)	**NCJW**	National Council of Jewish Women (Ecuador)
NCH	National Children's Home	**NCJWA**	National Council of Jewish Women of Australia
NCH	National Council on the Humanities (U.S.A.)	**NCK**	Nationale Confederatie van het Kaderpersoneel (Belgium) = CNC
NCHA	National Care Homes Association	**NCL**	National Chemical Laboratory (India)
NCHEE	National Council for Home Economics Education	**NCLA**	National Council for the Lay Apostolate
NCHM	National Center for Housing Management (U.S.A.)	**NCLA**	National Council of Local Administrators of Vocational Education and Practical Arts (U.S.A.)
NCHP	Navale et Commerciale Havraise Peninsulaire (Madagascar)	**NCLB**	Nederlandse Christelijke Landarbeidersbond

NCLC	National Consumer Law Center (U.S.A.)	**NCNA**	National Council on Noise Abatement (U.S.A.)
NCLC	National Council of Labour Colleges	**NCNA**	New China News Agency
NCLE	National Congress on Languages in Education	**NCNC**	National Captive Nations Committee (U.S.A.)
NCLIS	National Commission of Libraries and Information Science (U.S.A.)	**NCNC**	National Council for Nigeria and the Cameroons (Nigeria)
NCLR	National Council for Labor Reform (U.S.A.)	**NCNE**	National Campaign for Nursery Education
NCLR	National Council for Land Reform (U.S.A.)	**NCNIS**	National Committee of Navigational Instruments Standardization (China)
NCLS	National Council of Land Surveyors (U.S.A.)	**NCNL**	Nasionale Chemiese Navorsingslaboratorium (South Africa)
NCM	National College of Music	**NCNW**	National Council of Negro Women (Senegal)
NCM	Nationale Coöperatieve Melkprodukten-verkoopvereniging	**NCO**	National Council of Obesity (U.S.A.)
NCM	Nederlandse Credietverzekering Maatschappij	**NCO**	Nationale Commissie Voorlichting en Bewustwording Ontwikkelingssamenwerking
NCM	Nigerian Chamber of Mines	**NCOA**	National Council on the Ageing (U.S.A.)
NCM	Nippon Calculating Machine Company (Japan)	**NCOG**	National Centre for Organic Gardening
NCMA	National Childminding Association	**NCOI**	National Council for the Omnibus Industry
NCMA	National Concrete Masonry Association (U.S.A.)	**NCOPF**	National Council for One Parent Families
NCMA	National Contract Management Association (U.S.A.)	**NCOR**	National Committee for Oceanographic Research (Pakistan)
NCMB	Nigerian Cocoa Marketing Board	**NCOS**	Nationaal Centrum voor Ontwikkelingssamenwerking
NCMB	Nordic Council for Marine Biology = NKMB	**NCOS**	National Committee for Oceanic Sciences
NCMC	National Coalition for Marine Conservation (U.S.A.)	**NCOS**	Netherlands Christelijk Ondernemersverbond voor het Schildersbedrijf
NCME	National Council on Measurement in Education (U.S.A.)	**NCOV**	Nederlands Christelijk Ondernemers Verbond
NCMH	National Centre for Macromolecular Hydrodynamics	**NCP**	National Car Parks
NCMH	National Committee for Mental Hygiene (U.S.A.)	**NCP**	National Coalition Party (Mozambique)
NCMI	National Committee Against Mental Illness (U.S.A.)	**NCP**	National Conference of Priests
		NCP	National Convention Party (Gambia)
NCMP	National Commission for Manpower Policy (U.S.A.)	**NCP**	National Council of Psychotherapists
NCMP	National Commission on Materials Policy (U.S.A.)	**NCP**	National Country Party (Australia)
		NCP	Nepali Communist Party
NCMR	National Center for Marine Research (Greece)	**NCP**	Nepali Congress Party
		NCP	New Communist Party
NCMV	Nationaal Christelijk Middenstandsverbond (Belgium)	**NCP**	Non-Consultative Party
NCN	National Coalition for Neighbourhoods	**NCPA**	National Cottonseed Products Association (U.S.A.)
NCNA	National Children's Nurseries Association (Éire)	**NCPAC**	National Conservative Political Action Committee (U.S.A.)

NCPADD	National Committee for the Prevention of Alcoholism and Drug Dependency (U.S.A.)	**NCRI**	National Coastal Resources Research and Development Institute (U.S.A.)
NCPB	National Cereals and Produce Board (Kenya)	**NCRIr**	Society of Iridologists
NCPC	National Committee for the Protection of Consumers	**NCRL**	National Chemical Research Laboratory (South Africa)
NCPD	National Council for Population and Development	**NCRLC**	National Catholic Rural Life Conference (U.S.A.)
NCPERL	National Coalition for Public Education and Religious Liberty (U.S.A.)	**NCROPA**	National Campaign for the Reform of the Obscene Publications Acts
NCPF	National Collection of Pathogenic Fungi (PHLS)	**NCRP**	National Committee on Radiation Protection and Measurements (U.S.A.)
NCPG	National Catholic Pharmacists Guild of the United States	**NCRP**	National Council for Research and Planning (U.S.A.)
NCPGF	National Center for Postsecondary Governance and Finance (U.S.A.)	**NCRP**	New Christian Romania Party= PNRC
NCPI	National Conference of Priests of Ireland	**NCRRHA**	National Confederation of Registered Rest Home Associations
NCPJB	Nederlandse Christelijke Plattelands Jongeren Bond	**NCRT**	National College of Rubber Technology
		NCRV	Nederlandse Christelijke Radio Vereniging
NCPL	National Centre for Programmed Learning	**NCRVE**	National Center for Research in Vocational Education (U.S.A.)
NCPLA	National Council for Patent Law Associations (U.S.A.)	**NCRY**	National Commission on Resources for Youth (U.S.A.)
NCPPB	National Collection of Plant Pathogenic Bacteria (MAFF)	**NCS**	National Chrysanthemum Society
NCPPR	National Center for Public Policy Research (U.S.A.)	**NCS**	National Corrosion Service (DTI)
		NCS	Norwegian Computer Society
NCPS	National Commission on Product Safety (U.S.A.)	**NCSA**	National Center for Supercomputing Applications (U.S.A.)
NCPT	National Conference on Power Transmission (U.S.A.)	**NCSA**	North Central Sociological Association
NCPTA	National Confederation of Parent Teacher Associations	**NCSAC**	National Conservation Strategy Advisory Council
NCPUA	National Committee on Pesticide Use in Agriculture (Canada)	**NCSBCS**	National Conference of States on Building Codes and Standards (U.S.A.)
NCQHC	National Committee on Quality Health Care (U.S.A.)	**NCSC**	National Child Safety Council (U.S.A.)
		NCSC	National Companies and Securities Commission (Australia)
NCQR	National Council for Quality and Reliability	**NCSCA**	National Council of Speciality Contractors Associations (U.S.A.)
NCR	Nationale Coöperatieve Raad voor Land- en Tuinbouw	**NCSD**	Nordens Centrala Sparbanksorgans Delegation
NCRCB	National Committee on Racism in Children's Books	**NCSE**	National Council for Special Education (*now* NASEN)
NCRD	National Council for Research and Development (Israel)	**NCSF**	National Cold Storage Federation (*now* CSDF)
NCRE	National Conference on Research in English (U.S.A.)	**NCSH**	National Clearinghouse for Smoking and Health (U.S.A.)
NCRFW	National Commission on the Role of Filipino Women	**NCSI**	National Council for Stream Improvement (U.S.A.)
		NCSJ	National Commission on Social Justice
		NCSJ	National Council for Soviet Jewry

NCSL	National Conference of Standards Laboratories (U.S.A.)	**NCTL**	National Commercial Temperance League
NCSMC	National Council for the Single Mother and her Child (Australia)	**NCTM**	National Council of Teachers of Mathematics (U.S.A.)
NCSP	National Soil Conservation Program	**NCTR**	National Center for Toxicological Research (U.S.A.)
NCSR	National Centre of Systems Reliability (UKAEA)	**NCTSI**	National Council of Technical Service Industries (U.S.A.)
NCSR	National Council for Scientific Research (Lebanon, Zambia)	**NCTTF**	Northern Counties Textile Trades Federation
NCSR	National Council for Social Research (South Africa)	**NCTU**	Nangarhar Council of Trade Unions (Afghanistan)
NCSR	National Council of the Slovak Republic	**NCTU**	National Council of Trade Unions (Poland) = OPZZ
NCSS	National Center for Social Statistics (U.S.A.)	**NCTU**	Northern Carpet Trades Union
NCSS	National Council for School Sports	**NCTV**	National Coalition on Television Violence (U.S.A.)
NCSS	National Council for the Social Studies (U.S.A.)	**NCTYL**	National College for the Training of Youth Leaders
NCSSFL	National Council of State Supervisors of Foreign Languages (U.S.A.)	**NCU**	National Communications Union
NCST	National Council for Science and Technology (Nepal)	**NCU**	National Cyclists' Union
		NCU	Northern Cricket Union of Ireland
NCSTTO	National Council for the Supply and Training of Teachers Overseas	**NCUA**	National Credit Union Administration (U.S.A.)
NCSW	National Conference on Social Welfare (U.S.A.)	**NCUI**	National Cooperative Union of India
NCT	National Centre for Tribology	**NCUMC**	National Council for the Unmarried Mother and her Child
NCT	National Chamber of Trade		
NCT	National Childbirth Trust	**NCUR**	National Committee for Utilities Radio (U.S.A.)
NCTA	National Cable Television Association (U.S.A.)	**NCURA**	National Council of University Research Administrators (U.S.A.)
NCTA	National Council for Technological Awards	**NCVA**	National Council for Vocational Awards (Éire)
NCTAEP	National Committee on Technology, Automation and Economic Progress	**NCVCCO**	National Council of Voluntary Child Care Organisations
NCTC	National Collection of Type Cultures (PHLS)	**NCVO**	National Council for Voluntary Organisations
NCTE	National Council for Textile Education (U.S.A.)	**NCVQ**	National Counciol for Vocational Qualifications
NCTE	National Council of Teachers of English (U.S.A.)	**NCVVV**	Nederlandse Christelijke Vereniging van Verpleegkundigen en Verzorgenden
NCTET	National Council for Teacher Education and Training	**NCVYS**	National Council for Voluntary Youth Services
NCTF	National Check Traders' Federation	**NCW**	National Council of Women of Great Britain
NCTI	National Commission for Trade and Industry (Bhutan)	**NCW**	Nederlands Christelijk Werkgeversverbond
NCTIP	National Committee on the Treatment of Intractable Pain (U.S.A.)	**NCWA**	National Children's Wear Association
NCTJ	National Council for the Training of Journalists	**NCWCC**	North Central Weed Control Committee (U.S.A.)

NCWCD	National Commission for Wildlife Conservation and Development (Saudi Arabia)
NCWD	National Council on Women and Development (Ghana)
NCWGB	National Council of Women of Great Britain
NCWID	National Committee on Women in Development (Malawi)
NCWK	National Council of Women in Kenya = MYWO
NCWM	National Conference on Weights and Measures (U.S.A.)
NCWNZ	National Council of Women of New Zealand
NCWPA	National Council for the Welfare of Prisoners Abroad
NCWPNG	National Council of Women of Papua New Guinea
NCWRF	National Collection of Wood Rotting Fungi
NCWS	National Council of Women's Societies (Nigeria)
NCWS	National Council of Women of Switzerland = ASF, BSF
NCWSA	National Council of Women of South Africa
NCWTD	National Centrum voor Wetenschappelijke en Technische Documentatie (Belgium)
NCWTM	National Council on Wholistic Therapeutics and Medicine (U.S.A.)
NCY	Nordic Center Youth = NCF
NCYC	National Collection of Yeast Cultures (AFRC)
NCYOF	National Catholic Youth Organizations Federation (U.S.A.)
NCZ	Nationale Coöperatieve Zuivelverkoopcentrale
ND	Nea Demokratia
ND	New Democracy (Serbia)
NDA	National Dairymens' Association
NDA	National Defence Army (Rwanda)
NDA	National Democratic Alliance (Hungary)
NDA	National Development Association
NDAB	National Drugs Advisory Board (Éire)
NDALTP	Nationale Dienst voor Afzet van Land- en Tuinbouwproduktion = ONDAH
NDAPTA	National Drivers Association for the Prevention of Traffic Accidents (U.S.A.)

NDB	National Development Bank (Botswana, Jamaica, Sri Lanka)
NDBC	National Dry Bean Council (U.S.A.)
NDBHL	National Deaf-Blind Helpers' League
NDBI	National Dairymen's Benevolent Institution
NDBL	National Deaf Blind League
NDBU	Belgische Nationale Dienst voor de Bervordering van de Uitvoer
NDC	National Dairy Council (Éire, U.K., U.S.A.)
NDC	National Defence Council (Japan)
NDC	National Democratic Congress (Grenada)
NDC	National Design Council (Canada)
NDC	National Development Company (Philippines)
NDC	National Development Corporation (Dominica, Éire, St. Lucia, Tanzania)
NDC	National Development Council (India, New Zealand)
NDC	National Diving Council for Scotland
NDC	National Documentation Centre of NRC (Sudan)
NDC	National Drilling Company (Abu Dhabi)
NDC	NATO Defense College = NADEFCOL
NDC	Norsk Designcentrum
NDC	Northern Development Company
NDCF	National Development Control Forum
NDCS	National Deaf Children's Society
NDCS-TIC	National Deaf Children's Technology Information Centre
NDD	Nationale Delcrederedienst (Belgium) = OND
NDDB	National Dairy Development Board (India)
NDDN	National Dry Deposition Network (U.S.A.)
NDF	National Democratic Front (Burma, Guyana, Philippines)
NDF	National Development Foundation (South Africa)
NDF	Nordic Development Fund
NDF	Norges Danselærer-Forbund
NDF	Norges Drosjeeier-Forbund
NDF	Norske Dramatikeres Forbund
NDFA	National Drama Festivals Association
NDFC	National Development Finance Corporation (Pakistan)

NDFS	National Deposit Friendly Society	**NDS**	Congregation of Notre Dame de Sion
NDFTA	National Dried Fruit Trade Association	**NDS**	Narodna Demokratska Stranka (Montenegro) = PDP
NDG	Norsk Dokumentasjonsgruppe		
NDHF	Norges Dame- og Herrefrisørmestres Forbund (*now* NFF)	**NDS**	National Dahlia Society
		NDS	Nordic Demographic Society
NDIA	Nationwide Driving Instructors Association	**NDSATsB**	Nezavisima Demokraticheska Sotsialisticheska Asotsiatsiya na Tsiganite v Bulgariya (Bulgaria) = IDSAGB
NDIC	National Defence Industries Council		
NDL	National Diet Library (Japan)		
NDLEA	Nigerian National Drug Law Enforcement Agency	**NDSB**	Narcotic Drugs Supervisory Body (UN)
		NDT	Dansk NDT-Forening
NDM	New Democratic Movement (Ghana)	**NDT**	National Development Team for People with Learning Disabilities
NDMC	National Diamond Mining Company (Sierra Leone)		
		NDT	National Nondestructive Testing Centre
NDMF	National Development and Management Foundation (South Africa)	**NDTA**	National Defense Transportation Association (U.S.A.)
NDMP	National Diarrhoea Management Programme (India)	**NDV**	Nederlandse Dendrologische Vereniging
		NDV	Nederlandse Dierkundige Vereniging
NDO	Nederlandse Drogisten Organisatie	**NDWA**	National Dog Wardens Association
NDP	Narodna Demokratska Partija / National Democratic Party (Macedonia)	**NE**	Narcotics Education (U.S.A.)
		NE	Nuclear Electric
NDP	National Democratic Party (Austria, Barbados, Egypt, Pakistan, Suriname)	**NEA**	National Economic Association (U.S.A.)
NDP	National Democratic Party (Poland) = SND	**NEA**	National Education Association (U.K., U.S.A.)
NDP	National Democratic Party (Romania)	**NEA**	National Energy Authority of Iceland
NDP	National Development Party (Montserrat)	**NEA**	National Exhibitors Association
		NEA	Neighhourhood Energy Action
NDP	Natsionalno-Demokraticheskaia Partiia	**NEA**	North of England Assembly of Local Authorities
NDP	New Democratic Party (Canada, St. Vincent)		
		NEA	Northern Examination Association
NDP	Vereniging De Nederlandse Dagbladpers	**NÉA**	Nouvelles Éditions Africaines (Senegal)
NDPA	National Decorating Products Association (U.S.A.)	**NEA**	Nuclear Energy Agency (OECD) = AEN
NDPC	National Democratic Policy Committee (U.S.A.)	**NEAATS**	North East Asia Association of Theological Schools (Japan)
NDPD	National-Demokratische Partei Deutschlands	**NEAB**	Northern Examinations and Assessment Board
NDPK	National Democratic Party of Kazakhstan	**NEAC**	New English Art Club
		NEACH	Northeast Association for Computers and the Humanities
NDPKC	National Domestic Poultry Keepers Council		
NDPL	National Democratic Party of Liberia	**NEADEC**	Near East Animal Production and Health Development Centre (Lebanon)
NDPP	Narodowo-Demokratyczna Partia Polski	**NEAFC**	North-East Atlantic Fisheries Commission = CPANE
NDR	Norddeutscher Rundfunk		
NDR	Normenausschuss Druck- und Reproduktionstechnik im DIN	**NEAHI**	Near East Animal Health Institute
		NEANDC	Nuclear Energy Agency Nuclear Data Committee
NDRI	National Dairy Research Institute (India)		
		NEAP	National Environmental Action Plan

NEARA	New England Antiquities Research Association (U.S.A.)
NEAVB	National Employers Association of Vehicle Builders
NEB	National Economic Board (Republic of Korea)
NEB	National Electricity Board of the States of Malaysia
NEB	National Energy Board (Canada)
NEB	National Enterprise Board
NEB	Nederlandse Eiercontrôle Bureau
NEBA	Nederlandse Katholieke Bond van Beroeps-Assurantiebezorgers
NEBAHAI	National Examinations Board for Agriculture, Horticulture and Allied Industries
NEBF	National Farm Bureau Federation (U.S.A.)
NEBOPA	Nederlandse Bond van Paardenslagers en Paardenvleesverkopende Bedrijven
NEBOSH	National Examination Board in Occupational Safety and Health
NEBSS	National Examinations Board for Supervisory Studies
NEBUPZA	Nederlands Bureau voor de Uitvoer an Granen, Zaden en Peulvruchten
NEBUTA	Nederlands Bureau voor Technische Hulp
NEC	National Economic Council (Pakistan, Philippines)
NEC	National Electoral Commission (Nigeria)
NEC	National Electronics Council
NEC	National Energy Commission (Thailand)
NEC	National Engineering Center (Philippines)
NEC	National Executive Committee, Labour Party
NEC	National Extension College
NEC	Nederlands Elektrotechnisch Comité
NEC	Nippon Electronic Company (Japan)
NEC	Northern Engineering Centre
NECA	National Electrical Contractors Association (U.S.A.)
NECA	Nigerian Employers Consultative Association
NECCCRW	Near East Christian Council Committee for Refugee Work
NECCO	Nigerian Engineering and Construction Company Limited
NECCTA	National Education Closed-Circuit Television Association (U.S.A.)
NECEA	National Engineering Construction Employers Association
NECET	N E Coast Engineering Trust (*ex* NECIES)
NECIES	North-East Coast Institution of Engineers and Shipbuilders (*now* NECET)
NECK	Nuclear Energy Committee of Kuwait
NECO	National Iranian Industry Export Company
NECO-BETRA	Nederlandse Christelijke Ondernemersbond Electrotechniek en Radio
NECSR	North East Coast Ship Repairers
NECTA	National Electrical Contractors Trading Association
NED	National Endowment for Democracy (U.S.A.)
NED	Nederlandse Emigratiedienst
NEDA	National Economic and Development Authority (Philippines)
NEDA	National Economic Development Association (U.S.A.)
NEDA	National Electronic Distributors Association (U.S.A.)
NEDA	National Electronics Development Association (New Zealand)
NEDA	National Environmental Development Association (U.S.A.)
NEDACO	Vereniging Nederlandse Dakpannenfabrikanten Corporatie
NEDC	National Economic Development Council (Belize, U.K.)
NedCBTB	Nederlandse Christelijke Boeren-en Tuindersbond
NEDECO	Nederlands Ingenieursbureau voor Buitenlandse Werken
NEDEK	Nederlandse Groep Elektrische Draad en Kabel
NEDELSA	Nederlandse Fabrieken van Electrische Schakelapparatuur
NEDER-GRES	Nederlandse Vereniging van Gresbuizenfabrikanten
NEDERF	Nederlandse Stichting ter Voorbereiding en Uitvoering van het Erfgewassenproject
NEDL	National Equine Defence League
NEDO	New Energy Development Organisation (Japan)

NEDSMELT	Nederlandse Vereniging van Kaassmelters
NEEB	North-East Engineering Bureau
NEEN	North East Environment Network
NEERI	National Electrical Engineering Research Institute (South Africa)
NEERI	National Environmental Engineering Research Institute (U.S.A.)
NEETU	National Engineering and Electrical Trades Union
NEF	Near East Foundation (U.S.A.)
NEF	New Economics Foundation
NEF	Nordisk Embedsmandkomité for Fiskerisporgmål
NEF	Nordiska Ekonomiska Forskningsrådet
NEF	Norges Eiendomsmeglerforbund
NEF	Norsk Elektroteknisk Forening
NEF	Norsk Epilepsiforbund
NEF	Norsk Etnologforening
NEFA	North East Forest Alliance
NEFARMA	Nederlandse Associatie van de Farmaceutische Industrie
NEFATO	Vereniging van Nederlandse Fabrikanten van Voedertoevoegingen
NEFC	Near East Forestry Commission = CFPO
NEFMA	NATO EFA Development, Production & Logistic Management Agency
NEFO	Nordjylland Elektricitetsforsyning
NEFSG	Northeastern Forest Soils Group (Canada and U.S.A.)
NEFTIC	Northeastern Forest Tree Improvement Conference (U.S.A.)
NEFYTO	Nederlandse Stichting voor Fytofarmacie
NEGI	National Federation of Engineering and General Ironfounders
NEH	National Endowment for the Humanities (U.S.A.)
NEHA	National Environmental Health Association (U.S.A.)
NEI	Nederlandsch Economisch Instituut
NEI	Nuclear Engineering International
NEIBR	Norsk Institutt for By- og Regionforskning
NEIDA	Network of Educational Innovation for Development in Africa (Senegal)
NEIG	Nuclear Electricity Information Group
NEIMME	North of England Institute of Mining and Mechanical Engineers
NEJS	Nordiska Ämbetsmannakommittén för Jord- och Skogbruksfrågor
NEK	Nordisk Komité for Konsumentspoørgsmal = NCCA, NAK
NEK	Norsk Elektroteknisk Komite
NEL	National Engineering Laboratory
NELSAK	Nuclear Power Plants Institution (Turkey)
NELSAT	National Association of Land Settlement Association Tenants
NEM	New Antilles Movement = MAN
NEMA	National Early Music Association
NEMA	National Electrical Manufacturers Association (U.S.A.)
NEMAL	National Egg Marketing Association Ltd
NEMEC	National Electronics & Microtechnology Education Centre
NEMEC	Nederlandse Fabrieken van Elektrische en Elektronische Meet- en Regelapparatuur
Nemego	Nederlandse Vereniging van Meubelgrassiers
NEMI	North European Management Institute (Norway)
NEMKO	Norges Elektriske Materiellkontrol
NEMOG	Groep Nederlandse Fabrieken van Elektrische Motoren en Generatoren
NEMRI	North Electro-Mechanical Research Institute (China)
NEMS	North of England Museums Service
NEMSA	North of England Mule Sheep Association
NEN	Stichting Nederlands Normalisatie-Instituut
NENAR-ACA	Near East and North Africa Regional Agricultural Credit Association
NENIG	Northern European Nuclear Information Group
NEO	New European Order (Spain)
NEOCAT	Netherlands Oriental Cat Club
NEODA	National Edible Oil Distributors Association
NEOS	New England Ophthalmological Society (U.S.A.)
NEP	National Education Program (U.S.A.)
NEP	New Economic Policy (Malaysia)
NEPA	National Environment Protection Agency (China)
NEPA	Nigerian Electric Power Authority

NEPA	Northeastern Pennsylvania Artificial Breeding Cooperative (U.S.A.)
NEPC	National Environment Protection Council
NEPDI	Northeast Electric Power Design Institute (China)
NEPO	National Energy Policy Office (Philippines)
NEPP	National Egg and Poultry Promotion
NEPPCO	Northeastern Poultry Producers Council (U.S.A.)
NEPRA	National Egg Producers Retail Association
NEPRO-PHARM	Nederlandse Vereninging van Fabrikanten van Pharmaceutische Producten
NEPTTE	National Federation of Post, Telephone and Telegraph Employees (India)
NEQA	National Education Qualifications Authority (New Zealand)
NERA	National Emergency Relief Administration (U.S.A.)
NERATU	Groep Nederlandse Fabrieken van Radio-, Televisie- en Muziekapparatuur
NERBA	New England Road Builders' Association
NERC	National English Rabbit Club
NERC	Natural Environment Research Council
NERC	Nuclear Energy Research Centre = CEEN
NERCSPS	North of England Rose, Carnation and Sweet Pea Society
NERDDC	National Energy Research Development and Demonstration Council
NERG	Nederlands Elektronica- en Radiogenootschap
NERO	National Energy Resources Organization (U.S.A.)
NERO	Near East Regional Office (FAO)
NERRS	New England Röntgen Ray Society (U.S.A.)
NERSA	Centrale Nucléaire Européenne à Neutrons Rapides
NES	National Eczema Society
NES	National Extension Service (India)
NES	Neurootology and Equilibrium Society
NES	Nordiska Ergonomisällskapet
NES	Numerical Engineering Society Ltd
NESA	Network Educational Science Amsterdam
NESBIC	Netherlands Students Bureau for International Cooperation
NESC	National Economic and Social Council (Éire)
NESC	Nuclear Engineering and Science Conference
NESCCO	Nigerian Engineering and Construction Company
NESDA	North East Scotland Development Authority
NESS	National Environmental Satellite Service (NOAA)
NEST	International Foundation for the Promotion of New and Emerging Sciences and Technologies
NEST	National Council for Voluntary Organisations (Environment Support Team)
NET	Nitrigin Éireann Teoranta
NET	Vereniging Nederlandse Eigen-Textieldruckers
NETA	North Eastern Traders' Association
NETAC	Nuclear Energy Trade Associations Conference
NETAL-COM	Groep Fabrieken van Professionele Telecommunicatie- en Radiocommunicatieapparatur in Nederland
NETFO	Netherlands Environment Technology Foundation
NETFS	National Educational Television Film Service (U.S.A.)
NETT	Network for Environment Technology Transfer (EU)
NETUMAR	Companhia de Navagação Marítima (Brazil)
NEUCC	Northern European University Computing Centre (Denmark)
NEV	Nederlandsche Entomologische Vereniging
NEVAC	Nederlandse Vacuumvereniging
NEVEC	Nederlandse Economische Vereniging voor de Confectie-Industrie
NEVECOL	Netherlands-Flemish Ecological Society
NEVEHAC	Nederlandse Vereniging van Handelaren in Chemicaliën
NEVEM	Nederlandse Vereniging voor Physical Distribution en Material Management
NEVEMA	Nederlandse Vereniging van Matrassenfabrikanten
NEVEPA	Vereniging van Nederlandse Papierzakken- Fabrikanten

NEVERCO	Vereniging van Verhuurders van Grandverzetmachines	**NFAC**	National Federation of Aerial Contractors
NEVESUCO	Nederlandse Vereniging voor de Suikerwerk- en Chocoladeverwerkende Industrie	**NFAC**	National Food and Agriculture Council (Philippines)
NEVEXPO	Nederlandse Vereniging van Exporteurs van Pootaardappelen	**NFAI**	Norwegian Society of Allergology and Immunopathology
NEVI	Nederlands Vlasinstituut	**NFAIS**	National Federation of Abstracting and Indexing Services (U.S.A.)
NEVIE	Nederlandse Vereniging voor Inkoop-Efficiency	**NFAIS**	National Federation of American Information Services
NEVIKI	Nehézvegyipari Kutató Intézet	**NFAPCS**	National Federation of Agricultural Pest Control Trades
NEVIM	Nederlandse Vereniging voor International Meubeltransport	**NFAS**	National Field Archery Society
NEVLAS	Nederlandse Vlas Associatie	**NFAW**	National Foundation of Australian Women
NEVO	Nederlandse Volksdansvereniging		
NEVOK	Nederlandse Vereniging van Ondernemers in het Kappersbedrift	**NFB**	National Federation of the Blind of the United Kingdom
NEVON	Nederlandse Vereniging van Ondernemers in het Natuursteenbedrijf	**NFBB**	National Federation of Beer Bottlers
NEVRA	Nederlandse Vereniging van Groothandelaren in Rioleringsartikelen	**NFBB**	Norsk Forening for Bolig- og Byplanlegging
NEWAC	NATO Electronic Warfare Advisory Committee	**NFBBB**	Nationale Federatie Beroepsverenigingen van Aannemers van Begrafenissen van België
NEWO	Nederlandse Electrotechnische Winkeliers Organisatie	**NFBC**	National Film Board of Canada
NEWSMA	North of England Wine & Spirits Merchants' Association	**NFBF**	Nationale Federatie van de Beroepsfotografie
NEXPRI	Nederlands Expertise Centruum voor Ruimtelijke Informatiererwerkig	**NFBF**	Norsk Fabrikkbetongforening
		NFBG	National Federation of Badger Groups
NEZPA	New Zealand Press Association	**NFBR**	National Foundation for Brain Research (U.S.A.)
NF	Nasjonalt Folkeparti (Norway)		
NF	National Front (Afghanistan, U.K.)	**NFBS**	National Forum on Bibliographical Standards
NF	Naturvetenskapliga Forskningsradet		
NF	Neue Forum	**NFBSS**	National Federation of Bakery Students' Societies
NF	Nieuw Front (Suriname)	**NFBT**	Norsk Forening for Bio-Medisinsk Teknikk
NF	Norsk Fagloererlag		
NF	Norsk Folkehjelp	**NFBTO**	National Federation of Building Trade Operatives
NFA	National Farmers Association (Éire)	**NFBU**	National Federation of Bus Users
NFA	National Federation of Anglers	**NFBUK**	National Federation of the Blind of the United Kingdom
NFA	National Fertilizer Association (U.S.A.)		
NFA	National Film Archive	**NFC**	National Fireplace Council
NFA	National Food Alliance	**NFC**	National Freight Consortium
NFA	National Food Authority	**NFC**	Northern Fisheries Committee
NFA	National Foremen's Association	**NFCA**	National Foster Care Association
NFA	National Foundry Association (U.S.A.)	**NFCADA**	National Family Council Against Drug Abuse (U.S.A.)
NFA	Nordens Folkliga Akademi (Sweden)		
NFA	Norsk Forening for Automatisering	**NFCB**	National Federation of Community Broadcasters (U.S.A.)
NFA	Not Forgotten Association		
NFAA	National Federation of Advertising Agencies	**NFCC**	National Foundation for Consumer Credit (U.S.A.)

NFCDA	National Federation of Civil Defence Associations of Great Britain and the Commonwealth
NFCF	National Federation of Cemetery Friends
NFCF	National Federation of City Farms
NFCG	National Federation of Consumer Groups
NFCGA	National Federation of Constructional Glass Associations
NFCI	National Federation of Clay Industries (*now* BCC)
NFCMA	National Fireplace Council Manufacturers Association
NFCO	National Federation of Community Organisations
NFCPG	National Federation of Catholic Physicians Guilds (U.S.A.)
NFCPO	National Forum of Catholic Parent Organizations (U.S.A.)
NFCR	National Foundation for Cancer Research (U.S.A.)
NFCS	National Federation of Construction Supervisors
NFCSIT	National Federation of Cold Storage and Ice Trades
NFCT	National Forum of Care Trusts
NFCTA	National Fibre Can and Tube Association (U.S.A.)
NFCTC	National Foundry Craft Training Centre
NFCU	National Federation of Claimants Unions
NFCU	National Federation of Construction Unions
NFCU	National Federation of Credit Unions
NFCWC	National Free Church Women's Council
NFD	Nueva Fuerza Democrática (Colombia)
NFDA	National Food Distributors Association (U.S.A.)
NFDC	National Federation of Demolition Contractors
NFDC	National Fertilizer Development Centre (U.S.A.)
NFDLF	Northern Frontier District Liberation Front (Somalia)
NFDSP	National Forum on Deafness and Speech Pathology (U.S.A.)
NFE	Nederlandse Vereniging van Fokkers van Edelpelsdieren
NFEA	National Federated Electrical Association
NFEC	National Foundation for Environmental Control (U.S.A.)
NFEGI	National Federation of Engineering and General Ironfounders
NFER	National Foundation for Educational Research in England and Wales
NFETA	National Foundry and Engineering Training Association
NFF	Narrow Fabrics Federation
NFF	National Farmers' Federation
NFF	National Federation of Fishmongers
NFF	National Froebel Foundation
NFF	Norges Farmaceutiske Förening
NFF	Norges Farvehandlerforbund
NFF	Norges Fotografforbund
NFF	Norges Frisørmesterforbund (*ex* NDHF)
NFF	Norsk Flygelederforening
NFF	Norsk Flyhistorisk Forening
NFF	Norsk Forening for Fjellsprengningsteknikk
NFF	Norsk Fruktgrossisters Forbund
NFF	Norske Fiskeredskapfabrikanters Förening
NFF	Norske Forskningsbibliotekars Förening
NFF	Norske Fotterapeuters Forbund
NFF	Norske Fysioterapeuters Forbund
NFFA	National Frozen Food Association (U.S.A.)
NFFC	National Federation of Fisheries Cooperatives (Republic of Korea)
NFFF	National Federation of Fish Friers
NFFMR	Nordisk Förening för Medisinsk Radiologi (Finland)
NFFO	National Federation of Fishermens Organisations
NFFPOW	National Federation of Far-Eastern Prisoners of War Clubs
NFFPT	National Federation of Fruit and Potato Trades
NFFQO	National Federation of Freestone Quarry Owners
NFFR	Norges Fiskeriforskningsråd
NFFTU	National Federation of Furniture Trade Unions
NFG	Nordwestdeutsche Futtersaatbaugesellschaft
NFGS	National Federation of Gramophone Societies (*now* FRM)

NFH	Nordisk Forening for Handicaptandvård	**NFM**	Nederlandse Federatie van Makelaars in Onroerende Goederen
NFHA	National Federation of Housing Associations	**NFMA**	National Fireplace Makers Association
NFHC	National Federation of Housing Co-operatives	**NFMA**	Needleloom Felt Manufacturers Association
NFHO	National Federation of Homophile Organisations	**NFMD**	National Foundation for Muscular Dystrophy (U.S.A.)
NFHSA	Non-Ferrous Hot Stampers Association	**NFME**	Nordic Federation for Medical Education = NFMU
NFHSM	National Federation of Hide & Skin Markets	**NFMLTA**	National Federation of Modern Language Teachers Association (U.S.A.)
NFHSMI	National Federation of Hide and Skin Markets Incorporated	**NFMPS**	National Federation of Master Printers in Scotland
NFI	National Fisheries Institute (U.S.A.)		
NFI	Naturfreunde-Internationale = IAN, IFN	**NFMR**	Norsk Forening för Medisinsk Radiologi
NFIC	National Fisheries Industry Council	**NFMS**	National Federation of Music Societies
NFIK	Norsk Forening for Industriell Kvalitetskontroll	**NFMS**	Norsk Forening for Medisinsk Strålingfysikk
NFIKB	Nationale Federatie der Immobilienkamers van België	**NFMSLCE**	National Federation of Master Steeplejacks and Lightning Conductor Engineers
NFIM	Norges Forbund for Internasjonale Møbeltransporter	**NFMTA**	National Federation of Meat Traders Associations
NFIR	National Federation of Indian Railwaymen	**NFMU**	Nordisk Federation för Medisinsk Undervisning = NFME
NFIR	Norsk Forening for Internasjonal Rett	**NFMWC**	National Federation of Master Window Cleaners
NFIS	Network of Fertilizer Information Systems (ESCAP/FAO-UNIDO/FADINAP)	**NFNC**	National Food and Nutrition Commission (Zambia)
NFISM	National Federation of Iron and Steel Merchants	**NFNL**	Nationale Fisiese Navorsingslaboratorium (South Africa)
NFIWFM	National Federation of Inland Wholesale Fish Merchants	**NFO**	Nederlandse Federatie van Onderwijsvakorganisaties
NFJI	Naturfreundejugend International (France) = IJAN, IYNF	**NFO**	Nederlandse Fruittelersorganisatie
NFK	Nordiska Fertiletsklubben = SASF	**NFOZ**	Narodowy Fundusz Ochrony Zdrowia
NFK	Norsk Forening for Kvalitet	**NFP**	Narodowy Front Polski (Poland) = PNF
NFK-DK	Nordisk Konservatorforbund, Den Danske Afdeling	**NFP**	National Fatherland Party (Estonia)
		NFP	National Federation Party (Fiji)
NFKHNB	Nationale Federatie der Kamers voor Handel en Nijverheid van België = FNCCIB	**NFP**	National Front for Progress (Solomon Islands)
NFKK	Nordisk Forening for Klinisk Kjemi	**NFP**	Nederlandse Federatie voor de Handel in Pootaardappelen
NFKPA	National Federation of Kidney Patients Associations	**NFPA**	National Federation of Pensioners' Associations (Éire)
NFL	National Forensic League (U.S.A.)		
NFL	Norske Fotoimportørers Landsforbund	**NFPA**	National Fire Protection Association (U.S.A.)
NFLA	National Farm Loan Association (U.S.A.)	**NFPA**	National Flaxseed Processors Association (U.S.A.)
NFLC	National Federation of Livestock Clubs		
NFLP	National Front for the Liberation of Palestine	**NFPA**	National Food Processors Association (U.S.A.)

NFPA	National Forest Products Association (U.S.A.)	**NFS**	Nordens Fagliga Samorganisation
NFPA	National Foster Parents Association	**NFS**	Nordisk Flagselskab
NFPA	Nevis Family Planning Association	**NFS**	Norsk Farmaceutisk Selskap
NFPB	Northern Friends Peace Board	**NFS**	Norsk Fysisk Selskap
NFPC	National Federation of Plastering Contractors (*now* FPDC)	**NFS & MC**	National Federation of Sailing and Motor Cruising Schools
NFPDC	National Federation of Painting and Decorating Contractors	**NFSA**	National Federation of Sea Anglers
NFPDHE	National Federation of Plumbers and Domestic Heating Engineers	**NFSA**	National Fertilizer Solutions Association (U.S.A.)
NFPEDA	National Farm and Power Equipment Dealers Association (U.S.A.)	**NFSA**	National Food Service Association (U.S.A.)
NFPF	Nordisk Förening för Pedagogisk Forskning	**NFSCCCU**	National Federation of Save and Credit Co-operative Credit Unions
NFPHC	National Federation of Permanent Holiday Camps	**NFSCSW**	National Federation of Societies for Clinical Social Work (U.S.A.)
NFPO	National Federation of Professional Organizations (U.S.A.)	**NFSE**	National Federation of the Self-Employed and Small Businesses
NFPO	National Federation of Property Owners	**NFSG**	National Front Support Group
NFPP	National Family Planning Program	**NFSH**	National Federation of Spiritual Healers
NFPS	Norse Film & Pageant Society	**NFSL**	National Front for the Salvation of Libya
NFPU	Nordiska Förbundet Psykisk Utveklingshaemning	**NFSP**	National Federation of Sub-Postmasters
NFPW	National Federation of Petroleum Workers (India)	**NFSPS**	National Federation of State Poetry Societies (U.S.A.)
NFPW	National Federation of Press Women (U.S.A.)	**NFSS**	National Federation of Sea Schools
NFPW	National Federation of Professional Workers	**NFSSM**	Network for Foreign Students and Student Mobility in Europe and North America
NFR	Narodowy Fundusz Reprywatyzacji	**NFSW**	National Federation of Sugar Workers (Philippines)
NFR	Naturvetenskapliga Forskningsradet (Sweden)	**NFSWMM**	National Federation of Scale and Weighing Machine Manufacturers
NFR	Nordisk Folke-Reso (Denmark)	**NFT**	National Federation of Textiles (U.S.A.)
NFR	Nordisk Förening för Rehabilitering	**NFT**	National Film Theatre
NFR	Statens Naturvetenskapliga Forskningsråd	**NFTA**	National Federation of Taxicab Associations
NFRB	Norsk Forening af Rådgivende i Bedriftsledelse	**NFTA**	National Feminist Therapist Association (U.S.A.)
NFRC	National Federation of Roofing Contractors	**NFTA**	National Fillings Trades Associations
NFRC	National Freight Rail Corporation	**NFTA**	Nitrogen Fixing Tree Association (U.S.A.)
NFRI	National Food Research Institute (South Africa)	**NFTC**	National Foreign Trade Council (U.S.A.)
NFRN	National Federation of Retail Newsagents, Booksellers and Stationers	**NFTF**	Norges Kvalitetstekmiske Forening
NFRR	Norsk Forening af Rådgivende Rasjonaliseringsfirmoeoer	**NFTMS**	National Federation of Terrazzo-Mosaic Specialists
NFRS	National Fancy Rat Society	**NFTsR**	Narodnyi Front Tsentra Rossii
NFS	National Federation of Shopmobility	**NFTU**	Nordisk Film og TV Union
		NFU	Nanjing Forestry University

NFU	National Farmers Union	**NGC**	National Guild of Co-operators
NFU	Nordiska Finansiella Utskottet	**NGC**	National Gypsy Council
NFU	Nordiska Försäkringsmanna Unione	**NGC**	Nederlands Graancentrum
NFUDCL	National Farmers Union Development Company Limited	**NGCAA**	National Golf Clubs Advisory Association
NFUS	National Farmers Union of Scotland	**NGCSA**	National Guild of Community Schools of the Arts (U.S.A.)
NFV	Norsk Forening for Vedlikehold		
NFVB	Nederlandse Federatie van Verenigingen van Bedrijfspluimveehouders	**NGDA**	National Game Dealers Association
		NGDC	National Geophysical Data Center (U.S.A.)
NFVE	Nordvestjysk Folkecenter for Vedvarende Energi	**NGEA**	National Gastroenterological Association (U.S.A.)
NFVL	National Federatie van Verenigingen van Laboratorium-assistenten (Belgium)	**NGEC**	National Gypsy Education Council
NFVLS	National Federation of Voluntary Literacy Schemes	**NGF**	Nederlands Genootschap voor Fysiotherapie
NFW	National Federation of Workers (Belize)	**NGF**	Nordiska Glastekniska Föreningen
NFW	Normenausschuss Feurwehrwesen im DIN	**NGF**	Norges Grossistforbund
		NGF	Norsk Gartnerforbund
NFWB	Nederlandse Federatie van Werkgevers-Organisaties in het Bontbedrijf	**NGF**	Norsk Geografisk Forening
		NGF	Norsk Geologisk Forening
NFWC	National Federation of Women's Clubs of the Philippines	**NGF**	Norsk Geoteknisk Forening
		NGF	Norsk Grafiskforbund
NFWG	National Federation of Wholesale Grocers and Provision Merchants	**NGFA**	National Grain and Feed Association (U.S.A.)
NFWI	National Federation of Women's Institutes	**NGH**	National Group on Homeworking
NFWO	Nationaal Fonds voor Wetenschappelijk Onderzoek (Belgium) = FNRS	**NGH**	Naturhistorische Gesellschaft zu Hannover
NFWPM	National Federation of Wholesale Poultry Merchants	**NGI**	Nederlands Genootschap voor Informatica
NFWS	National Ferret Welfare Society	**NGI**	Norsk Gerontologisk Institutt
NFYC	National Federation of Youth Clubs (Éire)	**NGI**	Norwegian Geotechnical Institute
		NGIZ	Nederlandsch Genootschap voor Internationale Zaken
NFYFC	National Federation of Young Farmers' Clubs	**NGK**	Nederduitse Gereformeerde Kerk (South Africa)
NGA	National Grain Authority		
NGA	National Graphical Association (*now* GPMU)	**NGL**	Naturforschende Gesellschaft Luzern
		NGL	Nederlands Genootschap van Leraren
NGAA	Natural Gasoline Association of America	**NGL**	Normenausschuss Gleitlager im DIN
		NGL	Norsk Galvano- Teknisk Landsforening
NGAC	National Greenhouse Advisory Committee	**NGL**	Norsk Grafisk Leverandørforening
NGB	National Garden Bureau (U.S.A.)	**NGLS**	United Nations Non-Governmental Liaison Service
NGB	Naturforschende Gesellschaft in Bern		
NGB	Nederlands Genootschaap voor Besliskunde	**NGMB**	Nigeria Groundnuts Marketing Board
		NGMC	National Grid Management Council
NGB	Nordic Gene Bank for Agricultural and Horticultural Plants	**NGMR**	Nederlands Genootschap voor Micrografie en Reprografie
NGBF	National Grocers' Benevolent Fund	**NGO Scheme**	National Gardens Open Scheme
NGC	National Gasohol Commission (U.S.A.)		

NGO-EC	Liaison Committee of Development NGOs to the European Communities = ONG-EC	**NH**	Norges Herredsforbund
		NH	Norges Husmorforbund
NGO/OPI	Committee of Non-Governmental Organizations associated with the UN Office of Public Information	**NHA**	National Horse Association of Great Britain
		NHA	National Housewives Association
NGOCD	NGO Committee on Disarmament	**NHAS**	National Hearing Aid Society (U.S.A.)
NGOMESA	NGO Management Network for East and Southern Africa	**NHBC**	National Health and Beauty Council
		NHBC	National House Building Council
NGOT	Natural Gas Organisation of Thailand	**NHBS**	National Horse Brass Society
NGPR	Nederlands Genootschap voor Public Relations	**NHC**	National Health Council (U.S.A.)
		NHC	National Heritage Council (Éire)
NGR	Nordiska Godtemplarrådet	**NHC**	National Hurricane Center (NOAA)
NGRC	National Greyhound Racing Club	**NHC**	National Hyperbaric Centre
NGRH	Nationale Groepering van Ruwe Huiden	**NHC**	Nederlandse Hardevezelconventie
NGRI	National Geophysical Research Institute (India)	**NHCC**	National Hebrew Culture Council (U.S.A.)
NGS	National Gardens Scheme	**NHEI**	National Health Education Institute of China
NGS	National Geographic Society (U.S.A.)	**NHF**	National Hairdressers Federation
NGS	National Geriatrics Society (U.S.A.)	**NHF**	Nicaragua Health Fund
NGS	Normenausschuss Graphische Symbole in DIN	**NHF**	Nordens Hydrografiske Forbund (Sweden) = GHEN, NHG
NGSA	National Grammar Schools Association	**NHF**	Nordic Handicap Federation
NGSC	National Greenhouse Steering Committee	**NHF**	Norges Handelstands Forbund
		NHF	Norske Havforskeres Forening
NGSDC	National Geophysical and Solar-Terrestrial Data Center (NOAA)	**NHG**	Natuurhistorisch Genootschap im Limburg
NGSF	Norges Glass-og Stentøihandleres Forbund	**NHG**	Nederlands Historisch Genootschap
		NHG	Nederlands Huisarten Genootschap
NGSI	National Geographical Society of India	**NHG**	Neue Helvetische Gesellschaft
NGSTIN	National Gardening Scientific and Technical Information Network (China)	**NHG**	Northern Hydrographic Group (Sweden) = GHEN, NHF
NGT	National Guild of Telephonists	**NHH**	Nordiska Högskolan Hushållsvetenskap
NGTC	National Grain Trade Council	**NHIC**	National Home Improvement Council
NGTE	National Gas Turbine Establishment (MOD)	**NHIF**	Norske Håndverks- og Industribedrifters Forbund
NGTM	National Guild of Transport Managers	**NHISK**	Koninklijke Academie en National Hoger Instituut voor Schone Kunsten
NGU	Norges Geologiske Undersökelse		
NGUT	National Group of Unit Trusts	**NHK**	Nippon Hose Koyokai (Japan Broadcasting Corporation)
NGV	Nederlands Genootschap van Vertalers		
NGV	Nederlandse Genealogische Vereniging	**NHL**	National Harmonica League
NGV	Nederlandse Genetische Vereniging	**NHL**	National Hockey League (Canada)
NGV	Nederlandse Geologische Vereniging	**NHL**	Nordiske Hjerte- og Lungshandikappedes Forbund
NGVA	Natural Gas Vehicle Association		
NGvF	Nederlands Genootsschap voor Fysiotherapie	**NHLA**	National Health Lawyers Association (U.S.A.)
NGZ	Naturforschende Gesellschaft in Zürich	**NHLA**	National Housewives League of America
NH	National Heritage: the Museums' Action Movement	**NHLBI**	National Heart, Lung and Blood Institute (U.S.A.)

NHLPA	National Hockey League Players' Association (Canada)
NHLS	National Hedge-Laying Society
NHM	Natural History Museum
NHM	Nederlandse Heidemaatschappij
NHMA	National Housewares Manufacturers Association (U.S.A.)
NHMF	National Heritage Memorial Fund
NHMO (HAWK)	NATO Hawk Management Office
NHMRC	National Health and Medical Research Council (Australia)
NHN	National Homes Network
NHO	Noeringslivets Hovedorganisasjon
NHO	Nordic Housing Companies' Organisation = NBO, ONCPUHE
NHOS	National House Owners Society
NHPIC	National Health Planning Information Center (U.S.A.)
NHPLO	NATO Hawk Production and Logistics Organization
NHR	Nederlandse Huishoudraad
NHR	Normenausschuss Heiz-und Raumlufttechnik im DIN
NHRC	National Hydraulic Research Center (Philippines)
NHRF	Norsk Hotell- og Restaurantforbund
NHRI	National Hydrology Research Institute (Canada)
NHRI	Northwest Hydrotechnical Research Institute (China)
NHRIN	Hunan Research Institute of Non-Ferrous Metals (China)
NHRV	Nederlandse Handelsreizigers en Handelsagent- Vereniging
NHS	International Society for the Prevention and Mitigation of Natural Hazards (Canada)
NHS	National Health Service
NHS	National Honey Show
NHS	Nederlandse Hartstichting
NHS CCC	NHS Centre for Coding & Classification
NHSA	National Handicapped Skiers Association
NHSE	National Health Service Executive
NHSM	National History Society of Malta
NHSS	National Home Study Council (U.S.A.)
NHSTA	National Health Service Training Authority
NHSTF	National Health Service Trust Federation
NHT	Nordiska Handikapptförbundet (Sweden)
NHTPC	National Housing and Town Planning Council
NHTSA	National Highway Traffic Safety Administration (U.S.A.)
NHV	Nordiska Halsovårds-Logskolan
NHW	Normenausschuss Hauswirtschaft im DIN
NI	Nautical Institute
NI	Norges Industriforbund
NI	Normenausschuss Informations-Verarbeitung
NI	Numismatics International (U.S.A.)
NIA	National Irrigation Administration (Philippines)
NIA	Nutrition Institute of America
NIAA	Nursery Industry Association of Australia
NIAAA	National Institute for Alcoholism and Alcohol Abuse (U.S.A.)
NIAAA	Northern Ireland Amateur Athletic Association
NIAB	National Institute of Agricultural Botany
NIABA	Netherlands Industrial and Agricultural Association
NIABC	Northern Ireland Association of Boys Clubs
NIABS	National Institute of Applied Behavioral Sciences (U.S.A.)
NIAC	Northern Ireland Amenity Council
NIACE	National Institute of Adult and Continuing Education
NIACRO	Northern Ireland Association for the Care and Resettlement of Offenders
NIACT	Northern Ireland Advisory Commitee on Telecommunications
NIAD	National Institute of Alcohol and Drugs (Netherlands)
NIADDK	National Institute of Arthritis, Diabetes, Digestive and Kidney Diseases (U.S.A.)
NIAE	National Institute for Architectural Education (U.S.A.)
NIAES	National Institute of Agro-Environmental Sciences (Japan)
NIAESS	National Institute of Agricultural Engineering Scottish Station

NIAG	NATO Industrial Advisory Group	**NIBIN**	Netherlands Instituut voor Beleids-Informatie
NIAH	National Institute of Animal Health (Japan)	**NIBM**	National Institute of Burn Medicine (U.S.A.)
NIAI	National Institute of Animal Industry (Japan)	**NIBRAC**	Northern Ireland Building Regulations Advisory Committee
NIAID	National Institute of Allergy and Infectious Diseases (U.S.A.	**NIBS**	Nippon Institute for Biological Science (Japan)
NIAM	Nederlands Instituut Agrarisch Marktonderzoek	**NIBSC**	National Institute for Biological Standards and Control
NIAM	Nederlands Instituut voor Audio-visuelle Media	**NIC**	National Industrialisation Company (Saudi Arabia)
NIAMAC	Chambre Nationale des Négociants en Gros et Agents Généraux en Machines de Fabrication, Matériel d'Émouteillage, d'Emballage et de Conditionnement pour Toutes Industries (Belgium)	**NIC**	National Informatics Centre (India)
		NIC	National Institute of Confederations
		NIC	National Insurance Company (Bahrain, Tanzania)
NIAO	Northern Ireland Audit Office	**NIC**	National Investment Commission (Liberia)
NIAPP	National Institute of Agricultural Planning and Projection (Vietnam)	**NICA**	National Institute of Conveyancing Agents
NIAR	National Institute of Agrobiological Resources (Japan)	**NICAMAR**	Compañia Nicaragüense Mercantil e Industrial de Ultramar
NIAS	National Institute of Agricultural Sciences (Japan)	**NICAP**	National Investigations Committee on Aerial Phenomena (U.S.A.)
NIAS	Netherlands Institute for Advanced Study in the Humanities and Social Sciences	**NICCE**	Northern Ireland Council for Continuing Education
NIAS	Nordic Institute of Asian Studies	**NICCI**	Northern Ireland Chamber of Commerce and Industry
NIAS	Northern Ireland Archery Society	**NICD**	National Institute of Communicable Diseases (India)
NIAT	Nanchong Institute of Aeronautical Technology	**NICD**	National Institute of Community Development (India)
NIAYC	Northern Ireland Association of Youth Clubs	**NICE**	National Institute of Ceramic Engineers (U.S.A.)
NIB	National Investment Bank (Ghana)	**NICEC**	National Institute of Careers, Education and Counselling
NIB	Nigeria International Bank		
NIB	Nordic Investment Bank (Finland)	**NICED**	Northern Ireland Council for Educational Development
NIBA	National Insurance Brokers Association (Éire)	**NICEIC**	National Inspection Council for Electrical Installation Contracting
NIBA	Northern Ireland Bankers Association	**NICEM**	National Information Centre for Educational Media (U.S.A.)
NIBE	Nederlands Instituut voor het Bank- en Effectenbedrijf	**NICER**	Northern Ireland Council for Educational Research
NIBEC	Northern Ireland Bio-engineering Centre	**NICF**	National Institute of Carpet Fitters
NIBEM	Nationaal Instituut voor Brouwgerst, Mout en Bier	**NICG**	Nationalised Industries Chairmen's Group
NIBH	National Institute of Biosciences and Human Technology (Japan)	**NICGB**	National Illumination Committee of Great Britain
NIBI	Nederlands Instituut van Biologen	**NICHA**	Northern Ireland Chest and Heart Association
NIBID	National Investment Bank for Industrial Development (Greece)		

NICHD	National Institute for Child Health and Human Development (NIH)	**NIDFA**	National Independent Drama Festivals Association
NICI	Nijmegen Institute for Cognition and Information (Netherlands)	**NIDI**	Nederlands Interuniversitair Demografisch Instituut
NICIA	Northern Ireland Coal Importers Association	**NIDIG**	Netherlands Instituut van Directeuren en Ingenieurs van Gemeentewerken
NICIAC	Northern Ireland Construction Industry Advisory Council	**NIDMAR**	Network for Instrument Development, Maintenance and Repair (ACGC, IDP)
NICIE	Northern Ireland Council for Integrated Education	**NIDO**	Nationaal Instituut voor Diergeneeskundige Onderzoek (Belgium)
NICLR	Northern Ireland Centre for Learning Resources	**NIDOC**	National Information and Documentation Centre (Egypt)
NICOD	Northern Ireland Council for Orthopaedic Development	**NIDR**	National Institute of Dental Research (NIH)
NICOL	National Insurance Corporation of Liberia	**NIDS**	Northern Ireland Deer Society
NICON	National Insurance Corporation of Nigeria	**NIDTF**	Northern Ireland Dairy Trade Federation
NICPME	Northern Ireland Council for Postgraduate Medical Education	**NIE**	National Institute of Education (U.S.A.)
		NIE	Northern Ireland Electricity
NICRA	National Ice Cream Retailers Association (U.S.A.)	**NIEB**	Nationaal Instituut voor de Extractiebedrijven (Belgium) = INIEX
NICS	Northern Ireland Civil Service	**NIEC**	National Import and Export Corporation (Zambia)
NICSA	Northern Ireland Civil Service Association		
NICSA	Northern Ireland Countryside Staff Association	**NIEC**	Northern Ireland Economic Council
		NIECC	National Industrial Energy Conservation Council (U.S.A.)
NICSO	NATO Integrated Communications System Organization	**NIECE**	Nigerian International Educational and Cultural Exchange Centre
NICSSE	National Information Centre for Social Science Education (Australia)	**NIED**	National Research Institute for Earth Science and Disaster Prevention (Japan)
NICTL AN	Scientific Research Centre for Technological Lasers (Russian Federation)	**NIEF**	National Ironfounding Employers Federation
NICVA	Northern Ireland Council for Voluntary Action	**NIEHS**	National Institute of Environmental Health Sciences (NIH)
		NIEL	Northern Ireland Environment Link
NID	National Institute of Design (India)	**NIEP**	National Institute for Economic Policy (South Africa)
NIDA	National Institute of Development Administration (Thailand)	**NIER**	National Institute for Educational Research (Japan)
NIDA	National Investment and Development Authority (Papua New Guinea)	**NIERC**	Northern Ireland Economic Research Centre
NIDA	Northern Ireland Development Authority	**NIES**	National Institute for Environmental Studies (Japan)
NIDB	Nigerian Industrial Development Bank		
NIDC	National International Development Corporations (India)	**NIES**	Northern Ireland Electricity Service
		NIESG	Northern Ireland Environmental Standards Group
NIDC	Nepal Industrial Development Corporation	**NIESR**	National Institute of Economic and Social Research
NIDC	Northern Ireland Development Council		
NIDCS	National Industrial Development Corporation of Swaziland	**NIF**	National Islamic Front (Afghanistan) = MMI

NIF	Neighbourhood Initiatives Foundation
NIF	Nordisk Forskningsinstitut for Maling og Trykfarver (Denmark)
NIF	Nordiska Institutet for Fargforskning
NIF	Nordiska Institutet for Folkdiktning
NIF	Norges Industriforbund
NIF	Norske Ingeniørforening
NIF	Norske Sivilingeniørers Forening
NIFA	National Islamic Front of Afghanistan = MAHAZ
NIFA	Nuclear Institute for Food and Agriculture (Pakistan)
NIFES	National Industrial Fuel Efficiency Service
NIFF	Nordiska Ickekommersielle Fonograproducenters Förening (Sweden)
NIFFT	National Institute of Foundry and Forge Technology (India)
NIFGA	Northern Ireland Fruit Growers Association
NIFHA	Northern Ireland Federation of Housing Associations
NIFHA	Northern Ireland Fishery Harbour Authority
NIFI	National Institute for the Foodservice Industry
NIFOR	National Information Office, Poona (India)
NIFOR	Nigerian Institute for Oil Palm Research
NIFP	National Institute of Fresh Produce
NIFS	National Institute for Farm Safety (U.S.A.)
NIG	Nuklear-Ingenieur-Gesellschaft
NIGC	National Insurance and Guarantee Corporation
NIGER-CEM	Nigerian Cement Company
NIGER-TOUR	Société Nigérienne pour le Développement du Tourisme et l'Hostellerie
NIGMS	National Institute of General Medical Services (NIH)
NIGP	National Institute of Governmental Purchasing (U.S.A.)
NIGPAS	Nanjing Institute of Geology and Palaeontology, Academia Sinica
NIGTA	Northern Ireland Grain Trade Association Ltd
NIH	National Institute of Hardware
NIH	National Institutes of Health (U.S.A.)
NIHAE	National Institute of Health Administration and Education (India)
NIHBC	Northern Ireland House Building Council
NIHC	Northern Ireland Housing Council
NIHCA	Northern Ireland Hotels and Caterers Association
NIHE	National Institute for Higher Education
NIHE	Northern Ireland Housing Executive
NIHJ	National Institutes of Health, Japan
NIHORT	National Horticultural Research Institute (Nigeria)
NIHP	National Institute of Public Health (Norway)
NIHRD	National Institute of Health Research and Development (Indonesia)
NIHS	National Institute of Hygienic Sciences (Japan)
NII	Natal Institute of Immunology (South Africa)
NII	Netherlands Industrial Institute
NII	Nuclear Installations Inspectorate (HSE)
NIIA	Nigerian Institute of International Affairs
NIIGB	Nauchno-Issledovatel'skii Institut Glaznykh Boleznei
NIIGGR	Nauchno-Issledovatel'skii Institut Geofizicheskikh i Geokhimicheskikh Metodov Razvedki
NIIKB	Nederlands Instituut voor Internationale Kulturele Betrekkingen
NIIM	Nauchno-Issledovatel'skii Institut Metalurgii
NIIO	National Iranian Industries Organisation
NIIP	National Institute of Industrial Psychology
NIIP	Nauchno-Issledovatel'skii Institut Pedagogiki
NIIR	National Institute of Industrial Research (Nigeria)
NIIS	Northern Ireland Information Service
NIIVKh	Nauchno-Issledovatel'skii Institut Vodnogo Khoziaistva
NIIVT	Nauchno-Issledovatel'skii Institut Vysokikh Temperatur
NIIZHN	Concrete and Reinforced Concrete Scientific Research, Design and Technology Institute (Russia)
NIJSI	Vereniging de Nederlandse Ijzer- en Staalproducerende Industrie

NIK	Najwyzska Izba Kontroli	**NIMO**	Nederlands Instituut voor Maatschappelijke Opbouw
NIK	Nordiska Industriläkarradet		
NIKKEI-REN	Nihon Keieisha Dantai Renmei (Japan)	**NIMPA**	Northern Ireland Master Painters Association
NIKKE-ICHO	Nihon Keizai Chosa Kyogikai (Japan)	**NIMPA**	Northern Ireland Master Plumbers Association
NIKKYOSO	Teachers' Union (Japan)	**NIMR**	National Institute for Medical Research
NIKO-TNO	Netherlands Institute for Carbohydrate Research	**NIMR**	National Institute for Medical Research (Tanzania)
NIL	Naczelna Izba Lekarska	**NIMRA**	National Industrial Materials Recovery Association
NIL	Nederlands Instituut voor Lastechniek		
NIL	Norske Interiørarkitekters Landsforening	**NIN**	Normenausschuss Instandhaltung im DIN
NILCO	National Instituut voor de Landbouwstudie in Congo	**NINA**	Northern Ireland Netball Association
		NINB	National Institute of Neurology and Blindness
NILFO	Norsk Innkjøpslederforbund		
NILGOSC	Northern Ireland Local Government Officers Superannuation Committee	**NIO**	National Institute of Oceanography (India)
NILI	Nederlands Instituut voor Landbouwkundige Ingenieurs	**NIO**	Nederlandse Investeringsbank voor Ontwikkelingslanden
NILN	Navorsingsinstituut vir die Leernywerheid (South Africa)	**NIO**	Nederlandse Vereniging voor een Nieuw Internationaal Ontwikkelingsbeleid
NILOC	Nederlands Instituut Lichamelijke Opvoeding Club	**NIO**	Northern Ireland Office
NILU	Norsk Institutt for Luftforskning	**NIOBO**	Société Nouvelle Industrie Ouelléenne du Bois (Ivory Coast)
NIM	National Institute of Metallurgy (South Africa)	**NIOC**	National Iranian Oil Company
		NIOM	Nordiska Instituttet för Odontologisk Materialprovning
NIM	Nationale Investerings Maatschappij (Belgium) = SNI		
		NIOPR	Nigerian Institute for Oil Palm Research
NIM	Nigerian Institute of Management	**NIOSH**	National Institute for Occupational Safety and Health (U.S.A.)
NIMA	Nederlands Instituut voor Marketing		
NIMA	Norsk Forbund for Innkjøp og Logistikk	**NIOZ**	Nederlands Instituut voor Onderzoek der Zee
NIMA	Northern Ireland Ministry of Agriculture	**NIP**	National Independence Party (Lesotho)
NIMA	Northern Ireland Musicians Association	**NIP**	National Institute of Polarology
NIMAC	Nicaragua Machinery Company	**NIP**	National Integration Party (Liberia)
NIMAWO	Nederlands Instituut voor Maatschapplijk Werk Onderzoek	**NIP**	Nederlands Instituut van Psychologen
		NIP	Network Information Project
NIMC	National Institute of Management Counsellors (U.S.A.)	**NIP**	Norsk Forening for Industriens Patent-ingeniører
NIMD	National Institute of Management Development (Egypt)	**NIPA**	National Institute of Public Administration (Bangladesh, Zambia)
NIMESS	Nauchno-Izsledovatelski Institut po Mekhanizatsia i Elektrifikatsia na Selskoto Stopanstvo (Bulgaria)	**NIPA**	National Institute of Public Administration (Pakistan)
		NIPA	Norsk Institutt for Personaladministrasjon
NIMH	National Institute of Medical Health (U.S.A.)		
		NIPA	Northern Ireland Police Authority
NIMH	National Institute of Medical Herbalists	**NIPA**	Northern Ireland Provincial Amalgamation of Racing Pigeon Societies
NIMH	National Institute of Mental Handicap		
NIMH	National Institute of Mental Health (NIH)		

NIPACO	Nigerian Industrial Products Agencies Company	**NIRFTA**	Northern Ireland Retail Fish Trade Association
NIPCO	Nile Petroleum Company (Egypt)	**NIRI**	National Information Research Institute (U.S.A.)
NIPDOK	Nippon Dokumentesyon Kyokai		
NIPF	Northern Ireland Polio Fellowship	**NIRIA**	Nederlandse Ingenieursvereniging
NIPF	Northern Ireland Poultry Federation	**NIRNS**	National Institute for Research in Nuclear Science
NIPG	Nederlands Instituut voor Praeventieve Geneeskunde	**NIRO**	Nederlandsche Indisch Instituut voor Rubberonderzoek
NIPH	National Institute of Poultry Husbandry	**NIROV**	Nederlands Instituut voor Ruimtelijke Ordening en Volkshuisvesting
NIPH	National Institute of Public Health (Norway)		
NIPL	Nederlands Instituut voor Personeelsleiding	**NIRR**	National Institute for Road Research (South Africa)
NIPM	National Institute of Public Management (U.S.A.)	**NIRRA**	Northern Ireland Radio Retailers Association
NIPMA	Northern Ireland Potato Marketing Board	**NIRRD**	National Institute for Rocket Research and Development (South Africa)
NIPO	Nederlands Instituut voor de Publieke Opinie en het Marktonderzoek	**NIRS**	National Institute of Radiological Sciences (Japan)
NIPORT	National Institute of Population Research and Training (Bangladesh)	**NIS**	National Intelligence Service (South Africa)
NIPPORO	Nihon Hoso Rodo Kumiai (Japan)	**NISA**	National Ice Skating Association
NIPR	National Institute for Personnel Research (South Africa)	**NISA**	Northern IrelandShows Association
NIPR	National Institute for Polar Research (Japan)	**NISBS**	National Institute of Social and Behavioral Science (U.S.A.)
NIPSA	Northern Ireland Public Service Alliance	**NISCON**	National Industrial Safety Conference (RoSPA)
NIQOA	Northern Ireland Quarry Owners Association	**NISD**	National Institute of Steel Detailing (U.S.A.)
NIR	Belgisch Nationaal Instituut voor Radio-Omroep	**NISEC**	National Institute for the Study of Educational Change (U.S.A.)
NIR	Norsk Forening for Industriell Rettsbeskyttelse	**NISEC**	Northern Ireland Schools Examinations Council
NIR	Northern Ireland Railways	**NISEE**	National Information Service for Earthquake Engineering (U.S.A.)
NIRA	National Institute for Research Advancement (Japan)	**NISER**	Nigerian Institute for Social and Economic Research
NIRC	National Industrial Relations Court	**NISH**	National Industries for the Severely Handicapped (U.S.A.)
NIRD	National Institute for Research in Dairying		
NIRD	National Institute of Rural Development (India)	**NISI**	National Institute of Sciences of India
		NISK	Norsk Institutt for Skogforskning, As (Norway)
NIRE	National Institute for Rehabilitation Engineering (U.S.A.)	**NISO**	National Industrial Safety Organisation (Éire)
NIREX	United Kingdom Nuclear Industry Radioactive Waste Executive	**NISO**	National Information Standards Organization (U.S.A.)
NIRF	National Irrigation Research Fund	**NISRA**	National Industrial Salvage and Recovery Association
NIRFI	Nizhegorodskii Nauchno-Issledovatelskii Radiofizicheskii Institut (Russian Federation)	**NISS**	National Institute for Standards (Egypt)
		NISS	National Institute of Social Sciences (U.S.A.)

NIST	National Institute of Science and Technology (Philippines)	**NIVA**	Northern Ireland Volleyball Association
NIST	National Institute of Standards and Technology (U.S.A.)	**NIVA**	Norwegian Institute for Water Research
NISTA	Northern Ireland Seed Trade Association	**NIVAG**	Nederlands Instituut van Aannemers Grootbedrijf
NISTADS	National Institute of Science, Technology and Development Studies (India)	**NIVAP**	Nederlands Instituut voor Afzetbevordering van Pootaardappelen
NISTI	North Institute for Scientific and Technical Information (China)	**NIVB**	Navorsingsinstituut vir die Visserybedryf (South Africa)
NISU	Nederlands-Indonesische Suiker Unie	**NIVE**	Nederland Vereniging voor Management
NISW	National Institute for Social Work	**NIVNO**	Nasionale Instituut vir Vuurpylnavorsing en – ontwikkeling (South Africa)
NISWT	National Institute for Social Work Training	**NIVOT**	National Research Institute of Vegetables, Ornamental Plants, and Tea (Japan)
NITA	National Intravenous Therapy Association (U.S.A.)		
NITA	Nicophilic Institute of Tobacco Antiquarians	**NIVRA**	Nederlands Instituut van Registeraccountants
NITA	Northern Ireland Textiles Association	**NIVT**	Northern Ireland Voluntary Trust
NITA	Northern Ireland Training Authority	**NIVV**	Nederlands Instituut voor Vredesvraagstukken
NITB	Northern Ireland Tourist Board	**NIWAR**	National Institute of Water and Atmospheric Research, Ltd (New Zealand)
NITC	Northern Ireland Technology Centre		
NITCs	National Information Transfer Centres	**NIWC**	Northern Ireland Water Council
NITEL	Nigerian Telecommunications Ltd.	**NIWMMA**	Northern Ireland Wholesale Merchants and Manufacturers Association
NITEX	Société Nigérienne des Textiles		
NITHC	Northern Ireland Transport Holding Company	**NIWO**	Stichting Nederlandsche Internationale Wegvervoer Organisatie
NITHO	Nederlands Instituut voor Toegepast Huishoudkundig Onderzoek	**NIWR**	National Institute for Water Research (South Africa)
NITIA	Northern Ireland Timber Importers' Association (*now* NITTA)	**NIWU**	National Industrial Workers Union (U.S.A.)
NITIE	National Institute for Training in Industrial Engineering (India)	**NIZC**	National Industrial Zoning Committee (U.S.A.)
NITO	Norges Ingeniørörganisasjon	**NIZO**	Nederlandsche Instituut voor Zuivelonderzoek
NITR	National Institute for Telecommunications Research (South Africa)	**NJ**	Norges Juristforbund
		NJ	Norsk Journalistlag
NITR	Nigerian Institute of Trypanosomiasis Research	**NJ2**	Nanjing Seismological Observatory
NITRO	National Income Tax Reform Organisation (Éire)	**NJA**	National Jewellers' Association
		NJA	National Jogging Association
NITTA	Northern Ireland Timber Trade Association (*ex* NITIA)	**NJA**	Nepal Journalists Association
		NJAC	National Joint Action Committee (Trinidad and Tobago)
NIV	Nederlands Instituut voor Volksvoeding		
NIV	Nederlandsche Internisten Vereniging	**NJAC**	National Joint Apprenticeship Council
NIVA	Nordiska Institutionen för Vidareutbildning inom Arbetsmiljöområdet	**NJBG**	Nederlandse Jeugdbond ter Bestudering van de Geschiedenis
NIVA	Norsk Institutt for Vannforskning	**NJC**	Approved Driving Instructors National Joint Council

NJC	National Joint Council for Local Authorities' Administrative, Professional, Technical and Clerical Services	**NKB**	Nordiska Kommittén för Byggbestämmelser
		NKC	National Kidney Centre
NJCBI	National Joint Council for the Building Industry Administrative Council	**NKC**	Nordiskt KonstCentrum
		NKE	Nordiskt Kollegium för Ekologi
NJCC	National Joint Consultative Committee of Architects, Quantity Surveyors and Builders	**NKF**	Norges Kjøtt og Flesksentral
		NKF	Norsk Kiropraktor Forening
		NKF	Norsk Klassiskforbund
NJCEI	National Joint Council for the Exhibition Industry	**NKF**	Norsk Kommunalteknisk Forening
		NKF	Norsk Korrosjonsteknisk Forening
NJF	Nationaal Jeugd Front	**NKFO**	Nordisk Kollegium for Fysisk Oceanografi
NJF	Nordiska Jordbruksforskares Förening		
		NKG	Nederlands Kunstenaarsgenootschap
NJF	Nordiska Journalist Förbundet	**NKG**	Nordiska Kommissionen för Geodesi
NJF	Norges Jernvarehandleres Forbund	**NKGF**	Norges Kvinnelige Gymnastikklærer-forening
NJFA	National Jazz Foundation Archive		
NJFF	Norsk Jord-og Fjellteknisk Forbund	**NKGG**	Nationales Komitee für Geodäsie und Geophysik
NJHC	Stichting Nederlandse Jeugherberg Centrale		
		NKI	Netherlands Cancer Institute
NJIC	National Joint Industrial Council	**NKI**	Norges Kjemiske Industrigruppe
NJKF	Norges Jordskriftekandidat forening	**NKI**	Növényvédelmi Kutató Intézet
NJLS	Norges Jordskriftedommer- og Landmålersamband	**NKI**	Vereniging de Nederlandse Koeltechnische Industrie
NJM	New Jewel Movement (Grenada)	**NKIF**	Norsk Kjemisk Industriarbeiderforbund
NJMC	Justice for Mineworkers Campaign	**NKIM**	Nederlands Kali-import Mij
NJMF	Norsk Jern- og Metallarbeiderforbund	**NKJ**	Nordisk Kontraktorgan for Jordbrugsforskning
NJN	Nederlandse Jeugdbond voor Natuurstudie		
		NKJF	Norsk Konfedsjons Teknisk Forbund
NJPA	New Jersey Pharmaceutical Association (U.S.A.)	**NKK**	Nordkalottkommittén = PKK
		NKK	People's Congress of Kazakhstan
NJSHS	New Jersey State Horticultural Society (U.S.A.)	**NKKM**	Norske Kunst- og Kulturhistoriske Museer
NJSPE	New Jersey Society of Professional Engineers (U.S.A.)		
		NKL	Norges Kooperative Landsforening
NJSV	Nationalistisch Jong-studentenverbond (Belgium)	**NKLB**	Noord-Nederlandse Cooperatieve Eierhandel
NJSZT	Neumann János Szamitégéptudományi Táraság	**NKLF**	Norges Kolonial- og Landhandelforbund
NJU	Nordiska Järnvägsmanna-Unionen	**NKMB**	Nordisk Kollegium för Marinbiologi = NCMB
NJUG	National Joint Utilities Group (U.K., U.S.A.)		
		NKOV	Nederlands Katholiek Ondernemers Verbond
NJV	Nederlandse Juristen- Vereniging		
NK	Naczelny Komitet	**NKP**	Narodno-Konstitutsionnaia Partiia
NKA	National Karting Association	**NKP**	Norges Kommunistiske Parti
NKA	Nordiska Kontaktorganet för Atomenergifrågor	**NKR**	Nordiska Kommunaltjänstemannarådet
		NKRF	National Kidney Research Fund
NKAPE	Nederlandse Katholieke Aannemers-en Patroonsbond	**NKS**	Nederlandse Kastelenstichting
		NKS	Nordisk Kaktus Selskab
NKB	Nederlandse Kermisbond	**NKS**	Nordisk Kirkeligt Studieråd

NKS	Nordisk Kontakt om Statsbyggeri	**NLD**	National League for Democracy (Burma)
NKS	Nordiska Kommitten för Kärnsäkerhedforskning	**NLDCSEA**	National Libraries and Documentation Centre, South East Asia
NKS	Nordiska Kvinnosaksföreningars Samorganisation	**NLEC**	National Law Enforcement Council (U.S.A.)
NKS	Norsk Keramisk Selskap	**NLF**	National Law Foundation (U.S.A.)
NKS	Norsk Kjemisk Selskap	**NLF**	National Liberal Federation
NKS	Norske Kommuners Sentralförbund	**NLF**	National Liberation Front (Yemen)
NKT	Nordiska Kommittén för Trafiksäkerhetsforskning	**NLF**	Nordisk Luftpostsamler Forening
NKT	Normenausschuss Kommunale Technik im DIN	**NLF**	Norges Lastebileier-Forbund
NKTF	Nordiska Kommittén för Transportekonomisk Forskning	**NLF**	Norsk Landbruksakademikerforbund
NKTF	Norges Karttekniske Forbund	**NLF**	Norske Litotrykkeriers Forening
NKTF	Norges Kvalitetstekniske Forening	**NLFR**	Nordisk Laederforskningsråd
NKU	Nordisk Katolsk Utvicklingshjelp	**NLGC**	Nauru Local Government Council
NKV	Nederlands Katholiek Vakverbond	**NLGF**	National Lesbian and Gay Federation (Éire)
NKV	Nederlands Klassiek Verbond	**NLH**	Norges Landbrukshogskole
NKV	Nordisk Kollegium for Viltforskning	**NLHE**	National Laboratory for Higher Education (U.S.A.)
NKV	Nordiska Kommittén för Vägtrafiklagstiftning	**NLHS**	Neo Lao Hak Sat = LPF
NKVT	Nederlandsche Katholieke Vereniging van Ondernemers in de Textielhandel	**NLI**	National Library of Ireland
NKW	Naczelny Komitet Wykonawczy	**NLI**	Norsk Lokalhistorisk Institutt
NKWV	Nederlands Katholiek Werkgevers Verband	**NLKF**	Nordisk Læder Kemiker Forening
NKZZ	Niezalezny Krajowy ZwiØazek Zawodowy	**NLL**	National Land League (Éire)
NL	Norsk Lærerlag	**NLL**	Norsk Logopedlag
NLA	National Library of Australia	**NLM**	National Library of Medicine (U.S.A.)
NLA	National Lime Association (U.S.A.)	**NLM**	Nederlandse Luchtvaart Maatschappij
NLA	Nigerian Library Association	**NLMC**	National Labour Management Council
NLAC	National Landcare Advisory Committee	**NLMC**	Nordic Labour Market Committee = NAUT
NLAPW	National League of American Pen Women	**NLMGB**	National Liberation Movement of Guinea-Bissau
NLB	National Library for the Blind	**NLN**	Nordiska Låkemedelsnämnden
NLB&D	National League of the Blind and Disabled	**NLNE**	National League of Nursing Education (U.S.A.)
NLBI	National League of the Blind of Ireland	**NLO**	National Liberal Organisation
NLC	National Land Council (Australia)	**NLOGF**	National Lubricating Oil and Grease Federation
NLC	National League of Cities (U.S.A.)	**NLP**	National Liberal Party (Lebanon, Romania)
NLC	National Liberal Club	**NLP**	National Liberation Party (Gambia)
NLC	National Library of Canada	**NLP**	Natural Law Party
NLC	Nigerian Labour Congress	**NLPC**	National Libyan Petroleum Company (Libya)
NLCA	Norwegian Lutheran Church of America	**NLPGA**	National Liquid Petroleum Gas Association (U.S.A.)
NLCB	National Lottery Charities Board		
NLCIF	National Light Castings Ironfounders' Federation	**NLR**	National Lucht en Ruimtevaartlaboratorium

NLRB	National Labor Relations Board (U.S.A.)	**NMBA**	National Marine Bankers Association (U.S.A.)
NLRC	Narrottam Lalbhai Research Centre (India)	**NMBS**	Nationale Maatschappij der Belgische Spoorwegen = SNCB
NLRY	Nordic Liberal and Radical Youth (Sweden)	**NMC**	National Marketing Council
NLS	National Library of Scotland	**NMC**	National Mastitis Council (U.S.A.)
NLS	Nordiska Lärerorganisationers Samråd	**NMC**	National Meteorological Center (U.S.A.)
NLS	Norges Landsforbund for Sukkersyke	**NMC**	National Milling Corporation (Tanzania)
NLSB	National Land Survey Board (Sweden)	**NMC**	National Minorities Council (Poland) = RMN
NLSMB	National Live Stock and Meat Board (U.S.A.)	**NMC**	National Motorcycle Council
NLSPA	National Live Stock Producers Association (U.S.A.)	**NMC**	National Mouse Club
NLTF	Norsk Landbruksteknisk Forening	**NMC**	National Museum of Canada
NLU	Naturvåordsverkets Limnologiska Undersökning	**NMC**	National Music Council (U.S.A.)
NLU	Nordisk Lastebil Union	**NMC**	National Music Council of Great Britain
NLVA	National Licensed Victuallers Association	**NMC**	Norman Moore Centre
NLVF	Norges Landbruksvitenskapelige Forskningsrad	**NMCA**	National Meat Canners Association (U.S.A.)
NLW	National Library of Wales	**NMCIR**	Network of Man-Computer Interaction Research (IUPsyS) = MACINTER
NM	National Movement (Poland) = RN	**NMCT**	National Movement of the Crimean Tatars
NM	New Majority (Peru)	**NMDA**	National Medical and Dental Association (U.S.A.)
NM	Norges Mållag	**NMDA**	National Metal Decorators Association (U.S.A.)
NM	Normenstell Marine im DIN	**NMDIS**	National Music and Disability Information Service
NM	Norsk Musikerforbund	**NMEA**	National Marine Education Association (U.S.A.)
NM	Society of Nuclear Medicine	**NMEA**	National Marine Electronics Association (U.S.A.)
NM	Vereniging tot Behoud van Natuurmonumenten in Nederland	**NMERI**	National Mechanical Engineering Research Institute (South Africa)
NM-BYGG	Scandinavian Committee on Materials Research and Testing, Subcommittee on Building	**NMES**	Northern Mill Engine Society
		NMF	Norges Markedforbund
NMA	Lloyds Underwriters Non-Marine Association	**NMF**	Norsk Meteorologforening
NMA	National Management Association (U.S.A.)	**NMFB&AEA**	National Master Farriers, Blacksmiths and Agricultural Engineers Association
NMA	National Meat Association (U.S.A.)	**NMFS**	National Marine Fisheries Service (U.S.A.)
NMA	National Medical Association (U.S.A.)	**NMFTB**	National Music for the Blind
NMA	National Midwives Assocation (U.S.A.)	**NMHA**	National Mental Health Association (U.S.A.)
NMA	National Museum of Australia		
NMA	Needlemakers Association	**NMHC**	National Materials Handling Centre
NMA	Nordic Midwives Association	**NMHF**	Norges Musikkhandlerforbund
NMAA	National Machine Accountants Association (U.S.A.)	**NMHRA**	National Mobile Homes Residents Association
NMAB	Natural Materials Advisory Board of the National Academy of Sciences (U.S.A.)		
NMAC	National Medical Audiovisual Center (U.S.A.)		

NMIA	National Meteorological Institute of Athens (Greece)	**NMS**	Norwegian Dairies Sales Centre
NMK	Norse Marconi Kompani	**NMSC**	Nonferrous Metals Society of China
NMKL	Nordisk Metodik-Komité for Levnedsmidler	**NMSM**	National Sheet Music Society (U.S.A.)
		NMSN	National Miners Support Network
NMKN	Nationale Maatschappij voor Krediet aan de Nijverheid (Belgium) = SNCI	**NMSP**	New Mon State Party (Burma)
		NMSS	National Multiple Sclerosis Society (U.S.A.)
NML	National Federation of Norwegian Milk Producers	**NMT**	National Meningitis Trust
NML	National Metallurgical Laboratory (India)	**NMT**	Nordic Mobile Telephone Network
NML	Norske Melkeprodusenters Landsforbund	**NMTAS**	National Milk Testing and Advisory Service
NML	Norske Murmestres Landsforening	**NMTBA**	National Machine Tool Builders' Association (U.S.A.)
NMLF	Norsk Maling- of Lakkteknisk Forening	**NMTF**	National Market Traders Federation
NMLH	National Museum of Labour History	**NMTF**	National Metal Trades Federation
NMLK	National Movement for the Liberation of Kosovo = NPOK	**NMTFA**	National Master Tile Fixers' Association
NMLL	Norsk Musikklaereres Landsforbund	**NMTS**	National Milk Testing Service (U.S.A.)
NMM	National Minority Movement	**NMU**	Nordisk Musiker Union
NMN	Asocio por la Enkonduko de Nova Biologia Nomenklaturo = AINBN	**NMU**	Nordisk Musikkforleggerunion
		NMV	Nederlandse Malacologische Vereniging
NMNH	National Museum of Natural History (U.S.A.)	**NMV**	Nederlandse Museum Vereniging
		NMV	Nederlandse Mycologische Vereniging
NMO	Nederlandse Melkhandelaren Organisatie	**NN.UU**	Naciones Unidas = ONU, UN
NMO	Nordisk Malermester Organisation	**NNA**	National Newspaper Association (U.S.A.)
NMOC	National Marketing Organisation Committee	**NNA**	Nigerian National Alliance
NMOC	National Meteorological Operations Centre	**NNA**	Norwegian Nurses Association = NSF
		NNAF	Norges Astma-og Allergiforbund
NMPA	National Music Publishers Association (U.S.A.)	**NNBOB**	Nieuwe Nederlandse Bond van Ondernemers in het Bouwbedrijf
NMPF	National Milk Producers Federation (U.S.A.)	**NNC**	National Nuclear Corporation (U.S.A.)
		NNC	Noord-Nederlandse Co-operative
NMPU	Nordisk Musikpedagogisk Union	**NNDC**	National Nuclear Data Center (U.S.A.)
NMR	National Minority Roundtable (Hungary) = KK	**NNDC**	New Nigeria Development Company
		NNDP	Namibia National Democratic Party
NMR	Nordisk Ministerråd = PMN	**NNDTC**	National Nondestructive Testing Centre
NMRC	National Microelectronics Research Centre (Éire)	**NNEB**	National Nursery Examination Board
		NNF	Namibia National Front
NMS	National Malaria Society (U.S.A.)	**NNF**	Nordisk Neurokirurgisk Forening
NMS	National Manpower Service (Éire)	**NNF**	Norsk Nopatisk Forening
NMS	National Marine Services (Abu Dhabi)	**NNF**	Northern Nurses Federation (Sweden) = SSN
NMS	National Museums of Scotland		
NMS	Natural Medicines Society	**NNFA**	National Nutritional Foods Association (U.S.A.)
NMS	Nigerian Meteorological Service	**NNGA**	Northern Nut Growers Association (U.S.A.)
NMS	Norsk Metallurgisk Selskap		
NMS	Norske Meieriers Salgs Sentral	**NNH**	Nordiska Nämnden för Handikappfrågor = NCD

NNI	Nederlands Normalisatie-Instituut
NNIL	Northern Nigeria Investments Limited
NNKYL	Nuorten Naisten Kristillisten Yhdistysten Liitto
NNLC	Ngwane National Liberatory Congress (Swaziland)
NNML	Norske Naturhistoriske Museers Landsforbund
NNN	Nannies need Nannies Association
NNOC	Nigerian National Oil Corporation
NNP	New National Party (Grenada)
NNP	Vereniging 'De Nederlandse Nieuwsbladpers'
NNPA	National Newspaper Publishers Association (U.S.A.)
NNPC	Nigerian National Petroleum Corporation
NNRB	National Neurological Research Bank (U.S.A.)
NNRC	Neutral Nations Repatriation Commission
NNRI	National Nutrition Research Institute (South Africa)
NNRO	Norske Nasjonalkomite for Rasjonell Organisasjon
NNS	Neonatal Society
NNTO	Nepal National Teachers Organisation
NNU	Nanjing Normal University
NNU	Northern Naturalists' Union
NNV	Nederlandse Natuurkundige Vereniging
NNV	Norges Naturvernforbund
NO	National Offensive / Nationale Offensive / Narodowa Ofensywa (Poland)
NO	Nos Oiseaux: Société Romande pour l'Étude et la Protection des Oiseaux (Switzerland)
NO-RE--Farm Felleskontoret	Association of Foreign Pharmaceutical Manufacturers (Norway)
NOA	National Opera Association (U.S.A.)
NOA	National Optometric Association (U.S.A.)
NOA	National Orchestra Association (U.S.A.)
NOAA	National Oceanic and Atmospheric Administration (U.S.A.)
NOAACP	National Organization of African, Asian and Caribbean People
NOACM	Nordic Association for Computational Mechanics
NOAH	National Office of Animal Health Ltd
NOAO	National Optical Astronomy Observatories (U.S.A.)
NOB	Nationale Organisatie voor het Beroepsgoederenvervoer Wegtransport
NOB	Nederlandse Omroepproductie Bedrijf
NOB	Nederlandse Orde van Belastingadviseurs
NOBI	Norsk Bioingeniørforbund
NOBIM	Norsk forening for Bildebehandling og Mønstergjenkjenning
NOBIN	Nederlands Orgaan voor de Bevordering van de Informatie-verzorging
NOBLAN-CAM	La Nouvelle Blanchisserie du Cameroun
NOBRA	Nouvelles Brasseries Africaines (Cameroon)
NOC	National Oil Corporation (Libya)
NOC	Nederlands Olympisch Comité
NOCI	Nederlandse Organisatie voor Chemische Informatie
NOCIL	National Organic Chemical Industries (India)
NOCOCA	Nouvelle Confiserie Camerounaise
NOCUS	Nord Computer Users Society
NOD	Norsk Oseanografisk Datasenter
NODA	National Operatic and Dramatic Association
NODA UK	National Owner Drivers Association
NODAF	Non au Droit d'Affamer
NODC	National Oceanographic Data Centre (U.S.A.)
NODCO	National Oil Distribution Company (Qatar)
NODM	National Organisation for Dance and Mime
NOE	Nouvel Ordre Européen
NOEA	National Outdoor Events Association
NOEL	National Organization of Episcopalians for Life (U.S.A.)
NOEM	Netherlands Oil and Gas Equipment Manufacturers
NOF	Nordisk Odontologisk Förening
NOF	Nordisk Ortopedisk Förening
NOF	Norsk Oftalmologisk Förening
NOF	Norsk Oppfinnerforening
NOFA	National Organic Farmers Association (U.S.A.)
NOFAKI	Norges Farmasoytisk-Kjemiske Industriforening

NOFM	Nederlandse Overzeese Financierings-Maatschappij	**NOMOFO**	Norske Motoroverhalings-verksteders Forbund
NOFPP	National Family Planning and Population Office (Tunisia) = ONFP	**NOMUS**	Nämnderna för Nordiskt Musiksamarbete
NOFTIG	Nordisk Förening för Tillämpad Geofysik (Sweden)	**NONAS**	Negros Occidental National Agricultural School (Philippines)
NÖG	Nationalökonomische Gesellschaft (Austria)	**NONIA**	Newfoundland Outport Nursing and Industrial Association
NOG	Nederlandse Oogheelkundig Gezelschap	**NOOSA**	National Out of School Alliance Ltd
NOGA	National Osteopathic Guild Association (U.S.A.)	**NOP**	Narodowe Odrodzenie Polski (Poland) = NRP
NOGA	Nederlandse Organisatie van Glasassuradeuren	**NOP**	National Order Party (Turkey)
NoHaKa	Nederlandse Organisatie van Handelaren in de Kantoormachinebranche	**NOP**	Nederlandse Organisatie van Pluimveehouders
		NOP-N	Nordiska Publiceringsnämnden för Naturvetenskap = NPBS
NOHS	National Occupational Hygiene Service	**NOP-S**	Nordiska Publiceringsnämnden för Samhällsvetenskapliga Tidskrifter
NOHSC	National Occupational Health and Safety Commission	**NOPA**	National Office Products Association (U.S.A.)
NOIA	National Ocean Industries Association (U.S.A.)	**NOPA**	Nordic Union of Popular Writers
NOIC	National Oceanographic Instrumentation Centre (U.S.A.)	**NOPA**	Norwegian Society of Popular Composers, Authors and Arrangers
NOIL	Naval Ordnance Inspection Laboratory	**NoPEF**	Nordiska Projektexportfonden
NOISE	National Organisation for Initiatives in Social Education	**NOPH**	Nordisk Publiseringsnemd Humanistiske Tidskrifter
NOISE	National Organization to Ensure a Sound-controlled Environment (U.S.A.)	**NOPHO**	Nordic Society for Pediatric Hematology and Oncology
NOK	National Olympisches Komitee für Deutschland	**NOPO**	Norske Potetindustrier
NØK	Nordisk Økonomisk Kvaegavl	**NOPPMB**	Nigeria Oil Palm Produce Marketing Board
NOKIL	Norske Kinoleverandørers Landsforbund	**NOPSA**	Nordic Political Science Association
NOKYO	Union of Agricultural Cooperatives (Japan)	**NOR**	Nordisk Organ for Reinforskning
NOL	Nederlandse Organisatie van Loonconfectionnairs	**NORAD**	North American Aerospace Defense Command
NOLA	National Off-Licences Association	**NORAD**	Norwegian Agency for International Development
NOLPE	National Organisation on Legal Problems of Education (U.S.A.)	**NORAID**	Irish Northern Aid Committee (U.S.A.)
NOLS	National Organisation of Labour Students	**NORC**	National Opinion Research Center (U.S.A.)
NOLU	Nederlandse Organisatie van Leesportefeuille Uitgevers	**NORCAM-TOUR**	Agence Camérounaise de Tourisme
NOM	Natur- och Miljo (Finland)	**NORCAP**	National Organisation for Counselling Adoptees and their Parents
NOMESKO	Nordiska Medicinska Statistiska Kommissionen	**NORCOFEL**	Normalisation et Commercialisation des Fruits et Légumes (International)
NOMI	Norges Medisinalindustris Felleskontor	**NORD**	Natsionalno-Osvoboditelnoe Russkoe Dvizhenie
NÖMI	Növénytermesztési és Minosito Intézet		
NOMMA	National Ornamental Metal Manufacturers Association (U.S.A.)	**NORD**	Nordiskt Orienteringsråd

NORD-FORSK	Nordiska Samarbetsorganisationen för Tekniskvetenskaplig Forskning	**NORMAC**	Northern Prawn Fishery Management Committee
NORDAF	Nordiska Annonsörföreningarnas Förbund	**NORPRO**	Norwegian Committee on Trade Procedures
Nordbåt	Nordiska Båtrådet	**NORS**	Norwegian Operational Research Society
NORDEK	Organisation for Nordic Economic Cooperation	**NORSAM**	Nordisk Samråd for Eldreomsorg
NORDEL	Organ för Nordiskt Elsamarbete	**NORVAC**	Norsk VVS Energi- og Miljøteknisk Forening
NordEMS	Nordic EnvironmentaL Mutagen Society (Finland)	**NORVEN**	Comisión Venezolana de Normas Industriales
NORDGU	Nordic Council of the International Good Templar Youth Federation	**Norw CIGR**	Norske Avdeling av CIGR
NORDIA-TRANS	Foreningen for Nordisk Dialyse og Transplantation Personale	**NORWAID**	Norwegian Aid Society for Refugees and International Development
NORD-ICOM	Nordic Documentation Centre for Mass Communication Research	**NORWIDA**	North West Industrial Development Association
NORD-INFO	Nordic Council for Scientific Information and Research Libraries (Finland)	**NOS**	Joint Board for the Nordic Research Councils in the National Sciences
NORD-IPRO	Nordiska Handelsprocedurorganet	**NOS**	National Osteoporosis Society
		NOS	Nederlandse Omroepprogramma Stichting
NORDITA	Nordisk Institutt för Teoretisk Atomfysik	**NOS**	Nordiska Odontologiskastudent-kaerna = CNDS
NORDKEM	Nordiskt Samprojekt för Klimisk Kemi	**NOS**	Nordiske Oppfinnerforeningers Samarbeidsorganisasjon = CBNIA
NORD-PLAN	Nordiska Institutet för Samhällsplanering	**NOS-H**	Nordisk Samenarbeidsnämnden Humanistick Forskning
NORD-POST	Nordiska Postföreningen = NPU, UPPN	**NOS-M**	Nordiska Samarbetsnämnden för Medicinsk Forskning
NORD-REFO	Nordiska Institutet för Regionalpolitisk Forskning	**NOS-N**	Samarbetsnämnden för de Nordiska Naturvetenskapliga
NORDSAM	Nordiska Samarbetskommittén för Internationall Politik Inklusive Konflikt- och Fredsforskning	**NOS-S**	Nordiska Samarbetsnämnden för Samhällsforskning
NORDTEL	Nordic Cooperation on Telecommunications	**NOS-S**	Nordiske Samarbeidsnemnden Samfundsforskning
NORD-TEST	Samnordiskt Organ Inon Provningsområdet	**NOSA**	National Occupational Safety Association (South Africa)
Nordvision	Nordic Television Cooperation = NV	**NOSA**	Nordic Association for Aerosol Science
NORD-VOLC	Nordiska Vulcanologiska Institut (Iceland) = NVI	**NOSALF**	Nordiska Samfundet för Latin Amerika Forskning
NORG	Nederlandse Organisatie voor de Radio Groothandel	**NOSAMF**	Nordiska Samarbetskommitten för Arktisk Medicinsk Forskning
NORINCO	China North Industries Corporation	**NOSC**	National Olympic and Sports Congress (South Africa)
NORIT	Nordisk Institutt for Informasjonsteknologi	**NOSE-BRIMA**	Nouvelle Société d'Exploitation des Briqueteries du Mali
NORMA	Nordiska Samarbets-Kommittén Namnforskning	**NOSHEB**	North of Scotland Hydro-Electric Board
NORMA-DECO	Société Nouvelle Organisation pour le Meuble l'Agencement et la Décoration (Ivory Coast)	**NOSIE**	NODC Ocean Science Information Exchange (U.S.A.)
		NOSO	Norsk Sosionomforbund

NOSOCO	Nouvelle Société Commerciale du Gabon
NOSOCO	Nouvelle Société Commerciale Sénégalaise
NOSON-TRAM	Nouvelle Société Nationale des Transports Mauritaniens
NOSOSEPE	Nouvelle Société Sénégalaise de Pêche
NOSOSKO	Nordiska Socialstatistikkommittén
NOSTA	Nordic Society for Thermal Analysis
NOSTAC	Nordic Society for Thermal Analysis and Calorimetry
NOT	Naczelna Organizacja Techniczna
NOTA	National Organisation of Trade Unions (Uganda)
NOTU	National Organisation of Trade Unions (Uganda)
NOTU	Nederlandse Organisatie van Tijdschrift Uitgevers
NOU	Nederlandse Ornithologische Unie
NOUVEL-LECARE-MOCI	Carrelage, Revêtement, Mosaïque de la Côte d'Ivoire
NOUVEL-LESACAR	Nouvelle Société Abidjanaise de Carrelage (Ivory Coast)
NOUVEL-LESIACA	Société Ivoirienne d'Ananas et de Conserves Alimentaires
NOUW	National Organisation of Unemployed Workers
NOV	Nederlandse Organisatie van Verloskundigen
NOV	Nederlandse Orthopaedische Vereniging
NOVA	Nederlandse Orde van Advocaten
NOVA-TRANS	Société Nouvelle d'Exploitation de Transports Combinés
NOvAA	Nederlandse Orde van Accountants-Administratieconsultenten
NOVACAP	Companhia Urbanizadora da Nova Capital (Brazil)
NOVAKA	Nederlandse Vereniging van Ondernemers-Vakhandelaren in Kantoorinrichting en Administratiemiddelen
NOVI	Nederlands Opleidingsinstituut voor Informatica
NOVIB	Netherlands Organization for International Development Corporation
NOVO	Nederlandse Organisatie van Oliehandelaren
NOVOAH	Network of Voluntary Organizations in AIDS/HIV
NOVOK	Nederlandse Organisatie van Olie- en Kolenhandelaren
NOVU	Nederlandse Orde van Uitvinders
NOW	National Organization for Women (U.S.A.)
NOW	Nederlandse Ondernemersverbond in de Woninginrichtings- en Meubeleringsbedrijven
NOW	New Opportunities for Women Programme (EC)
NOW-a	Niezalezna Oficyna Wydawnicza
NOWEA	Nordwestdeutsche Ausstellungs-Gesellschaft
NOZHI	Independent Association of Women Initiatives (Russia)
NP	Nacionalista Party (Philippines)
NP	National Party (Australia, Papua New Guinea, South Africa)
NP	National Party (Montenegro)
NP	National Party (Poland) = SN
NP	Norsk Presseforbund
NPA	Civil Service Administration (Japan)
NPA	National Packaging Association (Australia)
NPA	National Parks Association
NPA	National Party of Australia
NPA	National Pasta Association (U.S.A.)
NPA	National Pawnbrokers' Association
NPA	National Peoples Army
NPA	National Perinatal Association (U.S.A.)
NPA	National Pharmaceutical Association (U.K., U.S.A.)
NPA	National Pigeon Association
NPA	National Pipeline Authority (Australia)
NPA	National Pistol Association
NPA	National Planning Association (U.S.A.)
NPA	National Playbus Association
NPA	National Podiatry Association (U.S.A.)
NPA	National Portage Association
NPA	National Psychological Association (U.S.A.)
NPA	National Publishing Administration of China
NPA	New Peoples Army (Philippines)
NPA	Newspaper Publishers Association
NPA	Nine Pin Association (GFR)
NPA	Nordic Planetarium Association
NPAC	National Plantations Advisory Committee

NPAC	Newcastle Photovoltaics Applications Centre
NPAC	Northeast Parallel Architectures Center (U.S.A.)
NPACI	National Production Advisory Council on Industry
NPANSW	National Parks Association of New South Wales
NPAP	National Psychological Association for Psychoanalysis (U.S.A.)
NPAQ	National Parks Association of Queensland
NPAS	National Property Advisory Group (NHS)
NPAT	National Petroleum Authority of Thailand
NPAV	Nederlandse Patholoog Anatomen Vereniging
NPB	National Parole Board (Canada)
NPB	National Productivity Board (Singapore)
NPBA	National Pig Breeders' Association
NPBA	National Prefabricated Building Association
NPBS	Nordic Publishing Board in Science = NOP-N
NPC	National Packaging Confederation
NPC	National Parents Council (Éire)
NPC	National Patent Council (U.S.A.)
NPC	National Peace Council
NPC	National Peach Council (U.S.A.)
NPC	National Peanut Council (U.S.A.)
NPC	National Pensioners' Convention
NPC	National Peoples Congress (China)
NPC	National Petrochemical Co. (Iran)
NPC	National Petroleum Council (U.S.A.)
NPC	National Pharmaceutical Council (U.S.A.)
NPC	National Population Council
NPC	National Postcode Centre
NPC	National Postgraduate Committee
NPC	National Potato Council (U.S.A.)
NPC	National Power Corporation (Philippines)
NPC	National Primary Centre
NPC	National Productivity Council (India)
NPC	NATO Parliamentarians' Conference
NPC	Nauru Phosphate Corporation
NPC	Northern People's Congress (Nigeria)
NPC	Northern Petroleum Company (Iraq)
NPCA	National Paint and Coatings Association (U.S.A.)
NPCA	National Parks and Conservation Association (U.S.A.)
NPCA	National Pest Control Association (U.S.A.)
NPCC	National Petroleum Construction Company (Abu Dhabi)
NPCC	National Projects Construction Corporation (India)
NPCCE	National Pollution Control Conference and Exposition
NPCGB	National Pool Council of Great Britain
NPCWGQA	National Pharmaceutical Consultative Working Group on Quality Assurance
NPD	Narodno-Pravoslavnoe Dvizhenie
NPD	Nationaldemokratische Partei Deutschlands
NPDC	National Patent Development Corporation (U.S.A.)
NPDMC	National Property Development and Management Company (Tanzania)
NPDN	Nordic Public Data Network
NPEC	National Pay Equity Campaign
NPESA	National Printing Equipment and Supply Association (U.S.A.)
NPF	National Poetry Foundation
NPF	Nederlandse Pluimvee Federatie
NPF	Normenausschuss Pigmente und Füllstoffe im DIN
NPF	Norsk Papirindustriarbeiderforbund
NPF	Norsk Plantevern Forening
NPF	Norsk Plastforening
NPF	Norsk Plastikkirurgisk Forening
NPF	Norsk Psykiatrisk Forening
NPF	Norsk Psykologforening
NPF	Norske Patentingeniørers Forening
NPF-PAMIAT	"Pamiat" – Natsionalno-Patrioticheskii Front
NPFA	National Playing Fields Association
NPFAP	NGOs Popular Forum in Asia and the Pacific
NPFC	Northwest Pacific Fisheries Commission
NPFI	National Plant Food Institute
NPFL	National Patriotic Front of Liberia
NPFRC	North Pacific Fisheries Research Centre (NMFS)

NPG	National Portrait Gallery	**NPRC**	National Provisional Ruling Council (Sierra Leone)
NPG	Nederlands Psychoanalytisch Genootschap	**NPRC**	Nederlandsche Particuliere Rijnvaartcentrale
NPG	Nezavisimyi Profsoiuz Gorniakov	**NPRC**	Nigerian Petroleum Refining Company
NPG	Nuclear Planning Group (NATO)	**NPRCA**	Norwegian Public Relations Consultants Association
NPGMP	Na'amat Pioneras Grupo Shalom Mane Prutzchi (Peru)	**NPRL**	National Physical Research Laboratory (South Africa)
NPI	National Productivity Institute (South Africa)	**NPRNP**	Nezavisimyi Professionalnyi Soiuz Rasprostranitelei Neformalnoi Pressy
NPI	Norsk Produktivitetsinstitut	**NPRS**	Norske Public Relations Klubb
NPIC	National Play Information Centre	**NPRT**	Nauru Phosphate Royalties Trust
NPIS	National Poisons Information Service	**NPS**	National Philatelic Society
NPK	National Partij Kombinatie (Suriname)	**NPS**	National Poetry Secretariat
NPKA	National Paving and Kerb Association	**NPS**	National Pony Society
NPL	National Physical Laboratory	**NPS**	Nationale Partij Suriname
NPL	Nederlandse Vereniging voor Produktieleiding	**NPS**	Nature Photographic Society
NPL	Norsk Planteskolelag	**NPS**	Normenausschuss Persönliche Schutzausrüstung und Sicherheits-Kennzeichnung im DIN
NPL	Norske Papirhandlers Landsforbund	**NPS**	Norsk Parapsykologisk Selskap
NPL	Norske Pelsskinneksportørers	**NPS**	Norsk Pediatrisk Selskap
NPM	National Association of Pastoral Musicians (U.S.A.)	**NPSU**	Nuclear Plant Safety Unit
NPM	National Prisoners' Movement	**NPSV**	Nezavisimyi Profsoiuz Voennosluzhashchikh
NPM	Nazionalen Prirodonauchen Muzei (Bulgaria)	**NPTA**	National Paper Trade Association (U.S.A.)
NPN	National Party of Nigeria	**NPTC**	National Proficiency Tests Council
NPO	Nederlandse Pluimvee Organisatie	**NPTP**	Namibia Primary Teachers' Programme
NPOK	Narodni Pokret za Oslobodjenje Kosova (Serbia) = NMLK	**NPU**	Newspaper Press Union of South Africa
NPP	Abu Dhabi National Plastic Pipe Fabrication Company	**NPU**	Nordic Postal Union = NORDPOST, UPPN
NPP	National Peasant Party (Serbia)	**NPU**	Nordisk Privatskole Union
NPP	National Peasants' Party (Romania)	**NPUP**	National Progressive Unionist Party (Egypt)
NPP	National People Party (Netherlands Antilles) = PNP	**NPV**	Nederlandse Planteziektenkundige Vereniging
NPP	National People's Party (South Africa)	**NPWA**	National Pure Water Association
NPP	New Patriotic Party (Ghana)	**NQA**	National Quoits Association
NPP	Nigerian People's Party	**NQBA**	National Quality Bacon Association
NPP-CD	National Peasants' Party – Christian Democrat (Romania)	**NQCC**	North Queensland Conservation Council
NPPA	National Panel Products Association	**NQCRRP**	North Queensland Community Rainforest Reforestation Program
NPPS	National Plants Preservation Society	**NQIC**	National Quality Information Centre
NPPTB	National Pig Progeny Testing Board	**NQNC**	North Queensland Naturalists Club (Australia)
NPR	Narodnaia Partiia Rossii	**NQRC**	North Quadrophonic Radio Committee (U.S.A.)
NPR	National Public Radio (U.S.A.)		
NPR	Peoples Consultative Assembly (Indonesia)		
NPRA	National Petroleum Refiners Association (U.S.A.)		

NR	Narodna Rada (Ukraine)	**NRC**	Nuclear Research Center (Iran)
NR	Nezavisimaia Rossiia	**NRCA**	Natural Resources Council of America
NR	Nordska Radet = NC, PN	**NRCC**	National Registry in Clinical Chemistry (U.S.A.)
NR	Norsk Redaktørforening		
NRA	Naczelna Rada Adwokacka	**NRCC**	National Republican Congressional Committee (U.S.A.)
NRA	National Registration Authority for Agricultural and Veterinary Chemicals		
		NRCC	National Research Council of Canada = CNRC
NRA	National Resistance Army (Uganda)		
NRA	National Restaurant Association (U.S.A.)	**NRCCL**	Norwegian Research Centre for Computers and Law
NRA	National Retreat Association	**NRCCLS**	National Resource Center for Consumers of Legal Services (U.S.A.)
NRA	National Rifle Association		
NRA	National Rivers Authority	**NRCD**	National Resource Centre for Dance
NRA	National Roads Authority (Éire)	**NRCL**	Natural Resources Conservation League of Victoria (Australia)
NRA	National Rounders Association		
NRA	National Rustproofers Association	**NRCP**	National Rainforest Conservation Program (DEST)
NRAA	National Rifle Association of America		
NRAC	National Research Advisory Council (New Zealand)	**NRCP**	National Research Council of the Philippines
NRAC	National Resource Analysis Center (U.S.A.)	**NRCPS**	National Research Council on Peace Strategy (U.S.A.)
NRAC	National Rural Advisory Council (Australia)	**NRCRI**	National Root Crops Research Institute, Umudike (Nigeria)
NRAO	National Radio Astronomy Observatory (U.S.A.)	**NRCSL**	National Research Center on Student Learning (U.S.A.)
NRB	National Rehabilitation Board (Éire)	**NRCST**	National Referral Center for Science and Technology (U.S.A.)
NRB	National Religious Broadcasters (U.S.A.)		
NRB	National Roads Board (New Zealand)	**NRCSTD**	National Research Center for Science and Technology for Development (China)
NRB	Natsionalno-Respublikanskii Blok		
NRBA	National Radio Broadcasters Association (U.S.A.)	**NRDB**	Natural Rubber Development Association (Malaysia)
NRBA	National Registered Builders Association	**NRDC**	National Register Drainage Contractors
NRC	National Rail Corporation	**NRDC**	National Research Development Corporation (India, U.K.)
NRC	National Reconciliation Council (Mali)		
NRC	National Reformation Council (Sierra Leone)	**NRDC**	Natural Resources Defense Council (U.S.A.)
NRC	National Regulatory Commission (U.S.A.)	**NREA**	Natural Resources and Energy Agency (MITI)
NRC	National Republican Convention (Nigeria)	**NREC**	National Resource Evaluation Center (U.S.A.)
NRC	National Research Center (Egypt)	**NREC**	National Rural Enterprise Centre
NRC	National Research Council (Canada, Iceland, Sudan, U.S.A.)	**NRECA**	National Rural Electric Cooperative Association (U.S.A.)
NRC	National Rural Center (U.S.A.)	**NREN**	National Research and Education Network
NRC	Niger River Commission		
NRC	Nippon Research Center (Japan)	**NRF**	Nordic Recycling Federation
NRC	Nuclear Regulatory Commission (U.S.A.) = USNRC	**NRF**	Nordisk Retsodontologisk Förening
		NRF	Nordiska Reklamebyra Förbundet
		NRF	Norges Rasjonaliserings-förbund

NRF	Norges Rutebileierforbund		NRLA	Nordic Research Librarians' Association = NVBF
NRF	Norsk Renholdsverks-Forening		NRLC	National Research Laboratory for Conservation of Cultural Property (India)
NRF	Norsk Renseriforening			
NRF	Norske Radiofabrikanters Förbund			
NRF	Norske Regnskapsbyraers Forening		NRLCC	Nordic Research Libraries' Committee of Co-operation
NRF	Norske Roergrossisters Forening			
NRFC	National Rail Freight Corporation		NRLM	National Research Laboratory of Metrology (Japan)
NRFF	National Research Foundation for Fertility (U.S.A.)			
			NRLO	Nationale Raad voor Landbouwkundig Onderzoek
NRHA	National Roller Hockey Association			
NRHP	National Register of Hypnotherapists and Psychotherapists		NRM	National Resistance Movement (Uganda)
NRI	Natural Resources Institute (ODA)		NRMA	National Retail Merchants Association (U.S.A.)
NRIAE	National Research Institute of Agricultural Engineering (Japan)			
NRIAG	National Research Institute of Astronomy and Geophysics (Egypt)		NRMA	National Roads and Motorists Association (Australia)
			NRMC	National Records Management Council (U.S.A.)
NRIC	National Reserves Investigation Committee			
			NRMDP	Natural Resource Management and Development Project
NRIC	National Resource Information Centre			
NRIES	Nanjing Research Institute of Environmental Science		NRMG	Nederlands Rekenmachine Genootsschap
NRIET	Nanjing Research Institute of Electronics Technology		NRMTC	Nordoff-Robbins Music Therapy Centre
			NRP	National Rebirth of Poland = NOP
NRIH	National Research Institute of Health (Ethiopia)		NRP	National Religious Party (Israel)
NRIM	National Research Institute for Metals (Japan)		NRP	Nevis Reformation Party (St Christopher and Nevis)
			NRP	New Republic Party (South Africa)
NRIMS	National Research Institute for Mathematical Sciences (South Africa)		NRP	Nordiska Rikspartiet
			NRPB	National Radiological Protection Board
NRIND	National Research Institute for Nutritional Diseases (South Africa)		NRPC	National Railroad Passenger Corporation (U.S.A.)
NRIO	National Research Institute for Oceanology (South Africa)		NRRA	Northern Regional Research Laboratory (U.S.A.)
NRIOD	National Research Institute for Occupational Diseases (South Africa)		NRRD	Natural Resources Research Division (UNESCO)
NRK	Norges Rode Kors		NRRDC	National Resources Research and Development Corporation
NRK	Normenausschuss Rundstahlketten im DIN			
			NRRF	Norges Registrerte Revisorers Forening
NRK	Norsk Rikskringkasting		NRRI	Natural Resources Research Institute (U.S.A.)
NRK	Norwegian Broadcasting Corporation			
NRL	Naval Research Laboratory (U.S.A.)		NRRL	Norsk Radio Relae Liga
NRL	Norske Radio/TV-handleres Landsforbund		NRS	Navy Records Society
			NRS	Nederlandsche Rundvee Stamboek
NRL	Norske Rørleggerbedrifters Landsforening		NRSA	National Remote Sensing Agency (India)
NRL	Norwegian Reindeer Herders			
NRL	Nutrition Research Laboratory (India)		NRSC	National Remote Sensing Centre
NRL"S"	Niezalezny Ruch Ludowy "Solidarność"		NRSCP	National Reserves System Cooperative Program (ANCA)

NRTA	Niagara Resort and Tourist Association (Canada)	**NSAS**	National Smoke Abatement Society
NRTC	National Road Transport Commission	**NSAV**	Nederlandse Sociologische en Antropologische Vereniging
NRTC	National Rural Telecommunications Co-operative (U.S.A.)	**NSB**	National Shipping Board (India)
NRU	Nederlandse Radio-Unie	**NSB**	National Small Business Association (U.S.A.)
NRV	Nederlandsche Reologische Vereinigung	**NSB**	National Standards Board (Ghana)
NRVC	National Religious Vocations Centre	**NSB**	Norges Statsbaner
NS	Narodnoe Soglasie	**NSB**	Nouvelle Société du Bois (Gabon)
NS	National Society of Paints, Sculptors and Printmakers	**NSB**	Nuclear Safety Bureau (Japan)
		NSBA	National School Band Association
NS	Natural Sciences Department of UNESCO	**NSBA**	National Silica Brickmakers' Association
NS	Navigation Society (China)	**NSBC**	North Sea Bird Club
NS	Nederlandse Spoorwegen	**NSBN**	Nordisk Samverkan Bygd Natur
NS	Newcomen Society	**NSBP**	National Smallholder and Bourgeois Party (Hungary)
NS	Nutrition Society	**NSC**	Namibia Support Committee
NSA	Naczelny Sąd Administracyjny	**NSC**	National Safety Council (Éire, India, U.S.A.)
NSA	National Sawmilling Association		
NSA	National Security Agency (U.S.A.)	**NSC**	National Salvation Council (Chad)
NSA	National Sheep Association	**NSC**	National Science Council (Taiwan)
NSA	National Shellfisheries Association (U.S.A.)	**NSC**	National Security Council (Turkey, U.S.A.)
NSA	National Skating Association of Great Britain	**NSC**	National Seeds Corporation (India)
		NSC	National Snorkellers Club
NSA	National Slag Association (U.S.A.)	**NSC**	National Sporting Club
NSA	National Socialist Alliance (Canada)	**NSC**	National Sports Congress (South Africa)
NSA	National Sound Archive (BL)	**NSC**	National Stone Centre
NSA	National Sprint Association Limited	**NSC**	Nicaragua Solidarity Campaign
NSA	Nederlands Studenten Akkoord	**NSC**	Nippon Steel Corporation (Japan)
NSA	Neurosurgical Society of America	**NSC**	Nuclear Society of China
NSA	Norsk Selskap for Aldersforskning	**NSC**	Nutrition Society of Canada
NSA	Norsk Svineavlslag	**NSCA**	National Safety Council of Australia
NSA	Norwegian Gerontological Society	**NSCA**	National Society for Clean Air
NSA	Nuclear Stock Association	**NSCA**	Natural Sausage Casing Association
NSAA	National Sulphuric Acid Association	**NSCAA**	National Society for Children and Adults with Autism (U.S.A.)
NSAC	National Society of Accountants for Cooperatives (U.S.A.)	**NSCC**	National Specialist Contractors' Association
NSACS	National Society for Abolition of Cruel Sports	**NSCEO**	National Society of Chief Executive Officers (U.S.A.)
NSAE	National Society of Architectural Engineers (U.S.A.)	**NSCG**	Narodna Stranka Crne Gore (Montenegro) = PPM
NSAFF	National Society Against Factory Farming	**NSCG**	Neue Schweizerische Chemische Gesellschaft
NSAI	National Standards Authority for Ireland	**NSCIA**	National Supervisory Council for Intruder Alarms
NSALG	National Society of Allotment and Leisure Gardeners	**NSCMA**	Natural Sausage Casings Manufacturers Association
NSAP	National Socialist Action Party		

NSCN	Nationalist Socialist Council of Nagaland (India)
NSCR	National Society for Cancer Relief
NSCSA	National Shipping Company of Saudi Arabia
NSCWA	Nigerian Society of Cost and Works Accountants
NSDA	National Space Development Agency (Japan)
NSDAP-AO	National Socialistische Deutsche Arbeiterpartei – Auslands Organisation (U.S.A.)
NSDB	National Science Development Board (Philippines, U.S.A.)
NSDC	National Space Development Centre (Japan)
NSDN	National Street Drinking Network
NSDO	National Seed Development Organisation
NSE	National Society for Epilepsy
NSE	Nigerian Society of Engineers
NSEAD	National Society for Education in Art and Design
NSEI	Norsk Selskap for Elektronisk Informasjonsbehandling
NSEL	Chambre Nationale Syndicale des Experts du Grand Duché de Luxembourg
NSERC	National Sciences and Engineering Research Council (Canada)
NSERI	National Solar Energy Research Institute (U.S.A.)
NSESG	North Sea Environmental Study Group
NSF	National Salvation Front (Romania, Russia)
NSF	National Sanitation Foundation (U.S.A.)
NSF	National Schizophrenia Fellowship (U.K., U.S.A.)
NSF	National Science Foundation (U.S.A.)
NSF	National Softball Federation
NSF	National Squash Federation
NSF	Nederlandse Sport Federatie
NSF	Nordiska Skattevetenskapliga Forskningsrådet
NSF	Norges Sporthandleres Forbund
NSF	Norges Standardiserings-forbund
NSF	Norges Støperitekniske Forening
NSF	Norsk Skuespillerforbund
NSF	Norsk Statsvitenskapelig Forening
NSF	Norsk Sykepleierforbund = NNA

NSF	Norske Siviløkonomers Forening
NSFA	Nordic Swimming Federations Association
NSFF	Norsk Selskap for Fotografi
NSFG	Nouvelle Société Forestière du Gabon
NSFGA	Nova Scotia Fruit Growers Association (Canada)
NSFGB	National Ski Federation of Great Britain
NSFI	Norges Skipsforskinings-institutt
NSFK	Nordisk Samarbeidsråd for Kriminologi
NSFNET	National Science Foundation Network (U.S.A.)
NSFPA	Nova Scotia Fish Packers Association
NSFRC	National Soil and Fertiliser Research Committee (U.S.A.)
NSG	National Security Guard (India)
NSG	National Socialist Group
NSG	Norsk Sau- og Geitalslag
NSG	Nouvelle Société du Gabon
NSG	Nuclear Suppliers Group
NSGA	National Sand and Gravel Association (U.S.A.)
NSGF	Norsk Samfunns-Geografisk Forening
NSGPMA	National Salt Glazed Pipe Manufacturers' Association
NSGV	Nederlandse Sint Gregorius Verenging
NSH	Nouvelle Société Helvétique
NSHC	North Sea Hydrographic Commission
NSHSC	National Self-Help Support Centre (NCVO)
NSI	NASA Science Internet
NSI	National Security Intelligence (Bangladesh)
NSI	National Sugar Institute (India)
NSI	Neytandasamtökin (Iceland)
NSI	Norsk Senter for Informatikk
NSI	Nuclear Society International, Moscow
NSIA	National Security Industrial Association (U.S.A.)
NSIA	National Softwood Importers Association
NSIC	National Small Industries Corporation (India, Tanzania)
NSIC	National Spinal Injuries Centre
NSICC	North Sea International Chart Commission
NSIDK	Nederlandse Stichting Informatie en Dokumentatiecentrum voor die Kartografie

NSIS	Nova Scotia Institute of Science (Canada)	**NSO**	Norsk Selskap for Optometri
NSIWP	National Socialist Irish Workers Party	**NSOA**	Nouvelles Savonneries de l'Ouest Africain (Senegal)
NSIWP	Nationalist Socialist Icelandic Workers' Party	**NSODCC**	North Sumatra Oil Development Corporation (Japan)
NSJ	Nautical Society of Japan	**NSOR**	Netherlands Society for Operational Research
NSK	Nihon Shinbun Kyokai (Japan)		
NSK	Nordisk Strafferetskomité	**NSOSG**	North Sea Oceanographic Study Group
NSKIP	Nordiska Samarbets-Kommitten för Internationell Politik, Inklusive Konflikt- och Fredsforskning	**NSP**	National Salvation Party (Turkey) = MSP
		NSP	National Seoposengwe Party (South Africa)
NSKO	Nationaal Secretariaat van het Katholiek Onderwijs	**NSP**	National Society of Painters
		NSP	Nederlandse Sport Pers
NSL	National Science Library (India)	**NSP**	New Socialist Party of Montenegro
NSL	National Socialist League (U.S.A.)	**NSP**	Nylands Svenska Lantbruks-Producentförbund
NSL	National Sporting League		
NSL	Nordiska Stichting voor Leprabestrijding	**NSPA**	National Socialist Party of America
		NSPA	National Society of Public Accountants (U.S.A.)
NSL	Norsk Sykehusadministrasjons Landsforbund	**NSPA**	Nova Scotia Pharmaceutical Association (Canada)
NSL	Norske Skofabrikkers Landssammenslutning	**NSPB**	National Society to Prevent Blindness (U.S.A.)
NSLA	Nova Scotia Library Association (Canada)	**NSPCC**	National Society for Prevention of Cruelty to Children
NSLF	Norsk Skog-og Landarbeiderforbund	**NSPE**	National Society of Professional Engineers (U.S.A.)
NSLF	Norske Sporveiers og Lokalbaners Forening	**NSPI**	National Society for Performance and Instruction (U.S.A.)
NSM	National Socialist Movement (U.S.A.)	**NSPI**	National Society for Programmed Instruction (U.S.A.)
NSM	Normenausschuss Sachmerkmale im DIN	**NSPKU**	National Society for Phenylketonuria and Allied Disorders
NSMF	Norske Sykkel- og Mopedfabrikanters Forening	**NSPRI**	Nigerian Stored Products Research Institute
NSMI	National Sports Medicine Institute		
NSMP	National Society of Master Patternmakers (*now* PMMMA)	**NSPS**	National Society of Professional Sanitarians (U.S.A.)
NSMP	National Society of Mural Painters (U.S.A.)	**NSPS**	National Society of Professional Surveyors (U.S.A.)
NSMPA	National Screw Machine Products Association (U.S.A.)	**NSPS**	National Sweet Pea Society
		NSQA	Natural Slate Quarries Association
NSMR	National Society for Medical Research (U.S.A.)	**NSQT**	National Society for Quality through Teamwork
NSMT	National Society of Master Thatchers	**NSR**	Nederlandse Studenten Raad
NSN	NASA Science Network	**NSR**	Nordisk Skuespillerad
NSNA	National Student Nurses Association (U.S.A.)	**NSR**	Nordiska Skogsarbetsstudieernas Råd
NSNS	National Society of Non-Smokers	**NSRA**	National Scooter Riders Association
NSO	National Solar Observatory (U.S.A.)	**NSRA**	National Smallbore Rifle Association
NSO	Nederlandse Sigarenwinkeliers-Organisatie	**NSRA**	National Society for Research into Allergy
NSO	Nezavisle Slovensky Obory		

NSRA	Nuclear Safety Research Association (Japan)		**NSSP**	Nava Sama Samaja Party (Sri Lanka)
NSRBA	Nova Scotia Road Builders Association		**NSSTE**	National Society of Sales Training Executives (U.S.A.)
NSRC	National Science Research Council (Canada)		**NSTA**	National Science Teachers' Association (U.S.A.)
NSRC	National Shoe Retailers' Council		**NSTAG**	National Science and Technology Analysis Group
NSRDC	National Standards Reference Data Center (U.S.A.)		**NSTC**	National Science and Technology Centre
NSRE Centre	National Society's Religious Education Centre		**NSTC**	New Science and Technology Council (Australia)
NSRF	Norges Statsautoriserte Revisorers Forening		**NSTF**	Norges Skogteknikeforbund
NSRF	Nova Scotia Research Foundation (Canada)		**NSTM**	Nordiska Skeppsteknika Mote
NSRFC	Nova Scotia Research Foundation Corporation		**NSTT**	Netherlands Society for Trenchless Technology
NSRG	Northern Science Research Group (Canada)		**NSTU**	Nova Scotia Teachers Union
NSRI	National Sea Rescue Institute (South Africa)		**NSU**	National Spiritualists Union
			NSU	Nordisk Samorganisasjon for Jordbruksfaglig og Kulturelt Ungdomsarbeid
NSRI	Nelspruit Subtropical Research Institute (South Africa)		**NSU**	Nordisk Sommeruniversitet
NSRP	National States Rights Party (U.S.A.)		**NSU**	Nordisk Sportsfiskerunion
NSRT	North South Round Table (SID)		**NSVV**	Nederlandse Stichting voor Verlichtingskunde
NSS	National Secular Society		**NSWA**	National Small Woods Association
NSS	National Security Service (Maldives)		**NSWEPA**	New South Wales Environment Protection Authority
NSS	National Speleological Society (U.S.A.)			
NSS	Noonan Syndrome Society		**NSWFC**	New South Wales Forestry Commission
NSS	Nordisk Kommittén för Samordning av Elektriska Säkerhetsfrågor		**NSWMA**	National Solid Wastes Management Association (U.S.A.)
NSS	Nordiska Socionomförbund Samarbetskommitte		**NSWNA**	New South Wales Nurses' Association (Australia)
NSS	Nordiska Statistiska Sekretariatet		**NSWNPWS**	New South Wales National Parks and Wildlife Service
NSSA	National School Sailing Association			
NSSA	National Scooter Sport Association		**NSWPP**	National Socialist White Peoples Party (Canada)
NSSA	National Sensitive Sites Alliance			
NSSB	National Social Service Board (Éire)		**NSWWP**	National Socialist White Workers Party (U.S.A.)
NSSC	National Soil Survey Committee (Canada)			
NSSDC	National Space Science Data Center (NASA)		**NSZZ**	Niezalezny Samorządny Związek Zawodowy
NSSE	National Society for the Study of Education (U.S.A.)		**NSZZRI**	Niezalezny Samorządny Związek Zawodowy Rolników Indywidualnych
NSSFC	National Severe Storms Forecast Center (NOAA)		**NT**	National Trust
			NT	Nederlands Textielinstituut
NSSL	National Seed Storage Laboratory (U.S.A.)		**NT**	Nga Tamatoa (New Zealand)
			NT	Nordisk Turistråd
NSSL	National Surveyors' Softball League		**NT**	Nordiske Tegnere
NSSLHA	National Student Speech Language and Hearing Association (U.S.A.)		**NT**	North Calotte Tourist Council
			NTA	National Technical Association (U.S.A.)

NTA	National Telecommunications Agency (U.S.A.)		**NTG**	Nederlandse Tandheelkundig Genootschap
NTA	National Tennis Association (U.S.A.)		**NTH**	Nordiska Tryckkäriskommissionen
NTA	National Transportation Agency of Canada		**NTH**	Norges Tekniske Hogskole
			NTHF	Norske Turisthotellers Forening
NTA	New Towns Association		**NTI**	Norsk Treteknisk Institutt
NTA	Nigerian Television Authority		**NTIA**	National Telecommunications Information Administration (U.S.A.)
NTA-TIA	National Tax Association – Tax Institute of America		**NTIAM**	National Swedish Testing Institute for Agricultural Machinery
NTB	A/S Norsk Telegrambyrå			
NTC	National Textile Corporation (India)		**NTID**	National Technical Institute for the Deaf (U.S.A.)
NTC	National Turfgrass Council			
NTC	Nigerian Tobacco Company		**NTIS**	National Technical Information Service (U.K., U.S.A.)
NTC	Nippon Telecommunications Consulting Committee (Japan)			
			NTK	Nordiska Teaterkommittén = NTC
NTC	Nordic Theatre Comittee = NTK		**NTK**	Normenausschuss Transportkette im DIN
NTCS	National Textile Corporation of Swaziland			
			NTL	Norsk Tjenestemannstag
NTDA	National Trade Development Association		**NTLPGK**	Norsk Teknisk LPG Komité
			NTMA	National Treasury Management Agency (Éire)
NTDA	National Tyre Distributors Association			
NTDPMA	National Tool, Die and Precision Machining Association		**NTN**	National Trends Network (U.S.A.)
			NTNF	Norges Teknisk-Naturvitenskapelige Forskningsråd
NTDRA	National Tire Dealers and Retreaders Association (U.S.A.)			
			NTO	National Tenants Organisation
NTEA	National Tax Equality Association (U.S.A.)		**NTO**	Nederlandse Tegelhandelaren-Organisatie
NTEC	National Traction Engine Club			
NTET	National Traction Engine Trust		**NTO**	Nordic Tele Organisation
NTETA	National Traction Engine and Tractor Association		**NTO**	Nordisk Toltiyenestemannsorganisajon
			NTOG	National Tourist Organisation of Greece
NTF	National Television Fund		**NTOM**	National Tourist Organisation of Malta
NTF	National Trainers Federation		**NTOS**	Natural Therapeutic and Osteopathic Society and Register
NTF	National Training Federation (*ex* NATG)			
			NTP	National Turkmen Party
NTF	Nationalföreningen för Trafiksakerhetens Främjande		**NTPC**	National Technical Planning Committee (Sudan)
NTF	Nordisk Thoraxkirurgisk Forening		**NTPS**	National Turf Protection Society
NTF	Nordisk Transportarbeiderfederasjon		**NTR**	Nordiska Trafiksäkerhetsrådet
NTF	Nordiska Textillaraförbundet		**NTR**	Nordiska Träskyddsrådet = CNPB, NWPC
NTF	Norges Tekstilkjöpmenns Forbund			
NTF	Norsk Tannlaegeforening		**NTR**	Nordiska Tulladministrativa Rådet
NTF	Norske Takpappfabrikkers Felleskontor		**NTRA**	National Television Rental Association
NTFA	National Track and Field Association (U.S.A.)		**NTRA**	National Tenants and Residents Association
NTFC	National Television Film Council (U.S.A.)		**NTRA**	National Tyre Recycling Association
			NTRC	National Tenants Resource Centre
NTFI	Norsk Tekstil Forsknings Instituut		**NTRC**	National Transport Research Center (Pakistan)
NTFMFS	National Tile Faience and Mosaic Fixers' Society			
			NTRF	National Tenants & Residents Federation

NTRI	National Timber Research Institute (CSIR) (South Africa)	**NTWH**	National Theater Workshop for the Handicapped (U.S.A.)
NTRL	National Telecommunications Research Laboratory (South Africa)	**NTZ**	Nederlandse Vereniging voor de Teelt van en de Handel in Tuinbouwzaden
NTRS	National Therapeutic Recreation Society (U.S.A.)	**NU**	Nahdatul Ulama (Indonesia)
NTS	Narodno-Trudovoi Soiuz	**NU**	Natur og Ungdom
NTS	Narodno-Trudovoi Soiuz Rossiiskikh Solidaristov	**NU**	Ningxia University
		NUAAW	National Union of Agricultural and Allied Workers
NTS	National Trust for Scotland	**NUAB**	Italian National Union against Blasphemy
NTS	Nederlandsche Televisie Stichting		
NTS	Nordiska Tidningsutgivarnas Samarbetsnämnd	**NUAE**	National Union of Afghanistan Employees
NTS	Norske Trevarefabrikkers Servicekontor	**NUAT**	Nordisk Union for Alkoholfri Trafik
NTS	Nouvelle Teinturerie du Sénégal	**NUB**	National Union of Blastfurnacemen, Ore Miners, Coke Workers and Kindred Trades
NTS	Tsentralen Suvet na Nauchno-Tekhnicheskite Suyuzi		
NTS CV	NTS Conservation Volunteers	**NUBEGW**	National Union of Building, Engineering and General Workers (Zambia)
NTSA	National Technical Services Association (U.S.A.)		
NTSA	National Transportation Safety Association (U.S.A.)	**NUC**	National Universities Commission (Nigeria)
NTSA	National Tuberous Sclerosis Association (U.S.A.)	**NUCAPS**	National Union of Civil & Public Servants
NTSAD	National Tay-Sachs and Allied Diseases Association (U.S.A.)	**NUCC**	National Unemployed Centres Combine
		NucE	Institution of Nuclear Engineers
NTSB	National Transportation Safety Board (U.S.A.)	**NUCEA**	National University Continuing Education Association (U.S.A.)
NTSC	National Television Systems Committee (U.S.A.)	**NUCIW**	National Union of Commercial and Industrial Workers (Zambia)
NTSEA	National Trade Show Exhibitors Association	**NUCL**	National Union of Liberal Clubs
NTSK	Nordiska Tele-Satelit Kommitten	**NUCLE-BRAS**	Empresas Nucleares Brasileiras
NTSN	National Threatened Species Network	**NUCLE-NOR**	Centrales Nucleares del Norte (Spain)
NTT	Nippon Telephone and Telegraph (Japan)	**NUCLEX**	International Nuclear Industrial Fair and Technical Meetings
NTTA	National Traders Traffic Association		
NTTF	Norsk Tekstil Teknisk Forbund	**NUCPS**	National Union of Civil and Public Servants
NTTK	Nordisk Turisttrafik-Kommitte		
NTTPC	Nippon Telegraph and Telephone Public Corporation (Japan)	**NUCR**	Nouvelle Union Corporative des Résineux
NTU	Nordisk Trafikkskole Union	**NUCS**	National Union of Club Stewards
NTU	Nordiska Tullmannaunionen	**NUCUA**	National Union of Conservative and Unionist Associations
NTUC	National Trades Union Congress (Singapore)	**NUDA&GO**	National Union of Domestic Appliance and General Operatives
NTUC	Nyasaland Trade Union Congress	**NUDBTW**	National Union of Dyers, Bleachers and Textile Workers
NTUCB	National Trade Union Congress of Belize		
NTUG	Nordic Tandem Users' Group	**NUDE**	National Union of Domestic Employees – Trinidad and Tobago

NUDO	National United Democratic Organisation (Namibia)
NUDT	National Union of Democratic Teachers (Jamaica)
NUDW	National Democratic Workers Union (Barbados) (*ex* BACSA)
NUEC	National Union Executive Committee
NUF	Norges Urmakerforbund
NUFAG	Northern Union of Farmers' Groups (Thailand)
NUFCOR	Nuclear Fuels Corporation (South Africa)
NUFCW	National Union of Funeral and Cemetery Workers
NUFFIC	Netherlands Universities Foundation for International Co-operation
NUFLAT	National Union of the Footwear, Leather and Allied Trades (*now* KFAT)
NUFO	Norsk Undervisningsforbund
NUFTIC	Nuclear Fuels Technology Information Center (ORNL)
NUGPO	Nordic Universities Group on Physical Oceanography
NUGS	National Union of Ghana Students
NUGSAT	National Union of Gold, Silver and Allied Trades
NUHKW	National Union of Hosiery and Knitwear Workers (*now* KFAT)
NUHSO	National Union of Home Secretary Operatives
NUI	National University of Ireland
NUI	Netware Users International
NUISY	National Union of Iraqi Students and Youth (U.K.)
NUIW	National Union of Insurance Workers
NUJ	National Union of Journalists
NUKFAT	National Union of Knitwear, Footwear and Apparel Trades (Éire, U.K.)
NUL	National Urban League (U.S.A.)
NULC	National Union of Liberal Clubs
NULMW	National Union of Lock and Metal Workers
NULO	National Union of Labour Organisers
NUM	National Union of Manufacturers
NUM	National Union of Mineworkers
NUMAB	Nederlandsche Unie van Metaalgieterijen en Aanwerwante Bedrijven
NUMAS	National Union of Manufacturers Advisory Service, Ltd

NUMAST	National Union of Marine, Aviation and Shipping Transport Officers
NuMOV	Nah- und Mittelost- Verein
NUMS	Niezalezna Unia Młodziezy Szkolnej
NUMSA	National Union of Mineworkers South Africa
NUNW	National Union of Namibian Workers
NUOD	Nationale Unie der Openbare Diesten (Belgium) = UNSP
NUP	National Unity Party (Burma)
NUP	National Unity Party (TRNC) (Cyprus)
NUPAAWP	National Union of Plantation, Agricultural and Allied Workers of the Philippines
NUPAW	National Union of Plantation and Agricultural Workers (Zambia)
NUPBPW	National Union of Printing, Bookbinding and Paper Workers
NUPE	National Union of Public Employees
NUPGE	National Union of Provincial Government Employes (Canada)
NUPI	Norsk Utenrikspolitisk Institutt
NUPJ	National Union of Private Journalists (Cameroon)
NUPRD	National Union for Psychiatric Research and Development
NUPW	National Union for Public Workers (Barbados)
NUPW	National Union of Plantation Workers (Malaysia)
NUR	National Union of Railwaymen
NURA	National Union of Ratepayers Associations
NURA	National Union of Residents' Associations
NUREP	National Uranium Resource Evaluation Program (U.S.A.)
NURT	National Union of Retail Tobacconists
NUS	National Union of Seamen
NUS	National Union of Students
NUSAC	Nuclear Science Advisory Committee (U.S.A.)
NUSAS	National Union of South African Students
NUSMW-CHDE	National Union of Sheet Metal Workers Coppersmiths, Heating and Domestic Engineers
NUSMWI	National Union of Sheet Metal Workers of Ireland
NUSS	National Union of School Students

NUT	National Union of Teachers	**NVB**	Nederlandse Vereniging van Bleekmiddelen-Fabrikanten
NUTAE	Nuffield Unit of Tropical Animal Ecology (East Africa)	**NVB**	Nederlandse Vereniging van Bouwondernemers
NUTEC	Norwegian Underwater Technology Centre	**NVB**	Nederlandse Vereniging voor Biochemie
NUTG	National Union of Townswomen's Guilds	**NVB**	Nederlandse Vissersbond
NUTGW	National Union of Tailors and Garment Workers	**NVBA**	Nederlandse Vereniging van Bedrijfsarchivarissen
NUTI	Nationale Unie van Technisch en IndustrieelIngenieurs (Belgium) = UNIT	**NVBB**	Nationale Vereniging voor Beveiliging tegen Brand = ANPI
NUTN	National Union of Trained Nurses	**NVBF**	Nordiska Vetenskapliga Bibliotekarie Forbundet = NRLA
NUTS	National Union of Track Statisticians	**NVBL**	Nederlandse Vereniging ter Bevordering van het Levensverzekeringswezen
NUU	New Universal Union (Iran)		
NUU	Nordiska Ungkonservative Unionen = NYCU	**NVBS**	Nederlandse Vereniging ter Bevordering van het Spaarkasbedrijf
NUUW	National Union of Unemployed Workers	**NVBV**	Nationaal Verbond van Belgische Verpleegsters
NUVB	National Union of Vehicle Builders	**NVC**	Nederlands Verpakkingscentrum
NUVIBB	Nationale Unie der Vrije en Intellektuele Beroepen van België = UNPLIB	**NVC**	Nederlands Vrouwen Comité
		NVC	Nederlandse Vereniging voor Celbiologie
NUVO	Nederlandse Unie van Opticiens	**NVCC**	Nederlandse Vereniging voor Cosmetische Chemie
NUVU	Nederlandse Unie van Ondernemers in het Uitvaartverzorgingsbedrijf	**NVCCP**	National Voluntary Council for Children's Play
NUWA	National Unemployed Workers Association	**NVD**	Nederlandse Vereniging van Dansleraren
NUWDAT	National Union of Wallcoverings, Decorative and Allied Trades	**NVD**	Nederlandse Vereniging van Diëtisten
NUWM	National Unemployed Workers Movement	**NVDAN**	Non-Violent Direct Action Network
		NVDO	Nederlandse Vereniging voor Diabetesonderzoek
NUWW	National Union of Women Workers		
NUWWM	National Union of Woodworkers and Woodcutting Machinists (Éire)	**NVE**	Nederlandse Vereniging voor Ergonomie
NV	Nordvision	**NVE**	Norges Vassdrags- og Energiverk
NVA	Nederlandse Vereniging van Antiquaren	**NVEM**	Nederlandse Vereniging voor Electronenmicroscopie
NVA	Nederlandse Vereniging van Assurantiebezorgers	**NVEV**	Nederlandse Vrouwen Electriciteitsvereniging
NVA	Nederlandse Vereniging voor Anesthesisten	**NVEW**	Nederlandse Vereniging van Electrotechnische Werkgevers
NVA	Nederlandse Vereniging voor Waterbeheer	**NVF**	National Vitamin Foundation (U.S.A.)
NVALT	Nederlandse Vereniging van Artsen voor Longziekten en Tuberkulose	**NVF**	Nederlandse Vereniging van Fruitteelers
		NVF	Nederlandse Vereniging voor Fotogrammetrie
NVATA	National Vocational Agricultural Teachers Association (U.S.A.)	**NVF**	Nordiska Vägtekniska Förbundet
		NVF	Norske Vaskeriers Forening
NVB	Nederlandse Vereniging van Bibliothecarissen, Documentalisten en Literatuuronderzoekers	**NVF**	Norske Ventilasjons-entreprenores Forening

NVFA	Nederlandse Vereniging voor Fysische Antropologie	**NVK**	Nederlandse Vereniging van Kindergeneeskunde
NVFF	Nederlandse Vereniging voor Fysiologie en Farmacologie	**NVK**	Nederlandse Vereniging voor Kartografie
NVFK	Nederlandse Vereniging-Federatie voor Kunststoffen	**NVK**	Nederlandse Vereniging voor Kriminologie
NVFL	Nederlandse Vereniging van Fabrikanten van Landbouwwerktuigen	**NVK**	Nordiska Vägtrafikkommitten
NVFS	Nederlandse Vereniging voor Fysiotherapie in de Sportgezondheidszorg	**NVKF**	Nederlandse Vereniging voor Klinische Fysica
NVG	Nederlands Verbond voor Vakvereningen	**NVKL**	Nederlandse Vereniging van Ondernemingen op het Gebied van de Koudetechniek en Luchtbehandeling
NVG	Nederlandse Vereniging voor Geodesie		
NVG	Nederlandse Vereniging voor Gerontologie	**NVKVV**	Nationaal Verband der Katholieke Vlaamse Verpleegkundigen en Vroedvrouwen
NVG	Nederlandse Vereniging voor Gezinscrediet	**NVL**	Nederlandse Vereninging van Levensverzekeraars
NVGA	National Vocational Guidance Association (U.S.A.)	**NVLA**	National Vehicle Leasing Association (U.S.A.)
NVGD	Nederlandsche Vereniging van Gramofoonplaten-handelaren	**NVLA**	National Viewers and Listeners Association
NVGGZ	Nationale Vereniging voor Geestelijke Gezondheidszorg	**NVLE**	Nederlandse Vereniging voor de Landelijke Eigendom
NVGI	Nederlandse Vereniging van Gramofoonplaten Importeurs en Fabrikanten	**NVLG**	Nederlandse Vereniging van Leveranciers van Grootkeukenapparatuur
NVGS	Nederlandse Vereniging voor Grafologie en Schrift-Expertise	**NVLM**	Nederlandse Vereniging van Leraren Maatschappijleer
NVGZ	Nederlandsche Vereniging van Grind- en Zandhandelaren	**NVLP**	Nederlandse Vereniging van Lucht- en Ruimtevaart-Publicisten
NVH	Nederlandse Vereniging van Hypotheekbanken	**NVLST**	Nederlandse Vereniging van Leder Scheikundigen en Technici
NVHB	Nationaal Verbond der Haarkappers van België = FNCB	**NVM**	Nederlandse Vereniging van Marktonderzoekers
NVHT	Nederlandse Vereniging voor Herpetologie en Terrariumkunde "Lacerta"	**NVM**	Nederlandse Vereniging van Meelfabrikanten
		NVM	Nederlandse Vuilafvoer Maatschappij
NVI	National Veterinary Institute (Belgium)	**NVM**	Northern Venture Mangers
NVI	Nordic Vulcanological Institute (Iceland) = NORDVOLC	**NVMA**	National Veterinary Medical Association
NVIB	Nederlandse Vereniging voor de Industriële Bakkerij	**NVMO**	Nederlandse Vereniging voor Medisch Onderwijs
NVIG	Nederlandse Vereniging van Leveranciers van Grootkeukeapparatuur	**NVMW**	Nederlandse Vereniging van Maatschappelijk Werkers
NVIR	Nederlands Vereniging voor Internationaal Recht	**NVNB**	Nederlandse Vereniging van Nachtveiligheidsdiensten en Bewakingsbedrijven
NVJ	Nederlandse Vereniging van Journalisten	**NVNI**	Nasionale Voedingnavorsingsinstituut (South Africa)
NVK	Nederlandse Vereniging van Keuken- en Voedingdeskundigen	**NVO**	Nationalist View Organisation (Turkey)
		NVO	Nederlandse Vereniging van Ongediertebestrijdingsbedrijven

NVOB	Nederlandse Vereniging van Ondernemers op Brandbeveil Gebied
NVOF	Nordiska Vendrarhemorganisationernas Förbund
NVOG	Nederlandse Vereniging van Ondernemers in het Graveerbedrijf
NVON	Nederlandse Vereniging voor het Onderwijs in de Natuurwetenschappen
NVOS	Nederlandse Vereniging voor Orthodontische Studie
NVOZ	Nederlandse Vereniging van Ongevallen- en Ziektenverzekeraars
NVP	Nationale Volkspartij (Netherlands Antilles) = PNP
NVP	Nederlandse Vereniging voor Parasitologie
NVP	Nederlandse Vereniging voor Personeelsbeleid
NVPH	Nederlands Vereniging van Postzegelhandelaren
NVPI	Nederlandse Vereniging van Producenten en Importeurs van Beeld- en Geluidsdragers
NVPsa	Nederlandse Vereniging voor Psychoanalyse
NVPU	Nederlandse Vereniging van Polyurethaanhardsschuim-fabrikanten
NVR	Nederlandse Vereniging van Rheumatologen
NVR	Nederlandse Vereniging van Rubber- en kunststaffabrikanten
NVR	Nederlandse Vereniging voor Ruimtevaart
NVRD	Nederlandse Vereniging van Radio en TV Detailhandelaren
NVRD	Nederlandse Vereniging van Reinigingsdirecteuren
NVRL	Nederlandse Vereniging van Radiologisch Laboranten
NVRN	Non-Violent Resistance Network
NVS	National Vegetable Society
NVS	Nederlandse Vereniging van Schoolmeubelfabrikanten
NVS	Nederlandse Vereniging voor Stralingshygiene
NVS	Nepali Vidyanthi Sangh
NVSH	Nederlandse Vereniging voor Seksuele Hervorming
NVSI	National Vaccine and Serum Institute (China)
NVSKPT	Naational Verbond der Syndikale Kamer der Praktici in de Tandheelkunde (Belgium)
NVT	Nederlands Verbond van Tussenpersonen
NVT	Nederlands Vereniging Ondernemers in de Textielhandel
NVT	Nederlandse Vereniging van Toneelkunstenaars
NVT	Nigerian Television Authority
NVTG	Nederlandse Vereniging van Time-Sharing-Gebruikers
NVTG	Nederlandse Vereniging voor Tropische Gneeskunde
NVTL	Nederlandse Vereniging Techniek in de Landbouw
NVTO	Nederlandse Vereniging voor Tekenonderwijs
NVTS	Nederlandse Vereniging van Technici op Scheepvartgebied
NVU	Nederlandse Vereniging voor Urologie
NVU	Nederlandse Volksunie
NVUA	Nederlandse Vereniging van Universiteits Artsen
NVV	Nationaal Verbond der Vlaswevers (Belgium)
NVV	Nederlands Verbond van Vakverenigigen
NVVA	Nederlandse Vereniging van Automobielassuradeuren
NVVA	Nederlandse Vereniging van Verpleeghuisaartsen
NVVB	Nationale Vereniging voor Beveiliging tegen Brand (Belgium)
NVvE	Nederlandse Vereniging voor Ergonomie
NVvGT	Nederlandse Vereniging van Gieterijtechnici
NVVI	Nederlandse Vereniging voor Immunologie
NVvIJ	Nederlandse Vereniging van Handelaren in Ijzerwaren
NVvIR	Nederlandse Vereniging voor Informatica en Recht
NVVK	Nederlandse Vereniging voor Kleurenstudie
NVVK	Nederlandse Vereniging voor Koeltechniek
NVVK	Nederlandse Vereniging voor Koude
NVVK	Nederlandse Vereniging voor Veligheidskunde

NVVL	Nederlandse Vereniging voor Luchttransport	**NWAC**	National Women's Action Committee – Trinidad and Tobago
NVvL	Nederlandse Vereniging voor Luchtvaarttechniek	**NWAF**	National Womens Aid Federation
NVVL	Nederlandse Vereniging voor Voedingsleer en Levensmiddelentechnologie	**NWB**	Normenausschuss Waagenbau im DIN
		NWC	New World Coalition (U.S.A.)
		NWCA	National Women Citizens Associations
NVvM	Nederlandse Vereniging van Modelmakerijen	**NWCAF**	North West Councils Against Fluoridation
NVvM	Nederlandse Vereniging voor Microbiologie	**NWCC**	National Weed Committee of Canada
NVvN	Nederlandse Vereniging van Neurochirurgen	**NWCC**	National Women's Consultative Council
		NWCP	Noxious Weeds Control Program
NVVS	Nederlandse Vereniging van Sportvissersfederaties	**NWDA**	National Wholesale Druggists Association (U.S.A.)
NVvT	Nederlandse Vereniging van Tandartsen	**NWEB**	North Western Electricity Board
NVVT	Nederlandse Vereniging van Veiligheidstechnici	**NWEMG**	North West European Microbiological Group
NVVT	Nederlandse Vereniging van Verftechnici	**NWEPC**	North West Economic Planning Council
NVvV	Nederlandse Vereniging voor Vlaggenkunde	**NWF**	National Wildlife Federation (U.S.A.)
		NWF	Native Woodland Forum
NVvV	Nederlandse Vereniging voor Voetverzorging	**NWF**	Norske Wallboard-fabrikkers Forening
NVVW	Nederlandse Vereniging tot Verbetering van het Welsumer	**NWFP**	North West Frontier Province (Pakistan)
NVvW	Nederlandse Vereniging van Wiskundeleraren	**NWGA**	National Wholesale Grocers Alliance (Éire)
NVWB	Nederlandse Vereniging van Wegenbouwers	**NWGA**	National Wool Growers Association (South Africa, U.S.A.)
NVWE	Nederlandse Vereniging van Electrotechnische Wergevers	**NWGB**	North Western Gas Board
		NWGCN	National Working Group on Coastal Management
NVWFT	Nederlandse Vereniging voor de Wetenschappelijke Film en Televisie	**NWIB**	Northwestern Institute of Botany (China
NVWH	Nederlandse Vereniging van Werkgevers in het Heibedrijf	**NWIEE**	Northwest China Research Institute of Electronic Equipment
NVWS	Nederlandse Vereniging vor Weer- en Sterrenkunde	**NWKV**	Nasionale Wolkekersvereniging van Suid-Afrika
NVZ	Nederlandse Vereniging van Zeepfabrikanten	**NWM**	Normenausschuss Werkzeugmaschinen im DIN
NVZAB	Nationaal Verbond de Zelfstandige Arbeiders van België = CNTIB	**NWMA**	National Woodwork Manufacturers Association (U.S.A.)
NVZD	Nederlandse Vereniging van Ziekenhuisdirekteuren	**NWMC**	National Wool Marketing Corporation (U.S.A.)
NVZE	Nederlandse Vereniging van Ziekenhuisekonomen	**NWML**	National Weights and Measures Laboratory
NVZT	Nederlandse Vereniging van Ziekenhuis Technici	**NWN**	National Women's Network for International Solidarity
		NWNU	North Western Naturalists Union
NW&SCA	National Water and Soil Conservation Organisation (New Zealand)	**NWO**	National Women's Organisation (Seychelles)
NWAA	North Wales Arts Association	**NWOA**	National Woodland Owners Association (U.S.A.)

NWP	Nationalist Workers Party (New Zealand)
NWP	Nederlandse Werkgroep van Prakitzjins in de Natuurlijke Geneeskunst
NWP	North West Playwrights
NWPC	Nordic Wood Preservation Council = CNPB, NTR
NWPO	Northwest Pacific Oceanographers
NWPU	National Wildlife Protection Unit (ANCA)
NWR	National Womens Register
NWRA	National Water Resources Association (U.S.A.)
NWRI	National Water Research Institute (Canada)
NWRLS	North Western Regional Library System
NWSA	National Welding Supply Association (U.S.A.)
NWSA	National Women's Studies Association (U.S.A.)
NWSC	National Water Safety Committee
NWSC	National Water Safety Congress (U.S.A.)
NWSDA	National Womens Self Defence Association
NWSIAH	North Western Society for Industrial Archaelogy and History
NWT	Normenausschuss Wärmebehandlungstechnik Metallischer Werkstoffe im DIN
NWTA	National Waterways Transport Association
NWTB	National Women's Talent Bank (Éire)
NWTEC	National Wool Textile Export Corporation
NWU	National Workers Union (Jamaica)
NWW	New Ways to Work
NXCSTI	Ningxia Commercial Science and Technology Institute
NY	Norske Yrkestegnere
NYA	National Youth Agency
NYAB	National Youth Advisory Board (U.S.A.)
NYAB	Radio National Youth Association of Bhutan
NYAM	New York Academy of Medicine
NYAM	New York Academy of Music
NYAS	New York Academy of Sciences
NYB	National Youth Bureau
NYCC	National Youth Campaigns Committee (Labour Party)

NYCI	National Youth Council of Ireland
NYCU	Nordic Young Conservative Union = NUU
NYES	New York Entomological Society
NYF	National Youth Federation (Éire)
NYF	Nordic Youth Foundation
NYHA	National Yacht Harbour Association
NYHA	New York Heart Association
NYK	Nippon Yusen Kaisha (Japan)
NYL	Norges Yrkeslaererlag
NYL	Pohjola Norden Yhdistysten Liitto = FNF
NYLC	National Young Life Campaign
NYMAC	National Young Managers Advisory Committee (BIM)
Nymex	New York Mercantile Exchange
NYO	National Youth Orchestra
NYOS	National Youth Orchestra of Scotland
NYSE	New York Stock Exchange
NYSEM	New York Society of Electron Microscopists
NYSPA	New York State Pharmaceutical Association
NYSSIM	New York State Society of Industrial Medicine
NYT	Landsforeningen Norske Yrkestegners
NYUIMS	New York University Insitute of Mathematical Sciences
NYZS	New York Zoological Society
NZ	Normenansschuss Zeichungswesen im DIN
NZ-UKCCI	New Zealand United Kingdom Chamber of Commerce and Industry (U.K.)
NZAA	New Zealand Archaeological Association
NZAB	New Zealand Association of Bacteriologists
NZAEC	New Zealand Atomic Energy Committee
NZAEI	New Zealand Agricultural Engineering Institute
NZAGDC	New Zealand Art Gallery Directors Council
NZAP	New Zealand Antarctic Program
NZAPMB	New Zealand Apple and Pear Marketing Board
NZART	New Zealand Association of Radio Transmitters
NZASA	New Zealand Association of Social Anthropologists

NZASc	New Zealand Association of Scientists		**NZIFST**	New Zealand Institute of Food Science and Technology
NZB	Netherlands Dairy Bureau			
NZBTO	New Zealand Book Trade Organization		**NZIIA**	New Zealand Institute of International Affairs
NZCC	New Zealand Chambers of Commerce			
NZCER	New Zealand Council for Educational Research		**NZIM**	New Zealand Institute of Management
			NZIMP	New Zealand Institute of Medical Photography
NZCH	Nacionalna Zajednica Crnogorca Hrvatske (Croatia) = NCCM		**NZInstW**	New Zealand Institute of Welding
			NZIP	New Zealand Institute of Physics
NZCS	New Zealand Computer Society		**NZIRE**	New Zealand Institute of Refrigeration Engineers
NZCTU	New Zealand Council of Trade Unions			
NZD	Nationale Zuiveldienst (Belgium) = ONL		**NZJCB**	New Zealand Joint Communications Board
NZDA	New Zealand Department of Agriculture		**NZLA**	New Zealand Library Association
NZDA	New Zealand Dietetic Association		**NZLP**	New Zealand Labour Party
NZDCS	New Zealand Department of Census and Statistics		**NZLS**	New Zealand Limnological Society
			NZMPB	New Zealand Meat Producers Board
NZDLS	New Zealand Department of Lands and Survey		**NZMS**	New Zealand Mathematical Society
			NZMS	New Zealand Meteorological Service
NZDP	New Zealand Democratic Party		**NZMSS**	New Zealand Marine Sciences Society
NZDSIR	New Zealand Department of Scientific and Industrial Research		**NZNAC**	New Zealand National Airways Corporation
NZEI	New Zealand Educational Institute		**NZNCOR**	New Zealand National Committee on Oceanic Research
NZEI	New Zealand Electronics Institute			
NZERDC	New Zealand Energy Research Development Committee		**NZNP**	New Zealand National Party
			NZNRAC	New Zealand National Research Advisory Council
NZES	New Zealand Ecological Society			
NZF	Norsk Zoologisk Forening		**NZOI**	New Zealand Oceanographic Institute
NZFL	New Zealand Federation of Labour		**NZP**	New Zealand Party
NZFMRA	New Zealand Fertilizer Manufacturers Research Association		**NZPA**	New Zealand Ports Authority
			NZPCE	New Zealand Prestressed Concrete Institute
NZFP	New Zealand Forest Products Ltd			
NZFPA	New Zealand Family Planning Association		**NZPOA**	New Zealand Purchasing Officers Association
NZFRI	New Zealand Forest Research Institute		**NZPsS**	New Zealand Psychological Society
NZFS	New Zealand Forest Service		**NZPTU**	New Zealand Printing and Related Trades Industrial Union of Workers
NZGA	New Zealand Grassland Association			
NZGenS	New Zealand Genetical Society		**NZR**	Nationale Ziekenhuisraad
NZGS	New Zealand Geographical Society		**NZR**	New Zealand Railways
NZHS	New Zealand Hydrological Society		**NZR**	Vereniging Nationale Ziekenhuisraad
NZIA	New Zealand Institute of Architects		**NZRFU**	New Zealand Rugby Football Union
NZIA	New Zealand Ireland Association		**NZS**	Niezalezne Zrzeszenie Studentów
NZIAS	New Zealand Institute of Agricultural Science		**NZSA**	New Zealand Society of Accountants
			NZSA	New Zealand Statistical Association
NZIC	New Zealand Institute of Chemistry		**NZSAP**	New Zealand Society of Animal Production
NZIE	New Zealand Institution of Engineers			
NZIER	New Zealand Institute of Economic Research		**NZSCA**	New Zealand Soil Conservation Association
NZIF	New Zealand Institute of Foresters		**NZSDST**	New Zealand Society of Dairy Science and Technology

NZSGP	New Zealand Self-Government Party	**OAC**	Oceanic Affairs Committee
NZSI	New Zealand Standards Institute	**OAC**	Outdoor Advertising Council
NZSLO	New Zealand Scientific Liaison Office	**OAC**	Overseas Automotive Club (U.S.A.)
NZSSS	New Zealand Society of Soil Science	**OACI**	Organización de la Aviación Civil Internacional; Organisation de l'Aviation Civile Internationale (UN) = ICAO, MOGA
NZV	Nederlandse Zoötechnische Vereiniging		
NZVA	New Zealand Veterinary Association		
NZVC	Nieuwe Zachte Vezel Combinatie	**OACIS**	Oregon Advanced Computing Institute (U.S.A.)
NZWCC	New Zealand Weed Control Conference		
NZWHN	New Zealand Women's Health Network	**OACV**	Opération Arachide et Cultures Vivrières (Mali)
NZWIRI	New Zealand Wool Industries Research Institute	**OAD**	Ordo Augustiniensum Discalceatorum
NZWPA	New Zealand Wholesale Pharmaceutical Association	**OADS**	Organisation Arabe de Défence Sociale contre le Crime (Morocco) = AOSD
NZWWF	New Zealand Waterside Workers Federation	**ÖAeV**	Österreichische Aerosol-Vereinigung
NZZR	Niezalezny Związek Zawodowy Rolników	**OAF**	Oljeselskapenes Arbeidgiverforening
		OAG	Gesellschaft für Natur-und Völkerkunde Ostasiens
		OAGB	Osteopathic Association of Great Britain
		ÖAGG	Österreichischer Arbeitskreis für Gruppentherapie und Gruppengynamik

O

		ÖAGM	Österreichische Arbeitsgemeinschaft für Mustererkennung
OA	Officers Association		
OA	Overeaters Anonymous	**OAH**	Organization of American Historians
OAA	Obstetric Anaesthetists Association	**OAI**	Országos Allategészégügyi Intézet
OAA	Ontario Association of Architects (Canada)	**OAIA**	Organisation des Agences d'Information d'Asie = OANA
OAA	Opticians Association of America	**OAIC**	Office Algéerien Interprofessionel des Céréales
OAA	Organisation d'Assurances Africaines		
OAA	Organización de las Naciones Unidas para la Aminentación y la Agricultura = FAO	**OAJ**	Opettajien Ammattijärjestö
		ÖAK	Österreichische Apothekerkammer
		ÖÄK	Österreichische Ärztekammer
OAA	Orient Airlines Association (Philippines)	**ÖAKT**	Österreichische Arbeitsreise für Tiefenpsychologie
OAA	Outdoor Advertising Association of Great Britain	**OAL**	Office of Arts and Libraries
OAAA	Outdoor Advertising Association of America	**ÖAL**	Österreichischer Arbeitsring für Lärmbekämpfung
OAAA	Outdoor Advertising Association of Australia Inc.	**OALA**	Organización Agustiniana Latinoamérica
ÖAAB	Österreichischer Arbeiter-und Angestelltenbund	**OAMA**	Oil Appliance Manufacturers Association
OAAC	Outdoor Advertising Association of Canada	**OAMCAF**	Organisation Africaine et Malagache du Café
OAAS	Ontario Association of Agricultural Societies (Canada)	**OAMJTB**	Organisation pour l'Afrique des Mouvements de Jeunesse et du Travail Bénévole
OAAU	Organisation for Afro-American Unity = OUAA		
		OAMPI	Office Africain et Malagache de la Propriété Intellectuelle
OAB	Ordem dos Advogados do Brasil		
OAB	Organisation Africaine de Bois (Gabon) = ATO	**ÖAMTC**	Österreichischer Automobil-Motorrad und Touring-Club

OANA	Organisation of Asian News Agencies = OAIA
OANM	Organisation Arabe de Normalisation de Métrologie (Egypt)
OAP	Office Algérien de Publicité
OAP	Organisation Asiatique de la Productivité
OAPEC	Organization of Arab Petroleum Exporting Countries = OPAEP
OAPNA	Organization of Asian-Pacific News Agencies
OAR	Ordo Augustinianorum Recollectorum
ÖAR	Österreichische Arbeitsgemeinschaft für Rehabilitation
OAS	Ohio Academy of Science (U.S.A.)
OAS	Oklahoma Academy of Science
OAS	Organisation of American States = OEA
OAS	Secret Army Organisation (Algeria)
OASA	Organisation Arabe des Sciences Administratives = AOAS
OASIS	Oasis AIDS Care Centre
OASRR	Organisation Afro-Asiatique pour la Reconstruction Rurale = AARRO
OAT	Organisation Arabe du Travail = ALO
OATUU	Organisation of African Trade Union Unity = OUSA
OAU	Organisation of African Unity = OUA
OAU/STRC	Scientific, Technical and Research Commission of the Organization of African Unity
ÖAV	Österreichische Arbeitsgemeinschaft für Volksgesundheit
ÖAV	Österreichischer Alpenverein
ÖAV	Österreichischer Apothekerverband
ÖAV	Österreichischer Astronomischer Verein
ÖAW	Österreichische Akademie der Wissenschaften
OB	Ordnance Board (U.S.A.)
OBAA	Oil Burning Apparatus Association
OBAE	Office des Bois de l'Afrique Équatoriale (Gabon)
OBAP	Office Belge pour l'Accroissement de la Productivité
OBAR	Office Béninois de l'Aménagement Rural
ÖBB	Österreichische Bundesbahnen
OBC	Oceania Basketball Confederation
OBC	Oeuvre Belge du Cancer
OBC	Old Bottle Club of Great Britain
OBCE	Office Belge du Commerce Extérieur

OBEA	Office Belge de l'Économie et de l'Agriculture
OBEMAP	Office Béninois des Manutentions Portuaires
OBEMINES	Office Béninois des Mines
OBESSU	Organising Bureau of European School Student Unions
ÖBG	Österreichische Bodenkundliche Gesellschaft
OBI	Office du Baccalauréat International = IBO
OBK	Office des Bauxites de Kindia (Guinea)
OBK	Organisation pour l'Aménagement et le Développement du Bassin de la Rivier Kagera = KBO
OBN	Ondernemersbond Bestratingsbedrijven Nederland
OBOP	Ośrodek Badania Opinii Publicznej
OBR	Ośrodek Badawczo Rozwojowy
OBRA	Overseas Broadcasting Representatives Association
OBS	Ośrodek Badań Społecznych
OBS	Obshto-Bulgarski Suyuz (Bulgaria) = ABU
OBSA	Organización Boliviana de Sanidad Agropecuária
OBV	Országos Bányagépyártó Vállalat
OCA	Olympic Council of Asia
OCA	Organización de las Cooperativas de América
OCA	Organization of Chinese Americans (U.S.A.)
OCAA	Office Central des Associations Agricoles du Finistère et des Côtes-du-Nord
OCAB	Overseas Correspondents Association Bangladesh
OCAC	Coordinating Office of Assistance for Country Women (Chile)
OCarm	Ordo Fratrum Beatissimae Mariae Virginis de Monte Carmelo
OCAS	Organization of Central American States = ODECA, OECA
OCATOUR	Office Centrafricain de Tourisme
OCAW	Oil, Chemical and Atomic Workers International Union (U.S.A.)
OCB	Office Congolais des Bois
OCB	Offshore Certification Bureau
OCB	Organisation Camérounaise de la Banane

OCBN	Organisation Commune Bénin-Niger des Chemins de Fer et des Transports
OCC	International Offshore Craft Conference
OCC	Office du Café et du Cacao (Congo)
OCC	Offshore Construction Council
OCCA	Oil and Colour Chemists Association (U.K., U.S.A.)
OCCDP	Organisation Catholique Canadienne pour le Développement et la Paix = CCODP
OCCEAC	Organisation Commune pour la Coopération Économique en Afrique Centrale (Zaïre)
OCCF	Office Commun des Consummateurs de la Ferrailles
OCCGE	Organisation de Coordination et de Coopération pour la Lutte contre les Grands Endémies
OCCIDEN-TAL	Organisation Universelle de Langue Internationale
OCCPMP	Office Centrafricain de Commercialisation des Pierres et Métaux Précieux
OCD	Ordo Fratrum Discalceatorum Beatae Virginis Mariae de Monte Carmelo
OCDA	Organización Demócrata Cristiana de América
OCDE	Organización para la Cooperación y el Desarrollo Económico; Organisation de Coopération et de Développement Économique = OECD, OESO
OCDE-AIE	OCDE Agencie Internationale de l'Énergie
OCE	Office de Commercialisation et d'Exportation (Morocco)
OCEAC	Organisation de Coordination pour la Lutte Contre des Endémies en Afrique Centrale
OCEAN	Organisation Communautaire Européenne d'Avitalleurs de Navires (EU)
OCEC	Oficio Central de Educación Católicos (Chile)
OCEPA	Organizacion Comercial Ecuatoriana de Productos Artesanales
OCER	Office Congolais de l'Entretien Routier
OCFF	Ordre des Conseils Fiscaux de France et d'Outre-Mer
OCFT	Office du Chemin de Fer Transcamerounais
ÖCG	Österreichische Computer Gesellschaft
OCH	Office Congolais de l'Habitat
OCI	Office of Computer Information (U.S.A.)
OCI	Oficina Central de Información (Venezuela)
OCI	Organisation de la Conférence Islamique (Saudi Arabia) = OIC
OCI	Organisation du Commerce International
OCIBU	Office des Cultures Industrielles du Burundi
OCIC	Office Chérifien Interprofessionel des Céréales (Morocco)
OCIC	Organisation Catholique Internationale du Cinéma et de Audiovisuel
OCIMF	Oil Companies International Marine Forum
OCINAM	Office-Cinématographiques National du Mali
OCIPE	Office Catholique d'Information sur les Problémes Européens
OCIR	Office des Cultures Industrielles de Rwanda
OCIR	Organisation de la Coopération de l'Industrie des Roulements à Bille = OCRBI, OSPP
OCIRU	Office des Cafés Indigénes du Rwanda et Burundi
OCIS	Oxford Centre for Islamic Studies
OCist	Ordo Cisterciensis
OCK	brona Cywilna Kraju
OCLAE	Organización Continental Latinoamericana de Estudiantes
OCLC	On-line Computer Library Center (U.S.A.)
OCM	Ordo Constantini Magni
OCMLP	Organização Comunista Marxista-Leninista de Portugal
OCMLR	Organisation Communiste Marxiste-Leniniste de la Réunion
OCMR	Ontario Centre for Materials Research
OCN	Office of the Commissioner of Namibia
OCNM	Organization of the Crimean Tatar National Movement
OCOM	Oficina Central de Organización y Metodos (Chile)
OCORA	Office de Coopération Radiophonique
OCP	Office Chérifien des Phosphates (Morocco)
OCP	Offices des Céréales Panifiables (Syria)

OCP	Onchocerciasis Control Program (WHO)	**ODCA**	Organización Demócrata Cristiana de América
OCPCA	Oil and Chemical Plant Constructors Association	**ODCAS**	Oficiul de Informare Documentara pentru Constructii Arhitectura si Sistematizare
OCPLACS	Ontario Cooperative Program in Latin American and Caribbean Studies	**ODDM**	Organizacion pro Desarrollo de los Derechos de la Mujer (Puerto Rico)
OCR	Ordo Cisterciensium Reformatorum	**ODE**	Organisatie voor Duurzame Energie
OCRA	Office Commercial du Ravitaillement et de l'Agriculture (Belgium)	**ODECA**	Organización de Estados Centroamericanos = OCAS, OECA = CACSO
OCRA	Office de Coopération Radiophonique		
OCRBI	Organization for Cooperation in the Roller Bearings Industry = OCIR, OSPP	**ODECABE**	Organización Deportiva Centroamericana y del Caribe (Mexico)
OCRPI	Office Central de Répartition des Produits Industriels	**ODEF**	Office National de Développement et d'Exploitation des Ressources Forestières (Togo)
OCRS	Organisation Commune des Régions Sahariennes	**ODEF**	Organizacion de Desarrollo Empresarial Femenino (Honduras)
OCRTA	Office du Chemin de Fer Transgabonais		
OCS	Office of the Chief Scientist	**ODEP**	Office d'Exploitation des Ports (Morocco)
OCS	Oriental Ceramic Society		
OCS	Overseas Communication Service (India)	**ODEPA**	Oficina de Planificación Agrícola (Chile)
OCSHA	Obra de la Cooperación Sacerdotal Hispanoamericana	**ODEPA**	Organización Deportiva Panamericana = PASO
OCSO	Ordo Cisterciensium Strictioris Observantiae	**ODEPLAN**	Oficina de Planificación Nacional (Chile)
OCT	Office du Commerce de la Tunisie	**ODESSA**	Organisation der Ehemaligen SS-Angerhörigen (Germany)
OCTI	Office Central des Transports Internationaux Ferroviaires	**ODETTE**	Organisation for Data Exchange by Teletransmission in Europe
OCTRA	Office du Chemin de Fer Transgabonais (Gabon)	**ÖDG**	Österreichische Dermatologische Gesellschaft
OCTRF	Ontario Cancer Treatment and Research Foundation (Canada)	**ODI**	Office pour le Développement Industriel (Morocco)
OCU	Organización de Consumidores y Usuarios	**ODI**	Open Door International for the Economic Emancipation of the Woman Worker
OCUFA	Ontario Confederation of University Faculty Associations (Canada)		
OCW	Opzoekingscentrum voor de Wegenbouw (Belgium)	**ODI**	Organisation Interaméricaine de Défense
ODA	Civic Democratic Alliance (Czech Republic)	**ODI**	Overseas Development Institute
		ODIHR	Office for Democratic Institutions and Human Rights (EU)
ODA	Offa's Dyke Association		
ODA	Official Development Assistance (OECD)	**ÖDK**	Österreichische Dentistenkammer
		ODM	Organizacion pro Derechos de la Mujer (Puerto Rico)
ODA	Ontario Dental Association (Canada)		
ODA	Overseas Development Administration	**ODNRI**	Overseas Development Natural Resources Institute
ODA	Overseas Doctors Association in the United Kingdom		
		ODOMEL	Odiki Omospondia tis Ellados = GRF
ODBA	Oregon Dairy Breeders Association (U.S.A.)	**ODP**	Ocean Drilling Program (U.S.A.)
ODC	Overseas Development Council (U.S.A.)	**ODP-MT**	Organisation pour la Démocratie Populaire – Mouvement du Travail (Burkina Faso)

ODPA	Organization of Democratic and Popular Action (Morocco)
ODPR	Office of the Data Protection Registrar
ODRS	Organización Desarrollo Rio Senegal
ODS	Civic Democratic Party (Czech Republic)
ODS	Obcanská demokratická strana
ODS	Oficina del Defensor del Soldado
ODSA	Overseas Development Service Association
ODSBA	Oxford Down Sheep Breeders Association
ODSC	Oficina de Desarrollo de Seguros Cooperativos (ACI, ICA, IGB, MKA) = BCDA, CIDB
ODTA	Organisation pour le Développement du Tourisme en Afrique (Togo)
ODUCAL	Organización de Universidades Católicas de América Latina
ÖDV	Österreichischer Detektiv-Verband
ÖDV	Österreichischer Drogistenverband
OE	Organisation Européenne
OE-CMT	Organisation Européenne de la Confédération Mondiale du Travail
OE-FISEC	Organisation Européenne – Fédération Internationale Sportive de l'Enseignement Catholique
OE-GIAPEC	Organisation Européenne – Groupement International des Associations de Parents d'Élèves de l'Enseignement Catholique
OEA	Office of European Associations in Higher Education (Belgium)
OEA	Ophthalmic Exhibitors Association
OEA	Organisation of Europe Aluminium-Smelters = OEAS
OEA	Organización de los Estados Americanos = OAS
OEAS	Organisation Europäischer Aluminium Schmelzhutten = OEA
OEB	Association Européenne des Bateliers = ESO
OEB	Ondervakgroep Export van Bloembollen
OEB	Organisation Européenne des Brevets = EPA, EPO, VEB
OEBC	Organisation Européenne de Biologie Cellulaire = ECBO
OEBI	Oficina de Estadisticas Balleneras Internacionales = BIWS, BSBI
OEBM	Organisation Européenne de Biologie Moléculaire = EMBO
OEC	Organisation Européenne pour la Qualité = EOQ
OEC	Overseas Employment Corporation (Pakistan)
OECA	Organisation des États Centro-Américains = OCAS, ODECA
OECD	Organisation for Economic Co-operation and Development = OCDE, OESO
OECD-IEA	OECD International Energy Agency = OECD-AIE
OECEI	Oficina de Estudio para la Colaboración Económica Internacional (Argentina)
OECF	Overseas Economic Cooperation Fund of Japan
OECL	Ordre des Experts Comptables Luxembourgeois
OECL	Organisation Européenne des Industries de la Conserve de Légumes
OECO	Organisation des États des Caraïbes Orientales = OECS
OECS	Organisation of Eastern Caribbean States (St Lucia) = OECO
OECT	Organisation Européenne Coopération Touristique
OECT	Organisation Européenne du Commerce de Gros en Textile
ÖED	Österreichischer Entwicklungsdienst
OEDA	Occupational and Environmental Diseases Association
OEE	Országos Erdészeti Egyesület
OEEPE	Organisation Européenne d'Études Photogrammétriques Expérimentales
OEF	Oxford Economic Forecasting
ÖEG	Österreichische Ethnologische Gesellschaft
ÖEG	Österreichische Exlibris-Gesellschaft
ÖEGBPT	Österreichische Gesellschaft für Bioprozesstechnik
OEHA	Office of Environmental and Health Affairs (World Bank)
OEHI	Organisai Exportir Hasilbumi Indonesia
OEI	Organisation Européenne d'Information
OEI	Organización de Estados Iberoamericanos para la Educación, la Ciencia y la Cultura = BEI, IABE
OEICTO	Association of European Tomato Processing Industries

OEIPS	Office of Engineering and Information Processing Standards (U.S.A.)
OEITFL	Organisation Européenne des Industries Tranformatices de Fruits et Légumes
ÖEKV	Österreichischer Energiekonsumenten-Verband
OEMSA	Optical Equipment Manufacturers & Suppliers Association
OEPP	Organisation Européenne et Méditerranéenne pour la Protection des Plantes = EPPO
OeRK	Oekumenischer Rat der Kirchen = CMI, COE, WCC
OERTC	Organisation Européenne de Recherche sur le Traitement du Cancer = EORTC
OES	Offshore Engineering Society
OES	Organization of European Saw-Mills = EOZ, EOZ
OESAD	Wildpeace-Organisation Européenne de Secours aux Animaux en Détresse
OESO	Organisatie voor Economische Samenwerking en Ontwikkeling = OCDE, OECD
OESO	Organisation Internationale d'Études Statistiques pour les Maladies de l'Oesophage
ÖET	Österreichische Ethnologische Gesellschaft
OETB	Offshore Energy Technology Board
OÉTI	Országos Élelmezés és Táplálkozástudományi Intézet
OEVA	Office de l'Expérimentation et de la Vulgarisation Agricoles (Tunisia)
OF	Operation Friendship
OFA	Office Arabe de Presse et de Documentation (Syria)
OFA	Ontario Film Association
OFAES	Oriental Fine Arts Exchange Society (China)
ÖFAI	Österreichisches Forschungsinstitut für Artificial Intelligence
OFALAC	Office Algérien d'Action Économique et Touristique
OFAR	Office of Foreign Agricultural Relations (U.S.A.)
OFAT	Oficina Fiscalizadora de Algodon y Tabaco (Paraguay)
OFBEC	Office Franco-Britannique d'Études et de Commerce
OFC	Oceania Football Confederation (New Zealand)
OFC	Overseas Food Corporation
OFCA	Organisation des Fabricants de Produits Cellulosiques Alimentaires de la CEE
OFCF	Overseas Farmers Co-operative Federation Ltd
OFE	Organization de Flora Europaea = FEO
OFEDES	Office des Eaux du Sous-Sol (Niger)
OFEMA	Office Français d'Exportation de Matériel Aéronautique
OFERMAT	Office Français de Coopération pour les Chemins de Fer et les Matériels d'Équipement
OFEROM	Office Central des Chemins de Fer d'Outre- Mer
OFESAUTO	Oficina Española de Aseguradores de Automoviles
OFESZ	Association of Reconciliation of Interests in Higher Education (Hungary)
OFET	Organisation Française d'Enseignement de la Télédetection
OFFA	One Fund For All
OFFER	Office of Electricity Regulation
OFFI	Orszagos Fordito es Forditashitelesito Iroda (Hungary)
OFFINTAC	Offshore Installations Technical Advisory Committee
OFFSET	Offshore Engineering Team (NEL)
OFG	Organic Farmers and Growers Ltd
ÖFG	Österreichische Forschungsgesellschaft für Philatelie und Postgeschichte
OFGAS	Office of Gas Supply
OFHB	Organisation des Femmes Handicapées du Benin
OFI	Orientation à la Faction Internationale
OFI	Oxford Forestry Institute
OFIA	Optical Frame Importers Association
OFIAMT	Office Fédéral de l'Industrie, des Arts et Métiers et du Travail (Switzerland)
OFICEMA	Oficina Central Maritima
OFIGAN	Oficina Nacional de Gandería (Costa Rica)
Ofines	Oficina Internacional de Información y Observación del Español
OFINTAC	Offshore Installations Technical Advisory Committee
OFIPLAN	Oficina de Planificación (Costa Rica)
OFITEC	Office Tunisien de l'Expansion Commerciale et du Tourisme
OFITOMEP	Office International de Reseignements des Fabricants de Toiles Métalliques pour Papeteries

OFLA	Office des Fruits et Légumes d'Algérie		**ÖGA**	Österreichischer Gartenarchitekter
ÖFLEI	Verband Österreichischer Fleischervereinigungen		**OGABI**	Omnium Gabonais de Développement Immobilier
ÖFLM	Österreichischer Fliesenverband		**ÖGAI**	Österreichische Gesellschaft für Artificial Intelligence
OFLOT	Office of the National Lottery		**ÖGAM**	Österreichische Gesellschaft für Allgemeinmedzin
OFM	Ordo Fratrum Minorum			
OFM Cap	Ordo Fratrum Minorum Capuccinorum		**OGAPROV**	Office Gabonais d'Amélioration et de Production de Viande
OFM Conv	Ordo Fratrum Minorum Conventualium			
OFN	Organization for Flora Neotropica		**OGAR**	Omnium Gabonais d'Assurances et de Réssurances
OFNACER	Office National des Céréales (Burkina Faso)		**ÖGB**	Österreichischer Gewerkschaftsbund
OFNACOM	Office National du Commerce (Congo)		**ÖGBD**	Österreichische Gesellschaft für Dokumentation und Bibliographie
OFOBA	Oils, Fats and Oilseeds Brokers Association (Netherlands)		**OGBL**	Onofhaengege Gewerkschaftsbond-Letzburg (Luxembourg)
OFR	Oliebranchens Fællesrepræsentation			
OFR	United Front of Workers		**ÖGBMT**	Österreichische Gesellschaft für Biomedizinische Technik
OFRANEH	Organización Fraternal Negra (Honduras)		**OGBTP**	Office Général du Bâtiment et des Travaux Publics
OFRB	Organisation des Femmes Révolutionnaires de Bénin		**OGC**	Oregon Graduate Centre
OFRS	Office Français de Recherches Sous-Marines		**ÖGCF**	Österreichische Gesellschaft für China-Forschung
OFS	Ordine Francescano Secolare = SFO, TOF		**OGD**	Observatoire Géopolitiques des Drogues (France)
ÖFSE	Österreichische Forschungsstifung für Entwicklungshilfe		**OGDC**	Oil and Gas Development Corporation (Pakistan)
Ofsted	Office for Standards in Education		**ÖGDI**	Österreichische Gesellschaft für Dokumentation und Information
OFT	Office of Fair Trading			
OFT	Oljeeldningstekniska Föreningen		**ÖGE**	Österreichische Gesellschaft für Elektronenmikroskopie
OFTEC	Oil Firing Technical Association for the Petroleum Industry		**ÖGE**	Österreichische Gesellschaft für Ernährungsforschung
OFTEL	Office of Telecommunications		**OGEA**	Organisation & Gestion de l'Enterprise Agricole
OFTEL	Office Technique des Éleveurs			
OFTH	Országos Földügyi és Térképészeti Hivatal, Földmérési és Térképészeti Föosztály		**ÖGEFA**	Österreichische Gesellschaft für Arbeitstechnik und Betriebstrationalisierung
OFV	Opplysningsrådet for Veitrafikkers		**ÖGEFUE**	Österreichische Gesellschaft zur Förderung von Umweltschutz und Energieforschung
ÖFVK	Österreichischer Fachverband für Volkskunde			
OFW	Opportunities for Women		**ÖGEW**	Österreichische Gesellschaft für Erdölwissenschaften
Ofwat	Office of Water Services			
OFY	Operation Feed Yourself (Ghana)		**OGF**	Oslo Geofysikeres Forening
ÖFZS	Österreichisches Forschungszentrum Seibersdorf		**ÖGFKM**	Österreichische Gesellschaft für Filmwissenschaft, Kommunikations- und Medienforschung
OG	Openly Gay			
OG	Organisation Gestosis (Switzerland)			
OG	Orientalische Gesellschaft (Austria)		**ÖGfM**	Österreichische Gesellschaft für Musik
OGA	Organic Growers Association		**ÖGfRV**	Österreichische Gesellschaft für Rechtsvergleichung
ÖGA	Österreichische Gesellschaft für Archéologie			

ÖGFT	Österreichische Gesellschaft für Weltraumforschung und Flugkörpertechnik
ÖGFU	Österreichische Gesellschaft für Unfallchirurgie
ÖGFW	Österreichische Gesellschaft für Angewandte Fremdenverkehrswissenschaft
ÖGfZP	Österreichische Gesellschaft für Zerstörungs-freie Prüfung
ÖGG	Österreichische Geographische Gesellschaft
ÖGG	Österreichische Geologische Gesellschaft
ÖGG	Österreichische Gesellschaft für Geomechanik
ÖGH	Österreichische Gesellschaft für Holzforschung
ÖGHMP	Österreichische Gesellschaft für Hygiene Mikrobiologie und Präventivmedizin
ÖGI	Österreichische Gesellschaft für Informatik
ÖGI	Österreichisches Giesserei-Institut
OGIL	Organizzazione Generale Italiano del Lavoro
ÖGKC	Österreichische Gesellschaft für Klinische Chemie
OGL	Ordre des Géomètre Luxembourgeois
ÖGLE	Österreichische Gesellschaft für Langfristige Entwicklungsforschung
ÖGMAC	Österreichische Gesellschaft für Mikrochemie und Analytische Chemie
OGN	Orah Group Na'amat (Australia)
ÖGNU	Österreichische Gesellschaft für Natur und Umweltschultz
ÖGO	Österreichische Gesellschaft für Ökologie = ASE
ÖGOR	Österreichische Gesellschaft für Operational Research
ÖGP	Österreichische Gesellschaft für Politikwissenschaft
ÖGP	Österreichische Gesellschaft für Psychologie
OGPI	Omskii Gosudarstvennyi Pedagogicheskii Institut
ÖGPMR	Österreichische Gesellschaft für Physikalische Medizin und Rehabilitation
ÖGPW	Österreichische Gesellschaft für Politikwissenschaft

Ogras	Ogeagras Chonradh na Gaeilge (Éire)
ÖGRR	Österreichische Gesellschaft für Raumforschung und Raumplanung
OGS	Ontario Geological Survey
OGS	Osservatorio Geofisico Sperimentale (Italy)
ÖGS	Österreichische Gesellschaft für Schweisstechnik
ÖGS	Österreichische Gesellschaft für Soziologie
ÖGS	Österreichische Gesellschaft für Sprachheilpädagogik
ÖGS	Österreichische Gesellschaft für Strassenwesen
ÖGSI	Österreichische Gesellschaft für Statistik und Informatik
ÖGTP	Österreichische Gesellschaft für Tropenmedizin und Parasitologie
ÖGUF	Österreichische Arbeitsgemeinschaft für Ur- und Frühgeschichte
ÖGV	Österreichische Gesellschaft für Vogelkunde
ÖGV	Österreichischer Geflügel- Wirtschafts-Verband
ÖGV	Österreichischer Gewerbeverein
ÖGVT	Österreichische Gesellschaft zur Förderung der Verhaltensforschung-modifikation und Verhaltenstherapie
OH	Obcanské hnuti
OH	Ordo Hospitalarius Sancti Ioannis de Deo = FBF
OH&S	Occupational Health and Safety
OHA	Ontario Horticultural Association (Canada)
OHA	Oral History Association (U.S.A.)
OHAC	Occupational Health Advisory Committee
OHAPEOS	Association Internationale de Sciences Expérimentales ou d'Érudition, Ppures et Appliquées, pour un Humanisme Objectif
OHE	Office of Health Economics
OHE	Országos Humánpolitikai Egyesület
ÖHFI	Österreichisches Holzforschungsinstitut
ÖHG	Österreichische Himalaya-Gesellschaft
ÖHG	Österreichische Humanistische Gesellschaft für die Steiermark
OHI	Organisation Hydrographique Internationale = IHO
OHIM	Office for Harmonization in the Internal Market (EU)

OHKI	Országos Húsipari Kutatointézet	**OICI**	Oficina Internacional Católica de la Infancia = BICE, ICCB, IKBK
ÖHKV	Österreichischer Heilbäder- und Kurorteverband	**OICI**	Omnium Immobilier de Côte d'Ivoire
OHMCI	Office of Her Majesty's Chief Inspectors of Schools in Wales	**OICI**	Organización Interamericana de Cooperación Intermunicipal = IAMO
OHP	Ochotnicze Hufce Pracy	**OICJ**	Office of International Criminal Justice
OHP	Operational Hydrology Program	**OICM**	Office Intercantonal de Contrôle des Médicaments (Switzerland)
OHPDA	Occupational Hygiene Product Distributors Association	**OICM**	Organisation Internationale pour la Coopération Médicale
ÖI	Österreichisches Ökologie-Institut	**OICN**	Organisation Internationale du Caoutchouc Naturel = INRO
OIA	Oceanic Industries Association (U.S.A.)	**OICNM**	Organisation Intergouvernementale Consultative de la Navigation Maritime
OIA	Organización Internacional del Azucar = ISO, OIS	**OICRF**	Office International du Cadastre et Régime Foncier
OIAC	Oil Industry Advisory Committee	**OICS**	Organe International de Contrôle des Stupéfiants = INCB, JIFE
OIAC	Organisation Inter-Africaine du Café = IACO	**OICS**	Organisation Internationale de Coopération pour la Santé = IOCHC, MMI
ÖIAG	Österreichische Industrieholding Aktiengesellschaft	**OICV**	Organisation Internationale des Commissions de Valeurs = IOSCO
ÖIAV	Österreichischer Ingenieur- und Architekten- Verein	**OID**	Ofensiva de la Izquierda Democrática (Bolivia)
ÖIB	Österreichischer Imkerbund	**OID**	Oficina de Informacion Diplomatica
ÖIBF	Österreichisches Institut für Bibliotheksforschung, Dokumentations- und Informationswesen	**OID**	Organisation Interaméricaine de Défense = IADB, JID
OIBT	Organisation Internationale des Bois Tropicaux = ITTO OIMT	**OIDB**	Oil Industry Development Board India
OIC	Oceans Institute of Canada	**OIDEL**	Organisation Internationale pour le Développement de la Liberté d'Enseignement
OIC	Optical Information Council	**OIDICh**	Oficiul de Informare Documentara pentru Industria Chimica
OIC	Ordo de Imitatione Christi		
OIC	Organisation Internationale Catholique	**OIDMM**	Office Internationale de Documentation de Médecine Militaire = IODMM
OIC	Organización de la Izquierda Comunista	**OIE**	Office International des Epizootics = IOE
OIC	Organización Interamericana del Café = IACO	**OIE**	Oficina Internacional de Educación (Switzerland) = BIE, IBE, MBD
OIC	Organization of the Islamic Conference (Saudi Arabia) = OCI	**OIE**	Organisation Internationale des Employeurs = IOE
OICA	Organisation Internationale des Constructeurs d'Automobiles	**ÖIE**	Österreichischen Informationsdienst für Entwicklungspolitik
OICC	Organisation of Islamic Capitals and Cities	**OIEA**	Office International pour l'Enseignement Agricole
OICCC	Office International du Cacao, du Chocolat et de la Confiseríe = IOCCC	**OIEA**	Organismo Internacional de Energia Atómica = AIEA, IAEA
OICD	Organisation Internationale des Sciences Chimiques pour le Développement = IOCD	**OIEC**	Office International de l'Enseignement Catholique = CIEO
OICD	Overseas Institute for Community Development (Éire)	**OIEC**	Organization for International Economic Cooperation
OICE	Associazione delle Organizzazioni di Ingegneria e di Consulenza Tecnico-Economica		
OICE	Organización Interamericana de Cooperación Económica		

OIEP	Office International d'Échange de Produits
OIETA	Office Inter-États du Tourisme Africain
ÖIF	Österreichisches Institut für Formgebung
ÖIFB	Österreichisches Institut für Bibliotheksforschung, Dokumentations und Informationswesen
ÖIFR	Österreichisches Institut fur Raumplanung
OIH	Országos Idegenforgalmi Hivatal / Hungarian Tourist Board
OIIC	Oil Investments International Corporation (Libya)
OIJ	Organisation Internationale des Journalistes = IOJ, MOZ, OIP
OIJAI	Obedinennyi Institut Iadernykh Issledovanii = JINR
OILB	Organisational Internationale de Lutte Biologique contre les Animaux et les Plantes Nuisibles = IOBC
OILC	Offshore Industry Liaison Committee
OIM	Organisation Internationale des Mineurs = IMO
OIM	Organisation Internationale pour les Migrations = IOM
OIML	Organisation Internationale de Métrologie Légale = ILMO
OIMR	Oficina Internacional de Mecanica de las Rocas (WMC) = BIMT, IBG, IBSM, MBMGP
OIMT	Organización Internacional de las Maderas Tropicales = ITTO, OIBT
OINA	Organisation Internationale Nouvelle Acropole = IONA
OIP	Organisation Internationale de la Paléobotanique = IOP
OIP	Organisation Internationale de Psychophysiologie = IOP
OIP	Organización Iberoamericana de Pilotos
OIP	Organización Internacional de Periodistas = IOJ, MOZ, OIJ
OIP	Société Belge d'Optique et d'Instruments de Précision
OIPC	Organisation Internationale de Protection Civile = ICDO
OIPC	Organización Internacional de Policia Criminal = ICPO, IKPO, INTERPOL
OIPF	Organisation Internationale de Placement Familiale = IFCO
OIPN	Office International pour la Protection de la Nature
OIPP	Organisation Internationale de la Presse Périodique
OIPQA	Oficina Internacional Permanente de Quimica Analitica para los Alimentos Humanos y Animales
OIR	Oficina Interamericana de Radio
ÖIR	Österreichisches Institut für Raumplanung
OIRC	Organisation Internationale de Recherche sur le Cerveau
OIRP	Organisation Internationale de Régies Paléobotaniques
OIRSA	Organismo Internacional Regional de Sanidad Agropecuária (El Salvador) = RIOPPAH
OIRT	Organisation Internationale de Radiodiffusion et Télévision
OIS	Organisation Internationale du Sucre = ISO, OIA
OISA	Office of International Science Activities (NSF)
OISCA	Organisation for Industrial, Spiritual and Cultural Advancement
OISE	Ontario Institute for Studies in Education (Canada)
OISS	Organización Iberoamericana de Seguridad Social
OISTAT	Organisation Internationale des Scénographes, Techniciens et Architectes de Théâtre = IOSTTA
OISTV	Organisation Internationale pour la Science et la Technique du Vide = IOVST
OIT	Ośrodek Informacji Turystycznej
OIT	Organisation Ibéroaméricaine de Télévision
OIT	Organisation International du Travail; Organización Internacional del Trabajo = IAO, ILO
OITAF	Organizzazione Internazionale dei Trasporti a Fune
OITP	Oficina Internacional de los Textiles y las Prendas de Vestir = ITCB
OIUC	Organización Internacional de las Uniones de Consumidores = IOCU
OIUCC	Offshore Industry Unions Co-ordinating Committee
OIUNT	Organisation Internationale d'Unification des Néologismes Terminologiques = IOUTN, MOUNT
OIV	Office International de la Vigne et du Vin

OIV	Office Internationale de la Viande = IMS, OPIC	**OKP**	Ogólnopolski Komitet Pokoju
ÖIV	Österreichisches Institut für Verpackungswesen	**OKSV**	Obshchestvennyi Komitet Spaseniia Volgi
OIWP	Oil Industry Working Party (OECD)	**ÖKTG**	Österreichische Kerntechnische Gesellschaft
ÖIZ	Österreichisches INIS-Zentrum	**OKTH**	Országos Környezet- és Természetvédelmi Hiyatal
OJCE	Orchestre des Jeunes de la Communauté Européenne = ECYO	**ÖKV**	Österreichischer Krankenpflegeverband
OJCIPF	Organisation Japonaise pour la Coopération Internationale en Matière de Planification Familiale = JOICFP	**ÖKW**	Österreichisches Kuratorium für Wirtschaftlichkeit
		OL	Ovnstøperienes Landforening
OJD	Office de Justification de la Diffusion	**OLA**	Open Learning Agency (Canada)
OJE	Organización Juvenil Española	**OLA**	Organic Living Association
OJIF	Ordre des Jurisconsultes Internationaux de France	**OLACEFS**	Organización Latinoamericana y del Caribe de Entidades Fiscalizadoras Superiores
OJM	Mozambique Youth Organization		
OJRB	Organisation de la Jeunesse Révolutionnaire de Bénin	**OLADE**	Organización Latinoamericana de Energía
OJSTP	Organização da Juventude de São Tomé e Principe	**OLAFABA**	Organización Latinoamericana de Fabricantes de Bebidas Alcoholicas (Uruguay)
OJU	Oceania Judo Union (Australia)		
OK	Oljekonsumenternas Förbund	**OLANI**	Office du Lait du Niger
OK	Oppikoulunopettajien Keskujärjestö	**OLAVI**	Organización Latinoamericana de Vivienda y Desarrollo de los Asentamientos Humanos (Ecuador)
ØK	Østasiatiske Kompagni = EAC		
OKŁ	Obywatelski Krąg Łemków "Hospodar" (Poland) = CCL		
		OLAVU	Organización Latinoamericana del Vino y de la Uva
ÖKB	Österreichischer Komponisterbund		
OKDIA	OK-Dinghy International Association (Germany)	**OLCP-EA**	Organisation de Lutte Contre le Criquet Pélerin dans l'Est Africain = DLCO-EA
ÖKEV	Österreicherischer Klub für Englische Vorstehkunde	**OLDE-PESCA**	Organización Latinoamericana de Desarrollo Pesquero (Peru)
OKFJN	Ogólnopolski Komitet Frontu Jedności Narodu	**OLEE**	Obshchestvo Liubitelei Estestvoznaniia i Etnografii
ÖKG	Österreichische Kardiologische Gesellschaft	**OLF**	Oromo Liberation Front (Ethiopia)
OKGT	Országos Köolaj- és Gázipari Tröszt	**OLG**	Office of Local Government
ÖKI	Öntözési Kutató Intézet	**OLIa RAN**	Division of Literature and Language, Russian Academy of Sciences
ÖKI	Österreichisches Kunstoffinstitut	**ÖLIZ**	Österreichisches Literaturzentrum
ÖKISTA	Österreichisches Komitee für Internationalen Studieaustausch	**OLLT**	Office of Libraries and Learning Technologies (U.S.A.)
OKISz	Ipari Szövetkezetek Országos Szövetsége / Hungarian Industrial Association	**OLM**	Ordo Libanensis Maronitarum
		ÖLMA	Östschweizerisch Land- und Milchwirtschaftliche Austellung
OKK	Obywatelskie Konwenty Konsultacyjne	**OLMB**	Open Learning Management Board (Northern Ireland)
ÖKL	Österreichische Krebsliga		
ÖKL	Österreichisches Kuratorium für Landtechnik	**OLME**	Federation of Secondary Teachers of Greece
OKL	Osuuspankkien Keskusliitto	**OLML**	Our Lady's Missionary League
OKP	Obywatelski Komitet Parlamentarny	**OLP**	Organisation de Libération de la Palestine = PLO

ÖLV	Österreichischer Lehrerverband
OLY	Oulun Luonnonystäväin Yhdistys ry
OM	Ordo Minimorum
OMA	Oilskin Manufacturers Association of Great Britain
OMA	Organization of Angolan Women
OMA	Oriental Music Association (China)
OMA	Overall Manufacturers Association of Great Britain
OMAAEEC	Organisation Mondiale des Anciens et Anciennes Élèves de l'Enseignement Catholique
OMAI	Organisation Mondiale Agudas Israel = AIWO
OMASD	Office of Management Appraisal and Systems Development (U.S.A.)
OMB	Office of Management and Budget
OMB	Organisation Moderne du Bureau (Ivory Coast)
OMB	Organizazione Mondiale per il Bambino (Switzerland) = OME, WOC, WOK
ÖMB	Österreichischer Museumbund
OMBKE	Országos Magyar Bányászati és Kohaszati Egyesület
OMBVI	Office Malien du Bétail et de la Viande
OMC	Consejo General de Colegios Oficiales de Médicos de España
OMC	Office Congolais des Matériaux de Construction
OMC	Office Mauritanien des Céréales
OMC	Organisation Mondiale Culturelle
OMC	Organisation Mondiale du Commerce = ITO
OMC	Organización Medica Colegial
OMCA	Offshore Manufacturers' & Constructors' Association
OMCAL	Organizacion de Mujeres Carmen Lyra (Costa Rica)
OMCT	Organisation Mondiale contre la Torture
OMCV	Organization of Women of Cape Verde
OMDA	Organisation Mondiale des Droits de l'Animal = WORA
OMDES	Oriental Music & Drawing Exchange Society (China)
OME	Organisation Mondiale de l'Emballage = WPO
OME	Organisation Mondiale pour l'Enfant (Switzerland) = OMB, WOC, WOK
OME	Organización Mundial de Exploradores

OMEASE	Organisation des Ministres d'Éducation de l'Asie du Sud-Est = SEAMEO
OMECOMS	Organisation pour le Mécanographie la Compatibilité et la Secretariat (Ivory Coast)
OMEM	Oficina Mundial de Estadísticas del Metal = WBMS
OMEP	Organisation Mondiale pour l'Éducation Préscolaire = WOECE
OMERAD	Office of Medical Education Research and Development (U.S.A.)
Omex	Orient-Mediterranean Express
ÖMF	Österreichische Mineralöl-Verwaltung
OMF	Overseas Missionary Fellowship
OMFP	Officine Meccan. Ferroviarie Pistoiesi
ÖMG	Österreichische Mathematische Gesellschaft
ÖMG	Österreichische Mineralogische Gesellschaft
ÖMG	Österreichische Mykologische Gesellschaft
OMGE	Organisation Mondiale de Gastro-Entérologie
OMI	Congregatio Missionarium Oblatorum BMV Immaculatae
OMI	Organisation Maritime Internationale = WMO
OMIDELAC	Organización de Militares por la Democracia, la Integración y la Liberación de América Latina y Caribe
OMIDOT	Organisation Mondiale pour l'Information sur le Don d'Organes ou de Tissus Humains
OMIG	Opencast Mining Intelligence Group
OMIKK	Országos Muszaki Információs Központés Könyvtár
OMIPE	Office Mondial d'Information sur les Problèmes d'Environnement = WOIEP
OMJM	Orchestre Mondial des Jeunesses Musicales
OMKDK	Országos Müszaki Könyvtár és Dokumentációs Központ
OMM	Ordo Maronita Beatae Virginis Mariae
OMM	Organisação da Mulher Mocambicana
OMM	Organisation Météorologique Mondiale; Organización Meterológica Mundial = WMO, WOM
OMMSA	Organisation of Museums, Monuments and Sites in Africa (Ghana)

OMNIS	Office Militaire National pour les Industries Stratégiques (Madagascar)
OMO	Offshore Mining Organisation (Thailand)
OMOI	Obedinena Makedonska Organizatsiya Ilinden (Bulgaria) = UMO
ÖMOLK	Österreichischer Molkerei -und Käsereiverband
OMONIA	Bashkimia Demokratik i Minoritet Grek (Albania) = DUGM
OMPA	Organización para el Mejoramiento de la Producción Azucarera (Cuba)
OMPH	Organisation Mondiale des Personnes Handicapés = DPI, OMPI
OMPI	Organisation Mondiale de la Propriété Intellectuelle
OMPI	Organización Mundial de Personas Impedidas = DPI, OMPH
OMPP	Organisation Mondiale de la Presse Périodique
ÖMR	Österreichischer Musikrat
OMRS	Orders and Medals Research Society
OMS	Office of Marketing Services (U.S.A.)
OMS	Organización Mundial de la Salud; Organisation Mondiale de la Santé = WHO
OMS	Oriental Missionary Society International
OMSC	Organisation Mondiale pour la Systématique et la Cybernétique = WOSC
ÖMSG	Österreichische Multiple Sklerose Gesellschaft
OMSTEP	Organisation des Femmes de Sao Tome et Principe
OMSTP	Organizaçao das Mulheres de Sao Tomé e Principe
OMSZ	Országos Meteorológiai Szolgálat
OMT	Oficina Municipal de Transportes
OMT	Organización Mundial del Turismo = VTO, WTO
OMTh	Organisation Mondiale du Thermalisme (SITH) = WHO
OMTKI	Országos Munkavédelmi Tudományos Kutató Intézet
OMTUR	Organizacja Młodziezy Towarzystwa Uniwersytetu Robotniczego
OMV	Congregatio Oblatorum Beatae Mariae Virginis
ÖMV	Österreichische Mineralöl-Verwaltung
ÖMV	Österreichische Mineralölvertriebsgesellschaft
OMVA	Office de Mise en Valeur Agricole (Morocco)
OMVG	Organisation pour la Mise en Valeur du Fleuve Gambie
OMVS	Organisation pour la Mise en Valeur du Fleuve Sénégal
OMVVM	Office de Mise en Valeur de la Vallée de la Medjerda (Tunisia)
OMW	Oberrheinische Mineralölwerke GmbH
ÖN	Österreichisches Normungsinstitut
ONA	Office of National Assessments
ONA	Oman News Agency
ONA	Omnium Nord Africain (Morocco)
ONA	Organización Nacional Agraria (Peru)
ONAA	Office National Anti-Acridien
ONAA	Oficina Nacional de Apoyo Alimentario (Peru)
ONAAC	Office National d'Alphabétisation et d'Action Communautaire (Haiti)
ONAB	Office National du Bois (Benin)
ONAC	Office National d'Approvisionnement et du Commercialisation (Djibouti)
ONAC	Office National du Commerce Extérieur (Burkina Faso)
ONACO	Office National de Commercialisation des Vins (Algeria)
ONADER	Office National du Développement Rural (Gabon)
ONAF	Office National d'Affrètements (Central Africa)
ONAF	Office National des Abattoirs et Frigorifiques (Togo)
ONAF	Office National des Forêts (Congo)
ONAFEX	Office National des Foires et Expositions (Algeria)
ONAH	Office National des Hydrocarbures (Guinée)
ONAJ	Oficina Nacional de Asesoria Juridica (Peru)
ONAPO	Office National des Produits Oléicoles (Algeria)
ONAR	Organización Nacional de Acción Revolucionaria (Mexico)
ONAREM	Office National des Ressources Minières (Niger)
ONAREP	Office National de Recherches et d'Exploitations Petrolières (Morocco)
ONAREST	Office National de la Recherche Scientifique et Technique (Cameroon)

ONARUM	Office National des Ressources Minières (Niger)
ONAT	Office National Algérien de l'Animation de la Promotion et de l'Information Touristique
ONATHO	Office National du Tourisme et de l'Hôtellerie (Benin)
ONATHOL	Office National du Tourisme et de l'Hôtellerie (Guinea)
ONATOUR	Office de la Tourbe de Burundi
ONATRA	Office National des Transportes au Zaïre
ONATRATE	Oficina Nacional de Transporte Terrestre (Dominican Republic)
ONB	Office National du Bois (Burundi)
ÖNB	Österreichische Nationalbibliothek
ÖNB	Österreichischer Naturschutzbund
ONBG	Office National des Bois du Gabon
ONC	Office National du Commerce (Burundi, Congo)
ONCA	Office National de Commercialisation Agricole (Gabon)
ONCE	Organización Nacional de Ciegos Españoles
ONCFG	Office National des Chemins de Fer de Guinée
ONCFM	Office National des Chemins de Fer du Maroc
ONCPA	Office Nationale de Commercialisation des Produits Agricoles (Central Africa, Congo)
ONCPB	Office National de Commercialisation de Produits de Base (Cameroon)
ONCPUHE	Organisation of Nordic Cooperative and Public Utility Housing Enterprises = NBO, NHO
ONCV	Office National de Commercialisation des Produits Viti-Vinicoles (Algeria)
OND	Office National des Diamants (Central Africa)
OND	Office National du Ducroire (Belgium) = NDD
ONDAH	Office National des Débouchés Agricoles et Horticoles (Belgium) = NDALTP
ONDEPA	Organización Nacional de Profesionales Agropecuários (Colombia)
ONDEPJOV	Oficina Nacional de Pueblos Jóvenes (Peru)
ONDR	Office National de Développement Rural (Chad)
ONE	Office National des Eaux (Burkina Faso)
ONEM	Office National de l'Emploi (Belgium)
ONEP	Office National de l'Eau Potable (Morocco)
ONEPI	Office National de l'Édition, de Presse et d'Imprimerie (Benin)
ONERA	Office National d'Études et de Recherches Aérospatiales
ONERN	Oficina Nacional de Evaluacion de Recursos Naturales (Peru)
ONERSOL	Office National de l'Énergie Solaire (Niger)
ONF	Office National des Forêts (France, Central Africa)
ONFC	Oman National Fisheries
ONFP	Office National Famille et Population (Tunisia) = NOFPP
ÖNG	Österreichische Gesellschaft für Nuclearmedizin
ÖNG	Österreichische Numismatische Gesellschaft
ONG-EC	Comité de Liaison des ONG pour le Développement auprès des Communautés Européennes = NGO-EC
ONGC	Oil and Natural Gas Commission (India)
ONGT	Organisation Non-Gouvernementale de Portée Transnationale
ONHA	Office National de l'Huilerie d'Abèche (Chad)
ONI	Office National d'Immigration
ONI	Office National des Irrigations (Morocco)
ONI	Otdel Nauchnoi Informatsii
ONIB	Office National Interprofessionnel du Blé
ONIBEV	Office National Interprofessionnel du Bétail et des Viandes
ONIC	Office National Interprofessionnel des Céréales
ONIC	Oman National Insurance Company
ONISEP	Office National d'Information sur les Enseignements et les Professions
ONJ	Organização Nacional das Jornalistas (Mozambique)
ONK	Obshchestvo Nauchnogo Kommunizma
ÖNK	Österreichische Notariatskammer
ONL	Office National du Lait et de ses Dérivés (Belgium) = NZD

ONL	Office National du Logement (Burundi)
ONM	Office National Météorologique
ONM	Organisation des Nationalistes Mauritaniens = MNO
ONMR	Office National de la Modernisation Rurale (Morocco)
ONOC	Oceania National Olympic Committees (Australia)
ÖNORM	Österreichischer Normenausschuss
ONP	Office National des Pêches (Tunisia)
ONP	Office National des Ports (Algeria)
ONPB	Office National de Pharmacie du Bénin
ONPB-KSNPS	Obshcherossiiskii Natsionalno-Patrioticheskii Blok – Koordinatsionnyi Sovet Narodno-Patrioticheskikh Sil
ONPI	Office Notarial Permanent d'Échange International
ONPPC	Office National de Produits Pharmaceutiques et Chimiques (Niger)
ONPU	Oficina Nacional de Planeamiento y Urbanismo (Peru)
ONR	Obóz Narodowo-Radykalny
ONR	Office of Naval Research (U.S.A.)
ONR	Organization for National Reconstruction (Antigua and Barbuda)
ÖNR	Österreichisch Medizinische Gesellschaft für Neuraltherapie nach Huneke-Regulationsforschung
ONRA	National Office of Agrarian Reform (Algeria)
ONRAP	Oficina Nacional de Racionalizacion y Capacitacion de la Administracion Publica (Peru)
ONRD	Office National de la Recherche et du Développement (Zaïre)
ONRI	Orde van Nederlandse Raadgevende Ingenieurs
ONRR	Office National Rail-Route (Guinea)
ONS	Offshore North Sea Technology Conference
ONS	Oriental Numismatic Society
ONSER	Organisme National de Sécurité Routière
ONSS	Office National de la Sécurité Sociale (Belgium) = RSZ
ONSSF	Organisation Nationale des Syndicats de Sages-Femmes
ONT	Office National du Tourisme (Algeria, Luxembourg, Niger)
ONTF	Office National des Travaux Forestiers (Algeria)
ONTIP	Otdel Nauchno Tekhnicheskoi Informatsii i Propagandy
ONTIPI	Otdel Nauchnoi, i Tekhnicheskoi, Ekonomicheskoi i Patentnoi Informatsii
ONU	Organisation des Nations Unies; Organización de las Naciones Unidas = NN.UU, UN
ONUCA	United Nations Observer Group for Central America (Nicaragua)
ONUDI	Organización de las Naciones Unidas para el Desarrollo Industrial; Organisation des Nations Unies pour le Développement Industriel = UNIDO
ONUG	Office des Nations Unies à Genève = UNOG
ONUMOZ	UN Operation in Mozambique
ONUSAL	United Nations Mission in El Salvador
ONUST	Organisme des Nations Unies Chargé de la Surveillance de la Trève (en Palestine) = UNTSO
OOA	Orde van Organisatiekundigen en Adviseurs
OOA	Organisationen til Oplysning om Atomkraft
OOAA	Organismos Autónomos Administrativos
ÖOG	Österreichische Ophthalmologische Gesellschaft
OOKDK	Országos Orvostudományi Konyvtar es Dokumentacios (Hungary)
OOMER	Organisation Oncologique Méditerranéenne d'Enseignement et de Recherche
OOMOTO	Universal Love and Brotherhood Association (Japan)
OOP	Oddziałowa Organizacja Partyjna
OOPEC	Office for the Official Publications of the European Communities
OOPM	Organización Politico Militar (Paraguay)
OOPS	Organismo de Obras Públicas y Socorro de las Naciones Unidas para los Refugiados de Palestina en el Cercano Oriente = UNRWA
OOR	Obedinena Organizatsiya Roma (Bulgaria) = URO
ÖOSI	Österreichisches Ost-und Sudosteuropa-Institut
OP	Oesterreichisches Patentamt
OP	Operação de Produção (Mozambique)
OP	Ordo Fratrum Praedicatorum

OP-17	Organisation Populaire de 17 Septembre (Haiti)
OPA	Oil and Pipelines Agency
OPAC	Office des Produits Agricoles de Costermansville (Zaïre)
OPAC	Operations Planning Advisory Committee
OPAD	Abel Djassi Pioneer Organization (Cape Verde)
OPAEP	Organisation des Pays Arabes Exportateurs de Pétrole (Kuwait) = OAPEC
OPAF	Organisation Panafricaine de la Famille = PAFO
OPAK	Office des Produits Agricoles du Kivu (Zaïre)
ÖPAK	Österreichische Patentanwaltskammer
OPAL	Ocean Process Analysis Laboratory (U.S.A.)
OPALC	Organización de Pre-Inversión de América Latina y el Caribe = POLAC
OPALS	Organisation Panafricaine de Lutte contre le SIDA
OPAM	Office des Produits Agricoles du Mali
OPANAL	Organismo para la Proscripción de las Armas Nucléares en la América Latina
OPAPE	Organisation Panafricaine de la Profession Enseignante (Ghana) = AATO
OPAS	Occupational Pensions Advisory Service
OPAS	Organização Panamericana da Saúde (OAS) = OPS, PAHO
OPAT	Office des Produits Agricoles du Togo
OPATSI	Operative Plasterers and Allied Trades Society of Ireland
OPB	Occupational Pensions Board
OPB	Overseas Projects Board (DTI)
OPC	Office of the Parliamentary Counsel
OPC	Overseas Press Club of America
OPCA	Ornamental Plant Collections Association (Australia)
OPCI	Oficina de Promoción de Comercio e Inversiones (Andean Pact)
OPCMIA	Operative Plasterers and Cement Masons International Association of the United States and Canada
OPCS	Office of Population Censuses and Surveys
OpD	Opus Dei
OPDR	Oldenburg Portugiesische Dampfschiffs Rhederei
OPE	Office de Promotion de l'Enterprise (Burkina Faso)
OPE	Omilos Pedagogikon Erevon Kyprou
OPE	Organisation Peuples Européens
OPEC	Organization of Petroleum Exporting Countries = OPEP
OPECNA	OPEC News Agency
OPEI	Office National de Promotion d'Entreprise Ivoirienne
OPEIU	Office and Professional Employees International Union (U.S.A.)
OPEM	Office National pour la Promotion de l'Exportation (Petites et Moyennes Entreprises)
OPEN	Office de Promotion de l'Entreprise Nigérienne
OPEN	Organisation des Producteurs d'Électricité Nucléaire
OPEP	Organisation des Pays Exportateurs de Pétrole = OPEC
OPET	Organisation for the Promotion of Energy Technologies (EU)
ÖPEV	Österreichischer Patentinhaber- und Erfinderverband
OPF	Organisation Panafricaine des Femmes = PAWO
OPFCA	Ornamental Pool and Fountain Constructors Association
ÖPG	Österreichische Paléontologische Gesellschaft
ÖPG	Österreichische Physikalische Gesellschaft
OPGC	Oil Palm Growers Council (Malaysia)
OPIC	Oficina Permanente Internacional de la Carne = IMS, OIV
OPIC	Overseas Private Investment Corporation (U.S.A.)
OPICBA	Office Professonnal des Industries et Commerces du Bois et de l'Ameublement
OPINA	Opinión Nacional (Venezuela)
OPIRG	Ontario Public Interest Research Group
OPITB	Offshore Petroleum Industry Training Board
OPJM	Organización de Pioneros Jose Marti (Cuba)
OPKA	Original Pearly Kings and Queens Association

OPLC	Organización para la Liberación de Cuba (U.S.A.)
OPM	Opera Pontificialia Missionariorum
OPM	Organisasi Papua Merdeka
OPM	Organización Primero de Marzo (Paraguay)
OPMA	Ophthalmic Prescription Manufacturers Association
OPMA	Oriented Polypropylene Film Manufacturers Association (Belgium)
OPMA	Overseas Press and Media Association
OPMO	Oddziały Prewencyjne Milicji Obywatelskiej
OPMT	Organizacion Puertorriquena de la Mujera Trabajadora (Puerto Rico)
OPNT	Office des Ports Nationaux Tunisiens (Tunisia)
OPO	Obshtestvo Peti Oktomvri (Bulgaria) = FOS
OPOCE	Office des Publications Officielles des Communautés Européennes
OPOR	Obshchestvenno-Politicheskoe Obedinenie "Rabochii"
OPOSA	Organizacion de la Patata del Pirineo Occidental
OPOYAZ	Obshchestvo Izucheniia Teorii Poeticheskogo Iazyka
OPP	Office of Polar Programs (U.S.A.)
OPPEM	Organizacion para la Protección de las Plantas en Europa y en el Mediterráneo
OPPI	Organisation of Pharmaceutical Producers of India
OPPS	Oxford Project for Peace Studies
OPR	Organisation du Peuple Rodriguais (Mauritania)
OPraem	Ordo Praemonstratensis CRP
OPRAF	Office of Passenger Rail Franchising
ÖPRG	Österreichische Public-Relations-Gesellschaft
OPRGA	Office des Ports et Rades du Gabon
OPRIZ	Otdel Patentovedeniia, Ratsionalizatsii i Izobretatel'stva
OPS	Office of Public Service (Cabinet Office)
OPS	Ophthalmic Photographers Society
OPS	Organisation Panaméricaine de la Santé (OAS)= OPAS, PAHO
OPS-MSD	Organizacion Panamericana de la Salud – Programa Mujer, Salud y Desarrollo (Costa Rica)
OPS/OMS-MSD	Oficina Panamericana de la Salud – Organizacion Mundial de la Salud – Programa Mujer, Salud y Desarrollo (Costa Rica)
OPSC	Oil and Protein Seed Centre (South Africa)
OPSIS	National Association for the Education, Training and Support of Blind and Partially Sighted People
OPSS	Office of Public Service and Science
OPSU	Planning Office of the National Council of Venezuelan Universities
OPT	Optimum Population Trust
OPT	Otechestvena Partiya na Truda (Bulgaria) = FPL
OPTA	Offshore Petroleum Training Association
OPTIMA	Organization for the Phyto-Taxonomic Investigation of the Mediterranean Area (Germany)
OPTULA	Oikeuspoliittinen Tutkimuslaitos
OPUS	Office des Publications Scientifiques de Langue Française
OPUS	Organisation for Promoting Understanding in Society
OPUS	Organisation of Parents under Stress
OPUS	Organisation of Professional Users of Statistics (U.K., U.S.A.)
OPV	Organisação da Policia Voluntaria (Mozambique)
OPVN	Office des Produits Vivriers du Niger
OPW	Office of Public Works (Éire)
ÖPWG	Österreichische Gesellschaft für Politikwissenschaft
ÖPWZ	Österreichisches Produktivitäts -und Wirtschftlichkeitszentrum
OPYRWA	Office du Pyrèthre au Rwanda
ÖPZ	Österreichisches Produktivitäts-Zentrum (Austria)
OPZZ	Ogólnopolskie Porozumienie Związków Zawodowych
OR	Odinic Rite
OR	Order of the Road
ÖR	Österreichischer Rundfunk = ORF
OR(I)C	Oceanographic Research (International) Committee
OR2000	Ocean Rescue 2000
ORA	Office des Renseignements Agricoles
ORA	Organisation Régionale Asienne (CISL)
ORAF	Organisation Régionale Africaine (CISL)

ORAIHA	Organisation Régionale de l'AIH pour l'Afrique = HAROA
ÖRAK	Österreichischer Rechtsanwaltkammertag
ORAN	Organisation Régionale Africaine de Normalisation (Kenya) = ARSO
ORANA	Organisme de Recherches sur l'Alimentation et la Nutrition Africaine
ORAP	Organisation Régionale de l'Orient pour l'Administration Publique = EROPA
ORB	Observatoire Royal de Belgique
ORC	Ordo Canonicorum Regularium Sanctae Crucis
ORC	Organisation of Railways Cooperation = OSShD, OSZD
ORC	Overseas Research Center (U.S.A.)
ORCA	Organisme Européen de Recherches sur la Carie
ORCA	Regional Office for Central America (IUCN)
ORCALC	Oficina Regional de Cultura de la UNESCO para América Latina y el Caribe (Cuba)
ORD	Organisme Régional de Développement du Nord Mossi (Burkina Faso)
ORDEN	Organización Democrática Nacionalista (El Salvador)
ORDINEX	Organisation International des Experts
ORE	Office for Research and Experiments
ORE	Office of Research and Evaluation (U.S.A.)
ORE	Organisation Régionale de la FDI pour l'Europe = ERO
ORE	Organisation Régionale Européenne (CISL)
OREALC	Oficina Regional de Educación para América Latina y el Caribe (Chile)
OREAM	Organisation d'Études d'Aires Métropolitains
OREPOC	Office Régional des Produits Oléicoles du Centre (Algeria)
ORES	European Society for Opinion Surveys and Market Research (Denmark)
ORESCO	Overseas Research Council
ORF	Ontario Research Foundation (Canada)
ÖRF	Österreichischer Rundfunk = ÖR
ORFS	Office of Registrar of Friendly Societies (Éire)
ORG	Oxford Research Group
ORGALIME	Organisme de Liaison des Industries Métalliques Européennes
ORGANI-BIO	Organisation Nationale Interprofessionnelle des Bioindustries
ORGATEC	Société Africaine d'Études Techniques (Senegal)
ORGECO	Organisation Générale des Consommateurs
ORI	Ocean Research Institute (Japan)
ORI	Ordre des Ingénieurs-Conseils et des Bureaux d'Ingénierie
ORIA	Oriental Rug Importers Association of America
ORIS	Office des Rayonnements Ionisants (CEA)
ORISE	Oak Ridge Institute for Science Education (U.S.A.)
ORIT	Organización Regional Interamericana del Trabajo (ICFTU)
ÖRK	Österreichische Rektorenkonferenz
ORL	Odrodzony Ruch Ludowy
ORLEIS	Office Régional Laïque d'Éducation par l'Image et par le Son
ORMUSA	Organizacion de Mujeres Salvadorenas para la Paz
ORNAMO	Association of Finnish Designers
ORNES	Organisatie van Nederlandse Speelgoedleveranciers
ORNL	Oak Ridge National Laboratory (U.S.A.)
ORPA	Organización Revolucionaria del Pueblo Armado (Guatemala)
ORPO	Office Régional des Produits Oléicoles du Centre (Algeria)
ORRA	Oriental Rug Retailers of America
ORRRC	Outdoor Recreation Resources Review Commission (Australia)
ORSA	Operations Research Society of America
ORSEC	Organisation Séjours Châteaux
ORSER	Office for Remote Sensing of Earth Resources (U.S.A.)
ORSI	Operations Research Society of India
ORSI	Operations Research Society of Ireland
ORSI	Operations Research Society of Italy
ORSIS	Operations Research Society of Israel
ORSJ	Operations Research Society of Japan
ORSOC	Operational Research Society
ORSS	Operational Research Society of Singapore
ORST	Operational Research Society of Turkey
ORSTOM	Office de la Recherche Scientifique et Technique d'Outre-Mer

ORT	Obsługa Ruchu Turystycznego	**OSCA**	United Kingdom Optical Sensors Collaborative Association
ORT	Organisation – Reconstruction – Travail, Union Mondiale	**OSCAR**	Organization for Sickle Cell Anaemia Research
ORT	Organisation for Rehabilitation by Training	**OSCAS**	Office of Statistical Coordination and Standards (Philippines)
ORT	Organización Revolucionaria de Trabajadores	**OSCE**	Office Statistique des Communautés Européennes = EUROSTAT, SOEC
ORTB	Office de Radiodiffusion et de Télévision de Bénin (Benin)	**OSCE**	Organization for Security and Co-operation in Europe (*ex* CSCE)
ORTF	Office de la Radiodiffusion-Télévision Française	**OSCOM**	Oslo Commission
ORTHO	American Orthopsychiatric Association	**OSCS**	Ordine Secolare dei Carmelitani Scalzi
ORTHO-BANDA	Vereniging tot het Behartigen van de Belangen van de Nederlandse Orthopedisten en Bandagisten	**OSD**	Offshore Safety Division (Health and Safety Executive)
ORTHOMA	Nederlandse Bond van Orthopaedisch Maatschoenmakers	**OSE**	Obras Sanitarias del Estado (Uruguay)
ORTM	Office de Radiodiffusion et Télévision de Mauritanie	**OSE**	Organismos Sidirodromon Ellados
ORTN	Office de Radio-diffusion-Télévision du Niger	**OSE**	Union Mondiale pour la Protection de la Santé des Populations Juives et Oeuvres de Secours aux Enfants
ORTPA	Oven-Ready Turkey Producers Association	**OSEA**	Ophthalmological Society of East Africa (Kenya)
ORTPN	Office Rwandais du Tourisme et des Parcs Nationaux	**OSEB**	Orissa State Electricity Board (India)
ORTS	Office de Radiodiffusion-Télévision du Sénégal	**OSEC**	Office Suisse d'Expansion Commerciale
ORV	Operation Romanian Villages	**ÖSEV**	Österreichischer Sekretärinnen-Verband
OS	Oceanography Society	**OSFS**	Oblati di Santi Francesco di Sales
OS	Omnibus Society	**ÖSG**	Österreichische Statistiche Gesellschaft = ASS
OS	Ordnance Survey Office	**OSGAP**	Office of the UN Secretary-General in Afghanistan and Pakistan
OS	Orthopaedic Society (China)	**OSGB**	Orchid Society of Great Britain
OS3	Organisation Suisse – Tiers Monde	**ÖSGK**	Österreichische Studiengesellschaft für Kybernetik = ASCS
OSA	Ochranný Svaz Autorský	**OSH**	Ordo Sancti Hieronymi
OSA	Offshore Supply Association	**OSHA**	Occupational Safety & Health Administration (U.S.A.)
OSA	Optical Society of America	**OSHE**	Office pour le Soutien de l'Habitat Économique (Ivory Coast)
OSA	Ordo Fratrum Sancti Augustini	**OSHIG**	Occupational Safety and Health Information Group
OSA	Organic Soil Association of Southern Africa	**OSHR**	Organisme Spécialisé d'Habitat Rural
OSACI	Oeconomisch Studie- en Actiecentrum voor Investeringen	**OSHT**	Oxford Society for Historical Theology
OSAS	Offshore Advisory Service (THE)	**OSI**	Congregation Oblatorum Sancti Ioseph = OSJ
OSAS	Overseas Service Aid Scheme	**OSIC**	International Offshore Suppliers Information Centre
OSAT	Office for the Study of Automotive Transportation (U.S.A.)	**OSIC**	Overseas Spinning Investment Company
OSB	Ordo Sancti Benedicti	**OSIM**	Oficiul De Stat Pentru Inventii Si Marci
OSBM	Order of the Basilians of St Macrina	**OSIS**	Office of Science Information Service (U.S.A.)
OSC	Ocean Sciences Centre (Canada)		
OSC	Ordo Sanctae Crucis		

OSJ	Congregation of the Oblates of St Joseph = OSI
OSJ	Ordre Souverain de Saint Jean de Jérusalem
OSJD	Organisation for the Collaboration of Railways (Poland)
OSL	International Order of Saint Luke the Physician
OSLAM	Organización de Seminarios Latinoamericanos
OSLJ	Ordre Militaire et Hospitalier de Saint Lazare de Jérusalem
OSM	Ordo Servorum Mariae
OSM	Organisation Sioniste Mondiale = WZO
OSMA	Opera Svizzera dei Monumenti d'Arte
OSME	Ornithological Society of the Middle East
OSMS	Občanské Shromáždění Moravy a Slezska (Czech Republic) = MSCA
OSNN	Osnivanje Slovačka Narodna Nasledstva (Serbia) = SNHF
OSNZ	Ornithological Society of New Zealand
OSO	"Omonia" Sociopolitical Organization = DUGM = BDMG (Albania)
OSO	Ochotnicza Straz Pozarna
OSO	Offshore Supplies Office
OSP	Obedinenie Samoupravliaiushchikhsia Profsoiuzov
OSP	Oficina Sanitaria Panamericana (Venezuela)
OSPAA	Organisation de la Solidarité des Peuples Afro-Asiatiques = AAPSO
OSPAAAL	Organisation de Solidarité des Peuples d'Afrique, d'Asie et d'Amérique Latine (Cuba)
OSPP	Organizatisija Sotrudnichestva Podshipnikovoj Promyshennosti = OCIR, OCRBI
OSPPE	Ordo Fratrum Sancti Pauli Primi Eremitae
OSR	Organisation for Scientific Research (Indonesia)
OSRB	Overseas Services Resettlement Bureau
OSRO	Office for Special Relief Operations (FAO)
OSS	Odontologiska Sällskapet i Stockholm
OSS	Office of Space Science (NASA)
OSS	Orden Seglar de los Siervos de Maria
OSSC	Oil Spill Service Centre
OSShD	Organisation für die Zusammenarbeit der Eisenbahnen = ORC, OSZD
OSSR	Hermanas Oblatas del Santissimo Redentor
OSSR	Ordo Sanctissimi Redemptoris
OSSREA	Organization for Social Science Research in Eastern Africa (CODESRIA) (Ethiopia)
OSST	Ordo Sanctissimae Trinitatis
OST	Office of Science and Technology
OST	Organisation Scientifique du Travail
OSTB	Offshore Safety and Technology Board
OSTIV	Organisation Scientifique et Technique Internationale du Vol à Voile
OSTiW	Ośrodek Sportu, Turystyki i Wypoczynku
OSTP	Office of Scientific and Technical Personnel (OECD)
ÖStV	Österreichischer Stahlbauverband
OSUK	Opthalmological Society of the United Kingdom
OSUKA	Empresa Acucareira Centro (Angola)
ÖSV	Österreichischer Schriftstellerverband
OSW	Office of the Status of Women
OSZD	Organizatisiia Sotrudnichestva Zheleznykh Dorog = ORC, OSShD
OSZH	National Co-operative Credit Institute (Hungary)
OSZT	Országos Szövetkezeti Tanács
OT	Genootschap Onze Taal
OTA	Office of Technology Assessment (U.S.A.)
OTA	Operation Town Affiliations (U.S.A.)
OTA	Orthodontic Technicians Association
OTAAI	Oficina Ténica de Asuntos Agrícolas Internacionales (Venezuela)
OTAC	Organisation des Travailleurs de l'Afrique Centrale (OATUU) (Zaïre) = OTUCA
OTAF	Office of Technology Assessment and Forecast (U.S.A.)
OTAN	Organisation du Traité de l'Atlantique-Nord; Organización del Tratado del Atlántico Norte = NATO
OTAN	Organisation of Tropical American Nematologists (Puerto Rico)
OTAO	Organisation des Travailleurs de l'Afrique Ouest (Niger) = OTUWA
OTAPARCS	Office de Tourisme de l'Artisanat et des Parcs Nationaux (Mauritania)
OTAR	Overseas Tariffs and Regulations Section (DTI)

OTB	Office du Thé du Burundi
OTC	Office of Technical Cooperation (UN)
OTC	Organisation for Trade Co-operation
OTC(A)	Overseas Telecommunications Commission (Australia)
OTCA	Overseas Technical Cooperation Agency (Japan)
OTCD	Christian Democratic Youth Organization (Moldova)
OTD	Office des Terres Domaniales (Tunisia)
OTDOGS	Opposition to Destruction of Open Green Space
OTE	Organisation des Transports Européens
OTE	Organismos Telepikoinonion tes Elladas
OTE	State Hellenic Telecommunications
OTEI	Ordnance Technology Engineering Research Institute (China)
ÖTG	Österreichische Tribologische Gesellschaft
OTH	Országos Találmányi Hivatal
ÖThG	Österreichische Theatertechnische Gesellschaft
OTI	Organización de la Televisión Iberoamericana
OTI	Organizzazione Tecnica Internazionale
OTIF	Organisation Intergouvernementale pour les Transports Internationaux Ferroviaires
OTIPI	Associazione Italiana delle Agenzie di Pubblicità Servizio Completo
OTIU	Overseas Technical Information Unit (DTI)
OTK	Co-operative Wholesale Association (Finland)
OTK	Obrona Terytorialna Kraju
OTLC	Overhead Transmission Line Contractors Association
OTM	Objectif Tiers Monde (Luxembourg)
OTM	Organização dos Trabalhadores Moçambicanos
OTP	Office Togolais des Phosphates
OTP	Országos Takarékpénztár
OTP	Ozone Trends Panel
OTPN	Opolskie Towarzystwo Przyjaciół Nauk
OTR	Office des Transports par Route (Belgium)
OTRACO	Office d'Exploitation des Transports Coloniaux (Zaïre)
OTS	Office of Thrift Supervision (U.S.A.)
OTS	Organization for Tropical Studies (Costa Rica)
OTS	Organization for Tropical Studies (U.S.A.)
OTTS	Organisation of Teachers of Transport Studies
OTU	Organisation pour le Tourisme Universitaire
OTUA	Office Technique pour l'Utilisation de l'Acier
OTUCA	Organisation of Trade Unions of Central Africa (OATUU) (Zaïre) = OTAC
OTUS	Office Tunisien de Standardisation
OTUWA	Organisation of Trade Unions of West Africa = OTAO
ÖTVV	Österreichischer Transport-Versicherungs-Verband
OU	Open University
OUA	Organisation de l'Unité Africaine; Organización de la Unidad Africana = OAU
OUAA	Organización de la Unidad Afroamericana = OAAU
OUAAT	Organisation Universelle d'Associations d'Agents de Tourisme
OUI	Organización Universitaria Interamericana = IOHE
OULG	Organisation Unifiée pour la Libération de la Guinée
OULIPO	Oeuvroir de Littérature Potentielle
OUR	Organización de Unidad Revolucionaria (Bolivia)
OUSA	Organisation de l'Unité Syndicale Africaine (Ghana) = OATUU
OUT	Organização Unida de Trabalhadores
OV	Optometristen Vereniging
ÖVA	Gesellschaft für den Volkskundeatlas in Österreich
OVA	Organisation des Villes Arabes (Kuwait) = ACO
OVA Jork	Ostbauversuchsanstalt Jork (Germany)
OVAC	Overseas Visual Aids Centre
ÖVAF	Österreichische Vereinigung für Agrarwissenschaftliche Forschung
OVB	Onafhankelijk Verbond van Bedrijfsorganisaties
OVE	Organisationen for Vedvarende Energi (Denmark)
ÖVE	Österreichister Verband für Elektrotechnik

OVEIP	Organisatie Vernigde Exporteurs van Indonesische Producten
ÖVFG	Österreichischer Verband für Flüssiggas
ÖVG	Österreichische Gesellschaft für Vermessung und Geoinformation = ASG
ÖVG	Österreichische Verkehrswissenschaftliche Gesellschaft
ÖVGBWS	Österreichischer Verband Gemeinnütziger Bau-, Wohnungs- und Siedlungsvereinigungen
ÖVGW	Österreichische Vereinigung für das Gas- und Wasserfach
OVH	Országos Vizugyi Hivatal (Hungary)
OVIBAR	Office de la Valorisation de la Bananeràie Rwandaise
OVIBER	Országos Vizügyi Beruházási Vállalat
OVIRJ	Organisatie van Rand- en Ijsselmeervissers
OVM	Onderlinge Verzekeringsmaatschappij
ÖVP	Österreichische Volkspartei
ÖVQ	Österreichische Vereinigung für Qualitätssicherung
OVR	Opération Villages Roumains
ÖVS	Österreichischer Verband für Strahlenschutz
ÖVSHG	Österreichische Vereinigung des Sanitär- und Heizungsgrosshandels
ÖVZ	Österreichisches Verpackungszentrum
OWA	One World Action
OWAEC	Organization for West African Economic Co-operation
ÖWB	Öffentliche Wissenschaftliche Bibliothek
OWC	Order of Woodcraft Chivalry
OWEN	East-West European Women's Network
OWF	Oceania Weightlifting Federation
ÖWG	Österreichische Werbegesellschaft
OWG	Outdoor Writers' Guild
OWL	Observers of Wildlife
OWLA	One World Linking Association
OWN	Older Women's Network (Australia)
OWP	Odrodzone Wojsko Polskie
OWRC	Ontario Water Resources Commission (Canada)
OWTC	Orkney Water Test Centre
OWTU	Oilworkers Trade Union (Trinidad and Tobago)
ÖWV	Österreichisches Wasserwirtschafts Verband
ÖWWV	Österreicherischer Wasserwirtschaftsverband
OXEXPORT	Landbrugets Kvaeg- og Kødsalg
OXFAM	Oxford Committee for Famine Relief
OYC	Ocean Youth Club
OYJ	Opettajien Yhteisjärjestö
OZACAF	Office Zaïrois du Café
ÖZEPA	Österreichische Vereinigung der Zellstoff und Papierchemiker und Techniker
OZI	Obywatelskie Zrzeszenie Inteligencji

P

P&GWA	Pottery and Glass Wholesalers Association
P&S	Pike & Shot Society
P-2	Propaganda Due (Italy)
P-S	Plast-Sammenslutningen
PA	Direction de la Production Agricole
PA	Paintmakers Association of Great Britain
PA	Palaeontological Association
PA	Parapsychological Association (U.S.A.)
PA	Partido Andalucista
PA	Patients' Association
PA	Pedestrians Association
PA	People's Alliance (Iceland) = AB
PA	People's Association (Singapore)
PA	Pizza Association
PA	Politics Association
PA	Popular Alliance = AP
PA	Postcard Association
PA	Press Association
PA	Prisoners Abroad
PA	Proprietary Association (U.S.A.)
PA	Protestant Alliance
PA	Psoriasis Association
PA	Publishers Association
PAA	Państwowa Agencja Atomistyki
PAA	Pacific Arts Association (New Zealand)
PAA	Paper Agents Association
PAA	Pharmaceutical Association of Australia
PAA	Population Association of America
PAA	Poster Advertising Association (Éire)
PAA	Potato Association of America
PAA	Proprietary Association of Australia

PAAA	Pan American Association of Anatomy	**PACC**	Pesticides and Agricultural Chemicals Committee
PAAAC	Pan-American Agricultural Aviation Centre	**PACC**	Prestwick Airport Consultative Committee
PAABS	Pan-American Association of Biochemical Societies	**PACCIOS**	Conseil Régional Panaméricain (CIOS)
PAAECI	Pan-American Association of Eductional Credit Institutions = APICE	**PACDIS**	Pacific Area Communicable Disease Information Service (Philippines)
PAAI	Poster Advertising Association of Ireland	**Pace**	Pacific America Container Service (U.S.A.)
PAANS	Pan-African Association of Neurological Sciences	**PACE**	Parental Alliance for Choice in Education
PAAO	Pan American Association of Ophthalmology (U.S.A.)	**PACE**	Philippine Association of Civil Engineers
PAAO	Pan-American Association of Academic and Research Libraries	**PACE**	Planetary Association for Clean Energy = AMEN
PAAT	Professional Association Alexander Teachers	**PACE**	Project for Advice Counselling and Education
PAAT	Programa Ampliado de Asistencia Técnica (NN.UU) = ETAP	**PACE**	Protestant and Catholic Encounter (Northern Ireland)
PAB	Public Affairs Bureau (DEST)	**PACEHOPE**	Fachverband de Papier-, Zellulose-, Holzstoff- und Pappenindustrie Österreichs
PABIAC	Paper and Board Industry Advisory Committee		
PABS	Pan American Biodeterioration Society (U.S.A.)	**PACES**	Political Action Committee for Engineers and Scientists (U.S.A.)
PAC	Civic Alliance Party (Romania)	**PACG**	Professional Association of Certified Graphologists / Psychologists = BGG/P
PAC	Packaging Committee of Canada		
PAC	Pacto de Alianza de Centro (Chile)	**PACGSR**	Pan-American Center for Geographical Studies and Research = CEPEIGE
PAC	Pan-Africanist Congress		
PAC	Pan-American Committee	**PACIP**	Pacific and Asia Council of Indigenous Peoples (U.S.A.)
PAC	Pan-American Highway Congress		
PAC	Partenariat Afrique Canada	**PACNEWS**	Pacific News Service (Solomon Islands)
PAC	Patrullas Autodefensa Civil (Guatemala)	**PACOIL**	Compania Petrolera del Pacifico S.A. (Ecuador)
PAC	Permanent Agricultural Committee (ILO)	**PACONA**	Parti pour la Conscience Nationale (Zaïre)
PAC	Pesticide Analysis Advisory Committee	**PACOR**	Pan-African College of Radiographers (Zimbabwe)
PAC	Planning Appeals Commission (Northern Ireland)	**PACOREDO**	Partido Comunista de la Republica Dominicana
PAC	Population Association of China		
PAC	Productivity Advisory Council (South Africa)	**PACR**	Civic Alliance of Romania
		PACRA	Pottery and Ceramics Research Association (New Zealand)
PAC	Provincial Armed Constabulary (India)	**PACREP**	Pan African Centre for Research on Peace, Development and Human Rights (Nigeria)
PAC	Public Accounts Committee		
PAC	Public Archives of Canada = APC		
PACA	Public Art Commissions Agency	**PACS**	Primary Agricultural Credit Societies (India)
PACBA	Pan-African Christian Broadcast Association		
		PACSA	People Against Child Sex Abuse
PACBROAD	Pacific Broadcasting Training and Development Project (PIBA)	**PACSC**	Pesticides and Agricultural Chemicals Standing Committee

PACT	Private Agencies Collaborating Together (U.S.A.)
PACT	Protestant Adoption Society and Single Parent Counselling Service (Ireland)
PACTS	Parliamentary Advisory Council for Transport Safety
PACWA	Pan African Christian Women Alliance (Kenya)
PAD	Pacific Australia Direct Line (U.S.A.)
PAD	Partido Acción Democrática (El Salvador)
PAD	Port Autonome de Dakau Sénégal
PADEC	Pan African Association for Community Development (Senegal)
PADEP	Peasant Agricultural Development Programme (Ethiopia)
PADF	Pan American Development Foundation = FUPAD
PADI	People Action for Development India
PADI	Professional Association of Diving Instructors
PADIN	Partido Integración Nacional (Peru)
PADIS	Pan-African Documentation and Information System (UN)
PADMU	Pakistan Desertification Monitoring Unit
PADO	Pan-African Development Organisation (Gambia) = PAIS, PAISACD
PADOG	Plan d'Aménagement et d'Organisation Générale de la Région Parisienne
PADRR	Democratic Alliance Party of Romania
PADT	Public Art Development Trust
PADU	Protected Areas Data Unit (WCMC)
PAEAC	Parliamentary Association for Euro-Arab Cooperation = APCEA
PAEC	Pakistan Atomic Energy Commission
PAEC	Philippines Atomic Energy Commission
PAEF	Pan-African Employers' Federation
PAEF	Polish-American Enterprise Fund
PAF	Papierindustriens Arbeidsgiverforening
PAF	Petroleumbranschens Arbetsgivareförbund
PAF	Police de l'Air et des Frontières
PAF	Prosjekt Alternativ Framtiel
PAF	Public Art Forum
PAFA	Pan-Albanian Federation of America
PAFA	Pan-American Festival Association
PAFAMS	Pan-American Federation of Associations of Medical Schools (Venezuela) = FEPAFEM
PAFATU	Pan-African Federation of Agricultural Trade Unions = FEPASA
PAFAWAG	Państwowa Fabryka Wagonów
PAFC	Philippine-American Financial Commission
PAFIE	Pacific Asian Federation of Industrial Engineering (India)
PAFLU	Philippine Association of Free Labour Unions
PAFMDC	Pan American Foot-and-Mouth Disease Center (Brazil) = PANAFTOSA
PAFO	Pan-African Family Organisation = OPAF
PAFOS	Pan African Federation of Oto-Rhino-Laryngological Societies (IFOS)
PAG	Państwowy Arbitraz Gospodarczy
PAG	Plant Advisory Group (IUCN and WWF)
PAG	Protein-Calorie Advisory Group of the United Nations System = GCP
PAGART	Polska Agencja Artystyczna
PAGB	Poultry and Egg Producers Association of Great Britain
PAGB	Proprietary Association of Great Britain
PAGED	Polska Agencja Eksportu Drewna
PAGENACI	Participation Générale Africaine de la Côte-d'Ivoire
PAGS	Parti de l'Avant-Garde Socialiste (Algeria)
PAGV	Stichting Proefstation voor de Akkerbouw en de Groenteteelt in de Vollegrond (Netherlands)
PAHA	Polish American Historical Association
PAHEF	Pan American Health and Education Foundation (U.S.A.)
PAHMC	Pan-American Homeopathic Medical Oongress
PAHO	Pan American Health Organization (OAS) = OPAS, OPS
PAHO-CENDES	Pan-American Health Organization Center for Development Studies
PAI	Parti Africain de l'Indépendance (Senegal)
PAI	Polska Agencja Informacyjna
PAI	Polska Agencja Interpress
PAIA	Pan American Implant Association
PAICV	Partido Africano da Independência de Cabo Verde
PAID	Pan-African Institute for Development = IPD

PAIDA	Pan American Infectious Diseases Association = PAIDS
PAIDS	Pan American Infectious Diseases Society = PAIDA
PAIGC	Partido Africano da Independência de Guiné e Cabo Verde (Guinea-Bissau)
PAIGH	Pan-American Institute of Geography and History (OAS)= IPGH, PIGH
PAIL	Procedural Aspects of International Law Institute (U.S.A.)
PAIN	Parents against Injustice
PAIN	Parti Agricole et Industriel National (Haiti)
PAIN	Prisoners Advice and Information Network
PAINCI	Participations Industrielles de Côte-d'Ivoire
PAIS	Pan-African Islamic Society for Agro-Cultural Development (Gambia) = PADO, PAISACD
PAIS	Partido Amplio de Izquierda Socialista (Chile)
PAIS	Public Affairs Information Service (U.S.A.)
PAISA	Partido Auténtico Institucional Salvadoreño
PAISACD	Pan-African Islamic Society for Agro-Cultural Development (Gambia) = PADO, PAIS
PAJ	Petroleum Association of Japan
PAJ	Pontificia Accademia dell'Immacolata (Vatican)
PAJ	Press Association of Jamaica
PAJOCA	Angolan Youth, Workers and Peasant Alliance Party
PAK	Kurdish Freedom Party
PAK	Panhellenic Liberation Movement (Greece)
PAL	Parents Anonymous London
PAL	Perceptual Alternatives Laboratory (U.S.A.)
PAL	Philippine Airlines
PAL	Planning Aid for London
PAL	Polska Akademia Literaty
PAL	Polska Armia Ludowa
PALA	Partido Laborista (Panama)
PALCO	Pan-American Liaison Committee of Women's Organizations
PALIKA	Parti de Libération Kanak (New Caledonia)
PALIPE-HUTU	Party for the Liberation of the Hutu People (Burundi)
PALM-EVEAS	Palmiers et Hévéas du Gabon
PALMO	Partido Liberal e Democrático de Moçambique
PALSS	Physical and Life Sciences Society (South Africa)
PALU	Progressive Arbeiders en Landbouwers Unie (Suriname)
PAM	People's Action Movement (St. Christopher and Nevis)
PAM	Programme Alimentaire Mondial = PMA, WFP
PAMA	Pan-American Medical Association
PAMA	Press Advertisement Managers Association
PAMAL	Plantations Pamol du Caméroun
PAME	Pankyprio Ananeotiko Metopo (Cyprus)
PAMEE	Philippine Association of Mechanical and Electrical Engineers
PAMI	Pontificia Accademia Mariana Internationalis (Vatican)
PAMI	Proyecto de Apoyo para la Salud Materno Infantil (Guatemala)
PAMM	British Ceramic Plant and Machinery Manufacturers Association
PAMWA	Pan American Medical Women's Alliance
PAN	Partido Acción Nacional (El Salvador, Mexico)
PAN	Partido de Ação Nacionalista (Brazil)
PAN	Pesticides Action Network
PAN	Plan Nacional de Alimentacion y Nutricion (Colombia)
PAN	Polska Akademia Nauk
PANA	Pan Arab News Agency
PANA	Pan-African News Agency
PANA	Pan-Asian News Agency
PANA	Philippine Association of National Advertisers
PANABAF	Pan-African Federation of Bank Employees (Libya)
PANABANK	Banco Panamericano (Panama)
PANAC	Plantations Association of Nigeria and the Cameroons
PANACH	Panafrican Chemical Industries (Ivory Coast)
PANACOM	Pan-African Workers of Commerce (Congo)

PANAF-TOSA	Centro Panamericano de Fiebre Aftosa (Brazil) = PAFMDC	**PAP**	People's Action Party (Papua New Guinea, Singapore)
PANAFCO	Panafrican Company (Togo)	**PAP**	People's Alliance Party (Solomon Islands)
PANAFTEL	Panafrican Telecommunication Network	**PAP**	Polska Agencja Prasowa
PANAGRA	Panorama Agricola Nacional de los Paises Latinoamericanos (Mexico)	**PAP**	Professional Association of Partners
PANAM	Pan American World Airways	**PAPA**	Pizza & Pasta Association
PANANEWS	Pan-Asia Newspaper Alliance (Singapore)	**PAPBC**	Pharmaceutical Association of the Province of British Columbia (Canada)
PANASA	Productos Alimentacios Nacionales (Costa Rica)	**PAPC**	Public Agricultural Production Corporation (Sudan)
PANASCO	Pan-African Students International Peace and Voluntary Services Organisation (Ghana)	**PAPCGS**	Pokret za Autonomni Pristup Crne Gore u Srbiju (Montenegro) = MMAAS
PANCAFE	Productores de Cafés Asociados (Mexico)	**PAPCHILD**	Pan Arab Project for Child Development
PAND International	Performers and Artists for Nuclear Disarmament International = PI	**PAPD**	Panhellenic Association of Private Detectives
PANESA	Pasture Network for Eastern and Southern Africa (ILCA)	**PAPE**	Pan-Pacific Association of Private School Education (Japan)
PANET	Panamerican Network of Medical Education and Health Information (PAFAMS, PAHO)	**PAPEC**	Société Africaine de Production d'Articles en Papier et d'Emballages en Carton (Burkina Faso)
PANGF	Pacific Alliance of National Gymnastic Federations	**PAPF**	Philippine Association for Permanent Forests
PANGIS	Pan African Network for a Geological Information System (France)	**PAPITEK**	Pusat Analisa Perkembangan IPTEK (Indonesia)
PANI	Patronato Nacional de la Infancia (Costa Rica)	**PAPMAD**	Papeteries de Madagascar
PANIDA	Société de Planification de Doala (Ivory Coast)	**Papo**	Partido de Acción Popular (Panama)
Panin	Pan Indonesia Bank	**PAPRI**	Pension & Population Research Institute
PANLAR	Pan-American League against Rheumatism	**PAPRICAN**	Pulp and Paper Research Institute of Canada
PANN	Professional Association of Nursery Nurses	**PAPU**	Pan-African Postal Union = UPAP
PANPA	Pacific Area Newspaper Publishers Association (Australia)	**PAR**	Partido Acción Renovadora (El Salvador)
PANPESAS	Confederación Panamericana de Levantamiento de Pesas = PAWC	**PAR**	Partido Aragones Regionalista
PANPRA	Parti Nationaliste Progressiste Révolutionnaire (Haiti)	**PARBICA**	Pacific Regional Branch of the International Council on Archives
PANSDOC	Pakistan National Scientific and Technology Documentation Centre	**PARC**	Pacific-Asia Resources Center (Japan)
PAO	Fédération des Associations de l'Industrie des Produits Dérivés de l'Avoine et de l'Orge dans la CEE	**PARC**	Pan Arab Research Center (Kuwait)
		PARC	Parallel Algorithm Research Centre
		PARCA	Pan American Railway Congress Association
PAOO	Philippine Academy of Opthalmology and Otolaryngology	**PARCOM**	Paris Commission
		PARD	Pakistan Academy for Rural Development
PAP	Partido Alianza Popular (Costa Rica)	**PARE**	People Against Racism in Education (U.S.A.)
PAP	Partido Aprista Peruano = APRA	**PARENA**	Partido de Renovacion Nacional (Chile)
		PAREX	European Programme of Cooperative Research in the Social Studies of Science

PARIBAS	Compagnie Financière de Paris et des Pays-Bas	**PASTIN-DUSTRIA**	Associazione Italiana fra gli Industriali Pastificatori
PARIBAS-CAMÉ-ROUN	Banque de Paris et Pays-Bas Caméroun	**PASTO-RALE**	Compagnie Pastorale Africaine (Caméroun)
PARIBAS-GABON	Banque de Paris et des Pays-Bas Gabon	**PASUS**	Pan-American Society of the United States
Paris Union	International Union for the Protection of Industrial Property = Union de Paris	**PAT**	Panhellenic Association of Translators
		PAT	Pin and Allied Trades Association
PARL	Prince Albert Radar Laboratory (Canada)	**PAT**	Polska Agencja Telegraficzna
PARLIG-AES	Parliamentary Liaison Group for Alternative Energy Strategies	**PAT**	Professional Association of Teachers
		PATA	Pacific Asia Travel Association (U.S.A.)
PARM	Partido Auténtico de la Revolución Mexicana	**PATA**	Proprietary Articles Trade Association
PARMÉ-HUTU	Parti du Mouvement de l'Émancipation Hutu (Rwanda)	**PATCH**	People Active Through Community Help (Éire)
PARTIZ-ANS	People Against Rio Tinto Zinc and its Subsidiaries	**PATH**	Program for Appropriate Technology in Health (PIACT)
PARVO	Professional and Academic Regional Visits Organisation	**PATIA**	Plant A Tree in Africa
		PATRA	Printing and Allied Trades' Research Association (U.S.A.)
PAS	Parti Islam Sa-Malaysia	**PATRAC**	Planning and Transportation Research Advisory Council
PAS	Poetry Association of Scotland		
PAS	Pontificia Academia Scientiarum	**PATS**	Philippine Aeronautics Training School
PAS	Prisoners' Advice Service	**PATU**	Pan African Telecommunications Union (Zaïre) = UPAT
PASA	Pacific Asian Studies Association		
PASA	Powder Actuated Systems Association (FBHTM)	**PATU**	Pan American Taekwondo Union (WTF)
		PAU	Pan-American Union (OAS) = UPA
PASB	Pan-American Sanitary Bureau (PAHO)	**PAU**	Polska Akademia Umiejętności
PASCAR	Pan African Society of Cardiology = SOPAC	**PAU**	Public Appointments Unit
		PAUJ	Pan African Union of Journalists
PASCO	Pan-Arab Shipping Company (Egypt)	**PAUSS**	Pacto de Unidad Sindical Solidaridad (Mexico)
PASCV	Pan American Society for Clinical Virology		
		PAV	Paksi Atomerömü Vállalat
PASEGES	Panellinios Synomospondia Enoseon Georgikon Synetairismon	**PAV**	Programme d'Assistance Volontaire (WMO) = VAP
PASLIB	Pakistan Association of Special Libraries	**PAVE**	Philippine Association for Vocational Education
PASM	Pan African Student Movement	**PAW**	Proefstation voor Akker- en Weidebouw
PASMA	Prefabricated Aluminium Scaffold Manufacturers Association	**PAWA**	Pan African Writers Association
		PAWA	Pan-American Women's Association
PASO	Pan American Sports Organisation = ODEPA	**PAWC**	Pan-American Weightlifting Confederation = PANPESAS
Paso	Partido Socialista (Honduras)	**PAWE**	Pakistan Association of Women Entrepreneurs
Pasoc	Partido de Acción Socialista		
PASOK	Panellinion Sosialistikon Kinema	**PAWF**	Pacific and Asian Women's Forum
PASPCR	PanAmerican Society for Pigment Cell Research	**PAWLA**	Pakistan Women Lawyers Association
		PAWO	Pan-African Women's Organisation = OPF
PASTIC	Pakistan Scientific and Technological Information Centre	**PAWORNET**	Pacific Women's Information/Communication Network (Fiji)

PAYM	Pan African Youth Movement = MPJ, PYM
PAY-MASTER	Office of HM Paymaster General
PAZA	Press Association of Zambia
PB	Papua Besena (Papua New Guinea)
PB	Pères Blancs = MAfr, WF
PBBA	Pro-Bessarabia and Bukovina Association (Romania) = APBB
PBC	Panamerican Badminton Confederation = CPB
PBC	People's Bank of China
PBCP	Political Bureau of the Communist Party
PBDC	Pacific Basin Development Council
PBDS	Parti Bangsa Dayak Sarawak
PBEC	Pacific Basin Economic Council (Australia)
PBF	Papirindustrielle Bedrifters Forbund
PBFA	Provincial Booksellers Fairs Association
PBFL	Planning for Better Family Living (FAO) = PVFM
PBI	Peace Brigades International
PBI	Programa Biológico Internacional = IBP
PBI	Programme Biologique Internationale = IBP
PBIC	Plant Breeding International Cambridge
PBM	Proefstation voor de Nederlandse Brouw-en Moutindustrie
PBMA	Plastics Bath Manufacturers Association
PBMCHRC	Pacific Basin Maternal and Child Health Resource Center (Guam)
PBO	Publiekrechtelijke Bedrijfsorganisatie (Netherlands)
PBP	Progressive Bosneger Partij (Suriname)
PBR	Państwowy Bank Rolny
PBR	Polski Bank Rozwoju
PBS	Pacific Biological Station (Canada)
PBS	Parti Bersatu Sabah (Malaysia) = SUP
PBS	Partia e Blerte Shqiptare
PBS	Philippine Broadcasting Service
PBS	Prayer Book Society
PBS	Public Broadcasting Service (U.S.A.)
PBSI	Indonesian Badminton Association
PBT	Party of Businessmen and Tradesmen (Czech Republic) = SPO
PBU	Pali Buddhist Union
PBVM	Sisters of the Presentation of the Blessed Virgin Mary
PBWG	Pakistan Bibliographical Working Group
PBZ	Peoples Bank of Zanzibar (Tanzania)
PC	Centre Accord (Poland)
PC	Partido Colorado (Uruguay)
PC	Partido Conservador (Colombia, Ecuador, Nicaragua)
PC	Paz y Cooperación
PC	Plaid Cymru (Wales)
PC	Polish Council (Czech Republic) = RP
PC	Popular Coalition = CP
PC	Porozumienie Centrum
PC	Press Council
PC	Printmakers' Council
PC	Progressive Conservative Party (Canada)
PCA	Packaging Council of Australia
PCA	Paperweight Collectors' Association
PCA	Parliamentary Candidates Association
PCA	Parochial Clergy Association (*now* ECA)
PCA	Partido Comunista de Argentina
PCA	Permanent Court of Arbitration (Netherlands)
PCA	Police Complaints Authority
PCA	Presidency of Civil Aviation (Saudi Arabia)
PCA	Prestressed Concrete Association
PCA	Print Council of America
PCA	Printed Circuit Association
PCA	Pro-Choice Alliance
PCA	Production Credit Association (U.S.A.)
PCA	Professional Cycling Association
PCA	Progressive Cultural Association
PCA	Proprietary Crematoria Association
PCA	Pulp Chemicals Association (U.S.A.)
PCAB	Programa de Cooperacion Andina para Bolivia
PCAC	Poultry Costings Advisory Council
PCAC	Professional Classes Aid Council
PCACT	Programa de Cultivos Alimenticios del Centro de Turriabla (Costa Rica)
PCAG	Petroleum Conservation Action Group (India)
PCARR	Philippines Council for Agricultural Resources and Research
PCB	Nederlandse Bond van Protestants-Christelijke Beroepsgoederenvervoeders
PCB	Parti Communiste de Belgique = KPB

PCB	Partido Comunista Brasileiro		**PCDMA**	Personal Computer Direct Marketers Association
PCB	Partido Comunista de Bolivia		**PCDNC**	Pontificium Consilium pro Dialogo cum Non Credentibus
PCBCI	Pedigree Cattle Breeders' Council of Ireland		**PCdoB**	Partido Comunista do Brasil
PCC	International Philatelic Press Club (U.S.A.)		**PCDPPP**	Pan Caribbean Disaster Preparedness and Prevention Project (PAHO, UNDRO)
PCC	Pacific Conference of Churches		**PCE**	Partido Comunista de España
PCC	Panama Canal Commission		**PCE**	Partido Conservador de Ecuador = PC
PCC	Panamerican Cultural Circle		**PCE-PCA**	Partido Comunista de Andalucia
PCC	Partido Comunista Cubano		**PCE-PCG**	Partido Comunista de Galicia
PCC	Partido Comunista de Colombia		**PCEM**	Parliamentary Council of the European Movement = CPME
PCC	Partit dels Comunistes de Catalunya		**PCER**	Partija za Celosna Emancipacija na Romite / Party for Complete Emancipation of Roma
PCC	Philippine Cotton Corporation			
PCC	Political Consultative Council (Russia)			
PCC	Pontificium Consilium de Cultura		**PCF**	Parti Communiste Français
PCC	Population Crisis Committee (U.S.A.)		**PCF**	Pontificium Consilium pro Familia
PCC	Press Complaints Commission		**PCFA**	Polytechnics and Colleges Funding Council
PCC	Print Collectors Club			
PCC	Program Coordinating Centre		**PCFA**	Precast Concrete Frame Association
PCCC	Pakistan Central Cotton Committee		**PCFRE**	Professional Council for Religious Education
PCCC	Penang Chinese Chamber of Commerce (Malaysia)		**PCG**	Parti Communiste Guadeloupéen
PCCDR	Conservative Christian Democratic Romanian Party		**PCG**	Period Costume Group
			PCG	Plant Charter Group
PCCGB	Photographic Collectors Club		**PCGG**	Philippine Commission on Good Government
PCCH	Partido Comunista Chileno			
PCCLAS	Pacific Coast Council on Latin American Studies		**PCGG**	Primary Care Group in Gynaecology
PCCMCA	Programa Cooperativo Centroamericano para el Mejoramiento de Cultivos Alimenticos (Mexico)		**PCH**	Państwowa Centrala Handlowa
			PCH	Partido Comunista de Honduras
			PCI	Pax Christi International
PCCS	Pontificium Consilium de Communicationibus Socialis		**PCI**	Population Council of India
			PCI	Press Council of India
PCCS	Primate Captive Care Society		**PCI**	Prospectors Club International (U.S.A.)
PCD	Christian Democratic Party (Moldova)		**PCIAC**	Petro-Canada International Assistance Corporation
PCD	Christian Party of Justice (Romania)			
PCD	Communist Party of Dahomey (Benin)		**PCID**	Pontifical Council for Inter-Religious Dialogue
PCD	Partido Comunista Dominicano (Dominican Republic)		**PCIF**	Printed Circuit Interconnection Federation
PCD	Partido Conservador Demócrata (Nicaragua)		**PCIFC**	Permanent Commission of the International Fisheries Convention = CPCIP
PCD	Partido da Convergência Democrática (Sao Tomé)			
PCD	Party of Christian Democrats (Poland)		**PCIJ**	Permanent Court of International Justice
PCD	Patriotic Coalition for Democracy (Guyana)		**PCIM**	Programa Cooperativo de Investigaciones de Maiz (Peru)
PCD	Pueblo, Cambio y Democracia (Ecuador)		**PCIRI**	Paint & Coatings Industry Research Institute (China)
PCdeN	Partido Comunista de Nicaragua			

PCIS	Period Cottage Improvement Society	**PCS**	Partido Comunista Salvadoreño
PCIZC	Permanent Committee of International Zoological Congresses	**PCS**	Partito Comunista Sammarinese
		PCS	Property Consultants Society
PCJ	Petroleum Corporation of Jamaica	**PCSAS**	Policy Committee for Scientific Agricultural Societies (U.S.A.)
PCJ	Sisters of the Poor Child Jesus		
PCJC	Pakistan Central Jute Committee	**PCSIR**	Pakistan Council of Scientific and Industrial Research
PCK	Polski Czerwony Krzyz		
PCL	Lebanese Communist Party	**PCST**	Pakistan Council for Science and Technology
PCL	Pontifical Council for the Laity		
PCM	Parti Communiste Martiniquais	**PCT**	Parti Communiste Tunisien
PCM	Partido Comunista Mexicano	**PCT**	Parti Congolais du Travail
PCMA	Plastic Crate Manufacturers Association	**PCT Union**	International Patent Cooperation Union (WIPO)
PCMA	Potato Chips Manufacturers Association	**PCTP**	Partido Comunista dos Trabalhadores Portugueses
PCMA	Precision Chain Manufacturers Association		
		PCU	Partido Comunista del Uruguay
PCMA	Professional Convention Management Association (U.S.A.)	**PCV**	Partido Comunista de Venezuela
		PCVM	Research Association of British Paint, Colour and Varnish Manufacturers
PCN	Partido Comunista de Nicaragua		
PCN	Partido Conservador de Nicaragua	**PCWPC**	Permanent Committee of the World Petroleum Congress
PCN	Partido de Conciliación Nacional (El Salvador)		
		PCWTU	Philippine Woman's Christian Temperance Union
PCN	Standing Committee of Nurses of the EC		
		PD	Democratic Party (Moldova)
PCO	Protestants Christelijke Onderwijsvakorganisatie	**PD**	Parti Démocratique (Luxembourg)
		PD	Partido Demócrata (Ecuador)
PCOB	Permanent Central Opium Board (UN)	**PD**	Plantenziektenkundige Dienst
PCOC	Partit Comunista Obrero de Catalunya	**PD**	Progressive Democrats (Éire)
PCOCA	Parti-Colour Oriental Cat Association	**PDA**	Agrarian Democratic Party (Moldova)
PCOE	Partido Comunista Obrero de España	**PDA**	Association of Management & Professional Staff Divers Section
PCP	Palestinian Communist Party		
PCP	Partido Comunista del Perú	**PDA**	Packaging Distributors Association
PCP	Partido Comunista Português	**PDA**	Panhellenic Dental Association
PCP	Partido Comunista Puertorriqueño	**PDA**	Parenteral Drug Association
PCP	Progressive Constitutional Party (Malta)	**PDA**	Partido Democrático Angolana
		PDA	Partido Democrático Arubano (Aruba)
PCP Centre	Centre for Personal Construct Psychology	**PDA**	Partit Democratic d'Andorra
PCPCI	Power Conversion Products Counci International	**PDA**	Party of Democratic Action (Bosnia – Herzegovina) = SDA
		PDA	Party of Democratic Action (Serbia)
PCPCU	Pontifical Council for Promoting Christian Unity	**PDA**	Photographic Dealers Association
		PDA	Plano de Desenvolvimento da Amazônia (Brazil)
PCPE	Partido Comunista del Pueblo Español		
PCPI	Parent Cooperative Preschools International	**PDA**	Population and Community Development Association (Thailand)
PCPI	Permanent Committee on Patent Information (WIPO)	**PDA**	Professional Designers' Association
		PDA	Pump Distributors Association of Great Britain
PCR	Parti Communiste Réunionnais		
PCR	Partido Comunista Revolucionaria (Argentina, Peru)	**PDA-M**	Party of Democratic Action-Montenegro = SDA-CG
PCS	Parti Chrétien-Social (Luxembourg) = CSV		

PDAF	Taiwan Provincial Department of Agriculture and Forestry	**PDIN**	Pusat Dokumentasi Ilmiah Nasional (Indonesia)
PDAK	Party of Democratic Action for Kosovo (Serbia) = SDAK	**PDIS**	Pusat Dokumentasi Ilmu-Ilmu Sosial (Indonesia)
PDB	Partei der Deutschsprachigen Belgier	**PDIUM**	Partito Democratico Italiano di Unité Monarchica
PDC	Pacte Democratic per Catalunya		
PDC	Parti Démocratique Chrétien (Burundi)	**PDIWT**	Planning & Design Institute for Water Transportation (China)
PDC	Parti Démocratique Congolais		
PDC	Partido da Democracia Cristão	**PDK**	Party of Democratic Kampuchea (Cambodia)
PDC	Partido Demócrata Cristão (Brazil)		
PDC	Partido Demócrata Cristiano (Argentina, Bolivia, Chile, Costa Rica, El Salvador, Honduras, Panama, Paraguay, Peru, Uruguay)	**PDL**	Party of the Democratic Left (Slovakia) = SDL
		PDLF	Pakistan Democratic Labour Federation
		PDM	Democratic Labour Party (Moldova, Romania)
PDC	Partisan Defence Committee		
PDC	Peru Debt Campaign	**PDM**	Partido Demócrata Mexicano
PDC	Population Documentation Center (UN)	**PDM**	Partit Demokratico Malti (Malta)
PDC	Productivity and Development Center (Philippines)	**PDM**	Peoples Democratic Movement (Guyana, Papua New Guines, Turks & Caicos Islands)
PDCA	Purebred Dairy Cattle Association (U.S.A.)		
		PDMS	Postal Direct Marketing Service
PDCG	Partido Democracia Cristiana Guatemalteca	**PDO**	Petroleum Development Oman
		PDO	Praktiserende Dyrlægers Organisation
PDCH	Parti Démocrate Chrétien Haïtien	**PDOIS**	People's Democratic Organisation for Independence and Socialism (Gambia)
PDCI	Parti Démocratique de la Côte d'Ivoire		
PDCN	Partido Democrático de Cooperación National (Guatemala)	**PDP**	Pakistan Democratic Party
		PDP	Partido del Pueblo (Panama) = PPP
PDCP	Private Development Corporation of the Philippines	**PDP**	Partido Demócrata Popular
		PDP	Partido Demócrata Progresista (Argentina)
PDCS	Partito Democrático Cristiano Sammarinese		
		PDP	Partido Democrático Popular (Ecuador)
PDD	Państwowy Dom Dziecka	**PDP**	Partija za Demokratski Prosperitet / Party for Democratic Prosperity (Macedonia)
PDDM	Pieuses Disciples du Divin Maître		
PDF	Pacific Dentistry Association		
PDF	Parti Démocrate Française	**PDP**	People's Democratic Party (Bulgaria) = PDV
PDF	People's Democratic Force (Bahamas)		
PDFLP	Popular Democratic Front for the Liberation of Palestine	**PDP**	People's Democratic Party (Burma)
		PDP	People's Democratic Party (Montenegro) = NDS
PDG	Parti Démocratique de Guinée		
PDG	Parti Démocratique Gabonais	**PDP**	People's Democratic Party (Uzbekistan)
PDG	Patent Documentation Group (Switzerland)	**PDP**	Popular Democratic Party (Puerto Rico)
		PDP	Porozumienie Demokratów Polskich
PDGE	Partido Democrático de Guinea Ecuatorial	**PDP**	Progressive Democratic Party (Montserrat)
PDI	Partai Demokrasi Indonesia	**PDP**	Progressive Democratic Party (Romania)
PDI	Participación Democrática de Izquierda (Chile)		
		PDPA	Bureau pour le Développement de la Production Agricole Outre-Mer
PDII	Pusat Dokumentasi dan Informasi Ilmiah (Scientific Documentation and Information Center, LIPI) (Indonesia)	**PDPA**	People's Democratic Party of Afghanistan

PDPELA-BAB	Pilipino Democratic Party
PDPK	Party of Democratic Progress of Kazakhstan
PDR	Parti Démocratique Progressif (Algeria)
PDR	Romanian Democratic Party
PDRE	People's Democratic Republic of Ethiopia
PDRI	Projeto de Desenvolvimento Rural Integrado (Brazil)
PDRMA	Portable Drill Rig Manufacturers Association (U.S.A.)
PDRU	Party of Democratic Rebirth of Ukraine
PDRY	People's Democratic Republic of the Yemen
PDS	Parkinson's Disease Society of the United Kingdom
PDS	Partei des Demokratischen Sozialismus
PDS	Parti Démocratique Sénégalais
PDS	Partia Demokratike të Shqipërisë (Albania) = DPA
PDS	Partido Demócrata Socialista (Panama)
PDS	Partido Democrático Social (Brazil)
PDS	Partito Democratico della Sinistra (Italy)
PDS	Pedagoško Društvo Srbije
PDS	Social Justice Party of Romania
PDS-R	Parti Démocratique Sénégalais – Renovation
PDSA	People's Dispensary for Sick Animals
PDSA	Provincial Department of Social Affairs (Taiwan)
PDSC	Population and Development Studies Centre (South Korea)
PDSP	Philippines Democratic Socialist Party
PDT	Partido Democrático Trabalhista (Brazil)
PDT	Powszechny Dom Towarowy
PDTS	Powell Duffryn Technical Services
PDU	Pacific Democrat Union
PDV	Partiya za Demokraticheski Vazkhod (Bulgaria) = PDP
PDVSA	Petroleos de Venezuela S.A. = Petroven
PE	Parlement Européen
PE	Partija Ekologjike (Albania) = EP
PEA	Physical Education Association of Great Britain and Northern Ireland
PEAB	Professional Engineers' Appointments Bureau
PEACE	Palestinian European Academic Cooperation in Education
PEACER	Petroleum Employers Advisory Council on Employee Relations
PEACESAT	Pan Pacific Educational and Cultural Exchange by Satellite Program (U.S.A.)
PEACH	Peace Ethics Animals and Consistent Human Rights
PEACS	Instítuto de Pesquisas e Experimentação Agropecuárias do Centro-Sul (Brazil)
PEAI	Physical Education Association of Ireland
PEAMUSE	Peabody Museum of Archaeology and Ethnology (U.S.A.)
PEAS	Printed Ephemera Society
PEC	Pan-African Employers' Confederation (Kenya)
PEC	Plain English Campaign
PECAM	Pêcheries Camérounaises
PECC	Pacific Economic Cooperation Conference (Singapore)
PECE	Pacto de Estabilidad y Crecimiento Económico (Mexico)
PECI	Plastiques et Elastomères de la Côte-d'Ivoire
PECTA	Programme des Emplois et des Compétences Techniques pour l'Afrique (ILO) = JASPA
PED	Emergency Preparedness and Disaster Relief Coordination Office
PED	Panellinia Enosi Diabitikon
PED	Petroleum Engineering Department
PED	Pôle Européen de Développement
PEDAÉP	Projet d'Expérimentation et de Démonstration en Arboriculture, Élevage et Pâturage (Tunisia)
PEEAFE	Panellinios Enosis Emporikon Antiprosopon Pharmakon Exoterikou
PEEM	Panel of Experts on Environmental Management for Vector Control (WHO/FAO/UNEP/UNCHS)
PÉEP	Federation des Parents d'Élèves de l'Enseignement Publique
PEER	Project of Equal Education Rights (U.S.A.)
PEF	European Pentecostal Fellowship
PEF	Palestine Exploration Fund (U.K.)
PEF	Panellinos Enosis Pharmekoviomichanias
PEF	Party of Economic Freedom (Russian Federation)

PEFC	Paper Exporters Freight Committee
PEFIA	Polyethylene Foam Manufacturers Association
PEFU	Panel of Experts on Fish Utilization (FAO)
PEGS	Groupe Européen de l'Industrie Pepetière pour les Affaires Sociales (Belgium)
PEGS	Pesticide Exposure Group of Sufferers
PEI	Petroleum Equipment Institute (U.S.A.)
PEIA	Poultry and Egg Institute of America
PEKEMAS	Parti Keadilan Masyarakat (Malaysia)
PEKSI	Persatuan Exportir Indonesia
PEL	Priests' Eucharistic League
PELNI	Pelayaran Nasional Indonesia
PELS	Locomotive 6201 "Princess Elizabeth Society Ltd"
PEM	People's Electoral Movement (Aruba)
PEMA	Packaging Equipment Manufacturers Association (*now* PPMA)
PEMA	Process Equipment Manufacturers Association (U.S.A.)
PEMARZA	Pêcherie Maritime Zaïroise
PEMETE	Panellinia Enosi Metapoiiton – Typoiiton Exagogeon Epitrapezion Elaion
PEMEX	Petróleos Mexicanos
PEN	Peninsula Environmental Network
PEN	Poets, Playwrights, Editors, Essayists and Novelists
PENCE	Protein Engineering Network of Centres of Excellence (Canada)
PENOMAH	Pest-Nógrád Megyei Allatforgalmi és Húsipari Vállalat
PEO	Pankypria Ergatiki Omospondia (Cyprus)
PEO	Professional Engineers Ontario
PEO	Programme Evaluation Organization (India)
PÉON	Commission pour la Production d'Énergie d'Origine Nucléaire
PEP	Personal Empowerment Programme
PEP	Puslitbang Ekonomi dan Pembangunan (Indonesia)
PEPAS	Western Pacific Regional Centre for the Promotion of Environmental Planning and Applied Studies (WHO)
PEPES	People Persecuted by Pablo Escobar
PEPL	Partido de Esperanza, Paz y Libertad (Colombia)

PEQUIVEN	Petroquímica de Venezuela
PER	Professional and Executive Recruitment (MSC)
PER	Romanian Ecologist Party
PERA	Production Engineering Research Association
PERBANAS	Perhimpunan Bank – Bank Nasional Swasta (Indonesia)
PERC	Party of the Economic Rebirth of Crimea
PERC	Political Economy Research Center (U.S.A.)
PERC	Psoriasis Education and Research Centre (Canada)
PERF	Police Executive Research Forum (U.S.A.)
PERI	Pakistan Economic Research Institute
PERIL-Europe	Association pour l'Expansion du Rôle International des Langues d'Europe Continentale
PERINASIA	Indonesian Society for Perinatology
PERME	Propellants Explosives and Rocket Motor Establishment (MOD)
PERNAS	Perbadanan Nasional Bhel (Malaysia)
PERSGA	Programme for the Environment of the Red Sea and Gulf of Aden (ALECSO) = RSGAEP
PERTA-MINA	Perusahaan Pertambangan Minyak Dan Gas Bumi Negara (Indonesia)
PERULAC	Compañía Peruana de Alimentos Lácteos
PERUM-TEL	Perusahaan Umum Telekomunikasi (Indonesia)
PERYÖN	Personel Yöneticileri Dernegi
PES	Party of European Socialists
PÉS	Société Plastique et Élastomère du Sénégal
PESA	Petroleum Equipment Suppliers Association (U.S.A.)
PESA	Progressive English Speaking Association (Israel)
PESC-ANGOLA	Empresa de Pesca de Angola
PESCA-PERU	Empresa Nacional de Pesca (Peru)
PESCAVE	Empresa Caboverdeana de Pescas (Cape Verde)
PESECO	Société de Pêche Sengalo-Coréenne
PESGB	Petroleum Exploration Society of Great Britain

PESL	Petroleum Exploration Society of Libya
PEST	People for Environmentally Sustainable Transport
PEST	Pressure for Economic and Social Toryism
PESTNET	Pest Management Research and Development Network (Kenya)
PET	Clinical Centre for Positron Emission Tomography
PET	Panellinois Enosis Technikon
PETA	People for the Ethical Treatment of Animals
PETA	Postal Equipment Trade Association
PETANS	Petroleum Training Association North Sea
PETCOR	Philippine Exporters Trading Corporation
PETMA	Portable Electric Tool Manufacturers Association
PETMARK	Petromin Marketing (Saudi Arabia)
PETRA/JNA	Jordan News Agency
PETRAN-GOL	Fina Petróleos de Angola
PETRAS	Polytechnic Educational Resources Advisory Service
PETRO-BRAS	Petróleo Brasileiro
PETRO-FéRTIL	Petrobrás Fertilizantes (Brazil)
PETRO-LUBE	Petromin Lubricating Oil Company (Saudi Arabia)
PETRO-MINAS	Empresa Nacional de Pesquisas e Exploração Petroliferas e Mineiras (Guinea-Bissau)
PETRO-PERU	Petróleos del Perú
PETRO-QUISA	Petrobrás Química (Brazil)
PETRO-SERVE	Petromin Services Department (Saudi Arabia)
PETRO-SHIP	Petromin Tankers and Mineral Shipping Company (Saudi Arabia)
PETRO-SUL	Sociedade Portuguesa de Refinacao de Petroleos
PETROBEL	Belayim Petroleum Company (Egypt)
PETROCI	Société Nationale d'Opérations Petrolières de la Côte d'Ivoire
PETROGAB	Société Nationale Pétrolière Gabonaise
Petrokemya	Arabian Petroleum Company (Saudi Arabia)
Petroliber	Compania Iberica Refinadora de Petroleos
Petrom	Romanian Oil Corporation
PETRO-MAR	Petroleos del Mar (Peru)
Petromisa	Petrobrás Mineração
PETROMOC	Empresa Nacional de Petroleos de Moçambique
PETRONAS	Petroleum Nasional (Malaysia)
PETRONIC	Empresa Nicaragüense del Petroleo (Nicaragua)
PETROPAR	Petróleos Paraguayos (Paraguay)
PETROPAR	Société de Participations Pétrolières (Mauritania)
PETROSEN	Société Nationale des Pétroles du Sénégal
Petroven	Petróleos de Venezuela = PDVSA
PETS	Pre-Eclamptic Toxaemia Society
PEU	Public Enterprise Unit (Swaziland)
PEVENCA	Pegamentos Venezolanos, C.A.
PEWEX	Przedsiębiorstwo Exportu Wewnętrznego
PF	Pagan Federation
PF	Patriotic Front (Zimbabwe)
PF	People First (Éire)
PF	Police Federation
PF	Polisario Front (Morocco)
PF	Polyteknisk Forening (Denmark)
PF & FS	Prisoners Families and Friends Service
PF-PNU	Party of Freedom – Party of National Unity (Slovakia) = SS-SNJ
PFA	Popular Flying Assocation
PFA	Popular Front of Azerbaijan
PFA	Power Fastenings Assocation
PFA	Pre-packed Flour Association (FDF)
PFA	Press Foundation of Asia (Philippines)
PFA	Professional Footballers' Association
PFA	Provincial Farmers Association (Taiwan)
PFA	Provincial Forestry Administration (Taiwan)
PFB	Provincial Food Bureau (Taiwan)
PFBA	Pila Federation of Barrio Associations (Philippines)
PFBC	Polled Friesian Breeders Club
PFBCA	Pennsylvania Farm Bureau Cooperative Association (U.S.A.)
PFCD	Christian Democratic Popular Front (Moldova)

PFCRN	Partido del Frente Cardenista de Reconstruccion Nacional (Mexico)	**PFSS**	Pet Fostering Service Scotland
PFCSz	Phralipe = PIGA (Testvériség) Független Cigány Szervezet (Hungary)	**PFTPM**	Promotion Fund of the Turkish Prime Ministry
PFE	Platform 'Fortress Europe'	**PFTTC**	Promotion Fund of the Turkiye Tunus Cad
PFE	Progetto Finalizzato Energetica (Italy)	**PFU**	Partie Feministe Unifié (Belgium)
PFEL	Pacific Far East Line (U.S.A.)	**PFZ**	Państwowy Fundusz Ziemi
PFF	Precast Flooring Federation	**PGA**	Parliamentarians Global Action
PFG	Polyteknisk Flyvegruppe (Denmark)	**PGA**	Power Generation Association
PFI	Papirindustriens Forskningsinstitutt	**PGA**	Prison Governors' Association
PFI	Polio Fellowship of Ireland	**PGA**	Professional Golfers Association
PFI	Prison Fellowship International (U.S.A.) = CCI	**PGA-NOC**	Permanent General Assembly of National Olympic Committees
PFL	Pacific Forum Line (SPF) (New Zealand)	**PGAH**	Pineapple Growers Association of Hawaii
PFL	Partido da Frente Liberal (Brazil)	**PGC**	Patent Glazing Conference
PFLC-GC	Popular Front for the Liberation of Palestine – General Command	**PGC**	Programa Grande Carajás (Brazil)
PFLO	Popular Front for the Liberation of Oman	**PGCA**	Patent Glazing Contractors Association
PFLP	Popular Front for the Liberation of Palestine	**PGEC**	Pharmaceutical Group of the European Community = GPCE
PFLP-GC	Popular Front for the Liberation of Palestine General Command	**PGG**	Professional Gardeners Guild
PFLT	People's Front of Liberation Tigers (Sri Lanka)	**PGI**	Institutet för Fiber- och Polymerteknologi (Sweden)
PFM	Political Freedom Movement	**PGI**	Plast- och Gummitekniska Institutet (Sweden)
PFMA	Pet Food Manufacturers Association	**PGI**	Pyrotechnics Guild International (U.S.A.)
PFMA	Phenolic Foam Manufacturers Association	**PGL**	Papirgrossistenes Landsforening
PFMA	Pressed Felt Manufacturers Association	**PGP**	Parti Gabonais du Progrès
PFMAI	Pet Food Manufacturers' Association of Ireland	**PGP**	Party for People's Government
PFN	Partido Frente Nacional (Costa Rica)	**PGPI**	Protein Grain Products International (U.S.A.)
PFN	Polski Front Narodowy	**PGR**	Państwowe Gospodarstwo Rolne
PFNP	Partido Federalista Nacionalista Popular (Panama)	**PGR**	Procuraduria General de la Republica (Mexico)
PFP	Partnership for Peace	**PGRC**	Plant Genetic Resource Centre
PFP	Progressive Federal Party (South Africa)	**PGRO**	Processors and Growers Research Organisation
PFPA	Pitch Fibre Pipe Association of Great Britain	**PGS**	Paget Gorman Society
PFPB	Panhellenic Federation of Publishers and Booksellers	**PGS**	Pressed Glassmakers Society of Great Britain
PFPUT	Pension Fund Property Unit Trust	**PGST**	Porozumienie Górnośląskich Stowarzyszeń i Towarzystw (Poland) = AUSSA
PFRA	Prairie Farm Rehabilitation Administration (Canada)	**PGT**	Partido Guatemalteco del Trabajo (Guatemala)
PFS	Palmerston Forts Society	**PGTV**	Pécsi Geodéziai és Térképészeti Vállalat
PFSF	Parents for Safe Food	**PGUM**	Polska Grupa Unii Międzyparlamentarnej

PH	Pueblos Hermanos
PHA	Pacific History Association (Australia)
PHA	Promotional Handling Association
PHA	Public Health Alliance
PHA	Public Health Association of Australia
PHA	Pullet Hatcheries Association
PHAB	Physically Handicapped and Able Bodied
PHAC	Patronato Hispano-Argentino de Cultura
PHAGRO	Bundesverband des Pharmazeutischen Grosshandels
PHARE	Assistance for Economic Restructuring in the Countries of Central and Eastern Europe (Belgium)
PHARE	Poland / Hungary Assistance for Restructuring Economies
PHARMA-CON	Stichting Pharmaceutische Kleinhandelsconventie
PHARMA-GABON	Société Pharmaceutique Gabonaise
PHARMA-MEGO	Federatie van Verenigingen van Groothandelaren in Pharmaceutische en Medische Artikelen
PHARMA-RIN	Office National de Pharmacie (Mauritania)
PHB	Owners of Historic Country Estates (Netherlands)
PHBGB	Poll Hereford Breeders of Great Britain
PHC	Pet Health Council
PHC	Public Health Committee
PHCA	Pig Health Control Association
PHCA	Private Hire Car Association
PHCA	Projeto Hidrologia e Climatologia da Amazonia (Brazil)
PHCI	Société Plantation et Huileries de Côte-d'Ivoire
PHDCCI	Punjab, Haryana and Delhi Chamber of Commerce and Industry
PHEU	Public Health Employees' Union (Afghanistan)
PHEWA	Presbyterian Health, Education and Welfare Association
PhGW	Photographische Gesellschaft in Wien
PHI	Conseil Intergouvernemental du Programme Hydrologique International (UNESCO) = IHP
PHILASAG	Philippine Association of Agriculturists
PHILCEM-COR	Philippine Cement Corporation
PHILCO-MAN	Philippines Council of Management
PHILCOA	Philippine Coconut Administration
PHILCUSA	Philippine Council for U.S. Aid
PHILNA-BANK	Philippine National Bank
PHILPRO	Philippine Committee on Trade Facilitation
PHILSA	Philippine Standards Association
PHILSUGIN	Philippine Sugar Institute
PHIVOLCS	Philippine Institute of Volcanology and Seismology
PHJC	Poor Handmaids of Jesus Christ
PHLS	Public Health Laboratory Service
PHLSB	Public Health Laboratory Service Board
PHOSBOU-CRAA	Phosphates de Boucraa (Morocco)
PHPA	Perlindungan Hutan dan Pelestrian Alam (Directorate General of Forest Protection and Nature Conservation, Ministry of Forestry) (Indonesia)
PHRG	Park Home Residents Guild
PHRG	Parliamentary Human Rights Group
PHRI	Port and Harbour Research Institute (Japan)
PHRI	Public Health Research Institute (U.S.A.)
PHS	Personhistoriska Samfundet
PhS	Philosophical Society of England
PHS	Plastics Historical Society
PHS	Police History Society
PHS	Postal History Society
PHS	Presbyterian Historical Society
PHS	Printing History Society
PHSA	Provincial Hospital Services Association
PHSI	Presbyterian Historical Society of Ireland
PHYTO-PHAR	Association Belge de l'Industrie des Produits Phytosanitaires
PI	Division of Plant Industry (CSIRO)
PI	Parents Initiative
PI	Performers and Artists for Nuclear Disarmament International = PAND International
PI	Population Institute (U.S.A.)
PI	Privacy International = WOPP
PIA	Pacific Islands Association (FSP)
PIA	Packaged Ice Association (U.S.A.)
PIA	Pakistan International Airlines
PIA	Partitioning Industry Association

PIA	Personal Investment Authority	**PICAGB**	Police Insignia Collectors Association of Great Britain
PIA	Photographic Importers Association	**PICC**	Paris International Conference on Cambodia
PIA	Pilots International Association		
PIA	Plastics Industries Association (Éire)	**PICC**	People's Insurance Company of China
PIA	Plastics Institute of America	**PICC**	Philippine International Convention Centre
PIA	Plastics Institute of Australia		
PIA	Printing Industries of America	**PICC**	Portuguese-Irish Chamber of Commerce
PIA	Program Implementation Agency (Philippines)	**PICC**	Provisional International Computation Centre
PIAC	Petroleum Industry Advisory Council	**PICEA**	Private Information Centre on Eastern Arabia (Belgium)
PIACC	Pacific Islands Association of Chambers of Commerce	**PICES**	North Pacific Marine Science Organization
PIACT	Program for the Introduction and Adaptation of Contraceptive Technology	**PICG**	Programme International de Corrélation Géologique = IGCP
PIACT	Programme International pour l'Amelioration des Conditions du milieu de Travail (OIT)	**PICIC**	Pakistan Industrial Credit and Investment Corporation
PIANC	Permanent International Association of Navigation Congresses = AIPCN, ISVSK	**PICMME**	Provisional Intergovernmental Committee for the Movement of Migrants from Europe = CIPMMG
PIAP	Przemystowy Instytut Automatyki i Pomiarów (Poland)	**PICO**	Partido Independiente de la Clase Obrera (Panama)
PIARC	Permanent International Association of Road Congresses = AIPCC, AIPCR	**PICOP**	Paper Industries Corporation of the Philippines
PIAWA	Printing Industry and Allied Workers' Union (Guyana)	**PICPA**	Philippine Institute of Certified Public Accountants
PIB	Petroleum Information Bureau	**PICUTPC**	Permanent and International Committee of Underground Town Planning and Construction
PIB	Piers Information Bureau		
PIBA	Pacific Islands Broadcasting Association (Vanuatu)	**PICV**	Permanent International Commission of Viticulture
PIC	Pacific Information Centre (USP) (Fiji) = IPS	**PID**	Democratic Left Party (Ecuador)
PIC	Petrochemical Industries Company (Kuwait)	**PID**	Panafrican Institute for Development, Geneva
PIC	Petroleum Industry Corporation (Burma)	**PID**	Partido Independiente Democrático (El Salvador)
PIC	Phosphate Investigation Commission (Nauru)	**PID**	Partido Institucional Democrático (Guatemala)
PIC	Population Investigation Committee	**PIDC**	Pakistan Industrial Development Corporation
PIC	Poultry Industry Conference		
PICA	Palestine Israelite Colonization Association (U.S.A.)	**PIDC**	Plano Integrado de Desenvolvimento Comunitário (Brazil)
PICA	Plastic Industrial Containers Association	**PIDC**	Precision Instrument Development Centre (Taiwan)
PICA	Police Insignia Collectors Association of Great Britain	**PIDC**	Programme International pour le Développement de la Communication; Programa Internacional para el Desarrollo de la Comunicacion (UNESCO) = IPDC
PICA	Private Investment Company for Asia (U.S.A.)		
PICAA	Permanent International Committee of Agricultural Associations	**PIDE**	Pakistan Institute of Development Economics

PIDP	Pacific Islands Development Program (EWC) (U.S.A.)	**PIMC**	Pineapple Industry Marketing Corporation (Malaysia)
PIDR	Programa Interamericano para el Desarrollo Rural (Costa Rica)	**PIME**	Pontificium Institutum pro Missionibus Exteris
PIDSA	Population Information and Documentation System for Africa (Ghana)	**PIME**	Promotora Internacional de Mercadeo Editorial (Colombia)
PIE	Paedophile Information Exchange	**PIMEC**	Programa Interamericano para Mejorar la Enseñanza de las Ciencias (OEA)
PIF	Philippine International Forum	**PIMES**	Programa Integrado de Mestrado em Economia e Sociologia (Brazil)
PIFA	Packaging and Industrial Films Association	**PIMOT**	Przemsłowy Instytut Motoryzacji
PIFC	Pakistan Industrial Finance Corporation	**PIMRIS**	Pacific Islands Marine Resources Information System (FFA, SOPAC, SPC, USP)
PIG	Państwowy Instytut Geologiczny		
PIG	Pipeline Industries Guild	**PIMS**	Pontifical Institute of Mediaeval Studies (Canada)
PIGA	"Phralipe " = PFCSz (Brotherhood) Independent Gypsy Association (Hungary)	**PIMS**	Pontificio Istituto di Musica Sacra
		PIN	Plano de Integração Nacional (Brazil)
PIGH	Pan-American Institute of Geography and History (OAS) = IPGH, PAIGH	**PIN RAS**	Palaeontological Institute of the Russian Academy of Sciences
PIH	Państwowa Inspekcja Handlowa	**PINA**	Pacific Islands News Association (Tonga)
PIH	Paintings in Hospitals		
PIH	Pan American Institute of Highways	**PINA**	Programa Integrado de Nutrición Aplicada (Colombia)
PIHM	Państwowy Instytut Hydrologiczno – Meteorologiczny	**PINAPA**	Panel on Interactions between the Neutral and Ionized Part of the Ionosphere
PIHZ	Polska Izba Handlu Zagranicznego		
PII	Indonesian Engineering Association	**PINGW**	Państwowy Instytut Naukowy Gospodarstwa Wiejskiego
PII	Programme Intergouvernemental d'Informatique (UNESCO) = IIP	**PINSER**	Les Petites Industries Sénégalaises Réunies
PIIA	Pakistan Institute of Industrial Accountants	**PINSTECH**	Pakistan Institute of Nuclear Science and Technology
PIIP	Programa Interamericano de Información Popular (Costa Rica)	**PINTEC**	Plastics Institute National Technical Conference
PIJP	Plastics Institute of Jilin Province	**PINU**	Partido de Innovación y Unidad (Honduras)
PIJR	Programa Interamericano para la Juventud Rural (Costa Rica)	**PINZ**	Plastics Institute of New Zealand
PIL	Pest Infestation Laboratory	**PIO**	Patronato de Igualdad de Oportunidades
PIL	Policia de Investigação Criminal (Mozambique)	**PIOS**	Państwowa Inspekcja Ochrony Środowiska
PILCAM	Société Camérounaise de Fabrication de Piles Électriques	**PIOSA**	Pan-Indian Ocean Science Association
PILOT	Panel on Instrumentation for Large Optical Telescopes	**PIP**	Packaging Institute of the Philippines
		PIP	Partido Independiente de Puerto Rico
PILS	Pacific Information and Library Services (Hawaii)	**PIP**	Policía de Investigaciones del Perú
PIM	Parti Integriste Musulman (Niger)	**PIP**	Progressive Independent Party (South Africa)
PIM	Plan Indicatif Mondial pour le Développement Agricole (FAO) = IWP	**PIP-PNR**	Polish Independence Party-Party of the New Right = PPN-PNP
PIMAG	Pharmaceutical Industry Medical Advisers Group (South Africa)		
PIMB	Przemyslowy Instytut Maszyn Budowlanych (Poland)	**PIPA**	Pacific Industrial Property Association

PIPPA	Pacific Islands Planned Parenthood Affiliation (Samoa)	**PIT**	Plano Intersindical de Trabajadores (Uruguay)
PIPS	Programme pour l'Échange International d'Informations sur les Politiques Scientifiques et Technologiques = SPINES	**PIT**	Punkt Informacji Turystyczrystycznej (Uruguay)
		PIT-CNT	Plenario Intersindical de Trabajadores – Convención Nacional de Trabajadores
PIR	Public Information Research (U.S.A.)	**PIT-PAT**	Pituitary Foundation
PIRA	Paper and Board, Printing and Packaging Industries Research Association	**PITA**	Pacific International Trapshooting Association (U.S.A.)
PIRA	Paper Industry Research Association (International)	**PITAC**	Pakistan Industrial and Technical Assistance Centre
PIRA	Provisional IRA	**PITB**	Petroleum Industry Training Board
PIRC	Pensions Investment Research Consultants	**PITC**	Philippine International Trading Corporation
PIRE	Pacific Institute for Research and Evaluation (U.S.A.)	**PIW**	Państwowy Instytut Wydawniczy
PIRI	Paint Industries Research Institute (South Africa)	**PIWR**	Państwowy Instytut Wydawnictw Rolniczych
PIRI	Paper Industrial Research Institute (China)	**PIZO**	Société Nationale de Distribution des Produits Pétroliers (Gabon)
PIRIMLI	Paper Industrial Research Institute (China)	**PJ**	Partido Justicialista (Argentina)
PIRINC	Petroleum Industry Research Foundation (U.S.A.)	**PJA**	Pakistan Jute Association
		PJA	Pipe Jacking Association
PIRM	Pacific Institute of Resource Management (New Zealand)	**PJG**	Het Psychiatrisch-Juridisch Gezelschap
PIRRCOM	Project for the Intensification of Regional Research on Cotton, Oilseeds and Millets (India)	**PJGN**	Plattelands Jongeren Gemeenschap Nederland
		PJMA	Pakistan Jute Mills Association
PIRSA	Psychological Institute of the Republic of South Africa	**PJPA**	Peasants' Justice Party of Afghanistan
PIS	Państwowa Inspekcja Sanitarna	**PJU**	Pan-American Judo Union
PISAI	Pontificio Istituto di Studi Arabi e d'Islamistica = IPEA	**PK**	Conservative Party (Poland)
		PKD	Partiia Konstitsionnykh Rossii
PISC	Philippines Internal Shipping Corporation	**PKD**	Polityczny Komitet Doradczy
		PKE	Polski Klub Ekologicany
PISC	Programme International sur la Sécurité des Substances Chimiques (OMS) = IPCS	**PKF**	Polska Kronika Filmowa
		PKG	Polski Komitet Geotechniki
		PKI	Partai Komunis Indonesia
PISC	Project for Inspection of Steel Components (EU)	**PKIU**	Printing and Kindred Industries Union (Australia)
PISM	Polski Instytut Spraw Międzynarodwych	**PKK**	Kurdish Workers Party
		PKK	Pohjoiskalotti-komiteta = NKK
PISPESCA	Asociación Colombiana de Piscicultura y Pesca	**PKK**	Prezydium Komisji Krajowej
		PKL	Państwowa Komisja Lokalowa
PIST	Państwowy Instytut Sztuki Teatralnej	**PKL**	Plast-och Kemikalieleverantörers Förening
PISUKI	Pacific Islands Society of the United Kingdom and Ireland	**PKL**	Polski Klub Literacki (PEN)
		PKLD	Parlamentarny Klub Lewicy Demokratycznej
PIT	Parque Indígena Tumucumaque (Brazil)	**PKMS**	Pertubohan Kebangsaan Melayu Singapura
PIT	Parti de l'Indépendance et du Travail (Senegal)	**PKN**	Polski Komitet Normalizacyji Miar i Jakosu

PKN	Polski Komitet Normalizacyjny	**PLAN**	People's Liberation Army of Namibia
PKO	Powszechna Kasa Oszczędności	**PLAN-ACRE**	Plano Integrado de Desenvolvimento do Estado do Acre (Brazil)
PKOL	Polski Komitet Olimpijski		
PKOSA	Polska Kasa Opieki Spółka Akcyjna	**PLANA-SEM**	Plano Nacional de Sementes (Brazil)
PKOZRiN	Polski Komitet Obrony Zycia, Rodziny i Narodu	**PLANATES**	Plano Nacional de Assisténcia Técnica a Suinicultura (Brazil)
PKP	Partito Kommunista ng Pilipinas	**PLANAVE**	Plano Nacional de Avicultura (Brazil)
PKP	Polskie Koleje Państwowe	**PLANER**	Plano Nacional de Extensão Rural (Brazil)
PKPS	Polski Komitet Pommogcy Społecznej		
PKR	Partiia Kommunistov Rossii	**PLANICYT**	Plan Nacional de Investigación Cientifica y Desarrollo Tecnologico
PKS	Państwowa Komunikacja Samochodowa	**PLANO**	Planejamento e Assesoria Limitada (Brazil)
PKS	Partia Kommuniste Shqiptare = ACP		
PKTF	Printing and Kindred Trades Federation	**PLANSA-BAR**	Plan de Saneamiento Basico Rural (El Salvador)
PKV	Verband der Privaten Krankenversicherung	**PLANTE-CAM**	Plantes du Caméroun
PKW	Państwowa Komisja Wyborcza	**PLANTI**	ASEAN Plant Quarantine Centre and Training Institute (Malaysia)
PKWN	Polski Komitet Wyzwolenia Narodowego		
PL	Parlamento Latino-Americano (Peru)	**PLASA**	Professional Lighting & Sound Association
PL	Partido Liberal (Brazil, Colombia, Honduras, Spain)	**PLASCO**	Latin American School of Social Sciences (Chile)
PL	Partido Liberal (Brazil, Paraguay, Peru, Spain)	**PLASMALI**	Société Malienne d'Exploitation de Matières Plastiques
PL	Progressive League	**PLAST-EUROFILM**	Fédération Européene des Producteurs de Films Plastiques
PL-1993	Liberal Party 1993 (Romania)		
PLA	Pakistan Library Association	**PLAST-EUROPAC**	Association Européenne des Fabricants d'Emballages Plastiques
PLA	Para Legal Association		
PLA	Partido Laborista Agrario (Panama)	**PLAST-EUROTEC**	Groupement Européen des Fabricants de Pièces Techniques Plastiques
PLA	Partido Liberal Auténtico (Panama)		
PLA	People's Liberation Army (China)	**PLAST-AFRIC**	Société Africaine de Transformation de Matières Plastiques (Burkina Faso)
PLA	Philippine Library Association		
PLA	Popular Liberation Army (Lebanon)	**PLASTI-LAGO**	Plasticos del Lago, C.A. (Venezuela)
PLA	Port of London Authority		
PLA	Private Libraries Association	**PLASTI-NIC**	Plásticos de Nicaragua
PLACART	Programa Latinoamericano de Comercializacion de Artesanias (Venezuela)		
		PLAT-FORM	Rail Users' Alliance
PLA-CONGO	Société des Placages du Congo	**PLB**	Pasaulio lietuviu bendruomene = WLC
		PLC	Partido Liberal Constitucionalista (Nicaragua)
PLADES	Sociedad Chilena de Planificacion y Desarrollo (Chile)		
		PLC	Plague Locust Commission
PLAFAM	Sociedad de Planificacion Familiar (Venezuela)	**PLCAA**	Professional Lawn Care Association of America
PLAL	Pro-Life Action League (U.S.A.)		
PLAMABO	Bond van Groothandelaren in Plaatmateriaal	**PLCAI**	Pipe Line Contractors Association International (U.S.A.)
PLAN	Foster Parents Plan International (U.S.A.)	**PLCW&TWU**	Power Loom Carpet Weavers and Textile Workers Union
PLAN	Partido Laboral Andino (Colombia)		

PLD	Free Democratic Party (Romania)	**PLRA**	Patrono de Leprosos de la Republica Argentina
PLD	Partido de la Liberación Dominicana (Dominican Reublic)	**PLRA**	Photo-Litho Reproducers Association
PLDR	Freedom and Romanian Democracy Party	**PLS**	Free Change Party (Romania)
		PLS	Parliamentary Liaison Services
PLDT	Philippine Long Distance Telephone Company	**PLS**	Partia Liberale Shqiptare = ALP
		PLS	Publishers Licensing Society
PLEMUU	Fundacion Plenario de Mujeres del Uruguay	**PLS-W**	Polish Peasant Party – Wilanow
		PLSA	Pacific Law and Society Association (U.S.A.)
PLF	Palestine Liberation Front		
PLF-UO	Peoples Liberation Front – Unified Organisation (Eritrea)	**PLSC**	Pakistan Labour Solidarity Committee
		PLT	Polskie Towarzystwo Lesne
PLH	Partido Liberal de Honduras	**PLTR**	Polskie Lekarskie Towarzystwo Radiologiczne
PLI	Partido Liberal Independiente (Nicaragua)		
		PLU	Partido Liberal Unificado (Paraguay)
PLI	Partito Liberale Italiano	**PLUNA**	Primeras Lineas Uruguayas de Navegación Aérea
PLIPDECO	Point Lisas Industrial Port Development Corporation		
		PLUS	Pharmaceutical Licences under Siege
PLL LOT	Polskie Linie Lotnicze LOT	**PLUS**	Prima Leben und Sparen
PLM	Association Internationale pour la Recherche en Pédagogie de la Langue Maternelle = MTE	**PLUS**	World Latvian Businessmen's Association
		PLUVA	Stichting voor Onderzoek van Pluimvee en Varkens
PLM	Peoples Liberation Movement (Montserrat)		
		PLWA	People Living With AIDS (Canada)
PLM	Progressive Labour Movement (Antigua)	**PM**	Policía Militar
		PM	Sisters of the Presentation of Mary
PLMR	Liberal Monarchist Party of Romania	**PM&C**	Department of Prime Minister and Cabinet (Australia)
PLN	Partido de Liberación Nacional (Costa Rica, El Salvador)		
		PM&O	Philippines, Micronesia and Orient Navigation Company (U.S.A.)
PLN	Partido Liberal Nacional (Panama)		
PLO	Palestine Liberation Organization = OLP	**PMA**	Mobile Military Police (Guatemala)
		PMA	Pacific Maritime Association
PLO	Polskie Linie Oceaniczne	**PMA**	Pakistan Medical Association
PLOPCziN	Polska Liga Obrony Praw Człowieka i Narodu	**PMA**	Pan-American Medical Women's Alliance
		PMA	Panhellenic Medical Association
PLOTE	Peoples Liberation Organisation of Tamil Eelam (Sri Lanka)	**PMA**	Personal Managers Association
		PMA	Pharmaceutical Manufacturers Association (U.S.A.)
PLP	Parliamentary Labour Party		
PLP	Parti Libéral Progressiste (Morocco)	**PMA**	Philippine Medical Association
PLP	Parti pour la Libération du Peuple (Senegal)	**PMA**	Polystyrene Moulders' Association (Éire)
PLP	Parti pour la Liberté et le Progrès (Belgium)	**PMA**	Programa Mundial de Alimentos = PAM, WFP
PLP	Progressive Labour Party (Bahamas, Bermuda, St. Lucia)	**PMA**	Property Managers Association
PLPCz	Polska Liga Praw Człowieka	**PMA Intl**	Photo Marketing Association International Ltd (ex APL)
PLR	Free Republican Party (Romania)		
PLR	Partido Liberal Radical (Ecuador, Paraguay)	**PMAA**	Promotion Marketing Association of America
PLRA	Partido Liberal Radical Auténtico (Paraguay) = ARLP		

PMAC	Pharmaceutical Manufacturers Association of Canada
PMAC	Provisional Military Administrative Council (Ethiopia)
PMAC	Purchasing Managers Association of Canada
PMACI	Projeto de Proteção ao Meio Ambiente e às Comunidades Indígenas (Brazil)
PMAESA	Port Management Association of Eastern and Southern Africa
PMAGB	Paint Makers Association of Great Britain (*now* BCF)
PMATA	Paint Manufacturers and Allied Trades Association
PMATA	Paper Makers Allied Trades Association
PMAWCA	Port Management Association of West and Central Africa
PMB	Pigs Marketing Board (Northern Ireland)
PMB	Popular Movement of Belarus
PMB	Potato Marketing Board
PMB	Print Measurement Bureau (Canada)
PMBC	Phuket Marine Biological Centre (Thailand)
PMC	Centre of Photographic Material (China)
PMC	Petites Missionnaires de la Charité = PSMdC
PMC	Philatelic Music Circle
PMC	Planning Ministers Council
PMC	Pomorski Meteoroloski Centar
PMC	Printmakers Council
PMDA	Pianoforte Manufacturers and Distributors Association
PMDA	Plastics Machinery Distributors Association
PMDB	Partido do Movimento Democrático Brasileiro
PMDC	Pakistan Minerals Development Corporation
PME	International Group for the Psychology of Mathematics Education
PME	Petites et Moyennes Entreprises
PME	Societas Pro Missionibus Exteris Provincias Québecensis (Canada)
PMEG	Perforated Metal Export Group
PMFC	Pacific Marine Fisheries Commission
PMH	Pari Mutuel sur les Hippodromes
PMH	Polska Marynarka Handlowa
PMI	Pensions Management Institute
PMIC	Programa Mundial de Investigaciones Climáticas (ICSU, WMO) = PMRC, WCRP
PML	Pakistan Muslim League
PML	Plymouth Marine Laboratory
PMLA	Production Music Librarians Association (U.S.A.)
PMLN	Partido Marxista-Leninista de Nicaragua
PMMA	Polymethylmethacrylate Producers' Association
PMMC	Precious Minerals Marketing Company (Sierra Leone)
PMMMA	Pattern, Model, & Mould Manufacturers Association (*ex* NSMP)
PMMS	Plainsong and Mediaeval Music Society (U.K., U.S.A.)
PMN	Partido de Mobilização Nacional (Brazil)
PMN	Pohjoismaiden Ministerineuvosto = NMR
PMR	Partido Mariateguista Revolucionario (Peru)
PMRC	Pakistan Medical Research Council
PMRC	Pohjoismaiden Ministerineuvosto = NMR
PMRC	Programme Mondial de Recherches sur le Climat (ICSU, WMO) = PMIC, WCRP
PMRI	Porous Media Research Institute (Canada)
PMSD	Parti Mauricien Social Démocrate
PMT	Partido Mexicano de los Trabajadores
PMU	Pari Mutuel Urbain
PMU	Pontifical Missionary Union
PMV	Pro Mundi Vita (Belgium)
PMW	Polska Marynarka Wojenna
PMWA	Philippine Medical Women's Association
PN	Partido Nacional (Honduras, Uruguay)
PN	Partit Nazzjonalista (Malta)
PN	Patrimonio Nacional
PN	Pohjoismaiden Neuvosts = NC, NR
PN	Produktivitetsnämnden
PN-2	National Police Intelligence Department (Guatemala)
PNA	Agrarian National Party (Romania)
PNA	Pakistan National Alliance
PNA	Palestine National Alliance

PNA	Palestine National Authority	**PNG**	Partido Nacionalista Gallego
PNA	Parti National Algérien	**PNGBC**	Papua New Guinea Banking Corporation
PNA	Polish Nobility Association		
PNAC	Place Names Advisory Committee (Wales)	**PNGDF**	Papua New Guinea Defence Force
		PNGTUC	Papua New Guinea Trade Union Congress
PNAD	Pesquisa Nacional por Amuestra Domiciliar (Brazil)		
		PNI	Indonesian Nationalist Party
PNAI	Provincial Newspapers Association of Ireland	**PNIC**	Pleasure Navigation International Joint Committee = CINP
PNB	Partido ng Bayan (Philippines)	**PNITC**	Pacific Northwest International Trade Council (U.S.A.)
PNB	Philippine National Bank		
PNBMS	Pacific Northwest Bird and Mammal Society (U.S.A.)	**PNL**	National Liberal Party (Moldova, Romania)
PNC	Palestine National Council	**PNL**	National Liberation Party (Costa Rica)
PNC	Parti National Caledonien	**PNL-CD**	National Liberal Party – Democratic Convention (Romania)
PNC	Partido Nacional Cristiano (Colombia)		
PNC	Peoples National Congress (Guyana)	**PNLA**	Palestine National Liberation Army
PNC-PNP	Polish National Commonwealth – Polish National Party = PWN-PSN	**PNLM**	Palestine National Liberation Movement
PNCA	Programa Nacional de Capacitación Agropecuária (Colombia)	**PNM**	People's National Movement (Trinidad and Tobago)
PND	Parti National Démocrate (Morocco)	**PNOC**	Philippine National Oil Company
PNDB	Brunei National Democratic Party	**PNP**	National Progressist Party (Romania)
PNDC	Christian Democratic National Party (Romania)	**PNP**	Partido Nacionalista Popular (Panama)
		PNP	Partido Nashonal di Pueblo (Netherlands Antilles)
PNDC	Partido Nacional de Democracia Centrista (Chile)		
PNDC	Programa Nacional de Desarrollo de la Comunidad (Guatemala)	**PNP**	Partido Nuevo Progresista (Puerto Rico)
		PNP	People's National Party (Jamaica)
PNDC	Provisional National Defence Council (Ghana)	**PNP**	Pro Niños Pobres (Luxembourg)
		PNP	Progressieve Nationale Partij (Suriname)
PNDD	National Democratic Party of Romania for Justice		
		PNP	Progressive National Party (Turks and Caicos Islands)
PNE	Party of National Equality (Montenegro) = SNJ		
		PNPF	"Pamiat" – Pravoslavnyi Natsionalnyi Patioticheskii Front
PNEA	Programma Nazionale di Ricerche in Antartide (Italy)	**PAMIAT**	
		PNPG	Parti National Populaire Guyanais (French Guiana)
PNEM	Partido Nacionalista Español de Melilla		
PNEU	Parents National Education Union	**PNR**	National Reunification Party (Romania)
PNEUROP	European Committee of Manufacturers of Compressors, Vacuum Pumps and Pneumatic Tools	**PNR**	National Royalist Party (Romania)
		PNR	Partido Nacionalista Renovador (Guatemala)
PNF	Palestine National Fund		
PNF	Parti Nationaliste Français	**PNR**	Partido Nacionalista Revolucionario (Ecuador)
PNF	Polish National Front = NFP		
PNFI	Petawawa National Forestry Institute (Canada)	**PNR**	Partij Nationalistische Republiek (Suriname)
		PNR	Romanian National Party
PNFS	Peak & Northern Footpaths Society	**PNRC**	New Christian Romanian Party
PNG	Papua New Guinea	**PNRC**	Partidul Noua Românîe Creştină (Romania) = NCRP

PNS	National Christian Party (Moldova)		**POCI**	Pontiac-Oakland Club International (U.S.A.)
PNSC	Pakistan National Shipping Corporation		**POCO**	Political Cooperation = CPE, EPC, EPS, EPZ
PNSD	Parti National pour la Solidarité et le Développement (Algeria)		**POCR**	Congregatio Piorum Operariorium Catechistarum Ruralium
PNSD	Plan Nacional sobre Drogas		**POE**	Parti Ouvrier Européen; Partito Operaio Europeo
PNSF	Palestine National Salvation Front			
PNSS	Philippine National Science Society		**POED**	Pancypria Organosi Ellinon Daskalon (Cyprus)
PNT	National Peasants' Party (Romania)			
PNT	Partido Nacionalista de los Trabajadores (Argentina)		**POED**	Post Office Engineering Department
			POEU	Post Office Engineering Union
PNTA	Pakistan National Tuberculosis Association		**PofB**	Ponies of Britain
			POG	Public Officers Group (Northern Ireland)
PNU	Party of National Unity (Albania)		**POGO**	Polar Orbiting Geophysical Observatory (U.S.A.)
PNU	Peasants' National Unity (Afghanistan) = BMI			
			POH	Polska Organizacja Harcerska
PNUC	Provisional National Unity Council (Romania)		**POKE**	Panellinios Organosis Kinimatografikon Epicheirision
PNUD	Programa de las Naciones Unidas para el Desarrollo; Programme des Nations Unies pour le Développement = UNDP		**POLAC**	Pre-investment Organization for Latin America and the Caribbean = OPALC
PNUE	Programme des Nations Unies pour l'Environnement = UNEP		**POLI-SARIO**	Frente Popular para el Liberación de Saguia El Hamra y Rio de Oro (Morocco)
PNUE/OIE	PNUE Département Industrie et Environnement = UNEP/IEO		**POLIS**	Network of Cooperation of the European Cities in Advanced Transport Telematics (CEC) (Belgium)
PNUMA	Chilean National Union for the Environment			
PNUMA	Programa de las Naciones Unidas para el Medio Ambiente = UNEP		**POLITE**	Preserve Our Local Independent Traders
			POLOAM-AZÔNIA	Program de Pólos Agropecuários e Agrominerais da Amazônia (Brazil)
PNV	Partido Nacional Vasco			
PNV	Partido Nacional Velasquista (Ecuador)		**POLONOR-OESTE**	Programa Integrado de Desenvolvimento do Noroeste do Brasíl
PNV	Partido Nacionalista Vasco			
PNWPSA	Pacific Northwest Political Science Association		**POM**	Państwowy Ośrodek Maszynowy
			POM	Polska Organizacja Młodziezowa
PNYME	Papir- és Nyomdaipari Müszaki Egyseület		**POMAG**	Société de Grands Magasins de Pointe-Noir (Congo)
PNZh	Profsoiuz Nezavisimykh Zhurnalistov		**POMC**	Parents of Murdered Children
PO	Project ORBIS		**POMO**	Production Oriented Maintenance Organization
POA	Pinball Owners Association			
POA	Prison Officers Association (Éire, U.K.)		**POMOA**	Provisional Office for Mass Organizational Affairs (Ethiopia)
POAAPS	Permanent Organisation for Afro-Asian Peoples Solidarity		**PONA**	Parti Ouvrier Nord-Américain
			POO	Parents Opposed to Opting Out
POAC	International Conference on Port and Ocean Engineering under Arctic Conditions		**POOL**	Ad hoc Group of Experts on Pollution of the Ocean Originating on Land (IOC)
POBL	Parti pour l'Organisation de la Bretagne Libre		**POP**	Partido de Orientación Popular (El Salvador)
POC	Public Oil Company (Sudan)		**POP**	Podstawowa Organizacja Partyjna
POC	Stichting Provinciale Onderzoekcentra		**POPA**	Property Owners Protection Association (U.S.A.)
POCH	Progressiven Organisationen der Schweiz			

POPED	Population Education Clearing House (PROAP) = RCHPE
POPEM	Peace Organisation of the People of Europe and the Mediterranean (Malta)
POPIN	Global Population Information Network
POPIN	UN Population Information Network
POPIN Africa	Population Information Network for Africa (POPIN)
POPIN-FORM	International Population Information Network (UN)
POPLAB	International Program of Laboratories for Population Statistics
POPS	Partners of Prisoners and Families Support Group
POR	Partido Obrero Revolucionario (Bolivia, Spain, Uruguay)
PORAM	Palm Oil Refiners Association of Malaysia
PORI	Public Opinion Research of Israel Ltd
PORIM	Palm Oil Research Institute of Malaysia
PORLA	Palm Oil Registration and Licensing Authority (Malaysia)
PORM-PST	Partido Obrero Revolucionario Marxista – Partido Socialista de los Trabajadores (Peru)
PORTO-BRAS	Empresa dos Portos do Brasil
POSAS	Patent Office Search and Advisory Service
POSL	Parti Ouvrier Socialiste Luxembourgeois = LSAP
POSMAS	Panellinios Osmospondia Somateion Mesiton Astikon Symbaseon
POST	Parliamentary Office of Science and Technology
POTELIN	Post Office Telectronic Institute (South Africa)
POU	Public Officers Union (Belize)
POUC	Post Office Unions Council
POUNC	Post Office Users' National Council
POUS	Partido Opérario de Unidade Socialista (Portugal)
POWAGOD	Prince of Wales Advisory Group on Disability
PP	Papua Party (Papua New Guinea)
PP	Partia Pracy
PP	Partido de los Pobres (Mexico)
PP	Partido Panameñista
PP	Partido Popular (Ceuta, Melilla, Spain)
PP	Phonographic Performance
PP	Poder Popular (Mozambique)
PP	Popular Party (Spain)
PP	Progressive Party (Iceland)
PPA	Pacific Planetarium Association (U.S.A.)
PPA	Pakistan Press Association
PPA	Parti du Peuple Algérien
PPA	Partido Panameñista Auténtico
PPA	Partido Patriótico Arubana (Aruba)
PPA	Partido Peronista Auténtico (Argentina)
PPA	Peat Producers Association of Great Britain and Ireland
PPA	Periodical Publishers Association
PPA	Piano Publicity Association
PPA	Pipe Products Association
PPA	Pipeline Protection Association
PPA	Pool Promoters Association
PPA	Potato Processors Association
PPA	Pre-school Playgroups Association
PPA	Process Plant Association
PPA	Professional Programmers Association (U.S.A.)
PPA	Progressive People's Alliance (Gambia)
PPAB	Programme and Policy Advisory Board (FAO)
PPAG	Planned Parenthood Association of Ghana
PPARC	Particle Physics and Astronomy Research Council
PPASA	Planned Parenthood Association of South Africa
PPASL	Planned Parenthood Association of Sierra Leone
PPAT	Planned Parenthood Association of Thailand
PPAUS	Peat Producers Association of the United States
PPAZ	Planned Parenthood Association of Zambia
PPBB	Parti Pesaka Bumiputera Bersatu (Malaysia)
PPBC	Plant Pathogenic Bacteria Committee
PPBF	Pan-American Pharmaceutical and Biochemical Federation
PPC	Parti Progressiste Congolais
PPC	Partido del Pueblo Costarricense
PPC	Partido Popular Cristiano (Peru)
PPC	People's Party of Crimea
PPCA	Power Plant Contractors Association

PPCA	Productivity Promotion Council of Australia	**PPI**	Professional Photographers of Israel Organization
PPCh	Polska Partia Chłopska	**PPI**	Progressive Policy Institute (U.S.A.)
PPCS	Primary Producers Co-operative Society (New Zealand)	**PPI**	Pulp and Paper International (Belgium)
PPCSEAPR	Plant Protection Committee for the South East Asia and Pacific Region (Thailand)	**PPIA**	American-Indonesian Friendship Association
PPD	Parti Populaire Djiboutien	**PPIAS**	Parent to Parent Information on Adoption Services
PPD	Partido Popular Democrático (Puerto Rico)	**PPIE**	Państwowe Przedsiębiorstwo Imprez Estradowych
PPD	Partido por la Democracia (Chile)	**PPII**	Public Policy Institute of Ireland
PPD	Party for Peace and Democracy (Republic of Korea)	**PPIP**	Philippine Poultry Improvement Plan
PPD	Provinciale Planologische Diensten	**PPIS**	Państwowe Przedsiębiorstwo Imprez Sportowych
PPDA	Produce Prepackaging Development Association	**PPITB**	Plastics Processing Industry Training Board
PPDC	Pig Production Development Committee (Northern Ireland)	**PPK**	Parliamentary Party of Kosovo = PSK
PPDHC	Partido Pro-Derechos Humanas en Cuba	**PPK**	Peasant Party of Kosovo
PPE	Parti Populaire Européen = EPP, EVP	**PPL**	Phonographic Performance Limited
PPEC	Panchayat Polity and Evaluation Committee (Nepal)	**PPLA**	Professional Photographic Laboratories Association
PPECB	Perishable Products Export Control Board (South Africa)	**PPLM**	Partido Progresista Liberal de Melilla
PPEIAC	Print and Printing Equipment Industries Association of China	**PPM**	Parti du Peuple Mauritanien
PPF	Peoples Police Force (Burma)	**PPM**	Parti Progressiste Martiniquais
PPFA	People's Pearl and Fishery Corporation (Burma)	**PPM**	Partido del Pueblo Mexicano
PPFA	Planned Parenthood Federation of America	**PPM**	Partido Popular Monárquico (Portugal)
PPFA	Plastic Pipe and Fittings Association (U.S.A.)	**PPM**	Patronato de Protección de la Mujer
PPFK	Planned Parenthood Federation of Korea	**PPM**	People's Party of Montenegro = NSCG
PPFN	Planned Parenthood Federation of Nigeria	**PPM**	Persatuan Perpustakaan Malaysia = LAM
PPFR	People's Party of Free Russia	**PPM**	Pusat Penelitian Marihat (Indonesia)
PPG	Gaugauz People's Party (Moldova)	**PPMA**	Pakistan Paint Manufacturers Association
PPG	Player Piano Group	**PPMA**	Petrol Pump Manufacturers Association
PPG	Polish Economic Programme (Poland)	**PPMA**	Plastic Pipe Manufacturers Association
PPG	Polska Partia Gospodarcza	**PPMA**	Processing & Packaging Machinery Association (*ex* PEMA)
PPG	Psychophysikalische Gesellschaft	**PPMA**	Produce Packaging and Marketing Association (*now* FPC)
PPGA	British Pot Plant Grower's Association	**PPMC**	People to People Music Committee (U.S.A.)
PPI	Pakistan Press International	**PPMC**	Produce Prepackaging Machinery Company
PPI	Pensioners for Peace International	**PPMF**	Pulp and Paper Manufacturers of Australia
PPI	Pickle Packers International (U.S.A.)	**PPMS**	Plastic Pipe Manufacturers' Society
PPI	Potash and Phosphate Institute (U.S.A.)	**PPN**	Parti Progressiste Nigérien
		PPN-PNP	Polska Partia Niepodległościowa – Partia Nowej Prawciy (Poland) = PIP-PNR

PPNEA	Protection and Preservation of Natural Environment in Albania	**PPSC**	Partido Popular Social Cristiano (El Salvador, Nicaragua)
PPP	Pakistan People's Party	**PPSCA**	Partido Popular Social Cristiano Auténtico (Nicaragua)
PPP	Palestinian People's Party		
PPP	Partai Persatuan Pembangunan (Indonesia)	**PPSEAWA**	Pan Pacific and Southeast Asia Women's Association
PPP	Partido del Pueblo de Panamá	**PPSF**	Palestine Popular Struggle Front
PPP	People's Political Party (St Vincent)	**PPSG**	Protein and Peptide Science Group
PPP	People's Progress Party (Papua New Guinea)	**PPSh**	Partia e Punes e Shqipërisë = AWP
		PPSiNS	Powszechna Partia Słowian i Narodów Sprzymierzonych (Poland) = UPSAN
PPP	People's Progressive Party (Gambia, Guyana, Malaysia)	**PPSML**	Pusat Penelitian Sumberdaya Manusia dan Lingkungan (Indonesia)
PPP	Program Powszechnej Prywatyzacji	**PPSR-D**	Polska Partia Socjalistyczna Rewolucyjno Demokratyczna
PPPB	Pusat Penelitian dan Pengembangan Biologi (Research and Development Center for Biology, LIPI) (Indonesia)		
		PPT	Parti Progressiste Tchadien
PPPEA	Pulp, Paper and Paperboard Export Association (U.S.A.)	**PPT**	Permanent People's Tribunal
		PPT	Pusat Penelitian Kependudukan dan Ketenagakerjaan (Indonesia)
PPPIP	Dhak Patiwat Phaochen Islam Pattani (Thailand)	**PPTiT**	Poczta Polska, Telegraf i Telefon
PPPL	Phak Pasason Pativat Lao	**PPTS**	Państwowe Przedsiębiorstwo "Totalizator Sportowy"
PPPO	Pusat Penelitian dan Pengembangan Oseanologi (Research and Development Center for Oceanology, LIPI) (Indonesia)		
		PPU	Peace Pledge Union
		PPU	Peasants' Party of Ukraine
PPPP	Polish Friends of Beer	**PPU**	People's Party of Ukraine
PPPRF	Pan Pacific Public Relations Federation	**PPUA**	Party of Popular Unity and Accord (Tajikistan)
PPPS	People Press Printing Society		
PPR	Politieke Partij Radikalen	**PPUG**	Professional Plant Users Group
PPR	Press and Public Relations Ltd.	**PPV**	Fachverband der Papier und Pappe Verarbeitenden Industrie (Austria)
PPRC	Pollution Prevention Research Center (U.S.A.)		
		PPWB	Prairie Provinces Water Board (Canada)
PPREC	Pulp and Paper Research and Education Center (U.S.A.)	**PPZ**	Polska Partia Zielonych
		PQ	Parti Quebécois (Canada)
PPRI	Policy Planning and Research Unit (Northern Ireland)	**PQAA**	Province of Quebec Association of Architects (Canada)
PPRIC	Pulp and Paper Research Institute of Canada	**PQD**	Partido Quisqueyano Demócrata (Dominican Republic)
PPS	Paediatric Pathology Society of Europe (Switzerland)	**PQP**	Productos Quimicos Panamericanos S.A. (Colombia)
PPS	Parti du Progrès et du Socialisme (Morocco)	**PQTUM**	Parque do Tumucumaque (Brazil)
PPS	Parti Popular Socialista (Mexico)	**PR**	Parti Républicain (France, Martinique, New Caledonia)
PPS	Partido Popular Salvadoreño	**PR**	Partido Radicale (Chile)
PPS	Peasant Party of Serbia	**PR**	Partido Reformista (Dominican Republic)
PpS	Photographes Professionels Suisses = SBF, FpS		
PPS	Polska Partia Socjalistyczna	**PR**	Partido Republicano (Panama)
PPSA	Pan-Pacific Surgical Association	**PR**	Partido Revolucionario (Guatemala)
PPSA	Point-to-Point Secretaries Association	**PR**	Partito Radicale
		PR	Public Relations Institute of Ireland

PR	Republican Party (Moldova)
PRA	Paint Research Association
PRA	Parti du Régroupement Africain (Burkina Faso)
PRA	Parti du Renouveau Algérien
PRA	Partido Revolucionario Auténtico (Bolivia)
PRA	Personnel Research Association (U.S.A.)
PRA	Petrol Retailers Association
PRA	Policy Research Associates
PRA	Port Rashid Authoity (Dubai)
PRA	Prairie Rail Authority (Canada)
PRA	Pre-Retirement Association of Great Britain and Northern Ireland
PRA	Psoriasis Research Association (U.S.A.)
PRA	Psychiatric Rehabilitation Association
PRAC	Pyrethrum Research Advisory Committee (Kenya)
PRAI	Planning Research and Action Institute (India)
PRAIÉN	Centre de Préparation Pratique aux Applications Industrielles de l'Énergie Nucléaire
PRAM	Practical Alternatives For Mums, Dads and Under-Fives
PRAMOS	Pravoslavnyi Monarkhicheskii Orden-Soiuz
PRAMS	Parent Resource and Mother Support
PRATRA	Philippines Relief and Trade Rehabilitation Administration
PRB	Partido de la Revolución Boliviana
PRB	Partido Republicano Brasileiro
PRB	Population Reference Bureau (U.S.A.)
PRC	Parti Républicain Caledonien
PRC	Parti Révolutionnaire Centrafricain
PRC	Partido Republicano Calderonista (Costa Rica)
PRC	People's Redemption Council (Liberia)
PRC	Peoples Republic of China
PRC	Permanent Representatives Committee of the European Communities = AStV, COREPER
PRC	Population Resource Centre (U.S.A.)
PRC	Postal Rate Commission (U.S.A.)
PRC	Projects Review Committee
PRCA	Public Relations Consultants Association
PRCD	Christian Democratic Revolution Party (Romania)
PRCR	Christian Republican Party of Romania
PRCS	Palestinian Red Crescent Society
PRD	Partido de la Revolucion Democrática (Mexico)
PRD	Partido Reformista Democrático (Melilla, Spain)
PRD	Partido Renovador Democrático (Portugal)
PRD	Partido Revolucionario Democrático (Panama)
PRD	Partido Revolucionario Dominicano
PRD	Polytechnic Research and Development Company (U.S.A.)
PRDM	Parti pour le Rassemblement Démocratique des Mahorais (Mayotte)
PRE	Fédération Européennes des Fabricants de Produits Réfractaires
PRE	Partido Roldosista Ecuatoriano
PRE	Programme de Reconstruction Européenne = ERP
PREAG	Preussen-Elektra AG
PREAL	Programme de Relations Politiques et de Coopération Euro-Amérique Latine
PREALC	Programa Regional del Empleo para América Latina y el Caribe (OIT)
PRECIS	Foreningen Public Relations Konsultforetag i Sverige
PRED	Education Project for Democracy (Chile)
PREDESUR	Programa Regional de Desarrollo del Sur (Ecuador)
PRef	Party of Reform (Moldova)
PRÉFAB-CAME-ROUN	Société de Préfabrication Camérounaise de Maisons Portuaires
PREFED	Programme Régional de Formation et d'Echanges pour le Développement (Rwanda)
PRELUDE	Programme de Recherche et de Liaison Universitaires pour le Développement (Belgium)
Premsoc	Premenstrual Society
PRÉPAL	Société Africaine de Préparations Alimentaires (Caméroun)
PREPS	Program of Research and Evaluation in Public Schools (U.S.A.)
PRESSBOF	Press Standards Board of Finance
PRF	Pain Relief Foundation
PRF	Partido Revolucionario Febrerista (Paraguay)

PRF	Party of Rights and Freedoms (Bulgaria)	**PRISCO**	Price Stabilisation Corporation (Philippines)
PRF	Petroleumhandelns Riksförbund	**PRISME**	Programme International de Soutien à la Maîtrise de l'Énergie (IEPF)
PRFRI	Pearl River Fisheries Research Institute (China)	**PRiTV**	Polskie Radio i Telewizja
PRG	Producer Responsibility Group	**PRIZE**	Program for Research in Information Systems Engineering (U.S.A.)
PRH	Partido Revolucionario Hondureño		
PRI	Partido Revolucionario Independiente (Dominican Republic)	**PRL**	Parti Réformateur Libéral (Belgium)
		PRL	Population Research Laboratory (Canada)
PRI	Partido Revolucionario Institucional (Mexico)	**PRL**	Prairie Research Laboratory Canada
PRI	Partito Repubblicano Italiano	**PRLA**	Puerto Rico Library Association
PRI	Party for Romani Integration (Slovakia) = SRI	**PRM**	Partidul România Mare (Romania) = GRP
PRI	Penal Reform International	**PRM**	Prezydium Rady Ministrów
PRI	Performance Registry International (U.S.A.)	**PRN**	Partido da Renovação Nacional (Brazil)
		PRN	Partido de la Revolución Nacional (Bolivia)
PRI	Petroleum Recovery Institute (Canada)	**PRN**	Proceso de Reorganización Nacional (Argentina)
PRI	Plastics and Rubber Institute		
PRI	Prévention Routière Internationale	**PRNU**	Party of Romanian National Unity = PUNR
PRI	Public Radio International (U.S.A.)		
PRI	Public Relations Institute of Ireland	**PRO**	Polskie Ratownictwo Okrętowe
PRID	Peace Research Institute, Dundas (Canada)	**PRO**	Prisoners' Rights Organisation (Éire)
		PRO	Public Record Office
PRIDE	Productive Rehabilitation Institute of Dallas for Ergonomics	**PRO CHILE**	Promotora de Exportacion de Chile
PRIDECO	Programa Integral de Desarrollo Comunal (El Salvador)	**Pro Deo**	International Association for the Promotion of Democracy under God
PRIDO	Puerto Rico Industrial Development Company	**PROA**	Plantations Réunies de l'Ouest Africain
		PROABRIL	Centro de Projectos Industriais (Brazil)
PRIH	Pineapple Research Institute of Hawaii	**PROAGRO**	Comisión Nacional de Promoción Agropecuário (Argentina)
PRII	Public Relations Institute of Ireland		
PRIISM	Pacific Research Institute for Information Systems and Management (U.S.A.)	**PROAP**	UNESCO Principal Regional Office for Asia and the Pacific (Thailand)
		PROAS	Productos Asfalticos, SA
PRIM-IFANO	Commission pour les Enfants Privés de Milieu Familial Normal (BICE)	**PROBE**	Poisons Research Organisation Benefitting the Environment
PRIMA	Paper and Related Industries Marketing Association (France)	**PROC**	Performing Rights Organisation of Canada = SDE
PRIN	Partido Revolucionairo de Izquierda Nacionalista (Bolivia)	**PROCACI**	Produits de Cacao de la Côte d'Ivoire
		PROCHI-MAD	Société des Produits Chimiques de Madagascar
PRIN	Peace Research Institute of Nigeria		
PRING	Partido Revolucionario de la Izquierda Nacional-Guieler (Bolivia)	**PROCHI-MIE**	Société Voltaïque de Produits Chimiques
PRINZ	Public Relations Institute of New Zealand	**PROCHILE**	Dirección General de Relaciones Económicas Internacionales (Chile)
PRIO	International Peace Research Institute in Oslo	**PROCIDA**	Société de Produits Chimiques Industriels et Agricoles
PRISA	Public Relations Institute of South Africa	**PROCOMA**	Promotion et Commercialisation Agricole (Ivory Coast)

PROCON	Productos de Concretos (Nicaragua)	**PROI**	Public Record Office of Ireland
PRODAC	Production Advisers' Consortium	**PROLAP**	Programa Latinoamericano de Actividades en Población
PROD-AROM	Syndicat National des Fabricants de Produits Aromatiques	**PROLUMA**	Produits Lubrificants de Madagascar
PROD-ASEN	Centro de Processamento de Dados do Senado (Brazil)	**PROM-IVOIRE**	Société Ivoirienne de Promotion
PRODECOR	Programa de Desenvolvimento do Comunitatos Ruralos (Brazil)	**PROM-ARCA**	Schweizerische Gesellschaft der Konsumgüterindustrie
PRODEFA	Foundation for the Rights of the Violence – International Secretariat	**PROMATT**	Syndicat des Professionnels du Travail Temporaire
PRODEHA	Protestants-Christelijke Bond van Detailisten in luxe en Huishoudellijke Artikelen	**PROMECA**	Programa de Mecanizacion Agropecuária (Honduras)
PRODEM	Project on Demilitarisation	**PROMED-LAC**	Regional Intergovernmental Committee for the Major Project in the Field of Education in Latin America and the Caribbean (Chile)
PRODEN	Proyecto para el Desarrollo Nacional (Chile)		
PRODES	Productores de Semillas	**PROMES**	Association Romande des Professionels de l'Energie (Switzerland)
PRODIS-ÉGES	Syndicat Professionnel des Producteurs d'Énergie et des Services Publics Autonomes	**PROMEX**	Promotora Mexicana de Comercio Exterior
		PROMICOL	Productos Minerales Colombianos Ltda
PROE	Programme Régional Océanien de l'Environnement (New Caledonia) = SPREP	**PROMO-GABON**	Agence Gabonaise de Promotion Industrielle et Artisanale
PROEXPO	Fondo de Promoción de Exportaciones (Colombia)	**PROMO-CET**	Promoção de Pesquisa Ciencia e Technologio do Estado de São Paulo (Brazil)
Prof BTM	Professional Business & Technical Management		
PROFAMIL	Association pour la Promotion de la Famille Haitienne	**PRO-MSTRA**	Production Methods and Stress Research Association (Netherlands)
PRO-FAMILIA	Asociación Dominicana Pro-Bienestar de la Familia (Dominican Republic)	**PRO-MUJER**	Proyecto de Estudios de la Mujer (Puerto Rico)
PRO-FAMILIA	Asociación Pro-Bienestar de la Familia Colombiana	**PRO-MUTAR**	Promocion de la Mujer Pastoral Social (Bolivia)
PRO-FAMILIA	Asociación Pro-Bienestar de la Familia Nicaraguense	**PRONAB**	Programa Nacional de Biotechnologia (Brazil)
Profeco	Procuraduria Federal del Consumidor (Mexico)	**PRONADI**	Chambre Syndicale Belge des Fabricants et Distributeurs de Produits Naturels et Diététiques
PROFO	Produksjonsteknisk Forskningsinstitutt		
PROFO-NICSA	Productora Forestal del Noreste de Nicaragua	**PRONAPA**	Programa Nacional de Pesquisas Arqueológicas (Brazil)
PRO-FRIJOL	Programa Cooperativo de Frijol de Centroamerica, Mexico y el Caribe (Costa Rica)	**PRONASE**	National Seed Production Agency (Mexico)
		PRONASOL	Programa Nacional de Solidaridad (Mexico)
PROFRIZA	Programa Frijol para la Zona Andina (Peru)	**PRONED**	Promotion of Non Executive Directors
PROG-NOSAG	European Centre for Applied Economic Research (Switzerland)	**PRO-NENCA**	Programa Nacional de Educación Nutricional y Complementación Alimentaria (Colombia)
PROGALVA	Association Belge pour la Promotion de la Galvanisation à Chaud	**PRONI**	Public Record Office of Northern Ireland
PROHUZA	Centre d'Études et d'Information des Problémes Humains dans les Zones Arides	**PROP**	Państwowa Rada Ochrony Przyrody
		PROP	Preservation of the Rights of Prisoners

PROPASI	Productores de Patata de Siembra	**PRS**	Prymasowska Rada Społeczna
Prosafe	Product Safety Enforcement Forum of Europe	**PRSA**	Public Relations Society of America
PROSAFE	Product Safety Forum of Europe (ECOSA)	**PRSC**	Partido Reformista Social Cristiano (Dominican Republic)
PROSALUS	ONG para la Promocion de la Salud en Paises en Desarrollo	**PRSC**	Partido Revolucionario Social Cristiano (Dominican Republic)
PROSEA	Plant Resources of South East Asia (Indonesia)	**PRSC**	Party Reform Steering Committee, Conservative Party
PROSEC	Association pour Favoriser la Diffusion des Appareils et Produits de Détection, de Protection et de Décontamination	**PRSP**	Public Relations Society of the Philippines
		PRSS	Slovensko PR Društvo
PROSIP	Promotora de Obras Sociales y de Instrucción Popular (Peru)	**PRT**	Partido Revolucionario de los Trabajadores (Costa Rica, Mexico, Panama, Peru)
PROTAAL	Proyecto Cooperativo de Investigacion sobre Tecnologia Agropecuário en América Latina	**PRT**	Partido Revolucionario de Trabajadores (Colombia)
		PRT	Prison Reform Trust
PROTERRA	Programa de Redistribuição de Terras e de Estimulos a Agro-industria do Norte e do Nordeste (Brazil)	**PRT**	Przedsiębiorstwo Robót Telekomunikalyjnych
		PRTA	Public Road Transport Association
PROVO	Stichting Proefbedrijf Voedselbestraling	**PRTC**	Partido Revolucionário de los Trabajadores Centro-americanos (El Salvador, Guatemala)
Proyecto BEIA	Bolsa Electronica Iberoamericana		
PRP	Parti de la Révolution Populaire (Zaïre)	**PRTC**	Princess Royal Trust for Carers
PRP	Parti Républicain Progressif (Algeria)	**PRTCH**	Partido Revolucionário de los Trabajadores Centro-americanos de Honduras
PRP	Partido de Renovación Puertorriqueño		
PRP	Partido Revolucionéria do Proletariado	**PRTCM**	Professional Register of Traditional Chinese Medicine (Éire)
PRP	Prevenção Rodoviária Portuguesa	**PRUA**	Party of Russian Unity and Accord
PRPB	Parti de la Révolution Populaire du Bénin	**PRUCIS**	Philippine Rural Community Improvement Society
PRPK	People's Revolutionary Party of Kampuchea	**PRURDCO**	Puerto Rico Undersea Research and Development Corporation
PRR	Party of Revolutionary Revival (Azerbaijan)	**PRVA**	Public Relations Verband Austria
		PRWNiD	Polski Ruch Wolnościowy "Niepodległość i Demokracja"
PRR	Petromin Riyadh Refinery (Saudi Arabia)		
PRR	Romanian Revolution Party	**PRZZ**	Państwowa Rada Związków Zawodowych
PRRM	Philippine Rural Reconstruction Movement	**PS**	Pain Society
PRS	Groupement National des Papetiers Répartiteurs Spécialisés	**PS**	Paleontological Society (U.S.A.)
		PS	Parapsychological Society (U.S.A.)
PRS	Paint Research Station	**PS**	Parti Socialiste (Belgium, France, Guadaloupe, Senegal)
PRS	Partia Republikane Shqiptare = ARP		
PRS	Partido Republicano Socialista (Brazil)	**PS**	Partido Socialista (Brazil, Portugal)
PRS	Partido Revolucionario Socialista (Mexico)	**PS**	Partido Socialista de Chile Unido
		PS	Pastel Society
PRS	Pattern Recognition Society (U.S.A.)	**PS**	Pharmaceutical Society of Great Britain
PRS	Performing Rights Society	**PS**	Photogrammetric Society
PRS	Pre-Raphaelite Society	**PS**	Physical Society
PRS	Protestant Reformation Society		

PS	Physiological Society		**PSC**	Parti Socialiste Caledonien
PS	Planetary Society		**PSC**	Partido Social Conservador (Colombia)
PS	Poetry Society		**PSC**	Partido Social Cristiano (Ecuador, Nicaragua)
PS	Polite Society		**PSC**	Partido Socialista Colombiano
PS	Protein Society		**PSC**	Partido Socialista Costarricense
PS	Socialist Party (Moldova)		**PSC**	Partido Socialista Cristão (Brazil)
PS(SA)	Photographic Society of Southern Africa		**PSC**	Peulvruchten Studie Combinatie
PS-1	Partido Socialista – Uno (Bolivia)		**PSC**	Pipe Smokers' Council
PSA	Pacific Science Association (Hawaii)		**PSC**	Pittsburgh Supercomputing Center
PSA	Pacific Seedsmens Association (U.S.A.)		**PSC**	Prairie Swine Centre Inc. (Canada)
PSA	Pakistan Sociological Association		**PSC**	Public Service Commission (Canada, Singapore)
PSA	Parti Solidaire Africain (Zaïre)		**PSC-PSOE**	Partido Socialista de Catalunya
PSA	Partido Socialista Argentino		**PSCAGNT**	Podhale Social-Cultural Association of Gypsies in Nowy Targ (Poland) = PSSKCwNT
PSA	Partido Socialista de Andalucia			
PSA	Passenger Shipping Association		**PSCH**	Parti Social Chrétien d'Haiti
PSA	Pastel Society of America		**PSCN**	Partido Socialcristiano Nicaragüense
PSA	Peace Studies Association		**PSD**	Parti Social Démocrate (Algeria, France, Madagascar)
PSA	Petites Soeurs de l'Assomption = HA, IA, LSA		**PSD**	Parti Socialiste Démocratique (Morocco)
PSA	Photographic Society of America		**PSD**	Partido Social Demócrata (Bolivia, Mexico, Nicaragua)
PSA	Phycological Society of America		**PSD**	Partido Social Democrático (Brazil, Portugal)
PSA	Pickles and Sauces Association		**PSD**	Partido Socialdemocracia (Chile)
PSA	Poetry Society of America		**PSD**	Partido Socialista Democrático (Guatemala)
PSA	Political Studies Association of the United Kingdom		**PSD**	Pesticides Safety Directorate
PSA	Poultry Science Association		**PSD**	Social Democratic Party (Moldova)
PSA	Prices Surveillance Authority		**PSDA**	Angolan Social Democratic Party
PSA	Product Safety Association (U.S.A.)		**PSDA**	Paper Sack Development Association
PSA	Promotional Sourcing Association		**PSDB**	Partido da Social Democracia Brasileira
PSA	Property Services Agency (DOE)		**PSDI**	Independent Social Democratic Party (Romania)
PSA	Public Service Alliance		**PSDI**	Partito Socialista Democratico Italiano
PSAC	Production Statistics Advisory Committee		**PSDIS**	Partito Socialista Democratico Independente Sanmarinese (San Marino)
PSAE	Philippine Society of Agricultural Engineers			
PSAI	Political Studies Association of Ireland		**PSDP**	Petites Soeurs des Pauvres = HDLP, IDP, LSP
PSAJ	Peace Studies Association of Japan		**PSDP**	Poveri Servi della Divina Providenza
PSAPR	Pathology Society of Asia and Pacific Region		**PSDR**	Romanian Social Democratic Party
PSAU	Plan de Suministros Alimentarios de Urgencia (PMA)		**PSE**	Panellinios Syndesmos Exagogeon
PSB	Partido Socialista Brasileiro		**PSE**	Partido Socialista Ecuatoriano
PSB	Partie Socialiste Belge = BSP		**PSE**	Phytochemical Society of Europe
PSC	Pacific Science Council		**PSEB**	Punjab State Electricity Board (India)
PSC	Palaeontological Society of China			
PSC	Palestine Solidarity Campaign			
PSC	Parti Social Chrétien (Belgium) = CVP			

PSERC	Public Sector Economics Research Centre	**PSM**	Physical Society of Moldova
PSEU	Public Service Executive Union (Éire)	**PSMA**	Power Supply Manufacturers' Association
PSEU	Public Services Employees' Union (Afghanistan)	**PSMA**	Pressure Sensitive Manufacturers Association
PSF	Parents for Safe Food	**PSMdC**	Piccole Suore Missionarie della Carità = PMC
PSFC	International Pacific Salmon Fisheries Commission	**PSME**	Partido Socialista de Melilla
PSFN	Polskie Stowarzyszenie Filmu Naukowego	**PSMSL**	Permanent Service for Mean Sea Level (FAGS)
PSG	Parti Socialiste Guyanais (French Guiana)	**PSN**	Partido Socialista Nicaragüense
PSG	Peru Support Group	**PSN**	Poor Sisters of Nazareth
PSG-PSOE	Partido Socialista de Galicia	**PSNA**	Phytochemical Society of North America
PSGB	Primate Society of Great Britain	**PSNC**	Parti Socialiste de la Nouvelle Caledonie
PSHSGB	Polar System History Society of Great Britain	**PSNC**	Pharmaceutical Services Negotiating Committee
PSI	Pakistan Standards Institution	**PSNI**	Pharmaceutical Society of Northern Ireland
PSI	Partito Socialista Italiano	**PSNZ**	Perinatal Society of New Zealand
PSI	Paul Scherrer Institute (Switzerland)	**PSOE**	Partido Socialista Obrero Español
PSI	Pharmaceutical Society of Ireland	**PSOE-A**	Partido Socialista de Andalucia
PSI	Policy Studies Institute	**PSOJ**	Private Sector Organisation of Jamaica
PSI	Population Services International (U.S.A.)	**PSP**	Pacifistich Socialistiche Partij
PSI	Psychological Society of Ireland	**PSP**	Parti Social pour le Progrès (Tunisia)
PSI	Public Services International = IÖD, ISKA, ISP	**PSP**	Parti Socialiste Progressiste (Lebanon)
PSI	Statisticians in the Pharmaceutical Industry	**PSP**	Partido Socialista de Perú
PSIA	Panellinios Syndesmos Idiotikon Astunomikon	**PSP**	Partido Socialista Puertorriqueño
PSIDC	Punjab State Industrial Development Corporation (India)	**PSP**	Pharmaceutical Society of Pakistan
		PSP	Policia Seguranía Pública (Portugal)
PSIF	Prison Service Industries and Farms	**PSP**	Popular Socialist Party
PSIL	Philippine Society of International Law	**PSPA**	Professional Sports Photographers Association
PSJ	Pharmaceutical Society of Japan	**PSPC**	Partido Socialista del Pueblo de Ceuta
PSK	Parlamentska Stranka Kosova (Serbia) = PPK	**PSPC**	Permanent South Pacific Commission
PSL	Environmental Study Center (Indonesia)	**PSPS**	Paddle Steamer Preservation Society
PSL	Parti Social-Libéral (Algeria)	**PSQC**	Philippine Society for Quality Control
PSL	Polish Peasant Party	**PSR**	Partido Socialista Revolucionário (Mexico, Peru)
PSL	Polskie Stronnictwo Ludowe	**PSRC**	Plastic Surgery Research Council (U.S.A.)
PSL-PL	Peasant Accord (Poland)		
PSM	Parti Socialiste Mauricien	**PSRM**	Parti Sosialis Rakyat (Malaysia)
PSM	Parti Socialiste Monegasque (Monaco)	**PSRN**	Partiia Soiuz Russkikh Natsionalistov
PSM	Parti Socialiste Monima (Madagascar) = VSM	**PSS**	Compagnie des Prêtres de Saint Sulpice
		PSS	Państwowa Spółdzielnia Spozywców
PSM	Partidul Socialist al Muncü (Romania) = SLP	**PSS**	Partia Socialiste e Shqipërisë (Albania) = SDP
		PSS	Partially Sighted Society

PSS	Partito Socialista Sammarinese
PSSA	Pharmaceutical Society of South Africa
PSSA	Photogrammetric Society of South Africa
PSSC	Philippine Social Science Council
PSSC	Pious Society of the Missionaries of St Charles = CS
PSSC	Police Science Society of China
PSSC	Public Service Satellite Consortium (U.S.A.)
PSSEW	Prosecuting Solicitors' Society of England and Wales
PSSF	Petites Soeurs de la Sainte-Famille
PSSG	International Printers Supply Salesmen's Guild (U.S.A.)
PSSI	Peace Science Society International
PSSKCwNT	Podhalańskie Stowarzyszenie Społeczno-Kulturalne Cyganów w Nowym Targu (Poland) = PSCAGNT
PSSM	Polish Society of Social Medicine = PTMS
PSSS	Philosophical Society for the Study of Sport
PSSS	Polish Society of Soil Science = PTG
PST	Mezhrespublikanskaia Partiia Svobodnogo Truda
PST	Parti Socialiste des Travailleurs (Algeria)
PST	Partido Socialista de los Trabajadores (Colombia, Mexico, Panama)
PST	Partido Socialista de Trabalhadores (Brazil)
PSTC	Pressure Sensitive Tape Council (U.S.A.)
PSU	Parti Socialiste Unifié
PSU	Partido Socialista Unido (Mexico)
PSU	Party of Serbian Unity
PSU	Public Service Union
PSU	Publications Services Unit (IUCN)
PSUB	Public Service Union of Belize
PSUC	Partit Socialista Unificat de Catalunya
PSUM	Partido Socialista Unificado de México
PSV	Progressieve Surinaamse Volkspartij
PSW	Public Service Watch
PSWTUF	Public Service Workers Trade Union Federation (Sri Lanka)
PSZ	Polskie Siły Zbrojne
PT	Partido de los Trabajadores (Costa Rica)
PT	Partido dos Trabalhadores (Brazil)
PT	Partiia Truda
PT	Polska Unia Socjaldemokratyczna
Pt-H	Partit tal-Haddiema (Malta) = MLP
PTA	Physikalisch- Technische Anstalt zu Braunschweig
PTA	Piano Tuners Association
PTA	Polskie Towarzystwo Akustyczne
PTA	Polskie Towarzystwo Archeologiczne = PTAiN
PTA	Polskie Towarzystwo Astronautyczne
PTA	Polskie Towarzystwo Astronomiczne
PTA	Post-Tensioning Association
PTA	Postcard Traders Association
PTA	Preferential Trade Area for East and Southern Africa = ESAPTA, ZEP
PTA	Printing Trades Alliance
PTA	Property Transfer Association
PTAC	Printing Technology Association of China
PTAiN	Polskie Towarzystwo Archeologiczne i Numizmatyczne = PTA
PTB	Parti du Travail de Belgique = PvdA
PTB	Partido Trabalhista Brasileiro
PTB	Pashtany Tejaraty Bank
PTB	Petit Train Bleu (Senegal)
PTB	Physikalisch- Technische Bundesanstalt
PTB	Polskie Towarzystwo Biometryczne
PTBBiMF	Polskie Towarzystwo Balneologii, Bioklimatologii i Medycyny Fizykalnej
PTBR	Polskie Towarzystwo Badań Radiacyjnych im Marii Skłodowskiej-Curie
PTC	Pacific Telecommunications Council
PTC	Peace Tax Campaign
PTC	Polskie Towarzystwo Chemiczne
PTC	Polskie Towarzystwo Cybernetyczne
PTC	Posts and Telecommunications Corporation (Zambia)
PTCA	Programme for Theology and Cultures in Asia
PTCG	Public Transport Campaign Group
PTCh	Polskie Towarzystwo Chemiczne
PTChD	Polskie Towarzystwo Chirurgów Dziecięcych
PTCMA	Plastic Tanks and Cisterns Manufacturers Association (*now* ATCM)
PTCR	Patent, Trademark and Copyright Research Institute (U.S.A.)

PTD	Polskie Towarzystwo Dermatologiczne	**PTK**	Pienteollisuuden Keskusliitto
PTDC	Pakistan Tourism Development Corporation	**PTK**	Polska Telefonia Komórkowa
		PTK	Polskie Towarzystwo Kardiologiczne
PTDL	Polskie Towarzystwo Diagnostyki Laboratoryjnej	**PTL**	Pohjoismainen Taideliitto = NKF
		PTL	Polskie Towarzystwo Leśne
PTE	Partido del Trabajo de España	**PTL**	Polskie Towarzystwo Lekarskie
PTE	Polskie Towarzystwo Entomologiczne	**PTL**	Polskie Towarzystwo Logopedyczne
PTEK	Polskie Towarzystwo Ekonomiczne	**PTL**	Polskie Towarzystwo Ludoznawcze
PTErg	Polskie Towarzystwo Ergonomiczne	**PTLS**	Polskie Towarzystwo Lingwistyki Stosowanej
PTES	People's Trust for Endangered Species		
PTF	Papirindustriens Tekniske Forening	**PTM**	Polskie Towarzystwo Matematyczne
PTF	Polskie Towarzystwo Farmakologiczne	**PTMS**	Polskie Towarzystwo Medycyny Społecznej = PSSM
PTF	Polskie Towarzystwo Filologiczne		
PTF	Polskie Towarzystwo Filozoficzne	**PTMTS**	Polskie Towarzystwo Mechaniki Teoretycznej i Stosowanej
PTF	Polskie Towarzystwo Fizyczne		
PTFarm	Polskie Towarzystwo Farmaceutyczne	**PTN**	Polskie Towarzystwo Nautologiczne
PTFit	Polskie Towarzystwo Fitopatologiczne	**PTN**	Polskie Towarzystwo Neofilologiczne
PTFM	Polskie Towarzystwo Fizyki Medyczne	**PTN**	Polskie Towarzystwo Neurologiczne
PTFP	Polskie Towarzystwo Funduszy Powierniczych	**PTN**	Polskie Towarzystwo Numizmatyczne
		PTNP	Polskie Towarzystwo Nauk Politycznych
PTG	Polskie Towarzystwo Głęboznawcze		
PTG	Polskie Towarzystwo Geograficzne	**PTNW**	Polskie Towarzystwo Nauk Weterynaryjnych
PTG	Polskie Towarzystwo Geologiczne		
PTGeof	Polskie Towarzystwo Geofizyczne	**PTNZ**	Polskie Towarzystwo Nauk Zywieniowych
PTGWO	Philippine Transport and General Workers Organisations		
		PTO	Patent and Trademark Office (U.S.A.)
PTH	Polskie Towarzystwo Higieniczne	**PTO**	Polskie Towarzystwo Okulistyczne
PTH	Polskie Towarzystwo Historyczne	**PTO**	Polskie Towarzystwo Onkologiczne
PTH	Polskie Towarzystwo Hydrobiologiczne	**PTO**	Polskie Towarzystwo Orientalistyczne
PTHiC	Polskie Towarzystwo Histochemików i Cytochemików	**PTOiTr**	Polskie Towarzystwo Ortopedyczne i Traumatologiczne
PTHiT	Polskie Towarzystwo Hematologów i Transfuzjologów	**PTOL**	Polskie Towarzystwo Otolaryngologiczne
PTHP	Polskie Towarzystwo Higieny Psychicznej	**PTOM**	Pays et Territoires d'Outremer (CE)
		PTP	Polskie Towarzystwo Pediatryczne
PTHZ	Polskie Towarzystwo Handlu Zagranicznego	**PTP**	Polskie Towarzystwo Pielęgniarskie = PNA
PTI	Polskie Towarzystwo Immunologiczne	**PTP**	Polskie Towarzystwo Przyrodników im Kopernika
PTI	Press Trust of India		
PTIA	Pet Trade and Industry Association	**PTP**	Polskie Towarzystwo Psychologiczne
PTIC	Patent and Trade Mark Institute of Canada	**PTPN**	Poznánskie Towarzystwo Przyjaciół Nauk
PTIDG	Presentation of Technical Information Discussion Group	**PTr**	Parti Travailliste (Mauritius)
		PTR	Partido Tercera República (Chile)
PTIO	Pesticides Technical Information Office (Canada)	**PTR**	Partido Trabhalista Renovador (Brazil)
		PTR	Physikalisch-Technische Reichsanstalt
PTIU	Public Transport Information Unit	**PTR**	Polskie Towarzystwo Radiologiczne
PTJ	Polskie Towarzystwo Językoznawcze	**PTR**	Polskie Towarzystwo Religioznawcze

PTR	Polskie Towarzystwo Rusycystyczne
PTRAC	Planning and Transport Research Advisory Council
PTRI	Philippine Textile Research Institute
PTS	Pali Text Society
PTS	Philatelic Traders Society
PTS	Polskie Towarzystwo Semiotyczne
PTS	Polskie Towarzystwo Socjologiczne
PTS	Polskie Towarzystwo Stomatologiczne
PTS	Polskie Towarzystwo Szpitalnictwa
PTS	Polymerteknisk Selskab
PTS	Protestant Truth Society
PTSA	Piano Trade Suppliers Association
PTT	Postes, Télégraphes, Télédiffusion
PTTI	Postal, Telegraph and Telephone International = ICTT, IPTT
PTTK	Polskie Towarzystwo Turystyczno-Krajoznawcze
PTTOX	Polskie Towarzystwo Toksykologiczne
PTU	Plumbing Trades Union
PTU	Polskie Towarzystwo Urologiczne
PTUC	Philippines Trade Union Council
PTUF	Palestine Trade Union Federation
PTUF	Professional Tennis Umpires Federation
PTWK	Polskie Towarzystwo Wydawców Ksiązek
PTWU	Postal and Telecommunications Workers Union (Éire)
PTZ	Polskie Towarzystwo Zootechniczne
PTZool	Polskie Towarzystwo Zoologiczne
PU	Coalición Pueblo Unido (Costa Rica)
PU	Peasants' Union (Slovenia)
PUA	Pacific Union Association
PUA	Partido de Unificación Anticomunista (Guatemala)
PUAID	Parti d'Unité Arabe Islamique-Démocratique (Algeria)
PUAS	Postal Union of the Americas and Spain = UPAE
PUB	Partido Unión Boliviana
PUB	Patriotic Union of Bonaire (Netherlands Antilles) = UPB
PUB	Public Utilities Board (Barbados, Singapore)
PUC	Conservative Humanist Party (Romania)
PUC	Pancyprian Union of Chemists
PUC	People's University of China
PUC/SP	Pontificia Universidad Católica de São Paulo (Brazil)
PUCA	Partido Unionista Centroamericana (El Salvador)
PUCH	Parti Unifié des Communistes Haïtiens
PUCh-D	Polska Unia Chrzescijańsko-Demokratyczna
PUCHE	Potchefstroom University for Christian Higher Education (South Africa)
PUCR	Partido Unión Civico Revolucionaria (Costa Rica)
PUDEMO	Peoples United Democratic Movement (Swaziland)
PUDINE	Programa Universitario de Desenvolvimento Industrial do Nordeste (Brazil)
PUDOC	Centrum voor Landbouwpublikaties en Landbouwdocumentatie
PUETO	Panhellenic Union of Exporters of Table Olives
PUFFS	Passengers United for Freedom to Smoke
PUK	Partia e Unitetit Kombëtar (Albania) = ANUP
PUK	Patriotic Union of Kurdistan (Iraq)
PUKO	Pan-American Union of Karatedo Organisations
PUL	Polish Union in Lithuania = LLS
PUL	Press Union of Liberia
PULO	Pattini United Liberation Organisation (Thailand)
PULPAPEL	Pulp and Paper Manufacturers Association (Philippines)
PULSE	Public and Local Services Efficiency Campaign (India)
PUM	Partido Unificado Mariateguista (Peru)
PUMC	Public Utilities Management Company (Kuwait)
PUMPA	Purine Metabolic Patients Association
PUN	Partido de Unión Nacional; Parti de l'Unité Nationale (Costa Rica, Honduras)
PUNR	Partidul Unității Naționale Române (Romania) = PRNU
PUNT	Partido Unico Nacional de los Trabajadores (Equatorial Guinea)
PUP	Parti de l'Unité Populaire (Tunisia)
PUP	Partido Union Popular (Costa Rica)
PUP	People's United Party (Belize)
PUP	People's Unity Party (Kazakhstan)

PUP	Progressive Unionist Party	**PW**	Positively Women
PUPiK	Przedsiębiorstwo Upowszechniania Prasy i Książki "Ruch"	**PWA**	Pakistan Welfare Association
		PWA	Pakistani Workers' Association
PUR	Republican Union Party (Romania)	**PWA**	Przegląd Wiadomości Agencyjnych
PURS	Partido de la Unión Socialista Republicana (Bolivia)	**PWC**	Peasants' Work Co-operatives (Yugoslavia)
PURSC	Partido Unido de la Revolución Socialista de Cuba	**PWC**	Peoples World Convention
		PWC	Preliminary Working Committee (China / Hong Kong)
PUSAF	Presses Universitaires et Scolaires d'Afrique (Ivory Coast)	**PWCA**	Peoples World Constituent Assembly
PUSC	Partido Unido Socialista Costarricense	**PWCB**	Provincial Water Conservancy Bureau (Taiwan)
PUSD	Pesticides Trust	**PWCC**	Postal Workers Co-ordination Committee
PUSD	Social Democratic Unity Party (Romania)	**PWF**	Pacific Whale Foundation (U.S.A.)
PUST	Pan-African Union of Science and Technology = UPST	**PWF**	Private Wagon Federation
		PWFA	Petroleum Workers Federation of Aruba
PUTRI	Indonesian Parks and Recreational Centres Association	**PWFS**	Prisoners Wives & Families Society
PUW	Proutist Universal Women	**PWG**	Permanent Working Group of European Junior Hospital Doctors
PV	Partido Verde (Brazil)		
PV	Partiia Vozrozhdeniia	**PWI**	Permanent Way Institution
PV-UK	British Photovoltaic Association	**PWI**	Persatuan Wartawan Indonesia
PVB	Provinciale Veevoederbureau	**PWiT**	Przedsiębiorstwo Wystaw i Targów
PVC	Partido de Veteranos Civiles (Dominican Republic)	**PWLB**	Public Works Loan Board
		PWM	Polskie Wydawnictwo Muzyczne
PVC	Provinciale Voedselcommissaris	**PWMA**	Photographic Waste Management Association
PvdA	Partij van de Arbeid (Belgium) = PTB		
PvdA	Partij van de Arbeit (Netherlands)	**PWN**	Polskie Wydawnictwo Naukowe
PVDP	Democratic Future of the Homeland Party (Romania)	**PWN-PSN**	Polska Wspólnota Narodowa Polskie Stronnictwo Narodowe (Poland) = PNC-PNP
PVFM	Planification pour une Vie Familiale Meilleure (FAO) = PBFL	**PWNDA**	Provincial Wholesale Newspaper Distributors Association
PVGA	Processed Vegetable Growers Association	**PWO**	Progressieve Werknemers Organisatie (Suriname)
PVI	Public Voice International	**PWPA**	Professors World Peace Academy (HSA-UWC, ICF)
PVM	Prisons Video Magazine Trust		
PVMA	Philippine Veterinary Medical Association	**PWPMA**	Philippine Welding Products Manufacturers Association
PVMA	Pressure Vessel Manufacturers Association (U.S.A.)	**PWPS**	Pure Water Preservation Society
PVOA	Passenger Vehicle Operators Association	**PWRB**	Pacific Women's Resource Bureau (SPC)
PVR	Partiia Vozrozhdeniia Rossii	**PWSA**	Prader-Willi Syndrome Association
PVSA	Peripheral Vascular Society of America	**PWSWA**	Processed Woodchip, Sawdust and Woodfloor Association
PVTA	Philippine Virginia Tobacco Administration	**PWTAG**	Pool Water Treatment Advisory Group
PVV	Partij voor Vrijheid en Vooruitgang (Belgium)	**PWU**	Provision Wholesalers Union (Malta)
PW	Parti Wallon (Belgium)	**PWU-MPS**	Polish Western Union-Movement of Polish Silesia = PZZ-RPS

PY	Party of Yugoslavs (Serbia)
PYBT	Prince's Youth Business Trust
PYM	Pan African Youth Movement = MPJ, PAYM
PYRESA	Prensa y Radio Española, S.A.
PYRM	Party of Yugoslavs in the Republic of Macedonia
PZA	Polski Związek Atletyczny
PZB	Polski Związek Bokserski
PZE	Polski Związek Eksperantystów
PZEM	Provinciale Zeeuwse Energie-Maatschappij (Netherlands)
PZF	Polski Związek Filatelistów
PZG	Polski Związek Gimnastyczny
PZH	Państwowy Zakład Higieny
PZHISRI	Panzhihua Iron and Steel Research Institute
PZHK	Polski Związek Hodowców Koni
PZHL	Polski Związek Hokeja na Łódzie
PZHT	Polski Związek Hokeja na Trawie
PZITB	Polski Związek Inzynierów i Techników Budownictwa
PZITS	Polskie Zrzeszenie Inzynierów i Techników Sanitarnych
PZJ	Polski Związek Jeżdziecki
PZK	Polski Związek Kajakowy
PZKol	Polski Związek Kolarski
PZKosz	Polski Związek Koszykówki
PZKS	Polski Związek Katolicko Społeczny
PZL	Polski Związek Łowiecki
PZLA	Polski Związek Lekkiej Atletyki
PZM	Polska Zegluga Morska
PZM	Polski Związek Motorowy
PZN	Polski Związek Narciarski
PZP	Pracownicza Kasa Zapomogowo – Pozyczkowa
PZPiT	Państwowy Zespół Pieśni i Tańca
PZPN	Polski Związek Pilki Noznej
PZPR	Polska Zjednoczona Partia Robotnicza
PZS	Polski Związek Szermierczy
PZTS	Polski Związek Tenisa Stołowego
PZTW	Polski Związek Towarzystw Wioslarskich
PZU	Państwowy Zakład Ubezpieczeń
PZW	Polski Związek Wedkarski
PZWS	Państwowe Zakłady Wydawnictw Szkolnych
PZZ	Polish Western Union
PZZ	Polski Związek Zapaśniczy
PZZ	Polski Związek Zeglarski
PZZ-RPŚ	Polski Związek Zachodni-Ruch Polskiego Śląska (Poland) = PWU-MPS

Q

Q Guild	Quality Guild
QAA	Quality Ash Association
QAFCO	Qatar Fertiliser Company
QANTAS	Queensland and Northern Territory Aerial Services (Australia)
QAPCO	Qatar Petrochemical Company
QARANC	Queen Alexandra's Royal Army Nursing Corps
QASCO	Qatar Steel Company
QATARGAS	Qatar Liquified Gas Company
QBC	Quality British Celery Association
QBS	Qatar Broadcasting Service
QBS	Quebec Bureau of Standards (Canada)
QBSA	Quarterly Bulletin on Solar Activity (IAU)
QCA	Quaker Concern for Animals
QCEA	Quaker Council for European Affairs
QCGA	Queensland Cane Growers' Association (Australia)
QCI	Queensland Confederation of Industry
QCIR	Queen's Centre for International Relations (Canada)
QEIM	Qinhuangdao Engineering & Research Institute for Ferrous Metallurgical Mines
QERI	Qingdao Electronics Research Institute
QETE	Quality Engineering Test Establishment (Canada)
QFRI	Queensland Fisheries Research Institute (Australia)
QGPC	Qatar General Petroleum Corporation
QI	Quota International (U.S.A.)
QIB	Qatar Islamic Bank
QIC	Quaker International Centre
QIMA	Queensland Institute of Municipal Administration
QKOA	Quarantine Kennel Owners' Association
QLS	Quantum Leap Society
QMA	Qatar Monetary Agency
QMC	Quekett Microscopical Club

QMP	Quality Milk Producers	**RA**	Ramblers Association
QMW	Queen Mary and Westfield College, University of London	**RA**	Referees Association
		RA	Refractories Association of Great Britain
QNA	Qatar News Agency		
QNB	Qatar National Bank	**RA**	Refugee Action
QNC	Qatar National Cement Company	**RA**	Religious of the Assumption
QNC	Queensland Naturalists Club (Australia)	**RA**	Rice Association
QNI	Queen's Nursing Institute	**RA**	Royal Academy of Arts
QNNTC	Qatar National Navigation and Transport Company	**RA**	Rural Action
		RA	The Reclamation Association
QOSMC	Qingdao Ocean Shipping Mariners' College	**RAA**	Regional Arts Association
		RAA	Rheumatism Association of ASEAN (Thailand)
QPS	Quaker Peace and Service		
QRISTHRA	Qiqihar Research Institute of Science and Technology, Harbin Railway Administration	**RAA**	Rice Growers' Association of Australia
		RAA	Royal Academy of Arts
		RAA	Royal Australian Artillery
QRPG	Quebec Rubber and Plastics Group (Canada)	**RAAD**	Rijks Zuivel-Agrarische Afvalwaterdienst
QSC	Al-Ahli Bank of Qatar	**RAAF**	Royal Australian Air Force
QSPP	Quebec Society for the Protection of Plants (Canada)	**RAAG**	Research Association of Applied Geometry (Japan)
QST	Quality Scottish Trout	**RAAM**	Refineria Argentina de Aceites Minerales
QTP	Quantum Theory Project (U.S.A.)		
QUANA	Authorized Newsagents Association of Queensland	**RAAS**	Racial Adjustment Action Society
		RAAS	Royal Amateur Arts Society
QUANTUM	Arbeitsgeminschaft für Quantifzierung und Methoden in der Historischen Sozialforschung	**RAAW**	Rural, Agricultural and Allied Workers
		RAB	Radio Advertising Bureau (U.S.A.)
QUB	Queen's University of Belfast (Northern Ireland)	**RAB**	Rationalisatie v. d. Arbeidstechniek in de Bosbouw
QUIM-BRASIL	Quimica Industrial Brasileira S.A.	**RAB**	Regional Arts Bureau
		RAB	Réseau Africain de Biosciences (Senegal) = ABN
QUIM-INICA	Distribuidora Quimica de Nicaragua, S.A.		
		RAB	Rijksarbeidsbureau
QUINA-CAM	Société Quinquina du Caméroun	**RABDF**	Royal Association of British Dairy Farmers
Quit	National Society of Non Smokers	**RABI**	Royal Agricultural Benevolent Institution
QUNG	Quaker United Nations Group		
QUNO	Quaker United Nations Office (U.S.A.)	**RABIN**	Netherlands Advisory Council for Libraries and Information Services
		RABL	Reial Acadèmia de Bones Lletres
	R	**RAC**	Resource Assessment Commission
		RAC	Royal Automobile Club
R&DSoc	Research and Development Society	**RAC**	Rubber Association of Canada
R&VA	Rating and Valuation Association (*now* IRRV)	**RAC MSA**	Royal Automobile Club Motor Sports Association
RA	Racecourse Association	**RACA**	Real Academia de Ciencias y Artes
RA	Radiocommunications Agency	**RACB**	Royal Automobile Club de Belgique
RA	Radionic Association	**RACE**	Real Automóvil Club de España

RACE	Research and Development in Advanced Communications Technologies in Europe (Turkey)	**RAF**	Regional Arab Federation of Associations for Voluntary Fertility Control
RACGP	Royal Australian College of General Practitioners	**RAF**	Regional Office for Africa (FAO)
RACI	Reale Automobile Club Italiano	**RAF**	Reklameatelierenes Forening
RACI	Royal Australian Chemical Institute	**RAF**	Rörledningsfirmornas Arbetsgivareförbund
RACMYP	Real Academia de Ciencias Morales y Politicas	**RAF**	Röte Armee Faktion
RACOG	Royal Australian College of Obstetricians and Gynaecologists	**RAF**	Royal Air Force
		RAFA	Royal Air Force Association
RACP	Royal Australasian College of Physicians	**RAFBF**	Royal Air Force Benevolent Fund
		RAFE	Regional Office for Asia and the Far East (FAO)
RACS	Royal Australasian College of Surgeons	**RAFES**	Royal Air Force Educational Service
RACSA	Radio Aeronautica de Cuba	**RAFGSA**	Royal Air Force Gliding and Soaring Association
RAD	Respect voor Arbeid en Democratie (Belgium) = UDRT	**RAFH**	Royal Air Force Historical Society
RAD	Royal Academy of Dancing	**RAFI**	Rural Advancement Fund International (U.S.A.)
RAD	Royal Association in Aid of Deaf People	**RAFOS**	Royal Air Force Ornithological Society
RADA	Royal Academy of Dramatic Art	**RAFR**	Regional Office for Africa (FAO)
RADAR	Rassemblement des Démocrates pour l'Avenir de la Réunion	**RAFSC**	Royal Air Force Staff College
RADAR	Royal Association for Disability and Rehabilitation	**RAFSC**	Royal Air Force Strike Command
		RAFT	Restoration of Appearance and Function Trust
RADD	Royal Association in Aid of the Deaf and Dumb	**RAG**	Radical Anthropology Group
RAdE	Rotaria Asocio de Esperantistoj	**RAG**	Rainforest Action Group
RADEV	Réseau Africain pour le Développement (Ethiopia)	**RAGA**	Regional Arquitectos de los Paises del Grupo Andino (Peru)
RADI	Réseau Africain pour le Développement Intégré (Senegal) = ANID	**RAGB**	Refractories Association of Great Britain
RADIO-BRAS	Empresa Brasiliera de Radiodifusão	**RAGB**	Restaurateurs Association
RADIUS	Religious Drama Society of Great Britain	**RAGE**	Radiotherapy Action Group Exposure
		RAGS	Recycling Advisory Group Scotland
RADIUS	Research and Development Institute of the United States	**RAH**	Real Academia de la Historia
RadTech Europe	European Association for the Advancement of Radiation Curing by UV, EB and Laser Beams	**RAHCAR**	Refugee Ad Hoc Campaign for Asylum Rights
		RAHS	Royal Australian Historical Society
RAE	Radiodifusión Argentina al Exterior	**RAI**	Nederlandse Vereniging de Rijwiel en Automobiel-Industrie
RAE	Real Academia Española	**RAI**	Radiotelevisione Italiano
RAE	Royal Aircraft Establishment	**RAI**	Rassemblement Arabique-Islamique (Algeria)
RAeC	Royal Aero Club of the United Kingdom	**RAI**	Reading Association of Ireland
RAEN	Russian Academy of the Natural Sciences	**RAI**	Restaurants Association of Ireland
		RAI	Royal Anthropological Institute
RAeS	Royal Aeronautical Society	**RAI**	Royal Archaeological Institute
RAF	Redernes Arbeidsgiverforening	**RAIA**	Royal Australian Institute of Architects

RAIC	Red Andina de Informacion Comercial (Peru)
RAIC	Royal Architectural Institute of Canada
RAID	Recherche, Aide, l'Intervention et Dissuasion
RAIMAZ	Records, Archives and Information Management Association of Zimbabwe
RAIPA	Royal Australian Institute of Public Administration
RAIPR	Royal Australian Institute of Parks and Recreation
RAIS	Rail Air International Service
RAIST	Réseau Africain d'Institutions Scientifiques et Techniques (Kenya) = ANSTI
RAIU	Réserve Alimentaire Internationale d'Urgence = IEFR
RAJAR	Radio Joint Audience Research
RAK	Rikets Allmanna Kartverk
RAM	Reform the Armed Forces Movement (Philippines)
RAM	Royal Academy of Music
RAMAC	Radio Marine Associated Companies
RAMC	Royal Army Medical Corps
RAMI	Royal Academy of Medicine in Ireland
RAMNAC	Radio Aids to Marine Navigation Application Committee
RAMS	Radikalnaia Assotsiatsiia za Mir i Svobody
RAN	Rainforest Action Network (U.S.A.) = IRFAN, TRAN
RAN	Régie du Chemin de Fer Abidjan-Niger
RAN	Rossiiskaia Akademiia Nauk = RAS
RAN	Royal Australian Navy
RANSA	Royal Australian Naval Sailing Association
RANZCP	Royal Australian and New Zealand College of Psychiatrists
RAOB	Royal Antediluvian Order of Buffalos
RAOC	Royal Army Ordnance Corps
RAOU	Royal Australasian Ornithologists Union
RAP	Radical Alternatives to Prison
RAP	Refugee Arrival Project
RAP	Rent Assessment Panel (Northern Ireland)
RAPA	FAO Regional Office for Asia and the Pacific
RAPAD	Research Association for Petroleum Alternatives Development (Japan)
RAPÉD	Réseau Africain pour la Participation des Églises au Développement (Congo) = ANCPD
RAPI	Royal Australian Planning Institute
RAPPANE	Réseau Africain pour la Prévention et la Protection contre l'Abus et la Négligence de l'Enfant (Kenya) = ANPPCAN
RAPR	Russian Association of Public Relations
RAPRA	Rubber and Plastics Research Association of Great Britain
RAR	Refinarias de Açúcar Reunidas
RARC	Ruakura Agricultural Research Centre (New Zealand)
RARDE	Royal Armament Research and Development Establishment
RARE	Rare Animal Relief Effort (U.S.A.)
RARE	Réseaux Associes pour la Recherche Européenne (*now* TERENA)
RAS	Recruitment and Assessment Services
RAS	Royal Aeronautical Society
RAS	Royal African Society
RAS	Royal Asiatic Society of Great Britain and Ireland
RAS	Royal Astronomical Society
RAS	Russian Academy of Sciences = RAN
RASA	Radiofusoras Asociadas (Mexico)
RASAC	Rural Assistance Scheme Advisory Committee
RASB	Royal Asiatic Society of Bengal
RASC	Royal Agricultural Society of the Commonwealth
RASC	Royal Astronomical Society of Canada = SRAC
RASCOM	Regional African Satellite Communication System for the Development of Africa (ITU)
RASD	Reference and Adult Services Division (ALA)
RASE	Royal Agricultural Society of England
RASILA	Rannikko-ja Sisävesiliikenteen Työnantajaliitto
RASK	Royal Agricultural Society of Kenya
RASNZ	Royal Astronomical Society of New Zealand
RASTBC	Research Association for Scientific and Technical Bulletins of China
RASU	Rangoon Arts and Science University
RASVY	Royal Australian Survey Corps
RAT	Résistance Armée Tunisienne

RATAU	Ukrainian Telegraph Agency
RATD	Register of Apparel and Textile Designers
RATEKSA	Radiobranchens Tekniske og Kommercielle Sammenslutning
RATP	Régie Autonome des Transports Parisiens
RAU	Rossiisko-Amerikanskii Universitet (Russia)
RAUC	Centre de Recherches en Architecture, Urbanisme, Construction
RAVIN-ARBENIN	Régie de Ravitaillement des Navires (Benin)
RAW	Rationalisierungs-Ausschusses der Deutschen Wirtschaft
RAW	Research and Analysis Wing (India)
RAWC	Radioactive Waste Co-ordinating Committee
RB	Redd Barna
RBA	Refined Bitumen Association
RBA	Reinsurance Brokers Association
RBA	Reserve Bank of Australia
RBA	Retail Book, Stationery and Allied Trades Employees Association
RBA	Romanian Banking Association
RBA	Royal Bhutanese Army
RBA	Royal Society of British Architects
RBA	Royal Society of British Artists (FBA)
RBAF	Royal Brunei Armed Forces
RBD	Red Barnet Danmark
RBDF	Royal Bahamian Defence Force
RBDP	Rehoboth Bevryder Demokratiese Party (Namibia)
RBDP	Rossiiskaia Burzhuazno-Demokraticheskaia Partiia
RBG	Royal Botanic Gardens, Kew
RBL	Royal British Legion
RBLS	Royal British Legion Scotland
RBNA	Royal British Nurses Association
RBOA	Residential Boat Owners Association
RBPF	Royal Bahamas Police Force
RBS	Rare Breeds Society
RBS	Royal Blind Society of New South Wales
RBS	Royal Botanical Society
RBS	Royal Society of British Sculptors
RBST	Rare Breeds Survival Trust
RBV	Rohrleitungsbauverband
RC	Rijksconsultentschap
RC	Romanian Cradle = VR
RCA	Race Course Association
RCA	Radio Corporation of America
RCA	Refractory Contractors' Association
RCA	Reinforced Concrete Association
RCA	Research Council of Alberta (Canada)
RCA	Residential Care Association
RCA	Retail Confectioners Association
RCA	Royal Cambrian Academy of Art
RCA	Royal Choral Society
RCA	Royal College of Art
RCA	Royal Company of Archers
RCA	Rural Crafts Association
RCAA	Royal Canadian Academy of Arts
RCAC	Regional Cultural Action Centre (ACI) = CRAC, RCCA
RCAF	Royal Canadian Air Force
RCAHMS	Royal Commission on the Ancient and Historical Monuments of Scotland
RCB	Romanian Commercial Bank
RCC	International Society of Reply Coupons Collectors
RCC	Regional Cultural Committee (CARICOM)
RCC	Retail Council of Canada
RCC	Revolutionary Command Council (Iraq)
RCC	Revolutionary Conservative Caucus
RCCA	Regional Centre for Cultural Action (ACI) = CRAC, RCAC
RCCC	Royal Caledonian Curling Club
RCCES	Research Centre for Canadian Ethnic Studies
RCCM	Research Council for Complementary Medicine
RCCO	Royal Canadian College of Organists
RCD	Rassemblement Constitutionnel Démocratique (Tunisia)
RCD	Rassemblement pour la Culture et la Démocratie (Algeria)
RCDM	Russian Christian Democratic Movement
RCDP	Romani Christian Democratic Party (Bulgaria) = RKhDP
RCDS	Ring Christlich-Demokratischer Studenten
RCE	Europäische Organisation für Soziale Gemeinschaftsverpflegung
RCE	Radio Cadena Española
RCE	Religious of Christian Education

RCE	Union Restaurants Collectifs Européens	**RCM**	Revolutionary Communist Maoists
RCEEA	Radio Communication and Electronic Engineering Association	**RCM**	Royal College of Midwives
		RCM	Royal College of Mines
RCEHMT	Regional Centre for Energy, Heat and Mass Transfer for Asia and Pacific (India)	**RCM**	Royal College of Music
		RCMA	Rubber Cultuur Maatschappij "Amsterdam"
RCEP	Royal Commission on Environmental Pollution	**RCMP**	Royal Canadian Mounted Police
RCEVH	Research Centre for the Education of the Visually Handicapped	**RCN**	Radio Cadena Nacional (Colombia, Mexico)
RCF	Redundant Churches Fund	**RCN**	Royal Canadian Navy
RCFM	Régie du Chemin de Fer du Mali	**RCN**	Royal College of Nursing
RCFS	Régie des Chemins de Fer du Sénégal	**RCNC**	Royal Corps of Naval Constructors
RCFSAP	Regional Commission on Food Security for Asia and the Pacific	**RCNYO**	UN Regional Commissions New York Office
RCFTU	Russian Confederation of Free Trade Unions	**RCO**	Royal College of Organists
		RCOA	Radio Club of America
RCG	Revolutionary Communist Group	**RCOA**	Refugee Council of Australia
RCGP	Royal College of General Practitioners	**RCOG**	Royal College of Obstetricians and Gynaecologists
RCGS	Royal Canadian Geographical Society = SGRC	**RCP**	Revolutionary Communist Party (U.K., U.S.A.)
RCGS	Royal Canadian Geological Society	**RCP**	Romanian Communist Party
RCHME	Royal Commission on the Historical Monuments of England	**RCP**	Royal College of Physicians of London
RCHPE	Regional Clearing House for Population Education (PROAP) = POPED	**RCPA**	Rice and Corn Production Administration (Philippines)
RCHS	Royal Caledonian Horticultural Society	**RCPath**	Royal College of Pathologists
RCI	Congregatio Rogationistarium a Corde Iesu = RCJ	**RCPB(M-L)**	Revolutionary Communist Party of Britain (Marxist-Leninist)
RCI	Radio Caraïbe Internationale (Martinique)	**RCPCC**	Rice and Corn Production Coordinating Council (Philippines)
RCI	Radio Chemical Inspectorate (DoE)	**RCPE**	Royal College of Physicians of Edinburgh
RCI	Recontres Creatives Internationales (Switzerland) = ICC	**RCPI**	Royal College of Physicians of Ireland
RCI	Research and Control Instruments Ltd	**RCPS**	Royal College of Physicians and Surgeons
RCI	Retail Confectioners International		
RCI	Romani Civic Initiative (Czech Republic) = ROI	**RCPSA**	Retired Civil and Public Servants' Association (Éire)
RCI	Royal Canadian Institute	**RCPSC**	Royal College of Physicians and Surgeons of Canada
RCIVS	Regional Conference on International Voluntary Service = CRSVI	**RCPSGlas**	Royal College of Physicians and Surgeons of Glasgow
RCJ	Rogationistes du Coeur de Jésus = RCI		
RCK	Research Centrum Kalkzandsteen Industrie	**RCPsych**	Royal College of Psychiatrists
RCL	Railway Conversion League	**RCR**	Royal College of Radiologists
RCLB	Revolutionary Communist League of Britain	**RCRDC**	Radio Components Research and Development Committee
RCM	République des Citoyens du Monde = CWC	**RCRF**	Rei Cretariae Romanae Fautores (Switzerland)

RCRME	Russian Commodity and Raw Materials Exchange	**RDCAP**	Research and Development Center for Applied Physics (Indonesia)
RCRP	Rape Counselling and Research Project	**RDCC**	Royal Dutch Cattle Company
RCS	Rainforest Conservation Society	**RDCG**	Research and Development for Geotechnology (Indonesia)
RCS	Royal Choral Society		
RCS	Royal College of Science	**RDCOT**	Regional Documentation Centre for Oral Tradition (Niger)
RCS	Royal College of Surgeons of England		
RCS	Royal Commonwealth Society	**RDD**	Rassemblement Démocratique Dahoméenne (Benin)
RCS	Rural Counselling Service		
RCSB	Royal Commonwealth Society for the Blind	**RDDR**	Rossiiskoe Dvizhenie Demokraticheskikh Reform
RCSC	Radio Components Standardization Committee	**RDE**	Groupe du Rassemblement des Démocrates Européens = ERD
RCSE	Research Centre for Surface Engineering	**RDEC**	Research Development and Evaluation Commission (Taiwan)
RCSEd	Royal College of Surgeons of Edinburgh	**RDF**	Rossiiskii Demokraticheskii Forum
RCSI	Royal College of Surgeons in Ireland	**RDG**	Republican Democratic Group
RCSS	Research Centre for Social Sciences	**RDG**	Revolutionary Democratic Group
RCSSMRS	Regional Centre for Services in Surveying, Mapping and Remote Sensing (ECA)	**RDL**	Rijeka Democratic League (Croatia)
		RDM	Ring Deutscher Makler – Verband der Immobilienberufe und Hausverwalter Bundesverband
RCT	Rehabilitation and Research Center for Torture Victims (Denmark)		
RCT	Revolutionary Communist Tendency	**RDMKI**	Rossiiskoe Molodezhnoe Dvizhenie "Kommunisticheskaia Initsiativa"
RCTA	Retail Confectioners and Tobacconists Association	**RDNP**	Rassemblement des Démocrates Nationaux Progressistes (Haiti)
RCTS	Railway Correspondence and Travel Society	**RDOEI**	Research and Development Organization for the Electrical Industry (India)
RCTV	Radio Caracas Televisión (Venezuela)		
RCUK	Resuscitation Council	**RDP**	Radical Democratic Party (Bulgaria)
RCV	Republica de Cabo Verde	**RDP**	Radiodifusão Portuguesa
RCVS	Royal College of Veterinary Surgeons	**RDP**	Rossiiskaia Demokraticheskaia Partiia
RCWP	Russian Communist Workers' Party	**RDPC**	Rassemblement Démocratique du Peuple Camérounais
RDA	Rassemblement Démocratique Africain (Ivory Coast, Niger)	**RdR**	Movement for the Republic (Poland)
RDA	Revolving Doors Agency	**RDS**	Democratic Social Movement (Poland)
RDA	Riding for the Disabled Association	**RDS**	Railway Development Society
RDA	Rijeka Democratic Alliance (Croatia) = RDS	**RDS**	Research Defence Society
		RDS	Riječki Demokratski Savez (Croatia) = RDA
RDA	Romanian Development Agency	**RDS**	Royal Drawing Society
RDB	Ring Deutscher Bergingenieure	**RDS**	Royal Dublin Society (Éire)
RDBA	Rural Design & Building Association	**RDSO**	Research Designs and Standards Organisation (India)
RDC	Rassemblement Démocratique Centrafricain	**RDTC**	Regional Dermatology Training Center (IFD) (Guatemala)
RDC	Red Deer Commission (Scotland)		
RDC	Research and Development Corporation	**RDTU**	Russian Dockers Trade Union
		RDW	Rijksdienst voor Werkvoorziening
RDC	Rural Development Commission	**RE**	Royal Engineers

RE	Royal Society of Painter-Etchers and Engravers	**RED**	Rurality – Environment – Development (Belgium)
Re-Pro	Guild of Recording Producers, Directors & Engineers	**REDA**	Ramo Editoriale degli Agricoltori
RE-SOLV	Society for the Prevention of Solvent and Volatile Substance Abuse	**REDA**	Rural Education & Development Association
RE-UNITE	Re-unite: National Council for Abducted Children	**RÉDAJA**	Recherches pour l'Éducation Affective des Jeunes en Afrique
REA	Registro de Economistas	**REDALC**	Information Network for Latin America and the Caribbean
REA	Réunion Européenne Automatisme		
REA	Rural Electrification Administration (U.S.A.)	**REDCA**	Regional Cooperative Network for Education & Research in Agricultural and Renewable Resources (Costa Rica)
REA	Russian Electors Association		
REAAA	Road Engineering Association of Asia and Australia	**REDCTU**	Russian Engine Crews Trade Union
REACH	Retired Executives Action Clearing House	**REDES**	Redes de Desarrollo del Sur; Réseau pour le Développement du Sud (Kenya) = SONED
REACT	Research, Education & Aid for Children with potentially Terminal Illness	**REDES-CA**	Red Regional de Organizaciones Ambientales no Gubernamentales para el Desarrollo Sostenido de Centroamérica (Nicaragua)
REAF	Rutebileiernes Arbeidsgiverforening		
REAL	Real-Aerovias do Brasil		
REAL	Research Extension Analytical Laboratory (U.S.A.)	**REDIAL**	Red Europea de Documentación y Información sobre América Latina
REAL	Road Emulsion Association Ltd.	**REDIMPA**	Representaciones y Distribuciones de Panama, S.A.
REAP	Resource Center for Efficient Agricultural Production (U.S.A.)	**REDINSE**	Red de Información Socio-Economica (Venezuela)
REBIA	Regional Building Institute for Africa	**RedLAES**	Latin American Network for Social Ecology
RÉBUS	Réseau des Bibliothèques Utilisant SIBIL	**REDP**	Regional Energy Development Programme (ESCAP, UNDP) (Thailand)
REC	Regional Environment Centre (Hungary)		
REC	Religious Education Council of England and Wales	**REDR**	Engineers for Disaster Relief
REC	Rural Electrification Corporation (India)	**REDUC**	Red Lationoamericana de Documentación en Educación
RECA	Research and Education Centre (Japan)		
RECAP	Research and Education Center for Architectural Preservation (U.S.A.)	**REÉ**	Comité Européen de Reconstruction Économique Européenne
RECAST	Research Centre for Applied Science and Technology (Nepal)	**REECA**	Renewable Energy and Environmental Conservation Association in Developing Countries
RECE	Representación Cubana del Exilio (U.S.A.) = CORE		
RECOBAA	Office of the Government Commissioner for Foreign Agricultural Affairs (Netherlands)	**REES**	Center for Russian and East European Studies (U.S.A.)
		REF	Railway Engineers Forum
REconS	Royal Economic Society	**REFA**	Real Estate Fund of America
RECOPE	Refinadora Costarricense de Petróleo, S.A.	**REFA**	Verband für Arbeitsstudien und Betriebsorganisation
RECSAM	Regional Centre for Education in Science and Mathematics SEAMEO) (Malaysia)	**REFESA**	Rede Ferroviéria Federal (Brazil)
		RÉGABON	Radio Électricité Gabonaise
RECTAS	Regional Centre for Training in Aerospace Surveys (ARSC)	**REGI-FERCAM**	Régie Nationale des Chemins de Fer du Caméroun
		Regia	Regia Anglorum

REGIC	Société Générale d'Industrie du Caméroun
REHIS	Royal Environmental Health Institute of Scotland
REHVA	Representatives of European Heating and Ventilating Associations
REI	Rat der Europaischen Industrieverbände = CEIF, CFIE
REIFEA	Réseau Européen Interuniversitaire de Formation des Enseignants Agricoles
REIS	Royal Environmental Institute of Scotland
REKU	Raditoren- en Ketel-Unie
REL	Riksförbundet für Electrikfieringen pa Landsbygden
RELAB	Red Latinoamericana de Ciencias Biológicas
RELARN	Russian Electronic Academic and Research Network
RELC	Regional English Language Centre (SEAMEO) (Singapore)
REMA	Retroreflective Equipment Manufacturers Association
REMA	Rotating Electrical Machines Association
REMASA	Remolques Maritimos, S.A.
REMAT	Research Center for Management of New Technology (U.S.A.)
REMAT	Research Centre for Management of New Technology (Canada)
REMC	Radio and Electronics Measurements Committee
REMP	Research Group for European Migration Problems
REMPEC	Regional Marine Pollution Emergency Response Centre for the Mediterranean Sea (Malta)
RÉNA	Réseau pour l'Éducation Nutritionnelle en Afrique (Belgium)
RENAMO	Resisténcia Nacional Moçambicana = MNR
RENAS-BMTC	Regional Network in Asia for Low Cost Building Materials, Technologies and Construction Systems (Philippines)
RENEL	Romanian Electricity Authority
RENFE	Red Nacional de los Ferrocarriles Españoles
RENGO	Private Sector Trade Union Confederation (Japan)
RENPAP	Regional Network on the Production, Marketing and Control of Pesticides for Asia and the Pacific

REntS	Royal Entomological Society of London
RENVA	Rengørings-og Vagtselskabernes Arbejdsgiverforening
REPC	Resource and Environmental Policy Centre
REPEM	Red de Educacion Popurar entre Mujeres (Colombia)
REPESA	Refineria de Petroleos de Escombreras, S.A.
REPIDISCA	Red Panamericana de Información y Documentación en Ingeniería Sanitaria y Ciencias del Ambiente (PAHO)
RePMA	Release Paper Manufacturers Association
RER	Réseau Express Régional
RERC	Rare Earth Research Conference (U.S.A.)
RERF	Radiation Effects Research Foundation (Japan)
RERIC	Regional Energy Resources Information Center (Thailand)
RES	Royal Economic Society
RES	Royal Entomological Society of London
RESACENT	Remote Sensing Applications Centre (Pakistan)
RESADOC	Réseau Sahélien d'Information et Documentation Scientifique et Technique
RESCARE	National Society for Mentally Handicapped People in Residential Care
RESCUE	Rescue Trust for British Archaeology
RESEDA	Réseau de Documentation en Économie Agricole
RESL	Royal Entomological Society of London
RÉSOPALM	Réseau Palmier Dattier et Oasis
RÉSPAO	Réseau d'Étude des Systèmes de Production en Afrique de l'Ouest (Burkina Faso) = WAFSRN
RESSG	Rural Economy and Society Study Group
REST	Relief Society of Tigre
RESTEC	Remote Sensing Technology Center of Japan
RESTII	Railway Engineering Scientific & Technical Information Institute (China)
RETD	Red Especial de Transmisión de Datos
RETI	Communauté de Travail des Régions de Tradition Industrielle
RETOUR	Réseau Européen des Télécommunications Opérationnelles Météorologiques

RETRA	Radio, Electrical and Television Retailers Associatior	**RFMF**	Royal Fijian Military Force
REU	FAO Regional Office for Europe	**RFNRE**	Revolving Fund for Natural Resources Exploration (UN)
REUR	Regional Office for Europe (FAO)	**RFO**	Radio-Télévision Française d'Outre-Mer
REVIMA	Société pour la Revision et l'Entretien du Materiel Aéronautique	**RFP**	Rassemblement des Forces Patriotiques (Chad)
REVOLT	Rural England Versus Overhead Live Transmissions	**RFR**	Rassemblement des Français pour la République
REWA	Revolutionary Ethiopian Women's Association	**RFS**	Robert Farnon Society
REYA	Revolutionary Ethiopian Youth Association	**RFS**	Royal Forestry Society
		RFSEW	Royal Forestry Society of England and Wales
RF	Radiobranchens Faellesrad	**RFSU**	Riksförbundet for Sexuell Uplysing
RF	Rossiyskaya Federatsiya	**RFSU**	Rugby Football Schools Union
RF	Rural Forum	**RFTF**	Retail Fruit Trade Federation
RFA	Renewable Fuels Association (U.S.A.)	**RFU**	Rugby Football Union
RFA	Rugby Fives Association	**RG**	Rada Główna
RFAC	Royal Fine Art Commission	**RG**	Renseignements Généraux
RFACS	Royal Fine Art Commission for Scotland	**RG**	Rio Group
RFBPA	Raw Fat and Bone Processors Association	**RGA**	Restricted Growth Association (*ex* ARRG)
RFBS	Ryeland Flock Book Society	**RGAHS**	Royal Guernsey Agricultural and Horticultural Society
RFBT	Romanian Bank of Foreign Trade	**RGDATA**	Retail Grocery, Dairy and Allied Trades Association (Éire)
RFC	Rajasthan Financial Corporation (India)		
RFC	Royal Forth Yacht Club	**RGE**	Rat de Gemeinden Europas = CCE, CEM
RFCWA	Regional Fisheries Commission for Western Africa (Ghana)	**RGI**	Royal Glasgow Institute of the Fine Arts
RFD	Rassemblement des Forces Démocratiques (Benin)	**RGNiSW**	Rada Główna Nauki i Szkolnictwa Wyższego
RFDMA	Rigid Foam Ducting Manufacturers Association	**RGO**	Royal Greenwich Observatory
RFDS	Royal Flying Doctor Service (Australia)	**RGOF**	Royal Gardeners' Orphan Fund
RFEA	Regular Forces Employment Association	**RGP**	Respublikanskaia Gumanitarnaia Partiia
		RGRE	Rat der Gemeinden und Regionen Europas = CCRE, CEMR, CMRE
RFF	Resources for the Future (U.S.A.)	**RGS**	Royal Geographical Society
RFFSA	Rêde Ferroviária Federal, S.A. (Brazil)	**RGSA**	Royal Geographical Society of Australasia
RFFU	Rundfunk-Fernseh-Film-Union		
RfH	Riksförbundet för Hembygdsvård	**RGW**	Rat für Gegenseitige Wirtschaftshilfe = CAME, CAEM, CMEA, SEV
RFHSM	Royal Free Hospital School of Medicine		
RFI	Richmond Fellowship International	**RHA**	Road Haulage Association
RFISE	Royal Federation of Independent Surveyors-Experts = FRGEI, KFSLE, KFZLE (Belgium)	**RHA**	Royal Hibernian Academy (Éire)
		RHAA	Royal Hibernian Academy of Arts
		RHACT	Red Hot AIDS Charitable Trust
RFJ	Relatives for Justice	**RHAS**	Rider Haggard Appreciation Society
RFL	Radio Free Lebanon	**RHASS**	Royal Highland and Agricultural Society of Scotland
RFL	Rugby Football League		
RFLW	Rijksfaculteit Landbouw-wetenschappen (Belgium)	**RHCG**	Research for Health Charities Group

RHE	Road Haulage Executive
RHEL	Rutherford High Energy Laboratory, Chilton
RHI	Racial Harmony International (U.K.)
RHistS	Royal Historical Society
RHMF	Registered Hide Markets Federation of Northern Ireland
RHS	Riksförbundet Hem och Skola
RHS	Robin Hood Society
RHS	Royal Horticultural Society
RHS	Royal Humane Society
RHS	Russian Heraldry Society
RHSI	Royal Horticultural Society of Ireland
RHSV	Royal Historical Society of Victoria (Canada)
RHT	Railway Heritage Trust
RHT	Rural Housing Trust
RI	Rehabilitation International
RI	Richelieu International (Canada)
RI	Rotary International
RI	Royal Institute of Painters in Water Colours
RI	Royal Institution of Great Britain
RI-ECA	Rehabilitation International – European Communities Association
RIA	Railway Industry Association of Great Britain
RIA	Research Institute of America
RIA	Robotic Industries Association (U.S.A.)
RIA	Rossiiskoe Informatsionnoe Agentsvo
RIA	Royal Irish Academy
RIA-Novosti	Rossiiskoe Informatsionnoe Agentstvo - Novosti
RIAA	Recording Industry Association of America
RIAC	Railways Industry Advisory Committee
RIAC	Royal Irish Automobile Club
RIACS	Research Institute for Advanced Computer Science (U.S.A.)
RIAD	Rencontres Internationales des Assureurs Défense
RIAI	Royal Institute of the Architects of Ireland
RIAL	Programa de Estudios Conjuntos sobre las Relaciones Internacionales de América Latina
RIAM	Royal Irish Academy of Music
RIAS	Research Institute for Animal Science (South Africa)
RIAS	Research Institute for Applied Sciences (Japan)
RIAS	Royal Incorporation of Architects in Scotland
RIAS	Rundfunk im Amerikanischen Sektor, Berlin
RIATS	Research Institute of Aerostructure Thermal Strength (China)
RIB	Racing Information Bureau
RIB	Research Institute of Brewing (Japan)
RIB	Rijksinkoopbureau (Netherlands)
RIBA	Royal Institute of British Architects
RIBI	Rotary International in Great Britain and Ireland
RIBLAC	Red de Informacion en Biosciencias para Latinoamerica y el Caribe (Venezuela) = BINLAC
RIBU	Russian Industrialists and Businessmen's Union
RIC	Race Industrial Consortium (Belgium)
RIC	Radio Industry Council
RIC	Railway Industry Council
RIC	Rare Earth Information Center (U.S.A.)
RIC	Rehabilitation Industries Corporation (India)
RIC	Rice Improvement Conference (PDAF)
RIC	Royal Institution of Cornwall
RICA	Research Institute for Consumer Affairs
RICA	Réseau d'Information Agricole
RICASIP	Research Information Center and Advisory Service on Information Processing (U.S.A.)
RICAT	Recherches Internationales Concertées dans l'Atlantique Tropical = ICITA
RICD	Research Institute of Chemical Defence (China)
RICE	Research and Information Center of Eritrea (U.S.A.)
RICE	Research Institute for the Care of the Elderly
RICE	Rice Information Cooperative Effort (Philippines)
RICM	Registre International Citoyens du Monde = IRWC
RICOB	Rice and Corn Board (Philippines)
RICOCI	Représentations Industrielles et Commerciales de l'Ouest de la Côte-d'Ivoire
RICS	Royal Institution of Chartered Surveyors

RICSS	Royal Institution of Chartered Surveyors in Scotland	**RILDD**	Research Institute of Launderers, Dry-cleaners and Dyers (New Zealand)
RIDA	Rural Industrial Development Authority (Malaysia)	**RILEM**	Réunion Internationale des Laboratoires d'Essais et de Recherches sur les Matériaux et les Constructions
RIDEM	Red de Informacion de los Derechos de la Mujer (Chile)	**RILKO**	Research into Lost Knowledge Organisation
RIEC	Research Institute for Estate Crops (Indonesia)	**RIM**	Revolutionary Internationalist Movement
RIÉDE	Réseau d'Information pour l'Éducation du Développement en Europe = EDECN	**RIMCU**	Research Institute of Mindanao Culture (Philippines)
Riep	Research Institute for Education Planning (South Africa)	**RIMDC**	Rajastan State Industrial and Mineral Development Corporation (India)
RIEPT	Red Internacional de Evaluación de Pastos Tropicales	**RIMTech**	Research Institute for the Management of Technology (U.S.A.)
RIÉS	Réseau International Énergie Solaire (IEPF)	**RIMTU**	Russian Independent Miners Trade Union
RIF	Rådgivende Ingeniørers Forening	**RIN**	Rijksinstituut voor Natuurbeheer
RIF	Svenska Reproindustri Föreningen	**RIN**	Royal Institute of Navigation
RIFALC	Red de Información Forestal para América Latina y el Caribe	**RINA**	Royal Institution of Naval Architects
RIFG	Résistance Internationale des Femmes contre la Guerre	**RINAVI**	Associazione Nazionale Industriali Riparatori Navali
RIGB	Royal Institution of Great Britain	**RINORD**	Consulting Engineers in the Nordic Countries
RIGEP	Red Iberoamericana de Instituciones de Formacion y Investigacion en Gerencia Publica (Venezuela)	**RINPO**	Research Institute of Nuclear Power Operation (China)
RIGM	Research Institute of Geology for Mineral Resources (China)	**RINSCA**	Regional Informatics Network in South and Central Asia
RIGPP	Research Institute of Geophysical Prospecting for Petroleum (China)	**RINSEAP**	Regional Informatics Network for Southeast Asia and the Pacific
RIHED	Regional Institute of Higher Education and Development (Singapore) = IRESD	**RINT**	Réseau International de Néologie et de Terminologie (Canada)
RIHES	Research Institute for Health Sciences (Thailand)	**RIOE**	Research Institute for Ocean Economics (Japan)
RIIA	Reuniones de Intercambio de Información Agropecuária (Argentina)	**RIOP**	Royal Institute of Oil Painters
RIIA	Royal Institute of International Affairs	**RIOPPAH**	Regional International Organisation for Plant Protection and Animal Health = OIRSA
RIIC	Rural Industries Innovation Center (Botswana)	**RIP**	Rijksinstituut voor Pluimveeteelt
RIIEC	Research Institute for International Economic Cooperation (China)	**RIPA**	Royal Institute of Public Administration
RIIPD	Réseau International d'Information sur la Prévention de la Délinquance = ICPIN	**RIPE**	Reseaux IP Europeenne
		RIPEN	Retiro Interdenominacional de Pastores Evangélicos de Nicaragua
RIJ	Romano Internationalno Jekhethanibe = CIR	**RIPHH**	Royal Institute of Public Health and Hygiene
RIL	Revolutionary Internationalist League	**RIPN**	Russian Institute for Public Networks
RIL	Suomen Rokennusinsinöörien Liitto	**RIPQPT**	Registro Internacional de Productos Quimicos Potencialmente Toxicos (UNEP) = IRPTC, RISCPT
RILC	Racing Industry Liaison Committee	**RIPS**	Radiotherapy Injured Patients Support
		RIPS	United Nations Regional Institute for Population Studies (Ghana)

RIR	Royal Irish Regiment	**RITLA**	Red de Información Tecnológica Latinoamericana (Brazil)
RIRDC	Rural Industry Research and Development Corporation	**RITM**	Research Institute for Tropical Medicine (Philippines)
RIS	Research and Information System for the Non-Aligned and other Developing Countries (India)	**RITSAAS**	Research Institute of Tea, Sichuan Academy of Agricultural Sciences
RIS	Resource Information Service	**RITT**	Research Institute of Telecommunications Transmission (China)
RISC	International Research Institute on Social Change		
RISC	Research Institute of Synthetic Crystals (China)	**RIVM**	National Institute of Public Health & Environmental Hygiene (Netherlands)
RISCPT	Registre International des Substances Chimiques potentiellement Toxiques (UNEP) = IRPTC, RIPQPT	**RIVO**	Rijksinstituut voor Visserijonderzoek (Netherlands)
RISCT	Research Institute for the Study of Conflict and Terrorism	**RIVRO**	Rijksinstituut voor Rassenonderzoek van Landbouwgewassen
RISDA	Rubber Industries Smallholders Development Authority (Malaysia)	**RIZA**	Rijksinstituut voor Zuivering van Afvalwater
RISE	Research and Information on State Education	**RJ**	Royal Jordanian National Airline
RISE	Research Institute for Studies in Education (U.S.A.)	**RJAA**	Royal Jordanian Air Academy
		RJAF	Royal Jordanian Air Force
RISEAP	Regional Islamic Dawah Council of South East Asia and the Pacific	**RJAHS**	Royal Jersey Agricultural and Horticultural Society
RISM	Répertoire International des Sources Musicales	**RJM**	Religious of Jesus and Mary
RISO	Rossiiskii Imperskii Soiuz – Orden	**RKD**	Rijksbureau voor Kunsthistorische Documentatie
RISP	Réseau International de Science et Paix (Canada) = SPIN	**RKF**	Rådvigande Kommittén Forskning
RISPA	Research Institute of the Sumatra Planters Association (Indonesia)	**RKhDD**	Rossiiskoe Khristianskoe Demokraticheskoe Dvizhenie
RISPAL	Latin American Research Network in Animal Production Systems	**RKhDP**	Roma Khristiyan Demokraticheska Partiya (Bulgaria) = RCDP
RISSB	Research Institute on the Sino-Soviet Bloc (U.S.A.)	**RKhDP**	Rossiiskaia Khristiansko-Demokraticheskaia Partiia
RISW	Royal Institution of South Wales	**RKJB**	Rooms-Katholieke Jonge Boerenstand
RIT	Recherches et Industries Thérapeutiques (Belgium)	**RKK**	Rådvigande Kommittén för Allmänkulturell Verksamhet
RITD	Red Iberoamericana de Transmisión de Datos	**RKK**	Rissho Kosei-Kai
RITENA	Reunión Internacional de Técnicos de la Nutrición Animal	**RKL**	Rationalisieriungs-Kuratorium für Landwirtschaft
RITES	Rail India Technical and Economic Services	**RKMN**	Ruch Katolickiej Młodzieży Niepodległościowej
RITF	Research Institute of Tropical Forestry (China)	**RKRP**	Rossiiskaia Kommunisticheskaia Rabochaia Partiia
RITIBMI	Research Institute of Technical Information, State Administration for Building Materials Industry (China)	**RKS**	Robotniczy Klub Sportowy
		RKSP	Rossiiskaia Konfederatsiia Svobodnykh Profsoiuzov
RITLA	Action Committee for the Establishment of a Latin American Network of Technological Information (Venezuela)	**RKTL**	Reichskuratorium für Technik in der Landwirtschaft
		RKU	Rådvigande Kommittén for Undervisning

RKW	Rationalisierungs-Kuratorium der Deutschen Wirtschaft		**RMAG**	Rocky Mountain Association of Geologists
RKW	Regionalna Komisja Wykonawcza		**RMAI**	Radio Manufacturers' Association of India
RL	Reproducørernes Landsforening			
RLAC	FAO Regional Office for Latin America and the Caribbean		**RMAS**	Royal Maritime Auxiliary Service
			RMB	Radio Marketing Bureau
RLAC	Red Latinoamericana de Abogados Católicos		**RMBC**	Regional Marine Biological Centre = CRBM
RLAF	Right Livelihood Awards Foundation		**RMBF**	Royal Medical Benevolent Fund
RLAT	Regional Office for Latin America (FAO)		**RMC**	Radio Monte-Carlo
			RMC	Regional Meteorological Centre (WMO)
RLB	Red Latinoamericana de Botanica			
RLC	Refugee Legal Centre		**RMC**	Republican Movement of the Crimea
RLC	Rijkslandbouwconsultentschap		**RMCC**	Royal Military College of Canada
RLD	Rijksluchtvaartdienst		**RMCS**	Royal Medical and Chirurgical Society
RLF	Ren Luft Foreningen		**RMCS**	Royal Military College of Science
RLF	Riksforbündet Landsbygdens Folk		**RMCU**	Royal Martyr Church Union
RLF	Royal Literary Fund		**RMDR**	Russian Movement for Democratic Reforms
RLG	Research Libraries Group (U.S.A.)			
RLH	Swedish Farmers Flax and Hemp Growers Association		**RME**	Religieuses en Mission Educative
			RMEA	Rubber Manfacturing Employers Association
RLL	Norske Radiofabrikanters Forbund			
RLL	Radio-Leverandorenes Landsforbund		**RMetS**	Royal Meteorological Society
RLL	Radioliikkeiden Liitto		**RMI**	Retail Motor Industry Federation (ex MAA)
RLLMA	Red Lead & Litharge Manufacturers' Association			
			RMI	Rocky Mountain Institute (U.S.A.)
RLPS	Royal Liverpool Philharmonic Society		**RMIT**	Royal Melbourne Institute of Technology
RLS	Rossiiskii Liberalnyi Soiuz			
RLSB	Royal London Society for the Blind		**RMK**	Raad voor het Midden-en Kleinbedrijf
RLSS	Royal Life Saving Society		**RMKI**	Részecske- és Magfizikai Kutató Intézet
RLTA	Recreation and Leisure Trades Association			
			RMM&CA	Road Markings and Contractors Manufacturers Association
RLVD	Rijkslandbouwvoorlichtingsdienst			
RLWS	Rijkslandbouwwinterscholen		**RMN**	Rada Mniejszości Narodowych (Poland) =NMC
RM	Rada Ministrów			
RM	Rossiia Molodaia		**RMNP**	Radical Moravian Nationalist Party = RMNS
RMA	Recreation Manager's Association of Great Britain			
			RMNS	Radikální Moravská Nacionálni Strana (Czech Republic) = RMNP
RMA	Retread Manufacturers Association			
RMA	Rijkscentrale voor Mechanische Administratie		**RMOC**	Rassemblement des Mouvements de l'Opposition des Comores
RmA	Riksförbundet mot Allergi		**RmP**	Riksföreningen mot Polio
RMA	Royal Monetary Authority (Bhutan)		**RMP**	Rio Mazan Project
RMA	Royal Musical Association		**RMPR**	Rassemblement Mahorais pour la République (Mayotte)
RMA	Rubber Manufacturers Association (U.S.A.)			
			RMR	Riksförbundet mot Reumatism
RMA	Rusk Manufacturers Association (now CIMA)		**RMS**	Records Management Society
			RMS	Royal Medical Society
			RMS	Royal Meteorological Society
			RMS	Royal Microscopical Society

RMS	Royal Society of Miniature Painters, Sculptors and Gravers
RMSM	Royal Military School of Music
RMT	National Union of Rail, Maritime and Transport Workers
RMTP	Regional Marine Turtle Management and Conservation Program
RN	Rada Narodowa
RN	Renovación Nacional (Chile)
RN	Resistencia Nicaragüense
RN	Rodoviaria Nacional (Portugal)
RN	Ruch Narodowy (Poland) = NM
RNA	Rassamblement National Arabe (Tunisia)
RNA	Romantic Novelists Association
RNA	Royal Naval Association
RNA	Royal Nepalese Army = SNJA
RNA	Royal Netherlands Army = KL
RNAA	Royal Norfolk Agricultural Association
RNAB	Regional Newspapers Advertising Bureau (Éire)
RNAM	Regional Network for Agricultural Machinery (Philippines)
RNARS	Royal Naval Amateur Radio Society
RNBS	Royal Naval Benevolent Society
RNBT	Royal Naval Benevolent Trust
RNBWS	Royal Navy Bird Watching Society
RNC	Regional Network Centre for East Africa of the International Training Network for Water and Waste Management (Kenya)
RNC	Romani National Congress (Czech Republic) = RNK
RNCC	Royal Northern & Clyde Yacht Club
RNCP	Rural Nature Conservation Program
RNCSMFE	Russian National Committee for Soil Mechanics and Foundation Engineering
RND	Rassemblement National Démocratique (Benin, Senegal)
RND	Rijksnijverheidsdienst
RNDFP PAMIAT	"Pamiat" – Russkii Narodno-Demokraticheskii Front Dvizheniia
RNDM	Religieuses de Notre-Dame des Missions
RNDT	Rassemblement Nationale Démocratique et Populaire du Tchad
RNE	Radio Nacional de España
RNEA	FAO Regional Office for the Near East
RNEA	Regional Office for the Near East (FAO)
RNES	Royal Navy Enthusiasts' Society
RNET	Régie Nationale des Eaux du Togo
RNF	Rossiiskii Narodnyi Front
RNG	Rhenische Naturforschende Gesellschaft e.V.
RNHA	Registered Nursing Home Association
RNHU	Royal National Homing Union
RNI	Rassemblement National des Indépendants (Morocco)
RNI	Rural Nutrition Institute (South Korea)
RNIB	Royal National Institute for the Blind
RNID	Royal National Institute for the Deaf
RNII	Raketnyi nauchno-issledovatel'skii Institut
RNIS	Réseau Numérique a l'Intégration de Services
RNK	Romský Národní Kongres (Czech Republic) = RNC
RNL	Riso National Laboratory (Denmark)
RNLAF	Royal Netherlands Air Force
RNLI	Royal National Lifeboat Institution
RNMDSF	Royal National Mission to Deep Sea Fishermen
RNPC	Régie Nationale des Palmeraies du Congo
RNPF	Respublikanskaia Partiia Rossiiskoi Federatsii
RNPR	Respublikanskaia Narodnaia Partiia Rossii
RNPTs	Russkii Natsionalno-Patrioticheskii Front
RNRAŚ	Ruch na Rzecz Autonomii Śląska (Poland) = MSA
RNRS	Royal National Rose Society
RNS	Royal Numismatic Society
RNSA	Royal Naval Sailing Association
RNSAS	Royal Netherlands Society for Agricultural Science
RNSHS	Royal Nova Scotia Historical Society (Canada)
RNSS	Royal Naval Scientific Service
RNSTS	Royal Naval Supply and Transport Service
RNT	Radiodiffusion Nationale Tchadienne
RNTP	Régie Nationale des Transports et des Travaux Publics (Congo)
RNU	Russian National Union
RNUP	Romanian National Unity Party
RNUR	Régie Nationale des Usines Renault

RNVR	Royal Naval Volunteer Reserve
RNYC	Royal Northern Yacht Club
RNZ	Radio New Zealand
RNZAC	Royal New Zealand Armoured Corps
RNZAF	Royal New Zealand Air Force
RNZAS	Royal Astronomical Society of New Zealand
RNZIH	Royal New Zealand Institute of Horticulture
RNZN	Royal New Zealand Navy
RO	Rusínska Obroda (Slovakia) = RR
ROA	Raad van Organisatie-Adviesbureaus
ROA	Racehorse Owners Association
ROA	Reinsurance Offices Association
ROAD	Ruch Obywatelski Akcja Demokratyczna
ROATA	Western African Animal Traction Network
ROBA	Regionaal Ontwikkelings Bureau Agrotechnologie
ROC	Regroupement des Officiers Communistes (Burkina Faso)
ROC	Royal Observer Corps
ROCAP	Regional Office for Central America and Panama (FAO)
ROCBA	Regional Office for Culture and Book Development in Asia (Pakistan)
ROCEP	Research Organisation for the Control of Environmental Pollution
ROCSOC	Republic of China Society of Cardiology
ROE	Royal Observatory Edinburgh
ROEDAC	Réseau Oecuménique pour l'Environnement et le Développement de l'Afrique Centrale (Congo) = ACEEDAC
ROI	Romská Občanská Iniciativa (Czech Republic) = RCI
ROL	Royal Overseas League
ROLTER	Manufactura del Calzado (Nicaragua)
ROM	Royal Ontario Museum
ROM-IVOIRE	Société de Commercialisation Ivoiro-Roumaine
ROMAZO	Vereningen van Rolluiken- Markeizen- en Zonweringbedrijven
Romgaz	Romanian National Gas Corporation
Rompres	Romanian Press Agency
ROM-TRANS	Association Roumaine pour Transports Routiers Internationaux

RONGEAD	Réseau des ONG Européennes sur les Questions Agro-Alimentaires et de Développement = ENAFOOD
RONS	Russkii Obshchenatsionalnyi Soiuz
ROP	Rada Ochrony Pracy
ROPME	Regional Organisation for the Protection of the Marine Environment (Kuwait)
ROPP	Rejonowe Ośrodki Pracy Partyjnej
RORC	Royal Ocean Racing Club
ROS	Rossiiskii Obshchenarodnyi Front
ROS	Russkii Obshchinyi Soiuz
ROSCM	Research Organisation of Ships Compositions Manufacturers
ROSCO	Road Operators Safety Council
ROSE-CARPE	North of England Rose, Carnation & Sweet Pea Society
ROSL	Royal Over-Seas League
RoSPA	Royal Society for the Prevention of Accidents
ROSTA	Regional Office for Science and Technology for Africa (UNESCO)
ROSTAS	Regional Office for Science and Technology for the Arab States (UNESCO)
ROSTE	Regional Office for Science and Technology for Europe (UNESCO) (Italy)
ROSTLAC	Regional Office for Science and Technology for Latin America and the Caribbean (UNESCO)
ROSTSCA	Regional Office for Science and Technology for South and Central Asia (UNESCO)
ROSTSEA	Regional Office for Science and Technology for South East Asia (UNESCO)
ROW	Rights of Women
ROWEA	Asociatia Româna Pentru Energia Vantului
RP	Rada Państwowa
RP	Rada Poláků (Czech Republic) = PC
RP	Republican Party (Bosnia-Herzegovina, Bulgaria)
RP	Republican Party / Republikanska Partija (Macedonia)
RP	Roma Parliament (Hungary) = MRP
RP	Royal Society of Portrait Painters
RP	Russkaia Partiia
RP	Rzeczpospolita Polska

RP-AR	Republican Party-Association for the Republic (Czech Republic) = RS-SR	**RPRA**	Rubber and Plastics Reclamation Association
RPA	Radio Paging Association	**RPRF**	Republican Party of the Russian Federation
RPA	Rationalist Press Association	**RPS**	Racial Preservation Society
RPA	Republica do Povo do Angola	**RPS**	Radical Philosophy Society
RPA	Rural Pharmacists Association	**RPS**	Radio Propagation Society (China)
RPA	Rural Preservation Association	**RPS**	Rare Poultry Society
RPA	Rwandan Patriotic Army	**RPS**	Royal Pharmaceutical Society
RPAA	Regional Planning Association of America	**RPS**	Royal Philanthropic Society
RPB	Sisters Adorers of the Precious Blood	**RPS**	Royal Philatelic Society
RPC	Research and Productivity Council (Canada)	**RPS**	Royal Philharmonic Society
RPC	Rijkspluimveeteeltconsulentschap	**RPS**	Royal Photographic Society
RPC	Romani Party of Croatia = SRH	**RPSI**	Railway Preservation Society of Ireland
RPCI	Retirement Planning Council of Ireland	**RPSL**	Royal Philatelic Society, London
RPCR	Rassemblement pour la Calédonie dans la République	**RPSS**	Respublikanskaia Partiia Svobody i Solidarnost
RPDP	Rossiiskaia Partiia Demokraticheskikh Preobrazovanii	**RPT**	Rassemblement du Peuple Togolais
RPDP/B	Rabochaia Partiia Diktatury Proletariata (Bolshevikov)	**RPT**	Reptile Protection Trust
		RPvZ	Rijksproefstation voor Zaadcontrôle
RPF	Reformatorische Politieke Federatie	**RPW**	Rada Porozumienia Narodowego
RPF	Romanian Popular Front = FPR	**RPW**	Rada Przekształceń Własnościowych
RPF	Rwandan Patriotic Front	**RPW**	Ruch Polityczny Wyzwolenie
RPFC	Royal Patriotic Fund Corporation	**RR**	Rada Robotnicza
RPFI	Asian Regional Cooperative Project on Food Irradiation	**RR**	Rörledningsfirmirnas Riksorganisation
		RR	Ruthenian Revival (Slovakia) = RO
RPFLP	Revolutionary Popular Front for the Liberation of Palestine (Lebanon)	**RRA**	Road Roller Association
		RRA	Rubber Research Association (Israel)
RPI	Registro de la Propiedad Industrial (Spain)	**RRC**	Rehabilitation Resource Centre
		RRC	Relief and Rehabilitation Commission (Ethiopia, Sudan)
RPIa	Revolutsionnye Proletarskie Iacheiki	**RRC**	Road Runners Club (U.K., U.S.A.)
RPK	Republican Party of Kazakhstan	**RRC**	Russian Research Center (U.S.A.)
RPM	Rastokhez Patriotic Movement (Tajikistan)	**RRCBC**	Regional Research Centre of the British Caribbean (Trinidad)
RPM	Republica Popular de Moçambique	**RRCH**	Registered Residential Care Homes
RPMA	Release Paper Manufacturers' Association	**RRF**	Registrerte Revisorers Forening
		RRI	Radio Republik Indonesia
RPNV	Russkaia Partiia Natsionalnogo Vozrozhdeniia	**RRI**	Rowett Research Institute
		RRI	Rubber Research Institute (Malaysia, Sri Lanka)
RPO	Reggae Philharmonic Orchestra		
RPP	Rassemblement Populaire pour le Progrès Djibouti	**RRII**	Rubber Research Institute of India
		RRIN	Rubber Research Institute of Nigeria
RPPITB	Rubber and Plastics Processing Industry Training Board	**RRISL**	Rubber Research Institute of Sri Lanka
		RRIU	Retail Clerks International Union
RPR	Rassemblement pour la République (France, French Guiana, Guadeloupe, Martinique, Réunion)	**RRIWB**	River Research Institute, West Bengal
		RRL	Radio Research Laboratory (Japan)
RPRA	Royal Pigeon Racing Association	**RRL**	Regional Research Laboratory (India)

RRLJ	Regional Research Laboratory, Jorhat (India)	**RSDA**	Road Surface Dressing Association
RRRPD	Réseau de Radio Rural des Pays en Développement = DCFRN	**RSDG**	Rassemblement Social-Démocrate Gabonais
RS	Royal Society	**RSDP**	Romanian Social Democratic Party
RS-SR	Republikánska Strana Sdruženi pro Republiku (Czech Republic) = RP-AR	**RSDR**	Royal Society for Disability & Rehabilitation
RSA	Racket Sports Association	**RSE**	Royal Society of Edinburgh
RSA	Refined Sugar Association	**RSEHN**	Real Sociedad Española de Historia Natural
RSA	Regional Science Association		
RSA	Regional Studies Association	**RSES**	Romanian Solar Energy Society = SRES
RSA	Relay Services Association of Great Britain	**RSF**	Real Sociedad Fotográfica
RSA	Renaissance Society of America	**RSF**	Reporters sans Frontières
RSA	Republic of South Africa	**RSF**	Riksförbundet för Sveriges Försvar
RSA	Royal Scottish Academy of Painting, Sculpture and Architecture	**RSF**	Riksförbundet Svensk Frukt
RSA	Royal Society of Arts	**RSF**	Russian Society of Foresters
RSA	Royal Society of Arts, Manufactures and Commerce	**RSFS**	Royal Scottish Forestry Society
		RSG	Robert-Schumann-Gesellschaft e.V.
RSA	Royal Society of Australia	**RSGAEP**	Red Sea and Gulf of Aden Environment Programme (ALECSO) = PERSGA
RSAA	Royal Society for Asian Affairs		
RSABI	Royal Scottish Agricultural Benevolent Institution	**RSGB**	Radio Society of Great Britain
		RSGS	Royal Scottish Geographical Society
RSAC	Royal Scottish Automobile Club	**RSH**	Royal Society for the Promotion of Health
RSACT	Risk and Systems Analysis for the Control of Toxics Program (U.S.A.)		
RSAI	Royal Society of Antiquaries of Ireland	**RSHG**	Radical Statistics Health Group
RSAMD	Royal Scottish Academy of Music and Drama	**RSHM**	Religious of the Sacred Heart of Mary = RSCM
		RSIA	Repetitive Strain Injury Association
RSAR	Retailers for Shop Acts Reform	**RSL**	Radio Saint Lucia
RSAS	Royal Surgical Aid Society	**RSL**	Returned Services League (Australia)
RSASA	Royal South Australian Society of Arts	**RSL**	Revolutionary Socialist League
RSAT	Real Sociedad Arqueólogica Tarraconense	**RSL**	Royal Society of Literature
RSBA	Royal Society of British Artists	**RSLPF**	Royal Saint Lucia Police Force
RSBS	Research School of Biological Sciences (ANU)	**RSM**	Royal School of Mines
		RSM	Royal Society of Medicine
RSBS	Royal Society of British Sculptors	**RSM**	Royal Society of Musicians
RSC	Refugee Support Centre	**RSMA**	Royal Society of Marine Artists (FBA)
RSC	Remote Sensing Centre (Egypt)	**RSMD**	Remote Sensing and Meteorological Applications Division (IAEA)
RSC	Royal Shakespeare Company		
RSC	Royal Society of Canada	**RSME**	Real Sociedad Matemática Española
RSC	Royal Society of Chemistry	**RSMG**	Rubber Stamp Manufacturers' Guild
RSCDS	Royal Scottish Country Dance Society	**RSMML**	Rajastan State Mines and Minerals Ltd (India)
RSCM	Religiose del Sacro Cuore di Maria = RSHM		
		RSN	Royal School of Needlework
RSCM	Royal School of Church Music	**RSNA**	Radiological Society of North America
RSD	Rassemblement des Socialistes et des Démocrates (Réunion)	**RSNC**	Royal Society for Nature Conservation
		RSNO	Royal Scottish National Orchestra
		RSNT	Railway Staffs National Tribunal

RSNT	Research Society for Natural Therapeutics
RSNTTD	Russian Society for Nondestructive Testing and Technical Diagnostics
RSNZ	Royal Society of New Zealand
RSP	Radioisotope Society of the Philippines
RSP	Rassemblement Socialiste Progressiste (Tunisia)
RSPB	Royal Society for the Protection of Birds
RSPBA	Royal Scottish Pipe Band Association
RSPCA	Royal Society for the Prevention of Cruelty to Animals
RSPP	Royal Society of Painter-Printmakers
RSPP	Royal Society of Portrait Painters (FBA)
RSPS	Research School of Pacific Studies (ANU)
RSPS	Royal Scottish Pipers Society
RSR	République Socialiste de Roumanie
RSR	Royal Sailors' Rests
RSRC	Rural Studies Research Centre
RSRE	Radar and Signals and Radar Establishment (MOD)
RSRIGS	Royal Society for the Relief of Indigent Gentlewomen of Scotland
RSS	Agrarian Party of Slovakia
RSS	Railway Society of Scotland
RSS	Rashtriya Swayamsewak Sangh (India) = RSSS
RSS	Rastriya Sambad Samiti (Nepal)
RSS	Remote Sensing Society
RSS	Robert Simpson Society
RSS	Royal Scientific Society (Jordan)
RSS	Royal Statistical Society
RSSA	Royal Scottish Society of Arts
RSSA	Royal Society of South Africa
RSSI	Royal Statistical Society of Ireland
RSSPCC	Royal Scottish Society for the Prevention of Cruelty to Children
RSSS	Rashtriya Swayam Sewak Sangh = RSS
RST	Rassemblement Socialiste Tunisien
RSTCA	Regional Sugarcane Training Centre for Africa (Mauritius)
RSTK	Robotnicze Stowarzyszenie Twórców Kultury
RSTM&H	Royal Society of Tropical Medicine and Hygiene
RSUA	Royal Society of Ulster Architects
RSV	Congregatio Religiosorum Sancti Vincentii a Paulo
RSV	Royal Society of Victoria
RSVP	Research Society for Victorian Periodicals (Canada, U.S.A.)
RSW	Prasa-Książka-Ruch
RSW	Royal Scottish Society of Painters in Water Colours
RSWG	Response Strategies Working Group (IPCC)
RSWGSC	RSWG Steering Committee
RSZ	Rijksdienst voor Sociale Zekerheid = ONSS
RTA	Comité de Coordination de la Route Trans-Africaine (Ethiopia) = TAH
RTA	Racehorse Transporters Association
RTA	Radiodiffusion Télévision Algérienne
RTA	Road Transport Association
RTA	Roofing Tile Association
RTA	Rose Trade Association
RTA	Rubber Trade Association (U.K., U.S.A.) (*now* AIRT)
RTAC	Roads and Transportation Association of Canada
RTAF	Royal Thai Air Force (Thailand)
RTB	Radiodiffusion-Télévision Belge = BRT
RTBF	Radio-Télévision Belge de la Communauté Culturelle Française
RTBI	National Association of Round Tables of Great Britain and Ireland
RTC	Resolution Trust Corporation (U.S.A.)
RTC	Rijkstuinbouwconsulentschap
RTC	River Transport Corporation (Sudan)
RTCEG	Rubber and Thermoplastic Cables Export Group
RTCH	National Conference of Road Transport Clearing Houses
RTCM	Radio Technical Commission for Maritime Services (U.S.A.)
RTCM	Register of Traditional Chinese Medicine
RTCMA	Rubber and Thermoplastic Cable Manufacturers Association
RTCS	Round Tower Churches Society
RTD	Radio-Télévision de Djibouti
RTE	Radio Telefís Éireann
RTEC	Retail Trades Education Council
RTEEB	Radio Television and Electronics Examination Board
RTG	Radiodiffusion Télévision Gabonaise
RTG	Radiodiffusion-Télévision Guinéenne

RTI	Radiodiffusion-Télévision Ivoirienne
RTI	Round Table International
RTITB	Road Transport Industry Training Board
RTL	Radio-Télé Luxembourg
RTM	Radio Television Malaysia
RTM	Radio-Télévision Malagasy
RTM	Radiodiffusion Télévision Marocaine
RTMA	Radio and Television Manufacturers Association (Canada, U.S.A.)
RTMDC	Research Trust for Metabolic Diseases in Children
RTNB	Radiodiffusion et Télévision Nationale du Burundi
RTP	Radio y Televisión Peruana
RTP	Radiotelevisão Portuguésa
RTP	Republican Turkish Party (TRNC)
RTPA	Régie de Transports de la Province de l'Atlantique
RTPI	Royal Town Planning Institute
RTR	Third Republic Movement (Poland)
RTRI	Railway Technical Research Institute (Japan)
RTRO	Reclamation Trades Research Organisation
RTS	Radio Television Seychelles
RTS	Risk Theory Society
RTS	River Thames Society
RTS	Royal Television Society
RTS	Royal Toxophilite Society
RTSA	Retail Trading Standards Association
RTSAN	Reclaim The Street Action Network
RTSP	Resources and Technical Services Division (ALA)
RTT	Radiodiffusion-Télévision Tunisienne
RTT	Régie des Télégraphes et des Téléphones / Régie van Telegrafie et van Telefonie (Belgium)
RTTC	Road Time Trials Council
RTUE	Recognition Technology Users Association (U.S.A.)
RTVE	Radiotelevisión Española
RTZ	Rio Tinto Zinc
RU-DATA	Radvigande Utskott i Datafragor
RUA	Romanian Unity Alliance
RUA	Royal Ulster Academy
RUAS	Royal Ulster Agricultural Society
RUBA	Rural Design and Building Association
RUBIAC	Rubber Industry Advisory Committee
RUBSSO	Rossendale Union of Boot, Shoe and Slipper Operatives
RUC	Royal Ulster Constabulary
RUCA	Rijksuniversitair Centrum Antwerpen (Belgium)
RUDT	Rassemblement pour l'Unité et la Démocratie Tchadienne
RUF	Refractory Users Federation
RUFI	Representantforeningen for Utlanska Farmaceutiska Industrier
RUFSAC	Société Rufisquoise de Fabrication de Sacs (Senegal)
RUHBC	Research Unit in Health and Behavioral Change
RUI	Resource Use Institute
RUIE	Russian Union of Industrialists and Entrepreneurs
RUKBA	Royal United Kingdom Benevolent Association
RUMS	Resource Use Management Subgroup (IPCC)
RUOG	Representación Unitaria de la Oposición Guatemalteca
RURAL	Society for the Responsible Use of Resources in Agriculture and on the Land
RURCON	Rural Development Consultancy for Christian Churches in Africa
RUSE	Research Unit for the Sociology of Education (Finland)
RUSHSAP	Regional Unit for Social and Human Sciences for the Asia Pacific Region (Unesco)
RUSI	Royal United Service Institute for Defence Studies
RusPC	Russian Party of the Crimea
RV	Radikale Venstre
RVA	Returned Volunteer Action
RVC	Rijksveeteeltconsulentschap
RVCI	Royal Veterinary College of Ireland
RVD	Rijksvoorlichtingsdienst
RVF	Svenska Renhållningsverksföreningen
RVIA	Recreational Vehicle Industry Association (U.S.A.)
RVIA	Royal Victorian Institute of Architects (Australia)
RVL	Rijksstation voor Landbouwtechniek (Belgium)
RVP	Council for Research in Values and Philosophy (U.S.A.)

RVP	Rijksvoorlichtingsdienst voor de Pluimveeteelt
RVS	Reifengewerbe-Verband der Schweiz
RW	Rassemblement Wallon (Belgium)
RWA	Race Walking Association
RWA	Raoul Wallenberg Association = RWF
RWANDEX	Rwanda Coffee Export Agency
RWAS	Royal Welsh Agricultural Society
RWC	Romanian World Congress = CMR
RWCAL	Romanian Working Commission of Applied Linguistics = GRLA
RWCC	Recycled Water Coordination Committee
RWDSU	Retail, Wholesale and Department Store Union (U.S.A.)
RWE	Rheinisch-Westfälisches Electrizitätswerk
RWEDP	Regional Wood Energy Development Programme (Thailand)
RWF	Raoul Wallenberg Foreningen = RWA
RWFCS	Red and White Friesian Cattle Society
RWI	Rhine-Westphalia Institute for Economic Research
RWIC	Rioja Wine Information Centre
RWL	Revolutionary Workers League
RWMAC	Radioactive Waste Management Advisory Committe
RWPG	Rada Wzajemnej Pomocy Gospodarczej
RWS	Royal Society of Painters in Water Colours
RYA	Royal Yachting Association
RYCB	Royal Yacht Club de Belgique
RYCO	Royal Yacht Club d'Ostende
RYMSA	Radiacion y Microondas
RZ	Rada Zakładowa
RZ	Russkoe Znamia
RZAL	Rotterdam – Zuid Amerika Lijn
RZC	Rijkszuivelconsulentschap
RŽOČZ	Rada Židovských Obcí Českých Zemí (Czech Republic) = CJCCL
RZS	Royal Zoological Society
RZSI	Royal Zoological Society of Ireland
RZSNSW	Royal Zoological Society of New South Wales
RZSS	Royal Zoological Society of Scotland
RZSSA	Royal Zoological Society of South Australia

S

S of M	Society of Metaphysicians
S&TA	Salmon and Trout Association
SČVU	Svaz Českych Vytvarnych Umelcu
S-2	Army Rural Intelligence Network (Guatemala)
SŁ	Stowarzyszenie Łemków (Poland) = LA
S4C	Sianel Pedwar Cymru
SA	Salvation Army
SA	Schweizerischer Apothekerverein
SA	Skogbrukets Arbeidsgiverforening
SA	Slovenian Alliance = SZ
SA	Société Africaine Radioélectrique
SA	Society of Actuaries (U.S.A.)
SA	Soeurs Auxiliatrices des Âmes du Purgatoire (France) = HHS
SA	Soil Association
SA	Sparebankenes Arbeidsgiverforening
SA	Sudan Airways
SA	Suomen Akatemia
SA	Superintendents' Association
SA	Svenska Agghandelsförbundet
SA	Svenska Akademien
SA	Svenska Akeriförbundet
SAA	Schweizerische Arbeitsgemeinschaft für Aphasie = CSA
SAA	Schweizerische Astronautische Arbeitsgemeinschaft
SAA	Scottish Aeromodellers Association
SAA	Scottish Archery Association
SAA	Scottish Assessors' Association
SAA	Shuaiba Area Authority (Kuwait)
SAA	Social Administration Association
SAA	Sociedad Argentina de Agronomia
SAA	Sociedad Argentina de Antropologia
SAA	Sociedad Argentina de Apicultores
SAA	Société Agricole de l'Agneby (Ivory Coast)
SAA	Société Algérienne d'Assurances
SAA	Société Auxiliare Africaine (Senegal)
SAA	Society for American Archaeology
SAA	Society of American Archivists
SAA	Society of Archer-Antiquaries
SAA	Society of Incorporated Accountants and Auditors (South Africa)
SAA	South African Airways

SAA	Standards Association of Australia	**SAAS**	Scottish Adoption Advice Service
SAA	Sub-Aqua Association	**SAAS**	Sichuan Academy of Agricultural Science
SAA	Svenska Aerosolföreningen		
SAAA	Scottish Agricultural Arbiters Association	**SAAS**	South African Archaeological Society
		SAAS	Southern Association of Agricultural Scientists (U.S.A.)
SAAA	Scottish Amateur Athletic Association		
SAAAS	South African Association for the Advancement of Science	**SAAT**	Société d'Aménagement et d'Activités Tertiaires
SAAB	Saudi Arabian Agricultural Bank	**SAATC**	Southern African Air Transport Council
SAAB	Svensk Aeroplan Aktiebolaget	**SAATVE**	South African Association for Technical and Vocational Education
SAABS	Scottish Action Against Blood Sports		
SAAC	Scottish Artists & Artist Craftsmen (ex SSWA)	**SAAU**	South African Agricultural Union
		SAAU	Système d'Approvisionnement Alimentaire d'Urgence (WFP) = EFSS
SAAC	Scottish Asian Action Committee		
SAACE	South African Association of Consulting Engineers	**SAAUW**	South African Association of University Women = SAVUV
SAAD	Society for the Advancement of Anaesthesia in Dentistry	**SAB**	Schweizerische Arbeitsgemeinschaft der Bergbauern
SAADCO	Saudi Arabian Agriculture and Dairy Company	**SAB**	Schweizerische Arbeitsgemeinschaft der Öffentlichen Bibliotheken
SAAEB	South African Atomic Energy Board	**SAB**	Schweizerische Arbeitsgemeinschaft für die Bergbevölkerung
SAAEVA	Southern Association for Agricultural Engineering and Vocational Agriculture (U.S.A.)		
		SAB	Sociedad Argentina de Biologia
		SAB	Sociedad Argentina de Botánica
SAAF	South African Air Force	**SAB**	Sociedad Arqueológica de Bolivia
SAAFOST	South African Association for Food Science and Technology	**SAB**	Société Africaine de Bonneterie (Ivory Coast)
SAAI	Sociedad Argentina de Alergia y Inmunopatologia	**SAB**	Société Africaine des Bois
		SAB	Society of Applied Bacteriology
SAAI	Speciality Advertising Association International (U.S.A.)	**SAB**	Stichting v. Aardappelbewaring
		SAB	Sveriges Allmänna Biblioteksförening
SAAMBR	South African Association for Marine Biological Research	**SABA**	Scottish Amateur Boxing Association
SAANZ	Sociological Association of Australia and New Zealand	**SABA**	South African Black Alliance
		SABA	South African Brick Association
SAAO	South African Astronomical Observatory	**SABAM**	Société Anonyme Belge des Auteurs, Compositeurs et Éditeurs de Musique
SAAP	Society for the Advancement of American Philosophy	**SABAP**	Southern African Bird Atlas Project
SAAP	Suid-Afrikaanse Arbeiders Party = SALP	**SABB**	Société d'Arrimage des Battures de Beauport (Canada)
SAAPE	Scottish Association of Advisers in Physical Education	**SABC**	Scottish Association of Boys Clubs
		SABC	Société des Brasseries du Caméroun
SAARA	Sociedad de Amigos del Arbol de la República Argentina	**SABC**	South African Broadcasting Corporation
SAARBS	South African Angora Ram Breeders Society	**SABCA**	Société Anonyme Belge de Constructions Aéronautiques
SAARC	South Asian Association for Regional Cooperation = ASACR	**SABCO**	Society for the Area of Biological and Chemical Overlap (Japan)
		SABE	Services Auxiliares de Barreaux Européens (Belgium)
SAARCI	Sindicato Autónomo Agenti Rappresentani Commercio Industria	**SABE**	Société Africaine d'Exploitation des Brevets Eries

SABE	Société Africaine des Bois de l'Est (Cameroon)
SABEA	Societa Alimentari Bevande e Affini
SABENA	Société Anonyme Belge d'Exploitation de la Navigation Aérienne
SABENI	Sociedad Agropecuária del Beni Ltda (Bolivia)
SABEPA	Société Anonyme Belge d'Exploitation de Photographie Aérienne
SABET	Scottish Association for Building Education and Training
SABEW	Saudi Basic Industries Corporation (Saudi Arabia)
SABHATA	Sand and Ballast Hauliers and Allied Trades Alliance
SABI	Société Africaine de Biscuiterie (Ivory Coast)
SABIC	Saudi Basic Industries Corporation (Saudi Arabia)
SABIC	Society for the Advancement of Brain Injured Children
SABIG	Société de Blanchisserie Industrielle du Gabon
SABL	Société des Sciences, Arts et Belles-Lettres de Bayeux
SABM	Société Africaine de Béton Manufacture
SABO	Société Agricole d'Abobo (Ivory Coast)
SABOGAB	Société des Bois du Gabon
SABR	Society for American Baseball Research
SABRA	Suid-Afrikaanse Bureau vir Rasse Aangeleenthede
SABRAO	Society for the Advancement of Breeding Researches in Asia and Oceania
SABRE	Sociedad Aleña Brasileira de Reflorestamento
SABRITA	South Africa-Britain Trade Association
SABS	Congregation of the Sisters of the Adoration of the Blessed Sacrament
SABS	South African Bureau of Standards
SABS	Southern Anti-Blood Sports Society
SABTS	South African Blood Transfusion Service
SAC	Advisory Committee on the Carriage of Dangerous Goods in Ships
SAC	Post Office Stamp Advisory Committee
SAC	Salmon Advisory Committee
SAC	Schweizer Alpen Club
SAC	Scientific Advisory Committee (IAEA)
SAC	Scottish Abortion Campaign
SAC	Scottish Agricultural College
SAC	Scottish Arts Council
SAC	Scottish Association for Counselling
SAC	Service de la Propriétarie Industrielle et Commerciale
SAC	Sociedad Agronómica de Chile
SAC	Sociedad Argentina de Criminologia
SAC	Sociedad de Agricultores de Colombia
SAC	Societas Apostolatus Catholici "Pallottini" = SCA
SAC	Société Africaine de Culture
SAC	Société d'Achat et de Commission
SAC	Society for Analytical Chemistry
SAC	Society of Applied Cosmetology
SAC	Southern Africa Coalition
SAC	Southern African Committee (U.S.A.)
SAC	State Advances Corporation (Australia)
SAC	Statistical Advisory Committee (FAO)
SAC	Structural Adjustment Committee
SAC	Student Abortion Campaign
SAC	Sugar Association of the Caribbean
SAC	Sveriges Arbetares Centralorganisation
SACA	Sabah Consumers Association (Malaysia)
SACA	Società per Azioni Construzioni Aeronavali
SACA	Société Agricole de Côte d'Afrique (Ivory Coast)
SACA	Société Auxiliare de Commerce Africain (Mali)
SACA	South African Cricket Association
SACA	Standards Association of Central Africa
SACAB	Scottish Association of Citizens Advice Bureaux
SACAC	South African Council for Automation and Computation
SACACT	Southern African Centre for Agricultural Credit Training (Swaziland)
SACAF	Société Centrafricaine du Sac
SACAM	Société Auxiliaire Coopérative de Crédit Agricole Mutuel
SACANGO	Southern African Committee on Air Navigation and Ground Operation
SACAR	Secretariat Européen d'Associations du Commerce Agricole Réunies
SACAR	Société Abidjanaise de Carrelages (Ivory Coast)
SACAV	Société Agro-Industrielle du Cap Vert (Senegal)

SACBC	Southern Africa Catholic Bishops Conference
SACBD	Scientific Advisory Committee on Biological Diversity
SACC	Société Camérounaise de Chaussures et Valises
SACC	Society of All Cargo Correspondents
SACC	South African Council of Churches
SACCA	Servicio Agrénomico de los Cultivadores de Caéa de Azécar (Venezuela)
SACCAR	Centre for Cooperation in Agricultural Research (SADCC)
SACCB	Société Anonyme des Cultures au Congo Belge
SACD	Société des Auteurs et Compositeurs Dramatiques
SACÉC	Société Africaine de Coopération Économique (Senegal)
SACÉL	Société Camérounaise Électronique
SACÉM	Société des Auteurs, Compositeurs et Éditeurs de Musique
SACEM	Syndicat des Cadres et Agents de Maitrise
SACEP	South Asia Cooperative Environment Programme (Sri Lanka)
SACEUR	Supreme Allied Commander Europe (NATO)
SACF	Sociedad Argentina de Ciencias Fisiologicas
SACFER	Société Africaine de Construction et de Fabrication d'Engins Roulants (Ivory Coast)
SACGB	Shark Angling Club
SACH	Sociedad Agronómica de Chile
SACHIA	Salone delle Techniche Chimiche nell'Industria e nell'Agricoltura
SACHIM	Société des Amis de la Maison de la Chimie
SACHR	Standing Advisory Commission on Human Rights
SACI	Société Africaine de Commerce et d'Industrie (Ivory Coast)
SACI	Society of the Agricultural Chemistry Industry (Japan)
SACI	South African Chemical Institute
SACIA	Société Africaine pour le Commerce l'Industrie et l'Agriculture
SACIA	Société Agricole Commerciale et Industrielle de l'Agneby (Ivory Coast)
SACICA	Société Agricole Commerciale et Industrielle de la Casamance (Senegal)
SACK	Scientific Advisory Committee on Kangaroos (ANCA)
SACL	South African Confederation of Labour
SACLANT	Supreme Allied Commander Atlantic (NATO)
SACLANT-CEN	SACLANT Undersea Research Centre
SACLAT	Standing Advisory Committee on Local Authorities and the Theatre
SACM	Sociedad de Autores y Compositores de Mexico
SACM	Société Abidjanaise de Constructions Méchaniques (Ivory Coast)
SACM	Société Africaine de Constructions Métallurgiques
SACM	Société Alsacienne de Constructions Mécaniques
SACMA	Société Anonyme de Construction de Moteurs Aéronautiques
SACO	Servicio Agricola Costarricensa, S.A.
SACO	Société Africaine de Cacao (Ivory Coast)
SACO	Société des Auteurs Congolais
SACO	Sveriges Akademikers Centralorganisation
SACOL	South African Confederation of Labour
SACOMAT	Société Africaine de Construction et Matériaux (Benin)
SACOMI	Société Africaine de Commerce et d'Industrie (Togo)
SACOR	Sociedade Anónima Concessionaría de Refinação de Petróleos em Portugal
SACOS	Società Azionaria Centrali Ortofrutticole Siciliane
SACOS	State Assurance Company of Seychelles
SACOT	Scottish Advisory Comitee on Telecommunications
SACOTRA	Société Africaine de Consignation et de Transit (Benin)
SACOTRA-TOGO	Société Africane de Cinsignation et de Transit, Togo
SACP	Scottish Agricultural Consultative Panel
SACP	Scottish Association of Children's Panels
SACP	South African Communist Party
SACP	State Administration of Commodity Prices (China)
SACPA	South African Cement Producers Association

SACPA	South Asian Catholic Press Association (India)	**SACV**	Schweizerische Artikelcode Vereinigung = ASCA
SACPE	South African Council for Professional Engineers	**SACVT**	Society of Air Cushion Vehicle Technicians (Canada)
SACPO	South African Coloured Peoples Organisation	**SACWA**	Society for the Advancement of Women's Studies (Kenya)
SACRA	Société Africaine de Courtage et de Représentation d'Assurances (Ivory Coast)	**SAD**	Scottish Action on Dementia
		SAD	Scottish Association for the Deaf
SACREXA	Société Africaine de Représentation, de Commercialisation et d'Exploitation Agricole (Ivory Coast)	**SAD**	Shiromani Akali Dal (India)
		SAD	Slovensko Arheološko Društvo
		SAD	Société Agricole de Diby (Ivory Coast)
SACRHEI	Standing Advisory Committee on Relations between Higher Education and Industry (Chemical Society)	**SAD**	Société Andine de Développement (Venezuela) = ADC, CAF
SACRO	Scottish Association for the Care and Resettlement of Offenders	**SAD**	Société des Artistes Decorateurs
		SAD	Spolecnost Antonina Dvoráka
SACRS	South Australian Centre for Remote Sensing	**SAD**	Srpsko Arheološko Društvo
		SADA	SAD Association
SACS	Sakata Agricultural Co-operative Society (Japan)	**SADA**	Sociedad Argentina de Apicultores
SACS	Société d'Analyse et de Conception de Systèmes	**SADACI**	Société Anonyme d'Applications de Chimie Industrielle (Belgium)
SACS	Swedish Agro Co-operative Services	**Sadaf**	Saudi Petrochemical Company (Saudi Arabia)
SACSEA	Supreme Allied Commander South East Asia		
		SADAG	Société Anonyme des Arts Graphiques
SACSIT	Scottish Association of Cold Storage and Ice Trades	**SADAIC**	Sociedad Argentina de Autores y Compositores de Música
SACT	Section Administrative de la Coopération Technique (UN)	**SADAR**	Société Anonyme d'Appareillage Radioélectrique
SACT	Société Algérienne de Constructions Téléphoniques	**SADARÉT**	Société Anglaise d'Études et de Réalisations d'Énergie et de Télécommunications
SACT	Société d'Affrètement, de Consignation et de Transit (Mauritania)	**SADAS**	Syllogos Architektonon Anotaton Scholon
SACTA	Société Agricole et de Collecte de Tabacs (Cameroon)	**SADC**	Southern African Development Community
SACTRA	Standing Advisory Committee on Trunk Road Assessment	**SADCC**	Southern African Development Coordination Conference
SACTU	South African Congress of Trade Unions	**SADCCAM**	Southern African Development Coordination Conference Museums Association (SADCC) (Zambia)
SACTW	South African Council of Transport Workers	**SADCO**	Société Africaine de Construction d'Accessoires Automobiles (Ivory Coast)
SACU	Scottish Auto-Cycle Union		
SACU	Sociedad de Avicultores y Cunicultores del Uruguay	**SADE**	Sociedad Argentina de Escritores
		SADE	Società Adriatica di Ellettricità
SACU	Society for Anglo-Chinese Understanding	**SADE**	Société Alsacienne de Développement et d'Expansion
SACU	South African Cricket Union		
SACU	Southern African Customs Union	**SADECO**	Seychelles Agricultural Development Corporation
SACUGS	South African Scientific Committee for the International Union of Geological Sciences	**SADEL**	Secretario Argentino de la Lano

SADELM	South Australian Department of Environment and Land Management = SADEP	**SADRA**	South African Development Research Association
SADEM	Société Africaine des Eaux Minérales (Ivory Coast)	**SADRAC**	South African Defence Research Advisory Committee
SADÉP	Société Auxiliaire pour la Diffusion des Éditions de Productivité	**SADRI**	Shanghai Aircraft Design & Research Institute
SADEP	South Australian Department of Environment and Planning = SADELM	**SADRI**	Social and Demographic Research Institute (U.S.A.)
SADER	Société Africaine de Déroulage des ets. Rougier et Fils (Gabon)	**SADWSS**	Scottish Association of Directors of Water and Sewerage Services
SADEYA	Sociedad Astronómica de España y América	**SAE**	Sociedad Anonima Española
		SAE	Société Auxiliaire d'Entreprise
SADF	South Australian Department of Fisheries	**SAE**	Society for the Advancement of Education (U.S.A.)
SADFA	South African Dyers and Finishes Association	**SAE**	Society of Assurance Executives
SADG	Société des Architectes Diplômés par le Gouvernement	**SAE**	Society of Automotive Engineers (U.S.A.)
SAD-GABON	Société Africaine pour le Développement (Gabon)	**SAE**	Sveriges Allmanna Exportförening
		SAEA	Society of Anaesthesiologists of East Africa (Kenya)
SADHEA	South African Dietetics and Home Economics Association	**SAEA**	South Asian Federation of Accountants
SADI	Société Africaine de Développement Industriel	**SAEC**	Société Abidjanaise d'Expansion Chimique (Ivory Coast)
SADI	Society of Approved Driving Instructors	**SAEC**	Société Africaine d'Expansion Chimique
SADIA	Société Africaine de Diffusion Industrielle et Automobile (Ivory Coast)	**SAEC**	Society of Automotive Engineers of China
SADIA	Société Auxiliaire de l'Industrie de l'Azote	**SAEC**	State Administration of Exchange Control (China)
SADIAMIL	Société Africaine du Développement de l'Industrie Alimentaire du Millet et du Sorgho (Niger)	**SAECO**	Société Africaine d'Entreprises Commerciales (Senegal)
		Saecs	Southern Africa Europe Container Service
SADIM	Société Anonyme pour le Développement Immobilier de Monaco	**SAÉD**	Société Africaine d'Études et de Développement
SADIO	Sociedad Argentina de Investigación Operativa	**SAED**	Société d'Aménagement et d'Exploitation des Terres du Delta du Fleuve Sénégal
SADITA	Société Africaine d'Importation et de Distribution de Tabacs et Articles Divers (Ivory Coast)	**SAÉFIC**	Société d'Études Financières et de Cautionnements
SADMIL	Société Africaine de Diffusion de Matériel Informatique et Logiciel (Ivory Coast)	**SAEGHT**	Société Africaine de Gestion Hôtelière et Touristique (Ivory Coast)
		SAÉI	Service des Affaires Économiques et Internationales
SADMN	Sociedad Argentina de Medicina Nuclear	**SAEL**	Sociedad Argentina de Estudios Lingüísticos
SADOI	Sociedad Argentina de Organización Industrial	**SAÉL**	Société Africaine d'Électricité
SADP	Scandinavian Association of Directory Publishers	**SAEMA**	Suspended Access Equipment Manufacturers Association
SADP	Syndicat Agricole de Défense Paysanne	**SAÉNA**	Syndicat des Accumulateurs Électriques Non Alcalins
SADR	Sahrawi Arab Democratic Republic		

SAENA	Syndicat des Fabricants Français de Piles Électriques
SAÉP	Société Africaine d'Éditions et de Publicité
SAEPC	Société Anonyme d'Explosifs et de Produits Chimiques
SAESA	Servicios Aéreos Especiales SA (Mexico)
SAESA	Sociedad Austral de Electricidad, S.A. (Chile)
SAEST	Society for the Advancement of Electrochemical Science and Technology (India)
SAET	Society of Automotive-Electrical Technicians
SAETA	Scottish Association of Educational Technology Advisers
SAETA	Sociedad Anonima Ecuatoriana de Transportes Aéreos (Eduador)
SAETA	Sociedad Anonima Emisorars de Television y Anexos (Uruguay)
SAÉTEG	Société Africaine d'Études Techniques d'Entreprises et de Gestion (Ivory Coast)
SAEWA	South African Electrical Workers Association
SAF	Scottish Athletic Federation
SAF	Singapore Air Force
SAF	Skibsfartens Arbeidsgiverforening
SAF	Skofabrikkenes Arbeidsgiverforening
SAF	Société Africaine Forestière (Ivory Coast)
SAF	Société Agricole de Foumbot (Cameroon)
SAF	Société Anonyme Française
SAF	Société Astronomique de France
SAF	Société des Agriculteurs de France
SAF	Society of American Florists
SAF	Society of American Foresters
SAF	Soundure Autogene Française
SAF	South African Foundation
SAF	Sports Aid Foundation
SAF	Svenska Aktiva Fastighetsmäklareförbundet
SAF	Svenska Anestesiologist Förening
SAF	Svenska Antikvariatföreningen
SAF	Svenska Arbetsgivareföreningen
SAF	Syndicat Général des Affineurs de France
SAFA	Scottish Amateur Football Association
SAFA	Société Africaine de Fournitures Automobiles (Sengal)
SAFA	Société Africaine Forestière et Agricole
SAFA	Société d'Achat France-Afrique
SAFA	South African Freedom Association
SAFA	Suomen Apteekkariliitto – Finlands Apotekareforbund
SAFA	Suomen Arkkitehtiliitto
SAFAA	Société Française d'Appareils Automatiques
SAFAD	Swedish Agency for Administrative Development
SAFAL	Société Africaine de Fonderie d'Aluminium
SAFAMI	Société Africaine de Fabrications Métalliques Industrielles (Ivory Coast)
SAFAR	Société Africaine de Fabrication des Automobiles Renault (Ivory Coast)
SAFARRIV	Société Africaine d'Assurances et de Réassurances en République de Côte d'Ivoire
SAFAS	Scottish Association of Flower Arrangement Societies
SAFB	Schweizerische Arbeitsgemeinschaft für Bevölkerungsfragen
SAFBAIL	Société Africaine de Crédit Bail (Ivory Coast)
SAFBPW	South African Federation of Business and Professional Women
SAFCA	Société Africaine de Fabrication de Cahiers
SAFCAC	Société Africaine pour le Caoutchouc, l'Automobile et le Cycle (Senegal)
SAFCO	Saudi Arabian Fertiliser Company
SAFCO	Société Africaine Colombani et Cie (Gabon)
SAFCO	Société Africaine de Conserveries (Ivory Coast)
SAFCO	Société Afrique Commerce (Benin)
SAFCO	Standing Advisory Committee on Fisheries of the Caribbean Organisation
SAFCOP	Société Africaine de Commercialisation des Produits de la Mer (Senegal)
SAFE	Braathens South American and Far East Airtransport (Norway)
SAFE	Security Facilities Executive
SAFE	Struggle Against Financial Exploitation
SAFE	Sustainable Agriculture, Food and Environment
SAFEA	Sportshall & Fitness Equipment Association

SAFEL	Société Agricole de Fruits et Légumes	**SAFRA**	Société Africaine d'Assurances (Senegal)
SAFEMCI	Société Africaine de Fabrication de Mousse et Matelas en Côte d'Ivoire	**SAFRÉCI**	Société Africaine d'Électricité et de Contrôle Industriel (Ivory Coast)
SAFÉR	Société d'Aménagement Foncier et d'Équipement Rural	**SAFRI**	Division of Forest Science and Technology (South Africa)
SAFF	Sub-Culture Alternative Freedom Foundation	**SAFRI**	Société Anonyme d'Aménagement Foncier et de Réalisations Immobilières
SAFFA	Schweizerische Ausstellung für Frauenarbeit	**SAFRIC**	Société Africaine de Confection (Ivory Coast)
SAFGRAD	Consultative Advisory Committee on Semi-Arid Food Grain Research and Development (OAU)	**SAFRICA**	Société Africaine d'Armement (Benin)
		SAFRICA	Société Africaine de Management (Ivory Coast)
SAFI	Sammenslutningen af Automobil-Fabrikanter og Importorer	**SAFRICO**	Société Africaine de Construction (Togo)
SAFI	Société Africaine de Fabrication Industrielle (Burkina Faso)	**SAFRINEX**	Société Africaine d'Exploitation Vinicole
SAFIC	Société Anonyme Française pour l'Importation du Caoutchouc	**SAFRIPA**	Société Africaine de Parfumerie
SAFIC	South Australian Fishing Industry Council	**SAFRITEX**	Société Africaine de Textile (Togo)
SAFICA	Société Africaine de Fabrication et d'Impression de Cahiers (Ivory Coast)	**SAFSR**	Society for the Advancement of Food Service Research (U.S.A.)
SAFICO	Société Abidjanaise de Fournitures pour l'Industrie et les Constructions en Côte d'Ivoire	**SAFT**	Société Africaine de Fabrications et de Transformation
		SAFT	Société d'Affrètement Maritime du Togo
SAFID	Sammenslutningen af Frugtpulpfabrikantereksportrer i Danmark	**SAFT**	Société des Accumulateurs Fixes et de Traction
SAFIÉ	Société Africaine d'Installations Électriques	**SAFTÉL**	Société Africaine d'Électronique et de Télécommunications
SAFIL	Société Africaine de Filterie (Cameroon)	**SAFTI**	Société Africaine de Transformation Industrielle (Ivory Coast)
SAFIL	South African Filtration Society	**SAFTO**	South African Foreign Trade Organization
SAFIM	Société d'Assistance pour la Formation et l'Insertion dans le Monde	**SAFUES**	South African Federation of University Engineering Students
SAFIN-ÉLEC	Société Africaine d'Injection et d'Électricité (Senegal)	**SAFV**	Sociedad Argentina de Fisiologia Vegetal
SAFIR	Société Africaine d'Assurances (Senegal)	**SAG**	Scandinavian Society of Geneticists
SAFIZ	Società Anonima Forniture Impianti Zootecnici	**SAG**	Schweizerische Astronomische Gesellschaft = SAS
SAFM	Société Africaine de Fabrication Métallique (Ivory Coast)	**SAG**	Screen Actors Guild
		SAG	Secretaria de Agricultura y Ganaderia (Mexico)
SAF-MARINE	South African Marine Corporation	**SAG**	Servicio Agrícola y Ganadero (Chile)
SAFO	Swedish Atomic Forum	**SAG**	Shell Aviation Guinée
SAFOD	Southern Africa Federation of the Disabled (Zimbabwe)	**SAG**	Société Agricole de Guinée
		SAG	Société Agricole du Gabon
SAFR	Schweizerische Arbeitsgemeinschaft für Raketentechnik	**SAG**	Stabilisatie Aannemers Groep
		SAG	Steroid Aid Group
SAFR	Schweizerische Arbeitsgemeinschaft für Raumfahrt	**SAG-BF**	Société Africaine de Groupage, Burkina Faso

SAG-CI	Société Africaine de Groupage Côte d'Ivoire		**SAGO**	Studie en Aktiegroep voor Ontwikkelingssamenwerking (Belgium)
SAGA	Sand and Gravel Association		**SAGOO**	Scientific Association of Greek Opticians – Optometrists
SAGA	Savonnerie du Gabon		**SÄGP**	Schweizerische Ärztegesellschaft für Psychotherapie = SMSP
SAGA	Schweizerische Aertzegesellschaft für Akupunktur		**SAGP**	Society for Ancient Greek Philosophy (U.S.A.)
SAGA	Schweizerische Akademische Gesellschaft der Anglisten = SAUTE		**SAGPCH**	Scottish Association of General Practitioner Community Hospitals
SAGA	Scottish Amateur Gymnastics Association		**SAGRO-COL**	Sociedad Agrológica Colombiana
SAGA	Société Suisse d'Études Anglaises		**SAGS**	Schweizerische Akademische Gesellschaft der Slavisten
SAGA	Society of American Graphic Artists		**SAGS**	South African Geographical Society
SAGAGB	Sand and Gravel Association of Great Britain		**SAGSET**	Society for the Advancement of Games and Simulations in Education and Training
SAGAPÉA	Société Gabonaise de Production, d'Élevage et Denrées Alimentaires (Gabon)		**SAGT**	Scottish Association of Geography Teachers
SAGASCO	South Australian Gas Company		**SAGTA**	School and Group Travel Association
SAGB	Schizophrenia Association of Great Britain		**SAGUF**	Schweizerische Arbeitsgemeinschaft für Umweltforschung
SAGB	Senior Advisory Group on Biotechnology (CEFIC)		**SAGW**	Schweizerische Akademie der Geistes- und Sozialwissenschaften = ASSH
SAGB	Shellfish Association of Great Britain		**SAGW**	Schweizerische Akademie der Geisteswissenschaften = ASSM
SAGB	Silk Association of Great Britain		**SAH**	Schweizerisches Arbeiterhilfswerk
SAGB	Skibob Association of Great Britain		**SAH**	Sociedad Argentina de Hematologia
SAGB	Spiritualist Association of Great Britain		**SAH**	Sociedad Argentina de Horticultura
SAGCA	Société Auxiliaire de Garantie et de Courtage d'Assurances (Senegal)		**SAH**	Society of American Historians
SAGD	Suid-Afrikaanse Geneeskundige Diens		**SAH**	Society of Architectural Historians
SAGE	Syndicat National des Fabricants d'Articles Galvanisés et Étamés		**SAH**	Sveriges Allmänna Hypoteksbank
SAGEC	Société Africaine de Génie Rurale (Burkina Faso)		**SAHC**	Scottish Association of Health Councils
SAGECCOM	Société Africaine de Génie Civil et de Constructions Métalliques		**SAHFOS**	Sir Alister Hardy Foundation for Ocean Science
SAGECO	Société Abidjanaise de Gérance et d'Exploitation Commercial (Ivory Coast)		**SAHGB**	Society of Architectural Historians of Great Britain
SAGEM	Société Africaine des Articles Galvanisés et Emaillés (Togo)		**SAHM**	Société Africaine des Halles Modernes
SAGÉM	Société d'Applications Géenérales d'Électricité et de Mécanique		**SAHO**	Société Abidjanaise d'Hôtellerie (Ivory Coast)
SAGETRA{FRANCE	Société Auxiliaire de Gestion d'Entreprises et de Transports		**SAHR**	Society of Army Historical Research
SAGGA	Scout and Guide Graduate Association		**SAHRDC**	South Asia Human Rights Documentation Centre (India)
SAGICAM	Société Agro-Industrielle du Caméroun		**SAHSA**	Servicio Aéreo de Honduras SA
SAGIM	Scandinavian Association for Gastrointestinal Motility (Denmark)		**SAHT**	Sallskapet for Agronomisk Hydroteknik
SAGIMO	Société Anonyme de Gestion et d'Investissement Immobiliers		**SAI**	Scout Association of Ireland
			SAI	Servicio Agricola Interamericana
			SAI	Shaanxi Archaeology Institute

SAI	Società Anonima Italiana		**SAIF**	Société Agricole d'Investissement Foncier
SAI	Società Assicuratrice Industriale		**SAIF**	Society of Allied & Independent Funeral Directors
SAI	Società Attori Italiani			
SAI	Société Africaine d'Importation (Ivory Coast)		**SAIF**	South African Industrial Federation
			SAIF	South African Institute of Forestry
SAI	Société Arabe d'Investissement (Saudi Arabia)		**SAIF**	South African Institute of Foundrymen
SAI	Society of Architectural and Industrial Illustrators		**SAIH**	Société Africaine Immobilière et Hôtelière
SAI	Sociological Association of Ireland		**SAIH**	Studentenes Akademikernes Internasjonale Hjelpefond
SAI	Southeast Asia Institute (U.S.A.)		**SAII**	Société Africaine d'Impressions Industrielles
SAI-Bank	Swiss-Albanian Iliria Bank			
SAIA	South Australian Institute of Architects		**SAIL**	Steel Authority of India Ltd
SAIAA	South African Institute of Assayers and Analysts		**SAILA**	South African Indian Library Association
SAIAeE	South African Institute of Aeronautical Engineers		**SAILIS**	South African Institute for Librarianship and Information Science
SAIAT	Società Attivita Immoblilari Ausliarie Telefoniche		**SAIM**	Società Agraria Industriale Meridionale
SAIB	Saudi Arabian Investment Bank		**SAIM**	South African Institute of Management
SAIB	Société Africaine d'Industrie et de Bonneterie (Ivory Coast)		**SAIMA**	Shipbuilding and Allied Industries Management Association
SAIB	Société Africaine des Industries du Bâtiment		**SAIME**	South African Institution of Mechanical Engineers
SAIC	SAARC Agricultural Information Centre (Bangladesh)		**SAIMM**	South African Institute of Mining and Metallurgy
SAIC	Scottish Agricultural Improvement Council		**SAIMR**	South African Institute for Medical Research
SAICA	Société Agricole et Industrielle de la Côte d'Afrique		**SAIO**	Sociedad Argentina de Investigacion Operativa (Argentina)
SAICCOR	South African Industrial Cellulose Corporation (Pty)		**SAIP**	Société d'Applications Industrielles de la Physique
SAICE	South African Institute of Civil Engineers		**SAIP**	South African Institute of Physics
SAIChemE	South African Institution of Chemical Engineers		**SAIP**	South African Institute of Printing
SAICI	Società Agricola Industriale della Cellulosa Italiana		**SAIPA**	Sociedad Argentina para la Investigación de Productos Aromaticos
SAICOS	Société Agricole Industrielle et Commerciale du Sénégal		**SAIPA**	South African Institute for Public Administration
SAIDA	South-East Asia Interdisciplinary Development Institute (Philippines)		**SAIPE**	South African Institute for Production Engineering
SAIDC	South African Inventions Development Corporation		**SAIRAC**	South African Institute of Refrigeration and Air-Conditioning
SAIE	Société Abidjanaise Import-Export (Ivory Coast)		**SAIRI**	Supreme Assembly of the Islamic Revolution of Iraq
SAIEE	South African Institute of Electrical Engineers		**SAIRR**	South African Institute of Race Relations
SAIET	Société Africaine d'Importation et d'Exportation Tchadienne		**SAIS**	Scientific Apparatus Information Service (U.S.A.)
			SAIS	Sociedades Agricoles de Interés Social (Peru)

SAIS	Società Agricola Italo Somalia		**SAL**	Society of Arabic Literature (China)
SAIS	South African Interplanetary Society		**SAL**	Svenska Amerika Linien
SAIS	Svenska AI-sállskapet / Swedish Artificial Intelligence Society		**SAL**	Sveriges Allmänna Lantbrukssallskap
SAISR	Society for American Indian Studies and Research (U.S.A.)		**SALA**	Sammenslutningen af Landbrugets Arbejdsgiverforeninger
SAISSA	Scottish Amateur Ice Speed Skating Association		**SALA**	South African Library Association
SAIT	Service d'Analyse de l'Information Technologique (CRIQ)		**SALALM**	Seminars on the Acquisition of Latin American Library Materials
SAIT	Sistema Andino de Informacion Tecnologica (Peru)		**SALB**	South African Library for the Blind
SAIT	Société Anonyme Internationale de Télégraphie Sans Fil (Belgium)		**SALC**	Southern Africa Labour Commission (Zambia)
SAITINT	South African Institute of Translators and Interpreters		**SALCI**	Société des Ananas de la Côte d'Ivoire
SAIV	South African Institute of Valuers		**SALF**	Société d'Andrologie de Langue Française
SAIVA	Société d'Importation et de Vente d'Alimentation (Congo)		**SALF**	Somali Abo Liberation Front (Ethiopia)
SAIW	South African Institute of Welding		**SALF**	Sveriges Agronom- och Lantbrukslärareforbund
SAJ	Savez Arhitekata Jugoslavije		**SALI-MAUREM**	Société Arabe Mauritano-Libienne de Pêche
SAJ	Shipbuilders Association of Japan			
SAJ	Sumo Association of Japan		**SALIC**	South Australian Land Information Council (State)
SAJ	Suomen Ammattijärjestö		**SALINTO**	Société des Salines du Togo
SAJA	Société des Amateurs de Jardins Alpins		**SALP**	Société Africaine de Librairie-Papeterie (Gabon)
SAJM	Schweizerische Arbeitsgemeinschaft für Jugendmusik und Musikerziehung		**SALP**	South African Labour Party = SAAP
SAK	Kuwait Investment Company		**SALRC**	Society for Assistance to Ladies in Reduced Circumstances
SAK	Samarbejdskomiteen for Fred og Sikkerhed (Denmark)		**SALS**	South African Logopedic Society
SAK	Stree Adhar Kendra (India)		**SALS**	Southern African Literature Society (Botswana)
SAK	Suomen Amattiyhdistysten Keskusliitto		**SALSC**	Scottish Association of Local Sports Councils
SAK	Suomen Ammattiliittojen Keskusjärjestö = FFC		**SALT**	Scottish Association for Language Teaching
SAK	Sveriges Allmänna Konstförening		**SALT**	Soviet-American Strategic Arms Limitation Talks
SAKELA	Société Agricole de L'Ekéla (Central Africa)			
SAKF	Svenska Akustikkonsulenters Förening		**SAM**	Samarbete För Fred
SAKM	Schweizerische Arbeitsgemeinschaft für Kieferchirurgie und Mundkrankheiten		**SAM**	Scottish AIDS Monitor
			SAM	Scottish Airline Museum
SAKO	Suomen Ammattikoulunopettajien Liitto		**SAM**	Scottish Association for Metals
SAL	Saskatchewan Accelerator Laboratory (Canada)		**SAM**	Sociedad Aeronáutica de Medellín Consolidada (Colombia)
SAL	Schweizerische Arbeitsgemeinschaft für Logopädie		**SAM**	Sociedad Agronómica Mexicana
			SAM	Società Aerea Mediterrania
SAL	Sociedad Anonima Laboral		**SAM**	Société Africaine de Menuiserie (Ivory Coast)
SAL	Société Astronomique de Liège			
SAL	Société d'Archéologie Lorraine et du Musée Historique Lorrain		**SAM**	Société des Americanistes
			SAM	Société des Auxiliaires des Missions (Belgium)

SAM	Society for Anaerobic Microbiology	SAMH	Scottish Association for Mental Health
SAM	Society for the Advancement of Management (U.S.A.)	SAMI	Société Africaine de Matériel Industriel (Gabon, Chad)
SAM	South African Museum, Capetown	SAMIA	Société Arabe des Industries Métallurgiques Mauritano-Koweitienne
SAM	South Australian Museum		
SAMA	Al-Jubail Fertiliser Company (Saudi Arabia)	SAMIN	Société Arabe des Mines d'Inchiri (Mauritania)
SAMA	Saudi Arabian Monetary Agency	SAMIPAC	Société Auxiliare et Minière du Pacifique
SAMA	Scientific Apparatus Makers of America		
SAMA	Scottish Agricultural Machinery Association	SAMIR	Société Anonyme Marocaine de l'Industrie du Raffinage (Morocco)
SAMA	Scottish Amateur Music Association	SÄMM	Schweizerische Ärztegesellschaft für Manuelle Medizin
SAMA	Scottish Association of Manufacturers Agents	SAMM	Société d'Applications des Machines Motrices
SAMA	Shock Absorber Manufacturers Association	SAMM	Support after Murder and Manslaughter
SAMA	Société des Amis du Musée de l'Armée	SAMMA	Société d'Acconage et de Manutention en Mauritanie
SAMA	South African Museums Association		
SAMA	South Australia Museum, Adelaide	SAMNAM	Nordiska Körkomittén
SAMACO	Save Malawi Committee	SAMNAM	Samradet for Nordisk Amatormusik (Denmark)
SAMAL	Svenska Amerika-Mexico Linien		
SAMAO	Société Auxiliare de Matériel pour l'Afrique Occidentale (Ivory Coast)	SAMOA	Société Agence Maritime de l'Ouest Africain (Cameroon, Ivory Coast, Senegal)
SAMARCO	Saudi Maritime Company (Saudi Arabia)	SAMOGA	Société d'Aménagement de la Moyenne Garonne
SAMAREC	Saudi Arabian Marketing and Refining Company	SAMPA	Services d'Approvisionnement en Moyens de Production Agricole
SAMB	Scottish Association of Master Bakers	SAMPE	Society for the Advancement of Material and Process Engineering (U.S.A.)
SAMB	Scottish Association of Master Blacksmiths		
SAMB	United Kingdom Liaison Committee for Sciences Allied to Medicine and Biology	SAMPM	Scottish Association of Milk Products Manufacturers
		SAMRA	South African Market Research Association
SAMBA	Saudi American Bank (Saudi Arabia)		
SAMC	Scottish Association of Manufacturing Coppersmiths	SAMRI	Sichuan Research Institute of Agricultural Machinery
SAMC	South African Medical Corps	SAMS	Scandinavian Analog Computer Society
SAMDA	Société Agricole Mutuelle d'Assurance	SAMS	Scottish Association for Marine Science
SAMDC	South African Medical and Dental Council	SAMS	Sichuan Academy of Medical Sciences
		SAMS	Société d'Application de Mécanisation des Semis
SAMDU	South African Milk Distributors Union		
SAME	Society of American Military Engineers	SAMS	South African Mathematical Society
SAMED	Production Society of the Children of Palestinian Martyrs	SAMS	South American Missionary Society
		SAMS	Swiss Academy of Medical Sciences = ASSM, SAMW
SAMER	Société d'Armement et de Manutention de la Mer Rouge (Djibouti)		
		SAMSA	Silica and Moulding Sands Association
SAMÉS	Société Anonyme de Machines Électrostatiques	SAMSA	South African Mathematical Sciences Association (Zimbabwe)
SAMG	Sociedad Argentina de Mineria y Geologia	SAMTAS	Supervisory and Management Training Association of Singapore

SAMTÉL	Société Marocaine de Télécommunications
SAMV	Schweizerischer Autolackierermeister Verband
SAMW	Schweizerische Akademie der Medizinischen Wissenschaften = ASSM, SAMS
SAN	Science Association of Nigeria
SAN	Seeds Action Network International (GRAIN)
SAN	Servicios Aéreos Nacionales (Ecuador)
SAN	Société Alimentaire de la Nomba (Gabon)
SAN	Society for Ancient Numismatics
SANA	Scottish Anglers National Association
SANA	Società Anonima Navigazione Aerea
SANAA	Servicio Autónomo Nacional de Acueductos y Alcantarillados (Honduras)
SANAE	South African National Antarctic Expedition
SANAS	Service d'Alimentation et Nutrition Appliquée du Sénégal
SANBRA	Sociedade Algodoeira do Nordeste Brasileiro
SANCA	South African National Council on Alcoholism and Drug Dependence
SANCAR	South African National Committee for Antarctic Research
SANCC	South African National Consumers Council
SANCGASS	South African National Committee for Geomagnetism, Aeronomy and Space Sciences
SANCI	South African National Committee on Illumination
SANCOLD	South African National Committee on Large Dams
SANCOR	South African National Committee for Oceanographic Research
SANCOT	South African National Committee on Tunnelling
SANCST	Saudi Arabian National Centre of Science and Technology
SANCU	South African National Consumer Union
SANCWEC	South African National Committee of the World Energy Conference
SAND	Scotland Against Nuclear Dumping
SANDF	South African National Defence Force (formerly MK and SADF)
SANDS	Stillbirth and Neo-natal Death Society
SANE	Schizophrenia: A National Emergency
SANE	Swedish American News Exchange
SANEF	Société des Autoroutes du Nord et de l'Est de la France
SANF	Société des Autoroutes du Nord de la France
SANFP	Scottish Association for Natural Family Planning
SANGO	South-Asia Association of Non-Governmental Organisations (Pakistan)
SANGORM	South African National Group of the International Society for Rock Mechanics
SANLAM	Suid-Afrikaanse Nasionale Lewensassuransie-maatskappy
SANNC	South African Native National Congress
SANP	Sociedad de Anatomia Normal y Patológica (Argentina)
SANROC	South African Non-Racial Olympics Committee
SANSA	Servicios Aéreos Nacionales (Costa Rica)
SANTA	South African National Tuberculosis Association
SANU	Srpska Akademija Nauka i Umetnosti
SANZ	Standards Association of New Zealand
SAO	Scottish Association of Opticians
SAO	Société Académique d'Archéologie, Sciences et Arts du Département de l'Oise
SAO	Société Agricole de l'Ouest (Ivory Coast)
SAO	South-East Asian Outreach
SAOA	South Australian Ornithological Association
SAOL	Sugar Association of London
SAONIC	Section Algérienne de l'Office National Interprofessionnel des Céréales
SAOS	Scottish Agricultural Organisation Society
SAOS	South African Ornithological Society
SAP	Nouvelle Société Africaine des Plastiques (Guinea)
SÄP	Schweizerische Ärztegesellschaft für Psychotherapie
SAP	Seychelles Agence de Presse
SAP	Social Action Party (Thailand)
SAP	Socialistisk Arbejderparti (Denmark)
SAP	Sociedad Agronómica de Panamá

SAP	Sociedad Argentina de Pediatria		**SAPCAM**	Société Africaine de Représentation (Burkina Faso)
SAP	Sociedade Anatómica Portuguesa		**SAPCO**	Société d'Aménagement de la Petite Côte
SAP	Société Africaine de Pétroles			
SAP	Société Africaine de Pneumatiques (Burkina Faso)		**SAPCS**	Société Africaine des Produits Chimiques Shell (Ivory Coast)
SAP	Société Africaine des Peaux		**SAPCT**	Scottish Association of Painting Craft Teachers
SAP	Société Agricole de Prévoyance			
SAP	Société d'Anthropologie de Paris		**SAPD**	Sammenslutringen af Praktiserande Dyroloeger
SAP	Society for Applied Philosophy			
SAP	Society of Analytical Psychology		**SAPEB**	Syndicat des Artisans et des Petites Entreprises du Bâtiment
SAP	South African Police			
SAP	South Asia Partnership		**SAPEC**	Syndicat des Fabricants d'Appareils de Production d'Eau Chaude par le Gaz
SAP	Stowarzyszenie Autorów Polskich			
SAP	Structural Adjustment Programme (Nigeria)		**SAPÉCO**	Société Africaine de Promotion Économique
SAP	Swedish Social Democratic Party		**SAPÉF**	Société Africaine de Publicité et d'Éditions Fusionnées
SAPA	Société Abidjanaise de Plantations d'Ananas (Ivory Coast)			
SAPA	Société Africaine des Pêches de l'Atlantique (Senegal)		**SAPEGA**	Société d'Approvisionnement et de Pêche du Gabon
SAPA	Société d'Application de Peintures en Afrique (Congo)		**SAPÉLEC**	Société Africaine des Piles Électriques (Ivory Coast)
SAPA	South African Poultry Association		**SAPEM**	Société Africaine d'Applications Plastiques et de Mousse (Senegal)
SAPA	South African Press Association			
SAPA	South African Psychological Association		**SAPÉM**	Société d'Applications Pneumatiques Électriques et Méchaniques
SAPABA	Société Agropastorale du Bandama (Ivory Coast)		**SAPH**	Société Africaine de Plantations d'Hévéas (Ivory Coast)
SAPAC	Société Anonyme de Pêche, d'Armement et de Conservation		**SAPHO**	Société Africaine de Promotion Hôteliere (Burkina Faso)
SAPACI	Société des Papeteries de Côte d'Ivoire		**SAPHY-DATA**	Systems for Acquisition, Transmission and Processing of Hydrological Data
SAPAF	Société Agro-Pastrole de Fouladou (Senegal)		**SAPI**	Société Africaine de Pêche Industrielle
SAPAL	Société Africaine de Produits Alimentaires (Senegal)		**SAPICAM**	Société Agropastorale et Industrielle du Caméroun
SAPAM	Society of African Physicists and Mathematicians		**SAPIT**	Société Alsacienne pour l'Industrie Textile
SAPAM	Special Action Programme on Administration and Management in Africa (ECA)		**SAPM**	Scottish Association of Paint Manufacturers
			SAPM	Syndicat pour l'Amélioration de la Production Mulassière
SAPAR	Associazione Nazionale Sezioni Apparecchi per Pubbliche Attrazioni Ricreative		**SAPN**	Société Agricole et Pastorale du Niari (Zaïre)
SAPAR	Société Appareillage Électrique		**SAPO**	South African Post Office
SAPB	Société d'Application Pharmaceutique et Biologique		**SAPPCO**	Saudi Plastic Products Company (Saudi Arabia)
SAPC	Scottish Accident Prevention Council		**SAPPI**	South African Pulp and Paper Industries Ltd
SAPC	Société Africaine de Plomberie et Couverture		**SAPRAL**	Société Africaine de Produits Alimentaires (Ivory Coast)

SAPRESSE	Société Africaine de Presse, d'Édition et de Publicité (Senegal)
SAPRI	Società per Azione Produttori Riso Italiana
SAPRIC	Société d'Approvisionnement et de Réprésentation Industrielle et Commerciale (Ivory Coast)
SAPRIM	Société Abidjanaise de Promotions Industrielles et Immobilières (Ivory Coast)
SAPRO	Société Anonyme de Pipeline à Produits (Switzerland)
SAPRO-CHIM	Société Africaine de Produits Chimiques (Congo)
SAPRO-LAIT	Société Africaine de Produits Laitiers
SAPROC	Société d'Achats de Produits du Caméroun
SAPROCSY	Société Africaine de Produits Chimiques et de Synthèse (Ivory Coast)
SAPS	Science and Plants for School
SAPS	Servico de Alimentação da Previdencia Social (Brazil)
SAPT	Scottish Association for Public Transport
SAPT	Société Africaine de Photogrammetrie et de Topographie
SAPT	Société d'Astronomie Populaire de Toulouse
SAPTCO	Saudi Public Transport Company (Saudi Arabia)
SAPTF	Scottish Anti-Poll Tax Federation
SAPV	Suid-Afrikaanse Pluimvee Vereniging
SAQ	Schweizerische Arbeitsgemeinschaft für Qualitätsförderung = ASPQ
SAR	Cambridge Society for the Application of Research
SAR	School of American Research (U.S.A.)
SAR	Schweizerische Arbeitsgemeinschaft für Rehabilitation
SAR	Search and Rescue (Indonesia)
SAR	Secteurs d'Améliorations Rurales (Algeria)
SAR	Société Africaine de Raffinage
SAR	Société Africaine de Ravitaillement (Congo)
SAR	Société Africaine de Représentation (Burkina Faso)
SAR	Société Suisse d'Anesthésiologie et de Réanimation
SAR	South African Railways
SAR	Svenska Arkitekters Riksförbund
SARA	Scottish Amateur Rowing Association
SARA	Scottish Anti-Racist Alliance
SARA	Società Assicurazioni Rishi Automobilistici
SARA	Society of American Registered Architects
SARA	Southeastern Association for Research in Astronomy (U.S.A.)
SARAM	Société d'Applications Radioélectriques à l'Aéronautique et à la Marine
SARANF	Société d'Anaesthésie et de Réanimation d'Afrique Noire Francophone (Benin)
SARB	Société d'Alimentation et de Recherches Biologiques
SARBICA	South-East Asian Regional Branch of the International Council on Archives
SARC	Scientific and Applied Research Centre (Qatar)
SARC	South Asia Regional Council (U.S.A.)
SARCCUS	Southern African Regional Committee for the Conservation and Utilisation of the Soil
SARCEA	South African Reinforced Concrete Engineers Association
SARCO	Saudi Arabian Refining Company
SARD	Swedish Agency for Research Cooperation with Developing Countries
SARDA	Search and Rescue Dog Association
SARDA	Society for Aid and Rehabilitation of Drug Addicts (Hong Kong)
SAREC	Swedish Agency for Research Cooperation with Developing Countries
SARECA	Société Africaine de Réprésentation (Burkina Faso)
SARECO	Société Africaine de Restauration Collective (Ivory Coast)
SARÉPA	Société Africaine de Recherches et d'Études pour Aluminium
SARF	South African Road Federation
SARF	Sveriges Annons-och Reklambyraers Förbund
SARFU	South African Rugby Football Union
SARGAS	Station Avicole de Recherches Génétiques Appliquées à la Sélection
SARH	Secretaría de Agricultura y Recursos Hidráulicos (Mexico)
SARI	Shenyang Aerodynamics Research Institut

SARI	Shenyang Automation Research Institute
SARI	Société Africaine de Répresentations Industrielles
SARIGECO	Société Sanaga Rice Corporation (Cameroon)
SARIS	Scottish Agricultural Research Institutes
SARL	South African Radio League
SARM	Scottish Anti-Racist Movement
SARMA	Société Anonyme de Récupération des Matériaux Abîmés
SARMAG	Société Africaine de Ravitaillement Maritime et d'Approvisionnements Généraux (Ivory Coast)
SARMN	Société Allemande de Radiobiologie et de Médicine Nucléaire
SARN	Scottish Animal Rights Network
SAROC	Société Anonyme des Réalisateurs d'Oeuvres Cinématographiques
SAROJ	Savez Astronautickih i Raketnih Organizacija Jugoslavije = YARS
SARP	Stowarzyszenie Architektów Polskich
SARRA	South Asia Rural Reconstruction Association
SARS	Safety and Reliability Society
SARS	Scots Ancestry Research Society
SARST	Société Auxiliare de la Recherche Scientifique et Technique
SARTEX	Schweizerische Arbeitsgemeinschaft für Textil-Kennzeichnung
SARTOC	Southern Africa Regional Tourism Council
SARUPRI	Indonesian Plantation Workers Trade Union
SARV	Suomen Arvostelijain Liitto ry
SARY	Suomen Autorengasyhdistys
SAS	Scandinavian Airlines System
SAS	Schweizerischer Arbeitgeberverband für das Schneidergewerbe
SAS	Scottish Australian Society
SAS	Shoqata e Arumunëve të Shqipërisë (Albania) = AAA
SAS	Slovak Academy of Sciences = SAV
SAS	Slovenská Archeologická Společnost při SAV
SAS	Società Adriatica di Scienze
SAS	Société Africaine des Silicates
SAS	Société Astronomique de Suisse = SAG
SAS	Society for Applied Sociology
SAS	Society for Applied Spectroscopy
SAS	Society for Armenian Studies
SAS	Solomone Ano Sagufenua
SAS	Special Air Service
SAS	Spolok Architektov Slovenska
SAS	Surfers Against Sewage
SAS	Svenska Akustiska Sällskapet
SASA	Scottish Agricultural Science Agency
SASA	Scottish Amateur Snooker Association
SASA	Scottish Amateur Swimming Association
SASA	Semilleros Argentinos S.A.
SASA	Slovenian Academy of Sciences and Arts = SZAU
SASA	South African Sugar Association
SASAC	South African Council for Automation and Computation
SASAP	South African Society of Animal Production
SASAR	Singapore Association of Shipbuilders and Repairers
SASCAR	South African Scientific Committee for Antarctic Research
SASCO	Singapore and Australia Shipping Company
SASCO	South Asia Science Cooperation Office (UNESCO)
SASCP	South African Society of Crop Production
SASD	Scottish Association for the Study of Delinquency
SASF	Salvation Army Students' Fellowship
SASF	Scandinavian Association for the Study of Fertility = NFK
SASF	South Asia Sports Federation
SASFA	South Australian Shark Fishermen's Association
SASG	South Asia Solidarity Group
SASI	Southern Association of Science and Industry (U.S.A.)
SASIF	Société Africaine de Soudages, Injections Forages
SASIF	South Asian Service Industries Forum
SASIF-CI	Société Africaine de Soudages, Injections Forages de Côte d'Ivoire
SASIO	Field Science Co-operation Office for South Asia
SASJZ	Schweizerische Arbeitsgemeinschaft für Schul- und Jugendzahnpflege

SASK	Suid-Afrikaanse Seinkorp
SASLI	Scottish Association of Sign Language Interpreters for the Deaf
SASLO	South African Scientific Liaison Office
SASM	Society for Automation in the Sciences and Mathematics (U.S.A.)
SASMA	Silk and Art Silks Mills Association (India)
SASMAL	South African Sugar Millers Association
SASMI	Sindicato Autónomo Scuola Media Italiana
SASMIRA	Silk and Artificial Silk Mills Research Association (India)
SASO	Saudi Arabia Standards Organization
SASO	South African Students Association
SASOL	South African Coal, Oil and Gas Corporation
SASP	Scandinavian Association for the Study of Pain
SASP	South African Society of Physiotherapy
SASPRSC	South African Society for Photogrammetry, Remote Sensing and Cartography
SASS	Scottish Agricultural Statistics Service
SASS	Shandong Academy of Social Sciences
SASS	Shanghai Academy of Social Sciences
SASS	Sichuan Academy of Social Sciences
SASS	Sir Arthur Sullivan Society
SASS	Société Académique des Slavistes Suisses
SASSA	Schweizerische Arbeitsgemeinschaft der Schulen für Sozialarbeit = CSESS
SAST	Swiss Association for Space Technology = ASTS, SVWT
SASTA	South African Sugarcane Technologists Association
SASV	Scottish Association for the Speaking of Verse
SAT	Sennacieca Asocio Tutmonda
SAT	Société Abidjanaise de Torrefaction (Ivory Coast)
SAT	Société Abidjanaise de Transport (Ivory Coast)
SAT	Société Africaine de Toxicologie
SAT	Société Africaine de Transit
SAT	Société Africaine de Transports Routiers (Mali)
SAT	Société Anonyme de Télécommunications
SAT	Société Archéologique de Touraine
SATA	Conference of Southern African Telecommunications Administrations (Mozambique)
SATA	Sociedade Açoriana de Transportes Aéreos
SATA	Société Africaine de Transit et d'Affrètement (Cameroon, Congo, Gabon, Ivory Coast, Senegal)
SATA	Société Anonyme de Transport Aérien (Switzerland)
SATA	Student Air Travel Association
SATAC	Société d'Applications Techniques Agricoles et Caoutchoutières (Ivory Coast)
SATAL	Société Agricole Togolaise Arabe Libyenne
SATAM	Société Anonyme pour Tout Appareillages Mécaniques
SATC	Société Abidjanaise de Tissus et Confections (Ivory Coast)
SATC	Société d'Applications Techniques au Caméroun
SATCC	Southern African Transport and Communications Commission
SATCO	Servicio Aéreo de Transportes Commerciales (Peru)
SATÉ	Société Africaine de Travaux et d'Études (Ivory Coast)
SATE	Swiss Association of Teachers of English
SATEC	Salon International du Textile et du Cuir (Morocco)
SATÉC	Société Africaine de Traitements Électro-Chimiques (Senegal)
SATEC	Société d'Aide Technique et de Coopération
SATEC	Société d'Assistance Technique et de Crédit
SATEF	Société d'Assistance Technique pour l'Exploitation Forestière (Ivory Coast)
SATÉL	Société Africaine des Techniques Électroniques (Benin)
SATELIT	Société Autonome des Télécommunications International du Togo
SATENA	Servicio Aéreo a Territorios Nacionales (Colombia)
SATERCO	Société Anonyme de Terrassements et de Constructions (Belgium)
SATÉT	Société Africaine de Travaux et d'Études Topographiques (Congo)

SATÉT-GABON	Société Gabonaise de Travaux et d'Études Topographiques	**SATS**	Scottish Association of Track Statisticians
SATÉTCA-MÉROUN	Société Camérounaise de Travaux et d'Études Topographiques	**SATS**	South African Transport Services
SATEX-CI	Société Africane de Textiles de Côte d'Ivoire	**SATT**	Société Africaine de Travaux et de Transports (Ivory Coast)
SATF	Société de Anciens Textes Français	**SATU**	South African Typographical Union
SATFA	Support around Termination for Abnormality	**SATUCC**	Southern African Trade Union Coordination Council (OATUU) (Lesotho)
SATG	Schweizerische Automobiltechnische Gesellschaft	**SATURN**	Scientific and Technological Updating in Remote Networks (Netherlands)
SATI	Société Africaine pour le Traitement de l'Information (Togo)	**SATW**	Schweizerische Akademie der Technischen Wissenschaften
SATI	Société Anonyme de Transports Isothermes (Belgium)	**SATW**	Society of American Travel Writers
SATI	Société d'Application des Techniques Industrielles (Cameroon)	**SAU**	Social Affairs Unit
SATI-CI	Société Africaine de Transit et d'Affrètement (Ivory Coast)	**SAUDI-LUBE**	Petromin Lube Oil Blending and Grease Manufacturing Plant (Saudi Arabia)
SATICAM	Société d'Approvisionnement et de Techniques pour l'Industrie au Caméroun	**SAUK**	Scoliosis Association United Kingdom
		SAUK	Suid-Afrikaanse Uitsaaikorporasie
SATIPS	Society of Assistant Teachers in Preparatory Schools	**SAUR-AFRIQUE**	Société d'Aménagement Urbain et Rural pour l'Afrique
SATK	Suid-Afrikaanse Toeristekorporasie	**SAUSSC**	Southern African Universities Social Science Conference
SATL	Suomen Autoteknillinen Liitto	**SAUTE**	Swiss Association of University Teachers of English = SAGA
SATM	Société Africaine de Transit Mory et Cie (Senegal)	**SAUU**	South African Underwater Union
SATMACI	Société d'Assistance Technique pour la Modernisation Agricole de la Côte d'Ivoire	**SAV**	Schweizerischer Altphilogenverband = ASPC
SATMAR	South African Torbanite Mining and Refining Company	**SAV**	Schweizerischer Anwaltsverband = FSA
		SAV	Schweizerischer Apothekerverein = SSF, SSPH
SATOA	South African Technical Officials Association	**SAV**	Slovenska Akadémie Vied
SATOM	Société de Travaux d'Outre-Mer	**SAV**	Svenska Arbetsgruppen för Världsfederation
SATOM-IVOIRE	Société Anonyme de Travaux d'Outre-Mer en Côte d'Ivoire	**SAVA**	South African Veterinary Association
SATPLAS-TIQUES	Société Africaine pour le Travail des Plastiques (Cameroon)	**SAVA**	Verband Schweizerischer Annoncen-Verwaltungen und Agenturen
SATRA	Shoe and Allied Trades Research Association	**SAVANA**	Société Agro-Industrielle de Production de Concentré de Tomate et de Jus de Fruits (Burkina Faso)
SATRA	Société Abidjanaise de Transit (Ivory Coast)	**SAVCO**	Servicios Aéreos Virgen de Copacabana (Bolivia)
SATRAF	Société Africaine de Transport Frigorifique (Burkina Faso)	**SAV-CONGO**	Savonnerie du Congo
SATRAM	Société Africaine de Travaux Maritimes et Fluviaux (Ivory Coast)	**SAVE**	Save Britain's Heritage
		SAVE	Society of American Value Engineers (U.S.A.)
SATRO	Science and Technology Regional Organisation (SCSST)	**SAVEC**	Société Africaine de Vente et de Consignation (Ivory Coast)
		SAVFAN	Standing Advisory Committee on Food and Nutrition (Caribbean)

SAVI	Society for the Advancement of the Vegetable Industry (Philippines)
SAVI	Suid-Afrikaanse Vertalersinstituut
SAVIA	Sociedad Agronomical Viveros Industriales Argentinos
SAVIÉM	Société Anonyme de Véhicules Industriels et d'Équipements Méchaniques (Ivory Coast)
SAVIMAR	Société Sénégalaise d'Avitaillement et de Manutention
SAVR	Special Army Volunteer Reserve
SAVS	Scottish Anti-Vivisection Society
SAVSS	Scottish Association of Victim Support Schemes
SAVUV	Suid-Afrikaanse Vereniging van Universiteits Vroue = SAAUW
SAW	Sächsische Akademie der Wissenschaften zu Leipzig
SAW	Scottish Association of Writers
SAW	Society of Architects in Wales
SAW&F	Woods and Forests Department of South Australia
SAWA	Scottish Amateur Wrestling Association
SAWA	Scottish Asian Women's Association
SAWA	Screen Advertising World Association (U.K., U.S.A.)
SAWAU	South African Women's Agricultural Union
SAWCAA	Soil and Water Conservation Association of Australia
SAWEK	Suid-Afrikaanse Akademie vir Wetenskap en Kuns
SAWGU	South African Wattle Growers Union
SAWI	Society for Animal Welfare in Israel
SAWIC	South African Water Information Centre
SAWJ	Scottish Association of Watchmakers and Jewellers
SAWL	Singapore Association of Women Lawyers
SAWMA	Soil and Water Management Association
SAWP	Society of American Wood Preservers
SAWPA	South African Wood Processing Association
SAWTRI	South African Wool Textile Research Institute
SAY	Scottish Asian Youths
SAY	Suomen Anestesiologiyhdistys
SAYC	Scottish Association of Youth Clubs
SAYCO	South African Youth Congress

SAYFC	Scottish Association of Young Farmers' Clubs
SAzK	Schweizerische Ärtzekommission für Notfallhilfe und Rettungswesen
SAZU	Slovenska Akademoja Znanosti in Umetnosti
SB	Special Branch
SB	Statistisches Bundesamt
SB	Subterranea Britannica
SB	Sugar Bureau
SBA	School Bookshop Association
SBA	Scottish Basketball Association
SBA	Scottish Beekeepers' Association
SBA	Scottish Biomedical Association
SBA	Scottish Bonsai Association
SBA	Scottish Bowling Association
SBA	Small Business Administration (U.S.A.)
SBA	Smaller Businesses Association
SBA	Sociedade Brasileira de Agronomia
SBA	Société Belge d'Astronomie, de Météorologie et de Physique du Globe
SBA	Society of Botanical Artists
SBA	Steam Boat Association of Great Britain
SBAAT	Scottish Business Achievement Award Trust
SBAC	Société des Tabacs, Cigares et Cigarettes J. Bastos de l'Afrique Centrale
SBAC	Society of British Aerospace Companies
SBAIMA	Ship Building and Allied Industries Management Association
SBAO	Schweizerischer Berufsverband für Augenoptik und Optometrie
SBAP	Schweizerischer Berufsverband für Angewandte Psychologie
SBARMO	Scientific Ballooning and Radiations Monitoring Organization
SBAT	Service Botanique et Agronomique de Tunisie
SBAT	Sociedade Brasileira de Autores Tetrais
SBAT	Supplementary Benefit Appeal Tribunal
SBB	Schweizerische Bundesbahnen
SBB	Small Business Bureau
SBB	Sociedade Botanica de Brasil
SBB	Sociedade Brasileira de Microbiologia
SBB	Société Belge de Biochemie = BVB
SBB	Société Belge de Biologie
SBB	Société Belge des Bétons
SBB	Société des Brasseries de Bouaké (Ivory Coast)

SBB	Société des Briqueterie et de Bois du Bandama (Ivory Coast)
SBBA	Scottish Boat Builders Association
SBBC	Shell Better Britain Campaign
SBBC	Société Belge de Biologie Clinique = BUKB
SBBMF	Societas Biochimica Biophysica et Microbiologica Fenniae
SBBNFSA	SBBNF Sailmakers Association
SBC	Scottish Beef Club
SBC	Singapore Broadcasting Corporation
SBC	Sociedade Brasileira de Cartografia
SBC	Société Bibliographique du Canada
SBC	Stamp Bug Club
SBC	Swedish Farmers Beet Growers Association
SBC	Swiss Broadcasting Corporation
SBCA	Scottish Building Contractors Association
SBCBC	Société des Bitumes et Cut-backs du Caméroun
SBCC	Société Belge de Chimistes Cosmétologues
SBCCPA	Sociedade Brasileira de Criadores de Cães Pastores Alemães
SBCI	Sociedade Brasileira de Cultura Inglêsa
SBCN	Stichting Broedercongregaties in Nederland
SBD	Société Belge de Démographie
SBD	Société des Bauxite de Dabola (Guinea)
SBDI	Société Belge de Droit International
SBDV	Schweizerische Berufsdirigenten-Verband
SBE	Sociedade Brasileira de Entomologia
SBE	Société Belge d'Ergologie
SBÉ	Société Belge des Électriciens
SBE	Society of Business Economists
SBÉE	Société Belge d'Études d'Expansion
SBÉE	Société Béninoise d'Électricité et d'Eau
SBEF	Scottish Building Employers' Federation
SBEF	Svenska Byggnadsentreprenérföreningen
SBET	Society of British Esperantist Teachers
SBETC	Small Business Export Trade Corporation (U.S.A.)
SBF	Schweizer Berufsfotografen = PpS, FpS
SBF	Sociedade Brasileira de Floricultura
SBF	Société Botanique de France
SBF	Société Burundaise de Financements
SBF	Southern Brick Federation
SBF	Svenska Bageriförbund
SBF	Svenska Barnmorskeförbundet
SBF	Svenska Bergsmannaföreningen
SBF	Svenska Bibliotekariesamfundet
SBF	Svenska Brandförsvarsföreningen
SBF	Svenska Busstrafikförbundet
SBF	Sveriges Begravningsentreprenörers Förbund
SBF	Sveriges Bildelsgrossisters Förening
SBF	Sveriges Biografägareförbund
SBF	Sveriges Biokemiska Forening
SBF	Sveriges Bryggmästare Förening
SBFD	Society of British Flight Directors
SBFV	Schweizerischer Berufsfischerverband
SBG	Schweizerische Botanische Gesellschaft
SBG	Schweizerischer Berufsgärtnerverband
SBG	Sociedade Brasileira de Geologia
SBG	Société Belge de Géologie
SBG	Stichting Bevordering Galvanotechniek
SBGE	Société Belge de Gastro-Entérologie
SBGI	Society of British Gas Industries
SBGW	Städtische Büchereien der Gemeinde Wien (Austria)
SBH	Société de Biomètrie Humaine
SBH	Stichting voor Banistiek en Heraldiek
SBH	Suiuz na Bulgarskite Khudozhnitsi
SBHATA	Sand and Ballast Hauliers and Allied Trade Alliance
SBHED	Sociedade Brasileira de Herbicides e Ervas Daninhas
SBHO	Société des Brasseries du Haut-Ogooué (Gabon)
SBHS	Strict Baptist Historical Society
SBHV	Schweizerischer Briefmarkenhändler-Verband
SBI	Società Botanica Italiana
SBI	Société Belge d'Investissement International = BMI
SBI	Société des Bois Ivoiriens
SBI	Society for Burn Injuries (China)
SBI	Statens Byggeforskningsinstitut (Denmark)
SBI	Sveriges Bokbinderiföreningen
SBIA	Société Belge des Ingénieurs de l'Automobile
SBIF	Svenka Byggnads-Industriförbundet

SBIT	Société Belge des Ingénieurs Techniciens
SBK	Schweizer Berufsverband der Krankenschwestern und Krankenpfleger = ASI
SBKA	Scottish Beekeepers' Association
SBKV	Schweizerischer Bäcker-Konditorenmeister Verband
SBL	Skibsbyggerienes Lansforening
SBL	Society of Biblical Literature
SBL	Society of Black Lawyers
SBL	Suomen Bensiinikauppiaitten Liitto
SBLAM	Syndicat Belge de la Librairie Ancienne et Moderne
SBLE	Sino-British Lijiang Expedition
SBM	Sociedad Botánica de México
SBM	Société Belge des Mécaniciens
SBM	Société Brazzavilloise de Magasins (Congo)
SBM	Société de Biologie de Montréal (Canada)
SBM	Société des Bains de Mer (Monaco)
SBMÉ	Société Belge de Microscopie Électronique
SBMI	Société Belge de Médecine Interne
SBMS	Shoqata "Bratska" e Maqedonave të Shqipërisë (Albania) = BPAMA
SBMV	Sociedade Brasileira de Medicina Veterinaria
SBN	Schweizerischer Bund für Naturschutz = LSPN
SBN	Stichting Bouwistorie Nederland
SBNS	Society of British Neurological Surgeons
SBO	Stichting Bloedroepen Onderzoek
SBOM	Société des Brasseries de l'Ogooué Maritime (Gabon)
SBOT	Société Belge de Chirurgie Orthopédique et de Traumatologie
SBP	Société Belge de Pédologie = BBV
SBP	Société Belge de Photogrammétrie
SBP	Société Belge de Physique
SBP	Société Belge de Psychologie = BVP
SBP	Society of Biological Psychiatry (U.S.A.)
SBP	Stowarzyszenie Bibliotekarzy Polskich
SBPC	Sociedade Brasileira para o Progresso da Ciencia
SBPF	Société Belge des Professeurs de Français
SBPH	Société Belge des Physiciens des Hôpitaux
SBPIM	Society of British Printing Ink Manufacturers (*now* BCF)
SBPM	Society of British Paint Manufacturers
SBPR	Sociedad de Bibliotecarios de Puerto Rico
SBPR	Society for Back Pain Research
SBPTC	Société Belge de Photogrammétrie, de Télédéction et de Cartographie
SBPV	Schweizerischer Baukpersonalverband
SBQ	Sociedade Brasileira de Química
SBR	Société Belge Radio-Électrique
SBR	Society for Biological Rhythm (Puerto Rico)
SBR	Stichting Bouwresearch
SBR	Svenska Byggnadsingenjörers Riksförbund
SBR	Sveriges Besinshandlares Riksförbund
SBR	Sveriges Biodlares Rijksförbund
SBREC	Sugar Beet Research and Education Committee
SBRF	Sveriges Bokförings-och Revisionsbyraers Förbund
SBRM	Societatea de Botanica din Republica Moldova
SBRS	Sheep Breeding Research Station (India)
SBS	Save British Science Society
SBS	Schweizerischer Berufsverband der Sozialarbeiter und Erzicher = ASAS
SBS	Slovenská Botanická Společnost při SAV
SBS	Sociedad Brasileira de Silvicultura
SBS	Southall Black Sisters
SBS	Special Broadcasting Service (Australia)
SBS	Superintendencia de Banca y Seguros (Peru)
SBS	Svenska Bibliotekariesamfundet
SBSA	Scottish Board Sailing Association
SBSA	Standard Bank of South Africa
SBSB	Society of British Snuff Blenders
SBSC	Spark Biotechnology Sector Committee (Canada)
SBSI	Sugar Beet Seed Institute (Iran)
SBSMP	Société Bernoulli pour la Statistique Mathématique et la Probabilité
SBSTTA	Subsidiary Body on Scientific, Technical and Technological Advice

SBTB	Statens Bibliotek og Trykkeri for Blinde	**SC/GEO**	UNESCO Division of Earth Sciences
SBTC	Sino-British Trade Council	**SC/HYD**	UNESCO Division of Water Sciences
SBTD	Society of British Theatre Designers	**SC/OCE**	UNESCO Division of Marine Sciences
SBTG	Schweizerischer Berufsverband für Tanz und Gymnastik	**SC/SER**	UNESCO Division of Scientific Research on Higher Education
SBU	Schweizer Barkeeper Union	**SC/STP**	UNESCO Divison of Science Technology Problems
SBU	Schweizerische Butter Union		
SBU	Scottish Badminton Union	**SC/TER**	UNESCO Division of Technological Research on Higher Education
SBU	Sociedades Biblicas Unidas = ABU, UBS, WBG	**SCA**	Scottish Canoe Association
SBU	Sumitomo Bayer Urethane (Japan)	**SCA**	Scottish Cashmere Association
SBUAM	Société Belge des Urbanistes et Architectes Modernistes	**SCA**	Scottish Chess Association
		SCA	Scottish Council for Arbitration
SBUF	Svenska Baptistamfundets Ungdomsförbund	**SCA**	Scottish Council on Alcohol
		SCA	Scottish Courts Administration
SBV	Schweizerischer Bank Verein	**SCA**	Scottish Croquet Association
SBV	Schweizerischer Bauernverband	**SCA**	Sea Cadet Association
SBV	Schweizerischer Baumeisterverband = SSE, SSIC	**SCA**	Sectional Chamber Association
SBV	Schweizerischer Bedienungspersonal-Verband	**SCA**	Selangor Consumers Association (Malaysia)
SBV	Schweizerischer Bergführerverband	**SCA**	Shadow Communications Agency
SBV	Schweizerischer Bierbrauerverein	**SCA**	Social Care Association
SBV	Schweizerischer Bootbauer-Verband	**SCA**	Sociedad Cientifica Argentina
SBV	Schweizerischer Brennstoffhändler Verband = UNC	**SCA**	Societatea Culturală Aromână (Romania) = ACS
SBV	Schweizerischer Buchdruckerverein	**SCA**	Société Centrale d'Apiculture
SBV	Schweizerischer Büchsenmacher Verband = ASA	**SCA**	Société Commerciale Africaine
		SCA	Société des Ciments d'Abidjan (Ivory Coast)
SBV	Speologisch Verband van België		
SBV	Stitching voor Bodemkartering	**SCA**	Society of Cardiovascular Anesthesiologists (U.S.A.)
SBV-EH	Shokata e Bashkimit Vullnetar – Enver Hoxha	**SCA**	Society of Company and Commercial Accountants
SBVV	Schweizer Buchhändler und Verleger Verein	**SCA**	Society of the Catholic Apostolate = SAC
SBWA	Standard Bank of West Africa	**SCA**	Specialist Cheesemakers Association
SBWK	Schweizerische Bauwirtschaftskonferenz	**SCA**	Sprayed Concrete Association
SC	Fratres a Sacratissimo Corde Iesu	**SCA**	Standing Committee of Analysts to review methods for Quality Control of the Water Cycle
SC	Servants of Charity = CSC, SdC		
SC	Society of Cartographers	**SCA**	Standing Committee on Agriculture
SC-IBP	Special Committee for the International Biological Programme	**SCA**	Steel Cladding Association
		SCA	Suez Canal Authority
SC-IDNDR	Special Committee for the International Decade on Natural Disaster Reduction	**SCA**	Suspended Ceilings Association
		SCA	Svenska Cellulose Aktiebolaget
SC-IGBP	Scientific Committee for the International Geosphere-Biosphere Programme	**SCAA**	School Curriculum and Assessment Agency (*ex* NCC)
SC/ECO	UNESCO Division of Ecological Sciences	**SCAAF**	Société Centrale d'Approvisionment des Agriculteurs de France

SCAAP	Special Commonwealth African Assistance Plan	**SCAM**	Sociétés Coopératives Agricoles Marocaines
SCAARF	Scottish Combined Action Against Racism & Fascism	**SCAM**	Steering Committee Against AZT Malpractice
SCAB	Sociedad Cooperativa de Agrónomos de Bolivia	**SCAMAP**	South and Central Asian Medicinal and Aromatic Plants Network
SCAB	Société Centrale d'Architectes de Belgique	**SCAMAP**	Syndicat des Cadres et Agents de Maîtrise de l'Aéroport de Paris
SCABA	Scottish Chartered Accountants Benevolent Association	**SCAMP**	Scottish Association of Magazine Publishers
SCAC	Scottish Countryside Activities Council	**SCAMTRA**	Société Camérounaise de Manutention, de Transport et de Transit
SCAC	Soil Conservation Advisory Committee		
SCAD	Société Centrafricaine de Déroulage	**SCAN**	Sistemas de Computacion y Analisis (Ecuador)
SCADOA	Service Commun d'Armements Desservant l'Ouest Africain	**SCAN**	Small Computers in the Arts Network (U.S.A.)
SCADU	Student Community Action Development Unit	**SCAN-AUSTRAL**	Scandinavian Australia Carriers Ltd (Norway)
SCAÉI	Syndicat des Constructeurs d'Appareillage Électrique d'Installations	**SCAN Test**	Scandinavian Pulp, Paper and Board Testing Committee
SCAEPA	Society for Computer Applications in Engineering, Planning and Architecture (U.S.A.)	**Scandia-transplant**	Nordic Committee on Kidney Transplantation
		SCANDLAS	Scandinavian Federation for Laboratory Animal Science
SCAÉR	Société de Crédit Agricole et d'Équipement Rurale (Mali)	**SCANDOC**	Scandinavian Documentation Centre (U.S.A.)
SCAF	Compagnie des Scieries Africaines (Ivory Coast)	**SCANN**	South Coast Against Nuclear Navies
SCAF	Société Centrale d'Aviculture de France	**SCANVAC**	Scandinavian Federation of Heating, Air Conditioning and Sanitary Engineering Associations
SCAFA	Scottish Child and Family Alliance		
SCAFA	Société Centrafricaine d'Affrètement et d'Acconage	**SCAO**	Standing Conference of Atlantic Organizations
SCAFR	Société Centrale d'Aménagement Foncier Rural	**SCAP**	Schweizerische Gesellschaft für Angewandte Geographie
SCAGMSO	Social-Cultural Association of the German Minority in Silesian Opole (Poland) = TSKMNŚO	**SCAP**	Sociedade de Ciencias Agrárias de Portugal
		SCAP	Société Centrale d'Aquiculture et de Pêche
SCAHT	Scottish Churches Architectural Heritage Trust	**SCAP**	States Cooperative Assistance Program (ANCA)
SCAHUR	Société Congolaise d'Aménagement de l'Habitat Urbain et Rurale	**Scapa**	Scottish Campaign for Public Angling
SCALA	Society of Chief Architects of Local Authorities	**SCAPA**	Sociedade de Comercialização e Apoio à Pesca Artesanal (Cape Verde)
SCALMS	Syndicat des Constructeurs d'Appareils de Levage, de Manutention et de Matériels de Stockage	**SCAPCAN**	Coopérative Agricole des Planteurs de Café Arabica du Ndé (Cameroon)
SCALOM	Société Camérounaise de Location de Matériel et de Travaux Publics	**ScAPS**	Scandinavian Association of Paediatric Surgeons = NBF
SCALOP	Standing Committee on Antarctic Logistics and Operations	**SCAR**	Scandinavian Council for Applied Research
SCAM	Société Commerciale d'Applications Mécanographiques	**SCAR**	Scientific Committee on Antarctic Research (ICSU) = CCIA, CSRA

SCAR	Society for Computer Applications in Radiology	**SCBK**	Société Congolaise des Brasseries Kronenbourg
SCAR	Standing Committee on Agricultural Research (EU) = CPRA	**SCBM**	Société Camérounaise de Béton Manufacture
SCAR	Student Campaign for Animal Rights	**SCBRO**	Society of Chief Building Regulation Officers (*now* DSABRO)
SCARA	Syndicat de Compagnies Assurant les Risques Automobiles (Belgium)	**SCBT**	Société Canadienne de Biologie Théorique = CSTB
SCARF	Sickle Cell Anaemia Research Foundation	**SCC**	Sarawak Chamber of Commerce (Malaysia)
SCARF	Standing Committee of the Australian Forestry Council	**SCC**	Scandinavian Clothing Council
SCARF	Supporters Campaign Against Racism in Football	**SCC**	Scandinavian Collectors Club
SCARM	Standing Committee on Agriculture and Resource Management	**SCC**	Science Council of Canada
		SCC	Scottish Churches Council
SCARO-MINES	Société Centrafricano Roumaine des Mines	**SCC**	Scottish Consumer Council
		SCC	Sea Cadet Corps
SCART	Syndicat de Constructeurs d'Appareils Radio-Récepteurs et Téléviseurs	**SCC**	Servicio Colombiano de Comunicacion – Social Circulo de Mujeres (Colombia)
SCAS	Society for Companion Animal Studies	**SCC**	Silhouette Collectors' Club
		SCC	Sisters of Christian Charity
SCAS	South Carolina Academy of Science	**SCC**	Société Canadienne de Chimie = CSC
SCASA	Servicio Cooperativo Agricola Salvadoreño Americano	**SCC**	Société Suisse des Chimistes-Cosméticiens
SCASS	Standing Conference of Arts & Social Sciences	**SCC**	Society of Cheese Connoisseurs
		SCC	Society of Cosmetic Chemists (U.S.A.)
SCAT	Société Centrafricaine des Tabacs	**SCC**	Society of Cost Consultants
SCATS	Standing Conference for the Advancement of Counselling, Training & Supervision	**SCC**	Species Survival Commission (IUCN)
		SCC	Standards Council of Canada
		SCC	Standing Conference of Consultatives (Angling and Fisheries)
SCAUL	Standing Conference of African University Libraries	**SCC**	Structural Concrete Consortium
SCAV	Soil Conservation Association of Victoria	**SCC**	Swedish Cooperative Centre
		SCC	Sylvac Collectors' Club
SCB	Schweizerische Chemische Gesellschaft	**SCCA**	Scottish Consumer Credit Association
SCB	Sociedad Cubana de Botánica	**SCCA**	Society of Company and Commercial Accountants (*now* IComA)
SCB	Société Camérounaise de Banque		
SCB	Société Chimique de Belgique	**SCCA**	Sound & Communications Contractors' Association
SCB	Société d'Étude et de Développement de la Culture Bananière (Ivory Coast)	**SCCAC**	Society for Conceptual and Contents Analysis by Computer (Germany)
SCB	Société de Chimie Biologique		
SCB	Société des Ciments du Bénin	**SCCAN**	Special Co-ordinating Committee of ASEAN Nations
SCB	Society for the Conservation of Biology	**SCCAPE**	Scottish Council for Commercial, Administrative and Professional Education
SCB	Solicitors Complaints Bureau		
SCB	Speedway Control Board		
SCB	Statistika Centralbyran	**SCCC**	Scottish Consultative Committee on the Curriculum
SCBÉ	Société Camérounaise des Bois Équatriaux		
SCBE	Société Canadienne des Brevets et d'Exploitation Limitée	**SCCDM**	Société Commerciale Camérounaise de Distribution Moderne

SCCE	Société Camérounaise de Conditionnement et d'Entreposage	**SCE**	Sociedad Colombiana de Economistas
SCCF	Scottish Conservative Christian Forum	**SCÉ**	Société Camérounaise d'Équipement
SCCF	Société Centrale Canine de France	**SCE**	Society of Chemical Engineers (Japan)
SCCH	Sociedad Cientifica de Chile	**SCE**	Society of Computational Economics
SCCI	Société pour le Compoundage en Côte d'Ivoire	**SCEA**	Scottish Civic Entertainment Association
SCCL	Scottish Council for Civil Liberties	**SCÉAM**	Symposium des Conférences Épiscopales d'Afrique et de Madagascar = SECAM
SCCM	Society of Critical Care Medicine	**SCEAR**	Scientific Committee on the Effects of Atomic Radiation (U.S.A.)
SCCOM	Société de Courtage et de Consignation Maritime	**SCÉB**	Société Canadienne des Études Bibliques = CSBS
SCCP	Sabah Chinese Consolidated Party (Malaysia)	**SCEC**	Scottish Community Education Council
SCCR	Society for Cross-Cultural Research (U.S.A.)	**SCÉC**	Société Canadienne des Études Classiques = CAC
SCCR	Stanford Centre for Chicano Research (U.S.A.)	**SCEC**	Sunshine Coast Environment Council
SCCS	Sociedad Colombiana de la Ciencia del Suelo	**SCECSAL**	Standing Conference of Eastern, Central and Southern African Librarians
SCCS	Standing Committee of Caribbean Statisticians (CARICOM)	**SCÉÉ**	Société Canadienne pour l'Étude de l'Éducation = CSSE
SCCTP	Société Camérounaise de Construction et de Travaux Publics	**SCÉES**	Société Central des Études et des Enquêtes Statistiques
SCCVO	Scottish Council for Community and Voluntary Organisations	**SCEF**	Société Camérounaise d'Exploitation Forestière
SCD	Scottish Council on Disability	**SCÉFL**	Société Camérounaise Équatoriale de Fabrication de Lubrifiants
SCD	Service de Coopération au Développement	**SCÉIO**	Société Canadienne pour l'Étude de l'Intelligence par Ordinateur = CSCSI
SCD	Slovene Christian Democrats	**SCÉL**	Société Coopérative d'Édition et de Librairie
SCD-ETE	Sociaux Démocrates Chrétiens – Entente Toutes Ethnies (New Caledonia)	**SCELO**	State Committee for the Establishment of Law and Order (Burma) = SLORC
SCDA	Scottish Community Drama Association	**SCEME**	Scottish Companies Exporting to the Middle East
SCDA	Sound & Communications Distributors Association (SCIF)	**SCEME**	Society of Chief Electrical and Mechanical Engineers in Local Government
SCDC	Scottish Cooperatives Development Committee	**SCEMSC**	Standing Conference of Ethnic Minority Senior Citizens
SCDEC	Société Camérounaise de Diffusion et d'Exploitation Cinématographique "Le Miffi"	**SCÉP**	Société Continentale d'Éditions et Périodiques
SCDH	Supreme Council for the Defence of the Homeland (Afghanistan)	**SCEPAG**	Société pour le Conditionnement et l'Exportation des Produits Agricoles (Madagascar)
SCDP	Schweizerischer Verband Diplomierter Psychiatrieschwestern und-pfleger	**SCEPS**	Strategic and Corporate Europlanners Society (Belgium)
SCDP	Slovak Christian Democratic Party = SKDS	**SCÉR**	Société Canadienne des Études Renaissance = CSRS
SCDP	Société Camérounaise de Dépôts Pétroliers	**SCERA**	Senate Committee on Environment, Recreation and the Arts
SCE	Nordisk Enzymkommitte; Scandinavian Committee on Enzymes		

SCÉRDI	Société Civile d'Études et de Recherches dans les Domaines de l'Innovation	**SCHA**	Scottish Catholic Historical Association
SCÉRI	Société Camérounaise d'Échanges et de Répresentations Industrielles	**SCHE**	Sociedad Chilena de Entomologia
		SCHÉ	Société Canadienne de l'Histoire de l'Église = CSHC
SCESO	Société de Cabotage et d'Entreposage du Sud-Ouest (Gabon)	**SCHEC**	Société Canadienne de l'Histoire Catholique = CCHA
SCET	Scottish Council for Educational Technology	**SCHF**	Sociedad Chilena de Fisica
SCÉT	Société Centrafricaine d'Équipement Touristique	**SCHG**	Sociedad Chilena de Genética
		SCHHG	Sociedad Chilena de Historia y Geografia
SCÉT	Société Centrale pour l'Équipement du Territoire (Algeria)	**SCHHN**	Sociedad Chilena de Historia Natural
SCET	Society of Civil Engineering Technicians	**SCHI**	Southern California Horticultural Institute (U.S.A)
SCETA	Société de Contrôle et d'Exploitation des Transport Auxiliaires	**SCHJ**	Société Canadienne de l'Histoire Juive = CJHS
SCETT	Standing Committee for the Education and Training of Teachers in the Public Sector	**SCHM**	International Commission for a History of the Scientific and Cultural Developments of Mankind
SCEU	Science and Culture Employees' Union (Afghanistan)	**SCHMC**	Society of Catering and Hotel Management Consultants
SCF	Save the Children Fund	**SCHN**	Société Canadienne d'Histoire Naturelle
SCF	Société de Comptabilité de France	**SCHNBT**	Sociedad Chilena de Nutrición, Bromatologia y Toxicologia
SCF	Spanish Cycling Federation		
SCF	Standing Committee on Fishing	**SCHO**	Société Canadienne d'Histoire Orale = COHA
SCF	Standing Committee on Forestry		
SCF	Svenska Civilekonomföreningen	**SCHP**	Sociedad Chilena de Parasitologia
SCFA	Save the Children Fund Australia	**SCHPA**	Sociedad Chilena de Producción Animal
SCFCÉF	Syndicat des Constructeurs Française de Condensateurs Électrique Fixes	**SCHPM**	Société Canadienne d'Histoire et de Philosophie des Mathématiques
SCFCS	Standing Committee on the Free Circulation of Scientists (Sweden)	**SCHPS**	Société Canadienne d'Histoire et de Philosophie des Sciences = CSHPS
SCG	Socialist Campaign Group	**SCHQ**	Sociedad Chilena de Quimica
SCGA	Sugar Cane Growers Association (Australia)	**SChr**	Societas Christi pro Emigrantibus Polonis
SCGAF	Société Centrale de Gestion des Agriculteurs de France	**SCHS**	Salford Centre for Housing Studies
SCGB	Ski Club of Great Britain	**SCHS**	Scottish Church History Society
SCGB	Société des Caoutchoucs de Grand-Béreby (Ivory Coast)	**SCHS**	Slovenská Chemická Spolecnost pri SAV
SCGC	Société Canadienne de Génie Chimique = CSHCE	**SChV**	Schweizerischer Chemiker-Verband
		SCHVPT	Southern Counties Historic Vehicle Preservation Trust
SCGI	Société Congolaise de Gaz Industriels	**SCI**	Congregatio Sacerdotum a Sacro Corde Iesu
SCGR	Société Canadienne de Génie Rural = CSAE		
		SCI	Sea Containers Inc.
SCGSN	Socialist Campaign Group Supporters Network	**SCI**	Service Civil Internationale = IVS, IZD
		SCI	Shipping Corporation of India
SCh	Samopomoć Chłopska	**SCI**	Società Chimica Italiana
SCH	Saudi Consulting House (Saudi Arabia)	**SCI**	Société Camérounaise Industrielle
		SCI	Société de Chemie Industrielle

SCI	Society of Chemical Industry
SCI	Society of Chiropodists in Ireland
SCI	Society of Composers, Inc.
SCI	Southern Cross International (U.K.)
SCI	Steel Construction Institute
SCI	Stein Collectors International (U.S.A.)
SCI	Swaythling Club International
SCI	Swedish Ceramic Institute
SCI/TAP	Sister Cities International Municipal and Technical Cooperation Program (U.S.A.)
SCIA	Servicio Cooperativo Interamericano de Agricultura
SCIA	Société Commerciale et Immobilière de l'Atlantique (Benin)
SCIAF	Scottish Catholic International Aid Fund
SCIBP	Special Committee for the International Biological Programme (ICSU)
SCIC	Saskatchewan Council for International Cooperation
SCIC	Société Centrale Immobilière de la Caisse des Dépôts
SCICA	Société Climique et Industrielle Camérounaise
SCID	Scotland's Campaign Against Irresponsible Drivers
SCIDA	Servicio Cooperativo Interamericano de Agricultura (Guatemala)
SCIDE	Servicio Cooperativo Interamericano de Educación (Bolivia)
SCIDT	Scottish Country Industries Development Trust
SCIEC	Société Civil Immobilière des Entrepôts de Coton
SCIEC	Syndicat des Commerçants Importateurs et Exportateurs du Caméroun
SCIÉFAM	Syndicat des Entreprises de Commerce International d'Équipement et Fournitures pour Automobiles
SCIENCE	Société des Consultants Indépendants et Neutres de la Communauté Européenne
SCIEP	Société Civile Immobilière d'Entrepôts Portuaires (Cameroon)
SCIES	South China Institute for Environmental Sciences
SCIF	Congregation of Bethlehemite Religious Women, Daughters of the Sacred Heart
SCIF	Servicio Cooperativo Interamericano de Irrigación, Vias de Communicación e Industrias (Peru)
SCIF	Sound and Communications Industries Federation
SCIFE	Servicio Cooperativo Interamericano de Fomento Económico (Panama, Peru)
SCII	Svenska Centralkommitten for Internationalla Ingenjörskongresser
SCIJ	Ski-Club International Journalists
SCILT	Scottish Centre for Information Language Teaching
SCIMA	Syndicat des Constructeurs et Constructeurs-Installateurs de Matériel Aéraulique
SCIMO	Société Commerciale et Industrielle pour la Métropole et Outre-Mer
SCIMPEX	Syndicat des Commerçants Importateurs et Exportateurs de l'Afrique de l'Ouest
SCIMPOS	Société Camérounaise d'Injection et de Modelage de Produits Organiques et Synthétiques
SCiP	Society for Computers in Psychology
SCIP	Syndicat des Cadres de I'Industrie du Pétrole
SCIPA	Servicio Cooperativo Inter-Americano de Producción de Alimentos
SCIPAG	Syndicat des Constructeurs de Machines pour les Industries du Papier, du Carton et des Arts Graphiques
SCIPLAC	Sciages et Placages Centrafricains
SCIPP	Santa Cruz Institute for Particle Physics
SCIPS	Servicio Cooperativo Interamericano Plan del Sur (Peru)
SCIR	Society of Cardiovascular and Interventional Radiology
SCIR	Syndicat Central d'Initiatives Rurales (France)
SCIRI	Supreme Council of the Islamic Revolution in Iraq
SCIS	Scottish Council of Independent Schools
SCIS	Sociedad de Comerciantes e Industriales Salvadoreños
SCISP	Servicio Cooperativo Interamericano de Salud Pública (Paraguay)
SCITEC	Association of the Scientific Engineering and Technological Community of Canada
SCITS	Servicio de Comercio de la Industria Textil Sedara
SCIV	Society of Chemical Industry of Victoria (Australia)
SCIVU	Scientific Council of the International Vegetarian Union
SCJ	Congregatio Sacerdotum a Sacro Corde Jesu

SCJM	Soeurs de la Charité de Jésus et Marie = ZLJM
SCK	Studiecentrum voor Kernenergie (Belgium) = CEN
SCKN-CONGO	Société Commerciale du Kouilou-Niari
SCL	Society for Caribbean Linguistics
SCL	Society for Computers and Law
SCL	Society of Construction Law
SCL	Society of County Librarians
SCLC	Scottish Child Law Centre
SCLFM	Society of Chain Link Fencing Manufacturers
SCLP	Scientists Committee on Loyalty Problems (U.S.A.)
SCLT	Scottish Civil Liberties Trust
SCLV	Socialist Campaign for a Labour Victory
SCM	Sociedad Colombiana de Matemátacis
SCM	Société Camérounaise de Minoterie
SCM	Société Camérounaise Michelin
SCM	Société de Chirurgie de Montréal (Canada)
SCM	Society of Coal Merchants
SCM	Society of Community Medicine
SCM	Sous-Commission de Coordination des Questions Forestières Méditerranéennes (FAO)
SCM	Student Christian Movement of Great Britain and Ireland
SCMA	Scottish Carpet Manufacturers' Association
SCMA	Scottish Cement Merchants Association
SCMA	Service Cinématographique du Ministère de l'Agriculture
SCMA	Society of Cinema Managers of Great Britain and Ireland, Amalgamated
SCMA	Sound & Communications Manufacturers' Association
SCMA	Stilton Cheese Makers Association
SCMAC	Scottish Catholic Marriage Advisory Council
SCMB	Société de Construction Métalliques de Bouké (Gabon)
SCMDI	Shenyang Coal Mine Design Institute
SCMESS	Society of Consulting Marine Engineers and Ship Surveyors
SCMM	Sisters of Charity of Our Lady Mother of Mercy
SCMM-K	Medical Mission Sisters – Kenya
SCMRTC	Sino-Canadian Mariculture Research and Training Centre
SCMT	Standing Committee of Ministers Responsible for Transportation (CARICOM)
SCMU	Scottish Commercial Motormen's Union
SCMU	Species Conservation Monitoring Unit (WCMC)
SCMV	Schweizerischer Coiffeurmeister-Verband
SCN	Sisters of Charity of Nazareth
SCND	Scottish Campaign for Nuclear Disarmament
SCNEA	Sealing Commission for the Northeast Atlantic
SCNI	Sports Council for Northern Ireland
SCNP	Scottish Council for National Parks
SCNR	Scientific Committee of National Representatives (SHAPE)
SCNVYO	Standing Conference of National Voluntary Youth Organisations
SCNWA	Sealing Commission for the Northwest Atlantic
SCO	Scottish Committee of Optometrists
SCOA	Société Commerciale de l'Ouest Africain
SCoA(SA)	Society of Company Accountants (South Africa)
SCOB	Syndicat de la Chimie Organique de Base
SCOBA	Standing Conference of the Canonical Orthodox Bishops in the Americas (U.S.A.)
SCOCLIS	Standing Conference of Co-operative Library and Information Services
SCODA	Standing Conference on Drug Abuse
SCODHE	Standing Conference on Dance in Higher Education
SCODI	Société des Conserves de Côte d'Ivoire
SCOFÉT	Syndicat des Constructeurs de Fours et d'Équipements Thermiques
SCoFF	Southern Counties Folk Federation
SCOG	Sociedad Colombiana de Obstricia y Ginecologia
SCOHLZA	Standing Committee of Head Librarians of Zambia
SCOLAG	Scottish Legal Action Group
SCOLARÉ	Association Internationale pour l'Utilisation des Langues Régionales à l'École (Belgium) = AIULRE

SCOLARÉ	Southern Council on Latin American Studies (U.S.A.)	**SCOT**	Scottish Confederation of Tourism
SCOLMA	Standing Conference on Library Materials on Africa	**SCOT**	Syrian Company for Oil Transport
		SCOTA	Scottish Offshore Training Association
SCOM	Société Centrale d'Organisation et Méthodes	**SCOTT**	Shipping Corporation of Trinidad and Tobago
SCOMAD	Service de Contrôle du Conditionnement de Madagascar	**SCOTTIE**	Society for the Control of Troublesome and Toxic Industrial Emissions
ScoMIA	Scottish Marine Industries Association	**SCOTVEC**	Scottish Vocational Education Council
SCONMEL	Standing Conference for Mediterranean Librarians	**SCOUTT**	Standing Committee of University Teachers ofTurkish Studies
SCONUL	Standing Conference of National and University Libraries	**SCOYO**	Standing Conference of Youth Organisations in Northern Ireland
SCOOP	Standing Committee on Official Publications (LA)	**SCP**	Scottish Communist Party
		SCP	Scottish Conservation Projects Trust
SCOOP	State Consultant Company for Oil Products	**SCP**	Sdruzení Ceskych Prekladatelú
		SCP	Social Credit Party (Canada)
SCOP	Société Coopératives Ouvrières de Production	**SCP**	Sociedad Cientifica de Paraguay
		SCP	Société Camérounaise de Publications
SCOP	Standing Conference of Principals	**SCP**	Société Camérounaise des Peaux
SCOPA	Seed Crushers & Oil Processors Association	**SCP**	Société Canadienne de Phytopathologie
		SCP	Société Chérifienne des Pétroles (Morocco)
SCOPAL	Standing Conference of Pacific Librarians	**SCP**	Société du Canal de Provence et d'Aménagement de la Région Provençale
SCOPE	Scientific Committee on Phosphates in Europe		
SCOPE	Scientific Committee on Problems of the Environment (ICSU) = CSPE	**SCP**	Society of Christian Philosophers
		SCP	Society of Clinical Psychiatrists
SCOPE	Scottish Council for Opportunities in Play Experience	**SCP**	Species Conservation Program (SSC)
		SCP	Spiritual Counterfeits Project (U.S.A.)
SCOPE	Standing Committee on Professional Exchange (Denmark)	**SCP**	Standing Conference of Principals
		SCP	Sudanese Communist Party
SCOPE	Standing Conference of Public Enterprises (India)	**SCP**	Supreme Council for Planning (Qatar)
		SCP	Syndicat des Constructeurs de Pompes
SCOR	Scientific Committee on Oceanic Research (ICSU) = CCIO, CSRO	**SCPA**	Scottish Cashmere Producers Association
SCOR	Société Commerciale de Réassurance	**SCPA**	Scottish Clay Pigeon Association
SCOR	Society & College of Radiographers	**SCPA**	Société Commerciale des Potasses d'Alsace
SCOR	Specialized Center of Research in Ischemic Heart Disease (U.S.A.)	**SCPA**	Société Commerciale des Potasses et de l'Azote
SCORE	Scottish Core of Retired Executives		
SCORE	Senior Corps of Retired Executives (U.S.A.)	**SCPC**	Société Camérounaise de Collecte des Peaux et Cuirs
SCOS	Standing Conference on Organisational Symbolism	**SCPC**	Stamp Collecting Promotion Council
		SCPDCIHE	Standing Conference of Principals and Directors of Colleges and Institutes of Higher Education
SCOSAC	Standing Committee on Sexually Abused Children		
SCOSS	Standing Committee on Structural Safety	**SCPE**	Secrétariat Catholique pour le Problèmes Européens
SCOSTEP	Scientific Committee on Solar Terrestrial Physics (ICSU) = CIUPST	**SCPL**	Société Camérounaise Pierre Lemonniers

SCPM	Silwood Centre for Pest Management		**SCRF**	Stanford Center for Reservoir Forecasting (U.S.A.)
SCPMA	Statiuhea de Cercetari pentru Plante Medicinale si Aromatice		**SCRI**	Scottish Crop Research Institute
SCPME	Standing Committee on Postgraduate Medical Education		**SCRI**	Shanghai Carpet Research Institute
			SCRIB	Steel Can Recycling Information Bureau
SCPR	Scottish Council of Physical Recreation		**SCRL**	Supreme Council of the Republic of Lithuania = LRAT
SCPR	Social and Community Planning Research		**SCRM**	Societatea de Chimie din Republica Moldova
SCPRI	Service Central de Protection contre les Rayonnements Ionisants		**SCRMA**	Surface Coating Synthetic Resin Manufacturer Association
SCPS	Scottish Centre for Pollen Studies		**SCRN**	Sociedad Colombia de Recursos Naturales
SCQS	Society of Chief Quantity Surveyors in Local Government		**SCRO**	Société Canadienne de Recherche Opérationelle = CORS
SCR	Société Centrale de Répresentation		**SCRP**	Syndicat de la Crémerie de la Région Parisienne
SCR	Society for Cardiovascular Radiology (U.S.A.)		**SCRS**	Standing Committee on Research and Statistics (NAFO)
SCR	Society for Cooperation in Russian and Soviet Studies (*ex* Society for Cultural Relations with the U.S.S.R.)		**SCRTA**	Steel Casting Research and Trade Association
SCR	Southern Council of Research (U.S.A.)		**SCS**	Science Council of Singapore
SCRA	Scottish Countryside Rangers Association		**SCS**	Scottish Crime Squad
			SCS	Singapore Civil Service
SCRA	Secteur Côtier des Recherches Agronomiques		**SCS**	Société Camérounaise de Sacherie
			SCS	Société Commerciale Sénégalaise
SCRAC	Standing Conference of Regional Advisory Councils for Further Education		**SCS**	Society for Computer Simulation (U.S.A.)
SCRAL	Sociedad Cooperativa Rural Argentina Ltda.		**SCS**	Society of Cosmetic Scientists
			SCS	Soil Conservation Service (U.S.A.)
SCRAM	Scottish Campaign to Resist the Atomic Menace		**SCS**	Solidarité Canada Sahel
			SCS	State Conservation Strategy
SCRATA	Steel Castings Research and Trade Association		**SCS**	Swiss Cooks Society = SKV, SSC
SCRC	Spanish Colonial Research Center (U.S.A.)		**SCS NWE**	Service Children's Schools (North West Europe)
SCRCC	Soil Conservation and Rivers Control Council (New Zealand)		**SCSA**	Scottish Cold Storage Association
SCRDC	Settle-Carlisle Railway Development Company		**SCSA**	Société Canadienne de Sociologie et d'Anthropologie
SCRE	Scottish Council for Racial Equality		**SCSA**	Soil Conservation Society of America
SCRE	Scottish Council for Research in Education		**SCSA**	Statiunea Centrala pentru Sericicultura si Apicultura (Romania)
SCRÉ	Syndicat des Constructeurs de Relais Électriques		**SCSA**	Strip Curtain Suppliers Association
SCREAM	Society for the Control and Registration of Estate Agents and Mortgage Brokers		**SCSA**	Supreme Council for Sports in Africa = CSSA
SCRÉM	Syndicat National de Commerce du Radio de la Télévision et de l'Équipement Ménager		**SČSA**	Svaz Československych Architektu
			SCSC	Soeurs de Charité de la Sainte Croix
SCRF	Scripps Clinic & Research Foundation (U.S.A.)		**SCSC**	Standing Committee on Soil Conservation

SCSCSP	Social-Cultural Society of Czechs and Slovaks in Poland = TSKLCZSwP	**SCTE**	Society of Cable Television Engineers (U.K., U.S.A.)
SCSH	Scottish Council for the Single Homeless	**SCTET**	Standing Conference for Technician Engineers and Technicians
SCSI	Société Canadienne de Santé Internationale = CSIH	**SCTHP**	Syndicat des Constructeurs de Transmissions Hydrauliques et Pneumatiques
SCSI	Society for Computer Simulation International	**SCTN**	Société Agricole pour le Contrôle e la Descendance des Taureaux de Race Normande
SCSIO	South China Sea Institute of Oceanology		
SCSJP	Social-Cultural Society of Jews in Poland = TSKŻwP	**SCTNB**	Société Commerciale des Techniques Nouvelles de Bâtiment
SCSK	Shellfish Commission for the Skagerrak-Kattegat	**SCTR**	Standing Conference on Telecommunications Research
SČSKU	Svaz Českych Skaladatelu a Koncertních Umelcu	**SCTT**	Société Commerciale de Transports Transatlantiques
SCSL	Sisters of Charity of St Louis	**SCTTAO**	Société Commerciale de Transports Trans-atlantiques Afrique Occidentale
SCSP	Scottish Council for Single Parents		
SCSPS	Standing Committee on the Safeguard of the Pursuit of Science (ICSU)	**SCTTCI**	Société Commerciale de Transports Transatlantiques Côte- d'Ivoire
SCSS	Scottish Council of Social Service	**SCU**	Scottish Cricket Union
SCSS	Standing Committee on Structure and Statutes (ICSU)	**SCU**	Scottish Crofters Union
		SCU	Scottish Cyclists Union
SCSST	Standing Conference on Schools Science and Technology	**SCUA**	Scottish Conservative and Unionist Association
SCT	Société Camérounaise des Tabacs	**SCUE**	Standing Conference on University Entrance
SCT	Société Canadienne de Théologie = CTS	**SCUIO**	Standing Conference of University Information Officers
SCT	Société Cotonnière Transocéanique		
SCT	Société de Chimie Thérapeutique	**SCUMRA**	Société Centrale de l'Uranium et des Minerais et Métaux Radioactifs
SCT	Society of Cardiological Technicians	**SCUP**	Society for College and University Planning (Canada, U.S.A.)
SCT	Society of Commercial Teachers		
SCT	Society of County Treasurers	**SCVANYO**	Standing Conference of Voluntary Youth Organizations
SCTA	Scottish Clay Target Association		
SCTA	Scottish Commercial Travellers Association	**SCVIR**	Society of Cardiovascular and Interventional Radiology
SCTA	Scottish Corn Trade Association Limited	**SCVM**	Service Central des Ventes du Mobilier de l'État
SCTA	Société Camérounais de Transport et d'Affrètement	**SCVO**	Scottish Council for Voluntary Organisations
SCTA	Society for Computing & Technology in Anaesthesia	**SCWG**	Scottish Co-Operative Women's Guild
SCTC	Société Camérounaise de Tissus et Confection KM	**SCWO**	Singapore Council of Women's Organizations
SCTC	Société Canadienne de Technologie Chimique = CSCT	**SCWO**	Standing Conference of West Indian Organisations in Great Britain
SCTC	Société Commerciale Transocéanique des Conteneurs	**SCWO**	Standing Conference of Women's Organisations
SCTCI	Scottish Centre for Technology for the Communication Impaired	**SCWR**	Scientific Committee on Water Research (ICSU)

SCWS	Scottish Co-operative Wholesale Society
SCYA	Scottish Christian Youth Assembly
SCYCOM-IMPEX	Syndicat des Industries de l'Afrique Équatoriale
SD	Democratic Party (Poland)
SD	Socialdemokratiet
SD	Stronnictwo Demokratyczne
SD&BBA	Soft Drink and Beer Bottlers Association (Éire)
SDA	Samnordisk Dokumentation for Arbederbeskyttelses-forskrifter (Denmark)
SDA	Schweizerische Depeschenagentur
SDA	Scottish Darts Association
SDA	Scottish Decorators' Association
SDA	Scottish Development Agency
SDA	Seventh Day Adventists General Conference
SDA	Société de l'Aérotrain
SDA	Stranka Demokratske Akcije (Bosnia-Herzegovina) = PDA
SDA	Syndicat de la Distillerie Agricole
SDA-CG	Stranka Demokratske Akcije–Crna Gora (Montenegro) = PDA-M
SDAC	Standing Dental Advisory Committee (NHS)
SDAI	Syndicat National de la Distribution pour l'Automobile et l'Industrie
SDAJ	Savez Drustava Anatoma Jugoslavije
SDAK	Stranka Demokratske Akcije Kosova (Serbia) = PDAK
SDAM	Social Democratic Alliance of Macedonia
SDAR	Savez Drustava Arhivskih Radnika Jugoslavije
SDASA	Scottish Deaf Amateur Sports Association
SDAT	Sociedad Dásonómica de la América Tropical
SDB	Società Salesiana di Santi Giovanni Bosco
SDBA	Soft Drink Bottlers' Association (Bahamas)
SDBO	Société de Banque Ocidentale
SdC	Servi della Carità = SC
SDC	Society of Designer-Craftsmen
SDC	Society of Dyers and Colourists
SDC	Sudan Development Corporation
SDC	Sustainable Development Commission
SDCA	Society of Dyers and Colourists of Australia
SDCC	State Drugs Crime Commission (Australia)
SDCGB	Square Dance Callers of Great Britain
SDCMRI	Shandong Coal Mining Research Institute
SDCVJ	Savez Drustava za Cistocu Vazduha Jugoslavije
SDE	Société Dakaroise d'Entreposage (Senegal)
SDE	Société de Droits d'Execution du Canada = PROC
SDEA	Shop and Display Equipment Association
SDECE	Service de Documentation Extérieure et de Contre-Espionnage
SDEJ	Savez Drustava Ekologa Jugoslavije
SdeM	Siervas de María
SDF	Sammenslutningen af Danmarks Forsknings-biblioteket
SDF	Scottish Decorators Federation
SDF	Scottish Disability Foundation
SDF	Self-Defence Forces (Japan)
SDF	Serbian Democratic Forum (Croatia) = SDF
SDF	Sikkim Democratic Front (India)
SDF	Social Democratic Federation (Japan)
SDF	Srpski Demokratski Forum / Serbian Democratic Forum (Croatia)
SDF	Svenska Dataföreningen
SDFM	Section Départementale des Fermiers et Métayers
SDG	Schweizerische Diabetes Gesellschaft = ASD
SDG	Société de Diamant de Guinée
SDGJ	Savez Drustva Geneticara Jugoslavije
SDHBS	South Devon Herd Book Society
SDI	Secours Dentaire International
SDI	Service de Documentation et de l'Information (Benin)
SDI	Sociedad para el Desarrollo Internacional
SDI	Società Dantesca Italiana
SDIA	Soap and Detergent Industry Association
SDIA	Socialist and Democratic Interafrican = IAS, IASD, SIA

SDIA	Susila Dharma International Association (SUBUD)	**SDP**	Social Democratic Party (Azerbaijan, Kosovo)
SDIC	Scientific and Technical Documentation and Information Center (China)	**SDP**	Social Democratic Party (Japan)
SDIC	Société de Développement Industriel du Caméroun	**SDP**	Social Democratic Party (Romania)
SDIÉ	Syndicat Français des Distributeurs de Papiers et Cartons d'Impression et d'Écriture	**SDP**	Stowarzyszenie Dziennikarzy Polskich
		SDP	Suomen Sosialidemokraattinen Puolue
		SDP	Swaziland Democratic Party
SDIG	Société pour le Développement de l'Industrie du Gaz	**SDP-BH**	Social Democratic Party of Bosnia-Herzegovina
SDIH	Société Dakaroise Immobilière et d'Habitation (Senegal)	**SDPA**	Social Democratic Party of Albania
		SDPCh	Sotsial-Demokraticheskaia Partiia Chuvashii
SDIT	Service de Documentation et d'Information Techniques de l'Aéronautique	**SDPD**	Sotsial-Demokraticheskaia Partiia Dagestana
		SDPE	Sistema de Direccion y Planificacion de la Economia (Cuba)
SDK	Schweizerische Direkoren-Konferenz Gewerblicher Berufs-und Fachschulen = CSD	**SDPK**	Social Democratic Party of Kazakhstan
		SDPM	Serbian Democratic Party of Montenegro = SDSCG
SDK	Slovensko Kemijsko Drustvo	**SDPM**	Social Democratic Party of Macedonia
SDK	Société de Kinésithérapie	**SDPM**	Société Dakaroise des Pétroles Mory (Senegal)
SDKOJ	Savez Drustava Radnika Kozarske i Kozarsko Preradivacke Industrije Jugoslavije	**SDPR**	Social Democratic Party of Reformers / Socijaldemokratska Partija Reformatora (Montenegro)
SDL	Democratic Left Party (Czech Republic)		
SDL	Strana Demokratickej Lavice (Slovakia) = PDL	**SDPR**	Sotsial-Demokraticheskaia Partiia Rossii
		SDPR	Sotsial-Demokraticheskaia Partiia Rossiiskoi Federatsii
SDL	Syndicat des Distillateurs-Liquoristes de Belgique	**SDPS**	Social Democratic Party of Slovenia
SDLP	Social Democratic and Labour Party (Northern Ireland)	**SDPU**	Social Democratic Party of Ukraine
		SDR	Sisters of the Divine Redeemer
SDM	Seychelles Democratic Movement	**SDR**	Slovenska Odborova Rada
SDMA	Surgical Dressings Manufacturers' Association (GFR) = BVM	**SDR**	Société de Développement Régional (Belgium, France)
SDMA	Surgical Dressings Manufacturers' Association (U.K.)	**SDR**	Society for Dance Research
SDMFAJ	Savez Drustava Matematicara, Fizicara i Astronoma Jugoslavije	**SDRA**	Société pour le Développement de la Riviéra Africaine (Ivory Coast)
SDMJ	Savez Drustava Mikrobiologa Jugoslavije	**SDRB**	Société de Développement Régional de Bruxelles (Belgium)
SDMO	Société de Diffusion de Moteurs de l'Ouest	**SDRP**	Socjaldemokracja Rzeczypospolitej Polskiej
SDN	Escuela Militar de Ingenieros (Mexico)	**SDS**	Servizio di Documentazione Spaziale
SDN	Sustainable Development Network (UNDP)	**SDS**	Sisters of the Divine Saviour
		SDS	Slavisticno Drustvo Slovenije
SDNS	Scottish Daily Newspaper Society	**SDS**	Societas Divini Salvatoris
SDP	Serbian Democratic Party (Bosnia-Herzegovina, Croatia) = SDS	**SDS**	Sozialistischer Deutscher Studentenbund
SDP	Serbian Democratic Party of Croatia	**SDS**	Space Documentation Service (ESRO/NASA)
SDP	Sisters of Divine Providence, Münster		

SDS	Special Distribution Services (Éire)	**SEA**	Service Employers Association (U.S.A.)
SDS	Srpska Demokratska Stranka (Bosnia-Herzegovina, Croatia) = SDP	**SEA**	Servicio de Extensión Agraria
		SEA	Servicios Especiales Aéros (Colombia)
SDS	Svenska Dermatologiska Sällskapet	**SEA**	Shipbuilding Exports Association
SDSA	Scottish Down's Syndrome Association	**SEA**	Slag Employers Association
SDSC	San Diego Supercomputer Center	**SEA**	Socialist Educational Association
SDSC	Strategic and Defence Studies Centre (Australia)	**SEA**	Sociedad Entomológica Argentina
		SEA	Sociedad Española de Acustica
SDSCG	Srpska Demokratska Stranka Crne Gore (Montenegro) = SDPM	**SÉA**	Société d'Électronique de d'Automatisme
SDSS	Social Democratic Party of Slovenia	**SÉA**	Société d'Équipement pour l'Afrique (Gabon)
SDSTA	Section Technique de l'Armée, Documentation Technique et Scientifique	**SÉA**	Société d'Études Ardennaises
		SÉA	Société Équatoriale d'Assurances
SDT	Society of Dairy Technology	**SEA**	Society for Economic Anthropology
SDTA	Scottish Dance Teachers Alliance	**SEA**	Society for Electronic Access
SDTF	Scottish Dairy Trade Federation	**SEA**	Southern Economic Association
SDTI	Société pour le Développement Touristique Interafricain (Benin)	**SEA**	Stazione di Entomologia Agraria
		SEA	Survival Education Association (U.S.A.)
SDTIM	Society for the Development of Techniques in Industrial Marketing	**SÉA**	Système des Écoles Associées appliquant un Programme d'Éducation pour la Coopération Internationale et la Paix = ASP
SDTU	Sign and Display Trades Union		
SDTZJ	Savez Drustava za Tehniku Zavarivanja Jugoslavije		
SDUHS	Social and Democratic Union of Hungarians in Slovakia = SDZMS	**SEAAC**	South-East Asia Air Command
		SÉABF	Société d'Équipement pour l'Afrique, Burkina Faso
SDUK	Society for the Diffusion of Useful Knowledge	**SÉAC**	Société d'Équipement pour l'Afrique, Caméroun
SDUSA	Social Democrats USA	**SEAC**	South-East Asia Command
SDV	Schweizerischer Dachdeckermeister Verband	**SÉACC**	Société de Coordination d'Études et d'Analyse des Coûts de Production (Ivory Coast)
SDV	Schweizerischer Detaillistenverband		
SDV	Schweizerischer Drogisten-Verband	**SEACEN**	South-East Asian Central Banks
SDV	Societas Divinarum Vocationum	**SEACFMO**	Société d'Exploitation de l'Alliance de Constructeurs Français de Machines-Outils
SDV	Stichting Doelmatig Verzinken		
SDVIVT	Savez Drustava Veterinara i Veterinarskih Tehnicara (*now* HVK)		
		SÉACI	Société d'Équipement pour l'Afrique, Côte d'Ivoire
SDVO	Soiuz Dukhnovnogo Vozrozhdeniia Otechestva	**SÉACO**	Société d'Équipement pour l'Afrique (Congo)
SDW	Schutzmeinschaft Deutscher Wald	**SEACON**	Southeast Asia Consortium
SDZMS	Sociálny a Demokratický Zväz Mad'arov na Slovensku (Slovakia) = SDUHS	**SEACORE**	Southeast Asia Communications Research
		SEACPA	Southeast Asian Catholic Press Association (Indonesia)
SE	Scottish Enterprise		
SE	Society of Engineers	**SEAD**	Scottish Education and Action for Development
SE	Solidaridad Española		
SE(S)TA	Sheffield Engineers' (Small) Tools Manufacturers' Association	**SEADAG**	South-East Asia Development Advisory Group (U.S.A.)
SEA	Science and Education Administration (U.S.A.)		

SEADD	South-East Asia Development Division (ODA)	**SEAP**	South-East Asia Project (IUCN)
SEADZ	Southeastern Agricultural Development Zone (Ethiopia)	**SEAP-CENTRE**	South East Asia Centre for the Promotion of Trade, Investments and Tourism (Japan)
SEAeIC	Sociedad Española de Alergología e Inmunología Clinica	**SEAPA**	Seaports Authority (Saudi Arabia)
SEAES	South East Asian Ergonomics Society	**SEAPAL**	South East Asia and Pacific League against Rheumatism
SEAF	Special Emergency Assistance Fund for Drought and Famine in Africa (OAU)	**SEAPEX**	South-East Asia Petroleum Exploration Society
SEAF	Sveriges Elektrik- och Elektronikagenters Förening	**SEAQ**	Swedish Association for Quality = SFK
SEAFDA	South East Asian Forum for Development Alternatives	**SEARCA**	Southeast Asian Regional Centre for Graduate Study and Research in Agriculture (Philippines)
SEAFDEC	Southeast Asian Fisheries Development Centre (Thailand)	**SEARCC**	South-East Asia Regional Computer Conference
SEAFIS	South East Asian Fisheries Information System	**SEARCF**	Société d'Encouragement pour l'Amélioration des Races de Chevaux en France
SÉAG	Société d'Équipement pour l'Afrique-Gabon	**SEARI**	Shanghai Electrical Apparatus Research Institute
SEAGS	South East Asia Geotechnical Society (Thailand)	**SEARICE**	South East Asian Institute for Community Education
SEAGST	South East Asia Graduate School of Theology	**SEARNG**	SE Asian Region Network for Geosciences
SEAISI	South East Asia Iron and Steel Institute	**SEARO**	Regional Office for South-East Asia (WHO)
SEAL	Society for Economic Analysis	**SEARS**	South and East Asian Regional Section (IOBC)
SEAL	Society of English & American Lawyers	**SEARSO-LIN**	South East Asia Rural Social Leadership Institute (Philippines)
SEAL	Solar Energy Applications Laboratory (U.S.A.)	**SEAS**	Centre for South-East Asian Studies
SEALION	Sea Level Instrumentation and Observation Network	**SEAS**	Centre for Southeast Asia Studies of Kyoto University (Japan)
SEALPA	South-East Asia Lumber Producers Association	**SEAS**	Scientific Exploration of the Atlantic Shelf
SEAM	Scandinavian East Asia Mission	**SEAS**	Scottish Export Assistance Scheme
SEAM	Servico de Equipos Agricolas Mecanizados (Chile)	**SEAS**	SHARE Europe
SEAMA	Small Electrical Appliance Marketing Association	**SEAS**	SHARE European Association (Switzerland)
SEAMEO	Southeast Asian Ministers of Education Organisation (Thailand) = OMEASE	**SEAS**	Social and Educational Association for Seafarers (U.S.A.)
SEAMEO-BIOTROP	Southeast Asian Regional Centre for Tropical Biology	**SÉAS**	Société d'Équipement pour l'Afrique, Sénégal
SEAMIC	South-East Asian Medical Information Centre (Japan)	**SEAS**	South of England Agricultural Society
SEAMS	South-East Asia Mathematical Society	**SEAS**	Svenska Solenergiföreningen
SEAN	Servicio Escolar de Alimentación y Nutrición	**SEASA**	South East Asia Shariah Association
SÉAN	Société d'Équipement pour l'Afrique-Niger	**SEASCO**	South-East Asia Science Co-operation Office = CCCAS
SEAP	Save the Environment from Atomic Pollution (Canada)	**SEASEE**	South East Asia Association on Seismology and Earthquake Engineering

SEASPECT	South-East Asian Specialists Group of Cooperative Training	**SEBOIS**	Société Sénégalaise Industrielle du Bois
SEASSE	Southeast Asian Society of Soil Engineering (Thailand)	**SEBRIMA**	Société d'Exploitation des Briqueteries du Mali
SEAT	Sociedad Española de Automóviles de Turismo	**SEBRO**	Servicebyråernas Branschorganisation
SEAT	Società Elenchi Ufficiali degli Abbonati al Telefono	**SEBT**	Société d'Exportation des Bois Tropicaux (Ivory Coast)
SEATAC	South East Asian Agency for Regional Transport and Communications Development	**SEBT**	South-Eastern Brick and Tile Federation
		SEC	Polski Ośrodek Kultury Europejskiej
		SEC	Scottish Evangelistic Crusade
SEATAG	South East Asia Trade Advisory Group	**SEC**	Secondary Examinations Council
SEATRAD	Southeast Asia Tin Research and Development Centre	**SEC**	Secretaria de Educação e Cultura (Brazil)
		SEC	Securities and Exchange Commission (Taiwan, U.S.A.)
SÉAVOM	Société d'Études et d'Applications Video-Optique Mécanique	**SEC**	Sindicato de Educadores Costarricenses
SEB	Securities Exchange of Barbados	**SEC**	Skye Environmental Centre
SEB	Sociedad Española de Bioquímica	**SÉC**	Société d'Échanges Commerciaux (Ivory Coast)
SEB	Société d'Exploitation des Briqueteries		
SEB	Société d'Exploitation du Parc à Bois de Bélabo (Cameroon)	**SÉC**	Société des Écrivains Canadiens
		SEC	Société Européenne de Cardiologie = ESC
SÉB	Société Équatoriale des Bois (Gabon)		
SEB	Society for Economic Botany (U.S.A.)	**SEC**	Société Européenne de Culture = ESC
SEB	Society for Experimental Biology	**SEC**	Société Européenne de la Contraception = ESC
SEB	Society for Experimental Botany		
SEB	Syndesmos Ellinon Biomichanon	**SEC**	Solar Energy Commission (Saudi Arabia)
SÉB	Syndicat des Éditeurs Belges		
SEB	Syndicat des Exploitants de Bauxite	**SEC**	State Electricity Commission of Victoria (Australia)
SEBA	Société Sénégalaise d'Exploitation des Bois Africains	**SEC**	Syndicat des Emballages Commerciaux
SEBA	Stichting Exploitatie en Bescherming Auteursrechten	**SECA**	Société d'Exploitation de Constructions Aéronautiques
SEBACAM	Société d'Études des Bauxites du Caméroun	**SECA**	Société pour l'Expansion Commerciale Africaine (Togo)
SEBAF	Société d'Exploitation des Bois Africains (Ivory Coast)	**SECA**	Student Education Commission of Asia (Hong Kong)
SEBATÉQ	Société Sénégalaise de Bâtiments, de Terrassements et d'Équipements	**SÉCA**	Syndicat d'Études des Centrales Atomiques
SÉBC	Société d'Éleveurs de Bovins Canadiens	**SECAB**	Secretária Ejecutiva Permanente del Convenio "Andrés Bello" (Peru)
SEBC	Societe d'Exploitation des Bois du Caméroun	**SECAM**	Société d'Exploitation des Cadres Maritimes
SEBI	Société d'Exportation des Bois Ivoiriens	**SECAM**	Symposium of Episcopal Conferences of Africa and Madagascar = SCEAM
SEBM	Society for Experimental Biology and Medicine	**SÉCAN**	Société d'Études et de Constructions Aéro-Navales
SEBO	Société d'Embouteillage des Bois Ivoiriens (Ivory Coast)	**SECAP**	Secrétariat Européen des Concessionnaires d'Autoroutes à Péage
SEBO	Société Sénégalaise d'Embouteillage de Boissons	**SECAP**	Servicio Ecuatoria de Capacitación Profesional
SEBOGA	Société pour l'Expansion des Boissons Hygiéniques au Gabon	**SECAR**	Société Européenne de Chirurgie Arthrite

SECARTYS	Servicio de Exportación de Electrónica	**SECPANE**	Servicio Cooperativo Peruano-Norteamericano de Educación
SECAS	Sociedad de Estudiantes de Ciencias Agronómicas Salvadoreñas	**SÉCPIA**	Société d'Étude Chimiques pour l'Industrie et l'Agriculture
SECCA	Société d'Exploitation Cinématographique du Caméroun	**SECPRE**	Sociedad Española de Cirurgia Plastica, Reparadora y Estetica
SECCAN	Science and Engineering Clubs of Canada	**SÉCRE**	Société d'Études et de Constructions
SECCI	Scottish Employers Council for the Clay Industries	**SÉCREN**	Société d'Études de Constructions et Réparations Navales (Madagascar)
SECEA	Servico Comercial de la Industria Textil Algodonera	**SECRI**	Shanghai Electronic Component Research Institute
SECED	Society for Earthquake and Civil Engineering Dynamics	**SECS**	Sociedad Española de Ciencia del Suelo
SECEGSA	Sociedad Española de Estudios para la Comunicacion Fija a traves del Estrecho de Gibraltar	**SÉCT**	Société des Écrivains de Cinéma et de Télévision
		SÉCTA	Société d'Études de Chemie et de Thérapie Appliquées
SECEM	Sociedad Española Construcciónes Electro-Mecanicas	**SECTAB**	Section Spécialisée pour le Tabac (COPA)
SECF	Société des Experts Comptables Français	**SECTEP**	Sociedade de Escritores
SECF-FASEN	Société d'Expertise Comptable Fiduciaire France-Afrique- Sénégal	**SED**	Scottish Education Department
		SED	Sozialistische Einheitspartei Deutschlands
SÉCI	Société d'Équipement de la Côte d'Ivoire	**SÉDA**	Société d'Éditions Documentaires Agricoles
SECI	Société d'Exploitation de Carrières Ivoiriennes	**SÉDA**	Société d'Études pour le Développement de l'Afrique (Cameroon)
SECJ	Service Européen de Coopération pour les Jeunes	**SÉDA**	Société d'Études pour le Développement de l'Automatisme
SECMA	Société d'Exploitation Cinématographique Africaine	**SEDAC**	Secretariado Episcopal de América Central y Panama
SECMA	Stock Exchange Computer Managers Association	**SEDAC**	Socioeconomic Data and Applications Center (CIESIN)
SÉCN	Société d'Études des Caissons Nucleaires	**SÉDAD**	Société d'Étude et Développement des Applications Dérivées Électroniques et Méchaniques
SECO	Bureau de Contrôle pour la Sécurité de la Construction en Belgique		
SECO-BRAH	Société d'Encouragement de la Culture des Orges de Brasserie et des Houblons en France	**SÉDAGRI**	Société d'Étude et de Développement Agricole
		SÉDAM	Société d'Études et de Développement des Aéroglisseurs Marins, Terrestres et Amphibies
SECOFI	Secretaría de Comercio y Fomento Industrial (Mexico)		
SECOINSA	Sociedad Española de Comunicaciones de Informatica, S.A.	**SEDAN**	Foreningen af Producenter i Danmark af Levnedsmidler Bestemt til Soerlig Ernoering
SECOLAS	Southeastern Council on Latin American Studies (U.S.A.)		
SECOM	Sociedad Española de Cirurgia Oral y Maxilofacial	**SEDAR**	Sociedad Española de Anestesiología y Reanimación
SECOTOX	International Society of Ecotoxicology and Environmental Safety	**SEDEC**	Social and Economic Development Centre, Colombo (Sri Lanka)
		SÉDÉC	Société d'Édition, de Documentation Économique et Commerciale
SÉCOTRAP	Société d'Études et de Contrôle de Travaux Publics (Ivory Coast)	**SEDECOS**	Secretaríado de Comunicación Social (Chile)

SÉDÉIPÉS	Société d'Études et d'Édition d'Information Politiques, Économiques et Sociales	**SEDIVER**	Société Européenne d'Isolateurs en Verre
SÉDÉIS	Société d'Études et de Documentation Économiques Industrielles et Sociales	**SEDNI**	Syndicat des Entrepreneurs de Dragages de Navigation Intérieure
SEDENA	Secretaría de la Defensa Nacional (Mexico)	**SEDO**	Sociedad Española de Optica
SEDEPAC	Servicio, Desarrollo y Paz (Mexico)	**SEDOS**	Servizio di Documentazione e Studi
SÉDERCAL	Société d'Équipement et de Développement Rural de la Nouvelle-Calédonie	**SÉDPA**	Société d'Édition et de Diffusion de la Presse Agricole
SÉDÉS	Société pour l'Étude et le Développement Économique et Social	**SEDUE**	Secretaría de Desarrollo Urbano y Ecología (Mexico)
SEDHA	Secretariat for Dental Health in Africa	**SEDUV**	Secretaria de Estado de Desarrollo Urbano y Vivienda (Argentina)
SEDI	Commission on the Study of the Earth's Deep Interior (U.S.A.)	**SEE**	Save Eyes Everywhere; British Council for the Prevention of Blindness
SEDI	Shaanxi Engineering Investigation and Design Institute	**SÉE**	Société d'Études et d'Expansion (Belgium)
SÉDIA	Société d'Étude de Développement Industriel et Agricole (Algeria)	**SÉÉ**	Société des Électriciens, des Électroniciens et des Radioélectriciens
SÉDIA	Société d'Études et de Distribution Inter-Africaines (Ivory Coast)	**SEE**	Society of Electronic Engineers (India)
SÉDIAC	Société pour l'Étude et le Développement de l'Industrie, de l'Agriculture et du Commerce (Burkina Faso)	**SEE**	Society of Environmental Engineers
		SÉE-NIGER	Sociéte d'Études et Entreprise d'Équipements au Niger
SÉDIBRA	Syndicat National d'Étude et de Défense des Intérêts de la Brasserie Française	**SEÉA**	Société Européenne d'Énergie Atomique = EAES
		SEEBIS	Soviet and East European Business Information Service
SEDIC	Sociedad Española de Documentación e Información Científica	**SEEC**	Scottish Environmental Education Council
SEDICAL	Société d'Exploitation et de Distribution de Carburants et de Lubrifiants (Ivory Coast)	**SEEC**	Sociedad Española de Estudios Clásicos
		SEÉCF	Société d'Encouragement à l'Élevage du Cheval Français
SEDICOS	Société Sénégalaise de Distribution, de Commerce et de Stockage	**SÉEÉ**	Société d'Études et Entreprise d'Équipements (Ivory Coast)
SEDICSS	Société Sénégalaise pour le Développement Industriel et Commercial du Sine Saloum	**SÉÉÉN**	Société pour les Économies d'Énergies et les Énergies Nouvelles
SEDIEX	Société Sénégalaise de Distribution Import-Export	**SEEEYYKT**	Syllogos Embokrikon Epicheiriseon Eidon Ygienis Ydraulikon Kai Thermanseos
SEDIGAS	Sociedad para el Estudio y Desarrollo de l'Industria del Gas	**SÉÉF**	Service des Études Économiques et Financières
SEDIMA	Syndicat National des Entreprises de Service et Distribution du Machinisme Agricole	**SEEF**	Society of Electronics Engineers, Finland
		SÉEG	Société d'Énergie et d'Eau du Gabon
SEDIS	Société Sénégalaise d'Importation et Distribution	**SEEI**	Southwest Electronic Engineering Institute (China)
SEDISI	Sociedad Española para et Desarrollo de las Industrias de Servicos de Informatica	**SÉÉN**	Syndicat d'Études de l'Énergie Nucléaire
		SEEP	Sociedad Española para el Estudio de los Pastos
		SÉERI	Société d'Études et de Réalisation Immobilières (Ivory Coast)

SÉES	Sociéte d'Études et d'Entreprises Sidérurgiques
SÉÉT	Société d'Études et d'Équipements
SEETCI	Société d'Exploitation d'Engins de Terrassement en Côte d'Ivoire
SEÉTPB	Société d'Entreprise d'Équipement de Travaux Publics et de Bâtiments (Ivory Coast)
SEF	Scottish Environmental Forum
SEF	Shipbuilding Employers Federation
SEF	Société d'Ethnologie Française
SEF	Société Entomologique de France
SEF	Société Ethnographique de France
SEF	Soiuz Evropeiskikh Foniatrov = UEP, UPE
SEF	Svenska Elversföreningen
SEF	Svenska Exlibrisföreningen
SEF	Syndicat des Exportateurs Suisses de Fromage
SEFA	Genossenschaft Schweizerischer Strassenemulsions-Fabrikanten
SEFA	South East Forest Alliance
SEFA	Syndicat Européen des Fûts en Acier
SEFAC	Société d'Exploitation Forestière et Agricole du Caméroun
SEFCA	Société des Entrepôts Frigorifiques de la Casamance (Senegal)
SÉFCO	Société d'Études Folkloriques de Centre-Ouest
SEFE	Suomen Ekonomiliitto
SEFEL	Secrétariat Européen des Fabricants d'Emballages Métalliques Légers (Belgium)
SEFERIF	Société d'Exploitation des Mines du Rif (Morocco)
SEFI	Société Européenne d'Ingénierie Financière = EFEC
SEFI	Société Européenne pour la Formation des Ingénieurs = ESEE
SEFI	Syndicat des Entrepreneurs Françaises Internationaux
SEFI	Syndicat des Entreprises Françaises de Travaux Publics à Vocation Internationale
SEFIC	Société d'Exploitations Forestières et Industrielles du Caméroun
SÉFIM	Société d'Études Financières et Meunières
SEFIPA	Société Européenne de Financement et de Participation
SEFN	Société d'Exploitation Forestière du Noum (Cameroon)
SEFRAN	Syndicat des Embouteilleurs de France
SEFRULEG	Société Sénégalaise des Fruits et Légumes
SEFS	Société d'Exploitation des Frigorifiques Survif (Mauritania)
SEFT	Society for Education in Film and Television
SEG	Saatgut-Erzeuger-Gemeinschaft Schleswig-Holstein
SEG	Schweizeriche Entomologische Gesellschaft = SES
SEG	Schweizeriche Ethnologische Gesellschaft = SSE
SEG	Sénégalaise d'Entreprise Générale
SEG	Société d'Exploitations Gabonaises
SEG	Société Européenne de Graphologie; Sociedad Europea de la Ciencia del Grafismo = EGF, EGS, ESHP, ESS, EVS, SEPS
SEG	Society of Economic Geology (U.S.A.)
SEG	Society of Exploration Geologists (U.S.A.)
SEG	Society of Exploration Geophysists
SEG	Sveriges Elgrossisters Förening
SEG	Verband Schweizerischer Eier- und Geflügelverwertungs- Genossenschaften
SÉGA	Société d'Études Gabonaises
SEGA	Société d'Exploitation de Gravières en Afrique
SÉGAP	Société d'Études pour l'Exploitation des Calcaires, Gypses, Argiles et Pouzzolanes de Madagascar
SÉGAZ-CAM	Société d'Études pour la Mise en Valeur du Gaz Naturel Camérounaise
SEGB	South Eastern Gas Board
SEGBA	Servicios Eléctricos del Gran Buenos Aires (Argentina)
SEGCA	Societas Europaea Gladstoniana Celticorum cum Amicis
SEGD	Society of Environmental Graphic Designers (U.S.A.)
SEGÉC	Syndicat Nationale Eau, Gas, Électricité des Cadres et Techniciens
SEGÉCAM	Entreprise Générale d'Électricité Camérounaise
SEGENI	Société Générale Sénégalaise pour le Négoce et l'Industrie
SEGESA	Seguros Generales S.A. (Paraguay)

SÉGÉSA	Société d'Études Géographiques, Économiques, et Sociologiques Appliquées	**SEICI**	Société d'Exportation et d'Importation de la Côte d'Ivoire
SEGI	Société Exploitation de Granit Ivoirien	**SÉIE**	Société d'Études de l'Industrie de l'Engrenage
SÉGIT	Syndicat des Éditeurs, Grossistes et Importateurs de Tapis	**SEIF**	Svenska Elektroingejors-föreningen
SEGOA	Société Sénégalaise d'Oxygène et d'Acetylène	**SEIFA**	Società Esportazione Importazione Fertilizanti Azotati
SÉGOR	Société d'Études de Gestion et d'Organisation (Cameroon)	**SEIFSA**	Steel and Engineering Industries Federation of South Africa
SÉGRAM	Société Équatoriale de Grands Magasins	**SEIM**	Sociedad Española de Informática Médica
SÉGRANI	Société d'Étude pour la Création d'une Usine de Graines au Niger	**SÉIMAD**	Société d'Équipement Immobilier de Madagascar
SEGyG	Sociedad Española de Geriatria y Gerontologia	**SEIMP**	Service Européen Information Ministérielle Parlementaire
SEH	Sociedad Española de Horticultura	**SÉIN**	Société d'Électronique Industrielle et Nucléaire
SEH	Societas Europaea Herpetologica	**SEIN**	Société d'Encouragement pour l'Industrie Nationale
SEH	Société Européenne d'Hematologie	**SEINA**	Société Européenne d'Instruments Numériques et Analogiques
SEHOMA	Société de Conseil et d'Expansion Commerciale Hollando-Malienne	**SEINAM**	Solar Energy Institute of North America
SEI	Secretaria Especial de Informática (Brazil)	**SEIO**	Sociedad de Estadistica e Investigación Operativa
SEI	Service d'Expérimentation et d'Information (INRA)	**SÉIR**	Société Sénégalaise d'Énergie et d'Irrigation
SEI	Sibirskii Energeticheskii Institut (Russia)	**SEITA**	Société Nationale d'Exploitation Industrielle des Tabacs et des Allumettes
SEI	Socialist Educational International		
SEI	Società Editrice Internazionale	**SÉJ**	Société des Études Juives
SEI	Societas Ergophthalmologica Internationalis	**SÉJÉF**	Société d'Études Juridiques Économiques et Fiscales
SEI	Société Générale d'Entreprises Immobilières et de Investissements (Belgium)	**SEJF**	Sri Lankan Environmental Journalists Forum
SEI	Société Sénégalaise d'Entreprises Industrielles	**SEK**	Schweizerischer Exportkaderverband
SEI	Society for Environmental Improvement	**SEK**	Svenska Elektiska Kommissionen
SEI	Syndicat de l'Emballage Industriel	**SEK**	Synomospondia Ergaton Kyprou
SÉIB	Société d'Électricité Industrielle et Bâtiments (Benin)	**SEKAPLAS**	Association of Greek Plastic Boat Manufacturers
SÉIB	Société Électrique et Industrielle du Baol (Senegal)	**SEKE**	Synetairistike Enosis Kapnoparagogon Ellados
SEIC	School Education International Centre	**SEKOM**	Sredneevropeyskii Tsentr Dokumentatsii Issledovaniiy Sredstv Massovoy Informatsii i Propagandy = CECOM
SÉIC	Société d'Études et d'Informations Charbonnières		
SÉIC	Société Électrique et Industrielle de la Casamance (Senegal)	**SEKRIMA**	Fivondrononam Ben'ny Sendika Kristianina Malagasy
SEIC	State Economics Information Centre (China)	**SEKV**	Schweizerische Einkäufer-Vereinigung
SEICAJA	Société d'Exploitation Industrielle et Commerciale Afro-Japonaise (Ivory Coast)	**SEL**	Safety Engineering Laboratory
		SEL	Scouts Esperanto League; Skolta Esperanto-Ligo

SEL	Societas Europea Lepidopterologica
SEL	Suomen Elocuvatoimistojen Liitto
SELA	Sistema Económico Latinoamericano (Venezuela)
SÉLAF	Société d'Études Linguistiques et Anthropologiques de France
SÉLAF	Société pour l'Études des Langues Africains
SELASI	Secretariado Latinoamericano de la Compañía de Jesús
SELAVIP	Fédération Internationale de Services Latino-Américains et Asiatiques de Promotion de l'Habitation Populaire
SELC	Schweizerischer Ex Libris Club
SELE	Syllogos Engegrimenon Logiston-Elegton Ellados
SÉLÉC	Société d'Étude des Électrocompresseurs
SElec	Society of Electroscience
SELF	Société d'Ergonomie de Langue Française
SÉLF	Syndicat des Écrivains de Langue Française
SELNI	Società Elettronucleare Italiana
SELSA	Servicio de Luchas Sanitarias (Argentina)
SELTA	Swedish-English Literary Translators Association
SELV	Société Eurafricaine de Location de Voitures (Ivory Coast)
SEM	Schweizerischer Engros-Möbelfabrikantenverband
SEM	Sociedad Española de Microbiología
SEM	Société Européenne des Mycobactériologistes
SEM	Society for Experimental Mechanics (U.S.A.)
SEM	Syndesmos Epistimonon Michanikon Kyprou
SÉM	Syndicat des Établissements Multiplicateurs de Semences Fourragères Sélectionnées
SEMA	Greek Midwives Association
SEMA	Secretaria Especial do Meio Ambiente (Brazil)
SÉMA	Société d'Équipement de Matériel Aéronautique (Congo)
SÉMA	Société d'Études de Mathématiques Appliquées
SÉMA	Société Équipement du Mali

SEMA	Spray Equipment Manufacturers Association
SEMA	Storage Equipment Manufacturers' Association
SEMABLE	Secteur de Modernisation d'Agriculture, Ble (Chad)
SÉMAK	Société d'Ébenisterie Menuiserie de l'Ancien Koumassi (Ivory Coast)
SEMA-PROC	Société Sénégalo-Malienne d'Import-Export des Produits du Cru
SÉMARP	Société d'Étude du Marché du Plateau (Ivory Coast)
SÉMATSEN	Société d'Équipement et de Matériels du Sénégal
SEMBACHI	Associazione Italiana Produttori Seme Bachi
SEMCA	South Eastern Marquee Contractors Association (*ex* MCA)
SEMCMA	Société Malienne d'Études et de Construction de Matériel Agricole
SEMCYC	Sociedad Española de Mecánica del Suelo y Cimentaciones
SEMDA	Surveying Equipment Manufacturers and Dealers Association
SEME	Sociedad Española de Microscopia Electrónica
SEMÉ	Société Belge de Microscopie Électronique = BVEM
SEMERC	Special Education Microelectronics Resource Centre
SEMF	Servicio para la Exportación de Material Ferroviario
SEMFA	Scottish Electrical Manufacturers' and Factors' Association
SEMG	Spring Makers' Export Group
SEMI	Semiconductor Equipment and Materials International (Belgium)
SÉMI	Société d'Ébénisterie et de Menuiserie Ivoirienne
SEMI	Société des Eaux Minérales Ivoiriennes
SEMIS	Société Européenne de Mini Informatique et des Systèmes
SEMKO	Svenska Elektriska Materielkontrollanstalten
SEMLH	Société d'Entraîde des Membres de la Légion d'Honneur
SEMM	Société Européenne de Matériels Mobiles
SÉMO	Société Belgo-Française d'Énergie Nucléaire Mosane

SEMPA	Syndicat des Entrepreneurs de Manutention du Port d'Abidjan (Ivory Coast)	**SENCICO**	Servicio Nacional de Capacitacion para la Industria de la Construccion (Peru)
SEMPE	Sociedad de Equipos Mecanicos y Productos Especializados (Honduras)	**SEND**	Scientists and Engineers for National Development (U.S.A.)
SEMPISA	Société Sénégalaise pour les Entreprises Maritimeset la Pêche Industrielle	**SENDA**	Société Sénégalaise de Développement Agricole
SEMR	Scottish Earth Mysteries Research	**SENDET**	Servicio Nacional de Detenidos (Chile)
SÉMRAD	Syndicat des Industries de l'Électronique Médicale et de la Radiologie	**SENDOS**	Servicio Nacional de Obras Sanitarias (Chile)
SEMRY	Société d'Expansion et de Modernisation de la Riziculture de Yagoua (Cameroon)	**SENE**	Servicio Nacional de Empleo (Panama)
		SENE-PHARMA	Société Pharmaceutique Sénégalaise
SEMS	Sociedad Española de Mecánica del Suelo	**SENE-TRANS-CARS**	Société Sénégalaise de Transports par Cars
SÉMT	Société d'Études de Machines Thermiques	**SENE-TRANSFIL**	Société Sénégalaise du Transformation du Fil de Métal
SEMY	Syndesmos Ergostasiarchon Michanikis Ypodimatopoias	**SENE-GALAP**	Société Sénégalaise de Diffusion d'Appareils Électriques
SEMZA	Association Professionnelle Belge des Négociants Préparateurs en Semences Agricoles	**SENÉLEC**	Société Sénégalaise de Distribution d'Énergie Électrique
		SENE-MBAL	Société Sénégalaise d'Emballages
SEN	Social Ecology Network	**SENE-MECA**	Société Sénégalaise de Mécanique
SEN	Sociedad Nuclear Española		
SENA	Servicio Nacional de Aprendizaje (Colombia)	**SENE PESCA**	Société Sénégalaise pour l'Expansion de la Pêche Côtière, Surgélation et Conditionnement des Aliments
SÉNA	Société d'Énergie Nucléaire Franco-Belge des Ardennes	**SENFOR**	Servicio Nacional de Formación Profesional (Paraguay)
SÉNA	Société d'Études Numismatiques et Archéologiques	**SENGAZ**	Société Sénégalaise de Gaz
SENABI	National Scientific and Technical Library and Documentation Services (South America)	**SENICOM**	La Sénégalaise Industrielle Commerciale
SENAC	Serviço Nacional de Aprendizagem Comercial (Brazil)	**SENICUA**	Servizio per gli Elenchi Nominativi dei Lavoratori e per i Contributi Unificati in Agricultura
SENAI	Serviço Nacional de Aprendizagem Industrial (Brazil)	**SENIMCO**	Société Sénégalaise Immobilière et Commerciale
SENALFA	Servicio Nacional de Lucha contra la Fiebre Aftosa (Paraguay)	**SENINFOR**	Société Sénégalaise de Travaux Informatiques
SENAM	Société Sénégalaise de Navigation Maritime	**SENN**	Società Elettronucleare Nazionale
SENAMA	Servicio Nacional de Maquinaria Agricola (Peru)	**SENNAC**	Special Educational Needs – National Advisory Council
SENAPET	Servicio Nacional de Programación y Evaluación Ténica (INTA)	**SENOTEL**	Société Anonyme de Construction et de Gestion Immobilière en Hôtelière
SENAPI	Servicio Nacional de Artesanias y Pequeñas Industrias (Panama)	**SENPA**	Servicio Nacional de Productos Agrarios
SENATI	Servicio Nacional de Aprendizaje y Trabajo Industrial (Peru)	**SENSE**	Scottish Environmental Network for a Sustainable Economy
SENCE	Servicio Nacional de Capacitacion y Empleo (Chile)	**SENSE**	The National Deafblind and Rubella Association

SENT	Sion Evangelisation Centre for National Training	**SEPBC**	Société d'Exploitation des Parcs à Bois du Caméroun
SÉNTA	Société d'Études Nucléaires et de Techniques Avancées	**SEPC**	Société d'Exploitation de Produits de Côte d'Ivoire
SENTOKYO	Senmon Toshokan Kyogikai (Japan)	**SEPCAÉ**	Société d'Engrais et Produits Chimiques d'Afrique Équatoriale
SÉO	Société des Études Océaniennes		
SEO	Society of Education Officers	**SÉPCEM**	Société d'Étude pour la Promotion de la Culture et l'Exploitation du Maïs au Caméroun
SEOC	Sindicato de Empleados y Obreros del Comercio (Paraguay)		
SÉOF	Société d'Études Ornithologiques de France	**SEPCM**	Société d'Engrais et de Produits Chimiques de Madagascar
SEOL	Suomen Erikois-Optikkojen Liitto	**SEPCO**	Services Electronic Parts Co-Ordinating Committee
SEORL	Sociedad Española de Otorrinolaringologia y Patologia Cervicofacial	**SEPD**	Sociedad Española de Patología Digestiva
SEP	Secretaria de Educación Pública (Mexico)	**SÉPE**	Secretariat pour l'Étude des Problèmes de l'Eau
SEP	Sociedad Ecuatoriana de Planificacion	**SEPÉCAT**	Société Européenne de Production de l'Avion École de Combat et d'Appui Tactique
SEP	Sociedad Entomológica del Perú		
SEP	Sociedad Española de Pscicoanálisis	**SEPÉRI**	Société Européenne pour l'Étude des Relations Internationales = ESSIR
SÉP	Société des Écoles Polytechniques		
SÉP	Société Équatoriale Pharmaceutique	**SÉPFA**	Société d'Études pour la Promotion Financière d'Activités Agro-Alimentaires (Senegal)
SEP	Société Européenne de Planification à Long Terme		
SEP	Société Européenne de Pneumologie	**SEPFA**	South-East Professional Fishermen's Association
SEP	Société Européenne de Propulsion	**SÉPIA**	Société d'Études de Protection des Installations Atomiques
SEP	Society of Experimental Psychologists (U.S.A.)		
SEP	Stowarzyszenie Elektryków Polskich	**SÉPIA**	Société d'Études et de Production Industrielle en Afrique
SEPA	Science Education Programme for Africa	**SEPL**	South European Pipe Line Company
SEPA	Scottish Environment Protection Agency	**SEPLA**	Seminario Permanente Latinoamérica
		SEPLA	Sindicato Español de Pilotos de Lineas Aereas
SÉPA	Société d'Éditions et de Publications Agricoles	**SEPLA**	Société d'Exploitation des Plantes Médicinales et Tropicales (Caméroun)
SEPA	Société Européenne de Paramétrologie	**SEPLA-CODI**	Secretaría de Planeamiento, Coordinación y Difusión (Uruguay)
SEPAB	Section on Experimental Psychology and Animal Behaviour (IUBS)		
SEPAM	Société d'Exploitation des Produits Animaux du Mali	**SEPLIS**	Secrétariat Européen des Professions Libérales, Indépendantes et Sociales (Belgium)
SEPAMA	Société d'Exploitation des Produits d'Arachides du Mali	**SEPM**	Society of Economic Palentologists and Mineralogists (U.S.A.)
SEPANI	Société d'Exploitation des Produits d'Arachides du Niger	**SEPMI**	Sociedad de Educación Patriotico-Militar (Cuba)
SÉPARC	Société d'Études pour la Promotion de l'Architecture et des Oeuvres d'Oscar Niemeyer	**SEPOGA**	Société d'Exploitation des Produits Oléagineux du Gabon
		SEPOM	Société d'Exploitation des Produits Oléagineux du Mali
SEPAS	Servicio Evangelico Peruano de Associación Social		
SEPBA	Société d'Exploitation du Parc à Bois d'Abidjan (Ivory Coast)	**SEPOR**	Service des Programmes des Organismes de Recherche

SEPP	Société d'Entreposage de Produits Pétroliers (Congo)
SÉPP	Société d'Étude de la Prévision de la Plantification (Switzerland)
SEPR	Sociedad Española de Proteccion Radiologica
SÉPR	Société d'Étude de la Propulsion par Réaction
SÉPROCI	Société d'Études et de Promotion de Côte d'Ivoire
SEPS	Società Europea di Psicologia della Scrittura = EGF, EGS, ESHP, ESS, EVS, SEG
SEPT	Serviço de Estatistica de Previdencia e Trabalho (Brazil)
SÉPT	Société d'Étude de Psychodrame Pratique et Thérapeutique
SEQA	Sociedad Española de Quimicos Analítica
SEQC	Sociedad Española de Quimica Clinica
SEQC	Sociedad Española de Quimicos Cosmeticos
SÉR	Service d'Économie Rurale (Luxembourg)
SER	Sociaal Economische Raad
SER	Sociedad Española de Radiodifusion
SER	Sociedad Española de Rehabilitación
SER	Société Européenne de Radiologie
SER	Society for Ecological Restoration
SER	Society for Educational Reconstruction
SER	Society for Epidemiological Research
SER	Svenska Elektroingenjörers Riksförening
SER	Sveriges Schaktentreprenörers Riksförbund
SERA	Scottish Educational Research Association
SERA	Socialist Environment and Resources Association
SÉRA	Société d'Études et de Réalisation Agricoles
SERADIS	Société Sénégalaise de Représentation, d'Approvisionnement et de Distribution
SÉRAI	Société d'Études de Recherches et d'Applications pour l'Industrie (Belgium)
SÉRAM	Service d'Études et de Recherches Antimalariennes (Zaïre)
SERAO	Société de Réalisations en Afrique de l'Ouest (Ivory Coast)
SERAS	Société d'Exploitation des Ressources Animales du Sénégal
SÉRAT	Société d'Études de Réalisations et d'Applications Techniques
SÉRB	Société d'Études et de Recherches Biologiques
SERB	Société Européenne de Radiobiologie
SERC	Science and Engineering Research Council
SÉRC	Service d'Étude et de Recherches de la Circulation Routière
SERC	Structural Engineering Research Centre (India)
SERCA	Servicios de Carga Aérea (Costa Rica)
SERCA	Société d'Exploitation de la République Centrafricaine
SERCE	Syndicat des Entrepreneurs de Réseaux, de Centrales et et d'Équipement Industriel Électriques
SERCÉL	Société d'Exploitation et de Recherches Électroniques
SÉRCH	Société d'Études et de Recherches pour la Connaissance de l'Homme
SERCO-METAL	Servicio Técnico Comercial de Construcciones Metálicas de Calderaria
SERCOBE	Servicio Tecnico Comercial de Construcciones de Beienes de Equipo
SERCOM	Station d'Essais et de Recherches de la Construction Métallique (Belgium)
SÉRDI	Société d'Étude et de Réalisation pour le Développement Industriel (Madagascar)
SÉREB	Société pour l'Étude et la Réalisation des Engins Balistiques
SÉRECCI	Société d'Études, de Recherches et d'Exploitation de Carrières de Côte d'Ivoire
SERÉL	Société d'Exploitation et de Recherches Électroniques
SEREM	Sociedad Española de Radiologia y Electrologia Médicas y de Medicina Nuclear
SÉRÉNA	Société d'Études pour le Développement de la Petite et Moyenne Réparation Navale à Dakar (Senegal)
SERENA	Société Européenne pour la Promotion des Systèmes Réacteurs Rapides au Sodium
SEREPCA	Société ELF de Recherches et d'Exploitation des Pétroles du Caméroun

SÉRES	Société d'Études et de Recherches en Sciences Sociales	**SÉRS**	Société d'Étude et Recherche Sociologiques
SÉRÉS	Société d'Études et Réalisation d'Équipements Spéciaux	**SERT**	Society of Electronic and Radio Technicians
SÉRES	Société d'Études Rurales et Sociales	**SERTAF**	Services Techniques Africains Côte d'Ivoire
SERGS	Sociedade de Engenharia do Rio Grande do Sul (Brazil)	**SÉRTEC**	Société d'Études et de Réalisations Techniques en Afrique Centrale (Cameroon)
SERH	Société d'Entreprises et de Réalisations Hydrauliques (Burkina Faso)	**SÉRTI**	Société d'Études et de Réalisation pour le Traitement de l'Information
SERI	Solar Energy Research Institute of ERDA (U.S.A.)	**SERTUC**	South East Region TUC
SÉRIC	Société d'Études et de Réalisation pour l'Industrie Caféière et Cacaoyère (Ivory Coast)	**SERUG**	Seminarie voor Toegepaste Economie bij de Rijksuniversiteit te Gent (Belgium)
SÉRICC	Société d'Études et de Recherches pour l'Industrie et le Commerce Camérounais	**SERVIU**	Servicio de Vivienda y Urbanismo Metropolitano (Chile)
SERICICO	Société Séricole de Côte d'Ivoire	**SES**	Samarbetsorginisationen for Emballagefragor i Skandinavien; Skandinaviska Emballage Selskapet
SERIMA	Société d'Entretien et de Réparation Industriels de Matériel Aéronautique		
SERL	Services Electronics Research Laboratory	**SES**	Scientific Exploration Society
		SES	Scottish Economic Society
SERM	Sociedad Española de Radiologia y Electrologia Médicas y de Medicina Nuclear	**SES**	Scottish Equipment Suppliers
		SÉS	Société des Études Socialistes = SSS
		SES	Société Entomologische Suisse = SEG
SÉRM	Société d'Études et de Recherches Minières de Madagascar	**SES**	Société Européenne de Semences (Belgium)
SÉRMIS	Société d'Études et de Recherches Minières du Sénégal	**SES**	Solar Energy Society
SERMOTO	Servicio Ténico-Comercial de Fabricantes y Montadores de Motocicletas	**SES**	Studies and Expansion Society (Belgium) = SEE, SFG
		SES	Suomen Egyptologinen Seura
SERNAM	Service National des Messageries	**SES**	Swedish Engineers Society (U.S.A.)
SERNAM	Servicio Nacional de la Mujer (Chile)	**SÉSA**	Société d'Études des Systèmes d'Automation
SERNAP	Secretaria de Recursos Naturales y Pesca (Chile)	**SESC**	Serviço Social do Comércio (Brazil)
SERNATUR	Servicio Nacional de Turismo (Chile)	**SESC**	Space Environment Services Center (U.S.A.)
SERNAUTO	Asociación Española de Fabricantes de Equipos y Componentes para Automoción	**SESC**	Systems Engineering Society of China
		SESCO	Société Européenne des Semiconducteurs
SERO	Sveriges Energiföreningars Riksorganisation	**SESD**	Society of Experimental Station Directors (U.S.A.)
SERPAJ	Service for Peace and Justice	**SESDA**	Secretariat de Santé Dentaire de l'Afrique
SERPAJ-AL	Servicio Paz y Justicia en América Latina (Ecuador)	**SÉSEP**	Société d'Études et de Soins pour les Enfants Paralysés
SERPAL	Servicio Radiofónico America Latina	**SESI**	Serviço Social de Industria (Brazil)
SERPEX	Servicio Peruano de Exportaciones	**SESI**	Solar Energy Society of Ireland
Serpro	Serviço Federal de Processamento de Dados (Brazil)	**SESK**	Verband Schweizerischer Schachtelkäsefabriken
SERRED	European Association of Reconditioners and Dealers in Drums		

SESKO	Suomen Sähköteknillinen Standardisoimisyhdistys SESKO ry
SESN	Sindicato dos Escritórios e Serviços do Norte
SESN	Società Elvetica di Scienze Naturali (Switzerland)
SESO	Studiecentrum voor Economisch en Sociaal Onderzoek
SESP	Serviço Especial de Saúde Pública (Brazil)
SESP	Société d'Entreposage de San Pedro (Ivory Coast)
SESP	Society for Experimental Social Psychology (U.S.A.)
SESR	Société Européenne de Sociologie Rurale = ESRS
SESRTCIC	Statistical, Economic and Social Research and Training Centre for Islamic Countries = CRSESFPI
SÉSS	Société d'Économie et de Sciences Sociales
SESS	Society of Ethnic and Special Studies (U.S.A.)
SÉSSIA	Société d'Études, de Constructions de Souffleries Simulateurs et Intrumentation Aérodynamique
SÉSUAM	Société d'Études Sucrières en Afrique et à Madagascar
SÉSUBF	Société d'Études Sucrières de Burkina Faso
SET	Securities Exchange of Thailand
SET	Serviço de Expansão do Trigo (Brazil)
SET	Société d'Encouragement au Tourisme
SÉT	Société d'Études et de Travaux Topographiques (Burkina Faso)
SET	Society for Environmental Therapy
SET	Society for Experimental Therapy
SET	Wirtschaftsverband Stahlbau und Energie-Technik
SETA	Scottish Egg Trade Association
SETA	Società Esercizi Telefonici Ausiliari
SÉTA	Société d'Équipements Techniques et Automobiles (Cameroon)
SETA-UITA	Syndicat Européen des Travailleurs de l'Alimentation, de l'Hôtellerie et des Branches Connexes dans l'UITA = EAL-IUL, ECF-IUF
SÉTACI	Société Ivoirienne d'Équipements Techniques et Automobiles
SÉTADEC	Société d'Études pour l'Amélioration, le Développement et l'Équipement des Collectivités Locales
SÉTAO	Société d'Études et de Travaux pour l'Afrique de l'Ouest (Ivory Coast)
SÉTAO	Société d'Études et de Travaux pour l'Afrique Occidentale
SÉTAP	Société pour l'Étude Technique d'Aménagement Planifiés
SÉTAT	Société d'Études Techniques et d'Aménagement du Territoire (Togo)
SETCa	Syndicat des Employés, Techniciens et Cadres de Belgique = BBTK
SETCI	Société d'Extrusion et de Tissage de Côte d'Ivoire
SÉTCO	Société d'Éditions Techniques Coloniales
SÉTEG	Société d'Électricité, de Téléphone et d'Eau du Gabon
SETEL	Société Européenne de Téléguidage
SÉTÉM	Société d'Études et de Travaux Électromécaniques (Mauritania)
SETENAVE	Estaleiros Navais de Setúbal
SETFIA	South East Trawl Fishery Industry Association
SETFP	Syndicat de l'Extrusion et de la Transformation des Films Plastiques
SETI	Société Européenne pour le Traitement de l'Information
SÉTIAC	Société des Éditions Techniques Industrielles, Agricoles et Commerciales
SÉTIMEG-GABON	Société d'Études, de Travaux et de Gestion du Gabon
SÉTM	Société d'Études et de Travaux Mécanographiques
SETMAC	South East Trawl Ministerial Advisory Committee
SETN	Sindicato dos Engenheiras Técnicos do Norte
SÉTP	Société d'Équipement et de Travaux Publics (Mali)
SETP	Society of Experimental Test Pilots (U.S.A.)
SÉTR	Société d'Étancheité et Travaux de Revêtements (Ivory Coast)
SÉTRA	Service d'Études Techniques des Routes et Autoroutes
SÉTRA-CONGO	Société d'Études et des Travaux au Congo
SÉTRAPEM	Société Équatoriale de Travaux Pétroliers Maritimes (Gabon)

SÉTU	Société d'Équipement des Terrains Urbains (Ivory Coast)
SÉTU	Société d'Études et de Travaux pour l'Uranium
SÉTUBA	Société d'Études et de Travaux pour l'Utilisation du Béton Armé (Cameroon, Central Africa)
SEU	Sindicato Español Universitario
SEUL	Service Européen des Universitaires Latinoaméricains
SEUM	Société d'Exploitation d'Usines Métallurgiques
SEUSS	South-Eastern Union of Scientific Societies
SEV	Schweizerischer Eisenbahner-Verband
SEV	Schweizerischer Elektrotechnischer Verein = ASE
SEV	Syndesmos Ellinon Viomichanon
SEVIC	Société d'Embouteillage de Vin au Caméroun
SEVIMA	Société d'Exploitation de la Viande à Madagascar
SEVMA-CAM	Société d'Exploitation et de Valorisation des Marbes, Cipolins et Aragonites à Madagascar
SEVPÉN	Service de Vente des Publications de l'Éducation Nationale
SEW/OGBL	Syndicat Education et Sciences de la Confédération Syndicale Indépendante du Luxembourg
SEWA	Self Employed Women's Association (India)
SEWAA	South East Wales Arts Association
SEXACAM	Société d'Exploitation Agro-Pastorale du Caméroun
SEYCO	Selección Comercio de Patata
SEYCOM	Seychelles National Commodity Company
SEYTIM	Seychelles Timber Company
SEZEB	Société d'Ethnozoologie et d'Ethnobotanique
SÉZID	Société d'Équipement des Zones d'Industrialisation Décentralisée
SF	Filii Sacrae Familiae
SF	Sågwerksförbundet
SF	Sinn Féin (Ireland)
SF	Socialistisk Folkeparti
SF	Sosioløkonomenes Forening
SF	Stone Federation
SF	Suomen Fyysikkoseura = FPS
SF2M	Société Française de Métallurgie et de Matériaux
SFA	Scientific Film Association
SFA	Scottish Football Association
SFA	Securities and Futures Authority
SFA	Shetland Fishermen's Association
SFA	Small Farmers Association
SFA	Small Firms' Association (Éire)
SFA	Société Française d'Acoustique
SFA	Société Française d'Archéologie
SFA	Syndicat Français des Adhésifs
SFA/CT	Service de la Formation Aéronautique et du Contrôle Technique
SFAA	Scottish Field Archery Association
SFAA	Society of Fine Art Auctioneers
SFAAW	Stove Furnace and Allied Appliance Workers International (U.S.A.)
SFAC	Social Fund Advisory Committee (EU)
SFAC	Solid Fuel Advisory Confederation (Éire)
SFAE	Swiss Federation for Adult Education = FSEA, SYEB
SFAF	Société Française des Analystes Financiers
SFAI	Steel Furnace Association of India
SFAJ	Société Française d'Architecture de Jardins
SFAK	Selskabet for Analytisk Kemi
SFAR	Société Française d'Anesthésie et de Réanimation
SFAS	Solid Fuel Advisory Service
SfB	Sanarbetskommittèn för Byttnadsfragor
SFB	Schweizerischer Fotografenbund
SFBBM	Société Française de Biochimie et de Biologie Moléculaire
SFBC	Société Française de Biologie Clinique
SFBD	Société Française de Biologie et de Dietetique
SFBIU	Scottish Farm Buildings Investigation Unit
SFBP	Société Française des Pétroles BP
SFBSiI	Społeczny Fundusz Budowy Szkół i Internatów
SFC	Saudi Fisheries Company (Saudi Arabia)
SFC	Scottish Film Council
SFC	Securities and Futures Commission (Hong Kong)
SFC	Société Française de Cardiologie

SFC	Société Française de Céramique	**SFÉ**	Société Française des Électriciens
SFC	Société Française de Chimie	**SFE**	Syndicats des Fonctionnaires Européens = BIEA, UIECS, VIEB
SFC	Société Française de Cosmétologie		
SFC	Société Française des Chrysanthèmistes	**SFÉA**	Société Française d'Études Agricoles
SFC	Standing Federation Committee (West Indies)	**SFÉC**	Société de Fabrication d'Éléments Catalytiques
SFC	Standing Finance Committee (ICSU)	**SFEC**	Student Forum of the EC (Belgium)
SFC	State Financial Corporations (India)	**SFÉCA**	Société Française d'Étude du Comportement Animal
SFCA	Sudan Fertility Care Association		
SFCA	Syndicat Français des Colles et Adhésifs	**SFÉCMAS**	Société Française d'Étude et de Construction de Matériels Aéronautiques Spéciaux
SFCI	Société Française de Chirurgie Infantile		
SFCM	Société Française de Chronométrie et de Microtechnique	**SFÉDS**	Société Française d'Étude du XVIII Siécle
SFCM	Société Française de Commerce à Madagascar	**SFEDTP**	Société Française d'Entreprises de Dragages et de Travaux Publics
SFCP	Société Française de Chirurgie Pédiatrique	**SFÉÉ**	Société Française d'Études pour l'Électricité
SFCPR	Société Française de Chirurgie Plastique et Reconstructive	**SFEE**	Sydesmos Pharmakeftikon Epicheiriseon Ellados
SFCS	Small Farmers' Co-Operative Society	**SFÉMI**	Société Française d'Équipement Minier et Industriel
SFCT	Syndicat Française des Produits Cosmétiques et de Toilette		
		SFÉN	Société Française d'Énergie Nucléaire
SFD	Saudi Fund for Development (Saudi Arabia)	**SFÉNA**	Société Française d'Équipements pour la Navigation Aérienne
SFD	Slovensko Farmaceutsko Drustvo	**SFEP**	Scottish Federation of Egg Packers
SFD	Société Forestière de Dolisie (Congo)	**SFEP**	Society of Freelance Editors and Proofreaders
SFD	Société Française du Dahlia		
SFD	Society of Film Distributors	**SFEPA**	Syndicat des Fabricants d'Explosifs et de Produits Accessoires
SFDA	Small Farmers Development Agency (India)	**SFÉR**	Société Française d'Économie Rurale
SFDAS	Société Française de Droit Aérien et Spatial	**SFÉR**	Société Française des Électriciens et Radio-Électriciens
SFDG	Société Française de Graphologie	**SFÉRB**	Syndicat des Fabricants d'Émulsions Routières de Bitume
SFDI	Société Française pour le Droit International		
SFDL	Société Forestière du Dja et Lobo (Cameroon)	**SFERMA**	Société Française d'Entretien et de Réparation de Matériel Aéronautique
SFDMC	Société Française des Microtechniques et de Chronométrie	**SFEU**	Scottish Further Education Unit
		SFÉV	Syndicat Française des Éleveurs de Visons
SFDMLL	Schweizerischer Fachverband der Diplomierten Medizinischen Laborantinnen und Laboranten = APSLLMD		
		SFF	Samfundet för Fastighetsvärdering
		SFF	Scottish Fishermen's Federation
SFDN	Svensk Förening för Näringslära	**SFF**	Scottish Flag Fund
SFE	Scottish Financial Enterprise	**SFF**	Society of Filipino Foresters
SFE	Société Financière Européenne	**SFF**	Svenska Fabriksbetong Föreningen
SFÉ	Société Française d'Égyptologie	**SFF**	Svenska Folkbibliotekarie Förbundet
SFÉ	Société Française d'Électrologie Médicale	**SFF**	Svenska Försäkringsföreningen
		SFF	Svenska Fotgrafernas Förbund
		SFF	Svenska Frisörförening

SFF	Svenska Fysioterapeutiska Föreningen
SFF	Sveriges Filatelist-Förbund
SFF	Sveriges Författarförbund
SFFC	Scottish Federation of Fishermen's Cooperatives
SFFCCP	Syndicat Français des Fournisseurs pour Coiffeurs et Coiffeurs Parfumeurs
SFFF	Societas pro Fauna et Flora Fennica
SFFL	Svensk Förening för Foniatri och Logopedi
SFfR =	Svensk Fürening für Radiofysik = SSRP
SFG	Sigmund Freud Gesellschaft (Austria)
SFG	Société Française de Gynécologie
SFG	Studien- und Förderungsgesellschaft (Belgium) = SEE, SES
SFGV	Schweizerischer Frauengewerbeverband
SFGWMA	Scottish Federation of Grocers and Wine Merchants Associations
SFH	Samfundet för Hembygdsvard
SFH	Société Française Hoechst
SFH	Studiengesellschaft für Hochspannungsanlagen
SFHA	Scottish Federation of Housing Associations
SFHCA	Somalia Family Health Care Association
SFHEA	Scottish Further and Higher Education Association
SFHM	Société Française d'Histoire de la Médecine
SFHOM	Société Française d'Histoire d'Outre-Mer
SFHR	Society for Film History Research
SFHV	Schweizerischer Fischhändler-Verband
SFI	Società Filosofica Italiana
SFI	Société Financière et d'Investissements du Sénégal
SFI	Société Financière Internationale (ONU) = CFI, IFC
SFI	Société Française d'Ichtyologie
SFI	Société Française d'Immunologie
SFI	Société Française des Amateurs d'Iris
SFI	Svenska Finlands Idrottsförbund
SFIA	Sea Fish Industries Authority
SFIA	Société Forestière et Industrielle de l'Azobé (Cameroon)
SFIAC	Scottish Federation of Independent Advice Centres
SFIB	Small Firms Information Bureau

SFIB	Syndicat National des Fabricants d'Ensembles de Information et des Machines de Bureau
SFIC	Société et Fédération Internationale de Cardiologie = ISFC
SFICÉ	Syndicat des Industries de Pièces Détachées et Accessoires Radio-Électriques et Électroniques
SFID	Société Forestière et Industrielle de la Doumé (Cameroon)
SFIÉ	Syndicat des Fabricants d'Isolants pour l'Électricité
SFIG	Syndicat des Fabricants Industriels de Glaces, Sorbets et Crèmes Glacées
SFIL	Société Forestière et Industrielle de la Lokoundje (Cameroon)
SFIL	Société Philosophique de Louvain
SFIM	Société de Fabrication d'Instruments de Mesure
SFIM	Svenska Forbundet for Internationaler Möbeltransporter
SFIO	Section Française Internationale Ouvrière
SFIR	Svenska Föreningen för Industrielle Rattsskydd
SFIS	Small Firms Information Service (of DTI)
SFIS	Société Forestière et Industrielle de la Sangha (Cameroon)
SFIT	Swiss Federal Institute of Technology
SFITV	Société Française des Ingénieurs Techniciens du Vide
SFK	Svenska Förbundet för Kvalitet = SEAQ
SFKK	Svensk Förening för Klinisk Kemi
SFL	Satens Forskningskommitté för Lantmannagbyggnader
SFL	Scandinavian Ferry Lines
SFL	Scottish Football League
SFL	Socialists for Labour
SFL	Statens Forskingsstasjoner i Landbruk (Norway)
SFL	Suomen Farmasia Liitto
SFL	Svenska Facklärarförbundet
SFL	Svenska Finlands Lärarförbund
SFL	Sveriges Fotolevantörers Förbund
SFLA	Solicitors' Family Law Association
SFM	Scarboro Foreign Mission Society
SFM	Sociedad Forestal Mexicana
SFM	Société Française de Malacologie
SFM	Société Française de Mesothérapie

SFM	Société Française de Métallurgie (*now* SF2M)
SFM	Société Française de Musicologie
SFMA	Scottish Flour Millers' Association
SFMA	Scottish Furniture Manufacturers Association
SFMC	Société Française de Minéralogie et Cristallographie
SFME	Société Française de Médecine Esthétique
SFME	Société Française de Microscopie Électronique
SFMF	Scottish Fish Merchants Federation
SFMG	Société Française de Médecine Générale
SFMGV	Schweizerischer Fahrrad- und Motorrad- Gewerbe- Verband = USMCM
SFMI	Société Française de Moteurs à Induction
SFMR	Société Forestière Marcel Régnier (Congo)
SFMRI	Shaanxi Forestry Machinery Research Institute
SFMS	Société Forestière du Maine Sénégal
SFMS	Société Française de Médecine du Sport
SFMT	Scottish Federation of Merchant Tailors
SFMT	Société Française de Médecine du Trafic
SFMTA	Scottish Federation of Meat Traders Associations
SFN	Sea of Faith Network
SFN	Société Française de Numismatique
SfN	Society for Neuroscience
SFNC	Société Française de Neurochirurgie
SFNI	Suikerfabrieknavorsingsinstituut (South Africa)
SFO	San Fernando Observatory (U.S.A.)
SFO	Scottish Fishermen's Organisation
SFO	Secular Franciscan Order = OFS, TOF
SFO	Serious Fraud Office
SFO	Société Française d'Ophthalmologie
SFO	Société Française d'Ostéopathie
SFOC	Société Forestière de l'Ouest Caméroun
SFOK	Społeczny Fundusz Odbudowy Kraju
SFOM	Société Financière pour les Pays d'Outre-Mer
SFOM	Société Française d'Optique et de Mécanique
SFOP	Scottish Friends of Palestine
SFOS	Société Française d'Organo-Synthèse
SFP	Société Française de Pédagogie
SFP	Société Française de Phoniatrie
SFP	Société Française de Photogrammétrie
SFP	Société Française de Photographie
SFP	Société Française de Physique
SFP	Société Française de Psychologie
SFP	Société Française des Paysagistes
SFP	Stowarzyszenie Filmowców Polskich
SFP	Svenska Folkpartiet (Finland)
SFPA	Science Fiction Poetry Association (U.S.A.)
SFPA	Structural Fire Production Association
SFPA	Sudan Family Planning Association
SFPB	Syndicat Française des Produits Cosmétiques et de Toilette
SFPC	Société Française de Pharmacie Clinique
SFPE	Scottish Food Promotion Executive
SFPE	Society of Fire Protection Engineers (U.S.A.)
SFPH	Société Française des Physiciens d'Hôpital
SFPH	Svenska Föreningen för Psykisk Hälsovård
SFPRI	Sichuan Family Planning Research Institute
SFPTOL	Sekcja Foniatryczna (PTOL)
SFR	Skogsägareföreningarnas Riksförbund
SFR	Société Française de Radioprotection
SFR	Société Française des Roses
SFR	Société Française Radioélectrique
SFR	Svenska Fargeritekniska Riksförbundet
SFR	Svenska Försäkringsbolags Riksförbund
SFR	Sveriges Färghandlares Riksförbund
SFR	Sveriges Fiskares Riksförbundet
SFR	Sveriges Förskollärares Riksförening
SFRI	Shaanxi Fisheries Research Institute
SFRL	Syndicat des Fabricants de Réactifs de Laboratoire
SFRMA	Synthetic Fibre Rug Manufacturers Association
SFRP	Société Française de Radioprotection
SFS	Föreningen Svensk Fjäderfaskötsel
SFS	Samfundet Finland-Sovjetunionen
SFS	Savez Filatelista Srbije
SFS	Schweizerischer Fachverband für Schweiss-und Schneidmaterial
SFS	Société Française de Sociologie

SFS	Society for French Studies	SFVL	Suomen Filmivalmistajien Liitto
SFS	Suomen Standardisoimisliitto	SFW	Schweizerische Fachgruppe für Wärmebehandlung
SFS	Svenska Fornskriftsällskapet		
SFS	Svenska Fysikersamfundet	SFWA	Science Fiction Writers of America
SFS	Sveriges Förenade Studentkårer	SFWA	Southern Fleece Washers Association
SFSA	Scottish Federation of Sea Anglers	SFY	Suomen Filosofinen Yhdistys
SFSA	Scottish Field Studies Association	SFZ	Slovenské Filozofické Združenie = SPA
SFSA	Steel Founders' Society of America	SFZ	Sozialwisenschaftliches Forschungszentrum
SFSC	Société Française de Sexologie Clinique		
SFSR	Socialist Federation of Soviet Republics	SG	Institutum Fratrum Instructionis Christianae a Sancto Gabriele
SFT	Société Forestière Tropicale (Ivory Coast)	SG	Showmen's Guild of Great Britain
SFT	Société Française des Télécommunications	SG	Siege Group
		SG	Siol nan Gaidheal
SFT	Société Française des Thermiciens	SG	Société Générale
SFT	Société Française des Traducteurs	SGA	Sand and Gravel Association
SFT	Society of Feed Technologists	SGA	Schweizerische Gesellschaft für Agrarwirtschaft und Agrarsoziologie
SFTAH	Society for the Autistically Handicapped		
		SGA	Schweizerische Gesellschaft für Akustik
SFTAS	Syndicat Français des Textiles Artificiels et Synthétiques	SGA	Schweizerische Gesellschaft für Anthropologie
SFTB	Schweizerischer Filmtechniker-Vereinigung	SGA	Schweizerische Gesellschaft für Asienkunde
SFTC	Sea Fisheries Training Council	SGA	Schweizerische Gesellschaft für Aussenpolitik = ASPE
SFTM	Société Française de Transports Maritimes	SGA	Schweizerische Gesellschaft für Automatik = ASSPA
SFTP	Science for the People (U.S.A.)		
SFTP	Société Française des Tubes Pneumatiques	SGA	Scientific Glassware Association
		SGA	Scottish Games Association
SFTSA	Scottish Forest Tree Seed Association	SGA	Scottish Glass Association
SFTV	Schweizerischer Filmtechnikerinnen- und Filmtechnikerverband = ASTF	SGA	Société de Géologie Appliquée aux Gîtes Minéraux
		SGA	Société Gabonaise d'Assainessement
SFTV	Verband Gewerbsmässiger Ferntransportunternehmer der Schweiz	SGA	Société Générale d'Alimentation (Zaïre)
SFU	Shanghai Fisheries University	SGA	Société Géologique de l'Afrique = GSA
SFU	Société de Fluoration de l'Uranium	SGA	Society of Graphic Artists
SFU	Société Française des Urbanistes	SGAA	Schweizerische Gesellschaft für Astrophysik und Astronomie = SSAA
SFUSA	Society of Swiss Friends of the U.S.A.		
SFUZO	Svitova Federacija Ukrainskih Zinocih Organizacij = WFUWO	SGAA	Stained Glass Association of America
		SGACC	Sécrétariat Général à l'Aviation Civile et Commerciale
SFV	Schweizerische Franchising-Vereiningung	SGAE	Österreichische Studiengesellschaft für Atomenergie
SFV	Schweizerischer Feuerwehrverband		
SFV	Schweizerischer Forstverein	SGAE	Schweizerische Gesellschaft für Anthropologie und Ethnologie
SFV	Schweizerischer Fremdenverkehrsverband	SGAE	Sociedad General de Autores Españoles
SFV	Société Française du Vide	SGAÉI	Société Gabonaise d'Aménagement et d'Équipement Immobiliers
SFV	Svenska Folkdansens Vänner		
SFVH	Svenska Föreningen för Vetenskaplig Homeopati	SGAG	Schweizerische Gesellschaft für Angewandte Geographie

SGAI	Schweizerische Gesellschaft für Allergologie und Immunologie = SSAI		**SGCC**	Société Générale des Coopératives de Consommation
SGAICO	Swiss Group for Artificial Intelligence and Cognitive Science		**SGCCI**	Société Générale Commerciale de Côte d'Ivoire
SGAM	Schweizerische Gesellschaft für Allgemeinmedizin		**SGCÉ**	Syndicat Général de la Construction Électrique
SGAP	Society for Growing Australian Plants		**SGCH**	Sociedad de Genética de Chile
SGAR	Schweizerische Gesellschaft für Anästhesiologie und Reanimation = SSAR		**SGCH**	Sociedad Geológica de Chile
			SGCI	Schweizerische Gesellschaft für Chemische Industrie = SSIC, SSCI
SGATAR	Study Group on Asian Tax Administration and Research (Republic of Korea)		**SGCICP**	Syndicat Général des Commerces et Industries du Caoutchouc et des Plastiques
SGAV	Sindicato Gremial de Artistas de Variedades (El Salvador)		**SGCP**	Scottish Graduate Careers Programme
SGB	Schweizerische Gesellschaft für Betriebswissenschaft		**SGCTMA**	Syndicat Général des Constructeurs de Tracteurs et Machines Agricoles
SGB	Schweizerische Gesellschaft für Biochemie = SSB		**SGD**	Stichting Gezondheidsdienst voor Dieren
SGB	Schweizerische Graphologische Berufsvereinigung		**SGD**	Swiss Graphic Designers
SGB	Schweizerischer Gewerkschaftsbund		**SGDH**	Savez Geografskih Drustava Hrvatske (*now* HGD)
SGB	Scottish Gas Board		**SGDL**	Société des Gens de Lettres de France
SGB	Sociedad Geográfica Brasileira		**SGDN**	Secrétariat Général de la Défense Nationale
SGB	Sociedad Geológica Boliviana			
SGB	Société des Bois du Gabon		**SGE**	Schweizerische Gesellschaft für Ernährungsforschung = SSRN
SGB	Société Générale de Banane			
SGB	Société Géologique de Belgique		**SGE**	Société Gabonaise d'Entreposage
SGBA	Société Générale de Banque aux Antilles (Martinique)		**SGE**	Société Gabonaise d'Entreprises
			SGEÉM	Société Générale d'Entreprises Électromécaniques (Mali)
SGBB	Schweizerische Gesellschaft für Balneologie und Bioklimatologie = SSMTC		**SGÉF**	Secrétariat Général de l'Épiscopat Français
SGBCI	Société Générale de Banque en Côte d'Ivoire		**SGÉN**	Syndicat Général de l'Éducation Nationale
SGBF	Schweizerische Gesellschaft für Boden- und Felsmechanik		**SGEP**	Syndicat Général de l'Enseignement Public
SGBFP	Schweizerische Gesellschaft für Photogrammetrie, Bildanalyse und Fernerkundung = SSPIT		**SGEPP**	Société Gabonaise d'Entreposage de Produits Pétroliers
			SGEVE	Synomospondia Geniki Epangelmation kai Viotechnon
SGBI	Schoolmistresses and Governesses Benevolent Institution		**SGF**	Scottish Growers Federation
			SGF	Société Géologique de France
SGBM	Société Gabonaise de Béton Manufacturée		**SGF**	Studiengemeinschaft für Fertigbau
			SGF	Svenska Gasföreningen
SGBS	Société Générale de Banques au Sénégal		**SGF**	Svenska Geofysiska Föreningen
			SGF	Svenska Geotekniska Föreningen
SGBT	Schweizerische Gesellschaft für Biomedizinische Technik		**SGF**	Sveriges Galvanotekniska Förening
			SGF	Sveriges Gjuteritekniska Förening
SGC	Service Générale de Contrôle (Belgium)		**SGF**	Sveriges Gummitekniska Förening = SKG
SGC	Sociedad Geográfica de Colombia			

SGFA	Society of Graphic Fine Art
SGFF	Schweizerische Gesellschaft für Familienforschung
SGFF	Syndicat Général des Fondeurs de France et Industries Connexes
SGFHTF	Syndicat Général des Fabricants d'Huile et de Tourteaux de France
SGFT	Schweizerische Gesellschaft für Feintechnik
SGG	Schweizerische Geisteswissenschaftliche Gesellschaft
SGG	Schweizerische Genossenschaft für Gemüsebau
SGG	Schweizerische Geologische Gesellschaft = SGS
SGG	Schweizerische Gesellschaft für Genetik = SSG
SGG	Schweizerische Gesellschaft für Gynäkologie = SSG
SGG	Schweizerische Graphologische Gesellschaft
SGgG	Schweizerische Geographische Gesellschaft
SGGG	Société Générale du Golfe de Guinée
SGGMN	Schweizerische Gesellschaft für Geschichte der Medizin und der Naturwissenschaften = SSHMSN
SGGO	Studiekring voor Grasland- en Groenvoederonderzoek
SGGP	Schweizerische Gesellschaft für Geschichte der Pharmazie
SGGP	Schweizerische Gesellschaft für Gesundheitspolitik
SGH	Schweizerische Gesellschaft für Hämatologie = SSH
SGH	Schweizerische Gesellschaft für Höhlenforschung = SSS
SGHC	Société des Grands Hôtels du Caméroun
SGHCV	Société des Grands Hôtels du Cap-Vert
SGI	Servicio Geodésico Interamericano
SGI	Società Geologica Italiana
SGI	Society for Gynecologic Investigation (U.S.A.)
SGI	Soka Gakkai International
SGI	Statens Geotekniska Institut
SGI	Swedish Geotechnical Institute
SGICF	Syndicat Général de l'Industrie Cotonnière Française
SGIEO	Sistema Global Integrado de Servicios Oceánicas = IGOSS, SMISO
SGIJ	Syndicat Général de l'Industrie du Jute
SGIM	Schweizerische Gesellschaft für Innere Medizin
SGIO	Special Group on International Organisations (OECD)
SGIPA	Syndicat Général de l'Industrie du Plastique Armé
SGIPR	Syndicat Général de l'Industrie des Plastiques Renforcés
SGIS	Safer Glazing Information Service
SGISO	Sistema Global de Servicios Oceanicos = IGOSS, SGIEO, SMISO
SGIT	Savez Gradevinskih Inzenera i Tehnicara Jugoslavije
SGK	Samband Grunnskólakennara
SGK	Schweizerische Gesellschaft der Kernfachleute = SOSIN
SGK	Schweizerische Gesellschaft für Kartografie
SGK	Schweizerische Gesellschaft für Kristallographie
SGK	Stichting Verkoopkantoor voor Gras- en Klavermeel
SGKB	Schweizerische Gesellschaft für Kaufmännisches Bildungswesen = ASES, SSEB
SGKC	Schweizerische Gesellschaft für Klinische Chemie = SSCC
SGKGS	Schweizerische Gesellschaft für Kulturgüterschutz = SSPBC, SSPCP
SGKJP	Schweizerische Gesellschaft für Kinder- und Jugendpsychiatrie = SSPEA
SGKV	Studiengesellschaft für den Kombinierten Verkehr
SGKZ	Schweizerische Gesellschaft für Klinische Zytologie
SGL	Schweizerische Gesellschaft für Lehrerinnen- und Lehrerbildung *(ex* SPV)
SGL	Schweizerische Gesellschaft für Logistik
SGM	Schweizerischer Verband der Grosshändler und Importeure der Motorfahrzeugbranche
SGM	Service Géologique de Madagascar
SGM	Société Gabonaise de Mécanique
SGM	Société Générale des Minerais (Belgium)
SGM	Society for General Microbiology

SGMA	Soup and Gravy Manufacturers Association
SGMB	Société Géologique et Minéralogique de Bretagne
SGMC	State Gold Mining Corporation (Ghana)
SGMGA	Scottish Glass Merchants and Glaziers Association
SGMT	Schweizerische Gesellschaft für Microtechnik = ASMT
SGMT	Société Générale des Moulins du Togo
SGN	Section de Génie Nucléaire de l'Association Suisse pour l'Énergie Atomique
SGN	Servicio Geológica Nacional (Colombia, Nicaragua, Salvador)
SGN	Société Gabonaise de Négoce
SGNB	Schweizerische Gesellschaft für ein Neues Bodemrecht
SGNF	Syndicat Général et National du Froid
SGO	Schweizerische Gesellschaft für Onkologie = SSO
SGO	Société Général Optique
SGOA	Schweizerische Gesellschaft für Orientalische Altertumswissenschaft = SSOEM, SSOME, SSPOA
SGOEM	Schweizerische Gesellschaft für Optik und Elektronen-Mikroskopie
SGOIP	Syndicat Général de l'Optique et des Instruments de Précision
SGOMSEC	Scientific Group on Methodologies for the Safety Evaluation of Chemicals
SGOP	Syndicat Générale des Ouates et Pansements
SGP	Schweizerische Gesellschaft für Personalfragen
SGP	Schweizerische Gesellschaft für Phlebologie
SGP	Schweizerische Gesellschaft für Photogrammetrie = SSP
SGP	Schweizerische Gesellschaft für Psychiatrie = SSP
SGP	Schweizerische Gesellschaft für Psychologie und ihre Anwendungen = SSP
SGP	Serviços Geológicos de Portugal
SGP	Sociedad Geológica del Perú
SGP	Staatkundig Gereformeerde Partij
SGP	Stowarzyszenie Geodetów Polskich
SGP	Stowarzyszenie Geomorfologów Polskich = APG
SGP	Stowarzyszenie Germanistów Polskich
SGP	Syndicat des Graphologues Professionnels
SGPA	Scottish General Publishers Association
SGPA	Stained Glass Professionals Association (U.S.A.)
SGPC	Shiromani Gurdwara Parbandhak Committee (India)
SGPF	Sveriges Glas- och Porslinshandlareförbund
SGPFBM	Syndicat Générale des Producteurs Fournisseurs de Bois aux Mines
SGPLA	Schweizerische Gesellschaft für Phoniatrie, Logorädie und Audiologie
SGPMR	Schweizerische Gesellschaft für Physikalische Medizin und Rheumatologie
SGPP	Schweizerische Gesellschaft für Praktische Psychologie
SGPSM	Schweizerischer Gesellschaft für Psychosomatische Médizin
SGR	Schweizerische Gesellschaft für Rheumatologie
SGR	Scientists for Global Responsibility
SGR	Sveriges Golvhandlares Riksförbund
SGRB	Société Générale des Représentants de Belgique
SGRC	Société Géographique Royale du Canada = RCGS
SGRNM	Schweizerische Gesellschaft für Radiologie und Nuklearmedizin
SGS	Schweizerische Gesellschaft für Soziologie = SSS
SGS	Slovenská Geografická Spoločnost
SGS	Società Generale Semiconduttori
SGS	Société Gabonaise de Services
SGS	Société Générale de Surveillance (France, Switzerland)
SGS	Société Géologique Suisse = SGG
SGS	Stage Golfing Society
SGS	Svenska Gymnastiklararesällskapet
SGSG	Schweizerische Gesellschaft für ein Soziales Gesundheitswesen
SGSH	Société Générale Suisse d'Histoire = AGGS, SGSS
SGSM	Schweizerische Gesellschaft für Sportmedizin = SSMS
SGSPM	Schweizerische Gesellschaft für Sozial- und Préventivmedizin
SGSS	Schweizerische Gesellschaft für Skandinavische Studien

SGSS	Società Generale Svizzera di Storia = AGGS, SGSH
SGSV	Schweizerische Gesellschaft für Statistik und Informatik
SGT	Schweizerische Galvano-technische Gesellschaft
SGT	Société de Groupage et de Transit
SGT	Société des Garde-Temps (Switzerland)
SGT	Société Guinéenne de Transport
SGT	Society of Glass Technology
SGTC	Société Gabonaise de Transports et Carrières
SGTE	Société Camérounaise de Grands Travaux de l'Est
SGTÉ	Société Générale de Techniques et d'Études
SGTICES	Sindicato General de Trabajadores de la Industria de la Construcción, Similares y Conexos de El Salvador
SGTK	Schweizerische Gesellschaft für Theaterkultur
SGTM	Société Générale Transport Maritime
SGTP	Schweizerische Gesellschaft für Tropenmedizin und Parasitologie
SGTS	Scottish Gaelic Texts Society
SGU	Schweizerische Gesellschaft für Umweltschutz = SPA, SPE
SGU	Scottish Gliding Union
SGU	Scottish Golf Union
SGU	Sveriges Geologiska Undersökning
SGUF	Schweizerische Gesellschaft für Ur- und Frühgeschichte = SSPA
SGV	Schweizerische Gesellschaft für Volkskunde
SGV	Schweizerischer Geflügelzuchtverband
SGV	Schweizerischer Gewerbeverband = USAM
SGV-NOK	Ständige Generalversammlung der Nationalen Olympischen Komitees
SGW	Schweizerische Gesellschaft Praktizierender Wirtschaftsberater
SGWCPFA	Spencer Gulf and West Coast Prawn Fishermen's Association
SGY	Suomen Geoteknillinen Yhdistys
SHA	Saskatchewan Horticultural Association
SHA	Scottish Hardware Association
SHA	Scottish Hockey Association
SHA	Secondary Heads Association
SHA	Socialist Health Association

SHA	Sociedad de Historia Argentina
SHA	Société Hôtelière de l'Air (Niger)
SHA	Society of Heraldic Arts
SHA	Swiss Hotel Association
SHAA	Society of Hearing Aid Audiologists
SHAC	London Housing Aid Centre (SHAC)
SHAC	Société Havraise Africaine de Commerce (Ivory Coast)
SHAC	Society for the History of Alchemy and Chemistry
SHACT	Scottish Housing Associations Charitable Trust
SHAD	Société Havraise Africaine de Décorticage (Ivory Coast)
SHADA	Haitian – American Society for Agricultural Development
SHADE	St. Helena Aviation Development Group
SHAF	Société de l'Histoire de l'Art Français
SHAFR	Society for Historians of American Foreign Relations
SHAL	Société d'Histoire et d'Archéologie de la Lorraine
SHALCO	Sharjah Liquefied Petroleum Gas Company (UAE)
SHALTA	Skin, Hide and Leather Trades Association
SHAO	Shanghai Astronomical Observatory
SHAPA	Solids Handling and Processing Association
SHAPE	Supreme Headquarters, Allied Powers, Europe (NATO)
SHARACO	Saudi Hotels and Resort Areas Company (Saudi Arabia)
SHARP	Self Help Addiction Recovery Programme
SHARP	Society for the History of Authorship, Reading and Publishing
SHAS	Scottish Hospitals Advisory Service
SHAS	Smallholders' Advisory Service (Malaysia and Sri Lanka)
SHAS	Société d'Histoire de l'Art en Suisse = GSK, SSAS
SHAT	Sociedad Horticola para América Tropical (Costa Rica)
SHB	Svenska Handelsbanken
SHBTh	Society of Health and Beauty Therapists (*ex* NFHB)
SHCF	Saint Hubert Club de France
SHCG	Social History Curators Group

ShChit	Rossiiskii Soiuz Sotsialnoi Zashchity Voennosluzhashchikh, Voennoobiazannykh i Chlenov ikh Semei	**SHIC**	Société Hôtelière et Immobilière du Congo
SHCP	Secretaria de Hacienda y Credito Publico (Mexico)	**SHIN-RENGO**	Trade Union Federation (Japan)
SHD	Société d'Histoire du Droit	**SHIO**	Sveriges Hantverks- och Industriorganisation
SHD	State Hydro-Electric Department (New Zealand)	**SHIP**	Sociedade Historica da Independéncia de Portugal
SHDA	Société d'Histoire des Droits de l'Antiquité	**SHIV**	Schweizerischer Handels- und Industrieverein = USCI
SHE	Society for Health Education	**SHIV**	Schweizerischer Holzindustrie-Verband
SHE	Society for History Education (U.S.A.)	**SHJPF**	Société d'Horticulture et des Jardins Populaires de France
SHECC	Scottish Health Education Coordinating Committee	**SHK**	Schweizerische Hochschulkonferenz = CUS
SHEDA	Storage and Handling Equipment Distributors' Association	**SHK**	Stowarzyszenie Harcerstwa Katolickiego
SHEDCO	Shariah Economic Development Corporation (UAE)	**SHL**	Suomen Hautaustoimistojen Liitto
SHEFC	Scottish Higher Education Funding Council	**SHL**	Suomen Huonekalukauppiatten Liitto
SHELBEN-INREX	Société Shell Béninoise de Recherches et d'Exploitation	**SHLF**	Société d'Histoire Littéraire de la France
SHELL-CAMREX	Société Shell Camérounaise de Recherches et d'Exploitation	**SHLM**	Society of Hospital Linen Service and Laundry Managers
SHELL-IVOREX	Société Shell Ivoirienne de Recherches et d'Exploitation	**SHLTA**	Skin, Hide & Leather Traders' Association
SHELL-NIGEREX	Société Shell Nigérienne de Recherches et d'Exploitation	**SHM**	Société de la Haute Mondah (Gabon)
SHELL-CENT-RAFREX	Société Shell Centrafricaine de Recherches d'Exploitation	**SHM**	Société des Hôtelleries du Mali
		SHM	Société des Hôtels Meridien
SHF	Société Hippique Française	**SHMIS**	Society of Headmasters of Independent Schools
SHF	Société Hydrotechnique de France	**SHN**	Servicio de Hidrografia Naval (Argentina)
SHF	Svenska Historiska Föreningen	**SHN**	Société des Huileries du Niger
SHF	Sveriges Handelsagenters Förbund	**SHNC**	Société Hôtelière Nord-Caméroun
SHFF	Scottish House Furnishers Federation	**SHO**	Self Help Organisation
SHFF	Société Historique et Folklorique Française	**SHOC**	Sheltered Housing Owners' Confederation of Scotland
SHFL	Sveriges Hogre Flickskolors Laraförbund	**SHOM**	Service Hydrographique et Océanographique de la Marine
SHG	Schweizerische Heilpédagogische Gesellschaft = ASA	**SHOT**	Society for the History of Technology
SHG	Schweizerische Heraldische Gesellschaft	**SHP**	Social Democratic Populist Party
		SHP	Société d'Histoire de la Pharmacie
SHGF	Scottish Hang-Gliding Federation	**SHP**	Sosyal Demokrat Halkei Parti (Turkey)
SHHD	Scottish Home and Health Department	**SHPA**	Solids Handling & Processing Association
Shhh	Self-help for hard of hearing people (U.S.A.)	**SHPF**	Société de l'Histoire du Protestantisme Français
SHIA	Swedish Organisation of the Handicapped International Aid Foundation	**SHPN**	Société Hellénique pour la Protection de la Nature = EEPV, HSPN
		SHR	Sisters of the Holy Redeemer

SHR	Société Hippique Rurale
SHR	Sveriges Hotell- och Restauranagförbund
SHRC	Shopping Hours Reform Council
SHRG	Scottish Homosexual Rights Group
SHRH	Servicio Hidráulico de la República Haitiana
SHRI	Sikh Human Rights Internet
SHRO	Sudan Human Rights Organisation
SHS	Schweizer Heimatschutz
SHS	Scottish History Society
SHS	Shire Horse Society
SHS	Social History Society of the United Kingdom
SHS	Socialist History Society
SHS	Stowarzyszenie Historyków Sztuki
SHS	Suomen Hammaslääkäriseura
SHS	Suomen Historiallinen Seura ry
SHSBF	Société des Huiles et Savons de Burkina Faso
SHSK	Schweizerische Häutschäden-Kommission
SHSN	Société Helvétique des Sciences Naturelles = SNG
SHSO	Sveriges Handverks och Småindustriorganisation
SHSPC	Scottish Health Service Planning Council
SHSR	Society For Humanity and Social Reform
SHTF	Sveriges Handelsträdgardmästareförbund
SHTJ	Savez Hamicara i Tehnologa Jugoslavije
SHTM	Société des Hôtelleries et du Tourisme du Mali
SHTS	Société Ivoirienne d'Alimentation et de Commerce
SHU	Scottish Hockey Union
SHU	Société Hippique Urbaine
SHU	Státni Hydrometeorologicky Ustáv
SHV	Schweizer Hotelier-Verein
SHV	Schweizerischer Hafnermeisterverband, Ofenbau- und Plattengeschäfte
SHV	Schweizerischer Handelslehnerverein
SHV	Schweizerischer Hebammen-Verband
SHVA	Scottish Health Visitors Association
SHY	Suomen Henkilökuntalehtien Yhdistys
SHY	Suomen Hypnoosiyhdistys
SI	Saintpaulia International (U.S.A.)
SI	Schweizer Informatiker Gesellschaft
SI	Silver Institute (U.S.A.)
SI	Skýrslutoeknifélag Íslands
SI	Smithsonian Institution (U.S.A.)
SI	Socialist International
SI	Societas Iesu = SJ
SI	Society of Indexers
SI	Solidaridad Internacional
SI	Soroptomist International
SI	Sotsialisticheskaia Initsiativa
SI	Statens Industreverk
SI	Survival International
SI	Sveriges Industriförbund
SI/A	Soroptimist International of the Americas
SI/E	Soroptomist International of Europe
SI/SWP	Soroptimist International of the South West Pacific
SI3T	Industries Françaises du Téléphone, du Télégraph et de leurs Applications Télématiques
SIA	Sajudzio informaciju agentura
SIA	Saskatchewan Institute of Agrologists (Canada)
SIA	Schweizerischer Ingenieur- und Architeken-Verein
SIA	Securities Industry Association
SIA	Semiconductor Industry Association
SIA	Service Innovation Action
SIA	Singapore International Airlines
SIA	Socialist Interafrican = IAS, IASD, SDIA
SIA	Società Italiana di Audiologia
SIA	Société d'Informatique Appliquée
SIA	Société d'Investissements Africains
SIA	Société des Ingénieurs de l'Automobile
SIA	Société Immobilière Agricole
SIA	Société Internationale Arthurienne
SIA	Société Interprofessionnelle de l'Aviculture et des Produits de Bassecour
SIA	Société Ivoirienne d'Assurances
SIA	Société Suisse des Ingénieurs et des Architectes
SIA	Society of Industrial Accountants
SIA	Society of Insurance Accountants (U.S.A.)
SIA	Society of Investment Analysts

SIA	Solidarité Internationale Antifasciste	**SIAN**	Société Industrielle d'Adjamé Nord (Ivory Coast)
SIA	Solvents Industry Association		
SIA	Spinal Injuries Association	**SIAN**	Société Industrielle et Agricole du Niari (French Equatorial Africa)
SIA	Sugar Industry Authority (Jamaica)		
SIA-CONGO	Société Industrielle et Agricole du Congo	**SIAP**	Sociedad Interamericana de Planificación = SIP
SIAAR	Swiss Institute of Allergy and Asthma Research	**SIAP**	Società Italiana di Anatomia Patologica
SIAB	Sociedad de Ingenieros Agrónomos de Bolivia	**SIAP**	Société Industrielle Africaine de Plastiques
SIAB	Stiftung für Internationalen Austauch in den Bergen (France)	**SIAP**	Société Ivoirienne d'Avitaillements Portuaires
SIAC	Secretariado Interamericano de Acción Católica	**SIAP**	Statistical Institute for Asia and the Pacific = ISAP
SIAC	Società Italiana Acciaierie Cornigliano	**SIAPA**	Società Italo-Americana Prodotti Anti-Parassitari
SIAC	Società Italiana Additivi per Carburanti	**SIAPAP**	Société Industrielle et Agricole de la Pointe-à-Pitre (Guadeloupe)
SIAC	Société Internationale des Artistes Chrétiens = ISCA	**SIAPE**	Société Industrielle d'Acide Phosphorique et d'Engrais (Tunisia)
SIACE	Scottish Institute for Adult and Continuing Education	**SIAR**	Société de la Surveillance Industrielle
SIACO	Société Ivoirienne d'Alimentation et de Commerce	**SIAR**	Société Immobilière de l'Autoroute (Ivory Coast)
SIAD	Service de l'Information pour l'Appui au Développement (UN)	**SIAR**	Stiftelsen Företagsadministrativ Forskning
SIAD	Società Italiana Autori Drammatici	**SIARCA**	Società Internazionale di Assicurazioni e Riassicurazioni
SIAE	Scottish Institute of Agricultural Engineering	**SIARCT**	Syndicat International des Auteurs de Radio, Cinéma et Télévision = IWG
SIAE	Sociedad Iberoamericana de Administración de Educación = ISEA	**SIARM**	Société Ivoirienne d'Approvisonnement et de Restauration Maritime
SIAE	Società Italiana degli Autori ed Editori	**SIAS**	Sammenslutningen af Indendøørs Arkitekter i Skandinavien
SIAE	Società Italiana per l'Antropologia e la Etnologia	**SIAS**	Scandinavian Institute of African Studies = NAI
SIAÉB	Société Industrielle d'Agriculture et d'Élevage de Boumango (Gabon)	**SIAS**	Shanghai Institute of Animal Schistosominsis
SIAEG	Sociedad Ibero Americana de Endoscopia Ginecologica (Brazil)	**SIAS**	Shenyang Institute of Agricultural Sciences
SIAEN	Sociedad Iberoamericana de Estudios Numismáticos	**SIAS**	Société Industrielle et Agricole de la Somme
SIAEX	Société d'Achat d'Exportation	**SIAS**	Société Ivoirienne Azar et Salame
SIAF	Società Italiana di Audiologia e Foniatria	**SIAS**	Society of Insurance Accountants and Secretaries (South Africa)
SIAF	Société des Ingénieurs Agronomes de France	**SIAT**	Secrétariat International pour les Applications de la Téléinformatique
SIAG	Société Industrielle et Automobile de Guinée	**SIAT**	Società Italiana Assicurazioni Trasporti
SIAL	Salon International de l'Alimentation	**SIAT**	Société Industrielle et Agricole du Congo
SIAM	Society for Industrial and Applied Mathematics (U.S.A.)		
SIAMF	Société Internationale des Amis d'Musique Française	**SIAT**	Société Industrielle et Agricole du Tabac Tropical (Congo)

SIAT	Société Ivoirienne Agricole de Tiassale
SIAT	Société Ivoirienne d'Assistance Technique
SIATRAC-CI	Société Inter-Africaine de Transit et de Consignation en Côte d'Ivoire
SIATSA	Servicios para la Investigación Agricola Tropical (Honduras)
SIAV	Schweizerischer Ingenieure- und Architektenverein
SIB	Securities and Investments Board
SIB	Shipbuilding Industry Board
SIB	Società Italiana de Biometrie
SIB	Società Italiana di Biochimica
SIB	Société Immobilière du Bénin
SIB	Société Industrielle de Biscuiterie (Burkina Faso)
SIB	Société Ivoirienne de Banque
SIB	Society of Independent Businesses
SIB	Special Investigations Branch, Military Police
SIB	Statens Institut för Byggnadsforskning (Sweden)
SIBA	Scottish Indoor Bowling Association
SIBA	Services Insurance Brokers Association
SIBA	Société Industrielle des Blanchisseries Africaines (Ivory Coast)
SIBAF	Société Industrielle de Fabrication d'Aliments de Bétail (Ivory Coast)
SIBAF	Société Industrielle des Bois Africains (Cameroon)
SIBAG	Société d'Industries de Bois au Gabon
SIBAGEC	Société Ivoirienne de Bâtiment de Génie Civil
SIBC	Société Internationale de Biologie Clinique = SIBIOC
SIBC	Solomon Islands Broadcasting Corporation
SIBEGIQ	Syndicate Belge des Grossistes et Importateurs en Quincailliers
SIBESA	Syndicat de l'Industrie Belge d'Enregistrements Sonores et Audio-Visuels
SIBEV	Société Interprofessionnelle du Bétail et des Viandes
SIBH	Society for the Interpretation of Britain's Heritage
SIBICOB	Société Industrielle de Biscuiterie et Confiserie du Bénin
SIBIOC	Société Internationale de Biologie Clinique = SIBC
SIBM	Société Internationale de Biologie Mathématique
SIBM	Société Ivoirienne de Béton Manufacturé
SIBMAS	Société Internationale des Bibliothèques et Musées des Arts du Spectacle
SIBMN	Società Italiana di Biologia e Medicina Nucleare
SIBO	Società Italiana di Bioterapia e di Omeopatica
SIBOC	Securities and Investments Board of Control
SIBP	Shanghai Institute of Biological Products
SIBP	Société Ivoirienne des Pétroles BP
SIBRAS	Société Industrielle de Brasseries du Sénégal
SIBTI	Société Ivoiro-Belge de Transactions Internationales
SIBU	Scandinavian Independent Baptist Union = FB
SIC	Schweizerischer Verband von Comestibles- Importeuren und Händlern
SIC	Science Information Council (NSF) (U.S.A.)
SIC	Società Italiana Canzioni
SIC	Società Italiana Chimici
SIC	Società Italiana di Chemioterapia
SIC	Società Italiana di Chirurgia
SIC	Società Italiana di Criminologia
SIC	Société Immobilière du Caméroun
SIC	Société Immobilière du Canal (Ivory Coast)
SIC	Société Immobilière et Commerciale (Senegal)
SIC	Société Industrielle des Cacaos (Cameroon)
SIC	Société Industrielle et Commerciale de San-Pedro (Ivory Coast)
SIC	Société Intercontinentale des Containers
SIC	Société Internationale de Cardiologie = ISC
SIC	Société Internationale de Chirurgie = ISS
SIC	Société Internationale de Criminologie
SIC	Société Ivoirienne de Cinéma
SICA	Société d'Intérêt Collectif Agricole
SICA	Société Immobilière de la Côte d'Afrique
SICA	Société Industrielle Centrafricaine

SICA	Société Industrielle de l'Est Camérounaise	**SICC**	Société Suisse des Ingénieurs en Chauffage et Climatisation
SICA	Société Internationale de Coopératives Agricoles	**SICC-CI**	Société Industrielle et Commerciale de Chaussures en Côte d'Ivoire
SICA	Society of Industrial and Cost Accountants of Canada	**SICCA-CAOS**	Société Industrielle Camérounaise des Cacaos
SICAB	Société Industrielle Camérounaise de Bois	**SICCS**	Società Italiana di Citologia Clinica e Sociale
SICABAG	Société d'Intérêt Collectif Agricole de Guadeloupe	**SICERI**	Shanghai Internal Combustion Engine Research Institute
SICABAM	Société Coopérative d'Intérêt Collectif Agricole de la Martinique	**SICF**	Scottish International Children's Festival
SICABLE	Société Ivoirienne de Câbles	**SICFA**	Société Industrielle et Commerciale Franco-Africaine
SICABO	Société Industrielle Camérounaise de Bonneterie	**SICH**	Sociedad Internacional de la Ciencia Horticola = ISHS, SISH
SICABO	Société Ivoirienne de Carrosserie Bois	**SICI**	Société Immobilière et Commerciale Ivoirienne
SICADE	Società Italiana Costruzione Apparecchi Domestici e Industriali	**SICI**	Société Immobilière pour le Commerce et l'Industrie
SICAÉ	Société d'Intérêt Collectif Agricole d'Électricité	**SICICAM**	Société Civile Immobilière Camérounaise
SICAF	Société Industrielle de Couvertures Africaines	**SICIND**	Società Incremento Cotonicolo Industriale nella Daunia
SICAF	Société Ivoirienne de Crédit Automobile et de Financement	**SICIPA**	Société Ivoirienne de Commerce International, de Promotion et d'Assistance
SICAF	Société Ivoirienne de Culture d'Ananas Frais	**SICL**	Société Industrielle et Commerciale de Louga (Senegal)
SICAG	Société Industrielle Commerciale et Agricole de Guinée	**SICLAC**	Socialist International Committee for Latin America and the Caribbean (SI)
SICAHR	Société d'Intérêt Collectif d'Habitat Rural	**SICLIM**	Société Ivoirienne de Froid Ménager
SICAP	Servicio Interamericano de Cooperacion Agricole en Panamá	**SICM**	Secretariat International des Citoyens du Monde = ISWC
SICAP	Société Italo-Congolaise d'Armement et de Pêche	**SICM**	Società Italiana di Chirurgia della Mano
SICAPEB	Société d'Intérêt Collectif Agricole des Planteurs et Producteurs-Exportateurs de Bananas (Guadeloupe)	**SICM**	Société Ivoirienne de Ciments et Matériaux
SICAR	Société de Courtage d'Assurances et de Réassurances (Ivory Coast)	**SICMA**	Société Industrielle de Construction de Matériel d'Automobiler (Cameroon)
SICASSO	Société d'Intérêt Collectif Agricole des Sylviculteurs du Sud-Ouest	**SICMA**	Syndicat National des Industries des Ciments Carrières et Matériaux de Construction
SICAV	Société d'Investissement à Capital Variable	**SICN**	Société Industrielle Commerciale Nigérienne
SICB	Società Italiana de Biologia	**SICN**	Société Industrielle de Combustible Nucléaire
SICB	Standing Intergovernmental Copper Body	**SICND**	Société Immobilière du Comptoir National du Diamant (Cameroon)
SICC	Shell International Chemical Company	**SICO-NIGER**	Société Industrielle et Commerciale du Niger
SICC	Singapore International Chamber of Commerce	**SICO-PECHE**	Société Ivoirienne de Coopération Internationale pour la Pêche
SICC	Società Italiana di Chimica e Scienze Cosmetologiche		

SICOB	Salon International d'Informatique, Télématique, Communication Organisation du Bureau et Bureautique
SICOC	Syndicat des Ingénieurs-Conseils en Organisation et Conseillers de Direction
SICOCAM	Société Industrielle et Commerciale du Caméroun
SICOD	Service Interconsulaire du Commerce et de la Distribution
SICODI	Société d'Investissement de Côte d'Ivoire
SICODIS	Société Ivoirienne de Conditonnement et de Distribution
SICOFEG	Société des Ingénieurs-Conseils de France en Génie Civil
SICOFEM	Société Ivoirienne de Confections Féminines et Masculines
SICOGERE	Société Ivoirienne de Copropriété et de Gérance
SICOGI	Société Ivoirienne de Construction et de Gestion Immobilière
SICOM	Società Italiana Construzioni e Montaggi
SICOM	State Industrial and Investment Corporation of Maharashtra (India)
SICOMAD	Société Industrielle de la Côte Ouest de Madagascar
SICOMAR	Société Ivoirienne de Consignation, de Manutention et d'Armement
SICOMED	Société Ivoirienne de Construction Médicale
SICOPAR	Société Ivoirienne de Pièces Automobiles et de Réprésentation
SICOPHAR	Société Industrielle du Coton Pharmaceutique
SICOR	Société Ivoirienne de Coco Râpé
SICORÉS	Société Internationale de Coopération pour Réalisations Économiques et Sociales
SICOS	State Insurance Company of Somalia (Djibouti)
SICOSB	Syndicat de l'Industries Chimiques Organiques de Synthèse et de la Biochimie
SICOT	Société Internationale de Chirurgie Orthopédique et de Traumatologie
SICOTP	Société Ivoirienne Commerciale Ouvrière de Travaux Publics et de Bâtiments
SICOTP	Société Ivoirienne de Construction et de Travaux Publics
SICOTRAC	Sindicato de Conductores de Transporte Colectivo (Panama)
SICOVAM	Société Interprofessionnelle pour la Compensation des Valeurs Mobilières
SICPAD	Société Industrielle Centrafricaine des Produits Alimentaires et Dérivés
SICPRE	Società Italiana di Chirurgia Plastica Ricostruttiva ed Estetica
SICRUS	Société Ivoirienne de Crustaces
SICS	Sociedad Internacional de las Ciencias del Suelo = AISS, IBG, ISSS
SICS	Société Internationale des Conseillers de Synthèse
SICT	Shanghai Institute of Computing Technology
SICT	Shenyang Institute of Computer Technology
SICT	Société Industrielle Chimique de Tiko (Cameroon)
SICT	Société Industrielle et Commerciale du Tchad
SICTA	Société Ivoirienne de Contrôles Techniiques Automobiles et Industriels
SICTU	Solomon Island Council of Trade Unions
SICU	Servicios Internacionales Cooperativas Universitarias
SICVERL	Syndicat des Industries de la Caravane, des Véhicules et Résidences de Loisir
SID	Föreningen Svenska Industridesigner
SID	Schweizerischer Verband Industrial Designers
SID	Society for Information Display (U.S.A.)
SID	Society for International Development
SID	Society for Investigative Dermatology (U.S.A.)
SID	Special- og Industriarbejderforbundet i Danmark
SIDA	Società Italiana di Asicurazioni
SIDA	Swedish International Development Authority
SIDAB	Scottish Industrial Development Advisory Board
SIDABT	Société Industrielle pour le Dévelopment Automobile au Bénin et au Togo
SIDAC	Socialist International Disarmament Advisory Council
SIDAL	Société Ivoirienne d'Ascenseurs et d'Appareils de Levage

SIDALC	Sistema de Informacion y Difusion de los Organismos de Integracion y Cooperacion de America Latina y el Caribe	**SIDERO-PERU**	Empresa Siderúrgica del Perú
SIDAM	Société Ivoirienne d'Assurances Mutuelles	**SIDERSA**	Empresa Siderúrgica Boliviana
SIDB	Société Industrielle des Bois (Congo)	**SIDES**	Sistema de Información y Documentación para la Educación Superior
SIDC	Sunspot Index Data Centre (WDC) (Belgium) = WDC-C	**SIDES**	Società Italiana di Dermatologia e Sifilografia
SIDC	Swaziland Industrial Development Corporation	**SIDeS**	Società Italiana pro Deontologia Sanitaria
SIDCI	Société Ivoirienne de Distribution Commerciale et Industrielle	**SIDÉST**	Société Indépendante de Documentation et d'Éditions Scientifiques et Techniques
SIDE	Secretaría de Información del Estado (Argentina)	**SIDETRA**	Société Industrielle de Déroulage et de Tranchage (Congo)
SIDE	Service de l'Information et de Documentation sur l'Eau	**SIDEV**	Società Italiana di Dermatologia e Venereologia
SIDE	Société Industrielle de Découpage et d'Emboutissage	**SIDEX**	Intergrated Iron and Steel Works (Romania)
SIDEA	Società Italiana di Economia Agraria	**SIDF**	Saudi Industrial Development Fund (Saudi Arabia)
SIDÉB	Société Ivoirienne de Distribution et d'Équipement de Bureaux	**SIDF**	Société Ivoirienne de Développement et de Financement
SIDEC	Société Sénégalaise d'Importation, de Distribution et d'Exploitation Cinématographique	**SIDH**	Sociedad Internacional para los Derechos Humanos = AIDH, IGH, ISHR
SIDEC	Stanford International Development Education Centre (U.S.A.)	**SIDI**	Société Ivoirienne de Développement Industriel
SIDECI	Société Ivoirienne pour le Développement de la Construction Industrialisée	**SIDIAMIL**	International Company for the Development of Food Industries using Sorghum and Millet (Africa)
SIDÉCO	Société Ivoirienne de Distribution Économique	**SIDIC**	Service International de Documentation Judéo-Chrétienne
SIDEF-COOP	Sociedad Interamericana de Desarrollo de Financiamiento Cooperativo	**SIDICO**	Groupement Sénégalais pour l'Importance et la Distribution du Cola
SIDÉLAF	Société Ivoirienne d'Électrification	**SIDIEF**	Société Ivoirienne de Distribution et d'Exploitation de Films
SIDEM	Société Ivoirienne d'Entreprises Maritimes	**SIDIGA**	Société d'Importation et de Distribution du Gabon
SIDÉMA	Société Ivoirienne d'Électroménager et d'Ameublement	**SIDIMAG**	Société Ivoirienne de Marchandises Générales
SIDEPAR	Siderúrgica de Paraguay	**SIDIMEX**	Société Ivoirienne de Distribution et d'Import-Export
SIDEPI	Seminario Internacional de Desarrollo Pesquero-Industrial (Peru)	**SIDIPROM**	Société Ivoirienne de Distribution des Produits de la Mer
SIDER	Entreprise Nationale de Sidérurgie (Algeria)	**SIDirSS**	Sindicato Italiano Dirigenti Servizi Sanitari
SIDER-AFRIC	Centre d'Information et de Promotion des Produits Sidérurgiques et des Tubes d'Acier Français en Afrique	**SIDITEX**	Société Internationale pour le Développement de l'Industrie Textile (Cameroon)
SIDER-BRAS	Siderurgica Brasileira	**SIDM**	Società Italiana di Musicologia
SIDER-MEX	Siderúrgica Mexicana		

SIDO	Small Industries Development Organization (Tanzania)
SIDO	Small-scale Industries Development Organization (Zambia)
SIDO	Société Internationale pour le Développement des Organisations
SIDO	Société Interprofessionnelle de Oléagineux
SIDODEM	Société Industrielle et Commerciale pour le Développement du Maïs en Côte d'Ivoire
Sidor	Siderúrgica del Orinoco (Venezuela)
SIDP	Seed Industry Development Programme (FAO)
SIDP	Society of Infectious Diseases Pharmacists
SIDPA	Sindicato Industrial de Dulces y Pastas Alimenticias (El Salvador)
SIDRAG	Société Ivoirienne de Dragage
SIDRO	Société Internationale d'Énergie Hydro-Électrique
SIDS	Société Internationale de Défense Sociale = ISSD
SIDSFI	SIDS Family International
SIDUO	Societas Internationalis Diagnostica Ultrasonica Ophthalmologia = ISUDO
SIdVdG	Società Italiana della Viola da Gamba
SIE	Secretariat International de l'Eau
SIE	Servicios Industriales Especiales (UNIDO)
SIE	Società Italiana di Endocrinologia
SIE	Società Italiana di Ergonomia
SIÉ	Société Internationale d'Électrochimie = ISE
SIE	Société Internationale d'Esthétique
SIEB	Société pour l'Importation et l'Exportation de Métaux Précieux au Bénin
SIEBEG	Société Ivoirienne d'Exploitation des Bois en Grumes
SIEC	Société Internationale pour l'Enseignement Commercial
SIEC	Société Ivoirienne d'Expansion Commerciale
SIECA	Secretaría Permanente del Tratado General de Integración Económica Centroamericana (CACM)
SIECA-PRODI	Société Ivoirienne d'Exportation de Café et de Produits Divers
SIÉCC	Société Internationale d'Étude des Cultures Comparées
SIÉCD	Société Internationale d'Éducation Continue en Dentisterie = ISCED
SIECOP	Scientific Information and Education Council of Physicians (U.S.A.)
SIECOT	Société Ivoirienne d'Entreprise de Construction et Travaux
SIECUS	Sex Information and Education Council of the U.S.
SIÉD	Société Ivoirienne d'Ébénisterie et de Décoration
SIEDS	Società Italiana di Economia Demografia e Statistica
SIÉDS	Société Internationale d'Étude du Dix-Huitiéme Siècle = ISECS
SIÉÉ	Société Ivoirienne d'Installation et d'Équipement Électriques
SIEF	Société Internationale d'Ethnographie et de Folklore
SIEG	Société Ivoirienne d'Exploitation de Graviers
SIÉHT	Société Ivoirienne d'Équipement Hôtelier et Touristique
SIÉIC	Secrétariat International Élèves Ingénieurs Catholiques
SIELOR	Société Ivoirienne d'Emballages Métalliques
SIEM	Società Italiana per l'Educazione Musicale
SIEM	Société Ivoirienne d'Emballages Métalliques
SIEMI	Société d'Importation et d'Exportation de Matériel Industriel (Cameroon, Central Africa)
SIEMPA	Syndicat des Importateurs-Exportateurs de Matières Premières Aromatiques
SIÉN	Société Internationale d'Études Néroniennes
SIEP	Regional Information Service on Population Education (UNESCO)
SIEPA	Société Ivoirienne d'Exportation de Produits Agricoles
SIÉPM	Société Internationale pour l'Étude de la Philosophie Médiévale
SIEPP	Société Ivoirienne d'Entreposage de Produits Pétroliers
SIÉRE	Syndicat des Industries Électroniques de Reproduction et d'Enregistrement
SIÉRI	Société Ivoirienne d'Études et de Réalisations Industrielles
SIEROMCO	Sierra Leone Ore and Metal Company
SIÉRS	Société Industrielle d'Études et Réalisations Scientifiques

SIÉRTA	Société Ivoirienne d'Études et du Réalisation de Travaux Agricoles
SIES	Sindicato de la Industria Electrica de El Salvador
SIES	Società Italiana di Ergonomia Stomatologica
SIES	Société Industrielle d'Engrais au Sénégal
SIES	Soils and Irrigation Extension Service (Australia)
SIESC	Secrétariat International des Enseignants Secondaires Catholiques
SIESC	Society for International Education, Science and Culture (Taiwan)
SIÉSCA	Société Ivoirienne d'Élevage, de Salaison et de Conserve Alimentaire
SIESO	Society of Industrial Emergency Service Officers
SIET	Scottish International Education Trust
SIÉT	Société Internationale d'Écologie Tropicale
SIÉTA	Société Internationale d'Études et de Travaux en Afrique (Ivory Coast)
SIETAR	Society for Intercultural Educational Training and Research (U.S.A.)
SIÉTH	Société Ivoirienne d'Équipement Hôtelier et Touristique
SIETHO	Société Ivoirienne d'Expansion Touristique et Hôtelière
SIÉTI	Société Ivoirienne d'Études Techniques et d'Information
SIETI	Société Ivoirienne de Vêtements sur Mesures Industrielles
SIEU	Service Employees International Union (U.S.A.)
SIEUSÉ	Secrétariat International de l'Enseignement Universitaire des Sciences de l'Éducation
SIEX	Superintendencia de Inversiones Extranjeras (Venezuela)
SIEXI	Société Ivoirienne d'Exportation et d'Importation
SIF	Selskabets for Industriel Fornigivning
SIF	Smøreolje Importørenes Forening
SIF	Sociedad Iberoamericana de Filosofia (Spain)
SIF	Società Italiana di Farmacologia
SIF	Società Italiana di Fisiologia
SIF	Società Italiana di Scienze Farmaceutiche

SIF	Società Italiana Fisica
SIF	Société de Soudages, Injections, Forages
SIF	Société Idiste Française
SIF	Société Ivoirienne de Financement
SIF	Society for Individual Freedom
SIF	Society of Irish Foresters
SIFA	Société Industrielle et Forestière des Allumettes
SIFA	Société Industrielle pour la Fabrication des Antibiotiques
SIFA	Statens Institutt for Alkohol- og Narkotikaforskning (Norway)
SIFAC	Sociedade Industrial de Formas e Artefactos para Calçado
SIFAC	Société Industrielle Forestière en Afrique Centrale
SIFACOL	Société Ivoirienne de Fabrication de Colles et Liants (Ivory Coast)
SIFAÉMA	Société Industrielle de Fabrication des Attributs d'Équipement Militaires et Administratifs (Senegal)
SIFAL	Société Ivoirienne de Fabrication de Lubrifiants
SIFAMED	Union Intersyndicale des Fabricants des Industries Medico – Chirurgicales et Dentaires et de Matériel pour Handicapés Physiques
SIFB	Society of Industrial Furnace Builders
SIFBEC	Société Ivoirienne de Fabrication de Bouchons et Emballages Couronnés
SIFCCA	Société Industrielle Forestière et Commerciale Camérounaise
SIFCI	Société Industrielle et Forestière de Côte d'Ivoire
SIFCODE	Société Ivoirienne de Fabrication Conditionnement et Distribution
SIFD	Società Italiana del Flauto Dolce
SIFD	Society for International Folk Dancing
SIFEL	Società Italiana di Foniatria e Logopedia
SIFÉL	Société Ivoirienne de Fabrication d'Élastiques
SIFÉLEC	Société Ivoirienne de Fabrication de Matériel Électrique et de Compteurs à Eau
SIFEMBAL	Société Ivoirienne de Fûts et d'Emballages
SIFERCOM	Société Ivoirienne d'Entreprise et de Construction Métallique

SIFET	Società Italiana di Fotogrammetria e Topografia
SIFF	Société Ivoirienne Farhat Frères
SIFF	Statens Institutt for Folkehelse (Norway)
SIFF	Syndicat des Industries Françaises du Fibres-Ciment
SIFIDA	Société Internationale Financière pour les Investissements et le Développement en Afrique
SIFMA	Société Ivoirienne de Fabrication et de Montage Automobile
SIFO	Small Industries Finance Office (Thailand)
SIFO	Società Italiana di Farmacia Ospedaliera
SIFO	Société Internationale de Fluorophotometrie Oculaire = ISOF
SIFO	Statens Institutt for Forbruksforskning (Norway)
SIFO	Svenska Institutet för Opinionsundersökningar
SIFOS	Sindicato de Fotografos Salvadoreños
SIFPAF	Syndicat des Industriels Fabricants de Pâtes Alimentaires de France
SIFRA	Société Industrielle des Fruits Africains (Guinea)
SIFRA-BRIC	Société Industrielle de Fabrication (Senegal)
SIFRAM	Société Ivoirienne de Fabrication de Remorques et de Transformations Métalliques
SIFRIA	Société Immobilière de l'Aluminium (Africa)
SIFROID	Société Industrielle de Froid du Bénin
SIFS	Società Suizzera degli Insegnanti di Filosofia delle Scuole Secondarie = SPES, VSPM
SIFT	Shanghai Institute of Foreign Trade
SIFUD	Société Internationale Francophone d'Uro-Dynamique
SIG	Schweizerische Industrie Gesellschaft
SIG	Service d'Information Géologique
SIG	Società Italiana di Glottologia
SIG	Société Ivoirienne de Gaufretterie
SIGA	Società Italiana di Genetica Agraria
SIGAM	Société Ivoirienne de Garage et Matériels Automobiles
SIGAMA	Société Italo-Gabonaise des Marbres
SIGB	Ski Industries of Great Britain
SIGBI	Soroptimist International of Great Britain and Ireland
SIGE	Società Italiana di Gastroenterologia = ISGE
SIGE	Società Italiana di Genetica e Eugenica
SIGE	Società Italiana Gestione Elicotteri
SIGE	Société Internationale de Gastro-Entérologie
SIGEBAN	Sindicato de la Industria General de Empleados Bancarios y Asociaciones de Ahorro y Préstamo (El Salvador)
SIGEFOR	Société Ivoirienne de Gestion et d'Exploitation Forestière
SIGÉLEC	Société Industrielle de Générateurs Électriques (Senegal)
SIGÉS	Société Ivoirienne de Gestion, d'Études et de Services
SIGESO	Sub-commitee, Intelligence German Electronics Signals Organisation
SIGEXA	Société Ivoirienne de Gestion et d'Exploitation Automobile
SIGEXE	Société Ivoirienne de Gestion et d'Exploitation d'Engins
SIGG	Società Italiana di Gerontologia e Geriatria
SIGI	Société Ivoirienne de Gestion Immobilière
SIGM	Società Italiana di Ginnastica Medica,Medicina Fisica e Riabilitazione
SIGMA	Chambre Syndicale des Importateurs de Matériel de Génie et de Manutention (Belgium)
SIGMA	Sealed Insulating Glass Manufacturers Association (U.S.A.)
SIGMA	Société Industriale Générale de Mécanique Appliquée
SIGMA	Station Internationale de Géobotanique Méditerranéenne et Alpine
SIGN	Special Interest Group Network
SIGP	Société Industrielle de la Grande Pêche
SIGRA	Sociedad Industrial de Grasas Vegetales (Colombia)
SIGRAG	Société Industrielle d'Exploitation des Granits Guinéens
SIGRAV	Società Italiana di Relatività Generale e Fisica della Gravitazione
SIGTTO	Society of International Gas Tanker and Terminal Operators
SIGUE	Society for Developments in Guinea
SIGWEB	Special Interest Group on the World Wide Web, United Kingdom and Ireland
SIH	Schweizerisches Institut für Hauswirtschaft

SIH	Société Internationale d'Hématologie = ISH	**SIK**	Svenska Institutet för Könserveringsförskning
SIH	Société Ivoirienne d'Hôtellerie	**SIKA-**	Société Industrielle du Karitè (Mali)
SIH	Society for Italic Handwriting	**MALI**	
SIH	Svenska Kommitten för Internationell Hjälprersamhet	**SIKR**	Société Internationale de Keratoplastie Refractive = CITA, IRSK
SIHFLÉS	Société Internationale pour l'Histoire du Français Langue Étrangère ou Seconde	**SIL**	Sähköinsinöriliitto
		SIL	Secrétariat International de la Laine = IWS
SIHM	Société Internationale d'Histoire de la Médecine = ISHM	**SIL**	Service International des Latitudes
SIHS	Scottish Industrial Heritage Society	**SIL**	Shenyang Municipal Institute of Landscape Gardening
SIHTCO	Société Ivoirienne Hôtelière et Touristique de le Comoé	**SIL**	Societas Internationalis Limnologiae Theoreticae et Applicae = AIL, IAL, IATAL, IVL
SII	Security Institute of Ireland		
SII	Société d'Imprimerie Ivoirienne	**SIL**	Société Internationale de la Lèpre = ILA
SII	Société Interaméricaine d'Invetissement = CII, ICC	**SIL**	Suomen Ilmailuliitto
		SIL	Syndicat de l'Industrie Laitière de l'Est
SII	Standards Institution of Israel	**SILA**	Svenska International Luftlinien Aktiebolaget
SIIA	Sichuan Industrial Institute of Antibiotics		
SIIAÉC	Secrétariat International des Ingénieurs, des Agronomes et des Cadres Économiques Catholiques	**SILA-NIERO**	Sindacato Nazionale dell'Industria Laniera Italiana
		SILAF	Sindacato Italiano Lavoratori Appalti Ferroviari
SIII	Società Italiana di Immunologia e di Immunopatologia	**SILAF**	Società Italiana per Lavori Agricoli e Forestali
SIIMP	Societa internazionale di Ipnosi Medica e Psicologica (U.S.A.) = ISMPH	**SILAF**	Société Ivoirienne Ammar Frères
		SILAP	Sindacato Nazionale Dipendenti Ministero del Lavori Pubblici
SIIS	Shanghai Institute for International Studies		
SIIT	Servicio Iberoamericano de Informacion sobre la Traduccion	**SILAS**	Singapore Integrated Library Automation System
		SILC	Société Internationale de Littérature Courtoise = ICLS
SIITS	Società Italiana di Immunoematologia e Trasfusione del Sangue		
		SILCA	Sindacato Italiano Lavoratori Cappellai ed Affini
SIIV	Schweizerischer Immobilien-Interessen-Verband		
		SILCO	Société Ivoiro-Libanaise de Commerce
SIJADEP	Secrétariat Internationaal des Juristes pour l'Amnistie et la Démocratie en Paraguay; Secretariado Internacional de Juristas para la Amnistia y la Democracia en el Paraguay	**SILF**	Société Internationale de Linguistique Fonctionnelle
		SILF	Sveriges Inköpsledares Förbund
		SILHOD	Sichuan Institute of Labour Hygiene and Occupational Diseases
SIJAU	Secrétariat International des Juristes pour l'Amnistie en Uruguay; Secretariado Internacional de Juristas por la Amnistia en Uruguay	**SILIN**	Société Interprofessionnelle des Graines et Huiles de Lin
		SILOC	Société Ivoirienne de Location
SIK	Samband Islenskra Kristnibodsfelaga	**SILOM**	Société d'Investissements Laitiers Outre-Mer
SIK	Schweizerische Informatikkonferenz = CSI		
		SILOM	Société Ivoirienne de Location de Matériel
SIK	Schweizerisches Institut für Kunstwissenschaft		
		SILOVE	Société Ivoirienne de Location et de Vente
SIK	Société Immobilière de Koutou (Congo)		

SILP	Sindacato Italiano Lavoratori del Petrolio
SILP	Sindacato Italiano Lavoratori Postelegrafonici
SILP	Société Internationale de Linguistique Psychologique
SILS	Société d'Investissements Libano-Sénégalaise
SIM	Samband Íslenskra Myndlistarmanna
SIM	Servicio de Inteligencia Militar (Chile)
SIM	Servicio e Investigación Militar
SIM	Servicio Industriel de la Marina (Peru
SIM	Shaanxi Institute of Engineering
SIM	Shanghai Institute of Metallurgy
SIM	Singapore Institute of Management
SIM	Società Italiana di Metapsichica
SIM	Società Italiana di Microbiologia
SIM	Société Industrielle des Métaux (Burkina Faso)
SIM	Société Internationale de la Moselle
SIM	Société Internationale de Métaphysique
SIM	Société Internationale de Musicologie = IGMW, IMS
SIM	Société Sénégalaise d'Investissements Maritimes
SIM	Society for Industrial Microbiology (U.S.A.)
SIM	Standards Institute of Malaysia
SIM	Sudan Interior Mission (U.K.)
SIMA	Salon International de la Machine Agricole
SIMA	Scientific Instrument Manufacturers Association of Great Britain
SIMA	Società Italiana di Meteorologia Applicata
SIMA	Société d'Importation et d'Exportation Centrafricaine
SIMA	Société Industrielle de Matériel Agricole
SIMA	Société Ivoirienne de Menuiserie et d'Ameublement
SIMA	Steel and Industrial Managers Association
SIMA-FRUIT	Société Interprofessionnelle Maritime et Fruitière (Ivory Coast)
SIMA-TRANS	Société Ivoirienne de Magasinage et de Transport
SIMAC	Société Immobilière d'Afrique Centrale
SIMAC	Société Ivoirienne d'Importation de Matériaux de Construction
SIMACO	Société Ivoirienne de Matériaux de Construction
SIMAJ	Scientific Instrument Manufacturers Association of Japan
SIMAP	Société Ivoirienne de Matériaux de Plomberie
SIMAQ	Syndicat des Négociants Importateurs Métropolitaines
SIMAR	Société Industrielle de Machines Agricoles Rotatives (Switzerland)
SIMAR	Société Ivoirienne de Maroquinerie
SIMAR	Société Ivoiro-Marocaine et Indienne d'Import-Export
SIMAREP	Société Ivoirienne de Matériels de Reprographie
SIMAS	Shanghai Institute of Metallurgy, Academia Sinica
SIMAS	Sodalizio Internazionale Massimista Assistenza Sociale
SIMAVIN	Société d'Importation Africaine Vinicole
SIMBA	Singaporean & Malaysian British Association
SIMC	Société Internationale de Médecine de Castastrophe = ISDM
SIMC	Société Internationale pour la Musique Contemporaine = ISCM
SIMC	Société Italienne des Musiciens et Compositeurs
SIMCA	Société Industrielle de Mécanique et de Carosserie Automobile
SIMCO	Société Immobilière et de Constructions du Tchad
SIMCOS	Sindicato de Trabajadores de los Medios de Comunicación (Guatemala)
SIMCOSS	Société Immobilière et Commerciale du Siné-Saloum
SIMDER	Syndicat National du Matériel de Dessin, Beaux-Arts, Reprographie
SIME	Ministerio de la Industria Sidero-Mecanico (Cuba)
SIMEA	Società Italiana Meridionale Energia Atomica
SIMEA	Société Ivoirienne de Montage et d'Exploitation Automobile
SIMÉCO	Société Ivoirienne de Menuiserie, d'Ébénisterie et de Constructions Immobilières
SIMEE	Shanghai Institute of Mechanical and Electrical Engineering
SIMÉÉCT	Syndicat des Industries Métallurgiques Électriques, Électroniques et Connexes de Toulouse

SIMÉI	Société Ivoirienne de Matériaux Étanches et Isolants	**SIMPA**	Société Industrielle Moderne de Plastiques Africaines
SIMEX	Singapore International Monetary Exchange	**SIMPEX**	Syndicat des Commerçants Importateurs et Exportateurs (Benin, Gabon, Ivory Coast)
SIMEX	Sociedad de Inversiones Mobiliarias en el Exterior	**SIMPICSA**	Société Ibéro-Mauritanienne de Promotion Industrielle et Commerciale
SIMEXCO	Société Ivoirienne d'Importation, d'Exportation et de Commission	**SIMPL**	Scientific, Industrial and Medical Photographic Laboratories
SIMFER	Società Italiana di Medicina Fisica e Riabilitazione	**SIMPOL**	Société Ivoirienne de Mousse Polyester
SIMFR	Solidarité Internationale des Maisons Familiales Rurales (Belgium)	**SIMPP**	Society of Independent Motion Picture Producers (U.S.A.)
SIMG	Societas Internationalis Medicinae Generalis = IGAM, ISGP	**SIMPRO-FRANCE**	Comité Français pour la Simplification de Procédures du Commerce Internationale
SIMGBM	Società Italiana di Microbiologia Generale e Biotecnologia Microbiche	**SIMPROH**	Sindicato de Motoristas Profesionales de Honduras
SIMH	Société Internationale de Médecine Hydrologique	**SIMPS**	Società Italiana di Medicina Preventiva e Sociale
SIMHA	Société Internationale de Mycologie Humaine et Animale = ISHAM	**SIMR**	Seriously Ill for Medical Research
SIMI	Società Italiana di Medicina Interna	**SIMRA**	Scientific Instruments Manufacturers Research Association
SIMI	Società Italiana Macchine Idrauliche	**SIMS**	Skandinaviska Simuleringssällskapet
SIMI	Societa Italo-Svizzeva Metalli Iniettati	**SIMS**	Società Italiana di Medicina Sociale
SIMI	Société Ivoirienne de Machettes Industrielles	**SIMS**	Societal Institute of the Mathematical Sciences (U.S.A.)
SIMI	Society of the Irish Motor Industry	**SIMS**	Students International Meditation Society (U.S.A.)
SIML	Società Italiana di Medicina del Lavoro	**SIMSA**	Savings Institutions Marketing Society of America
SIMLA	Società Italiana di Medicina Legale e delle Assicurazioni	**SIMSA**	Sociedad Industrial Molinera S.A. (Bolivia)
SIMMA	Syndicat des Industries de Matériels de Manutention	**SIMSI**	Società Italiana di Medicina Subacquea ed Iperbarica
SIMO	Société Industrielle des Mineris de l'Ouest	**SIMT**	Società Italiana di Medicina del Traffico
SIMO	Société Ivoirienne des Matériels d'Organisation	**SIMV**	Syndicat de l'Industrie du Médicament Vétérinaire
SIMOCA	Société Industrielle du Moyen-Orient au Caméroun	**SIN**	Schweizerisches Institut für Nuclearforschung
SIMOG	Società Italiana Medici e Operatori Geriatrici	**SIN**	Società Italiana di Nefrologia
SIMON	Syndicat des Industries Mécaniques d'Outre-Mer	**SIN**	Società Italiana di Neurochirurgia
SIMOPA	Société Industrielle Moderne de Parfumerie (Ivory Coast)	**SIN**	Società Italiana di Neurologia
SIMOVAR	Société Ivoirienne de Navigation Maritime	**SIN**	Société Industrielle et Navale
SIMP	Società Italiana di Medicina Psicosomatica	**SIN**	Society for International Numismatics (U.S.A.)
SIMP	Società Italiana di Mineralogia e Petrologia	**SIN**	Spanish International Network (U.S.A.)
SIMP	Stowarzyszenie Inżynierów i Techników Mechaników Polskich	**SINA**	Scottish Independent Nurseries Association
		SINA	Settlements Information Network Africa
		SINA	Shellfish Institute of North America

SINA	Sociedad Ibérica de Nutrición Animal		**SINEG**	Société Ivoirienne de Négoce
SINA-DIMID	Sindacato Nazionale Dipendenti Ministerio Difesa		**SINEPRO**	Société Ivoirienne de Négoce et de Produits
SINACMA	Sindacato Nazionale Dipendenti Corte dei Conti e Magistrature		**SINFAC**	Syndicat Interprofessionnel des Fabricants d'Articles Manufacturés pour Chassures
SINADEPS	Sistema Nacional de Propiedad Social (Peru)		**SINFDOK**	Statens Rad for Vetenskaplig Information och Dokumentation
SINADI	Sistema Nacional de Informacion (Peru)		**SINFOCA**	Société d'Informatique du Caméroun
SINAF	Sindacato Nazionale Dipendenti Ministerio Agricultura e Foreste		**SINN**	Société d'Imprimerie Nationale du Niger
SINAGI	Sindacato Nazionale Giornalai d'Italia		**SINO**	Société Internationale de Neuro-opthalmologie = ISNO
SINAM-EQUIP	Sindicato Nacional de Motoristas de Equipo Pesado de Honduras		**SINO-CHART**	China National Chartering Corporation
SINAMIL	Sindacato Nazionale Dipendenti Ministerio dei Lavoro e Previdenza Sociale		**SINO-TRANS**	China National Trade Transportation Corporation
SINAMOS	Sistema Nacional de Apoyo a la Movilización Social (Peru)		**SINOMA**	Sindicato Nacional de Obreros Metalurgicos y Afines (Paraguay)
SINAPI	Sindacato Nazionale Ministerio Pubblica Istruzione		**Sinopec**	China Petroleum Corporation
SINART	Sistema Nacional de Radio y Televisión Cultural (Costa Rica)		**SINORG**	Société Internationale d'Études de Recherches et d'Organisation
SINASCEL	Sindacato Nazionale Scuola Elementare		**SINP**	Saha Institute of Nuclear Physics (India)
SINATRAC	Sindicato Nacional de Trabajodores de la Construccion (Paraguay)		**SINPA**	Société d'Intérêt National des Produits Agricoles (Madagascar)
SINCATEX	Société Industrielle Camérounaise de Textiles		**SINPE**	Società Italiana di Nutrizione Parenterale ed Enterale
SINCO	Société Internationale de Commerce (Cameroon)		**SINPI**	Società Italiana di Neuropsichiatria Infantile
SINCOA	Société Industrielle et Commerciale Africaine (Cameroon)		**SINPR**	Suzhon Institute of Nuclear Power Research
SINCOE	Sindacato Nazionale Dipendenti Ministerio Industria e Commercio Estero		**SINR**	Shanghai Institute of Nuclear Research
			SINS	Sindacato Scuola non Statale
SINCOLIT	Société Industrielle et Commerciale de Literie (Senegal)		**SINS**	Società Italiana di Neurosontologia
SIND	Société Internationale de Neuroscience du Développement = ISDN		**SINT-ARMEL**	Sociedade Internacional de Armaçoes e Maquinas
SIND	Statens Industriverk		**SINTAGRO**	Syndicate of Banana Plantation Workers (Colombia)
SINDAF	Sindacato Nazionale Dipendenti Amministrazione Finanziarie		**SINTEF**	Stiftelsen for Industriell og Teknisk Forskning
SINDEP	Sindicato Democrático de Professores		**SINTRA**	Société Industrielle des Nouvelles Techniques Radioélectriques et de l'Électronique Française
SINDICOM	Sindicato Nacional das Empresas Distribuidoras de Combustivos (Brazil)		**SINUTTRA**	Sindicato de Trabajadores del Transporte (Panama)
SINDIFER	Sindacato Direttivi e Dirigenti		**SIO**	Sindacato Italiano Ostetriche
SINDIGAS	Sindicato Nacional Empresas Distribuidoras Gas Liquefeito Petroleo (Brazil)		**SIO**	Sisustusarkitehdit
			SIO	Società Italiana d'Optometria
			SIO	Surinaamse Islamitische Organisatie
SINEÉ	Société d'Intérêt National de l'Eau et de l'Électricité (Madagascar)		**SIOC**	Shanghai Institute of Organic Chemistry

SIOCMF	Società Italiana di Odontostomatologia e Chirurgia Maxillo-Facciale
SIOD	Sindacato Italiano Odontotecnici Diplomati
SIOEChCF	Società Italiana di Otorinolaringologia e Chirurgia Cervico Facciale
SIOFA	Société Interprofessionnelle des Oléagineux Fluides Alimentaires
SIOFM	Shanghai Institute of Organo-Fluorine Materials
SIOG	Società Italiana di Ostetricia e Ginecologia
SIOH	Shanghai Institute of Ornamental Horticulture
SIOI	Società Italiana di Odontoiatria Infantile
SIOI	Società Italiana per l'Organizzazione Internazionale
SIOM	Shanghai Institute of Optics and Fine Machinery
SIOP	Société Internationale d'Oncologie Pédiatrique
SIOP	Société Ivoirienne d'Opérations Pétrolières
SIOSA	Sicula Oceanic S.A.
SIOT	Società Italiana di Ortopedia e Traumatologia
SIP	Interamerican Society of Psychology = IASP
SIP	Saskatchewan Institute of Pedology (Canada)
SIP	Servicio de Investigación Prehistórica y Museu de Prehistoria
SIP	Sindacato Italiano Pescatori
SIP	Sindicato de la Industria Pesquera (El Salvador)
SIP	Sindicato Industriales de Panamá
SIP	Sociedad Interamericana de Planificación (Puerto Rico) = SIAP
SIP	Sociedad Interamericana de Prensa = IAPA
SIP	Sociedad Interamericana de Psicologia = IASP
SIP	Società Italiana di Parapsicologia
SIP	Società Italiana di Pediatria
SIP	Società Italiana di Psichiatria
SIP	Società Italiana per l'Esercizio Telefonico
SIP	Société Industrielle des Plastiques (Mali)
SIP	Société Internationale de Placements
SIP	Society for Invertebrate Pathology (U.S.A.)
SIP	Society of Irish Playwrights
SIPA	Servicio de Investigación y Promotión Agropecuária (Peru)
SIPA	Società Italiana di Patologia Aviare
SIPA	Société d'Importation de Pièces Automobiles (Ivory Coast)
SIPA	Société Immobilière Peyrissac Africauto (Senegal)
SIPA	Société Industrielle de Produits Africains
SIPAC	Société Ivoirienne de Produits Agricoles et Comestibles
SIPACCI	Société Ivoirienne de Préfabriques et d'Accessoires Industriels
SIPAG	Société Industrielle de Planification de Guinée
SIPAG	Syndicat des Instituteurs, Professeurs et Agents de la Guadeloupe
SIPAG	Syndicat National des Importateurs d'Équipements pour les Industries Papetières et Graphiques
SIPAI	Sociedad Italo-Peruana Agricola Industrial (Peru)
SIPAI	Società Italiana di Psicoterapia Analitica Immaginativa
SIPAI	Società per l'Incremento della Produzione Avicola Italiana
SIPAI	Société Internationale de Promotion Agro-Industrielle (Cameroon)
SIPAK	Vereniging van Groothandelaren in Sisalpaktouw
SIPAL	Société Industrielle de Préparations Alimentaires (Togo)
SIPAMA	Servico de Inspeção dos Producos Agropecuários e Materiais Agricolas (Brazil)
SIPAOC	Società Italiana di Patologia e di Allevamento degli Ovini e dei Caprini
SIPAR	Société Ivoirienne de Pêche et d'Armement
SIPARCO	Société Industrielle de Parfumerie et de Cosmétique (Senegal)
SIPARCO-CI	Société Industrielle de Parfumerie et de Cosmétiques (Ivory Coast)
SIPARÉ	Syndicat des Industries de Pièces Détachées et Accessoires Radio-Électriques et Électroniques
SIPC	Società Italiana di Psicopedagogia Clinica

SIPC	Société Interprofessionnelle pour la Production des Cocons, Graines de Vers à Soie et de Soie Grège en France
SIPCA	Saudi International Petroleum Carriers Limited (Saudi Arabia)
SIPCA	Société Industrielle de Produits Chimiques et Aromatiques (Cameroon)
SIPCAM	Società Italiana Prodotti Chimici e per l'Agricoltura, Milano
SIPCI	Société Ivoirienne de Promotion Commerciale et Industrielle
SIPCMF	Società Italiana di Odontostomatolgia e Chirurgia Maxillo-Faciale
SIPCO	Société Ivoirienne de Produits Congelés
SIPCO-CHIM	Société Inter-Africaine pour la Commercialisation des Products Chimiques (Ivory Coast)
SIPDA	Société Ivoirienne de Pièces Détachées
SIPE	Fundação Instítuto de Pesquisas Económicas (Brazil)
SIPE	Società Italiana di Psicoterapie Energetiche
SIPE	Société Industrielle de Plastiques et Emballages (Mauritania)
SIPÉ	Société Internationale de Psychologie de l'Écriture = IGSP, IHPS, SIPS
SIPE	Société Internationale de Psychopathologie de l'Expression = ISAP
SIPEC	Société Industrielle des Pêches du Caméroun
SIPEC	Syndicat des Importateurs de Surfaces Sensibles Photographiques et Cinématographiques
SIPECA	Service d'Information Pastorale Européenne Catholique (Belgium)
SIPECO	Société Internationale de Pêche et de Commerce (Mauritania)
SIPEGA	Société Industrielle des Pêches du Gabon
SIPER	Sénégalaise d'Industrie des Peintures et Revêtement
SIPEV	Société Industrielle de Peintures et Vernis (Ivory Coast)
SIPF	Svenska Industriens Patluntingenjörers Föreningen
SIPG	Société Internationale de Participations et de Gestion (Congo)
SIPG	Société Internationale de Pathologie Géographique = ISGP
SIPHAC	Société Industrielle Pharmaceutique du Caméroun
SIPHO	Société Immobilière de Promotion d'Études et de Réalisations Hôtelières (Ivory Coast)
SIPI	Scientists Institute for Public Information (U.S.A.)
SIPI	Shanghai Institute of Pharmaceutical Industry
SIPI	Società Italiana di Psicologia Individuale
SIPIC	Société Ivoirienne de Promotion Immobilière, Industrielle et de Construction
SIPL	Société Industrielle de Produits Laitiers (Senegal)
SIPLAST	Société Industrielle de Plastique (Ivory Coast)
SIPLOA	Société Ivoirienne de Plomberie et d'Adduction
SIPMAD	Société Industrielle de Pêche à Madagascar
SIPMAG	Société Ivoirienne de Papiers et Matériels d'Arts Graphiques
SIPO	Swiss Intellectual Property Office
SIPOA	Servico de Inspeção de Produtos de Origem Animal (Brazil)
SIPOA	Société Industrielle Pharmaceutique de l'Ouest Africain
SIPP	Society of Irish Plant Pathologists
SIPPA	Società Italiana Pubblicita Per Azioni
SIPRA	Société Ivoirienne de Productions Animales
SIPRAG	Société Ivoirienne de Promotion Agricole
SIPRC	Society of Independent Public Relations Consultants
SIPRI	Stockholm International Peace Research Institute
SIPRIM	Société Ivoirienne de Promotion et de Réalisations Immobilières
SIPRO-COM	Comité pour la Simplification des Procédures du Commerce International
SIPROBEL	Société Ivoirienne de Produits de Beauté
SIPROGIM	Société Ivoirienne de Promotion et de Gestion Immobilière
SIPROSEM	Société Ivoirienne de Production de Sel Marin
SIPS	Società Internazionale di Psicologia della Scrittura = IGSP, IHPS, SIPE
SIPS	Società Internazionale di Psicologia dello Sport = ISSP

SIPs	Società Italiana di Psicologia	**SIRÉC**	Syndicat International pour la Régénération de l'Écran
SIPS	Società Italiana di Psicologia Scientifica	**SIREDIS**	Société Ivoirienne de Représentation et de Distribution
SIPS	Società Italiana per il Progresso delle Scienze	**SIREMAR**	Sicilia Regionale Marittima
SIPS	Société Industrielle de Papeterie au Sénégal	**SIREP**	Société Internationale pour la Recherche et l'Exploitation du Pétrole (Chad)
SIPSEC	Syndicat des Importateurs de Produits Pétrolifères du Sud-Est et du Centre de la France	**SIRI**	Società Italiana per la Robotica Industriale
SIPT	Società Italiana di Psicosintesi Terapeutica	**SIRI**	Société Internationale pour la Réadaptation des Invalides
SIPT	Société Internationale de Photogrammétrie et Télédétection = IGPF, ISPRS	**SIRI**	Sugar Industry Research Institute (Mauritius)
SIPTU	Service, Industrial, Professional and Technical Union (Éire)	**SIRIC**	Société Ivoirienne de Représentation Industrielle et Commerciali
SIPV	Società Italiana di Patologia Vascolare	**SIRIM**	Standards and Industrial Research Institute of Malaysia
SIQ	Swedish Institute for Quality	**SIRIP**	Société Irano-Italienne de Pétrole
SIR	Service International de Recherches (CICR) = ISD, ITS	**SIRIRI**	Entreprise d'État d'Assurances et de Réassurances (Central African Republic)
SIR	Sociedad Internacional Rorschach = IGROF, IRS		
SIR	Società Italiana Resine	**SIRM**	Società Italiana di Radiologia Medica
SIR	Société Internationale Renardienne = IRS	**SIRM**	Società Italiana per le Ricerche de Mercata
SIR	Société Ivoirienne de Raffinage	**SIRM**	Società Italiana Radio-Marittima
SIR	Svenska Inredningsarkitekters Riksförbund	**SIRM**	Société Internationale Robert Musil (GFR)
SIRA	Scientific Instrument Research Association	**SIRMCE**	Société Internationale pour la Recherche sur les Maladies de Civilisation et l'Environnement = ISRCDVS, SIRAGVI
SIRA	Sénégalaise d'Importation de Représentation Automobile et d'Équipement		
SIRAID	Scientific Instrument Research Association Information and Data Service	**SIRMN**	Società Italiana di Radiologia Medica e Medicina Nucleare
SIRAMA	Société Siramamy Malagasy	**SIRNv**	Société Internationale de Recherches Neurovégétatives
SIRASVI	Société Internationale pour la Recherche sur l'Alimentation et les Substances Vitales = ISRCDVS, SIRMCE	**SIROT**	Société Internationale de Recherches Orthopédique et Traumatologique
		SIROW	Southwest Institute for Research on Women (U.S.A.)
SIRC	Security Intelligence Review Committee (Canada)	**SIRP**	Shanghai Institute of Rubber Products
SIRC	Socialist International Research Council	**SIRP**	Society of Independent Roundabout Proprietors
SIRCA	Société Industrielle de République Centrafricaine	**SIRPINC-CI**	Société Internationale de Représentation de Produits Industriels, Navals et Commerciaux de Côte d'Ivoire
SIRCE	Società per l'Incremento Rapporti Commerciali con l'Estero		
SIRCOFAM	Station Internationale de Recherche contre la Faim dans le Monde	**SIRS**	Sick and Indigent Roomkeepers Society (Éire)
SIREBAT	Société Ivoirienne de Revêtement et de Bâtiment	**SIRT**	Société Interprofessionnelle du Raison de Table
		SIRTC	Société Internationale de Recherche contre la Tuberculose et le Cancer

SIRTI	Società Italiana Reti Telfoniche Interurbane
SIS	Samband Islenzkra Samvinnufélaga
SIS	Scientific Instrument Society
SIS	Scotch-Irish Society of the United States of America
SIS	Secret Intelligence Service
SIS	Seguros e Inversiones (El Salvador)
SIS	Service International d'Informations Sousmarines
SIS	Società Italiana di Stomatologia
SIS	Società Italiani di Statistica
SIS	Société d'Informatique et de Systèmes Compagnie Bancaire
SIS	Société Française des Ingénieurs en Soudage
SIS	Société Immobilière du Sénégal
SIS	Société Internationale Scotiste = ISS
SIS	Société Ivoirienne de Spectacles
SIS	Special Industrial Services (UNIDO)
SIS	Svenska Interplanetariska Sallskapet
SIS	Sveriges Standardiseringskommission
SIS	Système d'Information du Sahel
SISA	Scottish Ice Skating Association
SISA	Scottish Industrial Sports Association
SISA	Sitram International Shipping Agencies (Ivory Coast)
SISA	Società Italiana per le Scienze Ambientali
SISA	Società Italiana per lo Studio dell'Arteriosclerosi
SISAC	Serials Industry Systems Advisory Committee (U.S.A.)
SISAC	Società Italiana per lo Studio dell'Antichità Classica
SISAC	Société Industrielle du Sac (Senegal)
SISAG	Société Ivoiro-Suisse Abidjanaise de Granit (Ivory Coast)
SISCA	Società Italiana per lo Studio della Cancerogenesi Ambientale ed Epidemologia dei Tumori
SISCOMA	Société Industrielle Sénégalaise de Constructions Mécaniques et de Matériels Agricoles
SISCOMS	Secrétariat International Spiritain de Communications Sociales par l'Audio-Visuel
SISCOT	Security Industry Steering Committee on Taurus
SISD	Scottish Information Service for the Disabled
SISE	Secretariado Internacional Sindicatos Espectáculo = ISETU, ISGKU, SISS
SISE	Società Italiana degli Storici dell'Economia
SISEP	Société Ivoirienne de Soufflage et Emballage Plastique
SISF	Società Italiana di Scienze Farmaceutiche
SISGAC	Scottish Industrial Safety Group Advisory Council
SISH	Société Internationale de la Science Horticole = ISHS, SICH
SISI	Small Industries Service Institute (India)
SISIMLI	Scientific Institute of Shoemaking Industry, Ministry of Light Industry (China)
SISIR	Singapore Institute for Standards and Industrial Research
SISMAR	Société Industrielle Sahelienne de Mécaniques, de Materièls Agricoles et de Representations (Senegal)
SISMES	Società Italiana di Statistica Medico-Sanitaria
SISN	Società Italiana di Scienze Naturali
SISP	Schweizerische Interessengemeinschaft f.d. Schutz von Pflanzenneuheiten
SISPA	Società Italiana Studio e Prevenzione dell'Alcoolismo
SISR	Société Internationale de Sociologie des Religions = ISSR
SISRI	Shanghai Iron & Steel Research Institute
SISS	Secrétariat International des Syndicats du Spectacle = ISGTU, ISGKU, SISE
SISS	Società Italiana Serbatoi Speciali
SISS	Société Internationale de la Science du Sol
SISSY	Schools' Information Service on Sexuality
SISTAC	Scottish Industrial Safety Training Advisory Council
SISU	Sichaun International Studies University
SISUGA	Société d'Investissements Sucrière du Gabon
SISV	Secrétariat International du Service Volontaire
SISV	Società Italiana delle Scienze Veterinarie
SISWO	Stichting Interuniversitair Instituut voor Sociaalwetenschappelijk Onderzoek

SIT	Salone Internazionale della Tecnica
SIT	Samband Islenzkra Trygginafélaga
SIT	Servicio de Información Técnica (Ecuador)
SIT	Singapore Improvement Trust
SIT	Sociedade Internacional de Trânsitos Lda
SIT	Société Industrielle du Togo
SIT	Société Industrielle Thanry (Ivory Coast)
SIT	Société Interafricaine de Transport
SIT	Société Intercontinentale de Transactions
SIT	Société Ivoirienne de Transit
SIT	Society of Industrial Tutors
SIT	Society of International Treasurers
SITA	Sociedade Internacional de Trilogia Analitica = ISAT
SITA	Società Internazionale Tommaso d'Aquino
SITA	Société Industrielle de Transports Automobiles
SITA	Société Internationale de Télécommunications Aéronautiques
SITA	Students International Travel Association
SITAB	Société Ivoirienne des Tabacs
SITAF	Société Industrielle des Transport Automobiles Africains (Ivory Coast)
SITAF-TOGO	Société Inter-Africaine de Transit et d'Affrètement
SITAL	Sociedade Industrial de Tintos e Anticorrosives Lda.
SITAM	Société Industrielle des Tabacs Malgaches
SITAO	Société Immobilière et Touristique de l'Afrique de l'Ouest
SITB	Shipping Industry Training Board
SITB	Société Industrielle de Travaux de Bureaux
SITB	Société Ivoirienne de Transformation du Bois
SITC	Società Svizzera degli Ingegneri Termici e Climatici = SWKI
SITCA	Secretaria de Integración Turistica Centroaméricana
SITCP	Société Industrielle Togolaise de Caoutchouc et de Plastique
SItE	Società Italiana di Ecologia
SITE	Society for Information Technology and Teacher Education
SITE	Society of Incentive Travel Executives
SITEF	Société Ivoirienne de Tâcheronnage et d'Exploitation Forestière
SITÉL	Société Belge des Ingénieurs des Télécommunications et d'Électronique
SITEL	Société Ivoirienne de Télécommunications
SITÉLESC	Syndicat des Industries de Tubes Électroniques et Semiconducteurs
SITÉM	Société Industrielle des Travaux Électro-Mécaniques
SITEMSH	Société Internationale de Traumatologie de Ski et de Médecine des Sports d'Hiver
SITENAPU	Sindicato de Trabajadores de la Empresa Nacional de Puertos (Peru)
SITÉP	Société Italo-Tunisienne de Tubes Électroniques et Semiconducteurs
SITÉR	Société Ivoirienne de Techniques Électroniques et Radio
SITGórn	Stowarzyszenie Inżynierów i Techników Górnictwa
SITH	Société Internationale de Technique Hydrothermale
SITI	Fachverband Sitzmöbel-und Tischindustrie
SITI	Schweizerisches Institut für Technische Information
SITI	Sezione Imprese Traslochi Internazionali
SITIM	Société Internationale des Techniques d'Imagerie Mentale
SITJ	Savez Inzenjera i Tehnicara Jugoslavije
SITKom	Stowarzyszenie Inżynierów i Techników Komunikacji
SITLiD	Stowarzyszenie Inżynierów i Techników Leśnictwa i Drzewnictwa
SITMA	Société des Ingénieurs et Techniciens du Machinisme Agricole
SITMI	Société Ivoirienne de Travaux et Matériels Informatiques
SITO	Société Immobilière Togolaise
SITO	Société Industrielle de Traitement des Oléagineux (Burkina Faso)
SITO	Société Ivoirienne des Transports de l'Ouest
SITO	Stowarzyszenie Naukowo-Techniczne Inżynierów i Techników Ogrodnictwa
SITOFA	Société des Industries de Transformation des Oléagineux Fluides Alimentaires

SITP	Société Internationale de Thérapie Psychomotrice (Belgium)
SITP	Société Ivoirienne de Transports Publics
SITPC	Syndicat des Industries de la Transformation de la Pellicule Cellulosique
SITPChem	Stowarzyszenie Inżynierów i Techników Przemysłu Chemicznego
SITPH	Stowarzyszenie Inżynierów i Techników Przemysłu Hutniczego
SITPMB	Stowarzyszenie Inżynierów i Techników Przemysłu Materiałów Budowlanych
SITPNiG	Stowarzyszenie Naukowe-Techniczne Inżynierów i Techników Przemysłu Naftowego i Gazowniczego
SITPP	Stowarzyszenie Inżynierów i Techników Przemysłu Papierniczego (*now* APP, SPP)
SITPRO	Simplification of International Trade Procedures Board
SITPRO-NETH	Netherlands Committee for the Simplification of International Trade Procedures
SITPSpoż	Stowarzyszenie Naukowo-Techniczne Inżynierów i Techników Przemysłu Spożywczego
SITPW	Stowarzyszenie Inżynierów i Techników Przemysłu Wlokienniczego
SITR	Stowarzyszenie Naukowo-Techniczne Inżynierów i Techników Rolnictwa
SITRA	Sindicato dos Transportes Rodoviáries e Afins
SITRA	Société Ivoirienne de Travaux
SITRA	South India Textile Research Association
SITRA	Specialist Information Training Resource Agency for Single Person Housing
SITRAC	Société Industrielle de Transformation Centrafricaine
SITRACEL	Société Industrielle de Traitement de Cellulose (Cameroon)
SITRACI	Société Ivoirienne de Transactions Internationales
SITRACO	Société Interprofessionnelle de Transit et de Commissariat en Douane (Ivory Coast)
SITRAL	Société Ivoirienne de Transformation de l'Aluminium
SITRAM	Société Industrielle de Transformation des Métaux (Central Africa)
SITRAM	Société Ivoirienne de Transport Maritime
SITRAN-BOIS	Société Ivoirienne de Transformation de Bois
SITRAPAR	Sindicato de Trabajadores de Paraguay Refrescos
SITRATELH	Sindicato de Trabajadores de Telecomunicaciones de Honduras
SITRI	Shaanxi International Trade Research Institute
SITS	Società Italiana Telecommunicazione Siemens
SITS	Société Internationale de Transfusion Sanguine = ISBT
SITS	Syndicat Général des Industries pour le Traitement des Surfaces
SITT	Syndicat des Industries Téléphoniques et Télégraphiques
SITTEF	Société Ivoirienne de Travaux Topographiques et Fonciers
SITTH	Savez Inzenjera i Tehnicara Tekstilaca Hrvatske
SITUMER	Société d'Ingénierie du Tunnel sous la Mer
SITVAR	Syndicat National des Industries Transformateurs de Vanille et des Elements Aromatiques Naturels au Chimiques
SITWM	Stowarzyszenie Inżynierów i Techników Wodnych i Melioracyjnych
SIU	Social Investigation Unit (RSPCA)
SIU	Società Italiana di Urologia
SIU	Société Internationale d'Urologie = ISU
SIU	Statehood and Independence for Ukraine
SIU-PR	Seafarers International Union of Puerto Rico
SIUB	Société Ivoirienne d'Usinage des Bois
SIUCEP	Suzhou Institute of Urban Construction and Environmental Protection
SIUI	Sverdslovskii Iuridicheskii Institut
SIUNA	Seafarers International Union of North America
SIUPA	Solomon Islands United Party
SIV	Schweizerischen Inserenten-Verband
SIV	Société Immobilière de la Volta
SIV	Société Sénégalaise pour l'Industrie du Vêtement
SIV-MAILLE	Société Ivoirienne de la Maille

SIVA	Société Industrielle de Vêtements en Afrique
SIVA	Société Ivoirienne d'Agriculture
SIVAK	Société Ivoirienne Agricole et Industrielle du Kenaf
SIVB	Society for In-Vitro Biology
SIVÉ	Société Ivoirienne d'Importation de Véhicules et d'Ééquipments
SIVÉLEC	Société Ivoirienne d'Électricité
SIVÉLEF	Société Ivoirienne des États Lefort-Francheteau
SIVELP	Sindicato Italiano Veterinari Liberi Professionisti
SIVEM	Société Ivoirienne d'Emballage
SIVENG	Société Ivoirienne d'Engrais
SIVIÉ	Société Ivoirienne d'Installations Électriques
SIVIT	Société des Industries de la Viande du Tchad
SIVO	Société Immobilière Voltaïque (Burkina Faso)
SIVO-PLAST	Société Ivoirienne de Plastique
SIVO-TRANS	Société Ivoirienne de Transports
SIVOA	Société Ivoirienne d'Oxygène et d'Acetylène
SIVOCLIM	Société Ivoirienne de Climatisation
SIVOITEX	Société Industrielle Ivoirienne de Textile
SIVOM	Société Ivoirienne d'Opérations Maritimes
SIVOMA	Société Ivoiro-Marocaine d'Alimentation
SIVOMAR	Société Ivoirienne de Navigation Maritime
SIVSAJ	Service International Volontaire Solidarité Amitié Jeunesse
SIVT	Shenyang Institute of Vacuum Technology
SIW	Sektion Informationswissenschaft (DGD)
SIW	Socialist International Women
SIW	Stichting Internationale Werkkampen
SIWA	Scottish Inland Waterways Association
SJ	Society of Jesus = SI
SJA	Society for Japanese Arts (Netherlands)
SJAC	Society of Japanese Aerospace Companies
SJAC	Society of Japanese Arts and Crafts (Netherlands)
SJBI	Scottish Joint Breast-feeding Initiative
SJC	Sisters of St. Joseph of Cluny
SJCRE	Scottish Joint Committee on Religious Education
SJDM	Society for Judgment and Decision Making
SJF	Scottish Judo Federation
SJF	Svenska Journalistförbundet
SJF	Syndicat des Journalistes Français
SJH	Society of Jewellery History
SJHL	Suomen Jalkojenhoitajain Liitto
SJIA	Saint Joan's International Alliance = AIJA
SJJA	Scottish Ju-Jitsu Association
SJK	Svenska Jordbrukskreditkassan
SJL	Suomen Journalistiliitto
SJOC	Society of Japanese Oil Chemists
SJPA	Syndicat des Journalistes de la Presse Agricole
SJT	Soeurs de Saint Joseph de Tarbes
SJU	Schweizerische Journalisten Union = USG, USJ
SJUF	Scandinavisk Judish Ungdomsförbundet
SJZ TRI	Shijiazhuang Textile Research Institute
SK	Schweizerische Käseunion
SK	Sealed Knot
SK	Soiuz Kazakov – Vserossiiskii Soiuz Kazakov
SK	Superklubo Internacia
SK	Svenska Kartongförpackningsföreningen
SK	Svenska Kemistsamundet
SKA	Scottish Knitwear Association
SKAF	Schweizerische Katholische Arbeitsgemeinschaft für Ausländerfragen
SKAF	Sveriges Konst- och Antikhandlarförening
SKAFF	Skadeforsikringsforeningen
SKAFOR	Skadeforsikringsselskapenes Forening
SKAG	Verband Schweizerischer Konzessionierter Automobilunternehmungen
SKäL	Suomen Kätilöliitto
Skantel	St. Kitts and Nevis Telecommunications Limited
SKAT	Schweizerische Kontaktstelle für angepasste Technik (Switzerland)
SKB	Schweizerischer Konsumentenbund

SKB	Svenska Kuvertfabrikanters Branschrad	**SKL**	Sveriges Kemisk- Tekniska Leverantorförening
SKBF	Schweizerische Koordinationsstelle für Bildungsforschung	**SKLE**	Hellenic Association of Social Workers
SKBSiI	Społeczny Komitet Budowy Szkól i Internatów	**SKLFS**	State Key Laboratory of Fire Science (China)
SKBT	Syndicale Kamer van de Belgische Tuinbouw	**SKLMMW**	State Key Laboratory of Millimeter Waves (China)
SKC	Scottish Kennel Club	**SKMNiE**	Sejmowa Komisja Mniejszości Narodowych i Etnicznych
SKC	Scottish Knitwear Council	**SKMV**	Schweizerischer Kaminfegermeisterverband
SKD	Slovensko Kemijsko Drustvo		
SKD	Soiuz Konstitutsionnykh Demokratov	**SKN**	Społeczny Komitet Nauki
SKDL	Suomen Kansan Demokraattinen Liitto	**SKO**	Sejmowa Komisja Obrony
SKDS	Slovenská Krest'anskodemokratická Strana (Slovakia) = SCDP	**SKOL**	Suomen Konsulttitoimistojen Liitto
SKF	Svensk Kirurgisk Förening	**SKP**	Stowarzyszenie Księgarzy Polskich
SKF	Svenska Kullagerfabriken AB	**SKP**	Suomen Kommunistinen Puolue
SKF	Svenska Kylfirmors Förening	**SKP-Y**	Suomen Kommunistinen Puolue – Yhtendisyys
SKFA	Scottish Keep Fit Association		
SKFB	Skandinaviska Kreatursförsäkringsbolaget	**SKR**	Spółdzielcze Kółko Rolnicze
		SKR	Svenska Kemiingenjörers Riksförening
SKFB	Sveriges Köpmannaförbund	**SKR**	Svenska Kosmetologers Riksförbund
SKFPA	St. Kitts-Nevis Family Planning Association	**SKR**	Sveriges Konstföreningars Riksförbund
		SKRI	Shanghai Knitting Research Institute
SKG	Schwedische Kunstkautschukgesellschaft = SGF	**SKS**	Schweizerische Konferenz für Sicherheit im Strassenverkehr = CSR
SKHL	Siipikarjanhoitajain Liitto	**SKS**	Stiftung für Konsumentenschutz (Switzerland)
SKHS	Suomen Kirkkohistoriallinen Seura		
SKI	Schweizerisches Krankenhausinstitut	**SKS**	Suomalaisen Kemistien Seura
SKI	Street Kids International (Canada)	**SKS**	Suomalaisen Kirjallisuuden Seura
SKI	Szölészeti Kutató Intézet	**SKS**	Svenska Keramiska Sällskapet
SKIF	Svenska Konsultföreningen	**SKT**	Verband Schweizerischer Kammgarnweber, Tuch-und Decken-Fabrikanten
SKIK	Sveriges Kemiska Industrikontor Kemikontoret		
		SKTA	Shetland Knitwear Trades Association
SKILL	National Bureau for Students with Disabilities (formerly National Bureau for Handicapped Students)	**SKTF**	Svensk Kommunal-Tekniska Föreningen
		SKTF	Sveriges Kvalitetstekniska Förening
Skill-UK	Society for the Promotion of Vocational Training and Education	**SKTH**	Savez Kemicara i Tehnologa Hrvatske
		SKTL	Suomen Kähertäjäliitto ry
SKIP	Svaz Knihovníku a Informačních Pracovníku ČR	**SKTL**	Suomen Kähertäjätyönantajaliitto
		SKTY	Suomen Kunnallisteknillinen Yhdistys
SKIV	Schweizerischer Kioskinhaber-Verband	**SKTY**	Suomen Kuntatekniikan Yhdistys
SKJP	Vereinigung Schweizerischer Kinder- und Jugendpsychologen = ASPEA	**SKV**	Schweizerischer Kaninchenzucht-Verband
SKK	Stichting Kernvootstuwing Koopvaardijschepen	**SKV**	Schweizerischer Kaufmännischer Verein
SKKS	Suomen Kemian Seura	**SKV**	Schweizerischer Kochverband = SSC, SCS
SKL	Schweizerische Krebsliga		
SKL	Suomen Kiinnteistönvälittäjäin Liitto	**SKV**	Schweizerischer Küfermeisterverband
SKL	Suomen Kristellinen Liitto	**SKV**	Schweizerischer Reklame-Verband

SKVC	Schweizerischer Konditor-Confiseurmeisterverband		**SLAGH**	Secretariado Latino-Americano de Grupos Homosexuales (Brazil)
SKVL	Suomen Kiinteistönvälittäjäin Liitto		**SLAIA**	Sociedad Latinoamericana de Ingenerios Agriculturos
SKVS	Svenska Konsulterande VVS-Ingenjörers Förening		**SLAIP**	Sociedad Latinoamericana de Investigación Pédiatrica
SKY	Suimen Kasvatusopillinen Yhdistys			
SKY	Suomen Kielitieteellinen Yhdistys ry		**SLAIS**	Slovenian Artificial Intelligence Society
SKY	Suomen Kirurgiyhdistys		**SLAKSJ**	Supreme Ladies Auxiliary Knights of St. John (U.S.A.)
SKY	Suomen Kuljetustaloudellinen Yhdistys			
SKZV	Schweizerischer Kanarien-Züchter Verband		**SLAM**	Sierra Leone Alliance Movement
			SLAM	Syndicat National de la Librairie Ancienne et Moderne
SL	Sendero Luminoso (Peru)		**SLAMI**	Société Agricole Minière et Industrielle (Madagascar)
SL	Spartacist League			
SL	Stronnictwo Ludowe		**SLAMS**	Syndicat des Constructeurs d'Appareils de Levage, de Manutention et de Matériels de Stockage
SL	Suomen Lääkintavoimistelijaliitto = FF			
SL	Sveriges Lantbruksförbund			
SL	Sveriges Lararförbund		**SLAN**	Sociedad Latinoamericana de Nutrición
SLA	Sammenslutningen av Landbrukets Arbeidsgiverforeningen		**SLANT**	School Library Association of the Northern Territory (Australia)
SLA	Scaffold Lashings Association		**SLAO**	Société Linguistique de l'Afrique Occidentale = SOAL, WALS
SLA	School Libraries Association			
SLA	Scottish Library Association		**SLAP**	Sociedad Latinoamericana Patolgia
SLA	Skogs- och Lantbruksakademien		**SLAS**	Scottish Law Agents Society
SLA	Sleep-Learning Association		**SLAS**	Society for Latin American Studies
SLA	Small Landowners Association		**SLASH**	Scottish Local Authorities Special Housing Group
SLA	Socialist Lecturers Alliance			
SLA	South Lebanon Army		**SLAT**	Harmony for Latvia
SLA	Special Libraries Association (U.S.A.)		**SLAT**	Sociedad Latinoamericana de Tiroides = LATS
SLA	State Land Administration (China)			
SLA	Surinamese Liberation Army		**SLAVCA**	Sindacato Nazionale Lavoratori Vetro e Ceramica
SLA	Svenska Lantarbetsgivareforeningen			
SLAA	Society for Latin American Anthropology (U.S.A.)		**sLB**	Left Bloc Party (Czech Republic)
			SLB	Schweizerischer Lithographenbund
SLaby	Suomen Laboratorio-Loitajayhdistys		**SLB**	Société Lagunaire des Bois (Ivory Coast)
SLAC	Stanford Linear Accelerator Centre (U.S.A.)			
			SLBC	Société Luxembourgeoise de Biologie Clinique
SLAC	Structures Lamellées d'Afrique Centrale			
SLACE	Society of Local Authority Chief Executives		**SLBC**	Sri Lankan Broadcasting Company
			SLBGA	Saint Lucia Banana Growers Association
SLACES	Syndicat de la Librairie Ancienne et du Commerce de l'Estampe en Suisse			
			SLC	Scottish Land Court
SLAD	Society of London Art Dealers		**SLC**	Scottish Law Commission
SLADE	Sociedad Latinoamericano de Estrategia (Colombia)		**SLC**	Société de Législation Comparée
			SLC	Society of Lithuanian Culture = LKD
SLADE	Society of Lithographic Artists, Designers, Engravers and Process Workers		**SLC**	Svenska Lantbruksproducenternas Centralförbund
			SLCD	Service Laïque de Coopération au Développement
SLAET	Society of Licensed Aircraft Engineers and Technologists (RAeS)		**SLCh**	Christian Peasant Alliance (Poland)

SLCP	Standing Liaison Committee of Physiotherapists within the EEC (Denmark) = CPLK	**SLHCT**	Sociedad Latinoamericana de Historia de las Ciencas y la Tecnologia = LASHST
SLD	Srpsko Lekarsko Drustvo	**SLHR**	Society for Life History Research (U.S.A.)
SLDP	Sierra Leone Democratic Party		
SLDTU	Social and Liberal Democrat Trade Unionists	**SLHS**	Scottish Labour History Society
		SLICAJ	Sindicato Libre e Independiente de los Cuerpos de la Administración de Justicia
SLE	Societas Linguistica Europaea		
SLE	Society of Logistics Engineers (U.S.A.)		
SLEAT	Society of Laundry Engineers and Allied Trades	**SLICE**	St. Louis Institute of Consulting Engineers (U.S.A.)
		SLIGA	Société Laitière Industrielle du Gabon
SLEN	Sociedad Luso-Española de Neurocirugia	**SLIM**	Société Librairie Imprimerie Messagerie (Tunisia)
SLENA	Sierra Leone News Agency		
SLESR	Société des Librairies de la Suisse Romande	**SLIMTRI**	Shangahi Light Industry Machinery Technical Research Institute
SLF	Eidgenössisches Institut für Schnee- und Lawinenforschung (Switzerland)	**SLIP**	Sociedad Latinoamericana de Investigadores en Papas (Venezuela)
SLF	Sammenslutningen af Lokalhistoriske Foreninger	**SLiR**	Société de Linguistique Romane
		SLIRI	Shanghai Light Industry Research Institute (China)
SLF	Scottish Landowners Federation		
SLF	Skandinaviska Lackteknikers Förbund	**SLITUF**	Sri Lanka Independent Trade Union Federation
SLF	Skolledarförbundet		
SLF	Svenska Laboratieassistent Föreningen	**SLjSRH**	Savez Ljevaca SR Hrvatske
SLF	Svenska Lantbrukstjänstemannaförbundet	**SLL**	Skotøy-og Loervareindustriens Leverandørforening
SLF	Svenska Sjukvards Leverantörers Förening	**SLL**	Society of Labour Lawyers
		SLL	Statens Lantbrukskemiska Laboratorium (Sweden)
SLF	Sveriges Läkreförbund		
SLF	Sveriges Lantmätareförening	**SLL**	Suomen Lääkäriliitto = FLF
SLFP	Sri Lanka Freedom Party	**SLLA**	Scottish Lime and Limestone Association
SLFUW	Sri Lanka Federation of University Women		
		SLLA	Sierra Leone Library Association
SLFV	Schweizerischen Landfrauenverbandes	**SLLA**	Sri Lanka Library Association
SLFY	Suomen Logopedis-Foniatrinen Yhdistys	**SLLC**	Sierra Leone Labour Congress
		SLLW	Société de Langue et de Littérature Wallonnes (Belgium)
SLG	Schweizerische Lichttechnische Gesellschaft = USL		
SLG	Socialist Labour Group	**SLm**	Society of Limners
SLG	Socialist Lesbian Group	**SLM**	Surinaamse Luchtvaart Maatschappij
SLGA	Scottish Ladies Golfing Association	**SLMA**	Steel Lintel Manufactures Association
SLgE	Schweizerische Liga gegen Epilepsie = LSCE	**SLMC**	Sri Lanka Muslim Congress
		SLMH	Schweizerischer Verband des Schmiede-, Landmaschinen-, Metall- und Holzewerbes
SLGIU	Scottish Local Government Information Unit		
SLGL	Schweizerische Liga gegen den Lärm	**SLMM**	Sindicato Libre de la Marina Mercante
SLH	Selskabet for Levnedsmiddelteknologiog-hygiene	**SLMWAK**	Sierra Leone Muslim Women's Association – Kankaylay
SLH	Sociedad Latinoamericana de Heptatalogia	**SLN**	Sveriges Lärares Nykterhetsförbund
		SLO	Stichting Landbourwhuishoudkundig Onderzoek

SLOA	Steam Locomotive Operators Association	**SLSTIC**	Sri Lanka Science and Technology Information Centre
SLORC	State Law and Order Restoration Council (Burma)	**SLSW**	Verband Schweizerischer Langlauf- und Ski-Wanderschulen
SLORL	Société Latine d'Oto-Rhino-Laryngologie	**SLT**	International Sacred Literature Trust (COREC) = SLTI
SLOT	Sociedad Latinoamericana de Ortopedía y Traumatolía	**SLTA**	Scottish Lawn Tennis Association
SLOV-UNION	National Union of Slovaks	**SLTA**	Scottish Licensed Trade Association
		SLTA	Sri Lanka Tourist Association
SLP	Scottish Labour Party	**SLTB**	Society for Low Temperature Biology
SLP	Serbian Liberal Party	**SLTC**	Society of Leather Technologists and Chemists (South Africa, U.K.)
SLP	Socialist Labor Party (Romania) = PSM		
SLP	Socialist Labour Party (Egypt)	**SLTI**	Sacred Literature Trust International (COREC) = SLT
SLP	Société de Linguistique de Paris	**SLV**	Schweizerischer Landmaschinen-Verband
SLP	St. Lucia Labour Party		
SLP	Stowarzyszenie Litwinów w Polsce (Poland) = ALP	**SLV**	Schweizerischer Landwirtschaftlichen Verein
SLPA	Sri Lanka Ports Authority	**SLV**	Schweizerischer Lederhändler-Verband = USMC
SLPCz	Studencka Liga Praw Człowieka		
SLPh	Société Luxembourgeoise de Philosophie	**SLV**	Schweizerischer Lehrerverein
		SLV	Schweizerischer Lichtspieltheater-Verband
SLPM	Sindikata e Lire dhe e Pavarur e Minatoreve (Albania) = FIMU		
		SLV	Society of Licensed Victuallers
SLPMB	Sierra Leone Produce Marketing Board	**SLV**	Statens Livsmedelsverk (Sweden)
SLPPA	St. Lucia Planned Parenthood Association	**SLVL**	Suomen Liike-ja Virkanaisten Liitto = FYF
SLPTA	Sri Lanka Pharmaceutical Traders' Association	**SLVS**	Slovenská Literánovedná Společnost
		SLY	Suomen Laatuyhdistys
SLR	Société Linguistique Romane	**SLY**	Suomen Lintutieteellinen Yhistys
SLR	Svenska Lantmännens Riksförbund	**SM**	Shoqata e Malazezëve (Albania) = AM
SLR	Sveriges Lassmedsmästares Riksförbund	**SM**	Slovak Motherland = MS
		SM	Slovenska Matica
SLR	Sveriges Leksakshandlares Riksförbund	**SM**	Societas Mariae
SLRP	Society for Strategic and Long Range Planning (U.S.A.)	**SM**	Society of Miniaturists
		SM	Soeurs Maristes
SLRS	Sexual Law Reform Society	**SM**	Stowarzyszenie Mazurskie (Poland) = MA
SLS	Scots Language Society		
SLS	Slovenská Lekárska Spolecnost	**SM**	Svaz Mad'arů (Czech Republic) = UH
SLS	Society of Landscape Studies	**SMA**	Salt Manufacturers' Association
SLS	Stephenson Locomotive Society	**SMA**	Schools Music Association
SLS	Suomen Lahetysseura	**SMA**	Seasoning Manufacturers Association (*now* SSA)
SLS	Svenska Läkaresällskapet		
SLS	Svenska Landsbygdens Studieförbund	**SMA**	Servicio Meteorológico de Angola
SLS	Svenska Litteratursällskapet i Finland	**SMA**	Sheffield Metallurgical Association
SLSA	Socio-Legal Studies Association	**SMA**	Singapore Manufacturers Association
SLSA	St. Lawrence Seaway Authority (Canada)	**SMA**	Singapore Medical Association
		SMA	Societas Missionum ad Afros
SLSA-GB	Surf Life Saving Association of Great Britain	**SMA**	Société Méditerannéenne d'Acupuncture

SMA	Society for Medieval Archaeology	**SMBK**	Schweizerischer Verband des Milch-, Butter- und Käsehandels
SMA	Society of Motor Auctions		
SMA	Society of Museum Archaeologists	**SMBPA**	Société Malienne de Biscuiterie et Pâtes Alimentaires
SMA	Society of Sales Management Administrators		
		SMBV	Schweizerischer Motorbootunternehmer-Verband
SMA	St. Mungo Association		
SMA	Stage Management Association	**SMC**	School Meals Campaign
SMA	Steel Merchants Association	**SMC**	Schweizerische Marketing Club
SMA	Sugar Manufacturers' Association (Jamaica)	**SMC**	Scottish Mountaineering Club
		SMC	Scottish Museums Council
SMA	Suomen Maisema-Arkkitehdit	**SMC**	Sealant Manufacturers Conference (*now* BASA)
SMA	Survey & Mapping Alliance		
SMA	Swiss Museums Association = AMS, VMS	**SMC**	Sociedad de Matemática de Chile
		SMC	Sociedad Mexicana de Cactalogia
SMAA	Scottish Modern Arts Association	**SMC**	Société Martiniquaise de Construction
SMAC	Society of Management Accountants of Canada	**SMC**	Société Mathématique du Canada = CMS
SMAC	Standing Medical Advisory Committee (NHS)	**SMC**	Société Scierie, Menuiserie et Charpenterie
SMAE	Society of Model Aeronautical Engineers	**SMC**	Sveriges Möbelhandlares Centralförbund
SMAG	Société Meunière et Avicole du Gabon	**SMCADT**	Société de Manutention de Carburants Aviation Dakar-Yoff (Senegal)
SMAI	Soup Manufacturers' Association of Ireland		
		SMCE	Sociedad Mexicana de Computación Electrónica
SMAK	Svensk Matpotatiskontroll		
SMAN	Scottish Medical Aid for Nicaragua	**SMCI**	Sciages et Moulures de Côte d'Ivoire
SMAP	Solidarity Movement of Afghan People	**SMCI**	Société Mauritanienne pour le Commerce et l'Industrie
SMAR	Société Mauritanienne d'Assurances et de Réassurances		
		SMCP	Société Mauritanienne pour la Commercialisation du Poisson
SMARA	Servicio Meterolologico de la Armada Argentina		
		SMCPP	Société Mauritanienne de Commercialisation des Produits Pétroliers
SMATA	Sindicato de Mecanicos y Afines del Transporte Automotor (Argentina)		
		SMCS	Sociedad Mexicana de la Ciencia del Suelo
SMAUI	Sales, Marketing and Administrative Union of Ireland		
		SMDBiB	Stowarzyszenie Miłośników Dawnej Broni i Barwy
SMB	Sociedad Meteorológica de Bolivia		
SMB	Societas Missionum Exterarum de Bethlehem in Helvetia	**SMDM**	Society for Medical Decision Making
		SMDN	Société Minière du Niger
SMB	Société Mathématique de Belgique	**SMDP**	Staff Movement for Disarmament and Peace (UN)
SMB	Société Mauritanienne de Banque		
SMB	Société Médicale de Biothérapie	**SMDRI**	Shanghai Metallurgical Design & Research Institute
SMB	Société Multinationale de Bitumes (Ivory Coast)		
		SMDSM	Systeme Mondial de Détresse et de Sécurité en Mer = GMDSS
SMB	Society for Mathematical Biology		
SMB	Society of Marriage Bureaux	**SME**	Sindicato Mexicano de Electricistas
SMB	Society of Missionaries of Bethlehem	**SME**	Sociedad Mexicana de Entomologia
SMB	Sujuz na Matematitsite v Bulgarija	**SME**	Society of Manufacturing Engineers (U.S.A.)
SMBA	Scottish Marine Biological Association		
SMBF	Scottish Musicians' Benevolent Fund	**SME**	Society of Military Engineers (U.S.A.)

SME	Society of Mining Engineers (AIME)
SME	Stichting Milieu-Educatie
SME	Stichting Mondiaal Alternatief
SME	Système Monétaire Européen = EMS, EWS
SMEC	Société Malienne d'Entreprises et de Constructions
SMÉCMA	Société Malienne d'Études et de Construction de Matériel Agricole
SMECOMA	Landbouwmechanisatiebedrijven
SMEE	Society of Model and Experimental Engineers
SMEI	Sales and Marketing Executives International (U.S.A.)
SMEITS	Savez Masinskih i Elektrotehnickih Inzenjera i Tehnicara i Srbije
SMEP	Société de Maroquinerie et d'Emballages Plastiques (Cameroon)
SMEP	Society for Multivariate Experimental Psychology
SMÉPC	Société Suisse des Maîtres des Écoles Professionnelles Commerciales = VLKB
SMER	Société Médicale Internationale d'Endoscopie et de Radio-Cinématographie
SMERT	Société Malienne d'Exploitation des Ressources Touristiques
SMF	Chambre Syndicale Nationale des Constructeurs et Constructeurs-Installateurs de Matériels et d'Équipements Frigorifiques
SMF	Sint-Maartensfonds (Belgium)
SMF	Social Market Foundation
SMF	Sociedad Mexicana de Fitogenética
SMF	Sociedad Mexicana de Fitopatologia
SMF	Société Mathématique de France
SMF	Société Météorologique de France
SMF	Svenska Missionsförbundet
SMF	Sveriges Mykologiska Förening
SMFF	Svenska Musikförläggare Föreningen
SMFI	Shanxi Man-Made Fibre Institute
SMFMA	Sprayed Mineral Fiber Manufacturers Association (U.S.A.)
SMG	Poor Servants of the Mother of God
SMG	Schweizerische Mathematische Gesellschaft
SMG	Schweizerische Multiple Sklerose Gesellschaft
SMG	Schweizerische Musikforschende Gesellschaft
SMG	Sociedad Minera del Guainía (Colombia)
SMG	Société des Matériaux du Gabon
SMG	Southall Monitoring Group
SMGC	Scottish Marriage Guidance Council
SMGE	Sociedad Mexicana de Geografica y Estadistica
SMGI	Société Mauritanienne des Gaz Industriels
SMGS	Socialist Countries Convention on Transport of Goods by Rail
SMGV	Schweizerischer Maler- und Gipsermeister-Verband = ASMPP
SMGV	Schweizerischer Modergewerbe-Verband
SMHÉ	Société Mauritanienne d'Hotellerie et Épicerie
SMHI	Sveriges Meteorologiska och Hydrologiska Institut
SMHN	Sociedad Mexicana de Historia Natural
SMHS	Scottish Military Historical Society
SMI	Shanghai Maritime Institute
SMI	Sindacato Musicisti Italiani
SMI	Social Marketing International Association (Mexico)
SMI	Sveriges Möbelindustriförbund
SMI	Swiss Meteorological Institute
SMI	Syndicat National des Constructeurs de Maisons Individuelles
SMIA	Scottish Music Industry Association
SMIA	Sheet Metal Industries Association
SMIA	Social Marketing International Association
SMIC	Scottish Music Information Centre
SMIC	Surveying and Mapping Industry Council
SMIC	Syndicat des Fabricants de Meubles Métalliques Industriels et Commerciaux
SMICO	Société Minière du Congo
SMID	Sammenslutningen af Medieforskere i Danmark
SMIDA	Small Manufacturing Industries Development Association
SMIE	Société Mauritanienne d'Importation et d'Exportation
SMIER	Société Médicale Internationale d'Endoscopie et de Radiocinématographie
SMIF	Sveriges Motorcykel-och Mopedimportöres Förbund

SMILE	Society for Music in Leisure & Education	**SMNA**	Safe Manufacturers National Association (U.S.A.)
SMIS	Society for Management Information Systems (U.S.A.)	**SMNDA**	Scottish Motor Neurone Disease Association
SMIS	Urad SZ za Standardizacijo in Meroslovje	**SMO**	Society of Museum Officers
SMISB	Société Mauritanienne des Industries Secondaires du Bâtiment	**SMOL**	Suomen Musiikinopettajain Liitto
		SMOM	Sovrano Militare Ordine di Malta
SMISO	Système Mondial Intégré de Services Océaniques = IGOSS, SGIEO SGISO	**SMOT**	Svobodnoe Mezhprofessionalnoe Obedinenie Trudiashchikhsia
SMIVAC	Société de Mise en Valeur de la Corse	**SMP**	Sociedad Mexicana de Parasitologia
SMKL	Suomen Metsäteollisuuden Keskusliitto	**SMP**	Societas Lusitana pro Missionibus
SML	Scottish Militant Labour	**SMP**	Society of Mural Painters
SML	Stichting Machinale Landbouw (Suriname)	**SMP**	Suomen Maaseudun Puolue
		SMPA	Scottish Master Patternmakers Association
SML	Suomen Maarakentajien	**SMPA**	Scottish Master Plasterers Association
SML	Suomen Markkinopintillitto	**SMPC**	Scottish Milk Publicity Council
SML	Suomen Matkaluliitto	**SMPC**	Société Marocaine des Produits Chimiques
SML	Suomen Mehiläishoitajain Liitto		
SML	Suomen Museoliitto	**SMPE**	Society of Marine Port Engineers (U.S.A.)
SML	Suomen Musiikkioppilaitosten Liitto		
SML	Suomen Muusikkojen Liitto ry	**SMPG**	Schweizerische Mineralogische und Petrographische Gesellschaft
SMLDA	Société Mauritano-Libyenne de Développement Agricole	**SMPI**	Société Mauritanienne de Presse et d'Impression
SMLT	Société du Metro Léger de Tunis	**SMPI**	Société Moderne du Pneumatique Ivoirien
SMM	Servico Meteorológica de Mocambique		
SMM	Sociedad Matemática Mexicana = MMS	**SMPI**	Société Monégasque du Promotion International
SMM	Societas Mariae Monfortana		
SMM	Society of Mary and Martha	**SMPMA**	Sausage and Meat Pie Manufacturers Association
SMM	Sucreries Marseillaises de Madagascar		
SMMB	Scottish Milk Marketing Board	**SMPMF**	Scottish Metal and Plumbers' Merchants' Federation
SMMCZ	Sociedad Mexicana de Medicina y Cirugía Zootécnicas	**SMPS**	Society of Master Printers of Scotland (*now* SPEF)
SMMD	Sociedades Mediadores en el Mercado de Dinero	**SMPTE**	Society of Motion Picture and Television Engineers (U.S.A.)
SMMI	Salésiennes Missionnaires de Marie Immaculée	**SMPV**	Schweizerischer Musikpädagogischer Verband = SSPM
SMMSA	Scottish Master Monumental Sculptors Association	**SMR**	Serbian Movement for Renewal
SMMT	Society of Motor Manufacturers and Traders	**SMR**	Société Musicale de la Russie = ARMS
		SMR	Societatea Micologicâ din România
SMMV	Schweizerischer Mechanikermeister-Verband	**SMR**	Society for Medicines Research
SMMY	Suomen Myynti-ja Mainosyhdistys	**SMR**	Society of Manufacturers Representatives (U.S.A.)
SMN	Scientific and Medical Network		
SMN	Servicio Meterológico Nacionál (Argentina, Mexico)	**SMR**	Society of Mary Reparatrix
		SMR	Svenska Mejeriernas Riksförening
SMN	Servicio Minero Nacional (Argentina)	**SMR**	Svenska Mekanister Riksförening
SMN	Société des Mélasses du Niari (Zaïre)	**SMR**	Swedish Dairies Association

SMRA	Scottish Milk Records Association		**SMT**	Sammenslutningen af Maskinfabrikker for Troeindustrien
SMRAB	Safety in Mines Research Advisory Board		**SMT**	Société de Micro-Informatique et de Télécommunications
SMRC	Scottish Motor Racing Club		**SMT**	Society for Music Theory
SMRC	Society of Miniature Rifle Clubs		**SMT**	Statiunea de Masini si Tractorare (Romania)
SMRC	Stoneham Museum and Research Centre (Kenya)		**SMTA**	Scottish Motor Trade Association
SMRI	Sugar Milling Research Institute (South Africa)		**SMTA**	Sewing Machine Trade Association (U.K., U.S.A.)
SMRP	Society for Medieval and Renaissance Philosophy (U.S.A.)		**SMTA**	Society for Music Teacher Education (U.S.A.)
SMRRF	Strategic Metals Recovery Research Facility (U.S.A.)		**SMTF**	Scottish Milk Trade Federation
SMRTB	Ship and Marine Requirements Technology Board		**SMTH**	Société Mauritaniene de Tourisme et d'Hôtellerie
SMRU	Sea Mammal Research Unit (NERC)		**SMTL**	Suomen Muoviteollisuusliitto = FIPIF
SMS	Scheepvaart Maatschappij Suriname		**SMTS**	Scottish Machinery Testing Station
SMS	School of Mathematical Sciences (ANU)		**SMTT**	Société Minière de Tassa n'Taghalgue (Niger)
SMS	Shipwrecked Mariners' Society		**SMTUC**	Socialist Movement Trade Union Committee
SMS	Slovenská Meteorolická Společnost			
SMS	Socialist Movement Scotland		**SMTY**	Suomen Materiaalitaloudellinen Yhdistys
SMS	Société Mathématique Suisse			
SMS	Society of Master Saddlers		**SMU**	Schweizerische Metall-Union = USM
SMS	Society of Model Shipwrights		**SMU**	Shanghai Medical University
SMS	Strategic Management Society		**SMU**	Surinaamse Mijnwerkers Unie
SMS	Suomen Maataloustieteellinen Seura		**SMUH**	Secrétariat des Missions d'Urbanisme et d'Habitat
SMS	Suomen Metsätietellinen Seura			
SMS	Svenska Matematikersamfundet / Swedish Mathematical Society		**SMUJ**	Savez Muzickih Umetnika Jugoslavije
			SMUSE	Socialist Movement for the United States of Europe
SMS	Sveriges Målarmästareförening			
SMS	Swiss Mycological Society		**SMUV**	Schweizerischer Metall- und Uhrenarbeiterverband
SMS	Syndicat National des Fabricants de Matériels de Soudage		**SMV**	Schweizerischer Markt-Verband
			SMV	Schweizerischer Mieterverband
SMS	Verband Schweizer Marketing- und Sozialforscher = ASSEM		**SMV**	Schweizerischer Milchwirtschaftlicher Verein
SMSA	Silica & Moulding Sands Association		**SMV**	Schweizerischer Musikerverband = USDAM
SMSF	Scottish Motor Sport Federation			
SMSH	Societe Médicale Suisse d'Homéopathie		**SMW**	Sheet Metal Workers International Association
SMSM	Soeurs Missionnaires de la Société de Marie = MMS		**SMW**	Society for the Ministry of Women
			SMWBA	Scottish Master Wrights and Builders Association
SMSP	Société Médicale Suisse de Psychothérapie = SAGP			
SMSR	Société des Meuniers de la Suisse Romande		**SMWS**	Scottish Malt Whisky Society
			SMY	Suomen Matemaattinen Yhdistys ry
SMSR	Society of Master Shoe Repairers		**SMY**	Suomen Metsäyhdistys ry
SMST	Scottish Maritime Sailing Trust		**SMY**	Suomen Muinaismuistoy Yhdistys
SMSW	State Medical Society of Wisconsin (U.S.A.)		**SN**	Statens Naturvardsverk

SN	Stronnictwo Narodowe (Poland) = NP
SN	Svenska Naturskyddsforeningen
SN	Sveriges Naturvetareförbund
SNA	Scottish Netball Association
SNA	Sindacato Nazionale Agenti di Assicurazione
SNA	Sindicato Nacional dos Arquitectos
SNA	Sociedad Nacional de Agricultura (Chile)
SNA	Sociedade Nacional de Agricultura (Brazil)
SNA	Société Nationale Aérospatiale
SNA	Société Nationale d'Acclimatation
SNA	Société Nationale d'Assurances (Algeria)
SNA	Stichting voor de Nederlandse Archeologie
SNA	Suburban Newspapers of America
SNA	Surinaams Nieuws Agentschaap (Suriname)
SNA	Syndicat National d'Apiculture
SNAA	Servicio Nacional de Acueductos y Alcantarillado (Costa Rica)
SNAA	Syndicat National des Aviculteurs Agréés
SNABM	Syndicat National des Adjuvants pour Bétons et Mortiers
SNABV	Syndicat National des Agences et Bureaux de Voyages
SNAC	Société Nouvelle d'Assurances du Caméroun
SNAC	Syndicat National des Auteurs et Compositeurs
SNACA	Scottish National Angling Clubs Association (*now* SANA)
SNACGIL	Sindacato Nazionale Artisti (CGIL)
SNACGP	Syndicat National des Armateurs de Chalutiers de Grande Pêche
SNACH	Sociedad Nacional de Agricultura de Chile
SNACI	Société Nouvelle d'Assurances de Côte d'Ivoire
SNACMA	Snack, Nut and Crisp Manufacturers Association
SNACO	Syndicat National du Commerce, de la Distribution et du Conditionnement des Oeufs
SNAD	Sindacato Nazionale Autori Drammatici
SNADAP	Syndicat National de la Domicile et des Actions Promotionnelles

SNADIGG	Sindacato Nazionale Dipendenti Ministerio Grazie e Giustizia
SNADIR-TEP	Sindacato Nazionale Autonomo Dipendenti Radio Television Private
SNAF	Société Nationale des Antiquaries de France
SNAF	Société Nationale des Architectes de France
SNAFIC	Seychelles National Fishing Company
SNAFID	Slovak National Agency for Foreign Investment and Development
SNAFOP	Société Nationale pour le Développement Forestier (Benin)
SNAG	Sindacato Nazionale Automono Giornalai
SNAG	Society of North American Goldsmiths
SNAGE	Syndicat National des Affineurs de Gruyère et d'Emmental
SNAGFA	Syndicat National des Agents et Groupeurs de Fret Aérien
SNAGIP	Sindacato Nazionale Autonomo Giornalisti Pubblicisti
SNAI	Sindacato Nazionale Agenzie Ippiche
SNAI	Società Nazionale Agricola Industriale (Somalia)
SNAI	Syndicat National des Architectes d'Intérieur
SNALS	Sindacato Nazionale Autonomo Lavoratori Scuola
SNAM	Società Nazionale Metanodotii
SNAM	Syndicat National des Agents Maritimes
SNAM	Syndicat National des Articles Métalliques et de leurs Dérivés
SNAME	Society of Naval Architects and Marine Engineers (U.S.A.)
SNANSC	Society of Neurosurgical Anaesthesia and Neurological Supportive Care
SNAP	Sarawak National Party
SNAP	Servicia Nacional de Agua Potable y Saneamiento Rural (Argentina)
SNAP	Société Industrielle des Nouvelles Applications des Matières Plastiques (Cameroon)
SNAP	Syndicat National des Agences de Publicité
SNAP	Syndicat National des Artistes Professionnels
SNAPAMR	Syndicat National de la Presse Agricole et du Monde Rurale
SNAPO	Syndicat National de la Publicité par l'Objet

SNAPP	Syndicat National des Agences de Presse Photographiques
SNAQ	Syndicat National Angora Qualité
SNAR	Société Nationale d'Assurances et Réassurances (Guinea, Niger)
SNAS	Singapore National Academy of Science
SNAS	Syndicat National du Commerce de Gros des Appareils Sanitaires, de Canalisation et de Chauffage
SNASA	Sociedad Nacional de Agricultura (Mexico)
SNASA	Syndicat National des Agents de Sociétés d'Auteurs
SNASDP	Syndicat National des Annuaires et Supports Divers de Publicité
SNASE	Sindacato Nazionale Autonomo Scuola Elementare
SNASP	Serviço Nacional de Segurança Popular (Mozambique)
SNAT	Société National d'Acconage et de Transit (Gabon)
SNAT	Société Nationale de l'Artisanat Traditionnel (Algeria)
SNATPA	Syndicat National de l'Action Technique et Professionnelle Agricole
SNAV	Sindacato Nazionale Attrazionisti Viaggianti
SNAV	Société Nouvelles des Ateliers de Venissieux
SNB&RTU	Screw, Nut, Bolt & Rivet Trade Union
SNBA	Société Nationale des Beaux-Arts
SNBATI	Syndicat National du Béton Armé et des Techniques Industrialisées
SNBBR	Section Nationale des Bailleurs de Baux Ruraux
SNBC	Syndicat National des Bouilleurs de Cru Producteurs de Fruits et Professions Connexes
SNBG	Société Nationale des Bois du Gabon
SNBP	Société Nigérienne des Pétroles BP
SNBP	Syndicat National des Fabricants de Bouillons et Potages
SNBSL	Société Nouvelle de la Banque de Syrie et du Liban (Lebanon)
SNBTF	Scottish National Building Trades Federation
SNBTS	Scottish National Blood Transfusion Service
SNC	Cameroon National Society
SNC	Slovak National Council
SNC	Société en Nom Collectif
SNC	Société Nationale de Cinématographie (Senegal)
SNC	Société Nationale de Colombiculture
SNC	Société Nationale de Confection (Mauritania)
SNC	Société Nationale de Construction
SNC	Société Nationale du Caméroun
SNC	Société Navale Caennaise
SNC	Société Nigérienne de Cimenterie
SNC	Supreme National Council (Cambodia)
SNC	Syndicat National des Chaines d'Hôtels et de Restaurants
SNC	Syndicat National des Cidriers et Fabricants d'Eau-de-Vie de Cidre
SNC	Syndicat National du Cinema
SNC-BOIS	Société Nationale du Caméroun-Bois
SNC3M	Syndicat Nationale des Constructeurs de Moules, Modèles et Maquettes
SNCA	Scottish National Camps Association
SNCA	Société Nationale de Construction Aéronautique
SNCAO	Société Nationale de Construction Aéronautique de l'Ouest
SNCAO	Syndicat National du Commerce de l'Antiquité et de l'Occasion
SNCAR	Syndicat National des Courtiers d'Assurance et de Réassurances
SNCASE	Société Nationale de Construction Aéronautique du Sud-Est
SNCASO	Société Nationale de Construction Aérienne du Sud-Ouest
SNCB	Société Nationale des Chemins de Fer Belges = NMBS
SNCCI	Sindacato Nazionale Critici Cinematografici Italiani
SNCDC	Syndicat National des Commerçants Détaillants en Confiserie
SNCDS	Société Nouvelle Conserveries du Sénégal
SNCDV	Société Navale Chargeurs Delmas-Vieljeux
SNCE	Société Nouvelle des Conduits d'Eau (Morocco)
SNCEA	Syndicat National des Cadres d'Exploitations Agricoles (CGA)
SNCEOOA	Syndicat National des Cadres, Employés et Ouvriers des Organisations Agricoles (CGA)
SNCF	Sindacato Nazionale Commercianti di Francobolli

SNCF	Société Nationale des Chemins de Fer Français	**SNCTA**	Syndicat National des Contrôleurs du Trafic Aérien
SNCF	Syndicat National des Chirurgiens Français	**SNCTN**	Syndicat National des Cadres et Techniciens du Notariat
SNCFA	Société Nationale des Chemins de Fer Algériens	**SNCTR**	Syndicat National du Commerce des Tubes et Raccords
SNCFS	Société Nationale des Chemins de Fer de Sénégal	**SNCV**	Société Nationale des Chemins de Fer Vicinaux (Belgium)
SNCFT	Société Nationale des Chemins de Fer Tunisiens	**SNCV**	Société Nouvelle de Confiserie de Vridi (Benin)
SNCGÉPVO	Syndicat National du Commerce en Gros des Équipements, Pièces pour Véhicules et Outillages	**SNCZ**	Société Nationale des Chemins de Fer Zaïrois
SNCGO	Syndicat National du Commerce des Graines Oléagineuses	**SND**	Sisters of Notre Dame
		SND	Stronnictwo Narodowo-Demokratyczne (Poland) = NDP
SNCH	Syndical National des Cadres Hospitaliers	**SND**	Syndicat National du Décolletage
SNCI	Société Nationale de Crédit à l'Industrie (Belgium) = NMKN	**SNDA**	Scottish National Dictionary Association
SNCI	Société Nationale de Crédit et d'Investissement (Luxembourg)	**SNDA**	Sunday Newspaper Distributing Association
SNCIC	Société Nouvelle du Commerce et de l'Industrie du Caméroun	**SNDA**	Syndicat National des Dénaturateurs d'Alcool
SNCIMIP	Syndicat National des Constructeurs et Installateurs de Matériels Industriels et Plastiques	**SNDdeN**	Soeurs de Notre-Dame de Namur
		SNDE	Société Nationale de Distribution d'Eau (Congo)
SNCLF	Société de Neuro-Chirurgie de Langue Française	**SNDE**	Society for Nonlinear Dynamics and Econometrics
SNCM	Syndicat National des Chaînes Mécaniques	**SNDE**	Syndicat National du Découpage et de l'Emboutissage
SNCMF	Syndicat Nationale des Courtiers Maritimes de France	**SNDF**	Syndicat National des Déshydrateurs de France
SNCP	Société Nigérienne de Collecte des Cuirs et Peaux	**SNDH**	Slovenské Národné Demokratické Hnutie (Slovakia) = SNDM
SNCP	Syndicat National des Conseils en Publicité	**SNDM**	Sestri Sluzebnici Neporocnoi Divi Marii = LCM
SNCP	Syndicat National du Commerce du Porc	**SNDM**	Slovak National Democratic Movement = SNDH
SNCPS	Syndicat National du Commerce des Produits Sidérurgiques	**SNDM**	Société Nouvelle des Distilleries de Mamers
SNČR	Sindikát Novináru České Republiky	**SNDM**	Syndicat National des Directeurs de Mutualité
SNCRP	Syndicat National des Conseils en Relations Publiques	**SNDOPA**	Syndicat National des Directeurs d'Organismes Professionnels Agricoles
SNCS	Syndicat National des Fabricants de Café Soluble	**SNDSDCA**	Syndicat National des Directeurs et Sous-Directeurs de Coopératives Agricoles
SNCS-FEN	Syndicat National des Chercheurs Scientifiques (FEN)		
SNCST	Saudi National Centre for Science and Technology (Saudi Arabia)	**SNE**	Sociedad Nuclear Española
		SNÉ	Société Nationale d'Énergie (Congo)
SNCT	Société Nationale Centrafricaine de Travaux et de Transport	**SNE**	Société Nationale des Eaux (Burkina Faso)

SNÉ	Syndicat National de l'Édition
SNE	Syndicat National des Emballeurs
SNE	Syndicat National des Enseignants (Luxembourg)
SNEA	Société Nationale d'Encouragement à l'Agriculture
SNEA	Société Nationale d'Exploitation Agricole (Central Africa)
SNEA	Société Nationale Elf Aquitaine
SNÉALC	Syndicat National d'Élevage et d'Amélioration du Lapin de Chair
SNEB	Société Nationale d'Exploitation des Bois (Congo)
SNEC	Société Nationale des Eaux du Cameroun
SNÉC	Syndicat National de l'Équipement de la Cuisine
SNEC	Syndicat National de l'Exploitation d'Équipments Thermiques et de Génie Climatique
SNÉCMA	Société Nationale d'Étude et de Construction et Moteurs d'Avion
SNECTI	Syndicat National des Entrepreneurs et Constructeurs en Thermique Industrielle
SNED	Sindacato Nazionale Estesisti Diplomati
SNÉD	Société Nationale d'Études et de Développement (Mali)
SNED	Syndicat National des Négociants Embouteilleurs et Distributeurs en Vins et Spiritueux de France
SNÉDIVU	Syndicat National des Éditeurs des Cartes Postales Vues
SNEÉT	Société Nationale des Eaux et d'Électricité du Togo
SNEF	Syndicat National de l'Estampage et de la Forge
SNEFAC	Société Nouvelle d'Entreprises Franco-Africaines de Constructions (Congo)
SNEFCA	Syndicat National des Entreprises du Froid et du Conditionnement de l'Air
SNEFP	Syndicat National des Experts Forestiers Patentes
SNÉGMA	Société Nationale d'Étude et de Construction Moteurs d'Aviation
SNÉI	Société Nouvelle d'Éditions Industrielles
SNEIL	Secretariat of the Nordic Energy Information Libraries
SNEK	Union of People's Unity of Kazakhstan
SNÉL	Société Nationale d'Électricité (Zaïre)
SNEL	Société Nouvelle des Entreprises Lacombe (Mauritania)
SNELPIF	Sindacato Nazionale Esperti Laureati Propagandisti Industrie Farinaceutiche
SNEMA	Société Nationale des Eaux Minérales Algériennes
SNEN	Société Nouvelle des Entreprises Navalon (Niger)
SNEP	Société Nationale des Entreprises de Presse
SNÉP	Syndicat National de l'Éducation Physique
SNEP	Syndicat National des Cadres de l'Enseignement Privé
SNÉPA	Syndicat National de l'Édition Phonographique et Audiovisuelle
SNÉPÉ	Société Nigérienne d'Étude pour la Production de l'Élevage
SNEPMA	Syndicat National de l'Enseignement Professionnel et Ménager Agricole
SNEPP	Syndicat National des Extrudeurs de Profilés Plastiques
SNEPT	Syndicat National des Exploitants de la Publicité Transport
SNERDI	Shanghai Nuclear Engineering Research and Design Institute
SNÉRI	Société Nationale d'Études de Gestion de Réalisations et d'Exploitations Industrielles (Algeria)
SNES	Syndicat National de l'Enseignement Secondaire
SNES	Syndicat National des Enseignements de Second Degré
SNESup	Syndicat National de l'Enseignement Supérieur
SNET	Syndicat National de l'Enseignement Technique
SNETAP	Syndicat National de l'Enseignement Technique Agricole Public
SNETI	Syndicat National des Entrepreneurs de Travaux Immergés
SNETP	Syndical National des Enseignements Techniques et Professionelles
SNF	Svenska Naturskyddsföreningen
SNF	Svenska Numismatiska Föreningen
SNF	Syndicat National des Industries et Commerces de la Récupération de la Ferraille
SNFA	Syndicat National de la Construction des Fenêtres, Façades et Activités

SNFBM	Syndicat National des Fabricants de Boîtes, Emballages et Bouchages Métalliques		**SNG**	Syndicat National des Graphistes
			SNGC	Stichting Nederlands Graancentrum
SNFBTE	Scottish National Federation of Building Trades Employers		**SNGÉ**	Société Nationale Gabonaise d'Études
			SNGM	Servicio Nacional de Geologia y Mineria (Ecuador)
SNFC	Société Nationale des Chemins de Fer Français		**SNGP**	Syndicat National des Graphistes Publicitaires
SNFC	Syndicat National des Fabricants de Confitures		**SNGP**	Syndicat National des Grossistes Distributeurs en Produits de Parfumerie et Accessoires de Toilette
SNFCCM	Syndicat National des Fabricants de Crèmes et Conserves de Marrons		**SNGTN**	Société Nationale des Grand Travaux du Niger
SNFÉPPA	Syndicat National des Fabricants d'Étires et de Profilés Pleins en Acier		**SNH**	Scottish Natural Heritage
SNFÉV	Syndicat Français des Éleveurs de Visons		**SNH**	Société Nationale de l'Habitat (Central Africa)
SNFFS	Syndicat National des Fabricants de Fruits au Sirop		**SNH**	Société Nationale des Hydrocarbures (Cameroon)
SNFGE	Société Nationale Français de Gastro-Entérologie		**SNHBM**	Société Nationale des Habitations à Bon Marché (Belgium)
SNFL	Syndicat National des Fabricants de Liqueurs		**SNHF**	Slovak National Heritage Foundation = OSNN
SNFM	Section Nationale des Fermiers et des Métayers		**SNHF**	Société Nationale d'Horticulture de France
SNFPA	Syndicat National des Fabricants de Produits Abrasifs		**SNHMV**	Syndicat National des Hybrideurs et Métisseurs Viticoles
SNFPAS	Syndicat National des Fabricants de Produits Aromatiques de Synthèse		**SNHTPC**	Scottish National Housing and Town Planning Council
SNFQ	Syndicat National des Fabricants de Quincaillerie		**SNI**	Serviço Nacional de Informações (Brazil)
SNFR	Syndicat National des Fabricants de Ressorts		**SNI**	Sistema Nacional de Investigadores (Mexico)
SNFS	Syndicat National des Fabricants de Sirops		**SNI**	Sociedad Nacional de Industrias (Peru)
SNFS	Syndicat National des Fabricants de Sucre de France		**SNI**	Società Numismatica Italiana
			SNI	Société Nationale d'Investissement (Belgium) = NIM
SNFTRP	Syndicat National des Fabricants de Tuyaux et Raccords en Polyoléfines		**SNI**	Société Nationale d'Investissement du Caméroun
SNFU	National Farmers Union of Scotland		**SNI**	Société Nationale d'Investissement et Fonds Annexes (Togo)
SNFV	Syndicat National des Fabricants de Vinaigres		**SNI**	Société Nationale d'Investissements (Madagascar, Morocco, Tunisia)
SNG	Schweizerische Naturforschende Gesellschaft = SHSN		**SNI**	Studieselskapet for Norsk Industri
SNG	Schweizerische Neurologische Gesellschaft		**SNI**	Syndicat National des Indepéndants
SNG	Schweizerische Numismatische Gesellschaft = SSN		**SNI**	Syndicat National des Instituteurs et Institutrices (France, French Guiana)
SNG	Scottish Neuroscience Group		**SNIA**	Servicio Nacional de Investigaciones Agropecuárias (Panama)
SNG	Senckenbergische Naturforschende Gesellschaft		**SNIA**	Sindacato Nazionale Istruzione Artistica
SNG	Sodruzhestvo Nezavissimikh Gosudarstv = CIS, CIE, GUS, WNP		**SNIA**	Société Nationale Industrielle Aérospatiale

SNIA	Syndicat National des Industriels de l'Alimentation Animale
SNIACE	Sociedad Nacional Industrias Aplicaciones Celulosa Española
SNIB	Syndicat National des Instituts de Beauté
SNIC	Singapore National Institute of Chemistry
SNIC	Société Nationale des Industries Chimiques (Algeria)
SNICL	Syndicat National de l'Industrie et du Commerce des Lubrifiants
SNID	Sindacato Nazionale Ingegneri Docenti
SNIDA	Syndicat National des Installateurs d'Antennes
SNIE	Sindacato Nazionale Insegnanti Elementari
SNIÉ	Syndicat National des Industries de l'Émail
SNIECV	Syndicat National des Industries Extractives pour la Céramique et la Verrerie
SNIEL	Syndicat National des Importateurs et Exportateurs de Livres
SNIÉM	Syndicat National des Importateurs d'Équipement Ménager
SNiF	Stichting Nederlandse Uienfederatie
SNIF	Syndicat National des Industriels Forains
SNIFI	Société Nouvelle d'Isolation Thermique, Frigorifique et d'Insonorisation (Ivory Coast)
SNII	Serikat Nelajan Islam Indonesia
SNIL	Suomen Neuvottelevien Insinöörien Liitto
SNILPI	Sindacato Nazionale Ingegneri Liberi Professionisti Italiani
SNIM	Servicio Nacional de Informacion de Mercados (Mexico)
SNIM-SEM	Société Nationale Industrielle et Minière et Société d'Économie Mixte (Mauritania)
SNIMA	Service de Normalisation Industrielle Marocaine
SNIMaBI	Syndicat National des Importateurs de Matériels de Bureau et d'Informatique
SNIO	Servicio Nacional de Instrumentación Oceanográfica (Mexico)
SNIP	Syndicat National de l'Industrie Pharmaceutique
SNIP	Syndicat National Interprofessionnel de Porc

SNIPEF	Scottish and Northern Ireland Plumbing Employers Federation
SNIPOT	Société Nationale Interprofessionnelle de la Pomme de Terre
SNIPV	Syndicat National de l'Industrie Pharmaceutique Vétérinaire
SNIR	Fédération Française des Syndicats Nationaux des Industries Radioélectriques et Électroniques
SNIRA	Syndicat National des Industries de Récupérations Animales
SNIRI	Snickerifabrikernas Riksförbund
SNIV	Syndicat National des Industriels de la Viande
SNIVTF	Syndicat National des Importateurs par Voies Terrestres et Fluviales
SNJ	Stranka Narodne Jednakost (Montenegro) = PNE
SNJ	Syndicat National des Journalistes
SNJA	Shahi Nepal Jangdi Adda
SNKO	Svaz Německých Kulturních Organizací (Czech Republic) = UGCA
SNL	Serviço Nacional de Lepra (Brazil)
SNL	Société des Naturalistes Luxembourgeois
SNLA	Scottish National Liberation Army
SNLB	Société Nationale des Industries des Lièges et du Bois (Algeria)
SNLF	Sveriges Nykterhetsuäens Landsförbund
SNLF	Syndicat National du Laminage à Froid du Feuillard d'Acier
SNLS	Swaziland National Library Service
SNLVLD	Syndicat National des Loueurs de Voitures "Longue Durée'"
SNM	Seychelles National Movement
SNM	Sindacato Nazionale Medici
SNM	Sociedad Nacional de Mineria (Chile)
SNM	Société Nationale de Musique
SNM	Society of Nuclear Medicine (China)
SNM	Somali National Movement
SNM	Stichting Natuur en Milieu
SNMA	Scottish Net Manufacturers' Association
SNMA	Servicios Nacionales de Meteorologia y Aerofotografica (Peru)
SNMAC	Société Nouvelle Malienne Cinématographique
SNMAC	Standing Nursing and Midwifery Advisory Committee (NHS)

SNMC	Société Nationale des Matériaux de Construction (Algeria, Morocco)
SNMETAL	Société Nationale de Constructions Métalliques (Algeria)
SNMF-SMSN	Syndicat National des Médecins Français Spécialistes des Maladies du Système Nerveux
SNMG	Syndicat National de la Mécanique Générale
SNMH	Servicio Nacional de Meteorologia e Hidrologia (Ecuador)
SNMI	Syndicat National de la Mécanique Industrielle d'Usinage et de Constructions Spéciales
SNMM	Syndicat National des Constructeurs de Menuiserie, Murs-Rideaux et Cloisons Métalliques
SNMM	Syndicat National du Mobilier Métallique
SNMOF	Syndicat National des Médecins Ostéothérapeutes Français
SNMP	Syndicat National du Moulage et de la Transformation des Feuilles et Films Plastiques
SNMRMA	Syndicat National des Marchands Réparateurs de Machines Agricoles
SNMV	Sindicato Nacional dos Médicos Veterinários (Portugal)
SNN	Syndicat National des Notaires
SNO	Scottish National Orchestra
SNO	Société Navale de l'Ouest
SNO	Srpska Narodna Obnova (Serbia) = SNR
SNOAT	Société Nouvelle d'Ouvrages d'Art et Travaux (Ivory Coast)
SNOF	Société National d'Oléiculture de France
SNöFO	Sveriges Snöfordonleverantörer
SNOOF	Syndicat National des Opticiens Optométristes de France
SNOP	Secrétariat National de l'Opinion Publique
SNP	Samnordisk Planteforedling
SNP	Scottish National Party
SNP	Serbian National Party (Croatia) = SNS
SNP	Servicio Nacional de Pesca (Argentina)
SNP	Sindicato Nacional de Paisanos (Paraguay)
SNP	Slovak National Party = SNS
SNP	Slovenian National Party = SNS
SNP	Sociedad Nacional de Pesqueria (Peru)
SNP	Society for Natural Philosophy (U.S.A.)
SNP-IVFM	Syndicat National des Professeurs des Instituts Universitaires de Formation des Maîtres
SNPA	Scottish Newspaper Proprietors Association
SNPA	Serviço Nacional de Pesquisas Agrónomicas
SNPA	Société National des Pétroles d'Aquitaine
SNPa	Syndicat National de la Parfumerie (Belgium)
SNPA	Syndicat National des Plastiques Alvéolaires
SNPA&ER	Service National de la Production Agricole et de l'Ensignement Rurale (Haiti)
SNPAA	Syndicat National des Producteurs d'Alcool Agricole
SNPBR	Section National des Preneurs de Baux Ruraux
SNPC	Secretaria Nacional de Planificación y Coordinación (Bolivia)
SNPCRT	Syndicat National de la Publicité Cinématographique, Radiophonique et Télévisée
SNPD	Syndicat National de la Publicité Directe
SNPDEN	Syndicat National des Personnels de Direction de l'Education Nationale
SNPDES	Syndicat National des Personnels de Direction de l'Enseignement Secondaire
SNPE	Société Nationale des Poudres et Explosifs
SNPÉ	Syndicat National des Triturateurs-Conditionneurs de Poivres et Épices
SNPÉN	Syndicat National des Professeurs des Écoles Normales d'Instituteurs
SNPEP	Syndicat National Professionnel des Engrais Phosphates
SNPETD	Syndicat National Professionnel des Entrepreneurs de Travaux de Drainage
SNPF	Syndicat National des Pédiatres Français
SNPF	Syndicat National des Producteurs de Fraisiers
SNPH	Syndicat National des Psychiatres des Hôpitaux
SNPI	Servicio Nacional de Productividad Industrial (Spain)

SNPI	Syndicat National des Emballages Commerciaux et Industriels		**SNRA**	Société Nigérienne de Réparations Automobiles
SNPIC	Syndicat National des Professionnels de l'Information et de la Communication des Entreprises et Collectivités		**SNRC**	Israel Atomic Energy Commission
			SNRMP	Syndicat National des Régérateurs de Matières Plastiques
SNPL	Syndicat National des Pilots de Ligne		**SNRSS**	Societatea Nationalà Românà pentru Stiinta Solului
SNPLV	Syndicat National de la Promotion et de la Publicité sur le Lieu de Vente		**SNRTMS**	Syndicat National des Revêtements et Traitements des Métaux et Substrats
SNPMI	Syndicat National des Producteurs de Mortiers Industriels		**SNS**	Samarbetsnämnden för Nordisk Skogsforskning
SNPMT	Syndicat National Professionnel des Médecins du Travail		**SNS**	Sindacato Nazionale Scrittori
SNPN	Servicio Nacional de Parques Nacionales (Argentina)		**SNS**	Slovenska Nacionalña Stranka (Slovenia) = SNP
SNPN	Société Nationale de Protection de la Nature et d'Acclimatation de France		**SNS**	Slovenská Národná Strana (Slovakia) = SNP
SNPNC	Syndicat National du Personnel Navigant Commercial		**SNS**	Société Nationale de Sidérurgie (Algeria)
SNPNH	Syndicat National des Producteurs de Nouveautés Horticoles		**SNS**	Srpska Narodna Stranka (Croatia) = SNP
SNPO	Society for Nonprofit Organizations (U.S.A.)		**SNS**	Studieförbundet Näringsliv och Samhälle
SNPOQ	Syndicat National des Producteurs d'Oeufs de Qualité		**SNSAF**	Syndicat National des Spécialistes Apicoles de France
SNPP	Société Nationale Publicité Presse		**SNSBI**	Society for Name Studies in Britain & Ireland (*ex* INS)
SNPP-PAMIAT	"Pamiat" – Soiuz za Natsionalno-Proportsionalnoe Predstavitelstvo		**SNSC**	Scottish National Ski Council
SNPPA	Syndicat National du Profilage des Produits Plats en Acier		**SNSEMPAC**	Société Nationale de Semouleries, Meuneries, Fabriques de Pâtes Alimentaires et Couscous (Algeria)
SNPPFOC	Syndicat National des Producteurs de Plantes de Fraisiers Officiellement Contrôlés		**SNSF**	Swiss National Science Foundation
SNPPT	Société Nationale de la Petite Propriété Terrienne (Belgium)		**SNSH**	Syndicat National des Succursalistes de l'Habillement
SNPQR	Syndicat National de la Presse Quotidienne Régionale		**SNSM**	Sindacato Nazionale Scuola Media
			SNSO	Syndicat National des Entreprises du Second Oeuvre du Bâtiment
SNPR	Stichting der Nederlandse Prester Religieuzen		**SNSO-GATRA**	Société Nouvelle Société Gabonaise de Travaux
SNPT	Société Nationale de Promotion Touristique (Senegal)		**SNSP**	Società Napoletana di Storia Patria
SNPTVT	Syndicat National des Producteurs et Transformateurs de Verre Textile		**SNSPRCS**	Scottish National Sweet Pea, Rose and Carnation Society
SNPU	Social National Party of Ukraine		**SNSRC**	Swedish Natural Science Research Council
SNPVAC	Sindicato Nacional de Pessoal de Vôo da Aviação Civil			
SNR	Serbian National Renewal = SNO		**SNSS**	School Natural Science Society
SNR	Societatea Numismatica Românà		**SNST**	Société Nationale pour la Vente des Scories Thomas
SNR	Society for Nautical Research			
SNRA	Scottish National Rifle Association		**SNT**	Secretaria Nacional de Transportes (Brazil)
SNRA	Servicio Nacional de Reforma Agraria (Bolivia)		**SNT**	Sindacato Nazionale Tabacchine

SNT	Société Nationale des Transports (Tunisia)
SNT	Société Navale Transafricaine (Ivory Coast)
SNTA	Société Nationale des Tabacs et Allumettes (Algeria)
SNTA	Société Nigérienne de Transport Automobile
SNTA	Syndicat National des Transporteurs Aériens
SNTASCRM	Sindicato Nacional de Trabajadores de Autotransportes, Similares y Conexos de la Republica Mexicana
SNTC	Sindicato Nacional de Transportes y Comunicaciones
SNTE	Sindicato Nacional de Trabajadores de la Educación (Mexico)
SNTF	Société Nationale des Transports Ferroviaires (Algeria)
SNTF	Société Nigérienne des Transports Fluviaux et Maritimes
SNTF	Syndicat National des Téléphériques et Téléskis de France
SNTFM	Société Nigérienne des Transportes Fluviaux et Maritimes
SNTI	Société Nationale de Tomates Industrielles (Senegal)
SNTITPCH	Stowarzyszenie Naukowo-Techniczne Inżynierów i Techników Przemysłu Chemicznego
SNTITPP	Stowarzyszenie Naukowo-Techniczne Inżynierów i Techników Przemysłu Papierniczego
SNTITR	Stowarzyszenie Naukowo-Techniczne Inzynierów i Techników Rolnictwa
SNTL	Statui Nakladatelstvi Technicke Literatury
SNTM-CNAN	Société Nationale des Transports Maritimes et Compagnie Nationale Algérienne de Navigation
SNTM-HYPROC	Société Nationale des Transports Maritimes des Hydrocarbures et des Produits Chimiques
SNTM-MSRM	Sindicato Nacional de Trabajadores Mineros, Metalúrgicos y Similares de la República Mexicana
SNTN	Société Nationale des Transports Nigériens
SNTP	Société Nationale de Travaux Publics
SNTP	Société Nationale de Travaux Publics et Particuliers (Senegal)
SNTPC	Scottish National Town Planning Council
SNTR	Société Nationale des Transports Routiers (Algeria, Togo)
SNTRI	Société Nationale de Transport Rural et Interurbain (Tunisia)
SNTRPCVR	Syndicat National des Fabricants de Tubes et Raccords en Polychlorure de Vinyle Rigide
SNTS	Det Store Nordske Telegraf-Selskab
SNTS	Société Nationale de Transfusion Sanguine
SNTS	Studiorum Novi Testamenti Societas
SNTU	Société Nigérienne de Transport Urbain
SNTUC	Singapore National Trade Union Congress
SNTV	Société Nationale pour le Transport des Voyageurs (Algeria)
SNTZ	Syndicat National des Travailleurs Zaïrois
SNU	Shandong Normal University
SNU	Spiritualists National Union
SNUG	Scottish Network Users' Group
SNV	Schweizerische Normen-Vereinigung
SNV	Schweizerische Notarenverband = FSN
SNVBA	Scottish National Vehicle Builders Association
SNVF	Syndicat National des Vétérinaires Français
SNVI	Société Entreprise Nationale de Véhicules Industriels (Algeria)
SNVPF	Syndicat National des Vétérinaires Praticiens Français
SNVR	Stichting Nederlandse Vrouwelijke Religieuzen
SNVV	Stichting voor de Nederlandse Vlasteelt en Vlasbewerking
SNWM	Scottish National War Memorial
SO-ACT	Society of Action for Children in Tower Blocks
SOA	Scottish Orienteering Association
SoA	Society of Authors
SOA	State Oceanic Administration (China)
SOAA	Solus Outdoor Advertising Association
SOACO	Société Ouest-Africaine de Cosmétique (Ivory Coast)
SOADIP	Société Africaine de Diffusion et de Promotion (Senegal)
SOAE	State Organization for Administration and Employment Affairs (Iran)

SOAEM	Société Ouest-Africaine d'Entreprises Maritimes (Cameroon, Congo, Gabon, Ivory Coast, Mauritania, Senegal)
SOAH	Syndicat de l'Outillage Agricole et Horticole
SOAI	Service des Organisations Aeronautiques Internationales
SOAL	Société Ouest-Africaine de Linguistique = SLAO, WALS
SOAM	Société d'Oxygène et d'Acetylène de Madagascar
SOAM	Société Ouest Africaine de Malherbologie = WAWSS
SOAP	Société Ouest-Africaine de Presse (Senegal)
SOAP	Society for Obstetric Anesthesia and Perinatology (U.S.A.)
SOAS	School of Oriental and African Studies
SOB	Schweizerische Organisation der Berufstanzlehrer
SOB	Sociedade de Olericultura do Brasil
SOBAB	Société Béninoise d'Automobile et de Divers
SOBAB	Société des Bois D'Abngourou (Ivory Coast)
SOBAMAD	Société Bananière de Madagascar
SOBCOT	Société Belge de Chirurgie Orthopédique et de Traumatologie
SOBECOV	Société de Stockage et de Commercialisation des Produits Vivriers (Burundi)
SOBEDI	Société Béninoise pour le Développement Industriel
SOBEFACO	Société Béninoise de Fabrication de Confiserie
SOBEGI	Société Béninoise des Gaz Industriels
SOBELAIR	Société Belge de Transports par Air
SOBEMAC	Société Béninoise des Matériaux de Construction
SOBÉMAP	Société Belge d'Économie et de Mathématique Appliquée
SOBEPALH	Société Béninoise de Palmier à Huile
SOBEPAR	Société Béninoise de Parfumerie
SOBEPEC	Société Béninoise de Peinteurs et Colorants
SOBE-PROM	Société Béninoise des Produits de la Mer
SOBER	Sociedade Brasileira de Economistas Rurais
SOBESEL	Société Béninoise du Sel
SOBETEX	Société Béninoise des Textiles
SOBE-VECO	Société Ophthalmologique Belge des Verres de Contact
SOBHD	Scottish Official Board of Highland Dancing
SOBIPO	Société Bretonne Interprofessionnelle de la Pomme de Terre
SOBIT	Société Belge des Ingénieurs Techniciens
SoBLA	Sociedad de Biofísicos Latinoamericanos
SOBOA	Société des Brasseries de l'Ouest Africain (Senegal)
SOBOCA	Société des Bois du Sud-Ouest Caméroun
SOBOCI	Société des Boissons Hygiéniques de la Côte d'Ivoire
SOBOL-COM	Sociedad Boliviana de Computacion
SOBOMA	Société des Boissons de Mauritanie
SOBOMBA	Société des Bois de la Manzan (Ivory Coast)
SOBRAGA	Société des Brasseries du Gabon
SOBRAMIL	Sociedade Brasileira de Mineração Limitada
SOBS	Society of Bookbinders
SOC	Scottish Ornithologists Club
SOC	Sociedad Odontológica de Concepción (Chile)
SOC	Solidaritat d'Obrers Catalans
SOC	Specialised Oceanographic Centre
SOC	Sveriges Oljeväxtodlares Centralförening
SOCA	Société des Compteurs Africains (Ivory Coast)
SOCA	Société Olympic Centrafricaine pour le Diamant et Métaux Précieux
SOCA	Submarine Old Comrades Association
SOCA-FRUITS	Société Camérounaise de Conserveries de Fruits
SOCA-METAL	Société Camérounaise de Constructions Métalliques
SOCA-MEXIM	Société Camérounaise d'Exportation et d'Importation
SOCA-PECHE	Société Africaine d'Armement et de Pêche (Ivory Coast)
SOCA-PHARM	Société Camérounaise Pharmaceutique
SOCA-TRACOP	Société Camérounaise de Transactions Commerciales de Produits

SOCAB	Société Agricole du Bandama (Ivory Coast)
SOCABAIL	Société Camérounaise de Bois
SOCABOL	Société Camérounaise de Boissons et Liqueurs
SOCABU	Société d'Assurances du Burundi
SOCABU	Société de Caoutchouc Butyl
SOCACAO	Société Camérounaise de Cacao
SOCACI	Société Commerciale et Agricole de la Côte d'Ivoire
SOCACIG	Société Centraficaine de Cigarettes
SOCACOT	Société Camérounaise de Commerce et de Transport
SOCADA	Société Camérounaise pour le Développement de l'Automobile
SOCADA	Société Centrafricaine de Développement Agricole
SOCADEM	Société Camérounaise d'Emballages Métalliques
SOCADÉP	Société Camérounaise d'Édition et de Publicité
SOCADÉP	Société Camérounaise de Diffusion d'Énergie Portable
SOCADI	Société Centrafricaine de Diamant Industriel
SOCADIA	Société Camérounaise de Diffusion d'Automobiles
SOCADIS	Société Camérounaise de Distribution
SOCAEM	Société Ouest Africaine d'Entreprises Maritimes
SOCAF	Société Commerciale Africaine (Ivory Coast)
SOCAFER	Société Camérounaise de Plomberie et de Ferronnerie
SOCAFI	Société Camérounaise Forestière et Industrielle
SOCAFRIC	Société Camérounaise de Froid et Représentation Industrielle et Commerciale
SOCAGI	Société Centrafricaine des Gaz Industriels
SOCAHIT	Société Camérounaise Hôtelière, Immobilière et Touristique
SOCAL	Société de Conserveries Alimentaires (Burkina Faso)
SOCAL	Standard Oil Company of California (U.S.A.)
SOCALTRA	Société Alsacienne d'Études et Travaux
SOCAM	Société Camérounaise de Menuiserie
SOCAM	Société Commerciale Africaine d'Importation (Ivory Coast)
SOCAM	Société des Conserves Alimentaires du Mali
SOCAM-GEPAR	Société Camérounaise de Gestion et de Participation
SOCAMAC	Société Camérounaise de Manutention et d'Acornage
SOCAMBO	Société Camérounaise Industrielle du Bois
SOCAMCO	Société Camérounaise de Conserveries
SOCAMCY	Société Camérounaise de Cycles
SOCAME	Société Camérounaise des Engrais
SOCAMER	Société Camérounaise de Travaux de Mer
SOCANA	Société Camérounaise de Navigation
SOCANT	Society of Antiquaries of London
SOCAO	Société des Carrières de l'Ouest (Burkina Faso)
SOCAP	Société Africaine de Promotion (Ivory Coast)
SOCAP	Société Camérounaise le Distribution et de Vente des Produits Pétroliers
SOCAP	Society of Consumer Affairs Professionals in Business
SOCAPALM	Société Camérounaise des Palmeraies
SOCAPÉ	Société Camérounaise de Presse et d'Éditions
SOCAPOL	Société Camérounaise de Polyurétane
SOCAPRA	Société de Production Animales (Cameroon)
SOCAPRAL	Société Gabonaise de Produits Alimentaires
SOCAPROD	Société Camérounaise de Production et de Diffusion de Boissons Hygiéniques
SOCAPS	Société Camérounaise de Produits Shell
SOCAR	Société Caméroun d'Assurances et de Réassurances
SOCAREC	Société Africaine de Rectification
SOCAREC	Société de Carrelage du Centre (Ivory Coast)
SOCARIC	Société Camérounaise de Représention Industrielle et Commerciale
SOCARSEL	Société Camérounaise de Raffinage de Sel
SOCARTO	Société Camérounaise de Cartonnages de Fournitures de Matériel Scolaire et Bureau
SOCAS	Société de Conserves Alimentaires du Sénégal
SOCASEP	Société Camérounaise de Sepultures et Transports Spéciaux

SOCATCI	Société Caoutchoucs de Côte d'Ivoire
SOCATEX	Société Camérounaise de Textiles
SOCATI	Société Centrafricaine de Telecommunications Internationales
SOCATRAF	Société Centrafricaine de Transports Fluviaux
SOCATRAL	Société Camérounaise de Transformation de l'Aluminium
SOCAVER	Société Camérounaise de Verrerie
SOCAVO	Société Camérounaise de Traitement de Vocanga
SOCBRO	Society of Chief Building Regulation Officers
SOCCA	Société Camérounaise de Crédit Automobile
SOCCDÉ	Société Commerciale Camérounaise pour le Développement de l'Économie
SOCCOM	Société Camérounaise de Construction Métallique
SOCÉA	Société Charentaise d'Équipements Aéronautiques
SOCÉCO	Société Camérounaise d'Études et de Constructions
SOCEF	Société de Construction et d'Exploitation d'Installations Frigorifiques en Côte d'Ivoire
SOCEFI	Société Centrafricaine d'Exploitation Forestières et Industrielle
SOCÉI	Société de Coordination d'Études et d'Ingéniérie (Cameroon)
SOCEN-TRACO	Société Centrafricaine de Commerce Général
SOCEPPAR	Sociedade Cerealista Exportadora de Produtos Paranaenses (Brazil)
SOCFI	Société d'Organisation de Congrès Français et Internationaux
SOCFI	Société d'Oto-Rhino-Laryngologie et de Chirurgie Cervico-Faciale des Pays Francophones
SOCGPA	Seed, Oil, Cake and General Produce Association
SOCHIM	Société Chimique et Industrielle Sénégalaise
SOCI-FRANCE	Société Immobilière Française (Central Africa)
SOCI-GABON	Société Commerciale et Industrielle au Gabon
SOCI-PECHE	Société Côte Ivoirienne de Pêche
SOCI-TRABAR	Société Commerciale et Industrielle des Transporteurs de Banjoun Réunis (Cameroon)
SOCI-TRACAM	Société Camérounaise Interprofessionelle pour la Fourniture des Traverses et de Bois Débites au Transcamerounais
SOCIA	Société pour l'Industrie Atomique
SOCIACI	Société Commerciale et Industrielle Africaine de Côte d'Ivoire
SOCIAGRI	Société Ivoirienne d'Expansion Agricole
SOCICA	Société Cinématographique Africaine
SOCICAB	Société Ivoirienne de Construction pour l'Aménagement de Buyo
SOCICO	Société Cimentière du Congo
SOCIDA	Société Commerciale et Industrielle Dakaroise (Senegal)
SOCIDA	Société Ivoirienne pour le Développement de l'Automobile
SOCIDIS	Société Ivoirienne d'Importation et de Distribution
SOCIDO	Société de Développement de la Région d'Odienné (Ivory Coast)
SOCIEX	Société Ivoirienne d'Import-Export
SOCIGA	Société de Cigarettes Gabonaise
SOCIM	Société Centrafricaine d'Investissements Immobiliers
SOCIM	Société de Constructions et l'Industries de la Mauritanie
SOCIM	Société des Ciments du Sud-Ouest (Ivory Coast)
SOCIMA	Société des Ciments du Mali
SOCIMAF	Société Commerciale et Immobilière de l'Afamba (Cameroon)
SOCIMEX	Société d'Importation et d'Exportation de l'Océan Indien (Madagascar)
SOCIPAR	Société Ivoirienne de Participation
SOCIPÉC	Société Ivoirienne de Participations Économiques
SOCIPRA	Société Industrielle de Peintures et Renouvellement (Ivory Coast)
SOCIPRA-GABON	Société Industrielle de Peinture et Ravalement (Gabon)
SOCITAF	Société Civile Immobilière pour l'Industrie Textile en Afrique (Ivory Coast)
SOCITAS	Société Ivoirienne de Textiles Artificiels et Synthétiques
SOCITOUR	Société Casamançaise d'Investissement Touristique (Senegal)
SOCIVER	Société Ivoirienne de Verrerie
SOCIVEX	Société Ivoirienne d'Exportation

SocInfo	CTI Centre for Sociology & the Policy Sciences
SOCO-FRACIM	Société Commerciale Franco-Africaine des Ciments
SOCO-FROID	Société Congolaise de Conservation et de Congélation
SOCO-MECAM	Société de Constructions Métalliques Camérounaises
SOCO-MÉTAL	Société de Construction Métallique (Mauritania)
SOCO-TRANS	Société Congolaise de Transports
SOCO-TRANS	Société Coopérative des Transporteurs de Grand-Bassam
SOCO-AGRO	Sociedad de Operaciones Agropecuárias (Chile)
SOCOBA	Société de Construction de Bâtiments (Gabon)
SOCOBIA	Société Commerciale de la Bia (Ivory Coast)
SOCOBLE	Société Coopérative des Producteurs de Blé
SOCOBO	Société Continentale de Bonneterie (Cameroon)
SOCOBOIS	Société Congolaise des Bois
SOCOCE	Société Commercial du Centre-Ouest (Ivory Coast)
SOCOCIM	Société Ouest Africaine des Ciments
SOCODE-BAS	Société Commerciale pour le Développement de la Basse-Sanaga
SOCODI	Société Congolaise de Disques
SOCODIM	Société Commerciale d'Importation (Benin, Niger)
SOCOFFA	Société Commerciale et Financière Franco-Africaine
SOCOFIDE	Société Congolaise de Financement du Développement
SOCOFIN	Société Commerciale de Produits Fins (Gabon)
SOCOFRA	Société Commerciale Français (Congo)
SOCOGA	Société Commerciale Gabonaise
SOCOGIF	Société de Constructions Giraudel Frères (Ivory Coast)
SOCOGIM	Société de Construction et de Gestion Immobilière de Mauritanie
SOCOL	Société de Construction d'Entreprises Générales (Belgium)
SOCOLOR	Sociedad Colombiana de Orquideologia
SOCOM-ÉLEC-IVOIRE	Société Commerciale de Matériel Électrique (Ivory Coast)
SOCOMA	Société des Conserves du Mali
SOCOMAB	Société Conglaise de Manutention des Bois au Port de Pointe-Noire
SOCOMAF	Société pour le Conditionnement de Maïs Français
SOCOMAR	Société Commerciale et Maritime (Senegal)
SOCOMAT	Société Camérounaise de Matériaux et de Travaux
SOCOMI	Société Commerciale de Mimongo (Gabon)
SOCOMID	Société de Caution Mutuelle des Industries Diverses
SOCOMINE	Société de Coopération Minière et Industrielle
SOCOMO	Société Commerciale Moderne (Senegal)
SOCONAR	Société Commerciale de Narsons (Benin)
SOCOPA	Société Co-opérative des Produits Agricoles (Zaïre)
SOCOPRÉ	Société Sénégalaise de Commercialisation des Produits de l'Élevage
SOCOPRISE	Société Africaine d'Entreprises Industrielles et Immobilières (Congo)
SOCORAM	Société de Constructions Radio-Électriques du Mali
SOCOSAC	Société Commerciale et Industrielle du Sac (Senegal)
SOCOTA	Société Commerciale de Transports Trans-Atlantiques Côte d'Ivoire
SOCOTEC	Société de Contrôle Technique (Cameroon, Gabon, Ivory Coast)
SOCOTEL	Société Mixte pour le Développment de la Technique de la Communication dans le Domaine des Télécommunications
SOCOTP	Société de Constructions et de Travaux Publics (Gabon,Senegal)
SOCPO	Society of Chief Personnel Officers in Local Government
SocPU	Socialist Party of Ukraine
SOCRPRO	Society of County and Regional Public Relations Officers
SOCS	Society of County Secretaries
SOCSA	Specialised Organic Chemicals Sector Association
SOCUDEF	Sociedad Cinetifica Cubana para el Desarrollo de la Familia
SOCUSAM	Société Sucrière du Caméroun

SOD	Samarskoe Obshchestvo Durakov
SODAB	Société pour le Développement de l'Aquaculture en Bretagne
SODAC	Société Dakaroise des Arts Graphiques
SODACAP	Société de Distribution d'Articles en Caoutchouc et Plastique (Ivory Coast)
SODACO	Société Daher et Cie (Ivory Coast)
SODACOM	Société Dakaroise de Construction Métallique (Senegal)
SODAFÉ	Société pour le Développement de l'Afrique Équatoriale
SODAGRI	Société de Développement Agricole et Industriel de Sénégal
SODAIF	Société des Décorateurs et Architectes d'Intérieurs Français
SODAK	Société Dakaroise de Négoce (Senegal)
SODAP-CI	Société d'Application des Synthèses Techniques et Commerciales en Côte d'Ivoire
SODARÉP	Société Dakaroise de Réprésentation (Senegal)
SODATRA	Société Dakaroise de Transit (Senegal)
SODÉ-CINAF	Société d'Études et Promotion de la Cinéma Afrique
SODÉ-COTON	Société de Développement du Coton (Cameroon)
SODÉ-FITEX	Société de Développement des Fibres Textiles (Senegal)
SODE-GESCA	Société de Gestion de Services Communs du Groupe Descours et Cabaud
SODÉ-NICOB	Société de Développement Regional de la Vallée du Niari et de Jacob (Congo)
SODEA	Société de Développement Agricole (Morocco)
SODÉAM	Société de le Développement de l'Électricité en Afrique et à Madagascar
SODÉC	Société de Décorticage (Senegal)
SODÉCAO	Société pour le Développement de Cacao (Cameroon)
SODECI	Société de Distribution d'Eau de la Côte d'Ivoire
SODECO	Sakhalin Oil Development Corporation (Japan)
SODECO	Société Dakaroise d'Entreprises et de Construction (Senegal)
SODÉCO	Société pour le Développement du Commerce (Benin)
SODÉFEL	Société pour le Développement de la Production des Fruits et Légumes (Ivory Coast)
SODÉFOR	Société pour le Développement des Plantations Forestières (Ivory Coast)
SODÉL	Société pour Développement des Applications de l'Électricité
SODELAC	Société pour le Développement de la Région du Lac (Chad)
SODÉLÉC	Société d'Études de l'Économie de Consummation
SODÉMI	Société pour le Développement Minier de la Côte d'Ivoire
SODÉ-NKAM	Société de Développement du Perimètre de Mise en Valeur Agricole Yambassi-Bafang (Cameroon)
SODEP	Sosyal Demokrasi Partisi (Turkey)
SODÉPA	Société de Développement et d'Exploitation des Productions Animales (Cameroon)
SODÉPAC	Société de Développement de la Pêche Artisanale des Comores
SODÉPALM	Société d'État pour le Développement du Palmier à Huile (Ivory Coast)
SODÉPRA	Société pour le Développement des Productions Animales (Ivory Coast)
SODÉPRIC	Société de Développement de Promotion Immobilière Industrielle Commerciale et Financière de Caméroun
SODÉRA	Société de Développement des Ressources Animales (Benin)
SODÉRAG	Société de Développement Regional Antilles-Guyane
SODÉRIM	Société Développement de la Riziculture dans la Plaine des Mbo (Cameroon)
SODÉRN	Société Anonyme d'Études et Réalisations Nucléaires
SODÉ-SUCRE	Société pour le Développement des Plantations de Cannes a Sucre, l'Industrialisation et la Commercialisation du Sucre (Ivory Coast)
SODÉTAM	Société pour le Développement des Voyages et du Tourisme en Afrique et à Madagascar
SODÉTEG	Société d'Études Techniques et d'Entreprises Générales
SODÉTO	Société des Détergents du Togo
SODÉTO	Société Sénégalaise de Développement Touristique
SODÉTRA	Société de Débardage et de Transport (Ivory Coast)

SODÉTRAF	Société pour le Développement du Transport Aérien en Afrique
SODÉTRAM	Société d'Études pour Réalisations en Outre-Mer
SODÉVA	Société de Développement et de Vulgarisation Agricole (Senegal)
SODEX	Société d'Exploitation (Gabon)
SODEXAFRIC	Société d'Exploitation de Magasins en Centrafrique
SODEXPORT	Association Française pour la Diffusion du Livre Scientifique, Technique et Médical
SODEXPAD	Société d'Exploitation, d'Expérimentation et de Promotion des Produits Agricoles et Derivés (Burkina Faso)
SODÉZONN	Société de Développement de la Zone Njock-Nkoué (Cameroon)
SODFEMA	Société de Crédit pour le Développement de la Martinique
SODIACAM	Société de Distribution Alimentaire du Caméroun
SODIAM	Société Centrafricaine du Diamant
SODIAN	Sociedad para el Desarrollo Industrial de Andalucia
SODIAR	Sociedad para el Desarrollo Industrial de Aragon
SODIC	Société de Développement Ivoirien de la Construction (Ivory Coast)
SODIC	Société pour la Conversion et le Développement Industriels
SODICAL	Sociedad para el Desarrollo Industrial de Castilla y Leon
SODICAMANN	Sociedad para el Desarrollo Industrial de Castilla-La Mancha
SODICAN	Sociedad para el Desarrollo Industrial de las Islas Canarias
SODIDA	Société de Gestion du Domaine Industriel de Dakar (Senegal)
SODIEX	Sociedad para el Desarrollo Industrial de Extremadura
SODIGA	Sociedad para el Desarrollo Industrial de Galicia
SODIKA	Société de Gestion du Domaine Industriel de Kaolack (Senegal)
SODIM-TP	Société de Distribution de Matériel de Travaux Publics (Gabon)
SODIMA	Société de Diffusion des Marques
SODIMA	Société de Distribution de Matériel Automobile et Technique (Senegal)
SODIMAF	Société de Distribution des Grandes Marques pour l'Afrique (Ivory Coast)
SODIMIZA	Société de Développement Industriel et Minier de Système
SODIMPEX	Société Commerciale d'Import-Export (Ivory Coast)
SODIP	Société pour la Diffusion de la Presse (Belgium)
SODIPHAC	Société de Diffusion Pharmaceutique en Afrique Centrale
SODIRÉP	Société de Diffusion et de Répresentation (Ivory Coast)
SODIS	Société de Diffusion Industrielle et Scientifique (Ivory Coast)
SODISHUL	Société de Distribution d'Huile
SODITAL	Société de Développement de l'Industrie Touristique en Algérie
SODITGA	Société pour le Développement Industriel et Touristique du Gabon
SODIZI	Société du Domaine Industriel de Ziguinchoi (Senegal)
SODOMEI	Nihon Rodo Kumiai Sodomei (Japan)
SODPRO	Society of District Council Public Relations Officers
SODRE	Servicio Oficial de Difusión Radio-Television y Espectáculos (Uruguay)
SODT	Swiss Office for the Developement of Trade
SOE	Societas Ophthalmologica Europaea = EOS
SOE	Société d'Optometrie d'Europe
SOEC	Statistical Office of the European Communities = EUROSTAT, OSCE
SOÉCO	Société d'Équipement et de Construction (Senegal)
SOEKOR	Southern Oil Exploration Corporation (South Africa)
SOÉLACI	Société d'Élevage et d'Agriculture de Côte d'Ivoire
SOF	Société Ornithologique de France
SOF	Society of Floristry
SOF	Sveriges Ornitologiska Förening
SOF	Syndicat des Osiéristes Français
SOFAA	Society of Fine Art Auctioneers
SOFACO	Société Africain de Fabrication, de Formulation et de Conditionnement (Ivory Coast)
SOFAIGUI	Society for Development of Agricultural and Industrial Products of Guinea
SOFAM	Société Franco-Africaine de Métallurgie (Senegal)
SOFAMI	Société de Fabrication Métallique Ivoirienne

SOFARA	Société Forestière Agricole des Ruraux Africains(Cameroon)
SOFAS	Sonnenenergie-Fachverband Schweiz
SOFASA	Sociedad de Fabricantes de Automotores S.A. (Colombia)
SOFBA	Société Française des Bois Africain
SOFCA	Société Française de Compléments Alimentaires
SOFCOT	Société Française de Chirurgie Orthopédique et de Traumatologie
SOFECAM	Société d'Exploitation Forestière du Caméroun
SOFFO	Société Financière pour la France et les Pays Outre-Mer
SOFHT	Society of Food Hygiene Technology
SOFI-DESIT	Société Financière Sénégalaise pour le Développement de l'Industrie et du Tourisme
SOFI-SEDIT	Société Financière Sénégalaise pour le Développement de l'Industrie et du Tourisme
SOFIBEL	Société Forestière et Industrielle de Belabo (Cameroon)
SOFIBOI	Société Forestière et Industrielle des Bois Ivoiriens (Ivory Coast)
SOFICA	Société de Fourniture pour l'Industrie et les Constructions Africaines (Senegal)
SOFICA	Société Financière de Courtage et d'Assurance (Ivory Coast)
SOFICA	Société Forestière Industrielle et Commerciale (Cameroon)
SOFICAL	Société de Financement Industriel Commercial et Agricole
SOFICO	Société pour l'Exploration des Fibres Locales (Zaïre)
SOFIDAK	Société pour la Foire Internationale de Dakar (Senegal)
SOFIDÉ	Société Financière de Développement (Zaïre)
SOFIDÉCA	Société de Financement et de Développement de de l'Économie Agricole
SOFIDEG	Société Financière de Développement de la Guyane (French Guiana)
SOFIFA	Société Financière et Immobilière Franco-Africaine
SOFIHDES	Société Financière Haïtienne de Développement
SOFIMEC	Société de Fibres et de Mécanique (Cameroon)
SOFINA	Société Financière de Transports et d'Entreprises Industrielles (Belgium)
SOFIO	Société Française des Ingénieurs pour la France d'Outre-Mer
SOFIOM	Société Française des Ingénieurs d'Outre-Mer
SOFIRAD	Société Financière de Radiodiffusion
SOFIRAN	Société Française des Pétroles d'Iran
SOFIT	Société de Financement Touristique (Senegal)
SOFITEX	Société de Filage et Texturation (Ivory Coast)
SOFLU-MAR	Société d'Armement Fluvial et Maritime
SOFMA	Société Française de Matériels d'Armement
SOFOCAM	Société Forestière du Caméroun
SOFOCI	Société Forestière de la Côte d'Ivoire
SOFOFA	Sociedad de Fomento Fabril (Chile)
SOFOR	Société Forestière (Gabon)
SOFOTE	Société Forestière de la Téné (Ivory Coast)
SOFRA-TOME	Société Française d'Études et de Réalisation Nucléaires
SOFRAGI	Société Française de Gestion et d'Investissement
SOFRA-MAS	Société Française de Médecine Aérospatiale (ex SFPMAC)
SOFRA-MER	Société Française d'Achats pour l'Outre-Mer
SOFRAS	Société Française d'Archéologie Soumerine
SOFRATOP	Société Française de Travaux Topographiques et Photogrammétriques
SOFRAVIN	Société Française des Vins (Senegal)
SOFRE-AVIA	Société Française d'Études et de Réalisation d'Équipements Aéronautiques
SOFRÉ-MINES	Société Française d'Études Minière
SOFRÉ-RAIL	Société Française d'Études et de Realisations Ferroviaires
SOFRÉ-COM	Société Française d'Études et de Réalisations d'Équipements de Télécommunications
SOFRÉGAZ	Société Française d'Études Gaz
SOFRÉLEC	Société Française d'Études Électrique
SOFREP	Société Française de Recherches et d'Exploitation Pétrolières
SOFRES	Société Française d'Enquêtes par Sondage
SOFRÉSID	Société Française d'Études Sidérurgique

SOFRÉTU	Société Française d'Études et de Réalisations de Transports Urbains
SOFR-EXAM	Société Française d'Exportation de Matérials Naval et Militaires
SOFRI-NORD	Société des Entrepôts Frigorifiques (Senegal)
SOFRIGAB	Société Frigorifique Gabonaise
SOFRIGAL	Société des Frigorifiques du Sénégal
SOFRIMA	Société des Frigorifiques de Mauretanie
SOFRIMA	Société Frigorifique Martiniquaise
SOFRINA	Société Française pour l'Industrie en Afrique
SOFRU-LEM	Société d'Exportation de Fruits et Légumes du Mali
SOFRUMA	Société Marocaine de Navigation Fruitière
SOFT UK	Support Organisation for Trisomy 13/18 and Related Disorders
SOG	Schweizerische Gesellschaft für Ornithologie, Geflügel-, Kaninchen-und Taubenzucht
SOG	Schweizerische Ophthalmologische Gesellschaft
SOG	Südosteuropa-Gesellschaft
SOGA-CÉRAM	Société Gabonaise de Céramique
SOGA-FERRO	Société Gabonaise des Ferro-Alliage
SOGA-FINEX	Société Gabonaise de Financement et d'Expansion
SOGA-LIVRE	Société Gabonaise du Livre
SOGA-STAFF	Société Gabonaise de Staff Afrique
SOGA-TRAM	Société Gabonaise de Transport Maritime
SOGA-TRANCO	Société Gabonaise de Transit et de Consignation
SOGABAIL	Société Gabonaise de Crédit Bail
SOGABOL	Société Gabonaise des Oléagineux
SOGACA	Société Gabonaise de Crédit Automobile
SOGACAM	Société Gabonaise de Cabotage Maritime et Fluvial
SOGACAR	Société Gabonaise de Carrières
SOGACCO	Société Gabono-Koréenne de Commerce (Gabon)
SOGACEL	Société Gabonaise de Cellulose
SOGACHIM	Société Gabonaise de Chimie
SOGAD	Société Gabonaise d'Amenagements et de Décoration

SOGA-DECO	Société Gabonaise de Conditionnement
SOGAEX	Société Gabonaise d'Exportation
SOGAFER	Société Gabonaise Ferroviaire
SOGAFRIC	Société Gabonaise Froid et Représentation Industrielles et Commerciales
SOGAFUTS	Société Gabonaise de Fûts
SOGAID	Société Gabonaise d'Agence Immobilière et de Déménagement
SOGALIM	Société Gabonaise de Leasing Immobilière
SOGAMAR	Société Gabonaise de Marbre et Matériaux
SOGAMÉ	Société Gabonaise de Matériel et d'Équipement
SOGA-MIRÉ	Société Gabonaise de Miroiterie et Ébénisterie
SOGANET	Société Gabonaise d'Entretien et de Travaux
SOGANI	Société des Gaz Industriels du Niger
SOGAPAR	Société Gabonaise de Participation et de Développement
SOGAR-PAR	Société Gabonaise de Participation et de Développement
SOGARA	Société Gabonaise de Raffinage
SOGARDIC	Société Gabonaise de Représentation et de Distribution Commerciale
SOGAREC	Société Gabonaise de Rectification et de Mécanique Générale
SOGAREM	Société Gabonaise de Recherches et d'Exploitations Minières
SOGARÉS	Société Gabonaise de Réalisation de Structures
SOGARI	Société Gabonaise de Réalisations Industrielles
SOGAS	Stichting Samenwerkende Organisaties van Detaillisten in Gasapparaten
SOGAT	Society of Graphical and Allied Trades (*now* GPMU)
SOGATOL	Société Gabonaise de Tôles et Produits Sidérurgiques
SOGATOR	Société Gabonaise de Torréfaction
SOGE-FINANCE	Société Générale de Financement et de Participations en Côte d'Ivoire
SOGE-SETRA	Société Sénégalaise de Bâtiments et Travaux Publics
SOGE-TOCAM	Société de Gestion pour le Tourisme au Cameroun
SOGEBE	Société Générale du Bénin

SOGÉC	Société Gabonaise d'Électrification et de Canalisation		**SOGESCI**	Société Belge pour l'Application des Méthodes Scientifique de Gestion
SOGEC	Société Générale pour le Commerce (Senegal)		**SOGEST**	Société de Gestion de Huilerie et Savonnerie Blohorn (Ivory Coast)
SOGECA	Société Générale de Crédit Automobile (Senegal)		**SOGETA**	Société de Gestion des Terres Agricoles (Morocco)
SOGECIM	Société pour la Gestion Commerciale et Industrielle par la Mécanographie		**SOGÉTA**	Société Générale des Techniques Agricoles (Burkina Faso)
SOGECO	Société Générale de Consignation et d'Entreprises Maritimes (Mauritania)		**SOGÉTÉC**	Société Générale de Topographie, Photogrammétrie et d'Études de Génie Civil (Senegal)
SOGECOR	Société de Gestion et de Conseil en Organisation		**SOGÉTÉL**	Société Génerale de Travaux et Constructions Électriques (Burkina Faso)
SOGÉCOS	Société Générale de Constructions et Travaux (Cameroon)		**SOGÉTHA**	Société Génerale des Techniques Hydro-Agricoles (Tunisia)
SOGÉDÉM	Société Gabonaise d'Étude et de Développement Maritimes		**SOGÉTRA**	Société Générale de Travaux (Belgium)
SOGEDIA	Société de Gestion et de Développement des Industries Alimentaires (Algeria)		**SOGÉTRAF**	Société Générale de Travaux et de Représentations en Afrique (Ivory Coast)
SOGEF	Société de Gestion d'Entrepéts Frigorifiques en Côte d'Ivoire		**SOGÉV**	Société Générale du Vide
SOGEFI-BAILCI	Société Générale de Financement par le Crédit-Bail du Côte d'Ivorie		**SOGEXSA**	Sociedad de Gestión de las Unidades de Exportación de Almendras y Avellanas
SOGEFIHA	Société de Gestion Financière de l'Habitat (Ivory Coast)		**SOGGO**	Société Guinéenne de Gynécologie et Obstétrique
SOGÉFOR	Société Générale des Forces Hydro-Électriques du Katanga		**SOGI**	Société Gabonaise Industrielle
SOGÉL	Société Gabonaise d'Élevage		**SOGICI**	Société Générale d'Industrie en Côte d'Ivoire
SOGÉLEM	Société Générale d'Électricité de Mauritainie		**SOGIEXCI**	Société Générale d'Importation et d'Exportation de de Côte d'Ivoire
SOGEM	Société de Gestion Moderne		**SOGIMET**	Société des Garages Intégrés pour la Mécanique, l'Électricité et la Télerie (Ivory Coast)
SOGEMA	Société de Gestion de Matériel (Ivory Coast)		**SOGIMEX-SVP**	Société Générale d'Import-Export, Études et Tous Services (Ivory Coast)
SOGÉMAT	Société Gabonaise d'Équipement et de Matériel Automobile		**SOGIP**	Société Générale pour l'Industrialisation de la Pêche
SOGÉP	Société Générale d'Études et de Planification		**SOGIP-IVOIRE**	Société Générale pour l'Industrialisation de la Pêche en Côte d'Ivoire
SOGEPAL	Société de Gestion et de Participations d'Industries Alimentaires		**SOGISMA**	Société des Gaz Industriels de Madagascar
SOGEPRO	Société de Gestion et de Programmation (Cameroon)		**SOGITEX**	Société Générale des Industries Textiles (Tunisia)
SOGEPSA	Société Générale Européenne d'Entreprises et de Promotion		**SOGIUP**	Société Guinéenne des Pétroles (Guinea)
SOGER-CAM	Société de Serrurerie Camérounaise		**SOGRÉAH**	Société Grenobloise d'Études et d'Application Hydrauliques
SOGÉRAO	Société Générale de Représentations Industrielles et de Travaux Publics (Benin)		**SOGT**	Société d'Obstétrique et du Gynécologie de Toulouse
SOGERCA	Société pour l'Entreprise de Réacteurs et de Centrales Atomiques		**SOH**	Stichting Oecumenische Hulp
SOGERMA	Société Girondine d'Entretien et de Réparation de Matériel Aéronautique		**SOHA**	Société Hôtelière de l'Atlantique (Benin)

SOHATA	Société Immobilière et Hôtelière d'Afrique (Ivory Coast)
SOHICO	Société Hôtelière et Immobilière de Cocody (Ivory Coast)
SOHIMA	Société Hôtelière et Immobilière de Madagascar
SOHLI	Société Hôtelière du Littoral (Cameroon)
SOHN	Society of Occupational Health Nursing
SOHORA	Société des Hôtels de la Riviéra Africaine (Ivory Coast)
SOHOTCI	Société Hôtelière et Touristique de Côte d'Ivoire
SOHYO	Nihon Rodo Kumiai Sohyogikai (Japan)
SOI	Schweizerisches Ost Institut
SOI	Società Oftalmologica Italiana
SOI	Società Ornitologica Italiana
SOI	Società Orticola Italiana
SOI	Special Olympics International (U.S.A.)
SOI	Standards Organisation of Iran
SOI	State Oceanographic Institute (Russia)
SOIDAH	Société Industrielle d'Habillement du Dahomey
SOIDI	Société Ivoirienne de Distribution
SOIPA	Società Italiana di Parassitologia
SOIPAC	Società Italiana di Patologia Clinica
SOIVRE	Servicio Oficial de Inspección, Viliancia y Regulación de la Exportaciones
SOK	Służba Ochrony Kolei
SOK	Suomen Osuuskauppojen Keskuskunta
SOK	Svenska Organisations Konsulters Förening
SOKINABU	Société d'Économie Mixte pour l'Exploitation du Quinquina au Burundi
SOKL	Suomen Osuuskauppojen Keskusliitto
SOKSI	Sentral Organisasi Karjawan Sosialis Indonesia
SOL	Soma Horkoton Logiston
SOL	Suomen Opettajain Liitto
SOLAC	Sociedad Latinoamericana de Estudios sobre America Latina y el Caribe
SOLACE	Society of Local Authority Chief Executives
SOLADO	Société de Laminage de Douala (Cameroon)
SOLAGRAL	Solidarites Agricoles et Alimentaires (France)
SOLALIBO	Société Malienne de Boissons Gazeuses
SOLANI	Société Latière du Niger
SOLAR	Sociedad Latinoamericana de Estudios sobre América Latina y el Caribe (Mexico)
SOLAS	Society for Laboratory Animal Science = GV
SOLCA	Sociedad de Lucha contra el Cáncer (Ecuador)
SOLCAP	Society of Leisure Consultants & Publishers
SOLEN	Société Internationale de Location d'Engins
SOLERAS	Solar Energy Research Joint Cooperation Program (Saudi Arabia, U.S.A.)
SOLET	Società Orveitana Essiccazione e Lavorazione dei Tabacchi
SOLF	Sveriges Optikleverantöres Förening
SOLI-DARIOS	Consejo de Fundaciones Americanas de Desarrollo
SOLIBRA	Société de Limonaderies et Brasseries d'Afrique (Ivory Coast)
SOLICAM	Société Textil du Caméroun pour le Linge de Maison
SOLICO	Société Limonadière de la Côte du Bénin
SOLIMA	Société Libyo-Malienne de Développement de l'Élevage et d'Exploitation du Bétail (Mali)
SOLIMA	Solitany Malagasy (Madagascar)
SOLIMAC	Société Libano-Ivoirienne de Matériaux de Construction
SOLINCI	Société de Lingerie de Côte d'Ivoire
Solo	National Federation of Solo Clubs
SOLO-TRAFER	Société Larraine de Travaux Ferroviaires (Ivory Coast)
SOLS	Scottish Organisation of Labour Students
ŚOM	Światowa Organizacja Meteorologiczna
SOM	Society of Metaphysicians
SOM	Society of Occupational Medicine
SOMA	GAFTA Soya Bean Meal Futures Association
SOMA	Sharing of Missionaries Abroad
SOMA	Société d'Oto-rhino-laryngologique du Maghreb Arabe
SOMA	Société Maritime de Madagascar
SOMA	Society of Medical Authors
SOMA-COTRET	Société Mauritanienne de Commerce, de Transport, de Représentation et de Transit

SOMA-QUIRÉ	Société Mauritanienne de Quincaillerie et de Représentation	**SOMATRA**	Société Malienne de Transports
SOMACA	Société Marocaine de Constructions Automobiles	**SOMA-TRAC**	Société Mauritanienne de Distribution de Matériel de Travaux Publics
SOMACI	Société de Mobilier et d'Agencement de Côte d'Ivoire	**SOMAU-LAITMC**	Société Mauritanienne de Laiterie et Matériels de Construction
SOMACI	Société Mamadon Sada-Diallo et Frères (Mali)	**SOMAUR-AL**	Société Mauritanienne de Allumettes
SOMACO	Société Nationale de Commerce (Madagascar)	**SOMDIAA**	Société Multinationale de Développement pour les Industries Alimentaires et Agricoles
SOMACOM	Société de Manutention et de Consignation Maritime (Réunion)	**SOMEA**	Società per la Matematica e l'Economia Applicate
SOMACOM	Société Maritime et Commerciale (Gabon)	**SOMEB**	Société de Mise en Bouteilles des Eaux de Bénichab (Mauritania)
SOMA-COTP	Société Mauritanienne de Construction et de Travaux Publics	**SOMÉC**	Société Mutuelle d'Études et de Coopération Industrielles
SOMADÉC	Société Mauritanienne de Développement et de Commerce	**SOMEC-AFRIQUE**	Société pour la Mécanisation des Entreprises de Centrafrique
SOMADÉP	Société Mauritanienne de Diffusion d'Énergie Portable	**SOMECAF**	Société d'Ateliers Mécaniques Africains
SOMAF	Société Malienne de l'Automobile et du Froid	**SOMENO**	Société des Menuiseries du Nord (Cameroon)
SOMAF	Société Marbrière Africaine	**SOMÉPI**	Société Mauritanienne d'Études et de Promotion Industrielles
SOMAFAM	Société Malienne de Fabrication d'Articles Métalliques	**SOMÉRA**	Société Monégasque d'Exploitation et d'Études de Radiodiffusion
SOMAFI	Société Martiniquaise de Financement	**SOMÉT**	Société Maroc d'Études
SOMA-FRÉC	Société Malienne de Froid et d'Électricité	**SOMÉTER**	Société Mauritanienne d'Études Techniques et de Représentation
SOMAGA	Société Marseillaise du Gabon	**SOMFA**	Soya Bean Meal Futures Association
SOMAIR	Société des Mines de l'Air (Niger)	**SOMI-BUROM**	Société Mixte, Minière et Industrielle Roumano-Burundaise
SOMALAC	Société Malgache Lac Alaotra (Madagascar)	**SOMICI**	Société d'Exploitation des Eaux Minérales de Côte d'Ivoire
SOMAL-IBO	Société Malienne de Boissons Gazeuses	**SOMICOA**	Société Maritime et Industrielle de la Côte Occidentale d'Afrique
SOMAP	Société Marocaines de Prévoyance	**SOMIEX**	Société Malienne d'Importation et d'Exportation
SOMAPA	Société Malienne de Parfumerie		
SOMA-PECHE	Société Malgache de Pêcherie (Madagascar)	**SOMIFER**	Société des Mines de Fer de Mekambo (Gabon)
SOMAPIL	Société Malienne des Piles Électriques	**SOMIMA**	Société Minière de Mauritanie
SOMA-PRIM	Société Malienne de Promotion Industrielle et Immobilière	**SOMINCI**	Société Minière de Côte d'Ivoire
		SOMIP	Société Mauritanienne des Industries de la Pêche
SOMARCA	Société Maritime Cassamançaise (Senegal)	**SOMIPEX**	Société Mauritanienne d'Importation, d'Exportation et de Représentation
SOMAREM	Société Mauritanienne de Représentation de Marques	**SOMIR**	Société Mauritanienne des Industries de Raffinage
SOMASAC	Société Malienne de Sacherie		
SOMASER	Société Maritime de Service	**SOMIREN**	Socieded Mixta Siderurgia Argentina
SOMAT	Société Maritime Atlantique du Togo	**SOMIREN**	Società Minerali Radioatttivi Energia Nucleare
SOMATEM	Société de Fabrication Industrielle de Matelas et de Mobilier (Gabon)		

SOMIRWA	Société des Mines du Rwanda
SOMISA	Sociedad Mixta Siderúrgica Argentina
SOMITAM	Société Minière de Tambao (Burkina Faso)
SOMIVA	Société pour la Mise en Valeur Agricole de la Corse
SOMMÉP	Syndicat de l'Outillage à Main et des Machines Électro-Portatives
SOMOACI	Société Agence Maritime de l'Ouest Africain Côte d'Ivoire
SOMOTEC	Société de Moteurs et Techniques (Ivory Coast)
SOMRA	Somali Relief Association
SoN	Society of Nematologists
SONA-COME	Société Nationale de Constructions Mécaniques (Algeria)
SONA-PECHE	Société Nationale d'Armement et de Pêche
SONA-PRESSE	Société Nationale de Presse et d'Édition (Gabon)
SONA-TRACH	Société Nationale pour la Recherche, la Production, le Transport, la Transformation et la Commercialisation des Hydrocarbures (Algeria)
SONABA	Société Nationale du Bâtiment (Chad)
SONAC	Société Nationale de la Céramique Artisanale et Industrielle du Bénin
SONACEB	Société Nationale de Commercialisation et d'Exportation de Bénin
SONACO	Société Nationale Agricole pour le Coton (Benin)
SONACO	Société Nationale de Commerce (Madagascar)
SONACO	Société Nationale de Conditionnement (Ivory Coast)
SONACO	Société Nationale de Construction (Congo)
SONACO-TRAP	Société Nationale de Construction et de Travaux Publics (Benin)
SONACOB	Société Nationale de Commercialisation des Bois et Dérivés (Algeria)
SONACOB	Société Nationale de Construction de Bâtiments (Senegal)
SONACOM	Société Nationale de Commerce (Togo)
SONACOM	Société Nationale de Commercialisation des Plantes Médicinales (Cameroon)
SONACOP	Société Nationale de Commercialisation des Produits Pétroliers (Benin)
SONACOS	Société Nationale de Commercialisation des Oléagineux du Sénégal
SONACOT	Société Nationale de Commercialisation du Tchad
SONAD	Sociétés Régionales d'Aménagement et de Développement (Togo)
SONADER	Société Nationale de Développement Rural (Benin, Mauritania)
SONADIG	Société Nationale d'Investissements du Gabon
SONADIS	Société Nouvelle pour l'Approvisionnement et la Distribution au Sénégal
SONAÉ	Société Nationale d'Équipement (Benin)
SONAFEL	Société Nationale pour le Développement des Fruits et Légumes (Benin)
SONAFI	Société Nationale de Financement (Ivory Coast)
SONAFOR	Société Nationale des Forages (Senegal)
SONAFRIG	Société Nationale des Frigorifiques (Senegal)
SONAGA	Société Nationale de Garantie et d'Assistance au Commerce (Senegal)
SONAGAR	Société Nationale Gabonaise d'Assurances et de Réassurances
SONAGECI	Société Nationale de Génie Civil (Ivory Coast)
SONAGEL	Sociedade Nacional de Combustiveis de Angola
SONAGIM	Société Nationale pour la Gestion Immobilière (Benin)
SONAGRI	Société Nationale pour la Production Agricole (Benin)
SONAMA	Société Nationale de Manutention (Algeria)
SONAMÉL	Société Nationale de Matériels Électriques et Électroménagers
SONAMI	Sociedad Nacional de Minería (Chile)
SONAMIF	Société Nationale des Mines de M'Fouati (Congo)
SONAMIS	Société Nationale Minière de Sounka-Koka-Moeka (Congo)
SONAM-VIE	Société Nationale d'Assurances Mutuelles-Vie (Senegal)
SON-ANGOL	Sociedade Nacional de Combustíveis de Angola
SONAP	Sociedad de Navegación Petrolera (Chile)
SONAP	Sociedade Nacional de Petroleos
SONAP	Société Nationale de Papeterie et de Librairie (Benin)

SONAP	Société Nationale des Articles de Papeterie (Central Africa)	**SONE-PRESS**	Société Nationale d'Édition et de Presse (Burkina Faso)
SONAPH	Société Nationale pour le Développement de la Palmeraie et des Huileries (Togo)	**SONE-PRESS**	Société Nationale de Presse, d'Édition et de Publicité (Senegal)
SONAPRA	Société Nationale pour la Promotion Agricole (Benin)	**SONEAB**	Société Nationale d'Exploitation des Arachides de Bouche (Senegal)
SONA-PRESS	Société Nationale de Presse, d'Édition et de Publicité (Senegal)	**SONED**	Southern Networks for Development (Kenya) = REDES
SONAR	Société Nationale d'Assurances et de Réassurances (Benin, Burkina Faso, Ivory Coast)	**SONÉD-Afrique**	Société Nouvelle des Études de Développement en Afrique (Senegal)
SONAR	Société Nationale du Monde Rural (Senegal)	**SONÉDIT**	Société Nigérienne d'Études, de Diffusions Industrielle et de Technique
SONARA	Société Nationale de Raffinage (Cameroon)	**SONEES**	Société Nationale d'Exploitation des Eaux du Sénégal
SONARA	Société Nigérienne de Commercialisation de l'Arachide	**SONEG**	Société Nationale d'Entreprise Générale (Senegal)
SONARAF	Société Nationale de Raffinage (Benin)	**SONÉL**	Société Nationale d'Électricité du Caméroun
SONARAM	Société Nationale de Recherches et d'Explorations Minières (Algeria)	**SONÉL**	Société Nationale d'Élevage (Congo, Système)
SONAREC	Société Nationale de Récupération (Senegal)	**SONÉLEC**	Société Nationale d'Eau et d'Électricité (Mauritania)
SONAREM	Société Nationale de Recherches et d'Exploitations Minières (Algeria)	**SONÉLEC**	Société Nationale de Fabrication et de Montage du Matériel Électrique (Algeria)
SONAREM	Société Nationale de Recherches et d'Exploration Minières (Mali)	**SONÉLGAZ**	Société Nationale de l'Électricité et du Gaz (Algeria)
SONAS	Société Nationale d'Assurances (Zaïre)	**SONÉPI**	Société Nationale d'Études et de Promotion Industrielle (Senegal)
SONAS	Society of Naval Architects of Singapore	**SONERAN**	Société Nigérienne d'Exploitation des Ressources Animales
SONASID	Société Nationale de Sidérurgie (Morocco)	**SONETE**	Sociedade Nacional de Estudos e Financiamento de Empreendimentos Ultramarinos (Portugal)
SONASUT	Société Nationale Sucrière du Chad	**SONETRA**	Société Nationale d'Entreprises et de Travaux Publics (Mali)
SONATAM	Société Nationale des Tabacs et Allumettes du Mali		
SONATEL	Société Nationale des Télécommunications du Sénégal	**SONETRA**	Société Sénégalaise de Transit
SONATITE	Société Nationale des Travaux d'Infrastructure des Télécommunications (Algeria)	**SONEXI**	Société Nigérienne d'Exploitation Cinématographique
		SONG	Société l'Okoumé de la N'gounie (Gabon)
SONATRAB	Société Nationale de Transformation du Bois	**SONHOTEL**	Société Nigérienne de l'Hôtellerie
SONATRAC	Société Nationale de Transit et de Consignation (Benin)	**SONI-CÉRAM**	Société Nigérienne de Produits Céramiques
SONATRAM	Société Nationale de Transports Maritimes (Gabon)	**SONI-TEXTIL**	Société Nouvelle Nigérienne des Textiles
SONATRAM	Société Nationale de Travaux Maritime (Algeria)	**SONIAH**	Société Nationale d'Irrigation et d'Aménagement Hydro-Agricole (Benin)
SONAVOCI	Société Nationale Voltaïque du Cinéma		
SONDA	Sociedad Nacional de Procesamiento de Datos (Chile)	**SONIBATP**	Société Nigériénne de Bâtiment et de Travaux Publics

SONIC	Société Nationale des Industries de la Cellulose (Algeria)
SONICA	Société Nigérienne de Crédit Automobile
SONICAR	Société Nigérienne de Carrelage
SONICHAR	Société Nigérienne du Chabon d'Anou Araren (Niger)
SONICO	Société Nationale pour l'Industrie et le Commerce (Burkina Faso)
SONICOB	Société Nationale d'Industrialisation et de Commercialisation du Bétail (Mauritania)
SONICOG	Société Nationale pour l'Industrie des Corps Gras (Benin)
SONIDA	Société Nigérienne pour le Développement de l'Automobile
SONIDEP	Société Nigérienne de Produits Pétroliers (Niger)
SONIFAC	Société Nigérienne de Fabrication de Couvertures (Niger)
SONIFAME	Société Nigérienne de Fabrications Métalliques
SONIMCO	Société Nationale d'Impression en Continu (Senegal)
SONIMEX	Société Nationale d'Importation et d'Exportation (Mauritania)
SONIPAL	Société Nigérienne pour la Production d'Allumettes
SONIPEC	Société Nationale des Industries des Peaux et Cuirs (Algeria)
SONIPLA	Société Nigérienne de Plastique
SONIPRIM	Société Nigérienne de Primeurs
SONITAN	Société Nigérienne de Tannerie
SONITEX	Société Nationale des Industries Textiles (Algeria)
SONITO	Société Nationale d'Intervention sur le Marché de la Tomate
SONITRA	Société Nationale Ivoirienne de Travaux
SONNA	Somali National News Agency
SONOCO	Son Optique Compagnie (Ivory Coast)
SONO-CRAF	Société Nouvelle des Comptoirs Réunis d'Afrique
SONOFILM	Société Nouvelle pour la Production, la Distribution et l'Exploitation Cinématographique (Cameroon)
SONOTREF	Société Nouvelle de Transports et d'Exploitation Forestière (Ivory Coast)
SONRA	Society of Newfoundland Radio Amateurs
SONUCI	Société Nigérienne d'Urbanisme et de Construction Immobilière

SOOJ	Society of Ophthalmological Optics of Japan
SOOP	Société Odontologique de Paris
SOOP	State Organisation for Oil Products (Iraq)
SOP	Société d'Ophthalmologie de Paris
SOPA	Society of Professional Archeologists (U.S.A.)
SOPAB	Société des Pansements du Bénin
SOPAC	Société de Papiers et Cahiers du Niger
SOPAC	Société de Pêche et d'Affrètement du Caméroun
SOPAC	Société Panafricaine de Cardiologie = PASCAR
SOPAC	South Pacific Applied Geoscience Commission (Fiji)
SOPAC	South Pacific News Service (New Zealand)
SOPAD	Société de Produits Alimentaires et Diététiques
SOPADA	Société de Plomberie, Adduction, Distribution, Assinissement (Cameroon)
SOPANATA	Sociedade Portuguesa de Navios Tanques
SOPANI	Société de Parfumerie Nigérienne
SOPAO	Société de Pêche de l'Afrique Occidentale
SOPAPECI	Société Générale d'Armement et de Pêche de Côte d'Ivoire
SOPARCA	Société de Fabrication de Parfumerie au Caméroun
SOPAR-CAM	Société de Participations Camérounaises
SOPARCO	Société Africaine de Parfumerie et de Conditionnement (Mali)
SOPAR-MOD	Société des Parfums Modernes du Tchad
SOPE	Copyright Protection Society (Greece)
SOPÉCAM	Société de Presse et d'Éditions du Caméroun
SOPECI	Société de Peinture en Côte d'Ivoire
SOPECO	Société Sénégalaise de Pêche et de Commercialisation
SOPECOBA	Société des Pêcheries Coloniales à la Baleine
SOPEKAM	Société de Pêche de Kamsar (Guinea)
SOPÉLA	Société pour la Promotion de l'Élevage en Afrique (Senegal)
SOPÉLEM	Société d'Optique, Précision, Électronique et Mécanique

SOPEMÉA	Société pour le Perfectionnement des Matériels et Équipements Aérospatiaux	**SORA**	Svenska Operationsanalysföreningen
SOPESEA	Société des Pêcheries Sénégalaises de l'Atlantique	**SORAD**	Société Radiologie d'Abidjan (Ivory Coast)
SOPESINE	Société des Pêcheries du Siné Saloum (Senegal)	**SORAM**	Société de Représentation d'Assurance Maritime (Senegal)
SOPETOGO	Société Pêcherie Togolaise	**SORARAF**	Société de Répresentation d'Assurances et de Réassurances Africaines (Chad)
SOPEXA	Société pour la Promotion de l'Exportation des Produits Agricoles et Alimentaires	**SORCA**	Société de Recherche Operationelle et d'Économie Appliquée (Belgium)
SOPEXCI	Société pour l'Expansion du Commerce et de l'Industrie (Benin)	**SORÉAS**	Syndicat des Fabricants d'Organes et d'Équipement Aéronautiques et Spatiaux
SOPHIE	Save Our Pets' History In Eternity (U.S.A.)	**SORÉCAM**	Société de Réchapage du Caméroun
SOPIM	Société de Promotion Immobilière de la Côte d'Ivoire	**SORÉCI**	Société d'Organisation Économique et Industrielle (Ivory Coast)
SOPIMA	Société des Piles de Madagascar	**SORECOM**	Société de Représentations Industrielles Commerciales et Maritimes (Senegal)
SOPOCAM	Société Portuaire au Caméroun	**SORÉCOM-IVOIRE**	Société Ivoirienne de Révision et d'Expertise Comptable
SOPOTEC	Société Pompes et Techniques (Ivory Coast)		
SOPREP	Sociedade Portuguesa de Relações Publicas	**SOREFAME**	Sociedades Reunidas Fabricações Metalicas (Portugal)
SOPRESCO	Société de Prestations de Services et de Consignation (Mauritania)	**SORÉLÉG**	Société de Réparations et d'Électricité de Garoua (Cameroon)
SOPREXI	Société de Promotion et d'Exploitation Industrielle Centrafrique	**SORÉM**	Société de Réalisation Électro-Mécanique (Ivory Coast)
SOPRIA	Société d'Étude et de Financement pour la Promotion des Industries Agricoles et de l'Alimentation	**SOREMI**	Société des Recherches et d'Exploitation Minières (Burkina Faso)
SOPRIVO	Société de Produits Ivoiriens	**SOREP**	Société de Recherches Pharmaceutiques (Cameroon)
SOPRO-DAVCI	Société d'Études pour la Production de l'Avocat en Côte d'Ivoire	**SOREPCI**	Société de Représentation Commerciale et Industrielle de Côte d'Ivoire
SOPRO-CAM	Société des Produits du Caméroun	**SORÉPÉL**	Société de Réparation Électromécanique (Ivory Coast)
SOPROGI	Société pour la Promotion et la Gestion Industrielle	**SOREPZA**	Société de Recherche et d'Exploitation des Pétroles au Système
SOPROLE	Sociedad Productores de Leche, S.A. (Chile)	**SORG**	Statospheric Ozone Review Group
		SORIN	Società Richerche ed Impianti Nucleari
SOPROSEN	Société de Promotion Sénégalaise	**SORIPA**	Société de Transformation Industrielle des Produits Agricoles (Ivory Coast)
SOQUI-MICH	Sociedad Química y Minera de Chile		
SOR	Sectie Operationele Research	**SORIS**	Specialised Organics Information Service
SOR	Servicio Oficial de Radiodifusión (Argentina)	**SORMA**	Société de Représentation et de Manufacture (Ivory Coast)
SOR	Société des Produits Laitiers du Togo	**SOROCI**	Société Routièr de Côte d'Ivoire
SOR	Society for Occupational Research (U.S.A.)	**SORSA**	Spatially-Oriented Referencing Systems Association
SOR	Society of Rheology (U.S.A.)	**SORUGAL**	Société Rufisquoise de Glace Alimentaire (Senegal)
SoR	Society of Roadcraft		
SOR	Sveriges Legitimerade Optikers Riksförbund	**SOS**	International Federation of Bloodgivers Organisations

SOS	Save Our Sarajevo
SOS	Save Our Seatrout (Éire)
SOS	Save our Shires
SOS	Slovenská Orientalistická Společnost
SOS	Society of Schoolmasters
SOS	Stars Organisation for Spastics
SOS	Svenska Optik Sällskapet / Swedish Optical Society
SOSA-CONGO	Société Commerciale Africaine de Congo
SOSAC	Société des Spécialités Agricoles et Chimiques
SOSACHIM	Société Industrielle de Produits Sanitaires Adhésifs et Chimiques (Senegal)
SOSAP	Société Sénégalaise d'Armement à la Pêche
SOSATCO	Société Sénégalaise d'Assistance Technique et de Conseil de Gestion
SOSC	Smithsonian Oceanographic Sorting Centre (U.S.A.)
SOSÉ-TRAUR	Société Sénégalaise de Travaux Urbains et Ruraux
SOSÉA	Société Sénégalaise d'Électronique Appliquée
SOSÉCHAL	Société Sénégalaise de Châlutage
SOSÉCI	Société Sénegalaise pour le Commerce et l'Industrie
SOSÉCO-PAR	Société Sénégalaise de Commerce et de Participation
SOSÉCOD	Société Sénégalaise pour le Commerce et le Développement
SOSÉCODA	Société Sénégalaise de Courtages et d'Assurances
SOSÉCOLA	Société Sénégalaise des Colas
SOSÉDA	Société Sénégalaise pour le Développement de l'Automobile
SOSÉDÉCO	Société Sénégalaise pour le Développement Commercial
SOSÉDI	Société Sénégalaise de Distribution
SOSÉFIL	Société Sénégalaise de Filterie
SOSÉG	Société Sénégalaise d'Amaillage et de Galvanisation
SOSÉKAP	Société Sénégalo-Koweitienne d'Armement et de Pêche (Senegal)
SOSÉLF	Société Sénégalaise des États Louis Feltrin
SOSÉMAR	Société Sénégalaise de Marbre Industriel
SOSÉPRA	Société Sénégalaise pour la Promotion de l'Artisanat d'Art
SOSÉTAM	Société Sénégalaise de Tannerie-Mégisserie
SOSÉTER	Société Sénégalaise de Terassements
SOSÉTRA-PROMER	Société Sénégalaise pour le Traitement des Produits de la Mer
SOSÉX-CATRA	Société Sénégalaise d'Exploitation de Carrières et de Transports
SOSIN	Société Suisse des Ingénieurs Nucléaires = SGK
SOSPRÉC	Société Sénégalaise de Promotion Économique
SOSTL	Sosiaalityöntekjäin Liitto
SOSU-BF	Société Sucrière (Burkina Faso)
SOSU-SOUROU	Société Sucrière Voltaïque de Sourou
SOSU-TCHAD	Société Sucrière du Tchad
SOSUCAM	Société Sucrière du Caméroun
SOSUHO	Société Sucrière du Haut-Ogooué (Gabon)
SOSUMA	Société Sucrière de Mauritanie
SOSUMAV	Société Sucrière de la Mahavavy
SOSUMO	Société Sucrière du Maso (Burundi)
SOT	Society of Organ Transplantation (China)
SOT	Society of Ornamental Turners
SOTA	Société Coopérative pour l'Achat du Tabac (Switzerland)
SOTA	Société des Transports Africains
SOTACI	Société de Tubes d'Acier et Aluminium en Côte d'Ivoire
SOTAGRI	Société Togolaise d'Agro-Industrie
SOTCON	Société Togolaise d'Étanchéité et de Carrelage
SOTEC	Sociedad Chilena de Tecnologia para el Desarrollo
SOTECO-BÉNIN	Société Technico-Commerciale du Bénin
SOTÉD	Société Togolaise d'Études de Développement
SOTEGA	Société Industrielle Textile du Gabon
SOTELEC	Société Mixte pour le Développement de la Technique des Télécommunications sur Câbles
SOTEMA	Société Textile de Majunga (Madagascar)
SOTEXCO	Société des Textiles du Congo
SOTEXI	Société Industrielle Textile de Côte d'Ivoire
SOTEXKA	Société Textile de Kaolack (Senegal)

SOTEXMA	Société Togolaise d'Exploitation de Matériel
SOTIBAS-IMPAFRIC	Société de Teinture, Blanchissement, Apprêts et d'Impressions Africaines (Senegal)
SOTICI	Société de Transformation Industrielle de Côte d'Ivoire
SOTIPA	Société de Transformation Industrielle du Papier (Ivory Coast)
SOTO-PROMER	Société Togolaise des Produits de la Mer
SOTO-TÔLES	Société Togolaise de Galvanisation de Tôles
SOTOCA	Société Industrielle et Commerciale Togolaise du Café
SOTOCAM	Société de Topographie au Caméroun
SOTOCO	Société Togolaise du Coton
SOTO-HOMA	Société Touristique et Hôtelière de Madagascar
SOTOM	Société de Topographie de Madagascar
SOTOMA	Société des Tabacs et Oléagineaux de Madagascar
SOTOMA	Société Togolaise de Marberie
SOTOMA-COSARL	Société Togolaise de Matériels de Construction Import- Export
SOTOMA-TÉRIAUX	Société Togolaise de Matériaux
SOTONAM	Société Togolaise de Navigation Maritime
SOTOPLAN	Société Togolaise de Plantation
SOTOTRAC	Société Togolaise de Transit et de Consignation
SOTRA	Société des Transports Abidjanais (Ivory Coast)
SOTRABCI	Société de Travaux Publics et de Bâtiments Côte d'Ivoire
SOTRABO	Société de Transformation du Bois
SOTRABOI	Société de Transformation des Bois Ivoiriens
SOTRAC	Société des Transports en Commun du Cap Vert (Senegal)
SOTRACI	Société de Transit de Côte d'Ivoire
SOTRA-COB	Société de Transit et de Consignation du Bénin
SOTRAHO	Société des Travaux du Haut-Ogoué (Gabon)
SOTRALGA	Société de Transformation de l'Aluminium du Gabon
SOTRAM	Société de Transformation des Métaux (Benin)
SOTRA-MIL	Société de Transformation du Mil et du Sorgho (Niger)
SOTRA-NORD	Société Camérounaise du Nord-Caméroun
SOTRAVIL	Société des Transports des Villes (Gabon)
SOTREC	Société des Tréfileries et Clouteries de la Côte d'Ivoire
SOTRÉC	Société Technique de Recherches et d'Études pour la Construction
SOTREF	Société Tropicale d'Exploitation Forestière (Cameroons, Ivory Coast)
SOTREP	Société Tchadienne de Réalisation et d'Entreprise de Pneumatiques
SOTROPAL	Société Tropicale des Alumettes (Ivory Coast)
SOTROPCO	Société Tropicale de Commerce
SOTS	Society for Old Testament Study (U.K., U.S.A.)
SOTSPROF	Obedinenie Sotsialnykh Professionalnykh Soiuzov
SOTUC	Société de Transports Urbains du Caméroun
SOU	Scandinavian Ornithological Union; Skandinaviske Ornitologiske Union
SOUR	Slozena Organizacija Udruzenog Rada
SOV	Schweizerischer Obstverband = FUS
SOV	Schweizerischer Optiker-Verband = ASO
SOV	Schweizerischer Orientteppichändler-Verband
SOV	Slovensku Oslobodzovací Vybor (GFR)
SOVA	Society of Voluntary Associates
SOVA-NORD	Société de Valorisation de l'Anacardier du Nord
SOVEA	Société Voltaïque d'Exploitation Automobile
SOVEA-CHAUS-SURES	Société de Vente en Afrique (Ivory Coast)
SOVÉC	Société Voltaïque d'Étanchéité et de Carrelage
SOVEG	Société Voltaïque d'Engineering et de Gestion
SOVEMA	Société Verrerie Malagasy (Madagascar)
SOVÊMAN	Société de Vêtements Manufacturés (Gabon)
SOVERCO	Société des Verreries du Congo
SOVERES	Société Voltaïque de Revêtement et Sanitaire (Burkina Faso)

SOVETCO	Société pour la Vente de Thons Congéles (Ivory Coast)	SP	Senterpartiet (Norway)
SOVETIV	Société de Vêtements Ivoiriens	SP	Servi Sancti Paracliti
SOVIAMAD	Société des Viandes de Madagascar	SP	Shining Path
SOVIC	Société Voltaïque de l'Industrie de la Chaussure (Burkina Faso)	SP	Slavianskaia Partiia
SOVICA	Société Voltaïque d'Intervention et de Coopération avec l'Agriculture	SP	Socialistische Partij (Belgium)
SOVIMAS	Société Voltaïque d'Importation Azar et Salam	SP	Society of Protozoologists (U.S.A.)
SOVINCI	Société des Vins de la Côte d'Ivoire	SP	Sotsialisticheskaia Partiia
SOVINCO	Société des Vins du Congo	SP	Statens Provningsanstalt (Sweden)
SOVINGAB	Société des Vins du Gabon	SP	Stronnictwo Pracy
SOVINTO	Sodas et Vins du Togo	SP	Svobodnye Profsoiuzy

SP — Senterpartiet (Norway)
SP — Servi Sancti Paracliti
SP — Shining Path
SP — Slavianskaia Partiia
SP — Socialistische Partij (Belgium)
SP — Society of Protozoologists (U.S.A.)
SP — Sotsialisticheskaia Partiia
SP — Statens Provningsanstalt (Sweden)
SP — Stronnictwo Pracy
SP — Svobodnye Profsoiuzy

SOVETCO — Société pour la Vente de Thons Congéles (Ivory Coast)
SOVETIV — Société de Vêtements Ivoiriens
SOVIAMAD — Société des Viandes de Madagascar
SOVIC — Société Voltaïque de l'Industrie de la Chaussure (Burkina Faso)
SOVICA — Société Voltaïque d'Intervention et de Coopération avec l'Agriculture
SOVIMAS — Société Voltaïque d'Importation Azar et Salam
SOVINCI — Société des Vins de la Côte d'Ivoire
SOVINCO — Société des Vins du Congo
SOVINGAB — Société des Vins du Gabon
SOVINTO — Sodas et Vins du Togo
SOVO-STOCK — Société Voltaïque de Stockage (Burkina Faso)
SOVOBRA — Société Voltaïque de Brasseries (Burkina Faso)
SOVOCA — Société Voltaïque de Crédit Automobile
SOVODA — Société Voltaïque pour le Développement de l'Automobile (Burkina Faso)
SOVOG — Société Voltaïque de Groupage
SOVOGI — Société Voltaïque de Gestion Immobilière (Burkina Faso)
SOVOIC — Société Voltaïque Industrielle et Commerciale (Burkina Faso)
SOVOL-PLAS — Société Voltaïque de Plastique
SOVOLCI — Société Voltaïque de Commerce et d'Industrie (Burkina Faso)
SOVOLDIA — Société Voltaïque de Diffusion Industrielle et Automobile (Burkina Faso)
SOVOL-FOR — Société Voltaïque de Forage (Burkina Faso)
SOVOL-SEM — Société Voltaïque d'Entreprise de Serrurerie Menuiserie Métallique et Charpente
SOVOLTA — Société Voltaïque de Tanneries et des Industries du Cuir (Burkina Faso)
SOVOMEA — Société Voltaïque de Montage et d'Exploitation Automobile (Burkina Faso)
SOVOPI — Société Voltaïque de Pointerie Industrielle (Burkina Faso)
SOY — Suomen Ostopäälliköiden Yhdistys
SOZ — Společnost pro Ochranu před Zářením
SOZIR — Société Zaïro-Italienne de Raffinage
SP — Commission Internationale de Phare du Cap Spartel

SP-W — Solidarność Polsko-Węgierska
SPA — Föreninger Sveriges Praktiserande Arkitekter
SPA — Saudi Press Agency
SPA — Scottish Petanque Association
SPA — Scottish Pipers Association
SPA — Scottish Pistol Association
SPA — Scottish Publishers Association
SPA — Screen Printing Association International
SPA — Servicio de Promocion Artesanal
SPA — Singapore People's Alliance
SPA — Slovak Philosophical Society = SFZ
SPA — Socialist Party of Australia
SPA — Sociedade Portuguesa de Autores
SPA — Società Svizzera per la Protezione dell'Ambiente = SGU, SPE
SPA — Society of Parliamentary Agents
SPA — Society of Personality Assessment (U.S.A.)
SPA — Society of Psychological Anthropology (U.S.A.)
SPA — Society of Public Administration (U.S.A.)
SPA — Society of Public and other Official Analysts (FUMPO)
SPA — Society of St Peter Apostle for Native Clergy
SPA — Software Producers Association (U.S.A.)
SPA — Southern Pine Association (U.S.A.)
SPA — State Property Agency (Hungary)
SPA — Strathclyde Poverty Alliance
SPA — Sumatra Planters Association (Indonesia)
SPA — Supreme People's Assembly (Democratic People's Republic of Korea)
SPA — Surinaamse Partij van de Arvid

SPA	Syndicate de la Presse Agricole
SPA	Systems and Procedures Association (U.S.A.)
SPAA	Scottish Passenger Agents' Association
SPAA	Screen Production Association of Australia
SPAAC	Syndicat du Personnel Africain de l'Aéronautique Civile
SPAAR	Special Programme for African Agricultural Research
SPAB	Society for the Protection of Ancient Buildings
SPABC	South Pacific Association of Bible Colleges (Australia)
SPAC	Salinity Program Advisory Council (ex SPPAC)
SPAC	Shoqata Patriotike Atdhetare "Çamëria" (Albania) = CPPA
SPAC	Standing Pharmaceutical Advisory Committee (NHS)
SPACE	Society for Private and Commercial Earth Stations (U.S.A.)
SPACEM	Sociedad Puertorriqueña de Autores, Compositores y Editores Musicales
SPACHEE	South Pacific Action Committee for Human Ecology and the Environment (Fiji)
SPACLALS	South Pacific Association for Commonwealth Literature and Language Studies (Australia)
SPADE	Société des Plantations d'Ananas de Divo (Ivory Coast)
SPAÉ	Service de la Production Aéronautique (DTCA)
SPAE	Sociedade Portuguesa de Antropologia e Etnologia
SPAÉF	Société des Pétrole d'Afriques Équatoriale Française
SPAF	Svenska Allmänflygförening
SPAF	Syndicat de la Presse Artistique Française – Association des Historiens et Critiques d'Art
SPAF	Verband Schweizerischer Fabrikanten, Lieferanten und Agenten von Sportartkeln
SPAFA	SEAMEO Project in Archeology and Fine Arts (Thailand)
SPAG	Syndicat des Produits Alimentaires en Gros
SPAGP	Stowarzyszenie Polskich Artystów Grafików Projektantów

SPAI	Screen Printing Association International
SPAI	Service Professionnel Agricole International (APCA)
SPAIC	Sociedade Portuguesa de Alergologia e Imunologia Clínica
SPAID	Society for the Prevention of Asbestosis and Industrial Diseases
SPAK	Shoqata Patriotike Atdhetare Kosova (Albania) = KPPA
SPAL	Société des Produits Alimentaires (Togo)
SPALDA	Scottish Peat and Land Development Association
SPAM	Society for the Publication of American Music
SPAM	Stowarzyszenie Polskich Artystów Muzyków
SPAN	Société des Plantations d'Ananas de Nianda (Ivory Coast)
SPAN	Space Physics Analysis Network
SPANA	Society for the Protection of Animals in North Africa
SPANCI	Syndicat Professionel des Amateurs de Navigation Côtière
SpARC	Space Automation and Robotics Center (U.S.A.)
SPARCENT	Space and Atmospheric Research Centre (Pakistan)
SPARK	Seminarium (Into the Psyche, Architecture and Rural Knowledge)
SPARMO	Solar Particles and Radiations Monitoring Organisation
SPARS	Society of Professional Audio Recording Studios (U.S.A.)
SPARTECA	South Pacific Regional Trade and Economic Co-Operation Agreement (Australia, New Zealand)
SPAS	Chambre Syndicale des Producteurs d'Aciers Fins et Spéciaux
SPASAI	South Pacific Association of Supreme Audit Institutions (Tonga)
SPASK	Service Provincial de l'Agriculture de Sud Kivu (Zaïre)
SPATA	Swimming Pool and Allied Trades Association
SPATF	South Pacific Appropriate Technology Foundation (New Guinea)
SPATiF	Stowarzyszenie Polskich Artystów Teatru i Filmu
SPB	Sociedad Peruana de Botánica

SPB	Sociedade Portuguesa de Bioquimica
SPB	Suiuz na Prevodachite y Bulgariya = BTU
SPBA	Scottish Pipe Band Association
SPBC	Society of Professional Business Consultants (U.S.A.)
SPBEA	South Pacific Board for Educational Assessment
SPBP	Society for the Preservation of Birds of Prey
SPBR	Society for Back Pain Research
SPBW	Society for the Preservation of Beers from the Wood
SPC	Seed Production Committee
SPC	Sherry Producers' Committee
SPC	Sociedade Portuguesa de Commercialização
SPC	Société de Provenderies du Cameroon
SPC	Société Française de Céramique
SPC	Society of Pension Consultants
SPC	South Pacific Commission = CPS
SPC	Southern Petroleum Company (Iraq)
SPC	Soy Protein Council (U.S.A.)
SPC	Special Political Committee
SPC	Special Premiers Conference
SPC	State Planning Commission (Albania)
SPC	Swiss Publishers Corporation
SPC	Syrian Petroleum Company
SPCC	South Pacific Cosmedical Centre (Tahiti)
SPCG	Socijalistička Partija Crne Gore (Montenegro) = SPM
SPCI	Société de Promotion Commerciale Ivoirienne
SPCI	Svenska Pappers- och Cellulosaingeniörsföreningen
SPCK	Society for Promoting Christian Knowledge
SPCMA	Scottish Pre-Cast Concrete Manufacturers' Association
SPCN	Société de Produits Chimiques du Niger
SPCO	Service Pharmaceutique des Caraïbes Orientales = ECDS
SPCS	Sociedade Portuguesa da Ciência da Solo
SPCT	Société de Promotion Commerciale et Touristique (Senegal)
SPCV	Sociedade Portuguesa de Ciências Veterinárias

SPD	Society for Pediatric Dermatology (U.S.A.)
SPD	Sozialdemokratische Partei Deutschlands
SPD	Svenska Privatdetektivförbundet
SPDC	Société du Palace de Cocody (Ivory Coast)
SPDE	Syndicat Professionnel des Distributeurs d'Eaux et Exploitants de Réseaux d'Assainissement
SPDF	Seychelles People's Defence Force
SPDJ	Social Democratic Party of Japan
SPDR	Social Democracy Party of Romania
SPE	Sociedade Portuguesa de Espeleologia
SPE	Société des Plantations d'Elima (Ivory Coast)
SPÉ	Société Sénégalaise de Plomberie et d'Équipement
SPE	Société Suisse pour la Protection de l'Environnement = SGU, SPA
SPE	Society for Photographic Education
SPE	Society of Petroleum Engineers (AIME)
SPE	Society of Plastic Engineers (U.S.A.)
SPE	Society of Professors of Education (U.S.A.)
SPEA	Sales Promotion Executives Association (U.S.A.)
SPEA	Scottish Physical Education Association
SPEAKE	Syndicat Professionnel des Entrepreneurs d'Asphalte et d'Étanchéité
SPÉC	Société de Prospection Électrique Schlumberger
SPEC	Society for Pollution and Environmental Control (Canada)
SPEC	South Pacific Bureau for Economic Cooperation (Fiji)
SPÉCCA	Société Pour l'Équipement de Carrières et la Commercialisation de Concassé en Afrique (Ivory Coast)
SPÉCI	Société de Presse et d'Édition de la Côte d'Ivoire
SPECI-CHAMBRE	Chambre Syndicale des Fabricants et Concessionnaires de Spécialités Pharmaceutiques
SPECR	Societas Europaea Physiologiae Clinicae Respiratoriae
Speed	Scottish Partnership in Electronics for Effective Distribution
SPEF	Scottish Plumbing Employers Federation

SPEF	Scottish Print Employers Federation (*ex* SMPS)
SPEF	Svenska Putsentreprenörföreningen
SPEIN	Syndicat Patronal des Entreprises et Industries du Niger
SPEIO	Associação Portuguesa de Estatistica e Investigação Operacional
SPÉL	Société Provisoire de l'Économique Laitière
SPEM	Sociedade Portuguesa de Esclerose Múltipla
SPÉM	Société de Presse et d'Édition de Madagascar
SPEMD	Sociedade Portuguesa de Estomatologia e Medicina Dentaria
SPÉO	Société de Presse et d'Édition Ovine
SPÉPE	Secrétariat Permanent pour l'Étude des Problèmes de l'Eau
SPÉR	Syndicat des Industries de Matériel Professionnel Électronique et Radioélectrique
SPERI	Shanghai Power Equipment Research Institute
SPES	Sociedade Portuguesa de Energia Solar
SPES	Société Suisse des Professeurs de Philosophie de l'Enseignement Secondaire = SIPS, VSPM
SPES	South-Place Ethical Society
SPÉTI	Société de Production des Équipements Techniques et l'Industrie (Mauritania)
SPF	Sasakawa Heiwa Zaidan
SPF	Science Policy Foundation
SPF	Scottish Pensioners Forum
SPF	Scottish Pharmaceutical Federation
SPF	Scottish Police Federation
SPF	Sociedade Portuguesa de Fisica
SPF	Société des Poètes Français
SPF	Société Pomologique de France
SPF	Société Préhistorique Française
SPF	South Pacific Forum
SPF	Svensk Pilotförening
SPF	Svenska Pappershandlareföreningen
SPF	Svenska Prästförbundet
SPF	Svenska Psykiatriska Föreningen
SPF	Sveriges Papersindustriförbund
SPF	Sveriges Personaladministrativa Förening
SPF	Sveriges Plastförbund
SPF	Sveriges Pomologiska Förening
SPF	Syndicat des Psychiatres Française
SPFA	Scottish Pelagic Fishermens Association
SPFA	Société des Palmeraies de la Ferme Suisse (Cameroon)
SPFA	Société des Professeurs Français en Amérique
SPFB	Chambre Syndicale des Producteurs de Fontes Brutes
SPFE	Society for the Preservation of the Fauna of the Empire
SPFF	Syndicat des Propriétaires Forestiers de France
SPFGBS	Syndicat des Producteurs Français des Graines de Betterave à Sucre
SPFV	Schweizerischer Pelz-Fachverband
SPG	Schweizerische Philosophische Gesellschaft = SSP
SPG	Schweizerische Physikalische Gesellschaft = SSP
SPG	Small Press Group of Great Britain
SPG	Sociedade Portuguesa de Gastrenterologia
SPG	Sociedade Portuguesa de Geotecnia
SPG	Special Protection Group (India)
SPGB	Socialist Party of Great Britain
SPH	Société Philatélique Hellénique = HPS
SPH	Société Protectrice Humains
SPH	Society of Public Health
SPHAN	Secretaria do Património Histórico e Artístico Nacional (Brazil)
SPHB	Société des Plantations du Haut-Bsamoun (Cameroon)
SPHB	Société des Plantations et Huileries de Bingerville (Ivory Coast)
SPHC	Société de Plantations d'Hévéas et de Cafeiers (Central Africa)
SPHEF	Société des Physiciens des Hôpitaux d'Expression Française
SPHN	Société de Physique et d'Histoire Naturelle de Genève
SPHS	Society for the Promotion of Hellenic Studies (U.S.A.)
SPHU	Société Propriétaire de l'Hôtel de l'Union (Senegal)
SPhV	Schweizerischer Photographenverband = USF, USP
SPI	Secrétariats Professionnels Internationaux = ITS
SPI	Serviço de Proteção aos Indios (Brazil)
SPI	Shaanxi Physics Institute

SPI	Società Psicoanalitica Italiana
SPI	Société pour l'Informatique
SPI	Society of Photographic Illustrators (U.S.A.)
SPI	Society of Practitioners of Insolvency
SPI	Society of Professional Investigators (U.S.A.)
SPI	Society of the Plastics Industry (U.S.A.)
SPI	Sports Philatelists International
SPI	Sports Promotion International
SPI	Svenska Petroleum Institutet
SPIADH	Syndicat Professionnel des Industries Annexes ou Dérivées de la Houille dans le Pas-de-Calais
SPIB	Society of Power Industry Biologists (U.S.A.)
SPIC	Société de Participations Industrielles et Commerciales
SPIC	Society of the Plastics Industry of Canada
SPIC	Southern Petrochemical Industries Corporation (U.S.A.) (India)
SPIC-MACAY	Society for the Promotion of Indian Classical Music and Culture Amongst the Young
SPICRIM	Société pour la Participation Industrielle et Commerciale pour la Représentation Industrielle en Mauritanie
SPICA	Société Industrielle de Produits Chimiques et Aromatiques (Cameroon)
SPICE	Stanford Program on International and Cross-Cultural Education (U.S.A.)
SPICMA	Special Projects in Christian Missionary Areas
SPIDÉL	Société pour l'Informatique et Documentation Électronique
SPIDS	Syndicat Professional des Industries du Sénégal
SPIE	International Society of Photo-optical Instrumentation Engineers
SPIE	Secrétariat Professionnel International de l'Enseignement = IFFTU, IVFL
SPIEA	Syndicat Professionnel de l'Industrie des Engrais Azotés
SPIF	Société de Participations Industrielles et Financières pour la France et l'Afrique
SPIFDA	South Pacific Islands Fisheries Development Agency
SPIGED	Syndicat Professional des Industries des Goudrons et Dérivés
SPIH	Syndicat des Producteurs Independants de Houblons
SPII	Scottish Pig Industry Initiative
SPII	Seed and Plant Improvement Institute (Iran)
SPIL	Society for the Promotion and Improvement of Libraries (India)
SPIMMCC	Syndicat Patronal des Industries Métallurgiques, Mécaniques et Connexes du Calvados
SPIN	Science for Peace International Network (Canada) = RISP
SPINES	Science and Technology Policies Information Exchange System = PIPS
SPIO	Spitzenorganisation der Filmwirtschaft
SPIRE	South Pacific Institute for Renewable Energy (Polynesia, Tahiti) = IERPS
SPIREX	South Pole Infrared Explorer (U.S.A.)
SPIRIM	Société Ivoirienne de Promotion et de Réalisations Immobilières
SPIS	Senate Permanent Investigating Subcommittee (U.S.A.)
SPITJ	Savez Poloprivrednih Inzenjera i Technicara Jugoslavije
SPIVHLB	Société Propriétaire du Village Hôtel de la Langue de Barbarie (Senegal)
SPK	Saporamean Kampuchea
SPK	Savezna Privredna Komara, Savat za Ugostiteljstvo
SPK	Schweizerische Gesellschaft der Psychotherapeuten für Kinder und Jugendliche
SPK	Socialist Party of Kazakhstan
SPK	Socialist Party of Kurdistan (Iraq)
SPK	Suomen Kommunistinen Puolue
SPKC	Small Pig Keepers Council
SPL	Socialist Party of Labour (Romania)
SPLA	Scottish Poetry Library Association
SPLA	Sudan Peoples Liberation Army
SPLASH	Single Parent Links and Special Holidays
SPLF	Society for the Preservation of Life from Fire
SPLM	Sudan People's Liberation Movement
SPM	Shoqata Politike Mëmëdheu (Albania) = MPA
SPM	Socialist Party of Macedonia
SPM	Socialist Party of Montenegro = SPCG
SPM	Sociedade Portuguesa de Matematica
SPM	Société des Pétroles de Madagascar

SPM	Society of Pharmaceutical Medicine
SPM	Society of Prospective Medicine (U.S.A.)
SPM	Somali Patriotic Movement
SPMA	Scottish Modern Pentathlon Association
SPMA	Sewage Plant Manufacturers Association
SPMA	Shoe Pattern Manufacturers Association (U.S.A.)
SPMA	Society for Post-Medieval Archaeology
SPMA	Sterilization Packaging Materials Association
SPMBNI	Seed Potato Marketing Board for Northern Ireland
SPMC	Society of Professional Management Consultants (U.S.A.)
SPMC	Syndicat des Petits et Moyens Commerçants du Niger
SPMF	Syndicat des Producteurs de Miel de France
SPMFR	Sociedade Portuguesa de Medicina Fisica & Reabilitação
SPML	Sociedade Portuguesa de Medicina Laboratorial
SPMM	Société des Produits de Mer Mauritaniens
SPMP	Syndicat Professionnel des Producteurs de Matières Plastiques
SPMRL	Sulphite Pulp Manufacturers Research League (U.S.A.)
SPN	Sociedade Portuguesa de Numismática
SPNI	Society for the Protection of Nature (Israel)
SPNM	Society for the Promotion of New Music
SPNR	Society for the Promotion of Nature Reserves
SPNT	Society for the Promotion of Nutritional Therapy
SPÖ	Socialistische Partei Österreichs
SPO	Society of Planning Officials (U.S.A.)
SPO	Srpski Pokret Obnove (Serbia) = SRM
SPO	Strana Podnikatelů a Obchodníků (Czech Republic) = PBT
SPO(FDO)	Soiuz Pionerskikh Organizatsii (Federatsii Detskikh Organizatsii)
SPOA	Scottish Plant Owners' Association
SPOA	Scottish Prison Officers' Association
SPOAE	Société de Production Alimentaire et d'Industrie (Benin)
SPOCC	South Pacific Organizations Coordinating Committee
SPOD	Association to Aid the Sexual and Personal Relationships of People with a Disability
SPOF	Svenska Patentombuds Föreningen
SPOFA	Leverantöföreningne för Sport- och Fritidsartiklar
SPOOF	Society for the Perpetration of Outrageous Farces
SPOOM	Syndicat des Producteurs d'Oléagineux d'Outre-Mer
SPORE	Society for the Preservation of the Rain-forest Environment
SPORT-SCAN	Sports Sponsorship Computer Analysis
SPOT	Sociedade Portuguesa de Ortopedia e Traumatologia
SPP	Secretaría de Programación y Presupuesto (Mexico)
SPP	Seed Potato Promotions of Northern Ireland
SPP	Sindicato de Periodistas del Paraguay
SPP	Slovene People's Party
SPP	Sociedade Portuguesa de Psicanálise
SPP	Society for Pediatric Psychology (U.S.A.)
SPP	Soiuz Proletarskikh Pisatelei
SPP	Stowarzyszenie Papierników Polskich = APP
SPP	Stowarzyszenie Pisarzy Polskich
SPP	Swaziland Progressive Party
SPPA	Scottish Pre-School Playgroup Association
SPPA	Serviço de Pesquisas de Patologia Animal (Brazil)
SPPA	Singapore Planned Parenthood Association
SPPA	South Pacific Ports Association
SPPAC	Salinity Pilot Program Advisory Council (now SPAC)
SPPC	Shokata Politike-Patriotike Çamëria (Albania) = CPPA
SPPC	Society of Plant Protection of China
SPPEF	Société pour la Protection des Paysages et de l'Esthétique de la France
SPPF	Sécretariat Permanent des Peuples Francophones (Canada)
SPPF	Seychelles People's Progressive Front
SPPF	Sociedade Portuguesa de Pastagens e Forragens

SPPI	Syndicat des Producteurs Phonographiques Indépendants
SPPL	Saathiaranagroat Prachhathippetay Prachhachhon Lao = LPDR
SPPRI	Sichuan Pulp and Paper Research Institute
SPQ	Sociedade Portuguesa de Química
SPQR	Senatus Populusque Romanus
SPR	Incorporated Society for Psychical Research
SPR	Sociedade Portuguesa de Reumatologia
SPR	Société Pédagogique de la Suisse Romande
SPR	Society for Pediatric Radiology
SPR	Society for Pediatric Research (U.S.A.)
SPR	Society for Psychical Research
SPR	Society for Psychophysiological Research (U.S.A.)
SPR	Society of Property Researchers
SPR	Studievereniging voor Psychical Research
SPR	Sveriges Pälsdjursuppfodares Riksförbund
SPR	Sveriges Parfymhandlares Riksförbund
SPR	Sveriges Public Relations Förening
SPRC	Society for Prevention and Relief of Cancer
SPRCA	Scottish Public Relations Consultants Association
SPRCAC	South Pacific Regional Civil Aviation Council (SPF) (Fiji)
SPRD	Soiuz Potomkov Rossiiskogo Dvorianstva
SPRDA	Solid Pipeline Research and Development Association (Canada)
SPRED	Society of Picture Researchers and Editors
SPREP	South Pacific Regional Environment Programme (New Caledonia) = PROE
SPRF	Schweizer Public-Relations-Forum
SPRG	Schweizerische Public Relations Gesellschaft = SSRP
SPRI	Scott Polar Research Institute
SPRIÉ	Société de Préfabrication, Revêtement Isolation, Étanchéité (Senegal)
SPRINT	Strategic Programme for Innovation and Technology Transfer (CEC)
SPRL	Society for the Promotion of Religion and Learning
SPRM	Societatea Protozoologicâ din Republica Moldova
SPROA	Société des Plantations Réunies de l'Ouest Africain (Ivory Coast)
SPRU	Science Policy Research Unit
SPRV	Schweizerischer Personalzeitungs-Redaktorenverband = ARJES
SPS	Saint Patrick's Society for the Foreign Missions
SPS	Scottish Prison Service
SPS	Serikat Penerbit Sirratkabar
SPS	Socialist Party of Serbia
SPS	Socialistička Partija Srbije (Serbia) = SSP
SPS	Société de Savon et Produits Similaires (Senegal)
SPS	Society of Pelvic Surgeons (U.S.A.)
SPS	Society of Portrait Sculptors
SPS	Stichting Planbureau Suriname
SPSA	Society of Philippine Surgeons of America
SPSAS	Société de Peintres, Sculpteurs et Architectes Suisses = GSMBA
SPSBS	Shetland Pony Stud Book Society
SPSDM	Society for the Philosophical Study of Dialectical Materialism (U.S.A.)
SPSF	Syndicat des Pisciculteurs-Salmoniculteurs de France
SPSI	All-Indonesia Union of Workers
SPSI	Society for the Promotion of Scientific Industry
SPSL	Society for the Protection of Science and Learning
SPSM	Society for the Philosophical Study of Marxism (U.S.A.)
SPSP	Somali Revolutionary Socialist Party
SPSS	Syndicat des Producteurs de Semences Sélectionnées
SPSSI	Society for the Psychological Study of Social Issues (U.S.A.)
SPSSR	Syndicat du Personnel Social des Services Sociaux Ruraux
SPT	Brancheforeningen for Soebe-Parfumeri-, Toilet- og Kemisk- Tekniske Artikler
SPT	Société Sénégalaise de Publicité et de Tourisme
SPT	Society of Photo-Technologists (U.S.A.)
SPT	Sotsialisticheskaia Partiia Trudiashchikhsia
SPT	Sveriges Personaltidningsförening
SPTA	Scottish Provision Trade Association

SPTA	Small Potteries Trade Association	**SPZR**	Party of Entrepreneurs, Tradesmen and Farmers of the Czech Republic
SPTC	Single Parent Travel Club	**SQAB**	Society for Quantitative Analyses of Behavior
SPTDP	South Pacific Telecommunications Development Programme (SPF) (Fiji)	**SQBLA**	Scotch Quality Beef and Lamb Association
SPTIY	Suomen Puuteollisuss-insinöörien Yhdistys	**SQER**	Société Québécoise pour l'Étude de la Religion
SPTL	Society of Public Teachers of Law in Great Britain and Northern Ireland	**SQI**	Sociedad de Quimica Industrial
SPTL	Suomen Pesuteollisuusliitto	**SQM**	Sociedad Química de México
SPTT	Sovet Promyshlennosti, Transporta i Torgovli	**SQP**	Sociedad Química del Perú
		SQR	Syndicat des Quotidiens Régionaux
SPTVC	Secteur Professionnel Textile-Vêtement- Chaussure	**SQRA**	Singapore Quality and Reliability Association
SPTW	Society for Promoting the Training of Women	**SQUASH**	Squatters Action for Secure Homes
SPU	Scientific Programs Unit (ANCA)	**SR**	Sågverkens Riksförbund
SPU	Serviço de Património da União (Brazil)	**SR**	Svobodnaia Rossiia
SPUC	Society for the Protection of the Unborn Child	**SRA**	Science Research Associates (U.S.A.)
		SRA	Scottish Records Association
SPUMS	South Pacific Underwater Medicine Society	**SRA**	Scottish Rifle Association
		SRA	Sea Ranger Association
SPUR	Singapore Planning Urban Research Group	**SRA**	Secretaria de la Reforma Agraria (Mexico)
SPURS	Special Program for Urban and Regional Studies of Developing Areas (U.S.A.)	**SRA**	Shooters' Rights Association
		SRA	Singapore Robot Association
		SRA	Snail Racing Association
SPV	Hanyang Special Auto Research Institute (China)	**SRA**	Social Research Association
		SRA	Sociedad Rural Argentina
SPV	Schweizer Pressephotographen Verband = ASPP	**SRA**	Société de Recherche Appliquée à l'Éducation
SPV	Schweizerische Schlachtvieh Produzentenverband	**SRA**	Société de Représentation et d'Agréage (Congo)
SPV	Schweizerischer Pädagogischer Verband (*now* SGL)	**SRA**	Society of Research Administration
SPV	Schweizerischer Pédicure Verband	**SRA**	Speedway Riders' Association
SPV	Schweizerischer Pferdezuchtverband	**SRA**	Squash Rackets Association
SPV	Schweizerischer Physiotherapeuten-Verband	**SRA**	State Rail Authority (Australia)
SPV	Schweizerischer Podologen Verband = ASP	**SRAA**	Société Royale d'Astronomie d'Anvers (Belgium)
SPVEA	Superintendência de Valorização Econômica da Amazônia	**SRAAP**	Subcentro Regional de Artesanias y Artes Populares (Guatemala)
SPVS	Society of Practising Veterinary Surgeons (BVA)	**SRAB**	Société Royale des Beaux-Arts (Belgium)
SPWLA	Society of Professional Well Log Analysts	**SRAC**	Société Royale d'Astronomie du Canada = RASC
SPY	Suomen Paperi-Insinöörien Yhdistys	**SRAD**	Société Romande des Auteurs Dramatiques
SPY	Suomen Puutavarakauppiasyhdistys	**SRAG**	Sydney Rainforest Action Group
SPyV	Secretaria de Proteccion y Vialidad (Mexico)	**SRAIN**	Société de Représentations Automobiles et Industrielles au Niger

SRAM	Regional Secretariat of Catholic Education for Africa and Madagascar (SECAM)		**SRCL**	Service Rural de Culture et Loisirs
SRAMA	Spring Research and Manufacturers Association		**SRCMA**	Steel Radiator and Convector Manufacturers' Association
SRAP	Scottish Rent Assessment Panel		**SRCOA**	Société Routière Colas de l'Ouest Africain
SRAPL	Société Romande d'Audiophonologie et de Pathologie du Langage		**SRCRA**	Shipowners Refrigerated Cargo Research Association
SRAT	Section Région d'Afrique Tropicale (IOBC)		**SRD**	Safety and Reliability Directorate (UKAEA)
SRAT	Société de Recherches et d'Applications Techniques		**SRD**	Stichting Rationele Distributie
SRB	Schweizerische Republikanische Bewegung = MRS		**SRDA**	Scottish Retail Distributors Association
			SRDC	Shopfitting Research and Development Council
SRB	Sociedad Rural Boliviana		**SRDC**	Sudan Rural Development Company
SRB	Sociedade Rural Brasileira		**SRDC**	Sugar Research and Development Corporation
SRB	Statens Rad for Byggnadsforskning			
SRBA	Société Royale Belge d'Astronomie, de Météorologie et de Physique du Globe		**SRDFC**	Sudan Rural Development Finance Company
SRBB	Société Royale de Botanique de Belgique		**SRDG**	Software Research and Development Group (Canada)
SRBÉ	Société Royale Belge des Électriciens = KBVE		**SRE**	Society of Reliability Engineers (U.S.A.)
SRBG	Société Royale Belge de Géographie		**SREM**	School of Resource and Environmental Management (ANU)
SRBGE	Société Royale Belge de Gastro-Entérologie		**SRÉPB**	Société Royale d'Économie Politique de Belgique
SRBII	Société Royale des Ingénieurs et des Industriels (Belgium)		**SRES**	School for Resource and Environmental Studies (Canada)
SRBMD	Société Royale Belge de Médecine Dentaire = KBVT		**SRES**	Science Rondo Esperantistaj Studentoj
SRBMPR	Société Royale Belge de Médecine Physique et de Réhabilitation = KBVFGR		**SRES**	Societatea Română de Energie Solară = RSES
			SRÉSA	Société de Recherche Économique et Sociologique en Agriculture
SRC	Scientific Research Council (Iraq)		**SRF**	Scottish Republican Forum
SRC	Scientific Research Council (Jamaica)		**SRF**	Self Realization Fellowship (U.S.A.)
SRC	Sex Race and Class (Black and Third World Women's Discussion and Study Group)		**SRF**	Svenska Reklambyra Forbundet
			SRF	Svenska Resebyraföreningen
			SRF	Sveriges Rationaliseringsförbund
SRC	Sheriff Court Rules Council		**SRF**	Sveriges Redareförening
SRC	Shri Ram Centre for Industrial Relations (India)		**SRF**	Sveriges Redovisningskonsultors Förbund
SRC	Social Research Center (Egypt)			
SRC	Social Research Centre (Cyprus, Hong Kong)		**SRF**	Syndicat des Riziculteurs de France
			SRFB	Société Royale Forestière de Belgique = KBBM
SRC	Société Royale du Canada = RSC			
SRC	Synchrotron Radiation Center (U.S.A.)		**SRFCAM**	Section de Recherches Forestières au Caméroun
SRCC	Société Nationale pour la Renovation et le Développement de la Cacoyère et de Cafetière Togolaise		**SRFD**	Society for the Rehabilitation of the Facially Disfigured (U.S.A.)
SRCI	Société Routière Colas de la Côte d'Ivoire		**SRFT**	Societatea Română de Fotogrammetrie și Teledecţie

SRG	Schweizerische Radio und Fernsehgesellschaft
SRG	Socialist Review Group
SRG	Socialist Revolutionary Group of Ireland
SRGB	Sports Retailers (*ex* FSGD)
SRGC	Scottish Rock Garden Club
SRGU	Soiuz Rabotnikov Gosudarstvennykh Uchrezhdenii
SRH	Société Sénégalaise de Régénération des Huiles Minérales
SRH	Stranka Roma Hrvatske (Croatia) = RPC
SRHE	Society for Research into Higher Education
SRHSB	Society for Research into Hydrocephalus and Spina Bifida
SRI	Ski Retailers International (U.S.A.)
SRI	Soil Research Institute (Ghana)
SRI	Strana za Rómsku Integráciu (Slovakia) = PRI
SRI	Sugar Research Institute (Australia)
SRIA	Scottish Record Industry Association
SRIAM	Shanghai Research Institute of Acupuncture & Meridian
SRICI	Shanghai Research Institute of Chemical Industry
SRICI	Shenyang Research Institute of Chemical Industry
SRIET	Shanghai Research Institute of International Economy and Trade
SRIIHOD	Shenyang Research Institute of Industrial Hygiene and Occupational Diseases
SRIMT	Shanghai Research Institute for Microwave Technology
SRiPB	Soiuz Real'nykh i Potentsial'nykh Bezrabotnykh (Belarus)
SRIPT	Shanghai Research Institute of Printing Technology
SRIS	Safety Research Information Service (U.S.A.)
SRIS	Science Reference and Information Service (BL)
SRISS	Shanghai Research Institute of Sports Science
SRIT	Section d'Études et Fabrications des Télécommunications
SRIT	Sikkim Research Institute of Tibetology
SRITD	Shanghai Research Institute of Tool & Die Technology
SRL	Schweizerische Rheumaliga
SRL	Sociedad de Responsabilidad Limitada
SRL	Society of Romance Languages (U.S.A.)
SRL	Sound Research Laboratories
SRL	Surveillance Research Laboratory (Australia)
SRL	Sveriges Radioleverantörer
SRL	Vereinigung der Stadt-, Regional- und Landesplaner
SRLA	Scottish Recreational Land Association
SRLF	Société de Réanimation de Langue Française
SRLF	Syndicat des Représentants Littéraires Français
SRLR	Societatea Româna de Linguistica Romanica
SRM	International Spiritual Regeneration Movement (U.K.)
SRM	Serbian Renewal Movement = SPO
SRMA	Spring Research Manufacturers Association
SRNA	Shipbuilders and Repairers National Association
SRO	Scottish Record Office
SRO	Society of Registration Officers
SRON	Space Research Organization Netherlands
SRP	Serbian Radical Party (Montenegro) = SRS
SRP	Serengeti Research Project (Tanzania)
SRP	Society for Radiological Protection
SRP	Society for Recorder Players
SRP	Subcarpathian Republican Party (Ukraine)
SRPA	Squash Rackets Professional Association
SRPBA	Scottish River Purification Boards Association
SRPMME	Society for Research in the Psychology of Music and Music Education
SRPO	Science Resources Planning Office (U.S.A.)
SRPS	Scottish Railway Preservation Society
SRR	Società Retorumantscha (Switzerland)
SRR	Sveriges Radiohandlares Riksförbund
SRRA	Sudan Relief and Rehabilitation Agency
SRS	Scottish Record Societty
SRS	Scottish Reformation Society

SRS	Scottish Rhododendron Society
SRS	Service de la Recherche Sociologique (Switzerland)
SRS	Srpska Radikalna Stranka (Montenegro) = SRP
SRS	Surgical Research Society
SRS	Svenska Revisoramfundet
SRS	Swiss Railways Society
SRSAG	Supra Regional Services Advisory Group
SRSBIA	Ship Repairers and Ship Builders Independent Association
SRSD	Society of Record Sleeve Designers
SRSP	Scottish Republican Socialist Party
SRSP	Somali Revolutionary Socialist Party
SRT	Société Routière du Togo
SRTI	Société de Recherches Techniques et Industrielles
SRTI	Société de Rénovation et Technique Industrielle (Gabon)
SRTPA	Syndicat des Redacteurs Techniques de la Presse Agricole
SRTR	Société de Radiodiffusion et de Télévision de la Suisse Romande
SRU	Savez Rutenca i Ukrajinca (Serbia) = ARU
SRU	Scottish Research into UFOs
SRU	Scottish Rugby Union
SRU	Société du Raffinage d'Uranium
SRUBLUK	Society for the Reinvigoration of Unremunerative Branch Lines in the United Kingdom
SRV	Schweizerischer Reklame-Verband
SRV	Schweizerischer Richtervereinigung = ASG, ASM
SRWN	Społeczna Rada Wydawnictów Niezaleznych
SRWS	Scottish Rights of Way Society
SRY	Suomen Radiologiyhdistys
SRZA	Société Royale Zoologique d'Anvers = KMDA
SRZB	Société Royale Zoologique de Belgique
SS	Department of Social Sciences (UNESCO)
SS	Sdružení Slováků (Czech Republic) = UOS
SS	Societas Ancillarum Sanctissimi Sacramenti
SS	Spastics Society

SS	Společnost Slováků (Czech Republic) = COS
SS	Stereoscopic Society
SS	Sveriges Slakteriförbund (Sweden)
SS DVT	Slovenská Spoločnosť pre Dejiny Vied a Techniky pri SAV
SS-SNJ	Strana Slobody-Strana Národnej Jednoty (Slovakia) = PF-PNU
SS/ENV	UNESCO Division of Human Settlements and Socio-Cultural Environment
SS/ETD	UNESCO Division of Study Development
SS/HR	UNESCO Division of Human Rights Peace
SS/PH	UNESCO Philosophy Division
SS/POP	UNESCO Population Division
SS/YTH	UNESCO Youth Division
SSA	Forskningsstiftelsen Skogsarbeten
SSA	School Secretaries Association
SSA	Scottish Schoolmasters Association
SSA	Scottish Skateboard Association (now FOSS)
SSA	Scottish Sound Archive
SSA	Seasoning and Spice Association (ex SMA, STA)
SSA	Seismological Society of America
SSA	Semiotic Society of America
SSA	Shan State Army (Burma)
SSA	Side-Saddle Association
SSA	Silver Steel Association
SSA	Sisters of St. Anne
SSA	Slovenská Spoločnosť pre Akost
SSA	Social Security Administration
SSA	Società Svizzera degli Albergatori
SSA	Société Suisse Amerikanisten-Gesellschaft
SSA	Society for the Study of Addiction
SSA	Society of Scottish Artists
SSA	Statistical Society of Australia
SSA	Svenska Sockerfabriks Aktiebolaget
SSAA	Scottish Schools Athletic Association
SSAA	Société Suisse d'Astrophysique et d'Astronomie = SGAA
SSAC	Scandinavian Society for Antimicrobial Chemotherapy
SSAC	Scottish Society for Autistic Children
SSAC	Scottish Sub-Aqua Club
SSAC	Social Security Advisory Committee

SSAD	Scottish Sports Association for the Disabled	**SSC**	Supply and Services Canada
SSAÉ	Service Social d'Aide aux Émigrants	**SSC**	Surgical Society of China
SSAE	Société Suisse d'Anthropologie et d'Ethnologie	**SSCA**	Scottish Ship Chandlers Association
		SSCA	Social Science Computing Association
SSAF	Scottish Salmon Angling Federation (S&TA)	**SSCC**	Congregatio Sacrorum Cordium Iesu et Mariae necnon adorationis perpetuae Sanctissimi Sacramenti Altaris
SSAFA	Soldiers' Sailors' and Airmen's Families Association	**SSCC**	Scottish Sporting Car Club
SSAG	Svenska Sällskapet för Antropologi och Geografi	**SSCC**	Société Suisse de Chimie Clinique = SGKC
SSAI	Société Suisse d'Allergologie et d'Immunologie = SGAI	**SSCH**	Soeurs de l'Enfance de Jésus et Marie de Sainte Chrétienne
SSAO	Société Shell de l'Afrique Occidentale	**SSCI**	Sociétés de Construction de Meubles Métalliques
SSAR	Société Suisse d'Anesthésiologie et de Réanimation = SGAR	**SSCI**	Sociétés de Service et Conseil en Informatique
SSAR	Society for the Study of Amphibians and Reptiles	**SSCI**	Swiss Society of Chemical Industries = SGCI, SSIC
SSAS	Società di Storia dell'Arte in Svizzera = GSK, SHAS	**SSCIA**	Scottish Spinal Cord Injury Association
SSAS	Society for South Asian Studies	**SSCJ**	Sisters of the Sacred Heart of Jesus
SSATS	Social Security Appeal Tribunals	**SSCLE**	Society for the Study of the Crusades and the Latin East
SSB	Scottish Salmon Board		
SSB	Securities Supervisory Board (Republic of Korea)	**SSCM**	Société Surgerienne de Constructions Mécaniques
SSB	Société Suisse de Biochimie = SGB	**SSCM**	Soeur Servantes du Saint-Coeur de Maria
SSBA	Scottish Schools Basketball Association	**SSCME**	Societas Sancti Columbani pro Missionaribus ad Exteros
SSBA	Scottish Spina Bifida Association	**SSCN**	Society for the Study and Conservation of Nature (Malta)
SSBMB	Slovenská Společnost pre Biochémiu a Mokekulárnu Biológiu	**SSCP**	Society for a Science of Clinical Psychology
SSC	Missionary Sisters of St. Columban		
SSC	Scottish Schoolboys' Club	**SSCR**	Scottish Society for Conservation and Restoration
SSC	Scottish Ski Club		
SSC	Scottish Society of Composers	**SSCR**	Scottish Society for Crop Research
SSC	Scottish Sports Council	**SSCRI**	Southern Subtropical Crops Research Institute (China)
SSC	Seismological Society of China		
SSC	Società Storica Catanese	**SSCSoc**	Society of Solicitors of the Supreme Courts of Scotland
SSC	Societas Presbyterorum Sancti Ioseph Benedicti Cottolengo	**SSCVYO**	Scottish Standing Conference of Voluntary Youth Organisations
SSC	Société Suisse de Chimie = SCG	**SSD**	Svoboda i Dostoinstvo
SSC	Société Suisse de Cristallographie	**SSDC**	Society of Stage Directors and Choreographers (U.S.A.)
SSC	Société Suisse des Cuisiniers = SKV		
SSC	Species Survival Commission (IUCN)	**SSDF**	Somali Salvation Democratic Front
SSC	Spectroscopy Society of Canada	**SSDT**	Society of Soft Drink Technologists (U.S.A.)
SSC	St Columban's Foreign Mission Society		
SSC	State Services Commission (New Zealand)	**SSE**	Services CCI pour la Sécurité de l'Entreprise (U.K.)
SSC	Statistical Society of Canada / Société Statistique du Canada	**SSE**	Société Suisse d'Ethnologie = SEG

SSÉ	Société Suisse des Écrivains		**SSFA**	Scottish Schools Football Association
SSE	Société Suisse des Entrepreneurs = SBV, SSIC		**SSFA**	Shetland Salmon Farmers' Association
SSE	Society for Scientific Exploration		**SSFA**	Stainless Steel Fabricators Association (*now* BSSA)
SSE	Society of Saint Edmund (U.S.A.)		**SSFC**	Social Science Federation of Canada
SSEA	Société Suisse des Exploitants d'Autotaxis et de Voitures de Remise		**SSFC**	Société Suisse des Fabriques de Cartonnages
SSEB	South of Scotland Electricity Board		**SSFD**	Société Sénégalaise de Fabrication et de Distribution
SSEB	Swiss Society for Business Education = ASEC, SGKB		**SSFF**	Skogbrukets of Skogindustrienes Forskningsforening
SSEC	Secondary School Examinations Council		**SSFF**	Solid Smokeless Fuels Federation
SSEC	Social Science Education Consortium (U.S.A.)		**SSFF**	Svenska Sällskapet för Fotogrammetri och Fjarranalys
SSÉC	Société Sucrière d'Études et de Construction (Belgium)		**SSFI**	Shanghai Synthetic Fibre Research Institute
SSEES	School of Slavonic and East European Studies		**SSFM**	Scandinavian Society of Forensic Medicine
SSEF	Sveriges Städentreprenörers Förbund		**SSFMAC**	Southern Shark Fishery Management Advisory Committee
SSEG	Scottish Solar Energy Group		**SSFO**	Scandinavian Society of Forensic Odontology = NROF
SSEPC	Société Sénégalaise d'Engrais et de Produits Chimiques		**SSFODF**	Syndicat des Spécialistes Français en Orthopédie Dento-Faciale
SSERC	Scottish Schools Equipment Research Centre		**SSFTA**	Scottish Soft Fruit Trade Association
SSÉS	Société Suisse pour l'Énergie Solaire		**SSG**	ONU Syndicat des Services Généraux = GSU
SSET	State Science, Environment and Technology Department (India)		**SSG**	Schweizerische Sprachwissenschaftliche Gesellschaft = SSL
SSF	Scottish Software Federation			
SSF	Scottish Surfing Federation		**SSG**	Società di Studi Geografici
SSF	Sildolje- og Sildemelindustriens Forskningsinstitiutt (Norway)		**SSG**	Société Suisse de Génétique = SGG
SSF	Società Svizzera di Farmacia = SAV, SSPH		**SSG**	Société Suisse de Gynécologie = SGG
			SSG	Société Suisse pour la Géothermie = SVG
SSF	Societas Scientiarum Fennica			
SSF	Society for the Study of Fertility		**SSG**	Society of Saint Gregory
SSF	Society of Shoe Fitters		**SSGA**	Scottish Salmon Growers Association
SSF	Somali Salvation Front		**SSGA**	Scottish Shellfish Growers Association
SSF	Statens Samfundsvidenskabelige Forskningsrad (Denmark)		**SSGA**	Société Suisse de Géographie Appliquée
SSF	Stiftelsen Svensk Skeppsforskning		**SSGBP**	Society of Snuff Grinders, Blenders and Purveyors
SSF	Svensk Sjuksköterskeförening			
SSF	Svensk-Sudanska Föreningen		**SSGM**	Scandinavian Society for Genitourinary Medicine
SSF	Svenska Slöjdföreningen			
SSF	Svenska Stämpelfabrikanföreningen		**SSH**	Société Suisse d'Hématologie = SGH
SSF	Sveriges Skogsvårdsförbund		**SSH**	Société Suisse des Hôteliers
SSF	Sveriges Stärkelsproducenters Förening		**SSHA**	Scottish Special Housing Association
SSF	Sveriges Stenindustri Förbund		**SSHA**	Social Science History Association (U.S.A.)
SSF	Sveriges Stuvareförbund			
SSF	Syndicat des Récoltants et Commerçants des Graines de Semences d'Essences Forestières		**SSHA**	Société Scientifique d'Hygiène Alimentaire

SSHB	Society for the Study of Human Biology (U.K., U.S.A.)
SSHC	Society to Support Home Confinement
SSHM	Scottish Society for the History of Medicine
SSHM	Society for the Social History of Medicine
SSHMSN	Société Suisse d'Histoire de la Médecine et des Sciences Naturelles = SGGMN
SSHOP	Scottish Society for the History of Photography
SSHRC	Social Sciences and Humanities Research Council (Canada)
SSI	Sculptors' Society of Ireland
SSI	Service Social International; Servicio Social Internacional = ISS
SSI	Società Speleologica Italiana
SSI	Societatea de Ştiinţe Istorice din România
SSI	Society of Scribes and Illuminators (U.K., U.S.A.)
SSI	Statens Strålskyddsinstitute
SSI	Stichting Sprenger Instituut
SSI	Svenska Samfundet för Informationsbehandling
SSIA	Ship Repairers and Ship Builders Independent Association
SSIA	South Sudan Independent Army
SSIC	Società Svizzera degli Impresari-Costruttori = SBV, SSE
SSIC	Société Suisse des Industries Chimiques = SGCI, SSCI
SSID	Service Specialisé d'Informatique Documentaire (CE)
SSIDA	Steel Sheet Information and Development Association
SSIDC	Small Scale Industries Development Corporation (India)
SSIEM	Society for the Study of Inborn Errors of Metabolism
SSIF	Sveriges Skogsindustriförbund
SSIGE	Société Suisse de l'Industrie du Gaz et des Eaux = SVGW
SSIH	Société Suisse pour l'Industrie Horlogère (Switzerland)
SSIL	Shaybani Society of International Law
SSIL	Société Suisse d'Industrie Laitière
SSIMF	Società Svizzera degli Insegnanti di Matematica e Fisica = VSMP, SSPMP
SSIMF	Società Svizzera dei Insegnanti di Matematica e Fisica = SSPMP, VSMP
SSIP	Sozialwissenschaftlicher Studienkreis für Internationale Probleme
SSISI	Statistical and Social Inquiry Society of Ireland
SSISS	Società Svizzera degli Scuole Secondarie = SSPES, VSG
SSIV	Schweizerischer Spenglermeister- und Installateurverband
SSJ	Savez Sindikata Jugoslavije
SSJ	Societas Sodalium Sancti Josephi a Sacro Corde
SSJE	Society of St. John the Evangelist
SSJG	Sisters of St. John of God
SSK	Sentral di Sindikatonan di Korsou (Netherlands Antilles)
SSKT	Slovenská Spoločnost pre Kybernetiku a Informatiku
SSL	Società Storica Locarnese
SSL	Société Suisse de Linguistique = SSG
SSL	Société Suisse des Liquoristes
SSL	Space Systems Laboratory, University of Maryland
SSL	Suomen Sairaanhoitajaliitto = FSF
SSL	Suomen Sanomalehtimiesten Liitto (*now* SJL)
SSLF	Sveriges Livsmedelshandlareförbund
SSLH	Society for the Study of Labour History
SSLRC	Soil Survey and Land Research Centre
SSM	Fachverband Schweizerischer Sussgetränke- und Mineralwasser-Industrien
SSM	Slovenská Spoločnost pre Mechaniku
SSM	Societatea de Ştiinţe Matematice din România
SSM	Societatea de Stiinte Matematice
SSM	Société des Sciences Médicales du Grand-Duché de Luxembourg
SSM	Syndikat Schweizerischer Medienschaffender
SSMA	Scottish Steel Makers' Association
SSMA	Stainless Steel Manufacturers Association
SSMA	State Servants (& Allied) Motoring Association
SSMA	Sterilised Suture Manufacturers Association
SSMAF	Société Suisse des Mensurations et Améliorations Foncières = SVVK

SSMC	Société Suisse des Maîtres Charpentiers = SZV
SSMD	Société Suisse des Maîtres de Dessin = GSZ
SSME	Society for the Study of Medical Ethnics
SSMG	Société Suisse de Médecine Générale = SGAM
SSMG	Société Suisse des Maîtres de Gymnastique
SSMH	Scottish Society for the Mentally Handicapped
SSMI	Sisters Servants of Mary Immaculate; Soeurs Servantes de Marie Immaculée = ABVMI
SSMI	Société Suisse des Maîtres Imprimeurs
SSMLL	Society for the Study of Mediaeval Languages and Literature
SSMMES	Société Suisse des Maîtres de l'Enseignement Secondaire = SSMMSM, SVMM
SSMMSM	Società Svizzera dei Maestri di Musica delle Scuole Medie = SSMMES, SVMM
SSMS	Société Suisse des Médecine du Sport = SGSM
SSMSR	Société Suisse de Mécanique des Sols et des Roches = SGBF
SSMTC	Société Suisse de Médecine Thermale et Climatique = SGBB
SSMUTA	Sheet and Strip Metal Users' Technical Association
SSN	Sociedad Silvicola Nacional (Cuba)
SSN	Société Suisse de Numismatique = SNG
SSN	Sykepleiernes Samarbeid i Norden = NNF
SSND	School Sisters of Notre Dame
SSNR	Society for the Study of Neuronal Regulation
SSNS	Scottish Society for Northern Studies
SSNTA	Scottish Seed and Nursery Trade Association
SSO	Société Suisse d'Odonto-Stomatologie
SSO	Société Suisse d'Oncologie = SGO
SSOEM	Swiss Society for Optic and Electron Microscopy = SGOEM, SSOME
SSOL	Suomen Silmäoptikkojen Liitto
SSOMÉ	Société Suisse d'Optique et de Microscopie Électronique = SGOEM, SSOEM
SSOMV	Schweizerischer Schuhmacher- und Orthopädieschuhmachermeister-Verband
SSOO	Société Suisse pour l'Optique et l'Optométrie = SBAO
SSP	Scandinavian Society for Psychopharmacology
SSP	Scottish Socialist Party
SSP	Scottish Society of Playwrights
SSP	Serbian Socialist Party = SPS
SSP	Sipah-e-Sahaba-e-Pakistan
SSP	Società Storica Pisana
SSP	Societas a Sancto Paulo Apostolo
SSP	Société Suisse de Pédologie = BGS
SSP	Société Suisse de Philosophie = SPG
SSP	Société Suisse de Photogrammétrie = SGP
SSP	Société Suisse de Physique = SPG
SSP	Société Suisse de Psychiatrie = SGP
SSP	Société Suisse de Psychologie et Psychologie Appliquée = SGP
SSP	Society for Scholarly Publishing (U.S.A.)
SSP/ZLP	Writers' Association (Poland)
SSPA	Société de Plastique Africain
SSPA	Société Suisse de Préhistoire et d'Archéologie / Società Svizzera di Preistoria e d'Archeologia = SGUF
SSPBA	Scottish SP Bookmakers' Association
SSPBC	Société Suisse pour la Protection des Biens Culturels = SGKGS, SSPCP
SSPC	Missionary Sisters of St. Peter Claver
SSPCA	Scottish Society for the Prevention of Cruelty to Animals
SSPCA	Steel Structures Painting Council of America (U.S.A.)
SSPCP	Swiss Society for the Protection of Cultural Property = SGKGS, SSPBC
SSPDC	Scottish Seed Potato Development Council
SSPE	Spolek Sberatelu a Prátel Exlibris v Praze
SSPEA	Société Suisse des Psychiatres d'Enfants et d'Adolescents = SEKJP
SSPES	Société Suisse des Professeurs de l'Enseignement Secondaire
SSPFM	Special Society of Package and Food Machinery (China)
SSPH	Société Suisse de Pharmacie

SSPIT	Société Suisse de Photogrammétrie, d'Analyse d'Image et de Télédétection = SGBPF
SSPL	Société Suisse des Patrons Lithographes
SSPM	Société Suisse de Pédagogie Musicale
SSPMP	Société Suisse des Professeurs de Mathématique et de Physique
SSPP	Scandinavian Society for Plant Physiology (Denmark)
SSPP	Société Sénégalaise de Presse et de Publications
SSPP	Society for the Study of Physiological Patterns
SSPP	Southern Society for Philosophy and Psychology
SSPR	Société Suisse de Public Relations
SSPS	Missionary Sisters Servants of the Holy Spirit = HSMS
SSPS	Sheffield Sawmakers' Protection Society
SSpSDAP	Sisters Servants of the Holy Spirit of Perpetual Adoration
SSPT	Société Sénégalaise des Phosphates de Thiès
SSPV	Scottish Society for the Prevention of Vivisection
SSPV	Société Suisse de Physiologie Végétale
SSPWB	Scottish Society for the Protection of Wild Birds
SSQ	Subversive Street Queers
SSR	Société Suisse de Radiodiffusion et Télévision
SSR	Society for the Study of Reproduction
SSR	Sveriges Skogsägareföreningars Riksförbund
SSR	Sveriges Skorstensfejaremästares Riksförbund
SSR	Sveriges Snickeriföretageres Riksförbund
SSR	Sveriges Socionomers Personal- och Förvaltningstjänstemäns Riksforbund
SSRA	Scottish Seaweed Research Association
SSRA	Scottish Squash Rackets Association
SSRB	Soil Survey Research Board (AFRC)
SSRC	Social Science Research Council (Philippines, U.S.A.)
SSRC	Social Sciences Research Center (Cameroon)
SSRC	Social Systems Research Center (U.S.A.)
SSRCC	Social Science Research Council of Canada = CCRSS
SSRD	Social Science Research and Development Corporation (U.S.A.)
SSRE	Society for Social Responsibility in Engineering
SSRG	Schweizerische Studiengesellschaft für Rationellen Guterumschlag
SSRI	Shaanxi Sericultural Research Institute
SSRI	Social Science Research Institute (Japan)
SSRI	Social Science Research Institute (U.S.A.)
SSRMA	Small Scale Rubber Manufacturers Association (Sri Lanka)
SSRN	Société Suisse de Recherches sur la Nutrition = SGE
SSRP	Société Suisse de Relations Publiques = SPRG
SSRP	Swedish Society of Radiation Physics = SFfR
SSRS	Society for Social Responsibility in Science (U.K., U.S.A.)
SSRT	Société Sénégalaise de Réalisation Touristique
SSRU	Social Science Research Unit (Swaziland)
SSS	Congregatio Presbyterorum a Sanctissimo Sacramento
SSS	Scandinavian Surgical Society (Sweden)
SSS	Ship Stamp Society
SSS	Simplified Spelling Society
SSS	Slovenská Sociologická Spoločnost
SSS	Société Suisse de Sociologie = SGS
SSS	Société Suisse de Spéléologie = SGH
SSS	Society for Slovene Studies
SSS	Society of Socialist Studies = SES
SSS	Soiuz Sovetskikh Stalinistov
SSS	Southern Sociological Society
SSS	Sunday Shakespeare Society
SSS	Suomen Säätöteknillinen Seura
SSS	Suomen Sukutukimusseura
SSS	Svenska Spannmalsföreningarnas Samorganisation
SSSA	Scottish Salmon Smokers Association
SSSA	Scottish Schools Swimming Association
SSSA	Soil Science Society of America
SSSA	Synthetic Sports Surfaces Association
SSSB	Society for the Study of Social Biology

SSSC	Soil Science Society of China
SSSCS	Society of Solicitors in the Supreme Courts of Scotland
SSSD	Scandinavian Society for the Study of Diabetes
SSSEA	Soil Science Society of East Africa
SSSF	Sodra Sveriges Skogagares Forbund
SSSH	Société Suisse des Sciences Humaines
SSSI	Society for the Study of Simbiotic Interaction (U.S.A.)
SSSI	Soil Science Society of Ireland
SSSP	Società Siciliana per la Storica Patria
SSSP	Society for the Study of Social Problems (U.S.A.)
SSSP-Sr	Società Siracusana di Storia Patria
SSSR	Society for the Scientific Study of Religion (U.S.A.)
SSSRI	Shanghai Ship and Shipping Research Institute (China)
SSSU	Scottish Speed Skating Union
SSSWP	Seismological Society of the South-West Pacific (New Zealand)
SST	Scottish Scenic Trust
SST	Scottish Sculpture Trust
SST	Société Sénégalaise des Tabacs
SST	Society of Surveying Technicians
SST	Yrkesförbundet Svenska Sjukvårdstjänstemän
SSTA	Scottish Secondary Teachers Association
SSTA	Secondary School Teachers Association of Malta
SSTAB	Société Sénégalaise de Transformation et d'Application du Bois
SSTEF	Svenska Sägwerks- och Trävareuxportföreningen
SSTL	Suomen Sähkötukkuliikkeiden Liitto
SSTS	Kilroy Travel International
SSTV	Sistema Sandinista de Televisión (Nicaragua)
SSU	Species Services Unit (of the Bureau of Meteorology)
SSU	Sveriges Socialdemokratiska Ungdomsförbund
SSUH	Sveriges Studerande Ungdoms Helnykterhetsförbund
SSV	Schweizerische Schiffahrtsvereinigung
SSV	Schweizerischer Sachversicherungsverband

SSV	Schweizerischer Samenhändleverband = ASMG
SSV	Schweizerischer Schriftstellerverband
SSV	Schweizerischer Spiegelglasverband
SSV	Schweizerischer Städteverband
SSV	Seljačka Stranka Vojvodine (Serbia) = FPV
SSVC	Services Sound and Vision Corporation
SSVC	Société Suisse des Voyageurs de Commerce = VRKS
SSWA	Scottish Society of Women Artists (*now* SAAC)
SSWA	Scottish Solway Wildfowlers' Association
SSWEG	Stainless Steel Wire Export Group
SSWG	Supplementary Strategies Working Group (AEC)
SSWIA	Stainless Steel Wire Industry Association
SSZ	Société Suisse de Zoologie = SZG
SSZ	Society of Systematic Zoology (U.S.A.)
ST	Missionari Servi della Santissima Trinità = MSSST
ST	Société Théosophique (India) = TG, TS
ST	Svensk Trycheriföreningen
ST	UNESCO Office of Statistics
ST-ECF	Space Telescope – European Coordinating Facility
ST/SF	Stop Tyndall/Stop the Fascists
STA	Sail Training Association
STA	Science and Technology Agency (Japan)
STA	Scottish Textile Association
STA	Scottish Trampoline Association
STA	Scottish Typographical Association
STA	Slovenska Tiskovna Agencija
STA	Socialist Teachers Association
STA	Sociedad de Tecnicos de Automoción
STA	Société de Télécommunications Africaines
STA	Société de Travail Aérien (Algeria)
STA	Société des Transports Aériennes (Mali)
STA	Société des Transports Africaines (Senegal)
STA	Society of Topographic Arts
STA	Solar Trade Association
STA	Spice Trade Association (*now* SSA)
STA	Supersonic Tunnel Association (Sweden)

STA	Swimming Teachers Association	**STAR**	Society for the Transportation and Aid of Respondents
STA	UNESCO Staff Association	**STAR**	Stress and Anxiety Research Society
STAA	Student Travel Association of Asia (Japan)	**STARDI**	Station de Recherches Bioécologiques Forestières de Dimonika (Congo)
StAAA	Saint Andrew's Ambulance Association	**STARÉC**	Société Technique d'Application et de Recherche Électronique
STAC	Southern Technology Applications Center (U.S.A.)	**STARÉP**	Société Transgabonaise d'Approvisionnement et de Représentation
STACA	Servicio Tecnico Agricola Colombiano Americano		
STACO	Society of Telecommunications Administrative and Controlling Officers	**STARLab**	Space, Telecommunications and Radioscience Laboratory (U.S.A.)
STACRES	Standing Committee on Research and Statistics (FAO)	**START**	Skin Treatment and Research Trust
STAEI	Société de Transit, Affrètement Export – Import (Senegal)	**STAS**	Oficiul de Stat pentru Standarde (Romania)
STAF	Stoppmébelindustrins Arbetgivareförbund	**STAT**	Society of Teachers of the Alexander Technique
STAFIM	Société Tunisienne Automobile, Financière, Immobilière et Maritime	**STATEC**	Service Central de la Statistique et des Études économiques (Luxembourg)
STAG	Soils, Trees and Grass Program (CSIRO)	**STATOIL**	Norwegian State Oil Company
StAGN	Ständiger Ausschuss für Geographische Namen	**STAUK**	Seed Trade Association of the United Kingdom
STAJ	Science and Technology Agency of Japan	**STAUK**	Sugar Traders Association of the United Kingdom
STAL-PECHE	Société Togolaise Arabe Libyenne de Pêche	**STAV**	Stiftelsen for Administrativ Vidareutbildning
STALMET	Stål- og Metallvare-fabrikkens Merkantile Landsforening	**STB**	Save the Bush Project (ANCA)
		STB	Scottish Tourist Board
STAMICO	State Mining Corporation (Tanzania)	**STB**	Société Togolaise de Boissons
STAMVIE	Société Tropicale d'Assurances Mutuelles et Vie (Ivory Coast)	**STB**	State Taxation Board (China)
		STBA	Statistisches Bundesamt
STAN	Servicio Técnico Agrícola de Nicaragua	**STBE**	Society of Teachers in Business Education
STANAV-FORCHAN	NATO Standing Naval Force Channel		
		STBP	Société Togolaise des Pétroles BP
STANAV-FORLANT	NATO Standing Naval Force Atlantic	**STBV**	Steinkohlen Bergbauverein
		STC	Scandinavian Trade Centre
STANPA	Agrupación Nacional de Fabricantes de Perfumería y Afines	**STC**	SHAPE Technical Centre
		STC	Société des Textiles et Chaussures (Benin)
STAPO	Staatspolizei (Austria)		
STAR	Saudi Technology and Research Consulting Centre (Saudi Arabia)	**STC**	Society for Technical Communication (U.S.A.)
STAR	Société Tananarivienne de Réfrigération et de Boissons Gazeuses (Madagascar)	**STC**	Solidaridad de Trabajadores Cristianos (Nicaragua)
		STC	Solidaridad de Trabajadores Cubanos
STAR	Société Tchadienne d'Assurances et de Réassurances	**STC**	Standard Telephones and Cables
STAR	Société Technique d'Acception en Réassurances	**STC**	Stowarzyszenie Techników Cukrowników
STAR	Society for Test Anxiety Research (Netherlands)	**STC**	Surgical Textiles Conference
		STC	Sveriges Trä- och Byggvaruhandlares Centralförbund

STCAN	Service Technique des Constructions et Armes Navales
STCAU	Service Technique Central d'Aménagement et d'Urbanisme
STCB	State Trading Corporation of Bhutan
STCG	Super Tension Cables Group
STCI	Société de Transports de la Côte d'Ivoire
STCTP	Société Togolaise de Commerce et de Travaux Publics
STCVS	Society of Thoracic and Cardiovascular Surgeons of Great Britain and Ireland
STD	Société Togolaise de Diesel
STD	Société Tunisienne de Diffusion
STD	Society of Teachers of the Deaf
STD	Society of Typographic Designers
STDN	Sociedade de Turismo e Diversoses de Macau
STDV	Schweizerischer Textildetaillisten-Verband = ASDT
STE	Société Française des Téléphones Ericsson
STE	Société Togolaise d'Entreposage
STE	Society of Telecom Executives
STE	Society of Test Engineers
STÉA	Société des Travaux d'Électrification et d'Adduction (Benin)
STEBT	Société de Transformation et d'Exploitation des Bois Tropicaux (Ivory Coast)
STEC	Société Technique d'Entreprises Chimiques
STEC	Storage and Transport of Explosives Committee (India)
STÉCI	Société de Travaux d'Équipement de la Côte d'Ivoire
STECLA	Standing Technological Conference of European Local Authorities
STECTA	Société Technique et Commerciale des Canalisations Souterraines en Tubes d'Acier
STEDI	Shanghai Tunnel Engineering Design Institute
STÉÉ	Société Tchadienne d'Énergie Électrique
STEÉL	Société de Travaux d'Éléctricité du Languedoc
STEEP	Centre on Science, Technology and Energy Policy
STEEP	Société Tchadienne d'Entreposage de Produits Pétroliers
STEF	Société des Transports et Entrepôts Frigorifiques
STEFO	Sveriges Tecknares och Formgivares Riksförbund
STEG	Scottish Thistle Export Group
STEG	Sindicato de Trabajadores de la Educación en Guatemala
STEG	Société Tchadienne d'Entreprises Générales
STÉG	Société Tunisienne de l'Électricité et du Gaz
STÉL	Société de Traitements Électrolytiques et Électrothermiques
STEL	Studenta Tutmonda Esperantista Liga
STEM	Society for Teachers of Emergency Medicine (U.S.A.)
STEM	Studiecentrum Technologie, Energie, Milieu (Belgium)
STEMI	Société de Transports et Manutentions Industriels
STÉMO	Société Technique d'Études Mécaniques et d'Outillage
STEMPRA	Science, Technology, Engineering, Medicine, Public Relations Association
STEMRA	Stiching Exploitatie Mechanische Rechten Auters
STEN	Société Togolaise des Engrais
STÉP	Société Togolaise d'Électronique Parby
STEP	Solar-Terrestrial Energy Programme
STEPAN	Science and Technology Policy Asian Network (Australia)
STEPC	Société Tropicale d'Engrais et de Produits Chimiques (Ivory Coast)
STEPS	St. Paul's Expeditioners
STER	Stichting Ether Reclame
STÉRO	Société Technique d'Études Recherches et Organisation
STES	Suomen Tekoälyseura ry = FAIS
STET	Società Torinese Esercizi Telefonici
STF	Scandinavian Transport Workers Federation
STF	Skipsteknisk Forbund
STF	Sociedad Colombiana de Transporte Ferroviario
STF	Société Touristique de Fleuve (Senegal)
STF	Søfartsteknisk Forening
STF	Statsautoriserte Translatørers Forening
STF	Svenska Taxiförbundet
STF	Svenska Teknologföreningen

STF	Svenska Turistföreningen
STF	Sveriges Takpappfabrikanters Förening
STF	Sveriges Tandläkarförbund
STFC	Scientific and Technical Fisheries Committee (EU) = CSTP
STFI	Svenska Träforskingsinstitutet
STG	Schiffbautechnische Gesellschaft
STG	Suomen Taidegraafikot
STGA	Scottish Tourist Guides Association
STH	Société Togolaise d'Hôtellerie
STH	Société Togolaise des Hydrocarbures
SThG	Schweizerische Theologische Gesellschaft
STI	Schweizerisches Tiefkühl-Institut
STI	Scottish Trade International
STI	Société de Transports Internationaux (Mali)
STI	Société Tchadienne d'Investissement
STI	Statens Teknologiske Institutt
STI	Stredisko Technickych Informaci
STI	Svenska Träskyddsinstitutet
STI	Swiss Tropical Institute
STIA	Sindicato de Trabajadores de la Industria Aeronautica (Mexico)
STIAF	Svensk Träindustriarbare-förbundet
STIB	Société de Transformation Industrielle des Bois (Ivory Coast)
StiBoka	Stichting voor Bodemkartering
STIC	Société Technique Industrielle Camérounaise
STICA	Servicio Técnico Inter-Americano de Cooperación Agrícola (Costa Rica)
STICERD	Suntory-Toyota International Centre for Economics
STICPA	Société Tchadienne Industrielle et Commerciale de Produits Animales
STICUSA	Nederlandse Stichting voor Culturele Samenwerking met Suriname en de Nederlandse Antillen
Stigmatines	Pauvres Filles des Sacrés Stigmates de Saint François d'Assise
STIL	Service Technique Interprofessionnel du Lait
STIM	Föreningen Svenska Tönsattaras Internationella Musikbyra
STIMA	Société de Techniques Industrielles et Maritimes (Ivory Coast)
STIMAT	Société pour le Transport Ivorien Maritime, Aérien, Terrestre
STIPEI	Sci-Tech Information and Publications for Engineering Industry (China)
STIPEL	Società Telefonica Interregionale Piemontese e Lombarda
STISEC	Scientific and Technological Information Services Enquiry Committee (New Zealand)
STISSS	Sindicato de Trabajadores del Institúto Salvadoreño del Seguro Social
STITAS	Sindicato de Trabajadores de la Industria Textil de Algodón, Sintéticos, Acabados Textiles, Similares y Conexos (El Salvador)
STJ	Society of Saint Teresa of Jesus
STK	Soiuz Trudovykh Kollektivov
STK	Statens Trykningskontor
STK	Suomen Työnantajain Keskusliitto
STKL	Suomen Turkiseläinten Kasvattajain Liitto
STKS	Sumalainen Teologinen Kirjallisuusseura
STL	Standard Telecommunication Laboratories
STL	Suomen Teatterliitto
STL	Suomen Tukkukauppiaiden Liitto
STL	Suoment Teollisuusliitto
STLD	Society of TV Lighting Directors
STLV	Schweizerischer Turnlehrer-Verein
STLY	Suomen Teollisuus-Lääketieteen Yhdistys
STM	International Group of Scientific, Technical and Medical Publishers
STM	Soyuz Trudovoy Molodezhi
STMHV	Schweizerischer Taxi- und Mietwagenhalter- Verband
STMP	Société Togolaise Maritime et Portuaire
STMSA	Scottish Timber Merchants and Sawmillers Association
STN	Syndicat des Transportateurs du Niger
STN	Szczecińske Towarzystwo Naukowe
STNA	Scottish Teachers Nursing Association
STO	Scottish Tenants' Organisation
STO	Społeczne Towarzystwo Oświatowe
STO	State Trading Organisation (Malaysia)
STOA	Scottish Training Officers' Association
STOCA	Société Togolaise de Crédit Automobile
STOCACI	Société de Stockage de Côte d'Ivoire
STOERI	Shantou Optics & Electronics Research Institute

STO-MAREY	Société Togolaise des Mareyeurs
STONIC	Section Tunisienne de l'Office National Interprofessional des Céréales
STOP	Stop the Destruction of the World
STOP	Stowarzyszenie Techniczne Odlewników Polskich
STOPA	Stiching Overname Pootaardappelen
STOPP	Society of Teachers Opposed to Physical Punishment
STOR	Sveriges Tankrengörings- och Oljeskadesaneringfirmors Risksförening
STOWA	Scottish Tug-of-War Association
STP	Institution of Polish Engineers in Great Britain
STP	Société Togolaise des Plastiques
STPC	Société des Tannaries et Peausseries du Caméroun
STPC	Society of Technical Presentation and Communication
STPCM	Secrétariat Technique Permanent de la Conférence des Ministres de l'Éducation Nationale des États d'Expression Française d'Afrique et de Madagascar
StPEMI-RAN	St. Petersburg Economic-Mathematical Institute, Russian Academy of Sciences
StPFIEA-RAN	St. Petersburg Branch, Miklukho-Maklai Institute of Ethnology and Anthropology, Russian Academy of Sciences
StPFIIET-RAN	St. Petersburg Branch, Vavilov Institute of the History of the Natural Sciences, Russian Academy of Sciences
StPFIRI-RAN	St. Petersburg Branch, Institute of Russian History, Russian Academy of Sciences
StPFIS-RAN	St. Petersburg Branch, Institute of Sociology, Russian Academy of Sciences
STPG	Société de Travaux Publics, Gabon
StPILI-RAN	St. Petersburg Institute of Linguistic Studies, Russian Academy of Sciences
STPN	Société des Transports Publics de Nouakschott (Mauritania)
STPRM	Sindicato de Trabajadores Petroleros de la República Mexicana
STPS	Secretaria del Trabajo y Prevision Social (Mexico)
STPT	Society of Town Planning Technicians
STPTC	Standard Tar Products Testing Committee

STR	Sindicato dos Trabalhadores Rurais (Brazil)
STR	Society for Theatre Research
STR	Sveriges Tandteknikers Riksförbund
STR	Sveriges Trafkkbilägares Rijksorganisation
STR	Sveriges Trähusfabrikers Riksförbund
STRA	Scottish Textile Research Association
STRA	Scottish Trekking & Riding Association
STRC	Scientific, Technical and Research Commission (OAU) = CSTR
STRG	Scottish Tory Reform Group
STRI	Icelandic Council for Standardisation
STRI	Smithsonian Tropical Research Institute (Panama)
STRI	Sports Turf Research Institute
STRIM	Société Technique de Rechereches Industrielles et Mécaniques
STRIVE	Society for the Preservation of Rural Industry and Village Enterprises
STRM	Sindicato de Telefonistas de la República Mexicana
STRO	Scandinavian Tire and Rim Organization
STRP	Société Tessinois de Relations Publiques
STRU	Science and Technology Research Unit (Swaziland)
STS	Samtök Tónlistarskólastjóra
STS	Scottish Tartans Society
STS	Scottish Text Society
STS	Skibsteknisk Selskab
STS	Société Textile Sénégalaise
STS	Suomen Taiteilijaseura ry
STS	Suomen Teknillinen Seura
STSA	Science Technology and Society Association
STSD	Society of Teachers of Speech and Drama
STSF	Scottish Target Shooting Federation
STSG	Scottish Transport Studies Group
STSN	Società Ticinese di Scienze Naturali
STSN	Società Toscana di Scienze Naturali
STSO	Société des Transports du Sud-Quest (Ivory Coast)
STT	Sacred Trees Trust
STT	Scottish Tree Trust
STT	Société Textile du Tchad
STT	Société Togolaise des Tabacs

STT-FNB	Oy Suomen Tietotoimisto – Finska Notisbyrån	**SU**	Sindicato Unitario
STTA	Scottish Table Tennis Association	**SU**	Supporters Union
STTA	Scottish Timber Trade Association	**SU-SFU**	Svensk Ungdom – Svenska Folkpartiets Ungdomsorganisation
STTA	Service Techniques des Télécommunications de l'Air	**SUA**	Seamen's Union of Australia
STTEA	Screw Thread Tool Export Association	**SUAB**	Svenska Utvecklingsaktiebolaget
STTF	Svensk Turisttrafikförbundet	**SUACI**	Service d'Utilité Agricole à Compétence Interdépartementale
STTIF	Sveriges Tval-och Tvättmedelsindustriförening	**SUAD**	Service d'Utilité Agricole pour le Développement
STTL	Suomen Tekstiilitekninen Liitto = VAVI	**SUBAW**	Scottish Union of Bakers and Allied Workers
STTMA	Screw Thread Tool Manufacturers Association	**SUBUD**	Susila Budhi Dharma
STTS	Scottish Tramway and Transport Society	**SUC**	Société d'Usinage du Café (Ivory Coast)
STU	Styrelsen for Teknisk Utvekling	**SUC**	Society of University Cartographers
STUA	Scottish Trust for Underwater Archaeology	**SUCAM**	Superintendência da Campanha de Saúde Pública (Brazil)
STUC	Scottish Trades Union Congress	**SUCE**	Scottish Universities Council on Entrance
STUK	Säteilyturvakeskus (Finland)		
STULM	Stichting tot Uitvoering van Landbouw Maatregelen	**SUCEE**	Socialist Union of Central-Eastern Europe
STUMOKA	Studiekring voor Moderne Kantoortechniek	**SUCESU**	Sociedade de Usairios de Computadores Electronicos e Equipments Subsidiaros (Brazil)
STUSID	Société Tuniso-Séoudienne d'Investissement et de Développement (Tunisia)	**SUCO**	Service Universitaire Canadien Outre-Mer = CUSO
STUVA	Studiengesellschaft für Untererdische Verkehrsanlagen	**SUCO**	Sucrerie du Congo
		SUCOMA	Sugar Corporation of Malawi
STV	Schweizerische Tonkünstlerverein = AMS	**SUCP**	Société des Usines Chimiques de Pierrelatte
STV	Schweizerischer Technischer Verband = UTS	**SUCRAL**	Société Sucrière de la Région Centrale (Togo)
STV	Schweizerischer Transport-Versicherungs Verein	**SUCRP**	Société des Usines Chimiques Rhône-Poulenc
STV	Scottish Television	**SUCSE**	Scottish Universities Council on Studies in Education
STV	Sisters of St. Thomas of Villanova		
STV	Société de Transports Vergraud (Ivory Coast)	**SUDAM**	Superintendência do Desenvolvimento da Amazônia (Brazil)
STV	Solidaridad de Trabajadores Vascos	**SUDAP**	Superintendência da Agricultura e Produção (Brazil)
STV	Svenska Tekniska Vetenskapsakademien i Finland	**SUDEC**	Superintendência do Desenvolvimento do Ceará (Brazil)
STVS	Surinaamse Televisie Stichting	**SUDEC**	Superintendência do Desenvolvimento Economico e Cultural (Brazil)
STW	Stichting voor de Technische Wetenschappen (Netherlands)	**SUDECO**	Superintendência do Desenvolvimento da Região Centro Oeste (Brazil)
STY	Suomen Tuulivoimayhdistys ry		
SU	Religieuses de la Compagnie de Sainte-Ursule	**SUDÉL**	Groupe Régional pour la Coordination de la Production et du Transport de l'Énergie entre l'Autriche, la Grèce, l'Italie et la Yougoslavie
SU	Scripture Union		
SU	Sindicato Unido de Trabajadores del Central Romana (Dominican Republic)		

SUDELPA	Superintendência do Desenvolvimento do Litoral Paulista (Brazil)
SUDENE	Superintendência do Desenvolvimento do Nordeste (Brazil)
SUDEPE	Superintendência do Desenvolvimento da Pesca (Brazil)
SUDESUL	Superintendência do Desenvolvimento da Região Sul (Brazil)
SUDHEVEA	Superintendência do Desenvolvimento da Hevea Brasileira
SUDUJ	Savez Udruzenja Dramskih Umetnika Jugoslavije
SÜDV	Schweizerischer Übersetzer- und Dolmetscherverband = ASTI
SUE	Sociedad Uruguaya de Entomologia
SUEPO	Staff Union of the European Patent Office = IGEPA, USOEB
SUERF	Société Universitaire Européenne de Recherches Financières
SUF	Svenska Uppfinnareföreningen
SUFJ	Savez Udruzenja Folklorista Jugoslavije
SUFOI	Skandinavisk UFO Information
SUFRAMA	Superintendência da Zona Franca de Manaus (Brazil)
SUGC	Sindicato Unificado de la Guardia Civil
SUHAF	Sveriges Universitets- och Högskoleamanuensers Förbund
SUI	Seamen's Union of Ireland (Éire)
SUI	Speleological Union of Ireland
SUISA	Schweizerische Gesellschaft für die Rechte der Urheber Musikalischer Werke
SUKKJ	Savez Udruzenja za Krivicno Pravo i Kriminologiju Jugoslavije
SUKOL	Suomen Kieltenopettajien Liitto
SULUJ	Savez Udruženja Likovnih Umetnika Jugoslavije
SULVI	Suomen Lämpö- Ja Vesijohtoteknillinen-Yhdistys
SUM	Servicio Universitario Mundial = EUM, WUS
SUM-CMA	Society of Ultrasound in Medicine, Chinese Medical Association
SUMAC	Sheffield University Metals Advisory Centre
SUMED	Arab Petroleum Pipelines Company (Egypt)
SUMOC	Superintendência da Moneda e Crédito (Brazil)
SUMUJ	Savez Udruzenja Muzickih Umetnika Jugoslavije
SUN	Symbols, Units and Nomenclature Commissions (IUPAP)
SUN	Symphony of United Nations (U.S.A.)
SUNA	Sudan News Agency
SUNAB	Superintendencia Nacional do Abastecimiento (Brazil)
SUNAMAM	Superintendência Nacional da Marinha Mercante (Brazil)
SUNCA	Sindicato Unico Nacional de la Construccion y Anexos (Uruguay)
SUNFED	Special United Nations Fund for Economic Development = FENUDE
SUNIA	Sindicato Unitario Nazionale Inquilini Assegnatari
SUNIST	Serveur Universitaire National pour l'Information Scientifique et Technique
SUNKLO	Suomen Näytelmäkirjailijaliitto
SUNSTAR	Stanford University Network for Space Telescience Applications Research (U.S.A.)
SUNTRACS	Sindicato Unico Nacional de Trabajadores de la Construcción y Similares (Panama)
SUNTU	Sindicato Unico Nacional de Trabajadores Universitarios (Mexico)
SUNY	State University of New York
SUP	Sabah United Party (Malaysia) = PBS
SUP	Socialist Unity Party (New Zealand)
SUPA	Society of University Patent Administrators (U.S.A.)
SUPARCO	Space and Upper Atmosphere Research Committee (Pakistan)
SUPE	Federación de Sindicatos Unidos Petroleros del Estado (Argentina)
SUPER-INDUST-RIA	Superintendencia de Industria y Comercio (Colombia)
SUPER-SOCIE-DADES	Superintendencia de Sociedades (Colombia)
Super-JANET	Super Joint Academic Network
SUPK	Samaj Unnayan Prasikshan Kendra (Bangladesh)
SUPLAN	Sub-secretaria de Planejamento e Orçamento Ministério da Agricultura (Brazil)
SUPO	Suojelupoliisi
SUPOPP	Státní Ustav Památkové rece a Ochrany Prírody v Praze

SUPP	Sarawak United People's Party (Malaysia)	**SVA**	Scottish Volleyball Association
SURALCO	Suriname Aluminium Company	**SVA**	Ständiger Veterinärauschuss (EWG) = CVP, SVC
SURIF	Sukamandi Research Institute for Food Crops (Indonesia)	**SVA**	Statens Veterinärmedicinska Anstalt (Sweden)
SURRC	Scottish Universities Research and Reactor Centre	**SVAC**	Scottish Valuation Advisory Council
SUS	Schweizerischer Verband des Seilbahnunternhmungen	**SVAE**	Schweizerischer Verband der Auto-Elektriker
SUS	Suomalais- Ugrilainen Seura	**SVAJ**	Schweizerische Vereinigung der Agrarjournalisten = ASGA, ASJA
SUSA	Serviço de Unidades Sanitárias Aéreas (Brazil)	**SVAJ**	Schweizerische Vereinigung der Automobil-Journalisten = AJSA, ASGA
SUSC	Suore della Santa Unione dei Sacri Cuori	**SVAM**	Società per lo Sviluppo Agricolo del Mezzogiorno
SUSEP	Superintendência de Seguros Privados (Brazil)	**SVB**	Schweizerischer Berband für Berufsberatung
SUSTA	Scottish Union of Students Travel Association	**SVBF**	Schweizerischer Verband für das Arbeitsstudium = ASET, ASSL
SUT	Sociedade Unificada de Tabacos de Angola	**SVBL**	Schweizerische Vereinigung zur Förderung der Betriebsberatung in der Landwirtschaft
SUT	Society for Underwater Technology		
SUTC	Sindicato Unión de Trabajadores de la Construcción (El Salvador)	**SVBM**	Société Voltaïque de Béton Manufacturé (Burkina Faso)
SUTEP	Sindicato Unico de Trabajadores en la Educación de Perú	**SVBM**	Société Voltaïque du Bois et Matériaux (Burkina Faso)
SUTERM	Sindicato Unico de Trabajadores Electricistas de la República Mexicana	**SVBP**	Société Voltaïque des Pétroles BP (Burkina Faso)
SÜTEV	Somogy Megyei Süto- és Édesipari Vällalat	**SVBU**	Schweizerischer Verband für Beruflichen Unterricht = USEP, USIP
SUTIN	Sindicato Unico de Trabajadores de la Industria Nuclear (Mexico)	**SVC**	Sociedad Venezolana de Cardiologia
SUTISS	Sindicato Unico de Trabajadores de la Industria Siderúrgica (Venezuela)	**SVC**	Standing Veterinary Committee (EU) = CVP, SVA
SUTRA-BANC	Sindicato Unico de Trabajadores Bancarios del Distrito Federal y Estado Miranda (Venezuela)	**SVC**	Svejescentralen
		SVC	Svenska Västkustfiskarnas Centralförbund
SUTRA-HIERRO	Sindicato Unico de Trabajadores del Hierro (Venezuela)	**SVCC**	Schweizerischer Verein der Chemiker-Coloristen
SUTRA-SFCO	Sindicato de Trabajadores de la Standard Fruit Company (Honduras)	**SVCF**	Schweizerischer Verband der Cementwarenfabrikanten
SUVA	Schweizerische Unfallversicherungs-Anstalt	**SVCN**	Sociedad Venezolana de Ciencias Naturales
SV	Schweizerischer Floristenverband	**SVCP**	Société Voltaïque des Cuirs et Peaux
SV	Society of Virology (China)	**SVCR**	Svenska Centralkommittén för Rehabilitering
SV	Stifterverband für die Deutsche Wissenschaft	**SVCS**	Sociedad Venezolana de la Ciencia del Suelo
SVA	Schweizerische Vereinigung für Altertumswissenschaft = ASEA	**SVD**	Schweizerische Vereinigung für Datenverarbeitung
SVA	Schweizerische Vereinigung für Atomenergie = ASPEA	**SVD**	Schweizerische Vereinigung für Direktwerbung

SVD	Schweizerische Vereinigung für Dokumentation	**SVFPCC**	Service de Vente en France des Publications des Communautés Européennes
SVD	Schweizerischer Drogisten-Verband	**SVFW**	Schweizerische Vereinigung für Flugwissenschaften
SVD	Societas Verbi Divini	**SVG**	Schweizerische Vereinigung für Geothermie = SSG
SVDB	Schweizerischer Verein für Druckbehälter-überwachung	**SVG**	Schweizerische Vereinigung für Gesundheitstechnik
SVDHTL	Schweizerischer Verband der Dozenten en Höheren Technischen Lehranstalten = ASPETS, ASPSTS	**SVG**	Sociedad Venezolana de Geólogos
SVDK	Schweizerischer Verband Diplomierter Krankenschwestern und Krankenpfleger	**SVG Television**	St. Vincent and the Grenadines Television
SVDPR	Svobodnaia Demokraticheskaia Partiia Rossii	**SVGLP**	St. Vincent and the Grenadines Labour Party
SVDS	Schweizerische Verein für die Deutsche Sprache	**SVGP**	Schweizerischer Verband der Gartenbauproduzenten
SVE	Schweizerische Vereinigung für Ernährung	**SVGU**	Schweizerischer Verband der Glas- und Gebäudereinigungs- Unternehmer
SVE	Sociedad Venezolana de Entomologia	**SVGW**	Schweizerischer Verein von Gas- und Wasserfaches = SSIGE
SVE	Society of Vector Ecologists (U.S.A.)	**SVH**	Société Vétérinaire Hellénique = EKE, HVMS
SVEA	Schweizerischer Verband Evangelischer Arbeiter und Angestellter	**SVHA**	Société Vaudoise d'Histoire et d'Archéologie
SVEABUND	Svenska Väg-och Vattenbyggarnas Arbetgivareförbund	**SVI**	Schweizerische Vereinigung für Informatik = FSI
SVEB	Schweizerische Vereinigung für Erwachsenenbildung = FSEA, SFAE	**SVI**	Schweizerischer Verein für Instandhaltung
SveBeFo	Stiftelsen Svensk Bergteknisk Forskning	**SVI**	Vereinigung Schweizeriches Verpackungsinstitut
SVEBIO	Svenska Bioenergiföreningen	**SVI**	Vereinigung Schweizerischer Verkehrsingenieure
SVEBRA	Svenska Brandredskaps föfeningen	**SVIA**	Schweizerischer Verband der Ingenieur-Agronomen
SVEFF	Sveriges Färgfabrikanters Förening	**SVIA**	Sociedad Venezolana de Ingenieros Agrónomos
SVEMEK	Svets Mekaniska Arbetsgirareförbundet		
SVEPM	Society for Veterinary Epidemiology and Preventive Medicine	**SVIAL**	Schweizericher Verband der Ingenieur-Agronomen und der Lebensmittelingenieure = ASIAT
SVERB	Schweizerischer Verband Diplomierter Ernährungsberaterinnen = ASDD	**SVIDIDH**	Schweizerischer Verband der Dental-Industrie und des Dental-Handels = ASICD
SVERTEX	Sveriges Textilindustriförbund		
SVF	Schweizerischer Fachverband für Gemeinschaftsverpflegung	**SVIF**	Sociedad Venezolana de Ingenieros Forestales
SVF	Schweizerischer Vereinigung von Fäbereifachleuten	**SVIH**	Sociedad Venezolana de Ingenieria Hidráulica
SVF	Stiftelsen für Värmeteknisk Forskning		
SVF	Svenska Vägföreningen	**SVIL**	Schweizerische Vereinigung für Innerkolonisation und Industrielle Landwirtschaft
SVF	Sveriges Varvsindustriförening		
SVF	Sveriges Veterinärförbund		
SVF	Svetstekniska Föreningen	**SVIM**	Sociedad Venezolana de Minas y Metalurgicos
SVFBJ	Schweizerische Vereinigung Freier Berufsjournalisten		
SVFJ	Schweizerischer Verband der Filmjournalistinnen und Filmjournalisten = ASJC, ASGC		

SVIMSA	Schweizerischer Verband der Innendekorateure, des Möbel- fachhandels und der Sattler = ASMAIS, USADIS
SVIMU	Associazione Italiana per lo Sviluppo della Ricera nelle Macchine Utensili
SVIPA	Swiss Viewdata Information Providers Association
SVIQ	Sociedad Venezolana de Ingenieros Químicos
SVIT	Schweizerischer Verband der Immobilien- Treuhänder
SVK	Schweizerische Vereinigung für Kleintiermedizin = ASMPA
SVK	Schweizerischer Verband der Krankenpflegerinnen und Krankenpfleger = ASIA
SVKAZ	Schweizerischer Verband Kantonal Approbrierter Zahnärzte
SVKS	Schweizerischer Verband der Klavierbauer und- Stimmer
SVKW	Schweizerischer Verband der Konfektions- und Wäsche- Industrie
SVL	Suomen Vaatturliito
SVL	Suomen Vähittäiskauppiasliitto
SVL	Suomen Valokuvaajain Liitto
SVLFC	Schweizerische Vereinigung der Lack- und Farbenchemiker
SVLP	St. Vincent Labour Party
SVLR	Schweizerische Vereinigung für Luft- und Raumrecht = ASDA
SVLT	Schweizerischer Verband für Landtechnik = ASATA, ASETA
SVM	Service Volontaire Mennonite (Germany)
SVM	Stichting voor Melkhygiëne
SVMF	Sveriges Vertgmaskinaffärers Förening
SVMIU	Associazione Italiana per lo Svipuppo della Ricerca nelle Machine Utensili
SVMM	Schweizerische Vereinigung der Musiklehrer an Mittelschulen = SSMMES, SSMMSM
SVMT	Schweizerischer Verband für die Materialprüfungen der Technik
SVMTRA	Schweizerische Vereinigung Medizinisch Technischer Radiologieassistenten = ASTRM
SVMY	Suomen Vene- ja Mootoriyhdistys
SVN	Scheepvaartvereniging Noord
SVO	Association for Military Revival (Czechoslovakia)
SVO	Soiuz Vozrozhdeniia Otechestva
SVO	Stiching voor Oliehoudende Zaden
SVO	Stiching voor Veevoedings Onderzoek
SVOB	Schweizerischer Verband der Orthopädisten und Bandagisten
SVOI	Staatsveeartenijkundig Onderzoekings Instituut
Svomas	Svobodniie gosudarstvennye khudozhestvenniie masterskie
SVOR	Schweizerische Vereinigung für Operations Research = ASRO
SVOT	Schweizer Verband der Orthopädie- Techniker
SVOT	Schweizerische Vereinigung für Neuzeitliche Obst- und Traubenenverwertung
SVP	Schweizerischer Predicure-Verband
SVP	Schweizerischer Verband Staalich Anerkanneter Physiotherapeuten
SVP	Sociedad Venezolana de Planificación
SVP	Society of Saint Vincent de Paul
SVP	Society of Vertebrate Paleontology (U.S.A.)
SVP	Sosialistisk Venstreparti (Norway)
SVP	Stiching voor Plantenveredeling
SVP	Studiekring voor Plantenveredeling
SVP	Südtiroler Volkspartei
SVPC	Syndicat des Entreprises de Vente par Correspondance
SVPCE	Société Voltaïque de Peintures, Colorants et Emballages
SVPCI	Société Voltaïque de Promotion Commerciale et Industrielle
SVPF	Société Vétérinaire Pratique de France
SVPG	Schweizerisches Verband für Photo- Handel und -Gewerbe = ASCAP
SVPP	Schweizerisches Vereinigung für Parapsychologie
SVPPA	St. Vincent Planned Parenthood Association
SVQ	Sociedad Venezolana de Quimica
SVR	Russian Intelligence Service
SVR	Svenska Väg- och Vattenbyggares Riksförbund
SVS	Schweizerische Verein für Schweisstechnik = ASS
SVS	Société des Vétérinaires Suisses
SVS	Society for Vascular Surgery (U.S.A.)
SVS	Society of Visiting Scientists

SVS	Svenska Vitterhetssamfundet		**SVZ**	Scheepvaartvereniging Zuid
SVS	Sveriges Standardisering-Kommission		**SVZ**	Sociedad Veterinaria de Zootecnia de España
SVSF	Sveriges Vetenskapliga Specialbiblioteks Förening		**SW**	Samaritans Worldwide
SVSN	Société Vaudoise des Sciences Naturelles (Switzerland)		**SWA**	Scotch Whisky Association
			SWA	Scottish Whitebait Association
SVSP	Schweizerische Vereinigung für Sozialpolitik = ASPS		**SWA**	Society of Women Artists
			SWA	Solo Wargamers Association
SVST	Slovenská Vysoká Skola Techniká		**SWA**	Sozialwissenschaftliche Arbeitsgemeinschaft (Austria)
SVT	Schweizerische Vereinigung für Tierzucht		**SWA**	Sports Writers' Association
SVT	Soqosoqo ni Vakavulewa ni Taukei (Fiji)		**SWA**	Steel Window Association
			SWAA	Society for Women and AIDS in Africa
SVTB	Schweizerische Vereinigung Technischer Bühnenberufe = ASTT		**SWAAA**	Scottish Women's Amateur Athletic Association
SVTF	Svenska Teknologföreningen		**SWABC**	South West African Broadcasting Corporation
SvTF	Sveriges Tandvårdschefsförening			
SVTM	Schweizerischer Verband der Tapezierermeister-Detailhandels		**SWACO**	South West Africa Company
			SWAFAC	South West Atlantic Fisheries Advisory Commission
SVTR	Société Voltaïque des Transports Routiers			
			Swal	Scandinavian West Africa Line (Sweden)
SVTRA	Schweizerische Vereinigung Technischer Röntgenassistentinnen und Röntegenassistenten		**Swalec**	South Wales Electricity
			SWAN	Scottish Women's Action Network
SVU	Slovenská Výtvarná Únia		**SWAN**	Society for Wildlife Art of the Nations
SVUL	Suomen Valtakunnan Uhreiluliitto		**SWANU**	South West African National Union
SVUOM	Statní Vyzkumny Ustav Ochrany Materiálu G.V. Akimova		**SWANUF**	South West Afica National United Front
			SWAP	Save, Waste and Prosper Ltd
SVV	Schweizerischer Versicherungsverband		**SWAP**	Scottish Women Against Pornography
SVV	Studiecentrum voor Vredesvraagstukken (Netherlands)		**SWAP**	Spat Women's Association for Progress (Dominica)
			SWAPO	South West Africa Peoples Organisation
SVVIA	Schweizerischer Verband der Versicherungs-Inspektoren und-Agenten		**SWAPO-D**	South West Africa Peoples Organisation of Namibia – Democrats
SVVK	Schweizerischer Verein für Vermessungswesen und Kulturtechnik		**SWARBICA**	South and West Asian Regional Branch of the International Council on Archives
			SWATF	South West Africa Territory Force
SVVLD	Schweizerische Vereinigung der Veterinär-Labordiagnostiker		**SWB**	Schweizerischer Werkbund
SVW	Schweizerischer Verband für Waldwirtschaft = ASEF		**SWBA**	South Wales Brewers Association
			SWBOAT	Swedish Boating Industries Association
SVW	Schweizerischer Verband für Wohnungswesen = USAL		**SWC**	Slovak World Congress
SVWG	Schweizerische Verkehrwissenschaftliche Gesellschaft = ASET, ASST		**SWCAA**	Soil and Water Conservation Association of Australia
			SWCC	Saline Water Conversion Corporation (Saudi Arabia)
SVWS	Schweizerischer Verband der Wirkerei- und Strickerei-Industrie		**SWCL**	Scottish Wildlife and Countryside Link
SVWT	Schweizerische Vereinigung für Weltraumtechnik = ASTS, SAST		**SWCRD**	Soil and Water Conservation Research Division (U.S.A.)
SVY	Suomen Voimalaitosyhdistys		**SWCS**	Soil and Water Conservation Society

SWCSC	Soil and Water Conservation Society of China
SWDA	Scottish Wholesaler Druggists Association
SWDR	Southern Women Democratic Reaction (Brazil)
SWE	Society of Women Engineers (U.S.A.)
SWE	Society of Wood Engravers
SWEB	South Western Electricity Board
SWEG	South West Energy Group
SWEPRO	Swedish Committee on Trade Procedures
SWET	Society of West End Theatres
SWF	Svenska Wallboardföreningen
SWFA	Scottish Women's Football Association
SWFPA	Scottish White Fish Producers Association
SWFUK	Sturge Weber Foundation
SWG	Science Working Group (IPCC)
SWG	Society of Women Geographers (U.S.A.)
SWG	Songwriters Guild of Great Britian
SWGA	Société des Exportateurs de Vins Suisses
SWGB	South Western Gas Board
SWGC	Special World Geophysical Centre
SWGM	Spanish World Gospel Mission (U.S.A.)
SWHA	Scottish Women's Hockey Association
SWHIHR	Society of West Highland & Island Historical Research
SWHV	Schweizerischer Weinhändlerverband
SWI	Scottish Woollen Industry
SWI	Sealant and Waterproofers Institute (U.S.A.)
SWIBA	Scottish Womens Indoor Bowling Association
SWIE	South Wales Institute of Engineers
SWIEE	South West China Research Institute of Electronic Equipment
SWIF	Svenska Wellappindustriföreningen
SWIFT	Society for Worldwide Interbank Financial Telecommunication (Belgium)
SWIFT	Society of Worldwide Interbank Telecommunication
SWIM	Social Workers in Mental Handicap (Éire)
SWINPC	China Southwest Institute of Nuclear Physics and Chemistry
SWIP	Society for Women in Philosophy (U.S.A.)
SWIRA	Swedish Industrial Robot Association
SWIRECO	Southwestern Institute of Radio Engineers Conference and Electronics Show (U.S.A.)
SWISS-MECH-ANIC	Schweizerischer Verband Mechanisch-Technischer Betriebe
SWISSAIR	Schweizweische Luftverkehr AG
SWISSPRO	Swiss Group on the Simplification of International Trade Procedures
SWKI	Schweizerischer Verein von Wärme- und Kilmaingenieuren = SITC
SWLA	Society of Wildlife Artists
SWLG	Scottish Wild Land Group
SWMA	Scottish Wirework Manufactures Association
SWMA	Solid Waste Management Association (U.S.A.)
SWMA	Steel Wool Manufacturers Association
SWMT	Schweizerischer Verband für die Materialprüfungen der Technik
SWO	Surinaamse Werknemers Organisatie
SWOA	Scottish Woodland Owners Association
SWOV	Stichting Wetenschappelijk Onderzoek Veerkeersveiligheid
SWP	Socialist Workers Party
SWP	Society for Women in Plastics (U.S.A.)
SWP	Stowarzyszenie Włokienników Polskich
SWP	Stowarzyszenie Wynalazców Polskich
SWPA	Steel Works Plants Association
SWPCA	Swiss Water Pollution Control Association = ASPEE, ASSPA, ASTEA, VSA
SWPiN	Stowarzyszenie Wydawców Prywatnych i Niezaleznych
SWPP	Stowarzyzenie Wspierania Porządku Publicznego
SWPP Ltd	Society of Wedding & Portrait Photographers
SWPRS	West Palaearctic Regional Section (IOBC)
SWR	Schweizerischer Wissenschaftsrat
SWRC	Social Work Research Centre
SWRI	Scottish Women's Rural Institutes
SWRLS	South Western Regional Library System
SWS	Society of Wetland Scientists
SWS	Sozialwissenschaftliche Studiengesellschaft (Austria)
SWSA	Scottish Water Ski Association

SWSF	Society for a World Service Federation (U.S.A.)
SWSGS	South-West Scotland Grass Society
SWSO	Social Welfare Services Office (Éire)
SWST	Society of Wood Science and Technology
SWT	Scottish Wildlife Trust
SWTMA	Scottish Woollen Trade Mark Association
SWUN	Stichting Verkgroep Urrodynamica Nederland
SWV	Schweizerischer Wasserwirtschaftsverband
SWV	Schweizerischer Webeblatt-Fabrikanten-Verband
SWV	Schweizerischer Wirteverband
SWVC	Sociaal Werkgevers-Verbond voor de Confectie-Industrie
SWWFC	South Wales Wholesale Fruit Centre
SWWJ	Society of Women Writers and Journalists
SWWS	Sarawak Women for Women Society
SX Pia	Societas Sancto Francisci Xaverii pro Exteris Missionibus
SYBAZ	Syndicat du Bâtiment du Zaïre
SYBÉLEC	Syndicat Belge d'Études et de Recherches Électroniques
SYBESCO	Syndicat Belge des Scories Thomas
SYBESI	Syndicat Belge pour le Séparation Isotopique
SYBÉTRA	Syndicat Belge d'Entreprises à l'Étranger
SYCÂBÉL	Syndicat Professionnel des Fabricants de Fils et Câbles Électriques
SYCACÉL	Syndicat des Fabricants Français de Conduits et Accessoires pour Canalisations Électriques
SYCÉF	Syndicat des Constructeurs Français de Condensateurs Électriques Fixes
SYCÉP	Syndicat des Industries de Composants Électroniques Passifs
SYCLOPA	Chambre Syndicale du Commerce en Gros des Produits Laitiers et Avicoles du Marché d'Intérêt National de Rungis
SYCOM-IMPEX	Syndicat des Commerçants Importateurs et Exportateurs (Central African Republic, Congo)
SYCOMÉL	Syndicat National des Constructeurs Français de Matériel et Équipement Laitier Industriel
SYCOMOM	Syndicat des Constructeurs Belge de Machines-Outils pour le Travail des Métaux
SYCOSER	Syndicat des Constructeurs et Constructeurs-Installateurs
SYFAC	Syndicat des Fabricants d'Aliments Composés pour l'Alimentation Animale
SYFACAR	Chambre des Fabricants des Négociants en Papiers d'Emballage et Cartons en Gros (Belgium)
SYFAMÉR	Syndicat National des Fabricants de Moteurs, Matériel Naval, Équipements de Bords et Remorques pour la Navigation de Plaisance
SYFÉD	Système Francophone d'Édition et de Diffusion
SYFFOB	Syndicat des Fabricants Français d'Outillage Mécanique à Bois
SYFODIA	Syndicat des Fabricants d'Outillage et de Produits à Base de Diamant
SYGÉCAM	Syndicat Général des Constructeurs et Concepteurs d'Équipements pour les Industries de la Chimie, de Emballage et du Conditionnement, de l'Alimentation, du Lait et ses Dérivés et Industries Annexes
SYHA	Scottish Youth Hostels Association
SYL	Somali Youth League
SYL	Sverges Yngre Läroverkslärares Förening
SYLAITEX	Syndicat du Commerce d'Exporatation de Produits Laitiers et Avicoles
SYLF	Sverges Yngre Läkares Förening
SYM	Salesian Youth Movement = MGS, MJS
SYMA	Syndicat des Constructeurs de Machines pour l'Alimentation
SYMACAP	Syndicat des Constructeurs Français de Matériel pour le Caoutchouc et les Matières Plastiques
SYMACO	Syndicat des Constructeurs de Matériels de Conditionnement
SYMAFO	Chambre Syndicale des Fabricants et Négociants en Machines et Fournitures pour Chassures (Belgium)
SYMAP	Syndicat de la Machine-Outil, de l'Assemblage et de la Productique Associée
SYMATEX	Syndicat des Constructeurs Belges de Machines Textiles
SYMCA	Syndicat des Constructeurs de Machines et Appareils pour les Industries Chimiques et Industries de l'Alimentation

SYMCAP	Syndicat des Constructeurs Français de Matériel pour le Caoutchouc et les Matières Plastiques
SYMCO	Syndicat des Constructeurs de Matériels de Conditionnement
SYME-CORA	Syndicat de la Mesure du Contrôle et de la Régulation Automatique
SYMSO	Syndicat des Fabricants de Mobilier Industriel et Commercial et de Systèmes d'Organisation
SYNABATI	Syndicat National des Fabricants et Constructeurs de Bâtiments Industrialisés
SYNACIB	Syndicat National des Commerçants et Industriels Africains du Bénin
SYNACO-BOIS	Syndicat National des Constructeurs Français de Machines à Bois et Outillages Annexes
SYNACO-MEX	Syndicat National du Commerce Extérieur des Céréales
SYNAD	Syndicat National des Producteurs de Béton Prêt à l'Emploi
SYNAFA	Syndicat National des Fabricants d'Aliments pour les Animaux
SYNAFEG	Syndicat National des Fabricants d'Emmental et de Gruyères
SYNAGRA	Syndicat National du Commerce des Céréales et Légumes Secs (Belgium)
SYNAMAP	Syndicat National des Manufacturers d'Articles de Protection
SYNAMÉ	Syndicat National de la Mesure Électrique et Électronique
SYNAP	Syndicat National des Attachés de Presse Professionnels
SYNAPE-MEIN	Syndicat National des Petites et Moyennes Enterprises et Industries Nigériennes
SYNAQ	Syndicat National d'Amélioration de la Qualité pour les Coopératives Agricoles
SYNASAV	Syndicat National des Services Après-Vente, Appareils Producteurs d'Eau Chaude, de Chauffage, Ménagers et Connexes
SYNAVOL	Syndicat National des Abattoirs de Volailles
SYNCOBEL	Syndicale Kamer der Fabrikanten van Confectie van België
SYNCOPAC	Syndicat National des Coopératives Préparant des Aliments Composés
SYNCOPEX	Syndicat National des Coopératives Agricoles Exportatrices
SYNDAGRI	Syndicat des Employeurs Agricoles (Ivory Coast)
SYNDES-MOS	World Fellowship of Orthodox Youth
SYNDI-CALU	Syndicat National des Fabricants d'Articles de Ménage en Aluminium
SYNDI-CHAM-PAGNE	Chambre Syndicale des Agents Accrédités par les Maisons de Champagne de Marque
SYNDI-CUIR	Syndicat Général des Cuirs et Dérivés (Belgium)
SYNDI-MINES	Syndicat des Entreprises Minières du Gabon
SYNDI-SCOTCH	Chambre Syndicale des Agents Accrédités de Scotch Whisky (Belgium)
SYNDIGEL	Syndicat National des Négociants en Produits Surgelés, Congelés et en Glaces
SYNDUS-TREF	Syndicat des Industries de l'Afrique Équatorial (Congo)
SYND-USTRICAM	Syndicat des Industriels du Caméroun
SYNECOT	Syndicat National des Fabricants d'Engrenages et Constructeurs d'Organes de Transmission
SYNÉG	Syndicat National de l'Équipement des Grandes Cuisines
SYNÉRCAU	Syndicat National d'Études de la Recherche pour les Coopératives Agricoles et Leurs Unions
SYNERVA	Syndicat National d'Études de Revision et de Vulgarisation des Coopératives Agricoles
SYNPA	Syndicat National des Producteurs d'Additifs Alimentaires
SYNTÉC	Chambre Syndicale des Société d'Études et de Conseils
SYNTE-CAM	Société Camérounaise pour la Fabrication des Tissus Synthétiques
SYP	Society of Young Publishers
SYPAL	Syndicat National des Fabricants et Fabricants Distributeurs de Palettes en Bois
SYPAOA	Syndicat Patronal et Artisanal de l'Ouest Africain (Senegal)
SYR	Sveriges Yrkesfruktodlares Riksförbund
SYS	Society of Young Scientists (India)
SYSNA	Société des Systems d'Aides à la Navigation
SYTEMÉL	Syndicat des Constructeurs de Turbines et Matériels Énergétiques Lourds

SYTRA-MINES	Syndicat des Constructeurs de Matériels pour Mines et Travaux Souterrains
SZ	Green Party (Czech Republic)
SZ	Slovenska Zveza (Slovenia) = SA
SZAK	Stowarzyszenie Zołnierzy Armii Krajowej
SZAMOK	International Computer and Information Centre (Hungary)
SZAU	Slovenská Akademija Znanosti i Umetnosti = SASA
SZBK	Szegedi Biologiai Központja
SZBV	Schweizer und Züricher Buchhändlerverein
SzDSz	Alliance of Free Democrats (Hungary)
SzDSz	Szerb Demokratikus Szövetség (Hungary) = DFS
SZEF	Szakszervezet Együttmüködési Fóruma
SZF	Schweizerische Vereinigung für Zukunftforschung
SZF	Société Zoologique de France
SZFKI	Szilárdtestfizikai Kutató Intézet
SZG	Schweizerische Zoologische Gesellschaft = SSZ
SZG	Schweizerische Zwirnerei-Genossenschaft
SZH	Schweizerische Zentrale für Handelsförderung
SZhP	Soiuz Zhenshchin-Predprinimatelei
SZIKKTI	Szilikátipari Központi Kutató és Tervezo Intézet
SZKFI	Magyar Szénhidrogénipari Kutató – Fejlesztö Intézet
SZKI	Számítástechnikai Kutató intézet és Innóvácios Központ
SZN	Stazione Zoologica di Napoli
SZOPK	Slovensky Zvaz Ochrancov Prirody a Krajiny
SZOT	Magyar Szakszervezetek Országos Tanácsa
SZS	Savezni Zavod za Standarizaciju
SZS	Schweizerische Zentralstelle für Stahlbau
SZS	Slovenská Zoologická Společnost
SZSP	Socjalistyczny Związek Studentów Polskich
SzT	Szentkorona Társulat (Hungary) = HCS
SZTAKI	Számítástechnikai és Automatizálási Kutató Intézet
SZU	Sociedad Zoológica del Uruguay
SZV	Schweizerische Zahntechnike Vereinigung
SZV	Schweizerischer Saatzuchtverband = FSS
SZV	Schweizerischer Zeitungsverlegerverband
SZV	Schweizerischer Zimmermeisterverband = SSMC
SZVT	Szervezési és Vezetési Tudományos Társaság
SZZV	Schweizerischer Ziegenzuchtverband

T

T&RA	Tennis and Rackets Association
T&TPC	Trinidad and Tobago Management Development and Productivity Centre
T2000	Transport 2000 Ltd
TA	Telecom Australia
TA	Territorial Army
TA	Tidningarnas Arbetsgivareförening
TA	Transport Association
TA	Tricycle Association
TAA	Technical Assistance Administration (UNDP) = AAT
TAA	Ticket Agents Association
TAA	Timber Arbitrators Association of the United Kingdom
TAA	Trans-Antarctic Association
TAA	Trans-Atlantic Agreement
TAA	Trans-Australia Airlines
TAA	Transportation Association of America
TAA	Tropical Agriculture Association
TAAF	Terres Australes et Antarctiques Françaises
TAAG	Linhas Aéreas de Angola
TAALS	The American Association of Language Specialists
TAAN	Transworld Advertising Agency Network
TAASII	Tianjin Academy of Agricultural Science Information Institute
TAB	Technical Assistant Board (UNDP) = BAT
TAB	Transporto Aériens du Bénin
TABA	Société Agricole Tchadienne de Collecte et de Traitement des Tabacs
TABA	Timber Agents and Brokers Association of the United Kingdom
TABA	Transportes Aéreos de Buenos Aires (Argentina)

TABA	Transportes Aéreos Regionais da Bacia Amazônica (Brazil)	**TAF**	Transportøkonomisk Förening
TABAMEX	Tabacos Mexicanos	**TAFF**	Take-Away and Fast Food Federation
TABMAC	The All British Martial Arts Council	**TAFIC**	Tasmanian Fishing Industry Council
TAC	Technical Assistance Committee (UNESCO)	**TAG**	Arthrogryposis Group
		TAG	Commonwealth Technical Assistance Group
TAC	The Aeroplane Collection	**TAG**	The American Group of CPA Firms
TAC	Theatres Advisory Council	**TAG**	Towpath Action Group
TAC	Tobacco Advisory Council (*now* TMA)	**TAGB**	Transportes Aéreos da Guine-Bissau
TAC	Trades Advisory Council of British Jewry	**TAH**	Trans-African Highway Co-ordinating Committee = RTA
TAC	Transitional Authority in Cambodia (UN)	**TAHA**	Trans-African Highway Authority = ARTA
TAC	Transkei Airways Corporation (South Africa)	**Tahis**	Transportes Aéreos Hispanos, S.A.
TAC	Transportes, Aduanas y Consignaciones	**TAHPERD**	Texas Association of Health, Physical Education, Recreation and Dance
TACAC	Trans Atlantic Committee on Agricultural Change	**TAI**	Transport Africain International (Togo)
TACADE	Teachers Advisory Council on Alcohol and Drug Education	**TAIB**	Trans-Arabian Investment Bank (Bahrain)
TACAP	Chambre Syndicate Nationale des Enterprises de Transports et de Services Auxiliaires des Collectivités et Administrations Publiques	**TAIC**	Tokyo Atomic Industrial Consortium (Japan)
		TAIDEC	Togo Agro Industrial Development Corporation
TACHD	Association for Children with Heart Disorders	**TAK**	Taal-Aktie Komitee (Belgium)
		TAK	Türk Ajansi Kibris (Cyprus)
TACIN	Town and Country Information Network	**TAKI**	MTA Talajtani és Agrokémiai Kutató Intézete (Hungary)
TACMA	Association of Control Manufacturers		
TACNNR	Turkish Association for the Conservation of Nature and Natural Resources	**TAKIS**	Tutmonda Asocio pri Kibernetiko Informatiko, kaj Sistemiko
		TALES	Association of Library Equipment Suppliers
TACT	Association of Corporate Trustees	**TALIRO**	Tanzania Livestock Research Organisation
TACT	Tories Against Cruise and Trident		
TACTRI	Taiwan Agricultural Chemicals and Toxic Substances Research Institute	**TALMA**	Truck and Ladder Manufacturers Association
TACV	Transportes Aéreos de Cabo Verde	**TAM**	Technical Association of Malaysia
TACW	Technische Advies Commissie voor de Waterkeringen	**TAM**	Televisora Andina de Mérida (Venezuela)
TAD	Tribunal de Abitraje Deportivo = CAS, TAS	**TAM**	Teresian Apostolic Movement = MTA
		TAM	Tovarna Avtomobilov in Motorjev
TAE	Istituto di Metodi e Processi Chimici per la Trasformazione e l'Accumulo dell'Energia (Italy)	**TAM**	Transportes Aéreos Militares (Bolivia, Paraguay)
		TAMBA	Twins and Multiple Births Association
TAE	Turkiye Atom Enerjisi Kurumu (Turkey)	**TAMCO**	Société des Transports, d'Automobile et de Mécanique au Congo
TAEC	Thai Atomic Energy Commission for Peace (Thailand)	**TAMDA**	Timber and Allied Materials Development Association (South Africa)
TAF	Angling Foundation		
TAF	Norske Travarefabrikkers Arbeidsgiverförening		
TAF	Trädgardsbranschens Arbetsgivareförbund	**TAME**	Transportes Aéreos Militares Ecuatorianos

TAMOR	Turkish Association of Marketing and Opinion Research	**TARA**	Teachers Anti-Racist Alliance
Tampa	Transportes Aéreos Mercantiles Panamericanos (Colombia)	**TARC**	Trace Analysis Research Centre (Canada)
TAMTI	Textile Academy, Ministry of Textile Industry (China)	**TARC**	Tropical Agricultural Research Center (Japan)
TAMTU	Tanzania Machinery Testing Unit	**TARD**	Türk Anesteziyoloji ve Reanimasyon Dernegi
TAMU	Transportes Aéreas Militares Uruguayes	**TARGET**	Team to Advance Research for Gas Energy Transformation (U.S.A.)
TAMWA	Tanzania Media Women Association	**TARI**	Taiwan Agricultural Research Institute
TAN	Linea Aerea Transportes Aéreos Neuquen (Argentina)	**TARL**	Texas Archaeological Research Laboratory (U.S.A.)
TAN	Third Age Network	**TAROM**	Romania State Airline
TAN	Transportes Aéreos Nacionales (Honduras)	**TAROM**	Transporturi Aeriene Rômane (Romania)
TANCA	Technical Assistance to Non-Commonwealth Countries	**TARS**	Technical Assistance Recruitment Service (UN)
TanD	Towns and Development (Netherlands)	**TARS**	The Arthur Ransome Society
TANDOC	Tanzania National Documentation Centre	**TARSA**	Linea Aerea Transporte Aereo Rioplatense (Argentina)
TandRA	Tennis & Rackets Association	**TAS**	Aviation Society
TANEA	Towards A New Education Act	**TAS**	Tennessee Academy of Science (U.S.A.)
TANESCO	Tanzania Electric Supply Company	**TAS**	Traditional Acupuncture Society
TANIC	Tabacalera Nicaragüense, S.A.	**TAS**	Tribunal Arbitral du Sport = CAS, TAD
TANISEN	Les Tanmaries Industrielles Sénégalaises	**TASC**	Centre for Technology and Social Change
TANJUG	Yugoslav News Agency	**TASCA**	Training and Supervision in Counselling and Related Areas Association
TANTUR	Ecumenical Institute for Theological Research (Israel)	**TASHA**	Tranquilliser Anxiety Stress Help Association
TAO	Technical Assistance Operations (UNDP) = DOAT	**TASMA**	Tanzania Sisal Marketing Board
TAP	Svenska Tapetfabrikanternas Förening	**TASO**	Television Allocation Study Organisation (U.S.A.)
TAP	Technical Advisory Panel (UN)	**TASPO**	Thalacker Allgemeine Samen- und Pflanzen Offerte
TAP	Technical Advisory Point (DTI)		
TAP	Technical Assistance Program (U.S.A.)	**TASR**	Tlačova Agentúra Slovenskej Republiky / News Agency of the Slovak Republic
TAP	Towarzystwo Anaestezjologów Polskich		
TAP	Transportes Aéreos Portugueses	**TASS**	Tianjin Academy of Social Sciences
TAP	Tunis Afrique Presse (Tunisia)	**TAT**	Tourism Authority of Thailand
TAP	Turystyczna Agencja Prasowa	**TAT**	Transport Aérien Transrégional
TAPA	Tanzania African Parents Association	**TAT**	Transportes Aéreos de Timor
TAPI	Technology Application and Promotion Institution (Philippines)	**TAT**	Tree Advice Trust
		TATHS	Tool and Trades History Society
TAPI	Tropical Agricultural Products Institute (Thailand)	**TAUN**	Technical Assistance of the United Nations
TAPOL	Indonesia Human Rights Campaign	**TAUS**	Tobacco Association of the United States
TAPPI	Technical Association for the Pulp and Paper Industry (U.S.A.)		
TAPRI	Tampere Peace Research Institute (Finland)	**TAVRA**	Territorial Auxiliary and Volunteer Reserve Associations
TAPS	Traditional Arts Projects Ltd		

TAWU	Transport and Allied Workers' Union (Kenya)	**TCAC**	Technical Committee on Agricultural Chemicals
TAZARA	Tanzania-Zambia Railway Authority	**TCAC**	William V.S. Tubman Center of African Culture (Liberia)
TBA	Tea Brokers' Association London	**TCARC**	Technical Centre for Agricultural and Rural Cooperation (ACP)
TBA	Tea Buyers Association		
TBA	Teaching Brothers' Association	**TCAS**	Three Counties Agricultural Society
TBA	Test Boring Association (U.S.A.)	**TCC**	Technical Change Centre
TBA	The Buying Agency	**TCC**	Technological Change Committee
TBA	Thoroughbred Breeders Association	**TCC**	Telecommunications Corporation (Jordan)
TBA	Tropical Biology Association		
TBBA	Thai-British Business Association	**TCC**	Textile Conservation Centre
TBC	Technology & Business Centre	**TCC**	Toxic Chemicals Committee
TBCC	Tom Baker Cancer Centre (Canada)	**TCC**	Transport and Communications Commission (UN)
TBD	Telemática e Banco de Dados Lda		
TBD	Türk Belediyecilik Dernegi	**TCCA**	Textile and Clothing Contractors Association
TBD	Turkiye Bilisim Dernegi = TIS		
TBE	Fédération Européenne des Fabricants de Tuiles et de Briques	**TCCA**	Thana Central Cooperative Association (Bangladesh)
TBF	Teachers Benevolent Fund	**TCCA**	Turkish Cypriot Cultural Association
TBG	Tidy Britain Group	**TCCB**	Test and County Cricket Board
TBI	Theodor Bilharz Research Institute (Egypt)	**TCCE**	Turkish Chamber of Civil Engineers = IMO
TBL	The Bad Life (Venezuela) = LMV	**TCCP**	Tissue Culture for Crops Project (U.S.A.)
TBMA	Timber Building Manufacturers Association	**TCD**	Trinity College, Dublin (Éire)
TBMSG	Trailokya Bauddha Mahasangha Sahayak Gana = AOBO, FWBO	**TCDD**	Türkiye Cumhuriyeti Devlet Demiryollari Isletmesi Genel Müdürlügü
TBNI	Technology Board for Northern Ireland		
TBOAA	Tuna Boat Owners Association of Australia	**TCDRI**	Tianjin Cement Industry Design and Research Institute
TBP	Türk Birligi Partisi (Cyprus)	**TCE**	Tribunal de Contas do Estado (Brazil)
TBPA	Tenpin Bowling Proprietors Association	**TCEA**	Training Centre for Experimental Aerodynamics (NATO)
TBS	Tanzanian Bureau of Standards		
TBS	Trinitarian Bible Society	**tCF**	Charity Forum
TBTAK	Scientific and Technical Research Council of Turkey	**TCF**	Compassionate Friends
		TCF	Technical Cooperation Fund
TC	Religiosi Terziari Cappuccini	**TCF**	Touring Club de France
TC	Tandem Club	**TCGA**	Tanzania Coffee Growers Association
TC	Taraxacum Club (Netherlands)	**TChP**	Towarzystwo Chirurgów Polskich
TC	Trilateral Commission	**TCI**	Tall Clubs International (U.S.A.)
TC	Trusteeship Council (UN)	**TCI**	Tasmanian Confederation of Industries
TC	Typhoon Committee (ESCAP, WHO)	**TCI**	Touring Club Italiano
TCA	Tertiary Colleges Association	**TCI**	Traffic Clubs International (U.S.A.)
TCA	Textile Converters Association	**TCI**	Transafricaine Côte d'Ivoire
TCA	Tile Council of America	**TCI**	Tree Council of Ireland
TCA	Tissue Culture Association (U.S.A.)	**TCI**	Trust Companies Institute (South Africa)
TCAA	Technical Communication Association of Australia	**TCIL**	Telecommunications Consultants India Ltd

TCJCC	Trades Councils' Joint Consultative Committee		**TD&RA**	Twist Drill and Reamer Association
TCK	Travaux de Constructions Kritikos (Cameroon)		**TDA**	Tableware Distributors' Association
TCL	Tanzania Creameries Ltd		**TDA**	Textile Distributors' Association (U.K., U.S.A.)
TCL	Trinity College of Music, London		**TDA**	Timber Development Association
TCL	Tsumet Corporation Ltd		**TDA**	Timber Drying Association
TCM	Trustul Centrolelor Mecanice		**TDA**	Trade Development Authority (India)
TCMA	Telephone Cable Makers Association		**TDB**	Trade and Development Board (UNCTAD)
TCMB	Tomato and Cucumber Marketing Board		**TDC**	Tourist Development Corporation of Malaysia
TCMB	Turkiye Cumhuriyet Merkez Bankasi		**TDC**	Trade Development Council (Hong Kong)
TCMD	Transnational Corporations and Management Division		**TDC**	Transportation Development Centre (Canada)
TCMIS	Trade Control Measures Information System (UNCTAD)		**TDC**	Türk Diabet Cemiyeti
TCMR	Trafford Centre for Medical Research		**TDCK**	Technisch Documentatiecentrum voor de Krijgsmacht
TCN	Tekniska Nomenklaturcentralens		**TDF**	Télédiffusion de France
TCNA	Tube Council of North America		**TDFL**	Tanzania Development Finance Company Ltd
TCO	Thunderstorm Census Organisation		**TDG**	Timeshare Developers Group
TCO	Tjänstemännens Centralorganisation		**TDI**	The Democracy International
TCOED	Training Centre for Oil Exploration and Development (China)		**TDI**	Turkiye Denizcilik Isletmeleri = TML
TCOT	Transit Congo-Oubanqui-Tchad		**TDK**	Tokyo Denki Kagaku
TCP	Trading Corporation of Pakistan		**TDK**	Türk Dil Kurumu
TCPA	Tantawangalo Catchment Protection Association		**TDM**	Teledifusão de Macau
TCPA	Town and Country Planning Association		**TDP**	Tajik Democratic Party
TCR	Société Tesseries Commerciale et Represéntation (Ivory Coast)		**TDP**	Teluga Desam Party (India)
TCRC	Telecommunications Research Centre (India)		**TDP**	Turkish Democratic Party / Turska Demokraticheska Partiya (Bulgaria)
TCRC	Tobacco Chemists Research Conference (U.S.A.)		**TDPI**	Tasmanian Department of Primary Industry
TCRI	Tobacco and Cotton Research Institute (South Africa)		**TDR**	Special Programme for Research and Training in Tropical Diseases (UNDP, World BANK, WHO)
TCS	Technology Club of Syracuse (U.S.A.)		**TDS**	Third Dimension Society of Great Britain
TCS	Token Corresponding Society			
TCSP	Tourism Council of the South Pacific		**TDSF**	Tasmanian Department of Sea Fisheries
TCSP	Tourist Council of the South Pacific		**TDTC**	Türk Dis Tabipleri Cemiyeti
TCT	Tasmanian Conservation Trust		**TDWG**	Taxonomic Databases Working Group for Plant Sciences (IUCN)
TCTS	Trans-Canada Telephone System			
TCVD	Technical Committee on Veterinary Drugs		**TE**	Internationale Konferenz für die Technische Einheit im Eisenbahnwegsen = UT
TCWF	Tibetan Children's Welfare Fund			
TCZB	Turkiye Cumhuriyeti Ziraat Bankasi		**TE**	Transfrigoroute Européen
TD	Pères de Timon David		**TEA**	Training and Employment Agency (DED)
TD	Towns and Development (Netherlands)			
TD	Treasury Department (U.S.A.)		**TEA**	Trans-European Airways (Belgium)

TEAC	Technical Education Advisory Council	**TEED**	Training, Enterprise and Education Directorate
Teagasc	Agriculture and Food Development Authority (Éire)	**TEES**	Texas Engineering Experiment Station
TEAHA	Trans-East-African Highway Authority (Ethiopia)	**TEF**	Textile Employers Federation
TEAM	The European Atlantic Movement (U.K.)	**TEFO**	Svenska Textilforskningsinstitutet
TEAR	The Evangelical Alliance Relief Fund	**TEGEWA**	Verband der Textilhilfsmittel-Lederhilfsmittel-, Gerbstoff- und Waschrohstoff-Industrie
TEB	Türk Eczacilari Birligi	**TEGMA**	Terminal Elevator Grain Merchants Association (U.S.A.)
TEBA	Tutmonde Esperantista Biblioteka Asocio	**TEGOVOFA**	European Group of Valuers of Fixed Assets
TEC	Tasmanian Environment Centre	**TÉIS**	Telecom Éireann Information Systems (Éire)
Tec	The Executive Committee	**TEJA**	Tutmonda Esperantista Jurnalistica Asocio
TEC	Total Environment Centre		
TECA	Trans-Europa Compañia de Aviación SA	**TEJO**	Tutmonda Esperantista Junulara Organizo
TECDA	Thai Environmental and Community Development Association	**TEK**	Finnish Association of Graduate Engineers
TECHION	Israel Institute of Technology	**TEK**	Turkiya Elektrik Kurumu
TECHN-OCEAN	Société Technique pour l'Océanologie	**TEK**	Turkiye Ekonomi Kurumu
TECHNI-CHAR	Association pour le Perfectionnement Technique des Appareils Domestiques d'Utilisation du Charbon (Belgium)	**TEKES**	Technology Development Centre (Finland)
TECHNI-COL	Association pour le Perfectionnement Technique des Appareils Domestiques d'Utilisation des Combustibles Liquides (Belgium)	**TEKO**	Sveriges Textil-och Konfektionsindustriförbund
		TEL	Tutmonda Ekumena Ligo
		TELAM	State News Agency (Argentina)
TECHNIC-ATOME	Société Technique pour l'Énergie Atomique	**TELCO**	Teta Engineering and Locomotive Co. Ltd. (India)
TECHNIP	Compagnie Française d'Études et de Construction	**TELCOR**	Dirección General de Telecommunicaciónes y Correos (Nicaragua)
TECHNO-NET	Asia Network for Industrial Technology Information and Extension (Singapore)	**TELE-TCHAD**	Chad Government Television
TECH-NOSET-ASIA	Asian Network for Industrial Technology Information and Extension	**TELE-DIREKTOR-ATET**	Norwegian Broadcasting Authority
TECHWARE	Technology for Water Resources (Belgium)	**TELECOM**	Empresa Nacional de Telecomunicaciones (Colombia)
TECN-IBERIA	Asociación Española Empresas de Estudios y Proyectos	**TELEMIG**	Telecomunicacões do Minas Gerais (Brazil)
TECNI-FUEGO	Asociación Técnica del Fuego	**TELEPARA**	Telecomunicacões do Pará (Brazil)
TECO	Tanzania Extract Company	**TELI**	Technisch-Literarische-Gesellschaft
TECO	Technical Cooperation Committee (OECD)	**TELIMALI**	Télécommunications Internationales du Mali
TECTRO	Société de Techniques Tropicales	**Telmex**	Telefonos de Mexico
TED	Thyroid Eye Disease	**TELO**	Tamil Eelam Liberation Organisation (Sri Lanka)
TEDCO	Thames Estuary Development Company		
TEDIS	Trade Electronic Data Interchange System (CEC) = EEC-TEDIS	**TEM**	Trans-European North-South Motorway Project (ECE) (Switzerland)

TEMA	Telecommunication Engineering and Manufacturing Association
TEMA	Texas Medieval Association
TEMPUS	Trans-European Mobility Scheme for University Studies (CEC, ETF) (Belgium)
TEN	Pool Trans-Euro-Nuit (Germany)
TEN	Third World Tourism European Ecumenical Network
TEPCO	Tokyo Electric Power Company (Japan)
TEPSA	Trans-European Policy Studies Association
TERC	Technic-Economic Research Center (China)
TERC	Tropical Ecosystems Research Centre (Australia)
TERENA	Trans-European Research and Education Networking Association (*ex* EARN, RARE)
TERG	Technical Education Resources Group
TERMIA	International Association of Terminology (Canada)
TermNet	International Network for Terminology
TERN	Training for Evaluation and Repair of Non-Traditional Buildings
TERN	Transnational European Rural Network (Belgium)
TERRASUL	Departamento de Terras e Colonização de Mato Grosso do Sul (Brazil)
TESA	Event Suppliers Association
TESA	Television and Electronics Service Association
TESCO	Hungarian International Scientific Co-operation Bureau
TESEM	Televisión Esmeraldeña Compañia de Economía Mixta (Ecuador)
TESOL	Teachers of English to Speakers of other Languages (U.S.A.)
TESSI-FIBRE	Associazione Tessiture Italiane Fibre Artificiali e Sintetiche
TESSI-LABIT	Associazione Italiana degli Industrali dell'Abbigliamento
TESSIL-VARI	Associazione Nazionale Produttori Tessili Vari e del Cappello
TETOC	Technical Education and Training Organisation for Overseas Countries (ODA)
TEVA	Tutmonda Esperantista Vegetara Asocio
TEVEC	Televisao Experimental de Cabo Verde
TEXIMEI	Textilipari Minöségellenörzö Intézete (Hungary)

TEXKAM	Institute of Mechanical Engineering (Bulgaria)
Texnicsa	Textilera de Nicaragua, S.A.
TEXTANG	Empresa Texteis de Angola
TEXTEL	Trinidad and Tobago Telecommunications Company
TEXTICAM	Société Textile du Caméroun
TF	Textile Foundation (U.S.A.)
TF	Trafiktekniska Föreningen
TFA	Taiwan Forest Administration (China)
TFA	Tenant Farmers' Association
TFA	Texas Forestry Association (U.S.A.)
TFA	Textile Finishers' Association
TFA	The Freedom Association
TFA	Track and Field Association (U.S.A.)
TFAI	Trade Fair Authority of India
TFAO	Tilapia Food Aid Organisation (Belgium)
TFAP	Tropical Forestry Action Plan
TFC	Tasmanian Forestry Commission
TFCA	Federation of Community Associations
TFCRI	Tropical Fish Culture Research Institute (Malaysia)
TFD	Tobaksarbejderforbund i Danmark
TFDL	Technisch Fysische Dienst voor de Landbouw
TFF	Tekniska Fysikers Förening
TFF	Transnationella Stiftelsen för Freds-och
TFIC	Federation of Image Consultants Ltd
TFiF	Tekniska Foreningen i Finland
TFK	Transportforskningskommissionen
TFMRC	Thermo-Fluid Mechanics Research Centre
TFNC	Tanzania Food and Nutrition Centre
TFOF	Taxi Fleet Operators' Federation (*now* LMCPA)
TFP	Bureau Tradition, Famille, Propriété pour le Canada
TFP	Tradição, Familia e Propriedade (Brazil)
TFP	Tradición, Familia y Propriedad (Venezuela)
TFPA	Television and Film Production Asociation
TFPA	Tonga Family Planning Association
TFR	Tribunal Federal de Recursos (Brazil)
TFRI	Taiwan Fisheries Research Institute
TFRI	Tianjin Fisheries Research Institute
TFRI	Transnational Family Research Institute (U.S.A.)

TFSK	Turkish Federated State of Kibris (Cyprus)	**THS**	Hovercraft Society
		THS	Hydrographic Society
TFSR	Tools For Self Reliance	**THSG**	Transport and Health Study Group
TFTA	Traditional Farmfresh Turkey Association	**THT**	Terrence Higgins Trust
		THW	Bundesanstalt Technisches Hilfswerk
TFTDWU	Taiwan Federation of Textile and Dyeing Workers Union	**THY**	Türk Hava Yollari
		THY	Turun Historiallinen Yhdistys
TG	Theosophische Gesellschaft = ST, TS	**THYT**	Teollisuudenharjoittajain Yleinen Ryhmä
TG	Townswomen's Guilds		
TGA	Tianjin Geological Academy	**TI**	Tawhid Islami (Lebanon)
TGA	Timber Growers Association	**TI**	Textile Institute
TGA	Touristische Gemeinschaft der Alpenlander (Switzerland)	**TI**	Toastmasters International
		TI	Tónskáldafélag Íslands
TGA	Tropical Growers Association	**TIA**	Taxation Institute of Australia
TGD	Timeshare Developers' Group	**TIA**	Telecommunications Industry Association
TGEW	Timber Growers, England and Wales Ltd		
		TIA	Trans-International Airlines (U.S.A.)
TGF	Tekstilgrossistenes Forbund	**TIAC**	Transport Industries Advisory Council (Australia)
TGI	Tory Green Initiative		
TGIA	Toy and Giftware Importers Association (*now* BTIDA)	**TIAC**	Travel Industry Association of Canada
		TIAFT	International Association of Forensic Toxicologists
TGLP	Tribal Grazing Land Policy (Botswana)		
TGLR	Tasmanian Gay and Lesbian Rights	**TIAR**	Tratado Interamericano de Asistencia Recíproca
TGNA	Turkish Grand National Assembly		
TGNU	Transitional Government of National Unity (Namibia)	**TIB**	Société Transivoirienne des Bois
		TIB	Tanzania Investment Bank
TGS	Texas Geographic Society (U.S.A.)	**TIBÉA**	Société Travaux Isolation-Bâtiment Étanchéité-Afrique (Congo)
TGSA	Tropical Grassland Society of Australia		
TGUK	Timber Growers United Kingdom Ltd.	**TIBO**	Träindustrins Branschorganisation
TGV	Schweizerischer Transportgewerbeverband	**TIC**	Tantalum Niobium International Study Centre (Belgium)
		TIC	Technical Information Center (China)
TGWU	Transport and General Workers' Union	**TIC**	Timber Industries Confederation
THA	Tanzania Harbours Authority	**TIC**	Tribune Internationale des Compositeurs (IMC)
THA	Thai Hotels Association		
THAI	Thai Airways International	**TIC**	Tyre Industry Council
THB	Tanzania Housing Bank	**TICA**	Thermal Insulation Contractors Association
THB	Traditional Housing Bureau		
THD	Türk Hemsireler Dernegi	**TICA**	Tourism International Cooperative and Associated = UITCA
THE	Technical Help to Exporters (BSI)		
THERE	Technology with Home Economics Resources in Education (*ex* HERE)	**TICCI**	Technical Information Centre for Chemical Industry (India)
		TICCIH	The International Committee for the Conservation of the Industrial Heritage
THET	Tropical Health and Education Trust		
THFP	Homeless Furniture Project	**TICERI**	Tianjin Internal Combustion Engine Research Institute
THG	Telecommunications Heritage Group		
THGK	Harita Genel Komutanligi	**TICOM**	Texas Institute for Computational Mechanics
THL	Teollisuudenharjoittajain Liitto		
THL	Tieteenharjoittajain Liitto	**TICST**	Trent International Centre for School Technology
THRA	Tasmanian Historical Research Association		

TIDA	Technology and Industry Development Authority (Australia)
TIDA	Travel and Industrial Development Association
TIDO	Trabajo, Investigacion, Desarrollo y Organizacion de la Mujer (Argentina)
TIE	Transnationals Information Exchange
TIES	International Environmetric Society
TIF	Theatre Investment Fund
TIF	Tilapia International Foundation
TiFC	Towarzystwo im Fryderyka Chopina
TIFR	Tata Institute of Fundamental Research (India)
TIG	Télécommunications Internationales Gabonaises
TIGA	Transport Issues Group Australia
TIHR	Tavistock Institute Human Relations
TII	European Association for the Transfer of Technologies, Innovation and Industrial Information (Luxembourg)
TIIAL	The International Institute of Applied Linguistics
TIJI	Tribune Internationale des Jeunes Interprètes (IMC) = IRP
TIK	Türkiye Isçi Köylü
TILC	Trotskyist International Liaison Committee
TILP	Tekhnologicheskii Institut Legkoi Promyshlennosti
TILT	Tianjin Institute of Laser Technology
TIMCON	Timber Packaging and Pallet Confederation
TIME	Thai International Maritime Enterprises
TIME	Training in Moral Education
TIMS	Institute of Management Sciences (U.S.A.)
TIMSA	Thermal Insulation Manufacturers and Suppliers Association
TINFO	Tieteellisen Informoinnin Neuvosto
TINTUC	Trinidad and Tobago National Trade Union Congress
TIP	Towarzystwo Internistów Polskich
TIP	Turkish Labour Party
TIPA	Tibetan Institute of Performing Arts
TIPA	Trade and Investment Promotion Agency (Botswana)
TIPER	Tanzanian Italian Petroleum Refinery Co.
TIPS	Teaching Improvement Project System (U.S.A.)
TIPS	Technological Information Pilot System (UNDP) (Italy)
TIRDO	Tanzania Industrial Research and Development Organization
TIRF	Traffic Injury Research Foundation of Canada
TIRR	Institute for Rehabilitation and Research (U.S.A.)
TIRU	Traitement Industriel des Résidus Urbains
TIS	Trade Information System on Barriers to Trade Among Developing Countries
TIS	Turkish Informatics Society = TBD
TISC	Textile Industry Support Campaign
TISCO	Tata Iron and Steel Company (India)
TISK	Türkiye Isveren Sendikalari Konfederasyonu
TISL	Telecommunications and Information Systems Laboratory (U.S.A.)
TISPOC	Trent Institute for the Study of Popular Culture (Canada)
TISTI	Tianjin Institute of Scientific and Technical Information
TISTR	Thailand Institute of Scientific and Technological Research
TIT	Tudományos Ismeretterjesztö Társulat
TITP	Tianjin Institute of Technical Physics
TITUS	Textile Information Treatment Users Service
TIU	Telecommunications International Union
TJA	Table Jellies Association
TJK	Türkiye Jeoloji Kurumu
TJP	Tehrik-e-Jafria-e-Pakistan
TKD	Türk Kütüphaneciler Dernegi
TKI	Tejgazdasági Kíserleti Intézet
TKI	Textilipari Kutató Intézet
TKKF	Towarzystwo Krzewienia Kultury Fizycznej
TKKS	Towarzystwo Krzewienia Kultury Swieckiej
TKL	Teollisuuden Keskusliitto
TKN	Towarzystwo Kursów Naukowych
TKP	Türkiye Komünist Partisi
TKV	Tieteellisten Kirjastorjen Virkailijat
TKWP	Towarzystwo Krzewienia Wiedzy Praktycznej
TL	Trehusindustriens Landsforbund
TL	Trelasthandlernes Landsforbund

TL	Turistvognmoendenes Landsorganisation
TLA	Thai Library Association
TLA	Toy Libraries Association
TLC	Trade Leaders Club (Portugal, U.S.A.)
TLDPC	Tidal Land Development Planning Commission (Taiwan)
TLIF	Traktor- og Landbruksmaskin-Importörenes Forening
TLJW	Stichting Technisch Landbouw Jongerenwerk
TLLF	Tekniska Läroanstalternas Larareforbund (Finland) = TOOL
TLMA	Tunnel Lining Manufacturerss Association
TLMI	The Leprosy Mission International
TLP	Tasmania Labour Party
TLP	Telefones de Lisboa e Porto
TLRI	Taiwan Livestock Research Institute
TLRS	Tramway and Light Railway Society
TLS	Tekniska Litteratursällskapet
TM	Taukei Movement (Fiji)
TM	Tiedotusmiehet
TM	Transcendental Meditation
TMA	Telecommunications Managers' Association
TMA	Theatrical Management Association
TMA	Tobacco Manufacturers Association (*ex* TAC)
TMA	Trans-Mediterranean Airways (Lebanon)
TMA	Trinidad Manufacturers Association
TMA	Turkish Management Association
TMAF	Tribune de la Musique Africaine (Ivory Coast) = AFMR
TMAG	Tasmania Museum and Art Gallery
TMAS	Tribune de Musique de l'Asie = ASMR
TMB	Tobacco Marketing Board (Zimbabwe)
TMBA	Twins and Multiple Births Association
TMC	Tourism Ministers Council
TMC	Turkish Mountaineering Club
TMCA	Titanium Metals Corporation of America
TMD	Turk Matematik Dernegi / Turkish Mathematical Society
TME	Toy Manufacturers Europe (Belgium)
TMG	Tape Manufacturers' Group
TMHiZK	Towarzystwo Milošników Historii i Zabytków Krakowa

TMI	Transport Medical Institute (Bulgaria)
TMIS	Technical Meetings Information Service (U.S.A.)
TMJP	Towarzystwo Milošników Języka Polskiego
TML	Turkish Maritime Lines = TDI
TMM	Towarzystwo Milošników Muzyki
TMMB	Türkiye Muhendisler ve Mimarlar Birligi
TMMOB	Turk Mühendis ve Mimar Odalari Birligi
TMO	Toprak Mahsulleri Offisi
TMPDF	Trade Marks Patents & Designs Federation
TMS	The Minerals, Metals & Materials Society
TMS	Tramway Museum Society
TMSA	Technical Marketing Society of America
TMSA	Telephone Manufacturers of South Africa
TMSC	Tobacco Manufacturers Standing Committee
TMT	Turk Mudata Teskilat (Cyprus)
TMTE	Textilpari Müszaki és Tudományos Egyesület
TN	Towarzystwo Naukowe
TNA	Tamil National Army (Sri Lanka)
TNAI	Trained Nurses Association of India
TNAUK	Talking Newspaper Association of the United Kingdom
TNB	Tenaga Nasional Berhad (Malaysia)
TNC	Tekniska Nomenklaturcentralen
TNC	The Nature Conservancy (U.S.A.)
TNC	Theatres National Committee
TNC	Trade Negotiations Committee (GATT)
TNDC	Thai National Documentation Centre
TNE	National Electoral Tribunal (Honduras)
TNEK	Türkiye Nükleer Enerji Kurumu
TNI	Transnational Institute (Netherlands)
TNIP	Transkei National Independence Party (South Africa)
TNO	Organisatie voor Toegepast Natuurweten-schappelijk Onderzoek
TNOIK	Towarzystwo Naukowe Organizacji i Kierownictwa
TNP	The National Party (Grenada)
TNP	Towarzystwo Naukowe Płockie
TNRC	Tianjin Nuclear Radiation Center
TNT	Tendencia Nacionalista de Trabajo (Honduras)

TNT	Towarzystwo Naukowe w Toruniuț
TNV	Tribal National Volunteer (India)
TNWU	Tunisian National Women's Union
TO	Time Off for Women
TOA	Toilers Organisation of Afghanistan
TOAA	Trawler Owner's Association of Australia
TOBETON	Société Togolaise de Béton
TOCOA	Toyota Commerical Agency (Gabon)
TODA	The Open Door Association
TODIREP	Société Togolaise de Diffusion et de Représentation
TOES	The Other Economic Summit (U.S.A.)
TOES	The Other Europe Summit
TOF	Tertius Ordo Sancti Francisci = OFS, SFO
TøF	Transportøkomisk Forening
TOF	Türk Otolarengoloji Federasyonu
TOFFS	Over Fifties Association
TOFINSO	Société Toulousaine Financière et Industrielle du Sud-Ouest
TOFS	Tracheo-Oesophageal Fistula Support
TOGA	Tropical Ocean and Global Atmosphere Programme (WRCP)
TOGO-FRUIT	Société Nationale de Développement de la Culture Fruitière (Togo)
TOGO-GRAIN	Office National des Produits Vivriers (Togo)
TOGO-METAL	Industrie Togolaise pour la Fabrication et la Vente de Meubles
TOGOGAZ	Société Togolaise des Gaz Industriels
TOGO--PROM	Société Togolaise de Promotion pour le Développement
TOGOTEX	Compagnie Togolaise des Textiles
TOH	Programme on Tobacco or Health (WHO)
TOK	Türk Orotmatik Kontrol Kumumu
TOL	Tree of Life
TOLA	Theater of Latin America (U.S.A.)
TOLE-GALVA	Groupement des Producteurs Français de Tôle Galvanisée
TOLES-IVOIRE	Société de Galvanisation de Tôles en Côte d'Ivoire
TOLEYIS	Turkiye Otel, Lokanta ve Eglence Yerleri Isei Sendikalari Federasyonu
TOM	Tertius Ordo Minimorum
TOM	Troops Out Movement
TOOL	Technische Ontwikkelingslanden
TOOL	Technologie Overdracht Ontwikkelingslanden
TOOL	Teknillisten Offilaitosten Opettajainliitto = TLLF
TOP RAKSU	General Directorate of Soil Conservation and Irrigation (Turkey)
TOPS	Theatre Organ Preservation Society
TOR	Tertius Ordo Regularis Sancti Francisci
TORP	Tertiary Oil Recovery Project (U.S.A.)
TORRO	Tornado and Storm Research Organisation
TORVENCA	Tornillos Venezolanos, C.A.
TOSD	Third Order Secular of St Dominic
TOSG	Tour Operators' Study Group
TOSHIBA	Tokio Shibaura
TOT	Tatar Public Centre
TOT	Telephone Organization of Thailand
TOT	Termelöszövetkezetek Országos Tanácsa
TOUC	Teleordering Users Council
TOURAC	Association Internationale Auxiliaire des Touring Clubs de l'Afrique Centrale
TOURESTO	Combinatie van Restaurateurs in Nederlands
TOURIS-MAD	Société Hôtelière et Touristique de Madagascar
TOW	Transport On Water Association
TOWA	Tug-of-War Association
TOZ	Towarzystwo Opieki nad Zwierz¿etami
TPA	Taiwan Pineapple Association
TPA	Tea Packers' Association
TPA	Tea Producers' Association
TPA	Televisão Popular de Angola
TPA	The Pizza Association
TPA	Tribunales Populares Antisomocistas (Nicaragua)
TPA	Turkish Peace Association
TPA	Tutmonda Parolspuro-Asocio
TPAF	Tracheotomy Patients Aid Fund
TPAS	Tenant Participation Advisory Service for England
TPAS	Trade Promotion Advisory Service (GATT)
TPC	Psychotherapy Centre
TPC	Tall Persons Club of Great Britain
TPC	Thai Packaging Centre
TPC	Trade Practices Commission
TPD	Towarzystwo Przyjaciół Dzieci
TPDC	Tanzania Petroleum Development Corporation
TPDF	Trade Marks Patents and Designs Federation

TPEPR	Tajikistan Party of Economic and Political Renewal
TpF	Talepoedagogisk Forening
TPFCC	Trans Pacific Fisheries Consultative Committee = CCPTP
TPG	Portman Group
TPG	Trésorier Payeur Général
TPGS	Thermal Power Generation Society (China)
TPI	Tropical Products Institute
TPIS	Tropical Pesticides Information Service
TPLA	Turkish People's Liberation Army
TPLF	Tigre People's Liberation Front (Ethiopia)
TPN	Towarzystwo Przyjaciół Nauk w Przemysłu
TPP	Turkish People's Party (Kosovo)
TPPA	Trade and Professional Publishers' Association (Éire)
TPPC	Timber Packaging and Pallet Confederation
TPPN	Towarzystwo Przyjaźni Polsko-Norweskiej
TPPR	Towarzystwo Przyjaźni Polsko-Radzieckiej
TPR	Tribunaux Populaires Révolutionnaires (Burkina Faso)
TPR	Trust for the Protection of Reptiles
TPRC	Thermophysical Properties Research Center (U.S.A.)
TPRC	Trade Policy Research Centre
TPRI	Thermal Power Research Institute (China)
TPRI	Tropical Pesticides Research Institute (Tanzania)
TPRI	Tropical Products Research Institute
TPRM	Thai Peoples Revolutionary Movement
TPS	Tax Payers Society
TPS	Thomas Paine Society
TPSL	Työväen ja Pienviljelijain Sosialidemokraattinen Liitto
TPTPA	Table Poultry and Turkey Producers Association
TPU	Threatened Plants Unit (IUCN)
TR	Teatrarnas Riksförbund
TR	Textilgrossisternas Riksförbund
TR	Trudovaia Rossiia
TRA	Taiwan Railway Administration
TRA	The Reclamation Association

TRA	Throughbred Racing Association (U.S.A.)
TRAC-TIONÉL	Société de Traction et d'Électricité (Belgium)
TRACO-GRAS	Association Belge des Transformateurs de Corps Gras Industriels
TRADA	Timber Research and Development Association
TRADEMO	Tradicionalismo Democrático (Paraguay) = MTC
TRADEVCO	Liberian Trading and Development Bank
TRAFO	Transportmateriel-Foreningen
TRAG	Tamil Refugee Action Group
TRAGASA	Empresa de Transformacion Agraria
TRAINMAR	Training Development in the Field of Maritime Transport (UNCTAD, UNDP)
TRAM	Teatr Rabochey Molodezhi
TRAMA-GRAS	Transformateurs de Matières Grasses
TRAMÉT	Groupement du Négoce International et du Traitement Industriel des Déchets Métalliques
TRAN	Tropical Rainforest Action Network = IRFAN, RAN
TRANET	Transnational Network for Appropriate/Alternative Technologies (U.S.A.)
TRANS-BENIN	Société des Transports Routiers du Bénin
TRANS-COBOIS	Commercialisation des Bois en Provenance de Centrafrique, Caméroun, Gabon (Congo)
TRANS-CODI	Société Transcontinentale de Diffusion Industrielle (Senegal)
TRANS-COFER	Société de Transport Complémentaire du Chemin de Fer (Cameroon)
TRANS-COGANTS	Société Transcontinentale des Gants (Senegal)
TRANS-COGAZ	Société Transcontinentale des Gaz de Pétrole BP
TRANS-ÉQUAT	Société de Transit Équatorial (Cameroon)
TRANS-GROUP	Transafricaine Groupage (Ivory Coast)
TRANS-NIGER	Nigerian Airlines
TRANSB-EUROP	European Federation of Butter Processing Industries
TRANSCAM	Société Camérounaise des Entreprises Bourdin et Chaussée

TRANSCAP	Société Eurafricaine de Voyages, de Transit et de Camionnage Portuaire
TRANS-FRIA	Société de Transport et d'Approvisionnement de l'Aluminium (Africa)
Transimport	Empresa Central de Abastecimiento y Venta de Equipos de Transportes Pesadas y sus Piezas (Cuba)
TRANSMER	Société de Transformation des Produits de la Mer (Ivory Coast)
Transnave	Transportes Navieros Ecuatorianos
TRANSNUC-LÉAIRE	Société pour les Transports de l'Industries Nucléaire
TRANSUD	Société des Transports du Sud de Madagascar
TRAPIL	Société des Transports Petroliers par Pipe-Line
TRAVAIL	BIT Département Conditions Milieu Travail
TRB	Tobacco Research Board (Zimbabwe)
TRC	Technical Reports Centre (DTI)
TRC	Telecommunications Research Center (U.S.A.)
TRC	Textile Research Council
TRC	Trade Relations Council of the United States
TRDA	Timber Research and Development Association
TRDB	Tanzanian Rural Development Bank
TRDC	Tana River Development Company (Kenya)
TRE	Telecommunications Research Establishment
TREAT	Trust for Education and Research on the Arms Trade
TREDA	Technology Research & Economy Development Academy (China)
TREE	Trends in Ecology and Evolution
TREUHAND	Treuhandanstalt
TRF	Trädgårdsnäringens Riksförbund
TRF	Trail Riders Fellowship
TRF	Tropical Forests Program (IUCN)
TRFA	Trussed Rafter Fabricators' Association
TRG	Tertiary Research Group
TRG	Tory Reform Group
TRI	Tape Respondents International
TRI	Tea Research Institute (China, Sri Lanka)
TRI	Textile Research Institute (U.S.A.)
TRI	Thrombosis Research Institute
TRI	Tin Research Institute
TRI	Tribal Research Institute and Training Centre (India)
TRI	Tropical Resources Institute (U.S.A.)
TRI	Trucking Research Institute (U.S.A.)
TRI-UN	Department of Trusteeship and Information from Non-Self Governing Territories
TRIBOIS	Société de Transformation Industrielle du Bois (Ivory Coast)
TRIC	Television and Radio Industries Club
TRICOMAD	Société Industrielle des Tricotages de Madagascar
TRIDO	Table Ronde Internationale pour le Développment de l'Orientation
TRIEA	Tea Research Institute of East Africa
TRIGC	Tea Research Institute Guangdong Academy of Agricultural Sciences
TRIMALCA	Latin American and Caribbean Music Rostrum
TRIN-DELAM	Société Camérounaise de Travaux Industriels pour l'Électricité
TRIN-DÉLCI	Travaux Industriels pour l'Électricité Côte d'Ivoire
TRIN-TOPEC	Trinidad and Tobago Petroleum Company
TRINDÉL	Travaux, Industriels pour l'Électricité
TRINTOC	Trinidad and Tobago Oil Company
TRIP	The Road Information Program (U.S.A.)
TRITURAF	Société Ivoirienne pour la Trituration de Graines Oléagineuses et le Raffinage d'Huiles Végétales
TRITWE	Tianjin Research Institute of Water Transport Engineering
TRL	Transport Research Laboratory
TRN	Taiga Rescue Network (Sweden)
TRNC	Turkish Republic of North Cyprus
TROA	Toilers' Revolutionary Organization of Afghanistan
TROBI	Tree Register of the British Isles
TROPARC	Center for Tropical and Subtropical Architecture Planning and Construction (U.S.A.)
TROPIC	Société des Forges Tropicales (Cameroon)
TROPMED	Tropical Medicine and Public Health Project (SEAMEO)
TROPMED-EUROP	Council of Directors of Institutes of Tropical Medicine in Europe

TROS	Televisie Radio Omroep Stichting	**TSBA**	Trustee Savings Banks Association
TRRB	Trade Relations Research Bureau	**TsBR**	Tsentral'nyi Bank Rossii
TRRC	Textile Resource and Research Center (U.S.A.)	**TSC**	Taiwan Sugar Corporation
		TSC	Tea Society of China
TRRL	Transport and Road Research Laboratory (DTI)	**TSC**	Theosophy Science Centre
		TSC	Turkey Solidarity Campaign
TRS	Tobacco Research Station (New Zealand)	**TSE**	Tribunal Superior Eleitoral (Brazil)
		TSE	Türk Standartlari Enstitüsü
TRS	Tree-Ring Society (U.S.A.)	**TsEMI**	Tsentral'nyi Ekonomichesko-Matematicheskii Institut
TRSC	Thailand Remote Sensing Center		
TRT	Télécommunications Radioélectriques et Téléphoniques	**TsEMI RAN**	Central Economic-Mathematical Institute, Russian Academy of Sciences
TRT	Three Revolutions Teams Movement (Democratic People's Republic of Korea)	**TSF**	Compagnie Générale de Télégraphie sans Fil
		TSFA	The Securities and Futures Authority
TRT	Transport Trust	**TSG**	Tibet Support Group
TRT	Türkiye Radyo Televizyon Kurumu	**TSGA**	Tanzania Sisal Growers Association
TRTA	Télécommunications Radioélectriques et Téléphoniques Africaines	**TSGB**	Tensor Society of Great Britain
		TSI	The Sulphur Institute (U.S.A.)
TRUE	Trust for Urban Ecology	**TSIA**	Trading Stamp Institute of America
TRZZ	Towarzystwo Rozwoju Ziem Zachodnich	**TsIK**	Central Electoral Commission (Russia)
		TSK	Tokyo Senpaku Kaisha Ltd.
TS	Theosophical Society = ST, TG	**TSK**	Tradgardnäringens Standardiseringskommitté
TS	Tolkien Society		
TS	Tourism Society	**TSKŻwP**	Towarzystwo Społeczno-Kulturalne Żydów w Polsce (Poland) = SCSJP
TSA	Telecommunications Staff Association		
TSA	Textile Services Association	**TSKB**	Turkiye Sinai Kalinma Bankasi
TSA	The Securities Association	**TSKhA**	Timirazev Agriculture Academy
TSA	Tourette Syndrome Association	**TSKL-CZSwP**	Towarzystwo Społeczno-Kulturalne Czechów i Słowaków w Polsce (Poland) = SCSCSP
TSA	Trust for the Study of Adolescence Ltd		
TSA	Tuberous Sclerosis Association of Great Britain	**TSKMNŚO**	Towarzystwo Społeczno-Kulturalne Mniejszości Niemíeckiej na Śląsku Opolskim (Poland) = SCAGMSO
TSA	United Kingdom Land & Hydrographic Survey Association		
		TSL	Treuhandstelle der Schweizenischen Lebensmittelimporteure
TSAC	Therapeutic Substances Advisory Committee (Éire)		
		TSM	Towarzystwo Swiadomego Macierzynstwa
TsAGI	Tsentral'nyi Aero-Gidrodinamicheskii Institut		
		TSMA	Traffic Safety Markings Association
TsAKA	Tsentral'nyi Arkhiv Krasnoi Armii	**TSP**	Tropical Stored Products (TPI)
TsAL	Tsentral'naia Akkumuliatornaia Laboratoriia	**TSRU**	Tuberculosis Surveillance Research Unit (Netherlands)
		TSS	Towarzystwo Szkoly Swieckiej
TsAM	Tsentral'nyi Apparat Ministerstva	**TSS**	Turner's Syndrome Society
TsAO	Tsentral'naia Aerologicheskaia Observatoriia	**TSSA**	Transport Salaried Staffs' Association
		TsSBS	Tsentral'nyi Sibirskii Botanicheskii Sad
TSAP GOOS	Technical and Scientific Advisory Panel for GOOS	**TsSDF**	Tsentral'naia Studiia Dokumental'nykh Fil'mov (Russia)
TSB	Taonan Sugar Beet Breeding Station		
TSB	Textile Statistics Bureau	**TsSK**	Tsentral'nyi Sportivnyi Klub (Russia)
TSBA	Teeswater Sheep Breeders' Association		

TsSML	Tsentral'naia Sudebno-Meditsinskaia Laboratoriia (Russia)
TsSMP	Tsentral'nyi Sovet Mongol'skikh Profsoiuzov (Mongolia)
TsSU	Tsentral'noe Staticheskoe Upravlenie
TST	Tribunal Superior do Trabalho (Brazil)
TSTFA	Tasmania Sashimi Tuna Fishermens's Association
TsUNKhU	Tsentral'noe Upravlenie Narodokhoziaistvennogo Ucheta
TSV	Turkiye Evre Surunlari = EPFT
TT	Transport Trust
TT REG	Teetotallers Register
TTA	Tanzania Tea Authority
TTA	Teacher Training Agency
TTA	Teknillisten Tieteiden Akatemia
TTAW	Table Tennis Association of Wales
TTC	Tanzania Tourist Corporation
TTC	Tea Trade Committee
TTC	Timeshare Council
TTC	Transit Transports Camérounais
TTCC	Test Card Circle
TTDC	Thana Training and Development Centre (Bangladesh)
TTEA	Thai Timber Exporters Association
TTEC	Thai Technical and Economic Cooperation Office
TTEG	Telephone and Telegraph Engineering Guild
TTF	Timber Trade Federation
TTF	Transporttekniska Foreningen
TTF	Treindustries Tekniske Forening
TTFC	Textile Technical Federation of Canada
TTGA	Tanzania Tea Growers' Association
TTHM	Türk Teknik Haberlesme Merkezi
TTIA	Timber Trade Industrial Association (Australia)
TTIC	Taiwan Tea Improvement Committee
TTIRI	Tianjin Textile Industry Research Institute
TTIS	Translation and Technical Information Services
TTK	Teknisen Tukkukaupan Keskusliitto
TTK	Türk Tarih Kurumu
TTLC	Trinidad and Tobago Labour Congress
TTOK	Türkiye Turing ve Otomobil Kurumu
TTRA	Tourist Trophy Riders Association
TTRA	TT Riders' Association
TTRI	Telecommunications Technical Training and Research Institute (Egypt)
TTS	Transport Ticket Society
TTTA	Timber Trade Training Association
TTWMB	Taiwan Tobacco and Wine Monopoly Bureau
TU	Svenska Tidningsutgivareföreningen
TUA	Telecommunications Users Association
TUA	Tractor Users Association
TUA	Traders' Union of Afghanistan
TUAC	Trade Union Advisory Committee (OECD) = CSC
TUBA	Turkiye Bilimler Akademisi / Turkish Academy of Sciences
TUBCS	Trade Union Badge Collectors Society
TUBE	The Union of Bookmakers Employees
TÜBITAK	Türkiye Bilimsel ve Teknik Arastirma Kurumu
TUC	Trades' Union Congress (Ghana, Guyana, Jamaica, U.K.)
TUCAL	Tunisienne de Conserves Alimentaires
TUCC	Transport Users Consultative Committee
TUCM	Trades Union Congress of Malawi
TUCN	Trades Union Congress of Nigeria
TUCND	Trade Union Campaign for Nuclear Disarmament
TUCP	Trade Union Congress of the Philippines
TUCRIC	Trade Union Community Resource and Information Centre
TUCSA	Trades Union Council of South Africa
TUCSICC	Trade Union Congress Steel Industry Consultative Committee
TUDA	Trade Union Disability Alliance
TUF	Tokyo University of Fisheries
TUFEC	Thailand-Unesco Fundamental Education Centre
TUFHA	Tuvalu Family Health Association
TUFL	Trade Unionists For Labour
TUFMAC	Uganda Fish Marketing Corporation
TUFML	TU Trust Managers Ltd
TUFMW	Trade Union Federation of Militia Workers (Russia)
TUFP	Trade Union Friends of Palestine
TUI	Teachers Union of Ireland
TUI	Trade Unions International of Public and Allied Employees = UIS

TUIAFPW	Trade Unions International of Agricultural, Forestry and Plantation Workers = MOPTSLKP, UISTABP, UISTAFP
TUIREG	Trade Union International Research and Education Group
TUIs	Trade Union Internationals = UIS
TUIWC	Trade Union International of Workers in Commerce = UISTC
TUIWE	Trade Unions International of Workers in Energy = UISTE
TUKI	Taasisi ya Uchunguzi wa Kiswahili (Tanzania)
TULF	Tamil United Liberation Front (Sri Lanka)
TULINK	Trade Union and Labour Ireland Network
TUNI	Trade Union Network on Ireland
TUNL	Triangle Universities Nuclear Laboratory (U.S.A.)
TUP	Towarzystwo Urbanistów Polskich
TUP	Trickle Up Program
TUPLAN	Textil Uruguaya de Productos de Lana
TUR	Towarzystwo Uniwersytetu Robotniczego
TÜRDOK	Türk Bilimensel ve Teknik Dokumentasyon Merkezi
TURI	Toxics Use Reduction Institute (U.S.A.)
TURiL	Towarzystwo Uniwersytetów Robotniczych i Ludowych
TÜRK-IS	Türkiye Isçi Sendikalari Konfederasyonu Genel Baskanligi
TÜRK-SEN	Kibris Türk Isçi Sendikalari Federasyonu (TRNC)
TURN	Trade Unions Regional Network
TÜRSAB	Türkiye Seyahat Acentalari Birligi
TURU(S)	Trade Union Research Unit (Scotland)
TÜSIAD	Türk Sanayicileri ve Isadamlari Dernegi
TUSM	World Federation of Ukrainian Student Organizations of Michnowsky
TUTB	European Trade Union Technical Bureau for Health and Safety
TÜV	Vereinigung der Technischen Überwachungs-Verein (Austria)
TUWTW	Trade Union of Water Transport Workers (Russia)
TVA	Tegleverkenes Arbeidsgiverforening
TVA	Tennessee Valley Authority (U.S.A.)
TVE	Televisão Experimental (Mozambique)
TVE	Televisión Española
TVE	Television Trust for the Environment
TVF	Teknisk-Vetenskaplig Forkning
TVHB	Türk Veteriner Hekimleri Birliği
TVK	Toimihenkilö-ja Virkamiesjärjestöjen Keskusliitto
TVN	Theosofische Vereniging in Nederland
TVNZ	Television New Zealand
TVRI	Yayasan Televisi Republik Indonesia
TVS	Technical Valuation Society (U.S.A.)
TVS	Theatervereine der Schweiz
TVT	Television of Thailand
TVU	Thames Valley University
TVVL	Nederlandse Technische Vereniging voor Installaties in Gebouwen
TWA	Tibetan Women's Association
TWA	Trans-World Airlines (U.S.A.)
TWARO	Textile Workers Asian Regional Organisation
TWAS	Third World Academy of Sciences (Italy)
TWAU	Transvaal Women's Agricultural Union (South Africa)
TWEC	Isaac N. Thut World Education Center (U.S.A.)
TWF	Third World First
TWF	Third World Forum = FTM
TWG	Third World Group (Malta)
TWI	The Welding Institute = WI
TWICO	Tanzania Wood Industries Corporation
TWIF	Tug of War International Federation
TWIG	Towarzystwo Wspierania Inicjatyw Gospodarczych
TWIN	Third World Information Network
TWK	Polskie Towarzystwo Walki z Kalectwem
TWL	Nederlandse Technische Vereniging voor Verwarming ewn Luchtbehandeling
TWL	The Women's Lobby (South Africa)
TWM	Third World Media (U.K.)
TWMAE W	Third World Movement Against the Exploitation of Women (Philippines)
TWN	Third World Network (Malaysia)
TWNSO	Third World Network of Scientific Organisations (Italy)
TWOWS	Third World Organization for Women in Science (Italy)
TWOZ	Commissie voor Toegepast Wetenschappelijk Onderzoek in de Zeevisserij (Belgium)

TWP	Committee for the Provision of Technical Assistance for the Welfare of the People (Thailand)
TWP	Towarzystwo Wiedzy Powszechnej
TWR	Trans World Radio
TWS	Tasmanian Wilderness Society
TWS	The Wilderness Society
TWS	Wildlife Society
TWSA	Theatrical Wardrobe Suppliers Association
TWSC	Third World Studies Center (Philippines)
TWU	Theatre Writers' Union
TWU	Tobacco Workers Union
TWU	Transport Workers Union (Guyana)
TWUA	Transport Workers' Union of America
TWWP	Towarzystwo Wolnej Wszechnicy Polskiej
TZF	Technische Zentralstelle der Deutschen Forstwirtschaft
TZR	Tanzania-Zambia Railway Authority

U

U3A	Third Age Trust/University of the Third Age
UA	Ulkomaakaupan Agenttiliitto
UA	Underwater Association for Scientific Research (U.K., U.S.A.)
UA	Urostomy Association
UAA	Union des Architectes Africains
UAA	Union des Avocats Arabes
UAA	United Arab Airlines (Egypt)
UAA	Urban Affairs Association (U.S.A.)
UAAEE	United Arab Atomic Energy Establishment
UAAS	Ukrainian Academy of Arts and Sciences (U.S.A.)
UAAS	Union Africaine des Artistes des Spectacles = UAPA
UAB	Union Arabe des Bourses de Valeur = UASE
UAB	Union of Arab Banks
UAB	Universities Appointments Board
UABS	Union of American Biological Societies
UAC	Stichting ter Bevordering van een Uniforme Artikel Codering
UAC	Ulster Automobile Club

UAC	Union Africaine des Chemins de Fer (Ethiopia) = UAR
UAC	Union of Arab Chemists
UAC	United Africa Company
UACB	Union des Agglomérés di Ciment de Belgique
UACC	Universal Autograph Collectors Club
UACE	Unión Americana Catolica de Educadores
UACEE	Union de l'Artisanat de la CEE
UACES	University Association for Contemporary European Studies
UACF	Union Arabe des Chemins de Fer = AUR
UACh	Universidad Autónoma de Chiapas (Mexico)
UACL	United Aircraft of Canada Ltd
UACO	United Africa Company
UACP	Union des Agences et Conseils en Publicité
UACS	Union des Associations Cinématographiques Suisses
UACVAO	Union des Associations de Chantiers de Volontaires de l'Afrique de l'Ouest = UWAVWA
UADE	Union Africaine de Distributeurs d'Eau = UAWS
UADI	Unión Argentina de Asociaciónes de Ingenieros
UADW	Universal Alliance of Diamond Workers = AUOD, WVD
UAE	United Arab Emirates
UAF	Uganda Air Force
UAFA	Union Arabe du Fer et de l'Acier = AESU, AISU
UAFA	Union of Arab Football Associations
UAG	Österreichische Arbeitsgemeinschaft für Ur- und Frühgeschichte
UAG	Union d'Assurances du Gabon
UAG	Universidad Autónoma de Guadalajara (Mexico)
UAHS	Ulster Architectural Heritage Society (Northern Ireland)
UAI	Union Académique International = IUA
UAI	Union Astronomique Internationale = IAU
UAI	Union d'Action Internationale (PME)
UAI	Union des Associations Internationales = UIA
UAIA	Union des Agences d'Information Africaines

UAIC	Unité d'Afforestation Industrielle du Congo	**UAR**	Union Asiatique de Radiodiffusion (Japan)
UAIDe	Users of Automatic Information Display Equipment (U.S.A.)	**UAR**	Union of African Railways = UAC
UAJ	Udruzenje Anesteziologas Jugoslavije	**UAR**	Uniunea Arhitecţilor din România
UAJ	Union of African Journalists = UJA	**UAR**	Uniunea Armenilor din România (Romania) = AUR
UAJ	Union of Arab Jurists	**UARCEE**	Union des Associations des Riziers de la CEE
UAK	Union Africaine de Karate		
UAL	United Air Lines (U.S.A.)	**UAREP**	Universities Associated for Research and Education in Pathology (U.S.A.)
UAM	Universidad Autónoma de Madrid		
UAM	Universidad Autónoma Metropolitana (Mexico)	**UARN**	Union des Chambres Artisanales du Bâtiment
UAMBD	Union Africaine et Mauricienne des Banques de Développement	**UARP**	Union des Associations Romandes de Pédicures
UAMDB	Union Africaine de Management des Banques pour le Développement (Benin)	**UAS**	Ulster Archaeological Society
		UAS	Union of African States
		UAS	Universidad Autónoma de Sinaloa (Mexico)
UAMS	Ukrainian Academy of Medical Sciences (U.S.A.)	**UAS**	University of Agricultural Sciences (India)
UAMS	Union Africaine de Médecine du Sport	**UASC**	United Arab Shipping Company (Kuwait)
UAN	United Animal Nations (Switzerland)		
UANA	Unión Amateur de Natación de las Américas = ASUA	**UASE**	Union of Arab Stock Exchanges = UAB
		UASIF	Union des Associations Scientifiques et Industrielles Françaises
UAOD	United Ancient Order of Druids		
UAOS	Ulster Agricultural Organisation Society (Northern Ireland)	**UASJ**	Union of African Sports Journalists
		UASP	Unidad de Acción Sindical y Popular (Guatemala)
UAP	IFLA International Programme for Universal Availability of Publications	**UASTM**	Universidad Agraria de la Selva de Tingo María (Peru)
UAP	Unabhängige Arbeiterpartei – Deutsche Sozialisten	**UAT**	Union Aéromaritime de Transport
UAP	Union des Assurances de Paris	**UAT**	Union of African Towns =UCA, UVA
UAP	Union of African Parliaments = UPA	**UATI**	Union des Associations Techniques Internationales = UITA
UAP	Union of Arab Pharmacists		
UAP	Uniunea Artistilor Plastici	**UAU**	Union of Architects of Ukraine
UAP	Universidad Autónoma de Puebla (Mexico)	**UAU**	Universities Athletic Union
UAPA	Union des Agences de Presse Africaines	**UAUW**	Uganda Association of University Women
UAPA	Union of African Performing Artists = UAAS	**UAW**	International Union of United Automobile, Aerospace and Agricultural Workers of America
UAPF	Union des Amateurs à la Pêche de France		
UAPNA	Union des Administrations Portuaires du Nord de l'Afrique	**UAW**	Union of Australian Women
		UAWS	Union of African Water Suppliers = UADE
UAPS	Union for African Population Studies (Dakar) = UEPA	**UAWU**	University and Allied Workers Union (Jamaica)
UAPS	Union of Arab Pediatric Societies = USAP	**UBA**	Ulusal Basin Ajansi (Turkey)
UAPT	Union Africaine des Postes et Télécommunications	**UBA**	Umweltbandsamt
		UBA	Union Belge de l'Automatique
UAPT	United Association for the Protection of Trade	**UBA**	Union Belge des Annonceurs

UBA	Union of Burma Airways
UBAC	Union Bancaire en Afrique Centrale
UBAF	Union des Banques Arabes et Françaises
UBAH	Union des Branches Annexes de l'Horlogerie (Switzerland)
UBB	Unie van Beveilings-en Bewakingspersoneel
UBCIM	IFLA Universal Bibliographic Control and International MARC Programme
UBD	Institut für Umwelt-Boden-Deponie-Analytik
UBE	Union Bouddhique d'Europe
UBEC	Union of Banana Exporting Countries = UPEB
UBESA	Unión de Bananeros Ecuatorianos
UBF	Universal Buddhist Fellowship (U.S.A.)
UBFTG	Union Belge des Fabricants de Téles Galvanisées
UBG	Union Belge des Géomètres-Experts Immobiliers
UBI-D	Union Beratender Ingenieure e.V.
UBIC	Union Belge des Installateurs en Chauffage Central, Ventilation et Tuyauteries
UBIL	Union Bretonne des Industriels Laitiers
UBJ	Udruzenje Banaka Jugoslavije
UBJET	Union Belge des Journalistes et Ecrivains du Tourisme
UBKA	Ulster Bee Keepers' Association
UBNIL	Union des Industriels Laitiers de Basse-Normandie
UBOS	Union de la Bijouterie et de l'Orfèvrerie Suisse
UBP	United Bermuda Party
UBPP	Union Belge des Prisonniers Politiques
UBS	Union Belge des Sérigraphes
UBS	United Bible Societies = ABU, SBU, WBG
UBSD	Union of Bosnian Social Democrats
UBT	Union Togolaise de Banque
UBUR	Unión de Bancos del Uruguay
UBZI	Unie der Belgische Zuivelindustrie
UC	Union Caledonienne
UC	Unión Civica (Uruguay)
UC	University of California
UCA	Uganda Cooperative Alliance
UCA	Ulster Chemists Association
UCA	Ulster Curers Association
UCA	Uniao das Cidades Africanas = UAT, UVA
UCA	United Council on Alcohol and other Drugs
UCA	Universidad Centroamericana 'José Simeón Cañas' (El Salvador)
UCAAF	Union des Coopératives Agricoles et Alimentaires Françaises
UCACE	Universities Council for Adult and Continuing Education
UCAD	Union Centrale des Arts Décoratifs
UCAÉYL	Union des Coopératives d'Élevage de l'Yonne-Loiret
UCAF	Utilities' Contractor Associations' Federation
UCAHM	Union Cinéastes Huitistes Mondiaux
UCAI	Unione Cattolica Artisti Italiani
UCAL	União das Cooperativas Abastacedoras de Leite de Lisboa
UCAL	Unión de Cinematecas de América Latina (Mexico)
UCALMA	Union Coopérative Agricole Laitière de la Manche
UCAM	Universidad Nacional Autónoma de México
UCAN	Union des Coopératives Agricoles de Noyon
UCAN	Union of Catholic Asian News
UCAO	Union Chimique de l'Ouest-Africain (Guinée)
UCAP	Union Catholique Africaine de la Presse
UCAP	United Coconut Association of the Philippines
UCAR	Union des Coopérative Agricoles Romandes
UCAR	University Corporation for Atmospheric Research (U.S.A.)
UCASEF	Union Nationale des Coopératives Agricoles de Semances Fourragères
UCASPOR	Union des Coopératives Agricoles du Silo Portuaire de Rouen
UCAT	Universidad Católica de Chile
UCATT	Union of Construction, Allied Trades and Technicians
UCB	Ufficio Centrale Brevetti
UCB	Uganda Commercial Bank
UCB	Uitvoer Contrôle-Bureau
UCB	Union Camérounaise des Brasseries
UCB	Union Chimique Belge
UCB	Union Congolais de Banques

UCB	Union Nationale des Coopératives Agricoles de Transformation de Betterave	**UCDP**	Ukrainian Christian Democratic Party
		UCE	Union de Consumidores de España
UCBSA	United Cricket Board of South Africa	**UCE**	Unione Suisse de Contrôle des Installations sous Pression
UCBT	Union for the Tropical Wood Trade of the EEC Countries	**UCECOM**	Uniunea Centrala a Cooperativelor Mestesugaresti
UCC	Ulster Countryside Committee		
UCC	Union Corporative de la Couleur	**UCeDé**	Unión del Centro Democrático (Argentina)
UCC	Union de la Critique du Cinéma (Belgium)	**UCÉI**	Union des Centres d'Échanges Internationaux
UCC	Union des Conseils des Chargeurs Africains (Ivory Coast)	**UCÉMA**	Usine Céramique du Mali
		UCEP	Union Colombiana de Empresas Publicitarias
UCC	University College, Cork (Éire)		
UCCA	Union Cotonnière Centrafricaine	**UCEPA**	Unidad de Comercio Exterior de Productos Agricolas (Venezuela)
UCCA	Union des Conseils des Chargeurs Africains (MINCONMAR)	**UCÉRC**	Union des Centres d'Études Rurales par Correspondance
UCCA	Universities Central Council on Admissions (*now* UCAS)		
		UCESM	Union des Conférences Européennes des Supérieurs Majeurs
UCCAEP	Unión Costarricensense de Cámaras y Asociaciones de la Empresa Privada		
		UCET	Universities Council for the Education of Teachers
UCCAO	Union Central des Coopératives Agricoles de l'Ouest (Cameroon)	**UCÉVER**	Union Nationale des Grossistes en Céramique et Verrerie
UCCBRA	University College Cardiff Bee Research Association		
		UCF	Ulster Cancer Foundation
UCCC	Ukrainian Civic Congress of the Crimea	**UCF**	Union Culturelle Française
UCCD	Union des Producteurs Belges de Chaux Calcaires, Dolomies et Produits Connexes	**UCF**	Union des Chausseurs Français
		UCF	Unions Chrétiennes Féminines
		UCF	United Cooperative Farmers Inc. (U.S.A.)
UCCE	Union des Capitales de la Communauté Européenne		
		UCF	United Counties Farmers Ltd
UCCÉGA	Union des Chambres de Commerce et Établissements Gestionnaires d'Aéroports	**UCFAF**	Union Centrale des Syndicats Agricoles de France
		UCFI	Union Cattolica Farmacisti Italiani
UCCET	Union of Chambers of Commerce, Industry, Maritime Commerce and Commodity Exchanges of Turkey	**UCG**	Universidade Católica de Goiás (Brazil)
		UCG	University College, Galway (Éire)
		UCH	Union Nationale des Chambres Syndicates d'Entreprises en Génie Climatique
UCCI	Union Carbide Côte d'Ivoire		
UCCI	Union Catholique Coopération Interraciale		
UCCI	Union Cavalleria Cristiana Internazionale	**UCI**	Ufficio Centrale Italiano
		UCI	Union Canine Internationale
UCCI	Unión de Ciudades Capitales Iberoamericanas	**UCI**	Union Cycliste Internationale = ICU
		UCI	Union des Cadres et Ingénieurs (CGT-FO)
UCCLA	Uniao das Cidades Capitais de Língua Portuguesa		
		UCI	Unione Cattolica Infermieri
UCCMA	Union des Caisses Centrales de la Mutualité Agricole	**UCI**	Unione Coltivatori Italiana
		UCI	Université Coopérative Internationale
UCD	University College, Dublin (Éire)	**UCIC**	Unione Cattolica Italiana Commercianti
UCDEC	Union Chrétienne Démocrate d'Europe Centrale = CDUCE, UDCEC	**UCIC**	Unione Costruttori Impianti di Combustione

UCICIS	Union Construttori Italiani Carrelli Industriali Semoventi ed Affini	**UCLA**	University of California at Los Angeles (U.S.A.)
UCID	União Caboverdiana Independente e Democrática	**UCLAP**	Unión Católica Latinoamericana de la Prensa (Uruguay)
UCID	Union Cristiana Imprenditori Dirigenti	**UCLG**	United Cement, Lime, Gypsum and Allied Workers International Union (U.S.A.)
UCIDT	União Catolica de Industriais e Dirigentes de Trabalho		
UCIÉ	Union Centrale des Industries Électrotechniques	**UCLMS**	University College London Medical School
UCIFA	Union Centralschweizerischer Cigarrenfabrikanten	**UCM**	Universal Christian Movement
		UCM	Universidad Complutense de Madrid
UCIIM	Union Cattolica Italiana Insegnati Medi	**UCMA**	Unione Costruttori Macchine Alimentari
UCIL	Uranium Corporation of India		
UCIMU	Unione Construttori Italiani Macchine Utensili	**UCMR**	Uniunea Compozitorilor şi Muzicologilor din România
UCINA	Union Cinématographique Africaine	**UCMTF**	Union des Constructeurs de Matériel Textile de France
UCINA	Unione Nazionale Cantieri e Industrie Nautiche ed Affini	**UCN**	Unión Cívica Nacional (Dominican Republic)
UCIP	Union Catholique Internationale de la Presse = ICUP, IKUP	**UCN**	Union del Centro Nacional (Guatemala)
UCIP	Union de Comercio la Industria y la Producción (Argentina)	**UCNOD**	União Coordenadora Nacional dos Organismos de Deficientes
UCIR	University Centers for International Rehabilitation (U.S.A.)	**UCNS**	Universities Council for Non-Academic Staff
UCIS	University Center for International Studies (U.S.A.)	**UCNW**	University College of North Wales, Bangor
UCISA	Universities and Colleges Information Systems Association	**UCODIMA**	Union Commerciale de Diffusion de Marques
UCISA-SDG	UCISA Staff Development Group	**UCODIS**	Union pour le Commerce et la Distribution des Grandes Marques
UCISAHG	UCISA Hardware Group		
UCISAMISG	UCISA Management and Information Services Group	**UCOMA**	Union des Commerçants Maliens
		UCOMAF	Union Commerciale Africaine
UCISANG	UCISA Networking Group	**UCOMESA**	Unione Costruttori Macchine Edili, Stradali, Minerari ed Affini
UCISASG	UCISA Software Group		
UCISATLIG	UCISA Teaching, Learning and Information Group	**UCONAL**	Unión de Cooperativas Nacionales (Colombia)
UCISP	Unione Costruttori Italiani Strumenti per Pesare	**UCOPOM**	Union Européenne du Commerce de Gros des Pommes de Terre
UCISS	Union Catholique Internationale de Service Social = CIUSS, IKVSA, KIUMW	**UCOPS**	Universal Coterie of Pipe Smokers (U.S.A.)
		UCOR	Uranium Enrichment Corporation (South Africa)
UCIT	Unione Cattolica Italiana Tecnici		
UCJF	Union Chrétienne des Jeunes Filles = YWCA	**UCOWR**	Universities Council on Water Resources (U.S.A.)
UCJG	Alliance Universelle des Unions Chrétiennes de Jeunes Gens = ACDG. ACJ, CVJM, YMCA	**UCPE**	Unit of Comparative Plant Ecology (NERC)
		UCPL	Union Centrale des Producteurs de Lait (Switzerland)
UCL	Uganda Creameries Ltd		
UCL	Union Chemical Laboratories (Taiwan)	**UCPMI**	Union des Consommateurs de Produits Métallurgiques et Industriels
UCL	University College, London		

UCPTÉ	Union pour la Coordination de la Production et du Transport de l'Électricité	**UDACI**	Unione Donne di Azione Cattolica Italiana
UCR	Union Centriste et Radicale	**UDAL**	Union de Universidades de America Latina (Mexico)
UCR	Unión Cívica Radical (Argentina)	**UDAP**	Unit for the Development of Alternative Products
UCRAO	Rothney Astrophysical Observatory (Canada)	**UDC**	Christian Democratic Union Party (Romania)
UCRIF	Union des Centres de Rencontres Internationales en France	**UDC**	Uganda Development Corporation
UCRIFER	Unione Costruttori e Riparatori Ferrotramviari	**UDC**	Union Démocratique Centrafricaine (Central African Republic)
UCRIMM	Unione Costruttori e Riparatori Materiale Mobile Ferrotramviario	**UDC**	Union du Centre
UCRP	Ukrainian Conservative Republican Party	**UDC**	Union pour la Démocratie Congolaise
		UDC	Unity-in-Diversity Council (U.S.A.)
UCS	Unión Comunal Salvadoreña	**UDCCA**	Union Démocrate Chrétienne Amérique Centrale
UCS	Union des Centrales Suisses de l'Électricité	**UDCEC**	Unión Democrática Cristiana de Europa Central = CDUCE, UCDEC
UCS	Union des Coopératives de Semences	**UDD**	Association pour l'Utilisation et la Diffusion de la Documentation
UCSA	Union des Confédérations Sportives Africaines	**UDD**	Union for Democracy and Development (Gabon)
UCSE	Union des Chambres Syndicales de l'Est	**UDDA**	Unione Democratica Dirigenti d'Azienda
UCSI	Union Cattolica Stampa Italiana	**UDDIA**	Union Démocratique de Défense des Intérêts Africains
UCSIP	Union des Chambres Syndicales de l'Industrie du Pétrole	**UDE**	Union Démocratique Européenne = EDU
UCSMB	Union des Carrièrers et Scieries de Marbres de Belgique	**UDEAC**	Union Douanière et Économique de l'Afrique Centrale
UCSTE	Unión Confederal de Sindicatos de Trabajadores de la Enseñanza	**UDÉAO**	Union Douaniere des États de l'Afrique de l'Ouest
UCTA	United Commercial Travellers' Association of Great Britain and Ireland	**UDEC**	Union d'Entreprises Camérounaises
UCTAT	Union des Co-opératives de Travaux Agricoles de Tunisie	**UDEC**	Union d'Entreprises de Constructions (Ivory Coast)
UCTF	Union Culturelle et Technique de Langue Française	**UDEC**	Union Professionnelle des Diplômés Experts Comptables
UCTLV	United Committee for the Taxation of Land Values	**UDÉCÉVER**	Union Européenne des Détaillants en Céramique et Verrerie
UCV	Universidad Central de Venezuela	**UDÉCMA/ KMTP**	Union Démocratique Chrétien Malgache
UCW	Union of Communication Workers		
UCW	University College of Wales, Aberystwyth	**UDECO**	Umm Al-Dalkh Development Company (Abu Dhabi)
UCWRE	Underwater Countermeasures and Weapons Research Establishment	**UDÉF**	Union des Éditeurs Français
UD	Unia Demokratyczna	**UDÉFA**	Union de la Distribution des Équipements et Fournitures pour Automobiles
UD	Union Démocratique (New Caledonia)		
UDA	Ulster Defence Association	**UDÉL**	Union des Éditeurs de Littérature
UDA	Union des Annonceurs	**UDÉLAV**	Union Pour la Défense de la Lavande et du Lavandin
UDA	United Democratic Alliance (Lesotho)		
UDACE	Unit for the Development of Adult and Continuing Education (NIACE)		

UDELPA	Union del Pueblo Adelante (Argentina)
UDEM	Union des Entreprises Métropolitaines
UDEMAG	Union de Empleados Profesionales de Ministerio de Agricultura y Ganaderia (Costa Rica)
UDÉPAC	Union Professionnelle des Détaillants en Porcelain et Cristaux (Belgium)
UDERC	Union des Dirigeantes d'Entreprise de la Région Choletaise
UDES	Union de Dirigentes de Empresas Salvadoreñas
UDET	Union de Docentes de Educación Tecnica (Argentina)
UDEV	Union des Dirigeants d'Entreprise de la Vendée
UDF	Ulster Defence Force
UDF	Union of Democratic Forces (Bulgaria)
UDF	Union pour la Démocratie Française (France, French Guiana, Guadeloupe, Martinique, New Caledonia, Réunion)
UDF	United Democratic Front (Namibia, South Africa)
UDFP	Democratic Union of Progressive Forces
UDI	Unión Demócrata Independiente (Chile)
UDI	Union Démocratique Internationale = IDU
UDI	Unione Donne Italiane
UDIA	United Dairy Industry Association (U.S.A.)
UDIAS	Union des Constructeurs et Importateurs d'Appareils Scientifiques, Médicaux et de Contrôle (Belgium)
UDIL	University Directors of Industrial Liaison
UDIMÉC	Union des Industries Métallurgiques, Électriques et Connexes et Connexes de l'Isere
UDIMÉRA	Union des Industries Métallurgiques et Électriques de la Région Rhône-Alpes
UDIMMÉ	Union des Importateurs de la Métallurgie, de la Mécanique et de l'Électronique
UDIPÉ	Union pour le Développement Industriel et la Promotion Économique
UDISTP	Uniao Sindical dos Trabalhadores de Sao Tomé e Principe
UDK	Union Deutscher Künstleragenten
UDLP	United Dominica Labour Party
UDM	Union Démocratique Mauricienne
UDM	Union Démocratique Mauritanienne
UDM	Union des Démocrates Martiniquais
UDM	Union of Democratic Mineworkers
UDMR	Uniunea Democratică a Maghiarilor din România (Romania) = DUHR
UDMTR	Uniunea Democratică a Musulmanilor Turci din România (Romania) = MTDUR
UDN	Union Democrática Nacional (El Salvador)
UDN-FARN	Union Democrática Nicaragüense – Fuerza Armadas Revolucionarias Nicaragüenses
UDO	United Display Organization (Switzerland)
UDP	Institut International pour l'Unification du Droit Privé
UDP	União Democrática Popular
UDP	Unidad Democrática Popular (Peru)
UDP	Union Democrática Popular (Bolivia, Ecuador)
UDP	United Democratic Party (Belize, Lesotho, Sierra Leone)
UDP	Urban Development Program (Canada)
UDP	Usines Béninoises de Préfabrication
UDPM	Ugandan Democratic Peoples Movement
UDPM	Union Démocratique du Peuple Malien
UDPS	Union pour la Démocratie et de Progrès Social (Zaïre)
UDR	Ulster Defence Regiment (Northern Ireland)
UDR	União Democrática Ruralista (Brazil)
UDR	Union Démocratique Républicaine
UDR	Union for Democratic Reforms (Ukraine)
UDRR	Uniunea Democratică Romilor din România (Romania) = DURR
UDRT	Union Démocratique pour le Respect du Travail (Belgium) = RAD
UDS	Union des Dentistes et Stomatologistes de Belgique
UDS	Uniunea Democratică a Sîrbilor (Romania) = DUS
UDSC	Uniunea Democratică a Slovacilor şi Cehilor (Romania) = DUSC
UDSSD	Union des Sociétés Suisses de Développement
UDT	União Democrática Timorense
UDT	Unión Democrática de Trabajadores (Chile)

UDT	United Dominions Trust		**UEEA**	Union Européenne des Exploitants d'Abbattoirs du Commerce de Bétail et de la Viande
UDU	Union Démocratique Unioniste (Tunisia)		**UEÉB**	Union des Exploitations Électriques de Belgique = VEB
UDUAL	Unión de Universidades de América Latina		**UEÉJ**	Union Européenne des Étudiants Juifs = EUJS
UDV	Union Démocratique Voltaïque (Burkina Faso)		**UEF**	Union Europäischer Forstberufsverbände
UE	Edinstvo Movement (Moldova)		**UEF**	Union Européenne des Fédéralistes
UEA	Union Européenne de l'Ameublement = EFF, EMV		**UEF**	Union Européenne Féminine = EFU, EUW
UEA	Union Européenne des Aveugles = EBU		**UEF**	Union of European Foresters
UEA	Universala Esperanto-Asocio		**UEFA**	Union of European Football Associations
UEA	University of East Anglia		**UEFDC**	Union Européenne des Femmes Démocrates-Chrétienne = UEMDC
UEA	University of East Asia (Macao)		**UÉFE**	Union Économique Fédérale Européenne
UÉAC	Union des États de l'Afrique Centrale		**UEFPC**	Union Européenne des Federations du Personnel Communal = EULAS
UEADM	Union Européenne des Associations de Délégués Médicaux		**UEFS**	Unione Europea delle Farmacie Sociali = EUSA, EUSMCP, EUSP, UEPS, VESA
UÉAE	Union des Étudiants Africains d'Europe		**UEFTU**	Union of European Foresters Trade Unions
UEAI	Union Européenne d'Arabisants et Islamisants = EUAIS		**UEGGSP**	Union Européenne Groupements Grossistes Specialisés en Papeterie
UEAPME	Union Européenne de l'Artisanat et des Petites et Moyennes Entreprises		**UEHMSU**	Union Européenne d'Hygiène et de Médecine Scolaires et Universitaires = EUSUHM
UEATC	Union Européenne pour l'Agrément Technique dans la Construction		**UEHP**	Union Européenne de l'Hospitalisation Privée
UEB	Ufficio Europeo dei Brevetti = EPA, EPO, OEB		**UEI**	Union of Educational Institutions
UEB	Union Europäischer Bankpersonalverbände		**UEIC**	United East India Company
UEB	Union Européenne de Badminton = EBU		**UEIF**	Union Européenne Industrielle et Financière
UÉBL	Union Économique Belgo-Luxembourgeoise = BLEU		**UEIG**	Union des Expéditeurs Internationaux de Grèce
UEC	Union Européenne de Chaudières = EBA, EHV		**UEIL**	Union Européenne des Indépendants en Lubrifiants
UEC	Union Européenne de la Carrosserie		**UEITP**	Union Européenne des Industries de Transformation de la Pomme de Terre
UECBV	Union Européenne du Commerce du Bétail et de la Viande		**UEJ**	Union Européenne de Judo
UECGPT	Union Européenne du Commerce de Gros des Pommes de Terre		**UEJDC**	Union Européennes des Jeunes Démocrates-Chrétiens = EUJCD, EUYCD
UECL	Union Européenne des Constructeurs de Logements		**UEL**	Universidade Estadual de Londrina (Brazil)
UECL	Union Professionnelle des Experts Comptables Libéraux		**UELDC**	Unione Europea dei Lavoratori Democratici Cristiani = EUCDA, EUCDW, UETDC
UECR	Union des Ententes et Communautés Rurales			
UED	Union Européenne de Douane			
UEDC	Union Européenne des Démocrates Chrétiennes = CDEU, ECDU			
UEDSPI	Union Européenne des Syndicats pour Indépendants			

UÉLF	Union des Éditeurs de Langue Française
UÉM	Union Économique et Monétaire = EMU
UEM	Union Européenne de Malacologie = EMU
UÉM	Union Évangélique Mondiale = AEM, WEF
UEMASS	Union Européenne de Médecine d'Assurance et de Sécurité Sociale
UEMD	Unione Europea dei Medici Dentisti = EUD, EUZ, UEPMD
UEMDC	Union Europea de Mujeres Demócrata Cristianas = UEFDC
UEMO	Union Européenne des Médecins Omnipracticiens
UEMOA	Union des Exposants de Machines et d'Outillage Africoles
UEMS	Union Européenne de Médecine Sociale
UEMS	Union Européenne des Médecins Spécialistes
UEMTA	Union Européenne contre l'Emploi Abusif des Animaux = EUMT
UEMV	Union Européenne des Miroitiers Vitriers
UENCPB	Union Européenne des Négociants en Cuirs et Peaux Bruts
UENDC	Union Européenne des Négociant Détaillants en Combustibles
UENF	Union Européenne des Non Fumeurs
UEO	Union de l'Europe Occidentale = WEU
UEP	Union Européenne de Pédopsychiatres
UEP	Union of European Phoniatricians = SEF, UPE
UÉPA	Union pour l'Étude de la Population Africaine (Dakar) = UAPS
UEPC	Union Européenne des Promoteurs-Constructeurs
UEPG	European Aggregates Association
UEPGH	Union Européenne des Portiers des Grandes Hôtels
UEPMD	Union Européenne de Practiciens de Médecine Dentaire = EUD, EUZ, UEMD
UEPS	Union Européenne de la Presse Sportive
UEPS	Union Européenne des Pharmacies Sociales = EUSA, EUSMCP, EUSP, UEFS, VESA
UEPS	United Elvis Presley Society
UEPSMC	Union Européenne des Pharmacies Sociales Mutualistes et Coopératives (Belgium)
UER	Union Européenne de Radiodiffusion = EBU
UERP	Union Européenne de Relations Publiques = EUPRISO
UESD	União da Esquerda Socialista Democrática (Portugal)
UESEG	United Earth Sciences Exploration Group
UESEM	Union Européenne des Sources d'Eaux Minérales Naturelles du Marché Commun
UESLA	Unione Europea dei Sindacati Liberi e Autonomi
UET	United Engineering Trustees (U.S.A.)
UET	Université Européenne du Travail
UET	Urban Environment Trust
UETDC	Union Européenne des Travailleurs Démocrates Chrétiens = EUCDA, EUCDW, UELDC
UETU	Union Européenne des Théâtres Universitaires
UEU	Ulemaailmne Eesti Uhing = WAE
UEVE	Union Européenne des Vétérinaires Enseignants
UEVF	Union Européenne des Vétérinaires Fonctionnaires = EASVO
UEVH	Union Européenne des Vélodromes d'Hiver
UEVH	Union Européenne des Vétérinaires Hygiénistes
UEVHA	Union Européenne des Vétérinaires Hygiénistes de l'Alimentation
UEVO	Union Européenne des Vétérinaires Engagées Outremer
UEVP	Union Européenne des Vétérinaires Practiciens
UEW	European Union of Electrical Wholesalers
UF	United Force (Guyana)
UF	United Front (Sri Lanka)
UFA	Upholstery Fillings Association
UFAB	Union Française d'Agriculture Biologique
UFAC	Union des Fabricants d'Aliments Composés
UFAC	Unione Feminile di Azione Cattolica
UFAC	Universidade Federal do Acre (Brazil)
UFACD	Union des Fabricants d'Appareils de Cuisine et de Chauffage Domestique
UFACEFAM	Union Fraternelle des Anciens Combattants d'Expression Française Africains et Malgaches

UFALEX	Union des Exportateurs Français de Demiproduits en Aluminium
UFARAL	Union des Fournisseurs des Artisans de l'Alimentation (Belgium)
UFAS	Union des Associations d'Assistants Sociaux Francophones (Belgium)
UFAW	Universities Federation for Animal Welfare
UFB	Union des Femmes Burundaises
UFB	Union Française de Banque
UFBA	Universidade Federal da Bahia (Brazil)
UFC	Union Fédérale des Consommateurs
UFC	Union Française des Céréales
UFC	Université Fédérale du Caméroun
UFC	Universities Funding Council
UFCAC	Union Fédérale des Coopératives Agricoles de Céréales
UFCC	Union Fédérale de la Coopération
UFCE	Union Fédéraliste des Communautés Ethniques Européennes = FUEN, FUEV, UFNE
UFCS	Union Féminine Civique et Sociale
UFD	Union des Forces Démocratiques (Algeria)
UFDC	Union des Femmes Démocrates-Chrétiennes = UMFDC, WUCDW
UFDI	Union Française des Designers Industriels
UFE	Union des Féculeries de Pommes de Terre (CE)
UFE	Union des Finanzpersonals in Europa
UFE	Union des Frères Enseignants
UFÉ	Union Famille-École
UFE	Union Foraine Européenne = ESU
UFEA	Union Financière pour l'Europe et l'Afrique
UFÉA	Union Française pour l'Équipement Agricole
UFEMAT	Union Européenne des Fédérations Nationales des Négociants en Matériaux de Construction
UFER	Mouvement International pour l'Union Fraternelle entre les Races et les Peuples
UFESAS	Universal Fair and Exhibition Service
UFF	Ulster Freedom Fighters
UFF	Ulster Furniture Federation
UFF	Universidade Federal Fluminense (Brazil)
UFF	Women's Rights Bureau (France)
UFFI	Union Foncière et Financière
UFG	Union Française des Géologues
UFI	Union des Foires Internationales
UFI	Union Française d'Information
UFI	Union Française Immobilière
UFI	Union Francophone des Ingénieurs Industriels et Ingénieurs Techniciens (UNIT) (Belgium)
UFIB	Unione Federazioni Italiani Bocce
UFIDÉC	Union pour l'Information et la Défense des Consommateurs (Belgium)
UFIE	Union Française des Industries Exportatrices de Biens de Consommation
UFIIB	Union Fédérale des Associations d'Ingénieurs Industriels de Belgique
UFINAL	Union Financière pour le Développement des Industries Alimentaires
UFINEX	Union pour la Financement et l'Expansion du Commerce International
UFIP	Union de Funcionarios Independientes de Prisiones
UFIPTÉ	Union Franco-Ibérique pour la Production et le Transport de l'Électricité
UFJT	Union des Foyers des Jeunes Travailleurs
UFK	Universala Framasona Ligo (Belgium)
UFL	Underraettelser fraan Flygledningen
UFLC	Union Internationale des Femmes Libérales Chrétiennes = IALRW
UFM	Union des Femmes de la Méditerranée
UFMAT	Union des Fédérations Nationales des Négociantes en Matériaux de Construction de la CEE
UFMG	Universidade Federal de Minas Gerais (Brazil)
UFMT	Universidade Federal do Mato Grosso (Brazil)
UFMUB	Union des Femmes Musulmanes du Benin
UFNA	Union Française pour la Nutrition et l'Alimentation
UFNE	Unión Federalista de Nacionalidades Europeas = FUEN, FUEV, UFCE
UFO	Union Forestière de l'Ogooué (Gabon)
UFOCA	Union Forestière Camérounaise
UFOD	Union Française des Organismes de Documentation

UFORA	Unidentified Flying Objects Research Association	**UGAF**	Union des Groupements Apicoles Français
UFOTECH	Union des Fournisseurs de Textiles aux Collectives Hospitalières	**UGAI**	Unione Giornalisti Aerospaziali Italiani
UFP	Union des Forces Populaires (Benin)	**UGAL**	Union des Groupements d'Achat de l'Alimentation (Belgium) = AROWF, UGEL
UFPa	Universidade Federal do Pará (Brazil)		
UFPDG	Union des Femmes (PDG) (Gabon)	**UGAT**	Union Générale de l'Agriculture Tunisienne
UFPE	Universidad Federal de Pernambuco		
UFPHF	Union des Fabricants de Papiers Héliographiques de France	**UGB**	Union Gabonaise de Banque
		UGB	Unión Guerrera Blanca (El Salvador)
UFPIPIA	Union des Fabricants pour la Promotion Internationale de la Propriété Industrielle et Artistique	**UGBF**	Union Générale de la Brasserie Française
		UGC	University Grants Commission (India)
UFPR	Universidade Federal do Parana (Brazil)	**UGC**	University Grants Committee (New Zealand)
UFRC	Ulster Federation of Rambling Clubs		
UFRGS	Universidade Federal do Rio Grande do Sul (Brazil)	**UGCA**	Union of German Cultural Associations (Czech Republic) = SNKO
UFRJ	Universidade Federal do Rio de Janeiro (Brazil)	**UGCAA**	Union Générale des Coopératives Agricoles d'Approvisionnement
UFRO	International Union of Forest Research Organisations	**UGCAC**	Union Générale des Coopératives Agricoles de Céréales
UFRRJ	Universidade Federal Rural do Rio de Janeiro (Brazil)	**UGCAF**	Union Générale des Coopératives Agricoles Françaises
UFRS	Universidade Federal do Rio Grande do Sul (Brazil)	**UGCI**	Unione Giuristi Cattolici Italiani
		UGCW	United Glass and Ceramic Workers of America
UFSAM	Union Féminine Suisse des Arts et Métiers		
UFSC	Universidade Federal de Santa Catarina (Brazil)	**UGEA**	Union des Groupements pour l'Exploitation Agricole
		UGÉAN	Union Générale des Étudiants d'Afrique Noire
UFSS	Union Française des Syndicats Séricicoles		
UFT	Union des Fédérations de Transports	**UGÉC**	Union Générale des Étudiants Congolaises
UFTA	United Farmers Trading Agency		
UFTAA	Universal Federation of Travel Agents Associations = FUAAV	**UGECO-BAM**	Union Générale des Coopératives Bananières du Mungo (Cameroon)
UFTF	Union des Fabricants de Tapis de France	**UGÉG**	Union Générale des Étudiants Guineens
UFTIW	Union of Forestry and Timber Industry Workers (Bulgaria)	**UGEL**	Union der Genossenschaftlichen Einkaufs-Organisationen für Lebensmittel = AROWF, UGAL
UFU	Ulster Farmers' Union		
UFUCH	Unión de Federaciones Universitarias de Chile	**UGÉM**	Union Générale des Étudiants du Mároc
		UGÉMA	Union Générale des Étudiants Muselmans d'Algérie
UFV	Independent Women's Association (Germany)		
		UGÉT	Union Générale des Étudiants de Tunisie
UFW	United Farm Workers of America		
UFW	United Furniture Workers of America	**UGEXPO**	Union Générale des Exposants de Matériels et de Produits Destinés à Agriculture (Belgium)
UFY	Uusfilologinen Yhdistys		
UGAA	Union Générale Arabe d'Assurance = FGAA, GAIF	**UGGI**	Union Géodésique et Géophysique Internationale = IUGG
UGAASA	Union General de Autores y Artistas de el Salvador	**UGI**	Union Géographique Internationale = IGU

UGICT	Union Genéralé des Ingénieurs, Cadres et Techniciens	**UH**	Union of Hungarians (Czech Republic) = SM
UGIMA	Unione Generale degli Industriali Apuani del Marmo ed Affini	**UHA**	Union der Hörgeräte-Akustiker
		UHDY	Union of Hungarian Democratic Youth (Romania) = UTDM
UGLC	University of Glasgow Language Centre	**UHF**	Ulster Historical Foundation
UGOCP	Union General Obrero Campesina y Popular (Mexico)	**UHP**	Union Hospitalière Privée
UGOJ	Udruzenje Ginekologa – Opstetricara Jugoslavije	**UHRA**	Uganda Human Rights Activists
		UHS	Unitarian Historical Society
UGPFE	Union des Groupements de Prévoyance des Fonctionnaires Européens	**UHSG**	Unemployment and Health Study Group
		UI	International Union of Graphic Reproduction Industries
UGS	Union Générale des Savonneries		
UGSA	Union Générale Sidérurgie Arabe	**UI**	Understanding Industry
UGSBF	Union Générale des Syndicats de la Brasserie Française	**UI**	Uranium Institute
		UI	Utrikespolitiska Institutet
UGSCAP	Union of German Social-Cultural Associations in Poland = ZNSSKP	**UIA**	Argentine Industrial Union
		UIA	Ultrasonic Industry Association
UGSR	Uniunea Generala a Sindicatelor din România	**UIA**	Union Immobilière Africaine (Congo)
		UIA	Unión Industrial Argentina
UGSS	Union of Local and Non Local General Service Staff of the Food and Agriculture Organisation of the United Nations	**UIA**	Union Internationale Antiraciste
		UIA	Union Internationale contre l'Alcoolisme = IUA
		UIA	Union Internationale des Architectes = IUA
UGT	Société Urbaine Gabonaise de Travaux		
UGT	União General de Trabalhadores	**UIA**	Union Internationale des Avocats
UGT	Unión General de Trabajadores (Puerto Rico, Spain, Uruguay)	**UIA**	Union of International Associations = UAI
UGTA	Union Générale des Travailleurs Algériens	**UIAA**	Union Internationale des Associations d'Alpinisme
UGTB	Union Générale des Travailleurs du Bénin	**UIAA**	Union Internationale des Assureurs Aéronautiques = IUAI
UGTC	General Workers' Union of Cuba	**UIADPÉ**	Union Internationale des Agents de Diffusion, Presse, Édition
UGTC	Union Générale des Travailleurs du Centrafrique	**UIAÉ**	Union Industrielle pour l'Afrique Équatoriale
UGTCI	Union Générale des Travailleurs de Côte d'Ivoire	**UIAÉÉH**	Union Internationale des Anciens Élèves des Écoles Hôtelières
UGTD	Unión General de Trabajadores Dominicanos	**UIAF**	Union Interprofessionnelle de l'Angora Français
UGTM	Union Générale des Travailleurs du Mauritanie	**UIAGM**	Union Internationale des Associations de Guides de Montagne = IVBV
UGTM	Union Générale des Travailleurs Marocains	**UIAMS**	Union Internationale d'Action Morale et Sociale = IUMS
UGTP	União General dos Trabalhadores Portugueses	**UIAOM**	Union Internationale des Agriculteurs de l'Outre-Mer
UGTS	Union Générale des Travailleurs du Sénégal	**UIAP**	Union Intérfédérale des Armateurs à la Pêche
UGTT	Union Générale des Travailleurs Tunisiennes	**UIAPME**	Union Internationale de l'Artisanat et des Petites et Moyennes Entreprises = IACME, IGU
UGWU	United General Workers' Union (Belize)		

UIAPPA	Union Internationale des Associations de Prévention de la Pollution Atmosphérique = IUAPPA
UIAT	Union Internationale des Syndicats des Industries de l'Alimentation et du Tabac = IUFDT
UIATU	Union of Independent Albanian Trade Unions = BSPS
UIB	Unie der Immobiliënberoepen van België = UPI
UIB	Union Internationale de Biochemie = IUB
UIB	Union Internationale des Maîtres Boulangers
UIBA	Unión Iberoamericana de Colegios y Agrupaciones de Abogados
UIBÉB	Union Internationale des Bègues Éliminant leur Bégaiement (Belgium)
UIBPA	Union Internationale de Biophysique Pure et Appliquée =IUPAB
UIBWM	Trade Unions International of Workers of Building, Wood and Building Materials Industries = UITBB
UIC	Ufficio Italiano dei Cambi
UIC	Unified Information Council (Israel)
UIC	Union des Industries Chimiques
UIC	Union Industrielle pour le Caméroun
UIC	Union Internationale des Chemins de Fer = IUR
UIC	Union of Independent Companies
UIC CR	Union of Towns and Communities of the Czech Republic
UICAMO	Universidade Estadual de Campinas (Brazil)
UICB	Unión Internacional de Ciencias Biológicas = IUBS, UISB
UICB	Union Internationale des Centres du Bâtiment
UICC	Union Internationale Contre le Cancer = IUAC
UICCIA	Unione Italiana della Camere di Commercio, Industria, Artigiano, Agricoltura
UICF	Unión Internacional de Ciencias Fisiológicas = IUPS, UISP
UICG	Unión Internacional de Ciencias Geológicas = IUGS, UISG
UICGF	Union Internationale du Commerce en Gros de la Fleur
UICI	Union Interprofessionnelle du Commerce et de l'Industrie

UICN	Alliance Mondial pour la Nature = IUCN
UICP	Union Internationale de la Couverture et Plomberie = IURPC
UICPA	Union Internationale de Chimie Pure et Appliquée = IUPAC, UIQPA
UICR	Union Internationale des Chauffeurs Routières
UICTMR	Union Internationale Contre la Tuberculose et les Maladies Respiratoires = IUATLD
UID	Union Internationale Dendrologie
UIDA	Union Internationale des Organisations de Détaillants de la Branche Alimentaire = IFGA, IVLD
UIDC	Union Internationale de Culture
UIDC	Union Internationale des Directeurs Commerciaux
UIDIA	Union Internationale de Interlinguistic Service
UIDJZ	Union Internationale des Directeurs de Jardins Zoologiques = IUDZG
UIE	Institute for Education (UNESCO)
UIE	UNESCO Institute for Education (Germany) = IUE, UIP
UIE	Union Industrielle et d'Entreprise
UIÉ	Union Internationale d'Électrothermie = IUE
UIÉ	Union Internationale des Éditeurs = IPA, IVU
UIÉ	Union Internationale des Étudiants = ISB, IUS, MSS
UIEC	Union Industrielle et d'Entreprise pour le Congo
UIEC	Union Internationale de l'Exploitation Cinématographique = IUCE
UIECS	Union of International and European Civil Servants = BIEA, SFE, VIEB
UIÉIS	Union Internationale pour l'Étude des Insectes Sociaux
UIÉOA	Union Internationale des Études Orientales et Asiatiques
UIEP	Union Internationale des Entrepreneurs de Peinture
UIÉS	Union Internationale d'Éducation pour la Santé = IUGE, IUHE
UIÉSP	Union Internationale pour l'Étude Scientifique de la Population = IUSSP
UIÉV	Université Internationale d'Été de Versailles

UIFA	Union Internationale des Femmes Architectes =IUWA	**UIJDC**	Union Internationale de Jeunesse Démocrate Chrétienne = IUJCD, IUYCD, UIGDC
UIFAB	Union Internationale des Fédérations des Amateurs de Billard	**UIJPLF**	Union Internationale des Journalistes et de la Presse de Langue Française
UIFI	Union Internationale des Fabricants d'Imperméables = IRC	**UIJS**	Union Internationale de la Jeunesse Socialiste = IUSY
UIFL	Union Internationale des Fédérations de Détaillants en Produits Laitiers	**UIL**	Union Internationale Loisirs
UIFPA	Union Internacional de Fisica Pura y Aplicada = IUPAP, UIPPA	**UIL**	Unione Italiana del Lavoro
UIG	Union Industrielle de Gruyère	**UILAS**	Unione Italiana Lavoratori Assicurazioni
UIG	Union Interprofessionnelle de la Guadeloupe	**UILB**	Union de l'Industrie Laitière Belge
UIGA	Unione Italiana Giornalisti dell'Automobile	**UILC**	Unione Italiana Lavoratori Chimici
UIGDC	Unione Internazionale del Giovani Democratici Cristiani = IUJCD, IUYCD, UIJDC	**UILDEP**	Federazione Nazionale Dipendenti Enti Pubblici
		UILDM	Unione Italiana Lotta alla Distrofia Muscolare
UIGG	Unión Internacional de Geodesia y Geofisica = IUGG, UGGI	**UILE**	Union Internationale pour la Liberté d'Enseignement
UIGSE	Union Internationale des Guides et Scouts d'Europe	**UILI**	Union Internationale des Laboratoires Indépendants
UIHJ	Union Internationale des Huissiers de Justice et Officiers Judiciaires	**UILIAS**	Unione Italiana Lavoratori Industie Alimentari Saccariferi
UIHL	Union Internationale de l'Humanisme Laïque = IHEU	**UILJ**	Union Internationale pour les Livres de Jeunesse
UIHMSU	Union Internationale d'Hygiène et de Médecine Scolaires et Universitaires = IUSUHM	**UILM**	Unione Italiana Lavoratori Metallurgici
		UILT	Unione Italiana Lavoratori della Terra
		UILTA-TEP	Unione Italiana Lavatori Trasporti Ausiliari Traffico e Portuali
UIHP	Union Internationale de l'Hospitalisation Privée = IUIH, IUPH, IUPNH	**UILTCS**	Unione Italiana Lavatori Turismo Commercio e Servizi
UIHPS	Union Internationale d'Histoire et de Philosophie des Sciences = IUHPS	**UIM**	Union Industrielle et Maritime
UII	Union des Intellectuels Indépendants	**UIM**	Union Internationale des Magistrats
UII	Union Internationale Immobilière	**UIM**	Union Internationale des Maires
UIIDÉ	Union Internationale des Infirmières Diplômées d'État = IURN	**UIM**	Union Internationale Monarchiste = IMU
		UIM	Union Internationale Motonautique
UIIG	Union Internationale de l'Industrie du Gaz = IGU	**UIM**	Unione Italiana Marittimi
UIIOM	Union Intersyndicale des Industries d'Outre-Mer	**UIMC**	Union Internationale des Services Médecaux des Chemins de Fer = IURMS
UIIPI	Unione Italiana Lavatori Pubblico Impiego	**UIMEC**	Unione Italiana Mezzadri e Coltivatori Diretti
UIJ	Union des Industriels du Jura	**UIMJ**	Union Internationale des Maisons de Jeunesse (FIJC)
UIJ	Union Internationale des Journalistes = IUAJ	**UIMM**	Union des Industries Métallurgiques et Minières
UIJA	Union Internationale des Journalistes Agricoles = IUAJ	**UIMNPC**	Union des Industries Métallurgiques du Nord et du Pas-de-Calais
UIJC	Universities and Industry Joint Committee	**UIMP**	Universidad Internacional Menendez Pelayo

UIMTCT	Union Internationale de Médecine Thermale et de Climatothalassothérapie = IUTCT
UIMVT	Union Internationale contre les Maladies Vénériennes et les Treponematoses = IUVDT
UINF	Union Internationale de la Navigation Fluviale = IBU, IUIN
UINL	Union Internationale du Notariat Latin = IULN
UIO	Union Internationale des Oenologues
UIOA	International Union for Applied Ornithology
UIOF	Union Internationale des Organismes Familiaux = IUFO
UIOG	Union Internationale de Orphelins de Guerre
UION	Uniunea Internationala pentru Ocrotirea Naturii (Romania)
UIOOPT	Union Internationale des Organisations Officielles de Propagande Touristique
UIP	UNESCO-Institut für Pädagogik = IUE, UIE
UIP	Union Industrial Paraguaya
UIP	Union Internationale d'Associations de Propriétaires de Wagons Particuliers
UIP	Union Internationale de Patinage = ISU
UIP	Union Internationale Paysanne
UIP	Union Interparlementaire = IPU
UIP	Universidad Iberoamericana de Postgrado
UIPA	Union Interparlementaire Arabe (Syria) = Arab AIPU
UIPC	Unione Italiana per il Progresso della Cultura
UIPCG	Union Internationale de la Pâtisserie, Confiserie, Glacerie
UIPDÉ	Union Internationale des Producteurs et Distributeurs d'Énergie Électrique
UIPGH	Union Internationale des Portiers des Grands Hôtels
UIPI	Union Internationale de la Propriété Immobilière = IUPO
UIPMB	Union Internationale de Pentathlon Moderne et Biathlon
UIPP	Union des Industries de la Protection des Plantes
UIPPA	Union Internationale de la Presse Professionnelle d'Ameublement
UIPPA	Union Internationale de Physique Pure et Appliquée = IUPAP
UIPPI	Union Internationale pour la Protection de la Propriété Industrielle = IUPIP
UIPRÉ	Union Internationale de la Presse Radiotechnique et Électronique
UIPVT	Union Internationale contre le Péril Vénérien et les Tréponematoses = IUVDT
UIQPA	Unión Internacional de Quimica Pura y Aplicada = IUPAC, UICPA
UIR	Union der Internationalen Rheinschiffahrt = IRU, UNIR
UIR	Union Internationale de Radio-diffusion
UIR	Union Internationale des Radioécologistes (Belgium) = IUR
UIR	Union Interprofessionnelle des Résineux
UIRD	Union Internationale de la Résistance et de la Déportation
UIRR	Union International de Transport Combinés Rail-Route
UIS	Union Internationale de la Spéléologie = IUS
UIS	Union Internationale de Secours = IRU
UIS	Union Internationale des Syndicats des Travailleurs de la Fonction Publique et Assimilés = TUI
UIS	Union Internationale des Syndicats des Travailleurs des Industries Alimentaires, Tabacs, Hôtels et Branches Connexes
UIS	Union of Insurance Staffs
UIS	Unions Internationales des Syndicats = TUIs
UIS	Universidad Industrial de Santander (Colombia)
UISA	United Inventors and Scientists of America
UISAE	Union Internationale des Sciences Anthropologiques et Ethnologiques = IUAES, UNICAE
UISB	Union Internationale des Sciences Biologiques = IUBS, UICB
UISG	Union Internationale des Sciences Géologiques = IUGS, UICG
UISG	Union Internationale des Supérieurs Générales
UISG	Unione Italiana Stampa Giovanile
UISIF	Union Internationale des Sociétés d'Ingénieurs Forestiers = IUSF
UISJP	Ustredni Informacní Stredisko pro Jaderny Program

UISLAF	Unione Internationale dei Sindicati dei Lavoratori Agricoli e Forestali
UISM	Union Internationale des Sociétés de Microbiologie = IUMS
UISMM	Union Internationale des Syndicats des Industries Métallurgiques et Mécaniques
UISN	Union Internationale des Sciences de la Nutrition = IUNS
UISP	Union Internationale des Sciences Physiologiques = IUPS, UICF
UISP	Union Internationale des Syndicats de la Police = IUPA
UISPP	Union Internationale des Sciences Préhistoriques et Protohistoriques = IUPPS
UISPTT	Union Internationale Sportive des Postes, des Téléphones et des Télécommunications
UISTA	Unione Italiana Stampa Tessile e dell' Abbigliamento
UISTABP	Union Internacional de Sindicatos de Trabajadores de la Agricultura, de los Bosques y de las Plantaciones = MOPTSLKP, TUIAFPW, UISTAFP
UISTAFP	Union Internationale des Syndicats des Travailleurs de l'Agriculture, des Forêts et des Plantations = MOPTSLKP, TUIAFPW, UISTABP
UISTAV	Union Internationale pour la Science, la Technique et les Applications du Vide = IUVFTA, IUVSTA
UISTC	Union Internationale des Syndicats des Travailleurs du Commerce = TUIWC
UISTÉ	Union Internationale des Syndicats des Travailleurs de l'Énergie = TUIWE
UISTICPS	Union Internationale des Syndicats des Travailleurs des Industries Chimiques, du Pétrole et Similaires
UIT	Unión de Industrias Textiles (el Salvador)
UIT	Union des Industries Textiles
UIT	Union Internationale de Tir
UIT	Union Internationale des Télécommunications = ITU
UIT	Université Internationale de Technologie = ITU
UITA	Unión Internacional de Associaciones de Trabajadores de Alimentos y Ramos Afines = IUF, IUL
UITA	Union Internationale des Travailleurs de l'Alimentation et des Branches Connexes = IUF, IUL
UITA	Union of International Technical Associations = UATI
UITBB	Union Internationale des Syndicats des Travailleurs du Bâtiment, du Bois et des Matériaux de Construction = UIBWM
UITF	Union des Ingénieurs et des Techniciens Utilisant la Langue Française
UITP	Union Internationale des Transports Publics
UITUA	Union of Independent Trade Unions of Albania
UIU	Upholsterers International Union of North America
UIV	Union Internationale des Villes et Pouvoirs Locaux = IGV, IULA
UIVB	Union Interprofessionnelle des Vins du Beaujolais
UIWU	United Israel World Union
UIZ	Unió Ibérica de Zoos (Spain)
UJ	Ursulines de Jésus
UJA	Udruženje Jugoslovenskih Arhitekata
UJA	Union des Journalistes Africains (Zaïre) = UAJ
UJA	Union of Journalists of Afghanistan
UJAF	Union de la Jeunesse Agricole et France
UJAO	Union des Journalistes de l'Afrique de l'Ouest
UJC	Unión de Jóvenes Comunistas (Cuba)
UJE	Union de Jeunesse Européenne
UJJEF	Union Journaux et Journalistes d'Entreprise de France
UJM	Uniunea Jurnaliştilor din Moldova
UJNR	United States-Japan Cooperative Program in Natural Resources
UJPDG	Union des Jeunes du PDG (Gabon)
UJSA	Union des Journalistes Sportifs Africains = ASJU
UJSC	Union de la Jeunesse Socialiste Congolaise
UJW	Union of Jewish Women (Zimbabwe)
UJWSA	Union of Jewish Women of South Africa
UK CEE	United Kingdom Centre for European Education
UK CEED	United Kingdom Centre for Economic and Environmental Development
UK GER	United Kingdom Global Environmental Research Office
UKA	United Kingdom Alliance
UKA	United Klans of America

UKACC	United Kingdom Automatic Control Council	**UKCCFSR**	United Kingdom Co-ordinating Committee for Food Science and Technology
UKADLO	United Kingdom Association of Direct Labour Organisations	**UKCDG**	United Kingdom Chemometrics Discussion Group
UKAEA	United Kingdom Atomic Energy Authority	**UKCIC**	United Kingdom CALS Industry Council
UKAEAT	United Kingdom Atomic Energy Authority Technology	**UKCMET**	United Kingdom Council for Music Education and Training
UKAEL	United Kingdom Association for European Law	**UKCOSA**	United Kingdom Council for Overseas Student Affairs
UKAFFP	United Kingdom Association of Frozen Food Producers	**UKCRS**	United Kingdom Controlled Release Society
UKAFIS	United Kingdom Association of the FIS	**UKCSBS**	United Kingdom Civil Service Benefit Society
UKAFMM	United Kingdom Association of Fish Meal Manufacturers	**UKCTA**	United Kingdom Commercial Travellers Association
UKAIIM	United Kingdom Association for Image and Information Management	**UKCVCC**	United Kingdom Computer Virus Control Centre
UKAM	Composers and Authors Union (Malta)	**UKDA**	United Kingdom Dairy Association
UKAMBY	United Kingdom Association of Manufacturers of Bakers Yeast	**UKEASMA**	United Kingdom EAS Manufacturers Association
UKAN	Narcolepsy Association	**UKEB**	United Kingdom Ecolabelling Board
UKAN	United Kingdom Advocacy Network	**UKELA**	United Kingdom Environmental Law Association
UKAPE	United Kingdom Association of Professional Engineers	**UKEMS**	United Kingdom Environmental Mutagen Society
UKAPTD	United Kingdom Association of Professional Teachers of Dancing	**UKEP**	United Kingdom Egg Producers' Association
UKASA	United Kingdom Agricultural Students Association	**UKERNA**	United Kingdom Education and Research Networking Association
UKASS	United Kingdom Association of Suggestion Schemes	**UKF**	Unie van Kunstmestfabrieken
UKASTA	United Kingdom Agricultural Supply Trade Association	**UKFA**	United Kingdom Fellmongers Association
UKB	Samenwerkingsverband van de Universiteits- en Hogeschoolbibliotheken en de Koninkijke Bibliotheek	**UKFBPW**	United Kingdom Federation of Business and Professional Women
UKBG	United Kingdom Bartenders Guild	**UKFC**	United Kingdom Fortifications Club
UKBICC	United Kingdom Baking Industry Consultative Committee	**UKFCC**	United Kingdom Federation for Culture Collections
UKBSA	United Kingdom Board Sailing Association	**UKFDDA**	United Kingdom Freight Demurrage & Defence Association
UKCA	United Kingdom Coffee Association	**UKFFCA**	United Kingdom Freight Forwarders Container Association
UKCBDA	United Kingdom Carbon Block Distributors Association	**UKFJB**	United Kingdom Federation of Jazz Bands
UKCC	United Kingdom Central Council for Nursing, Midwifery and Health Visiting	**UKFR**	United Kindgom Feline Register
UKCCD	United Kingdom Council for Computing Development	**UKFSP**	United Kingdom Foundation for the Peoples of the South Pacific
UKCCECS	United Kingdom Co-ordinating Committee for Examinations in Computer Studies	**UKGPA**	United Kingdom Glycerine Producers Association

UKHA	United Kingdom Harp Association	**UKOLN**	United Kingdom Office for Library Networking
UKHA	United Kingdom Housekeepers Association	**UKOLUG**	United Kingdom Online Users Group
UKHCA	United Kingdom Home Care Association	**UKOOA**	United Kingdom Offshore Operators' Association
UKHEF	United Kingdom Home Economics Federation	**UKOP**	United Kingdom Oil Pipelines
UKHIA	United Kingdom Herbal Infusions Association	**UKOWLA**	United Kingdom One World Linking Association
UKHIS	United Kingdom Hazard Information Service	**UKPA**	United Kingdom Pilots Association
UKI	Uniono Katolik Idista	**UKPIA**	United Kingdom Petroleum Industry Association
UKIAS	United Kingdom Immigrant Advisory Service	**UKPMA**	United Kingdom Preserves Manufacturers Association
UKIC	United Kingdom Institute for Conservation of Historic and Artistic Works	**UKPTF**	United Kingdom Provision Trade Federation
UKIPA	United Kingdom and Ireland Particleboard Association (*now* WPPF)	**UKRA**	United Kingdom Reading Association
UKISC	United Kingdom Industrial Space Committee	**UKRA**	United Kingdom Renderers Association
UKISES	United Kingdom Section of the International Solar Energy Society	**UKRAS**	United Kingdom Railway Advisory Service
UKISSB	United Kingdom Iron and Steel Statistics Bureau	**UKRC**	United Kingdom Reclamation Council
UKITO	United Kingdom Information Technology Organisation	**UKREP**	United Kingdom Permanent Representation (EC)
UKITSEC	United Kingdom Information Technology Security	**UKRSA**	United Kingdom Rett Syndrome Association
UKJAID	United Kingdom Jewish Aid and International Development	**UKS**	United Kingdom Skeptics
UKJGA	United Kingdom Jute Goods Association	**UKS**	Writers Union of Serbia
UKJSA	United Kingdom Jet Ski Association	**UKSA**	United Kingdom Shareholders Association
UKLEO	United Kingdom Laser & Electro-Optics Trade Association	**UKSA**	United Kingdom Sponsoring Authority for the Exchange of Young Agriculturists
UKMANZRA	United Kingdom Manufacturers and New Zealand Representatives Association	**UKSABA**	United Kingdom South Africa Business Association (*ex* UKSATA)
UKMBCN	United Kingdom Molecular Biology of Cancer Network	**UKSATA**	United Kingdom South African Trade Association (*now* UKSABA)
UKMCA	United Kingdom Module Constructors' Association (*now* OMCA)	**UKSCC**	United Kingdom Spoon Collectors Club
UKMHMG	United Kingdom Mechanical Health Monitoring Group	**UKSE**	United Kingdom Seeds Executive
		UKSG	United Kingdom Serials Group
UKMO	United Kingdom Meteorological Office	**UKSIA**	United Kingdom Sugar Industry Association
UKOBA	United Kingdom Outboard Boating Association	**UKSIF**	United Kingdom Social Investment Forum
UKOGL	United Kingdom Onshore Geophysical Library	**UKSM**	United Kingdom Scientific Mission
		UKSMA	United Kingdom Sugar Merchants' Association
		UKSPA	United Kingdom Science Park Association
		UKSS	United Kingdom Simulation Society
		UKTA	United Kingdom Tea Association

UKTA	United Kingdom Trade Agency for Developing Counties
UKTCA	United Kingdom Transplant Coordinators Association
UKTSSA	United Kingdom Transplant Support Services Authority
UKUF	United Kingdom Unicycle Federation
UKUSA	United Kingdom United States of America Agreement
UKUUG	United Kingdom Unix Systems Users Group
UKW	United Kingdom Weighing Federation
UKWAL	United Kingdom West Africa Line
UKWGF	United Kingdom Wool Growers Federation
UKWMO	United Kingdom Warning and Monitoring Association
UKWWA	United Kingdom Wood Wool Association
UL	Union Latine (France)
UL	Union Libéral
UL	United List (Slovenia)
UL	Universala Ligo
ULA	Uganda Library Association
ULA	Ulster Launderers Association
ULA	Union der Leitenden Angestellten
ULABEL	Union Professionelle des Loueurs de Voiteurs sans Chauffeur de Belgique
ULAC	Unión Latinamericana de Ciegos
ULACETS	Unión Latinoamericana contra las Enfermedades de Transmisión Sexual
ULADE	Unión Latino American del Embalaje
ULAJE	Unión Latinoamericana de Juventudes Ecuménicas
ULAST	Unión Latino Americana de Sociedades de Tisiologia
ULATEM	Unión Latinoamericana de Tenis de Mesa = LATTU
ULB	Bratianu Liberal Union (Romania)
ULB	Union Laitière de Bamako (Mali)
ULBA	Universal Love and Brotherhood Association (Japan)
ULC	Union de la Lutte Communiste (Burkina Faso)
ULC	Union Luxembourgeoise des Consommateurs
ULCC	University of London Computer Centre
ULCRA	Unión Latinoamericana y del Caribe de Radiodifusión

ULDRR	Democratic and Free Union of Romanis of Romania
ULE	Unión Liberal Española
ULE	Unión Liberal Europea
ULF	Sveriges Universitetslärarförbundet
ULF	United Left Front (Sri Lanka)
ULFA	United Liberation Front of Assam
ULI	Union pour la Langue Internationale Ido
ULM	Unión Latinoamericana de Motociclismo (Venezuela)
ULPS	Union of Liberal and Progressive Synagogues
ULT	United Lodge of Theosophists
ULTAB	Brazilian Agricultural Workers Union
ULU	Union of Latin American Universities
ULUPUDS	Udruženje Likovnih Umetnika Primenjenih Umetnosti i Dizajnera Srbije
ULV	Universele Liga Brijmetselaren
ULYA	Union of Labour Youth of Albania
UMA	Union des Médecins Arabes
UMA	Union du Maghreb Arabe = AMU
UMA	Union Marocaine de l'Agriculture
UMA	Unión Matemática Argentina / Argentinian Mathematical Union
UMA	Union Mathématique Africaine
UMA	Union Mondiale des Aveugles = WBU
UMA	Universidad Modular Abierta (El Salvador)
UMA	Utenti Motori Agricoli
UMAA	Union Mondiale des Anciennes Élèves de l'Assomption
UMAÉC	Union Monétaire de l'Afrique Équatoriale et du Caméroun
UMAH	Union Mondiale d'Avancée Humaine
UMAI	Unión Mexicana de Asociaciones de Ingenieros
UMALCA	Unión Matemética de América Latina y el Caribe/Mathematical Union of Latin America and the Caribbean
UMALCO	Union al-Qaiwain Aluminium Company (UAE)
UMAP	Unidades Militaries de Ayuda a la Producción (Cuba)
UMARCO	Union Maritime et Commercial (Cameroon, Ivory Coast, Senegal)
UMATI	Uzazi na Malezi Bora Tanzania
UMB	Union Médicale Balkanique
UMB	Union Mondiale de Billard

UMBC	United Malayan Banking Corporation		**UMIB**	Unit of Marine Invertebrate Biology (NERC)
UMC	United Methodist Church (U.S.A.)		**UMIMA**	Union Malienne d'Industries Maritimes
UMC	Upper Mantle Committee (U.S.A.)		**UMIMA**	Union Mauritanienne d'Industries Maritimes
UMCA	Unión Monetaria Centroamericana (El Salvador)		**UMIST**	University of Manchester Institute of Science and Technology
UMCA	Universities Mission to Central Africa		**UMJL**	Union Mondiale pour un Judaïsme Libéral
UMCA	Uraba, Medellin and Central Airways Incorporated (Colombia)		**UML**	United Marxist-Leninist Party (Nepal)
UMCC	United Maritime Consultative Council		**UMLP**	Union Mondiale des Libres Penseurs = WUF. WUFT
UMCTM	Union Nationale des Industries des Machines pour Chaussures, Tannerie et Maroquinerie		**UMM**	Université Maritime Mondial; Universidad Marítima Mundial = UMI, WMU
UMD	Unia Młodziezy Demokratycnej		**UMML**	Union Médicale de la Méditerranée Latine = LMMU
UMD	Unión Militar Democrática		**UMNO**	United Malays' National Organisation
UMD	University of Maryland		**UMNO**	New UMNO (Malaysia)
UMDH	Union Mondiale des Hommes (Belgium)		**(BARU)**	
UMDSJ	Udruženje Madžara za Našu Domovinu, Srbiju i Jugoslaviju (Serbia) = AHFSY		**UMNS**	Union Mondiale des Nationaux Socialistes = WUNS
UME	Union Malacological Europaea = EMU		**UMO**	Ilinden United Macedonian Organization – OMOI (Bulgaria)
UMEA	Universala Medicina Esperanto Asocio		**UMO**	Union of Muslim Organisations of the United Kingdom and Éire
UMEC	Union Mondiale des Enseignants Catholiques = WUCT		**UMOA**	Union Monétaire Ouest Africaine = WAMU
UMÉJ	Union Mondiale des Étudiants Juifs = WUJS		**UMOAN**	Union Mondiale des Juifs Originaires d'Afrique du Nord
UMEL	Union Médecine Européenne Libérale		**UMOFC**	Union Mondiale des Organisations Féminines Catholiques = WKFO, WUCWO
UMEMPS	Union of Middle East Mediterranean Paediatric Societies = USPMOM			
UMF	Umbrella Makers Federation		**UMOSBÉSL**	Union Mondiale des Organisations Syndicales sur Base Économique et Sociale Libérale = WULTUO
UMFA	United Mineworker's Federation of Australia			
UMFDC	Union Mondiale des Femmes Démocrates-Chrétiennes = UFDC, WUCDW		**UMP**	Uganda Meat Packers Ltd
			UMP	Union Mondiale des Professions = WUP
UMFR	Union Mondiale des Femmes Rurales = ACWW		**UMP**	Upper Mantle Project (U.S.A.)
UMI	Union de Melillenses Independientes (Melilla)		**UMPA**	Union de Mujeres Paraguayas
			UMPB	Union Professionnelle des Maîtres Photograveurs Belges
UMI	Union Mathématique Internationale = IMU		**UMPC**	Uganda Milk Processing Company
UMI	Union Monarchica Italiana		**UMPF**	Union Mondiale de la Presse Féminine
UMI	Union Mondiale des Intellectuels		**UMPH**	Union Mondiale des Sociétés d'Histoire Pharmaceutique
UMI	Unión Mundial pro Interlingua			
UMI	Unione Matematica Italiana		**UMPL**	Union Mondiale des Professions Libérales
UMI	Unione Micologica Italiana			
UMI	Université Maritime Internationale = UMM, WMU		**UMPL**	Union Mondiale Polonais Libres Leurs Amis Liberté
UMI	University Microfilms International (U.S.A.)			

UMPS	Union Mondiale des Pionniers de Stockholm = WUSP	**UNAC**	Union Nationale des Anciens Combattants
UMRCC	Universities Mobile Radio Research Corporation	**UNAC**	United Nations Association in Canada
UMRL	Uniunea Mondiala a Românilor Liberi = WUFR	**UNAC**	United Nations Auxiliary Commission
		UNACA	Unión Nacional de Astronomia y Ciencias Afines
UMS	Union des Meuniers Suisses		
UMS	Union Maraîchère Suisse = USPV, VSGP	**UNACAFE**	Unión Nacional Agricola de Cafeteros (Mexico)
UMS	Union Suisse des Marchands Forains	**UNACAP**	Union Nationale des Coopératives Apicoles
UMSR	Universal Movement for Scientific Responsibility = MURS	**UNACAST**	United Nations Advisory Committee on the Application of Science and Technology to Development
UMT	Union Marocaine du Travail		
UMTA	Union Marocaine du Travail Autonome	**UNACC**	United Nations Administrative Committee and Co-ordination
UMTA	Urban Mass Transportation Association (U.S.A.)	**UNACI**	Union Africaine pour le Commerce et l'Industrie en Côte d'Ivoire
UMVF	Union Mondiale des Voix Françaises		
UMVP	Union Mondiale des Villes de la Paix = ICPU, WUCP, WUPT	**UNACIL**	United Africa Commercial and Industrial Ltd
UMWA	United Mine Workers of America	**UNACO OPRL**	Unión Nacional de Cooperativas (Costa Rica)
UMYS	Union of Maghreb Youth and Students	**UNACOMA**	Unione Nazionale Costruttori Macchine Agricole
UN	Unión Nacional		
UN	United Nations = NN.UU, ONU	**UNACOOPH**	Unión Nacional de Cooperativas Populares de Honduras
UN SMDP	United Nations and Related Agencies Staff Movement for Disarmament and Peace = SMDP	**UNADA**	United Nations Atomic Development Authority
UN-ECE	United Nations Economic Commission for Europe	**UNADE**	Unión Nacional Democrática (Panama)
		UNADI	United Nations Asian Development Institute
UN/CAA	United Nations Centre Against Apartheid	**UNADIF**	Union Nationale des Associations des Déportes Internés et Familles de Disparus
UN/ECLAC	United Nations Economic Commission for Latin America and the Caribbean		
UNA	Uganda News Agency	**UNAÉA**	Union Européenne des Anciens et Anciennes Élèves de l'Enseignement Catholique
UNA	Ukrainian National Assembly		
UNA	Union Nationale de l'Aviculture et des Productions Rattachées	**UNAEC-Europe**	Union Européenne des Anciens et Anciennes Élèves de l'Enseignement Catholique
UNA	Union Nationale des Agriculteurs (Tunisia)		
UNA	Unione Nazionale dell'Avicoltura	**UNAF**	Union Nationale de l'Apiculture Française
UNA	United Nations Association = ANU	**UNAF**	Union Nationale des Associations Familiales
UNA	Universidad Nacional Abierta (Venezuela)	**UNAFAM**	Union Internationale des Amis et Familles de Malades Mentaux
UNA SDU	United Nations Association Sustainable Development Unit	**UNAFEI**	United Nations Asia and Far East Institute for the Prevention of Crime and the Treatment of Offenders (Japan)
UNA-USA	United Nations Association of the USA		
UNAA	United Nations Association of Australia		
UNAAF	Union Nord Africaine Agricole et Financière	**UNAFIMA**	Union Nationale des Associations de Formation et d'Information Mutualistes Agricoles
UNAAFR	Union Nationale des Associations d'Aides Familiales Rurales		

UNAFPA	Union des Associations des Fabricants de Pâtes Alimentaires (CE)	**UNAP**	Union Nationale des Attachés de Presse
UNAFR	Union Nationale des Aides Familiales Rurales	**UNAPACE**	Unione Nazionale Aziende Auto-Produttrici e Consumatrici di Energia Elettrica
UNAFRI	United Nations African Institute for the Prevention of Crime and the Treatment of Offenders	**UNAPC**	Union Nationale des Attachés de Presse-Professionnels de la Communication
UNAG	Union Nacional de Agricultores y Ganaderos (Nicaragua)	**UNAPDI**	United Nations Asian and Pacific Development Institute (Thailand)
UNAG	Union Professionnelle des Agents en Bois de Belgique	**UNAPHAL**	Union Nationale des Pharmaciens Luxembourgeois
UNAG	Verband Schweizerischer Zeitungsgenturen und Büchergrossisten	**UNAPL**	Union Nationale des Associations de Professions Libérales
UNAGA	Unión Nacional de Asociaciones Ganaderas (Colombia)	**UNAPSA**	Union of National African Paediatric Societies and Associations
UNAGAR	Union Nationale des Agents Généraux d'Assurances Retraités	**UNAR**	Unione Associazioni Regionali
UNAI	Union Nazionale delle Associazioni Italiane	**UNARC**	University of Alexandria Research Centre (Egypt)
UNAIS	United Nations Association International Service	**UNARDOL**	United Nations Assistance for the Reconstruction and Development of Lebanon
UNAIYS	United Nations Association International Youth Service	**UNASCA**	Unione Nazionale Autoscuole e Studi di Consulenza Automobilistica
UNAL	UNESCO Network of Associated Libraries	**UNASCO**	União Nacional das Associações de Cooperativas (Brazil)
UNALOR	Union Allumettière Équatoriale (Cameroon)	**UNAT**	Union Nationale des Agriculteurs Tunisiens
UNAM	Union Nationale des Analystes Médicales (Belgium)	**UNAT**	Union Nationale des Associations de Tourisme
UNAM	Universidad Nacional Autónoma de México	**UNAT**	Unione Nazionale Artisti Teatrali
UNAM	University of Namibia	**UNATAC**	Union d'Assistance Technique pour l'Automobile et la Circulation Routière
UNAMAZ	Association of Amazonian Universities (Brazil)	**UNATCA**	Union Nationale des Associations de Techniciens du Conseil Agricole
UNAMC	United Nations Advance Mission in Cambodia	**UNATEB**	Union Nationale des Techniciens Biologistes
UNAMIC	United Nations Advance Mission in Cambodia = MIPRENUC	**UNATECH**	Union Européenne pour la Promotion des Formations Techniques dans les Métiers de l'Hôtellerie
UNAMIR	United Nations Assistance Mission to Rwanda	**UNATI**	Union Nationale des Artisans et Travailleurs Indépendants
UNAMO	Union Nacional Mocambicana	**UNAU**	Unione Nazionale Assistenti Universitari
UNAN	Universidad Nacional Autónoma de Nicaragua	**UNAULA**	Universidad Autónoma Latinoamericana (Colombia)
UNANEM II	United Nations Angola Verification Mission II	**UNAVCA**	Union Nationale des Associations de Vulgarisation et de Conseillers Agricoles
UNAO-FBA	Union Nationale des Anciens des Armées d'Occupation et des Forces Belges en Allemagne	**UNAVEM**	United Nations Angola Verification Mission
UNAP	Union Nationale des Artistes Professionnels des Arts Plastiques et Graphiques (Belgium)	**UNAVIC**	United Nations Audiovisual Information Centre (Canada)

UNB	Universidade Nacional de Brasília	**UNCATA**	Union Nationale des Coopératives Agricoles des Traitements Antiparasitaires
UNBSA	United Nations Bureau of Social Affairs		
UNBTAO	United Nations Bureau of Technical Assistance Operations	**UNCC**	Union Nacional de Colegios Católicos (Dominican Republic)
UNC	Unión Nacional Campesina (El Salvador, Nicaragua)	**UNCC**	Union Nationale des Commissaires aux Comptes
UNC	Unión Nacional de Campesinos (Honduras)	**UNCC**	Union Nigérieene de Crédit et de Coopération
UNC	Union Nationale des Combattants	**UNCDCV**	Union Nationale des Caves et Distilleries Coopératives Vinicoles
UNC	Union Nouvelle Caledonienne		
UNC	Union Suisse des Négociants en Combustibles = SBV	**UNCDF**	United Nations Capital Development Fund = FENU, FNUDC
UNC	Unione Nazionale Chinesiologi	**UNCEA**	Union Commerciale pour l'Europe et l'Afrique
UNC	Unione Nazionale Consumatori		
UNC	United National Congress (Trinidad)	**UNCED**	United Nations Conference on Environment and Development
UNC	United National Convention (Ghana)		
UNC	United Nations Command (Republic of Korea)	**UNCÉF**	Union Nationale des Caisses d'Épargne de France
UNC	Universidad Nacional de Colombia	**UNCÉIA**	Union Nationale des Coopératives d'Élevage et d'Insémination Artificielle
UNCA	United Nations Correspondents Association		
		UNCEM	Unione Nazionale Comuni ed Enti Montani
UNCAA	Union Nationale des Coopératives Agricoles d'Approvisionnement	**UNCG**	University of North Carolina at Greensboro
UNCAC	Union National des Coopératives Agricoles de Céréales	**UNCGABV**	Union Nationale des Coopératives et Groupement Agricoles de Bétail et de Viande
UNCAC	Union Nationale de Coopératives Agricoles Chanvrières		
UNCAF	Union Nationale des Caisses d'Allocations Familiales	**UNCHBP**	Centre for Housing, Building and Planning (UN)
UNCAFL	Union Nationale des Coopératives Agricoles de Fruits et Légumes	**UNCHE**	United Nations Conference on the Human Environment
UNCAH	Unión Nacional de Campesinos Auténticos de Honduras	**UNCHS**	United Nations Centre for Human Settlements (Kenya)
UNCAL	Union National de Comités d'Action Lycéens	**UNCI**	Union Nacional de Comercio e Industria (Colombia)
UNCAMB	Union Nationale des Coopératives Agricoles de Meunerie et de Meunerie-Boulangerie	**UNCI**	Unione Nazionale Chimici Italiani
		UNCIET	Unione Nazionale Costruttori Impianti Elettrici e Telefonici
UNCAMTC	Union Nationale des Coopératives Agricoles de Meunerie et de Transformation des Céréales	**UNCIP**	United Nations Commission for India-Pakistan
UNCAP	National Union of the Agricultural Production Cooperatives of Romania	**UNCITRAL**	United Nations Commission on International Trade Law = CNUDCI, CNUDMI
UNCAP	Union National des Commerçants Artisans et Professions Libérale	**UNCJIN**	United Nations Criminal Justice Information Network
UNCARR	Union National des Comités d'Action Renovation Rurale	**UNCL**	Union Nationale des Cafetiers-Limonadiers
UNCASTD	United Nations Advisory Comittee on the Application of Science and Technology to Development	**UNCL**	Union Nationale des Coopératives Laitières
		UNCL	Union Nationale pour la Course au Large

UNCLS	United Nations Conference on the Law of the Sea	**UNDC**	Union Nationale pour la Démocratie aux Comores
UNCO	United Nations Civilian Operations Mission (Zaïre)	**UNDCC**	United Nations Development Cooperation Cycle
UNCOD	United Nations Conference on Desertification	**UNDCP**	United Nations International Drug Control Programme
UNCOK	United Nations Commission on Korea	**UNDD**	Union Nationale pour la Défense de la Démocratie (Burkina Faso)
UNCON	United Nations Council for Oppressed Nations = UNPO	**UNDEL**	Unione Nazionale Dipendenti Enti Locali
UNCOPUOS	United Nations Committee on the Peaceful Uses of Outer Space (United Nations)	**UNDESIPA**	United Nations Population Info. Network, UN Population Division
UNCP	Ukrainian National Conservative Party	**UNDHA**	United Nations Department of Humanitarian Affairs
UNCP	United Nations Conference of Plenipotentiaries	**UNDOF**	United Nations Disengagement Observer Force = FNUOD, FNUOS
UNCRD	United Nations Centre for Regional Development (Japan) = CNUDR	**UNDP**	Union National Democratic Party (Burma)
UNCSAI	Unione Nazionale Costruttori Serramenti in Alluminio e Leghe Pregiate	**UNDP**	Union Nationale pour la Démocratie et le Progrès (Benin)
UNCSAT	United Nations Conference on the Application of Science and Technology for the Benefit of Less Developed Areas	**UNDP**	United National Democratic Party (Antigua & Barbuda)
		UNDP	United Nations Development Programme = PNUD
UNCSCMP	Union Nationale des Chambres Syndicales de Charpente, Menuiserie et Parquets	**UNDRO**	United Nations Disaster Relief Office
		UNDTCD	United Nations Department of Technical Cooperation for Development
UNCSDHA	United Nations Centre for Social Development and Humanitarian Affairs = UNOV/CSDHA	**UNDTI**	Unione Nazionale Diplomati Tecnici Italiani
UNCSTD	United Nations Committee on Science and Technology for Development	**UNE**	Union Nacional de Educadores (Ecuador)
UNCTAD	United Nations Conference on Trade and Development = CNUCED	**UNE**	University of New England
		UNÉA	Union Nationale des Étudiants Algériens
UNCTC	United Nations Centre on Transnational Corporations	**UNEAC**	Unión de Escritores y Artistas de Cuba
UNCULTA	Unión Nacional de Cultivadores de Tabaco (Venezuela)	**UNEAC**	Union Européenne des Anciens et Anciennes Élèves de l'Enseignement Catholique
UNCURK	United Nations Commission for the Unification and Rehabilitation of Korea = CNUURC	**UNEAP**	Union Nationale de l'Enseignement Agricole Privé
UNCVDC	Union Nationale des Coopératives Viticoles et Distilleries Coopératives	**UnEAS**	Union of European Accountancy Students = UNECS
UND	Uluslararasi Nakliyeciler Dernegi	**UNEB**	Union Nationale des Industries Françaises de l'Emballage Utilisant le Bois
UND	Unión Nacional Democrática (El Salvador)		
UND	Union Nationale et Démocratique (Monaco)	**UNÉBECE**	Association d'Utilisateurs et Négociants Belges de Combustibles
UNDA	International Catholic Association for Radio and Television	**UNEBIF**	Union Européenne des Fabricants de Bijouterie Fantasie
UNDAL	Union Nazionale des Distillateurs Agricoles Luxembourgeois	**UNEC**	Unión Nacional Educación Católica (Uruguay)

UNÉC	Union Nationale des Établissements Catholiques (Burkina Faso)	**UNÉM**	Union Nationale des Étudiants Marocains
UNEC	United Nations Education Conference	**UNEMAF**	Union des Employers Agricoles et Forestiers (Ivory Coast)
UNECA	Union de Empresas Constructoras Caribe (Cuba)	**UNEMI**	Union Editori di Musica Italiani
UNECA	Union Européenne des Fondeurs et Fabricants de Corps Gras Animaux	**UNÉMO**	Union Nationale des Étudiants du Mozambique
UNECA	Union Nationale des Experts Comptables Agricoles	**UNEO**	United Nations Emergency Operation
UNECA	United Nations Economic Commission for Africa	**UNÉP**	Union Nationale des Éleveurs de Porcs
Unecamoto	Unión de Empresas de Camiones y Motores (Cuba)	**UNEP**	Union Nationale des Entrepreneurs du Paysage
UNECI	Union of European Community Industries	**UNEP**	United Nations Environmental Programme = PNUE, PNUMA
UNECIA	Universities of England Consortium for International Activities	**UNEP/CMS**	Secretariat of the Convention on the Conservation of Migratory Species of Wild Animals = CMS
UNECOLAIT	Union Européenne du Commerce Laitier	**UNEP/IEO**	UNEP Industry and Environment Office = PNUE/OIE
UNECS	Union Européenne desExperts Compatables Stagiaires = UnEAS	**UNEPA**	Unión Económica Patagónica (Argentina)
UNECTES	Union Européenne des Conseillers Techniques et Scientifiques	**UNEPNET-LAC**	UNEP Network for Latin America and the Carribean
UNED	Union Nationale des Exploitants de Décharges	**UNEPSA**	Unión Española de Entidades Aseguradoras, Reaseguradoras y de Capitalizacion
UNED	United Nations Environment and Development	**UNEPSA**	Union of National European Pediatric Societies and Associations
UNED	Universidad Nacional de Enseñanza a Distancia	**UNERP**	Union Nationale Experts en Relations Publiques
UNEDA	United Nations Economic Development Administration	**UNESCO**	United Nations Educational Scientific and Cultural Organisation
UNEDBAS	UNESCO Regional Office of Education in the Arab States (Jordan)	**UNESCO/LDS**	UNESCO Library and Documentation Service = LDS
UNEDIC	Union Nationale pour l'Emploi dans l'Industrie et le Commerce	**UNESCO ROBDAP**	Regional Office for Book Development in Asia and the Pacific
UNÉEPF	Union Nationale des Éditeurs-Exportateurs de Publications Périodiques Françaises	**UNESCO ROEAO**	Unesco Regional Office for Education in Asia and Oceania (Thailand)
UNÉESA	Union Nationale des Étudiants de l'Enseignement Supérieur Agricole	**UNESCO ROSTAS**	UNESCO Regional Office for Science and Technology in the Arab States (France)
UNÉF	Union Nationale des Étudiants de France	**UNESCO ROSTLAC**	UNESCO Regional Office for Science and Technology for Latin America and the Caribbean (Uruguay)
UNEFA	Union de Escuelas Familiares Agrarias	**UNESCO ROSTSCA**	UNESCO Regional Office of Science and Technology of South and Central Asia (India)
UNEFICO	Universal Engineering and Finance Corporation (Switzerland)		
UNEGA	Union Européenne des Fondeurs et Fabricants de Corps Gras Animaux	**UNESCO ROSTSEA**	UNESCO Regional Office for Science and Technology in South East Asia (Indonesia)
UNÉK	Uniion Nationale des Étudiants Kamerunais	**UNESDA**	Union des Associations de Boissons Gazeuses des Pays Membres de la CEE
UNELCA	Union Electrica de Canarias		

UNESEM	Union Européenne des Sources d'Eaux Minérales Naturelles du Marché Commun	**UNHCR**	United Nations High Commissioner for Refugees = ACNUR, HCR
UNESID	Union de Empresas y Entidades Siderurgicas	**UNHHSF**	United Nations Habitat and Human Settlements Foundation
UNESP	Universidade Estadual Paulista "Júlio de Mesquita Filho" (Brazil)	**UNHQ**	United Nations Headquarters
		UNHRC	United Nations Human Rights Commission
UNESPA	Unión Española de Entidades Aseguradores, Reaseguradoras y de Capitalización	**UNI**	Ente Nazionale Italiano di Unificazione
		UNI	União das Nações Indígenas (Brazil)
UNETAP	United Nations Expanded Technical Assistance Program	**UNI**	Union Nationale des Indépendants (Burkina Faso)
UNETAS	United Nations Emergency Technical Aid Service	**UNI**	Union Nationale Interuniversitaire
		UNI	Union Nationale pour l'Indépendance (Djibouti)
UNETPSA	United Nations Educational and Training Programme for Southern Africa	**UNI**	United News of India
UNETT	Union Nationale des Entreprises de Travail Temporaire	**UNI-FRUTIS**	Union Nationale Interprofessionnelle des Fruits, Légumes et Pommes de Terre
UNEUROP	Association Économique Européenne	**UNI-GRAINS**	Union Financière pour le Développement de l'Économie Céréalière
UNEXSO	International Underwater Explorers Society	**UNI-VENCA**	Unión Venezolana Criadores de Aves
UNF	Ungdommens Naturvidenskabelige Forening		
UNFA	Union Nationale des Femmes Algériennes	**UNI VIANDES-**	Union Nationale Interprofessionnelle des Viandes
UNFAO	United Nations Food and Agriculture Organisation	**UNIA**	Union des Ingénieurs Diplômés des Écoles Nationales Supérieures Agronomiques
UNFB	United Nations Film Board	**UNIA**	Union Nationale des Industries Agricoles
UNFC	Unitied Nations Food Conference		
UNFDAC	United Nations Fund for Drug Abuse Control = FNULAD	**UNIA**	Unione Italiana Autoriparatori
		UNIADU-SÉC	Union Internationale des Associations de Diplômés Universitaires en Sciences Économiques et Commerciales
UNFICYP	United Nations Peace-Keeping Force in Cyprus		
UNFN	United Nations Fund for Namibia	**UNIAPA**	Union Iberoamericana de Padres de Familia
UNFP	Union Nationale des Forces Populaires (Morocco)	**UNIAPAC**	Union Internationale Chrétienne des Dirigeants d'Entreprise
UNFPA	United Nations Fund for Population Activities = FNUAP	**UNIAPRAVI**	Union Interamericana para la Vivienda
UNFRFJ	Union Nationale des Foyers Ruraux de la Famille et des Jeunes	**UNIARTE**	Unión Nacional de Industriales y Artesanos (Venezuela)
UNFSTD	United Nations Fund for Science and Technology for Development	**UNIATEC**	Union Internationale des Associations Techniques Cinématographiques = IUTCA
UNFT	Union Nationale des Femmes de Tunisie		
UNGA	United Nations General Assembly	**UNIBA**	Unione Nazionale Industrie Bigiotterie ed Affini
UNGDA	Union Nationale des Groupements de Distillateurs d'Alcool	**UNIBAN**	Union de Bananeros (Colombia)
		UNIBERO	Universidades Iberoamericanas Europeas
UNGEGN	United Nations Group of Experts on Geographical Names = GENUNG		
UNGP	Union Nationale des Grandes Pharmacies	**UNIBEV**	Union Nationale Interprofessionelle du Bétail et des Viandes

UNIBEX	Union des Brasseries Belges d'Exportation
UNIBG	Union Nazionale Industriali Bevande Gassate
UNIBID	UNISIST International Centre for Bibliographic Descriptions (UNESCO)
UNIC	Union Internationale des Cinémas
UNIC	Union Nationale Interprofessionnelle du Cheval
UNIC	Unione Nazionale Industria Conciaria
UNIC	United International Club (U.S.A.)
UNIC	United Nations Information Centre = CINU
UNICA	Association of Caribbean Universities and Research Institutes (Puerto Rico)
UNICA	European Capitals Universities Network (Belgium)
UNICA	Union Internationale du Cinéma Non-professionnel
UNICA	Universidad Nacional, Institúto Colombiano Agropecuário
UNICA	Universidades e Institútos del Caribe
UNICAE	Union Internacional de Ciencias Antropológicas y Etnologicas = IUAES, UISAE
UNICAF	Union d'Importationes Industrielles et Commerciales Africains
UNICAFE	Union Industrielle des Cafés (Ivory Coast)
UNICAPEC	Unione Nazionale Italiana Collegi Associazioni Periti, Esperti e Consultenti
UNICC	United Nations International Computing Centre
UNICE	Union des Confédérations de l'Industrie et des Employeurs d'Europe
UNICEB	Unione Nazionale Importatori Carni e Bestiame
UNICEF	United Nations Children's Fund
UNICEM	Union Nationale des Industries de Carrieres et Matériaux de Construction
UNICEMA	Union Nationale des Industriels, Commerçants et Entrepreneurs de Mauritanie
UNICER	União Cervejeira
UNICERE-ALES	Union Nationale Interprofessionnelle des Céréales
UNICÉTA	Union Nationale des Ingénieurs des Centres d'Études Techniques Agricoles
UNICHAD	Union Interprofessionnelle du Tchad
UNICHAL	Union Internationale des Distributeurs de Chaleur
UNICHOCO	Union des Chambers Syndicales des Chocolatiers Confiseurs Fabricants Détaillants
UNICI	Union Internationale des Cinéastes Indépendants
UNICID	Union Nationale Interprofessionnelle Cidricole
UNICLIMA	Union Intersyndicale des Constructeurs de Matériel Aéraulique
UNICME	Union Nazionale Importatorie Commercianti Motoveicoli Esteri
UNICO	Union Industrielle et Commerciale de l'Ouest de la Côte d'Ivoire
UNICO-CYM	Union Internationale du Commerce et de la Réparation du Cycle et du Motocycle
UNICOMA	Union des Coopératives du Morbihan et le Loire-Atlantique
UNICOMAR	Union Commerciale et Maritime (Mauritania)
UNICOMAT	Union Intersyndicale des Constructeurs de Matériel Aéraulique, Thermique et Frigorifique
UNICOMER	Union des Comptoirs d'Outre-Mer
UNICON-SERVE	Union Nationale Interprofessionnelle de la Conserve
UNICONGO	Union Patronale et Interprofessionnelle du Congo
UNICOOP	Union Coopérative de Viticulteurs Charentais
UNICOS	Union Internationale pour la Coopération au Développement = IUDC
UNICRI	United Nations Interregional Crime and Justice Research Institute
UNICUIR	Unione Internationale des Négociants en Cuir
UNIDI	Unione Nazionale delle Industrie Dociarie Italiane
UNIDIR	United Nations Institute for Disarmament Research
UNIDO	United Nations Industrial Development Organisation = ONUDI
UNIDROIT	Institut Internationale pour l'Unification du Droit Privé = IIUPL
UNIECE	Economic Commission for Europe
UNIÉCO	Union Internationale d'Écoles par Correspondance
UNIEG	Unie van de Industrieén der Europese Gemeenschap

UNIEG	Unione Nazionale Industrie Editoriali e Grafiche
UNIEM	Union Nationale des Entrepreneurs-Menuisiers et Charpentiers (Belgium)
UNIEMA	Union des Industries et Entreprises de Mauritanie
UNIENET	United Nations International Emergency Network (UNDRO)
UNIÉNSA	Union des Ingénieurs Diplômés des Écoles Nationales Supérieurs Agronomiques
UNIEP	Union Internationale des Entrepreneurs de Peinture = IUMP
UNIFA	Union Nationale des Industries Français de l'Ameublement
UNIFAM	Union Nacional de Fabricantes de Alfombras, Moquetas, Revestimientos eI Industrias Afines y Auxiliares
UNIFE	Union des Industries Ferroviaires Européennes
UNIFEM	United Nations Development Fund for Women
UNIFICYP	United Nations Interim Force in Cyprus
UNIFIL	United Nations Interim Force in Lebanon = FINUL, FPNUL
UNIFL	Union Nationale Interprofessionnelles des Fruits et Légumes
UNIFLAC	Centro Universitario Franco-Latinoamericano
UNIFO-DENT	Union Professionnelle des Négociants en Fournitures Dentaires de Belgique
UNIG	Union Nationale Industrielle du Gruyere et de l'Emmental
UNIGABON	Union Interprofessionnelle Économique et Sociale du Gabon
UNIGAZ	Union Togolais des Gaz
UNIGRA	Union des Industries Graphiques et du Livre (Belgium)
UNIKOM	UN-Iraq-Kuwait Observation Mission
UNIKOM	Union des Komoriens
UNIL	United Nordic Importers Ltd (Denmark)
UNILOC	United Nations International Labour Organizations Committee
UNILOIRE	Union des Industriels Laitiers des Pays de Loire
UNILSE	Union des Industriels Laitiers du Sud-Est
UNIM	Union Nationale des Industries de la Manutention dans les Ports Français
UNIMA	Union Internationale de la Marionette
UNIMA	Union Nazionale Imprese di Meccanizzazione Agricola
UNIMES	Union des Importateurs-Exportateurs Sénégalaise
UNIMETAL	Union Nationale des Petites et Moyennes Enterprises du Métal (Belgium)
UNIMO	Union Nigérienne de Fabrique de Mousse
UNIN	Institute for Namibia (Zambia)
UNINAT	Union des Industries de Matériaux Naturels
UNINCCA	Universidad Incca de Colombia
UNINCO	Union Internationale des Corps Consulaires
UNIND	União das Nações Indígenas (Brazil)
UNINSA	Union de Siderurgicas Asturianus SA (Spain)
UNIO	United Nations Information Organisation
UNIOCON-CIARIA	Unione Nazionale Industria Conciaria
UNIOM	Union Nationale Interprofessionnelle des Oléagineux Métropolitains
UNION	Union of European Practitioners in Industrial Property
Union de Berne	Union d'Assureurs des Crédits et des Investissements Internationaux = Berne Union
Union de Berne	Union Internationale pour la Protection des Oeuvres Littéraires et Artistiques = Berne Union
Union de Paris	Union Internationale pour la Protection de la Propriété Industrielle = Paris Union
UNION-BIRRA	Union Italiana Fabricanti Birra e Malto
UNION-CHIMICA	Unione Nazionale Piccole e Medie Industrie Chimiche ed Affini
UNION-FLEURS	Union Internationale du Commerce de Gros en Fleurs
UNION-LEGNO	Unione Nazionale Piccole e Medie Industrie del Legno
UNION-PELLI	Unione Nazionale Commercio Pelli e Cuoi
UNION-PLAST	Unione Nazionale Industrie Materie Plastiche
UNION-RISO	Unione Italiana dell'Industria Risiera
UNION-TESSILE	Unione Nazionale Piccole e Medie Industrie Tessili

UNIONALI-MENTARI	Union Italiana Piccole e Medie Industrie Alimentari	**UNISA**	Unidad de Servicios para Fomentar la Participacion de la Mujer Hondurena
UNIP	Union Nationale Interprofessionnelle des Protéagineux	**UNISA**	Unione Nazionale Italiana Sindacati Autonomi
UNIP	United National Independence Party (Zambia)	**UNISA**	Unione Nazionale Italiana Stampatori Acciaio
UNIPAC	UNICEF Procurement Assembly Centre (Denmark)	**UNISCAN**	British-Scandinavian Economic Committee
UNIPAC	Union Industrielle des Fabricants de Papiers et Cartons	**UNISCAT**	United Nations Expert Committee on the Application of Science and Technology
UNIPACO	Union Paraguaya de Cooperativas		
UNIPAG	Union des Professionnels des Arts Graphiques	**UNISIST**	UNESCO-ICSU Joint Project to Study the Feasibility of a World Information System
UNIPAR	Union de Participations de France et d'Outre-Mer	**UNISIST**	Universal System for Information in Science and Technology
UNIPEDÉ	Union Internationale des Producteurs et Distributeurs d'Énergie Électrique	**UNISTOCK**	Union Professionnelle des Stockeurs de Céréales dans la CEE
UNIPHAR	Union des Industries et Commerces Pharmaceutiques	**UNISYNDI**	Union Intersyndicale d'Entreprises et d'Industries de l'Ouest Africain
UNIPI	Unione Industriali Pastai Italiani	**UNIT**	Union Nationale des Ingénieurs Diplômés de l'Enseignement Supérieur Technique et de l'Enseignement Supérieur Agricole (Belgium)
UNIPLPL	Union Nationale Interprofessionnelle de Propagande pour le Lait et les Produits Laitiers (France)		
UNIPOL	Union des Industries de Produits Oléagineux	**UNIT**	Union Nationale des Ingénieurs Industriels et Ingénieurs Techniciens (Belgium) = NUTI
UNIPRESSE	Union pour l'Expansion de la Presse Française dans le Monde	**UNITA**	União Nacional para a Independência Total de Angola
UNIPRO	Unione Nazionale delle Industrie di Profumeria Cosmesi, Saponi da Toilette e Affini	**UNITAB**	Internationalen Union der Tabakspflanzer
UNIPRO-LAIT	Union Nationale Interprofessionnelle des Produits Laitiers	**UNITAM**	Union Intersyndicale des Fabricants d'Articles pour la Table, le Ménage et Activités Connexes
UNIPYME	Union de la Pequeña y Mediana Empresa	**UNITAN**	Union de la Tannerie et de la Mégisserie Belge
UNIR	Unidad Nacional de Izquierda Revolucionaria (Mexico)	**UNITAP**	United Nations Intermunicipal Technical Assistance Programme
UNIR	Unión de Izquierda Revolucionaria (Peru)	**UNITAR**	United Nations Institute for Training and Research
UNIR	Union de la Navigation Internationale du Rhin = UIR, IRU	**UNITEC**	Union Togolaise de Commerce
UNIR	Union Nationale pour l'Indépendance et la Révolution (Chad)	**UNITEC**	University Information Technology Corporation (U.S.A.)
UNIRÉ	Unione Nazionale Incremento Razza Équine	**UNITESA**	Union Nazionale dell'Istruzione Tecnica e Professionale
UNIRIZ	Union Nationale Interprofessionnelle du Riz	**UNITHAI**	United Thai Shipping Corporation
UNIRS	Union Nationale des Institutions de Retraite des Salariés	**UNITI**	Bundesverband Mittelständischer Mineralölunternehmen
UNIS	United Nations Information Service	**UNITOP**	Union Nationale des Industries de Transmissions Oléo-Hydrauliques et Pneumatiques
UNIS	United Nations International School (U.S.A.)		

UNITRA	Union pour l'Industrie et les Travaux Publics (Senegal)
UNITRAS-COL	Union de Trabajadores del Transporte de Colombia
UNIVCC	Union Nationale Intercoopérative des Vins de Consommation Courante
UNIVENSA	Unión Industrial Venezolana
UNIVIGNE	Union Nationale Interprofessionnelle de la Vigne
UNIVOL-AILLE	Union Nationale Interprofessionnelle de la Volaille
UNIVSERV	United Nations International Voluntary Service Fund
UNJA	Union Nationale de la Jeunesse Algérienne
UNJIU	Joint Inspection Unit of the United Nations
UNJSPB	United Nations Joint Staff Pension Board
UNKRA	United Nations Korean Reconstruction Agency
UNLA	Uganda National Liberation Army
UNLA	Unione Nazionale per la Lotta Contra l'Analfabatismo
UNLC	United Nations Liaison Committee
UNLG	Union Nationale des Livres Généalogiques
UNM	Unon de Normalisation de la Mécanique
UNM	Urad pro Normalizaci a Mereni
UNMC	United Nations Mediterranean Commission
UNMÉ	Union Nationale des Maisons de l'Élevage
UNMEM	United Nations Middle East Mission = MNUOM
UNMFAR	Union Nationale des Maisons Familiales d'Apprentissage Rural
UNMFC	United Nations Monetary and Financial Conference
UNMIH	United Nations Mission in Haiti
UNMOGIP	United Nations Military Observer Group in India and Pakistan
UNMRÉFO	Union Nationale des Maisons Familiales Rurales pour l'Éducation et l'Orientation
UNO	Unión Nacional Obrista (Peru)
UNO	Union Nacional Opositora (Nicaragua)
UNO	United Nations Organisation = UN
UNOAI	Union Nationale des Ouvriers Agricoles Indépendants
UNOASD	United Nations Outer Space Affairs Division
UNOB	Union Nationale des Opticiens de Belgique
UNOC	Unión Nacional Obrero-Campesina (El Salvador)
UNOCA	Office for the Coordination of United Nations Humanitarian and Economic Assistance Programmes Relating to Afghanistan (UN)
UNOCCÉR	Union Nationale des Offices de Compatibilité et des Centres d'Économie Rurale
UNOD	Nationale Unie der Openbare Diensten = UNSP
UNOE	Union Nationale des Oenologues
UNOEOA	United Nations Office for Emergency Operations in Africa
UNOG	United Nations Office at Geneva = ONUG
UNOH	Union Nationale des Ouvriers d'Haiti
UNOLE-ARIA	Associazione Nazionale dell' Industria Olearia
UNOLS	University-National Oceanographic Laboratory System (U.S.A.)
UNOMIG	United Nations Observer Mission in Georgia
UNOMIL	United Nations Observer Mission in Liberia
UNOMOZ	United Nations Operation in Mozambique
UNOOB	Union Nationale des Optométristes et Opticiens de Belgique
UNORCA	Union Nacional de Organizaciones Regionales Campesinas Autónomas (Mexico)
UNOSOM II	United Nations Operation in Somalia II
UNOSTRA	Union Nationale des Organisations Syndicales de Transporteurs Routiers Automobiles
UNOTC	United Nations Office of Technical Co-operation
UNOV	United Nations Office at Vienna
UNOV/ CSDHA	United Nations Office at Vienna/UN Centre for Social Development and Humanitarian Affairs = UNCSDHA
UNOY	United Nations of Youth
UNP	Ukrainian National Party
UNP	Unification National Party (Democratic People's Republic of Korea)
UNP	Union Nacional de Periodistas (Ecuador)

UNP	United National Party (Sri Lanka)
UNPA	Union National des Paysans Algériens
UNPA	United Nations Postal Administration = APNU
UNPAAERD	United Nations Program of Action of African Economic Recovery and Development
UNPADI	Unión Panamericana de Asociaciónes de Ingeneiros
UNPAL	Unión Nacional de Productores de Aceite de Limón (Mexico)
UNPASA	Unión Nacional de Productors de Azúcar de Caña (Mexico)
UNPBF	Union Nationale des Producteurs Belges de Films
UNPC	Union Nationale des Professionnels de la Comptabilité
UNPEG	Unión Nacional de Produtores y Exportadores de Garbanzo (Mexico)
UNPF	Union Nationale des Pharmacies de France
UNPF	Unione Nazionale Produttori Film
UNPFA	United Nations Fund for Population Activities
UNPJF	Union Nationale des Producteurs et Distributeurs de Jus de Fruits et de Légumes (France)
UNPLIB	Union Nationale des Professions Libérales et Intellectuelles de Belgique = NUVIBB
UNPO	Unrepresented Nations' and Peoples' Organization (Netherlands) = UNCON
UNPOC	United Nations Peace Observation Commission
UNPRG	Union Nationale du Personnel en Retraite de la Gendarmerie
UNPROFOR	United Nations Protection Force
UNPVF	Union Nationale des Peintres-Vitriers de France
UNRAE	Unione Nazionale Rapresentanti Autoveicoli Estri
UNRÉP	Union Nationale Rurale d'Éducation et de Promotion
UNRFNRE	United Nations Revolving Fund for Natural Resource Exploration
UNRISD	United Nations Research Institute for Social Development
UNRST	Union Nationale des Revêtements de Sol et du Tapis
UNRTD	United Nations Resources and Transport Division
UNRWA	United Nations Relief and Works Agency for Palestine Refugees in the Near East = OOPS
UNRWI	United Nations Representative for West Irian
UNSA	Unione Nazionale Sindacati Autonomi
UNSAC	United Nations Scientific Advisory Committee
UNSC	United Nations Security Council
UNSC	United Nations Social Commission
UNSCC	United Nations Standards Co-ordinating Committee
UNSCCUR	United Nations Scientific Conference on the Conservation and Utilisation of Resources
UNSCEAR	United Nations Scientific Committee on the Effects of Atomic Radiation
UNSCH	Universidad Nacional de San Cristobal de Huamanga (Peru)
UNSCO	United Nations Special Commission to the Balkans
UNSDD	United Nations Social Development Division
UNSDRI	United Nations Social Defence Research Institute (Italy)
UNSÉ	Union Nationale des Syndicats d'Étang
UNSEA	Ufficio Nazionale Statistico Economico dell'Agricoltura
UNSEPF	Union Nationale des Syndicats d'Entrepreneurs Paysagistes de France
UNSEPRF	Union Nationale des Syndicats d'Entrepreneurs Paysagistes et Reboiseurs de France
UNSFA	Union Nationale des Syndicats Français d'Architectes
UNSFL	Union Nationale des Syndicats de Fabricants de Lunetterie
UNSI-TRAGUA	Unión de Sindicatos de Trabajadores de Guatemala
UNSO	United Nations Statistical Office
UNSO	United Nations Sudano-Sahelian Office = BNUS
UNSOF	Union Nationale des Syndicats d'Opticiens de France
UNSP	Union Nationale des Services Publics (Belgium)
UNSR	United Nations Space Registry
UNST	Union Nationale des Syndicats du Tchad
UNSTB	National Union of Workers' Trade Unions of Benin

UNSU	United Nations Staff Union
UNSU	United Nations Study Unit
UNSW	University of New South Wales
UNT	Union Nationale Tchadienne
UNTA	União Nacional de Trabalhadores Angolanos
UNTA	Unión Nacional de Trabajadores Agriculturas (Mexico)
UNTAA	United Nations Technical Assistance Administration = AATNU
UNTAB	United Nations Technical Assistance Board
UNTAC	United Nations Transitional Authority in Cambodia
UNTAC	Universidad Nacional de Tacna (Peru)
UNTACDA	Inter-Agency Coordinating Committee for the Transport and Communications Decade in Agrica (UN)
UNTAG	United Nations Transition Assistance Group (Namibia)
UNTAM	United Nations Technical Assistance Mission
UNTAP	United Nations Technical Assistance Program
UNTC	Union Nationale des Travailleurs Congolais
UNTC	Union Nationale des Travailleurs du Caméroun
UNTC	United Nations Trusteeship Council
UNTC-CS	União Nacional dos Trabalhadores de Cabo Verde-Central Sindical
UNTÉL	Union Nationale des Syndicats des Tissus Élastiques
UNTFAD	United Nations Trust Fund for African Development
UNTFDPP	United Nations Trust Fund for Development Planning and Projections = FASNUPPD
UNTFSA	United Nations Trust Fund for South Africa
UNTFSD	United Nations Trust Fund for Social Development = FASNUDS, FFNUDS
UNTG	Uniao Nacional dos Trabalhadores de Guiné (Guinea-Bissau)
UNTM	Union Nationale des Travailleurs du Mali
UNTM	Union Nationale des Travailleurs du Maroc
UNTRA	Union of National Radio and Television Organisations of Africa
UNTRACH	Unión de Trabajadores de Chile
UNTS	Unidad Nacional de Trabajadores Salvadoreños
UNTS	Union Nationale des Travailleurs Sénégalais
UNTSO	United Nations Technical Special Operations
UNTSO	United Nations Truce Supervision Organisation = ONUST
UNTT	Union Nationale des Travailleurs Togolais
UNTZA	Union Nationale des Travailleurs du Zaïre
UNU	Uganda National Union
UNU	Ukrainian Nationalist Union
UNU	United Nations University (Japan)
UNU/INRA	UNU Institute for Natural Resources in Africa = INRA
UNU/WI-DER	UNU World Institute for Development Economics Research of the United Nations University
UNUCI	Unione Nazionale Ufficiali in Congedo d'Italia
UNV	United Nations Volunteers = VNU
UNVDA	Société de Développement de la Haute Vallée du Noun (Cameroon)
UNVFVT	United Nations Voluntary Fund for Victims of Torture
UNVR	National Union for the Victory of the Revolution (Romania)
UNWDC	United Nations World Disarmament Campaign
UNWG	United Nations Women's Guild
UNY	United Nations of Yoga
UNYOM	United Nations Yemen Observation Mission
UOA	Underground Officials Association of South Africa
UOA	United Ostomy Association (U.S.A.)
UOASE	Union des Organisations Agricoles du Sud-Est
UOC	Federación Unidad Obrero Campesina (Chile)
UOE	Unidad de Operaciones Especiales
UOF	Union Ovine de France
UOI	Union Obrera Independiente (Mexico)
UOIF	Union des Organisations Internationales non Gouvernementales Établies en France
UOIW	United Optical and Instrument Workers of America

UOM	Union Obrera Metalurgica de la Republica Argentina	**UPADI**	Union Panamericana de Asociaciones de Ingenieros
UOP	Urząd Ochrony Państwa	**UPAE**	Union Postal de las Americas y España = PUAS
UOS	Union of Slovaks (Czech Republic) = SS	**UPAf**	Union Postale Africaine
UOSS	Union des Offices Suisse de Statistiques = UUSS, VSSA	**UPAFI**	Union Professionnelle d'Agents, Fabricants et Importateurs Exclusifs d'Objets d'Art et de Cadeaux (Belgium)
ÚOÚD	Úřad pro Ochranu Ústavy a Demokracie	**UPAM**	United Planters' Association of Malaya
UOVS	Universiteit van die Oranje Vrystaat (South Africa)	**UPANIC**	Unión de Productores Agropecuários de Nicaragua
UP	Umma Party (Sudan)	**UPAO**	Union Postale de l'Asie et de l'Océanie
UP	Unidad Popular (Chile)	**UPAP**	Union Panafricaine des Postes = PAPU
UP	Union de Pagesos	**UPASI**	United Planters' Association of Southern India
UP	Union des Propriétaires du Grand-Duché de Luxembourg	**UPAT**	Union Panafricaine des Télécommunications (Zaïre) = PATU
UP	Union of Labour (Poland)		
UP	Union Pacific	**UPAV**	Union Professionnelle Belge des Agences des Voyages
UP	Unión Patriótica (Colombia)		
UP	Union Pétrolié (Switzerland)	**UPAVE**	Unión de Productores de Azúcar de Venezuela
UP	Union Popular (Costa Rica) = PUP		
UP	Unión Popular (Peru)	**UPB Unión**	Patriótico Bonairiano (Netherlands Antilles)
UP	Unione Petrolifera		
UP	United Party (Papua New Guinea)	**UPBAN**	Union Professionnelle Belge des Approvisionneurs de Navires
UP	Unity Party (Liberia)		
UP	University for Peace (Costa Rica)	**UPBIF**	Union Professionnelle Belge des Industriels du Froid
UP	Urząd Patentowy		
UPA	Uganda Peoples Army	**UPBMO**	Union Professionnelle Belge des Médecins Ophthalmologistes
UPA	União das Populacões de Angola		
UPA	Union des Parlements Africains = APU	**UPBOB**	Union Professionnelle des Bandagistes et Orthopédistes de Belgique
UPA	Unión Panamericana = PAU		
UPA	Union Postale Africaine = APU/ATU	**UPBPP**	Union Professionnelle Belge de la Police Privée
UPA	Union Postale Arabe = APU		
UPA	Union Professionelle des Architectes (Belgium)	**UPC**	Unidad Popular Castellana
		UPC	Union des Pelleteries et Confectionneurs en Fourrure
UPA	Union Royale Professionelle des Architectes Diplômes des Instituts Supérieurs d'Architecture Saint-Luc de Belgique = BUA	**UPC**	Union des Producteurs de Caoutchouc Natural
		UPC	Union du Peuple Corse (Corsica)
UPA	Unions Professionnelles Agricoles (Belgium)	**UPC**	Union pour construire (New Caledonia)
		UPC	Universidad Politecnica de Cataluña
UPA	United Printers Association	**UPCA**	Union Professionnelle des Coopératives Agricoles (Belgium)
UPA	Utenti Pubblicità Associati		
UPAA	University Photographers Association of America	**UPCA**	University of the Philippines College of Agriculture
UPAB	Fédération des Unions Professionneles Agricoles de Belgique	**UPCID**	Union Partonale du Commerce et de l'Industrie du Douaisis
UPACCIM	Union des Ports Autonomes et des Chambres de Commerce et d'Industrie Maritimes	**UPCIL**	Union Interfédérale des Producteurs, des Coopératives et des Industriels Laitiers

UPCL	Union Professionnelle des Promoteurs de Logements et d'Aménagement du Territoire (Belgium)
UPCRA	Union of Peasant Co-operatives of the Republic of Afghanistan
UPD	Una Proposta Diversa
UPD	Unidad Popular Democrática (El Salvador)
UPD	Union des Patriotes Démocratiques (Haiti)
UPDAL	Union Professionnelle de Commerce de Gros des Produits Laitiers Laitiers Indigénes et d'Importation autre que Beurre et Fromage (Belgium)
UPDBF	Union Professionnelle des Distributeurs Belges de Films
UPDEA	Union of Producers and Distributors of Electric Power in Africa
UPDEC	Union Professionnelle des Diplômés Comptables
UPDM	Union Démocratique du Peuple Malien (Mali)
UPDP	Ukrainian Peasants' Democratic Party
UPÉ	Union de la Presse Étrangère en Belgique
UPE	Union des Phoniatres Européens = SEF, UEP
UPEA	Union Professionnelle des Entreprises d'Assurances (Belgium)
UPEB	Unión de Paises Exportadores de Banano (Panama) = UBEC
UPEC	Uttar Pradesh Export Corporation (India)
UPECL	Union Professionnelle des Experts Comptables Libéraux
UPEDI	Union Professionnelle des Entreprises de Travail Intérimaire
UPÉFE	Union de la Presse Économique et Financière Européenne
UPEI	Union Pétrolière Européenne Indépendante
UPEPI	Union des Praticiens en Propriété Industrielle
UPET	Ufficio per la Esportazione Tobacco
UPETITA	Union Professionnelle des Entreprises de Travaux d'Isolation ThermiqueI et Acoustique (Belgium)
UPETTC	Union Professionnelle des Exploitants de Taxis et de Taxis-Camionnettes
UPEX	Union Professionnelle des Experts en Automobiles de Belgique

UPF	Union Progresista de Fiscales
UPF	United Patriotic Front (U.S.A.)
UPFC	Uttar Pradesh Financial Corporation (India)
UPG	Union du Peuple Gabonais
UPG	Union du Peuple Guinéen
UPGA	United Progressive Grand Alliance (Nigeria)
UPGWA	International Union United Plant Guard Workers of Amercia
UPHA	United Professional Horsemen's Association
UPHR	Unity Party for Human Rights (Albania) = BDN
UPI	Ulkopoliittinen Instituutti
UPI	Union des Professions Immobilières de Belgiques = UIB
UPI	United Press International
UPIA	Union Pharmaceutique Inter-Africaine
UPICO	Union Patronale de l'Industrie et du Commerce de l'Oise
UPIGO	Union Professionnelle Internationale des Gynécologues et Obstétriciens
UPIL	Union des Pharmaciens d'Industrie Luxembourgeoise
UPIP	Union des Pharmaciens de l'Industrie Pharmaceutique (Belgium) = VAPI
UPIPL	Union des Pharmaciens de l'Industrie Pharmaceutique du Grand-Duché de Luxembourg
UPIR	Uttar Pradesh Irrigation Research Institute (India)
UPIU	United Paperworkers International Union
UPL	International Insitute for the Unification of Private Law
UPL	Union des Pilotes d'Aviation du Grand-Duché de Luxembourg
UPLAC	Union des Producteurs de Levure-Aliment de la CEE
UPLB	University of the Philippines Los Banos
UPLF	Union Professionnelle des Logopèdes Francophones
UPLG	Union Populaire pour la Libération de la Guadeloupe
UPM	Unión del Pueblo Melillense (Melilla)
UPM	Union Progressiste Mélanesienne (New Caledonia)
UPM	United People's Movement (St. Vincent)
UPMC	Urban Planning Ministers Conference

UPMRC	Union of Palestinian Relief Committees
UPN	Union de Periodistas de Nicaragua
UPN	Union del Pueblo Navarro
UPN	Unity Party of Nigeria
UPOA	Ulster Public Officers Association
UPONI	Universidad Politecnica de Nicaragua
UPOV	International Union for the Protection of New Varieties of Plants
UPOV	Union Internationale pour la Protection des Obtentions Végétales
UPP	United Peasants' Party = ZSL
UPP	United People's Party (Bangladesh)
UPP	United Peoples Party (Nigeria)
UPPB	Union de la Presse Périodique Belge
UPPIC	Union Syndicale Interprofessionnelle pour la Promotion de la Conserve
UPPN	Union Postale des Pays du Nord = NORDPOST
UPQÉI&F	Union de la Presse Quotidienne, Économique, Industrielle et Financière
UPR	Unia Polityki Realnej
UPR	Union Professionnelle des Représentants de Commerce de Belgique
UPR	Union Professionnelle des Transports Publics Routiers
UPRDiMW	Unia Polityki Realnej, Dziekanii i Młodziezy Wszechpolskiej
UPREL	Union Professionnelle Belge des Conseillers et des Cadres Supérieurs en Relations Publiques
UPRF	Union Professionnelle Belge du Commerce des Fromages
UPROCA	Union Professionelle des Producteurs du Caoutchouc (Belgium)
UPRONA	Union pour le Progrès National (Burundi)
UPROTAB	Union Professionnelle Nationale des Importateurs Négociants, Commissionnaires, Courtiers et Agents en Tabacs en Feuilles en Belgique
UPS	Union of Professional Staff (UN)
UPS	Union Producteurs Suisses
UPS	Union Progressiste Sénégalaise
UPS	Università Pontificia Salesiana
UPSA	Union Professionnelle Suisse de l'Automobile
UPSAN	Universal Party of Slavs and Allied Nations (Poland) = PPSiNS
UPSEB	Uttar Pradesh State Electricity Board (India)
UPSFEC	Union Professionnelle des Sociétés Fiduciaires d'Expertise Comptable
UPSIC	Uttar Pradesh Small-Scale Industries Corporation (India)
UPSIDC	Uttar Pradesh State Industrial Development Corporation (India)
UPSJF	Union Professionnelle des Sociétés Juridiques et Fiscales
UPSOA	Union Postale du Sud et de l'Ouest de l'Asie
UPSS	United Postal Stationery Society (U.S.A.)
UPSSC	Uttar Pradesh State Sugar Corporation
UPST	Union Panafricaine de la Science et de la Technologie = PUST
UPSTC	Uttar Pradesh State Textile Corporation (India)
UPTCS	Union of Professional and Technical Civil Servants (Éire)
UPTD	Union Professionnelle des Teinuriers-Dégraisseurs (Belgium)
UPTRI	Union Professionnelle Belge des Transporteurs Routiers Internationaux
UPU	Universal Postal Union = WPV
UPV	Unión Popular Venezolana
UPV	Union Professionelle Vétérinaire (Belgium)
UQ	University of Queensland
URA	Union des Remorqueurs d'Abidjan (Ivory Coast)
URA	Universities Research Association (U.S.A.)
URACA	Unione Regionale Associazioni Campane Albergatori
URAI	Union des Représentations Automobiles et Industrielles (Gabon)
Uralmash	Ural'skiy zavod tiazhelogo mashinostroeniia
URAMEX	Uranio Mexicano
URANEX	Groupement d'Intérêt Économique pour la Commercialisation de l'Uranie
URAPABOL	Comisión Mixta Permanente Uruguay-Paraguay-Bolivia (Paraguay)
URBANI-COM	Association Internationale Urbanisme et Commerce
URBED	Urban and Economic Development Group
URBT	Centre de Recherches dur les Ressources Biologiques Terrestres (Algeria)

URC	Union du Ressemblement et du Centre (Guyana)
URC	United Reformed Church
URCA	Société de l'Uranium Centrafricain
URCAM	Union Régionale des Coopératives du Midi
URCC	Union Régionale des Coopératives Cidricoles
URCCE	Union des Régions des Capitales de la Communauté Européenne
URD	Unidad Revolucionaria Demócrata (Guatelama)
URD	Union des Remorqueurs de Dakar (Senegal)
URD	Unión Republicana Democrática (Venezuela)
URDA	Unité Régionale de Développement de l'Agriculture
URDC	Union pour une République Démocratique aux Comores
URDU	Urban Regional Development Unit (ACOSS)
URE	Union de Radioaficionados Españoles
URE-CSAV	Ustav Radiotechniky a Elektroniky CSAV
UREF	Université des Réseaux d'Expression Française
UREGÉR	Union pour la Recherche et l'Expansion de la Gestion et de l'Économie Rurale
UREMG	Universidade Rural do Estado de Minas Gerais (Brazil)
URENCO	Uranium Enrichment Company (Denmark/Netherlands/U.K.)
UREP	University Research Expeditions Program (U.S.A.)
URF	Union des Services Routiers des Chemins de Fer Européens
URF	United Revolution Front (Ghana)
URFC	Union Révolutionnaire des Femmes Congolaises
URG	Union des Religieux de Grèce
URGA	Unión Recibidores de Granos y Anexos (Argentina)
URGCI	Union Romande des Gérants et Courtiers en Immeubles
URI	Université Radiophonique et Télévisuelle Internationale
URIA	Unione Romana degli Ingeneri e Architetti
URIMÉPAC	Union Régionale des Industries Métallurgiques, Électriques et Connexes Provence-Côte d'Azur-Corse
URISA	Urban and Regional Information Systems Association (U.S.A.)
URJ	Union Romande de Journaux (Switzerland)
URLAC	Union Régionale Laitière Agricole Coopératives
URM	Urząd Rady Ministrów
URMA	Union Romande de Moulins Agricoles (Switzerland)
URNG	Unidad Revolucionaria Nacional Guatemalteca
URO	Union des Remorquers de l'Océan
URO	United Roma Organization (Bulgaria) = OOR
URO	Ustredni Rada Odbicu
UROG	Union Internationale des Orphelins de Guerre
URO-GABON	Union des Remorqueurs de l'Océan Gabon
UROME	Union Royale Belge pour les Pays d'Outre-mer et l'Europe Unie
URP	Ukrainian Republican Party
URP	Unión Revolucionario del Pueblo (Honduras)
URPE	Union des Résistants pour une Europe Unie
URPE	Union for Radical Political Economics (U.S.A.)
URSA	Tähtitieteellinen Yhdistys Ursa ry
URSI	Union Radio-Scientifique Internationale = IURS
URSSAF	Union pour le Recouvrement des Cotisations de la Sécurité Sociale et les Allocations Familiales
URT	Union des Religieux et des Religieuses de Turquie
URTI	Université Radiophonique et Télévisuelle Internationale
URTNA	Union des Radiodiffusions et Télévisions Nationales d'Afrique
URTS	Union des Religieuses de Terre Sainte
URTU	United Road Transport Union
URW	United Rubber, Cork, Linoleum and Plastic Workers of America
URZA	Unité de Recherche sur les Zones Arides (Algeria)
USA	Union Syndicale Agricole (Morocco)

USAAPEB	Union Syndicale Ardennaise des Artisans et Petites Entreprises du Bâtiment
USAAW	Union of Schools, Agricultural and Allied Workers (Jamaica)
USAB	United States Activities Board (IEEE)
USAB	United States Animal Bank
USABF	United States Amateur Baseball Federation
USAC	United States Auto Club
USACASP	Union des Société d'Assurances et de Capitalisation par Actions du Secteur Privé
USADIS	Unione Svizzera Arredatori d'Interni e Sellai = ASMAIS, SVIMSA
USAEC	United States Atomic Energy Commission
USAF	United States Air Force
USAF	United States Aquaculture Federation
USAFCRL	U.S. Air Force Cambridge Research Laboratories
USAHA	United States Animal Health Association
USAID	United States Agency for International Development
USAIRE	United States of America Aerospace Industries Representatives in Europe
USAL	Union Suisse des Acheteurs de Lait
USAL	Union Suisse pour l'Amélioration du Logement = SVW
USAL	Universidad Salvadoreña
USAM	Union des Syndicats Autonomes de Madagascar
USAM	Union Suisse des Arts et Métiers = SGV
USAP	Union des Sociétés Arabes de Pédiatrie = UAPS
USAP	United States Antarctic Program
USAR	Union des Syndicats Agricoles Romands (Switzerland)
USARCI	Unione Sindicate Autonomi Agenti Rappresentanti Commercio Industria
USARP	United Nations Antarctic Research Programme
USAVC	United States Army Vehicle Club (U.K.)
USB	Union Schweizerischer Briefumschlagfabriken
USB	Union Sénégalaise de Banques pour le Commerce et l'Industrie
USBA	United States Badminton Association
USBA	United States Brewers Association
USBC	United States Bureau of Census
USBE	Universal Serials and Book Exchange (U.S.A.)
USBF	United States Baseball Federation
USBLM	United States Bureau of Land Management
USBM	United States Bureau of Mines
USBN	United States Bureau of Navigation
USBR	United States Bureau of Reclamation
USBSA	United States Beet Sugar Association
USC	Union Suisse des Coopératives de Consommation
USC	Unione Svizzera dei Cartolai
USC	United Somali Congress
USC	Universidad de San Carlos (Guatemala)
USC	Uphill Ski Club of Great Britain
USCA	Union Syndicale des Courtiers en Assurances (Belgium)
USCAP	Union Syndicate des Cadres du Pétrole
USCAPAT	Union des Sociétés de Commercialisation d'Achat de Produits Agricoles du Togo
USCAR	United States Civil Administration, Ryukyu Islands
USCAS	South American Union of Societies of Cardiology; Union Sud-Américaine des Sociétés de Cardiologie
USCB	United Saudi Commercial Bank (Saudi Arabia)
USCC	United States Catholic Conference
USCCHO	United States Conference of City Health Officers
USCCI	United States Chamber of Commerce in Ireland
USCF	United States Chess Federation
USCI	Union Suisse du Commerce et de l'Industrie = SHIV
USCIAA	United States Committee of the International Association of Art
USCIB	United States Council for International Business
USCICSW	United States Committee of the International Council on Social Welfare
USCIGW	Union of Salt, Chemical and Industrial General Workers
USCL	United Society for Christian Literature
USCL	US Coalition for Life
USCO	Union Steel Corporation (South Africa)
USCSC	United States Civil Service Commission

USCSC	United States Cuban Sugar Council
USCV	Union Scientifique Continentale du Verre (Belgium)
USCWF	United States Council for World Freedom
USDA	Union Suisse des Acheteurs
USDA	United States Department of Agriculture
USDAM	Union Suisse des Artistes Musiciens
USDAW	Union of Shop, Distributive and Allied Workers
USDC	Uganda Society for Disabled Children
USDC	Union Svizzera dei Compratori
USDC	United States Defense Committee
USDC	United States Department of Commerce
USDD	United States Department of Defense
USDGA	United States Durum Growers Association
USDI	United States Department of the Interior
USDJ	United States Department of Justice
USDL	United States Department of Labor
USDOE	United States Department of Energy
USDPU	United Social Democratic Party of Ukraine
USE	Unidad de Servicios Especiales (Peru)
USE	United Students for Europe
USÉF	Union Sociale Économique de France
USEI	Union Syndicale Euratom, Ispra
USEK	Union Syndicale Euratom, Karlsruhe
USELPA	Usinas Eletricas do Paranapanema (Brazil)
USEM	Confederación de Unions Sociales de Enpresarios Mexicanos
USEMA	United States Electronic Mail Association
USEP	Union Suisse pour l'Enseignement Professionnel = SVBU, USIP
USEPA	United States Environmental Protection Agency
USER	Urban Social Environmental Research
USERC	United States Enviroment and Resources Council
USERP	United Scientists for Environmental Responsibility and Protection
USES	United States Employment Service
USF	International Union of Societies of Foresters (Finland)
USF	Unione Svizzera dei Fotografi = SPhV, USP
USFA	Ulster Sea Fishermen's Association
USFB	Union Suisse des Fabricants de Boîtes de Montres
USFEC	Union Professionelle des Sociétés Fiduciaires d'Expertise Comptable
USFGC	United States Feed Grains Council
USFHTF	Union Syndicate des Fabricants d'Huile et de Torteaux de France
USFI	Unione Stampa Filatelica
USFI	United Secretariat of the Fourth International
USFJ	Union Suisse des Fabricants de Jouets
USFJ-CFDT	Union Syndicale des Journalistes Français
USFLF	Union Syndicale des Fabricants de Limes de France
USFMC	Union Syndicale des Fabricants de Matières Colorantes et d'Hydrosulfites
USFO	Union Syndical Francaise du Carton Ondulé
USFP	Union Socialiste des Forces Populaires (Morocco)
USFS	United States Forest Service
USFWS	United States Fish and Wildlife Service
USG	Union of Superiors-General (Vatican)
USG	Union Socialiste Gabonaise
USG	Union Suisse de la Glace Polie
USG	Unione Svizzera dei Giornalisti = SJU, USJ
USGA	United States Golf Association
USGEB	Union Schweizerischer Gesellschaften für Experimentalle Biologie = USSBE
USGF	United States Gymnastics Federation
USGOS	Union des Stockeurs de Graines Oléagineuses de Semences
USGPO	United States Government Printing Office
USGS	United States Geological Survey
USH	Udruženje Srba Hrvatske (Serbia) = ASC
USHF	Union Syndicale de l'Huilerie Français
USHL	United States Hockey League
USHR	Union des Sociétés Historiques du Rhône
USI	União Sindical Independente (Brazil)
USI	Union of Students in Ireland
USI	United Schools International (India)
USI	Ustav Stavebních Informací
USIA	United States Information Agency
USIC	Union Suisse des Industriels en Carrosserie

USIC	United States Industrial Council
USIÉ	Union Suisse des Installateurs-Électriciens = VSEI
USIÉM	Union des Syndicats d'Intérêt Économique Madagasque
USIHR	United States Institute of Human Rights
USIHS	Ulster Society for Irish Historical Studies
USIMA	Union Sénégalaise d'Industries Maritimes
USINEN	Société Ivoirienne d'Usinage
USIO	Union Syndicale Interprofessionnelle Oléicole
USIP	Unione Svizzera per l'Insegnamento Professionale = SVBU, USEP
USIPA	Union des Syndicats des Industries des Produits Amylacés et de leurs Dérivés
USIPE	Unidad Sectorial de Investigacion y Planificacion Educativa (Guatemala)
USIPU	United States Interparliamentary Union
USIRF	Union Syndicale des Industries Routières Françaises
USITA	United States Independent Telephone Association
USITC	United States International Trade Commission
USITHAM	Union Syndicale des Industries Textiles, Habillement et Annexes du Midi
USITT	United States Institute for Theatre Technology
USJ	Udruzenje Stomatologa Jugoslavije
USJ	Union Suisse des Journalistes = SJU, USG
USJF	Union Syndicale des Journalistes Français
USJF	United States Judo Federation
USJF	United States Justice Foundation
USJTC	United States, Japan Trade Council
USL	Union Suisse pour la Lumière = SLG
USLS	Ulster-Scots Language Society
USLV	Union des Schweizerischen Lichtspieltheater-Verbände
USM	Union des Semouliers de Maïs
USM	Union des Supérieurs Majeurs (Switzerland)
USM	Union des Syndicats de Monaco
USM	Union Suisse du Métal = SMU
USMA	Underfeed Stoker Makers Association
USMA	United States Maritime Administration
USMA	United States Metric Association
USMA	United States Monopoly Association
USMAP	Union Syndicale de la Maîtrise du Pétrole
USMB	Union des Supérieurs Majeurs en Burkina Faso
USMB	Union Suisse des Marchands de Beurre
USMC	Union Suisse des Marchands de Chaussures
USMC	Union Suisse des Marchands de Cuir
USMCM	Union Suisse de Marchands et Mécaniciens de Cycles et Motocycles = SFMGV
USMF	Union Syndicale des Médecins Français
USMI	Unione Superiore Maggiori d'Italia
USMIRFA	União des Superioras Maiores dos Institútos Religiosos Femininos de Angola
USMLA	United States Maritime Law Association
USMLS	United States Museum Librarian Society
USMMASA	Union Scientifique Mondiale des Médecins Acupuncteurs et des Sociétés d'Acupuncture
USMSR	Union des Supérieures Majeures de Suisse Romande
USMT	Union Sportive Métropolitaine
USNC/TAM	United States National Committee on Theoretical and Applied Mechanics
USNDC	United States Nuclear Data Committee
USNEF	Union Syndical National des Exploitations Frigorifiques
USNM	United States National Museum
USNO	United Sabah National Organization (Malaysia)
USNPS	United States National Parks Service (U.S.A.)
USNRC	United States Nuclear Regulatory Commission = NRC
USNSA-USNTCE OOPA	United States Naval Sailing Association Union des Syndicats Nationaux de Techniciens, Cadres, Employés et Ouvriers des Organisations Professionnelles Agricoles
USO	Unión Sindical Obrero (Colombia, Spain)
USOCA	United States Office of Consumer Affairs
USOE	United States Office of Education

USOEB	Union Syndicale de l'Office Européenne des Brevets = IGEPA, SUEPO
USOF	United States Orienteering Federation
USOO	United States Oceanographic Office
USOS	Universitaire Stichting voor Ontwikkelingssamenwerking (Belgium)
USP	Union Suisse des Papetiers
USP	Union Suisse des Photographes = SPhV, USF
USP	Universidade de São Paulo (Brazil)
USP	University of the South Pacific
USPA	United States Passport Agency
USPC	Ulster Society for the Preservation of the Countryside
USPC	United States Pharmacopoeial Convention
USPCA	Ulster Society for the Prevention of Cruelty to Animals
USPE	Utah Society of Professional Engineers
USPES	Union of the Societies for the Protection of the Environment = ZVOS
USPG	United Society for the Propagation of the Gospel
USPHS	United States Public Health Service
USPI	Union des Sociétés et Groupements Professionnels Indochinois
USPI	Union Suisse des Professionels de l'Immobilier
USPI	Unione della Stampa Periodica Italiana
USPK	United Socialist Party of Kurdistan (Iraq)
USPM	Union des Syndicats Patronaux de Madagascar
USPMOM	Union des Sociétés de Pédiatre du Moyen-Orient et de la Méditerranée = UMEMPS
USPO	United States Patent Office
USPR	United States Public Radio
USPS	United States Postal Service
USPSA	University of South Pacific Students' Association
USPTA	United States Physical Therapy Association
USPV	Unione Svizzera dei Produtti di Verdura = UMS, VSGP
USR	Union Suisse des Industries Graphiques de Reproduction
USRA	United States Railway Associaton
USRA	University Space Research Association (U.S.A.)
USRC	Union in Support of the Republic of Crimea
USRM	Union Suisse des Reconstructeurs de Moteurs
USRP	Unia Socjaldemokracji Rzeczpospolitej Polskiej
USRT	Union Suisse des Installateurs Concessionnaires en Radio et Télévision = VSRT
USS	Union de Seifen-und Waschmittlefabrikanten der Schweiz
USS	Union Syndicale Suisse
USS	United Seamen's Service (U.S.A.)
USSA	Union Suisse des Syndicats Autonomes
USSA	United States Sports Academy
USSASA	University Science Students Association of South Africa
USSBE	Union des Sociétés Suisses de Biologie Expérimentale = USGEB
USSCC	University Social Sciences Council Conference (East Africa)
USSEA	United States Scientific Export Association
USSEA	United States Space Education Association
USSF	United States Soccer Federation
USSI	Union des Sociétés Suisses d'Ingénieurs-Conseils
USSI	Union Stampa Sportiva Italiana
USSM	Uniunea Societàtilor de Stiinte Medicale
USSPEI	Unions Syndicales des Services Publics Européens et Internationaux
UST	Union des Entreprises Suisses de Transports Publics = VST
UST	Union of Speech Therapists
UST	Union Suisse des Fabricants de Tubes d'Emballage et de Boîtes en Aluminium
USTA	United States Tennis Association
USTA	United States Trademark Association
USTB	Union Syndicale des Travailleurs Burkinabès
USTC	United States Tourist Council
USTD	United States Treasury Department
USTÉL	Union Syndicale du Tréfilage, Étirage et Laminage à Froid de l'Acier
USTI	Unione Stampa Turistica Italiana
USTIL	Syndicat National des Fabricants d'Utensiles Industriels de Laiterie
USTN	Union des Syndicats des Travailleurs du Niger

USTTA	United States Table Tennis Association	UTE	Administración Nacional de las Usinas y Transmisiones Electricas del Estado (Uruguay)
USTTA	United States Travel and Tourism Administration	UTÉ	Union Technique de l'Électricité
USTV	Union Syndicale des Travailleurs Voltaïques	UTE	Universidad Ténica del Estado (Chile)
USU	Upper Silesian Union (Poland) = ZG	UTE	Usinas Electricas los Telefonos del Estado (Uruguay)
USUARIOS	Asociación de Usuarios del Transporte Maritimo, Terrestre y Aereo del Istmo Centroamericano	UTEHA	Unión Tipográfica Editorial Hispano Americana (Mexico)
USUCA	United Steelworkers Union of Central Africa	UTEK	Föreningen Underhållsteknik
USVB	Union Syndicale Vétérinaire Belge	UTET	Unione Tipografioco-Editrice Torinese
USVBA	United States Volley Ball Association	UTEXI	Union Textile de Côte d'Ivoire
USVC	Union Suisse Des Fabricants de Vernis et de Couleurs	UTF	Union des Transporteurs de Ferkessedougou (Ivory Coast)
USWA	United Steelworkers of America	UTG	Union des Travailleurs Guyanais (French Guiana)
USWD	Undersurface Warfare Division	UTGC	Uganda Tea Growers Corporation
USYRU	United States Yacht Racing Union	UTH	Union Touristique et Hôtelière
USYS	Union of Socialist Youth of Slovenia	UTHE	Union des Établissements Thermaux de la Communauté Européenne (Italy)
UT	Conférénce Internationale pour l'Unité Technique des Chemins de Fer = UT	UTI	Union Technique Interprofessionnelle des Fédérations Nationales du Bâtiment et des Travaux Publiques
UT	Union of Youth (Moldova)	UTI	Union Télégraphique Internationale
UT	University of Tasmania	UTI	Union Thérapeutique Internationale = IUT
UTA	Ulster Transport Authority	UTI	Unione Tabacchicoltori Italiani
UTA	Union des Transports Aériens	UTIAS	Institute for Aerospace Studies (Canada)
UTA	Unit Trust Association	UTICA	Union Tunisienne de l'Industrie, du Commerce et de l'Artisanat
UTAC	Union Technique de l'Automobile et du Cycle	UTICI	Union Technique des Ingénieurs Conseils
UTAFRIQ	Union Trading Afrique (Ivory Coast)	UTIFAR	Unione Tecnica Italiana Farmacisti
UTAL	Universidad de los Trabajodores de América Latina (Venezuela)	UTIP	Union Technique Intersyndicale Pharmaceutique
UTB	Union des Travailleurs du Burundi	UTIS	Uganda Technical Information Service
UTB	Union Togalaise de Banque		
UTBA	Unión de Trabajadores Bananeros del Atlántico (Costa Rica)	UTIS	Unione Totoricevitori Italiani Sportivi
UTC	Unión de Trabajadores del Campo (El Salvador)	UTIT	Unión de Trabajadores de la Industria Textil del Distrito Federal y Estado Miranda (Venezuela)
UTC	Union des Torréfacteurs de Café (Belgium) = VVK	UTK	Ustav Technickej Kybernetiky (SAV)
UTC	Unitary Tax Campaign	UTLA	Universidad Tecnica Latinoamericana (El Salvador)
UTCGA	Union Tunisienne de la Confédération Générale de l'Agriculture	UTLS	Union des Travailleurs Libres Sénégalais
UTCPTT	Union Internationale des Organismes Touristiques et Culturels des Postes et des Télécommunications		
UTDA	Ulster Tourist Development Association	UTM	Union des Travailleurs de Mauritanie
UTDC	Urban Transportation Development Corporation (Canada)	UTM	Union Trading Monaco
UTDM	Uniunea Tineretului Democratic Maghiar (Romania) = UHDY	UTM	Universidad Tecnologica del Magdalena (Colombia)

UTMM	Union Technique des Constructeurs de Menuiserie Métallique (Belgium)
UTN	Unit Tenaga Nuklear (Malaysia)
UTO	United Towns Organization = FMCU, FMVJ
UTO	Universal Tourism Organisation
UTOP	United Technological Organisations of the Philippines
UTP	Union des Transports Publics
UTPA	United Turf Producers Association
UTPA	Usine de Traitement de Produits Agricoles (Ivory Coast)
UTPUR	Union des Transports Publics Urbains et Régionaux
UTR	Union des Travailleurs du Rwanda
UTRAC-TEXCO	Unión de Trabajadores Textiles de Colombia
UTRACUN	Unión de Trabajadores de Cundinamarca (Colombia)
UTRADEC	Unión de Trabajadores Estatales de Colombia
UTRAM	Union des Transitaires et Agents Maritimes du Sine' Saloum (Senegal)
UTRAM-MICOL	Union de Trabajadores Metalúrgicos y Mineros de Colombia
UTRAVAL	Unión de Trabajadores del Valle (Colombia)
UTRIN	Ustvedi Technického Rozvoja a Informaci
UTS	Union des Tanneries Suisses
UTS	Union Technique Suisse
UTSMA	United Terminal Sugar Market Association
UTU	Ulster Teachers Union
UTU	Universidad del Trabajo del Uruguay
UTU	Urban Theology Unit
UTUC	United Trades Union Congress (India)
UTW	Union of Textile Workers
UTWA	United Textile Workers of America
UTWB	Union of Turkish Women in Britain
UTZ	Union Nationale des Travailleurs Zaïroises
UUA	Unisys Users Association
UUC	Ulster Unionist Council (Northern Ireland)
UUP	Union of Ukrainians in Poland = ZUP
UUR	Union of Ukrainians in Romania / Uniunea Ucrainienilor din România
UURCS	Union of Ukrainians and Ruthenians in Czechoslovakia = ZURČS
UURWAW	United Union of Roofers, Waterproofers and Allied Workers (U.S.A.)
UUSS	Unione degli Uffici Svizzeri di Statistica = UOSS, VSSA
UV	Union Valenciana
UVA	Unon des Villes Africaines (Senegal) = UAT, UCA
UVAT	Unie van Assurantietussenpersonen
UVATERV	Ut-és Vasúttervezo Vállalat
UVCB	Union des Villes et Communes Belges = VBSG
UVE	Union Végé Européenne
UVF	Ulster Volunteer Force
UVL	Institutet for Vatten-och Luftvard-forskning
UVL	Ungarischer Verband für Logistik = MLBKT, HLA
UVLI	Ustav Vedeckych Lekarskych Informaci
UVM	Union des Villes Méditérranées
UVNC	Ustav pro Vyzkum Vyssi Nervové Cinnosti pri Univerzite Palackého
UVOCAM	Union Voltaïque des Coopératives Agricoles et Maraîchères (Burkina Faso)
UVOH	Union of Voluntary Organisations for the Handicapped (Éire)
UVOS	Ustredni Vybor Odborového Svazu Pracovniku Obchodu
UVOS	Utlandska Vin- och Spritproducenters Ombud i Sverige
UVP	Union des Importateurs de Verre Plat (Switzerland) = VFG
UVP	Ustav pro Vyzkum a Vyuzití Paliv
UVS	Union Voltaïque de Transport
UVSG	Ultra Violet Spectrometry Group
UVTEI	Ustredí Vedeckych, Technickych a Ekonomickych Informaci
UVTP	Union des Usagers de Véhicules de Transport Privé
UWA	University of Western Australia
UWAP	Union of Writers of the African Peoples
UWAVWA	Union of West African Voluntary Workcamps Association (Ghana) = UACVAO
UWB	Universal White Brotherhood; Universelle Weisse Bruderschaft (France) = FBU
UWC	Unemployed Workers' Charter
UWC	United World Colleges International
UWE	University of the West of England

UWE	University Women of Europe = GEFDU
UWÉA	Union Walloune des Écrivains et des Artistes
UWEAMA	Under Water Equipment & Apparel Manufacturers' Association
UWESO	Uganda Women's Effort to Save Orphans
UWH/WCS	Universal World Harmony World Council of Service = HMU/CMS
UWI	University of the West Indies
UWM	United World Mission (U.S.A.)
UWMA	United Women's Muslim Association (Kenya)
UWMAS	United Wallpaper Merchants Association of Scotland
UWP	Unia Własności Pracowniczej
UWP	United Workers Party (St. Lucia)
UWP	Up With People (U.S.A.)
UWRA	Urban Water Research Association
UWRC	Urban Wildlife Research Center (U.S.A.)
UWS	University of Western Sydney
UWT	Union of Tanzania Women
UWT	Union of Women Teachers
UWT	United World Educational and Research Trust
UWT	Urban Wildlife Trust
UWUSA	United Workers' Union of South Africa
UY	Universal Youth = JU
UZD	Umetnostnozdodovinsko Drustvo Slovenije
UZRA	United Zionist Revisionists of America

V

V	Venstre (Denmark)
V&A	Victoria and Albert Museum
VA	Volunteers in Asia (U.S.A)
VAA	Verband angestellter Akademiker der Chemischen Industrie
VAAD	Konfederatsiia Evreiskikh Organizatsii i Obshchin
VAAJ	Veterinary Association for Arbitration and Jurisprudence
VAAM	Vereinigung für Allgemeine und Angewandte Mikrobiologie
VAB	Voluntary Agencies Bureau
VABB	Vereniging van Archivarissen en Bibliothecarissen van België = AABB

VABI	Vereniging voor Automatisering in de Bouw en Installatietechniek
VABMV	Voennaia Akademiia Bronetankovykh i Mekhanizirovannykh Voisk
VABTV	Voennaia Akademiia Bronetankovykh Voisk
VAC	Vente-Achat-Coopération
VAC	Verbond van Nederlandse Fabrikanten van Asbestcementwaren
VACD	Voluntary Associations for Community Development (Canada)
VACO	Vereniging van Bandenspecialisten in Nederland
VAD	Directia Aprovizfionarii si Desfacerii
VAD	Vereingung von Afrikanisten in Deutschland
VADIZO	Vsesoiuznyi Avtomobil'no – Dorozhnyi Institut Zaochnogo Obucheniia
VADZI	Vsesoiuznyi Avtomobil'no – Dorozhnyi Zaochnyi Institut
VAE	Vereingung der Automobil-Experten der Schweiz = FEA
VAEU	Vereinigung der Arbeitgeberverbände Energi-und versorgungswirtschaftlicher Unternehmungen
VAG	Vernacular Architecture Group
VAGA	Visual Arts & Galleries Association (*ex* AGA)
VAGVF	Vsesoiuznaia Akademiia Grazhdanskogo Vozdushnogo Flota
VAGWW	Vereniging Aanemers Grond-, Water-en Wegenbouw
VAHA	Vereniging Fabrieken van Aluminium Huishoudelijke Artikelen
VAHVA	Vahinkovakuutusyhdistys
VAK	Verband der Aufbau-und Geräte-Industrie für Kommunalzwecke
VAKIF-BANK	Türkiye Vakiflar Bankasi
VAKOLA	Valtion Maatalousteknologian Tutkimuslaitos (Finland)
VALCO	Volta Aluminium Co. (Ghana)
VAM	Vereniging voor Algemene Machinehandel
VAMH	Voluntary Association for Mental Health
VAMMR-KKA	Voennaia Akademiia Mekhanizatsii i Motorizafsii Raboche- Krest'ianskoi Krasnoi Armii
VAMZhKh	Vsemirnaia Assotsiatsiia Molodykh Zhenshchin Khristianok

VAN	Vereniging van Archivarissen in Nederland	**VATEVA**	Vaatetuseollisuuden Keskuslitto
VAN	Voluntary Arts Network	**VAV**	Schweizerischer Verband Akademicher Volks-und Betriebwissenschafter = ASE
VAÖ	Verband der Agrarjournalisten in Österreich	**VAV**	Svenska Vatten-och Avloppsverksföreningen
VAÖ	Verband der Akademikerinnen Österreichs	**VAV**	Värjays ja Vlimeistysjaosto = STTL
VAÖ	Verband der Antiquare Österreichs	**VAV**	Vlaamse Architecten Vereniging
VAP	Verband Schweizerischer Anschussgeleise- und Privatgüterwagenbesitzer	**VAVI**	Vereniging voor de Aardappelverwerkende Industrie
VAP	Verein der Ausländischen Presse	**VAVPS**	Vysshii Akademicheskii Voenno Pedagogicheskii Sovet
VAP	Voluntary Assistance Programme (WMO) = PAV	**VAWO**	Vereniging van Academici bij het Wetenschappelijk Onderwijs
VAPI	Vereniging der Apotekers van de Pharmaceutische Industrie (Belgium) = UPIP	**VBA**	Coöperatieve Vereniging Verenigde Bloemen veilingen Aalsmeer
VAPM	Vserossiiskaia Assotsiatsiia Proletarskikh Muzykantov	**VBA**	Verband der Berguns-und Abschleppunternehmen Deutschlands
VAPP	Vserossiiskaia Assotsiatsiia Proletarskikh Pisatelei	**VBA**	Vereniging der Belgische Aannemers van Werken van Burgerlijke Bouwkunde (Belgium) = ADEB
VAPS	Vysshii Akademicheskii Voenno-pedagogicheskii Soviet	**VBAM**	Vereniging der Belgische Aannemers van Montagewerk
VAR	Vereniging voor Administratief Recht	**VBB**	Vattenbyggnadsbyran
VAR	Vereniging voor Agrarisch Recht	**VBB**	Veenkoloniale Boerenbond
VARA	Vereniging voor Arbeiders Radio-Amateurs	**VBB**	Verein der Bibliothekare an Öffentlichen Bibliotheken
VARIG	Viação Aéreo Rio Grandense (Brazil)	**VBBA**	Vietnam-British Business Association
VARIM	Vattenreningsgruppen inom Sveriges Mekanförbund	**VbBV**	Verband Beratender Betriebs- und Volkswirte, Wirtschaftsjuristen und Sachverstandiger
VARME-FORSK	Stiftelsen för Värmeteknisk Forskning	**VBC**	Vereningen Bedrijfsleven Curacao
VARS	Visual Artists Rights Society	**VBD**	Versuchanstalt für Binnenschiffbau e. V. – Forschungsinstitut für Flachwasserhydrodynamik
VAS	Vasectomy Advancement Society of Great Britain	**VBE**	Nederlandse Vereniging van Boseigenaren
VAS	Verband der Auslandsbanken in der Schweiz	**VBE**	Verband Bildung und Erziehung
VASAMF	Vsemirnyi Antisionistskii Antimasonskii Front "Pamiat"	**VBEFA**	Vehicle Builders Employees' Federation of Australia
VASCA	Electronic Valve and Semi-Conductor Manufacturers Association	**VBF**	Vinegar Brewers Federation
VASF	Verband der Angestelten des Schweizer Fernsehens	**VBI**	Verband der Beleuchtungs-Industrie (Switzerland)
VASKhNIL	Vsesoiuznoe Ordena Lenina i Ordena Trudovogo Krasnogo Znameni Akademiia Selskokhoziaistvennykh Nauk Imeni V. I. Lenina	**VBI**	Verein Beratender Ingenieure
		VBI	Vereniging van Blikverwekende Industrieën
VASP	Viação Aéreo São Paulo (Brazil)	**VBIÖ**	Verband Beratender Ingenieure Österreichs
VATE	Victorian Association for the Teaching of English (Australia)	**VBK**	Verband der Deutschen Bodenbelags-, Kunststoff- Folien- und Beschichtungs-Industrie

VBK	Verwertungsgesellschaft Bild-Künst (Germany)	**VBT**	Vetenskapliga Bibliotekens Tjänstemannaforening
VBK	Verwertungsgesellschaft Bildender-Künstler (Austria)	**VbU**	Verband Bergbaulicher Unternehmen und Bergbauverwandter Organisationen
VBKD	Verband Bildender Künstler Deutschlands	**VBV**	Vereinigung Beratender Betriebs-und Volkswirte
VBKKB	Verbond der Belgische Kamers van Koophandel in het Buitenland = FCCBE	**VBV**	Vereniging Band-, Vlecht- en Kantindustrie
VBLA	Verband der Arbeitnehmer in Handels-, Transport-und Lebensmittelbetrieben der Schweiz	**VBV**	Vereniging voor Bedrijfsvoorlichting
		VBVB	Vereniging ter Bevordering van het Vlaamse Boekwezen
VBLA	Verband der Christlichen Angestellten der Schweiz	**VBW**	Vereniging voor Bitumineuze Werken
VBLJ	Vereniging van Belgische Landbouw-Journalisten	**VBZ**	Verband der Lieferanten für Brandschutz, Zivilschutz und Erste Hilfe
VBMWG	Vereniging van de Belgische Medische Wetenschappelijke = ASSMB	**VBZV**	Verband der Bayerischer Zeitungsverleger
VBN	Verbond der Belgische Nijverheid	**VC**	Vereinigung Cockpit e.V.
VBN	Vereniging van Bedrijfsredacteuren in Nederland	**VC&GCA**	Victoria Cross and George Cross Association
VBN	Vereniging van Betonmortelfabrikanten in Nederland	**VCA**	Vehicle Certification Agency
		VCAA	Veteran and Classic Aeroplane Association
VBN	Vereniging van Boeren en Pluimveefokbedrijven in Nederland	**VCB**	Verband Deutscher Betriebswirte
VBN	Vereniging voor Bedrijfsrestaurateurs in Nederland	**VCC**	Veteran Car Club of Great Britain
		VCG	Vereniging tot Behartiging v. d. Belangen v. Coöperatieve Grasdrogerijen
VBNA	Vereniging ter Behartiging van den Nederlandschen Aardappelhandel		
VBNN	Society for Nature Conservation in the Netherlands	**VCH**	Verband Christlicher Hospize
		VCI	Variety Clubs International (U.S.A.)
VBÖ	Verband der Baustoffhändler Österreichs	**VCI**	Verband der Chemischen Industrie
VBO	Verbond van Belgische Ondeernemingen = FEB	**VCIOM**	National Public Opinion Research Centre (Russia)
VBO	Vereinigung für Bankbetriebsorganisation	**VCL**	Vereinigung Christlicher Leher an den Höheren Schulen Österreichs
VBO	Vereniging Belge des Omnipraticiens = GBO	**VCM**	Vereniging van Coöperative Melkinrichtingen
VBP	Verband Bayerischer Papierfabriken	**VCMA**	Vacuum Cleaner Manufacturers Association (U.S.A.)
VBP	Vlaamse Bond van Postzegelverzamelaars		
VBRA	Vehicle Builders and Repairers Association	**VCN**	New Communist Party of the Netherlands
VBS	Verbond der Belgische Beroepsverenigingen van Geneesheren-Specialisten = GBS	**VCN**	Vereniging van Classici in Nederland
		VCOAD	Voluntary Committee on Overseas Aid and Development
VBS	Verein der Buchbindereien der Schweiz = FSR	**VCP**	Vêtements et Chemiserie de Paris (Ivory Coast)
VBS	Vereniging van Blauwe Steen	**VCP**	Voluntary Cooperation Program (WMO)
VBSG	Vereniging van Belgische Steden en Gemeenten = UVCB	**VCPA**	Vintage & Classic Power Craft Association
		VCPLA	Veterinary College of the People's Liberation Army of China

VCPS	Video Copywright Protection Society		**VDCh**	Verein Deutscher Chemiker
VCRA	Veterans Cycle Racing Association		**VDD**	Berufsverband Dokumentation Information Kommunikation
VCRS	Verband Chemischer Reingungsanstalten der Schweiz		**VDD**	Industrieverband Bitumen- Dach-und Dichtungsbahnen
VCS	Voluntary and Christian Service		**VDD**	Verband der Datenverarbeiter
VCSA	Vintage & Classic Sailing Association		**VDD**	Verband Deutscher Drogisten
VCT	Vintage Carriages Trust		**VDD**	Vereinigung der Drahtflechterein
VCTA	Victorian Commercial Teachers Association (Australia)		**VdDB**	Verein der Diplom-Bibliothekare an Wissenschaftlichen Bibliotheken
VCTV	Verbond der Coöperatieve Tuinbouwveilingen		**VDDF**	Verein Deutscher Düger-Fabrikanten
VCU	Vereinigung Christlicher Unternehmer der Schweiz		**VDDI**	Verband der Deutschen Dental-Industrie
VCU	Vereniging van Christelijke Uitgevers		**VddI**	Verband der Deutschen Ingenieurwissenschaftler
VCUÖ	Verband Christlicher Unternehmer Österreichs		**VDDI**	Verband Deutscher Diplom-Ingenieure
VCV	Vlaamse Chemische Vereniging (Belgium)		**VDDS**	Vereinigung Diplomieter Kaufleute des Detailhandels der Schweiz
VCW	Vereniging van Constructiewerkplaatsen		**VDDW**	Verband der Deutschen Wasserzählerindustrie
VCW	Vereniging van Werkgevers in de Chemische Wasserijen en Ververijen		**VDE**	Verband Deutscher Elektrotechniker
VD	Veeartsenijkundige Dienst		**VDEfa**	Verein Deutscher Emailfachleute
VDA	Schweizerischer Verband Diplomieter Arztegehilfinnen		**VDEh**	Verein Deutscher Eisenhüttenleute
VDA	Verband der Automobilindustrie		**VDEI**	Verband Deutscher Eisenbahn-Ingenieure
VDA	Verband Deutscher Agrarjournalisten		**VDEL**	Verband Deutsche Esperanto-Lehrer
VDA	Verband Deutscher Antiquare		**VDEN**	Vereniging van Directeuren van Electriciteitsbedrijven in Nederland
VDA	Verband Deutscher Architekten		**VDEW**	Vereinigung Deutscher Elektrizitätswerke
VdA	Verein Deutscher Archivare		**VDF**	Verband der Deutschen Fassgrosshandels
VDAI	Verband der Deutschen Automatenindustrie		**VDF**	Verband der Deutshcen Faserplattenindustrie und verwandter Betriebe
VdB	Verband der Bautenschutzmittel-Industrie		**VDF**	Verband Deutschen Fruchtsaft-Industrie
VdB	Verband der Druchfarbenindustrie		**VDF**	Verband Deutscher Feuerverzinkerein
VDB	Verband Deutscher Badebetriebe		**VDF**	Verband Deutscher Flugleiter
VDB	Verband Deutscher Bestattungsunternehmen e.V.		**VDF**	Verein Deutscher Färber
VDB	Verband Deutscher Biologen		**VDF**	Volunteer Defence Force (St. Christopher and Nevis)
VDB	Verein Deutscher Bibliothekare		**VDFP**	Village Developoment Fund Project (Mali)
VDB	Verein Deutscher Buchbinderein für Verlag und Industrie		**VDG**	Verein Deutscher Giessereifachleute
VDBeV	Verband Deutscher Badeärtze e.V.		**VDG**	Vereinigung Deutscher Gewässerschutz
VDBF	Verband der Briefumschlag-und Papierausstattungs-Fabriken		**VdGS**	Viola da Gamba Society
VDBI	Verband der Deutschen Bestattungswäsche-Industrie		**VdGV**	Verband Deutschschweizerischer Gartenbauvereine
VdBNW	Verband der Bibliotheken des Lander Nordrhein-Westfalen		**VDH**	Verband Deutscher Häutehändler
VDC	Verband Deutscher Fachschulchemiker		**VDH**	Verband Deutscher Heilbrunnen

VDH	Verein Deutscher Holzeinfuhrhäuser		**VDM**	Verband Deutscher Marktforscher
VDH	Vereinigung Deutscher Harfenisten e.V.		**VDM**	Verband Deutscher Meteorologen
VDI	Verband der Importeure van Kraftfahrzeugen		**VDM**	Verband Deutscher Mineralbrunnen
VDI	Verein Deutscher Ingenieure		**VdM**	Verband Deutscher Motorjournalisten
VDI-GET	Verein Deutscher Ingenieure Gesellschaft Energietechnik		**VdM**	Verband Deutscher Musikschulen
VDI-TGA	Verein Deutscher Ingenieure-Gesellschaft Technische Gebäudeausrüstung		**VDMA**	Verband Deutscher Maschinen- und Anlagenbau e.V.
VDID	Verband Deutscher Industrie-Designer		**VDMA**	Verein Deutscher Machinebauanstalten
VDIG	Vereinigung Deutsch-Italienischer Gesellschaften		**VDMK**	Gewerkschaft der Musikerzieher und Konzertierender Künstler
VDIK	Verband der Importeure von Kraftfahrzeugen		**VDN**	Verband Deutscher Nähmaschinehändler
VDK	Verband des Draftfahrzeughandels		**VDNA**	Verband Deutscher Naturfoscher und Ärzte
VDK	Verband Deutsche Künstler		**VDO**	Vereinigung Deutscher Ordensoberen
VDK	Verband Deutscher Dokumentar-und Kurzfilmproduczenten		**VDP**	Bundesverband Deutscher Privatschulen
VDKC	Verband Deutscher Konzertchöre e.V.		**VDP**	Gruppe der Zellbast-und Konsumpackpapier-Hersteller
VDKF	Verband Deutscher Kälte-Klima-Fachleute		**VDP**	Verband der Deutschen Parkett-Industrie
VDKF	Verband Deutscher Kur-und Fremdenverkehrsfachbetriebe		**VDP**	Verband Deutscher Papierfabriken
VDKM	Vytauto Didziojo karo muziejus		**VDP**	Verband Deutscher Pradikätsweingüter
VDKS	Verband Deutscher Kapitäne und Schiffsoffziere		**VDP**	Verenigde Democratische Partijen (Suriname)
VDL	Verband der Deutschen Lokomotivindustrie		**VDP**	Vereniging van Personeelsdirekteurs = ADP (*ex* CDSP)
VdL	Verband der Lackindustrie		**VDPD**	Vereinigung der Directeurs van Personeeldiensten (Belgium) = CDSP
VDL	Verband Deutscher Akademiker für Landwirtschaft, Ernährung und Landespflege		**VDPh**	Verband Deutscher Physiotherapeuten
VDL	Verband Deutscher Diplomandwirte		**VDPI**	Verband der Deutschen Photographischen Industrie
VDL	Verband Deutscher Luftfahrttechniker		**VDPI**	Verband Deutscher Post-Ingenieure
VDL	Vereinigung Deutscher Landesschafzuchtverbände		**VdPÖ**	Verband der Professoren Österreichs
VDL	Vereniging van Fabrikanten en Importeurs van Direct Gestookte Luchtverwarmers		**VDPW**	Verband der Patentwirtschaftler = ANCOPI, LITCA
VDLU	Verband Deutscher Luftfahrt-Unternehmen		**VDR**	Verband Deutscher Realschullehrer
			VDR	Verband Deutscher Reeder
VDLUFA	Verband Deutscher Landwirtschaftlicher Untersuchungs- und Forschungsanstalten		**VDRG**	Verband Deutscher Rundfunk- und Fernseh-Fachgrosshändler
			VDRI	Verein Deutscher Revisions-Ingenieure
VDM	Verband der Deutschen Milchwirtschaft		**VDRJ**	Vereinigung Deutscher Reisejournalisten
VDM	Verband der Deutschen Möbelindustrie		**VDRZ**	Verband Deutscher Rechenzentren
VdM	Verband der Mineralfarbenindustrie		**VDS**	Verband Deutscher Schiffswerften
VdM	Verband der Motorjournalisten e.V.		**VDS**	Verband Deutscher Schirmfachgeschäfte
VDM	Verband Deutscher Makler für Grundbesitz und Finanzierungen		**VDS**	Verband Deutscher Schulmusikerzieher
			VDS	Verband Deutscher Sonderschulen e.V. – Fachverband für Behindertenpädogogik

VDS	Verband Deutscher Studienschaften	**VE**	Vereinigle Energiewerke
VDS	Vereinigung Deutscher Sägewerksverbände	**VEA**	Nederlandse Vereniging voor Erkende Adverteniebureaux
VDS	Vereinigung von Verbänden der Deutschen Sanitärwirtschaft	**VEA**	Valve Engineering Association
		VEA	Verband der Energie-Abnehmer
VDSB	Verein Deutschschweizerischer Bienenfreunde	**VEA**	Vereinigung von Fabriken Elektrothermischer Apparate (Switzerland)
VDSG	Verband Deutscher Schulgeographen e.V.		
		VEA	Vereniging der Experten in Automobielen
VDSI	Verein Deutscher Sicherheitsingenieure	**VEAWI**	Vereinigung der Europäischen Aluminiumwaren-Industrie (France) = EAHMA, FEAMA
VDSM	Internationaler Verband der Stadt-Sport- und Mehrzweckhallen		
VDSS	Verband Deutscher Schiffahrtssachverständiger	**VEB**	Vereinigung Evangelischer Bucherein
		VEB	Vereniging der Electriciteitbedrijven België = UEEB
VDSt	Verband Deutscher Städtestatistiker		
VDst	Verband Deutscher Stahlwarenhändler	**VEB**	Vereniging Effectenbescherming
VDT	Verband des Deutschen Tischlerhandwerks	**VEBI**	Vereniging voor de Verbruiker en de Beroepsmensen van de Informatie Verwerking in België = ASAB
VDT	Verband Deutscher Tapetenfabrikanten		
VDT	Verband Deutscher Techniker		
VDTL	Verband Deutscher Tauchlehrer e.V.	**VEBIDAK**	Vereniging van Bitumineuze Dakbedekkingsbedrijven
VdTUV	Vereinigung der Technischen Überwachungs-Vereine	**VEBO**	Vereniging voor Brouwerij Onderzoek en Onderwijs
VDU	Verband der Deutschen Uhrenindustrie		
VDÜ	Verband Deutschsprachiger Übersetzer Literarischer und Wissenschaftlicher Werke	**VEBUKU**	Vereinigung der Buchantiquare and Kupferstichhändler der Schweiz
		VEBV	Verband Evangelischer Buchhandlungen und Verlage der Schweiz
VDU	Vytauto Didziojo Universitetas		
VDV	Verband der Versandgeschäfte	**VECE**	Coöperative Verkoopcentrale voor Eieren
VDV	Verband Deutscher Vermessungs-ingenieure		
		VECO	Vereniging van op Coöperatieve Grondslag werkende Afzetorganisaties voor Zaaizaad en Pootgoed
VDVM	Verein Deutscher Versicherungsmakler		
VdW	Verband der Wagonindustrie		
VDW	Verband der Wellpappen-Industrie	**VECOL**	Empresa Colombiana de Productos Veterinarios
VdW	Verband Deutschen Fruchtwein-und Fruchtschaumwein-Industrie	**VECOR**	Vanderbijl Engineering Corporation (South Africa)
VDW	Verband Deutscher Weinexporteure		
VDW	Verband Deutscher Werkzeugmaschinenfabriken	**VECTA**	Vereniging van Ondernemers van Concertbureaux
VDWW	Vereinigung Deutscher Werks-und Wirtschaftsarchivare	**VECTU**	Svenska Vechopressens Tidningustgivareförening
VDZ	Verband des Deutscher Zweiradhandels	**VED**	Verband der Exhibition-Designer
VDZ	Verband Deutscher Zeitschriftenverleger	**VED**	Verkerks- und Energiewirtschaftsdepartement (Switzerland)
VDZ	Verein Deutscher Zeitschriftenverleger		
VDZ	Verein Deutscher Zementwerke		
VDZ	Verein Deutscher Zuckertechniker	**VEDAG**	Verband Deutschschweizerischer Ärtegesellschaften
VdZ	Vereinigung von Verbänden der Deutschen Zentralheizungswirtschaft		
		VEDC	Victorian Economic Development Corporation (Australia)
VDZI	Verband Deutscher Zahntechniker-Innungen Bunderinnungsverband	**VEDC**	Vitreous Enamel Development Council

VEDEWA	Vereinigung der Wasserversorgungsverbände und Gemeinden mit Wasserwerken
VEEN	Vereniging van Exploitanten van Electriciteitsbedrijven in Nederland
VEF	Vereniging van Emaillefabrieken
VEG	Bundesverband des Elektro-Grosshandels
VEG	Verband Österreichischer Elektro-Grossändler
VEG	Vereniging van Exploitanten van Gasbedrijven
VEGA	Vegetable Growing Association of America
VEGA	Vegetarian Economy and Green Agriculture
VEGAT	Verband Schweizerischer Garn-und Tricotveredler
VEGIN	Vereniging van Exploitanten van Gasbedrijven in Nederland
VEGRO-COS	Nederlandse Vereniging van Groothandelaren in Cosmetica en Parfumerieën
VEGROS	Vereniging Groothandel Goud, Zilver, Uurwerken en Aanverwante Artikelen
VEHAVLAS	Vereniging der Handelaars in Vlasvezels
VEIB	Vereniging van Electotechnische Installatiebedrijven
VEICB	Vereniging der Electrische Industriële Centrales van België
VEIMMAVO	Vereniging van Importeurs van en Handelaren in Machines voor de Zuivel-Dranken-Voedings- en Genot-middelenindustrie
VEK	Veterana Esperentista Klubo (Germany)
VELA	Vereinigung Leitender Angestellten
VELEBI	Vereniging van Leraren in de Biologie
VELEDES	Schweizerischer Verband der Lebensmittel-Detaillisten
VELF	Verwaltung für Ernährung, Landwirtschaft und Forsten
VELINES	Vereniging van Leraren in Natuur- en Scheikunde
VELKD	Vereinigte Evangelisch-Lutherische Kirche Deutschlands
VEMI	Vereniging van Importeurs en Fabrikanten van en Groothandelaren in Melkwinning- en Bewaarapparatuur
VEMI	Vereniging van Muziekinsturmenthandelaren
VENALUM	Venezolana de Aluminio
VENCER-AMICA	Venezolana de Ceramicas
VENE-AGRO	Sociedad Venezolana de Exportaciones Agricolas
VENEDAK	Vereniging van Nederlandse Dakrolfabrikanten
VENEFAB	Vereniging van Nederlandse Fabrikanten van Bestrijdingsmiddelen
VENEPAL	Venezolana du Pulpa y Papel
VENESO	Organisations Voie Européenne Nord-Est/Sud-Ouest
VENEXA	Vereniging van Nederlandse Exporteurs van Aardappelen
VENG	Vereinigung zur Erforschung der Neueren Geschichte e.V.
VENO	Verbond Algemene Exporthandel
VENO	Verbond van Exporterende Nederlandse Ondernemingen
VEÖ	Verband der Elektrizitätswerke Österreichisches
VEO	Vsesoiuznoe Entomologischeskoe Obshchestvo pri Akademie Nauk
VEPAVE	Vereniging van Papierverwerkers
VERAS	Vereinigung Schweizerischer Asphaltunternehmungen
VERBISKO	Vereniging van Fabrikanten van Banket, Beschuit, Biscuit, Koek en Aanverwante Produkten
VERE-MABEL	Groupement Belge des Vendeurs-Réparateurs de Tracteurs et Machines Agricoles
VERI	Vineyard Environmental Research Institute (U.S.A.)
VERINVI	Vereniging van Vis Invoerders
VERNOF	Vereniging van Nederlandse Fabrikanten van Eetbare Oliën en Vetten
VERTGLAS	Genossenschaft der Schweizerischen Glasgrosshändler
VERTIC	Verification Technology Information Centre
VERTRIKO	Vereniging van Tricot- en Kousenfabrikanten
VERVOEX	Vereniging van Oesterwekers en Exporteurs
VES	Voluntary Emergency Service
VES	Voluntary Euthanasia Society
VESA	Verband des Europäischen Sozialen Apoteken = EUSA, EUSMCP, EUSP, UEFS, UEPS
VESEIGA	Verband Schweizerischer Seidengarnfarbereien

VESKA	Verband Schweizerischer Krankenanstalten	**VFGI**	Verband der Schweizerischen Fabrikanten, Grossisten und Importeurs der
VESKOF	Vereinigung Schweizerischer Kontrollfirmen für Sämereien	**VFHA**	Vanuatu Family Health Association
VESLIC	Association of Swiss Leather Chemists and Technologists	**VFI**	Verband der Schweizerischen Industrie Flexibler Verpackung
VESTRA	Verband Schweizerischer Unternehmungen für Strassenbeläge	**VFI**	Verkfrædingafélag Islands
		VFI	Vintners' Federation of Ireland
VESW	Vereniging van Experts op Scheeps- en Werktuigkundig gebied in Nederland	**VfK**	Verein freiberuflicher Krankenpflege
		VFK	Verein zur Förderung Moderner Kunst e.V.
VETER-MON	Veterinarios Sin Fronteras	**VfK**	Vereinigung für Kristallographie in der Gesellschaft für Geologische Wissenschaften
VETOMAG	Vetomagtermeitetö és Értékesitö Vällalat		
VETRUNI-ONE	Union Nazionale Trasformatori e Distributori Vetro Piano	**VFK**	Vereniging van Fourage-en Kunstmesthandelaren
VETSALL	Veterinarians Alliance	**VFK**	Vereniging van Nederlandse Fabrieken van Ketels, Drukhouders en Tanks
VEV	Vereniging ter Bevordering van de Export van Vleeswaren Vleesconserven	**VfLA**	Verein für Leitende Angestellte
VEV	Vlaams Economische Verbond	**VFM**	Verband der Fahrrad-und Motorradindustrie
VEW	Vereinigte Elektrizitatswerke Westfalen		
VEWIN	Vereniging van Exploitanten van Waterleidingsbedrijven in Nederland	**VFMA**	Verband der Führungskräfte der Metall- und Electroindustrie
VF	Sveriges Verkstadsförening	**VFMG**	Vereinigung der Freunde der Mineralogie und Geologie
VF	Vestlandske Fartybyggjarlag		
VFA	Vereinigung Freischaffender Architekten Deutschlands	**VFN**	Vereniging van Financieringsondernemingen in Nederland
VFB	Vacances Franco-Brittaniques		
VFB	Vereniging van Fabrikanten van Bakkerij-Installaties	**VFO**	Vereniging Fabrieks leveranciers Oudpapier
VFDB	Vereinigung zur Föderung des Deutschen Brandschutzes	**VFP**	Verband der Fellgrossisten und Pelzkonfektionäre
VFDM	Vsemirnaia Federatsiia Demokraticheskoy Molodezhi = FMJD, WBDJ, WFDY	**VFP**	Vereenigde Feministische Partij (Belgium)
		VFP	Vereinigung für Finanzpolitik (Switzerland)
VFF	Verband der Fenster-und Fassadenhersteller	**VFP**	Vsemirnaia Federatsiia Profsoiuzov = FSM, WFTU, WGB
VFFS	Schweizerischer Verband der Freiberuflichen Fahrzeugsachverständigen	**VFR**	Verband der Radio Fernsch-und Elektro-Fachhandels Österreichs
VFG	Verband der Flachgasimporteure (Switzerland) = UVP	**VFRC**	Valley Forge Research Center (U.S.A.)
VFG	Verein zur Föderung der Forschung für die Graphischen Gewerbe und die Verwandten Wirschaftszweige (Austria)	**VfrK**	Verband der früheren Kaftoffelbrennereien und Sonstigen Eigenbrennereien Ost-und Mitteldeutschlands
VFG	Verein zur Föderung der Giesserei-Industrie	**VfS**	Gesellschaft für Wirtschafts- und Sozialwissenschaften – Verein für Socialpolitik
VFG	Versuchanstalt für Getreideverwertung	**VfV**	Verein für Volkskunde
VFGI	Verband der Flachglasimporteure	**VFVP**	Vietnam Friendship Village Project

VFW	Vereinigte Flugtechnische Werke	**VGN**	Vereniging van Gasfabrikanten in Nederland
VFWL	Verein zur Förderung der Wasser-und Lufthygiene (Switzerland) = ASHEA, ASIAA	**VGN**	Vereniging van Geschiedensleraren in Nederland
VFWU	Verband Freier Wohnungsunternehmen	**VGÖ**	Vereinigte Grünen Österreich
VGA	Verein für Geschichte der Arbeiterbewegung	**VGRO**	Vereniging van Grafische Reproductie Ondernemingen
VGAAD	Vereniging van Grootwinkelbedrijven in Alcoholhoudende en AlcoholvrijeI Dranken	**VGS**	Verband Schweizerischer Gärtnermeister
VGAS	Verband Galvanischer Anstalten der Schweiz	**VGS**	Vereniging van Gespecialiseerde Schoolleveranciers
VGB	Technische Vereinigung der Grosskraftwerks-betreiber	**VGS**	Volksgesundheit Schweiz
VGB	Vereinigung der Grosskraftwerksbetreiber	**VGSB**	Vereniging van Grootwinkelbedrijven in Speciale Branches
VGB	Vereniging van Groothandelaren in Brandstoffen	**VGSW**	Verein für Geschichte der Stadt Wien (Austria)
VGC	Vintage Glider Club of Great Britain	**VGT**	Nederlandse Vereniging van Groothandelaren in Tandheelkundige Benodigdheden
VGCT	Verein für Gerberei-Chemie und-Technik		
VGD	Verband der Geschichtslehrer Deutschlands	**VGT**	Verband des Garagen-und Tankstellengewerbes
VGD	Verband Gewerbetreibender des Direktvertriebs im Medienbereich zur Wahrung und Förderung ihrer Berufsinteressen	**VGT**	Vereniging Gasturbine
		VGV	Vereniging van Gespecialiseerde Vloerenbedrijven
VGD	Vereniging van de Grote Distributieondernemingen van België	**VGW**	Verband der Deutschen Gas- und Wasserwerke
VGG	Verband der Hersteller von Gewerblichen Geschirrspülmaschinen	**VGW**	Verening van Groothandelaren Woningtextiel
VGHM	Vereniging voor de Groothandel in Huishoudelijke Artikelen en Metaalwaren	**VH**	Versuchsanstalt der Hefeindustrie
		VHA	Vision Homes Association
VGIFUW	Virginia Gildersleeve International Fund for University Women (IFUW)	**VHB**	Verband der Hersteller von Bauelementen für wärmetechnische Anlagen
VGIG	Vereniging voor de Groothandel in Gasverwarmings- en Verbruikstoestellen en Andere Verwarmingstoestellen	**VHF**	Veterinaeærhygienisk Forening
		VHI	Verband der Deutschen Holzewerkstoff-Industrie
VGKL	Verband des Deutschen Gross-und Aussenhandels für Krankenpflege und Laborbedarf	**VHI**	Voluntary Health Insurance Board (Éire)
		VHK	Verband der Hersteller von Konditoreihilfstoffen
VGL	Schweizerische Vereinigung für Gewésserschutz and Lufthygiene	**VHN**	Vereniging van Houtimpregneerinrichtingen in Nederland
VGM	Verband Gross-Städtischer Milchversorgungsbetriebe		
VGN	Verein für Geschichte der Stadt Nürnberg	**VHOB**	Vereinigung Höherer Ordensoberen der Brüderorden und Kongregationen Deutschlands
VGN	Vereniging Gereedschapsfabrieken in Nederland		
		VHOD	Vereinigung Höherer Ordensoberinnen Deutschlands
VGN	Vereniging van Docenten in Geschiedenis en Staatsriching in Nederland	**VHOK**	Vereniging van Handelaren in Oude Kunst in Nederland
		VHP	Nederlandse Vereniging voor de Handel in Pluimvee en Wild

VHP	Vereinigung der Höheren Beamten der Deutschen Bundespost	**VIDC**	Vienna Institute for Development and Cooperation
VHP	Vishawa Hindu Parishad	**VIDEA**	Victoria International Development Association (Canada)
VHP	Vooruitstrevende Hervormings Partij (Suriname)	**VIDES**	Volontariat International Femmes Éducation Développement (Belgium)
VHPI	Verband der Schweizerishcen Holzverpackungs-und Palettenindustrie	**VIDO**	Veterinary Infectious Disease Organisation (Canada)
VHPZ	Vereniging Hoger Personeel Zuivelindustrie	**VIDRA**	Institutul de Cercetari pentru Legumicultura si Floricultura
VHR	Vereniging voor de Handel in Rubberartikelen	**VIE**	Victorian Institute of Engineers (Australia)
VHS	Vereniging Fabrieken van Hang- en Sluitwerk	**VIEB**	Verband der Internationalen und Europäischen Beamtem = BIEA, SFE, UIECS
VHV	Vereinigung der Holzhandelsverbände	**Vienna Centre**	European Coordination Centre for Research and Documentation in Social Sciences = Centre de Vienne
VHVH	Nederlandse Vereniging van Handelaren in Verwarmings- en Huishoudijke Apparaten Apparaten		
VHVP	Nederlandse Verniging voor de Handel en Verwerking van Pluimvee, Wild en Tamme Konijnen	**VIEW**	Visually Impaired Empowering Women (New Zealand)
		VIF	Svenska Värmeisolermaterial-fabrikanterna
VHW	Verband Hochschule und Wissenschaft im Deutschen Beamtembund	**VIF**	Verband von Importeuren der Fisch-und Fischproduktenbranche
VHZ	Vereniging voor de Handel in Landbouwzaaizaden	**VIF**	Verkstadindustrins Internordiska Forskningskommitté
VHZMK	Vereinigung der Hochschullehrer für Zahn-, Mund- und Kieferheilkunde	**VIF**	Voix de l'Informatique Francophone
VHZV	Verband Hessischer Zeitungsverleger	**VIFKA**	Vereniging van Importeurs en Fabrikanten van Kantoormachines
VIA	Internationale Vereinigung des Tapetenhandels	**VIFPA**	Virgin Islands Family Planning Association
VIA	Variety Initiatives for Disabled Access	**VIGPA**	Nederlandse Vereniging van Importeurs van en Groothandelaren in Glas, Porcelan en Aardewerk
VIA	Videotex Industry Association		
VIAR	Volcani Institute of Agricultural Research (Israel)	**VIIIa**	Military Institute of Foreign Languages (Russia)
VIASA	Sociedad Venezolana Internacional de Aviación, S.A.	**VIIR**	Vlaamse Interuniversitaire Raad (Belgium)
VIB	Nederlandse Vereniging in het Isolatiebedrijf	**VIK**	Vereinigung Deutscher Kraftwirtschaft
VIB	Vereniging van Importeurs van Bouwmaterialen	**VIK**	Vereinigung Schweizerischer Industrieller Kartonverabeiter
VIB	Voedselvoorzienings in en Verkoopbureau	**VILF**	Verband der Ingenieure des Lack- und Farbenfaches
VIBÖ	Vereinigung Industrieller Bauunternehmungen Österreichs	**VILLA**	Ventes Immobilières de Logement et de Lotissements en Afrique (Congo)
VICA	Vocational Industrial Clubs of America	**VILS**	Verband Schweizerischer Industrielleferanten für Schrott
VICOM	International Association of Visual Communications Management		
VICORP	Virgin Islands Corporation	**VIMAG**	Vereniging van Importeurs van Machinegereedschappen voor de Metaalbewerking
VID	Vereniging van Ingenieurs van Defensie		
VIDA	Victorian Institute for Dryland Agriculture (Australia)	**VIMETAAL**	Vereniging van Importeurs van Gereedschapswerktuigen

VIMHOUT	Vereniging van Importeurs van en Handelaren
VIMKO	Vereniging van Importeurs van Koelmachines en Koelkasten
VIMPO-STAAL	Vereniging van Handelaren in Speciaalstaal
VIMPOL	Vereniging van Importeurs van Landbouwwerktuigen
VIMPOLTU	Vereniging van Importeurs van en Groothandelaren in Land- en Tuinbouwmachines
VIMTU	Vereniging van Importeurs van Tuinbouwwerktguigen
VINACON-TROL	Vietnam National Export-Import Goods Control Company
VINAFPA	Vietnam Family Planning Association
VIP	Verein der Industriefilmproduzenten
VIP	Vereniging Importeurs Pneumastische Werktuigen
VIPEP	Asociación de Vivienda Propia del Empleado Publico (Peru)
VIPOSA	Viviendas Populares S.A. (El Salvador)
VIPS	Verband der Industriepatentandwälten der Schweiz = ACBIS
VIPS	Vereinigung der Importeure Pharmazeutischer Spezialtäten (Switzerland)
VIR	Vereniging Informatie en Recherche-Bureauhouders
VIRA	Vereniging voor Internationale Relaties
VIRI	Voice and/or Vision of the Islamic Republic of Iran
VIRO	Netherlands United Nations Association
VIRO	Vereniging van Internationale Rechtsorde
VIRO	Vlaams Instituut voor Ruimtelijke Ordening
VIS	Veterinary Investigation Service
VIS	Volontariato Internazionale per lo Sviluppo
VISACAM	Société des Viandes et Salaisons du Caméroun
Visfederatie	Federatie van Organisaties op het Gebied van de Groothandel en Be- en Verwerking van Vis
VITA	Volunteers for International Technical Assistance (U.S.A.)
VITAR	Veterinary Institute for Tropical and High Altitude Research (Peru)
VITIAZ	"Vitiaz" – Molodezhnyi Pravoslavnyi Monarkhicheskii Kapitul
VITM	Party for National Unity
VITUKI	Vízgazdálkodási Tudományos Kutatóközpont
VIV	Food Import Bureau (Holland)
VIV	Verband Industrieverbundener Versicherungs- Vermittler
VIV	Verband Schweizer Vieh-Importeure
VIV	Vereniging van Importeurs van Verbrandingsmortoren
VIWF	Koninklijk Verbond van de Industrie van Waters en Frisdranken (Belgium) = FIEB
VKaL	Verein Katholischer Deutscher Lehrerinnen
VKB	Verband Katholischer Verleger-und Buchhändler
VKD	Verband der Köche Deutschlands
VKE	Verband Kuntstofferzeugende Industrie und Verwandt Gebiete
VKF	Vereinigung Kantonaler Feuerversicherungen
VKF	Vereinigung Schweizerischer Kabel-Fabriken
VKF	Vereniging van Kartonnagefabrikanten in Nederland
VKFA	Vereinigung Kantonaler Feuerversicherungsanstalten
VKG	Verband der Kraftfahrzeugteile-und Zweirad-Grosshändler
VKhuTeIn	Vysshii Gosudarstvennyi Khudozhestvenno-Tekhnicheskii Institut
VKI	Groep Verwarmings- en Kookapparatenindustrie
VKI	Vandkvalitetsinstituttet (Denmark)
VKI	Verband Kunstoff Verarbeitender Industriebetriebe der Schweiz
VKI	Verein für Konsumenten Information (Austria)
VKI	Vereniging Klei Industrie
VKIFD	Von Karman Institute for Fluid Dynamics (Belgium) = IVKDF
VKL	Vereniging van Katholieke Leraren "Sint-Bonaventura"
VKL	Vereniging van Kleuterschool Leveranciers
VKÖ	Verband der Köche Österreichs
VKR	Wissenschaftliche Vereinigung zur Pflege des Konsumenten-Schutzrechts (Switzerland)
VKS	Verband Kommunaler Städereinigungsbetriebe

VKV	Vlaams Kinesitherapeuten Verbond
VKWB	Verband Kirchlich- Wissenschaftlicher Bibliotheken
VLA	Vereniging Fabrieken van Luchttechnische Apparaten
VLAM	Vereniging van Leveranciers van Audio-Visuele Media
VLB	Versuchs-und Lehranstalt für Braurei in Berlin
VLDP	Vanguard for Liberation and Democracy Party (Guyana)
VLET	Vereniging van Leveranciers van Electrotechnische Toestellen
VLG	Vereniging van Leveranciers voor de Galvano-Techniek
VLGN	Verband Landwirtschaftlicher Genossenschaften der Nordwestschweiz
VLGZ	Verband Landwirtschaftlicher Genossenschaften der Zentralschweiz
VLHT	Vereniging van Laboratoriumhoudende Tandtechnici in Nederland
VLK	Verband der Landwirtschaftkammern
VLK	Verband der Leitenden Krankenhausärzte Deutschlands
VLKB	Schweizerischer Verband der Lehrer an Kaufmännischen Berufsschulen = SMEPC
VLKNO	Verein für Landeskunde von Niederösterreich
VLL	Nederlandse Vereniging van Leraren in Landbouw-Mechanica
VLM	Vereniging Logistiek Management
VLM	Vereniging van Leveranciers van Merkspeelgoed
VLMS	Vintage Light Music Society
VLMW	Voralberger Landesmuseumsverein
VLN	Vereniging tot Bevordering v. d. Landbouwtuigpaardfokkerij in Nederland
VLP	Schweizerische Vereinigung für Landesplanung = ASPAN
VLRF	Vereinigung der lieferanten der Radio- und Fernsehbranche
VLRP	Vitamin Laboratories of Roche Products (Australia)
VLSF	Verband der Lastwagen-Spediteure und Ferntransportunternehmer (Switzerland)
VLSF	Versuchs- und Lehranstalt für Spiritusfabrikation und Fermentationstechnologie in Berlin
VLT	Vereniging van Loonveredilingsbedrijven voor de Textielindustrie
VLTA	Veterans' Lawn Tennis Association of Great Britain
VLV	Voice of the Listener & Viewer (*ex* VOL)
VLVB	Verband von Lieferanten Versilbenter Bestecke (Switzerland)
VLW	Bundesverband der Lehrer an Wirtschaftsschulen
VLWZ	Verband Lampenschirm-Wohnraumleuchten-und Zubehö-Industrie
VMA	Vlaamse Management Associatie
VMAI	Veterinary Medical Association of Ireland
VMB	Vereniging van Metaalbeschermingsbedrijven
VMBI	Vereniging voor Medische en Biologische Informatieverwerking
VMCC	Vintage Motor Cycle Club
VMCCA	Vintage Motor Car Club of America
VMD	Vereniging Milieudefensie
VMD	Veterinary Medicines Directorate
VMF	Vieilles Maisons Françaises
VMG	Voluntary Movement Group
VMHK	Vereniging voor het Museum van Hedendaagse Kunst te Gent vzw (Belgium)
VMI	Vereniging van Metaal-Industrieén
VMI	Visión Mundial Internacional (U.S.A.)
VMM	Vegetarian Matchmakers
VMM	Veille Météorologique Mondial = WWW
VMM	Volunteer Missionary Movement
VMNICM	Vaikunth Mehta National Institute of Cooperative Management (India)
VMÖ	Verband der Marktforscher Österreichs
VMO	Vereniging van Marktonderzoekbureaux
VMO	Vlaamse Militanten Orde (Belgium)
VMPA	Vancouver Museums and Planetarium (Canada)
VMPA	Verband der Materialprüfungsämter
VMR	Vereniging van Metalen-Ramenfabrikanten
VMRO-DP	Vnatrešna Makedonska Revolucionerna Organizacija-Demokratska Partija (Macedonia) = IMRO-DP

VMRO-DPMNE	Vnatrešna Makedonska Revolucionerna Organizacija-Demokratska Partija za Makedonsko Nacionalno Edinstvo (Macedonia) = IMRO-DPMNU
VMRO-N	Vútreshna Makedonska Revolyutsionna Organizatsiysa – Nezavisim (Bulgaria) = IMRO-I
VMRO-OMD	Vútreshna Makedonska Revolyutsionna Organizatsiya-Obedinenie na Makedonskite Druzhestva (Bulgaria) = IMRO-UMS
VMS	Verband der Museen der Schweiz = AMS, SMA
VMS	Victorian Military Society
VMSÖ	Verband für Medizinischer Strahlenschutz in Österreich
VMT	Vereniging der Mond- en Tandartsen van België
VMVM	Verbond der Middelgrote Verzekeringsmaatschappijen
VNA	Vereniging van de Nederlandse Aardolie-Industrie
VNA	Vietnam News Agency
VNAB	Vereninging Nederlandse Assurantiebeurs
VNCI	Vereniging van de Nederlandse Chemische Industrie
VNG	Verbond van de Nederlandse Groothandel
VNG	Vereniging van Nederlandse Gemeenten
VNG	Vereniging van Nederlandse Golfkartonfabrikanten
VNG	Vereniging van Nederlandse Grasdrogerijen
VNGF	Vereniging van Kleuterschool Leveranciers
VNIGNI	All-Russian Research Geological Oil Institute
VNIIL	Vserossiiskii Nauchno-Issledovatelskii Institut Lupina
VNIIOENG	Vsesoiuznyi Nauchno-issledovatel'skii Institut Organizatsii Upravleniia i Ekonomiki Neftegazovoi Promyshlennosti
VNJ	Vlaams-Nationaal Jeugdverbond (Belgium)
VNK	Vereniging Nederlandse Kerftabakindustrie
VNK	Vereniging van Nederlandse Kunsthistorici
VNK	Vereniging voor Japanse Kunst
VNKI	Vereniging van Nederlandse Kolenimporteurs
VNM	Vereniging Nederlandse Fabrieken van Melktransportkannen
VNM	Vereniging Nederlandse Motorenrevisiebedrijven
VNM	Vereniging voor Nederlandse Muziekgeschiedenis
VNMF	Vereniging van Nederlandse Mengvoederfabrikanten
VNO	Verbond van Nederlandse Ondernemingen
VNOF	Vsesoiuznoe Nauchnoe Obshchestvo Farmatsevov
VNOLO	Vsesoiuznoe Nauchnoe Obshchestvo Otorinolaringologov
VNOO	Vsesoiuznoe Nauchnoe Obshchestvo Oftal'mologov
VNP	Verein Naturschutzpark
VNP	Vereninging van Nederlandsche Papierfabrikanten
VNR	Verband Norddeutscher Rechenzentren
VNR	Vereniging van Nederlandse Reformhuizen
VNRC	Vegetarian Nutritional Research Centre
VNRTC	Viet-Nam Radio and Television Commission
VNS	Verenigde Nederlandse Slijters
VNS	Violet Needham Society
VNT	Vereniging van Nederlandse Toneelgezelschappen
VNU	Volontaires des Nations Unies; Voluntarios de las Naciones Unidas = UNV
VNV	Veremiging van Nederlandse Verkeersvliegers
VNV	Vereniging van Nederlandse Vleeswaren- en Vleeconservenfabrikanten
VNZ	Vereniging van Nederlandse Fabrikanten van Zuivelwerktuigen
VÖA	Verband Österreichischer Archivare
VÖÄ	Vereinigung Österreichischer Ärzte
VOA	Vereniging voor Bedrijfskunde
VOA	Vereniging voor Organisatie en Arbeidskunde
VOA	Veterinary Officers' Association (Éire)
VÖAG	Verband des Österreichischen Automatengewerbes
VÖB	Verband Öffentlicher Banken

VÖB	Vereinigung Österreichischer Betriebs- und Organisationsberater
VÖB	Vereinigung Österreichischer Bibliothekare
VÖBB	Verband Österreichischer Banken und Bankiers
VOC	Vereniging voor Ordinatie en Classificatie
VOCA	Visiting Orchestras Consultative Association
VOCAL	Victims Of Clergy Abuse Link-up (U.S.A.)
VOCAL	Victims of Crime and Leniency (U.S.A.)
VOCAL	Voluntary Organisations Communications and Language
VÖCh	Verein Österreichischer Chemiker
VÖCHICHT	Verein Österreichischer Chemieingenieure und Chemotechniker
VOCOSS	Voluntary Organisations Co-operating in Overseas Social Service
VOCTECH	Regional Centre for Vocational and Technical Education (SEAMEO)
VODG	Voluntary Organizations Disability Group
VOE	Verband oberer Angestellter der Eisen- und Stahlindustrie
VÖEST	Vereingtie Österreichische Eisen- und Stahlwerke AG
VOF	Verband der Fabrikanten von Technischen Ölen, Fetten und Verwandten Produkten
VÖF	Verband Österreichischer Fernfrächter
VOFG	Verband Ostschweizerischer Fleckviehzuchgenossenschaften
VÖFVL	Verband Österreichischer Flugverkehrsleiter
VOFyToZ	Vereniging voor Studie en Onderzoek over Fytopatologie en Toegepaste Zoologie (Belgium) = AERZAP
VÖG	Verein Österreichischer Giessereifachleute
VOGIN	Nederlandse Vereiniging van Gebruikers van Online Informatiesystemen
VÖGT	Verband Österreichscher Grüfuttertrocknungsanlagen
Vohil	Vereniging Regionale Importeurs en Groothandelaren in Land- en Tuinbouwmachines
VÖI	Verband Österreichische Giessereifachleute
VÖI	Verband Österreichische Ingenieure
VÖI	Vereinigung Österreichischer Industrieller
VOICE	Voluntary Organizations in a Citizen's Europe (ECAS) (Belgium)
VOIS	Vsemirnaia Organizatsiia Intellektualnoi Sobstvennosti = OMPI, WIPO
VÖK	Vereinigung Österreichischer Kunststoffverarbeiter
VOKh	Vsesoiuznoe Nauchnoe Obshchestvo Khirurgov
VOL	Voice of the Listener (*now* VLV)
VÖLB	Verein Österreichischer Lebensmittel- und Biotechnologen
VOLBRI-CÉRAM	Société Voltaïque de Briqueterie et de Céramique
VOLFRI	Société Voltaïque de Friperie
VOLG	Verband Ostschweizerischer Landwirtschaftlicher Genossenschaften
VOLPROF	Centre for Voluntary Sector and Not-for-Profit Management
VÖLT	Verein Österreichischer Ledertechniker
VOLTAP	Société Voltaïque de Diffusion d'Appareils Électriques
VOLTAVIN	Société des Vins (Burkina Faso)
VOLTEX	Société Voltaïque des Textiles (Burkina Faso)
VOLTOA	Société Voltaïque d'Oxygène et d'Acetylène
VOM	Vereniging voor Oppervlaktetechnieken van Metalen
VÖN	Verband der Österreichischen Neuphilologen
VON	Vereniging van Opleidingsinstituten voor Verplegende en Verzorgende Beroepen
VON	Vereniging voor Oppervlaktetechnieken Metalen
VON	Vereningen van Orgelvouwers in Nederland
VONJY	Vonjy Iray Tsy Mivaky (Madagascar)
VONS	Committee for the Defence of Persons Unjustly Persecuted (Czechoslovakia)
VOO	Vereniging voor Openbaar Onderwijs
VOO	Veronica Omroep Organisatie
VOP	Stichting tot Bevordering van de Vakopleiding voor de Handel in Pluimvee, Wild en Tamme Konijnen
VOPEG	Verenging voor de Ontwikkeling en de Promotie van de Europese Gedachte (Belgium)

VOPH	Verband Österreichischer Philatelisten-Vereine
VÖR	Vereinigung des Österreichischen Rübenbauerorganisationen
VORI	Viticultural and Oenological Research Institute (South Africa)
VOSCO	Vietnam Ocean Shipping Company
VOSH-International	Volunteer Optometric Services to Humanity International (U.S.A.)
VÖT	Verband des Österreichischen Transportgewerbes
VOT	Voice of Turkey
VÖTC	Verein Österreichischer Textilchemiker und Coloristen
VÖV	Verband Öffentlicher Verkehrsbetriebe
VÖV	Verband Österreichischer Volkshochschulen
VOV	Vereiniging van Openbare Verzorgingsinstellingen = AEPS
VÖVV	Verband Österreichischer Volksbücherein und Volksbibliothekare
VOW	Vereniging van Ondernemers in Wandbekleding
VÖWA	Verband Österreichischer Wirtschaftsakademiker
VÖZ	Verband Österreichischer Zeitungsherausgeber
VÖZ	Verband Österreichischer Ziegelwerke
VÖZ	Verein Österreichischern Zementfabrikanten
VP	Vanuaaku Pati (Vanuata)
VPA	Vegetable Protein Association
VPA	Virginia Pharmaceutical Association
VPB	Vereniging van Particuliere Beveiliginsorganisaties
VPBS	Verband Papier, Bürobedarf und Schreibwaren in der Hauptgemeinschaft des Deutschen Einzelhandels
VPC	Veterinary Products Committe (MAFF)
VPCA	Vereniging der Publiciteitschefs der Adverteerders van België
VPCM	Vereniging van Protestants-Christelijke Metallindustriëlen in Nederland
VPD-"OTCHIZNA"	"Otchizna" – Vserossiiskoe Patoticheskoe Dvizhenie
VPDP	Vereniging der Directeurs van Personeeldiensten
VPI	Nederlandse Vereniging van Producenten en Importeurs van Wegen- en Waterbouwmaterialen
VPIN	Verband Papier Pappe und Kunstoff verabeitende Industrie Niedersachsens
VPK	Vaensterpartiet Kommunisterna
VPL	Vereniging Parkevloeren Leveranciers
VPL	Video Performance Limited
VPLC	Vereniging van Pluimveeselecteurs in Dienst van Landbouw -coöperaties
VPM	Nederlandse Vereniging van Fabrikanten van Verbanstoffen, Pleisters en Maandverband
VPMG	Vintage Plant & Machinery Preservation Group
VPN	Verein für Psychiatric and Neurologie (Austria)
VPN	Verejnosț proti násiliu
VPOD	Schweizerishcer Verband des Personals Offentlicher Dienste
VPP	Deutscher Verband der Patentingenieure und Patentassessoren
VPRA	Vereniging van Public Relations Adviesbureaus
VPRB	Verbond der Papier en Karton Recuperatie Bedrijven = FERP
VPRC	Video Packaging Review Committee
VPRO	Vrijzinnig Protestantse Radio-Omroep
VPS	Verband Privater Städtereinigingsbetriebe
VPSG	Verband Schweizerischer Papier- und Papierstoff-Fabrikanten
VPT	Verband Physikalische Therapie
VPU	Vilniaus pedagoginis Universitetas
VR	Vatra Românească (Romania) = RC
VR	Vatra Romaneasca Union (Romania)
VRA	Nederlandse Vereniging van Artsen voor Revalidatie en Physische Geneeskunde
VRA	Visual Resources Association
VRA	Volta River Authority (Ghana)
VRB	Vereniging van Religieus-Wetenschappelijke Bibliothecarissen (Belgium)
VRF	Verband der Radio, Fernseh-und Elektro-Fachhandels Österreichs
VRH	Verband der Reformwaren-Hersteller
VRH	Volunteer Reading Help
VRIN	Vereniging van Revalidatiecentra in Nederland
VRIS	Voting Reform Information Service
VRKD	Verband Reisender Kaufleute Deutschlands

VRKÖ	Verband Reisender Kaufleute Österreichs		**VSB**	Verband Schweizerischer Bücher- Steuer- Treuhanderexperten = ASE, ASP
VRKS	Verband Reisender Kaufleute der Schweiz		**VSB**	Verein zum Schutz der Bergwelt e.V.
VRLÖ	Verband der Russische-Lehrer Österreichs		**VSB**	Vereinigung Schweizerischer Bibliothekare = ASB
VRM	Vereinigung der Regierungsbaumeister des Machinenwesens 'Motor'		**VSB**	Vereinigung Schweizerischer Bohrfirmen = AISP, ASEF
VRRI	Vocational and Rehabilitation Research Institute (Canada)		**VSB**	Vereniging Surinaams Bedrijfsteven
VRS	Virtual Reality Society		**VSB**	Vereniging voor Strategische Beleidvorming
VS	The Victorian Society		**VSBF**	Verband Schweizerischer Blechemballagen-Fabrikanten
VS	Vegetarian Society		**VSBH**	Verband Schweizerischer Baumaterial-Händler = ASMMC
VS	VenstreSocialisterne (Denmark)			
VS	Verband Deutscher Schriftsteller		**VSBH**	Vereinigung Schweizerischer Buchdruck-Hilfsarbeiter
VS	Verkhovnyi Soviet Rossiiskoi Federatsii		**VSBM**	Verband Schweizerischer Baumaschinen- Fabrikanten und Händler
VSA	Föreningen Värmlands Skogarbetsstudier			
VSA	Verband für Simmentaler Alpfleckviehzucht und Alpwirtschaft		**VSBN**	Vereinigung Schweizerischer Bettfedernfabriken
VSA	Verband Schweizerischer Abwasserfachleute = ASPEE, ASSPA, ASTEA, SWPCA		**VSBPF**	Verband Schweizerischer Bürsten-und Pinselfabrikanten
			VSBS	Verband Schweizerischer Bildhauer-und Steinmetzmeister
VSA	Verband Schweizerischer Annonce-Expeditionen		**VSBW**	Vereinigung Schweizerischer Bahnhofwirte
VSA	Vereinigung Schweizerischer Akkumulatorenfabrikanten		**VSC**	Verband Schweizerischer Carbesitzer
VSA	Vereinigung Schweizerischer Angestelltenverbände		**VSCC**	Vintage Sports Car Club
VSA	Vereinigung Schweizerischer Archivare = AAS		**VSCF**	Verein Schweizerischer Cartonnage-Fabriken
VSA	Vereinigung Schweizerischer Aviatikjournalisten		**VSchM**	Verband Schweizerischer Müller
VSA	Vintage Sailing Association		**VSCI**	Verband der Schweizerischer Carosserie-Industrie = USIC
VSA	Voluntary Service Abroad		**VSCTU**	Vereinigung Schweizerischer Chemischreinigungs- und Textilpflege-Unternehmen = ASENET
VSAB	Verband Schweizerischer Altstoffhandels Betriebe			
VSAI	Vereinung Schweizerischer Automobil-Importeure		**VSD**	Verband der Schweizer Druckindustrie
VSAK	Verband Schweizer Antiquare und Kunsthändler		**VSD**	Verband des Schweizerischen Darmhandels
VSAZ	Verband Schweizerischer Anzeiger-Zeitungen		**VSD**	Verband Schweizerischer Düngerhändler
VSB	Schweizerische Vereinigung zum Schutz und zur Föderung des Berggebietes		**VSd**	Verein Schweizerdeutsch
			VSD	Verein Schweizerischer Deutschlehrer
			VSD	Vereinigung Schweizerischer Druckfarbenfabrikanten
VSB	Schweizerischer Bierbrauverein		**VSE**	Verband der Schweizerischen Edelsteinbranche
VSB	Verband Schweizer Badekurorte			
VSB	Verband Schweizerischer Baumschulbesitzer		**VSE**	Verband Schweizerischer Eisengiessereien

VSE	Verband Schweizerischer Eisenwarenhändler = AQS		**VSG**	Verband Schweizerischer Graphiker
VSE	Verband Schweizerischer Ergotherapeuten = ASE		**VSG**	Verband Schweizerischer Graphologen
VSE	Vereniging Slachpluimvee-Export		**VSG**	Verband Schweizerischer Grastrocknungsbetriebe
VSE	Vereniging van Schipper-Eignaren		**VSG**	Verein Schweizerischer Gymnasiallehrer = SSISS, SSPES
VSEF	Verband Schweizersicher Edelmetallwaren-Fabrikanten = AFSBO		**VSG**	Vereinigung voor Sportgeneeskunde
VSEI	Verband Schweizerische Elektro-Installationsfirmen = USIE		**VSGB**	Vereinigung Schweizerischer Glashandels- und Glasverabeitungsbetriebe
VSEMK	Verband Schweizerischer Edelstahl-, Metall- und Kunststoffändler = GSMAMP		**VSGF**	Vereinigung Schweizerischer Gasherd-Fabrikanten
VSF	Värme- och Sanitetstekniska Föreningen i Finland		**VSGg**	Verein Schweizerischer Geographielehrer = ASPG
VSF	Verband Schweizeischer Seidenstoff-Fabrikanten		**VSGH**	Verband Schweizerischer Geflügelhalter
VSF	Verband Schweizerischer Filialunternehmungen		**VSGI**	Verband Schweizerischer Geflü- und Wild-Importeure
VSF	Verband Schweizerischer Förster = ASF		**VSGN**	Vereinigung Schweizerischer Grosshandelsfirmen in Abféllen von Nichteisenmetallen
VSF	Vereinigung des Schweizerischen Farbenfachhandels		**VSGP**	Verband Schweizerischer Gemüseproduzenten = UMS, USPV
VSF	Vereinigung Schweizerischer Filmkritiker		**VSGT**	Verband Schweizerischer Gummi- und Thermoplast- Industrieller
VSF	Vereinigung Schweizerischer Formularhersteller = ASFF		**VSGU**	Verband Schweizerischer Generalunternehmer = ASEG
VSF	Vereinigung Schweizerischer Futtermittelfabrikanten		**VSH**	Verband Schweizerischer Hadernsortiewerke
VSF	Vétérinaires sans Frontières		**VSH**	Verband Schweizerischer Hartschotterwerke
VSFA	Victoria State Forestry Association (Australia)		**VSH**	Verband Schweizerischer Heuhandelsfirmen
VSFAV	Verband Schweizerischer Film und AV-Produzenten		**VSH**	Vereinigung Schweizerischer Hafermühlen
VSFBR	Verband Schweizerischer Fabrikanten van Besen aus Reisig		**VSHB**	Verband Schweizerischer Holzbildhauer
VSFE	Verband Schweizerischer Fabrikanten von Einbauküchen		**VSHF**	Verband Schweizerischer Holzbearbeitungsmaschinen- und Werkzeug-Fabrikanten
VSFF	Verband Schweizerischer Fleischwaren-Fabrikanten		**VSHF**	Verband Schweizerischer Holzwarenfabrikanten
VSFK	Verein Schweizerischer Fabrikanten von Kunstoffpackungen		**VSHL**	Verband Schweizerischer Heizungs- und Lüftungsfirmen = ASCV, ASIRA
VSG	Verband des Schweizerischen Spirituosengewerbes		**VSI**	Bundesverband des Sanitär-Fachhandels
VSG	Verband Schweizerischer Garn-und Gewebe-Exporteure		**VSI**	Vegetarian Society of Ireland
VSG	Verband Schweizerischer Gärtnermeister		**VSI**	Verband Schmierfett-Industrie
VSG	Verband Schweizerischer Gaswerke		**VSI**	Verband Schweizerischer Immobilienbureaux
VSG	Verband Schweizerischer Gerberein		**VSI**	Verband Schweizerischer Isolierfirmen
VSG	Verband Schweizerischer Goldschmiede		**VSI**	Verband Selbständiger Ingenieure
			VSI	Vereinigung Schweizer Innenarchitekten

VSI	Vinnuveitandasamband Islands
VSI	Voluntary Service International (Éire)
VSIA	Verband Schweizerischer Industrie-Lieferanten für Altpapier
VSIA	Verband Selbständiger Ingenieure und Architekten
VSIEA	Vereinigung Schweizerischer Importeure Elektrischer Apparate
VSIG	Vereinigung des Schweizerischen Import-und Grosshandels
VSJ	Verband der Schweizer Journalisten
VSJE	Vereinigung Schweizerischen Import- und Edelmetallbranchen
VSK	Verband Schweizerischer Konsumvereine
VSKB	Vereniging voor het Theologisch Bibliothecariaat
VSKE	Verband Schweizerischer Käseeporteure
VSKF	Verband Schweizerischer Kachelofenfabrikanten
VSKF	Verein Schweizerischer Kondensatoren-Fabrikanten
VSKI	Verband der Schweizerischen Keramischen Industrie
VSKM	Verband Schweizerischer Kundenmüller
VSKPS	Verband Schweizerischer Kunstoff-, Press und Spritzwerke
VSL	Verband Schweizerischer Firmen für Linoleum und Spezialbodenbeläge
VSL	Verband Schweizerischer Keinen-Industrieller
VSL	Verband Schweizerischer Lagerhäuser
VSLB	Verein Schweizerischer Lithographiebesitzer
VSLF	Verband Schweizerischer Lack-und Farbenfabrikanten
VSLF	Vereinigung Schweizerischer Leichtbauplattenfabrikanten
VSLG	Verband des Schweizerischen Leder-Grosshandels
VSLG	Verband Schweizerischer Grossisten für Linoleum und Spezialbodenbeläge
VSLG	Verband Schweizerischer Leasing-Gesellschaften
VSLG	Vereinigung Schweizerischer Lebensverischerungs-Gesellschaften
VSLIB	Verband Schweizerischer Leiferanten der Inneausstatungs-und Bettwaren-Branche
VSLR	Verband Schweizerischer Lichtpaus-und Reprografie-Betriebe
VSLT	Verband Schweizerischer Fachgeschäfte für Linoleum Spezialboden-beläge und Teppiche
VSM	Verband Schweizer Metzgermeister
VSM	Verband Schweizerischer Marmor- und Granitwerke
VSM	Verband Schweizerischer Messerschmiedmeister und verwandter Berufsgruppen
VSM	Verband Schweizerischer Mineralquellen
VSM	Verein Schweizerischer Maschinen-Industrieller
VSM	Vereiniging Fabrikanten van Stalen Kantoor- en Bedrijfsmeubelen
VSM	Vereinigung Schweizerischer Modehäuser
VSM	Vondrona Sosialista Monima (Madagascar)
VSM	Vsemirnyi Sovet Mira = CMP, WFR, WPC
VSMB	Verband Schweizerischer Modellbaubetriebe
VSMBD	Verband Schweizerischer Mercerie- und Bonneterie-Detaillisten
VSMF	Verband Schweizerischer Marktforscher = ASSEM
VSMF	Verein Schweizerischer Metallwarenfabrikanten
VSMG	Verband Schweizerischer Metallgiesserein
VSMP	Verein Schweizerischer Mathematik- und Physiklehrer = SSIMF, SSPMP
VSMR	Verband Schweizerischer Motor-Revisionsbetriebe
VSMWH	Verband des Schweizerischen Maschinen-und Werkzeughandels
VSN	Vasuki Seva Nilayam (India)
VSN	Vereinigung Schweizerischer Naturwissenschaftslehrer
VSN	Vereniging Smeerolieondernemingen Nederland
VSN	Volontaires de la Sécurité National (Haiti)
VSÖ	Verband der Sicherheitsunternehmungen Österreichs
VSO	Vereinigung Schweizerischer Offsetdruckereien
VSO	Vienna Symphony Orchestra
VSO	Voluntary Service Overseas

VSOD	Vin of Spiritus Organisationen i Danmark	**VSS**	Verband Schweizerischer Studentenschaften
VSP	Gesellschaft für Wirtschafts- und Sozialwissenschaften Verein für Sozialpolitik	**VSS**	Vereinigung Schweizerischer Büromaschinenhändler
VSP	Verband Schweizerischer Papeteristen	**VSS**	Vereinigung Schweizerischer Schlauchfabrikanten
VSP	Verband Schweizerischer Patentanwälte = ASCPI, ASPA	**VSS**	Vereinigung Schweizerischer Siebdrukerien
VSP	Verband Schweizerischer Pferdemetzgerein	**VSS**	Vereinigung Schweizerischer Strassenfachleute
VSP	Verband Schweizerischer Pflasterermeister	**VSSA**	Verband Schweizerischer Statisticher Amter = UOSS. UUSS
VSP	Verein der Schweizer Presse	**VSSB**	Verband Schweizerischer Schloss- und Beschlägefabrikanten
VSP	Vereingung Schweizer Petroleum-Geologen und Ingenieure	**VSSB**	Verband Schweizerischer Spielwaren-Beschlägefabrikanten
VSPG	Verband Schweizerischer Papier-Grossisten	**VSSE**	Verband Schweizerischer Schreib- und Exporteure
VSPK	Vsesoiuznyi Sotsialno-Politicheskii Klub	**VSSF**	Verband Schweizerischer Schallplatten-Fachgeschäfte
VSPM	Schweizerischer Verband der Philosophielehrer au Mittelschulen = SIFS, SPES	**VSSF**	Verband Schweizerischer Spielwarenfabrikanten
VSPPF	Verband Schweizerischer Papier-und Papierstoff-Fabrikanten	**VSSF**	Vereinigung Schweizerischer Stickerei-Fabrikanten
VSPV	Verband Schwizerischen Philatelistenvereine	**VSSJ**	Verband Schweizer Sportjournalisten = ASJS
VSR	Verband Schweizerischer Rolladen-und Storenfabriken	**VSSL**	Verband Schweizerischer Schallplatten-Lieferanten
VSR	Vereinigung Schweizerischer Reproduktionsbetriebe	**VSSM**	Verband Schweizerischer Schreinermeister und Möbelfabrikanten
VSR	Vereniging Fabrieken van Staalplaat Radiatoren	**VSSÖ**	Verband der Sportausrüster und Sportautikelerzeuer Österreichs
VSRA	Veteran Speedway Riders Association	**VSSS**	Verband Schweizerischer Schreib- und Siebdruckereien
VSRD	Verband Schweizer Reform- und Diätfachgeschäfte	**VSSTF**	Verband Schweizerischer Sperrholz-und Tischleplatten-Fabrikanten
VSRF	Verein Schweizerischer Rauchtabak-Fabrikanten	**VSSU**	Verband Schweizerischer Schiffahrtsunternehmungen
VSRLF	Verband Schweizerischer Reiseartikel-und Lederwaren-Fabrikanten	**VSSZ**	Verein Schweizerischer Seidenzwirner
VSRT	Verband Schweizerischer Radio- und Televisionsfachgeschäfte = USRT	**VST**	Verband Schweizerischer Tapetenhandelsfirmen = MSP
VSRV	Vsesoiuznyi Soviet Roditelei Voennosluzhashchikh	**VST**	Verband Schweizerischer Teigwarenfabrikanten
VSS	Verband des Schweizerischen Spirituosengewerbes = FSS	**VST**	Verband Schweizerischer Transportanstalten
VSS	Verband Scheizerischer Schrott-Verbraucher	**VST**	Verband Schweizerischer Transportunternehmungen des Öffentlichen Verkehrs = UST
VSS	Verband Schweizerischer Schuhindustrieller	**VST**	Vereinigung Schweizerischer Teppichhändler
VSS	Verband Schweizerischer Schirmfabrikanten	**VST**	Vereinigung Schweizerischer Tiefbauunternehmer = ASILP, ASTP
VSS	Verband Schweizerischer Schmierölimporteurs		

VSTF	Verein Schweizerischer Teppichfabrikanten	**VSWN**	Verband für Sicherheit in der Wirtschaft Norddeutschland
VSTG	Verband Schweizerischer Teppich-Grossisten	**VSWS**	Verband Schweizerischer Woll-und Seidenstoff-Fabrikanten
VSTG	Verband Schweizerischer Topfpflanzen- und Schnittblumengärtnerein	**VSZ**	Verband Schweizerischer Zigarrenfabrikanten
VSTH	Verband Schweizerischer Tabakhändler	**VSZ**	Vysdká Skola Zemedelská
VSTH	Verband Schweizerischer Technischer Händler	**VSZKGF**	Verein Schweizerischer Zement-, Kalk- und Gips-Fabrikanter
VSTH	Verband Schweizerischer Traubensafthersteller	**VSZS**	Verband Schweizerischer Ziegel- und Steinfabrikanten = ASFBT
VSTI	Verein Schweizerischer Textilindustrieller	**VSZV**	Verein Südwestdeutscher Zeitungsverleger
VSTV	Verband der Schweizerischen Textil-Veredlungs-Industrie	**VTA**	Verband der Teer- und Asphaltmischwerke
VSU	Verband Schweizerischer Uhren- und Bijouteriefachgeschäfte	**VTA**	Video Trade Association
VSU	Verband Selbständige Unternehmen der Nährmittelindustrie	**VTA**	Vodka Trade Association (*now* GVA)
VSUK	Vegetarian Society of the United Kingdom	**VTB**	Vereniging voor het Theologisch Bibliothecariaat
VSUO	Vyzkumny a Slechtitelsky Ustav Obilnársky	**VTB**	Vlaamse Toeristenbond
VSUZ	Vyzkumny a Slechtitelsky Ustav Zelinarsky	**VTCC**	Verein der Textil-Chemiker und Coloristen
VSV	Verband der Schweizerischen Volkshochschulen = AUPS	**VTCVG**	Vereniging Technische Commissie Vloeibaar Gas
VSV	Verband des Schweizerischen Versandhandels	**VTFF**	Verband Technischer Betriebe für Film- und Fernsehen
VSV	Verband Schweizerischer Verkehrsverein	**VTG**	Verband Schweizer Tierarzneimittelgrossisten
VSV	Vereinigung Selbständiger Berlagsvertreter	**VTI**	Statens Väg-och Transportforskningsinstitut
VSVM	Verband der Schweizer Versandmetzgereien	**VTI**	Vereniging van Textiel-Inkoopcombinaties
VSVM	Vereinigung Schweizerischer Versicherungsmathematiker	**VTL**	Finnish Association of PR Agencies
VSVT	Verband Schweizerischer Vermessungstechniker	**VTMSZ**	Vezetési Tanácsadók Magyarországi Szövetsége
VSVVS	Vereinigung Schweiz Versuchs-und Vermittlungsstellen für Saatkartoffeln	**VTO**	Vereniging van Textielondernemingen in Nederland
VSW	Verband des Speditions-gewerbes Baden-Württemberg	**VTO**	Vsemirnaja Turisticheskaja Organizatsija = OMT, WTO
VSW	Verband Schweizerischer Werbegesellschaften	**VTOT**	All-Union Tatar Public Centre
VSWF	Vereinigung Schweizerischer Weisskalkfabrikanten	**VTR**	Verband Schweizerischer Unternehmungen für Tankreinigungen
VSWK	Verband der Schweizerischen Waren- und Kaufhäuser	**VTS**	Vereinigung der Tiefdruckanstalten der Schweiz
VSWM	Vereniging Fabrikanten van Stalen Woningmeubelen	**VTT**	Valtion Teknillinen Tutkmuskeskus
		VTU	Vilniaus technikos Universitetas
		VTY	Virkamiesten ja Työntekijäin Yhteisjärjestö
		VU	Vaterländische Union (Liechtenstein)
		VÜ	Verband der Übersetzungsbüros

VU	Vilniaus Universitetas
VU	Volksunie (Belgium)
VUBI	Verband Unabhängig Beratender Ingenieurfirmen
VUC	Vanguardia Unitaria Comunista (Venezuela)
VUCH	Vyzkumny Ustav Chmelarsky
VUGPT	Vyzkumny Ustav Gumárenské a Plastikárské Technologie
VUHZ	Vyzkumny Ustav Hutnictví Zeleza
VUK	Vyzkumny Ustav Kozedélny
VULH	Vyskumny Ustav Lesného Hospodárstva
VULP	Vyskumny Ustav Lúk a Pasienkov
VUM	Vyzkumny Ustav Mlékárensky
VUMP	Vyzkumny Ustav Masného Prumyslu
VUNB	Vereniging van Uitgevers van Nederlandstalige Boeken
VUPC	Vyskumny Ustav Papiera a Celulózy
VUPP	Vyskumny Ustav Prumysly Papirenského
VUPVR	Vyzkumny Ustav Podoznalectva a Vyzivy Rastlín
VUR	Vereinigung für Umweltrecht (Switzerland)
VUSE	Vyzkumny Ustav Silnoproude Elektrotechniky
VUTP	Vyzkumny Ustav Tabakového Priemyslu
VUUV	Vyzkumny Ustav Upravy Vod
VUV	Vyskumny Ustav Vodohosppodársky
VUVA	Vyskumny Ustav Vystavby a Architektury
VUVc	Vyzkumny Ustav Vcelarsky
VUVH	Vyzkumny Ustav Vodného Hospodárstva
VUZ	Vyskumny Ustav Zváracsky = WRI
VUZT	Vyzkumny Ustav Zemedelské Techniky Praha
VVA	Vee an Vlees Aankoopbureau
VvA	Vereniging voor Arbeidsrecht
VVAA	Nederlandse Vereniging van Artsen
VVB	Vereinigung der Versieherungs-Betriebswirte
VVBAD	Vlaamse Vereniging voor het Bibliotheek-, Archief- en Documentatie-wesen
VVBADP	Vlaamse Vereniging van Bibliotheek-, Archief- en Documentatiepersoneel
VVBAP	Vlaamse Vereniging van Bibliotheek- en Archiefpersoneel
VVCW	Vereniging voor Calvinistische Wijsbegeerte
VVD	Volkspartij voor Vrijheid en Democratie
VVDA	Verlegerverband Deutscher Anzigenblätter
VVDF	Vereniging van Drukinkfabrikanten
VVDO	Vakgroep Voedilngsmiddelen van Dierlijke Oorsprong
VVE	Vereniging voor Economie vzw (Belgium)
VVF	Verband Vollpappe-Kartonagen
VVF	Vlaamse Vereniging voor Familiekunde
VVG	Vlaamse Vereniging voor Gastroenterologie
VVHDKM	Vereniging der Vrienden van de Historische Dienst van de Krijgmacht
VVIA	Vlaamse Vereniging voor Industriele Archeologie vzw
VVK	Verband Vollpappe-Kartonagen
VVK	Verbond van Koffiebranders (Belgium) = UTC
VVK	Verein für Visuelle Kommunikation e.V.
VVK	Verein für Volkskunde (Austria)
VVKS	Vlaams Verbond der Katholieke Scouts
VvL	Nederlandse Vereniging voor Logica en Wijsbegeerte der Exacte Wetenschappen
VVL	Vlaamse Vereniging voor Logopedisten
VvL/VvS	Vereniging van Letterkundigen; Vakbond van Schrijvers
VVM	Vereniging tot Voorlichting van de Zelfstandige Molenaar
VVMA	Vereniging van Medische Analisten
VVN	Verbond van Verzekeraars
VVO	Verband der Versicherungsunternehmen Österreichs
VVO	Verbond van Vlaams Overheidspersoneel
VVS	Kungliga Vetenskaps-och Vitterhets-Samhället i Göteborg
VVS	Norsk Forening for Varme-, Ventilasjon-of Sanitærteknikk
VVS	Svenska Rörgrossistförening
VVS	Vereniging voor Statistiek
VvS	Vereniging voor Statistiek
VVSTI	Verband der Vorarlberger Stickereiindustrie
VVT	Verbond der Vlaamse Tandartsen
VvU	Vereinigung von Unternehmerinnen
VVV	Vliegtuigeienaars-en Vlieëniersvereniging
VVVF	Vereniging van Verf-en Drukinktfabrikanten

VVVF	Vereniging van Vernis-en Verffabrikanten in Nederland
VVVH	Vereiniging van Verfhandelaren in Nederland
VVW	Vlaamse Vereniging voor Watertoerisme
VVZM	Vereniging voor Zuivelindustrie en Melkhygiène
VWA	Bundesverband Deutscher Verwaltungs- und Wirtschafts-Akademien
VWA	Vereinigung der Werbeleiter und Werbeassistenten
VWC	Virtual Worlds Consortium (U.S.A.)
VWF	Verband der Wissenschaftler an Forschungsinstituten
VWFA	Verband Unabhängiger Wirtschafts-, Finanz -und Anlageberater
VWGÖ	Verband der Wissenschaftlichen Gesellschaften Österreichs
VWI	Verband Deutscher Wirtschaftsingenieure
VWI	Vereniging van Weegwerktuig-Industrieë
VWJ	Vereinigung der Wirtschaftsjuristen in der Bundesrepublik Deutschland
VWN	Vereniging voor Waterleidingbelangen in Nederland
VWO	Verbond van Wetenschappelijke Onderzoekers
VWS	Versuchsanstalt für Wasserbau und Schiffbau (Germany)
VZB	Vereniging van Zelfbedienings-Bedrijven
VZH	Nederlandse Bond van Verzenhandelaren in Groenten en Fruit
VZI	Verband der Zigarettenpapier Verarbeitenden Industrie
VZLPS	Veće za Zastitu Ljudskih Prava i Sloboda (Serbia) = CPHRF
VZLS	Verband Zahntechnischer Laboratorien der Schweiz = ALPDS
VZLU	Vyzkumny a Zkusební Letecky Ustav

W

W&E	CSIRO Division of Wildlife and Ecology
WA	Willwriters Association
WAA	Water Authorities Association
WAA	Water Services Association

WAA	Western Association of Africanists (U.S.A.)
WAA	World Atlatl Association (U.S.A.)
WAAA	Women's Amateur Athletic Association
WAAC	World Academy of Arts and Culture (U.S.A.)
WAACC	Western Australian Automobile Chamber of Commerce
WAAE	World Association for Adult Education
WAAER	World Association for the Advancement of Educational Research
WAALD	West African Association of Agricultural Librarians and Documentalists
WAAP	World Association for Animal Production = AMPA, AMZ, WVT
WAAS	World Academy of Art and Science
WAATI	West African Association of Theological Institutions
WAAVP	World Association for the Advancement of Veterinary Parasitology
WAB	Wales Advisory Body for Local Authority Higher Education
WAB	World Association for Buiatrics = AMB, WGB
WABA	Welsh Amateur Basketball Association
WABA	Welsh Amateur Boxing Association
WABA	West African Banks Association (Sierra Leone) = ABAO
WAC	Water Allocation Council (New Zealand)
WAC	Water Appeals Commission (Northern Ireland)
WAC	West African Committee (U.K.)
WAC	Women's Advisory Committee of the British Standards Institution
WACA	Western Agricultural Chemicals Association (U.S.A)
WACA	World Airlines Clubs Association
WACA	World Association of Center Associates (U.S.A.) = AMAC
WACACT	West African Centre for Agricultural Credit Training (Sierra Leone)
WACAF	West and Central African Action Plan
WACC	World Africa Chamber of Commerce
WACC	World Association for Christian Communication = AMCC
WACH	West African Clearing House (AACB) (Sierra Leone) = CCAO
WACMR	West African Council for Medical Research

WACN	West African College of Nursing (WAHC)	**WAFC**	West African Fisheries Commissioner (FAO)
WACN	Women Awareness Centre Nepal	**WAFC**	Workers' Autonomous Federation of China
WACO	World Air Cargo Organisation		
WACOJ	World Affairs Council of Jerusalem (Israel)	**WAFE**	Womens Aid Federation (England)
		WAFRI	West African Fisheries Research Institute
WACP	West African College of Physicians		
WACRAL	World Association of Christian Radio Amateurs and Listeners	**WAFRU**	West African Fungicide Research Unit
		WAFSRN	West African Farming Systems Research Network (Burkina Faso) = RESPAO
WACRI	West African Cacao Research Institute (Ghana)		
WACS	West African College of Surgeons = COAC	**WAFUNIF**	World Association of Former United Nations Interns and Fellows
Wacs	West Australian Coastal Shipping Commission	**WAG**	Women's Action Group (Zimbabwe)
		WAGA	Welsh Amateur Gymnastic Association
WACS	World Association of Cooks' Societies = FMSC, WDK	**WAGC**	World Amateur Golf Council
		WAGGGS	World Association of Girl Guides and Girl Scouts = AMGE, AMGS
WACU	West African Customs Union		
WACY2000	World Association for Celebrating Year 2000	**WAGR**	Western Australian Goverment Railways
WAD	World Association of Detectives	**WAHC**	West African Health Community
WADA	Wum Area Development Agency (Cameroon)	**WAHLI**	Indonesian Wildlife Forum
		WAHO	World Arabian Horse Organization
WADB	West African Development Bank (Togo) = BOAD	**WAHS**	West African Health Secretariat
WADE	World Association of Document Examiners	**WAHVM**	World Association for the History of Veterinary Medicine = AMHMV, WGGVM
WADIS	West African Development Information System (PADIS) = CDIAO	**WAI**	Weltverband der Arbeitnehmer in Industriebetrieben = FMTI, WFIW, WIB
WADP	World Association for Dynamic Psychiatry		
WAE	World Association of Estonians (U.S.A.)	**WAIA**	World Association of Introduction Agencies
		WAICA	West African Insurance Companies Association (Liberia)
WAEC	West African Examinations Council		
WAEO	World Aerospace Education Organisation	**WAIF**	World Adoption International Fund
		WAIFOR	West African Institute for Oilpalm Research (Nigeria)
WAEP	World Association for Element-Building and Prefabrication		
WAEPA	Worldwide Assurance for Employees of Public Agencies	**WAIIC**	Western State Agricultural and Industrial Investment Company (Nigeria)
WAER	World Association for Educational Research (Belgium) = AMSE	**WAIP**	World Association for Infant Psychiatry
		WAIPAD	World Association for Infant Psychiatry and other Disciplines
WAF	Wojskowa Agencja Fotograficzna		
WAF	Women Against Fundamentalism	**WAISER**	West African Institute of Social and Economic Research
WAFA	Wikalat Anbaa' Filastiniya		
WAFA	World Association of Flower Arrangers	**WAITR**	West African Institute for Trypanosomiasis Research
WAFAH	West African Federation of Associations for the Advancement of Handicapped Persons = FOAPH	**WAITRO**	World Association of Industrial and Technological Research Organisations
WAFB	Workers Aid for Bosnia	**WAJ**	World Association of Judges

WAJA	West African Journalists Association
WAJAL	West African Joint Agency Ltd
WAK	Catholic Electoral Committee (Poland)
WAKL	West Asia Kontena Line (Singapore)
WAL	World Association of Lawyers
WALA	West African Library Association
WALP	World Association of Law Professors (U.S.A.)
WALS	West African Linguistic Society = SLAO, SOAL
WALS	World Association of Law Students (U.S.A.)
WAM	Wojskowa Akademia Medyczna
WAM	Working Association of Mothers
WAMDEV-IN	West African Management Development Institutions Network (Nigeria)
WAMF	Welsh Amateur Music Federation
WAMITAB	Waste Management Industry Training and Advisory Board
WAMLA	West African Modern Language Literature Association = ALVAO
WAMRU	West African Maize Research Unit
WAMS	World Association of Military Surgeons
WAMT	Women and Manual Trades
WAMU	West African Monetary Union = UMOA
WAMY	World Assembly of Muslim Youth
WAND	Caribbean Women and Development Unit (Barbados)
WANO	World Association of Nuclear Operators
WANOPC	World Association of Nuclear Power Operators (France)
WAO	Women's Aid Organization (Malaysia)
WAO	World Association for Orphans and Abandoned Children
WAOS	Welsh Agricultural Organisation Society
WAOW	Women Against the Ordination of Women
WAP	Wojskowa Akademia Polityczna
WAP	Women's Action for Palestine
WAPC	Women Against Pit Closures
WAPDA	Water and Power Development Authority (Pakistan)
WAPET	West Australian Petroleum (Pty) Ltd.
WAPF	West African Pharmaceutical Federation
WAPMC	West African Postgraduate Medical College (Nigeria)
WAPOR	World Association for the Public Opinion Research = AMROP
WAPR	World Association of Psychosocial Rehabilitation = AMRP
WAPRI	World Association of Pulp and Papermaking Research Institute
WAPTT	World Association for Professional Training in Tourism = AMFORT
WAR	White Aryan Resistance (U.S.A.)
WAR	Women Against Rape
WAR	Workers Against Racism
WARBICA	West African Regional Branch of the International Council on Archives
WARC	Women's Amateur Rowing Council
WARC	World Administrative Radio Conferences
WARC	World Alliance of Reformed Churches = ARM
WARCS	West African Regional Computer Society (Nigeria)
WARDA	West African Rice Development Association = ADRAO
WARM	Wood and Solid Fuel Association of Retailers and Manufacturers
WARMER	World Action for Recycling Materials and Energy From Rubbish
WARN	Worldwide Accelerated Response Network (Amnesty)
WARPATH	World Association to Remove Prejudice Against the Handicapped (U.S.A.)
WARRC	World Acaricide Resistance Reference Centre
WARRS	West African Rice Research Station
WAS	Washington Academy of Sciences (U.S.A.)
WAS	Witwatersrand Agricultural Society (South Africa)
WAS	World Aquaculture Society
WAS	World Archaeological Society
WAS	World Association for Sexology
WASA	Welsh Amateur Swimming Association
WASA	West African Science Association= ASOA
WASA	West African Shippers Association = ASAO
WASAC	Welsh Association of Sub Aqua Clubs
WASCO	National Water and Soil Conservation Organisation (New Zealand)
WASH	Women Against Sexual Harassment
WASID	Water and Soil Investigation Department (Pakistan)
WASME	World Assembly of Small and Medium Enterprises

WASOG	West African Society of Gastroenterology (Ghana)	**WAWA**	West African Women's Association
WASP	West African Society for Pharmacology	**WAWE**	World Association of Women Entrepreneurs = FCEM
WASP	World Association for Social Psychiatry	**WAWE**	World Association of Women Executives = FCE
WASP	World Association of Societies of Pathology Anatomic and Clinical	**WAWF**	World Association of World Federation = AUFM, MUFM
WASPRU	West African Stored Products Research Unit	**WAWR**	Workers Army of the Welsh Republic
WASWC	World Association of Soil and Water Conservation	**WAWSS**	West African Weed Science Society = SOAM
WAT	Wojskowa Akademia Techniczna	**WAWV**	World Association of Wildlife Veterinarians
WATA	World Association of Travel Agencies	**WAY**	World Assembly of Youth = AMJ
WATAO	Worldwide Agricultural Technical Assistance Organization	**WAYC**	Welsh Association of Youth Clubs
WATBRU	West African Timber Borer Research Unit	**WB**	Weather Bureau
		WB	Weltausschuss für Berufsaktion (WVA)
WATCH	Watch Trust for Environmental Education	**WB**	World Brotherhood = FM
WATCH	Women Acting Together for Change (Nepal)	**WBA**	Welsh Bowling Association
WATCH	World Assembly of Technical and Creative Humorists = AMCSH	**WBA**	Weltbund der Angestellten = FME, WFCW, WVB
WATCIM	Waterloo Centre for Integrated Manufacturing (Canada)	**WBA**	World Bowling Association
WATOC	World Association of Theoretically Oriented Chemists	**WBA**	World Boxing Association = AMB
		WBAO	Wissenschaftliche Vereinigung für Augenoptik und Optometrie
WATTE	West African Tropical Testing Establishment	**WBAT**	World Bank Administrative Tribunal (U.S.A.)
WAVA	World Association of Veteran Athletes	**WBC**	Workers' Beer Company
WAVA	World Association of Veterinary Anatomists = AMAV, WV	**WBC**	World Boxing Council
		WBC	World Business Council (U.S.A.)
WAVAW	Women Against Violence Against Women	**WBCA**	Weltbewegung der Christlichen Arbeiter = MMTC, WMCW
WAVE	World Association of Veterinary Educators	**WBCS**	Welsh Black Cattle Society
WAVES	Women's Audio Visual Education Scheme	**WBDJ**	Weltbund der Demokratischen Jugen = FMJD, VFDM, WFDY
WAVFH	World Association of Veterinary Food Hygienists = AMVHA	**WBF**	World Bridge Federation
		WBFC	West Bengal Financial Corporation (India)
WAVMI	World Association of Veterinary Microbiologists, Immunologists and Specialists in Infectious Diseases = AMVMI	**WBFF**	World Bonsai Friendship Federation (Japan)
		WBG	Weltbund der Bibelgesellschaften = ABU, SBU, UBS
WAVP	World Association of Veterinary Pathologists = AMPV	**WBG**	Wiener Beethoven Gesellschaft
WAVPPBT	World Association of Veterinary Physiologists, Pharmacologists, Biochemists and Toxicologists = AMFFBTV, AMPPBTV	**WBG**	Wiener Bibliophilen Gesellschaft
		WBIT	World Bank of International Terms = BMTI
		WBL	Nederlandse Vereniging tegen Water-, Bodem- en Luchtverontreiniging
WAVSFDP	World Association of Veterinary Specialists in Fish Diseases and Productions	**WBMS**	World Bureau of Metal Statistics = OMEM

WBN-MMUMA	West Bengal Non-ferrous Metal Merchants and Utensils Merchants Association (India)	**WCC**	World Council of Churches = CMI, COE, OeRK
WBO	World Boxing Organisation	**WCC**	World Council of Clergymen (U.S.A.)
WBRA	Wagon Building & Repairing Association	**WCC**	World Crafts Council = CMAO
		WCC	World Cultural Council
WBRI	Wheat and Barley Research Institute (South Korea)	**WCCA**	West Cameroon Cooperative Association
WBS	Wassmann Biological Society (U.S.A.)	**WCCA**	Wholesale Cash and Carry Association
WBS	Wellington Botanical Society (N.Z.)	**WCCC**	World Convention of Churches of Christ (U.S.A.)
WBSC	World Buddhist Sangha Council (China)	**WCCES**	World Council of Comparative Education Societies = CMAEC
WBU	Welsh Badminton Union		
WBU	Welsh Baseball Union	**WCCI**	World Council for Curriculum and Instruction (U.S.A.) = CME, WFB
WBU	World Blind Union = UMA		
WBV	Schweizerischer Weinbauverein	**WCCL**	Welsh Council for Civil Liberties
WBW	World Bowling Writers (U.S.A.)	**WCCLGF**	Welsh Consultative Council on Local Government Finance
WC	Wildflower Club		
WC	Women's Centre (India)	**WCCS**	World Chamber of Commerce Service (U.S.A.)
WCA	Wholesale Caterers' Alliance		
WCA	Women's Cricket Association	**WCD**	Welsh Council for the Disabled
WCA	Wood Carvers Association	**WCDA**	Women and Child Development Association (India)
WCA	Wool Council of Australia		
WCA	World Calendar Association	**WCDM**	Welsh Committee on Drug Misuse
WCA	World Citizens Assembly = AMC	**WCDMP**	World Climate Data and Monitoring Program
WCA	World Communication Association (U.S.A.)		
		WCDP	World Climate Data Program
WCACA	World Christian Anti-Communist Association (Taiwan)	**WCED**	World Commission on Environment and Development (UN) = CMED
WCADL	Weaker Community's Action for Development and Liberation (India)	**WCET**	World Council of Enterostomal Therapy Nurses
WCAP	World Climate Applications Program	**WCEU**	World Christian Endeavour Union
WCARRD	World Conference on Agrarian Reform and Rural Developments = CMRADR	**WCF**	Commonwealth Weightlifting Federation
WCASP	World Climate Applications and Services Program	**WCF**	World Congress of Faiths
		WCF	World Curling Federation
WCB	World Council for the Biosphere (FEC) (Switzerland)	**WCFBA**	World Catholic Federation for the Biblical Apostolate = KWBF
WCB-ISEE	World Council for the Biosphere-International Society for Environmental Education	**WCFU**	World Congress of Free Ukrainians
		WCG	Women of the Church of God (Antigua-Barbuda)
WCBA	Weltbewegung der Christlichen Arbeiter	**WCGA**	World Computer Graphics Association
WCBA	Women Cooperative Business Association (Nigeria)	**WCGLJO**	World Congress of Gay and Lesbian Jewish Organizations (U.S.A.)
WCC	Wales Craft Council	**WCGR**	Waterloo Centre for Groundwater Research (Canada)
WCC	Welsh Consumer Council = CDC		
WCC	Women's Co-ordination Council (India)	**WCH**	World Congress of Herpetology
WCC	World Cheerleader Council (U.S.A.)	**WCI**	Wildlife Conservation International (U.S.A.)
WCC	World Climate Conference (WMO) = CMC	**WCIA**	Watch & Clock Importers' Association (*now* BHF)

WCIC	Kalyanamitra Women's Communication and Information Centre (Indonesia)
WCIE	World Centre for Islamic Education
WCIP	World Climate Impacts Programme
WCIP	World Council of Indigenous Peoples = CMPI
WCIRP	World Climate Impact Assessment and Response Strategies Program
WCISP	World Climate Impact Studies Program
WCJCC	World Confederation of Jewish Community Centres
WCJCS	World Conference of Jewish Communal Service
WCL	Women for Caribbean Liberation
WCL	World Confederation of Labour = CMT, WVA
WCLC	World Christian Life Community = CVX, GCL
WCLR	Wadsworth Center for Laboratories and Research (U.S.A.)
WCMA	Wiping Cloth Manufacturers Association
WCMC	World Conservation Monitoring Centre (IUCN, UNEP)
WCMMF	World Congress of Man-Made Fibres
WCMT	Winston Churchill Memorial Trust
WCN	Women's Centre of Nigeria
WCNDT	World Conference on Non-Destructive Testing
WCOTP	World Confederation of Organisations of the Teaching Profession = CMOPE
WCP	World Climate Programme (WMO)
WCP	World Council of Peace
WCP	World Court Project
WCPA	White Christians Patriots Association (Canada)
WCPA	World Constitution and Parliament Association
WCPS	World Confederation of Productivity Science
WCPT	World Confederation of Physical Therapy
WCR	Welsh Community Resistance
WCRA	Women's Cycle Racing Association
WCRP	World Climate Research Programme (ICSU, WMO) = PMIC, PMRC
WCRP	World Conference on Religion and Peace
WCRRD	World Conference on Agrarian Reform and Rural Development (FAO)
WCRZZ	Wszechzwiązkowa Centralna Rada Związków Zawodowych
WCS	Wilkie Collins Society
WCSC	World Correctional Service Center (U.S.A.)
WCSC	World Council of Service Clubs
WCSM	Worshipful Company of Spectacle Makers
WCSZ	Wildlife Conservation Society of Zambia
WCT	Women Caring Trust
WCT	World Confederation of Teachers = CSME, WVL, WVOP
WCTA	Wholesale Confectionery and Tobacco Trade Alliance)
WCTA	World Committee for Trade Action = CMAP
WCTR	World Conference on Transport Research = CMRT
WCTTA	Wholesale Confectionery and Tobacco Trade Alliance
WCTU	Women's Christian Temperance Union
WCU	Welsh Chess Union
WCU	World Conservation Union
WCV	World Coalition Against Vivisection = CMAV
WCVA	Wales Council for Voluntary Action
WCYMSC	World Council of Young Men's Service Clubs
WDA	Well Drillers Association
WDA	Welsh Development Agency
WDA	World Dredging Association = WODA
WdB	Weltbund der Weltföderalisten
WDB	Wine Development Board
WDC	World Darts Council
WDC	World Data Centre
WDC	World Disarmament Campaign
WDC-C	World Data Centre – C for Sunspot Index (Belgium) = SIDC
WDCA	World Diving Coaches Association
WDCM	World Data Centre on Microorganisms
WDCS	Whale & Dolphin Conservation Society
WDCs	World Data Centre Systems (ICSU)
WDDTY	What Doctors Don't Tell You
WDEI	Wuhan Digital Engineering Institute
WDF	World Darts Federation
WDF	World Draughts Federation = FMJD
WDFF	Women's Division – Federated Farmers of New Zealand

WDFSA	World Federation of Direct Selling Associations
WDIC	Women's Development and Information Center (Bolivia)
WDK	Weltbund der Kochverbände = FMSC, WACS
WDK	Wirtschaftsverband der Deutschen Kautschukindustrie
WDL	Wages Due Lesbians
WDL	White Defence League
WDM	World Development Movement (U.K.)
WDR	Westdeutscher Rundfunk
WDRC	World Data Referral Centre (France)
WDRSG	Workplace Deaths Relatives Support Group
WDS	Women's Design Service
WE	Women in Enterprise
WE	World Evangelism (U.S.A.)
WE&FA	Welsh Engineers' & Founders' Association
WEA	Royal West of England Academy
WEA	Workers' Educational Association
WEAAP	Western European Association for Aviation Psychology (Belgium)
WEAN	Women's Earth Action Network
WEAP	World Environment Action Plan
WEB	Werkgeversvereniging Elektriciteitsbedrijven
WEBA	World Educational Broadcasting Assembly
WEC	World Energy Conference = CME
WEC	World Engineering Conference
WEC	World Environment Centre
WECAFC	Western Central Atlantic Fishery Commission (FAO) = COPACO
WECI	World Evangelisation Crusade International = CEM, CPM, WEK
WECT	World Encyclopaedia of Contemporary Theatre
WED	Women's Enterprises Development (Kenya)
WED	World Energy Development (Gabon)
WEDA	Western Dredging Association
WEDA	Wholesale Egg Distributors Association
WEDA	Wholesale Engineering Distributors Association
WEDC	Water, Engineering and Development Centre
WEDG	Wood Energy Development Group
WEDNET	Women, Environment and Development Network (Kenya)
WEE	Weltbund für Erneurung der Erziehung
WEED	Weltwirtschaft, Ökologie und Entwicklung
WEETAG	Women's Employment, Education, and Training Advisory Group
WEF	World Education Fellowship = LIEN
WEF	World Evangelical Fellowship (Switzerland) = AEM, UEM
WEFC	West European Fisheries Conference
WEG	Wirtschaftsverband Erdöl- und Erdgasgewinnung
WEI	Western European Institute for Wood Preservation = IEO
WEI	World Enviroment Institute = IME
WEK	Weltweiter Evangelisations-Kreuzzug = CEM, CPM, WECI
WEL	Women's Electoral Lobby (Australia)
WEM	Western European Metal Trades Employers Organization
WEMA	Wirtschaftverband Eisen- Maschinen- und Apparatebau
WEN	The Women's Environmental Network
WEN	Work and Economy Network in the European Churches
WEN	World Environment News
WEP	Whole Earth Party (Australia)
WEP International	Women's Exchange Programme International = WIEN
WEPARM	Werkgroep Export Propaganda Agrarisch Reproduciemateriaal
WEPCO	Western Desert Petroleum Company (Egypt)
WEPZA	World Export Processing Zone Association = AMZFI
WERC	Waste Management Education and Research Consortium
WERC	Women's Education and Research Centre (Sri Lanka)
WERI	Water and Energy Research Institute of the Western Pacific – University of Guam
WES	Welding Engineering Society (Japan)
WES	Western Equestrian Society
WES	Women's Engineering Society
WES	Writing Equipment Society
WEST	Western Earth Science Technologies (U.S.A.)
WESTPAC	IOC Sub-Commission for the Western Pacific

WETT	Women's Educational Training Trust
WETUC	Workers Educational Trade Union Committee
WEU	Western European Union = UEO
WEVA	World Electric Vehicle Association (Canada) = FMPVE
WEVA	World Equine Veterinary Association
WEXAS	World Expeditionary Association
WF	Wallboardfabrikkenes Felleskontor
WF	White Fathers = MAfr, PB
WFA	Weightlifting Federation of Africa
WFA	Western Front Association
WFA	White Fish Authority
WFA	Women's Football Association
WFA	Workers' Film Association
WFA	World Federation of Advertisers = FMA
WFA	World Friendship Association (U.S.A.)
WFAC	Working for a Charity
WFAC	World Federal Authority Committee
WFAFW	World Federation of Agricultural and Food Workers = FeMTAA, WFALA, WFLVA
WFALA	Weltföderation der Agrar- und Lebensmittelarbeiter = FeMTAA, WFAFW, WFLVA
WFALW	Weltbund Freiheitlicher Arbeitnehmerverbände auf Liberaler Wirtschaftsgrundlage = UMOSBESI, WULTUO
WFAMS	World Federation of Acupuncture-Moxibustion Societies (China)
WFAPS	World Federation of Associations of Pediatric Surgeons
WFAS	World Federation of Acupuncture Soiceties
WFB	Weltrat für Bildung = CME, WCCI
WFB	Wirtschaftsförderung Berlin
WFB	World Fellowship of Buddhists
WFBMA	Woven Fabric Belting Manufacturers Association
WFBSC	World Federation of Building Service Contractors
WFBTMA	World Federation of Baton Twirling and Majorettes Associations
WFBWU	World Federation of Building and Woodworkers Unions = FMCB, FMTCM, WFWBI, WVBH
WFBY	World Fellowship of Buddhist Youth
WFC	World Feminist Commission
WFC	World Food Council (UN) = CMA
WFCC	World Federation for Culture Collections = FMCC
WFCS	World's Fair Collectors Society (U.S.A.)
WFCW	World Federation of Clerical Workers = FME, WBA, WVB
WFD	World Federation of the Deaf = FMS
WFD	Wytwórnia Filmów Dokumentalnych
WFDA	Wholesalers Floorcovering Distributors Association
WFDB	World Federation of Diamond Bourses (Belgium)
WFDC	World Foundation for Deaf Children (Italy)
WFDF	World Flying Disc Federation
WFDFI	World Federation of Developing Financial Institutions = FEMIDE
WFDRA	Wallcovering, Fabric & Decor Retailers Association (*ex* WPWRA)
WFDWRHL	World Federation of Doctors Who Respect Human Life
WFDY	World Federation of Democratic Youth = FMJD, WBDJ
WFE	Women for Freedom in Europe
WFED	World Foundation for Environment and Development
WFEO	World Federation of Engineering Organisations = FMOI
WFF	World Friendship Federation
WFF	Wytwórnia Filmów Fabularnych
WFFL	World Federation of Free Latvians
WFFLTA	World Federation of Foreign-Language Teachers' Associations = FIPLV
WFFM	World Federation of Friends of Museums (Belgium) = FMAM
WFGA	Women's Farm and Garden Association
WFH	Wages for Housework
WFH	World Federation of Healing
WFH	World Federation of Hemophilia
WFH	World Federation of Hungarians = MVSz
WFHA	Welsh Federation of Housing Associations
WFHA-AVSC	World Federation of Health Agencies for the Advancement of Voluntary Surgical Contraception
WFHC	Wages for Housework Campaign
WFHJ	World Federation of Hungarian Jews
WFI	Wheat Flour Institute (U.S.A.)

WFI	Wirtschaftsförderungsinstitut (Austria)	**WFS**	Wimmin for Survival (Australia)
WFIC	World Federation of Investment Clubs	**WFS**	Women for Socialism
WFIJI	World Federation of International Juridical Institutions	**WFS**	World Food Security
		WFS	World Future Society (U.S.A.)
WFIM	World Federation of Islamic Missions (Pakistan)	**WFSA**	World Federation of Societies of Anaesthesiologists
WFIMC	World Federation of International Music Competitions = FMCIM	**WFSBP**	World Federation of Societies of Biological Psychiatry
WFIS	World Federation of Iranian Students	**WFSEC**	World Fellowship of Slavic Evangelical Christians
WFIW	World Federation of Industry Workers = FMTI, WAI, WIB		
WFL	Women's Freedom League	**WFSF**	World Future Studies Federation
WFLOE	Women For Life On Earth	**WFSGI**	World Federation of the Sporting Goods Industry
WFLRY	World Federation of Liberal and Radical Youth = FMJLR	**WFSS**	Welsh Folk Song Society
		WFSW	World Federation of Scientific Workers = FMTS, WFW
WFLVA	Weraldfederatie van Landbouw en Voedingsarbeiders = FeMTAA, WFAFW, WFALA	**WFT**	Winged Fellowship Trust
		WFT	World Federation of Transylvania (Hungary) = EVSz
WFME	World Federation for Medical Education = FMEM	**WFTC**	World Federation of Therapeutic Communities
WFMH	World Federation for Mental Health = FMSM	**WFTJW**	World Federation of Travel Journalists and Writers
WFMLTA	World Federation of Modern Language Teachers Association	**WFTST**	World Foundation for the Transnationalization of Specialised Terminology (IOUTN)
WFMW	World Federation of Methodist Women		
WFN	World Federation of Neurology = FMN	**WFTT**	World Federation of Twinned Towns
WFNMB	World Federation of Nuclear Medicine and Biology	**WFTU**	World Federation of Teachers Unions
		WFTU	World Federation of Trade Unions = FSM, VFP, WGB
WFNMW	World Federation of Trade Unions of Non-Manual Workers = FMTNM	**WFTUNMW**	World Federation of Trade Unions Non-Manual Workers
WFNS	World Federation of Neurosurgical Societies	**WFTV**	Women in Film and Television
WFO	Wytwórnia Filmów Oświatowych	**WFU**	Women's Farming Union
WFOT	World Federation of Occupational Therapists	**WFUCA**	World Federation of UNESCO Clubs and Associations = FMACU
WFP	White Flag Party (Burma)	**WFUMB**	World Federation for Ultrasound in Medicine and Biology
WFP	World Federation of Parasitologists		
WFP	World Food Programme (UN, FAO) = PAM, PMA	**WFUNA**	World Federation of United Nations Associations = FMANU
WFPHA	World Federation of Public Health Associations	**WFUWO**	World Federation of Ukrainian Women's Organisations = SFUZO
WFPMA	World Federation of Personnel Managers Associations	**WFV**	Werkfeuerwehrverband
		WFW	Weltföderation der Wissenschaftler = FMTS, WFSW
WFPMM	World Federation of Proprietary Medicine Manufacturers = FMFSGP		
WFPPA	World Forensic Psychiatry and Psychology Association	**WFW**	Women for Women (Bangladesh)
		WFWBI	World Federation of Trade Unions for the Wood & Building Industries = FMCB, FMTCM, WFWBU, WVBH
WFPT	World Federation for Physical Therapy		
WFR	Weltfriedensrat = CMP, VSM, WPC		
WFS	Wild Flower Society	**WG**	Het Wiskundig Genootschap

WG-GGI	Working Group on Geodesy and Geographic Information		**WGOC**	World Government Organisations Coalition
WGA	Wild Goose Association (U.S.A.)		**WGPSN**	Working Group for Planetary System Nomenclature
WGA	Working Group on Agriculture (SCF)		**WGRA**	Western Governmental Research Association
WGA	Writers Guild of America		**WGS**	World Geodetic System
WGAE	World Government of the Age of the Enlightenment (U.S.A.)		**WGTh**	Wissenschaftliche Gesellschaft für Theologie
WGARCR	Working Group Against Racism in Children's Resources		**WGU**	Welsh Golfing Union
WGAS	Wholesale Grocers Association of Scotland		**WGWC**	World Government of World Citizens = WSA
WGB	Weltgesellschaft für Buiatrik = AMB, WAB		**WGWDA**	Working Group for the Worldwide Development of Astronomy
WGB	Weltgewerkschaftsbund = FSM, VFP, WFTU		**WGWPC**	World Goverment World Peace Centre
WGB	Werkgeversvereniging Gasbedrijven		**WH&HSA**	Welsh Hospital and Health Services Association
WGC	World Gold Council (Switzerland)		**WHA**	Welsh Hockey Association
WGC	World Gospel Crusades (U.S.A.)		**WHA**	Western Horsemen's Association of Great Britain
WGDAA	Working Group on Encouraging International Development of Antarctic Astronomy		**WHAC**	Welsh Housing Associations Council
WGE	Wissenschaftliche Gesellschaft für Europarecht		**WHAC**	World Hemophilia AIDS Center (U.S.A.)
WGEID	Working Group on Enforced or Involuntary Disappearances (UN)		**WHAG**	World Hemophilia Action Group
WGF	Women's Gas Federation and Young Homemakers		**WHAM**	Women, Heritage & Museums
WGfF	Westdeutsche Gesellschaft für Familienkunde		**WHAT**	World Humanity Action Trust
			WHC	Women's Health Concern
WGFSK	Wiener Gesellschaft zur Föderung der Schönen Künste (Austria)		**WHC**	World Hereford Council (Canada)
WGGB	Writers Guild of Great Britain		**WHC**	World Heritage Committee =CPM
WGGVM	Weltgesellschaft für Geschichte der Veterinärmedizin		**WHCSA**	Welsh Health Comon Services Agency
WGL	Wijsgerig Gezelschap te Leuven		**WHEDA**	Women's Health and Economic Development Association (Nigeria)
WGM	Wirtschaftsverband Grosshandel Metallhalbzeug		**WHERNIN**	Women's Health Research Network in Nigeria
WGM	World Gospel Mission (U.S.A.)		**WHES**	World Hunger Education Service (U.S.A.)
WGMA	Wire Goods Manufacturers Association			
WGMA	Wissenschaftlich-Technisch Gesellschaft für Mess- und Automatisierungstechnik		**WHF**	World Heritage Fund (UNESCO)
			WHF	World Hindu Federation = VHP
			WHGS	Wyoming Historical and Geological Society (U.S.A.)
WGMS	World Glacier Monitoring Service (IUGG)		**WHI**	Welsh Hearing Institute
WGNE	Working Group on Numerical Experimentation		**WHIC**	Women's Health Information Centre
			WHISC	Women's Health Information and Support Centre
WGNRR	Women's Global Network for Reproductive Rights		**WHL**	World Hypertension League
			WHMA	Womens Home Missionary Association
WGOC	World Goverment Organisations Coordinating Council		**WHO**	World Health Organisation = OMS
			WHO	World Hydrothermal Organisation (SITH) = OMTh

WHO-LEMSIP	Laboratory for Experimental Medicine & Surgery in Primates (WHO)	**WIBA**	Welsh Indoor Bowls Association
		WIBAS	Wuhan Institute of Botany, Academia Sinica
WHO-PAHO-CARET	Caribbean Epidemiology Centre (Trinidad-Tobago)	**WIBC**	Women's International Bowling Congress (U.S.A.)
WHO-PAHO-ECO	Pan American Centre for Human Ecology and Health (Mexico)	**WIBHHV**	Wereld Instituut voor de Bescherming van de Hoge Hoedanigheid der Voeding
		WIBP	Wuhan Institute of Biological Products
WHO-PAHO-LACRIP	Latin American Cancer Research Information Project	**WIC**	West Indian Committee (U.K.)
		WICA	Witches International Craft Association (U.S.A.)
WHO-TOH	WHO Programme on Tobacco or Health	**WICAT**	World Institute for Computer Assisted Teaching (U.S.A.)
WHO/EURO	WHO Regional Office for Europe	**WICBC**	West Indies Cricket Board of Control
WHO/IRC	WHO International Reference Centre for Community Water Supply and Sanitation = CIR	**WICBE**	World Information Centre for Bilingual Education = CMIEB
WHO/SEAR-HELLIS	WHO South-East Asia Region Health Literature, Library and Information Services Network	**WICC**	Women's Inter-Church Council
		WICC	World Information Clearing Centre (Switzerland) = CMI
WHO-PEPAS	Western Pacific Regional Centre for Promotion of Enviroment Planning and Applied Studies (Malaysia)	**WICCE**	Women's International Cross Cultural Exchange
		WICF	Women's International Cultural Federation = FICF
WHOC	Welsh Housing Consultative Committee	**WICHE**	Western Interstate Commission for Higher Education (U.S.A.)
WHPU	Welsh Homing Pigeon Union	**WID**	Women in Development (Botswana)
WHRA	Welwyn Hall Research Association	**WID**	World Institute on Disability (U.S.A.)
WHRC	World Health Research Center	**WIDAB**	Welsh Industrial Development Advisory Board
WHS	Wesley Historical Society		
WHSC	West Highland Steamer Club	**WIDE**	Women in Development Europe (ICDA)
WHSRN	Western Hemisphere Shorebird Reserve Network (U.S.A.)	**WIDER**	World Institute for Development Economics Research = UNU/WIDER
WHTL	Verband der Handels-, Transport- und Lebensmittelarbeiter der Schweiz	**WIDF**	Women in Development Foundation (Philippines)
WHY	Why Helpless Youngsters	**WIDF**	Women's International Democratic Federation = FDIF, FDIM, IDFF, MDFZ
WI	Federation of Women's Institutes of Northern Ireland	**WIEC**	World Institute of Ecology and Cancer = IMEC
WI	Welding Institute = TWI	**WIEN**	Women's International Exchange Network = WEP INternational
WIA	Willow Importers' Association		
WIA	Windward Islands Airways = Winair	**WIF**	Worldview International Foundation (Sri Lanka)
WIA	Wool Importers Association		
WIA	World Interfaith Association	**WIFO**	Österreichisches Institut für Wirtschaftsforschung
WIAC	Women's International Art Club		
WIACO	World Insulation Acoustics Congress Organisation	**WIFOL**	Windward Islands Federation of Labour (Netherlands Antilles)
WIAMH	World Islamic Association for Mental Health (Egypt)	**WIG**	Verband Schweizerischer Wein-Importgrossisten
WIAS	West Indies Associated States		
WIB	Wereldfederatie van Werknemers met Industriële Bedrijven = FMTI, WAI, WFIW	**WIG**	Weltverband der Industriegewerkschaften = FEMOSI, FEMUSI, WOFIWU

WIGS	Women in German Studies
WIIST	Wuhan Information Institute of Science and Technology (China)
WIIU	Workers International Industrial Union
WIJ	Women in Journalism
WIL	Workers International League
WILD	International Wilderness Leadership Foundation
WILDAF	Women in Law and Development in Africa
WILPF	Women's International League for Peace and Freedom = IFFF, LIFPL, LIMPL
WIM	Wirtschaftsvereinigung Industrielle Meerestechnik
WIM	Women in Management
WIM	Women in Media
WIM	Women In Medicine
WIMA	Women's International Motorcycle Association
WIMA	World International Medical Association
WIML	Wojskowy Instytut Medycyny Lotniczej
WIMPS	Women in Moving Pictures
WIN	Women's International Network (U.S.A.)
WINA	Women's Institute for New Awareness (India)
Winair	Windward Islands Airways = WIA
WINAP	Women's Information Network for Asia and the Pacific
WINBAN	Windward Islands Banana Growers Association
WINFOL	Windward Islands Federation of Labour
WING	Women's Immigration and Nationality Group
WING	Work Injured Nurses Group
WIO	Women's International ORT
WIOC	West Indies Oil Company (Antigua)
WIP	Women in Publishing
WIP	Work Group Indigenous Peoples
WIPHN	Women's International Public Health Network (U.S.A.)
WIPL	Women Into Public Life
WIPM	West Indian Peoples Movement (Netherlands Antilles)
WIPO	World Intellectual Property Organisation = OMPI, VOIS
WIPOG	Wirtschaftpolitische Gesellschaft
WIPTC	Womens International Professional Tennis Council
WIR	White Irish Resistance
WIRA	Wax Importers and Refiners Association (U.S.A.)
WIRA	Wool Industries Research Association Technology Group
WIRF	Women's International Religious Fellowship (U.S.A.)
WIRFMD	Wellcome Institute for Research into Foot and Mouth Disease
WIRSPA	West Indies Rum and Spirit Producers Association
WIS	Wheat Information Service (Japan)
WIS	World Institute of Science (Belgium) = IMS
WISA	West Indies Sugar Association
WISC	West Indian Standing Conference
WISCO	West Indies Shipping Corporation
WISCO	West Indies Sugar Company
WISDA	Wirtschaftsgruppe Schweizerischer Dachpappenfabriken
WISDOM	Women in Service Development Organisation and Management (Gambia)
WISE	Welsh, Irish, Scots, English
WISE	World Information Service on Energy (Netherlands)
WISH	Women in Special Hospitals
WISI	World Information System on Informatics
WISICA	West Indies Sea Island Cotton Association
WISMIC	WVF International Socio-Medical Information Centre (Norway)
WISPA	Women's International Squash Players' Association = DVSPA, WISRF
WISRF	Women's International Squash Rackets Federation = WISPA, DVSPA
WISSHES	World Institute of Safety Security Health Environment Specialists (Philippines)
WISU	Wuhan Iron and Steel University
WIT	Women in Theology
WIT	Women into Information Technology Foundation Ltd
WITA	Women's International Tennis Association
WITAG	West Indies Trade Advisory Group
WITI	International Network of Women in Technology

WITMA	Western Indian Tile Manufacturers Association (India)	**WLSA**	Women and Law in Southern Africa Project
WITS	Women in Technology and Science (Éire)	**WLSC**	Women's Legal Status Committee (South Africa)
WIWA	West Indian Women's Association	**WLTA**	Welsh Lawn Tennis Association
WIZ	Wissenchaftliches Informationzentrum	**WLTBU**	Watermen, Lightermen, Tugmen and Bargemen's Union
WIZO	Women's International Zionist Organisation	**WLU**	World Liberal Union
WJA	World Jurist Association of World Peace through Law Center (U.S.A.)	**WLZM**	World Labour Zionist Movement
WJC	World Jewish Congress = CJM	**WMA**	Southern African Wildlife Management Association
WJCB	World Jersey Cattle Bureau	**WMA**	Wallcovering Manufacturers Association (U.K., U.S.A.)
WJEC	Welsh Joint Education Committee	**WMA**	Washer Manufacturers' Association of Great Britain
WJFITB	Wool, Jute and Flax Industry Training Board	**WMA**	Waterbed Manufacturers Association (U.S.A.)
WJG	Wiener Juristische Gesellschaft (Austria)	**WMA**	Waterheaters Manufacturers Association
WKA	Warp Knitters Association	**WMA**	Weather Modification Association
WKFO	Weltunion der Katholischen Frauen-Organisationen = UMOFC, WUCWO	**WMA**	Welding Manufacturers Association
WKOK	Wojewódzki Komitet Obrony Kraju	**WMA**	Wellington Mathematical Association (New Zealand)
WKP	Wojewódzka Komisja Przedjazdowa	**WMA**	Wikalat al-Maghreb al Arabi (Morocco)
WKS	Bundesversuchs- und Forschungsanstalt für Warme- Kalte- und Stromungstechnik (Austria)	**WMA**	Workers' Music Association
		WMA	Working Mothers' Association
WKS	Wojskowy Klub Sportowy	**WMA**	World Media Association
WL	Women's League (Zambia)	**WMA**	World Medical Association = AMM
WLA	Welsh Lacrosse Association	**WMA**	World Modeling Association (U.S.A.)
WLA	World Literary Academy	**WMAA**	World Martial Arts Association (U.S.A.)
WLC	World Lithuanian Community = PLB	**WMARC**	World Maritime Administrative Radio Conference
WLD	Women Liberal Democrats	**WMC**	World Methodist Council
WLF	Women's Liberal Federation	**WMC**	World Mining Congress
WLFD	World League for Freedom and Democracy (Republic of Korea)	**WMC**	World Muslim Congress
WLG	Witwatersrand Landbougenootskap	**WMCCSA**	World Masters Cross Country Ski Association
WLHB	Women's League of Health and Beauty	**WMCIU**	Working Men's Club & Institute Union
WLL	Women's League of Latvia = LSL	**WMCRI**	Wuhan Maritime Communication Research Institute
WLN	Western Library Network (U.S.A.)	**WMCW**	World Movement of Christian Workers = MMTC, WBCA
WLPGF	World Liquefied Petrol Gas Forum = FMGPL		
WLPGF	World LPG Forum = FMGPL	**WMF**	Waste Management Forum
WLPSA	Wild Life Preservation Society of Australia	**WMF**	World Memorial Fund for Disaster Relief
WLRA	World Leisure and Recreation Association	**WMF**	World Mercy Fund
WLRI	World Life Research Institute (U.S.A.)	**WMFT**	Westdeutscher Medizinischer Fakultätentag
WLS	Welsh Language Society		
WLS	World Life Saving (U.S.A.)	**WMG**	Waste Managers Guild
WLSA	Welsh Land Settlement Association	**WMG**	World Mind Group (Canada)

WMHS	World Methodist Historical Society (U.S.A.)
WMI	Wildlife Management Institute (U.S.A.)
WMIA	Woodworking Machinery Importers Association of America
WMM	World Movement of Mothers = MMM
WMMA	Woodworking Machinery Manufacturers Association of America
WMO	World Meteorological Organisation = OMM, WOM
WMOAS	Women's Migration and Oversea Appointments Society
WMPL	World Mission Prayer League (U.S.A.)
WMR	World Medical Relief (U.S.A.)
WMRA	Woollen Mills Research Association (New Zealand)
WMRG	Water Management Research Group (ICSU)
WMRP	Women's Media Resource Project
WMS	Welsh Mines Society
WMSA	Woodworking Machinery Suppliers Association
WMTS	World Medical Tennis Society
WMU	World Maritime University = UMI, UMM
WMW	Women's Media Watch (Jamaica)
WMWFG	World Movement for World Federal Government
WN	World Neighbors (U.S.A.)
WN-CAELA	Women's Network of the Council for Adult Education in Latin America
WNA	Welsh Netball Association
WNA	World Nature Association (U.S.A.)
WNAS	Women's National Advisory Service
WNAS	Women's Nutritional Advisory Service
WNBA	World Ninepin Bowling Association (FIQ) = NPA
WNC	Women's National Commission
WNCCC	Women's National Cancer Control Campaign
WNFIP	Women for A Nuclear-Free and Independent Pacific
WNLF	Women's National Liberal Federation
WNNR	Wetenskaplike en Nywerheids-Navorsingsraad (South Africa)
WNP	Wspólnota Niepodległych Państw = CEI, CIS, GUS, SNG
WNPC	White Nile Petroleum Company (Sudan)
WNR	World New Religion (U.S.A.)
WNRM	Women in Natural Resources Management Program (IUCN)
WNTBN	Women's Nuclear Test Ban Network
WOAR	Women Organised Against Rape
WOBA	Werkgroep Onderzoek Bestrijding Aardappelcystenaaltjes
WOBO	World Organisation of Building Officials
WOC	World Organization for the Child (Switzerland) = OME, OMB, WOK
WOC	World Orthopaedic Consern
WOCCU	World Council of Credit Unions
WOCE	World Ocean Circulation Experiment
WOCID	World Council of Islamic Dawah
WOCTP	World Confederation of Organisations of the Teaching Profession
WODA	World Organization of Dredging Associations = WDA
WODC	World Ozone Data Centre (WHO) (Canada)
WODCON	World Dredging Conference
WOECE	World Organisation for Early Childhood Education = OMEP
WOF	World Organisation for the Family
WOFIWU	World Federation of Industrial Workers' Unions = FEMOSI, FEMUSI, WIG
WOFPP	Women's Organisation for Political Prisoners
WOFUNA	World Federations of United Nations Associations
WOG	Wielka Organizacja Gospodarcza
WOG	Working for Organic Growers (*ex* WWOOF)
WOGSC	World Cybernetics and Systems Organization
WOHP	World Organization for Human Potential (U.S.A.)
WOIEP	World Office of Information on Environmental Problems = OMIPE
WOJAC	World Organization of Jews from Arab Countries
WOJD	World Organization of Jewish Deaf
WOK	Weltorganization für das Kind (Switzerland) = OMB, OME, WOC
WOLA	Washington Office on Latin America
WOM	Weltorganisation für Meteorologie = OMM, WMO
WOMP	World Order Models Project (U.S.A.)
WONA	Web Offset Newspaper Association

WONAAC	Women's National Abortion Action Campaign (New Zealand)	**WPA**	Wire Products Association
WONARD	Women's Organization of the National Association of Retail Druggists (U.S.A.)	**WPA**	Working Peoples Alliance (Guyana)
		WPA	World Pheasant Association
		WPA	World Phytotherapy Association
WONCA	World Organisation of National Colleges, Academies and Academic Associations of General Practitioners and Family Physicians	**WPA**	World Psychiatric Association = AMP
		WPB	Workers Party of Barbados
		WPBS	Welsh Plant Breeding Station
		WPBSA	World Professional Billiards and Snooker Association
WONPA	World Organisation of Negro Plastic Arts	**WPC**	Welsh Pricing Committee
WONZ	Women Outdoors New Zealand	**WPC**	World Peace Council = CMP, VSM, WFR
WOOLTAC	Wool Textile and Clothing Industry Action Committee	**WPC**	World Petroleum Congress = CMP
WOOMB	World Organisation of Ovulation Method Billings	**WPC**	World Print Council
WOP	Wojska Ochrony Pogranicza	**WPCC**	Water Pollution Control Council (New Zealand)
WOPK	Wojska Obrony Powiętrznej Kraju	**WPCF**	Water Pollution Control Federation (U.S.A.)
WOPP	World Organisation for the Protection of Privacy = PI	**WPCS**	Welsh Pony and Cob Society
WOPR	Wodne Ochotnicze Pogotowie Ratunkowe	**WPCS**	White Park Cattle Society
		WPE	Workers Party of Ethiopia
WORA	World Organisation for the Rights of Animals = OMDA (India)	**WPEC**	World Plan Executive Council
WORI	World Order Research Institute (U.S.A.)	**WPF**	World Peace Foundation (U.S.A.)
WORLD-DIDAC	World Organisation of Manufacturers and Distributors of Educational Materials	**WPFC**	Commission for Fisheries Research in the West Pacific
		WPFC	World Press Freedom Committee (U.S.A)
WOSA	Workers' Organisation for Socialist Action (South Africa)	**WPG**	Workers Power Group
WOSC	World Organisation of Systems and Cybernetics = OMSC	**WPGA**	Womens' Professional Golf Association
WOSIC	Watchmakers of Switzerland Information Centre	**WPGET**	Women Professional Golfers' European Tour
WOSM	World Organisation of the Scout Movement	**WPH**	Wojskowe Przedsiębiorstwo Handlowe
WOTRO	Stichting voor Wetenschappelijk Onderzoek van de Tropen	**WPI**	World Institute for Advanced Phenomenological Research and Learning; World Phenomenology Institute
WOVO	World Organisation of Volcano Observatories (IAVCEI)	**WPI**	World Press Institute (U.S.A.)
WOW	War On Want	**WPJ**	Workers Party of Jamaica
WOW	Wider Opportunities for Women	**WPK**	Wirtschaftsprüferkammer
WOW	Women against the Ordination of Women	**WPLTC**	World Peace Through Law Center
		WPM	World Presbyterian Missions
WOW	Women on Water (New Zealand)	**WPN**	Vereniging Warmbloed Paardenstamboek in Nederland
WOW	World of Water		
WOWI	Women on Words and Images (U.S.A.)	**WPNA**	World Proof Numismatic Association (U.S.A.)
WP	Wisma Putra (Malaysia)	**WPO**	Water Programs Office (EPA) (U.S.A.)
WP	Wojsko Polskie	**WPO**	World Packaging Organization= =OME
WP	Workers Party (Ireland)	**WPO**	World Ploughing Organization
WPA	Water Polo Association	**WPOA**	Western Pacific Orthopaedic Association

WPoCC	Working Party on Co-operative Communications (ICA)
WPoCLIDO	Working Party of Cooperative Librarians and Documentation Officers
WPPF	Wood Panel Products Federation (*ex* UKIPA)
WPRA	Waste Paper Recovery Association
WPRL	Water Pollution Research Laboratory
WPRO	Western Pacific Regional Office (WHO)
WPS	International Association of Word Processing Specialists
WPS	Wireless Preservation Society and National Wireless Museum
WPS	World Population Society (U.S.A.)
WPSA	Wildlife Preservation Society of Australia
WPSA	World's Poultry Science Association = AVI
WPSC	Western Pacific Society of Chemotherapy (Malaysia)
WPSMA	Welsh Plate and Steel Makers Association
WPTI	Wildlife-Preservation Trust International (U.S.A.)
WPU	Women's Protestant Union
WPV	Weltpostverein = UPU
WPVP	Working People's Vanguard Party (Guyana)
WPW	Wilki Prus Wschodnich (Poland) = EPW
WPWRA	Wallpaper, Paint and Wallcovering Retailers Association (*now* FDRA)
WPY	Workers' Party Youth (Éire)
WQF	Wider Quaker Fellowship (U.S.A.)
WR	World Runners = WRF
WRA	Windsurfing Retailers Association
WRAC	Waste and Recycling Advisory Committee (ANZEC)
WRAC	Water Resources Advisory Committee (Australian Environment Council)
WRAC	Women's Royal Army Corps
WRADAC	Water Research Association Distribution Analogue Centre
WRAF	Women's Royal Air Force
WRAG	Welsh Railways Action Group
WRAPSD	World Rehabilitation Association for the Psycho-Socially Disabled
WRB	Water Resources Board
WRBS	Wholesale and Retail Bakers of Scotland

WRC	Water Research Centre
WRC	Women's Resource Centre
WRC	World Relief Corporation (U.S.A.)
WRC	World Romani Congress
WRCC	Wildlife Research Co-ordinating Committee (East Africa)
WRDC	White Rose Dollmakers' Circle
WRDC	Wool Research and Development Corporation
WRDP	Women's Research and Development Project (Tanzania)
WREC	Wire Rope Export Conference
WREN	World Radio for Environment and Natural Resources
WRF	World Rehabilitation Fund
WRF	World Runner Foundation
WRG	Waterway Recovery Group
WRI	War Resisters International = IdK, IOT, IRG
WRI	Warwick Research Institute
WRI	Welding Research Institute (India)
WRI	Welfare Research Incorporated (U.S.A.)
WRI	Work Research Institute (Norway)
WRI	World Research Incorporated (U.S.A.)
WRI	World Resources Institute (IIED) (U.S.A.)
WRIPT	Wuhan Research Institute of Posts and Telecommunications
WRK	Westdeutsche Rektorenkonferenze
WRM	World Rainforest Movement
WRMF	World Radio Missionary Fellowship
WRN	Wojewódzka Rada Narodowa
WRN	Woman Returners Network
WRNS	Women's Royal Naval Service
WRO	Weed Research Organisation (AFRC)
WRON	Wojskowa Rada Ocalenia Narodowego
WRONZ	Wool Research Organization of New Zealand
WRP	Workers Revolutionary Party
WRP(N)	Workers Revolutionary Party (Namibia)
WRP(NL)	Workers Revolutionary Party (News Line)
WRP(WP)	Workers Revolutionary Party (Workers Press)
WRPC	Water Resources Planning Commission (Taiwan)
WRPDB	Western Regional Production Development Board (Nigeria)
WRRC	Water Resources Research Centre (Pakistan)

WRRC	Women's Research and Resources Centre
WRRI	Water Resources Research Institute (U.S.A.)
WRRIC	Women's Reproductive Rights Information Centre
WRRS	World Relief Refugee Services (U.S.A.)
WRRU	Water Resources Research Unit (Ghana)
WRS	War Relief Services (U.S.A.)
WRSA	World Rabbit Science Association
WRSIC	Water Resources Scientific Information Center (U.S.A.)
WRSP	Welsh Republican Socialist Party
WRST	World Rainforest Survival Trust
WRU	Welsh Rugby Union
WRU	Western Reserve University (U.S.A.)
WRU	Work Research Unit (ACAS)
WRVS	Women's Royal Voluntary Service
WRZZ	Wojewódzka Rada Związków Zawodowych
WS	Society of Writers to H.M. Signet
WS	The Wilderness Society
WS	Web Society
WS	Wereldsolidariteit (Belgium)
WSA	Vereinigung der Walzstahlverabeiter
WSA	Wasser und Schiffahrtsampt
WSA	Water Services Association
WSA	Wine & Spirit Association of Great Britain & Northern Ireland
WSA	Womensport Australia
WSA	Work Sciences Association
WSA	World Service Authority
WSA	World Society of Anesthesiology
WSA	World SUBUD Association) (*ex* SBIF)
WSAC	Water Space Amenity Committee
WSAEW	Water Services Association of England and Wales
WSAI	Wine & Spirit Association of Ireland
WSAS	Wine and Spirit Association of Scotland
WSAVA	World Small Animal Veterinary Association = AMVPA
WSB	World Scout Bureau
WSBBA	Welsh Schools Basketball Association
WSC	Welfare State Campaign
WSC	Western Sahara Campaign
WSC	World Spiritual Council
WSC	World Squash Council = ISTB
WSCA	Welsh Schools Cricket Association
WSCAR	Wisconsin Center for Space Automation and Robotics (U.S.A.)
WSCF	World Student Christian Federation = CSW, FUACE, FUMEC
WSCM	Supreme World Council for Masajid (Saudi Arabia)
WSE	Western Society of Engineers (U.S.A.)
WSE	World Society of Ekistics
WSET	Wine and Spirit Education Trust
WSET	Writers and Scholars Educational Trust (U.S.A.)
WSEU	Weaving and Sewing Employees' Union (Afghanistan)
WSF	Women's Sports Foundation
WSF	World Schizophrenia Fellowship
WSF	World Scout Foundation
WSF	World Sephardi Federation = FSM
WSF	World SF: International Organisation of Science Fiction and Fantasy Professionals
WSF	World Strengthlifting Federation (India)
WSFA	Wood and Solid Fuel Association of Retailers and Manufacturers
WSFARM	Wood and Solid Fuel Association of Retailers and Manufacturers
WSFC	Women's Solid Fuel Council
WSFHA	Western Samoa Family Health Association
WSFS	World Science Fiction Society (U.K.)
WSG	International Wool Study Group
WSG	Wiener Sprachgesellschaft
WSG	Women's Study Group (Tanzania)
WSGF	Welsh Seed Growers Federation
WSK	Wytwórnia Sprzętu Komunikacyjnego
WSL	Weltbund zum Schutze des Lebens
WSLF	Western Somali Liberation Front (Ethiopia)
WSM	Workers Solidarity Movement
WSMP	Wissenschaftliche Sozietät Musikpädogogik e.V.
WSO	Weather Service Office
WSO	World Safety Organization
WSO	World Sikh Organisation
WSO	World Simulation Organization
WSOC	Wider Share Ownership Council
WSPA	Women's Squash Players' Association = WISPA, WISRF
WSPA	World Society for Protection of Animals
WSPNZ	World Socialist Party of New Zealand

WSPU	Women's Social and Political Union	**WTMF**	Wool Textile Manufactures Federation
WSPU	World Scout Parliamentary Union (Republic of Korea)	**WTMU**	Wildlife Trade Monitoring Unit (WCMC)
WSRA	Women's Squash Rackets Association	**WTN**	Worldwide Television News
WSRO	World Sugar Research Organisation	**WTN**	Wrocławskie Towarzystwo Naukowe
WSRP	Welsh Socialist Republican Party	**WTO**	World Tourism Organization = OMT, VTO
WSRS	Wildlife Sound Recording Society		
WSS	World Ship Society	**WTO**	World Trade Organisation
WSSA	Weed Science Society of America	**WTP**	World Tape Pals (U.S.A.)
WSSA	Welsh Secondary Schools Association	**WTR**	Groupe de Travail Internationale sur la Toxicologie des Additifs du Caoutchouc (Belgium)
WSSEA	Weed Science Society for Eastern Africa (Kenya)		
WSSFN	World Society for Stereotatic and Functional Neurosurgery	**WTRD**	Water Treatment Research Division (South Africa)
WSSI	Weed Science Society of Indonesia	**WTRO**	Wool Textile Research Council
WSSRC	World Sailing Speed Record Council	**WTT**	World Teacher Trust (India)
WSTA	World Secretariat for Trade Action – WCL (Belgium)	**WTUSL**	Women's Temperance Union of Sri Lanka
WSTEC	Western Samoa Trust Estates Corporation	**WTYF**	World Theosophical Youth Federation
		WU	Women's Union
WSV	World Society of Victimology	**WU**	World Union (India)
WSW	Wojskowa Słuzba Wewnętrzna	**WU**	World University (WUR)
WSWA	Weed Society of Australia	**WUA**	Women's Union of Albania = BGS
WTA	Wholesale Traders' Association	**WUA**	Workers' Unions' Association (Sudan)
WTA	World Transport Agency	**WUCDW**	World Union of Christian Democratic Women = UFDC, UMFDC
WTAA	World Trade Alliance Association		
WTB	Wales Tourist Board	**WUCP**	World Union of Cities for Peace = ICPU, UMVP, WUPT
WTCA	World Trade Centres Association		
WTCC	Wet Tropics Consultative Committee	**WUCT**	World Union of Catholic Teachers = UMEC, WUKAL
WTCM	Wetenschappelijk en Technisch Centrum van de Metaalverwerkende Nijverheid = CRIF (Belgium)	**WUCWO**	World Union of Catholic Women's Organisations = UMOFC, WKFO
		WUF	Welt-Union der Freidenker = UMLP, WUFT
WTF	World Taekwondo Federation (Republic of Korea)		
		WUF	Western United Front (Fiji)
WTFDA	Worldwide TV-FM DX Association (U.S.A.)	**WUF**	World Underwater Federation = CMAS
WTG	Welt-Tierärztegesellschaft = AMV, WVA	**WUFR**	World Union of Free Romanians = UMRL
WTI	Water Transportation Institute (China)	**WUFT**	World Union of Free Thinkers = UMLP, WUF
WTI	Wirtschaftlich-Technischer Informationsdienst (Austria)	**WUG**	Wyższy Urząd Górniczy
WTIEC	World Tourism Information Exchange Centre (WTO) (Spain)	**WUJS**	World Union of Jewish Students = UMEJ
WTIF	Wall Tie Installers Federation	**WUKAL**	Wereldunies van Katholieke Leerkrachten = UMEC, WUCT
WTIS	World Trade Information Service (U.S.A.)	**WUKO**	World Union of Karatedo Organisations
WTLMF	Warszawskie Towarzystwo Lekarzy Medycyny Fizykalnej	**WULTUO**	World Union of Liberal Trade Union Organisations = UMOSBESL, WFALW
WTMA	Welded Tool Manufacturers Association	**WUM**	World Union Movement

WUNS	World Union of National Socialists =UMNS
WUP	World Union of Professions = UMP
WUPJ	World Union for Progressive Judaïsm
WUPO	World Union of Pythagorean Organisations
WUPT	World Union of Peace Towns = ICPU, UMVP, WUCP
WUR	World University Roundtable
WUS	World University Service = EUM, SUM
WUS-DK	WUS Danish National Committee
WUSA	World University Service in Australia
WUSC	World University Service in Canada = EUMC
WUSL	Women's United Service League
WUSP	World Union of Stockholm Pioneers = UMPS
WUUA	World Union for a Universal Alphabet
WUUN	Women United for United Nations
WV	Weltvereinigung der Veterinäranatomen = AMAV, WAVA
WVA	Welsh Volleyball Association
WVA	Weltverband Arbeitnehmer = CMT, WCL
WVA	Wereld Verbond van de Arbeid= CMV, WCL
WVA	Wirtschaftsverband Asbest
WVA	World Veterinary Association = AMV, WTG
WVAO	Wissenschaftliche Vereinigung für Augenoptik und Optometrie
WVB	Wereldverbond van Beambten = FME, WBA, WFCW
WVB	Wirtschaftsvereinigung Bergbau = WBA, WFCW
WVBH	Weltband der Bau-und Holzarbeiterorganisationen = FMCB, FMTCM, WFBWU, WFWBI
WVD	Wereldverbond van Diamantbewerkers = AUOD, UADW
WVEFG	Werkgemeenschap van Europese Grensgebieden = AEBR, AGEG, ARFE
WVER	Westvlaamse Ekonomische Raad
WVF	World Veterans Federation = FMAC
WVGM	Wirtschaftliche Vereinigung Grosshandel Metallhalbfabrikate
WVI	World Vision International Switzerland
WVI	World Vision of Ireland
WVIB	Wirtschaftsverband Industrieller Unternehmen Baden
WVL	Weltverband der Lehrer = CSME, WCT, WVOP
WVL	West Vancouver Laboratory (Canada)
WVLI	Wirtschaftsvereinigung der Lebensmittelindustrie
WVOP	Wereldvakverbond van Onderwijzend Personeel = CSME, WCT,WVL
WVPA	World Veterinary Poultry Association = AMVA
WVRSC	Wholesale Vegetable and Root Seeds Committee
WVT	Weltvereinigung für Tierproduktion = AMPA, AMZ, WAAP
WVV	Wissenschaftlicher Verein für Verkehrswesen e.V.
WVZ	Wirtschaftliche Vereinigung Zucker
WWA	War Widows Association of Great Britain
WWA	Welsh Water Authority
WWA	Woven Wire Association
WWANZ	Widows and Widowers' Association of New Zealand
WWB	Women's World Banking
WWC	World Water Conference (UN)
WWC	World's Wristwrestling Championship (U.S.A.)
WWCA	Asociación Femenina Trabajo y Cultura (Costa Rica)
WWCC	Western Weed Control Conference (U.S.A.)
WWCTU	World's Woman's Christian Temperance Union
WWD	Women for World Disarmament
WWF	Worldwide Fund for Nature
WWFA	Waterside Workers' Federation of Australia
WWFI	Worldwide Fund for Nature International
WWG	Österreichische Werbewissenschaftliche Gesellschaft
WWGBP	World Working Group on Birds of Prey and Owls (Germany)
WWHA	Welsh Women's Hockey Association
WWI	Werkgroep van Winkelinrichtingsbedrijven
WWJ	W. W. Jacobs Appreciation Society
WWOOF	Willing Workers On Organic Farms (Ireland)
WWOOF	Working Weekends on Organic Farms (*now* WOG)

WWP	World Wide Peace
WWPP	World Women Parliamentarians for Peace
WWREA	Wire & Wire Rope Employers' Association
WWSMA	Wood Wool Slab Manufacturers Association
WWSSF	Women's World Summit Foundation (Switzerland)
WWSSN	World Wide Standard Seismic Network
WWT	Wildfowl & Wetlands Trust
WWTA	Welsh Weight Training Association
WWTA	Woollen and Worsted Trades Association
WWTA	World Welly-throwing Association
WWTNC	West Wales Trust for Nature Conservation
WWTT	Worldwide Tapetalk (U.K.)
WWU	Wire Workers' Union
WWW	Wirtschaftsverband Werbeagenturen Werbemittler
WWW	Women Welcome Women
WWW	World Weather Watch (WMO) = VMM
WWWC	World Without War Council
WXILI	Wuxi Institute of Light Industry
WYAAA	World Youth Action Against Apartheid
WYC	World Youth Choir (FIJM)
WYFL	World Youth Freedom League
WYSF	Woollen Yarn Spinners Association
WZB	Wissenschaftszentrum Berlin
WZL	Laboratorium für Werkzeugmaschinen und Betriebslehre (Germany)
WZO	World Zionist Organisation (Israel) = OSM
WZO	World Zoroastrian Organisation
WZOA	Women's Zionist Organisation of America
WZZ	Wolne Związki Zawodwe

X

XAAS	Xinjiang Academy of Agricultural Sciences
XCDRI	Xi'an Coal Design and Research Institut
XHRI	Xi'an Highway Research Institute
XIH	Xi'an Institute of Highways
XIN	Xizang Institute for Nationalities

XISS	Xavier Institute of Social Service (India)
XNU	Xinjiang Normal University
XPI	Xinjiang Petroleum Institute

Y

YAA	Yachtsmens Association of America
YAAS	Yunnan Academy of Agricultural Sciences
YAD	Yoneylem Arastirmasi Dernegi
YAF	Young Americans for Freedom
YANPET	Saudi Yanbu Petrochemical Company (Saudi Arabia)
YAPLO	Yorkshire Association of Power Loom Workers
YAR	Yemen Arab Republic
YARS	Yugoslav Astronautical and Rocket Society = SAROJ
YASGB	Youth Association of Synagogues in Great Britain
YAT	Yugoslavian Air Transport = JAT
YATAMA	Indian Organizations Opposed To Sandinistas
YBDSA	Yacht Brokers, Designers and Surveyors Association
YBRD	Yemen Bank for Reconstruction and Development (YAR)
YC	Young Conservative Organisation
YCA	Yacht Charter Association
YCA	Yacht Cruising Association
YCES	Yeongnam Crop Experiment Station (South Korea)
YCF	Yacht Club de France
YCF	Yacimientos Carboniferos Fiscales (Argentina)
YCIF	Yacht Club de l'Île de France
YCL	Young Communist League
YCNAC	Young Conservatives National Advisory Committee
YCND	Youth Campaign for Nuclear Disarmament
YCS	International Young Catholic Students = JEC, KSJ
YCUK	Youth Call (International) UK
YCUK	Youth Clubs UK
YCW	International Young Christian Workers = JOC, JOCI

YD	Youth Defence	**YIG**	Yunnan Institute of Geography
YDA	Youth Development Association	**YIMI**	Yunnan Institute of Medical Information
YDC	Youth for Development and Cooperation	**YIP**	Youth International Party (U.S.A.)
YDCW	Ymgyrch Diogelu Cymru Wledig	**YJA**	Yachting Journalists' Association
YDS	Yorkshire Dialect Society	**YJA**	Young Journalists' Association
YEA	Yanhee Electricity Authority (Thailand)	**YJWK**	Patriotic Women's Association of Kurdistan
YEE	Youth and Environment Europe (Denmark)	**YKI**	Ytkemiska Institutet (Sweden)
YEF	Young European Federalists = JEF	**YKRI**	Yingkou Knitting Research Institute
YEF	Youth and Environment Europe	**YLE**	Oy Yleisradio Ab
YEM	Young European Movement	**YLGN**	Young Labour Green Network
YEMINCO	Yemen Oil and Mineral Industrial Company (YAR)	**YMBA**	Yacht and Motor Boat Association
		YMCA	Young Men's Christian Association = ACDG, ACJ, CVJM, UCJG
YEMROCK	National Company for Industrial and Construction Materials (YAR)	**YMCF**	Yacht Motor Club de France
YEN	Youth of European Nationalities = JCEE, JEV	**YMS**	Yanzhou Coal Mine Design & Research Institute
		YMU	Yemeni Workers' Union
YENED	Ypiressia Enimerosseos Enoplon Dhynameon	**YMYWHA**	Young Mens and Young Womens Hebrew Association (U.S.A.)
YES	Young Entomologists Society	**YNA**	Young Newspaper Executives Association (*ex* Young Newspaperman's Association)
YES	Young Europeans for Security (Netherlands)		
YES	Youth for Environment and Service (U.S.A.)	**YNA**	Yugoslav National Army
		YOAN	Youth of All Nations (U.S.A.)
YET	Young Explorers Trust	**YOC**	Young Ornithologists' Club
YEU	Youth for Exchange and Understanding (Germany)	**YOL**	Yleinen Ossuskauppojen Liitto
		YOMINCO	Yemen Oil and Mineral Resources Corporation (Yemen)
YEWF	Young Europeans for World Freedom		
YFC	Young Farmers' Club	**YOU**	Young Officers' Union (Philippines)
YFCI	Youth for Christ International = JFC, JPC	**YPC**	Yemen Petroleum Company (YAR)
		YPF	Yacimientos Petrolíferos Fiscales Sociedad del Estado (Argentina)
YFEC	Youth Forum of the European Communities = FJCE		
		YPFB	Yacimientos Petrolíferos Fiscales Bolivianos
YFRI	Yellow Sea Fisheries Research Institute (China)	**YPSCE**	Young People's Society for Christian Endeavour
YFU	Youth For Understanding International Exchange (U.S.A.)	**YPTENC**	Young People's Trust for the Environment and Nature Conservation
YGEC	Yemen General Electricity Corporation (YAR)	**YPTES**	Young People's Trust for Endangered Species
YHA	Yacht Harbour Association	**yr Urdd**	Urdd Gobaith Cymru
YHA	Youth Hostels Association	**YRC**	Youth Rights Campaign
YHANI	Youth Hostel Association of Northern Ireland	**YRE**	Youth Against Racism in Europe
		YRS	Yuen Ren Society for the Promotion of Chinese Dialect Fieldwork
YHC	Young Herpetologists Club		
YICAM	Société Yoo-Hoo Industries of Cameroon	**YRSRI**	Yangtze River Scientific Research Institute
YIED	Yunnan Provincial Institute of Epidemic Diseases Control and Research (China)	**YS**	Yamashita-Shinnikion Steamship Company (Japan)

YSA	Young Socialist Alliance
YSAU	Young Swimmers Athletic Union
YSF	Yoruba Solidarity Front
YSKOR	Suid-Afrikaanse Yster en Staal Industriële Korporasie Beperk
YSMBE	Yugoslav Society for Medical and Biological Engineering
YSP	Yemeni Socialist Party
YSRI	Sugarcane Research Institute, Yunnan Academy of Agricultural Sciences
YTA	Young Theatre Association
YTCRI	Yunnan Tropical Crops Research Institute
YTP	Yeni Türkiye Partisi
YUBIN	Jugoslovenski Bibliograsko-Informacijski Institut
Yucan	Yugoslav Canada Line (Yugoslavia)
YUTEL	Yugoslav TV Network
YVA	Young Vietnamese Association
YWCA	Young Women's Christian Association = UCJF
YWFD	Young World Food and Development (FAO)
YWPG	Young World Promotion Group (FAO)
YZPCI	Yang Zi Petrochemical Co Research Institute

Z

Z	Zentralsparkasse und Kommerzialbank Wien (Austria)
ZAAA	Zambia Amateur Athletics Association
ZAAS	Zhejiang Academy of Agricultural Sciences
ZADCA	Zinc Alloy Die Casters' Association
ZADCO	Zakum Development Company (Abu Dhabi)
ZADI	Zentralstelle für Agrardokumentation und Information
ZAED	Zentralstelle für Atomkernenergie Dokumentation
ZAKR	Związek Polskich Autorów i Kompozytorów Rozrywkowych
ZALAHUS	Zala Megyei Allatforgalmi és Hüsipari Vállalat
ZAM	Zentralinstitut für Arbeitsmedizin
ZAMEFA	Metal Fabricators of Zambia
ZAMS	Zhejiang Academy of Medical Sciences

ZAMWA	Zambia Media Women's Association
ZANA	Zambia News Agency
ZANU-PF	Zimbabwe African National Union – Patriotic Front
ZANU-S	Zimbabwe African National Union – Sithole
ZAP	Zaaizaadvereniging Anna-Paulowna
ZAP	Związek Polskich Artystów Plastyków
ZAPI	Société Régionale de Développement des Zones d'Actions Prioritaires Intégrés de l'Est (Cameroon)
ZAR	Zentrale Arbeitsgemeinschaft Österreicher Rinderzüchter
ZAR	Związek Artystów Rzeżbiarzy
ZARD	Zambia Association for Research and Development
ZASP	Związek Artystów Scen Polskich
ZASTI	Zambia Air Services Training Institute
ZAV	Zentralarbeitsgemeinschaft des Strassenverkehrsgewerbes
ZAV	Zentralstelle für Arbeitsvermittlung
ZAVAR	Institut Za Varilstvo (Yugoslavia)
ZAW	Zentralausschuss der Werbewirtschaft
ZB	Związek Bezdomnych
ZBHD	Zambia Broken Hill Development Co.
ZBI	Zentralverband Berufsständischer Ingenieurvereine
ZBW	Zentralkellerei Badischer Winzergenossenschaften
ZBZ	Zentrum Berlin für Zukunftsforschung
ZC	Zangger Committee
ZCCM	Zambia Consolidated Copper Mines
ZCCT	Zoo Check Charitable Trust
ZChN	Zjednoczenie Chrześcijańsko-Narodowe (Poland) = CNU
ZCS	Zim Container Service (Israel)
ZCSD	Zambia Council for Social Development
ZCTCM	Zhejiang College of Traditional Chinese Medicine
ZCTU	Zambia Congess of Trade Unions
ZCTU	Zimbabwe Congress of Trade Unions
ZDA	Zimbabwe Development Association
ZDA	Zinc Development Association
ZDAS	Zveza Društev Arhitektov Slovenije
ZDB	Zentralverband des Deutschen Baugewerbes
ZDB	Zimbabwe Development Bank
ZDF	Zweites Deutsches Fernsehen

ZDG	Zentralverband der Deutschen Geflügelwirtschaft		**ZFA**	Zentral-Fachausschuss für die Druckindustrie
ZDH	Zentralverband des Deutschen Handwerks		**ZFD**	Zentralverband der Medizinischen Fusspfleger Deutschlands
ZDI	Zentralverband Deutscher Ingenieure		**ZFIV**	Zentrales Forschungsinstitut des Verkehrswesens
ZDK	Zentralverband des Kraftfahrzeuggewerbes		**ZfKf**	Zentrum für Kulturforschung (Germany)
ZDK	Zentralverband Deutscher Kaninchen- züchter		**ZFMA**	Zip Fastener Manufacturers Association (India, U.K.)
ZDP	Zentralverband Deutscher Pelztierzéchter eV		**ZFRI**	Zhejiang Forestry Research Institute
ZDS	Zentralverband Deutscher Schiffsmakler		**ZFV**	Deutsche Zentrale für Fremdenverkehr
ZDSLU	Zveza Društev Slovenskih Likovnih Umetnikov		**ZFV**	Zentralinstitut für Versuchstierzucht (Germany)
ZDV	Zentralverband des Deutschen Vulkaniseur Handwerks		**ZFW**	Zentralinstitut für Festkörperphysik und Werkstofforschung
ZDVTS	Zveza Društev za Varilno Tehniko Slovenije		**ZG**	Związek Górnośląski (Poland) = USU
ZE	Združenje na Egipčanite (Macedonia) = EAC		**ZGA**	Zambia Geographical Association
ZECER	Zhejiang Provincial Institute of Estuarine and Coastal Engineering Research		**ZGDS**	Zveva Geografskih Drustev Slovenije
			ZGSBP	Zarząd Główny Stowarzyszenia Bibliotekarzy Polskich
ZECPI	Zhejiang Provincial Economic Construction Planning Institute		**ZGSKP**	Zarząd Główny Społecznego Komitetu Przeciwalkoholowego
Zefal	Zim Eilat Far East Australia Line (Israel)		**Zhenotdel**	Otdel po Rabote sredi Zhenshchin
ZELL- CHEMING	Verein der Zellstoff-und Papier- Chemiker und Ingenieure		**ZHI**	Stichting v.d. Nederlandse Zelfstandige Handel en Industrie
ZEN EIEN	Zenkoku Eiga Engeki Rodo Kumiai (Japan)		**ZHOS**	Zveza Hortikulturnih Organizacij Slovenije
ZENKO	Zen Nihon Kinzoku Kozan Rodo Kumiai Rengokai (Japan)		**ZHP**	Związek Harcerstwa Polskiego
ZENNOH	National Federation of Agricultural Cooperatives Associations (Japan)		**ZHR**	Związek Harcerstwa Rzeczypospolitej
			ZhSBND	Zhenshchiny za Sotsialishicheskoe Budushchee Nashikh Detei
ZENRO	Zen Nihon Rodo Kumiai Kiagi (Japan)		**ZHW**	Zakład Higieny Weterynaryjnej
ZENSEN- DOMEI	Zenkoku Sen-i Sangyo Rodo Kumiai Domei (Japan)		**ZHZ**	Zuid-Hollandse Zuivelbond
ZENTEI	Zen Teishin Rodo Kumiai (Japan)		**ZI**	Zinc Institute (U.S.A.)
ZENT- GENO	Zentralverband der Genossenschaftlichen Grosshandels- und Dienstleistungsunternehmen		**ZI**	Zonta International (U.S.A.)
			Ziana	Zimbabwe Inter-African News Agency (U.S.A.)
ZÉP	Zone d'Échanges Préférentielle pour l'Afrique Orientale et Australe = ESAPTA, PTA		**ZIB**	Konrad-Zuse-Zentrum für Informationstechnik Berlin (Germany)
			ZIDA	Zentrum für Information und Dokumentation der Aussenwirtschaft
ZEPH	Zambia Educational Publishing House		**ZIF**	Zentralinstitut für Fertigungstechnik
ZESCO	Zambia Electricity Supply Corporation		**ZIF**	Zentrum für Interdisziplinäre Forschung (Germany)
ZEV	Zuivel-Export-Vereniging		**ZIH**	Żydowski Instytut Historyczny w Polsce
ZF	Zionist Federation of Great Britain and Ireland		**ZIID**	Zentralinstitut für Information und Dokumentation
			ZIM	Zimbabwe Institute of Management

ZIMCO	Zambia Industrial and Mining Corporation	**ZLPRI**	Zhejiang Leather and Plastics Research Institute
ZIMED	Zhejiang Institute of Mechanical and Electrical Design	**ZMB**	Zentrale für Maikäfer-Bekampfungsaktionen
ZIMP	Zaochnyi Institut Metalloobrabatyvaiushchei Promyshlennosti	**ZMCh**	Związek Młodziezy Chrzescijańskiej
		ZMD	Zentralstell für Maschinell Dokumentation
ZINCOM	Zambian Industrial and Commercial Association	**ZMD**	Związek Młodziezy Demokratycznej
ZINS	Zionist Information Service (U.S.A.)	**ZMM**	Združenie na Makedonci Muslimani (Macedonia) = AMM
ZIP	Zhengzhou Institute of Pomology (China)	**ZMP**	Zentrale Markt- und Preisberichtstelle der Deutschen Landwirtschaft
ZIPA	Zimbabwe People's Army	**ZMP**	Związek Młodziezy Polskiej
ZIPK	Zaochnyi Institut Povysheniya Kvalifikatsii	**ZMPD**	Zrzeszenie Międzynarodowych Przewozników Drogowych w Polsce
ZIS	Zentralinstitut für Schweisstechnik	**ZMRI**	Zhejiang Mariculture Research Institute
ZISP	Zaochnyi Institut Stroitel'noi Promyshlennosti	**ZMRI**	Zhejiang Metallurgical Research Institute
ZIST	Zaochnyi Institut Sovetskoi Torgovlii	**ZMS**	Związek Młodziezy Socjalistycznej
ZITF	Zimbabwe International Trade Fair	**ZMW**	Związek Młodziezy Wiejskiej
ZITS	Zveza Inzenirjev in Tehnikov Slovenije	**ZMWRP**	Związek Młodziezy Wiejskiej Rzeczypospolitej Polskiej "Wici"
ZIV	Zentrale Informationsstelle für Verkehr in der Deutschen Verkehrswissenschaftlichen	**ZNA**	Zimbabwe National Army
		ZNCC	Zimbabwe National Chambers of Commerce
ZIW	Związek Inwalidów Wojennych	**ZNFPC**	Zimbabwe National Family Planning Council
ZJFC	Zhejiang Forestry College		
ZKB	Zuivel Kwaliteitscontrôle Bureau	**ZNMS**	Związek Niezaleznej Młodziezy Socjalistycznej
ZKF	Zentralverband Karosserie- und Fahrzeugtechnik	**ZNP**	Związek Nauczycielstwa Polskiego
ZKI	Spolok Slovenských Knihovníkov	**ZNSSKP**	Związek Niemieckich Stowarzyszeń Społeczno-Kulturalnych w Polsce (Poland) = UGSCAP
ZKI	Zentralinstitut für Kybernetik und Informationsprozesse		
ZKI	Zväz Slovenskych Knihovníkov a Informatikov	**ZNTB**	Zambia National Tourist Bureau
		ZNZ	Zuid-Nederlandse Zuivelbond
ZKiOR	Związek Kółek i Organizacji Rolniczych	**ZOA**	Zentralverband der Organisationen des Automaten-Aufstell-Gewerbes
ZKM	Zentrum für Kunst und Medientechnologie Karlsruhe	**ZOA**	Zionist Organisation of America
		ZOLIC	Zona Libre de Industrial y Comercio Santo Tomas de Castilla (Guatemala)
ZKP	Związek Kompozytorów Polskich		
ZKR	Zentral Kommission für die Rheinschiffahrt= CCNR, CCR	**ZOO**	Société Royale di Zoologie d'Anvers (Belgium)
ZŁ	Zjednoczenie Łemków (Poland) = LU	**ZOPA**	Zinc Oxide Producers Association (Belgium)
ZLA	Zambia Library Association	**ZOSP**	Związek Ochotniczych Strazy Pozarnych
ZLA	Zimbabwe Library Association		
ZLDI	Zentralstelle für Luftfahr-dokumentation und Information	**ZOZ**	Zespół Opieki Zdrowotnej
		ZP	Zegluga Polska
ZLJM	Zusters van Liefde van Jezus en Maria = SCJM	**ZPAF**	Związek Polskich Artystów Fotografików
ZLP	Związek Literatów Polskich		

ZPAP	Związek Polskich Artystów Plastyków		**ZTG**	Zentralverband des Tankstellen-und Garagengewerbes
ZPC	Zaaizaad en Pootgoed Cooperatieve		**ZTRS**	Zambia-Tanzania Road Services (Zambia)
ZPDA	Zinc Pigment Development Association		**ZUA**	Lietuvos zemes ukio akademija = LAA, LZUA
ZPHT	Zrzeszenie Polskich Hoteli Turystycznych			
ZPP	Zjednoczenie Przemysłu Piwowarskiego		**ZUM**	Zimbabwe Unity Movement
ZPP	Zrzeszenie Prawników Polskich		**ZUMA**	Zentrum für Umfragen, Methoden und Analysen (Germany)
ZPP	Związek Patriotów Polskich			
ZPTL	Zrzeszenie Polskich Towarzystw Lekarskich		**ZUP**	Związek Ukraińców w Polsce (Poland) = UUP
ZPTM	Zrzeszenie Polskich Towarzystw Medycznych		**ZUPO**	Zimbabwe United Peoples Organisation
ZRIME	Zhengzhou Research Institute of Mechanical Engineering		**ZURČS**	Zväz Ukrajincov a Rusínov v Česko-Slovensku (Slovakia) = UURCS
ZRMK	Zavod za Raziskavo Materiala in Konstrukcij		**ZUS**	Zakład Ubezpieczeń Społecznych
ZRP	Związek Rzemiosła Polskiego		**ZUU**	Zemedelsky Ustav Ucetnicko-sprayoredny
ZS	Agrarian Party (Czech Republic)		**ZV**	Zentralverband der Auskunfteien und Detekteien
ZS	Zrzeszenie Sportowe			
ZSA	Zululand Swaziland Association (U.K.)		**ZVA**	Zentralverband der Augenoptiker
ZSA	Zväz Slovenskych Architektov (*now* SAS)		**ZVDH**	Zentralverband des Deutschen Dachdeckerhandwerks Fachverband Dach- Wand- und Abdichtungstechnik
ZSCh	Związek Samopomocy Chłopskiej		**ZVEH**	Zentralverband der Deutschen Electrohandwerke
ZSCM	Združenie na Srbi i Crnogorci vo Makedonija (Macedonia) = ASMM		**ZVEI**	Zentralverband der Elektrotechnischen Industrie
ZSI	Zhejiang Shipbuilding Institute			
ZSI	Związek Spółdzielni Inwalidów		**ZVFIFU**	Zentralverband Forstindustrie und Forstunternehem
ZSIG	Zürcherische Seidenindustrie-Gesellschaft		**ZVG**	Zentralverband der Deutschen Gemüs-, Obst- und Gartenbau
ZSITS	Zveza Strojnih Inženirjev in Tehnikov Slovenije		**ZVI**	Zentrale Verkaufsleitung (DB)
ZSKBIP	Zväz Slovenskych Knihovnikov Bibliografov Informacnych Pracovnikov		**ZVI**	Zentralverband der Ingenieure des Offentlichen Dienstes in Deutschland
ZSL	United Peasant Party (Poland)		**ZVK**	Zentralverband der Krankengymnasten
ZSL	Zjednoczone Stronnictwo Ludowe		**ZVK**	Zentralverband des Kraftfahrzeughandwerks
ZSL	Zoological Society of London			
ZSMP	Związek Socjalistycznej Młodziezy Polskiej		**ZVM**	Zentralverband Deutscher Mechaniker-Handwerke
ZSN	Zemské Shromáždění Němců (Czech Republic) = GLA		**ZVOS**	Zveza Društev za Varstvo Okolja v Sloveniji = USPES
ZSN	Zoological Stations of Naples		**ZVR**	Zentralverband des Raumausstatterhandwerks
ZSP	Zrzeszenie Studentów Polskich			
ZSS	Związek Spółdzielni Spozywców		**ZVSHK**	Zentralverband Sanitär- Heizungs- und Klimatechnik
ZSSA	Zoological Society of Southern Africa		**ZVSM**	Zentralverband Schweizerischer Milchproduzenten = UCPL
ZTA	Związek Teatrów Amatorskich			
ZTDC	Zimbabwe Tourist Development Corporation		**ZVSU**	Zentralverband Schweizerischer Uhrmacher

ZWO	Nederlandse Organisatie voor Zuiverwetenschappelijk Onderzoek	**ZZ**	Związek Zawodowe
ZWRCN	Zimbabwe Women's Resource Centre and Network	**ZZF**	Zentralverband Zoologischer Fachbetriebe Deutschlands
ZYI	Zhongyuan Research Institute of Electronics Technology	**ZZM**	Związek Zawodowy Metalówców
		ZZPRz	Związek Zawodowy Pracowników Rzemiosła